the Next EXIT®

INTERSTATE HIGHWAY GUIDE

2014

THE MOST ACCURATE INTERSTATE HIGHWAY SERVICE GUIDE EVER PRINTED™

the Next EXIT® will save time, money and frustration.

This tool will help you find services along the USA interstate Highways like nothing you have ever used.

GAS STATIONS • RESTAURANTS • RV CAMPING • HOTELS • AND MUCH MORE

PO Box 888
Garden City, UT 84028
www.theNextExit.com

the Next Exit®
USER GUIDE

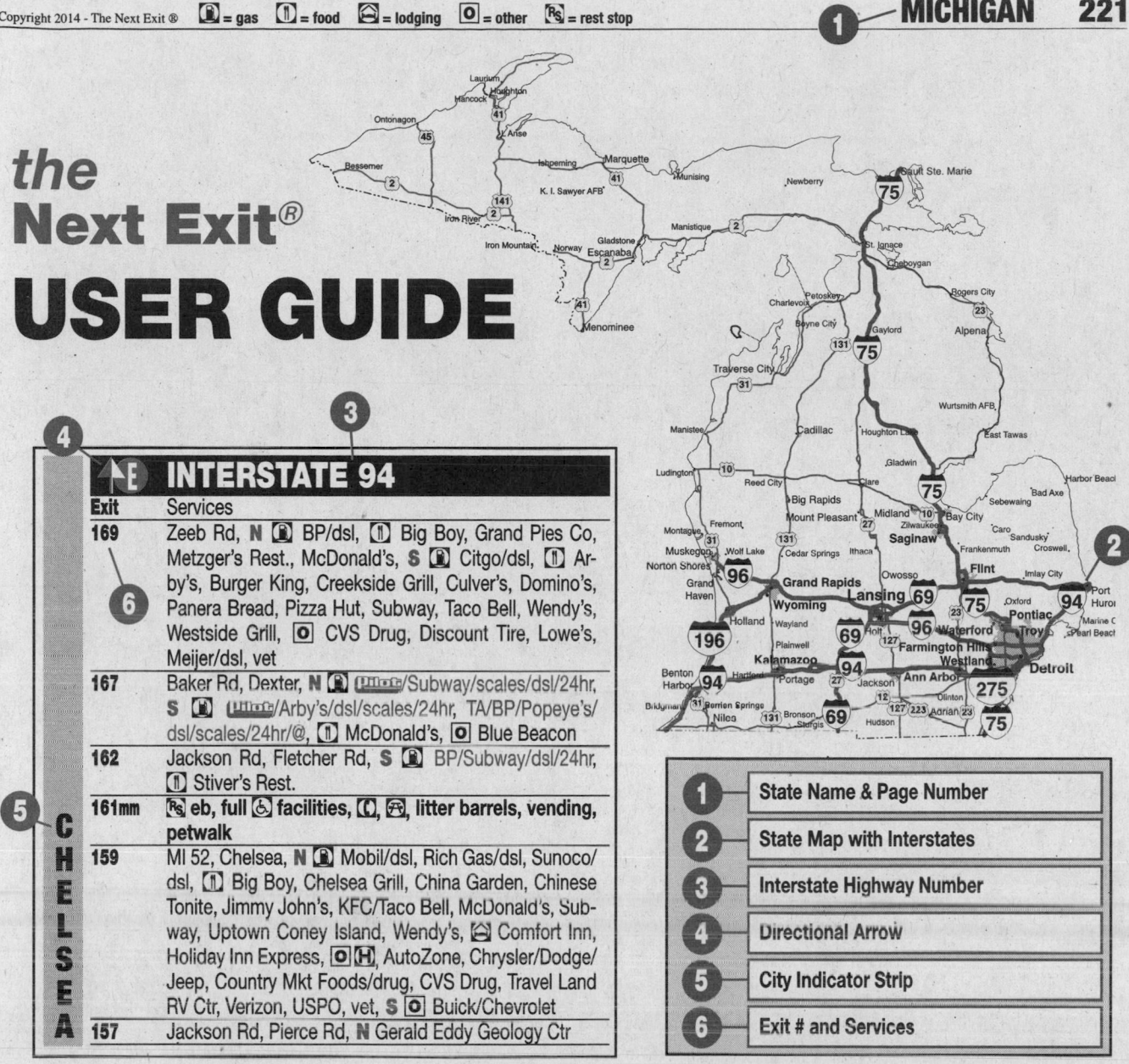

❹ ⬆🅴 INTERSTATE 94 ❸

Exit	Services
169	Zeeb Rd, **N** 🅟 BP/dsl, 🍴 Big Boy, Grand Pies Co, Metzger's Rest., McDonald's, **S** 🅟 Citgo/dsl, 🍴 Arby's, Burger King, Creekside Grill, Culver's, Domino's, Panera Bread, Pizza Hut, Subway, Taco Bell, Wendy's, Westside Grill, 🅞 CVS Drug, Discount Tire, Lowe's, Meijer/dsl, vet
167	Baker Rd, Dexter, **N** 🅟 ▥▥▥/Subway/scales/dsl/24hr, **S** 🅟 ▥▥▥/Arby's/dsl/scales/24hr, TA/BP/Popeye's/dsl/scales/24hr/@, 🍴 McDonald's, 🅞 Blue Beacon
162	Jackson Rd, Fletcher Rd, **S** 🅟 BP/Subway/dsl/24hr, 🍴 Stiver's Rest.
161mm	🆁🆂 eb, full ♿ facilities, 🚻 🎁 litter barrels, vending, petwalk
159	MI 52, Chelsea, **N** 🅟 Mobil/dsl, Rich Gas/dsl, Sunoco/dsl, 🍴 Big Boy, Chelsea Grill, China Garden, Chinese Tonite, Jimmy John's, KFC/Taco Bell, McDonald's, Subway, Uptown Coney Island, Wendy's, 🛏 Comfort Inn, Holiday Inn Express, 🅞🅷 AutoZone, Chrysler/Dodge/Jeep, Country Mkt Foods/drug, CVS Drug, Travel Land RV Ctr, Verizon, USPO, vet, **S** 🅞 Buick/Chevrolet
157	Jackson Rd, Pierce Rd, **N** Gerald Eddy Geology Ctr

❺ C H E L S E A

❶	**State Name & Page Number**
❷	**State Map with Interstates**
❸	**Interstate Highway Number**
❹	**Directional Arrow**
❺	**City Indicator Strip**
❻	**Exit # and Services**

Exit

Most states number exits by the nearest mile marker(mm). A few states use consecutive numbers, in which case mile markers are given in ( ). Mile markers are the little green vertical signs beside the interstate at one mile intervals which indicate distance from the southern or western border of a state. Odd numbered interstates run north/south, even numbered run east/west.

Services

Services are listed alphabetically by category 🅟=gas 🍴=food 🛏=lodging 🆁🆂=rest stop 🅞=other services including camping.

"🅷" indicates an exit from which a hospital may be accessed, but it may not be close to the exit.

Services located away from the exit may be referred to by "access to," or "to" and a distance may be given.

A directional notation is also given, such as **N**, **S**, **E** or **W**

Directional Arrows

Follow exits DOWN the page if traveling from North to South or East to West, UP the page if traveling South to North or West to East.

the Next EXIT® USER GUIDE

TABLE OF CONTENTS

Abbreviations & Symbols used in the Next EXIT ®

Abbrev.	Meaning	Abbrev.	Meaning
AFB	Air Force Base	pk	park
B&B	Bed&Breakfast	pkwy	parkway
Bfd	Battlefield	rest.	restaurant
Ctr	Center	nb	northbound
Coll	College	sb	southbound
Cyn	canyon	eb	eastbound
dsl	diesel	wb	westbound
$	Dollar	SP	state park
Mem	Memorial	SF	state forest
Mkt	Market	Sprs	springs
Mtn	Mountain	st	street, state
mm	mile marker	sta	station
N	north side of exit	TPK	Turnpike
S	south side of exit	USPO	Post Office
E	east side of exit	vet	veterinarian
W	west side of exit	whse	warehouse
NM	National Monument	@	truckstop (full service)
NHS	Nat Hist Site	red print	RV accessible
NWR	Nat Wildlife Reserve	♿	Handicapped accessible
NF	National Forest	☎	Telephone
H	Hospital		Gas
✈	Airport		Food
⊞	Picnic Tables		Lodging
NP	National Park		Other
NRA	Nat Rec Area	Rs	Rest Stop / Rest Area

For Trans Canada Highway (TCH) information and more, please visit us on the web at *www.thenextexit.com*

Deadhead

by Mark Watson - Winter 2014

The Honda and I merged onto Interstate 495, crossed over the Potomac by way of the Woodrow Wilson Bridge then followed Interstate 95 as it hurries away south from Washington, DC. The morning rush was over yet traffic rolled relentlessly through thick suburbia cushioning the capital. Soon we were cruising comfortably past Woodbridge and Quantico toward Richmond on three lanes at 74 mph, and having finally extracted ourselves from the beltway swamp our spirits improved with each expiring mile. Interstate 95 from Richmond to Washington is one of the busiest stretches of highway in America. It is a route I have driven so many times I cannot remember them all, except for that very first time...

In the early 1960's, my oldest brother survived an enlistment with the United States Marine Corps, saw some of the world and then settled into a career as an operator for a national transportation company. At first he lived overlooking the Iwo Jima Monument near Arlington, and then on the Maryland side of the nation's capital. Our frequent visits from SC to DC so familiarized me with every important site around the seat of government that before long I was irreverently climbing onto Lincoln's knees and crawling all over Jefferson's feet giving nary a thought to the solemn nature of these sacred shrines. In those days freedom to climb and crawl on holy ground was an unquestioned liberty, I concluded, because I owned the place.

My brother was also a free thinker. For instance, whenever we came to town he saw no problem with me accompanying him to work as he drove passengers from downtown Washington to all points north. If the bus was not full, I sat in the row immediately behind him next to the window. If there were no extra seats, I stood outside until the paying passengers all had places, then plopped down on a pillow beside him in the aisle. In my mind, it was the best seat in the house and nobody ever made a comment or even frowned at the arrangement. It was my brother who first drove me through the Lincoln Tunnel into New York City and showed me the Empire State Building, tall cotton for a small town southern boy. It was my brother who pointed out Barbara Fritchie's house in Frederick, Maryland. And it was my brother who took me to Philadelphia, the 'City of Brotherly Love', and Gettysburg, where the War was lost or won, depending on your perspective.

I was a little disappointed when he moved to Richmond even though it made traveling to his house easier. Washington had attractions that Richmond could never match, but I still rode with him day or night, whenever the dispatcher called to notify him that his rotation was approaching. At age 15, I was excited to hear the phone ring at midnight summoning us to the terminal where he was directed to his destination. The best of all situations, I thought, was when he was assigned to drive a completely empty bus from one city to another simply to balance out capacity. A 'deadhead' meant that the two of us had the entire vehicle all to ourselves.

Such a call came late one night a month short of my 16th birthday, and off to the lot we went to claim our carrier with my enthusiasm leading the way. We learned that our mission was to deadhead from Richmond to Washington in the quiet hours between two and four o'clock AM, the perfect plan if you had asked me. Only we two would be on that trip and almost no one else would be driving on newly constructed Interstate 95 as it connected the cities one hundred miles apart by

Continued Next Page

DEADHEAD

four broad lanes of fresh concrete. But nobody asked me anything until about ten miles out of Richmond when my brother called me to come and stand by his side as we headed north.

"Come here, Boy," he said. Then as now, I had a name which he almost never referenced, maybe because he was much older and to remind me of my place. I came there. "Look here," he continued, and I looked there. "This is the accelerator, and this is the brake, see?" I saw. "Hold it between those two white lines, it's just like driving Daddy's tractor." And then with one smooth motion he stepped out from under the wheel and pushed me into the drivers seat. The huge transport began to lose momentum so he added, "now hold it right on 70 because if you don't the highway patrol will notice and stop you to see what is wrong." So I pressed on the pedal and off toward Washington we went.

They both were controlled by a steering wheel but after that the comparison to Dad's tractor weakened considerably. Just as I was settling into my new job I discovered a mirror which provided a view of the bus' interior. That is when I saw my brother seated near the back calmly writing out reports. "Will I need to change gears?" I bravely asked. "Shouldn't," he answered. "What do I do when I see Washington coming?" I ventured. "Let me know," he replied without looking up, "but we won't have to worry about that for another hour or so." Then he went back to reporting and I went back to driving.

By and by the lights of the Capital flickered into view and right on cue my brother appeared and took the wheel. Relieved, I watched the next half hour as he nimbly threaded us through the streets toward the station, amazed at how easily he maneuvered around corners and down narrow lanes, at last pulling precisely into the correct gate. "See?" he said, "nothing to it." As the doors swung open I heard over the public address speakers, "Four-thirty to Richmond, gate five!"

"Yes!" I thought, "yes, we are!"

Without that experience in the middle of the night 50 years ago, the whole trip might have passed from memory with no residue much like any other event, just another adventure among so many. Deadheading means something very different to me now but the only real mark it left is the recurring dream I have every few years. I am driving again anxiously through the streets of Washington, DC, wondering when my brother will finish his reports, horrified at changing lanes, terrified of turning and petrified at the thought of parking the long bus. Just when everything seems hopeless he always arrives, takes the wheel and calmly steers us safely home.

Disclaimers:
Do not attempt!
Any resemblance to real persons in this story,
    living or dead, is purely coincidental.
One of the characters in this tale is deceased and
    the other ought to be a mature adult.
The statute of limitations on foolhardiness
    never expires, but on an experience like this,
    it probably does.

DEADHEAD

⬆E INTERSTATE 10

Exit	Services
66.5mm	Alabama/Florida state line
66mm	**Welcome Ctr full** ♿ **facilities,** 🅟, **vending,** ⛲ **litter barrels, petwalk**
53	rd 64, Wilcox Rd, **N** 🅖 BP/Oasis/Chester's/Stuckey's/Subway/dsl/scales/24hr/@, ⊙ Riverside RV Park, Styx River Resort, **S** 🅖 Chevron/dsl, Outpost/dsl, ⊙ Azalea Acres RV Park, Hilltop RV Park (1.5 mi), Wilderness RV Park, fireworks
44	AL 59, Loxley, **N** 🅖 Loves/Arby's/dsl/scales/24hr, 🛏 Bay Inn, **S** 🅖 Chevron/dsl, Exxon/dsl, RaceWay/dsl, 🍴 Burger King, Hardee's, McDonald's, Waffle House, 🛏 Loxley Motel (3mi), WindChase Inn, ⊙ to Gulf SP
38	AL 181, Malbis, **N** 🍴 CA Dreaming, Chick-fil-A, Cracker Barrel, Hibachi Grill, Logan's Roadhouse, McDonald's, Moe's SW Grill, Olive Garden, Panera Bread, Poor Mexican, Ruby Tuesday, Starbucks, Stix Asian, Taco Bell, Wendy's, Wintzell's Oyster House, 🛏 Best Western, Country Inn&Suites, Holiday Inn Express, La Quinta, ⊙ Advance Parts, Barnes&Noble, Belk, Best Buy, Dillard's, $Tree, Goodyear/auto, Michael's, Old Navy, Petsmart, Publix, Ross, Tuesday Morning, Verizon, Walgreens, World Mkt, **S** 🅖 Chevron/dsl, Shell/LA Subs, Texaco/dsl, 🍴 Burger King, Don Carlos, Firehouse Subs, Mellow Mushroom, Zaxby's, 🛏 Malbis Motel (1mi), ValuePlace, ⊙ Urgent Care, AT&T, Honda, Hyundai, Lowe's, Nissan, Sam's Club/gas, Toyota/Scion, Walmart
35	US 90, US 98, **N** 🅖 BP, Shell, 🍴 Beef O'Brady's, China Fun, 🛏 Courtyard, Fairfield Inn, ⊙ Bass Pro Shops, Books-A-Million, JC Penney, Kohl's, Rite Aid, USPO, **S** 🅖 Exxon/dsl, Shell, 🍴 Arby's, Bangkok Thai, Baumhower's, Burger King, Domino's, Dragon City Buffet, El Rancho Mexican, Firehouse Subs, 5 Guys Burgers, Grand Buffet, Hooters, IHOP, Longhorn Steaks, Los Tacos, Marble Slab, McAlister's Deli, McDonald's, O'Charley's, Papa John's, Pizza Hut, Smoothie King, S China Rest., Starbucks, Subway, Taco Bell, Top of the Bay, Waffle House, Wendy's, Zaxby's, 🛏 Comfort Suites, Eastern Shore Motel, Hampton Inn, Hilton Garden, Homewood Suites, Microtel, ⊙ �H, AT&T, Dick's, GNC, Hobby Lobby, Hancock Fabrics, Home Depot, Office Depot, Radio Shack, SteinMart, TJ Maxx, to Blakeley SP
30	US 90/98, Battleship Pkwy, same as 27
27	US 90/98, Battleship Pkwy, Gov't St, **S** 🍴 Capt's Table Seafood, Felix's Fish Camp, R&R Seafood, Tacky Jack's Rest, Word's Rest, 🛏 Battleship Inn, ⊙ Lap's Grocery, to USS Alabama
26b	Water St, Mobile, downtown, **N** 🛏 Adventure Inn, Hampton Inn, Holiday Inn, Quality Inn, Renaissance, to Visitors Ctr
26a	Canal St (from eb), same as 26b
25b	Virginia St, Mobile, **N** 🅖 Shell/dsl
25a	Texas St (from wb, no return)

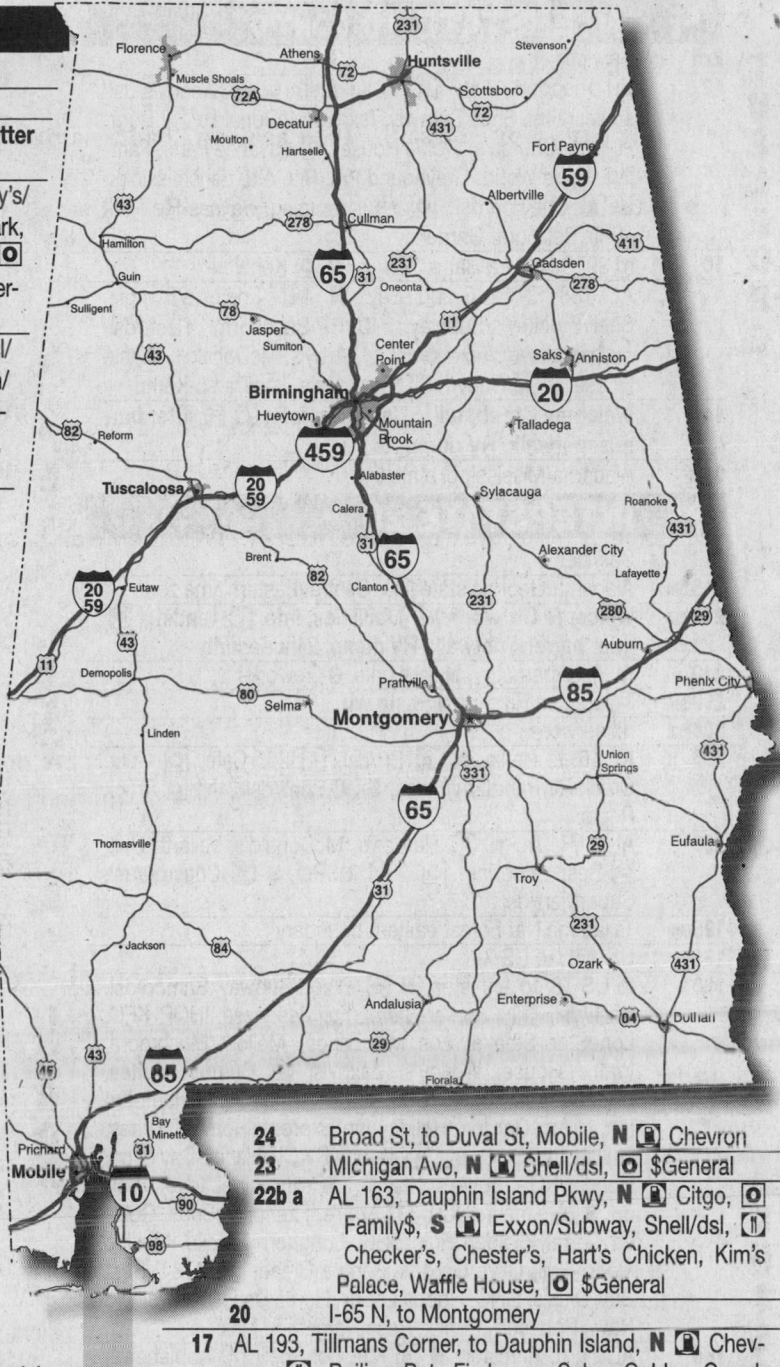

24	Broad St, to Duval St, Mobile, **N** 🅖 Chevron
23	Michigan Avo, **N** 🅖 Shell/dsl, ⊙ $General
22b a	AL 163, Dauphin Island Pkwy, **N** 🅖 Citgo, ⊙ Family$, **S** 🅖 Exxon/Subway, Shell/dsl, 🍴 Checker's, Chester's, Hart's Chicken, Kim's Palace, Waffle House, ⊙ $General
20	I-65 N, to Montgomery
17	AL 193, Tillmans Corner, to Dauphin Island, **N** 🅖 Chevron, 🍴 Boiling Pot, Firehouse Subs, Golden Corral, IHOP, Ruby Tuesday, Ryan's, Zaxby's, ⊙ �H, Big 10 Tire, Deep South RV Ctr, Lowe's, Office Depot, Radio Shack, Walmart/Subway
15b a	US 90, Tillmans Corner, to Mobile, **N** 🅖 Chevron, RaceWay, Shell, 🍴 Arby's, Burger King, Checker's, Domino's, Hooters, KFC, McDonald's, Papa John's, Pizza Hut, Popeye's, Russell's BBQ, Subway, Taco Bell, Waffle House, 🛏 Baymont Inn, Best Value Inn, Comfort Suites, Days Inn, EconoLodge, Hampton Inn, Holiday Inn, InTown Suites, La Quinta, Motel 6, Quality Inn, Red Roof Inn, Rodeway Inn, Super 8, Wingate Inn, ⊙ AutoZone, BigLots, CarQuest, $General, $Tree, Family$, Mike's Transmissions, O'Reilly Parts, Rite Aid, Sears Essentials, Walgreens, vet, **S** 🅖 Chevron, Exxon, Kangaroo, RaceWay/dsl, Shell/dsl, 🍴 Hardee's, Waffle House, ⊙ Advance Parts, B&R RV Ctr, Johnnys RV Ctr, Peterbilt, auto repair, tires, transmissions, USPO, vet

MOBILE

INTERSTATE 10 CONT'D

Exit	Services
13	to Theodore, **N** 🔲 Clark/dsl, 🏬/Wendy's/dsl/scales/24hr, Shell/Subway, Texaco/McDonald's, 🍴 Burger King, Church's, Waffle House, ⬛ Advance Parts, Family$, Food World, Greyhound Prk, Rite Aid, transmissions, **S** 🔲 Chevron/dsl, ⬛ I-10 Kamping, Paynes RV Park (4mi), Bellingraf Gardens
10	rd 39, Bayou La Batre, Dawes, **N** ⬛ Kenworth
4	AL 188 E, to Grand Bay, **N** 🔲 Energize/Blimpie, Shell/Stuckey's/Subway, TA/BP/Buckhorn Rest./dsl/scales/24hr/@, Texaco/dsl, 🍴 Arby's, McDonald's, Waffle House, **S** 🔲 Chevron, 🍴 Hardee's, ⬛ Trav-L-Kamp
1mm	**Welcome Ctr eb, full** ♿ **facilities, info,** 🚰, 🏧, **litter barrels, petwalk, RV dump**
0mm	Alabama/Mississippi state line

INTERSTATE 20

Exit	Services
215mm	Alabama/Georgia state line, Central/Eastern time zone
213mm	**Welcome Ctr wb, full** ♿ **facilities, info,** 🚰, **vending,** 🏧, **litter barrels, petwalk, RV dump, 24hr security**
210	AL 49, Abernathy, **N** fireworks, **S** fireworks
209mm	Tallapoosa River, **weigh sta wb**
208mm	no services
205	AL 46, to Heflin, **N** 🔲 BP/dsl, 🍴 205 Cafe, ⬛ Cane Creek RV Park (2mi), tires, **S** 🔲 Shell/dsl/24hr, ⬛ Truck Repair
199	AL 9, Heflin, **N** 🍴 Hardee's, McDonald's, Vallarta Grill, 🛏 Best Value Inn, ⬛ Ford, USPO, **S** 🔲 Chevron/dsl, SuperMart/dsl
198mm	Talladega Nat Forest eastern boundary
191	US 431, to US 78
188	to US 78, to Anniston, **N** 🔲 Exxon/Subway, Samco/dsl, Shell/dsl, 🍴 Cracker Barrel, Fuji Japanese, IHOP, KFC, LoneStar Steaks, Los Mexicanos, Mellow Mushroom, Waffle House, Wendy's, Zaxby's, 🛏 Comfort Suites, Country Inn&Suites, Courtyard, Fairfield Inn, Hampton Inn, Hilton Garden, Holiday Inn Express, Home 2 Suites, Quality Inn, Sleep Inn, ⬛ Dandy RV Ctr, Harley-Davidson, Honda, KOA, Lowe's, Nissan, O'Reilly Parts, Toyota/Scion, **S** 🔲 Chevron/dsl, 🍴 Arby's, Firehouse Subs, Golden Corral, Golden Rule BBQ, Longhorn Steaks, Mexico Lindo Grill, Olive Garden, Panera Bread, ⬛ AT&T, Best Buy, Dick's, GNC, Hobby Lobby, Home Depot, Kohl's, Old Navy, Petsmart, Publix, Ross, Target, TJ Maxx
185	AL 21, to Anniston, **N** 🔲 MapCo, Shell, 🍴 Applebee's, Arby's, Burger King, Capt D's, CiCi's Pizza, China Luck, Hardee's, HoneyBaked Ham, Jack's Rest., Logan's Roadhouse, McAlister's Deli, McDonald's, O'Charley's, Papa John's, Pizza Hut, Red Lobster, Shoney's, Sonic, Starbucks, Super Buffet, Taco Bell, Waffle House, Western Sizzlin, 🛏 Best Value Inn, Liberty Inn, Red Carpet Inn, ⬛ Advance Parts, BooksAMillion, CVS Drug, Dillard's, $General, Firestone/auto, JC Penney, Martin's Foods, Rite Aid, Sears/auto, Verizon, to Ft McClellan, **S** 🔲 Chevron/dsl, Delta Express, Kangaroo/dsl/scales, Murphy USA/dsl, RaceWay, Valero/Subway/dsl, 🍴 Chick-fil-A, Outback Steaks, Waffle House, Wendy's, 🛏 Comfort Inn, EconoLodge, Key West Inn, Motel 6, Super 8, ⬛ 🅷, Walmart, tires/repair
179	AL 202, to US 78, to Munford, Coldwater, **N** 🔲 Chevron/Subway/dsl, 🍴 China King, Jack's Rest., ⬛ Anniston Army Depot, $General, Rite Aid, Winn Dixie, **S** 🔲 Texaco/dsl

Exit	Services
173	AL 5, Eastaboga, **S** 🔲 MapCo/cafe, 🍴 DQ/Stuckey's, ⬛ to Speedway/Hall of Fame
168	AL 77, to Talladega, **N** 🔲 Citgo/dsl, Marathon/KFC/Taco Bell, QV/Domino's, 🍴 Jack's Rest, Waffle House, **S** 🔲 AOC/Burger King, Chevron/Subway/dsl, Race City TC/diner/dsl/scales, 🍴 McDonald's, MT Grill, Rana's Mexican, 🛏 Comfort Inn, Days Inn, McCaig Motel, ⬛ to Speedway, Hall of Fame
165	Embry Cross Roads, **N** 🔲 Hi-Tech/dsl, 🏬/Subway/dsl/scales/24hr, ⬛ Paradise Island RV Park, **S** 🔲 165 TP/Huddle House/dsl, I-20TrkStp/rest./dsl/scales/24hr, 🍴 JR's BBQ, 🛏 McCaig Motel
164mm	Coosa River
162	US 78, Riverside, **N** ⬛ Safe Harbor RV Park, **S** 🔲 Texaco/dsl, 🛏 Best Value Inn/rest
158	US 231, Pell City, **N** 🔲 Marathon/dsl, Murphy USA/dsl, 🍴 Arby's, Chick-fil-A, Cracker Barrel, El Cazador, Golden Rule BBQ, Jade E Chinese, Krystal, Wendy's, Zaxby's, 🛏 Comfort Suites, Hampton Inn, Holiday Inn Express, ⬛ **Urgent Care**, City Tire, $Tree, Home Depot, Radio Shack, Walgreens, Walmart/Subway, **S** 🔲 Chevron, Shell/dsl, Texaco/dsl, 🍴 Akita Japanese, Burger King, Hardee's, Jack's Rest., KFC, McDonald's, Pell City Steaks, Pizza Hut, Subway, Taco Bell, Waffle House, 🛏 Quality Inn, ⬛ 🅷, AutoZone, CVS Drug, $General, Ford, Fred's, Verizon
156	US 78 E, to Pell City, **S** 🔲 Chevron/dsl, Shell/dsl
153	US 78, Chula Vista
152	Cook Springs
147	Brompton, **N** 🔲 Citgo, Valero TC/dsl/scales/24hr, **S** 🔲 Chevron/dsl
144	US 411, Leeds, **N** 🔲 BP/dsl, RaceWay/dsl, Shell/Subway, 🍴 Arby's, Bojangles, Burger King, Cracker Barrel, Krystal, Logan's Roadhouse, Milo's Burgers, Pizza Hut, Ruby Tuesday, Waffle House, Wendy's, 🛏 Best Western, Comfort Inn, Super 8, ⬛ $Tree, Food Giant, RV camping, **S** 🔲 Chevron, RaceWay/dsl, 🍴 Capt D's, Chick-fil-A, El Cazador Mexican, Guadalajara Jalisco Mexican, Hardee's, KFC, Little Caesars, McDonald's, Supreme East Buffet, Taco Bell, Waffle House, 🛏 Days Inn, ⬛ AT&T, AutoZone, $General, Lowe's, O'Reilly Parts, Radio Shack, Walgreens, Walmart/Subway
140	US 78, Leeds, **N** ⬛ Distinctive Outlets/famous brands, **S** 🔲 Chevron, Marathon, 🍴 Subway, 🛏 Best Value Inn, Hampton Inn, ⬛ Bass Pro Shop
139mm	Cahaba River
136	I-459, S to Montgomery, Tuscaloosa
135	US 78, Old Leeds Rd, **N** 🔲 Shell, ⬛ B'ham Race Course
133	US 78, to Kilgore Memorial Dr, (wb return at 132), **N** 🔲 Chevron, Exxon/dsl, 🍴 Golden Rule BBQ, Hamburger Heaven, Jack's, Krystal, Waffle House, 🛏 Best Value Inn, Siesta Motel, same as 132, **S** 🔲 BP, 🍴 McDonald's, Zaxby's, 🛏 Hampton Inn, Holiday Inn Express, Quality Inn, ⬛ Sam's Club/dsl, Tire Ctr
132b a	US 78, Crestwood Blvd, **N** 🔲 Chevron, Exxon/dsl, 🍴 Golden Rule BBQ, Hamburger Heaven, Jack's, Krystal, Subway, Villa Fiesta Mexican, Waffle House, 🛏 Best Value Inn, Siesta Motel, ⬛ Aamco, $General, O'Reilly Parts, same as 133, **S** 🔲 Chevron, Exxon, Marathon/dsl, Shell, Texaco, 🍴 Arby's, Bojangles, Burger King, Capt D's, Chick-fil-A, El Cazador Mexican, Hacienda Mexican, IHOP, KFC, Logan's Roadhouse, McDonald's, Milo's Burgers, New China Buffet, Olive Garden, Pizza Hut,

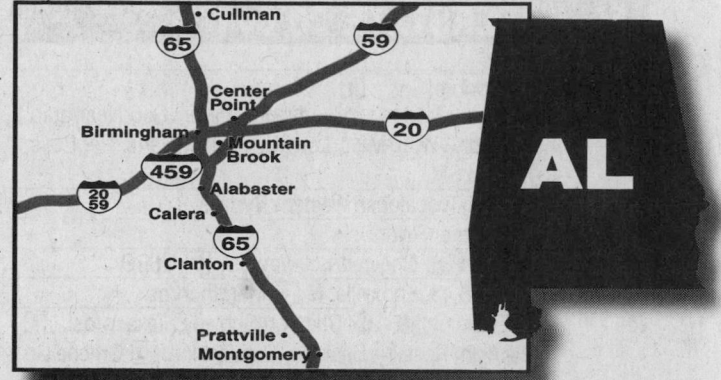

🅴 INTERSTATE 20 CONT'D

Exit	Services
132b a	Continued
	Starbucks, Taco Bell, Wendy's, 🛏 Delux Inn, Garden Suites, USA Lodge, 🄾 🄷 Advance Parts, Aldi Foods, $Tree, Firestone/auto, Home Depot, K-Mart, Office Depot, Radio Shack, Ross, TJ Maxx, Tuesday Morning, Walgreens, Walmart
130b	US 11, 1st Ave, **N** 🅖 Chevron, Marathon, Petro, 🄾 AutoZone, Piggly Wiggly, **S** 🅖 Exxon/dsl, 🍴 McDonald's, Pacific Seafood, 🛏 Relax Inn, Sky Inn
130a	I-59 N, to Gadsden

I-59 S and I-20 W run together from B'ham to Meridian, MS

Exit	Services
129	Airport Blvd, **N** 🛏 Clarion, 🄾 ✈, **S** 🅖 BP, Shell/dsl, 🍴 Hardee's, Kabob House, 🛏 Best Inn, Holiday Inn
128	AL 79, Tallapoosa St, **N** 🅖 Kangaroo/Subway/dsl/scales, Exxon/Wings/dsl
126b	31st St, **N** 🅖 Shell, Texaco/dsl, 🍴 McDonald's, 🄾 Family$
126a	US 31, US 280, 26th St, Carraway Blvd, **N** 🍴 Church's, KFC, Rally's
125b	22nd St, **N** 🍴 Subway, 🛏 Sheraton, Westin
125a	17th St, to downtown
124b a	I-65, S to Montgomery, N to Nashville
123	US 78, Arkadelphia Rd, **N** 🅖 Chevron, Jet-Pep, 🚆/Wendy's/dsl/scales/24hr (0.5mi), Shell/dsl, 🍴 Popeye's, 🛏 Days Inn, **S** 🄾 🄷, to Legion Field
121	Bush Blvd (from wb, no return) Ensley, **N** 🅖 BP, Exxon
120	AL 269, 20th St, Ensley Ave, **N** 🅖 Jet-Pep, 🍴 KFC, 🄾 Honda, **S** 🅖 BP, 🄾 🄷, Toyota/Scion
119b	Ave I (from wb)
119a	Lloyd Noland Pwky, **N** 🅖 Chevron/dsl, Sunoco/dsl, 🍴 Burger King, Fairfield Seafood, McDonald's, Subway, **S** 🅖 Mobil, Texaco, 🄾 🄷
118	AL 56, Valley Rd, Fairfield, **S** 🅖 Shell, 🍴 Papa John's, 🛏 Best Inn, 🄾 Urgent Care, Advance Parts, Home Depot, Radio Shack
115	Allison-Bonnett Memorial Dr, **N** 🅖 Marathon, RaceWay/dsl, Shell/dsl, 🍴 Church's, Jack's, Los Reyes, Subway, Zaxby's, 🄾 Advance Parts, O'Reilly Parts, USPO
113	18th Ave, to Hueytown, **S** 🅖 Chevron/dsl, Marathon, 🍴 McDonald's
112	18th St, 19th St, Bessemer, **N** 🅖 RaceWay/dsl, Shell, 🍴 Jack's Rest., 🄾 tire/repair, **S** 🅖 Chevron, Sunoco/dsl, 🍴 KFC, Muffaletta's Italian, Rally's, Sykes BBQ, 🄾 Advance Parts, FMS Drug, Lowe's, NAPA, O'Reilly Parts, Walgreens
110	AL Adventure Pkwy, **N** AL Adventure Funpark, **S** 🄷
108	US 11, AL 5 N, Academy Dr, **N** 🅖 Marathon, 🍴 Applebee's, Carnation Buffet, Catfish Cabin, Cracker Barrel, Waffle House, 🛏 Best Western, Comfort Inn, Country Inn&Suites, Fairfield Inn, Holiday Inn Express, Quality Inn, ValuePlace, 🄾 Chevrolet, Chrysler/Dodge/Jeep, Nissan, **S** 🅖 BP, Texaco/Church's/dsl, 🍴 Burger King, Domino's, Jade Garden, Little Caesars, McDonald's, Milo's Burgers, Ruby Tuesday, Sonic, Wendy's, Zaxby's, 🛏 Best Value Inn, Economy Inn, Hampton Inn, Motel 6, 🄾 🄷, Aldi Foods, BigLots, $Tree, Ford, PepBoys, Radio Shack, Verizon, Walmart/Subway, to civic ctr
106	I-459, N to Montgomery
104	Rock Mt Lakes, **S** 🅖 ⊕FLYING J/Subway/dsl/LP/24hr
100	to Abernant, **N** 🅖 ♥Loves/McDonald's/Subway/dsl/scales/24hr, 🄾 McCalla Camping, **S** 🅖 BP, Exxon, Petro/Chevron/rest./dsl/scales/24hr/@, 🄾 $General, Tannehill Ironworks Camping, Tannehill SP (3mi)

Exit	Services
97	US 11 S, AL 5 S, to W Blocton, **S** 🅖 Chevron/KFC/dsl, Exxon/Subway/dsl, Shell, Texaco/dsl, 🍴 Jack's Rest. La Tortilla, 🄾 Cahaba River NWR
89	Mercedes Dr, **N** 🛏 Greystone Inn, **S** 🄾 Mercedes Auto Plant
86	Vance, to Brookwood, **N** 🅖 BP/Huddle House/Subway/dsl, Shell/dsl/rest./24hr
85mm	🆁🆂 both lanes, full 🚻 facilities, 🅲, vending, 🗑, litter barrels, petwalk, RV dump
79	US 11, University Blvd, Coaling, **S** 🅖 Chevron/dsl, Texaco
77	Cottondale, **N** 🅖 Chevron/McDonald's, TA/BP/Subway/Taco Bell/dsl/scales/@, Wilco/Wendy's/dsl/scales/24hr, 🍴 Arby's, Pizza Hut, Ruby Tuesday, 🛏 Hampton Inn, Microtel, 🄾 Blue Beacon, SpeedCo, USPO, **S** Chevrolet
76	US 11, E Tuscaloosa, Cottondale, **N** 🅖 BP, Chevron, Shell/dsl, 🍴 Burger King, Cracker Barrel, Waffle House, 🛏 Centerstone Inn, Howard Johnson, ValuePlace, Western Motel, Wingate Inn, 🄾 Sunset 2 RV Park, transmissions, **S** 🅖 🚆/Subway/dsl/scales/24hr, Texaco/dsl, 🛏 Rodeway Inn
73	US 82, McFarland Blvd, Tuscaloosa, **N** 🅖 BP/dsl, Chevron/dsl, Marathon, RaceWay, Shell/dsl, 🍴 Applebee's, Arby's, Buffalo Wild Wings, Burger King, Capt D's, Chick-fil-A, Chipotle, 5 Guys Burgers, Full Moon BBQ, Jason's Deli, Kobe Japanese, Krispy Kreme, Krystal, Longhorn Steaks, Moe's SW Grill, O'Charley's, Olive Garden, Panera Bread, Popeye's, Red Lobster, Shrimp Basket, TCBY, Waffle House, 🛏 Best Western, Best Value Inn, Comfort Suites, Guest Lodge, Holiday Inn Express, Masters Inn, 🄾 🄷, Aamco, Advance Parts, AT&T, Barnes&Noble, Belk, Belle Foods, Best Buy, CVS Drug, Firestone/auto, Goodyear/auto, Home Depot, JC Penney, Michael's, Old Navy, PepBoys, Rite Aid, Sears/auto, SteinMart, Target, Verizon, vet, **S** 🅖 Jet-Pep, Marathon, 🍴 Checker's, Cheddar's, Chili's, Grand Buffet, Guthrie's, Hardee's, KFC, Logan's Roadhouse, McDonald's, Papa John's, Pizza Hut, Sonic, Subway, Taco Bell, Taco Casa, 🛏 Ambassador Inn, Candlewood Suites, Country Inn&Suites, Days Inn, EconoLodge, La Quinta, Motel 6, Quality Inn, Ramada Inn, Super 8, 🄾 Books-A-Million, Chrysler/Dodge/Jeep, $General, $Tree, FoodWorld, NAPA, Office Depot, Rite Aid, Sam's Club/gas, TJ Maxx, U-Haul, Walmart/Subway
71b	I-359, Al 69 N, to Tuscaloosa, **N** 🄾 🄷, U of AL, to Stillman Coll
71a	AL 69 S, to Moundville, **S** 🅖 Chevron, Citgo, MapCo/dsl, Shell/dsl, 🍴 Arby's, Chick-fil-A, Costa BBQ, Hooters, IHOP, OutBack Steaks, Pizza Hut, Ryan's, Waffle House, Wendy's, Zaxby's, 🛏 Baymont Inn, Courtyard, Fairfield 🄾 $General, repair/tires

(Left margin vertical labels: BIRMINGHAM, BESSEMER; Right margin vertical label: TUSCALOOSA)

AL

⬆E INTERSTATE 20 CONT'D

Exit	Services
71a	Continued Inn, Hilton Garden, ⊡ Advance Parts, Goodyear/auto, Kia/Mazda/VW, K-Mart, Lowe's, O'Reilly Parts, PepBoys, to Mound SM
68	Northport-Tuscaloosa Western Bypass
64mm	Black Warrior River
62	Fosters, N 🅖 Chevron/Subway/dsl, ⊡ USPO
52	US 11, US 43, Knoxville, N 🅖 Marathon/dsl
45	AL 37, Union, S 🅖 Chevron/Subway, Texaco/dsl, 🍴 South Fork Rest, 🛏 Best Inn, Comfort Inn, ⊡ Greene Co Greyhound Park
40	AL 14, Eutaw, N ⊡ to Tom Bevill Lock/Dam, S 🅖 BP, 🅗
39mm	🅟🅢 wb, full 🚻 facilities, 🅲, vending, 🖼 litter barrels, petwalk, RV dump
38mm	🅟🅢 eb, full 🚻 facilities, 🅲, vending, 🖼 litter barrels, petwalk, RV dump
32	Boligee, N 🅖 BP/rest./dsl/24hr, S 🅖 Chevron/Subway/dsl
27mm	Tombigbee River, Tenn-Tom Waterway
23	rd 20, Epes, to Gainesville
17	AL 28, Livingston, S 🅖 Chevron/Subway/dsl, Shell/dsl, Texaco/L&B/dsl/24hr, 🍴 Burger King, McDonald's, Pizza Hut, 🛏 Comfort Inn, Western Inn, ⊡ repair/24hr
8	AL 17, York, S 🅖 BP/New Orleans Grill/dsl/scales/@, 🛏 Best Inn, ⊡ 🅗
1	to US 80 E, Cuba, N 🅖 Rocking Chair Trkstp/Rest./dsl/, S 🅖 Chevron, Citgo/rest./dsl
.5mm	Welcome Ctr eb, full 🚻 facilities, 🅲, vending, 🖼 litter barrels, petwalk, RV dump
	I-20 E and I-59 N run together from Meridian, MS to B'ham
0mm	Alabama/Mississippi state line

⬆E INTERSTATE 22 (FUTURE)

Exit	Services
93	rd 77, (I-22 future begins/ends)
91	rd 105, to Brookside
89	rd 65, to Adamsville, Graysville
87	rd 112, to Graysville
85	US 78, Birmingham
81	rd 45, W Jefferson
78	rd 81, Dora, Sumiton, N 🅖 TJ's/dsl
72	rd 61, Cordova
70	rd 22, Cordova, Parish
65	Bevill Ind Pkwy, Jasper, N 🅖 RaceWay/dsl, 🛏 Hampton Inn (3mi), ⊡ 🅗, to Walker Co Lake, S 🅖 ❤Loves / McDonald's/Subway/dsl/scales/24hr, ⊡ Buick/Cadillac/Chevrolet/GMC
63	AIL 269, Jasper, Parish, N 🅖 Chevron/deli/dsl
61	AL 69, Jasper, Tuscaloosa, N 🅖 RJ's
57	AL 118 E, Jasper, S 🅖 Chevron, Exxon, 🍴 Panter's Place Rest
52	AL 118, Carbon Hill, S 🛏 Shadowbrook Inn
46	rd 11, Carbon Hill, Nauvoo, S 🅖 Shell
39	AL 13, Natural Bridge, Eldridge
34	AL 233, Glen Allen, Natural Bridge
30	AL 129, Brilliant, Winfield, S 🅖 Shell/deli/dsl, Texaco/deli/dsl, 🛏 EconoLodge, Hampton Inn
26	AL 44, Brilliant, Guin, S 🛏 Holiday Inn Express, other: 🅗
22	rd 45
16	US 43, US 278, Hamilton, Guin, S 🅖 Shell/deli/dsl

14	Hamilton, N 🅖 Texaco/dsl, 🍴 Huddle House, 🛏 Days Inn (1mi), EconoLodge (1mi), Keywest Inn
11	AL 17, Hamilton, Sulligent, N 🅖 Citgo/dsl, ⊡ 🅗
7	Hamilton, Weston, N 🅗
3	rd 33
0mm	Alabama/Mississippi State Line

⬆N INTERSTATE 59

Exit	Services
241.5mm	Alabama/Georgia state line, Central/Eastern time zone
241mm	Welcome Ctr sb, full 🚻 facilities, 🅲, vending, 🖼 litter barrels, petwalk, RV dump
239	to US 11, Sulphur Springs Rd, E ⊡ camping
231	AL 40, AL 117, Hammondville, Valley Head, E ⊡ DeSoto SP, camping (5mi), W 🅖 Victory Fuel
224	49th St, to Ft Payne
222	US 11, to Ft Payne, E 🅖 Delta, ⊡ Chevrolet, 1 mi E 🍴 Arby's, Hardee's, Jack's Rest., KFC, Krystal, New Asian Buffet, Pizza Hut, SteviB's Pizza, Subway, 🛏 Country Hearth Inn, ⊡ Foodland/dsl, W 🅖 JetPep/dsl, 🍴 Waffle King
218	AL 35, Ft Payne, E 🍴 Capt D's, DQ, Don Chico Mexican, Jack's, Jefferson's Burgers, McDonald's, New China, Papa John's, Quiznos, Taco Bell, Wendy's, Western Sizzlin, Zaxby's, ⊡ Advance Parts, AutoZone, BigLots, Buick/GMC, Chrysler/Dodge/Jeep, $General, O'Reilly Parts, W 🅖 Kangaroo/dsl, MapCo, Murphy USA/dsl, Victory Fuel, 🍴 Burger King, Chow King, Cracker Barrel, Hardee's, Ryan's, Ruby Tuesday, Santa Fe Steaks, Subway, Waffle House, 🛏 Days Inn, EconoLodge, Hampton Inn, Holiday Inn Express, ⊡ 🅗, AT&T, $Tree, Ford/Lincoln, GNC, K-Mart, Lowe's, Radio Shack, Verizon, Walgreens, Walmart, Will's Creek RV Park
205	AL 68, Collinsville, E 🅖 Delta, 🍴 Jack's Rest., 🛏 Traveler's Inn, ⊡ to Little River Canyon, Weiss Lake, W 🅖 BP/dsl, MapCo
188	AL 211, to US 11, Gadsden, E 🅖 Jet-Pep, ⊡ Noccalula Falls Camping, W 🅖 Clean Fuels/dsl/E85
183	US 431, US 278, Gadsden, E 🅖 Jet-Pep/dsl, Shell, Texaco/dsl, 🍴 Magic Burger, Waffle House, 🛏 Days Inn, Rodeway Inn, Travelodge, ⊡ st police, W 🅖 Chevron, Exxon, Jet-Pep, 🍴 Krystal, McDonald's, Pizza Hut, Subway, Taco Bell
182	I-759, to Gadsden
181	AL 77, Rainbow City, to Gadsden, E 🅖 Petro/rest./dsl/scales/24hr/@, 🍴 Ezell's Fishcamp, 🛏 Days Inn, W 🅖 Citgo, Kangaroo/dsl, Murphy Express/dsl, Pure/dsl, 🍴 Arby's, Bubba Rito's SW Grill, Cracker Barrel, Domino's, Hardee's, Los Arcos, Lucky Wok, Old Mexico Grille, Ray's BBQ, Ruby Tuesday, Subway, Waffle House, Wendy's, 🛏 Best Western, Comfort Suites, Fairfield Inn, Hampton Inn, Holiday Inn Express, ⊡ $General, $Tree, O'Reilly Parts, Radio Shack, Walmart/Papa John's
174	to Steele, E 🅖 ❤Loves/Subway/Chester's/dsl/scales/24hr, W 🅖 JetPep/dsl, Shell/rest/dsl
168mm	🅟🅢 sb, full 🚻 facilities, 🅲, vending, 🖼 litter barrels, petwalk, RV dump
166	US 231, to Ashville, Oneonta, E 🅖 BP, W 🅖 Texaco/dsl, 🍴 Jack's Rest., Huddle House, Subway
165mm	🅟🅢 nb, full 🚻 facilities, 🅲, vending, 🖼 litter barrels, petwalk, RV dump
156	AL 23, to US 11, Springville, to St Clair Springs, W 🅖 Citgo/dsl, 🍴 Azteca's Mexican, China Stix, Hardee's, Pizza Hut, Waffle House, ⊡ AT&T, Curves, $Tree, Walmart/Subway

FT PAYNE

GADSDEN

🔼🔽 INTERSTATE 59 CONT'D

Exit	Services
154	AL 174, Springville, to Odenville, **W** 🅖 Chevron, MapCo, Shell/dsl, Valero/Subway, 🍴 Choppin Block Rest., Huck's Ribshack, Jack's Rest., McDonald's, Sal's Rest., Smokin Grill BBQ, 🅞 vet
148	to US 11, Argo, **E** 🅖 BP
143	Mt Olive Church Rd, Deerfoot Pkwy, **E** 🅖 Chevron/dsl/CNG, Shell/dsl (1mi), 🅞 Publix (1mi)
141	to Trussville, Pinson, **E** 🅖 Bama Gas, Shell/Subway/dsl, Texaco/dsl, 🍴 Applebee's, Cracker Barrel, LoneStar Steaks, McDonald's, Papa John's, Pizza Hut, Taco Bell, Waffle House, Wendy's, 🏨 Comfort Inn, Holiday Inn Express, Quality Inn, 🅞 Harley-Davidson, **W** 🅖 BP, Chevron, Shell/dsl, 🍴 Arby's, Buffalo Wild Wings, Burger King, Chick-fil-A, Costa's Italian, DQ, East Buffet, Frontera Grill, Jack's, Konomi Japanese, Krystal, Little Caesars, Milo's Burgers, Moe's SW Grill, Momma Goldberg's Deli, Palace Asian, Paul's Hotdogs, Ruby Tuesday, Seafood&Chicken Box, Whataburger, Zaxby's, 🅞 Ace Hardware, Advance Parts, Aldi Foods, AT&T, BigLots, CVS Drug, $Tree, GNC, K-Mart, Kohl's, Marshalls, Office Depot, Petsmart, Sam's Club/gas, Walgreens, Walmart/Subway, vet
137	I-459 S, to Montgomery, Tuscaloosa
134	to AL 75, Roebuck Pkwy, **W** 🅖 Chevron, Marathon/Kangaroo, Murphy USA/dsl, Shell/dsl, 🍴 Arby's, Burger King, Chick-fil-A, Krystal, McDonald's, Milo's Burgers, Pizza Hut, Ruby Tuesday, Taco Bell, Waffle House, 🏨 Best Inn, 🅞 🅷, Aldi Foods, AT&T, CVS Drug, $Tree, GNC, Honda, NTB, O'Reilly Parts, Rite Aid, V Tires, Walgreens, Walmart
133	4th St, to US 11 (from nb), **W** 🍴 Papa John's, 🅞 $General, Suzuki, USPO, same as 134
132	US 11 N, 1st Ave, **E** same as 131, **W** 🅖 Chevron, Shell, 🍴 Krispy Kreme, 🅞 city park
131	Oporto-Madrid Blvd (from nb), **E** 🅖 Chevron, Marathon/Subway, 🍴 Church's, Little Caesars, Rally's, 🅞 CVS Drug, Family$, O'Reilly Parts, U-Haul, same as 132
130	I-20, E to Atlanta, W to Tuscaloosa

I-59 S and I-20 W run together from B'ham to Mississippi. See Alabama Interstate 20.

🔼🔽 INTERSTATE 65

Exit	Services
366mm	Alabama/Tennessee state line
365	AL 53, to Ardmore, **E** 🅖 Pure, 🏨 Budget Inn
364mm	**Welcome Ctr sb, full ♿ facilities, info, ☎, vending, 🚮, litter barrels, petwalk, RV dump**
361	Elkmont, **W** 🅖 BP/dsl, HQ/rest./dsl, 🍴 Momma D's Rest., 🅞 antiques, repair
354	US 31 S, to Athens, **W** 🅖 Chevron, Texaco/dsl, 🍴 Capt D's, China Dragon, Domino's, Jack's Rest., Little Caesars, McDonald's, Pizza Hut, Rooster's Cafe, Subway, 🏨 Mark Motel, 🅞 🅷, Advance Parts, CVS Drug, $General, K-Mart, Northgate RV Park, Piggly Wiggly, Rite Aid, Walgreens, city park
351	US 72, to Athens, Huntsville, **E** 🅖 Exxon, RaceWay, Shell/Subway, Texaco/dsl, 🍴 Burger King, Clark's Rest., Cracker Barrel, Lawler's BBQ, McDonald's/RV Parking, New China Buffet, Pepper's Deli, Waffle House, Wendy's, 🏨 Country Hearth Inn, Hampton Inn, Quality Inn, Travel Inn, 🅞 AT&T, Publix, Russell Stover, Verizon, vet, **W** 🅖 BP, Citgo/dsl, Murphy USA, 🍴 Applebee's, Arby's,

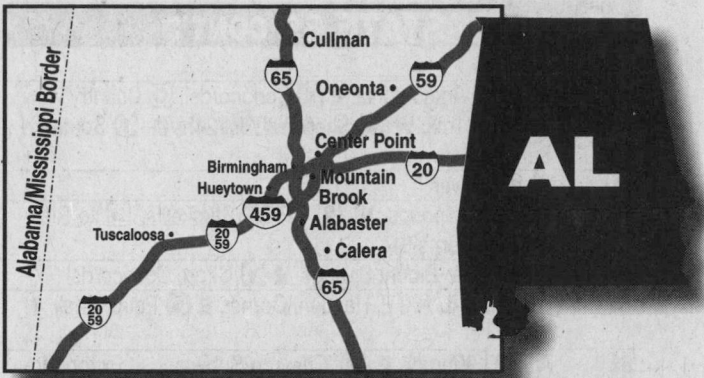

Exit	Services
351	Continued Bojangles, Burger King, Catfish Cabin, Casa Blanca Mexican, Chick-fil-A, Hardee's, KFC, Krystal, Logan's Roadhouse, Papa John's, Papa Murphy's, Pizza Hut, Ruby Tuesday, Shoney's, Sonic, Starbucks, Steak-Out, Subway, Taco Bell, Zaxby's, 🏨 Best Western, Days Inn, Holiday Inn Express, Sleep Inn, Super 8, 🅞 🅷, Advance Parts, Big 10 Tire, Chevrolet, Chrysler/Dodge/Jeep, $General, $tree, Ford/Lincoln, Goodyear/auto, Lowe's, O'Reilly Parts, Radio Shack, Staples, Verizon, Walmart, to Joe Wheeler SP
347	Brownsferry Rd, Huntsville, **W** Swan Creek RV Park
340b	I-565, to Huntsville, to Alabama Space & Rocket Ctr
340a	AL 20, to Decatur, **W** 🅖 Chevron/dsl, RaceWay, **2 mi W** 🏨 Courtyard, Hampton Inn, Holiday Inn
337mm	Tennessee River
334	AL 67, Priceville, to Decatur, **E** 🅖 BP/dsl, RaceWay/dsl, 🍴 JW's Steaks, 🏨 Days Inn, Super 8, 🅞 $General, **W** 🅖 Chevron, 🍴 Subway/Wendy's/dsl/scales/24hr, 🍴 Burger King, DQ, Hardee's, Krystal, McDonald's/playplace, Smokehouse BBQ, Waffle House, 🏨 Comfort Inn, 🅞 🅷, Hood RV Ctr
328	AL 36, Hartselle, **E** 🍴 Cracker Barrel, **W** 🅖 BP, Cowboys/dsl, Jet-Pep/dsl, Shell, 🍴 Huddle House, 🏨 Country Hearth Inn
325	Thompson Rd, to Hartselle
322	AL 55, to US 31, to Falkville, Eva, **E** 🅖 BP/Chester's/dsl, **W** 🅖 Chevron, Loves/McDonald's/Subway/dsl/scales/24hr, 🍴 Full House Rest., 🅞 $General
318	US 31, to Lacon, **E** 🅖 BP/DQ/Stuckey's, 🏨 Lacon Motel
310	AL 157, Cullman, West Point, **E** 🅖 BP, Conoco/Subway/dsl, Exxon, Shell/dsl, Texaco/Wendy's/dsl, 🍴 Arby's, Backyard Burger, Burger King, Cracker Barrel, Denny's, KFC, McDonald's, New China, Ruby Tuesday, Taco Bell, Waffle House, 🏨 Best Western, Comfort Suites, Hampton Inn, Holiday Inn Express, Quality Inn, Sleep Inn, 🅞 🅷, Buick/GMC, Ford/Lincoln, Piggly Wiggly, **W** 🅖 BP/dsl, Exxon/dsl, 🏨 Super 8
308	US 278, Cullman, **E** 🏨 Days Inn, **W** 🅖 Chevron, 🅞 flea mkt
304	AL 69 N, Good Hope, to Cullman, **E** 🅖 Exxon/dsl, Jet-Pep, Shell/rest/dsl/scales, 🍴 Hardee's, Jack's Rest., Waffle House, 🏨 EconoLodge, 🅞 🅷, Good Hope Camping, Kountry Mile RV Ctr, dsl/rv repair, **W** 🅖 Jet-Pep, to Smith Lake Camping, 🅞 $General
301mm	**🆁🆂 both lanes, full ♿ facilities, ☎, vending, 🚮, litter barrels, petwalk, RV dump**
299	AL 69 S, to Jasper, **E** 🅞 Millican RV Ctr, **W** 🅖 Dodge City/Conoco/rest./dsl/scales/24hr, HQ, Shell/McDonald's/dsl, Texaco/dsl, 🍴 Jack's Rest., Subway, 🅞 CarQuest

Vertical side labels: ATHENS · DECATUR · CULLMAN

AL

⬆N INTERSTATE 65 CONT'D

Exit	Services
291	AL 91, to Arkadelphia, **E** 🅟 Conoco/dsl, 🅞 Country View RV Park (1mi), **W** 🅟 Shell/rest./dsl/24hr/@, 🍴 Southern Sunrise Cafe
291mm	Warrior River
289	to Blount Springs, **W** 🅟 BP/DQ/Stuckey's, 🅞 to Rickwood Caverns SP
287	US 31 N, to Blount Springs, **E** 🅟 Citgo, Conoco/dsl
284	US 31 S, AL 160 E, Hayden, Corner, **E** 🅟 Petro, Shell, **W** tires
282	AL 140, Warrior, **E** 🅟 Chevron/Subway/dsl, Exxon/McDonald's, FuelZ/dsl, 🍴 Hardee's, Pizza Hut, Taco Bell, **W** 🅟 BP
281	US 31, to Warrior, **E** 🅞 Chevrolet
280	to US 31, to Warrior, **E** 🅞 Chevrolet
279mm	Warrior River
275	to US 31, Morris
272	Mt Olive Rd, **W** 🅟 Shell/dsl, **W** 🅟 BP/dsl, Chevron/dsl, 🍴 Jack's Rest., 🅞 $General
271	Fieldstown Rd, **E** 🅟 BP/Circle K, Chevron/dsl, Exxon, Murphy USA/dsl, RaceWay/dsl, 🍴 Arby's, Chick-fil-A, China Garden, Guthrie's Diner, Habanero's Mexican, Jim'n Nick's BBQ, KFC, Little Caesars, McDonald's, Milo's Burgers, Pasquales Pizza, Pizza Hut, Ruby Tuesday, Ryan's, Sonic, Subway, Taco Bell, Waffle House, Wendy's, Zaxby's, 🏨 Microtel, 🅞 Advance Parts, AT&T, AutoZone, $General, $Tree, Hobby Lobby, Kia, NAPA, Publix, Radio Shack, Verizon, Walgreens, Walmart/McDonald's, **W** 🅟 Shell/dsl, 🍴 Cracker Barrel, 🏨 Best Western
267	Walkers Chapel Rd, to Fultondale, **E** 🅟 Chevron/dsl, JetPep, Murphy Express/dsl, Shell/Subway/dsl, 🍴 Applebee's, Arby's, Burger King, Casa Fiesta, Chick-fil-A, Chili's, China One, Domino's, Firehouse Subs, 5 Guys Burgers, Fullmoon BBQ, Hardee's, Jack's Rest., Logan's Roadhouse, McDonald's, O'Charley's, Outback Steaks, Stix Asian, Waffle House, Whataburger, Zaxby's, 🏨 Comfort Suites, Fairfield Inn, Hampton Inn, Holiday Inn Express, La Quinta, 🅞 AAA, AT&T, Best Buy, Books-A-Million, CVS Drug, $General, GNC, JC Penney, Lowe's, O'Reilly Parts, Rite Aid, Ross, Target, Verizon, Volvo Trucks, Winn-Dixie, USPO, Urgent Care, **W** 🅟 Chevron/dsl, 🍴 Porky's Pride BBQ
266	US 31, Fultondale, **E** 🅟 Chevron/dsl, 🏨 Super 8
265	I-22 W, to Memphis
264	41st Ave, **W** 🅟 ⭐FLYING J/Denny's/dsl/LP/scales/24hr
263	33rd Ave, **E** 🅟 Chevron/dsl, 🏨 Apex Motel, **W** 🅟 Exxon
262b a	16th St, Finley Ave, **E** 🅟 BP, Marathon/dsl, Shell/dsl, 🅞 Kenworth, **W** 🅟 Chevron, Fuel City/dsl, Mobil/dsl/scales, 🍴 Capt D's, McDonald's, Popeye's
261b a	I-20/59, E to Gadsden, W to Tuscaloosa
260b a	6th Ave N, **E** 🅟 BP, Shell, Texaco, 🍴 Mrs Winner's, 🏨 Tourway Inn, 🅞 Chevrolet, Chrysler/Dodge/Jeep, Hyundai, Nissan, Subaru, **W** 🅟 Chevron/dsl, 🅞 Tire Pros, to Legion Field
259b a	University Blvd, 4th Ave, 5th Ave, **E** 🅟 Chevron/dsl, 🍴 Capt D's, McDonald's, Ted's Cafeteria, 🅞 🏥, **W** 🅟 Chevron/dsl, 🅞 Goodyear
258	Green Springs Ave, **E** 🅟 Chevron, Shell, Sunoco/dsl, 🍴 Exotic Wings
256b a	Oxmoor Rd, **E** 🅟 Exxon, Mobil/dsl, Shell, 🍴 Acapulco Grill, Alfredo's Pizza, Burger King, Domino's, Firehouse

---

B I R M I N G H A M

Exit	Services
256b a	Continued Subs, Hunan Rest., KFC, Krystal, McDonald's, Paw Paw Patch, San Miguel Mexican, Tai Pei Bistro, The Baskits, Zaxby's, 🏨 Howard Johnson, 🅞 Urgent Care, Aldi Foods, AutoZone, BigLots, Firestone/auto, Food World, Goodyear/auto, K-Mart, Midas, Office Depot, Omega Tire Pros, PepBoys, Publix, Tuesday Morning, Walmart Mkt, **W** 🅟 Chevron, Texaco/dsl, 🍴 Hamburger Heaven, Hardee's, Jim'n Nick's BBQ, Waffle House, 🏨 Best Value Inn, Comfort Inn, EconoLodge, Motel 6, Quality Inn, Super 8, 🅞 Batteries+, Valley Tire, vet
255	Lakeshore Dr, **E** 🅟 BP/Circle K, 🅞 🏥, to Samford U, **W** 🅟 Chevron, Shell, 🍴 Arby's, Chili's, Chick-fil-A, Costas BBQ, Hooters, IHOP, Landry's Seafood, McAlister's Deli, McDonald's, Milo's Burger, Moe's SW Grill, Mr Wang's, O'Charley's, Okinawa Grill, Outback Steaks, Starbucks, Subway, Taco Bell, Taco Casa, Wendy's, 🏨 Best Western, Candlewood Suites, Country Inn&Suites, Drury Inn, Extended Stay, Hampton Inn, Hilton Garden, Holiday Inn, La Quinta, Residence Inn, Sun Suites, TownePlace Suites, 🅞 AT&T, $Tree, Goodyear/auto, Hobby Lobby, Lowe's, Old Navy, Radio Shack, Sam's Club/gas, Verizon, Walmart/ Subway
254	Alford Ave, Shades Crest Rd, **E** 🅟 Chevron, 🅞 vet, **W** 🅟 BP/dsl, Shell/dsl
252	US 31, Montgomery Hwy, **E** 🅟 Chevron, Shell, Sunoco, Texaco/dsl, 🍴 Arby's, Backyard Burger, Bruster's, Capt D's, ChuckECheese's, Hardee's, Ichiban Japanese, Milo's Burger, Waffle House, 🏨 Baymont Inn, Days Inn, 🅞 🏥, Aamco, GMC, PepBoys, NAPA, Verizon, Volvo, VW, vet, **W** 🅟 Exxon/dsl, Shell, Sunoco/dsl, 🍴 Burger King, Chick-fil-A, Dave's Deli, FishMkt Rest., Full Moon BBQ, Golden Rule BBQ, Habanero's Mexican, Krispy Kreme, Krystal, Mandarin House, Mexico Lindo, McDonald's, Outback Steaks, Papa John's, Papa Murphy's, Salvatore's Pizza, Starbucks, Subway, Waffle House, 🏨 EconoLodge, 🅞 Acura, Advance Parts, Books-A-Million, Buick, Cadillac, Chevrolet, Chrysler/Dodge/Jeep, $Tree, Firestone, Goodyear/auto, Honda, Hyundai, Mr Transmission, Nissan, Publix, Rite Aid, Staples, TJ Maxx, vet
250	I-459, to US 280
247	rd 17, Valleydale Rd, **E** 🅟 BP/Circle K, 🍴 Hardee's, Jeffersons Wings, 🅞 Goodyear/auto, Lowe's, **W** 🅟 Marathon, RaceWay/dsl, Shell/dsl, 🍴 Arby's, Backyard Burger, IHOP, Milo's Burgers, Papa John's, RagTime Café, Subway, Waffle House, Zapatas Mexican, 🏨 Fairfield Inn, Homewood Suites, InTown Suites, La Quinta, 🅞 O'Reilly Parts, Rite Aid, Publix, Walgreens, vet
246	AL 119, Cahaba Valley Rd, **E** 🅞 to Oak Mtn SP, **W** 🅟 Chevron, Kangaroo/Subway/dsl/scales, Murphy USA/dsl, RaceWay/dsl, Shell, 🍴 Applebee's, Arby's, Burger King, Capt D's, Chick-fil-A, Cracker Barrel, DQ, Dunkin Donuts, Ezell's Fishcamp, Flame's Steakhouse, Golden Corral, Hooters, Johnny Ray's BBQ, KFC, Krystal, Margarita Grill, McAlister's Deli, McDonald's, Pizza Hut, Purple Onion, Ruby Tuesday, Shoney's, Sonic, Taco Bell, TX Roadhouse, 2 Pesos Mexican, Waffle House, Wendy's, Whataburger, 🏨 Best Western, Comfort Suites, Fairfield Inn, Hampton Inn, Holiday Inn Express, Quality Inn, Ramada, Sleep Inn, Travelodge, ValuePlace, 🅞 🏥, Advance Parts, AutoZone, $Tree, Firestone/auto, Harley-Davidson, Kia, Mazda, NAPA, O'Reilly Parts, Verizon, Walmart

H O O V E R

F U L T O N D A L E

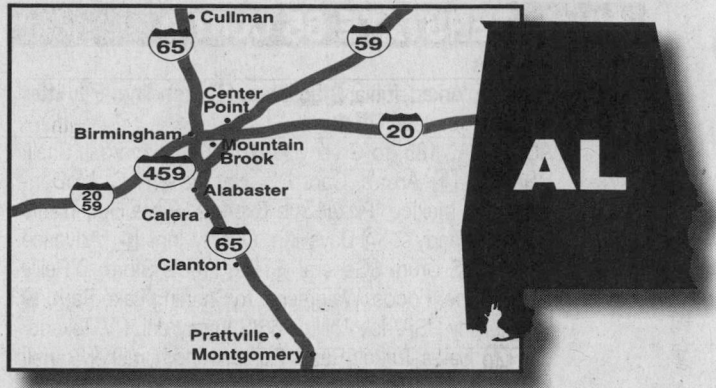

INTERSTATE 65 CONT'D

PELHAM

Exit	Services
242	rd 52, Pelham, **E** 🅿 Chevron/dsl, Exxon/dsl, Shell/dsl, 🍴 Johnny Ray's BBQ, Subway, Ⓞ CVS Drug, Publix, **W** 🛏 Shelby Motel (2mi), Ⓞ🅷, Good Sam Camping (1mi)
238	US 31, Alabaster, Saginaw, **E** 🅿 Murphy USA/dsl, 🍴 Arby's, Buffalo Wild Wings, Chick-fil-A, DQ, Firehouse Subs, Full Moon BBQ, Habanero's Mexican, HoneyBaked Ham, Jim'n Nick's BBQ, Longhorn Steaks, McDonald's, Mizu Japanese, Moe's SW Grill, Momma Goldberg Deli, O'Charley's, Olive Garden, Panda House, Panera Bread, Ruby Tuesday, Starbucks, Steak'n Shake, Taco Bell, 🛏 Candlewood Suites, Ⓞ **Urgent Care**, AT&T, Belk, Best Buy, Books-A-Million, $Tree, GNC, JC Penney, Lowe's, NTB, Old Navy, Petsmart, Radio Shack, Ross, Target, TJ Maxx, Walmart/Subway, **W** 🅿 Cannon, Chevron/dsl, Shell/dsl, 🍴 Waffle House, Whataburger, **2 mi W** 🛏 Shelby Motel, Ⓞ🅷
234	Shelby County ✈, **E** 🅿 BP/Subway/dsl, **W** 🅿 Chevron/dsl, Shell/dsl, Ⓞ Buick/GMC, Camping World RV Ctr, vet
231	US 31, Saginaw, **E** 🅿 GasBoy, Murphy USA/dsl, Shell, 🍴 Bojangles, Capt D's, Cracker Barrel, Ezell's Catfish Cabin, McDonald's, Milo's Burgers, Subway, Taco Bell, Waffle House, Zaxby's, Zopapan Mexican, 🛏 Hampton Inn, Quality Inn, Ⓞ AT&T, Burton RV Ctr, $Tree, Publix, Radio Shack, Rolling Hills RV Park, Verizon, Walmart/Subway, **W** 🍴 3D Dogs Cafe
228	AL 25, to Calera, **E** 🅿 Marathon/dsl, Shell/dsl, 🛏 Best Value Inn, **W** 🅿 Chevron/dsl, 🍴 Hardee's (1mi), Subway, Ⓞ $General, Family$, to Brierfield Iron Works SP (15mi)
227mm	Buxahatchie Creek
219	Union Grove, Thorsby, **E** 🅿 Chevron/dsl, Exxon/Subway/dsl, Ⓞ Peach Queen Camping, **W** 🅿 Shell/dsl, 🍴 Jack's Rest., Smokey Hollow Rest.
213mm	Ⓡ both lanes, full Ⓖ facilities, 🍴 vending, 🚻 litter barrels, petwalk, RV dump

CLANTON

Exit	Services
212	AL 145, Clanton, **E** 🅿 Chevron/dsl, Ⓞ Nissan, Toyota/Scion, **W** 🅿 Texaco/Subway, Headco/dsl, Ⓞ🅷, Buick/Chevrolet/GMC, Chrysler/Dodge/Jeep, One Big Peach
208	Clanton, **E** 🅿 💙Loves/Arby's/dsl/scales/24hr, Ⓞ Higgins Ferry RV Park (8mi), **W** 🅿 Exxon/dsl, 🍴 Shoney's, 🛏 Clanton Inn, Ⓞ Dandy RV Park/Ctr, Heaton Pecans, KOA
205	US 31, AL 22, to Clanton, **E** 🅿 Jet-Pep/dsl/E85, Shell/dsl, Texaco/dsl, 🍴 McDonald's, Waffle House, Whataburger, 🛏 Best Western, Days Inn, Holiday Inn Express, Scottish Inn, Ⓞ Peach Park, to Confed Mem Park (9mi), **0-2 mi W** 🅿 Chevron/dsl, Murphy USA/dsl, Shell/dsl, 🍴 Boomerang's Grill, Burger King, Capt D's, Jack's Rest., KFC, New China Buffet, Pizza Hut, San Marcos Mexican, Subway, Taco Bell, Wendy's, Zaxby's, 🛏 Key West Inn, Ⓞ $General, $Tree, Durbin Farms Mkt, Verizon, Walmart
200	to Verbena, **E** 🅿 Texaco/dsl, **W** 🅿 Sunoco
195	Worlds Largest Confederate Flag
186	US 31, Pine Level, **E** Ⓞ Confederate Mem Park (13mi), **W** 🅿 Chevron/dsl, Exxon/dsl, Texaco/Subway/dsl, 🍴 Shann's Kitchen, 🛏 Knights Inn, Ⓞ🅷
181	AL 14, to Prattville, **E** 🅿 Chevron/dsl, Entec/dsl, 🍴 Jack's, **W** 🅿 BP, Diamond/DQ/dsl, Marathon/Kangaroo, QV, 🍴 Cracker Barrel, Los Toros, McDonald's, Ruby Tuesday, Subway, Waffle House, Wendy's, 🛏 EconoLodge, Hometowne Suites, La Quinta, Quality Inn, Super 8, Ⓞ🅷

MILLBROOK

Exit	Services
179	US 82 W, Millbrook, **E** 🅿 Chevron/dsl, 🛏 Country Inn&Suites, Key West Inn, Sleep Inn, Ⓞ K&K RV Ctr/Park, **0-2 mi W** 🅿 Liberty, Murphy Express/dsl, RaceWay/dsl, Shell/dsl, 🍴 Applebee's, Arby's, Beef'O'Brady's, Bruster's, Burger King, Capt. D's, Chick-fil-A, CiCi's Pizza, City Buffet, El Patron, Firehouse Subs, Hardee's, IHOP, Jim'n Nick's BBQ, KFC, Krystal, Las Casitas Mexican, Logan's Roadhouse, Longhorn Steaks, McAlister's Deli, McDonald's, Mellow Mushroom, Mexico Tipico, Moe's SW Grill, O'Charley's, Olive Garden, Outback Steaks, Popeye's, Ryan's, Shoney's, Sonic, Steak'n Shake, Subway, Waffle House, Zaxby's, 🛏 Baymont Inn, Courtyard, Days Inn, Hampton Inn, Holiday Inn Express, Howard Johnson, Rodeway Inn, Ⓞ **Urgent Care**, AT&T, AutoZone, Bass Pro Shops, Belk, Best Buy, BigLots, Books-A-Million, Chevrolet, CVS Drug, $General, $Tree, Firestone/auto, Food World, Ford, GNC, Hobby Lobby, Home Depot, JC Penney, K-Mart, Kohl's, Lowe's, Michael's, Office Depot, O'Reilly Parts, PepBoys, Petsmart, Publix, Ross, Target, TJ Maxx, Verizon, Walmart, vet
176	AL 143 N (from nb, no return), Millbrook, Coosada
173	AL 152, North Blvd, to US 231
172mm	Alabama River
172	Clay St, Herron St, **E** 🛏 Embassy Suites, Hampton Inn, Renaissance Hotel, **W** 🅿 Chevron/dsl
171	I-85 N, Day St

MONTGOMERY

Exit	Services
170	Fairview Ave, **E** 🅿 Citgo/Subway, Gas Depot, 🍴 Church's, McDonald's, Wing Master, Ⓞ Advance Parts, AutoZone, CVS Drug, Family$, O'Reilly Parts, Piggly Wiggly, Rite Aid, **W** 🅿 Exxon, Ⓞ Calhoun Foods, Family$
169	Edgemont Ave (from sb), **E** 🅿 Liberty
168	US 80 E, US 82, South Blvd, **E** 🅿 BP/dsl, Entec/dsl, Kangaroo/dsl, TA/Marathon/Country Pride/dsl/24hr/@, 🍴 Arby's, Burger King, Capt D's, KFC, McDonald's, Popeye's, Pizza Hut, Taco Bell, Waffle House, 🛏 Best Inn, Economy Inn, Ⓞ🅷, **W** 🅿 Chevron/dsl, RaceWay/dsl, Shell/Subway/dsl, 🍴 DQ, Hardee's, Wendy's, 🛏 Candlelight Inn, Comfort Inn, Days Inn, KeyWest Inn, Magnuson Inn
167	US 80 W, to Selma
164	US 31, Hyundai Blvd, Hope Hull, **E** 🅿 Liberty, Saveway/dsl/scales/24hr, 🛏 Lakeside Hotel, Ⓞ Montgomery Camping, auto repair, **W** 🅿 BP, Chevron, Liberty/Subway, 🍴 Burger King, Waffle House, 🛏 Best Western, Comfort Suites, Hampton Inn, Holiday Inn, Motel 6, Ⓞ auto repair
158	to US 31, Tyson, **E** 🅿 BP/DQ/Stuckey's, Ⓞ Montgomery South RV Park, **W** 🅿 FLYING J/Denny's/dsl/scales/24hr
151	AL 97, to Letohatchee, **E** 🅿 Marathon/dsl, **W** 🅿 BP, PaceCar/dsl
142	AL 185, to Ft Deposit, **E** 🅿 Shell/dsl, USA/dsl, 🍴 Priester's Pecans, Subway, Ⓞ auto parts, **W** 🅿 Chevron

AL

GREENVILLE · EVERGREEN · ATMORE

INTERSTATE 65 CONT'D

Exit	Services
133mm	🅁ˢ both lanes, full ♿ facilities, 🍴, vending, 🕮, litter barrels, petwalk, RV dump
130	AL10 E, AL 185, to Greenville, **E** 🚰 Chevron/dsl, Shell, USA/dsl, 🍴 Arby's, Capt D's, Hardee's, KFC, McDonald's, Old Mexico, Pizza&Sub Express, Pizza Hut, Waffle House, Wendy's, 🛏 Days Inn, Quality Inn, Ⓞ Advance Parts, CVS Drug, $General, $Tree, Fred's Store, O'Reilly Parts, Super Foods, Walgreens, to Sherling Lake Park, **W** 🚰 Murphy USA/dsl, Phillips 66/Subway/dsl, QV, Texaco/dsl, 🍴 Bates Turkey Rest., Burger King, Cracker Barrel, Krystal, Ruby Tuesday, Shoney's, Sonic, Taco Bell, Vallarta Mexican, 🛏 Best Western, Comfort Inn, Hampton Inn, Holiday Inn Express, Jameson Inn, Ⓞ AT&T, Chevrolet, Verizon, Walmart/Subway
128	AL 10, to Greenville, Pine Apple, **E** 🚰 Shell/Smokehouse/dsl, Ⓞ Ⓗ, **W** 🚰 BP
114	AL 106, to Georgiana, **E** Ⓞ Hank Williams Museum, **W** 🚰 BP, Chevron, Ⓞ auto repair
107	rd 7, to Garland
101	to Owassa, **E** 🚰 BP/dsl, **W** 🚰 Exxon/dsl, Ⓞ Owassa RV Park, dsl repair
96	AL 83, to Evergreen, **E** 🚰 Chevron, Shell, 🍴 Burger King, Hardee's, KFC/Taco Bell, McDonald's, Ⓞ Ⓗ, **W** 🚰 Spirit/Subway/dsl, 🍴 Black Angus Rest., Pizza Hut, Waffle House, 🛏 Best Value Inn, Comfort Inn, Days Inn
93	US 84, to Evergreen, **W** 🚰 BP/dsl, ♥Loves /Arby's/dsl/scales/24hr
89mm	🛏 sb, full ♿ facilities, 🍴, vending, 🕮, litter barrels, petwalk, RV dump
85mm	🛏 nb, full ♿ facilities, 🍴, vending, 🕮, litter barrels, petwalk, RV dump
83	AL 6, to Lenox, **E** 🚰 Marathon, Ⓞ RV Park (4mi)
77	AL 41, to Range, Brewton, Repton, **W** 🚰 Shell/dsl
69	AL 113, to Flomaton, **E** 🚰 Jet-Pep/Subway/dsl, Chevron/dsl, Shell/dsl/scales/24hr, Ⓞ dsl repair, **W** 🚰 Minute Stop/dsl, 🍴 Huddle House
57	AL 21, to Atmore, **E** 🚰 Chevron/dsl, Exxon/dsl, 🍴 Hardee's, McDonald's, Wrangler Steaks, 🛏 Hampton Inn, Holiday Inn Express, Muskogee Inn, Ⓞ Wind Creek Indian Gaming, **W** 🚰 BP/dsl, Ⓞ to Kelley SP
54	Escambia Cty Rd 1, **E** 🚰 BP/Subway/dsl, Ⓞ to Creek Indian Res
45	to Perdido, **W** 🚰 Chevron/dsl
37	AL 287, Gulf Shores Pkwy, to Bay Minette, **E** 🚰 BP, Ⓞ Ⓗ
34	to AL 59, to Bay Minette, Stockton
31	AL 225, to Stockton, **E** Ⓞ to Blakeley SP, Confederate Mem Bfd, **W** 🚰 Shell/Subway/dsl, Ⓞ Landing RV Park (2mi)
29mm	Tensaw River
28mm	Middle River
25mm	Mobile River
22	Creola, **E** River Delta RV Park (1mi), marine ctr, truck repair
19	US 43, to Satsuma, **E** 🚰 Chevron/dsl/24hr, 🚂 /Arby's/dsl/scales/24hr, 🍴 McDonald's, Pintoli's Italian (2mi), Waffle House, 🛏 La Quinta, **W** 🚰 Chevron, Shell/dsl, Ⓞ I-65 RV Park (1.5mi)
15	AL 41, **E** 🚰 Chevron, Shell/Pizza Inn/dsl, 🍴 China Chef, Church's, Godfather's Pizza, Pizza Hut, Ⓞ Family$, Food World, O'Reilly Parts, Rite Aid, Walgreens, **W** 🚰 Circle K, Shell/Subway/dsl, Ⓞ $General

MOBILE

Exit	Services
13	AL 158, AL 213, to Saraland, **E** 🚰 Murphy USA/dsl, Shell/dsl, 🍴 Krystal, Ruby Tuesday, Waffle House, Wintzell's Oyster House, 🛏 Best Western, Comfort Suites, Days Inn, EconoLodge, Microtel, Quality Inn, Ⓞ Radio Shack, Walmart/McDonald's, **Urgent Care**, **W** 🚰 Exxon/Subway, 🛏 Hampton Inn, Holiday Inn Express, Ⓞ to Chickasabogue Campground
10	W Lee St, **E** 🚰 Kangaroo, Shell/Subway, 🍴 Huddle House, 🛏 Best Inn
9	I-165 S, to Mobile, to I-10 E
8b a	US 45, to Prichard, **E** 🚰 Chevron/Circle K/dsl, Shell/dsl, Texaco/dsl, 🍴 Church's, 🛏 Star Motel, Ⓞ $General, tires/repair, **W** 🚰 BP, Citgo/dsl, 1st Stop, Pride Trkstp/dsl/scales, RaceWay/dsl, Texaco/dsl, 🍴 Burger King, Domino's, Golden Egg Café, McDonald's, Pizza Hut, Ⓞ CVS Drug, $General, vet
5b	US 98, Moffett Rd, **E** 🚰 Exxon/dsl, Texaco/dsl, 🍴 Burger King, Church's, McDonald's, Saucy Q BBQ, Sub King, Ⓞ Big 10 Tire, **W** 🍴 Hardee's, 🛏 Super 8, Ⓞ auto repair
5a	Spring Hill Ave, **E** 🚰 Shell/dsl, 🍴 McDonald's, Ⓞ Ⓗ Big 10 Tire, Mr Transmission, **W** 🚰 Chevron, Shell/dsl, 🍴 Hibachi Express, Starbucks, Subway, Waffle House, Zaxby's, 🛏 Extended Stay America, Wingate Inn
4	Dauphin St, **E** 🚰 BP/Circle K/dsl, Shell/Summit, 🍴 Checker's, Chick-fil-A, Cracker Barrel, Hong Kong Rest., Krystal, McDonald's, Popeye's, Subway, Taco Bell, Waffle House, Wendy's, 🛏 Comfort Inn, Comfort Suites, Red Roof Inn, Rodeway Inn, Ⓞ Buick/GMC, $General, FoodWorld, Lowe's, Mercedes, Rite Aid, Tuesday Morning, Walmart/McDonald's, same as 3 & 5a, **W** Ⓞ Ⓗ
3	Airport Blvd, **E** 🚰 Shell, 🍴 Burger King, Cane's, Izume Japanese, Logan's Roadhouse, Macaroni Grill, Morrison's Cafeteria, Piccadilly's, Starbucks, Wendy's, 🛏 Marriott, Ⓞ Ⓗ, Acura/Jaguar/Infiniti, Belk, Best Buy, BigLots, Cadillac, Dillard's, $Tree, Firestone/auto, Ford, Goodyear/auto, Harley-Davidson, Honda, JC Penney, Land Rover, Marshall's, Nissan, Old Navy, Sam's Club, Sears/auto, Staples, Target, mall, **W** 🚰 GasCo/dsl, Shell, 🍴 American Cafe, Arby's, Baumhowers, Big Apple Chinese, Boiling Pot, Burger King, Carrabba's, ChuckeCheese, Denny's, El Chico, Firehouse Subs, GolBerg's Deli, Honeybaked Ham, Hooters, IHOP, Lenny's Subs, Los Rancheros Mexican, Marble Slab, Newk's Cafe, O'Charley's, Olive Garden, Osaka Japanese, Panera Bread, Popeye's, Quiznos, Red Lobster, Ruby Tuesday, Starbucks, Subway, Taco Bell, 🛏 Ashberry Suites, Baymont Inn, Best Value Inn, Courtyard, Days Inn, Drury Inn, EconoLodge, Fairfield Inn, Family Inn, Hampton Inn, Hilton Garden, Holiday Inn, InTowne Suites, La Quinta, Motel 6, Quality Inn, Residence Inn, ValuePlace, Ⓞ Books-A-Million, $General, $Tree, Fresh Mkt Foods, Home Depot, Jo-Ann Fabrics, Office Depot, PepBoys, Petsmart, Radio Shack, Ross, SteinMart, TJ Maxx, U-Haul, Walgreens, to USAL
1b a	US 90, Government Blvd, **E** 🚰 Raceway/dsl, 🍴 McAlister's Deli, Steak'n Shake, 🛏 Emerald Palms, Ⓞ Audi/Porsche/VW, BMW, Chevrolet, Chrysler/Jeep, Dodge, Kia, Lexus, Lincoln/Volvo, Toyota/Scion, **W** 🚰 Shell/dsl, 🍴 Waffle House, 🛏 Rest Inn
0mm	I-10, E to Pensacola, W to New Orleans

I-65 begins/ends on I-10, exit 20.

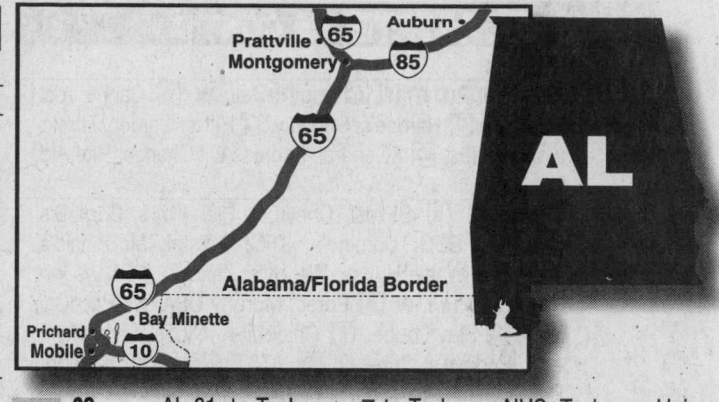

	INTERSTATE 85
Exit	**Services**
80mm	Alabama/Georgia state line, Chattahoochee River
79	US 29, to Lanett, E 🅰 BP/Circle K, Murphy USA, 🍴 Arby's, Burger King, Capt D's, Chuck's BBQ, KFC, Krystal, Little Caesars, McDonald's, Pizza Hut, San Marcos Mexican, Subway, Taco Bell, Waffle House, Wendy's, Wing Stop, ⊙ 🇭, Advance Parts, $General, $Tree, Verizon, Walmart, repair, to West Point Lake, W 🅰 JetPep, QV, Raceway/dsl, 🍴 Domino's, Sonic, 🛏 Days Inn, EconoLodge, ⊙ AutoZone, CVS Drug, Kroger, O'Reilly Parts, vet
78.5mm	Welcome Ctr sb, full 🚻 facilities, 🅲, vending, 🚮 litter barrels, petwalk
77	AL 208, to Huguley, E 🅰 Jet Pep/Church's/dsl, Shell/Circle K, 🍴 Waffle House, 🛏 Holiday Inn Express, ⊙ Chevrolet, Chrysler/Dodge/Ford/Lincoln, auto repair, W 🛏 Hampton Inn, ⊙ fireworks
76mm	Eastern/Central time zone
70	AL 388, to Cusseta, E 🅰 BigCat/dsl, Trvl Plaza/Shell/rest/dsl/scales/24hr/@
66	Andrews Rd, to US 29
64	US 29, to Opelika, E 🅰 Sunoco/dsl, W 🅰 Tiger/dsl
62	US 280/431, to Opelika, E 🅰 Chevron/dsl, Eagle/dsl, Liberty, Shell/Circle K/Church's/dsl, 🍴 Burger King, Durango Mexican, McDonald's, Subway, Wok'n Roll Rest., 🛏 Best Value Inn, Days Inn, EconoLodge, Knights Inn, Quality Inn, Super 8, ⊙ Lakeside RV Park (4.5mi), W 🅰 GrubMart, JetPep, 🍴 Capt. D's, Cracker Barrel, Sizzlin Steaks, Waffle House, 🛏 Comfort Inn, Travelodge, ⊙ Buick/Chevrolet/GMC, Chrysler/Dodge/Jeep, Ford, H&W Tire, Harley-Davidson, Jeep, USA Stores/famous brands
60	AL 51, AL 169, to Opelika, E 🅰 RaceWay/dsl, 🍴 Hardee's, ⊙ $General, W 🅰 Lo-Buck's, ⊙ 🇭, auto repair
58	US 280 W, to Opelika, E 🛏 Hampton Inn, Holiday Inn Express, ⊙ golf, museum, W 🅰 Shell/Subway/dsl, 🍴 Arby's, Brick Oven Pizza, Buffalo Wild Wings, Chick-fil-A, El Patrone Mexican, Huddle House, Jim Bob's, Moe's SW Grill, Logan's Roadhouse, Longhorn Steaks, O'Charley's, Olive Garden, Sonic, Starbucks, Waffle House, Zaxby's, 🛏 Fairfield Inn, Microtel, Motel 6, ⊙ 🇭, Best Buy, Books-A-Million, Dick's, Hobby Lobby, Home Depot, Kohl's, Kroger/dsl, Lowe's, Office Depot, Old Navy, PetCo, Ross, Target, TJ Maxx, World Mkt, Urgent Care
57	Glenn Ave, W 🅰 Exxon, QV, 🍴 Provino's Italian, Shakey's Pizza, Waffle House, Wendy's, 🛏 Hilton Garden, University Motel, ⊙ Sam's Club/gas
51	US 29, to Auburn, E 🅰 Shell, 🛏 Hampton Inn, ⊙ Cadillac/Chevrolet, Leisure Time RV Park/Camping, Nissan, Toyota/Scion, to Chewacla SP, W 🅰 Chevron/Subway/dsl, Murphy USA, 🍴 Arby's, Burger King, El Dorado Mexican, Firehouse Subs, Hong Kong Buffet, Krystal, Little Caesars, McDonald's, Philly Connection, Pizza Hut, Ruby Tuesday, Sonic, Taco Bell, Waffle House, Wendy's, Zaxby's, 🛏 Catfish Cabin, EconoLodge, Holiday Inn Express, Microtel, Quality Inn, Sleep Inn, ⊙ Advance Parts, $General, Ford/Lincoln, Walmart, Winn-Dixie, to Auburn U, tires/repair, Urgent Care, vet
50	Cox Rd
44mm	℞s both lanes, full 🚻 facilities, 🅲, vending, 🚮 litter barrels, petwalk, RV dump, 24hr security
42	US 80, AL 186 E, Wire Rd, E ⊙ to Tuskegee NF, dsl repair/tires, W 🅰 Torch 85/rest./dsl/24hr

38	AL 81, to Tuskegee, E to Tuskegee NHS, Tuskegee University
32	AL 49 N, to Tuskegee, E 🅰 BP/dsl
26	AL 229 N, to Tallassee, E 🅰 Shell/Guthrie's/dsl, W 🇭
22	US 80, to Shorter, E 🅰 BP/dsl, Marathon/dsl, Petro/Chevron/rest./dsl/scales/24hr, 🛏 Days Inn
16	Waugh, to Cecil, E 🅰 BP/Subway/dsl, ⊙ auto repair
11	US 80, AL 110, to Mitylene, to Mt Meigs, E 🅰 Exxon/Subway/dsl, Liberty/dsl, 🍴 Anthony's Rest., Bruster's, Burger King, Cracker Barrel, Jose's Grill, McDonald's, Top China, Waffle House, 🛏 Candlewood Suites, Comfort Inn, Country Inn&Suites, Fairfield Inn, Holiday Inn Express, Sleep Inn, ⊙ Home Depot, Walmart/Subway, auto repair, W 🅰 Chevron/dsl, 🛏 Microtel
9	AL 271, to AL 110, to Auburn U/Montgomery, E 🍴 Arby's, Boardwalk Burgers, BoneFish Grill, Chick-fil-A, Chili's, 5 Guys Burgers, Guthrie's, Ixtapa Mexican, Mimi's Cafe, Moe's SW Grill, Panera Bread, Red Robin, Ruby Tuesday, Sonic, Starbucks, TX Roadhouse, Wendy's, Zoe's Kitchen, 🛏 Hampton Inn, Staybridge Suites, ⊙ AT&T, Books-A-Million, Costco/gas, Dick's, Dillard's, EarthFare Foods, Jo-Ann Fabrics, Kohl's, Michael's, Old Navy, Petsmart, Radio Shack, Ross, Target, Verizon, World Mkt, Urgent Care, vet, W 🇭
6	US 80, US 231, AL 21, East Blvd 0-2 mi E 🅰 Chevron, Exxon/dsl, RaceWay/dsl, Shell, 🍴 Arby's, Arriba Mexican, Baumhowers, Burger King, Carrabba's, Chick-fil-A, Golden Corral, Hardee's, Jason's Deli, KFC, Longhorn Steaks, Los Cabos, Los Vaqueros Mexican, McDonald's, Ming's Garden, Olive Garden, Panera Bread, Piccadilly's, Popeye's, Rock Bottom Cafe, Ruby Tuesday, Schlotzsky's, Shogun Japanese, Starbucks, Subway, Sushiyama, Taco Bell, Waffle House, Wendy's, Zaxby's, 🛏 Best Inn, Comfort Inn, Country Inn&Suites, Courtyard, Extended Stay America, La Quinta, Quality Inn, Red Roof Inn, Residence Inn, Rodeway Inn, Sleep Inn, SpringHill Suites, Studio+, ValuePlace, Wingate Inn, ⊙ Acura, Best Buy, Books-A-Million, $General, Family$, Ford/Lincoln, Fresh Mkt Foods, Home Depot, Honda, Hyundai, Lowe's, Office Depot, PetCo, Radio Shack, Subaru, TJ Maxx, Walmart/McDonald's, Winn-Dixie, USPO, W 🅰 BP, Chevron, Liberty, Shell, 🍴 Arby's, Buffet City, Capt D's, Guthrie's, Hardee's, Hibaci Buffet, IHOP, Krispy Kreme, Krystal, McDonald's, Outback Steaks, Shoney's, Stevi B's Pizza, Taco Bell, Waffle House, 🛏 Baymont Inn, Budgetel, Comfort Suites, Drury Inn, Express Inn, Motel 6, Ramada Inn, ⊙ Audi/VW, BMW, Buick/Cadillac, Chevrolet, Chrysler/Dodge/Jeep, $General, Firestone/auto, Fred's Store, Infiniti, JC Penney, Kia, Lexus, Mercedes, Nissan, Sam's Club/gas, Sears/auto, Toyota, mall, to Gunter AFB

AL AZ

INTERSTATE 85 CONT'D

Exit	Services
4	Perry Hill Rd, **E** 🍴 Chappy's Deli, **W** 🅿 Cannon/dsl, Chevron, 🍴 Hardee's, Subway, 🛏 Hilton Garden, Homewood Suites, 🅾 $General, Express Oil Change, Rite Aid, vet
3	Ann St, **E** 🅿 BP/dsl, Chevron, 🍴 Arby's, Capt D's, Country's BBQ, Domino's, KFC, Krystal, McDonald's, Taco Bell, Waffle House, Wendy's, Zaxby's, 🛏 Days Inn, 🅾 Big 10 Tire, **W** 🅿 Entec, Murphy USA/dsl, PaceCar, Ztec, 🛏 Stay Lodge, 🍴 Chick-fil-A, CiCi's Pizza, Hardee's, Popeye's, Subway, 🅾 AT&T, $Tree, Office Depot, Radio Shack, Ross, Verizon, Walmart/Subway
2	Forest Ave, **E** CVS Drug, **W** 🄷
1	Court St, Union St, downtown, **E** 🅿 BP/dsl, Exxon/dsl, **W** to Ala St U
0mm	**I-85 begins/ends on I-65,** exit 171 in Montgomery

INTERSTATE 459 (BIRMINGHAM)

Exit	Services
33b a	I-59, N to Gadsden, S to Birmingham
32	US 11, Trussville, **N** 🅿 BP/24hr, **S** 🅿 BP, Chevron/dsl/24hr, RaceWay/dsl/24hr, Shell/dsl, 🍴 Arby's, Chili's, China Palace, Coldstone, Firehouse Subs, Habanero's Rest., Hooters, Jack's Rest., Jim'n Nick's BBQ, KFC, Lee Garden, Logan's Roadhouse, McDonald's, Red Robin, Starbucks, Subway, Waffle House, Wendy's, 🛏 Courtyard, Hampton Inn, Hilton Garden, 🅾 AT&T, Belk, Best Buy, Big 10 Tires, Books-A-Million, Buick/GMC, Harley-Davidson, Home Depot, JC Penney, Lowe's, Mazda, Michael's, Old Navy, Staples, Target, TJ Maxx, Verizon
31	Derby Parkway, **N** 🅾 B'ham Race Course
29	I-20, E to Atlanta, W to Birmingham
27	Grants Mill Rd, **N** 🛏 Hampton Inn, 🅾 Fiat, **S** 🅿 Chevron/dsl, 🅾 Audi/Porsche, BMW/Lexus, Chrysler/Dodge/Jeep, Land Rover, Mini
23	Liberty Parkway, **S** 🍴 Billy's Grill, DQ, Tazaki's Greek, 🛏 Hilton Garden
19	US 280, Mt Brook, Childersburg, **N** 🅿 Chevron, 🍴 CA Pizza Kitchen, Cheesecake Factory, Flemings Rest., Macaroni Grill, Panera Bread, PF Chang's, Village Tavern, 🅾 Barnes&Noble, **0-3 mi S** 🅿 BP/Circle K, Chevron, Exxon, RaceWay.dsl, Shell, 🍴 Arby's, Baha Burger, Burger King, Carrabba's, Chick-fil-A, Chili's, Chipotle Mexican, Cracker Barrel, DQ, Edgar's Rest., Fox&Hound Grille, Full Moon BBQ, Hamburger Heaven, Hooters, IHOP, Jade Palace, Jason's Deli, Joe's Crabshack, Kobe Japanese, Logan's Roadhouse, Longhorn Steaks, Lloyd's Rest., Max's Deli, McAlister's Deli, McDonald's, Milo's Burgers, Ming's Chinese, Outback Steaks, Pablo's, Papa John's, Petruccelli's Italian, Pizza Hut, Ralph&Kacoos, Schlotzsky's, Shogun Japanese, Subway, Superior Grill, Suria 280, Taco Bell, Taziki's Greek, TCBY, Tilted Kilt, Wendy's, Zaxby's, 🛏 Best Western, Candlewood Suites, Courtyard, Drury Inn, Fairfield Inn, Hampton Inn, Hilton, Holiday Inn Express, Homestead Suites, Homewood Suites, Hyatt Place, La Quinta, Marriott, Residence Inn, SpringHill Suites, Wingate Inn, 🅾 AT&T, Best Buy, BigLots, Books-A-Million, Curves, CVS Drug, Dick's, Firestone/auto, Fresh Mkt Foods, Goodyear/auto, Hancock Fabrics, Home Depot, Kohl's, Lowe's, Michael's, NTB, PetCo, Petsmart, Ross, Staples, SteinMart, Target, TJMaxx, Verizon, Walgreens, Walmart, vet

Exit	Services
17	Acton Rd, **N** 🅿 Shell/dsl/24hr, 🍴 Krystal, McDonald's, **S** 🛏 Comfort Inn
15b a	I-65, N to Birmingham, S to Montgomery
13	US 31, Hoover, Pelham, **N** 🅿 BP, Chevron, Citgo, Exxon, Shell, 🍴 Burger King, Chick-fil-A, Dave's Deli, Fish Mkt Rest., Full Moon Cafe, Golden Rule BBQ, Habanero's, Krispy Kreme, Krystal, McDonald's, Outback Steaks, Papa John's, Quiznos, Salvatori's Pizza, Starbucks, Subway, 🛏 Days Inn, 🅾 **Urgent Care**, Acura, AutoZone, Books-A-Million, Buick, Cadillac, Chevrolet, $Tree, Firestone/auto, Goodyear/auto, Honda, Hyundai, Mr Transmission, Nissan, Publix, Rite Aid, Staples, TJ Maxx, vet, **S** 🅿 Jet-Pep, Shell/dsl/24hr, 🍴 Arby's, Bonefish Grill, CA Pizza Kitchen, Carino's, Chipotle Mexican, Guthrie's, J Alexander's Rest., Jason's Deli, Jim'n Nicks BBQ, McDonald's, Michael's Steaks, Moe's SW Grill, Olive Garden, Panera Bread, Pizza Hut, Quiznos, Ruby Tuesday, Shula's Steaks, Starbucks, Subway, Taco Bell, Ted's MT Grill, Top China, Wendy's, 🛏 Courtyard, Days Inn, Embassy Suites, Hampton Inn, Hyatt Place, Microtel, Residence Inn, Wynfrey Hotel, 🅾 Barnes&Noble, Belk, Best Buy, Big 10 Tire, Bruno's Foods, Costco/gas, CVS Drug, Dick's, Hancock Fabrics, Home Depot, Infiniti, JC Penney, Jo-Ann Fabrics, Macy's, Marshall's, Mercedes, Michael's, NTB, Office Depot, Petsmart, Ross, Sam's Club/gas, Sears/auto, Smart Car, Tuesday Morning, Verizon, Walmart (1mi), mall
10	AL 150, Waverly, **N** 🅿 Chevron (1mi), Shell (1mi), 🍴 Frontera Mexican Grill, 🅾 $Tree, Kohl's, PetCo, Target, **S** 🅿 BP/dsl/24hr, Exxon, 🛏 Hampton Inn, Hyatt Place, 🅾 **Urgent Care**, Ford, Toyota, Walgreens, Publix/deli
6	AL 52, to Bessemer, **N** 🅿 BP/dsl, **S** 🅿 BP, Jet-Pep, Texaco/Taco Bell, 🍴 Arby's, China Wok, Domino's, Hickory Grill, McDonald's, Pizza Hut, Quiznos, Subway, Waffle House, Wendy's, 🛏 Sleep Inn, 🅾 $General, CVS Drug, TrueValue, Winn-Dixie, RV Camping
1	AL 18, Bessemer, **N** 🅿 Exxon, Shell/dsl, 🍴 Burger King, Chick-fil-A, East Palace, Full Moon BBQ, Habanero's Mexican, Logan's Roadhouse, McAlister's Deli, Taco Bell, 🅾 AT&T, GNC, JC Penney, Publix, Ross, Target, Verizon, **S** 🅿 BP/dsl, 🍴 Bojangles, China King, McDonald's, Momma's Rest., San Antonio Grill, Subway, Zaxby's, 🅾 Advance Parts, CVS Drug, Piggly Wiggly, to Tannehill SP
0mm	**I-459 begins/ends on I-20/59,** exit 106

ARIZONA

INTERSTATE 8

Exit	Services
178b a	**I-10, I-8 begins/ends on I-10,** exit 199, E to Tucson, W to Phoenix
174	Trekell Rd, to Casa Grande, **2-4 mi N** 🅾 🄷, gas, food, lodging
172	Thornton Rd, to Casa Grande, **5-8 mi N** gas, food, Francisco Grande Resort, Holiday Inn
171mm	Santa Cruz River
169	Bianco Rd
167	Montgomery Rd
163mm	Santa Rosa Wash
161	Stanfield Rd
151	AZ 84 E, Maricopa Rd, to Stanfield, **S** 🅿 Vija Trkstp/dsl, 🅾 Saguaro RV Park

Side labels: HOOVER, BESSEMER, BIRMINGHAM

INTERSTATE 8 CONT'D   ⑮

Exit	Services
151mm	picnic area wb, 🚻, litter barrels
149mm	picnic area eb, 🚻, litter barrels
144	Vekol Rd
140	Freeman Rd
119	Butterfield Trail, to AZ 85, I-10, Gila Bend, **N** 🅿️ Shell/dsl/scales/RV Park/24hr, 🍴 Cafe Charro Mexican, Subway, 🏨 America's Choice Inn, 🅾️ Augie's RV Park, **3 mi N** 🅿️ Shell/Cafe Charro/Noble Roman's/Subway/dsl, 🍴 DQ, Little Italy, 🏨 Best Western, Space Age/rest, Yucca Motel, 🅾️ $General
117mm	Sand Tank Wash
115	AZ 85, to Gila Bend, **1-2 mi N** 🅿️ ❤️Loves/Taco Bell/dsl/scales/24hr, Circle K, Texaco/dsl, 🍴 Burger King, McDonald's, 🏨 Best Western, El Coronado Motel, Yucca Motel, 🅾️ 🅷 Family$, Goodyear/auto, NAPA, Wheel Inn RV park
111	Citrus Valley Rd
106	Paloma Rd
102	Painted Rock Rd **11 mi N** Painted Rock Petroglyph Site
87	Aqua Caliente Rd, Sentinel Rd, Sentinel, Hyder, **N** 🅿️ Sentinel Gen Store/dsl, 🅾️ RV Camping
85mm	Ⓡ🅢 wb, full 🚻 facilities, 🍴, 🚻, litter barrels, vending, petwalk
84mm	Ⓡ🅢 eb, full 🚻 facilities, 🍴, 🚻, litter barrels, vending, petwalk
78	Spot Rd
73	Aztec **4 mi S** Oasis RV Park/dump
67	Dateland, **S** 🅿️ Texaco/Quiznos/dsl, 🅾️ Oasis RV Park/dump
56mm	Ⓡ🅢 both lanes, full 🚻 facilities, 🍴, 🚻, litter barrels, vending, petwalk
54	Ave 52 E, Mohawk Valley
42	Ave 40 E, to Tacna, **N** 🅿️ Chevron/dsl/24hr, 🏨 Chaparral Motel
37	Ave 36 E, to Roll
30	Ave 29 E, Wellton, **N** 🅿️ Circle K/gas, 🏨 Desert Motel, 🅾️ Tier Drop RV Park, **S** 🅿️ Chevron/dsl, 🍴 Beach Club Grill, Chen's Chinese, Desert Pizza, Jack-in-the-Box, Quiznos, 🏨 Microtel, 🅾️ Coyote Wash Mkt
24mm	Ligurta Wash
23mm	Red Top Wash
22mm	parking area/litter barrels both lanes
21	Dome Valley, **N** 🅾️ Ligurta Sta RV park, Yuma Proving Ground (16mi)
17mm	insp sta eb
15mm	Fortuna Wash
14	Foothills Blvd, **N** 🅾️ Sundance RV Park, **S** 🍴 Domino's, Foothills Eatery, Mi Fajita, 🅾️ Foothill Hardware, Foothills RV Park, The Grocery Store/gas/dsl, auto/RV care/lube ctr

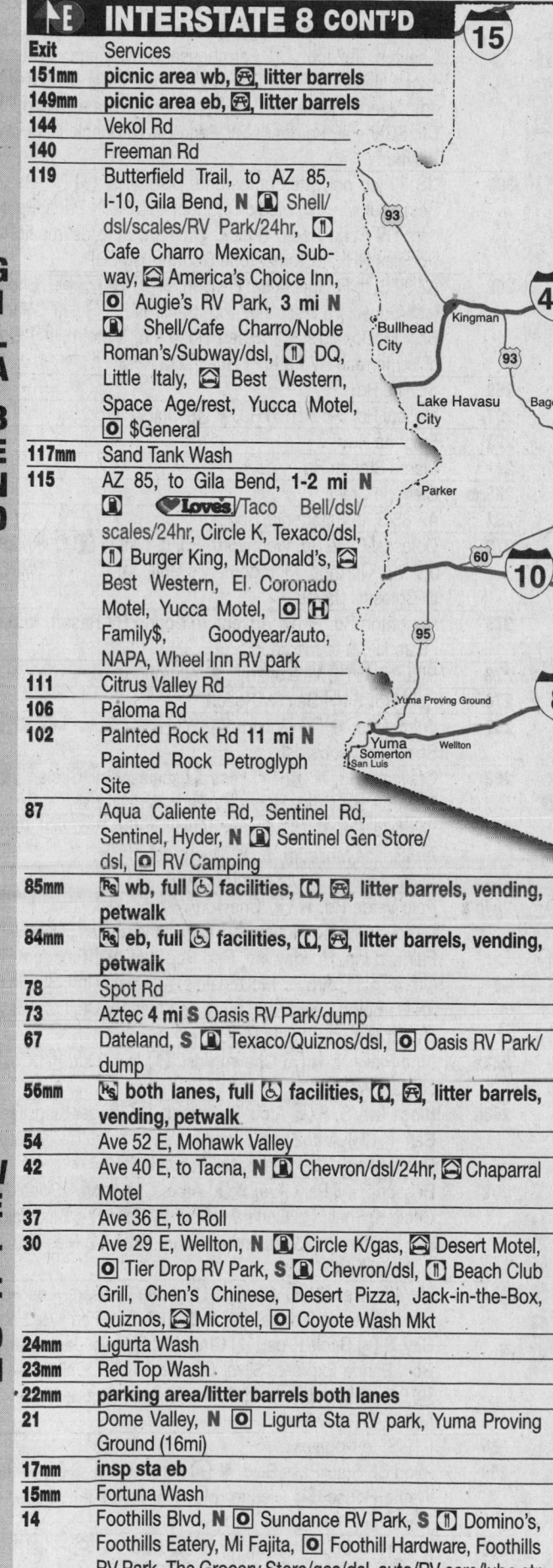

12	Fortuna Rd, to US 95 N, **N** 🅿️ Chevron/dsl, ⚡FLYING J/Barney's/dsl/scales/24hr, 🍴 DayBreakers Cafe, Jack-in-the-Box, Pizza Hut, 🏨 Comfort Inn, Courtesy Inn, 🅾️ Caravan RV Park, Oasis RV Park, Shangri La RV Park, **S** 🅿️ Shell/Burger King/dsl, 🍴 Applebee's, A&W/KFC, Daboyz Pizza, DQ, Subway, 🏨 Microtel, 🅾️ Big O Tire, Checker Parts, Curves, $General, Family$, Fry's Foods, Radio Shack, Walgreens, **Urgent Care**
9	32nd St, to Yuma, **S** 🍴 Del Taco, Jack-in-the-Box, Panda Express, 🅾️ Sun Vista RV Park, **Walmart**
7	AZ 195, Araby Rd, **N** 🅿️ Circle K/dsl, **S** 🅿️ Chevron/Jack-in-the-Box/dsl, Circle K/dsl, 🅾️ RV World, Sun Vista RV Park, to AZWU
3	AZ 280 S, Ave 3E, **N** 🍴 Arby's, 🏨 Candlewood Suites, Holiday Inn Express, **S** 🅿️ ❤️Loves/Chester's/Subway/dsl/scales/24hr, 🍴 Sonic, 🅾️ Harley-Davidson, to Marine Corp Air Sta
2	US 95, 16th St, Yuma, **N** 🅿️ Circle K, 🍴 Ah-So Steaks, Buffalo Wild Wings, Burrito Grill, Chili's, ChuckeCheese, Coldstone Creamery, Cracker Barrel, Del Taco, Denny's, Famous Dave's BBQ, Food Ct, Hawaiian BBQ, In-N-Out, Jack-in-the-Box, Kneaders, Logans Roadhouse, Mimi's Cafe, Olive Garden, Panda Express, Penny's, Diner, Red Lobster, Starbucks, Subway, 🏨 Best Western, Days Inn,

GILA BEND

WELLTON

YUMA

AZ

YUMA

⭢🄴 INTERSTATE 8 CONT'D

Exit	Services
2	Continued
	Fairfield Inn, Hampton Inn, Holiday Inn, Homewood Suites, La Fuente Inn, Motel 6, OakTree Inn, Shilo Inn/rest., SpringHill Suites, TownePlace Suites, Wingate Inn, 🄾 AT&T, Best Buy, Dillards, $Tree, JC Penney, Jo-Ann Fabrics, Kohl's, Marshall's, Old Navy, PetsMart, Ross, Sam's Club/gas, Target, auto/tire repair, **S** 🅖 Arco/dsl/24hr, Chevron/Blimpie/dsl, Shell, 🍴 Applebee's, Burger King, Carl's Jr, Chretin's Mexican, IHOP, Jack-in-the-Box, McDonald's, Golden Corral, Outback Steaks, TX Roadhouse, Village Inn Pizza, Wendy's, 🛏 Comfort Inn, Motel 6, Radisson, Super 8, 🄾 H, BigLots, Family$, Home Depot, KIA, Radio Shack, Staples
1.5mm	**weigh sta both lanes**
1	Giss Pkwy, Yuma, **N** 🄾 to Yuma Terr Prison SP, **S on 4th Ave E** 🅖 Chevron, Circle K/gas, 🍴 Jack-in-the-Box, Yuma Landing Rest., 🛏 Best Western, Hilton Garden
0mm	Arizona/California state line, Colorado River, Mountain/Pacific time zone

⭢🄴 INTERSTATE 10

Exit	Services
391mm	Arizona/New Mexico state line
390	Cavot Rd
389mm	📷 **both lanes, full** ♿ **facilities,** 🍴, 🅿, **litter barrels, vending, petwalk**
383mm	**weigh sta eb, weigh/insp sta wb**
382	Portal Rd, San Simon
381mm	San Simon River
378	Lp 10, San Simon, **N** 🅖 4K Trkstp/Chevron/Noble Romans/Quiznos/dsl/scales/24hrs/@, 🄾 auto/dsl/RV repair
366	Lp 10, Bowie Rd, **N** 🅖 Shell/dsl, **S** 🄾 Alaskan RV park
362	Lp 10, Bowie Rd, **N** gas, lodging, camping, **S** to Ft Bowie NHS
355	US 191 N, to Safford
352	US 191 N, to Safford, same as 355
344	Lp 10, to Willcox, **N** 🄾 Lifestyle RV Resort
340	AZ 186, to Rex Allen Dr, **N** 🅖 TA/Shell/Popeye's/Subway/dsl/scales/24hr/@, 🛏 Holiday Inn Express, Super 8, 🄾 Magic Circle RV Park, Stout's CiderMill, **S** 🅖 Alco, Circle K, Doc's/Plaza Rest/dsl, Texaco/dsl, 🍴 Burger King, McDonald's, Pizza Hut, 🛏 Days Inn, Motel 6, Quality Inn, 🄾 H, Ace Hardware, Alco, AutoZone, Beall's, $General, Family$, Hometown Grocery, Medicine Shoppe, Radio Shack, Safeway, Grande Vista RV Park, auto/tire/RV repair, to Chiricahua NM
336	AZ 186, Willcox, **S** 🅖 Chevron/dsl/LP, **1-3 mi S** 🛏 Royal Western Lodge, 🄾 Ft Willcox RV Park, Life Style RV Park
331	US 191 S, to Sunsites, Douglas, **S** 🄾 to Cochise Stronghold
322	Johnson Rd, **S** 🅖 Shell/DQ/dsl/gifts
320mm	📷 **both lanes, full** ♿ **facilities,** 🍴, 🅿, **litter barrels, vending, petwalk**
318	Triangle T Rd, to Dragoon, **S** lodging, camping
312	Sibyl Rd
309mm	Adams Peak Wash
306	AZ 80, Pomerene Rd, Benson, **1-2 mi S** 🅖 Circle K, 🍴 86 Cafe, 🄾 CarQuest, Pato Blanco Lakes RV Park, Silver Legacy RV Park, repair
305mm	San Pedro River

WILCOX

BENSON

TUCSON

Exit	Services
304	Ocotillo St, Benson, **N** 🍴 Denny's, Jack-in-the-Box, 🛏 Days Inn, Super 8, 🄾 Benson RV Park, KOA, **S** 🅖 Chevron, Texaco, 🍴 Farmhouse Rest, Magaly's Mexican, Palatianos Rest, Subway, Wendy's, 🛏 Best Western, QuarterHorse Inn, 🄾 H, Ace Hardware, Dillon RV Ctr, $General, Pardner's RV Park, Radio Shack, Safeway, Walmart
303	US 80 (eb only), to Tombstone, Bisbee, **S** 🅖 🍴 Reb's Rest., Subway, 🄾 Medicine Shoppe, O'Reilly Parts, Pardners RV Park, Radio Shack, Walmart, auto/dsl/repair, to Douglas NHL, to Tombstone Courthouse SHP
302	AZ 90 S, to Ft Huachuca, Benson, **S** 🅖 ♥Loves /Chester's/Subway/dsl/scales/24hr, Shell/dsl, 🍴 KFC/Taco Bell, McDonald's, 🛏 Desert Rose Inn, Motel 6, 🄾 Cochise Terrace RV Park, Ft Huachuca NHS
299	Skyline Rd
297	Mescal Rd, J-6 Ranch Rd, **N** 🄾 QuickPic/dsl
292	Empirita Rd
291	Marsh Station Rd
288mm	Cienega Creek
281	AZ 83 S, to Patagonia, Sonoita
279	Colossal Cave Rd, Wentworth Rd, **0-1 mi N** 🅖 QuikMart, 🍴 DQ, Quiznos, Montgomery's Grill, 🄾 Curves, USPO, to Colossal Caves
275	Houghton Rd, **N** 🄾 Adventure Bound RV Resort, to Saguaro NP, **S** to fairgrounds
273	Rita Rd, **N** 🅖 Valero (2mi), **S** fairgrounds
270	Kolb Rd, **S** 🄾 Bay RV Resort
269	Wilmot Rd, **N** 🅖 Chevron/A&W/dsl, 🛏 Travel Inn, **S** 🅖 Shell/pizza/subs/dsl
268	Craycroft Rd, **N** 🅖 TTT/rest/dsl/scales/24hr, Circle K, Mr T/dsl/LP, 🄾 Crazy Horse RV Park, **S** dsl repair
267	Valencia Rd, **N** 🅖 Chevron/Jack-in-the-Box, 🄾 Pima Air&Space Museum, **S** 🅖 Valero/dsl, 🄾 ✈
265	Alvernon Way, Davis-Monthan AFB
264b a	Palo Verde Rd, **N** 🅖 Chevron/Wendy's/dsl, Circle K, 🍴 Denny's, Waffle House, 🛏 Crossland Suites, Days Inn, Fairfield Inn, Holiday Inn, Red Roof Inn, 🄾 Freedom RV Ctr, **S** 🅖 🍴 Arby's, McDonald's, 🛏 Quality Inn, Studio 6, 🄾 Camping World RV Resort, La Mesa RV Ctr, Lazy Days RV Ctr/Resort, Pedata RV Ctr
263b	Kino Pkwy N, **N** 🅖 Chevron/dsl, 🍴 In-N-Out, 🄾 Costco/gas, Walmart
263a	Kino Pkwy S, **S** 🅖 Arco, Shamrock, 🍴 Burger King, Taco Bell, 🄾 H, AutoZone, $Tree, Fry's Foods, O'Reilly Parts, Radio Shack, Walgreens, to Tucson Intn'l ✈
262	Benson Hwy, Park Ave, **S** 🅖 Arco, Chevron/McDonald's, Circle K, Shell, 🍴 Carl's Jr., Country Folks, 🛏 Best Value Inn, Western Inn, Windemere Hotel, 🄾 7-11, Mack/Volvo Trucks, USPO
261	6th/4th Ave, **N** 🅖 GasCo, 🍴 Little Caesars, Los Portales, 🛏 EconoLodge, 🄾 Discount Tire, Family$, Food City, **S** 🅖 Circle K/dsl, 🍴 Church's, El Indio, Jack-in-the-Box, Panda Express, Silver Saddle Steaks, Whataburger, 🛏 Lazy 8 Motel, 🄾 Big O Tire, El Super Foods, Family$, Midas, O'Reilly Parts
260	I-19 S, to Nogales
259	22nd St, Starr Pass Blvd, **N** 🅖 Circle K/dsl, **S** 🍴 Kettle, Waffle House, 🛏 Clarion, Motel 6, Regal Inn, Super 8, Travel Inn, Travelodge
258	Congress St, Broadway St, **N** 🅖 Circle K, 🛏 Hotel Tuscan, Inn Suites, **S** 🍴 Carl's Jr, 🛏 Days Inn, Howard John

INTERSTATE 10 CONT'D

TUCSON

Exit	Services
258	Continued son, Motel 6, River Park Inn, Travelodge
257a	St Mary's Rd, N H, S Arco, Shell, Burger King, Denny's, Furr's Cafeteria, Jack-in-the-Box, Country Inn&Suites, Ramada Ltd., Pima Comm Coll
257	Speedway Blvd, N Best Western, H, Victory Motorcycles, U of AZ, S Arco/dsl, Old Town Tucson, museum
256	Grant Rd, N Sonic, auto/dsl repair, S Circle K, QT/dsl, Shell, Arby's, IHOP, KFC, Las Cazuelita's, Waffle House, Comfort Inn, Grant Inn, Hampton Inn, Holiday Inn Express, Super 8, Ace Hardware
255	AZ 77 N, to Miracle Mile
254	Prince Rd, N U-Haul, tires, S Kenworth, Prince of Tucson RV Park, golf
252	El Camino del Cerro, Ruthrauff Rd, N Arco, Ruthrauff RV Ctr, S Chevron/Jack-in-the-Box
251	Sunset Rd
250	Orange Grove Rd, N Arco, Circle K, Domino's, Firehouse Subs, Subway, Wendy's, Petsmart, Sprouts Mkt, Staples, **N on Thornydale** Burger King, Culver', Golden Corral, Tulioberto's, Big O Tire, Costco/gas, Home Depot, Parts+
248	Ina Rd, N Chevron/dsl, Circle K/dsl, Shell/dsl, Carl's Jr, ChickeNuevo, Chinese Box, Chuy's, DQ, Eegee's Cafe, Hooters, Jack-in-the-Box, Lupita's Cafe, McDonald's, Peter Piper's Pizza, Starbucks, Taco Bell, Waffle House, InTown Suites, Motel 6, BigLots, CarQuest, CVS Drug, Discount Tire, $Tree, Fry's Foods/dsl, Goodyear/auto, Hancock Fabrics, Lowe's, Michael's, 99¢ Store, Office Depot, PepBoys, Radio Shack, Target, U-Haul, Walgreens, S Circle K, Denny's, Starbucks, Best Western, Red Roof Inn, Travelodge, Freedom RV Ctr, Harley-Davidson
246	Cortaro Rd, N Circle K/Arby's/dsl, QT/dsl, IHOP, Wendy's, S Shell/dsl, Boston's Rest, Burger King, Chili's, Cracker Barrel, Eegee's Rest., In-N-Out, KFC/Taco Bell, Little Caesars, McDonald's, New Town Asian, Panda Express, Starbucks, Subway, TX Roadhouse, Days Inn, Comfort Inn, Holiday Inn Express, La Quinta, Super 8, Ace Hardware, Batteries+, GNC, Kohl's, O'Reilly Parts, Verizon, Walmart/McDonald's, USPO, access to RV camping
244	Twin Peaks Rd
242	Avra Valley Rd, S Saguaro NP (13mi), RV camping, airport
240	Tangerine Rd, to Rillito, N A-A RV Park, S USPO
236	Marana, S Chevron/dsl/LP, Circle K, Sun RV Park, auto repair
232	Pinal Air Park Rd, S Pinal Air Park
228mm	wb pulloff, to frontage rd
226	Red Rock, S USPO
219	Picacho Peak Rd, N Shell/DQ, Shell/dsl, S Ostrich Ranch, Pichaco Peak RV Park, to Picacho Peak SP
212	Picacho (from wb), N Premium Gas/tires, USPO S KOA
211b	AZ 87 N, AZ 84 W, to Coolidge, S KOA
211a	Picacho (from eb), S KOA, state prison
208	Sunshine Blvd, to Eloy, N Pilot/Subway/dsl/scales/24hr, dsl repair, S FLYING J/Denny's/dsl/scales/24hr, Blue Beacon

CASA GRANDE

Exit	Services
203	Toltec Rd, to Eloy, N Circle K/dsl, Shell/McDonald's/playplace/24hr, Carl's Jr, El Caballito Mexican, Best Value Inn, Red Roof Inn, Super 8, Desert Valley RV Park, dsl/tire repair, S TA/A&W/Taco Bell/dsl/24hr/@, Pizza Hut, truckwash
200	Sunland Gin Rd, Arizona City, N Petro/Iron Skillet/dsl/scales/24hr/@, Pride/Subway/dsl/24hr, Burger King, Eva's Mexican, Days Inn, Travelodge, Blue Beacon, Eagle Truckwash, Las Colinas RV Park, S Loves/Arby's/Baskin-Robbins/dsl/24hr, Golden 9 Rest., Motel 6, Speedco Lube
199	I-8 W, to Yuma, San Diego
198	AZ 84, to Eloy, Casa Grande, N Robson Ranch Rest./golf, S Casa Grande Outlets/famous brands
194	AZ 287, Florence Blvd, to Casa Grande, N Chick-fil-A, Culver's, In-N-Out, Mimi's Cafe, Olive Garden, Rubio's, Subway, Dillard's, GNC, JC Penney, Kohl's, Marshall's, Michael's, Old Navy, Petsmart, Radio Shack, Ross, Staples, Sunscape RV Park (7mi), Target, Verizon, Walgreens, World Mkt, **0-2 mi S** Arco/dsl, Chevron/Little Caesars, Circle K/gas, Shell/DQ, A&W, Arby's Burger King, Carl's Jr, Chili's, China Buffet, Chipotle Mexican, Church's, Coldstone, Cracker Barrel, Del Taco, Denny's, Eegee's, Golden Corral, IHOP, JB's, LJ Silver, Macayo's Mexican, Panda Express, Papa Murphy's, Peter Piper Pizza, Sonic, Starbucks, Subway, Taco Bell, Best Western, Comfort Inn, Holiday Inn Express, Legacy Suites, Mainstay Suites, Super 8, H, Ace Hardware, AutoZone, CVS Drug, Discount Tire, $Tree, Encore Camping (2mi), Fiesta Grande RV Resort, Fry's Food/drug, Home Depot, Jo-Ann Fabrics, Lowe's, Tuesday Morning, Walgreens, Walmart/McDonalds, **Urgent Care**
190	McCartney Rd, N to Central AZ Coll
185	AZ 387, to Coolidge, Florence, S Eva's Mexican (6mi), Fransisco Grande, Holiday Inn, Fry's Food/gas (6mi), Val Vista RV camping (3mi), hwy patrol, to Casa Grande Ruins NM
183mm	**rest area wb, full facilities, litter barrels, vending, petwalk**
181mm	**rest area eb, full facilities, litter barrels, vending, petwalk**
175	AZ 587 N, Casa Blanca Rd, Chandler, Gilbert, S Shell/dsl
173mm	Gila River
167	Riggs Rd, to Sun Lake, N Shell (3mi), Akimel Smoke Shop
164	AZ 347 S, Queen Creek Rd, to Maricopa, N to Chandler airport, gas
162b a	Wild Horse Pass Rd, Sundust Rd, N Loves /Ar

AZ

AZ

CHANDLER

🔷E INTERSTATE 10 CONT'D	
Exit	**Services**
162b a	Continued by's/dsl/scales/24hr, 🍴 McDonald's, ⊙ Beaudry RV Ctr, **S** 🚹 Chevron, 🛏 Wildhorse Pass Hotel/Casino, ⊙ Firebird Sports Park, Gila River Casino
161	AZ 202 E, Pecos Rd
160	Chandler Blvd, to Chandler, **N** 🚹 Chevron/dsl, Circle K, 🍴 Burger King, Denny's, Marie Callender's, Whataburger, 🛏 Fairfield Inn, Hampton Inn, Homewood Suites, Motel 6, Radisson, Red Roof Inn, Super 8, ⊙ Aamco, Firestone/auto, Harley-Davidson, to Compadre Stadium, Williams AFB, **S** 🚹 Chevron, Circle K, 7-11, 🍴 Applebee's, Arriba Mexican, Carl's Jr, Cracker Barrel, Del Taco, Dunkin Donuts, Hooters, Jersey Mike's, Starbucks, Waffle House, Wendy's, 🛏 Holiday Inn Express, Extended Stay America, InTown Suites, La Quinta, ⊙ 🅷, AutoZone, CVS Drug, Discount Tire, Kohl's
159	Ray Rd, **N** 🚹 Circle K, Shell/dsl, 🍴 Buca Italian, Carrabba's, Charleston's Rest., Chipotle Mexican, El Pollo Loco, 5&Diner, Fleming's Steaks, In-N-Out, Jasons Deli, Jilly's Rest., McDonald's, Outback Steaks, Paradise Cafe, Red Lobster, Roy's Cafe, Rumbi Grill, Starbucks, Tejas, Tomaso's Italian, 🛏 Courtyard, ⊙ BMW, Chevrolet, Ford, Home Depot, Lexus, Lowe's Whse, Mercedes, PetsMart, Sam's Club/gas, **S** 🚹 Shell, Circle K/dsl, 🍴 Boston Mkt, IHOP/24hr, Jack-in-the-Box, Macaroni Grill, Mimi's Café, On-the-Border, Peter Piper Pizza, Pizza Hut, Rock Bottom Rest., Rubio's, Sweet Tomatoes, Wendy's, 🛏 Extended Stay America, ⊙ Barnes&Noble, Best Buy, CVS Drug, JC Penney, Jo-Ann Fabrics, Michael's, Old Navy, PetCo, Ross, SteinMart, Target, Urgent Care
158	Warner Rd, **N** 🚹 Circle K/dsl, QT, 🍴 Port of Subs, ⊙ Dick's, **S** 🚹 Arco, Circle K/dsl, 🍴 Burger King, ChuckeCheese, DQ, Macayo's Mexican, Malaya Mexican, McDonald's, Nello's Pizza, Panda Garden, Quizno's, Ruffino's Italian, ⊙ Ace Hardware, Basha's Foods, Big 10 Tire, Goodyear/auto, vet
157	Elliot Rd, **N** 🚹 Chevron, Shell/Circle K, 🍴 Applebee's, Arby's, Baja Fresh, Burger King, Coco's, Crackers Cafe, Crazy W Buffet, Dayton's Place, HoneyBear's BBQ, Kabab Palace, Kobe Japanese, Moe's SW Grill, Olive Garden, Panda Express, Quizno's, Red Robin Rest., Souper Salad, Sonic, Starbucks, Subway, Taco Bell, The Groves, Wendy's, YC Mongolian Grill, Yupha's Kitchen, 🛏 Country Inn&Suites, ⊙ Acura, Buick, Cadillac/GMC, Costco/gas, Discount Tire, Dodge, $Tree, Ford/Lincoln, Honda, Nissan, PetsMart, Savers, Staples, Toyota/Scion, Walmart, Urgent Care, **S** 🚹 Shell/Circle K, 🍴 Baskin-Robbins, Cactus Jack's, KFC, Mesquite Broiler, McDonald's, Sub Factory, 🛏 Clarion, Grace Inn, ⊙ Checker Parts, Safeway, Walgreens
155	Baseline Rd, Guadalupe, **N** 🚹 Shell/Circle K/Popeye's/dsl, 🍴 Carl's Jr, ClaimJumper, 5& Diner, Joe's Crabshack, KFC, McDonald's, Poliberto's Tacos, Rainforest Cafe, Taco Bell, Waffle House, Wendy's, 🛏 Best Western, Candlewood Studios, Holiday Inn Express, InnSuites, Ramada, Residence Inn, SpringHill Suites, TownePlace Suites, ⊙ AutoZone, AZ Mills/Famous Brands, CVS Drug, Food City, Home Depot, JC Penney Outlet, Marshall's, Pro Auto Parts, Ross, Walgreens, **S** 🚹 Arco, QT, 7-11, 🛏 Homestead Suites, 🍴 Aunt Chilada's Mexican, China Town, Denny's, Sonic, Subway, ⊙ Fry's Electronics, Fry's Foods

PHOENIX

154	US 60 E, AZ 360, Superstition Frwy, to Mesa, **N** ⊙ to Camping World (off Mesa Dr)
153b	Broadway Rd E, **N** 🍴 Denny's, 🛏 Comfort Suites, Courtyard, Homestead Suites, Quality Inn, Red Roof Inn, Sheraton, ⊙ to Diablo Stadium, **S** 🚹 Chevron/dsl, Shell/Circle K/Del Taco/24hr, 🍴 Panda Express, Papa John's, Pizza Hut, Port of Subs, Taco Bell, Whataburger, 🛏 Hampton Inn, Homewood Suites, ⊙ Staples
153a	AZ 143 N, **N** 🍴 Denny's, 🛏 Courtyard, Fairfield Inn, Hilton, Holiday Inn, La Quinta, Sleep Inn, ⊙ to Diablo Stadium, **S** same as 153b
152	40th St, **N** 🚹 Shell/dsl, ⊙ U Phoenix, **S** 🚹 Shell/Circle K, 🍴 Burger King, Quiznos
151mm	Salt River
151b a	28th St, 32nd St, University Ave, **N** 🍴 Waffle House, 🛏 Drury Inn, Extended Stay America, Hilton Garden, Holiday Inn Express, ⊙ AZSU, U Phoenix, **S** 🚹 Circle K, 🍴 McDonald's
150b	24th St E (from wb), **N** Air Nat Guard, 🛏 Motel 6, **S** 🛏 Best Western/rest.
150a	I-17 N, to Flagstaff
149	Buckeye Rd, **N** ⊙ Sky Harbor ✈
148	Washington St, Jefferson St, **N** 🚹 Chevron/dsl, Shell, Tiemco/dsl, 🍴 Carl's Jr, McDonald's, 🛏 Motel 6, Sterling Hotel, ⊙ to Sky Harbor ✈, **S** 🚹 Circle K, ⊙ 🅷
147b a	AZ 51 N, AZ 202 E, to Squaw Peak Pkwy
146	16th St, **N** 🚹 Shell/Circle K, 🍴 Filiberto's Mexican, 🚹 Circle K, Shamrock/dsl, 🍴 Church's, Jack-in-the-Box, Salsita's Mexican, ⊙ 🅷, Ranch Mkt
145	7th St, **N** 🍴 McDonald's, Sonic, Starbucks, Subway, Taco Bell, Whataburger, ⊙ Safeway Foods, Walgreens, **S** 🚹 Circle K, Shell, Sinclair/dsl, 🍴 Quiznos, 🛏 Courtyard, Holiday Inn Express, Hyatt, Sheraton, Springhill Suites, ⊙ 🅷, to Chase Field
144	7th Ave, **N** 🚹 Circle K, 🍴 Peiwei Asian, Starbucks, **S** 🚹 Circle K, ⊙ central bus dist
143c	US 60, 19th Ave (from wb) downtown
143b a	I-17, N to Flagstaff, S to Phoenix
142	27th Ave (from eb, no return), **N** 🛏 Comfort Inn
141	35th Ave, **N** 🍴 Jack-in-the-Box, Rita's Mexican, **S** 🚹 Shell/Circle K
140	43rd Ave, **N** 🚹 Circle K/dsl, 7-11, Shell, 🍴 KFC, Filiberto's Mexican, Pizza Hut, Salsita's Mexican, Subway, 🛏 ValuePlace Hotel, ⊙ AutoZone, Fry's Mercado/gas, 99¢ Store, Radio Shack, Walgreens
139	51st Ave, **N** 🚹 Chevron/dsl, Circle K, 🍴 Burger King, Domino's, El Pollo Loco, McDonald's, Sonic, Waffle House, 🛏 Best Value Inn, Budget Inn, Crossland Suites, Holiday Inn, InTown Suites, La Quinta, Motel 6, Red Roof Inn, Travelodge, ⊙ Discount Tire, Food City, 7-11, **S** 🚹 QT/dsl/scales, Shell/dsl, 🍴 Carl's Jr, IHOP, Port of Subs, Taco Bell, 🛏 I-10 West Hotel, Super 8, Travelers Inn
138	59th Ave, **N** 🚹 Circle K, Shamrock, 🍴 Los Armandos Mexican, Subway, ⊙ AutoZone, Checker Parts, Family$, 7-11, Walgreens, **S** 🚹 Liberty/Chester's/dsl/24hr, 🍴 Waffle House, ⊙ Blue Beacon/scales
137	67th Ave, **N** 🚹 QT, Circle K/dsl, Shell/dsl, 🍴 Church's, **S** 🚹 *FLYING J*/Denny's/dsl/LP/24hr
136	75th Ave, **N** 🚹 Chevron/dsl, Circle K/dsl, 🍴 A&W/LJ Silver, CiCi's Pizza, Coco's, Denny's, Great China, IHOP, Lin's Buffet, McDonald's, Olive Garden, Red Lobster, Starbucks, Subway, TX Roadhouse, Wendy's, Whataburg

INTERSTATE 10 CONT'D

Exit	Services

P H O E N I X

136 Continued
er, 🅞 AT&T, Big O Tire, Dillards, Home Depot, Lowe's, PetsMart, Radio Shack, Ross, Sears, Staples, Target, Walmart, **S** 🅖 Arco/24hr

135 83rd Ave, **N** 🅖 Circle K/dsl, 🍴 Arby's, Burger King, Jack-in-the-Box, Waffle House, 🏨 Comfort Suites, Premier Inn, Victory Inn, 🅞 K-Mart, Sam's Club/gas

134 91st Ave, Tolleson, **N** 🅖 Circle K/dsl

133b Lp 101 N

133a 99th Ave, **N** 🅖 Chevron/dsl, 🍴 Baja Fresh, Carrabba's, Chick-fil-A, Chipotle Mexican, ClaimJumper, HoneyBaked Ham, Ichiban Rest., Island's Burgers, McDonald's, Peter Piper Pizza, Red Robin, Rumbi Grill, Starbucks, Subway, Village Inn, 🏨 Courtyard, 🅞 Best Buy, Costco/gas, Discount Tire, GNC, Hobby Lobby, Marshall's, Old Navy, PetCo, Verizon, **Urgent Care**, **S** 🍴 🚂 /Subway/Wendy's/dsl/scales/24hr, 🅞 CarMax, Chevrolet

132 107th Ave, **N** 🅞 Walgreens, **S** 🅞 Chrysler/Jeep, Dodge, Dodge, Honda, Hyundai, Kia, Nissan, Subaru, Suzuki, Toyota/Scion, VW

131 Avondale Blvd, to Cashion, **N** 🅖 Circle K/dsl, **S** 🍴 Jack-in-the-Box, Panda Express, Ruby Tuesday, 🏨 Hilton Garden, Homewood Suites, 🅞 Fresh&Easy, Staples, to Phoenix Intnl Raceway

129 Dysart Rd, to Avondale, **N** 🅖 Chevron/dsl, Shell/Circle K/dsl, 🍴 Big Apple Rest., Buffalo Wild Wings, Chick-fil-A, In-N-Out, Jack-in-the-Box/24hr, Mimi's Cafe, NYPD Pizza, Ono Hawaiian BBQ, Palermo's Pizza, Panda Express, Papa Murphy's, Peiwei Asian, Starbucks, Subway, Taco Bell, Tagliani Italian, Tomo Japanese, 🏨 Holiday Inn Express, 🅞 AT&T, AutoZone, Discount Tire, JC Penney, Jo Ann Fabrics, Fry's Foods, Kohl's, Lowe's, PetsMart, Sprouts Mkt, Tuesday Morning, Verizon, Walmart, vet, **S** 🅖 QT, 🍴 A&W/LJ Silver, Bamboo Palace, Black Bear Diner, Del Taco, Filiberto's Mexican, Golden Corral, IHOP, KFC, McDonald's, Peter Piper Pizza, Subway, Waffle House, Whataburger, Yoshinoya, 🏨 Quality Inn, Super 8, 🅞 Brakemasters, Food City, Home Depot, Pepboys, Sam's Club/gas, Walgreens

128 Litchfield Rd, **N** 🅖 Circle K, 🍴 Applebee's, Black Angus Steaks, Carl's Jr, Chili's, Chipotle Mexican, Cracker Barrel, Denny's, Macaroni Grill, Macavo's Mexican, McDonald's, McGrath's Fishouse, Rossati's Pizza, Starbucks, Subway, TGIFriday's, Wendy's, Wildflower Bread Co., 🏨 Hampton Inn, Holiday Inn Express, Residence Inn, 🅞🏥 Barnes&Noble, Best Buy, Circle K, Michael's, Ross, Target, Wigwam Resort/rest (3mi), to Luke AFB, **S** 🅖 Circle K/dsl, 🍴 Arby's, Burger King, JB's, Schlotsky's, Taco Bell, 🏨 Best Western, TownePlace Suites, 🅞 AutoZone, BigLots, Buick/GMC, Checker Parts, Ford, Fry's Food/drug

127 Bullard Ave

126 PebbleCreek Pkwy, to Estrella Park, **N** 🅖 Barro's Pizza, Olive Garden, Paradise Cafe, Red Lobster, Rubio's, Starbucks, Taco Bell, 🅞 Basha's Foods, Old Navy, PetCo, Staples, TJ Maxx, Walgreens, **S** 🅖 Horizon, 🍴 Augie's Grill, Bro's Pizza, Jack-in-the-Box, McDonald's, Panda Express, Papa Murphys, Senor Taco, Subway, Yan's Chinese, 🏨 Comfort Suites, 🅞 Ace Hardware, Fletcher Tire, Radio Shack, Safeway Foods/dsl, Walgreens, Walmart, **Urgent Care**, vet

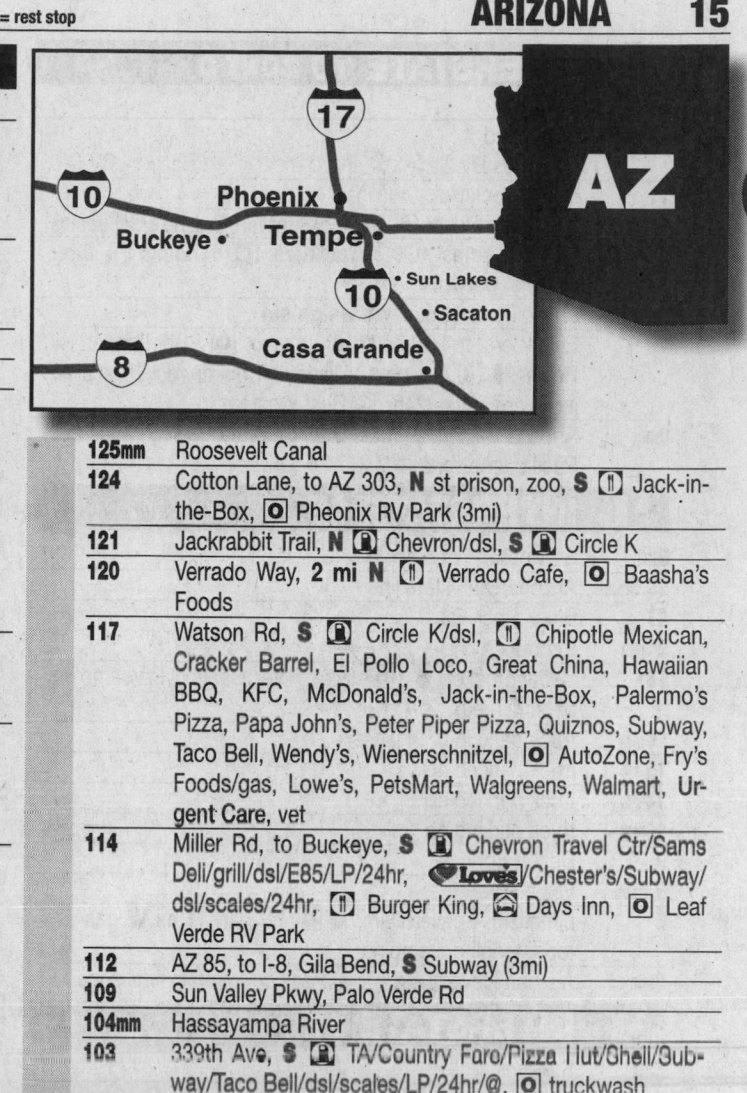

125mm Roosevelt Canal

124 Cotton Lane, to AZ 303, **N** st prison, zoo, **S** 🍴 Jack-in-the-Box, 🅞 Phoenix RV Park (3mi)

121 Jackrabbit Trail, **N** 🅖 Chevron/dsl, **S** 🅖 Circle K

120 Verrado Way, **2 mi N** 🍴 Verrado Cafe, 🅞 Baasha's Foods

117 Watson Rd, **S** 🅖 Circle K/dsl, 🍴 Chipotle Mexican, Cracker Barrel, El Pollo Loco, Great China, Hawaiian BBQ, KFC, McDonald's, Jack-in-the-Box, Palermo's Pizza, Papa John's, Peter Piper Pizza, Quiznos, Subway, Taco Bell, Wendy's, Wienerschnitzel, 🅞 AutoZone, Fry's Foods/gas, Lowe's, PetsMart, Walgreens, Walmart, Urgent Care, vet

114 Miller Rd, to Buckeye, **S** 🅖 Chevron Travel Ctr/Sams Deli/grill/dsl/E85/LP/24hr, Loves/Chester's/Subway/dsl/scales/24hr, 🍴 Burger King, 🏨 Days Inn, 🅞 Leaf Verde RV Park

112 AZ 85, to I-8, Gila Bend, **S** Subway (3mi)

109 Sun Valley Pkwy, Palo Verde Rd

104mm Hassayampa River

103 339th Ave, **S** 🅖 TA/Country Fare/Pizza Hut/Shell/Subway/Taco Bell/dsl/scales/LP/24hr/@, 🅞 truckwash

98 Wintersburg Rd

97mm Coyote Wash

95.5mm Old Camp Wash

94 411th Ave, Tonopah, **S** 🅖 Chevron/dsl, Mobil/dsl, Shell/Cafe Charro/Noble Roman's/Subway/dsl/LP/24hr, 🍴 Tonopah Joe's Rest., 🏨 Mineral Wells Motel, 🅞 Saddle Mtn RV Park, tires/repair, USPO

86mm 🆁🆂 both lanes, full ♿ facilities, 🅒, 🏕, litter barrels, petwalk, vending

81 Salome Rd, Harquahala Valley Rd

69 Ave 75E

53 Hovatter Rd

52mm 🆁🆂 both lanes, full ♿ facilities, 🅒, vending, 🏕, litter barrels, petwalk

45 Vicksburg Rd, **N** 🅖 Zip TC/HotStuff/dsl/scales/LP/24hr, 🍴 Cactus Cafe, **S** 🅖 Valero/dsl/rest./scales/24hr, 🅞 Jobski's dsl Repair/towing, Kofa NWR, RV Park, tires

31 US 60 E, to Wickenburg, **12 mi N** 🅞 food, camping

26 Gold Nugget Rd

19 Quartzsite, to US 95, Yuma, **N** 🅖 Arco/dsl, Chevron/dsl, Shell/dsl, 🍴 Taco Mio, 🅞 Beall's, Family$, Roadrunner Foods, RV camping

18mm Tyson Wash

17 US 95, AZ 95, Quartzsite, **N** 🅖 Mobil/Burger King/LP, 🚂DQ/Subway/dsl/scales/24hr, 🍴 Best Mexican, Carl's Jr, McDonald's, Quartzsite Yacht Grill, 🅞 RV camping, tires/repair, **S** 🅖 Loves/Chester's/Subway/dsl/24hr, 🏨 Super 8, 🅞 Desert Gardens RV Park

Q U A R T Z S I T E

▶E INTERSTATE 10 CONT'D

Exit	Services
17	Continued
	Lifestyles RV Ctr
11	Dome Rock Rd
5	Tom Wells Rd, N [gas] Texaco/SunMart/Quizno's/dsl/scales
4.5mm	[Rs] both lanes, full [&] facilities, [C], vending, [litter] litter barrels, petwalk
3.5mm	eb AZ Port of Entry, **wb weigh sta**
1	Ehrenberg, to Parker, N [gas] Texaco, [O] River Lagoon RV Resort, S [gas] ⒻLYING J/Wendy's/Cookery/dsl/LP/scales/lube/repair/tires/24hr, [lodging] Best Western
0mm	Arizona/California state line, Colorado River, Mountain/Pacific time zone

▶N INTERSTATE 15

Exit	Services
29.5mm	Arizona/Utah state line
27	Black Rock Rd
21mm	turnout sb
18	Cedar Pocket, S [O] Virgin River Canyon RA/camping, parking area
16mm	truck parking both lanes
15mm	truck parking nb
14mm	truck parking nb
10mm	truck parking nb
9	Desert Springs
8.5mm	Virgin River
8	Littlefield, Beaver Dam, E [O] RV park, **1 mi W** gas/dsl, food, lodging, camping
0mm	Arizona/Nevada state line, Pacific/Mountain time zone

▶N INTERSTATE 17

Exit	Services
341	McConnell Dr, **I-17 begins/ends**, N [gas] Chevron/dsl, Conoco/dsl, Giant/dsl, Mobil/dsl, Circle K, Shell, Texaco/Wendy's/dsl, [food] Arby's, August Moon Chinese, Baskin-Robbins, Buffalo Wild Wings, Burger King, Buster's Rest., Carl's Jr, Chili's, China Garden, Chipotle Mexican, Coco's, Coldstone, DQ, Del Taco, Denny's, Domino's, 5 Guys Burgers, Freddy's Steakburgers, IHOP, Jack-in-the-Box, KFC, Little Caesars, Mandarin Buffet, McDonald's, Native New Yorker, Ni Marco's Pizza, Olive Garden, Panda Express, Papa John's, Papa Murphy's, Picazzo's Pizza, Peter Piper Pizza, Pizza Hut, Quiznos, Red Lobster, Sizzler, Starbucks, Subway, Taco Bell, [lodging] Best Inn, Budget Inn, Canyon Inn, Comfort Inn, Courtyard, Country Inn, Days Inn, Drury Inn, EconoLodge, Embassy Suites, Executive Inn, Fairfield Inn, Hampton Inn, Knights Inn, La Quinta, Motel 6, Quality Inn, Ramada Ltd, Rodeway Inn, SpringHill Suites, Super 8, [O] [H], AT&T, Barnes&Noble, Basha's Foods, Discount Tire, $Tree, Hastings Books, Jo-Ann Crafts, Kohl's, Michael's, O'Reilly Parts, Petsmart, Ross, Safeway, Staples, Target, Verizon, Walgreens, Walmart, auto/RV repair
340b a	I-40, E to Gallup, W to Kingman
339	Lake Mary Rd (from nb), Mormon Lake, E [gas] Circle K/dsl, [lodging] AZ Mtn Inn, access to same as 341
337	AZ 89A S, to Sedona, Ft Tuthill RA, W [food] camping
333	Kachina Blvd, Mountainaire Rd, E [food] Mountainaire Rest. (1mi), [lodging] Abineau B&B, W [gas] Shell/Subway/dsl, [O] city park
331	Kelly Canyon Rd

Exit	Services
328	Newman Park Rd
326	Willard Springs Rd
322	Pinewood Rd, to Munds Park, E [gas] Shell/dsl, Woody's/dsl, [food] Lone Pine Rest., [O] Motel in the Pines, golf, W [gas] Chevron/dsl, [food] Pine Woody's Pizza, [O] Munds RV Park
322mm	Munds Canyon
320	Schnebly Hill Rd
317	Fox Ranch Rd
316mm	Woods Canyon
315	Rocky Park Rd
313mm	scenic view sb, litter barrels
306	Stoneman Lake Rd
300mm	runaway truck ramp sb
298	AZ 179, to Sedona, Oak Creek Canyon, **7-15 mi W** [food] Burger King, Cowboy Club Rest., Joey's Bistro, [lodging] Belrock Inn, Diamond Resort, Hilton, La Quinta, Radisson/cafe, Wildflower Inn, [O] Rancho Sedona RV Park
297mm	[Rs] both lanes, full [&] facilities, [C], [litter], litter barrels, vending, petwalk
293mm	Dry Beaver Creek
293	Cornville Rd, McGuireville Rd, to Rimrock, E [gas] McGuireville, [food] Creek Side Grill, W [gas] Conoco/Beaver Hollow/dsl, 76/dsl, [food] El Patio Grill
289	Middle Verde Rd, Camp Verde, E [gas] Chevron/dsl, [food] Sonic, The Gathering Rest., [lodging] Cliff Castle Hotel/casino/rest., [O] to Montezuma Castle NM, W [O] Distant Drums RV Park
288mm	Verde River
287	AZ 260, to AZ 89A, Cottonwood, Payson, E [gas] Shell/Subway/dsl/RV dump/LP/24hr, [food] Burger King, DQ, Denny's, Famous Pizza, Los Betos Mexican, McDonald's, Starbucks, Taco Bell, [lodging] Comfort Inn, Days Inn, Super 8, [O] Territorial RV Park (1mi), Trails End RV Park, Zane Grane RV Park (9mi), W [gas] Chevron/Wendy's/dsl/24hr, [O] to Jerome SP, RV camping
285	Camp Verde, Gen Crook Tr, **3 mi E** [food] Rio Verde Mexican, [lodging] Territorial Town Inn, [O] Zane Gray RV Park (9mi), Trail End RV Park, to Ft Verde SP
281mm	safety pullout area nb
278	AZ 169, Cherry Rd, to Prescott
269mm	Ash Creek
268	Dugas Rd, Orme Rd
265.5mm	Agua Fria River
262b a	AZ 69 N, Cordes Jct Rd, to Prescott, E [gas] Chevron, Shell/Noble Roman's/Subway/dsl/LP/24hr, [food] Cafe Charo, McDonald's, [lodging] Cordes Jct Motel/RV Park
262mm	Big Bug Creek
259	Bloody Basin Rd, to Crown King, Horsethief Basin RA
256	Badger Springs Rd
252	Sunset Point, **W** scenic view/ [Rs] both lanes, full [&] facilities, [C], [litter], litter barrels, vending
248	Bumble Bee, W [O] Horsethief Basin RA
244	Squaw Valley Rd, Black Canyon City, E [food] Kid Chilleen's BBQ/Steaks, W [gas] Shell, [food] Beni's Pizza, Byler's Amish Kitchen, [O] Bradshaw Mtn RV Resort (2mi)
243.5mm	Agua Fria River
242	Rock Springs, Black Canyon City, E KOA (1mi), W [gas] Chevron/dsl, 76, Shell, [food] Beni's Pizza, Byler's Kitchen, Rock Springs Café, [lodging] Bradshaw Mtn RV Resort, Mtn Breeze Motel
239.5mm	Little Squaw Creek
239mm	Moore's Gulch

Side margins: AZ • SEDONA • CAMP VERDE • FLAGSTAFF

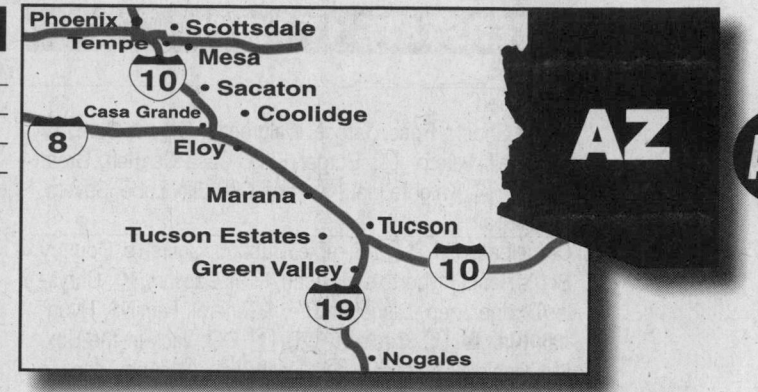

⬆N INTERSTATE 17 CONT'D

Exit	Services
236	Table Mesa Rd
232	New River, E 🍴 RoadRunner Rest.
231.5mm	New River
229	Anthem Way, Desert Hills Rd, E ⛽ Circle K, 🍴 Legend's Grill, McDonald's, Pizza Hut, Rosati's Pizza, Starbucks, Subway, Taco Bell, Wendy's, 🅾 Anthem RV Ctr, CVS Drug, Safeway, **Urgent Care**, vet, W ⛽ Chevron/dsl, Circle K/dsl, 🍴 Del Taco, Denny's, Fresca's Mexican, Subway, 🛏 Hampton Inn, 🅾 Anthem Outlets/famous brands/food court, Discount Tire, $Store, Harley-Davidson, O'Reilly Parts, Tobias Auto, U-Haul, Walmart
227	Daisy Mtn Dr, E ⛽ Circle K/dsl, 🍴 Cafe Province, Domino's, Jack-in-the-Box, Roberto's Mexican, Starbucks, Subway, 🅾 CVS Drug, Fry's Foods, Verizon
227mm	Dead Man Wash
225	Pioneer Rd, W 🅾 Pioneer RV Park, Pioneer AZ Museum
223	AZ 74, Carefree Hwy, to Wickenburg, E ⛽ Chevron, 🍴 AZool Grill, Chili's, Denny's, Good Egg Cafe, In-N-Out, McDonald's, Ray's Pizza, Starbucks, Subway, Taco Bell, 🅾 Albertson's/Osco, GNC, Home Depot, Kohl's, Staples, W 🅾 Cibola Vista Camping (11mi)
222	Senora Blvd
220	Dixileta (from nb)
219	Jomax Rd
218	Happy Valley Rd, E ⛽ Circle K/dsl, Shell, 🍴 Applebee's, Bajio, Buffalo Wild Wings, Burger King, Carl's Jr, Chipotle Mexican, Coldstone, IHOP, Jack-in-the-Box, Jersey Mike's Subs, Joey's Hotdogs, Johnny Rocket's, Logan's Roadhouse, L&L Hawaiian BBQ, Mellow Mushroom Pizza, Olive Garden, Panda Express, Paradise Cafe, PF Chang's, Rays Pizza, Red Robin, Sauce Pizza, Shane's Ribshack, Smash Burger, Starbucks, Subway, TGIFriday's, 🛏 Courtyard, Hampton Inn, Homewood Suites, Residence Inn, 🅾 Barnes&Noble, Best Buy, Big O Tire, Dick's, $Tree, Lowe's, O'Reilly Parts, PetCo, Ross, Staples, TJ Maxx, Verizon, Walmart, World Mkt, vet
217	Pinnacle Peak Rd, E 🛏 Drury Inn, 🅾 Phoenix RV Park
215a	Rose Garden Ln, same as 215b
215b	Deer Valley Rd, E ⛽ Shell/Circle K, 🍴 Arby's, Armando's Mexican, Culvers, Dunkin Donuts, Jack-in-the-Box, McDonald's, Sonic, Taco Bell, Wendy's, 🅾 Little Dealer RV Ctr, W ⛽ Arco/dsl, Circle K/dsl, 🍴 Cracker Barrel, Denny's, Times Square Italian, Waffle House, 🛏 Days Inn, Extended Stay America, 🅾 🏨 U-Haul
214c	AZ 101 loop
214b	Yorkshire Dr, W 🍴 In-N-Out, Jack-in-the-Box, 🛏 Budget Suites, 🅾 🏨 Costco/gas, W on 27th Ave ⛽ 7-11, 🍴 El Patron Mexican, 5&Diner, Pizza Hut, Wendy's, 🅾 Michael's, Petsmart, Ross, Target
214a	Union Hills Dr, E ⛽ Circle K/dsl, Valero, W ⛽ Arco, 🛏 Comfort Inn, Sleep Inn, Studio 6
212b a	Bell Rd, Scottsdale, to Sun City, E ⛽ Chevron/dsl, Circle K, QT, Shell/dsl, 🍴 Big Apple Rest., Caramba Mexican, IHOP, Jack-in-the-Box, LJ Silver, McDonald's, Schlotzsky's, Shenanigan's Grill, Waffle House, 🛏 Fairfield Inn, Motel 6, Super 8, 🅾 AAA, Big O Tire, Chevrolet, Chrysler/Jeep/Dodge, Discount Tire, Fiat, Ford, Hyundai, Kohl's, Lincoln, Mazda, Nissan, O'Reilly Parts, Sam's Club/gas, Toyota/Scion, U-Haul, Volvo, Walmart, W 🍴 Applebee's, Denny's, Hooters, Native New Yorker, 🛏 Red Roof Inn, 🅾 Fry's Foods/dsl

211	Greenway Rd, E 🛏 Embassy Suites, La Quinta, 🅾 7-11
210	Thunderbird Rd, E ⛽ Circle K/dsl, Valero/dsl/LP, 🍴 Asian Cafe, Barro's Pizza, Jack-in-the-Box, Macayo's Mexican, Pizza Hut/Taco Bell, Subway, Tulioberto's, Wendy's, 🅾 CVS Drug, Home Depot, Walgreens, W ⛽ QT, 🍴 Jamba Juice, McDonald's, Port of Subs, Whataburger, 🛏 Days Inn, 🅾 Best Buy, Fry's Electronics, Lowe's, **Urgent Care**
209	Cactus Rd, W ⛽ Chevron/dsl, 7-11, 🍴 China Harvest, Pedro's Mexican, 🛏 Holiday Inn, 🅾 Food City
208	Peoria Ave, E 🍴 Fajita's, Outback Steaks, Pappadeaux, Sweet Tomatoes, TGIFriday's, 🛏 Candlewood Suites, Comfort Suites, Crowne Plaza, Extended Stay America, Homewood Suites, Hyatt Place, W ⛽ QT, 🍴 Black Angus, Buffalo Wild Wings, Burger King, Cane's, Chili's, China Chan, Chipotle Mexican, Coldstone, Culvers, Fat Burger, Hibachi Grill, In-N-Out, Jason's Deli, Mimi's Cafe, Mi Pueblo, Old Country Buffet, Olive Garden, Peter Piper Pizza, Red Lobster, Robeks, Sizzler, Souper Salad, Starbucks, Swenson's Ice Cream, Subway, TX Roadhouse, Wendy's, Whataburger, 🛏 Premier Inn, 🅾 Barnes&Noble, Dillard's, Discount Tire, $Tree, Firestone/auto, Macy's, Michael's, PetCo, Petsmart, Ross, Sears/auto, Staples, Verizon, mall
208.5mm	Arizona Canal
207	Dunlap Ave, E ⛽ Circle K, Shell/dsl, 🍴 Blimpie, Cousin's Subs, Domino's, Fajitas, Fuddrucker's, Jack-in-the-Box, Outback Steaks, Steaken Burger, Subway, Sweet Tomatoes, Wong's, 🛏 Budget Lodge, Comfort Suites, Courtyard, Homestead Suites, Mainstay Suites, Sheraton, SpringHill Suites, TownPlace Suites, 🅾 Aamco, CVS Drug, Firestone, **Urgent Care**, W ⛽ Chevron/dsl, 🍴 Denny's, Schlotzsky's, Subway, 🛏 ValuePlace, 🅾 Midas, U-Haul, repair
206	Northern Ave, E ⛽ Circle K/dsl, Shell/dsl, 🍴 Boston Mkt, Burger King, Del Taco, Denny's, Dunkin Donuts, El Pollo Loco, Gyros House, Los Compadres, McDonald's, Papa John's, Pizza Hut, Starbucks, Subway, Uncle Tony's Pizza, 🛏 Best Western, 🅾 Albertson's/Osco, Walgreens, W ⛽ Arco, QT, 🍴 Bobby Q's, DQ, 🛏 Motel 6, Residence Inn, Super 8, 🅾 $General, K-Mart, vet
205	Glendale Ave, E ⛽ QT, 7-11, 🍴 Burger King, Pizza Patron, Subway, 🅾 Ace Hardware, Circle K, Fry's Foods/dsl, repair, transmissions, vet, W ⛽ Circle K/dsl, 🍴 Jack-in-the-Box, Lenny's Burger, 🅾 O'Reilly Parts, 7-11, Walgreens, to Luke AFB
204	Bethany Home Rd, E ⛽ Arco, Chevron, Shell/Church's/dsl, 🍴 Carl's Jr, Dunkin Donuts, KFC, McDonald's, Pizza Hut/Taco Bell, Papa Joe's, Subway, Tulioberto's Mexican, Whataburger, 🅾 🏨 BigLots, Costco, $Tree, JC Penney,

AZ

P H O E N I X

⬆N INTERSTATE 17 CONT'D

Exit	Services
204	Continued
	Radio Shack, Ross, Target, Walgreens, **Urgent Care**, **W** 🅖 Shell, Valero, 🍴 Burger King, Casa Carmen, Great Dragon, 🛏 Knights Inn 🅞 Food City, Jiffy Lube, Savers, auto repair
203	Camelback Rd, **E** 🍴 Blimpie, Cubano, Church's, Country Boy's Rest., Filiberto's Mexican, Little Caesars, 🅞 Chrysler/Dodge/Jeep, Discount Tire, $General, Family$, Hyundai, Kia, **W** 🅖 Circle K, QT, 🍴 DQ, Jack-in-the-Box, McDonald's, TacoMex, 🛏 Quality Inn, 🅞 AutoZone, to Grand Canyon U
202	Indian School Rd, **E** 🅖 Arco/dsl, 🍴 Domino's, Federico's Mexican, Pizza Hut, Subway, 🅞 Ace Hardware, CVS Drug, Food City, Little RV Ctr, **W** 🅖 Shell, Sinclair/dsl, Valero/dsl, 🍴 JB's Rest, Wendy's, 🛏 Motel 6, Travel Inn, 🅞 7-11, Wide World of Maps
201	Thomas Rd, **E** 🅖 Chevron/McDonald's/playplace, 🍴 Arby's, Denny's, Dunkin Donuts, Jack-in-the-Box, Starbucks, 🛏 Days Inn, La Quinta, 🅞 Circle K, **W** 🅖 QT, 🍴 Carl's Jr, Subway, 🅞 NAPA
200b	McDowell Rd, Van Buren, **E** 🅞 Purcell's Tire, **W** 🛏 Knights Inn
200a	I-10, W to LA, E to Phoenix
199b	Jefferson St (from sb), Adams St (from nb), Van Buren St (from nb), **E** 🅖 Circle K, 🍴 Jack-in-the-Box, 🅞 to st capitol, **W** 🅖 Circle K/gas, 🍴 La Canasta Mexican, Salsita's Mexican, 🅞 Penny Pincher Parts, PepBoys
199a	Grant St
198	Buckeye Rd (from nb)
197	US 60, 19th Ave, Durango St, **E** 🍴 Jack-in-the-Box, Whataburger, to St Capitol
196	7th St, Central Ave, **W** 🅖 Shell/dsl
195b	7th St, Central Ave, **E** 🅖 Big Tiger/dsl, Circle K/dsl, 🍴 Jack-in-the-Box, McDonald's, Taco Bell, 🛏 EZ 8 Motel/rest., 🅞 🄷, NAPA Care
195a	16th St (from sb, no EZ return), **E** 🍴 Burger King, 🅞 Food City, to Sky Harbor ✈
194	I-10 W to AZ 151, to Sky Harbor ✈

I-17 begins/ends on I-10, exit 150a

⬆N INTERSTATE 19

T U C S O N

Exit	Services
I-19 uses kilometers (km)	
101b a	I-10, E to El Paso, W to Phoenix. **I-19 begins/ends on I-10, exit 260**
99	AZ 86, Ajo Way, **E** 🅖 Circle K, 🍴 Eegee's Cafe, Hamburger Stand, Peter Piper Pizza, Pizza Hut, Subway, Taco Bell, Wienerschnitzel, 🅞 Fry's Foods, GNC, Goodyear/auto, U-Haul, Walgreens, auto repair, vet, **W** 🅖 Circle K, QT/dsl, Shell, 🍴 Bamboo Terrace, Burger King, Church's, Domino's, Little Caesars, 🅞 🄷, **Urgent Care**, Family$, Food City, Jiffy Lube, to Old Tucson, museum
98	Irvington Rd, **E** 🅖 Arco, 🍴 TX Roadhouse, 🅞 Fry's Foods/drug/dsl, 99¢ Store, **W** 🅖 Chevron, 🍴 Buffalo Wild Wings, China Olive Buffet, Coldstone, Hana Tokyo, McDonald's, Olive Garden, Panda Express, Peter Piper Pizza, Red Lobster, Starbucks, Subway, 🅞 **Urgent Care**, AT&T, Best Buy, Discount Tire, $Tree, Family$, Food City, Home Depot, JC Penney, Marshall's, Michael's, Office Depot, Old Navy, Petsmart, Ross, Target, Verizon

G R E E N   V A L L E Y

A M A D O

Exit	Services
95b a	Valencia Rd, **E** 🅖 Circle K, Shell, 🍴 Church's, Donut Wheel, Jack-in-the-Box, Little Caesars, McDonald's, Peter Piper Pizza, Sonic, Subway, Whataburger, Yokohama Asian, 🅞 Aamco, AutoZone, Brake Masters, $General, $Tree, Food City, Family$, Jiffy Lube, Walgreens, USPO, to ✈, **W** 🅖 Chevron/dsl, Circle K/dsl, 🍴 Arby's, Baskin-Robbins/Dunkin Donuts, Burger King, Carl's Jr, Chili's, China Dragon, Denny's, El Taco Tote, Golden Corral, Grand Buffet, Hamburger Stand, Little Caesars, Papa John's, Papa Murphy's, Pizza Hut, Subway, Taco Bell, Wendy's, 🅞 **Urgent Care**, BigLots, Big O Tire, CVS Drug, Lowe's, 99¢ Store, Radio Shack, Walgreens, Walmart, repair, transmissions
92	San Xavier Rd, **W** 🅞 to San Xavier Mission
91.5km	Santa Cruz River
87	Papago Rd
80	Pima Mine Rd, **E** 🍴 Agave Rest., Diamond Casino
75	Helmut Peak Rd, to Sahuarita, **E** 🅖 Shell/dsl/e-85, 🅞 Asian Sky Rest, El Charro Cafe, Mama's Hawaiian BBQ, McDonald's, Starbucks, Subway, 🅞 Fry's Foods/drug, USPO
69	US 89 N, Duval Mine Rd., Green Valley, **E** 🍴 Carl's Jr., Denny's, Little Caesars, Panda House, Pizza Hut, Rigoberto's, Subway, 🅞 BigLots, Fletcher's Repair, 99¢ Store, O'Reilly Parts, Radio Shack, Ross, Verizon, Walgreens, Walmart/Subway, **W** 🅖 Circle K, Texaco/DQ/dsl, 🍴 Arby's, Burger King, DQ, Domino's, Papa Murphy's, Starbucks, Taco Bell, 🛏 Holiday Inn Express, 🅞 **Urgent Care**, Big O Tire, Curves, Ford/Hyundai, Green Valley RV Resort, NAPA, Safeway/gas, Titan Missile Museum, USPO, vet
65	Esperanza Blvd, to Green Valley, **E** 🅖 Shell/repair/dsl, **W** 🅖 Texaco/dsl, 🍴 AZ Family Rest., La Placita Mexican, 🛏 Best Western/rest, Comfort Inn, 🅞 Ace Hardware, Family$, Walgreens
63	Continental Rd, Green Valley, **E** 🍴 Quail Valley Rest., 🅞 golf, USPO, **2 mi E** 🅞 San Ignacio Golf Club/rest., **W** 🅖 Chevron/HotStuff Pizza, 🍴 KFC, Los Agave's, Mama's Kitchen, McDonald's, Starbucks, Trivettie's Rest., 🅞 CVS Drug, Merle's Parts, Safeway, TrueValue, Verizon, Walgreens, repair/tires, to Madera Cyn RA
56	Canoa Rd, **W** 🛏 San Ignacio Inn, Wyndham Resort
54km	🅡🅢 **both lanes, full** 🛏 **facilities,** 🍴, 🛏, **litter barrels, vending, petwalk**
48	Arivaca Rd, Amado, **2-3 mi E** 🛏 Amado Inn, 🅞 Mtn View RV Park, Rex Ranch Resort, **W** 🍴 Cow Palace Rest., 🅞 Amado Mkt/gas, JJ's Auto Repair
42	Agua Linda Rd, to Amado, **E** 🅞 Mtn View RV Park
40	Chavez Siding Rd, Tubac, **E** 🅞 Tubac Golf Resort
34	Tubac, **E** 🅖 El Mercado, 🍴 Elvira's Cafe, Maria's Grill, Tubac Hamburgers, Tubac Pizza, 🅞 Tubac Golf Resort, Tubac Mkt, USPO, to Tubac Presidio SP
29	Carmen, Tumacacori, **E** gas, food, lodging, 🅞 to Tumacacori Nat Hist Park
25	Palo Parado Rd
22	Pec Canyon Rd
17	Rio Rico Dr, Calabasas Rd, **W** 🅖 Chevron/dsl/LP, 🍴 Hua Mei Chinese, Nickles Diner, Wood Oven Pizza, 🛏 Esplendor Resort, 🅞 IGA Foods, JC Auto Repair/Lube, USPO, vet
12	AZ 289, to Ruby Rd, **E** 🅖 ▨/Wendy's/dsl/scales/24hr, **W** 🅞 to Pena Blanca Lake RA
8	AZ 82 (exits left from sb, no return), Nogales, **E** 🅖 Circle K, 🅞 Mi Casa RV Park

INTERSTATE 19 CONT'D

Exit	Services
4	AZ 189 S, Mariposa Rd, Nogales, **E** ⓖ FasTrip/dsl, ⓕ Bella Mia Rest., China Buffet, ChinaStar, City Salads, DQ, Jack-in-the-Box, KFC, Little Caesars, McDonald's, Panda Express, Subway, Taco Bell, ⓛ Motel 6, Super 8, ⓞ AutoZone, Batteries+, Buick/GMC, Chevrolet, $General, $Tree, Ford, Home Depot, JC Penney, K-Mart, NAPA, Buick/GMC, Ross, Safeway, Walgreens, Walmart/McDonald's (N Grand Ave), **W** ⓖ Circle K/dsl, ⓕ Carl's Jr, IHOP, ⓛ Best Western, Candlewood Suites, Holiday Inn Express, ⓞ Mexico Insurance
1b	Western Ave, Nogales
1a	International St
0km	**I-19 begins/ends in Nogales**, Arizona/Mexico Border, **1/2 mi** ⓖ Circle K, Jr's Fuel Depot/dsl, Shell, ⓕ Burger King, Church's, Jack-in-the-Box, McDonald's, Peter Piper Pizza, Pizza Hut, Subway, ⓞ AutoZone, CarQuest, Family$, Food City, NAPA, O'Reilly Parts, PepBoys, museum

INTERSTATE 40

Exit	Services
359.5mm	Arizona/New Mexico state line
359	Grants Rd, to Lupton, **N** Welcome Ctr/Ⓡ **both lanes, full** ♿ **facilities,** ⓕ, Ⓡ, **litter barrels, petwalk,** ⓖ Speedy's/dsl/rest./24hr, ⓞ Tee Pee Trading Post/rest., YellowHorse Indian Gifts
357	AZ 12 N, Lupton, to Window Rock, **N** ⓞ USPO
354	Hawthorne Rd
351	Allentown Rd, **N** ⓞ Chee's Indian Store, Indian City Gifts
348	St Anselm Rd, Houck, **N** ⓞ Ft Courage Food/gifts
347.5mm	Black Creek
346	Pine Springs Rd
345mm	Box Canyon
344mm	Querino Wash
343	Querino Rd
341	Ortega Rd, Cedar Point, **N** ⓖ Armco/gas/gifts
340.5mm	insp/weigh sta both lanes
339	US 191 S, to St Johns, **S** ⓖ Conoco/dsl, ⓞ Family$, RV Park, USPO
333	US 191 N, Chambers, **N** ⓖ Rte 66 Gas/dsl, ⓞ to Hubbell Trading Post NHS, USPO, **S** ⓖ Mobil/dsl, ⓛ Chieftain Inn/rest.
330	McCarrell Rd
325	Navajo, **S** ⓖ Shell/Subway/Navajo Trading Post/dsl/24hr
323mm	Crazy Creek
320	Pinta Rd
316mm	Dead River
311	Painted Desert, **N** ⓖ Chevron, ⓞ Petrified Forest NP, Painted Desert
303	Adamana Rd, **N** ⓞ Stewarts/gifts, **S** ⓞ Painted Desert Indian Ctr
302.5mm	Big Lithodendron Wash
301mm	Little Lithodendron Wash
300	Goodwater
299mm	Twin Wash
294	Sun Valley Rd, **N** Root 66 RV camping, **S** ⓞ Knife City
292	AZ 77 N, to Keams Canyon, **N** ⓖ Conoco/Burger King/dsl/24hr, ⓞ dsl repair
289	Lp 40, Holbrook, **N** ⓖ Chevron/dsl, Hatch's/dsl, ⓕ Denny's, Jerry's Rest., Mesa Rest., ⓛ Best Inn, Best Western, Comfort Inn, Days Inn, EconoLodge, Motel 6, Ramada Ltd, Sahara Inn, Travelodge, ⓞ Goodyear

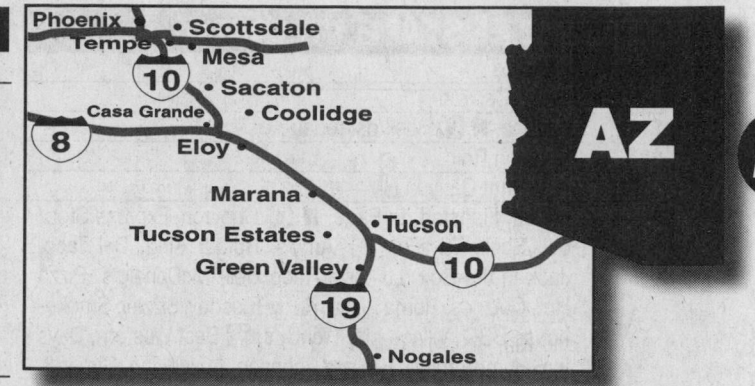

Exit	Services
286	Navajo Blvd, Holbrook, **N** ⓖ Chevron/dsl, Circle K, Maverik/dsl, ⓕ Aliberto's Mexican, Burger King, Hilltop Cafe, KFC, McDonald's, Pizza Hut, Taco Bell, ⓛ Holiday Inn Express, Super 8, 66 Motel, ⓞ Alco, $General, KOA, OK RV Park, O'Reilly Parts, **S** ⓖ Chevron/dsl, Fuel Express/dsl, Jack's/repair/LP, MiniMart/gas, Speedy Dsl, ⓕ DQ, Rte 66 Cafe, ⓛ Best Value, El Rancho Motel/rest., Knights Inn, ⓞⒽ, Dodge/Ford/Lincoln, Scotty & Son Repair, SW Transmissions, museum, rockshops
285	US 180 E, AZ 77 S, Holbrook **1 mi S** ⓖ Giant/dsl, ⓕ Butterfield Steaks, Wayside Mexican, ⓛ Best Western, Economy Inn, Globetrotter Hotel, Wigwam Motel, ⓞ Best Hardware, Family$, Safeway, repair, ✈ / Ⓡ /litter barrels, to Petrified Forest NP
284mm	Leroux Wash
283	Perkins Valley Rd, Golf Course Rd, **S** ⓖ Fuel Express/dsl/rest./scales/24hr/@
280	Hunt Rd, Geronimo Rd, **N** ⓞ Geronimo Trading Post
277	Lp 40, Joseph City, **N** ⓖ ♥Loves/Chester's/Subway/scales/dsl/24hr, **S** ⓞ to Cholla Lake CP, RV camping
274	Lp 40, Joseph City, **N** gas, food, lodging, RV camping
269	Jackrabbit Rd, **S** ⓞ Jackrabbit Trading Post
264	Hibbard Rd
257	AZ 87 N, to Second Mesa, **N** ⓞ to Homolovi Ruins SP, camping, **S** ⓞ trading post
256.5mm	Little Colorado River
255	Lp 40, Winslow, **N** ⓖ Winslow Fuel/dsl, ⓞ Mi Pueblo Mexican, ⓛ Best Western, ⓞ Take-A-Rest RV Park, **S** ⓖ ✈FLYING J/Denny's/dsl/LP/scales/RV Dump/24hr, ⓕ Sonic, ⓞ Chrysler/Dodge/Jeep, Nissan, ✈
253	N Park Dr, Winslow, **N** ⓖ Chevron, Maverik/dsl, ⓕ Arby's, Capt Tony's Pizza, Denny's, Pizza Hut, ⓞ $General, Ford, O'Reilly Parts, Walmart/truck parking, tires/lube, **S** ⓕ Alfonso's Mexican, KFC, LJ Silver/Taco Bell, McDonald's, Subway, ⓛ Motel 6, Oak Tree Inn, Quality Inn, ⓞⒽ Family$, NAPA
252	AZ 87 S, Winslow, **S** ⓖ Shell/dsl, ⓕ Entre Chinese, ⓛ Best Value, Rest Inn, Super 8, The Lodge
245	AZ 99, Leupp
239	Meteor City Rd, Red Gap Ranch Rd, **S** ⓞ Meteor City Trading Post, to Meteor Crater
235mm	Ⓡ **both lanes, full** ♿ **facilities, info,** ⓕ, Ⓡ, **litter barrels, petwalk**
233	Meteor Crater Rd, **S** ⓖ Mobil/Meteor Crater RV Park/dump, ⓞ to Meteor Crater NL
230	Two Guns
229.5mm	Canyon Diablo
225	Buffalo Range Rd
219	Twin Arrows

AZ

FLAGSTAFF

INTERSTATE 40 CONT'D

Exit	Services
218.5mm	Padre Canyon
211	Winona, **N** 🅟 Shell/dsl/repair
207	Cosnino Rd
204	to Walnut Canyon NM
201	US 89, Flagstaff, to Page, **N** 🅟 Chevron, Express Stop/dsl, Shell, Texaco, 🍽 Arby's, Burger King, Del Taco, Jack-in-the-Box, LJ Silver/Taco Bell, McDonald's, Pizza Hut, Quiznos, Roma Pizza, Ruby Tuesday, Sizzler, Smokehouse BBQ, Village Inn, Wendy's, 🛏 Best Western, Days Inn, Hampton Inn, Howard Johnson, Luxury Inn, Super 8, 🅞 🏥, Best Buy, CVS Drug, Dillard's, Discount Tire, Family$, Flagstaff RV Ctr/LP, Goodyear/auto, Home Depot, JC Penney, KOA, Marshall's, Old Navy, O'Reilly Parts, PetCo, PitStop Lube, Safeway/dsl, Sears/auto, Toyota, World Mkt, auto repair, mall, **S** 🅟 Mobil/dsl, 🛏 Residence Inn
198	Butler Ave, Flagstaff, **N** 🅟 Chevron, Conoco/dsl, Shell, 🍽 Burger King, Country Host Rest., Cracker Barrel, Denny's, Hogs Rest., McDonald's, Outback Steaks, Sonic, Taco Bell, 🛏 EconoLodge, Holiday Inn Express, Howard Johnson, Motel 6, Quality Inn, Ramada, Rodeway Inn, Super 8, Travelodge, 🅞 Ace Hardware, NAPA, Sam's Club/gas, U-Haul, Walmart, vet, **S** 🅟 Mobil, Sinclair/Little America/dsl/motel/@, 🍽 Black Bart's Steaks/RV Park
197.5mm	Rio de Flag
195b	US 89A N, McConnell Dr, Flagstaff, **N** 🅟 Chevron/dsl, Conoco/dsl, Giant/dsl, Mobil/dsl, Circle K, Shell, Texaco/Wendy's/dsl, 🍽 Arby's, August Moon Chinese, Baskin-Robbins, Buffalo Wild Wings, Burger King, Buster's Rest., Carl's Jr, Chili's, China Garden, Chipotle Mexican, Coco's, Coldstone, DQ, Del Taco, Denny's, Domino's, 5 Guys Burgers, Freddy's Steakburgers, IHOP, Jack-in-the-Box, KFC, Little Caesars, Mandarin Buffet, McDonald's, Native New Yorker, Ni Marco's Pizza, Olive Garden, Panda Express, Papa John's, Papa Murphy's, Picazzo's Pizza, Peter Piper Pizza, Pizza Hut, Quiznos, Red Lobster, Sizzler, Starbucks, Subway, Taco Bell, 🛏 Best Inn, Budget Inn, Canyon Inn, Comfort Inn, Courtyard, Country Inn, Days Inn, Drury Inn, EconoLodge, Embassy Suites, Executive Inn, Fairfield Inn, Hampton Inn, Knights Inn, La Quinta, Motel 6, Quality Inn, Ramada Ltd, Rodeway Inn, SpringHill Suites, Super 8, 🅞 🏥, AT&T, Barnes&Noble, Basha's Foods, Discount Tire, $Tree, Hastings Books, Jo-Ann Crafts, Kohl's, Michael's, O'Reilly Parts, Petsmart, Ross, Safeway, Staples, Target, Verizon, Walgreens, Walmart, auto/RV repair
195a	I-17 S, AZ 89A S, to Phoenix
192	Flagstaff Ranch Rd
191	Lp 40, to Grand Canyon, Flagstaff, **5 mi N** 🅟 Chevron, Maverik, Whistle Stop/dsl, 🍽 Galaxy Diner, 🛏 Best Value, Budget Host, Comfort Inn, Days Inn, EconoLodge, Radisson, Super 8, Travelodge, Travel Inn, 🅞 CarQuest, Checker Parts, Chevrolet/Cadillac, Home Depot, Kia, Kit Carson RV Park, vet, Woody Mtn Camping
190	A-1 Mountain Rd
189.5mm	Arizona Divide, elevation 7335
185	Transwestern Rd, Bellemont, **N** 🅟 ⛽ /McDonald's/Subway/dsl/scales/24hr/@, 🛏 Motel 6, **S** 🅞 Camping World, Harley-Davidson/Roadside Grill
178	Parks Rd, **N** 🅟 Texaco/dsl
171	Pittman Valley Rd, Deer Farm Rd, **S** 🛏 Ranch Resort
167	Garland Prairie Rd, Circle Pines Rd, **N** 🅞 KOA

WILLIAMS

SELIGMAN

165	AZ 64, to Williams, Grand Canyon, **N** 🅟 Texaco (8mi), Shell/dsl (4mi), 🅞 KOA (4mi), **S** 🛏 Super 8 (1mi)
163	Williams, **N** 🅟 Chevron/dsl, 🛏 Quality Inn, 🅞 Canyon Gateway RV Park, to Grand Canyon, **S** 🅟 Circle K, Mobil/dsl, Mustang/dsl, Conoco, 🍽 Jack-in-the-Box, KFC, McDonald's, Pine Country Rest., Pizza Factory, Pizza Hut, Pancho's Mexican, Red Garter Rest, Rod's Steaks, Rosa's Cantina, Rte 66 Diner, Taco Bell, Twisters Soda Fountain, 🛏 El Rancho Motel, Grand Canyon Railway Hotel, Holiday Inn, Howard Johnson, Knights Inn, Mountainside Motel, Rodeway Inn, Rte 66 Inn/cafe, Travelodge, 🅞 CarQuest, USPO, same as 161
161	Lp 40, Golf Course Dr, Williams, **N** RV camping, **0-3 mi S** 🅟 Circle K, Conoco/dsl/LP, Shell, 🍽 DQ, Denny's, Jessica's Rest., Pizza Factory, Rolando's Mexican, 🛏 AZ Motel, Best Western, Best Value, Budget Host, Canyon Country Inn, Comfort Inn, Days Inn, Grand Canyon Hotel, Highlander Motel, Motel 6, Super 8, Westerner Motel, 🅞 🏥, Family$, Safeway, Railside RV Ranch, to Grand Canyon Railway
157	Devil Dog Rd
155.5mm	safety pullout wb, litter barrels
151	Welch Rd
149	Monte Carlo Rd, **N** 🅞 dsl repair
148	County Line Rd
146	AZ 89, to Prescott, Ash Fork, **N** 🅟 Mobil/dsl, Shell/dsl, 🍽 Ranch House Cafe, 🛏 Ash Fork Inn
144	Ash Fork, **N** 🛏 Ash Fork Inn, 🅞 Grand Canyon RV Park, museum, USPO, **S** 🅟 Chevron/Piccadilly's/dsl, Texaco/dsl/RV Park, 🅞 auto/RV repair
139	Crookton Rd, to Rte 66
123	Lp 40, to Rte 66, Seligman, **N** 🅟 Shell, **1 mi N** 🅟 Chevron/A&W, Mustang/dsl, 🍽 Copper Cart Cafe, Lilo's Rest., 🛏 Canyon Lodge, Stagecoach 66 Motel/pizza, Supai Motel, 🅞 KOA (1mi), to Grand Canyon Caverns, USPO, repair, (same as 121), **S** 🅟 Chevron/Subway/dsl/24hr
121	Lp 40, to Rte 66, Seligman, **1 mi N** 🅟 Chevron/A&W, Mustang/dsl, 🍽 Copper Cart Cafe, Lilo's Rest., Roadkill Cafe, 🛏 Canyon Lodge, Route 66 Motel/pizza, Supai Motel, 🅞 KOA (1mi), to Grand Canyon Caverns, USPO, repair (same as 123)
109	Anvil Rock Rd
108mm	Markham Wash
103	Jolly Rd
96	Cross Mountain Rd
91	Fort Rock Rd
87	Willows Ranch Rd
86mm	Willow Creek
79	Silver Springs Rd
75.5mm	Big Sandy Wash
73.5mm	Peacock Wash
71	US 93 S, to Wickenburg, Phoenix
66	Blake Ranch Rd, **N** 🅟 Petro/Mobil/Iron Skillet/dsl/rest./scales/24hr/@, 🅞 Blake Ranch RV Park, Blue Beacon, SpeedCo Lube
60mm	Frees Wash
59	DW Ranch Rd, **N** 🅟 💙Loves /Chester's/Subway/dsl/scales/24hr, 🅞 Hualapai Mtn Park, truckwash
57mm	Rattlesnake Wash
53	AZ 66, Andy Devine Ave, to Kingman, **N** 🅟 Chevron, ⬧FLYING J/dsl/LP/scales/24hr, Terrible's/dsl, Texaco,

INTERSTATE 40 CONT'D

KINGMAN

Exit	Services
53	Continued
	🍴 Arby's, Burger King, Denny's, Jack-in-the-Box, McDonald's, Pizza Hut, Taco Bell, 🛏 Days Inn, EconoLodge, 1st Value Inn, Motel 6, Silver Queen Motel, Super 8, Travelodge, 🅾 🅷, Basha's Foods, Freightliner, Goodyear, K-Mart, KOA (1mi), Outdoorsman RV Ctr/Service, TireWorld, dsl/tire repair, S 🅿 Mobil/dsl, Shell/repair, 🍴 ABC Chinese, JB's, Lo's Chinese, Oyster's Mexican, Sonic, 🛏 Best Value Inn, Best Western, Comfort Inn, Days Inn, High Desert Inn, Holiday Inn Express, Lido Motel, Rodeway Inn, Rte 66 Motel, SpringHill Suites, 🅾 Chrysler/Dodge/Jeep, Kia, NAPA, Sunrise RV Park, Uptown Drug
51	Stockton Hill Rd, Kingman, N 🅿 Arco/24hr, Chevron, Circle K/dsl, 🍴 Chili's, Cracker Barrel, Del Taco, Golden Corral, IHOP, In-N-Out, KFC, Panda Express, Papa John's, Palace Buffet, Papa Murphy, Scotty's Rest., Sonic, Starbucks, Subway, Taco Bell, 🛏 Hampton Inn, 🅾 AT&T, AutoZone, AZ RV Depot/repair, BigLots, BrakeMasters, Buick/Chevrolet, CVS Drug, $General, $Tree, Ford/Lincoln, Home Depot, Honda, Hyundai, Oil Can Henry's, O'Reilly Parts, PetCo, Petsmart, Ross, Safeway/gas, Smith's Foods/dsl, Staples, Superior Tire, TrueValue, Walgreens, Walmart, vet, S 🅿 Circle K, 🍴 Alfonso's Mexican, Kingman Co Steaks, Little Caesars, Pizza Hut, 🅾 CarQuest, Family$, Hastings Books, JC Penney, Radio Shack, Safeway/gas, Sears
48	US 93 N, Beale St, Kingman, N 🅿 Chevron/dsl, Mobil/dsl, 76/dsl, Shell/dsl, TA/Country Pride/Popeye's/dsl/scales/24hr/@, Texaco/dsl, USA/Subway/dsl, Woody's, 🍴 Wendy's, 🛏 Budget Inn, Economy Inn, Tristate Inn,

YUCCA

Exit	Services
48	Continued
	🅾 Urgent Care, 4A Tire/auto/RV repair, S 🅿 Chevron/Quiznos/dsl, 🍴 Calico's Rest., Carl's Jr, 🛏 AZ Inn, Motel 6, 🅾 Ft Beale RV Park, city park, Mohave Museum
46.5mm	Holy Moses Wash
44	AZ 66, Oatman Hwy, McConnico, to Rte 66, S 🅿 Crazy Fred's/café/dsl, 🅾 Canyon West RV Camping (3mi), truckwash
40.5mm	Griffith Wash
37	Griffith Rd
35mm	Black Rock Wash
32mm	Walnut Creek
28	Old Trails Rd
26	Proving Ground Rd, S 🅾 AZ Proving Grounds
25	Alamo Rd, to Yucca, N USPO
23mm	🆁 both lanes, full ♿ facilities, 🍴, 🆁, litter barrels, vending, petwalk
21mm	Flat Top Wash
20	Santa Fe Ranch Rd
18.5mm	Illavar Wash
15mm	Buck Mtn Wash
13.5mm	Franconia Wash
13	Franconia Rd
9	AZ 95 S, to Lake Havasu City, Parker, London Br, S 🅿 Chevron/dsl, Loves/Carl's Jr/Subway/dsl/scales/24hr, Wendy's/dsl/scales/24hr, 🅾 Havasu RV Park, Prospectors RV Resort
4mm	weigh sta both lanes
2	Needle Mtn Rd
1	Topock Rd, to Bullhead City, Oatman, N gas, food, camping, to Havasu NWR
0mm	Arizona/California state line, Colorado River, Mountain/Pacific time zone

ARKANSAS

INTERSTATE 30

LITTLE ROCK

Exit	Services
143b a	I-40, E to Memphis, W to Ft Smith, I-30 begins/ends on I-40, exit 153b
142	15th St, S 🅿 Super Stop/dsl
141b	US 70, Broadway St, downtown, N 🅿 Exxon, US Fuel/dsl, 🍴 Burger King, 🅾 Verizon Arena, U-Haul, S 🅿 Citgo, Valero/dsl, 🍴 KFC/LJ Silver, McDonald's, Popeye's, Taco Bell, Wendy's
141mm	Arkansas River
141a	AR 10, Cantrell Rd, Markham St, wb only, to downtown
140	9th St, 6th St, downtown, N 🅿 Exxon/dsl, Phillips 66, Shell, 🍴 Pizza Hut, 🛏 Holiday Inn, 🅾 USPO, S 🅿 SuperStop, 🛏 Comfort Inn
139b	I-630, downtown
139a	AR 365, Roosevelt Rd, N 🅿 Exxon, 🍴 Sim's BBQ, 🅾 AutoZone, S 🅿 Shell, 🅾 Family$, Kroger, NAPA
138b	I-530 S, US 167 S, US 65 S, to Pine Bluff
138a	I-440 E, to Memphis 🅾
135	W 65th St, N 🅿 Exxon/dsl, MapCo, Shell/dsl, 🛏 Days Inn, S 🛏 Rodeway Inn
134	Scott Hamilton Dr, S 🅿 Exxon/dsl, 🛏 Best Value Inn, Motel 6
133	Geyer Springs Rd, N 🅿 Exxon, Hess, 🍴 Church's, Sonic, Subway, S 🅿 Exxon, Phillips 66, Shell, 🍴 Arby's,

MABLEVALE

Exit	Services
133	Continued
	Burger King, El Chico, KFC, Little Caesars, McDonald's, Panda Chinese, Rallys, Shark's Rest., Taco Bell, Waffle House, Wendy's, 🛏 Baymont Inn, Best Western, Comfort Inn, Quality Inn, Rest Inn, 🅾 Advance Parts, Family$, Goodyear/auto, Kroger/gas, Radio Shack, Walgreens
132	US 70b, University Ave, N 🅿 RaceWay/dsl, SuperStop, Valero, 🛏 Best Value Inn, 🅾 Chevrolet, S 🍴 Luigi's Pizza
131	McDaniel Dr, N 🅾 U-Haul, S 🛏 Knights Inn, Super 7 Inn, 🅾 Firestone
130	AR 338, Baseline Rd, Mabelvale, N 🛏 Best Inn, 🅾 Harley-Davidson, Suzuki, S 🅿 Shell/Popeye's, 🍴 Applebee's, China Buffet, Dixie Cafe, McDonald's, #1 Buffet, Pizza Hut, Sonic, Taco Bueno, Wendy's, 🅾 AT&T, Crain RV Ctr, Chevrolet, $Tree, Home Depot, Walmart/Subway
129	I-430 N
128	Otter Creek Rd, Mabelvale West, N 🅿 Loves/Hardee's/Subway/dsl/scales/24hr, S 🅿 Exxon/dsl, 🛏 La Quinta, 🅾 🅷, Goodyear
126	AR 111, County Line Rd, Alexander, N 🅿 Phillips 66/dsl, Shell/dsl, S 🅿 Citgo/Subway, 🅾 Cherokee RV Park/dump (4mi)
123	AR 183, Reynolds Rd, to Bryant, Bauxite, N 🅿 Murphy USA/dsl, Shell, SuperStop, 🍴 Arby's, Backyard Burgers, Burger King, Catfish Barn, Cracker Barrel, D-Light Chinese, Domino's, Firehouse Subs, IHOP, KFC, Papa

AR

↱E INTERSTATE 30 CONT'D

Exit	Services
123	Continued Murphy's, Pizza Hut, Quiznos, Ruby Tuesday, Subway, TaMolly's, Waffle House, 🏨 Best Value Inn, Comfort Inn, Hampton Inn, Holiday Inn Express, Hometown Hotel, La Quinta, Vista Inn, ⊙ AT&T, AutoZone, $Tree, Radio Shack, Walgreens, Walmart/Subway, **S** ⛽ Conoco/dsl, Exxon/dsl, 🍴 Chick-fil-A, Little Caesars, Logan's Roadhouse, McDonald's, Mi Ranchito, Sonic, Taco Bell, Wendy's, Zaxby's, 🏨 Super 8, ⊙ $General, Lowe's, O'Reilly Parts, USPO
121	Alcoa Rd, **N** ⛽ Citgo, 🏪/Subway/dsl/scales/24hr/@, 🍴 McDonald's, Taco Bueno, ⊙ Chrysler/Dodge/Jeep, Fiat, Firestone, **S** 🍴 Chili's, McAlister's Deli, Moe's SW Grill, Sakura Japanese, Sonic, Starbucks, Subway, ⊙ AT&T, Best Buy, Buick/GMC, GNC, Kohl's, Old Navy, PetCo, Target
118	Congo Rd, **N** 🍴 Applebee's, Brown's Rest, CiCi's, Dixie Café, Patrone Mexican, Santa Fe Grill, ⊙ Chevrolet/Hummer, Curves, Home Depot, Williams Tire, **S** ⛽ Exxon, 🍴 Burger King, 🏨 Days Inn, Ramada Inn, ⊙ Ford, I-30 Travel Park, RV City, USPO
117	US 64, AR 5, AR 35, **N** ⛽ Shell, 🍴 Denny's, IHOP, Papa John's, Pizza Hut, Waffle House, 🏨 Best Inn, Best Western, EconoLodge, **S** ⛽ Exxon, Fina, Murphy USA, Shell, Valero, 🍴 Arby's, Backyard Burger, Buffet City, Burger King, Capt D's, Chicken Express, Colton's Steaks, IHOP, KFC, La Hacienda Mexican, McDonald's, Pasta Jack's Italian, Rib Crib, Sonic, Subway, Taco Bell, Wendy's, Western Sizzlin, 🏨 Days Inn, ⊙ H, Advance Parts, AT&T, AutoZone, BigLots, $General, $Tree, Fred's, GNC, Hastings Books, Kroger, Office Depot, O'Reilly Parts, Radio Shack, Tuesday Morning, Verizon, Walgreens, Walmart
116	Sevier St, **N** ⛽ Citgo/dsl, Shell/dsl, 🍴 Hunan Place Chinese, 🏨 Troutt Motel, **S** ⛽ Phillips 66, 🏨 Capri Inn
114	US 67 S, Benton, **S** ⛽ Valero/McDonald's/dsl, 🍴 Sonic
113mm	**insp sta both lanes**
111	US 70 W, Hot Springs, **N** ⊙ Cloud 9 RV Park, to Hot Springs NP
106	Old Military Rd, **N** ⛽ Fina/JJ's Rest./dsl/scales/@, **S** ⊙ JB'S RV Park
99	US 270 E, Malvern, **N** H
98b a	US 270, Malvern, Hot Springs, **N** 🏨 Super 8, **S** ⛽ Murphy USA/dsl, Phillips 66/dsl, Shell/dsl, Valero/Baskin-Robbins, 🍴 Burger King, Chile Peppers, Cotija Mexican, El Parian, Great Wall Buffet, McDonald's, Pizza Hut, Sonic, Subway, Taco Bell, Waffle House, Wendy's, Western Sizzlin, 🏨 Best Value Inn, Comfort Inn, Holiday Inn Express, Super 8, ⊙ H, AutoZone, Buick/GMC, Chevrolet, $General, $Tree, Ford, O'Reilly Parts, Radio Shack, Verizon, Walmart/Subway, city park, USPO
97	AR 84, AR 171, **N** ⊙ Lake Catherine SP, RV camping
93mm	🅿️ (both lanes exit left), full ♿ facilities, 🍴, 🏕️, litter barrels, vending, petwalk
91	AR 84, Social Hill
83	AR 283, Friendship, **S** ⛽ Shell/dsl
78	AR 7, Caddo Valley, **N** ⛽ Conoco/dsl/scales/24hr, Valero/dsl, Shell/dsl, 🍴 Cracker Barrel, 🏨 Holiday Inn Express, ⊙ Arkadelphia RV Park, to Hot Springs NP, **S** ⛽ Exxon/Subway/dsl, Phillips 66, Shell/dsl, 🍴 McDonald's, Taco Bell, TaMolly's Mexican, Waffle House, Wendy's, 🏨 Best

BENTON

MALVERN

ARKADELPHIA

HOPE

78	Continued Value Inn, Best Western, Comfort Inn, Days Inn, Hampton Inn, Motel 6, Quality Inn, Super 8, ⊙ De Gray SP
73	AR 8, AR 26, AR 51, Arkadelphia, **N** ⛽ Citgo/dsl, Shell/Stuckey's, 🍴 Chicken Express, Domino's, Great Wall Buffet, McDonald's, Western Sizzlin, ⊙ AT&T, $Tree, Radio Shack, Verizon, Walmart/Subway, to Crater of Diamond SP, **S** ⛽ Exxon/dsl, Shell, 🍴 Andy's Rest., Burger King, Little Italy, Mazzio's Pizza, Subway, Taco Tico, ⊙ H, Ace Hardware, AT&T, AutoZone, Brookshire Foods, Curves, $General, Fred's, O'Reilly Parts, Walgreens, tires/repair, vet
69	AR 26 E, Gum Springs
63	AR 53, Gurdon, **N** ⛽ South Fork Trkstp/Citgo/rest./dsl, 🏨 Best Value Inn, **S** ⛽ Shell/rest/dsl, ⊙ to White Oak Lake SP
56mm	🅿️ both lanes, full ♿ facilities, vending, 🏕️, litter barrels, vending, petwalk
54	AR 51, Gurdon, Okolona
46	AR 19, Prescott, **N** ⛽ Valero/Horizon/cafe/dsl/24hr, ⊙ Crater of Diamonds SP (31mi), White Oaks SP, **S** ⛽ ♥Love's/Hardee's/dsl/scales/24hr, 🍴 Los Agave's Mexican
44	AR 24, Prescott, **N** ⛽ TA/Country Fare/Subway/Taco Bell/dsl/scales/24hr/@, **S** ⛽ Norman's 44 Trkstp/rest/dsl/scales/@, 🏨 Best Value Inn, ⊙ H, truckwash, to S Ark U
36	AR 299, to Emmett
31	AR 29, Hope, **N** ⛽ Shell/dsl, 🍴 Uncle Henry's BBQ, 🏨 Relax Inn, Village Inn/RV park, ⊙ st police, **S** ⛽ Exxon/dsl, Valero/dsl, 🍴 KFC, 🏨 Best Value Inn, ⊙ H
30	AR 4, Hope, **N** ⛽ Murphy USA, Valero/dsl, 🍴 Dos Loco Gringos, 🏨 Best Western, Hampton Inn, Holiday Inn Express, Super 8, ⊙ Verizon, Walmart/Subway, Millwood SP, **S** ⛽ Exxon/Baskin-Robbins/Wendy's, Shell, 🍴 Amigo Juan Mexican, Burger King, Little Caesars, McDonald's, Panda Chinese, Pizza Hut, Sonic, Subway, Taco Bell, Waffle House, 🏨 Days Inn, ⊙ H, AT&T, AutoZone, Buick/Chevrolet/GMC, Bumper Parts, $Tree, Fred's, Ford, O'Reilly Parts, Super 1 Foods/gas, Walgreens, Old Washington Hist SP
26mm	**weigh sta both lanes**
18	rd 355, Fulton, **N** ⛽ Red River Trkstp/dsl
17mm	Red River
12	US 67 (from EB), Fulton
7mm	**Welcome Ctr eb, full ♿ facilities, info, 🍴, 🏕️, litter barrels, vending, petwalk**
7	AR 108, Mandeville, **N** ⛽ ✈FLYING J/Denny's/dsl/LP/24hr, 🏨 Sunrise RV Park, ⊙ truckwash
3	AR 549
2	US 67, AR 245, Texarkana, **N** ⛽ Shell/Circle K/dsl, RoadRunner/dsl, **S** 🍴 T-Town Diner, ⊙ Nick's RV Ctr
1	US 71, Jefferson Ave, Texarkana, **N** 🏨 Holiday Inn Express, ⊙ KOA, **S** 🏨 Country Host Inn
0mm	Arkansas/Texas state line

↱E INTERSTATE 40

Exit	Services
285mm	Arkansas/Tennessee state line, Mississippi River
284mm	**weigh sta wb**
281	AR 131, **S** to Mound City
280	Club Rd, Southland Dr, **N** ⛽ 🏪/Wendy's/dsl, **S** ⛽ BP, ✈FLYING J/Denny's/dsl/LP/24hr, ♥Love's/Subway/

INTERSTATE 40 CONT'D

Exit	Services
280	Continued dsl, Petro/Iron Skillet/dsl/24hr/@, 🍴 KFC/Taco Bell, McDonald's, Waffle House, 🛏 Best Western, Deluxe Inn, Express Inn, Super 8, ⊙ Blue Beacon, SpeedCo Lube
279a	I-55 S (from eb)
279b	Ingram Blvd, **N** 🛏 Budget Host, Days Inn, Red Roof Inn, ⊙ Ford, Southland Racetrack, U-Haul, **S** 📟 Citgo/dsl, Phillips 66, 🍴 Cupboard Rest., Waffle House, 🛏 Best Value Inn, EconoLodge, Hampshire Inn, Holiday Inn, Motel 6, Ramada, Relax Inn
278	AR 77, 7th St, Missouri St, **N** 📟 Shell/dsl, **Welcome Ctr/** 🅿️s, 🛏, **litter barrels, petwalk, full** ♿ **facilities, S on 7th St** 📟 Comfort Suites, Quality Inn, **S on Missouri** 📟 Exxon, MapCo, Phillips 66/dsl, Shell, 🍴 Applebee's, Bonanza, Burger King, Domino's, Krystal, Lenny's Subs, McDonald's, Mrs. Winners, Papa John's, Pizza Hut, Popeye's, Shoney's, Subway, Taco Bell, Wendy's, 🛏 Howard Johnson, ⊙ H, $Tree, Goodyear/auto, Kroger/gas, Radio Shack, Verizon, Walgreens, Walmart, auto repair
277	I-55 N, to Jonesboro
276	AR 77, Rich Rd, to Missouri St (from eb only), **S** 📟 Exxon, MapCo, Murphy Express/dsl, Phillips 66/dsl, Shell, 🍴 Applebee's, Bonanza, Burger King, Domino's, Krystal, Lenny's Subs, McDonald's, Mrs. Winners, Papa John's, Pizza Hut, Popeye's, Shoney's, Subway, Taco Bell, Wendy's, 🛏 Howard Johnson, ⊙ H, $Tree, Goodyear/auto, Kroger/gas, Radio Shack, Verizon, Walgreens, Walmart, auto repair, same as 278
275	AR 118, Airport Rd, **S** 📟 Shell/DQ, 🍴 Huddle House, ⊙ city park, Urgent Care
274mm	weigh sta eb, parking area wb
271	AR 147, to Blue Lake, **S** 📟 BP/dsl, Exxon/Chester's, ⊙ to Horseshoe Lake, RV camping, tires
265	US 79, AR 218, to Hughes
260	AR 149, to Earle, **N** 📟 Citgo/Subway, TA/Country Pride/Burger King/Taco Bell/dsl/scales/24hr/@, Valero/dsl, 🛏 Relax Inn, Shell Lake Motel, ⊙ Shell Lake Camping, **S** 📟 Shell, ⊙ dsl repair
256	AR 75, to Parkin, **N** Parkin Archeological Park (12mi)
247	AR 38 E, to Widener
245mm	St Francis River
243mm	🅿️s wb, full ♿ facilities, vending, 🗑 litter barrels, petwalk
242	AR 284, Crowley's Ridge Rd, **N** ⊙ H, to Village Creek SP, camping
241b a	AR 1, Forrest City, **N** 📟 Citgo/DQ/dsl, Shell/Popeye's/

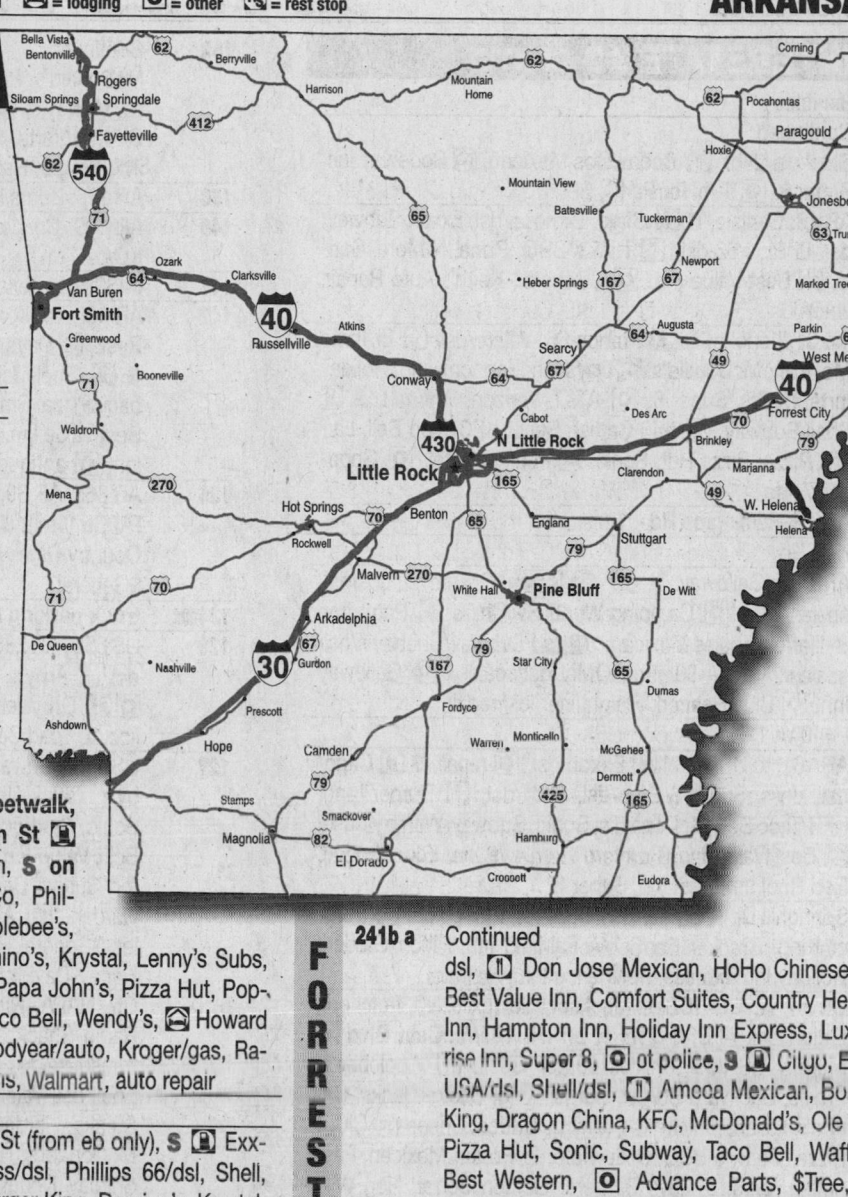

Exit	Services
241b a	Continued dsl, 🍴 Don Jose Mexican, HoHo Chinese, Wendy's, 🛏 Best Value Inn, Comfort Suites, Country Hearth Inn, Days Inn, Hampton Inn, Holiday Inn Express, Luxury Inn, Sunrise Inn, Super 8, ⊙ ot police, **S** 📟 Citgo, Exxon, Murphy USA/dsl, Shell/dsl, 🍴 Amoca Mexican, Bonanza, Burger King, Dragon China, KFC, McDonald's, Ole Sawmill Cafe, Pizza Hut, Sonic, Subway, Taco Bell, Waffle House, 🛏 Best Western, ⊙ Advance Parts, $Tree, Food Giant, Fred's Drug, O'Reilly Parts, Save-A-Lot Foods, Verizon, Walmart, Walgreens
239	AR 1, to Wynne, Marianna
235mm	🅿️s eb, full ♿ facilities, 🍴 vending, 🗑 litter barrels, petwalk
234mm	L'Anguille River
233	AR 261, Palestine, **N** 📟 ♥Loves/Chester's/Subway/dsl/scales/24hr, 🛏 Rest Inn, **S** 📟 Citgo/dsl, 🍴 Head's Cafe
221	AR 78, Wheatley, **N** 📟 SweetPea/dsl/repair, **S** 📟 BP/Pitstop/diner/dsl, MapCo/Subway/dsl
216	US 49, AR 17, Brinkley, **N** 📟 Citgo, Mobil/dsl, ⊙ KFC/Taco Bell, Los Piños Mexican, 🛏 Best Inn, Days Inn, EconoLodge, Motel 6/RV Park, ⊙ dsl repair, **S** 📟 Exxon/Baskin-Robbins/dsl, MapCo/dsl, Shell, 🍴 Gene's BBQ, McDonald's, New China, Pizza Hut, Sonic, Subway, Waffle House, 🛏 Heritage Inn/RV Park, ⊙ Bumper Parts, $General, Family$, Fred's, Kroger, O'Reilly Parts
205mm	Cache River
202	AR 33, to Biscoe
200mm	White River
199mm	🅿️s both lanes, full ♿ facilities, vending, 🗑 litter barrels, no 🍴
193	AR 11, to Hazen, **N** 📟 Exxon/Chester's, **S** 📟 Citgo/dsl,

WEST MEMPHIS — **FORREST CITY** — **BRINKLEY** — **AR**

🛡E	**INTERSTATE 40 CONT'D**

AR

L O N O K E

Exit	Services
193	Continued
	Shell/dsl/24hr, 🍴 Cocos Dos Mexican, 🛏 Rodeway Inn, Super 8, ⊙ T-rix RV Park,
183	AR 13, Carlisle, **S** 📰 Citgo, Conoco/dsl, Exxon/Subway/dsl, Phillips 66/dsl, 🍴 Nick's BBQ, Pizza 'N More, Sonic, 🛏 Best Value Inn, ⊙ $General, Keith's Auto Repair, NAPA
175	AR 31, Lonoke, **N** 📰 Phillips 66, Valero/dsl, 🍴 El Torito Mexican, McDonald's, 🛏 Days Inn, Economy Inn, Holiday Inn Express, Super 8, ⊙ AT&T, Verizon, Walmart, **S** 📰 Shell/Subway, 🍴 I-40 Catfish Rest., KFC/Taco Bell, Larry's Pizza, Pizza Hut, Sonic, 🛏 Perry's Motel, ⊙ Goodyear/auto
169	AR 15, Remington Rd
165	Kerr Rd
161	AR 391, Galloway, **N** 📰 Love's/Chester's/subs/dsl/scales/24hr, ⊙ Camping World RV Ctr, **S** 📰 Petro/Iron Skillet/dsl/scales/24hr/@, ▥/Subway/Chester's/dsl/scales/24hr, IA-80 TruckOMat/dsl/scales, 🛏 Galloway Inn, ⊙ Blue Beacon, Freightliner, dsl repair
159	I-440 W, **S** 🔧

L I T T L E   R O C K

Exit	Services
157	AR 161, to US 70, **N** 📰 Exxon/dsl, ⊙ repair, **S** 📰 Citgo/dsl, Hess, Super S Stop/dsl, Shell/dsl, 🍴 Burger King, KFC/Taco Bell, McDonald's, Sonic, Subway, Waffle House, 🛏 Best Value Inn, Comfort Inn, Days Inn, EconoLodge, Red Roof Inn, Rest Inn, Super 8
156	Springhill Dr, **N** 📰 Murphy USA/dsl, Phillips 66, 🍴 Burger King, Cracker Barrel, 🛏 Fairfield Inn, Hilton Garden, Holiday Inn Express, Residence Inn, Walmart
155	US 67 N, US 167, to Jacksonville (exits left from eb), Little Rock AFB, **0-3 mi N on US 167/McCain Blvd** 📰 Murphy USA/dsl, Phillips 66/dsl, Shell, 🍴 Applebee's, Arby's, Backyard Burger, Burger King, Cactus Jacks, Carino's Italian, Chick-fil-A, Chili's, ChuckECheese's, CiCi's Pizza, Corky's BBQ, Dixie Cafe, El Porton Mexican, Firehouse Subs, 5 Guys Burgers, Golden Corral, Hog Wild Cafe, Hooters, IHOP, Jason's Deli, Jimmy John's, Kanpai Japanese, Little Caesars, McDonald's, Old Chicago Pizza, Olive Garden, On-the-Border, Outback Steaks, Panera Bread, Pizza Hut, Rally's, Red Lobster, Sonic, Subway, Taco Bell, TGIFriday's, TX Roadhouse, US Pizza, Waffle House, Wendy's, 🛏 Comfort Inn, Hampton Inn, Hilton Garden, Holiday Inn Express, La Quinta, Super 8, ⊙ 🅗, Aamco, AT&T, Barnes&Noble, Best Buy, BigLots, Books-A-Million, Buick/GMC, Chevrolet, Chrysler/Dodge/Jeep, Dillard's, $Tree, Firestone/auto, Ford, Gander Mtn, Home Depot, Honda, Hyundai, JC Penney, KIA, Lincoln, Lowe's, Mazda, Michael's, Nissan, Office Depot, PepBoys, PetCo, Petsmart, Sam's Club/gas, Sears/auto, Steinmart, Target, TJ Maxx, Toyota/Scion, Verizon, VW, Walmart, mall, vet
154	to Lakewood (from eb)
153b	I-30 W, US 65 S, to Little Rock
153a	AR 107 N, JFK Blvd, **N** 📰 Exxon, Mapco, Shell, 🍴 Schlotzsky's, 🛏 Best Value Inn, ⊙ vet, **S** 📰 Exxon, 🍴 Royal Buffet, Waffle House, 🛏 Best Western, Bugetel, Hampton Inn, Holiday Inn, Motel 6, Simply Home Suites, ⊙ 🅗, USPO
152	AR 365, AR 176, Camp Pike Rd, Levy, **N on Camp Robinson Rd** 📰 Exxon, EZ Mart, Phillips 66, Shell, 🍴 Burger King, Dixie Pig, KFC, Little Caesars, Mexico Chiquito,

Exit	Services
152	Continued
	McDonald's, Pizza Hut, Sonic, Subway, Taco Bell, US Pizza, Wendy's, ⊙ AutoZone, Family$, Fred's, Kroger/gas, O'Reilly Parts, **S** 📰 Shell, 🍴 Chicken King, ⊙ 🅗, Family$, Kroger, Radio Shack
150	AR 176, Burns Park, Camp Robinson, **S** ⊙ info, camping
148	AR 100, Crystal Hill Rd, **N** 📰 Shell, **S** 📰 Citgo/dsl, ⊙ KOA
147	I-430 S, to Texarkana
142	AR 365, to Morgan, **N** 📰 Phillips 66, Valero/dsl, 🍴 I-40 Rest., 🛏 Days Inn, ⊙ Bumper Parts, Trails End RV Park, **S** 📰 Shell/dsl, 🍴 KFC/Taco Bell, McDonald's, Razorback Pizza, Smokeshack BBQ, Subway, Waffle House, 🛏 Best Value Inn, Hampton Inn, Holiday Inn Express, Quality Inn, ⊙ antiques
135	AR 365, AR 89, Mayflower, **N** 📰 Hess/dsl, ⊙ Mayflower RV Ctr (1mi), **S** 📰 Exxon/dsl, Valero, 🍴 Sonic, Stroud's Country Diner, Tampico Mexican, ⊙ Big Star Food/Drug, $General
134mm	**truck parking both lanes**
129	US 65B, AR 286, Conway, **S** 📰 Citgo/dsl, Exxon, MapCo/dsl, 🍴 Arby's, Subway, 🛏 Budget Inn, Continental Motel, ⊙ 🅗, Chrysler/Dodge/Jeep, Honda, Toyota/Scion, st police, to Toad Suck SP
127	US 64, Conway, **N** 📰 Exxon, Satterfield, Shell, 🍴 Arby's, Chick-fil-A, Chili's, Denny's, Logan's Roadhouse, Sonic, Starbucks, Subway, TGIFriday's, Waffle House, 🛏 Best Value Inn, Best Western, Country Inn&Suites, Comfort Suites, Days Inn, Economy Inn, Hampton Inn, Hilton Garden, ⊙ AT&T, Belk, Best Buy, Buick/GMC, Chevrolet, $General, Firestone/auto, Ford, GNC, Goodyear/auto, Harley-Davidson, Home Depot, Hyundai, Kohl's, Moix RV Ctr, NAPA, Nissan, Old Navy, O'Reilly Parts, Petsmart, Radio Shack, Staples, Target, TJ Maxx, Verizon, repair/transmissions, to Lester Flatt Park, vet, **S** 📰 RaceWay, Shell/dsl, Valero/dsl, 🍴 Burger King, Church's, Colton's Steaks, Hardee's, Jimmy John's, Kings Steaks, LJ Silver, McDonald's, New China, Pizza Inn, Rally's, Saigon Rest., Shipley Doughnuts, Sonic, Taco Bell, Tokyo Japanese, Wendy's, Whole Hog Cafe, 🛏 Kings Inn, ⊙ AutoZone, BigLots, Family$, Fred's Drugs, Hancock Fabrics, Hobby Lobby, Kroger/gas, Walgreens, tires
125	US 65, Conway, **N** 📰 Conoco/dsl, Exxon/Subway/dsl, Shell/dsl/24hr, 🍴 China Town, Cracker Barrel, El Acapulco Mexican, La Hacienda Mexican, MktPlace Deli, McDonald's, 🛏 Quality Inn, ⊙ $Tree, JC Penney, Office Depot, Sears, **S** 📰 Citgo, Mobil/dsl, Murphy USA, Sinclair, 🍴 Backyard Burger, Burger King, CiCi's Pizza, Dixie Cafe, Firehouse Subs, Hart's Seafood, IHOP, McAlister's Deli, Mexico Chiquito, New China, Outback Steaks, Panera Bread, Ruby Tuesday, Sonic, Starbucks, Subway, Waffle House, Wendy's, 🛏 Candlewood Suites, Fairfield Inn, Holiday Inn, Holiday Inn Express, Howard Johnson, La Quinta, Microtel, Motel 6, Stacy Motel, Super 8, ⊙ 🅗, Advance Parts, $General, Hastings Books, Lowe's, Walmart, tires
124	AR 25 N, to Conway, **S** 📰 Hess, Shell/dsl, 🍴 Catfish&More, DQ, KFC, Mazzio's, Popeye's, ⊙ 🅗, U-Haul
120mm	Cadron River
117	to Menifee
112	AR 92, Plumerville, **N** 📰 Exxon/dsl, **S** 📰 Country Store dsl, ⊙ USPO

C O N W A Y

🆘 INTERSTATE 40 CONT'D

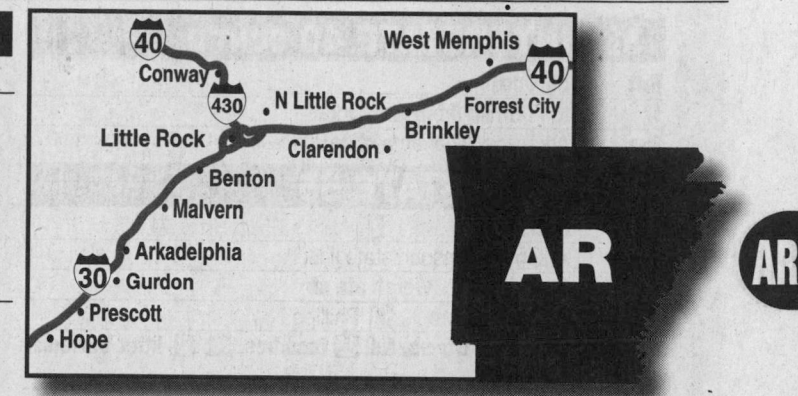

Exit	Services
108	AR 9, Morrilton, **S** 🅖 Murphy USA, Shell/Pizza Pro/dsl, Valero, 🍴 Bonanza, Chop Stix, Hardees, McDonald's, Ortega's Mexican, Pizza Hut, Sonic, Subway, Waffle House, Wendy's, 🛏 Holiday Inn Express, Super 8, 🅞 🅗 Ace Hardware, AT&T, Chrysler/Dodge/Jeep, $General, Ford/Lincoln, Kroger, NAPA, Verizon, Walmart, to Petit Jean SP (21mi), RV camping
107	AR 95, Morrilton, **N** 🅞 Best Value Inn, 🅞 I-40/107 RV Park, **S** 🅖 ♥Loves/Subway/dsl/24hr, Shell, 🍴 Mom&Pop's Waffles, Morrilton Drive Inn, Yesterdays Rest., 🛏 Days Inn, 🅞 Bumper Parts
101	Blackwell, **N** 🅖 Blackwell TrkStp/Citgo/Domino's/diner/dsl/scales/24hr, 🅞 Utility Trailer Sales
94	AR 105, Atkins, **N** 🅖 Exxon/Subway/dsl, Shell/McDonald's/dsl, 🍴 Berky's Diner, El Parian Mexican, Sonic, 🅞 $General, repair, **S** 🅞 Sexton Foods
88	Pottsville, **S** 🍴 Pottsville Country Cafe, 🅞 truck repair/wash
84	US 64, AR 331, Russellville, **N** 🅖 ⓕFLYING J/Denny's/dsl/scales/LP/24hr, Shell/dsl, 🅞 Ivys Cove RV Retreat, trucklube, **S** 🅖 Phillips 66, 🅖/Subway/Wendy's/dsl/scales, 🍴 CiCi's Pizza, Hardee's, Hunan Chinese, McDonald's, Sonic, Waffle House, 🛏 Comfort Inn, Quality Inn, 🅞 🅗 AutoZone, Belk, Buick/Chevrolet/GMC, Chrysler/Dodge/Jeep, $Tree, JC Penney, Hastings Books, Hobby Lobby, Hyundai, K-Mart, Lowe's, Nissan, Petsmart, Staples, TJ Maxx, Toyota, USPO
83	AK 326, Weir Rd, **S** 🅖 Murphy USA/dsl, Phillips 66, 🍴 DQ, McAlisters Deli, Popeye's, Ryan's, Starbucks, Subway, Taco Bueno, 🛏 Comfort Inn, 🅞 AT&T, AutoZone, Curves, $General, Ford, Mazda, NAPA, O'Reilly Parts, Verizon, Walmart
81	AR 7, Russellville, **N** 🅖 SuperStop/dsl, 🍴 CJ's Burgers, 7-40 Rest., 🛏 Motel 6, 🅞 Outdoor RV Ctr/Park, **S** 🅖 Exxon/dsl, Phillips 66/dsl/24hr, Shell, 🍴 Arby's, Burger King, Colton's Steaks, Cracker Barrel, Dixie Café, IHOP, La Huerta Mexican, New China, Ruby Tuesday, Subway, Waffle House, 🛏 Best Value, Best Western, Days Inn, Economy Inn, Fairfield Inn, Hampton Inn, Hawthorn Park Inn, La Quinta, Super 8, 🅞 to Lake Dardanelle SP, RV camping,
80mm	Dardanelle Reservoir
78	US 64, Russellville, **S** 🍴 Fat Daddy's BBQ, 🅞 🅗 Darrell's Mkt, Mission RV Park, to Lake Dardanelle SP
74	AR 333, London
72mm	🆁🆂 wb, full ♿ facilities, 🅒, 🚻, litter barrels, vending, petwalk
70mm	overlook wb lane, litter barrels
68mm	🆁🆂 eb, full ♿ facilities, 🅒, 🚻, litter barrels, vending, petwalk
67	AR 315, Knoxville, **S** 🅖 Citgo, Knoxville Mkt, 🅞 USPO
64	US 64, Clarksville, Lamar, **S** 🅖 Valero/Pizza Pro/dsl, 🅞 Dad's Dream RV Park
58	AR 21, AR 103, Clarksville, **N** 🅖 Shell/dsl, Valero, 🍴 Emerald Dragon Chinese, KFC, Larry's Pizza, McDonald's, Pasta Grill, Pizza Hut, Sonic, Subway, Taco Bell, Waffle House, 🛏 Best Western, Executive Inn, Quality Inn, Super 8, 🅞 🅗 Buick/Chevrolet, $General, **S** 🅖 Murphy USA/dsl, 🍴 Arby's, China Fun, Wendy's, 🅞 Chrysler/Dodge/Jeep, $Tree, Ford, Walmart/Subway
57	AR 109, Clarksville, **N** 🅖 Fuel Stop/dsl, 🍴 Subway, 🅞 Family$, Harvest Foods/drug, **S** 🅖 Shell/Chester's/dsl, 🅞 TrueValue, repair
55	US 64, AR 109, Clarksville, **N** 🍴 Crosswoods Rest., Hardee's, 🛏 Days Inn, Hampton Inn, Holiday Inn Express, **S** 🅖 Exxon/dsl, 🍴 Jackson Family Steaks, 🅞 Radio Shack, st police
47	AR 164, Coal Hill
41	AR 186, Altus, **S** 🍴 Swiss Family Rest., Wiederkehr Rest., 🅞 Pine Ridge RV Park, winery
37	AR 219, Ozark, **S** 🅖 ♥Loves /Subway/dsl/scales/24hr, Shell/McDonald's/dsl, 🍴 KFC/Taco Bell, 🛏 Days Inn, 🅞 🅗
36mm	🆁🆂 both lanes, full ♿ facilities, 🅒, 🚻, litter barrels, petwalk
35	AR 23, Ozark, **S** 🅖 Valero/Subway/dsl, 🍴 Hillbilly Hideout Rest, **3 mi S** 🍴 Hardee's, Subway, 🛏 Ozark Inn, Oxford Inn, 🅞 🅗 Aux Arc Park (5mi), to Mt Magazine SP (20 mi)
24	AR 215, Mulberry, **S** Vine Prairie Park
20	Dyer, **N** 🅖 Conoco/dsl, 🅞 Freightliner/Western Star, **S** 🅖 Phillips 66/dsl, Shell/dsl, 🛏 Mill Creek Inn
13	US 71 N, Alma, **N** 🅖 Phillips 66/dsl, Shell, 🍴 Burger King, Catfish Hole, China Fun, Cracker Barrel, KFC, La Fiesta Mexican, Mazzio's, Pizza Parlor, Subway, Taco Bell, 🛏 Comfort Inn, Meadors Inn, 🅞 Crabtree RV Ctr/Park, Curves, $General, KOA (2mi), O'Reilly Parts, to U of AR, Lake Ft Smith SP, **S** 🅖 Murphy USA/dsl, Shamrock, Valero/dsl, 🍴 Braum's, El Trio, Geno's Pizza, McDonald's, Sonic, 🛏 Days Inn, 🅞 Alma Drug, AT&T, C&H Tires, CV's Foods, Harp's Foods, Walgreens, Walmart
12	I-540 N, to Fayetteville, **N** 🅞 to Lake Ft Smith SP
9mm	weigh sta both lanes
7	I-540 S, US 71 S, to Ft Smith, Van Buren, **S** 🅗
5	AR 59, Van Buren, **N** 🅖 Citgo/dsl, Murphy USA/dsl, Phillips 66, 🍴 Arby's, Burger King, Chili's, China Buffet, Domino's, Firehouse Subs, Frank's Italian, Golden Wok, La Fiesta Mexican, McDonald's, Popeye's, Zaxby's, 🛏 Best Western, Hampton Inn, 🅞 Advance Parts, AT&T, Cooley's Tire, $Tree, Radio Shack, Lowe's, NAPA, Verizon, Walmart, USPO, **S** 🅖 Shell/dsl/24hr, 🍴 Braum's, Big Jake's Steaks, Geno's Pizza, Home Run Pizza, KFC/Taco Bell, La Fresas Mexican, Rick's Rib House, Sonic, Subway, Waffle House, Wendy's, 🛏 Holiday Inn Express, Motel 6, Sleep Inn, Super 8, 🅞 CV's Foods, $General, Grizzle Tire, Outdoor RV Ctr, Walgreens, truckwash
3	Lee Creek Rd, **N** 🅖 Shell, 🅞 Park Ridge Camping
2.5mm	Welcome Ctr eb, full ♿ facilities, info, 🅒, 🚻, litter barrels, vending, petwalk

Left margin labels: MORRILTON RUSSELLVILLE

Right margin labels: CLARKSVILLE VAN BUREN

⬆E INTERSTATE 40 CONT'D

Exit	Services
1	to Ft Smith (from wb), Dora
0mm	Arkansas/Oklahoma state line

⬆N INTERSTATE 55

Exit	Services
72mm	Arkansas/Missouri state line
72	State Line Rd, **weigh sta sb**
71	AR 150, Yarbro
68mm	**Welcome Ctr sb, full** ♿ **facilities,** 🅿, 🖼, **litter barrels, petwalk**
67	AR 18, Blytheville, **E** 🅿 Murphy Express/dsl, 🍽 Burger King, Subway, Waffle Inn, Zaxby's, 🛏 Best Value Inn, Days Inn/RV park, Ⓞ $Tree, Lowe's, Verizon, Walmart/Subway, **W** 🅿 Citgo/dsl, QuikStop/dsl, Shell, 🍽 Cotton Patch Buffet, El Acapulco Mexican, GreatWall Chinese, Grecian Steaks, Hardee's, McDonald's, Olympia Steaks, Perkins, Pizza Inn, 7 Mayors Rest, Sonic, Subway, Taco Bell, Wendy's, 🛏 Comfort Inn, Fairview Suites, Hampton Inn, Holiday Inn, Quality Inn, Super 8, Ⓞ 🅷, AT&T, AutoZone, CarQuest, Family$, Fred's, Ford/Lincoln, JC Penney, Nissan, Toyota
63	US 61, to Blytheville, **E** Ⓞ Shearins RV Park (2mi), **W** 🅿 Dodge's Store/dsl, Exxon/Baskin-Robbins/Chester's/Pizza Hut/dsl, Shell/McDonald's/dsl, 🛏 Best Western, Relax Inn, Ⓞ 🅷, truckwash
57	AR 148, Burdette, **E** Ⓞ NE AR Coll
53	AR 158, Victoria, Luxora
48	AR 140, to Osceola, **E** 🅿 Mobil/dsl, Shell/Baskin-Robbins/Chester's/dsl, Ⓞ Cotton Inn Rest., Huddle House, 🛏 Days Inn, Deerfield Inn, EconoLodge, Fairview Inn, **3 mi E** 🍽 McDonald's, Pizza Inn, Sonic, Subway, Ⓞ 🅷
45mm	truck parking nb, litter barrels
44	AR 181, Keiser
41	AR 14, Marie, **E** Ⓞ to Hampson SP/museum
36	AR 181, to Wilson, Bassett
35mm	truck parking sb, litter barrels
34	AR 118, Joiner
23b a	US 63, AR 77, to Marked Tree, Jonesboro, ASU, **E** 🅿 Citgo/chicken/pizza
21	AR 42, Turrell, **W** 🅿 Exxon/rest./dsl/scales/24hr
17	AR 50, to Jericho
14	rd 4, to Jericho, **E** 🅿 Citgo/dsl/scales/24hr, **W** 🅿 Citgo/Stuckey's, Ⓞ Chevrolet, KOA
10	US 64 W, Marion, **E** 🅿 Citgo/Baskin-Robbins/Subway/scales, Shell/McDonald's, 🍽 Ameca Mexican, KFC/Taco Bell, Sonic, Tops BBQ, 🛏 Comfort Inn, Hallmarc Inn, Ⓞ $General, Family$, Mkt Place Foods, Marion Tire/repair, USPO, **W** 🅿 JP Mkt, Shell, 🍽 Burger King, Colton's Steaks, Mi Pueblo, Wendy's, Zaxby's, 🛏 Best Western, Journey Inn, Ⓞ AutoZone, Neats Repair, to Parkin SP (23mi)
9mm	truck parking nb, **weigh sta sb**
8	I-40 W, to Little Rock
	I-55 and I-40 run together 3 mi. See I-40, exits 278-279b
5	(279 b from I-40), Ingram Blvd, **E** 🍽 Margaritas Mexican, 🛏 Days Inn, Homegate Inn, Knights Inn, Red Roof Inn, Ⓞ Ford, Southland Racetrack, U-Haul, **W** 🅿 Citgo/dsl, Shell/dsl, 🍽 Cupboard Rest., Waffle House, 🛏 Best Value Inn, EconoLodge, Hampshire Inn, Holiday Inn, Motel 6, Ramada, Relax Inn

4	King Dr, Southland Dr, **E** 🅿 ✈FLYING J/Denny's/dsl/LP/scales/RV dump, ⊂Love's⊃/Subway/dsl/scales/@, Petro/Iron Skillet/rest./dsl/24hr/@, ▭/Subway/Wendy's/dsl/scales/24hr, 🍽 KFC/Taco Bell, McDonald's, 🛏 Best Western, Deluxe Inn, Express Inn, Super 8, Ⓞ Blue Beacon, SpeedCo Lube, **W** 🍽 Poncho's Mexican, 🛏 Sunset Inn
3b a	US 70, Broadway Blvd, AR 131, Mound City Rd (exits left from nb), **W** 🛏 Budget Inn
2mm	**weigh sta nb**
1	Bridgeport Rd
0mm	Arkansas/Tennessee state line, Mississippi River

⬆N INTERSTATE 430 (LITTLE ROCK)

Exit	Services
13b a	I-40. **I-430 begins/ends on I-40, exit 147.**
12	AR 100, Maumelle, **W** 🅿 Citgo, Ⓞ O'Reilly Parts, NAPA, vet
10mm	Arkansas River
9	AR 10, Cantrell Rd., **W** Maumelle Park, Pinnacle Mtn SP
8	Rodney Parham Rd, **E** 🅿 Conoco, Shell, 🍽 Arby's, Baskin-Robbins, El Chico, Firehouse Subs, KFC, McAlister's Grill, McDonald's, Mt Fuji Japanese, New China Buffet, Sonic, Starbucks, Subway, Taco Bell, Terri Lynn's BBQ, US Pizza, 🛏 La Quinta, Ⓞ Advance Parts, AutoZone, $Days, $General, Drug Emporium, Kroger, Walgreens, **W** 🅿 Exxon, 🍽 Burger King, Chili's, Chizi's Pizza, Chuck-eCheese, Dixie Cafe, Dominos, Franke's Café, Heavenly Ham, LoneStar Steaks, Olive Garden, Shorty Small's Ribs, Wendy's, 🛏 Best Western, Ⓞ Firestone/auto, GNC, K-Mart, Radio Shack, USA Drug, Whole Foods Mkt, vet
6	I-630, Kanis Rd, Markham St, to downtown, **E** 🍽 McDonald's, 🛏 Candlewood Suites, Comfort Inn, Motel 6, SpringHill Suites, **W** 🅿 Exxon, 🍽 Cozymel's Grill, Denny's, Famous Dave's BBQ, IHOP, Jason's Deli, Kobe Japanese, Lenny's Subs, Macaroni Grill, McAlister's Deli, Mimi's Cafe, On-the-Border, PF Chang's, Shotgun Dan's Pizza, Starbucks, Taco Bell, Waffle House, Wendy's, 🛏 Courtyard, Crowne Plaza, Embassy Suites, Extended Stay America, Jameson Inn, La Quinta, Ramada Ltd, Ⓞ AT&T, Barnes&Noble, Best Buy, PetsMart, Walmart
5	Kanis Rd, Shackleford Rd, **E** 🍽 Cracker Barrel, Panda Garden, Samurai Steaks, TX Roadhouse, 🛏 Candlewood Suites, Comfort Inn, Motel 6, SpringHill Suites, Towneplace Suites, Ⓞ Gordman's, JC Penney, **W** 🅿 Shell, 🍽 Krispy Kreme, 🛏 Hampton Inn, Holiday Inn Select, La Quinta, Residence Inn, Studio+, Wingate Inn, Ⓞ 🅷, Lexus
4	AR 300, Col Glenn Rd, **E** 🍽 Subway, Wendy's, 🛏 Holiday Inn Express, ValuePlace Hotel, Ⓞ Toyota/Scion, **W** 🅿 Valero/Burger King/dsl, Ⓞ Honda, Hyundai, Jaguar, Land Rover, Mazda, Mercedes, Nissan
1	AR 5, Stagecoach Rd, **E** 🍽 Our Place Grill, **W** 🅿 Phillips 66, Valero, 🍽 Grandpa's Catfish, Jordan's BBQ, Subway, Ⓞ Tires
0mm	I-30. **I-430 begins/ends on I-30, exit 129.**

⬆N INTERSTATE 440 (LITTLE ROCK)

Exit	Services
11	**I-440 begins/ends on I-40, exit 159.**
10	US 70, **W** Ⓞ Peterbilt
8	Faulkner Lake Rd, **W** 🅿 Pioneer/dsl
7	US 165, to England, **S** Agricultural Museum, Toltec

BLYTHEVILLE   LITTLE ROCK

AR

Copyright 2014 - The Next Exit ®   🅖 = gas   🅕 = food   🅛 = lodging   🅞 = other   🆁🆂 = rest stop

INTERSTATE 440 (LITTLE ROCK) CONT'D

Exit	Services
7	Continued
	US 165 Mounds SP, Willow Beach SP
6mm	Arkansas River
5	Fourche Dam Pike, LR Riverport, **N** 🅖 Exxon, Shell/Subway, 🅕 McDonald's, 🅛 Travelodge, 🅞 Kenworth, **S** 🅖 Phillips 66/dsl, Valero/dsl
4	Lindsey Rd
3	Bankhead Dr, **N** 🅛 Comfort Inn, 🅞 LR ⊙, **S** 🅖 Valero, 🅕 Boston's Rest., Waffle House, 🅛 Days Inn, Holiday Inn, Holiday Inn Express
1	AR 365, Springer Blvd, **S** Little Rock Ntl Cemetery
0mm	**I-440 begins/ends on I-30, exit 138.**

INTERSTATE 540 (FAYETTEVILLE)

Exit	Services
93	US 71B, Bentonville, **I-540 begins/ends on US 71 N.**
88	AR 72, Bentonville, Pea Ridge, **E** 🅖 Conoco, 🅕 River Grille, 🅛 Courtyard, Simmon's Suites, **W** 🅖 Kum&Go/dsl, 🅕 Smokin' Joe's Ribs, 🅞 Walmart Visitors Ctr
86	US 62, AR 102, Bentonville, Rogers, **E** 🅛 TownePlace Suites, 🅞 Sam's Club/gas, Walmart Mkt, Pea Ridge NMP, **W** 🅖 Phillips 66/McDonald's/dsl, Shell/dsl, 🅕 Arby's, Sonic, Subway, Taco Bell, 🅛 ValuePlace
85	US 71B, AR 12, Bentonville, Rogers, **E** 🅖 Conoco/dsl, 🅕 Abuelo's, Applebee's, Arby's, Atlanta Bread, Bob Evans, Carino's Italian, Chick-fil-A, Chili's, Colton's Steaks, Copeland's Rest., Dixie Café, Famous Dave's, Freddy's Burgers, IHOP, Logan's Roadhouse, McDonald's, Napoli's Pizza, On-the-Border, Outback Steaks, Quiznos, Red Robin, Sonic, Starbucks, 🅛 Candlewood Suites, Country Inn&Suites, Fairfield Inn, Hampton Inn, Homewood Suites, Hyatt Place, Mainstay Suites, Residence Inn, 🅞 AT&T, Barnes&Noble, Belk, Firestone/auto, Kohl's, Lowe's, Marshalls, Office Depot, Old Navy, PetCo, Ross, Staples, Verizon, Beaver Lake SP, Prairie Creek SP, **W** 🅖 Kum&Go, Murphy Express/dsl, Phillips 66/dsl, 🅕 Braum's, Buffalo Wild Wings, Denny's, Firehouse Subs, HoneyBaked Ham, Joe's Italian, Jonny Brusco's Pizza, Krispy Kreme, Lenny's Subs, Lin's Garden, Mama Fu's Asian, McAlister's Deli, Panera Bread, Shogun Japanese, Starbucks, Subway, Taco Bueno, Village Inn, Waffle House, Whole Hog Cafe, Zaxby's, 🅛 Best Western, Comfort Suites, Days Inn, DoubleTree Hotel, EconoLodge, Hilton Garden, Holiday Inn Express, La Quinta, Microtel, Motel 6, SpringHill Suites, Suburban Lodge, Super 8, 🅞 🅗 Urgent Care, Buick/GMC, Chevrolet, Christian Bros Auto, Honda, Hyundai, Kia, Mazda, Nissan, Toyota/Scion
83	AR 94 E, Pinnacle Hills Pkwy, **E** 🅖 Phillips 66, 🅕 After 5 Grill, Bariola's Pizza, ChuckECheese's, Dickey's BBQ, Firehouse Subs, 5 Guys Burgers, Genghis Grill, Jimmy John's, Mojitos Mexican, Olive Garden, Panda Express, Qdoba, Red Lobster, Slim Chickens, Starbucks, Steak'n Shake, Taco Bell, 🅞 🅗 Home Depot, Horse Shoe Bend Park, Walgreens, **W** 🅕 Bonefish Grill, Carrabba's, Crabby's Seafood Grill, Coldstone, Grub's Grille, Mellow Mushroom, Ruth's Chris Steaks, Subway, The Egg&I, Tropical Smoothie, 🅛 Embassy Suites, Holiday Inn, Staybridge Suites, ALoft
82	Promenade Blvd, **E** 🅕 Fish City Grill, Food Pavilion, Houlihan's, PF Changs, 🅞 🅗 AT&T, Best Buy, Cabela's, Dil

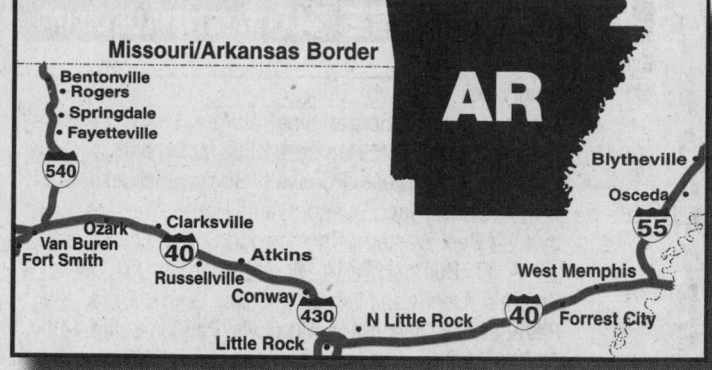

82	Continued
	lard's, Fresh Mkt, GNC, Gordman's, Hancock Fabrics, JC Penney, Old Navy, Target, TJMaxx, **W** 🅞 Walmart Mkt/dsl
81	Pleasant Grove Rd, **E** 🅖 Murphy USA/dsl, 🅕 Backyard Burger, Chick-fil-A, Golden Corral, Mad Pizza, McDonald's, Starbucks, Subway, Taco Bueno, 🅞 Firestone/auto, Walgreens, Walmart, **W** 🅖 Casey's/dsl
78	AR 264, Lowell, Cave Sprgs, Rogers, **E** 🅖 Kum&Go, Shell, 🅕 Arby's, Dickey's BBQ, Domino's, DQ, KFC, LJ Silver, Mazzio's Pizza, McDonald's, Sonic, Subway, Taco Bell, 🅞 Super 8, 🅞 AT&T, Camping World RV Ctr, $General, **W** 🅖 Kum&Go/dsl
76	Wagon Wheel Rd, **E** 🅖 Shell/Subway/dsl, 🅞 to Hickory Creek Park
73	Elm Springs Rd, **E** 🅖 Kum&Go/dsl, VP/dsl, 🅕 Eureka Pizza, Patrick's Burgers, 🅛 ValuePlace, 🅞 Chevrolet, Family$, **W** 🅖 Shell/dsl
72mm	**weigh sta nb**
72	US 412, Springdale, Siloam Springs, **E** 🅖 Conoco, Phillips 66/Subway, 🅕 Applebee's, Bleu Monkey Grill, Braum's, Denny's, Golden Dragon Buffet, Guadalajara Grill, Joe's Italian, Little Caesars, Mkt Place Rest., McDonald's, Sonic, Taco Bell, Waffle House, Wendy's, Western Sizzlin, 🅛 DoubleTree Hotel, Extended Stay America, Fairfield Inn, Hampton Inn, Holiday Inn, La Quinta, Residence Inn, Royal Inn, Sleep Inn, Super 8, 🅞 AT&T, Big O Tire, $General, Harp's Mkt, Kenworth/Volvo Trucks, Lowe's, Office Depot, O'Reilly Parts, Radio Shack, Verizon, Walmart Mkt, Walgreens, **W** 🅖 Murphy Express/dsl, ▭/Burger King/dsl/scales/24hr, 🅕 Arby's, Buffalo Wild Wings, Cracker Barrel, Jose's Mexican, McDonald's, Quiznos, Rib Crib, Subway, Taco Bueno, 🅞 BigLots, Buick/GMC, Harp's Mkt/dsl, Hobby Lobby, vet
71mm	**weigh sta sb**
69	Johnson Mill Blvd, **1-2 mi E** 🅕 Chick-fil-A, Eureka Pizza, Fire Mtn Grill, Hooters, Inn at the Mill Rest, James Rest, Shogun Japanese, 🅛 Inn at the Mill, TownePlace Suites
67	US 71B, Fayetteville, **E** 🅗
66	AR 112, Garland Ave, **E** 🅖 Phillips 66/dsl, 🅛 Motel 6, **W** 🅞 Acura, Chevrolet, Fiat, Honda, Sam's Club/gas, Toyota/Scion
65	Porter Rd
64	AR 16 W, AR 112 E, Wedington Dr, **E** 🅕 Eureka Pizza (2mi), **W** 🅖 Murphy Express/dsl, Phillips 66/McDonald's/dsl, 🅕 Boar's Nest BBQ, El Matador Mexican, Gusano's Pizza, IHOP, Pizza Hut, Sonic, Subway, Taco Bell, 🅛 Comfort Inn, Hilton Garden, Holiday Inn Express, Homewood Suites, 🅞 Harp's Food/gas, Walmart Mkt, vet
62	US 62, AR 180, Farmington, **E** 🅖 Phillips 66, Shell, 🅕

(Left margin, vertical text:) BENTONVILLE

(Right margin, vertical text:) FAYETTEVILLE

AR CA

FARMINGTON

⬆N INTERSTATE 540 (FAYETTEVILLE) CONT'D

Exit	Services
62	Continued
	Arby's, Braum's, Burger King, Burger Shack, Charlie's Chicken, Chick-fil-A, Hardee's, KFC, McDonald's, Mexico Viejo, Panda Express, Popeye's, Sonic, Starbucks, Subway, Taco Bell, Taco Bueno, Waffle House, Wendy's, Zaxby's, 🅛 Best Western, Candlewood Suites, EconoLodge, 🅞 AT&T, Bumper Parts, **W** 🅖 Murphy USA/dsl, 🅕 Braum's, Denny's, Firehouse Subs, Gino's Pizza, King Pizza, Lucy's Diner, Papa Murphy's, Pavilion Buffet, Ruby Tuesday, 🅛 Guesthouse Inn, Hampton Inn, Quality Inn, Regency 7 Motel, Super 8, Travelodge, ValuePlace, 🅞 Aldi Foods, AutoZone, $Tree, Lowe's, Radio Shack, Verizon, Walgreens, Walmart
61	US 71, to Boston Mtn Scenic Lp, sb only

60	AR 112, AR 265, Razorback Rd, **E** 🅛 Staybridge Suites, 🅞 Southgate RV Park, to U of AR
58	Greenland, **W** 🅖 Phillips 66/McDonalds/dsl/scales/24hr, 🅕 Sonic
53	AR 170; West Fork, **E** 🅖 Harp's/dsl, 🅞 Harp's Mkt, Winn Creek RV Resort (4mi), **W** to Devils Den SP
45	AR 74, Winslow, **W** to Devils Den SP
41mm	Bobby Hopper Tunnel
34	AR 282, to US 71, Chester, **W** USPO
29	AR 282, to US 71, Mountainburg, **1 mi E** 🅞 $General, to Lake Ft Smith SP
24	AR 282, to US 71, Rudy, **E** 🅖 Shell/dsl, 🅕 Red Hog BBQ, 🅞 KOA, Boston Mtns Scenic Lp
21	Collum Ln
20	(from sb) to US 71, **E** 🅖 Shell, 🅕 KFC, Taco Bell, 🅛 Comfort Inn, Days Inn

I-540 N begins/ends on I-40, exit 12.

CALIFORNIA

YREKA

⬆N INTERSTATE 5

Exit	Services
797mm	California/Oregon state line
796	Hilt, **W** 🅖 State Line Service/café/gas
793	Bailey Hill Rd
791mm	inspection sta sb
790	Hornbrook Hwy, Ditch Creek Rd
789	A28, to Hornbrook, Henley, **E** 🅖 Chevron/dsl/LP, 🅞 Blue Heron RV Park/rest., 🅞 to Iron Gate RA
786	CA 96, Klamath River Hwy, **W** 🆁🆂 **both lanes, full ♿ facilities, info,** 🅞, 🅛, **litter barrels, petwalk,** to Klamath River RA
782mm	Anderson Summit, elev 3067
780mm	vista point sb
779mm	Shasta River
776	Yreka, Montague, **E** 🅛 Holiday Inn Express, 🅞 Yreka RV Park, **W** 🅖 USA/dsl, 🅕 Casa Ramos Mexican, Puerto Vallarta, 🅛 Mtn View Inn, Super 8, 🅞 Ray's Foods
775	Miner St, Central Yreka, **W** 🅖 Chevron/dsl, Texaco/dsl, 🅕 China Dragon, Gold Rush Burger, Grandma's House, Purple Plum Rest., RoundTable Pizza, 🅛 Best Western, Budget Inn, EconoLodge, Klamath Motel, Relax Inn, Rodeway Inn, Yreka Motel, 🅞 🅗, Ace Hardware, Baxter Parts, CarQuest, Clayton Tire, Honda, Rite Aid, Shop Smart Foods, USPO, museum
773	CA 3, to Ft Jones, Etna, **E** 🅞 Les Schwab, Trailer Haven RV Park, truck repair, **W** 🅖 Shell/dsl, 🅕 BlackBear Diner, Burger King, Carl's Jr, McDonald's, Pizza Factory, Subway, Taco Bell, 🅛 Baymont Inn, Comfort Inn, Motel 6, 🅞 🅗, AAA, AT&T, $Tree, Ford/Lincoln, JC Penney, NAPA, O'Reilly Parts, Radio Shack, Raley's Foods, Walmart, CHP, **1 mi W** 🅖 Valero/dsl, 🅕 KFC
770	Shamrock Rd, Easy St, **W** 🅖 Beacon/LP, Fuel 24/7/dsl, 🅞 RV camping
766	A12, to Gazelle, Grenada, **E** 🅖 76/dsl, **W** 🅖 Texaco/dsl, 🅞 RV camping
759	Louie Rd
753	Weed Airport Rd, 🆁🆂 **both lanes, full ♿ facilities,** 🅛, **litter barrels,** 🅞, **petwalk**
751	Stewart Springs Rd, Edgewood, **E** 🅛 Lake Shasta RA/RV camp (2mi), **W** 🅞 RV camp (7mi)

WEED

MT SHASTA

DUNSMUIR

748	to US 97, to Klamath Falls, Weed, **E** 🅖 Chevron, Shell, dsl, Spirit/dsl, 🅕 Ellie's Cafe, Pizza Factory, Subway, 🅛 Hi-Lo Motel/rest., Motel 6, Summit Inn, Townhouse Motel, 🅞 NAPA, Ray's Foods, auto repair, golf, RV camping
747	Central Weed, **E** same as 748, 🅞 auto repair, **W** Coll of Siskiyou
745	S Weed Blvd, **E** 🅖 Chevron/dsl, Shell/dsl, 🅖/Subway/dsl/scales/24hr, 🅕 Burger King, Dos Amigos Mexican, McDonald's/RV parking, Silva's Rest., Taco Bell, 🅛 Comfort Inn, Quality Inn, Sis-Q Inn, 🅞 Friendly RV Park
743	Summit Dr, Truck Village Dr
742mm	Black Butte Summit, elev 3912
741	Abrams Lake Rd, **E** 🅞 Schwab Tire, **W** 🅛 Abrams Lake RV Park
740	Mt Shasta City (from sb), **E** 🅖 Pacific Pride/dsl/LP, 🅛 Cold Creek Inn
738	Central Mt Shasta, **E** 🅖 Chevron/dsl, Shell/dsl/LP, Spirit/dsl, 🅕 BlackBear Diner, Burger King, KFC/Taco Bell, RoundTable Pizza, Subway, 🅛 Best Western/Treehouse Rest., Mt Shasta Inn, Travel Inn, 🅞 🅗, Best Hardware, NAPA, O'Reilly Parts, Radio Shack, Ray's Foods, Rite Aid, Verizon, USPO, visitors info, **W** 🅛 Mt Shasta Resort/rest., Lake Siskiyou RV Park, Sisson Museum
737	Mt Shasta City (from nb), **E** 🅕 Casa Ramos, Chen&Lee's Chinese, LaiLai Chinese, Lily's Rest., Piemont Italian, 🅛 Alpine Lodge, Choice Inn, Evergreen Lodge, Swiss Holiday Lodge, 🅞 McCloud RV Park, same as 738
736	CA 89, to McCloud, to Reno, **E** 🅛 Swiss Holiday Lodge
735mm	weigh sta sb
734	Mott Rd, to Dunsmuir
732	Dunsmuir Ave, Siskiyou Ave, **E** 🅕 Penny's Diner, 🅛 Oak Tree Inn, **W** 🅖 Chevron/dsl, 🅛 Acorn Inn, Cedar Lodge
730	Central Dunsmuir, **E** 🅕 Burger Barn, Cornerstone Cafe, Dumsmuir Brewery Rest., Hot Dog Depot, Pizza Factory, 🅛 Dunsmuir Inn, Hotel Dunsmuir/Rest., 🅞 True Value, Value King Foods, USPO, **W** 🅖 Chevron/dsl/LP, 🅕 Hitching Post, Micki's Burgers, 🅛 Cave Springs Motel, 🅞 city park
729	Dunsmuir, **E** 🅕 Manfredi's/deli/dsl, 🅛 Dunsmuir Lodge, tires, to hist dist
728	Crag View Dr, Dunsmuir, Railroad Park Rd, **W** 🅞 Railroad Park Motel/RV Park

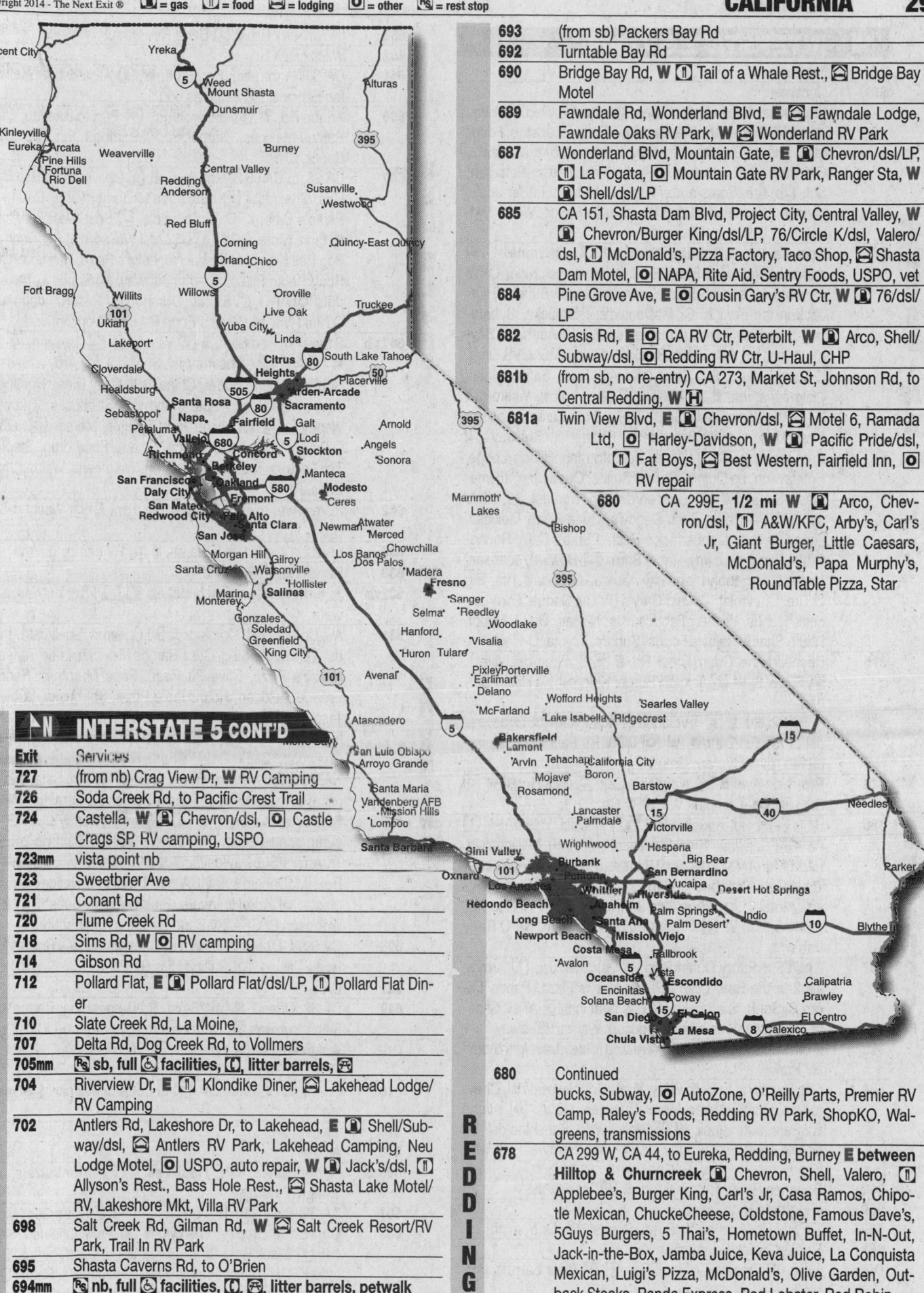

693	(from sb) Packers Bay Rd
692	Turntable Bay Rd
690	Bridge Bay Rd, **W** 🍴 Tail of a Whale Rest., 🏕 Bridge Bay Motel
689	Fawndale Rd, Wonderland Blvd, **E** 🏕 Fawndale Lodge, Fawndale Oaks RV Park, **W** 🏕 Wonderland RV Park
687	Wonderland Blvd, Mountain Gate, **E** 🅿 Chevron/dsl/LP, 🍴 La Fogata, 🄾 Mountain Gate RV Park, Ranger Sta, **W** 🅿 Shell/dsl/LP
685	CA 151, Shasta Dam Blvd, Project City, Central Valley, **W** 🅿 Chevron/Burger King/dsl/LP, 76/Circle K/dsl, Valero/dsl, 🍴 McDonald's, Pizza Factory, Taco Shop, 🏕 Shasta Dam Motel, 🄾 NAPA, Rite Aid, Sentry Foods, USPO, vet
684	Pine Grove Ave, **E** 🄾 Cousin Gary's RV Ctr, **W** 🅿 76/dsl/LP
682	Oasis Rd, **E** 🄾 CA RV Ctr, Peterbilt, **W** 🅿 Arco, Shell/Subway/dsl, 🄾 Redding RV Ctr, U-Haul, CHP
681b	(from sb, no re-entry) CA 273, Market St, Johnson Rd, to Central Redding, **W** 🄷
681a	Twin View Blvd, **E** 🅿 Chevron/dsl, 🏕 Motel 6, Ramada Ltd, 🄾 Harley-Davidson, **W** 🅿 Pacific Pride/dsl, 🍴 Fat Boys, 🏕 Best Western, Fairfield Inn, 🄾 RV repair
680	CA 299E, **1/2 mi W** 🅿 Arco, Chevron/dsl, 🍴 A&W/KFC, Arby's, Carl's Jr, Giant Burger, Little Caesars, McDonald's, Papa Murphy's, RoundTable Pizza, Star

CA

INTERSTATE 5 CONT'D

Exit	Services
727	(from nb) Crag View Dr, **W** RV Camping
726	Soda Creek Rd, to Pacific Crest Trail
724	Castella, **W** 🅿 Chevron/dsl, 🄾 Castle Crags SP, RV camping, USPO
723mm	vista point nb
723	Sweetbrier Ave
721	Conant Rd
720	Flume Creek Rd
718	Sims Rd, **W** 🄾 RV camping
714	Gibson Rd
712	Pollard Flat, **E** 🅿 Pollard Flat/dsl/LP, 🍴 Pollard Flat Diner
710	Slate Creek Rd, La Moine,
707	Delta Rd, Dog Creek Rd, to Vollmers
705mm	℞ₛ sb, full 🛆 facilities, 🍴 litter barrels, 🏕
704	Riverview Dr, **E** 🍴 Klondike Diner, 🏕 Lakehead Lodge/RV Camping
702	Antlers Rd, Lakeshore Dr, to Lakehead, **E** 🅿 Shell/Subway/dsl, 🏕 Antlers RV Park, Lakehead Camping, Neu Lodge Motel, 🄾 USPO, auto repair, **W** 🅿 Jack's/dsl, 🍴 Allyson's Rest., Bass Hole Rest., 🏕 Shasta Lake Motel/RV, Lakeshore Mkt, Villa RV Park
698	Salt Creek Rd, Gilman Rd, **W** 🏕 Salt Creek Resort/RV Park, Trail In RV Park
695	Shasta Caverns Rd, to O'Brien
694mm	℞ₛ nb, full 🛆 facilities, 🍴🏕 litter barrels, petwalk

R E D D I N G

| 680 | Continued
bucks, Subway, 🄾 AutoZone, O'Reilly Parts, Premier RV Camp, Raley's Foods, Redding RV Park, ShopKO, Walgreens, transmissions |
| 678 | CA 299 W, CA 44, to Eureka, Redding, Burney **E between Hilltop & Churncreek** 🅿 Chevron, Shell, Valero, 🍴 Applebee's, Burger King, Carl's Jr, Casa Ramos, Chipotle Mexican, ChuckeCheese, Coldstone, Famous Dave's, 5Guys Burgers, 5 Thai's, Hometown Buffet, In-N-Out, Jack-in-the-Box, Jamba Juice, Keva Juice, La Conquista Mexican, Luigi's Pizza, McDonald's, Olive Garden, Outback Steaks, Panda Express, Red Lobster, Red Robin, |

CA

⬆N INTERSTATE 5 CONT'D

Exit	Services

REDDING

678 Continued
Starbucks, Subway, Taco Bell, 🛏 Motel 6, Red Lion Inn, 🅞 AT&T, Barnes&Noble, Best Buy, BigLots, Costco, Food-Maxx, Home Depot, JC Penney, Kohl's, Macy's, Michael's, Old Navy, Office Depot, O'Reilly Parts, PetCo, Petsmart, Schwab Tire, Sears/auto, Target, TJ Maxx, Trader Joe's, Verizon, Walmart/McDonald's, WinCo Foods, World Mkt, vet

677 Cypress Ave, Hilltop Dr, Redding, **E** 🅖 Chevron/dsl, 76/dsl, Valero/dsl, 🍴 Black Bear Diner, Burger King, Carl's Jr, Coldstone, Del Taco, Denny's, Grand Buffet, IHOP, Jack-in-the-Box, KFC, McDonald's, Starbucks, Subara-ma, Taco Bell, Togo's, Umstead's BBQ, Wendy's, 🛏 Bay-mont Inn, 🅞 AutoZone, Buick/Cadillac/GMC, CVS Drug, K-Mart, Lowe's, 99¢ Store, Rite Aid, Ross, Safeway/gas, Walgreens, vet, **E on Hilltop** 🅖 Chevron/dsl, Valero/dsl, 🍴 Cattlemen's Rest., Gibb's Grille, Jade Garden, Logan's Roadhouse, Marie Callender's, Pizza Hut, Subway, 🛏 Best Western, Comfort Inn, Hampton Inn, Hilltop Lodge, Holiday Inn, La Quinta, Oxford Suites, Quality Inn, Towne-Place Suites, **W** 🅖 Beacon/dsl, Chevron/dsl, 76, USA/dsl, 🍴 CA Cattle Rest, Denny's, Guadalajara Mexican, Little Caesars, Lumberjack's Rest., Perko's Cafe, Round-Table Pizza, Subway, Taco Barn, 🛏 Howard Johnson, Motel 6, Vagabond Inn, 🅞 Aamco, America's Tire, Big O Tire, Chevrolet, Cousin Gary's RV Ctr, Dodge, Ford/Lin-coln, Honda, Jo-Ann Fabrics, Kia, Nissan, Office Depot, Radio Shack, Raley's Foods, Subaru, Toyota, U-Haul

675 Bechelli Lane, Churn Creek Rd, **E** 🅖 Chevron/dsl, Valero, 🛏 Super 8, **W** 🅖 Texaco/Burger King/dsl, 🛏 Hilton Garden

673 Knighton Rd, **E** 🅖 TA/Country Pride/Pizza Hut/Popeye's/dsl/LP/scales/24hr/@, **W** 🅞 JGW RV Park (3mi), Sacramento River RV Park (3mi)

670 Riverside Ave, **E** 🍴 Woodside Grill, 🛏 Gaia Hotel, **W** 🅞 B&B RV Ctr, Camping World RV Ctr

ANDERSON

668 Balls Ferry Rd, Anderson, **E** 🅖 Shell/dsl, Valero/dsl, 🍴 A&W/KFC, Burger King, El Mariachi Mexican, McDonald's, Papa Murphy's, Peacock Chinese, Perko's Cafe, Round-Table Pizza, Starbucks, Subway, Taco Bell, 🛏 Best West-ern, Motel 6, 🅞 $Tree, Les Schwab Tire, NAPA, Rite Aid, Safeway/dsl, **W** 🍴 Players Pizza, Taco Barn, 🅞 O'Reilly Parts

667 CA 273, Factory Outlet Blvd, **W** 🅖 Shell/dsl, 🍴 Arby's, Jack-in-the-Box, Luigi's Pizza, Mary's Pizza, Panda Ex-press, Sonic, Starbucks, 🛏 Baymont Inn, 🅞 AT&T, Shas-ta Outlets/famous brands, Verizon, Walmart/Subway

665 (from sb) Cottonwood, **E** 🛏 Alamo Motel, Travelers Motel/RV Park

664 Gas Point Rd, to Balls Ferry, **E** 🅖 Cottonwood/dsl, Chev-ron/dsl/LP, 🛏 Alamo Motel, Travelers Motel, 🅞 Alamo RV Park, auto repair, **W** 🅖 Holiday/dsl, Sunshine/dsl, 🍴 Eagles Nest Pizza, Subway, 🅞 Ace Hardware, Holiday Foods

662 Bowman Rd, to Cottonwood, **E** 🅖 Texaco/dsl

660mm **weigh sta both lanes**

659 Snively Rd, Auction Yard Rd, (Sunset Hills Dr from nb)

657 Hooker Creek Rd, Auction Yard Rd

656mm 🆁🆂 **both lanes, full** ♿ **facilities,** 🚻, 🍴, **litter barrels, pet-walk**

RED BLUFF

653 Jellys Ferry Rd, **E** 🛏 Bend RV Park/LP

652 Wilcox Golf Rd

651 CA 36W (from sb), Red Bluff, **W** 🅖 Arco/dsl, 🛏 Holiday Inn Express, 🅞 same as 650

650 Adobe Rd, **W** 🅖 Chevron/dsl, 🍴 Burrito Bandito, Casa Ramos Mexican, Starbucks, 🛏 Hampton Inn, 🅞 Home Depot, CHP

649 CA 36, to CA 99 S, Red Bluff, **E** 🅖 Chevron/dsl, Red Bluff Gas, Shell/dsl, 🍴 Applebee's, Burger King, Del Taco, Perko's Cafe, KFC, McDonald's, 🛏 Best Western, Com-fort Inn, Motel 6, **W** 🅖 USA/dsl, Valero/dsl, 🍴 Denny's, Egg Roll King, Los Mariachis, Luigi's Pizza, Riverside Grill, RoundTable Pizza, Shari's, Subway, 🛏 Super 8, Travelo-dge, 🅞 AT&T, CVS Drug, Durango RV Resort, Foodmaxx, O'Nite RV Park, River's Edge RV Park, Verizon, vet

647a b S Main St, Red Bluff, **E** 🅖 Valero/dsl, 🛏 Days Inn, 🅞🅗, **W** 🅖 Arco/dsl, Chevron/dsl, Shell/dsl, 🍴 Arby's, Baskin-Robbins, China Buffet, China Doll, Cozy Diner, Domino's, Jack-in-the-Box, Papa Murphy's, Starbucks, Subway, Wendy's, 🛏 American Inn, Triangle Motel, 🅞 GNC, O'Reilly Parts, Radio Shack, Raley's Food/drug, Staples, Tire Factory, True Value, Verizon, Walgreens, Walmart/Mc-Donald's

642 Flores Ave, to Proberta, Gerber **1 mi E** 🅞 Walmart Dist Ctr

636 rd A11, Gyle Rd, to Tehama, **E** 🅞 RV camping (7mi)

633 Finnell Rd, to Richfield

632mm 🆁🆂 **both lanes, full** ♿ **facilities,** 🚻, 🍴, **litter barrels, pet-walk**

CORNING

631 A9, Corning Rd, Corning, **E** 🅖 Chevron, Shell/dsl/LP, 76/dsl, 🍴 Burger King, Casa Ramos Mexican, Little Caesars, Marco's Pizza, Olive Pit Rest., Papa Murphy's, Rancho Grande Mexican, RoundTable Pizza, Starbucks, Subway, Taco Bell, 🛏 American Inn, Best Western, Economy Inn, 7 Inn Motel, Super 8, 🅞 Ace Hardware, AutoZone, Buick/Chevrolet, Clark Drug, $Tree, Ford, Heritage RV Park, NAPA, O'Reilly Parts, Radio Shack, Rite Aid, Safeway, Ve-rizon, auto repair, **W** 🍴 Giant Burger, 🛏 Corning RV Park

630 South Ave, Corning, **E** 🅖 🟦Loves/Denny's/dsl/LP/dump/scales/24hr, Petro/Iron Skillet/dsl/scales/24hr/@, TA/Arby's/Subway/dsl/scales/24hr/@, 🍴 Jack-in-the-Box, McDonald's, 🛏 CA Inn, Days Inn, Holiday Inn Ex-press, 🅞 Ace Hardware, Blue Beacon, SpeedCo Lube, Woodson Br SRA/RV Park (6mi), truck wash/lube

628 CA 99W, Liberal Ave, **W** 🅖 Chevron/dsl, 🛏 Rolling Hills Hotel/Casino, 🅞 Rolling Hills RV Park

621 CA 7

619 CA 32, Orland, **E** 🅖 76/dsl, 🍴 Burger King, Berry Patch Rest., Subway, 🛏 Orlanda Inn, 🅞 AutoZone, CVS Drug, Walgreens, **W** 🅖 Shell/dsl, 🍴 Taco Bell, 🅞 Old Orchard RV Park, Parkway RV Park

618 CA 16, **E** 🅖 Shell/dsl, 🍴 El Potrero Mexican, 🛏 Orland Inn

614 CA 27

610 Artois

608mm 🆁🆂 **both lanes, full** ♿ **facilities,** 🚻, 🍴, **litter barrels, pet-walk, RV dump**

607 CA 39, Blue Gum Rd, Bayliss, **2 mi E** 🛏 Blue Gum Motel

603 CA 162, to Oroville, Willows, **E** 🅖 Arco, Chevron, Shell/dsl, 🍴 Black Bear Diner, Burger King, Casa Ramos, Den-ny's, KFC, La Cascada Mexican, McDonald's, RoundTable Pizza, Starbucks, Subway, Taco Bell, Wong's Chinese, 🛏

⛽ = gas 🍽 = food 🛏 = lodging ⊙ = other 🅡ₛ = rest stop

⬆N INTERSTATE 5 CONT'D

Exit	Services
603	Continued
	Baymont Inn, Holiday Inn Express, Days Inn/RV parking, Motel 6, Super 8, Travelodge, ⊙ H, CHP, W 🍽 Nancy's Café/24hr, ⊙ Walmart, RV Park (8mi), 🔄
601	rd 57, E ⛽ 76/dsl
595	Rd 68, to Princeton, E to Sacramento NWR
591	Delevan Rd
588	Maxwell (from sb), access to camping
586	Maxwell Rd, E ⊙ Delavan NWR, W ⛽ Chevron, 🛏 Maxwell Inn/rest., ⊙ Maxwell Parts
583	🅡ₛ both lanes, full ♿ facilities, 🚰, 🛒, litter barrels, petwalk
578	CA 20, Colusa, W ⛽ Shell/Orv's Cafe/dsl, ⊙ H, hwy patrol
577	Williams, E ⛽ Shell/Baskin-Robbins/Togo's/dsl, 🍽 Carl's Jr, Subway, Taco Bell, 🛏 Ramada Inn, W ⛽ Chevron/dsl, 76/dsl, Shell/dsl, 🍽 Burger King, Denny's, Granzella's Rest., Louis Cairo's Rest., McDonald's/RV parking, Straw Hat Pizza, Williams Chinese Rest., 🛏 Granzella's Inn, Motel 6, Quality Inn, StageStop Motel, Travelers Inn, ⊙ H, NAPA, Shop'n Save Foods, USPO, camping, hwy patrol, **Urgent Care**
575	Husted Rd, to Williams
569	Hahn Rd, to Grimes
567	frontage rd (from nb), to Arbuckle, W ⛽ Chevron/dsl
566	to College City, Arbuckle, E ⊙ Ace Hardware, USPO, W ⛽ J&J/dsl
559	Yolo/Colusa County Line Rd
557mm	🅡ₛ both lanes, full ♿ facilities, 🚰, 🛒, litter barrels, petwalk
556	E4, Dunnigan, E ⛽ Chevron/dsl/LP, 76/dsl, 🍽 Jack-in-the-Box, 🛏 Best Value Inn, Motel 6, ⊙ Farmers Mkt Deli, W 🛏 Camper's RV Park/golf (1mi)
554	rd 8, E ⛽ 🍽/Wendy's/dsl/scales/24hr, ⊙ Oasis Grill, 🛏 Hacienda Motel, ⊙ HappyTime RV Park, W ⛽ United TP/dsl
553	I-505 (from sb), to San Francisco, callboxes begin sb
548	Zamora, E ⛽ Shell/dsl
542	Yolo, 1 mi E gas
541	CA 16W, Esparta, Woodland, 3 mi W ⊙ H
540	West St, W ⛽ Arco, 🍽 Denny's
538	CA 113 N, E St, Woodland, E 🛏 Valley Oaks Inn, W ⛽ Arco/dsl, Chevron/dsl, 🍽 Perry's, 🛏 Best Western
537	CA 113 S, Main St, to Davis, E ⊙ Buick/Cadillac/Chevrolet/GMC, same as 536, W ⛽ Chevron/dsl, 🍽 Carl's Jr, Denny's, McDonald's, Sonic, Subway, Taco Bell, Wendy's, 🛏 Days Inn, Motel 6, Quality Inn, ⊙ $Tree, Food4Less
536	rd 102, E on Main St ⛽ Arco, Chevron, 🍽 Applebee's, Jack-in-the-Box, McDonald's, Quiznos, Subway, 🛏 Hampton Inn, Holiday Inn Express, ⊙ America's Tire, Home Depot, Staples, Walmart/McDonald's, museum, same as 537, W 🍽 In-N-Out, Panda Express, Red Robin, Spoon Me, Starbucks, Subway, ⊙ Best Buy, Costco/gas, Michael's, Target, Verizon
531	rd 22, Sacramento
530mm	Sacramento River
529mm	🅡ₛ sb, full ♿ facilities, 🚰, 🛒, litter barrels, petwalk
528	Airport Rd, E ⛽ Arco, ⊙ ✈, food
525b	CA 99, to CA 70, to Marysville, Yuba City

California/Oregon Border
Yreka
⑤ Weed
  Mount Shasta
  Dunsmuir
  Central Valley
Redding
Anderson
  Red Bluff
  Corning
  Orland
⑤

CA

CA

Exit	Services
525a	Del Paso Rd, E ⛽ Chevron, 🍽 A&W/KFC, IHOP, In-N-Out, Jack-in-the-box, Jamba Juice, Malabar Rest., Panera Bread, Panda Express, Sizzler, Starbucks, Straw Hat Pizza, Taco Bell, Wienerschnitzel, 🛏 Hampton Inn, Holiday Inn Express, Homewood Suites, ⊙ Rite Aid, Safeway Foods/dsl, W 🍽 Subway, 🛏 Sheraton, ⊙ Walgreens
524	Arena Blvd, E 🍽 Subway, ⊙ Power Balance Arena, W 🍽 RoundTable Pizza, Starbucks, ⊙ Bel-Air Food/Drug/dsl
522	I-80, E to Reno, W to San Francisco
521b a	Garden Hwy, West El Camino, W ⛽ Shell/dsl, 🍽 Carl's Jr, Jack-in-the-Box, Jamba Juice, Starbucks, Subway, Togo's/Baskin-Robbins, 🛏 Courtyard, Hilton Garden, Residence Inn, SpringHill Suites
520	Richards Blvd, E ⛽ Chevron/dsl, 🍽 Grill Master's Steaks, McDonald's, Sekou's BBQ, 🛏 Governor's Inn, Hawthorn Suites, Ramada Ltd, Super 8, W ⛽ Arco, Shell, 🍽 Coyote Jct Mexican, 🛏 Best Value Inn, Best Western, Comfort Suites, Days Inn, La Quinta, Motel 6, ⊙ waterfront park
519b	J St, Old Sacramento, E 🍽 Denny's, 🛏 Holiday Inn, Vagabond Inn, W 🛏 Embassy Suites, ⊙ Railroad Museum
519a	Q St, downtown Sacramento, W 🛏 Embassy Suites, to st capitol
518	US 50, CA 99, Broadway, E services downtown
516	Sutterville Rd, E ⛽ Land Park/dsl, 76/dsl, 🍽 La Bou Cafe, Macau Cafe, ⊙ Sunflower Mkt, Wm Land Park, zoo
515	Fruitridge Rd, Seamas Rd
514	43rd Ave, Riverside Blvd (from sb), E ⛽ 76/repair
513	Florin Rd, E ⛽ Arco, Chevron, 🍽 Rosalinda's Mexican, RoundTable Pizza, Sizzling Wok, ⊙ Bel Air Foods, CVS Drug, $Tree, O'Reilly Parts, **Urgent Care**, W 🍽 Burger King, Coldstone, JimBoy's Tacos, L&L Hawaiian BBQ, Panda Garden, Shari's, Starbucks, Subway, Wings Stop, ⊙ AAA, Marshall's, Nugget Mkt, Radio Shack, Rite Aid
512	CA 160, Pocket Rd, Meadowview Rd, to Freeport, E ⛽ Shell/dsl, Valero/dsl, 🍽 IHOP, KFC/LJ Silver, McDonald's, Starbucks, Wendy's, ⊙ AT&T, Home Depot, Staples, Walgreens, vet
508	Laguna Blvd, E ⛽ Chevron/McDonald's/dsl, 76/Circle K/dsl/LP, Shell, 🍽 A&W/KFC, Starbucks, Subway, Wendy's, 🛏 Extended Stay America, Hampton Inn, ⊙ Jiffy Lube, Laguna Tire, U-Haul
506	Elk Grove Blvd, E ⛽ Arco/dsl, Chevron/dsl, Shell, 🍽 Carl's Jr, Nick-N-Willy's Pizza, Pete's Grill, Vallarta Mexican, Wasabi Grill, 🛏 Holiday Inn Express
504	Hood Franklin Rd
498	Twin Cities Rd, to Walnut Grove

(left margin, vertical: WILLIAMS · DAVIS *)*
(right margin, vertical: SACRAMENTO *)*

⛽ = gas 🍴 = food 🛏 = lodging Ⓞ = other 🅿️ = rest stop   Copyright 2014 - The Next Exit ®

⬆N INTERSTATE 5 CONT'D

Exit	Services
493	Walnut Grove Rd, Thornton, **E** ⛽ CFN/dsl, Chevron/Subway/dsl
490	Peltier Rd
487	Turner Rd
485	CA 12, Lodi, **E** ⛽ Arco/Subway/dsl/24hr, Chevron/dsl, ⭐FLYING J/Denny's/dsl/scales/24hr, 76/Rocky's Rest./dsl/scales/24hr, Shell/dsl, 🍴 Burger King, Carl's Jr, McDonald's, Taco Bell, 🛏 Best Western, Microtel, Ⓞ Blue Beacon, Flag City RV Resort, Profleet Trucklube, **W** Ⓞ KOA (5mi)
481	Eight Mile Rd, **W** ⛽ Chevron/Jack-in-the-Box/dsl, 🍴 Baskin-Robbins, Del Taco, Hawaiian BBQ, Jalapeno's, Jamba Juice, McDonald's, MooMoo's Burgers, Panda Express, Panera Bread, RoundTable Pizza, Sonic, Starbucks, Strings Italian, Subway, Wendy's, Ⓞ AAA, AT&T, Jo-Ann Fabrics, KOA, Kohl's, Lowe's, Office Depot, Petsmart, Ross, Target, Verizon, Walmart
478	Hammer Lane, Stockton, **E** ⛽ Arco, 76/dsl, 🍴 Adalberto's Mexican, Carl's Jr, KFC, Little Caesars, McDonald's, Subway, Ⓞ AutoZone, Radio Shack, Rally's Foods, Walgreens, **W** ⛽ Chevron/dsl, QuikStop, 🍴 Jack-in-the-Box, Lupe's Mexican, Taco Bell
477	Benjamin Holt Dr, Stockton, **E** ⛽ Arco, Chevron/dsl, QwikStop, 🍴 Pizza Guys, 🛏 Motel 6, Ⓞ Quikstop, **W** ⛽ 7-11, 🍴 Casa Flores, Eddie's Pizza, Fon Wong Chinese, Lumber Jack's Rest., McDonald's, Subway/TCBY, Ⓞ Ace Hardware, Marina Foods, vet
476	March Lane, Stockton, **E** ⛽ 7-11, 🍴 Applebee's, Carl's Jr, Denny's, El Torito, Jack-in-the-Box, McDonald's, Marie Callender's, Olive Garden, Red Lobster, StrawHat Pizza, Taco Bell, Toot Sweets Bakery, Wendy's, 🛏 Comfort Inn, Hilton, Ⓞ CVS Drug, Marshall's, SMart Foods, **W** ⛽ 76/dsl, 🍴 Carrow's Rest., In-N-Out, Italian Cuisine, Jamba Juice, Krispy Kreme, RoundTable Pizza, Old Spaghetti Factory, Starbucks, Subway, Wong's Chinese, 🛏 Courtyard, Extended Stay America, La Quinta, Quality Inn, Residence Inn, Ⓞ Home Depot
475	Alpine Ave, Country Club Blvd same as 474 b
474b	Country Club Blvd (from nb), **E** ⛽ 76/dsl, **W** ⛽ Shell/Subway/dsl, 7-11, Ⓞ BigLots, Safeway/gas
474a	Monte Diablo Ave
473	Pershing Ave (from nb), **W** ⛽ Arco, 🛏 Red Roof Inn
472	CA 4 E, to CA 99, Fresno Ave, downtown
471	CA 4 W, Charter Way, **E** ⛽ Chevron/dsl, Shell, United, 🍴 Burger King, Denny's, Little Ceasars, McDonald's, Quiznos, 🛏 Days Inn, Ⓞ O'Reilly Parts, **W** ⛽ 76/dsl/scales/24hr, Valero/Subway, 🍴 Jack-in-the-Box, Taco Bell, 🛏 Motel 6, Ⓞ Les Schwab Tire, truck repair
470	8th St, Stockton, **W** ⛽ CA Stop/dsl, Shell/Subway/dsl, 🛏 I-5 Inn
469	Downing Ave, **W** 🍴 China Express, Lou's Chinese, Mtn Mike's Pizza, Subway, Ⓞ AutoZone, Food4Less/gas
468	French Camp, **E** ⛽ 76/Togo's/dsl, Ⓞ Pan Pacific RV Ctr, **W** Ⓞ Ⓗ
467b	Mathews Rd, **E** ⛽ J&L Mkt/dsl, Ⓞ tires/repair, **W** Ⓞ Ⓗ
467a	El Dorado St (from nb)
465	Roth Rd, Sharpe Depot, **E** ⛽ FL/dsl, Ⓞ Freightliner, Kenworth, truck/rv repair
463	Lathrop Rd, **E** ⛽ Chevron/dsl/LP, Joe's Trkstp/Texaco/Togo's/dsl/scales, TowerMart/dsl, Valero/dsl, 🍴 Baskin-

Exit	Services
463	**Continued** Robbins, CK Grill, China Wok, Little Ceasars, Mi Kasa Japanese, Royal Pizza, Starbucks, Subway, 🛏 Best Western, Comfort Inn, Days Inn, Holiday Inn Express, Ⓞ Harley-Davidson, SaveMart Mkt, Walgreens, **W** Ⓞ Dos Reis CP, RV camping
462	Louise Ave, **E** ⛽ Arco/dsl, Shell, 🍴 A&W/KFC, Carl's Jr, Denny's, Golden Bowl, Jack-in-the-Box, McDonald's, Mtn Mike's Pizza, Quiznos, Taco Bell, 🛏 Hampton Inn, Quality Inn, Ⓞ Mossdale CP, **W** Ⓞ Target
461	CA 120, to Sonora, Manteca, **E** Ⓞ Oakwood Lake Resort Camping, to Yosemite
460	Mossdale Rd, **E** ⛽ Arco/dsl, **W** 🍴 fruit stand/cafe
458b	I-205, to Oakland (from sb, no return)
458a	11th St, to Tracy, Defense Depot, **2 mi W** ⛽ gas/dsl/food
457	Kasson Rd, to Tracy, **W** ⛽ Valley Pacific/dsl
452	CA 33 S, Vernalis
449b a	CA 132, to Modesto, **E** Ⓞ The Orchard Campground
446	I-580 (from nb, exits left, no return)
445mm	**Westley** 🅿️ **both lanes, full** ♿ **facilities,** 🏕 **, litter barrels,** Ⓒ**, RV dump, petwalk**
441	Ingram Creek, Howard Rd, Westley, **E** ⛽ Chevron/dsl, Joe's Trvl Plaza/dsl/scales/24hr, 76/dsl, Triangle TruckStp/dsl, 🍴 Antojito's Mexican, Carl's Jr, McDonald's, Subway, 🛏 Best Value Inn, Days Inn, EconoLodge, Holiday Inn Express, **W** ⛽ Shell/dsl, 🍴 Ingram Creek Rest., fruits, Ⓞ truck repair
434	Sperry Ave, Del Puerto, Patterson, **E** ⛽ Chevron, 76/Subway/dsl, 🍴 A&W/KFC, Carl's Jr, Denny's, El Rosal Mexican, Golden Lion Chinese, Jack-in-the-Box, Lamp Post Pizza, Starbucks, Strings Italian, 🛏 Best Western, Ⓞ Kit Fox RV Park
430mm	vista point nb
428	Fink Rd, Crow's Landing
423	Stuhr Rd, Newman, **5 mi E** food, lodging, Ⓞ Ⓗ, RV camping
422mm	vista point sb
418	CA 140E, Gustine
409	weigh sta both lanes
407	CA 33, Santa Nella, **E** ⛽ Arco/Subway, ❤Loves/Del Taco/dsl/scales/24hr, TA/Buckhorn Rest./Popeye's/dsl/scales/24hr/@, 🍴 Carl's Jr, Andersen's Rest, Wendy's, 🛏 Best Western/Andersen's, Holiday Inn Express, **W** ⛽ Chevron, Rotten Robbie/dsl/scales, Shell/Circle K/Jack-in-the-Box/dsl, Valero/dsl, 🍴 Denny's, In-N-Out, McDonald's, Quiznos, Starbucks, Taco Bell, 🛏 Hotel de Oro, Motel 6, Ⓞ Santa Nella RV Park
403b a	CA 152, Los Banos, **6 mi E** Ⓞ Ⓗ, **W** ⛽ Petro/dsl/24hr (1mi), Ⓞ KOA, San Luis RV Park
391	CA 165N, Mercy Springs Rd, **E** Ⓗ, **W** ⛽ Shell
388mm	vista point (from nb)
386mm	🅿️ **both lanes, full** ♿ **facilities,** Ⓒ**,** 🏕**, litter barrels, petwalk**
385	Nees Ave, to Firebaugh, **W** ⛽ Chevron/CFN/Subway/dsl/scales
379	Shields Ave, to Mendota
372	Russell Ave
368	Panoche Rd, **W** ⛽ Chevron/McDonald's, Mobil/Taco Bell/dsl, 76/dsl, Shell/dsl, 🍴 Apricot Tree Rest., Fosters Freeze, Subway, 🛏 Best Western, Ⓞ country store
365	Manning Ave, to San Joaquin
357	Kamm Ave

⬆N INTERSTATE 5 CONT'D

Exit	Services
349	CA 33 N, Derrick Ave
337	CA 33 S, CA 145 N, to Coalinga
334	CA 198, to Lemoore, Huron, **E** 🅿 Shell/Subway/dsl/24hr, 🛏 Harris Ranch Inn/rest., **W** 🅿 Chevron, 76, Valero/dsl, 🍴 Burger King, Carl's Jr, Denny's, McDonald's, Oriental Express Chinese, Taco Bell, 🛏 Best Western, Motel 6, Travelodge, 🅾🅷
325	Jayne Ave, to Coalinga, **W** 🅿 Arco, Shell/Baja Fresh/dsl, 🛏 Sommerville RV Park/LP, 🅾🅷
320mm	🆁🆂 both lanes, full ♿ facilities, 🅲, 🖼, litter barrels, petwalk
319	CA 269, Lassen Ave, to Avenal, **W** 🅿 Hillcrest TP/76/dsl/scales/24hr
309	CA 41, Kettleman City, **E** 🅿 CFN/dsl, Chevron/McDonald's, Mobil/Starbucks/dsl/24hr, 76/Subway/TCBY, Shell/dsl, Valero/dsl, 🍴 Carl's Jr, Denny's, In-N-Out, Jack-in-the-Box, Pizza Hut/Taco Bell, 🛏 Best Western, Super 8, 🅾 Travelers RV Park
305	Utica Ave
288	Twisselman Rd
278	CA 46, Lost Hills, **E** 🅿 Buford Star Mart/dsl/LP, 🅾 to Kern NWR, **W** 🅿 Chevron/dsl, Loves/Arby's/dsl/scales/24hr, Mobil/McDonald's/dsl/LP, Wendy's/dsl/scales/24hr, 76/Quiznos, Shell/Pizza Hut/Subway/Taco Bell/dsl, Valero/dsl, 🍴 Carl's Jr, Denny's, Jack-in-the-Box, McDonald's, 🛏 Days Inn, Motel 6, 🅾 K&S Truck Wash, Lost Hills RV Park
268	Lerdo Hwy, to Shafter
262	7th Standard Rd, Rowlee Rd, to Buttonwillow
259mm	**Buttonwillow** 🆁🆂 both lanes, full ♿ facilities, 🅲, 🖼, litter barrels, petwalk
257	CA 58, to Bakersfield, Buttonwillow, **E** 🅿 Arco/dsl, Bruce's/dsl/wash, Chevron/dsl, 76/Circle K/Quiznos/dsl, TA/Pizza Hut/Taco Bell/dsl/scales/24hr/@, Shell/dsl, 🍴 Carl's Jr, Denny's, McDonald's, Starbucks, Subway, Tita's Mexican, Willow Ranch BBQ, 🛏 EconoLodge, Knights Inn, Motel 6, 🅾 Castro's Tire/Truckwash, **W** 🅿 Valero/dsl
253	Stockdale Hwy, **E** 🅿 Chevron/dsl, Shell/dsl/24hr, 🍴 IHOP, Jack-In-the-Box, 🛏 Best Western, Vagabond Inn, **W** 🅾 Tule Elk St Reserve
246	CA 43, to Taft, Maricopa, 🅾 to Buena Vista RA
244	CA 119, to Pumpkin Center, **E** 🅿 Mobil/dsl, **W** 🅿 Chevron/dsl/LP
239	CA 223, Bear Mtn Blvd, to Arvin, **E** 🅾 Bear Mtn. RV Resort, **W** 🅾 to Buena Vista RA, RV camping
234	Old River Rd
228	Copus Rd, **E** Murray Farms Mkt
225	CA 166, to Mettler, **2-3 mi E** gas/dsl, food
221	I-5 and CA 99 (from nb, exits left, no return)
219b a	Laval Rd, Wheeler Ridge, **E** 🅿 TA/Chevron/Popeye's/Subway/scales/@, 🍴 Burger King, Pizza Hut, Taco Bell, 🛏 Microtel, 🅾 Blue Beacon, **W** 🅿 Chevron/dsl, Mobil/dsl, Petro/Iron Skillet/Subway/dsl/scales/24hr/@, 🍴 Baskin-Robbins, Chipotle Mexican, Del Taco, In-N-Out, McDonald's, Panda Express, Starbucks, Subway, Wendy's, Yogurtland, 🛏 Best Western
218	truck weigh sta sb
215	Grapevine, **E** 🅿 Valero/dsl, 🍴 Denny's, Jack-in-the-Box, **W** 🅿 Shell/dsl, 🍴 Don Perico Grill, 🛏 Ramda Ltd.
210	Ft Tejon Rd, **W** 🅾 to Ft Tejon Hist SP, towing/repair

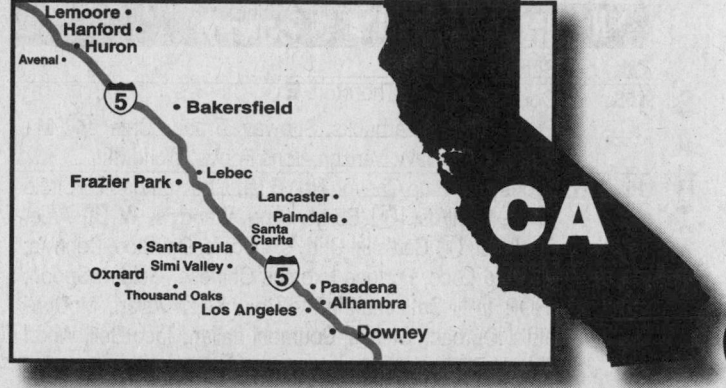

	Exit	Services
	209mm	brake check area nb
	207	Lebec Rd, **W** 🅾 USPO, CHP, antiques, towing
	206mm	🆁🆂 both lanes, full ♿ facilities, 🅲, vending, 🖼 litter barrels, petwalk
F T T E J O N	205	Frazier Mtn Park Rd, **W** 🅿 Chevron/Subway/dsl/24hr, ✈FLYING J/Denny's/dsl/LP/24hr/@, 76, Shell/Quiznos/dsl/LP, 🍴 Jack-in-the-Box, Los Pinos Mexican, 🛏 Holiday Inn Express, Motel 6, 🅾 NAPA, auto repair/towing, to Mt Pinos RA
	204	Tejon Pass, elev 4144, **truck brake insp sb**
	202	Gorman Rd, to Hungry Valley, **E** 🅿 Chevron/dsl/LP, 76/dsl, 🍴 Carl's Jr, El Grullense, Ranch House Rest., 🛏 EconoLodge, **W** 🅿 Shell, 🍴 McDonald's, 🅾 auto repair
	199	CA 138 E, Lancaster Rd, to Palmdale
	198b a	Quail Lake Rd, CA 138 E (from nb)
	195	Smokey Bear Rd, Pyramid Lake, **W** 🅾 Pyramid Lake RV Park
	191	Vista del Lago Rd, **W** 🅾 visitors ctr
	186mm	brake inspection area sb, motorist callboxes begin sb
	183	Templin Hwy, **W** 🅾 Ranger Sta, RV camping
C A S T A I C	176b a	Lake Hughes Rd, Parker Rd, Castaic, **E** 🅿 7-11, Castaic Trkstp/dsl/24hr, Wendy's/dsl/scales/24hr/@, Shell/dsl, 🍴 Baskin-Robbins, Burger King, Mike's Diner, Carl's Jr, Denny's, Domino's, El Pollo Loco, Fosters Freeze, Jersey Mikes, McDonald's, Mike's Diner, Panda Express, Pizza Factory, Popeye's, Starbucks, Subway, Telly's Drive-in, Vinny's Pizza, Wok's Chinese, 🛏 Castaic Inn, Days Inn, Rodeway Inn, 🅾 Benny's Tire/repair, Castaic Lake RV Park, $Tree, O'Reilly Parts, Ralph's Food, Rite Aid, vct, to Castaic Lake, **W** 🅿 Mobil, 76/repair, 🍴 Jack-in-the-Box, Taco Bell, 🅾 Walgreens, auto repair
	173	Hasley Canyon Rd, **W** 🍴 Amici Pizza, Las Delicias, Pizza Hut, Subway, 🅾 Ralph's Foods
	172	CA 126 W, to Ventura, **E** 🛏 Courtyard, Embassy Suites
	171mm	weigh sta nb
	171	Rye Canyon Rd (from sb), **W** 🅿 Chevron, Shell, 🍴 Del Taco, Jack-in-the-Box, Jimmy Deans, Starbucks, Subway, Tommy's Burgers, 🅾 6 Flags
	170	CA 126 E, Magic Mtn Pkwy, Saugus, **E** 🍴 Denny's, Geisha Japanese, Sam's Grille, Starbucks, 🛏 Best Western/rest., Holiday Inn Express, **W** 🅿 Chevron/dsl, 🍴 El Torito, Game Day Cafe, Marie Callender's, Red Lobster, Wendy's, 🛏 Hilton Garden, 🅾 Six Flags of CA
	169	Valencia Blvd, **W** 🍴 Fat Burger, Nick'n Willy's Pizza, Panda Express, Robeks, Starbucks, Subway, 🅾 Albertson's, Sav-On, Verizon
	168	McBean Pkwy, **E** 🅾🅷, **W** 🍴 Baskin-Robbins, Cabo Cabana, Chili's, ChuckeCheese, ClaimJumper, Jamba Juice, Jersey Mikes Subs, Macaroni Grill, Mamma Mia Italian,

INTERSTATE 5 CONT'D

Exit	Services
168	Continued
	Pick up Stix, Starbucks, Subway, Urbane Cafe, 🅞 Michael's, Old Navy, Verizon, Vons Foods, WorldMkt
167	Lyons Ave, Pico Canyon Rd, **E** 🅖 Chevron/dsl, 76/Circle K/dsl, Shell/dsl, 🍴 Burger King, Wendy's, **W** 🅖 Arco, Shell/dsl, 🍴 Carl's Jr, Chuy's, Coco's, Del Taco, Denny's, El Pollo Loco, Fortune Express Chinese, Golden Spoon, IHOP, In-N-Out, Jack-in-the-Box, Kinza Asian, McDonald's, Outback Steaks, Spumoni Italian, Taco Bell, Wood Ranch BBQ, Yamato Japanese, 🏠 Comfort Suites, Extended Stay America, Fairfield Inn, Hampton Inn, La Quinta, Residence Inn, 🅞 AT&T, Camping World RV Ctr, GNC, Jiffy Lube, Marshall's, Petsmart, Ralph's Foods, Ross, Staples, SteinMart, Tire World, Walmart/McDonald's
166	Calgrove Blvd
162	CA 14 N, to Palmdale
161b	Balboa Blvd (from sb)
160a	I-210, to San Fernando, Pasadena
159	Roxford St, Sylmar, **E** 🅖 Chevron/dsl, Mobil/dsl, 🍴 Denny's/24hr, McDonald's, 🏠 Good Nite Inn, Motel 6
158	I-405 S (from sb, no return)
157b a	SF Mission Blvd, Brand Blvd, **E** 🅖 Arco, Chevron, Mobil/dsl, 76, Shell, 🍴 Carl's Jr, In-N-Out, Little Caesars, New Asia, Pollo Gordo, Popeye's, Subway, Taco Bell, Winchell's, 🅞 🏠, Honda, Rite Aid
156b	CA 118
156a	Paxton St, Brand Ave (from nb), **E** 🅖 Shell/dsl, 🅞 7-11
155b	Van Nuys Blvd (no EZ nb return), **E** 🅖 Eagle, 🍴 Jack-in-the-Box, KFC/LJ Silver, McDonald's, Pizza Hut, Popeye's, 🅞 Discount Parts, USPO, **W** 🍴 Domino's, 🅞 auto repair
155a	Terra Bella St (from nb), **E** 🅖 Arco
154	Osborne St, to Arleta, **E** 🅖 Arco, Chevron/dsl, 🍴 El Pollo Loco, Knight's Pizza, Papa's Tacos, 🅞 AutoZone, BigLots, Food4Less, Superior Grocers, Target, **W** 🅖 Mobil/Burger King, 76, 🅞 7-11
153b	CA 170 (from sb), to Hollywood
152a	Sheldon St, **E** 🍴 Big Jim's Rest., 🅞 Big O Parts, 🏠, auto repair
152	Lankershim Blvd, Tuxford, **E** 🅖 Superfine/dsl/scales
151	Penrose St
150b	Sunland Blvd, Sun Valley, **E** 🅖 Mobil, 76/dsl, 🍴 Acapulco Rest., Carl's Jr, El Pollo Loco, Old Time Burgers, Quiznos, Subway, Town Café, Yoshinoya, 🏠 Economy Inn, 🅞 Ralph's Foods, 7-11, **W** 🅖 76, Shell, 🍴 Big Boy, McDonald's
150a	GlenOaks Blvd (from nb), **E** 🅖 Superior/dsl, 🏠 Willows Motel
149	Hollywood Way, **W** 🅖 Shell/dsl, 🅞 U-Haul, ☞
148	Buena Vista St, **E** 🏠 Hampton Inn, **W** 🅖 76/dsl, 🍴 Jack-in-the-Box, 🏠 Quality Inn, Ramada Inn
147	Scott Rd, to Burbank, **E** 🅖 Sevan/dsl, **W** 🍴 Hometown Buffet, Krispy Kreme, Outback Steaks, Panda Express, Starbucks, Wendy's, 🏠 Courtyard, Extended Stay America, 🅞 Best Buy, Lowe's, Marshall's, Michael's, Staples, Target, Verizon
146b	Burbank Blvd, **E** 🅖 76/repair, 🍴 Baskin-Robbins, CA Pizza Kitchen, Carl's Jr, Chevy's Mexican, ChuckeCheese, Corner Cafe, Harry's Rest., Hooters, IHOP, In-N-Out, McDonald's, Pizza Hut, Popeye's, Quiznos, Robek's Juice, Shakey's Pizza, Starbucks, Subway, Taco Bell, Tommy's

Exit	Services
146b	Continued
	Burgers, Yoshinoya, 🏠 Holiday Inn, 🅞 Barnes&Noble, Curves, CVS Drug, Henry's Mkt, K-Mart, Loehmanns, Macy's, Office Depot, Old Navy, Ralph's Foods, Ross, Sears, **W** 🍴 McDonald's, Subway, 🅞 Costco/gas, Discount Tire
146a	Olive Ave, Verdugo, **E** 🍴 Black Angus, BJ's Rest., 🏠 Holiday Inn, 🅞 Radio Shack, USPO, **W** 🅞🏠, Chevrolet, Metro RV Ctr, 7-11
145b	Alameda Ave, **E** 🅖 Chevron, 🍴 Baskin-Robbins/Togo's, Del Taco, Habit Burgers, Starbucks, 🅞 CarMax, CVS Drug, Home Depot, Ralph's Foods, Trader Joes, Walgreens, **W** 🅖 Arco, Shell, 🏠 Burbank Inn, 🅞 U-Haul
145a	Western Ave, **W** 🅞 Gene Autrey Museum
144 b a	CA 134, Ventura Fwy, Glendale, Pasadena
142	Colorado St
141a	Los Feliz Blvd, **E** 🅞🏠, **W** 🅞 Griffith Park, zoo
140b	Glendale Blvd, **E** 🅖 76, Valero, 🍴 Starbucks, Subway, 🅞 auto repair, **W** 🅖 Valero
140a	Fletcher Dr (from sb)
139b a	CA 2, Glendale Fwy
138	Stadium Way, Figueroa St, **E** 🅖 Chevron, Thrifty, Valero, 🍴 IHOP, McDonald's, 🅞 Home Depot, **W** 🅞 to Dodger Stadium
137b a	CA 2, Glendale Fwy, **W** 🅖 76
136b	Broadway St (from sb), **W** 🅖 76
136a	Main St, **E** 🅖 Chevron/24hr, 76, 🍴 Chinatown Express, Jack-in-the-Box, McDonald's, Mr Pizza, 🅞🏠, Parts+
135c	I-10 W (from nb), Mission Rd (from sb), **E** 🅖 Chevron, 76/dsl, 🍴 Jack-in-the-Box, McDonald's, 🅞🏠
135b	Cesar Chavez Ave, **W** 🅞🏠
135a	4th St, Soto St, **E** 🅖 76/dsl, Shell/Subway/dsl, **W** 🅖 Arco/dsl, 🅞 city park
134b	Ca 60 E (from sb), Soto St (from nb)
134a	CA 60 W, Santa Monica Fwy
133	Euclid Ave (from sb), Grand Vista (from nb), **E** 🅖 Arco, USA/dsl, **W** 🅖 Mobil, Shell, 🅞🏠
132	Calzona St, Indiana St, **E** 🅖 Arco/dsl
131b	Indiana St (from nb), **E** 🅖 Arco/dsl, Valero/dsl
131a	Olympic Blvd, **E** 🍴 McDonald's, **W** 🍴 Jack-in-the-Box, King Taco, 🅞🏠
130c b	I-710 (exits left from nb), to Long Beach, Eastern Ave, **E** 🍴 McDonald's
130a	Triggs St (from sb), **E** 🅞 outlet mall, **W** 🍴 Denny's/24hr, 🏠 Destiny Inn
129	Atlantic Blvd N, Eastern Ave (from sb), **E** 🍴 Carl's Jr, Fresca's Mexican, Panda Express, Ruby's Diner, Starbucks, Subway, 🏠 Doubletree, 🅞 Hyundai, outlets/famous brands, **W** 🍴 Denny's, Steven's Steaks
128b	Washington Blvd, Commerce, **E** 🅖 Chevron/dsl, repair/24hr, 🍴 McDonald's, 🏠 Doubletree, Crowne Plaza Hotel/casino, 🅞 Costco, outlets/famous brands, **W** 🅖 Arco, 🍴 Del Taco, Subway
128a	Garfield Blvd, **E** 🏠 Commerce/Hotel/casino, 🅞 Home Depot, Office Depot, **W** 🅖 76
126b	Slauson Ave, Montebello, **E** 🅖 Shell, Valero/dsl, 🍴 Ozzie's Diner, Quiznos, Starbucks, 🏠 Quality Inn, Super 8, **W** 🅖 Arco, 🍴 Denny's, 🏠 Budget Inn, Ramada Inn
126a	Paramount Blvd, Downey, **E** 🅖 Shell/Jack-in-the-Box/ds
125	CA 19 S, Lakewood Blvd, Rosemead Blvd, **E** 🅖 Mobil, Thrifty, 🍴 Arthurs Cafe, Foster's Freeze, Sam's Burgers, Starbucks, Taco Bell, 🏠 EconoLodge, **W** 🍴 Chin Wok, Chris&Pitt's BBQ, McDonald's, Subway, 🅞 Ralph's Foods

⬆N INTERSTATE 5 CONT'D

Exit	Services
124	I-605
123	Florence Ave, to Downey, **E** 🅿 Mobil, **W** 🅾 Honda, repair
122	Imperial Hwy, Pioneer Blvd, **E** 🅿 Chevron, 🍴 Applebees, Habit Burgers, IHOP, Jack-in-the-Box, McDonald's, Subway, Wendy's, Wood Grill Buffet, 🅾 Firestone/auto, Rite Aid, Target, **W** 🅿 Chevron, 7-11, 🍴 Alberts Mexican, Denny's, HongKong Express, Panda King, Pizza Hut, Rally's, Shakey's Pizza, Sizzler, Wienerschnitzel, 🛏 Comfort Inn, Keystone Motel, Rodeway Inn, 🅾 Toyota/Scion, Walmart
121	San Antonio Dr, to Norwalk Blvd, **E** 🍴 IHOP, Jack-in-the-Box, McDonald's, Outback Steaks, Starbucks, Wood Grill Buffet, 🛏 Doubletree Inn, 🅾 Rite Aid, Target, **W** 🅿 76, 🅾 auto repair
120b	Firestone Blvd (exits left from nb)
120a	Rosecrans Ave, **E** 🅿 Valero/dsl, 🍴 Jim's Burgers, KFC, Little Caesars, Starbucks, Taco Joe, 🅾 🅷 BigSaver Foods, **W** 🅿 Arco/24hr, 🍴 El Pollo Loco, Fosters Freeze, 🛏 Guesthouse Inn, 🅾 Camping World RV Ctr, El Monte RV Ctr, Tune-Up Masters
119	Carmenita Rd, Buena Park, **E** 🅿 Arco, 🍴 Burger King, 🅾 Ford Trucks, Lowe's, **W** 🍴 Galaxy Burgers 🛏 Budget Inn, Dynasty Suites
118	Valley View Blvd, **E** 🍴 Carl's Jr, Elephant Bar Rest, In-N-Out, Northwoods Rest, Red Robin, Subway, 🛏 Extended Stay America, Holiday Inn Select, Residence Inn, 🅾 Staples, **W** 🅿 Chevron, 🍴 Burger King, El Pollo Loco, 🅾 Thompson's RV Ctr, to Camping World
117	Artesia Blvd, Knott Ave, **E** 🅿 Chevron, 76/24hr, 🛏 Extended Stay America, 🅾 CarMax, **W** 🅾 Chrysler, Knotts Berry Farm, to Camping World RV Ctr
116	CA 39, Beach Blvd, **E** 🅿 Chevron, 🅾 🅷 Acura, BMW, Buick/GMC, CarMax, Honda, Hyundai, Mercedes, Nissan, Toyota/Scion, VW, **W** 🅿 Chevron, 🍴 Arby's, Black Angus, Denny's, Fuddruckers, KFC, Pizza Hut, Subway, Wendy's, 🛏 Holiday Inn, Red Roof Inn, 🅾 Stater Bros, Target, to Knotts Berry Farm
115	Manchester (from nb), same as 116
114b	CA 91 E, Riverside Fwy, **W** to 🍴
114a	Magnolia Ave, Orangethorpe Ave, **E** 🅿 Mobil/dsl, 🍴 Burger King, Burger Town, Taco Bell, 🅾 Harley-Davidson
113c	CA 91 W (from nb)
113b a	Brookhurst St, LaPalma, **E** 🅿 Chevron/dsl, 🍴 Subway, **W** 🅿 Arco, Texaco/dsl, 🍴 Carl's Jr., Quiznos, Starbucks, 🅾 Home Depot, Staples
112	Euclid St, **E** 🅿 Arco, 🍴 IHOP, Marie Callender's, McDonald's, Starbucks, Taco Bell, Wendy's, 🅾 AAA, PetCo, Ross, 7-11, TJ Maxx, Walmart, **W** 🅿 Mobil, 76, 🍴 Burger King, Charley's Subs, Denny's, KFC/LJ Silver, Subway, 🅾 Radio Shack, Target, Verizon
111	Lincoln Ave, to Anaheim, **E** 🍴 El Triunfo Mexican, La Casa Garcia Mexican, Ruby's Diner, Starbucks, Subway, 🅾 vet, **W** 🅾 Discount Auto Repair
110b	Ball Rd (from sb) **E** 🅿 Chevron/dsl, 7-11, Shell, 🍴 Burger King, El Pollo Loco, McDonald's, Shakey's Pizza, Starbucks, Taco Bell, Subway, 🛏 Best Inn, Best Value Inn, Days Inn, Hotel Menage, 🅾 Anaheim RV, Traveler's World RV Park, **W** 🅿 Arco/24hr, Shell/dsl, 🛏 Best Western, Budget Inn, Holiday Inn, Rodeway Inn, Sheraton, Travelodge, 🅾 Camping World RV Ctr, Disneyland, USPO

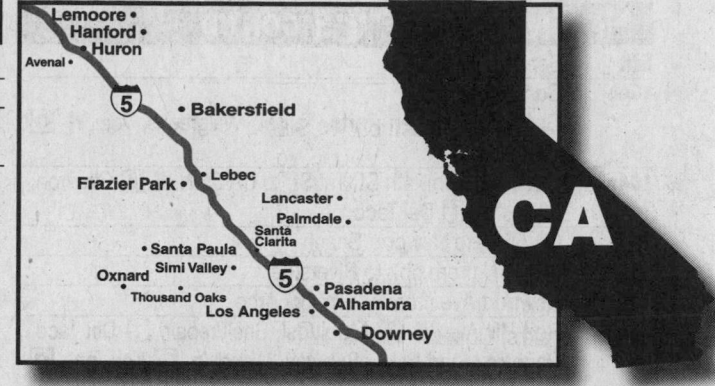

Exit	Services
110a	Harbor Blvd, **E** 🅿 Chevron, Shell, 🍴 Carrow's, Shakey's Pizza, Taco Bell, 🛏 Days Inn, EconoLodge, Frontier Harbor Hotel, Hotel Menage, Ramada Ltd, 🅾 Anaheim Harbor RV Park, **0-2 mi W** to Disneyland, 🍴 Acapulco Mexican, Captain Kidd's, Coldstone, Del Sol, Dennys, IHOP, McDonald's, Millie's Rest., Mimi's Cafe, Mortons Steaks, Overland Sage BBQ, Quiznos, Tony Roma's, 🛏 Anaheim Resort, Best Inn, Best Western, Candy Cane Inn, Camelot Inn, Carousel Inn, Castle Inn Suites, Clarion, Courtyard, Desert Inn, Fairfield Inn, Hampton Inn, Hilton Garden, Howard Johnson, ParkVue Inn, Portofino Inn, Ramada Inn, Red Lion, Saga Inn, Sheraton, Travelodge, Tropicana Inn, same as 109
109	Katella Ave, Disney Way, **E** 🅿 Arco, 🍴 Baskin-Robbins, Carl's Jr, Catch Seafood, Denny's, El Torito, McDonald's, Mr Stox Dining, Panda Express, Subway, Togo's, 🛏 Angel Inn, TownePlace Suites, 🅾 Angels Stadium, **W** 🅿 Chevron, 🍴 Bubba Gump Shrimp, CA Pizza Kitchen, Cheesecake Factory, Del Taco, McCormick&Schmick, PF Chang's, Roy Roy's, Subway, 🛏 Arena Inn, Best Value Inn, Comfort Inn, Desert Palms Suites, Extended Stay America, Hilton, Holiday Inn Express, Little Boy Blue, Marriott, Peacock Suites, Ramada Inn, Residence Inn, Riviera Motel, Staybridge Suites, Super 8, Worldmark, 🅾 7-11, to Disneyland
107c	St Coll Blvd, City Drive, **E** 🍴 Del Taco, 🛏 Hilton Suites, **W** 🛏 Doubletree Hotel
107b a	CA 57 N, Chapman Ave, **E** 🍴 Burger King, Del Taco, Denny's, 🛏 Holiday Inn, Motel 6, Quality Inn, **W** 🅿 Chevron, 🍴 Krispy Kreme, Lucille's BBQ, Taco Bell, Wendy's, 🛏 Ayer's Inn, DoubleTree, 🅾 🅷 Best Buy
106	CA 22 W (from nb), Garden Grove Fwy, Bristol St
105b	N Broadway, Main St, **E** 🅿 7-11, 🍴 Baskin-Robbins, CA Pizza Kitchen, Carl's Jr, Chili Pepper Mexican, Corner Bakery, El Torito, FoodCourt, Habit Burgers, Jamba Juice, Manhattan Steaks, McCormick&Schmicks, Papa Johns, Pat&Oscars, Polly's Café, Rubio's Grill, Starbucks, Subway, Taco Bell, Togo's, 🛏 Days Inn, Red Roof Inn, 🅾 🅷 Barnes&Noble, CVS Drug, JC Penney, Macy's, Nordstrom's, Staples, Verizon, mall, **W** 🛏 Golden West Motel, Travel Inn, 🅾 Bowers Museum
105a	17th St, **E** 🅿 76/dsl/24hr, 🍴 Hometown Buffet, IHOP, McDonald's, 🅾 Chevrolet, CVS Drug, Food4Less, Walgreens, same as 104b, **W** 🅿 Chevron, 🍴 YumYum Donuts, 🅾 7-11
104b	Santa Ana Blvd, Grand Ave, **E on Grand** 🍴 Denny's, Hometown Buffet, IHOP, KFC/LJ Silver, Marie Callender, McDonald's, Pizza Hut/Taco Bell, Popeye's, Starbucks, Subway, Taco Sinaloa, 🅾 Big O Tire, CVS Drug, $TREE

↑N INTERSTATE 5 CONT'D

Exit	Services
104b	Continued
	Goodyear, Kragen Parts, Target, Walgreens, vet, **W** 🅞 KIA, Suzuki
104a	(103c from nb), 4th St, 1st St, to CA 55 N, **E** 🅟 Chevron, Shell, 76, 🍴 Del Taco
103b	CA 55 S, to Newport Beach
103a	CA 55 N (from nb), to Riverside
102	Newport Ave (from sb), **W** 🅟 Arco
101b	Red Hill Ave, **E** 🅟 Mobil/dsl, Shell/repair, 🍴 Del Taco, Denny's, Starbucks, Subway, Wendy's, 🛏 Key Inn, 🅞 BigLots, U-Haul, **W** 🅟 Arco/24hr, Chevron/24hr, 76, 🍴 Pizza Shack, Taco Bell, 🅞 7-11, Stater Bros
101a	Tustin Ranch Rd, **E** 🍴 McDonald's, 🅞 Acura, Buick/GMC, Cadillac, Chrysler/Dodge/Jeep, Costco, Ford/Lincoln, Hyundai, Infiniti, Lexus, Mazda, Nissan, Toyota/Scion
100	Jamboree Rd, **E** 🅟 Shell, 🍴 Baja Fresh, BJ's Rest., Buca Italian, Burger King, CA Pizza, Carl's Jr, Chick-fil-A, Corner Bakery, Daphne's Greek, DQ, El Pollo Loco, IHOP, In-N-Out, Jamba Juice, JinJin Asian, Lazy Dog Cafe, Macaroni Grill, On the Border, Panda Express, Panera Bread, Pick-up Stix, Quiznos, Red Robin, Rubio's, Starbucks, Subway, Taco Bell, Taco Rosa, 🅞 AAA, AT&T, Barnes&Noble, Best Buy, Costco, Dick's, Henry's Mkt, Home Depot, Loehmann's, Lowe's, Old Navy, Petsmart, Radio Shack, Ralph's Foods, Rite Aid, Ross, Target, TJ Maxx, Verizon
99	Culver Dr, **E** 🅟 Shell/24hr, 🅞 vet
97	Jeffrey Rd, **E** 🅟 Arco, 🍴 Baskin-Robbins, Juice-it-Up, La Salsa, Starbucks, Subway, 🅞 Albertson's, Kohl's, **W** 🅟 76/dsl, 🍴 Thai Cafe, 🅞 Ranch Mkt Foods, Verizon, vet
96	Sand Canyon Ave, Old Towne, **W** 🅟 76/dsl, 🍴 Denny's, Jack-in-the-Box, Knowlwood Burgers, Tiajuana's Rest., 🛏 La Quinta, 🅞 🏥 Traveland USA RV Park
95	CA 133 (**toll**), Laguna Fwy, N to Riverside, S Laguna Beach
94b	Alton Pkwy, **E** 🅟 Shell/Subway/dsl, 🍴 Cabo Grill, Carl's Jr, Quiznos, Starbucks, 🍴 Homestead Suites, **W** 🍴 CA Pizza, Cheesecake Factory, Chipotle Mexican, Dave&Buster's, Johnny Rockets, Panda Express, PF Chang's, Wahoo's Fish Tacos, Wood Ranch, Yardhouse Rest., 🛏 Doubletree Inn, 🅞 Barnes&Noble, Macy's, Nordstrom, Old Navy, Target
94a	I-405 N (from nb)
92b	Bake Pkwy, same as 92a
92a	Lake Forest Dr, Laguna Hills, **E** 🅟 Chevron/24hr, Shell/dsl, 🍴 Buffalo Wild Wings, Del Taco, Jack-in-the-Box, McDonald's, Panera Bread, Pizza Hut, RoundTable Pizza, Subway, Taco Bell, The Hat, 🛏 Best Value Inn, Holiday Inn, Irvine Suites Hotel, Quality Inn, 🅞 America's Tire, Buick/GMC, Chrysler/Dodge/Jeep, Ford/Lincoln, Honda, Hyundai, Mazda, Nissan, Subaru, Volvo, VW, **W** 🅟 Chevron/24hr, Shell, 🍴 Carl's Jr, Coco's, Del Taco, McDonald's, Quiznos, Subway, 🛏 Comfort Inn, Courtyard, 🅞 AZ Leather, Best Buy, BMW/Mini
91	El Toro Rd, **E** 🅟 Chevron/dsl, USA, 🍴 Arby's, Asia Buffet, Baskin-Robbins, Cafe Rio, Chipotle Mexican, Chronic Tacos, Denny's, El Pollo Loco, Flamebroiler, Fuddrucker's, Hooters, Jack-in-the-Box, Lucille's BBQ, McDonald's, Mr Wok, Panda Express, PeiWei Asian, Quiznos, Scarantino's Rest., Sizzler, Starbucks, Subway, Tommy's Burgers,

LAGUNA HILLS / MISSON VIEJO / CAPISTRANO

Exit	Services
91	Continued
	Wendy's, 🅞 CVS Drug, Firestone/auto, Home Depot, 99¢ Store, PetCo, PetsMart, Ralph's Foods, Ross, Staples, **W** 🅟 Chevron/dsl/24hr, Shell/24hr, 76/Circle K, 🍴 BJ's Rest., Carrow's, El Torito, In-N-Out, King's Fishhouse, LoneStar Steaks, Nami Seafood, Starbucks, Woody's Diner, 🛏 Laguna Hills Lodge, 🅞 🏥, CVS Drug, Firestone/auto, JC Penney, Just Tires, Macy's, Marshall's, Sears/auto, Trader Joe's, Walgreens, USPO, mall
90	Alicia Pkwy, Mission Viejo, **E** 🍴 Del Taco, Denny's, Subway, 🅞 Albertson's, America's Tire, CVS Drug, $Tree, Kragen Parts, Target, **W** 🅟 Chevron, 76/dsl, 🍴 Carl's Jr, It's a Grind, Togo's, Wendy's, 🅞 AAA, BigLots, Mazda, vet
89	La Paz Rd, Mission Viejo, **E** 🅟 Arco/24hr, Shell, 🍴 Chronic Tacos, Pizza Hut, Starbucks, Taco Bell, TK Burgers, 🅞 Albertson's/Sav-On, vet, **W** 🅟 76, 🍴 Claim Jumper Rest., DQ, Flamingos Mexican, Hot Off the Grill, Jack-in-the-Box, Krispy Kreme, La Salsa, McDonald's, Outback Steaks, Spasso's Italian, Starbucks, Subway, Villa Roma, Wienerschnitzel, Yamato Japanese, 🛏 Hills Hotel, 🅞 Best Buy, Curves, Goodyear/auto, Jo-Ann Fabrics, PetCo, 7-11, **Urgent Care**, to Laguna Niguel Pk
87	Oso Pkwy, Pacific Park Dr, **E** 🅟 Chevron/repair, 76/dsl/repair, 🍴 Carl's Jr, Starbucks, Subway, 🛏 Fairfield Inn, 🅞 golf
86	Crown Valley Pkwy, **E** 🅟 Arco, Chevron, 76, 🍴 Buffalo Wild Wings, Chili's, Coco's, Islands Grill, 🅞 🏥, Macy's, mall, vet, **W** 🅟 Chevron/dsl, 🅞 Aamco, Costco/gas
85b	Avery Pkwy, **E** 🅟 Shell/dsl, 🍴 Alberto's Mexican, Carrow's, Del Taco, Jack-in-the-Box, Mongolian BBQ, Papa John's, Starbucks, Subway, 🅞 Acura, America's Tire/auto, Audi/Infiniti, Jaguar/Land Rover, Lexus, Parts+, World Mkt, **W** 🅟 Chevron, Shell/dsl/24hr, 🍴 A's Burgers, Carl's Jr, In-N-Out, 🛏 Best Value Laguna Inn, 🅞 Aamco, Cadillac/GMC, Costco/gas, Firestone/auto, Hyundai, Mercedes
85a	CA 73 N (**toll**)
83	Junipero Serra Rd, to San Juan Capistrano, **W** 🅟 Shell, Spirit/service/dsl
82	CA 74, Ortego Hwy, **E** 🅟 Chevron/dsl, 76, Shell, 🍴 Bad to the Bone BBQ, Ballpark Pizza, Bravo Burgers, Denny's, Subway, 🛏 Best Western, 🅞 vet, **W** 🅟 Chevron/24hr, 🍴 Arby's, Carl's Jr, Del Taco, Jack-in-the-Box, KFC, Marie Callender's, McDonald's, Oeeshi Japanese, Pedro's Tacos, Quiznos, RoundTable Pizza, Ruby's Cafe, Starbucks, Taco Bell, 🛏 Cedar Creek Inn, Mission Inn, 🅞 Capistrano Trading Post, GNC, Marshall's, Ralph's Foods, Ross, TrueValue, San Juan Capistrano Mission
81	Camino Capistrano, **E** 🅞 VW, **W** on Capistrano 🅟 Chevron, 🍴 El Adobe Rest., El Pollo Loco, Eng's Chinese, KFC, Papa John's, Pizza Hut, Ricardo's Mexican, Starbucks, 🅞 Aamco, BigLots, Costco, Ford, Goodyear/auto, Honda, KIA, Nissan, PetCo, PetsMart, Radio Shack, Rite Aid, Ross, Staples, Toyota/Scion, Vons Foods, San Juan Capistrano SP (1mi), CHP, **Urgent Care**
79	CA 1, Pacific Coast Hwy, Capistrano Bch, Capistrano, **1 mi W** 🅟 Arco/24hr, 76/dsl, 🍴 A's Burgers, Carl's Jr, Del Taco, Denny's, Jack-in-the-Box, JuiceSpot, McDonald's, Rib Joint, Subway, 🛏 DoubleTree, Harbor Inn, Holiday Inn Express, 🅞 Ralph's Foods, Rite Aid, USPO, vet
78	Camino de Estrella, San Clemente, **E** 🅟 76/dsl, 🍴 Carl's

🅿 = gas 🍴 = food 🛏 = lodging 🅾 = other ℞ₛ = rest stop

◤N INTERSTATE 5 CONT'D

Exit	Services
78	**Continued** Jr, China Well, Coldstone, Crispins, Flame Broiler, Jamba Juice, Melting Pot, Papa Murphy's, RoundTable Pizza, Rubio's, Starbucks, Subway, Wahoo's Fish Taco, 🅾 🅗 AT&T, CVS Drug, Ralph's Foods, Stater Bros Foods, Trader Joe's, vet, **W** 🅿 Arco/dsl, 🍴 Las Golondrinas, 🅾 BigLots, Kragen Parts, Sears Essentials
77	Ave Vista Hermosa
76	Ave Pico, **E** 🅿 Mobil, 🍴 Buono Pizza, Carrow's, Golden Spoon, Juice it Up, McDonald's, Panda Express, 🅾 Albertson's/Sav-On, GNC, **W** 🅿 Chevron, Shell/dsl, 🍴 Bad to the Bone BBQ, BurgerStop, Del Taco, Denny's/24hr, Pick-up-Stix, Pizza Hut, Stuft Pizza, Subway, 🛏 Holiday Inn Express, 🅾 Curves, 99¢ Store, Staples, Tuesday Morning, USPO, tires/repair, vet
75	Ave Palizada, Ave Presidio, **W** 🅿 Valero, 🍴 Baskin-Robbins, Coffee Bean, Mr. Pete's Burgers, Sonny's Pizza, Subway, Starbucks, Taka-O Japanese, 🛏 Holiday Inn, 🅾 7-11, TrueValue
74	El Camino Real, **E** 🅿 Chevron/dsl/24hr, 🍴 El Mariachi Rest., Pipes Cafe, 🛏 Budget Lodge, San Clemente Inn, Tradewinds Motel, 🅾 vet, same as 75, **W** 🅿 Exxon, 76/dsl, 🍴 FatBurger, KFC, Pizza Hut/Taco Bell, Subway, Taste Of China, Tommy's Rest./24hr, 🅾 Kragen Parts, Radio Shack, Ralph's Foods, 7-11
73	Ave Calafia, Ave Magdalena, **E** 🅿 76/dsl, Shell, 🍴 Jack-in-the-Box, Molly Bloom's Cafe, Pedro's Tacos, Sugar Shack Cafe, 🛏 Budget Inn, Calafia Beach Motel, C-Vu Inn, Hampton Inn, LaVista Inn, San Clemente Motel, Travelodge, 🅾 San-O Tire, 7-11, repair, **W** to San Clemente SP
72	Cristianitos Ave, **E** 🍴 Cafe Del Sol, Carl's Jr., 🛏 Comfort Suites, Carmelo Motel, 🅾 San Mateo RV Park/dump, **W** 🅾 to San Clemente SP
71	Basilone Rd, **W** 🅾 San Onofre St Beach
67mm	**weigh sta both lanes**
66mm	viewpoint sb
62	Las Pulgas Rd
59mm	**Aliso Creek ℞ₛ both lanes, full 🚻 facilities, 🅒, vending, 📧, litter barrels, petwalk, RV dump**
54c	Oceanside Harbor Dr, **W** 🅿 Chevron, Mobil, 🍴 Burger King (1mi), Del Taco, Denny's/24hr, 🛏 GuestHouse Inn, Holiday Inn Express, Sandman Hotel, Travelodge, The Bridge Motel, 🅾 to Camp Pendleton
54b	Hill St (from sb), to Oceanside, **W** 🅿 Chevron, Mobil, 🍴 Carrow's Rest., Denny's, 🛏 GuestHouse Inn, Holiday Inn Express, Travelodge
54a	CA 76 E, Coast Hwy
53	Mission Ave, Oceanside, **E** 🅿 Arco/24hr, Mobil/dsl, 🍴 Alberto's Mexican, Arby's, Armando's Tacos, Burger King, China Star, Jack-in-the-Box, KFC, McDonald's, Mission Donuts, 🛏 Quality Inn, Ramada, 🅾 CarQuest, NAPA, PepBoys, Valu+ Foods, **W** 🍴 El Pollo Loco, Panda Express, Subway, Wendy's, 🅾 99¢ Store, Office Depot, Radio Shack
52	Oceanside Blvd, **E** 🍴 Alberto's Mexican, Domino's, IHOP, McDonald's, Papa John's, Pizza Hut, Starbucks, Subway, Taco Bell, Wienerschnitzel, 🅾 Boney's Foods, CVS Drug, Ralph's Foods, CHP, **W** 🅿 Oceanside/dsl, 🛏 Best Western Oceanside
51c	Cassidy St (from sb), **W** 🅿 7-11, Mobil, 76, 🅾 🅗
51b	CA 78, Vista Way, Escondido, **E** 🅿 Chevron/dsl/24hr, 76/Circle K, Shell, 🍴 Applebee's, Boston Mkt, Burger King, Carl's Jr, Chili's, ChuckeCheese, Fuddrucker's, Golden Taipei, Hooters, Macaroni Grill, McDonald's, Mimi's Café, Olive Garden, Outback Steaks, QuikWok, Rubio's, Starbucks, Subway, Wendy's, 🛏 Holiday Inn Express, 🅾 Best Buy, CVS Drug, $Tree, Firestone, Henry's Mkt, JC Penney, Macy's, Marshall's, Michael's, PetCo, Sears/auto, Staples, Stater Bros Foods, Target, Tuesday Morning, Vons Foods, Walmart/auto, World Mkt, **W** 🍴 Hunter Steaks
51a	Las Flores Dr
50	Elm Ave, Carlsbad Village Dr, **E** 🅿 Shell/24hr, 🍴 Lotus Thai Bistro, **W** 🅿 Carlsbad/dsl/LP, Valero, 🍴 Al's Cafe, Carl's Jr, Denny's/24hr, Jack-in-the-Box, KFC/Taco Bell, Mikko Japanese, 🛏 Extended Stay America, Motel 6, 🅾 Albertson's, TrueValue
49	Tamarack Ave, **E** 🅿 Chevron/24hr, 76/dsl, 🍴 Village Kitchen, 🛏 Comfort Inn, Rodeway Inn, Travel Inn, 🅾 GNC, Rite Aid, Vons Foods, **W** 🅿 Arco, 🍴 Hensley's Grill
48	Cannon Rd, Car Country Carlsbad, **E** 🅾 Acura, Buick, Cadillac/Chevrolet, Ford, Honda, Lexus, Lincoln, Mazda, Mercedes, Toyota, VW
47	Carlsbad Blvd, Palomar ⤵ Rd, **E** 🅿 Chevron, Mobil/dsl, 7-11, 🍴 BJ's Rest., Carl's Jr, Islands Burgers, Panda Express, Pat&Oscar's Rest., PF Chang's, Subway, Strauss Brewery Rest., Taco Bell, TGIFriday's, 🛏 Holiday Inn, Motel 6, 🅾 Carlsbad Ranch/Flower Fields, Chrysler/Dodge/Jeep, Costco/gas, Ford, outlet mall, **W** 🅿 Shell/dsl, 🍴 ClaimJumper Rest., Marie Callender's, McDonald's, 🛏 Hilton Garden, 🅾 S Carlsbad St Bch
45	Poinsettia Lane, **W** 🅿 Chevron, 🍴 Benihana, El Pollo Loco, Golden Spoon, Jack-in-the-Box, Pick-Up Stix, Starbucks, Subway, 🛏 La Quinta, Motel 6, Quality Inn, Ramada, 🅾 Ace Hardware, Porsche/Volvo, Ralph's Foods, Rite Aid
44	La Costa Ave, **E** vista point, **W** 🅿 Chevron/dsl
43	Leucadia Blvd, **E** 🛏 Howard Johnson, **W** 🅿 Shell/service
41b	Encinitas Blvd, **E** 🅿 Chevron/dsl, O'Brien Sta., Valero, 🍴 Coco's Cafe, Del Taco, Gusto Trattoria, HoneyBaked Ham, Oggi's Pizza, 🅾 CVS Drug, NAPA, to Quail Botanical Gardens, vet, **W** 🅿 Shell, 🍴 Denny's, Little Caesar's, Subway, Wendy's, 🛏 Best Western/rest., Days Inn, 🅾 PetCo
41a	Santa Fe Dr, to Encinitas, **E** 🅿 Shell, 🍴 Carl's Jr, El Nopalito, Papa Toni's Pizza, 🅾 7-11, **W** 🍴 Today's Pizza, 🅾 🅗, Rite Aid, Vons Foods, vet
40	Birmingham Dr, **E** 🅿 Chevron, Valero, 🍴 Mandarin City,

Side labels (left column): **SAN CLEMENTE**, **OCEANSIDE**

Side labels (right column): **CARLSBAD**, **ENCINITAS**

Side tab: **CA**

CA

LA JOLLA

⬆N INTERSTATE 5 CONT'D

Exit	Services
40	Continued
	🏠 Holiday Inn Express, W 🅖 Arco/24hr
39mm	viewpoint sb
39	Manchester Ave, E 🅖 76, 🅞 to MiraCosta College
37	Lomas Santa Fe Dr, Solana Bch, E 🍴 Baskin-Robbins, Pizza Nova, Samurai Rest., Starbucks, 🅞 Ross, Vons Foods, We-R-Fabrics, W 🅖 Mobil, 🍴 Carl's Jr, Golden Spoon, Jamba Juice, Panda Express, Panera Bread, RoundTable Pizza, Starbucks, Togo's, 🅞 CVS Drug, Discount Tire, GNC, Henry's Foods, Marshall's, Staples
36	Via de La Valle, Del Mar, E 🅖 Chevron, Mobil, 🍴 Chevy's Mexican, Coffee Bean, McDonald's, Milton's Deli, Pappachino's Italian, Paradise Grille, Pasta Pronto, Pick-Up Stix, Taste of Thai, 🅞 Albertson's/SavOn, PetCo, Radio Shack, W 🅖 Arco/24hr, Shell/dsl, 🍴 Denny's, FishMkt Rest., Red Tracton's Rest., 🏠 Hilton, 🅞 racetrack
34	Del Mar Heights Rd, E 🅖 Shell/dsl, W 🍴 7-11, 🍴 Elijah's Rest., Jack-in-the-Box, Mexican Grill, 🅞 CVS Drug, Vons Foods, vet
33	Carmel Mtn Rd, E 🅖 Arco, Shell/repair, 🍴 Taco Bell, Tio Leo's Mexican, 🏠 DoubleTree Hotel, Hampton Inn, Marriott
32	CA 56 E, Carmel Valley Rd
31	I-805 (from sb)
30	Sorrento Valley Rd, new exit
29	Genesee Ave, E 🅞 🏥
28b	La Jolla Village Dr, E 🍴 Italian Bistro, 🏠 Embassy Suites, Hyatt, Marriott, 🅞 🏥 to LDS Temple, W 🅖 Mobil/dsl, 🍴 BJ's Grill, CA Pizza Kitchen, Chipotle Mexican, Dominos, Elijah's Deli, El Torito, Flame Broiler, Islands Burgers, Mrs Gooch's, Pick-Up Stix, RockBottom Café, Rubio's, TGI-Friday's, 🏠 Sheraton, 🅞 🏥, AT&T, Best Buy, CVS Drug, Marshall's, PetsMart, Radio Shack, Ralph's Foods, Ross, Staples, Whole Foods Mkt, Trader Joe's
28a	Nobel Dr (from nb), E 🏠 Hyatt, 🅞 LDS Temple, W same as 28b
27	Gilman Dr, La Jolla Colony Dr
26b	CA 52 E
26a	La Jolla Rd (from nb)
23b	CA 274, Balboa Ave, 1 mi E 🅖 Shell, 🍴 Del Taco, 🅞 Albertson's, W 🅖 Mobil, 76/repair, 7-11, 🍴 McDonald's, In-N-Out, Rubio's, Wienerschnitzel, 🏠 Days Inn, Holiday Inn Express, Mission Bay Inn, San Diego Motel, 🅞 🏥, Discount Tire, Express Tire, Ford, Nissan, Toyota/Scion, Mission Bay Pk
23a	Grand Ave, Garnet Ave, same as 23b
22	Clairemont Dr, Mission Bay Dr, E 🅖 Arco, Shell, 🏠 Best Western, 🅞 Chevrolet/VW, W to Sea World Dr
21	Sea World Dr, Tecolote Dr, E 🅖 Shell, 🏠 Seaside Inn, Aamco, CarQuest, Circle K, PetCo, W 🏠 Hilton, 🅞 Old Town SP, Seaworld
20	I-8, W to Nimitz Blvd, E to El Centro, CA 209 S (from sb), to Rosecrans St
19	Old Town Ave, E 🅖 Arco/24hr, Shell, 🏠 Courtyard, La Quinta
18b	Washington St, E 🏠 Comfort Inn
18a	Pacific Hwy Viaduct, Kettner St
17b	India St, Front St, Sassafras St, E 🅖 Mobil, Rte 66 Gas, W 🅞 🏠, civic ctr
17a	Hawthorn St, Front St, W 🅖 Exxon/dsl, 🏠 Holiday Inn, Motel 6, Radisson, 🅞 🏥

SAN DIEGO AREA

SAN YSIDRO

16b	6th Ave, downtown
16a	CA 163 N, 10th St, E 🅞 AeroSpace Museum, W 🅖 Shell, 🍴 Del Taco, Jack-in-the-Box, McDonald's, 🏠 Days Inn, Downtown Lodge, El Cortez Motel, Holiday Inn, Marriott, 🅞 🏥
15c b	CA 94 E (from nb), Pershing Dr, B St, civic ctr
15a	CA 94 E, J St, Imperial Ave (from sb),
14b	Cesar Chavez Pkwy
14a	CA 75, to Coronado, W toll rd to Coronado
13b	National Ave SD, 28th St, E 🍴 Little Caesar's, Starbucks, Subway, 🅞 AutoZone, W 🅖 Shell, 🍴 Burger King, Del Taco, El Pollo Loco
13a	CA 15 N, to Riverside
12	Main St, National City
11b	8th St, National City, E 🅖 Arco, Shell/24hr, 🍴 Jack-in-the-Box, 🏠 Holiday Inn, Howard Johnson, Ramada Inn, Super 8, Value Inn, W 🅖 Chevron/dsl
11a	Harbor Dr, Civic Center Dr
10	Bay Marina, 24th St, Mile of Cars Way, 1/2 mi E 🍴 Denny's, In-N-Out
9	CA 54 E
8b	E St, Chula Vista, E 🏠 Motel 6, W 🍴 Anthony's Fish Grotto, 🏠 GoodNite Inn
8a	H St
7b	J St (from sb)
7a	L St, E 🅖 7-11, 76, Shell/dsl, 🍴 Mandarin Chinese, 🏠 Best Western, 🅞 AutoZone, NAPA, Parts+, Office Depot
6	Palomar St, E 🅖 Arco, 🍴 China King, Del Taco, DQ, HomeTown Buffet, KFC, Little Caesar's, McDonald's, Subway, 🏠 Palomar Inn, 🅞 Food4Less, Office Depot, 7-11, E on Broadway 🍴 Jack-in-the-Box, KFC, Panda Express, Quizno's, Yoshinoya, 🅞 Costco/gas, Michael's, Ross, Target, Walmart
5b	Main St, to Imperial Beach, E 🅖 Arco, 🍴 AZ Chinese
5a	CA 75 (from sb), Palm Ave, to Imperial Beach, E 🅖 Arco, 🍴 Armando's Mexican, Papa John's, Wahshing Chinese, 🅞 Discount Tire, 7-11, Soto's Transmissions, W 🅖 Arco, 7-11, Shell/repair/24hr, Thrifty, 🍴 Boll Weevil Diner, Burger King, Carl's Jr, Carrow's, Coldstone Creamery, El Chile Mexican, Los Pancho's Tacos, McDonald's, Rally's, Red Hawk Steaks, Roberto's Mexican, Subway, Taco Bell, Wienerschnitzel, 🏠 Super 8, Travelodge, 🅞 AutoZone, CVS Drug, Home Depot, Jiffy Lube, 99¢ Store, Von's Foods
4	Coronado Ave (from sb), E 🅖 Chevron/service, Shell/service, 🍴 Denny's, Taco Bell, 🏠 EZ 8 Motel, 🅞 7-11, W 🅖 Shell/dsl, 🏠 Day's Inn, 🅞 to Border Field SP
3	CA 905, Tocayo Ave, W 🅖 7-11
2	Dairy Mart Rd, E 🅖 Arco/24hr, Circle K, 🍴 Burger King, Carl's Jr, Coco's, KFC, McDonald's, Roberto's Mexican, 🏠 Americana Inn, Best Value, Super 8, Valli-Hi Motel, 🅞 CarQuest, Radio Shack, Pacifica RV Resort
1b	Via de San Ysidro, E 🅖 Chevron, Exxon, Mobil, 76, 🅞 Max's Foods, NAPA, W 🅖 Chevron, 🍴 Denny's, KFC, 🏠 Economy Inn, Knights/RV park, Motel 6
1a	I-805 N (from nb), Camino de la Plaza (from sb), E 🍴 Burger King, El Pollo Loco, Jack-in-the-Box, KFC, McDonald's, Subway, 🏠 Flamingo Motel, Gateway Inn, Holiday Motel, Travelodge, 🅞 AutoZone, W 🍴 Achiato Mexican, Gingling House Chinese, IHOP, Iron Wok, McDonald's, Pizza Hut/Taco Bell, Sunrise Buffet, 🅞 Baja Duty-Free, K-Mart, Ross, Marshall's, factory outlet, border parking

⬆N INTERSTATE 5 CONT'D

Exit	Services
0	US/Mexico Border, California state line, customs, **I-5 begins/ends**

⬆E INTERSTATE 8

Exit	Services
172.5mm	California/Arizona state line, Colorado River, Pacific/Mountain time zone
172	4th Ave, Yuma, **N** Ft Yuma Casino, **S** 🅿 Chevron, Circle K, 🍴 Jack-in-the-Box, Yuma Landing Rest., 🛏 Best Western, Hilton Garden, 🅾 Rivers Edge RV Park, to Yuma SP
170	Winterhaven Dr, **S** Rivers Edge RV Park
166	CA 186, Algodones Rd, Andrade, **S** Cocopah RV Resort/golf, Quechan Hotel/Casino, to Mexico
165mm	**CA Insp/weigh Sta**
164	Sidewinder Rd, **N** st patrol, **S** 🅿 Shell/LP, 🅾 Pilot Knob RV Park
159	CA 34, Ogilby Rd, to Blythe
156	Grays Well Rd, **N** Imperial Dunes RA
155mm	🆁🆂 **both lanes (exits left), full facilities,** 🛗 **litter barrels, petwalk**
151	Gordons Well
146	Brock Research Ctr Rd
143	CA 98, to Calexico, Midway Well
131	CA 115, VanDerLinden Rd, to Holtville, **5 mi N** gas, food, lodging, RV camping
128	Bonds Corner Rd
125	CA 7 S, Orchard Rd, Holtville, **4 mi N** gas/dsl, food
120	Bowker Rd
118b a	CA 111, to Calexico, **1 mi N** 🅿 Shell/dsl/café/scales, 🅾 RV park, tires/truckwash
116	Dogwood Rd, **S** 🅿 Arco, 🍴 Carino's, Chili's, ChuckeCheese, Denny's, Famous Dave's BBQ, Fortune Garden, Jack-in-the-Box, Sombrero Mexican, Starbucks, 🛏 Fairfield Inn, TownePlace Suites, 🅾 Americas Tire, Best Buy, Dillard's, $Tree, JC Penney, Macy's, Marshall's, Michael's, Old Navy, PetCo, Ross, Sears/auto, Staples, mall
115	CA 86, 4th St, El Centro, **N** 🅿 Arco/24hr, Chevron/dsl, 7-11/dsl, Shell/dsl, 🍴 Carl's Jr, China Express, Exotic Thai, Jack-in-the-Box, Manila Lumpia, McDonald's, Mexicali Taco, 🛏 Holiday Inn Express, Motel 6, 🅾 El Sol Mkt, U Haul, **S** 🅿 Mobil/dsl/scales, On the Go/Subway, 🍴 IHOP, In-N-Out, Taco Bell, 🛏 Best Western, Comfort Inn, Rodeway Inn, 🅾 AutoZone, Home Depot, Honda/Hyundai, Lucky Foods, Desert Trails RV Park
114	Imperial Ave, El Centro, **0-3 mi N** 🅿 Arco, Chevron/dsl, 7-11/dsl, Shell, USA/dsl, 🍴 Applebee's, Burger King, Carl's Jr, Carrow's, Church's, Del Taco, Denny's, Domino's, El Pollo Loco, Farmer Boys, Golden Corral, Jack-in-the-Box, KFC, Little Caesars, McDonald's, Mexicali Grill, Pizza Hut, Quiznos, Rally's, Scribble's Rest, Sizzler, Sonic, Subway, Taco Bell, TasteeFreez Burgers, Wendy's, 🛏 Clarion, EconoLodge, Howard Johnson, Knights Inn, SuperStar Inn, Vacation Inn/RV Park, 🅾 Americas Tire, AutoZone, Costco/gas, $Tree, Food4Less, Ford, Goodyear/auto, K-Mart, Kragen Parts, Lowe's, 99¢ Store, Nissan, PepBoys, Radio Shack, Rite Aid, Staples, Target, Toyota/Scion, Von's Foods, Walgreens, Walmart, st patrol
111	Forrester Rd, to Westmorland
108mm	**Sunbeam** 🆁🆂 **both lanes, full** 🛗 **facilities,** ⬆, 🛗 **litter barrels, petwalk, RV dump**

Exit	Services
107	Drew Rd, Seeley, **N** Sunbeam RV Park, to Sunbeam Lake, **S** Rio Bend RV Park
101	Dunaway Rd, Imperial Valley, elev 0 ft, **N** st prison
89	Imperial Hwy, CA 98, Ocotillo, **N** 🅾 USPO, **S** 🅿 Texaco/dsl, 🅾 RV camping, museum
87	CA 98 (from eb), to Calexico
81mm	runaway truck ramp, eb
80	Mountain Springs Rd
77	In-ko-pah Park Rd, **N** 🔧, towing
75mm	brake insp area eb, 🔧
73	Jacumba, **S** 🅿 Chevron/dsl, Shell/Subway/dsl/24hr, 🅾 RV camping
65	CA 94, Boulevard, to Campo, **S** 🅿 MtnTop/dsl, 🛏 Lux Inn, 🅾 auto repair, USPO, to McCain Valley RA (7mi)
63mm	Tecate Divide, elev 4140 ft
62mm	Crestwood Summit, elev 4190 ft
61	Crestwood Rd, Live Oak Springs, **S** 🅿 Golden Acorn Trkstp/casino/dsl, 🛏 Live Oak Sprs Country Inn, 🅾 Outdoor World RV Camp, info
54	Kitchen Creek Rd, Cameron Station, **S** food, RV camping
51	rd 1, Buckman Spgs Rd, to Lake Morena, **S** gas/dsl/LP, food, lodging, RV camping, Lake Morena CP (7mi), Potrero CP (19mi), 🆁🆂 **both lanes, full** 🛗 **facilities,** 🔧, 🛗, **litter barrels, petwalk, RV dump**
48	**insp sta, wb**
47	rd 1, Sunrise Hwy, Laguna Summit, elev 4055 ft, **N** to Laguna Mtn RA
45	Pine Valley, Julian, **N** 🍴 Calvin's Rest., Frosty Burger, Major's Diner, 🛏 Pine Valley Inn, 🅾 Curves, Mtn Mkt, Pine Valley/gas, to Cuyamaca Rancho SP, city park, USPO, vet
44mm	Pine Valley Creek
42mm	elev 4000 ft
40	CA 79, Japatul Rd, Descanso, **N** 🍴 Descanso Rest., 🅾 to Cuyamaca Rancho SP
37mm	vista point eb, elev 3000 ft
36	E Willows, **N** Alpine Sprs RV Park, Viejas Indian Res, casino
33	W Willows Rd, to Alpine, **N** Alpine Sprs RV Park, Viejas Outlets/famous brands, casino, same as 36, **S** ranger sta
31mm	elev 2000 ft
30	Tavern Rd, to Alpine, **N** 🅿 Chevron/dsl, Valero/dsl, **S** 🅿 76/Circle K, Shell, 🍴 Carl's Jr, La Carreta, Little Caesars, Mediterraneo Grill, Ramon's BBQ, Subway, 🛏 Ayre's Inn, 🅾 Ace Hardware, CVS Drug, Daniel's IGA Mkt, Rite Aid, TrueValue, city park
27	Dunbar Lane, Harbison Canyon, **N** 🅾 RV camping, Flinn Sprgs CP
25mm	elev 1000 ft
24mm	🔧

🅖 = gas ⓕ = food 🛏 = lodging ⓞ = other 🆁🆂 = rest stop   Copyright 2014 - The Next Exit ®

INTERSTATE 8 CONT'D

Exit	Services
23	Lake Jennings Pk Rd, Lakeside, **N** 🅖 Arco/Jack-in-the-Box/dsl/24hr, to Lake Jennings CP, ⓞ RV camping, **S** 🅖 7-11, ⓕ Burger King, Karla's Mexican, Marechiaro's Pizza
22	Los Coches Rd, Lakeside, **N** 🅖 Eagle/dsl/LP, 7-11, Valero, ⓕ Albert's Mexican, Danny's Pizza, Laposta Mexican, Mike's NY Pizza, ⓞ RV camping/dump, **S** 🅖 Shell/dsl, ⓕ Denny's, Giant NY Pizza, McDonald's, Panda Express, Subway, Taco Bell, ⓞ Radio Shack, Vons Foods, Walmart
20b	Greenfield Dr, to Crest, **N** 🅖 Chevron/dsl, Valero/dsl, ⓕ Jack-in-the-Box, Marita's Mexican, McDonald's, Panchos Tacos, Pernicano's Pizza, Subway, ⓞ 🄷, Albertson's, AutoZone, Curves, Ford, 99¢ Store, RV camping, 7-11, auto repair, st patrol, **Urgent Care**, **S** 🅖 Mobil/dsl/LP
20a	E Main St (from wb, no EZ return), **N** 🛏 Budget Inn, ⓞ Ford, Vacationer RV Park, repair, **S** 🅖 Arco, ⓞ Cadillac
19	2nd St, CA 54, El Cajon, **N** 🅖 Arco/24hr, Chevron/dsl, Exxon/dsl, ⓕ Marechio's Italian, ⓞ CVS Drug, NAPA, Vons Foods, repair, **S** 🅖 On the Go, Shell, ⓕ Arby's, Burger King, Carl's Jr, Estrada's Mexican, Fred's Burgers, IHOP, Jack-in-the-Box, KFC, McDonald's, Pizza Hut, Popeye's, Quiznos, Subway, Taco Bell, Taco Shop, 🛏 Best Value Inn, ⓞ CarQuest, Firestone/auto, Jiffy Lube, PepBoys, PetCo, Ralphs Foods, Radio Shack, Rite Aid, Walgreens
18	Mollison Ave, El Cajon, **N** 🅖 Chevron, ⓕ Denny's, 🛏 Best Western, Days Inn, **S** 🅖 Arco/24hr, QuickTrip/dsl, ⓕ Taco Bell, 🛏 Super 8
17c	Magnolia Ave, CA 67 (from wb), to Santee, **N** 🅖 Arco, ⓕ Black Angus, Del Taco, Jack-in-the-Box, Panda Express, ⓞ Food4Less, Target, mall, **S** 🅖 Shell/service, ⓕ Panda Express, Perry's Cafe, Red Brick Pizza, Rubio's, 🛏 Motel 6, Rodeway Inn, ⓞ Nudo's Drug, Ross
17b	CA 67 (from eb), same as 17 a&c
17a	Johnson Ave (from eb), **N** ⓕ Applebee's, Boston Mkt, Burger King, Carl's Jr, Coco's, KFC, LJ Silver, McDonald's, On the Border, Pat&Oscars, Rubio's, Sizzler, Subway, ⓞ Best Buy, Big Boy, Big O Tire, Chevrolet, CVS Drug, $Tree, Goodyear/auto, Home Depot, Honda, JC Penney, Macy's, Marshall's, Office Depot, PetsMart, Sears/auto, Subaru, Toyota/Scion, Walmart, mall, **S** ⓞ Aamco, KIA, vet
16	Main St, **N** 🅖 Arco/24hr, ⓕ Denny's/24hr, Sombrero Mexican, 🛏 Relax Inn, ⓞ 7-11, **S** 🅖 Chevron/dsl, Super Star, ⓞ Nissan, brakes/transmissions
15	El Cajon Blvd (from eb), **N** 🛏 Quality Inn, **S** 🅖 Exxon/dsl, ⓕ Wrangler BBQ, ⓞ BMW
14c	Severin Dr, Fuerte Dr (from wb), **N** 🅖 Arco/24hr, ⓕ Anthony's Fish Grotto, Charcoal House Rest., 🛏 Holiday Inn Express, **S** ⓕ Brigantine Seafood Rest.
14b a	CA 125, to CA 94
13b	Jackson Dr, Grossmont Blvd, **N** 🅖 Chevron, ⓕ Arby's, Casa de Pico, Chili's, Chipotle Mexican, ChuckeCheese, ClaimJumper, Fuddrucker's, Jamba Juice, McDonald's, Olive Garden, Panda Express, Panera Bread, Red Lobster, Rubio's, Schlotsky's, Starbucks, ⓞ 🄷, Barnes&Noble, Best Buy, CVS Drug, $Tree, Kragen Parts, Macy's, 7-11, Staples, Target, Trader Joes, Walmart, mall, USPO, **S** 🅖 76, ⓕ Honeybaked Ham, Jack-in-the-Box, ⓞ Discount Tire, Ford, Hyundai, Ralph's Foods, VW
13a	Spring St (from eb), El Cajon Blvd (from wb), **N** ⓞ Chrys

13a	Continued ler/Jeep, Dodge, **S** ⓕ La Salsa Mexican, Starbucks, Subway, 🛏 Hitching Post, ⓞ AutoZone, 99¢ Store
12	Fletcher Pkwy, to La Mesa, **N** 🅖 Shell, ⓕ Chipotle Mexican, McDonald's, Pick Up Stix, 🛏 Heritage Inn, Holiday Inn, ⓞ Costco, 7-11, **S** ⓕ El Torito, La Salsa Mexican, Starbucks, 🛏 Motel 6, ⓞ Chevrolet, 99¢ Store, San Diego RV Resort
11	70th St, Lake Murray Blvd, **N** 🅖 Shell/dsl, ⓕ Subway, ⓞ truck/RV repair, **S** 🅖 Shell/7-11/dsl, ⓕ Aiken's Deli, Denny's, Marie Callender's, ⓞ 🄷
10	College Ave, **N** 🅖 Chevron/dsl, ⓞ Windmill Farms Mkt, **S** ⓞ 🄷, to SDSU
9	Waring Rd, **N** ⓕ Nicolosi's Italian, 🛏 Days Inn, Quality Inn
8	Fairmount Ave (7 from eb), to Mission Gorge Rd, **N** 🅖 Arco/24hr, Mobil/dsl, 7-11, ⓕ Arby's, Black Angus, Carl's Jr, Chili's, Coco's, El Pollo Loco, Jack-in-the-Box, Jamba Juice, McDonald's, Rally's, Roberto's Tacos, Rubio's, Sombrero Mexican, Starbucks, Subway, Szechuan Chinese, Togo's, Wendy's, 🛏 Super 8, ⓞ 🄷, Aamco, CVS Drug, Discount Tire, Home Depot, Honda, NAPA, Rite Aid, Toyota/Scion, Tuesday Morning, Vons Foods
7b a	I-15 N, CA 15 S, to 40th St
6b	I-805, N to LA, S to Chula Vista
6a	Texas St, Qualcomm Way, **N** ⓕ Dave&Buster's, same as 5
5	Mission Ctr Rd, **N** 🅖 Chevron, ⓕ Carl's Jr, Chevy's Mexican, Chipotle Mexican, Fuddrucker's, Hooters, In-N-Out, Jack-in-the-Box, King's Fishouse, Maggie Moo's, Mimi's Cafe, On The Border, Outback Steaks, Panda Express, Pick-Up Stix, Peiwei Asian, Robex Juice, Subway, Taco Bell, 🛏 Marriott, Sheraton, ⓞ Best Buy, Chevrolet, Lincoln, Macy's, Marshall's, Michael's, Nordstrom Rack, Old Navy, Staples, Target, mall, **S** 🅖 Arco/24hr, ⓕ Benihana, Denny's, El Torito, Wendy's, 🛏 Comfort Suites, Hilton, La Quinta, Sheraton, ⓞ Mazda, Suzuki
4c b	CA 163, Cabrillo Frwy, **S** to downtown, zoo
4a	Hotel Circle Dr (from eb), CA 163 (from wb)
3a	Hotel Circle, Taylor St, **N** ⓕ Hunter Steaks, Kelly's Steaks, 🛏 Comfort Suites, Crowne Plaza, Handlery Hotel, Motel 6, Town&Country Motel, ⓞ golf, **S** 🅖 Arco, ⓕ Adam's Cafe, Albie's Rest., Ricky's Rest., Tickled Trout, Valley Kitchen, 🛏 Best Western, Comfort Inn, Courtyard, Days Hotel, DoubleTree Inn, Extended Stay America, Hawthorn Suites, Hilton, Howard Johnson, King's Inn/rest., Mission Valley Hotel, Ramada Inn, Residence Inn, Super 8, Travelodge, Vagabond Inn, ⓞ Chrysler/Jeep, vet
2c	Morena Blvd (from wb)
2b	I-5, N to LA, S to San Diego
2a	Rosecrans St (from wb), CA 209, **S** 🅖 Chevron, ⓕ Burger King, Chipotle Mexican, Del Taco, In-N-Out, Jack-in-the-Box, McDonald's, Panda Express, Starbucks, 🛏 Super 8, ⓞ BigLots, PetsMart, Staples
1	W Mission Bay Blvd, Sports Arena Blvd (from wb), **N** to SeaWorld, **S** 🅖 Arco, ⓕ Arby's, Chick-fil-A, Denny's, Jack-in-the-Box, McDonald's, Phil's BBQ, Red Lobster, Taco Bell, Wendy's, 🛏 Heritage Inn, Holiday Inn Express, Ramada Ltd, ⓞ CVS Drug, Home Depot, U-Haul
0mm	**I-8 begins/ends on Sunset Cliffs Blvd, N** Mission Bay Park, **1/4 mi W** 🅖 Exxon, Shell, ⓕ Jack-in-the-Box, Kaiserhof Cafe

Left margin: CA / EL CAJON

Right margin: SAN DIEGO AREA / POINT LOMA

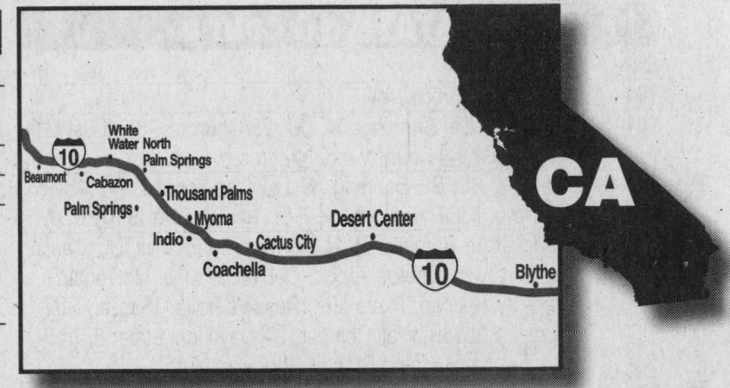

✈E	**INTERSTATE 10**
Exit	Services
245mm	California/Arizona state line, Colorado River, Pacific/Mountain time zone
244mm	inspection sta wb
243	Riviera Dr, **S** 🅾 KOA
241	US 95, Intake Blvd, Blythe, **N** 🅿 Mobil/dsl, 🍴 Steaks'n Cakes Rest., Sunset Grille, 🛏 Days Inn, Rodeway Inn, 🅾 Burton's RV Park, auto/RV repair/24hr, to Needles, **S** McIntyre Park
240	7th St, **N** 🅿 EZ Mart, 76/dsl, 🍴 Foster's Freeze, Starbucks, 🛏 Astro Motel, Blue Line Motel, Budget Inn, Knights Inn, 🅾 Albertson's, AutoZone, Ford, Rite Aid, repair
239	Lovekin Blvd, Blythe, **N** 🅿 Mobil/Subs/dsl, Shell/Quiznos, 🍴 Carl's Jr, Del Taco, Domino's, Jack-in-the-Box, La Casita Dos, McDonald's, Pizza Hut, Popeye's, Rosita's Mexican, Sizzler, Starbucks, Wang's Chinese, 🛏 Best Value Inn, Best Western, Budget Host, Hampton Inn, Regency Inn, Willow Inn, 🅾 🅷, Ace Hardware, Checker Parts, $Tree, Goodyear/auto, K-Mart/Little Caesars, Radio Shack, Verizon, **S** 🅿 Chevron/dsl/24hr, 76/dsl, Shell/DQ/dsl, Valero, 🍴 Burger King, Casa de Maria Mexican, Denny's, KFC, Subway, Taco Bell, 🛏 Comfort Suites, Holiday Inn Express, Motel 6, Super 8, 🅾 Buick/Chevrolet, city park
236	CA 78, Neighbours Blvd, to Ripley, **N** 🅿 Valero/dsl, **S** to Cibola NWR
232	Mesa Dr, **N** 🅿 76/dsl/rest./scales/24hr/@, Valero/Subway/dsl, 🅾 ✈
231	**weigh sta wb**
222mm	Wileys Well Rd, **N** 🆁🆂 **both lanes, full ♿ facilities, 🚻, 🛆 litter barrels, petwalk, S to st prison**
217	Ford Dry Lake Rd
201	Corn Springs Rd
192	CA 177, Rice Rd, to Lake Tamarisk, **N** 🍴 Desert Ctr Cafe, 🅾 camping
189	Eagle Mtn Rd
182	Red Cloud Rd
177	Hayfield Rd
173	Chiriaco Summit, **N** 🅿 Chevron/Foster's Freeze/dsl/24hr, 🍴 Chiriaco Rest, 🅾 Patton Museum, truck/tire repair
168	to Twentynine Palms, to Mecca, Joshua Tree NM
162	frontage rd
159mm	**Cactus City 🆁🆂 both lanes, full ♿ facilities, 🛆 litter barrels, petwalk**
147mm	0 ft elevation
146	Dillon Rd, to CA 86, to CA 111 S, Coachella, **N** 🅿 Chevron/24hr, Loves/Carl's Jr/dsl/24hr, 🍴 Del Taco, **S** 🅿 Chevron/Jack-in-the-Box, TA/Arco/Arby's/Taco Bell/dsl/24hr/@, 🅾 Spotlight Casino
145	(from eb), CA 86 S
144	CA 111 N, CA 86 S, Indio, **N** 🛏 Holiday Inn Express, 🅾 Classic RV Park, Fantasy Sprgs Casino/Hotel/Cafe
143	Jackson St, Indio, **N** 🍴 Jack-in-the-Box, KFC, McDonald's, Panda Express, Subway, Taco Bell, 🅾 BigLots, CVS Drug, $Tree, Fletcher's Tire, Home Depot, Marshall's, PetCo, Ross, Target, Walgreens, WinCo Foods, **S** 🅾 Circle K
142	Monroe St, Central Indio, **N** 🅾 RV camping, **S** 🅿 Circle K, 76, Shell/dsl/LP, 🍴 Mexicali Cafe, Taco Jalisco, 🛏 Quality Inn
139	Jefferson St, Indio Blvd, **N** 🅾 Shadow Hills RV Resort, hwy patrol
137	Washington St, Country Club Dr, to Indian Wells, **N** 🅿 Arco/24hr, Chevron, 🍴 Burger King, Burger Time, Coco's, Del Taco, Mario's Italian, Popeye's, Starbucks, Winchell's, 🛏 Comfort Suites, Motel 6, 🅾 Buick/GMC, Ford/Lincoln, Honda, McMahon's RV Ctr, 1000 Trails RV Park, Rite Aid, Stater Bros, Toyota/Scion, VW, Walgreens, **S** 🅿 Mobil/dsl, 76/Circle K, 🍴 Baskin-Robbins/Togo's, Carl's Jr, Chicken Pie Factory, China Wok, Domino's, Goody's Cafe, Lili's Chinese, Pizza Hut, Quiznos, Subway, Taco Shop, Wendy's, 🛏 Embassy Suites, 🅾 Firestone/auto, Goodyear/auto
134	Cook St, to Indian Wells, **S** 🅿 Arco, Mobil, 🍴 Applebees, Carl's Jr, Dogo's Hot Dogs, Firehouse Grill, Jack-in-the-Box, Starbucks, Subway, 🛏 Courtyard, Hampton Inn, Hilton/Homewood Suites, Residence Inn
131	Monterey Ave, Thousand Palms, **N** 🅿 Arco/24hr, 🍴 Jack-in-the-Box, **S** 🍴 Clark's Cafe/Food Mkt, Del Taco, El Pollo Loco, IHOP, McDonald's, Panda Express, Quiznos, Red Robin, Starbucks, Subway, Taco Bell, Wendy's, 🅾 America's Tire, Costco/gas, Curves, Home Depot, Kohls, PetsMart, Sam's Club/gas, Verizon, Walmart
130	Ramon Rd, Bob Hope Dr, **N** 🅿 Chevron/24hr, ⊕FLYING J/dsl/LP/rest./24hr, Shell/dsl, Valero, 🍴 Carl's Jr, Casa de Pasta, Del Taco, Denny's, Guerro Mexican, In-N-Out, McDonald's, 🛏 Red Roof Inn, 🅾 truckwash, **S** 🅾 🅷, Agua Caliente Casino/rest.
126	Date Palm Dr, Rancho Mirage, **S** 🅿 Arco/24hr, Mobil, Valero, 🍴 La Palapa Mexican, 🅾 RV Camping
123	Palm Dr, to Desert Hot Sprgs, **N** 🅿 Arco, Chevron/Jack-in-the-Box, 🅾 Caliente Springs Camping, **3 mi S** to Gene Autry Trail
120	Indian Ave, to N Palm Sprgs, **N** 🅿 76/Circle K, Shell, 🍴 Denny's, 🛏 Motel 6, **S** 🅿 Chevron, 🚚/DQ/Wendy's/dsl/scales/24hr, 🍴 Jack-in-the-Box, 🅾 🅷
117	CA 62, to Yucca Valley, Twentynine Palms, to Joshua Tree NM
114	Whitewater, many windmills
113mm	🆁🆂 **both lanes, full ♿ facilities, 🚻, 🛆 litter barrels**
112	CA 111 (from eb), to Palm Springs
110	Haugeen-Lehmann
106	Main St, to Cabazon, **N** 🅿 Shell/dsl, 🍴 Burger King, Wheel Inn Rest., **S** 🅿 Valero/Circle K/dsl
104	Cabazon, same as 103
103	Fields Rd, **N** 🅿 Chevron, TC/A&W/dsl, 🍴 McDonald's, Ruby's Diner, 🅾 Hadley Fruit Orchards, Premium Outlets/famous brands, Morongo Reservation/casino
102.5mm	**Banning weigh sta both lanes**

(Vertical side labels: **BLYTHE**, **INDIO**, **PALM SPRINGS**)

[gas] = gas [food] = food [lodging] = lodging [other] = other [rest stop] = rest stop

CA

INTERSTATE 10 CONT'D

BANNING

BEAUMONT

REDLANDS

Exit	Services
102	Ramsey St (from wb)
101	Hargrave St, Banning, N [gas] 76/Church's, Shell/dsl/LP, Valero/dsl, [lodging] Country Inn, [other] tires
100	CA 243, 8th St, Banning, N [gas] Chevron/dsl, [food] Ahloo Chinese, IHOP, Jack-in-the-Box, [other] Rite Aid, S [other] KOA
99	22nd St, to Ramsey St, N [gas] Arco/24hr, Shell, [food] Carl's Jr, Carrow's, Chelos Tacos, Del Taco, KFC, McDonald's, Pepe's Mexican, Pizza Hut, Russo's Italian, Sizzler, Starbucks, Subway, Wall Chinese, [lodging] Days Inn, Super 8, Travelodge, [other] Banning RV Ctr, Goodyear/auto
98	Sunset Ave, Banning, N [gas] Chevron/dsl, [food] Domino's, Gramma's Kitchen, Gus Jr #7 Burger, [lodging] Holiday Inn Express, [other] Ace Hardware, AutoZone, BigLots, Buick/Chevrolet/GMC, Ray's RV Ctr, Rio Ranch Mkt, repair, vet
96	Highland Springs Ave, N [gas] Arco/24hr, Chevron, Shell, [food] Applebee's, Burger King, Denny's, Jack-in-the-Box, Orchid Thai, Papa John's, Subway, Wendy's, [lodging] Hampton Inn, [other] [H], Do-It Hardware, Food4Less, Kragen Parts, Stater Bros Foods, Walgreens, S [gas] Mobil, [food] Carl's Jr, Chili's, El Pollo Loco, La Casita, McDonald's, Palermo's Pizza, Panda Express, Quiznos, Rubio's, Starbucks, Wienerschnitzel, [other] Albertson's, Best Buy, Curves, GNC, Home Depot, K-Mart, Kohls, PetCo, Rite Aid, Ross, Staples, Walmart/Subway, hwy patrol
95	Pennsylvania Ave (from wb), Beaumont, N [food] Jasmine Thai, [lodging] Rodeway Inn, [other] AutoZone, Miller RV Ctr, Tom's RV Ctr
94	CA 79, Beaumont, N [gas] Arco, 76/dsl, [food] Baker's DriveThru, Hawaiian BBQ, McDonald's, Popeye's, YumYum Donuts, [lodging] Best Western, Best Value Inn, [other] NAPA, S [food] Del Taco, Denny's, [other] RV camping
93	CA 60 W, to Riverside
92	San Timoteo Canyon Rd, Oak Valley Pkwy, N [gas] Chevron, [food] Figero's Pizza, [lodging] Holiday Inn Express, [other] Rite Aid, golf, S golf
91mm	**[rest stop] wb, full [handicapped] facilities, [phone], [picnic], litter barrels, petwalk**
90	Cherry Valley Blvd, N [other] truck/tire repair
89	Singleton Rd (from wb), to Calimesa
88	Calimesa Blvd, N [gas] Arco/24hr, Chevron/dsl, Shell, [food] Best Wok, Burger King, Carl's Jr, Denny's, Isabella's Italian, McDonald's, Subway, Taco Bell, Tang's Chinese, [lodging] Calimesa Inn, [other] Fresh&Easy Foods, Stater Bros Foods, Walgreens, S [food] Big Boy, Jack-in-the-Box
87	County Line Rd, to Yucaipa, N [gas] FasTrip/gas, Shell/dsl, [food] Baker's DriveThru, Del Taco, [other] auto repair/tires
86mm	**Wildwood [rest stop] eb, full [handicapped] facilities, [phone], [picnic], litter barrels, petwalk**
85	Live Oak Canyon Rd, Oak Glen
83	Yucaipa Blvd, N [gas] Arco/dsl/24hr, Chevron, Mobil, [food] Baker's DriveThru, Starbucks, S [food] Subway
82	Wabash Ave (from wb)
81	Redlands Blvd, Ford St, S [gas] 76
80	Cypress Ave, University St, N [H], to U of Redlands
79b a	CA 38, 6th St, Orange St, Redlands, N [gas] Chevron, Thrifty, [lodging] Budget Inn, Stardust Motel, [other] Stater Bros Foods, S [gas] 76, Shell, [food] Chipotle Mexican, Denny's, Domino's, Eureka Burger, Open Kitchen Chinese, Phoenicia Greek, Rubio's, Togo's, Sizzler, Starbucks, Subway, [other] Kragen Parts, NAPA, Office Depot, Trader Joe's, Von's Foods
77c	(77b from wb) Tennessee St, N [food] Shakey's Pizza, [other]

SAN BERNARDINO

Exit	Services
77c	Continued Home Depot, Toyota/Scion, S [gas] Shell, [food] Arby's, Bakers DriveThru, Carl's Jr, Coco's, El Burrito, El Pollo Loco, Papa John's, Subway, Taco Bell, [lodging] Ayers Hotel, Comfort Suites, Dynasty Suites, Howard Johnson, [other] Ford, USPO
77b	(77c from wb) CA 30, to Highlands
77a	Alabama St, N [gas] 76/Circle K, [food] Canton Bistro, Chili's, Chick-fil-A, Coldstone Creamery, Denny's, Famous Dave's BBQ, Hawaiian BBQ, Jamba Juice, Macaroni Grill, Magic Wok, Mr. Tortilla, Noodle 21 Asian, Qdoba Mexican, Red Robin, Starbucks, Subway, Tom's Charburgers, [lodging] Best Value Inn, Super 8, [other] Barnes&Noble, GNC, JC Penney, Jo-Ann Superstore, Kohl's, Marshall's, Michael's, PetCo, Target, Verizon, VW, U-Haul, S [gas] Chevron, Shell, [food] Del Taco, IHOP, Marie Callender's, McDonald's, Mona Lisa Pizza, Nick's Burgers, Old Spaghetti Factory, Quizno's, Slim's BBQ, Starbucks, Zabella's Mexican, [lodging] Country Inn&Suites, GoodNite Inn, [other] Aamco, BigLots, Chevrolet, CVS Drug, Discount Tire, $Tree, Goodyear/auto, K-Mart, Lowe's, 99¢ Store, Nissan, PepBoys, 7-11, Tuesday Morning
76	California St, N [food] Mill Creek Rest., [other] funpark, museum, S [gas] Arco/24hr, Shell/LP/24hr, [food] Applebee's, Bravo Burger, Jose's Mexican, Panda Express, Subway, Wienerschnitzel, Wendy's, [other] AT&T, Food4Less, Just Tires, Mission RV Park, Radio Shack, Verizon, Walmart
75	Mountain View Ave, Loma Linda, N [gas] Valero/dsl, S [food] Domino's, FarmerBoys Burgers, Lupe's Mexican, Subway
74	Tippecanoe Ave, Anderson St, N [gas] Thrifty, [food] CA Pizza Kitchen, Chipotle Mexican, Coldstone Creamery, Denny's, Elephant Bar Rest., El Pollo Loco, Hawaiian BBQ, In-N-Out, Jack-in-the-Box, Jamba Juice, Panera Bread, Pick-Up Stix, Ruby Tuesday, Starbucks, Subway, Tasty Goody, [lodging] American Inn, Fairfield Inn, Residence Inn, [other] Costco/gas, Sam's Club, Staples, Verizon, S [gas] 76/dsl, [food] Baker's DriveThru, Del Taco, HomeTown Buffet, KFC, Napoli Italian, Wienerschnitzel, [other] Harley-Davidson, Honda, Hyundai, transmissions, to Loma Linda U
73b a	Waterman Ave, N [gas] 76, Shell/dsl/24hr, [food] Baja Fresh, Black Angus, Chili's, ChuckeCheese, ClaimJumper, Coco's, Crabby Bob's, El Torito, IHOP/24hr, King Buffet, Lotus Garden Chinese, Mimi's Café, Olive Garden, Outback Steaks, Panda Express, Pat&Oscar's, Red Lobster, Sizzler, Souplantation, Starbucks, TGIFriday's, [lodging] Best Western, Days Inn, Hilton, Hilton Garden, La Quinta, Quality Inn, Super 8, [other] Best Buy, Home Depot, Office Depot, PetsMart, S [gas] Arco/24hr, [food] Burger King, Carl's Jr, Gus Jr Burger #8, McDonald's, Popeye's, Starbucks, Taco Bell, [lodging] Motel 6, [other] Camping World RV Service/supplies, El Monte RV Ctr, repair
72	I-215, CA 91
71	Mt Vernon Ave, Sperry Ave, N [gas] 7-11, Trkstp/dsl/LP, [lodging] Colony Inn, Colton Motel, [other] brake/muffler, repair
70b	9th St, N [gas] Mobil, [food] Burger King, Denny's, McDonald's, P&G Burgers, Subway, [lodging] Hampton Inn, [other] Bumper Parts, Stater Bros Foods, USPO
70a	Rancho Ave, N [food] Del Taco, Jack-in-the-Box, KFC/Taco Bell, Wienerschnitzel
69	Pepper Dr, N [gas] Valero, [food] Baker's DriveThru
68	Riverside Ave, to Rialto, N [gas] Arco, Chevron, I-10 Trkstp/dsl/scales, [food] Burger King, Coco's, El Pollo Loco, HomeTown Buffet, Jack-in-the-Box, McDonald's, Starbucks,

INTERSTATE 10 CONT'D

SAN BERNARDINO

Exit	Services
68	Continued
	Subway, Taco Joe's, 🏠 American Inn, Empire Inn, Super 8, 🅾 Big O Tire, Walmart, dsl repair, S 🍴 76/Circle K/dsl
66	Cedar Ave, to Bloomington, N 🅿 Arco/24hr, Valero, 🍴 Baker's DriveThru, FarmerBoys Burgers, Pizza Hut/Taco Bell, Subway, 🅾 USPO, S 🍴 Citgo/7-11
64	Sierra Ave, to Fontana, N 🅿 Arco/24hr, Mobil, Shell, Valero, 🍴 Applebee's, Arby's, Billy J's Rest., Burger King, China Cook, ChuckeCheese, DQ, Denny's, Del Taco, El Gallo Giro, In-N-Out, Jack-in-the-Box, KFC, Little Caesars, McDonald's, Millie's Kitchen, 1 China, Pancho Villa's, Papa John's, Pizza Hut/Taco Bell, Popeye's, Sizzler, Spire's Rest., Subway, 3 Hermanos, Wendy's, Wienerschnitzel, Yoshinoya, 🏠 Best Value Inn, EconoLodge, Motel 6, Valley Motel, 🅾🏨 AT&T, BigLots, CVS Drug, $Tree, Fiesta Foods, Food4Less, GNC, Honda, Just Tires, Kia, K-Mart, Kragen Parts, PepBoys, Radio Shack, Rite Aid, Stater Bros Foods, Verizon, S 🍴 Brandon's Diner, China Buffet, Circle K, Del Taco, El Gran Burrito, Shakey's Pizza, Tasty Goody, 🏠 Hilton Garden, 🅾 AutoZone, 99¢ Store, Ross, Target
63	Citrus Ave, N 🅿 Gasco, 76, 🍴 Baker's DriveThru, Subway, 🅾 Ford, S 🅿 Arco, 7-11/dsl
61	Cherry Ave, N 🅿 Arco, Chevron/dsl, Trucktown Trkstp/dsl/24hr/@, Valero, 🍴 Carl's Jr, Del Taco, Jack-in-the-Box, 🏠 Circle Inn Motel, 🅾 Ford Trucks, S 🅿 North American Trkstp/dsl, 3 Sisters Trkstp/dsl/@, 76/Circle K, 🍴 Farmer Boy's Rest., La Chaquita, Mariscos Mexican, 🅾 Peterbilt
59	Etiwanda Ave, Valley Blvd
58b a	I-15, N to Barstow, S to San Diego

ONTARIO

57	Milliken Ave, N 🅿 Arco/24hr, Chevron, Mobil/Albertos Mexican/dsl, 76/dsl, Shell, 🍴 Applebee's, Arby's, Baja Fresh, BJ's Rest., Boston's, Burger King, Carl's Jr, Chevy's Mexican, Chipotle, Coco's, Coldstone, Dave&Buster's, Del Taco, El Pollo Loco, Famous Dave's BBQ, Fat Burger, Fuddruckers, Hooters, IHOP, In-n-Out, Jack-in-the-Box, Jamba Juice, KFC, Krispy Kreme, McDonald's, Mkt Broiler, New City Buffet, NY Grill, Olive Garden, Outback Steaks, Rain Forest Cafe, Red Lobster, Rubio's, Sonic, Starbucks, Subway, Tokyo Tokyo, Wendy's, Wienerschnitzel, Wing Place, 🏠 Ayre's Suites, Country Inn&Suites, Courtyard, Hampton Inn, Hilton Garden, Holiday Inn Express, Homewood Suites, Hyatt, TownePlace Suites, 🅾 America's Tire, Best Buy, Big O Tire, Carmax, Costco/gas, JC Penney, Jo-Ann Fabrics, Kohl's, Marshalls, Ontario Mills Mall, Petsmart, Sam's Club/gas, Staples, Target, Verizon, S 🍴 TA/Shell/Pizza Hut/Subway/Taco Bell/dsl/rest./24hr/@, Rodeway Inn
56	Haven Ave, Rancho Cucamonga, N 🅿 Mobil, 🍴 Benihana, Black Angus, Pizza Factory, 🏠 Aloft Hotel, Best Western, Extended Stay America, Hilton, La Quinta, Ontario Grand Suites, S 🍴 Panda Chinese, TGIFriday's, 🏠 Fairfield Inn
55b a	Holt Blvd, to Archibald Ave, N 🅿 Arco, Mobil/dsl, 🍴 Baker's Drive-thru, Burgertown USA, Hawaiian BBQ, Subway, Weinerschnitzel
54	Vineyard Ave, N 🅿 76/Circle K, 🍴 Carl's Jr, Del Taco, El Pollo Loco, Great China, Pizza Hut/Taco Bell, Popeye's, Quiznos, Rocky's Pizza, 🅾 AutoZone, Ralph's Foods,

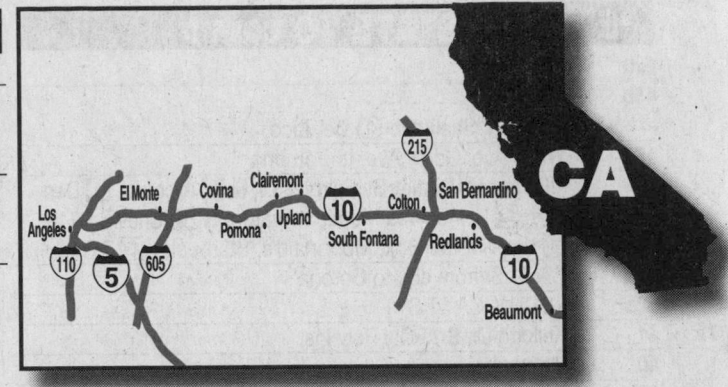

54	Continued
	Rite Aid, Stater Bros Foods, S 🅿 Mobil, 76, Valero, 🍴 Basil Rest., Cowboy Bugers, Denny's, Garden Square Rest., In-N-Out, Jack-in-the-Box, Marie Callenders, Quiznos, Rosa's Italian, Spires Rest., Yoshinoya Japanese, Wendy's, 🏠 Ayers Suites, Best Western, Comfort Suites, Countryside Suites, DoubleTree Inn, Holiday Inn, Motel 6, Ontario ✈ Inn, Quality Inn, Ramada Inn, Red Roof Inn, Residence Inn, Sheraton, 🅾 Buick/Cadillac/Chevrolet/GMC, USPO, to ✈
53	San Bernardino Ave, 4th St, to Ontario, N 🅿 Arco, 7-11, 76, Shell, 🍴 Burger King, Carl's Jr, Jack-in-the-Box, 🏠 EconoLodge, Motel 6, 🅾 K-Mart, Radio Shack, S 🅿 Arco/24hr, 76, Valero, 🍴 Denny's, Little Caesars, Subway, YumYum Donuts, 🏠 Days Inn, Rodeway Inn, 🅾 Jax Mkt, city park
51	CA 83, Euclid Ave, to Ontario, Upland, N 🅾🏨
50	Mountain Ave, to Mt Baldy, N 🅿 Chevron, Mobil/dsl, Shell/dsl, 🍴 Carrow's, Denny's, El Torito, Fresh&Easy, HoneyBaked Ham, Mimi's Café, Mi Taco, Rubio's, Subway, Trader Joe's, Wendy's, 🏠 Super 8, 🅾 AT&T, CVS Drug, $Tree, Home Depot, Kohl's, Michaels, Radio Shack, Staples, S 🅿 76/dsl, 🍴 Baskin-Robbins, Carl's Jr, Chopstix, Coldstone, Jo-Anne's Cafe, Pizza Hut, Quiznos, Roundtable Pizza, Starbucks, Wingnuts, 🅾 Albertsons, Rite Aid, USPO, vet

MONTCLAIR

49	Central Ave, to Montclair, N 🍴 Carl's Jr., Chipotle Mexican, Del Taco, El Pollo Loco, Hometown Buffet, John's Incredible Pizza, McDonald's, Panda Garden Buffet, Pizza Hut, Quiznos, Starbucks, Subway, Taco Bell, 🅾 America's Tire, AT&T, AutoZone, Barnes&Noble, Best Buy, Firestone/auto, Giant RV Ctr, Goodyear/auto, Harley-Davidson, JC Penney, Just Tires, Macy's, 99¢ Store, PepBoys, PetCo, Ross, Sears/auto, Target, Tuesday Morning, mall, vet, same as 48, S 🅿 Chevron, Thrifty, 🍴 Alberto's Mexican, Fulin Chinese, Jack-in-the-Box, LJ Silver, Subway, Wienerschnitzel, 🅾 Acura/Honda/Infiniti, Costco/gas, Nissan, 7-11, Stater Bro's
48	Monte Vista, N 🅿 Shell, 🍴 Acapulco Mexican, Applebee's, Chilis, Black Angus, Elephant Bar Rest., Macaroni Grill, Olive Garden, Red Lobster, 🅾🏨 Nordstrom's, Macy's, mall, same as 49
47	Indian Hill Blvd, to Claremont, N 🅿 Mobil, 🍴 BC Cafe, Garden Square, 🏠 Claremont Lodge, Howard Johnson, S 🅿 Chevron/McDonald's, 76/dsl, 🍴 Burger King, Carl's Jr, Denny's, In-N-Out, Norm's Rest., RoundTable Pizza, Starbucks, World Famous Grill, 🅾 7-11, Toyota/Scion
46	Towne Ave, N 🅿 76/dsl, 7-11, 🍴 Jack-in-the-Box
45b	Garey Ave, to Pomona, N 🅿 Arco, 🅾🏨 vet, S 🅿

🅖 = gas   🅕 = food   🛏 = lodging   🅞 = other   🆁🆂 = rest stop   Copyright 2014 - The Next Exit ®

➤🅔 INTERSTATE 10 CONT'D

CA

COVINA

Exit	Services
45b	Continued Chevron, Shell/dsl, 🅕 Del Taco
45	White Ave, Garey Ave, to Pomona
44	(43 from eb) Dudley St, Fairplex Dr, **N** 🅖 Arco/dsl, 🅕 Denny's, 🛏 LemonTree Motel, Sheraton, **S** 🅖 Chevron/24hr, 🅕 Jack-in-the-Box, McDonald's, Starbucks, 🅞 7-11
42b	CA 71 S (from eb), to Corona
42a	I-210 W, CA 57 S
41	Kellogg Dr, **S** to Cal Poly Inst
40	Via Verde
38b	Holt Ave, to Covina, **N** 🅕 Hamiltons Steaks, 🛏 Radisson
38a	Grand Ave, **N** 🅖 Arco/dsl, United, 🅕 Baily's Rest, Denny's, 🛏 Best Western
37b	Barranca St, Grand Ave, same as 37a, **N** 🅖 76, Shell/dsl, 🅕 BJ's Rest., Carinos, Carl's Jr, Chili's, Chipotle Mexican, Dockside Grill, El Torito, Habit Burgers, Hooters, Islands Burgers, Marie Callender, Mariposa Mexican, Starbucks, 🛏 Best Western, Clarion, Fairfield Inn, Hampton Inn, 🅞 Albertsons, CVS Drug, Dick's, IKEA, Marshalls, Office Depot, Old Navy, Petsmart, Target, Verizon, **S** 🅕 In-N-Out, McDonald's, 🛏 Days Inn, 5 Star Inn
37a	Citrus Ave, to Covina, same as 37b, **N** 🅖 Chevron, 🅕 Buffalo Wild Wings, Burger King, Del Taco, IHOP, Jack-in-the-Box, Millie's Rest., Starbucks, Subway, TGIFriday's, Yum Yum Donuts, 🅞 Acura, Albertsons, Baja Ranch Foods, Buick/GMC, CVS Drug, KIA, Marshall's, Nissan, VW, **S** 🅖 76/autocare, 🅕 Classic Burger, 🅞🅗 Cadillac
36	CA 39, Azusa Ave, to Covina, **N** 🅖 Arco/24hr, 76/dsl, 🅕 Dennys, Green Field Brazillian, McDonald's, Norm's Rest., Papa John's, Quiznos, Subway, 🅞 BigLots, Chrysler/Dodge/Jeep, CVS Drug, Food4Less, Stater Bros, **S** 🅖 Mobil, Shell/dsl, 🅕 Carrow's, 🅞 Audi, Chevrolet, Ford, Honda, Hummer, Mercedes, Toyota
35	Vincent Ave, Glendora Ave, **N** 🅖 76/dsl/autocare, **S** 🅖 76, 🅕 Applebee's, Baja Fresh, CA Pizza Kitchen, Elephant Bar Rest., Fresh&Easy, Grand Buffet, Jamba Juice, Panera Bread, Pizza Hut, Red Robin, Starbucks, Subway, Weinerschnitzel, 🅞 Best Buy, Big O Tire, Firestone, JC Penney, Macy's, Sears/auto, Verizon, mall, USPO
34	Pacific Ave, **N** 🅖 76, **S** 🅖 Mobil, Valero, 🅞🅗 Discount Tire, K-Mart, Sears Outlet, mall, same as 35
33	Puente Ave, **N** 🅖 Chevron, 🅕 Denny's, Farmer Boy's, Guadalajara Grill, McDonald's, Panda Express, Sizzler, Starbucks, 🛏 Courtyard, Motel 6, 🅞 AT&T, Home Depot, Verizon, Walmart, **S** 🅖 Valero/dsl, 🛏 Regency Inn, 🅕 Jack-in-the-Box, 🅞 Harley-Davidson, U-Haul
32b	Francisquito Ave, to La Puente, **N** 🅖 V&G, 🅞 hwy patrol, **S** 🅖 76, 🅕 Carl's Jr, In-N-Out, Wienerschnitzel, 🛏 Grand Park Inn
32a	Baldwin Pk Blvd, **N** 🅖 Chevron/McDonald's, 🅕 Burger King, Fronteiras, IHOP, Jack-in-the-Box, Papa Johns, Pizza Hut/Taco Bell, Starbucks, Subway, Wok'n Go, Yum Yum Donuts, 🅞🅗 CVS Drug, Food4Less, Target, transmissions, **S** 🅕 In-N-Out
31c	(31b from wb) Frazier St, **N** 🅞 7-11
31b a	(31a from wb) I-605 N/S, to Long Beach
30	Garvey Ave, **S** 🅖 Rte 66
29b	Valley Blvd, Peck Rd, **N** 🅖 Chevron, 🅕 Baskin-Robbins, Carl's Jr., Denny's, Hometown Buffet, Jamba Juice, KFC, Papa Johns, Shakey's Pizza, Subway, Taco Bell,

EL MONTE

LOS ANGELES AREA

Exit	Services
29b	Continued Yoshinoya, 🛏 Motel 6, 🅞 Honda, Hyundai, Lexus, Nissan, Radio Shack, Sears Essentials, Staples, Toyota/Scion, Walgreens, **S** 🅕 McDonald's, Pepe's Seafood, Tommy's Burgers
29a	S Peck Rd (from eb)
28	Santa Anita Ave, to El Monte, **S** 🅖 76/dsl, 🅞 7-11, vet
27	Baldwin Avenue, Temple City Blvd, **S** 🅖 Arco/24hr, 🅕 Denny's, same as 26b a
26b	CA 19, Rosemead Blvd, Pasadena, **N** 🅕 Coldstone, Denny's, IHOP, Jamba Juice, Mayumba Cuban, Subway, 🛏 Knights Inn, 🅞 $Tree, GNC, Goodyear/auto, Office Depot, Radio Shack, Target, **S** 🅕 Del Taco, Jack-in-the-Box, Quiznos, Starbucks
26a	Walnut Grove Ave
25b	San Gabriel Blvd, **N** 🅖 Shell, 🅕 Carl's Jr, Pizza Hut/Taco Bell, Popeye's, Wienerschnitzel, 🛏 Budget Inn, **S** 🅖 7-11
25a	Del Mar Ave, to San Gabriel, **N** 🅖 76, 🅞 auto repair, 🅖 Arco, Chevron/dsl, 🛏 Rodeway Inn
24	New Ave, to Monterey Park, **N** 🅕 KFC, to Mission San Gabriel
23b	Garfield Ave, to Alhambra, **S** 🅖 Arco, 🛏 Grand Inn, 🅞 🅗
23a	Atlantic Blvd, Monterey Park, **N** 🅖 Mobil, 76, 🅕 Pizza Hut, Popeye's, Starbucks, 🅞🅗, **S** 🛏 Best Western, 🅞 Ralph's Foods, auto repair
22	Fremont Ave, **N** 🅗, tuneup, **S** 🅕 Papa Johns, 🅞 7-11
21	I-710, Long Beach Fwy, Eastern Ave (from wb)
20b a	Eastern Ave, City Terrace Dr, **S** 🅖 Chevron/service, Mobil, 🅕 Burger King, McDonald's
19c	Soto St (from wb), **N** 🅖 Chevron/dsl, 🅕 Burger King, 🅞 🅗, city park, **S** 🅖 Mobil, 76
19b	I-5 (from wb), US 101 S, N to Burbank, S to San Diego
19a	State St, **N** 🅗
17	I-5 N
16b	I-5 S (from eb)
16a	Santa Fe Ave, San Mateo St, **S** 🅖 76/dsl, 🅞 Penske Trucks, industrial area
15b	Alameda St, **N** 🅖 76/dsl, 🅕 Jack-in-the-Box, to downtown, **S** industrial area
15a	Central Ave, **N** 🅖 Shell/repair
14b	San Pedro Blvd, **S** industrial
14a	LA St, **N** conv ctr, **S** 🅕 El Pollo Loco, McDonald's, 🅞 Urgent Care, 99¢ Store, O'Reilly Parts, Radio Shack, Rite Aid
13	I-110, Harbor Fwy
12	Hoover St, Vermont Ave, **N** 🅖 Mobil, 🅕 Burger King, McDonald's, Subway, 🅞 AutoZone, Honda, PepBoys, Rite Aid, **S** 🅖 Arco, Chevron, 76, 🅕 Jack-in-the-Box, Papa Johns, Yoshinoya, 🅞 Ralph's Foods
11	Normandie Ave, Western Ave
10	Arlington Ave, **N** 🅖 Chevron, 76
9	Crenshaw Blvd, **S** 🅖 Chevron, Mobil, 76, Thrifty, 🅕 El Pollo Loco, McDonald's, Pizza Hut/Taco Bell, Subway, Yoshinoya, 🅞 U-Haul
8	La Brea Ave, **N** 🅖 Valero/dsl, 🅞 USPO, **S** 🅖 Chevron, 🅞 AutoZone
7b	Washington Blvd, Fairfax Ave, **S** 🅖 Mobil, same as 8
7a	La Cienega Blvd, Venice Ave (from wb), **N** 🅖 Chevron/24hr, Mobil, 🅕 Carl's Jr., Del Taco, 🅞 Firestone/auto, **S** 🅕 Subway, 🅞 Aamco
6	Robertson Blvd, Culver City, **N** 🅖 Chevron, Valero, 🅕

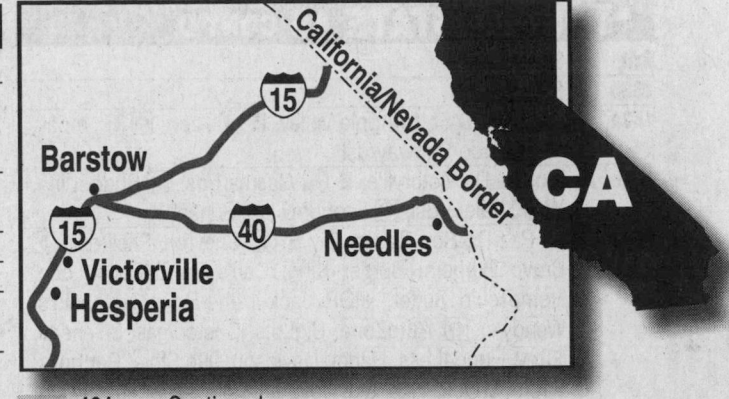

INTERSTATE 10 CONT'D

Exit	Services
6	Continued
	Domino's, Taco Bell, 🅾 EZ Lube, Goodyear, S 🍴 Del Taco, 🅾 Albertsons, CVS Drug, Ross
5	National Blvd, N 🅶 76, United Oil, 🍴 Starbucks, Subway, Taco+, 🅾 Rite Aid, Von's Foods, S 🅶 Arco
4	Overland Ave, S 🅶 Mobil/dsl
3b a	I-405, N to Sacramento, S to Long Beach
2c b	Bundy Dr, N 🅶 Chevron, Shell/dsl, 🍴 Taco Bell, 🅾 Cadillac/GMC, Staples
2a	Centinela Ave, to Santa Monica, N 🍴 Taco Bell, S 🍴 McDonald's, Trader Joe's, 🛏 Santa Monica Hotel
1c	20th St (from wb), Cloverfield Blvd, 26th St (from wb), N 🅶 Arco, 76/dsl, Shell/repair, 🅾 🅷
1b	Lincoln Blvd, CA 1 S, N 🅶 Mobil, 🍴 Arbys, Denny's, Jack-in-the-Box, McDonald's, Norm's Rest., Starbucks, 🛏 Holiday Inn, 🅾 BrakeMasters, Jo-Ann Fabrics, Sears, Toyota, Tuesday Morning, Vons Foods, USPO, S 🅶 Chevron/dsl, Mobil, 76, Shell, World Gas, 🍴 Dominos, Hawaiian BBQ, Jack-in-the-Box, Subway, Taco Bell, Tommy's Burgers, 🛏 Doubletree Suites, 🅾 EZ Lube, Firestone/auto, 7-11, U-Haul
1a	4th, 5th, (from wb), N 🅾 Sears, mall
0	Santa Monica Blvd, to beaches, **I-10 begins/ends on CA 1.**

INTERSTATE 15

Exit	Services
298	California/Nevada state line, services located at state line, Nevada side
291	Yates Well Rd
286	Nipton Rd, E Mojave Nat Preserve, to Searchlight
281	Bailey Rd
276mm	**brake check area for trucks, nb**
272	Cima Rd, E 🅶 Shell/cafe/dsl/towing
270mm	**Valley Wells 🆁🆂 both lanes, full ♿ facilities, 🚻, 🏞, litter barrels, petwalk**
265	Halloran Summit Rd
259	Halloran Springs Rd
248	to Baker (from sb), same as 246
246	CA 127, Kel-Baker Rd, Baker, to Death Valley, W 🅶 Arco, Chevron/Taco Bell, 76/dsl, Shell/Jack-in-the-Box/dsl, Valero/A&W/Pizza Hut/Subway/TCBY, Valero/DQ/Quiznos/dsl, 🍴 Arby's, Big Boy Rest., Burger King, Carl's Jr, Del Taco, Dennys, IHOP, Mad Greek Café, 🛏 BunBoy Hotel, Will's Fargo Motel, 🅾 Alien Fresh Jerky, Baker Mkt Foods, Country Store, World's Tallest Thermometer, USPO, repair
245	to Baker (from nb), same as 246
239	Zzyzx Rd
233	Rasor Rd, E 🅶 Shell/Rasor Sta/dsl/towing/24hr
230	Basin Rd
221	Afton Rd, to Dunn, W 🅾 Mini Mkt
217mm	**🆁🆂 both lanes, full ♿ facilities, 🚻, 🏞, litter barrels, petwalk**
213	Field Rd
206	Harvard Rd, to Newberry Springs
198	Minneola Rd, W gas/dsl
197mm	**agricultural insp sta sb**
196	Yermo Rd, Yermo
194	Calico Rd
191	Ghost Town Rd, E 🅶 Arco/24hr, Mohsen Oil Trkstp/

Exit	Services
191	Continued
	dsl/24hr, 🍴 Jack-in-the-Box, Peggy Sue's 50s Diner, Penny's Diner, 🛏 OakTree Inn, W 🅶 Shell/dsl/24hr, 76, 🅾 Calico GhostTown (3mi), KOA
189	Ft Irwin Rd
186	CA 58 W, to Bakersfield, W 🍴 Idle Spur Steaks
184	E Main, Barstow, Montera Rd (from eb), to I-40, E 🅶 76/dsl, 🍴 Grill It, Hollywood Subs, McDonald's, Mega Tom's Burgers, Panda Express, Popeye's, Starbucks, Straw Hat Pizza, 🛏 Best Western, Travelodge, S of I-40 🅶 Arco, 🅾 Walmart/McDonald's/auto, W 🅶 Chevron, Circle K, Shell/dsl, Thrifty/dsl, Valero, 🍴 Burger King, Carl's Jr, China Town Buffet, Coco's, Del Taco, Denny's, FireHouse Italian, IHOP, Jack-in-the-Box, Jenny's Grill, Little Caesars, LJ Silver, Sizzler, Taco Bell, Wienerschnitzel, 🛏 Astrobudget Motel, Best Motel, Budget Inn, CA Inn, Days Inn, Desert Inn, EconoLodge, Economy Inn, Motel 6, Quality Inn/rest, Ramada Inn, Rodeway Inn, Super 8, 🅾 AutoZone, $Tree, Family$, 99¢ Store, O'Reilly Parts, Radio Shack, U-Haul/LP, Von's Foods, vet
184a	I-40 E (from nb), **I-40 begins/ends**
183	CA 247, Barstow Rd, E 🅶 Circle K, Valero/dsl, 🍴 Pizza Hut, Jimenez Mexican, Subway, 🅾 $General, Rite Aid, W 🅶 Chevron, 🅾 🅷, Food4Less, Mojave River Valley Museum, st patrol
181	L St, W Main, Barstow, W 🅶 Chevron, Thrifty, 🍴 Foster's Freeze, 🛏 Best Value Inn, Holiday Inn Express, 🅾 Home Depot, NAPA, tires/towing
179	CA 58, to Bakersfield
178	Lenwood, to Barstow, E 🅶 Arco/dsl, Chevron, ⛽FLYING J/Denny's/dsl/24hr, Shell/dsl, 76/dsl, Valero, 🍴 Arby's, Big Boy, Burger King, Carl's Jr, Chili's, Chipotle Mexican, Del Taco, El Pollo Loco, In-N-Out, Jack-in-the-Box, Panda Express, Starbucks, Subway, Tommy's Burgers, 🛏 Comfort Suites, Country Inn&Suites, Hampton Inn, Holiday Inn Express, 🅾 Blue Beacon, Old Navy, Tanger Outlet/famous brands/food ct, W 🅶 Loves/Chester's/Godfather's/dsl/scales/24hr/@, 🅶 Subway/dsl/scales/24hr, TA/Shell/Country Fare/Subway/dsl/scales/24hr/@, 🍴 McDonald's, 🛏 Days Inn, 🅾 Zippy Lube, repair, truckwash
175	Outlet Ctr Dr, Sidewinder Rd
169	Hodge Rd
165	Wild Wash Rd
161	Dale Evans Pkwy, to Apple Valley
157	Stoddard Wells Rd, to Bell Mtn
154	Stoddard Wells Rd, to Bell Mtn, E 🅾 Shady Oasis Camping/LP, W 🅶 Mobil, 76/dsl, 🍴 Frankie's Diner, 🛏 Motel 6, Queens Motel
153.5mm	Mojave River

SANTA MONICA

BAKER

BARSTOW

LENWOOD

CA

🔼N INTERSTATE 15 CONT'D

V I C T O R V I L L E

H E S P E R I A

Exit	Services
153b	E St
153a	CA 18 E, D St, to Apple Valley, **E** 🅖 Arco, 🅞 🏥, repair, **W** 🅖 Arco/Subway/dsl
151b	Mojave Dr, Victorville, **E** 🅖 Gasmart/dsl, 🏠 Budget Inn, **W** 🅖 Valero/dsl, 🏠 Economy Inn, Sunset Inn
151a	La Paz Dr, Roy Rogers Dr, **E** 🅖 Chevron, Shell/dsl, 🍴 Bravo Burgers, Burger King, Carl's Jr, El Pollo Loco, HomeTown Buffet, IHOP, Jack-in-the-Box, McDonald's, Wendy's, 🅞 AutoZone, BigLots, Costco/gas, $General, $Tree, Food4Less, Harley-Davidson, 99¢ Store, Pepboys, Radio Shack, Rite Aid, Toyota/Scion, same as 144, **W** 🅖 Arco, 🍴 Carl's Jr, Domino's, Farmer Boys, Golden ChopStix, Hawaiian BBQ, In-N-Out, Panda Express, Papa John's, Starbucks, Subway, Taco Grande, 🅞 Americas Tire, Buick/GMC, Chrysler/Dodge/Jeep, Home Depot, Honda, Kia, Nissan, Stater Bros, Verizon, Walgreens, Win-Co Foods
150	CA 18 W, Palmdale Rd, Victorville, **E** 🍴 Baker's Drive-Thru, Burger King, Denny's, KFC, Richie's Diner, 🏠 Greentree Inn, Red Roof Inn, **W** 🅖 Arco, Circle K, 🍴 Coco's, Del Taco, House of Joy, La Casita Mexican, McDonald's, Pizza Hut, Raul's Mexican, Starbucks, Subway, Taco Bell, Tom's Rest., 🏠 Ambassador Inn, Budget Inn, Days Inn, 🅞🏥, Aamco, AutoZone, CVS Drug, Ford, Hyundai, Kamper's Korner RV, Mazda, Target, Town&Country Tire, vet
147	Bear Valley Rd, to Lucerne Valley, **0-2 mi E** 🅖 Arco, Chevron, Mobil, 76/Circle K/dsl, 🍴 Arby's, Baker's Drive-Thru, Blimpie, Burger King, Carl's Jr, Del Taco, Dragon Express, John's Pizza, KFC, Los Alazanes Mexican, Los Toritos, Marie Callender's, McDonald's, Panda Express, Red Robin, Starbucks, Steer'n Stein, Subs'n Salads, Tacos Mexico, Wienerschnitzel, 🏠 Comfort Suites, Day&Night Inn, EconoLodge, Extended Studio Hotel, Hilton Garden, La Quinta, Super 8, Travelodge, 🅞 Affordable RV Ctr, America's Tire, AutoZone, Firestone/auto, Food4Less, Home Depot, Michael's, O'Reilly Parts, Range RV, Rite Aid, Scandia Funpark, Tire Depot, Tire Guys, Vallarta Foods, Walmart/McDonald's/auto, vet, **W** 🅖 Arco, Chevron/dsl, 76/Circle K, Valero/dsl, 🍴 Applebee's, Archibald's Drive-Thru, Baja Fresh, Baskin-Robbins, Carino's, Chili's, Chipotle Mexican, ChuckeCheese, Del Taco, El Pollo Loco, El Tio Pepe Mexican, Farmer Boy's Rest., Freddy's Custard, Giuseppe's, Jack-in-the-Box, Little Caesar's, McDonald's, Mimi's Cafe, Olive Garden, Outback Steaks, Pancho Villa's, Red Lobster, RoadHouse Grill, Sonic, Starbucks, Subway, Tokyo Steaks, Wendy's, 🏠 Hawthorn Suites, 🅞 AAA, Albertson's, AT&T, Barnes&Noble, Best Buy, CVS Drug, Goodyear/auto, Hobby Lobby, JC Penney, Kohl's, Lowe's, Macy's, 99¢ Store, Petsmart, Rite Aid, Stater Bros., Verizon, Walgreens, Walmart, mall
143	Main St, to Hesperia, Phelan, **E** 🅖 Chevron/dsl, Shell/Popeye's/dsl, Valero/Alberto's, 🍴 Arby's, Burger King, Del Taco, Denny's, IHOP, In-N-Out, Jack-in-the-Box, Quiznos, Starbucks, 🏠 Courtyard, SpringHill Suites, **W** 🅖 Arco/dsl, 76/dsl, 🍴 Baker's Drive-thru, Farmer Boys, Golden Corral, Subway, 🏠 Holiday Inn Express, Motel 6, 🅞 Desert Willow RV Park, GNC, Jo-Ann Fabrics, Marshall's, Radio Shack, Ross, SuperTarget, Verizon, **Urgent Care**
141	US 395, Joshua St, Adelanto, **W** 🅖 Arco/dsl, 🍴/Wen

Exit	Services
141	Continued dy's/dsl/scales/24hr, 🍴 Outpost Café, 🅞 Zippy Lube, repair, RV supply ctr, truck/RV wash
138	Oak Hill Rd, **E** 🅖 Chevron/dsl, 🍴 Summit Inn Café, **W** 🅞 Oak Hills RV Village/LP
137mm	Cajon Summit, elevation 4260, **brake check sb**
131	CA 138, to Palmdale, Silverwood Lake, **E** 🅖 Chevron, 🍴 McDonald's, 🅞 Silverwood SRA, **W** 🅖 76/Circle K/Del Taco/LP, Shell/Subway/dsl/LP, 🏠 Best Western
130mm	**weigh sta both lanes,** elevation 3000
129	Cleghorn Rd
124	Kenwood Ave
123	I-215 S, to San Bernardino, **E** 🅖 Arco, to Glen Helen Park
122	Glen Helen Parkway
119	Sierra Ave, **W** 🅖 Arco/dsl, Chevron/dsl, Shell/Del Taco/dsl, Valero/dsl, 🍴 Jack-in-the-Box, McDonalds, 🅞 to Lytle Creek RA
116	Summit Ave, **E** 🅖 Chevron, 7-11, 🍴 Chili's, Coldstone, Del Taco, El Ranchero, Hawaiian BBQ, Jack-in-the-Box, Juice It Up, Little Beijing, Little Caesars, Panera Bread, Quiznos, Roundtable Pizza, Starbucks, Subway, Taco Bell, Wendy's, 🅞 CVS Drug, GNC, Kohl's, Marshall's, Michael's, Petsmart, Ross, Staples, Stater Bros, Target, Verizon
115b a	CA 210, Highland Ave, **E** to Lake Arrowhead
113	Base Line Rd, **E** 🅖 USA, 🍴 Denny's, Jack-in-the-Box, Logans Roadhouse, Pizza Hut, Rosa Maria's, Starbucks, 🏠 Comfort Inn
112	CA 66, Foothill Blvd, **E** 🅖 Chevron, 🍴 Asia Buffet, ClaimJumper, Golden Spoon, In-N-Out, Panda Express, Subway, Taco Bell, Tutti Frutti Yogurt, Wienerschnitzel, 🅞 $City, Food4Less, Jiffy Lube, Radio Shack, Walmart, **1-2 mi W** 🅖 Chevron/dsl, 76/dsl, 🍴 Baker's, Buffalo Wild Wings, Carino's, Cheesecake Factory, Chick-fil-A, Chipotle Mexican, Del Taco, Denny's, El Pollo Loco, El Torito, Flemings Steaks, The Hat Grill, Islamadora Fish Co, Jack-in-the-Box, Joe's Crab Shack, Johnny Rockets, Kings Fishouse, Lucille's BBQ, Old Spagetti Factory, Paisano's Rest., PF Chang's, Popeyes, Red Robin, Richie's Diner, Shakey's Pizza, Starbucks, TGIFriday's, Wendy's, 🏠 Sheraton 4 Points, 🅞 AT&T, AutoZone, Bass Pro Shops, Best Buy, Discount Tire, Fresh&Easy Mkt, Home Depot, JC Penney, Macy's, Office Depot, Sears Grand
110	4th St, **E** 🅖 Arco/dsl, 🍴 Baker's, Subway, **W** 🅖 Arco, Chevron/Alberto's Mexican/dsl, 76/dsl, Shell/dsl, 🍴 Applebee's, Arby's, Baja Fresh, Baskin-Robbins, BJ's Rest., Boston's, Burger King, Carl's Jr, Chevy's Mexican, Chick-fil-A, Chipotle, Chop Sticks, Chu Chinese, Coco's, Coldstone, Daphne's Greek, Del Taco, Denny's, El Pollo Loco, Famous Dave's BBQ, Fat Burger, Fuddruckers, Hooters, IHOP, In-N-Out, Jack-in-the-Box, Jamba Juice, Juice It Up, KFC, Krispy Kreme, Lazy Dog Cafe, McDonald's, Mkt Broiler, New City Buffet, NY Grill, Olive Garden, Oporto Chicken Burgers, Outback Steaks, Panera Bread, Quiznos, Rain Forest Cafe, Red Brick Pizza, Red Lobster, Rubio's, Sonic, Starbucks, Subway, Tokyo Tokyo, Tokyo Wako, Wendy's, Wienerschnitzel, Wing Place, 🏠 Ayre's Suites, Country Inn&Suites, Courtyard, Hampton Inn, Hilton Garden, Holiday Inn Express, Homewood Suites, Hyatt Place, TownePlace Suites, 🅞 America's Tire, Costco/gas, $Tree, JC Penney, Jo-Ann Fabrics, Kohl's, Marshall's, Ontario Mills Mall, Petsmart, Sam's Club/gas, Staples, Target, Tire Pros, Verizon

C U C A M O N G A

↑N INTERSTATE 15 CONT'D

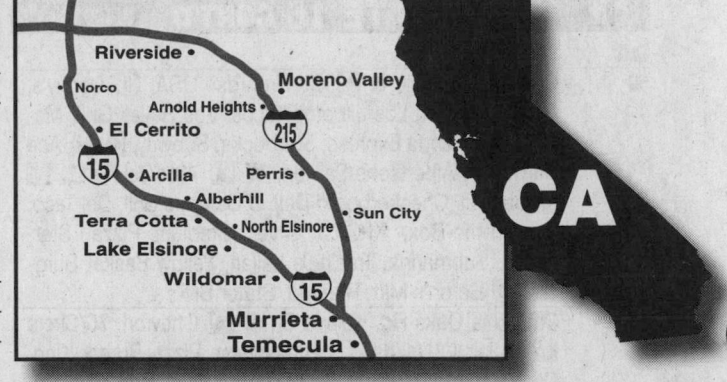

ONTARIO

Exit	Services
109b a	I-10, E to San Bernardino, W to LA
108	Jurupa St, E 📑 Chevron/dsl, 🍴 Burger King, Del Taco, El Gran Burrito, Starbucks, Subway, ⊙ Affordable RV, BMW, Chrysler/Dodge/Jeep, Family RV Ctr, Fiat, Honda, Hyundai, Lexus, Mazda, Mini, Nissan, Subaru, Toyota/Scion, Volvo, VW, W 📑 Arco, 🍴 Carl's Jr, ⊙ Ford, Kia, Scandia funpark
106	CA 60, E to Riverside, W to LA
105	Cantu-Galleano Ranch Rd
103	Limonite Ave, E 🍴 Alberto's Mexican, Carl's Jr, Del Taco, Denny's, 5 Guys Burgers, Hawaiian BBQ, Jamba Juice, Subway, ⊙ Lowe's, Michael's, PetCo, Ross, W 📑 Chevron, 🍴 Applebee's, Carino's, Coldstone, El Gran Burrito, Farmer Boys, Golden Chop Sticks, Golden Spoon, Johnny Rockets, L&L BBQ, Little Caesars, McDonald's, On-the-Border, Panda Express, Pick Up Stix, Quiznos, Red Brick Pizza, Starbucks, Subway, Taco Bell, Tasty Chinese, Tutti Frutti Yogurt, Wendy's, ⊙ AT&T, Best Buy, GNC, Home Depot, Kohl's, Nestle Tollhouse, Petsmart, Radio Shack, Ralph's Foods/gas, Staples, Target, TJ Maxx, Verizon, Vons Foods/gas, Walgreens, **Urgent Care**

NORCO

Exit	Services
100	6th St, Norco Dr, Old Town Norco, E 📑 Chevron, 76/dsl, 🍴 Jack-in-the-Box, McDonald's, Starbucks, ⊙ Rite Aid, W 📑 Arco, Valero/dsl, 🍴 Big Boy, Norco's Burgers, Senior Tacos, Wienerschnitzel, Zaky's Kabob, 🛏 Knights Inn, ⊙ Brake Masters, Jiffy Lube, USPO, vet
98	2nd St, W 📑 Mobil, Shell/dsl, Thrifty, 🍴 Baja Fish Tacos, Burger Basket, Burger King, Carl's Jr, Del Taco, Domino's, In-N-Out, Magic Wok, Pizza Hut, Polly's Cafe, Sizzler, Subway, ⊙ Ace Hardware, America's Tire, $Tree, Mazda, Norco Tires, 7-11, Stater Bros
97	Yuma Dr, Hidden Valley Pkwy, E 📑 7-11, 🍴 Baja Fresh, Chick-fil-A, Fat Burger, Hot Dog Shoppe, Shogun Japanese, Starbucks, Subway, ⊙ Kohl's, Stater Bros, Walgreens, W 📑 Chevron, 76/dsl, Shell/dsl, 🍴 Alberto's Mexican, Burger City Grill, Carl's Jr, Chipotle, DQ, Denny's, Domino's, 5 Guys Burgers, Hawaiian BBQ, Hickory Joe's BBQ, Jamba Juice, Jack-in-the-Box, Jersey Mikes, KFC, Magic Wok, McDonald's, Miguel's Jr, Papa John's, Pizza Hut/Taco Bell, Rodrigo's Mexican, Rubio's, Starbucks, 🛏 Hampton Inn, Howard Johnson Express, ⊙ Albertson's/Sav-On, America's Tire, AT&T, AutoZone, BigLots, GNC, K-Mart, O'Reilly Parts, Radio Shack, Staples, Target, Verizon, Walgreens
96b a	CA 91, to Riverside beaches
95	Magnolia Ave, E 📑 Chevron/Jack-in-the-Box/dsl, 🍴 Islands Burgers, Lonestar Steaks, Shamrock's Grill, 🛏 Residence Inn, ⊙ AAA, Lowe's, Office Depot, W 📑 Mobil/Circle K, Shell, 🍴 Baskin-Robbins, Burger King, Coco's, Golden China, Jersey's Pizza, Little Caesars, McDonald's, Sizzler, Subway, 🛏 Holiday Inn Express, ⊙ AT&T, CVS Drug, $Tree, El Tapatio Mkt, O'Reilly Parts, Rite Aid, Stater Bros Foods
93	Ontario Ave, to El Cerrito, E 📑 Shell/dsl, 🍴 Sombrero Mexican, Starbucks, ⊙ Mtn View Tire, vet, W 📑 Arco, Chevron, 76/Circle K, 🍴 Chopstix, Denny's, Eatza Pizza, El Pollo Loco, Hawaiian BBQ, In-N-Out, Jack-in-the-Box, Juice It Up, KFC, Magic Wok, McDonald's, Miguel's Jr, Papa John's, Porky's Pizza, Quiznos, Rubio's, Subway, Taco Bell, Tommy's Burgers, Wienerschnitzel, 🍴 Sprin

EL CERRITO

Exit	Services
93	Continued gHill Suites, ⊙ Albertson's/Sav-On, America's Tire, AutoZone, CVS Drug, Fresh&Easy Mkt, Home Depot, Long's Drug, Radio Shack, Sam's Club/gas, USPO, Walmart, vet
92	El Cerrito Rd
91	Cajalco Rd, E 🍴 BJ's Grill, Bubba Jack's Roadhouse, Buffalo Wild Wings, Chick-fil-A, Chili's, 5 Guys Burgers, Jamba Juice, King's Fish House, Macaroni Grill, Panera Bread, Starbucks, Wendy's, ⊙ AT&T, Barnes&Noble, Best Buy, Kohl's, Marshall's, Michael's, Old Navy, PetCo, Ross, See's Candies, Staples, Target, World Mkt, W 📑 Mobil/dsl, 🍴 Jack-in-the-Box, Juice It Up, NY Pizza, Subway, ⊙ Stater Bros, vet
90	Weirick Rd, Dos Lagos Dr, E 📑 Arco/dsl, 🍴 Citrus City Grille, Miguel's, Tap's Rest., TGIFriday's, Wood Ranch BBQ, ⊙ 7 Oaks Gen Store, Trader Joe's
88	Temescal Cyn Rd, Glen Ivy, E 📑 Shell, W 📑 Arco/dsl, 🍴 Carl's Jr, Tom's Farms/BBQ
85	Indian Truck Trail, W 🍴 Pizza Hut, Starbucks, Subway, ⊙ Von's Foods/dsl, CVS Drug
81	Lake St
78	Nichols Rd, W 📑 Arco/dsl, ⊙ Outlets/famous brands

LAKE ELSINORE

Exit	Services
77	CA 74, Central Ave, Lake Elsinore, E 📑 Arco, Chevron, Mobil/Circle K/dsl, 🍴 Archibald's, Burger King, Chili's, Del Taco, Douglas Burgers, Hawaiian BBQ, Juice It Up, Panda Express, Submarina, Taco Del Mar, Tom's Chili-Burgers, Wendy's, ⊙ AT&T, Costco/gas, $Tree, Lowe's, Petsmart, Staples, Valvoline, W 🍴 El Pollo Loco, Farmer Boys, Golden Chop Stix, IHOP, McDonald's, Papa John's, Starbucks, Subway, Wienerschnitzel, ⊙ Home Depot, 99¢ Store, PetCo, Target, Verizon, Walgreens
75	Main St, Lake Elsinore, W 📑 Main St Gas/dsl, 🍴 Gina's Rest., ⊙ Circle K, tires/repair
73	Railroad Cyn Rd, to Lake Elsinore, E 📑 Shell/Circle K/dsl, 76/7-11, 🍴 Alberto's Mexican, Denny's, El Pollo Loco, In-N-Out, KFC, Peony Chinese, Starbucks, 🛏 Holiday Inn Express, ⊙ Albertson's, GNC, Jiffy Lube, O'Reilly Parts, Verizon, Von's Foods, Walmart/McDonald's, **Urgent Care**, vet, W 📑 Arco, Chevron, Mobil/Circle K/dsl, 🍴 Annie's Cafe, Cafe China, Carl's Jr, Coco's, Del Taco, Don Jose's Mexican, King Kabob, Kokoro Japanese, Los Gallos Mexican, McDonald's, My Buddies Pizza, Pizza Hut, Sizzler, Subway, Taco Bell, Vincenzo's, 🛏 Best Western Lake Elsinore, Quality Inn, Travel Inn, ⊙ AutoZone, BigLots, Buick/GMC, Chevrolet, CVS Drug, Express Tire/auto, Firestone/auto, Ford, NAPA, Radio Shack, Rite Aid, 7-11, Stater Bro's, Walgreens, vet
71	Bundy Cyn Rd, W 📑 Arco, 🍴 Jack-in-the-Box
69	Baxter Rd, E 🍴 Pizza Factory

📵 = gas 🍴 = food 🏠 = lodging 🅞 = other 🅟 = rest stop   Copyright 2014 - The Next Exit ®

⬆N INTERSTATE 15 CONT'D

Exit	Services
68	Clinton Keith Rd, **E** 📵 Chevron/dsl, USA, 🍴 Denny's, Golden Spoon, Los Jilbetos Tacos, Los Reyes Grill, McDonald's, Panda Express, Starbucks, Subway, 🅞🏠 Ace Hardware, Albertsons/Sav-on, **W** 📵 Arco/dsl, 7-11, 🍴 Arriba Grill, Checkerboard Deli, D'Canter's Grill, Del Taco, Jack-in-the-Box, KFC/LJ Silver, Stadium Pizza, Starbucks, Submarina, Tresino's Italian, Yellow Basket Burgers, 🅞 Baron's Mkt, Rite Aid, Stater Bro's
65	California Oaks Rd, Kalmia St, **E** 📵 Chevron, 76/Circle K/dsl, Shell/7-11/dsl, 🍴 Big Cheese Pizza, Burger King, Carl's Jr, Chili's, Chiptole Mexican, DQ, Jade Chinese, Jamba Juice, Jersey's, Jimenez Mexican, KFC, Little Caesars, Papa John's, Starbucks, Subway, Wings'N Things, 🏠 Comfort Inn, 🅞 Albertson's/Sav-On, AutoZone, Express Tire, $Tree, O'Reilly Parts, Radio Shack, Ralphs, Rite Aid, Target, Tuesday Morning, Walgreens, vet, **W** 📵 Arco/dsl, Chevron, 🍴 Applebee's, Carrow's, Chick-fil-A, Farmer Boys, Jack-in-the-Box, Juice it Up, Pick Up Stix, Sizzlin Steer, Subway, Taco Bell, 🅞 America's Tire, Giant RV Ctr, Kohl's, Lowe's, Office Depot, PetCo, Verizon, fun ctr
64	Murrieta Hot Springs Rd, to I-215, **E** 📵 7-11, Shell/dsl, 🍴 Alberto's Mexican, Buffalo Wild Wings, Carl's Jr, El Pollo Loco, Hungry Bull, Richie's Diner, Rubio's, Sizzler, Starbucks, Wendy's, 🅞 Ralph's Foods, Rite Aid, Ross, Sam's Club/gas, Walgreens, **W** 📵 7-11, Shell/Popeye's/dsl, 🍴 Arby's, Chuy's, Coldstone, Denny's, IHOP, Jersey Mike's Subs, McDonald's, Los Jilbertos, Panda Express, Starbucks, Subway, Tom's Burgers, Wienerschnitzel, 🅞 AAA, American Tire Depot, AT&T, Best Buy, BigLots, Home Depot, 99¢ Store, Petsmart, Staples, Walmart/McDonald's
63	I-215 N (from nb), to Riverside
61	CA 79 N, Winchester Rd, **E** 📵 Chevron, 76/dsl, 🍴 Baja Fresh, Baskin-Robbins/Togo's, BJ's Rest., Burger King, CA Pizza Kitchen, Carl's Jr, Chick-fil-A, Chipotle Mexican, Coldstone, Del Taco, El Torito, 5 Guys Burgers, Harry's Grill, Hometown Buffet, Islands Burgers, Jamba Juice, Lucille's BBQ, Macaroni Grill, McDonald's, Mimi's Cafe, Ming's, Olive Garden, On-the-Border, Outback Steaks, Panda Express, Panera Bread, PF Chang's, Pick Up Stix, Red Lobster, Red Robin, Roadhouse Grill, Shakey's Pizza, Shogun Chinese, Souplantation, Starbucks, Sub City, Subway, Taco Bell, TGIFriday's, Tilted Kilt, Wahoo's, Wok Inn, Yellow Basket Hamburgers, 🅞 America's Tire, AT&T, AutoZone, Barnes&Noble, Big O Tire, Costco/gas, CVS Drug, $Tree, Express Tire, Food4Less, GNC, Hobby Lobby, JC Penney, Jo-Ann Fabrics, K-Mart, Lowe's, Macy's, Office Depot, Old Navy, 99¢ Store, PepBoys, PetCo, Radio Shack, Ramona Tire, Sears/auto, See's Candies, Sprouts Mkt, TJ Maxx, Trader Joe's, Verizon, WinCo Foods, World Mkt, **W** 📵 Arco, Chevron/dsl, 🍴 Arby's, Banzai Japanese, Del Taco, El Pollo Loco, Farmer Boys, In-N-Out, Jack-in-the-Box, Serrano's Grill, Simply Sharon's Rest., Starbucks, Subway, Super China, Tacos El Gallo, Vail Ranch Steakhouse, Wendy's, 🏠 Best Western, Extended Stay America, Fairfield Inn, Holiday Inn Express, La Quinta, Quality Inn, 🅞 Hyundai, NAPA, Richardson's RV Ctr, st patrol, tires/repair
59	Rancho California Rd, **E** 📵 Arco, Mobil/Circle K/dsl, Shell/dsl, 🍴 Black Angus, Chili's, ClaimJumper, Del

Exit	Services
59	Continued Taco, Golden Spoon, Little Caesars, Marie Callender's, Pat&Oscar's Rest., Peony Chinese, Pizza Hut, RoundTable Pizza, Rubio's, Starbucks, Subway, 🏠 Embassy Suites, 🅞 BigLots, CVS Drug, Michael's, Target, Verizon, Von's Foods, **Urgent Care**, vet, **W** 📵 Chevron, 76/Circle K/dsl, 🍴 Alberto's Mexican, Denny's, McDonald's, Mr Kabob Grill, Penfold's Cafe, Rosa's Café, Starbucks, Vince's Spaghetti, 🏠 Hampton Inn, Motel 6, Rancho California Inn, Rodeway Inn, SpringHill Suites, 🅞 USPO, to Old Town Temecula
58	CA 79 S, to Indio, Temecula, **E** 📵 Mobil/Circle K/dsl, Valero/Circle K/dsl, 🍴 Carl's Jr, Del Taco, Domino's, Francesca's Italian, Golden Bowl Asian, In-N-Out, Starbucks, other, Ace Hardware, America's Tire, CVS Drug, 7-11, Valvoline, **W** 📵 Arco, Shell/dsl, 🍴 Baskin-Robbins, Eldorado Mexican, Hungry Howie's, Leinzo Charro Mexican, Wienerschnitzel, 🏠 Ramada Inn, 🅞 Express Tire, HarleyDavidson
55mm	**check sta nb**
54	**Rainbow Valley Blvd, 2 mi E** gas, food, **W CA Insp Sta**
51	Mission Rd, to Fallbrook, **W** 🏠
46	CA 76, to Oceanside, Pala, **E** 🅞 RV camp, **W** 📵 Mobil/Circle K, 🏠 La Estancia Inn, 🅞 Palamesa Mkt
44mm	San Luis Rey River
43	Old Hwy 395
41	Gopher Canyon Rd, Old Castle Rd, **1 mi E** 🏠 Welk Resort, 🅞 RV camping, gas
37	Deer Springs Rd, Mountain Meadow Rd, **W** 📵 Arco
34	Centre City Pkwy (from sb)
33	El Norte Pkwy, **E** 📵 Arco, Shell/dsl, 🍴 Arby's, DQ, IHOP, Starbucks, 🏠 Best Western, 🅞 CVS Drug, Express Tire/auto repair, Radio Shack, Von's Foods, RV Resort, vet, **W** 📵 76/dsl/repair, Circle K, 🍴 Jack-in-the-Box, Killer Pizza, Subway, Wendy's, 🅞 Von's Foods, vet
32	CA 78, to Oceanside
31	Valley Pkwy, **E** 📵 Arco, 🍴 Chili's, ChuckeCheese, Cocina del Pharro, McDonald's, Olive Garden, Panda Express, Rock'N Jenny's Subs, Thai Kitchen, 🅞🏠 Barnes&Noble, Michael's, Meineke, PetCo, **Urgent Care**, **W** 📵 Express, 🍴 Applebee's, Burger King, Carl's Jr, Chipotle Mexican, Coco's, Del Taco, El Pollo Loco, 5 Guys Burgers, In-N-Out, Jamba Juice, Mike's BBQ, Panera Bread, Soup Plantation, Starbucks, Subway, Wendy's, 🏠 Comfort Inn, Holiday Inn Express, 🅞 Albertson's, AT&T, BigLots, Dick's, Dodge, Home Depot, Lexus, Long's Drug, Ross, 7-11, Staples, Target, TJ Maxx, Verizon, World Mkt
30	9th Ave, Auto Parkway, **E** 🅞 Infiniti, Mercedes, **W** same as 31
29	Felicita Rd
28	Centre City Pkwy (from nb, no return), **E** 🍴 Center City Café, 🏠 EconoLodge, 🅞 vet
27	Via Rancho Pkwy, to Escondido, **E** 📵 Chevron/dsl, Shell, 🍴 BJ's Rest., Macaroni Grill, On-the-Border, Panera Bread, 🅞 JC Penney, Macy's, Nordstrom, Sears/auto, San Diego Animal Park, Target, **W** 📵 Shell/Quiznos/dsl, 🍴 McDonald's, Starbucks, Subway, 🅞 Verizon
26	W Bernardo Dr, to Highland Valley Rd, Palmerado Rd
24	Rancho Bernardo Rd, to Lake Poway, **E** 📵 Arco, Mobil/Circle K, 🍴 Pizza Hut, Soup Plantation, Starbucks, Stirfresh, Sub Marina, Subway, Taco Shop, 🏠 Hilton Garden, 🅞 AT&T, Barons Mkt, Von's Foods, **W** 📵 76/Circle K,

CA

M U R R I E T A

T E M E C U L A

E S C O N D I D O

🔼 INTERSTATE 15 CONT'D

Exit	Services
24	Continued
	Shell/repair, 🅕 Elephant Bar Rest., Hooters, Starbucks, 🅛 Holiday Inn Express, Radisson
23	Bernardo Ctr Dr, **E** 🅖 Chevron, 🅕 Burger King, Carl's Jr, Coco's, Denny's, Jack-in-the-Box, Little Caesars, Panda Buffet, Quiznos, Robeks Juice, RoundTable Pizza, Rubio's, 🅞 CVS Drug, Express Tire/auto, Firestone/auto, Radio Shack, vet
22	Camino del Norte
21	Carmel Mtn Rd, **E** 🅖 Chevron, Shell/dsl, 🅕 Baskin-Robbins, Boston Mkt, CA Pizza Kitchen, Carl's Jr, Cheeburger Cheeburger, Chick-fil-A, China Fun, Chipotle Mexican, ClaimJumper, El Pollo Loco, Habit Burgers, In-N-Out, Islands Burgers, Jamba Juice, Joey's BBQ, Marie Callender's, McDonald's, Olive Garden, Quiznos, Panda Express, Panera Bread, Pat&Oscar's, Rubio's, Sombrero Mexican, Subway, Taco Bell, TGIFriday's, Wendy's, 🅛 Residence Inn, 🅞 AT&T, Barnes&Noble, Best Buy, Costco, GNC, Home Depot, Marshall's, Michael's, PetCo, Radio Shack, Ralph's Foods, Rite Aid, Ross, Sears Outlet, Sprouts Mkt, Staples, Trader Joe's, Valvoline, Verizon, USPO, **W** 🅖 Chevron, 🅕 Jack-in-the-Box, Starbucks, 🅞 Albertson's, Big O Tire, Office Depot, 7-11
19	CA 56 W, Ted Williams Pkwy
18	Rancho Penasquitos Blvd, Poway Rd, **E** 🅖 Arco, 🅕 Alvero's Mexican, Papa John's, 🅞 AAA, **W** 🅖 Mobil/dsl, 76/dsl, 🅕 IHOP, McDonald's, Mi Ranchito Mexican, MXN Cafe, NY Pizza, Starbucks, Subway, 🅛 La Quinta, 🅞 7-11
17	Mercy Rd, Scripps Poway Pkwy, **E** 🅖 USA/dsl, 🅕 Chili's, Nugent's Fire Grille, Wendy's, 🅛 Residence Inn, SpringHill Suites, **W** 🅖 Chevron, 🅕 KFC, Que Pasa Mexican, Starbucks
16	Mira Mesa Blvd, to Lake Miramar, **E** 🅕 Bruski Burgers, ChuckeCheese, Denny's, Filippi's Pizza, Golden Crown Chinese, Lucio's Mexican, Pizza Hut, Shozen BBQ, Sombrero Mexican, 🅛 Comfort Suites, Holiday Inn Express, 🅞 Curves, Trader Joe's, USPO, **W** 🅖 Arco, Shell, 🅕 Applebee's, Arby's, Buca Italian, Coldstone, El Patron, In-N-Out, Islands Burgers, Jack-in-the-Box, Jamba Juice, Jersey Mike's Subs, McDonald's, Mimi's Café, MXN Mexican, On the Border, Pat&Oscar's Rest., Panera Bread, Pick Up Stix, Popeye's, Rubio's, Starbucks, Subway, 🅞 Albertson's/Sav-On, AT&T, AutoZone, Barnes&Noble, Best Buy, BigLots, CVS Drug, Discount Tire, GNC, Home Depot, Old Navy, Ralph's Foods, Rite Aid, Ross, Tuesday Morning, USPO
15	Carroll Canyon Rd, to Miramar College, **E** 🅕 Carl's Jr, Subway
14	Pomerado Rd, Miramar Rd, **W** 🅖 Arco/dsl, Chevron/dsl, Mobil, Shell/dsl, 🅕 Carl's Jr, Chin's Rest., IHOP, Rice King, Subway, 🅛 Best Western, Holiday Inn, Quality Inn, 🅞 Audi/Porsche, Land Rover, aviation museum, vet
13	Miramar Way, US Naval Air Station
12	CA 163 S (from sb), to San Diego
11	to CA 52
10	Clairemont Mesa Blvd, **W** 🅕 Boll Weevil Rest., Carl's Jr, CK Mediterranean, Giovanni's Pizza, Jack-in-the-Box, La Salsa, McDonald's, Mr. Chick's Rest., Palomino's Mexican, Panda Express, Quiznos, Robeks, Rubio's, Spice

10	Continued
	House Cafe, Starbucks, Subway, Sunny Donuts, Taco Bell, Togo's, Wendy's, 🅞 7-11, vet
9	CA 274, Balboa Ave
8	Aero Dr, **W** 🅖 Arco, Chevron, 7-11, 🅕 Baskin-Robbins/Togo's, Jack-in-the-Box, McDonald's, Papa John's, Pick Up Stix, Rubio's, Sizzler, SmashBurger, Starbucks, Submarina, Subway, Taco Bell, 🅛 Holiday Inn, 🅞 AT&T, $Tree, Express Tire/auto, Fry's Electronics, Petsmart, Radio Shack, Verizon, Von's Foods, Walmart/McDonald's
7b	Friars Rd W, **W** 🅕 Coldstone, Dragon Chinese, IHOP, Islands Burgers, Luna Grill, McDonald's, Oggi's Pizza, Playa Grill, Starbucks, Subway, 🅞 Costco/gas, Lowe's, San Diego Stadium
7a	Friars Rd E
6b	I-8, E to El Centro, W to beaches
6a	Adams Ave, downtown
5b	El Cajon Blvd, **E** 🅖 Pearson/dsl/E85/NG, 🅕 Subway, 🅞 Carquest, **W** 🅖 Chevron/dsl, United Oil, 🅕 Church's, 🅞 PepBoys
5a	University Ave, **E** 🅖 Chevron/dsl, 🅕 Burger King, Jack-in-the-Box
3	I-805, N to I-5, S to San Ysidro
2b	(2c from nb) CA 94 W, downtown
2a	Market St, downtown
1c	National Ave, Ocean View Blvd
1b	(from sb) I-5 S, to Chula Vista
1a	(from sb) I-5 N. **I-15 begins/ends on I-5**

🔼 INTERSTATE 40

Exit	Services
155	California/Arizona state line, Colorado River, Pacific/Mountain time zone
153	Park Moabi Rd, to Rte 66, **N** boating, camping
149mm	**insp both lanes**
148	5 Mile Rd, to Topock, Rte 66 (from eb)
144	US 95 S, E Broadway, Needles, **N** 🅖 Chevron/dsl, Mobil, Shell/dsl/LP, 🅕 Domino's, 🅞 Basha's Foods, Harris Repair/towing, Rite Aid, **S** 🅛 Best Value Inn, 🅞 $Tree, Stout Tires/repair
142	J St, Needles, **N** 🅖 76, Valero/dsl, 🅕 Jack-in-the-Box, McDonald's, 🅛 Travelers Inn, 🅞 Big O Tire, NAPA, **S** 🅕 Denny's, 🅛 Days Inn, Motel 6, 🅞 🅗
141	W Broadway, River Rd, Needles, **N** 🅕 River City Pizza, 🅛 Best Motel, Desert Mirage Inn, River Valley Motel, **S** 🅖 Chevron/dsl, Mobil/dsl, Shell/DQ/dsl, 🅕 Carl's Jr, China Garden, River Cafe, Taco Bell, Wagon Wheel Rest., 🅛 Best Western, Budget Inn, Needles Inn, Relax Inn, Rio Del Sol Inn, 🅞 auto/RV/tire/repair

(side labels: CARMEL MTN, MIRA MESA, SAN DIEGO AREA, NEEDLES)

🅖 = gas 🍴 = food 🛌 = lodging 🅞 = other 🅡ₛ = rest stop   Copyright 2014 - The Next Exit ®

⬆️🅔 INTERSTATE 40 CONT'D

Exit	Services
139	River Rd Cutoff (from eb), **N** rec area, Hist Rte 66, 🅞 KOA, Desert View RV Park
133	US 95 N, to Searchlight, to Rte 66
120	Water Rd
115	Mountain Springs Rd, High Springs Summit, elev 2770
107	Goffs Rd, Essex, **N** gas/dsl/food, Hist Rte 66
106mm	🅡ₛ **both lanes, full ♿ facilities,** 🚻, 🛇, **litter barrels, pet-walk**
100	Essex Rd, Essex, **N** to Providence Mtn SP, Mitchell Caverns
78	Kelbaker Rd, to Amboy, E Mojave Nat Preserve, Kelso, **S** Hist Rte 66, 🅞 RV camping (14mi)
50	Ludlow, **N** 🅖 76/DQ, **S** 🅖 Chevron/dsl, 🍴 Ludlow Cafe, 🛌 Ludlow Motel
33	Hector Rd, to Hist Rte 66
28mm	🅡ₛ **both lanes, full ♿ facilities,** 🚻, 🛇, **litter barrels, pet-walk**
23	Ft Cady Rd, to Newberry Spgs, **S** 🅞 Newberry Mtn RV Park, Twins Lake RV Park (8mi)
18	Newberry Springs, **S** 🅖 Chevron/Subway/dsl/LP
12	Barstow-Daggett ✈️, **N** 🅞
7	Daggett, **N** 🅞 RV camping (2mi), to Calico Ghost Town
5	Nebo St (from eb), to Hist Rte 66
2	USMC Logistics Base, **N** 🛌 Pennywise Inn
1	E Main St, Montara Rd, Barstow, **N** 🅖 76/dsl, 🍴 Grill It, Hollywood Subs, McDonald's, Panda Express, Popeye's, Starbucks, Tom's Burgers, 🛌 Best Western, Travelodge, **1 mi N** 🅖 Chevron, Circle K, Shell/dsl, Thrifty/dsl, Valero, 🍴 Burger King, Carl's Jr, China Town Buffet, Coco's, Del Taco, Denny's, FireHouse Italian, IHOP, Jack-in-the-Box, Jenny's Grill, Little Caesars, LJ Silver, Sizzler, Taco Bell, Wienerschnitzel, 🛌 Astrobudget Motel, Best Motel, Budget Inn, CA Inn, Days Inn, Desert Inn, EconoLodge, Economy Inn, Motel 6, Quality Inn/rest, Ramada Inn, Rodeway Inn, Super 8, 🅞 AutoZone, $Tree, Family$, 99¢ent Store, O'Reilly Parts, Radio Shack, U-Haul/LP, Von's Foods, vet, **S** 🅖 Arco, 🅞 Walmart/McDonald's/auto
0mm	**I-40 begins/ends on I-15 in Barstow**

⬆️🅔 INTERSTATE 80

Exit	Services
208	California/Nevada state line
201	Farad
199	Floristan
194	Hirschdale Rd, **N** to Boca Dam, Stampede Dam, **S** RV Park
191mm	(from wb) **weigh sta, inspection sta**
190	Overland Trail
188	CA 89 N, CA 267, to N Shore Lake Tahoe, **N** 🅞 USFS, **S** same as 186
186	Central Truckee (no eb return), **S** 🅖 Beacon, 76, 🍴 Best Pies Pizzeria, Burger Me, Casa Baeza Mexican, El Toro Bravo Mexican, Wagon Train Café, 🛌 Hilltop Lodge, Truckee Hotel
185	CA 89 S, to N Lake Tahoe, **N** 🍴 DQ, Jiffy's Pizza, Nik'n Willies Pizza, Panda Express, Port of Subs, RoundTable Pizza, Starbucks, Zano's Pizza, 🅞 🏥 Urgent Care, Ace Hardware, NAPA, New Moon Natural Foods, Radio Shack, Rite Aid, Safeway Foods, 7-11, hwy patrol, **S** 🅖 Shell/dsl, 🍴 Bill's Rotisseire, KFC, McDonald's, Subway,
185	Continued Village Pizzaria, 🅞 CVS Drug, SaveMart Foods, auto repair, to Squaw Valley, RV camping
184	Donner Pass Rd, Truckee, **N** 🅖 Shell/dsl, 🍴 La Bamba Mexican, Pizza Shack, Truckee Pizza, 🛌 Sunset Inn, **S** 🅖 Chevron/dsl, 76, 🍴 Taco Bell, 🛌 Truckee Donner Lodge, 🅞 chain service, to Donner SP, RV camp/dump
181mm	vista point both lanes
180	Donner Lake (from wb), **S** 🛌 Donner Lake Village Resort
177mm	Donner Summit, elev 7239, 🅡ₛ **both lanes, full ♿ facilities, view area,** 🚻, 🛇, **litter barrels, petwalk**
176	Castle Park, Boreal Ridge Rd, **S** 🛌 Boreal Inn/rest., 🅞 Pacific Crest Trailhead, skiing
174	Soda Springs, Norden, **S** 🅖 Beacon/dsl, 🍴 Summit Rest., 🛌 Donner Summit Lodge, 🅞 chain services
171	Kingvale, **S** 🅖 Shell
168	Rainbow Rd, to Big Bend, **S** 🛌 Rainbow Lodge/rest., 🅞 RV camping
166	Big Bend (from eb)
165	Cisco Grove, **N** 🅞 RV camp/dump, skiing, snowmobiling, **S** 🅖 Valero/24hr, 🅞 chain services
164	Eagle Lakes Rd
161	CA 20 W, to Nevada City, Grass Valley
160	Yuba Gap, **S** 🅞 snowpark, 🚻, 🛇, boating, camping, skiing
158	Laing Rd, **S** 🛌 Sierra Woods Lodge/café
157mm	**brake check area, wb**
158a	Emigrant Gap (from eb), **S** 🛌 Sierra Woods Lodge/café
156	Nyack Rd, Emigrant Gap, **S** 🅖 Shell/Burger King/dsl, 🍴 Nyack Café
156mm	brake check area
155	Blue Canyon
150	Drum Forebay
148b	Baxter, **N** 🅞 RV camping, chainup services, food, 🚻
148a	Crystal Springs
146	Alta
145	Dutch Flat, **N** 🍴 Monte Vista Rest., **S** 🅖 Tesoro/dsl, 🅞 RV camping, chainup services, hwy patrol
144	Gold Run (from wb), **N** gas/dsl, food, 🚻, chainup
143mm	🅡ₛ **both lanes, full ♿ facilities,** 🚻, 🛇, **litter barrels, pet-walk**
143	Magra Rd, Gold Run, **N** chainup services
140	Magra Rd, Rollins Lake Rd, Secret Town Rd
139	Rollins Lake Road (from wb) RV camping
135	CA 174, to Grass Valley, Colfax, **N** 🅖 76/dsl, 🍴 Colfax Max Burgers, McDonald's, Pizza Factory, Starbucks, Taco Bell, TJ's Roadhouse, 🛌 Colfax Motel, 🅞 1Buck+, Sierra Mkt Foods, NAPA, **S** 🅖 Chevron/dsl, Valero/dsl, 🍴 Shang Garden Chinese, Subway, 🅞 Best Hardware
133	Canyon Way, to Colfax, **S** 🍴 Dine'n Dash Cafe, 🅞 Chevrolet, Plaza Tire
131	Cross Rd, to Weimar
130	W Paoli Lane, to Weimar, **S** 🅖 Weimar Store/dsl
129	Heather Glen, elev 2000 ft
128	Applegate, **N** 🅖 Applegate Gas/dsl/LP, 🅞 chainup services
125	Clipper Gap, Meadow Vista, **N** Oliver's Gas
124	Dry Creek Rd
123	Bell Rd
122	Foresthill Rd, Ravine Rd, Bowman, **N** 🅞 RV camping/dump, **S** 🍴 Burger King, La Bonte's Rest., Sizzler, Starbucks, Subway, TioPepe Mexican, 🛌 Best Western, Quality Inn, same as 121

Side tabs: CA, BARSTOW, TRUCKEE, TRUCKEE, COLFAX

INTERSTATE 80 CONT'D

Exit	Services
A U B U R N 121	(from eb)Lincolnway, Auburn, **N** 🅖 Arco, Flyers/dsl, Valero, 🍴 Denny's, JimBoy's Tacos, Maria's Tacos, Taco Bell, Wienerschnitzel, 🏨 Comfort Inn, Foothills Motel, Motel 6, Super 8, **S** 🅖 Arco, Beacon/dsl, Chevron/dsl, Gas&Shop, Shell/dsl, 🍴 Burger King, Burrito Shop, Carl's Jr, Hawaiian BBQ, Jack-in-the-Box, Joe Caribe Bistro, KFC, La Bonte's Rest., McDonald's, Pete's Grill, Sierra Grill, Sizzler, Starbucks, Subway, 🏨 Best Western, Quality Inn, 🅞 Ikeda's Mkt, Raley's Foods, Verizon
120	Russell Ave (from wb), to Lincolnway from eb, same as 121
119c	Elm Ave, Auburn, **N** 🅖 76/dsl, Shell, 🍴 Foster's, 🏨 Holiday Inn, 🅞 CVS Drug, Grocery Outlet, Rite Aid, SaveMart Foods, Staples, Verizon
119b	CA 49, to Grass Valley, Auburn, **N** 🅖 76, Shell, 🍴 In-N-Out, 🏨 Holiday Inn, 🅞 Staples
119a	Maple St, Nevada St, Old Town Auburn, **S** 🅖 Valero, 🍴 Mary Belle's, Tiopete Mexican
118	Ophir Rd (from wb)
116	CA 193, to Lincoln, **S** 🅞 truck repair
115	Indian Hill Rd, Newcastle, **N** 🅞 transmissions, **S** 🅖 Flyers/dsl, Valero/dsl, 🍴 Denny's, CHP
112	Penryn, **N** 🅖 76/dsl, Valero/Subway/dsl, 🍴 Cattle Baron's Cafe, Houston's Steaks
110	Horseshoe Bar Rd, to Loomis, **N** 🍴 Burger King, RoundTable Pizza, Starbucks, Taco Bell, 🅞 Raley's Food
109	Sierra College Blvd, **N** 🅖 Chevron/McDonald's/dsl, 7-11, 🍴 Carl's Jr, 🅞 Camping World RV Ctr, Eads RV Ctr
R O C K L I N 108	Rocklin Rd, **N** 🅖 Valero, 🍴 Adalberto's Mexican, A&W/KFC, Arby's, Baskin-Robbins, Denny's, Golden Dragon, Jack-in-the-Box, Jamba Juice, Papa Murphy's, Quiznos, RoundTable Pizza, Starbucks, Subway, Taco Bell, 🏨 Days Inn, Heritage Inn, Howard Johnson, 🅞 CVS Drug, GNC, Land Rover, Mercedes, Porsche, Radio Shack, Safeway Foods, **S** 🅖 Arco, 🍴 Little Caesar's, 🏨 Rocklin Park Hotel, 🅞 vet
106	CA 65, to Lincoln, Marysville, **1 mi N on Stanford Ranch Rd** 🅖 Arco, Chevron, 76, Shell, 🍴 Applebee's, BJ's Rest, Buca Italian, Carl's Jr, Cheesecake Factory, IHOP, Jack-in-the-Box, KFC, McDonald's, Mimi's Cafe, Olive Garden, On-the-Border, PF Changs, Red Robin, Subway, 🏨 Comfort Suites, Coutyard, Hyatt Place, Homewood Suites, 🅞 AutoZone, Barnes&Noble, Best Buy, Costco, Goodyear/auto, JC Penney, Macy's, Marshall's, Michael's, Nordstrom's, Old Navy, Ross, Staples, Whole Foods Mkt
105b	Taylor Rd, to Rocklin (from eb), **N** 🍴 Cattlemen's Rest., **S** 🅖 Chevron, 76/Burger King/dsl, 🍴 Islands Burgers, Subway, Tahoe Joe's, 🏨 Fairfield Inn, Hilton Garden, Holiday Inn Express, Larkspur Suites, Residence Inn, 🅞 🄷 SaveMart Foods, funpark
105a	Atlantic St, Eureka Rd, **S** 🅖 76, Shell/Circle K, 🍴 Chicago Fire Rest, In-N-Out, Panda Express, Taco Bell, Wendy's, 🏨 Marriott, 🅞 🄷 America'sTire, Buick/GMC, Carmax, Chevrolet, Ford, Home Depot, Hyundai, Lexus, Mazda, Nissan, Petsmart, Subaru, Target, Toyota/Scion, VW, Walmart, mall
103b a	Douglas Blvd, **N** 🅖 Arco/dsl, Chevron, 76/dsl, 🍴 Burger King, Carolina's Mexican, McDonald's, Starbucks, 🏨 Extended Stay America, Heritage Inn, Residence Inn, 🅞 🄷 Ace Hardware, BigLots, Big O Tire, BrakeMasters, $Tree,

Exit	Services
C I T R U S H E I G H T S 103b a	Continued Firestone, Goodyear, Kragen Parts, Radio Shack, Rite Aid, Sunflower Mkt, Trader Joe's, **S** 🅖 Shell, 🍴 Carl's Jr, Carrow's, Denny's, Outback Steaks, Subway, 🏨 Hampton Inn, Orchid Suites, 🅞 Fry's Electronics, Office Depot, Target
102	Riverside Ave, Auburn Blvd, to Roseville, **N** 🅖 Arco/dsl, Chevron/dsl, 🍴 Starbucks, Subway, 🅞 auto repair, vet, **S** 🅖 76, Shell, Tower, Valero/dsl, 🍴 Baskin-Robbins, CA Burgers, DQ, Grand China, Jack-in-the-Box, 🅞 AutoZone, BMW Motorcycles, $World, K-Mart, NAPA, Schwab Tire, Village RV Ctr, transmissions/auto repair
100	Antelope Rd, to Citrus Heights, **N** 🅖 76, 🍴 Carl's Jr, Giant Pizza, McDonald's, Papa Murphy's, Popeye's, RoundTable Pizza, Subway, Taco Bell, Wendy's, 🅞 $Tree, O'Reilly Parts, Raley's Foods, 7-11, vet
100mm	weigh sta both lanes
98	Greenback Lane, Elkhorn Blvd, Orangevale, Citrus Heights, **N** 🍴 Carl's Jr, Little Caesar's, McDonald's, Pizza Hut, Subway, Taco Bell, 🅞 CVS Drug, Radio Shack, Safeway Foods
96	Madison Ave, **N** 🅖 Chevron/dsl, Valero/dsl, 🍴 Brookfield's Rest., Denny's, El Zarape Mexican, Jack-in-the-Box, Mongolian BBQ, Starbucks, 🏨 Motel 6, Super 8, 🅞 funpark, to McClellan AFB, **S** 🅖 Arco, 76, Shell/dsl, 🍴 Boston Mkt, Burger King, Chipotle Mexican, El Pollo Loco, IHOP, In-N-Out, Jack-in-the-Box, McDonald's, Panda Express, Starbucks, Subway, Wienerschnitzel, 🏨 Holiday Inn, La Quinta, 🅞 Acura, AT&T, Chevrolet, Ford, Office Depot, PepBoys, Schwab Tire, 7-11, Target, Verizon, Walgreens
95	CA 99 S
94b	Auburn Blvd
94a	Watt Ave, **N** 🅖 Arco, 76/dsl, 🍴 Golden Corral, KFC, 🏨 Days Inn, Motel 6, 🅞 Firestone/auto, McClellan AFB, **S** 🅖 Arco, Chevron, Shell, 🍴 CheeseSteak, China Taste, Denny's, Jimboy's Tacos, Starbucks, Subway, Wendy's, 🏨 Great Value Inn
93	Longview Dr
92	Winters St
91	Raley Blvd, Marysville Blvd, to Rio Linda, **N** 🅖 Arco, Chevron, **S** 🅞 Mkt Basket Foods, Valley Tires, USPO
90	Norwood Ave, **N** 🅖 Arco/Jack-in-the-Box, Valero, 🍴 Golden China, McDonald's, RoundTable Pizza, Starbucks, Subway, 🅞 Rite Aid, Viva Foods
S A C R A M E N T O 89	Northgate Blvd, Sacramento, **N** 🅞 Fry's Electronics, **S** 🅖 Arco, Circle K, Shell, 🍴 Carl's Jr, Classic Burgers, El Pollo Loco, IHOP, KFC, LJ Silver, McDonald's/playplace, Starbucks, Subway, Taco Bell, 🏨 Extended Stay America,

🅶 = gas 🍴 = food 🛏 = lodging ⊙ = other 🆁🆂 = rest stop   Copyright 2014 - The Next Exit ®

⨊ INTERSTATE 80 CONT'D

Exit	Services

SACRAMENTO

89 Continued
Quality Inn, ⊙ BigLots, Foodsco Foods, Kragen Parts, PepBoys, Schwab Tire

88 Truxel Rd, **N** 🅶 Chevron, Shell/dsl, 🍴 Applebee's, BJ's Rest, Canyon Creek Grill, Carino's Italian, Chili's, Chipotle Mexican, Del Taco, Hooters, In-N-Out, Jamba Juice, Logan's Roadhouse, Mongolian BBQ, On the Border, Panera Bread, Qdoba, Rubio's, Starbucks, 🛏 Staybridge Suites, ⊙ Arco Arena, Barnes&Noble, Best Buy, GNC, Home Depot, Michael's, Old Navy, Petsmart, Radio Shack, Raley's Depot, Ross, Staples, Target, Walmart, World Mkt, mall

86 I-5, N to Redding, S to Sacramento, to CA 99 N

85 W El Camino, **N** 🅶 Chevron/Subway/dsl/24hr, 49er Trk-stp/Silver Skillet/dsl/scales/24hr/@, 🍴 Burger King, 🛏 Fairfield Inn, Super 8

83 Reed Ave, **N** 🅶 76/dsl, 🍴 Hawaiian BBQ, Jack-in-the-Box, Los Amigo's, Quizno's, Panda Express, Starbucks, Subway, 🛏 Extended Stay America, Hampton Inn, ⊙ dsl repair, **S** 🅶 Arco/24hr, Shell/McDonald's/dsl, 🍴 In-N-Out, Taco Bell, ⊙ Home Depot, Walmart Super Ctr

82 US 50 E, W Sacramento

81 Enterprise Blvd, W Capitol Ave, W Sacramento, **N** 🅶 Chevron/dsl/24hr, Valero/dsl, 🍴 Eppie's Rest/24hr, 🛏 Granada Inn, **S** 🅶 7-11, 🍴 Denny's, JR's BBQ, Starbucks, Subway, ⊙ KOA

78 Rd 32A, E Chiles Rd, **S** Fruit Stand

75 Mace Blvd, **N** 🅶 Arco, **S** 🅶 Chevron/24hr, Valero/dsl, 🍴 Burger King, Cindy's Rest., McDonald's, Mtn Mike's Pizza, Subway, Taco Bell/24hr, 🛏 Howard Johnson, Motel 6, ⊙ Chevrolet, Chrysler/Dodge/Jeep, Ford, Honda, Nissan, Nugget Mkt Foods, Schwab Tire, Toyota/Scion, Tuesday Morning, to Mace Ranch

DAVIS

73 Olive Dr (from wb, no EZ return)

72b a Richards Blvd, Davis, **N** 🅶 Shell/24hr, 🍴 Caffe Italia, In-N-Out, Redrum Burger, 🛏 University Park Inn, ⊙ NAPA, **S** 🅶 Chevron, 🍴 Applebee's, Del Taco, IHOP, KFC, Wendy's, 🛏 Comfort Suites, Hotel Davis, ⊙ Jiffy Lube, Kragen Parts

71 to UC Davis

70 CA 113 N, to Woodland, **N** 🄷

69 Kidwell Rd

67 Pedrick Rd, **N** 🅶 Chevron/dsl, 76/LP, ⊙ produce

66b Milk Farm Rd (from wb)

66a CA 113 S, Currey Rd, to Dixon, **S** 🅶 Arco, CFN/dsl, Shell/dsl, Valero/Popeye's/dsl, 🍴 Cattlemen's Rest., Jack-in-the-Box, Papa Murphy's, Subway, Taco Del Mar, Wendy's, 🛏 Comfort Suites, ⊙ Walmart

64 Pitt School Rd, to Dixon, **S** 🅶 Chevron/24hr, Valero/24hr, 🍴 Arby's, Asian Garden, Burger King, Chevy's Mexican, Denny's, IHOP, Little Ceasar's, Maria's Mexican, Mary's Pizza, McDonald's, Pizza Guys, Quizno's, Solano Bakery, Starbucks, Subway, Taco Bell, 🛏 Best Western, Microtel, ⊙ Curves, Ford, Kragen Parts, Safeway/dsl

63 Dixon Ave, Midway Rd, **N** 🅶 Truck Stp/dsl, **S** 🅶 Chevron/LP/lube, USA/24hr, 🍴 Carl's Jr, Mr Taco, 🛏 Super 8, ⊙ Dixon Fruit Mkt, RV Dump

60 Midway Rd, Lewis Rd, Elmyra, **N** Produce Mkt, RV camping

59 Meridian Rd, Weber Rd

57 Leisure Town Rd, **N** ⊙ 🄷, Camping World, **S** 🅶 Arco,

VACAVILLE

57 Continued
Chevron, KwikStop/dsl, 76/McDonald's, 🍴 Black Oak Rest., Island Grill, Jack-in-the-Box, King's Buffet, Omlette Bistro, Popeye's, Quizno's, 🛏 Best Value, Extended Stay America, Fairfield Inn, Holiday Inn Express, Motel 6, Quality Inn, Residence Inn, ⊙ Buick/GMC, Chevrolet, Chrysler/Dodge/Jeep, Harley-Davidson, Home Depot, Honda, Kohl's, Nissan, Toyota, VW

56 I-505 N, to Winters,

55 Nut Tree Pkwy, Monte Vista Dr, Allison Dr, **N** 🅶 7-11, 76/Circle K, Valero, 🍴 Amici Pizza, Arby's, Burger King, Denny's, Elephant Bar Rest., Hisui Japanese, IHOP, Jamba Juice, McDonald's, Murillo's Mexican, Nations Burger, Panera Bread, Pelayo's Mexican, Rubio's, Subway, Taco Bell, Wendy's, 🛏 Best Value Inn, Best Western, Super 8, ⊙ 🄷, America's Tire, Best Buy, Big O Tire, Firestone/auto, Lowe's Whse, Nugget Foods, Old Navy, Petsmart, See's Candies, U-Haul, transmissions, **S** 🅶 Arco/24hr, Chevron/24hr, 🍴 Applebee's, Baja Fresh, BJ's Grill, Black Oak Rest., Carl's Jr, Chevy's Mexican, Chili's, Coldstone Creamery, Fresh Choice Rest., In-N-Out, Jack-in-the-Box, Jamba Juice, KFC, Mel's Diner, Olive Garden, Omlette Bistro, Popeye's, Quizno's, Starbucks, String's Italian, Tahoe Joe's Steaks, TGIFriday, Togo's, 🛏 Comfort Suites, Courtyard, Fairfield Inn, Holiday Inn Express, Motel 6, Residence Inn, ⊙ GNC, Jo-Ann Fabrics, Marshall's, Michael's, PetCo, GMC, Radio Shack, Ross, Safeway, Sam's Club, Staples, Target, Vacaville Stores/famous brands, Walmart/auto

54b Mason St, Peabody Rd, **N** 🅶 Chevron, Valero, 🍴 A&W/LJ Silver, 🛏 Hampton Inn, ⊙ NAPA, Schwab Tire, **S** 🅶 USA, 🍴 Domino's, Starbucks, Subway, ⊙ Costco/gas, 7-11

54a Davis St, **N** 🅶 Chevron/McDonald's, 🍴 Outback Steaks, 🛏 Hampton Inn **S** 🅶 QuikStop, ⊙ WinCo Foods, repair

53 Merchant St, Alamo Dr, **N** 🅶 Chevron, Shell/dsl, Valero, 🍴 Bakers Square, Baldo's Mexican, Baskin-Robbins, Lyon's/24hr, RoundTable Pizza, Subway, Tin Tin Buffet, 🛏 Alamo Inn, ⊙ BigLots, vet, **S** 🅶 76/dsl, 🍴 Jack-in-the-Box, KFC, McDonald's, Pizza Hut, Starbucks, ⊙ Radio Shack

52 Cherry Glen Rd (from wb)

51b Pena Adobe Rd, **S** 🛏 Ranch Hotel

51a Lagoon Valley Rd, Cherry Glen

48 N Texas St, Fairfield, **S** 🅶 Arco/24hr, Chevron, Shell, 🍴 El Pollo Loco, Jim Boy's Tacos, RoundTable Pizza, Panda Express, Starbucks, Subway, Texas Roadhouse, ⊙ Longs Drugs, Raley's Foods

FAIRFIELD

47 Waterman Blvd, **N** 🍴 Dynasty Chinese, Loard's Icecream, RoundTable Pizza, Starbucks, Strings Italian, ⊙ Chevrolet/Cadillac, Safeway, to Austin's Place, **S** to Travis AFB, museum

45 Travis Blvd, Fairfield, **N** 🅶 Arco/24hr, Chevron/24hr, 🍴 Baskin-Robbins, Burger King, Denny's, In-N-Out, McDonald's, Peking Rest., Subway, Taco Bell, 🛏 Courtyard, Motel 6, ⊙ Raley's Foods, Harley-Davidson, Ford, Hyundai, Nissan, PetCo, CHP, **S** 🍴 BizWiz Tasty Burgers, Carino's Italian, Chevy's Mexican, Chipotle Mexican, Coldstone Creamery, FreshChoice Rest., Marie Callender's, Mimi's Café, Panda Express, Quizno's, Redbrick Pizza, Red Lobster, Starbucks, 🛏 Hilton Garden, ⊙ 🄷, Barnes&Noble, Best Buy, Cost+, JC Penney, Macy's, Michael's, Ross, Sears/auto, Trader Joe's, World Mkt, mall

⮤ INTERSTATE 80 CONT'D

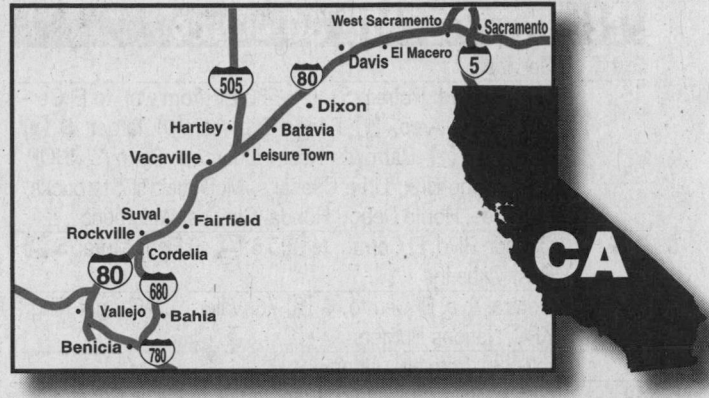

Exit	Services
44	W Texas St, same as 45, Fairfield, **N** 🅟 Shell/dsl, Valero/dsl, 🍴 ChuckeCheese, Gordito's Mexican, Starbucks, 🛏 Extended Stay America, 🅾 Staples, **S** 🅟 Valero, 🍴 Baldo's Mexican, McDonald's, Paleyo's Mexican, Scenario's Pizza, 🅾 Acura/Honda, Chrysler/Jeep/Dodge, FoodMaxx, Home Depot, Hyundai, Infiniti, Mitsubishi, Nissan, Target, Toyota, Volvo, Walgreens
43	CA 12 E, Abernathy Rd, Suisun City, **S** 🅾 Budweiser Plant, Walmart
42mm	**weigh sta both lanes,** 🍴
41	Suisan Valley Rd, **N** 🛏 Homewood Suites, Staybridge Suites, **S** 🅟 Arco/24hr, Chevron, 76/dsl/24hr, Shell/dsl, Valero, 🍴 Arby's, Bravo's Pizza, Burger King, Carl's Jr, Denny's, Green Bamboo, Jack-in-the-Box, McDonald's, Starbucks, Subway, Taco Bell, Wendy's, 🛏 Best Western, Comfort Inn, Days Inn, Fairfield Inn, Holiday Inn Express, 🅾 Ray's RV Ctr, Scandia FunCtr
40	I-680 (from wb)
39b	Green Valley Rd, I-680 (from eb), **N** 🍴 Hawaiian BBQ, Peloyas Mexican, RoundTable Pizza, Starbucks, Sticky Rice Bistro, Subway, 🛏 Homewood Suites, Staybridge Suites, 🅾 Costco/gas, Longs Drug, Safeway, TJ Maxx, **S** 🅟 Arco
39a	Red Top Rd, **N** 🅟 76/Circle K/24hr, 🍴 Jack-in-the-Box
36	American Canyon Rd
34mm	🆁🆂 wb, full 🅰 facilities, info, 🍴, 🛏, litter barrels, petwalk, vista parking
33b a	CA 37, to San Rafael, Columbus Pkwy, **N** 🅟 Chevron/dsl, 🍴 Baskin-Robbins, Carl's Jr., 🛏 Best Western, Courtyard, 🅾 funpark, **S** same as 32
32	Redwood St, to Vallejo, **N** 🅟 76, 🍴 Denny's, Panda Garden, 🛏 Best Inn, Motel 6, 🅾🅷, **S** 🅟 Arco, BonFair, Shell, 🍴 Applebee's, Black Angus, Chevy's Mexican, Coldstone Creamery, IHOP, Jamba Juice, Lyon's Rest., McDonald's, Mtn. Mike's Pizza, Olive Garden, Panda Express, Red Lobster, Rubio's, Starbucks, Subway, Taco Bell, Wendy's, 🛏 Comfort Inn, Ramada Inn, 🅾 AutoZone, Best Buy, Cadillac/Chevrolet, Costco/gas, Hancock Fabrics, Home Depot, Honda, Hyundai, Longs Drug, Marshall's, Mazda, Michael's, Old Navy, PepBoys, PetCo, Radio Shack, Ross, Safeway, Toyota
31b	Tennessee St, to Vallejo, **S** 🅟 Valero/dsl, 🍴 Jack-in-the-Box, Pacifica Pizza, Pizza Guys, 🛏 Great Western Inn, Quality Inn, 🅾 Grocery Outlet
31a	Solano Ave, Springs Rd, **N** 🍴 Burger King, Church's, El Rey Mexican, Taco Bell, 🛏 Deluxe Inn, Relax Inn, 🅾 Rite Aid, U-Haul, **S** 🅟 Chemco, Chevron, Grand Gas, Quik-Stop, 🍴 DQ, Domino's, Pizza Hut, Starbucks, Subway, Wok, 🛏 Islander Motel, 🅾 Island Pacific Foods, Kragen Parts
30c	Georgia St, Central Vallejo, **N** 🅟 Safeway/gas, **S** 🅟 Shell/Starbucks/dsl, 🍴 McDonald's, 🛏 California Motel
30b	Benicia Rd (from wb), **S** 🅟 Shell/dsl, 🍴 McDonald's, Starbucks
30a	I-780, to Martinez
29b	Magazine St, Vallejo, **N** 🅟 BPG, 🍴 Starbucks, Subway, 🛏 Budget Inn, El Rancho, 7 Motel, 🅾 Tradewinds RV Park, **S** 🍴 McDonald's, 🛏 Travel Inn, 🅾 7-11
29a	CA 29, Maritime Academy Dr, Vallejo, **N** 🅟 Chevron/dsl/24hr, 5 Star Gas, 🍴 Subway, 🛏 Motel 6, Vallejo Inn
28mm	**toll plaza, pay toll from eb**
27	Pomona Rd, Crockett, **N** 🍴 Dead Fish Seafood, vista point
26	Cummings Skyway, to CA 4 (from wb), to Martinez
24	Willow Ave, to Rodeo, **N** 🍴 Straw Hat Pizza, Subway, 🅾 Safeway/24hr, USPO, **S** 🅟 76/Circle K/dsl, 🍴 Burger King, Mazatlan, Starbucks, Willow Garden Chinese
23	CA 4, to Stockton, Hercules, **N** 🅟 Shell, 🍴 Extreme Pizza, Jack-in-the-Box, Starbucks, 🅾 Radio Shack, **S** 🍴 McDonald's, RoundTable Pizza, Subway, Taco Bell, 🅾 BigLots, Curves, Home Depot, Lucky Foods, Rite Aid, USPO
22	Pinole Valley Rd, **S** 🅟 Arco/24hr, Chevron/dsl, 🍴 Jack-in-the-Box, Jamba Juice, NY Pizza, Red Onion Rest., Subway, 🅾 7-11, Trader Joe's, Walgreens
21	Appian Way, **N** 🅟 Pinole Express, 🍴 China Delite, McDonald's, Pizza Hut, 🅾 Kragen Parts, Longs Drug, Safeway, **S** 🅟 Valero/dsl, 🍴 Burger King, Carl's Jr, Coldstone Creamery, Hawaiian BBQ, HomeTown Buffet, HotDog Sta, KFC, Krispy Kreme, In-N-Out, Panda Express, Papa Murphy's, RoundTable Pizza, Sizzler, Starbucks, Subway, Taco Bell, Wendy's, Wing Stop, 🛏 Days Inn, Motel 6, 🅾 AutoZone, Best Buy, $Tree, K-Mart, Lucky Foods, Radio Shack
20	Richmond Pkwy, to I-580 W, **N** 🅟 Chevron, 🍴 Ground Round Rest., IHOP, McDonald's, Me&Ed's Pizza, Subway, 🅾 Barnes&Noble, Chrysler/Dodge/Jeep, Ford, 99¢ Store, Petsmart, Ross, **S** 🅟 Chevron, Shell/dsl, 🍴 Applebee's, Chuck Steak, In-N-Out, Krispy Kreme, Outback Steaks, Panda Express, RoundTable Pizza, 🅾 FoodMaxx, Kragen Parts, Old Navy, Michael's, Staples, Target
19b	Hilltop Dr, to Richmond, **N** 🅟 Chevron, 🍴 Chevy's Mexican, Olive Garden, Red Lobster, Tokyo Rest., 🛏 Courtyard, Extended Stay America, 🅾 Firestone, JC Penney, Jo-Ann Fabrics, Macy's, Nissan, Sears/auto, Walmart, mall, **S** 🅟 Hilltop Fuel/dsl
19a	El Portal Dr, to San Pablo, **S** 🅟 SMP, 🍴 McDonalds, Mtn. Mike's Pizza, KFC, Subway, 🅾 Raley's Foods, Walgreens
18	San Pablo Dam Rd, **N** 🅟 Chevron, 🍴 Burger King, Denny's, El Pollo Loco, Empire Buffet, Jack-in-the-Box, Jamba Juice, Nations Burgers, Popeye's, RoundTable Pizza, Starbucks, Subway, Taco Bell, 🛏 Holiday Inn Express, 🅾🅷, AutoZone, $Tree, FoodMaxx, Lucky Foods, Walgreens, **S** 🅾 CamperLand RV Ctr
17	Macdonald Ave (from eb), McBryde Ave (from wb), Richmond, **N** 🅟 Arco/24hr, 🍴 Burger King, Church's, **S** 🅟 Chevron/24hr, 🍴 Wendy's, 🅾 Safeway, auto repair
16	San Pablo Ave, to Richmond, San Pablo, **S** 🅟 Chevron, 🍴 KFC, LJ Silver, Subway, Wendy's, 🅾 Safeway

VALLEJO **RICHMOND**

➤E INTERSTATE 80 CONT'D

Exit	Services
15	Cutting Blvd, Potrero St, to I-580 Br (from wb), to El Cerrito, **N** 🅖 Arco, 🍴 Panda Express, 🅞 Target, **S** 🅖 Chevron, 🍴 Carrow's Rest., Church's, Denny's, IHOP, Jack-in-the-Box, Little Ceasar's, McDonald's, Starbucks, 🅞 $Tree, Home Depot, Honda, Staples, Walgreens
14b	Carlson Blvd, El Cerrito, **N** 🅖 76, 🛏 40 Flags Motel, **S** 🛏 Best Value Inn
14a	Central Ave, El Cerrito, **S** 🅖 76, Valero, 🍴 Burger King, KFC, Nations Burgers
13	to I-580 (from eb), Albany
12	Gilman St, to Berkeley, **N** Golden Gate Fields Racetrack, **S** 🅞 Target
11	University Ave, to Berkeley, **S** 🅖 76, University Gas, 🛏 La Quinta, 🅞 to UC Berkeley
10	CA 13, to Ashby Ave
9	Powell St, Emeryville, **N** 🅖 Shell, 🍴 Chevy's Mexican, 🛏 Hilton Garden, **S** 🅖 76, 🍴 Burger King, CA Pizza Kitchen, Denny's, Elephant Bar/Grill, Jamba Juice, PF Chang's, Starbucks, Togo's, 🛏 Courtyard, Sheraton, Woodfin Suites, 🅞 Barnes&Noble, Old Navy, Ross, Trader Joe's
8c b	Oakland, to I-880, I-580
8a	W Grand Ave, Maritime St
7mm	**toll plaza wb**
5mm	SF Bay
4a	Treasure Island (exits left)
2c b	Fremont St, Harrison St, Embarcadero (from wb)
2a	4th st (from eb), **S** 🅖 Shell
1	9th st, Civic Ctr, downtown SF
1b a	**I-80 begins/ends on US 101 in SF**

➤E INTERSTATE 110 (LOS ANGELES)

Exit	Services
21	**I-110 begins/ends on I-10.**
20c	Adams Blvd, **E** 🅞 Audi, Chevron, Chrysler/Dodge/Jeep, Mercedes, Nissan, Office Depot, VW, LA Convention Ctr.
20b	37th St, Exposition Blvd, **W** 🅖 Chevron/McDonald's, 🛏 Radisson, 🅞 Chevrolet
20a	MLK Blvd, Expo Park, **W** 🅖 Chevron, 🍴 McDonald's, Subway
19b	Vernon Ave, **E** 🅖 Mobil, 🍴 Tacos El Gavilan, **W** 🅖 76/24hr, Shell, 🍴 Burger King, Jack-in-the-Box, 🅞 Rite Aid, Ross
18b	Slauson Ave, **E** 🅖 Mobil, **W** 🅖 76
18a	Gage Blvd, **E** 🅖 Arco, 🍴 Church's, Hercules Burgers
17	Florence Ave, **E** 🅖 Shell, 🍴 Jack-in-the-Box, **W** 🅖 Chevron, Valero, 🍴 Burger King, Little Caesars, McDonald's, Pizza Hut, Subway
16	Manchester Ave, **E** 🅖 Arco, 🍴 El Pollo Loco, Little Caesars, McDonald's, Subway, Winchell's, 🅞 AutoZone, **W** 🅖 76/Circle K, 🍴 Church's, Jack-in-the-Box, Tam's Burgers, Popeye's
15	Century Blvd, **E** 🅖 Arco, Shell/Subway/dsl, 🍴 Burger King, McDonald's, **W** 🅖 76/dsl
14b	Imperial Hwy, **W** 🅖 Chevron/dsl, 🍴 McDonald's, Jack-in-the-Box
14a	I-105
13	El Segundo Blvd, **E** 🍴 Dominos, Taco Bell, **W** 🅖 Mobil, Shell, 🛏 Executive Inn
12	Rosecrans Ave, **E** 🅖 Arco/24hr, Valero, **W** 🅖 Chevron/

12	Continued McDonald's, Valero, 🍴 Jack-in-the-Box, KFC/LJ Silver, Pizza Hut, Popeye's, Subway, Yoshinoya, 🅞 Chief Parts, 7-11, casino
11	Redondo Beach Blvd, **E** 🍴 McDonald's, **W** 🅖 Mobil, 🅞 🄷, casino
10b a	CA 91, 190th St, **W** 🅖 Arco, 🍴 Carl's Jr, Jack-in-the-Box, Krispy Kreme, McDonald's, Pizza Hut/Taco Bell, Subway, 🅞 Food4Less, Ranch Mkt, Sam's Club
9	I-405, San Diego Fwy
8	Torrance Blvd, Del Amo, **E** 🍴 Burger King, Chile Verde, Hawaiian BBQ, Starbucks, 🅞 K-mart, **W** 🅖 Mobil, Shell, Subway/dsl
7b	Carson St, **E** 🍴 KFC, 🛏 Cali Inn, 🅞 vet, **W** 🅖 76, Shell, 🍴 FatBurger, Hong Kong Deli, In-N-Out, Jack-in-the-Box, Louis Burgers, McDonalds, Pizza Hut, Polly's Pies, Starbucks, Subway, Wienerschnitzel, 🅞 🄷, Autozone, Carson Drug, Costsaver Mkt, O'Reilly Parts, Rite Aid
5	Sepulveda Blvd, **E** 🍴 McDonald's, 🅞 Albertson's, Home Depot, Staples, Target, **W** 🅖 Arco/24hr, Chevron, Mobil, 🍴 Burger King, Carl's Jr, McDonald's, Pizza Hut/Taco Bell, Popeye's, Starbucks, Subway, 🛏 Motel 6, 🅞 AT&T, $Tree, Food4Less, 99¢ Store, Rite Aid, Ross
4	CA 1, Pacific Coast Hwy, **E** 🅖 Arco, 76, 🍴 Jack-in-the-Box, Pizza Hut, Wienerschnitzel, **W** 🅖 Circle K, United/dsl, 🍴 Del Taco, Denny's, El Pollo Loco, Subway, 🛏 Best Western, 🅞 🄷, Discount Parts, PepBoys, Rite Aid, transmissions
3b	Anaheim St, **W** 🅖 Mobil/dsl, Thrifty, 🅞 radiators, **W** Conoco/Phillips Refinery
3a	C St
1b	Channel St, **W** 🅖 Arco, Chevron, 🍴 Subway, 🅞 Home Depot, 7-11, Target
1a	CA 47, Gaffey Ave
0mm	**I-110 begins/ends**

➤E INTERSTATE 205 (TRACY)

Exit	Services
12	**I-205 begins wb, ends eb, accesses I-5 nb**
9	MacArthur Dr, Tracy, **S** gas Chevron/Jack-in-the-Box/Subway/dsl, 🅞 Prime Outlet Ctr/famous brands
8	Tracy Blvd, Tracy, **N** 🅖 Chevron, 76/Mean Gene's Burger/dsl, Shell/dsl, 🍴 Denny's, 🛏 Holiday Inn Express, Motel 6, **S** 🅖 Arco, 🍴 Arby's, Burger King, In-N-Out, McDonald's, McHenry's Rest., Milano Pizza, Nations Burgers, Pizza Guys, Starbucks, Straw Hat Pizza, Subway, Wendy's, Wok King, 🛏 Best Western, Microtel, Quality Inn, 🅞 🄷, CVS Drug, Mi Pueblo Mkt, O'Reilly Parts, CHP
6	Grant Line Rd, Antioch, **N** 🅖 Chevron/dsl, 🍴 Applebee's, Burger King, Cavey's Grille, Chevy's Mexican, Famous Dave's BBQ, Golden Corral, Hometown Buffet, IHOP, Jamba Juice, Olive Garden, Panda Express, RoundTable Pizza, Rubio's, Sonic, Starbucks, Strings Italian, Subway, Taco Bell, TX Roadhouse, Wienerschnitzel, 🛏 Extended Stay America, Fairfield Inn, Hampton Inn, Squeeze Inn, 🅞 America's Tire, AT&T, Barnes&Noble, Best Buy, Chevrolet, Chrysler/Dodge/Jeep, Costco/gas, Ford, Home Depot, Honda, Hyundai, JC Penney, Les Schwab Tire, Macy's, Marshall's, Michael's, Nissan, PetCo, Petsmart, Ross, Sears/auto, See's Candies, Staples, Target, Toyota/Scion, Verizon, Walmart/McDonald's/auto, WinCo Foods, World Mkt, mall, **S** 🅖 Arco, 7-11, 76/dsl, Shell/dsl, 🍴 A&W/KFC, Black Bear Diner, Carl's Jr, Chili's, Hawaiian BBQ,

🅖 = gas 🅕 = food 🅗 = lodging 🅞 = other 🆁🆂 = rest stop

⬆E INTERSTATE 205 (TRACY)

Exit	Services
6	Continued
	Mtn Mike's Pizza, Popeye's, Taco Del Mar, 🅞 Rite Aid
4	11th St (from eb), to Tracy, Defense Depot
2	Mtn House Pkwy, to I-580 E
0mm	I-205 begins eb/ends wb, accesses I-580 wb.

⬆E INTERSTATE 210 (PASADENA)

Exit	Services
74	I-215 N to Barstow S to San Bernardino
73	State St, University Pkwy, N 🅖 Thrifty, Valero
71	Riverside Ave, N 🅕 Carl's Jr, Del Taco, Starbucks, Subway, 🅞 Fresh&Easy, Ralph's Foods, Rite Aid, Walgreens, S 🅖 Arco, 🅕 Jack-in-the-Box, 🅞 7-11
70	Ayala Dr, S 🅞 Target
68	Alder Ave
67	Sierra Ave, N 🅕 Applebee's, Carl's Jr, Dickie's BBQ, El Pollo Loco, Hawaiian BBQ, Jamba Juice, Mimi's Cafe, Panda Express, Pizza Hut, Teo's Mexican, Subway, 🅞 Costco/gas, $Tree, Lowe's Whse, S 🅞 Chevrolet, Nissan
66	Citrus Ave, N 🅕 El Gran Burrito, FarmerBoys Rest., Marble Slab Creamery, Pick Up Stix, Quizno's, Red Brick Pizza, Wienerschnitzel, 🅞 Home Depot, Ralph's Foods, Walgreens
64	Cherry Ave
63	I-15 N to Barstow, S to San Diego
62	Day Creek Blvd, S 🅖 Arco/dsl, Shell, 🅕 Chinese Food, Jack-In-the-Box, Marble Slab Creamery, Pizza Factory, Starbucks, Wendy's, 🅞 Ralph's Foods
60	Milliken Ave, S 🅖 Mobil, 🅕 Taco Bell, 🅞 Albertsons, CVS Drug, Kragen Parts
59	Haven Ave, N 🅖 Mobil, 76, 7-11, 🅕 Del Taco, Domino's, Jack-in-the-Box, McDonald's, Subway, Teo's Mexican, 🅞 Trader Joe's, Vons Foods, Walgreens
58	Archibald Ave, S 🅕 Blimpie, Barboni's Pizza, Carl's Jr, 🅞 Stater Bros, vet
57	Carnelion St, S 🅖 76, 🅕 Baskin-Robbins, Del Taco, El Ranchero Mexican, Papa John's, Starbucks, 🅞 Radio Shack, Rite Aid, Vons Foods, Walgreens
56	Campus Ave, S 🅕 Carl's Jr, Chick-fil-A, Golden Spoon Yogurt, Hawaiian BBQ, IHOP, Jamba Juice, Magic Wok, Qdoba Mexican, Quizno's, Starbucks, Subway, 🅞 Albertsons, Goodyear, Home Depot, Kohl's, Office Depot, Petsmart, Target
54	Mtn Ave, Mount Balde
52	Baseline Rd
50	Towne Ave
48	Fruit St, LaVerne, S 🅖 Shell, 🅕 El Pollo Loco, Magic Wok, McDonald's, Myiabi, Panda Express, Pizza Hut, Quizno's, Round Table Pizza, Rubio's, Subway, 🅞 Kohl's, Marshall's, Office Depot, Pet Depot, Vons Foods, U of LaVerne, vet
47	Foothill Blvd, LaVerne, N 🅖 Mobil/Taco Bell, 🅕 Denny's, S 🅖 Chevron/dsl, Shell, 🅕 IHOP, Starbucks, Togo's, 🅞 GNC, Radio Shack
46	San Dimas Ave, N San Dimas Canyon CP
45	CA 57 S
44	Lone Hill Ave, Santa Ana, S 🅖 Chevron, 🅕 Baja Fresh, Chili's, Coco's, In-N-Out, Subway, Wendy's, 🅞 Barnes&Noble, Best Buy, Chevrolet, Chrysler/Dodge/Jeep, Ford, Home Depot, Hyundai, Kohl's, Old Navy, Petsmart, Sam's Club/gas, Staples, Toyota, Walmart/auto

Exit	Services
43	Sunflower Ave
42	Grand Ave, to Glendora, N 🅖 76, Valero/dsl, 🅕 Denny's, 🅞 🅗
41	Citrus Ave, to Covina
40	CA 39, Azusa Ave, N 🅖 Arco/24hr, Chevron, Mobil, Shell/Del Taco, 🅕 Jack-in-the-Box, 🅗 Rodeway Inn, Super 8, S 🅖 Chevron, Valero, 🅕 Baskin-Robbins, In-N-Out, Marquez Mexican, 🅗 Best Value, 🅞 Rite Aid, 7-11
39	Vernon Ave (from wb), same as 38
38	Irwindale, N 🅖 Arco, 🅕 Carl's Jr, Denny's, FarmerBoys Rest., McDonald's, Shanghai Buffet, Taco Bell, 🅞 Costco/gas, NAPA
36b	Mt Olive Dr
36a	I-605 S
35b a	Mountain Ave, N 🅖 Arco, Chevron 🅕 Denny's, Old Spaghetti Factory, Tommy's Hamburgers, Wienerschnitzel, 🅗 Oak Park Motel, 🅞 Best Buy, BMW/Mini, CarMax, Buick/Chevrolet, Ford, Honda, Infiniti, Nissan, Staples, Subaru, Target, Walgreens, S 🅕 IHOP, Panda Express, Roasty Toasty Chicken, Senor Fish, Subway, 🅞 Home Depot, Ross, Walmart
34	Myrtle Ave, S 🅖 Chevron, 76, 🅕 Jack-in-the-Box
33	Huntington Dr, Monrovia, N 🅖 Shell/dsl, 🅕 Acapulco Rest., Applebee's, Black Angus, Burger King, Chili's, ChuckeCheese, Domino's, LeRoy's Rest., McDonald's, Mimi's Cafe, Panda Express, Popeye's, Quizno's, RoundTable Pizza, Rubio's, Starbucks, 🅗 Courtyard, 🅞 GNC, King Ranch Foods, Marshall's, Office Depot, Pepboy's, Radio Shack, Rite Aid, Trader Joe's, S 🅖 Chevron, 🅕 Baja Fresh, BJ's Grill, Capistrano's, ClaimJumper, Daphne's Rest., Derby Rest., Fusion Grill, Golden Dragon, Macaroni Grill, Olive Garden, Outback Steaks, Red Lobster, Sesame Grill, Soup Plantation, Starbucks, Subway, Taisho Rest., Togo's, Tokyo Wako, 🅗 Double Tree, Embassy Suites, Extended Stay America, Hampton Inn, Hilton Garden, Homestead Suites, OakTree Inn, Residence Inn, SpringHill Suites
32	Santa Anita Ave, Arcadia, N 🅖 Arco, 76, 🅕 KFC, McDonald's, Pizza Hut, Subway, 🅞 Ralph's Foods, Rite Aid, S 🅖 Chevron/dsl, 🅕 In-N-Out, 🅞 carwash
31	Baldwin Ave, to Sierra Madre
30b a	Rosemead Blvd, N 🅖 Arco, 76/dsl, 🅕 Boston Mkt, ChuckeCheese, Jamba Juice, Starbucks, 🅞 CVS Drug, EZ Lube, Marshall's, Ralph's Foods, Rite Aid, Sears/auto, Whole Foods Mkt, S 🅖 76, 🅕 Coco's, Jack-in-the-Box, 🅗 Days Inn, 🅞 Big O Tires
29b a	San Gabriel Blvd, Madre St, N 🅖 76, 🅕 Chipotle Mexican, El Torito, Starbucks, Togo's, 🅞 Best Buy, Old Navy, Petsmart, Ross, S 🅖 76, 🅕 Jack-in-the-Box, 🅗 Best

S A N D I M A S

M O N R O V I A

CA

🔵E INTERSTATE 210 (PASADENA) CONT'D

PASADENA

Exit	Services
29b a	Continued Western, Holiday Inn Express, Quality Inn, 🅾 Buick/Chevrolet/GMC, Cadillac, Hyundai, Jiffy Lube, Land Rover, Staples, Target, Toyota
28	Altadena Dr, Sierra Madre, **S** 🅿 Chevron, Mobil, 🅾 Just Tires
27 b	Allen
27 a	Hill Ave
26	Lake Ave, **N** 🅿 Mobil, 🅾 Jo-Ann Fabrics
25b	CA 134, to Ventura
25a	Del Mar Blvd, CA Blvd, CO Blvd (exits left from eb)
24	Mountain St
23	Lincoln Ave, **S** 🛏 Lincoln Motel, 🅾 auto repair
22b	Arroyo Blvd, **N** 🍴 Jack-in-the-Box, **S** to Rose Bowl
22a	Berkshire Ave, Oak Grove Dr
21	Gould Ave, **S** 🅿 Arco, 🍴 Dominos, McDonald's, RoundTable Pizza, Trader Joes, 🅾 Firestone, Just Tires, Ralph's Foods
20	CA 2, Angeles Crest Hwy
19	CA 2, Glendale Fwy, **S** 🅾🅷
18	Ocean View Blvd, to Montrose
17b a	Pennsylvania Ave, La Crescenta, **N** 🅿 76, Shell, Valero, 🍴 Baja Fresh, Burger King, Domino's, Starbucks, Subway, Togo's, Wienerschnitzel, 🅾 GNC, Nissan, Office Depot, Ralph's Foods, Rite Aid, Toyota, Vons Foods, Walgreens, USPO, **S** 🅾 Gardenia Mks/deli, 7-11
16	Lowell Ave
14	La Tuna Cyn Rd
11	Sunland Blvd, Tujunga, **N** 🅿 Mobil, 76, Shell, 🍴 Coco's, Jack-in-the-Box, KFC, Sizzler, Yum Yum Donuts, 🅾 Ralph's Foods, Rite Aid, 7-11, city park
9	Wheatland Ave
8	Osborne St, Lakeview Terrace, **N** 🍴 Ranch Side Cafe, 🅾 7-11
6a	Paxton St
6b	CA 118
5	Maclay St, to San Fernando, **S** 🅿 Chevron, 76/dsl, 🍴 El Pollo Loco, KFC, McDonald's, Quizno's, Subway, Taco Bell, 🅾 Home Depot, Office Depot, Radio Shack, Sam's Club
4	Hubbard St, **N** 🅿 Chevron, 🍴 Denny's, Yum Yum Donuts, 🅾 AutoZone, Radio Shack, Rite Aid, Valley Foods, **S** 🅿 Mobil/dsl, Shell, 🍴 El Caporal Mexican, Jack-in-the-Box, Shakey's Pizza, Subway, 🅾 Vons Foods
3	Polk St, **S** 🅿 Arco, Chevron/24hr, 🍴 KFC, 🅾🅷, 7-11
2	Roxford St, **N** 🅿 Arco/dsl, 🍴 Topia Pizza/Subs, 🅾🅷, Jiffy Lube, **S** 🛏 Country Side Inn
1c	Yarnell St
1b a	I-210 begins/ends on I-5, exit 160.

🔼N INTERSTATE 215 (RIVERSIDE)

Exit	Services
55	I-215 begins/ends on I-15.
54	Devore, **E** 🅿 Arco/dsl, Shell, **W** 🍴 Tony's Diner
50	Palm Ave, Kendall Dr, **E** 🅿 Arco, 7-11, 🍴 Albertacos, Burger King, Mico Cocina Mexican, Starbucks, Subway, **W** 🍴 Denny's
48	University Pkwy, **E** 🅿 Chevron/dsl, 76/Circle K, 🍴 Alberto's, Baskin Robbins/Togo's, Carl's Jr, Del Taco, Domino's, IHOP, KFC, Little Ceasars, McDonald's, Papa John's,

SAN BERNARDINO

Exit	Services
48	Continued Starbucks, Subway, Wienerschnitzel, 🅾 AT&T, Jiffy Lube, Radio Shack, Ralph's Foods, Staples, **W** 🅿 Arco, Mobil/dsl/LP, 🍴 Jack-in-the-Box, Pizza Hut/Taco Bell, 🛏 Days Inn, Motel 6, 🅾 Verizon, Walmart/Subway
46c b	27th St, **E** golf, **W** golf
46a	CA 210 W, Highland Ave
45b	Musciape Dr, **E** 🅿 Shell/dsl, Thrifty, 🍴 Jack-in-the-Box, 🅾 Chevrolet, Home Depot, SavOn Foods, Stater Bros
45a	CA 210 E, Highlands
44b	Baseline Rd
44a	CA 66 W, 5th St, **E** 🍴 In-N-Out, 🛏 Best Value Inn, Country Inn, EconoLodge, Golden Star Inn, Rodeway Inn
43	2nd St, Civic Ctr, **E** 🅿 Arco, Chevron/dsl, 🍴 China Hut, Del Taco, In-N-Out, McDonald's, Pizza Hut/Taco Bell, Starbucks, 🛏 Best Value Inn, 🅾 Ford, Food4Less, Marshall's
42b	Mill St, **E** 🍴 Carl's Jr, Del Taco, Jack-in-the-Box, McDonald's, 🅾 AutoZone, **W** 🅿 Shell, 🍴 Yum-yum Donuts
42a	Inland Ctr Dr, **E** 🅿 Chevron/dsl, 🍴 Carl's Jr, Jack-in-the-Box, Wienerschnitzel, 🅾 AutoZone, Gottschalk's, Kragen Parts, Macy's, Sears/auto, mall
41	Orange Show Rd, **E** 🅿 Arco, Chevron, Exxon, 🍴 Denny's, Pancho Villa Mexican, Subway, 🛏 Knights Inn, Travelodge, 🅾 BigLots, Chrysler/Dodge/Jeep, Firestone/auto, Kelly Tire, Radio Shack, 99¢ Store, Target, **W** 🅾 Hyundai, Isuzu, Kia, Mazda, Mitsubishi, Nissan, Scion, Suzuki, Toyota
40b a	I-10, E to Palm Springs, W to LA
39	Washington St, Mt Vernon Ave, **E** 🅿 Arco, 5 Point/repair, 76/Circle K, 🍴 Baker's Drive-Thru, China Town, DQ, George's Burgers, Siquio's Mexican, Taco Joe's, Starbucks, 🛏 Colton Inn, 🅾 BigLots, Goodyear/auto, Jiffy Lube, **W** 🍴 Buffet Star, Burger King, Carl's Jr, Del Taco, Denny's, Graziano's Pizza, Hot Taco, Jack-in-the-Box, McDonald's, Starbucks, Subway, Taco Patron, 🛏 Red Tile Inn, 🅾 GNC, 99¢ Store, Radio Shack, Ross, Walmart/auto, multiple RV dealers
38	Barton Rd, **E** 🅿 Arco, Shell/Circle K/dsl, 🍴 Miguel's Mexican, Quiznos, 🅾 AutoZone, Stater Bros., **W** 🍴 Demetri's Burgers, 🅾 vet
37	La Cadena Dr, (Iowa Ave from sb), **E** 🅿 Shell/dsl, 🍴 Jack-in-the-Box, YumYum Rest., 🛏 Holiday Inn Express
36	Center St, to Highgrove, **E** 🅿 Chevron/Subway/dsl, **W** 🅿 Valero/dsl
35	Columbia Ave, **E** 🅿 Arco/dsl, **W** 🅾 Circle K
34b a	CA 91, CA 60, Main St, Riverside, to beach cities
33	Blaine St, 3rd St, **E** 🅿 76, Shell, Valero, 🍴 Baker's Drive-Thru, Jack-in-the-Box, Starbucks, 🅾 K-Mart, Stater Bros., Valvoline
32	University Ave, Riverside, **W** 🅿 Mobil/dsl, Shell, Thrifty, 🍴 Canton Chinese, Carl's Jr, Coco's, Denny's, Domino's, Gus Jr, IHOP, Jack-in-the-Box, Little Ceasars, Pizza Hut, Quiznos, Rubio's, Santana's Mexican, Starbucks, Subway, Taco Bell, Wienerschnitzel, 🛏 Comfort Inn, Courtyard, Motel 6, 🅾 AT&T, Food4Less, O'Reilly Parts, Radio Shack, Rite Aid, Walgreens
31	MLK Blvd, El Cerrito
30b	Central Ave, Watkins Dr
30a	Fair Isle Dr, Box Springs, **W** 🅿 76/Circle K/Subway/dsl, 🍴 Jack-in-the-Box, 🅾 Ford, Nissan
29	CA 60 E, to Indio, **E on Day St** 🅿 Arco, Shell/dsl, 🍴

RIVERSIDE

N↑ INTERSTATE 215 (RIVERSIDE) CONT'D

Exit	Services
29	Continued Applebee's, Baker's Drive-Thru, Burger Boss, Carl's Jr, Chick-fil-A, El Pollo Loco, Golden Chop Stix, Hawaiian BBQ, Home Town Buffet, Hooters, Jamba Juice, Jason's Deli, John's Pizza, McDonald's, Mimi's Cafe, Olive Garden, Outback Steaks, Panda Express, Panera Bread, Portillo's Hot Dogs, Qdoba Mexican, Quiznos, Red Robin, Rubio's, Starbucks, Subway, Wendy's, Wienerschnitzel, 🛏 Ayres Hotel, Hampton Inn, 🄾 Best Buy, Costco/gas, $Tree, Home Depot, JC Penney, Jo-Ann Fabrics, Lowe's, Macy's, Marshall's, Michael's, 99¢ Store, Old Navy, PetCo, Petsmart, Sears/auto, Staples, Target, Verizon, Walmart, WinCo Foods, World Mkt, mall
28	Eucalyptus Ave, Eastridge Ave, E 🍴 Bravo Burgers, Hooters, 🄾 Sam's Club/gas, Target, Walmart, same as 29
27b	(27c from sb), Alessandro Blvd, E 🅐 Arco/dsl, 🄾 Big O Tire, auto repair, W 🅐 Chevron, 🍴 Farmer Boys
27a	Cactus Ave to March ARB, E 🅐 Chevron/dsl, 76/dsl, 🍴 Carl's Jr
25	Van Buren Blvd, E 🄾 March Field Museum, W 🄾 Riverside Nat Cen.
23	Harley Knox Blvd, E 🄾 auto repair
22	Ramona Expswy, **1 mi** E **on Perris Blvd** 🅐 Arco, Chevron, Mobil/Circle K, Shell/Subway/dsl, 🍴 Farmer Boys, Harry's Cafe, Papa John's, Starbucks, Valentino's Plzza, W 🅐 Arco/dsl/scales/24hr, 76/Circle K/dsl/LP, 🍴 Jack-in-the-Box
19	Nuevo Rd, E 🅐 Arco, Chevron/dsl, Mobil/Circle K, 🍴 Baskin-Robbins, Burger King, Carl's Jr, China Palace, Del Taco, El Pollo Loco, IHOP, Jenny's Rest., McDonald's, Pizza Hut, Sizzler, Starbucks, Subway, 🄾 AutoZone, Big-Lots, Food4Less, GNC, O'Reilly Parts, Radio Shack, Rite Aid, Stater Bros Foods, Walmart
17	CA 74 W, 4th St, to Perris, Lake Elsinore, E 🅐 Shell, W 🅐 Chevron, 🍴 Del Taco, Denny's, Jack-in-the-Box, Jimenez Mexican, Little Caesar's, Popeye's, 🛏 Holiday Inn Express, 🄾 AutoZone, Chrysler/Dodge/Jeep/Kia
15	CA 74 E, Hemet, E 🛏 Sun Leisure Motel
14	Ethanac Rd, E 🍴 KFC/Taco Bell, 🄾 Richardson's RV, W 🅐 Circle K/dsl, 76/dsl, 🍴 Carl's Jr, Del Taco, Ono Hawaiian BBQ, Starbucks, Subway, 🄾 Just Tires, Home Depot, Verizon, WinCo Foods
12	McCall Blvd, Sun City, E 🅐 Valero/dsl, 🍴 Wendy's, 🛏 Best Value Inn, Motel 6, 🄾 H, W 🅐 Chevron/dsl, United Oil, 🍴 Coco's, McDonald's, Santana's Mexican, Subway, 🄾 Rite Aid, Von's Foods, Walgreens
10	Newport Rd, Quail Valley, E 🅐 Shell/Del Taco/dsl, 🍴 Cathay Chinese, Jack-in-the-Box, Papa John's, Subway, Taco Bell, 🄾 AutoZone, $Tree, GNC, Ralph's Foods, Ross, W 🅐 76/Circle K/dsl, 🍴 Baskin-Robbins, BJ Rest., Chipotle Mexican, In-N-Out, Miguel's Mexican, NY Pizza, Panda Express, Panera Bread, Red Robin, Starbucks, Subway, TX Roadhouse, Yellow Basket Cafe, 🄾 AT&T, Best Buy, Kohl's, Lowe's, Michael's, Old Navy, PetCo, Radio Shack, Staples, SuperTarget, TJ Maxx, Verizon, Urgent Care
7	Scott Rd, E 🅐 Arco/dsl, 7-11, 🍴 Carl's Jr, Del Taco, Jack-in-the-Box, Subway, Wood Rock Fire Pizza, 🄾 Albertson's/SavOn, Verizon, Walgreens
4	Clinton Keith Rd, W 🍴 Del Taco, Juice It Up, Starbucks, Subway, 🄾 Mtn View Tire, Target, Walgreens
2	Los Alamos, E 🅐 Shell, 🍴 Board'z Grill, In-N-Out, Miguel's Jr Mexican, Peony Chinese, Sebastian's Italian, Taco Bell, 🄾 USPO, W 🅐 Mobil/Circle K/dsl, 🍴 Chuck-eCheese, Jack-in-the-Box, McDonald's, Pizza Hut, Starbucks, Subway, TJ's Pizza, 🄾 CVS Drug, Stater Bros., vet
1	Murrieta Hot Springs, E 🅐 7-11, Shell/dsl, 🍴 Alberto's Mexican, Buffalo Wild Wings, Carl's Jr, El Pollo Loco, Hungry Bull, Richie's Diner, Rubio's, Sizzler, Starbucks, Wendy's, 🄾 Ralph's Foods, Rite Aid, Ross, Sam's Club/gas, Walgreens, W 🍴 Richie's Diner, Starbucks,
0mm	I-215 begins/ends on I-15.

Side labels: PERRIS, MURRIETA, SAN FRANCISCO

↑E INTERSTATE 280 (BAY AREA)

Exit	Services
58	4th St, **I-280 begins/ends**, N 🄾 Whole Foods Mkt, S 🅐 Shell
57	7th St, to I-80, downtown
56	Mariposa St, downtown
55	Army St, Port of SF
54	US 101 S, Alemany Blvd, Mission St, E 🅐 Shell
52	San Jose Ave, Bosworth St (from nb, no return)
51	Geneva Ave
50	CA 1, 19th Ave, W 🅐 Chevron, 🄾 to Bay Bridge, SFSU
49	Daly City, E 🅐 76/dsl/LP, 🄾 Toyota, Walgreens, W 🅐 Arco, 🍴 Carl's Jr, Domino's, IHOP, In-N-Out, Krispy Kreme, McDonald's, Val's Rest., 🛏 Hampton Inn
47a	Serramonte Blvd, Daly City (from sb), E 🅐 Silver Gas, 🄾 Cadillac, Chevrolet, Ford, Home Depot, Honda, Nissan, Target, W 🅐 Olympian, 76, 🍴 Boston Mkt, Elephant Bar Rest., McDonald's, Sizzler, Starbucks, 🄾 Macy's, Longs Drugs, Office Depot, PetsMart, Ross, Target
47b	CA 1, Mission St (from nb), Pacifica, E 🍴 Hawaiian BBQ, RoundTable Pizza, Sizzler, 🄾 H, Chrysler/Jeep/Dodge, Drug Barn, Fresh Choice Foods, Home Depot, Infiniti, Isuzu, Jo-Ann Fabrics, Lexus, Mitsubishi, Nordstrom's, PetCo, Target, mall
46	Hickey Blvd, Colma, E 🅐 Chevron/dsl/24hr, Shell, W 🅐 Shell/dsl/24hr, 🍴 Boston Mkt, Celia's Rest., Koi Palace, Moonstar, Outback Steaks, Sizzler, 🄾 Ross, 7-11
45	Avalon Dr (from sb), Westborough, W 🅐 Arco/24hr, Valero/dsl, 🍴 Denny's, McDonald's, Subway, 🄾 Pak'n Save Foods, Walgreens/24hr, Skyline Coll
44	(from nb)
43b	I-380 E, to US 101, to SF ✈
43a	San Bruno Ave, Sneath Ave, E 🍴 Au's Kitchen, Baskin-Robbins, Carl's Jr, Jamba Juice, Quizno's, Starbucks, Taco Bell, 🄾 GNC, Longs Drugs, Mollie Stones Mkt, Radio Shack, W 🅐 Chevron, 76, 🍴 Baker's Square, 🄾 7-11

📶E INTERSTATE 280 (BAY AREA) CONT'D

Exit	Services
42	Crystal Springs (from sb), county park
41	CA 35 N, Skyline Blvd (from wb, no EZ return), to Pacifica **1 mi W** 📶 Chevron
40	Millbrae Ave, Millbrae, **E** 📶 Chevron
39	Trousdale Dr, to Burlingame, **E** 🏠
36	Black Mtn Rd, Hayne Rd, **W** golf, vista point
36mm	**Crystal Springs** Ⓡ **wb, full** 🚻 **facilities,** 🚮**, picnic table, litter barrels, petwalk**
35	CA 35, CA 92W (from eb), to Half Moon Bay
34	Bunker Hill Dr
33	CA 92, to Half Moon Bay, San Mateo
32mm	vista point both lanes
29	Edgewood Rd, Canada Rd, to San Carlos, **E** Ⓞ 🏠
27	Farm Hill Blvd, **E** Ⓞ Cañada Coll, 🚮
25	CA 84, Woodside Rd, Redwood City, **1 mi W** 📶 Chevron/dsl, 🍴 John Bentley's Rest., Buck's Rest., Ⓞ Robert's Mkt, USPO
24	Sand Hill Rd, Menlo Park. **1 mi E** 📶 Shell, 🍴 Starbucks, Ⓞ Longs Drug, Safeway
22	Alpine Rd, Portola Valley, **E** Ⓞ 🏠, **W** 📶 Shell/autocare, 🍴 Red Lotus Cafe, RoundTable Pizza, Ⓞ Curves
20	Page Mill Rd, to Palo Alto, **E** 🏠, to Stanford U
16	El Monte Rd, Moody Rd
15	Magdalena Ave
13	Foothill Expswy, Grant Rd, **E** 📶 Chevron/24hr, 🍴 Starbucks, Woodpecker Grill, Ⓞ Rite Aid, Trader Joe's, **W** Ⓞ to Rancho San Antonio CP
12b a	CA 85, N to Mtn View, S to Gilroy
11	Saratoga, Cupertino, Sunnyvale, **E** 📶 Chevron, 🍴 Carl's Jr, Quizno's, 🏠 Cupertino Inn, Ⓞ Goodyear, Michael's, Rite Aid, TJ Maxx, repair, **W** 📶 Chevron, Dianza Gas, 76, USA, 🍴 BJ's Rest., Outback Steaks, 🏠 Cypress Hotel, Ⓞ Apple Computer HQ, PetsMart
10	Wolfe Rd, **E** 📶 Arco/24hr, 🍴 Teppan Steaks, Starbucks, 🏠 Courtyard, Hilton Garden, Ⓞ Ranch Mkt, **W** 📶 76, 🍴 Alexander Steaks, Benihana, Vallco Dynasty Chinese, Ⓞ FreshChoice Foods, JC Penney, Jiffy Lube, Sears/auto, Vallco Fashion Park
9	Lawrence Expswy, Stevens Creek Blvd (from eb), **N** 🍴 El Pollo Loco, McDonalds, Mtn Mikes Pizza, Panda Express, Quizno's, Starbucks, Ⓞ Safeway, Marshalls, Ⓞ Land Rover, Nissan, **S** 📶 Rotten Robbie, 76, 🍴 IHOP, Subway, 🏠 7-11, Woodcrest Hotel
7	Saratoga Ave, **N** 📶 Arco/24hr, Chevron/24hr, 🍴 Black Angus, Burger King, Garden City Rest., Happi House, Lion Rest., McDonald's, Taco Bell, Ⓞ Cadillac, Chevrolet, Ford, Goodyear, Jiffy Lube, PepBoys, 7-11, **S** 📶 76, Shell, Valero, 🍴 Applebee's, Tony Roma's, 🏠 MoorPark Hotel
5c	Winchester Blvd, Campbell Ave (from eb)
5b	CA 17 S, to Santa Cruz, I-880 N, to San Jose
5a	Leigh Ave, Bascom Ave
4	Meridian St (from eb), **N** 📶 76, Ⓞ Big O Tire, FoodMaxx, **S** 📶 Chevron, 🍴 KFC, Subway, Wienerschnitzel, Ⓞ 7-11
3b	Bird Ave, Race St
3a	CA 87, **N** 🏠 Hilton, Holiday Inn, Hotel Sainte Claire, Marriott
2	7th St, to CA 82, **N** conv ctr
1	10th St, 11th St, **N** Ⓞ 7-11, Ⓞ to San Jose St U
0mm	**I-280 begins/ends on US 101.**

📶N INTERSTATE 405 LOS ANGELES

Exit	Services
73	I-5, N to Sacramento, I-5, S to LA
72	Rinaldi St, Sepulveda, **E** 📶 Chevron/dsl, 76, 🍴 Arby's, McDonald's, Presidente Mexican, Subway, Ⓞ 🏠, Nissan, Toyota, **W** 📶 Shell, 🏠 Best Value Inn
71	CA 118 W, Simi Valley
70	Devonshire St, Granada Hills, **E** 📶 Arco, GasMart/dsl, 76, 🍴 Holiday Burger, Millie's Rest., Papa John's, Quiznos, Safari Room Rest., Subway, Ⓞ Bare's RV Ctr, Radio Shack, Ralph's Foods, Rite Aid, Verizon, Vons Foods
69	Nordhoff St, **E** 📶 Mobil/dsl, 🍴 China Wok, Coldstone, Del Taco, KFC, Panda Express, Pollo Campero, 7 Mares, Starbucks, 🏠 Hillcrest Inn, Ⓞ Marshalls, 7-11, Vallarta Foods, Walgreens, **W** 📶 Arco, 76/dsl, 🍴 Jack-in-the-Box, Pizza Hut
68	Roscoe Blvd, to Panorama City, **E** 📶 76/dsl, Shell, 🍴 Burger King, Country Folks Rest., Denny's, Galpin Rest., Jack-in-the-Box, Little Caesars, McDonald's, Panda Express, Taco Bell, Yoshinoya, 🏠 Holiday Inn Express, Ⓞ AutoZone, Ford, Lincoln, Jaguar/Volvo, 7-11, U-Haul, **W** 📶 Chevron/dsl, Shell/dsl, 🍴 Tommy's Burgers, 🏠 Motel 6
66	Sherman Blvd, Reseda, **E** 📶 Chevron, Mobil/LP, 🍴 Golden Chicken, KFC, McDonald's, Starbucks, 🏠 Motel 6, Ⓞ BigLots, CVS Drug, Jon's Foods, **W** 📶 76/dsl/24hr, 🍴 Taco Bell, Ⓞ 🏠, USPO
65	Victory Blvd, Van Nuys, **E on Sepulveda** 🍴 Carl's Jr, El Pollo Loco, Jack-in-the-Box, Subway, Wendy's, Ⓞ CVS Drug, El Monte RV Ctr, Costco/gas, Office Depot, PepBoys, Staples, **W on Victory** 📶 Arco/24hr, Ⓞ 🏠
64	Burbank Blvd, **E** 📶 Chevron, Shell, 🍴 Denny's, 🏠 Best Western, Hampton Inn, Ⓞ Target
63b	US 101, Ventura Fwy
63a	Ventura Blvd (from nb), **E** 📶 Mobil, 🍴 Cheesecake Factory, El Pollo Loco, Ⓞ Whole Foods Mkt, mall, **W** 📶 76, 🍴 Ameci Pizza, CA Chicken Cafe, Corner Bakery Cafe, IHOP, McDonald's, 🏠 Courtyard, Valley Inn
63a	Valley Vista Blvd (from sb)
61	Mulholland Dr, Skirvall Dr
59	Sepulveda Blvd, Getty Ctr Dr, **W** to Getty Ctr
57	Sunset Blvd, Morega Dr, **E** 📶 Chevron/24hr, 76/dsl, Ⓞ to UCLA, **W** 🏠 Luxe Hotel
56	Waterford St, Montana Ave (from nb)
55c b	Wilshire Blvd, **E** downtown, **W** Ⓞ 🏠
55a	CA 2, Santa Monica Blvd, **E** 📶 Chevron, Mobil, Shell, Thrifty, 🍴 Coffee Bean, Jack-in-the-Box, Jamba Juice, Quiznos, Starbucks, Winchell's, Yoshinoya, Zankau Chicken, Ⓞ Firestone/auto, 7-11, LDS Temple, Staples, vet, **W** 📶 Chevron/dsl, 76/24hr, 🍴 Subway, 🏠 Holiday Inn Express
54	Olympic Blvd, Peco Blvd, **E** 📶 Mobil, 🍴 Islands Burgers, Jack-in-the-Box, La Salsa, Norm's Rest., Stabucks, Ⓞ Barnes&Noble, Nordstroms, **W** 🍴 Big Tomy's Rest., Ⓞ Best Buy, Marshall's, Ⓞ USPO
53	I-10, Santa Monica Fwy
52	Venice Blvd, **E** 📶 Chevron/service, Shell/dsl, 🍴 Carl's Jr, Subway, 🏠 Ramada, Ⓞ 7-11, services on Sepulveda, **W** 📶 SP/dsl, 🍴 FatBurger
51	Culver Blvd, Washington Blvd, **E** 🍴 Dear John's Café, Taco Bell, Ⓞ vet, **W** 📶 76/repair
50b	CA 90, Slauson Ave, to Marina del Rey, **E** 📶 Arco/24hr,

(vertical side text left: SAN JOSE, CA)
(vertical side text right: LOS ANGELES AREA)

⬆N INTERSTATE 405 (LOS ANGELES) CONT'D

Exit	Services
50b	Continued

50b 🅕 Del Taco, El Pollo Loco, HoneyBaked Ham, Shakey's Pizza, Winchell's, 🅞 BigLots, $Tree, Firestone/auto, Goodyear/auto, Just Tires, Office Depot, Old Navy, Staples, transmissions, **W** 🅖 76, 🅕 Denny's, 🅞 Albertson's

50a Jefferson Blvd (from sb), **E** 🅕 Coco's, Jack-in-the-Box, 🅞 PetsMart, Rite Aid, Target, **W** to LA ✈

49 Howard Hughes Pkwy, to Centinela Ave, **E** 🅖 Chevron/dsl, Mobil/dsl, 🅕 BJ's Brewhouse, Quiznos, Sizzler, 🅛 Courtyard, Sheraton, 🅞 Best Buy, CVS Drug, Ford, Honda, JC Penney, Macy's, Marshall's, Target, mall, **W** 🅖 Chevron, 🅕 Dinah's Rest., Habuki Japanese, Islands Burgers, Marie Callender's, Rubio's, Starbucks, Subway, Wild Thai, 🅛 Extended Stay America, Radisson, 🅞 Howard Hughes Ctr, Nordstrom

48 La Tijera Blvd, **E** 🅖 Mobil/sl, 🅕 Burger King, ChuckeCheese, El Pollo Loco, Jamba Juice, KFC, McDonald's, Starbucks, Subway, Taco Bell, TGIFriday's, 🅛 Best Western, 🅞 CVS Drug, 99¢ Store, Ralph's Foods, Ross, Vons Foods, **W** 🅖 Chevron/dsl/24hr, 76/Circle K, 🅕 Buggy Whip Rest., Wendy's, 🅞 USPO

47 CA 42, Manchester Ave, Inglewood, **E** 🅖 76/Circle K/dsl/24hr, 🅕 Carl's Jr, Subway, 🅛 Best Western, Economy Inn, 🅞 7-11, repair, **W** 🅖 Arco, Circle K, Shell, 76, Valero, 🅕 Arby's, Burger King, Denny's, El Pollo Loco, Jack-in-the-Box, Louis Burgers, 🅛 Days Inn, 🅞 CarMax, Chrysler/Dodge/Jeep, Home Depot, Hyundai

46 Century Blvd, **E** 🅖 Chevron/dsl, 🅕 Casa Gamino Mexican, El Pollo Loco, Flower Drum Chinese, Hawaiian BBQ, Little Caesars, Panda Express, Rally's, 🅛 Best Value Inn, Best Western, Comfort Inn, Motel 6, Tivoli Hotel, 🅞 LAX Transmissions, 7-11, **W** 🅖 Arco/24hr, Chevron/dsl, 76/Circle K, Shell, 🅕 Carl's Jr, Denny's, McDonald's, Pizza Hut/Taco Bell, 🅛 Hampton Inn, Hilton, Holiday Inn, Marriott, La Quinta, Travelodge, Westin Hotel, 🅞 to LAX

45 I-105, Imperial Hwy, **E** 🅖 76/dsl, Shell, Valero, 🅕 El Pollo Loco, El Tarasco Mexican, KFC/Taco Bell, Jack-in-the-Box, McDonald's, 🅛 Best Value Inn, Candlewood Suites, Holiday Inn Express, 🅞 J&S Transmissions, repair, **W** 🅕 Wild Goose Rest./Theater (1mi)

44 El Segundo Blvd, to El Segundo, **E** 🅖 Chevron/24hr, Thrifty, Valero, 🅕 Burger King, Christy's Donuts, Cougars Burgers, Jack-in-the-Box, Jase Burgers, Subway, 🅛 El Segundo Inn, 🅞 transmissions, **W** 🅕 Denny's, 🅛 Ramada Inn

43b a Rosecrans Ave, to Manhattan Beach, **E** 🅖 76, Shell, 🅕 Denny's, El Pollo Loco, Pizza Hut, Starbucks, Subway, 🅞 Best Buy, CVS Drug, Food4Less, Ford/Lincoln, Home Depot, Marshall's, Michael's, Office Depot, Ross, **W** 🅖 Thrifty, 🅕 Cafe Rio, Carl's Jr, Chipotle Mexican, Flemings Rest., Hawaiian BBQ, Houston's, Luigi's Rest., Macaroni Grill, McDonald's, Qdoba Mexican, Robeks Juice, Sansai Japanese, Starbucks, Subway, 🅛 Ayres Hotel, Hyatt, TownePlace Suites, SpringHill Suites, 🅞 AT&T, Barnes&Noble, Costco/gas, CVS Drug, Fresh&Easy, Nissan, Office Depot, Old Navy, Staples, Trader Joe's, VW

42b Inglewood Ave, **E** 🅖 Shell, 🅕 Baskin-Robbins, Del Taco, Denny's, Domino's, In-N-Out, Quiznos, 🅞 CVS Drug, Marshall's, PetCo, Vons Foods, **W** 🅖 76, Shell/dsl/24hr, 🅕 La Salsa Mexican, Subway, 🅞 99¢ Store, repair

42a CA 107, Hawthorne Blvd, **E** 🅖 Chevron, 🅕 Carl's Jr, Jack-in-the-Box, Little Caesars, McDonald's, Panda Express, Papa John's, Wendy's, Wienerschnitzel, 🅛 Baymont Inn, Best Western, Days Inn, 🅞 CVS Drug, Kragen Parts, 99¢ Store, PepBoys, Radio Shack, Value+ Foods, vet, **W** 🅖 Arco/24hr, Chevron/dsl, Thrifty, 🅕 Boston Mkt, Marie Callendar's, Quiznos, Sizzler, Starbucks, Subway, Taco Bell, Yoshinoya, 🅞 AutoZone, Macy's, Nordstom

40b Redondo Beach Blvd (no EZ sb return), Hermosa Beach, **E** 🅖 Arco/24hr, 76, 🅕 ChuckeCheese, Jack-in-the-Box, 🅞 golf, **W** 🅕 RoundTable Pizza, Starbucks, 🅞 AutoZone, Curves, CVS Drug, Urgent Care

40a CA 91 E, Artesia Blvd, to Torrance, **W** 🅖 Chevron, 🅒 Carl's Jr, Starbucks, YumYum Donuts

39 Crenshaw Blvd, to Torrance, **E** 🅖 Arco/24hr, Shell, 🅕 Burger King, El Pollo Loco, McDonald's, 🅞 Ralph's Foods, USPO, **W** 🅖 Mobil/dsl, Shell/Subway/dsl, 🅞 Jiffy Lube

38b Western Ave, to Torrance, **E** 🅖 Arco, Chevron, 76/dsl, 🅕 Del Taco, Denny's, Hong Kong Express, Local Place, Papa John's, Quiznos, Starbucks, Wendy's, Yorgo's Burgers, 🅛 Dynasty Inn, 🅞 Albertson's/Sav-On, Curves, GNC, Toyota/Scion, **W** 🅖 Mobil, 🅕 Mill's Rest., 🅛 Courtyard, 🅞 Lexus

38a Normandie Ave, to Gardena, **E** 🅛 Comfort Inn, **W** 🅖 Shell/dsl, 🅕 Big Island BBQ, Carl's Jr, Chile Verde Mexican, Hong Kong Cafe, Pizza Hut/Taco Bell, Quiznos, Starbucks, Subway, Wienerschnitzel, 🅛 Extended Stay America, 🅞 $Tree, Walmart

37b Vermont Ave (from sb), **W** 🅛 Holiday Inn, 🅞 hwy patrol

37a I-110, Harbor Fwy

36 Main St (from nb)

36mm **weigh sta both lanes**

35 Avalon Blvd, to Carson, **E** 🅖 Chevron, Mobil, 🅕 Carson Buffet, Chili's, ChuckeCheese, Denny's, 5 Guys Burgers, FoodCourt, Jack-in-the-Box, Jamba Juice, McDonald's, Panda Express, Panera Bread, Pizza Hut, Quiznos, Sensai Grill, Shakey's Pizza, Sizzler, Starbucks, Tokyo Grill, Tony Roma, WingStop, 🅛 Clarion, 🅞 America's Tire, AT&T, Bestway Foods, Firestone/auto, Goodyear/auto, Ikea, JC Penney, Just Tires, PepBoys, Radio Shack, Sears/auto, Target, Verizon, mall, USPO, **W** 🅖 Arco/24hr, Mobil, 🅕 Carl's Jr, McDonald's, 🅞 Kia, Kragen Parts, Ralph's Foods

34 Carson St, to Carson, **E** 🅛 EconoLodge, **W** 🅖 Mobil, 76/dsl/24hr, 🅕 Carl's Jr, Jack-in-the-Box, Subway, 🅛 DoubleTree Inn

33b Wilmington Ave, **E** 🅖 Mobil/dsl, 🅕 Carson Burgers, **W** 🅖 Chevron/Jack-in-the-Box/dsl, Shell/Subway/dsl, 🅕

Vertical margin labels: HAWTHORNE (left), TORRANCE (center), CARSON (center-lower)

CA

⬆N INTERSTATE 405 (LOS ANGELES) CONT'D

Exit	Services
33b	Continued
	Del Taco, Spires Rest., 🅞 Chevrolet/Hyundai, Honda, Nissan, Toyota/Scion
33a	Alameda St
32d	Santa Fe Ave (from nb), E 🅖 Arco/24hr, W 🅖 Chevron/24hr, United/dsl, 🍴 Fantastic Burgers
32c b	I-710, Long Beach Fwy
32a	Pacific Ave (from sb)
30b	Long Beach Blvd, E 🅖 Arco/dsl, 🍴 Subway, 🅞 7-11, W 🅖 Exxon, 🅞 H
30a	Atlantic Blvd, E 🅖 Chevron/dsl, 🍴 Arby's, Carl's Jr, Denny's/24hr, El Torito, Jack-in-the-Box, Polly's Cafe, 🅞 CVS Drug, NAPACare, Staples, Target, Walgreens, vet, W 🅞 H, $Tree, Home Depot, PetCo, Ross
29c	Orange Ave (from sb), W 🅞 Dodge/GMC/Nissan
29b a	Cherry Ave, to Signal Hill, E 🅖 Mobil/dsl, 🍴 Fantastic Burgers, 🅞 Ford, Lincoln, Mazda, auto repair, W 🅖 76, 🅞 America's Tire, Best Buy, BMW/Mini, Buick, Dodge, Firestone, Honda, Mercedes, Nissan
27	CA 19, Lakewood Blvd, E 🏠 Marriott, 🅞 ✈, W 🅖 Chevron, Shell/24hr, 🍴 Spires Rest., 🏠 Extended Stay America, Holiday Inn, Residence Inn, 🅞 H, Ford, Goodyear/auto
26b	Bellflower Blvd, E 🅖 76, 🍴 Burger King, Carl's Jr, Denny's, Jamba Juice, KFC, Papa John's, Subway, Togo's, 🅞 Ford, K-Mart, Lowe's, W 🅖 Chevron, Mobil/dsl, Shell, 🍴 Baja Fresh, Hof's Hut, IHOP, McDonald's, Pick-Up Stix, Quiznos, Wendy's, 🅞 H, BigLots, CVS Drug, Goodyear/auto, Rite Aid/24hr, Sears, See's Candies, Target, USPO
26a	Woodruff Ave (from nb)
25	Palo Verde Ave, W 🅖 76, 🍴 Dave's Burgers, Del Taco, Domino's, Pizza Hut/Taco Bell, Starbucks, Subway
24b	Studebaker Rd (from sb)
24a	I-605 N
23	CA 22 W, 7th St, to Long Beach
22	Seal Beach Blvd, Los Alamitos Blvd, E 🅖 Chevron/repair/24hr, Mobil/dsl, 76/dsl, 🍴 Baja Fresh, CA Pizza Kitchen Daphne's Greek, Hot Off the Grill, Islands Burgers, Jamba Juice, KFC, Kobe Japanese, Macaroni Grill, Marie Callenders, Peiwei Asian, Pick-Up Stix, Quiznos, Rubio's, Spaghettini Grill, Starbucks, Z Pizza, 🏠 Ayres Hotel, 🅞 AT&T, CVS Drug, GNC, Kohl's, Marshall's, Ralph's Foods, Sprouts Mkt, Target, **1 mi** W 🅖 Chevron, 76/dsl, 🍴 Carl's Jr, Del Taco, Domino's, 🏠 Hampton Inn
21	CA 22 E, Garden Grove Fwy, Valley View St, E 🅞 Ford
19	Westminster Ave, to Springdale St, E 🅖 Arco/24hr, Chevron/dsl, 76/Circle K, Thrifty, 🍴 Café Westminster, Carl's Jr, In-N-Out, KFC, McDonald's, 🏠 Knights Inn, Motel 6, Travelodge, 🅞 America's Tire, AutoZone, BigLots, Home Depot, Kragen Parts, Radio Shack, Rite Aid, Ross, 7-11, W 🅖 Chevron/dsl/24hr, 🍴 Starbucks, Subway, 🏠 Best Western, Courtyard Inn, 🍴 Ranchito Mkt
18	Bolsa Ave, Golden West St, W 🅖 Mobil/dsl, 76, 🍴 Coco's, El Torito, IHOP, Jack-in-the-Box, Outback Steaks, Rodrigo's Mexican, Starbucks, Wendy's, 🅞 CVS Drug, $Tree, JC Penney, Jo-Ann Fabrics, Jons Foods, Macy's, Sears/auto, Target, mall
16	CA 39, Beach Blvd, to Huntington Bch, E 🅖 Chevron, Shell, 🍴 Jack-in-the-Box, Subway, 🏠 Super 8, 🅞 H, PepBoys, Toyota, U-Haul, W 🅖 Mobil/service, 🍴 Arby's,

C O S T A   M E S A

Exit	Services
16	Continued
	BJ's Rest., Buca Italian, Burger King, CA Pizza Kitchen, Chipotle Mexican, Panera Bread, Islands Burgers, Jack-in-the-Box, Macaroni Grill, Marie Callender's, McDonald's, Popeye's, Quiznos, Starbucks, Subway, 🏠 Comfort Suites, 🅞 AT&T, Barnes&Noble, Big O Tire, Chrysler/Dodge/Jeep, Firestone/auto, Kohl's, Office Depot, See's Candies, Staples, Target, Verizon, Whole Foods Mkt
15b a	Magnolia St, Warner Ave, E 🍴 Del Taco, Sizzler, 🅞 Fresh&Easy, W 🅖 Chevron, Mobil, 🍴 Carrow's, Magnolia Café, Starbucks, Tommy's Burgers, 🏠 Days Inn, 🅞 CVS Drug, Grocery Outlet, 7-11, Tuesday Morning, Winchell's
14	Brookhurst St, Fountain Valley, E 🅖 Arco/24hr, Chevron, Mobil, Shell, 🍴 Alerto's Mexican, Carl's Jr, Coco's, Del Taco, KFC, Taco Bell, 🏠 Courtyard, Residence Inn, 🅞 America's Tire, Sam's Club/gas, Thompson's RV Ctr, W 🅖 Arco, 76/dsl, Shell/dsl, 🍴 Applebee's, Black Angus, Chop Stix, ClaimJumper, Coco's, Coldstone, Corner Bakery Cafe, Islands Burgers, Mandarin, Mimi's Cafe, Quiznos, Rubio's, Starbucks, Subway, Togo's, Wendy's, 🅞 H Albertson's, Office Depot, Ralph's Foods, Rite Aid, TJ Maxx, vet
12	Euclid Ave, E 🍴 Cancun Fresh, Carl's Jr, Coffee Bean, FlameBroiler, Panda Express, Pita Fresh Grill, Quiznos, Souplantation, Starbucks, Subway, Taco Bell, Z Pizza, 🅞 H, Big Lots, Costco/gas, $Tree, PetsMart, Staples, Tire Whse
11b	Harbor Blvd, to Costa Mesa, E 🍴 Hooters, 🏠 La Quinta, W 🅖 Arco, Chevron, Mobil, Shell/dsl, 7-11, 🍴 Burger King, Denny's, Domino's, El Pollo Loco, IHOP, Jack-in-the-Box, KFC, LJ Silver, McDonald's, Subway, 🏠 Costa Mesa Inn, Motel 6, Super 8, Vagabond Inn, 🅞 Acura/Dodge, Albertson's, Big O Tire, Buick, Cadillac, Chevrolet, Ford/Lincoln, Honda, Infiniti, JustTires, Mazda, Radio Shack, Rite Aid, Target, Vons Foods, Winchell's
11a	Fairview Rd, E 🅞 Barnes&Noble, Best Buy, Marshall's, Nordstrom's, Old Navy, W 🅖 Chevron, 76, Shell, 🍴 Del Taco, Jack-in-the-Box, Round Table Pizza, Taco Bell, 🅞 CVS Drug, Kragen Parts, Stater Bros
10	CA 73, to CA 55 S (from sb); Corona del Mar, Newport Beach
9b	Bristol St, E 🅖 Chevron/dsl, 🍴 Antonello's Italian, Baja Fresh, Baskin-Robbins, Boudin SF Cafe, Capital Grill, Carrow's, Chick-fil-A, China Olive, Chipotle Mexican, ClaimJumper, Corner Bakery, Darya Persian, In-N-Out, Jack-in-the-Box, Jade Palace, Maggiano's Rest., McDonald's, Morton's Steaks, Pat&Oscar's, Pizza Hut, Quiznos, Red Robin, Sabores Mexican, Scott Seafood, South Coast Rest, Starbucks, Subway, Z Pizza, Ztejas Rest, 🏠 Marriott Suites, Westin Hotel, 🅞 BigLots, Bloomingdale's, CVS Drug, Firestone/auto, GNC, Macy's, Michael's, Office Depot, PetCo, Radio Shack, Rite Aid, Ross, Sears/auto, Staples, Target, TJ Maxx, Trader Joe's, Vons Foods, World Mkt, mall, W 🅖 Chevron/dsl, 76/Circle K/dsl, 🍴 Del Taco/24hr, El Pollo Loco, McDonald's, Orchid Rest., Subway, Wahoo's Fish Taco, 🏠 Hanford Hotel, Hilton, 🅞 PepBoys, 7-11, vet
9a	CA 55, Costa Mesa Fwy, to Newport Bch, Riverside
8	MacArthur Blvd, E 🅖 Chevron, Mobil/Subway, 🍴 Carl's Jr, El Torito, McCormick&Schmick's, McDonald's, Quiznos, Starbucks, 🏠 Crowne Plaza, Embassy Suites, 🅞

🧭 INTERSTATE 405 (LOS ANGELES) CONT'D

IRVINE

Exit	Services
8	Continued
	Pepperdine U, **W** 🅖 Chevron, 🍴 El Torito, Gulliver's Ribs, IHOP, 🏨 Atrium Hotel, Hilton, to ✈
7	Jamboree Rd, Irvine, **E** 🅖 Shell, 🍴 Andrei's Rest., Burger King, Soup Plantation, 🏨 Courtyard, Hyatt, Residence Inn, **W** 🍴 CA Pizza Kitchen, Daily Grill, FatBurger, Flamebroiler, Houston's, Melting Pot, Ruth's Chris Steaks, Starbucks, Subway, Taleo Mexico, Wahoo's Fish Taco, 🏨 Marriott, 🅾 Office Depot
5	Culver Dr, **W** 🅖 Alfie's Gas, Chevron/dsl, 🍴 Carl's Jr, Subway, 🅾 Ace Hardware, Rite Aid, Wholesome Foods Mkt
4	Jeffrey Rd, University Dr, **E** 🅖 Chevron, Circle K/gas, 🍴 Baja Fresh, Coffee Bean, Daphney's Greek, El Cholo Cantina, El Pollo Loco, Golden Spoon, Juice It Up, McDonald's, NY Pizza, Peiwei Asian, Pick-Up Stix, Pomodoro Italian, Starbucks, Togo's, Z Pizza, 🅾 🏨 Ace Hardware, CVS Drug, Gelson's Mkt, Office Depot, Ralph's Foods, Walgreens, **W** 🅖 Mobil/dsl, 🍴 IHOP, Korean BBQ, Subway, 🅾 Curves, Ralph's Foods, vet
3	Sand Canyon Ave, **E** 🏨, **W** 🅖 Arco/dsl, 🏨 Crystal Jade Asian, Lucca Cafe, Mitsui Grill, Red Brick Pizza, Sharkey's Mexican, Starbucks, Subway, Thai Bamboo, 🅾 Albertson's, Starbucks, CVS Drug
2	CA 133, to Laguna Beach, **E** 🏨 DoubleTree Inn
1c	Irvine Center Dr, **E** 🍴 Cheesecake Factory, Chipotle Mexican, Dave&Buster's, Oasis Cafes, Panda Express, PF Chang's, Wahoo's Fish Tacos, 🅾 Barnes&Noble, Macy's, Nordstrom, Target, **W** 🅖 7-11, 🍴 Burger King, La Salsa, NY Deli, 🅾 Big O Tire
1b	Bake Pkwy, **W** 🅾 Carmax, Toyota
1a	Lake Forest
0mm	I-405 begins/ends on I-5, exit 132.

🧭 INTERSTATE 505 (WINTERS)

Exit	Services
33	I-5. I-505 begins/ends on I-5.
31	CA 12A
28	CA 14, Zamora
24	CA 19
21	CA 16, to Esparto, Woodland, **W** 🅖 Guy's Food/fuel, 🍴 La Plazita
17	CA 27
15	CA 29A
11	CA 128 W, Russell Blvd, **W** 🅖 Chevron/24hr, Interstate/dsl, 🍴 RoundTable Pizza, Subway, 🅾 Lorenzo's Mkt, vet
10	Putah Creek Rd, no crossover, same as 11
6	Allendale Rd
3	Midway Rd, **E** 🅾 RV camping
1c	Vaca Valley Pkwy
1b	I-80 E. I-505 begins/ends on I-80.

🧭 INTERSTATE 580 (BAY AREA)

Exit	Services
79	I-580 begins/ends, accesses I-5 sb.
76b a	CA 132, Chrisman Rd, to Modesto, **E** 🅖 76/dsl, 🅾 RV camping (5mi)
72	Corral Hollow Rd
67	Patterson Pass Rd, **W** 🅖 76/dsl/24hr
65	I-205 (from eb), to Tracy

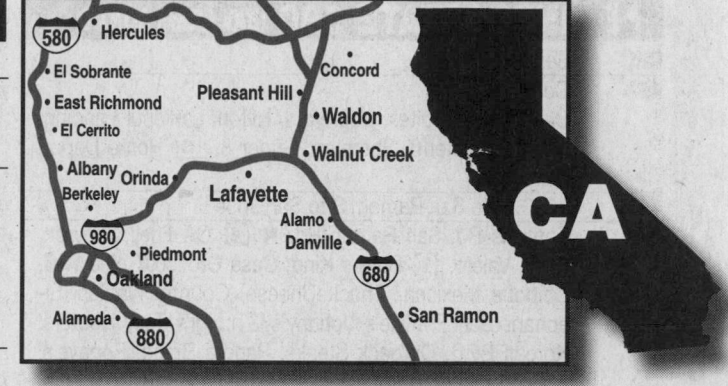

Exit	Services
63	Grant Line Rd, to Byron
59	N Flynn Rd, Altamont Pass, elev 1009, **S** Brake Check Area, many wind-turbines
57	N Greenville Rd, Laughlin Rd, Altamont Pass Rd, to Livermore Lab, **S** 🅖 Chevron/Subway/dsl, 🏨 Best Western, La Quinta, 🅾 Harley-Davidson
56mm	**weigh sta both lanes**
55	Vasco Rd, to Brentwood, **N** 🅖 Arco, Chevron, QuikStop/dsl, 76, Shell/dsl/deli, 🍴 A&W/KFC, McDonald's, **S** 🅖 Citgo/7-11, Valero/dsl, 🍴 Blimpie, Jack-in-the-Box, Taco Bell, 🏨 Quality Inn
54	CA 84, 1st St, Springtown Blvd, Livermore, **N** 🅖 Chevron, 🏨 DoubleTree Hotel, Holiday Inn, Motel 6, Springtown Inn, 🅾 7-11, **S** 🅖 Shell, 76/24hr, Valero/Circle K, 🍴 Applebee's, Arby's, Burger King, Chevy's Mexican, Chili's, Crazy Buffet, IHOP, Italian Express, McDonald's, Panda Express, Starbucks, Subway, Taco Bell, Togo's, 🅾 America's Tire, Longs Drug, Lowe's Whse, Office Depot, Radio Shack, Ross, Safeway/gas, Target
52	N Livermore Ave, **S** 🅖 Chevron/Jack-in-the-Box, Citgo/7-11, 🍴 Baja Fresh, Coldstone Creamery, In-N-Out, Popeye's, Quizno's, String's Itallan, 🏨 Hawthorn Suites, 🅾 Home Depot, Honda, Schwab Tire, Walmart/auto
51	Portola Ave, Livermore (no EZ eb return)
50	Airway Blvd, Collier Canyon Rd, Livermore, **N** 🅖 Shell/dsl, 🍴 Baskin-Robbins, Wendy's, 🏨 Courtyard, Hampton Inn, Hilton Garden, Holiday Inn Express, Residence Inn, 🅾 Costco Whse/gas, **S** 🍴 Cattlemen's Rest., Chicago Pizza, Starbucks, 🏨 Extended Stay America, 🅾 Chrysler/Jeep, Ford/Lincoln, Mazda, 7-11
48	El Charro Rd, O'Fallon Rd
47	Santa Rita Rd, Tassajara Rd, **N** 🅾 Buick/GMC Safeway Foods, **S** 🅖 Shell, 🍴 Bakers Square, Korea Garden, McDonald's, Quizno's, Subway, Taco Bell, TGI Friday, Thai Quisine, 🅾 Acura, BMW, Cadillac, GMC, Hummer, Infiniti, Lexus, Long's Drug, MiniCooper, Mitsubishi, Rose Pavilion Trader Joe's, Volvo
46	Hacienda Dr, Pleasanton, **N** 🅖 Shell, 🍴 Applebee's, Black Angus, Fuddruckers, Macaroni Grill, Mimi's Cafe, On-the-Border, Papa John's, Woks Up, 🏨 AmeriSuites, 🅾 Barnes&Noble, Best Buy, Ford, Old Navy, TJ Maxx, **S** 🍴 Red Robin, 🅾 🏨 Kohl's, Staples, Walmart/auto
45	Hopyard Rd, Pleasanton, **N** 🅖 76/Circle K, Minimart, Shell/dsl, 🏨 Hilton, Holiday Inn Express, 🅾 America's Tire, Dodge, El Monte RV Ctr, Goodyear, Honda, Nissan, Office Depot, Pak'n Sav, RV Ctr, U-Haul, Toyota, **S** 🅖 Chevron, Shell/dsl, 🍴 Arby's, Burger King, Chef India, Chevy's Mexican, Chili's, Denny's, El Balazo, In-N-Out, Nations Burgers, Pleasant Asian, Starbucks, Taco Bell, 🏨

LIVERMORE

PLEASANTON

🅖 = gas 🍴 = food 🛏 = lodging 🅾 = other 🆁🆂 = rest stop   Copyright 2014 - The Next Exit ®

⬆️🅴 INTERSTATE 580 (BAY AREA) CONT'D

CA

CASTRO VALLEY

Exit	Services
45	Continued Candlewood Suites, Courtyard, Hilton, Larkspur Landing, Marriott, Motel 6, Sheraton, Super 8, 🅾 Home Depot, Mercedes
44b	I-680, N to San Ramon, S to San Jose
44a	Foothills Rd, San Ramon Rd, **N** 🅖 CA Fuel, Chevron, Shell, Valero, 🍴 Burger King, Casa Orozco, China Wall, Chipotle Mexican, ChuckeCheese, Country Waffles, Elephant Bar, Frankie's Johnny's & Luigi's Too, Hooters, Korean BBQ, Outback Steaks, Panera Bread, Popeye's, RoundTable Pizza, Starbucks, 🛏 Radisson, 🅾 Big Lots, Curves, $Tree, Kragen Parts, Long's Drug, Marshall's, Michael's, PetCo, PetsMart, Ranch Mkt Foods, Ross, Target, **S** 🍴 Cheesecake Factory, PF Chang's, 🛏 Marriott, Residence Inn, Sheraton, 🅾 JC Penney, Macy's, Nordstrom's, Sears, mall
39	Eden Canyon Rd, Palomares Rd, **S** 🅾 rodeo park
37	Center St, Crow Canyon Rd same as 35, **S** 🅖 Arco /24hr, Chevron/dsl/, 76/dsl, Quikstop, 🍴 McDonald's, Starbucks, Subway
35	Redwood Rd (from eb), Castro Valley, **N** 🅖 Chevron, 76/dsl, Shell/dsl, 🍴 Baker's Square, Chipotle Mexican, KFC, McDonald's, Quizno's, RoundTable Pizza, Sizzler, Taco Bell, Wendy's, 🅾 Comfort Suites, Holiday Inn Express, 🅾 Goodyear, Longs Drug, Lucky Foods, NAPA, Radio Shack, Rite Aid, Safeway, Walgreens
34	I-238 W, to I-880, CA 238, **W off I-238** 🍴 McDonald's, Jack-in-the Box, 🅾 Chrysler/Jeep, 99¢ Store
33	164th Ave, Miramar Ave, **E** 🅖 Chevron/dsl, Valero, 🛏 Fairmont Inn
32	150th Ave, Fairmont, **E** 🅾🅷, **W** 🅖 Shell, 76/dsl, 🍴 Arby's, Burger King, Carrows, Chili's, Denny's, McDonald's, RoundTable Pizza, Starbucks, Tito's Cafe, 🅾 Goodyear, Kohl's, Long's Drug, Macy's, Pepboys, Staples, Target
31	Grand Ave (from sb), Dutton Ave, **W** 🅖 Coast, 🅾 Rite Aid
30	106th Ave, Foothill Blvd, MacArthur Blvd, **W** 🅖 Arco, 🍴 Church's
29	98th Ave, Golf Links Rd, **E** 🅖 Shell, 🅾 Oakland Zoo, **W** 🅖 76, Valero
27b	Keller Ave, Mtn Blvd, **E** repair
27a	Edwards Ave (from sb, no EZ return), **E** US Naval 🅷
26a	CA 13, Warren Fwy, to Berkeley (from eb)
26b	Seminary Rd, **E** Observatory/Planetarium, **W** 🅖 Arco/24hr
25b a	High St, to MacArthur Blvd, **E** 🅖 76, 🍴 Subway, Razzo's Pizza, 🅾 Kragen Parts, Lucky Foods, USPO, **W** 🅖 76, 🅾 Walgreens
24	35th Ave (no EZ sb return), **E** 🅖 76, 🍴 Taco Bell, **W** 🅖 Chevron, QuikStop, 76
23 .	Coolidge Ave, Fruitvale, **E** 🅖 Shell/24hr, 🍴 China Gourmet, McDonald's, Subway, 🅾 Longs Drug, Farmer Joe's, Radio Shack
22	Park Blvd, **E** 🅖 Shell, **W** 🅖 Arco, Quikstop, 🅾🅷
21b	Grand Ave, Lake Shore, **E** 🅖 Chevron/dsl, 76/24hr, 🍴 KFC, Subway, 🅾 Long's Drug, Trader Joe's, Walgreens, USPO, **W** 🅖 Chevron/dsl/24hr
21a	Harrison St, Oakland Ave, **E** 🅖 Quikstop, **W** 🅾 Honda
19d c	CA 24 E, I-980 W, to Oakland
19b	West St, San Pablo Ave, **E** 🛏 Extended Stay America, 🅾 Best Buy, Home Depot, Jo-Ann Fabrics, Michael's, Office Depot

OAKLAND AREA

Exit	Services
19a	I-80 W
18c	Market St, to San Pablo Ave, downtown
18b	Powell St, Emeryville, **E** 🅖 76, 🍴 Burger King, CA Pizza Kitchen, Denny's, Elephant Bar/Grill, Jamba Juice, PF Chang's, Starbucks, Togo's, 🛏 Courtyard, Sheraton, Woodfin Suites, 🅾 Barnes&Noble, Old Navy, Ross, Trader Joe's, **W** 🅖 Shell, 🍴 Chevy's Mexican, 🛏 Hilton Garden
18a	CA 13, Ashby Ave, Bay St, same as 18b
17	University Ave, Berkeley, **E** 🅖 76, University Gas, 🛏 La Quinta, 🅾 to UC Berkeley
16	Gilman St, **E** 🅾 Golden Gate Fields Race Track, **W** 🅾 Target
13	Albany St, Buchanan St (from eb)
12	Central Ave (from eb), El Cerrito, **E** 🅖 Shell, Valero, **W** 🅾 Costco/gas
11	Bayview Ave, Carlson Blvd, **E** 🅖 76
10b	Regatta Blvd, **E** 🅖 Golden Gate/dsl
10a	S 23rd St, Marina Bay Pkwy, **E** 🅖 Stop and Save/dsl, 🍴 Subway, **W** 🍴 Cafe Tiatro, El Molchaete, Quizno's, Wing Stop, 🅾 Longs Drugs
9	Harbour Way, Cutting Blvd, **E** 🅖 Arco, **W** food:Burger King
8	Canal Blvd, Garrard Blvd, **W** 🅖 Chevron/dsl, 🛏 Days Inn
7b	Castro St, to I-80 E, Point Richmond, downtown industrial
7a	Western Drive (from wb), Point Molate
5mm	**Richmond-San Rafael Toll Bridge**
2a	Francis Drake Blvd, to US 101 S, **E** 🛏 Extended Stay Deluxe, 🅾 BMW, Home Depot
1b	Francisco Blvd, San Rafael, **E** 🅖 Beacon, Circle K, Francisco, 🍴 Burger King, La Croissant, 🛏 Motel 6, Travelodge, 🅾 Mazda, tires, U-Haul, **W** 🍴 Subway, Wendy's, 🅾 Office Depot, USPO, to San Quentin
1a	US 101 N to San Rafael, **I-580 begins/ends on US 101.**

⬆️🅴 INTERSTATE 605 (LOS ANGELES)

Exit	Services
27c	Huntington Dr, **I-605 begins/ends.** 🅖 Mobil, 🍴 Subway, 🅾 CVS Drug, Fresh&Easy Foods
27	I-210
26	Arrow Hwy, Live Oak, **E** Santa Fe Dam, **W** Irwindale Speedway
24	Lower Azusa Rd, LA St
23	Ramona Blvd, **E** 🅖 Mobil, 🍴 Del Taco/24hr
22	I-10, E to San Bernardino, W to LA
21	Valley Blvd, to Industry, **E** 🅖 Chevron/Chester's/Subway/dsl, 76, 🍴 El Charro, Las Milpas Mexican, 7 Mares Rest., Winchell's Donuts, 🛏 Valley Inn
19	CA 60, Pamona Fwy
18	Peck Rd, **E** 🅖 Shell, **W** 🅾 Ford Trucks
17	RoseHills Rd, **W** Sports Arena
16	Beverly Blvd
15	Whittier Blvd, **E** 🅖 Arco, 76/dsl, 🍴 Carl's Jr, Taco Bell, YumYum Donuts, 🛏 GoodNite Inn, 🅾 7-11, **W** 🅖 Chevron, Shell, 🍴 DQ, Pizza Hut, Shakey's Pizza, Starbucks, Subway, Taco's Mexico, Tommy's Burgers, 🛏 Howard Johnson, 🅾 AutoZone, Rite Aid
14	Washington Blvd, to Pico Rivera, **E** 🅾 Firestone/auto
13	Slauson Ave, **E** 🅖 Arco, Mobil, 🍴 Denny's, 🛏 Motel 6, **W** 🅷
12	Telegraph Rd, to Santa Fe Springs, **E** 🅖 Chevron, 76, 🍴 Del Taco, Jack-in-the-Box, KFC, Subway, Taco Bell, Yoshinoya, 🅾 Urgent Care, **W** 🅖 Arco/dsl

▶️N INTERSTATE 605 (LOS ANGELES) CONT'D

Exit	Services
12mm	I-5
11	Florence Ave, to Downey, **E** 🅿️ Mobil, 🅾️ Cadillac, Chevrolet, Honda
10	Firestone Blvd, **E** 🅿️ 76, 🍴 ChuckeCheese, KFC, McDonald's, Norm's Burgers, Sam's Burgers, Subway, 🏠 Best Western, 🅾️ Audi/BMW/Porsche, Costco, Food-4Less, 99¢ Store, Staples, Verizon, Walgreens, **W** 🅿️ Chevron/repair, 🍴 Starbucks, 🅾️ Chrysler/Dodge/Jeep, Office Depot, Target
8	I-105, Imperial Hwy, **E** 🅿️ 76, 🍴 Domino's, KFC, LJ Silver, McDonald's, Pizza Hut/Taco Bell, 🅾️ CVS Drug, Food4Less, **W** 🅿️ Arco
9	Rosecrans Ave, to Norwalk, **E** 🅿️ Chevron, Mobil, 🍴 Del Taco, Little Caesars, McDonald's, Subway, 🅾️ 🏥 Food Basket Foods, Fresh&Easy, Walgreens, vet, **W** 🍴 Carrow's Rest, 🏠 Motel 6
7	Alondra Blvd, **E** 🅿️ Chevron, 7-11, 🍴 A&W, Alondra's Mexican, Frantone's Rest., KFC, Red Chili, 🅾️ CVS Drug, Home Depot, Staples, **W** 🅿️ Shell/Subway/24hr, 🍴 Del Taco
6	CA 91
5	South St, **E** 🍴 BJ's Rest., CA Pizza Kitchen, Carl's Jr, Chick-fil-A, Coco's, Coldstone, 5 Guys, Hometown Buffet, Jamba Juice, Lazy Dog Cafe, Luecille's BBQ, Panda Express, Panera Bread, Quiznos, Red Robin, Starbucks, 🅾️ AT&T, Firestone, Macy's, Nordstrom's, Sears/auto, Target, Verizon, mall, **W** 🅿️ Shell/service, Valero, 🅾️ Acura, Buick/GMC, Chevrolet, Chrysler/Dodge/Jeep, Ford, Honda, Hyundai, Infiniti, KIA, Lexus, Mazda, Nissan, Smartcar, Suzuki, Toyota/Scion, VW
4	Del Amo Blvd, to Cerritos, **E** 🍴 Del Taco, Omega Burgers, Starbucks, 🅾️ Ralph's Foods, **W** 🅿️ Mobil
3	Carson St, **E** 🅿️ Price Saver/dsl, 76, 🍴 Alberto's Mexican, Jack-in-the-Box, KFC, Little Caesar's, McDonald's, Pizza Hut, Popeye's, Subway, Taco Bell, Wienerschnitzel, 🏠 Lakewood Inn, 🅾️ CVS Drug, Food4Less, O'Reilly Parts, Price Right Foods, 7-11, **W** 🅿️ Chevron/Subway/dsl, 🍴 Carl's Jr, Chick-fil-A, Denny's, Del Taco, El Pollo Loco, El Torito, FoodCourt, In-N-Out, Island's Burgers, Jack-in-the-Box, Leucille's BBQ, Panda Express, Roadhouse Grill, Starbucks, SuperMex, TGIFriday's, Yashi Japanese, 🅾️ America's Tire, Barnes&Noble, Lowe's, Michael's, Old Navy, Petsmart, Radio Shack, Ross, Staples, Sam's Club, Walmart/auto
1	Katella Ave, Willow St, **E** 🅿️ Shell, 🍴 Madera's Steaks, McDonald's, Polly's Cafe, Starbucks, 🅾️ 🏥 Rite Aid, **W** Eldorado Regional Park
0mm	**I-605 begins/ends on I-405.**

▶️N INTERSTATE 680 (BAY AREA)

Exit	Services
71b a	I-80 E, to Sacramento, W to Oakland, **I-680 begins/ends on I-80.**
70	Green Valley Rd (from eb), Cordelia, **N** 🅿️ Arco am/pm, 🅾️ Costco/gas, Longs Drug, Safeway
69	Gold Hill Rd, **W** 🅿️ TowerMart/dsl
65	Marshview Rd
63	Parish Rd
61	Lake Herman Rd, **E** 🅿️ Arco/Jack-in-the-Box/dsl, **W** 🅿️ Gas City/dsl, Shell/Carl's Jr/dsl/24hr, 🅾️ vista point

Exit	Services
60	Bayshore Rd, industrial park
58	I-780, to Benicia, **toll plaza**
56	Marina Vista, to Martinez
55mm	**Martinez-Benicia Toll Br**
54	Pacheco Blvd, Arthur Rd, Concord, **W** 🅿️ 76, Shell/dsl
53	CA 4 E to Pittsburg, W to Richmond
52	CA 4 E, Concord, Pacheco, **E** 🍴 Hometown Buffet, Marie Callender's, Starbucks, Taco Bell, 🏠 Crowne Plaza, Holiday Inn, 🅾️ Chevrolet, Ford, Hyundai, Infiniti/VW, Sam's Club, Toyota, Trader Joe's, USPO, **W** 🅿️ Grand Gas, Shell/24hr, 76, 🍴 Denny's, McDonald's, Wendy's, 🅾️ AutoZone, Barnes&Noble, Firestone, K-Mart, Kragen Parts, Pepboys, Safeway Foods, Schwab Tire, Target, Toyota
51	Willow Pass Rd, Taylor Blvd, **E** 🍴 Benihana Rest., Buffet City, Claim Jumper, Denny's, Elephant Bar Rest., El Torito, Fuddruckers, Grissini Italian, Jamba Juice, Panera Bread, Quizno's, Sizzler, 🏠 Hilton, 🅾️ Cost+, Old Navy, Willows Shopping Ctr, **W** 🍴 Baja Fresh, Red Robin, 🅾️ JC Penney, Macy's, Sears/auto
50	CA 242 (from nb), to Concord
49b	Monument Blvd, Gregory Lane (from sb), **E** 🅿️ Valero/dsl, 🍴 Country Waffles, Panda Express, Rubio's, Starbucks, 🅾️ Kohl's, Marshall's, **W** 🅿️ Chevron, 🍴 Boston Mkt, Jack-in-the-Box, McDonald's, Nations Burgers, Pizza Hut, Red Brick Pizza, Taco Bell, 🏠 Courtyard, Hyatt, 🅾️ Big O Tire, Grocery Outlet, Lucky Foods, Michael's, Radio Shack, Rite Aid, Ross, Safeway Foods, Staples, Tuesday Morning
49a	Contra Costa Blvd (from nb)
48	Treat Blvd, Geary Rd, **E** 🅿️ Chevron, 🍴 Back 40 BBQ, Heavenly Cafe, Subway, 🏠 Embassy Suites, Extended Stay America, 🅾️ Best Buy, Office Depot, 7-11, **W** 🅿️ Chevron, Shell, 🍴 Black Angus, Primavera Pasta, Quizno's, Starbucks, Wendy's, Yan's China Bistro, 🅾️ Walgreens
47	N Main St, to Walnut Creek, **E** 🅿️ Chevron, 🍴 Fuddrucker's, Jack-in-the-Box, Taco Bell, 🏠 Marriott, Motel 6, Walnut Cr Motel, 🅾️ Cadillac, Chevrolet, Chrysler/Dodge/Jeep, Harley-Davidson, Honda, Jaguar, Land Rover, Mercedes, Nissan, Target, **W** 🅿️ 76/7-11/dsl/24hr, 🍴 Domino's, 🅾️ NAPA, Porsche
46b	Ygnacio Valley Rd
46a	SR-24 W
45b	Olympic Blvd, Oakland
45a	S Main St, Walnut Creek, **E** 🏥
44	Rudgear (from nb)
43	Livorna Rd
42b a	Stone Valley Rd, Alamo, **W** 🅿️ Chevron, Shell/dsl, 🍴 Papa Murphy's, Starbucks, Subway, Taco Bell, Xenia's,

= gas = food = lodging = other = rest stop Copyright 2014 - The Next Exit ®

CA

INTERSTATE 680 (BAY AREA) CONT'D

SAN RAMON

Exit	Services
42b a	Continued Curves, Longs Drugs, Rite Aid, Safeway, 7-11, vet
41	El Pintado Rd, Danville
40	El Cerro Blvd
39	Diablo Rd, Danville, E 76/24hr, Chinese Cuisine, Taco Bell, Walgreens, Mt Diablo SP (12mi), W Diablo
38	Sycamore Valley Rd, E Shell, Denny's, Best Western, W 76/dsl, Valero/dsl
36	Crow Canyon Rd, San Ramon, E Shell, Burger King, Carl's Jr, Chili's, Cheesesteak, El Ballazo, Jamba Juice, Max's Diner, O'Zachary's Rest., Starbucks, Subway, Extended Stay America, , Big O Tire, Costco, Lucky Foods, Marshall's, Office Depot, PetCo, Rite Aid, Sea's Candies, USPO, W Chevron/repair/24hr, 76, Shell/autocare, Valero, Chipotle Mexican, Giuseppe's Italian, In-N-Out, McDonald's, Nation's Burger's, Quizno's, Subway, Taco Bell, Togo's, Hotel Sierra, Home Depot, Jo-Ann Fabrics, Longs Drug, Safeway, 7-11, Staples, repair/tires, vet
34	Bollinger Canyon Rd, E Valero, Baja Fresh, El Ballazo, Izzy's Steaks, Subway, Marriott, Residence Inn, Long's Drug, Target, Whole Foods, W Chevron, Applebee's, Chevy's Mexican, Marie Callender's, Courtyard, Homestead Village
31	Alcosta Blvd, to Dublin, E 76/7-11, W Chevron, Shell/dsl, DQ, Mtn Mike's Pizza, McDonalds, Papa John's, Rulu's Cafe, Subway, Taco Bell, Lucky Foods, Walgreens
30	I-580, W to Oakland, E to Tracy
29	Stoneridge, Dublin, E Hilton, W Cheesecake Factory, PF Chang's, Taco Bell, JC Penney, Macy's, Nordstrom's, Sears, mall
26	Bernal Ave, Pleasanton, E Shell/Jack-in-the-Box, Lindo's Mexican
25	Sunol Blvd, Pleasanton
21 b a	CA 84, Calvaras Rd, Sunol, W to Dumbarton Bridge
20	Andrade Rd, Sheridan Rd (from sb), E Sunol Super Stp/dsl
19mm	**weigh sta nb**
19	Sheridan Rd (from nb)
18	Vargas Rd
16	CA 238, Mission Blvd, to Hayward, E Shell, McDonald's, W
15	Washington Blvd, Irvington Dist, E QuikStop
14	Durham Rd, to Auto Mall Pkwy, W 76/Circle K/ Subway/24hr, Shell/Jack-in-the-Box, Fry's Electronics, Home Depot, Walmart
12	CA 262, Mission Blvd, to I-880, Warm Springs Dist, W 76, Valero, Burger King, Carl's Jr, Denny's, KFC, RoundTable Pizza, Starbucks, Subway, Taco Bell, Extended Stay America, GNC, Longs Drug, Radio Shack, Ross, Safeway, 7-11, Walgreens
10	Scott Creek Rd
9	Jacklin Rd, E Bonfare Mkt, W Shell
8	CA 237, Calaveras Blvd, Milpitas, E Shell/repair, 76, Domino's, Flames CoffeeShop, RoadTable Pizza, Sizzler, Subway, Exectuive Inn, Oceans SuperMkt, 7-11, W Shell, El Torito, Giorgio's Italian, It's a Grind, Lyon's Rest., McDonald's, Red Lobster,

SAN JOSE

8	Continued Embassy Suites, Extended Stay America, Longs Drug, Lucky Foods, Safeway, Staples
6	Landess Ave, Montague Expswy, E Arco, Chevron, 76, Burger King, Jack-in-the-Box, McDonald's, Taco Bell, Togo's, Wienerschnitzel, Firestone, Lucky Foods, Radio Shack, Rite Aid, Target, Walgreens
5	Capitol Ave, Hostetter Ave, E Shell, Carl's Jr, Popeye's, SaveMart Foods, W Valero, Jiffy Lube
4	Berryessa Rd, E Arco/24hr, USA, Valero/repair, Denny's, Lee's Sandwiches, McDonald's, Taco Bell, AutoZone, Longs Drug, Safeway
2b	McKee Rd, E 76, Chevron, Shell, Burger King, HomeTown Buffet, Pizza Hut, Quizno's, Starbucks, Togo's, Wienerschnitzel, $Tree, PaknSave Foods, Ross, Target, Walgreens, W World Gas, Baskin-Robbins, Foster's Freeze, Lee's Sandwiches, McDonald's, RoundTable Pizza, Yum Yum Doughnut, Wendy's, , Kohl's
2a	Alum Rock Ave, E Shell/dsl/24hr, Jack-in-the-Box, Taco Bell, W Chevron, 76/24hr, Carl's Jr
1d	Capitol Expswy
1c	King Rd, Jackson Ave (from nb), E L&D Gas, Shell, El Gallo Giro, Jamba Juice, Kings Burger, Panda Express, Starbucks, Super Buffet, Taco Bell, Target, Walgreens
1b	US 101, to LA, SF
1a	(exits left from sb) I-680 begins/ends on I-280.

INTERSTATE 710 (LOS ANGELES)

LOS ANGELES AREA

Exit	Services
23	I-710 begins/ends on Valley Blvd, E Arco
22b a	I-10
20c	Chavez Ave
20b	CA 60, Pamona Fwy, W Shell, E King Taco, Monterrey Hill Rest.
20a	3rd St
19	Whittier Blvd, Olympic Blvd, W Shell, McDonald's
17b	Washington Blvd, Commerce, W Commerce Trkstp/dsl/rest.
17a	Bandini Blvd, Atlantic Blvd, industrial
15	Florence Ave, E Alfredo's Mexican, Applebee's, Coldstone, El Pescador Mexican, El Pollo Loco, IHOP, KFC, McDonald's, Panda Express, Quiznos, Red Brick Pizza, Starbucks, Subway, Taco Bell, Yoshinoya, Comfort Inn, $Tree, Food4Less, Marshall's, Rite Aid, Ross, casino, W truck repair
13	CA 42, Firestone Blvd, E Arco, Burger King, Denny's, McDonald's, Panda Express, Subway, Guesthouse Inn, El Super Foods, Ford, GNC, Radio Shack, Sam's Club, Target
12b a	Imperial Hwy, E Shell/dsl, Abierto's Mexican, Carl's Jr., El Pollo Loco, Subway, W Chevron/dsl, 76, Shell, KFC, McDonald's, Panda Express, Pizza Patron, Starbucks, Subway, Taco Bell, Winchell's, Wienerschnitzel, AutoZone, Manny's Repair, Radio Shack, Valu+ Foods, Walgreens
11b a	I-105
10	Rosecrans Ave
9b a	Alondra Ave, E Chevron/dsl, Jack-in-the-Box, Home Depot
8b a	CA 91
7b a	Long Beach Blvd, E Chevron, Mobil, United/dsl, Valero, El Ranchito Mexican, McDonald's, Sizzler, CVS Drug, W Arco/24hr, Jack-in-the-Box, Mocasalitos, Subway, Luxury Inn

FREMONT

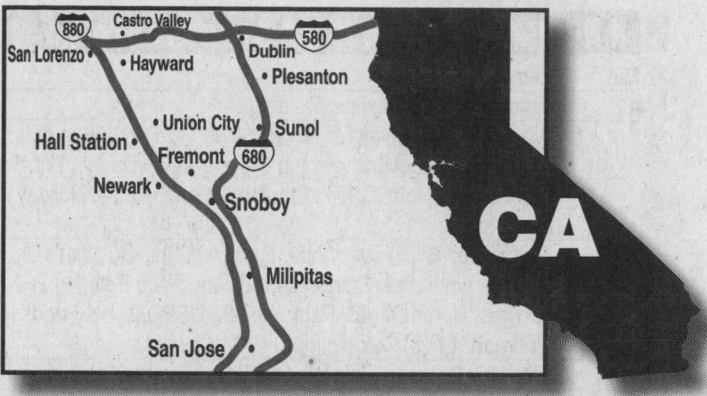

INTERSTATE 710 (LOS ANGELES) CONT'D

Exit	Services
6	Del Amo Blvd
4	I-405, San Diego Freeway
3b a	Willow St, **E** [gas] Arco, Chevron, [food] Baskin-Robbins, Chee Chinese, Dominos, Pizza Hut, [other] Radio Shack, Walgreens, **W** [gas] Arco, 76, [food] KFC, Little Caesars, Popeye's, [other] AutoZone, Big Saver Foods
2	CA 1, Pacific Coast Hwy, **E** [gas] Arco/mart, Chevron, Mobil, 76/dsll, [food] Hong Kong Express, KFC, McDonald's, [lodging] Beacon Inn, Don Chente Tacos, King Taco, La Mirage Inn, Travel Eagle Inn, [other] Ranch Mkt, auto repair, **W** [gas] 76/service, Shell/Carl's Jr/dsl, PCH Trkstp/dsl, [food] Alberto's Mexican, Golden Star Rest., Jack-in-the-Box, McDonald's, Taco Bell, Tom's Burgers, Winchell's, [lodging] Hiland Motel, SeaBreeze Motel, [other] TrueValue, truckwash
1d	Anaheim St, **W** [gas] Speedy Fuel, [other] dsl repair/scales
1c	Ahjoreline Dr, Piers B, C, D, E, Pico Ave
1b	Pico Ave, Piers F-J, Queen Mary
1a	Harbor Scenic Dr, Piers S, T, Terminal Island, **E** [lodging] Hilton
0mm	**I-710 begins/ends in Long Beach**

INTERSTATE 780 (VALLEJO)

BENICIA

Exit	Services
7	**I-780 begins/ends on I-680.**
6	E 5th St, Benicia, **N** [gas] Fast&Easy, **S** [gas] Citgo/7-11, Valero/dsl, [food] China Garden, [other] Big O Tire, repair, vet
5	E 2nd St, Central Benicia, **N** [gas] Valero, [lodging] Best Western, **S** [food] McDonald's, Pappa's Rest.
4	Southampton Rd, Benicia, **N** [food] Asian Bistro, Burger King, Coldstone Creamery, Country Waffles, Jamba Juice, Rickshaw Express, RoundTable Pizza, Starbucks, Subway, [other] Ace Hardware, Radio Shack, Raley's Foods, vet
3b	Military West
3a	Columbus Pkwy, **N** [gas] Shell, [food] Burger King, Napoli Pizza, Subway, [other] Jiffy Lube, Longs Drugs, **S** to Benicia RA
1d	Glen Cove Pkwy, **N** Hwy Patrol, **S** [food] Baskin-Robbins, Subway, Taco Bell, [other] Safeway
1c	Cedar St
1b a	**I-780 begins/ends on I-80.**

INTERSTATE 805 (SAN DIEGO)

Exit	Services
28mm	I-5 (from nb). **I-805 begins/ends on I-5.**
27.5	CA 56 E (from nb)
27	Sorrento Valley Rd, Mira Mesa Blvd
26	Vista Sorrento Pkwy, **E** [gas] Mobil/dsl, Shell, [food] Chili's, Jamba Juice, McDonald's, Starbucks, [lodging] Country Inn, Courtyard, Holiday Inn Express, [other] Staples
25b a	La Jolla Village Dr, Miramar Rd, **1 mi E** [gas] 76/dsl, [other] Discount Tire, Firestone, **W** [food] Coast Cafe, Cozymel's Cantina, Donovan's Grill, Harry's Grill, Miami Grill, PF Chang's, [lodging] Embassy Suites, Marriott, [other] [H], Macy's, Nordstom's, Sears, mall
24	Governor Dr
23	CA 52
22	Clairemont Mesa Blvd, **E** [gas] Chevron, Mega/Subway/dsl, Shell, [food] Arby's, Burger King, Carl's Jr, Coco's, Godfather Rest., McDonald's, Players Grill, Quizno's, Rubio's Grill, Souplantation, Starbucks, Tommy's Burgers, [other] Food-4Less, Ford, Jiffy Lube, Ranch Mkt, Sears Essentials, Walmart, **W** [gas] Arco/24hr, [food] Joe's Pizza, Mr. Bon's Rest,

SAN DIEGO AREA

Exit	Services
22	Continued VIP Oriental Buffet, [lodging] Best Western, CA Suites, Motel 6
21	CA 274, Balboa Ave, **E** [gas] Arco, Chevron, Exxon/dsl, 76, Shell, [food] Applebee's, Islands Burger, Jack-in-the-Box, [other] Albertson's/SavOn, Balboa AutoCare, Chevrolet, Dodge
20	CA 163 N, to Escondido
20a	Mesa College Dr, Kearney Villa Rd, **W** [H]
18	Murray Ridge Rd, to Phyllis Place
17b	I-8, E to El Centro, W to beaches
16	El Cajon Blvd, **E** [gas] Arco/24hr, Ultra, [food] [other] Pancho Villa Mkt, **W** [gas] North Park Gas, 76, [food] Carl's Jr, Jack-in-the-Box, Starbucks, Subway, Wendy's
15	University Ave, **E** [gas] Chevron, [food] Subway, [other] Radio Shack, **W** [gas] Exxon, Thrifty/dsl, [food] Starbucks, [other] CVS Drug, Walgreens
14	CA 15 N, 40th St, to I-15
13b	Home Ave, MLK Ave
13a	CA 94
12b	Market St
12a	Imperial Ave, **E** [gas] Exxon, Homeland Gas/dsl, **W** [food] Domino's, KFC/LJ Silver, Sizzler, Starbucks, [other] Home Depot, 99¢ Store
11b	47th St
11a	43rd St, **W** [food] Giant Pizza, Jack-in-the-Box, [other] AutoZone, CVS Drug, Northgate Mkt
10	Plaza Blvd, National City, **E** [food] Chow King, DQ, Dragon Garden Chinese, McDonald's, Pizza Hut, Popeye's, Starbucks, Winchell's, [other] [H], AutoZone, Firestone/auto, Ralph's Foods, Walgreens, Well's Drug, vet, **W** [gas] Thrifty Gas, [food] Family House Rest., IHOP, Sizzler, [lodging] Comfort Inn, Stardust Inn, [other] Big Lots, CVS Drug, Discount Tire, Jo-Ann Fabrics
9	Sweetwater Rd, **E** [food] Applebee's, Outback Steaks, [other] JC Penney, 7-11, **W** [gas] Chevron/dsl, [food] Ben's Rest., Carl's Jr, Denny's, Hanaoka Japanese, La Placita Mexican, L&L BBQ, Pizza Hut, Starbucks, Subway, Taco Bell, [other] Curves, Goodyear, Longs Drug, Staples
8	CA 54
7c	E St, Bonita Rd, **E on Bonita Plaza Rd** [food] Applebee's, [food] Outback Steaks, Pat&Oscar's Rest., [other] JC Penney, Macy's, mall, **W** [gas] Chevron, Shell, [food] Burger King, Denny's, Loves Rest., [lodging] La Quinta, Ramada Inn, [other] RV Park
7b a	H St, **E** [gas] Carmalor Gas, [food] China China, Coldstone Creamery, Jack-in-the-Box, Subway, Taco Bell, [other] Longs Drug, Marshall's, Vons Foods, mall, RV camping
6	L St, Telegraph Canyon Rd, **E** [gas] Canyon Fuel/dsl, [food] Mandarin Canyon, McDonald's, Starbucks, Subway, [other] [H], Rite Aid, Olympic Training Ctr, RV camping, **W** [gas] Thrifty, [other] 7-11

⬆️N INTERSTATE 805 (SAN DIEGO) CONT'D

Exit	Services
4	Orange Ave, **E** Olympic Training Ctr
3	Main St, Otay Valley Rd, **E** 🅖 Shell, 🅕 Panda Express, Souplantation, 🅞 Chevrolet, Chrysler/Jeep/Dodge, Ford, Kohl's, PetsMart, Scion, Staples, Toyota, **W** 🅛 Holiday Inn Express
2	Palm Ave, **E** 🅖 Arco/24hr, Chevron/24hr, 🅕 Carl's Jr, Hometown Buffet, Starbucks, Subway, Taco Bell, 🅞 Big O Tires, Home Depot, Radio Shack, USPO, Von's Foods, Walmart, **W** 🅖 76/dsl, 🅕 KFC, McDonald's
1b	CA 905, **E** Brown Field ✈, Otay Mesa Border Crossing
1a	San Ysidro Blvd, **E** 🅖 Arco, Shell, 🅛 Travelodge, Factory2U, Kragen Parts, Longs Drug, 99¢ Store, U-Haul, **W** 🅖 Chevron, Exxon, Mobil, 76, 🅕 Denny's, McDonald's, Si Senor Mexican, 🅛 Motel 6

I-805 begins/ends on I-5.

⬆️N INTERSTATE 880 (BAY AREA)

Exit	Services
46b a	I-80 W (exits left). I-80 E/580 W.
44	7th St, Grand Ave, downtown
42b a	Broadway St, **E** 🅕 KFC, 🅛 Marriott, **W** 🅛 Jack London Inn, 🅞 to Jack London Square
41a	Oak St, Lakeside Dr downtown
40	5th Ave, Embarcadero, **E** 🅕 Burger King, **W** 🅕 Quizno's, Starbucks, 🅛 Executive Inn, Homewood Suites, Motel 6
39b a	29th Ave, 23rd Ave, to Fruitvale, **E** 🅖 Shell, 🅕 Boston Mkt, Burger King, DonutStar, Popeye's, Starbucks, 🅞 AutoZone, Lucky Foods, Office Depot, Radio Shack, **W** 🅖 7-11
38	High St, to Alameda, **E** 🅛 Bay Breeze Inn, Coliseum Motel, 🅞 El Monte RV Ctr, **W** 🅖 Shell/dsl, 🅕 McDonald's, 🅞 Home Depot
37	66th Ave, Zhone Way, **E** coliseum
36	Hegenberger Rd, **E** 🅖 Arco/24hr, Shell/dsl, 🅕 Burger King, Chubby Freeze, Denny's, Jack-in-the-Box/24hr, McDonald's, Taco Bell, 🅛 Day's Hotel, Fairfield Inn, La Quinta, Motel 6, Quality Inn, 🅞 Pak'n Save Foods, GMC/Volvo, Freightliner, **W** 🅖 76/Circle K/dsl, Shell, 🅕 Carrows Rest., Francesco's Rest., Hegen Burger, In-N-Out, Jamba Juice, Panda Express, Quizno's, Red Barn Pizza, Starbucks, Subway, Wing Stop, 🅛 Best Western, Courtyard, Econolodge, Hilton, Holiday Inn, Holiday Inn Express, Marriott, Park Plaza Motel, 🅞 Harley-Davidson, Infiniti, Lexus, Walmart/auto, to Oakland ✈
35	98th Ave, **W** ✈
34	Davis St, **W** 🅖 Shell/Burger King, 🅕 Hawaiian BBQ, Jamba Juice, Starbucks, Togo's, 🅞 Costco/gas, Home Depot, Office Depot, See's Candy, Walmart/McDonald's
33b a	Marina Blvd, **E** 🅖 Valero, 🅕 Jack-in-the-Box, La Salsa Mexican, Panda Express, Starbucks, Taco Bell, 🅞 Buick/GMC, Chevrolet, Ford, Honda, Hyundai, Kia, Marshall's, Nissan, Nordstrom's, Radio Shack, Volvo, **W** 🅖 Flyers/dsl, 🅕 A&W/KFC, DairyBelle, Denny's
32	Washington Ave (from nb), Lewelling Blvd (from sb), **W** 🅖 Arco, 76, TechCo, 🅕 Hometown Buffet, Jack-in-the-Box, McDonald's, Papa Murphy's, Subway, 🅛 Nimitz Motel, 🅞 Big Lots, Big O Tire, Food Maxx, GNC, Home Depot, Longs Drugs, 99¢ Store, Radio Shack, Safeway/24hr, Walgreens/24hr, same as 30
31	I-238 (from sb), to I-580, Castro Valley

Exit	Services
30	Hesperian Blvd, **E** 🅖 76, 🅕 KFC, In-N-Out, Quizno's, Starbucks, 🅞 Kragen Parts, Walmart, Wheelworks Repair, **W** 🅖 Arco, Chevron, 76, 🅕 Black Angus, Hometown Buffet, 🅛 Hilton Garden, Nimitz Inn, 🅞 BigLots, Food Maxx, Longs Drugs, Lucky Foods, 99¢ Store, Radio Shack, USPO, vet, same as 32
29	A St, San Lorenzo, **E** 🅖 76/Circle K, 🅕 McDonald's, 🅛 Best Western, 🅞 Costco, tires/repair, **W** 🅖 KB/dsl, 76/Circle K, Valero, 🅕 Burger King, Carrow's, Chef Ming, Hawaiian BBQ, Jamba Juice, Pizza Hut, Starbucks, Subway, 🅛 Days Inn, Heritage Inn, La Quinta, MainStay Suites, Phoenix Lodge, 🅞 $Tree, Home Depot, Mi Pueblo Foods, Target
28	Winton Ave, **W** 🅖 Chevron, Valero/dsl, 🅕 Applebee's, Coldstone Creamery, Elephant Bar/Grill, Hawaiian BBQ, Hometown Buffet, Marie Callendar's, Mimi's Cafe, Olive Garden, Panda Express, Panera Bread, Sizzler, Subway, 🅞 Firestone/auto, Goodyear/auto, JC Penney, Kragen Parts, Macy's, Ross, Sears/auto, mall
27	CA 92, Jackson St, **E** 🅖 Beacon, 76, Valero/24hr, 🅕 Asian Wok, Baskin-Robbins, Hawaiian BBQ, Mnt Mike's Pizza, Nations Burgers, Papa Murphy's, Popeye's, Starbucks, Subway, Taco Bell, 🅞 Grocery Outlet, Longs Drug, Lucky Foods, Radio Shack, Safeway, 7-11, Walgreens, **W** San Mateo Br
26	Tennyson Rd, **E** 🅖 All American/dsl, 76, 🅕 Jack-in-the-Box, KFC, RoundTable Pizza, 🅞 Kragen Parts, Walgreens, **W** 🅖 76, 🅞 🅗
25	Industrial Pkwy (from sb), **E** 🅖 Industrial/dsl, 🅕 Lite Wok, Quizno's, Starbucks, **W** 🅛 Pheonix Lodge
24	Whipple Rd, Dyer St, **E** 🅖 Chevron/dsl/24hr, 76, 🅕 Country Waffles, Del Taco, Denny's, McDonald's, Panda Express, Taco Bell, Wing Stop, 🅛 Best Value Inn, Motel 6, 🅞 FoodMaxx, Home Depot, PepBoys, Target, **W** 🅖 Shell, 🅕 Applebee's, Baskin-Robbins, Burger King, Chili's, FreshChoice, Fuddrucker's, In-N-Out, IHOP, Jamba Juice, Jollibee, Krispy Kreme, La Salsa Mexican, Pasta Pormadora, Starbucks, Texas Roadhouse, TGIFriday, Togo's, Tony Roma's, 🅛 Extended Stay America, Holiday Inn Express, 🅞 Best Buy, Lowe's Whse, Lucky Foods, Michael's, PetCo, Radio Shack, Walmart/auto
23	Alvarado-Niles Rd (same as 24) **E** 🅖 Shell, 🅛 Crowne Plaza, 🅞 7-11, **W** 🅖 Shell, 🅞 Walmart/auto
22	Alvarado Blvd, Fremont Blvd, **E** 🅕 Phoenix Garden Chinese, Subway, 🅛 Motel 6, 🅞 Lucky Foods
21	CA 84 W, Decoto Rd to Dumbarton Br, **E** 🅖 7-11, 🅕 McDonald's, 🅞 Walgreens
19	CA 84 E, Thornton Ave, Newark, **E** 🅞 U-Haul, **W** 🅖 Chevron/dsl/24hr, Shell, 🅕 Carl's Jr, KFC, Mtn Mike's Pizza, Taco Bell, 🅞 BigLots, Home Depot, 7-11
17	Mowry Ave, Fremont, **E** 🅖 Chevron/dsl, QuikStop, 76/Circle K, Valero, 🅕 Applebee's, Burger King, Chinese Buffet, Denny's, HoneyBaked Ham, KFC, Olive Garden, Starbucks, Subway, T&D Sandwiches, 🅛 Best Western, Extended Stay Deluxe, Residence Inn, 🅞 🅗 Lucky Foods, **W** 🅖 76, 🅕 Arby's, BJ's Rest., Bombay Garden, El Burro Mexican, Jack-in-the-Box, McDonald's, Red Robin, Subway, Taco Bell, TK Noodles, 🅛 Chase Suites, Comfort Inn, EZ 8 Motel, Homewood Suites, Motel 6, Towneplace Suites, 🅞 Firestone, Goodyear/auto, JC Penney, Jiffy Lube, Lion Mkt., Macy's, Mazda, Sears/auto, Target, TJ Maxx, mall

⬆N INTERSTATE 880 (BAY AREA) CONT'D

Exit	Services
16	Stevenson Blvd, **E** ☐ Arco/dsl, Shell, ☐ Jack-in-the-Box, Outback Steaks, **W** ☐ Chevron, ☐ Chevy's Mexican, ChuckeCheese, Palm Gardens Rest., Starbucks, Togo's, ☐ Hilton, ☐ FoodMaxx, Ford, Harley-Davidson, Nissan, Tuesday Morning, Walmart
15	Auto Mall Pkwy, **E** ☐ Arco, Chevron, ☐ Subway, **W** ☐ Shell/dsl, ☐ Applebee's, Asian Pearl, Carino's, Chipotle Mexican, ClaimJumper, Coldstone Creamery, Dickey's BBQ, Hawaiian BBQ, In-N-Out, Jamba Juice, Panda Express, Panera Bread, PF Chang's, Quizno's, Rubio's, Starbucks, Subway, Tandoori Grill, Wendy's, Wing Stop, ☐ BMW, Chrysler/Dodge/Jeep, Costco/gas, Honda, Jo-Ann Fabrics, Jaguar, Kia, Kohl's, Land Rover, Lexus, Lowes Whse, Mercedes, Office Depot, Old Navy, Porsche, Radio Shack, Staples, Toyota, Volvo
14mm	**weigh sta both lanes**
13	Fremont Blvd, Irving Dist, **W** ☐ Valero/Subway, ☐ McDonald's, SmartBrew, ☐ GoodNite Inn, Homestead Suites, La Quinta, Marriott
13a	Gateway Blvd (from nb), **E** ☐ Holiday Inn Express
12	Mission Blvd, **E** to I-680, ☐ 76, Valero, ☐ Carl's Jr, Denny's, Jack-in-the-Box, KFC, Togo's, ☐ Holiday Inn Express, Quality Inn, ☐ Longs Drugs, Safeway, 7-11, Walgreens, **W** ☐ Courtyard, Hampton Inn, Hyatt Place
10	Dixon Landing Rd, **E** ☐ McDonald's, ☐ Residence Inn, ☐ 7-11
8b	CA 237, Alviso Rd, Calaveras Rd, to McCarthy Rd, Milpitas, **E** ☐ CA Fuel, 76, ☐ Burger King, Carl's Jr, Chili Palace, Denny's, Lee's Sandwiches, Marie Callender's, ☐ Best Western, Days Inn, Travelodge, ☐ BigLots, Kragen Parts, SaveMart Foods, 7-11, Walgreens, vet, **W on McCarthy Rd** ☐ Chevron, ☐ Applebee's, Black Angus, HomeTown Buffet, Happi House, In-N-Out, Jamba Juice,

SAN JOSE (vertical label, left margin)

8b	Continued Macaroni Grill, McDonald's, On the Border, Pasta Pomodoro, RedBrick Pizza, Starbucks, Subway, Taco Bell, ☐ Crowne Plaza, Hampton Inn, Hilton Garden, Homestead Suites, Larkspur Landing Hotel, Staybridge Suites, ☐ Best Buy, GNC, Michael's, Petsmart, RanchMkt Foods, Ross, Walmart/McDonald's/auto
8a	Great Mall Parkway, Tasman Dr, **E** ☐ Toyota
7	Montague Expswy, **E** ☐ Shell/dsl, Valero, ☐ Jack-in-the-Box, ☐ Sleep Inn, ☐ U-Haul, **W** ☐ Chevron/dsl, ☐ Dave&Buster's, ☐ Beverly Heritage Hotel, Sheraton
5	Brokaw Rd, **E** ☐ Lowe's Whse, **W** ☐ Ford Trucks, Fry's Electronics, CHP
4d	Gish Rd (nb only), **W** ☐ auto/dsl repair/transmissions
4c b	US 101, N to San Francisco, S to LA
4a	1st St, **E** ☐ 76, Shell/repair, ☐ Subway, **W** ☐ 76, ☐ Cathay Chinese, Denny's/24hr, Empire Buffet, Genji Japanese, ☐ Clarion, Comfort Suites, Days Inn, Executive Inn, EZ 8 Motel, Holiday Inn Express, Homestead Suites, Radisson, Red Roof Inn, Vagabond Inn, Wyndham Garden, ☐ 7-11
3	Coleman St, **E** ☐ Valero/dsl, ☐ Quizno's, **W** ☐
2	CA 82, The Alameda, **W** ☐ Shell/repair, ☐ Starbucks, Subway, Taco Bell, ☐ Best Western, Santa Clara Inn, St. Francis Hotel, Sterling Motel, Valley Inn, ☐ Safeway, Santa Clara U
1d	Bascom Ave, to Santa Clara, **W** ☐ Rotten Robbie/dsl, Valero, ☐ Burger King
1c	Stevens Creek Blvd, San Carlos St, **E** ☐ Valero/dsl, Valley/dsl, ☐ Valley Park Hotel, ☐ ☐, **W** ☐ 76, ☐ Arby's, CheeseCake Factory, Jack-in-the-Box, RoundTable Pizza, ☐ Audi/VW, Best Buy, Ford, Goodyear/auto, Lexus, Longs Drugs, Macy's, Nordstrom's, Old Navy, Safeway, 7-11, Subaru, mall
1b	I-280. **I-880 begins/ends on I-280**
1a	Ca 17 to Santa Cruz.

SAN JOSE (vertical label, right margin)

CA   **CO** (side tab)

COLORADO

⬆N INTERSTATE 25

Exit	Services
299	Colorado/Wyoming state line
296	point of interest both lanes
293	to Carr, Norfolk
288	Buckeye Rd
281	Owl Canyon Rd, **E** KOA Campground, truck repair
278	CO 1 S, to Wellington, **W** ☐ Kum&Go/dsl, Loaf'N Jug/dsl, Shell/dsl, ☐ Burger King, McDonald's, Subway, Taco John's, ☐ Days Inn, ☐ Bella Mkt, Family$, USPO, vet
271	Mountain Vista Dr, **W** Budweiser Brewery
269b a	CO 14, to US 87, Ft Collins, **E** ☐ CF&G Cookhouse, McDonald's, ☐ Guesthouse Inn, **W** ☐ Conoco, Shell/dsl, ☐ Denny's, Hacienda Real, Waffle House, ☐ Comfort Inn, Days Inn, La Quinta, Motel 6, 9 Motel, Plaza Inn, Sleep Inn, Super 8, ☐ RV Service, U-Haul, truck repair, vet, to CO St U, **2 mi W** ☐ Valero, ☐ DQ, Papa John's, Qdoba Mexican, ☐ Home Depot, Radio Shack, Walmart
268	Prospect Rd, to Ft Collins, **W** ☐ ☐, **Welcome Ctr**, ☐ **both lanes, full** ☐ **facilities, litter barrels,** ☐ **petwalk**
267mm	**weigh sta both lanes**
266mm	st patrol

FT COLLINS (vertical label, left margin)

265	CO 68 W, Timnath, **E** ☐ Murphy USA/dsl, ☐ Walmart/Subway, **W** ☐ Shell/dsl, **2-3 mi W** ☐ Austin's Grill, Carrabba's, Coldstone, Firehouse Subs, 5 Guys Burgers, Golden Corral, Huhot Chinese, Chipotle, IHOP, Macaroni Grill, McAlister's Deli, Old Chicago, Outback Steaks, Panera Bread, Papa John's, Qdoba, Quizno's, SmashBurger, Starbucks, Subway, Texas Roadhouse, Village Inn Rest., ☐ Cambria Suites, Courtyard, Hampton Inn, Hiltson Garden, Marriott, Residence Inn, ☐ AT&T, Lowe's, Office Depot, Safeway/gas, Sam's Club, Target, Verizon, Walgreens, World Mkt
262	CO 392 E, to Windsor, **E** ☐ Conoco/dsl, 7-11/dsl, Shell/Subway/dsl, ☐ Arby's, Pueblo Viejo, Taco John's, ☐ AmericInn, Super 8, **W** ☐ Powder River RV Ctr
259	Crossroads Blvd, **E** ☐ Shell/dsl, ☐ Boot Grill, Carl's Jr, Nordy's, Qdoba Mexican, Palomino Mexican, Perkins, Subway, ☐ Candlewood Suites, Embassy Suites, Holiday Inn Express, ValuePlace Inn, **W** ☐ Hooters, ☐ BMW, Buick/GMC, Chevrolet, Harley-Davidson, Hyundai, Mercedes, Mini, Subaru, to ☐
257b a	US 34, to Loveland, **E** ☐ 7-11/dsl, Shell/dsl, ☐ Biaggi Italian, BoneFish Grill, Cafe Athens, Culver's, On-the-Border, PF Chang's, Red Robin, Rock Bottom Rest., Star

↑N INTERSTATE 25 CONT'D

CO | **LOVELAND** | **LONGMONT** (left margin)

BROOMFIELD THORNTON DENVER AREA (right margin)

Exit	Services
257b a	Continued

257b a Continued
bucks, 🅾 AT&T, Barnes&Noble, Best Buy, Dick's, GNC, Macy's, See's Candies, Verizon, **W** 🚮 Conoco/dsl, 🍴 Arby's (2mi), Buffalo Wild Wings, Carino's Italian, Chick-fil-A, Chili's, Chipotle Mexican, Cracker Barrel, IHOP, Jimmy Johns, KFC/Taco Bell, LoneStar Steaks, McDonald's, Mimi's Cafe, Noodles&Co, Old Chicago, Panera Bread, Qdoba, Starbucks, Subway, Wendy's, 🛏 Best Western, Fairfield Inn, Hampton Inn, Residence Inn, Super 8 (2mi), 🅾 Ⓗ, JoAnn Fabrics, Loveland Outlets/famous brands, Loveland RV Resort, Marshall's, Old Navy, Petsmart, Ross, Sportsman's Whse, Staples, Target, museum, to Rocky Mtn NP

255 CO 402 W, to Loveland

254 to CO 60 W, to Campion, **E** 🚮 Johnson's Corner/Sinclair/café/dsl/scales/motel/24hr, 🛏 Budget Host, 🅾 RV retreat/service

252 CO 60 E, to Johnstown, Milliken, **W** 🚮 Loaf'n Jug/Subway/dsl

250 CO 56 W, to Berthoud, **W** Berthoud B&B, to Carter Lake

245 to Mead

243 CO 66, to Longmont, Platteville, **E** 🚮 Conoco/dsl, Kum&Go/dsl, Shell/7-11, 🍴 Rancheros, Red Rooster Rest., 🅾 Big John's RV Ctr, Camping World/K&C RV Ctr, tires, **W** to Rocky Mtn NP, to Estes Park

241mm St Vrain River

240 CO 119, to Longmont, **E** 🚮 Shell/7-11/dsl, 🍴 Burger King, Carl's Jr, Del Taco, Good Times Grill, Pizza Hut, Popeye's, Qdoba, Quiznos, Starbucks, Wendy's, 🛏 Best Western, Comfort Suites, Value Place Inn, 🅾 Century RV Ctr, Home Depot, Kia, Lexus, Toyota/Scion, Transwest RV Ctr, **W** 🚮 Conoco/dsl/scales/24hr, 7-11/Subway/dsl, Shell/Circle K/dsl, 🍴 Arby's, McDonald's, Pizza Hut/Taco Bell, Waffle House, 🛏 Best Value Inn, Days Inn, 1st Inn, Quality Inn, Super 8, 🅾 Ⓗ, Valley Camper RV Ctr, museum, truckwash, to Barbour Ponds SP

235 CO 52, Dacono, **E** 🚮 Kum&Go/dsl, 🅾 Ford, **W** 🚮 Conoco/McDonald's/dsl/LP, 🍴 Pepper Jacks Grille, Starbucks, Subway, 🅾 Harley-Davidson, to Eldora Ski Area

232 to Erie, Dacono

229 CO 7, to Lafayette, Brighton, **E** 🍴 Buffalo Wild Wings, Chick-fil-A, Chili's, Famous Dave's BBQ, Goodtimes Burgers, Gunther Toody's, La Fogata, Starbucks, Subway, Village Inn, 🅾 AT&T, Costco/gas, Dick's, Home Depot, Petsmart, Sears Grand

228 E-470, **tollway**, to Limon

226 144th Ave, **E** Cabela's, **W** 🍴 HuHot Mongolian, Marco's Pizza, Mimi's Cafe, Mooyah Burgers, Red Robin, Starbucks, 🅾 Ⓗ, AT&T, $Tree, GNC, JC Penney, Macy's, Old Navy, REI, Ross, Staples, Target, Verizon

225 136th Ave, **W** 🚮 Valero/dsl, 🍴 Big Burrito, Carl's Jr, KFC/LJ Silver's, Starbucks, Subway, 🅾 Advance Parts, Lowe's, Walmart/McDonald's

223 CO 128, 120th Ave, to Broomfield, **E** 🚮 Conoco, Valero/dsl, 🍴 Applebee's, Burger King, Café Rio, Chipotle Mexican, Chick-fil-A, Coldstone, Damon's, Fazoli's, Jim'N Nick's BBQ, Jimmy John's, Krispy Kreme, LoneStar Steaks, McDonald's, Panda Express, Pizza Hut, Olive Garden, Outback Steaks, Panera Bread, Smash Burger, Sonic, Starbucks, Subway, TGIFriday's, 🛏 DoubleTree,

223 Continued
EconoLodge, Hampton Inn, Holiday Inn Express, Ramada Inn, 🅾 Albertson's, Barnes&Noble, Big O Tire, Brakes+, CarQuest, Discount Tire, $Tree, Meineke, Michael's, O'Reilly Parts, PetCo, Sprouts Mkt, Target, Tires+, Walgreens, vet, **W** 🚮 Conoco/dsl, Shell/Circle K/Popeye's/dsl, Valero/dsl, 🍴 CB Potts Rest., Chili's, Cracker Barrel, DQ, Hooters, Laguna's Mexican, Perkins, Qdoba, Starbucks, Subway, Village Inn Rest., Wendy's, 🛏 Comfort Suites, Cottonwood Suites, Extended Stay America, Fairfield Inn, La Quinta, Super 8

221 104th Ave, to Northglenn, **E** 🚮 Conoco, 🍴 Buffalo Wild Wings, Burger King, CiCi's Pizza, DQ, Denny's, Firehouse Subs, Old Chicago, Qdoba, Starbucks, Subway, Texas Roadhouse, 🅾 Ⓗ, Gander Mtn, GNC, Home Depot, King's Soopers, Tires+, Walgreens, **W** 🚮 7-11, Shell/Circle K/dsl, 🍴 Blackeyed Pea, Cinzzetti's Italian, GoodTimes Burger, Gunther Toody's, McDonald's, Red Lobster, Seoul BBQ, Starbucks, Taco Bell, 🅾 Best Buy, Fiat, Firestone/auto, Ford, Goodyear/auto, Hyundai, Jo-Ann Fabrics, Lowe's, Marshalls, Office Depot, Petsmart, Radio Shack, Ross, Subaru

220 Thornton Pkwy, **E** 🍴 Golden Corral, Rico Pollo, 🅾 Ⓗ, AT&T, Sam's Club/gas, Walmart, Thornton Civic Ctr, **W** 🚮 Shell, Valero/dsl, Western/dsl, 🍴 Subway

219 84th Ave, to Federal Way, **E** 🚮 Shell/dsl, Valero/dsl, 🍴 Arby's, McDonald's, Sonic, Starbucks, Subway, Taco Bell, Taco Star, Waffle House, 🅾 O'Reilly Parts, **W** 🚮 Econogas, Valero/dsl, 🍴 Burger King, DQ, El Fogon, McDonald's, Pizza Hut, Popeye's, Santiago's Mexican, Village Inn Rest., 🛏 Motel 6, 🅾 Ⓗ, AutoZone, CarQuest, Discount Tire, Meineke, Save-A-Lot

217 US 36 W (exits left from nb), to Boulder, **W** 🚮 Chevron, 🅾 Chevrolet

216b a I-76 E, to I-270 E

215 58th Ave, **E** 🍴 Burger King, McDonald's, Steak Escape, Taco John's, Wendy's, 🛏 Comfort Inn, **W** 🚮 Conoco/dsl, Shamrock/dsl/LP, 🛏 Super 8

214c 48th Ave, **E** coliseum, 🔄, **W** 🍴 Village Inn Rest., 🛏 Holiday Inn, Quality Inn

214b a I-70, E to Limon, W to Grand Junction

213 Park Ave, W 38th Ave, 23rd St, downtown, **E** 🚮 Conoco, 7-11, Shell, 🍴 Denny's, Domino's, McDonald's, Starbucks, Quizno's, 🛏 La Quinta, 🅾 Goodyear, **W** 🛏 Regency Inn, Town&Country Motel

212c 20th St, downtown, Denver, **W** 🍴 Pagliacci's Italian

212b a Speer Blvd, **E** downtown, museum, **W** 🚮 Conoco, Shell, 🛏 Ramada Inn, Residence Inn, Super 8, Travel Inn

211 23rd Ave, **E** funpark

210c CO 33 (from nb)

210b US 40 W, Colfax Ave, **W** 🍴 Denny's, KFC, 🛏 Ramada Inn/rest., Red Lion Inn, 🅾 Mile High Stadium

210a US 40 E, Colfax Ave, **E** civic center, downtown, U-Haul

209c 8th Ave, **E** 🛏 Motel 7, 🅾 Bob's Auto Parts

209b 6th Ave W, US 6, **W** 🛏 Day's Inn

209a 6th Ave E, downtown, Denver

208 CO 26, Alameda Ave (from sb), **E** 🚮 Shamrock/dsl, 🍴 Burger King, Denny's, 🅾 Home Depot, same as 207b **W** 🚮 Conoco

207b US 85 S, Santa Fe Dr, same as 208

207 a Broadway, Lincoln St, **E** 🍴 Griff's Burgers, 🅾 USPO

206b Washington St, Emerson St, **E** 🅾 WildOats Mkt/café, **W** 🅾 Ⓗ

▲N INTERSTATE 25
CONT'D

Exit	Services
206a	Downing St (from nb)
205b a	University Blvd, **W** to U of Denver
204	CO 2, Colorado Blvd, **E** ⛽ Conoco, Shamrock, 7-11, Shell, Sinclair, 🍴 Arby's, Asian Grill, Black Eyed Pea, Boston Mkt, GoodTimes Grill, Hooters, KFC, Lazy Dog Café, McDonald's, Noodles&Co, Pizza Hut, Starbucks, Subway, Taco Bell, Village Inn Rest., Wild Oats Cafe, 🛏 Cherry Creek, Day's Inn, Fairfield Inn, Hampton Inn, Lowes Denver, Ramada, Ⓞ AAA, Barnes&Noble, Best Buy, Chevrolet/Buick, Mercedes/BMW, Ross, Safeway Foods, VW, Walgreens, **W** ⛽ Conoco, 🍴 A&W/KFC, Dave&Buster's, Denny's, McDonald's, Perkins, 🛏 La Quinta
203	Evans Ave, **E** ⛽ Conoco, 🍴 Big Papa's BBQ, Breakfast Inn, McDonald's, Palace Chinese, Quiznos, 🛏 Rockies Inn, Ⓞ AutoZone, Discount Tire, NAPA, Walgreens, **W** 🛏 Cameron Motel, Ⓞ Ford
202	Yale Ave, **W** ⛽ Shamrock
201	US 285, CO 30, Hampden Ave, to Englewood, Aurora, **E** ⛽ Conoco/Circle K/LP, Phillips 66, Shamrock, Sinclair, 🍴 Ajuuai Rest, Applebee's, Boston Mkt, Chicago Grill, Chili's, Domino's, Einstein Bros, McDonald's, Mexican Grill, Noodles&Co, NY Deli, Old Chicago, On-the-Border, Qdoba, Starbucks, Subway, 🛏 Embassy Suites, Marriott, Sheraton, TownePlace Suites, Ⓞ Discount Tire, King's Sooper Foods, Walgreens, Whole Food Mkt, vet, **W** ⛽ Conoco, 🍴 Aurelio's Pizza, Burger King, Starbucks, Ⓞ Safeway
200	I-225 N, to I-70
199	CO 88, Belleview Ave, to Littleton, **E** ⛽ Sinclair, 🍴 Chipotle Mexican, Harvest Rest., Off Belleview Grill, Pancake House, Panera Bread, Sandwiches+, Starbucks, Tosh's Hacienda Rest., Wendy's, 🛏 Hyatt Place, Hyatt Regency, Marriott, Wyndham, **W** ⛽ Conoco, Shamrock, 🍴 McDonald's, Pappadeaux Café, Paradise Valley Grill, Pizza Hut, Taco Bell, 🛏 Day's Inn, Extended Stay America, Holiday Inn Express, HomeStead Village, Ramada, Super 8
198	Orchard Rd, **E** 🍴 Del Frisco's Steaks, Shepler's, **W** ⛽ Shell/Circle K, 🍴 Quizno's, 🛏 Hotel Denver Tech, Ⓞ 🄷
197	Arapahoe Blvd, **E** ⛽ Conoco, Shell/Circle K, 🍴 A&W, Arby's, Bro's BBQ, Burger King, Carlos Miguel's, Del Taco, Dickie's BBQ, El Parral, Gunther Toody's Rest., Hoong's Palace, KFC, Mr. Panda, Outback Steaks, Pat's Cheesesteak, Pizza Hut, Sonic, Subway, Wendy's, 🛏 Candlewood Suites, Courtyard, Homestead Suites, Sleep Inn, Ⓞ Big A Parts, Buick, Cadillac, Chrysler, Discount Tire, Ford, GMC, Home Depot, Honda, Hyundai, Jeep, Lowe's

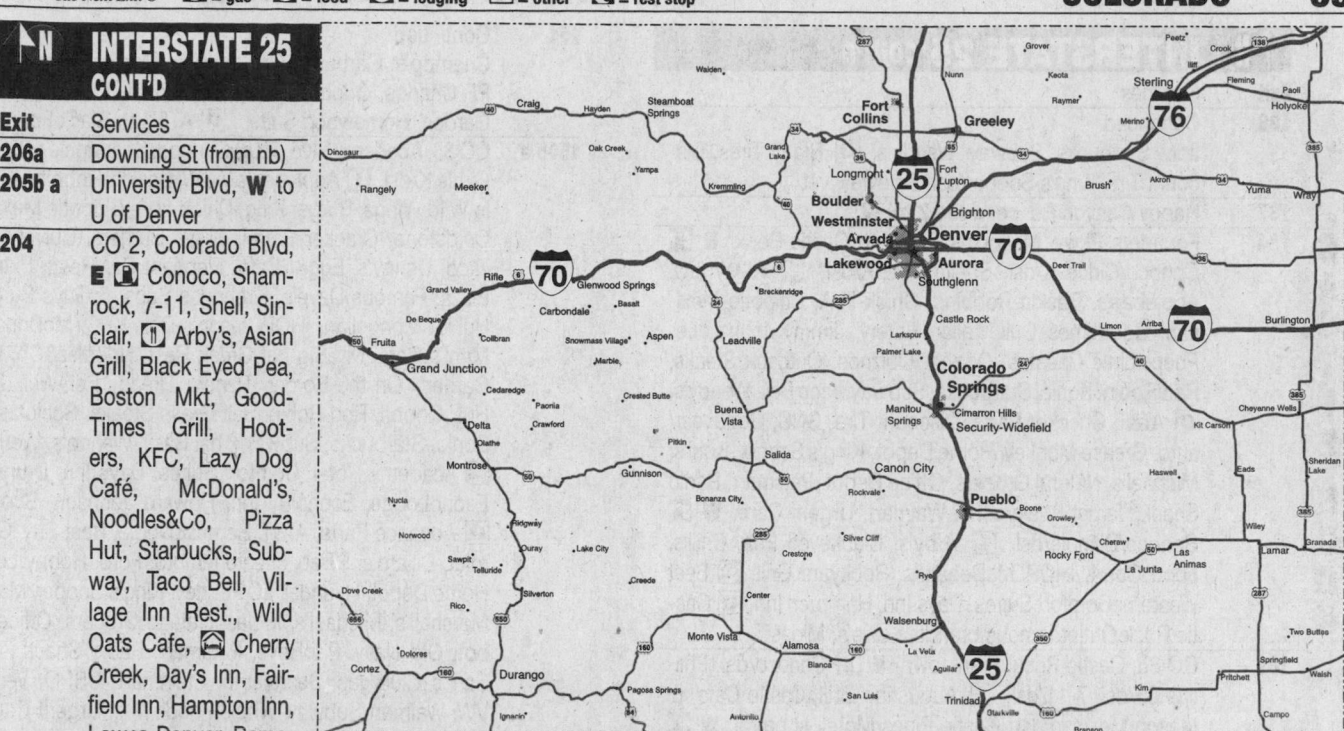

197	Continued Whse, Mazda, Nissan, Scion, Subaru, Target, Toyota, USPO, Walmart, **W** ⛽ Phillips 66, Shamrock, Shell, 🍴 Arby's, Blackeyed Pea, Boston Mkt, Chipotle Mexican, DQ, Einstein Bro's, Elephant Bar Rest., Jamba Juice, KFC, Macaroni Grill, McDonald's, Mongolian BBQ, Papa John's, Qdoba, Quizno's, Red Robin, Souper Salad, Sushi Moon, Taco Bell, 🛏 Residence Inn, Wingate Inn, Ⓞ Albertson's, Barnes&Noble, Brakes+, Curves, Firestone/auto, Goodyear/auto, Office Depot, Sav-On
196	Dry Creek Rd, **E** 🍴 IHOP, Landry's Seafood, Maggiano's Italian, Trail Dust Steaks, 🛏 Best Western, Bradford Suites, Country Inn Suites, Days Inn, Holiday Inn Express, Homestead Suites, La Quinta, Quality Inn, Ramada Ltd, Studio+, **W** 🛏 Drury Inn
195	County Line Rd, **E** 🛏 Courtyard, Residence Inn, **W** ⛽ Conoco, 🍴 Buffalo Wild Wings, Burger King, CA Pizza Kitchen, Champ's Rest., Chick-fil-A, Fleming's Rest., PF Changs, Red Robin, Rock Bottom Brewery/Cafe, Starbucks, Thai Basil, 🛏 Hyatt Place, Ⓞ Barnes&Noble, Best Buy, Costco/gas, Dillard's, Home Depot, JC Penney, JoAnn Fabrics, Michaels, Nordstrom's, PetsMart
194	CO 470 W, CO 470 E **(tollway)**, **1 exit W on Quebec** 🍴 Arby's, ClaimJumper, Country Buffet, LoneStar Steaks, McDonald's, TGIFriday's, 🛏 Comfort Suites, Fairfield Inn, Hyatt Place, Ⓞ Barnes&Noble, Firestone, Home Depot, PepBoys, Sam's Club, Walmart
193	Lincoln Ave, to Parker, **E** ⛽ Shamrock, 🍴 Carraba's, PanAsia Bistro, Hacienda Colorado, 🛏 Candlewood Suites, Extended Stay America, Hilton Garden, **W** ⛽ Conoco/dsl, 🍴 Chipotle Grill, Chili's, Heidi's, McDonald's, Pizza Hut/Taco Bell, Starbucks, Subway, 🛏 Hampton Inn, Marriott, Ⓞ 🄷, Cabela's, Discount Tire, Safeway
192	Ridgegate Pkwy
191	no services
190	Surrey Ridge
188	Castle Pines Pkwy, **W** ⛽ Conoco, Shell/Circle K/Popeye's/24hr, 🍴 Cafe De France, La Dolce Vita, Little

D E N V E R   A R E A

CASTLE ROCK

INTERSTATE 25 CONT'D

Exit	Services
188	Continued
	Italy, Starbucks, Subway, Wendy's, Big O Tires, Discount Tire, King's Sooper/dsl, Safeway, vet
187	Happy Canyon Rd, **services 2 mi W**
184	Founders Pkwy, Meadows Pkwy, to Castle Rock, **E** Conoco/Cirlce K/dsl, Shell/Circle K/dsl, A&W/KFC, Applebee's, Baskin-Robbins, Chick-fil-A, Chipotle Mexican, Goodtimes Grill, Italian Eatery, Jimmy John's, Le-Peep, Little Caesars, Qdoba, Quiznos, Outback Steaks, Red Robin, Sonic, Starbucks, Subway, Taco Bell, Wendy's, AT&T, Checker Parts, Discount Tire, GNC, Goodyear/auto, Grease Monkey, Home Depot, King's Sooper, Kohl's, Michael's, Natural Grocers, Office Depot, Petsmart, Radio Shack, Target, Walgreens, Walmart, **Urgent Care**, **W** Conoco/Blimpie/dsl, Arby's, Blackeyed Pea, Chili's, Food Court, IHOP, McDonald's, Rockyard Grill, Best Western, Comfort Suites, Days Inn, Hampton Inn, Castle Rock Outlet/famous brands, Lowe's, Midas
182	CO 86, Castle Rock, Franktown, **E** Conoco/dsl, Phillips 66/dsl, 7-11/dsl, Augustine Grill, Castle Cafe, El Meson Mexican, Castle Pines Motel, st patrol, **W** Shell/Circle K/dsl, Valero/dsl, Burger King, Domino's, Guadalajara Mexican, Jack-in-the-Box, McDonald's, Old West BBQ, Santiago's Mexican, Village Inn, Waffle House, Wendy's, Castle Inn, Quality Inn, Super 8, NAPA
181	CO 86, Wilcox St, Plum Creek Pkwy, Castle Rock, **E** Conoco, Valero/dsl, Western/dsl, DQ, Papa John's, Papa Murphy's, Pizza Hut, Quiznos, Starbucks, Subway, Taco Bell, Castle Rock Motel, AutoZone, Big O Tire, Buick/Chevrolet/GMC, Chrysler/Dodge/Jeep, Ford, Midas, Safeway/gas, Tuesday Morning, Walgreens, USPO
174	Tomah Rd, **W** Yogi Bear's Campground

LARKSPUR

173	Larkspur (from sb, no return), **1 mi W** Conoco/Larkspur Cafe/dsl/
172	Upper Lake Gulch Rd, Larkspur, **2 mi W** Conoco/dsl/ , Larkspur Pizza Cafe
167	Greenland
163	County Line Rd
162.5mm	Monument Hill, elev 7352
162mm	**weigh sta both lanes**
161	CO 105, Woodmoor Dr, **E** Conoco, Papa John's, Sundance Mtn Lodge/rest, CO Hts RV Park (2mi), **W** Conoco/Circle K/dsl, 7-11, Arby's, La Casa Fiesta New Mexican, Domino's, McDonald's, Rosie's Diner, Starbucks, Subway, Taco Bell, Village Inn, Big O Tire, Natural Grocers, Safeway/dsl, Walgreens, USPO
158	Baptist Rd, **E** Shell/Circle K/Popeye's/dsl/24hr, Borriello Bros. Pizza, Chili's, Coldstone, Freddy's Steakburgers, Fusion Cuisine, McDonald's, Papa Murphy's, Subway, TX Roadhouse, Fairfield Inn, AutoZone, Christian Bros. Auto, Discount Tire, GNC, Home Depot, King's Sooper, Kohl's, O'Reilly Parts, Petsmart, Staples, Verizon, Walgreens, Walmart/Subway, **Urgent Care**, **W** Shamrock/dsl/scales
156b	N Entrance to USAF Academy, **W** visitors center
156a	Gleneagle Dr, **E** mining museum
153	InterQuest Pkwy, **E** Cheddar's, Hampton Inn, Residence Inn
152	scenic overlook on sb
151	Briargate Pkwy, **E** 7-11, Biaggi's, CA Pizza Kitchen

COLORADO SPRINGS

151	Continued
	Champp's, Garbanzo Grill, Maggie Moo's, Panera Bread, PF Changs, Qdoba, Starbucks, Ted's MT Grill, Hilton Garden, Homewood Suites, AT&T, to Black Forest
150b a	CO 83, Academy Blvd, **E** Conoco, Shamrock/dsl, Shell/Circle K/dsl, Applebee's, A&W, Baskin-Robbins, Buffalo Wild Wings, Burger King, Chick-fil-A, Chipotle Mexican, Coldstone, Cracker Barrel, Crave Burgers, Culver's, Del Taco, Denny's, Egg&I Café, Elephant Bar Rest., Extreme Pizza, Famous Dave's, Firehouse Subs, 5 Guys Burgers, HuHot Mongolian, IHOP, Jason's Deli, KFC, McDonald's, Mimi's Café, My Big Fat Greek Rest, Noodles&Co, Olive Garden, On-the-Border, Panera Bread, Pei Wei, Pizza Hut, Qdoba, Red Robin, Salt Grass Steaks, Schlotzsky's, Sonic, Starbucks, Subway, Thai Basil, Wahoo's, Wendy's, Academy Hotel, Comfort Suites, Days Inn, Drury Inn, EconoLodge, Economy Inn, Howard Johnson, Super 8, Advance Parts, AT&T, Barnes&Noble, Best Buy, Chevrolet, Dillard's, $Tree, Firestone/auto, Ford, Hobby Lobby, Home Depot, Hyundai, JC Penney, King's Sooper, Macy's, Marshall's, Michael's, Midas, Natural Grocers, Office Depot, Old Navy, PepBoys, Petsmart, Radio Shack, Ross, Sam's Club/gas, Sears/auto, Steinmart, USPO, Verizon, VW, Walmart/Subway, Whole Foods Mkt, **Urgent Care**, to Peterson AFB, **W** S Entrance to USAF Academy
149	Woodmen Rd, **E** Carl's Jr, Carraba's, Nissan, **W** Shell/Circle K, Old Chicago Pizza, Hooters, Outback Steaks, TGIFriday's, Zio's Italian, Comfort Inn, Embassy Suites, Fairfield Inn, Hampton Inn, Holiday Inn Express, Microtel, Staybridge Suites
148	Corporate Ctr Dr, Nevada Ave, **E** BJ's Rest, Chipotle Mexican, Panera Bread, Smash Burger, Costco/gas, Harley-Davidson, Kohl's, Lowe's, vet, **W** Shell/Circle K, Zane's Steaks, Crestwood Suites, Extended Stay America, Hyatt House, Marriott, to Rodeo Hall of Fame
146	Garden of the Gods Rd, **E** Conoco/7-11, Shell/Circle K/dsl, Carl's Jr, Caspian Cafe, Drifter's Burgers, McDonald's, Best Value Inn, La Quinta, Aamco, Emergicare, **W** Conoco/Circle K, 7-11, Shamrock/dsl, Shell/dsl, Applebee's, Blackeyed Pea, Chick-fil-A, Jimmy John's, Mollica's Italian, Souper Salad, Sonic, Subway, Taco Bell, Village Inn, Wendy's, Days Inn, Hyatt Place, Quality Inn, Super 8, Discount Tire, to Garden of Gods, vet
145	CO 38 E, Fillmore St, **E** 7-11, Shamrock/dsl, Western/dsl, Arby's, Carl's Jr, DQ, Lucky Dragon, McDonald's, Subway, Taco Bell, Budget Host, H, Advance Parts, **W** Conoco/dsl, Shell/Circle K/dsl, Waffle House, Motel 6, Super 8
144	Fontanero St
143	Uintah St, **E** 7-11, Uintah Fine Arts Ctr
142	Bijou St, Bus Dist, **E** Hilton, Firestone/auto, visitor info, **W** Denny's, Clarion, Quality Inn, Family$, 7-11
141	US 24 W, Cimarron St, to Manitou Springs, **W** Conoco/dsl, Shell/7-11/dsl, Arby's, Capt D's, La Casita Mexican, McDonald's, Popeye's, Sonic, Subway, TX Roadhouse, Acura, Audi, AutoZone, Brakes+, Buick/GMC, Cadillac, Chevrolet, Chrysler/Dodge/Jeep, Discount Tire, Ford, Grease Monkey, Hobby Lobby, Hyundai, Just Brakes, Kia, Lexus, Lincoln, Mazda, Meineke, Mercedes, NAPA, Office Depot, Porsche, Radio Shack, Subaru, Toyota/Scion, Volvo, VW, Walmart/McDonald's, to Pikes Peak

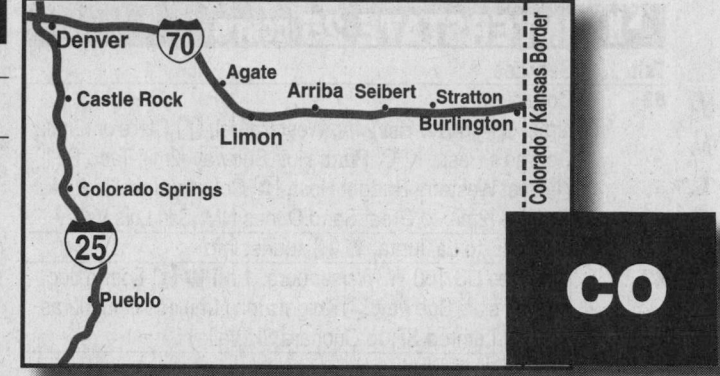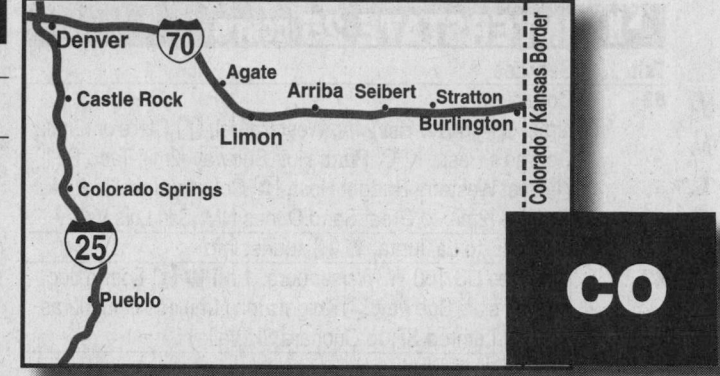

INTERSTATE 25 CONT'D

Exit	Services
140b	US 85 S, Tejon St, **E** ⊙ Peerless Tires, **W** ⛽ Conoco/dsl, ⊙ access to same as 141
140a	Nevada Ave, **E** 🛏 Chateau Motel, Howard Johnson, ⊙ Tire King, **W** ⛽ 7-11, Shamrock, 🍴 Arcio's Mexican, Burger King, China Kitchen, KFC, IHOP, McDonald's, Mollica's Italian, Noodles&Co, Panera Bread, Rancho Alegre Mexican, Schlotzsky's, Starbucks, Subway, Taco Bell, Taco Express, Wendy's, 🛏 Chief Motel, Rodeway Inn, Sunsprings Motel, Travel Star Inn, ⊙ Big O Tire, $Tree, Home Depot, Michael's, Midas, Natural Grocers, Office Depot, O'Reilly Parts, Petsmart, Ross, Safeway Foods, Sears, Tuesday Morning, Walgreens, tires/repair, USPO, access to auto dealers at 141
139	US 24 E, to Lyman, Peterson AFB
138	CO 29, Circle Dr, **E** ⛽ Conoco, Shell/Circle K/dsl, 🍴 McDonald's, 🛏 Crowne Plaza, Days Inn, Super 8, ⊙ Kohl's, 🐾, zoo, **W** ⛽ 7-11, 🍴 Arby's, Buffalo Wild Wings, Burger King, Carrabba's, Carl's Jr, Chili's, ChuckeCheese, Culver's, Denny's, Fazoli's, Macaroni Grill, Outback Steaks, Smoothie King, Village Inn, Subway, 🛏 Best Western, Comfort Inn, Courtyard, DoubleTree Hotel, Fairfield Inn, Hampton Inn, La Quinta, Residence Inn, ⊙ AT&T, Batteries+, GNC, PetCo, Radio Shack, Target
135	CO 83, Academy Blvd, **E** to Cheyenne Mtn SP, to 🐾, **W** Ft Carson
132	CO 16, Wide Field Security, **E** ⛽ ♥Loves /Subway/dsl, ⊙ Camping World RV Ctr, KOA
128	to US 85 N, Fountain, Security, **E** ⛽ Loaf'n Jug/Subway/dsl, 7-11, 🍴 Grand China, ⊙ USPO, **W** ⛽ Tomahawk/Shell/rest/dsl/24hr/@, 🛏 Fountain Inn, Super 8
125	Ray Nixon Rd
123	no services
122	to Pikes Peak Meadows, **W** Pikes Peak Intn'l Raceway
119	Rancho Colorado Blvd
116	county line rd
115mm	🅿 nb, full ♿ facilities, 🗑 litter barrels, petwalk
114	Young Hollow
112mm	🅿 sb, full ♿ facilities, 🗑 litter barrels, petwalk
110	Pinon
108	Purcell Blvd, Bragdon, **E** ⛽ racetrack, **W** KOA
106	Porter Draw
104	Eden, **W** ⛽ ♥Loves/Subway/dsl/scales/24hr
102	Eagleridge Blvd, **E** ⛽ Loaf'n Jug/dsl, 🍴 Burger King, Subway, TX Roadhouse, 🛏 Holiday Inn Express, ⊙ Big O Tire, Home Depot, Sam's Club/gas, **W** ⛽ Shell/dsl, 🍴 Asian Flower Bistro, Buffalo Wild Wings, Cactus Flower Mexican, Carino's, Chili's, Cracker Barrel, IHOP, Starbucks, Taco Star, Village Inn, 🛏 Best Western, Comfort Inn, EconoLodge, Hampton Inn, La Quinta, Ramada, Wingate Inn, ⊙ Best Buy, Kohl's, Old Navy, PetCo, Harley-Davidson, frontage rds access 101
101	US 50 W, Pueblo, **E** 🍴 Coldstone, Country Buffet, Denny's, Ruby Tuesday, Souper Salad, Subway, 🛏 Sleep Inn, ⊙ Barnes&Noble, Dillard's, JC Penney, Petsmart, Ross, Sears/auto, Target, TJ Maxx, U-Haul, Verizon, Walmart, mall, **W** ⛽ Loaf'n Jug/dsl, 7-11, Shell/dsl, Valero, 🍴 Applebee's, Arby's, Blackeyed Pea, Carl's Jr, China Rest., Chipotle Mexican, Country Kitchen, DJ's Steaks, DQ, Domino's, Fazoli's, Golden Corral, Jack-in-the-Box, Little Caesars, Manhattan's Pizza, McAlister's Deli, McDonald's,

101	Continued
	Noodles&Co, Olive Garden, Papa John's, Papa Murphy's, Pass Key Rest., Pizza Hut, Popeye's, Red Lobster, Starbucks, Subway, SW Grill, Taco Bell, Wendy's, 🛏 Clarion, Days Inn, Howard Johnson, Motel 6, Quality Inn, Rodeway Inn, Super 8, ⊙ Aamco, Advance Parts, Albertson's, AT&T, AutoZone, Brakes+, Chevrolet, Chrysler/Dodge/Jeep, Discount Tire, EmergiCare, Ford, Hyundai, Kia, K-Mart, Lowe's, Mazda, NAPA, Nissan, O'Reilly Parts, Staples, Subaru, Toyota, Walgreens, vet, frontage rds access 102
100b	29th St, Pueblo, **E** 🍴 Country Buffet, KFC, Mongolian Grill, Ruby Buffet, ⊙ Car Dr, $Tree, Hobby Lobby, King's Sooper Foods, Natural Grocers, Peerless Tires, Tires-4Less, Tuesday Morning, **W** ⛽ Conoco, 🍴 Sonic, 🛏 USA Motel, ⊙ Grease Monkey, Safeway
100a	US 50 E, to La Junta, **E** ⛽ Loaf'n Jug, Shell, 🍴 Little Caesars, McDonald's, Pizza Hut, Wendy's, ⊙ AutoZone, Family$, Goodyear, Save-A-Lot Foods, Walgreens
99b a	Santa Fe Ave, 13th St, downtown, **W** 🍴 Subway, Taco Bell, Wendy's, 🛏 Bramble Tree Inn, Guesthouse Inn, Travelers Motel, ⊙ 🅷 Buick/Cadillac/GMC, CarQuest
98b	CO 96, 1st St, Union Ave Hist Dist, Pueblo, **W** ⛽ Loaf'n Jug, 🍴 Carl's Jr, 🛏 Cambria Suites, Marriott
98a	US 50E bus, to La Junta, **W** ⛽ Phillips 66/dsl, 🍴 Sonic
97b	Abriendo Ave
97a	Central Ave, **W** ⛽ Shamrock, 🍴 McDonald's
96	Indiana Ave, **W** ⊙ 🅷
95	Illinois Ave (from sb), **W** to dogtrack
94	CO 45 N, Pueblo Blvd, **W** ⛽ Loaf'n Jug/dsl, Western/dsl, 🍴 Subway, Taco Bell, 🛏 Hampton Inn, Microtel, ⊙ Forts RV Park, fairgrounds/racetrack, to Lake Pueblo SP
91	Stem Beach
88	Burnt Mill Rd
87	Verde Rd
83	No Services
77	Hatchet Ranch Rd, Abbey Rd
74	CO 165 W, Colo City, **E** ⛽ Shamrock/deli/dsl/24hr, 🍴 Obie's BBQ, ⊙ KOA, **W** ⛽ Sinclair/Subway/dsl, 🍴 Los Cuervo's, Max's Rest., 🛏 Days Inn/rest., 🅿 both lanes, full ♿ facilities, 🚻, vending, 🗑 litter barrels, petwalk
71	Graneros Rd
67	to Apache
64	Lascar Rd
60	Huerfano
59	Butte Rd
56	Redrock Rd
55	Airport Rd
52	CO 69 W, to Alamosa, Walsenburg, **W** ⛽ Loaf'n Jug/dsl

🅖 = gas 🍴 = food 🛏 = lodging 🅞 = other 🆁🆂 = rest stop Copyright 2014 - The Next Exit ®

W A L S E N B U R G **T R I N I D A D** **B U R L I N G T O N**

🅒🅞

▲N	**INTERSTATE 25** CONT'D
Exit	Services
52	Continued
	(2mi), Shell/A&W/dsl/24hr, Western/dsl, 🍴 Carl's Jr (2mi), George's Rest., KFC, Pizza Hut, Subway (2mi), Taco Bell, 🛏 Best Western, Budget Host, 🅞 Country Host RV Park, Family$ (2mi), to Great Sand Dunes NM, San Luis Valley
50	CO 10 E, to La Junta, W 🇭, tourist info
49	Lp 25, to US 160 W, Walsenburg, **1 mi** W 🅖 Loaf'n Jug, 🍴 Carl's Jr., Subway, 🛏 Knights Inn (4mi), Rio Chucharas Inn, 🅞 Lathrop SP, to Cuchara Ski Valley
42	Rouse Rd, to Pryor
41	Rugby Rd
34	Aguilar
30	Aguilar Rd, W rv park, truck/tire repair
27	Ludlow, W Ludlow Memorial
23	Hoehne Rd
18	El Moro Rd, W 🆁🆂 both lanes, full 🚻 facilities, 🏕 litter barrels, petwalk
15	US 350 E, Goddard Ave, E 🍴 Burger King, Pizza Hut, 🛏 Super 8, 🅞 🇭, AutoZone, Big R Ranch Store, Family$, W 🅖 Shell/dsl, 🛏 Frontier Motel/café
14	Commercial St, downtown, Trinidad, same as 13b
13b	Main St, Trinidad, E CO Welcome Ctr, 🅖 Shell/Subway/dsl, 🍴 KFC/Taco Bell, McDonald's, Sonic, 🅞 CarQuest, Safeway Foods/dsl, Trinidad Motor Inn, W 🍴 DQ, Great Wall Chinese, Wonderful House Chinese, 🅞 RV camping, to Trinidad Lake, Monument Lake
13a	Santa Fe Trail, Trinidad, E 🛏 Best Western, 🅞 RV camping
11	Starkville, E 🅖 Shell/Wendy's/dsl/24hr, 🍴 Taquila's Mexican, 🛏 Budget Inn, Budget Summit Inn, Holiday Inn, 🅞 Bigg's RV Park, to Santa Fe Trail, **weigh/check sta**, W 🛏 La Quinta, Quality Inn/rest, 🅞 Big O Tire, Grease Monkey, O'Reilly Parts, Toyota, Walmart
8	Springcreek
6	Gallinas
2	Wootten
1mm	scenic area pulloff nb
0mm	Colorado/New Mexico state line, Raton Pass, elev 7834, **weigh sta sb**

▲E	**INTERSTATE 70**
Exit	Services
450mm	Colorado/Kansas state line
438	US 24, Rose Ave, Burlington, N 🅖 Conoco/dsl, 🛏 Hi-Lo Motel, Sloan's Motel, 🅞 🇭, Buick/Cadillac/Chevrolet/GMC, CarQuest, $General, Family$, Ford/Lincoln, NAPA, Safeway Foods, S 🅖 Shell/Reynaldo's Mexican/dsl/24hr, 🅞 Bonny SRA, RV Camping, truck repair
437.5mm	**Welcome Ctr wb, full 🚻 facilities, info, 🅒🅞, 🏕, litter barrels, petwalk, historical site**
437	US 385, Burlington, N 🅖 Conoco/dsl, Western/dsl, 🍴 Arby's, Burger King, Denny's, McDonald's, Pizza Hut, Route Steaks, Subway, 🛏 Best Value Inn, Burlington Inn, Chaparral Motel, Comfort Inn, Western Motel, 🅞 🇭, Alco, to Bonny St RA, S 🛏 Best Western/rest
429	Bethune
419	CO 57, Stratton, N 🅖 Cenex/dsl, Conoco/dsl, 🍴 Dairy Treat, 🛏 Claremont Inn/café, I-70 Inn, 🅞 Marshall Ash Village Camping, Trails End Camping
412	Vona, **1/2 mi** N gas, 🅒🅞

L I M O N

405	CO 59, Seibert, N Shady Grove Camping, S 🅖 Conoco/dsl, 🅞 tire repair
395	Flagler, N 🅖 Loaf'N Jug/dsl, 🍴 I-70 Diner, Subway, 🛏 Little England Motel, 🅞 Flagler SWA, NAPA, RV camping, S 🅖 Cenex/dsl 🅞 golf
383	Arriba, N 🅖 DJ/café/dsl, motel, S 🆁🆂 both lanes full 🚻 facilities, 🏕, litter barrels, point of interest, petwalk, RV camping
376	Bovina
371	Genoa, N point of interest, gas, food, 🅒🅞, S 🇭
363	US 24, US 40, US 287, to CO 71, to Hugo, Limon **13 mi** S 🇭
361	CO 71, Limon, N 🅞 Ace Hardware, Chrysler/Dodge/Jeep, S 🅖 Conoco/dsl, Shell/Wendy's/dsl, 🍴 Golden China, Pizza Hut, 🛏 1st Inn Gold, Knights Inn, 🅞 Alco, KOA, st patrol, RV camping, vet
360.5mm	**weigh/check sta both lanes**
359	to US 24, to CO 71, Limon, N 🅖 ❤FLYING J/IHOP/dsl/scales/LP/24hr, 🅞 dsl repair, RV camping, S 🅖 Phillips 66, Qwest/dsl, TA/Shell/Subway/Country Pride/dsl/scales/24hr/@, 🍴 Arby's, Denny's, McDonald's, Oscar's Grill, 🛏 Comfort Inn, EconoLodge, Holiday Inn Express, Quality Inn, Super 8, TS Inn, 🅞 camping
354	No Services
352	CO 86 W, to Kiowa
348	to Cedar Point
340	Agate, **1/4 mi** S gas/dsl, 🅒🅞
336	to Lowland
332mm	🆁🆂 wb, full 🚻 facilities, info, 🅒🅞, 🏕, litter barrels, vending, petwalk
328	to Deer Trail, N 🅖 Phillips/dsl, S 🅖 Shell/dsl, 🅞 USPO
325mm	East Bijou Creek
323.5mm	Middle Bijou Creek
322	to Peoria
316	US 36 E, Byers, N 🅖 Sinclair, 🛏 Budget Host, 🅞 Thriftway Foods/Drug, S 🅖 Tri Valley, 🍴 Country Burger Rest., 🅞 USPO
310	Strasburg, N 🅖 Conoco/dsl, Ray's, 🍴 Patio Cafe, Subway, 🛏 Strasburg Inn, 🅞 Country Gardens RV Camping (3mi), KOA, NAPA, Western Hardware, dsl/auto repair, USPO
306mm	Kiowa, Bennett, N 🆁🆂 both lanes, full 🚻 facilities, 🅒🅞, 🏕, litter barrels, petwalk
305	Kiowa (from eb)
304	CO 79 N, Bennett, N 🅖 Conoco/Hotstuff Pizza/dsl, ❤Love's/McDonald's/dsl/scales/24hr, 🍴 Chesters, China Kitchen, High Plains Diner, Starbucks, Subway, 🅞 Family$, King Soopers Foods/dsl, USPO, S 🅞 Ace Hardware
299	CO 36, Manila Rd, S 🅖 Shamrock/dsl
295	Lp 70, Watkins, N 🅖 Shell/Tomahawk/rest/dsl/24hr/@, 🍴 Biscuit's Cafe, Lulu's Cafe, 🛏 Country Manor Motel, 🅞 USPO
292	CO 36, Airpark Rd
289	E-470 **Tollway**, 120th Ave, CO Springs
288	US 287, US 40, Lp 70, Colfax Ave (exits left from wb)
286	CO 32, Tower Rd, N 🅖 Murphy Express/dsl, 🍴 Chili's, Chipotle Mexican, Del Taco, McAlister's Deli, Starbucks, Wendy's, 🅞 Best Buy, Brakes+, Discount Tire, $Tree, GNC, Home Depot, Les Schwab Tire, Office Depot, O'Reilly Parts, PetCo, Verizon, Walmart/Subway
285	Airport Blvd, N Denver Int ✈, S 🅖 ❤FLYING J/Denny's/dsl/scales/24hr, Shell/McDonald's/dsl, 🛏 Comfort Inn, Crystal Inn, 🅞 Harley-Davidson
284	I-225 N (from eb)

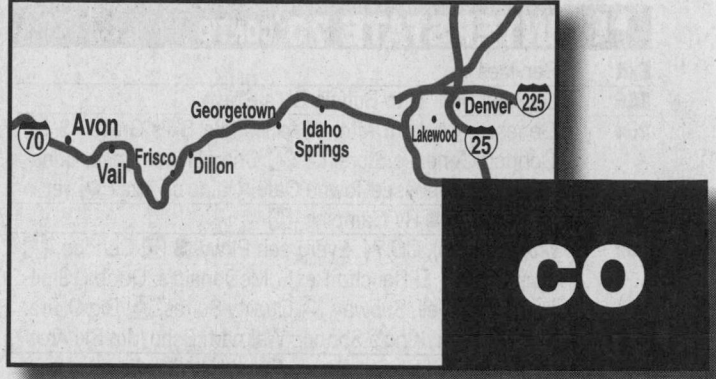

INTERSTATE 70 CONT'D

Exit	Services
283	Chambers Rd, **N** 📵 Conoco, Shell/Circle K/Popeye's, 🍴 A&W/KFC, Anthony's Pizza, Applebees, Chicago Grill, Jimmy John's, LJ Silver/Taco Bell, Outback Steaks, Pizza Hut, Qdoba, Sonic, Subway, Ted's MT Grill, Urban Sombrero, Wendy's, 🛏 A Loft, Cambria Suites, Country Inn&Suites, Crowne Plaza, Hampton Inn, Hilton Garden, Homewood Suites, Hyatt Place, Marriott, Residence Inn, Sleep Inn, ◯ Tires+, U-haul, **S** 📵 Shamrock, 🍴 Burger King, 🛏 Crossland Suites, ◯ America East RV Ctr
282	I-225 S, to Colorado Springs
281	Peoria St, **N** 📵 Conoco, 7-11, Shell/dsl, 🍴 Burger King, Del Taco, Domino's, El Patron Mexican, GoodTimes Burgers, McDonald's, Peoria Grill, Subway, 🛏 Drury Inn, La Quinta, Timbers Motel, ◯ Big O Tire, Family$, **S** 📵 Conoco/dsl, Shamrock/dsl, 🍴 Bennett's BBQ, Chester's Grill, Church's, Denny's, Ho Mei Chinese, Pizza Hut/Taco Bell, Real Deminas Mexican, Subway, Waffle House, Wendy's, 🛏 Motel 6, Quality Inn, Star Hotel, Stay Inn, ◯ Curves, Goodyear/auto, Tires For Less, auto/RV repair, vet
280	Havana St, **N** 🛏 Embassy Suites
279	I-270 W, US 36 W (from wb), to Ft Collins, Boulder
278	CO 35, Quebec St, **N** 📵 Sapp Bros/Sinclair/Subway/dsl/@, TA/dsl/rest./24hr/@, 🍴 Coldstone, Del Taco, Jim'n Nick's BBQ, Marco's Pizza, Olive Garden, Qdoba, Red Lobster, Starbucks, TGIFriday's, Wahoo's, 🛏 Best Inn, Comfort Inn, Studio Suites, ◯ AT&T, Bass Pro Shops, JC Penney, Macys, Old Navy, Super Target, Verizon, mall, **S** 🍴 Arby's, Buffalo Wild Wings, Country Buffet, Famous Dave's BBQ, Jimmy John's, IHOP, McDonald's, Panda Express, Panera Bread, Papa John's, Red Robin, Sonic, Subway, 🛏 Courtyard, DoubleTree Hotel, Holiday Inn, Red Lion Inn, Renaissance Inn, Super 8, ◯ AT&T, GNC, Home Depot, Office Depot, Radio Shack, Ross, Sam's Club/gas, Tires+, Walgreens, Walmart/Subway
277	to Dahlia St, Holly St, Monaco St, frontage rd
276b	US 6 E, US 85 N, CO 2, Colorado Blvd, **S** 📵 Conoco/Subway/dsl, 🍴 Carl's Jr, Domino's, KT'S BBQ, Starbucks
276a	Vasquez Ave, **N** 📵 (Loves)/Wendy's/dsl/scales/24hr, 🛏 Colonial Motel, Western Inn, ◯ Blue Beacon, Ford/Mack Trucks, **S** 📵 7-11, 🍴 Burger King
275c	York St (from eb), **N** 🛏 Colonial Motel
275b	CO 265, Brighton Blvd, Coliseum, **N** 📵 7-11
275a	Washington St, **N** 🍴 Pizza Hut, **S** 📵 Conoco, 🍴 McDonald's, Quiznos, Subway
274b a	I-25, N to Cheyenne, S to Colorado Springs
273	Pecos St, **N** ◯ CO Ranch Mkt, Family$, True Value, **S** 📵 7-11, 🍴 Quiznos, ◯ transmissions
272	US 287, Federal Blvd, **N** 📵 Conoco/dsl, Sinclair, 🍴 Burger King, Goodtimes Burgers, Little Caesar's, McCoy's Rest., McDonald's, Pizza Hut, Rico Pollo, Subway, Taco Bell, Village Inn, Winchell's, Wendy's, 🛏 Motel 6, ◯ Advance Parts, $Tree, tires, **S** 📵 Conoco/Circle K, 🍴 El Padrino Mexican, Popeye's, Starbucks, 🛏 Howard Johnson
271b	Lowell Blvd, Tennyson St (from wb)
271a	CO 95, **S** funpark
270	Sheridan Blvd, **N** 📵 Shell/dsl, **S** 🍴 El Paraiso Mexican, ◯ Family$, Firestone/auto, Radio Shack, fun park, repair
269b	I-76 E (from eb), to Ft Morgan, Ft Collins
269a	CO 121, Wadsworth Blvd, **N** 📵 Conoco, 7-11, Shell, 🍴 Alamos Verdes Mexican, Anthony's Pizza, Applebee's,

DENVER AREA (side tab)

Exit	Services
269a	Continued
	Bennet's BBQ, Burger King, Chipotle Mexican, Coldstone, El Tapatio, Fazoli's, Gunther Toody's Diner, IHOP, Kukoro Japanese, LoneStar Steaks, McDonald's/playplace, Red Robin, Ruby Tuesday, Smiling Moose Deli, Starbucks, Subway, Taco Bell, TX Roadhouse, ◯ Advance Parts, Brakes+, Costco/gas, Discount Tire, $Tree, Goodyear/auto, Home Depot, Lowe's, Office Depot, Petsmart, Radio Shack, Sam's Club, Tires+, city park, mall, **Urgent Care**
267	CO 391, Kipling St, Wheat Ridge, **N** 📵 Conoco, Shell/Carl's Jr/Circle K/dsl, 🍴 Burger King, Einstein Bros, Furr's Dining, Jack-in-the-Box, Lil Nick's Pizza, Margarita's Mexican, Panda Express, Qdoba, Quiznos, Starbucks, Subway, 🛏 American Inn, Motel 6, ◯ Cadillac/Chevrolet, Chrysler/Jeep, GNC, NAPA, 7-11, Target, Verizon, repair, vet, **S** 📵 Conoco/Circle K, Phillips 66, Shell, 🍴 Pizza Hut/Taco Bell, Smokin' Joe's Grill, Village Inn, Winchell's, 🛏 Affordable Inn, Best Value Inn, Comfort Inn, Holiday Inn Express, Ramada, ◯ Ketelesen RV Ctr
266	CO 72, W 44th Ave, Ward Rd, Wheat Ridge, **N** 📵 Conoco/dsl, ◯ transmissions, **S** 📵 Shamrock/dsl, TA/rest./scales/dsl/24hr/@, 🛏 Howard Johnson, ◯ RV America
265	CO 58 W (from wb), to Golden, Central City
264	Youngfield St, W 32nd Ave, **N** 📵 Conoco/Circle K, 🍴 Denny's, GoodTimes Burgers, 🛏 La Quinta, **S** 🍴 Abrusci's Italian, Chili's, DQ, McDonald's, Old Chicago Pizza, Pizza Hut/Taco Bell, Qdoba, SmashBurger, Starbucks, Subway, ◯ Camping World RV Ctr, King's Sooper/24hr, Petsmart, Tuesday Morning, Walgreens, Walmart
263	Denver West Blvd, **N** 🛏 Marriott/rest., **S** 🍴 Coldstone, Jamba Juice, Keg Steaks, Macaroni Grill, McGrath's Fishouse, Mimi's Cafe, Qdoba, ◯ Barnes&Noble, Best Buy, Office Depot, Old Navy, Whole Foods Mkt, same as 262
262	US 40 E, W Colfax, Lakewood, **N** 📵 Sinclair/dsl, 🍴 Jack-in-the-Box, Little Ricky's Cafe, Subway, 🛏 Hampton Inn, ◯ Buick/GMC, Camping World RV Ctr, Chrysler/Jeep, Dodge, Home Depot, Honda, Hyundai, Kohl's, NAPA, PetCo, Staples, Subaru, U-Haul, transmissions, vet, **S** 📵 Shell/Circle K/dsl/LP, 🍴 Chipotle Mexican, Hops Brewery, Jamba Juice, Mimi's Cafe, On-the-Border, Outback Steaks, Pei Wei Asian, Quiznos, Wendy's, 🛏 Courtyard, Days Inn/rest., Holiday Inn, Mtn View Inn, Residence Inn, ◯ Chevrolet, Lexus, Old Navy, Target, Toyota, mall, same as 263
261	US 6 E (from eb), W 6th Ave, to Denver
260	CO 470, to Colo Springs
259	CO 26, Golden, **N** 📵 Conoco, 🛏 Hampton Inn (2mi), ◯ Heritage Sq Funpark, **S** Music Hall, to Red Rocks SP
257mm	runaway truck ramp eb

WHEATRIDGE (side tab) **LAKEWOOD** (side tab)

⅀E INTERSTATE 70 CONT'D

CO / **IDAHO SPRINGS** / **SILVERTHORNE**

Exit	Services
256	Lookout Mtn, **N** to Buffalo Bill's Grave
254	Genesee, Lookout Mtn, **N** to Buffalo Bill's Grave, **S** 🅖 Conoco/Genesee Store, LP, 🍴 Chart House Rest., Christie's Rest., Genesee Towne Cafe, Guido's Pizza, 🄾 vet
253	Chief Hosa, **S** RV Camping, 🄾
252	(251 from eb), CO 74, Evergreen Pkwy, **S** 🅖 Conoco, 🍴 Burger King, El Rancho Rest., McDonald's, Qdoba, Smiling Moose Deli, Subway, 🛏 Quality Suites, 🄾 Big O Tire, Home Depot, King's Sooper, Walmart, Echo Mtn Ski Area
248	(247 from eb), Beaver Brook, Floyd Hill, **S** antiques
244	US 6, to CO 119, to Golden, Central City, Eldora Ski Area
243	Hidden Valley
242mm	tunnel
241b a	rd 314, Idaho Springs West, **N** 🅖 Conoco/McDonald's/dsl, Sinclair, Shell/dsl, Western/dsl/e85, 🍴 Carl's Jr, Cherry Blossom Chinese, Marion's Rest., Quiznos, Smokin' Yards BBQ, Starbucks, Subway, Wildfire Rest., 🛏 Argo Inn, Columbine Inn, H&H Motel, Idaho Springs Hotel, JC Motel, Marion's Rest., 6&40 Motel, 🄾 CarQuest, Safeway Foods/Drug, USPO
240	CO 103, Mt Evans, **N** 🅖 Kum&Go/dsl, Shell, Sinclair/dsl, 🍴 Azteca Mexican, Beaujo's Pizza, Buffalo Rest., Jiggie's Cafe, Main St Rest., Mangia Italian, Picci Pizza, Tommy Knocker Grill, 2 Bros Deli, West Winds Cafe, same as 241, **S** to Mt Evans
239	Idaho Springs, **S** 🄾 camping
238	Fall River Rd, to St Mary's Glacier
235	Dumont (from wb)
234	Downeyville, Dumont, **N** 🅖 Conoco/Subway/dsl, 🍴 Burger King, Starbucks, 🄾 ski rentals, **weigh sta both lanes**
233	Lawson (from eb)
232	US 40 W, to Empire, **N** to Berthoud Pass, Rocky Mtn NP, Winterpark/Sol Vista ski areas
228	Georgetown, **S** 🅖 Conoco/Subway/dsl, Shell/dsl, Valero, 🍴 Mountain Buzz Cafe, 🛏 Chateau Chamonix, Super 8, 🄾 visitors ctr
226.5mm	scenic overlook eb
226	Georgetown, Silver Plume Hist Dist, **N** 🄾 Buckley Bros Mkt, repair
221	Bakerville
220mm	Arapahoe NF eastern boundary
219mm	parking area (eb only)
218	no services
216	US 6 W, Loveland Valley, Loveland Basin, ski areas
214mm	Eisenhower/Johnson Tunnel, elev 11013
213mm	parking area eb
205	US 6 E, CO 9 N, Dillon, Silverthorne, **N** 🅖 Conoco/dsl, 7-11, Shell/7-11/dsl, 🍴 Asian Oven, China Gourmet, Chipotle Mexican, Dominos, Mint Cafe, Mtn Lyon Café, Murphy's Cafe, Quiznos, Village Inn, Wendy's, 🛏 Days Inn, 1st Interstate Inn, La Quinta, Luxury Suites, Quality Inn, Silver Inn, 🄾 Buick/Cadillac/Chevrolet/GMC, CarQuest, Chrysler/Dodge/Jeep, Ford, Old Navy, Outlets/famous brands, Subaru, Target, TrueValue, **S** 🅖 Shamrock, Shell/dsl, 🍴 Arby's, Bamboo Garden, Blue Moon Deli, Burger King, Dam Brewery/Rest., DQ, Fiesta Mexican, Jimmy John's, McDonald's, Nick'n Willy's Pizza, Noodles&Co, Pizza Hut, Qdoba, Red Mtn Grill, Ruby Tuesday, SmashBurger, Smiling Moose Cafe, Starbucks, Subway, Sunshine Cafe, 🛏

FRISCO / **AVON** / **EAGLE**

Exit	Services
205	Continued Comfort Suites, Dillon Inn, Super 8, 🄾 City Mkt Foods/gas, Outlets/famous brands, Natural Grocery, Tuesday Morning, Verizon, Walgreens, vet
203.5mm	scenic overlook both lanes
203	CO 9 S, to Breckenridge, Frisco, **S** 🅖 Conoco/Wendy's/dsl, 7-11, Shell, Valero/dsl, 🍴 A&W, KFC, Carlos Miguel's Mexican, Hacienda Real Mexican, Q4U BBQ, Starbucks, Subway, Szechuan Chinese, Taco Bell, 🛏 Alpine Inn, Best Western, Holiday Inn, Ramada Ltd, Summit Inn, 🄾 Big O Tire, NAPA, Radio Shack, Safeway Foods, Walmart/McDonald's, vet, to Breckenridge Ski Area, RV Resort (6mi)
201	Main St, Frisco, **S** 🅖 Loaf N' Jug, 🍴 Alpine Deli, Backcountry Brew Pub, Boatyard Pizzaria, Butterhorn Cafe, Cowboy Pizza, Log Cabin Cafe, Lost Cajun Rest., Rainbow Ct Rest., 🛏 Blue Spruce Inn, Frisco Lodge, Hotel Frisco, Snowshoe Motel, 🄾 Bighorn Reservations, RV camping, museum/visitor info, USPO, to Breckenridge Ski Area
198	Officers Gulch, emergency callbox
196mm	scenic area (wb only)
195	CO 91 S, to Leadville, 1 mi **S** 🅖 Conoco/dsl, 🍴 Quiznos, 🛏 Copper Lodging, 🄾 to Copper Mtn Ski Resort
190	**S** 🆁🆂 **both lanes, full** ♿ **facilities,** 🄾, 🖼, **litter barrels**
189mm	Vail Pass Summit, elev 10662 ft, parking area both lanes
180	Vail East Entrance, 🄾, services **3-4 mi S**
176	Vail, **S** 🄾🄷, ski info/lodging
173	Vail Ski Area, **N** 🅖 Phillips 66, Shell/dsl, 🍴 Bearfish Grill, Gohanya Chinese, McDonald's, Qdoba, Subway, Taco Bell, Wendy's, 🛏 Holiday Inn, Roost Lodge, 🄾 Ace Hardware, City Mkt Foods/deli, Safeway Food/Drug, 7-11, USPO, **S** 🅖 Conoco/dsl/LP, 🛏 Black Bear Inn, Marriott/Streamside Hotel
171	US 6 W, US 24 E, to Minturn, Leadville, **N** 🄾 Ski Cooper ski area, **2 mi S** 🅖 Shell, 🍴 Magusto's Italian, Minturn Steaks, 🛏 Minturn Inn, 🄾 RV Camping, USPO
169	Eaglevale (from wb), no return
168	William J. Post Blvd, **S** 🍴 Zaccazai Cafe, 🄾 Home Depot, Walmart/McDonald's
167	Avon, **N** 🅖 Conoco/7-11/dsl, Shell, 🍴 Pizza Hut, 🄾 Goodyear, vet, **S** 🍴 Burger King, Denny's, Domino's, Fiesta Jalisco Mexican, Panda City, Pazzo's Pizza, Starbucks, Subway, 🛏 Avon Ctr Lodge, Christie Lodge, Comfort Inn, Sheraton, Westin, 🄾 City Mkt/drugs, GNC, Office Depot, to Beaver Creek/Arrowhead Ski, ski info, **Urgent Care**, USPO
163	Edwards, **S** 🆁🆂 **both lanes, full** ♿ **facilities,** 🖼, **litter barrel, RV dump,** 🅖 Conoco/dsl, Shell/Wendy's/dsl, 🍴 Cafe Milano, Cosmos BBQ, Dish Cafe, Gashouse Rest., Gore Range Brewery, Marble Slab Creamery, Marko's Pizza, Old Forge Pizza, Smiling Moose, Subway, Zino's Italian, 🛏 Riverwalk Inn, 🄾 Villiage Mkt, to Arrowhead Ski Area, USPO
162mm	scenic area eb
159mm	Eagle River
157	CO 131 N, Wolcott, **N** to Steamboat Ski Area
147	Eagle, **N** 🅖 Kum&Go/pizza/dsl, 🍴 Burger King, Starbucks, 🛏 AmericInn, Comfort Inn, Holiday Inn Express, 🄾 City Mkt Foods, **S** 🅖 Conoco/dsl, Sinclair/Subway/dsl, 🍴 Eagle Diner, El Pariente, Gourmet China, Grand Ave Grill, Moe's Original BBQ, Pazzo's Pizzaria, Taco Bell, Wendy's, 🛏 Eagle Lodge&Suites, Silverleaf Suites, 🄾 Costco/gas (3mi), USPO, 🆁🆂 **both lanes, full** ♿ **facilities, info**

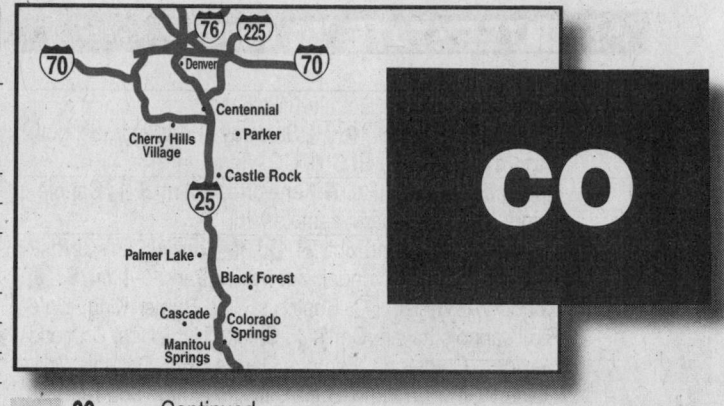

↑E INTERSTATE 70 CONT'D

Exit	Services
140	Gypsum, **S** 💷 Kum&Go, Shell, 🍴 Columbine Mkt Deli, Ritten House Rest., Salsa's Mexican, 🅾 auto/truck repair, ✈, USPO, **3 mi S** River Dance Resort camping
134mm	Colorado River
133	Dotsero, **N** 🅾 River Dance RV Camping (3mi)
129	Bair Ranch, **S** 🆁🆂 **both lanes, full** ♿ **facilities**, ✈, **litter barrels, petwalk**
128.5mm	parking area eb
127mm	tunnel wb
125mm	tunnel
125	to Hanging Lake (no return eb)
123	Shoshone (no return eb)
122.5mm	exit to river (no return eb)
121	to Hanging Lake, Grizzly Creek, **S** 🆂 **both lanes, full** ♿ **facilities**, ✈, **litter barrels,**
119	**No Name, 🆁🆂 both lanes, full** ♿ **facilities, RV camping, rafting**
118mm	tunnel
116	CO 82 E, to Aspen, Glenwood Springs, **N** 💷 Conoco/dsl, Shell/dsl, 🍴 Chomp's Rest., Fiesta Guadalajara, KFC, Qdoba, Subway, Tequilas Rest., Village Inn, 🛏 Best Western, Glenwood Springs Inn, Hampton Inn, Holiday Inn Express, Hotel Colorado, Ramada Inn, Silver Spruce Motel, Starlight Motel, 🅾 Land Rover, NAPA, Toyota, Hot Springs Bath, funpark, **0-2 mi S** 💷 Conoco, Phillips 66/dsl, Shamrock/dsl, Shell, Sinclair, 🍴 Arby's, Bears Loft Rest., China Town, Domino's, Little Ceasar's, McDonald's, 19th St Diner, Pizza Hut, Rib City Grill, Starbucks, Subway, Taco Bell, Taipei Japanese, Wendy's, 🛏 Caravan Inn, Cedar Lodge, Frontier Lodge, Hotel Denver, 🅾 🅷 Alpine Tire, AutoZone, B.Thornal DDS, City Mkt Foods, Curves, NAPA, Office Depot, Rite Aid, Safeway Foods, 7-11, Walmart, USPO, city park, to Ski Sunlight
115mm	🆁🆂 **eb, full** ♿ **facilities**, ✈, **litter barrels**
114	W Glenwood Springs, **N** 💷 Phillips 66/dsl, 7-11, Shell, 🍴 Burger King, Jilbirtito's Mexican, Porker's BBQ, Rte 6 Grill House, Vicco's Charcoal Burger, 🛏 Affordable Inn, Best Value Inn, Ponderosa Motel, Red Mtn Inn, Rodeway Inn, 🅾 AT&T, Big O Tire, Checker Parts, Ford, JC Penney, K-Mart, Radio Shack, Staples, Subaru, Verizon, mall, **S** 💷 Conoco/DQ/dsl, 🍴 Chili's, Moe's SW Grill, Russo's Pizza, Starbucks, 🛏 Courtyard, Glenwood Suites, Quality Inn, Residence Inn, 🅾 Audi/VW, Harley-Davidson, Lowe's, PetCo, Target, **Urgent Care**
111	South Canyon
109	Canyon Creek
108mm	parking area both lanes
105	New Castle, **N** 💷 Conoco/dsl, Kum&Go/dsl, 🍴 McDonald's, New Castle Diner, Subway, 🛏 Rodeway Inn, 🅾 City Mkt Foods/deli, Elk Creek Campground (4mi), **S** 🅾 Best Hardware
97	Silt, **N** 💷 Conoco/dsl/24hr, Kum&Go, Phillips 66/dsl, 🛏 Red River Inn, 🅾 auto repair, to Harvey Gap SP, **S** 🍴 Red Brick BBQ, 🛏 Holiday Inn Express, Ruby River Cabins, 🅾 Heron's Nest RV Park
94	Garfield County Airport Rd
90	CO 13 N, Rifle, **N** 🆁🆂 **both lanes, full** ♿ **facilities**, ✈, **litter barrels, RV dump**, NF Info, 🅾 Conoco, Kum&Go, Phillips 66/dsl, Shell, 🍴 KFC, 🛏 Winchester Motel (1mi), 🅾 USPO, Rifle Gap SP, **S** 💷 Kum&Go, Phillips 66/Sub
90	Continued way/dsl, Shell, 🍴 Burger King, Domino's, Little Caesar's, McDonald's/playplace, Rib City Grill, Sonic, Starbucks, Taco Bell, 🛏 Comfort Inn, Hampton Inn, La Quinta, Red River Inn/rest., Rusty Cannon Motel, 🅾 🅷, Checker Parts, Radio Shack, Walmart/Subway
87	to CO 13, West Rifle
81	Rulison
75	Parachute, **N** 🆁🆂 **both lanes, full** ♿ **facilities, info**, 🎁, ✈, **litter barrels, petwalk**, 💷 Sinclair/dsl, Shell/dsl/24hr, 🍴 El Tapatio Mexican, Hong's Garden Chinese, Outlaws Rest., Subway, 🛏 Comfort Inn, Parachute Inn, 🅾 NAPA, Radio Shack, Verizon, USPO, vet, **S** 💷 Phillips 66/Domino's/dsl, Shell/Wendy's, Sinclair, 🛏 Candlewood Suites, Holiday Inn Express, 🅾 Family$, RV Park (4mi), True Value
63mm	Colorado River
62	De Beque, **N** 💷 CFN Fuel, Kum&Go/Subway/dsl, 🅾 food, 🎁, auto repair
50mm	parking area eastbound, Colorado River, tunnel begins eastbound
49mm	Plateau Creek
49	CO 65 S, to CO 330 E, to Grand Mesa, Powderhorn Ski Area
47	Island Acres St RA, **N** CO River SP, RV camping, **S** 💷 Conoco/rest./dsl
46	Cameo
44	Lp 70 W, to Palisade, **3 mi S** gas, food, lodging
43.5mm	Colorado River
42	US 6, Palisade, **1 mi S** Fruitstand/store, gas, 🛏 Wine Country Inn, 🅾 wineries
37	to US 6, to US 50 S, Clifton, Grand Jct, **0-1 mi S** 💷 Conoco/dsl, Maverik/dsl, Shamrock/dsl, Sinclair, 🍴 Burger King, Cactus Canyon, Chin Chin Oriental, Dos Hombres, Jimmy Johns, KFC, Little Caesar's, McDonald's/playplace, Papa Johns, Papa Murphy's, Pizza Hut, Qdoba, Sonic, Starbucks, Subway, Taco Bell, Wendy's, 🛏 Best Western, 🅾 Ace Hardware, AutoZone, Checker Parts, City Mkt Food/gas, Curves, Family$, Murdoch's Store, USPO, Walgreens, Walmart (2mi), repair
31	Horizon Dr, Grand Jct, **N** 💷 Shell/dsl, 🍴 Enzo's Pizza, Las Palmas Mexican, Pepper's Rest., Village Inn, Wendy's, 🛏 Best Value Inn, Clarion, Comfort Inn, Courtyard, Grand Vista Hotel, Holiday Inn, La Quinta, Motel 6, Ramada Inn, Residence Inn, 🅾 Harley-Davidson, USPO, Zarlingo's Repair, ✈, **S** 💷 Conoco/Subway/dsl, Shell/dsl, 🍴 Applebee's, Burger King/playland, Denny's, Good Pastures Rest., Herford Steaks, Nick'n Willy's Pizza, Pizza Hut, Sang Garden, Starbucks, Taco Bell, 🛏 Affordable Inn, Best Western, Country Inn, Doubletree Hotel, Mesa Inn,

Left margin (vertical): GLENWOOD SPRINGS ... RIFLE

Right margin (vertical): PARACHUTE ... GRAND JCT

Right tab: CO

⬆️🅴 INTERSTATE 70 CONT'D

Exit	Services
31	Continued Quality Inn, Super 8, 🅞 🄷, Safeway Food/drug/gas, golf, visitors ctr, to Mesa St Coll, CO NM
28	Redlands Pkwy, 24 Rd, **N** Kenworth, **0-2 mi S** 🏠 Candlewood Suites, city park, same as 26
26	US 6, US 50, Grand Jct, **N** 🅖 ❤Love's/Carl's Jr/dsl/Scales/24hr, 🅞 Hyundai, Jct W RV Park, **0-4 mi S** 🅖 Conoco/A&W/dsl, 🍴 Boston's Grill, Burger King, Cafe Rio, Carino's Italian, Carl's Jr, Chick-fil-A, Chili's, Chipotle Mexican, Coldstone, Famous Dave's BBQ, Genghis Grill, Golden Corral, Grand Buffet, IHOP, Jimmy John's, McDonald's/playplace, Olive Garden, Outback Steaks, Papa Murphys, Qdoba, Red Lobster, Red Robin, Schlotzky's, Sonic, Starbucks, Subway, Taco Bell, Wendy's, 🏠 Holiday Inn Express, West Gate Inn, 🅞 AutoZone, Barnes&Noble, Best Buy, Big O Tire, Buick/Chevrolet, Cabela's, Chrysler/Dodge/Jeep, City Mkt, $Tree, Ford, Freightliner, Hobby Lobby, Home Depot, Honda, JC Penney, Kohl's, Lowe's, Michael's, Mobile City RV Park, Nissan, Office Depot, Old Navy, PetCo, Petsmart, Rite Aid, Ross, Sam's Club/gas, Scott RV Ctr, Sears/auto, Subaru, Suzuki, Target, Toyota, Verizon, Walmart/McDonald's, mall
19	US 6, CO 340, Fruita, **N** 🅖 Conoco/dsl, 🍴 Burger King, Munchie's Burgers/Pizza, 🏠 Balanced Rock Motel, 🅞 🄷, City Mkt Foods/deli/24hr, USPO, Walgreens, **S** Welcome Ctr, full ♿ facilities, 🅒, 🏞, litter barrels, RV dump, petwalk, 🅖 Conoco/Subway/dsl/24hr, Shell/Wendy's/dsl/24hr, 🍴 Dragon Treasure Chinese, El Tapatio Mexican, McDonald's/playplace, Rib City Grill, Taco Bell, 🏠 Comfort Inn, La Quinta, Super 8, 🅞 Monument RV Park, Peterbilt/Volvo, Verizon, dinosaur museum, to CO NM, vet
17mm	Colorado River
15	CO 139 N, to Loma, Rangely, **N** to Highline Lake SP, gas/dsl, 🅒
14.5mm	**weigh/check sta both lanes, 🅒**
11	Mack. **2-3 mi N** gas/dsl, food
2	Rabbit Valley, to Dinosaur Quarry Trail
0mm	Colorado/Utah state line

⬆️🅴 INTERSTATE 76

Exit	Services
185mm	**I-76 begins/ends on NE I-80, Exit 102**
184mm	Colorado/Nebraska state line
180	US 385, Julesburg, **N** 🅖 Shell, 🍴 Subway, 🏠 Budget Host, 🅞 🄷, **Welcome Ctr/** 🆁🆂 **both lanes, full** ♿ **facilities, info, RV dump, S** 🅖 Conoco/dsl
172	Ovid
165	CO 59, to Haxtun, Sedgwick, **N** Lucy's Cafe
155	Red Lion Rd
149	CO 55, to Fleming, Crook, **S** 🅖 Sinclair/dsl/café
141	Proctor
134	Iliff
125	US 6, Sterling, **0-3 mi N** 🅖 Cenex/dsl, Sinclair, 🍴 Arby's, Bamboo Garden, Burger King, Domino's, DQ, KFC/LJ Silver, McDonald's, Old Town Bistro, Papa Murphy's, Pizza Hut, Sonic, Subway, Taco Bell, Taco John's, Village Inn, Wendy's, 🏠 Best Western, 1st Interstate Inn, 🅞 🄷, AutoZone, Buick/Chevrolet, Chrysler/Dodge/Jeep, $General, $Tree, Ford/Lincoln, Goodyear/auto, Home Depot, NAPA, O'Reilly Parts, Radio Shack, Sun Mart Foods, Verizon,

Exit	Services
125	Continued Walgreens, Walmart, N Sterling SP, museum, st patrol, USPO, 🆁🆂 **both lanes** ♿ **facilities,** 🏞 **litter barrels, petwalk, vending, RV dump, S** 🅖 Reata/Quiznos/dsl, 🍴 Country Kitchen, 🏠 Comfort Inn, Ramada Inn, Super 8, Travelodge, 🅞 RV Camping
115	CO 63, Atwood, **N** 🅖 Sinclair/dsl, 🅞 🄷, **S** 🍴 Steakhouse
102	Merino
95	Hillrose
92	to US 6 E, to US 34, CO 71 S
90b a	CO 71 N, to US 34, Brush, **N** 🅖 Tomahawk Trkstp/Shell/rest./dsl/24hr, 🍴 China Buffet, Pizza Hut, Wendy's, 🏠 Econolodge, **S** 🅖 Conoco/dsl, 🍴 McDonald's, 🏠 Microtel
89	Hospital Rd, **S** 🄷, golf
86	Dodd Bridge Rd
82	Barlow Rd, **N** 🅖 Conoco/dsl, 🍴 Maverick's Grill, 🏠 Comfort Inn, Rodeway Inn, **S** 🅖 Reata/Quiznos/dsl/scales, USA/dsl, 🍴 Burger King, 🅞 $Tree, Walmart/Subway
80	CO 52, Ft Morgan, **N** 🅞 City Park, Golf, RV Camping, **S** 🅖 Conoco/dsl, Maverik/dsl, Sinclair/dsl, Western/dsl, 🍴 Arby's, DQ, McDonald's, Sonic, Subway, Taco John's, Wonderful House Chinese, 🏠 Central Motel, Hampton Inn, Sands Inn, Super 8, 🅞 🄷, AutoZone, Toyota, Verizon, Walgreens
79	CO 144, to Weldona, (no wb return)
75	US 34 E, to Ft Morgan, **S** 🅖 Shell/pizza/dsl, 🍴 Embers Rest., 🏠 Clarion, 🅞 st patrol
74.5mm	**weigh sta both lanes**
73	Long Bridge Rd
66b	US 34 W (from wb), to Greeley
66a	CO 39, CO 52, to Goodrich, **N** 🅖 Phillips 66/dsl, 🅞 RV Camping, to Jackson Lake SP, **S** 🅖 Sinclair/cafe/dsl/e-85, 🅞 🆁🆂 **both lanes, full** ♿ **facilities,** 🏞 **litter barrels, petwalk, vending**
64	Wiggins (from eb)
60	to CO 144 E, to Orchard
57	rd 91
49	Painter Rd (from wb)
48	to Roggen, **N** 🅖 Conoco/dsl, **S** 🅞 USPO
39	Keenesburg, **S** 🅖 Shell/dsl, 🍴 Rooster's Rest., 🏠 Keene Motel
34	Kersey Rd
31	CO 52, Hudson, **N** 🅖 ❤Love's/Subway/Carl's Jr/scales/24hr/dsl, **S** 🅖 Conoco/dsl, Shell/dsl, 🍴 El Faro Mexican, Pepper Pod Rest., 🅞 RV camping, USPO
25	CO 7, Lochbuie, **N** 🅖 Shell/dsl
22	Bromley Lane, **N** 🅖 Valero/dsl, 🍴 KFC/LJ Silver, Wendy's, 🏠 Hampton Inn (4mi), 🅞 🄷, Lowe's, **S** Barr Lake SP
21	144th Ave, Eagle Blvd, **N** 🍴 Buffalo Wild Wings, Chick-fil-A, Chili's, Heidi's Deli, McDonald's, Quiznos, Subway, Taco Bell, 🏠 Candlewood Suites, Holiday Inn Express, 🅞 🄷, Dick's, $Tree, GNC, Home Depot, JC Penney, Kohl's, Michael's, Office Depot, Petsmart, Ross, Target, Verizon
20	136th Ave, **N** Barr Lake RV Park, same as 21
18	E-470 **tollway**, to Limon (from wb)
16	CO 2, Sable Blvd, Commerce City, **N** 🅖 Shell/diner/dsl/24hr/@, to Denver 💬
12	US 85 N, to Brighton (exits left from eb), Greeley

🏁E INTERSTATE 76 CONT'D

Exit	Services
11	96th Ave, **N** dsl repair, **S** Buick/GMC
10	88th Ave, **N** 🅖 Shell/dsl, 🏨 La Quinta, Super 8, **S** flea mkt
9	US 6 W, US 85 S (no EZ wb return), Commerce City, **S** 🅞 Freightliner, transmissions, st patrol
8	CO 224, 74th Ave (no EZ eb return) **1 mi N** NAPA
6b a	I-270 E, to Limon, to I-25 N, to 🔁
5	I-25, N to Ft Collins, S to Colo Springs
4	Pecos St
3	US 287, Federal Blvd, **N** 🅖 Shamrock/dsl, **S** 🅞 Advance Parts, Family$, vet
1b	CO 95, Sheridan Blvd
1a	CO 121, Wadsworth Blvd, **N** 🅖 Conoco, Phillips 66, 7-11/gas, 🍴 Alamos Verdes Mexican, Applebee's, Bennet's BBQ, Burger King, Chipotle Mexican, Coldstone Creamery, Fazoli's, Gunther Toody's Diner, IHOP, Koro Japanese, LoneStar Steaks, McDonald's/playplace, Red Robin, Ruby Tuesday, Starbucks, Subway, Taco Bell, 🅞 Advance Parts, Brakes+, Costco/gas, Discount Tire, $Tree, Goodyear/auto, Home Depot, Lowe's Whse, Office Depot, Petsmart, Radio Shack, Sam's Club, Tires+, mall
0mm	**I-76 begins/ends on I-70, exit 269b.**

🏁N INTERSTATE 225 (DENVER)

Exit	Services
12b a	I-70, W to Denver, E to Limon
10	US 40, US 287, Colfax Ave, **E** 🅖 Conoco/dsl, Phillips 66, 7-11, Shell, Sinclair, 🍴 Arby's, Burger King, Del Taco, DQ, KFC, McDonald's, Pizza Hut/Taco Bell, Popeye's, Starbucks, Subway, Wendy's, Village Inn, 🅞 Aamco, Advance Parts, Chevrolet, Family$, King's Sooper/gas, K-Mart, NAPA, RV camping, Walgreens, **W** 🅖 Conoco/dsl, 🍴 Anthony's, Carlbou Coffee, Chipotle Mexican, Noodles&Co, Spicy Pickle, 🅞🏥, Curves, U-Haul
9	Co 30, 6th Ave, **E** 🅖 Conoco/dsl, 🍴 Denny's, 🏨 Super 8, ValuePlace Inn, 🅞 Hobby Lobby, **W** 🅖 Phillips 66/dsl, 🅞🏥
8	Alameda Ave, **E** 🅖 Conoco, Shamrock, 🍴 Atlanta Bread, Baja Fresh, Benny's Cafe, BJ's Rest., Chili's, Fat

8	Continued
	Burger, Jamba Juice, L&L BBQ, Macaroni Grill, Mimi's Cafe, Panda Express, Starbucks, TGIFriday, Wingstop, 🅞 Barnes&Noble, Dillards, Gordman's, JC Penney, Macys, Old Navy, Petsmart, Ross, Sears/auto, Super Target, **W** 🅖 Conoco/dsl, Shell/Circle K, 🅞 $Tree
7	Mississippi Ave, Alameda Ave, **E** 🍴 Arby's, Bono's BBQ, Burger King, CiCi's, Chubby's Mexican, ChuckeCheese, Fazoli's, Guadalajara Mexican, Schlotsky's, Sonic, Subway, Village Inn, 🏨 Best Western, Holiday Inn Express, La Quinta, 🅞 Best Buy, Burlington Coats, Home Depot, JoAnn Fabrics, Sam's Club/gas, Tires +, Walmart, **W** 🍴 IHOP, McDonald's, Senor Ric's, Waffle House, 🅞 AutoZone, 7-11, Office Depot, Pepboys, PetCo
5	Iliff Ave, **E** 🅖 7-11, 🍴 Applebee's, Boston Mkt, Carrabba's, Fuddrucker's, Hibachi Japanese, Joe's Crabshack, Outback Steaks, Rosie's Diner, Ruby Tuesday, Sweet Tomatoes, TX Roadhouse, 🏨 Comfort Inn, Crestwood Suites, Extended Stay Deluxe, Fairfield Inn, Homestead Suites, Motel 6, **W** 🅖 Phillips 66, 🍴 Dragon's Boat, Subway, 🏨 DoubleTree
4	CO 83, Parker Rd, **E** 🏨 Red Lion, 🅞 Cherry Creek SP, **W** 🅖 Phillips 66/dsl, 🍴 Big Burrito, Bent Noodle, DQ, Little Caesars, Popeyes, Starbucks, Subway, Table Steaks, Taco Bell, Wendy's, 🅞 $Tree, Firestone/auto, King Sooper/dsl, 7-11
2b	no services
2	DTC Blvd, Tamarac St, **W** 🅖 Conoco, 🍴 La Fogata Mexican, Quizno's, Sonic, 🅞 Curves, Goodyear, 7-11, vet
1b a	I-25, **I-225 begins/ends on I-25, exit 200**

🏁E INTERSTATE 270 (DENVER)

Exit	Services
4	I-70
3	**N** 🅖 TA/Burger King/Country Pride/Popeye's/Pizza Hut/dsl/24hr/@, **S** 🅖 Sapp Bros/Sinclair/Subway/dsl/@
2b a	US 85, CO 2, Vasquez Ave, **N** 🍴 Arby's, Carls Jr, Chipotle Mexican, GoodTimes Grill, KFC/LJ Silver, McDonald's, Taco John's, Wendy's 🅞 TDS, Walgreens, Walmart
1b	York St
1a	I-76 E, to Ft Morgan
1c	I-25 S, to Denver

CONNECTICUT

🏁E INTERSTATE 84

Exit	Services
98mm	Connecticut/Massachusetts state line
74 (97)	CT 171, Holland, **S** 🍴 Traveler's Book Rest., 🅞 RV camping
95mm	weigh sta wb
73 (95)	CT 190, Stafford Springs, **N** 🅞 camping (seasonal), motor speedway, st police
72 (93)	CT 89, Westford, **N** 🏨 Red Carpet Inn, camping (seasonal)
71 (88)	CT 320, Ruby Rd, **S** 🅖 TA/Shell/Burger King/Country Pride/dsl/scales/24hr/@, 🍴 Dunkin Donuts, 🏨 Rodeway Inn
70 (86)	CT 32, Willington, **N** 🅞🏥, **S** 🅖 Mobil/dsl, Sunoco/dsl, 🅞 RV Camping
85mm	🆁🆂 both lanes, full 🏨 facilities, info, 🚻, vending, 🦮, litter barrels, petwalk, campers

69 (83)	CT 74, to US 44, Willington, **S** gas, food, 🚾, RV camping, st police
68 (81)	CT 195, Tolland, **N** 🅖 Gulf/dsl, Mobil, 🍴 Dunkin Donuts, Papa T's Rest., Subway, 🅞 NAPA, RV camping, **S** 🅖 Citgo, 🅞 Big Y Foods, Radio Shack
67 (77)	CT 31, Rockville, **N** 🅖 Mobil, Shell, 🍴 Beni's Grill, Burger King, China Taste, Dunkin Donuts, McDonald's, Subway, 🅞🏥, RV Camping, **S** Nathan Hale Mon
66 (76)	Tunnel Rd, Vernon
65 (75)	CT 30, Vernon Ctr, **N** 🅖 Mobil/dsl, Shell, 🍴 Brick Oven Pizza, Burger King, Joy Luck, KFC, Lotus Rest., Oki Asian, Rein's Deli, Vernon Diner, 🏨 Howard Johnson, Quality Inn, 🅞 CarQuest, Firestone/auto, K-Mart, Meineke, Stop&Shop/gas
64 (74)	Vernon Ctr, **N** 🅖 Mobil/24hr, Sunoco, 🍴 Angellino's Italian, Anthony's Pizza, Denny's, Dunkin Donuts, Friendly's, McDonald's, 99 Rest., Rita's Custard, Taco Bell, Wood'n

(vertical text: VERNON CTR)

INTERSTATE 84 CONT'D

WINDSOR

HARTFORD

Exit	Services
64 (74)	Continued Tap, [lodging] Holiday Inn Express, [other] AutoZone, CVS Drug, $Tree, GNC, Goodyear/auto, PriceChopper, Staples, TJ Maxx, vet, **S** [lodging] Motel 6
63 (72)	CT 30, CT 83, Manchester, S Windsor, **N** [food] Applebee's, Azteca Mexican, Chipotle Mexican, Dunkin Donuts, McDonald's, HomeTown Buffet, Longhorn Steaks, Outback Steaks, Panera Bread, Red Robin, Starbucks, TGIFriday's, [lodging] Courtyard, Residence Inn, [other] AT&T, Barnes&Noble, Best Buy, Dick's, JC Penney, Macy's, Marshall's, PetCo, Sears/auto, Walgreens, Walmart, same as 62, **S** [gas] Shell/dsl, Sunoco/dsl, Xtra, [food] Misaki Buffet, Shea's Grill, [lodging] Baymont Inn, Best Value Inn, Extended Stay America, Motel 6, [other] [H], Big Y Mkt, Hyundai, Kohl's, Nissan, Subaru, Toyota/Scion, U-Haul
62 (71)	Buckland St, **N** [gas] Mobil/Dunkin Donuts/dsl, [food] Bonefish Grill, Boston Mkt, Boston's, Chili's, Friendly's, Hooters, Johnny Rocket's, KFC, Moe's SW Grill, Olive Garden, Taco Bell, Starbucks, Ted's MT Grill, Tullycross Tavern, [lodging] Fairfield Inn, Hampton Inn, [other] BigLots, $Tree, Home Depot, Jo-Ann Fabrics, Lowe's, Michael's, PetsMart, Sam's Club, Target, mall, same as 63, **S** [gas] Xtra/dsl, [food] Buffalo Wild Wings, Carrabba's, ChuckeCheese, Dunkin Donuts, Golden Dragon, McDonald's, Sonic, Subway, TX Roadhouse, Wendy's, [other] BJ's Whse/gas, Firestone/auto, GNC, Honda, USPO
61 (70)	I-291 W, to Windsor
60 (69)	US 6, US 44, Burnside Ave (from eb)
59 (68)	I-384 E, Manchester
58 (67)	Roberts St, Burnside Ave, **N** [food] Margarita's Grill, [lodging] Comfort Inn, Ramada, **S** [gas] Mobil, Sunoco, [food] Dunkin Donuts, [other] Cabelas
57 (66)	CT 15 S, to I-91 S, Charter Oak Br
56 (65)	Governor St, E Hartford, **S** [airport]
55 (64)	CT 2 E, New London, downtown
54 (63)	Old State House, **N** [other] Chevrolet, Ford, Lincoln, Lexus
53 (62)	CT Blvd (from eb), **S** [lodging] Holiday Inn
52 (61)	W Main St (from eb) downtown
51 (60)	I-91 N, to Springfield
50 (59.8)	to I-91 S (from wb), **N** [lodging] Ramada, **S** [lodging] Hilton, Residence Inn
48 (59.5)	Asylum St, downtown, **N** [lodging] Ramada, **S** [lodging] Holiday Inn Express, [other] [H]
47 (59)	Sigourney St, downtown, **N** Hartford Seminary, Mark Twain House
46 (58)	Sisson St, downtown (from wb, exits left), UConn Law School
45 (57)	Flatbush Ave (from wb, exits left)
44 (56.5)	Prospect Ave, **N** [gas] Mobil, Shell/dsl, [food] Burger King, D'angelo's, Hibachi Grill, McDonald's, Prospect Pizza, Wendy's, [other] ShopRite Foods
43 (56)	Park Rd, W Hartford, **N** to St Joseph Coll
42 (55)	Trout Brk Dr (exits left from wb), to Elmwood
41 (54)	S Main St, ElmwoodAmerican School for the Deaf
40 (53)	CT 71, New Britain Ave, **S** [gas] Shell, Sunoco, [food] Brio Grille, Burger King, CA Pizza, Chili's, China Pan, Chipotle Mexican, Dunkin Donuts, McDonald's, Olive Garden, Panera Bread, PF Chang's, Red Robin, Starbucks, Subway, Wendy's, [lodging] Courtyard, [other] Barnes&Noble, Best Buy, JC Penney, Macy's, Michael's, Nordstrom, Office Depot,
40 (53)	Continued Old Navy, PetCo, Radio Shack, Sears/auto, Target, TJ Maxx, Trader Joe's, Verizon, mall
39a (52)	CT 9 S, to New Britain, Newington, **S** [H]
39 (51.5)	CT 4, (exits left from eb), Farmington, **N** [H]
38 (51)	US 6 W (from wb), Bristol, **N** [gas] same as 37
37 (50)	Fienemann Rd, to US 6 W, **N** [gas] Shell, [food] Dunkin Donuts, Stonewell Rest., Subway, [lodging] Hampton Inn, Marriott, **S** [lodging] Extended Stay America
36 (49)	Slater Rd (exits left from eb), **S** [H]
35 (48)	CT 72, to CT 9 (exits left from both lanes), New Britain, **S** [H]
34 (47)	CT 372, Crooked St, **N** [gas] Gulf/dsl, Sunoco, [food] Applebee's, Friendly's, McDonald's, Starbucks, [lodging] Fairfield Inn, [other] Big Y Mkt, Dick's, Ford/Lincoln, Kohl's, Lowe's, Marshall's, Old Navy, Petsmart, VW
33 (46)	CT 72 W, to Bristol (exits left from eb)
32 (45)	Ct 10, Queen St, Southington, **N** [gas] Cumberland Farms, Exxon, Shell/dsl, [food] Bertucci's, Buffalo Wild Wings, Burger King, Chili's, D'angelos, Denny's, Dunkin Donuts, JD's Rest., KFC, Liberty Pizza, Luenhop, McDonald's, Moe's SW Grill, Outback Steaks, Puerto Vallarta, Ruby Tuesday, Starbucks, Subway, Taco Bell, [lodging] Motel 6, [other] [H], CVS Drug, $Tree, GNC, Home Depot, PetCo, Radio Shack, 7-11, ShopRite Foods, Staples, TJ Maxx, TownFair Tire, **S** [gas] Hess, Mobil, Sunoco, [food] Aziagos Italian, Dunkin Donuts, El Sombrero, Friendly's, Nordelli's Cafe, Pizza Hut, Rita's Custard, Subway, TD Homer's Grill, Wendy's, Wood'n Tap Grill, [lodging] Days Inn, Holiday Inn Express, Knights Inn, [other] Advance Parts, AT&T, Firestone, Midas, Monro, PriceChopper Foods, Rite Aid, Walmart
31 (44)	CT 229, West St, **N** [gas] Mobil, Sunoco/dsl, [other] Lowe's, Target, **S** [gas] Citgo, Valero, [food] Dunkin Donuts, Giovanni's Pizza, Subway, [lodging] Residence Inn
30 (43)	Marion Ave, W Main, Southington, **N** ski area, **S** [gas] Mobil/dsl, [other] [H]
29 (42)	CT 10, from wb, exits left, Milldale
41.5mm	**[rest stop] eb, full [handicapped] facilities, info, [phone], [picnic], litter barrels, petwalk**
28 (41)	CT 322, Marion, **S** [gas] Fleet/dsl, Mobil, TA/Country Pride/Pizza Hut/Popeye's/Taco Bell/dsl/scales/24hr/@, [food] Blimpie, Burger King, DQ, Dunkin Donuts, Manor Inn Rest., Subway, Young Young Chinese, [lodging] Comfort Suites, EconoLodge, [other] Home Depot, repair
27 (40)	I-691 E, to Meriden
26 (38)	CT 70, to Cheshire, **N** [food] Blackie's Cafe
25a (37)	Austin Rd, **N** [gas] Winzz/dsl, [food] Asian Garden, Subway, [other] Costco/gas, Kohl's, funpark
25 (36)	Harper's Ferry Rd, Reed Dr, Scott Rd, E Main St, **N** [gas] Gulf/dsl, Mobil/dsl, [food] Dunkin Donuts, Subway, [other] NAPA, **S** [gas] Gulf, [food] Burger King, Dunkin Donuts, Friendly's, Golden Wok, McDonald's, Nino's Rest., Subway, [lodging] Quality Inn, [other] Aldi Foods, BJ's Whse/gas, Cadillac/Chevrolet, CVS Drug, Super Stop&Shop/gas
23 (33.5)	CT 69, Hamilton Ave, **N** [food] Bertucci's, Buffalo Wild Wings, Chili's, HomeTown Buffet, IHOP, McDonald's, Olive Garden, TGIFriday's, [other] [H], Barnes&Noble, JC Penney, Macy's, Michael's, Save-a-Lot Foods, Sears/auto, mall, **S** [gas] Shell, [food] Dunkin Donuts
22 (33)	Baldwin St, Waterbury, **N** [gas] Gulf, [lodging] Courtyard, [other] [H], USPO, same as 23
21 (33)	Meadow St, Banks St, **N** [gas] Citgo, 7-11, **S** [gas] Exxon/dsl, [other] Home Depot, PetsMart

SOUTHINGTON

MARION

CT

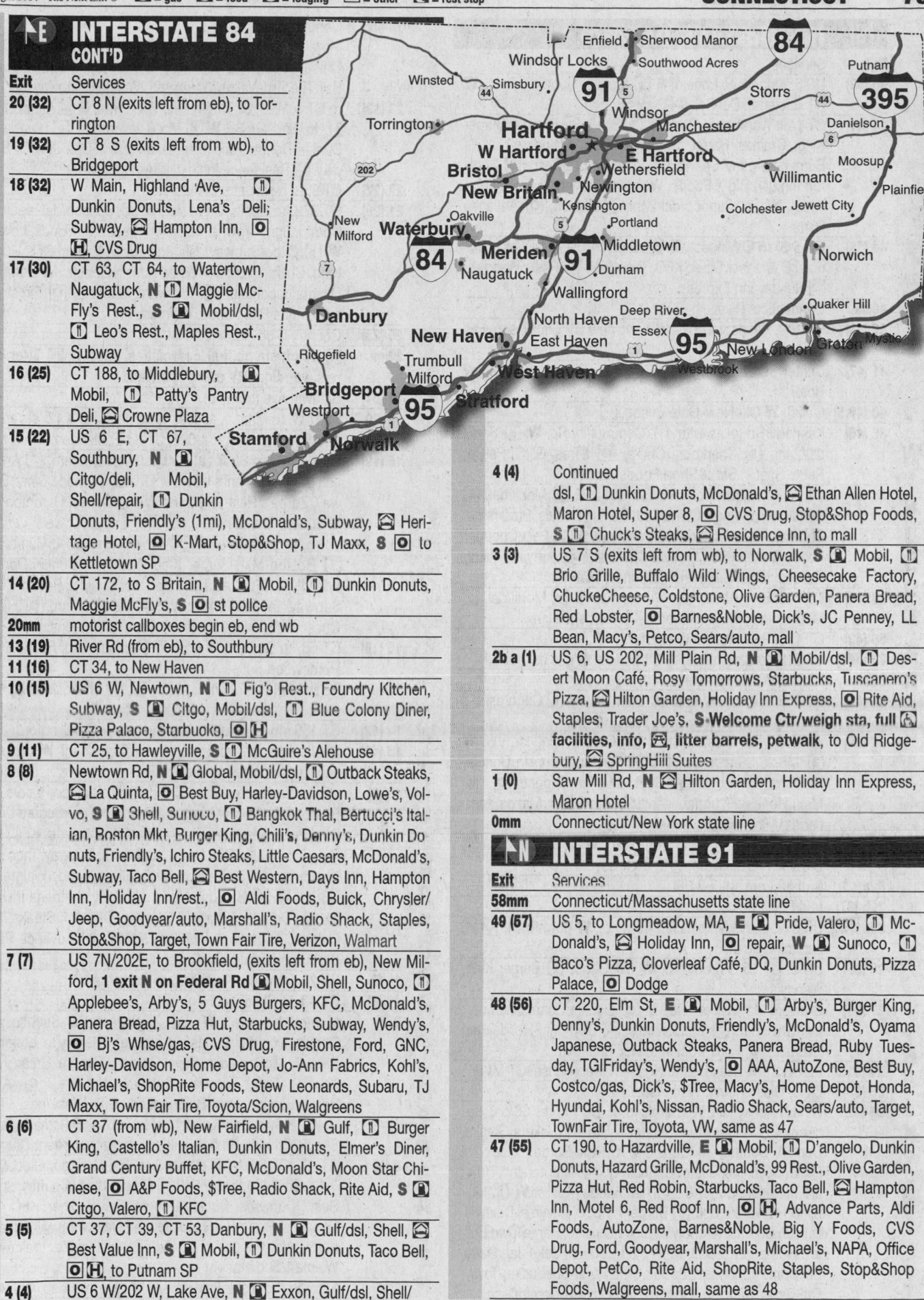

SOUTHBURY

▲E INTERSTATE 84
CONT'D

Exit	Services
20 (32)	CT 8 N (exits left from eb), to Torrington
19 (32)	CT 8 S (exits left from wb), to Bridgeport
18 (32)	W Main, Highland Ave, 🅕 Dunkin Donuts, Lena's Deli; Subway, 🅛 Hampton Inn, 🅞 🄷, CVS Drug
17 (30)	CT 63, CT 64, to Watertown, Naugatuck, **N** 🅕 Maggie Mc-Fly's Rest., **S** 🅖 Mobil/dsl, 🅕 Leo's Rest., Maples Rest., Subway
16 (25)	CT 188, to Middlebury, 🅖 Mobil, 🅕 Patty's Pantry Deli, 🅛 Crowne Plaza
15 (22)	US 6 E, CT 67, Southbury, **N** 🅖 Citgo/deli, Mobil, Shell/repair, 🅕 Dunkin Donuts, Friendly's (1mi), McDonald's, Subway, 🅛 Heritage Hotel, 🅞 K-Mart, Stop&Shop, TJ Maxx, **S** 🅞 to Kettletown SP
14 (20)	CT 172, to S Britain, **N** 🅖 Mobil, 🅕 Dunkin Donuts, Maggie McFly's, **S** 🅞 st police
20mm	motorist callboxes begin eb, end wb
13 (19)	River Rd (from eb), to Southbury
11 (16)	CT 34, to New Haven
10 (15)	US 6 W, Newtown, **N** 🅕 Fig's Rest., Foundry Kitchen, Subway, **S** 🅖 Citgo, Mobil/dsl, 🅕 Blue Colony Diner, Pizza Palace, Starbucks, 🅞 🄷
9 (11)	CT 25, to Hawleyville, **S** 🅕 McGuire's Alehouse
8 (8)	Newtown Rd, **N** 🅖 Global, Mobil/dsl, 🅕 Outback Steaks, 🅛 La Quinta, 🅞 Best Buy, Harley-Davidson, Lowe's, Volvo, **S** 🅖 Shell, Sunoco, 🅕 Bangkok Thai, Bertucci's Italian, Boston Mkt, Burger King, Chili's, Denny's, Dunkin Donuts, Friendly's, Ichiro Steaks, Little Caesars, McDonald's, Subway, Taco Bell, 🅛 Best Western, Days Inn, Hampton Inn, Holiday Inn/rest., 🅞 Aldi Foods, Buick, Chrysler/Jeep, Goodyear/auto, Marshall's, Radio Shack, Staples, Stop&Shop, Target, Town Fair Tire, Verizon, Walmart
7 (7)	US 7N/202E, to Brookfield, (exits left from eb), New Milford, **1 exit N on Federal Rd** 🅖 Mobil, Shell, Sunoco, 🅕 Applebee's, Arby's, 5 Guys Burgers, KFC, McDonald's, Panera Bread, Pizza Hut, Starbucks, Subway, Wendy's, 🅞 Bj's Whse/gas, CVS Drug, Firestone, Ford, GNC, Harley-Davidson, Home Depot, Jo-Ann Fabrics, Kohl's, Michael's, ShopRite Foods, Stew Leonards, Subaru, TJ Maxx, Town Fair Tire, Toyota/Scion, Walgreens
6 (6)	CT 37 (from wb), New Fairfield, **N** 🅖 Gulf, 🅕 Burger King, Castello's Italian, Dunkin Donuts, Elmer's Diner, Grand Century Buffet, KFC, McDonald's, Moon Star Chinese, 🅞 A&P Foods, $Tree, Radio Shack, Rite Aid, **S** 🅖 Citgo, Valero, 🅕 KFC
5 (5)	CT 37, CT 39, CT 53, Danbury, **N** 🅖 Gulf/dsl, Shell, 🅛 Best Value Inn, **S** 🅖 Mobil, 🅕 Dunkin Donuts, Taco Bell, 🅞 🄷, to Putnam SP
4 (4)	US 6 W/202 W, Lake Ave, **N** 🅖 Exxon, Gulf/dsl, Shell/
4 (4)	Continued dsl, 🅕 Dunkin Donuts, McDonald's, 🅛 Ethan Allen Hotel, Maron Hotel, Super 8, 🅞 CVS Drug, Stop&Shop Foods, **S** 🅕 Chuck's Steaks, 🅛 Residence Inn, to mall
3 (3)	US 7 S (exits left from wb), to Norwalk, **S** 🅖 Mobil, 🅕 Brio Grille, Buffalo Wild Wings, Cheesecake Factory, ChuckeCheese, Coldstone, Olive Garden, Panera Bread, Red Lobster, 🅞 Barnes&Noble, Dick's, JC Penney, LL Bean, Macy's, Petco, Sears/auto, mall
2b a (1)	US 6, US 202, Mill Plain Rd, **N** 🅖 Mobil/dsl, 🅕 Desert Moon Café, Rosy Tomorrows, Starbucks, Tuscanero's Pizza, 🅛 Hilton Garden, Holiday Inn Express, 🅞 Rite Aid, Staples, Trader Joe's, **S Welcome Ctr/weigh sta, full 🅛 facilities, info, 🆁🆂, litter barrels, petwalk,** to Old Ridgebury, 🅛 SpringHill Suites
1 (0)	Saw Mill Rd, **N** 🅛 Hilton Garden, Holiday Inn Express, Maron Hotel
0mm	Connecticut/New York state line

▲N INTERSTATE 91

Exit	Services
58mm	Connecticut/Massachusetts state line
49 (57)	US 5, to Longmeadow, MA, **E** 🅖 Pride, Valero, 🅕 McDonald's, 🅛 Holiday Inn, 🅞 repair, **W** 🅖 Sunoco, 🅕 Baco's Pizza, Cloverleaf Café, DQ, Dunkin Donuts, Pizza Palace, 🅞 Dodge
48 (56)	CT 220, Elm St, **E** 🅖 Mobil, 🅕 Arby's, Burger King, Denny's, Dunkin Donuts, Friendly's, McDonald's, Oyama Japanese, Outback Steaks, Panera Bread, Ruby Tuesday, TGIFriday's, Wendy's, 🅞 AAA, AutoZone, Best Buy, Costco/gas, Dick's, $Tree, Macy's, Home Depot, Honda, Hyundai, Kohl's, Nissan, Radio Shack, Sears/auto, Target, TownFair Tire, Toyota, VW, same as 47
47 (55)	CT 190, to Hazardville, **E** 🅖 Mobil, 🅕 D'angelo, Dunkin Donuts, Hazard Grille, McDonald's, 99 Rest., Olive Garden, Pizza Hut, Red Robin, Starbucks, Taco Bell, 🅛 Hampton Inn, Motel 6, Red Roof Inn, 🅞 🄷, Advance Parts, Aldi Foods, AutoZone, Barnes&Noble, Big Y Foods, CVS Drug, Ford, Goodyear, Marshall's, Michael's, NAPA, Office Depot, PetCo, Rite Aid, ShopRite, Staples, Stop&Shop Foods, Walgreens, mall, same as 48

CT

WINDSOR AREA

ROCKY HILL

⬆N INTERSTATE 91 CONT'D

Exit	Services
46 (53)	US 5, King St, to Enfield, **E** 🅖 Mobil, 🍴 Astro's Rest., **W** 🍴 Hacienda Del Sol, 🛏 Super 8
45 (51)	CT 140, Warehouse Point, **E** 🅖 Shell, 🍴 Blimpie, Burger King, Cracker Barrel, Dunkin Donuts, Friendly's, Jake's Burgers, Jimmy Chen's Chinese, Sofia's Rest., 🛏 Comfort Inn, 🅞 Big Y Foods, Walmart/Subway, to Trolley Museum, **W** 🅖 Sunoco/dsl/24hr, 🛏 Clarion, 🅞 Advance Parts
44 (50)	US 5 S, to E Windsor, **E** 🅖 Sunoco/dsl, 🍴 Dunkin Donuts, E Windsor Diner, KFC, Taco Bell, Tj's Rest., Wendy's, 🛏 Holiday Inn Express
49mm	Connecticut River
42 (48)	CT 159, Windsor Locks, **E** Longview RV Ctr, **W** same as 41
41 (47)	Center St (exits with 39), **W** 🍴 Ad's Pizzaria, 🛏 Bradley Hotel
40 (46.5)	CT 20, **W** Old New-Gate Prison, 🚳
39 (46)	Kennedy Rd (exits with 41), Community Rd, **W** 🅖 Shell/dsl/24hr, 🍴 Charkoon, Chili's, 🅞 $Tree, GNC, PetCo, Radio Shack, Stop&Shop Foods, Target
38 (45)	CT 75, to Poquonock, Windsor Area, **E** 🅖 Mobil/dsl, 🍴 Buffalo Wild Wings, China Sea, Dunkin Donuts, Pizzarama, Subway, 🅞 to Ellsworth Homestead, AT&T, PriceChopper Foods, Verizon, **W** 🍴 River City Grill, 🛏 Courtyard, Hilton Garden, Hyatt Summerfield Suites, Marriott
37 (44)	CT 305, Bloomfield Ave, Windsor Ctr, **E** 🅖 Mobil/dsl, 🍴 McDonald's, **W** 🅖 Sunoco, 🛏 Residence Inn
36 (43)	CT 178, Park Ave, to W Hartford
35b (41)	CT 218, to Bloomfield, to S Windsor, **E** gas/dsl, food
35a	I-291 E, to Manchester
34 (40)	CT 159, Windsor Ave, **E** 🅖 Shell/dsl, **W** 🅖 Citgo/dsl, 🛏 Flamingo Inn, RanchHouse Rest., 🅞 🏩
33 (39)	Jennings Rd, Weston St, **E** 🅞 Cadillac, Jaguar, VW, **W** 🅖 Mobil, Sunoco/dsl, 🍴 Burger King, Dunkin Donuts, McDonald's, Subway, 🛏 Best Value Inn, Super 8, 🅞 CarMax, Honda, Hyundai, Infiniti/Toyota/Scion, Mazda, Mercedes, Mini, Nissan, Subaru
32b (38)	Trumbull St (exits left from nb), **W** to downtown, 🛏 Crowne Plaza, Hilton, 🅞 🏩, Goodyear
32a	(exit 30 from sb), I-84 W
29b (37)	I-84 E, Hartford
29a (36.5)	US 5 N, CT 15 N (exits left from nb), **W** downtown, 🅞 🏩 capitol, civic ctr
28 (36)	US 5, CT 15 S (from nb), **W** 🅖 Citgo, 🍴 Burger King, Wendy's
27 (35)	Brainerd Rd, Airport Rd, **E** 🅖 Dunkin Donuts/Subway/dsl, Shell/dsl, 🍴 McDonald's, 🛏 Days Inn, Holiday Inn Express, 🅞 Ford Trucks, to Regional Mkt
26 (33.5)	Marsh St, **E** Silas Deane House, Webb House, CT MVD
25 (33)	CT 3, Glastonbury, Wethersfield
24 (32)	CT 99, Rocky Hill, Wethersfield, **E** 🅖 Phillips 66/dsl, Sunoco, 🍴 Angry Olive, Chuck's Steaks, Dakota Steaks, Dunkin Donuts, McDonald's, On-the-Border, Rockyhill Pizza, Saybrook Seafood, Subway, 🛏 Hampton Inn, Howard Johnson, Super 8, 🅞 Aldi Foods, Kohl's, **W** 🅖 Mobil, Shell, Valero/dsl, 🍴 Burger King, D'angelo's, Denny's, Dunkin Donuts, Friendly's, Ginza Cuisine, HomeTown Buffet, Humphrey's Grill, KFC, Red Lobster, Sake Japanese, Sapporro Japanese, Sophia's Pizzaria, Starbucks, Townline Diner, Wendy's, Wood-n-Tap Grill, 🛏 Comfort Inn,

WALLINGFORD

NEW HAVEN

Exit	Services
24 (32)	Continued Motel 6, 🅞 CVS Drug, $Tree, Goodyear/auto, Marshalls, Office Depot, Radio Shack, Stop&Shop, TJMaxx, Town-Fair Tire, TrueValue, Walgreens, Walmart/Subway
23 (29)	to CT 3, West St, Rocky Hill, Vet Home, **E** 🛏 Marriott, 🅞 🏩, to Dinosaur SP, **W** 🅖 Mobil, Valero/dsl, 🍴 D'angelo's, Dunkin Donuts, Michelangeo's Pizza, Papa John's, Subway, 🛏 Residence Inn, 🅞 IGA Foods, vet
22 (27)	CT 9, to New Britain, Middletown
21 (26)	CT 372, to Berlin, Cromwell, **E** 🅖 Sunoco/dsl/repair, 🛏 Comfort Inn, Crowne Plaza, 🅞 Krauszer's Foods, Lowe's, **W** 🅖 Citgo/Subway/dsl, Mobil/dsl, 🍴 Baci Grill, Burger King, Chili's, Cromwell Diner, Dunkin Donuts, McDonald's, Oyama Japanese, 🛏 Courtyard, Super 8, 🅞 Firestone/auto, Price Rite Foods, Walmart, vet
20 (23)	Country Club Rd, Middle St
22mm	🆁🆂 weigh sta nb, full 🚽 facilities, info, 🅟, 🛢, litter barrels, vending, RV dump, petwalk
19 (21)	Baldwin Ave (from sb)
18 (20.5)	I-691 W, to Marion, access to same as 16 & 17, ski area
17 (20)	CT 15 N (from sb), to I-691, CT 66 E, Meriden
16 (19)	CT 15, E Main St, **E** 🅖 Gulf/dsl, Mobil, Valero, 🍴 American Steaks, Gianni's Rest., NY Pizza, Olympos Diner, Subway, Zorba's Rest., 🛏 Candlewood Suites, Hampton Inn, Sheraton, The Meridan Inn, 🅞 Family$, Lowe's, Verizon, Volvo, **Urgent Care**, **W** 🅖 BP/dsl, Getty/dsl, Gulf/repair, 🍴 Boston Mkt, Burger King, Dominos, Dunkin Donuts, Friendly's, KFC, Les' Dairy Bar, McDonald's, Ramini Pizza, Subway, Taco Bell, Wendy's, 🛏 Comfort Inn, 🅞 🏩CarQuest, CVS Drug, Hancock's Drug, Walgreens, vet
15 (16)	CT 68, to Durham, **E** golf, **W** 🛏 Courtyard, Fairfield Inn, Homewood Suites
15mm	🆁🆂 sb, full 🚽 facilities, info, 🅟, 🛢, litter barrels, petwalk
14 (12)	CT 150 (no EZ return), Woodhouse Ave, Wallingford
13 (10)	US 5 (exits left from nb), Wallingford, **2 mi W on US 5** services, to Wharton Brook SP
12 (9)	US 5, Washington Ave, **E** 🅖 Shell, Sunoco, Valero, 🍴 Boston Mkt, Burger King, D'angelo's, DQ, Droogie's Pizza, Dunkin Donuts, Friendly's, Jade City Chinese, KFC, McDonald's, Rustic Oak Rest., Starbucks, Subway, Taco Bell, Wendy's, 🅞 CVS Drug, Stop&Shop Food, Walgreens, USPO, **W** 🅖 Gulf/dsl, Mobil, 🍴 Arby's, Athena II Diner, Dunkin Donuts, Greatwall Chinese, Outback Steaks, Thai Cuisine, 🛏 Holiday Inn/Harry's Grill, 🅞 Advance Parts, BigY Foods/drug, CarQuest, vet
11 (7)	CT 22 (from nb), North Haven, same as 12
10 (6)	CT 40, to Cheshire, Hamden
9 (5)	Montowese Ave, **W** 🅖 Berkshire/dsl, Sunoco, 🍴 Dunkin Donuts, Dynasty Chinese, Friendly's, Longhorn Steaks, McDonald's, Olive Garden, Panera Bread, Red Lobster, Ruby Tuesday, Subway, Wendy's, 🅞 AT&T, Barnes&Noble, Best Buy, BigLots, BJ's Whse/gas, $Tree, GNC, Home Depot, Michael's, PetCo, Petsmart, Radio Shack, Staples, Target, TJMaxx, Verizon, **Urgent Care**
8 (4)	CT 17, CT 80, Middletown Ave, **E** 🅖 Citgo, Global/dsl, 7-11, Shell, Sunoco/24hr, 🍴 Burger King, Country House Rest., Dominos, Dunkin Donuts, Exit 8 Diner, KFC, McDonald's, Pizza Hut/Taco Bell, 🛏 Days Inn, 🅞 Advance Parts, Aldi Foods, AT&T, AutoZone, Lowe's, Walgreens, Walmart/Subway, vet
7 (3)	Ferry St (from sb), Fair Haven, **W** 🅖 Hess/dsl, 🅞 NAPA

⬆N INTERSTATE 91 CONT'D

Exit	Services
6 (2.5)	Willow St (exits left from nb), Blatchley Ave, **E** repair
5 (2)	US 5 (from nb), State St, Fair Haven, **E** 🍴 New Star Diner
4 (1.5)	State St (from sb), downtown
3 (1)	Trumbull St, downtown, **W** Peabody Museum
2 (.5)	Hamilton St, downtown, New Haven
1 (.3)	CT 34W (from sb), New Haven, **W** 🅷, downtown
0mm	I-91 begins/ends on I-95, exit 48.

⬆N INTERSTATE 95

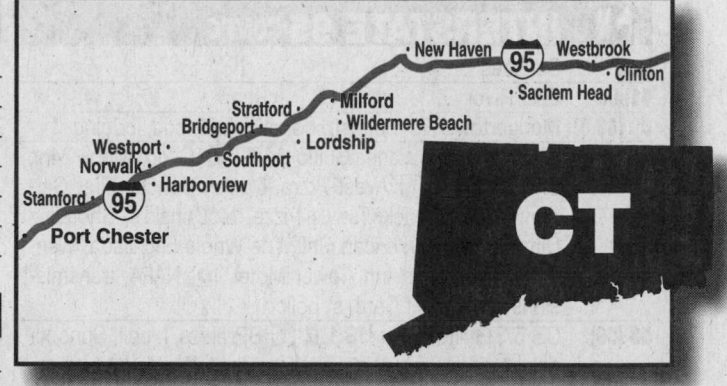

Exit	Services
94mm	Connecticut/Rhode Island state line
93 (111)	CT 216, Clarks Falls, **E** 🅴 Shell/dsl/repair, 🍴 Dunkin Donuts, Subway, to Burlingame SP, **W** 🅴 Mobil/Dunkin Donuts/dsl, 🚚Shell/Stuckey's/Roy Rogers/Sbarro's/dsl/scales/24hr, 🍴 McDonald's, 🛏 Budget Inn, Stardust Motel
92 (107)	CT 2, CT 49 (no EZ nb return), Pawcatuck, **E** 🅴 Shell, 🍴 Dunkin Donuts, 🛏 La Quinta, 🅾 🅷, Stop&Shop, **W** 🛏 Cedar Park Suites, 🅾 FoxWoods (8mi), KOA
91 (103)	CT 234, N Main St, to Stonington, **E** 🅾🅷
90 (101)	CT 27, Mystic, **E** 🅴 Mobil/Domino's/Dunkin Donuts/dsl, 🍴 Boathouse Rest., Equinox Diner, 5 Guys Burgers, Friendly's, Go Fish, McDonald's, Starbucks, Steak Loft, Ten Clams, 🛏 EconoLodge, Hilton, Holiday Inn Express, Howard Johnson, Hyatt Place, 🅾 Curves, Mystic Outlet Shops, Verizon, aquarium, **W** 🅴 Shell/Subway/dsl, 🍴 Dunkin Donuts, Jakes Burgers, Pizza Grille, Thai 1, 🛏 Comfort Inn, Days Inn, Hampton Inn, Ramada Inn, Residence Inn, 🅾 Chevrolet, Chrysler/Dodge/Jeep, Ford, RV camping, TrueValue, VW
89 (99)	CT 215, Allyn St, **W** camping (seasonal)
89mm	scenic overlook
88 (98)	CT 117, to Noank, **E** ⛴, **W** 🍴 Octagon Steaks, Starbucks, 🛏 Marriott
87 (97)	Sharp Hwy (exits left from sb), Groton, **E** 🛏 Hampton Inn, 🅾 to Griswold SP, ⛴
86 (96)	rd 184 (exits left from nb), Groton, **E** 🍴 Applebees, 99 Rest., 🛏 Hampton Inn, Knights Inn, 🅾 Walgreens, **W** 🅴 Cory's/dsl, Hess, Mobil, Shell/dsl, 🍴 Chinese Kitchen, Dunkin Donuts, Flanagan's Diner, Groton Rest., KFC, NY Pizza, Russell's Ribs, Subway, Taco Bell, 🛏 Best Western, Groton Inn, Super 8, 🅾 Advance Parts, $Tree, GNC, Honda, Kia, Kohl's, Midas, Stop&Shop, Verizon, to US Sub Base
85 (95)	US 1 N, Groton, downtown, **E** 🅾 NAPA
84 (94)	CT 32 (from sb), New London, downtown
83 (92)	CT 32, New London, **E** to Long Island Ferry
82a (90.5)	frontage rd, New London, **E** 🅴 Mobil, 🍴 Panda Buffet, Pizza Hut, 🅾 AutoZone, NSA Foods, Radio Shack, Staples, TownFair Tire, Verizon, same as 82, **W** 🍴 Chili's, ChuckeCheese, Outback Steaks, 🛏 Clarion, SpringHill Suites, 🅾 Marshall's, Petsmart, ShopRite Foods, same as 82
82 (90)	CT 85, to I-395 N, New London, **W** 🅴 Mobil/Dunkin Donuts, 🍴 Coldstone, FoodCourt, Longhorn Steaks, Olive Garden, Panera Bread, Ruby Tuesday, Subway, Wendy's, 🅾 Best Buy, Dick's, Home Depot, JC Penney, Macy's, Michael's, PetCo, Sears/auto, Target, Verizon, mall
90mm	weigh sta both directions
81 (89.5)	Cross Road, **W** 🛏 Rodeway Inn, 🅾 BJ's Whse/gas, Lowe's, Walmart/McDonald's

Exit	Services
80 (89.3)	Oil Mill Rd (from sb), **W** 🛏 Rodeway Inn
76 (89)	I-395 N (from nb, exits left), to Norwich
75 (88)	US 1, to Waterford
74 (87)	rd 161, to Flanders, Niantic, **E** 🅴 Cory's/repair, Citgo/dsl, Mobil, 🍴 Burger King, Country Gourmet, Dunkin Donuts, Illiano's Grill, Quiznos, Shoreline Rest., Starbucks, 🛏 Best Value Inn, Hilltop Inn, Motel 6, Sleep Inn, 🅾 Ford, Stop&Shop, Tires+, **W** 🅴 Shell, 🍴 5 Guys Burgers, Flanders Pizza, Flanders Seafood, Kings Garden Chinese, McDonald's, Nanami Japanese, Shack Rest., Smokey O'Grady's BBQ, Yummy Yummy Pizza, 🅾 Curves, CVS Drug, IGA Foods, Rite Aid, TrueValue, RV camping, vet
74mm	🆁🆂 sb, full ♿ facilities, st police
73 (86)	Society Rd
72 (84)	to Rocky Neck SP, **2 mi E** food, lodging, RV camping, to Rocky Neck SP
71 (83)	4 Mile Rd, River Rd, to Rocky Neck SP beaches, **1 mi E** camping (seasonal)
70 (80)	US 1, CT 156, Old Lyme, **W** 🅴 Shell/dsl, 🍴 Morning Glory Cafe, Subway, 🛏 Old Lyme Inn/dining, 🅾 Big Y Foods, Rite Aid, Griswold Museum, USPO, vet
69 (77)	US 1, CT 9 N, to Hartford, **W** 🍴 Bangkok Sushi, 🛏 Comfort Inn, 🅾 antiques, vet
68 (76.5)	US 1 S, Old Saybrook, **E** 🅴 Irving/dsl, Mobil, 🍴 Cloud 9 Deli, Pat's Country Kitchen, **W** 🅾 Buick/GMC, Chevrolet/Nissan, Chrysler/Dodge/Jeep, Kia, Mazda, NAPA, VW
67 (76)	CT 154, Elm St (no EZ sb return), Old Saybrook, **E** 🍴 Pasta Vita Itaian, same as 68
66 (75)	to US 1, Spencer Plain Rd, **E** 🅴 Citgo/dsl, 🍴 Blue Crab Steaks, Brick Oven Pizza, Cuckoo's Nest Mexican, DQ, Dunkin Donuts, Fogo Grill, Luigi's Italian, Mike's Deli, Pizza Palace, Sal's Pizza, Samurai Japanese, Siagon City, Tiberio's Italian, 🛏 Days Inn, EconoLodge, Saybrook Motel, Super 8, 🅾 Benny's Mkt, transmissions, vet
65 (73)	rd 153, Westbrook, **E** 🅴 Mobil/Dunkin Donuts, Valero, 🍴 Cafe Rotier, Cristy's Rest., Denny's, Subway, Westbook Deli, 🅾 Honda, Old Navy, Tanger Factory Stores/famous brands, Toyota/Scion, Walgreens, USPO
64 (70)	rd 145, Horse Hill Rd, Clinton
63 (68)	CT 81, Clinton, **E** 🅴 Shell, **1 mi E on US 1** 🅴 Shell/dsl/LP, Sunoco/dsl, 🍴 Chips Rest., McDonald's, Piccadeli Sta., 🅾 CVS Drug, USPO, vet, **W** 🍴 Coldstone, Dunkin Donuts, 🅾 AT&T, Clinton Crossing Premium Outlets/famous brands, PetCo
62 (67)	**E** to Hammonasset SP, RV camping, beaches
66mm	service area both lanes, Mobil/dsl, McDonald's, atm
61 (64)	CT 79, Madison, **E** 🅴 Gulf, Shell, Sunoco, 🍴 Cafe Alegre, Starbucks, Subway, Village Pizza, 🅾 CVS Drug, Stop&Shop, USPO

Vertical labels: MYSTIC, GROTON, NIANTIC, OLD SAYBROOK. **CT**

⬆N INTERSTATE 95 CONT'D

Exit	Services
61mm	East River
60 (63.5)	Mungertown Rd (from sb, no return), **E** food, lodging
59 (60)	rd 146, Goose Lane, Guilford, **E** ⛽ Citgo, Mobil/24hr, Shell/DQ/dsl, 🍴 Avest Pizza, Dunkin Donuts, First Garden Chinese, Nick&Tony's Pizza, McDonald's, Shoreline Diner, Splash American Grill, The Whole Enchilada, Wendy's, 🛏 Comfort Inn, Tower Motel, Ⓞ NAPA, transmissions, **W** Urgent Care, st police
58 (59)	CT 77, Guilford, **on US 1 E** ⛽ BP, Hess, Mobil, Sunoco/dsl, Ⓞ CVS Drug, Walgreens, to Henry Whitfield Museum, **W** st police
57 (58)	US 1, Guilford, **E** Ⓞ Extra/Dunkin Donuts/dsl, **W** Ⓞ Land Rover
56 (55)	rd 146, to Stony Creek, **E** 🛏 Rodeway Inn, **W** ⛽ Mobil, Shell/dsl, TA/Popeye's/Starbucks/Subway/dsl/scales/24hr/@, 🍴 Dunkin Donuts, Friendly's, USS Chowderpot, 🛏 Baymont Inn, Best Value Inn, Ⓞ Freightliner, Stop&Shop Foods, Verizon
55 (54)	US 1, **E** ⛽ Branford/repair, Cumberland, Global, 🍴 Hornet's Nest Deli, Lynn's Rest, Marco Pizzaria, Rita's Custard, Sapori d'Italia, TNT Seafood Grill, 🛏 Holiday Inn Express, Motel 6, Ⓞ Ford, Walgreens, vet, **W** ⛽ Gulf, Mobil/Dunkin Donuts/dsl, 🍴 Brother's Deli, Chuck's Margarita Grill, Gourmet Wok, Parthenon Diner, Su Casa Mexican, 🛏 Days Inn
54 (53)	Cedar St, Branford, **E** ⛽ Citgo/repair, Mobil, 🍴 Dragon East Chinese, Dunkin Donuts, La Luna Ristorante, Ⓞ AAA, Hyundai, Staples, Subaru, **W** Krauszer's Foods
52mm	**service area both lanes,** Mobil/dsl/24hr, McDonald's, pizza, atm
52 (50)	rd 100, North High St, **E** Ⓞ to Trolley Museum, **W** st police
51 (49.5)	US 1, Easthaven, **E** ⛽ Hess/dsl, Sunoco, Valero/dsl, 🍴 Boston Mkt, Chili's, 🛏 Quality Inn, Ⓞ Chevrolet, Lexus, TJ Maxx, Verizon, **W** 🍴 Dunkin Donuts, Wendy's, Ⓞ AutoZone, CarMax, Home Depot, USPO
50 (49)	Woodward Ave (from nb), **E** Ⓞ US Naval/Marine Reserve, Ft Nathan Hale
49 (48.5)	Stiles St (from nb)
48 (48)	I-91 N, to Hartford
47 (47.5)	CT 34, New Haven, **W** ⛽ Mobil/Dunkin Donuts/dsl, 🍴 Brazi's Italian, Greek Olive Diner, 🛏 La Quinta, Ⓞ Ikea, Long Warf Theater, same as 46
46 (47)	Long Wharf Dr, Sargent Dr, **E** 🍴 Leon's Rest., **W** ⛽ Mobil/Dunkin Donuts/dsl, 🍴 Brazi's Italian, Greek Olive Diner, 🛏 La Quinta, Ⓞ Ikea, Long Warf Theater
45 (46.5)	CT 10 (from sb), Blvd, **W** ⛽ BP, 🍴 Dunkin Donuts, McDonald's, same as 44
44 (46)	CT 10 (from nb), Kimberly Ave, **E** 🛏 Super 8, **W** ⛽ BP, 🍴 Dunkin Donuts, McDonald's, same as 45
43 (45)	CT 122, 1st Ave (no EZ return), West Haven, **W** ⛽ 1st Fuel/dsl, 🍴 China Sea, Ⓞ 🄷 to U of New Haven
42 (44)	CT 162, Saw Mill Rd, **E** 🍴 Pizza Hut, 🛏 EconoLodge, **W** ⛽ Mobil, Shell, 🍴 American Steaks, Dan's Dog House, Denny's, Dunkin Donuts, Friendly's, Starbucks, Subway, TX Roadhouse, 🛏 Best Western, Hampton Inn, Ⓞ Aldi Foods, Walmart
41 (42)	Marsh Hill Rd, to Orange
41mm	**service area both lanes,** ⛽ Mobil/dsl, 🍴 McDonald's
40 (40)	Old Gate Lane, Woodmont Rd, **E** ⛽ Citgo/dsl, 🍴🛏/

Exit	Services
40 (40)	Continued Wendy's/dsl/scales/24hr, Shell, Sunoco, 🍴 Cracker Barrel, Duchess Rest., Dunkin Donuts, Gipper's Rest., Presto's Rest., 🛏 Hilton Garden, Mayflower Motel, Quality Inn, Ⓞ Blue Beacon, Lowe's, 7-11
39 (39)	US 1, to Milford, **E** ⛽ BP, Cumberland Farms/dsl, 🍴 Athenian Diner, Chicago Grill, Friendly's, Hooters, 🛏 Howard Johnson, Super 8, Ⓞ CVS Drug, Firestone/auto, Mazda/Volvo, ShopRite Foods, Walgreens, **W on US 1** ⛽ Mobil, 🍴 Arby's, Boston Mkt, Buffalo Wild Wings, Burger King, Chili's, Chipotle Mexican, Dunkin Donuts, Hometown Buffet, HoneyBaked Ham, KFC, McDonald's, Michelangelo Pizza, Panera Bread, Red Robin, Subway, Taco Bell, Ⓞ Acura, Advance Parts, AT&T, Barnes&Noble, BigLots, Costco/gas, Dick's, JC Penney, Jeep, Jo-Ann Fabrics, Macy's, Marshall's, Michael's, Old Navy, PetCo, Rite Aid, Sears/auto, Staples, Target, TownFair Tire, USPO, Walmart/Subway, Whole Foods Mkt, mall
38 (38)	CT 15, Merritt Pkwy, Cross Pkwy
37 (37.5)	High St (no ez nb return), **E** ⛽ Gulf, Sunoco, USA, 🍴 Kimberly Diner, Ⓞ 7-11, Toyota/Scion
36	Plains Rd, **E** ⛽ Mobil, 🛏 Hampton Inn
35 (37)	Bic Dr, School House Rd, **E** ⛽ Citgo, 🍴 Armellino's Italian, Wendy's, 🛏 Fairfield Inn, Ⓞ AutoZone, Buick/GMC, Chevrolet, Chrysler/Dodge/Jeep, Dennis' Parts, Ford/Lincoln, Honda, Kia, K-Mart, Land Rover, Nissan, Stop&Shop Foods/gas, Subaru, Walgreens, **W** 🛏 Red Roof Inn, SpringHill Suites
34 (34)	US 1, Milford, **E on US 1** 🍴 Dunkin Donuts, Gourmet Buffet, McDonald's, Pizza Hut, Subway, Taco Bell, 🛏 Devon Motel, Ⓞ $Tree, Hyundai, Radio Shack, Walgreens
33 (33.5)	US 1 (from nb, no EZ return), CT 110, Ferry Blvd, **E** ⛽ Shell/dsl, Sunoco, 🍴 Brazilian Steaks, Bridgehouse Rest., Danny's Drive-In, Savin Rock Grill, Subway, Ⓞ BJ's Whse, PetCo, Staples, **W** 🍴 McDonalds, 99 Rest., Ⓞ Home Depot, Marshall's, Shaw's Foods, ShopRite Foods, Stop&Shop Foods, Walmart/Subway
32 (33)	W Broad St, Stratford, **E** ⛽ USA/Subway/dsl, **W** ⛽ Gulf, 🍴 Dunkin Donuts
31 (32)	South Ave, Honeyspot Rd, **E** ⛽ Gulf/Dunkin Donuts, 🛏 Comfort Inn, **W** ⛽ Citgo/dsl, Ⓞ NAPA, TownFair Tire, VIP Service Ctr
30 (31.5)	Lordship Blvd, Surf Ave, **E** ⛽ Shell, Sunoco/dsl, 🍴 Dunkin Donuts, 🛏 Ramada/rest., **W** ⛽ Massey/dsl
29 (31)	rd 130, Stratford Ave, Seaview Ave, **W** 🄷
28 (30)	CT 113, E Main St, Pembrook St
27 (29.5)	Lafayette Blvd, downtown, **W** 🍴 Dunkin Donuts, Subway, Ⓞ 🄷, Barnum Museum
27a (29)	CT 25, CT 8, to Waterbury
26 (28)	Wordin Ave
25 (27)	CT 130 (from sb, no EZ return), State St, Commerce Dr, Fairfield Ave, **E** ⛽ BP, Santa/dsl/repair, 🍴 Wendy's, Ⓞ Audi, Buick, Infiniti, Mercedes, Porsche, Smart Car, Stop&Shop, USPO, **W** ⛽ Prime, 🍴 McDonald's, Ⓞ transmissions
24 (26.5)	Black Rock Tpk, **E** 🍴 Blackrock Oyster Bar, Fairfield Pizza, Sweet Basil, 🛏 Best Western, Ⓞ BJ's Whse/Subway, Lexus, Porsche, Staples, USPO, Verizon, **W** ⛽ Gulf, Ⓞ Firestone/auto, Nissan
23 (26)	US 1, Kings Hwy, **E** ⛽ Sunoco/dsl, Ⓞ CVS Drug, Home Depot, Whole Foods Mkt
22 (24)	Round Hill Rd, N Benson Rd

⬆️N INTERSTATE 95 CONT'D

Exit	Services
23.5mm	**service area both lanes**, 🅿️ Mobil/dsl, 🍴 FoodCourt (sb), McDonald's
21 (23)	Mill Plain Rd, **E** 🅿️ Citgo/dsl, Mobil, 🍴 Avellino's Italian, DQ, Rawley's Drive-In, Starbucks, Subway, The Shack Grill, Wilson's BBQ, 🅾️ Hemlock Hardware, Rite Aid
20 (22)	Bronson Rd (from sb)
19 (21)	US 1, Center St, **W** 🅿️ BP, Shell/dsl, 🍴 Athena Diner, Baskin-Robbins/Dunkin Donuts, Friendly's, Subway, 🛏️ Westport Inn, 🅾️ Balducci's Mkt, Curves, Honda, Stop&Shop, TownFair Tire, Verizon, Walgreens
18 (20)	to Westport, **E** Sherwood Island SP, beaches, **W** 1 mi on US 1 🅿️ Citgo, Gulf, Mobil, 🍴 Angelina's Trattoria, Arby's, Arcudi's Rest., Bertucci's Italian, McDonald's, Sherwood Diner, Starbucks, Subway, 🅾️ Barnes&Noble, Marshall's, Radio Shack, Toyota/Scion, Walgreens, st police, vet
17 (18)	CT 33, rd 136, Westport, **W** 🅾️ FastStop Mart
16 (17)	E Norwalk, **E** 🅿️ Citgo, Mobil, Shell/dsl, Sunoco, 🍴 Baskin-Robbins/Dunkin Donuts, Eastside Café, Penny's Diner, Subway, 🅾️ Rite Aid, **W** 🅿️ Stew Leonard's Mkt
15 (16)	US 7, to Danbury, Norwalk, **E** 🅿️ Shell, 🅾️ Walgreens, **W** 🅿️ Getty
14 (15)	US 1, CT Ave, S Norwalk, **E** st police, **W** 🅿️ Shell/Dunkin Donuts, 🍴 Burger King, Driftwood Diner, Post Road Diner, Rowley's Tavern, Sierra Grill, Silver Star Diner, Wendy's, 🅾️ 🇭, Barnes&Noble, Best Buy, Kohl's, Old Navy, Petsmart, Radio Shack, ShopRite Foods, Stop&Shop, TJ Maxx, TownFair Tire, same as 13
13 (13)	US 1 (no EZ return), Post Rd, Norwalk, **W** 🅿️ Mobil, Shell, Sunoco, 🍴 American Steaks, Bertucci's, Chipotle Mexican, Darien Diner, Friendly's, John's Rest., KFC, McDonald's, 🛏️ DoubleTree Hotel, 🅾️ AT&T, Costco, Home Depot, Land Rover, Staples, Walmart, vet, same as 14
12.5mm	**service area nb**, Mobil/dsl, McDonald's
12 (12)	rd 136, Tokeneke Rd (from nb, no return), **W** 🍴 deli
11 (11)	US 1, Darien, **E** 🅿️ BP, 🛏️ Chuck's Steaks, 🅾️ Chevrolet, Nissan, vet, **W** 🅿️ Gulf, 🍴 Panera Bread, 🅾️ BMW, Whole Foods Mkt
10 (10)	Noroton, **W** 🅿️ BP, Shell, 🅾️ vet
9.5mm	**service area sb**, 🅿️ Mobil/dsl, 🍴 McDonald's
9 (9)	US 1, rd 106, Glenbrook, **E** 🛏️ Best Value Inn, 🅾️ Mini, **W** 🅿️ Gulf, 🍴 Chin's Chinese, Dunkin Donuts, McDonald's, Subway, 🅾️ cat vet
8 (8)	Atlantic Ave, Elm St, **E** U-Haul, **W** 🅿️ Sunoco, 🛏️ Marriott, 🅾️🇭
7 (7)	CT 137, Atlantic Ave, **W** 🛏️ Hampton Inn, Marriott, 🍴 PF Chang's, 🅾️ Barnes&Noble, USPO, same as 8
6 (6)	Harvard Ave, West Ave, **E** 🅿️ Gulf, 🍴 City Limits Diner, 🛏️ La Quinta, 🅾️ Advance Parts, Petsmart, Subaru, USPO, **W** 🅿️ Shell, 🛏️ Super 8, 🅾️🇭
5 (5)	US 1, Riverside, Old Greenwich, **W** 🅿️ A&P, BP, Shell, 🍴 Boston Mkt, Corner Deli, Hunan Cafe, McDonald's, Mo's Burger Joint, Starbucks, Subway, Taco Bell, 🛏️ Hyatt Regency, 🅾️ CVS Drug, GNC, Staples, Walgreens, USPO
4 (4)	Indian Field Rd, Cos Cob, **W** 🅾️ Bush-Holley House Museum
3 (3)	Arch St, Greenwich, **E** Bruce Museum, **W** 🅿️ Shell, 🅾️🇭 Lexus
2mm	**weigh sta nb**
2 (1)	Delavan Ave, Byram
0mm	Connecticut/New York state line

(left margin, vertical: NORWALK · GREENWICH)

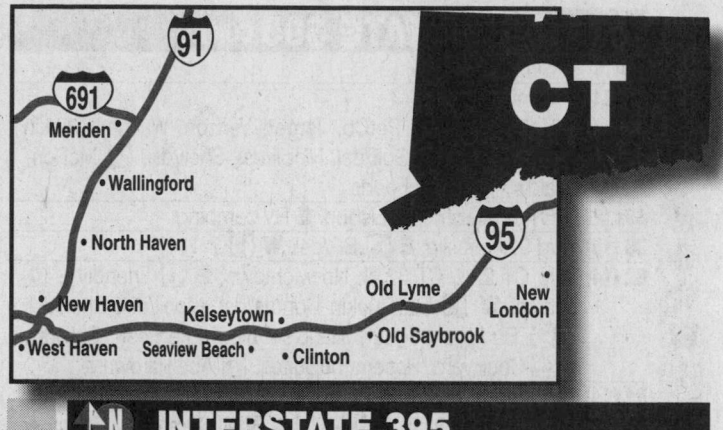

⬆️N INTERSTATE 395

Exit	Services
55.5mm	Connecticut/Massachusetts state line
100 (54)	E Thompson, to Wilsonville
99 (50)	rd 200, N Grosvenor Dale, **E** W Thompson Lake Camping (seasonal)
98 (49)	to CT 12 (from nb, exits left), Grosvenor Dale, same as 99
97 (47)	US 44, to E Putnam, **E** 🍴 Dunkin Donuts, Empire Buffet, McDonald's/playplace, Subway, Wendy's, 🅾️ Advance Parts, BigLots, CVS Drug, $Tree, Giant Pizza, GNC, Radio Shack, Sears Essentials, Stop&Shop/gas, **W** 🅿️ Shell/dsl/repair, Sunoco, 🅾️ Walmart/Subway
96 (46)	to CT 12, Putnam, **W** 🍴 Casa Mariachi, 🛏️ King's Inn, 🅾️ 🇭
95 (45)	Kennedy Dr, to Putnam, **E** Ford, **W** 🇭
94 (43)	Ballouville, **W** 🍴 Gold Eagle Rest., 🛏️ Comfort Inn, 🅾️ truck parts
93 (41)	CT 101, to Dayville, **E** 🅿️ Shell/dsl, 🍴 Burger King, China Garden, Domino's, Dunkin Donuts, Nuccio's Pizza, Subway, Yamoto Japanese, Zip's Diner, 🅾️ Aldi Foods, $Tree, Walgreens, Wibberley Tire/repair, **W** 🅿️ Mobil/dsl, Xtra/dsl, 🍴 Dunkin Donuts, McDonald's, Mozzarella's Grill, 99 Rest., 🅾️ AT&T, GNC, Lowe's, Michael's, PetCo, Target, TJ Maxx, Staples, Stop&Shop, Verizon, city park
92 (39)	to S Killingly, **W** 🍴 Dunkin Donuts, Giant Pizza, 🅾️ Bonneville Drug, st police
91 (38)	US 6 W, to Danielson, to Quinebaug Valley Coll
90 (36)	to US 6 E (from nb), to Providence
35mm	Rs **both lanes, full ♿ facilities**, 🅿️ Mobil/dsl
89 (32)	CT 14, to Sterling, Central Village, **E** 🅿️ Best Way, Gulf/repair, 🍴 Johnny's Rest., Pizza Pizzazz, 🅾️ Rite Aid, RV camping, USPO, **W** 🅿️ 7-11/dsl, Shell/Dunkin Donuts/dsl, 🍴 Music Lady Cafe, Subway, 🛏️ Knights Inn, 🅾️ transmissions
88 (30)	CT 14A to Plainfield, **E** RV camping (seasonal), **W** 🅿️ Mobil
87 (28)	Lathrop Rd, to Plainfield, **E** 🅿️ Shell/Domino's/dsl, 🍴 Dunkin Donuts, HongKong Star Chinese, Subway, Wendy's, 🛏️ Holiday Inn Express, Quality Inn, 🅾️ Big Y Foods, Ford, Hyundai, Mazda, Mercedes, Radio Shack, **W** 🅿️ Gulf, Sunoco/dsl, 🍴 Bakers Dozen Cafe, Eli's Steaks, McDonald's, 🅾️ Advance Parts, Curves, CVS Drug
86 (24)	rd 201, Hopeville, **E** Hopeville Pond SP, RV camping
85 (23)	CT 164, CT 138, to Pachaug, Preston, **E** 🅿️ Petro Max/Dunkin Donuts/dsl, 🅾️ Curves, $Tree, RV camping, **W** 🛏️ AmericInn
84 (21)	CT 12, Jewett City, **E** 🍴 Chili's, Panera Bread, Ruby Tuesday, 🅾️ Aldi Foods, AT&T, Dick's, GNC, Home Depot,

(right margin, vertical: PUTNAM · PLAINFIELD; right edge tab: CT)

⬆N INTERSTATE 395 CONT'D

Exit	Services
84 (21)	Continued
	Kohl's, Lowe's, PetCo, Target, Verizon, Walmart/Dunkin Donuts, **W** 🅿 Gulf/dsl, Mobil/dsl, Shell/dsl, 🍴 McDonald's, 🅾 Val-U Foods
83a (20)	CT 169 (from nb), Lisbon, **E** RV camping
83 (18)	rd 97, Taftville, **E** 🅿 BP/dsl, **W** 🅿 7-11
82 (14)	to CT 2 W, CT 32 N, Norwichtown, **E** 🍴 Friendly's, 🅾 tires, **W** 🅿 BP/Dunkin Donuts/dsl, Mobil/dsl, Shell/dsl, 🍴 Buddy's Dugout, Illiano's Grill, Prime Rest., Subway, 🛏 Courtyard, Rosemont Suites, 🅾 Ace Hardware
81 (14)	CT 2 E, CT 32 S, Norwich, **E** 🏥, to Mohegan Coll
80 (12)	CT 82, Norwich, **E** 🅿 Mobil, Shell, Xtra/dsl, 🍴 Burger King, Chinese Buffet, Dunkin Donuts, Friendly's, KFC/Taco Bell, McDonald's, Mr Pizza, 99 Rest., Papa Gino's, Subway, Wendy's, 🅾 Jo-Ann Fabrics, Rite Aid, ShopRite Foods, Staples, TJ Maxx, TownFair Tire, Verizon, **W** 🛏 Holiday Inn, 🅾 Big Y Foods, Walmart, RV Camping
79a (10)	CT 2A E, to Ledyard, **E** to Pequot Res
8.5mm	nb st police, 🅾, sb Mobil/dsl, 🆁🆂 full facilities
79 (6)	rd 163, to Uncasville, Montville, **1 mi E** 🅿 Mobil/dsl, 🍴 Dunkin Donuts, Friendly Pizza, McDonald's, Subway, 🅾 Rite Aid, Tri-Town Foods, repair
78 (5)	CT 32 (from sb, exits left), to New London, RI Beaches
77 (2)	CT 85, to I-95 N, Colchester, **1/2 mi E** 🅿 Shell/dsl, Dunkin Donuts, 🛏 Oakdell Motel
0mm	I-95. **I-395 begins/ends on I-95, exit 76.**

⬆E INTERSTATE 691

Exit	Services
I-691 begins/ends on I-91	
12 (12)	Preston Ave
11 (11)	I-91 N, to Hartford
10 (11)	I-91 S, to New Haven, CT 15 S, W Cross Pkwy
9	Berlin Tpk
8 (10)	US 5, Broad St, **N** 🅿 Citgo, Cumberland, Irving, Shell/dsl, 🍴 Broad St Pizza, Chinese Gourmet, DQ
7 (9)	downtown (no ez wb return), Meriden, **S** 🅿 Citgo
6 (8)	Lewis Ave (from wb, no EZ return), to CT 71, **N** 🍴 Ruby Tuesday, 🅾 🏥, Best Buy, Dick's, Macy's, JC Penney, Macy's, Old Navy, Sears/auto, Target, mall, **S** 🅿 7-11, 🍴 Subway
5 (7)	CT 71, to Chamberlain Hill (from eb, no EZ return), **N** 🅾 🏥, Best Buy, Target, mall, **S** 🅿 7-11/gas, 🍴 McDonald's, Subway
4 (4)	CT 322, W Main St (no re-entry from eb), **N** 🅿 Sunoco, 🍴 Dunkin Donuts, Hubbard Park Pizza, 🅾 🏥
3mm	Quinnipiac River
3 (1)	CT 10, to Cheshire, Southington, **N** 🍴 Sam's Clams Rest., Tony's Rest.
2 (0)	I-84 E, to Hartford
1 (0)	I-84 W, to Waterbury
I-691 begins/ends on I-84	

DELAWARE

⬆N INTERSTATE 95

Exit	Services
23mm	Delaware/Pennsylvania state line, motorist callboxes for 23 miles sb
11 (22)	to I-495 S, DE 92, Naamans Rd, **E** 🍴 China Star, 🅾 Burlington Coats, $General, Jo-Ann Fabrics, K-Mart, WaWa, **W** 🅿 Gulf/dsl, 🍴 KFC/Taco Bell, Quiznos, 🛏 Holiday Inn Select, 🅾 Home Depot, Radio Shack, Rite Aid
10 (21)	Harvey Rd (no nb return)
9 (19)	DE 3, to Marsh Rd, **E** 🍴 Dunkin Donuts, Lamberti's Italian, Starbucks, 🅾 Rockwood Museum, to Bellevue SP, st police
8b a (17)	US 202, Concord Pike, to Wilmington, **E** 🅾 Home Depot, to Brandywine Park
7b a (16)	DE 52, Delaware Ave
6 (15)	DE 4, MLK Blvd, **E** 🍴 Joe's Crabshack, McDonald's, 🅾 AAA, Fresh Grocer Foods, Rite Aid, **W** 🅿 Gulf, 🅾 Family$
5c (12)	I-495 N, to Wilmington, to DE Mem Bridge
5b a (11)	DE 141, to US 202, to New Castle, Newport, **E** 🛏 Quality Inn (3mi)
4b a (8)	DE 1, DE 7, to Christiana, **E** 🍴 Brio Tuscan Grille, CA Pizza Kitchen, Cheesecake Factory, Don Pablo, Food-Court, JB Dawson's Rest., Panera Bread, Ruby Tuesday, 🅾 Barnes&Noble, Costco, Dick's, JC Penney, Macy's, Michael's, Nordstrom, PetCo, Target, mall, **W** 🍴 Applebee's, Bugaboo Creek Steaks, Cheeseburger Paradise, Chili's, Dunkin Donuts, Firebird's Grill, Marble Slab Creamery, Michael's Rest., Old Country Buffet, Olive Garden, Quiznos,

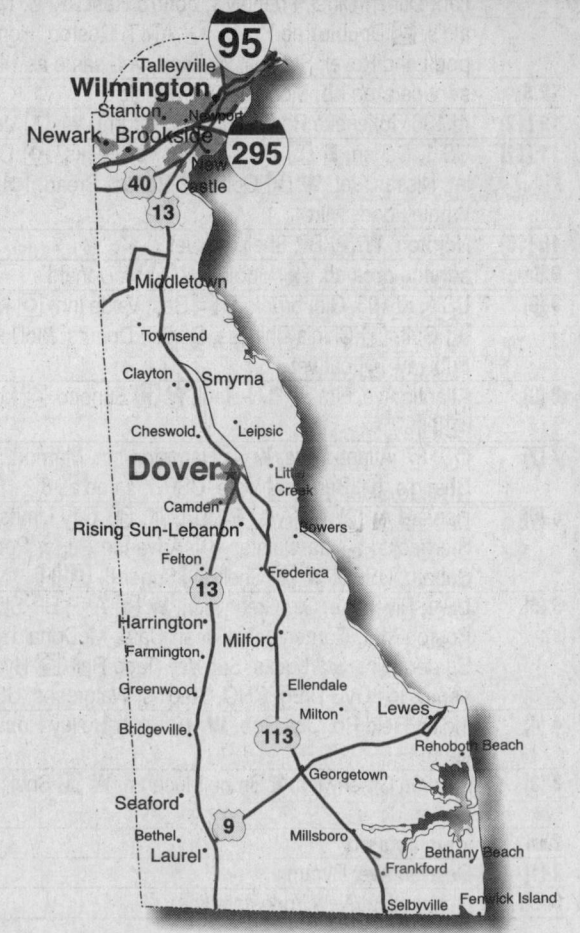

⬆N INTERSTATE 95 CONT'D

Exit	Services
4b a (8)	Continued
	Red Lobster, 🛏 Country Inn&Suites, Courtyard, Days Inn, Fairfield Inn, Hilton, Homestead Suites, Red Roof Inn, 🅾 🅗, AAA, Best Buy, Home Depot, Office Depot, Petsmart, TJ Maxx, Verizon, casino/racetrack
3b a (6)	DE 273, to Newark, Dover, **E** 🅿 BP, Exxon/dsl, 🍽 Bertucci's, Bob Evans, Boston Mkt, Ciao Pizza, Famous Dave's BBQ, Red Robin, Olive Grill Italian, Shell Hammer's Grille, Wendy's, 🛏 Ramada Inn, Residence Inn, Staybridge Suites, TownePlace Suites, 🅾 Acme Foods, Boscov's, Jo-Ann Fabrics, Old Navy, Staples, Walgreens, **W** 🅿 Getty, Shell/dsl, 🍽 Denny's, Dunkin Donuts, Pizza Hut, 🛏 Comfort Inn, EconoLodge, Holiday Inn Express, 🅾 7-11
5mm	**service area both lanes** (exits left from both lanes), info, 🅿 Sunoco/dsl, 🍽 Baja Fresh, Burger King, Famiglia, Popeye's, Starbucks, Z-Mkt
1b a (3)	DE 896, to Newark, to U of DE, Middletown, **W** 🅿 Exxon, Gulf/dsl, Shell/dsl, Sunoco, 🍽 Boston Mkt, China Garden, Dunkin Donuts, 896 Diner, Friendly's, Mario's Pizza, Matilda's Rest, McDonald's, TGIFriday's, 🛏 Best Value Inn, Courtyard (3mi), Embassy Suites, Homewood Suites, Howard Johnson, Sleep Inn, 🅾 DE Tire Ctr
1mm	**toll booth, st police**
0mm	Delaware/Maryland state line, motorist callboxes for 23 miles nb

⬆N INTERSTATE 295 (WILMINGTON)

Exit	Services
15mm	Delaware/New Jersey state line, Delaware River, Delaware Memorial Bridge

14.5mm	**toll plaza**
14	DE 9, New Castle Ave, to Wilmington, **E** 🅿 BP, Citgo, 🍽 Giovanni's Cafe, 🅾 Advance Parts, Family$, Firestone/auto, Harley-Davidson/rest., Rite Aid, SuperFresh Foods, **W** 🅿 Shell, Super/dsl, 🍽 Dunkin Donuts, McDonald's, 🛏 Budget Inn, Motel 6, SuperLodge
13	US 13, US 40, to New Castle, **E** 🅿 BP, Hess, Sunoco/dsl, Shell/dsl, WaWa, 🍽 Applebee's, Arby's, Arner's Rest, Burger King, DogHouse, Dove Diner, Dunkin Donuts, Hadfield's Seafood, Hooters, IHOP, KFC, Lonestar Steaks, McDonald's, Pizza Hut, Popeye's, Season's Pizza, Subway, Taco Bell, TGIFriday's, Wendy's, 🛏 EconoLodge, Quality Inn, Super 8, 🅾 Acura, AutoZone, BJ's Whse/gas, Chevrolet, Chrysler/Jeep/Dodge, Cottman Transmissions, $Tree, Fiat, Ford, Home Depot, Hyundai, Lincoln, Mazda, Nissan, PathMark Foods, PepBoys, Radio Shack, Ross, Save-a-Lot, 7-11, Staples, Toyota/Scion, Walgreens, Walmart, repair, **W** 🅿 WaWa/dsl, 🍽 Dunkin Donuts, 🛏 Clarion, 🅾 Ford Trucks, Freightliner, Lowe's
12	I-495, US 202, N to Wilmington
I-295 begins/ends on I-95	

⬆N INTERSTATE 495

Exit	Services
11mm	I-95 N. **I-495 begins/ends on I-95.**
5 (10)	US 13, Phila Pike, Claymont, **W** 🅿 BP, Exxon/dsl, Sunoco/dsl, 🍽 Arby's, Boston Mkt, Dunkin Donuts, McDonald's, 🛏 Milan Motel, 🅾 Family$, Food Lion, USPO
4 (5)	US 13, rd 3, Edgemoor Rd, to Fox Point Park
3 (4)	12th St
2 (3)	rd 9A, Terminal Ave, Port of Wilmington
1 (1)	US 13, **E** 🅿 WaWa/dsl, 🍽 Dunkin Donuts, 🛏 Clarion, 🅾 Ford Trucks, Lowe's
0mm	I-95 S. **I-495 begins/ends on I-95.**

FLORIDA

⬆E INTERSTATE 4

Exit	Services
132	I-95, S to Miami, N to Jacksonville, FL 400. **I-4 begins/ends on I-95, exit 260b**
129	to US 92 (from eb, exits left)
126mm	🆁🆂 eb, 🆁🆂 litter barrels, no security
118	FL 44, to DeLand, **N** 🅿 BP/dsl, 🛏 Howard Johnson, 🅾 🅗
116	Orange Camp Rd, Lake Helen
114	FL 472, to DeLand, Orange City, **N** 🅾 Clark Campground (1mi), to Blue Sprgs SP
111b a	Deltona, **N** 🅿 Hess/dsl, RaceTrac/dsl, Shell/Circle K, 🍽 Baskin-Robbins/Dunkin Donuts, Bob Evans, Chick-fil-A, Chili's, Denny's, Jimmy John's, KFC, Papa John's, Perkins, Pizza Hut, Quiznos, Ruby Tuesday, Sonic, Sonny's BBQ, Steak'n Shake, Subway, Taco Bell, Tijuana Flats, Zaxby's, 🛏 Holiday Inn Express, 🅾 🅗, Urgent Care, $General, Firestone/auto, Home Depot, Lowe's, Office Depot, Publix/deli, Save-A-Lot Foods, Tire Kingdom, Tires+, Verizon, Walgreens, Walmart, **S** 🅿 Chevron/repair, 🍽 Wendy's, 🅾 Family$, Publix, Walgreens
108	Dirksen Dr, DeBary, Deltona, **N** 🅿 Chevron, 🍽 Burger King, IHOP, 🛏 Hampton Inn, **S** 🅿 Kangaroo, 🍽 McDonald's, Subway, Waffle House, 🛏 Best Western, 🅾 Publix (2mi)

Exit	Services
104	US 17, US 92, Sanford, **N** 🍽 Captains Cove Rest., 🅾 La Mesa RV Ctr, **S** 🅿 Citgo/Subway
101c	rd 46, to Mt Dora, Sanford, **N** 🅿 7-11, 🍽 Tijuana Flats, 🅾 Ace Hardware, Ford, **S** 🅿 Chevron/dsl, Mobil, Murphy USA/dsl, RaceTrac, 7-11, 🍽 Baskin-Robbins/Dunkin Donuts, Big Boy, Burger King, Cracker Barrel, Denny's, Don Pablo, Firehouse Subs, Hooters, Joe's Crabshack, LJ Silver/Taco Bell, Logan's Roadhouse, McDonald's, Olive Garden, Outback Steaks, Panda Express, Panera Bread, Red Brick Pizza, Red Lobster, Rte 46 Smokehouse, Smokey Bones BBQ, Steak'n Shake, Subway, Wendy's, 🛏 Comfort Inn, Days Inn, SpringHill Suites, Super 8, 🅾 🅗, Urgent Care, Aldi Foods, Beall's, Belk, Best Buy, Big 10 Tire, BJ's Whse/gas, Books-A-Million, CVS Drug, Dillard's, $Tree, GNC, Goodyear/auto, Harley-Davidson, JC Penney, Jo-Ann Fabrics, Macy's, Marshall's, Michael's, Old Navy, PetCo, Ross, Sears/auto, Target, Tire Kingdom, Tuffy Auto, Verizon, Walmart, World Mkt, mall
101a b	rd 46a, FL 417 **(toll)**, FL 46, Sanford, Heathrow, **N** 🍽 Applebee's, Carlos'n Charley's, Crisper's, FishBones, Moe's SW Grill, Papa Joe's Pizza, Rikka Asian Bistro, Ruth's Chris Steaks, Shula's 347 Grill, Subway, Vamonos, 🛏 Hampton Inn, Marriott, Residence Inn, Westin, 🅾 Urgent Care, Publix, Walgreens, **S** 🅾 Acura, CarMax, CVS Drug, Honda, Kohl's, Sam's Club/gas, 7-11, Toyota/Scion

Left margin: **NEWARK** (I-95 section), **SANFORD** (I-4 section)

Right margin tab: **DE / FL**

INTERSTATE 4 CONT'D

Exit	Services
98	Lake Mary Blvd, Heathrow, **N** 🅖 Shell, 🍴 Luigino's Italian, Panera Bread, Peach Valley Cafe, Stonewood Grill, Subway, 🛏 Courtyard, Hyatt Place, 🄾 CVS Drug, Verizon, Walgreens, Winn-Dixie, **S** 🅖 BP/24hr, Chevron/24hr, Citgo, Mobil/dsl, 7-11, 🍴 Arby's, Baskin-Robbins/Dunkin Donuts, Bob Evans, Boston Mkt, Burger King, Checkers, Chick-fil-A, Chili's, Chipotle Mexican, Chop Stix, Domino's, Firehouse Subs, Frank&Naomi's, KFC, Krystal, Longhorn Steaks, Macaroni Grill, McDonald's, Panera Bread, Papa John's, Papa Joe's Pizza, Pizza Hut/Taco Bell, Quiznos, Starbucks, Steak'n Shake, Subway, Taste of China, Uno, Wendy's, WingZone, 🛏 Candlewood Suites, Extended Stay America, Hilton Garden, Homestead Suites, Homewood Suites, La Quinta, 🄾 Advance Parts, Albertsons, AT&T, Family$, Gander Mtn, Goodyear, Home Depot, K-Mart, Office Depot, Petsmart, Publix, Radio Shack, Staples, Target, Tires+, TJ Maxx, Walgreens, USPO, mall, vet
95mm	🆁🆂 both lanes, full ♿ facilities, 🛢 vending, 🗑 litter barrels, petwalk, 24hr security
94	FL 434, to Winter Springs, Longwood, **N** 🅖 Hess/dsl, Mobil/dsl, 7-11, 🍴 Burger King, East Buffet, Imperial Dynasty, Kobe Japanese, Melting Pot Rest., Miami Subs, Panera Bread, Papa Joe's Pizza, Starbucks, Tijuana Flats, Wendy's, 🛏 Comfort Inn, 🄾 CVS Drug, Publix, **S** 🍴 Bonefish Grill, Boston Mkt, Carmela's Rest., Crisper's, Pickle's NY, 🛏 Candlewood Suites, 🄾 🄷
92	FL 436, Altamonte Springs, **N** 🅖 7-11, Shell/Circle K/dsl, 🍴 Bojangles, Boston Mkt, Checkers, Chick-fil-A, Chipotle Mexican, ChuckeCheese, Cracker Barrel, Kobe Japanese, Little Caesars, Longhorn Steaks, McDonald's, Olive Garden, Perkins, Pollo Tropical, Popeye's, Red Lobster, Sweet Tomatoes, Taco Bell, TGIFriday's, Waffle House, WingHouse, 🛏 Days Inn, Hampton Inn, Hotel Altamonte, Quality Suites, Remington Inn, Residence Inn, SpringHill Suites, 🄾 Urgent Care, Best Buy, CVS Drug, Family$, Firestone/auto, Goodyear/auto, Tire Kingdom, U-Haul, Walgreens, **S** 🅖 BP, Citgo, Hess/dsl, Mobil/dsl, 🍴 Bahama Breeze, Burger King, Chili's, Denny's, Dunkin Donuts, Elephant Bar, 5 Guys Burgers, Jason's Deli, Mimi's Cafe, Moe's SW Grill, Orlando Alehouse, Panda Express, Pizza Hut, Starbucks, Steak'n Shake, Subway, Wendy's, 🛏 Embassy Suites, Hilton, Homestead Suites, 🄾 🄷, Advance Parts, Albertsons, Barnes&Noble, CVS Drug, Dillard's, JC Penney, Marshall's, Michael's, Office Depot, PetCo, Publix, Ross, Sears/auto, TJMaxx, vet
90b a	FL 414, Maitland Blvd, **N** 🅖 7-11, 🍴 Applebee's, Chick-fil-A, Oak Grill, Wendy's, 🛏 Extended Stay America, Extended Stay Deluxe, Homewood Suites, Sheraton, **S** Maitland Art Ctr
88	FL 423, Lee Rd, **N** 🅖 7-11, 🍴 Arby's, Burger King, Del Frisco, IHOP, Little Caesars, LJ Silver/Taco Bell, McDonald's, Nick&Gina's Italian, Popeye's, Quiznos, 🛏 Countryside Inn, InTown Suites, La Quinta, Motel 6, 🄾 Aamco, Family$, Firestone/auto, Home Depot, Land Rover, Mini, Ross, Save-A-Lot Foods, Tires+, VW, **S** 🅖 Chevron/dsl, Sunoco, 🍴 Denny's, 🄾 BMW
87	FL 426, Fairbanks Ave (no eb re-entry), **N** 🅖 Hess/Blimpie/Dunkin Donuts/Godfather's/dsl, 1mi **S** 🍴 Burger King, Chick-fil-A, Chipotle Mexican, Pizza Hut/Taco Bell, Popeye's, Steak'n Shake, Subway, Wendy's, 🄾 Walgreens

86	Par St (from eb, no re-entry), **S** 🅖 Shell/Circle K
85	Princeton St, **S** 🅖 Chevron, 7-11, 🄾 🄷
84	FL 50, Colonial Dr, Ivanhoe Blvd, **N** 🛏 Crowne Plaza
83b	US 17, US 92, FL 50, Amelia St (from eb), **N** 🛏 Crowne Plaza
83a	FL 526 (from eb), Robinson St, **N** 🛏 Sheraton
83	South St (from wb) downtown
82c	Anderson St E, Church St Sta Hist Dist downtown
82b	Gore Ave (from wb), **S** 🄷, downtown
82a	FL 408 (**toll**), to FL 526
81b c	Kaley Ave, **S** 🅖 Mobil, 🄾 🄷
81a	Michigan St (from wb), **N** 🅖 Citgo/dsl
80b a	US 17, US 441 S, US 92 W, **S** 🅖 Citgo, Chevron, RaceTrac, Shell, Sunoco, 🍴 Checkers, Gyros, McDonald's, Subway, 🛏 Days Inn, 🄾 Aldi Foods, AutoZone, Goodyear/auto, Save-A-Lot Foods, Walgreens
79	FL 423, 33rd St, John Young Pkwy, **N** 🛏 Ramada Inn, 🄾 Harley-Davidson, **S** 🅖 RaceTrac/dsl, 🍴 IHOP, 🛏 Days Inn
78	Conroy Rd, **N** 🅖 7-11, **S** 🍴 BJ's Rest., Bloomingdale's, Elephant Bar Rest., Green's Grill, Krispy Kreme, McDonald's, Mimi's Cafe, Moe's SW Grill, Olive Garden, Panda Express, Pollo Tropical, Subway, TGIFriday's, Village Tavern, Waffle Shop, Wendy's, Zaxby's, 🄾 AT&T, Best Buy, BJ's Whse, Dick's, $Tree, Home Depot, Infiniti/Smart, Macy's, Marshall's, Mercedes, Old Navy, PetCo, Super Target, mall
77	FL 527, FL TPK (**toll**)
75b a	FL 435, International Dr (exits left from both lanes), **N** 🅖 Mobil, 🍴 Cracker Barrel, Denny's, TGIFriday's, 🛏 Days Inn, DoubleTree Motel, Fairfield Inn, Holiday Inn, Hyatt Place, 🄾 to Universal Studios, **S** 🅖 Chevron, 7-11, 🍴 Bamboo Rest., Black Angus Steaks, Denny's, Great Western Steaks, IHOP, Ponderosa, Red Lobster, Sizzler, Sweet Tomatoes, 🛏 Best Western, Clarion, Court of Flags Hotel, EconoLodge, Hampton Inn, Hilton Garden, Holiday Inn Express, Homewood Suites, Howard Johnson, International Gateway Inn, Lakefront Inn, Las Palmas Hotel, Motel 6, Rodeway Inn, Sheraton, Super 8, multiple hotels & resorts, 🄾 Bass Pro Shops, Belz Outlet/famous Brands, Books A Million, Office Depot, Walgreens
74b	Universal Studios (from wb)
74a	FL 482, Sand Lake Rd, **N** 🅖 Chevron, 7-11, 🍴 Alexander's Rest., Chick-fil-A, McDonald's, Timpano Italian, Wendy's, multiple restaurants, 🛏 Comfort Suites, 🄾 K-Mart, Publix, Whole Food Mkt, Walgreens, Walmart, **S** 🅖 BP, Chevron, Mobil, 7-11, Shell/Circle K/dsl, 🍴 Asian Buffet, Bahama Breeze, Buffalo Wild Wings, Burger King, Cattleman's Steaks, Charley's Steaks, Checkers, Chili's, CiCi's Pizza, China Jade, Crabhouse, Denny's, Fish Bones Rest., Friendly's, Golden Corral, Houlihan's, IHOP, Italianni's, Kobe Japanese, Lobster Feast, McDonald's, Miller's Alehouse, Ming Court, Olive Garden, Perkins, Pizza Hut, Ponderosa, Popeye's, Sizzler, TGIFriday's, Tony Roma's, Uno, Vito's Chophouse, Wendy's, Wild Bean Cafe, 🛏 Best Western, Castle Hotel, Courtyard, Comfort Inn, Crowne Plaza, EconoLodge, Embassy Suites, Fairfield Inn, Hampton Inn, Holiday Inn, Homewood Suites, Howard Johnson, Hyatt Place, La Quinta, Marriott, Masters Inn, Microtel, Peabody Hotel, Quality Inn, Radisson Inn, Ramada Inn, Red Roof Inn, Residence Inn, Rodeway Inn, Rosen Suites, Staybridge Suites, Wyndham Garden, 🄾 🄷, Harley-Davidson, Ripley's Believe-it-or-not!, Stouffer Resort, Walgreens, RV Park

🢁 INTERSTATE 4 CONT'D

Exit	Services
72	FL 528 E (**toll**, no eb re-entry), to Cape Canaveral, **N** USPO, **S** to 🍴
71	Central FL Pkwy (from eb no re-entry), **S** 🅟 Chevron, 🍴 Wendy's, 🛏 Hilton Garden, Renaissance Resort, Residence Inn, to SeaWorld
68	FL 535, Lake Buena Vista, **N** 🅟 Mobil/dsl, 7-11, Shell/Circle K/dsl, 🍴 AleHouse, Amici Italian, Black Angus Steaks, Buffalo Wild Wings, Burger King, Chevy's Mexican, Chili's, China Buffet, CiCi's Pizza, Denny's, Dragon Super Buffet, El Patron, Flipper's Pizzaria, Fuddrucker's, Giordano's, Havana's Cuisine, Hooters, IHOP, Joe's Crabshack, Johnnie's Rest., Kobe Japanese, Macaroni Grill, McDonald's, Olive Garden, Perkins, Pizza Hut, Qdoba, Quiznos, Red Lobster, Shoney's, Sizzler, Steak'n Shake, Subway, Sweet Tomatoes, Taco Bell, The Crabhouse, TGIFriday's, Uno, 🛏 Comfort Inn, Country Inn&Suites, Courtyard, DoubleTree, Embassy Suites, Extended Stay Deluxe, Hampton Inn, Hawthorn Suites, Hilton, Hilton Gargen, Holiday Inn, Holiday Inn Express, Homewood Suites, Hyatt Hotel, Orlando Vista Hotel, Quality Inn, Radisson, Residence Inn, Sheraton, StayBridge Suites, ⊙ Gooding's Foods/drug, Walgreens, USPO, **S** 🅟 Chevron, 7-11, Shell/dsl, 🍴 Applebee's, Bahama Breeze, Carrabba's, Chick-fil-A, CiCi's Pizza, Dunkin Donuts, Golden Corral, Landry's Seafood, LoneStar Steaks, Panera Bread, Santa Fe Steaks, Starbucks, Wendy's, 🛏 Blue Heron Resort, Buena Vista Suites, Courtyard, Fairfield Inn, Holiday Inn Resort, Marriott Village, Residence Inn, Sheraton, SpringHill Suites, ⊙ CVS Drug, Orlando Premium Outlets, Verizon, Walgreens
67	FL 536, to Epcot, **N** DisneyWorld, **1 mi S** 🅟 7-11, 🍴 Asian Harbor, 🛏 Buena Vista, Marriott, ⊙ CVS Drug, to 🍴, multiple resorts
65	Osceola Pkwy, to FL 417 (**toll**), **N** to DisneyWorld, Epcot, Animal Kingdom, and Wide World of Sports
64b a	US 192, FL 536, to FL 417 (**toll**), to Kissimmee, **N** 🅟 7-11, to DisneyWorld, MGM, **0-3 mi S** 🅟 Mobil/dsl, RaceTrac/dsl, 7-11, 🍴 Applebee's, Arby's, Bob Evans, Boston Lobster Feast, Burger King, Charley's Steakhouse, Checkers, Chick-fil-A, Chili's, Chinese Buffet, CiCi's Pizza, Cracker Barrel, Denny's, Domino's, Dunkin Donuts, Golden Corral, IHOP, Joe's Crabshack, Kabuki Oriental, KFC, Kobe Japanese, Krispy Kreme, Logan's Roadhouse, Longhorn Steaks, Macaroni Grill, McDonald's, Ocean 11 Rest., Olive Garden, Pacino's Italian, Panda Express, Papa John's, Perkins, Pizza Hut, Ponderosa, Quiznos, Red Lobster, Rio Mexican Grill, Ruby Tuesday, Sizzlin Grill, Smokey Bones BBQ, Starbucks, Subway, Taco Bell, TGIFriday's, Uno, Waffle House, Wendy's, 🛏 Best Inn, Celebration Suites, Comfort Suites, Days Inn, Holiday Inn, Howard Johnson, Knight Inn, Masters Inn, Mona Lisa Hotel, Motel 6,
64b a	Continued Orlando Palms, Parkway Resort, Quality Suites, Ramada, Radisson, Red Roof Inn, Rodeway Inn, Sun Inn, Super 8, Seralago Hotel, Travelodge, ⊙ Ⓗ AT&T, Camping World RV Ctr, CVS Drug, $General, Harley-Davidson, Jo-Ann Fabrics, Marshall's, Publix, Target, Walgreens, USPO, factory outlet/famous brands
62	FL 417 (**toll**, from eb), World Dr, **N** to DisneyWorld, **S** Celebration, to 🍴
60	Fl 429 N (**toll**), Apopka
58	FL 532, to Kissimmee, **N** 🅟 BP, 7-11, 🍴 Chili's, China One, McDonald's, Pizzaria, Subway, 🛏 Championship Gate Resort, ⊙ Publix, Walgreens, **S** 🍴 Dunkin Donuts (1mi), 🛏 Reunion Resort (2mi)
55	US 27, to Haines City, **N** 🅟 7-11, Sunoco/dsl, 🍴 Burger King, Cracker Barrel, Denny's, McDonald's, Waffle House, Wendy's, 🛏 Comfort Inn, Hampton Inn, Holiday Inn Express, Super 8, ⊙ Ford, FL Camp Inn (5mi), **S** 🅟 BP/dsl, Marathon, RaceWay/dsl, 7-11, Shell/dsl/service, 🍴 Bob Evans, CiCi's Pizza, Grand China, Perkins, Sake Steaks, Subway, 🛏 Days Inn, Microtel, Quality Inn, Southgate Inn, ⊙ Ⓗ Belk, Best Buy, Books-A-Million, Deer Creek RV

📣 = gas 🍴 = food 🛏 = lodging ⊙ = other Ⓡ🅢 = rest stop   Copyright 2014 - The Next Exit ®

◀E INTERSTATE 4 CONT'D

Exit	Services
55	Continued
	Resort, Dick's, $Tree, GNC, JC Penney, KOA, Michael's, Petsmart, Ross, Staples, Target, Theme World RV Park, Verizon, to Cypress Gardens, tourist info
48	rd 557, to Winter Haven, Lake Alfred, S 📣 BP/dsl
46mm	Ⓡ🅢 both lanes, full 🚻 facilities, 🚰 vending, 🚮 litter barrels, petwalk, 24hr security
44	FL 559, to Auburndale, S 📣 BP/dsl/scales/24hr, ❤Loves/Arby's/dsl/scales/24hr
41	FL 570 W toll, Auburndale, Lakeland
38	FL 33, to Lakeland, Polk City
33	rd 582, to FL 33, Lakeland, N 📣 BP, Exxon/24hr, 7-11, 🍴 Applebee's, Cracker Barrel, 5 Guys Burger, McDonald's, Starbucks, Wendy's, 🛏 Crestwood Suites, Country Inn&Suites, Days Inn, Jameson Inn, Hampton Inn, La Quinta, Quality Inn, Ramada, Sleep Inn, ⊙ BMW, CVS Drug, GNC, Publix, S 📣 BP/dsl, 🍴 Waffle House, 🛏 ValuePlace, ⊙🅷 Harley-Davidson, Lakeland RV Resort, Nissan
32	US 98, Lakeland, N 📣 BP, Mobil, Murphy USA/dsl, 7-11, 🍴 Asian Buffet, Checkers, Chili's, ChuckeCheese, CiCi's Pizza, DQ, Domino's, Dunkin Donuts, Golden Corral, Hooters, IHOP, KFC, Ling's Buffet, LJ Silver, McDonald's, Moe's SW Grill, Olive Garden, Outback Steaks, Panera Bread, Papa John's, Place Garden, Red Lobster, Smokey Bones BBQ, Sonny's BBQ, Starbucks, Steak'n Shake, Subway, Taco Bell, TGIFriday's, Wendy's, Zaxby's, 🛏 Comfort Inn, La Quinta, Royalty Inn, ⊙ Advance Parts, Aldi Foods, AT&T, AutoZone, Barnes&Noble, Beall's, Belk, Best Buy, CVS Drug, Dillard's, $General, Firestone/auto, Goodyear/auto, JC Penney, JoAnn Fabrics, Lowe's, Macy's, PepBoys, PetCo, Publix, Sam's Club/gas, Sears/auto, Staples, Sweetbay Foods, Target, Tire Kingdom, Tires+, Verizon, Walgreens, Walmart (2mi), vet, S 📣 Coastal, RaceTrac/dsl, 7-11, Sunoco/dsl, 🍴 Bob Evans, Burger King, Denny's, LJ Silver, McDonald's, Popeye's, Waffle House, 🛏 Howard Johnson, Motel 6, ⊙🅷 AutoZone, Beall's, Chrysler/Dodge, Family$, Home Depot, NAPA, U-Haul
31	FL 539, to Kathleen, Lakeland, N 📣 Shell/Circle K, 🍴 Romeo's Pizza, Suwbay, Wendy's, ⊙ Publix/dsl, Walgreens, S hist dist
28	FL 546, to US 92, Memorial Blvd, Lakeland, S 📣 Shell/Circle K/dsl, Sunoco, 🍴 Hardee's
27	FL 570 E toll, Lakeland
25	County Line Rd, S 📣 Citgo/dsl, Shell/Circle K/Subway, 🍴 McDonald's, Wendy's, 🛏 Fairfield Inn, ⊙ FL Air Museum
22	FL 553, Park Rd, Plant City, N ⊙ Chevrolet, S 📣 Shell/Circle K/Subway, 🍴 Arby's, Burger King, Denny's, Popeye's, 🛏 Comfort Inn, Holiday Inn Express
21	FL 39, Alexander St, to Zephyrhills, Plant City S on FL 39 📣 BP/dsl, Shell/dsl, 🛏 Days Inn, Red Rose Inn/rest.
19	FL 566, to Thonotosassa, N 📣 BP, S 📣 RaceTrac/dsl, 🍴 Applebee's, BuddyFreddy's Rest., Carrabba's, Lin's Chinese, Little Caesars, McDonald's, Mi Casa, OutBack Steaks, Pizza Hut/Taco Bell, Sonny's BBQ, Starbucks, Subway, Waffle House, ⊙🅷 AT&T, $General, Publix, Walgreens
17	Branch Forbes Rd, N 📣 Marathon, Sunoco, ⊙ Dinosaur

Exit	Services
17	Continued
	World, S 📣 BP, Shell/Circle K/Subway/dsl, ⊙ Advance Parts, AutoZone
14	McIntosh Rd, N 📣 BP/dsl, ⊙ Longview RV Ctr, Windward RV Park (2mi), S 📣 RaceWay/dsl, 7-11/dsl, 🍴 Burger King, McDonald's/playplace, ⊙ Bates RV Ctr, East Tampa RV Park
12mm	weigh sta both lanes
10	rd 579, Mango, Thonotosassa, N 📣 ⏻FLYING J/Denny's/dsl/LP/scales/24hr, Sunoco, TA/Arby's/Popeye's/dsl/scales/24hr/@, 🍴 Bob Evans, Cracker Barrel, 🛏 Country Inn&Suites, Hampton Inn, ⊙ Camping World RV Ctr, Ford/Lincoln, Hillsboro River SP, Lazy Day's RV Ctr, Rally RV Park, S 📣 Shell/Circle K/dsl, 🍴 Hardee's, Subway, Wendy's, 🛏 Masters Inn
9	I-75, N to Ocala, S to Naples
7	US 92W, to US 301, Hillsborough Ave, N 📣 Chevron/dsl, Mobil, 🍴 Waffle House, ⊙ Knights Inn, ⊙ Hard Rock Hotel/casino, S 📣 BP, Citgo, Hess/Dunkin Donuts/Quiznos, 🍴 5 Guys Burgers, WingHouse, 🛏 Comfort Suites, Holiday Inn Express, La Quinta, Red Roof Inn, ⊙ FL Expo Fair
6	Orient Rd (from eb)
5	FL 574, MLK Blvd, N 🍴 McDonald's, ⊙ truck/rv wash, S 📣 BP, Mobil, Sunoco/Subway, 🍴 Wendy's, 🛏 Fairfield Inn, ⊙ Kenworth
3	US 41, 50th St, Columbus Dr (exits left from eb), N 📣 Chevron/dsl, Shell/Subway/dsl, 🛏 Best Value Inn, Days Inn, Quality Inn, ⊙ to Busch Gardens, S 📣 Sunoco/dsl, 🍴 Checkers, Church's, KFC, McDonald's, Salem's Subs, Subway, Taco Bell, 🛏 Howard Johnson, ⊙ Urgent Care, Advance Parts, Family$, Save-A-Lot, Sweetbay Foods
1	FL 585, 22nd, 21st St, Port of Tampa, S 📣 Sunoco, 🍴 Burger King, McDonald's, ⊙ museum
0mm	I-4 begins/ends on I-275, exit 45b.

◀E INTERSTATE 10

Exit	Services
363mm	I-10 begins/ends on I-95, exit 351b.
362	Stockton St, to Riverside, S 📣 BP, Gate, ⊙🅷
361	US 17 S (from wb), S 📣 BP, Gate
360	FL 129, McDuff Ave, S 📣 BP, 🍴 Popeye's
359	Luna St, to Lenox Ave (from wb)
358	FL 111, Cassat Ave, N 📣 Hess/Godfather's/Quiznos/dsl, Shell/Subway/dsl, 🍴 Burger King, McDonald's, Popeye's, Wendy's, ⊙ AutoZone, Mr Transmission, S 📣 BP, RaceWay/dsl, 🍴 Baskin-Robbins/Dunkin Donuts, Domino's, Gorgi's BBQ, Pizza Hut, Taco Bell, Wendy's, ⊙ Advance Parts, Discount Tire, Lowe's, Walgreens
357	FL 103, Lane Ave, N 📣 Hess/dsl, 🍴 Andy's Sandwiches, 🛏 Knights Inn, Stars Rest Inn, S 📣 BP, Shell/dsl, 🍴 Applebee's, Cross Creek Steaks, Hardee's, KFC, Lee's Dragon, McDonald's, Piccadilly's, 🛏 Diamond Inn, Executive Inn, Sleep Inn, ⊙ Carquest, CVS Drug, Firestone/auto, Home Depot, Office Depot, PepBoys
356	I-295, N to Savannah, S to St Augustine
355	Marietta, N 📣 Exxon, S 📣 Hess/Dunkin Donuts/Godfather's/Quiznos/dsl, Shell/dsl, 🍴 Domino's
351	FL 115, Chaffee Rd, to Cecil Fields, N 📣 Kangaroo/dsl, ⊙ Rivers RV Ctr, S 📣 Chevron, KwikChek, Shell/Subway/dsl, 🍴 Cracker Barrel, King Wok, McDonald's, Mr Chubby's Wings, Perard's Italian, Wendy's, 🛏 Best Western, Fairfield Inn, Hampton Inn, Holiday Inn Express, ⊙

Vertical side labels: LAKELAND | MANGO | TAMPA | JACKSONVILLE | FL

INTERSTATE 10 CONT'D

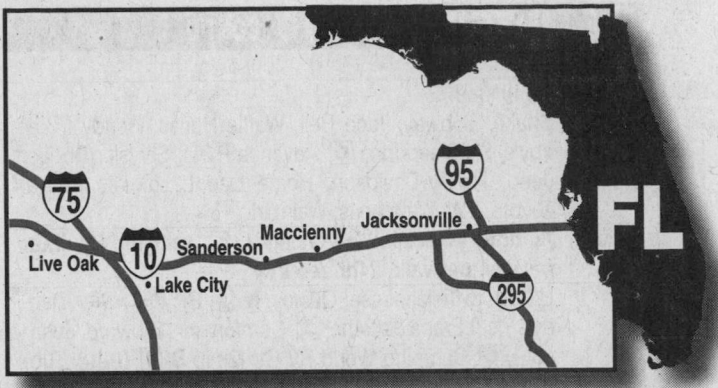

Exit	Services
351	Continued
	Family$, Winn-Dixie
350	FL 23, Cecil Commerce Ctr Pkwy
343	US 301, to Starke, Baldwin, **S** 🅖 Chevron, 🚚/Subway/dsl/scales/24hr, TA/Shell/Arby's/dsl/scales/24hr/@, 🅕 Burger King, McDonald's, Waffle House, 🏠 Best Western, 🅞 NAPA
336	FL 228, to Maxville, Macclenny, **N** 🅖 Murphy USA/dsl, 🅕 Starbucks, 🅞🅷 Walmart/Subway, fireworks
335	FL 121, to Lake Butler, Macclenny, **N** 🅖 BP/dsl, Kangaroo, 🅕 China Dragon, Crystal River Seafood, Domino's, Hardee's, KFC, McDonald's, Pier 6, Pizza Hut, Subway, Taco Bell, Waffle House, Wendy's, Woody's BBQ, Zaxby's, 🏠 American Inn, 🅞🅷 Advance Parts, AutoZone, $General, $Tree, Save-A-Lot Foods, Walgreens, Winn-Dixie, Verizon, USPO, repair, **S** 🅖 RaceWay/dsl, Exxon/dsl, 🅕 Burger King, China Buffet, San Jose Mexican, 🏠 EconoLodge, Travelodge
333	rd 125, Glen Saint Mary, **N** 🅖 Citgo/dsl/24hr
327	rd 229, to Raiford, Sanderson, **1 mi N** gas
324	US 90, to Olustee, Sanderson, **S** 🅖 Citgo/dsl, to Olustee Bfd, Osceola NF
318mm	🆁🆂 both lanes, full ♿ facilities, 🅒, vending, 🗑, litter barrels, petwalk, 24hr security
303	US 441, Lake City, to Fargo, **N** 🅖 Chevron/dsl, 🅞 Lake City Camping (1mi), Oaks'n Pines RV Park, **S** 🅖 Shell/dsl, Sunoco/dsl, 🅕 Huddle House, 🏠 Days Inn, 🅞🅷
301	US 41, to Lake City, **N** 🅖 Busy Bee/dsl, 🅞 to Stephen Foster Ctr, **S** 🅞🅷
296b a	I-75, N to Valdosta, S to Tampa
294mm	🆁🆂 both lanes, full ♿ facilities, 🅒, vending, 🗑, litter barrels, petwalk, 24hr security
292	rd 137, to Wellborn
283	US 129, to Live Oak, **N** 🅖 Penn/dsl, to Boys Ranch, **S** 🅖 BP, Chevron/dsl, Exxon/dsl, Murphy USA/dsl, Shell/dsl, 🅕 China Buffet, Huddle House, Krystal, McDonald's, Subway, Taco Bell, Waffle House, Wendy's, Zaxby's, 🏠 Best Western, EconoLodge, Holiday Inn Express, 🅞🅷 $Tree, Lowe's, Verizon, Walmart
275	US 90, Live Oak, **N** to Suwannee River SP, **S** 🅞🅷
271mm	truck insp sta both lanes
269mm	Suwannee River
265mm	🆁🆂 both lanes, full ♿ facilities, 🅒, vending, 🗑, litter barrels, petwalk, 24hr security
264mm	weigh sta both lanes
262	rd 255, Lee, **N** to Suwannee River SP, **S** 🅖 Jimmy's/Chevron/Red Onion Grill/dsl/scales/24hr/@, 🅛Loves/Arby's/dsl/scales/24hr
258	FL 53, **N** 🅖 Chevron/McDonald's/dsl, Mobil/DQ/Subway/Wendy's/dsl/scales/24hr, 🅕 Denny's, Waffle House, 🏠 Best Western, Days Inn, Super 8, 🅞🅷, **S** 🏠 Deerwood Inn, 🅞 Jellystone Camping, Madison Camping
251	FL 14, to Madison, **N** 🅖 Mobil/Arby's/24hr, 🅞🅷
241	US 221, Greenville, **N** 🅖 Mobil/DQ
234mm	🆁🆂 both lanes, full ♿ facilities, 🅒, 🗑, litter barrels, petwalk, 24hr security
233	rd 257, Aucilla, **N** 🅖 Shell/dsl
225	US 19, to Monticello, **N** 🅞 Camper's World Camping, **S** 🅖 BP, Chevron/McDonald's/dsl, Mobil/Arby's/dsl, Sunoco/dsl, 🅕 Huddle House, 🏠 Days Inn, Super 8, 🅞 A
225	Continued
	Stones Throw RV Park, KOA, dogtrack
217	FL 59, Lloyd, **S** 🅖 BP/rest/dsl/scales/24hr, Shell/Subway/dsl, 🏠 EconoLodge, 🅞 truckwash
209b a	US 90, Tallahassee, **N** 🏠 Staybrige Suites, **S** 🅖 Circle K/dsl, Shell/Subway/dsl, 🅕 Eastern Chinese, Waffle House, 🏠 Best Western, Country Inn&Suites, 🅞 Publix, Tallahassee RV Park, auto museum
203	FL 61, US 319, Tallahassee, **N** 🅖 BP/dsl, Shell/Circle K, USA, 🅕 Applebee's, Baskin-Robbins/Dunkin Donuts, Bonefish Grill, Firehouse Subs, 5 Guys Burgers, Genghis Grill, Jimmy John's, McDonald's, Moe's SW Grill, Panda Buffet, Panera Bread, Popeye's, Sonny's BBQ, Starbucks, Subway, Taco Bell, Waffle House, Wendy's, 🅞 AT&T, Books-A-Million, CVS Drug, Discount Tire, $Tree, Fresh Mkt Foods, GNC, Hobby Lobby, Publix, Radio Shack, SteinMart, SuperLube, TJ Maxx, Walgreens, Walmart (3mi), **S** 🅖 BP, Citgo, 🅕 Calico Jack's Oyster Bar, Carrabba's, Chick-fil-A, Los Amigos, McDonald's, Osaka Japanese, Outback Steaks, Steak'n Shake, Subway, Ted's MT Grill, TGIFriday's, Village Inn, Zaxby's, 🏠 Cabot Lodge, Courtyard, Hampton Inn, Hilton Garden, Residence Inn, Sheraton, Studio+, 🅞🅷 Urgent Care, Advance Parts, Goodyear/auto, Home Depot, Infiniti, Office Depot, Petsmart, U-Haul, vet
199	US 27, Tallahassee, **N** 🅖 Chevron/dsl, Kangaroo/dsl, McKenzie/dsl, 🅕 Burger King, Domino's, McDonald's, Papa John's, Pizza Hut, Subway, Taco Bell, Waffle House, 🏠 Baymont Inn, Country Inn&Suites, Days Inn, Fairfield Inn, Holiday Inn, Microtel, Quality Inn, 🅞 Ace Hardware, Advance Parts, Big Oak RV Park (2mi), CVS Drug, $General, Family$, Walgreens, Walmart, Winn-Dixie, USPO, vet, **S** 🅖 Chevron/dsl, Shell/Circle K, USA/dsl, 🅕 Arby's, Boston Mkt, Chick-fil-A, China Buffet, Chuck-ECheese, Cracker Barrel, Crystal River Seafood, DQ, Denny's, El Jalisco, Firehouse Subs, Golden Corral, Hooters, IHOP, Julie's Rest, Kacey's Rest, KFC, Krispy Kreme, Little Caesars, Longhorn Steaks, McDonald's, Melting Pot, Ole Times Buffet, On-the-Border, Papa John's, Red Lobster, Shoney's, Sonic, Sonny's BBQ, Starbucks, Subway, TCBY, Whataburger, Wendy's, Zaxby's, 🏠 Best Value Inn, EconoLodge, Guesthouse Inn, Howard Johnson, La Quinta, Red Roof Inn, Rodeway Inn, Super 8, 🅞 Advance Parts, AT&T, AutoZone, Barnes&Noble, Belk, CVS Drug, $Tree, PepBoys, Publix, Staples, Sun Tire, Tuffy Auto, U-Haul, Verizon, Walgreens, city park, vet
196	FL 263, Tallahassee, **S** 🅖 Chevron/dsl, Inland/dsl, Shell/dsl, Stop'n Save Gas, 🅕 Applebee's, Checker's, Dunkin Donuts, Firehouse Subs, KFC, McDonald's, Sonic, Steak'n

FL

QUINCY

➤ INTERSTATE 10 CONT'D

Exit	Services
196	Continued Shake, Subway, Taco Bell, Waffle House, Wendy's, Zaxby's, 🏠 Sleep Inn, ⊙ Advance Parts, Chrysler/Dodge/Jeep, Harley-Davidson, Home Depot, Lowe's, Mazda, Toyota, VW, Walgreens, Walmart, 🔧
194mm	🅁🆂 both lanes, full ♿ facilities, 🚰 vending, 🗑 litter barrels, petwalk, 24hr security
192	US 90, to Tallahassee, Quincy, N ⛽ BP, ⚜FLYING J/Denny's/dsl/LP/scales/24hr, 🏠 Comfort Inn, Howard Johnson, ⊙ Camping World RV Ctr (2mi), S ⛽ 🅻🅾🆅🅴🆂/Subway/dsl/scales/24hr, 🍴 Waffle House, 🏠 Best Western
181	FL 267, Quincy, 1 mi N ⛽ Murphy USA/dsl, 🍴 Domino's, Mayflower Chinese, ⊙ H,Walmart, S ⛽ BP/dsl, Pure, 🏠 Hampton Inn, Holiday Inn Express, Parkway Inn, to Lake Talquin SF
174	FL 12, to Greensboro, N ⛽ BP/dsl, Shell/Burger King/dsl
166	rd 270A, Chattahoochee, N to Lake Seminole, to Torreya SP, S ⛽ Shell/dsl, ⊙ KOA (1mi)
161mm	🅁🆂 both lanes, full ♿ facilities, 🚰 vending, 🗑 litter barrels, petwalk, 24hr security
160mm	Apalachicola River, central/eastern time zone
158	rd 286, Sneads, N Lake Seminole, to Three Rivers SP
155mm	weigh sta both lanes
152	FL 69, to Grand Ridge, Blountstown, N ⛽ BP, Exxon/dsl
142	FL 71, to Marianna, Oakdale, N ⛽ Murphy USA/dsl, 🅻🅾🆅🅴🆂/Arby's/dsl/scales/24hr, 🍴 Beef'O'Brady's, Burger King, Firehouse Subs, Hong Kong Chinese, KFC, Pizza Hut, PoFolks, Ruby Tuesday, San Marco's Mexican, Sonny's BBQ, Waffle House, 🏠 American Inn, Comfort Inn, Days Inn, Fairfield Inn, Marianna Inn, Microtel, Quality Inn, Super 8, ⊙ H, AT&T, $Tree, Lowe's, Verizon, Walmart/Subway, to FL Caverns SP (8mi), S ⛽ Chevron/dsl, Sunoco/dsl, TA/Pizza Hut/Popeye's/Taco Bell/dsl/scales/24hr/@, 🍴 DQ, McDonald's, 🏠 Best Value Inn, ⊙ Dove Rest RV Park
136	FL 276, to Marianna, N ⊙ to FL Caverns SP (8mi)
133mm	🅁🆂 both lanes, full ♿ facilities, 🚰 🗑 litter barrels, petwalk, 24hr security
130	US 231, Cottondale, N ⛽ BP/dsl, Chevron, 🍴 Hardee's, Subway, S ⛽ 🄻oves/Chester's/McDonald's/dsl/scales/24hr/@, RaceWay/dsl

CHIPLEY

Exit	Services
120	FL 77, to Panama City, Chipley, N ⛽ BP/dsl, Exxon/Burger King/Stuckey's, Murphy USA/dsl, Shell/dsl, 🍴 Arby's, Cancun Mexican, Hardee's, Hungry Howie's, Jin-Jin Chinese, KFC, McDonald's, Pizza Hut, Sonic, Subway, Waffle House, Wendy's, 🏠 Comfort Inn, Days Inn/rest., Executive Inn, Quality Inn, Super 8, ⊙ H, Advance Parts, $General, $Tree, NAPA, O'Reilly Parts, Save-A-Lot Foods, Verizon, Walmart, S Falling Water SP
112	FL 79, Bonifay, N ⛽ Chevron, Citgo/Tom Thumb/dsl, Exxon/dsl, 🍴 Burger King, Hardee's, Hungry Howie, McDonald's, Pizza Hut, Simbo's Rest, Subway, Waffle House, 🏠 Bonifay Inn, Economy Lodge, Holiday Inn Express, Tivoli Inn, ⊙ H, FL Springs RV Camping, Fred's, repair, S Panama City Beach
104	rd 279, Caryville
96	FL 81, Ponce de Leon, N ⊙ $General, to Ponce de Leon SRA, Vortex Spring Camping (5mi), S ⛽ BP/dsl, 87 Depot/Subway/dsl, Exxon/dsl, ⊙ Ponce de Leon Motel, 🅁🆂 both lanes, full ♿ facilities, 🚰, 🗑 litter barrels, petwalk, 24hr security

CRESTVIEW

Exit	Services
85	US 331, De Funiak Springs, N ⛽ Chevron/dsl, Murphy USA/dsl, 🍴 Arby's, Beef O'Brady's, Burger King, Hungry Howie's, McLain's Steaks, Pizza Hut, Sonic, Subway, Waffle House, 🏠 Best Value Inn, Regency Inn, Sundown Inn, Super 8, ⊙ H, AT&T, $General, $Tree, Lowe's, Verizon, Walgreens, Walmart, Winn-Dixie, winery, S ⛽ BP, 87 Depot/dsl, Emerald Express/dsl, 🍴 KFC, McDonald's, Whataburger, 🏠 Best Western, ⊙ H, camping (3mi)
70	FL 285, to Ft Walton Bch, Eglin AFB, N ⛽ RaceWay/dsl, S 🏠 Rodeway Inn, ⊙ Dixie RV Ctr, repair
60mm	🅁🆂 both lanes, full ♿ facilities, 🚰 vending, 🗑 litter barrels, petwalk, 24hr security
56	FL 85, Crestview, Eglin AFB, N ⛽ BP/dsl, Mobil/Chester's/dsl, 🍴 Applebee's, Beef O'Brady's, Burger King, Capt D's, Chill Frozen Yogurt, China 1, Dunkin Donuts, Golden Asian, Hungry Howie's, Hunon Chinese, Lenny's Subs, McDonald's, Mia's Italian, Ryan's, Sonic, Starbucks, Steve&Joe's Diner, Taco Bell, 🏠 Country Inn&Suites, EconoLodge, ⊙ H, Urgent Care, Advance Parts, AT&T, AutoZone, BigLots, $General, GNC, Lowe's, Publix, Radio Shack, Staples, Verizon, Walgreens, Walmart, S ⛽ Citgo/Tom Thumb/dsl, Exxon/dsl, 🍴 Arby's, Coach-n-Four Steaks, Cracker Barrel, Hardee's, Hooters, LaRumba Mexican, Waffle House, Wendy's, Whataburger, 🏠 Baymont Inn, Best Value Inn, Comfort Inn, Hampton Inn, Holiday Inn Express, Jameson Inn, Rodeway Inn, Super 8, ⊙ Buick/GMC, Chevrolet, Ford, museum, RV camping
45	rd 189, to US 90, Holt, N ⛽ Chevron (1mi), ⊙ to Blackwater River SP, Eagle's Landing RV Park, S River's Edge RV Park (1mi)
31	FL 87, to Ft Walton Beach, Milton, N ⛽ Exxon/dsl, 🍴 Waffle House, 🏠 Holiday Inn Express, ⊙ Blackwater River SP, KOA, S ⛽ BP, Shell/dsl, 🏠 Comfort Inn, Red Carpet Inn
31mm	🅁🆂 both lanes, full ♿ facilities, 🚰, 🗑 litter barrels, petwalk, 24hr security
28	rd 89, Milton, N H
27mm	Blackwater River
26	rd 191, Bagdad, Milton, N ⛽ Shell/Circle K/dsl, ⊙ H, $General, S ⛽ Chevron/DQ/Stuckey's, ⊙ Pelican Palms RV Park
22	N FL 281, Avalon Blvd, N ⛽ RaceWay/dsl, Tom Thumb, 🍴 Capt Pete's Oyster House, McDonald's, S ⛽ Shell/Circle K/Subway/dsl, 🍴 Waffle House, 🏠 Red Roof Inn, ⊙ Avalon Landing RV Park (3mi)
18mm	Escambia Bay
17	US 90, Pensacola, N ⛽ BP/dsl, S ⛽ Exxon/DQ, 🏠 Quality Inn/rest.
14mm	truck inspection sta

PENSACOLA

Exit	Services
13	FL 291, to US 90, Pensacola, N ⛽ BP, Exxon, Shell/dsl, 🍴 Arby's, Capt D's, Denny's, DQ, La Hacienda Mexican, McDonald's, Santino's Cafe, Subway, Taco Bell, Waffle House, 🏠 Comfort Inn, Holiday Inn, La Quinta, Motel 6, Villager Lodge, ⊙ CVS Drug, $Tree, Food World, Ross, U-Haul, Walgreens, S 🍴 ChuckECheese, Fazoli's, HoneyBaked Ham, Los Rancheros Mexican, Shrimp Basket Rest, Waffle House, Wendy's, Whataburger, 🏠 Baymont Inn, Best Value Inn, Courtyard, Extended Stay America, Fairfield Inn, Hampton Inn, Mainstay Suites, Red Roof Inn, Super 6 Inn, TownePlace Suites, ⊙ H, Belk, Books-A-Million, $General, Firestone/auto, Hobby Lobby, JC Penney, Jo-Ann Fabrics, PepBoys, Petsmart, Radio Shack, Sears/auto, TJ Maxx, U-Haul

INTERSTATE 10 CONT'D

Exit	Services
12	I-110, to Pensacola Hist Dist, Islands Nat Seashore
10b a	US 29, Pensacola, **N** 🅰 Kangaroo/dsl/scales, Murphy USA/dsl, 🍴 Church's, Hardee's, Ryan's, Sonic, Vallarta Mexican, Waffle House, 🅾 Advance Parts, AT&T, AutoZone, Carpenter's RV Ctr, $Tree, GNC, Office Depot, O'Reilly Parts, Radio Shack, Tires+, Walmart, **0-2 mi S** 🅰 RaceWay/dsl, Shell/Circle K, Tom Thumb, 🍴 Burger King, Capt D's, Founaris Bro's Greek, IHOP, McDonald's, Pizza Hut, Ruby Tuesday, Smokey's BBQ, Waffle House, Wendy's, Whataburger, 🏠 Best Value Inn, Days Inn, Executive Inn, Howard Johnson, Key West Inn, Luxury Suites, Motel 6, Pensacola Inn, Quality Inn, Ramada Inn, Travelodge, 🅾 Buick/Cadillac/GMC, Chevrolet, Dodge/Jeep, Ford, Harley-Davidson, Honda, Hyundai, Kia, Lincoln, Mazda, NAPA, Nissan, Subaru, Suzuki, Toyota/Scion, funpark
7b a	Fl 297, Pine Forest Rd, **N** 🅰 Chevron, 🍴 Beef'O'Brady's, Starbucks, Wendy's, 🏠 Best Western, Comfort Inn, Garden Inn, Value Place, 🅾 Publix, Tall Oaks Camping, transmissions, **S** 🅰 BP, Raceway/dsl, Tom Thumb, 🍴 Burger King, Cracker Barrel, Figaro's Pizza, Hardee's, McDonald's, Ruby Tuesday, Sonny's BBQ, Subway, Waffle House, Wayne's Diner, 🏠 Country Inn&Suites, Holiday Inn Express, Microtel, Quality Inn, Red Roof Inn, 🅾 Food World/24hr, Big Lagoon SRA (12mi), museum
5	US 90 A, **N** 🅰 Kangaroo/Subway/dsl, Shell/Circle K, 🍴 Beef'O Brady's, Hershey's Ice Cream, Starbucks, Wendy's, 🅾 AT&T, Publix/gas, Walgreens, **S** Leisure Lakes Camping
4mm	Welcome Ctr eb, full 🅱 facilities, info, 🅲 vending, 🆁, litter barrels, petwalk, wi-fi, 24hr security
3mm	weigh sta both lanes
1mm	inspection sta eb
0mm	Florida/Alabama state line, Perdido River

INTERSTATE 75

Exit	Services
471mm	Florida/Georgia state line. Motorist callboxes begin sb.
469mm	Welcome Ctr sb, full 🅱 facilities, info, 🅲 vending, 🆁, litter barrels, petwalk
467	FL 143, Jennings, **E** 🅾 Budget Lodge, **W** 🅰 Exxon/dsl, 🏠 Jennings House Inn, N Florida Inn, 🅾 Jennings Camping, fireworks
460	FL 6, Jasper, **E** 🅰 BP/Burger King, Indian River Fruit/gas, Penn Oil/Huddle House/dsl, 🏠 7 Oaks Inn, **W** 🅰 Shell/dsl, Sunoco/dsl, 🍴 Sheffield's Country Kitchen, 🏠 Scottish Inn, 🅾 Suwanee River SP
451	US 129, Jasper, Live Oak, **E** 🅰 Loves/Arby's/dsl/scales/24hr, Mobil/DQ/Subway/dsl, **W** 🅰 BP/Lester's Grill/dsl, 🅾 Suwanee Music Park (4mi), to FL Boys Ranch
448mm	weigh sta both lanes
446mm	insp sta both lanes
443mm	Historic Suwanee River
439	to FL 136, White Springs, Live Oak, **E** 🅰 Gate/dsl/e-85, Shell/dsl, 🍴 McDonald's, 🅾 Lee's Camping (3mi), Suwanee RV Camping (4mi), to S Foster Ctr, **W** 🏠 Best Value Inn
435	I-10, E to Jacksonville, W to Tallahassee
427	US 90, to Live Oak, Lake City, **E** 🅰 BP/dsl, Chevron/dsl, Exxon, Gas'n Go, Murphy USA/dsl, Shell/dsl, 🍴 Applebee's, Arby's, Burger King, Cedar River Seafood,
427	Continued Cracker Barrel, Domino's, Elliano's Coffee, El Potro, Firehouse Subs, Hardee's, Gondolier Italian, IHOP, Ken's BBQ, Krystal, McDonald's, Moe's SW Grill, Ole Times Buffet, Papa John's, Pizza Hut, Player's Club, Red Lobster, Ruby Tuesday, Sonny's BBQ, Starbucks, Steak'n Shake, Subway, Taco Bell, TX Roadhouse, Waffle House, Wasabi, Wendy's, Zaxby's, 🏠 Best Inn, Budget Inn, Cypress Inn, Days Inn, Driftwood Inn, Holiday Inn, Jameson Inn, Piney Woods Motel, Ramada Ltd, Rodeway Inn, Scottish Inn, 🅾 Ⓗ, Advance Parts, AT&T, AutoZone, Belk, BigLots, CVS Drug, Ford/Lincoln, Home Depot, Inn&Out RV Park, JC Penney, Kia, Lowe's, Petsmart, Publix, Radio Shack, Tire Kingdom, TireMart, TJ Maxx, Toyota/Scion, Verizon, Walgreens, Walmart, mall, **W** 🅰 BP, Chevron/dsl, Shell, Sunoco, 🍴 Bob Evans, China One, Waffle House, 🏠 Best Western, Best Value Inn, Cabot Lodge, Comfort Suites, Country Inn&Suites, EconoLodge, Fairfield Inn, Gateway Inn, Hampton Inn, Red Roof Inn, Travelodge, 🅾 Cadillac/Chevrolet, Camping World RV Ctr, Carquest, Chrysler/Dodge/Jeep, $General, Family$, Harvey's Foods, Nissan, vet
423	FL 47, to Ft White, Lake City, **E** 🅰 Shell/dsl, 🅾 Mack/Volvo Trucks, **W** 🅰 BP/dsl, Exxon/dsl, Stop-N-Go/USPO, 🍴 Little Caesars, Subway, 🏠 Motel 8, Super 8, 🅾 Casey Jones RV Park, $General, Freightliner
414	US 41, US 441, to Lake City, High Springs, **E** 🅰 Chevron/dsl, Exxon, Pitstop, 🏠 Traveler's Inn, Travelodge, **W** 🅰 BP/dsl, Shell/Wendy's/dsl, 🍴 Subway, 🅾 antiques, tires/repair, to O'Leno SP (5 mi)
413mm	🆁🆂 both lanes, full 🅱 facilities, 🅲, vending, 🆁, litter barrels, petwalk, 24hr security
409mm	Santa Fe River
404	rd 236, to High Springs, **E** 🅰 Chevron/fruits/gifts, Citgo/dsl, Sunoco, **W** High Springs Camping
399	US 441, to High Sprs, Alachua, **E** 🅰 BP, Kangaroo, 🍴 Domino's, McDonald's, Moe's SW Grill, Pizza Hut, Sonny's BBQ, Subway, Taco Bell, Waffle House, 🏠 EconoLodge, Quality Inn, 🅾 Advance Parts, AT&T, CVS Drug, $General, Family$, Hitchcock's Foods, Lowe's, Traveler's Campground (1mi), Walgreens, vet, **W** 🅰 Chevron, Kangaroo/Wendy's, Mobil/PizzaVito/dsl, 🍴 KFC, Mason's Grill, 🏠 Best Value Inn, Royal Inn
390	FL 222, to Gainesville, **E** 🅰 Chevron/dsl, Kangaroo/Subway/dsl, Marathon/McDonald's/dsl, 🍴 Burger King, La Fiesta Mexican, Pomodoro Cafe, Sonny's BBQ, Wendy's, 🅾 Publix, Walgreens, **W** 🅰 BP/DQ/Dunkin Donuts/dsl, 🏠 Best Western, 🅾 Harley-Davidson, vet
387	FL 26, to Newberry, Gainesville, **E** 🅰 BP, Chevron/dsl,

🅖 = gas 🍴 = food 🛏 = lodging 🅞 = other 🆁🆂 = rest stop   Copyright 2014 - The Next Exit ®

↑N INTERSTATE 75 CONT'D

Exit	Services
387	Continued

GAINESVILLE

Sunoco, Shell/dsl, 🍴 BJ's Rest., Bono's BBQ, Boston Mkt, Burger King, Dunkin Donuts, FoodCourt, Honey-Baked Ham, Jason's Deli, LJ Silver, Macaroni Grill, McAlister's Deli, McDonald's, Mr Tequila's Grill, Perkins, Red Lobster, Ruby Tuesday, Starbucks, Subway, Wendy's, 🛏 La Quinta, 🅞🅷 Belk, Books-A-Million, Dillard's, JC Penney, Macy's, Office Depot, PetCo, Sears/auto, SteinMart, Verizon, to UF, mall, **W** 🅖 BP, Chevron/dsl, Exxon/dsl, Marathon/dsl, 🍴 Asian Cafe, El Norteno's Mexican, Hardee's, Krystal, Moe's SW Grill, Napolatanos Rest., Pizza Hut, Taco Bell, Waffle House, 🛏 Baymont Inn, Days Inn, EconoLodge, Gainesville Hotel, 🅞 Advance Parts, $Tree, Goodyear/auto, Home Depot, Jo-Ann Fabrics, K-Mart, PepBoys, Publix, TJ Maxx, Walgreens, tires/repair, vet

384 FL 24, to Archer, Gainesville, **E** 🅖 Chevron/dsl, Exxon/dsl, Shell, 🍴 Arby's, Asian Wok, Backyard Burger, BoneFish Grill, Burger King, Checkers, Chick-fil-A, Chili's, Chipotle Mexican, Chuy's Mexican, CiCi's Pizza, Cody's Roadhouse, Coldstone, DQ, Dunkin Donuts, Firehouse Subs, 5 Guys Burgers, Gainesville Alehouse, Genghis Grill, KFC, McAlister's Deli, McDonald's, Moe's SW Grill, Olive Garden, Outback Steaks, Panera Bread, Papa John's, Pizza Hut, Sonny's BBQ, Starbucks, Steak'n Shake, Subway, Taco Bell, TX Roadhouse, TGIFriday's, Tijuana Flats, Waffle House, Wendy's, Willy's Mexican Grill, Wing House, Zaxby's, 🛏 Cabot Lodge, Comfort Inn, Courtyard, Extended Stay America, Hampton Inn, Hilton Garden, Homewood Suites, Motel 6, Red Roof Inn, Residence Inn, Sleep Inn, SpringHill Suites, Super 8, 🅞 Barnes&Noble, Best Buy, CarQuest, CVS Drug, Discount Tire, $Tree, Firestone/auto, GNC, Kohl's, Lowe's, Michael's, Old Navy, Petsmart, Publix, Radio Shack, Ross, Target, Tuffy Auto, Verizon, Walgreens, Walmart, **W** 🅖 Marathon/dsl, 🍴 Cracker Barrel, 🛏 Country Inn&Suites, Holiday Inn Express, 🅞 Sunshine RV Park, to Bear Museum

382 FL 121, to Williston, Gainesville, **E** 🅖 Marathon/dsl, Mobil/dsl, 🍴 1st Wok, Little Caesars, McDonald's, Subway, 🅞 Publix, USPO, **W** 🅖 BP/dsl, Chevron/dsl, Kangaroo/dsl, 🍴 43rd St Deli, 🛏 Quality Inn, Rodeway Inn, ValuePlace, 🅞 Fred Bear Museum

381mm 🆁🆂 both lanes, full ♿ facilities, 🅲, vending, 🗑, litter barrels, petwalk, 24hr security

374 rd 234, Micanopy, **E** 🅖 BP, Chevron/dsl, 🅞 antiques, to Paynes Prairie SP, **W** 🛏 Micanopy Inn, 🅞 repair

368 rd 318, Orange Lake, **E** 🅖 Chevron, Jim's/BBQ, Petro/BP/Iron Skillet/dsl/scales/24hr/@, 🍴 Wendy's, 🅞 Grand Lake RV Park (3mi), **W** Ocala N RV Camping

358 FL 326, **E** 🅖 Marathon/McDonald's/dsl, 🚛/Arby's/dsl/scales/24hr, 🚛/Wendy's/dsl/scales/24hr, Sunoco/FL Citrus Ctr/dsl, 🅞 Freightliner, auto/truck repair, **W** 🅖 Chevron/dsl, ♥Love's/Chester's/Subway/dsl/scales/24hr, 🍴 DQ

354 US 27, to Silver Springs, Ocala, **E** 🅖 BP/dsl, RaceTrac/dsl, 🍴 Burger King, Rascal's BBQ, 🛏 Golden Palms Inn, **W** 🅖 BP/dsl, Chevron/dsl, Shell/dsl, 🍴 Blanca's Cafe, China Taste, McDonald's, Roma Rest., Subway, Swampy's Grill, 🛏 Budget Host, Comfort Suites, Days Inn, Howard Johnson, Ramada, 🅞 AT&T, $General, Family$, GNC,

OCALA

354 Continued
Nelson's Trailers, Oaktree Village Camping, Publix, Walgreens, Winn-Dixie

352 FL 40, to Silver Springs, Ocala, **E** 🅖 Chevron, Mobil/dsl, RaceTrac/dsl, Sunoco/dsl, 🍴 Dunkin Donuts, McDonald's, Pizza Hut/Taco Bell, Subway, Wendy's, Zaxby's, 🛏 Amadeus Inn, Days Inn/café, Economy Inn, Motor Inn/RV, 🅞 Family$, to Silver River SP (8mi), **W** 🅖 Shell/dsl, Texaco/dsl, 🍴 Denny's, Golden Coast Buffet, Waffle House, 🛏 Red Roof Inn, Super 8, Travelodge, 🅞 Gander Mtn, Holiday Trav-L Park

350 FL 200, to Hernando, Ocala, **0-2 mi E** 🅖 BP/dsl, Citgo/dsl, Texaco/dsl, 🍴 Applebee's, Arby's, Bob Evans, Boston Mkt, Burger King, Carrabba's, Checkers, Chick-fil-A, Chili's, ChuckECheese, City Buffet, Cody's Roadhouse, Coldstone, Crispers, Domino's, El Toreo Mexican, Firehouse Subs, 5 Guys Burgers, Golden Corral, Guadalajara Mexican, Hardee's, House of Japan, Krystal, Lee's Chicken, Logan's Roadhouse, McDonald's, Moe's SW Grill, Ocean Buffet, Olive Garden, Outback Steaks, Papa John's, Panera Bread, Red Lobster, Ruby Tuesday, Shane's Rib Shack, Smoothie King, Starbucks, Sonic, Sonny's BBQ, Stevie B's Pizza, Subway, Taco Bell, Wendy's, Zaxby's, 🛏 Country Inn&Suites, Hilton, La Quinta, 🅞🅷 Urgent Care, Acura, Advance Parts, Aldi Foods, Belk, Best Buy, Books-A-Million, Chevrolet, CVS Drug, Discount Tire, $Tree, Goodyear/auto, Hobby Lobby, Home Depot, Honda, Hyundai, JC Penney, Jo-Ann Fabrics, Kia, Lowe's, Macy's, Mazda, Michael's, Nissan, Office Depot, O'Reilly Parts, PepBoys, Petsmart, Publix, Ross, Sears/auto, Staples, SteinMart, Target, Tire Kingdom, TJ Maxx, Toyota, Tuffy Auto, Verizon, Walgreens, Walmart, **W** 🅖 BP/dsl, Chevron, 🍴 Bonefish Grill, Burger King, Cracker Barrel, Dunkin Donuts, KFC, McAlister's Deli, McDonald's, Mimi's Cafe, Panera Bread, Starbucks, Steak'n Shake, Tijuana Flats, Waffle House, Yamato Japanese, 🛏 Best Western, Courtyard, Fairfield Inn, Hampton Inn, Holiday Inn, Homewood Suites, Residence Inn, 🅞🅷 AT&T, Barnes&Noble, BMW, Buick/GMC, Cadillac, Camper Village RV Park, Dick's, Dillard's, Kohl's, Ocala RV Park, Old Navy, PetCo, Porsche, Sam's Club/gas, Tires+, Verizon, VW, Walgreens, vet

346mm 🆁🆂 both lanes, full ♿ facilities, 🅲, vending, 🗑, litter barrels, petwalk, 24hr security

341 rd 484, to Belleview, **E** 🅖 Chevron/fruit, Citgo/Baskin-Robbins/Dunkin Donuts, Exxon/dsl, Shell/dsl, 🍴 Cracker Barrel, KFC/Taco Bell, Sonny's BBQ, Zaxby's, 🛏 Microtel, Sleep Inn, 🅞 FL Citrus Ctr, drag racing museum, **W** 🅖 🚛/DQ/Wendy's/dsl/scales/24hr, 🍴 McDonald's, Subway, Waffle House, 🛏 Hampton Inn, 🅞 Ocala Sun RV Resort, outlets

338mm weigh sta both lanes

329 FL 44, to Inverness, Wildwood, **E** 🅖 Marathon/dsl, Sunoco/DQ, Wilco/Hess/Steak'n Shake/dsl/scales/24hr, 🍴 Burger King, McDonald's, Waffle House, Wendy's, 🅞 FL Citrus Ctr, Wild Wood RV Park, **W** 🅖 Citgo/dsl/repair/24hr, 🚛/dsl/scales/24hr, TA/BP/Pizza Hut/Popeye's/Subway/dsl/scales/24hr/@, 🍴 IHOP, KFC, 🛏 Best Value Inn, Days Inn, Super 8, Villager Lodge, 🅞 truck-wash, truck repair

328 FL TPK (from sb), to Orlando

321 rd 470, to Sumterville, Lake Panasoffkee, **E** 🅖 Spirit/deli/dsl/scales/24hr, 🅞 Coleman Correctional, **W** 🅖 Chevron/7-11/dsl, Mobil/Hardee's/Subway/dsl

INVERNESS

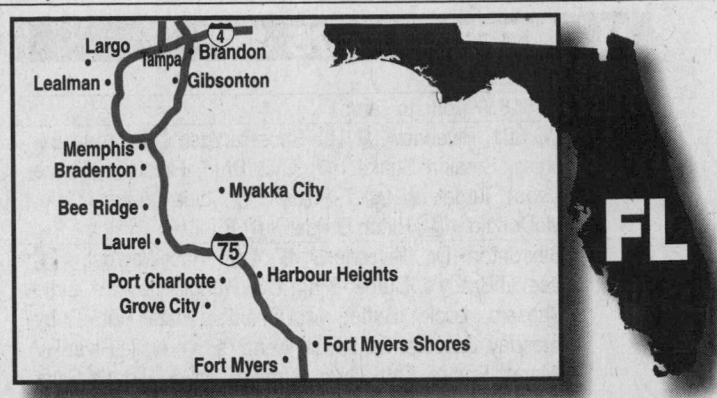

INTERSTATE 75 CONT'D

Exit	Services
314	FL 48, to Bushnell, E 🅟 Citgo, Murphy USA/dsl, Shell/Circle K/Subway, Texaco, 🍴 Hong Kong Chinese, KFC/Taco Bell, McDonald's, Wendy's, 🛏 Rodeway Inn, 🅞 AutoZone, BlueBerry Hill RV Camp, $Tree, Red Oaks Camp (1mi), Verizon, Walmart, vet, to Dade Bfd HS, W 🅟 Shell/dsl, Sunoco/dsl, 🍴 Beef'O'Brady's, Sonny's BBQ, Waffle House, 🛏 Microtel, 🅞 Flagship RV Ctr
309	rd 476, to Webster, E Breezy Oaks RV Park (1mi), Sumter Oaks RV Park (1mi)
307mm	🆁🆂 both lanes, full 🚻 facilities, 🅒 coffee, vending, 🍽 litter barrels, petwalk, 24hr security
301	US 98, FL 50, to Dade City, E 🅟 RaceTrac/dsl, 🍴 Beef'O'Brady's, Cracker Barrel, Denny's, McDonald's, Quinzos, Subway, Waffle House, Wendy's, 🛏 Days Inn, Holiday Inn Express, 🅞 Advance Parts, $General, Tall Pines RV Park, Winn-Dixie, W 🅟 Chevron/dsl, 🍴 Burger King, 🛏 Hampton Inn, Microtel, Quality Inn, 🅞 🅗
293	rd 41, to Dade City, E 🅟 Citgo (2mi), 🅞 to Sertoma Youth Ranch, W 🅞 Travelers Rest Resort RV Park
285	FL 52, to Dade City, New Port Richey, E 🅟 🄵 FLYING J/Denny's/dsl/LP/scales/24hr, 🅞 🅗, Blue Beacon, W 🅟 Citgo/dsl/scales/24hr, 🍴 Waffle House
279	FL 54, to Land O' Lakes, Zephyrhills, E 🅟 Hess/Dunkin Donuts/Godfather's/Quiznos/dsl, 🍴 Applebee's, Burger King, Gonna China, Papa's John's, Pizza Hut/Taco Bell, Sonny's BBQ, Subway, Waffle House, Wendy's, Winner's Grill, 🅞 Ace Hardware, Beall's, Fiat, Ford, Happy Days RV Camping (9mi), Kia, Leasure Days RV Park (7mi), Nissan, Publix, Ralph's RV Camping (7mi), Toyota/Scion, Walgreens, vet, to Hillsborough River SP (18mi), W 🅟 Marathon, Mobil/Dunkin Donuts, 7-11, Shell/Circle K/dsl, 🍴 Beef'O'Brady's, Buffalo's, Cracker Barrel, DQ, Hungry Howie's, Marco's Pizza, McDonald's, Outback Steaks, Remington's Steaks, Shanghai Chinese, 🛏 Best Western, Comfort Inn, Holiday Inn Express, Sleep Inn, 🅞 Urgent Care, Advance Parts, AT&T, Best Buy, CVS Drug, Dick's, $Tree, Encore RV Camping, GNC, Goodyear/auto, Honda, Hyundai, Mazda, Michael's, Petsmart, Quail Run RV Camping, Ross, Tire Kingdom, TJ Maxx, Tuffy Auto, Verizon
277mm	🆁🆂 both lanes, full 🚻 facilities, 🅒 vending, 🍽 litter barrels, petwalk, 24hr security
275	FL 56, Land O Lakes, Tarpon Springs, E 🅟 BP/Dunkin Donuts/dsl, 🍴 TX Roadhouse, 🛏 Hampton Inn, 🅞 Mini, Publix (2mi), W 🅟 Shell/dsl, 🅞 Walgreens
274	I-275 (from sb), to Tampa, St Petersburg
270	rd 581, Bruce B Downs Blvd, E 🅟 Hess/dsl, Mobil, 7-11, Shell/Circle K/Taco Bell/dsl, 🍴 Baskin-Robbins/Dunkin Donuts, Boston Mkt, Chick-fil-A, Chili's, Coldstone, DQ, Firehouse Subs, Jimmy John's, KFC, Kobe Japanese, Liang's Asian Bistro, Macaroni Grill, McDonald's, Moe's SW Grill, Panera Bread, Papa John's, Pizza Hut, Ruby Tuesday, Selmon's Cafe, Starbucks, Steak'n Shake, Subway, Tijuana Flats, TGIFriday's, Wendy's, 🛏 Holiday Inn Express, Wingate Inn, 🅞 Urgent Care, Best Buy, CVS Drug, GNC, Home Depot, Kauffman Tire, Michael's, Publix, Radio Shack, Tires+, Verizon, Walgreens, Walmart, W 🅟 7-11, 🍴 McDonald's, Olive Garden, Panda Buffet, Red Lobster, Stonewood Grill, 🛏 SpringHill Suites, 🅞 BJ's Whse/gas, CVS Drug, $Tree, Jo-Ann Fabrics, Lowe's, Petsmart, Ross, Staples, USPO
266	rd 582A, Fletcher Ave, W 🅟 Shell/Circle K/dsl, 🍴 Baskin-Robbins/Dunkin Donuts, Bob Evans, Lenny's Subs, Starbucks, Wendy's, 🛏 Courtyard, Extended Stay America, Fairfield Inn, Hampton Inn, Hilton Garden, Holiday Inn Express, Residence Inn, Sleep Inn, 🅞 🅗
265	FL 582, Fowler Ave, Temple Terrace, E 🅞 Happy Traveler RV Park, flea mkt, W 🅟 BP, Sunoco, Value/dsl, 🍴 IHOP, Marco's Pizza, 🛏 Ramada Inn, 🅞 to USF, to Busch Gardens
261	I-4, W to Tampa, E to Orlando
260b a	FL 574, to Mango, Tampa, E 🅟 Chevron, Citgo/dsl, Shell/Circle K/Subway, 🍴 Baskin-Robbins/Dunkin Donuts, China Wok, Quiznos, Waffle House, 🅞 SweetBay Foods, Walgreens, W 🅟 BP, Mobil, 🛏 Residence Inn, Sheraton, Staybridge Suites
257	FL 60, Brandon, E 🅟 Chevron, Citgo/dsl, Mobil/dsl, Shell/Circle K, Sunoco, 🍴 Anthony's Pizza, Arby's, Brandon Ale House, Boston Mkt, Buffalo Wild Wings, Burger King, Checkers, Cheescake Factory, Chili's, Chuck-ECheese, DQ, Denny's, Dunkin Donuts, Firehouse Subs, 5 Guys Burgers, Grill Smith Grill, Jesse's Steaks, Jimmy John's, Kabuki Japanese, KFC, Kobe Japanese, Krispy Kreme, Little Caesars, LJ Silver, Macaroni Grill, McDonald's, Moe's SW Grill, Olive Garden, Outback Steaks, Panda Express, Panera Bread, Papa John's, Popeye's, Qdoba, Quiznos, Red Lobster, Salad Works, Smokey Bones BBQ, Smoothie King, Steak'n Shake, Subway, Tia's TexMex, Tops China Buffet, Tres Amigos Mexican, Waffle House, Wendy's, Wing House, 🛏 Holiday Inn Express, HomeStead Suites, La Quinta, 🅞 🅗, Urgent Care, Aamco, Advance Parts, AT&T, AutoZone, Barnes&Noble, Best Buy, Books-A-Million, CVS Drug, Dick's, Dillard's, $General, $Tree, Family$, Firestone/auto, JC Penney, Kia, Kohl's, K-Mart, Macy's, Marshall's, Michael's, Office Depot, PepBoys, PetCo, Petsmart, Publix, Radio Shack, Ross, Sam's Club/gas, Sears/auto, Staples, Target, Tires+, TJ Maxx, Tuffy Auto, U-Haul, Walgreens, mall, E on Causeway Blvd 🅟 Mobil, 🍴 Buca Italian, Cheddars, Chick-fil-A, Crispers, Longhorn Steaks, McDonald's, Starbucks, Steak'n Shake, 🅞 Cadillac, Costco/gas, Fiat, JoAnn Fabrics, Kohl's, Lowe's, Petsmart, Publix, Walmart, W 🅟 Citgo/dsl, Marathon, Shell, 🍴 Beef O'Brady's, Bob Evans, Burger King, Hooters, McDonald's, Sonny's BBQ, Subway, Sweet Tomatoes, Wendy's, 🛏 Best Western, Comfort Suites, Country Inn&Suites, Courtyard, Embassy Suites, Fairfield Inn, Homewood Suites, La Quinta, Motel 6, Red Roof Inn, SpringHill Suites, 🅞 Buick/GMC, Chevrolet, Chrysler/Dodge/Jeep, Ford, Harley-Davidson, Home Depot, Honda, Hyundai, Mazda, Nissan, Office Depot, Toyota/Scion, VW

[gas] = gas [food] = food [lodging] = lodging [other] = other [rest stop] = rest stop

Copyright 2014 - The Next Exit ®

INTERSTATE 75 CONT'D

Exit	Services
256	FL 618 W (**toll**), to Tampa
254	US 301, Riverview, **E** [gas] RaceTrac/dsl, [food] Panda Express, Steak'n Shake, [other] CVS Drug, Firestone, Home Depot, Target, **W** [gas] 7-11/dsl, [food] China 1, Crazy Cafe, McDonald's, [lodging] Hilton Garden, [other] Publix
250	Gibsonton Dr, Riverview, **E** [gas] RaceWay/dsl, [food] Beef'O'Brady's, Burger King, DQ, Hungry Howie's, Little Caesars, Lucky Buffet, McDonald's, Pizza Hut, Ruby Tuesday, Subway, Taco Bell, Wendy's, [other] Alafia River RV Resort, Beall's, CVS Drug, $Tree, Family$, Hidden River RV Resort (4mi), Lowe's, Save-a-Lot, Walgreens, Winn-Dixie, USPO, **W** [gas] Murphy USA/dsl, [other] Walmart/McDonald's
246	rd 672, Big Bend Rd, Apollo Bch, **E** [gas] Hess/Dunkin Donuts/Godfather's Pizza/Quiznos/dsl, 7-11, [food] Applebee's, Beef'O'Brady's, Buffalo Wild Wings, Burger King, China Taste, East Coast Pizza, 5 Guys Burgers, Little Caesars, McDonald's, Panera Bread, Pita, Poppi's Pizza, Sakura Japanese, Sonic, Starbucks, Subway, Qdoba, Village Inn, Wendy's, [other] **Urgent Care**, Ace Hardware, Advance Parts, AT&T, AutoZone, Beall's, $Tree, Firestone/auto, GNC, Goodyear/auto, Publix, Sam's Club/gas, Sweetbay Foods, Tire Choice, Tuffy Auto, Verizon, Walgreens, vet, **W** [gas] Shell/Dunkin Donuts/dsl
240b a	FL 674, Sun City Ctr, Ruskin, **E** [gas] Shell, [food] Beef'O'Brady's, Bob Evans, Burger King, Denny's, Hungry Howie's, Pizza Hut, Seafood Dive, Sonny's BBQ, Subway, Taco Bell, Wendy's, [lodging] Comfort Inn, [other] [H], Beall's, GNC, Home Depot, Radio Shack, SunLake RV Resort (1mi), to Little Manatee River SP, **W** [gas] Circle K/dsl, Hess/dsl, RaceTrac/dsl, [food] China Wok, KFC, McDonald's, [lodging] Ruskin Inn, [other] BigLots, NAPA, auto repair
237mm	**[rest stop] both lanes, full [handicapped] facilities, [phone], vending, [picnic], litter barrels, petwalk, 24hr security**
229	rd 683, Moccasin Wallow Rd, to Parrish, **E** Little Manatee Sprs SRA (10mi), **W** [other] Circle K, Fiesta Grove RV Park (3mi), Frog Creek RV Park (3mi), Terra Ceia RV Village (2mi), Winterset RV Park (3mi)
228	I-275 N, to St Petersburg
224	US 301, to Bradenton, Ellenton, **E** [gas] Mobil, RaceWay/dsl, Shell/Circle K/dsl, [food] Applebee's, Checkers, GioPizza, Hungry Howie's, Kings Wok, McDonald's, Peach's Rest., Ruby Tuesday, Subway, Wendy's, Woody's River Grill, [lodging] Hampton Inn, Sleep Inn, [other] Ace Hardware, Beall's, $General, $Tree, Ellenton Outlets/famous brands, GNC, Just Brakes, K-Mart, Publix, Walgreens, USPO, **W** [gas] Pilot/dsl, [food] Anna Maria's, Crabtrap Seafood, Waffle House, [lodging] GuestHouse Inn, Ramada Ltd
220b a	FL 64, to Zolfo Springs, Bradenton, **E** Lake Manatee SRA, **W** [gas] BP/dsl, Citgo/dsl, RaceTrac/dsl, Shell/Circle K/dsl, [food] Burger King, Cracker Barrel, D. Americo's Pizza, Dunkin Donuts, KFC/LJ Silver, McDonald's, Sonny's BBQ, Subway, Waffle House, Wendy's, [lodging] Best Western, Comfort Inn, Days Inn, EconoLodge, Motel 6, [other] [H], Dream RV Ctr, Encore RV Resort (1mi), Harley-Davidson, Toyota/Scion, Walmart
217b a	FL 70, to Arcadia, **E** [gas] Hess/Godfather's/Quiznos/dsl, [food] Burger King, Crispers, [lodging] Wingate Inn, [other] Goodyear/auto, Sweetbay Foods, Walmart/Subway, **W** [gas] BP/Dunkin Donuts/dsl, 7-11/dsl, Shell/Circle K, [food] Applebee's, Arby's, Bangkok Tokyo, Bob Evans, Bogey's Rest., Chick-fil-A, Dawson's Rest, DQ, Hungry Howie's, LJ Silver/Taco Bell, McDonald's, Papa John's, Peppermill Eatery, Rice Bowl, Starbucks, Subway, [lodging] Country Inn&Suites, [other] Beall's, CVS Drug, $Tree, Lowe's, Pleasant Lake RV Resort, Publix, Tire Kingdom, Tires+, Tuffy Auto, Verizon, vet
213	University Parkway, to Sarasota, **E** [gas] Mobil/dsl, [food] Chili's, Ms JC Garden, Monty's Pizza, Pizza Hut, Quiznos, [lodging] Fairfield Inn, Holiday Inn, [other] [H], **Urgent Care**, GNC, Publix, Walgreens, **W** [food] Bellacino's, BoneFish Grill, Buffalo Wild Wings, Carrabba's, Chipotle Mexican, 5 Guys Burgers, Jason's Deli, Jersey Mike's Subs, Jimmy John's, John Dough Cafe, Moe's SW Grill, Pei Wei, Red Elephant Grill, Ruby Tuesday, Selmon's Rest., Starbucks, Stonewood Grill, Sweet Tomatoes, Tijuana Flats, Wendy's, [lodging] Comfort Suites, Hampton Inn, [other] Beall's, Best Buy, BJ's Whse/gas, CVS Drug, $Tree, Fresh Mkt Foods, Home Depot, Jo-Ann Fabrics, Kohl's, Marshall's, Michael's, Old Navy, PetCo, Ross, SteinMart, Target, Verizon, to Ringling Museum
210	FL 780, Fruitville Rd, Sarasota, **E** [other] Sun-N-Fun RV Park (1mi), **W** [gas] BP/dsl/LP, Mobil/7-11/dsl, RaceTrac/dsl, Sav-On/dsl, Shell, [food] Applebee's, Bob Evans, Burger King, Cafe Italia, Checkers, Chick-fil-A, Don Pablo's, Dunkin Donuts, Firehouse Subs, KFC, Longhorn Steaks, McDonald's, Peking Tokyo, Perkins, Starbucks, Subway, Super Buffet, Taco Bell, Trader Vic's Grill, [lodging] AmericInn, Homewood Suites (2mi), [other] Advance Parts, AT&T, $Tree, CVS Drug, GNC, Lowe's, Office Depot, Publix, Radio Shack, Sam's Club, Target, Tire Kingdom, Tuffy Auto, Verizon, Winn-Dixie
207	FL 758, Sarasota, **W** [gas] BP/Subway/dsl, Marathon/Dunkin Donuts/Subway, [food] Arby's, Cafe Amalfi, Chili's, Fortune Buffet, MadFish Grill, McDonald's, Panera Bread, Pizza Hut, Sarasota Alehouse, Starbucks, Steak'n Shake, Taco Bell, [lodging] Hampton Inn, [other] [H], Beall's, Home Depot, Publix, Radio Shack, Verizon, Walgreens, Walmart, to Selby Botanical Gardens (8mi), vet
205	FL 72, to Arcadia, Sarasota, **E** Myakka River SP (9mi), **W** [gas] BP/dsl, Mobil/7-11/dsl, Shell/Circle K, [food] Applebee's, Burger King, Chick-fil-A, Dunkin Donuts, Gecko's Grill, Just Pizza, KFC, McDonald's, Quiznos, Starbucks, Subway, Waffle House, Wendy's, Wings&Weenies, [lodging] Comfort Inn, Days Inn, Holiday Inn Express, [other] Acura, AT&T, Beall's, BMW, CVS Drug, Jaguar, Land Rover, Lexus, Lotus, Mercedes/Smart, Publix, Tire Kingdom, Turtle Beach Camping (8mi), Walgreens, Windward Isle RV Park, UPSO, vet
200	FL 681 S (from sb), to Venice, Osprey, Gulf Bchs
195	Laurel Rd, Nokomis, **E** [gas] BP/USPO/dsl, [food] Subway, [other] CVS Drug, **W** [other] Encore RV Park (2mi), Scherer SP (6mi)
193	Jaracanda Blvd, Venice, **W** [gas] Hess/Godfather's/Quiznos/dsl, RaceTrac/dsl, [food] BrewBurgers, Ping's Chinese, Cracker Barrel, McDonald's, [lodging] Best Western, Fairfield Inn, Holiday Inn Express, [other] [H], CVS Drug, Publix, Verizon
191	rd 777, Venice Rd, to Englewood, **W** [other] Encore RV Park (3mi), KOA (6mi), to Myakka SF (9mi)
182	rd 771, Sumter Blvd, to North Port
179	rd 779, Toledo Blade Blvd, North Port, **1-2 mi W** [gas] Mobil/Subway/dsl, Shell/Burger King, [other] [H], Publix

FL

BRADENTON

SARASOTA

VENICE

⬆N INTERSTATE 75 CONT'D

Exit	Services
170	rd 769, to Arcadia, Port Charlotte, **E** 🚗 Murphy USA/dsl, RaceTrac/dsl, 7-11/dsl, 🍴 Applebee's, 🛏 Hampton Inn, Holiday Inn Express, 🅾 Lettuce Lake Camping (7mi), Riverside Camping (5mi), Walmart, **W** 🚗 Hess/dsl, Mobil/Circle K/DQ/dsl, Shell/Circle K/Dunkin Donuts, 🍴 Burger King, Cracker Barrel, DQ, Domino's, McDonald's, Peach Garden, Quiznos, Starbucks, Subway, Taco Bell, Top China, Waffle House, Wendy's, 🛏 Country Inn&Suites, La Quinta, Sleep Inn, 🅾 H, Ace Hardware, Advance Parts, Beall's, Curves, CVS Drug, $General, $Tree, Publix, Walgreens, Winn-Dixie, USPO, vet
167	rd 776, Port Charlotte
164	US 17, Punta Gorda, Arcadia, **E** 🚗 Chevron/7-11/dsl, RaceWay/dsl, Shell/Circle K/dsl, 🍴 King House Chinese, Subway, RV camping, vet, 🅾 $General, Winn-Dixie, **W** 🍴 Fisherman's Village Rest. (2mi), 🅾 H
161	rd 768, Punta Gorda, **E** 🅿️ both lanes, full ♿ facilities, 🅲, vending, 🗑 litter barrels, petwalk, 24hr security, **W** 🚗 BP/DQ/Subway, Murphy USA/dsl, 🚛 Arby's/dsl/scales/24hr, Sunoco/dsl, 🍴 Burger King, McDonald's, Pizza Hut, Waffle House, Wendy's, 🛏 Best Value Inn, Knights Inn, 🅾 Encore RV Park (2mi), Walmart
160mm	**weigh sta both lanes**
158	rd 762, Tropical Gulf Acres, Tuckers Grade, **E** Babcock-Wells Wildlife Mgt Area
143	FL 78, to Cape Coral, N Ft Myers, **E** 🚗 Marathon/dsl, 🅾 Seminole Camping (1mi), Up the River Camping, **W** 🛏 Encore RV Camping
141	FL 80, Palm Bch Blvd, Ft Myers, **E** 🚗 Marathon, Sunoco/dsl, 🍴 Cracker Barrel, Waffle House, 🛏 Comfort Inn, ValuePlace, **W** 🚗 Hess/Dunkin Donuts/dsl, Mobil, 7-11, 🍴 Domino's, Hardee's, KFC, Papa John's, Popeye's, Sonny's BBQ, Subway, Taco Bell, 🅾 BigLots, CVS Drug, $General, North Trail RV Ctr, Radio Shack, Save-A-Lot, USPO, vet
139	Luckett Rd, Ft Myers, **E** 🅾 Camping World RV Service/supplies, Cypress Woods RV Resort, **W** 🚗 🚛/Subway/dsl/scales/24hr/@
138	FL 82, to Lehigh Acres, Ft Myers, **E** 🚗 7-11/dsl, 🛏 Hyatt Place, **W** 🚗 Mobil/dsl, Sunoco/dsl, 🅾 Peterbilt
136	FL 884, Colonial Blvd, Ft Myers, **E** 🛏 Candlewood Suites, Holiday Inn Express, 🍴 Bajio, Buffalo Wild Wings, 5 Guys Burgers, Starbucks, Subway, 🅾 Best Buy, Books-A-Million, GNC, Home Depot, PetCo, Ross, Staples, Target, **W** 🚗 BP, Marathon/dsl, Murphy USA/dsl, 7-11, Shell/Circle K/dsl, 🍴 Applebee's, Bob Evans, Burger King, Chick-fil-A, Chili's, Golden Corral, LJ Silver/Taco Bell, McDonald's, Panda Express, Steak'n Shake, Subway, TX Roadhouse, 🛏 ValuePlace, 🅾 H, AT&T, Beall's, BJ's Whse/gas, $Tree, Hobby Lobby, Kohl's, Lowe's, Petsmart, Publix, Tire Choice/auto, Verizon, Walmart/McDonald's
131	rd 876, Daniels Pkwy, to Cape Coral, **E** 🅿️ both lanes, full ♿ facilities, 🅲, vending, 🗑 litter barrels, petwalk, 24hr security, 🚗 BP/Dunkin Donuts/Subway/dsl, RaceTrac/dsl, 🍴 Cracker Barrel, Fat Katz, 🛏 Comfort Inn, Floridian 🍴 Inn, Grand Stay, 🅾 CVS Drug, Porsche, 🍴, **W** 🚗 Hess/Dunkin Donuts/dsl, RaceWay/dsl, 7-11, Shell/Circle K/dsl, 🍴 Arby's, Beef'O'Brady's, Burger King, DQ, Denny's, Mac Daddy's, McDonald's, New China, Papa John's, Rib City, Sports Page Grill, Subway, Taco Bell,

Exit	Services
131	**Continued** Waffle House, Wendy's, 🛏 Baymont Inn, Best Western, Hampton Inn, La Quinta, Quality Inn, SpringHill Suites, Travelodge, 🅾 H, CVS Drug, Dream RV Ctr, Publix, Tire Choice/auto, Tuffy Auto, Walgreens
128	Alico Rd, San Carlos Park, **E** 🚗 7-11, 🍴 Aurelio's Pizza, Bar Louie, Carrabba's, Chick-fil-A, Connor's Steaks, Elevation Burger, Famous Dave's BBQ, Miller's Alehouse, Longhorn Steaks, McDonald's, Moe's SW Grill, Olive Garden, Outback Steaks, Pincher's Crabshack, Pita Pit, Red Robin, 🛏 Courtyard, Hilton Garden, Holiday Inn, Homewood Suites, Residence Inn, 🅾 AT&T, Bass Pro Shop/Islamorada Fish Co, Belk, Best Buy, Costco/gas, Dick's, $Tree, GNC, JC Penney, Jo-Ann Fabrics, Marshall's, PetCo, Ross, Staples, Target, Verizon, **W** 🚗 Hess/Dunkin Donuts/dsl, 7-11/dsl
123	rd 850, Corkscrew Rd, Estero, **E** 🚗 BP/Dunkin Donuts/dsl, Chevron/7-11/dsl, 🍴 Beef'O'Brady's, China Gourmet, Marsala's Italian, McDonald's, Naples Flat Bread, Perkins, Subway, 🅾 CVS Drug, Johnson Tire/auto, Miramar Outlet/famous brands, Publix, **W** 🚗 Hess/Dunkin Donuts/dsl, 7-11, Shell/Blimpie/dsl, 🍴 Applebee's, Arby's, Rib City, Ruby Tuesday, Subway, 🛏 Embassy Suites, Hampton Inn, 🅾 Chevrolet, Lowe's, Tire Choice/auto, Koreshan SHS (2mi), Woodsmoke RV Park (4mi)
116	Bonita Bch Rd, Bonita Springs, **E** 🚗 Mobil, Valero/7-11/dsl, 🍴 Subway, 🅾 Advance Parts, AT&T, Publix, Tire Choice/auto, **W** 🚗 Chevron/dsl, Hess/Dunkin Donuts/dsl, Shell/McDonald's, 🍴 Waffle House, 🛏 Best Western, 🅾 CVS Drug, Home Depot, Imperial Bonita RV Park, Tire Kingdom, Walgreens, to Lovers Key SP (11mi)
111	rd 846, Immokalee Rd, Naples Park, **E** 🚗 Mobil/dsl, 7-11, 🍴 Bob Evans, Burger King, Chili's, L'Appetite Pizza, Panera Bread, 🛏 Hampton Inn, 🅾 Staples, Target, World Mkt, **W** 🚗 Shell/Circle K/dsl, 🍴 Bella's Pizza, Subway, 🅾 H, Publix, Verizon, Walmart/McDonald's, to Delnor-Wiggins SP
107	rd 896, Pinebridge Rd, Naples, **E** 🚗 BP/McDonald's/dsl, 🍴 China Garden, Giovanni Ristorante, Starbucks, Subway, 🅾 H, Publix, Walgreens, vet, **W** 🚗 Chevron/dsl, RaceTrac/dsl, Shell/Circle K/dsl, 🍴 Burger King, 5 Guys Burgers, Hooters, IHOP, Perkins, Senor Tequilas, Sophia's Rest., Starbucks, Waffle House, 🛏 Best Western, Hawthorn Suites, Spinnaker Inn, 🅾 Harley-Davidson, Johnson Tire/auto, Nissan, Tire Choice/auto, vet
105	rd 886, to Golden Gate Pkwy, Golden Gate, **E** 🍴 Subway, 🅾 CVS Drug, **W** 🍴 to 🍴, zoo
101	rd 951, to FL 84, to Naples, **E** 🚗 BP/Subway/pizza, 🛏 Fairfield Inn, SpringHill Suites, 🅾 H, **W** 🚗 BP/dsl, Circle

(Side margin labels: PUNTA GORDA, FT MYERS, CAPE CORAL, ESTERO, NAPLES)

🅖 = gas 🍽 = food 🏨 = lodging 🅞 = other 🆁🆂 = rest stop   Copyright 2014 - The Next Exit ®

🔼N INTERSTATE 75 CONT'D

Exit	Services
101	Continued
	K, Mobil/dsl, Shell/dsl, 🍽 BBQ Place, Cracker Barrel, McDonald's, Subway, Taco Bell, Waffle House, 🏨 Comfort Inn, Days Inn, La Quinta, Super 8, 🅞 AT&T, Club Naples RV Ctr, $Tree, Endless Summer RV Park (3mi), KOA
100mm	**toll plaza eb**
80	FL 29, to Everglade City, Immokalee, **W** 🅞 Big Cypress NR, Everglades NP, Smallwoods Store
71mm	Big Cypress Nat Preserve, hiking, no security,
63mm	**W** 🆁🆂 both lanes, full ♿ facilities, 🍵 vending, 🗑 litter barrels, petwalk, 24hr security
49	rd 833, Snake Rd, Big Cypress Indian Reservation, **E** 🅖 Miccosukee Service Plaza/deli/dsl, 🅞 museum, swamp safari
41mm	**rec area eb**, 🗑 litter barrels
38mm	**rec area wb**, 🗑 litter barrels
35mm	**W** 🆁🆂 rec area both lanes, full ♿ facilities, 🍵 vending, 🗑 litter barrels, petwalk, 24hr security
32mm	**rec area both lanes**, 🗑 litter barrels
25mm	**toll plaza wb, motorist callboxes begin/end**
23	US 27, FL 25, Miami, South Bay
22	FL 84 W, NW 196th, Glades Pkwy, **W** 🅞 Publix, same as 21
21	FL 84 W (from nb), Indian Trace, **W** 🅖 BP/dsl, 🍽 Las Rikuras, Papa John's, Spain's Cuisine 🅞 $Days
19	I-595 E, FL 869 (toll), Sawgrass Expswy
15	Royal Palm Blvd, Weston, Bonaventure, **W** 🅖 Chevron, Mobil, 🍽 Carolina Ale House, El Mariachi, Flanigan's Rest, Il Toscano Rest., La Granja, Lucille's Cafe, Offerdahl's Grill, Pollo Tropical, Sir Pizza, Wendy's, 🏨 Comfort Suites, Courtyard, Residence Inn, 🅞 🏥, Meineke, Tires+, USPO
13b a	Griffin Rd, **E** 🅖 Shell/dsl, 🍽 Burger King, DQ, Donato's Rest., Outback Steaks, Subway, Waffle House, 🅞 Goodyear/auto, Publix, vet, **W** 🅖 7-11/dsl, Tom Thumb/dsl, 🍽 Anthony's Pizza, Bone Fish Grill, Chick-fil-A, Chili's, Coldstone, Domino's, Dunkin Donuts, HoneyBaked Ham, Jimmy John's, McDonald's, Panera Bread, Pei Wei, Pizza Heaven, Starbucks, Weston Diner, 🅞 AT&T, Fiat, Home Depot, Honda, Hyundai, Nissan/Volvo, Office Depot, Publix, Radio Shack, Toyota/Scion, Walgreens, vet
11b a	Sheridan St, **E** 🅖 Chevron, 🍽 Cracker Barrel, Wendy's, 🏨 Hampton Inn, Holiday Inn Express, 🅞 🏥 (3mi), Audi, BMW, Piccolo Park, **W** 🅖 Shell/dsl, 🍽 Applebee's, Bistro 555, China One, Coldstone, Little Caesars, McDonald's, Original Pancake House, Romeus Cuban, Subway, TGIFriday's, 🅞 Urgent Care, Firestone/auto, GNC, Lowe's, Publix, Verizon, Walgreens, vet
9b a	FL 820, Pine Blvd, Hollywood Blvd, **E** 🅖 BP, Shell, 🍽 Boston Mkt, Brio Italian, Brimstone Woodfire Grill, Cheesecake Factory, Chick-fil-A, Chili's, Fuddrucker's, HoneyBaked Ham, Jason's Deli, La Granja, Latin-American Grill, Lime Mexican Grill, Macaroni Grill, McDonald's, RA Grill, Sal's Italian, Starbucks, Stir Crazy, Subway, The Pub, Tijuana Flats, Village Tavern, Wendys, 🅞 🏥, Barnes&Noble, BJ's Whse/gas, Dick's, Dodge, Mercedes, Old Navy, Petsmart, Publix, Radio Shack, Verizon, Walgreens, Walmart, USPO, **W** 🅖 BP/dsl, Citgo/dsl, Shell, 🍽 Burger King, Chick-fil-A, Chipotle Mexican, Elevation Burger, KFC/Taco Bell, La Granja, Las Vegas Cuban,

(left vertical label) **WESTON**

(FL badge at left margin)

9b a	Continued
	McDonald's, Marco's Pizza, Panda Express, Sal's Italian, SmashBurger, Starbucks, Sweet Tomatoes, Wendy's, 🅞 Acura, Advance Parts, AT&T, AutoZone, Costco/gas, CVS Drug, GNC, Lexus, Publix, Sedano's Foods, Subaru, Tires+, Walgreens, Whole Foods Mkt
7b a	Miramar Pkwy, **E** 🅖 Chevron, 🍽 Baskin-Robbins/Dunkin Donuts, Cancun Grill, La Carreta, McDonald's, Pollo Tropical, Quiznos, Sal's Italian, Starbucks, Subway, Tijuana Flats, Wendy's, 🏨 Courtyard, Hilton Garden, Residence Inn, Wingate Inn, 🅞 $Tree, Publix, Walgreens, USPO, **W** 🅖 Shell, 🍽 Benihana, Chick-fil-A, Chili's, Coldstone, McDonald's, Orient Chef, Panera Bread, Starbucks, Subway, Yummy Asian, 🅞 🏥, AT&T, CVS Drug, Home Depot, Marshall's, Office Depot, Ross, SuperTarget, Winn-Dixie, city park
5	to FL 821 (from sb), FL TPK (toll)
4	FL 860, NW 186th, Miami Gardens Dr, **E** 🅖 BP, Chevron, 🍽 Carrabba's, Chicken Kitchen, Dunkin Donuts, McDonald's, Starbucks, Subway, 🅞 AT&T, CVS Drug, GNC, Publix/deli, Sedanos Foods, vet
2	NW 138th, Graham Dairy Rd, **W** 🅖 Mobil, Shell/dsl, 🍽 China Casa, China Wok, IHOP, Latin Cuban Cafe, Little Caesars, McDonald's, Starbucks, Subway, Wendy's, 🅞 🏥, GNC, Publix, Walgreens, vet
1b a	**I-75 begins/ends on FL 826**, Palmetto Expswy, multiple services on FL 826.

🔼N INTERSTATE 95

Exit	Services
382mm	Florida/Georgia state line, St Marys River, motorist callboxes begin/end.
381mm	**inspection sta both lanes**
380	US 17, to Yulee, Kingsland, **E** 🅖 Osprey RV Park, **W** 🅖 Shell, 🏨 American Inn
378mm	**Welcome Ctr sb, full ♿ facilities, 🍵 vending, 🗑 litter barrels, petwalk, 24hr security**
376mm	**weigh sta both lanes**
373	FL 200, FL A1A, to Yulee, Callahan, Fernandina Bch, **E** 🅖 Flash/Krystal, Sunoco, 🍽 Burger King, KFC/Pizza Hut, DQ, McDonald's, Wendy's, 🏨 Comfort Inn, Holiday Inn Express, Nassau Holiday Motel (3mi), 🅞 RV Camping (3mi), to Ft Clinch SP (16mi), **W** 🅖 BP/Subway/dsl, Exxon/dsl
366	Pecan Park Rd, **W** Flea&Farmer's Mkt, Pecan Park RV Camping
363b a	Duval Rd, **E** 🅖 Mobil/7-11, 🍽 Arby's, Boston's, Buffalo Wild Wings, Buffalo's Philly, Chick-fil-A, Chili's, Coldstone, Cracker Barrel, 5 Guys Burgers, Green Papaya, Hardee's, Jimmy John's, Logan's Roadhouse, McDonald's, Olive Garden, Panda Express, Panera Bread, Pollo Tropical, Red Lobster, Salsaritas, Starbucks, Sticky Fingers, Subway, Taco Bell, Wasabi, 🏨 A Loft, 🅞 Urgent Care, AT&T, AutoZone, Best Buy, Dick's, Discount Tire, $Tree, Gander Mtn, GNC, Goodyear/auto, Lowe's, Marshall's, Michael's, Old Navy, Petsmart, Ross, Verizon, Walgreens, Walmart/Subway, **W** 🅖 BP/dsl, Chevron, Exxon/dsl, Sunoco/Subway, 🍽 Denny's, Longhorn Steaks, Millhouse Steaks, Ruby Tuesday, Waffle House, Zaxby's, 🏨 Airport Inn, Best Western, Comfort Suites, Country Hearth Inn, Courtyard, Crowne Plaza, Fairfield Inn, Hampton Inn, Hilton Garden, Hyatt Place, Jacksonville Plaza Hotel, Jaxport Inn, Microtel, Quality Inn, Red Roof Inn, Residence Inn, SpringHill

(right vertical labels) **MIAMI** / **JACKSONVILLE**

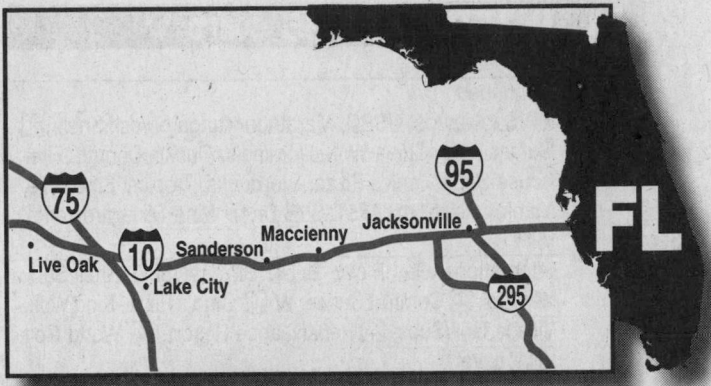

⬆N INTERSTATE 95 CONT'D

Exit	Services
363b a	Continued
	Suites, Travelodge, Wingate Inn, 🅞 Gore's RV Ctr, ✈
362b a	I-295 S, FL 9A, to Blount Island, Jacksonville
360	FL 104, Dunn Ave, Busch Dr, E 🅖 Gate/dsl, 🍴 Hardee's, Waffle House, 🛏 Executive Inn, 🅞 Sam's Club/gas, USPO, W 🅖 BP/dsl, Chevron, Hess, RaceTrac/dsl, Shell/dsl, 🍴 Arby's, Burger King, Capt D's, Checker's, China Buffet, Country Cabin Rest., Firehouse Subs, KFC, Krystal, Little Caesars, McDonald's, New China, Pizza Hut, Popeye's, Sonny's BBQ, Starbucks, Subway, Taco Bell, Wendy's, 🛏 EconoLodge, La Quinta, Motel 6, 🅞 Aamco, Advance Parts, BigLots, CVS Drug, $Tree, Family$, Marshall's, Office Depot, PepBoys, Publix, Radio Shack, Tires+, Walgreens
358b a	FL 105, Broward Rd, Heckscher Dr, E zoo, W 🅖 BP/dsl, 🛏 USA Inn
357mm	Trout River
357	FL 111, Edgewood Ave, W 🅖 BP/dsl, Texaco/dsl
356b a	Fl 115, FL 117, Lem Turner Rd, Norwood Ave, E 🍴 Hardee's, W 🅖 BP/dsl, Hess/Dunkin Donuts, RaceWay/dsl, Shell, 🍴 Burger King, Checker's, Golden EggRoll, Ho-Ho Chinese, Krystal, Popeye's, Subway, Taco Bell, 🅞 Advance Parts, Save-A-Lot, Tires+, Walgreens
355	Golfair Blvd, E 🅖 Shell, 🍴 McDonald's, 🅞 Publix, W 🅖 Chevron/dsl, RaceWay/dsl
354b a	US 1, 20th St, to Jacksonville, to AmTrak, MLK Pkwy
353d	FL 114, to 8th St, E 🍴 McDonald's, 🅞 🄷, Walgreens
353c	US 23 N, Kings Rd, downtown
353b	US 90A, Union St, Sports Complex, downtown
353a	Church St, Myrtle Ave, Forsythe St, downtown
352d	I-10 W, Stockton St (from sb), Lake City
352c	Monroe St (from nb) downtown
352b a	Myrtle Ave (from nb) downtown
351d	Stockton St, 🄷, downtown
351c	Margaret St, downtown
351b	I-10 W, to Tallahassee
351a	Park St, College St, 🄷, to downtown
351mm	St Johns River
350b	FL 13, San Marco Blvd, E 🄷
350a	Prudential Dr, Main St, Riverside Ave (from nb), to downtown, E 🅖 BP, 🛏 Extended Stay America, Hampton Inn, Wyndham, W 🍴 Panera Bread, 🛏 Hilton Garden
349	US 90 E (from sb), to beaches downtown, W 🛏 Super 8
348	US 1 S (from sb), Philips Hwy, W 🛏 Scottish Inn, Super 8, 🅞 Volvo
347	US 1A, FL 126, Emerson St, E 🅖 Chevron/dsl, Shell, 🍴 Hot Wok, 🅞 Advance Parts, Family$, O'Reilly Parts, W 🅖 BP/dsl, Gate/dsl, Hess/dsl, 🍴 McDonald's, Taco Bell, 🛏 Emerson Inn, 🅞 Chevrolet, Goodyear/auto
346b a	FL 109, University Blvd, E 🅖 Exxon/dsl, Hess/dsl, Shell, 🍴 Capt D's, Checkers, DQ, El Potro Mexican, Firehouse Subs, Happy Garden Chinese, Huddle House, Korean BBQ, Krystal, Pizza Hut, Popeye's, Ying's Chinese, 🅞 🄷 Ace Hardware, CarQuest, CVS Drug, Family$, Firestone/auto, NAPA, Tire Kingdom, Tires+, Sun Tire, Winn-Dixie, W 🅖 BP/dsl, Chevron, RaceTrac, 🍴 Arby's, Baskin-Robbins/Dunkin Donuts, Burger King, Famous Amos, KFC, McDonald's, Papa John's, Sonny's BBQ, Taco Bell, Wendy's, Whataburger, Woody's BBQ, 🛏 Days Inn, Ramada Inn, Super 8, 🅞 Family$, U-Haul, auto repair
345	FL 109, University Blvd (from nb), E 🅖 Chevron, Gate/dsl/24hr, Hess/Blimpie/Godfather's Pizza/dsl, 🍴 Bono's BBQ, Schnitzel House, 🅞 🄷
344	FL 202, Butler Blvd, E 🅖 Gate/dsl, 🍴 Dave&Buster's, 🛏 Best Western, Candlewood Suites, EconoLodge, Holiday Inn Express, Homestead Suites, Howard Johnson, Marriott, Radisson, 🅞 🄷, USPO, W 🅖 BP/dsl, Shell, 🍴 Applebee's, Baskin-Robbins/Dunkin Donuts, Chick-fil-A, Cracker Barrel, Hardee's, McDonald's, Quiznos, Sonic, Starbucks, Waffle House, Wendy's, Whataburger/24hr, Zaxby's, 🛏 Courtyard, Extended Stay Deluxe, Fairfield Inn, Jameson Inn, La Quinta, Microtel, Red Roof Inn, Wingate Inn
341	FL 152, Baymeadows Rd, E 🅖 BP/dsl, Gate/dsl, Shell/dsl, 🍴 Arby's, Chili's, CiCi's Pizza, Hardee's, Krystal, Omaha Steaks, Panda Express, Quiznos, Subway, 🛏 Bay Meadows Inn, Comfort Suites, Embassy Suites, Holiday Inn, HomeStead Suites, 🅞 Advance Parts, Tires+, Walgreens, Winn-Dixie, W 🅖 Kangaroo, Shell, 🍴 Al's Pizza, Bamboo Creek, Chicago Pizzaria, Denny's, Gator's Seafood, IHOP, KFC, Larry's Subs, Little Caesars, McDonald's, Pagoda Chinese, Red Lobster, Taco Bell, Wendy's, Woody's BBQ, 🛏 Best Inn, Homewood Suites, La Quinta, Motel 6, Quality Inn, Residence Inn, Sheraton, Studio 6, Sun Suites, 🅞 BJ's Whse/gas, CVS Drug, Discount Tire, $Tree, Goodyear/auto, Harley-Davidson, Lowe's, Office Depot
340	FL 115, Southside Blvd (from nb) E on FL 115 🅖 Kangaroo/dsl, 🍴 5 Guys Burgers, Longhorn Steaks, 🅞 AT&T, Home Depot, Michael's, Petsmart, Target, same as 339
339	US 1, Philips Hwy, E 🅖 Kangaroo/dsl, RaceTrac, 🍴 Arby's, Bono's BBQ, Buca Italian, Burger King, Chick-fil-A, Coldstone, McDonald's, Mikado, Moe's SW Grill, Olive Garden, Ruby Tuesday, Starbucks, Taco Bell, 🅞 Belk, Best Buy, Chevrolet, Dillard's, $Tree, Ford, JC Penney, Mazda, Nissan, Sears/auto, Tire Kingdom, Toyota, Walmart, mall, W 🅖 BP/dsl, 🍴 Benito's Italian, Steak&Shake, Subway
337	I-295 N, to rd 9a, Orange Park, Jax Beaches
335	Old St Augustine Rd, E 🍴 Applebee's, Starbucks, 🛏 Courtyard, 🅞 🄷, W 🅖 Gate/dsl, Shell, 🍴 Bamboo Wok, Bono's BBQ, Chili's, Daruma Steaks, 5 Guys Burgers, McDonald's, Panera Bread, Subway, Tijuana Flats, Zaxby's, 🛏 Hampton Inn, 🅞 AT&T, GNC, Goodyear/auto, Kohl's, Publix, Verizon, Walgreens, vet
331mm	🆁 both lanes, full 🛇 facilities, 🄲, vending, 🛆 litter barrels, petwalk, 24hr security
329	rd 210, Green Cove Springs, Ponte Vedra Beach, E 🍴 ▨▨/McDonald's/dsl/scales/24hr, Sunoco/fruit, TA/Shell/Subway/dsl/scales/24hr/@, 🍴 Waffle House, W 🅖

JACKSONVILLE

🅖 = gas 🍴 = food 🛏 = lodging 🅞 = other 🆁🆂 = rest stop Copyright 2014 - The Next Exit ®

INTERSTATE 95 CONT'D

Exit	Services

329 Continued
BP/Subway/dsl/USPO, Marathon/Kangaroo/dsl, Shell, 🍴 Burger King, China Wok, Domino's, Dunkin Donuts, Firehouse Subs, Jenk's Pizza, Starbucks, Tropical Smoothie, Yummy Asian, 🅞 AT&T, CVS Drug, Winn-Dixie, fireworks, vet

323 International Golf Pkwy, **E** 🅖 BP/dsl/USPO, Shell/Subway/dsl, 🛏 Comfort Suites, **W** 🍴 Cino's Pizza, King Wok, Village Grill/Subs, 🛏 Renaissance Resort, 🅞 World Golf Village, vet

318 FL 16, Green Cove Sprgs, St Augustine, **E** 🅖 BP/DQ/dsl, Gate/dsl/fruit, Kangaroo/dsl, Shell, 🍴 Burger King, Dunkin Donuts, Krystal, McDonald's, NY Diner, Subway, 🛏 Best Value Inn, Comfort Inn, Courtyard, Fairfield Inn, Holiday Inn Express, La Quinta, Quality Inn, 🅞 Camping World RV Ctr, Cadillac, Ford/Lincoln, Gander Mtn, Gore's RV Ctr, St Augustine Outlets/Famous Brands, **W** 🅖 Exxon, RaceTrac/dsl, 🍴 A-1 Chinese, Cracker Barrel, Denny's, Giovanni's Italian, IHOP, KFC, LemonGrass Asian, Ruby Tuesday, Sonny's BBQ, Taco Bell, Wendy's, 🛏 Best Western, Days Inn, Hampton Inn, Ramada Ltd, Super 8, Wingate Inn, 🅞 St Augustine Outlets, Verizon, RV camping, funpark

311 FL 207, St Augustine, **E** 🅖 Chevron, Hess/Subway/dsl, RaceTrac/dsl, 🅞 🅷 Indian Forest RV Park (2mi), Indian River Fruit, KOA (7mi), St Johns RV Park, flea mkt/fireworks, to Anastasia SP, **W** 🅖 Mobil/dsl/repair, 🛏 Quality Inn

305 FL 206, to Hastings, Crescent Beach, **E** 🅖 ✈FLYING J/Denny's/Subway/dsl/LP/scales/24hr, 🅞 to Ft Matanzas NM, truck repair, **W** 🍴 truck repair

302mm 🆁🆂 both lanes, full 🅷 facilities, 🅲, vending, 🅰 litter barrels, petwalk, 24hr security

298 US 1, to St Augustine, **E** 🅖 BP/dsl, Indian River Fruit, Sunoco, 🅞 to Faver-Dykes SP, **W** 🅖 Mobil/DQ/dsl, Sunrise/dsl

289 to FL A1A (toll br), to Palm Coast, **E** 🅖 Kangaroo/dsl, Mobil/7-11, RaceTrac/dsl, Shell, 🍴 China Express, Colletti's Italian, Cracker Barrel, Denny's, Dunkin Donuts, Grand China, KFC, McDonald's, Salsa's Mexican, Starbucks, Wendy's, 🛏 Best Western, Fairfield Inn, Microtel, Sleep Inn, 🅞 Beall's, CVS Drug, Publix, Staples, Walgreens, vet, **W** 🅖 Chevron, Citgo, Shell, Kangaroo/dsl, 🍴 Baskin-Robbins/Dunkin Donuts, Bob Evans, Brusters, China King, China One, Golden Corral, HoneyBaked Ham, Houligan's, Joe's NY Pizza, Nathan's Cafe, Outback Steaks, Perkins, Ruby Tuesday, Sakura Japanese, Sonny's BBQ, Steak'n Shake, Subway, Taco Bell, Wendy's, 🛏 Days Inn, 🅞 Advance Parts, AutoZone, Beall's, Belk, CVS Drug, $General, Ford, Home Depot, Kohl's, Lowe's, Publix, Radio Shack, Tire Kingdom, Tuffy Auto, Verizon, Walgreens, Walmart, Winn-Dixie, USPO

286mm weigh sta both lanes, 🅲

284 FL 100, to Bunnell, Flagler Beach, **E** 🅖 Mobil/dsl, Valero/dsl, 🍴 Burger King, Domino's, McDonald's, Oriental Garden, Subway, Woody's BBQ, 🛏 Hampton Inn, Holiday Inn Express, 🅞 Ace Hardware, Curves, Russell Stover's, Winn-Dixie, vet, **W** 🅖 BP, 🅞 Dunkin Donuts, Panera Bread, Red Lobster, 🛏 Hilton Garden, 🅞 🅷 Chevrolet, Chrysler/Dodge/Jeep

278 Old Dixie Hwy, **E** 🅖 7-11, 🍴 King Chinese, Plantation Grill, 🅞 Bulow RV Park (3mi), Publix, to Tomoka SP, **W** 🅖 BP/dsl, 🍴 Joe's Pizza, 🛏 Country Hearth Inn, 🅞 Holiday Travel Park, vet

273 US 1, **E** 🅖 Chevron, RaceTrac/dsl, 🍴 McDonald's, Waffle House, 🛏 Econo Inn, La Quinta, 🅞 Giant Rec RV Ctr, fruit/fireworks, **W** 🅖 Exxon/Burger King, ♥Loves/Arby's/dsl/scales/24hr, 🍴 Daytona Pig Stand BBQ, DQ, Houligan's, 🛏 Days Inn, Daytona Hotel, Motel 6, Scottish Inn, Super 8, 🅞 Encore RV Park, Harley-Davidson

268 FL 40, Ormond Beach, **E** 🅖 Chevron/dsl, Hess/dsl, 🍴 Applebee's, Boston Mkt, Chili's, Chick-fil-A, Crispers, Denny's, Dustin's BBQ, Houligan's, Mama Mia's Pizza, Papa John's, Starbucks, Steak'n Shake, Subway, Taco Bell, Takeya Steaks, The Dish, Wendy's, Wok&Roll, 🛏 Sleep Inn, 🅞 🅷 AT&T, Beall's, Discount Tire, $General, $Tree, GNC, Lowe's, Publix, Ross, Tire Kingdom, Walmart, Whole Foods Mkt, USPO, vet, to Tomoka SP, **W** 🅖 BP/Dunkin Donuts, Mobil/dsl, RaceTrac/dsl, 7-11, Texaco, 🍴 Cracker Barrel, Little Italy, McDonald's, Salsa's Mexican, 🛏 Hampton Inn, Jameson Inn, 🅞 Walgreens

265 LPGA Blvd, Holly Hill, Daytona Beach, **E** 🅖 7-11, Shell/Circle K/Dunkin Donuts/dsl, 🍴 Vince Carter Rest, Wendy's, 🅞 CVS Drug, **W** 🛏 Holiday Inn, 🅞 BMW, Chrysler/Dodge/Jeep, Fiat, Ford, Lincoln, Mazda, Nissan, VW

261b a US 92, to DeLand, Daytona Bch, **E** 🅖 Citgo/dsl, Hess/Quiznos/Dunkin Donuts/dsl, RaceTrac, RaceWay/dsl, 7-11, Sunoco, 🍴 Applebee's, Asian Grill, BJ's Rest., Bob Evans, Buffalo Wild Wings, Burger King, Carrabba's, Checkers, Chick-fil-A, Chili's, Chipotle Mexican, Cracker Barrel, Dickey's BBQ, Daytona Ale House, Denny's, Firehouse Subs, 5 Guys Burgers, Gators, Hooters, Jersey Mike's Subs, Jimmy John's, KFC, Krystal, Longhorn Steaks, McDonald's, Olive Garden, Outback Steaks, Panera Bread, Piccadilly, Quiznos, Red Lobster, Ruby Tuesday, Subway, Taco Bell, Tijuana Flats, Waffle House, Wendy's, Winghouse, 🛏 Comfort Suites, Hampton Inn, Hilton Garden, Holiday Inn Express, Homewood Suites, La Quinta, Quality Inn, Ramada Inn, Residence Inn, 🅞 🅷 AT&T, Barnes&Noble, Beall's, Best Buy, BigLots, Books-A-Million, Dick's, Dillard's, $Tree, Firestone/auto, Hobby Lobby, Home Depot, JC Penney, Jo-Ann Fabrics, K-Mart, Macy's, Marshall's, Michael's, Old Navy, PepBoys, PetCo, Petsmart, Sears/auto, Staples, SteinMart, Target, TJMaxx, Tuesday Morning, Verizon, World Mkt, mall, to Daytona Racetrack, **W** 🅖 BP/dsl, 🍴 IHOP, McDonald's, 🛏 Days Inn, Super 8, 🅞 KOA, flea mkt

260b a I-4, to Orlando, FL 400 **E**, to S Daytona, **E** 🅖 Chevron/dsl, Citgo/7-11

256 FL 421, to Port Orange, **E** 🅖 BP, Shell/Circle K, 🍴 Applebee's, Bob Evans, Boston Mkt, Burger King, Chick-fil-A, Chili's, Daily Grind Burgers, Denny's, Dustin's BBQ, Golden Corral, KFC, Marble Slab Creamery, McDonald's, Monterrey Grill, Panera Bread, Papa John's, Quiznos, Smoothie King, Sonny's BBQ, Stonewood Grill, TGIFriday's, Tijuana Flats, 🛏 Country Inn&Suites, La Quinta, 🅞 BigLots, CVS Drug, Daytona Beach RV Park, Home Depot, Lowe's, Save-a-Lot, Super Target, Tuffy Auto, Walgreens, Walmart, vet, **W** 🅖 BP, Citgo, 7-11, 🍴 China Chef, Coldstone, 5 Guys Burgers, Gatti's Pizza, Malibu Beach Grill, McDonald's, Olive Garden, Red Brick Pizza, Red Robin, Subway, Takara Steaks, TX Roadhouse, Wen

🅖 = gas   🍴 = food   🛏 = lodging   🅞 = other   ℞ = rest stop

⬆N INTERSTATE 95 CONT'D

Exit	Services
256	Continued dy's, 🅞 AT&T, Belk, $Tree, GNC, Kohl's, Marshall's, Michael's, PetCo, Publix, Walgreens, Whole Foods Mkt
249b a	FL 44, to De Land, New Smyrna Beach, **E** 🅖 Shell/dsl/fruit, 🅞 New Smyrna RV Camp (3mi), **W** 🅖 Chevron/dsl, 🍴 McDonald's, 🅞 Walmart/Subway
244	FL 442, to Edgewater, **E** 🅖 BP/dsl, 🅞 truck repair
231	rd 5A, Scottsmoor, **E** 🅖 BP/Stuckey's/dsl, 🅞 Crystal Lake RV Park
227mm	℞ sb, full 🚻 facilities, 🍴 vending, 🛒 litter barrels, petwalk, 24hr security
225mm	℞ nb, full 🚻 facilities, 🍴 vending, 🛒 litter barrels, petwalk, 24hr security
223	FL 46, Mims, **E** 🅖 Chevron (2mi), RaceWay/dsl, 🍴 McDonald's, **W** 🅖 BP, Shell, 🅞 KOA/LP, Seasons RV Park
220	FL 406, Titusville, **E** 🅖 BP/dsl, Shell/Hungry Howie's/dsl, 🍴 Beef'O'Brady's, 1st Wok, Kelsey's Pizza, McDonald's, Subway, Valentino's Rest, Wendy's, 🛏 Super 8, 🅞 🅗, Advance Parts, AT&T, $General, GNC, Publix, Tires+, Walgreens, to Canaveral Nat Seashore
215	FL 50, to Orlando, Titusville, **E** 🅖 BP/KFC/dsl, Circle K, Mobil/Subway/dsl, Murphy USA/dsl, Shell/DQ/dsl, 🍴 Buddy Freddy's, Burger King, Denny's, Durango Steaks, McDonald's, Panda Express, Quiznos, Sonny's BBQ, Taco Bell, Waffle House, Wendy's, 🛏 Best Western, Ramada Inn, 🅞 Aldi Foods, Ford, GNC, Home Depot, Lowe's, Marshall's, PetCo, Radio Shack, Staples, Target, Tire Kingdom, Walmart, to Kennedy Space Ctr, **W** 🍴 Cracker Barrel, IHOP, 🛏 Days Inn, Fairfield Inn, Hampton Inn, Holiday Inn, Quality Inn, 🅞 Christmas RV Park (8mi), Great Outdoors RV/golf Resort
212	FL 407, to FL 528 **toll (no re-entry sb)**
208	Port St John
205	FL 528 **(toll 528)**, to Cape Canaveral & Cape Port AFS
202	FL 524, Cocoa, **E** 🅖 Shell/dsl, 🅞 Museum of History&Science, **W** 🅖 BP/dsl, 🛏 Days Inn
201	FL 520, to Cocoa Bch, Cocoa, **E** 🅖 BP/dsl, Chevron, 🅖/Subway/dsl/scales/24hr, 🍴 IHOP, Waffle House, 🛏 Best Western, Motel 6, 🅞 🅗, Sams Club/gas, fireworks, **W** 🅖 Chevron/dsl, Shell/Burger King, Sunoco/dsl, 🍴 McDonald's, 🛏 Holiday Inn Express, 🅞 Camping World RV Ctr
195	FL 519, Fiske Blvd, **E** 🅖 Mobil/dsl, 7-11, 🍴 Dominico Italian, Ruby Tuesday, 🛏 Swiss Inn, 🅞 🅗, Discount Tire, Lowe's, Space Coast RV Park
191	rd 509, to Satellite Beach, Viera, **E** 🅖 BP, Hess/dsl, 7-11, Sunoco/dsl, 🍴 Bob Evans, Carrabba's, Chick-fil-A, DQ, Denny's, Domino's, Firehouse Subs, McDonald's, Papa John's, Perkins, Sonny's BBQ, Tropical Smoothie, Uno Grill, Wendy's, 🛏 Hampton Inn, Holiday Inn, 🅞 Urgent Care, AT&T, CVS Drug, Publix, Radio Shack, Tires+, Tuffy Auto, Walgreens, zoo, to Patrick AFB, **W** 🅖 Chevron/dsl, Murphy USA, 🍴 Asian Too, Asian Wok, Burger King, Chili's, Cracker Barrel, Coldstone, 5 Guys Burgers, Longhorn Steaks, Melting Pot, Mimi's Cafe, Moe's SW Grill, Panera Bread, Pita Pit, Pizza Gallery, Starbucks, Steak'nShake, Subway, 🛏 La Quinta, 🅞 🅗, AT&T, Belk, Books-A-Million, $Tree, GNC, Hobby Lobby, Kohl's, Lexus, Michael's, Office Depot, Old Navy, PetCo, Ross, SuperTarget, Tire Kingdom, Verizon, Walmart/McDonald's, World Mkt

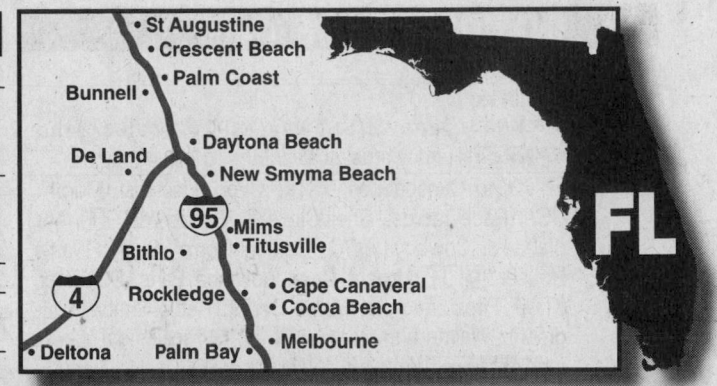

Exit	Services
188	FL 404, Patrick AFB, Satellite Beach
183	FL 518, Melbourne, Indian Harbour Beach, **E** 🅖 BP, Chevron/Baskin-Robbins/Dunkin Donuts/dsl, RaceTrac/dsl, 7-11, 🅞 🅗, AT&T, art museum, **W** Flea Mkt
180	US 192, to Melbourne, **E** 🅖 BP/dsl, Circle K, Mobil/dsl, RaceTrac/dsl, 7-11, Sunoco/dsl, 🍴 ChuckECheese, Denny's, IHOP, Waffle House, 🛏 Best Value Inn, Budget Inn, Days Inn, EconoLodge, Fairfield Inn, Hampton Inn, Holiday Inn Express, 🅞 🅗, Ace Hardware, Lowe's, Sam's Club/gas, Volvo, fireworks, vet
176	rd 516, to Palm Bay, **E** 🅖 BP/dsl, Citgo, Murphy USA/dsl, 7-11, 🍴 Baskin Robbins/Dunkin Donuts, Bob Evans, Chick-fil-A, Cracker Barrel, Denny's, Golden Corral, Starbucks, 🛏 Jameson Inn, 🅞 Aldi Foods, BJ's Whse/gas, GNC, Harley-Davidson, Office Depot, Walmart, Walgreens, vet, **W** 🅖 Mobil/dsl, 7-11, Shell, 🍴 Buffalo Wild Wings, Burger King, 5 Guys Burgers, Long Doggers, Longhorn Steaks, McDonald's, Michelli's Pizzeria, Moe's SW Grill, Panera Bread, Subway, Wendy's, 🅞 AT&T, CVS Drug, Discount Tire, $Tree, Kohl's, Marshall's, Michael's, PetCo, Publix, Ross, Target, Walgreens
173	FL 514, to Palm Bay, **E** 🅖 RaceTrac/dsl, Shell, Sunoco/dsl, 🛏 Holiday Inn Express, 🅞 🅗, Firestone/auto, Ford, truck/RV repair, **W** 🅖 Hess/Quiznos, Mobil/dsl, Sunoco, 🍴 Arby's, Burger King, IHOP, Japanese Buffet, McDonald's/playplace, Panda Express, Sonny's BBQ, Subway, Taco Bell, TX Roadhouse, Waffle House, Wendy's, 🛏 Comfort Suites, Motel 6, 🅞 Urgent Care, Advance Parts, Beall's, BigLots, CVS Drug, $General, Home Depot, Lowe's, Publix, Tire Kingdom, Verizon, Walgreens, Walmart, USPO
168mm	℞ both lanes, full 🚻 facilities, 🍴 vending, 🛒 litter barrels, petwalk, 24hr security
156	rd 512, to Sebastian, Fellsmere, **E** 🅖 BP/DQ/Stuckey's/dsl, Chevron/McDonald's, RaceWay/dsl, 🅞 🅗, Encore RV Park, Sebastian Inlet SRA, Vero Bch RV Park (8mi), **W** 🅞 Marsh Landing Camping, St Sebastian SP
147	FL 60, Osceola Blvd, **E** 🅖 BP/Dunkin Donuts/dsl, Citgo/dsl, Mobil/dsl, 7-11, Sunoco, TA/BP/Popeye's/Subway/dsl/scales/24hr/@, Texaco/dsl, Valero/dsl, 🍴 IHOP, Wendy's, 🛏 Best Value Inn, Comfort Suites, Howard Johnson, Knights Inn, Vero Beach Resort, 🅞 🅗, Hyundai, USPO, vet, **W** 🅖 Shell/dsl, 🍴 Cracker Barrel, McDonald's, Steak'n Shake, 🛏 Country Inn&Suites, Hampton Inn, Holiday Inn Express, 🅞 Vero Beach Outlets/famous brands
138	FL 614, Indrio Rd, 3 mi **E** 🅞 Oceanographic Institute
133mm	℞ both lanes, full 🚻 facilities, 🍴 vending, 🛒 litter barrels, petwalk, 24hr security
131b a	FL 68, Orange Ave, **E** 🅞 🅗, to Ft Pierce SP, **W** 🅖

↖N INTERSTATE 95 CONT'D

Exit	Services
131b a	Continued
	⛟FLYING J/Denny's/Subway/dsl/LP/scales/24hr, ▬Loves/Hardee's/dsl/scales/24hr, Ⓞ Blue Beacon
129	FL 70, to Okeechobee, E 🅿 Citgo, Hess/dsl, Murphy USA, RaceTrac/dsl, Shell/Circle K, Sunoco/dsl, 🍴 Applebee's, Cowboys BBQ, Golden Corral, Sonic, Waffle House, Ⓞ 🅷 Urgent Care, Advance Parts, $General, $Tree, Firestone/auto, Home Depot, Radio Shack, Walgreens, Walmart, truck tires, W 🅿 BP/scales/dsl, Chevron, ▬Loves/Arby's/dsl/24hr/@, Mobil/Dunkin Donuts/Subway, ▭▭/McDonald's/dsl/scales/24hr, 🍴 Burger King, Cracker Barrel, La Granja, LJ Silver, KFC, McDonald's, Red Lobster, Steak'n Shake, Waffle House, Wendy's, 🛏 Best Value Inn, Best Western, Comfort Suites, Fairfield Inn, Hampton Inn, Holiday Inn Express, La Quinta, Motel 6, Quality Inn, Rodeway Inn, Sleep Inn, Treasure Coast Inn, Ⓞ Indian River Fruit, Treasure Coast RV Park, to FL TPK, UF R&E Ctr
126	rd 712, Midway Rd, E 🅿 BP/Subway/dsl
121	St Lucie West Blvd, E 🅿 BP/Dunkin Donuts, Mobil/7-11, Murphy USA/dsl, 7-11, Shell/Subway/dsl, 🍴 Arby's, Bob Evans, Burger King, Carrabba's, Chili's, Chipotle Mexican, Duffy's Grill, Frank&Al's Pizza, Friendly's, Hokkaido, Hurricane Grill, IHOP, Jimmy John's, KFC, Little Caesars, McDonald's, Moe's SW Grill, Outback Steaks, PA BBQ, Panda Express, Panera Bread, Ruby Tuesday, Starbucks, Stevi B's Pizza, Taco Bell, TGIFriday's, Wendy's, 🛏 Hampton Inn, Holiday Inn Express, Residence Inn, SpringHill Suites, Ⓞ 🅷 Urgent Care, AT&T, Beall's, CVS Drug, $Tree, Outdoor Resorts Camping (2mi), PetCo, Publix/deli, Ross, Staples, SteinMart, Tires+, Tire Kingdom, Verizon, Walgreens, Walmart, USPO, W 🅿 Mobil/dsl, 🛏 Hilton Garden, MainStay Suites, Sheraton Resort, Ⓞ PGA Village
120	Crosstown Pkwy
118	Gatlin Blvd, to Port St Lucie, E 🅿 BP/dsl/LP, Chevron/Dunkin Donuts/Subway/dsl, Shell, Sunoco/e-85, 🍴 McDonald's, Taco Bell, Ⓞ AutoZone, Home Depot, Sam's Club/gas, Tires+, Walgreens, Walmart, vet, W 🍴 Longhorn Steaks, McDonald's, Olive Garden, Subway, Tropical Smoothie, 🛏 Homewood Suites, Ⓞ 🅷 GNC, Michael's, Old Navy, Petsmart, Publix, Radio Shack, Target, TJ Maxx
114	Becker Rd
112mm	weigh sta sb
110	FL 714, to Martin Hwy, Palm City, Stuart, E 🅷
106mm	🅁ˢ both lanes, full 🚻 facilities, 🍴, vending, 🦮 litter barrels, petwalk, 24hr security
102	Rd 713, High Meadow Ave, Palm City, Stuart
101	FL 76, to Stuart, Indiantown, E 🅿 Chevron/dsl, Sunoco/dsl, 🍴 Baskin-Robbins/Dunkin Donuts, Cracker Barrel, McDonald's, 🛏 Courtyard, Holiday Inn Express, Ⓞ 🅷 Publix, Walgreens, city park, W 🅿 Marathon/DQ/dsl, Valero/dsl, Ⓞ RV camping
96	rd 708, to Hobe Sound, E Dickinson SP (11mi), RV camping
92mm	weigh sta nb
87b a	FL 706, to Okeechobee, Jupiter, E 🅿 Citgo, Mobil/dsl, Shell/dsl, Sunoco, 🍴 Applebee's, Cheeseburgers&More, Duffy's Rest., Dunkin Donuts, 5 Guys Burgers, Giuseppe's, IHOP, Jersey Mike's Subs, KFC, McDonald's, Panera

87b a	Continued
	Bread, Pollo Tropical, Rancho Chico, Sonny's BBQ, Starbucks, Subway, Taco Bell, Tomato Pie, YumYum, 🛏 Comfort Inn, Fairfield Inn, Ⓞ 🅷 Urgent Care, Advance Parts, BMW, Books-A-Million, GNC, Home Depot, PepBoys, Publix, Tire Kingdom, Walgreens, Walmart, Winn-Dixie, to Dickinson SP, hist sites, museum, vet, W 🅿 Sunoco, Ⓞ RV camping, to FL TPK
83	Donald Ross Rd, E 🅿 BP/Subway, Shell/deli, 🍴 McDonald's, 🛏 Hampton Inn, Holiday Inn Express, Homewood Suites, Ⓞ 🅷 AT&T, CVS Drug, Walgreens, stadium
79c	FL 809 S (from sb), Military Tr, W to FL TPK, same services as 79b
79a b	FL 786, PGA Blvd, E 🅿 Shell, 🍴 Chili's, TGIFriday's, Yardhouse Rest, 🛏 Hilton Garden, Marriott, Ⓞ 🅷 Best Buy, Michael's, PetCo, Publix, Whole Foods Mkt, W 🅿 Shell/dsl, 🍴 Cantina Laredo, China Kitchen, Chipotle Mexican, J Alexanders, Outback Steaks, 3 Forks Rest, 🛏 DoubleTree Hotel, Embassy Suites, Ⓞ CVS Drug, Publix
77	Northlake Blvd, to W Palm Bch, E 🅿 BP, Hess/Dunkin Donuts, Shell/dsl, 🍴 Aladdin Grill, Applebee's, Arby's, Burger King, Checkers, Chick-fil-A, Giovanni's Rest, Jimmy John's, KFC, La Granja, Little Caesars, McDonald's, Miami Subs, Panera Bread, Pollo Tropical, Starbucks, Taco Bell, Ⓞ 🅷 AT&T, Buick/Chevrolet/GMC, Chrysler/Dodge/Jeep, Costco, CVS Drug, $Tree, Family$, Ford, Gander Mtn, Home Depot, Hyundai, K-Mart, Lowe's, PepBoys, Ross, Staples, Target, Verizon, VW, Walgreens, vet, W 🅿 Chevron/dsl, Shell, Sunoco/dsl, Valero, 🍴 Duffy's Grill, Dunkin Donuts, Original Pancakes, Papa John's, Pizza Hut, Wendy's, 🛏 Inn of America, Ⓞ Advance Parts, CVS Drug, Radio Shack, Publix, Verizon, Winn-Dixie, vet
76	FL 708, Blue Heron Blvd, E 🅿 BP/dsl, Shell/dsl, 🍴 Wendy's, 🛏 Travelodge, Ⓞ Honda, Kia, Nissan, Walgreens, W 🅿 BP, Chevron/dsl, Cumberland Farms, RaceTrac/dsl, Texaco/dsl, 🍴 Burger King, Denny's, McDonald's, 🛏 Super 8
74	FL 702, 45th St, E 🍴 Burger King, IHOP, 🛏 Days Inn, Ⓞ 🅷 Urgent Care, Cadillac, Walgreens, W 🅿 RaceTrac, 🍴 Cracker Barrel, McDonald's, Pollo Tropical, Subway, Taco Bell, Wendy's, 🛏 Courtyard, Extended Stay Deluxe, Holiday Inn Express, Homewood Suites, Red Roof Inn, Residence Inn, SpringHill Suites, Ⓞ Family$, FoodTown, Goodyear/auto, Harley-Davidson, Sams Club/gas, Walmart
71	Lake Blvd, Palm Beach, E 🅿 BP, Mobil/7-11/dsl, 🍴 McDonald's, Wendy's, 🛏 Best Western, Ⓞ 🅷 Best Buy, Firestone/auto, Home Depot, JC Penney, Target, Tire Kingdom, W 🅿 Texaco/dsl, Valero, 🍴 Carrabba's, Chick-fil-A, Chipotle Mexican, Hooters, Manzo Italian, Palm Tree Cafe, Sweet Tomatoes, 🛏 Comfort Inn, La Quinta, Ⓞ Urgent Care, Walgreens, vet
70b a	FL 704, Okeechobee Blvd, E 🍴 McCormick&Schmicks, Ruth's Chris Steaks, 🛏 Marriott, Ⓞ museum, W 🅿 BP/dsl, Chevron/dsl, Hess, Mobil/dsl, Shell, Texaco/dsl, Valero/dsl, 🍴 Arby's, Burger King, Checkers, Denny's, Firehouse Grill, IHOP, McDonald's, Pizza Hut, Pollo Tropical, Starbucks, Subway, Taco Bell, Ⓞ AT&T, Audi/Porsche, BMW/Mini, Chevrolet, $Tree, Firestone/auto, GNC, Hyundai, Mercedes, Michael's, Office Depot, Old Navy, Petsmart, Staples, Verizon, VW
69b	W to 🖂

Side tabs: OKEECHOBEE · FL · W PALM BEACH · PALM BEACH

⬆🅽 INTERSTATE 95 CONT'D

Exit	Services
69a	Belvedere Rd, **W** 🅿 BP, Shell, 🍴 Burger King, IHOP, Wendy's, 🛏 Best Western, Courtyard, Crowne Plaza, DoubleTree, Hampton Inn, Hilton Garden, Holiday Inn/rest., Studio 6
68	US 98, Southern Blvd, **E** 🅿 Texaco, 🅾 CVS Drug, Publix, Radio Shack, **W** 🛏 Hilton
66	Forest Hill Blvd, **W** 🅿 Chevron/dsl, Sunoco, 🍴 Bellante's Pizza, 🅾 Advance Parts
64	10th Ave N, **W** 🅿 BP, Citgo, 🍴 China Empire, Dunkin Donuts, Flanigans Grill, Wendy's, 🅾 CarQuest, CVS Drug, Family$, Ford, President Foods, Ross, Tires+, Walgreens, Walmart/Subway, vet
63	6th Ave S, **W** 🏥
61	FL 812, Lantana Rd, **E** 🅿 Shell, 🍴 Domino's, Dunkin Donuts, Golden Wok, KFC, Little Caesars, McDonald's, Pearl's Rest, Riggin's Crabhouse, Subway, 🛏 Motel 6, 🅾 Ace Hardware, CVS Drug, $General, Publix, 7-11, **W** 🅾 🏥, Costco/gas
60	Hypoluxo Rd, **E** 🅿 BP, Mobil/dsl, Shell/dsl, 🍴 IHOP, Popeye's, Subway, Taco Bell, Wendy's, 🛏 Best Value Inn, Comfort Inn, Super 8, 🅾 Family$, Sam's Club, Tires+, Tire Kingdom, Tire Pros, Winn-Dixie, **W** 🅿 Valero/dsl, 🍴 Anchor Inn Rest, 🅾 Advance Parts
59	Gateway Blvd, **W** 🅿 Mobil/7-11/dsl, 🍴 Bonefish Grill, Boynton Alehouse, Carrabba's, Chili's, Firehouse Subs, Friendly's, Golden Phoenix Chinese, Greek Cafe, McDonald's, Starbucks, Subway, Tropical Smoothie, 🛏 Hampton Inn, 🅾 AT&T, CarMax, CVS Drug, Kohl's, Publix, Ross, Tuesday Morning, vet
57	FL 804, Boynton Bch Blvd, **E** 🅿 Marathon/dsl, 🍴 KFC, 🛏 Boynton Beach Inn, 🅾 🏥, USPO, **0-2 mi W** 🅿 BP, Mobil, Shell, 🍴 Applebee's, Burger King, Checkers, Chick-Fil-A, Dunkin Donuts, Golden Corral, KFC, La Granja, Little Caesars, Sonic, Starbucks, Steak'n Shake, Subway, TGIFriday's, Wendy's, 🅾 Barnes&Noble, BJ's Whse/gas, CVS Drug, Dick's, Dillard's, GNC, JC Penney, Macy's, Office Depot, Old Navy, PetCo, Petsmart, Publix, Radio Shack, Sears, 7-11, SteinMart, TJ Maxx, Walmart, USPO, vet
56	Woolbright Rd, **E** 🅿 Shell, Valero, 🍴 Boynton Diner, McDonald's, Subway, 🅾 🏥, Jo-Ann Fabrics, Publix, 7-11, Walgreens, Winn-Dixie, vet, **W** 🅿 RaceTrac/dsl, 🍴 Burger King, Cracker Barrel, Dunkin Donuts, 🅾 Advance Parts, Bravo Foods, Home Depot, Lowe's, Staples, Walgreens
52b a	FL 806, Atlantic Ave, **W** 🅿 Chevron/dsl, Shell/dsl, 🍴 Dunkin Donuts, Sandwich Man, Silver Wok, 🅾 🏥, Tires+, Verizon, Walgreens, transmissions, vet
51	rd 782, Linton Blvd, **E** 🅿 Shell, 🍴 Applebee's, Arby's, Chipotle Mexican, DQ, Duffy's Grill, IHOP, KFC, McDonald's, Outback Steaks, Pollo Tropical, Steak'n Shake, Subway, Taco Bell, Wendy's, 🅾 AT&T, Chevrolet, Ford, Home Depot, Marshall's, Michael's, Mercedes, Petsmart, Publix, Ross, Staples, Target, Tire Kingdom, Verizon, **W** 🅿 Shell, 🍴 Little Caesars, 🅾 🏥, Urgent Care, Family$, Monterrey's Mkt
50	Congress Ave, **W** 🅿 Mobil, 🛏 Hilton Garden, Residence Inn
48b a	FL 794, Yamato Rd, **E** 🅿 Mobil, 🍴 Panera Bread, 🅾 CVS Drug, vet, **W** 🅿 Chevron/dsl, Mobil, 🍴 Blue Fin,

Exit	Services
48b a	Continued
	Dunkin Donuts, Jersey Mike's Subs, Jimmy John's, McDonald's, Miller's Alehouse, Quiznos, Sal's Italian, Starbucks, Subway, Wendy's, 🛏 DoubleTree, Embassy Suites, Guest Suites, Hampton Inn, SpringHill Suites, TownePlace Suites
45	FL 808, Glades Rd, **E** 🅿 Chevron/dsl, 🍴 J Alexander's Rest, Jamba Juice, PF Changs, 🛏 Fairfield Inn, 🅾 Barnes&Noble, CVS Drug, Whole Foods Mkt, museum, **W** 🅿 BP, 🍴 Brewzzi Cafe, Brio Italian Grill, CA Pizza Kitchen, Capital Grille, Cheesecake Factory, Chili's, Chipotle Mexican, Coldstone, Hooters, Houston Rest., Macaroni Grill, Maggiano's Italian, Moe's SW Grill, Morton Steaks, Pinon Grill, Quiznos, Rosso Italian, Season's Rest, Starbucks, Stephane's, Stir Crazy, Subway, Wendy's, 🛏 Courtyard, Holiday Inn, Marriott, Wyndham Garden, 🅾 Macy's, Nordstrom, Publix, Sears/auto
44	Palmetto Park Rd, **E** 🅿 Valero/dsl, 🍴 Denny's, Dunkin Donuts, Red's BBQ, Subway, Taco Bell, Tomasso's Pizza, 🅾 AT&T, K-Mart, Publix, museums, **W** 🍴 McDonald's (2mi)
42b a	FL 810, Hillsboro Blvd, **E** 🅿 BP, Shell/dsl, 🍴 Hook Fish&Chicken, McDonald's, Popeye's, Wendy's, 🛏 Hampton Inn, Hilton, La Quinta, 🅾 Advance Parts, **W** 🅿 Chevron/dsl, Mobil/dsl, 🍴 Boston Mkt, Checkers, Dunkin Donuts, Subway, 🛏 Holiday Park Hotel, La Quinta, 🅾 CVS Drug, Home Depot, Walgreens
41	FL 869 (**toll**), SW 10th, to I-75, **E** 🅿 Mobil/7-11, 🍴 Cracker Barrel, Pizza Express, 🛏 Extended Stay America, **W** 🛏 Best Western, Comfort Suites
39	FL 834, Sample Rd, **E** 🅿 BP, Chevron/dsl, Hess/dsl, Shell/dsl, 🍴 Taco Bell, 🅾 🏥, $General, Save-A-Lot, U-Haul, **W** 🅿 Chevron, Citgo/dsl, Mobil/dsl, Solo/dsl, Sunoco/dsl, 🍴 Burger King, Checkers, IHOP, La Granja, McDonald's, Miami Subs, Subway, 🅾 CarMax, Costco/gas, CVS Drug, Family$, Seabra Foods, 7-11, vet
38b a	Copans Rd, **E** 🅿 BP/7-11, 🍴 McDonald's, Subway, 🅾 Land Rover, Mercedes, PepBoys, Porche/Audi, Walmart, **W** 🅿 Chevron, Valero/dsl, 🅾 Home Depot, NAPA
36b a	FL 814, Atlantic Blvd, to Pompano Beach, **E** 🅿 RaceTrac/dsl, 🍴 KFC/Pizza Hut/Taco Bell, Miami Subs, **1 mi W** 🅿 BP, Chevron, Mobil/dsl, Murphy USA/dsl, 🍴 Baskin-Robbins/Dunkin Donuts, Burger King, Golden Corral, KFC/LJ Silver, McDonald's, Pollo Tropical, Subway, Wendy's, 🅾 Chevrolet/Mazda, CVS Drug, $Tree, Radio Shack, Walgreens, Walmart, USPO, to FL TPK, Power Line Rd has many services
33b a	Cypress Creek Rd, **E** 🅿 BP, Hess, 7-11, 🍴 Duffy's Diner, 🛏 Extended Stay America, Hampton Inn, Westin Hotel, **W**

(vertical text in margin: POMPANO BEACH)

⛽ = gas   🍴 = food   🏨 = lodging   Ⓞ = other   🅛s = rest stop   Copyright 2014 - The Next Exit ®

⬆N INTERSTATE 95 CONT'D

Exit	Services
33b a	Continued ⛽ Hess, Shell/repair, 🍴 Arby's, Burger King, Carlucci's Italian, Champp's Grill, Chili's, 5 Guys Burgers, Hooters, Longhorn Steaks, McDonald's, Moonlite Diner, Subway, Sweet Tomatoes, Wendy's, 🏨 Courtyard, La Quinta, Marriott, Sheraton Suites, Ⓞ **Urgent Care**, AT&T, GNC, Jaguar, Office Depot, Tires+
32	FL 870, Commercial Blvd, Lauderdale by the Sea, Lauderhill, E 🍴 Subway, W ⛽ BP, Circle K, Mobil/dsl, Shell, Sunoco/dsl, 🍴 Dunkin Donuts, KFC, McDonald's, Miami Subs, Subway, Waffle House, 🏨 Holiday Inn Express, Red Roof Inn, Universal Palms Motel, Ⓞ Advance Parts, BJ's Whse/gas, Tire Kingdom, auto repair
31b a	FL 816, Oakland Park Blvd, E ⛽ Chevron, Mobil/dsl, Petro America/dsl, 7-11, 🍴 BBQ Jacks, Burger King, Checkers, Denny's, Domino's, Dunkin Donuts, Little Caesars, McDonald's, Miami Subs, Primanti Bros, Subway, Taco Bell, 24 Diner, Wendy's, Ⓞ Advance Parts, K-Mart, Lowe's, Publix, Radio Shack, Walgreens, W ⛽ BP/dsl, RaceTrac/dsl, Shell, Texaco, Valero, 🍴 Burger King, Checkers, Baskin-Robbins/Dunkin Donuts, IHOP, KFC, McDonald's, Pizza Hut, Subway, 🏨 Days Inn, Ⓞ $General, Home Depot, Toyota/Scion, Walgreens, USPO, vet
29b a	FL 838, Sunrise Blvd, E ⛽ BP, Shell, Sunoco/dsl/e-85, Valero/dsl, 🍴 Burger King, Krystal, Miami Subs, Popeye's, Ⓞ Advance Parts, AutoZone, Family$, Winn-Dixie, auto repair/tires, to Birch SP, W ⛽ BP, Exxon/dsl, Marathon, Shell, Valero, 🍴 China Bowl, Church's, KFC, McDonald's, Snapper's Fish&Chicken, Subway, Ⓞ 🅗, Family$
27	FL 842, Broward Blvd, Ft Lauderdale, E 🅗
26	I-595 (from sb), FL 736 (from nb), Davie Blvd, W to ✈
25	FL 84, E ⛽ Marathon/dsl, RaceTrac/dsl, 7-11, Sunoco/dsl, Texaco, Valero, 🍴 Dunkin Donuts, Li'l Red's BBQ, McDonald's, Ruby Chinese, Subway, Wendy's, 🏨 Best Western, Candlewood Suites, Holiday Inn Express, Motel 6, Sky Motel, Ⓞ BigLots, $Tree, Firestone/auto, Radio Shack, U-Haul, Winn-Dixie, W 🏨 Ramada Inn, Red Carpet Inn, Rodeway Inn
24	I-595 (from nb), to I-75, E to ✈
23	FL 818, Griffin Rd, E 🏨 Hilton, Sheraton, W ⛽ Mobil, 🍴 Subway, 🏨 Courtyard, Fairfield Inn, Homewood Suites, Ⓞ Bass Pro Shops, N Trail RV Ctr, Publix
22	FL 848, Stirling Rd, Cooper City, E ⛽ Mobil, 🍴 AleHouse Grill, Burger King, Dave&Buster's, Chipotle Mexican, McDonald's, Moonlite Diner, Quiznos, Red Lobster, Sal's Italian, Sweet Tomatoes, Taco Bell, TGIFriday's, Wendy's, Yum Berry Yogurt, 🏨 Comfort Inn, Hampton Inn, Hilton Garden, Hyatt House, Hyatt Place, La Quinta, SpringHill Suites, Ⓞ Advance Parts, BJ's Whse, GNC, Home Depot, K-Mart, Marshall's, Michael's, Old Navy, Petsmart, Radio Shack, Ross, Verizon, to Lloyd SP, W 🍴 Las Vegas Cuban, Mr M's Sandwiches, Subway, 🏨 Best Western, Ⓞ CVS Drug, PepBoys, Tire Kingdom, Walgreens, Winn-Dixie, vet
21	FL 822, Sheridan St, E ⛽ BP, Chevron/dsl, Cumberland Farms/gas, same as 22, W ⛽ Shell, 🍴 Denny's, 🏨 Days Inn, Holiday Inn
20	FL 820, Hollywood Blvd, E ⛽ Shell, 🍴 IHOP, Miami Subs, 🏨 Hollywood Gateway Inn, Ⓞ Goodyear/auto, Office Depot, U-Haul, vet, W ⛽ BP, Chevron/dsl, 🍴 Bos

Exit	Services
20	Continued ton Mkt, China Hollywood, Coldstone, Firehouse Subs, Mama Fu's Asian, McDonald's, Offerdahl's Grill, Quiznos, Taco Bell, Starbucks, Subway, Waffle Works, Wendy's, Ⓞ 🅗, Publix, Radio Shack, Target, Verizon, Walgreens
19	FL 824, Pembroke Rd, E ⛽ Shell, W ⛽ Giant
18	FL 858, Hallandale Bch Blvd, E ⛽ Exxon, 7-11, Shell, 🍴 Baskin-Robbins/Dunkin Donuts, Burger King, Denny's, IHOP, KFC, La Granja, Little Caesars, McDonald's, Miami Subs, Pollo Tropical, Subway, Wendy's, Won Ton Garden, 🏨 Best Western, Ⓞ 🅗, Family$, Goodyear/auto, Tire Kingdom, Walgreens, Winn-Dixie, vet, W ⛽ BP/dsl, RaceTrac/dsl, Ⓞ Advance Parts
16	Ives Dairy Rd, E 🅗, mall, W ⛽ BP/7-11, 🍴 Subway
14	FL 860, Miami Gardens Dr, N Miami Beach, E 🅗, Oleta River SRA, W ⛽ BP, Valero/dsl
12c	US 441, FL 826, FL TPK, FL 9, E ⛽ BP, Chevron, Hess/dsl, 7-11, Valero, 🍴 Baskin-Robbins/Dunkin Donuts, Burger King, McDonald's, Wendy's 🏨 Holidays Hotel, Ⓞ 🅗, PepBoys
12b	US 441 (from nb), same as 12c
12a	FL 868 (from nb), FL TPK N
11	NW 151st (from nb), W ⛽ Sunoco/dsl, 🍴 McDonald's, Ⓞ Advance Parts, Winn-Dixie, services on US 441 N
10b	FL 916, NW 135th, Opa-Locka Blvd, W ⛽ Chevron, CR/dsl, Liberty, 🍴 Checkers, Subway
10a	NW 125th, N Miami, Bal Harbour, W ⛽ Shell, 🍴 Burger King, Wendy's
9	NW 119th (from nb), W ⛽ BP/McDonald's, 🍴 KFC, Pollo Tropical, Popeye's, Ⓞ Advance Parts, AutoZone, CVS Drug, Family$, Walgreens, Winn-Dixie
8b	FL 932, NW 103rd, E ⛽ Shell, Texaco, Ⓞ 7-11, W ⛽ BP, Sunoco, 🍴 Baskin-Robbins/Dunkin Donuts, Bravo Foods, $General
8a	NW 95th, E ⛽ BP, W ⛽ CR/dsl, Mobil/dsl, 🍴 McDonald's, Ⓞ 🅗, Advance Parts, Walgreens
7	FL 934, NW 81st, NW 79th, E ⛽ BP/dsl, Chevron/dsl, W ⛽ Sunoco, 🍴 Checkers
6b	NW 69th (from sb)
6a	FL 944, NW 62nd, NW 54th, W 🍴 China Town, McDonald's, Subway, Wing Stop, Ⓞ Family$, Presidente Mkt, Walgreens
4b a	I-195 E, FL 112 W (toll), Miami Beach, E downtown, W ✈
3b	NW 8th St (from sb)
3a	FL 836 W (toll) (exits left from nb), W 🅗, to ✈
2d	I-395 E (exits left from sb), to Miami Beach
2c	NW 8th, NW 14th (from sb), Miami Ave, E Port of Miami
2b	NW 2nd (from nb), downtown Miami
2a	US 1 (exits left from sb), Biscayne Blvd, downtown Miami
1b	US 41, SW 7th, SW 8th, Brickell Ave, E ⛽ Chevron, Citgo, 🍴 Burger King, Graziano's, McDonald's, Munchies, Subway, Wendy's, 🏨 Extended Stay America, Hampton Inn, Ⓞ CVS Drug, GNC, Publix, W ⛽ Shell, 🍴 Papa John's, Pepper's Mexican Grill
1a	SW 25th (from sb), downtown, to Rickenbacker Causeway, E Ⓞ museum, to Baggs SRA
0mm	**I-95 begins/ends on US 1, 1 mi S** ⛽ BP, 🍴 Quiznos

⬆N INTERSTATE 275 (TAMPA)

Exit	Services
59mm	**I-275 begins/ends on I-75, exit 274.**
53	Bearss Ave, E ⛽ Citgo/dsl, Ⓞ Carmax, W ⛽ Chevron/dsl, Marathon/Dunkin Donuts, RaceTrac/dsl, Shell, 🍴 Burger King, IHOP, McDonald's, Subway, 🏨 Vista Inn, Ⓞ

FL

F T L A U D E R D A L E

H O L L Y W O O D

M I A M I

INTERSTATE 275 (TAMPA) CONT'D

Exit	Services
53	Continued
	Aldi Foods, BigLots, CVS Drug, GNC, Ross
52	Fletcher Ave, **E** 🅖 BP, Citgo/dsl, Hess, RaceTrac/dsl, Shell/dsl, Sunoco, 🍴 Arby's, Bruno's Pizza, Church's, DQ, Hoho Chinese, Krystal, Little Caesars, McDonald's, Popeye's, 🛏 Days Inn, 🅞 🅗, Aldi Foods, AutoZone, Family$, Toyota/Scion, to USF, **W** 🅖 BP, Citgo, Mobil, 🍴 Dunkin Donuts, 🛏 Super 8, 🅞 Advance Parts, Cadillac, Family$, Jaguar, Save-A-Lot, Sweetbay Foods
51	FL 582, Fowler Ave, **E** 🅖 BP, Citgo/dsl, GK, Mobil/dsl, Shell/Circle K, 🍴 A&W/LJ Silver, Baskin-Robbins/Dunkin Donuts, Burger King, Checkers, Chili's, China Buffet, Chipotle Mexican, Denny's, Firehouse Subs, 5 Guys Burgers, Jason's Deli, Jimmy John's, KFC, Longhorn Steaks, McAliter's Deli, McDonald's, Panera Bread, Pizza Hut, Quiznos, Sonic, Steak'n Shake, Subway, Taco Bell, TGI-Friday's, Tia's TexMex, Waffle House, Wendy's, 🛏 Clarion, Embassy Suites, Howard Johnson, Hyatt Place, La Quinta, Wingate Inn, 🅞 Advance Parts, AT&T, CarQuest, CVS Drug, $General, $Tree, Family$, Firestone/auto, Macy's, O'Reilly Parts, Sears/auto, 7-11, Sweetbay Foods, Verizon, Walgreens, **W** 🛏 Economy Inn, Motel 6, Rodeway Inn, 🅞 Audi, BMW
50	FL 580, Busch Blvd, **E** 🅖 BP, Chevron, Citgo, 🍴 Arby's, McDonald's, Olive Garden, Popeye's, Red Lobster, Sonny's BBQ, Subway, Taco Bell, 🛏 Days Inn, Holiday Inn Express, La Quinta, Red Roof Inn, 🅞 AutoZone, Busch Gardens, $General, Family$, Walgreens, **W** 🅖 Chevron/dsl, 🍴 Burger King, Pizza Hut, 🅞 Advance Parts, CVS Drug, $Tree, Firestone/auto, Home Depot, Meineke, Radio Shack, Walmart Mkt
49	Bird Ave (from nb), **W** 🅖 Shell, 🍴 Checkers, KFC, McDonald's, Wendy's, 🅞 $General, K-Mart, Save-A-Lot
48	Sligh Ave, **E** 🅖 BP, Sunoco, 🅞 USPO, **W** 🅞 zoo
47b a	US 92, to US 41 S, Hillsborough Ave, **E** 🅖 Circle K, Marathon, Mobil/dsl, 🍴 Burger King, Checkers, McDonald's, Popeye's, Subway, Wendy's, 🅞 Advance Parts, Ross, Walgreens, vet, **W** 🅖 BP, Shell/Circle K, 🍴 Papa John's, Starbucks, 🛏 Dutch Motel
46b	FL 574, MLK Blvd, **E** 🅖 BP, 🅞 Advance Parts, Sweetbay Foods, Walgreens, **W** 🅖 Chevron/dsl, 🍴 McDonald's, 🅞 🅗
46a	Floribraska Ave (from sb, no return)
45b	I-4 E, to Orlando, I-75
45a	Jefferson St, downtown E
44	Ashley Dr, Tampa St downtown W
42	Howard Ave, Armenia Ave, **W** 🅖 Texaco/dsl, 🍴 Popeye's
41c	Himes Ave (from sb), **W** RJ Stadium
41b a	US 92, Dale Mabry Blvd, **E** 🅖 BP, Marathon, Mobil/dsl, Shell/Circle K, 🍴 Brickhouse Grill, Burger King, Carrabba's, Chick-Fil-A, Don Pan Cuban, Donatello Italian, Grill Smith, IHOP, J.Alexanders Rest, Jersey Mike's Subs, Little Caesars, Pei Wei, Pizza Hut, Red Elephant Cafe, Ruby Tuesday, Shells Rest., Starbucks, Subway, Village Inn, 🛏 Best Western, Courtyard, Quality Inn, Tahitian Inn/cafe, 🅞 AT&T, Barnes&Noble, CVS Drug, Hancock Fabrics, Office Depot, Tire Kingdom, Verizon, to MacDill AFB, **W** 🅖 Marathon/Dunkin Donuts, 🍴 Burger King, Chili's, China 1, Crazy Buffet, Denny's, Jimmy John's, Joe's Pizza, Long

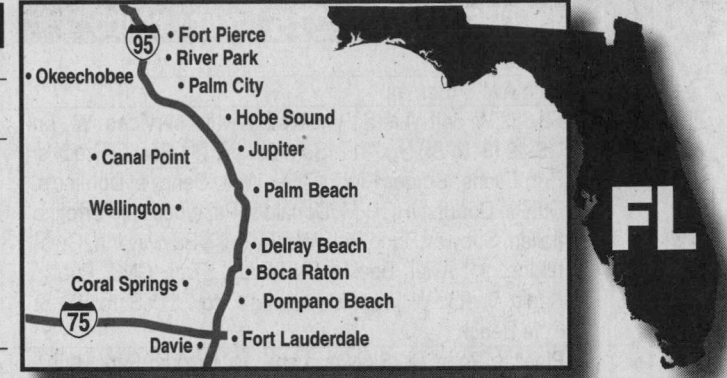

41b a	Continued
	horn Steaks, Macaroni Grill, McDonald's, Moe's SW Grill, Sonic, Sonny's BBQ, Subway, Sweet Tomatoes, Wendy's, 🛏 Hilton, Howard Johnson, Residence Inn, Stadium Inn, 🅞 Best Buy, Chrysler/Dodge/Jeep, Family$, Home Depot, K-Mart, Petsmart, Staples, SweetBay Foods, Target, Walmart, Whole Foods Mkt, to RJ Stadium
40b	Lois Ave, **W** 🅖 Marathon/dsl, 🍴 Charley's Rest., 🛏 DoubleTree Hotel, Sheraton
40a	FL 587, Westshore Blvd, **E** 🅖 BP, Chevron/dsl, Citgo/Subway, 🍴 Burger King, Chipotle Mexican, Gogo's Greek, Maggiano's Rest., McDonald's, Panera Bread, PF Chang's, Season's Grill, Starbucks, Taco Bell, Waffle House, 🛏 Crowne Plaza, Embassy Suites, 🅞 Goodyear, JC Penney, Macy's, Old Navy, PetCo, Sears/auto, Walgreens, **W** 🅖 Shell/Subway, 🍴 Blue Water Grill, Hurricane Grill, 🛏 Hampton Inn, Marriott, Ramada Inn, SpringHill Suites, Wyndham
39b a	FL 60 W, **W** 🍴 Outback Steaks, 🅞 to ✈
32	Fl 687 S, 4th St N, to US 92 (no sb re-entry)
31b a	9th St N, MLK St N (exits left from sb) info, ✈
30	FL 686, Roosevelt Blvd, **0-2 mi W** 🍴 Dascom's Chophouse, Bob Evans, Burger King, Chil-fil-A, Cracker Barrel, Kingfish Grill, McDonald's, Panchero's Mexican, Subway, Taco Bell, 🛏 Courtyard, EconoLodge, Executive Inn, Extended Stay America, Fairfield Inn, Hampton Inn, Holiday Inn, La Quinta, Marriott, Quality Inn, Sleep Inn, SpringHill Suites, 🅞 CVS Drug, Publix
28	FL 694 W, Gandy Blvd, Indian Shores, **0-2 mi W** 🅖 Citgo, Hess/dsl, WaWa/dsl, 🍴 Applebee's, BJ's Brewhouse, Bob Evans, Chili's, Cracker Barrel, Dunkin Donuts, Firehouse Subs, Godfather's, McDonald's, Pollo Tropical, Sonny's BBQ, Taco Bell, Wendy's, 🛏 La Quinta, 🅞 Bentley, Cadillac, Home Depot, Marshall's, Michael's, Office Depot, PetCo, Publix, Rolls Royce, Target, U-Haul
26b a	54th Ave N, **E** 🅖 Cracker Barrel, 🛏 Comfort Inn, Holiday Inn Express, **W** 🅖 RaceTrac/dsl, 🍴 Waffle House, 🛏 Knights Inn, La Quinta, 🅞 🅗, Harley-Davidson, NAPA
25	38th Ave N, to beaches, **E** 🍴 Chick-fil-A, Hooters, McDonald's, **W** 🅖 Citgo/dsl, 🍴 Burger King, Hardee's
24	22nd Ave N, **E** 🅖 Rally, 🅞 Sunken Gardens, **W** 🅖 Citgo/dsl, RaceTrac/dsl, 🍴 Taco Son, 🅞 Home Depot, Lowe's, Tommy's Auto Service
23b	FL 595, 5th Ave N, **E** 🅗
23a	I-375, **E** The Pier, Waterfront, downtown
22	I-175 E, Tropicana Field, **W** 🅗
21	28th St S, downtown
20	31st Ave (from nb), downtown
19	22nd Ave S, Gulfport, **W** 🅖 Chevron, Citgo, Shell, 🍴 Church's, KFC, 🅞 Bravo Foods, Family$

🅖 = gas 🍴 = food 🛏 = lodging 🅞 = other 🆁🆂 = rest stop   Copyright 2014 - The Next Exit ®

⬆N INTERSTATE 275 (TAMPA) CONT'D

Exit	Services
18	26th Ave S (from nb)
17	FL 682 W, 54th Ave S, Pinellas Bayway **services W on US 19 (34th St)** 🅖 7-11, Sunoco/dsl, 🍴 Beef'O'Brady's, Bob Evans, Burger King, China Wok, Denny's, Domino's, Dunkin Donuts, IHOP, McDonald's, Papa John's, Portofino Italian, Subway, Taco Bell, Wendy's, 🛏 Bayway Inn, Crystal Inn, 🅞 AT&T, Beall's, CVS Drug, $Tree, GNC, Publix, Radio Shack, Walmart/McDonald's, to Ft DeSoto Pk, St Pete Beach
16	Pinellas Point Dr, Skyway Lane, to Maximo Park, **E** 🛏 Holiday Inn Resort, **W** marina
16mm	toll plaza sb
13mm	N Skyway Fishing Pier, **W** 🆁🆂 **both lanes, full** ♿ **facilities,** 🍴, **vending,** 🗑 **litter barrels, petwalk**
10mm	Tampa Bay
7mm	S Skyway Fishing Pier, **E** 🆁🆂 **both lanes, full** ♿ **facilities,** 🍴, **vending,** 🗑 **litter barrels, petwalk**
6mm	toll plaza nb
5	US 19, Palmetto, Bradenton
2	US 41, (last nb exit before **toll**), Palmetto, Bradenton, **E** 🅞 Circle K, Fiesta Grove RV Resort, Frog Creek Campground, Terra Ceia Village Campground, Winterset RV Resort, **W** 🅖 BP/DQ/Subway/dsl
0mm	**I-275 begins/ends on I-75, exit 228.**

⬆N INTERSTATE 295 (JACKSONVILLE)

Exit	Services
61ba	**I-295 begins/ends on I-95, exit 337**
60	US 1, Philips Hwy, **E** 🅖 RaceTrac/dsl, 🅞 Buick/GMC, Honda, VW, **W** 🅖 BP, 🅞 Chevrolet, Ford, Mazda, Nissan
58	FL 9b
56	FL 152, Baymeadows Rd, **E** 🛏 Holiday Inn, 🅞 Chrysler/Dodge/Jeep, **W** 🅖 Shell, 🍴 Bubba Burger, Carrabba's, Hurricane Grill, Outback Steaks, Sticky Fingers, Tequila's Mexican, Tony D's Pizza, Wendy's, Hampton Inn, 🅞 Urgent Care, Publix, SteinMart, Verizon, Walgreens, vet
54	Gate Pkwy, **W** 🍴 Joey's Pizzeria, Melting Pot
53	FL 202, Butler Blvd, **1 mi W on Gate Pkwy** 🅖 Shell, 🍴 Bahama Breeze, BJ's Rest, Bono's BBQ, Brio Grille, Capital Grill, Cheesecake Factory, Chipotle Mexican, Maggiano's Italian, Mimi's Cafe, Panera Bread, Pei Wei, PF Chang's, Pollo Tropical, Panda Express, Seasons Rest, Wasabi, Wendy's, Zaxby's, 🛏 Sheraton, 🅞 Barnes&Noble, Best Buy, Costco, CVS Drug, Dick's, Dillard's, Target
52	U of NF Dr, Town Center Pkwy, **W** same as 53
51	US 90, Beach Blvd, **E** 🅖 Citgo, 🍴 Burger King, Dunkin Donuts, Gene's Seafood, Jimmy John's, **W** 🅖 Shell, 🍴 Arby's, KFC, McDonald's, Pizza Hut, Sonic, Taco Bell, 🛏 InTown Suites, 🅞 Advance Parts, $Tree, Walgreens, Winn-Dixie
49	St John's Bluff Rd (from nb), **E** 🅖 BP, Shell, 🍴 Papa John's, 🛏 Holiday Inn Express, InTown Suites, 🅞 Nissan
48	FL 10, to Atlantic Blvd
47	Monument Rd, **E** 🅖 Marathon/Kangaroo/dsl, 🍴 Mudville Grille, 🅞 vet, **W** 🅖 Gate/dsl, 🍴 Ruby Tuesday, 🛏 Courtyard, Hampton Inn, 🅞 Walmart
46	FL 116 E, Wonderwood Connector, Merrill Rd, **E** 🛏 Candlewood Suites
44mm	St John's River
41	FL 105, Heckscher Dr, Zoo Pkwy, **E** 🅖 Gate/dsl, **W** 🅖

Exit	Services
41	Continued Chevron/Kangaroo/dsl, 🍴 Wendy's, 🛏 Holiday Inn Express, 🅞 zoo
40	Alta Dr, **E** 🍴 3 Lions Grill, Viva Mexican
37	Pulaski Rd, **N** 🅖 Kangaroo/dsl
36	US 17, Main St, **N** 🅖 Kangaroo/dsl, 🍴 DQ, McDonald's, 🅞 Winn-Dixie, **S** 🍴 Subway
35b a	I-95, S to Jacksonville, N to Savannah.
	I-295 begins/ends on I-95, exit 362b.
33	Duval Rd, **W** 🍴
32	FL 115, Lem Turner Rd, **E** 🍴 China Wok, Larry's Subs, McDonald's (1mi), Subway, Wendy's, 🅞 Home Depot, Radio Shack, Walmart, **W** 🅞 Flamingo Lake RV Resort, Lakeside Cabins/RV Park
30	FL 104, Dunn Ave, **E** 🅖 Gate/dsl, Shell (1mi), 🍴 McDonald's (1mi), Wendy's (4mi), **W** 🅞 Big Tree RV Park
28b a	US 1, US 23, to Callahan, Jacksonville, **E** 🅖 Kangaroo, **W** 🅖 BP/DQ/dsl, Chevron/Subway/dsl, RaceTrac/dsl, auto repair
25	Pritchard Rd, **W** 🅖 Kangaroo/Subway/deli/dsl/24hr
22	Commonwealth Ave, **E** 🅖 BP/dsl, 🍴 Burger King, Hardee's, Waffle House, 🛏 Holiday Inn, 🅞 dogtrack, **W** 🍴 Wendy's, 🛏 Comfort Suites, Country Inn&Suites
21b a	I-10, **W** to Tallahassee, **E** to Jacksonville
19	FL 228, Normandy Blvd, **E** 🅖 BP/dsl/24hr, Murphy USA/dsl, 🍴 Arby's, Burger King, El Potro, Firehouse Subs, Golden Corral, Hot Wok, McDonald's, Panda Express, Papa John's, Sonic, Wendy's, 🅞 CVS Drug, $Tree, Radio Shack, Walgreens, Walmart, st patrol, **W** 🅖 BP, Hess/dsl, RaceTrac/dsl, Shell, 🍴 Famous Amos, Golden China, Hardee's, KFC, McDonald's, Pizza Hut, Popeye's, Whataburger, 🅞 Advance Parts, Curves, CVS Drug, Family$, K-Mart, Publix, Walgreens, Winn-Dixie
17	FL 208, Wilson Blvd, **E** 🅖 BP/Subway/dsl, Hess/Dunkin Donuts/dsl, 🍴 China Wok, Hardee's, McDonald's (1mi), 🅞 Advance Parts, $General, FL RV Ctr, **W** 🅖 Kangaroo
16	FL 134, 103rd St, Cecil Field, **E** 🅖 BP, Gate/dsl, Hess, Shell/dsl, 🍴 Applebee's, Arby's, Capt D's, Firehouse Subs, Krystal, Papa John's, Popeye's, Red Apple Asian, Sonic, Wendy's, Ying's Chinese, 🛏🄷 ity Inn, 🅞 Advance Parts, CVS Drug, $General, Goodyear/auto, NAPA, Radio Shack, Save-A-Lot Foods, Tires+, U-Haul, Walmart/McDonald's, **W** 🅖 BP, Chevron, Exxon/dsl, Kangaroo, Shell, 🍴 Burger King, DQ, Dunkin Donuts, IHOP, KFC, Little Caesars, McDonald's, Pizza Hut, Rosy's Mexican, Subway, Taco Bell, 🅞 Aamco, AutoZone, Family$, Goodyear/auto, O'Reilly Parts, Publix, SavRite Foods, Sun Tires, Walgreens, vet
12	FL 21, Blanding Blvd, **E** 🅖 BP, Hess/Blimpie/Dunkin Donuts/Godfather's/dsl, RaceWay/dsl, Texaco, 🍴 Burger King, Larry's Subs, McDonald's, Pizza Hut, Subway, Sunrise Cafe, 🅞 Acura, Audi, Best Buy, Buick/GMC, Cadillac, Chrysler/Dodge/Jeep, CVS Drug, $General, Ford, Honda, Hyundai, Lincoln, Lexus, Mazda, Mercedes, Nissan, Office Depot, Petsmart, Subaru, U-Haul, VW, Walgreens, USPO, **W** 🅖 BP, Kangaroo/dsl, Shell, 🍴 Applebee's, Arby's, Buffalo's, Burger King, Carrabba's, Chick-fil-A, Chili's, China Buffet, Chipotle Mexican, ChuckeCheese, Denny's, El Potro, 5 Guys Burgers, HoneyBaked Ham, Hooters, KFC, Kyodai Steaks, Longhorn Steaks, Olive Garden, Orange Park Ale House, Outback Steaks, Panda Express, Panera Bread, Papa John's, Red Lobster, Ruby

S T P E T E R S B U R G

J A C K S O N V I L L E

FL

INTERSTATE 295 (JACKSONVILLE) CONT'D

JACKSONVILLE

Exit	Services
12	Continued Tuesday, Smokey Bones, Sonic, Starbucks, Steak'n Shake, Sweet Tomatoes, Taco Bell, Ted's MT Grill, TGI-Friday's, Thai Garden, 🛏 Country Inn&Suites, Hampton Inn, La Quinta, Motel 6, Red Roof Inn, Suburban Lodge, Super 8, Ⓞ Ⓗ Advance Parts, AT&T, Belk, Books-A-Million, Dick's, Dillard's, Discount Tire, $Tree, Goodyear/auto, Home Depot, JC Penney, Jo-Ann Fabrics, Michael's, Old Navy, O'Reilly Parts, PepBoys, Publix, Sam's Club/gas, Sears/auto, Target, Tire Kingdom, Tires+, TJMaxx, Toyota, Verizon, Walgreens, mall
10	US 17, FL 15, Roosevelt Blvd, Orange Park, E 🛏 Best Western, W 🅿 BP, Chevron/dsl/24hr, Hess, RaceTrac/dsl, 🍴 Aron's Pizza, Cracker Barrel, Krystal, McDonald's, Ramirez Rest., Subway, Waffle House, Wendy's, 🛏 Comfort Inn, Days Inn, Fairfield Inn, Hilton Garden, Holiday Inn, Rodeway Inn, Ⓞ Ⓗ, CVS Drug, $General, General RV Ctr, Harley-Davidson, Save-A-Lot Foods, Sun Tire, Winn-Dixie, vet
7mm	St Johns River, Buckman Br
5b a	FL 13, San Jose Blvd, E 🅿 Chevron/DQ/dsl, Hess, 🍴 Arby's, Bob Evans, Bono's BBQ, Carrabba's, Domino's, Famous Amos, Firehouse Subs, 5 Guys Burgers, Hon

5b a	Continued eyBaked Ham, Krystal, McDonald's, Outback Steaks, Popeye's, Red Elephant Pizza, Smoothie King, Starbucks, Steak'n Shake, Subway, Tijuana Flats, Village Inn, Wendy's, 🛏 La Quinta, Ramada Inn, Ⓞ Urgent Care, Aamco, Advance Parts, BigLots, CVS Drug, Firestone/auto, K-Mart, Office Depot, PepBoys, Publix, Sun Tire, Target, Tire Kingdom, Tires+, Verizon, Walgreens, Whole Foods Mkt, auto repair, vet, W 🅿 BP, Citgo, Shell (1mi), 🍴 Al's Pizza, Brooklyn Pizza, Bruster's, Chili's, Chipotle Mexican, Golden China, Golden Corral, Hardee's, Krispy Kreme, Lee's Chicken, Mama Fu's, Mandarin Ale House, McDonald's, Moe's SW Grill, Osaka Grill, Panera Bread, Papa John's, Papa Murphy's, Pizza Hut, Subway, Taco Bell, Ⓞ Ace Hardware, Advance Parts, AT&T, AutoZone, Barnes&Noble, Books-A-Million, $Tree, Goodyear/auto, Marshall's, Michael's, NAPA, PetCo, Publix, Radio Shack, Staples, SteinMart, Tire Kingdom, TJMaxx, U-Haul, Walmart, Winn-Dixie, World Mkt
3	Old St Augustine Rd, E 🅿 BP, Shell, 🍴 Burger King, Little Caesars, Little China, McDonald's, Taco Bell, Wendy's, 🛏 Holiday Inn Express, Ⓞ CVS Drug, $General, $Tree, Family$, GNC, Hobby Lobby, Publix/deli, Winn-Dixie, W 🅿 Gate/dsl, Kangaroo/dsl, 🍴 Firehouse Subs, KFC, Rosy's Mexican, Subway, Vino's Pizza, Ⓞ Lowe's, Walgreens, vet

GEORGIA

FL GA

INTERSTATE 16

SAVANNAH

Exit	Services
167b a	W Broad, Montgomery St, Savannah, 0-1 mi N 🅿 Chevron, Enmark, Parker's, 🛏 Best Western, Courtyard, DoubleTree, Hampton Inn, Hilton Garden, Quality Inn, Residence Inn, Sheraton, Ⓞ S 🍴 Burger King, Popeye's, Wendy's, **I-16 begins/ends in Savannah.**
166	US 17, Gwinnet St, Savannah, Savannah Visitors Ctr
165	GA 204, 37th St (from eb), to Ft Pulaski NM, Savannah College
164b a	I-516, US 80, US 17, GA 21
162	Chatham Pkwy, S 🅿 Shell/dsl, 🍴 Kan Pai Japanese, Larry's Subs, Nicky's Pizza, Sunrise Rest., Ⓞ Kia, Lexus, Subaru, Toyota/Scion
160	GA 307, Dean Forest Rd, N 🅿 Shell/dsl, 🚏 Subway/dsl/scales, 🍴 Ronnie's Rest., Waffle House
157b a	I-95, S to Jacksonville, N to Florence
155	Pooler Pkwy, N 🅿 Murphy USA/dsl, 🍴 Jalapeno's Mexican, Papa John's, Subway, Ⓞ Lowe's, S 🅿 BP/dsl, to ✈
152	GA 17, to Bloomingdale
148	Old River Rd, to US 80
144mm	weigh sta both lanes
143	US 280, to US 80, S 🅿 El Cheapo/dsl, Zip'N Go/Subway/dsl
137	GA 119, to Pembroke, Ft Stewart
132	Ash Branch Church Rd
127	GA 67, to Pembroke, Ft Stewart, N 🅿 BP/dsl, Shell/dsl, 🍴 Bay South Rest., Ⓞ antiques
116	US 25/301, to Statesboro, N 🅿 Chevron/rest/dsl/scales/24hr, 🍴 Magnolia Springs SP (45 mi), to GA S U, S 🅿 Sunoco/dsl, 🛏 Scottish Inn

METTER

111	Pulaski-Excelsior Rd, S 🅿 Citgo/Grady's Grill/dsl, Ⓞ tires/repair
104	GA 22, GA 121, Metter, N 🅿 BP/dsl/scales/24hr, Chevron/dsl, Exxon, Shell/dsl, 🍴 Bevrick's Grille, Burger King, Chinese Buffet, DQ, Jomax BBQ, KFC/Taco Bell, Krispy Chic, McDonald's, Papa Buck's BBQ, Pond House Grill, Señor Luis, Subway, Village Pizza, Waffle House, Zaxby's, 🛏 American Inn, Best Value Inn, Days Inn, Scottish Inn, Ⓞ Ⓗ, Chevrolet, O'Reilly Parts, Rite Aid, to Smith SP, RV camping, S 🅿 Marathon/dsl, Phillips 66/dsl, Ⓞ Ford
101mm	Canoochee River
98	GA 57, to Stillmore, S 🅿 BP/dsl/24hr, Chevron/dsl, Ⓞ to Altahama SP
90	US 1, to Swainsboro, N 🅿 Marathon/dsl
88mm	Ohoopee River
84	GA 297, to Vidalia, N truck sales
78	US 221, GA 56, to Swainsboro
71	GA 15, GA 78, to Soperton, N 🅿 Chevron/dsl
67	GA 29, to Soperton, S 🅿 Chevron/dsl, Marathon/dsl, 🍴 Huddle House
58	GA 199, Old River Rd, East Dublin
56mm	Oconee River
54	GA 19, to Dublin, S 🅿 Chevron/dsl
51	US 441, US 319, to Dublin, N 🅿 BP/Stuckey's/Subway/dsl, Flash/gas, Neighbor's/dsl, 🚏 dsl/scales/24hr, 🍴 Arby's, Buffalo's Café, Burger King, KFC, McDonald's, Ruby Tuesday, Taco Bell, Waffle House, Wendy's, 🛏 Comfort Inn, Days Inn, EconoLodge, Hampton Inn, Holiday Inn Express, Jameson Inn, Quality Inn, Super 8, Travelodge, Ⓞ Ⓗ, Ace Hardware, Chrysler/Dodge/Jeep, $General, Steve's RV, S 🅿 Chevron/dsl, 🍴 Cracker Barrel, Longhorn Steaks, Zaxby's, 🛏 La Quinta, Ⓞ Pinetucky Camping (2mi), to Little Ocmulgee SP

DUBLIN

🅿 = gas 🍽 = food 🛏 = lodging 🅾 = other 🆁🆂 = rest stop   Copyright 2014 - The Next Exit ®

INTERSTATE 16 CONT'D

Exit	Services
49	GA 257, to Dublin, Dexter, **N** 🅿 Chevron/dsl, 🅾 🅷, **S** 🅿 💗Love's/Chester's/Subway/dsl/scales/24hr
46mm	🆁🆂 wb, full ♿ **facilities**, 🚻, 🏞, **litter barrels, vending, petwalk, RV dump**
44mm	🆁🆂 eb, full ♿ **facilities**, 🚻, 🏞, **litter barrels, vending, petwalk, RV dump**
42	GA 338, to Dudley
39	GA 26, to Cochran, Montrose
32	GA 112, Allentown, **S** 🅿 Chevron/dsl
27	GA 358, to Danville
24	GA 96, to Jeffersonville, **N** 🅿 Marathon/dsl, **S** 🅿 Exxon/Huddle House/dsl/24hr, 🛏 Ambassador Inn, 🅾 to Robins AFB, museum
18	Bullard Rd, to Jeffersonville, Bullard
12	Sgoda Rd, Huber, **N** 🅿 Marathon/dsl
6	US 23, US 129A, East Blvd, Ocmulgee, **N** 🅿 BP/Circle K/DQ, 🍽 McDonald's, Waffle House, 🛏 Days Inn (2mi), 🅾 to 🏥, GA Forestry Ctr, **S** 🅿 Chevron/Huddle House/dsl, Friendly Gus, 🍽 Subway
2	US 80, GA 87, MLK Jr Blvd, **N** 🛏 Marriott, 🅾 🅷, Ocmulgee NM, conv ctr, **S** 🅿 Marathon/dsl, 🅾 to Hist Dist
1b	GA 22, to US 129, GA 49, 2nd St (from wb), **N** 🅾 coliseum, **S** 🛏 Ramada, 🅾 🅷
1a	US 23, Gray Hwy (from eb), **N** 🅿 Citgo, Flash/dsl, Shell, 🍽 Arby's, Burger King, Chen's Wok, DQ, El Sombrero Mexican, Fincher's BBQ, Hong Kong Express, Krispy Kreme, Krystal, McDonald's, Papa John's, Subway, Taco Bell, Wendy's, 🅾 🅷, Attaway Tire, CVS Drug, Kroger, O'Reilly Parts, Radio Shack, U-Haul, Walgreens, **S** 🅿 Circle K, Exxon, Marathon/dsl, 🍽 Burger King, Checker's, Krystal, Pizza Hut, Waffle House, Zaxby's, 🛏 Ramada
0mm	I-75, S to Valdosta, N to Atlanta. **I-16 begins/ends on I-75, exit 165 in Macon.**

INTERSTATE 20

Exit	Services
202mm	Georgia/South Carolina state line, Savannah River
201mm	**Welcome Ctr wb, full** ♿ **facilities**, 🚻, **vending**, 🏞 **litter barrels, petwalk**
200	GA 104, Riverwatch Pkwy, Augusta, **N** 🅿 📠/Wendy's/dsl/24hr, 🍽 Waffle House, 🛏 Baymont Inn, Candlewood Suites, Comfort Suites, Jameson Inn, Microtel, Quality Inn, Sleep Inn, ValuePlace, **S** 🅾 Cabela's, Costco/gas
199	GA 28, Washington Rd, Augusta, **0-3 mi N** 🅿 BP, RaceWay, Shell/Circle K, Sprint, 🍽 Applebee's, Baskin-Robbins/Dunkin Donuts, Burger King, CA Dreaming, Capt D's, Checkers, Chick-fil-A, DQ, Domino's, Denny's, Firehouse Subs, Fujiyama Japanese, KFC, Krystal, Longhorn Steaks, McDonald's, Mi Rancho Mexican, Piccadilly, Pizza Hut, Rhinehart's Seafood, Starbucks, Steakout, Vera Cruz Mexican, Waffle House, Wife Saver Rest, Wild Wing Cafe, 🛏 Best Value Inn, Clarion, Courtyard, Days Inn, Hampton Inn, Hilton Garden, Homewood Suites, La Quinta, Masters Inn, Scottish Inn, Sheraton, Sunset Inn, Super 8, Travelodge, 🅾 AutoZone, Buick/GMC, Chrysler/Dodge/Jeep, Chevrolet, $Tree, Goodyear/auto, Hancock Fabrics, Hyundai, Infiniti, Lexus, Mazda, Mercedes, NAPA, Nissan, Toyota/Scion, Tuesday Morning, **S** 🅿 BP, Shell/Circle K/dsl, 🍽 Arby's, BoneFish Grill, Carrabba's, Crazy Turk's Pizza, 5 Guys Burgers, HoneyBaked Ham, Hooters, Krispy

Exit	Services
199	**Continued** Kreme, McDonald's, Moe's SW Grill, New Peking, Olive Garden, Outback Steaks, Red Lobster, Roadrunner Cafe, Shangri La, Straw Hat Pizza, Subway, Taco Bell, T-Bonz Steaks, TGIFriday's, Thai Jong Rest., Vallarta Mexican, Waffle House, Wendy's, Zaxby's, 🛏 Best Western, Country Inn&Suites, Guest Inn, Knights Inn, Motel 6, Parkway Inn, Ramada Inn, Staybridge Suites, Westbank Inn, 🅾 Aamco, AT&T, CVS Drug, $Tree, Firestone/auto, Fred's, Fresh Mkt Foods, Goodyear/auto, Kroger/dsl, Midas, PepBoys, Publix, SteinMart, Tire Kingdom, Verizon, Walgreens, vet
196b	GA 232 W, **N** 🅿 Enmark, Murphy Express/dsl, 🍽 Checkers, Golden Corral, Krystal, Marlin&Ray's, Ryan's, Salsa's Grill, Stevi B's Pizza, 🛏 Baymont Inn, Travel Inn, 🅾 Home Depot, Lowe's, O'Reilly Parts, Sam's Club/gas, Tire Kingdom, Walgreens, Walmart
196a	I-520, Bobby Jones Fwy, **S** 🅿 BP, 🍽 Atlanta Bread Co, Buffalo Wild Wings, Carolina Alehouse, Chick-fil-A, Chili's, Logan's Roadhouse, Macaroni Grill, McDonald's, O'Charley's, Panera Bread, Starbucks, Sticky Fingers, Subway, Waffle House, 🛏 DoubleTree Hotel, 🅾 🅷, Best Buy, Hobby Lobby, Michael's, Office Depot, Old Navy, Petsmart, Staples, Target, Tires+, Verizon, vet, to 🏥
195	Wheeler Rd, **N** 🅿 Sprint, 🅾 CarMax, **0-2 mi S** 🅿 BP/dsl, Shell/Circle K/Blimpie, 🍽 Guiseppe's Pizza, Sonic, 🛏 Days Inn, 🅾 🅷, Urgent Care, Harley-Davidson, Rite Aid
194	GA 383, Belair Rd, to Evans, **N** 🅿 Fuel Express, Shell/Circle K/dsl, Sprint, 🍽 Bojangles, Burger King, Hungry Howie's, Popeye's, Sun Kwong Chinese, Taco Bell, Waffle House, Wendy's, 🛏 GA Inn, 🅾 AT&T, Family$, Food Lion, Fun Park, **S** 🅿 BP/DQ/dsl, Fuel Express, 📠/Subway/dsl/24hr, 🍽 Amici Italian, Cracker Barrel, KFC, Steak'n Shake, Waffle House, 🛏 Best Suites, Best Value Inn, Best Western, Comfort Inn, EconoLodge, Hampton Inn, Hawthorn Suites, Holiday Inn, Howard Johnson, Motel 6, Quality Inn, Red Roof Inn, Super 8, Wingate Inn, 🅾 Goodyear/auto
190	GA 388, to Grovetown, **N** 🅿 TPS/dsl/scales/24hr, 🍽 Waffle House, **S** 🅿 Murphy Express/dsl, 🍽 Arby's, Jersey Mike's Subs, Mi Rancho, 🅾 Verizon, Walmart
189mm	**weigh sta both lanes**
183	US 221, to Harlem, Appling, **S** 🅿 Exxon/dsl, 🅾 to Laurel&Hardy Museum
182mm	🆁🆂 **both lanes, full** ♿ **facilities**, 🚻, **vending**, 🏞, **litter barrels, RV dump, petwalk**
175	GA 150, **N** 🅿 Chevron/rest/dsl/24hr, 🛏 Knights Inn, 🅾 to Mistletoe SP
172	US 78, GA 17, Thomson, **N** 🅿 💗Love's/Chester's/Subway/dsl/scales/24hr, 🍽 Waffle House, 🅾 Chrysler/Dodge/Jeep, **S** 🅿 BP/DQ/dsl, Circle K/Blimpie/dsl, M&A/dsl, RaceWay/dsl, Shell, 🍽 Amigo's Mexican, Arby's, Burger King, Checkers, Domino's, Habaneros Mexican, Kiosco Mexican, Krystal, LJ Silver, Lucky Chinese, McDonald's, MingWah Chinese, Pizza Hut, Popeye's, Ryan's, Taco Bell, Waffle House, Wendy's, Zaxby's, 🛏 Best Western, Comfort Inn, EconoLodge, Hampton Inn, Scottish Inn, 🅾 🅷, Urgent Care, Advance Parts, AutoZone, Bi-Lo, $General, Family$, O'Reilly Parts, Verizon, Walgreens
169	Thomson
165	GA 80, Camak

Side labels: OCMULGEE, MACON, AUGUSTA (left column); AUGUSTA, THOMSON (right column); GA

INTERSTATE 20 CONT'D

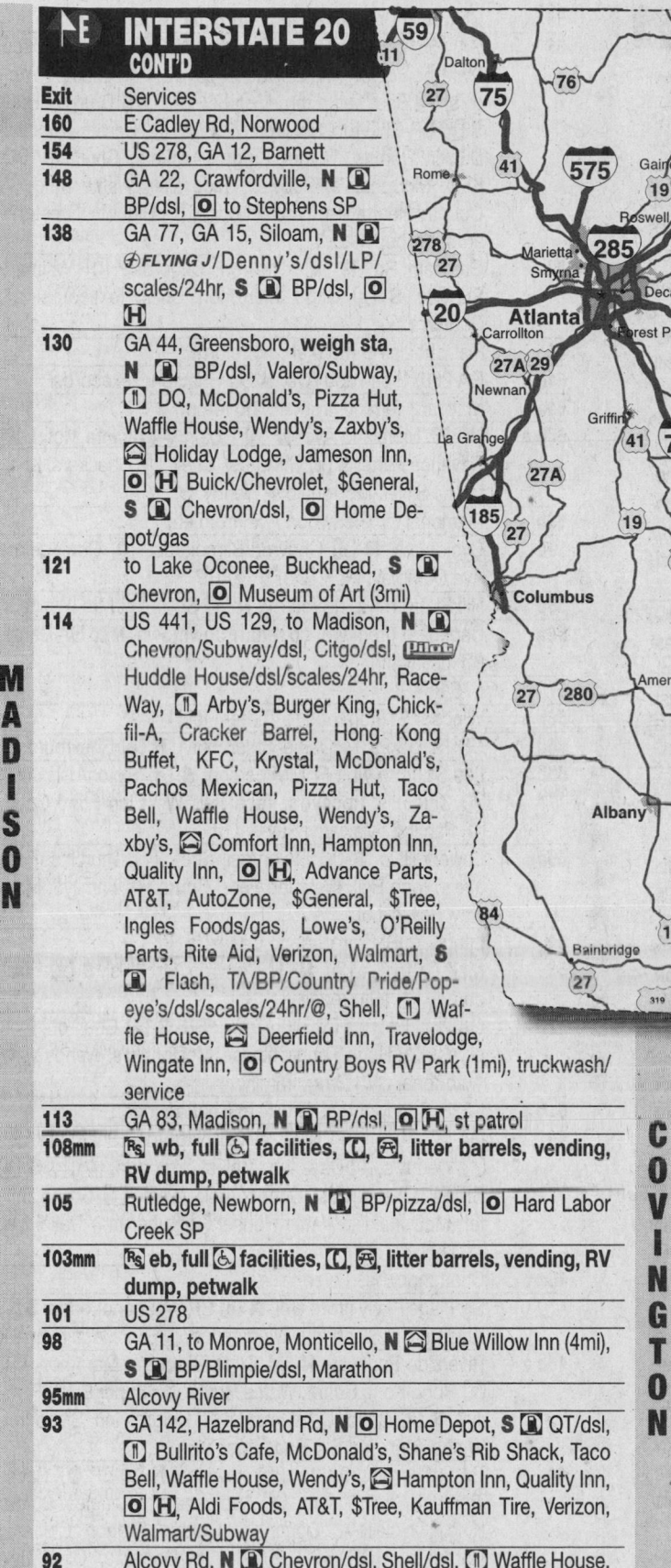

Exit	Services
160	E Cadley Rd, Norwood
154	US 278, GA 12, Barnett
148	GA 22, Crawfordville, N ⛽ BP/dsl, Ⓞ to Stephens SP
138	GA 77, GA 15, Siloam, N ⛽ FLYING J/Denny's/dsl/LP/scales/24hr, S ⛽ BP/dsl, Ⓞ H
130	GA 44, Greensboro, **weigh sta**, N ⛽ BP/dsl, Valero/Subway, 🍴 DQ, McDonald's, Pizza Hut, Waffle House, Wendy's, Zaxby's, 🛏 Holiday Lodge, Jameson Inn, Ⓞ H Buick/Chevrolet, $General, S ⛽ Chevron/dsl, Ⓞ Home Depot/gas
121	to Lake Oconee, Buckhead, S ⛽ Chevron, Ⓞ Museum of Art (3mi)
114	US 441, US 129, to Madison, N ⛽ Chevron/Subway/dsl, Citgo/dsl, Pilot/Huddle House/dsl/scales/24hr, RaceWay, 🍴 Arby's, Burger King, Chick-fil-A, Cracker Barrel, Hong Kong Buffet, KFC, Krystal, McDonald's, Pachos Mexican, Pizza Hut, Taco Bell, Waffle House, Wendy's, Zaxby's, 🛏 Comfort Inn, Hampton Inn, Quality Inn, Ⓞ H, Advance Parts, AT&T, AutoZone, $General, $Tree, Ingles Foods/gas, Lowe's, O'Reilly Parts, Rite Aid, Verizon, Walmart, S ⛽ Flash, TA/BP/Country Pride/Popeye's/dsl/scales/24hr/@, Shell, 🍴 Waffle House, 🛏 Deerfield Inn, Travelodge, Wingate Inn, Ⓞ Country Boys RV Park (1mi), truckwash/service
113	GA 83, Madison, N ⛽ BP/dsl, Ⓞ H, st patrol
108mm	Ⓡ wb, full ♿ facilities, 🍴 ,🚮, litter barrels, vending, RV dump, petwalk
105	Rutledge, Newborn, N ⛽ BP/pizza/dsl, Ⓞ Hard Labor Creek SP
103mm	Ⓡ eb, full ♿ facilities, 🍴 ,🚮, litter barrels, vending, RV dump, petwalk
101	US 278
98	GA 11, to Monroe, Monticello, N 🛏 Blue Willow Inn (4mi), S ⛽ BP/Blimpie/dsl, Marathon
95mm	Alcovy River
93	GA 142, Hazelbrand Rd, N Ⓞ Home Depot, S ⛽ QT/dsl, 🍴 Bullrito's Cafe, McDonald's, Shane's Rib Shack, Taco Bell, Waffle House, Wendy's, 🛏 Hampton Inn, Quality Inn, Ⓞ H, Aldi Foods, AT&T, $Tree, Kauffman Tire, Verizon, Walmart/Subway
92	Alcovy Rd, N ⛽ Chevron/dsl, Shell/dsl, 🍴 Waffle House, 🛏 Baymont Inn, Best Value Inn, Covington Lodge, Days Inn, Super 8, S H
90	US 278, GA 81, Covington, S ⛽ Citgo/dsl, QT, RaceWay/dsl, 🍴 Applebee's, Arby's, Bojangles, Capt D's, Checkers, Chick-fil-A, Covington Diner, Domino's, DQ, Hardee's, KFC, Krystal, Little Caesars, LJ Silver, Longhorn Steaks,

COVINGTON

Exit	Services
90	Continued Mama Maria's, McDonald's, Nagoya Japanese, Pacho's Mexican, Papa John's, Pizza Hut/Taco Bell, Stalvey's Rest., Stevi B's Pizza, Subway, Waffle House, Zaxby's, 🛏 Holiday Inn Express, Ⓞ Ace Hardware, Advance Parts, BigLots, Chevrolet, $General, Family$, Food Depot, Ingles Foods, Ford, GNC, K-Mart, Kroger/dsl, O'Reilly Parts, Radio Shack, Rite Aid, Walgreens, vet
88	Almon Rd, to Porterdale, N ⛽ Chevron/dsl, S ⛽ BP, Liberty, 🍴 McDonald's, Subway (2mi), Ⓞ Riverside Estates RV Camp, transmissions/repair
84	GA 162, Salem Rd, to Pace, N ⛽ BJ's Whse/gas, Marathon/dsl, S ⛽ Chevron/dsl, Citgo, QT, RaceWay/dsl, 🍴 Baskin-Robbins, Burger King, Dunkin Donuts, Hardee's, KFC, Los Bravos Mexican, McDonald's, Quiznos, Subway, Taco Bell, Waffle House, Wendy's, Ⓞ Advance Parts, Family$, Food Depot, Ingles/gas, Olympic Auto, O'Reilly Parts, PepBoys, Rite Aid
82	GA 138, GA 20, Conyers, N ⛽ BJ's/gas, BP, QT, 🍴 Applebee's, Bruster's, Chili's, ChuckECheese, Coldstone, Cracker Barrel, Don Tello's, Golden Corral, IHOP, O'Charley's, Outback Steaks, Red Lobster, Sonic, Subway, 🛏 Country Inn&Suites, Days Inn, Hampton Inn, Holi

◢E INTERSTATE 20 CONT'D

Exit	Services
82	Continued

day Inn Express, Jameson Inn, La Quinta, Super 8, 🅞 AT&T, Belk, Chevrolet, Ford, Harley-Davidson, Home Depot, Kohl's, Michael's, Office Depot, Old Navy, Petsmart, Staples, Tires+, U-Haul, Walmart, **S** 🅟 Chevron, Shell/dsl, ⑪ Arby's, Baskin-Robbins, Blimpie, Burger King, Capt D's, Checkers, Chianti Italian, Chick-fil-A, CiCi's Pizza, Daruma Japanese, Dunkin Donuts, Folk's Rest., Frontera Mexican, Glenn's BBQ, Grand Buffet, HoneyBaked Ham, Hooters, KFC, Krystal, LJ Silver, Mandarin Garden, McDonald's, Mellow Mushroom, Milano Cafe, Moe's SW Grill, Oakes Family Rest., Piccadilly's, Popeye's, Ruby Tuesday, Silver Dragon, Sonny's BBQ, Starbucks, Subway, Taco Bell, Waffle House, Wendy's, 🛏 Microtel, 🅞 Aldi Foods, BigLots, Discount Tire, Dodge, $General, $Tree, Firestone/auto, GNC, Goodyear/auto, Hobby Lobby, Honda, Hyundai, Jo-Ann Fabrics, Kia, Kroger/gas, NAPA, NTB, PepBoys, Publix, Radio Shack, Ross, Target, TJ Maxx, Verizon, Walgreens

80	West Ave, Conyers, **N** 🅟 Chevron, Shell/dsl, ⑪ DQ, Domino's, Mrs Winner's, Subway, Waffle House, 🛏 Best Value Inn, Motel 6, 🅞 Urgent Care, Conyers Drug, Family$, Meineke, Piggly Wiggly, **S** 🅟 QT, Texaco/dsl, ⑪ Fish House, Longhorn Steaks, McDonald's, 🛏 Comfort Inn, 🅞 Chrysler/Dodge/Jeep, Nissan, vet
79mm	parking area eb
78	Sigman Rd, **N** 🅟 Shell/dsl, Texaco, ⑪ Waffle House, **S** 🅞 Crown RV Ctr, st police
75	US 278, GA 124, Turner Hill Rd, **N** 🅟 BP/dsl, Citgo/dsl, **S** ⑪ Applebee's, Arizona's, Bruster's, Buffalo Wild Wings, Chick-fil-A, Chicken&Waffles, ChuckECheese, Dontello's Grill, Firehouse Subs, Flambeaux, Grand China, Kampai's Steaks, KFC, Marlin&Rays, McDonald's, Olive Garden, Panera Bread, Smokey Bones BBQ, Steak n'Shake, Subway, Zaxby's, 🛏 Comfort Inn, Comfort Suites, Fairfield Inn, Hilton Garden, Hyatt Place, 🅞 Best Buy, Dillard's, JC Penney, Kohl's, Macy's, Marshalls, PetCo, Rite Aid, Ross, Sam's Club/gas, Sears/auto, Staples, Target, Tires+, Toyota/Scion, Verizon, mall
74	Evans Mill Rd, GA 124, Lithonia, **N** 🅟 BP, Chevron, Shell, ⑪ Capt D's, McDonald's, Pizza Hut, SoulFood Rest., Subway, Wendy's, 🅞 Advance Parts, CVS Drug, O'Reilly Parts, **S** 🅟 Citgo/dsl, ⑪ Da-Bomb Wings/Seafood, DQ, Dudley's Rest., Krystal, Waffle House, 🛏 Microtel, 🅞 $General
71	Hillandale Dr, Farrington Rd, Panola Rd, **N** 🅟 QT/dsl, Shell, ⑪ Burger King, Checkers, KFC, McDonald's, Waffle House, Wings&Philly, 🛏 Budgetel, Super 8, 🅞 Family$, **S** 🅟 BP/dsl, Citgo, Murphy USA/dsl, Shell/dsl, ⑪ Dunkin Donuts, IHOP, Popeye's, Ruby Tuesday, Subway, Taco Bell/LJ Silver, Wendy's, 🛏 Red Roof Inn, 🅞 Lowe's, Publix, Radio Shack, Tires+, Verizon, Walgreens, Walmart/McDonald's
68	Wesley Chapel Rd, Snapfinger Rd, **N** ⑪ Capt D's, Checkers, Chick-fil-A, Church's, KFC, New China, Subway, Taco Bell, Waffle House, 🛏 Economy Inn, 🅞 $General, Home Depot, Kroger, **S** 🅟 Chevron/dsl, Mobil, QT, Shell/dsl, ⑪ Dragon Chinese, JJ's Fish& Chicken, McDonald's, Popeye's, 🛏 Super Inn, 🅞 Family$, NTB
67b a	I-285, S to Macon, N to Greenville
66	Columbia Dr (from eb, no return), **N** 🅟 Chevron
65	GA 155, Candler Rd, to Decatur, **N** 🅟 Chevron, Citgo, Marathon/dsl, ⑪ Pizza Hut, Popeye's, Red Lobster, Wendy's, 🛏 Best Value Inn, Motel 6, 🅞 CVS Drug, U-Haul, **S** 🅟 BP, Chevron, Shell/dsl, Texaco, ⑪ Baskin-Robbins/Dunkin Donuts, Burger King, Checkers, Church's, DQ, KFC, McDonald's, Subway, Taco Bell, Waffle King, 🛏 Country Hearth Inn, Sunset Lodge, 🅞 BigLots, Firestone/auto, Kroger, Macy's
63	Gresham Rd, **N** 🅟 Chevron, Citgo/dsl, 🅞 Walmart/Subway, **S** 🅟 Citgo, Marathon, Shell, Texaco/dsl, ⑪ Church's
62	Flat Shoals Rd (from eb, no return)
61b	GA 260, Glenwood Ave, **N** 🅟 Chevron, Texaco/dsl
61a	Maynard Terrace (from eb, no return)
60b a	US 23, Moreland Ave, **N** 🅟 Exxon, 🛏 Atlanta Motel, 🅞 Advance Parts, **S** 🅟 Citgo/dsl, Shell, ⑪ Checkers, Krystal, LJ Silver, McDonald's, Wendy's
59b	Memorial Dr, Glenwood Ave (from eb)
59a	Cyclorama, **N** 🅟 Chevron/Blimpie/dsl, 🅞 Confederate Ave Complex, MLK Site, **S** 🅟 BP
58b	Hill St (from wb, no return), **N** 🅟 Shell, ⑪ Mrs. Winners
58a	Capitol St (from wb, no return) downtown, **N** to GA Dome, **S** Holiday Inn
57	I-75/85
56b	Windsor St (from eb), to Turner Field
56a	US 19, US 29, McDaniel St (eb only), **N** 🅟 Chevron/dsl
55b	Lee St (from wb), Ft McPherson, **S** 🅟 Exxon/dsl, Shell, ⑪ Church's, Popeye's, Taco Bell, West Inn Food Court, 🅞 Family$, Maxway, Sav-A-Lot
55a	Lowery Blvd, **S** 🅟 Exxon/dsl, Shell, ⑪ Church's, Popeye's, Taco Bell, West Inn Food Court, 🅞 Family$, Maxway, Sav-A-Lot
54	Langhorn St (from wb), to Cascade Rd
53	MLK Dr, to GA 139, **N** 🅟 Chevron, Shell/dsl, **S** 🅟 Texaco/dsl, 🅞 auto repair
52b a	GA 280, Holmes Dr, High Tower Rd, **S** 🅟 Chevron, Exxon/dsl, ⑪ Hong Kong Chinese, McDonald's, Wendy's, 🅞 AutoZone, CVS Drug, Family$
51b a	I-285, S to Montgomery, N to Chattanooga
49	GA 70, Fulton Ind Blvd, **N** 🅟 Citgo/dsl, Shamrock/dsl, ⑪ Wendy's, 🛏 Days Inn, Majestick Lodge, 🅞 🕿, **S** 🅟 BP/dsl, Chevron/dsl, Sunoco/dsl, Valero, ⑪ Grand Buffet, McDonald's, Waffle House, 🛏 Super Inn, Travel Inn, 🅞 U-Haul
48mm	Chattahoochee River
47	Six Flags Pkwy (from wb), **N** 🅟 BP, 🛏 EconoLodge, **S** 🛏 Knights Inn, Sleep Inn, Wingate Inn, 🅞 Six Flags Funpark
46b a	Riverside Parkway, **N** 🅟 Citgo/Church's, Marathon, QT, ⑪ Hong Kong Buffet, Waffle House, 🛏 Super 8, 🅞 Family$, **S** 🅟 Citgo, ⑪ Wendy's, 🛏 Knights Inn, Sleep Inn, Wingate Inn, 🅞 Six Flags Funpark
44	GA 6, Thornton Rd, to Lithia Springs, **N** 🅟 BP, QT, RaceTrac/dsl, Shell, Valero, ⑪ Applebee's, Bojangles, Burger King, Chick-fil-A, Domino's, Golden Dragon Chinese, Hardee's, IHOP, KFC, Krystal, McDonald's, Olive Tree Rest., Popeye's, Ruby Tuesday, Shoney's, Sonic, Subway, Taco Bell, Waffle House, Wendy's, Zaxby's, 🛏 Budget Inn, Holiday Inn Express, Knight's Inn, Quality Inn, Suburban Lodge, 🅞 🕿, AT&T, Atlanta West Camping (2mi), Carmax, Chevrolet, $General, Ford, Home Depot, Honda, Hyundai, Kroger/gas, Nissan, Office Depot, Tires+, Veri

CONYERS — **LITHONIA** (side tab)

ATLANTA AREA (side tab)

GA (side tab)

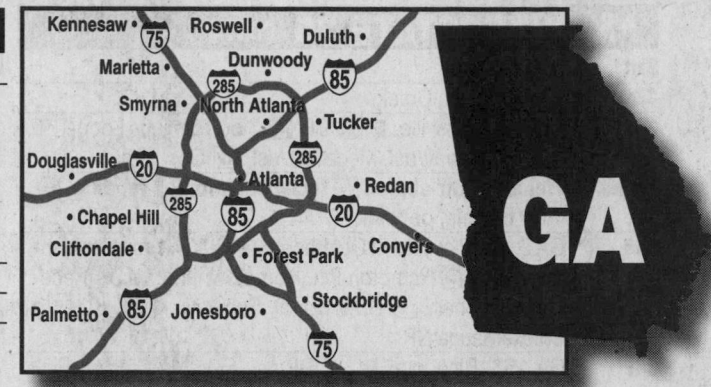

🔼🇪 INTERSTATE 20 CONT'D

Exit	Services
44	Continued
	zon, VW, Walgreens, vet, **S** 🅟 Shell, 🍴 Cracker Barrel, Fiesta Mexican, 🛏 Country Inn&Suites, Courtyard, Fairfield Inn, Hampton Inn, Hilton Garden, SpringHill Suites, Ⓞ Chrysler/Dodge/Jeep, Kia, Toyota, Walmart, to Sweetwater Creek SP
42mm	**weigh sta eb**
41	Lee Rd, to Lithia Springs, **N** 🅟 Marathon/dsl
37	GA 92, to Douglasville, **N** 🅟 RaceTrac/dsl, Shell/dsl, 🍴 Blimpie, Checker's, Chick-fil-A, Church's, DQ, Kenny's Rest., Krystal, Longhorn Steaks, Martin's Rest., McDonald's, Pizza Hut, Popeye's, Taco Bell, Waffle House, Wendy's, 🛏 Best Value Inn, Comfort Inn, Days Inn, EconoLodge, Quality Inn, Ramada Ltd, Royal Inn, Ⓞ 🄷, AutoZone, CVS Drug, Family$, Kroger/dsl, NAPA, O'Reilly Parts, Tires+, Walgreens, vet, **S** 🅟 Chevron/dsl, QT, 🍴 Waffle House, Ⓞ Aamco, Advance Parts, $General, Ingles Foods
36	Chapel Hill Rd, **N** 🄷, **S** 🅟 BP, QT, Shell/dsl 🍴 Arby's, Carrabba's, China Garden, Coldstone, 5 Guys Burgers, Joe's Crabshack, Johnny's Subs, Logan's Roadhouse, McDonald's, O'Charley's, Olive Garden, Outback Steaks, Panda Express, Provino's Italian, Shane's Rib Shack, Starbucks, TX Roadhouse, $3 Cafe, Waffle House, 🛏 Hampton Inn, Ⓞ Aldi Foods, Belk, BigLots, Dillard's, Discount Tire, $Tree, Firestone/auto, Hobby Lobby, JC Penney, Kohl's, Macy's, Marshall's, Michael's, Petsmart, Rite Aid, Ross, Sears/auto, Target, Verizon
34	GA 5, to Douglasville, **N** 🅟 RaceTrac/dsl, Texaco, 🍴 Cracker Barrel, Hibachi Cafe, Stevie B's Pizza, Waffle House, Williamson Bro's BBQ, Zaxby's, 🛏 Holiday Inn Express, La Quinta, Sleep Inn, Ⓞ Urgent Care, $Tree, Kauffman Tires, Sam's Club, Walmart, **S** 🅟 Chevron/dsl, Circle K, Shell, 🍴 Applebee's, Buffalo Wild Wings, Burger King, Chick-fil-A, ChuckECheese, DQ, Dunkin Donuts, El Tio Mexican, Fiesta Mexican, Folk's Rest., Golden Buddah, Golden Corral, HoneyBaked Ham, IHOP, KFC, King Buffet, Krystal, LJ Silver, McDonald's, Moe's SW Grill, Monterrey Mexican, Papa John's, Pizza Hut, Quiznos, Red Lobster, Seabreeze Seafood, S'more BBQ, Sonic, Subway, Taco Bell, Taco Mac, Waffle House, Wendy's, 🛏 InTown Suites, Ⓞ Advance Parts, AT&T, Best Buy, Home Depot, Jo-Ann Crafts, Kroger, Lowe's, NTB, Office Depot, PepBoys, Publix, Tuesday Morning, U-Haul, Walgreens, USPO, vet
30	Post Rd, **S** 🅟 Shell/dsl
26	Liberty Rd, Villa Rica, **N** 🅟 Shell/dsl, Swifty/dsl, 🍴 China Wok, Johnny's Pizza, McDonald's, Mex-Grill, Olive Tree Rest., Subway, Sumo Japanese, Waffle House, Ⓞ 🄷, $General, Publix, Walgreens, **S** 🅟 Chevron, Wilco/Hess/Godfather's Pizza/Subway/dsl/scales/24hr, 🛏 American Inn
24	GA 101, GA 61, Villa Rica, **N** 🅟 BP, RaceTrac/dsl, Shell/dsl, 🍴 Arby's, Chick-fil-A, Hardee's, KFC/Taco Bell, Krystal, Lin's Garden Chinese, McDonald's, Pizza Hut, Romero's Italian, Sonic, Stix Grill, Subway, Waffle House, Wendy's, 🛏 Comfort Inn, Days Inn, EconoLodge, Super 8, Ⓞ 🄷, Advance Parts, AT&T, AutoZone, CVS Drug, Ingles Foods, Rite Aid, Walgreens, **S** 🅟 QT, Shell/dsl, 🍴 Bojangles, Burger King, Capt D's, Domino's, El Ranchito Mexican, O'Charley's, Papa John's, Waffle House, Zaxby's, Ⓞ

(left margin vertical: DOUGLASVILLE   VILLA RICA)

Exit	Services
24	Continued
	Urgent Care, Chevrolet, $Tree, Home Depot, GNC, Radio Shack, Verizon, Walmart/Subway, to W GA Coll
21mm	Little Tallapoosa River
19	GA 113, Temple, **N** 🅟 *FLYING J*/dsl/scales/24hr, 🚚/Subway/Wendy's/dsl/scales/24hr/@, 🍴 El Tapatio's, Fortune Star Chinese, Hardee's, McDonald's, Waffle House, Ⓞ Ingles Foods/gas, Truck-o-Mat/scales
15mm	**weigh sta wb**
11	US 27, Bremen, Bowdon, **N** 🅟 Chevron/dsl, Murphy USA, Texaco, Valero, 🍴 Arby's, Capt D's, Checker's, Chopsticks Chinese, Cracker Barrel, Juanito's, KFC/Taco Bell, McDonald's, Papa John's, Subway, Waffle House, Wendy's, Zaxby's, 🛏 Days Inn, Holiday Inn Express, Hampton Inn, Microtel, Quality Inn, Ⓞ 🄷, Urgent Care, Advance Parts, $General, Ford, Ingles Foods/gas, Verizon, Walmart/McDonald's (1mi), **S** 🅟 BP/dsl, Kangaroo/dsl, 🍴 John Tanner SP
9	Waco Rd, **N** 🅻🅾🆅🅴🆂/Chesters/Subway/dsl/scales/24hr, Ⓞ Jellystone RV Park (2mi)
5	GA 100, Tallapoosa, **N** 🅟 Citgo/dsl/24hr, Victory/dsl, 🍴 Waffle House Ⓞ Big Oak RV park, **S** 🅟 Newhorn TrkStp/rest/dsl/24hr/@, 🚚/KFC/Taco Bell/dsl/scales/24hr, Robinson/Subway, 🍴 DQ, GA Diner, 🛏 motel, Ⓞ truck repair/wash, to John Tanner SP
1mm	**Welcome Ctr eb, full 🛏 facilities, 🅲, vending, 🗑, littor barrels, petwalk**
0mm	Georgia/Alabama state line, Eastern/Central time zone

🔼🇳 INTERSTATE 59

Exit	Services
	I-59 begins/ends on I-24, exit 167. For I-24, turn to Tennessee Interstate 24.
20mm	I-24, W to Nashville, E to Chattanooga
17	Slygo Rd, to New England, **W** 🅟 Midnite/dsl, Ⓞ KOA (2mi)
11	GA 136, Trenton, **E** 🅟 Chevron/dsl, Exxon/dsl, Marathon/Kangaroo, 🍴 Asian Garden, Guthrie's, Hardee's, McDonald's, Pizza Hut, Subway, 🛏 Days Inn, Ⓞ Advance Parts, CVS Drug, Family$, Ingles, O'Reilly Parts, to Cloudland Canyon SP, **W** 🅟 BP, Citgo/dsl, Marathon/Kangaroo/dsl, 🍴 Huddle House, Krystal, Little Caesars, Taco Bell, Wendy's, Ⓞ BiLo, $General, Food Outlet
4	Rising Fawn, **E** 🅟 Citgo, **W** 🅟 BP/dsl, 🚚/Subway/dsl/scales/24hr, Ⓞ camping
0mm	Georgia/Alabama state line, eastern/central time zone

🔼🇳 INTERSTATE 75

Exit	Services
355mm	Georgia/Tennessee state line

(right margin vertical: BREMEN; GA)

🅶 = gas   🍴 = food   🛏 = lodging   🅾 = other   🆁🆂 = rest stop   Copyright 2014 - The Next Exit ®

⬆🅽 INTERSTATE 75 CONT'D

Exit	Services
354mm	Chickamauga Creek
353	GA 146, Rossville, **E** 🅶 BP, 🛏 Cloud Springs Lodge, **W** 🅶 BP/Subway/dsl, MegaStar/dsl, 🅾 Costco/gas
352mm	**Welcome Ctr sb, full ♿ facilities, info, 🚻, vending, 🆇, litter barrels, petwalk**
350	GA 2, Bfd Pkwy, to Ft Oglethorpe, **E** 🅶 Chevron/dsl, Kangaroo/dsl, 🛏 Hampton Inn, Hometown Inn, **W** 🅶 RaceTrac/dsl, Shell, 🍴 BBQ Corral, Subway, 🅾 🏥 KOA, to Chickamauga NP
348	GA 151, Ringgold, **E** 🅶 BP/dsl, FM, 🍴 Cracker Barrel, Hardee's, KFC, Los Reyes Mexican, McDonald's, Pizza Hut, Subway, Taco Bell, Waffle House, 🛏 Holiday Inn Express, Super 8, 🅾 Advance Parts, AutoZone, CVS Drug, Chevrolet, Dunlap's RV Ctr, Ingles, Walgreens, **W** 🍴 Domino's, Guthries, New China, Wendy's, 🅾 Ace Hardware, Family$, Food Lion, Peterbilt, truck repair
345	US 41, US 76, Ringgold, **E** 🅶 BP, **W** 🅶 Chevron, Cochran's/Midnite/rest/dsl/scales/24hr/@, Kangaroo/Subway/dsl/scales/24hr, 🍴 Waffle House
343mm	**weigh sta both lanes**
341	GA 201, to Varnell, Tunnel Hill, **W** 🅶 Chevron, Shell, 🅾 carpet outlets
336	US 41, US 76, Dalton, Rocky Face, **E** 🅶 Murphy USA/dsl, RaceTrac/dsl, Shell, 🍴 Checkers, Waffle House, 🛏 EconoLodge, 🅾 🏥 Ford/Lincoln, Home Depot, Kohl's, PetCo, Walmart, **W** 🅶 BP/dsl, Exxon, 🍴 Los Pablos, Oyster Grill, Tijuana Mexican, Wendy's, 🛏 Baymont Inn, Guest Inn, Motel 6, Staylodge, Super 8, carpet outlets
333	GA 52, Dalton, **E** 🅶 BP/dsl, Exxon/dsl, RaceTrac/dsl, 🍴 Amici's Italian, Applebee's, Bruster's, Burger King, Capt D's, Chick-fil-A, CiCi's Pizza, Cracker Barrel, DQ, Five Guys Burgers, Fuji Japanese, IHOP, Jersey Mike's Subs, Kani Japanese, KFC, Los Pablos Mexican, LJ Silver, Longhorn Steaks, Los Pablos, McDonald's, O'Charley's, Outback Steaks, Panda Express, Panera Bread, Pizza Hut, Schlotzsky's, Shoney's, Sonic, Starbucks, Steak'n Shake, Taco Bell, Waffle House, Wendy's, 🛏 Best Inn, Days Inn, Hampton Inn, Travelodge, 🅾 AT&T, BigLots, Chevrolet, Chrysler/Jeep, $Tree, Harley-Davidson, K-Mart, Kroger/dsl, TJ Maxx, Tuesday Morning, Walgreens, **W** 🍴 Chili's, Red Lobster, Zaxby's, 🛏 Comfort Inn, Courtyard, Country Inn Suites, Holiday Inn, Holiday Inn Express, Jameson Inn, La Quinta, Quality Inn, Ramada, 🅾 NW GA Trade/Conv Ctr
328	GA 3, to US 41, **E** 🅶 BP/Kangaroo/dsl, 🚛/Arby's/dsl/scales/24hr, 🍴 Waffle House, Wendy's, 🛏 Best Value Inn, Super Motel, **W** carpet outlets
326	Carbondale Rd, **E** 🅶 🚛/McDonald's/Subway/dsl/scales, Smart/dsl, **W** 🅶 BP, Exxon
320	GA 136, to Lafayette, Resaca, **E** 🅶 ⚡FLYING J/Denny's/dsl/LP/24hr, 🅾 truckwash, truck repair/parts
319mm	Oostanaula River, 🚻 sb, full ♿ facilities, 🚻, vending, 🆇, litter barrels, petwalk
318	US 41, Resaca, **E** 🅶 Hess/Wilco/DQ/Wendy's/scales/dsl/24hr, 🍴 Hardee's, 🛏 Relax Inn, **W** 🅶 Pure, Shell/dsl, 🍴 Chuckwagon Rest., 🛏 Best Inn, Executive Inn
317	GA 225, to Chatsworth, **E** New Echota HS, Vann House HS, **W** 🅶 BP (1mi) 🛏 Express Inn
315	GA 156, Redbud Rd, to Calhoun, **E** 🅶 Citgo/dsl, Kangaroo, 🍴 Waffle House, 🅾 Food Lion, KOA (2mi), **W** 🅶

Side tabs (left column): **GA**, **DALTON**, **RESACA**

315	Continued BP/dsl, Liberty/Subway/dsl, Shell, 🍴 Arby's, Shoney's, 🛏 Ramada Ltd, 🅾 🏥 Rite Aid
312	GA 53, to Calhoun, **E** 🅶 Shell/dsl, 🍴 Cracker Barrel, Longhorn Steaks, 🛏 Days Inn, Country Inn&Suites, La Quinta, 🅾 Calhoun Outlets/famous brands, **W** 🅶 BP/Arby's, Chevron/dsl, Marathon/Kangaroo, Murphy USA, 🍴 Big John's Rest., Bojangles, Burger King, Capt D's, Checker's, Chick-fil-A, China Palace, DQ, Domino's, Eastern Cafe, El Nopal Mexican, Gondolier Pizza, Huddle House, IHOP, KFC, Krystal, Little Caesars, Los Reyes Mexican, LJ Silver, McDonald's, Papa's Pizza, Pizza Hut, Ryan's, Ruby Tuesday, Starbucks, Subway, Taco Bell, Tokyo Steaks, Wendy's, Zaxby's, 🛏 Guest Inn, Hampton Inn, Holiday Inn Express, Jameson Inn, Motel 6, Scottish Inn, 🅾 Advance Parts, AutoZone, $General, GNC, Goodyear/auto, Home Depot, Ingles, Kroger/gas, Office Depot, Walmart, vet
308mm	🆁🆂 nb, full ♿ facilities, 🚻, 🆇, litter barrels, vending, petwalk
306	GA 140, Adairsville, **E** 🅶 Cowboy's/dsl, QT/dsl/scales/24hrs, Shell, 🍴 Cracker Barrel, Wendy's, 🛏 Hampton Inn, 🅾 truck repair, **W** 🅶 Adairsville TP/dsl/scales, BP/dsl, Chevron/dsl, Exxon/dsl, 🍴 Burger King, Hardee's, McDonald's, Taco Bell, Waffle House, Zaxby's, 🛏 Best Western, Magnuson Inn, Quality Inn, Ramada Ltd, 🅾 Harvest Moon RV Park
296	Cassville-White Rd, **E** 🅶 🚛/McDonald's/Subway/dsl/scales, Pure, TA/BP/Burger King/Pizza Hut/Popeye's/Taco Bell/dsl/scales/24hr/@, Texaco, 🛏 Cartersville North Inn, 🅾 truckwash, **W** 🅶 Chevron, Marathon/dsl, Shell, 🛏 Best Inn, Howard Johnson, 🅾 KOA
293	US 411, to White, **E** 🅶 Sunoco/dsl, Texaco/dsl, 🛏 Quality Inn, **W** 🅶 Chevron/dsl, Horizon, Marathon, 🍴 AJ's Cafe, Waffle House, 🛏 Holiday Inn, 🅾 Harley-Davidson, RV camping, mineral museum, st patrol
290	GA 20, to Rome, **E** 🅶 Chevron/Subway/dsl, Exxon/dsl, Kangaroo/dsl, 🍴 Arby's, Fruit Jar Cafe, McDonald's, Wendy's, 🛏 Best Western, Country Inn Suites, EconoLodge, Motel 6, Ramada Ltd, Red Roof Inn, Super 8, **W** 🅶 BP, Murphy USA (1.5mi), Shell, 🍴 Cracker Barrel, Michael's BBQ, Pruitt's BBQ, Shoney's, Waffle House, 🛏 Days Inn, Hampton Inn, 🅾 🏥 RV camping (7mi), Walmart (1.5mi)
288	GA 113, Cartersville, **0-2 mi W** 🅶 BP/dsl, Exxon/Subway/dsl, 🍴 Applebee's, Burger King, Chick-Fil-A, Chili's, Gondolier Pizza, IHOP, KFC, Krystal, Las Palmas Mexican, Longhorn Steaks, McDonald's, Moe's SW Grill, Mrs Winner's, Pizza Hut, Publix, Red Lobster, Starbucks, Taco Bell, Waffle House, Wing Moon, 🛏 Fairfield Inn, Hampton Inn, Hilton Garden, Knights Inn, Quality Inn, 🅾 Belk, Chrysler/Dodge/Jeep, K-Mart, Kohl's, Kroger, Rite Aid, Staples, Target, to Etowah Indian Mounds (6mi)
286mm	Etowah River
285	Emerson, **E** 🅶 Sunoco, 🛏 Red Top Mtn Lodge, 🅾 to Allatoona Dam, to Red Top Mtn SP
283	Allatoona Rd, Emerson, **E** 🅶 Allatoona Landing Resort (2mi), camping, **W** 🅶 ♥Love's/McDonald's/Subway/dsl/scales/24hr, Sunoco (1mi)
280mm	Allatoona Lake
278	Glade Rd, to Acworth, **E** 🅶 BP/dsl, Shell, 🛏 Best Value, 🅾 McKinney Camping (3mi), to Glade Marina, **W** 🅶 Chevron, 🍴 Bojangles, Hong Kong Chinese, KFC,

Side tabs (right column): **CALHOUN**, **ADAIRSVILLE**

INTERSTATE 75 CONT'D

Exit	Services
278	Continued Krystal, Papa John's, Pizza Hut, Subway, Taco Bell, Waffle House, 🏠 Best Inn, 🅞 AutoZone, BigLots, Ingles/cafe, Rite Aid
277	GA 92, Acworth, **E** 🅖 BP, RaceTrac, 🍴 Hardee's, Shoney's, Waffle House, 🏠 Comfort Suites, La Quinta, Ramada Ltd, **W** 🅖 Chevron/dsl, Shell/DQ/dsl, 🍴 Bamboo Garden, China Chef, Domino's, McDonald's, Ricardo's Mexican, Sonic, Subway, Taco 2 Go, Waffle House, Wendy's, Zaxby's, 🏠 Best Western, Day's Inn, Econolodge, Motel 6, Super 8, 🅞 Advance Parts, CVS Drug, Goodyear/auto, Publix, Walgreens
273	Wade Green Rd, **E** 🅖 BP, Pure, RaceTrac, 🍴 Arby's, Burger King, Dunkin Donuts, Las Palmas Mexican, McDonald's, Mrs Winners, Papa John's, Pizza Hut/Taco Bell, Subway, Waffle House, 🏠 Magnuson Motel, Sleep Inn, 🅞 BigLots, GNC, Goodyear/auto, Publix, Rite Aid, **W** 🅖 Shell, Texaco/dsl, 🍴 BBQ Street, Coldstone, Johnny's Pizza/Subs, Quiznos, Starbucks, Wendy's, Wing Zone, 🅞 Home Depot, Kroger/gas, Walgreens
271	Chastain Rd, to I-575 N, **E** 🅖 Chevron, 🍴 CA Dreaming, Brewsters, Chick-Fil-A, Chilito's Mexican, Cracker Barrel, Dunkin Donuts, Firehouse Subs, Five Guys Burgers, Kayson's Grill, Little Zio, Los Reyes, McAlister's Deli, O'Charley's, Panda Express, Panera Bread, Sidelines Grille, Starbucks, Taco Mac, ToGo's/Baskin Robbins, Zaxby's, Zucca Pizza, 🏠 Best Western, Comfort Inn, Embassy Suites, Extended Stay America, Fairfield Inn, La Quinta, Residence Inn, Suburban Lodge, Super 8, 🅞 Goodyear/auto, Outlets Ltd Mall, **W** 🅖 Citgo, Swifty Save Gas/Blimpie, Shell/dsl, 🍴 Arby's, Mrs Winners, Waffle House/24hr, Wendy's, 🏠 Country Inn Suites, SpringHill Suites, Sun Suites, 🅞 museum
269	to US 41, to Marietta, **E** 🅖 Chevron/24hr, Shell, Texaco/dsl, 🍴 Applebee's, Burger King, Fuddrucker's, Highlands Grill, Honey Baked Ham, Longhorn Steaks, McDonald's, New China, Olive Garden, Pizza Hut, Provino's, Red Lobster, Shogun Japanese, Smoothie King, Smokey Bones, Starbucks, Subway, Twisted Taco, Waffle House, 🏠 Comfort Inn, Econolodge, Holiday Inn Express, La Quinta, Red Roof Inn, Super 8, 🅞 Barnes&Noble, Big 10 Tire, Firestone/auto, Home Depot, JC Penney, Macy's, Marshall's, Publix, Sears/auto, TJ Maxx, mall, **W** 🅖 BP, Exxon, 🍴 Bahama Breeze, Bailey's Grill, Bugaboo, Carrabbas, Copelands Grill, Creek Steaks, Chick-fil-A, Chili's, Chuck-eCheese, Coldstone, Golden Corral, Joe's Crabshack, Macaroni Grill, On-the-Border, Outback Steaks, Rafferty's, Starbucks, Steak'n Shake, Sweet Tomato, TGIFriday, Willy's Mexican, 🏠 Day's Inn, Hampton Inn, Hilton Garden, Quality Inn, Wingate Inn, 🅞 Best Buy, Buick/GMC, CarMax, Chevrolet, Costco/gas, Ford/Lincoln, Goodyear/auto, Jo-Anne Fabrics, Kia/Toyota, Nissan, Mitsubishi, NTB, Office Depot, Old Navy, PetsMart, Target, mall, to Kennesaw Mtn NP
268	I-575 N, GA 5 N, to Canton
267b a	GA 5 N, to US 41, Marietta
265	GA120, N Marietta Pkwy, **W** 🅖 Chevron, Shell/dsl, 🍴 Arbys, Bojangles, Chick-fil-A, KFC, 🏠 Days Inn, Sun Inn, Suburban Lodge, Travelers Motel
263	GA 120, to Roswell, **E** 🅖 Chevron/dsl/24hr, QT,

263	Continued Texaco/24hr, **W** 🅖 Exxon/dsl, RaceTrac, 🍴 Applebee's, Capt D's, China Kitchen, DQ, Hardee's, Haveli Rest., Piccadilly's, Subway, 🏠 Best Western, Crowne Plaza, Fairfield Inn, Hampton Inn, Marietta Motel, Ramada Ltd, Regency Inn, Super 8, Wyndham Garden, 🅞 U-Haul, Atl-Marietta RV Resort
261	GA 280, Delk Rd, to Dobbins AFB, **E** 🅖 Exxon, RaceTrac, Shell/McDonald's, 🍴 CC Cafeteria, China Wok, Hardee's, KFC/Taco Bell, Murphy's Deli, Ruby Tuesday, Spaghetti Whse, 🏠 Budget Inn, Courtyard, Drury Inn, Motel 6, Scottish Inn, Sleep Inn, Super 8, Travelers Inn, 🅞 Publix, **W** 🅖 BP, Chevron, 🍴 Cracker Barrel, D&B Rest., Waffle House, 🏠 Best Inn, Comfort Inn, Days Inn, Fairfield Inn, Holiday Inn, La Quinta, Quality Inn, Wingate Inn
260	Windy Hill Rd, to Smyrna, **E** 🅖 BP/dsl, 🍴 Boston Mkt, Famous Dave's, Fuddrucker's, Houston's Rest., Jersey Mike's Subs, Mellow Mushroom, NY Pizza, Pappasito's Cantina, Pappadeaux Seafood, Philly Cafe, Rose&Crown, Sal Grosso Brazilian, Schlotzsky's, Starbucks, Subway, TGIFriday, 🏠 Country Hearth Inn, EconoLodge, Extended Stay Deluxe, Hilton Garden, Hyatt, Marriott, Studio Lodge, 🅞 CVS Drug, USPO, **W** 🅖 Chevron, Citgo, Shell, 🍴 Arby's, Chick-fil-A, Fatburger, Halftime Grill, McDonald's, Panda Express, Popeye's, Starbucks, Waffle House, Wendy's, 🏠 Best Western, Country Inn&Suites, Courtyard, Days Inn, DoubleTree, Hilton, Masters Inn, Red Roof Inn, 🅞 🅷, Target
259b a	I-285, W to Birmingham, E to Greenville
258	Cumberland Pkwy, **W** 🍴 Chipotle Mexican, Copelands Rest., Hooters, Moe's SW Grill, Ray's On The River, Shane's Ribshack, Subway
257mm	Chattahoochee River
256	to US 41, Northside Pkwy
255	US 41, W Paces Ferry Rd, **E** 🅖 Chevron, Shell/dsl, 🍴 Blue Ridge Grill, Caribou Coffee, Chick-fil-A, Houston's Rest., McDonald's/playplace, OK Café, Pero's Pizza, Starbucks, Steak'n Shake, Taco Bell, Willy's Rest., 🅞 🅷, Ace Hardware, Publix, **W** 🅖 Exxon
254	Moores Mill Rd
252b	Howell Mill Rd, **E** 🅖 Shell, 🍴 Chick-fil-A, Domino's, McDonald's, Willy's Grill, 🅞 Goodyear, Publix, Rite Aid, USPO, **W** 🅖 Shell, 🍴 Arby's, Arthur's Italian, Chin Chin Chinese, Einstein Bro's, Kayson's, KFC/Pizza Hut, Mexican, Rest., Piccadilly, Sensational Subs, Starbucks, Subway, Taco Bell, US BBQ, Waffle House, Wendy's, 🏠 Budget Inn, Holiday Inn, 🅞 Ace Hardware, Firestone/auto, GNC, Just Brakes, Kroger, Office Depot, Petsmart, Ross, TJ Maxx, Walmart

Left margin: **ACWORTH**
Right margin: **MARIETTA SMYRNA ATLANTA**
GA

🛈N INTERSTATE 75 CONT'D

Exit	Services
252a	US 41, Northside Dr, **E** 🅖 🄷, **W** 🅖 Shell, 🍴 Krystal, Little Zio's, McDonald's, Waffle House, 🛏 Days Inn
251	I-85 N, to Greenville
250	Techwood Dr (from sb), 10th St, 14th St, **E** 🛏 Travelodge
249d	10th St, Spring St (from nb), **E** 🅖 BP, Chevron/24hr, 🍴 Checker's, Domino's, Pizza Hut, The Varsity, 🛏 Fairfield Inn, Regency Suites, Renaissance Hotel, Residence Inn, **W** 🍴 McDonald's, 🛏 Courtyard, Comfort Inn, 🄾 🄷, to GA Tech
249c	Williams St (from sb), downtown, to GA Dome
249b	Pine St, Peachtree St (from nb), downtown, **W** 🛏 Hilton, Marriott
249a	Courtland St (from sb), downtown, **W** 🛏 Hilton, Marriott, 🄾 GA St U
248d	Piedmont Ave, Butler St (from sb), downtown, **W** 🛏 Courtyard, Fairfield Inn, Radisson, 🄾 🄷, Ford, MLK NHS
248c	GA 10 E, Intn'l Blvd, downtown, **W** 🛏 Hilton, Holiday Inn, Marriott Marquis, Radisson
248b	Edgewood Ave (from nb), **W** 🄾 🄷, downtown, hotels
248a	MLK Dr (from sb), **W** st capitol, to Underground Atlanta
247	I-20, E to Augusta, W to Birmingham
246	Georgia Ave, Fulton St, **E** 🛏 Comfort Inn, Country Inn& Suites, Holiday Inn, 🄾 stadium, **W** 🅖 BP, 🍴 KFC, 🄾 to Coliseum, GSU
245	Ormond St, Abernathy Blvd, **E** 🛏 Comfort Inn, Country Inn& Suites, 🄾 stadium, **W** st capitol
244	University Ave, **E** 🅖 Chevron, Exxon, 🄾 NAPA, **W** 🍴 Mrs Winner's
243	GA 166, Lakewood Fwy, to East Point
242	I-85 S, to ✈
241	Cleveland Ave, **E** 🅖 BP, Chevron, 🍴 Checker's, Church's, McDonald's, Subway, 🛏 Palace Inn, 🄾 Advance Parts, K-Mart, **W** 🅖 Shell, Marathon, Phillips 66, Texaco, 🍴 Blimpie, Burger King, Krystal/24hr, Mrs Winners, 🛏 American Inn, Day's Inn, 🄾 CVS Drug, Kroger
239	US 19, US 41, **E** 🅖 Chevron/dsl, 🍴 Waffle House, 🄾 USPO, **W** 🅖 Texaco, 🍴 IHOP, McDonald's, Wendy's, 🛏 Best Western, to ✈
238b a	I-285 around Atlanta
237a	GA 85 S (from sb), **W** 🍴 Denny's, 🛏 Burger King, McDonald's, Waffle House, 🛏 Day's Inn, Day's Lodge
237	GA 331, Forest Parkway, **E** 🅖 BP, Chevron/dsl, Shell/McDonald's, 🍴 Burger King, Mr Taco, Subway, Waffle House, 🛏 Econolodge, 🄾 Farmer's Mkt, **W** 🅖 BP, 🍴 Denny's, 🛏 Day's Inn, Ramada Ltd
235	US 19, US 41, GA 3, Jonesboro, **E** 🅖 Chevron/dsl, Exxon/Subway/dsl, Phillips 66, Valero, 🍴 Waffle House, 🛏 Travelodge, **W** 🅖 BP, Shell, Texaco/dsl, 🍴 Applebee's, Burger King, Checker's, ChuckeCheese, Dunkin Donuts, Folk's Rest., Hooters, Krystal, Popeye's, Red Lobster, Tokyo Buffet, Waffle House, Zaxby's, 🛏 Best Value, Econolodge, Holiday Inn, Motel 6, 🄾 🄷, Office Depot, O'Reilly Parts
233	GA 54, Morrow, **E** 🅖 BP, Citgo, Marathon, 🍴 Cracker Barrel, IHOP, Krystal/24hr, Mrs Winner's, Papa Buffet, Taco Bell, Waffle House, Wendy's, 🛏 Best Western, Days Inn, Drury Inn, Red Roof Inn, 🄾 Walmart, **W** 🅖 Circle K, Exxon/24hr, 🍴 China Café, KFC, Lenny's Subs, McDonald's, Quizno's, Subway, Waffle House, 🛏 Hampton Inn, Quality Inn, 🄾 Acura, Best Buy, Costco/gas, Harley-Da

Exit	Services
233	Continued vidson, Macy's, Nissan, TJ Maxx, Toyota, Tuesday Morning
231	Mt Zion Blvd, **E** 🅖 QT, 🄾 Chrysler/Dodge/Jeep, Ford/Lincoln, Honda, **W** 🅖 Chevron, Exxon/dsl, Texaco/dsl, 🍴 Arby's, Boston's Rest., Brewster's, Burger Shack, Burger King, Chick-fil-A, Chili's, Joe's Crabshack, Longhorn Steaks, McDonald's, Mo-Joe's, Panda Express, Papa John's, Pizza Hut, Steak'n Shake, Subway, Truett's Rest., Waffle House, Wendy's, Wok Asian, 🛏 Country Inn&Suites, Extended Stay America, Sleep Inn, Sun Suites, 🄾 Barnes & Noble, Best Buy, Home Depot, Michael's, NTB, Old Navy, PetsMart, Publix, Ross, Target
228	GA 54, GA 138, Jonesboro, **E** 🅖 Exxon, Raceway/24hr, 🍴 Applebee's, Arby's, Broadway Diner, Burger King, Chick-fil-A, ChinChin Chinese, CiCi's, DQ, Frontera Mexican, Golden Corral, Honeybaked Ham, IHOP, KFC, Krystal, McDonald's, O'Charlie's, Piccadilly's, Subway, Taco Mac, Tokyo Seafood, Waffle House, Wendy's, 🛏 Best Western, Day's Inn, Comfort Inn, Holiday Inn, Howard Johnson, La Quinta, Hampton Inn, Holiday Inn, Motel 6, Red Roof Inn, 🄾 🄷, GNC, Goodyear, K-Mart, Kroger/dsl, Lowes Whse, Office Depot, Tires+, **W** 🅖 BP/24hr, Marathon, Sunoco/Wendy's, 🍴 Dragon Garden Chinese, Ranchero's Mexican, 🄾 CarMax, CVS Drug, Kohl's
227	I-675 N, to I-285 E (from nb)
224	Hudson Bridge Rd, **E** 🅖 Shell, Texaco/dsl, 🍴 Chick-fil-A, China Wok, DQ, KFC, La Hacienda, Outback Steaks, Pizza Hut, Starbucks, Subway, Waffle House, Wendy's, 🛏 Baymont Inn, 🄾 🄷, Publix, Rite Aid, Walgreens, **W** 🅖 Murphy USA/dsl, QT, 🍴 Arby's, China Cafe, Firehouse Subs, McDonald's, Mellow Mushroom, Subway, Taco Bell, Zaxby's, 🛏 Super 8, 🄾 Discount Tire, $Tree, Walmart/24hr
222	Jodeco Rd, **E** 🅖 BP, Citgo/24hr, Texaco, 🍴 Hardee's, Waffle House, **W** 🅖 BP, Chevron/dsl, Citgo, 🄾 Atlanta So. RV Camping
221	Jonesboro Rd, **E** 🅖 QT, 🄾 Kroger/gas, Kauffman Tire, **W** 🍴 Arby's, Burger King, Chili's, Cici's Pizza, Golden Corral, Hooter's, Logan's Roadhouse, Longhorn Steaks, Marble Slab Creamery, McDonald's, O'Charley's, Olive Garden, Quizno's, Red Lobster, Rocky's Pizza, Starbucks, Subway, Truett's Grill, Wendy's, 🛏 Fairfield Inn, 🄾 Belk, Best Buy, Books-A-Million, BJ's Whse/gas, Home Depot, Marshall's, Michael's, PetsMart, Radio Shack, Ross, Sam's Club/gas, Staples, Target
218	GA 20, GA 81, McDonough, **E** 🅖 BP, Murphy USA, QT, Texaco, 🍴 Applebee's, Arby's, Blimpie, Burger King, China Star, Cracker Barrel, DQ, KFC, IHOP, McDonald's, Moe's SW Grill, Mrs Winner's, OB's BBQ, Pizza Hut, Quizno's, Ruby Tuesday, Taco Bell, 3 Dollar Cafe, Tokyo Japanese, Waffle House, Wendy's, Zaxby's, 🛏 Best Inn, Best Western, Economy Inn, Hampton Inn, Motel 6, 🄾 Aamco, $General, Goodyear, Lowe's Whse, Office Depot, Rite Aid, Walmart, **W** 🅖 Citgo/dsl, RaceTrac, Shell/24hr, 🍴 Chick-fil-A, El Agade Mexican, Firehouse Subs, Fuddruckers, Starbucks, Subway, Waffle House, 🛏 Comfort Inn, Econolodge, Hilton Garden, Holiday Inn Express, Super 8, 🄾 JC Penney, Kohl's, Toyota
216	GA 155, McDonough, Blacksville, **E** 🅖 Shell, Sunoco/Backyard Burger, Texaco/dsl, 🍴 Blimpie, 🛏 Best Value, Budget Inn, Day's Inn, Roadway Inn, 🄾 Chevrolet,

Side tab labels: ATLANTA   GA   MORROW   JONESBORO   MCDONOUGH

⬆N INTERSTATE 75 CONT'D

Exit	Services
216	Continued
	Buick, Lincoln, GMC, **W** 🅖 BP/dsl, Chevron, Citgo, Citgo/dsl/24hr, Mystik/dsl, QT, 🍴 Da Vinci's Pizza, Krystal, Kuma Japanese, Legends Grill, Subway, Waffle House, 🛏 Country Inn&Suites, Quality Inn
212	to US 23, Locust Grove, **E** 🅖 BP/McDonald's/dsl, Chevron/Burger King, Citgo/dsl, JP, Marathon/Subway, Shell/dsl, 🍴 Capt D's, Country Steaks, Denny's, Gabino's Mexican, Huddle House, KFC/Pizza Hut/Taco Bell, Shane's Ribshack, Sunrise China, Waffle House, Wendy's, Zaxby's, 🛏 Economy Inn, Executive Inn, La Quinta, Ramada Ltd, Red Roof Inn, 🅞 Ingles/gas, NapaCare, Tanger Outlet/famous brands, **W** 🅖 Citgo/DQ/dsl, Exxon/dsl, 🛏 Comfort Suites, Scottish Inn, Sundown Lodge, Super 8, 🅞 Bumper Parts
205	GA 16, to Griffin, Jackson, **E** 🅖 BP, **W** 🅖 BP, Chevron/dsl, 🅞 Forest Glen RV Park, auto repair
201	GA 36, to Jackson, Barnesville, **E** 🅖 ♥Loves/McDonald's/dsl/grill/scales/24hr, TA/Subway/Taco Bell/dsl/scales/24hr/@, Wilco/Hess/DQ/Stuckey's/Wendy's/dsl/scales/24hr/@, 🅞 Blue Beacon, **W** 🅖 BP/dsl, ✈FLYING J/Denny's/dsl/LP/24hr, 🅞 Sagon RV Ctr, Speedco Lube, truckwash
198	Highfalls Rd, **E** 🅖 Exxon (1mi), 🍴 High Falls BBQ, Ken's Cafe, 🛏 High Falls Lodge, 🅞 HighFalls RV Park (1ml), High Falls SP
193	Johnstonville Rd, **E** 🅖 BP
190mm	weigh sta both lanes
188	GA 42, **E** 🅖 Shell/24hr, 🛏 Best Western, Budget Inn, 🅞 to Indian Spings SP, RV camping
187	GA 83, Forsyth, **E** 🛏 Econolodge, New Forsyth Inn, Regency Inn, **W** 🅖 BP/Circle K, Citgo/dsl, Marathon, Shell, 🍴 Burger King, Capt D's, China Inn, DQ, Hardee's, McDonald's, Pizza Hut, Subway, Taco Bell, Waffle House, Wendy's, 🛏 Day's Inn, Tradewinds Motel, 🅞 Advance Parts, Freshway Foods, O'Reilly Parts, Walmart
186	Tift College Dr, Juliette Rd, Forsyth, **E** Jarrell Plantation HS (18mi), KOA, **W** 🅖 BP/dsl, Chevron, Marathon, 🍴 Waffle House, 🛏 Holiday Inn/rest., Holiday Inn Express, Super 8, 🅞 H CVS Drug, Ingles/Deli
185	GA 18, **E** L&D RV Park (2mi), **W** 🅖 BP/Circle K/24hr, Shell/dsl, 🍴 Shoney's, 🛏 Comfort Inn, 🅞 Ford, repair, st patrol
181	Rumble Rd, to Smarr, **E** 🅖 BP/dsl/24hr, Shell/dsl/24hr
179mm	🆁🆂 sb, full 🅰 facilities, 🍴 vending, 🗑 litter barrels, petwalk
177	I-475 S around Macon (from sb)
175	Pate Rd, Bolingbroke (from nb, no re-entry)
172	Bass Rd, **E** 🍴 Pig in a Pit BBQ, McDonald's, Quizno's, Zaxby's, 🅞 Bass Pro Shop, **W** 🅖 Citgo/dsl/24hr, 🍴 Magarita's Mexican, Mellow Mushroom, 🍴 Homewood Suites, 🅞 Publix, to Museum of Arts&Sciences
171	US 23, to GA 87, Riverside Dr, **E** 🅖 BP, Marathon/dsl, 🍴 Bonefish Grill, Chili's, Jock&Jill's Grill, Mandarin Express, Sticky Fingers, 🅞 Acura, Barnes & Noble, Belk, Dillards, KIA, Mercedes, Subaru, Volvo, **W** 🍴 Cracker Barrel, 🅞 Lexus, Toyota/Scion, same as 169 W
169	to US 23, Arkwright Dr, **E** 🅖 Shell/Circle K/24hr, 🍴 Carrabba's, Logan's Roadhouse, Outback Steaks, Waffle House, Wager's Grill, 🛏 Candlewood Suites, Comfort Inn,

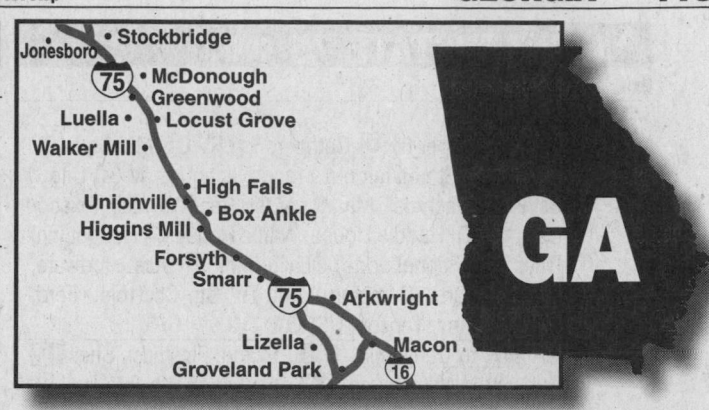

Exit	Services
169	Continued
	Country Inn & Suites, Courtyard, Fairfield Inn, Hampton Inn, Holiday Inn, La Quinta, Red Roof Inn, Residence Inn, Sleep Inn, Super 8, 🅞 Buick/Cadillac/GMC, **W** 🅖 BP/dsl, Chevron/24hr, Marathon/dsl, 🍴 Arby's, Burger King, Cheddar's, Cheng's Kitchen, Chick-fil-A, Corky Bells, Cracker Barrel, Dunkin Donuts, El Azteca Mexican, 5 Guys Burgers, Guiseppi's Italian, Hooters, KFC, Krystal, Longhorn Steaks, Mandarin Chinese, McDonald's, Papa John's, Papoulis' Gyros, Panera Bread, Pizza Hut, Shoki Japanese, Starbucks, Steak'n Shake, Steve B's Pizza, Subway, Taco Bell, Waffle House, 🛏 Baymont Inn, Best Inn, Extended Stay Deluxe, Quality Inn, Travelodge, Wingate Inn, 🅞 H Ace Hardware, Chrysler/Jeep/Dodge, $Tree, Hyundai, K-Mart, Kroger, Mazda, Publix, Radio Shack, same as 167
167	GA 247, Pierce Ave, **E** 🛏 Days Inn, **W** 🅖 BP/Circle K/dsl, Chevron, Conoco, Exxon, LoBucks Gas, Marathon/Subway/dsl, Shell, 🍴 Applebee's, Loco's Grill, Pier 97 Seafood, Pizza Hut, Red Lobster, San Marcos Mexican, Shogun Japanese, SteakOut Rest., Waffle House, 🛏 Best Western/rest., Comfort Inn, Holiday Inn Express, Howard Johnson, Motel 6, 🅞 ExperTire, Rite Aid
165	I-16 E, to Savannah
164	US 41, GA 19, Forsyth Ave, Macon, **E** 🍴 Sid's Rest., 🅞 hist dist, **W** 🅖 Citgo/dsl, 🅞 H museum
163	GA 74 W, Mercer U Dr, **E** 🛏 Hilton Garden, 🅞 to Mercer U, **W** 🅖 Citgo, Marathon/dsl
162	US 80, GA 22, Eisenhower Pkwy, **W** 🅖 BP, Chevron, Lolo Gas, 🍴 Burger King, Capt D's, Checker's, IHOP, Krispy Kreme, Krystal, LJ Silver, McDonald's, Mrs Winners, Subway, Taco Bell, Wendy's, 🛏 InTown Suites, 🅞 $Tree, Fred's, Meineke, Office Depot, O'Reilly Parts, PepBoys, Piggly Wiggly, Save-A-Lot Foods, Walgreens
160	US 41, GA 247, Pio Nono Ave, **E** 🅖 Flash/dsl, RaceWay/Dunkin Donuts/dsl, 🍴 Waffle House, **W** 🅖 BP, Enmark/dsl, 🍴 Arby's, DQ, KFC, McDonald's, Subway, Waffle House, 🅞 Advance Parts, $General, Family$, O'Reilly Parts, Piggly Wiggly, Raffield Tire, Roses, same as 162
156	I-475 N around Macon (from nb)
155	Hartley Br Rd, **E** 🅖 BP/KFC/dsl/24hr, 🍴 Subway, Waffle House, Wendy's, 🅞 Kroger/dsl, Verizon, **W** 🅖 Citgo/dsl, Exxon/dsl, Flash/DQ/dsl, 🍴 McDonald's, Zaxby's, 🛏 Best Value Inn, 🅞 Advance Parts, CVS Drug
153	Sardis Church Rd
149	GA 49, Byron, **E** 🅖 Chevron/dsl, Marathon/dsl, Shell/dsl, 🍴 Burger King, Denny's, GA Bob's BBQ, Krystal, McDonald's, Pizza Hut, Subway, Waffle House, Wendy's, Zaxby's, 🛏 Best Western, Comfort Suites, Holiday Inn

⬆N INTERSTATE 75 CONT'D

Exit	Services
149	Continued
	Express, Super 8, 🅾 Campers Inn RV Ctr, Mid-State RV Ctr, Peach Stores/famous brands, antiques, **W** 🅿 Citgo/dsl/24hr, Flash/dsl, Marathon/dsl, RaceWay/dsl, Texaco/dsl, 🍴 DQ, Huddle House, Waffle House, 🛏 Budget Inn, Days Inn, EconoLodge, Quality Inn, 🅾 Ace Hardware, Bumper Parts, Camping World RV Ctr, Chevrolet, Ford, O'Reilly Parts, Verizon, USPO
146	GA 247, to Centerville, **E** 🅿 Exxon, Flash/dsl, Shell, 🍴 Subway, Waffle House, 🛏 EconoLodge, Knights Inn, 🅾 🅷, to Robins AFB, museum, **W** 🅿 ⛽/Arby's/dsl/24hr
144	Russel Pkwy, **E** Robins AFB, aviation museum
142	GA 96, Housers Mill Rd, **E** 🅿 Chevron/dsl, 🅾 Ponderosa RV Park
138	Thompson Rd, **E** 🅿 Valero/dsl, 🅾 🅷, **W** ✈
136	US 341, Perry, **E** 🅿 Flash/dsl, Shell/dsl, 🍴 Burger King, Capt D's, Chick-fil-A, China House, KFC, Krystal, Long-horn Steaks, McDonald's, Pizza Hut, Red Lobster, Son-ny's BBQ, Steamers Seafood, Subway, Taco Bell, Waffle House, Wendy's, Zaxby's, 🛏 Best Inn, Great Inn, Hamp-ton Inn, Howard Johnson, Jameson Inn, Super 8, 🅾 🅷 Ace Hardware, Advance Parts, AT&T, Boland's RV Park, $Tree, GNC, Kroger/dsl, NAPA, Radio Shack, Verizon, Walmart, **W** 🅿 Chevron/dsl, Marathon/dsl, 🍴 Apple-bee's, Green Derby Rest., Grill Master BBQ, 🛏 Ashburn Inn, EconoLodge, Knights Inn, Passport Inn, Quality Inn, Ramada Inn, Roadway Inn
135	US 41, GA 127, Perry, **E** 🅿 Flash/dsl, Marathon, Shell, Texaco, 🍴 Cracker Barrel, DQ, Subway, Waffle House, 🛏 Best Western, Comfort Inn, Red Carpet Inn, Relax Inn, Travelodge, 🅾 Chrysler/Dodge/Jeep, Kia, GA Nat Fair, **W** 🅾 Fair Harbor RV Park, st patrol
134	South Perry Pkwy, **W** 🅿 Marathon, 🛏 Microtel, 🅾 Buick/Chevrolet/GMC, Priester's Pecans
127	GA 26, Henderson, **E** Twin Oaks Camping, **W** 🅿 Chevron
122	GA 230, Unadilla, **E** 🅿 Chevron/dsl, 🅾 Chevrolet/Ford, **W** 🛏 Red Carpet Inn
121	US 41, Unadilla, **E** 🅿 Borum/repair, Danfair, Flash/DQ/Stuckey's/dsl, Shell, 🍴 Country Boys BBQ, Subway, 🛏 Economy Inn, Scottish Inn, 🅾 Carquest, $General, Fam-ily$, Firestone, Piggly Wiggly, Southern Trails RV Resort, **W** 🅿 Citgo/rest./dsl/scales/24hr
118mm	🆁🆂 **sb, full** ♿ **facilities,** 🍴 **, vending,** ♨ **litter barrels, petwalk, RV dump**
117	to US 41, Pinehurst
112	GA 27, Vienna
109	GA 215, Vienna, **E** 🅿 ⛽/McDonalds/dsl/scales/24hrs, **W** 🅿 Citgo/dsl, Shell/Subway/dsl/e-85, Sunoco, 🍴 Huddle House, Popeye's, 🛏 Executive Inn, 🅾 🅷, an-tiques, Cotton Museum
108mm	🆁🆂 **nb, full** ♿ **facilities,** 🍴 **, vending,** ♨ **litter barrels, petwalk, RV dump**
104	Farmers Mkt Rd, Cordele
102	GA 257, Cordele, **E** 🅿 Sunoco/dsl, **W** 🍴 Pecan House, 🅾 🅷
101	US 280, GA 90, Cordele, **E** 🅿 Chevron, ⛽/Arby's/dsl/scales/24hr, Shell, 🍴 Denny's, Golden Corral, Waffle House, 🛏 Days Inn, Fairfield Inn, Holiday Inn Express, Ra-mada Inn, 🅾 Ford/Lincoln, st patrol, **W** 🅿 Flash, Gas'n Go, Pacecar Express, Sunoco, 🍴 Burger King,

101	Continued
	Capt D's, Cracker Barrel, Cutter's Steaks, DQ, Domino's, Hardee's, KFC, Krystal, Little Caesars, Los Compadres, McDonald's, New China, Pizza Hut, Sonic, Subway, Taco Bell, TJ's Rest, Wendy's, Zaxby's, 🛏 Ashburn Inn, Athens 8 Motel, Best Western, Comfort Inn, Hampton Inn, Quality Inn, Travelodge, 🅾 Ace Hardware, Advance Parts, Au-toZone, Belk, $General, $Tree, Harvey's Foods, Home De-pot, NAPA, O'Reilly Parts, Radio Shack, Save-A-Lot, Ve-rizon, Walgreens, Walmart, to Veterans Mem SP, J Carter HS
99	GA 300, GA/FL Pkwy, **E** 🍴 Citgo/DQ/dsl, **W** 🍴 Waffle House, 🛏 Country Inn&Suites, 🅾 to Chehaw SP
97	to GA 33, Wenona, **E** 🅾 Cordele RV Park, dsl repair, **W** 🅾 KOA, truckwash
92	Arabi, **E** 🅿 Shell/Plantation House, **W** 🅿 Citgo/dsl, 🅾 Southern Gates RV Park
85mm	🆁🆂 **nb, full** ♿ **facilities,** 🍴 **, vending,** ♨ **litter barrels, petwalk**
84	GA 159, Ashburn, **W** 🅿 Chevron/DQ/Subway/dsl/24hr, 🛏 Ashburn Inn/RV Park
82	GA 107, GA 112, Ashburn, **W** 🅿 BP, Shell, Sunoco/dsl, 🍴 KFC, McDonald's, Pizza Hut, Shoney's, Waffle House, Zaxby's, 🛏 Best Value Inn, Best Western, Days Inn, Super 8, 🅾 Auto Value Parts, Buick/Chevrolet/GMC, $General, Fred's, O'Reilly Parts, Piggly Wiggly, Rite Aid, to Chehaw SP
80	Bussey Rd, Sycamore, **W** 🅾 Allen's Tires
78	GA 32, Sycamore, **E** to Jefferson Davis Mem Pk (14mi)
76mm	🆁🆂 **sb, full** ♿ **facilities,** 🍴 **, vending,** ♨ **litter barrels, petwalk**
75	Inaha Rd
71	Willis Still Rd, Sunsweet, **W** 🅿 BP/dsl
69	Chula-Brookfield Rd, **E** 🅿 Sunoco/dsl, 🛏 Chula Carpet Inn
66	Brighton Rd
64	US 41, Tifton, **E** 🅿 BP/dsl, 🅾 🅷, $General, Harvey's Foods, **W** 🅿 Shell
63b	8th St, Tifton, **E** 🅿 Flash/dsl/e-85, 🍴 Los Compadres, 🅾 Publix, **W** 🍴 Pit Stop BBQ, 🅾 GA Museum of Agri-culture
63a	2nd St, Tifton, **E** 🅿 BP, Marathon, 🍴 Asahi Xpress, Checker's, El Cazador Mexican, Krystal, McDonald's, Pizza Hut, Ranchero's Grill, Red Lobster, Stevi B's Pizza, Subway, Taco Bell, Waffle House, 🛏 EconoLodge, Super 8, 🅾 Belk, Buick/Cadillac/GMC, $General, $Tree, JC Penney, K-Mart, **W** 🅿 Bob's/dsl, 🍴 Coyoacan Mexican, 🛏 Quality Inn, Travelodge
62	US 82, to US 319, Tifton, **E** 🅿 BP, Citgo, Flash/dsl, 🍴 Applebee's, Charles Seafood, Chili's, Cracker Barrel, DQ, Golden Corral, King Buffet, Logan's Roadhouse, Ole Times, Sonic, Tokyo Japanese, Waffle House, Zaxby's, 🛏 Comfort Inn, Country Inn&Suites, Fairfield Inn, Hampton Inn, Microtel, Tifton Inn, 🅾 Advance Parts, AutoZone, Big-Lots, Bumper Parts, $Tree, Family$, Ford/Lincoln, NAPA-Care, O'Reilly Parts, Pecan Outlet, Save-A-Lot, Staples, **W** 🅿 Exxon/Burger King, EZ Mart, Flash/dsl, Murphy USA/dsl, RaceWay/dsl, Shell/dsl, 🍴 Capt D's, Chick-fil-A, HogBones BBQ, Lin's Garden, Little Caesars, Loco's Grill, Longhorn Steaks, McDonald's, Oishi Japanese, Ruby Tuesday, Shoney's, Starbucks, Subway, Waffle House, Wendy's, 🛏 Days Inn, Hilton Garden, Rodeway

(left margin vertical: PERRY, GA, CORDELE)

(center margin vertical: WENONA, ASHBURN, TIFTON)

🅝 INTERSTATE 75 CONT'D

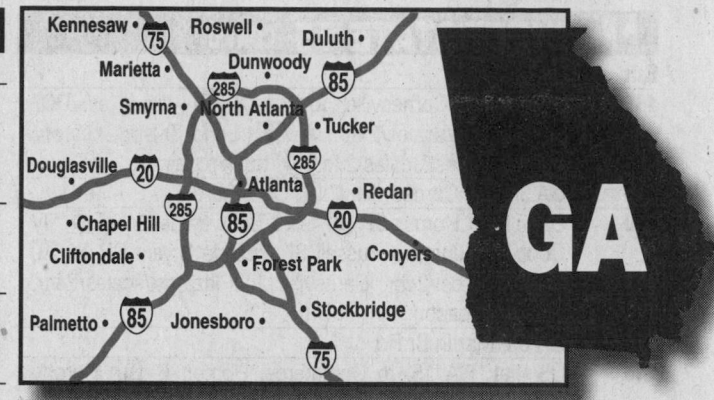

Exit	Services
62	Continued
	Inn, 🄾 **Urgent Care**, Chevrolet, Chrysler/Dodge/Jeep, $General, Honda, Lowe's, Radio Shack, Toyota, Verizon, Walmart/Subway
61	Omega Rd, **E** 🅖 Nissan, **W** 🅖 Shell/Stuckey's/Country Diner/pizza/dsl/24hr, 🛏 Motel 6, 🄾 Harley-Davidson, Pines RV Park
60	Central Ave, Tifton, **E** 🅖 Chevron, 🍴 Dragon 1 Chinese, **W** 🅖 Steak'n Shake/Subway/dsl/scales/24hr, 🄾 Blue Beacon, KOA
59	Southwell Blvd, to US 41, Tifton, **E** 🅖 ♥Loves/Hardee's/dsl/24hr
55	to Eldorado, Omega, **E** 🅖 Shell/Magnolia Plantation/dsl
49	Kinard Br Rd, Lenox, **E** 🅖 Dixie/dsl, 🛏 Knights Inn, **W** 🅖 BP/dsl/24hr, 🄾 repair
47mm	🆁🆂 **both lanes, full 🦽 facilities, 🚰 vending, 🗑 litter barrels, petwalk**
45	Barneyville Rd, **E** 🛏 Economy Inn
41	Rountree Br Rd, **E** 🅖 Citgo, **W** to Reed Bingham SP
39	GA 37, Adel, Moultrie, **E** 🅖 Citgo/dsl, Dixie Gas, Quick Gas, Shell/McDonald's/dsl, 🍴 DQ, Hardee's, Subway, Waffle House, 🛏 Scottish Inn, Super 8, 🄾 🄷, Ace Hardware, Advance Parts, $General, Family$, Harvey's Foods, Piggly Wiggly, O'Reilly Parts, Rite Aid, **W** 🅖 BP, Citgo/dsl/scales, 🍴 Burger King, Capt D's, China Buffet, IHOP, Taco Bell, Wendy's, Western Sizzlin, 🛏 Days Inn, Hampton Inn, 🄾 to Reed Bingham SP
37	Adel
32	Old Coffee Rd, Cecil, **E** 🅖 Citgo, 🛏 Stagecoach Inn, **W** 🅖 Chevron, 🄾 Cecil Bay RV Park
29	US 41 N, GA 122, Hahira, Sheriff's Boys Ranch, **E** 🍴 Subway, 🄾 NAPA, **W** 🅖 Big Foot TC/cafe/dsl/24hr, Citgo/dsl, 🛏 Hahira Inn
23mm	**weigh sta both lanes**
22	US 41 S, to Valdosta, **E** 🅖 BP, Shell/Subway/dsl, 🍴 Waffle House, 🛏 Best Western, 🄾 🄷, Buick/Chevrolet/GMC, Mazda, golf, **W** 🅖 Citgo/Stuckey's, 🍴 Burger King, DQ, 🛏 Days Inn, Howard Johnson
18	GA 133, Valdosta, **E** 🅖 Citgo/dsl, Exxon, Flash, Mobil, 🍴 Applebee's, Arby's, Atl. Bread Co, Brusters, Buffalo Wild Wings, Burger King, Chick-fil-A, Chili's, Cracker Barrel, Chow Town, CiCi's Pizza, Crystal River Seafood, Denny's, El Potro Mexican, El Toreo, Fazoli's, Green Iguana Cafe, Honeybaked Ham, Hooters, KFC, Krystal, Little Caesars, Longhorn Steaks, Marble Slab, McAlister's Deli, McDonald's, Olive Garden, Outback Steaks, Quiznos, Red Lobster, Ruby Tuesday, Sonny's BBQ, Starbucks, Steak'n Shake, Subway, Taco Bell, TX Roadhouse, Waffle House, Wendy's, Zaxby's, 🛏 Comfort Suites, Country Inn&Suites, Courtyard, Drury Inn, Hilton Garden, Holiday Inn Express, InTown Suites, Jameson Inn, Jolly Inn, La Quinta, Quality Inn, 🄾 AT&T, Belk, Best Buy, Books-A-Million, $Tree, Family$, Harvey's Foods, Hobby Lobby, Home Depot, JC Penney, Kohl's, Lowe's, Michael's, Office Depot, Old Navy, Petsmart, Publix, Ross, Sears/auto, Target, TJ Maxx, Tuesday Morning, Verizon, Walgreens, mall, repair, **W** 🅖 BP/dsl, RaceWay/dsl, Shell, 🛏 Days Inn, EconoLodge, Sleep Inn, Super 8, 🄾 RiverPark Camping, Toyota/Scion
16	US 84, US 221, GA 94, Valdosta, **E** 🅖 Big Foot/dsl, BP/dsl, Citgo/DQ/dsl, Danfair Express, Murphy Express/dsl,

Exit	Services
16	Continued
	Pure/dsl, Shell/dsl, 🍴 Aligatou Japanese, Bojangles, Bubba Jax Crab Shack, Burger King, Cheddar's, IHOP, McDonald's, Pizza Hut, Sonic, Waffle House, Wendy's, 🛏 Days Inn, Fairfield Inn, Hampton Inn, Holiday Inn, Motel 6, New Valdosta Inn, Quality Inn, Stay Inn, Super 8, Wingate Inn, 🄾 NAPA, Sam's Club/gas, Walmart/Subway, repair, to Okefenokee SP, **W** 🅖 Horizon/Backyard Burger/pizza, Shell/dsl/24hr, 🍴 Austin's Steaks, 🛏 Clarion, Knights Inn
13	Old Clyattville Rd, Valdosta, **W** Wild Adventures Park
11	GA 31, Valdosta, **E** 🅖 Subway/dsl/24hr/@, Wilco/Hess/Dunkin Donuts/Stuckey's/dsl/scales/24hr, 🍴 Waffle House, 🛏 Travelers Inn, 🄾 truckwash, **W** 🅖 BP, 🍴 Big Ed's BBQ, 🄾 $General
5	GA 376, to Lake Park, **E** 🅖 Citgo, Flash Foods/Stuckey's/dsl, RaceWay/dsl, Shell, 🍴 Chick-fil-A, Domino's, Farmhouse Rest., Krystal, Lin's Garden Chinese, Rodeo Mexican, Sonny's BBQ, Subway, Waffle House, Zaxby's, 🛏 Guesthouse Inn, Quality Inn, 🄾 $Tree, Eagles Roost Camping, Family$, Fred's, Horizon RV Ctr, Winn-Dixie, antiques, USPO, **W** 🅖 Citgo/dsl, Exxon/dsl, Shell/dsl, 🍴 Cracker Barrel, McDonald's, Pizza Hut, Taco Bell, Wendy's, 🛏 Ashburn Inn, Days Inn, Hampton Inn, Super 8, 🄾 KOA
3mm	**Welcome Ctr nb, full 🦽 facilities, 🚰 vending, 🗑 litter barrels, petwalk**
2	Lake Park, Bellville, **E** 🅖 Mobil/DQ, Shell/dsl, TA/BP/Arby's/dsl/scales/24hr/@, 🄾 SpeedCo, **W** 🅖 FLYING J/Denny's/Subway/dsl/LP/scales/24hr, 🛏 Motel 6, 🄾 lube/tires/wash
0mm	Georgia/Florida state line

🅝 INTERSTATE 85

Exit	Services
179mm	Georgia/South Carolina state line, Lake Hartwell, Tugaloo River
177	GA 77 S, to Hartwell, **E** 🅖 BP/gifts/dsl, 🍴 Dad's Grill, 🄾 to Hart SP, Tugaloo SP
176mm	**Welcome Ctr sb, full 🦽 facilities, info, 🚰, 🗑, litter barrels, vending, petwalk**
173	GA 17, to Lavonia, **E** 🅖 RaceTrac/dsl, 🍴 Blimpie, La Cabana Mexican, McDonald's, Subway, Taco Bell, Waffle House, 🛏 EconoLodge, Sleep Inn, 🄾 $General, Lavonia Foods, Rite Aid, **W** 🅖 Chevron/dsl, Exxon/dsl, 🍴 Burger King, Hardee's, Pizza Hut, Shoney's, Wendy's, Zaxby's, 🛏 Holiday Inn Express, Super 8, 🄾 Chrysler/Dodge/Jeep, Ford, to Tugaloo SP
171mm	**weigh sta nb**
169mm	**weigh sta sb**

Vertical left margin: A D E L / V A L D O S T A

Vertical right margin: L A V O N I A

GA

▶N INTERSTATE 85 CONT'D

Exit	Services
166	GA 106, to Carnesville, Toccoa, **E** 🅿 Wilco/Hess/DQ/Wendy's/dsl/scales/24hr, **W** 🅿 Echo Trkstp/Chevron/Echo Rest./dsl/scales/24hr, ⓞ truck repair
164	GA 320, to Carnesville, **E** 🅿 Chevron/dsl
160	GA 51, to Homer, **E** 🅿 Shell/Subway/dsl/24hr, ⓞ Ty Cobb Museum, to Russell SP, Victoria Bryant SP, **W** 🅿 ✈FLYING J/dsl/24hr, Carnsville TrvlPlaza/dsl/scales/24hr, ⓞ Blue Beacon
154	GA 63, Martin Br Rd
149	US 441, GA 15, to Commerce, Homer, **E** 🅿 Murphy USA, QT/dsl, TA/Buckhorn Rest/dsl/scales/24hr/@, 🍴 Capt D's, Denny's, El Azteca, Grand Buffet, Krispy Kreme, Longhorn Steaks, Outback Steaks, Pizza Hut/Taco Bell, Sonny's BBQ, Zaxby's, 🛏 Best Value Inn, Dandelion Inn, Hampton Inn, Scottish Inn, ⓞ🅷 $General, $Tree, Funopolis, GNC, O'Reilly Parts, Radio Shack, Walmart, **W** 🅿 BP/Krystal/dsl, Citgo, RaceTrac/dsl, 🍴 Applebee's, Arby's, Burger King, Checker's, Chick-fil-A, Cracker Barrel, DQ, 5 Guys Burgers, La Fiesta, La Hacienda, McDonald's, Pizza Hut, Ruby Tuesday, Ryan's, Sonic, Starbucks, Subway, Wendy's, 🛏 Best Inn, Best Western, Comfort Suites, Fairfield Inn, Holiday Inn Express, Howard Johnson, Jameson Inn, Motel 6, Quality Inn, Super 8, ⓞ Home Depot, Pritchett Tires, Tanger Outlet/famous brands
147	GA 98, to Commerce, **E** 🅿 ✈FLYING J/Dunkin Donuts/dsl/24hr, FuelMart/dsl, Valero, ⓞ🅷 **W** ⓞ Gulf
140	GA 82, Dry Pond Rd, **E** Freightliner, **W** RV & Truck Repair
137	US 129, GA 11 to Jefferson, **E** 🅿 RaceTrac/dsl, 🍴 Arby's, El Jinete Mexican, KFC/Taco Bell, McDonald's, Waffle House, Zaxby's, 🛏 Comfort Inn, ⓞ museum, **W** 🅿 QT/dsl/scales/24hr, 🍴 Burger King, Waffle House, Wendy's, ⓞ flea mkt
129	GA 53, to Braselton, **E** 🅿 Chevron/dsl, Shell/Golden Pantry/dsl, 🍴 La Hacienda Mexican, Waffle House, 🛏 Best Western, ⓞ USPO, **W** 🅿 📠/McDonald's/dsl/scales/24hr, 🍴 Cracker Barrel, Domino's, El Centinela, Stonewall's, Subway, Tea Garden Chinese, Wendy's, Zaxby's
126	GA 211, to Chestnut Mtn, **E** 🅿 Shell/dsl, 🍴 Subway, Waffle House, 🛏 Country Inn&Suites, **W** 🅿 BP/dsl, 🍴 Blimpie, Chateau Elan Winery/rest., China Garden, Papa John's, 🛏 Holiday Inn Express, ⓞ Publix, vet
120	to GA 124, Hamilton Mill Rd, **E** 🅿 BP, QT/dsl, 🍴 Arby's, Buffalo's Café, Burger King, Caprese Rest., Dos Copas Mexican, 5 Guys Burgers, McDonald's, Moe's SW Grill, Shane's Rib Shack, Starbucks, Subway, Wendy's, Zaxby's, ⓞ AT&T, Home Depot, Kohl's, Publix/Deli, RV World of GA (1mi), auto repair, vet, **W** 🅿 Chevron, Murphy USA/dsl, Shell/dsl, 🍴 Barbarito's, Chick-fil-A, Chili's, El Molcajate, Hardee's, Italy's Pizza, Little Caesars, ⓞ CVS Drug, O'Reilly Parts, Tires+, Walmart
115	GA 20, to Buford Dam, **E** 🅿 QT, **W** 🅿 QT/dsl, 🍴 Arby's, Bonefish Grill, Bruster's, Buck Head Pizza, Buffalo's Cafe, Burger King, Chick-fil-A, Chili's, Chipotle, Chuck-e-Cheese, Einstein's Bagels, Firehouse Subs, 5 Guy's Burgers, Genghis Grill, Kani House, Krispy Kreme, Longhorn Steaks, Liu's Buffet, Macaroni Grill, McDonald's, Mimi's Cafe, Moe's SW Grill, O'Charley's, Olive Garden, On-the-Border, Panda Express, PF Chang's, Provino's Italian, Red Lobster, Shogun Japanese, Sonny's BBQ, Starbucks,

115	Continued
	Steak n' Shake, Subway, Taco Mac, Ted's MT Grill, TGI-Friday's, Waffle House, Wendy's, 🛏 Country Inn&Suites, Courtyard, Hampton Inn, SpringHill Suites, Wingate Inn, ⓞ AT&T, Belk, Best Buy, Costco/gas, Dick's, Dillard's, Discount Tire, $Tree, Fiat, Firestone, Honda, Hyundai, JC Penney, Lowe's, Macy's, Mazda, Michael's, Nissan, Nordstrom's, PetCo, Petsmart, Radio Shack, Ross, Sam's Club/gas, Staples, Target, TJ Maxx, Toyota/Scion, Verizon, VW, Walmart, Mall of GA, to Lake Lanier Islands
113	I-985 N (from nb), to Gainesville
111	GA 317, to Suwanee, **E** 🅿 BP, Sims/dsl, 🍴 Applebee's, Arby's, Checker's, Chick-fil-A, Cracker Barrel, Dunkin Donuts, Oriental Garden, Outback Steaks, Philly Connection, Pizza Hut/Taco Bell, Subway, Waffle House, Wendy's, 🛏 Comfort Inn, Comfort Suites, Courtyard, Fairfield Inn, Mayqueen Hotel, Motel 6, Sun Suites, ⓞ CVS Drug, GNC, **W** 🅿 Chevron/dsl, Murphy USA/dsl, RaceTrac/dsl, Shell, 🍴 Atlanta Bread, CiCi's Pizza, HoneyBaked Ham, IHOP, KFC, McDonald's, Moe's SW Grill, Sonic, Subway, Taco Mac, 🛏 Budgetel, Super 8, ⓞ AT&T, $Tree, Lowe's, Office Depot, Tires&More, Walmart
109	Old Peachtree Rd, **E** 🅿 QT/dsl/24hr, 🍴 McDonald's, Mi Casa Mexican, 🛏 Hampton Inn, ⓞ Bass Pro Shops, $World, Publix, **W** 🍴 Califonia Dreaming, Chick-fil-A, China Delight, Firehouse Subs, 5 Guys Burgers, Jim&Nicks BBQ, Magnolia Bakery Cafe, Starbucks, Subway, Waffle House, 🛏 Hilton Garden, Holiday Inn, ⓞ Home Depot
108	Sugarloaf Pkwy (from nb), **E** 🛏 Hampton Inn, **W** 🍴 Carrabba's, Chick-fil-A, 🛏 Hilton Garden, Holiday Inn, ⓞ Gwinnett Civic Ctr
107	GA 120, to GA 316 E, Athens, **E** 🅿 Shell, 🍴 Burger King, Carino's, Jillian's, Zaxby's, ⓞ Bass Pro Shops, Books-a-Million, Burlington Coats, Discount Tire, Food Ct, Mercedes, Nieman-Marcus, Rite Aid, Ross, Saks 5th Ave, Sears, Suburban Tire, **W** 🅿 BP, Chevron, 🍴 China Gate, McDonald's, Roadhouse Grill, Subway, Waffle House, 🛏 La Quinta, Suburban Lodge
106	Boggs Rd (from sb, no return), Duluth, **W** 🅿 QT/dsl/24hr
104	Pleasant Hill Rd, **E** 🅿 Chevron/24hr, QT, Shell, Sim's/dsl, 🍴 Arby's, Bahama Breeze, Burger King, Chick-fil-A, East Pearl, Fung Mi Chinese, GA Diner, Golden House, Grand Buffet, Ida's Pizza Kitchen, Joe's Crabshack, Krispy Kreme, Lobster House, McDonald's, Moe's SW Grill, Popeye's, Quiznos, Starbucks, Stevie B's Pizza, Subway, TGIFriday's, Waffle House, Wendy's, 🛏 Candlewood Suites, Comfort Suites, Hampton Inn Suites, Holiday Inn Express, Marriott, Residence Inn, ⓞ Advance Parts, Best Buy, $General, $Tree, Family$, Home Depot, Publix, Walgreens, Urgent Care, **W** 🅿 BP/dsl, Chevron, Sim's/dsl, 🍴 Applebee's, Arby's, Bruster's, Burger King, Checker's, Chili's, Chipotle Mexican, Hooters, IHOP, Jimmy John's, KFC, McDonald's, Olive Garden, On the Border, Panda Express, Red Lobster, Ryan's, Starbucks, Steak'n Shake, Subway, Sweet Tomatoes, Taco Bell, Wendy's, 🛏 Courtyard, Days Inn, Extended Stay America, Holiday Inn, Hyatt Place, Quality Inn, Wingate Inn, ⓞ AT&T, Audi, Barnes&Noble, Batteries+, Belk, BMW, Buick/GMC, Firestone/auto, Fry's Electronics, Goodyear/auto, Honda, JC Penney, Jo-Ann Fabrics, KIA, Macy's, Marshall's, Nissan, Old Navy, PetCo, Rite Aid, Sears/auto, Staples, TJ Maxx, Toyota/Scion, Tuesday Morning, Verizon, mall
103	Steve Reynolds Blvd (from nb, no return), **W** 🅿 QT, Shell,

COMMERCE JEFFERSON — SUWANEE DULUTH ATLANTA AREA — GA

📙 = gas 🍴 = food 🛏 = lodging ⭕ = other Ⓡs = rest stop

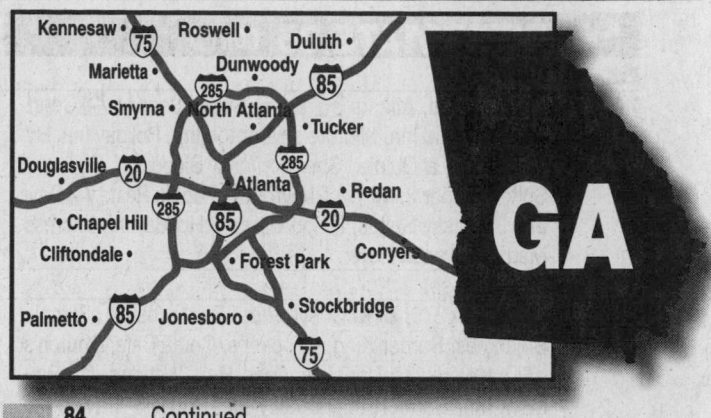

🔼N INTERSTATE 85 CONT'D

Exit	Services
103	Continued 🍴 Dave&Buster's, Waffle House, 🛏 InTown Suites, ⭕ Costco/gas, Kohl's, Petsmart, Sam's Club, Target, same as 104
102	GA 378, Beaver Ruin Rd, **E** 📙 Shell/dsl, QT, **W** 📙 Citgo
101	Lilburn Rd, **E** 📙 QT/dsl, Shell/dsl/24hr, 🍴 Blimpie, Bruster's, Burger King, Hong Kong Buffet, Krystal, KFC, Manhattan Pizza, McDonald's/playplace, Quiznos, Starbucks, Taco Bell, Waffle House, 🛏 Guesthouse Inn, InTown Suites, ⭕ Jones RV Park, **W** 📙 Chevron, Marathon, QT, 🍴 Arby's, El Indo Mexican, El Taco Veloz, Grand Buffet, Papa John's, Pizza Plaza, Subway, Waffle House, Wendy's, 🛏 Knights Inn, Red Roof Inn, ⭕ CarMax, Lowe's
99	GA 140, Jimmy Carter Blvd, **E** 📙 Phillips 66/dsl, Shell, 🍴 Checker's, Chick-fil-A, Cracker Barrel, Denny's, Dunkin Donuts, El Nortino Mexican, KFC, McDonald's, Papa John's, Pizza Hut/Taco Bell, Pollo Campero, Wendy's, 🛏 Best Inn, Courtyard, Horizon Inn, La Quinta, Motel 6, Ramada, Rite4Us Suites, ⭕ Advance Parts, Aldi Foods, Family$, U-Haul, Walgreens, **W** 📙 Chevron/24hr, Citgo/dsl, QT/dsl, 🍴 Barnacle's Grill, 5 Guys Burgers, Hong Kong Buffet, Pappadeaux Steak/seafood, Quiznos, Sonic, Waffle House, Wendy's, 🛏 Days Inn, Drury Inn, Country Inn&Suites, Microtel, ⭕ AutoZone, CarQuest, NTB, O'Reilly Parts, PepBoys
96	Pleasantdale Rd, Northcrest Rd, **E** 🍴 Burger King, 🛏 Peachtree Inn, **W** 📙 Exxon/dsl, QT/dsl, 🍴 Subway, Waffle House, 🛏 Atlanta Lodge
95	I-285
94	Chamblee-Tucker Rd, **E** 📙 Chevron/dsl, Shell, **W** 📙 QT/dsl, Shell, 🍴 DQ, Waffle House, 🛏 Motel 6, Super 8, ⭕ to Mercer U
93	Shallowford Rd, to Doraville, **E** 📙 Shell, 🍴 Blimpie, Hop Shing Chinese, ⭕ Publix, U-Haul, **W** 📙 Shell/dsl, 🛏 Quality Inn
91	US 23, GA 155, Clairmont Rd, **E** 📙 Chevron, Shell, 🍴 IHOP, Mo's Pizza, Popeye's, ⭕ IGA Foods, repair, **W** 📙 BP, 🍴 McDonald's, Mykonos Greek, Waffle House, 🛏 Marriott, Wingate Inn, ⭕ NTB, Sam's Club/dsl
89	GA 42, N Druid Hills, **E** 📙 Chevron/Subway/dsl, QT/dsl/24hr, Shell, 🍴 Arby's, Boston Mkt, Burger King, Chick-fil-A, Einstein Bro's, El Torero, Fortune Cookie, Jersey Mike's, Lettuce Souperise You, McDonald's, Moe's SW Grill, Piccadilly's, Starbucks, Taco Bell, Tin Roof Cantina, 🛏 Courtyard, ⭕ $Tree, Firestone/auto, GNC, Target, Walgreens, **W** 📙 Chevron/dsl, Exxon, Shell, 🍴 Atlanta Diner, HoneyBaked Ham, Krystal, Waffle House, 🛏 DoubleTree, Hampton Inn, Red Roof Inn, ⭕ CVS Drug, Just Brakes, vet
88	Lenox Rd, GA 400 N, Cheshire Br Rd (from sb), **E** 📙 Shell, 🛏 La Quinta
87	GA 400 N (from nb)
86	GA 13 S, Peachtree St, **E** 📙 BP, 🍴 Denny's, Wendy's, 🛏 Intown Inn, La Quinta, ⭕ Brake-O
85	I-75 N, to Marietta, Chattanooga
84	Techwood Dr, 14th St, **E** 📙 BP, Shell, 🍴 CheeseSteaks, La Bamba Mexican, Thai Cuisine, VVV Ristorante Italiano, 🛏 Best Western, Hampton Inn, Marriott, Sheraton, Travelodge, ⭕ Woodruff Arts Ctr, **W** 🍴 Blimpie, 🛏 Court

Exit	Services
84	Continued yard, Knights Inn, ⭕ CVS Drug, Dillard's, Office Depot, to Georgia Tech
249d	10th St, Spring St (from nb), **E** 📙 BP, Chevron/24hr, Shell, 🍴 Checker's, Domino's, Pizza Hut, Varsity Drive-In, 🛏 Fairfield Inn, Marriott, Regency Suites, Renaissance Hotel, Residence Inn, Wyndham Hotel, ⭕ Publix, to Mitchell House, **W** 🍴 McDonald's, 🛏 Courtyard, ⭕ Ⓗ, CVS Drug, to GA Tech
249c	Williams St (from sb), downtown, to GA Dome
249b	Pine St, Peachtree St (from nb), downtown, **E** 🛏 Reniassance Inn, ⭕ Ⓗ, to midtown, **W** downtown, hotels
249a	Courtland St (from sb), downtown, **W** 🛏 Hilton, Marriott, ⭕ GA St U
248d	Piedmont Ave, Butler St (from sb), downtown, **W** 🛏 Courtyard, Fairfield Inn, Radisson, ⭕ Ⓗ, Ford, MLK NHS
248c	GA 10 E, Intn'l Blvd, downtown, **W** 🛏 Hilton, Holiday Inn, Marriott Marquis, Radisson
248b	Edgewood Ave (from nb), **W** ⭕ Ⓗ, downtown, hotels
248a	MLK Dr (from sb), **W** st capitol, to Underground Atlanta
247	I-20, E to Augusta, W to Birmingham
246	Georgia Ave, Fulton St, **E** 🛏 Hampton Inn, Holiday Inn Express, ⭕ to Turner Stadium, **W** 🍴 KFC, ⭕ to Coliseum, GSU
245	Ormond St, Abernathy Blvd, **E** 🛏 Comfort Inn, Country Inn Suites, Hampton Inn, Holiday Inn Express, ⭕ Turner Stadium, **W** st capitol
244	University Ave, **E** 📙 Chevron/dsl, Exxon/dsl, 🍴 Subway, Wendy's, ⭕ NAPA
243	GA 166, Lakewood Fwy, to East Point
77	I-75 S
76	Cleveland Ave, **E** 📙 Citgo/dsl, Marathon, 🍴 Burger King, Krystal, Papa John's, ⭕ Ⓗ, AutoZone, BigLots, CVS Drug, $Tree, Family$, Kroger, Radio Shack, Walgreens, **W** 📙 Shell/dsl, Texaco/dsl, 🍴 Chick-fil-A, Church's
75	Sylvan Rd, **E** 📙 Phillips 66, Shell/dsl, 🍴 Chick-fil-A
74	Loop Rd Aviation Commercial Center
73b a	Virginia Ave, **E** 📙 Citgo/dsl, 🍴 Jonny's Pizza, Malone's Grill, McDonald's, Pizza Hut, Quiznos, Ruby Tuesday, Schlotsky's, Spondivit's Rest., Waffle House, Wendy's, Willy's Mexican, 🛏 Courtyard, Drury Inn, Hilton, Motel 6, Renaissance Hotel, Residence Inn, **W** 📙 Chevron/Subway, Shell, 🍴 Arby's, Blimpie, Giovanna's Italian, Happy Buddah Chinese, KFC, La Fiesta Mexican, Waffle House, 🛏 Comfort Inn, Country Inn&Suites, Crowne Plaza, DoubleTree, EconoLodge, Fairfield Inn, Hampton Inn, Hilton Garden, Holiday Inn, Hyatt Place, Ramada Inn, Wellesley Inn
72	Camp Creek Pkwy

ATLANTA AREA

ATLANTA AREA

GA

INTERSTATE 85 CONT'D

Exit	Services
71	Riverdale Rd, Atlanta ☒, **E** Ⓕ Ruby Tuesday, ☒ Courtyard, Fairfield Inn, Microtel, Hampton Inn, Holiday Inn, Hyatt Place, La Quinta, Sheraton/grill, Sleep Inn, Springhill Suites, Super 8, **W** Ⓖ Chevron, Ⓕ Joe's Rest., ☒ Days Inn, Embassy Suites, Hilton Garden, Holiday Inn Express, Marriott, Westin Hotel
70	I-85 (from sb)
69	GA 14, GA 279, **E** Ⓖ Chevron/dsl, Exxon/dsl, Ⓕ Blimpie, Bojangles, Burger King, Checker's, China Cafe, Church's, KFC, Krystal, McDonald's, Taco Bell, Wendy's, ☒ Baymont Inn, Comfort Inn, Quality Inn, Super 8, Travelodge, Wyndham Garden, Ⓞ CVS Drug, Goodyear/auto, U-Haul, **Urgent Care**, **W** Ⓖ Chevron/dsl, Texaco, Ⓕ Waffle House, ☒ EconoLodge
68	I-285 Atlanta Perimeter (from nb)
66	Flat Shoals Rd, **W** Ⓖ BP, Chevron/dsl, Shell/Blimpie, Ⓕ Supreme Fish Delight, Waffle House, ☒ Motel 6
64	GA 138, to Union City, **E** Ⓖ BP/dsl, RaceTrac/dsl, Ⓕ Waffle House, ☒ EconoLodge, Western Inn, Ⓞ BMW/Mini, Buick/GMC, Chevrolet, Chrysler/Dodge/Jeep, CVS Drug, Ford/Lincoln, Honda, Infiniti, Kia/Nissan, Lexus, Lincoln, Subaru, Toyota/Scion, **W** Ⓖ Chevron/dsl, QT, Shell/dsl, Ⓕ Arby's, Burger King, Capt D's, China Garden, Corner Cafe, IHOP, KFC, Krystal, McDonald's, Papa John's, Pizza Hut, Sonic, Subway, Taco Bell, Wendy's, Zaxby's, ☒ Best Western, Comfort Inn, Country Hearth Inn, Days Inn, Garden Inn, La Quinta, Microtel, Ⓞ Advance Parts, BigLots, $Tree, Firestone, Goodyear/auto, Kroger/dsl, NTB, O'Reilly Parts, PepBoys, Radio Shack, Sears/auto, Walgreens, Walmart/Subway, vet
61	GA 74, to Fairburn, **E** Ⓖ BP/Huddle House/dsl/scales/24hr, Citgo/dsl, RaceTrac/dsl, Shell, Ⓕ Chick-fil-A, Dunkin Donuts, McDonald's, Waffle House, Wendy's, Zaxby's, ☒ Country Inn&Suites, Hampton Inn, Holiday Inn Express, Sleep Inn, Wingate Inn, Ⓞ Tire Depot, vet, **W** Ⓖ Chevron/dsl, Citgo/Blimpie/dsl, ☒ Efficiency Motel
56	Collinsworth Rd, **W** Ⓖ Marathon/dsl, Shell, Ⓕ Frank's Rest., Ⓞ South Oaks Camping
51	GA 154, to Sharpsburg, **E** Ⓖ Phillips 66/dsl, Texaco/Blimpie, **W** Ⓖ Chevron/dsl, Shell/Subway/dsl, Ⓕ Waffle House
47	GA 34, to Newnan, **E** Ⓖ BP, Chevron/dsl, Marathon/Subway/dsl, QT, Shell, Ⓕ Applebee's, Arby's, Asian Chef, Capt D's, Chin Chin, Dunkin Donuts, Hooters, La Hacienda, Longhorn Steaks, Marco's Pizza, Me'n Ed's Pizza, Moe's SW Grill, Panda Express, Papa's Smokehouse, Red Lobster, Ruby Tuesday, Sprayberry's BBQ, Steak'n Shake, Stevie B's Pizza, TX Roadhouse, Waffle House, Wendy's, ☒ Country Inn&Suites, Hampton Inn, Springhill Suites, Ⓞ GNC, Goodyear, Hobby Lobby, Home Depot, Kauffman Tire, Kohl's, Lowe's, Petsmart, Ross, Walmart/McDonald's, **W** Ⓖ Exxon, Phillips 66, RaceTrac, Ⓕ Burger King, Chick-fil-A, Coldstone, Cracker Barrel, 5 Guys Burgers, Goldberg's Deli, Golden Corral, HoneyBaked Ham, IHOP, KFC, Krystal, Logli Mogli, Mama Lucia's, O'Charley's, Olive Garden, Panera Bread, Red Robin, Rockback Pizza, Shane's BBQ, Shoney's, Taco Bell, Taco Mac, Thai Heaven, Zaxby's, ☒ Best Western, Comfort Inn, La Quinta, Motel 6, Ramada, Ⓞ Ⓗ, AT&T, Barnes&Noble, Belk, Best Buy, BigLots, BJ's Whse, Buick/Cadillac/GMC, Chevrolet,

Exit	Services
47	Continued Dick's, Dillards, &General, $Tree, Ford/Lincoln, Hyundai, JC Penney, Just Brakes, Michael's, Office Depot, Old Navy, Publix, Radio Shack, Target, Tires+, TJ Maxx, Toyota/Scion, Verizon, Walgreens, USPO, vet
41	US 27/29, Newnan, **E** Ⓖ /Subway/Wendy's/dsl/scales/24hr, Ⓞ Little White House NHS, Roosevelt SP, **W** Ⓖ BP/dsl, Chevron, Phillips 66/dsl, Ⓕ Huddle House, McDonald's, Waffle House, ☒ Best Value Inn, Howard Johnson, Super 8, Ⓞ $General
35	US 29, to Grantville, **W** Ⓖ BP/dsl, Phillips 66/dsl
28	GA 54, GA 100, to Hogansville, **W** Ⓖ Chevron/dsl, ♥Loves/Arby's/dsl/scales/24hr, Shell/dsl, Ⓕ China Cafe, Intnat'l Cafe, McDonald's, Roger's BBQ, Subway, Waffle House, Wendy's, ☒ Garden Inn, Wood Stream Inn, Ⓞ Ingles
23mm	Beech Creek
22mm	**weigh sta both lanes**
21	I-185 S, to Columbus
18	GA 109, to Mountville, **E** Ⓖ Marathon/Domino's, ☒ Red Roof Inn, Wingate Inn, Ⓞ to FDR SP, Little White House HS, **W** Ⓖ BP/dsl, Circle K/dsl, RaceTrac/dsl, Shell/dsl, Texaco/dsl, Ⓕ Applebee's, Banzai Japanese, Burger King, Chick-fil-A, Cracker Barrel, IHOP, Juanito's Mexican, Longhorn Steaks, Los Nopales, McDonald's, Mi Casa Mexican, Moe's SW Grill, Ryan's, Starbucks, Subway, Waffle House, Wendy's, Zaxby's, ☒ Baymont Inn, Best Western, Comfort Inn, Country Inn&Suites, Holiday Inn Express, Jameson Inn, Super 8, Ⓞ AT&T, Belk, Chrysler/Dodge/Jeep, Ford/Lincoln, Home Depot, Honda, Hyundai, JC Penney, Verizon, RV Park (3mi), mall
14	US 27, to LaGrange, **W** Ⓖ Pure, Shell, Summit/dsl, ☒ Hampton Inn
13	GA 219, to LaGrange, **E** Ⓕ Waffle House, ☒ Days Inn, **W** Ⓖ /Subway/dsl/scales/24hr, Shell/dsl, Ⓕ Arbys, McDonald's, Ⓞ Ⓗ
10mm	Long Cane Creek
6	Kia Blvd, **W** Kia Plant
2	GA 18, to West Point, **E** Ⓖ Shell/dsl, Summit/dsl, ☒ Travelers Inn, **W** Ⓕ Subway (1.5), Ⓞ to West Point Lake, camping
.5mm	**Welcome Ctr nb, full ♿ facilities, Ⓒ, ☒, litter barrels, vending, petwalk**
0mm	Georgia/Alabama state line, Chattahoochee River

INTERSTATE 95

Exit	Services
113mm	Georgia/South Carolina state line, Savannah River
111mm	**Welcome Ctr/weigh sta sb, full ♿ facilities, info, Ⓒ, vending, ☒, litter barrels, petwalk**
109	GA 21, to Savannah, Pt Wentworth, Rincon, **E** Ⓖ Enmark/dsl, /McDonald's/Subway/dsl/scales/24hr, Ⓕ Waffle House, ☒ Country Inn&Suites, Hampton Inn, Mulberry Grove Inn, Wingate Inn, Ⓞ Peterbilt, **W** Ⓖ Flash/dsl, Murphy Express/dsl, Shell/Circle K/Blimpie/dsl, Ⓕ El Ranchito, Happy Wok, Island Grill, Monte's Pizza, Silverado Kitchen, Wendy's, Zaxby's, ☒ Comfort Suites, Days Inn, Holiday Inn Express, Quality Inn, Ramada Ltd, Savannah Inn, Sleep Inn, Super 8, Ⓞ CVS Drug, Family$, FoodLion, Whispering Pines RV Park (3mi)
107mm	Augustine Creek
106	Jimmy DeLoach Pkwy
104	Savannah ☒, **E** Ⓖ BP, Shell/Wendy's/dsl, Ⓕ Sam

GA

F A I R B U R N

N E W N A N

L A G R A N G E

S A V A N N A H

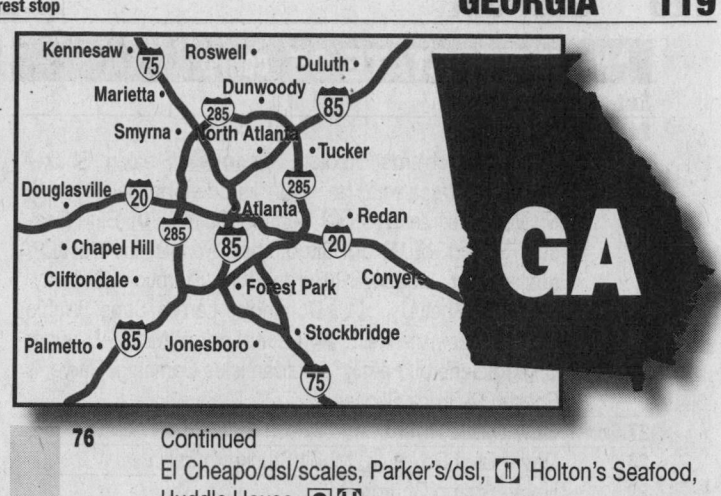 = gas   = food   = lodging   = other   = rest stop

⬆N INTERSTATE 95 CONT'D

Exit	Services

104 Continued

Sneed's Grill, Waffle House, 🛏Cambria Suites, Candlewood Suites, Comfort Suites, Country Inn&Suites, Fairfield Inn, Hampton Inn, Hawthorn Suites, Hilton Garden, Holiday Inn Express, Sheraton, SpringHill Suites, Staybridge Suites, TownePlace Suites, Wingate Inn, ⊙ to ✈ W ⛽ Murphy USA/dsl, Parkers/dsl, Shell/Subway, 🍴 Arby's, Cheddar's, Chick-fil-A, DQ, Fatz Cafe, Hilliard's Rest., Lemongrass Grill, Lenny's Subs, Longhorn Steaks, Mellow Mushroom, Ruby Tuesday, Shane's Rib Shack, Smokin' Hot BBQ, Sonic, Zaxby's, 🛏 Embassy Suites, Red Roof Inn, ⊙ **Urgent Care**, Goodyear, Home Depot, Publix, Sam's Club/gas, Savannah Tire, Verizon, Walmart/ McDonald's

102 US 80, to Garden City, **E** ⛽ BP/Baldinos Subs, Enmark/dsl, Flash/dsl, 🍴 Cracker Barrel, Dickey's BBQ, Dizzy Dean's, Guerrero, Hirenos Steaks, Huddle House, KFC, Krystal, Larry's Subs, Masato Japanese, McDonald's, Peking Chinese, Pizza Hut/Taco Bell, Waffle House, 🛏 Bradbury Suites, Jameson Inn, Microtel, Motel 6, Travelodge, ⊙ Camping World RV Ctr, Food Lion, Family$, to Ft Pulaski NM, museum, **W** ⛽ BP, Gate/Subway/dsl, Shell, Texaco, 🍴 Burger King, Domino's, Don's BBQ, El Potro Mexican, Hardee's, Italian Pizza, New China, Pizza Hut, Wendy's, Western Sizzlin, 🛏EconoLodge, Holiday Inn, La Quinta, Magnolia Inn, Savannah Conf Hotel, Sleep Inn, ⊙ NAPA, auto repair

99b a I-16, W to Macon, E to Savannah

94 GA 204, to Savannah, Pembroke, **E** ⛽ BP/dsl, Exxon, Murphy USA/dsl (2mi), Shell/dsl, 🍴 Applebee's, Cracker Barrel, Denny's, Hardee's, Houlihan's, IHOP, McDonald's, Perkins, Ruby Tuesday, Sonic, Tony Popa's, 🛏 Baymont Inn, Best Inn, Best Western, Clarion, Comfort Suites, Days Inn, EconoLodge, Fairfield Inn, Hampton Inn, Holiday Inn Express, Howard Johnson, La Quinta, Quality Inn, Red Roof Inn, San's Boutique Hotel, Scottish Inn, Sleep Inn, SpringHill Suites, Wingate Inn, ⊙ H Factory Stores/Famous Brands, GNC, Walmart (2mi), **W** ⛽ Chevron/dsl, Shell, 🍴 Hooters, JT's Grill, Shellhouse Rest, Subway, Waffle House, 🛏 Heritage Inn, Knights Inn, Microtel, Travel Inn, ⊙ Harley-Davidson, Savannah Oaks RV Park (2mi)

91mm Ogeechee River

90 GA 144, Old Clyde Rd, to Ft Stewart, Richmond Hill SP, **E** ⛽ Exxon/dsl, Parkers, 🍴 DQ, Jalapeno's, Pizza Hut, Starbucks, Subway, Zaxby's, ⊙ **Urgent Care**, AT&T, Kroger/deli/dsl, Verizon, **W** ⛽ ♥Loves/McDonald's/dsl/scales/24hr, Shell/dsl, ⊙ Gore's RV Ctr

87 US 17, to Coastal Hwy, Richmond Hill, **E** ⛽ BP, Chevron/dsl, RaceWay/dsl, 🍴 China 1, Denny's, Domino's, Fuji Japanese, Papa Murphy's, Smokin' Pig BBQ, Southern Image Rest., Steamer's Rest., Subway, Waffle House, 🛏 Days Inn, Motel 6, Royal Inn, Scottish Inn, Travelodge, ⊙ **Urgent Care**, Food Lion, **W** ⛽ El Cheapo, Exxon/McDonald's/dsl, TA/BP/Pizza Hut/Popeye's/dsl/scales/24hr/@, Shell/dsl, 🍴 Arby's, KFC/Taco Bell, Waffle House, Wendy's, 🛏 Best Western, Comfort Suites, EconoLodge, Hampton Inn, Quality Inn, Savannah South Inn, ⊙ KOA

85mm Elbow Swamp

80mm Jerico River

76 US 84, GA 38, to Midway, Sunbury, **E** hist sites, **W** ⛽

---

76 Continued

El Cheapo/dsl/scales, Parker's/dsl, 🍴 Holton's Seafood, Huddle House, ⊙ H

67 US 17, Coastal Hwy, to S Newport, **E** ⛽ Chevron/Subway/dsl, Citgo/dsl, El Cheapo, Shell/McDonald's, 🍴 Jones BBQ, ⊙ Harris Neck NWR, S Newport Camping (2mi), **W** ⛽ Texaco

58 GA 99, GA 57, Townsend Rd, Eulonia, **E** ⛽ BP/dsl, Citgo, ⊙ $General, USPO, **W** ⛽ Chevron/dsl, El Cheapo, Shell/Stuckey's/dsl, 🛏 Magnuson Inn, 7 Townsend Inn, ⊙ McIntosh Lake RV Park, Lake Harmony RV Park

55mm weigh sta both lanes, 🍴

49 GA 251, to Darien, **E** ⛽ Chevron, Mobil/dsl, 🍴 DQ, McDonald's, Waffle House, ⊙ Cathead RV Park, Ford, Inland Harbor RV Park, **W** ⛽ BP, El Cheapo/Larry's Subs/dsl/scales, Shell/Stuckey's/dsl, 🍴 Burger King, KFC/Taco Bell, Ruby Tuesday, Wendy's, 🛏 Comfort Inn, Days Inn, Hampton Inn, Quality Inn, Super 8, ⊙ Darien Outlets/famous brands

47mm Darien River

46.5mm Butler River

46mm Champney River

45mm Altamaha River

42 GA 99, **E** to Hofwyl Plantation HS

41mm Rs sb, full 🚻 facilities, info, 🍴, vending, 🗑 litter barrels, petwalk

38 US 17, GA 25, N Golden Isles Pkwy, Brunswick, **E** ⛽ RaceTrac/dsl, 🛏 Comfort Suites, Country Inn&Suites, Embassy Suites (2mi), Fairfield Inn, Hawthorn Inn, Holiday Inn, Microtel, ⊙ H, Nissan, **W** ⛽ BP, Chevron/dsl, Flash, Shell/dsl, 🍴 China Town, Denny's, Huddle House, Logan's Roadhouse, Toucan's, Subway, Waffle House, 🛏 Best Western, Courtyard, EconoLodge, Guest Cottage Motel, Hampton Inn, Quality Inn, Sleep Inn, ⊙ $General, Family$, Harley-Davidson, Harvey's Foods, Toyota/Scion

36b a US 25, US 341, to Jesup, Brunswick, **E** ⛽ Chevron/Subway/dsl, Exxon/dsl, RaceWay/dsl, 🍴 Cracker Barrel, IHOP, KFC, Krystal, McDonald's, Pizza Hut, Starbucks, Taco Bell, Wendy's, 🛏 Brunswick Park Motel, Days Inn, Howard Johnson, La Quinta, Red Roof Inn, ⊙ Jack's Tires, transmissions, **W** ⛽ Mr Pete's/dsl, Parker's/dsl, Sunoco/dsl, 🍴 Capt Joe's Seafood, China Lee, Huddle House, Larry's Subs, Sonny's BBQ, Waffle House, 🛏 Clarion, Comfort Inn, Magnuson Inn, Ramada Inn, Rodeway Inn, Super 8, ⊙ Advance Parts, CVS Drug, $General, Family$, Fred's, Winn-Dixie

33mm Turtle River

30mm S Brunswick River

29 US 17, US 82, GA 520, S GA Pkwy, Brunswick, **E** ⛽

🅖 = gas   🍴 = food   🛏 = lodging   🅞 = other   🆁🆂 = rest stop   Copyright 2014 - The Next Exit ®

⬆N INTERSTATE 95 CONT'D

Exit	Services
29	**Continued** Citgo Church's/dsl, Exxon, ♥Loves/Steak'n Shake/Subway/dsl/scales/24hr, 🍴 Huddle House, Krystal, McDonald's, Zaxby's, 🛏 Comfort Suites, 🅞 Blue Beacon, SpeedCo, **W** 🅖 Citgo, ✈FLYING J/Denny's/dsl/LP/scales/24hr, Goasis/BP/Burger King/Starbucks/Subway/dsl/24hr, Shell/dsl, 🍴 Domino's, Larry's Subs, Waffle House, Zachry's Rest, 🛏 EconoLodge, Microtel, Super 8, 🅞 $General, Family$, Golden Isles Camping, Harvey's Foods, TA Truck Service
27.5mm	Little Satilla River
26	Dover Bluff Rd, **E** 🅖 Mobil/Stuckey's/dsl
22	Horse Stamp Church Rd
21mm	White Oak Creek
19mm	Canoe Swamp
15mm	Satilla River
14	GA 25, to Woodbine, **W** 🍴 Chevron/Sunshine/rest/dsl/scales/24hr, 🛏 Stardust Motel (3mi)
7	Harrietts Bluff Rd, **E** 🅖 Exxon/dsl, Shell/Subway/e-85, **W** 🅖 BP/dsl, 🅞 Walkabout Camping/RV Park
6.5mm	Crooked River
6	Laurel Island Pkwy, **E** 🅖 Green Cedar/Shell/dsl
3	GA 40, Kingsland, to St Marys, **E** 🅖 BP/dsl, Chevron, El Cheapo, Exxon/Krystal, Mobil, Murphy USA/dsl, Shell/Subway, 🍴 Applebee's, Burger King, Chick-fil-A, China Wok, DQ, Dunkin Donuts, Hong Kong Buffet, KFC, Little Caesars, Longhorn Steaks, McDonald's, Papa John's, Ruby Tuesday, Sonny's BBQ, Taco Bell, Waffle House, Wendy's, Zaxby's, 🛏 Best Value Inn, Best Western, Comfort Inn, Country Inn&Suites, Days Inn, Fairfield Inn, Hawthorn Suites, Magnolia Inn, Microtel, Red Roof Inn, Rodeway Inn, Sleep Inn, 🅞🅷 Urgent Care, Buick/Chevrolet, Chrysler/Dodge/Jeep, CVS Drug, $Tree, Ford, GNC, K-Mart, Lowe's, NAPA, Publix, Radio Shack, Suzuki, Tire Kingdom, Verizon, Walgreens, Walmart, Winn-Dixie, to Crooked River SP, to Submarine Base, **W** 🅖 Flash/dsl, Petro/Popeye's/dsl/scales/24hr/@, RaceWay/dsl, Shell/dsl, 🍴 Cracker Barrel, Domino's, IHOP, Millhouse Steaks, Subway, Waffle House, 🛏 Clean Stay USA, Country Hearth Inn, EconoLodge, Hampton Inn, Jameson Inn, La Quinta, Springfield Suites, 🅞 Ace Hardware, Fred's, Kiki RV Park, **Welcome Ctr/info**
1	St Marys Rd, **E Welcome Ctr nb, full** 🛁 **facilities,** 🅞, **vending,** 🚮, **litter barrels, petwalk,** 🅖 Shell/dsl, 🍴 to Cumberland Is Nat Seashore, **W** 🅖 BP/dsl, Chevron/dsl, Wilco/Hess/Dunkin Donuts/Wendy's/dsl/scales/24hr, 🍴 Jack's BBQ, 🅞 GS RV Park, KOA
0mm	Georgia/Florida state line, St Marys River

⬆N INTERSTATE 185 (COLUMBUS)

Exit	Services
48	I-85. I-185 begins/ends on I-85.
46	Big Springs Rd, **E** 🅖 Shell/dsl, **W** 🅞 tires
42	US 27, Pine Mountain, **E** 🅖 Shell/dsl, Summit, 🍴 Waffle House, 🅞 Pine Mtn Camping, to Callaway Gardens, Little White House HS
34	GA 18, to West Point, **E** to Callaway Gardens
30	Hopewell Church Rd, Whitesville, **W** 🅖 Shell/dsl
25	GA 116, to Hamilton, **W** RV camping
19	GA 315, Mulberry Grove, **W** 🅖 Chevron/dsl/24hr

Exit	Services
14	Smith Rd
12	Williams Rd, **W Welcome Ctr/rest rooms,** 🅖 Summit/dsl, Shell, 🛏 Country Inn&Suites, Microtel
10	US 80, GA 22, to Phenix City, **W** Springer Opera House
8	Airport Thruway, **E** 🍴 China Moon, Great Wall, 🅞 $Tree, GNC, Home Depot, Walmart/Subway, **W** 🅖 BP/Circle K, Circle K, 🍴 Applebee's, Ben's Chophouse, Buffet City, Burger King, Capt D's, Hardee's, Houlihan's, IHOP, La Margarita Grill, McDonald's, Mikata Japanese, Pickle Barrel Cafe, River City Grill, Stevie B's Pizza, Taco Bell, 🛏 Comfort Suites, Doubletree, Extended Stay America, Hampton Inn, Sleep Inn, 🅞 BigLots, Hancock Fabrics, K-Mart, Office Depot
7	45th St, Manchester Expswy, **E** 🅖 Chevron, 🍴 Applebee's, Burger King, Carino's Italian, Krystal, Ruby Tuesday, 🛏 Courtyard, La Quinta, Super 8, 🅞 Best Buy, Cadillac/Chevrolet, Dillard's, JC Penney, Macy's, mall, **W** 🅖 BP, Chevron, Circle K, Marathon, 🍴 Arby's, China Express, Dunkin Donuts, Goldberg's Deli, Golden Corral, KFC, Logan's Roadhouse, Lucky China, McDonald's, Pizza Hut, Ryan's, Shogun Japanese, Sonic, Starbucks, Subway, Waffle House, 🛏 Fairfield Inn, Holiday Inn, TownePlace Suites, 🅞🅷, Advance Parts, Big 10 Tire, $General, Mr. Transmissions, Civil War Naval Museum, vet
6	GA 22, Macon Rd, **E** 🅖 Chevron/dsl, Circle K/dsl, 🍴 Bruster's, Burger King, DQ, KFC, Little Caesars, Taco Bell, 🛏 Best Western, Comfort Inn, Days Inn, 🅞 $General, Kia, Rite Aid, U-Haul, Walgreens, vet, **W** 🅖 Chevron/dsl, Shell, 🍴 American Deli, Capt D's, ChuckeCheese, Cici's Pizza, Country BBQ, Denny's, Firehouse Subs, Jimmy John's, Longhorn Steaks, McDonald's, Subway, Zaxby's, 🛏 Efficiency Lodge, La Quinta, 🅞 AT&T, CVS Drug, Freds Store, GNC, Goodyear, K-Mart, Publix, Radio Shack, Tuesday Morning, Verizon
4	Buena Vista Rd, **E** 🅖 BP, Circle K, Solo, 🍴 Burger King, Capt D's, Chef Lee Chinese, Checker's, Church's, Krystal, McDonald's, Papa John's, Pizza Hut, Subway, Taco Bell, Waffle House, Zaxby's, 🅞 AutoZone, $Tree, Firestone/auto, Goodyear/auto, O'Reilly Parts, Rainbow Foods, Walgreens, Walmart, Winn-Dixie, repair, USPO, vet
3	St Marys Rd, **E** 🛏 Microtel, 🍴 Domino's, 🅞 Family$, **W** 🅖 FuelTech/dsl, Shell/dsl, 🍴 Hardee's, Zeb's Seafood Chicken, 🅞 Ace Hardware, $General, Piggly Wiggly
1 b a	US 27, US 280, Victory Dr, 0-3 mi **W** 🅖 Chevron/dsl, Circle K, Liberty, RaceWay/dsl, 🍴 Arby's, Burger King, Capt D's, Checker's, Krystal, McDonald's, Papa John's, Sonic, Subway, Taco Bell, Wendy's, 🛏 Candlewood Suites, Columbus Inn, EconoLodge, Holiday Inn Express, Motel 6, Suburban Lodge, 🅞 Advance Parts, AutoZone, $General, Family$, Mkt Place Foods, Piggly Wiggly, **I-185 begins/ends.**

⬆N INTERSTATE 285 (ATLANTA)

Exit	Services
62	GA 279, S Fulton Hwy, Old Nat Hwy, **N** 🅖 Chevron, Texaco, 🍴 City Cafe, 🛏 Econolodge, **S** 🅖 Chevron, Exxon, Shell, 🍴 Blimpie, Burger King, Checker's, China Cafeteria, Church's, El Nopal Mexican, KFC/Pizza Hut, Krystal, Longhorn Steaks, McDonald's, Mrs Winner's, Popeye's, Subway, Taco Bell, Waffle House, Wendy's, 🛏 Clarion, Comfort Inn, Day's Inn, Howard Johnson, Motel 6, Quality Inn, 🅞 AutoZone, Cottman Transmissions, Curves, Family$, NAPA, U-Haul

(vertical left margin) **GA** **ST MARYS**

(vertical center margin) **COLUMBUS**

INTERSTATE 285 (ATLANTA)

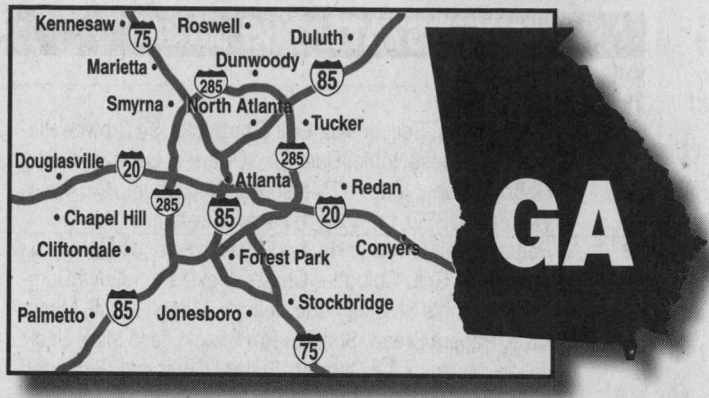

ATLANTA AREA

Exit	Services
61	I-85, N to Atlanta, S to Montgomery, **Services 1 mi N** GA I-85, exit 71. **E** 🍴 Ruby Tuesday, 🏨 Comfort Suites, Courtyard, GA Conv Ctr, Microtel, Hampton Inn, Sheraton/grill, Sleep Inn, Sumner Suites, Super 8, Wingate Inn, **W** 🏨 Comfort Inn, Day's Inn, Embassy Suites, Marriott, Quality Inn, Ramada, Super 8, Travelodge, Westin Hotel
60	GA 139, Riverdale Rd, **N** 🏨 Fairfield Inn (2mi), Microtel (2mi), Wingate Inn (2mi), **S** 🅖 Exxon, QT, Shell/dsl, 🍴 Checker's, Church's, KFC/LJ Silver, McDonald's, 🏨 Best Western, Country Inn&Suites, Day's Inn, Quality Inn, Ramada Inn, 🅞 Advance Parts, Aldi Foods, $General, Family$, U-Haul
59	Clark Howell Hwy, **N** air cargo
58	I-75, N to Atlanta, S to Macon (from eb), to US 19, US 41, to Hapeville, **S** 🅖 BP, Chevron/24hr, 🍴 Bojangles, Philly Connection, Subway, Waffle House, Wendy's, 🏨 Home Lodge Motel
55	GA 54, Jonesboro Rd, **N** 🏨 Super 8, **S** 🅖 BP, Citgo/dsl, Phillips 66, Shell/dsl, 🍴 Alondra's Mexican/Chinese, Capt D's, Church's, DaiLai Vietnamese, Golden Gate Chinese, LJ Silver, McDonald's, Subway, Taco Bell, 🅞 Home Depot, repair
53	US 23, Moreland Ave, to Ft Gillem, **N** 🅖 BP, Citgo, Conoco/dsl, **S** 🅖 Citgo, Shell, TA/dsl/24hr/@, 🍴 Popeye's, Wendy's, 🏨 Economy Inn
52	I-675, S to Macon
51	Bouldercrest Rd, **N** 🅖 BP, 🍴Wendy's/dsl/24hr, 🍴 A&W/LJ Silver, Hardee's, KFC/Pizza Hut, WK Wings, 🏨 DeKalb Inn, 🅞 Family$, Wayfield Foods, **S** 🅖 Chevron/dsl
48	GA 155, Flat Shoals Rd, Candler Rd, **N** 🅖 BP, Chevron, Marathon, Shell/dsl, Stop'n Go, 🍴 Arby's, Burger King, Checker's, DQ, KFC/Pizza Hut, McDonald's, Subway, Taco Bell, Waffle King, WK Wings, 🏨 Country Hearth Inn, Gulf American Inn, 🅞 BigLots, Macy's, Pep Boys, **S** 🅖 QT, Phillips 66, 🍴 Sonic
46b a	I-20, E to Augusta, W to Atlanta
44	GA 260, Glenwood Rd, **E** 🅖 Sunoco/dsl, 🏨 EconoLodge, **W** 🅖 Exxon/dsl, Texaco/dsl, Valero
43	US 278, Covington Hwy, **E** 🅖 Chevron/Subway, Citgo/dsl, 🍴 Waffle House, 🅞 U-Haul, **W** 🅖 BP, QT, RaceTrac/dsl, Shell/dsl, Texaco/dsl, 🍴 HoneyBaked Ham, Mrs Winner's, Wendy's, 🏨 Best Inn, 🅞 Advance Parts, Family$
42	(from nb) Marta Station
41	GA 10, Memorial Dr, Avondale Estates, **E** 🅖 Citgo, Shell/dsl, 🍴 Applebee's, Baskin-Robbins/Dunkin Donuts, Burger King, Church's, DQ, IHOP, Pancake House, Pizza Hut, Subway, Taco Bell, Waffle House, Wendy's, 🏨 Aloha Inn, Savannah Suites, United Suites, 🅞 **Urgent Care,** Advance Parts, Atl Tires, AutoZone, $Tree, Family$, Firestone/auto, GNC, Office Depot, Ross, U-Haul, transmissions
40	Church St, to Clarkston, **E** 🅖 Chevron, Shell/dsl, Texaco, 🅞 auto repair, **W** 🅞🅗
39b a	US 78, to Athens, Decatur
38	US 29, Lawrenceville Hwy, **E** 🅖 Phillips 66, QT/dsl, RaceTrac/dsl, 🍴 Waffle House, 🏨 Knights Inn, Super 8, 🅞🅗 **W** 🅖 Citgo/dsl, 🍴 Bruster's, 🏨 Masters Inn, Motel 6, 🅞 AutoZone, CVS Drug

Exit	Services
37	GA 236, to LaVista, Tucker, **E** 🅖 Chevron/dsl, Texaco, 🍴 Checkers, Folks Rest., IHOP, O'Charley's, Piccadilly's, Waffle House, 🏨 Comfort Suites, Days Inn, 🅞 Firestone, Target, **W** 🅖 BP/repair, Chevron, Citgo/dsl, Shell/dsl, 🍴 Arby's, Blackeyed Pea, Blue Ribbon Grill, Capt D's, Chick-fil-A, Chipotle, City Cafe, Coco Cabana Cuban, Dunkin Donuts, Eduardo's Mexican, HoneyBaked Ham, Jason's Deli, Kacey's Rest., Lucky Key Chinese, Madios Pizza, McDonald's, Mellow Mushroom, Panda Express, Red Lobster, Smoothie King, Starbucks, Wendy's, 🏨 Courtyard, DoubleTree, Holiday Inn, Quality Inn, 🅞 AT&T, Best Buy, $Tree, Goodyear/auto, JC Penney, Kohl's, Kroger, Macy's, Michael's, Office Depot, Petsmart, Publix, Sears/auto, TJ Maxx, Verizon, mall
34	Chamblee-Tucker Rd, **E** 🅖 Chevron, Texaco, 🍴 Galaxy Diner, Hunan Chinese, Jersey Mike's Subs, KFC/Taco Bell, Moe's SW Grill, S&S Cafeteria, $3 Cafe, Wendy's, 🏨 Motel 6, 🅞 Advance Parts, Goodyear, Kroger, Rite Aid, Verizon, **W** 🅖 Citgo, Shell, 🍴 Little Cuba, McDonald's, Subway, 🅞 BigLots, vet
33b a	I-85, N to Greenville, S to Atlanta
32	US 23, Buford Hwy, to Doraville, **E** 🅖 DP/dsl, 🍴 Burger King/playland, Checkers, Chick-fil-A, McDonald's, Waffle House, White Windmill Café, Zaxby's, 🅞 Advance Parts, Firestone/auto, Marshalls, PepBoys, auto repair, **W** 🅖 Citgo, QT/dsl, 🍴 McDonald's, Monterrey Mexican, Pestones Cuban, Subway, Tostones Cuban, Waffle House, 🏨 Comfort Inn, 🅞 $Tree, Meineke, transmissions
31b a	GA 141, Peachtree Ind, to Chamblee, **W** 🅖 Citgo/dsl, QT, 🍴 Arby's, Baskin-Robbins/Dunkin Donuts, Chick-fil-A, IHOP, McDonald's, Pizza Hut, Subway, Wendy's, 🅞 Acura, Advance Parts, Audi/VW, Brands Mart, Buick/GMC, Chevrolet, CVS Drug, Fiat, Firestone/auto, Ford, Honda, Hyundai, Kia, Lexus, Mazda, Mini, Office Depot, Porsche Toyota, Walgreens
30	Chamblee-Dunwoody Rd, N Shallowford Rd, to N Peachtree Rd, **N** 🅖 BP, Shell, Texaco/dsl, 🍴 Bagel&Co. Deli, Burger King, Guthrie's, Marco's Pizza, McDonald's, Starbucks, Subway, Waffle House, 🅞 Kroger, Tuesday Morning, **S** 🅖 Exxon/Blimpie/dsl, Mobil, Phillips 66/dsl, Shell, Valero/dsl, 🍴 Bombay Grill, La Botana Mexican, Mad Italian Rest., Papa John's, Taco Bell, Wendy's, Wild Ginger Thai, 🏨 Holiday Inn Select, Residence Inn, 🅞 vet
29	Ashford-Dunwoody Rd, **N** 🅖 BP, Exxon/Subway, 🍴 Brio Tuscan, Broken Egg, CA Pizza Kitchen, Capital Grille, Cheesecake Factory, Chili's, Firebird's Rest., Goldfish, Jason's Deli, J. Alexander's, Maddio's Pizza, Maggiano's Little Italy, McDonald's, McCormick&Schmick's, McKendrick Steaks, Olive Garden, PF Chang's, Popeye's,

ATLANTA AREA

GA

INTERSTATE 285 (ATLANTA)

Exit	Services
29	Continued Schlotzsky's, Seasons 32 Grill, Starbucks, 🛏 Crowne Plaza, Ⓞ Barnes&Noble, Best Buy, Dillard's, Goodyear/auto, Hobby Lobby, Macy's, Marshalls, Nordstrom, Old Navy, Walmart, USPO, mall, **S** Ⓞ Hilton Garden
28	Peachtree-Dunwoody Rd (no EZ return wb), **N** 🍽 Arby's, Chequer's Grill, Chipotle, Chuy's Mexican, 5 Guys Burgers, Fleming's Steaks, Fuddrucker's, Genghis Grill, Mimi's Café, Panera Bread, Shane's Rib Shack, Taco Mac, Uncle Julio's Mexican, 🛏 Comfort Suites, Courtyard, Extended Stay America, Extended Stay Deluxe, Fairfield Inn, Hampton Inn, Hilton Suites, Holiday Inn Express, Homestead Suites, La Quinta, Marriott, Microtel, Residence Inn, Sheraton, Westin, Ⓞ Costco/gas, Firestone/auto, Home Depot, Petsmart, Publix, Rite Aid, Ross, Target, TJ Maxx, Verizon, mall, **S** Ⓗ
27	US 19 N, GA 400, **2 mi N** LDS Temple
26	Glenridge Dr (from eb), Johnson Ferry Rd
25	US 19 S, Roswell Rd, Sandy Springs, **N** 🛢 BP, Shell/dsl, 🍽 Applebee's, Bobbys Burgers, Boston Mkt, Burger King, Chick-fil-A, Chipotle Mexican, Domino's, Dunkin Donuts, Egg Harbor Café, El Azteca Mexican, Firehouse Subs, 5 Guys Burgers, Hudson Grille, IHOP, Jason's Deli, Jimmy John's, Longhorn Steaks, Mandarin House, McDonald's, Mellow Mushroom, Moe's SW Grill, Pizza Hut, Ray's NY Pizza, Roasters, Ruth's Chris Steaks, SeaBass Kitchen, Smash Burger, Starbucks, Steak'n Shake, Subway, Taco Bell, Waffle House, Wendy's, 🛏 Comfort Inn, Ⓞ Ⓗ, **Urgent Care**, Aldi Foods, AT&T, CVS Drug, DeKalb Tire, $Tree, Hancock Fabrics, Lowe's, Marshalls, Mr Transmission, NAPA AutoCare, Office Depot, PepBoys, PetCo, Publix, Radio Shack, Target, Toyota, Trader Joe's, Tuesday Morning, Verizon, Walgreens, Whole Foods Mkt, **S** 🛢 Chevron/dsl, Citgo, Shell, 🍽 Barberitos, El Taco Veloz, Kobe Steaks, Seasons Rest., Starbucks, Subway, Taco Mac, Ⓞ **Urgent Care**, Publix, Staples, Target
24	Riverside Dr
22	New Northside Dr, to Powers Ferry Rd, **N** 🛢 Shell/Subway/dsl, **S** 🛢 BP, Chevron/dsl, 🍽 Blimpie, McDonald's, Peter Cheng's Chinese, Ray's Rest., Waffle House, 🛏 Candlewood Suites, Hawthorn Suites, Homestead Suites, Wyndham, Ⓞ CVS Drug, Publix, vet
21	(from wb), **N** 🛢 Shell, 🍽 Harry's Pizza, Homestead Village, Ⓞ BMW/Mini
20	I-75, N to Chattanooga, S to Atlanta (from wb), to US 41 N
19	US 41, Cobb Pkwy, to Dobbins AFB, **N** 🛢 BP, Chevron/24hr, Citgo, Shell, 🍽 Arby's, BBQ, Bruster's, Carrabba's, ChuckeCheese, Denny's, Dunkin Donuts, Hardee's, IHOP, Jade Palace, Joe's Crabshack, KFC, McDonald's, Olive Garden, Papa John's, Pizza Hut, Red Lobster, Steak'n Shake, Subway, Sunny's BBQ, The Border Mexican, Waffle House, Wendy's, Wingate Inn, 🛏 Hilton, Holiday Inn Express, Ⓞ Best Buy, Cadillac, Buick/Subaru, Chevrolet, Honda, Hyundai, Lexus, Marshall's, Michael's, Office Depot, PetsMart, Ross, Target, Walgreen, **S** 🛢 Chevron/24hr, 🍽 Buffalo's Café, Cheese Factory, Chipotle Mexican, Chick-fil-A, El Toro Mexican, Hooters, Jason's Deli, Johnny Rocket's, Longhorn Steaks, Maggiano's Italian, Malone's Grill, Olde Mill Steaks, PF Chang, Pizza Hut, Ruby Tuesday, Schlotsky's, 🛏 Courtyard

---

Exit	Services
19	Continued Homewood Suites, Renaissance Motel, Sheraton Suites, Stouffer Waverly Hotel, Sumner Suites, Ⓞ A&P, Barnes&Noble, Costco/gas, JC Penney, Macy's, Sears/auto, USPO, mall
18	Paces Ferry Rd, to Vinings, **N** 🍽 Panera Bread, 🛏 Fairfield Inn, La Quinta, **S** 🛢 QT/24hr, 🍽 Chick-fil-A, Subway, Willy's Grill, 🛏 Extended Stay Deluxe, Hampton Inn, Wyndham, other:, Goodyear/auto, Home Depot, Publix
16	S Atlanta Rd, to Smyrna, **N** 🍽 Five Guys Burgers, Waffle House, Zio's Italian, 🛏 Holiday Inn Express, Ⓞ Ⓗ, **S** 🛢 🍺/Wendy's/dsl/scales/24hr, Shell/dsl, Texaco, Ⓞ Kroger
15	GA 280, S Cobb Dr, **E** 🛢 Microtel, Ⓞ U-Haul, **W** 🛢 BP/dsl, RaceTrac, Shell, 🍽 Arby's/Mrs Winners, Checker's, Chick-fil-A, China Buffet, IHOP, Krystal/24hr, McDonald's, Subway, Taco Bell, Wendy's, Zaxby's, 🛏 AmeriHost, Comfort Inn, Country Inn Suites, Knight's Inn, Sun Suites, Ⓞ Ⓗ
14mm	Chattahoochee River
13	Bolton Rd (from nb)
12	US 78, US 278, Bankhead Hwy, **E** 🛢 Citgo/dsl, Petro/Iron Skillet/dsl/rest./scales/24hr/@, Shell/dsl/24hr, 🍽 Mrs Winner's, Ⓞ Blue Beacon, **W** 🛢 BP, Marathon
10b a	I-20, W to Birmingham, E to Atlanta (exits left from nb), **W** to Six Flags
9	GA 139, MLK Dr, to Adamsville, **E** 🛢 Phillips 66, Shell, 🍽 Mrs Winner's, Ⓞ Family$, Wayfield Foods, **W** 🛢 Chevron, Shell, 🍽 Checker's, Church's, Golden House Chinese, KFC/Taco Bell, McDonald's
7	Cascade Rd, **E** 🛢 Marathon, 🍽 Papa John's, Ⓞ Kroger, **W** 🛢 BP, Phillips 66, 🍽 Applebee's, China Express, KFC, McDonald's, Moe's SW Grill, Mrs Winner's, Pizza Hut, Quizno's, Starbucks, Subway, Up the Creek, Wendy's, Ⓞ Ⓗ, GNC, Home Depot, Publix, Radio Shack, Tires+
5b a	GA 166, Lakewood Fwy, **E** 🛢 Chevron, Shell, 🍽 Blimpie, Burger King, Capt D's, Checker's, IHOP, KFC, Taco Bell, Wendy's, Ⓞ Goodyear, Firestone, Kroger, Macy's, mall, **W** 🛢 BP, Citgo/dsl, RaceWay, Shell/dsl/24hr, 🍽 Church's, KFC, Mrs Winner's, Wendy's, 🛏 Deluxe Inn, Ⓞ VET, AutoZone, CVS Drug, Family$
2	Camp Creek Pkwy, to ✈, **E** 🛢 BP, Exxon, Texaco, 🍽 Checker's, McDonald's, Mrs Winner's, 🛏 Comfort Suites, **W** 🛢 🍽 American Deli, Brewster's, Carino's, Chick-fil-A, Jason's Deli, LongHorn Steaks, Panda Express, Red Lobster, Ruby Tuesday, Wendys, Ⓞ Barnes&Noble, BJ's Whse/gas, Lowes Whse, Marshall's, Old Navy, PetsMart, Publix, Ross, Staples, Target, Walgreens
1	Washington Rd, **E** 🛢 Texaco/dsl, **W** 🛢 Chevron, 🛏 Regency Inn

⬆N INTERSTATE 475 (MACON)

Exit	Services
16mm	I-475 begins/ends on I-75, exit 177.
15	US 41, Bolingbroke, **1 mi E** 🛢 Exxon/dsl/LP, Marathon/dsl
9	Zebulon Rd, **E** 🛢 Citgo, Murphy USA/dsl, Shell/Circle K/24hr, 🍽 Buffalo's Café, Chen's Wok, Chick-fil-A, JL's BBQ, Krystal, Margarita's Mexican, McAlister's Deli, McDonald's, NU Way Wieners, Papa John's, Pizza Hut, Sonic, Subway, Taco Bell, Taki Japanese, Waffle House, Wendy's, 🛏 Baymont Inn, Comfort Suites, Fairfield Inn, Sleep Inn, Ⓞ Ⓗ, Goodyear/auto, GNC, Kohl's, Kroger/gas, Krystal, Lowe's, Walgreens, Walmart, USPO, **W** 🛢

ATLANTA AREA

⬆N INTERSTATE 475 (MACON) CONT'D

Exit	Services
9	Continued Marathon, 🍴 Polly's Café, Zaxby's, Ⓞ Advance Parts, CVS Drug
8mm	🆁🆂 nb, full ♿ facilities, 🚰 vending, 🗑 litter barrels, petwalk
5	GA 74, Macon, **E** 🅟 RaceWay, 🍴 Waffle House, Ⓞ Harley-Davidson, to Mercer U, **W** 🅟 Flash/Subway/dsl, Texaco/Church's/dsl, 🍴 Capt D's, Wok&Roll Chinese, 🛏 Howard Johnson, Ⓞ $General, Food Lion, Tires+, vet, to Lake Tobesofkee
3	US 80, Macon, **0-2 mi E** 🅟 Marathon/dsl, Murphy USA/dsl, RaceWay, Spectrum/Circle K/Subway, Sunoco/dsl, 🍴 Applebee's, Burger King, Chick-fil-A, China Buffet, Cracker Barrel, DQ, Golden Corral, JL's BBQ, KFC, Krystal, Mc-Donald's, Ryan's, S&S Cafeteria, Sonny's BBQ, Taco Bell, Waffle House, Zaxby's, 🛏 Best Western, Country Hearth Inn, Days Inn, Discovery Inn, Economy Inn, Hampton Inn, Holiday Inn Express, La Quinta, Motel 6, Quality Inn, Ramada Inn, Red Roof Inn, Rodeway Inn, Super 8, Trav-elodge, ValuePlace, Villager Inn, Ⓞ Best Buy, BigLots, Books-A-Million, CVS Drug, Dick's, Dillard's, Firestone/auto, Home Depot, Honda, JC Penney, Kroger, Lowe's, Macy's, Marshall's, Michael's, Nissan, Old Navy, Petsmart, Ross, Sam's Club/gas, Sears/auto, Staples, Target, VW, Walmart/24hr, mall, **W** 🅟 Marathon/dsl, Shell/Circle K, 🍴 Burger King, 🛏 EconoLodge, Knights Inn, Scottish Inn
1	Hartley Bridge Rd, same as I-75 exit 156
0mm	I-475 begins/ends on I-75, exit 156.

⬆N INTERSTATE 575

Exit	Services
30 mm	I-575 begins/ends on GA 5/515.
27	GA 5, Howell Br, to Ball Ground
24	Airport Dr
20	GA 5, to Canton, **E** 🅟 BP, 🍴 Casey's rest., Chick-fil-A, Hooters, Ryan's, Stevi B's Pizza, Waffle Wouse, Wendy's, 🛏 Comfort Inn, Homestead Inn, Ⓞ Chevrolet, Toyota, Walmart/24hr, **W** 🅟 Citgo, RaceTrac, 🍴 Applebee's, Arby's, Cracker Barrel, Longhorn Steaks, McDonald's, O'Charley's, Outback Steaks, Panda Express, Red Lobster, Starbucks, Subway, Waffle House, Zaxby's, 🛏 Holiday Inn Express, Ⓞ Belk, Home Depot, Michaels, Publix, Radio Shack, Ross
19	GA 20 E, Canton
17	GA 140, to Roswell (from sb), Canton
16	GA 20, GA 140, **E** 🅟 Pure, **W** 🅟 Citgo, Shell, 🍴 BBQ, Burger King, KFC, Mandarin House, LJ Silver, Papa John's, Taco Bell, Waffle House, Ⓞ $General, K-Mart
14	Holly Springs, **E** 🅟 Citgo/dsl, 🍴 Domino's, Pizza Hut, 🛏 Pinecrest Motel, **W** 🅟 BP, Chevron, RaceTrac, Shell, 🍴 Subway, Viva Mexico, Wendy's, Zaxby's, Ⓞ Kroger, Publix, Walgreens
11	Sixes Rd, **E** 🅟 Chevron, QT, **W** 🅟 Citgo
8	Towne Lake Pkwy, to Woodstock, **E** 🅟 Citgo, Shell, 🍴 McDonald's, Waffle House, Waffle King/24hr, Ⓞ Ford, Hyundai, **W** 🅟 Phillips 66
7	GA 92, Woodstock, **E** 🅟 Chevron, QT, Shell, 🍴 Arby's, Burger King, Capt D's, Checker's, Chick-fil-A, DQ, Fire-house Subs, Folk's Kitchen, KFC, McDonald's, Moe's SW Grill, Mrs Winner's, O'Charley's, Resturante Mexico, Ruby

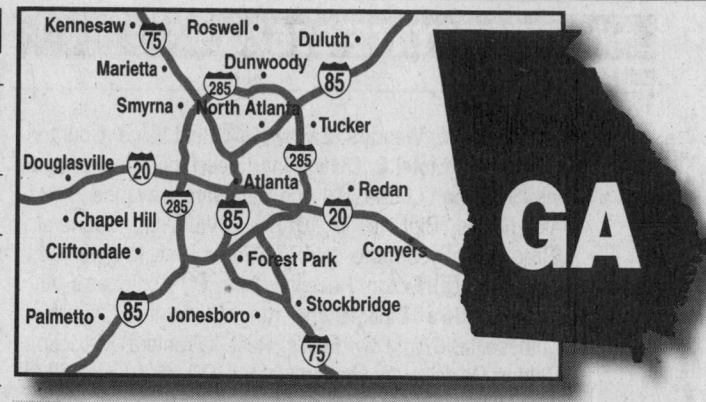

7	Continued Tuesday, Subway, Taco Bell, Waffle House, Wendy's, 🛏 Comfort Suites, Hampton Inn, Suburban Lodge, Ⓞ Big 10 Tire, Camping World, CVS Drug, Firestone/auto, Good-year/auto, Ingles, Just Brakes, **W** 🅟 BP, 🍴 Caribou Coffee, IHOP, Mi Casa Mexican, Schlotzky's, Steak'n Shake, Taco Mac, Ⓞ Atlanta Bread, Big Lots, BJ's Whse/gas, Discout Tire, Honda, Home Depot, Kohl's, Lowe's Whse, Office Depot, Old Navy, Target
4	Bells Ferry Rd, **W** 🅟 QT/24hr, Shell/dsl, 🍴 Arby's, Burger King, Ralph's Grill, Subway, Waffle House, other:
3	Chastain Rd, to I-75 N, **W** 🅟 Chevron, Citgo, Shell, 🍴 Arby's, Cracker Barrel, Mrs. Winner's, Los Reyes, O'Charley's, Panda Express, Sidelines Grill, Subway, ToGo's/Baskin Robbins, Waffle House, Wendy's, 🛏 Best Western, Comfort Inn, Country Inn&Suites, Fairfield Inn, Residence Inn, Springhill Suites, Suburban Inn, Ⓞ to Kennesaw St Coll
1	Barrett Pkwy, to I-75 N, US 41, **E** 🅟 Chevron, Murphy USA/dsl, QT, 🍴 Barnacle's Cafe, Buffalo Wild Wings, Burger King, Fuddruckers, KFC, Moe's SW Grill, Quizno's, Starbucks, Texas Roadhouse, Waffle House, Wendy's, Zaxby's, Ⓞ Atlanta Bread, Barnes&Noble, CVS Drug, $Tree, Firestone, Publix, Ross, SteinMart, Walmart/dsl, **W** 🅟 Shell, Texaco, 🍴 Applebee's, Fuddrucker's, McDonald's, Olive Garden, Provino's Italian, Red Lobster, Smokey Bones, Starbucks, Waffle House, 🛏 Comfort Inn, Crestwood Suites, Day's Inn, Holiday Inn Express, La Quinta, Ramada Ltd, Red Roof Inn, Ⓞ Big 10 Tire, Firestone/auto, Home Depot, Marshall's, Michael's, TJ Maxx, mall
0mm	I-575 begins/ends on I-75, exit 268.

⬆N INTERSTATE 675

Exit	Services
10mm	I-285 W, to Atlanta ✈, E to Augusta. **I-675 begins/ends on I-285, exit 52.**
7	Anvil Block Rd, Ft Gillem, **E** 🅟 BP, 🍴 Subway, **W** 🅟 Exxon
5	Forest Pkwy, **E** 🅟 Texaco/dsl, **W** 🅟 QT/dsl/scales, 🍴 McDonald's, Waffle House
2	US 23, GA 42, **E** 🅟 BP, Texaco, 🍴 Horizon/Backyard Burger, Mo-Joe's Café, **W** 🅟 Chevron/dsl, Citgo, 🍴 Teapot Chinese, Waffle House, other:, Family$, Food Depot, Goodyear/auto, USPO
1	GA 138, to I-75 N, Stockbridge, **E** 🅟 BP, Chevron/24hr, Citgo/dsl, Exxon, Murphy USA/dsl, QT, Shell, 🍴 Arby's, Burger King, Capt D's, Checker's, Church's Chicken, DQ, Dunkin Donuts, Golden Corral, Hong Kong Buffet, KFC, McDonald's, Papa John's, Pizza Hut, Popeye's, Taco Bell,

🅖 = gas   🍴 = food   🛏 = lodging   🄾 = other   🆁🆂 = rest stop   Copyright 2014 - The Next Exit ®

⬆N INTERSTATE 675 CONT'D

Exit	Services
1	Continued

Waffle House, Wendy's, Zaxby's, 🛏 Best Value, Country Hearth Inn, Motel 6, Quality Inn, Sleep Inn, Stockbridge Inn, Suburban Lodge, 🄾 Ace Hardware, Advance Parts, Aldi Foods, BigLots, Big10 Tire, CVS Drug, $General, $Tree, Goodyear/auto, NAPA, Radio Shack, Walmart, USPO, **W** 🅖 Exxon, Raceway/24hr, 🍴 Applebee's, Arby's, Broadway Diner, Burger King, Chick-fil-A, ChinChin Chinese, CiCi's, DQ, Folk's Rest., Frontera Mexican, Golden Corral, Honeybaked Ham, IHOP, KFC, Krystal, LJ Silver, McDonald's, Piccadilly's, Philly Connection, Shoney's, Subway, Taco Bell, Taco Mac, Tokyo Seafood, Waffle House, Wendy's, 🛏 Best Western, Day's Inn, Comfort Inn, Holiday Inn, La Quinta, Hampton Inn, Motel 6, Red Roof Inn, 🄾🄷, GNC, Goodyear, K-Mart, Kroger, Lowes Whse, Office Depot, Tires+

I-675 begins/ends on I-75, exit 227.

⬆N INTERSTATE 985 (GAINESVILLE)

Exit	Services

I-985 begins/ends on US 23, 25mm.

24	to US 129 N, GA 369 W, Gainesville, **N** 🄾🄷, GA Mtn Ctr, **S** 🅖 BP/Subway/dsl, Chevron/dsl, Citgo, 🍴 Double B Burger, Rabbit Trail Cafe,
22	GA 11, Gainesville, **N** 🅖 BP/dsl, Citgo, QT/24hr, 🍴 Burger King, McDonald's, 🛏 Best Western/rest., **S** 🅖 Chevron, Shell/dsl, 🍴 Waffle House, 🛏 Motel 6
20	GA 60, GA 53, Gainesville, **N** gas Citgo/dsl, 🍴 El Man

20	Continued

arca, McDonald's, Mrs Winners, 🛏 Best Value Inn, Hampton Inn, **S** 🅖 Kangaroo, 🍴 Subway, Waffle House

16	GA 53, Oakwood, **N** 🅖 BP, Citgo, 🍴 Arby's, Baskin-Robbins/Dunkin Donuts, Burger King, DQ, El Sombrero Mexican, Hardee's, KFC, McDonald's, Pizza Hut, Subway, Taco Bell, Waffle House, Zaxby's, 🛏 Admiral Benbow Inn, Country Inn Suites, Jameson Inn, 🄾 Chrysler/Jeep, CVS Drug, Food Lion, RV Ctr, Sam's Club, **S** 🅖 Citgo/dsl, QT/dsl, 🍴 Checker's, Krystal, Mrs Winners, Sonny's BBQ, Waffle House, Wendy's, 🛏 Comfort Inn, 🄾 AutoZone, Goodyear/auto, Publix, Walgreens
12	Spout Springs Rd, Flowery Branch, **N** 🅖 Exxon/dsl, **S** 🅖 BP/Subway, Chevron/dsl, 🍴 Burger&Shake, China Garden, CrossRoads Grill, Domino's, El Sombrero Mexican, TCBY, Thai Dish, other:, Publix
8	GA 347, Friendship Rd, Lake Lanier, **N** 🅖 BP, Chevron, Shell, Texaco, 🍴 Backyard Burger, Blimpie, Burger King, China Garden, Huddle House, McDonald's, Sonia's Mexican, Subway, 3rd Coast, Waffle House, Wendy's, Vinny's NY Grill, Zaxby's, 🄾 Advance parts, Publix, **S** Harley Davidson, Camper City RV Ctr
4	US 23 S, GA 20, Buford, **N** 🅖 QT, Shell, 🍴 Arby's, Burger King, Capt D's, Checker's, Golden Buddah, Golden Corral, Huddle House, IHOP, KFC, McDonald's, Saigon Bangkok, Taco Bell, Wendy's, Zaxby's, 🛏 Days Inn, Holiday Inn Express, 🄾 Ace Hardware, Buick/GMC, Dodge/Jeep, Home Depot, KIA, Tuesday Morning, **S** 🅖 BP, Chevron, Citgo, Texaco, 🍴 Ryan's, Sonny's BBQ, Waffle House, 🄾 $Tree, Expert Tire, Honda, Lowes Whse, Walmart
0mm	**I-985 begins/ends on I-85.**

IDAHO

⬆N INTERSTATE 15

Exit	Services
196mm	Idaho/Montana state line, Monida Pass, continental divide, elev 6870
190	Humphrey
184	Stoddard Creek Area, **E** Historical Site, RV camping, **W** Stoddard Creek Camping
180	Spencer, **E** 🅖 Opal Mtn Mine/gas, 🍴 Opal Country Café, 🄾 High Country Opal Store, RV Park
172	no services
167	ID 22, Dubois, **E** 🅖 Phillips 66/dsl, 🍴 Dubois Cafe, 🄾 USPO, city park, 🆁🆂 **both lanes, full 🚻 facilities, 🚰, 🏧, litter barrels, petwalk, W** to Craters NM, Nez Pearce Tr.
150	Hamer, **E** 🄾 Ron's Tire, USPO, Camus NWR, food, 🚰
143	ID 33, ID 28, to Mud Lake, Rexburg, **W** Sacajawea Hist Bywy, **weigh sta both lanes**
142mm	roadside parking, hist site
135	ID 48, Roberts, **E** 🅖 Exxon/cafe/dsl/LP, 🄾 city park
128	Osgood Area, **E** gas/dsl, camping (6mi)
119	US 20 E, to Rexburg, Idaho Falls, **E on Lindsay** 🅖 Sinclair/dsl, 🍴 Denny's, Jaker's Steaks, Outback Steaks, Sandpiper Rest., 🛏 Best Western, Guesthouse Inn, Hampton Inn, Hilton Garden, Hotel on the Falls, LeRitz Hotel, Safari Inn, Shilo Inn/rest., Super 8, 🄾 KOA, LDS Temple, Snake River RV Park/camping, same as 118, **W** 🅖 Chevron/dsl
118	US 20, Broadway St, Idaho Falls, **E** 🅖 Phillips 66/dsl, 🍴 Applebee's, Arctic Circle, Carl's Jr, Cedric's Rest.,

118	Continued

Chili's, Domino's, Famous Dave's BBQ, Jimmy John's, Olive Garden, Shari's Rest., Smitty's Pancakes, Starbucks, Wendy's, 🛏 Fairfield Inn, Hampton Inn, Hilton Garden, Residence Inn, 🄾🄷, Candy Jct, Ford, Harley-Davidson, LDS Temple, Verizon, Walmart/Subway, tires, same as 119, **W** 🅖 Exxon/dsl, Phillips 66/dsl, Sinclair/McDonald's, 🍴 Arby's, Burger King, 5 Buck Pizza, Hong Kong Rest., Jack-in-the-Box, Los Alberto's Mexican, O'Brady's, Papa Murphy's, Pizza Hut, Subway, 🛏 Comfort Inn, Motel 6, Motel West, 🄾 Albertsons, AutoZone, O'Reilly Parts, Walgreens

116	US 26, Sunnyside Rd, Ammon, Jackson, **E** 🛏 Yellowstone Motel, 🄾🄷, Sunnyside Acres RV Park, Toyota/Scion, zoo, **W** 🅖 Exxon/diesel, 🛏 Sleep Inn, 🄾 VW
113	US 26, to Idaho Falls, Jackson, **E** 🅖 Chevron/Burger King/dsl, ♥Loves/McDonald's/dsl/scales/24hr, Sinclair/Dad's/dsl/24hr/@, 🍴 Subway, 🄾🄷, Jack's Tires, Peterbilt, Sunnyside RV Park, Targhee RV Park
108	Shelley, Firth Area, **1 mi E** 🄾 RV Park/dump
101mm	🆁🆂 **both lanes, full 🚻 facilities, 🚰, 🏧, litter barrels, petwalk, geological site**
98	Rose-Firth Area
94.5mm	Snake River
93	US 26, ID 39, Blackfoot, **E** 🅖 Chevron, Maverik, Stinker/dsl, 🍴 Arby's, Burger King, Golden China, Homestead Rest., Italiano's, Little Caesars, McDonald's, Papa Murphy's, Pizza Hut, Rolberto's Mexican, Subway, Taco Bell,

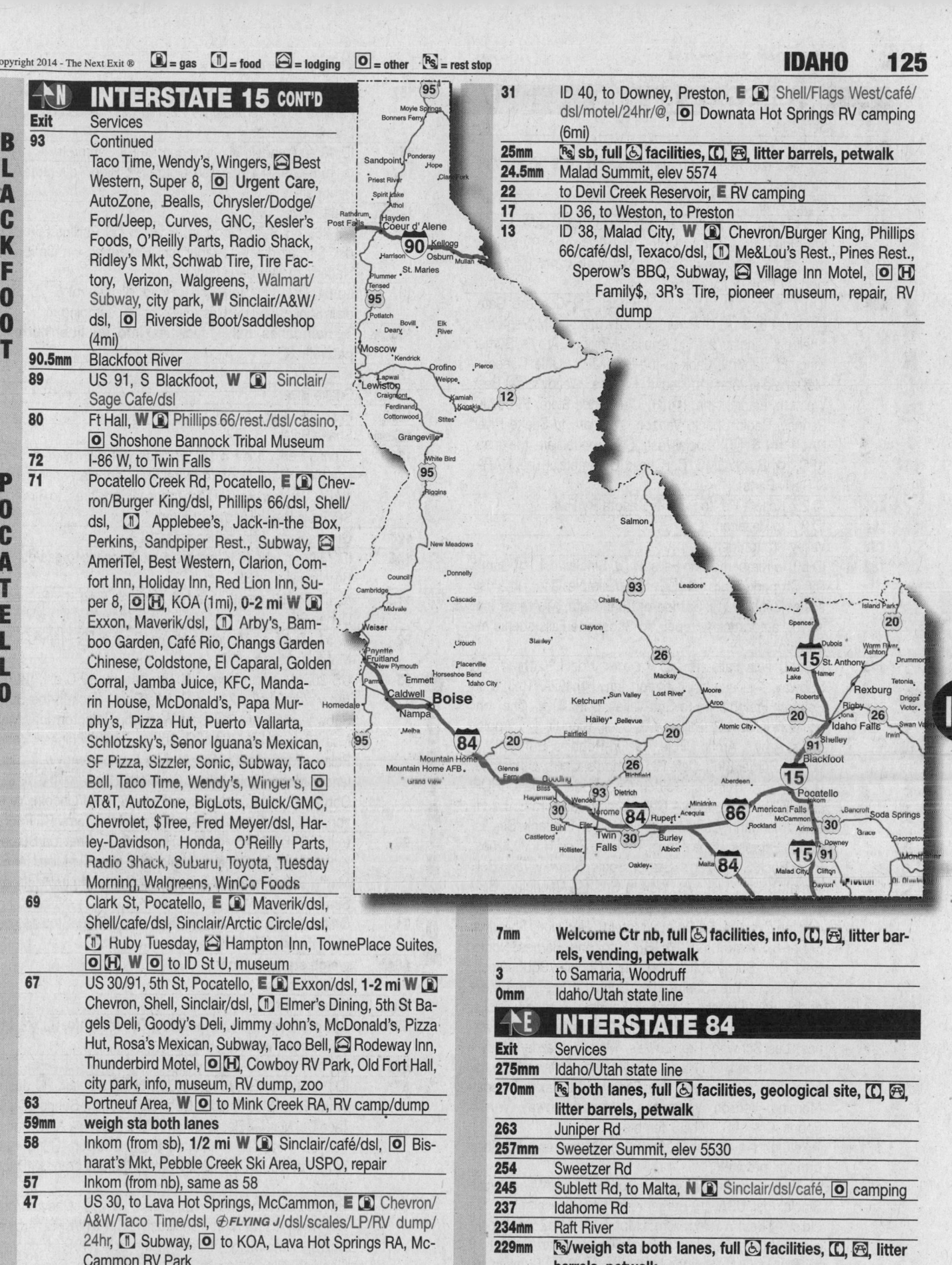

B L A C K F O O T	**P O C A T E L L O**

⬆N INTERSTATE 15 CONT'D

Exit	Services
93	Continued
	Taco Time, Wendy's, Wingers, 🛏 Best Western, Super 8, 🄾 Urgent Care, AutoZone, Bealls, Chrysler/Dodge/Ford/Jeep, Curves, GNC, Kesler's Foods, O'Reilly Parts, Radio Shack, Ridley's Mkt, Schwab Tire, Tire Factory, Verizon, Walgreens, Walmart/Subway, city park, **W** Sinclair/A&W/dsl, 🄾 Riverside Boot/saddleshop (4mi)
90.5mm	Blackfoot River
89	US 91, S Blackfoot, **W** 🅖 Sinclair/Sage Cafe/dsl
80	Ft Hall, **W** 🅖 Phillips 66/rest./dsl/casino, 🄾 Shoshone Bannock Tribal Museum
72	I-86 W, to Twin Falls
71	Pocatello Creek Rd, Pocatello, **E** 🅖 Chevron/Burger King/dsl, Phillips 66/dsl, Shell/dsl, 🍴 Applebee's, Jack-in-the Box, Perkins, Sandpiper Rest., Subway, 🛏 AmeriTel, Best Western, Clarion, Comfort Inn, Holiday Inn, Red Lion Inn, Super 8, 🄾 🄷, KOA (1mi), **0-2 mi W** 🅖 Exxon, Maverik/dsl, 🍴 Arby's, Bamboo Garden, Café Rio, Changs Garden Chinese, Coldstone, El Caparal, Golden Corral, Jamba Juice, KFC, Mandarin House, McDonald's, Papa Murphy's, Pizza Hut, Puerto Vallarta, Schlotzsky's, Senor Iguana's Mexican, SF Pizza, Sizzler, Sonic, Subway, Taco Bell, Taco Time, Wendy's, Winger's, 🄾 AT&T, AutoZone, BigLots, Buick/GMC, Chevrolet, $Tree, Fred Meyer/dsl, Harley-Davidson, Honda, O'Reilly Parts, Radio Shack, Subaru, Toyota, Tuesday Morning, Walgreens, WinCo Foods
69	Clark St, Pocatello, **E** 🅖 Maverik/dsl, Shell/cafe/dsl, Sinclair/Arctic Circle/dsl, 🍴 Ruby Tuesday, 🛏 Hampton Inn, TownePlace Suites, 🄾 🄷, **W** 🄾 to ID St U, museum
67	US 30/91, 5th St, Pocatello, **E** 🅖 Exxon/dsl, **1-2 mi W** 🅖 Chevron, Shell, Sinclair/dsl, 🍴 Elmer's Dining, 5th St Bagels Deli, Goody's Deli, Jimmy John's, McDonald's, Pizza Hut, Rosa's Mexican, Subway, Taco Bell, 🛏 Rodeway Inn, Thunderbird Motel, 🄾 🄷, Cowboy RV Park, Old Fort Hall, city park, info, museum, RV dump, zoo
63	Portneuf Area, **W** 🄾 to Mink Creek RA, RV camp/dump
59mm	weigh sta both lanes
58	Inkom (from sb), **1/2 mi W** 🅖 Sinclair/café/dsl, 🄾 Bisharat's Mkt, Pebble Creek Ski Area, USPO, repair
57	Inkom (from nb), same as 58
47	US 30, to Lava Hot Springs, McCammon, **E** 🅖 Chevron/A&W/Taco Time/dsl, ◈FLYING J/dsl/scales/LP/RV dump/24hr, 🍴 Subway, 🄾 to KOA, Lava Hot Springs RA, McCammon RV Park
44	Lp 15, Jenson Rd, McCammon, **E** access to food
40	Arimo, **E** 🅖 Sinclair/deli/dsl, 🄾 USPO
36	US 91, Virginia

Exit	Services
31	ID 40, to Downey, Preston, **E** 🅖 Shell/Flags West/café/dsl/motel/24hr/@, 🄾 Downata Hot Springs RV camping (6mi)
25mm	🆁🆂 sb, full 🅰 facilities, 🄲, 🄿, litter barrels, petwalk
24.5mm	Malad Summit, elev 5574
22	to Devil Creek Reservoir, **E** RV camping
17	ID 36, to Weston, to Preston
13	ID 38, Malad City, **W** 🅖 Chevron/Burger King, Phillips 66/café/dsl, Texaco/dsl, 🍴 Me&Lou's Rest., Pines Rest., Sperow's BBQ, Subway, 🛏 Village Inn Motel, 🄾 🄷 Family$, 3R's Tire, pioneer museum, repair, RV dump
7mm	Welcome Ctr nb, full 🅰 facilities, info, 🄲, 🄿, litter barrels, vending, petwalk
3	to Samaria, Woodruff
0mm	Idaho/Utah state line

⬆E INTERSTATE 84

Exit	Services
275mm	Idaho/Utah state line
270mm	🆁🆂 both lanes, full 🅰 facilities, geological site, 🄲, 🄿, litter barrels, petwalk
263	Juniper Rd
257mm	Sweetzer Summit, elev 5530
254	Sweetzer Rd
245	Sublett Rd, to Malta, **N** 🅖 Sinclair/dsl/café, 🄾 camping
237	Idahome Rd
234mm	Raft River
229mm	🆁🆂/weigh sta both lanes, full 🅰 facilities, 🄲, 🄿, litter barrels, petwalk
228	ID 81, Yale Rd, to Declo
222	I-86, US 30, E to Pocatello
216	ID 77, ID 25, to Declo, **N** 🅖 Phillips 66/FoodCourt/dsl, 🄾

🅡 = gas 🍴 = food 🛏 = lodging 🔲 = other 🆁🆂 = rest stop   Copyright 2014 - The Next Exit ®

➤Ｅ INTERSTATE 84 CONT'D

Exit	Services
216	Continued
	🅗, Village of Trees RV Park, to Walcott SP, **S** 🅡 Shell/Pit Stop Grill/dsl
215mm	Snake River
211	ID 24, Heyburn, Burley, **N** 🅡 Sinclair/A&W/café/dsl, 🍴 Wayside Cafe, 🛏 Tops Motel, 🔲 🅗, Country RV Village/park, **S** 🅡 ♥Loves♥/Carl's Jr./dsl/scales/24hr, 🔲 Riverside RV Park, truck repair
208	ID 27, Burley, **N** 🅡 Phillips 66/dsl, 🍴 Conner's Cafe, 🛏 Super 8, **S** 🅡 Chevron/Subway/dsl/24hr, Maverik/dsl, Shell/dsl, Sinclair/dsl, 🍴 Aguila's Mexican, Arby's, Burger King, El Caporal, Jack-in-the-Box, JB's, Little Caesars, McDonald's, Morey's Steaks, Perkins, Wendy's, 🛏 Best Western, Fairfield Inn, 🔲 🅗, Cal Ranch Store, $Tree, JC Penney, Radio Shack, Verizon, Walmart, to Snake River RA, **1 mi S** 🅡 Sinclair/dsl, 🍴 Guadalajara Mexican, KFC, 🔲 Buick/GMC, CarQuest, Commercial Tire, NAPA, O'Reilly Parts
201	ID 25, Kasota Rd, to Paul, **N** Kasota RV Park
194	ID 25, to Hazelton
188	Valley Rd, to Eden
182	ID 50, to Kimberly, Twin Falls, **N** 🅡 Sinclair/dsl, 🔲 Gary's RV Ctr/park/dump, **S** 🅡 Shell/Blimpie/Taco Time/dsl/scales/24hr/@, 🍴 Garden of Eden Cafe, 🛏 Amber Inn, 🔲 🅗, auto/truck/rv repair, to Shoshone Falls scenic attraction
173	US 93, Twin Falls, **N** 🅡 ⓕＦＬＹＩＮＧ Ｊ/dsl/LP/24hr/@, 🍴 Subway, 🛏 Days Inn, Comfort Inn, 🔲 KOA (1mi), Blue Beacon, Freightliner, to Sun Valley, **5 mi S** 🅡 Chevron/dsl, Exxon/dsl/LP, Phillips 66, Shell, Sinclair, 🍴 Applebee's, Arby's, Arctic Circle, Baskin-Robbins, Buffalo Wild Wings, Burger King, Cafe Rio, Carino's, Chili's, Coldstone, DQ, 5 Guys Burgers, Golden Corral, Idaho Joe's, IHOP, Jack-in-the-Box, Jakers Grill, Jamba Juice, KFC, La Fiesta, Mandarin Chinese, McDonald's, Outback Steaks, Panda Express, Papa John's, Perkins, Pizza Hut, Quiznos, River Rock Grill, Shari's, Sizzler, Sonic, Subway, Taco Bell, Tomato's Grill, Wendy's, Wok In Grill, 🛏 AmericInn, Best Western, Comfort Inn, Hampton Inn, Hilton Garden, Holiday Inn Express, La Quinta, Motel 6, Red Lion, Shilo Inn, Super 8, Weston Inn, 🔲 🅗, AutoZone, Barnes&Noble, Best Buy, Buick/GMC, Chevrolet, Chrysler/Dodge/Jeep, Commercial Tire, Costco/gas, Curves, $Tree, Fred Meyer/dsl, Ford/Lincoln, Hancock Fabrics, Hastings Books, Home Depot, Honda, Hyundai, JC Penney, Jo-Ann Fabrics, Les Schwab Tire, Lowe's, Macy's, Mazda/VW, Michael's, Nissan, Old Navy, O'Reilly Parts, Petsmart, Sears/auto, ShopKO, Target, Tire Factory, TJ Maxx, Tuesday Morning, Verizon, Walgreens, Walmart/Subway, WinCo Foods, Coll of S ID, LDS Temple
171mm	🆁🆂/**weigh sta eb, full** 🦽 **facilities, 🚻, vending, 🗑, litter barrels, petwalk**
168	ID 79, to Jerome, **N** 🅡 Chevron/dsl, Shell/Wendy's/dsl, Sinclair/dsl, USA, 🍴 Burger King, Little Caesars, McDonald's, 🛏 Best Western, Crest Motel, 🔲 AutoZone, Brockman RV Ctr, $Tree, Les Schwab Tire, Walmart/Subway, **2 mi N** 🍴 DQ, 🛏 Holiday Motel, 🔲 🅗, **S** 🍴 Subway, 🔲 Chevrolet, ID RV Ctr/marine
165	ID 25, Jerome, **N** 🅡 Sinclair/dsl, 🛏 Holiday Motel (1mi), 🔲 🅗, RV camping/dump

Exit	Services
157	ID 46, Wendell, **N** 🍴 Subway, **1 mi N** 🔲 🅗, CarQuest, Family$, Intermountain RV Park, **S** 🅡 Phillips 66/dsl, 🍴 Farmhouse Rest.
155	ID 46, to Wendell, **N** Intermountain RV Camp/ctr
147	to Tuttle, **S** 🔲 to Malad Gorge SP, High Adventure RV Park/cafe
146mm	Malad River
141	US 26, to US 30, Gooding, **N** 🅗, **S** 🅡 Phillips 66/café/dsl, Sinclair/dsl, 🛏 Amber Inn, Hagerman Inn (9mi), 🔲 Hagerman RV Village (8mi)
137	Lp 84, to US 30, to Pioneer Road, Bliss, **2 mi S** 🅡 Sinclair/Stinker/Oxbow Rest/dsl/24hr, 🔲 camping
133mm	🆁🆂 **both lanes, full** 🦽 **facilities, info, 🗑, litter barrels, petwalk, 🚻**
129	King Hill
128mm	Snake River
125	Paradise Valley
122mm	Snake River
121	Glenns Ferry, **1 mi S** 🅡 Shell/dsl, Sinclair/dsl, 🛏 Hansen Motel/cafe, Redford Motel, 🔲 Carmela Winery/rest., NAPA, Western Family Mkt, fudge factory, tires, to 3 Island SP, Trails Break RV camp/dump
120	Glenns Ferry (from eb) same as 121
114	ID 78 (from wb), to Hammett, **1 mi S** access to gas/dsl, to Bruneau Dunes SP
112	to ID 78, Hammett, **1 mi S** gas/dsl, food, to Bruneau Dunes SP
99	ID 51, ID 67, to Mountain Home, **2 mi S** 🛏 Maple Cove Motel, camping
95	US 20, Mountain Home, **N** 🅡 Chevron/KFC/dsl, ⬛⬛⬛/Arby's/dsl/scales/24hr, 🍴 AJ's Rest., Jack-in-the-Box, Subway, Wingers, 🛏 Best Western, Hampton Inn, Mtn Home Inn, **S** 🅡 USA, 🍴 Golden Crown Chinese, Jade Palace, McDonald's, Smoky Mtn Pizza, Wendy's, 🛏 Hilander Motel (1mi), Towne Ctr Motel (1mi), 🔲 🅗, AT&T, Chrysler/Dodge/Jeep, $Tree, Family$, Ford/Lincoln, Verizon, Walmart/Subway, visitors ctr, to Mtn Home RV Park
90	to ID 51, ID 67, W Mountain Home, **S** 🅡 Chevron/Burger King/dsl, 🍴 McDonald's (4mi), 🛏 to Hilander Motel (4mi), Maple Cove Motel (4mi), Towne Ctr Motel (4mi), 🔲 KOA
74	Simco Rd
71	Orchard, Mayfield, **S** 🅡 Sinclair/rest/StageStop Motel/dsl/24hr, 🔲 🚻, truckwash
66mm	**weigh sta both lanes**
64	Blacks Creek
Kuna	historical site
62mm	🆁🆂 **both lanes, full** 🦽 **facilities, OR Trail info, 🚻, 🗑, litter barrels, vending, petwalk**
59b a	S Eisenman Rd, Memory Rd
57	ID 21, Gowen Rd, to Idaho City, **N** 🅡 Sinclair, 🍴 Jack-in-the-Box, McDonald's, Quiznos, Subway, Sunrise Cafe, Taco Del Mar, 🛏 Best Western/NW Lodge, 🔲 Albertsons/Sav-On, Peterbilt, to Micron, **S** 🅡 Chevron, 🍴 Burger King, FoodCourt, 🔲 Boise Stores/famous brands, ID Ice World
54	US 20/26, Broadway Ave, Boise, **N** 🅡 Chevron/dsl, ⓕＦＬＹＩＮＧ Ｊ/dsl/LP/24hr, Shell/dsl, 🍴 A&W/KFC, Arby's, Chili's, Fiesta Mexican, Jack-in-the-Box, IHOP, Mongolian Noodles, Nick'n Willy's Pizza, Port Of Subs, Sonic, Starbucks, Subway, Wendy's, 🛏 Courtyard (3mi), 🔲 🅗, Big O Tire, Dowdie's Automotive, Fred Meyer, Goodyear/auto, Home Depot, Hyundai, Jo-Ann Fabrics, O'Reilly Parts,

(vertical margin labels: BURLEY, TWIN FALLS, MOUNTAIN HOME, ID)

🔼E INTERSTATE 84 CONT'D

Exit	Services
54	Continued
	PetCo, Radio Shack, Ross, ShopKO, Walgreens, vet, to Boise St U, **S** 🅖 TA/Buckhorn Rest/Taco Bell/Subway/dsl/24hr/@, 🅛 Shilo Inn, 🅞 Bretz RV Ctr, Kenworth, Mtn View RV Park
53	Vista Ave, Boise, **N** 🅖 Shell/dsl, Texaco/dsl, 🅕 Applebee's, Pizza Hut, 🅛 Boise Hotel, Comfort Suites, Extended Stay America, Fairfield Inn, Hampton Inn, Holiday Inn/rest., Holiday Inn Express, Super 8, 🅞 museums, st capitol, st police, zoo, **S** 🅖 Chevron/McDonald's, 🅕 Denny's, Kopper Kitchen, 🅛 Best Western, Comfort Inn, InnAmerica, Motel 6, Sleep Inn, 🅞🔆
52	Orchard St, Boise, **N** 🅖 Shell/dsl, 🅞 Fiat, Kia, Mazda/Nissan, GMC
50b a	Cole Rd, Overland Rd, **N** 🅖 Chevron/dsl, Shell, Sinclair, 🅕 Cancun Mexican, Eddie's Rest., McDonald's, Outback Steaks, Pizza Hut, Subway, Taco Bell, Taco Time, 🅞 Ace Hardware, LDS Temple, transmissions, **S** 🅖 Common Cents/dsl, Phillips 66/dsl, 🅕 A&W/KFC, Black Bear Diner, Burger King, Carino's, Carl's Jr, Chapala Mexican, Chuck-a-Rama, Cracker Barrel, Fuddruckers, Goodwood BBQ, Jamba Juice, McGrath's FishHouse, Legend's Grill, Lucky Palace Chinese, On the Border, Panda Express, Papa John's, Panda Express, Perky's Pizza, Pollo Ray, Port Of Subs, Primo's, Sonic, Starbucks, Tucano's Brazilian Grill, 🅛 Budget Host, Hampton Inn, Hilton Garden, Homewood Suites, Oxford Suites, 🅞 AT&T, Commercial Tire, Costco/gas, Dillon RV Ctr, Les Schwab Tire, Lowe's, Verizon, Walmart/McDonald's, vet
49	I-184 (exits left from eb), to W Boise, **N** 🅞🅗
46	ID 55, Eagle, **N** 🅖 Chevron/McDonald's/dsl, 🅕 Blimpie, Buffalo Wild Wings, Del Taco, Ketchn Burritos, Ling&Louis, Loo Beto's, Smash Burger, Starbucks, Subway, 🅛 Comfort Suites, Hampton Inn, Meridian Inn, 🅞🅗, **S** 🅖 Chevron/dsl, 🅕 Beef'O'Brady's, Chicago Connection, Dickey's BBQ, Don Diego Mexican, Jack-in-the-Box, Jimmy John's, Joy Garden, Moxie Java, Pita Pit, Port Of Subs, Qdoba, Quiznos, Rudy's Grill, Sakana Japanese, Taco Bell, TCBY, 🅛 Candlewood Suites, Courtyard, TownePlace Suites, 🅞 AAA, Harley-Davidson,
44	ID 69, Meridian, **N** 🅖 Chevron/dsl, Sinclair, 🅕 A&W/KFC, Blimpie, China Wok, DQ, McDonald's, Panda Express, Pizza Hut, Quiznos, Shari's, Starbucks, Subway, Taco Bell, Taco Time, Wendy's, 🅛 Best Western, Motel 6, 🅞 AT&T, Home Depot, Les Schwab Tire, Sierra Trading Post, Verizon, WinCo Foods, Urgent Care, **S** 🅖 Shell/dsl, 🅕 JB's, Papa John's, 🅛 Mr Sandman Motel, 🅞 Camping World RV Ctr, Ford, Lowe's, O'Reilly Parts, Walgreens, waterpark
42	Ten Mile Rd
38	Garrity Blvd, Nampa, **N** 🅖 Chevron/dsl, 🅕 Jack-in-the-Box, Port of Subs, 🅛 Hampton Inn, 🅞 Buick/GMC, Cadillac/Chevrolet, Chrysler/Dodge/Jeep, Ford, Hyundai, Kia, Nissan, Subaru, Swiss Village Cheese, Toyota/Scion, Verizon, Walmart/gas, **S** 🅖 Phillips 66/McDonald's/dsl, Shell/dsl, 🅕 A&W/KFC, Panda Express, Pizza Hut, Subway, 🅛 Holiday Inn Express, 🅞🅗 Garrity RV Park, JC Penney, Macy's, War Hawk Museum
36	Franklin Blvd, Nampa, **N** 🅖 Maverik, 🅕 Jack-in-the-Box, Noodles Rest., 🅛 Shilo Inn/rest., **S** 🅖 Chevron/dsl,

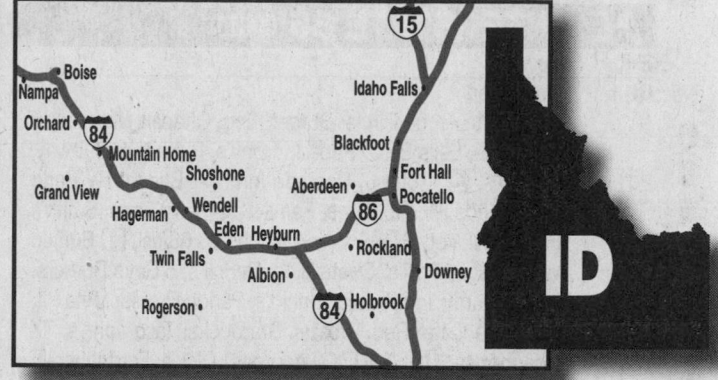

36	Continued
	Shell/Subway/dsl/RV dump/scales/4hr, 🅛 Sleep Inn, 🅞 🅗, Bish's RV Ctr, Freightliner, Honda, Mason Cr RV Park
35	ID 55, Nampa, **S** 🅖 Shell/dsl, 🅕 Denny's, 🅛 Rodeway Inn, Shilo Inn, Super 8
33b a	ID 55 S, Midland Blvd, Marcine, **N** 🅕 McDonald's, Olive Garden, Port of Subs, Qdoba Mexican, Sonic, Subway, TGIFriday's, Tulley's Coffee, Winger's, 🅛 Fairfield Inn, 🅞 AT&T, Best Buy, Costco/gas, Gordmans, Kohl's, Michael's, Old Navy, PetCo, Target, World Mkt, **S** 🅖 Shell/dsl, 🅕 Applebee's, Arby's, Baskin-Robbins, Blimpie, Buffalo Wild Wings, Carl's Jr, Coldstone, DQ, Golden Corral, IHOP, Jack-in-the-Box, Jade Garden, Jalapeno's Grill, Mongolian BBQ, Outback Steaks, Papa Murphy's, Quiznos, Red Robin, Shari's Rest, Skipper's, Smokey Mtn Grill, Subway, TX Roadhouse, Wendy's, 🅞 BigLots, Big O Tire, $Tree, Hastings Books, Home Depot, Jo-Ann Fabrics, K-Mart, Lowe's, NAPA, Radio Shack, Ross, Savers, ShopKO, Staples, Tire Factory, U-Haul, Verizon, Walgreens, WinCo Foods
29	US 20/26, Franklin Rd, Caldwell, **N** 🅖 🄵 FLYING J/Denny's/dsl/LP/scales/24hr, 🅞 Ambassador RV camping, RV dump, **S** 🅖 Sage/Sinclair/cafe/dsl/24hr, 🅕 Magic Recipe, 🅛 Best Western, La Quinta
28	10th Ave, Caldwell, **N** 🅖 Maverik, 🅞 city park, **S** 🅖 Chevron, Shell/dsl, 🅕 Carl's Jr, Fiesta Mexican, Jack-in-the-Box, KFC, Mr V's Rest., Pizza Hut, Subway, Wendy's, 🅛 Sundowner Motel, 🅞🅗, AutoZone, Paul's Food/Drug, Tire Factory, Walgreens
27	ID 19, to Wilder, **1 mi S** 🅖 Tesoro/dsl
26.5mm	Boise River
26	US 20/26, to Notus, **N** 🅞 Caldwell Campground, **S** 🅖 Sinclair/dsl
25	ID 44, Middleton, **N** 🅖 Shell/dsl, 🅕 44 Burgers/shakes, **S** Insp sta eb
17	Sand Hollow, **N** 🅕 Sand Hollow Café, 🅞 Country Corners RV Park
13	Black Canyon Jct, **S** 🅖 Sinclair/rest./motel/dsl/scales/24hr, 🄲
9	US 30, to New Plymouth
3	US 95, Fruitland, **N** 🅖 Chevron/A&W/dsl, **5 mi N** 🅞 Neat Retreat RV Park, to Hell's Cyn RA
1mm	Welcome Ctr eb, full ♿ facilities, info, 🄲, 🗑, litter barrels, petwalk
0mm	Idaho/Oregon state line, Snake River

🔼E INTERSTATE 86

Exit	Services
63b a	I-15, N to Butte, S to SLC. **I-86 begins/ends on I-15, exit 72.**
61	US 91, Yellowstone Ave, Pocatello, **N** 🅖 Exxon, Shell/dsl,

🅰 = gas   🍴 = food   🏠 = lodging   🅾 = other   🆁🆂 = rest stop   Copyright 2014 - The Next Exit ®

◄E INTERSTATE 86 CONT'D

POCATELLO

Exit	Services
61	Continued
	🍴 Arby's, Arctic Circle, Burger King, Chapala Mexican, 5 Mile Café, Lei's BBQ, Papa Murphy's, Pizza Hut, Subway, Wendy's, 🏠 Motel 6, Ramada Inn, 🅾 Budget RV Park, Crossroads RV Ctr, $Tree, Family$, O'Reilly Parts, Smith's Foods/dsl, vet, **S** 🅰 Exxon/dsl, Phillips 66/dsl, 🍴 Buffalo Wild Wings, Chili's, Costa Vida, Denny's, 5 Guys Burgers, IHOP, Jimmy John's, McDonald's, Panda Express, Pita Pit, Pizza Pie Café, Red Lobster, Starbucks, Taco John's, TX Roadhouse, 🅾 AT&T, Costco/gas, Dick's, Ford/Lincoln, Herbergers, Home Depot, JC Penney, Jo-Ann Fabrics, K-Mart/Little Caesars, Lowe's, PetCo, Radio Shack, Ross, Schwab Tire, Sears, ShopKo, Staples, TJ Maxx, Verizon, Walgreens, Walmart, dsl repair
58.5mm	Portneuf River
58	US 30, W Pocatello, **N** Batise Springs RV Park/dump
56	**N** Pocatello Reg ⤡, **S** 🍴 Sinclair/dsl/24hr
52	Arbon Valley, **S** 🅰 Phillips 66/Bannock Peak/dsl, 🅾 casino
51mm	Bannock Creek
49	Rainbow Rd
44	Seagull Bay
40	ID 39, American Falls, **N** 🅰 Phillips 66/dsl (1mi), Sinclair/dsl (1mi), 🍴 Pizza Hut, Subway, Tres Hermanos Mexican, 🏠 American Motel, 🅾 ⑂ Alco, Family$ (1mi), Jiffy Lube, NAPA, Schwab Tire, Willow Bay RV Park/dump, auto repair, to Am Falls RA, **S** 🏠 Hillview Motel
36	ID 37, to Rockland, American Falls, **2 mi N** 🅰 Shell/dsl, 🏠 Falls Motel, 🅾 ⑂, **2 mi S** Indian Springs RV Resort
33	Neeley Area
31mm	🆁🆂 wb, full 🚻 facilities, 🆑, 🛒, litter barrel, petwalk, vending, hist site
28	**N** 🅾 to Massacre Rock SP, Register Rock Hist Site, RV camping/dump
21	Coldwater Area
19mm	🆁🆂 eb, full 🚻 facilities, 🆑, 🛒, litter barrel, petwalk, vending, hist site
15	Raft River Area
1	I-84 E, to Ogden. **I-86 begins/ends on I-84, exit 222.**

◄E INTERSTATE 90

WALLACE

Exit	Services
74mm	Idaho/Montana state line, Pacific/Central time zone Lookout Pass elev 4680
73mm	scenic area/hist site wb
72mm	scenic area/hist site eb
71mm	runaway truck ramp wb
70mm	runaway truck ramp wb
69	Lp 90, Mullan, **N** 🅰 CFN/dsl, 🏠 Lookout Motel (1mi), 🅾 USPO, museum
68	Lp 90 (from eb), Mullan, same as 69
67	Morning District
66	Gold Creek (from eb)
65	Compressor District
64	Golconda District
62	ID 4, Wallace, **S** 🅰 Conoco, 🍴 Pizza Factory, 🏠 Brooks Hotel, Stardust Motel, 🅾 ⑂ Depot RV Park, Harvest Foods, TrueValue, museum, repair
61	Lp 90, Wallace, **S** 🅰 Conoco/dsl, 🍴 Pizza Factory, Wallace Sta Rest./gifts, 🏠 Brooks Hotel/rest., Molly B-Damm

Exit	Services
61	Continued
	Inn, Wallace Inn, 🅾 auto repair, info ctr, same as 62
60	Lp 90, Silverton, **S** 🏠 Molly B-Damm Inn, 🅾 RV camping
57	Lp 90, Osburn, **S** 🅰 76/dsl, 🅾 Blue Anchor RV Park, auto repair, USPO
54	Big Creek, **N** 🅾 Elk Creek Store/repair, hist site, rv dump
51	Lp 90, Division St, Kellogg, **N** 🅰 Conoco/dsl, 🏠 Trail Motel, 🅾 ⑂, Buick/Cadillac/Chevrolet/GMC, Chrysler/Dodge/Jeep, Schwab Tire, Stein's Foods, Sunnyside Drug, **S** 🍴 In Cahoots Cafe, Moose Creek Grill, 🅾 USPO, auto repair, museum

KELLOGG

50	Hill St (from eb), Kellogg, **N** 🍴 Humdinger Drive-In, Sunshine Rest., 🏠 Trail Motel, 🅾 Ace Hardware, NAPA, Stein's Foods, Sunnyside Drug, tires, **S** 🅰 Conoco/dsl, 🍴 Greek Deli, 🅾 Silver Mtn Ski/summer resort/rec area, Yoke's Foods, museum
49	Bunker Ave, **N** 🅰 Conoco/dsl, 🍴 McDonald's, Sam's Drive-In, Subway, 🏠 Silverhorn Motel/rest., 🅾 ⑂, **S** 🍴 Noah's Canteen, Silver Mtn Rest., 🏠 GuestHouse Inn, Morning Star Lodge, 🅾 Silver Mtn RA, museum, RV dump
48	Smelterville, **S** 🍴 Sands Cafe, 🅾 Tire Factory, Walmart
45	Pinehurst, **S** 🅰 Chevron/dsl/repair, Conoco/dsl, 🅾 By-the-way Camping, Harvest Foods, NAPA, TrueValue, USPO
43	Kingston, **N** 🅰 Conoco/dsl, 🍴 Snakepit Café, 🏠 Enaville Resort, RV camping, **S** 🅰 Exxon/dsl/rv dump, USPO
40	Cataldo, **N** 🍴 Mission Inn Rest., USPO, **S** RV Park
39.5mm	Coeur d' Alene River
39	Cataldo Mission, **S** 🅾 Old Mission SP, Nat Hist Landmark
34	ID 3, to St Maries, Rose Lake, **S** 🅰 Conoco/dsl, Rose Lake/dsl, 🍴 Rose Lake Cafe, 🅾 White Pines Scenic Rte
33mm	chain removal eb
32mm	chainup area/**weigh sta wb**
31.5mm	Idaho Panhandle NF, eastern boundary, 4th of July Creek
28	4th of July Pass RA, elev 3069, Mullan Tree HS, ski area, snowmobile area, turnout both lanes
24mm	chainup eb, removal wb
22	ID 97, to St Maries, L Coeur d' Alene Scenic ByWay, Wolf Lodge District, Harrison, **1 mi N** Wolf Lodge Camping, **S** 🅾 Lake Coeur d'Alene RV Park, Squaw Bay Resort (7mi)
20.5mm	Lake Coeur d' Alene
17	Mullan Trail Rd
15	Lp 90, Sherman Ave, Coeur d' Alene, **N** 🅾 forest info, Lake Coeur D' Alene RA/HS, **S** 🅰 Exxon/dsl, Tesoro/dsl, LP, Texaco, 🍴 Jimmy's Cafe, Michael D's Eatery, O'Shay's Rest., 🏠 Bates Motel, BudgetSaver Motel, Gedar Motel, El Rancho Motel, Holiday Motel, Japan House Suites, La Quinta, State Motel, 🅾 Peterson's Foods, NAPA Care, tourist info

COEUR d' ALENE

14	15th St, Coeur d' Alene, **S** 🅰 TAJ Mart, 🅾 Jordon's Grocery
13	4th St, Coeur d' Alene, **N** 🅰 A&D/dsl, 🍴 Atilano's Mexican, Carl's Jr, DQ, Davis Donuts, Denny's, Fiesta Mexican, IHOP, Jimmy John's, Little Caesars, Original Mongolian BBQ, Panda Express, Subway, Taco Time, Wendy's, 🏠 Comfort Inn, 🅾 AutoZone, BigLots, Costco/gas, Hastings Books, NAPA, Radio Shack, Schwab Tire, same as 12, **S** 🅰 Exxon/dsl, 🍴 Thai Bamboo
12	US 95, to Sandpoint, Moscow, **N** 🅰 Exxon/dsl, Holiday/dsl, Mobil, 🍴 Applebee's, Arby's, Burger King, Cafe Chulo Mexican, Casa de Oro, Chili's, Del Taco, Dragon

🔼E INTERSTATE 90 CONT'D

Exit	Services
12	Continued
	House Chinese, Elmer's, Garlic Jim's Pizza, MacKenzie River Pizza, McDonald's, Olive Garden, Panda Express, Perkins, Pizza Factory, Pizza Hut, Red Lobster, Skipper's, Taco Bell, Tomato St., TX Roadhouse, 🛏 Best Western, Guesthouse Inn, La Quinta, Motel 6, Shilo Suites, Super 8, ◉ AT&T, Best Buy, Buick/GMC, Cadillac, Discount Tire, Dodge, $Tree, Ford/Lincoln, Fred Meyer/dsl, GNC, Grocery Outlet, Harley-Davidson, Home Depot, JC Penney, Kia, K-Mart, Kohl's, Michael's, Office Depot, O'Reilly Parts, PetCo, Ross, Safeway/gas, Sears/auto, Super 1 Foods, Target, TireRama, TJ Maxx, Toyota/Scion, Tuesday Morning, U-Haul, Verizon, Walgreens, Walmart/Subway, S ⛽ Conoco, 🍴 Greek St Pizza, Jack-in-the-Box, Jamba Juice, Papa Murphy's, Qdoba Mexican, Quiznos, Schlotzsky's, Shari's, Starbucks, 🛏 AmeriTel, ◉ H, Albertson's/gas, AT&T, GNC, Rite Aid, ShopKO/drugs, Staples, same as 13
11	Northwest Blvd, N ⛽ Conoco/dsl, ◉ Lowe's, S ⛽ Exxon/dsl, Texaco, 🍴 Azteca Mexican, Coldstone, Outback Steaks, Porky G's BBQ, Red Robin, SF Sourdough, Starbucks, Subway, Ugly Fish Rest., 🛏 Days Inn, Hampton Inn, Holiday Inn Express, ◉ H, Honda, Riverwalk RV Park, Verizon
8.5mm	**Welcome Ctr/weigh sta eb, 🅿 both lanes, full ♿ facilities, info, 🚰, litter barrels, petwalk**
7	ID 41, to Rathdrum, Spirit Lake, N ⛽ Mirastar/dsl, 76/dsl, 🍴 Del Taco, La Cocina Mexican, Noodle Express, NY Pizza, Papa Murphy's, Pita Pit, Pizza Factory, Quiznos, Sonic, Starbucks, Subway, Wendy's, ◉ Chevrolet, Chrysler/Dodge/Jeep, $Tree, Hyundai, Mazda, Nissan, Radio Shack, Subaru, Walmart/Subway, Couer d'Alene RV Park, S ⛽ Chevron/dsl, 🍴 A&W/KFC, Capone's Grill, DQ, 🛏 Comfort Inn, ◉ truck repair, vet
6	Seltice Way, N ⛽ 7-11, 🍴 La Cabana Mexican, Pizza Hut, ◉ Super 1 Foods, Walgreens, S ⛽ Conoco/dsl/LP, 🍴 Denny's, Hot Rod Café, Little Caesars, McDonald's, Rancho Viejo Mexican, Taco Bell, Taco Time, ◉ Ace Hardware, Curves, O'Reilly Parts, TireRama, Trading Co

Exit	Services
6	Continued
	Foods, USPO, vet
5	Lp 90, Spokane St, Treaty Rock HS, N ⛽ Exxon/dsl, 76, 🍴 Domino's, Golden Dragon Chinese, Hunter's Rest., Rob's Seafood/burgers, Subway, WhiteHouse Grill, ◉ AutoZone, CarQuest, Perfection Tire/repair, Schwab Tire, Seltice RV Ctr, S ⛽ 76/Pacific Pride/dsl, 🍴 Rosa's Italian, 🛏 Red Lion Inn, ◉ visitors ctr
2	Pleasant View Rd, N ⛽ Exxon/dsl, *FLYING J*/Conoco/Subway/dsl/LP/scales/24hr, *Love's*/Carl's Jr/dsl/scales/24hr, 🍴 McDonald's, Toro Viejo Mexican, 🛏 Best Value Inn, ◉ Suntree RV Park, RV/truckwash, S ⛽ Exxon/Subway/dsl/24hr, 🍴 Zip's Drive-in, 🛏 Riverbend Inn, Sleep Inn, ◉ dogtrack
0mm	Idaho/Washington state line

🔼E INTERSTATE 184 (BOISE)

Exit	Services
6mm	**I-184 begins/ends on 13th St**, downtown ⛽ Shell, 🍴 Chandler's Steaks, 5 Guys Burgers, PF Chang's, 🛏 Hampton Inn, Safari Inn, The Grove, ◉ Office Depot, USPO
5	River St (from eb), W ⛽ Chevron, 🍴 McDonald's, ◉ Ford
4.5mm	Boise River
3	Fairview Ave, to US 20/26 E, W 🍴 Joe's Crabshack, McDonald's, Tepanyaki Japanese, 🛏 Boise Inn, Budget Inn, Riverside Hotel, Shiloh Inn, ◉ Commercial Tire
2	Curtis Rd, to Garden City, E ⛽ Shell, 🛏 Rodeway Inn, ◉ H
1b a	Cole Rd, Franklin Rd, E ⛽ Chevron/Subway, 🛏 Harrison Hotel, ◉ Acura/Honda, Dodge, Jaguar, Land Rover, Volvo, W ⛽ Sinclair, 🍴 Cafe Ole, Cafe Rio, Carl's Jr, Cheesecake Factory, Chili's, Hooters, Jack-in-the-Box, Jalapeno's, Keva Juice, Old Chicago Pizza, Olive Garden, Quiznos, Red Lobster, Red Robin, Shari's, Sizzler, Smash Burger, Starbucks, TGIFriday's, Wendy's, 🛏 Ameritel, Candlewood Suites, Residence Inn, ◉ AT&T, Audi/VW, Best Buy, Cabela's, Dillard's, JC Penney, Kohl's, Macy's, Michael's, Office Depot, Old Navy, PetCo, Petsmart, Ross, Sears/auto, Target, TJ Maxx, Verizon, mall, vet
0mm	**I-184 begins/ends on I-84, exit 49.**

ILLINOIS

🔼E INTERSTATE 24

Exit	Services
38mm	Illinois/Kentucky state line, Ohio River
37	US 45, Metropolis, N 🅿 both lanes, full ♿ facilities, info, vending, 🚰, litter barrels, petwalk, 0-2 mi S ⛽ BP/Quiznos/dsl, 🍴 Huddle House, KFC, McDonald's, Pizza Hut, Sonic, 🛏 Best Value Inn, Holiday Inn Express, Metropolis Inn, Motel 6, Super 8, ◉ H, Buick/Chrysler/Dodge/GMC/Jeep, Chevrolet, O'Reilly Parts, Plaza Tire, to Riverboat Casino, Ft Massac SP, camping
27	to New Columbia, Big Bay
16	IL 146, Vienna, N ⛽ Gambit Inn, S ⛽ BP/dsl, FastStop, Roc/dsl, 🍴 Dolly's Rest., DQ, Jumbo Grill, McDonald's, Newt's Pizza, Subway, 🛏 Limited Inn
14	US 45, Vienna, S camping
7	to Goreville, Tunnel Hill, N ⛽ Fast Stop/dsl, ◉ winery, S ◉ to Ferne Clyffe SP, camping

1	I-57, N to Chicago, S to Memphis. **I-24 begins/ends on I-57, exit 44.**

🔼N INTERSTATE 39

Exit	Services
	I-39 and I-90 run together into Wisconsin. See Illinois Interstate 90, exits 15mm through 1.
122b a	US 20 E, Harrison Ave, to Belvidere, W ⛽ Mobil, Road Ranger/Subway/dsl, 🍴 Arby's, Bergner's, Burger King, DQ, Granite City Rest., Lung Fung, Sonic, Taco Bell, TGIFriday's, ◉ AT&T, Barnes&Noble, BMW, Chevrolet, Collier RV Ctr, Goodyear/auto, Harley-Davidson, Hilander Foods/gas, JC Penney, Macy's, Menards, Sears/auto, Tires+, VW, Walgreens, mall, **last nb exit before toll rd**
119	US 20 W, Alpine Rd, to Rockford
116.5mm	Kishwaukee River
115	Baxter Rd, E ⛽ Shell/dsl/scales/24hr/@
111	IL 72, to Monroe Center, E ⛽ BP/Sunrise Family Rest./

ID
IL

BOISE

ROCKFORD

⬆N INTERSTATE 39 CONT'D

Exit	Services
111	Continued dsl/24hr, Marathon (1mi), 🍴 Roadhouse Rest. (1mi)
104	IL 64, to Oregon, Sycamore, **W** Grubsteakers Rest/truck parking (2mi)
99	IL 38, to De Kalb, Rochelle, **0-2 mi W** 🅿 BP/dsl, Petro/Iron Skillet/dsl/scales/RV Dump/@, Road Ranger/🌮/Subway/dsl/scales/24hr, Shell/dsl, 🍴 Arby's, Butterfly Rest, China Wok, Culver's, DQ, Little Ceasar's, McDonald's, New China, Taco Bell, Wendy's, 🛏 Baymont Inn, Comfort Inn, Holiday Inn Express, Super 8, 🅾 🏥, Blue Beacon, Curves, $General, Sullivan's Foods, Walgreens, Walmart
97b a	**I-88 tollway**, to Moline, Rock Island, Chicago
93	Steward
87	US 30, to Sterling, Rock Falls, **E** to Shabbona Lake SP, **W** Yogi Bear Camping (16mi)
84.5mm	🆁🆂 both lanes, full 🚻 facilities, 🅲, 🅵, litter barrels, vending, playground, petwalk
82	Paw Paw, **3 mi E** Casey's, **W** many wind turbines
72	US 34, to Mendota, Earlville, **W** 🅿 BP/Buster's Buffet/dsl/scales/24hr, Road Ranger/🌮/dsl/scales/24hr, 🍴 KFC/Taco Bell, McDonald's, 🛏 Comfort Inn, Super 8/truck parking, 🅾🏥
67.5mm	Little Vermilion River
66	US 52, Troy Grove, **E** KOA (1mi)
62.5mm	Tomahawk Creek
59b a	I-80, E to Chicago, W to Des Moines
57	US 6, to Peru, La Salle, **1-2 mi W** 🅿 Casey's, Shell/24hr, 🛏 Daniel's Motel, 🅾 city park
56mm	Illinois River, Abraham Lincoln Mem Bridge
54	Oglesby, **E** 🅿 BP, Casey's, Phillips 66/dsl, Shell/24hr, 🍴 Bella's Rest., Burger King, Delaney's Rest., KFC/Taco Bell, McDonald's, Root Beer Stand, Subway, 🛏 Best Western, Days Inn, 🅾 Starved Rock SP, **W** 🅿 ♥Loves♥/Hardee's/dsl/scales/24hr,
52	IL 251, to La Salle, Peru
51	IL 71, to Hennepin, Oglesby
48	Tonica, **E** 🅿 Casey's, 🅾 city park
41	IL 18, to Streator, Henry
35	IL 17, to Wenona, Lacon, **E** 🅿 BP/dsl, Casey's (2mi), Shell/Burger King/Subway/dsl/RV dump, 🛏 Super 8/truck parking, 🅾 NAPA
27	to Minonk, **E** 🅿 Casey's (2mi), Shell/Subway/Woody's Rest./dsl/24hr, 🛏 Motel 6, 🅾 NAPA
22	IL 116, to Peoria, Benson
14	US 24, to El Paso, Peoria, **E** 🅿 Freedom/dsl, Shell/Subway/dsl/24hr, 🍴 DQ, Hardee's/24hr, McDonald's, Oriental Buffet, Woody's Family Rest., 🛏 Days Inn, 🅾 Bushert's Hardware, El Paso RV Ctr, Ford, IGA Foods, NAPA, city park, USPO, **W** 🍴 Monical's Pizza, 🛏 Super 8, 🅾 $General, Hickory Hill Camping (4mi), antiques
9mm	Mackinaw River
8	IL 251, Lake Bloomington Rd, **E** Lake Bloomington, **W** 🅾 Evergreen Lake, to Comlara Park, RV camping
5	Hudson, **1 mi E** 🅿 Casey's
2	US 51 bus, Bloomington, Normal
0mm	**I-39 begins/ends on I-55, exit 164.**

⬆N INTERSTATE 55

Exit	Services
295mm	**I-55 begins/ends on US 41**, Lakeshore Dr, in Chicago.
293a	to Cermak Rd (from nb)

(vertical margin labels: **IL**, **OGLESBY**, **CHICAGO AREA**)

Exit	Services
292	I-90/94, W to Chicago, E to Indiana
290	Damen Ave, Ashland Ave (no EZ nb return), **E** 🅿 Marathon, Shell, 🅾 Target
289	to California Ave (no EZ nb return), **E** 🅿 Citgo, Speedway/dsl
288	Kedzie Ave, (from sb no ez return), **E** 🅿 Citgo
287	Pulaski Rd, **E** 🅿 Mobil/dsl, Shell, 🍴 Burger King, Domino's, Quiznos, Subway, 🅾 Advance Parts, Aldi Foods, Dodge, Family$, Honda, Pete's Mkt, Staples, Target, Walgreens
286	IL 50, Cicero Ave, **E** 🅿 Citgo/dsl, Marathon, Mobil, 🍴 Burger King, Dunkin Donuts, JJ Fish, McDonald's, Pepe's Mexican, Popeye's, Starbucks, Subway, 🅾 Family$, O'Reilly Parts, Walgreens, to 🚇
285	Central Ave, **E** 🅿 BP/dsl, Citgo, Marathon/Dunkin Donuts, 🍴 Burger King, Donald's HotDogs
283	IL 43, Harlem Ave, **E** 🅿 Shell, 🍴 Baskin-Robbins/Dunkin Donuts, Burger King, Domino's, El Pollo Loco, Little Caesars, Portillo HotDogs, Subway, 🅾 AT&T, AutoZone, Fannie May Candies, Walgreens
282b a	IL 171, 1st Ave, **W** 🅾 Brookfield Zoo, Mayfield Park
279b	US 12, US 20, US 45, La Grange Rd, **0-2 mi W** 🅿 BP, Mobil, Shell, 🍴 Al's Beef, Applebee's, Arby's, Baskin-Robbins/Dunkin Donuts, Boston Mkt, Brown's Chicken, Burger King, Cafe Salsa, Jimmy John's, Ledo's Pizza, LoneStar Steaks, McDonald's, Nancy's Pizza, NoNno's Pizza, Old Country Buffet, Panda Express, Pizza Hut, Popeye's, Subway, Taco Bell, Taco Tico, Time Out Grill, Via Bella, Wendy's, White Castle, 🛏 Best Western, Holiday Inn, La Grange Motel, 🅾 Aldi Foods, Best Buy, Buick/Cadillac/GMC, Chevrolet, Discount Tire, Dodge, $Tree, Firestone/auto, Ford, GNC, Honda, Jo-Ann Fabrics, Kohl's, Mazda, Menards, NAPA, Nissan, NTB, Office Depot, PepBoys, PetCo, Petsmart, Sam's Club/gas, Subaru, Suzuki, Target, Toyota/Scion, Verizon, VW, Walmart
279a	La Grange Rd, to I-294 **toll**, S to Indiana
277b	I-294 **toll** (from nb), S to Indiana
277a	I-294 **toll**, N to Wisconsin
276c	Joliet Rd (from nb)
276b a	County Line Rd, **E** 🍴 Capri Rest., China King, Ciazzi's Cafe, Cooper's Hawk, Max&Erma's, Moon Dance Diner, Salerno's Pizza, Starbucks, Subway, Topaz Rest., 🛏 Extended Stay America, Marriott, Quality Inn, 🅾 Brookhaven Mkt, Tuesday Morning, **W** 🛏 SpringHill Suites
274	IL 83, Kingery Rd, **E** 🅿 Shell, **W** 🅿 Mobil/dsl, Phillips 66/dsl, 7-11, Shell, 🍴 Bakers Square, Barnelli's Pasta, Buffalo Wild Wings, Burger King, Chipotle Mexican, Denny's, Domino's, Dunkin Donuts, Jamba Juice, Jimmy John's, Papa John's, Patio BBQ, Pei Wei, Portillo's HotDogs, Potbelly's Rest., Starbucks, Subway, Wendy's, 🛏 Holiday Inn, La Quinta, Red Roof Inn, Super 8, 🅾 AT&T, Firestone, Ford/KIA, K-Mart, Michael's, Radio Shack, Staples, Target, Verizon
273b a	Cass Ave, **W** 🅿 Shell, 🍴 La Notte Due Rest., Rosati's Pizza, Uncle Mao's Chinese, 🅾 vet
271b a	Lemont Rd, **E** 🛏 Extended Stay America, **W** 🅿 Shell
269	I-355 **toll**, to W Suburbs
268	(from sb only), Joliet, same as 267
267	IL 53, Bolingbrook, **E** 🅿 BP, Phillips 66/55 Trkstp/rest./dsl/scales/24hr/@, 🍴 McDonald's, 🛏 La Quinta, Ramada Ltd, Super 8, 🅾 Chevrolet, **W** 🅿 Shell/Circle K, Speedway/dsl, 🍴 A&W/LJ Silver, Burger King, Ched

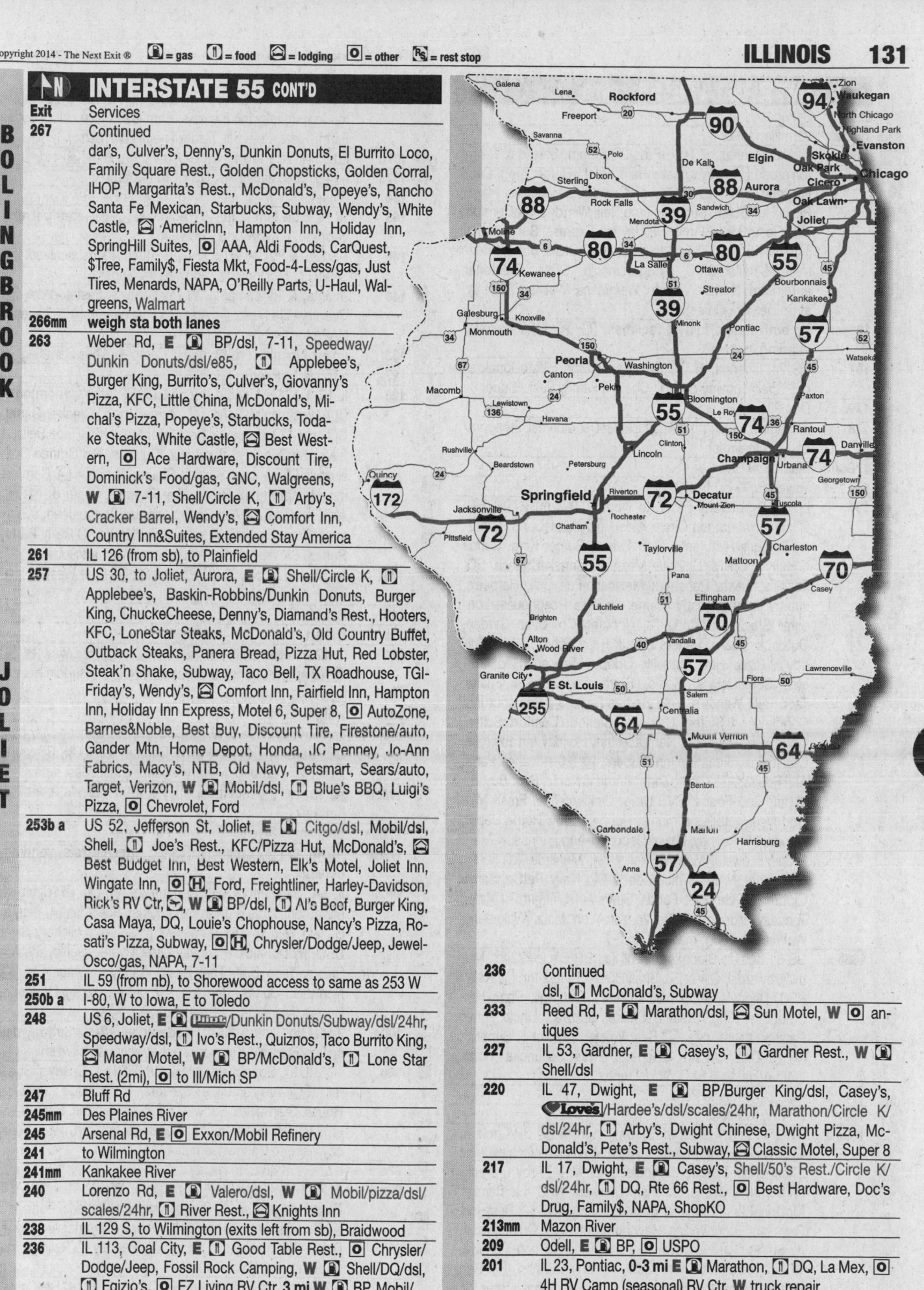

◆N INTERSTATE 55 CONT'D

Exit	Services
267	Continued
	dar's, Culver's, Denny's, Dunkin Donuts, El Burrito Loco, Family Square Rest., Golden Chopsticks, Golden Corral, IHOP, Margarita's Rest., McDonald's, Popeye's, Rancho Santa Fe Mexican, Starbucks, Subway, Wendy's, White Castle, 🛏 AmericInn, Hampton Inn, Holiday Inn, SpringHill Suites, 🅾 AAA, Aldi Foods, CarQuest, $Tree, Family$, Fiesta Mkt, Food-4-Less/gas, Just Tires, Menards, NAPA, O'Reilly Parts, U-Haul, Walgreens, Walmart
266mm	**weigh sta both lanes**
263	Weber Rd, **E** 🆁 BP/dsl, 7-11, Speedway/ Dunkin Donuts/dsl/e85, 🍴 Applebee's, Burger King, Burrito's, Culver's, Giovanny's Pizza, KFC, Little China, McDonald's, Michal's Pizza, Popeye's, Starbucks, Todake Steaks, White Castle, 🛏 Best Western, 🅾 Ace Hardware, Discount Tire, Dominick's Food/gas, GNC, Walgreens, **W** 🆁 7-11, Shell/Circle K, 🍴 Arby's, Cracker Barrel, Wendy's, 🛏 Comfort Inn, Country Inn&Suites, Extended Stay America
261	IL 126 (from sb), to Plainfield
257	US 30, to Joliet, Aurora, **E** 🆁 Shell/Circle K, 🍴 Applebee's, Baskin-Robbins/Dunkin Donuts, Burger King, ChuckeCheese, Denny's, Diamond's Rest., Hooters, KFC, LoneStar Steaks, McDonald's, Old Country Buffet, Outback Steaks, Panera Bread, Pizza Hut, Red Lobster, Steak'n Shake, Subway, Taco Bell, TX Roadhouse, TGI-Friday's, Wendy's, 🛏 Comfort Inn, Fairfield Inn, Hampton Inn, Holiday Inn Express, Motel 6, Super 8, 🅾 AutoZone, Barnes&Noble, Best Buy, Discount Tire, Firestone/auto, Gander Mtn, Home Depot, Honda, JC Penney, Jo-Ann Fabrics, Macy's, NTB, Old Navy, Petsmart, Sears/auto, Target, Verizon, **W** 🆁 Mobil/dsl, 🍴 Blue's BBQ, Luigi's Pizza, 🅾 Chevrolet, Ford
253b a	US 52, Jefferson St, Joliet, **E** 🆁 Citgo/dsl, Mobil/dsl, Shell, 🍴 Joe's Rest., KFC/Pizza Hut, McDonald's, 🛏 Best Budget Inn, Best Western, Elk's Motel, Joliet Inn, Wingate Inn, 🅾 Ⓗ Ford, Freightliner, Harley-Davidson, Rick's RV Ctr, 🔄 **W** 🆁 BP/dsl, 🍴 Al's Beef, Burger King, Casa Maya, DQ, Louie's Chophouse, Nancy's Pizza, Rosati's Pizza, Subway, 🅾 Ⓗ Chrysler/Dodge/Jeep, Jewel-Osco/gas, NAPA, 7-11
251	IL 59 (from nb), to Shorewood access to same as 253 W
250b a	I-80, W to Iowa, E to Toledo
248	US 6, Joliet, **E** 🆁🚛/Dunkin Donuts/Subway/dsl/24hr, Speedway/dsl, 🍴 Ivo's Rest., Quiznos, Taco Burrito King, 🛏 Manor Motel, **W** 🆁 BP/McDonald's, 🍴 Lone Star Rest. (2mi), 🅾 to Ill/Mich SP
247	Bluff Rd
245mm	Des Plaines River
245	Arsenal Rd, **E** 🅾 Exxon/Mobil Refinery
241	to Wilmington
241mm	Kankakee River
240	Lorenzo Rd, **E** 🆁 Valero/dsl, **W** 🆁 Mobil/pizza/dsl/scales/24hr, 🍴 River Rest., 🛏 Knights Inn
238	IL 129 S, to Wilmington (exits left from sb), Braidwood
236	IL 113, Coal City, **E** 🍴 Good Table Rest., 🅾 Chrysler/Dodge/Jeep, Fossil Rock Camping, **W** 🆁 Shell/DQ/dsl, 🍴 Egizio's, 🅾 EZ Living RV Ctr, **3 mi W** 🆁 BP, Mobil/
236	Continued
	dsl, 🍴 McDonald's, Subway
233	Reed Rd, **E** 🆁 Marathon/dsl, 🛏 Sun Motel, **W** 🅾 antiques
227	IL 53, Gardner, **E** 🆁 Casey's, 🍴 Gardner Rest., **W** 🆁 Shell/dsl
220	IL 47, Dwight, **E** 🆁 BP/Burger King/dsl, Casey's, 🔷Loves/Hardee's/dsl/scales/24hr, Marathon/Circle K/dsl/24hr, 🍴 Arby's, Dwight Chinese, Dwight Pizza, McDonald's, Pete's Rest., Subway, 🛏 Classic Motel, Super 8
217	IL 17, Dwight, **E** 🆁 Casey's, Shell/50's Rest./Circle K/dsl/24hr, 🍴 DQ, Rte 66 Rest., 🅾 Best Hardware, Doc's Drug, Family$, NAPA, ShopKO
213mm	Mazon River
209	Odell, **E** 🆁 BP, 🅾 USPO
201	IL 23, Pontiac, **0-3 mi E** 🆁 Marathon, 🍴 DQ, La Mex, 🅾 4H RV Camp (seasonal) RV Ctr, **W** truck repair

🅿 = gas   🍴 = food   🛏 = lodging   ⊙ = other   🆁🆂 = rest stop   Copyright 2014 - The Next Exit ®

↑N INTERSTATE 55 CONT'D

Exit	Services
198mm	Vermilion River
197	IL 116, Pontiac, **E** 🅿 BP/dsl, Freedom, Shell/dsl, Thornton's/dsl, 🍴 Arby's, Baby Bull's Rest., Burger King, Cafe Fontana, KFC, LJ Silver, McDonald's, Monical's Pizza, Pizza Hut Buffet, Subway, Taco Bell, Wendy's, 🛏 Comfort Inn, Fiesta Motel (1mi), Holiday Inn Express, Super 8, ⊙ 🄷, Aldi Foods, AT&T, AutoZone, Big R Store, Buick/Chevrolet, Cadillac/GMC, Dodge/Lincoln, $Tree, Firestone/auto, Ford, K-Mart, Verizon, Walgreens, Walmart/Subway, st police, **W** 🅿 FastStop
193mm	🆁🆂 **both lanes, full** ♿ **facilities,** 🅲, 🄿🄲, **litter barrels, vending, petwalk**
187	US 24, Chenoa, **E** 🅿 Casey's, Phillips 66/McDonald's/dsl, Shell/Subway/dsl, 🍴 Chenoa Family Rest., Super 8
179mm	Des Plaines River
178	Lexington, Lexington, **E** 🅿 BP/McDonalds/dsl, Freedom/dsl, **W** Chevrolet
178mm	Mackinaw River
171	Towanda, **E** 🅿 FastStop
167	Lp 55 S Veterans Pkwy, to Normal, **0-3 mi E** 🅿 BP/Circle K, Marathon/Circle K/dsl, 🍴 Applebee's, Blimpie, Biaggi's Ristorante, Bob Evans, Burger King, Carlos O'Kelly's, Chili's, Chipotle Mexican, ChuckeCheese, DQ, Fazoli's, Fiesta Ranchera Mexican, Fuji Grill, Hardee's, Jimmy John's, Krispy Kreme, Logan's Roadhouse, Lonestar Steaks, McDonald's, Noodles&Co, Olive Garden, Outback Steaks, Panera Bread, Papa John's, Papa Murphy's, Pizza Hut, Potbelly, Qdoba Mexican, Red Lobster, Schlotzsky's, Sonic, Starbucks, Steak'n Shake, Taco Bell, Wendy's, Wild Berries Rest., 🛏 Baymont Inn, Candlewood Suites, Chateau, Clarion, Comfort Suites, Courtyard, Days Inn, Hampton Inn, Holiday Inn Express, Quality Inn, Signature Inn, Super8, ⊙ 🄷, Advance Parts, Aldi Foods, AT&T, AutoZone, Barnes&Noble, Best Buy, BigLots, Cub Foods, CVS Drug, Dick's, $Tree, Fresh Mkt, Goodyear/auto, Gordman's, Hobby Lobby, Home Depot, Honda, JC Penney, Jewel-Osco, Jo-Ann Fabrics, K-Mart, Kroger, Lowe's, Macy's, Meijer/dsl, Menards, Michael's, Mitsubishi, NAPA, Office Depot, Old Navy, PetCo, Sam's Club/gas, Schnuck's Foods, Sears/auto, Target, TJ Maxx, Tuesday Morning, Tuffy, Verizon, Von Maur, Walgreens, Walmart/Subway, mall, vet, to ✈
165b a	US 51 bus, to Bloomington, **E** 🅿 BP/Circle K/24hr, Mobil/Arby's/dsl, Qik-n-EZ, Shell/Burger King/24hr, 🍴 A&W/KFC, Denny's, McDonald's, Moe's SW Grill, Pizza Hut, Smoothie King, Steak'n Shake, Subway, Uncle Tom's Pancakes, Wendy's, 🛏 Best Western, Motel 6, Super 8, ⊙ 🄷, Discount Tire, $General, $Tree, Schuncks Foods, Walgreens, to Ill St U, **W** dsl repair
164	I-39, US 51, N to Peru
163	I-74 W, to Peoria
160b a	US 150, IL 9, Market St, Bloomington, **E** 🅿 BP/Circle K, Citgo/dsl, Freedom/dsl, 🚚/Wendy's/dsl/scales/24hr, Shell/repair, TA/rest./dsl/scales/24hr/@, 🍴 Arby's, Cracker Barrel, Culver's, JJ Fish&Chicken, KFC, La Bamba, McDonald's, Popeye's, Subway, Taco Bell, 🛏 Best Inn, Days Inn, EconoLodge, Hawthorn Suites, La Quinta, Quality Suites, ⊙ 🄷, Advance Parts, Blue Beacon, Family$, **W** 🅿 Marathon/Circle K/dsl, Murphy USA/dsl, 🍴 Bob Evans, Fiesta Ranchera Mexican, Steak'n Shake/24hr, 🛏
160b a	Continued Comfort Suites, Country Inn&Suites, Fairfield Inn, Hampton Inn, Holiday Inn Express, Ramada Ltd, ⊙ Aldi Foods, Farm&Fleet, Peterbilt, Radio Shack, Walmart
157b	Lp 55 N, Veterans Pkwy, Bloomington, **E** ⊙ 🄷, to ✈
157a	I-74 E, to Indianapolis, US 51 to Decatur
154	Shirley
149	**W** 🆁🆂 **both lanes, full** ♿ **facilities,** 🅲, 🄿🄲, **litter barrels, vending, playground, petwalk**
145	US 136, **E** RV Ctr, **W** 🅿 Dixie/BP/tuckey's/dsl/scales/24hr, Shell, 🍴 McDonald's, Subway, 🛏 Super 8
140	Atlanta, **E** RV camping, **W** 🅿 Casey's, Faststop/dsl, 🍴 Country-Aire Rest., 🛏 America's Value Inn, ⊙ $General, NAPA
133	Lp 55, Lincoln, **2 mi E** ⊙ 🄷, Camp-A-While Camping
127	I-155 N, to Peoria
126	IL 10, IL 121 S, Lincoln, **0-2 mi E** 🅿 BP/Arby's, Thornton's/🚚/dsl/scales/24hr, 🍴 Burger King, Cracker Barrel, Culver's, DQ, Daphne's Rest., Hardee's, KFC/Taco Bell, LJ Silver, McDonald's, Pizza Hut, Quiznos, Rio Grande Grill, Rusty's Clubhouse, Steak'n Shake, Wendy's, 🛏 Comfort Inn, Hampton Inn, Holiday Inn Express, Super 8, ⊙ 🄷, Aldi Foods, AT&T, AutoZone, Chrysler/Dodge/Jeep, $General, $Tree, Family$, Ford/Lincoln, Kroger, O'Reilly Parts, Russell Stover, Verizon, Walgreens, Walmart/Subway
123	Lp 55, to Lincoln, **E** 🅿 Phillips 66, 🛏 Best Western, ⊙ 🄷
119	Broadwell
115	Elkhart
109	IL 123, Williamsville, **E** 🅿 Casey's, 🍴 Subway, **W** 🅿 Loves/McDonalds/dsl/scales/24hr, 🍴 Huddle House, ⊙ New Salem SHS
107mm	**weigh sta sb**
105	Lp 55, to Sherman, **W** 🅿 Casey's, 🍴 Cancun Mexican, DQ, Subway, ⊙ to Prairie Capitol Conv Ctr, Riverside Park Campground, Military Museum, hist sites, repair
103mm	🆁🆂 **sb, full** ♿ **facilities,** 🅲, 🄿🄲, **litter barrels, vending, petwalk**
102mm	Sangamon River
102mm	🆁🆂 **nb, full** ♿ **facilities,** 🅲, 🄿🄲, **litter barrels, vending, petwalk**
100b	IL 54, Sangamon Ave, Springfield, **W** 🅿 BP/Circle K, Marathon/Circle K, Murphy USA/dsl, Shell/dsl, 🍴 Arby's, Buffalo Wild Wings, Burger King, Culver's, Hickory River BBQ, McDonald's, Parkway Cafe, Ryan's, Sonic, Steak'n Shake, Taco Bell, Thai Basil, Wendy's, Wings Etc, 🛏 Northfield Suites, Ramada, ⊙ AT&T, Harley-Davidson, Lowe's, Menards, Walmart/Subway, ✈, to Vet Mem
100a	Il 54, E to Clinton, **E** 🅿 Road Ranger/🚚/Subway/dsl/scales/24hr, ⊙ Kenworth/Ryder/Volvo, truckwash
98b	I-72, IL 97, Springfield, **W** 🅿 BP/Circle K, Casey's, Shell/dsl, 🍴 Arby's, Little Caesars, McDonald's, Seafood House, Starbucks, Subway, 🛏 Best Rest Inn, Best Western, ⊙ 🄷, Ford Trucks, Goodyear, K-Mart, Walgreens, city park, to Capitol Complex
98a	I-72 E, US 36 E, to Decatur
96b a	IL 29 N, S Grand Ave, Springfield, **W** 🅿 Marathon/dsl, Road Ranger/dsl, 🍴 Burger King, Godfather's, Popeye's, 🛏 Red Roof Inn, Super 8, ⊙ Advance Parts, AutoZone, Buick/GMC, Hyundai, Isuzu, JC Penney, O'Reilly Parts, Shop'n Save, Volvo, museum
94	Stevenson Dr, Springfield, **E** KOA (7mi), **W** 🅿 BP/Circle

The left margin reads vertically: **PONTIAC · NORMAL · BLOOMINGTON** and **IL**

The right margin reads vertically: **LINCOLN · SPRINGFIELD**

▲N INTERSTATE 55 CONT'D

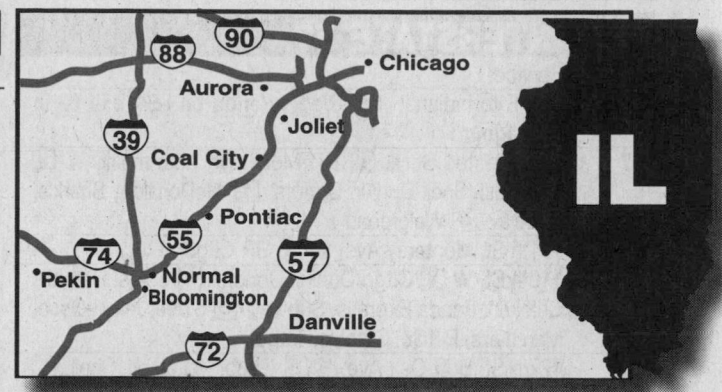

Exit	Services

SPRINGFIELD

94 Continued
K/Quiznos, Mobil/Subway/dsl, Ⓕ Antonio's Pizza, Applebee's, Arby's, Bob Evans, Cheddar's, Denny's, Di Piero's Italian, Gallina Pizza, Hardee's, Hooters, IHOP, La Fiesta Mexican, LJ Silver, McDonald's, Outback Steaks, Panera Bread, Red Lobster, Smokey Bones BBQ, Steak'n Shake, Taste of Tai, Ⓛ Candlewood Suites, Comfort Suites, Crowne Plaza, Days Inn/rest., Drury Inn, Hampton Inn, Hilton Garden, Holiday Inn Express, Microtel, Stevenson Inn, Ⓞ BigLots, CVS Drug, $General, GNC, Jo-Ann Fabrics, NAPA, Radio Shack, Walgreens, USPO, zoo (4mi)

92b a I-72 W, US 36 W, 6th St, Springfield, W Ⓐ Road Ranger/dsl, Thornton's, Ⓕ Arby's, Burger King, Chadito's Tacos, DQ, Golden Corral, Jimmy John's, KFC, McDonald's, New China, Pizza Hut, Sgt. Pepper's Cafe, Starbucks, Subway, Taco Bell, Ⓛ Route 66, Super 8, Travelodge/rest., Ⓞ Ⓗ AutoZone, CarX, County Mkt Foods, Family$, Lincoln, Mazda, Verizon, Walgreens, Walmart

90 Toronto Rd, E Ⓐ Qik-n-EZ/Wendy's/dsl, Shell/Circle K, Ⓕ Antonio's Pizza, Centrum Cafe, Cracker Barrel, China Express, McDonald's, Subway, Taco Bell, Ⓛ Baymont Inn, Motel 6, Ramada Ltd, Ⓞ Ⓗ

89mm Lake Springfield

88 E Lake Dr, Chatham, E Ⓞ to Lincoln Mem Garden/Nature Ctr, W Ⓐ JJ RV Park/camping (2mi), KOA

83 Glenarm, W JJ RV Park/camping (4mi)

82 Il 104, to Pawnee, E to Sangchris Lake SP, W Ⓐ Mobil/Auburn Trvl Ctr/Subway/scales/dsl/rest/24hr, Ⓕ Myra's Rest, Ⓞ antiques/crafts

80 Hist 66, Divernon, W Ⓞ antiques

72 Farmersville, W Ⓐ Jimmy's/Subway/dsl/24hr, Shell/24hr, Ⓛ Art's Motel/rest.

65mm Ⓡˢ both lanes, full Ⓗ facilities, Ⓒ, Ⓔ, litter barrels, vending, playground, petwalk

63 IL 48, IL 127, to Raymond

60 IL 108, to Carlinville, E Ⓞ Kamper Kampanion RV Park, truck parts, W Ⓐ Shell/dsl/LP/café, Ⓛ Magnuson Grand Hotel/cafe, Ⓞ antiques, to Blackburn Coll

56mm weigh sta nb

LITCHFIELD

52 IL 16, Hist 66, Litchfield, E Ⓐ BP, Casey's, Conoco/Jack-in-the-Box/dsl, Faststop/deli/dsl/scales, Murphy USA/dsl, Shell, Ⓕ A&W/LJ Silver, Angus Chophouse, Arby's, Ariston Café, Burger King, China Town, DQ, Denny's, Domino's, E-52 Patio N Grill, El Rancherito Mexican, Jubelt's Rest., KFC, Maverick Steaks, McDonald's, Pizza Hut, Ruby Tuesday, Taco Bell, Wendy's, Ⓛ Best Value Inn, Hampton Inn, Holiday Inn Express, Quality Inn, Super 8, Ⓞ Ⓗ Aldi Foods, AT&T, Buick/Cadillac/Chevrolet/GMC, $General, $Tree, Ford, Goodyear/auto, IGA Foods, NAPA, O'Reilly Parts, Radio Shack, Walgreens, Walmart/Subway, camping (8mi), W st police

44 IL 138, to Benld, Mt Olive, E Ⓐ Jimmy's, Ⓕ Crossroads Diner, Ⓞ Mother Jones Mon

41 to Staunton, E Country Classic Cars, W Ⓐ Casey's, Ⓕ DQ, Las Cabanas Mexican, Ⓛ Super 8, Ⓞ Ⓗ $General

37 Livingston, New Douglas, W Ⓐ BP/dsl/24hr, Ⓕ Gasperoni's Café, Ⓛ Country Inn/rest, Ⓞ IGA Foods, NAPA

33 IL 4, to Staunton, Worden, W Gas & Tires

30 IL 140, Hamel, E Innkeeper Motel, W Ⓐ Shell, Ⓕ Weezy's Grill

28mm Ⓡˢ both lanes, full Ⓗ facilities, Ⓒ, Ⓔ, litter barrels, vending, petwalk

23 IL 143, Edwardsville, E Ⓐ Phillips 66/dsl, W Red Barn Camping (apr-oct)

20b I-270 W, to Kansas City

20a I-70 E, to Indianapolis

I-55 S and I-70 W run together 18 mi

18 IL 162, to Troy, E Ⓐ Phillips 66/dsl, ⬛/Arby's/dsl/scales/24hr, TA/BP/Country Pride/dsl/scales/24hr/@, ZX, Ⓕ Burger King, China King, DQ, Domino's, Jack-in-the-Box, Little Caesar's, McDonald's/playplace, Pizza Man, Pizza Hut, Subway, Troy Rest., Ⓞ Ⓗ, Ace Hardware, $General, Speedco, SuperValu Foods, Walgreens, USPO, W Ⓐ Phillips 66/dsl/24hr, Ⓕ Callahan's Grill, Cracker Barrel, Imo's Pizza, Taco Bell, Ⓛ Congress Motel, Holiday Inn Express, Red Roof Inn, Super 8, Ⓞ Freightliner, Verizon

17 US 40 E, to Troy, to St Jacob

15b a IL 159, Maryville, Collinsville, 0-2 mi E Ⓐ Phillips 66/dsl, Shell, Zx Gas, Ⓕ Carisillo's Mexican, Fazzi's Rest., KFC, McDonald's, Sonic, Steak-Out, Ⓞ Aldi Foods, AutoZone, CVS Drug, $General, Family$, Ford/Lincoln, O'Reilly Parts, Walgreens, vet W Ⓛ EconoLodge

14mm weigh sta sb

COLLINSVILLE

11 IL 157, Collinsville, E Ⓐ Casey's, Ⓕ A&W/LJ Silver, Denny's, Golden Corral, Han's Buffet, Little Caesar's, McDonald's, Penn Sta Subs, Qdoba Mexican, St Louis Bread Co, Starbucks, Waffle House, Wendy's, Ⓛ Motel 6, Ⓞ AT&T, GNC, Home Depot, Midas, Radio Shack, Verizon, Walgreens, Walmart, W Ⓐ Motomart/dsl/24hr, Ⓕ Applebee's, Arby's, Bandana's BBQ, Bob Evans, Burger King, Culver's, DQ, Pizza Hut, Ponderosa, Ravanelli's Rest., Ruby Tuesday, Steak'n Shake, White Castle/24hr, Zapata's Mexican, Ⓛ Comfort Inn, Days Inn, DoubleTree Inn, Drury Inn, Extended Stay Suites, Fairfield Inn, Hampton Inn, Super 8, Ⓞ Buick/GMC, st police

10 I-255, S to Memphis, N to I-270

9 Black Lane (from nb, no return), E Fairmount RaceTrack

6 IL 111, Great River Rd, Fairmont City, E Ⓐ Phillips 66, Ⓛ Indian Mound Inn, Relax Inn, Royal Budget Inn, Cahokia Mounds SP, W Horseshoe SP

5mm motorist callboxes begin at 1/2 mi intervals nb

4b a IL 203, Granite City, E Ⓐ Phillips 66/dsl/24hr, Ⓛ Western Inn, W Ⓐ ⬛/Subway/Taco Bell/dsl/scales/24hr/@, Ⓕ Burger King, Ⓞ Gateway Int Raceway

3 Exchange Ave

2 I-64 E, IL 3 N, St Clair Ave

2b 3rd St

2a M L King Bridge, to downtown E St Louis

1 IL 3, to Sauget (from sb)

I-55 N and I-70 E run together 18 mi

0mm Illinois/Missouri state line, Mississippi River

Copyright 2014 - The Next Exit ®

INTERSTATE 57 (N)

CHICAGO

Exit	Services
358mm	I-94 E to Indiana. **I-57 begins/ends on I-94, exit 63 in Chicago.**
357	IL 1, Halsted St, **E** [gas] BP, Mobil, [other] auto repair, **W** [gas] Citgo/dsl, Shell/Dunkin Donuts, [food] McDonald's, Shark's, Subway, [other] Walgreens
355	111th St, Monterey Ave, **W** [gas] BP, Citgo
354	119th St, **W** [gas] Citgo/Dunkin Donuts, [food] Chili's, Harold's Chicken, Panda Express, Subway, [other] $Tree, Jewel-Osco, Marshall's, PetCo, Staples, Target
353	127th St, Burr Oak Ave, **E** [gas] Citgo, Marathon, Shell, [food] Burger King, Dillinger's Drive-In, McDonald's, Wendy's, [lodging] Motel 6, Plaza Inn, Red Roof Inn, [other] [H], Ace Hardware, Advance Parts, Aldi Foods, Family$, Walgreens, **W** [gas] BP, Citgo/dsl, [other] JJ Fish&Chicken
352mm	Calumet Sag Channel
350	IL 83, 147th St, Sibley Blvd, **E** [gas] Marathon/dsl, [food] Checker's, Dunkin Donuts, Harold's Chicken, McDonald's, Subway, [other] Aldi Foods, Family$, O'Reilly Parts, **W** [other] USPO
348	US 6, 159th St, **E** [gas] Citgo/dsl, Clark, Marathon/dsl, [food] Baskin-Robbins/Dunkin Donuts, Burger King, Harold's Chicken, McDonald's, Popeye's, Subway, Taco Bell, White Castle, [lodging] Comfort Inn, [other] AutoZone, BigLots, $Tree, Family$, U-Haul, Walgreens, auto repair, **W** [gas] Citgo/dsl, Mobil/dsl
346	167th St, Cicero Ave, to IL 50, **E** [gas] BP, Citgo/dsl, [food] Applebee's, Baskin-Robbins/Dunkin Donuts, Bee's Steaks, Harold's Chicken, McDonald's, Panda Express, Shark's Fish&Chicken, Sonic, Subway, Thom's BBQ, Wendy's, [lodging] Best Western Oak Forest, [other] Radio Shack, Verizon, Walmart/Subway, **W** [gas] Shell, [other] 7-11
345b a	I-80, W to Iowa, E to Indiana, to I-294 N **toll** to Wisconsin
342	Vollmer Rd, **E** [gas] Shell/Circle K/dsl, [other] [H]
340b a	US 30, Lincoln Hwy, Matteson, **E** [gas] BP, Citgo/dsl, [food] A&W/LJ Silver, Afusion Asian, Applebee's, Bocce's Grill, Burger King, ChuckeCheese, Cracker Barrel, Culver's, Dusties Buffet, Fuddrucker's, Hibachi Grill, IHOP, Jimmy John's, KFC, Knock-Outs Rest., McDonald's, Michael's Rest., Mr Benny's Rest., Olive Garden, Panda Express, Panera Bread, Pepe's, Perros Bros Gyros, Pizza Hut, Quiznos, Red Lobster, Shark's, Starbucks, Subway, Taco Bell, Wendy's, White Castle, [lodging] Best Value Inn, Country Inn&Suites, Hampton Inn, La Quinta, Matteson Hotel, [other] Aldi Foods, AT&T, Best Buy, Chrysler/Dodge/Jeep, Discount Tire, $Tree, Dominick's Foods, Firestone/auto, Home Depot, JC Penney, Marshall's, Menards, NTB, Old Navy, PepBoys, Prtsmart, Radio Shack, Sam's Club/gas, Sears/auto, Target, Verizon, Walgreens, Walmart, USPO, **W** [other] Buick/Cadillac/GMC, Ford/Lincoln, Honda, Hyundai, Kia, Nissan, Toyota/Scion, Walgreens
339	Sauk Trail, to Richton Park, **E** [gas] BP, Citgo/dsl, [food] Domino's, McDonald's, Uncle John's BBQ/Ribs, [other] Walgreens
335	Monee, **E** [gas] BP/Dunkin Donuts/Subway/dsl, Petro/Iron Skillet/dsl/e-85/scales/24hr/@, Pilot/McDonald's/dsl/scales/24hr, [food] Burger King, Lucky Burrito, Quiznos, Schoops Rest., [lodging] Best Western, Country Host Motel, Red Roof Inn, Super 8, [other] Blue Beacon
332mm	**Prairie View [rest stop] both lanes, full [handicapped] facilities, info, [phone], vending, [picnic], litter barrels, petwalk**
330mm	**weigh sta both lanes**
327	to Peotone, **E** [gas] Casey's, Shell/Circle K, [food] Bierstube

MATTESON

IL

BRADLEY

KANKAKEE

Exit	Services
327	Continued German, McDonald's/RV parking
322	Manteno, **E** [gas] Phillips 66/Subway, Shell/McDonald's, [food] Jimmy John's, KFC/Pizza Hut/Taco Bell, Monical's Pizza, Wendy's, [lodging] Country Inn&Suites, Howard Johnson, [other] Curves, Harley-Davidson, **W** [gas] BP/dsl
315	IL 50, Bradley, **E** [gas] F&F, Shell/Circle K/Burger King, [food] Buffalo Wild Wings, Cracker Barrel, LoneStar Steaks, McDonald's, Red Lobster, Ruby Tuesday, TGIFriday's, Tucci's Rest., White Castle, [lodging] Best Inn, Fairfield Inn, Hampton Inn, Holiday Inn Express, [other] Barnes&Noble, Best Buy, Chrysler/Dodge/Jeep, Dick's, JC Penney, Kohl's, Marshall's, Michael's, PetCo, Petsmart, Sears/auto, Staples, Target, Verizon, Walmart/Subway, mall, **W** [gas] Phillips 66/dsl, Shell/Circle K/dsl, Speedway/dsl, [food] Applebee's, Arby's, Bakers Square, Coyote Canyon, Denny's, El Campesino Mexican, IHOP, LJ Silver, Mancino's Pizza, McDonald's, Oberweis Ice Cream, Old Country Buffet, Panda Express, Pizza Hut/Taco Bell, Starbucks, Steak'n Shake, Subway, VIP's Rest., Wendy's, [lodging] Motel 6, Quality Inn, Super 8, [other] Aldi Foods, AutoZone, Brown RV Ctr, Buick/GMC, Chevrolet, $Tree, Hobby Lobby, Honda, Hyundai, Jo-Ann Fabrics, Kia, K-Mart, Lowe's, Menards, Nissan, Verizon, vet, to Kankakee River SP
312	IL 17, Kankakee, **E** [other] Twin River's Camping, **W** [gas] BP/dsl, Marathon/dsl, Shell/Circle K, [food] Cptn Hook's Fish&Chicken, McDonald's/RV parking, PoorBoy Rest., [other] [H], Advance Parts, Family$, Walgreens, auto repair
310.5mm	Kankakee River
308	US 45, US 52, to Kankakee, **E** [gas] Loves/Arby's/dsl/scales/24hr, [other] KOA (3mi), **W** [gas] Speedway/Dunkin Donuts/Subway/dsl, Gas Depot, [food] El Mexicano, KFC/Taco Bell, [lodging] Fairview Motel, Hilton Garden, [other] Aldi Foods, $Tree, Walmart/Subway, [airport]
302	Chebanse, **W** truck repair
297	Clifton, **W** [gas] Phillips 66/DQ/dsl, [food] CharGrilled Cheeseburgers
293	IL 116, Ashkum, **E** [gas] Shell/Subway/dsl, **W** [food] Loft Rest., [other] st police, tires
283	US 24, IL 54, Gilman, **E** [gas] Apollo/Marathon/dsl/scales/24hr, K&H Trkstp/BP/dsl/scales/24hr/@, Shell/dsl, [food] Burger King, DQ, McDonald's, Monical's Pizza, Red Door Rest., [lodging] Motel 6, Super 8, **W** [gas] Shell/Subway/dsl
280	IL 54, Onarga, **E** [gas] Casey's, Phillips 66, [other] USPO, **W** Lake Arrowhead RV camping
272	to Roberts, Buckley
268.5mm	**[rest stop] both lanes, full [handicapped] facilities, vending, [phone], [picnic], litter barrels, petwalk**
261	IL 9, Paxton, **0-1 mi E** [gas] Casey's, Phillips 66/dsl, [food] Hardee's, Monical's Pizza, Pizza Hut, Subway, [other] Buick/Cadillac/Chevrolet/GMC, Family$, IGA Foods, TrueValue, USPO, **W** [gas] BP, Marathon, [food] Country Garden Rest., [lodging] Paxton Inn
250	US 136, Rantoul, **0-1 mi E** [gas] BP/Circle K, Casey's/dsl, [food] Arby's, Baskin-Robbins/Dunkin Donuts, Burger King, Hardee's, KFC/Taco Bell, LJ Silver, McDonald's, Monical's Pizza, Papa John's, Red Wheel Rest., Subway, [lodging] Best Western, Days Inn, Super 8, [other] Chrysler/Dodge/Jeep, $General, Ford, NAPA, Walgreens, Walmart/Subway, camping, vet, to Chanute AFB
240	Market St, **E** [gas] Road Ranger/Pilot/McDonald's/dsl/scales, [other] D&W Lake Camping/RV Park, Kenworth/Volvo, truck/tire repair

🅝 INTERSTATE 57 CONT'D

Exit	Services
238	Olympian Dr, to Champaign, **W** 🅖 Mobil/dsl, 🍴 DQ, 🏨 Microtel, 🅞 RV/dsl repair
237b a	I-74, W to Peoria, E to Urbana
235b	I-72 W, to Decatur
235a	University Ave, to Champaign, **E** 🅗, U of Ill
232	Curtis Rd
229	to Savoy, Monticello, Tolono, **E** 🅖 Marathon/dsl
221.5mm	🆁🆂 both lanes, full ♿ facilities, 🍴, 🛆, litter barrels, vending, petwalk
220	US 45, Pesotum, **E** st police
212	US 36, Tuscola, **E** 🅖 FuelMart/dsl, **W** 🅖 Phillips 66/Circle K, 🚛/Road Ranger/dsl/scales/24hr, 🍴 Amish Land Country Buffet, Big Red Barn Rest, Burger King, DQ, Denny's, McDonald's, Monical's Pizza, Pantry Cafe, Pizza Hut, Subway, Tuscany Steaks, 🏨 Baymont Inn, Holiday Inn Express, Super 8, 🅞 Ford, IGA Foods, Radio Shack, ShopKO, Tanger Outlets/Famous Brands, Verizon
203	IL 133, Arcola, **E** 🏨 Best Western, **W** 🅖 Phillips 66/Subway/dsl, Sunrise/dsl, 🍴 DQ, Hen House, La Cazuela's Mexican, Monical's Pizza, 🏨 Arcola Inn, Comfort Inn, Knights Inn, 🅞 $General, NAPA, Rockome Gardens (5mi), city park, vet
192	CtyRd 1000 N, Rd 18
190b a	IL 16, to Mattoon, **E** 🅖 BP/dsl, 🅞 🅗, to E IL U, Fox Ridge SP, **W** 🅖 Huck's, Murphy USA/dsl, Phillips 66/Subway/dsl, 🍴 Alamo Steaks, Arby's, A&W/LJ Silver, Buffalo Wild Wings, Cody's Roadhouse, Cracker Barrel, Domino's, Don Sol Mexican, DQ, Fast Freddy's, Jumbo Buffet, KFC, Lee's Chicken, McDonald's/playplace, McHugh's, Papa Murphy's, Pizza Hut, Quiznos, Stadium Grill, Steak'n Shake, Super Jumbo Buffet, Taco Bell, Wendy's, 🏨 Baymont Inn, Comfort Suites, Days Inn, Hampton Inn, Holiday Inn Express, Super 8, 🅞 Aldi Foods, BigLots, CVS Drug, $General, $Tree, Home Depot, JC Penney, Petsmart, Sears, Staples, Verizon, Walgreens, Walmart/Subway
184	US 45, IL 121, to Mattoon, **E** 🅖 Phillips 66/Subway/dsl, **W** 🍴 McDonald's, 🏨 Budget Inn, Quality Inn, 🅞 to Lake Shelbyville
177	US 45, Neoga, **E** 🅖 FuelMart/Subway/dsl/e-85, 🅞 NAPA, **W** 🅖 Casey's (1mi), 🅞 $General
166.5mm	🆁🆂 both lanes, full ♿ facilities, vending, 🍴 s, 🛆 litter barrels, petwalk
163	I-70 E, to Indianapolis

I-57 S and I-70 W run together 6 mi

162	US 45, Effingham, **E** 🅖 Motomart, 🅞 Harley-Davidson, **W** 🅖 🚛/McDonald's/dsl/scales/24hr, 🍴 Foxx's Den Smokehouse, Subway, 🅞 Camp Lakewood (2mi), truck repair
160	IL 33, IL 32, Effingham, **E** 🍴 Domino's, Jimmy John's, LoneStar Steaks, Papa John's, Pizza Hut, 🏨 Comfort Inn, Fairfield Inn, Hampton Inn, 🅞 🅗, Aldi Foods, AutoZone, $General, Family$, K-Mart, Midas, Save-a-Lot, Verizon, vet, **W** 🅖 BP/Quiznos/dsl, ✈FLYING J/Denny's/dsl/LPscales/24hr, Marathon, Murphy USA/dsl, TA/Country Pride/Popeye's/dsl/@, 🍴 Arby's, Bangkok Thai, Buffalo Wild Wings, Burger King, Cracker Barrel, Denny's, El Rancherito Mexican, KFC, LJ Silver, McDonald's, Ryan's, Ruby Tuesday, Starbucks, Steak'n Shake, Subway, Taco Bell, TGIFriday's, Wendy's, 🏨 Country Inn&Suites, Days Inn, Hilton Garden, Holiday Inn Express, Motel 6, Rode

160	Continued way Inn, Super 8, 🅞 AT&T, Blue Beacon, Camp Lakewood RV Park, $Tree, Ford/Lincoln, Kohl's, Menards, Peterbilt, SpeedCo, Verizon, Walmart/Subway
159	US 40, Effingham, **E** 🅖 BP/dsl/24hr, Marathon/dsl, Phillips 66/dsl, 🍴 China Buffet, Culver's, Hardee's, Little Caesars, Niemerg's Rest, Subway, 🏨 Abe Lincoln Motel, Best Value Inn, Comfort Suites, EconoLodge, 🅞 O'Reilly Parts, Walgreens, tires/repair, **W** 🅖 Petro/Iron Skillet/dsl/24hr/@, 🏨 Best Western, 🅞 Blue Beacon, Truck-O-Mat/IA-80/scales/wash

I-57 N and I-70 E run together 6 mi

157	I-70 W, to St Louis
151	Watson, 5 mi **E** Percival Springs RV Park
150mm	Little Wabash River
145	Edgewood, **E** 🅖 Phillips 66
135	IL 185, Farina, **E** 🅖 BP/Subway/dsl, 🅞 $General, Ford
127	to Kinmundy, Patoka
116	US 50, Salem, **E** 🅖 Huck's/dsl, Shell/Circle K/dsl, Swifty, 🍴 Burger King, Domino's, Hardee's, La Cocina Mexican, LJ Silver, McDonald's, Pizza Hut, Pizza Man, Subway, Taco Bell, Village Garden, Wendy's, 🅞 🅗, AutoZone, Chrysler/Dodge/Jeep, CVS Drug, GMC, NAPA, O'Reilly Parts, Save-A-Lot, USPO, to Forbes SP, **W** 🅖 Murphy USA/dsl, Phillips 66/dsl, 🍴 Applebee's, Arby's, Denny's, KFC, 🏨 Comfort Inn, Guesthouse Inn, Salem Inn, Super 8, 🅞 AT&T, Buick/Chevrolet, $Tree, Ford, Salem Tires, Walmart, Carlisle Lake (23mi),
114mm	🆁🆂 both lanes, full ♿ facilities, 🍴, 🛆, litter barrels, vending, petwalk, playground
109	IL 161, to Centralia, **W** 🅖 Biggie's General Store/cafe/dsl
103	Dix, **E** 🍴 Austin's Rest, 🏨 Red Carpet Inn
96	I-64 W, to St Louis
95	IL 15, Mt Vernon, **E** 🅖 BP/dsl/24hr, Hucks, Marathon/Circle K, Phillips 66, 🍴 Agave Mexican, Bandana's BBQ, El Rancherito Mexican, Fazoli's, Grand Buffet, Hardee's, KFC, Little Caesar's, LJ Silver, McDonald's, Panda Express, Papa John's, Pizza Hut, Steak'n Shake, Subway, Taco Bell, Wendy's, Waffle Co, 🏨 Best Inn, Best Value Inn, Comfort Suites, Cozy Inn, Motel 6, Red Roof Inn, Super 8, 🅞 🅗, Aldi Foods, AutoZone, Chevrolet, CVS Drug, $Tree, Ford, Harley-Davidson, JC Penney, K-Mart, Kroger/dsl, O'Reilly Parts, Prompt Care, Radio Shack, Sears, Verizon, Walgreens, vet, **W** 🅖 Hucks/rest/dsl/scales/24hr, Marathon/Circle K, 🚛/Denny's/dsl/scales/24hr, Shell/Circle K, TA/Country Pride/Popeye's/dsl/24hr/@, 🍴 Applebee's, Arby's, Bob Evans, Buffalo Wild Wings, Burger King, Chili's, Cracker Barrel, Jimmy John's, Kriger's Grill, LoneStar Steaks, McDonald's, Ryan's, Sonic, Subway, 🏨

MATTOON   **EFFINGHAM**   **SALEM**   **MT VERNON**

🅖 = gas   🍴 = food   🛏 = lodging   🅞 = other   🆁🆂 = rest stop   Copyright 2014 - The Next Exit ®

🔼Ⓝ INTERSTATE 57 CONT'D

Exit	Services
95	Continued
	Days Inn, Fairfield Inn, Hampton Inn, Holiday Inn, Quality Inn, 🅞 Buick/Cadillac/GMC, $Tree, Freightliner, Kohl's, Lowe's, NAPA, Outlet Mall, Quality Times RV Park, Staples, Toyota, Verizon, Walmart, truckwash
94	Veteran's Memorial Dr, E 🄷
92	I-64 E, to Louisville
83	Ina, E 🅖 ⬥Loves/McDonald's/dsl/scales, Marathon/deli/dsl/scales/24hr, 🅞 Sherwood Camping (2mi), W to Rend Lake Coll
79mm	🆁🆂 sb, full ♿ facilities, info, vending, 🅒, 🗑, litter barrels, petwalk, playground
77	IL 154, to Whittington, E 🅖 Shell, 🅞 Whittington Woods RV Park, W 🍴 Gibby's Grill, 🛏 Seasons at Rend Lake Lodge/rest., 🅞 to Rend Lake, golf, Wayne Fitzgerrell SP
74mm	🆁🆂 nb, full ♿ facilities, vending, 🅒, 🗑, litter barrels, petwalk, playground
71	IL 14, Benton, E 🅖 Jumpin' Jimmy's/dsl, 🍴 Arby's, Hardee's, KFC/Taco Bell, Pizza Hut, 🛏 Days Inn/rest., Gray Plaza Motel, Super 8, 🅞 🄷, AutoZone, CVS Drug, KOA (1.5mi), O'Reilly Parts, Plaza Tire, W 🅖 BP/dsl, Murphy USA/dsl, Phillips 66/dsl/24hr, 🍴 Applebee's, Burger King, McDonald's, Subway, 🅞 Radio Shack, Verizon, Walmart, to Rend Lake
65	IL 149, W Frankfort, E 🅖 BP/dsl, Gas-4-Less, Marathon/dsl, Shell/dsl, 🍴 China Star, Dixie Cream Deli, Hardee's, La Fiesta Mexican, LJ Silver, Mike's Drive-In, Miranda's Rest., Sonic, Subway, 🛏 Gray Plaza Motel, 🅞 🄷, CarQuest, MadPricer Foods; repair, W 🅖 Casey's, 🍴 EEE BBQ, McDonald's, Pizza Hut, 🛏 Best Value Inn, 🅞 Buick/Chevrolet/GMC, $General, $Tree, K-Mart, Kroger, VF Factory Stores
59	to Herrin, Johnston City, E 🅖 ROC/dsl/e85, ZX/dsl, 🍴 DQ, McDonald's, Subway, 🅞 $General, NAPA, Sandy Drug, camping (2mi), W 🅞🄷, camping (4mi)
54 b a	IL 13, Marion, E 🅖 Phillips 66/dsl, 🍴 Arby's, Fazoli's, Hardee's, KFC, La Fiesta Mexican, LJ Silver, Papa John's, Pizza Hut, Quiznos, Subway, Tequila's Mexican, Wendy's, Western Sizzlin, 🛏 Days Inn, EconoLodge, 🅞 Aldi Foods, Advance Parts, AutoZone, Cadillac/Chevrolet, $General, Ford/Hyundai/Lincoln, Kroger/gas, Plaza Tire, Menards, Radio Shack, Sav-A-Lot Foods, Walgreens, USPO, W 🅖 Huck's/dsl, 🛢Subway/dsl/scales/24hr, 🍴 Applebee's, Asian Bistro, Backyard Burger, Bob Evans, Burger King, Hong Kong BBQ, Logan's Roadhouse, Mackie's Pizza, McAlister's Deli, McDonald's, O'Charley's, Panera Bread, Red Lobster, Ryan's, 17th St Grill, Sonic, Steak'n Shake, Taco Bell, Wok'n Roll Buffet, 🛏 Best Inn, Comfort Inn, Country Inn&Suites, Drury Inn, Fairfield Inn, Hampton Inn, Holiday Inn Express, Motel 6, Super 8, 🅞 🄷, Buick/Chevrolet/GMC, Chrysler/Dodge/Jeep, Dillard's, Harley-Davidson, Home Depot, Honda, Menards, Mercedes, Nissan, Sam's Club/gas, Sears/auto, Subaru, Target, Toyota/Scion, Verizon, Walmart/Subway, mall
53	Main St, Marion, E 🍴 DQ, 🛏 Motel Marion, 🅞🄷, Marion Camping/RV Park, NAPA, W 🅖 Motomart, 🍴 Cracker Barrel, HideOut Steaks, 🛏 Comfort Suites, Holiday Inn Express, Quality Inn
47mm	weigh sta both lanes
45	IL 148, 1 mi E 🅖 King Tut's Food/dsl, 🛏 Lake Tree Inn, 🅞 camping, dsl repair

Exit	Services
44	I-24 E to Nashville
40	Goreville Rd, E 🅞 Ferne Clyffe SP, camping, scenic overlook
36	Lick Creek Rd, W 🅞 vineyards
32mm	Trail of Tears 🆁🆂 both lanes, full ♿ facilities, info, 🅒 s, 🗑, litter barrels, vending, petwalk, playground
30	IL 146, Anna, Vienna, W 🅖 Fast Stop/dsl, 🅞🄷, auto/RV repair
25	US 51 N (from nb, exits left), to Carbondale
24	Dongola Rd, E 🅞 $General, W 🅖 BP/dsl
18	Ullin Rd, W 🅖 Fast Stop/dsl, 🍴 EEE BBQ, 🛏 Best Value Inn, 🅞 Chevrolet, st police
8	Mounds Rd, to Mound City, E 🅞 K&K AutoTruck/dsl/repair
1	IL 3, to US 51, Cairo, E 🛏 Belvedere Motel (2mi), Days Inn, 🅞 $General, Mound City Nat Cem (4mi), camping, W camping
0mm	Illinois/Missouri state line, Mississippi River

🔼Ⓔ INTERSTATE 64

Exit	Services
131.5mm	Illinois/Indiana state line, Wabash River
131mm	Skeeter Mtn Welcome Ctr wb, full ♿ facilities, 🅒, vending, 🗑, litter barrels, petwalk
130	IL 1, to Grayville, N 🅖 Casey's (2mi), Shell/dsl/24hr, 🍴 Subway, 🛏 Super 8, Windsor Oaks Inn/rest., 🅞 museum, Beall Woods St Park, S Season's Grill
124mm	Little Wabash River
117	Burnt Prairie, S 🅖 Marathon/dsl, 🍴 ChuckWagon Charlie's Café, 🅞 antiques
110	US 45, Mill Shoals
100	IL 242, to Wayne City, N 🅖 Marathon/dsl
89	to Belle River, Bluford
86mm	🆁🆂 wb, full ♿ facilities, 🅒, vending, 🗑, litter barrels, petwalk
82.5mm	🆁🆂 eb, full ♿ facilities, 🅒, vending, 🗑, litter barrels, petwalk
80	IL 37, to Mt Vernon 2 mi N 🅖 BP/Burger King/dsl/24hr, Hucks/dsl/24hr, 🛏 Royal Inn, 🅞 $General, camping
78	I-57, S to Memphis, N to Chicago
I-64 and I-57 run together 5 mi. See I-57, exits 95-94	
73	I-57, N to Chicago, S to Memphis
69	Woodlawn
61	US 51, to Centralia, Ashley
50	IL 127, to Nashville, N to Carlyle Lake, S 🅖 Citgo/rest/E-85/dsl, Little Nashville/Conoco/rest/dsl/scales/24hr, Shell/dsl/24hr, 🍴 McDonald's, 🛏 Best Western, 🅞🄷
41	IL 177, Okawville, S 🅖 🛢/Road Ranger/dsl/24hr, 🍴 Burger King, DQ, Pizza Man, Subway, 🛏 Original Springs Motel, Super 8, 🅞 $General, truck repair
37mm	Kaskaskia River
34	to Albers, 3 mi N 🅖 Casey's
27	IL 161, New Baden, N 🅖 Shell/dsl, 🍴 Good Ol Days Rest., McDonald's, Subway, 🅞 Chevrolet, $General
25mm	🆁🆂 both lanes, full ♿ facilities, info, 🅒, vending, 🗑, litter barrels, petwalk
23	IL 4, to Mascoutah, N 🅖 Mobil, 🛏 La Quinta, 3mi N 🍴 McDonald's, S 🍴
19 b a	US 50, IL 158, N 🅖 Motomart, 🍴 Schiappa's Italian, Subway, 🛏 Settle Inn, S 🅞🄷, to Scott AFB
18mm	weigh sta eb
16	to O'Fallon, Shiloh, N 🍴 Sonic, 🛏 Hilton Garden, 🅞 Urgent Care, CVS Drug, Harley-Davidson, S 🅖 Motomart/\

IL

INTERSTATE 64 CONT'D

Exit	Services
16	Continued dsl, 🍴 Applebee's, Arby's, Buffalo Wild Wings, China King, Coldstone, Cracker Barrel, 54th St. Grille, Golden Corral, Jimmy John's, Little Caesar's, McAlister's Deli, McDonald's, Qdoba Mexican, Quiznos, St. Louis Bread Co., Starbucks, TX Roadhouse, White Castle, 🛏 Drury Inn, Holiday Inn Express, Ⓞ AT&T, Dierbergs Foods, Dobb's Tire, Michael's, Radio Shack, Target, World Mkt
14	O'Fallon, **N** 🅖 Circle K, Motomart, Shell/24hr, 🍴 IHOP, Steak'n Shake/24hr, Subway, 🛏 Baymont Inn, Best Value Inn, Country Inn&Suites, Extended Stay America, Suburban Inn, Ⓞ Cadillac, Chevrolet, Ford, O'Reilly Parts, **S** 🅖 Casey's, 🍴 Chevy's Mexican, Culver's, DQ, Hardee's, Jack-in-the-Box, KFC, McDonald's, O'Charley's, Papa Murphy's, Royal Bamboo, Sake Grill, Taco Bell, 🛏 Candlewood Suites, Days Inn, Quality Inn, Ⓞ Aldi Foods, Home Depot, Honda, Hyundai, KIA, Mazda, Nissan, Petsmart, Sam's Club/gas, Toyota, VW, Walmart
12	IL 159, to Collinsville, **N** 🅖 Shell/Circle K, 🍴 Agostino's, Applebee's, Bob Evans, Houlihan's, Joe's Crabshack, Lotawata Creek Grill, Olive Garden, Red Lobster, TGIFriday's, 🛏 Best Western, Comfort Suites, Drury Inn, Fairfield Inn, Hampton Inn, Holiday Inn, Ramada Inn, Sheraton, Super 8, Ⓞ Fiat, Gordman's, **S** 🅖 BP, Motomart/dsl, 🍴 Arby's, Boston Mkt, Burger King, Capt D's, Casa Gallardo, Cheddar's, Chili's, Chipotle Mexican, ChuckE-Cheese, Domino's, Fazoli's, 5 Guys Burgers, Haley's Grill, Hometown Buffet, Honeybaked Ham, Imo's Pizza, Krispy Kreme, Logan's Roadhouse, Longhorn Steaks, LJ Silver, McAlister's Deli, McDonald's, Pizza Hut, Popeye's, Qdoba Mexican, Quiznos, Red Robin, Ruby Tuesday, Smokey Bones BBQ, Steak'n Shake, St. Louis Bread, Subway, Taco Bell, White Castle, Ⓞ Aamco, AT&T, Barnes&Noble, Best Buy, BigLots, Dillard's, Dobb's Tire, $Tree, Firestone/auto, Hobby Lobby, JC Penney, Jo-Ann Fabrics, K-Mart, Kohl's, Lowe's, Macy's, Marshall's, NTB, Office Depot, Old Navy, O'Reilly Parts, PetCo, Russell Stover, Schnuck's Foods, Sears/auto, TJ Maxx, Verizon, Walgreens, USPO
9	IL 157, to Caseyville, **N** 🅖 Huck's/dsl, Phillips 66/Subway/repair, 🍴 Jade Garden, 🛏 Western Inn, **S** 🍴 BP/dsl/repair, 🍴 Cracker Barrel, DQ, Domino's, McDonald's, Pizza Hut/Taco Bell, 🛏 Best Inn, Days Inn, Motel 6, Quality Inn
7	I-255, S to Memphis, N to Chicago
6	IL 111, Kingshighway, **N** 🅖 BP, Mobil/24hr, 🍴 Popeye's, 🛏 Econo Inn
5	25th St
4	15th St, Baugh
3	I-55 N, I-70 E, IL 3 N, to St Clair Ave, to stockyards
2b a	3rd St, **S** gas
1	IL 3 S, 13th St, E St Louis, **N** Casino Queen
0mm	Illinois/Missouri state line, Mississippi River

INTERSTATE 70

Exit	Services
156mm	Illinois/Indiana state line
154	US 40 W
151mm	weigh sta wb
149mm	🅡 wb, full 🚻 facilities, info, 🕿, 🖼, vending, litter barrels, petwalk

Exit	Services
147	IL 1, Marshall, **S** 🅖 Casey's (1mi), Jiffy/dsl/24hr, Marathon/Arby's/dsl, 🍴 Burger King, Los Tres Caminos, McDonald's, Pizza Hut, Sam's Steaks, Subway, Wendy's, 🛏 Lincoln Suites, Relax Inn, Super 8, Ⓞ Ford, Walmart, Lincoln Trail SP, antiques, camping
136	to Martinsville, **S** 🅖 Fast Stop/dsl/24hr
134.5mm	N Fork Embarras River
129	IL 49, Casey, **N** Ⓞ RV service, KOA (seasonal), **S** 🅖 BP/Subway/dsl, Casey's, Fast Stop/DQ, Marathon/Circle K/dsl, 🍴 Hardee's, McDonald's, Pizza Hut, 🛏 Comfort Inn, Ⓞ IGA Foods
119	IL 130, Greenup, **S** 🅖 Casey's, Marathon/dsl, 🍴 Backyard BBQ, Dandy Kitchen, DQ, Subway, 🛏 Budget Host, Greenup Motel, Ⓞ $General, camping, hist sites
105	Montrose, **N** Ⓞ Spring Creek Camping (1mi), **S** 🅖 BP/dsl, Marathon/dsl/24hr, 🛏 Fairview Inn, Red Carpet Inn
98	I-57, N to Chicago
I-70 and I-57 run together 6 mi. See Interstate 57, exits 159-162.
92	I-57, S to Mt Vernon
91mm	Little Wabash River
87mm	🅡 both lanes, full 🚻 facilities, info, 🕿 vending, 🖼, litter barrels, playground, petwalk, RV dump
82	IL 128, Altamont, **N** 🅖 Casey's, Jumpin Jimmy's/Subway/dsl/24hr, Marathon/dsl, 🍴 Dairy Bar, McDonald's, 🛏 Altamont Motel, Ⓞ city park, **S** 🛏 Super 8
76	US 40, St Elmo, **N** 🅖 Casey's, 🛏 Waldorf Motel, Ⓞ Timberline Camping (2mi)
71mm	weigh sta eb
68	US 40, Brownstown, **N** Ⓞ Okaw Valley Kamping, **S** truck repair
63.5mm	Kaskaskia River
63	US 51, Vandalia, **N** 🍴 Chuck Wagon Cafe, LJ Silver, 🛏 Days Inn, **S** 🅖 BP/Burger King/24hr, Casey's, Phillips 66, 🍴 Arby's, China Buffet, DQ, McDonald's, Pizza Hut, Rancho Nuevo Mexican, Sonic, Subway, Wendy's, 🛏 Jay's Inn, Travelodge, Ⓞ H, Aldi Foods, County Mkt Foods, city park, hist site
61	US 40, Vandalia, **N** 🅖 Fast Stop/Denny's/dsl/scales/24hr, **S** 🅖 Murphy USA/dsl, 🍴 KFC/Taco Bell, Ponderosa, 🛏 Holiday Inn Express, Ramada Ltd, Ⓞ AutoZone, Verizon, Walmart
52	US 40, Mulberry Grove, **N** 🅖 Jumpin Jimmy's/dsl, Ⓞ Timber Trail Camp-In (2mi), tires, **S** Cedar Brook Camping (1mi)
45	IL 127, Greenville, **N** 🅖 Jumpin Jimmy's/Domino's/dsl, Loves/Subway/dsl/scales/24hr, Shell/dsl/24hr, 🍴 Cunetto's Rest., Huddle House, KFC/Taco Bell, Lu-Bob's Rest., McDonald's, 🛏 EconoLodge, M Hotel, Super 8, 2 Acre Motel, Ⓞ H, Ford, **S** 🍴 La Hacienda Mexican, 🛏

⛽ INTERSTATE 70 CONT'D

Exit	Services
45	Continued
	Sleep Inn, Ⓞ American Farm Heritage Museum, RV Service, to Carlyle Lake
41	US 40 E, to Greenville
36	US 40 E, Pocahontas, **S** 🅖 Marathon/dsl/24hr, Phillips 66/dsl/24hr, 🍴 Funderburks Grill, 🛏 Lighthouse Lodge, Powhatan Motel/rest., Tahoe Motel, Ⓞ truck/tire repair
30	US 40, IL 143, to Highland, **S** 🅖 Shell/dsl/wi-fi/24hr, 🍴 Blue Springs Café, Ⓞ 🄷 Tomahawk RV Park (7mi)
26.5mm	**Silver Lake** 🆁🆂 **both lanes, full** ♿ **facilities,** 🚰, 🏕, **litter barrels, vending, petwalk**
24	IL 143, Marine, **4 mi S** 🍴 Ponderosa, 🛏 Holiday Inn Express, Ⓞ 🄷
21	IL 4, Lebanon
15b a	I-55, N to Chicago, S to St Louis, I-270 W to Kansas City
	I-70 and I-55 run together 18 mi. See Interstate 55, exits 1-18.
0mm	Illinois/Missouri state line, Mississippi River

⛽ INTERSTATE 72

Exit	Services
183mm	**1 mi E on University** 🅖 Thornton's/dsl, 🍴 Arby's, Burger King, La Bamba Mexican, McDonald's, Monical's Pizza, Original Pancakes, Pizza Hut, Sonic, Taco Bell, Taffie's Rest., TX Roadhouse, Village Inn Pizza, Ⓞ Advance Parts, Aldi Foods, AutoZone, CVS Drug, County Mkt Foods, Schnuck's Foods/gas, Walgreens
182b a	I-57, N to Chicago, S to Memphis, to I-74
176	IL 47, to Mahomet
172	IL 10, Clinton
169	White Heath Rd
166	IL 105 W, Market St, **N** Ford, Ⓞ 🄷, **S** 🅖 Mobil/Subway/dsl, 🍴 Red Wheel Rest., 🛏 Best Western, Foster Inn, Ⓞ city park, railway museum
165mm	Sangamon River
164	Bridge St, **1 mi S** 🅖 Mobil/dsl, 🍴 China Star, DQ, Hardee's, McDonald's, Monical's Pizza, Pizza Hut, Subway, Ⓞ 🄷, Buick/Chevrolet, Chrysler/Dodge/Jeep, $General, USPO
156	IL 48, to Weldon, Cisco, **S** Friends Creek Camping (may-oct) (3mi)
153mm	🆁🆂 **both lanes, full** ♿ **facilities,** 🚰, 🏕, **litter barrels, vending, petwalk**
152mm	Friends Creek
150	Argenta
144	IL 48, Oreana, **S** 🅖 ⛽/McDonald's/Subway/dsl/scales/24hr, 🛏 Sleep Inn, Ⓞ 🄷, Chrysler/Dodge, Honda, Hyundai, Tressley RV Ctr
141b a	US 51, Decatur, **N** 🅖 Shell/Circle K, 🍴 Applebee's, Buffalo Wild Wings, Cheddar's, Cracker Barrel, HomeTown Buffet, McDonald's, Mi Jalapeno, O'Charley's, Pizza Hut, Red Lobster, Steak'n Shake, Subway, Taco Bell, TX Roadhouse, 🛏 Baymont Inn, Country Inn&Suites, Fairfield Inn, Hampton Inn, Homewood Suites, Quality Inn, Ramada Ltd, Welcome Hotel, Ⓞ AT&T, Bergner's, Best Buy, Bon-Ton, Buick/Cadillac/GMC, $Tree, Harley-Davidson, JC Penney, Lowe's, Kohl's, Menards, Petsmart, Sears/auto, Staples, Von Maur, Verizon, mall, **S** 🍴 Arby's, Burger King, El Rodeo Mexican, Fuji Japanese, Monical's Pizza, Olive Garden, Panera Bread, Papa Murphy's, Starbucks,

Exit	Services
141b a	Continued
	Ⓞ 🄷, Jo-Ann Fabrics, Radio Shack, Sam's Club, Target, Verizon, Walgreens, Walmart/Subway
138	IL 121, Decatur, **S** 🄷
133b a	US 36 E, US 51, Decatur, **S** 🅖 Phillips 66/Subway/dsl, 🛏 Best Value Inn, Decatur Hotel/rest.
128	Niantic
122	to Mt Auburn, Illiopolis, **N** 🅖 FastStop/dsl
114	Buffalo, Mechanicsburg, **S** 🅖 Gas Depot/dsl (2mi), Ⓞ USPO
108	Riverton, Dawson
107mm	Sangamon River
104	Camp Butler, **2 mi N** 🛏 Best Rest Inn, Best Western, Lincoln Inn, Park View Motel, 🍴 Arby's, McDonald's, Starbucks, Ⓞ golf
103b a	I-55, N to Chicago, S to St Louis, Il 97, to Springfield
	I-72 and I-55 run together 6 mi. See Interstate 55, exits 92-98.
96	MacArthur Blvd, **N** 🍴 Quaker Steak, Ⓞ Scheels
93	IL 4, Springfield, **N** 🅖 Hucks, Thorntons/dsl, 🍴 Applebee's, Arby's, Bakers Square, Burger King, Cara BBQ, Chili's, Chipotle Mexican, Denny's, Ginger Asian, Hickory River, LoneStar Steaks, Longhorn Steaks, Los Rancheros Mexican, McDonald's, Noodles&Co, Olive Garden, Panda Express, Panera Bread, Sonic, Starbucks, Subway, Taco Bell, TGIFriday's, TX Roadhouse, Wendy's, 🛏 Courtyard, Fairfield Inn, Quality Inn, Sleep Inn, Ⓞ AT&T, Barnes&Noble, Best Buy, County Mkt Foods, Dick's, Discount Tire, Gordman's, Jo-Ann Fabrics, K-Mart, Kohl's, Lowe's, Menards, Michael's, Office Depot, Old Navy, PetCo, Petsmart, Sam's Club/gas, Sears/auto, Staples, St Fair Camping, Target, TJ Maxx, Verizon, Walgreens, Walmart, vet, **S** 🅖 Meijer/dsl/E85, 🍴 Bob Evans, Monical's Pizza, O'Charley's, Steak'n Shake, 🛏 Hampton Inn, Staybridge Suites, Ⓞ Cadillac, Chevrolet, Chrysler/Jeep, Fiat, Ford, Gander Mtn, Honda
91	Wabash Ave, to Springfield, **N** 🅖 Quik'n EZ, 🍴 Bella Milano, Buffalo Wild Wings, Culver's, Firehouse Subs, IHOP, Mimosa Thai, Ⓞ Kia, Nissan, Toyota, **S** Colmans RV Ctr
82	New Berlin, **S** 🅖 Phillips 66/Subway/dsl, Ⓞ $General
76	IL 123, to Ashland, Alexander
68	to IL 104, to Jacksonville, **2 mi N** 🅖 BP, Ⓞ 🄷
64	US 67, to Jacksonville, **N** 🅖 Clark/Quiznos/dsl/e-85, 🛏 Comfort Inn, Holiday Inn Express, Ⓞ 🄷, Hopper RV Ctr, **2 mi N** 🅖 BP/Circle K/dsl, Casey's, FastStop, 🍴 DQ, KFC, McDonald's, Ⓞ 🄷, CVS Drug, $General, Family$, Walgreens
60	to US 67 N, to Jacksonville, **6 mi N on IL 104** 🄷, gas, food, lodging
52	to IL 106, Winchester, **N** golf, **2 mi S** gas, food, lodging
46	IL 100, to Bluffs
42mm	Illinois River
35	US 54, IL 107, to Pittsfield, Griggsville, **4 mi N** gas, food, lodging, **S** Ⓞ 🄷, Jellystone Camping (6mi), st police
31	to Pittsfield, New Salem, **5 mi S** 🄷, gas, food, lodging, Jellystone Camping
20	IL 106, Barry, **S** 🅖 FastStop/dsl/24hr, Shell/dsl, 🍴 Rodger's St Cafe (1mi), Wendy's, Ⓞ antiques, winery
10	IL 96, to Payson, Hull
4a	I-172, N to Quincy
1	IL 106, to Hull
0mm	Illinois/Missouri state line, Mississippi River.
	Exits 157 & 156 are in Missouri.
157	to Hannibal, MO 179, **S** 🅖 Ayerco, BP, Phillips 66, Shell/

🏫 INTERSTATE 72 CONT'D

Exit	Services
157	Continued
	dsl, 🍴 Mark Twain Dinette, Subway, 🏨 Best Value Inn, Best Way Inn, Hotel Mark Twain, 🅾 auto repair, visitor info
156	US 61, New London, Palmyra. **I-72 begins/ends in Hannibal, MO on US 61.**, N 🅿 BP, Conoco/dsl, Murphy USA/dsl, 🍴 Burger King, Country Kitchen, Domino's, Golden Corral, Hardee's, LJ Silver, Maya Mexican, McDonald's, Mi Mexico, Pizza Hut, Royal Garden, Sonic, Subway, Taco Bell, 🅾 Aldi Foods, BigLots, $General, $Tree, Ford, JC Penney, Kroger, Lowe's, Radio Shack, Walmart, **0-2 mi S** 🅿 Ayerco, Shell/dsl, 🍴 Cassano's Subs, DQ, Gran Rio Mexican, Hardee's, Joe's Diner, KFC, Logue's Rest, Papa John's, Wendy's, 🏨 Days Inn, EconoLodge, Hannibal Inn, Holiday Inn Express, Mark Twain Motel, Motel 6, Super 8, 🅾 AutoZone, Buick/Chevrolet, Chrysler/Dodge/Jeep, County Mkt Foods, $General, Family$, Injun Joe's RV Camp, O'Reilly Parts, Walgreens

🏫 INTERSTATE 74

Exit	Services
221mm	Illinois/Indiana state line, Central/Eastern Time Zone
220	Lynch Rd, Danville, N 🅿 BP/dsl, Marathon/dsl (1mi), 🍴 Big Boy, 🏨 Best Western, Comfort Inn, Danville Inn, Fairfield Inn, Hampton Inn, Holiday Inn Express, Sleep Inn, Super 8
216	Bowman Ave, Danville, N 🅿 Mobil/dsl, Phillips 66/dsl, 🍴 Godfather's, KFC, 🅾 city park
215b a	US 150, IL 1, Gilbert St, Danville, N 🅿 BP, Casey's/dsl, Circle K/dsl, 🍴 Arby's, El Toro, La Potosina, LJ Silver, McDonald's, Pizza Hut, Steak'n Shake, Subway, Taco Bell, 🏨 Best Western, Days Inn, 🅾🏨 Aldi Foods, BigLots, Ford/Lincoln, S 🅿 Casey's/dsl, Marathon/Circle K/dsl, 🍴 Burger King, Green Jade Chinese, Mike's Grill, Monical's Pizza, Rich's Rest., 🅾 AutoZone, Big R, Buick/Chevrolet/GMC, $General, Family$, Forest Glen Preserve Camping (11mi), Toyota/Scion
214	G St, Tilton
210	US 150, MLK Dr, **2 mi N** 🅿 Marathon, 🍴 Little Nugget Steaks, 🅾🏨 to Kickapoo SP, S 🍴 PossumTrot Rest.
208mm	**Welcome Ctr wb, full 🏨 facilities, info, 🚻 s, 🅿, litter barrels, vending, petwalk**
206	Oakwood, S 🅿 Phillips 66/Subway/dsl/scales, Casey's (1mi), Oakwood TP/Shell/rest/dsl/scales/24hr, 🍴 McDonald's, 🅾 $General
200	IL 49 N, to Rankin
197	IL 49 S, Ogden, S 🅿 Phillips 66/Godfather's/dsl, 🍴 Rich's Rest., 🅾 city park
192	St Joseph, S 🍴 DQ, Monical's Pizza, 🅾 antiques
185	IL 130, University Ave
184	US 45, Cunningham Ave, Urbana, N 🅿 F&F, 🅾 Hyundai, Kia, Mazda, Toyota/Scion, VW, S 🅿 Marathon/Circle K/Subway/dsl, Shell, 🍴 Arby's, Cracker Barrel, Domino's, El Toro, Hickory River BBQ, McDonald's, MT Mike's Steaks, Steak'n Shake, 🏨 Eastland Suites, Motel 6, 🅾 $General, auto repair, vet
183	Lincoln Ave, Urbana, S 🅿 Circle K/dsl, Marathon/Circle K/dsl, Mobil/dsl, 🍴 Urbana Garden Rest., 🏨 Comfort Suites, Holiday Inn/rest., Holiday Inn Express, Ramada Inn, Sleep Inn, Super 8, 🅾🏨 Harley-Davidson, to U of IL
182	Neil St, Champaign, N 🍴 Alexander's Steaks, Bob Evans,

Exit	Services
182	Continued
	Chevy's Mexican, Food Court, McAlister's Deli, McDonald's, Old Chicago, Olive Garden, Panera Bread, Taco Bell, Zia's Italian, 🏨 Baymont Inn, La Quinta, Quality Inn, Red Roof Inn, Super 8, 🅾 Barnes&Noble, Bergner's, Cadillac/Chevrolet, Chrysler/Dodge/Jeep, Hobby Lobby, Gordman's, JC Penney, Kohl's, Macy's, Mercedes/Volvo, Office Depot, Old Navy, Sears/auto, TJ Maxx, mall, same as 181, S 🅿 Mobil, 🅾 Jo-Ann Fabrics
181	Prospect Ave, Champaign, N 🅿 Meijer/dsl, Murphy USA/dsl, 🍴 Applebee's, Best Wok, Buffalo Wild Wings, Burger King, Chili's, China Town, Culver's, Fazoli's, Hometown Buffet, LoneStar Steaks, Longhorn Steaks, O'Charley's, Oishi Asain, Outback Steaks, Panda Express, Penn Sta Subs, Red Lobster, Ruby Tuesday, Ryan's, Starbucks, Steak'n Shake, Subway, Wendy's, 🏨 Candlewood Suites, Country Inn&Suites, Courtyard, Drury Inn, Extended Stay America, Fairfield Inn, ValuePlace Hotel, Wingate Inn, 🅾 Advance Parts, AT&T, Best Buy, Dick's, $Tree, Lowe's, Menards, Michael's, Petsmart, Radio Shack, Sam's Club/gas, Staples, Target, Tires+, Walmart/Subway, same as 182, S 🅿 Freedom/dsl, Marathon/Circle K, Mobil/Jimmy John's, 🍴 Arby's, Dos Reales Mexican, Dunkin Donuts, LJ Silver, 🏨 Days Inn, EconoLodge, 🅾 CarX, $General, Home Depot, NAPA, Tire Barn, Walgreens
179b a	I-57, N to Chicago, S to Memphis
174	Lake of the Woods Rd, Prairieview Rd, N 🅿 BP, Casey's, Mobil/dsl, 🅾 Tin Cup RV Park, Lake of the Woods SP, auto repair, S 🅿 Marathon/Subway/dsl, 🍴 McDonald's
172	IL 47, Mahomet, N 🅾 R&S RV Sales, S 🅿 BP/dsl, Mobil/dsl, Shell/Domino's/dsl, 🍴 Azteca, Arby's, DQ, HenHouse Rest., Jr's Burgers&Custard, Los Zarapes, Monical's Pizza, Peking House, Subway, The Wok, 🏨 Heritage Inn, 🅾 Ace Hardware, CVS Drug, IGA Foods, NAPA, Walgreens, vet
166	Mansfield, S 🅿 BP/dsl, 🅾 Mansfield Gen. Store/Rest.
159	IL 54, Farmer City, S 🅿 Casey's, Huck's/Quiznos/dsl, 🍴 Family Rest., 🏨 Budget Motel, Days Inn, 🅾 NAPA, USPO, to Clinton Lake RA
156mm	🆁🆂 both lanes, full 🏨 facilities, 🚻, 🅿, litter larrels, vending, playground, petwalk
152	US 136, to Heyworth
149	Le Roy, N 🅿 BP, Freedom/dsl, ♥Love's/Arby's/dsl/scales/24hr, 🍴 Jack's Cafe, McDonald's, Roma Ralph's Pizza, Subway, 🏨 Holiday Inn Express, 🅾 Doc's Drug, $General, IGA Foods, NAPA, TrueValue, to Moraine View SP, S 🅿 Shell/Woody's Rest./dsl/scales/24hr, 🏨 Red Roof Inn, 🅾 Clinton Lake, camping
142	Downs, N 🅿 BP/Pizza/Subs/dsl/24hr, 🅾 USPO

Side markers: **DANVILLE** (left margin), **CHAMPAIGN** (center), **IL** (right)

INTERSTATE 74 CONT'D

Exit	Services
B L O O M I N G T O N	
135	US 51, Bloomington, **N** 🚽 BP/Circle K/dsl, Huck's/dsl, Mobil/dsl, 🍴 McDonald's, 🅾 $General, **S** 🚽 FastStop/dsl
134b[157]	Veterans Pkwy, Bloomington, **N** 🅾 🅷, to ✈
134a	I-55, N to Chicago, S to St Louis, I-74 E
	I-74 and I-55 run together 6 mi. See Interstate 55, exits 157b-160b a
127[163]	I-55, N to Chicago, S to St Louis, I-74 W to Peoria
125	US 150, to Bloomington, Mitsubishi Motorway
123mm	weigh sta wb
122mm	weigh sta eb
120	Carlock, **N** 🚽 BP/dsl/repair, 🍴 Carlock Rest., **S** Kamp Komfort Camping (Apr-Oct)
114.5mm	🆁🆂 **both lanes, full** ♿ **facilities, vending,** 🅲, 🅰, **litter barrels, petwalk**
113.5mm	Mackinaw River
112	IL 117, Goodfield, **N** 🚽 Shell/Subway/dsl, 🍴 Busy Corner Rest., 🅾 to Timberline RA, Jellystone Camping (1mi), Eureka Coll, Reagan Home
102b a	Morton, **N** 🚽 BP/rest/dsl, Mobil/Arby's/dsl/scales/24hr, 🍴 Burger King, Pizza Ranch, Cracker Barrel, Culver's, Hardee's, Ruby Tuesday, Steak'n Shake, Subway, Taco Bell, 🛏 Baymont Inn, Best Western, Days Inn, Holiday Inn Express, Quality Inn, Travelodge, 🅾 Freightliner, Walmart, **S** 🚽 Marathon/Circle K, Shell/Subway/dsl/24hr, 🍴 China Dragon, KFC, La Fiesta, Lin's Buffet, McDonald's, Monical's Pizza, 🅾 Chrysler/Dodge/Jeep, Curves, CVS Drug, $Tree, Ford, GMC, K-Mart, Kroger, O'Reilly Parts
101	I-155 S, to Lincoln
99	I-474 W ✈
98	Pinecrest Dr
96	95c (from eb), US 150, IL 8, E Washington St, E Peoria, **N** 🚽 Fast Stop, 🍴 Monical's Pizza, 🛏 Super 8, 🅾 O'Reilly Parts
95b	IL 116, to Metamora, **N** 🚽 Shell/dsl, 🍴 Burger King, 🛏 Hampton Inn, Paradise Hotel, 🅾 casino
95a	N Main St, Peoria, **S** 🚽 BP/24hr, 🍴 A&W/LJ Silver, Bob Evans, China Buffet, Firehouse Pizza, Grand Village Buffet, Godfather's Pizza, Hardee's, IHOP, Jimmy John's, Subway, Taco Bell, 🛏 Holiday Inn Express, Motel 6, 🅾 Aldi Foods, Advance Parts, Costco/gas, Curves, CVS Drug, Goodyear/auto, Kohl's, Kroger, Walgreens
P E O R I A	
94	IL 40, RiverFront Dr, **S** 🚽 Hucks/Godfather's/24hr, 🍴 Applebee's, Arby's, Buffalo Wild Wings, Chili's, Culver's, Grant City Grill, Logan's Roadhouse, Lorena's Mexican, Ming's Rest., Panera Bread, Papa John's, Quiznos, Schlotzky's, Steak'n Shake, TGIFriday's, TX Roadhouse, 🛏 Embassy Suites, 🅾 Lowe's, PetsMart, Radio Shack, Verizon, Walmart/Subway
93.5mm	Illinois River
93b	US 24, IL 29, Peoria, **N** 🚽 BP, **S** civic ctr
93a	Jefferson St, Peoria, **N** 🚽 BP, **S** 🍴 Chicago Grill, 🛏 Holiday Inn, Mark Twain Hotel, 🅾 to civic ctr
92b	Glendale Ave, Peoria, **S** 🅾 🅷, downtown
92a	IL 40 N, Knoxville Ave, Peoria, **S** 🛏 Holiday Inn, 🅾 🅷
91	University St, Peoria
90	Gale Ave, Peoria, **S** 🚽 Marathon, 🍴 Firehouse Pizza, 🅾 to Bradley U
89	US 150, War Memorial Dr, Peoria, **N on War Memorial** 🚽 BP/Circle K, Marathon/dsl, Shell, 🍴 Arby's, Avanti's

Exit	Services
89	Continued
	Rest., Baskin-Robbins/Dunkin Donuts, Beef O'Brady's, Bob Evans, Brickhouse Grille, Burger King, Chuck-eCheese, Hometown Buffet, IHOP, McDonald's, Mickie's Pizza, Panera Bread, Perkins/24hr, Pizza Hut, Red Lobster, Ruby Tuesday, Schlotsky's, Sonic, Steak'n Shake, Subway, Wendy's, 🛏 Baymont Inn, Comfort Suites, Courtyard, Extended Stay America, Grand Hotel, Jamison Inn, Red Roof Inn, Residence Inn, Sleep Inn, SpringHill Suites, Super 8, 🅾 AutoZone, Barnes&Noble, Best Buy, Cadillac, Chevrolet, Cub Foods, Hobby Lobby, JC Penney, Lowe's, Macy's, Michael's, NAPA, PetsMart, Sears/auto, Target, Tires+, U-Haul, Verizon, Walgreens, Walmart, mall, vet
88	to US 150, War Memorial Dr, same as 89
87b a	I-474 E, IL 6, N to Chillicothe, **E** ✈
82	Edwards Rd, Kickapoo, **N** 🚽 Mobil/dsl/service, Shell/Subway/dsl, 🍴 Jubilee Café, 🅾 to Jubilee Coll SP, **S** 🅾 USPO, Wildlife Prairie SP
75	Brimfield, Oak Hill, **N** 🚽 Casey's
71	to IL 78, to Canton, Elmwood
62mm	🆁🆂 **both lanes, full** ♿ **facilities,** 🅲, 🅰, **litter barrels, vending, petwalk**
61.5mm	Spoon River
54	US 150, IL 97, Lewistown, **N** 🅾 TravL Park Camping (1mi), **S** 🚽 Mobil/dsl (2mi)
51	Knoxville, **S** 🚽 BP/dsl, Phillips 66/Charley's Subs/dsl/scales, 🍴 Hardee's/24hr, McDonald's, 🛏 Super 8
G A L E S B U R G	
48b a	E Galesburg, Galesburg, **N** 🛏 Best Western, 🅾 Harley-Davidson, **S** 🚽 Beck's, BP/Circle K, HyVee/dsl, Mobil/dsl, 🍴 DQ, KFC, Hardee's, Jalisco Mexican, McDonald's, Pizza Hut, Subway, Taco Bell, 🛏 Holiday Inn Express, 🅾 Family$, Firestone, Goodyear, HyVee Foods, Sav-A-Lot Foods, Walgreens, to Sandburg Birthplace, Lincoln-Douglas Debates
46b a	US 34, to Monmouth, **N** 🅾 Nichol's dsl Service, **S** 🅾 🅷, 1 mi **S** 🍴 Buffalo Wild Wings, Chinese Buffet, Pepperonis Pizza, 🅾 Menards, Verizon, Walmart, vet
32	IL 17, Woodhull, **N** 🚽 BP/dsl, Shell/dsl/e-85/scales, 🍴 Homestead Rest., Subway, **S** 🅾 Shady Lakes Camping (8mi)
30mm	🆁🆂 **wb, full** ♿ **facilities, vending,** 🅰, **litter barrels,** 🅲 **s, playground, petwalk, RV dump**
28mm	🆁🆂 **eb, full** ♿ **facilities, vending,** 🅰, **litter barrels,** 🅲 **s, playground, petwalk, RV dump**
24	IL 81, Andover, **N** 🚽 Casey's (2mi), camping
14mm	I-80, E to Chicago, I-80/I-280 W to Des Moines
8mm	weigh sta wb
6mm	weigh sta eb
M O L I N E	
5b	US 6, Moline, **S** 🚽 Shell/dsl, 🍴 McDonald's, MT Jack's, 🛏 Best Inn, Country Inn&Suites, Days Inn, Hampton Inn, La Quinta, Motel 6, Ramada Inn, 🅾 ✈
5a	I-280 W, US 6 W, to Des Moines
4b a	IL 5, John Deere Rd, Moline, **N** 🚽 BP, Phillips 66, Shell/dsl, 🍴 Applebee's, Burger King, Carlos O'Kelly's, Culver's, Hungy Hobo, Panda Buffet, Panera Bread, Ryan's, Starbucks, Steak'n Shake, Subway, Wendy's, 🛏 Residence Inn, 🅾 Cadillac, Curves, $Tree, Lowe's, Radio Shack, Staples, Subaru, Tires+, Toyota/Scion, Volvo, Walmart, **S** 🚽 BP, 🍴 A&W/LJ Silver, Arby's, Buffalo Wild Wings, Denny's, IHOP, KFC, McDonald's, Miss Mamie's, New Mandarin Chinese, Qdoba Mexican, Taco Bell, Wen

⬆️E INTERSTATE 74 CONT'D

Exit	Services
4b a	Continued
	dy's, 🏨 Best Western, Comfort Inn, Fairfield Inn, Super 8, ⊙ Best Buy, Buick/GMC, Chevrolet, Dillards, $General, Firestone/auto, Ford/Lincoln, Goodyear/auto, Gordman's, Hancock Fabrics, JC Penney, Mazda, Nissan, Old Navy, PetCo, Sears/auto, Von Maur, Walgreens, Younkers, mall
3	23rd Ave, Moline, N 🏨 Economy Inn
2	7th Ave, Moline, S 🅿️ Cenex, ⊙ USPO, to civic ctr, riverfront
1	3rd Ave (from eb), Moline, S 🅿️ Cenex, 🏨 Stoney Creek Inn
0mm	Illinois/Iowa state line, Mississippi River. **Exits 4-1 are in Iowa.**
4	US 67, Grant St, State St, Bettendorf, N 🅿️ BP, Phillips 66/dsl, Shell, 🍴 Ross' Rest./24hr, Subway, 🏨 Traveler Motel, Twin Bridges Motel, ⊙ CarQuest, S 🍴 Village Inn Rest., 🏨 City Ctr Motel, ⊙ $General
3	Middle Rd, Locust St, Bettendorf, S 🅿️ BP, 🍴 China Taste, Grinders Rest., McDonald's, Starbucks, Subway, 🏨 Holiday Inn, ⊙ H, Hobby Lobby, Home Depot, Marshall's, Schuck's Foods, Walgreens
2	US 6 W, Spruce Hills Dr, Bettendorf, N 🅿️ BP/dsl, Phillips 66, 🍴 Domino's, Old Chicago Pizza, 🏨 Courtyard, EconoLodge, Ramada Inn, Super 8, The Lodge Hotel/rest., ⊙ U-Haul, S 🍴 Applebee's, Burger King, Godfather's, KFC, Panera Bread, Red Lobster, 🏨 Days Inn, Fairfield Inn, La Quinta, ⊙ Buick/Cadillac/GMC, Gander Mtn, Gordman's, Kohl's, Lowe's, PetCo, Sam's Club/gas, st patrol
1	53rd St, Hamilton, N 🅿️ BP, 🍴 Biaggi's Italian, Buffalo Wild Wings, Chili's, Coldstone, Dickey's BBQ, Granite City Rest., Maggle Moo's, Osaka Steaks, Panchero's Mexican, Red Robin, Ruby Tuesday, Symposium Cafe, IX Roadhouse, 🏨 Hampton Inn, Staybridge Suites, ⊙ H, Harley-Davidson, HyVee Foods, Michael's, Old Navy, TJ Maxx, Walgreens, S 🅿️ Murphy USA, Phillips 66, 🍴 Arby's, Azteca Mexican, Chick-fil-A, China Cafe, DQ, Dynasty Buffet, Golden Corral, Hungry Hobo, IHOP, La Rancherita, Noodles&Co., Qdoba Mexican, Sonic, Starbucks, Steak'n Shake, Subway, TGIFriday's, Village Inn Rest., Taco Bell, Wendy's, 🏨 Sleep Inn, ⊙ Aldi Foods, AT&T, Best Buy, $Tree, PetsMart, Staples, Target, Verizon, Walmart
0mm	**I-74 begins/ends on I-80, exit 298. Exits 1-4 are in Iowa.**

⬆️E INTERSTATE 80

Exit	Services
163mm	Illinois/Indiana state line
161	US 6, IL 83, Torrence Ave, N 🅿️ BP, 🍴 Burger King, Chili's, Culver's, Dixie Kitchen, Hooters, IHOP, Kenny's Ribs, Liang's Garden, New China Buffet, Oberweiss, Olive Garden, Shark's, Taco-Burrito's, Wendy's, 🏨 Comfort Suites, Days Inn, Extended Stay America, Holiday Inn Express, Howard Johnson Express, Red Roof Inn, Sleep Inn, Super 8, ⊙ Aldi Foods, AT&T, Best Buy, CarEx, Chrysler/Jeep, Curves, $General, $Tree, Dunkin Donuts, Fannie May Candies, Firestone/auto, Home Depot, Honda, JustTires, K-Mart, PepBoys, Radio Shack, Ultra Foods, Walmart, S 🅿️ Citgo, Marathon, Mobil, 🍴 China Chef, Burger King, DQ, Dunkin Donuts, Jonny's K's Cafe, McDonald's/playplace, Mr Gyros, Popolono's Italian, Sub

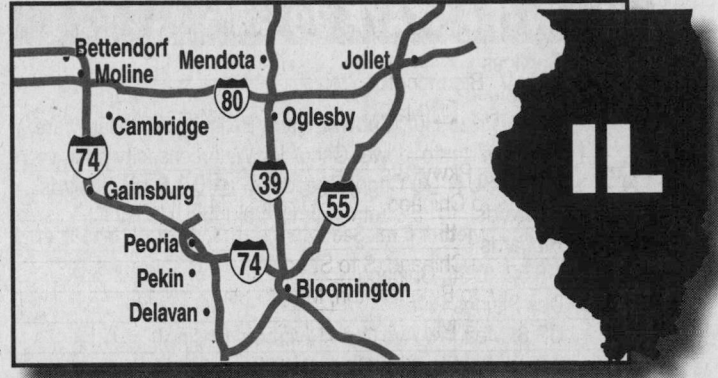

Exit	Services
161	Continued
	way, 🏨 Pioneer Motel, ⊙ Chevrolet, Petsmart, SunRise Foods, Tuesday Morning, Walgreens, vet
160b	I-94 W, to Chicago, **tollway begins wb**, ends eb
160a	IL 394 S, to Danville
159mm	Oasis, 🅿️ Mobil/dsl, 🍴 McDonald's, Panda Express, Starbucks, Subway
157	IL 1, Halsted St, N 🅿️ Citgo/dsl, Marathon/dsl, 🍴 Burger King, 🏨 Chicago Southland Hotel, Clarion, Comfort Inn, Comfort Suites, EconoLodge, Regency Inn, S 🅿️ Citgo, Delta Sonic, Shell, Speedway, 🍴 Applebee's, Athens Gyros, Arby's, Boston Mkt, Burger King, Chili's, Dunkin Donuts, Fannie May Candies, KFC, McDonald's, Panda Express, Pizza Hut, Popeye's, Starbucks, Subway, Taco Bell, Washington Square Rest., Wendy's, White Castle, 🏨 Homewood Hotel, Super 8, ⊙ Aldi Foods, AT&T, Best Buy, Chevrolet, Discount Tire, $Tree, Fanny May Candies, Firestone/auto, Goodyear/auto, Home Depot, Jewel-Osco, Jo-Ann Fabrics, K-Mart, Kohl's, Menards, PepBoys, PetCo, Radio Shack, Target, TJ Maxx, Walgreens
156	Dixie Hwy (from eb, no return), S 🅿️ Mobil, 🍴 Leona's Rest., ⊙ golf
155	I-294 N, **Tri-State Tollway, toll plaza**
154	Kedzie Ave (from eb, no return), N 🅿️ Speedway, S H
151b a	I-57 (exits left from both directions), N to Chicago, S to Memphis
148b a	IL 43, Harlem Ave, N 🅿️ Speedway/dsl, 🍴 Al's Beef, Buffalo Wild Wings, Burger King, Cracker Barrel, Culver's, Dunkin Donuts, Eggi Grill, Hamada of Japan, Pop's Italian Beef, Quizno's, Taco Fresco, Tin Fish Grill, Wendy's, 🏨 Comfort Suites, Fairfield Inn, Hampton Inn, Holiday Inn, La Quinta, Sleep Inn, Wingate Inn, S 🍴 Arby's, Boston's Grill, Subway, Taco Bell, TGIFriday's, ⊙ Best Buy, Carmax, Kohl's, Michael's, PetsMart, SuperTarget, ampitheater
147.5mm	weigh sta wb
145b a	US 45, 96th Ave, N 🍴 Arby's, Arrenello's Pizza, Baskin-Robbins/Dunkin Donuts, 4K Asian, Quizno's, Tokyo Steaks, TX Roadhouse, 🏨 Country Inn&Suites, Hilton Garden, ⊙ Harley-Davidson, 0-2 mi S 🅿️ BP, Clark, Gas City, Shell/Circle K/dsl/24hr, 🍴 A&W, Applebee's, Beggar's Pizza, DQ, Denny's, KFC, Mindy's Ribs, Nick's Rest., Rising Sun Chinese, Stoney Pt Grill, Subway, White Castle, Wendy's, 🏨 Super 8, ⊙ Brookhaven Foods, CVS Drug, Tuesday Morning, repair
143mm	weigh sta eb
140	SW Hwy, **I-355 N Tollway**, US 6 S
137	US 30, New Lenox, N 🍴 Williamson's Rest., ⊙ K-Mart, S 🅿️ Speedway/dsl, 🍴 Beggar's Pizza, Burger King, KFC, LJ Silver/Papa Joe's, McDonald's/playplace, Paisono's

🅶 = gas   🍽 = food   🛏 = lodging   🅾 = other   🆁🆂 = rest stop   Copyright 2014 - The Next Exit ®

INTERSTATE 80 CONT'D

Exit	Services
137	Continued
	Pizza, Pizza Hut, Subway, Taco Bell, 🅾 Ace Hardware, Goodyear/auto, Jewel-Osco/dsl, Walgreens, city park, vet
134	Briggs St, **N** 🅶 Citgo, Speedway, 🅾 🄷, **S** 🅶 Shell/dsl, Valero/dsl, 🅾 EZ Lube, Martin Camping, US RV Ctr
133	Richards St
132b a	US 52, IL 53, Chicago St
131.5mm	Des Plaines River
131	US 6, Meadow Ave, **N** to Riverboat Casino
130b a	IL 7, Larkin Ave, **N** 🅶 Clark, Delta Sonic/dsl, Marathon/24hr, Mobil, Shell/24hr, Speedway, 🍽 A&W/KFC, Baskin-Robbins/Dunkin Donuts, Boston Mkt, Bellagio Pizzaria, Bob Evans, Burger King, DQ, JJ Fish&Chicken, McDonald's, Quizno's, Steak'n Shake, Subway, Taco Bell, Wendy's, White Castle, 🛏 Budget Inn, Comfort Inn, Holiday Inn, Motel 6, Red Roof Inn, Super 8, 🅾 🄷, Aldi Foods, Cadillac/Chevrolet, Discount Tire, Ford, Goodyear/auto, K-Mart, Pepboys, Radio Shack, Sam's Club/gas, 7-11, to Coll of St Francis, vet, **S** 🅶 Citgo, 🅾 auto repair
127	Houbolt Rd, to Joliet, **N** 🅶 BP/deli, 7-11, 🍽 Arby's, Burger King, China Kitchen, Cracker Barrel, Dunkin Donuts, Heros Sports Grill, Jimmy John's, McDonald's, Papa&Nana's Pizza, 🛏 Fairfield Inn, Hampton Inn, Ramada Inn, 🅾 Riverboat Casino
126b a	I-55, N to Chicago, S to St Louis
125.5mm	Du Page River
122	Minooka, **N** 🅶 Citgo/dsl/24hr, **S** 🅶 BP/24hr, 🍽 Arby's/scales/dsl/24hr, 🍽 Baskin-Robbins/Dunkin Donuts, Gino Angelo's Pizza, KFC/LJ Silver, McDonald's/playplace, Subway, Taco Bell, Wendy's, 🅾 $General, 7-11
119mm	🆁🆂 wb, full 🅰 facilities, vending, 🄲 s, 🄰, litter barrels, playground, petwalk
117mm	🆁🆂 eb, full 🅰 facilities, vending, 🄲, 🄰, litter barrels, playground, petwalk
116	Brisbin Rd
112	IL 47, Morris, **N** 🅶 Marathon/dsl, TA/BP/Quiznos/scales/dsl/24hr/@, 🍽 Bellacino's, Chili's, IHOP, 🛏 Comfort Inn, Days Inn, Holiday Inn Express, Quality Inn, 🅾 $General, Menards, **S** 🅶 BP, Mobil, Phillips 66, Shell, 🍽 Burger King, Culver's, DQ, Dunkin Donuts, Hong Kong Chinese, KFC/LJ Silver, Maria's Ristorante, McDonald's, Morris Diner, Pizza Hut, Rosati's Pizza, Taco Bell, Wendy's, 🛏 Park Motel, Sherwood Oaks Motel, Super 8, 🅾 Aldi Foods, AT&T, Big R Store, Buick/Cadillac/Chevrolet, Curves, Fisher Parts, Ford, GMC, Jewel-Osco, Morris Drug, Radio Shack, Verizon, Walgreens, Walmart/Subway, to Stratton SP, transmissions/repair
105	to Seneca
97	to Marseilles, **S** 🅶 Shell/dsl, 🍽 Taco Time, 🅾 Four Star Camping, Glenwood Camping (4mi), to Illini SP, RV camping
93	IL 71, Ottawa, **N** 🅶 🍽/Road Ranger/Subway/dsl/scales/24hr, Shell/dsl, 🅾 Skydive Chicago RV Park (2mi), **S** 🍽 Hank's Farm Rest., 🅾 🄷
92.5mm	Fox River
90	IL 23, Ottawa, **N** 🅶 BP/Subway, 🍽 Arby's, Cracker Barrel, Taco Bell, 🛏 Hampton Inn, Holiday Inn Express, 🅾 AT&T, F&F, Ford/Kia/Lincoln, Honda, Toyota/Scion, Walmart/McDonald's, **S** 🅶 BP/dsl/LP, Thornton's/dsl 🍽

Exit	Services
90	Continued
	Culver's, Dunkin Donuts, KFC/LJ Silver, Papa Murphy's, Sunfield Rest., 🛏 EconoLodge, Fairfield Inn, Super 8, Surrey Motel, 🅾 🄷 Aldi Foods, $Tree, Harley-Davidson, Kroger, Radio Shack, USPO
81	IL 178, Utica, **N** 🅶 Loves/McDonald's/Subway/dsl/scales/24hr, 🅾 Hickory Hollow Camping, KOA (2mi), **S** 🅶 Shell/Jimmy Johns/dsl, 🛏 Starved Rock Inn, 🅾 to Starved Rock SP, repair, visitor info
79b a	I-39, US 51, N to Rockford, S to Bloomington
77.5mm	Little Vermilion River
77	IL 351, La Salle, **S** 🅶 FLYING J/Denny's/dsl/scales/24hr, 🍽 UpTown Grill (3mi), 🛏 Daniels Motel (1mi), 🅾 st police
75	IL 251, Peru, **N** 🅶 BP, Shell/rest./dsl/24hr, 🍽 Arby's, 4Star Rest., McDonald's, Olive Garden, Starbucks, Taco Bell, 🛏 Holiday Inn Express, Super 8, Welcome Inn, 🅾 Kohl's, Petsmart, Walmart/Dunkin Donuts/Subway, **S** 🅶 BP, Phillips 66, Shell, 🍽 Applebee's, Buffalo Wild Wings, Burger King, Culver's, DQ, IHOP, Jalepeno's Mexican, Jimmy John's, Master StirFry, McDonald's, Mi Margarita, Papa John's, Pizza Hut, Red Lobster, Steak'n Shake, Subway, Wendy's, 🛏 Fairfield Inn, Hampton Inn, La Quinta, 🅾 🄷, Aldi Foods, AT&T, AutoZone, BigLots, Buick/GMC, Chevrolet/Mercedes, Chrysler/Dodge/Jeep, CVS Drug, $Tree, Ford/Hyundai/Lincoln, Goodyear/auto, Hobby Lobby, Home Depot, HyVee Food/dsl, JC Penney, Jo-Ann Fabrics, Marshall's, Menards, Mercedes, NAPA, Nissan, O'Reilly Parts, Sears/auto, Staples, Target, Verizon, Walgreens
73	Plank Rd, **N** 🅶 Sapp Bros/Burger King/dsl/scales/@, 🍽 Big Apple Rest., 🅾 Barney's Lake Camping, Kenworth
70	IL 89, to Ladd, **N** 🅶 Casey's, **S** 🅶 BP (3mi), Shell (3mi), 🛏 Spring Valley Motel, 🅾 🄷, golf
61	I-180, to Hennepin
56	IL 26, Princeton, **N** 🅶 Road Ranger/🍽/scales/dsl/@, 🛏 Super 8, **S** 🅶 Beck's/Bigg's Chicken/dsl, BP, Shell/dsl, 🍽 Big Apple Rest., Burger King, Coffee Cup Rest., Culver's, KFC, McDonald's, Roma Italian, Subway, Wendy's, Wise Guys Grill, 🛏 AmericInn, Days Inn, EconoLodge, 🅾 🄷, AutoZone, Buick/Cadillac/Chevrolet, $General, O'Reilly Parts, Pennzoil, Sullivan's Food/gas/E-85, Walmart, antiques, vet
51mm	🆁🆂 both lanes, full 🅰 facilities, 🄲, 🄰, litter barrels, vending, playground, petwalk, RV dump
45	IL 40, **N** 🅾 to Ronald Reagan Birthplace (21mi), antiques, **S** 🍽 Sheffield Diner, 🅾 Hennepin Canal SP, camping
44mm	Hennepin Canal
33	IL 78, to Kewanee, Annawan, **N** 🅶 Shabbona RV Ctr/Camp (3mi), **S** 🅶 Cenex/dsl, FS/dsl/E-85, Shell/Subway/dsl, 🍽 Blackburn's Roadhouse, 🛏 Best Western, 🅾 to Johnson-Sauk Tr SP
27	to US 6, Atkinson, **N** 🅶 Casey's (1mi)
19	IL 82, Geneseo, **N** 🅶 BP/dsl, 🍽 Culvers, DQ, Hardee's, Happy Joe's Pizza, McDonald's, New China, Pizza Hut, Sweet Pea's Grill, Subway, 🛏 Geneseo Inn, Super 8 (2mi), 🅾 🄷, $General, Ford, Verizon, Walgreens, Walmart, **S** 🍽 Los Ranchitos Mexican
10	I-74, I-280, W to Moline, E to Peoria
9	US 6, to Geneseo, **N** 🍽 Lavender Crest Winery/Cafe, **S** 🅾 Niabi Zoo
7	Colona, **N** 🅶 Shell/dsl, 🍽 Country Fixins Rest.
5mm	Rock River

*(margin label: **IL**)*

*(margin label: **MORRIS**)*

*(margin label: **PERU**)*

Copyright 2014 - The Next Exit ®   🅟 = gas   🍴 = food   🛏 = lodging   🄾 = other   🆁🆂 = rest stop   **ILLINOIS   143**

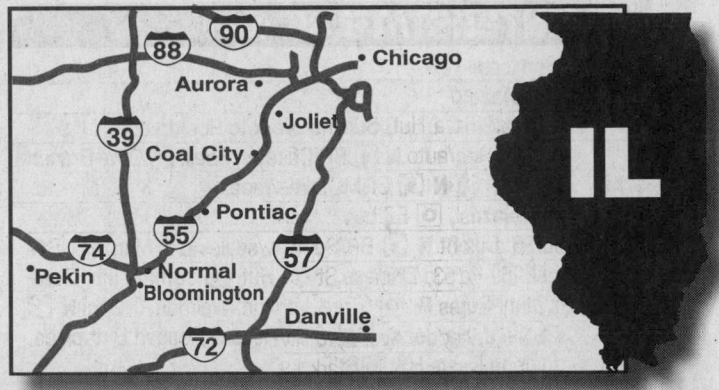

⛺E INTERSTATE 80 CONT'D

Exit	Services
4a	IL 5, IL 92, W to Silvis, **S** 🄾 Lundeen's Camping, st police
4b	I-88, IL 92, E to Rock Falls
2mm	weigh sta both lanes
1.5mm	Welcome Ctr eb, full 🅱 facilities, info, 🚻, 🄿, litter barrels, petwalk, scenic overlook
1	IL 84, 20th St, Great River Rd, E Moline, **N** 🅟 BP/dsl, 🍴 Bros Rest., 🄾 camping, The Great River Rd, **3 mi S** 🅟 BP, 🄾 camping
0mm	Illinois/Iowa state line, Mississippi River

⛺E INTERSTATE 88

Exit	Services
139.5mm	I-88 begins/ends on I-290.
139	I-294, S to Indiana, N to Milwaukee
138mm	toll plaza
137	IL 83 N, Cermak Rd, **N** 🍴 Clubhouse rest., Ditkas Rest., McDonald's, 🛏 Marriott, Renaissance Inn, 🄾 Barnes&Noble, Lord&Taylor, Macy's, Nieman-Marcus
136	IL 83 S, Midwest Rd (from eb), **N** 🅟 Shell/Circle K, 🍴 All-Stars Rest., Burger King, Capri Ristorante, Chipotle Mexican, Denny's, Dunkin Donuts, Eggstacy, Giordano's Rest., Jamba Juice, McDonalds, Noodles&Co, Quizno's, Redstones, Starbucks, Subway, Subway, 🛏 Holiday Inn, La Quinta, 🄾 AT&T, Costco/gas, Home Depot, Nordstrom's, Old Navy, TJ Maxx, Walgreens, World Mkt
134	Highland Ave (no EZ wb return), **N** 🍴 Baker's Square, Bouna Beef, Brio Grille, Buca Italian, Burger King, Capital Grille, Champps Grill, Cheeseburger Paradise, Cici's, Claimjumper Rest., Fuddruckers, Harry Caray's, Hooters, Joe's Crabshack, Kona Grill, Kyoto, McCormick & Schmick's, Miller's Steakhouse, Olive Garden, Panera Bread, PF Chang's, Portilo's Hotdogs, Potbelly's, Qdoba, Red Lobster, Rockbottom Brewery, Ruby Tuesday, Starbucks, Subway, Taylor Brewing Co, TGIFriday's, Uncle Milio's, Weber Grill, 🛏 Comfort Inn, Embassy Suites, Holiday Inn Express, Homestead Studios, Hyatt Place, Marriott, Red Roof Inn, Westin Hotel, 🄾 🄷, Best Buy, Firestone/auto, Home Depot, JC Penney, Kohl's, Marshall's, PetsMart, Vonmaur, mall, **S** 🍴 Parkers Ocean Grill
132	I-355 N (from wb)
131	I-355 S (from eb)
130	IL 53 (from wb), **1 mi N** 🅟 BP, Mobil, 🍴 McDonald's, 🄾 Walmart
127	Naperville Rd, **N** 🍴 Mullen's Grill, 🛏 Hilton, Wyndam, **S** 🅟 Mobil, 🍴 Buona Beef, Froots, HoneyBaked Ham, Jason's Deli, Maggiano's, McDonald's, Morton's Steaks, Pizza Hut, Subway, Taco Fresco, TGIFriday's, Wendy's, White Chocolate Grill, 🛏 Best Western, Courtyard, Days Inn, Fairfield Inn, Hampton Inn, Holiday Inn Select, 🄾 Dodge, Ford, Kia, Office Depot, Radio Shack, Subaru
125	Winfield Rd, **N** 🅟 BP, Mobil, 🛏 Hamton Inn, 🄾 🄷, Walgreens, **S** 🍴 Arby's, Atlanta Bread, Buffalo Wild Wings, CA Pizza Kitchen, Chipotle Mexican, Corner Bakery Cafe, GoRoma, Jamba Juice, Max&Erma's, McDonald's, Potbelly's, Red Robin, Rockbottom Brewery, Starbucks, Stir-Crazy Grill, 🛏 Hilton Garden, Springhill Suites, 🄾 Super-Target
123	IL 59, **N** 🅟 Gas City/dsl, 🍴 Omega Rest., 🄾 Carmax, **S** 🅟 BP, Mobil/dsl, Speedway, 🍴 Baskin Robbins/Dunkin Donuts, Caribou Coffee, Cracker Barrel, Danny's

Exit	Services
123	Continued Grill, Jimmy John's, Lee's Garden, Oberweis, Spicy Pickle, Starbucks, Steak'n Shake, Subway, TX Roadhouse, Wendy's, 🛏 Extended Stay America, Fairfield Inn, Red Roof Inn, Sleep Inn, SpringHill Suites, Towneplace Suites, 🄾 CVS Drug, 7-11, Walgreens
119	Farnsworth Ave, **N** 🅟 BP, Shell, 🍴 McDonald's, Millet's Grill, Papa Bear Rest., Quizno's, Sonic, Starbucks, 🛏 Fox Valley Inn, Motel 6, 🄾 Firestone/auto, Premium Outlets/Famous Brands, Walmart, **S** 🅟 Marathon, Phillips 66/dsl, Shell, Speedway, 🍴 Baskin-Robbins/Dunkin Donuts, Drive-Thru, Little Caesars, McDonald's, Mike&Denise's Pizza, Subway, Taco Bell, 🄾 AutoZone, Family$, Goodyear, 7-11, Walgreens
118mm	toll plaza
117	IL 31, IL 56, to Aurora, Batavia, **N** 🅟 Citgo/dsl, 🍴 A&W, 🄾 7-11, **S** 🅟 Mobil, Thornton's, 🍴 Arby's, Baskin-Robbins/Dunkin Donuts, Burger King, Culver's, Denny's, KFC, LJ Silver, McDonald's, Nikary's, Rest., Popeye's, Quizno's, Subway, Taco Bell, White Castle, 🛏 Baymont Inn, 🄾 🄷 Ace Hardware, AutoZone, Cermak Foods, $Store, Firestone, GNC, Jewel/Osco, Murray's Parts, Radio Shack, U-Haul, Walgreens
115	Orchard Rd, **N** 🍴 McDonald's, Subway, 🄾 Best Buy, Chrysler/Dodge/Jeep, Ford/Lincoln, Hyundai, JC Penney, Michaels, Nissan, PetCo, Subaru, Target, Woodman's/dsl, **0-2 mi S** 🅟 7-11, 🍴 A&W/KFC, Arby's, Buffalo Wild Wings, Chili's, Cold Stone, IHOP, Jimmy John's, Panera Bread, Papa Saverio's, Pizza Hut, Quizno's, Starbucks, Wendy's, 🛏 Candlewood Suites, Hampton Inn, Holiday Inn, 🄾 AT&T, CVS Drug, Discount Tire, Home Depot, Lowe's Whse, Office Depot, T-Mobile
114	IL 56W, to US 30 (from wb, no EZ return), to Sugar Grove
109	IL 47 (from eb), Elburn
94	Peace Rd, to IL 38, **N** 🄷
93mm	**Dekalb Oasis/24hr both lanes,** 🅟 Mobil/dsl, 🍴 McDonald's, Panda Express, Subway
92	IL 38, IL 23, Annie Glidden Rd, to DeKalb, **N** 🛏 Super 8, **2-3 mi N** 🅟 BP, Road Ranger/dsl, Marathon, Shell, 🍴 Aldorado, Baskin-Robbins, Blackstone Rest, Burger King, Chipotle Mexican, El Burrito Loco, Gyro's, Happy Wok Chinese, Jct Rest., KFC, LJ Silver, Lukulo's Rest., McDonald's, Molly's Eatery, Pagliai's Pizza, Pancake Rest., Panda Express, Papa John's, Potbelly, Pizza Hut, Pizza Pros, Pizza Villa, Quizno's, Starbucks, Subway, Taco Bell, Tom&Jerry's, Topper's Pizza, Vinny's Pizza, Wendy's, 🛏 Best Western, Magneson Inn, Travelodge, 🄾 $General, Ford, Illini Tire, Schnuck's Food/Drug, Walgreens, to N IL U

INTERSTATE 88 CONT'D

Exit	Services
86mm	toll plaza
78	I-39, US 51, S to Bloomington, N to Rockford
76	IL 251, Rochelle, N 🅖 BP, Casey's, Shell, 🍴 Olive Branch Rest., 🅞 🏥 Ford, GMC, tires/repair
56mm	toll plaza
54	IL 26, Dixon, N 🅖 BP/Subway/scales/dsl, Murphy USA/ dsl, 🍴 Panda Chinese, Pizza Hut, 🛏 Comfort Inn, Quality Inn, Super 8, 🅞 $Tree, Verizon, Walmart, 1-2 mi N 🍴 Culver's, Hardee's, 🅞 🏥 to Ronald Reagan Birthplace, to John Deere HS, to St Parks
44	US 30 (last free exit eb), N gas, food, lodging, 🅞 Leisure lake RV Ctr (2mi)
41	IL 40, to Sterling, Rock Falls, 1-2 mi N 🅖 Marathon, Mobil/dsl, Shell, 🍴 American Grill, Arby's, Arthur's Deli, Burger King, Candlelight Rest., Culver's, El Tapatio Mexican, First Wok Chinese, Gazi's Rest., Hardee's, KFC, McDonald's/playplace, Perna's Pizza, Pizza Hut, Red Apple Rest., Subway, 🛏 All Seasons Motel, Candlelight Inn, Country Inn&Suites, Holiday Inn, Super 8, 🅞 🏥 AutoZone, Country Mkt Foods, Curves, $General, Harley-Davidson, O'Reilly Parts, Sav-a-Lot, Walgreens, Walmart
36	to US 30, Rock Falls, Sterling
26	IL 78, to Prophetstown, Morrison, N 🅞 to Morrison-Rockwood SP
18	to Albany, Erie
10	to Port Byron, Hillsdale, S 🅖 Phillips 66/dsl, Shell/Mama J's Rest./scales/dsl/24hr
6	IL 92 E, to Joslin, N 🍴 Jammerz Roadhouse (2mi), S 🅞 Sunset Lake Camping (1mi)
2	Former IL 2
1b a	I-80, W to Des Moines, E to Chicago
0mm	IL 5, IL 92, W to Silvis, to Quad City Downs, Lundeen's Camping. I-88 begins/ends on I-80, exit 4b.

INTERSTATE 90

Exit	Services
0mm	Illinois/Indiana state line, Chicago Skyway Toll Rd begins/ends
1mm	US 12, US 20, 106th St, Indianapolis Blvd, N 🅖 Citgo, Mobil, Shell/dsl, 🅞 casino, S 🍴 Burger King, KFC, McDonald's, 🅞 Aldi Foods, Jewel-Osco, auto repair
2.5mm	🅖 Skyway Oasis, 🍴 McDonald's, 🅞 toll plaza
3mm	87th St (from wb)
4mm	79th St, services along 79th St and Stoney Island Ave
5.5mm	73rd St (from wb)
6mm	State St (from wb), S 🅖 Citgo
7mm	I-94 N (mile markers decrease to IN state line)
	I-90 E and I-94 E run together. See Interstate 94, exits 43b - 59a.
84	I-94 W, Lawrence Ave, N 🅖 BP
83b a	Foster Ave (from wb), N 🅖 BP, 🍴 Checker's, Dunkin Donuts, 🅞 Firestone/auto, Goodyear/auto, Walgreen
82c	Austin Ave, to Foster Ave
82b	Byrn-Mawr (from wb)
82a	Nagle Ave
81b	Sayre Ave (from wb)
81a	IL 43, Harlem Ave, S 🅖 BP, Shell
80	Canfield Rd (from wb), N 🅞 Walgreen
79b a	IL 171 S, Cumberland Ave, N 🅖 7-11, Marathon, 🍴 Hooters, McDonald's, Outback Steaks, Starbucks, 🛏 Holiday Inn, Marriott, SpringHill Suites, Westin Hotel, 🅞

Exit	Services
79b a	Continued
	Dominick's Foods, S 🍴 🛏 Ramada, Renaissance
78.5mm	River Road Plaza, N 🍴 McDonald's, 🛏 Marriott, Westin Hotel, S Hyatt
78mm	I-294, I-190 W, to O'Hare ✈
76mm	IL 72, Lee St (from wb), N 🛏 Extended Stay America, Quality Inn, Wyndham, S 🍴 McDonald's, 🛏 Best Western, Holiday Inn Express, Holiday Inn Select, Sheraton Gateway, Studio+
74.5mm	Des Plaines Oasis both lanes 🅖 Mobil/dsl/24hr, 🍴 McDonald's/24hr, Panda Express, Starbucks, Subway
73.5mm	Elmhurst Rd (from wb), S 🅖 Shell, 🍴 McDonald's, 🛏 Best Western, Comfort Inn, Days Inn, La Quinta, Microtel, Motel 6
70.5mm	Arlington Hts Rd, N on Algonquin 🅖 Shell, 🍴 Arby's, Baja Fresh, Birch River Grill, Buona Beef, Caribou Coffee, Chicago Pizza, Chili's, Chipotle Mexican, Denny's, Honey Baked Ham, Jimmy Johns, Magnum Steaks, McDonald's, Old Country Buffet, Panda Express, Pappadeaux Rest., Potbelly's, Steak'n Shake, Subway, Yanni's Greek Rest., 🛏 Courtyard, DoubleTree, Hyatt, Motel 6, Radisson, Red Roof Inn, Jameson Suites, 🅞 AT&T, GNC, Lowe's Whse, Meijer, NTB, Staples, Walmart, vet, S 🅖 Mobil, Shell, 🍴 Subway, 🛏 Sheraton
68mm	I-290, IL 53, N on Algonquin 🍴 Moretti's Italian, 🛏 Best Western, Embassy Suites, Holiday Inn, Holiday Inn Express, Renaissance Inn, 🅞 mall, 1 mi S on Golf Rd 🍴 CA Pizza Kitchen, Cheesecake Factory, Hooters, Joe's Crabshack, Olive Garden, Panera Bread, Red Robin, Ruby Tuesday, Starbucks, Subway, TGI Friday's, Uno, 🛏 Extended Stay America, Hyatt, Residence Inn, 🅞 AT&T, Firestone, JC Penney, Lord&Taylor, Macy's, Marshall's, Nordstrom, Sears/auto
65.5mm	Roselle Rd (from wb, no return), N 🅞 Medieval Times Funpark, S 🅖 Mobil, 🍴 Boston Mkt, Caribou Coffee, Chipotle Mexican, Denny's, Fox&Hound, Jimmy John's, KFC, La Magdalena, Melting Pot, Outback Steaks, Panda Express, Subway, Wendy's, 🛏 Country Inn&Suites, Extended Stay America, Holiday Inn Express, Homestead Suites, 🅞 Advance Parts, Audi, AutoZone, Buick/GMC, Carmax, Chrysler/Dodge/Jeep, Firestone, Hancock Fabrics, Jewel-Osco, Lexus, Mazda, Office Depot, O'Reilly Parts, PetCo, 7-11, TJ Maxx, Walgreens
62mm	Barrington Rd (from wb), N 🍴 Apple Villa Pancake House, Hunan Beijing, Jersey's Grill, Jimmy John's, Lucky Monk, Millrose Rest., Quiznos, Subway, 🛏 Hilton Garden, 🅞 vet, S 🅖 BP, 🍴 Chili's, IHOP, Macaroni Grill, McDonald's, Starbucks, Steak'n Shake, TGIFriday's, 🛏 Candlewood Suites, Comfort Inn, Hampton Inn, Hyatt Place, La Quinta, Red Roof Inn, 🅞 U-Haul
59.5mm	IL 59, N 🍴 Buffalo Wild Wings, Caribou Coffee, Chipotle Mexican, Claim Jumper Rest., Cooper's Hawk Rest., Jimmy John's, Moe's SW Grill, Noodles&Co, Panda Express, Panera Bread, Potbelly's, Red Robin, Ruth's Chris Steaks, Subway, Which Wich, 🛏 Marriott, 🅞 AT&T, Cabela's, CVS Drug, GNC, Michael's, Petsmart, Ross, Target, TJ Maxx, Verizon, World Mkt, to Poplar Creek Music Theatre
58mm	Beverly Rd (from wb)
56mm	IL 25, N 🛏 Lexington Inn, S 🅖 BP/dsl, Citgo, Shell/dsl, Speedway/dsl, 🍴 Arby's, Baker Hill Pancakes, Wendy's, 🅞 🏥 Advance Parts, NAPA AutoCare, city park
54.5mm	IL 31 N, N 🅖 BP, Thornton's, 🍴 Alexander's Rest., Baskin-Robbins/Dunkin Donuts, 🛏 Courtyard, Hampton

⬆E INTERSTATE 90 CONT'D

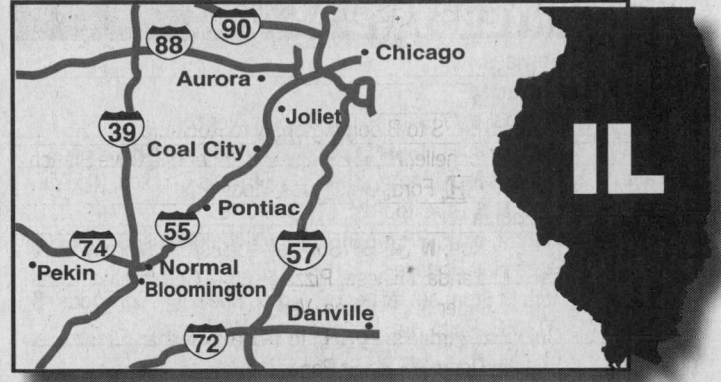

Exit	Services
54.5mm	Continued
	Inn, Holiday Inn, Quality Inn, Super 8, TownePlace Suites, **S** One for the Road Hotdogs
54mm	**Elgin Toll Plaza**, 🅒
52mm	Randall Rd, **N** 🅿 Shell, 🍴 Big Sammy's Hot Dogs, Burnt Toast, Cafe Roma, DQ, Jimmy John's, Jimmy's Charhouse, Mr Wok, Panera Bread, Rookies Grill, Starbucks, Tilted Kilt, Village Pizza, 🛏 Comfort Suites, Country Inn&Suites, 🅾 Honda, **S** 🅿 7-11, 🛏 Candlewood Suites, 🅾 🅗
46.5mm	IL 47, to Woodstock, **N** 🅾 Huntley Outlets/famous brands, Ford, General RV Ctr
42.5mm	US 20, Marengo, **N** 🅿 Citgo/Arrowhead Rest/dsl/scales/24hr, 🚂/Road Ranger/Subway/dsl/scales/24hr, TA/BP/Burger King/Popeye's/dsl/scales/24hr/@, 🍴 McDonald's, Wendy's, 🛏 Super 8, 🅾 museums, access to services at exit 46 (6mi), Ford, Huntley Outlets
38mm	**Marengo Toll Plaza** (from eb)
25mm	Genoa Rd, to Belvidere, **N** 🅿 Murphy USA/dsl, 🍴 Applebee's, Rosati's Pizza, Starbucks, Subway, 🅾 Verizon, Walmart/Blimpie, camping
24mm	**Belvidere Oasis both lanes** 🅿 Mobil/7-11/dsl/24hr, 🍴 Food Court, McDonald's, Panda Express, Starbucks, Subway, Taco Bell, 🅒
23.5mm	**Belvidere Toll Plaza**
18mm	Kishwaukee River
17.5mm	I-39 S, US 20, US 51, to Rockford, **S** funpark
15mm	US 20, State St, **N** 🅿 Mobil/dsl, Phillips 66/Subway/dsl, 🍴 Cracker Barrel, 🛏 Baymont Inn, Clocktower Best Western Resort, Days Inn, **0-2 mi S** 🅿 BP, Mobil/dsl, Road Ranger/dsl, 🍴 Applebee's, BeefaRoo, Buffalo Wild Wings, Burger King, Charley's Steaks, Chili's, China King, Chipotle Mexican, City Buffet, Coldstone, Denny's, Dos Reales, Fiesta Cancun, 5 Guys Burgers, Gerry's Pizza, Giovanni's Rest., Golden Corral, Hoffman House Rest., Honey Baked Ham, IHOP, Jimmy John's, Kochi Japanese, KFC/LJ Silver, LoneStar Steaks, Machine Shed Rest, McDonald's, Murphy's Grill, Noodles&Co, Old Chicago Grill, Old Country Buffet, Olive Garden, Outback Steaks, Panda Express, Panera Bread, Panino's Drive-Thru, Perkins, Pizza Hut/Taco Bell, PotBelly, Quiznos, Red Lobster, Red Robin, Ruby Tuesday, Starbucks, Steak'n Shake, Stone Eagle Tavern, Subway, ThunderBay Grille, TX Roadhouse, 🛏 Candlewood Suites, Comfort Inn, Courtyard, Extended Stay America, Fairfield Inn, Hampton Inn, Hilton Garden, Holiday Inn, Motel 6, Quality Suites, Radisson, Red Roof Inn, Residence Inn, Sleep Inn, Staybridge Suites, Studio+, Super 8, 🅾 🅗 Advance Parts, Aldi Foods, AT&T, Best Buy, BigLots, Buick/GMC, Chrysler/Dodge/Jeep, Dick's, Discount Tire, $Tree, GNC, Gordman's, Hancock Fabrics, Hobby Lobby, Home Depot, Hyundai, Iogli Mkt, JoAnn Fabrics, K-Mart, Kohl's, Lowe's, Marshall's, Michael's, Office Depot, Old Time Pottery, Old Navy, PetCo, Petsmart, Radio Shack, Ross, Sam's Club/gas, Target, Tuesday Morning, Valli Foods, Verizon, Walgreens, Walmart/McDonald's
12.5mm	E Riverside Blvd, Loves Park, **0-2 mi S** 🅿 Mobil/dsl, Phillips 66/dsl, Road Ranger/🚂/Subway/dsl, Shell, 🍴 Arby's, BeefARoo, Ciaobella, Culver's, DQ, Domino's, Japanese Express, KFC, McDonald's, Rosatti's Pizza, 2nd Cousin's Grill, Subway, Taco Bell, Wendy's, 🛏 Holi

Exit	Services
12.5mm	Continued
	day Inn Express, Quality Inn, 🅾 Audi/Honda/Mercedes, Autowerks, Farm&Fleet, Lexus, Toyota/Scion, Tuffy Auto, Walgreens, to Rock Cut SP, funpark
9mm	Il 173, **S** to Rock Cut SP
3.5mm	**S Beloit Toll Plaza**, 🅒
2	Rockton Rd, **S** 🅿 Loves/Hardee's/dsl/scales/24hr
1.5mm	**Welcome Ctr**/🆁🆂 eb, full 🛏 facilities, info, 🚻 litter barrels, 🅒, petwalk, playground, RV dump
1	US 51 N, IL 75 W, S Beloit, **N** 🅿 Road Ranger/McDonald's/dsl, **S** 🅿 Road Ranger/🚂/BeefARoo/Subway/dsl/E85/scales/24hr, *FLYING J*/Denny's/dsl/scales/24hr, 🛏 Best Western, Tollway Inn, 🅾 Finnegan's RV Ctr, Pearl Lake camping (2mi)
0mm	Illinois/Wisconsin state line

⬆E INTERSTATE 94

Exit	Services
77mm	Illinois/Indiana state line
I-94 and I-80 run together 3 mi. See Interstate 80, exit 161	
74[160]b	I-80/I-294 W
74a	IL 394 S, to Danville
73b a	US 6,159th St, **N** 🅿 Mobil, 🍴 Applebee's, Buffalo Wild Wings, Fuddrucker's, Outback Steaks, Panda Express, Quiznos, Rib Ribs, Sonic, Starbucks, Taco Bell, White Castle, 🅾 BigLots, Hyundai, JC Penney, Kia, Lincoln, Macy's, Marshall's, Michael's, Nissan, Office Depot, Old Navy, PetCo, Target, Toyota/Scion, USPO, vct, **S** 🅿 BP, Marathon, 🍴 Harold's Chicken, McDonald's, Popeye's, Rally's, Shark's, Subway, 🛏 Cherry Lane Motel, 🅾 Aldi Foods, Jewel-Osco, Stanfa Tire/repair
71b a	Sibley Blvd, **N** 🅿 Citgo, Mobil/dsl, Valero/dsl, 🍴 McDonald's, Nicky's Gyros, Popeye's, Quiznos, Shark's, Subway, 🛏 Baymont Inn, 🅾 Family$, Pete's Mkt, **S** 🅿 Clark, Marathon/dsl, Shell, 🍴 Baskin-Robbins/Dunkin Donuts, Burger King, KFC, Snapper's Chicken, Family Wendy's, White Castle, 🛏 Best Motel, 🅾 Advance Parts, AutoZone, $General, Fairplay Foods, Food4Less/gas, Menards, Radio Shack, Walgreens
70b a	Dolton Ave
69	(from eb), Beaubien Woods Forest Preserve
68b a	130th St
66b	115th St, **S** 🍴 McDonald's
66a	111th Ave, **S** 🅿 Citgo/dsl, Shell, 🅾 🅗 Firestone/auto
65	103rd Ave, Stony Island Ave
63	I-57 S (exits left from wb)
62	Wentworth Ave (from eb), **N** 🅿 Citgo, Mobil, 🍴 Subway
61b	87th St, **N** 🅿 BP, Shell, 🍴 Burger King, McDonald's, **S** 🍴 Stabucks, Subway, 🅾 AutoZone, Best Buy, Burlington Coats, $Tree, Food4Less, Home Depot, Jewel-Osco,

ELGIN · **ROCKFORD** · **CHICAGO AREA** · **IL**

 = gas   = food   = lodging   = other   = rest stop   Copyright 2014 - The Next Exit ®

INTERSTATE 94 CONT'D

CHICAGO AREA

Exit	Services
61b	Continued
	Marshall's, O'Reilly Parts, Staples, Verizon
61a	83rd St (from eb), N Shell, Subway, st police
60c	79th St, N Mobil, Shell, Brown's Chicken, Walgreens, S Citgo/dsl, Church's
60b	76th St, N BP, Mobil, Shell, Walgreens, S KFC/Pizza Hut, Popeye's
60a	75th St (from eb), N BP, Mobil, Shell, Aldi Foods, S KFC, Pizza Hut, Popeye's, Walgreens
59c	71st St, N BP, S McDonald's
59a	I-90 E, to Indiana Toll Rd
58b	63rd St (from eb), N Citgo, S Mobil
58a	I-94 divides into local and express, 59th St, S BP
57b	Garfield Blvd, N Al's Beef, Checker's, Grand Chinese Kitchen, Subway, Family$, Walgreens, S Citgo, Mobil, Shell/24hr, Wendy's,
57a	51st St
56b	47th St (from eb)
56a	43rd St, S BP/Subway/dsl, Citgo/dsl
55b	Pershing Rd
55a	35th St, S to New Comiskey Park
54	31st St
53c	I-55, Stevenson Pkwy, N to downtown, Lakeshore Dr
53b	I-55, Stevenson Pkwy, S to St Louis
52c	18th St (from eb), W Dominick's Foods
52b	Roosevelt Rd, Taylor St (from wb), N Citgo, Best Buy, Home Depot, Walgreens, Whole Foods Mkt
52a	Taylor St, Roosevelt Rd (from eb), N Citgo
51h-i	I-290 W, to W Suburbs
51g	E Jackson Blvd, downtown
51f	W Adams St, downtown
51e	Monroe St (from eb), downtown, S Crowne Plaza, Dominick's Foods, Walgreens
51d	Madison St (from eb), downtown, S Crowne Plaza, Dominick's Foods, Walgreens
51c	E Washington Blvd, downtown
51b	W Randolph St, downtown
51a	Lake St (from wb)
50b	E Ohio St, downtown, S Marathon
50a	Ogden Ave
49b a	Augusta Blvd, Division St, N Lexus, S BP, Shell, Pizza Hut
48b	IL 64, North Ave, N BP, S Valero, Mercedes
48a	Armitage Ave, N Best Buy, Kohl's, S Shell, Jaguar, Land Rover, Volvo
47c b	Damen Ave, N Citgo, car/vanwash
47a	Western Ave, Fullerton Ave, N Citgo, Burger King, Dunkin Donuts, Popeye's, Starbucks, Subway, Costco/gas, Home Depot, Jo-Ann Fabrics, Pepboys, Petsmart, Staples, Target, S Marathon
46b a	Diversey Ave, California Ave, N Citgo, S IHOP/24hr, Popeye's, Walgreens
45c	Belmont Ave, N Wendy's
45b	Kimball Ave, N Marathon/dsl, S Valero, Dunkin Donuts, Pizza Hut, Subway, Aldi Foods, Best Buy, Radio Shack, Walgreens
45a	Addison St
44b	Pulaski Ave, Irving Park Rd, N BP, Mobil
44a	IL 19, Keeler Ave, Irving Park Rd, N BP, Shell/24hr, to Wrigley Field

CHICAGO AREA

Exit	Services
43c	Montrose Ave
43b	I-90 W
43a	Wilson Ave
42	W Foster Ave (from wb), S Citgo, Marathon
41mm	Chicago River, N Branch
41c	IL 50 S, to Cicero, to I-90 W
41b a	US 14, Peterson Ave, N Whole Foods Mkt
39b a	Touhy Ave, N BP/dsl, Shell/Circle K, Cassidy Tire, Toyota/Scion, S BP, Citgo, Shell, Baja Fresh, Baskin-Robbins/Dunkin Donuts, Buffalo Wild Wings, Burger King, Chili's, Chipotle Mexican, ChuckeCheese, Jack's Rest./24hr, McDonald's, Noodles&Co, Outback Steaks, Quiznos, Red Robin, Sander's Rest., Starbucks, Subway, Holiday Inn, Barnes&Noble, Best Buy, Dick's, GNC, Jewel-Osco, Lee's Parts, Nissan, Office Depot, PepBoys, PetCo, Petsmart, Radio Shack, Walgreens, Walmart, vet
37b a	IL 58, Dempster St
35	Old Orchard Rd, N BP, Shell, Bloomingdale's, CA Pizza Kitchen, CheeseCake Factory, McCormick&Schmick's Rest., , Nissan, mall, S Ruby Tuesday, Extended Stay America, Hampton Inn
34c b	E Lake Ave, N BP, Omaha Steaks, Panda Express, Starbucks, Fresh Mkt Foods, GNC, S BP, Shell, DQ
34a	US 41 S, Skokie Rd (from eb)
33b a	Willow Rd, S BP, Shell, Starbucks, Dominick's Foods, Walgreens
31	E Tower Rd, S BMW, Carmax, Chrysler/Dodge/Jeep, Infiniti, Mercedes, Toyota/Scion, vet
30b a	Dundee Rd (from wb, no EZ return), S Citgo, Marathon, Barnaby's Rest., Morton's Steaks, Potbelly's, Ruth's Chris Steaks, Starbucks, Renaissance
29	US 41, to Waukegan, to **Tri-state tollway**
28mm	IL 43, Waukegan Rd, N BP, Shell, Baja Fresh, Old Country Buffet, Red Roof Inn, Embassy Suites, Best Buy, Home Depot, Jewel-Osco, NTB, Steinmart, TJ Maxx
26mm	I-294 S, Lake-Cook Rd (from sb), E J-Alexander's Rest, Hyatt
25mm	**Deerfield Rd toll plaza**
24mm	Deerfield Rd (from nb), W Mobil, Marriott Suites
22mm	IL 22, Half Day Rd, E La Quinta, W Homewood Suites
19mm	IL 60, Town Line Rd, E , W Hilton Garden, Residence Inn, Costco/gas
18mm	**Lake Forest Oasis both lanes**, E Mobil/7-11/dsl, KFC, McDonald's, Panda Express, Starbucks, Subway, Taco Bell, info
16mm	IL 176, Rockland Rd (no nb re-entry), E Harley-Davidson, to Lamb's Farm
14mm	IL 137, Buckley Rd, E to VA , Chicago Med School
11mm	IL 120 E, Belvidere Rd (no nb re-entry), E
10mm	IL 21, Milwaukee Ave (from eb, no eb re-entry), E Papa John's, , Six Flags
8mm	IL 132, Grand Ave, E Speedway/dsl, Baskin-Robbins/Dunkin Donuts, Burger King, ChuckeCheese, Cracker Barrel, Culver's, Golden Corral, Ichibahn, IHOP, Joe's Crabshack, Jimmy John's, KFC/LJ Silver, McDonald's, Moe's SW Grill, Oberweiss, Old Chicago Red Hots, Olive Garden, Outback Steaks, Rosati's Pizza, Starbucks, Subway, Best Western, Country Inn&Suites, Grand Hotel, Extended Stay America, Hampton Inn, Key Lime Cove

GURNEE

IL

⬆E INTERSTATE 94 CONT'D

G U R N E E

Exit	Services
8mm	Continued
	Resort, La Quinta, ◻ Six Flags Park, **0-2 mi** **W** ◻ Mobil, Shell/Circle K, ◻ Bakers Square, Boston Mkt, Chili's, Chipotle Mexican, Denny's, Giordano's Pizza, Jersey Mike's Subs, Jimano's Pizza, LoneStar Steaks, McDonald's, Noodles&Co, Panda Express, Panera Bread, Penn Sta Subs, Pizza Hut, Potbelly's, Red Robin, Red Lobster, Ruby Tuesday, Starbucks, Steak'n Shake, Taco Bell, TGIFriday's, Uno Grill, Wendy's, White Castle, ◻ Comfort Inn, Fairfield Inn, Holiday Inn, ◻ AT&T, AutoZone, Bass Pro Shops, Best Buy, Buick/GMC, Chrysler/Dodge/Jeep, $Tree, Dominick's Foods, Firestone/auto, Goodyear, Gurnee Mills Outlet Mall/famous brands, Home Depot, Honda, Hyundai, Jewel-Osco, Kohl's, Macy's, Menards, Michael's, Nissan, Old Navy, Petsmart, Radio Shack, Ross, Sam's Club, Sears Grand/auto, Target, TJ Maxx, Tuesday Morning, Verizon, VW, Walgreens, Walmart
5mm	**Waukegan toll plaza** ◻
2mm	IL 173 (from nb, no return), Rosecrans Ave, **E** to IL Beach SP
1b	US 41 S, to Waukegan (from sb), **E** ◻ I-94 RV Ctr
1a	Russell Rd, **W** ◻ Citgo/dsl/scales, TA/Country Pride/dsl/scales/24hr/@, ◻ Peterbilt
0mm	Illinois/Wisconsin state line

⬆N INTERSTATE 255 (ST LOUIS)

Exit	Services
I-255 begins/ends on I-270, exit 7.	
30	I-270, W to Kansas City, E to Indianapolis
29	IL 162, to Glen Carbon, to Pontoon Beach, Granite City
26	Horseshoe Lake Rd, **E** st police
25b a	I-55/I-70, W to St Louis, E to Chicago, Indianapolis
24	Collinsville Rd, **E** ◻ DP/24hr, ◻ Jack-in-the-Box, ◻ Shop'n Save, **W** Fairmount Racetrack
20	I-64, US 50, W to St Louis, E to Louisville, **services 1 mi E off I-64, exit 9.**
19	State St, E St Louis, **E** ◻ Western Inn, ◻ Holten SP
17b a	IL 15, E St Louis, to Belloville, Centreville, **E** ◻ Ⓙ FLYING J/Denny's/dsl/scales/24hr, **W** ◻ Phillips 66
15	Mousette Lane, **E** ◻, **W** ◻ Peterbilt
13	IL 157, to Cahokia, **E** ◻ Phillips 66, **W** ◻ BP/24hr, QT, ◻ Capt D's, China Express, Classic K Burgers, DQ, Domino's, Hardee's, Jade Garden, KFC, McDonald's, Pizza Hut, Popeye's, Rally's, Subway, ◻ Holiday Inn Express, ◻ Advance Parts, Aldi Foods, AutoZone, Buick/GMC, Cahokia RV Park, CarQuest, Curves, Dobb's Tires, Family$, $General, Schnuck's, Shop'n Save Foods, Walgreens, Walmart/drugs, Cahokia RV Parque (2mi)
10	IL 3 N, to Cahokia, E St Louis, **W** ◻ ZX/Subway/dsl
9	to Dupo, **W** ◻ BP
6	IL 3 S, to Columbia (exits left from sb), **E** ◻ Phillips 66, Shell/dsl/24hr, ◻ Hampton Inn (2mi), ◻ Chevrolet
4mm	**Missouri/Illinois state line, Mississippi River**
3	Koch Rd
2	MO 231, Telegraph Rd, **N** ◻ Conoco, Shell/Circle K, ◻ McDonald's, Pizza Hut/Taco Bell, Steak'n Shake, Waffle House, ◻ Advance Parts, $Tree, Radio Shack, Walmart, Jefferson Barracks Nat Cem, **S** ◻ CFM/dsl, Mobil, QT, Shell, ◻ China Wok, DQ, Imo's Pizza, ◻ Curves

C H I C A G O   A R E A

1d c	US 50, US 61, US 67, Lindbergh Blvd, Lemay Ferry Rd, accesses same as I-55 exit 197 E, **N** ◻ Phillips 66, ◻ Arby's, Buffalo Wild Wings, ChuckeCheese, CiCi's Pizza, Dillard's, Hometown Buffet, HoneyBaked Ham, Hooters, KFC, Krispy Kreme, Macaroni Grill, Noodles&Co, Qdoba Mexican, Quizno's, Station Subs, Steak'n Shake, St Louis Bread Co, Subway, Tucker's Place, ◻ Advance Parts, Best Buy, Costco/gas, Dillard's, Discount Tire, Dodge, Ford, Home Depot, JC Penney, Kia, K-Mart, Macy's, Marshall's, NTB, Sears/auto, Tuesday Morning, mall, **S** ◻ Phillips 66, ◻ Jack-in-the-Box, McDonald's, Rich & Charlie's Italian, White Castle, ◻ BigLots, $General, Firestone, Old Navy, Petsmart, Sam's Club/gas, Walgreens
1b a	I-55 S to Memphis, N to St Louis. **I-255 begins/ends on I-55, exit 196.**

INTERSTATE 270 (ST LOUIS)

See Missouri Interstate 270 (St Louis)

⬆E INTERSTATE 294 (CHICAGO)

Exit	Service
I-294 begins/ends on I-94, exit 74. Numbering descends from west to east.	
I-294 & I-80 run together 5 mi. See Interstate 80, exits 155-160.	
5mm	I-80 W, access to I-57
5.5mm	167th St, **toll booth,** ◻
6mm	US 6, 159th St, **E** ◻ Citgo, Clark, Marathon, Mobil/dsl, Shell/dsl, ◻ Aldi Foods, AutoZone, Walgreen, **W** ◻ BP, ◻ Baskin-Robbins/Dunkin Donuts, Burger King, McDonald's, Popeye's, Subway, Taco Bell, White Castle, ◻ Chicago Inn&Suites, ◻ AutoZone, $Tree, Family$, U-Haul, Walgreens
11mm	Cal Sag Channel
12mm	IL 50, Cicero Ave, **E** ◻ BP, 7-11, Shell/dsl, ◻ Dunkin Donuts, Subway, White Castle, ◻ Home Depot, **W** ◻ Shell/dsl, ◻ Boston Mkt, IHOP, Panda Express, Pizza Hut, Popeye's, Portillo's Dogs, Potbelly, Subway, ◻ Baymont Inn, Hampton Inn, Holiday Inn Express, ◻ Best Buy, NTB, PepBoys
18mm	US 12/20, 95th St, **E** ◻ Citgo, Marathon, ◻ Chick-fil-A, TX Corral, ◻ ◻, CarMax, Discount Tire, Mazda, Sears/auto, mall, **W** ◻ BP, 7-11, Shell, Speedway/dsl, ◻ Arby's, Baskin-Robbins, Burger King, Denny's, Dunkin Donuts, Jimmy John's, Les Bros Rest., McDonald's, Prime Time Rest., The Pit Ribhouse, Wendy's, ◻ Exel Inn, ◻ ◻ $Tree, Jewel-Osco, Walgreen
20mm	**toll booth,** ◻
22mm	75th St, Willow Springs Rd
23mm	I-55, Wolf Rd, to Hawthorne Park
25mm	**Hinsdale Oasis both lanes** ◻ Mobil/7-11/dsl, ◻ KFC/Taco Bell, McDonald's, Panda Express, Sbarro, Subway,

□ = gas   □ = food   □ = lodging   □ = other   RS = rest stop   Copyright 2014 - The Next·Exit ®

↑E INTERSTATE 294 (CHICAGO) CONT'D

Exit	Service
25mm	**Continued** McDonald's
28mm	US 34, Ogden Ave, **E** zoo, **W** □ BP, Shell/deli, □ Dunkin Donuts, Starbucks, McDonald's, □ **H**, Ferrari/Maserati, Firestone/auto, LandRover, Whole Foods Mkt
28.5mm	Cermak Rd (from sb, no return)
29mm	I-88 **tollway**
30mm	**toll booth,** □
31mm	IL 38, Roosevelt Rd (no EZ nb return), **E** □ Citgo/dsl, □ Hillside Manor Motel
32mm	I-290 W, to Rockford (from nb)
34mm	I-290 (from sb), to Rockford
38mm	**O'Hare Oasis both lanes** □ Mobil/7-11/dsl, □ KFC, McDonald's, Panda Express, Sbarro, Starbucks, Subway, Taco Bell, TCBY
39mm	IL 19 W (from sb), Irving Park Rd, **E** □ Clark, Marathon/dsl, □ 7-11, Walgreen, **1 mi E** □ BP/repair, Clark, □ DQ, Dunkin Donuts, McDonald's, Subway, Wendy's, □ Comfort Suites, □ Aldi Foods, **W** □ Candlewood Suites, Day's Inn, Hampton Inn, Howard Johnson, Sheraton
40mm	I-190 W, **E Services from I-90, exit 79** □ Mobil, □ McDonald's, □ Courtyard, Doubletree, Embassy Suites, Holiday Inn, Hotel Softel, Hyatt, Marriott, Radisson, Rosemont Suites, Westin
41mm	**toll booth,** □
42mm	Touhy Ave, **W** □ Mobil/service, □ Tiffany's Rest., □ Comfort Inn
43mm	Des Plaines River
44mm	Dempster St (from nb, no return), **E H, W** □ Dunkin Donuts, Subway
46mm	IL 58, Golf Rd, **E** □ Citgo/dsl, Shell, □ Omega Rest., Senoya Oriental, □ Wyndham, □ **H**, Best Buy, CVS Drug, Golf Mill Mall, Target, auto repair
49mm	Willow Rd, **W** □ TGIFriday's, □ Doubletree Suites, Courtyard, Fairfield Inn, Motel 6, **1 mi W on Milwaukee** □ BP, □ Burger King, Denny's, McDonald's, □ Wingate Inn
53mm	Lake Cook Rd (no nb re-entry), **E** □ Hyatt, □ Embassy Suites
	I-294 begins/ends on I-94.

↑N INTERSTATE 355

Exit	Services
30mm	**I-355 begins/end on I-290**
29	US 20 W Lakes St, **E** □ Citgo/dsl, Marathon, Shell, □ Applebee's, Baskin-Robbins/Dunkin Donuts, Culver's, Famous Dave's BBQ, Home Run Rest, IHOP, Jimmy John's, La Hacienda Mexican, Nana Hotdogs, Panera Bread, Ristorante de Marco's, Starbucks, Wok'n Fire, Zaza's Steaks, □ Hampton Inn, □ Midas, Verizon, Walmart, **W** □ Shell, □ Venuti's Rest
28	IL 64, E North Ave, **E** □ BP/Subway/dsl, Shell/Circle K, □ Burger King, McDonald's, Comfort Suites, Fairfield Inn, **W** □ Phillips 66, Speedway/dsl, □ Hilton Garden, Ramada, □ Art's RV Ctr, Goodyear
25	Roosevelt, **E** □ Mobil, □ Boston Mkt, Buffalo Wild Wings, Odyssey Greek, Pizza Hut, Roundhead Pizza, Starbucks, White Castle, Wolfy's Dogs, □ Crowne Plaza, □ AutoZone, Cadillac, $General, Jewel-Osco, K-Mart, Toyota/Scion, **W** □ Jimmy John's, □ Dominick's Foods, NAPA

22	IL 56, Butterfield Rd, **E** □ Brick House Rest, Buona Beef, Burger King, Cheese Burger Paradise, Chipotle Mexican, CiCi's Pizza, Fuddrucker's, Hooters, Melting Pot, Olive Garden, Panera Bread, Portillo, Qdoba, Red Lobster, Rita's Mexican, Ruby Tuesday, Subway, □ Comfort Inn, Holiday Inn Express, Marriott, Red Roof Inn, □ Best Buy, $Tree, Kohl's, Petsmart, Verizon, **W** □ Carlucci Italian, □ DoubleTree Suites, □ Home Depot, 7-11
20mm	**I-88 E/I-355 run together**
19	US 34, Ogden Ave, **E** □ Shell, □ Culver's, Jimmy John's, □ InTown Suites, □ AT&T, Buick/GMC, Chrysler/Dodge/Jeep, **W** Speedway/dsl, □ Baskin-Robbins/Dunkin Donuts, □ Extended Stay America, □ Chevrolet
18	Maple Ave, **1 mi E** □ BP, □ KFC/Taco Bell, McDonald's, □ Walgreens
16	63rd St, Hobson Rd, **E** □ Mobil, Thornton's/McDonald's, □ Steven's Rest, Subway, □ AutoZone, Dominick's Foods, GNC, Target, Walgreen's
15	W 75th St, **E** □ Mobil, □ Arby's, Bakers Square Rest, □ Home Depot, JC Penney Sam's Club/gas, **W** □ Marathon, Phillips 66, □ Dunkin-Donuts, El Burro Loco, McDonald's, Pizza Italiano, Sandpiper Rest, □ Jewel-Osco
14	87th St, Baughton Rd, **E** □ BP, Shell, □ Al's Pizza, Dunkin-Donuts, McDonald's, Subway, Wendy's, □ CVS Drug, Costco/gas, Staples, **W** □ Mobil, □ Buffalo Wild Wings, Famous Dave's BBQ, 5 Guys Burgers, Johnny Rockets, Longhorn Steaks, Panda Express, Potbelly, Starbucks, □ Barnes&Noble, Bass Pro Shops, Macy's, Meijer/gas, Verizon, Walgreens
12	I-55
8	127th St, **E** □ Phillips 66/dsl, □ Burger King, KFC, McDonald's, Starbucks, Subway, Taco Bell, □ Aldi Foods, Firestone/auto, Jewel-Osco, Jiffy Lube, Walgreens, USPO
6	IL 171, Archer Ave, 143rd St, **E** □ Kohl's, Target, vet
5	159th Ave, IL 7, Orland Park, Homer Glen, **E** □ Speedway/dsl, **W** Urgent Care
3mm	**toll booth,** both directions
1	US 6, **W** □
0mm	I-80 E, W. **I-355 begins/ends on I-80 exit 140**

↑E INTERSTATE 474 (PEORIA)

Exit	Services
15	I-74, E to Bloomington, W to Peoria
9	IL 29, E Peoria, to Pekin, **N** □ Shell/Arby's, Thornton's, □ Driftwood Pizza, DQ, Pizza Hut, Taco John's, □ Ragon Motel, □ Riverboat Casino (6mi), **S** □ Casey's, Shell/Subway/dsl, □ Denny's, KFC, McDonald's, Mickie's Pizza, □ Chrysler/Dodge/Jeep, Toyota
8mm	Illinois River
6b a	US 24, Adams St, Bartonville, **S** □ BP/dsl, Shell/24hr, □ Hardee's, KFC, McDonald's, Tyroni's Café
5	Airport Rd, **S** □ Phillips 66/e-85
3a	to IL 116, Farmington, **S** Wildlife Prairie Park
0b a	I-74, W to Moline, E to Peoria. **I-474 begins/ends on I-74, exit 87.**

INDIANA

↑E INTERSTATE 64

Exit	Services
124mm	Indiana/Kentucky state line, Ohio River
123	IN 62 E, New Albany, **N** □ Shell/Circle K, Sunoco, □ DQ, □ Firestone/auto, Save-A-Lot, U-Haul, **S** □ BP, Shell/Circle K, Valero, □ Lancaster's Deli, Subway, Waffle

(vertical text) CHICAGO AREA

(vertical text) IL / IN

(vertical text) PEORIA

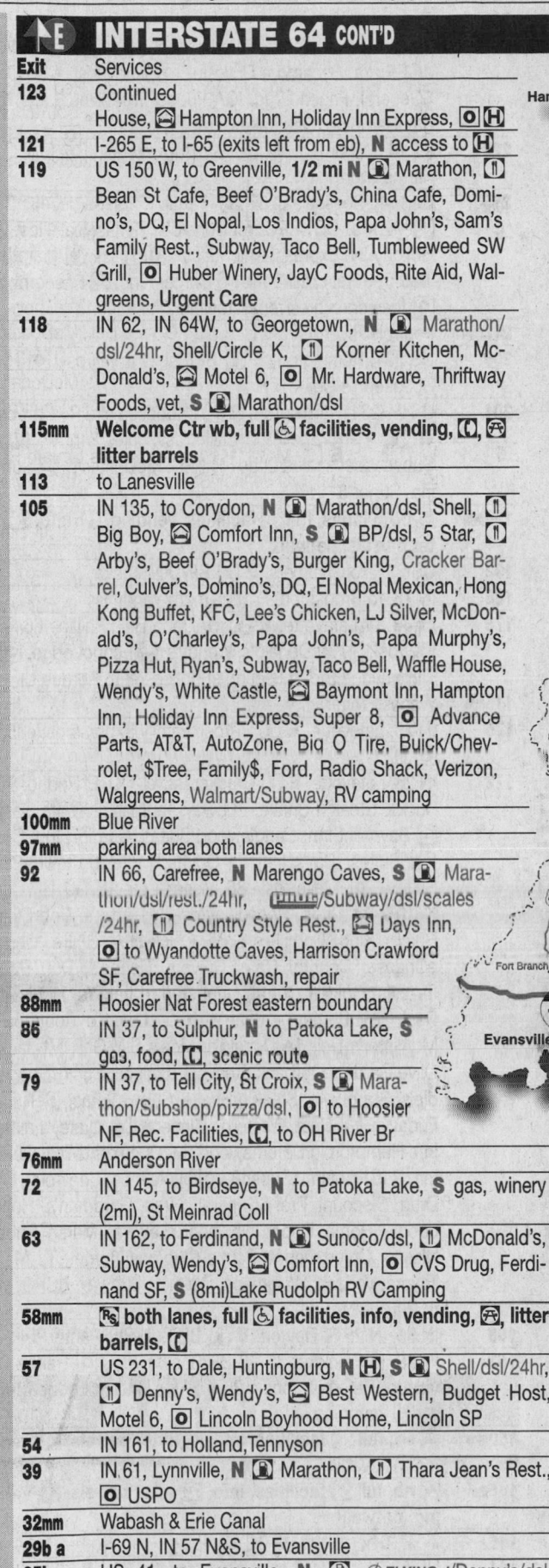

⬆️E INTERSTATE 64 CONT'D

Exit	Services
123	Continued
	House, 🛏 Hampton Inn, Holiday Inn Express, 🅾 🅷
121	I-265 E, to I-65 (exits left from eb), **N** access to 🅷
119	US 150 W, to Greenville, **1/2 mi N** 🅖 Marathon, 🍴 Bean St Cafe, Beef O'Brady's, China Cafe, Domino's, DQ, El Nopal, Los Indios, Papa John's, Sam's Family Rest., Subway, Taco Bell, Tumbleweed SW Grill, 🅾 Huber Winery, JayC Foods, Rite Aid, Walgreens, Urgent Care
118	IN 62, IN 64W, to Georgetown, **N** 🅖 Marathon/dsl/24hr, Shell/Circle K, 🍴 Korner Kitchen, McDonald's, 🛏 Motel 6, 🅾 Mr. Hardware, Thriftway Foods, vet, **S** 🅖 Marathon/dsl
115mm	**Welcome Ctr wb, full ♿ facilities, vending, 🆑, 🌲 litter barrels**
113	to Lanesville
105	IN 135, to Corydon, **N** 🅖 Marathon/dsl, Shell, 🍴 Big Boy, 🛏 Comfort Inn, **S** 🅖 BP/dsl, 5 Star, 🍴 Arby's, Beef O'Brady's, Burger King, Cracker Barrel, Culver's, Domino's, DQ, El Nopal Mexican, Hong Kong Buffet, KFC, Lee's Chicken, LJ Silver, McDonald's, O'Charley's, Papa John's, Papa Murphy's, Pizza Hut, Ryan's, Subway, Taco Bell, Waffle House, Wendy's, White Castle, 🛏 Baymont Inn, Hampton Inn, Holiday Inn Express, Super 8, 🅾 Advance Parts, AT&T, AutoZone, Big O Tire, Buick/Chevrolet, $Tree, Family$, Ford, Radio Shack, Verizon, Walgreens, Walmart/Subway, RV camping
100mm	Blue River
97mm	parking area both lanes
92	IN 66, Carefree, **N** Marengo Caves, **S** 🅖 Marathon/dsl/rest./24hr, ⛽ Subway/dsl/scales /24hr, 🍴 Country Style Rest., 🛏 Days Inn, 🅾 to Wyandotte Caves, Harrison Crawford SF, Carefree Truckwash, repair
88mm	Hoosier Nat Forest eastern boundary
86	IN 37, to Sulphur, **N** to Patoka Lake, **S** gas, food, 🆑 scenic route
79	IN 37, to Tell City, St Croix, **S** 🅖 Marathon/Subshop/pizza/dsl, 🅾 to Hoosier NF, Rec. Facilities, 🆑 to OH River Br
76mm	Anderson River
72	IN 145, to Birdseye, **N** to Patoka Lake, **S** gas, winery (2mi), St Meinrad Coll
63	IN 162, to Ferdinand, **N** 🅖 Sunoco/dsl, 🍴 McDonald's, Subway, Wendy's, 🛏 Comfort Inn, 🅾 CVS Drug, Ferdinand SF, **S** (8mi)Lake Rudolph RV Camping
58mm	🆁🆂 both lanes, full ♿ facilities, info, vending, 🌲 litter barrels, 🆑
57	US 231, to Dale, Huntingburg, **N** 🅷, **S** 🅖 Shell/dsl/24hr, 🍴 Denny's, Wendy's, 🛏 Best Western, Budget Host, Motel 6, 🅾 Lincoln Boyhood Home, Lincoln SP
54	IN 161, to Holland, Tennyson
39	IN 61, Lynnville, **N** 🅖 Marathon, 🍴 Thara Jean's Rest., 🅾 USPO
32mm	Wabash & Erie Canal
29b a	I-69 N, IN 57 N&S, to Evansville
25b a	US 41, to Evansville, **N** 🅖 ✈FLYING J/Denny's/dsl/ scales/24hr, ✦Loves/Wendy's/dsl/24hr, ⛽ Subway/ Taco Bell/dsl/24hr, 🛏 Baymont Inn, 🅾 Blue Bea

25b a	Continued
	con, truck repair/lube, **S** 🍴 Arby's, Denny's, McDonald's, Stoll's Amish Rest., 🛏 Best Western, Comfort Inn, Holiday Inn Express, Super 8, 🅾 st police, to U S IN
18	IN 65, to Cynthiana, **S** 🅖 Motomart/dsl/24hr
12	IN 165, Poseyville, **S** gas, dsl, 🍴 Red Wagon Rest., 🅾 Chevrolet, New Harmonie Hist Area/SP
7mm	**Black River Welcome Ctr eb, full ♿ facilities, 🆑, 🌲 litter barrels, petwalk**
5mm	Black River
4	IN 69 S, New Harmony, Griffin, **1 mi N** gas/dsl, food, motel, antiques, USPO, **S** Harmony St Park
2mm	Big Bayou River
0mm	Indiana/Illinois state line, Wabash River

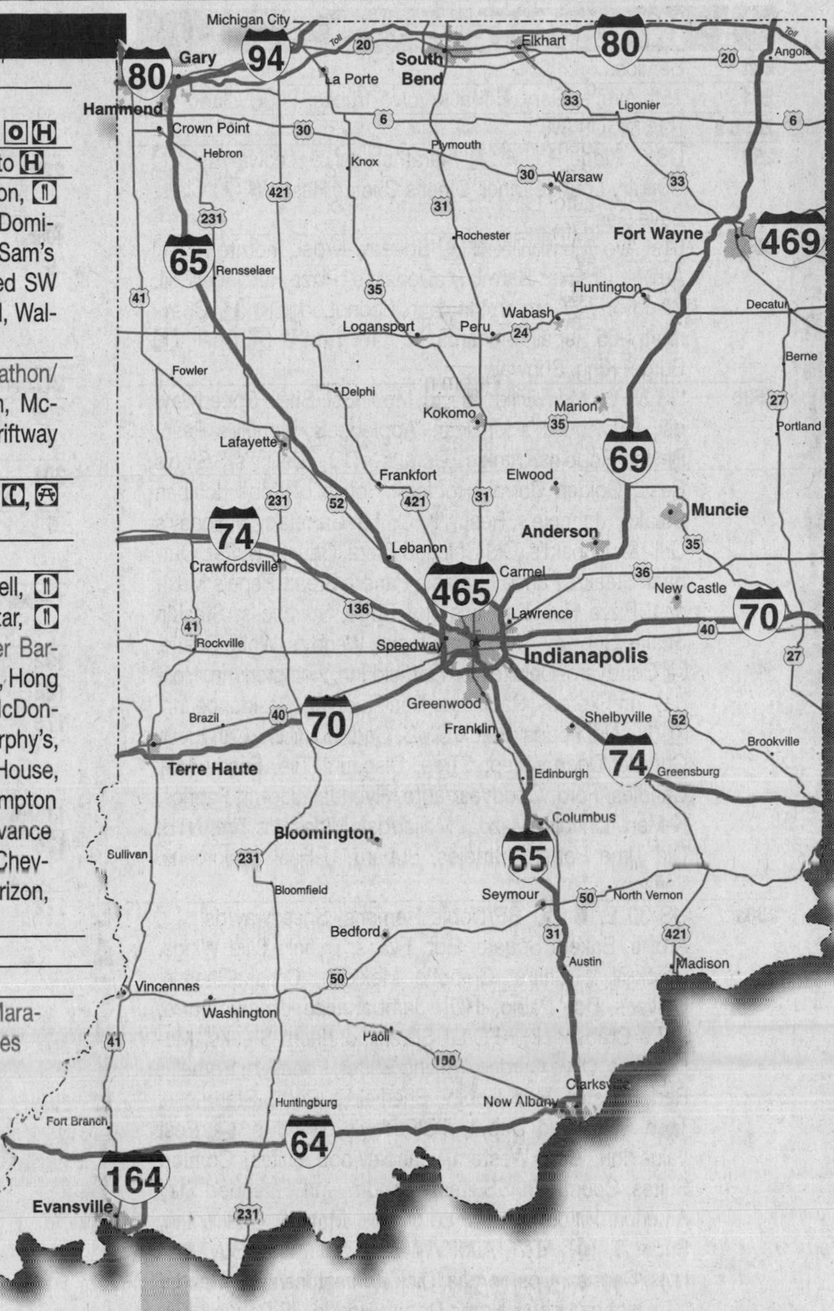

⬆️N INTERSTATE 65

Exit	Services
262	I-90, W to Chicago, E to Ohio, **I-65 begins/ends on US 12, US 20.**

CORYDON (vertical text, left margin)

⬆N INTERSTATE 65 CONT'D

Exit	Services
261	15th Ave, to Gary, **E** Mack/Volvo Trucks, **W** 🅿 Clark
259b a	I-94/80, US 6W
258	US 6, Ridge Rd, **E** 🅿 Marathon/dsl, Speedway/dsl, 🍴 Country Lounge Diner, Diner's Choice Rest., **W** 🅿 Clark, Save Gas
255	61st Ave, Merrillville, **E** 🅿 Speedway/dsl, Thornton's, 🍴 Arby's, Cracker Barrel, McDonald's, Pizza Hut/Taco Bell, Wendy's, 🛏 Comfort Inn, $Inn, EconoLodge 🅾 🅗, Chevrolet, I-65 Repair, Menards, Mr Tire, **1 mi W** 🅿 Shell, 🍴 Burger King, Subway
253b	US 30 W, Merrillville, **W** 🅿 Mobil/dsl, Shell, Speedway/dsl, 🍴 Abuelo's Mexican, Applebee's, Barnelli's Rest., Baskin-Robbins/Dunkin Donuts, DQ, Denny's, Gino's Rest., Golden Corral, Hooters, House of Kobe, Ichiban Steaks, Johnnie's Rest., KFC, La Carreta's, Maloney's Grill, McDonald's, Old Chicago Pizza, Oriental Buffet, Outback Steaks, Panda Express, Panera Bread, Pepe's Mexican, Pizza Hut, Portillo's Hot Dogs, Starbucks, Steak'n Shake, Subway, TX Corral Steaks, Wendy's, White Castle, 🛏 Courtyard, Deluxe Inn, Fairfield Inn, Hampton Inn, Holiday Inn Express, Radisson, Red Roof Inn, Residence Inn, 🅾 🅗, Aldi Foods, Buick/GMC, Cadillac, CarX, CarQuest, Chrysler/Dodge/Jeep, $Tree, Discount Tire, Fanny May Candies, Ford, Goodyear/auto, Hyundai, Jo-Ann Fabrics, K-Mart, Lincoln, Mazda, Meijer/dsl, Midas, Mr Tire, NTB, Old Time Pottery, Staples, Subaru, U-Haul, Walgreens, Verizon
253a	US 30 E, **E** 🅿 BP/Noble Romans, Speedway/dsl, 🍴 Arby's, Bakers Square, Bob Evans, Buffalo Wild Wings, Chick-fil-A, Chili's, Chipotle Mexican, ChuckeCheese, Culver's, Don Pablo, IHOP, Jamba Juice, Jimmy John's, Joe's Crabshack, KFC/LJ Silver, Longhorn Steaks, McDonald's, Olive Garden, Peking Buffet, Popeye's, Potbelly, Red Lobster, Red Robin, Sheffield's Rest., Starbucks, Taco Bell, Taco Depot, TGIFriday's, Wendy's, 🛏 Best Value Inn, Best Western, Candlewood Suites, Comfort Suites, Country Inn&Suites, Economy Inn, Extended Stay America, Hilton Garden, La Quinta, Motel 6, Quality Inn, Super 8, 🅾 AT&T, Audi/VW, AutoZone, Best Buy, BigLots, Carmax, Costco/gas, Dick's, Firestone/auto, Gander Mtn, Hobby Lobby, Home Depot, Honda, JC Penney, Kia, Kohl's, Lowe's, Macy's, Michael's, Nissan, Office Depot, Old Navy, PetCo, Petsmart, Sam's Club/gas, Sears/auto, Target, TJ Maxx, Tire Barn, Toyota/Scion, Tuesday Morning, Walmart/McDonald's, mall, vet
249	109th Ave, **W** 🍴 Beggars Pizza, China Garden, Golden Apple Rest., Jimmy John's, Oberweis Icecream, 🅾 GNC, Verizon, Walgreens
247	US 231, Crown Point, **W** 🅿 Mobil/dsl, 🅾 🅗, Vietnam Vet Mem
241mm	weigh sta sb
240	IN 2, Lowell, **E** 🅿 ⓕFLYING J/Denny's/dsl/24hr/@, Mobil/Burger King, 🚛/McDonalds/dsl/scales/24hr, 🍴 Arby's, Subway, 🛏 Comfort Inn, Super 8, 🅾 truck wash, **W** st police
234mm	Kankakee River
231mm	ⓡ **both lanes, full** 🦽 **facilities,** 🅲 **, info,** 🖼 **, litter barrels, vending, petwalk**
230	IN 10, Roselawn, **E** 🅿 Gas City/Kozy Kitchen/dsl/scales/24hr, 🚛Loves/Arby's/dsl/scales/24hr, **W** 🅿
230	Continued Family Express/e85, Marathon/Subway, 🍴 China Wok, J&J Pizza, Sycamore Drive-In, 🅾 CarQuest, CVS Drug, $General, Fagen Drug, IGA Foods, TrueValue, Lake Holiday Camping, Oak Lake Camping
220	IN 14, Winamac, **W** 🅿 BP/Subway/dsl, 🅾 Fair Oaks Farms Store
215	IN 114, Rensselaer, **E** 🅿 Family Express/dsl/e85/24hr, 🍴 Arby's, DQ, KFC, McDonald's, Rensselear Rest., 🛏 Holiday Inn Express, Knights Inn, 🅾 🅗, **W** 🅿 Marathon/Trail Tree Rest./dsl/24hr, 🍴 Burger King, 🛏 Economy Inn, 🅾 fireworks, tires/repair/towing/24hr
212mm	Iroquois River
205	US 231, Remington, **E** 🅿 BP/dsl, Crazy D/dsl, 🅾 🅗, to St Joseph's Coll
201	US 24/231, Remington, **E** 🅾 Caboose Lake RV Camping, **W** 🅿 Petro/Shell/Iron Skillet/dsl/scales/24hr/@, 🚛 Subway/dsl/scales/24hr, 🍴 KFC, McDonald's, 🛏 Sunset Inn, Super 8
196mm	ⓡ **both lanes, full** 🦽 **facilities, vending,** 🅲 **, info,** 🖼 **, litter barrels, petwalk**
193	US 231, to Chalmers, **E** 🅿 BP/DQ/Stuckey's
188	IN 18, to Brookston, Fowler, many windmills
178	IN 43, W Lafayette, **E** 🅿 GA/Taco Bell, Phillips 66/Subway/dsl, 🍴 McDonald's, Wendy's, 🛏 EconoLodge, 🅾 to Tippecanoe Bfd, museum, st police, **W** to Purdue U
176mm	Wabash River
175	IN 25, Lafayette, **E** 🅿 BP/dsl, Family Express/dsl/e85, **W** 🅾 🅗
172	IN 26, Lafayette, **E** 🍴 Cracker Barrel, DQ, El Rodeo, Starbucks, Steak'n Shake, Subway, Taj Mahal, White Castle, 🛏 Baymont Inn, Candlewood Suites, Comfort Inn, Comfort Suites, Days Inn, La Quinta, Motel 6, TownePlace Suites, 🅾 Meijer/dsl/e85, visitor's ctr, **W** 🅿 BP/Circle K/dsl/24hr, Citgo, Speedway/dsl, 🍴 Arby's, Bob Evans, Burger King, Camille's Cafe, Chick-fil-A, Chili's, ChuckeCheese, Country Cafe, Culvers, Denny's, Don Pablo, Fazoli's, Golden Corral, Grindstone Charlie's, Hour Time Rest., IHOP, Jimmy John's, KFC, Logan's Roadhouse, McAlister's Deli, McDonald's, Moe's SW Grill, Mt Jack's, Olive Garden, Outback Steaks, Pizza Hut, Sonic, Spagedie's, Starbucks, Steak'n Shake, Subway, Taco Bell, TGIFriday's, 🛏 Best Western, Clarion, Courtyard, Fairfield Inn, Hampton Inn, Homewood Suites, Knights Inn, Quality Inn, Red Roof Inn, Super 8, 🅾 🅗, Aamco, Chevrolet, CVS Drug, Discount Tire, $General, $Tree, Gordman's, Hobby Lobby, Home Depot, Hyundai, Lowe's, Marsh Foods, Nissan, Office Depot, Sam's Club/gas, Target, TJ Maxx, Toyota, Verizon, Walgreens, Walmart/Subway, USPO, vet, to Purdue U
168	IN 38, IN 25 S, Dayton, **E** 🅿 BP/Subway, Pantry/dsl
158	IN 28, to Frankfort, **E** 🅿 BP/Subway/dsl, 🅾 Harley-Davidson, Peterbilt, repair, **2 mi W** 🛏 Lincoln Lodge Motel, 🅾 🅗, camping
150mm	ⓡ **sb, full** 🦽 **facilities, info,** 🖼 **, litter barrels,** 🅲 **, vending, petwalk**
148mm	ⓡ **nb, full** 🦽 **facilities, info,** 🖼 **, litter barrels,** 🅲 **, vending, petwalk**
146	IN 47, Thorntown, **W** 🅗, camping
141	US 52 W (exits left from sb), Lafayette Ave, **E** 🅗
140	IN 32, Lebanon, **E** 🅿 BP/repair, Marathon/dsl, 🍴 Denny's, Depot Rest., McDonald's, White Castle, 🛏 Comfort

MERRILLVILLE

LAFAYETTE

IN

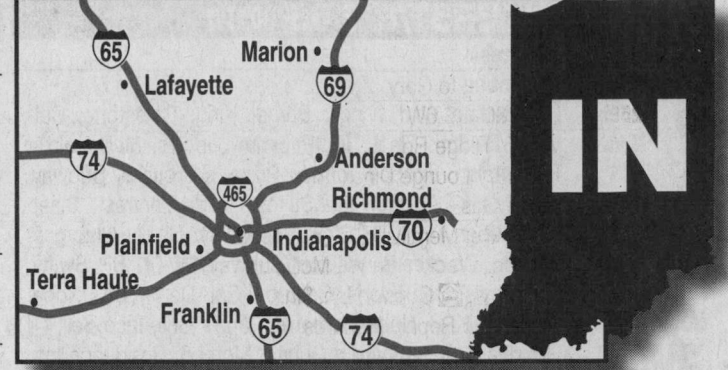

INTERSTATE 65 CONT'D

Exit	Services

L E B A N O N

140 Continued
Inn, ⊙ H, AutoZone, Goodyear/auto, Menards, O'Reilly Parts, Pomp's Tires, **W** ⊛ McClure/dsl/e85, Shell, ⊙ Arby's, Flapjacks Pancakes, KFC, Steak'n Shake, Subway, Taco Bell, ⌂ EconoLodge, Holiday Inn Express, Motel 6, Super 8, ⊙ truckwash

139 IN 39, Lebanon, **E** ⊛ GA/dsl, ⊙ Penn Sta Subs, Starbucks, Wendy's, **W** ⊛FLYING J/IHOP/dsl/LP/scales/24hr, ⊙ Donaldson's Chocolates

138 to US 52, Lebanon, **E** ⊛ BP/dsl

133 IN 267, Whitestown, **W** ⊛ ✦Loves/McDonald's/Subway/dsl/scales/24hr

130 IN 334, Zionsville, **E** ⊛ Marathon/Noble Roman's/Starbucks/Stuckey's/dsl/24hr, Shell/Circle K/Subway/dsl, ⊙ Burger King, El Rodeo Mexican, Fox's Pizza, Hong Kong House, McDonald's, Taco Bell, ⊙ H, CVS Drug, Lowe's, **W** ⊛ TA/BP/Popeye's/dsl/scales/24hr/@

129 I-865 E, to I-465 E, US 52 E (from sb)

126mm Fishback Creek

124 71st St, **1 mi E** ⊛ BP, ⊙ Bob Evans, Starbucks, Steak'n Shake, ⌂ Candlewood Suites, Courtyard, Hampton Inn, Hilton Garden, Residence Inn, Wingate Inn, **W** Eagle Creek Park

123 I-465 S, S to 🚻

I N D I A N A P O L I S   A R E A

121 Lafayette Rd, **E** ⊛ GA, Speedway/dsl, ⌂ Quality Inn, **W** ⊛ Shell/Circle K, ⊙ Applebee's, Arby's, Church's, Fazoli's, La Bamba Burritos, Wendy's, ⌂ Best Value Inn, ⊙ H, Batteries+, Discount Tire, $Tree, Family$, Kia, Mazda, NAPA, Nissan, PepBoys, Tire Barn, Toyota/Scion, Verizon, Walmart/Subway, same as 119

119 38th St (no nb return), **W** ⊛ Speedway/dsl, ⊙ ChuckeCheese, Fiesta Mexican, Hooters, KFC, McDonald's, O'Charley's, Papa John's, Penn Sta Subs, Pizza Hut, Popeye's, Red Lobster, Taco Bell, WTT Buffet, ⊙ Aldi Foods, Best Buy, Chevrolet, CVS Drug, Honda, Hyundai, Meijer/dsl, Radio Shack, Staples, Tires+, same as 121

117.5mm White River

117 MLK St (from sb), **W** ⊛ Marathon/dsl

116 29th St, 30th St (from nb)   Marian Coll

115 21st St, **E** ⊛ Shell/Circle K, ⊙ H, **W** museums, zoo

114 MLK St, West St, downtown

113 US 31, IN 37, Meridian St, to downtown, **E** ⊙ H

112a I-70 E, to Columbus

111 Market St, Michigan St, Ohio St, **E** ⊙ Hardee's, **W** ⊙ City Market, museum

110b I-70 W, to St Louis

110a Prospect St, Morris St, East St

109 Raymond St, **E** H, **W** ⊛ BP, Speedway/dsl, ⊙ Little Caesars, White Castle, ⊙ CVS Drug, Family$, Safeway

107 Keystone Ave, **E** ⊛ Mystik, ⌂ Best Value Inn, ⊙ H, **W** ⊛ Phillips 66/dsl, Speedway/dsl, Valero, ⊙ Big Kahuna Pizza, Burger King, Denny's, McDonald's, Subway, Wendy's, ⌂ Comfort Inn, ⊙ $General, Walmart Mkt, U of Indianapolis

106 I-465 and I-74

103 Southport Rd, **E** ⊛ BP/McDonald's, Shell/Circle K, ⊙ Arby's, Chick-fil-A, Chicago Grill, El Puerto, Hardee's, Hong Kong, Jimmy John's, Longhorn Steaks, Noble Roman's, O'Charley's, Panda Express, Panera Bread, Penn Sta Subs, Qdoba, Quiznos, Rally's, Starbucks, Taco Bell,

---

103 Continued
⊙ Aldi Foods, AT&T, Firestone/auto, Harley-Davidson, Home Depot, Kohl's, Menards, Meijer/dsl/e85, Radio Shack, Staples, Target, Verizon, **W** ⊛ Marathon/Circle K, Phillips 66, Speedway/dsl, ⊙ Bob Evans, Burger King, Carrabba's, Cheeseburger Paradise, Cracker Barrel, JT Johnson's Grill, KFC, McDonald's, Starbucks, Steak'n Shake, Subway, TX Roadhouse, Waffle House, Wendy's, ⌂ Best Western, Comfort Suites, Country Inn&Suites, Courtyard, Fairfield Inn, Hampton Inn, Jameson Inn, Quality Inn, Super 8, ⊙ H, 7-11

101 CountyLine Rd, **E** ⊙ Candlewood Suites, **W** ⊛ Murphy USA/dsl, ⊙ Buffalo Wild Wings, El Mason Mexican, Fireside Rest., Little Mexico, Pasquale's Pizza, Tokyo Buffet, ⌂ Hilton Garden, Holiday Inn Express, Value Place Hotel, ⊙ H, Gander Mtn, Kroger, Verizon, Walmart/Subway

G R E E N W O O D

99 Greenwood, **E** ⊛ Road Ranger/[ ]/Subway/dsl/scales/24hr, **W** ⊛ Marathon, Shell/Circle K, Sunoco, ⊙ Arby's, Bob Evans, Byrd's Cafeteria, China Wok, Denny's, McDonald's, Oaken Barrel Rest., Puerto Vallarta, Starbucks, Subway, Taco Bell, Waffle House, White Castle, ⌂ Baymont Inn, InTown Suites, Red Carpet Inn, Red Roof Inn, ⊙ H, Camping World RV Ctr, Sam's Club, vet

95 Whiteland, **E** ⊛ ⊛FLYING J/Denny's/scales/dsl/LP/RV dump/24hr, ⊙ Blue Beacon, SpeedCo, tires, **W** ⊛ ✦Loves/Arby's/dsl/scales/24hr, [ ]/McDonald's/dsl/scales/24hr/@, ⊙ Family RV Ctr

90 IN 44, Franklin, **W** ⊛ Marathon/Chester's/Subway/dsl, Shell/Circle K, ⊙ Burger King, El Torito, McDonald's/RV Parking, Waffle House, ⌂ Comfort Inn, Howard Johnson, Quality Inn, Red Carpet Inn, Super 8, ⊙ H, golf

85mm Sugar Creek

82mm Big Blue River

80 IN 252, to Flat Rock, Edinburgh, **W** ⊛ Shell/dsl, Sunoco/dsl

76b a US 31, Taylorsville, **E** ⊛ Shell/Circle K/dsl, Speedway/dsl, ⊙ A&W/KFC, Burger King, El Toreo Mexican, Waffle House, ⌂ Red Roof Inn, ⊙ H, Buick/Cadillac/Chevrolet/GMC, $ General, Toyota, **W** ⊛ Marathon, Thornton's/café/dsl, ⊙ Arby's, Cracker Barrel, Hardee's, Max&Erma's, McDonald's, MT Mikes, Ruby Tuesday, Snappy Tomato Pizza, Subway, Taco Bell, ⌂ Best Western, Comfort Inn, Hampton Inn, Hilton Garden, Holiday Inn Express, ⊙ Driftwood RV Camp, Goodyear, Harley-Davidson, Premium Outlets/famous brands, antiques, repair

73mm 🅿️ both lanes, full ♿ facilities, 🅿 vending, info, 🚮 litter barrels, petwalk

68mm Driftwood River

68 IN 46, Columbus, **E** ⊛ Shell/Circle K, Speedway/dsl,

🔼N INTERSTATE 65 CONT'D

Exit	Services
68	Continued
	🍴 Buffalo Wild Wings, Burger King, Coldstone, Culver's, Dimitri's Rest., IHOP, Jimmy John's, McDonald's, RuYi Asian, Snappy Tomato Pizza, Starbucks, Subway, Wendy's, 🛏 Comfort Inn&Suites, Holiday Inn/rest., Sleep Inn, Super 8, 🅾 🅷, AT&T, Menards, Sam's Club/gas, Verizon, Walgreens, Walmart/Subway, **W** 🅿 BP, Swifty, 🍴 Arby's, Bob Evans, Casa del Sol, Denny's, El Nopal Mexican, KFC, Noble Roman's, Papa's Grill, Taco Bell, 🛏 Courtyard, Days Inn, La Quinta, Motel 6, Residence Inn, 🅾 CVS Drug, $General, Jay-C Foods, to Brown Co SP
64	IN 58, Walesboro, **W** 🅿 Marathon/dsl, 🅾 to RV camping
55	IN 11, to Jonesville, Seymour
54mm	White River
51mm	**weigh sta both lanes**
50b a	US 50, Seymour, **E** 🅿 Marathon/Circle K/dsl, Swifty, TA/BP/Country Pride/dsl/24hr/@, 🍴 McDonald's, Waffle House, 🛏 Allstate Inn, Days Inn, EconoLodge, Motel 6, Super 8, **W** 🅿 Citgo/dsl, Shell/Circle K/dsl, Speedway/dsl, Sunoco/dsl, 🍴 Applebee's, Arby's, Buffalo Wild Wings, Buffet China, Burger King, Capt D's, Chili's, Cracker Barrel, Domino's, DQ, El Nopal Mexican, Hardee's, KFC, Little Caesars, LJ Silver, McDonalds, Papa John's, Pizza Hut, Rally's, Ryan's, Steak'n Shake, Subway, Taco Bell, Tumbleweed Grill, Wendy's, White Castle, 🛏 Fairfield Inn, Hampton Inn, Holiday Inn Express, Knights Inn, Quality Inn, 🅾 🅷, Advance Parts, Aldi Foods, AT&T, AutoZone, BigLots, Buick/Cadillac/Chevrolet/GMC, Chrysler/Dodge/Jeep, CVS Drug, $General, $Tree, Ford, GNC, Home Depot, Jay-C Foods, JC Penney, O'Reilly Parts, Radio Shack, Russell Stover Candies, Staples, Walgreens, Walmart/Subway, st police
41	IN 250, Uniontown, **E** tires, **W** 🅿 UnionTown/rest./dsl, 🅾 auto/truck repair
36	US 31, Crothersville, **E** 🅿 Shell, **W** 🅿 Marathon/dsl
34a b	IN 256, Austin, **E** 🅿 Shell/Circle K, 🅾 to Hardy Lake, Clifty Falls SP, **W** 🅿 Fuelmart/dsl/scales, Sunoco/Huddle House/dsl
29b a	IN 56, to Salem, Scottsburg, **E** 🅿 MotoMart, Speedway/dsl, 🍴 Burger King, Cracker Barrel, KFC, Mariann Rest., Papa John's, Ponderosa, Sonic, Subway, Taco Bell, 🛏 Best Value Inn, Holiday Inn Express, 🅾 🅷, Ace Hardware, Advance Parts, AutoZone, CVS Drug, O'Reilly Parts, **W** 🅿 Marathon, Murphy USA, Shell/Circle K, 🍴 Arby's, LJ Silver, McDonald's, Pizza Hut, Roadhouse USA, Waffle House, Wendy's, 🛏 Hampton Inn, Quality Inn, Super 8, 🅾 Big O Tire, Jellystone Camping (4mi), Radio Shack, Verizon, Walmart/Subway
22mm	🆁🆂 both lanes, full ♿ facilities, info, 🅿, 🍴, litter barrels, vending, petwalk
19	IN 160, Henryville, **E** 🅿 Marathon/Subway/dsl, Shell/Circle K, 🍴 Schuler's Rest., 🅾 Family$
16	Memphis Rd, Memphis, **E** 🅿 ♥Love's/McDonald's/Subway/dsl/scales/24hr, 🍴 Fill'n Station Cafe, **W** 🅿 ▨/Arby's/dsl/scales/24hr/@, 🅾 Customers 1st RV Ctr
9	IN 311, to New Albany, Sellersburg, **E** 🅿 BP, 5 Star Gas, Shell/Circle K, Swifty, 🍴 Arby's, Cracker Barrel, DQ, Quiznos, Waffle House, 🛏 Ramada Inn, 🅾 Carmerica/repair, Ford, O'Reilly Parts, st police, **W** 🅿 Marathon/Circle

Exit	Services
9	Continued
	K, 🍴 Burger King, El Nopal Mexican, McDonald's, Taco Bell, 🛏 Comfort Inn, 🅾 city park
7	IN 60, Hamburg, **E** 🅿 Clark/dsl, **W** 🍴 Cricket's Cafe, KFC/Pizza Hut, 🛏 Days Inn
6b a	I-265 W, to I-64 W, IN 265 E, New Albany
5	Veterans Parkway, **E** 🅿 Shell/Circle K, 🍴 Beef'O Brady's, 🅾 🅷, Tire Discounters **W** 🍴 Buffalo Wild Wings, Cheddars, Chick-fil-A, Chuy's Mexican, DQ, Famous Dave's, IHOP, Krispy Kreme, Longhorn Steaks, McAlister's Deli, Moe's SW Grill, Olive Garden, Panera Bread, Papa Murphy's, Pizza Hut, Ruby Tuesday, Stevie B's Burgers, Studio Pizza, Subway, Taco Bell, 🅾 AT&T, Bass Pro Shops, Best Buy, Chevrolet, Lowe's, Michael's, Old Navy, Old Time Pottery, Petsmart, Rite Aid, Sam's Club/gas, Staples, Target, Verizon, Walmart/Subway
4	US 31 N, IN 131 S, Clarksville, New Albany, **E** 🅿 Thorntons/Dunkin Donuts/dsl, 🍴 White Castle, 🛏 Value Place Inn, 🅾 Raben Tire, **W** 🅿 Speedway/dsl, 🍴 Applebee's, Arby's, Bob Evans, Burger King, Capt D's, ChuckeCheese, Denny's, Don Pablo, El Caporal, Fazoli's, Frisch's, Golden Corral, Hooters, Iguana Rest., Logan's Roadhouse, LJ Silver, McDonald's, O'Charley's, Outback Steaks, Papa John's, Rally's, Red Lobster, Steak'n Shake, Wendy's, 🛏 Best Western, Candlewood Suites, Hampton Inn, Suburban Lodge, 🅾 AT&T, AutoZone, BigLots, Books-A-Million, Buick/GMC, Dick's, Dillard's, $Tree, Firestone/auto, Ford, Hobby Lobby, Home Depot, Honda, JC Penney, Jo-Ann Fabrics, Kia, Kroger/gas, Office Depot, O'Reilly Parts, PepBoys, Sears/auto, Toyota/Scion, Tuesday Morning, USPO, VW, Walgreens
2	Eastern Blvd, Clarksville, **E** 🛏 Comfort Suites, Days Inn, Motel 6, Super 8, 🅾 🅷, U-Haul, **W** 🅿 Shell/Circle K, 🛏 Best Inn
1	US 31 S, IN 62, Stansifer Ave, **E** 🅿 Thorntons, 🍴 DQ, 🅾 🅷, Advance Parts, Walgreens, info ctr, **W** 🛏 Holiday Inn, 🅾 Stinnett RV Ctr
0	Jeffersonville, **E** 🅿 Thornton/Dunkin Donuts, 🍴 Hardee's, McDonald's, Waffle House, 🅾 🅷, Chrysler/Jeep, Hyundai, Nissan, Walgreens, to Falls of OH SP, **W** 🍴 Subway, 🛏 Fairfield Inn, Sheraton, TownePlace Suites
0mm	Indiana/Kentucky state line, Ohio River

🔼N INTERSTATE 69

Exit	Services
358mm	Indiana/Michigan state line
357	Lake George Rd, to IN 120, Fremont, Lake James, **E** 🅿 Petro/Iron Skillet/dsl/LP/scales/24hr/@, 🅾 Freightliner/Western Star Truck Repair, Kenworth, **W** 🅿 Marathon/dsl, ▨/Wendy's/dsl/scales/24hr, Shell/Subway/dsl, 🍴 McDonald's, Red Arrow Rest., 🛏 Holiday Inn Express, Redwood Inn, 🅾 Freemont Outlets/Famous Brands, GNC, **services on IN 120 E** 🛏 Comfort Inn, Hampton Inn, Travelers Inn, 🅾 golf/rest, **W** to Pokagon SP, Jellystone Camping (5mi)
356	I-80/90 **Toll Rd**, E to Toledo, W to Chicago
354	IN 127, to IN 120, IN 727, Fremont, Orland, **E** 🛏 Budgeteer Motel, Comfort Inn, Hampton Inn, Ramada, Travelers Inn, 🅾 Oak Hill RV camp, golf, **W** 🅿 Marathon/dsl, 🛏 Holiday Inn Express, 🅾 Freemont Outlets/Famous Brands, to Pokagon SP, Jellystone Camping (4mi)
350	rd 200 W, to Lake James, Crooked Lake, **E** 🅿 Sunoco/Subway/dsl, 🅾 fireworks, **W** 🅿 Marathon, Shell, 🍴 Ca

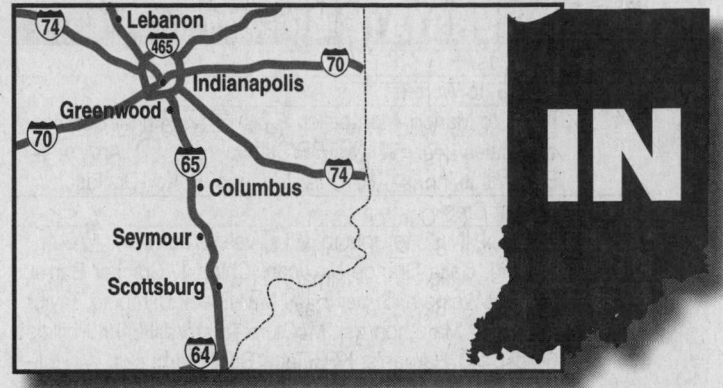

INTERSTATE 69 CONT'D

Exit	Services
354	Continued
	ruso's Rest., Tasty Pizza, 🅞 Marine Ctr
348	US 20, to Angola, Lagrange, **E** 🅟 Marathon/Subway/dsl, Speedway/Taco Bell/dsl, 🍴 McDonald's, 🏠 Happy Acres Camping (1mi), University Inn (2mi), 🅞 🅷, **W** 🅞 Circle B RV Prk (2mi)
345mm	Pigeon Creek
344mm	🅟ˢ sb, full ♿ facilities, info, 🛢, 🚰, litter barrels, vending, petwalk
340	IN 4, to Hamilton, Ashley, Hudson, **1 mi W** 🅟 Marathon/Ashley Deli/dsl
334	US 6, to Waterloo, Kendallville, **E** 🍴 Subway (1mi), **W** 🅟 BP/dsl, Marathon/dsl/24hr, 🍴 Maria's Pancakes
329	IN 8, to Garrett, Auburn, **E** 🅟 BP, GA, Lassus, Speedway/dsl, 🍴 Applebee's, Arby's, Bob Evans, Burger King, China Buffet, DQ, KFC, Little Caesars, McDonald's, Papa John's, Peking Buffet, Penguin Point Rest., Pizza Hut, Ponderosa, Richard's Rest., Starbucks, Steak'n Shake, Subway, Taco Bell, Wendy's, 🏠 Comfort Suites, Days Inn, Holiday Inn Express, La Quinta, Quality Inn, Super 8, 🅞 🅷, Ace Hardware, Advance Parts, AT&T, AutoZone, Buick/Chevrolet/RV Ctr, Chrysler/Dodge/Jeep, CVS Drug, $General, $Tree, Ford, GNC, Kroger/dsl, Radio Shack, Staples, Walmart/Subway, museum, **W** 🅟 Marathon/dsl, 🍴 Buffalo Wild Wings, Cracker Barrel, Paradise Buffet, 🏠 Hampton Inn, 🅞 Home Depot, Verizon
326	rd 11A, to Garrett, Auburn, **E** Kruse Auction Park, **W** camping
324mm	🅟ˢ nb, full ♿ facilities, info, 🚰, litter barrels, vending
317	Union Chapel Rd, **E** 🅷
316	IN 1 N, Dupont Rd, **E** 🅟 Lassus/Elmo's/dsl, Phillips 66/Burger King, 🍴 Arby's, Culver's, 🏠 Comfort Suites, Hampton Inn, 🅞 🅷, **W** 🅟 Speedway/dsl, 🍴 Bandito's Mexican, Bob Evans, Cozy Nook Cafe, Jimmy John's, Mancino's Grinders, McDonald's, Pine Valley Grill, Starbucks, Trolley Grill, 🏠 Baymont Inn, La Quinta
315	I-469, US 30 E, **W** 🏠 Value Place Hotel
312b a	Coldwater Rd, **E** 🅟 BP/dsl, Marathon, Sunoco, 🍴 Arby's, Chappell's, Chili's, Cork'N Cleaver, Hall's Factory Rest., Hunan Chinese, IHOP, Jimmy John's, Koto Japanese, Papa John's, Quiznos, Rally's, Red Lobster, Red River Steaks, Steak'n Shake, Taco Bell, Wendy's, 🏠 Hotel Ft Wayne, Hyatt Place, 🅞 $Tree, Hobby Lobby, Hyundai, JoAnn Fabrics, NAPA, O'Reilly Parts, PetCo, Tuesday Morning, Tuffy Auto, U-Haul, Walmart/Subway, **W** Dunkin Donuts
311b a	US 27 S, IN 3 N, **E** 🅟 Shell/dsl, Sunoco/dsl, 🍴 Arby's, Cheddar's, ChuckECheese's, DQ, Fazoli's, Golden Corral, Hall's Rest., McDonald's, Olive Garden, Quaker Steak&Lube, TGIFriday's, 🏠 Candlewood Suites, Stay Inn, TownePlace Suites, 🅞 Aldi Foods, Barnes&Noble, Chevrolet, Chrysler/Dodge/Jeep, Costco/gas, Discount Tire, Fiat, Ford/Lincoln, Hancock Fabrics, Honda, Infiniti, JC Penney, Macy's, Nissan, Sears, Toyota/Scion, Verizon, **W** 🅟 Lassus/Elmo's Pizza/dsl, Marathon, 🍴 Applebee's, Burger King, Cracker Barrel, Culver's, Golden China, IHOP, Logan's Roadhouse, McDonald's, Panda Express, Starbucks, Subway, Taco Bell, TX Roadhouse, 🏠 Best Value Inn, Courtyard, County Inn&Suites, Days Inn, EconoLodge, Extended Stay America, Fairfield Inn,

Exit	Services
311b a	Continued
	Guesthouse Motel, Hampton Inn, Quality Inn, Super 8, 🅞 Urgent Care, CVS Drug, Gander Mtn, Home Depot, Lowe's, Meijer/dsl/E85, Sam's Club/gas, Walgreens, VW
309b a	US 33, Goshen Rd, Ft Wayne, **E** 🅟 🚛/dsl/scales/24hr, Sunoco/dsl, 🍴 Liberty Diner, McDonald's, Pace Rest., 🏠 Clarion, Country Hearth Inn, Guest House Inn, Knights Inn, Motel 6, Red Roof Inn, Travel Inn, 🅞 🅷, Blue Beacon, NAPA, auto/dsl repair
305b a	IN 14 W, Ft Wayne, **E** 🅟 Lassus, Murphy USA, Shell/Subway/dsl, Speedway/dsl/LP, 🍴 Arby's, Biaggi's, Bob Evans, Burger King, Chick-fil-A, Chipotle Mexican, Coldstone, Eddy Merlot Rest., Flat Top Grill, Firehouse Subs, Great Wall Buffet, Logan's Roadhouse, McAlister's Deli, Noodles&Co., O'Charley's, Panda Express, Panera Bread, Papa Murphy's, Penn Sta Subs, Qdoba, Smokey Bones BBQ, Starbucks, Steak'n Shake, Subway, Tilted Kilt Eatery, Wendy's, 🏠 Klopfenstein Suites, 🅞 🅷, Acura, Advance Parts, AT&T, Audi/Porsche, Barnes&Noble, Best Buy, BigLots, BMW, Buick/GMC, Cadillac, Chevrolet, Chrysler/Dodge/Jeep, Dick's, $Tree, Ford/Lincoln, Hancock Fabrics, Harley-Davidson, Kia, Kohl's, Lexus, Lowe's, Marshalls, Mazda, Meijer/dsl, Menards, Michael's, NAPA, Old Navy, Petsmart, Radio Shack, Staples, Subaru, Target, Toyota/Scion, Tuesday Morning, Verizon, Volvo, Walmart, mall, vct, to St Francis U
302	US 24, to Jefferson Blvd, Ft Wayne, **E** 🍴 Subway (1mi), Taco Bell (1mi), 🏠 Extended Stay America, Hampton Inn, Residence Inn, 🅞 🅷, to IN Wesleyan U, **W** 🅟 Lassus, Marathon/dsl, 🍴 Applebee's, Arby's, Bob Evans, Buffalo Wild Wings, Carlos O'Kelly's, Coventry Tavern Rest., McDonald's, Naked Chopstix, Outback Steaks, Pizza Hut, Sara's Rest., Starbucks, Wendy's, Zesto Drive-In, 🏠 Best Western Luxury, Comfort Suites, Hilton Garden, Holiday Inn Express, Homewood Suites, Staybridge Suites, 🅞 Kroger, Meineke, Walgreens, st police
299	Lower Huntington Rd, **E** to 🅟ˢ
296b a	I-469, US 24 E, US 33 S, **E** to 🅟ˢ
286	US 224, to Huntington, Markle, **E** 🅟 Marathon (1mi), Phillips 66/Subway/dsl, 🍴 Daily Diner, DQ, Vinatelli's, 🏠 Guesthouse Inn, Super 8, 🅞 🅷, repair/tires, **W** to Huntington Reservoir, Roush Lake
280mm	**weigh sta sb**/parking area nb
278	IN 5, to Warren, Huntington, **E** 🅟 Phillips 66/dsl, 🏠 Huggy Bear Motel, **W** 🅟 Marathon/Subway/dsl, Sunoco/HomeTown Diner/dsl/scales/24hr, 🍴 McDonald's, Ugalde's Rest., 🏠 Best Value Inn, Comfort Inn, 🅞 🅷, RV Camping, fireworks, to Salamonie Reservoir
276mm	Salamonie River

⬆N INTERSTATE 69 CONT'D

Exit	Services
273	IN 218, to Warren
264	IN 18, to Marion, Montpelier, **E** 🅖 ♥Love's/McDonalds/dsl/scales/24hr, **W** 🅖 BP/Subway/dsl, 🍴 Arby's, 🛏 Best Value Inn, 🅞 🄷, Chrysler/Jeep, Harley-Davidson
260mm	Walnut Creek
259	US 35 N, IN 22, to Upland, **E** 🅖 Valero/Subway, 🍴 Burger King, Casa Grande Mexican, China 1, Cracker Barrel, 🛏 Best Western, Super 8, 🅞 Mar-Brook Camping, Taylor U, **W** 🅖 Marathon/dsl, McClure Trkstp/dsl/24hr, Phillips 66/dsl, 🍴 Hardee's, KFC/Taco Bell, Starbucks, 🛏 Holiday Inn Express, 🅞 to IN Wesleyan
255	IN 26, to Fairmount
250mm	🅡ₛ both lanes, full 🅱 facilities, info, ⓒ, 🄵, litter barrels, vending, pet walk
245	US 35 S, IN 28, to Alexandria, Albany, **E** 🅖 Petro/Shell/Iron Skillet/Subway/dsl/scales/24hr/@, 🅞 RV Camping
241	IN 332, to Muncie, Frankton, **E** 🅖 BP/dsl, 🅞 🄷, to Ball St U
234	IN 67, to IN 32, Chesterfield, Daleville, **E** 🅖 🚚 Subway/dsl/scales/24hr, Shell, 🍴 Arby's, Pizza Hut, Smokehouse BBQ, Taco Bell, Waffle House, White Castle, 🛏 Budget Inn, 🅞 🄷, **W** 🅖 McClure/dsl/E85, 🚚 Denny's/dsl/scales/24hr, Speedway/dsl, 🍴 McDonald's, Subway, 3rd Generation Pizza, Wendy's, 🛏 Travel Inn, 🅞 Timberline Valley Camping (3mi), flea mkt
226	IN 9, IN 109, to Anderson, **E** 🍴 A&W/KFC, Culver's, Golden Corral, MT Mike's, 🛏 Deluxe Inn, Hampton Inn, Holiday Inn Express, Quality Inn, 🅞 Meijer/dsl, Menards, visitors ctr, **W** 🅖 BP, Marathon/dsl, PayLess/dsl, Speedway/dsl, 🍴 Applebee's, Arby's, Bob Evans, Buffalo Wild Wings, Burger King, Cracker Barrel, Fazoli's, IHOP, Jimmy John's, LoneStar Steaks, Mayo Mexican, McDonald's, Olive Garden, Panda Express, Panera Bread, Papa Murphy's, Penn Sta Subs, Perkins, Pizza Hut, Poblanos Mexican, Qdoba, Quiznos, Red Lobster, Ruby Tuesday, Starbucks, Steak'n Shake, Subway, Taco Bell,. Waffle House, Wendy's, White Castle, 🛏 Best Western, Comfort Inn, Days Inn, Fairfield Inn, Motel 6, Super 8, 🅞 🄷, Aldi Foods, AT&T, Cadillac/Chevrolet, Chrysler/Dodge/Jeep, $General, $Tree, Freightliner, GNC, Hobby Lobby, Kohl's, Lowe's, Marshalls, Office Depot, Old Navy, O'Reilly Parts, Petsmart, Radio Shack, Target, Tire Barn, Toyota/Scion, Verizon, Walgreens, Walmart/Subway, to Anderson U, to Mounds SP
222	IN 9, IN 67, to Anderson, **W** 🅖 Speedway/dsl, 🍴 Skyline Chili, 🅞 🄷, st police
219	IN 38, Pendleton, **E** 🅖 Marathon, 🍴 Burger King, McDonald's, Subway, **W** 🅞 Pine Lakes Camping
214	IN 13, to Lapel, **E** 🅖 BP, 🍴 Waffle House, **W** 🅖 🚚 Subway/dsl/scales/24hr, 🅞 camping
210	IN 238, to Noblesville, Fortville, **E** 🅖 BP, 🍴 DQ, Starbucks, Taco Bell, Wendy's, 🅞 🄷, **W** 🍴 Bella Pizzeria, Coldstone, Famous Dave's, BBQ, 5 Guys Burgers, Houlihan's, McAlister's Deli, McDonald's, Mo's Cafe, Olive Garden, Panda Express, Paradise Cafe, Qdoba, Red Robin, Stone Creek Rest., 🛏 Cambria Suites, 🅞 AT&T, CVS Drug, Dick's, $Tree, Earth Fare Foods, Firestone/auto, GNC, JC Penney, Old Navy, Radio Shack, Sleepy Bear Camping, Steinmart, Verizon
205	IN 37 N, 116th St, to Noblesville, Fishers, **E** 🅖 BP, 🍴 La

205	Continued Fuente Mexican, Penn Sta Subs, Sunrise Cafe, 🅞 Urgent Care, Fresh Mkt, Kroger, **W** 🅖 Shell/Circle K, Speedway, 🍴 Coldstone, 5 Guys Burgers, Friaco's Mexican Grill, Greek Pizzaria, Handel's Ice Cream, Happy Dragon, Jet's Pizza, Marco's Pizza, Maya Mexican, McAlister's Deli, McDonald's, Moe's SW Grill, O'Charley's, Qdoba, Starbucks, Steak'n Shake, Subway, Wendy's, Wild Ginger Asian, 🛏 Hampton Inn, 🅞 AT&T, CVS Drug, Firestone/auto, Target
203	96th St, **E** 🅖 Marathon/dsl, Murphy USA/dsl, Shell/Circle K, 🍴 Applebee's, Blimpie, Cracker Barrel, Donato's Pizza, Dunkin Donuts, Extreme Pizza, IHOP, Jimmy John's, McDonald's, Noodles&Co., Panda Express, Panera Bread, Qdoba, Ruby Tuesday, Sahm's Grill, Starbucks, Steak'n Shake, Subway, Tiawana Flats, Wendy's, 🛏 AmericInn, Baymont Inn, Hilton Garden, Holiday Inn, Studio 6, 🅞 AT&T, Fry's, GNC, Kohl's, Marsh Food, Meijer/dsl, PepBoys, PetCo, Radio Shack, Staples, Tuesday Morning, Verizon, Walmart, **W** 🅖 Marathon/dsl, 🍴 Arby's, Bob Evans, Burger King, Cheeseburger Paradise, Culver's, DJ's Hotdogs, Izakya Japanese, La Cabana, Panda Express, Peterson's Steaks/seafood, Quiznos, Starbucks, Taco Bell, Wolfie's Grill, 🛏 Comfort Suites, Residence Inn, SpringHill Suites, Staybridge Suites, 🅞 Aldi Foods, $Tree, Home Depot, Menards, NAPA, Sam's Club/gas
201	82nd St, Castleton, **E** 🅖 Shell, 🍴 Boston Mkt, Burger King, Golden Corral, Jet's Pizza, O'Charley's, 🛏 $Inn, Drury Inn, Extended Stay, Hilton, Super 8, 🅞 🄷, CVS Drug, Lowe's, Walgreens, **W** 🅖 Speedway/dsl, 🍴 Applebee's, Arby's, Burger King, Castleton Grill, Charleston's Rest., Denny's, Domino's, Fazoli's, Formosa Buffet, Hooters, Houlihan's, Jimmy John's, Joe's Grille, KFC, LJ Silver, Longhorn Steaks, Los Cabos Mexican, McDonald's, Olive Garden, Penn Sta Subs, Pizza Hut, Rally's, Red Lobster, Skyline Chili, Starbucks, Stir Crazy, Subway, Taco Bell, Wendy's, 🛏 Candlewood Suites, Days Inn, Hampton Inn, Magnuson Hotel, Motel 6, 🅞 Aamco, Advance Parts, AutoZone, Best Buy, CarX, Dick's, Discount Tire, $Tree, Firestone/auto, Goodyear/auto, JC Penney, Macy's, Midas, O'Reilly Parts, Sears/auto, Tire Barn, Verizon, fireworks, mall
200mm	I-465 around Indianapolis. **I-69 begins/ends on I-465, exit 37, at Indianapolis.**

⬆E INTERSTATE 70

Exit	Services
156.5mm	Indiana/Ohio state line, **weigh sta**
156b a	US 40 E, Richmond, **N** 🅖 Petro/BP/Iron Skillet/dsl/24hr/@, 🛏 Fairfield Inn, 🅞 Blue Beacon, **S** 🅖 BP/White Castle, Murphy USA/dsl, Shell, Speedway/dsl, 🍴 A&W/LJ Silver, Applebee's, Arby's, Big Boy, Bob Evans, Buffalo Wild Wings, Burger King, Chili's, Chipotle Mexican, Cracker Barrel, Fazoli's, Golden Corral, Hacienda Mexican, IHOP, Jade House Chinese, KFC, McDonald's, MCL Cafeteria, O'Charley's, Pizza Hut, Rally's, Red Lobster, Starbucks, Steak'n Shake, Subway, Super China, Taco Bell, TX Roadhouse, 🛏 Best Western, Days Inn, Hampton Inn, Lee's Inn, Motel 6, Quality Inn, 🅞 Advance Parts, Aldi Foods, AT&T, Best Buy, BigLots, Buick/GMC, CarQuest, Chevrolet, Chrysler/Jeep, Dillard's, $General, $Tree, Expert Tire, Family$, Ford, Hastings Books, Hobby Lobby, Hyundai, JC Penney, Jo-Ann Fabrics, Kohl's, Kroger, Lowe's, Menards, Save-A-Lot Foods, Sears/auto, Tires+, Toyota/

Sidebar labels: **INDIANAPOLIS AREA**, **ANDERSON**, **RICHMOND**, **ID**

◄E INTERSTATE 70 CONT'D

Exit	Services
156b a	Continued Scion, Tuffy, U-Haul, Verizon, Walgreens, Walmart
153	IN 227, to Whitewater, Richmond, **2 mi N** Grandpa's Farm RV Park (seasonal)
151b a	US 27, to Chester, Richmond, **N** 🍴 Fricker's Rest., Ⓞ Honda, KOA, **S** 🅶 Shell, 🍴 Bob Evans, Burger King, Carver's Rest., China Buffet, McDonald's, Rally's, Subway, Taco Bell, Wendy's, 🛏 Comfort Inn, Super 8, Ⓞ Ⓗ, CVS Drug, Harley-Davidson, Meijer/dsl/E85
149b a	US 35, IN 38, to Muncie, **N** ♥Loves/Hardee's/dsl/scales/24hr, **S** 🅶 Shell/Quiznos/dsl, Ⓞ Raper RV Ctr
148mm	weigh sta wb
145	Centerville, **N** 🅶 BP/DQ/Stuckey's, 🛏 Super 8, Ⓞ Goodyear/truck repair, **S** Warm Glow Candles
145mm	Nolands Fork Creek
144mm	🆁🆂 wb, full ♿ facilities, info, vending, 🆖, 🅿, litter barrels, petwalk
141mm	Greens Fork River
137	IN 1, to Hagerstown, Connersville, **N** Amish Cheese, **S** 🅶 GA, Gas City/rest./dsl/24hr, Shell, 🍴 Burger King, McDonald's
131	Wilbur Wright Rd, New Lisbon, **S** 🅶 Shell/KFC/Taco Bell/dsl/scales/24hr/@, Ⓞ New Lisbon RV park
126mm	Flatrock River
123	IN 3, to New Castle, Spiceland, **N** 🛏 All American Inn (3mi), Holiday Inn Express (3mi), Ⓞ Ⓗ, **S** 🅶 ♦FLYING J/Denny's/Subway/dsl/LP/scales/24hr, Ⓞ tires/repair
117mm	Big Blue River
115	IN 109, to Knightstown, Wilkinson, **N** 🅶 GA/rest/dsl/scales/24hr, 🍴 Burger King, Ⓞ Jellystone Camping
107mm	🆁🆂 both lanes, full ♿ facilities, vending, 🆖, 🅿, litter barrels, petwalk
104	IN 9, Greenfield, Maxwell, **N** 🅶 GA/Miami Grill/dsl, **S** 🅶 GA, Murphy USA/dsl, Shell/Circle K, Sunoco/dsl, Swifty, 🍴 Applebee's, Arby's, Bamboo Garden, Bob Evans, Burger King, China Inn, Cracker Barrel, Culver's, El Rodeo Mexican, Hardee's, KFC, Little Caesars, McDonald's, Mi Casa Mexican, MT Mike's Steaks, Mozzi's Pizza, O'Charley's, Papa John's, Papa Murphy's, Penn Sta Subs, Pizza Hut, Ponderosa, Qdoba, Quiznos, Starbucks, Steak'n Shake, Subway, Taco Bell, Wendy's, White Castle, 🛏 Comfort Inn, Country Inn&Suites, $Inn, Hampton Inn, Holiday Inn Express, Quality Inn, Super 8, Ⓞ Ⓗ, Advance Parts, Aldi Foods, BigLots, Big O Tire, CVS Drug, $General, $Tree, GNC, Home Depot, Kroger/dsl, Marsh Foods, Radio Shack, Walgreens, Walmart
96	Mt Comfort Rd, **N** 🅶 GA/Subway/dsl, 🍴/Pizza Hut/dsl/scales/24hr, 🍴 Burger King, El Nopal, Wendy's, **S** 🅶 Shell/Circle K, 🍴 McDonald's, Ⓞ KOA (seasonal), Mt Comfort RV Ctr
91	Post Rd, to Ft Harrison, **N** 🅶 Citgo, 7-11, 🍴 Cracker Barrel, Denny's, Joe's Crabshack, McDonald's, Outback Steaks, Steak'n Shake, Wendy's, 🛏 InTown Suites, La Quinta, Ⓞ Lowe's, st police, **S** 🅶 Admiral, BP/dsl, Shell/dsl, Speedway, 🍴 Hardee's, KFC/Taco Bell, Waffle House, 🛏 Country Hearth Inn, Days Inn, Ⓞ CVS Drug, Family$, Home Depot, Marsh Foods
90	I-465 (from wb)
89	Shadeland Ave, I-465 (from eb), **N** 🅶 Marathon/dsl, 🍴 Bob Evans, 🛏 Comfort Inn, Hampton Inn, Holiday Inn Ex

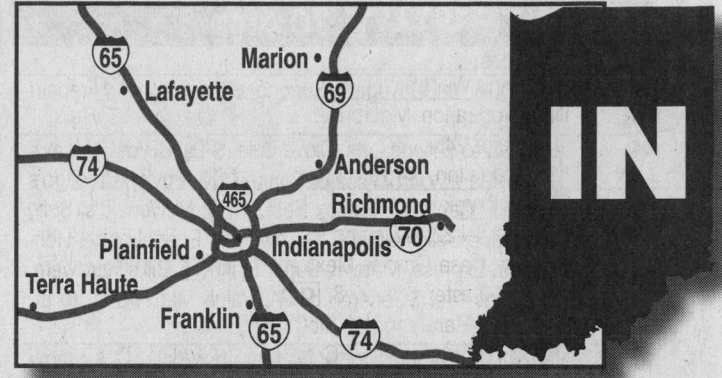

Exit	Services
89	Continued press, Motel 6, Ⓞ Toyota/Scion, U-Haul, **S** 🅶 Admiral/dsl, Circle K, Marathon, Shell, Speedway/dsl, 🍴 Arby's, Burger King, Damon's, 4Seasons Diner, Lincoln's Rest., McDonald's, Noble Roman's, Papa John's, Penn Sta Subs, Rally's, Red Lobster, Ryan's, Starbucks, Subway, Taco Bell, TX Roadhouse, Wendy's, White Castle, Zelma's Rest., 🛏 Best Value Inn, Candlewood Suites, Fairfield Inn, Knights Inn, La Quinta, Marriott, Quality Inn, Ramada Inn, Ⓞ Aamco, CarX, CVS Drug, Chevrolet, Chrysler/Dodge/Jeep, Honda, Kia, Kroger/gas, Mazda, Nissan
87	Emerson Ave, **N** 🅶 BP/McDonald's, Speedway/dsl, **S** 🅶 Shell, Ⓞ Ⓗ
85b a	Rural St, Keystone Ave, **N** fairgrounds
83b (112)	I-65 N, to Chicago
83a (111)	Michigan St, Market St, downtown, **S** 🍴 Hardee's
80 (110a)	I-65 S, to Louisville
79b	Illinois St, McCarty St, downtown
79a	West St, **N** 🅶 Speedway/dsl, 🛏 Comfort Inn, Holiday Inn Express, Hyatt, Staybridge Suites, Ⓞ Ⓗ, to Union Sta, Govt Ctr, Lucas Oil Stadium, zoo
78	Harding St, to downtown, **S** 🅶 Marathon, 🍴 Wendy's
77	Holt Rd, **N** 🍴 Steak'n Shake, **S** 🅶 Shell, 🍴 McDonald's, Ⓞ Ford Trucks
75	⤵ Expswy, to Raymond St (no EZ wb return), **N** 🅶 Marathon, Speedway/dsl, 🍴 Denny's, Indy's Rest., Library Rest, Waffle House, 🛏 Adam's Mark, Candlewood Suites, Courtyard, EconoLodge, Extended Stay Deluxe, Fairfield Inn, Hyatt Place, La Quinta, Quality Inn, Ramada, Residence Inn, Ⓞ NAPA, to ⤴
73b a	I-465 N/S, I-74 E/W
69	(only from eb), to I-74 E, to I-465 S
68	Six Points Rd, **N** 🍴 Subway, 🛏 Hampton Inn, Hilton Garden, Ⓞ ⤴
66	IN 267, to Plainfield, Mooresville, **N** 🅶 BP, Shell/Circle K, Speedway/dsl, Thornton's/dsl, 🍴 Arby's, Bob Evans, Burger King, Coachman Rest., Cracker Barrel, Denny's, Golden Corral, Hog Heaven BBQ, McDonald's, Quiznos, Steak'n Shake, Subway, White Castle, Wood Fire Grill, 🛏 Baymont Inn, Best Western, Budget Inn, Cambria Suites, Comfort Inn, Days Inn, Hampton Inn, Holiday Inn Express, Homewood Suites, Motel 6, Staybridge Suites, Super 8, ValuePlace Inn, Wingate Inn, Ⓞ Buick/GMC, Chateau Thomas Winery, Harley-Davidson
65mm	🆁🆂 both lanes, full ♿ facilities, info, vending, 🆖, 🅿, litter barrels, petwalk
59	IN 39, to Belleville, **N** 🅶 ♥Loves/McDonald's/Subway/dsl/scales/24hr, Ⓞ Ⓗ, **S** 🅶 TA/Country Pride/dsl/scales/24hr/@, truckwash

GREENFIELD

INDIANAPOLIS AREA

IN

🅖 = gas   🍴 = food   🏠 = lodging   🅞 = other   🆁🆂 = rest stop   Copyright 2014 - The Next Exit ®

INTERSTATE 70 CONT'D

Exit	Services
51	rd 1100W, S 🅖 Koger's/Sunoco/dsl/rest/24hr, 🅞 repair/towing/24hr
41	US 231, to Greencastle, Cloverdale, S 🅖 BP/dsl, Casey's (2mi), Marathon/dsl/scales/24hr, 🍴 Arby's, Chicago's Pizza, El Cantarito, Icebox Rest., KFC, McDonald's, Subway, Taco Bell, Wendy's, 🏠 Days Inn, EconoLodge, Holiday Inn Express, Motel 6, Super 8, 🅞 🏥, Bill's Hardware, Discount Tire, $General, NAPA, Value Mkt Foods, to Lieber SRA
37	IN 243, to Putnamville, S 🅖 Marathon/dsl, 🍴 A-Frame Cafe, 🅞 Misty Morning Campground (4mi), to Lieber SRA
23	IN 59, to Brazil, N 🅖 🚚/McDonald's/Subway/dsl/scales/24hr, 🅞 🏥, S 🅖 AM Best/Brazil Grill/dsl/scales/24hr/@, BP/Rally's/dsl, Road Ranger/🚚/Subway/dsl/scales, 🍴 Burger King, Family Table Rest., 🏠 Knights Inn
15mm	Honey Creek
11	IN 46, Terre Haute, N 🅖 🚚/Subway/dsl/scales/24hr, Thornton/dsl, 🍴 Burger King, McDonald's, lodging Holiday Inn Express, 🅞 🏥, S KOA
7	US 41, US 150, Terre Haute, N 🅖 Marathon/dsl, Thornton's/dsl, 🍴 Applebee's, Beef o'Brady's, Bob Evans, Cracker Barrel, China Buffet 8, Fazoli's, IHOP, LoneStar Steaks, Pasta House, Pizza Hut, Real Hacienda Mexican, Starbucks, Steak'n Shake, Sunrise Rest., TX Roadhouse, Tumbleweed SW Grill, 🏠 Best Value Inn, Comfort Suites, Days Inn, Drury Inn, EconoLodge, Fairfield Inn, PearTree Inn, Super 8, 🅞 AutoZone, Chrysler/Jeep, Kia, Mike's Mkt, O'Reilly Parts, S 🅖 Speedway/dsl, Thornton's/mart, 🍴 Arby's, Baskin-Robbins, Buffalo Wild Wings, Burger King, Cheeseburger Paradise, Crazy Buffet, DQ, Denny's, Garfield's Rest., Golden Corral, Hardee's, Ichiban Japanese, Jimmy John's, KFC, Little Caesar's, Los Tres Caminos, LJ Silver, McDonald's, Monical's Pizza, Olive Garden, Outback Steaks, Panda Garden, Panera Bread, Papa John's, Penn Sta. Subs, Rally's, Red Lobster, Ruby Tuesday, Ryan's, Starbucks, Subway, Taco Bell, TGIFriday's, Wendy's, White Castle, 🏠 Hampton Inn, Holiday Inn, Motel 6, SpringHill Suites, 🅞 🏥, Aldi Foods, AT&T, Best Buy, BigLots, BooksAMillion, Buick/Cadillac/GMC, Burlington Coats, Chevrolet, Dodge, $Tree, Ford, Gander Mtn., Goodyear/auto, Harley-Davidson, Hobby Lobby, Hyundai/Nissan, Jo-Ann Fabrics, K-Mart/gas, Kohl's, Kroger/gas, Lowe's, Macy's, NAPA, Old Navy, Petsmart, Sam's Club/gas, Sears/auto, Staples, Tire Barn, TJ Maxx, Verizon, Walgreens, Walmart
5.5mm	Wabash River
3	Darwin Rd, W Terre Haute, N to St Mary of-the-Woods Coll
1.5mm	Welcome Ctr eb, full ♿ facilities, info, 🏠 litter barrels, 🍴 vending, petwalk
1	US 40 E (from eb, exits left), to Terre Haute, W Terre Haute
.5mm	weigh sta, eb only
0mm	Indiana/Illinois state line

INTERSTATE 74

Exit	Services
171.5mm	Indiana/Ohio state line
171mm	weigh sta wb
169	US 52 W, to Brookville

(side vertical labels: TERRE HAUTE, GREENSBURG, SHELBYVILLE, IN)

Exit	Services
168.5mm	Whitewater River
164	IN 1, St Leon, N 🅖 Exxon/Noble Romans, Shell/dsl, S 🅖 BP/Blimpie/dsl
156	IN 101, to Sunman, Milan, S 🅖 Exxon/dsl
152mm	🆁🆂 both lanes, full ♿ facilities, 🍴, 🏠, litter barrels, vending, petwalk
149	IN 229, to Oldenburg, Batesville, N 🅖 Marathon, Shell/dsl, 🍴 China Wok, McDonald's, Pizza King, Subway, Toros Mexican, Wendy's, 🏠 Hampton Inn, 🅞 Urgent Care, Advance Parts, $General, Kroger/dsl, ShopKo, Verizon, S 🅖 BP, 🍴 Arby's, DQ, KFC/Taco Bell, La Rosa's Pizza, Steak'n Shake, Skyline Chili, 🏠 Comfort Inn, 🅞 🏥, CVS Drug, O'Reilly Parts
143	to IN 46, New Point, N 🅖 Petro/Iron Skillet/Subway/dsl/scales/24hr/@, S 🅖 BP, 🏠 Hwy 46 Inn
134b a	IN 3, to Rushville, Greensburg, S 🅖 BP/dsl, Marathon/DQ/Subway, Speedway/dsl, Swifty, 🍴 A&W, Arby's, Big Boy, Buffalo Wings, Burger King, Chili's, El Reparo Mexican, Great Wall Buffet, Jimmy John's, KFC/LJ Silver, Little Caesars, McDonald's, Papa John's, Taco Bell, Waffle House, Wendy's, 🏠 Baymont Inn, Holiday Inn Express, Quality Inn, 🅞 Aldi Foods, AutoZone, Buick/Chevrolet, Chrysler/Dodge/Jeep, CVS Drug, $General, $Tree, Ford, GNC, NTB, O'Reilly Parts, Radio Shack, Staples, TrueValue, Verizon, Walgreens, Walmart/Subway, repair, vet
132	US 421, to Greensburg, S 🅖 BP, 🏠 Hampton Inn, Holiday Inn Express (2mi)
130mm	Clifty Creek
123	Saint Paul, S 🅖 ♥Love's/McDonald's/Subway/dsl/scales/24hr, 🅞 repair, camping
119	IN 244 E, to Milroy
116	IN 44, to Shelbyville, Rushville, N 🅖 Marathon/Circle K/dsl, S 🅖 BP, Marathon, Murphy USA/dsl, Sunoco/dsl, Swifty, 🍴 Applebee's, Arby's, Bellacino's, Bob Evans, Buffalo Wild Wings, Burger King, China Buffet, China Inn, Denny's, Domino's, DQ, Dunkin Donuts, Fazoli's, Golden Corral, KFC, King Buffet, LJ Silver, McDonald's, Papa John's, Penn Sta Subs, Pizza Hut, Rally's, Starbucks, Subway, Taco Bell, Wendy's, White Castle, 🏠 Quality Inn, 🅞 🏥, Ace Hardware, Advance Parts, Aldi Foods, AT&T, AutoZone, BigLots, Chevrolet, $General, $Tree, Ford, GNC, Kroger/dsl, O'Reilly Parts, Radio Shack, Verizon, Walgreens, Walmart/McDonald's
115mm	Little Blue River
113mm	Big Blue River
113	IN 9, to Shelbyville, N 🅖 Speedway, 🍴 Cracker Barrel, Wendy's, S 🅖 Shell, Shell/Circle K/Subway/dsl (1mi), 🍴 McDonald's, Waffle House, 🏠 Comfort Inn, EconoLodge, Hampton Inn, Holiday Inn Express, Super 8, 🅞 🏥
109	Fairland Rd, N 🅖 🚚/McDonald's/dsl/scales/24hr, 🅞 Indiana Downs/casino, S 🅞 Brownie's Marine
103	London Rd, to Boggstown
102mm	Big Sugar Creek
101	Pleasant View Rd, N 🅖 Country Mark/dsl/repair
99	Acton Rd
96	Post Rd, N 🅖 Marathon/Subway/dsl/24hr, 🍴 McDonald's, S 🅖 Shell/Circle K/dsl, 🍴 Wendy's, 🅞 Chevrolet
94b a	I-465/I-74 W, I-465 N, US 421 N
	I-74 and I-465 run together 21 miles. See Interstate 465, Exits 2-16, and 52-53.
73b	I-465 N, access to same services as 16a on I-465
73a	I-465 S, I-74 E

⤴ INTERSTATE 74 CONT'D

BROWNSBURG

Exit	Services
71mm	Eagle Creek
68	Ronald Reagan Pkwy
66	IN 267, Brownsburg, **N** 🅖 Citgo/dsl, Shell/Circle K, 🍴 Applebee's, Asia Wok, Buffalo Wild Wings, Dunkin Donuts, Hardee's, Steak'n Shake, Subway, Tequila Mexican, 🏨 Hampton Inn, Holiday Inn Express, 🅞 Big O Tire, **S** 🅖 BP/dsl, Speedway/dsl, 🍴 Arby's, Asian Fusion, Bob Evans, Burger King, China's Best, HoWah, Hurricane Grill, Jimmy John's, KFC, Little Caesars, Los Toros Mexican, McDonald's, Papa Murphy's, Penn Sta Subs, Starbucks, Taco Bell, Wendy's, White Castle, 🏨 Comfort Suites, Super 8, 🅞 AT&T, $Tree, Firestone/auto, Ford, Kohl's, Kroger/gas, K-Mart, Lowe's, Radio Shack, Walmart/Subway, USPO
61	to Pittsboro, **S** 🅖 💟Loves/Godfather's/Subway/dsl/scales/24hr
58	IN 39, to Lebanon, Lizton, **S** 🅗
57mm	🆁🆂 both lanes, full ♿ facilities, 🚻, 🛢, litter barrels, vending, petwalk
52	IN 75, to Advance, Jamestown, **2 mi S** gas, food, camping
39	IN 32, to Crawfordsville, **S** 🅖 ⛽/Subway/dsl/scales/24hr
34	US 231, to Linden, **S** 🅖 BP/Circle K, GA, Marathon/dsl, 🍴 Burger King, McDonald's, Subway, 🏨 Candlewood Suites, Comfort Inn, Hampton Inn, Holiday Inn Express, Motel 6, Quality Inn, Ramada Ltd., Super 8, 🅞🅗, Buick/GMC, KOA (1mi), Sugar Creek Campground (4mi)
25	IN 25, to Wingate, Waynetown
19mm	weigh sta eb/parking area wb
15	US 41, to Attica, Veedersburg, **1 mi S** 🅖 Marathon/dsl, 🍴 Apple Tree Diner, 🅞 to Turkey Run SP, camping
8	Covington, **N** 🅖 Marathon, Valero/dsl, 🍴 Benjamin's, Overpass Pizza, 🅞 Ford, fireworks
7mm	Wabash River
4	IN 63, to Newport, **N** 🅖 ⛽/Arby's/dsl/scales/24hr, 🍴 Beefhouse Rest., Wendy's
1mm	Welcome Ctr eb, full ♿ facilities, info, 🚻, 🛢, litter barrels, vending, petwalk
0mm	Indiana/Illinois state line, Eastern/Central Time Zone

⤴ INTERSTATE 80/90

ELKHART

Exit	Services
157mm	Indiana/Ohio state line
153mm	toll plaza, litter barrels
146mm	TP both lanes 🅖 Mobil/dsl, 🍴 McDonald's
144	I-69, US 27, Angola, Ft Wayne, **N** 🅖 Petro/BP/dsl/scales/@, ⛽/Wendy's/dsl/scales, Shell/Subway/dsl, 🍴 Clay's Family Rest., Lake George Rest., McDonald's, Red Arrow Rest., 🏨 Redwood Inn, 🅞 Freightliner/Western Star/truck repair, **S** 🅖 Marathon/dsl, 🏨 Holiday Inn Express, 🅞 Freemont Outlet Shops/famous brands, GNC, **Services on IN 120 E** 🏨 Comfort Inn, Hampton Inn, Travelers Inn, 🅞 golf/rest, **W** to Pokagon SP, Jellystone Camping (5mi)
131.5mm	Fawn River
126mm	Ernie Pyle TP both lanes, 🅖 Mobil/dsl, 🍴 Hardee's, Red Burrito, 🅞 gifts, RV dump
121	IN 9, to Lagrange, Howe, **N** 🅖 Golden Buddha, 🏨 American Inn, Best Western, Hampton Inn, Travel Inn, 🅞🅗 (4mi), **2 mi N** 🅖 Marathon, Murphy USA/dsl, Speed
121	Continued way/dsl, 🍴 Applebee's, Burger King, Fiesta Mexican, Hot'n Now, KFC, King Dragon, Little Caesar's, McDonald's, Pizza Hut, Subway, Taco Bell, Wendy's, 🏨 Country Hearth Inn, Regency Inn, Sturgess Inn, 🅞 AT&T, Cadillac/Chevrolet, CarQuest, $Tree, Family$, Ford, GNC, K-Mart, Kroger, Radio Shack, Rite Aid, Walgreens, Walmart/Subway, **S** 🅖 Valero/dsl, 🏨 Holiday Inn Express, Super 8, 🅞🅗 (8mi)
120mm	Fawn River
108mm	trucks only 🆁🆂 both lanes
107	US 131, IN 13, to Middlebury, Constantine, **0-3 mi N** 🅖 Marathon/dsl, Speedway, 🍴 Country Table Rest., McDonald's, 🏨 Patchwork Quilt Inn, Plaza Motel, Tower Motel, 🅞 $General, Family$, **1 mi S** 🅖 BP/Blimpie/dsl, 🍴 Yup's DairyLand, 🏨 McKenzie House B&B, 🅞 Eby's Pines RV Park, KOA (apr-nov)
101	IN 15, to Goshen, Bristol, **0-2 mi S** 🅖 7-11, Speedway/dsl, 🍴 River Inn Rest., Subway, 🅞 Eby's Pines Camping (3mi), USPO
96	Rd 1, E Elkhart, **2 mi S** 🅖 BP/dsl, Marathon, 7-11, 🍴 Arby's, China Star, DQ, McDonald's, Subway, Taco Bell, 🅞 Ace Hardware, RV/MH Hall of Fame
92	IN 19, to Elkhart, **N** 🅖 Marathon, Phillips 66/Subway/dsl, 7-11, 🍴 Applebee's, Cracker Barrel, Golden Egg Pancakes, Perkins, Steak'n Shake, 🏨 Best Western, Candlewood Suites, Comfort Suites, Country Inn&Suites, Diplomat Motel, EconoLodge, Fairway Inn, Hampton Inn, Hilton Garden, Holiday Inn Express, Microtel, Quality Inn, Sleep Inn, Staybridge Suites, Turnpike Motel, 🅞 Aldi Foods, CVS Drug, $General, Elkhart Campground (1mi), GNC, K-Mart, Martin's Foods, Walgreens, tires, transmissions, **0-2 mi S** 🅖 Marathon/dsl, Shell, Speedway, 🍴 Arby's, Bob Evans, Burger King, Callahan's, Chicago Grill, Chubby Trout, Culver's, Da Vinci's Pizza, DQ, El Camino Royal, Jimmy John's, KFC, King Wha Chinese, LJ Silver, Marco's Pizza, Matterhorn Rest., McDonald's, North Garden Buffet, Olive Garden, Papa John's, Pizza Hut, Red Lobster, Ryan's, Subway, Taco Bell, TX Roadhouse, Wendy's, Wings Etc., 🏨 Budget Inn, Days Inn, Jameson Inn, Red Roof Inn, Super 8, 🅞🅗, Ace Hardware, Advance Parts, AT&T, AutoZone, CarQuest, $Tree, Family$, Lowe's, Menards, O'Reilly Parts, Radio Shack, Verizon, Walmart, vet
91mm	Christiana Creek
90mm	Schricker TP both directions, 🅖 BP/dsl, 🍴 Burger King, Pizza Hut, Starbucks, Z Mkt, 🅞 RV Dump, USPO
83	to Mishawaka, **N** 🅖 BP/dsl, Phillips 66/Subway/dsl, 🍴 Applebee's, Moe's SW Grill, 🏨 Country Inn&Suites, Hampton Inn, Red Roof Inn, 🅞 CVS Drug, $Tree, Mar

🅖 = gas   🍴 = food   🛏 = lodging   🅞 = other   🆁🆂 = rest stop   Copyright 2014 - The Next Exit ®

INTERSTATE 80/90 CONT'D

Exit	Services
83	Continued

shall's, Martin's Foods/gas, Menards, PetCo, Target, Walgreens, vet, **1-2 mi N on IN 23 W** 🍴 Barlouie, Famous Dave's BBQ, 5 Guys Burgers, Granite City Grill, King's Buffet, Olive Garden, Papa Murphy's, Pizza Hut, Subway, Wendy's, Wings Etc., 🛏 Fairfield Inn, Holiday Inn Express, Super 8, 🅞 Barnes&Noble, Best Buy, JC Penney, Macy's, Michael's, Sears/auto, KOA (mar-nov), mall, **2 mi S on Grape Rd & Main St** (off IN 23W) 🅖 Meijer/dsl, 🍴 Arby's, Bob Evans, Buffalo Wild Wings, Burger King, Carraba's, Chick-fil-A, Chili's, Chipotle Mexican, CiCi's Pizza, Culver's, Del Taco, Hacienta Mexican, Houlihan's, Hooters, IHOP, Jimmy John's, Krispy Kreme, Logan's Roadhouse, Mancino's Pizza, Max&Erma's, McDonald's, Old Country Buffet, Outback Steaks, Panera Bread, Papa Vino's Italian, Quiznos, Red Lobster, Red Robin, Sonic, Starbucks, Steak'n Shake, Subway, Taste of Asia, TGIFriday's, 🛏 Comfort Inn, Courtyard, Extended Stay America, Hyatt Place Hotel, Residence Inn, SpringHill Suites, Studio+, 🅞 🄷, Aldi Foods, Barnes&Noble, Buick/GMC/Hyundai, Christmas Tree Shop, Discount Tire, Hobby Lobby, Home Depot, Honda, Jo-Ann Fabrics, Kohl's, Lexus, Lowe's, Meijer/gas, Mercedes, Nissan, Office Depot, Old Navy, Petsmart, Sam's Club, TJ Maxx, VW, Walmart

77	US 33, US 31B, IN 933, South Bend, **N** 🅖 Admiral, Mobil/dsl, 🍴 Arby's, DQ, Eleni's Rest., Fazoli's, Marco's Pizza, McDonald's, Papa John's, Ponderosa, Starbucks, Steak'nShake, Subway, 🛏 Comfort Suites, Hampton Inn, Motel 6, Suburban Lodge, Waterford Lodge, 🅞 AutoZone, BMW, Mazda, NAPA, O'Reilly Parts, TrueValue, Walgreens, **2 mi N on frtge rd** 🅖 Meijer/dsl/24hr, Murphy USA, Phillips 66/Subway/dsl, 🍴 Applebee's, Burger King, Hacienda Mexican, Jimmy John's, KFC, McDonald's, Quiznos, Sonic, 🅞 Aldi Foods, $Tree, Meijer, Walmart, **S** 🅖 Marathon, Phillips 66/Subway/dsl, 🍴 American Pancake House, Bob Evans, HoPing House, Mikados Japanese, Perkins, Taco Bell, Wendy's, 🛏 Best Value Inn, Hilton Garden, Holiday Inn Express, Howard Johnson, Jameson Inn, Knights Inn, Microtel, Quality Inn, St Marys Inn, 🅞 🄷, vet, to Notre Dame
76mm	St Joseph River
72	US-31, to Niles, South Bend, **N** 🅖 ▨▨▨/Subway/dsl/scales/24hr, Speedway/Subway/dsl, 🛏 Super 8, **2 mi S on US 20** 🍴 4 Seasons Rest., McDonald's, Ponderosa, Taco Bell, Wendy's, 🛏 Days Inn, Quality Inn, 🅞 RV Ctr, to Potato Creek SP (20mi), 🆂🆁, st police
62mm	Eastern Time Zone/Central Time Zone
56mm	**TP both lanes**, BP/dsl, DQ, McDonald's, 🄲, RV dump, litter barrel
49	IN 39, to La Porte, **N** 🛏 Hampton Inn, **S** 🛏 Cassidy Inn & RV, 3mi **S** 🅖 Family Express, Phillips 66/dsl, 🍴 DQ, El Bracero Mexican, 🛏 Best Western, Blue Heron Inn, Holiday Inn Express, Super 8
39	US 421, to Michigan City, Westville, **S** Purdue U North Cent
38mm	**trucks only** 🆁🆂 **both lanes, litter barrels**
31	IN 49, to Chesterton, Valparaiso, **N** 🅖 Family Express, Phillips 66, Speedway/dsl, 🍴 Bob Evans, Clock Rest., 🛏 Hilton Garden, 🅞 CVS Drug, Goodyear, Sand Creek RV Park (3mi, Apr-Oct), WiseWay Foods, to IN Dunes Nat Lakeshore, **S** 🛏 Hampton Inn (8mi), Super 8 (8mi)

Exit	Services
24mm	toll plaza
23	Portage, Port of Indiana, **0-2 mi N** 🅖 Marathon, Shell, 🍴 Denny's, Mark's Grill, 🛏 Best Western, Days Inn, $Inn, Comfort Inn, Country Inn&Suites, Holiday Inn Express, Ramada Inn, Super 8, **S** 🅖 BP, Marathon, Speedway, 🍴 Burger King, CiCi's Pizza, Dunkin Donuts, DQ, El Contarito Mexican, First Wok Chinese, Jimmy John's, J&J's Pizza, KFC, Little Caesar's, McDonald's, Rosewood Rest., Starbucks, Subway, Wendy's, 🅞 Advance Parts, Ace Hardware, AutoZone, Family$, GNC, Town&Country Mkt, USPO, Walgreens
22mm	**TP both lanes**, info, 🅖 BP/dsl, 🍴 Hardee's, Red Burrito, 🅞 scales
21mm	**I-90 and I-80 run together eb, separate wb. I-80 runs with I-94 wb. For I-80 exits 1 through 15, see Indiana Interstate 94.**
21	I-94 E to Detroit, I-80/94 W, US 6, IN 51, Lake Station, **N** 🅖 Blue Ox/Subway/dsl/scales/24hr, ⚘FLYING J/Denny's/dsl/scales/24hr/@, TA/BP/Popeye's/dsl/scales/24hr/@, 🅞 Blue Beacon, **S** 🅖 ▨▨▨/Road Ranger/Subway/dsl/scales, 🍴 McDonald's
17	I-65 S, US 12, US 20, Dunes Hwy, to Indianapolis
14b	IN 53, to Gary, Broadway, **S** 🅖 Citgo
14a	Grant St, to Gary, **S** 🄷
10	IN 912, Cline Ave, to Gary, **N** 🆇, casino
5	US 41, Calumet Ave, to Hammond, **S** 🅖 Nice'n Easy, RaceCo, Speedway/dsl, 🍴 Arby's, Aurelio's Pizza, Dunkin Donuts, Johnel's Rest., KFC, McDonald's, Subway, Taco Bell, White Castle, 🛏 Quality Inn, Ramada Inn, Super 8, 🅞 Aldi Foods, AutoZone, Murray's Parts, Walgreens
3	IN 912, Cline Ave, to Hammond, to Gary Reg 🆇, **S** 🅖 BP
1.5mm	toll plaza
1mm	US 12, US 20, 106th St, Indianapolis Blvd, **N** 🅖 Citgo, Mobil, Shell/dsl, 🅞 casino, **S** 🍴 Burger King, KFC, McDonald's, 🅞 Aldi Foods, Jewel-Osco, auto repair
0mm	Indiana/Illinois state line

INTERSTATE 94

Exit	Services
46mm	Indiana/Michigan state line
43mm	**Welcome Ctr wb, full** ♿ **facilities, info,** 🄲, 🆇, **litter barrels, vending, petwalk**
40b a	US 20, US 35, to Michigan City, **N** 🍴 McDonald's (3mi), 🅞 🄷, **S** 🅖 Speedway/dsl
34b a	US 421, to Michigan City, **N** 🅖 BP/dsl, Citgo/dsl, Family Express/e-85, Speedway/White Castle/dsl, 🍴 Applebee's, Arby's, Asian Buffet, Baskin-Robbins/Dunkin Donuts, Bob Evans, Buffalo Wild Wings, Burger King, Chili's, Culver's, Damon's, Denny's, Dynasty Buffet, El Bracero Mexican, IHOP, KFC, LJ Silver, McDonald's, Olive Garden, Papa John's, Pizza Hut/Taco Bell, Quizno's, Red Lobster, Ryan's, Schoop's Rest., Sophia's Pancakes, Starbucks, Steak'n Shake, Subway, TX Corral, Wendy's, 🛏 ABC Motel, Clarion, Comfort Inn, Country Inn&Suites, Knights Inn, Microtel, Milan Inn, Quality Inn, Red Roof Inn, Super 8, Travel Inn, 🅞 🄷, Advance Parts, Aldi Foods, AutoZone, BigLots, Big R, CVS Drug, $General, $Tree, Fannie May Candies, Ford/Lincoln, Hobby Lobby, JC Penney, Jewel-Osco Drug/gas, JoAnn Fabrics, Lowe's, Meijer/dsl, Menards, NAPA, Office Depot, Radio Shack, Save-a-Lot, Sears/auto, Verizon, Walgreens, Walmart/Subway, **S** 🅖 Gas City/Subway/dsl/scales/e-85, 🅞 Buick/Chevrolet/GMC, Harley-Davidson

INTERSTATE 94 CONT'D

Exit	Services
29mm	weigh sta both lanes
26b a	IN 49, Chesterton, **N** to IN Dunes SP, **S** N BP/White Castle, Speedway/dsl, 1 Applebee's, A&W/KFC, Arby's, Burger King, DQ, Dunkin Donuts, El Salto Mexican, Jimmy John's, Little Caesar's, LJ Silver, McDonald's, Pizza Hut, Quizno's, Subway, Sunrise Rest., Taco Bell, Tao Chins, Third Coast Cafe, Wendy's, ⌂ Best Western, EconoLodge, Hilton Garden (3mi), Super 8, O Advance Parts, AutoZone, Jewel-Osco, K-Mart, Sand Cr Camping (5mi), Walgreens, to Valparaiso
22b a	US 20, Burns Harbor, **N** N Steel City Express/dsl/e-85/ scales/LP, TA/BP/Buckhorn Rest/Pizza Hut/Popeye's/ Subway/Taco Bell/dsl/scales/24hr/@, ⌂ Comfort Inn, O Blue Beacon, fireworks, **S** N Luke/dsl, 🏪McDonald's/Subway/dsl/scales/24hr, O Camp-Land RV Ctr, Chevrolet, Ford, Nissan, Toyota/Scion, fireworks, repair
19	IN 249, to Port of IN, Portage, **N** N Family Express/ dsl/e-85, 1 Deli Belly, Egg Face Grill, Longhorn Steaks, Quaker Steak&Lube, Starbucks, ⌂ Country Inn&Suites, O Bass Pro Shops, **S** N Marathon/dsl, Shell/Luke, 1 Denny's, Lure Burgers, Shenanigans Grill, ⌂ Best Western, Days Inn, Dollar Inn, Hampton Inn, Super 8, Travel Inn
16	access to I-80/90 **toll road** E, **I-90 toll road** W, IN 51N, Ripley St same as 15b&a
I-94/I-80 run together wb	
15b	US 6W, IN 51, **N** N BP, ✈FLYING J/Denny's/dsl/ scales/24hr/@, Blue Ox/Subway/dsl/scales/24hr, TA/BP/ Popeye's/Subway/dsl/scales/24hr/@, 1 McDonald's, O Blue Beacon, **N on US 20** N Dunes/Steel City/dsl/scales/ dsl repair, 1 Paradise Rest., Ponderosa, Wing Wah
15a	US 6E, IN 51S, to US 20, **S** N GoLo, Road Ranger/🏪/ Subway/dsl/scales/24hr, Shell/Luke, 1 Burger King, DQ, Papa John's, LJ Silver, Ruben's Café, Wendy's, O Ace Hardware, Walgreens
13	Central Ave (from eb)
12b	I-65 N, to Gary and **toll road**
12a	I-65 S (from wb), to Indianapolis
11	I-65 S (from eb)
10b a	IN 53, Broadway, **N** N Citgo, Gas for Less, 1 JJ Fish, **S** N Mobil, 1 DQ, Rally's
9	Grant St, **N** N Clark, 1 Chicago Hotdogs, O County Mkt Foods, Sav-a-Lot Foods, Walgreens, **S** N Citgo, ♥Loves/Denny's/dsl/scales/LP/24hr/@, Steel City/dsl/ scales/rest./24hr, 1 A&W/KFC, Burger King, Church's, Dunkin Donuts, J&J Fish, McDonald's, Subway, O Aldi Foods, AutoZone, CarX, $Tree, Fagen Drug, Firestone/ auto, Midas
6	Burr St, **N** N 🏪/Subway/dsl/scales/24hr/@, TA/ Chester's/Pizza Hut/Taco Bell/dsl/scales/24hr/@, 1 J&J Fish & Chicken, Philly Steaks, Rico's Pizza, O SpeedCo, **S** N Citgo/dsl/24hr
5	IN 912, Cline Ave, **S** N BP, Clark, Marathon, Speedway, 1 Arby's, DQ, Jedi's Garden Rest., KFC, McDonald's, Pizza Hut, Popeye's, Taco Bell, Wendy's, White Castle, ⌂ Best Western, Hometowne Lodge, Motel 6, Super 8, O $Tree, Fannie May Candies, K-Mart, Radio Shack
3	Kennedy Ave, **N** N Clark, Mobil/dsl, Speedway, 1 Burger King, Domino's, McDonald's, O Walgreens, repair, **S** N Citgo, 1 Cholie's Pizza, Cracker Barrel, Squigi's Pizza, Subway, Wendy's, ⌂ Courtyard, Fairfield Inn, Residence Inn, O **IN Welcome Ctr**, USPO

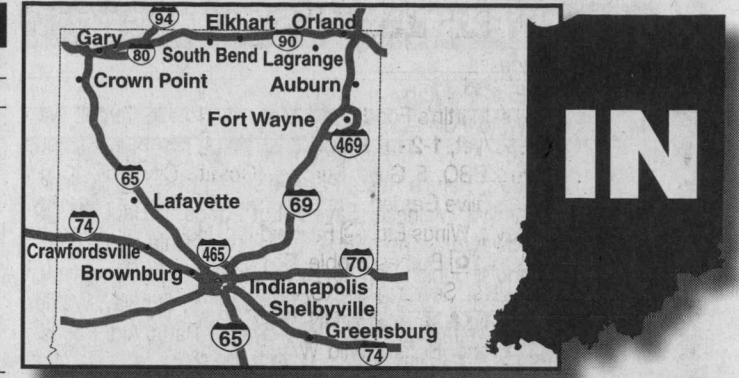

Exit	Services
2	US 41S, IN 152N, Indianapolis Blvd, **N** N GoLo, Luke, SavAStop, 1 Arby's, Dunkin Donuts, House Of Pizza, La Rosa, Papa John's, Pizza Hut, Popeye's, Rally's, Schoop's Burgers, Taco Bell, Wheel Rest., Woodmar Rest., O Car-Ex, Goodyear, Midas, vet, **S** N 🏪/scales/dsl/24hr, 1 White Castle, ⌂ Hammond Inn, O Aldi Foods, Cabela's
1	US 41N, Calumet Ave, **N** N BP/dsl, Gas City, 1 Barton's Pizza, Baskin-Robbins/Dunkin Donuts, Subway, O Walgreens, **S** N BP, Mobil/dsl, Marathon, Shell, 1 Arby's, Baskin-Robbins/Dunkin Donuts, Boston Mkt, Burger King, Canton House Chinese, Edwardo's Pizza, Fortune House, Munster Gyros, Subway, Taco Bell, Wendy's, O $Jct, Jewel-Osco, Radio Shack, Staples, Target, vet
0mm	Indiana/Illinois state line

INTERSTATE 465 (INDIANAPOLIS)

Exit	Services
I-465 loops around Indianapolis. Exit numbers begin/end on I-65, exit 108.	
53b a	I-65 N to Indianapolis, S to Louisville
52	Emerson Ave, I-74 W and I-465 S run together around S Indianapolis 21 miles., **N** N Marathon, Shell/Circle K, Speedway, 1 Asian Spice, Burger King, Denny's, Domino's, KFC, LJ Silver, Subway, Taco Bell, Wendy's, ⌂ Motel 6, O H, $General, Family$, **S** N Circle K, Shell/Circle K, Speedway/dsl, 1 Applebee's, Arby's, Bamboo House, Buffalo Wild Wings, China Buffet, DQ, Donato's Pizza, El Puerto Mexican, Fazoli's, Fujiyama, Hardee's, Hunan House, McDonald's, Papa John's, Pizza Hut, Ponderosa, Rally's, Starbucks, Steak'n Shake, Subway, Waffle House, Wendy's, White Castle/24hr, ⌂ Budget Inn, Holiday Inn, InnAmerica, La Quinta, Red Roof Inn, O Advance Parts, AutoZone, Curves, $Tree, GNC, Goodyear/auto, K-Mart, Kroger, Lowe's Whse, Marsh Foods, NAPA, Radio Shack, Walgreens, Walmart, vet
I-74 W and I-465 S run together around S Indianapolis 21 miles	
49	I-74 E, US 421 S
48	Shadeland Ave (from nb)
47	US 52 E, Brookville Rd, **E** N Marathon/Burger King, Speedway/dsl, 1 Bugsy's Grill, McDonald's, Subway, ⌂ Baymont Inn, O CVS Drug, vet
46	US 40, Washington St, **E** N Marathon, Phillips 66, Shell/ dsl, Speedway, 1 Arby's, Blueberry Hill Pancakes, China Buffet, Church's, LJ Silver, Olive Garden, Skyline Chili, Steak'n Shake, Yen Ching Chinese, O Advance Parts, AutoZone, $General, Ford, Meineke, O'Reilly Parts, Radio Shack, Target, **W** N Thornton's, 1 Applebee's, Bob Evans, Fazoli's, McDonald's, Subway, ⌂ Best Western, O Buick/GMC, Hyundai, K-Mart, PepBoys

INDIANAPOLIS AREA

GARY AREA

ⓡ = gas　Ⓕ = food　⌂ = lodging　Ⓞ = other　Ⓡs = rest stop　Copyright 2014 - The Next Exit ®

INTERSTATE 465 (INDIANAPOLIS) CONT'D

Exit	Services
44b	I-70 E, to Columbus
44a	I-70 W, to Indianapolis
42	US 36, IN 67 N, Pendleton Pike, **E** Ⓕ Chile Verde, Hardee's, Papa's Rest., Popeye's, Wendy's, Ⓞ $General, Family$, Meineke, Save-A-Lot Foods, U-Haul, **W** ⓡ Speedway/dsl, Thornton's, Ⓕ Arby's, Café Heidelberg, Domino's, Dunkin Donuts, KFC, LJ Silver, Los Rancheros, McDonald's, Pizza Hut/Taco Bell, Rally's, Subway, Waffle House, White Castle, Ⓞ Ⓗ Advance Parts, Aldi Foods, CVS Drug, Family$, Menards, O'Reilly Parts
40	56th St, Shadeland Ave, **E** ⓡ Marathon, to Ft Harrison SP
37b a	I-69, N to Ft Wayne, IN 37, **W** Ⓞ Ⓗ, services on frontage rds
35	Allisonville Rd, **N** Ⓕ Bravo Italian, Buca Italian, Buffalo Wild Wings, Dave&Buster's, Hardee's, Max&Erma's, MCL Cafeteria, Melting Pot, On-the-Border, Outback Steaks, ⌂ Courtyard, Ⓞ Costco/gas, Firestone/auto, Gander Mtn, JC Penney, Jo-Ann Fabrics, Macy's, Sear/auto, Target, Tires+, Van Maur, mall, **S** ⓡ Shell, Speedway/dsl, Ⓕ China Buffet, ChuckeCheese, 5 Guys Burgers, Panera Bread, Papa John's, Perkins/24hr, Qdoba, White Castle, ⌂ Jameson Inn, Ⓞ Marsh Foods, Michael's, Petsmart, Radio Shack, TJ Maxx, Trader Joe's
33	IN 431, Keystone Ave, **N** ⓡ BP/McDonald's, Marathon/dsl, Ⓕ Arby's, Bob Evans, Burger King, Penn Sta Subs, Ruth Chris Steaks, Subway, Ⓞ Acura, Audi, BMW/Mini, Chevrolet, Ford, Harley-Davidson, Honda, Hyundai, Infiniti, Nissan, Porsche, Scion/Toyota, Subaru, **S** Ⓕ Blimpie, Champ's, Cheesecake Factory, El Torito Grill, Fleming's Steaks, LePeep's Rest, Lulu's Rest, Maggiano's, Maggie Moo's Icecream, McAlister's Deli, PF Changs, Pizza Hut, Shanghai Lil, Starbucks, Sullivan's Steaks, TGIFriday's, ⌂ Hyatt Place, Marriott, Sheraton, Ⓞ Kohl's, Nordstrom's, mall
31	US 31, Meridian St, **N** ⌂ Courtyard, Jameson Inn, Radisson, Ⓞ Ⓗ, Cadillac, **S** ⓡ Shell/Circle K/dsl, Ⓕ Arby's, Granite City Rest, La Margarita, McAlister's Deli, McDonald's, Paradise Bakery/Cafe, Starbucks
27	US 421 N, Michigan Rd, **N** ⓡ Marathon, Phillips 66/dsl, Speedway/dsl, Ⓕ Applebee's, Bajio Mexican, Burger King, HoneyBaked Ham, Jimmy John's, Maggie Moo's Icecream, McDonald's, Noble Roman's, Red Robin, Subway, Wendy's, Wings Etc, ⌂ Country Inn&Suites, Red Roof Inn, Ⓞ AT&T, Best Buy, Buick/GMC, Chevrolet, Chrysler/Dodge/Jeep, Ford, Home Depot, Kohl's, Marshall's, PetCo, Target, Walgreens, **S** ⓡ Citgo/dsl, Shell/Circle K, Ⓕ Arby's, Burger King, Chic-fil-A, China Buffet, Chipotle Mexican, Cici's, Cracker Barrel, Denny's, El Meson Mexican, Famous Dave's, Hardee's, McAlister's Deli, McDonald's, Noodles&Co, O'Charley's, Outback Steaks, Panda Express, Papa Murphy's, Pizza Hut, Qdoba, Rally's, Ruby Tuesday, Steak'n Shake, Subway, Taco Bell, TX Roadhouse, Wendy's, White Castle, Yen Ching Chinese, ⌂ Best Western, Comfort Inn, Days Inn, Drury Inn, Embassy Suites, Extended Stay America, Extended Stay Deluxe, Holiday Inn, Homewood Suites, InTown Suites, La Quinta, Microtel, Residence Inn, Super 8, Ⓞ Aamco, Aldi Foods, BigLots, Costco/gas, Discount Tire, $General, $Tree, Firestone, GNC, JC Penney, Lowe's Whse, Office
27	Continued Depot, Radio Shack, Sam's Club/gas, Staples, Walgreens, Walmart
25	I-865 W, I-465 N to Chicago
23	86th St, **E** ⓡ BP, Speedway/dsl, Ⓕ Abuelo's, Applebee's, Arby's, Chili's, Coldstone Creamery, Jimmy John's, Longhorn Steaks, Macaroni Grill, Monical's Pizza, Noodles&Co, Panera Bread, Quizno's, Starbucks, Steak'n Shake, Subway, Taco Bell, Ted's MT Grill, Traders Mill Grill, Wendy's, ⌂ Fairfield Inn, Homestead Suites, InTown Suites, Ⓞ Ⓗ AT&T, Big-O Tires, BookAMillion, Marsh Foods, Michael's, Old Navy, Petsmart
21	71st St, **E** ⓡ BP, Ⓕ Bella Chino's Italian, Hardee's, McDonald's, Steak'n Shake, Subway, ⌂ Candlewood Suites, Clarion Inn, Courtyard, Hampton Inn, Holiday Inn Express, TownePlace Suites, Ⓞ Curves, **W** Ⓕ Bob Evans, LePeep's Rest, Los Agave's Mexican, Max&Erma's, Quizno's, Starbucks, ⌂ Hilton Garden, Residence Inn, Wingate Inn
20	I-65, N to Chicago, S to Indianapolis
19	56th St (from nb), **E** ⓡ Marathon, Speedway/dsl
17	38th St, **E** ⓡ BP, Marathon/dsl, Shell/Circle K/24hr, Speedway, Ⓕ ChuckeCheese, DQ, Domino's, El Maguey Mexican, Ginzo Japanese, Golden Corral, Hooters, Little Caesar's, LoneStar Steaks, LJ Silver, Machu Pichu Peruvian, O'Charley's, Penn Sta Subs, Popeye's, Red Lobster, Starbucks, Steak'n Shake, Subway, White Castle, World Buffet, ⌂ Best Value Inn, Ⓞ AutoZone, Best Buy, Chevrolet, CVS Drug, $Tree, Family$, Ford, Home Depot, Kroger/gas, Meijer, O'Reilly Parts, Radio Shack, Staples, Walgreens, **W** Ⓕ Arby's, Burger King, Chili's, Cracker Barrel, McDonald's, Mike's Subs, Pizza Hut/Taco Bell, Ruby Tuesday, TGIFriday's, ⌂ Ramada Ltd, Jameson Inn, Ⓞ Marsh Foods, Target

I-74 W and I-465 S run together around S Indianapolis 21 miles

16b	I-74 W, to Peoria
16a	US 136, to Speedway, **E** ⓡ Circle K, Shell/Circle K, Thornton's/dsl, Ⓕ Applebee's, Arby's, Buffalo Wild Wings, Denny's, Hardee's, KFC, LJ Silver, McDonald's, Quizno's, Papa Murphy's, Pizza Hut, Subway, Taco Bell, Wendy's, ⌂ Budget Inn, $Inn, Motel 6, Red Roof Inn, Ⓞ CVS Drug, $General, $Tree, Firestone/auto, Goodyear/auto, Kroger, Marsh Foods, PetCo, Radio Shack, **W** ⌂ Clarion
14b a	10th St, **E** Ⓕ Peking Chinese, Penn Sta, Pizza Hut, Wendy's, Ⓞ Ⓗ Lowe's Whse, **W** ⓡ GA/Subway, Shell/Circle K, Speedway/24hr, Ⓕ Arby's, Fazoli's, Hardee's, McDonald's, Rally's, Starbucks, Taco Bell, Ⓞ CVS Drug
13b a	US 36, Rockville Rd, **E** ⓡ Marathon, ⌂ Comfort Inn, Microtel, Sleep Inn, Wingate Inn, Ⓞ Sam's Club, **W** ⓡ Speedway/dsl/24hr, Ⓕ Bob Evans, ⌂ Best Western
12b a	US 40 E, Washington St, **E** Ⓕ Burger King, China Buffet, Church's, Fazoli's, McDonald's, Papa John's, Pizza Hut, Taco Bell, Wendy's, White Castle, Ⓞ Ace Hardware, Advance Parts, AutoZone, CVS Drug, $Tree, Family$, Kroger/gas, Speedway Parts, U-Haul, Walgreens, repair, **W** ⓡ Marathon/Circle K, Phillips 66/Noble Roman's/dsl, Thornton's/24hr, Ⓕ Arby's, Hardee's, KFC, LJ Silver, McDonald's, Pizza Hut, Steak'n Shake, Subway, ⌂ $Inn, Ⓞ Aamco, Goodyear, K-Mart, TireBarn
11b a	Sam Jones Expwy, **E** ⓡ Marathon, Ⓕ Denny's, Indy's Rest., Schlotzky's, Waffle House, ⌂ Adam's Mark Hotel,

INTERSTATE 465 (INDIANAPOLIS) CONT'D

Exit	Services
11b a	Continued Candlewood Suites, Courtyard, Day's Hotel, Econolodge, Extended Stay America, Extended Stay Deluxe, Fairfield Inn, Hyatt Place, La Quinta, Quality Inn, Ramada Inn, Residence Inn, W 🛏 Crowne Plaza, Radisson
9b a	I-70, E to Indianapolis, W to Terre Haute
8	IN 67 S, Kentucky Ave, E 🄷, W 🅿 BP/McDonald's/dsl, Swifty, Speedway/dsl, Shell, Subway, 🍴 Burger King, Culver's, Damon's, Denny's, KFC, 🛏 Country Inn&Suites
7	Mann Rd (from wb), E 🄷
4	IN 37 S, Harding St, N 🅿 Mr Fuel/dsl/scales, 🅿 Subway/dsl/scales/24hr, 🍴 Omelette Shoppe, 🛏 Best Inn, Quality Inn, 🄾 🄷, Blue Beacon, S 🅿 ⊕FLYING J /Denny's/dsl/LP/scales/24hr/@, Marathon, 🍴 Hardee's, McDonald's, Taco Bell, White Castle, 🛏 Knight's Inn, 🄾 Freightliner, SpeedCo, TruckoMat/scales
2b a	US 31, IN 37, E 🅿 BP/24hr, 🍴 Arby's, China Garden, CiCi's, Domino's, DQ, El Azabache, KFC, King Gyros, LJ Silver, MCL Cafeteria, Old Country Buffet, Penn Sta, Pizza Hut, Steak'n Shake, White Castle, 🄾 Advance Parts, Aldi Foods, AutoZone, Chrysler/Jeep, $General, $Tree, Family$, Firestone, GNC, Goodyear, Jiffy Lube, Kroger/gas, Lincoln, Office Depot, Radio Shack, Save-A-Lot, U-Haul, W 🅿 Speedway, 🍴 Bob Evans, Denny's, 8Lucky Buffet, McDonald's, Red Lobster, Subway, Taco Bell, Wendy's, 🛏 Best Value Inn, Comfort Inn, Holiday Inn Express, Ramada, Super 8, Travelore Inn, Travelodge, 🄾 CVS Drug, Walgreens
53b a	I-65 N to Indianapolis, S to Louisville

I-465 loops around Indianapolis. Exit numbers begin/end on I-65, exit 108.

INTERSTATE 469 (FT WAYNE) CONT'D

Exit	Services
31c b a	I-69, US 27 S, Auburn Road. **I-469 begins/ends.**
29.15mm	St Joseph River
29b a	Maplecrest Rd, W 🅿 Lassus/DQ/Subway/dsl, Marathon/dsl
25	IN 37, to Ft Wayne, W 🅿 Murphy USA/dsl, 🍴 Antonio's Pizza, Applebee's, Bob Evans, Buffalo Wild Wings, Cracker Barrel, DQ, Golden Corral, Steak'n Shake, Subway, Vince's Rest., Wendy's, Wings Etc, Zianos Italian, 🄾 AT&T, Discount Tire, Kohl's, Marshall's, Meijer/dsl, Menards, Michael's, Office Depot, Petsmart, Walgreens, Walmart/McDonald's
21	US 24 E
19b a	US 30 E, to Ft Wayne, E 🅿 ⊕FLYING J/Huddle House/Subway/dsl/LP/scales/24hr, Sunoco/Taco Bell/dsl, 🄾 Freightliner, Mack, Peterbilt, truck/tire repair, W 🅿 Marathon, 🍴 Garno's Italian, Golden Gate Chinese, Mancino's Grinders, Richard's Rest., Salvatori's Mexican, Zesto Drive-In, 🛏 Holiday Inn Express
17	Minnich Rd
15	Tillman Rd
13	Marion Center Rd
11	US 27, US 33 S, to Decatur, Ft Wayne, E 🅿 BP/Subway/dsl
10.5mm	St Marys River
9	Winchester Rd
6	IN 1, to Bluffton, Ft Wayne, E KOA, W to ✈
2	Indianapolis Rd, W to ✈
1	Lafayette Ctr Rd

IOWA

INTERSTATE 29

Exit	Services
152mm	Iowa/South Dakota state line, Big Sioux River
151	IA 12 N, Riverside Blvd, E 🅿 Casey's, 🄾 $General, Fareway Foods, Riverside Park, to Stone SP, Pecaut Nature Ctr
149	Hamilton Blvd, E 🅿 Conoco, 🍴 Horizon Rest, 🛏 Rodeway Inn, 🄾 JiffyLube, to Briar Cliff Coll, W **Iowa Welcome Ctr sb, full facilities**, 🍴 Bev's on the River Rest., 🛏 Hilton Garden, 🄾 Riverboat Museum
148	US 77 S, to S Sioux City, Nebraska, W 🅿 Casey's, Conoco/dsl, Sam's, 🍴 DQ, McDonald's, MiFamilia, Pizza Hut, Taco Bell, 🛏 Marina Inn, Regency Inn, 🄾 Advance Parts, Family $, O'Reilly Parts, camping/🄰
147b	US 20 bus, Sioux City, E 🅿 Sam's, 🍴 Arby's, Burger King, Chili's, Famous Dave's BBQ, Hardee's, IHOP, Perkins, 🛏 Holiday Inn, Ramada, Stoney Creek Inn, 🄾 🄷, Chevrolet, USPO, Walgreens
147a	Floyd Blvd, E 🅿 Valero, 🄾 Home Depot, W to Riverboat Casino
146.5mm	Floyd River
144b	I-129 W, US 20 W, US 75 S
144a	US 20 E, US 75 N, to Ft Dodge, **1 mi E on Lakeport Rd** 🅿 Casey's, Shell, 🍴 A&W/LJ Silver, Applebee's, Black Bear Diner, Buffalo Wild Wings, Burger King, Carlos'o Kelly's, ChuckeCheese, 5 Guys Burgers, Golden Corral, Hardee's, HuHot Chinese, Iron Hill Grill, Jimmy John's, McDonald's,
144a	Continued Olive Garden, Outback Steaks, Red Lobster, Red Robin, Starbucks, Taco Del Mar, TX Roadhouse, Tokyo Japanese, 🛏 Comfort Inn, Fairfield Inn, Holiday Inn Express, Quality Inn, 🄾 Barnes&Noble, Best Buy, Buick/Honda, Gordman's, Hobby Lobby, Hy-Vee Foods/gas, JC Penney, Jiffy Lube, Kohls, Lowe's, Michael's, Old Navy, Petsmart, Scheel's, Sears/auto, Staples, Target, Verizon, Younkers, **Urgent Care**
143	US 75 N, Singing Hills Blvd, E 🅿 Cenex/dsl, Murphy USA/dsl, 🅿 Moe's SW Grill/Subway/dsl/scales/24hr, 🍴 China Buffet, Culver's, Eldon's Rest., KFC, McDonald's, Pizza Hut, Quiznos, Taco John's, 🛏 AmericInn, Days Inn, Victorian Inn, 🄾 AT&T, Cadillac/GMC, $Tree, Ford/Kia, Mazda, Nissan, Sam's Club/gas, Subaru, Suzuki, Toyota/Scion, Verizon, Walmart/Subway, Sgt Floyd Mon, **Urgent Care**, vet, W 🅿 Loves/Subway/dsl/scales/24hr/@, 🍴 Wendy's, 🛏 Super 8, 🄾 Peterbilt, truckwash/repair
141	D38, Sioux Gateway ✈, E 🅿 Cenex, Phillips 66/dsl, Shell/dsl, 🍴 Aggies Rest., Pizza Ranch, Puerto Vallarta Mexican, Subway, 🛏 EconoLodge, 🄾 $General, W 🛏 Motel 6, 🄾 ✈, museum
139mm	🆁🆂 both lanes, full 🛏 facilities, 🍴 info, 🄰 litter barrels, RV dump, wireless internet
135	Port Neal Landing
134	Salix, W camping
132mm	weigh sta sb, ✈ parking only nb, 🄰 litter barrels
127	IA 141, Sloan, E 🅿 Casey's, Kum&Go/Subway/dsl, 🅿

®= gas   ⊕ = food   ☒ = lodging   ⊡ = other   ℞ = rest stop   Copyright 2014 - The Next Exit ®

◤N INTERSTATE 29 CONT'D

Exit	Services
127	Continued
	Homestead Inn, WinnaVegas Inn, ⊡ RV Park, **3 mi W** ® Heritage Express, ⊡ to Winnebago Indian Res/casino
120	to Whiting, **W** camping
112	IA 175, Onawa, **E** ® Conoco/Subway/dsl, Phillips 66/dsl, ⊕ DQ, McDonald's, Michael's Rest., ☒ Super 8, ⊡ Ⓗ, NAPA, On-Ur-Wa RV Park, Pamida, repair, **2 mi W** ⊡ KOA, Lewis&Clark SP, Keel Boat Exhibit
110mm	℞ **both lanes, full** ☒ **facilities,** ⊕, **info,** ⊠, **litter barrels, petwalk, RV dump, wireless internet**
105	E60, Blencoe
96mm	Little Sioux River
95	F 20, Little Sioux, **E** gas, ⊡ Loess Hills SF (9mi), **W** Woodland RV Park
92mm	Soldier River
91.5mm	℞ **both lanes, litter barrels, parking only**
89	IA 127, Mondamin, **1 mi E** ® Jiffy Mart/dsl, ⊕ K Crossing Cafe
82	F50, Modale, **1 mi W** ® Cenex/dsl
79mm	℞ **both lanes, full** ☒ **facilities, info,** ⊕, ⊠, **litter barrels, RV dump, wireless internet**
75	US 30, Missouri Valley, **E Iowa Welcome Ctr** (5mi), ® Shell/dsl/24hr, ⊕ Arby's, McDonald's, Penny's Diner, Subway, ☒ Oaktree Inn, ⊡ Ⓗ (2mi), to Steamboat Exhibit, **W** ® BP/dsl, Phillips 66/Jctn Cafe/dsl, ⊕ Burger King, Taco John's, ☒ Days Inn, Rath Inn, Super 8, ⊡ Buick/Chevrolet
72.5mm	Boyer River
72	IA 362, Loveland, **E** ® Phillips 66/dsl, **W** to Wilson Island SP (6mi)
71	I-680 E, to Des Moines
	I-29 S & I-680 W run together 10 mi.
66	Honey Creek, **W** RV Camping,
61b	I-680 W, to N Omaha. I-29 N & I-680 E run together 10 mi, **W** Mormon Trail Ctr
61a	IA 988, to Crescent, **E** to ski area
56	IA 192 S (sb only, exits left), Council Bluffs, **E** Ⓗ
55	N 25th, Council Bluffs, **E** ® Cenex/dsl, Sinclair
54b	N 35th St (from nb), Council Bluffs
54a	G Ave (from sb), Council Bluffs
53b	I-480 W, US 6, to Omaha (exits left from nb)
53a	9th Ave, S 37th Ave, Council Bluffs, **E** ® Phillips 66, Shell, ⊕ Hog Stop BBQ, ☒ Days Inn, **W** ⊡ Harrah's Hotel/Casino, RiverBoat Casino, camping
52	Nebraska Ave, **E** ® Phillips 66/dsl, ⊕ Quaker Steak, Ruby Tuesday, ☒ Comfort Suites, Holiday Inn Express, Microtel, SpringHill Suites, ValuePlace Inn, ⊡ Bass Pro Shops, **W** ☒ AmeriStar Hotel/casino, Hampton Inn, Holiday Inn
51	I-80 W, to Omaha
	I-29 and I-80 run together 3 miles. See Iowa Interstate 80, exits 1b-3.
48	I-80 E (from nb), to Des Moines, **E** Ⓗ
47	US 275, IA 92, Lake Manawa, **E** ⊡ Iowa School for the Deaf, **W** ⊕ Buffalo Wild Wings, Firehouse Subs, Freddy's, Longhorn Steaks, Olive Garden, Panda Express, Panera Bread, Pizza Ranch, ⊡ $Tree, Hobby Lobby, Kohl's, Petsmart, Radio Shack, Target, TJ Maxx, Verizon
42	IA 370, to Bellevue, **W** ⊡ K&B Saddlery, to Offutt AFB, truck parts

Exit	Services
38mm	℞ **both lanes, full** ☒ **facilities,** ⊕, **info,** ⊠, **litter barrels, RV dump, petwalk, wireless internet**
35	US 34 E, to Glenwood, **E** ⊕ McDonalds (4mi), ☒ Western Inn (4mi), ⊡ RV Park, **W** ® BP/rest/dsl, ☒ Bluff View Motel, ⊡ Harley-Davidson
32	US 34 W, Pacific Jct, to Plattsmouth
24	L31, to Tabor, Bartlett
20	IA 145, Thurman
15	J26, Percival, **1-2 mi E** gas/dsl
11.5mm	weigh sta nb
10	IA 2, to Nebraska City, Sidney, **E** to Waubonsie SP (5mi), **W** ® BP/Sapp Bros/Apple Barrel Rest/dsl/scales/24hr, Cenex/Godfathers/dsl/E85, Shell/Subway/dsl/scales/24hr, ⊕ Wendy's, ☒ Best Value Inn, Super 8, ⊡ Victorian Acres RV Park (3mi), Lewis&Clark Ctr (3mi), to Arbor Lodge SP, antiques, dsl/tire repair
1	IA 333, Hamburg, **1 mi E** ® Casey's/dsl, ⊕ Bootleggers Rest., ☒ Hamburg Motel, ⊡ Ⓗ, NAPA, Soda Fountain
0mm	Iowa/Missouri state line

◤N INTERSTATE 35

Exit	Services
219mm	Iowa/Minnesota state line
214	rd 105, to Northwood, Lake Mills, **E** ☒ Royal Motel (7mi), **W Welcome Ctr both lanes, full** ☒ **facilities,** ⊠, **litter barrels, vending, petwalk, RV dump, wireless internet,** ® BP/Burger King/dsl, ☒ Country Inn&Suites, Holiday Inn Express, ⊡ casino
212mm	**weigh sta sb,** ℞ **nb,** ⊠, **litter barrels**
208	rd A38, to Joice, Kensett, windmills
203	IA 9, to Manly, Forest City, to Pilot Knob SP
202mm	Winnebago River
197	rd B20, **8 mi E** Lime Creek Nature Ctr
196mm	℞ **both lanes, litter barrels, parking only**
194	US 18, to Mason City, Clear Lake, **E** ⊡ Ⓗ (8mi), Chevrolet, Freightliner, truck repair, **W** ® Casey's/dsl, ⟨⟩/Denny's/Subway/dsl/scales, Kum&Go/dsl, Shell/Wendy's/dsl, ⊕ Arby's, Cancun Mexican, Culver's, DQ, KFC/Taco Bell, McDonald's, Perkins, Pizza Hut, Rice House Chinese, Subway, ☒ AmericInn, Best Western/rest., Budget Inn, Microtel
193	rd B35, to Mason City, Emery, **E** ® Kum&Go/Taco John's/dsl/E-85, ☒ Super 8, ⊡ truckwash, **W** ⊡ Ford, to Clear Lake SP
190	US 18, rd 27 E, to Mason City
188	rd B43, to Burchinal
182	rd B60, to Rockwell, Swaledale
180	rd B65, to Thornton, **W** ® Cenex (2mi), ⊡ camping
176	rd C13, to Sheffield, Belmond
170	rd C25, to Alexander
165	IA 3, **E** ® Shell/dsl/rest., ☒ AmericInn (9mi), Hampton Motel (9mi), ⊡ Ⓗ (7mi)
159	rd C47, Dows, **W** ℞ **both lanes, full** ☒ **facilities info,** ⊕, ⊠, **litter barrels, petwalk, vending, RV dump, wireless internet,** Shell/Arby's/Godfather's/dsl/24hr
155mm	Iowa River
151	rd R75, to Woolstock
147	rd D20, to US 20 E
144	rd D25, Williams, **E** ® Boondocks Trkstp/cafe/dsl, Best Western, Boondocks Motel, ⊡ RV camping, **W** ® ⊛FLYING J/Trump's Rest/dsl/scales/24hr
142b a	US 20, to Webster City, Ft Dodge

Side tabs (left margin): MO VALLEY • COUNCIL BLUFFS
Side tab (right margin): CLEAR LAKE
IA

📵🔼 INTERSTATE 35 CONT'D		

Exit	Services
139	rd D41, to Kamrar
133	IA 175, to Jewell, Eldora, **W** 📵 Kum&Go/Subway/dsl
128	rd D65, to Stanhope, Randall, **5 mi W** Little Wall Lake Pk
124	rd 115, Story City, **W** 📵 Casey's, Kum&Go/dsl, 🍴 DQ, Happy Chef/24hr, McDonald's, Pizza Ranch, Royal Cafe, Subway, 🛏 Comfort Inn, Super 8, Viking Motel/rest, 🅾 Ford, Story City RV Ctr, VF Factory Stores/famous brands, Whispering Oaks Camping, antiques
123	rd E18, to Roland, McCallsburg
120mm	🆁ₛ nb, full ♿ facilities, info, 🚻, 🖼 litter barrels, vending, wireless internet, RV dump/scenic prairie area sb
119mm	🆁ₛ sb, full ♿ facilities, 🚻, 🖼 litter barrels, vending, wireless internet, RV dump
116	rd E29, to Story, **2 mi W** Story Co Conservation Ctr
113	13th St, Ames, **W** 📵 Kum&Go/Burger King/dsl/E-85, Phillips 66/Arby's, 🍴 Pizza Ranch, 🛏 Holiday Inn Express, Quality Inn, 🅾 �H Harley-Davidson, to USDA Vet Labs, ISU
111b a	US 30, to Nevada, Ames, **E** Twin Acres Campground (11mi), **W** 📵 Kum&Go/DQ/Subway/dsl, 🍴 El Azteca Mexican, 🛏 AmericInn, Comfort Inn, Country Inn&Suites, EconoLodge, Fairfield Inn, Hampton Inn, Microtel, Super 8, TownePlace Suites, 🅾 to IA St U
109mm	S Skunk River
106mm	weigh sta both lanes
102	IA 210, to Slater, **3 mi W** 🍴 Subway
96	to Elkhart, **W** to Big Creek SP (11mi), Saylorville Lake
92	1st St, Ankeny, **W** 📵 Kum&Go, QT, 🍴 Ankeny Diner, Applebee's, Arby's, Burger King, Cazador Mexican, Fazoli's, Guadalajara Mexican, KFC, Quiznos, Tokyo Steaks, Village Inn, 🛏 Best Western/rest., Days Inn, Fairfield Inn, Quality Inn, Super 8, 🅾 �H Goodyear/auto, O'Reilly Parts, Staples, Tires+, auto repair
90	IA 160, Ankeny, **E** 📵 Casey's, 🍴 Chip's Diner, Outback Steaks, 🛏 AmericInn, Comfort Inn, Country Inn&Suites, Courtyard, Holiday Inn Express, 🅾 Buick/GMC, **W** 📵

(left vertical labels: AMES, ANKENY; right vertical labels: DES MOINES)

90	Continued
	Casey's/dsl, 🍴 B-bops Rest., Buffalo Wild Wings, Burger King, Chili's, China Buffet, Culver's, El Charro, HuHot Chinese, IHOP, Jimmy John's, Marble Slab, McDonald's, Old Chicago, Panchero's Mexican, Panera Bread, Smash-Burger, Starbucks, Subway, Tasty Tacos, Wendy's, 🅾 AT&T, Best Buy, Big O Tires, Chevrolet, Chrysler/Dodge/Jeep, Ford, GNC, Home Depot, Jo-Ann Fabrics, Kohl's, Menards, Michael's, Petsmart, Radio Shack, Staples, Target, TJ Maxx, Tuesday Morning, Tuffy Auto, Verizon, Walgreens, Walmart/Subway, vet, to Saylorville Lake (5mi)
89	Corporate Woods Dr, **E** 🛏 Hampton Inn, **W** 🛏 ValuePlace
87b a	I-235, I-35 and I-80
72c	(124 from I-80) University Ave, See I-80, exit 124. **E** 📵 BP/MaidRite, 🍴 Applebees, Bakers Square, Chili's, Huhot Mongolian, Jason's Deli, KFC, Little Caesars, Macaroni Grill, McDonald's, Mi Mexico, Outback Steaks, Qdoba Mexican, RockBottom Rest/Brewery, TCBY, 🛏 Chase Suites, Courtyard, Days Inn, Sheraton, Super 8, Wildwood Lodge, 🅾 AT&T, Barnes&Noble, Best Buy, Home Depot, Kmart, Kohl's, Lowes, Marshall's, Office Depot, Petsmart, Target, Horizon, Whole Foods Mkt, World Mkt, **W** 📵 Kum&Go/Burger King, QT, 🍴 Biaggi's Rest, Boston's Caribou Coffee, Cracker Barrel, El Rodeo Mexican, Panera Bread, Red Rossa Pizza, Wendy's, Z'Marik's Cafe, 🛏 Best Western, Country Inn & Suites, La Quinta, 🅾 �H Granite CityFood, Walgreen's
	I-35 and I-80 run together 14 mi around NW Des Moines. See Iowa Interstate 80, exits 124-136.
72b	I-80 W
72a	I-235 E, to Des Moines
70	Civic Pkwy, Mills, **E** 📵 Kum&Go/McDonald's, 🍴 Fire Creek Grill, Legend's Grill, 🅾 Hy-Vee Foods/gas, Verizon, Walgreens, **W** 📵 Casey's/MaidRite/dsl, 🍴 Applebee's, BangBang Mongolian, BoneFish Grill, Buffalo Wild Wings, Caribou Coffee, Champp's Grill, Cheesecake Factory, Chick-fil-A, Cusina Italiana, Fleming's Rest., Fuddruckers, Iron Wok, Joe's Crabshack, Johnny's Italian Steaks,

⬆N INTERSTATE 35 CONT'D

Exit	Services
70	Continued
	Joseph's Steaks, Mimi's Cafe, Monterrey Mexican, O'Charly's, On-the-Border, Panda Express, Panera Bread, PF Chang's, Quiznos, Red Robin, Starbucks, Sticks Rest., 🛏 Courtyard, Drury Inn, Hilton Garden, Holiday Inn, Residence Inn, Ⓞ 🄷, Barnes&Noble, Best Buy, Costco/gas, Dillards, Kohl's, Lowe's, Old Navy, PetCo, Scheel's Sports, Target, TJ Maxx, Trader Joe's, Walmart
69b a	Grand Ave, W Des Moines
68.5mm	Racoon River
68	IA 5, **7 mi E** to ✈, to Walnut Woods SP
65	G14, to Norwalk, Cumming, **14 mi W** John Wayne Birthplace, Madison Co Museum
61mm	North River
56	IA 92, to Indianola, Winterset, **W** 🅿 Kum&Go/dsl, 🍴 Hitchin Post Grill, Ⓞ Diamond Trail RV Ctr
56mm	Middle River
53mm	🆁🆂 nb, litter barrels
52	G50, St Charles, St Marys, **W** 🅿 Casey's/dsl, Kum&Go, other, 14 mi: John Wayne Birthplace, museum
51mm	🆁🆂 sb, litter barrels, parking only
47	rd G64, to Truro, **W** 🅿 Kum&Go (1mi)
45.5mm	South River
43	rd 207, New Virginia, **E** 🅿 Kum&Go/Subway/dsl
36	rd 152, to US 69, **3 mi E** 🛏 Blue Haven Motel, Evergreen Inn, **W** st patrol
34	Clay St, Osceola, **W** 🅿 🚛/Subway/dsl/scales/24hr, Ⓞ Lakeside Casino Resort/camping
33	US 34, Osceola, **E** 🅿 Casey's/dsl/scales, 🍴 McDonald's, Pizza Hut, Subway, 🛏 Best Value Inn, Days Inn, Super 8, Ⓞ 🄷 Ford, Goodyear, Hy-Vee Foods, O'Reilly Parts, st patrol, tires, **W** 🅿 BP/Arby's/dsl, 🍴 KFC/Taco Bell, 🛏 AmericInn, Ⓞ Harley-Davidson, Walmart
32mm	🆁🆂 **both lanes, full** ♿ **facilities,** Ⓒ, 🚻, **litter barrels, vending, petwalk, RV dump, wireless internet**
31mm	**weigh sta nb,** parking area sb
29	rd H45
22	rd J14, Van Wert
18	rd J20, to Grand River
12	rd 2, Decatur City, Leon, **E** 🅿 Shell/dsl, **5 mi E** 🛏 Little River Motel, Ⓞ 🄷
7.5mm	Grand River
7mm	🆁🆂 **both lanes, full** ♿ **facilities, info,** Ⓒ, 🚻, **litter barrels, vending, petwalk, RV dump, wireless internet**
4	US 69, to Davis City, Lamoni, **E** to 9 Eagles SP (10mi), **W** 🅿 Casey's (2mi), Kum&Go/dsl/E-85, 🍴 Maid-Rite Cafe, Pizza Hut (2mi), QC Rest, Subway (2mi), 🛏 Best Value Inn, Chief Lamoni Motel, Ⓞ CarQuest, auto/truck repair, **IA Welcome Ctr**
0mm	Iowa/Missouri state line

⬆E INTERSTATE 80

Exit	Services
307mm	Iowa/Illinois state line, Mississippi River
306	US 67, to Le Claire, **N** 🅿 Phillips 66/dsl, 🍴 Hungry Hobo, McDonald's, Steventon's Rest., Subway, 🛏 Comfort Inn, Holiday Inn Express, Super 8, Ⓞ Slagles Foods, **1 mi N** 🅿 BP, 🍴 A&W (2mi), Ⓞ Buffalo Bill Museum, **S** 🅿 BP (2mi)
301	Middle Rd, to Bettendorf

Exit	Services
300mm	🆁🆂 **both lanes, full** ♿ **facilities,** Ⓒ, 🚻, **litter barrels, vending, petwalk, RV dump, WiFi**
298	I-74 E, to Peoria, **S** Ⓞ to 🄷, st patrol
295b a	US 61, Brady St, to Davenport, **N** 🅿 BP/dsl, Ⓞ Sears Auto Ctr, to Scott CP, **0-2 mi S** 🅿 BP, Phillips 66, Shell, 🍴 Burger King, Cracker Barrel, Happy Joe's Pizza, Hardee's, Hooters, Los Agaves Mexican, McDonald's, Mo Brady's Steaks, Papa John's, ThunderBay Grille, Village Inn Rest., 🛏 AmericInn, Best Western, Baymont Inn, Casa Loma Suites, Clarion, Country Inn&Suites, Motel 6, Quad City Inn, Quality Inn, Residence Inn, Super 8, Travelodge, Wickliffe Inn, Ⓞ AutoZone, CarQuest, $General, Hancock Fabrics, Honda, Hyundai, JC Penney, K-Mart, Kia, Lexus, Menards, Nissan, Sears/auto, Tires+, Toyota, US Adventures RV Ctr, Von Maur, VW, mall, vet
292	IA 130 W, Northwest Blvd, **N** 🅿 ⓕFLYING J/Denny's/dsl/LP/scales/24hr, ❤Loves/Arby's/dsl/scales/24hr, 🛏 Comfort Inn, Ⓞ Interstate RV Park (1mi), F&F, Peterbilt, truckwash, **S** 🅿 BP/McDonald's/dsl, Sinclair, 🍴 Machine Shed Rest., 🛏 Days Inn, Ⓞ Freightliner
290	I-280 E, to Rock Island
284	Y40, to Walcott, **N** 🅿 🚛/Arby's/dsl/24hr/scales, TA/IA 80/BP/DQ/Pizza Hut/Taco Bell/Wendy's/dsl/scales/24hr/@, 🍴 Gramma's Rest., 🛏 Comfort Inn, EconoLodge, Ⓞ Blue Beacon, IA 80 Trucking Museum, IA 80 Truck-o-Mat, SpeedCo Lube, tires, **S** 🅿 🚛/Subway/dsl/24hr, 🍴 McDonald's, 🛏 Days Inn, Ⓞ Cheyenne Camping Ctr, Walcott CB
280	Y30, to Stockton, New Liberty
277	Durant, **2 mi S** 🅿 Sinclair/dsl/E-85
271	US 6 W, IA 38 S, to Wilton
270mm	🆁🆂 **both lanes, full** ♿ **facilities, info,** Ⓒ, 🚻, **litter barrels, vending, petwalk, RV dump, WiFi**
268mm	parking areas
267	IA 38 N, to Tipton, **N** 🅿 Kum&Go/Subway/dsl/E-85, Ⓞ Cedar River Camping
266mm	Cedar River
265	to Atalissa, **S** 🅿 🚛/Chester's/dsl only/scales/24hr
259	to West Liberty, Springdale, **S** 🅿 BP/dsl/24hr, 🛏 EconoLodge, Ⓞ West Liberty Camping
254	X30, West Branch, **N** 🅿 BP/Quiznos/dsl, Casey's, Ⓞ Jack&Jill Foods, USPO, Hoover NHS, **S** 🅿 Kum&Go, 🍴 McDonald's, 🛏 Presidential Inn, Ⓞ Chrysler/Dodge/Jeep
249	Herbert Hoover Hwy, **N** winery (2mi), **S** 🍴 Wildwood Smokehouse, Ⓞ golf
246	IA 1, Dodge St, **N** 🅿 BP/A&W/Subway/dsl, 🛏 Clarion, **S** 🅿 Sinclair, 🍴 Bob's Pizza, 🛏 Travelodge
244	Dubuque St, Iowa City, **N** Coralville Lake, **S** 🄷, to Old Capitol, museum
242	to Coralville, **N** 🍴 River City Grille, 🛏 Hampton Inn, Holiday Inn, **S** 🅿 BP, Kum&Go/dsl, 🍴 Applebee's, Arby's, Bandana's BBQ, Burger King, DQ, Delago Mexican Cafe, Edge Water Grill, Hardee's, IA Riverpower Rest., Jade Sisters Rest., McDonald's, Milio's Sandwiches, Mondo's Cafe, Old Chicago Grill, Papa John's, Peking Buffet, Perkins, Sonic, Sparti's Gyros, Subway, Taco John's, 🛏 Best Western, Big Ten Inn, Comfort Inn, Days Inn, Fairfield Inn, Heartland Inn, IA Lodge, Marriott, Motel 6, Super 8, Ⓞ 🄷 Aamco, Walgreens, vet
240	IA 965, to US 6, Coralville, N Liberty, **N** 🅿 BP, Casey's/dsl, 🍴 Buffalo Wild Wings, Culver's, Jimmy John's, McDonald's, Steak'n Shake, TX Roadhouse, Village Inn, Wen

Side tab: **IA**

Side text (Interstate 35): **O S C E O L A**

Side text (Interstate 80): **D A V E N P O R T** ... **I O W A C I T Y**

INTERSTATE 80 CONT'D

Exit	Services
240	Continued
	dy's, 🏠 AmericInn, Country Inn&Suites, Suburban Lodge, 🅞 Colony Country Camping (3mi), Costco/gas, Gordmans, Harley-Davidson, Kohl's, Michael's, PetCo, TJ Maxx, Walgreens, Walmart/Subway, **S** 🅐 Casey's, 🍴 Caribou Coffee, Chili's, Coldstone, Food Court, Huhot Mongolian, IHOP, Jimmy John's, Noodles&Co, Old Country Buffet, Olive Garden, Outback Steaks, Panchero's Mexican, Papa Murphy's, Pizza Hut, Red Lobster, Starbucks, Taste of China, Which Which, 🏠 Comfort Suites, Holiday Inn Express, Residence Inn, 🅞 Ace Hardware, Barnes&Noble, Best Buy, Dillard's, Hobby Lobby, HyVee Foods/dsl, JC Penney, Lowe's, Radio Shack, Scheel's Sports, Sears/auto, Target, Tires+, U-Haul, Verizon, Younkers, mall
239b	I-380 N, US 218 N, to Cedar Rapids
239a	US 218 S
237	Tiffin, **N** 🅐 Kum&Go/Subway/dsl, 🍴 Jon's Rest (1mi) (seasonal)
236mm	🆁🆂 both lanes, full ♿ facilities, 🍴, 🛢, litter barrels, vending, RV dump, petwalk, wireless internet
230	W38, to Oxford, **N** 🅞 Sleepy Hollow Camping, Kalona Museum
225	US 151 N, W21 S, **N** to Amana Colonies, 🏠 Heritage Inn, **S** Welcome Ctr, 🅐 BP, Casey's, 🍴 Colony Village Rest., MaidRite Cafe, Little Amana Rest./Winery, 7 Villages Rest., Ox Yoke Rest., 🏠 Clarion, Motel 6
220	IA 149 S, V77 N, to Williamsburg, **N** 🅐 BP, Casey's/rest/dsl, 🍴 Arby's, McDonald's, Subway, 🏠 Best Western, Crest Motel, Super 8, 🅞 GNC, Old Navy, factory outlets/famous brands, **S** 🏠 Days Inn
216	to Marengo, **N** 🅐 Kum&Go/Subway/dsl, 🏠 Sudbury Court Motel (7mi), 🅞 🏥 (8mi)
211	to Ladora, Millersburg, **S** Lake IA Park (5mi)
208mm	🆁🆂 both lanes, full ♿ facilities, 🍴, vending, 🛢, litter barrels, petwalk, wireless internet, RV dump
205	to Victor
201	IA 21, to Deep River, **N** 🅐 ▭▭▭/Subway/dsl/scales/24hr, 🏠 Baymont Inn, **S** 🅐 KwikStar/Pinecone Rest./dsl/scales/24hr/@, truck repair
197	to Brooklyn, **N** RV camping
191	US 63, to Montezuma, **S** to Diamond Lake SP (9mi)
182	IA 146, to Grinnell, **0-2 mi N** 🅐 Casey's, Kum&Go/Subway/dsl/24hr, 🍴 Casa Margaritas, DQ, Grinnell Steakhouse, KFC, McDonald's, Pizza Ranch, Taco John's, 🏠 Best Western, Comfort Inn, Country Inn, Days Inn, Super 8, 🅞 🏥 (4mi), Ace Hardware, Buick/Chevrolet/GMC, $General, HyVee Foods, O'Reilly Parts, Verizon, Walmart, vet
180mm	🆁🆂 both lanes, full ♿ facilities, 🍴, vending, weather info, 🛢, litter barrels, petwalk, playground, RV dump (eb) wireless internet
179	IA 124, to Oakland Acres, Lynnville
175mm	N Skunk River
173	IA 224, Kellogg, **N** 🅐 Phillips 66/Best Burger/dsl/24hr, 🅞 Kellogg RV Park, Rock Creek SP (9mi), **S** 🅞 Pella Museum
168	SE Beltline Dr, to Newton, **1 mi N** 🅐 Casey's/dsl, Murphy USA/dsl, 🍴 Arby's, 🏠 Mid-Iowa Motel, 🅞 $Tree, Radio Shack, KOA (seasonal), Walmart, **S** 🅐 Loves/Chester's/McDonald's/dsl/scales, 🏠 AmericInn, 🅞 Iowa Speedway

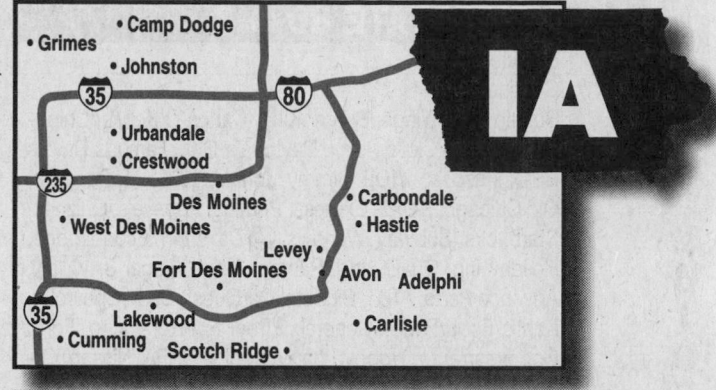

Exit	Services
164	US 6, IA 14, Newton, **N** 🅐 Casey's, Phillips 66/Subway/dsl, 🍴 Country Kitchen, Culver's, KFC/Taco Bell, MT Mikes, Okoboji Grill, Perkins, Pizza Ranch, Senor Tequila Mexican, 🏠 Days Inn, EconoLodge, Quality Inn, Super 8, 🅞 🏥, museum, **S** 🏠 Best Value Inn, 🅞 Cadillac/Chevrolet, to Lake Red Rock
159	F48, to Jasper, Baxter
155	IA 117, Colfax, **N** 🅐 BP/McDonald's, 🏠 Colfax Inn, Microtel, 🅞 Pitstop RV Camping, truck repair, **S** 🅐 Casey's, Kum&Go/Subway/dsl/24hr
153mm	S Skunk River
151	weigh sta wb
149	Mitchellville
148mm	🆁🆂 both lanes, full ♿ facilities, 🍴, 🛢, litter barrels, petwalk, vending, RV dump, wireless internet
143	Altoona, Bondurant, **0-2 mi S** 🅐 Casey's, Kum&Go, 🍴 Pizza Ranch, 🏠 Holiday Inn Express, 🅞 HyVee Foods
142b a	US 65, Hubble Ave, Des Moines, **S** 🅐 ⊕FLYING J/Max's Diner/dsl/scales/24hr/@, Git'n Go, 🍴 Big Steer Rest., Burger King, Culver's, Jethro's BBQ, KFC/Taco Bell, McDonald's/playplace, Pizza Hut, Subway, Taco John's, 🏠 Adventureland Inn, Best Western, Motel 6, Regency Inn, Settle Inn, 🅞 Adventureland Funpark, Blue Beacon, Freightliner, Peterbilt, camping, casino
141	US 6 W, US 65 S, Pleasant Hill, Des Moines, **S** 🍴 Uncle Buck's Grill, 🅞 Bass Pro Shops
137b a	I 35 N, I 235 S, to Des Moines
	I-80 W and I-35 S run together 14 mi.
136	US 69, E 14th St, Camp Sunnyside, **N** 🅐 BP/dsl, Casey's, 🍴 Bonanza Steaks, MT Mikes, 🏠 Budget Inn, Comfort Inn, Motel 6, Rodeway Inn, 🅞 Allied Tire, Shoppers, Volvo, antiques, **0-1 mi S** 🅐 Casey's/dsl, Star Gas, QT/Burger King/dsl/scales/24hr, 🍴 Arby's, Fazoli's, Hardee's, KFC, McDonald's, Papa Murphy's, Pueblo Viejo Mexican, Subway, Taco Bell, Taco John's, Village Inn, Wendy's, 🏠 Baymont Inn, Travelodge, 🅞 Advance Parts, Aldi Foods, AutoZone, CarX, $General, Family$, O'Reilly Parts, Tires+, TruckLube, USPO
135	IA 415, 2nd Ave, Polk City, **N** 🍴 Smokey D's BBQ, 🅞 Harley-Davidson, Rider Trucks, antiques, **S** 🅐 Git'n Go, QT, Shell, 🅞 🏥 Earl's Tire, NAPA, st patrol
133mm	Des Moines River
131	IA 28 S, NW 58th St, **N** 🅐 Casey's, QT, 🍴 Bandit Burrito, Chopsticks, DQ, El Mariachi Mexican, Greenbriar Rest., Jimmy John's, Pagliai's Pizza, Panera Bread, Sonic, Subway, VanDee's Icecream/Sandwiches, 🏠 AmericInn, 🅞 Ace Hardware, Acura, Audi/VW, Goodyear/auto, Hy-Vee Food, Verizon, USPO, vet, **S** 🅐 BP/dsl/LP/24hr, Casey's, QT, 🍴 Applebee's, Arby's, Bamboo Buffet, Bennigan's,

🚪 = gas   🍴 = food   🛏 = lodging   ⚪ = other   Ⓡˢ = rest stop   Copyright 2014 - The Next Exit ®

⛛E INTERSTATE 80 CONT'D

D E S M O I N E S

Exit	Services
131	Continued
	Buffalo Wild Wings, Burger King, Carlos O'Kelly's, Chipotle Mexican, Cici's Pizza, Daytona's Grill, Famous Dave's BBQ, Fazoli's, IHOP, Jimmy John's, KFC, McDonald's, Old Chicago, Panda Express, Perkins, Popeye's, Quiznos, Starbucks, Subway, Wendy's, 🛏 Days Inn, EconoLodge, Holiday Inn, Quality Inn, Ramada/Rest., Super 8, ⚪ 🏥, Advance Parts, AT&T, BigLots, CarQuest, CarX, Chevrolet, Dahl's Food/Fuel, $General, $Tree, Firestone/auto, Ford, Goodyear/auto, Hobby Lobby, Kohl's, NAPA, Nissan, Office Depot, Sears/auto, Staples, Target, Tires+, Toyota/Scion, Verizon, Younkers, mall, **Urgent Care**, vet
129	NW 86th St, Camp Dodge, **N** 🚪 Kum&Go, 🍴 Burger King, Coldstone, Garden Grill, Legends Grill, Maid-Rite Cafe, McDonald's, Okoboji Grill, Panchero's Mexican, Planet Sub, Quiznos, Starbucks, TX Roadhouse, Village Inn, 🛏 Hilton Garden, Stoney Creek Inn, TownePlace Suites, ⚪ Dahl's Foods, Verizon, **S** 🚪 Casey's, Kum&Go/dsl, 🍴 Arby's, B-Bops Burgers, Culver's, Friedrich's Coffee, Overtime Grill, Ruby Tuesday, 🛏 Holiday Inn Express, Microtel, ⚪ Walgreens
127	IA 141 W, Grimes, **N** 🚪 BP/dsl, QT/dsl, 🍴 MaidRite Cafe, McCoy's Grill, Subway, 🛏 AmericInn (3mi), ⚪ Kia/Suzuki, to Saylorville Lake, **S** 🚪 Kum&Go/E-85, 🍴 McDonald's, Quiznos, ⚪ Home Depot, Target
126	Douglas Ave, Urbandale, **N** 🚪 🚚/Grandma Max's/Subway/dsl/scales/24hr/@, Kum&Go/dsl, **S** 🍴 Dragon House, 🛏 EconoLodge, Extended Stay America, Villa Lodge, ⚪ Chevrolet
125	US 6, Hickman Rd, **N** 🚪 ♥Loves/Denny's/dsl/scales/LP/24hr, ⚪ Chrysler/Dodge/Jeep, Menards, **S** 🍴 IA Machine Shed Rest., Starbucks, 🛏 Clive Hotel, Comfort Suites, Sleep Inn, ⚪ AAA, Honda, Hyundai, to Living History Farms
124	(72c from I-35 nb), University Ave, **N** 🚪 Kum&Go/Burger King, QT, 🍴 Biaggi's Rest., Boston's, Caribou Coffee, Cracker Barrel, El Rodeo Mexican, Panera Bread, Red Rossa Pizza, Wendy's, Z'Marik's Cafe, 🛏 Best Western, Country Inn&Suites, La Quinta, ⚪ 🏥, Granite City Food, Walgreens, **S** 🚪 BP/MaidRite, 🍴 Applebee's, Bakers Square, Chili's, Huhot Mongolian, Jason's Deli, KFC, Little Caesars, Macaroni Grill, McDonald's, Mi Mexico, Outback Steaks, Qdoba Mexican, RockBottom Rest./brewery, TCBY, 🛏 Chase Suites, Courtyard, Days Inn, Sheraton, Super 8, Wildwood Lodge, ⚪ AT&T, Barnes&Noble, Best Buy, Home Depot, K-Mart, Kohl's, Lowe's, Marshall's, Office Depot, Petsmart, Target, Verizon, Whole Foods Mkt, World Mkt
	I-80 E and I-35 N run together 14 mi.
123b a	I-80/I-35 N, I-35 S to Kansas City, I-235 to Des Moines
122	(from eb)60th St, W Des Moines
121	74th St, W Des Moines, **N** 🍴 Biaggi's Rest., Panera Bread, Red Rossa Pizza, 🛏 Hampton Inn, Staybridge Suites, ⚪ 🏥, Granite City Foods, HyVee Food/gas, Walgreens, **S** 🚪 Kum&Go/Subway, 🍴 Arby's, Burger King, CK's, Culver's, McDonald's, Perkins, Quiznos, Taco John's, 🛏 Candlewood Suites, Fairfield Inn, Marriott, Motel 6, SpringHill Suites, vet
119mm	Ⓡˢ both lanes, full 🚻 facilities, info, vending, 🕴, 🛒, petwalk, RV dump, Wireless Internet

Exit	Services
117	R22, Booneville, Waukee, **N** 🍴 Organic Farm Rest., ⚪ Timberline Camping (2mi), **S** 🚪 Kum&Go/24hr, 🍴 Rube's Steaks, Waveland Rest. (2mi)
115mm	**weigh sta eb**
113	R16, Van Meter, **1 mi S** 🚪 Casey's, ⚪ Feller Museum, Veteran's Cemetary
112mm	N Racoon River
111mm	Middle Racoon River
110	US 169, to Adel, DeSoto, **N** camping (6mi), **S** 🚪 Casey's, Kum&Go/dsl/E-85, 🛏 Countryside Inn, Edgetowner Motel, ⚪ John Wayne Birthplace (14mi)
106	F90, P58, **N** KOA (apr-oct)
104	P57, Earlham, **S** 🚪 Casey's (2mi), 🍴 Master Griller (2mi)
100	US 6, to Redfield, Dexter, **N** 🚪 Casey's (2mi), 🍴 Drew's Chocolate (2mi)
97	P48, to Dexter, **N** 🚪 Casey's (2mi), camping
93	P28, Stuart, **N** 🚪 Casey's/dsl/scales, Kum&Go/dsl, 🍴 Burger King, McDonald's/playplace, Subway, 🛏 AmericInn, Super 8, ⚪ Chevrolet, $General, Hometown Foods, camping (7mi), city park, **S** 🚪 Phillips 66/dsl, 🍴 Country Kitchen, 🛏 Economy Inn, Edgetowner Motel, ⚪ NAPA
88	P20, Menlo
86	IA 25, to Greenfield, Guthrie Ctr, **S** ⚪ 🏥 (13mi), to Spring Brook SP
85mm	Middle River
83	N77, Casey, **1 mi N** 🚪 Kum&Go, ⚪ camping
80.5mm	Ⓡˢ both lanes, full 🚻 facilities, 🕴, 🛒, litter barrels, vending, petwalk, RV dump, wireless internet
76	IA 925, N54, Adair, **N** 🚪 Casey's/dsl, Kum&Go/Subway/dsl, 🍴 Happy Chef, 🛏 Adair Budget Inn, Super 8, ⚪ camping, city park
75	G30, to Adair
70	IA 148 S, Anita, **S** to Lake Anita SP (6mi)
64	N28, to Wiota
61mm	E Nishnabotna River
60	US 6, US 71, to Atlantic, Lorah, **S** 🚪 Phillips 66/dsl/24hr, 🛏 Best Value Inn
57	N16, to Atlantic, **S** 🏥 (7mi), Nelsen RV Ctr
54	IA 173, to Elk Horn, **6 mi N Welcome Ctr/Wireless Internet**, 🛏 AmericInn (6mi), ⚪ Windmill Museum, gas, food (7mi)
51	M56, to Marne
46	M47, Walnut, **N** 🚪 BP/McDonald's/dsl, 🍴 Emma Jean's Rest., 🛏 Super 8, to Prairie Rose SP (8mi), **S** 🚪 Kum&Go/pizza/dsl, 🛏 EconoLodge/RV Park, tires/repair
44mm	**weigh sta, wb**/parking area eb
40	US 59, to Harlan, Avoca, **N** 🚪 🚚/Phillips 66/Taco John's/MaidRite Cafe/dsl/24hr/scales, 🍴 CJ's Grill, Subway, 🛏 Motel 6, ⚪ 🏥 (12mi), truckwash, **S** 🚪 Casey's/dsl, Shell/dsl, 🍴 Embers Rest., 🛏 Acova Motel, Capri Motel, ⚪ Avoca Foods, Farmall-Land Museum (seasonal), Nishna Museum
39.5mm	W Nishnabotna River
34	M16, Shelby, **N** 🚪 BP/rest/dsl/E-85, Shell/Cornstalk Cafe/dsl, 🍴 DQ, Godfather's, 🛏 Shelby Country Inn/RV Park
32mm	Ⓡˢ both lanes, parking only
29	L66, to Minden, **S** 🚪 Phillips 66/A&W/dsl, 🛏 Mid-Town Motel (2mi), ⚪ winery (4mi)
27	I-680 W, to N Omaha
23	IA 244, L55, Neola, **S** 🚪 Kum&Go/dsl, ⚪ to Arrowhead Park, camping

IA

INTERSTATE 80 CONT'D

Exit	Services
20mm	Welcome Ctr eb/🅿 wb, full ♿ facilities, 🕿, 🚻, litter barrels, vending, petwalk, RV dump, Wireless Internet
17	G30, Underwood, **N** ⛽ Phillips 66/Subway/dsl/24hr, 🛏 Underwood Motel, ⓞ truck/tire repair
8	US 6, Council Bluffs, **N** ⛽ Phillips 66/dsl (1mi), ⓞ 🏥 (3mi), $General, K-Mart, **S** st patrol
5	Madison Ave, Council Bluffs, **N** ⛽ BP/dsl, 🍴 Burger King, FoodCourt, Great Wall Chinese, KFC, McDonald's, Papa Murphy's, Pizza Hut, Starbucks, Subway, 🛏 AmericInn, ⓞ HyVee Foods/drug, Sears/auto, Verizon, Walgreens, **S** ⛽ Cenex/DQ/dsl, Phillips 66, 🍴 Johnny's Cantina, Puerto Vallarta, Sam&Louie's Pizza, Village Inn Rest., 🛏 Western Inn, ⓞ No Frills Mkt, TrueValue
4	I-29 S, to Kansas City
3	IA 192 N, Council Bluffs, **N** to Hist Dodge House, **S** ⛽ Phillips 66/dsl, Shell/dsl, TA/dsl/scales/24hr@, 🍴 Applebee's, Beijing Rest., Burger King, Cracker Barrel, DQ, Fazoli's, Golden Corral, Hardee's, Huhot Mongolian, La Mesa Mexican, LJ Silver, McDonald's, Old River Pizza, Perkins, Red Lobster, Subway, Taco Bell, 🛏 Days Inn, Fairfield Inn, Motel 6, Settle Inn, ⓞ Advance Parts, Aldi Foods, Best Buy, Buick/GMC, Cadillac/Chevrolet, Chrysler/Jeep/Suzuki, Ford, Freightliner, Gordman's, Home Depot, Hyundai/Subaru, Kia, Menards, Nissan, Outdoor Recreation RV, Sam's Club/gas, U-Haul, Verizon, Walmart/Subway, truck/dsl repair
1b	S 24th St, Council Bluffs, **N** ⛽ BP, Casey's, ▨▨▨/Arby's/scales/dsl/24hr, Sapp Bros/Shell/Burger King/dsl, 🍴 Famous Dave's BBQ, Hooters, Quaker Steak&Lube, Ruby Tuesday, Uncle Buck's, 🛏 American Inn, Best Western, Country Inn&Suites, Hilton Garden, Holiday Inn Express, Microtel, SpringHill Suites, Super 8, ⓞ Bass Pro Shop, Blue Beacon, Camping World RV Ctr, Horseshoe RV Park, Peterbilt, SpeedCo, casino, **S** Welcome Ctr, full facilities, 🍴 Culver's, TX Roadhouse, ⓞ JC Penney, PetCo, ShopKO, Verizon
1a	I-29 N, to Sioux City
0mm	Iowa/Nebraska state line, Missouri River

INTERSTATE 235 (DES MOINES)

Exit	Services
15	I-80, E to Davenport
12	US 6, E Euclid Ave, **E** ⛽ Casey's, 🍴 Burger King, Dragon House Chinese, Papa John's, Perkins, Tasty Tacos, ⓞ $Tree, HyVee Foods/drug, Radio Shack, Walgreens, **W** ⛽ QT, ⓞ NAPA
11	Guthrie Ave, **W** ⛽ Kum&Go/dsl, ⓞ CarQuest
10a b	IA 163 W, E University Ave, Easton Dr
9	US 65/69, E 14th, E 15th, **N** ⓞ Walgreens, **S** ⛽ QT, 🍴 McDonald's, Quiznos, ⓞ🏥, st capitol, Urgent Care, zoo
8b	E 6th St, Penn Ave (from wb), **N** 🏥
8a	3rd St, 5th Ave, **N** 🛏 Holiday Inn, ⓞ🏥, **S** 🛏 Embassy Suites, Marriott, Quality Inn, ⓞ Conv Ctr
7	Keo Way
6	MLK Blvd/31st St, Drake U, Governor's Mansion, **S** 🚻
5b	42nd St, Science & Art Ctr, **N** ⛽ Git'n Go, 🍴 Papa John's, ⓞ Curves
5a	56th St (from wb), **N** golf
4	IA 28, 63rd St, to Windsor Heights, **S** Historic Valley Jct, zoo

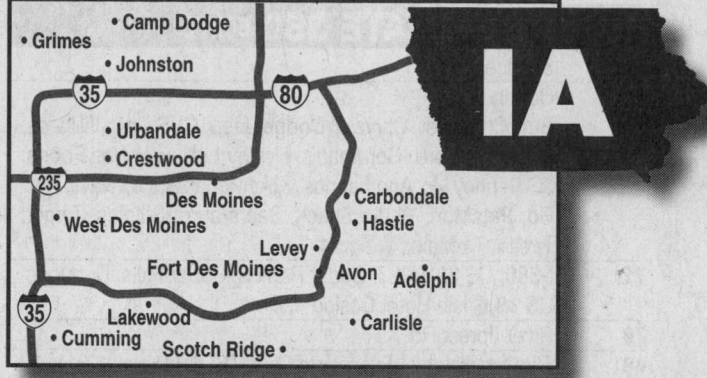

3	8th St, W Des Moines, **N** ⛽ Kum&Go, 🍴 B-Bop's Café, Burger King, Papa Murphy's, Starbucks, ⓞ HyVee Foods, PetCo, Sam's Club/gas, Walmart/Subway, **S** ⛽ BP, Kum&Go/dsl/E-85, 🍴 Jimmy John's, Lemongrass Thai, Raul's Mexican, Taste of Oriental, 🛏 Days Inn
2	22nd St, 24th St, W Des Moines, **N** ⛽ BP, Casey's, QT/dsl, 🍴 Arby's, Culver's, Famous Dave's BBQ, Hardee's, Hooters, LoneStar Steaks, SmashBurger, Taco Bell, Village Inn, 🛏 Studio+, ⓞ $Tree, Firestone/auto, Gordman's, Meineke, Michael's, Walgreens
1b	Valley West Dr, W Des Moines, **N** ⛽ BP/dsl, 🍴 Carlos O'Kelly's, Chipotle Mexican, Eastern Buffet, Hamilton's Rest., Jimmy John's, Noodles&Co, Olive Garden, Panera Bread, Red Lobster, Subway, 🛏 Valley West Inn, ⓞ AT&T, Best Buy, Home Depot, HyVee Foods, JC Penney, Marshall's, Target, Von Maur, Whole Foods Mkt, Younker's, mall
0mm	I-235 begins/ends on I-80, exit 123.

INTERSTATE 280 (DAVENPORT)

Exit	Services
18b a	I-74, US 6, Moline, **S** ⛽ Shell/dsl, 🍴 McDonald's, MT Jack's, 🛏 Best Inn, Country Inn&Suites, Days Inn, Econolodge, Hampton Inn, La Quinta, Quality Inn, Ramada Inn, ⓞ 🚻
15	Airport Rd, Milan, **N** 🍴 (1mi)MaidRite Café, Subway, ⓞ Buick/Chevrolet, Firestone
11b a	IL 92, to Andalusia, Rock Island, **S** KOA Camping
9.5mm	Iowa/Illinois state line, Mississippi River
8	rd 22, Rockingham Rd, to Buffalo
6	US 61, W River Dr, to Muscatine, **W** gas, camping
4	Locust St, rd F65, 160th St, **E** 🏥, to Palmer Coll, St Ambrose U, **W** ⛽ Shell/Dickey's BBQ/dsl
1	US 6 E, IA 927, Kimberly Rd, to Walcott, **3 mi E** ⛽ Murphy USA, 🍴 Applebee's, Culver's, Sonic, Steak'n Shake, Subway, Wendy's, ⓞ K-Mart, Walmart

INTERSTATE 380

Exit	Services
73mm	I-380 begins/ends on US 218, 73mm in Waterloo, **E** ⛽ BP/dsl, **W** ⛽ Clark, 🍴 Pizza Hut
72	San Marnan Dr, **W** 🍴 A&W/LJ Silver, Applebee's, Bonanza, Burger King, Carlos O'Kelly's, Coldstone, Hardee's, Godfather's, Golden China, IHOP, Jimmy John's, Olive Garden, Panera Bread, Pizza Hut, Red Lobster, Starbucks, Subway, Taco John's, 🛏 Baymont Inn, Candlewoods Suites, Comfort Inn, Country Inn&Suites, Days Inn, Fairfield Inn, Hampton Inn, Holiday Inn Express, Super 8, ⓞ Advance Parts, Aldi Foods, Barnes&Noble, Best

COUNCIL BLUFFS

DES MOINES

WATERLOO

IA

🅖 = gas   🍴 = food   🏠 = lodging   🅞 = other   🆁🆂 = rest stop   Copyright 2014 - The Next Exit ®

🔼🔽Ⓝ INTERSTATE 380 CONT'D

Exit	Services
72	Continued
	Buy, Chevrolet, Chrysler/Dodge/Jeep, CVS Drug, Dillards, $General, Ford, Gordman's, Hobby Lobby, HyVee Foods, JC Penney, Jo-Ann Fabrics, KIA, Menards, Old Navy, Pet-Co, PetsMart, Radio Shack, Sears/auto, Staples, Target, Tires+, TJ Maxx, Walmart
71	I-380, US 20, IA 27, Cedar Rapids, Cedar Falls, Dubuque US 18 **S** Isle Hotel/Casino
70	River Forest Rd
68	Elk Run Heights, Evansdale Dr, **E** 🅖 *FLYING J*/Denny's/dsl/scales/24hr, 🚛/RR/Junie's/Subway/dsl/scales/24hr/@, 🍴 Arby's, McDonald's, 🏠 Days Inn, 🅞 Freight-liner, Paine's RV Ctr, truckwash/repair
66	Gilbertville, Raymond
65	US 20 E, Dubuque
62	rd d-38, Gilbertville
55	rd v-65, Jesup, La Port, **W** 🅞 Hickory Hills Park, McFar-lane Park
54mm	**weigh sta sb**
51mm	**weigh sta nb**
49	rd d-48, Brandon, **1 mi W** gas, food
43	IA 150, Independence, Vinton, **E** 🅖 Phillips 66/dsl/24hr, 🏠 Inn Suites, 🅞 truckwash
41	Urbana, **E** 🅞 Lazy Acres RV Park, **W** 🅖 Casey's/dsl
35	rd w-36, Center Point, **E** 🅖 BP, Casey's, Sinclair/McDon-ald's/Subway/dsl/scales/24hr, **W** 🅖 Pleasant Creek SRA (5mi)
28	rd e-34, Robins, Toddville, **W** 🅞 Wickiup Outdoor Learn-ing Ctr (5mi)

(side label: CEDAR RAPIDS)

Exit	Services
25	Boyson Rd, Hiawatha, **E** 🅞 Ketelsen RV Ctr, **W** 🅖 BP, Casey's/Blimpie/Pizza, 🍴 Culver's, Pizza Wagon, 🅞 Toyota/Scion/VW
24	IA 100, Blairs Ferry Rd, **E** 🅖 KwikShop/dsl 🍴 Happy Chef, Hardee's, KFC, La Glorias Mexican, McDonald's, 🏠 Days Inn, Hawthorn Suites, 🅞 CVS Drug, HyVee Foods, **W** 🅖 Road Ranger, 🍴 Arby's, Burger King, Metro Buffet, Pizza Hut, Subway, Taco Bell, 🅞 Aldi Foods, AutoZone, GNC, Lowe's, Sam's Club/gas, Walmart
22	Glass Rd, 32nd st, **E** 🅖 KwikShop/dsl, 🍴 Papa Johns
21	H St, Cedar Rapids, downtown
20b	7th St E, Cedar Rapids, downtown, **E** 🅷
20a	US 151 Bus., **E** 🏠 Crowne Plaza
19b	1st Ave W, **W** 🏠 Best Western, 🅞 NAPA
18	Wilson Ave, museums
17	33rd ave SW, Hawkeye Downs, **W** 🅖 Casey's, 🍴 Burger King, McDonald's, Sonic, Taco Bell, Wendy's, 🏠 Clarion, Comfort Inn, Economy Inn, Hampton Inn, Heartland Inn, Holiday Inn Express, Motel 6, Red Roof Inn, Super 8
16	US 30 W, US 151 S, US 218 N, Tama
13	Ely, **W** 🅖 Casey's/A&W/dsl, Casey's/dsl/scales, 🍴 Mc-Donald's, 🏠 AmericInn, Country Inn&Suites, 🅞🛬
12mm	🆁🆂 **both lanes**, 🚻 **littler barrels**, 🅒 **petwalk, vending, RV Dump, wireless internet**
10	rd f-12, Shueyville, Swisher, **E** 🅖 BP/dsl, 🅞 Lake Mc-bride SP, **W** 🅖 Amana Colonies
8mm	Iowa River
4	rd f-28, North Liberty, **E** 🅖 BP/dsl, Casey's/Blimpie, Kum&Go/dsl (2mi), 🏠 Sleep Inn, 🅞 Colony Country RV Park (5mi)
0b a	I-80 E to Iowa City, W to Des Moines, **I-380 begins/ends on I-80**

KANSAS

🔼🔽Ⓝ INTERSTATE 35

Exit	Services
235mm	Kansas/Missouri state line
235	Cambridge Circle
234b a	US 169, Rainbow Blvd, **E** 🅖 QT, Phillips 66, 🍴 Apple-bee's, Arby's, Burger King, McDonald's, Rosedale BBQ, Sonic, Wendy's, 🏠 Best Western, Sun Inn, 🅞 KU MED CTR, **W** 🍴 KFC, LJ Silver, Taco Bell
233a	SW Blvd, Mission Rd
233b	37th Ave (from sb)
232b	US 69 N, **E** 🅖 QT, 🍴 Cici's, McDonald's, Taco Bell
232a	Lamar Ave, **E** 🅖 QT, 🏠 ValuePlace Inn
231b a	I-635 (exits left from sb)
230	Antioch Rd (from sb), **E** 🅖 QT
229	Johnson Dr, **E** 🅖 Phillips 66, 🍴 Arby's, Bob Evans, Chili's, Chipotle Mexican, McDonald's, Papa John's, Starbucks, 🅞 GNC, Hen House Mkt, Home Depot, Mar-shall's, Old Navy, Petsmart, Walgreens, **W** 🅖 Cenex/dsl
228b	US 56 E, US 69, Shawnee Mission Pkwy, **E** 🅖 Shell, 🍴 Caribou Coffee, Denny's, IHOP, Krispy Kreme, Pizza Hut, Taco Bell, 🏠 Drury Inn, Homestead Suites, Winsteads Suites, 🅞 BMW/Mini, Sears Grand, **W** 🅖 Valero, 🍴 A&W, LJ Silver, Panera Bread, Pizza Hut, Subway, Wen-dy's, 🅞 Cotman's Transmissions, Firestone, Ford, Good-year/auto, Jo-Ann Fabrics, Office Depot, O'Reilly Parts, Russell Stover, Walgreens

(side label: KANSAS CITY AREA)

Exit	Services
228a	67th St, **E** 🏠 Quality Inn, 🅞 CarMax, **W** 🅖 Phillips 66/Circle K/dsl, 🅞 Hyundai, Jaguar, Land Rover, Maserati, Mercedes, Porsche Smart, Toyota/Scion
227	75th St, **E** 🍴 McDonald's, 🏠 Extended Stay America, 🅞🅷 Acura, Walmart, vet, **W** 🅖 QT/dsl, 🍴 Domino's, Sonic, Subway, Taco Bell, 2 Amigos Mexican, Wendy's, 🏠 Hampton Inn, 🅞 Hyundai
225b	US 69 S (from sb), Overland Pkwy
225a	87th St, **E** 🅖 Phillips 66, 🍴 Green Mill Rest, 🏠 Holiday Inn, **W** 🅖 Phillips 66/Circle K/dsl, 🍴 Taco Bell, Zarda BBQ, 🅞 auto repair
224	95th St, **E** 🅖 Phillips 66/Circle K, Shell, 🍴 Applebee's, BD Mongolian BBQ, Burger King, Chick-fil-A, Chipotle Mexican, Denny's, Houlihan's, KFC, McDonald's, Mimi's Café, On-the-Border, Outback Steaks, Panda Express, Subway, Taco Bell, TGIFriday's, Winstead's Cafe, 🏠 Com-fort Inn, Crowne Plaza, Days Inn, Extended Stay America, Knight's Inn, La Quinta, Motel 6, Super 8, 🅞🅷 Advance Parts, Barnes&Noble, Best Buy, Dillard's, Firestone/auto, Hy-Vee Foods, JC Penney, Kohl's, Macy's, Nordstrom, Office Depot, PetCo, Sam's Club/gas, Target, mall, **W** 🅖 Phillips 66, 🍴 Mi Ranchito, 🅞 Costco/gas, O'Reilly Parts, U-Haul
222b a	I-435 W & E
220	119th St, **E** 🅖 Conoco/7-11, Phillips 66/Circle K, Shell, 🍴 A&W, Buffalo Wild Wings, Burger King, Chick-fil-A, Chipotle Mexican, Coldstone, Cracker Barrel, Dodge City

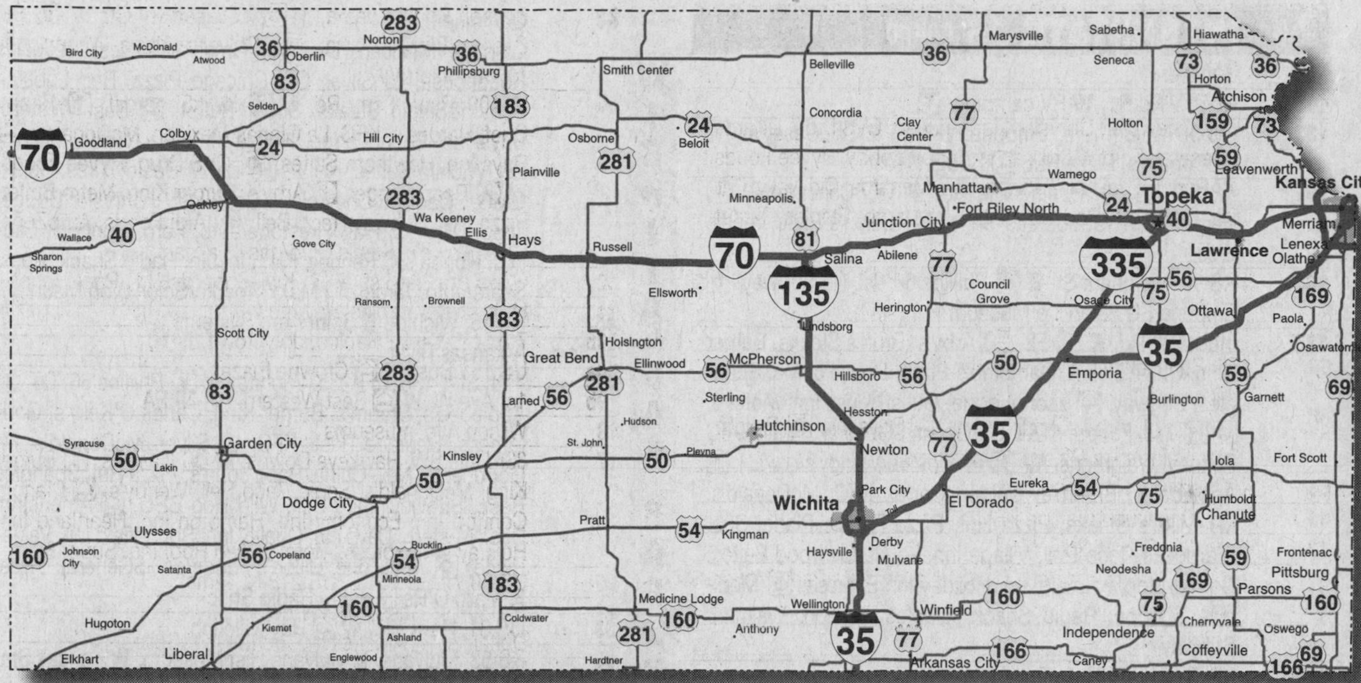

INTERSTATE 35 CONT'D

Exit	Services
220	Continued Steaks, Firehouse Subs, 5 Guys Burgers, Granite City Cafe, Greek Rest., Haru's Steak, IHOP, Jersey Mike's, Jimmy John's, Joe's Crabshack, La Parrilla, LJ Silver, Longhorn Steaks, McDonald's, Noodles&Co, OK Joe's BBQ, Old Chicago, Olive Garden, Panda Express, Panera Bread, Papa Murphy's, Pei Wei, Planet Sub, Popeye's, Red Lobster, Ruby Tuesday, Schlotzsky's, Starbucks, Steak'n Shake, Subway, Taco Bell, TX Roadhouse, Wei's Buffet, Zio's Italian, [lodging] Comfort Suites, Fairfield Inn, Hampton Inn, Hilton Garden, Residence Inn, SpringHill Suites, ValuePlace Inn, [other] AT&T, Best Buy, Chrysler/Dodge/Jeep, Dick's, Fiat, GNC, Goodyear/auto, Home Depot, Honda, Marshall's, Mazda, Michael's, NTB, Old Navy, Petsmart, Radio Shack, Target, U-Haul, Verizon, **W** [food] Houlihan's, Jason's Deli, Longhorn Steaks, Starbucks, [other] Bass Pro Shops
218	135th, Santa Fe St, Olathe, **E** [gas] Phillips 66/dsl, QT, [food] Applebee's, Burger King, Chapala Mexican, China Buffet, ChuckeCheese, Church's, Garozzo's Italian, McDonald's, Other Place Grill, Papa John's, Perkins, Pizza St, Quiznos, Sheridan's Custard, Subway, Taco Bell, [other] Ace Hardware, Aldi Foods, AutoZone, BigLots, CVS Drug, $General, $Tree, Ford/Lincoln, GNC, Goodyear, Hobby Lobby, Hy-Vee Foods, K-Mart, Kohl's, Lowe's, Office Depot, PriceChopper Foods, Tuesday Morning, vet, **W** [gas] QT, [food] El Camino Real, Taco Bell, Waffle House, Wendy's, [lodging] Rodeway Inn, [other] Aamco, Advance Parts, Buick/GMC, Chevrolet, Harley-Davidson, Hyundai, Kia, Meineke, O'Reilly Parts, Radio Shack, Subaru, Toyota/Scion, VW
217	Old Hwy 56 (from sb), same as 215
215	US 169 S, KS 7, Olathe, **E** [gas] Phillips 66/dsl, QT/dsl, [food] China Inn, Chipotle Mexican, Cilantro Mexican, IHOP, Jimmy John's, Outback Steaks, Panera Bread, Red Robin, Ryan's, [lodging] Candlewood Suites, Comfort Inn, [other] Aldi Foods, AT&T, Home Depot, Jiffy Lube, NTB, Target, **W** [gas] Shell/dsl/scales/24hr, [food] Applebee's, Burger King, Chili's,

OLATHE

Exit	Services
215	Continued 54th St Grill, FoodCourt, Red Lobster, McDonald's, Taco Bell, Waffle House, Wendy's, [lodging] Best Western, Days Inn, Holiday Inn, La Quinta, [other] [H], Mazda, mall
214	Lone Elm Rd, 159th St
213mm	**weigh sta both lanes**
210	US 56 W, Gardner, **W** [gas] Phillips 66/Circle K/dsl, [food] Arby's, Burger King, KFC, McDonald's, Mr Goodcents Subs, Pizza Hut, Subway, Taco Bell, Waffle House, [lodging] Super 8, [other] NAPA, Verizon, Walmart/Subway
207	US 56 E, Gardner Rd, **E** Olathe RV Ctr, **W** [gas] Phillips 66/dsl, Shell/dsl
202	Edgerton
198	KS 33, to Wellsville, **W** gas, food
193	Tennessee Rd, Baldwin
188	US 59 N, to Lawrence
187	KS 68, Ottawa, **W** [other] Central RV Ctr, vet, **W** [gas] Zarco/Phillips 66/dsl/E-85
185	15th St, Ottawa
183	US 59, Ottawa, **E** [gas] Loves/Hardee's/dsl/scales/24hr, **W** [gas] BP, Conoco/dsl, Ottawa/dsl, [food] Applebee's, Burger King, KFC, McDonald's, Old 56 Rest, Pizza Hut, Sirloin Stockade, Taco Bell, Wendy's, [lodging] Best Western, Comfort Inn, Days Inn, EconoLodge, Super 8, [other] [H], Advance Parts, CountryMart Foods, $General, $Tree, Walmart
182b a	US 50, Eisenhower Rd, Ottawa
176	Homewood, **W** RV camping
175mm	**[RS] both lanes, full [handicapped] facilities, [phone], [picnic], litter barrels, vending, petwalk, RV dump, wireless internet**
170	KS 273, Williamsburg, **W** gas, food
162	KS 31 S, Waverly
160	KS 31 N, Melvern
155	US 75, Burlington, Melvern Lake, **E** [gas] BP/Subway/dsl, TA/Shell/Wendy's/dsl/scales/24hr/@, [food] Beto Jct Rest., [lodging] Wyatt Earp Inn, [other] dsl repair
148	KS 131, Lebo, **E** [gas] Casey's, Cenex/dsl, [food] Lebo Diner, [lodging] Universal Inn, **W** to Melvern Lake
141	KS 130, Neosho Rapids, **E** NWR (8mi)
138	County Rd U

OTTAWA

KS

= gas = food = lodging = other = rest stop   Copyright 2014 - The Next Exit ®

⬆N INTERSTATE 35 CONT'D

Exit	Services
135	County Rd R1, **W** RV camping/
133	US 50 W, 6th Ave, Emporia, **1-3 mi E** Casey's, McDonald's, Pizza Hut, Budget Host
131	KS 57, KS 99, Burlingame Rd, **E** Conoco/dsl, Hardee's, Mr Goodcents Subs, Dillon's Food, repair, tires
130	KS 99, Merchant St, **E** Phillips 66/dsl, Subway, Emporia SU, Lyon Co Museum
128	Industrial Rd, **E** FL, Arby's, Bruff's Steaks, Burger King, China Buffet, Gambino's Pizza, House of Ma, Spangles, Subway, EconoLodge, GuestHouse Inn, Motel 6, Aldi Foods, AT&T, CarQuest, $General, Family$, JC Penney, Walgreens, **W** Phillips 66/Wendy's/dsl/LP, Applebee's, Braum's, Golden Corral, KFC, McDonald's, MT Mike's Steaks, Pizza Hut, Pizza Ranch, Planet Sub, Starbucks, Taco Bell, Village Inn, Candlewood Suites, Comfort Inn, Fairfield Inn, Holiday Inn Express, Medicine Shoppe, Radio Shack, Staples, Verizon, Walmart/Subway
127c	KS Tpk, I-335 N, to Topeka
127b a	US 50, KS 57, Newton, **E** FLYING J/Huddle House/ dsl/LP/scales/24hr, Shell, Arby's, China Buffet, Papa John's, Best Inn, Best Western/rest., Days Inn, Knights Inn, Super 8, Buick/Chevrolet, Chrysler/Dodge/Jeep, Ford/Lincoln, Kenworth, NAPA, Nissan, PriceChopper Foods, Tires4Less, Toyota, dsl repair, **W** Emporia RV Park
127mm	I-35 and I-335 KS Tpk, **toll plaza**, I-35 S and KS tpk S run together

I-35 S and KS Tpk S run together.

125mm	Cottonwood River
111	Cattle Pens
97.5mm	**Matfield Green Service Area** (both lanes exit left), Phillips 66/dsl, McDonald's
92	KS 177, Cassoday, **E** Fuel'n Service,
76	US 77, El Dorado N, **E** El Dorado SP, **3 mi E** Casey's, Pizza Hut, Taco Bell, Stardust Motel, Ace Hardware, Dillon's Foods/gas, $General, Walgreens, city park
71	KS 254, KS 196, El Dorado, **E** Conoco/dsl, Phillips 66/dsl, QT, Arbys, Braum's, Burger King, China Star Buffet, DD Family Rest, Freddy's Frozen Custard, Gambino's Pizza, KFC, Kountry Kettle, LJ Silver, McDonald's, Papa Murphy's, Pizza Hut, Playa Azul Mexican, Sonic, Spangles, Subway, Taco Tico, Best Western, Heritage Inn, Holiday Inn Express, Sunset Inn, Super 8, Buick/Cadillac, Bumper Parts, Deer Grove RV Park, $General, KS Oil Museum, O'Reilly Parts, Radio Shack, Walmart
65mm	**Towanda Service Area** (both lanes exit left), Phillips 66/dsl, McDonald's
62mm	Whitewater River
57	21st St, Andover, **W** golf,
53	KS 96, Wichita, **1 mi W on Kellogg** Phillips 66
50	US 54, Kellogg Ave, **E** McConnell AFB, **W** Comfort Inn, Fairfield Inn, GuestHouse Inn, Hampton Inn, Hawthorn Suites, Marriott, Motel 6, Studio+, Super 8, **E on Kellogg Ave** Conoco/Wendy's/dsl, Beijing Bistro, Burger King, Golden Corral, IHOP, McDonald's, Panda Express, Pizza Hut, Sonic, Subway, Taco Bell, Acura, AT&T, CarMax, Infiniti, Jaguar/Porsche, Lexus, Lowe's, Mazda, Michael's, Nissan, Suzuki, Verizon, VW, Walmart/Subway, **W on Kellogg Ave** BJ's Rest, Carlos Kelly's,

50	Continued
	Chipotle Mexican, Denny's, Green Mill Rest., Logan's Roadhouse, LJ Silver, Old Chicago Pizza, Red Lobster, Scotch&Sirloin Steaks, Super Buffet, Best Western, Days Inn, EconoLodge, Holiday Inn, La Quinta, Wichita Inn, Wichita Suites, VA , BMW, Bosley Tires, Buick/GMC, Cadillac/Chevrolet, CarQuest, Chrysler/Dodge/Jeep, Dillard's, Fiat, Firestone/auto, Ford, Hancock Fabrics, Honda, JC Penney, Kia, Lincoln, Radio Shack, Ross, Sears/auto, Target, TJ Maxx, Toyota/Scion, Von Maur
45	KS 15, Wichita, **E** Spirit Aero Systems
44.5mm	Arkansas River
42	47th St, I-135, to I-235, Wichita, **W** Phillips 66, QT, Applebee's, Braum's, Burger King, Carlos O'Kelly's, Godfather's, Heritage Rest, KFC, LJ Silver, McDonald's, Mr Goodcents, New China, Papa John's, Pizza Hut, Spangles Rest., Subway, Taco Bell, Wild Hog BBQ, AmericInn, Best Western, Days Inn, Quality Inn, Springfield Inn, ValuePlace, AutoZone, Dillon's Foods/dsl, $General, $Tree, K-Mart, O'Reilly Parts, Radio Shack
39	US 81, Haysville, **W** Haysville Inn
33	KS 53, Mulvane, **E** Mulvane Hist Museum, **W** Kansas Star Casino/Hotel, Wyldewood Winery
26mm	**Belle Plaine Service Area** (both lanes exit left), Phillips 66/dsl, McDonald's
19	US 160, Wellington, **3 mi W** KFC, McDonald's, Penny's Diner, OakTree Inn, Sunshine Inn, KOA
17mm	**toll plaza**

I-35 N and KS TPK N run together.

4	US 166, to US 81, South Haven, **E** Motel 6, repair/tires, **W** Oasis RV Park
1.5mm	**weigh sta nb**
0mm	Kansas/Oklahoma state line

⬆E INTERSTATE 70

Exit	Services
423b	3rd St, James St
423a	5th St
422d c	Central Ave, service rd
422b a	US 69 N, US 169 S
421b	I-670
421a	**S** railroad yard
420b a	US 69 S, 18th St Expswy, **N** Cenex, China Town, Jack-in-the-Box, Tapatio Mexican, SunFresh Foods
419	38th St, Park Dr, access to 10 motels
418b	I-635 N (eb only)
418a	I-635 S
417	57th St
415a	KS 32 E (from eb)
415b	to US 24 W, State Ave, Kansas City, **N on US 24** Conoco Phillips 66/dsl, Papa John's, Perkins, Taco Bell, Gables Motel, Chrysler/Jeep, Ford, Lowe's, Toyota/Scion
414mm	**vehicle insp sta wb**, parking area both lanes,
414	78th St, **N** QT/dsl, Wendy's, Days Inn, **N on US 40** Phillips 66, Arby's, Burger King, Capt D's, DQ, Hardee's, Lucky Chinese, McDonald's, Sonic, Subway, , Advance Parts, BigLots, Buick/GMC, $Tree, Firestone, Goodyear/auto, K-Mart, O'Reilly Parts, PriceChopper Foods, Tires+, Walgreens, **S** BP, American Motel, Comfort Inn
411b	I-435, access to Woodlands Racetrack, to KCI

KS

INTERSTATE 70 CONT'D

Exit	Services
411a	I-435 S
410	110th St, **N** 🏠 Great Wolf Lodge, 🅾 Cabela's, KS Speedway
225mm	**I-70 W and KS TPK W run together**
224	KS 7, to US 73, Bonner Springs, Leavenworth, **N** 🅿 Phillips 66/dsl, QT, 🍴 KFC/Taco Bell, Mazzio's, Subway, Waffle House, 🏠 Holiday Inn Express, Super 8, 🅾 museum, **S** 🅿 BP, 🍴 Arby's, Burger King, Evergreen Chinese, Goodcents Subs, McDonald's, Papa Murphy's, Pizza Hut, Subway, Taco John's, 🅾 AutoZone, Cottonwood RV Camp, $Tree, Ford, PriceChopper Foods, Radio Shack, TrueValue, Walgreens, Walmart/Subway, last free exit wb before KS TPK
217mm	**toll booth**
212	Eudora, Tonganoxie
209mm	**Lawrence Service Area** (both lanes exit left), **full facilities**, Phillips 66/dsl, McDonald's
204	US 24, US 59, to E Lawrence, **S** 🅿 Phillips 66/dsl, 🍴 Burger King, Sonic, 🏠 Motel 6, SpringHill Suites (1mi), 🅾 Harley-Davidson, Jellystone Camping, O'Reilly Parts
203mm	Kansas River
202	US 59 S, to W Lawrence, **S on US 40** 🅿 BP, Conoco/dsl, Phillips 66/dsl, 🍴 Burger King, Domino's, McDonald's, Panda Garden, Sonic, Spangles, Subway, Taco Bell, Taco John's, Wendy's, 🏠 Baymont Inn, Best Western, Days Inn, EconoLodge, Hampton Inn, Holiday Inn, Quality Inn, Rodeway Inn, Super 8, 🅾 🅷 Advance Parts, CarQuest, Dillon's Foods/gas, $General, to Clinton Lake SP, to U of KS
197	KS 10, Lecompton, Lawrence, **N** Perry Lake SP, **S** Clinton Lake SP
188mm	**Topeka Service Area, full 🚻 facilities**, Conoco/dsl, Dunkin Donuts, Hardee's, Pizza Hut, Taco Bell
183	I-70 W (from wb), to Denver
367mm	**toll plaza**
366	I-470 W, to Wichita
	I-70 E and KS TPK E run together
365	21st St, Rice Rd, access to Shawnee Lake RA
364b	US 40 E, Carnahan Ave, to Lake Shawnee
364a	California Ave, **0-1 mi S** 🅿 BP/dsl, Phillips 66/dsl, 🍴 Arby's, Baskin-Robbins, Burger King, Domino's, DQ, McDonald's, Pizza Hut, Subway, Tacos Mexicano, 🅾 Ace Hardware, Advance Parts, AutoZone, Dillon's Food/gas, $General, Family$, O'Reilly Parts, TrueValue, Walgreens, repair, vet
363	Adams St, downtown
362c	10th Ave (from wb), **N** 🏠 Ramada Inn, **S** 🅾 st capitol
362b a	to 8th Ave, downtown, **N** 🏠 Ramada, **S** 🅾 to St Capitol
361b	3rd St, Monroe St
361a	1st Ave, **S** Ryder
359	MacVicar Ave
358b a	Gage Blvd
357b a	Fairlawn Rd, 6th Ave, **S** 🅿 Conoco/dsl, Phillips 66, 🏠 Best Western, Holiday Inn/rest., Motel 6, 🅾 $General, NAPACare, zoo-rain forest, vet
356b a	Wanamaker Rd, **N** 🍴 Carino's, Red Robin, 🏠 Hyatt Place, 🅾 KS Museum of History, **S** 🅿 BP, Murphy Express/dsl, Phillips 66/dsl, 🍴 Applebee's, Arby's, Boston Mkt, Buffalo Wild Wings, Chili's, Chipotle Mexican, ChuckECheese, CiCi's Pizza, Coldstone, Coyote Canyon

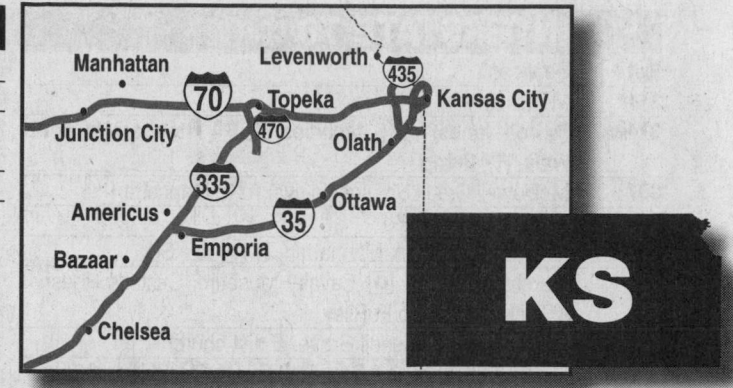

Exit	Services
356b a	Continued Café, Cracker Barrel, Denny's, Famous Dave's BBQ, Freddy's Steakburgers, Golden Corral, Hooters, Huhot Chinese, IHOP, Jason's Deli, Jersey Mike's Subs, Jimmy John's, Jose Pepper's, Longhorn Steaks, McDonald's, Mr Goodcents, Mr Stirfry, Old Chicago, Olive Garden, On-the-Border, Panera Bread, Papa John's, Perkins, Pizza Hut, Qdoba, Red Lobster, Sonic, Spangles, Starbucks, Steak'n Shake, Taco Bell, Taco John's, TX Roadhouse, Wendy's, 🏠 AmericInn, Baymont Inn, Candlewood Suites, Clubhouse Inn, Comfort Suites, Country Inn&Suites, Courtyard, Days Inn, Fairfield Inn, Hampton Inn, Holiday Inn Express, Motel 6, Quality Inn, Residence Inn, Sleep Inn, Super 8, ValuePlace, 🅾 AAA, Aldi Foods, AT&T, Barnes&Noble, Best Buy, Dick's, Dillard's, $Tree, Ford/Lincoln, Goodyear/auto, Hobby Lobby, Home Depot, JC Penney, K-Mart, Kohl's, Lowe's, Macy's, Menards, Michael's, Office Depot, Old Navy, PetCo, Radio Shack, Sam's Club/gas, Sears/auto, Suzuki, Target, Tuesday Morning, Verizon, Walmart/Subway, mall
355	I-470 E, US 75 S, to VA Med Ctr, Topeka air museum. **1 mi S** same as 356
353	KS 4 W, to Auburn Rd
351	frontage rd (from eb), Mission Creek
350	Valencia Rd
347	West Union Rd
346	Carlson Rd, to Rossville, Willard
343	Ranch Rd
342	Keene-Eskridge Rd access to Lake Wabaunsee
341	KS 30, Maple Hill, **S** 🅿 24-7/Subway/café/dsl/RV dump
338	Vera Rd, **S** 🅿 Valero/Baskin-Robbins/dsl
336mm	🆁🆂 (exits left from both lanes), full 🚻 facilities, 🅲, 🚮, litter barrels, RV parking, wireless internet, petwalk
335	Snokomo Rd, Paxico, Skyline Mill Creek Scenic Drive
333	KS 138, Paxico, **N** Mill Creek RV Park, winery
332	Spring Creek Rd
330	KS 185, to McFarland
329mm	**weigh sta both lanes**
328	KS 99, to Alma, **S** Wabaunsee Co Museum
324	Wabaunsee Rd, **N** Grandma Horners Store&Factory
322	Tallgrass Rd
318	frontage rd
316	Deep Creek Rd
313	KS 177, to Manhattan, **8 mi N** 🅿 Phillips 66, 🍴 Chili's, IHOP, Longhorn Steaks, McAlister's Deli, McDonald's, Olive Garden, Sonic, Taco Bell, TX Roadhouse, Wendy's, 🏠 Best Western, Candlewood Suites, Comfort Inn, Fairfield Inn, Hampton Inn, Hilton Garden, Motel 6, Quality Inn, Super 8, 🅾 Aldi Foods, JC Penney, Sears/auto, Walmart/Subway, to KSU

⬆️E INTERSTATE 70 CONT'D

Exit	Services
311	Moritz Rd
310mm	🅿️ both lanes, full ♿ facilities, 🚻, 🚰, litter barrels, petwalk, RV dump
307	McDowell Creek Rd, scenic river rd to Manhattan
304	Humboldt Creek Rd
303	KS 18 E, to Ogden, Manhattan, N 🅾 to KSU
301	Marshall Field, N 🅾 Cavalry Museum, Custer's House, KS Terr Capitol, to Ft Riley
300	US 40, KS 57, Council Grove, S hist church
299	Flinthills Blvd, to Jct City, Ft Riley, N 🛢 Phillips 66/dsl, 🍴 Stacy's Rest., 🛏 EconoLodge, Great Western Inn, Red Carpet Inn, Super 8
298	Chestnut St, to Jct City, Ft Riley, N 🛢 Shell/dsl/24hr, 🍴 Arby's, Cox Bros BBQ, Cracker Barrel, Family Buffet, Freddy's Steakburgers, La Fiesta, Mr Goodcents Subs, Pizza Hut, Taco Bell, 🛏 Best Western, Candlewood Suites, Courtyard, Holiday Inn Express, Quality Inn, 🅾 $General, $Tree, Verizon, Walmart/Subway
296	US 40, Washington St, Junction City, N 🛢 Casey's, Cenex/dsl, Phillips 66, Shell/dsl, 🍴 McDonald's, Peking Chinese, Senor Tequila Mexican, Sonic, Subway, 🛏 Budget Host/RV park, Comfort Inn, Hampton Inn, Howard Johnson, Knights Inn, Ramada Ltd, ValuePlace, 🅾 Cadillac/Chevrolet, Haas Tire, Harley-Davidson, city park, vet
295	US 77, KS 18 W, Marysville, to Milford Lake, N 🛢 Phillips 66/Sapp Bro's/A&W/dsl/24hr, 🛏 Motel 6, 🅾 🅷 RV Ctr, truckwash, S truckwash
294mm	🅿️ both lanes, full ♿ facilities, 🚻, 🚰, litter barrels, RV dump, petwalk
290	Milford Lake Rd
286	KS 206, Chapman, S 🛢 Cenex/dsl, 🅾 KS Auto Racing Museum, 1 mi S 🛢 Casey's
281	KS 43, to Enterprise, N 🛢 Shell/dsl, 🅾 4 Seasons RV Ctr/Park
277	Jeep Rd
275	KS 15, to Clay Ctr, Abilene, N 🍴 DQ, 🛏 Brookville Hotel/rest., Holiday Inn Express, S 🛢 KwikShop, 24-7/dsl, 🍴 Burger King, Green Acres Grill, M&R Grill, McDonald's, Pizza Hut, Sonic, Subway, 🛏 Best Value Inn, Budget Inn, Super 8, 🅾 🅷 Alco/gas, AutoZone, Buick/Cadillac/Chevrolet, CountryMart Foods, $General, O'Reilly Parts, Ricco Drug, to Eisenhower Museum
272	Fair Rd, to Talmage, S Russell Stover Candies
266	KS 221, Solomon
265mm	🅿️ both lanes, full ♿ facilities, 🚻, 🚰, litter barrels, vending, petwalk, RV dump
264mm	Solomon River
260	Niles Rd, New Cambria
253mm	Saline River
253	Ohio St, N RV park, S 🛢 🇫𝗹𝗬𝗜𝗡𝗚 𝗝/Huddle House/dsl/LP/scales/24hr, 🅾 🅷 Harley-Davidson, Kenworth
252	KS 143, 9th St, Salina, N 🛢 Petro/Shell/Starbucks/Wendy's/dsl/24hr/@, 24-7/Subway/dsl/24hr, 🍴 IHOP, Iron Skillet, McDonald's, 🛏 Best Inn, Days Inn, Holiday Inn Express, Howard Johnson, La Quinta, Motel 6, Super 8, 🅾 Blue Beacon, Freightliner, KOA, dsl repair, S 🛢 ⚡/Grandma Max/dsl/scales/24hr/@, 🛏 EconoLodge, Rodeway Inn
250b a	I-135, US 81, N to Concordia, S to Wichita

Exit	Services
249	Halstead Rd, to Trenton
244	Hedville, N Sundowner West RV Park (seasonal), S 🅾 Rolling Hills Park
238	to Brookville, Glendale, Tescott
233	290th Rd, Beverly
225	KS 156, to Ellsworth, S 🛢 D&S/pizza/dsl, 🅾 Ft Harker Museum, Ft Larned HS
224mm	🅿️ both lanes, full ♿ facilities, 🚻, 🚰, litter barrels, petwalk, RV dump
221	KS 14 N, to Lincoln
219	KS 14 S, to Ellsworth, S 🛢 Conoco/dsl
216	to Vesper
209	to Sylvan Grove
206	KS 232, Wilson, N 🛢 Travel Shoppe/rest., 🅾 RV Park, Wilson Lake (6mi), winery
199	Dorrance, N to Wilson Lake, S 🛢 Agco/dsl/food
193	Bunker Hill Rd, N 🛢 Conoco/Quiznos/dsl/24hr, to Wilson Lake WA
189	US 40 bus, Pioneer Rd, Russell
187mm	🅿️ both lanes, full ♿ facilities, 🚻, 🚰, litter barrels, RV dump, petwalk
184	US 281, Russell, N 🛢 Phillips 66/Fossil Sta./dsl, 24-7/dsl, 🍴 A&W, McDonald's, Meridy's Rest., Pizza Hut, Sonic, Subway, 🛏 Days Inn, Fossil Creek Hotel, Russell's Inn, Super 8, 🅾 🅷 Alco, CarQuest, $General, JJJ RV Park, Fossil Creek RV Park, st patrol
180	Balta Rd, to Russell
175	Gorham, 1 mi N 🛢 Co-Op/dsl
172	Walker Ave
168	KS 255, to Victoria, S 🛢 255 Diner/dsl, to Cathedral of the Plains
163	Toulon Ave
161	Commerce Parkway
159	US 183, Hays, N 🛢 Qwest/dsl, 🍴 Applebee's, Carlos O'Kelly's, Golden Corral, IHOP, Subway, Wendy's, 🛏 Best Western, Comfort Inn, Fairfield Inn, Hampton Inn, Holiday Inn Express, Sleep Inn, 🅾 AT&T, Chrysler/Dodge/Jeep, Ford/Lincoln, Harley-Davidson, Home Depot, Radio Shack, Toyota, Walmart/Subway, S 🛢 Conoco/dsl/24hr, ❤Loves, Phillips 66/dsl, Shamrock, 24-7/dsl, 🍴 Arby's, Burger King, China Garden, Emperial Garden, Freddy's Steakburgers, Jimmy John's, K's Diner, KFC, LJ Silver, Lucky Buffet, McDonald's, MT Mike's Steaks, Pheasant Run Pancakes, Pizza Hut, Smoothie King, Sonic, Subway, Taco Bell, Taco Grande, Vagabond Rest., Wendy's, Whiskey Creek Grill, 🛏 Baymont Inn, Best Value Inn, Days Inn, EconoLodge, Motel 6, Quality Inn, Ramada, Super 8, 🅾 🅷 Ace Hardware, Advance Parts, Chevrolet, Dillon's Foods/gas, $General, Firestone/auto, Hastings Books, JC Penney, O'Reilly Parts, Tires 4 Less, Verizon, Walgreens, st patrol
157	US 183 S byp, to Hays, S 🅾 museum, tourist info, to Ft Hays St U
153	Yocemento Ave
145	KS 247 S, Ellis, S 🛢 Casey's, ❤Loves/DQ/Subway/dsl/scales/24hr, 🛏 Days Inn, 🅾 to Chrysler Museum, Railroad Museum, RV camping, USPO
140	Riga Rd
135	KS 147, Ogallah, N 🛢 Frontier Selfserve/dsl, S to Cedar Bluff SP (13mi)
132mm	🅿️ both lanes, full ♿ facilities, 🚰, litter barrels, petwalk, RV dump

Vertical labels (left): JCT CITY, ABILENE, SALINA, KS
Vertical labels (right): RUSSELL, HAYS, ELLIS

⮝Ⓔ INTERSTATE 70 CONT'D

Exit	Services
128	US 283 N, WaKeeney, N 🛏 Super 8
127	US 283 S, WaKeeney, N 🍴 El Dos De Oros, Jade Garden Rest., McDonald's, Pizza Hut, 🛏 Best Western, KS Kountry Inn, 🅞 $General, city park, S 🅖 Conoco/Subway/dsl/24-7/Real Country Cafe/dsl/24hr, 🛏 EconoLodge, 🅞 KOA, antiques, auto repair
120	Voda Rd
115	KS 198 N, Banner Rd, Collyer
107	KS 212, Castle Rock Rd, Quinter, N 🅖 Sinclair/dsl, 🛏 Budget Host, 🅞 🏥, repair, S 🅖 Conoco/dsl/24hr, 🍴 DQ
99	KS 211, Park, 1 mi N 🅖 Sinclair/dsl
97mm	🆁🆂 both lanes, full ♿ facilities, 🚻, litter barrels, vending, petwalk, RV dump
95	KS 23 N, to Hoxie
93	KS 23, Grainfield, N 🅖 Sinclair/dsl
85	KS 216, Grinnell
79	Campus Rd
76	US 40, to Oakley, S 🅖 TA/Shell/Buckhorn Rest./Subway/dsl/e-85/scales/24hr/@, 🛏 EconoLodge (2mi), Relax Inn, Sleep Inn, 🅞 🏥, Blue Beacon, Fick Museum
70	US 83, to Oakley, N 🛏 Free Breakfast Inn, S 🅖 Phillips 66/dsl, 🍴 Colonial Steaks, 🅞 🏥, High-Plains RV Park, Prairie Dog Town, Fick Museum, antiques
62	rd K, Mingo, S 🅖 gas/dsl/🍴
54	Country Club Dr, Colby, N 🅖 ▭▭▭/Subway/dsl/scales/24hr, 🛏 Hampton Inn, 🅞 🏥, truck/dsl repair
53	KS 25, Colby, N 🅖 Conoco, 24-7/Subway/dsl, 🍴 Arby's, Burger King, China Buffet, McDonald's, MT Mike's Steaks, Pizza Hut, Sonic, Subway, Taco John's, 🛏 Days Inn, Holiday Inn Express, Motel 6, Quality Inn, Sleep Inn, Super 8, 🅞 🏥, Dillon's Foods/dsl, $General, Ford/Lincoln, Haas Tire, Prairie Museum, Quilt Cabin, Radio Shack, Walmart, dsl repair, RV park/antiques, trucklube/wash, visitors ctr, S 🅖 Petro/Phillips 66/scales/dsl/@, 🍴 Baskin-Robbins, City Limits Grill, Quiznos, Starbucks, Village Inn, 🛏 Comfort Inn, Knights Inn, 🅞 Chrysler/Dodge/Jeep, truck repair/wash
48.5mm	🆁🆂 both lanes, full ♿ facilities, 🚻, litter barrels, RV park/dump, vending, petwalk
45	US 24 E, Levant
36	KS 104, Drewster, N 🅖 Fuel Depot/dsl
35.5mm	Mountain/Central time zone
27	KS 253, Edson
19	US 24, Goodland, N 🍴 Pizza Hut, 🛏 Motel 7, 🅞 $General, KOA, High Plains Museum
17	US 24, KS 27, Goodland, N 🅖 Cenex/dsl, Conoco, Phillips 66/dsl, 🍴 DQ, McDonald's, Mexico #3, Reynaldo's Mexican, Subway, Taco John's, Wonderful House Chinese, 🛏 Best Value Inn, Comfort Inn, Days Inn, Motel 6, Super 8, 🅞 🏥, Chevrolet, CarQuest/Firestone, GMC, Walmart, S 🅖 24-7/dsl/scales, 🛏 Holiday Inn Express, 🅞 Mid-America Camping
12	rd 14, Caruso
9	rd 11, Ruleton
7.5mm	Welcome Ctr eb/🆁🆂 wb, full ♿ facilities, info, 🚻, 🚻, litter barrels, petwalk, vending, wireless internet, RV dump
1	KS 267, Kanorado, N gas, food
.5mm	weigh sta eb
0mm	Kansas/Colorado State Line

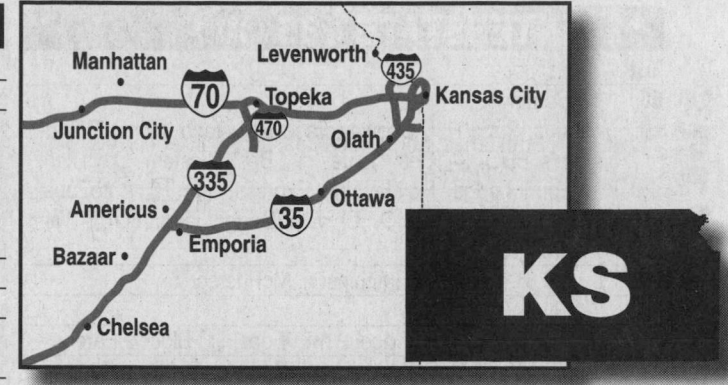

⮝Ⓔ INTERSTATE 135

Exit	Services
95b a	US 81 continues nb., I-70, E to KS City, W to Denver.
	I-135 begins/ends on I-70, exit 250.
93	KS 140, State St, Salina, E art ctr, museum
92	Crawford St, E 🅖 Gas4Less/dsl, KwikShop, Shell, Sinclair, 24-7/dsl, 🍴 Arby's, Braum's, Cotijas Mexican, Daimaru Steaks, Great Wall Chinese, Gutierrez Mexican, Hickory Hut BBQ, Jim's Chicken, KFC, McDonald's, Russell's Rest., Spangles, Subway, Taco Bell, Western Sizzlin, 🛏 AmericInn, Days Inn, Fairfield Inn, Knights Inn, Ramada Inn, Value Inn&Suites, 🅞 Advance Parts, Dillon's Foods, $General, K-Mart, Midwest Tires, NAPA, O'Reilly Parts, Radio Shack, Walgreens, W 🅖 Phillips 66/dsl, 🛏 Quality Inn
90	Magnolia Rd, E 🅖 Casey's, Phillips 66/dsl, 🍴 Apple-Tree Rest., Burger King, Carlos O'Kelly's, Chili's, Coyote Canyon Café, Domino's, Freddy's Burgers, Hog Wild BBQ, Hong Kong Buffet, IHOP, Jalisco Mexican, Longhorn Steaks, McDonald's, Mr Goodcents Subs, Papa Murphy's, Poncho's Mexican, Schlotzsky's, Sonic, Spangles, Starbucks, Subway, 🛏 Best Value Inn, Candlewood Suites, 🅞 Aldi Foods, AutoZone, BigLots, Cadillac/Chevrolet, Dick's, Dillard's, Dillon's Foods/dsl, $General, $Tree, Hobby Lobby, Honda, JC Penney, Jo-Ann Fabrics, Kohl's, Menard's, Old Navy, O'Reilly Parts, PetCo, Sears/auto, Subaru, Toyota, Tuesday Morning, Verizon, vet, W 🅖 Cenex/dsl
89	Schilling Rd, E 🅖 KwikShop/dsl, 🍴 Applebee's, Daimaru Steaks, Logan's Roadhouse, Olive Garden, Pizza Hut, Popeye's, Red Lobster, Tucson's Steaks, Wendy's, 🛏 Country Inn&Suites, Courtyard, Hampton Inn, 🅞 Lowe's, Sam's Club/gas, Target, Walmart/Subway, W 🅖 Casey's, 🛏 Best Western, Comfort Suites, Super 8
88	Water Well Rd, E 🛏 Sleep Inn, 🅞 Ford, Nissan
86	KS 104, Mentor, Smolan
82	KS 4, Falun Rd, Assaria, E 🅞 RV Camping
78	KS 4 W, Lindsborg, E to Sandz Gallery/Museum
72	Lindsborg, Roxbury, 4 mi E 🅞 McPherson St Fishing Lake, Maxwell WR, W 🅞 🏥, gas, food, lodging, camping, museum
68mm	🆁🆂 (both lanes exit left), full ♿ facilities, 🚻, 🚻, litter barrels petwalk, RV dump
65	Pawnee Rd
60	US 56, McPherson, Marion, W 🅖 Midway Gas/dsl, Phillips 66/dsl, 🍴 Applebee's, Arby's, Braum's, Freddy's Burgers, Golden Dragon Chinese, Hunan Chinese, KFC/LJ Silver, La Fiesta Mexican, McDonald's, MT Mike's, Per

KS

🅖 = gas 🍴 = food 🛏 = lodging 🅞 = other 🆁🆂 = rest stop   .Copyright 2014 - The Next Exit ®

⬆N INTERSTATE 135 CONT'D

Exit	Services
60	Continued
	kins, Pizza Hut, Subway, Taco Bell, Taco John's, Woodie's BBQ, 🛏 Best Value Inn,. Best Western, Days Inn, EconoLodge, Holiday Inn Express, 🅞 🄷, AutoZone, Buick/Cadillac/GMC, Chrysler/Dodge/Jeep, Ford, Walgreens, Walmart
58	US 81, KS 61, to Hutchinson, McPherson
54	Elyria
48	KS 260 E, Moundridge, **2 mi W** gas, 🍴 Block 2 Eatery
46	KS 260 W, Moundridge, **2 mi W** truck repair, gas, food
40	Lincoln Blvd, Hesston, **E** 🍴 Panda Kitchen, 🛏 AmericInn, 🅞 Cottonwood Grove RV Camping, **W** 🅖 Casey's/dsl/24hr, 🍴 El Cerrito Grill, Lincoln Perk Coffee, Pizza Hut, Sonic, Subway, 🛏 Best Value Inn, 🅞 city park
34	KS 15, N Newton, to Abilene, **E** 🅞 RV camping, **W** 🍴 Subway (1mi), Taco Bell (1mi), 🅞 Kauffman Museum
33	US 50 E, to Peabody (from nb)
31	1st St, Broadway St, **E** 🅖 Conoco/dsl/@, 🍴 Applebee's, CJ's Rest., Huddle House, KFC, 🛏 Days Inn, EconoLodge, 1st Inn, Holiday Inn Express, 🅞 Cadillac/Chevrolet, Chrysler/Dodge/Jeep, Ford/Lincoln, **W** 🍴 Braum's, MT Mike's, 🛏 Best Western/rest., Comfort Inn
30	US 50 W, KS 15 (exits left from nb), to Hutchinson, Newton, **W** 🅖 KwikShop/dsl, 🍴 Arby's, Papa Murphy's, Pizza Hut, Sonic, Subway, 🅞🄷, AutoZone, Buick/GMC, Dillon's Foods, $Tree, Radio Shack, R Tires, Verizon, Walmart
28	SE 36th St, **W** 🅖 Phillips 66/dsl, 🍴 Burger King, 🅞 Chisholm Trail Outlets/famous brands
25	KS 196, to Whitewater, El Dorado
23mm	🆁🆂 **both lanes, full 🚻 facilities, 🅒, 🏧, litter barrels, vending, petwalk, RV dump**
22	125th St
19	101st St, **W** 🅞 RV camping
17	85th St, **E** Valley Ctr, KS Coliseum
16	77th St, **E** 🛏 Sleep Inn, 🅞 Wichita Greyhound Park
14	61st St, **E** 🅖 QT/dsl, 🍴 Applebee's, Chopstix, Cracker Barrel, Pizza Hut, Spangles Rest., Subway, Taco Bell, Wendy's, 🛏 Comfort Inn, 🅞 Chevrolet, TrueValue, vet, **W**

Exit	Services
14	Continued
	🅖 Phillips 66/dsl, 🍴 KFC, McDonald's, 🛏 Quality Inn, Super 8, 🅞 Goodyear/auto
13	53rd St, **E** Freightliner, Harley-Davidson, Mack Trucks, **W** 🅖 Phillips 66/dsl, 🍴 Country Kitchen, 🛏 Best Western, Days Inn
11b	I-235 W, KS 96, to Hutchinson
11a	KS 254, to El Dorado
10b	29th St, Hydraulic Ave
10a	KS 96 E
9	21st St, **E** 🍴 Sonic, 🅞 $General, Wichita St U
8	13th St, **E** 🍴 Mel's Carryout, **W** 🍴 Dad's BBQ, Pig In Pig Out BBQ
7a	downtown
7b	8th St, 9th St, Central Ave., **E** School of Medicine
6b	1st St, 2nd St, downtown
5b	US 54, US 400, Kellogg Ave, **E** 🅖 QT/dsl, 🍴 Burger King, Chipotle Mexican, Jimmy John's, Subway, Taco Bueno, 🛏 Wichata Suites
5a	Lincoln St, **E** 🍴 DQ, **W** 🅖 QT
4	Harry St, **1 mi E** 🅖 QT, 🍴 Arby's, Bionic Burger, Burger King, Church's, Denny's, Jimmie's Diner, Jimmy's Egg, Little Caesars, LJ Silver, McDonald's, NuWay Drive-Thru, Poblano Mexican, Shanghai Chinese, Spangles Rest., Subway, Taco Bell, Wendy's, 🅞🄷, BigLots, CVS Drug, Firestone/auto, Goodyear/auto, **W** 🅖 BD-C/dsl
3	Pawnee Ave, **E** 🅖 QT, 🅞 Family$, O'Reilly Parts, **W** 🅖 Jumpstart/dsl, 🍴 Burger King, Pizza Hut, Spangles, 🛏 Pawnee Inn (1mi), 🅞 AutoZone, $General ·
2	Hydraulic Ave, **E** 🅖 QT, **W** 🍴 McDonald's, Subway
2mm	Arkansas River
1c	I-235 N, **2 mi W** Hilton
1b a	US 81 S, 47th St, **E** 🅖 QT, 🛏 Days Inn, Quality Inn, Super 8, **W** 🅖 Phillips 66, 🍴 Applebee's, Braum's, Burger King, Carlos O'Kelly's, Godfather's, Goodcents Subs, Heritage Rest, Hog Wild BBQ, KFC, LJ Silver, McDonald's, New China, Papa John's, Pizza Hut, Spangles Rest., Subway, Taco Bell, 🛏 Best Western, Springfield Inn, ValuePlace, 🅞 Air Capital RV Park, AutoZone, Dillon's Foods/dsl, $Tree, K-Mart, O'Reilly Parts, Radio Shack
0mm	**I-135 begins/ends on I-35, exit 42.**

KENTUCKY

⬆E INTERSTATE 24

Exit	Services
93.5mm	Kentucky/Tennessee state line
93mm	**Welcome Ctr wb, full 🚻 facilities, 🅒, 🏧, litter barrels, vending, petwalk**
91.5mm	Big West Fork Red River
89	KY 115, to Oak Grove, **N** to Jeff Davis Mon St HS, **S** 🅖 🚚/McDonald's/dsl/scales/24hr, Shell/dsl, 🅞 truck repair
86	US 41A, to Ft Campbell, Pennyrile Pkwy, Hopkinsville, **N** 🅖 Marathon/Chester's/dsl/scales/24hr, **S** 🅖 BP/dsl/24hr, ✈FLYING J/Denny's/dsl/LP/scales/24hr, 🚚/Subway/Wendy's/dsl/scales/24hr, 🍴 McDonald's, Waffle House, 🛏 Comfort Suites, Days Inn, Holiday Inn Express, Quality Inn, Sleep Inn, 🅞🄷, truck wash
81	Pennyrile Pky N, to Hopkinsville
79mm	Little River

Exit	Services
73	KY 117, to Gracey, Newstead
65	US 68, KY 80, to Cadiz, **S** 🅖 BP/dsl, Marathon/dsl, Shell/dsl/24hr, 🍴 Cracker Barrel, KFC, McDonald's, Subway, Taco Bell, Wendy's, 🛏 Broadbent Inn, Knights Inn, Super 7 Inn, Super 8, 🅞🄷, Chevrolet, golf, to NRA
56	KY 139, to Cadiz, Princeton, **S** 🅖 Marathon/dsl, 🅞 KOA (9mi), NRA
47mm	Lake Barkley
45	KY 293, to Princeton, Saratoga, **S** 🅖 Marathon/dsl, 🅞 Mineral Mound SP, RV Camping, to KY St Penitentiary
42	to W KY Pkwy, Elizabethtown
40	US 62, US 641, Kuttawa, Eddyville, **N** 🛏 Regency Inn, Relax Inn, 🅞 Mineral Mound SP, camping, **S** 🅖 BP/Wendy's/dsl/24hr, Huck's/Quiznos/dsl/scales/24hr, Marathon, 🍴 Huddle House, SW Grill, 🛏 Days Inn, Hampton Inn, 🅞 to Lake Barkley, KY Lake Rec Areas, camping
36mm	**weigh sta both lanes, 🅒**
34mm	Cumberland River

KS
KY

🅟 = gas 🍴 = food 🛏 = lodging 🄾 = other 🆁🆂 = rest stop

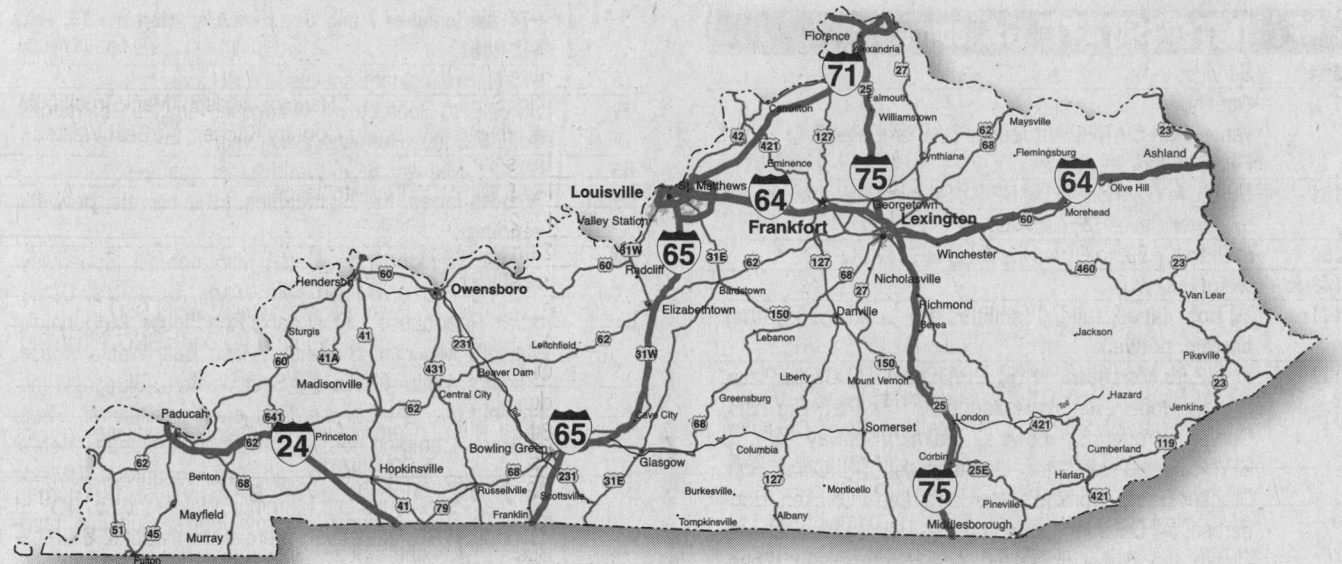

◤E INTERSTATE 24 CONT'D

Exit	Services
31	KY 453, to Grand Rivers, Smithland, **N** 🅟 BP/dsl, 🛏 Patti's Inn, **S** 🅟 Exxon/dsl, 🍴 Miss Scarlett's, 🛏 Best Value Inn, Grand Rivers Resort (3mi), Lighthouse Landing Resort, 🄾 Exit 31 RV Park, NRA
29mm	Tennessee River
27	US 62, to KY Dam, Calvert City, **N** 🅟 BP/dsl, 🍴 Cracker Barrel, DQ, Mama D's Italian, McDonald's, KFC, Waffle House, Willow Pond Rest., 🛏 Days Inn, KY Dam Motel, Super 8, 🄾 Cypress Lakes Camp, Freightliner, KOA, vet, **S** 🅟 Loves/Arby's/dsl/scales/24hr, 🍴 Subway, 🄾 truck repair
25b a	to Calvert City, Carroll/Purchase Pkwy, **Services 1 mi N**, **S** KY Lake RA
16	US 68, to Paducah, **S** 🅟 BP/Southern Pride/Subway/dsl/scales/24hr, 🄾 antiques, flea mkt
11	rd 1954, Husband Rd, to Paducah, **N** 🅟 Parkway/dsl, 🛏 Best Western, 🄾 Duck Creek RV Park, **S** 🄾 Harley-Davidson
7	US 45, US 62, to Paducah, **N** 🅟 BP/dsl, 🍴 Burger King, Taco Bell, 🄾 🄷, **S** Welcome Ctr both lanes, full ♿ facilities, 🚰 vending, 🎇 litter barrels, petwalk, 🅟 BP, Marathon/dsl, 🍴 Arby's, Backyard Burger, Chong's Chinese, Hardee's, KFC, Los Amigo's Mexican, McDonald's, Parker's Drive-In, Pizza Hut, Popeye's, Quiznos, Sonic, Waffle House, 🛏 Denton Motel, 🄾 K-Mart, O'Reilly Parts, Plaza Tires, SuperValu Foods/gas, Verizon
4	US 60, to Paducah, **N** 🅟 BP, 🍴 Applebee's, Bob Evans, Burger King, McDonald's, O'Charley's, Outback Steaks, Rafferty's, 🛏 Candlewood Suites, Courtyard, Days Inn, Drury Inn, Fairfield Inn, Hampton Inn, Holiday Inn Express, Residence Inn, Westowne Inn, 🄾 Hancock Fabrics, Toyota/Scion, **S** 🅟 BP, Murphy USA/dsl, Superway, 🍴 Arby's, Backwoods BBQ, Backyard Burger, Buffalo Wild Wings, Capt D's, c Chick-fil-A, Chong's Chinese, ChuckeCheese, Cracker Barrel, Domino's, El Chico's, Fazoli's, Hardee's, IHOP, Logan's Roadhouse, Los Amigos, McAlister's Deli, Olive Garden, Panera Bread, Pasta House, Penn Sta. Subs, Pizza Hut, Red Lobster, Ryan's, Sonic, Steak'n Shake, Taco Bell, TX Roadhouse, TGIFriday's, Tokyo Hibachi, Wendy's, 🛏 Comfort Suites, Country Inn&Suites,

P A D U C A H

Exit	Services
4	Continued
	Drury Suites, Motel 6, Paducah Inn, PearTree Inn, Thrifty Inn, 🄾 AAA, Advance Parts, Aldi Foods, AT&T, Best Buy, Books-A-Million, Dick's, Dillard's, Gander Mtn, Goodyear, Hobby Lobby, Home Depot, JC Penney, Kohl's, Lowe's, Michael's, Office Depot, Old Navy, Petsmart, Sam's Club/gas, Sears/auto, TJ Maxx, Tuesday Morning, Verizon, Walmart, mall
3	KY 305, to Paducah, **N** 🅟 Shell/dsl, 🛏 Best Value Inn, Comfort Inn/rest., EconoLodge, **S** 🅟 Cheers/Huddle House/pizza/subs/dsl/e85, Pilot/Subway/dsl/scales/24hr, 🍴 Yu's Kitchen, Waffle Hut, 🛏 Baymont Inn, 🄾 Fern Lake Camping
0mm	Kentucky/Illinois state line, Ohio River

◤E INTERSTATE 64

Exit	Services
192mm	Kentucky/West Virginia state line, Big Sandy River
191	US 23, to Ashland, **1-2 mi N** 🅟 Exxon, GoMart, Marathon/Subway/dsl, Speedway, 🍴 Arby's, Little Caesars, McDonald's, Waffle House, Wendy's, 🛏 Ramada Ltd, 🄾 🄷, Rite Aid, Foodland Foods, USPO
185	KY 180, Cannonsburg, **0-3 mi N** 🅟 BP/dsl, Shell/McDonald's/USPO, Superquik, 🍴 Arby's, Bob Evans, Burger King, DQ, KFC, Subway, Taco Bell, Waffle House, Wendy's, 🛏 Days Inn, Fairfield Inn, Hampton Inn, Holiday Inn Express, 🄾 $Tree, st police, Urgent Care, **S** 🅟 ⊕FLYING J/Denny's/dsl/LP/scales/24hr, 🄾 Hidden Valley Camping
181	181 US 60, to Princess, **N** 🅟 BP/dsl, **S** 🅟 Marathon/dsl
179	rd 67, Industrial Parkway, **N** 🄾 KOA
174mm	🆁🆂 eb, full ♿ facilities, 🚰 vending, 🎇 litter barrels, petwalk
173mm	🆁🆂 wb, full ♿ facilities, 🚰 vending, 🎇 litter barrels, petwalk
172	rd 1, rd 7, Grayson, **N** 🅟 Superquik/dsl/24hr, 🍴 A&W/LJ Silver, Huddle House, KFC, Pizza Hut, Shoney's, Subway, 🛏 Days Inn, Guesthouse Inn, Quality Inn, 🄾 Chrysler/Dodge/Jeep, $General, $Tree, Ford, K-Mart, Save-A-Lot Foods, Urgent Care, **S** 🅟 BP, Exxon/Hardees, Loves/Wendy's/scales/dsl/24hr, Marathon, Shell, Speedway, 🍴 Arby's, Biscuit World, China House, DQ, Little Caesar's, McDonald's, Taco Bell, Toro Loco, 🛏 Super 8, 🄾 Ad

G R A Y S O N

KY

R = gas　🍴 = food　🛏 = lodging　O = other　RS = rest stop　Copyright 2014 - The Next Exit ®

INTERSTATE 64 CONT'D

Exit	Services
172	Continued
	vance Parts, AT&T, AutoZone, $General, Family$, Food-Fair, Rite Aid, TrueValue
161	US 60, to Olive Hill, N R BP, 🛏 Spanish Manor Motel, O to Carter Caves SP, camping
156	rd 2, to KY 59, to Olive Hill, S R BP, 🍴 DQ
148mm	weigh sta wb
141mm	RS both lanes, full ♿ facilities, 🍴, vending, 🎒, litter barrels, petwalk
137	KY 32, to Morehead, N R BP/DQ/dsl, 🍴 CiCi's Pizza, Huddle House, Reno's Roadhouse, O AT&T, Big Lots, Curves, Kroger/dsl, Lowe's, Walmart/Subway, S R BP/McDonald's/dsl/24hr, Marathon/dsl, 🍴 China Star, Cracker Barrel, Domino's, Hardee's, Lee's Chicken, Ponderosa, 🛏 Days Inn, Hampton Inn, Holiday Inn Express, Quality Inn, Super 8, O H Ace Hardware, AutoZone, $General, Radio Shack, auto repair, st police
133	rd 801, to Sharkey, Farmers, N R Shell/dsl, S R BP/Subway/dsl, 🛏 Comfort Inn, O Outpost RV Park (4mi)
123	US 60, to Salt Lick, Owingsville
121	KY 36, to Owingsville, N R BP/dsl, Exxon, Valero/dsl, 🍴 DQ, McDonald's, Subway, O $General, Family$
113	US 60, to Mt Sterling, N R Shell/dsl, S R 🚚/McDonald's/Subway/dsl/scales/24hr
110	US 460, KY 11, Mt Sterling, N R Shell/Krystal/dsl, Valero, 🍴 Cracker Barrel, 🛏 Fairfield Inn, Ramada Ltd, O golf, S R Marathon/dsl, 🍴 Applebee's, Arby's, Burger King, City King Buffet, El Camino Real, Jerry's Rest., KFC, Lee's Chicken, LJ Silver, McDonald's, Waffle House, Wendy's, 🛏 Budget Inn, Days Inn/rest., O H AutoZone, Family$, O'Reilly Parts, USPO, S on KY 686 R Marathon/Circle K, 🍴 El Cancun, Hardee's, Little Caesar's, Pizza Hut, Taco Bell, O Advance Parts, Chevrolet, Chrysler/Dodge/Jeep, $Tree, Ford, JC Penney, Kroger, Lowe's, Verizon, Walmart/Subway
101	US 60
98.5mm	RS eb, full ♿ facilities, 🍴, vending, 🎒, litter barrels, petwalk
98	KY 402 (from eb), S Natural Bridge Resort SP
96b a	KY 627, to Winchester, Paris, N R BP/dsl, Marathon/96 Truck Plaza/dsl/rest./scales, S 🛏 Hampton Inn, Quality Inn, Royal Inn, O Buick/Chevrolet/GMC
94	KY 1958, Van Meter Rd, Winchester, N R Road Ranger/dsl/24hr, Shell/scales/dsl, 🛏 Best Value Inn, Holiday Inn Express, S R BP/dsl, Marathon, Murphy Express/dsl, Speedway/dsl, 🍴 Applebee's, Arby's, Big Boy, Burger King, Cantuckee Diner, Capt D's, Chester Hacienda, Domino's, Don Senor, DQ, El Camino Real, Fazoli's, Golden Corral, Great Wall Chinese, Hardee's, Jade Garden Chinese, KFC, Little Caesar's, McDonald's, Papa John's, Pizza Hut, Quiznos, Rally's, Sonic, Subway, Taco Bell, Taste Of China, Waffle House, Wendy's, 🛏 Best Western, O H, Advance Parts, AT&T, AutoZone, Chrysler/Dodge/Jeep, $General, $Tree, Ford, K-Mart, Kroger, Lowe's, Office Depot, O'Reilly Parts, Radio Shack, Rite Aid, Walgreens, Walmart/Subway, to Ft Boonesborough Camping, auto repair
87	KY 859, Blue Grass Sta
81	I-75 S, to Knoxville

I-64 and I-75 run together 7 mi. See Kentucky Interstate 75, exits 113-115.

Exit	Services
75	I-75 N, to Cincinnati access to KY Horse Park
69	US 62 E, to Georgetown, N antiques (6mi), to Georgetown Coll., S Equus Run Vineyards (2mi)
65	US 421, Midway, S R Waddy's/dsl, antiques
60mm	RS both lanes, full ♿ facilities, litter barrels, petwalk, vending
58	US 60, Frankfort, N R BP, Marathon/dsl, Speedway/dsl, 🍴 Arby's, Buffalo Wild Wings, Capt. D's, Cattleman's Roadhouse, DQ, Logan's Roadhouse, McDonald's, Miguel's Mexican, Starbucks, Taco Bell, Waffle House, Wendy's, White Castle, 🛏 Best Western, Bluegrass Inn, Fairfield Inn, O Chrysler/Dodge/Jeep, $General, $Tree, ElkHorn Camping (5mi), Ford/Lincoln, Honda, Kohl's, Kroger/gas, Michael's, Nissan, TireDiscounters, TJMaxx, Toyota/Scion, Tuesday Morning, Walgreens, to KY St Capitol, KYSU, to Viet Vets Mem, transmissions, S Cracker Barrel
55mm	Kentucky River
53b a	US 127, Frankfort, N R Marathon, Valero/dsl, 🍴 A&W/LJ Silver, Applebee's, Baskin-Robbins, Beef O'Brady's, Big Boy, Burger King, Capt D's, Carino's Italian, Chili's, China Buffet, DQ, Fazoli's, Ginza Japanese, Hardee's, KFC, Longhorn Steaks, McDonald's, O'Charley's, Panera Bread, Papa John's, Pizza Hut, Qdoba Mexican, Rio Grande Mexican, Shoney's, Sonic, Starbucks, Steak'n Shake, Subway, Taco Bell, Taco John's, Wendy's, 🛏 Best Value Inn, Days Inn, Hampton Inn, Holiday Inn Express, O H, Advance Parts, AT&T, BigLots, Big-O Tire, AutoZone, Family$, GNC, Goodyear/auto, JC Penney, K-Mart, Kroger/gas/24hr, Lowe's, Office Depot, Rite Aid, Verizon, Walgreens, Walmart/Subway, Ancient Age Tour, to KY St Capitol, st police, vet, S R BP/dsl, Marathon
48	KY 151, to US 127 S, S R BP/dsl, Valero/dsl, 🍴 Subway
43	KY 395, Waddy, N R FLYING J/Denny's/dsl/LP/scales/24hr, S R Loves/McDonald's/Subway/dsl/scales/24hr
38.5mm	weigh sta eb
35	KY 53, Shelbyville, N R Marathon, Shell/Circle K/dsl, Speedway/dsl, 🍴 Cracker Barrel, KFC, Little Caesar's, McDonald's (1mi), Taco Bell, Waffle House, O Advance Parts, Family$, Ford, Kroger/deli/dsl, Lake Shelby Camping (3mi), vet, S R Huck's, Valero, 🛏 Holiday Inn Express, O golf
32b a	KY 55, Shelbyville, 1-2 mi N R Murphy USA/dsl, Valero, 🍴 Arby's, Asian Buffet, Firefresh BBQ, KFC, McDonald's, Pizza Hut, Quiznos, Subway, Waffle House, Wendy's, 🛏 Best Western, Country Hearth Inn, Days Inn, O H, AutoZone, Big O Tire, Buick/Chevrolet/GMC, $Tree, Lowe's, Rolling Hills Camping (16mi), Walgreens, Walmart, S 🍴 Cattleman's Roadhouse, 🛏 Ramada, O Taylorsville Lake SP
28mm	RS eb, full ♿ facilities, info, 🍴, 🎒, litter barrels, vending, petwalk
28	KY 1848, Veechdale Rd, Simpsonville, N R 🚚/Wendy's/dsl/scales/24hr, 🍴 DQ, Subway, O golf, S R BP/dsl
19b a	I-265, Gene Snyder Fwy, N to Tom Sawyer SP
17	S Blankenbaker, N R Circle K, Shell/dsl, 🛏 Staybridge Suites, O Harley-Davidson, S R Marathon, Thornton's/dsl, 🍴 Arby's, BackYard Burger, Burger King, Cracker

MT STERLING

WINCHESTER

FRANKFORT

SHELBYVILLE

KY

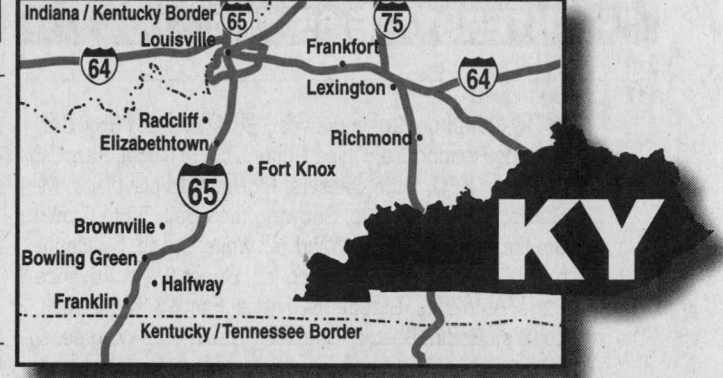

🛣️E INTERSTATE 64 CONT'D

Exit	Services
17	**Continued**
	Barrel, HomeTown Buffet, KFC, King Buffet, Kingfish Rest., LJ Silver/Taco Bell, Logan's Roadhouse, McDonald's, Penn Sta., Qdoba, Ruby Tuesday, Starbucks, Waffle House, Wendy's, 🏨 Candlewood Suites, Comfort Suites, Country Inn&Suites, Extended Stay America, Fairfield Inn, Hampton Inn, Hilton Garden, Holiday Inn Express, La Quinta, Microtel, Quality Inn, Sleep Inn, Wingate Inn, Ⓞ Lexus, Sam's Club/gas
15	Hurstbourne Pkwy, Louisville, 0-2 mi N Ⓡ Shell/Circle K/dsl, Speedway, Thorton's/dsl, 🍴 Arby's, Bob Evans, Bonefish Grill, Carrabba's, Chili's, Fazoli's, Great Harvest, IHOP, Jimmy John's, Macaroni Grill, McDonald's, Mimi's Cafe, Olive Garden, Panera Bread, Papa John's, PF Changs, Qdoba, Sichuan Garden, Skyline Chili, Starbucks, Subway, Tony Roma's, Waffle House, 🏨 Baymont Inn, Courtyard, Days Inn, Drury Inn, Holiday Inn, Hyatt Place, Red Roof Inn, Residence Inn, Ⓞ Barnes&Noble, Lowe's, Towery's Auto, Walgreens, S Ⓡ Kroger, Marathon, Meijer/dsl, 🍴 Applebee's, BD BBQ, Buca Rest., Burger King, China Buffet, ChuckeCheese, Coldstone, DQ, El Toro, Famous Daves, Home Run Burgers, Jason's Deli, J Gumbo's Cajun, Jumbo Grill, Longhorn Steaks, Lonestar Steaks, McAlister's Deli, McDonald's, Moe's SW Grill, O'Charley's, Old Chicago, Penn Sta. Subs, Piccadilly, Qdoba, Quiznos, Shogun Japanese, Smokey Bones BBQ, Starbucks, Steak'n Shake, Taco Bell, Taco Bueno, Tumbleweed SW Grill, Wendy's, White Castle, 🏨 Marriott, Red Carpet Inn, Ⓞ Autozone, Carmax, Chevrolet, $Tree, Hancock Fabrics, Home Depot, Honda, Infiniti, Kroger, Michael's, Office Depot, Radio Shack, Staples, Target, VW, Walgreens, Walmart/drugs
12b	I-264 E, Watterson Expswy, 1 exlt N on US 60 Ⓡ Chevron, 🍴 Arby's, Big Boy, BJ's Rest., CA Pizza, Cheesecake Factory, Cosina Italian, Fox&Hound, J Alexander's, Logan's Roadhouse, McDonald's, Outback Steaks, Panera Bread, Taco Bell, Wendy's, Ⓞ Acura, Best Buy, Dillard's, Ford/Lincoln, Goodyear/auto, JC Penney, Kia, Kohl's, Macy's, Staples, SteinMart, Vonmaur, Whole Foods Mkt, mall
12a	I-264 W, access to Ⓗ
10	Cannons Lane
8	Grinstead Dr, Louisville, S 🍴 KT Cafe, Jim Porter's Rest., gas
7	US 42, US 62, Mellwood Ave, Story Ave
6	I-71 N (from eb), to Cincinnati
5a	I-65, S to Nashville, N to Indianapolis
5b	3rd St, Louisville, N 🍴 Joe's CrabShack, S 🏨 Galt House Hotel, Marriott, 🍴 Kingfish Rest., ⒪Ⓗ
4	9th St, Roy Wilkins Ave, S KY Art Ctr, science museum, downtown
3	US 150 E, to 22nd St, S Ⓡ Marathon/dsl, Shell/Circle K, 🍴 DQ, McDonald's, Subway
1	I-264 E, to Shively, S ☎, zoo
0mm	Kentucky/Indiana state line, Ohio River

🛣️N INTERSTATE 65

Exit	Services
138mm	Kentucky/Indiana state line, Ohio River
137	I-64 W, I-71 N, I-64 E, W to Galt House, downtown
136c	Jefferson St, Louisville, E ⒪Ⓗ, Walgreens, W Ⓡ Shell,

Exit	Services
136c	**Continued**
	🍴 McDonald's, Papa John's, Subway, White Castle, 🏨 Courtyard, EconoLodge, Fairfield Inn, Hampton Inn, Hyatt, Marriott, SpringHill Suites, Ⓞ Tires+
136b	Broadway St, Chestnut St (from nb), E ⒪Ⓗ, NAPA, Walgreens, W Ⓡ Shell, Thornton's, 🍴 McDonald's, Rally's, Subway, White Castle, 🏨 Courtyard, Fairfield Inn, Hampton Inn, Hyatt, Marriott, Springhill Suites, Ⓞ Tires+, same as 136c
135	W. St Catherine, E Ⓡ Shell
134b a	KY 61, Jackson St, Woodbine St, W Ⓡ Shell/Circle K, 🏨 Days Inn, Quality Inn, Ⓞ Harley-Davidson
133b	US 60A, Eastern Pkwy, Taylor Blvd, E 🍴 Denny's, Pizza Mia, Snappy Tomato Pizza, Subway, W Ⓡ Marathon, 🍴 Cracker Barrel, McDonald's, Papa John's, 🏨 Country Hearth Inn, Ⓞ U of Louisville, Churchill Downs, museum
133b	Crittenden Dr (132from sb), E 🍴 Denny's, same as 133, W Ⓡ BP, 🍴 Arby's, Burger King, Cracker Barrel, Hall of Fame Cafe, 🏨 Country Inn&Suites, Hilton Garden, Holiday Inn, Ramada Inn, Super 8
131b a	I-264, Watterson Expswy, W Cardinal Stadium, Expo Center, ☎
130	KY 61, Preston Hwy, E on Ky 61 Ⓡ Shell/Circle K, Speedway/dsl, Thornton's, 🍴 Bob Evans, Burger King, Domino's, Fazoli's, KFC, Little Caesars, McDonald's, Papa John's, Popeyes, Rally's, Royal Garden Buffet, Subway, Taco Bell, Waffle House, Wendy's, 🏨 EconoLodge, Red Roof Inn, Super 8, Ⓞ Aamco, AutoZone, Big O Tire, BigLots, Chevrolet/Kia, Dodge, $General, Ford, O'Reilly Parts, PepBoys, Radio Shack, Sav-A-Lot Foods, Staples, Tires+, U-Haul
128	KY 1631, Fern Valley Rd, E Ⓡ BP, Marathon/Circle K, Thornton's/dsl, 🍴 Arby's, Big Boy, El Nopal Mexican, Hardee's, Indi's Rest., McDonald's, Outback Steaks, Shoney's, Subway, Taco Bell, Waffle House, Wendy's, White Castle, 🏨 Comfort Suites, Days Inn, Fern Valley Hotel, Holiday Inn, InTown Suites, Jameson Inn, Ⓞ Sam's Club/gas, Walgreens, W UPS Depot
127	KY 1065, outer loop, E TX Roadhouse, W 🍴 McDonald's/RV Parking, to Motor Speedway
125b a	I-265 E, KY 841, Gene Snyder Fwy
121	KY 1526, Brooks Rd, E Ⓡ BP, Marathon, 🍴 Arby's, Burger King, Cracker Barrel, McDonald's, Tumbleweed Grill, 🏨 Comfort Inn, Fairfield Inn, Holiday Inn Express, ⒪Ⓗ, Tinker's RV Ctr, W Ⓡ BP/dsl, ⛽Subway/Taco Bell/dsl/scales/24hr, 🍴 Waffle House, 🏨 Baymont Inn, EconoLodge, Hampton Inn, Quality Inn
117	KY 44, Shepherdsville, E Ⓡ Gulf, 🍴 Bearno's Pizza, Denny's, 🏨 Best Western/rest., Days Inn, Ⓞ KOA (2mi),

Ⓡ = gas Ⓕ = food 🏠 = lodging Ⓞ = other Ⓡˢ = rest stop   Copyright 2014 - The Next Exit ®

⬆N INTERSTATE 65 CONT'D

Exit	Services
117	Continued
	W Ⓡ Marathon, Speedway/dsl, Ⓕ Arby's, Big Boy, Cattlelands Roadhouse, China Buffet, DQ, El Nopal, Fazoli's, LJ Silver, KFC, Little Caesars, McDonald's/playplace, Mr Gatti's, Quiznos, Sonic, Subway, Taco Bell, Triple Crown Steaks, Waffle House, Wendy's, White Castle, 🏠 Country Inn&Suites, Motel 6, Sleep Inn, Super 8, Ⓞ Advance Parts, AutoZone, BigLots, $General, Family$, Kroger/gas, Lowe's, Radio Shack, Rite Aid, Sav-a-Lot, Walgreens, auto repair
116.5mm	Salt River
116	KY 480, to KY 61, **E** Ⓡ ♥Loves/Chester's/Subway/dsl/scales/24hr, Shell/dsl, Ⓞ House of Quilts, **W** Ⓡ Marathon/dsl, Ⓞ Grandma's RV Park/flea mkt
114mm	Ⓡˢ sb, full 🅰 facilities, Ⓒ, vending, 🏠, litter barrels, petwalk
112	KY 245, Clermont, **E** Ⓡ Shell/dsl, Ⓞ Jim Beam Outpost, Bernheim Forest, to My Old Kentucky Home SP
105	KY 61, Lebanon Jct, **W** Ⓡ ⛽/McDonald's/Subway/dsl/scales/24hr/@, 105 QuikStop/dsl, Ⓕ Vegas Lou's BBQ
102	KY 313, to KY 434, Radcliff, **W** to Patton Museum
94	US 62, Elizabethtown, **E** Ⓡ BP/dsl, Marathon/dsl, Ⓕ Denny's, Waffle House, White Castle, 🏠 Comfort Inn, Days Inn, Super 8, **W** Ⓡ BP/dsl, Speedway/dsl, Ⓕ Arby's, Burger King, Cracker Barrel, Chalupa's Mexican, Gatti's Pizza, HoneyBaked Ham, KFC/Taco Bell, McDonald's, Papa John's, Ruby Tuesday, Ryan's, Shoney's, Snappy Tomato Pizza, Stone Hearth, Subway, TX Outlaw Steaks, TX Roadhouse, Wendy's, 🏠 Baymont Inn, Best Western, Comfort Suites, Fairfield Inn, Hampton Inn, Holiday Inn Express, Howard Johnson, La Quinta, Motel 6, Ramada Inn, Ⓞ Ⓗ, Advance Parts, AutoZone, Crossroads Camping, $General, $Tree, Kroger/gas, Skagg's RV Ctr, Walgreens, USPO, st police, visitors ctr
93	to Bardstown, to BG Pky, **E** to My Old KY Home SP, Maker's Mark Distillery
91	US 31 W, KY 61, WK Pkwy, Elizabethtown, **E** Ⓡ Marathon/dsl, Ⓕ LJ Silver, Subway, 🏠 Bluegrass Inn, Budget Motel, Commonwealth Lodge, Ⓞ $General, to Lincoln B'Place, **W** Ⓡ Doug's/dsl, Marathon, Ⓕ Jerry's Rest., 🏠 KY Cardinal Inn, Roadside Inn, Ⓞ Ⓗ
90mm	weigh sta sb only
86	KY 222, Glendale, **E** Ⓡ ⛽/McDonalds/dsl/scales/24hr, Ⓞ Glendale Camping, trk repair, **W** Ⓡ Petro/Dunkin Donuts/dsl/scales/24hr/@, 🏠 Glendale Economy Inn, Ⓞ Blue Beacon
83mm	Nolin River
81	KY 84, Sonora, **E** Ⓡ Marathon/dsl, ⛽/Subway/dsl/scales/24hr, Ⓞ Blue Beacon, to Lincoln B'Place, **W** Ⓡ BP/dsl
76	KY 224, Upton, **E** Ⓡ Marathon/dsl, **W** to Nolin Lake
75mm	eastern/central time zone
71	KY 728, Bonnieville
65	US 31 W, Munfordville, **E** Ⓡ BP/Subway/dsl, FiveStar/dsl, Ⓕ DQ, El Mazatlan, King Buffet, Pizza Hut, McDonald's, Sonic, 🏠 Super 11, Ⓞ Advance Parts, $General, Family$, Fred's Store, IGA Foods, Pamida, Save-A-Lot, **W** Ⓡ Marathon/dsl, Shell, Ⓕ Country Kitchen, to Nolin Lake

Exit	Services
61mm	Ⓡˢ both lanes, full 🅰 facilities, info, Ⓒ, 🏠, litter barrels, vending, petwalk, Green River
58	KY 218, Horse Cave, **E** Ⓡ ♥Loves/McDonald's/dsl/scales/24hr/@, Ⓞ Ⓗ, **W** Ⓡ Gulf/dsl, Marathon/dsl/repair, 🏠 Country Hearth Inn, Hampton Inn, Ⓞ KOA, to Mammoth Cave NP
53	KY 70, KY 90, Cave City, **E** Ⓡ BP/dsl, Gulf/dsl/repair, JR's, Marathon/dsl, Shell, Ⓕ A&W/LJ Silver, Cracker Barrel, El Mazatlan, El Patron, KFC, McDonald's, Pizza Hut, Subway, Wendy's, 🏠 Best Value Inn, Best Western, Comfort Inn, Days Inn/rest., EconoLodge, Sleep Inn, Super 8, Ⓞ Ⓗ, $General, Barren River Lake SP (24mi), **W** Ⓕ Watermill Rest., Ⓞ Onyx Cave, Mammoth Cave NP, Jellystone Camping
48	KY 255, Park City, **E** Ⓡ Shell/dsl, Ⓞ $General, Park Mammoth Resort, **W** Diamond Caverns Resort, to Mammoth Cave NP
43	Nun/Cumberland Pky, to Barren River Lake SP
38	KY 101, Smiths Grove, **W** Ⓡ Exxon/dsl/scales, Marathon/Subway/dsl, Shell, Ⓕ Bestway Pizza, McDonald's, Wendy's, 🏠 Bryce Motel, Ⓞ $General, IGA Foods, Larry's Parts, auto repair, city park
36	US 68, KY 80, Oakland, (no nb return)
28	rd 446, to US 31 W, Bowling Green, **W** Ⓡ Shell/dsl, Ⓕ Hardee's, Jerry's Rest., Wendy's, 🏠 Continental Inn, Country Hearth Inn, Super 8, Value Lodge, Ⓞ Ⓗ, Corvette Museum/cafe, **3 mi W** to WKYU
26	KY 234, Bowling Green, **W** Ⓡ Shell/dsl, Ⓕ Subway, Ⓞ Ⓗ, IGA Foods
22	US 231, Bowling Green, **E** Ⓡ Exxon/dsl Keystop Gas, Shell, Ⓕ Catfish House, Cracker Barrel, Culver's, Denny's, Domino's, Godfather's, Hardee's, Mancino's Pizza, Motor City Grill, Ryan's, Sonic, Waffle House, Zaxby's, 🏠 Best Value Inn, Best Western, Comfort Inn, Days Inn, EconoLodge, Fairfield Inn, HomeTowne Suites, La Quinta, Microtel, Quality Inn, Ramada Inn, Sleep Inn, Ⓞ Camping World/Gander Mtn, $General, Harley-Davidson, **Urgent Care**, USPO, **W** Ⓡ Gulf/dsl, RaceWay, Shell/dsl, Speedway/dsl, Ⓕ Applebee's, Arby's, Beijing Chinese, Bob Evans, Bruster's, Buffalo Wild Wings, Burger King, Capt D's, ChuckeCheese, Chick-fil-A, China Buffet, Double-Dog's Chowhouse, Fazoli's, Great Harvest Bread, Guadalajara Grill, KFC, Krystal, Kyoto Steaks, Linzie's Sandwiches, Logan's Roadhouse, Longhorn Steaks, McDonald's, Moe's SW Grill, MT Grille, O'Charley's, Olive Garden, Outback Steaks, Panera Bread, Pizza Hut, Rafferty's, Red Lobster, Ruby Tuesday, Shogun Japanese, Smokey Bones BBQ, Sonic, Starbucks, Steak'n Shake, Subway, Taco Bell, TGIFriday's, Toots Rest., Waffle House, Wendy's, White Castle, Zaxby's, 🏠 Baymont Inn, Candlewood Suites, Country Inn&Suites, Courtyard, Drury Inn, Hampton Inn, Hilton Garden, Holiday Inn, Motel 6, News Inn, Red Roof Inn, Ⓞ Ⓗ, Advance Parts, AT&T, Barnes&Noble, Best Buy, BMW/Mercedes, Buick/GMC, Chevrolet, Chrysler/Jeep, Curves, CVS Drug, Dillard's, $General, Fisher Parts, Ford/Lincoln, Goodyear/auto, Hancock Fabrics, Hobby Lobby, Home Depot, Honda, JC Penney, K-Mart, KOA, Kia, Kohl's, Kroger/gas, Lowe's, Nissan, Office Depot, Old Navy, PetCo, Sam's Club/gas, Sears, Staples, Target, TJ Maxx, Toyota, U-Haul, Walgreens, Walmart/McDonald's, mall, **Urgent Care**
20	WH Natcher **Toll Rd**, to Bowling Green, access to W KY U, st police

E L I Z A B E T H T O W N

B O W L I N G G R E E N

KY

⬆N INTERSTATE 65 CONT'D

FRANKLIN

Exit	Services
6	KY 100, Franklin, **E** BP/dsl, Shell/dsl/24hr, 🅞 truckwash, **W** 🅖 ▦/Subway/dsl/scales/24hr, ▦/Wendy's/dsl/scales/24hr, 🛏 Comfort Inn, Days Inn, Knights Inn, 🅞 H, Bluegrass RV Park, Petrolube, SpeedCo, truck&tires/repair, truckwash
4mm	weigh sta nb
2	US 31 W, to Franklin, **E** ⊘FLYING J/Denny's/dsl/LP/scales/24hr, Keystop/Marathon/Burger King/dsl/24hr, **W** 🅖 BP/dsl, 🍴 Cracker Barrel, McDonald's, Oasis SW Grill, Waffle House, 🛏 Best Western, EconoLodge, Hampton Inn, Holiday Inn Express, Quality Inn, Super 8, 🅞 H, antiques
1mm	Welcome Ctr nb, full ♿ facilities, 🚻, vending, 🅟 litter barrels, petwalk
0mm	Kentucky/Tennessee state line

⬆N INTERSTATE 71

Exit	Services
	Kentucky/Ohio state line, Ohio River
	I-71 and I-75 run together 19 miles. See Kentucky Interstate 75, exits 175-192.
77[173]	I-75 S, to Lexington
75mm	weigh sta sb
72	KY 14, to Verona, **E** 🅖 BP/dsl, Marathon/dsl, 🅞 Oak Creek Camping (5mi)
62	US 127, to Glencoe, **E** 🅖 62 TrkPlaza/rest./dsl, **W** 🅖 BP/dsl/rest., 🛏 127 Motel
57	KY 35, to Sparta, **E** 🅖 Marathon/dsl, 🅞 Eagle Valley Camping (10mi), Sparta RV Park (3mi), **W** 🅖 BP/dsl, 🛏 Ramada, 🅞 KY Speedway
55	KY 1039, **W** 🅖 ♥Loves/McDonald's/Subway/dsl/scales/24hr, 🅞 KY Speedway, casino
44	KY 227, to Indian Hills, **W** 🅖 BP/dsl, Marathon/dsl, Murphy USA/dsl, 🍴 Arby's, Burger King, El Nopal, Hometown Pizza, KFC, McDonald's, New China, Subway, Taco Bell, Waffle House, 🛏 Best Western, Hampton Inn, Holiday Inn Express, Super 8, 🅞 H, AutoZone, Chevrolet, $General, Ford, Kroger/dsl, Sav-a-Lot Foods, Verizon, Walmart, Gen. Butler SP
43.5mm	Kentucky River
43	KY 389, to KY 55, English
34	US 421, New Castle, Bedford, Campbellsburg, **W** 🅖 BP/Subway/dsl, Marathon/dsl, 🅞 st police
28	KY 153, KY 146, to US 42, Pendleton, **E** 🅖 BP/dsl, Marathon/dsl, ▦/Subway/dsl/scales/24hr/@,**W** 🅖 ▦/McDonald's/scales/dsl/24hr
22	KY 53, La Grange, **E** 🅖 BP/dsl, Speedway/Rally's/dsl, 🍴 Applebee's, Beef O'Brady's, Burger King, Jumbo Buffet, Papa John's, Papa Murphy's, Ponderosa, Sonic, Waffle House, Wendy's, 🛏 Best Western-Ashbury, Holiday Inn Express, 🅞 H, AT&T, Big-O Tire, GNC, Kroger/gas, Radio Shack, Walgreens, Walmart/Subway, **Urgent Care**, **W** 🅖 Marathon/dsl, Swifty, 🍴 Arby's, Cracker Barrel, Domino's, DQ, El Nopal, Hometown Pizza, KFC, LJ Silver, McDonald's, Taco Bell, 🛏 Comfort Suites, Super 8, 🅞 Advance Parts, Buick/Chevrolet, Curves, Lee Tires, NAPA, Rite Aid, Sav-a-Lot, flea mkt, USPO, vet
18	KY 393, Buckner, **W** 🅖 Marathon/dsl, 🍴 Subway
17	KY 146, Buckner, **E** 🅞 Ford, **W** 🅖 Thornton's/dsl/24hr, 🅞 USPO, st police

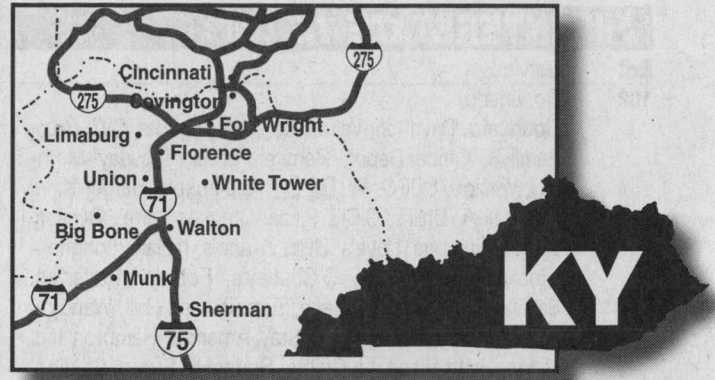

LOUISVILLE

Exit	Services
14	KY 329, Crestwood, Pewee Valley, Brownsboro, **E** 🅖 BP/dsl, 🍴 Starbucks, **2 mi E** 🍴 DQ, Hometown Pizza, McDonald's, Sonic, Subway
13mm	🆁🆂 both lanes, full ♿ facilities, 🚻, vending, 🅟 litter barrels, petwalk
9b a	I-265, KY 841, Gene Snyder Fwy, **E** 🅞 Costco/gas, to Sawyer SP
5	I-264, Watterson Expswy (exits left from sb), **E** to Sawyer SP
2	Zorn Ave, **E** VA H, **W** 🅖 BP, Shell/dsl, 🍴 El Nopal Mexican, KingFish Rest., 🛏 Ramada Inn, 🅞 WaterTower Art Museum
1b	I-65, S to Nashville, N to Indianapolis

⬆N INTERSTATE 75

COVINGTON

Exit	Services
193mm	Kentucky/Ohio state line, Ohio River
192	5th St (from nb), Covington, **E** 🅖 BP, Shell, Speedway, 🍴 Big Boy, Burger King, GoldStar Chili, McDonald's, Riverfront Pizza, Skyline Chili, Subway, Taco Bell, Waffle House, White Castle, 🛏 Courtyard, Extended Stay America, Holiday Inn, Radisson, 🅞 Lexus, Toyota/Scion, Riverboat Casino, **W** 🛏 Hampton Inn
191	12th St, Covington, **E** 🅞 H, museum, same as 192
189	KY 1072, Kyles Lane, **W** 🅖 BP/dsl, Marathon/dsl, Shell/dsl, 🍴 Big Boy, Skyline Chili, Substation II Subs, 🛏 Days Inn, Rodeway Inn, 🅞 Walgreens, same as 188
188	US 25, US 42, Dixe Hwy, **E** 🅖 Sunoco, 🍴 Subway, 🅞 GNC, Kroger, Tuesday Morning, **W** 🛏 Days Inn, Rodeway Inn, USA Hotel, 🅞 $Tree, same as 189
186	KY 371, Buttermilk Pike, Covington, **E** 🅖 BP/dsl, Marathon/DQ, 🍴 Graeter's Ice Cream, Oriental Wok, Papa John's, 🛏 Drawbridge Inn/rest., Montgomery Inn, Super 8, **W** 🅖 BP, Shell, Sunoco/dsl, 🍴 Arby's, Baskin-Robbins/Dunkin Donuts, Bonefish Grill, Burger King, Chipotle Mexican, Empire Buffet, GoldStar Chili, Jimmy John's, La Rosa's Pizza, McDonald's, Miyako Steaks, Outback Steaks, Papa Murphy's, Pizza Hut, Quiznos, Rima's Diner, Skyline Chili, Subway, 🅞 AT&T, Home Depot, Remke Foods, Staples, Verizon, Walgreens
185	I-275 E and W, **W** to 🔜
184	KY 236, Donaldson Rd, to Erlanger, **E** 🅖 BP, Marathon, 🍴 Double Dragon Oriental, **W** 🅖 Marathon, Speedway/dsl, Sunoco/Subway/dsl, 🍴 La Badeya Grill, Peecox Grill, Waffle House, 🛏 Comfort Inn, Country Hearth Inn, EconoLodge, Wingate Inn, 🅞 Goodyear/auto
182	KY 1017, Turfway Rd, **E** 🅖 BP/dsl, Shell, 🍴 Big Boy, China City, Lee's Chicken, McDonald's, Papa John's, Pizza Hut, Taco Bell, 3 Amigo's Mexican, Subway, 🛏 Clarion,

🅖 = gas 🍴 = food 🛏 = lodging 🅞 = other 🆁🆂 = rest stop Copyright 2014 - The Next Exit ®

⬆N INTERSTATE 75 CONT'D

Exit	Services
182	Continued
	Courtyard, Days Inn, ValuePlace, 🅞 BigLots, CVS Drug, Family$, Office Depot, Remke Foods, Tuesday Morning, Verizon, USPO, **W** 🅖 🍴 Applebee's, Burger King, Chick-fil-A, Chili's, CiCi's Pizza, Cracker Barrel, Dynasty Buffet, Famous Dave's BBQ, Karlo's Italian, Longhorn Steaks, Noodles&Co., O'Charley's, Potbelly, Rafferty's, Skyline Chili, Steak'n Shake, Tumbleweed Grill, Wendy's, 🛏 Comfort Inn, Extended Stay America, Hampton Inn, Hilton, Hyatt Place, La Quinta, SpringHill Suites, Studio+, 🅞🅷, Best Buy, Dick's, Home Depot, Kohl's, Lowe's, Meijer, Michael's, Petsmart, Radio Shack, Sam's Club, Target, Turfway Park Racing
181	KY 18, Florence, **E** 🅖 Speedway/dsl, Swifty, TA/Sunoco/Pizza Hut/Popeye's/dsl/24hr/@, 🍴 Waffle House, 🛏 Best Value Inn, Best Western, Heritage Inn, 🅞 Chevrolet, auto repair, vet, **W** 🅖 BP/dsl, Shell, Speedway, 🍴 Buffalo Wild Wings, Cheddars, City BBQ, El Rio Grande, Fazoli's, Hooters, IHOP, La Rosa's, Logan's Roadhouse, Panera Bread, Quiznos, Red Robin, 🛏 Microtel, Stay Lodge, 🅞 Buick/GMC, Chrysler/Jeep, $Tree, Dodge, Ford, Honda, Hyundai, K-Mart, Mazda, Nissan, Tire Discounters, Toyota/Scion, VW, Walmart
180a	Mall Rd (from sb), **W** 🍴 Asian Buffet, Chipotle Mexican, ChuckeCheese, Coldstone, GoldStar Chili, HoneyBaked Ham, Olive Garden, Pizza Hut, Qdoba, Quiznos, Skyline Chili, Smokey Bones BBQ, Starbucks, Subway, Taco Bell, 🅞 AAA, AT&T, Barnes&Noble, $General, $Tree, Hobby Lobby, JC Penney, JoAnn Fabrics, Kroger, Macy's, Old Navy, Sears/auto, Staples, TJ Maxx, Verizon, mall, **Urgent Care**, same as 180
180	US 42, US 127, Florence, Union, **E** 🅖 BP/dsl, Speedway/dsl, 🍴 Big Boy, Bob Evans, Burger King, Camino Real, Capt D's, Chipotle Mexican, Cielito Lino Mexican, Dunkin Donuts, Mai Thai, McDonald's, Rally's, Red Lobster, Subway, Wendy's, 🛏 Holiday Inn, Knights Inn, Motel 6, Quality Inn, Super 8, 🅞 Cadillac, Subaru, funpark, **W** 🅖 Marathon/dsl, Shell/dsl Speedway, 🍴 Arby's, KFC, LJ Silver, Little Caesars, Perkins, Ponderosa, Waffle House, White Castle, 🛏 Ramada Inn, Travelodge, 🅞 CarX, Midas, Old Time Pottery, PepBoys, Tire Discounters, Tires+, Walgreens
178	KY 536, Mt Zion Rd, **E** 🅖 BP/Rally's/dsl, Mobil, Shell/dsl, Sunoco/Subway/dsl, 🍴 Buffalo Bob's, GoldStar Chili, Hot Head Burritos, Jersey Mike's Subs, La Rosa's Pizza, Sonic, Steak'n Shake, 🅞 AT&T, AutoZone, Goodyear/auto, Kroger
177mm	**Welcome Ctr sb/ 🆁🆂 nb, full 🦽 facilities, 🅲, vending, 🚮 litter barrels, RV dump**
175	KY 338, Richwood, **E** 🅖 TA/BP/Country Pride/Taco Bell/dsl/24hr/@, 🚍/Subway/dsl/24hr, 🍴 Arby's, Burger King, White Castle, 🛏 Comfort Inn, 🅞 RV Park, **W** 🅖 BP/dsl, 🚍/Subway/dsl/scales/24hr, Shell/dsl, 🍴 GoldStar Chili, McDonald's, Penn Sta Subs, Skyline Chili, Waffle House, Wendy's, 🛏 EconoLodge, Holiday Inn Express, 🅞 to Big Bone Lick SP
173	I-71 S, to Louisville
171	KY 14, KY 16, to Verona, Walton, **E** 🅖 BP/dsl, Marathon/DQ/dsl, 🍴 China Moon, El Toro Mexican, McDonald's, Starbucks, Subway, Waffle House, 🅞 AT&T, AutoZone,

Exit	Services
171	Continued
	Kohl's, Kroger/dsl, Walton Drug, **W** 🅖 ⌖FLYING J/Denny's/dsl/scales/24hr, 🅞 Blue Beacon, Delightful Days RV Ctr, Oak Creek Camping (1mi), to Big Bone Lick SP
168mm	**weigh sta/rest haven sb**
166	KY 491, Crittenden, **E** 🅖 Gulf/dsl, Marathon/dsl, 🍴 McDonald's, 🅞 Chrysler/Dodge/Jeep, Cincinnati S Camping (2mi), **W** 🅖 Marathon/dsl, Shell/Gold Star Chili/dsl, 🍴 Subway, Wendy's, 🅞 Curves, $General
159	KY 22, to Owenton, Dry Ridge, **E** 🅖 BP, Marathon, Shell/dsl, 🍴 Arby's, Burger King, Happy Dragon Chinese, KFC/Taco Bell, LJ Silver, McDonald's, Pizza Hut, Skyline Chili, Subway, Waffle House, Wendy's, 🛏 Microtel, Super 8, 🅞 🅷, $General, O'Reilly Parts, Radio Shack, Walmart, **W** 🅖 Roadranger/dsl, Speedway/dsl, 🍴 Cracker Barrel, 🛏 Comfort Inn, Hampton Inn, 🅞 Camper Village, Dry Ridge Outlets/famous brands, Sav-A-Lot, Toyota/Scion, Tire Discounters
156	Barnes Rd, **E** 🅞🅷
154	KY 36, Williamstown, **E** 🅖 Marathon/dsl, Shell/dsl, 🅞 🅷 to Kincaid Lake SP, **W** 🅖 Marathon/dsl, 🍴 El Jalisco Mexican, 🛏 Best Value Inn, Days Inn
144	KY 330, to Owenton, Corinth, **E** 🅖 Marathon/dsl, Noble's Trk Plaza/rest./dsl, 🅞 camping, **W** 🅖 BP, 🍴 Danny's Diner, 🛏 3 Springs Motel
136	KY 32, to Sadieville, **W** 🅖 Marathon
130.5mm	**weigh sta nb**
129	rd 620, Cherry Blossom Wy, **E** 🅖 🚍/Wendy's/dsl/scales/24hr/@, 🍴 Waffle House, 🛏 Days Inn, Motel 6, **W** 🅖 🚍/McDonald's/dsl/scales/24hr, Shell
127mm	**🆁🆂 both lanes, full 🦽 facilities, 🅲, vending, 🚮 litter barrels, petwalk**
126	US 62, to US 460, Georgetown, **E** 🅖 Marathon, Murphy USA/dsl, 🍴 Applebee's, Asian Royal Buffet, Big Boy, Burger King, CiCi's, Golden Corral, Gold Star Chili, Jimmy John's, McDonald's, Mi Mexico, O'Charley's, Papa John's, Penn Sta Subs, Starbucks, Steak'n Shake, Subway, 🛏 Holiday Inn, 🅞 Kohl's, Lowe's, Tire Discounters, Verizon, Walmart/Subway, **Urgent Care**, vet, **W** 🅖 BP, Marathon, Shell/Subway, Speedway/dsl, 🍴 Chick-fil-A, Cracker Barrel, Fazoli's, KFC, Ruby Tuesday, Waffle House, 🛏 Best Western, Comfort Suites, Country Inn&Suites, Knights Inn, Fairfield Inn, Hampton Inn, Hilton Garden, Microtel, Quality Inn, Super 8, 🅞 🅷, Buick/Chevrolet, to Georgetown Coll, same as 125
125	US 460 (from nb), Georgetown, **E** 🅖 Gulf, Shell, 🍴 FatKats Pizza, 🛏 Knights Inn, **W** 🅖 Gulf/dsl, Swifty, 🍴 Arby's, DQ, Little Caesars, LJ Silver, Taco Bell, Wendy's, 🛏 Winner's Circle Motel, 🅞 Advance Parts, BigLots, K-Mart, Radio Shack, Outlets/Famous Brands, same as 126
120	rd 1973, to Ironworks Pike, KY Horse Park, **E** KY Horse Park Camping, **W** 🅖 Valero/dsl, 🅞🅷
118	I-64 W, to Frankfort, Louisville
115	rd 922, Lexington, **E** 🅖 Shell/Subway/dsl, 🍴 Cracker Barrel, McDonald's, Waffle House, 🛏 Fairfield Inn, Knights Inn, La Quinta, Sheraton, 🅞 SaddleHorse Museum (4mi), **W** 🅖 Marathon/dsl, 🍴 Cortland's Kitchen, Denny's, Happy Dragon Chinese, 🛏 Clarion, Embassy Suites, Marriott/rest., 🅞 museum
113	US 27, US 68, to Paris, Lexington, **E** 🅖 Marathon, Speedway, 🍴 Waffle House, 🛏 Ramada Inn, **W** 🅖 Marathon/dsl, Shell/dsl, Swifty, 🍴 Arby's, Burger King, Capt D's

FLORENCE

GEORGETOWN

KY

▲N INTERSTATE 75 CONT'D

LEXINGTON

Exit	Services
113	Continued
	DQ, Donato's Pizza, Fazoli's, Golden Corral, Hardee's, Horseshoes Grill, Little Caesars, McDonald's, Penn Sta Subs, Rally's, Taco Bell, 🛏 Catalina Motel, Days Inn, Red Roof Inn, 🅾 Advance Parts, AutoZone, Bluegrass RV Ctr, Chevrolet, CVS Drug, Northside RV Ctr, O'Reilly Parts, Walmart, to UK, Rupp Arena
111	I-64 E, to Huntington, WV
110	US 60, Lexington, **W** 🅿 Murphy USA/dsl, Shell/dsl, Speedway/dsl, Thorntons/dsl, 🍴 Arby's, Bajio, Bob Evans, Calistoga Cafe, Cane's Chicken, Cracker Barrel, McDonald's, Starbucks, Subway, Waffle House, Wendy's, 🛏 Baymont Inn, Best Western, Comfort Inn, Country Inn&Suites, Envoy Inn, Hampton Inn, Microtel, Motel 6, Ramada Ltd, Super 8, 🅾 🏥 Lowe's, Rite Aid, Walmart/Subway
108	Man O War Blvd, **E** 🅿 Shell, 🅾 Rite Aid, **W** 🅿 Marathon/dsl, Meijer/dsl, Shell/KFC/Wendy's, 🍴 Applebee's, Arby's, Backyard Burger, BD Mongolian Grill, BoneFish Grill, Carino's, Carrabba's, Cheddar's, Chick-fil-A, Chipotle Mexican, Domino's, Fazoli's, GoldStar Chili, IChing Asian, Logan's Roadhouse, Malone's, McDonald's, Old Chicago, Outback Steaks, Pizza Hut, Qdoba, Quiznos, Rafferty's, Red Lobster, Saul Good Rest., Show-Me's Rest., Starbucks, Steak'n Shake, Taco Bell, TGIFriday's, Waffle House, 🛏 Courtyard, Hilton Garden, Homewood Suites, Hyatt Place, Sleep Inn, 🅾 🏥 Audi, Barnes&Noble, Best Buy, BigLots, Dick's, GNC, Gordmans, Harley-Davidson, Kohl's, Marshall's, Michael's, Old Navy, Petsmart, Staples, Target, Tire Discounters, Walgreens
104	KY 418, Lexington, **E** 🅿 BP/Arby's/dsl, Shell/Hardee's, 🍴 Waffle House, 🛏 Best Western, Comfort Inn, Days Inn, EconoLodge, La Quinta, **W** 🅿 Marathon/dsl, Speedway/Subway, 🍴 Wendy's, 🅾 🏥
99	US 25 N, US 421 N, Clays Ferry
98mm	Kentucky River
97	US 25 S, US 421 S, Clay's Ferry
95	rd 627, to Boonesborough, Winchester, **E** 🅿 BP/dsl, Love's/Arby's/dsl/scales/24hr, 🍴 McDonald's, 🅾 Ft Boonesborough SP, camping, **W** 🅿 Shell/dsl/24hr
90	US 25, US 421, Richmond, **E** 🅿 Shell, 🍴 Cracker Barrel, 🛏 Knights Inn, La Quinta, Red Roof Inn, Super 7, **W** 🅿 BP, Exxon/Arby's/dsl, Marathon, Shell, Thorobred, 🍴 Big Boy, DQ, Hanger's Rest., Hardee's, Pizza Hut, Subway, Waffle House, Wendy's, 🛏 Days Inn, Super 8, 🅾 $General, NTB, USPO

RICHMOND

87	rd 876, Richmond, **E** 🅿 BP/dsl, Gulf, Marathon, Shell/dsl, Speedway/dsl, 🍴 A&W/LJ Silver, Arby's, Casa Fiesta Mexican, Domino's, Fazoli's, Fong's Chinese, Hardee's, Hooters, King Buffet, Lee's Chicken, Little Caesars, McDonald's, Papa John's, Penn Sta Subs, Pizza Hut, Qdoba, Rally's, Taco Bell, Waffle House, Wendy's, 🛏 Best Western, Country Hearth Inn, Quality Quarters Inn, 🅾 🏥 Ace Hardware, AT&T, BigLots, $General, Goodyear/auto, Rite Aid, Suzuki, to EKU, **W** 🅿 BP/dsl, Marathon/Circle K, 🍴 Bob Evans, Buffalo Wild Wings, Burger King, Chick-fil-A, Culver's, Koto Japanese, Logan's Roadhouse, Olive Garden, Panera Bread, Ryan's, Starbucks, Steak'n Shake, Subway, 🛏 Comfort Suites, Hampton Inn, Holiday Inn Express, Jameson Inn, 🅾 Belk, Hastings Books, JC Pen

BEREA

87	Continued
	ney, Meijer/dsl, Petsmart, Radio Shack, Tire Discounters, TJ Maxx, Verizon
83	to US 25, rd 2872, Duncannon Ln, Richmond, **E** 🅾 Bluegrass Army Depot
77	rd 595, Berea, **E** 🅾 🏥 KY Artisan Ctr/Cafe/Travelers Ctr, to Berea Coll, **W** 🅿 BP/Subway/dsl, Shell/dsl, 🍴 Pizza+, Rio Grande Mexican, Smokehouse Grill, 🛏 Country Inn&Suites, Days Inn
76	KY 21, Berea, **E** 🅿 BP, Marathon/Circle K, Shell/Burger King, Speedway/dsl, 🍴 A&W/LJ Silver, Arby's, Cracker Barrel, Dinner Bell Rest., Hong Kong Buffet, KFC, Mariachi Mexican, Mario's Pizza, McDonald's, Old Town Amish Rest., Papa John's, Pizza Hut, Subway, Taco Bell, WanPen Chinese/Thai, Wendy's, 🛏 Best Value Inn, Holiday Motel, Knights Inn, 🅾 🏥 $General, Radio Shack, Walmart, tires, Urgent Care, **W** 🅿 BP, Marathon/dsl, 76 Fuel/dsl, 🍴 Lee's Chicken, 🛏 Comfort Inn, EconoLodge, Fairfield Inn, 🅾 Oh! Kentucky Camping
62	US 25, to KY 461, Renfro Valley, **E** 🅿 Derby City/rest./dsl, Shell, 🍴 Hardee's, 🛏 Heritage Inn, 🅾 KOA (2mi), Renfro Valley RV Park/rest, **W** 🅿 BP, Marathon/Wendy's/dsl, Marathon/Chester's, Shell, 🍴 Arby's, Denny's, Godfather's/Subway, KFC, McDonald's, Rock Fire Steaks, 🛏 Days Inn, EconoLodge, 🅾 🏥 Rite Aid, to Big South Fork NRA, Lake Cumberland
59	US 25, to Livingston, Mt Vernon, **E** 🅿 BP, Shell/dsl, TravelCtr/dsl, 🍴 El Cazador Mexican, Pizza Hut, 🛏 Kastle Inn, **W** 🅿 BP, 🍴 Shakers Pizza, 🛏 Mtn View Inn
51mm	Rockcastle River
49	KY 909, to US 25, Livingston, **E** 🅾 Camp Wildcat BFD, **W** 🅿 49er/dsl/24hr, 🅾 RV Park, truck/tire repair

LONDON

41	rd 80, to Somerset, London, **E** 🅿 Speedway, 🍴 Arby's, Azteca Mexican, Burger King, KFC, McDonald's, Sonic, White Castle, 🛏 Days Inn, EconoLodge, Quality Inn, Red Roof Inn, Super 8, 🅾 🏥 Advance Parts, AutoZone, CVS Drug, $General, Family$, Kroger/deli, Parsley's Tire/repair, st police, **W** 🅿 BP/rest/dsl/24hr, Clark/dsl, Marathon/McDonald's, Shell/pizza, 🍴 Cracker Barrel, LJ Silver, Shiloh Roadhouse, Subway, Taco Bell, Waffle House, Wendy's, 🛏 Budget Host, Hampton Inn, 🅾 Dog Patch Ctr, Westgate RV Camping
38	rd 192, to Rogers Pkwy, London, **E** 🅿 BP/dsl, Marathon, Shell/Quiznos/dsl, Speedway/dsl, 🍴 Big Boy, Burger King, Capt D's, DQ, Dino's Italian, Domino's, El Dorado Mexican, Fazoli's, Golden Corral, Great Wall Chinese, Hardee's, Huddle House, Krystal, McDonald's, Pizza Hut, Ruby Tuesday, Starbucks, Steak'n Shake, Taco Bell, 🛏 Baymont Inn, Comfort Suites, Country Inn&Suites, Holi

KY

⬆N INTERSTATE 75 CONT'D

Exit	Services
38	Continued
	day Inn Express, Microtel, 🔲 🅷, Advance Parts, $Tree, E Kentucky RV Ctr, K-Mart, Kroger/dsl, Lowe's, Nissan, Office Depot, Peterbilt, Radio Shack, USPO, Verizon, Walgreens, Walmart/Subway, 🔄, camping, Rogers Pkwy to Manchester/Hazard, to Levi Jackson SP, W to Laurel River Lake RA
34mm	**weigh sta both lanes**, truck haven
30.5mm	Laurel River
29	US 25, US 25E, Corbin, E 🅖 Marathon, Murphy USA, 🚚/McDonald's/Subway/dsl/scales/24hr, Stop-N-Go, 🍴 DQ, David's Steaks, Huddle House, Mi Jalisco Mexican, Shoney's, Taco Bell, 🛏 Super 8, 🔲 Aldi Foods, Blue Beacon, Lowe's, Radio Shack, Walmart/Subway, to Cumberland Gap NP, W 🅖 BP/Krystal/dsl, 💗Love's/Hardee's/dsl/scales/24hr/@, Marathon, Shell/dsl, 🍴 Cracker Barrel, Sonny's BBQ, 🛏 Baymont Inn, Comfort Suites, Fairfield Inn, Hampton Inn, Knights Inn, 🔲 KOA, tires/repair, to Laurel River Lake RA
25	US 25W, Corbin, E 🅖 Speedway/dsl, 🍴 Applebee's, Buckner's Grill, Burger King, McDonald's, O'Mally's, Wendy's, 🛏 Country Inn&Suites, Days Inn, Holiday Inn Express, Landmark Inn, 🔲 🅷, auto repair/tires, W 🅖 Shell/24hr, 🍴 Arby's, El Dorado Mexican, Jade China Buffet, Subway, Waffle House, 🛏 Best Western, Mtn View Lodge, 🔲 to Cumberland Falls SP
15	US 25W, to Williamsburg, Goldbug, W 🅖 Shell, Xpress/dsl, 🔲 Cumberland Falls SP
14.5mm	Cumberland River
11	KY 92, Williamsburg, E 🅖 BP/dsl, Shell, 🍴 Arby's, El Dorado Mexican, Hardee's, KFC, Little Caesars, McDonald's, Pizza Hut, Sonic, Subway, Taco Bell, 🛏 Cumberland Inn, Scottish Inn, Super 8, 🔲 Advance Parts, AutoZone, $General, Family$, Radio Shack, Sav-A-Lot, Windham Drug, museum, W 🅖 Shell/dsl, 🚚/Wendy's/dsl/scales/24hr, 🍴 Burger King, Huddle House, Krystal, LJ Silver, 🛏 Hampton Inn, 🔲 Walmart, to Big South Fork NRA
1.5mm	**Welcome Ctr nb, full ♿ facilities, 🚻, vending, 🛒 litter barrels, petwalk**
0mm	Kentucky/Tennesee state line

⬆N INTERSTATE 275 (CINCINNATI)

Exit	Services
84	I-75, I-71, N to Cincinnati, S to Lexington, Louisville
83	US 25, US 42, US 127, S 🅖 Shell/dsl, Speedway, Thorntons, 🍴 Abuelo's Mexican, Burger King, Carrabba's, Coldstone, Donato's Pizza, 5 Guys Burgers, John Phillip's Rest., KFC, Max&Erma's, McAlister's Deli, McDonald's, Moe's SW Grill, Panera Bread, Pizza Hut, Starbucks, Subway, Taco Bell, Wendy's, 🔲 Dillard's, $Tree, GNC, K-Mart, Walgreens
82	rd 1303, Turkeyfoot Rd, S 🅷
80	KY 17, Independence, N 🅖 Speedway/dsl, United/dsl, 🍴 Arby's, Big Boy, Bob Evans, Buffalo Wild Wings, Burger King, Golden Corral, Hot Wok, Penn Sta Subs, Snappy Tomato Pizza, Subway, TX Roadhouse, Wendy's, 🔲 TireDiscounters, Walmart, S 🅖 Thorntons/dsl, 🍴 McDonald's, 🔲 Chevrolet
79	KY 16, Taylor Mill Rd, N 🅖 BP, Marathon, Speedway, 🍴

79	Continued
	Goldstar Chili, LJ Silver, McDonald's, Wendy's, 🔲 BigLots, CVS Drug, $Tree, Kroger/gas, Radio Shack, Walgreens, S 🅖 BP/dsl, 🍴 KFC/Taco Bell, McDonald's, Oriental Wok, Skyline Chili, Subway, 🔲 Remke's Foods
77	KY 9, Maysville, Wilder, N 🛏 Hampton Inn, S 🅖 Mobil/dsl, Thorntons/dsl, 🍴 DQ, Goldstar Chili, McDonald's, Waffle House
74a	Alexandria, to US 27, (exits left from sb)
74b	I-471 N, Newport, Cincinnati, N 🅷
73mm	OH/KY state line, OH River
72	US 52 W, Kellogg Ave, S 🅖 Marathon, 🔄
71	US 52 E, New Richmond
69	5 Mile Rd, W 🅖 BP/dsl, 🍴 Big Boy, IHOP, La Rosa's Mexican, McDonald's, TGIFriday's, Wendy's, 🔲 🅷, Kroger/gas
65	OH 125, Beechmont Ave, Amelia, E 🅖 Mobil/dsl, Shell, Speedway, 🍴 Hibachi Grill, Hooters, Red Lobster, Wendy's, 🛏 Motel 6, 🔲 CarX, Ford, Lowe's, Tires+, Walgreens, W 🅖 BP, Speedway/dsl, Marathon, 🍴 Big Boy, Bob Evans, Burger King, Butterbee's Grille, Chick-fil-A, Chipotle Mexican, Dos Amigo's Mexican, McDonald's, Olive Garden, Smokey Bones BBQ, Starbucks, White Castle, 🛏 Best Western, Days Inn, Red Roof Inn, 🔲 Aldi Foods, AT&T, BigLots, $Tree, Goodyear/auto, Hancock Fabrics, Home Depot, Honda, Kroger, Staples, Sumerel Tire/repair, Target, TireDiscounters, TJ Maxx, Toyota/Scion, Verizon
63b a	OH 32, Batavia, Newtown, E 🅖 Marathon, Mobil, Thornton's, 🍴 Applebee's, Cheeseburger Paradise, Chick-fil-A, CiCi's Pizza, City BBQ, Bob Evans, Burger King, Fuji Steaks, Golden Corral, KFC, LJ Silver, Longhorn Steaks, Max&Erma's, McDonalds, Panera Bread, Penn Sta Subs, Perkins, Pizza Hut, Popeye's, Skyline Chili, Taco Bell, White Castle, 🛏 Comfort Inn, Fairfield Inn, Hampton Inn, Holiday Inn, 🔲 Best Buy, Bigg's Foods, Dillard's, $Tree, Hobby Lobby, Jo-Ann Fabrics, Kohl's, Kroger, Meijer/dsl, Michael's, PepBoys, Petsmart, Sam's Club/gas, Sears/auto, Walmart, W 🅖 Exxon, Marathon, Speedway/dsl, Sunoco, 🍴 La Rosa's Mexican, Roy Rogers, 🔲 Kroger
59	OH 452, US 50, Milford Pkwy, Hillsboro, S 🅖 Mobil, 🍴 Buffalo Wild Wings, Cracker Barrel, Goldstar Chili, Mio's Pizza, Quaker Steak&Lube, Red Robin, Ruby Tuesday, TX Roadhouse, Subway, Wendy's, 🛏 Homewood Suites, 🔲 Office Depot, Petsmart, Target, Walmart
57	OH 28, Blanchester, Milford, 0-1 mi N 🍴 Applebee's, Arby's, Burger King, Chipotle Mexican, DQ, Dunkin Donuts, Goldstar Chili, IHOP, Panera Bread, Skyline Chili, Sonic, Subway, Steak'n Shake, Taco Bell, Wendy's, White Castle, 🔲 Home Depot, K-Mart, Kroger/gas, Lowe's, Meijer/dsl, S 🅖 Exxon, Shell, Speedway, Thorntons/dsl, 🍴 Big Boy, Bob Evans, Cazadore's Mexican, Hong Kong Wok, Little Caesar's, McDonald's, Putter's Grill, Quiznos, Roosters Grill, 🛏 Holiday Inn Express, 🔲 🅷, BigLots, CVS Drug, $Tree, Goodyear/auto, Kroger/gas, Tires+, USPO, vet
54	Wards Corner Rd, N 🅖 BP, S 🅖 Mobil/dsl, 🍴 Big Boy, Dominos, Goldstar Chili, Subway, 🛏 Hilton Garden
53mm	Little Miami River
52	Loveland, Indian Hill, N 🅖 Circle K/dsl, Marathon, Shell, Speedway/dsl, 🍴 Arby's, Burger King, Dragon Wok, Penn Sta Subs, Pizza Hut, Starbucks, Subway, Taco Bell, Wendy's, 🔲 CVS Drug, Verizon, VW, Walgreens
50	US 22, OH 3, Montgomery, N 🅖 Shell, 🍴 Buffalo Wild

⬆N INTERSTATE 275 (CINCINNATI) CONT'D

Exit	Services
50	Continued Wings, Chili's, DQ, Donato's Pizza, Melting Pot, Panera Bread, Starbucks, Subway, Taco Casa, Ⓞ Acura, GNC, Hyundai, Kroger, **S** Ⓖ BP/dsl, Shell, 🍴 Goldstar Chili, La Rosa's, McDonald's, Merlot's Rest., Quiznos, Skyline Chili, Wendy's, Ⓞ Ⓗ
49	I-71 N to Columbus, S to Cincinnati
47	Reed Hartman Hwy, Blue Ash, **S** 🍴 Chipotle, Jersey Mike's, Jimmy John's, Kanpai Japanese, Ruby Tuesday, 🛏 DoubleTree, Hyatt Place, Residence Inn
46	US 42, Mason, **N** Ⓖ BP, 🍴 Chipotle, KFC, McDonald's, Skyline Chili, Taco Bell, Wendy's, White Castle, 🛏 Holiday Inn, Motel 6, ValuePlace, Ⓞ Advance Parts, CVS Drug, Kroger, **S** Ⓖ Marathon/dsl, Shell, Speedway/dsl, UDF/dsl, 🍴 Arby's, Schezwan House, Waffle House, 🛏 Days Inn, Ⓞ Midas, Mr Transmission, Tire Discounters
44	Mosteller Rd, **N** 🍴 Subway, **S** 🛏 Homewood Suites
43b a	I-75, N to Dayton, S to Cincinnati
42	OH 747, Springdale, Glendale, **N** Ⓖ Sunoco, Thorntons, Ⓞ Staples, **S** Ⓖ Shell, 🍴 BJ's Brewhouse, Chipotle, Firehouse Subs, Jimmy John's, KFC, La Rositas, McDonald's, Skyline Chili, Steak'n Shake, TGIFriday's, Ⓞ BigLots, Chevrolet, Chrysler/Dodge/Jeep, Dillard's, Hobby Lobby, Macy's, Petsmart, Sears, Tires+
41	OH 4, Springdale Pkwy, **N** Ⓖ Mobil, Shell, Speedway/dsl, 🍴 Burger King, Hooters, Olive Garden, Pappadeaux, Roosters Rest., Skyline Chili, Wendy's, 🛏 La Quinta, Ⓞ Tire Discounters, **S** Ⓖ BP, UDF/dsl, 🍴 Beef'O'Brady's, DQ, Goldstar Chili, Outback Steaks, Subway, White Castle, 🛏 Extended Stay America, Howard Johnson, Super 8, Ⓞ Urgent Care, CVS Drug, Family$, O'Reilly Parts
39	Winton Rd, Winton Woods, **N** Ⓖ BP, 🍴 Bob Evans, Chipotle, Golden Corral, IHOP, McDonald's, Old Spaghetti Factory, Panera Bread, Red Lobster, Steak'n Shake, 🛏 Comfort Suites, Hampton Inn, Ⓞ Bass Pro Shops, CarMax, Home Depot, Kohl's, Meijer/dsl, PetCo, Tire Discounters, **S** Ⓖ Marathon/dsl, Shell/dsl, UDF/dsl, 🍴 Big Boy, Buffalo Wild Wings, Cancun Mexican, Cracker Barrel, Popeye's, Skyline Chili, Starbucks, Subway, Wendy's, 🛏
39	Continued Quality Inn, SpringHill Suites, Ⓞ AAA, Aldi Foods, $Tree, Kroger/gas, Tires+, Walgreens, Walmart
36	US 127, Hamilton, Mt Healthy, **N** Ⓖ BP/Circle K, Speedway, 🍴 Skyline Chili, Wendy's, **S** Ⓖ Shell/dsl, Sunoco, 🍴 Arby's, Big Boy, La Rosa's Pizza, Little Caesars, McDonald's, Rally's, Subway, Taco Bell, Ⓞ Advance Parts, Family$, O'Reilly Parts
33	US 27, US 126, Colerain Ave, **N** Ⓖ Speedway, 🍴 Burger King, Skyline Chili, Steak'n Shake, Wendy's, Ⓞ Colerain RV Ctr, Dick's, Hobby Lobby, Lowe's, Walmart/Subway, **S** Ⓖ Shell, 🍴 Arby's, Big Boy, Bob Evans, Burger King, Cheddar's, Chipotle, Firehouse Subs, 5 Guys Burgers, IHOP, KFC, LJ Silver, Longhorn Steaks, McDonald's, Olive Garden, Outback Steaks, Panera Bread, Pizza Hut, Qdoba, Red Lobster, Starbucks, Taco Bell, TGIFriday's, White Castle, Ⓞ Urgent Care, AT&T, Best Buy, JC Penney, Kia, Macy's, Marshalls, Meijer/dsl, Michael's, Old Navy, Tires+, Walgreens
31	Ronald Reagan Hwy, Blue Rock Rd
28	I-74, US 52, E to Cincinnati, W to Indianapolis
24	I-74, E to Cincinnati, W to Indianapolis
21	Kilby Rd, **W** Ⓞ Indian Springs Camping (3mi)
18 mm	Ohio/Indiana State Line
16	US 50, Greendale, Lawrenceburg, **W** Ⓖ Ameristop/dsl, Marathon/dsl, Shell/Circle K/Subway, 🍴 Buffalo's Cafe, Burger King, KFC, McDonald's, 🛏 Comfort Inn, Holiday Inn Express, Quality Inn, Riverside Inn, Ⓞ Buick/Chevrolet/GMC, Chrysler/Dodge/Jeep, Ford, TireDiscounters, Walgreens, casino
14mm	Kentucky/Indiana state line, Ohio River
11	Petersburg
8b a	KY 237, Hebron, **N** Ⓖ BP/DQ/dsl, Mobil/dsl, 🍴 Arby's, Beef'O'Brady's, China Wok, Edwardo's Pizza/Subs, El Marlachi, Jimmy John's, Penn Sta Subs, Vintage Deli, Wendy's, Ⓞ Remke's Foods, **S** Ⓖ Shell/Subway/dsl, 🍴 Bruster's, Burger King, Goldstar Chili, Waffle House
4a b	KY 212, KY 20, **N** Ⓖ ValAir Gas, 🛏 Comfort Suites, Country Inn&Suites, Hampton Inn, Marriott, **S** 🛏 DoubleTree, Ⓞ Ⓗ ♿
2	Mineola Pike, **N** Ⓖ Mobil/Rally's/Subway/dsl, 🛏 Holiday Inn, Quality Inn, **S** 🛏 Courtyard Inn, Residence Inn

LOUISIANA

⬆E INTERSTATE 10

Exit	Services
274mm	Louisiana/Mississippi state line, Pearl River
272mm	West Pearl River
270mm	**Welcome Ctr wb, full ♿ facilities, info, 📞, 🚻, litter barrels, petwalk, RV dump**
267b	I-12 W, to Baton Rouge
267a	I-59 N, to Meridian
266	US 190, Slidell, **N** Ⓖ RaceTrac/dsl, Shell/dsl, TA/dsl/rest./scales/24hr/@, Valero, 🍴 Arby's, Baskin-Robbins, Cane's Rest., Chesterfield Grill, Chick-fil-A, Copeland's Rest., Golden Dragon Chinese, KFC, Los Tres Amigos, McDonald's, Panda Express, Quiznos, Retro Grill, Shoney's, Sonic, Subway, Taco Bell, Wendy's, 🛏 Best Value Inn, Best Western, Deluxe Motel, Motel 6, Ⓞ Ⓗ, Curves, CVS Drug, Firestone/auto, Harley-Davidson, Hobby Lobby,
266	Continued Office Depot, O'Reilly Parts, PepBoys, Radio Shack, Rouses Mkt, U-Haul, Verizon, **S** Ⓖ Chevron/Subway/dsl, Murphy USA, RaceTrac/dsl, 🍴 Applebee's, Big Easy Diner, Cracker Barrel, McAlister's Deli, Outback Steaks, Ruby Tuesday, Sonic, Starbucks, TX Roadhouse, Waffle House, 🛏 Days Inn, La Quinta, Relax Inn, Value Inn, Ⓞ Ⓗ, AT&T, Home Depot, Lowe's, Walmart/Subway, repair/transmissions, casino, vet
265	US 190, Fremaux Ave
263	LA 433, Slidell, **N** Ⓖ Exxon, Shell/dsl, 🍴 China Buffet, Waffle House, 🛏 Hampton Inn, Super 8, Ⓞ Hyundai, repair, **S** Ⓖ Kangaroo/Subway/scales/dsl, Texaco/dsl, 🍴 McDonald's, Wendy's, 🛏 Holiday Inn, Ⓞ Buick/GMC, Chevrolet, Chrysler/Dodge/Jeep, Ford/Lincoln, Honda, Kia, Nissan, Pinecrest RV Park, Toyota/Scion, Slidell Factory Outlet/famous brands, KOA (1mi)

KY
LA

S L I D E L L

▲E INTERSTATE 10 CONT'D

Exit	Services
261	Oak Harbor Blvd, Eden Isles, N 🅖 Exxon/dsl, 🍴 Waffle House, 🛏 Sleep Inn, S 🅖 Shell/Subway/dsl, Ⓞ Bayou Country Store
255mm	Lake Pontchartrain
254	US 11, to Northshore, Irish Bayou, S 🅖 Texaco/dsl
251	Bayou Sauvage NWR, S swamp tours
248	Michoud Blvd
246b a	I-510 S, LA 47 N, S to Chalmette, N to Little Woods
245	Bullard Ave, N 🅖 Chevron, Shell, 🛏 Comfort Suites, Holiday Inn Express, Ⓞ Honda, S 🅖 Chevron, Shell, 🍴 Burger King, IHOP, KFC/Taco Bell, McDonald's, Papa John's, Subway, Super Cajun Seafood, 🛏 La Quinta, Motel 6, Ⓞ BigLots, Chrysler/Dodge/Jeep, Ford, Home Depot, Nissan, PepBoys, Rite Aid, Tire Kingdom, Toyota/Scion, Walgreens
244	Read Blvd, N 🅖 Shell, 🍴 McDonald's, S 🅖 EZ Stop/dsl, 🍴 Popeye's, Subway, Wendy's, 🛏 Best Value, Best Western, Days Inn, Ⓞ 🅷, Lowe's, Urgent Care
242	Crowder Blvd, N 🅖 Chevron S 🅖 Crowder Ctr, Exxon, 🍴 Subway, 🛏 Quality Inn, Ⓞ Walgreens
241	Morrison Rd, N 🅖 Big E-Z/dsl
240b a	US 90 E, Chef Hwy, Downman Rd, N 🅖 Shell/dsl, 🛏 Super 8, Ⓞ Chevrolet, U-Haul, USPO, S 🅖 Chevron/dsl, DZ, Ⓞ Delta Tires
239b a	Louisa St, Almonaster Blvd, N 🅖 Chevron/dsl, Fuel-Zone/dsl, 🍴 Burger King, Church's, McDonald's, Popeyes, Rally's, Subway, Taco Bell, Waffle House, Wendy's, 🛏 EconoLodge, Motel 6, Ⓞ $General, Family$, Goodyear/auto, Home Depot, Walgreens, Winn-Dixie, S 🅖 Day&Night/dsl
238b	I-610 W (from wb)
237	Elysian Fields Ave, N Ⓞ Lowe's
236c	St. Bernard Ave
236b	LA 39, N Claiborne Ave
236a	Esplanade Ave, downtown
235a	Orleans Ave, to Vieux Carre, French Qtr, S 🅖 Chevron, 🛏 Clarion, Marriott, Sheraton
235b	Poydras St, N 🅷, S to Superdome, downtown
234a	US 90A, Claiborne Ave, to Westbank, Superdome
232	US 61, Airline Hwy, Tulane Ave, N 🍴 Burger King, S on Carolton 🅖 Exxon, Shell, 🍴 KFC, McDonald's, Popeye's, Rallys, Ⓞ Family$, Pepboys, USPO, vet, to Xavier U
231b	Florida Blvd, WestEnd
231a	Metairie Rd
230	I-610 E (from eb), to Slidell
229	Bonnabel Blvd
228	Causeway Blvd, N 🅖 Exxon, Shell/dsl, 🍴 Burger King, Outback Steaks, PF Chang's, Red Lobster, TGIFriday's, 🛏 Best Western, Hampton Inn, Ramada, Ⓞ Dillard's, Macy's, Old Navy, Whole Foods Mkt, S 🅖 DZ, Exxon, 🍴 IHOP, 🛏 Courtyard, Days Inn, Extended Stay America, Holiday Inn, La Quinta, Residence Inn, Sheraton
226	Clearview Pkwy, Huey Long Br, N 🅖 Chevron/dsl, Exxon, 🍴 Cafe Dumonde, Chili's, Copeland's Cheesecake Bistro, Corky's BBQ, Don's Seafood Hut, Hooters, Jimmy John's, Popeye's, Quiznos, Semolina's, Starbucks, Taco Bell, Taco Tico, Webster's Rest., 🛏 Sleep Inn, Ⓞ Ford/Lincoln, Hancock Fabrics, Sears/auto, Target, Tire Kingdom, Walgreens, S 🅖 Chevron, Danny&Clyde, 🍴 Beijing Chinese, Burger King, Piccadilly, Shoney's, Smoothie

Exit	Services
226	Continued King, Subway, TCBY, 🛏 Sun Suites, Super 8, Ⓞ 🅷, AT&T, Buick/GMC, Firestone/auto
225	Veterans Blvd, N 🅖 Chevron, DZ, Shell, 🍴 Burger King, Cuco's Mexican, Denny's, McDonald's, Subway, 🛏 La Quinta, Ⓞ CVS Drug, Honda, Radio Shack, Rite Aid, Rouses Mkt, **Urgent Care**, S 🅖 DZ, Shell, 🍴 Casa Garcia, ChuckeCheese, Little Caesars, Louisiana Purchase Kitchen, New Orleans Burgers, O'Henry's, Popeye's, Subway, Tiffin Pancakes, Wendy's, 🛏 Evergreen Inn, Sheraton, Ⓞ Acura, Best Buy, BigLots, BMW, Chevrolet, $General, GNC, Home Depot, Jo-Ann Fabrics, Kia, K-Mart, Lexus, Nissan, Office Depot, PepBoys, Petsmart, TJ Maxx, Verizon, VW, Walgreens, Walmart, vet
224	Power Blvd (from wb)
223b a	LA 49, Williams Blvd, N 🅖 DZ/dsl, Exxon, Shell, 🍴 Cafe Dumonde, Cane's Chicken, Casa Tequila, Fisherman's Cove, IHOP, Papa's Pizza, Popeye's, Rally's, Sakura Asian, Subway, Taquiera Jalisco, Taco Bell, Wendy's, 🛏 Fairfield Inn, Ⓞ AutoZone, Dillards, $Tree, Family$, Ford, Macy's, Office Depot, PetCo, Rite Aid, Save-a-Lot Foods, Target, TrueValue, Walmart Mkt, S 🅖 Exxon/dsl, Shell, 🍴 American Pie Diner, Brick Oven, Dot's Diner, KFC/LJ Silver, McDonald's, Prime Time Steaks/Seafood, Sonic, Taco Tico, Subway, 🛏 📶 Inn, Comfort Suites, Contempra Inn, Country Inn&Suites, Crowne Plaza, DoubleTree, EconoLodge, La Quinta, Ⓞ CVS Drug, $General, Family$, Firestone/auto, Goodyear/auto, NAPA, Toyota/Scion, U-Haul, Winn-Dixie, USPO
221	Loyola Dr, N 🅖 Chevron, Circle K, Exxon/dsl, Shell/dsl, 🍴 Church's, McDonald's, Piccadilly, Popeye's, Rally's, Taco Bell, Ⓞ Advance Parts, Sam's Club/gas, S 🅖 Citgo/dsl, DZ, 🍴 Wendy's, 🛏 Sleep Inn, Ⓞ Family$, Super Foods, 📶, info
220	I-310 S, to Houma
214mm	Lake Pontchartrain
210	I-55N (from wb)
209	I-55 N, US 51, to Jackson, LaPlace, Hammond, N 🅖 Shell/Huddle House/casino/dsl, 🛏 Suburban Lodge, S 🅖 Chevron, Circle K/dsl, 🚛/Subway/dsl/24hr/scales, Shell/dsl, 🍴 Bully's Seafood, Burger King, McDonald's, Shoney's, Waffle House, Wendy's, 🛏 Best Western, Days Inn, Hampton Inn, Holiday Inn Express, Quality Inn
207mm	**weigh sta both lanes**
206	LA 3188 S, La Place, S 🅖 Shell/dsl, Ⓞ 🅷, Chrysler/Dodge/Jeep, Ford, Goodyear/auto
194	LA 641 S, to Gramercy, **4-6 mi** S 🅖 Chevron, Shell, Taylors/dsl, 🍴 Golden Grove Rest, McDonald's, Popeye's, Ⓞ 🅷, **11-15 mi** S plantations
187	US 61, N to Sorrento, S to Gramercy
182	LA 22, Sorrento, N 🅖 Shell/Popeye's/dsl, Texaco/dsl, S 🅖 Chevron/Subway/dsl/scales/24hr, SJ/dsl, 🍴 McDonald's, Subway, Waffle House, Ⓞ tourist info
179	LA 44, Gonzales, N 🅖 Exxon/Popingo's Cafe/dsl, **1 mi N** Ⓞ Buick/GMC, $General, Fred's Store, Walgreens
177	LA 30, Gonzales, N 🅖 Cracker Barrel/dsl, Shell, 🍴 Burger King, Jack-in-the-Box, McDonald's, Outback Steaks, Shoney's, Taco Bell, Waffle House, 🛏 Best Western, Budget Inn, Clarion, Highland Inn, Western Inn, Ⓞ 🅷, Home Depot, S 🅖 Chevron, RaceTrac/dsl, Shell/dsl, 🍴 Chili's, Cracker Barrel, Don's Seafood Hut, KFC, Popeye's, Sonic, Starbucks, Subway, Wendy's, 🛏 Hampton Inn, Holiday

🅿 = gas 🍴 = food 🏨 = lodging 🅾 = other ℞ = rest stop

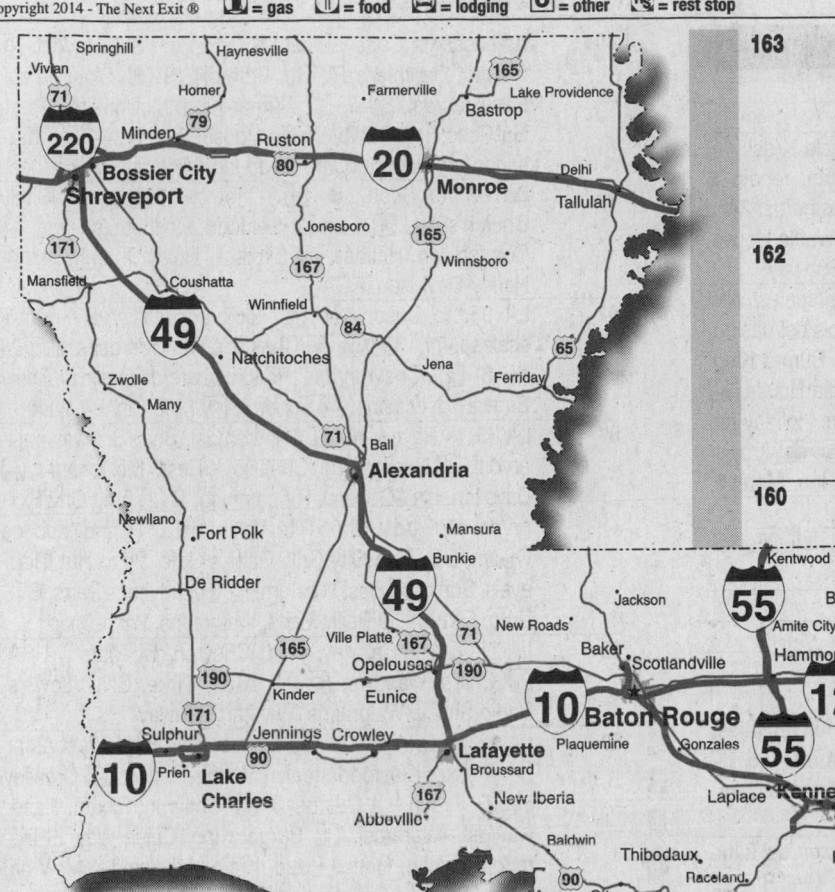

163 Continued
fice Depot, PetCo, Radio Shack Target, Verizon, **S** 🍴 Backyard Burger, Chili's, ChuckeCheese, Joe's Crabshack, TX Roadhouse, Zapata's Mexican, 🏨 Courtyard, Residence Inn, 🅾 BooksAMillion, Kohl's, Lowe's/Subway, Old Navy, Petsmart, Sam's Club/gas, Old Navy, TJ Maxx, Walmart/Subway

162 Bluebonnet Rd, **N** 🅿 Chevron/dsl, 🍴 Cadillac Cafe, Kabuki Japanese, 🏨 Quality Suites, 🅾 vet, **S** 🅿 Raceway, 🍴 BJ's Brewhouse, Bravo Italiano, Copeland's Cheesecake Bistro, J Alexander's, King Buffet, Logan's Roadhouse, Pluckers Wing Bar, Ralph&Kacoo's, Red Lobster, Sake Cafe, 🏨 Hyatt Place, 🅾 Best Buy, Dick's, Dillard's, JC Penney, Macy's, Sears/auto, Mall of LA, mall, World Mkt, 🏥

160 LA 3064, Essen Lane, **S** 🅿 Exxon, RaceTrac/dsl, Valero, 🍴 Burger King, Copeland's Bistro, Domino's, McDonald's, Piccadilly, Popeye's, Quiznos, Sakura Hibachi, Smoothie King, Subway, Taco Bell, Times Grill, Wasabi Grill, Wendy's, 🏨 Drury Inn, Fairfield Inn, Springhill Suites, 🅾 Albertson's, $General, Firestone, O'Reilly Parts, Rite Aid, Tire Kingdom, Walgreens, 🏥

159 I-12 E, to Hammond

158 College Dr, Baton Rouge, **N** 🅿 Valero, 🍴 Alabasha Café, Cane's, CiCi's, Coto Rest., Fox&Hound Grill, Hooters, Izzo's Grill, Jason's Deli, Mansurs Rest., Marble Slab Creamery, Melting Pot, On-the-Border, Ruby Tuesday, Subway, Sullivan's Rest., Waffle House, Wendy's, 🏨 Best Western, Chase Suites, Extended Stay America, Homewood Suites, Marriott, 🅾 🏥, Barnes&Noble, **S** 🅿 Chevron/24hr, Exxon, Shell/Circle K, 🍴 Casa Maria Mexican, Chick-fil-A, Chili's, Gino's Rest., Great Wall Chinese, IHOP, McDonald's, Ninfa's Mexican, Ruth's Chris Steaks, Sporting News Grill, Starbucks, Taco Bell, 🏨 Aspen Suites, Comfort Inn, Comfort Suites, Crowne Plaza, Embassy Suites, Hampton Inn, Holiday Inn, Holiday Inn Express, 🅾 Albertson's/SavOn, AutoZone, $Tree, Hobby Lobby, Office Depot, Radio Shack, Walgreens, Walmart/Subway

157b Acadian Thwy, **N** 🅿 Chevron, Shell/Circle K, 🍴 Mestizo's Grill, Rib's Rest., 🏨 La Quinta, Radisson, 🅾 🏥, **S** 🅿 Shell/Circle K, 🍴 Acme Oyster House, Coyote Blues Mexican, Outback Steaks, 🏨 Courtyard, 🅾 AT&T, CVS Drug, Tuesday Morning

157a Perkins Rd (from eb), same as 157b

156b Dalrymple Dr, **S** to LSU

156a Washington St

155c Louise St (from wb)

155b I-110 N, to Baton Rouge bus dist, 🅾

155a LA 30, Nicholson Dr, Baton Rouge, **N** Belle Hotel, **S** to LSU

🔽🔼 **INTERSTATE 10** CONT'D

Exit	Services
177	**Continued**
	Inn Express, Supreme Inn, TownePlace Suites, 🅾 Cabela's, Tanger/famous brands, Vesta RV Park
173	LA 73, to Geismar, Prairieville, **N** 🅿 Shell/dsl, **S** 🅿 Chevron/dsl, Conoco/dsl, Exxon/TCBY/dsl, Mobil/McDonald's/dsl, RaceTrac/dsl, 🍴 Burger King, Griffin Grill, Godfather's Pizza, Good Eats Cafe, Hot Wok, Las Palmas Mexican, Papa Murphy's, Pizza Hut, Popeye's, Smoothie King, Sonic, Subway, 🅾 Curves, Family$, Harvest Foods, Twin Lakes RV Park (1mi), Walgreens
166	LA 42, LA 427, Highland Rd, Perkins Rd, **N** 🅿 Chevron/Church's/dsl, Exxon/dsl, 🍴 Church's, Las Palmas Mexican, Popeye's, Sonic, Starbucks, Waffle House, 🅾 Goodyear/auto, Home Depot, funpark, **S** 🅿 Shell/BBQ, Texaco/dsl, 🍴 Subway
163	Siegen Lane, **N** 🅿 Chevron/dsl, RaceTrac/dsl, Shell/Circle K, 🍴 Arby's, Burger King, Cane's, Chee Burger, Chick-fil-A, China 1, CiCi's Pizza, Hooter's, IHOP, Jason's Deli, McAlister's, McDonald's, Olive Garden, Pancho's Mexican, Pizza Hut/Taco Bell, Quiznos, Ribs Chophouse, Smoothie King, Subway, Twin Peaks Rest., Waffle House, Whataburger, 🏨 Best Western, Days Inn, Hampton Inn, Holiday Inn Express, La Quinta, Microtel, Motel 6, Super 8, 🅾 Advance Parts, AT&T, BigLots, Cadillac, CarMax, $Tree, Firestone/auto, Harley-Davidson, Honda, Kia, Of

🅿 = gas   🍽 = food   🛏 = lodging   🅾 = other   🆁🆂 = rest stop   Copyright 2014 - The Next Exit ®

➤E INTERSTATE 10 CONT'D

Exit	Services
154mm	Mississippi River
153	LA 1, Port Allen, **N** 🅿 Chevron, Shell/Circle K/dsl, 🍽 Church's, 🅾 AutoZone, Family$, Kenworth, repair, **S** 🅿 Chevron, LA 1S Truck Plaza/Exxon/Casino/dsl/24hr, RaceTrac/dsl, 🍽 Quiznos, Smoothie King, Waffle House, 🛏 EconoLodge, 🅾 AT&T, $Tree, Walmart/Subway
151	LA 415, to US 190, **N** 🅿 Cash's Trk Plaza/dsl/scales/casino, Chevron, Exxon/dsl, Gold Mine/Domino's/dsl/casino, Nino's Trkstp/casino, Shell/Blimpie/dsl, 🍽 Burger King, KFC/Taco Bell, McDonald's, Popeye's, Waffle House, 🛏 Best Western, Comfort Suites, Hampton Inn, Holiday Inn Express, Quality Inn, West Inn, **S** 🅿 ♥Loves/Arby's/dsl/scales/24hr, Shell/dsl/24hr, 🛏 Audubon Inn, Motel 6, Super 8, 🅾 truck repair
139	LA 77, Grosse Tete, **N** 🅿 Shell/Subway/dsl, 🅾 Chevrolet, casino, **S** 🅿 Tiger/Conoco/dsl/rest./@
135	LA 3000, to Ramah
127	LA 975, to Whiskey Bay
126.5mm	Pilot Channel of Whiskey Bay
122mm	Atchafalaya River
121	**Butte La Rose, visitors ctr/🆁🆂, both lanes, full facilities, 🆁, litter barrels, vending, petwalk, tourist info, S** 🍽 Lazy Cajun Grill (2mi), 🅾 Frenchman's Wilderness Campground (.5mi)
115	LA 347, to Cecilia, Henderson, **N** 🅿 Exxon/dsl/24hr, Shamrock, Texaco/dsl, 🍽 Chicken on the Bayou, Landry's Seafood, 🛏 Holiday Inn Express, 🅾 casinos, **S** 🅿 Chevron/dsl, Exxon/Subway/dsl, Shell/McDonald's, Texaco/dsl, Valero, 🍽 Popeye's, Waffle House
109	LA 328, to Breaux Bridge, **N** 🅿 Shell/dsl, Texaco/grill/dsl/casino, 🛏 Microtel, 🅾 Poaches RV Park, **S** 🅿 Chevron/Popeye's/dsl, Exxon/Domino's/dsl, ♥Loves/Arby's/dsl/scales/24hr, 🍽 Burger King, City Buffet, Crazy Bout Cajun, McDonald's, Mulate's, Pizza Hut, Sonic, Taco Bell, Waffle House, Wendy's, Zapote Mexican, 🛏 Bayou Cabins B&B, Sona Inn, Super 8, 🅾 Chevrolet, $General, $Tree, Family$, Ford/Lincoln, O'Reilly Parts, Pioneer Camping, Walgreens, Walmart/Subway, Winn-Dixie, city park
108mm	**weigh sta both lanes**
104	Louisiana Ave, **S** 🍽 Chick-fil-A, Subway, Taco Bell, 🅾 AT&T, GNC, JC Penney, Office Depot, PetCo, Ross, Target
103b	I-49 N, to Opelousas
103a	US 167 S, to Lafayette, **US 167 S** 🅿 Chevron/dsl/24hr, Murphy USA/dsl, RaceTrac/dsl, Shell/dsl, Valero, 🍽 Checker's, KFC, McDonald's, Pizza Hut, Popeye's, Shoney's, Subway, Taco Bell, Waffle House, 🛏 Best Western, Comfort Inn, EconoLodge, Fairfield Inn, Holiday Inn, Howard Johnson, Jameson Inn, La Quinta, Quality Inn, Royal Inn, Super 8, TravelHost Inn, 🅾 🄷 Albertson's, CVS Drug, Home Depot, Super 1 Foods/gas, Walmart/Subway, transmissions
101	LA 182, to Lafayette, **N** 🅿 Chevron/McDonald's, TA/Country Pride/dsl/scales/24hr/@, Shell, Valero/Subway/dsl, 🍽 Burger King, Waffle House, Whataburger, 🛏 Red Roof Inn, **S** 🅿 Exxon, RaceTrac/dsl, Shell/dsl, Texaco, 🍽 Cracker Barrel, 🛏 Best Value Inn, Days Inn, Drury Inn, Hilton Garden (2mi), Peartree Inn, 🅾 🄷 $General, Family$, Kia/Suzuki, O'Reilly Parts
100	Ambassador Caffery Pkwy, **N** 🅿 Exxon/Subway/dsl, 🅾 Curves, Gauthier's RV Ctr, Peterbilt, **S** 🅿 Chevron/dsl, RaceTrac/dsl, Shell, 🍽 Burger King, McDonald's, Pizza Hut/Taco Bell, Sonic, Waffle House, Wendy's, 🛏 Ambassador Inn, Hampton Inn, Sleep Inn, Microtel, 🅾 🄷, tires
97	LA 93, to Scott, **S** 🅿 Chevron/McDonald's, Shell/Church's/dsl, 🍽 Fezzo's Seafood, Rochetto's Pizza, 🛏 Comfort Inn, Holiday Inn Express, Howard Johnson, 🅾 Harley-Davidson, KOA
92	LA 95, to Duson, **N** 🅿 Exxon/dsl/casino/RV dump/scales/24hr, ♥Loves/Chester's/Wendy's/dsl/scales/24hr, **S** 🅿 Chevron/dsl, Roadies/cafe/dsl/casino, Shell/Subway/dsl/casino, 🛏 Super 8, 🅾 Frog City RV Park
87	LA 35, to Rayne, **N** 🅿 Chevron/dsl, Shell/Subway/casino/dsl, 🍽 Burger King, Chef Roy's Rest., McDonald's, 🛏 Days Inn, 🅾 $General, RV camping, **S** 🅿 Frog City/Exxon/dsl, Mobil/dsl, Shop Rite, Valero/dsl, 🍽 Candyland Ice Cream, DQ, Frog City Grill, Gabe's Café, Pizza Hut, Popeye's, Sonic, 🛏 Best Western, 🅾 🄷, Advance Parts, CVS Drug, Family$, O'Reilly Parts, Walgreens, Winn-Dixie
82	LA 1111, to E Crowley, **S** 🅿 Chevron/dsl, Murphy USA, 🍽 Chili's, Wendy's, 🅾 🄷, AT&T, $Tree, GNC, Lowe's, Radio Shack, Walgreens, Walmart/Subway
80	LA 13, to Crowley, **N** 🅿 Conoco/Exit 80/dsl/rest./24hr, 🍽 Fezzo's Seafood/steaks, Waffle House, 🛏 Crowley Inn, Days Inn, La Quinta, **S** 🅿 Chevron, Exxon, Raceway/dsl, Valero/dsl, 🍽 Burger King, Cajun Way, El Dorado Mexican, Gatti's Pizza, KFC, McDonald's, Mr Wok, Pizza Hut, PJ's Grill, Popeye's, Sonic, Subway, Taco Bell, 🅾 AutoZone, Chrysler/Dodge/Jeep, $General, Family$, Ford, O'Reilly Parts, Radio Shack, Rite Aid, Verizon, Winn-Dixie
76	LA 91, to Iota, **S** 🅿 Petro/Shell/Subway/dsl/scales/24hr
72	Egan, **N** 🍽 Cajun Haven RV Park
65	LA 97, to Jennings, **S** 🅿 Shell/dsl/casino, 🛏 Best Value
64	LA 26, to Jennings, **N** 🍽 Los Tres Potrillos, 🛏 Boudreaux Inn, 🅾 RV Park, **S** 🅿 Exxon/dsl, EZ Mart, Murphy USA, Jennings Trvl Ctr/dsl/casino, Valero/dsl, 🍽 Burger King, Gatti's Pizza, General Wok Chinese, McDonald's, Pizza Hut, Popeye's, Shoney's, Sonic, Subway, Waffle House, Walker's Cajun Rest., Wendy's, 🛏 Days Inn, Hampton Inn, Red Carpet Inn, 🅾 🄷, AutoZone, Chrysler/Dodge/Jeep, $General, $Tree, Fred's Store, O'Reilly Parts, Radio Shack, Verizon, Walgreens, Walmart/Subway
59	LA 395, to Roanoke, **N** 🅿 Petos TrvlCtr/Chevron/dsl/scales/24hr
54	LA 99, Welsh, **S** 🅿 Circle R/Perky's Pizza, Cajun Lunch/dsl, Exxon/dsl/24hr, 🍽 Cajun Tales Seafood, DQ
48	LA 101, Lacassine, **S** 🅿 Exxon
44	US 165, to Alexandria, **N** 🅾 Quiet Oaks RV Park (10mi), **S** 🍽 Rabideaux's Cajun, 🅾 RV Park
43	LA 383, to Iowa, **N** 🅿 Exxon/Pit Grill/Quiznos/dsl/24hr, ♥Loves/Hardee's/dsl/scales/24hr, 🍽 Burger King, 🛏 Howard Johnson Express, La Quinta, 🅾 United RV Ctr, **S** 🅿 Citgo/dsl, Shell/McDonald's, Valero, 🍽 Fausto's Rest., Subway, 🅾 $General, I-10 Outlet/famous brands, Mkt Basket Foods, RV park
36	LA 397, to Creole, Cameron, **N** Jean Lafitte RV Park (2mi), I-10 RV Camping, Jellystone Camping, **S** 🅿 Cash Magic/grill/dsl/RV Dump, Chevron/dsl, 🛏 Red Roof Inn, 🅾 casino, RV Camping
34	I-210 W, to Lake Charles

CROWLEY

JENNINGS

LAFAYETTE

LA

INTERSTATE 10 CONT'D

LAKE CHARLES

Exit	Services
33	US 171 N, N [gas] Citgo, Conoco/dsl, Exxon/dsl, Murphy USA/dsl, Shell, Tobacco Place, Valero, [food] Burger King, Church's, Subway, Taco Bell, [lodging] Baymont Inn, Best Value, Comfort Suites, La Quinta, Richmond Suites, [other] AutoZone, $General, Family$, O'Reilly Parts, Walgreens, Walmart/McDonalds, to Sam Houston Jones SP, S [lodging] Holiday Inn Express, Motel 6, Treasure Inn
32	Opelousas St, N [gas] Exxon, S [lodging] Holiday Inn Express, Motel 6, Treasure Inn
31b	US 90 E, Shattuck St, to LA 14, N [gas] Shell/cafe/dsl/casino
31a	US 90 bus, Enterprise Blvd, S [food] Popeye's
30b	downtown
30a	LA 385, N Lakeshore Dr, Ryan St, N [gas] Exxon, [food] Steamboat Bill's Rest., Waffle House, [lodging] Days Inn, Oasis Inn, S [gas] Citgo, [food] Wendy's, [lodging] Best Suites
29	LA 385 (from eb), same as 30a
28mm	Calcasieu Bayou, Lake Charles
27	LA 378, to Westlake, N [gas] Chevron/dsl, Conoco/dsl, Shell/dsl, [food] Burger King, McDonald's, Popeye's, Sonic, Subway, [other] Bumper Parts, $General, O'Reilly Parts, to Sam Houston Jones SP, S [lodging] Inn at the Isle, [other] Riverboat Casinos
26	US 90 W, Southern Rd, Columbia, N [gas] Circle K/gas
25	I-210 E, to Lake Charles
23	LA 108, to Sulphur, N [gas] Circle K, Citgo, Exxon, Murphy USA, [food] Burger King, Cane's, Chili's, China Wok, McDonald's, Popeye's, Subway, Taco Bell, Wendy's, [lodging] Quality Inn, [other] $General, $Tree, Lowe's, Radio Shack, Walgreens, Walmart, S [gas] Cash Magic/dsl, Chevron/Jack-in-the-Box/dsl, Sulfur Trkstp/Citgo/dsl, [food] Cracker Barrel, Waffle House, [lodging] Best Western, Days Inn, Comfort Suites, Crossland Suites, Holiday Inn Express, Super 8, [other] casino, tires
21	LA 3077, Arizona St, N [gas] Conoco, Shell, [food] Boiling Point Cajun, China Taste, Papa John's, [other] AT&T, CVS Drug, $General, Ford, GNC, Kroger/gas, NAPA, Walgreens, vet, S [gas] Chevron/dsl, Valero/dsl/casino, [other] [H], Hidden Ponds RV Park
20	LA 27, to Sulphur, N [gas] Bayou, Chevron, Circle K, Conoco, Valero, [food] Burger King, Casa Ole Mexican, Cajun Charlie's, Checker's, Gatti's Pizza, Hollier's Cajun, Johnny T's Grill, McDonald's, Mr Bills Steaks, Pitt Grill Cajun, Popeye's, Subway, Taco Bell, Wendy's, [lodging] EconoLodge, Hampton Inn, Sulphur Inn, [other] Brookshire Bros/gas, Family$, Firestone/auto, Goodyear/auto, Jiffy Lube, S [gas] Conoco/dsl, Shell/dsl, [food] Navroskey's Burgers, Pizza Hut, Sonic, Waffle House, [lodging] Baymont Inn, Candlewood Suites, Fairfield Inn, Holiday Inn, La Quinta, Microtel, Wingate Inn, [other] [H], Stine, casino, to Creole Nature Trail
8	LA 108, Vinton, N [gas] Chevron/dsl, Exxon/dsl, [food] Cajun Cowboy's Rest., [other] V RV Park
7	LA 3063, Vinton, N [gas] Exxon/dsl, [food] Burger King, Sonic, Subway, [other] $General, casino, S [gas] Love's/Arby's/dsl/scales/24hr
4	US 90, LA 109, Toomey, N [gas] Cash Magic/dsl/grill/casino, Chevron/dsl/casino, [other] truck repair, S [gas] Cash Magic, Exxon/dsl, Shell/dsl/rest, [food] Subway, [other] RV Park, casinos
2.5mm	**weigh sta both lanes**

SULPHUR

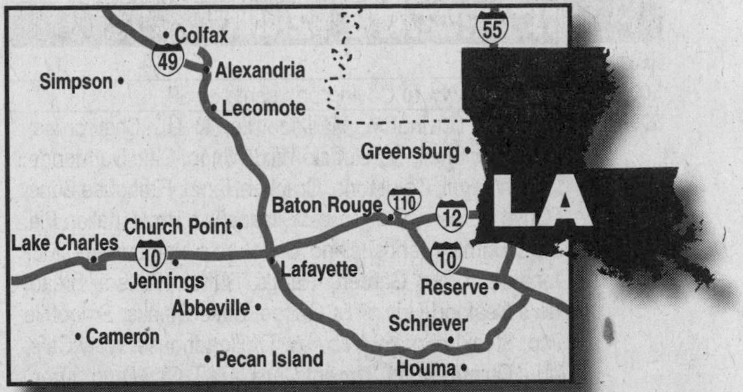
Colfax
55
49
Alexandria
Simpson
Lecomote
Greensburg
LA
Baton Rouge
110
12
Church Point
Lake Charles
10
Jennings
Lafayette
10
Reserve
Abbeville
Cameron
Schriever
Pecan Island
Houma

Exit	Services
1.5mm	**Welcome Ctr eb, full [handicapped] facilities, [phone], [picnic], litter barrels, petwalk**
1	(from wb), Sabine River Turnaround
0mm	Louisiana/Texas state line, Sabine River

INTERSTATE 12

COVINGTON

Exit	Services
85c	I-10 E, to Biloxi. **I-12 begins/ends on I-10, exit 267.**
85b	I-59 N, to Hattiesburg
85a	I-10 W, to New Orleans
83	US 11, to Slidell, N [gas] Chevron/dsl, Exxon/dsl, Valero/dsl, [food] Burger King, McDonald's, Sonic, Waffle House, [other] $General, S [gas] Shell/dsl, [other] [H]
80	Airport Dr, North Shore Blvd, N [gas] Kangaroo/Krystal/dsl, [food] IHOP, PJ's Coffee, Quiznos, Smoothie King, Sonic, [lodging] Comfort Inn, [other] AT&T, Petsmart, Ross, Target, S [gas] Chevron, Shell/dsl, [food] Burger King, Chili's, ChuckECheese's, McDonald's, Olive Garden, Pizza Hut/Taco Bell, Starbucks, Subway, Wendy's, Vera's Seafood, Zea Grill, [lodging] Candlewood Suites, Homewood Suites, La Quinta, [other] Best Buy, Dillard's, $Tree, Goodyear/auto, Home Depot, JC Penney, Marshalls, Office Depot, Sam's Club/gas, Sears/auto, Walgreens, Walmart, mall
74	LA 434, to Lacombe, N [gas] Chevron/Subway/dsl, [other] [H], Steve's RV Ctr, S Big Branch Marsh NWR
68	LA 1088, to Mandeville,
65	LA 59, to Mandeville, N [gas] Chevron/dsl, Danny&Clyde's/cafe, Shell, [food] Popeye's, Sonic, Subway, Waffle House, [lodging] Comfort Suites, [other] tourist info, S [gas] Kangaroo/Arby's/dsl, Texaco/Domino's/dsl, [food] Liu's Wok, McDonald's, PJ's Coffee, Quiznos, Wow Cafe, [other] Winn-Dixie, to Fontainebleau SP, camping, vet
63b a	US 190, Covington, Mandeville, N [gas] Chevron, Exxon, RaceTrac, Shell/Circle K, [food] Acme Oyster House, Albasha Greek, Applebee's, Baskin-Robbins, Burger King, Cane's, Chick-fil-A, CiCi's Pizza, Copeland's Grill, Don's Seafood, 4 Seasons Chinese, Garcias Mexican, HoneyBaked Ham, IHOP, Isabella's Pizza, Lee's Hamburgers, Mellow Mushroom Cafe, Mi Casa Mexican, Osaka Japanese, Outback Steaks, Picadilly, Rolly Polly Sandwiches, Sonic, Subway, Thai Chili, Waffle House, Wendy's, [lodging] Best Western, Clarion, Comfort Inn, Country Inn&Suites, Courtyard, Hampton Inn, Hilton Garden, Homewood Suites, Residence Inn, Staybridge Suites, Super 8, [other] Ace Hardware, AT&T, AutoZone, Books-A-Million, Chevrolet, Chrysler/Dodge/Jeep, CVS Drug, Firestone/auto, GNC, Home Depot, Honda, Hyundai, Lincoln, Lowe's, Nissan, Office Depot, Petsmart, Rouses Mkt, Subaru, Toyota, Verizon, Walmart, S [other] [H], st police, to New Orleans via **toll** causeway

⬦E INTERSTATE 12 CONT'D

Exit	Services
60	Pinnacle Pkwy, to Covington same as 59
59	LA 21, to Covington, Madisonville, **N** 🅿 Chevron/dsl, Kangaroo, Shell, 🍴 Buffalo Wild Wings, Cafe Du Monde, Carreta's Grill, Coldstone, Cracker Barrel, Firehouse Subs, 5 Guys Burgers, Golden Wok, Isabella's Pizza, Italian Pie, Izzo's Burrito, Jerk's Island Grill, Lee's Hamburgers, McDonald's, Olive Garden, Panda Buffet, Panera Bread, Pek's Seafood Grill, PJ's Coffee, Sake Steaks, Smoothie King, Steak'n Shake, Subway, TX Roadhouse, Wow Cafe, 🏨 La Quinta, ◻ 🅷 Urgent Care, AT&T, CVS Drug, $Tree, Hobby Lobby, Kohl's, Walgreens, Winn-Dixie, **S** 🅿 Texaco/Domino's, 🍴 Chick-fil-A, ChuckECheese's, Longhorn Steaks, Quiznos, Taco Bell, Wendy's, 🏨 Hampton Inn, Holiday Inn Express, ◻ AT&T, Belk, Best Buy, GNC, JC Penney, Marshall's, Michael's, Ross, Sam's Club/gas, Target, World Mkt, Fairview Riverside SP
57	LA 1077, to Goodbee, Madisonville, **S** 🅿 QuickWay/PoBoys/dsl, 🍴 Best Wok, Pizza Hut, PJ's Coffee, Subway, ◻ Family RV Park, to Fairview Riverside SP
47	LA 445, to Robert, **1-3 mi N** ◻ Jellystone Camping, to Global Wildlife Ctr
42	LA 3158, to ✈, **N** 🅿 Chevron/Quiznos/dsl/24hr, Texaco/dsl, 🍴 McDonald's, 🏨 Friendly Inn, **S** 🅿 Shell/Chester's/dsl, ◻ 🅷, Berryland RV Ctr
40	US 51, to Hammond, **N** 🅿 RaceTrac/dsl, Shell/Circle K, 🍴 Burger King, Cane's, China Garden, Church's, Coldstone, Don's Seafood, IHOP, Jimmy John's, McDonald's, Nagoya Rest, Olive Garden, Pizza Hut, Quiznos, Ryan's, Santa Fe Steaks, Smoothie King, Sonic, Subway, Taco Bell, Wendy's, 🏨 Best Western, Holiday Inn, Motel 6, Quality Inn, Supreme Inn, ◻ AT&T, Best Buy, Books-A-Million, Dillard's, Harley-Davidson, JC Penney, Rite Aid, Sears/auto, Target, TJ Maxx, U-Haul, Walgreens, Verizon, mall, **S** 🅿 Petro/Mobil/Subway/dsl/scales/24hr/@, ⬜/Arby's/dsl/scales/24hr, Shell/dsl, 🍴 Waffle House, 🏨 Colonial Inn, Days Inn, La Quinta, ◻ 🅷, Blue Beacon, $General, SpeedCo
38b a	I-55, N to Jackson, S to New Orleans
37mm	**weigh sta both lanes**
35	Pumpkin Ctr, Baptist, **N** 🅿 Exxon/dsl, Texaco, ◻ Dixie Camping World RV Service/Supplies, $General, Punkin RV Park (2mi), **S** 🅿 Chevron/Bayou Boyz/dsl
32	LA 43, to Albany, **N** 🅿 Big River/dsl, Chevron/Subway/dsl, Exxon/dsl, **S** 🅿 Potluck/dsl, ◻ to Tickfaw SP (11mi), tourist info
29	LA 441, to Holden, **N** 🅿 1Stop/dsl, ◻ Berryland Campers
22	LA 63, to Frost, Livingston, **N** 🅿 Chevron/dsl, 🍴 Hi-Ho BBQ, Subway, Wayne's BBQ, ◻ Carters Foods, Family$, Thrift Town Drug, **S** ◻ Lakeside RV Park (1mi)
19	to Satsuma, Colyell, **N** 🅿 Exxon/dsl
15	LA 447, to Walker, **N** 🅿 Murphy Express/dsl, Shell/Subway/dsl, Texaco/dsl, 🍴 Burger King, Domino's, Jack-in-the-Box, McDonald's, Papa John's, Papa Murphy's, Pizza Hut, Popeye's, Quiznos, Sherwood PoBoy's, Sonic, Taco Bell, Waffle House, Wendy's, 🏨 La Quinta, ◻ AutoZone, $General, $Tree, NAPA, O'Reilly Parts, Verizon, Walgreens, Walmart/Subway, Winn-Dixie, vet, **S** 🅿 Chevron/dsl
12	LA 1036, Juban Rd, **2 mi N** 🅿 Valero/dsl

10	LA 3002, to Denham Springs, **N** 🅿 Chevron, Circle K, RaceTrac/dsl, Shell/Circle K/dsl, 🍴 Arby's, Baskin-Robbins, Burger King, Cactus Café, Cane's, Chili's, Domino's, Don's Seafood, Gatti's Pizza, IHOP, McDonald's, Papa John's, Papi's Fajita, Pizza Hut, Popeye's, Ron's Seafood, Ryan's, Sonic, Starbucks, Subway, Taco Bell, Waffle House, Wendy's, 🏨 Best Western, Hampton Inn, Quality Inn, Western Inn, ◻ **Urgent Care**, Advance Parts, Albertsons, AT&T, AutoZone, CVS Drug, $General, $Tree, Home Depot, Meineke, Office Depot, O'Reilly Parts, PetCo, Radio Shack, Rite Aid, Tire Kingdom, Verizon, Walgreens, Walmart, **S** 🅿 ⬜/Subway/dsl/scales/24hr, Shell, 🍴 Backyard Burger, Hooters, Islamorada Fish Co, Longhorn Steaks, Piccadilly, VooDoo BBQ, 🏨 Days Inn, Highland Inn, ◻ Bass Pro Shops, Chrysler/Dodge/Jeep, Ford, KOA, Sam's Club/gas, Walgreens
8.5mm	Amite River
7	O'Neal Lane, **N** 🅿 Mobil, 🏨 La Quinta, Quality Inn, ◻ Hobby Lobby, Toyota/Scion, **S** 🅿 RaceTrac/dsl, Shell, Texaco/Subway/dsl, 🍴 Backyard Burger, China King, Las Palmas Mexican, Little Caesars, LoneStar Steaks, McDonald's, Pizza Hut/Taco Bell, Popeye's, Sonic, Waffle House, Wendy's, ◻ 🅷, AutoZone, $Tree, O'Reilly Parts, Radio Shack, Walgreens, Walmart/Subway
6	Millerville Rd, **N** 🅿 Chevron/dsl, 🍴 Chick-fil-A, Chili's, ◻ Best Buy, Lowe's, Office Depot, Petsmart, Super Target, **S** 🅿 Texaco/dsl, 🍴 Subway, Tiger Bait Grill, ◻ Ace Hardware
4	Sherwood Forest Blvd, **N** 🅿 Exxon, Shell/Circle K/dsl, 🍴 Burger King, ChuckECheese, Egg Roll King, Jack-in-the-Box, Kung Fu Buffet, McDonald's, Popeye's, Sonic, Subway, Taco Bell, Waffle House, 🏨 Crossland Suites, Red Roof Inn, Super 8, Value Place, ◻ Fred's, Goodyear/auto, Rite Aid, **S** 🅿 RaceTrac/dsl, Shell, 🍴 Baskin-Robbins, Cane's, Dunkin Donuts, Nagoya, Picadilly, Podnuh's BBQ, Sherwood PoBoys, 🏨 Calloway Inn, ◻ AT&T, auto care
2b	US 61 N, **N** 🅿 B-Quik/dsl, Chevron/dsl, Rende's/dsl, 🍴 Applebee's, Chinese Inn, Cracker Barrel, Little Caesars, McDonald's, Panda Buffet, Pizza Hut/Taco Bell, Subway, 🏨 Holiday Inn, Knights Inn, Magnuson Hotel, Microtel, Motel 6, Ramada Inn, Sleep Inn, ◻ Albertsons/gas, Dodge, $Tree, Marshall's, Michael's, Nissan, PepBoys, SteinMart, Toyota/Scion, Walgreens, Walmart Mkt, repair/transmissions
2a	US 61 S, **S** 🅿 Chevron, Circle K, Exxon/Circle K/dsl, Ride USA, 🍴 Burger King, China 1, Isabella's Pizza, McDonald's, Subway, Waffle House, 🏨 Deluxe Inn, ◻ Home Depot, Hyundai, Volvo
1b	LA 1068, to LA 73, Essen Lane, **N** 🅿 Shell/Circle K/dsl, 🍴 Cane's, McDonald's, VooDoo BBQ, ◻ 🅷, Family$, Hancock Fabrics, Hi-Nabor Foods, Radio Shack, vet
1a	I-10 (from wb). **I-12 begins/ends on I-10, exit 159 in Baton Rouge**

⬦E INTERSTATE 20

Exit	Services
189mm	Louisiana/Mississippi state line, Mississippi River
187mm	**weigh sta both lanes**
186	US 80, Delta, **S** 🅿 Chevron/Subway/dsl/24hr
184mm	🆁🆂 wb, full 🏨 facilities, 🄲, 🏨, litter barrels, petwalk, RV dump
182	LA 602, Mound
173	LA 602, Richmond

Side margins: HAMMOND   BATON ROUGE   LA

↑E INTERSTATE 20 CONT'D

Exit	Services
171	US 65, Tallulah, N 🅿 Chevron/Subway/dsl, Kangaroo/dsl, 🍴 McDonald's, Wendy's, 🏨 Days Inn, Super 8, ⓞ H, S 🅿 Exxon/dsl/scales, ♥Loves/Arby's/dsl/scales/24hr, TA/Country Pride/dsl/scales/24hr/@, Texaco, 🍴 Red Top Grill
164mm	Tensas River
157	LA 577, Waverly, N 🅿 Tiger Trkstp/rest./dsl/24hr, to Tensas River NWR, S Chevron/Hunt Bros Pizza/dsl/24hr, Shell/rest./dsl/24hr, ⓞ Casino
155mm	Bayou Macon
153	LA 17, Delhi, N 🅿 Chevron/Subway/dsl, Texaco/dsl, 🍴 Burger King, China Garden, Pizza Hut, Sonic, ⓞ H Brookshire's Foods, $General, Family$, Fred's, Verizon, USPO, S 🅿 Valero/dsl, 🏨 Best Western, Executive Inn
148	LA 609, Dunn
145	LA 183, rd 202, Holly Ridge
141	LA 583, Bee Bayou Rd
138	US 425, Rayville, N 🅿 Bud's, ⊞⊞⊞/Wendy's/dsl/scales/24hr, 🍴 Fox's Pizza, McDonald's, Sonic, 🏨 Days Inn, ⓞ H, AT&T, AutoZone, Brookshire's Foods, Buick/Chevrolet, $General, Family$, Verizon, Walmart, S 🅿 Chevron/Subway/dsl/24hr, Exxon/Circle K/Quiznos/dsl, RaceWay/dsl, 🍴 Big John's Rest., Popeye's, Waffle House, 🏨 Super 8
135mm	Boeuf River
132	LA 133, Start, N 🅿 Exxon/dsl
128mm	Lafourche Bayou
124	LA 594, Millhaven, N 🅿 EZ Mart/dsl, ⓞ st police, to Sage Wildlife Area
120	Garrett Rd, Pecanland Mall Dr, N 🅿 Chevron/dsl, 🍴 Applebee's, ChuckECheese, Copeland's Rest., Eastern Empire Buffet, IHOP, Longhorn Steaks, McAlister's, O'Charleys, Olive Garden, Red Lobster, Ronin Habachi, Sonic, 🏨 Courtyard, Residence Inn, TownePlace Suites, ⓞ AT&T, Belk, Best Buy, Dick's, Dillard's, $Tree, Firestone/auto, Home Depot, JC Penney, Kohl's, Michael's, Old Navy, PetCo, Petsmart, Ross, Sears/auto, Target, TJ Maxx, mall, S 🅿 Kangaroo/dsl, 🏨 Best Western, Days Inn, ⓞ Freightliner, Harley-Davidson, Lowe's, Pecanland RV Park, Sam's Club/gas, Ouachita RV Park
118b a	US 165, N 🅿 Valero/dsl, 🏨 Clarion, La Quinta, Stratford House Inn, ⓞ Hyundai, Kia, Nissan, to NE LA U, S 🅿 Chevron, Conoco/dsl, Exxon, Shell/Circle K, 🍴 Burger King, Capt D's, Church's, KFC, McDonald's, Popeye's, Sonic, Subway, Taco Bell, Wendy's, 🏨 Comfort Suites, Hampton Inn, Motel 6, Super 8
117b	LA 594, Texas Ave, N 🅿 Now Save/deli/dsl
117a	Hall St, Monroe, N H, Civic Ctr
116b	US 165 bus, LA 15, Jackson St, N H
116a	5th St, Monroe
115	LA 34, Mill St, N 🅿 Chevron, S ⓞ Clay's RV Service
114	LA 617, Thomas Rd, N 🅿 Murphy USA, RaceWay/dsl, 🍴 Burger King, Cane's, Capt D's, Cheddar's, Chick-fil-A, El Chico, El Chile Verde, 5 Guys Burgers, Grandy's, IHOP, KFC, McAlister's Deli, McDonald's, Papa John's, Papa Murphy's, Popeye's, Subway, Taco Bell, Waffle House, Wendy's, 🏨 Best Value Inn, Super 8, Wingate Inn, ⓞ H, AT&T, BigLots, Hobby Lobby, Office Depot, Rite Aid, Walgreens, Walmart/McDonald's, S 🅿 Chevron, Exxon/Circle K/Subway/dsl, 🍴 Buffalo Wild Wings, Chili's, Cracker

Exit	Services
114	Continued Barrel, El Sombrero, Genghis Grill, Hooters, Logan's Roadhouse, LoneStar Steaks, Outback Steaks, Peking Chinese, Pizza Hut, Ronin Hibachi, Sonic, Waffle House, 🏨 Best Western, Comfort Inn, Motel 6, Quality Inn, Red Roof Inn, ⓞ Firestone, Radio Shack
113	Downing Pines Rd, S 🏨 Hampton Inn, Hilton Garden, Holiday Inn Express, ⓞ Chrysler/Dodge/Jeep
112	Well Rd, N 🅿 Conoco, Shell/Circle K/dsl, Texaco/dsl, 🍴 Burger King, Domino's, McDonald's, Sonic, Subway, Taco Bell, Waffle House, Zaxby's, ⓞ Advance Parts, Walgreens, vet, S 🅿 ⊞⊞⊞/Subway/Wendy's/dsl/scales/24hr, ⓞ Pavilion RV Park
108	LA 546, to US 80, Cheniere, N 🅿 Shell/dsl
107	Camp Rd, rd 25, Cheniere
103	US 80, Calhoun, N 🅿 Chevron, Shell/rest/dsl/24hr, 🍴 Johnny's Pizza (1mi), 🏨 Avant Motel
101	LA 151, to Calhoun, S 🅿 Chevron/Huddle House/Subway/dsl, Exxon, 🍴 Sonic
97mm	🅿 wb, full 🚻 facilities, 🚰, 🅿, litter barrels, petwalk, RV dump
95mm	🅿 eb, full 🚻 facilities, 🚰, 🅿, litter barrels, petwalk, RV dump
93	LA 145, Choudrant, S 🅿 American, ⓞ Jimmy Davis SP, camping
86	LA 33, Ruston, N 🅿 Murphy USA, RaceWay/dsl, Shell/Circle K/Quiznos/dsl, Texaco/dsl, 🍴 Cane's Chicken, Chili's, Hot Rod BBQ, Huddle House, Log Cabin Grill, Logan's Roadhouse, Portico Grill, Ryan's, Sonic, Taco Bell, Whataburger, Z Buffet, 🏨 Comfort Inn, Days Inn, ⓞ AT&T, Buick/GMC, Cadillac/Chevrolet, Chrysler/Dodge/Jeep, $Tree, Ford/Lincoln, Fred's, Lowe's, Toyota, Walmart/Subway, vet, S 🅿 Spirit/dsl, 🏨 Fairfield Inn, Holiday Inn Express
85	US 167, Ruston, N 🅿 Chevron/Subway, Exxon, Shell/Circle K, 🍴 Applebee's, Burger King, Capt D's, Little Caesars, McDonald's, Peking Chinese, Wendy's, 🏨 Budget Lodge, Hampton Inn, Relax Inn, ⓞ $General, Office Depot, Radio Shack, Super 1 Foods, TrueValue, Walgreens, S 🅿 Texaco, Valero/dsl, 🍴 Pizza Hut, 🏨 Best Value Inn, Sleep Inn, ⓞ H, Advance Parts
84	LA 544, Ruston, N 🅿 Mobil/dsl, S 🅿 Chevron/dsl, Exxon, 🍴 Domino's, Johnny's Pizza, Pizza Inn, Starbucks, Subway, Waffle House, 🏨 Super 8
81	LA 149, Grambling, S 🅿 Chevron/Church's/dsl, Exxon, ⓞ to Grambling St U
78	LA 563, Industry, S 🅿 Texaco/dsl
77	LA 507, Simsboro
69	LA 151, Arcadia, N 🅿 Mobil/Burger King/dsl, 🍴 La Fo

LA

= gas   = food   = lodging   = other   = rest stop   Copyright 2014 - The Next Exit ®

⬆E INTERSTATE 20 CONT'D

Exit	Services
69	Continued
	gata Mexican, **S** Exxon/dsl, Gulf/dsl, Shell/Church's/dsl, McDonald's, Sonic, Subway, Days Inn, H Brookshire Foods, $General, Factory Stores/famous brands, Fred's, tires/repair
67	LA 9, Arcadia, **N** to Lake Claiborne SP, **S** Shell/dsl
61	LA 154, Gibsland, **N** to Lake Claibourne SP
55	US 80, Ada, Taylor
52	LA 532, to US 80, Dubberly, **N** Texaco/CJ's Diner/dsl
49	LA 531, Minden, **N** ♥Loves/Arby's/dsl/scales/24hr, Minden TrkStp/Shell/dsl/rest./24hr, Murphy USA, Quick-Draw/Subway/dsl, KFC (3mi), Pizza Hut (3mi), Taco Bell (3mi), Walmart (3mi), **S** truck/tire repair
47	US 371 S, LA 159 N, Minden, **N** Chevron/dsl, Exxon/dsl, Valero/dsl, Beanie&Bubba's Grill, Best Western, Exacta Inn/rest., Holiday Inn Express, Southern Inn, H, Ford, **S** to Lake Bistineau SP, camping
44	US 371 N, Cotton Valley, **N** Exxon/Huddle House/dsl, Crawfish Hole #2, Nicky's Cantina, Sonic, Minden Motel (2mi), Cinnamon Creek RV/camping, Family$, Lakeside RV Camping
38	Goodwill Rd, Ammo Plant, **S** Gulf/Rainbow Diner/dsl/24hr, truck/trailer repair
33	LA 157, Fillmore, **N** Texaco, **S** Exxon, Pilot, Arby's/dsl/scales/24hr, Waffle House, $General, Family$, Fred's, USPO, Lake Bistineau SP
26	I-220, Shreveport, **1 mi N** Raceway, Casino
23	Industrial Dr, **N** Exxon, Shell/Circle K, Valero/dsl, McDonald's, Sue's Country Kitchen, Popeye's, Taco Bell, Wendy's Ramada Inn, O'Reilly Parts, st police, **S** Mobil/dsl, EconoLodge, Southern RV Ctr
22	Airline Dr, **N** Citgo/dsl, Mobil/McDonald's/dsl, Shell/Circle K, Valero/dsl, Applebee's, Arby's, Burger King, Chili's, China Flag, ChuckeCheese, DQ, 5 Guys Burgers, Gatti's Pizza, IHOP, Johnny's Pizza, Logan's Roadhouse, Notini's Italian, Popeye's, Red Lobster, Shogun Steaks, Sonic, Starbucks, Subway, Taco Bell, Waffle House, Country Hearth Inn, Crossland Suites, Rodeway Inn, Super 8, Albertsons/gas, BigLots, Books-A-Million, CVS Drug, Dillard's, Firestone/auto, JC Penney, K-Mart, Meineke, Michael's, Office Depot, PepBoys, Sears/auto, Tuesday Morning, Verizon, Walgreens, mall, **S** Exxon/dsl, Capt John's, Church's, Outback Steaks, Quizno's, Microtel, Quality Inn, Red Carpet Inn, H, AutoZone, Fred's Store, Super1 Foods, to Barksdale AFB
21	LA 72, to US 71 S, Old Minden Rd, **N** Shell/Circle K, Valero, Chimi V's, Johnny's Pizza, McDonald's, Podnah's BBQ, Poncho's Mexican, Posado's Mexican, Ralph&Kacoo's, Subway, TX Roadhouse, Whataburger, Best Value Inn, Hampton Inn, Hilton Garden, Homewood Suites, La Quinta, MainStay Suites, TownePlace Suites, Audi/Mazda/Porsche, Bayou RV Ctr, $General, O'Reilly Parts, VW, **S** RaceWay, Waffle House, Wendy's, Days Inn, Motel 6, ValuePlace Inn, visitor info
20c	to US 71 S, to Barksdale Blvd
20b	LA 3, Benton Rd, same as 21
20a	Hamilton Rd, Isle of Capri Blvd, **N** Circle K, Wingate Inn, **S** Exxon, Bossier Inn, casino
19b	Traffic St, Shreveport, downtown, **N** lodging Courtyard, Bass Pro Shop, Chevrolet, casino, **S** casino

Exit	Services
19a	US 71 N, LA 1 N, Spring St, Shreveport, **N** Don's Seafood, Best Western, Hilton, Holiday Inn
18b-d	Fairfield Ave (from wb), downtown Shreveport, **S**
18a	Line Ave, Common St (from eb), downtown, **S** 1st Stop,
17b	I-49 S, to Alexandria
17a	Lakeshore Dr, Linwood Ave
16b	US 79/80, Greenwood Rd, **N** H, **S** Citgo/dsl, El Chico, Travelodge
16a	US 171, Hearne Ave, **N** Clark/dsl, Subway, H, **S** Raceway/dsl, KFC, Cajun Inn
14	Jewella Ave, Shreveport, **N** Phillips 66/dsl, Texaco/dsl, Valero, Burger King, Church's, McDonald's, Popeye's, Subway, Sonic, Whataburger, AutoZone, County Mkt Foods, Family$, O'Reilly Parts, Rite Aid, Super 1 Foods, Walgreens
13	Monkhouse Dr, Shreveport, **N** Bro's Cafe, Days Inn, Ramada, Residence Inn, Super 8, Value Inn, **S** Chevron/dsl, Citgo/dsl, Exxon/Subway/dsl, Monk House Seafood, Waffle House, Baymont Inn, Hampton Inn, Holiday Inn Express, Merryton Inn, Pelican Inn, Quality Inn, Regency Inn, to
11	I-220 E, LA 3132 E, to I-49 S
10	Pines Rd, **N** Gulf/dsl, DQ, Pizza Hut, Popeye's, Subway, **S** Circle K, Exxon/dsl, Murphy USA/dsl, Burger King, CiCi's Pizza, Cracker Barrel, Domino's, Dragon Chinese, IHOP, KFC, McDonald's, Nicky's Mexican, Papa John's, Sonic, Subway, Taco Bell, Waffle House, Wendy's, Whataburger, Comfort Suites, Courtyard, Fairfield Inn, La Quinta, Hilton Garden, Holiday Inn, Homewood Suites, Howard Johnson, Sleep Inn, ValuePlace Inn, CVS Drug, $General, $Tree, Family$, GNC, Home Depot, O'Reilly Parts, Radio Shack, Rainbow Foods, Rite Aid, Verizon, Walgreens, Walmart/Subway, USPO
8	US 80, LA 526 E, **N** Motel 6, Freightliner, **S** Chevron/dsl, Citgo/dsl, Petro/Shell/dsl/scales/@, Wendy's, Blue Beacon, Camper's RV Ctr/park, Tall Pines RV Park (1mi)
5	US 79 N, US 80, to Greenwood, **N** TA/Country Pride/Subway/dsl/scales/24hr/@, Shell, Country Inn, Mid Continent Motel, **S** $General, Southern Living RV Park
3	US 79 S, LA 169, Mooringsport, **S** ⓕFLYING J/Denny's/dsl/LP/scales/24hr, ♥Loves/Arby's/dsl/scales/24hr, Sonic, Alligator RV Park (4mi), SpeedCo
2mm	**Welcome Ctr eb, full ♿ facilities, 🚻, 🛏, litter barrels, petwalk, RV dump**
1mm	**weigh sta both lanes**
0mm	Louisiana/Texas state line

⬆N INTERSTATE 49

Exit	Services
I-49 begins/ends in Shreveport on I-20, exit 17.	
206	I-20, E to Monroe, W to Dallas
205	King's Hwy, **E** Cane's, McDonald's, Piccadilly's, Taco Bell, Dillard's, Sears/auto, mall, **W** Valero/dsl, Burger King, LJ Silver, Subway, Sleep Inn, H
203	Hollywood Ave, Pierremont Rd, **W** Chevron/dsl
202	LA 511, E 70th St, **E** RaceWay/dsl, **W** Circle K, SC Chicken, $General, Family$
201	LA 3132, to Dallas, Texarkana
199	LA 526, Bert Kouns Loop, **E** Chevron/Arby's/dsl/24hr, Exxon/Circle K, Burger King, KFC, Taco Bell, Wen

Side margins:
M I N D E N / **S H R E V E P O R T** / **G R E E N W O O D** / **S H R E V E P O R T**

LA

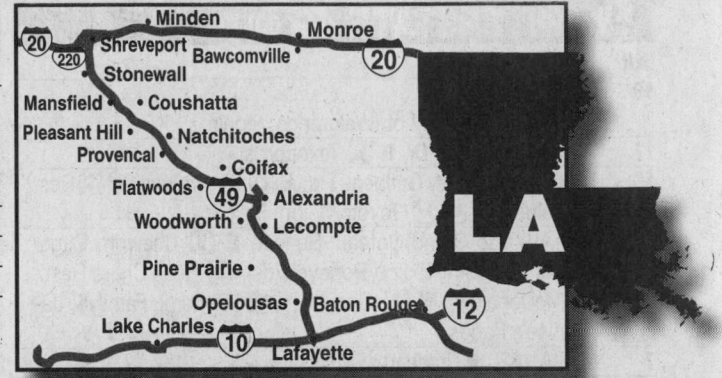

➤N INTERSTATE 49 CONT'D

Exit	Services
199	Continued
	dy's, 🛏 Comfort Inn, ⦿ Home Depot, **W** 🅖 RaceWay/dsl, Shell/dsl, 🍴 McDonald's, Sonic, Starbucks, Waffle House, ⦿ Brookshire Foods
196	Southern Loop
196mm	Bayou Pierre
191	LA 16, LA 3276, to Stonewall
186	LA 175, to Frierson, Kingston, **E** ⦿ Trailerhood RV Park (3mi), **W** 🅖 Relay Sta./rest./casino/dsl/scales, ⦿ Heart of Haynesville RV Park (7mi)
177	LA 509, to Carmel, **E** 🅖 Texaco/Eagles Trkstp/casino/dsl/rest., **W** ⦿ Hwy 509 RV Park (4mi)
172	US 84, to Grand Bayou, Mansfield, **W** New Rockdale RV Park (4mi), Civil War Site
169	Asseff Rd
162	US 371, LA 177, to Evelyn, Coushatta, Pleasant Hill
155	LA 174, to Ajax, Lake End, **W** ⦿ Country Livin' RV Pk, gas/dsl
148	LA 485, Powhatan, Allen
142	LA 547, Posey Rd
138	LA 6, to Natchitoches, **E** 🅖 French Mkt/cafe/dsl, RaceWay/dsl, 🍴 Popeye's, Wendy's, 🛏 Best Western, Comfort Suites, Days Inn, Holiday Inn Express, ⦿🅷, Walmart (5mi), **W** 🅖 Chevron/dsl, Exxon, Texaco/dsl, 🍴 Burger King, Huddle House, McDonald's, 🛏 EconoLodge, Hampton Inn, Quality Inn, ⦿ Nakatosh RV Park, to Kisatchie NF
132	LA 478, rd 620
127	LA 120, to Cypress, Flora, **E** 🅖 Exxon/dsl, ⦿ to Cane River Plantations
119	LA 119, to Derry, Cloutierville, **E** to Cane River Plantations
113	LA 490, to Chopin, **E** 🅖 Express Mart TrkStp/dsl
107	to Lena, **E** USPO
103	LA 8 W, to Flatwoods, **E** 🅖 Shell/dsl, **W** ⦿ to Cotile Lake, RV camping
99	LA 8, LA 1200, to Boyce, Colfax, **6 mi W** Cotile Lake RV Camping
98	LA 1 (from nb), to Boyce
94	rd 23, to Rapides Sta Rd, **E** 🅖 Rapides/dsl, **W LA Welcome Ctr, full ♿ facilities, litter barrels, petwalk, 🆁🆂, vending**, ⦿ I-49 RV Ctr
90	LA 498, Air Base Rd, **W** 🅖 Chevron/dsl/CNG/24hr, Exxon/Subway/dsl, Shell/dsl, Texaco/Eddie's BBQ/dsl, 🍴 Burger King, Cracker Barrel, McDonald's, 🛏 Comfort Suites, Hampton Inn, La Quinta, Super 8, Travel Express Inn, ⦿ Cabana RV Park
86	US 71, US 165, MacArthur Dr, **0-2 mi W** 🅖 Chevron, Conoco/dsl, Exxon/dsl, Mobil/dsl, Shell/Circle K/dsl, Texaco/dsl, 🍴 Anchor's Seafood Rest, Applebee's, Arby's, Burger King, Cane's, Cajun Landing Rest., Chick-fil-A, Church's, CiCi's Pizza, DQ, Dominos, Eddie's BBQ, El Reparo Mexican, Little Caesars, McDonald's, Outlaw's BBQ, Picadilly, Popeye's, Ryan's, Schlotzsky's, Sonic, Subway, Taco Bell, Taco Bueno, TX Roadhouse, 🛏 Alexandria Inn, Baymont Inn, Best Value Inn, Best Western, Candlewood Suites, Comfort Inn, EconoLodge, Guesthouse Inn, Holiday Inn Express, Motel 6, Quality Inn, Ramada Ltd, Super 8, Value Place Inn, ⦿ Advance Parts, AutoZone, BigLots, Buick/GMC, $General, Family$, Hastings Books, Kia, Kroger, NAPA, O'Reilly Parts, Rite Aid, Staples, Super 1 Foods
85b	Monroe St, Medical Ctr Dr (from nb), **E** 🅷
85a	LA 1, 10th St, MLK Dr, downtown
84	US 167 N, LA 28, LA 1, Pineville Expswy (no ez return nb)
83	Broadway Ave, **E** gas, **1 mi W** 🍴 Checker's, Sonic, Wendy's, ⦿ AutoZone, $Tree, Harley-Davidson, Radio Shack, Walmart
81	US 71 N, LA 3250, Sugarhouse Rd, MacArthur Dr (from sb), **W** same as 80 and 83
80	US 71 S, US 167, MacArthur Dr, Alexandria, **0-3 mi W** 🅖 Chevron/dsl, Exxon/dsl, Shell, 🍴 Buffalo Wild Wings, Burger King, Capt D's, Carino's Italian, Chili's, Copeland's Rest, IHOP, KFC, Logan's Roadhouse, McDonald's, Outback Steaks, Pizza Hut, Popeye's, Sonic, Subway, Taco Bell, 🛏 Courtyard, ⦿ Albertsons, Best Buy, Dillard's, $General, Family$, Ford/Lincoln, Hyundai, JC Penney, Marshall's, Mazda, Michael's, Old Navy, Petsmart, Sam's Club/gas, U-Haul, mall
73	LA 3265, rd 22, to Woodworth, **E** dsl repair, **W** 🅖 Exxon/Coops/dsl, ⦿ LA Conf Ctr, to Indian Creek RA, RV camping
66	LA 112, to Lecompte, **E** 🅖 Chevron/dsl, 🍴 Burger King, **W** 🅖 Exxon/dsl, ⦿ museum
61	US 167, to Meeker Turkey Creek, **E** to Loyd Hall Plantation (3mi)
56	LA 181, Cheneyville
53	LA 115, to Bunkie, **E** 🅖 Sammy's/Chevron/dsl/casino/24hr, 🛏 Howard Johnson
46	LA 106, to St Landry, **W** to Chicot SP
40	LA 29, to Ville Platte, **E** 🅖 Exxon/Cafe Mangeur/casino/dsl
35mm	**E** 🆁🆂/rec area both lanes, full ♿ facilities, 🆁🆂, litter barrels, vending, petwalk, RV dump
27	LA 10, to Lebeau
25	LA 103, to Washington, Port Barre, **W** 🅖 Citgo, Mobil, ⦿ Family$
23	US 167 N, LA 744, to Ville Platte, **E** 🅖 Chevron/Subway/Stuckey's/dsl/scales/casino, Texaco/dsl/casino, **W** 🅖 Exxon/dsl/casino, ⦿ visitors ctr
19b a	US 190, to Opelousas, **E** Evangeline Downs Racetrack, **W** 🅖 Exxon/dsl, Mobil/dsl, RaceTrac/dsl, ⦿🅷, CVS Drug, Lowe's, tourist info, USPO
18	LA 31, to Cresswell Lane, **E** 🅖 Murphy USA/dsl, 🍴 Casa Ole's, Little Caesars, 🛏 Comfort Inn, Holiday Inn, ⦿ Urgent Care, Chrysler/Dodge/Jeep, $Tree, Radio Shack, Verizon, Walmart/Subway, **W** 🅖 Chevron/dsl, Shell, Valero/dsl, 🍴 Burger King, Cane's, Cresswell Lane, Domino's, Gatti's Pizza, Hacienda Mexican, McDonald's, Peking Buffet, Pizza Hut, Subway, Taco Bell, Wendy's, 🛏 Days Inn, Super 8, ⦿ AT&T, Buick/GMC, Family$, Nissan, Piggly

NATCHITOCHES   ALEXANDRIA   OPELOUSAS   **LA**

INTERSTATE 49 CONT'D

Exit	Services
18	Continued
	Wiggly, Save-A-Lot, Walgreens, repair
17	Judson Walsh Dr, **E** Texaco/dsl
15	LA 3233, Harry Guilbeau Rd, **E** RV Brokers, **W** Best Value Inn, , Toyota/Scion, RV Ctr
11	LA 93, to Grand Coteau, Sunset, **E** Chevron, Citgo/rest./dsl/24hr, Exxon/Popeye's/dsl, Beau Chere Rest., McDonald's, **W** Subway, $General, Family$, Janise's Foods
7	LA 182, **W** Primeaux RV Ctr
4	LA 726, Carencro, **E** Urgent Care, Super 1 Foods/gas, **W** Chevron/Popeye's/dsl, Texaco/dsl, Burger King, King Wok, McDonald's, Economy Inn, $General, Don's Country Mart, Family$, Mack, Kenworth, USPO
2	LA 98, Gloria Switch Rd, **E** Chevron/deli/dsl, Chili's, IHOP, Prejean's Rest., Wendy's, Lowe's, **W** Shell/Church's/dsl, Domino's, Great Wall Buffet, Picante Mexican, Subway
1c	Pont Des Mouton Rd, **E** Exxon/dsl/LP, Texaco/dsl, Burger King, Motel 6, Plantation Inn, Walgreens, st police, **W** Ford
1ba	I-10, **W** to Lake Charles, **E** to Baton Rouge, **US 167 S** Chevron/dsl, Murphy USA/dsl, RaceTrac/dsl, Shell/dsl, Valero, Checker's, KFC, McDonald's, Popeye's, Shoney's, Subway, Taco Bell, Waffle House, Wendy's, Best Western, Comfort Inn, EconoLodge, Fairfield Inn, Holiday Inn, Howard Johnson, Jameson Inn, La Quinta, Quality Inn, Super 8, , CVS Drug, Home Depot, Radio Shack, Super 1 Foods/gas, Walmart/Subway, transmissions

I-49 begins/ends on I-10, exit 103.

INTERSTATE 55

Exit	Services
66mm	Louisiana/Mississippi state line
65mm	**Welcome Ctr sb, full facilities, tourist info, , , litter barrels, petwalk**
64mm	**weigh sta nb**
61	LA 38, Kentwood, **E** Chevron/dsl, Texaco, Jam Chicken, Popeye's, Sonic, , AutoZone, $General, Family$, Fred's, IGA Foods, Super$, **W** Kangaroo/dsl, Kangaroo/Subway/dsl
58.5mm	**weigh sta sb**
57	LA 440, Tangipahoa, **E** to Camp Moore Confederate Site
53	LA 10, to Greensburg, Fluker, **W**
50	LA 1048, Roseland, **E** Chevron/dsl, Subway (1mi)
46	LA 16, Amite, **E** Exxon/dsl, Murphy USA/dsl, RaceTrac/dsl, Burger King, Master Chef, McDonald's, Mike's Catfish, Panda Garden, Popeye's, Sonic, Subway, Waffle House, Wendy's, Comfort Inn, , AutoZone, $Tree, Fred's, O'Reilly Parts, Walgreens, Walmart/Subway, Winn-Dixie, to Bogue Chitto SP, **W** Amite Trkstp/grill/dsl (2mi), Ardillo's, Colonial Inn, Holiday Inn Express, Buick/Chevrolet/GMC
40	LA 40, Independence, **E** Best Stop, , **W** Indian Cr Camping (2mi)
36	LA 442, Tickfaw, **E** Chevron/dsl, camping, to Global Wildlife Ctr (15mi), **W** Exxon/dsl
32	LA 3234, Wardline Rd, **E** Chevron, Kangaroo/dsl, Texaco, Burger King, McDonald's, Popeye's, Sarita Grill,

32	Continued
	Sonic, Subway, Taco Bell, Wendy's, Lexington Inn, Tony's Tire
31	US 190, Hammond, **E** Exxon/Subway/dsl, Murphy USA/dsl, RaceTrac/dsl, Shell/dsl/scales/24hr, Applebee's, Baskin-Robbins, Buffalo Wild Wings, Burger King, Cane's, Chili's, CiCi's Pizza, Cracker Barrel, Firehouse Subs, Hi-Ho 1 BBQ, Lee's Burgers, McDonald's, Pizza Hut, Sonic, Starbucks, Taco Bell, Voodoo BBQ, Waffle House, Wendy's, Comfort Inn, Hampton Inn, Super 8, ValuePlace, Western Inn, , Aamco, Advance Parts, AT&T, AutoZone, Chrysler/Dodge/Jeep, CVS Drug, $General, $Tree, Family$, Hobby Lobby, LeBlanc's Foods Lowe's, Office Depot, Radio Shack, Ross, Sav-A-Lot Foods, Tuesday Morning, Walgreens, Walmart/Subway, Winn-Dixie
29b a	I-12, **W** to Baton Rouge, **E** to Slidell
28	US 51 N, Hammond, **E** Exxon, RaceTrac/dsl, Don's Seafood/Steaks, Great Wall Chinese, Magnuson Hotel, Motel 6, , Buick/GMC, Mitchell RV Ctr, Toyota/Scion, dsl repair
26	LA 22, to Springfield, Ponchatoula, **E** Chevron/dsl, Exxon/dsl, Shell/dsl, Burger King, China King, Hi-Ho BBQ, McDonald's/playplace, Papa John's, Pizza Hut, Popeye's, Smoothie King, Sonic, Subway, Waffle House, Wendy's, Microtel, AutoZone, Bohning's Foods, CVS Drug, Family$, Ford, O'Reilly Parts, Walgreens, Winn-Dixie, **W** Kangaroo/Domino's/dsl, Tickfaw SP (13mi)
23	US 51, Ponchatoula
22	frontage rd (from sb)
15	Manchac, **E** Middendorf Café, , swamp tours
7	Ruddock
1	US 51, to I-10, Baton Rouge, La Place, **S** Circle K/dsl, /Subway/dsl/24hr/scales, Shell/Huddle House/casino/dsl, Bully's Seafood, Burger King, McDonald's, Shoney's, Waffle House, Wendy's, Best Western, Days Inn, Hampton Inn, Holiday Inn Express, Quality Inn, Suburban Lodge

I-55 begins/ends on I-10, exit 209.

INTERSTATE 59

Exit	Services
11	**W** to Bogue Chitto NWR, Pearl River Turnaround
5b	Honey Island Swamp
5a	LA 3081, Pearl River, **E** Riverside TrvlCtr/dsl
3	US 11 S, LA 1090, Pearl River, 0-1 mi **W** Chevron/dsl, Interstate Fuels/dsl, Shell/Subway/dsl, Texaco, McDonald's, Sonic, Waffle House, Microtel, AutoZone, Family$, Jubilee Foods/drug, NAPA
1.5mm	**Welcome Ctr sb, full facilities, info, , , litter barrels, petwalk, RV dump**
1c b	I-10, **E** to Bay St Louis, **W** to New Orleans
1a	I-12 **W**, to Hammond. **I-59 begins/ends on I-10/I-12.**

INTERSTATE 220 (SHREVEPORT)

Exit	Services
	I-220 begins/ends on I-20, exit 26.
17b	I-20, **W** to Shreveport, **E** to Monroe
17a	US 79, US 80, **N** RaceWay, Shell/Circle K, McDonald's, Taco Bell, Waffle House, SpringHill Suites, LA Downs Racetrack/casino, **S** Chevron/Huddle House/dsl
15	Shed Rd

🅔 INTERSTATE 220 (SHREVEPORT) CONT'D

Exit	Services
13	Swan Lake Rd
12	LA 3105, Airline Dr, N 🅡 🍽 Baskin-Robbins, Chick-fil-A, Firehouse Subs, McAlister's Deli, Olive Garden, Papa Murphy's, Quiznos, Starbucks, Subway, TaMolly's, 🅞 🛏 AT&T, Belk, Best Buy, Petsmart, Ross, Target, Verizon, Walgreens, S 🅡 Exxon/dsl, Murphy USA/dsl, Shell/Circle K/Subway, Valero/dsl, 🍽 Applebee's, Burger King, Cane's, Capt D's, China Flag, CiCi's Pizza, Gatti's Pizza, McDonald's, Moe's SW Grill, Nicky's Rest., Ruby Tuesday, Ryan's, Sonic, Taco Bell, Trejo's Mexican, Wendy's, 🅞 $Tree, Home Depot, Lowe's, Radio Shack, Walmart, USPO, vet
11	LA 3, Bossier City, N 🅞 🛏 Buick/GMC, Ford, Harley-Davidson, Lexus, Suzuki, Toyota, RV Park, S 🅡 Chevron/dsl/24hr, 🅞 Chrysler/Dodge/Jeep, Nissan
7b a	US 71, LA 1, Shreveport, N 🅡 Citgo, Exxon/dsl, 🍽 Domino's, Rally's, Sonic, Subway, Waffle House, Whataburger/24hr, 🅞 Brookshire Foods/gas, Curves, $General, Walgreens, S 🅡 Chevron/24hr, RaceWay/dsl, Shell, 🍽 Burger King, Church's, KFC, Gumbo Daddy's, McDonald's, Podnah's BBQ, Popeye's, Taco Bell, Wen

Exit	Services
7b a	Continued dy's, 🅡 Royal Inn, 🅞 Advance Parts, AutoZone, County Mkt Foods, CVS Drug, Family$, O'Reilly Parts, Radio Shack, Rite Aid, U-Haul, repair/transmissions
5	LA 173, Blanchard Rd, S 🅡 Citgo
2	Lakeshore Dr, N 🅡 Citgo
1a	Jefferson Paige Rd, S 🛏 Best Western, Days Inn, Hampton Inn, Ramada Inn, Residence Inn, Super 8, Value Inn
1b c	I-20, E to Shreveport, W to Dallas. I-220 begins/ends on I-20, exit 11.

🅔 INTERSTATE 610 (NEW ORLEANS)

Exit	Services
I-610 begins/ends on I-10	
4	Franklin Ave (from eb)
3	Elysian fields, N 🛏, S 🅡 B Express, Shell, 🍽 Burger King, McDonald's, 🅞 Lowe's
2b	US 90, N Broad St, New Orleans St (from wb)
2c	Paris Ave (from wb, no return), S 🅡 Shell/24hr, Spur, 🍽 Popeye's
2a	St Bernard Ave (from eb), to LSU School of Dentistry auto racetrack
1a	Canal Blvd
1b	I-10, to New Orleans
I-610 begins/ends on I-10	

MAINE

🅝 INTERSTATE 95

Exit	Services
305mm	US/Canada border, Maine state line, US Customs. I-95 begins/ends.
305	US 2, to Houlton, E 🅞 Houlton ✈ DFA Duty Free Shop
303mm	Meduxnekeag River
302	US 1, Houlton, E 🅡 Irving/Circle K/dsl/24hr, 🍽 Burger King, KFC, McDonald's, Pizza Hut, Tang's Chinese, 🅞 🛏 IGA Foods, Mardens, Rite Aid, VIP Parts/service, W 🆁🆂 both lanes, full 🛏 facilities, 🚻, 🖼, litter barrels, petwalk, 🅡 Citgo/Subway/dsl, Irving/Circle K/dsl/scales/@, Shell/Dunkin Donuts/dsl, 🍽 Elmtree North, Tim Hortons, 🛏 Ivey's Motel, Shiretown Motel, 🅞 Family$, Ford/Lincoln, Shop'n Save, Toyota, Walmart, Arrowstook SP
301mm	B Stream
291	US 2, to Smyrna, E 🛏 Brookside Motel/rest.
286	Oakfield Rd, to ME 11, Eagle Lake, Ashland, W 🅡 Irving/Circle K/dsl, Valero/dsl, 🍽 A Place To Eat, 🅞 USPO
277mm	Mattawamkeag River, W Branch
276	ME 159, Island Falls, E 🅡 Porter's/rest., Dysarts Fuel, 🅞 Bishop's Mkt, USPO, W to Baxter SP (N entrance), RV camping
264	to ME 11, Sherman, E 🅡 Shell/dsl/LP/rest., W 🅡 Irving/Circle K/dsl, 🛏 Katahdin Valley Motel, 🅞 to Baxter SP (N entrance)
259	Benedicta (from nb, no re-entry)
252mm	scenic view Mt Katahdin, nb
247mm	Salmon Stream
244	ME 157, to Medway, E Millinocket, W 🅡 Irving/Circle K/dsl, 🛏 Gateway Inn, 🅞 🛏 Pine Grove Camping (4mi), USPO, vet, to Baxter SP (S entrance), city park
244mm	Penobscot River
243mm	🆁🆂 both lanes, full 🛏 facilities, 🚻, 🖼, litter barrels, petwalk
227	to US 2, ME 6, Lincoln, 4 mi E 🛏, gas, food, lodging, RV camping

Exit	Services
219mm	Piscataquis River
217	ME 6, Howland, E 🅡 Irving/95 Diner/dsl, 🍽 Jim & Jill's Grill, 🅞 95er Towing/repair, LP, camping
201mm	Birch Stream
199	ME 16 (no nb re-entry), to LaGrange
197	ME 43, to Old Town, E gas/dsl
196mm	Pushaw Stream
193	Stillwater Ave, to Old Town, E 🅡 Citgo/dsl, Irving/Circle K/dsl, Mobil/Subway/dsl, 🍽 Burger King, Dunkin Donuts, Governor's Rest., KFC/Taco Bell, McDonald's/playplace, Wendy's, 🛏 Black Bear Inn, 🅞 $Tree, IGA Foods, VIP Parts, mall
191	Kelly Rd, to Orono, 2-3 mi E gas, food, lodging, camping
187	Hogan Rd, Bangor Mall Blvd, to Bangor, E 🅡 Citgo, 🍽 Denny's, 🛏 Courtyard, Hilton Garden, 🅞 🛏 Audi/VW, Cadillac/Chevrolet, Chrysler/Dodge, Firestone/auto, Ford, GMC, Honda, Hyundai, Jeep, Mazda, Mercedes, Nissan, Sam's Club/gas, Subaru, Volvo, W 🅡 Citgo/dsl, Irving/Circle K/dsl, 🍽 Applebee's, Arby's, Bugaboo Creek Café, Burger King, Chicago Grill, Chili's, Dunkin Donuts, Green Tea Japanese, Happy China, KFC, Longhorn Steaks, McDonald's, Miguel's Mexican, 99 Rest., Olive Garden, Papa Johns, Pizza Hut, Quiznos, Starbucks, Subway, TX Roadhouse, Wendy's, 🛏 Bangor Motel, Comfort Inn, Country Inn, Hampton Inn, 🅞 Advance Parts, Best Buy, BigLots, Dick's, $Tree, Goodyear/auto, Harley-Davidson, Hannaford Foods, Home Depot, JC Penney, Jo-Ann Fabrics, K-Mart/Little Caesars, Kia, Kohl's, LL Bean, Lowe's, Macy's, Old Navy, PetCo, Sears/auto, Staples, Suzuki, Target, Verizon, VIP Parts, Walmart, mall, Urgent Care
186	Stillwater Ave, same as 187
185	ME 15, to Broadway, Bangor, E 🅡 Irving/Circle K/dsl, 🍽 Tri-City Pizza, 🅞 🛏, W 🅡 Citgo, Mobil, 🍽 Amato's, Coldstone/Tim Hortons, China Light, DQ, Governor's Rest., Jimmy V's Cafe, KFC, McDonald's, Pizza Hut, Subway, Taco Bell, 🅞 CarQuest, Hannaford Foods, Rite Aid,

⬆️Ⓝ INTERSTATE 95 CONT'D

Exit	Services
185	Continued TJ Maxx, Walgreens
184	ME 222, Union St, to Ohio St, Bangor, **E** 🅖 Citgo, Irving, 🅞 Rite Aid, **W** 🅖 Citgo, Exxon, Gulf, Mobil/dsl, 🍴 Burger King, Capt Nick's Rest., Dunkin Donuts, McDonald's, Nicky's Rest., Wendy's, 🛏 Sheraton, 🅞 $Tree, Hannaford Foods, Marshall's, Staples, RV Camping, to 🅡🅢
183	US 2, ME 2, Hammond St, Bangor, **E** 🅖 Citgo, 🍴 Papa Gambino's Pizza, Pipino's Mexican, 🅞 Corner Store, Fairmont Mkt, NAPA, TrueValue, **W** 🅡🅢
182b	US 2, ME 100 W, **W** 🅖 Irving/Subway/dsl, 🍴 Dunkin Donuts, Ground Round, Tim Hortons, 🛏 Days Inn, EconoLodge, Fairfield Inn, Holiday Inn, Howard Johnson, Motel 6, Ramada Inn, Super 8, Travelodge, 🅞 RV camping, VIP Parts/service
182a	I-395, to US 2, US 1A, Bangor, downtown
180	Cold Brook Rd, to Hampden, **E** Citgo, 🍴 Angler's Rest. (1mi), **W** 🅖 Citgo/dsl/24hr/@, Dysarts Fleet Fuel/dsl, 🛏 Best Western, 🅞 Mack, Volvo, dsl repair
178mm	🆁🆂 sb, full 🅰 facilities, info, 🅒, vending, 🖼 litter barrels, petwalk, wireless internet
177mm	Soudabscook Stream
176mm	🆁🆂 nb, full 🅰 facilities, info, 🅒, vending, 🖼 litter barrels, petwalk, wireless internet
174	ME 69, to Carmel, **E** 🅖 Citgo/dsl, **W** RV camping
167	ME 69, ME 143, to Etna
161	ME 7, to E Newport, Plymouth, **E** LP, **W** RV camping
159	Ridge Rd (from sb), to Plymouth, Newport
157	to US 2, ME 7, ME 11, Newport, **W** 🅖 Citgo, Irving/Circle K/dsl/24hr, Mobil/dsl, 🍴 Burger King, China Way, Dunkin Donuts, McDonald's, Pizza House, Pizza Hut, Sawyers Dairy Bar, Subway, Tim Hortons, 🛏 Lovley's Motel, 🅞 Aubuchon Hardware, Auto Value Parts, CarQuest, Chrysler/Dodge/Jeep, Rite Aid, Shop'n Save, Verizon, Walmart
151mm	Sebasticook River
150	Somerset Ave, Pittsfield, **E** 🅖 Irving, 🍴 Subway, 🛏 Pittsfield Motel, 🅞🅷 CarQuest, Chevrolet, Family$, Rite Aid, Shop'n Save Foods
138	Hinckley Rd, Clinton, **W** 🅖 ME Country Store/dsl
134mm	Kennebec River
133	US 201, Fairfield, **E** 🍴 Purple Cow Pancakes
132	ME 139, Fairfield, **W** 🅖 Irving/Circle K/Subway/dsl/scales/24hr
130	ME 104, Main St, Waterville, **E** 🅖 Citgo, 🍴 Arby's, Cappza's Pizza, Coldstone, Friendly's, Governor's Rest., McDonald's, Ruby Tuesday, Starbucks, Subway, Tim Horton, Wendy's, 🛏 Comfort Inn, Fireside Inn, Grand Hotel, 🅞 🅷, Advance Parts, Audi/Mazda/VW, Hannaford Foods, Home Depot, JC Penney, K-Mart, Mr Paperback, Radio Shack, Staples, Verizon, VIP Parts/service, Walmart
129mm	Messalonskee Stream
127	ME 11, ME 137, Waterville, Oakland, **E** 🅖 Circle K/dsl, Irving/dsl/24hr, Xpress/dsl, 🍴 Applebee's, Burger King, DQ, Dunkin Donuts, KFC/Taco Bell, McDonald's, Pad Thai, Papa John's, Pizza Hut, Sam's Italian, Subway, Super China, Weathervane Seafood, 🛏 Budget Host, EconoLodge, Hampton Inn, 🅞🅷, AutoZone, Buick/Chevrolet, Chrysler/Dodge/Jeep, CVS Drug, Hannaford Foods, Jo-Ann Fabrics, Marden's, Shaw's Foods/Osco Drug, Tire Whse, TJ Maxx, Toyota/Scion, **W** 🅖 Shell, 🅞 Aubuchon Hardware, CarQuest, Ford/Lincoln
120	Lyons Rd, Sidney

117mm	weigh sta both lanes
113	ME 3, Augusta, Belfast
112	ME 27, ME 8, ME 11, Augusta, **E** 🅖 Citgo, 🍴 DQ, Longhorn Steaks, Olive Garden, Panera Bread, Sam's Italian, Red Robin, Rooster's, Ruby Tuesday, Subway, 🛏 Civic Ctr Inn, 🅞 Barnes&Noble, Dick's, Home Depot, Kohl's, Old Navy, Radio Shack, Sam's Club, Staples, TownFair Tire, Verizon, Walmart, **W** 🅖 Irving/Circle K/dsl/24hr, 🍴 Great Wall Chinese, KFC/Taco Bell, 99 Rest., Wendy's, 🛏 Comfort Inn, Fairfield Inn, 🅞 Advance Parts
109	US 202, ME 11, ME 17, ME 100, Augusta, **E** 🅖 Citgo/Dunkin Donuts/dsl, Irving/Circle K/dsl, 🍴 Amato's Rest., Applebee's, Arby's, Burger King, Capital Buffet, China King, Damon's Italian, Domino's, DQ, Friendly's, KFC, Little Caesars, McDonald's, Pizza Hut, Subway, Tim Horton, Wendy's, 🛏 Senator Inn, 🅞 Best Buy, BigLots, $Tree, Family$, K-Mart, Lowe's, Petsmart, Radio Shack, Shaw's Foods/Osco Drug, Staples, Target, U-Haul, Verizon, VIP Parts, Walgreens, USPO, **W** 🅖 Valero, 🍴 Margarita's Mexican, TX Roadhouse, 🛏 Motel 6, Quality Inn, Super 8, 🅞 CarQuest, Chrysler/Dodge, Hyundai, Hannaford Foods, Jeep, Kia, Nissan, PetCo, Sears/auto, Subaru, Suzuki, TJ Maxx, Toyota/Scion
103	to I-295 S, ME 9, ME 126, to Gardiner, (from sb), **service plaza**, Citgo, Burger King, Hersheys, Quiznos, Starbucks ZMkt
102	to I-295 S, rd 9, rd 106, (from nb), **service plaza**, Citgo, Burger King, Hersheys, Quiznos, Starbucks ZMkt
100mm	**toll plaza**
86	to ME 9, Sabattus
84mm	Sabattus Creek
80	ME 196, Lewiston, **W on ME 196** 🅖 Gendron's/dsl, Getty/dsl, Mobil, Shell, Sunoco, 🍴 Burger King, Cathay Hut Chinese, Coldstone, D'angelo's, Dunkin Donuts, Governor's Rest., KFC/Taco Bell, McDonald's, Papa John's, Pepper&Spice Thai, Sam's Italian, Tim Horton, 🛏 Advance Parts, Motel 6, Ramada Inn, Super 8, 🅞🅷, $Tree, NAPA, Rite Aid, Staples, USPO
78mm	Androscoggin River
75	US 202, rd 4, rd 100, to Auburn, **E** 🅖 Irving/dsl, Mobil/Subway/dsl, 🍴 Danny Boy's Rest., Dunkin Donuts, 🛏 Fireside Inn, 🅞 RV Camping, **W** 🅷
71mm	Royal River
66mm	**toll plaza**
63	US 202, rd 115, rd 4, to ME 26, Gray, **E** 🅖 Gulf, Mobil, Sunoco, 🍴 China Gray, Dunkin Donuts, Goody's Pizza, Subway, McDonald's, 🅞 NAPA, TrueValue
59mm	**service plaza both lanes**, Citgo/dsl, Chicago Pizza, Starbucks, atm
55mm	Piscataqua River
53	to ME 26, ME100 W, N Portland, **E** 🅖 Irving/Circle K/Subway/dsl, 🍴 Bernie's Rest., Dunkin Donuts, 🅞🅷, Hannaford Foods
52	to I-295, US 1, Freeport
48	ME 25, to Portland, **E** 🅖 Citgo, 🍴 Applebee's, Asian Bistro, Full Belly Deli, Little Caesar's, Quiznos, Subway, 🛏 Portland Inn, 🅞 AT&T, BigLots, BJ's Whse/gas, Chevrolet, CVS Drug, Fiat, Jo-Ann Fabrics, Lowe's, Radio Shack, **W** 🅖 Citgo, Irving/Circle K/dsl, Mobil, 🍴 Amato's Rest., Burger King, Dunkin Donuts, Denny's, Friendly's, KFC/Taco Bell, McDonald's, Panera Bread, Pizza Hut, Ruby Tuesday, Seasons Grille, Wendy's, 🛏 Fireside Inn, Howard Johnson, Motel 6, Super 8, Travelodge, 🅞 Advance Parts, CarQuest, Ford, Harley-Davidson, Home Depot, Hyundai, Kohl's, Lexus/Toyota/Scion, Lincoln, NAPA,

Side labels: NEWPORT, WATERVILLE, ME, AUGUSTA, LEWISTON

⬆N   INTERSTATE 95 CONT'D

Exit	Services
48	Continued
	Shaw's Foods/Osco Drug, Sullivan Tire, Suzuki, Tire Whse, VIP Parts/service, vet
47	to ME 25, Rand Rd
47mm	Stroudwater River
46	to ME 22, Congress St, same as 45
45	to US 1, Maine Mall Rd, S Portland, **E** 🅐 Citgo/dsl, Sunoco, 🍴 Burger King, Bugaboo Creek Steaks, Chicago Grill, Chili's, Chipotle Mexican, ChuckeCheese, Coldstone, Cracker Barrel, Dunkin Donuts, FoodCourt, Friendly's, Great Wall Chinese, IHOP, Jimmy the Greek Rest., Longhorn Steaks, Macaroni Grill, McDonald's, Newick's Lobster House, Old Country Buffet, Olive Garden, On the Border, Panera Bread, Pizza Hut, Ruby Tuesday, Tim Horton, Weathervane Seafood, Wendy's, 🏨 Comfort Inn, Courtyard, Days Inn, EconoLodge, Fairfield Inn, Hampton Inn, Homewood Suites, Wyndham, 🅾 Best Buy, Dick's, $Tree, Hannaford Foods, Honda, JC Penney, Macy's, Michael's, Nissan, PetCo, Sears/auto, Staples, TJ Maxx, TownFair Tire, Verizon, mall, **W** 🍴 Applebee's, Starbucks, 🏨 Holiday Inn Express, Marriott, 🅾 Old Navy, Target
44	I-295 N (from nb), to S Portland, Scarborough, **1 mi E on ME 114** 🅐 Cumberland/Dunkin Donuts, 🍴 Chia Sen Chinese, KFC/Taco Bell, Little Caesars, Shogun Japanese, Subway, TX Roadhouse, 🏨 Residence Inn, TownePlace Suites, 🅾 🅷 Lowe's, NAPA, Sam's Club/gas, Shaw's Foods/Osco. Drug, VIP Parts/service, Walmart/Dunkin Donuts
42mm	Nonesuch River
42	to US 1, **E** 🏨 Courtyard, Homewood Suites, 🅾 Cabela's, Scarborough Downs Racetrack (seasonal)
36	I-195 E, to Saco, Old Orchard Beach, **E** 🏨 Hampton Inn, 🅾 KOA, Paradise Park Resort RV
35mm	**E** 🏨 Ramada Inn/Saco Hotel Conference Ctr
33mm	Saco River
32	ME 111, to Biddeford, **E** 🅐 Irving/Circle K/Subway/dsl, 🍴 Amato's Sandwiches, Dunkin Donuts, Ruby Tuesday, Wendy's, 🏨 Best Value Inn, Comfort Suites, 🅾 🅷 AAA, AutoZone, Osco Drug, Shaw's Foods, VIP Parts/Service, Walmart, **W** 🅐 Cumberland/dsl, 🍴 Applebees, Casa Fiesta Mexican, Kobe Japanese, Longhorn Steaks, Olive Garden, Panera Bread, 🅾 Best Buy, GNC, Home Depot, Kohl's, Lowe's, Old Navy, Petsmart, Staples, Target, TJ Maxx, TownFair Tire, Verizon
25mm	Kennebunk River
25	ME 35, Kennebunk Beach, **E** 🏨 Turnpike Motel
24mm	**service plaza both lanes**, sb Citgo/dsl, Burger King, Hersheys, Popeye's, Starbucks, Z Mkt, nb Citgo/dsl, Burger King, Hershey's, Sbarro's, Starbucks, Z Mkt, atm,
19.5mm	Merriland River
19	ME 9, ME 109, to Wells, Sanford, **W** to Sanford RA
7mm	Maine Tpk begins/ends, **toll booth**
7	ME 91, to US 1, The Yorks, **E** 🅐 Gulf, Irving/Circle K/dsl, Mobil/dsl, Shell, 🍴 China Bistro, Norma's Rest., Wildcat Pizza, 🏨 Best Western, Microtel, 🅾 🅷 Chrysler/Dodge/Jeep, Curves, Ford, Hannaford Foods, NAPA, Rite Aid, TrueValue, vet, last exit before toll rd nb
5.5mm	weigh sta nb
5mm	York River
4mm	weigh sta sb
3mm	**Welcome Ctr nb, full** ♿ **facilities, info,** 🅒 **vending,** 🅿, **litter barrels, petwalk**
2	(2 & 3 from nb), US 1, to Kittery, **E on US 1** 🅐 Irving/Circle K/dsl/scales, 7 11/dsl, 🍴 DQ, McDonald's, Subway, Sunrise Grill, Tasty Thai, Weathervane Seafood Rest., 🏨 Blue Roof Motel, Days Inn, Kittery Motel, Northeaster Hotel, Ramada Inn, 🅾 Outlets/Famous Brands, vet
1	ME 103 (from nb, no re-entry), to Kittery
0mm	Maine/New Hampshire state line, Piscataqua River

⬆N   INTERSTATE 295

Exit	Services
52mm	**I-295 begins/ends on I-95 exit 103**
51	ME 9, ME 126, to Gardiner, Litchfield, **toll plaza, W toll plaza, service plaza,** Citgo, Burger King, Hersheys, Quiznos, Starbucks, ZMkt
49	US 201, to Gardiner
43	ME 197, to Richmond, **E** 🅐 Irving/Quincey's Deli/dsl, 🍴 Dunkin Donuts, Subway
37	ME 125, Bowdoinham
31b a	ME 196, to Lisbon, Topsham, **E** 🅐 Irving/Circle K/Dunkin Donuts/Subway, Gibbs/dsl, 🍴 Arby's, Fairground Cafe, Little Caesars, McDonald's, 99. Rest., Romeo's Pizza, Ruby Tuesday, Starbucks, Tim Horton's, Wendy's, 🏨 Best Buy, Dick's, $Tree, Hannaford Foods, Home Depot, JoAnn Fabrics, PetCo, Radio Shack, Rite Aid, Target, Tire Whse, Toyota/Scion, Verizon, VIP Parts/service, **W** 🅐 Xpress Stop

ME

= gas   = food   = lodging   = other   = rest stop   Copyright 2014 - The Next Exit ®

INTERSTATE 295 CONT'D

Exit	Services
30mm	Androscoggin River
28	US 1, Bath, **1 mi E on US 1** Cumberland/Subway/dsl, Irving/dsl, Mobil/dsl, Shell, Amato's, McDonald's, Best Value Inn, Comfort Inn, Fairfield Inn, Knights Inn, Travelers Inn, H, Chevrolet/Mazda, Chrysler/Dodge, Ford, Jeep, repair
24	to Freeport (from nb), **services 1 mi E on US 1**
22	ME 125, to Pownal, **E on US 1** Irving/Circle K, Azure Cafe, Corsican Rest., Friendly's, Jameson Rest., McDonald's, Sam's Italian, Siano's Pizza, Starbucks, Subway, CVS Drug, LL Bean, USPO, outlets/famous brands, **W** to Bradbury Mtn SP
20	Desert Rd, Freeport, **E** Irving/Circle K, Antonia's Pizza, Buck's BBQ, Dunkin Donuts, Friendly's, Subway, Thai Garden Rest., Comfort Suites, Econolodge, Hampton Inn, Holiday Inn Express, Super 8, Shaw's Foods, outlets/famous brands, RV camping
17	US 1, Yarmouth, **E both lanes, full facilities, info**, Day's Takeout, Muddy Rudder Rest., Best Western, Ford, Delorme Mapping, **W** Citgo/dsl, Gulf/dsl, Dominos Pizza, McDonald's, Pat's Pizza, Ace Hardware, Hannaford Foods, NAPA, VIP Parts/service, vet
15	US 1, to Cumberland, Yarmouth, **W** Irving/dsl, Mobil, Romeo's Pizza, 233 Grill, Brookside Motel, AT&T, Rite Aid, Verizon
11	to I-95, ME Tpk (from sb)
10	US 1, to Falmouth, **E** Citgo/dsl, Irving/dsl, Dunkin Donuts, Foreside Rest., House of Pizza, Hugs Italian, Lo

Exit	Services
10	Continued tus Japanese, McDonald's, Ricetta's Pizza, Starbucks, Stony Field Cafe, Subway, Wendy's, Ace Hardware, Audi/VW, Mazda, Radio Shack, Rite Aid, Shaw's Foods, Walmart
9mm	Presumpscot River
9	US 1 S, ME 26, to Baxter Blvd
8	ME 26 S, Washington Ave, E U-Haul
7	US 1A, Franklin St, E AAA, CarQuest, Freightliner, NAPA, Walgreens
6b a	US 1, Forest Ave, **E** Citgo, H, Firestone/auto, USPO, **W** Mobil/dsl, Arby's, Burger King, Leonardo's Pizza, Stavro's Pizza, Whaddipita, CVS Drug, Hannaford Foods, U of SME
5b a	ME 22, Congress St, **E** Amato's Rest., Denny's, D'Angelos, Dunkin Donuts, Lang's Chinese, McDonald's, La Quinta, H, Sullivan Tire, **W** Citgo/Dunkin Donuts, Mobil/dsl, Anania's Italian, Clarion
3mm	Fore River
4	US 1 S, to Main St, to S Portland, US 1 S, **E services on US 1**
3	ME 9, to Westbrook St, no sb return, **W** Citgo/dsl, Irving/Circle K/dsl, Buffalo Wild Wings, Olive Garden, Outback Steaks, Seadog Brew Co., Subway, Wild Willy's Burger, Chevrolet, Home Depot, Marshalls
2	to US 1 S, S Portland, **services E on US 1** Irving/Circle K/dsl, Mobil, 7-11, Dunkin Donuts, Governor's Rest., Best Western, Howard Johnson, Knights Inn, Super 8, Discount Tire
1	to I-95, to US 1, multiple services E on US 1, same as 2
	I-295 begins/ends on I-95, exit 44.

MARYLAND

INTERSTATE 68

Exit	Services
82c	I-70 W, to Breezewood. **I-68 begins/ends on I-70, exit 1.**
82b	I-70 E, US 40 E, to Hagerstown
82a	US 522, Hancock, **N** Chevrolet, Chrysler/Dodge/Jeep, **S** Mobil/dsl, Sheetz, Hardee's, Pizza Hut, Park'n Dine, Subway, Weaver's Rest., Best Value Inn, Super 8, $General, Happy Hills Camping, Save-A-Lot Foods
77	US 40, MD 144, Woodmont Rd, **S** RV camping
75mm	runaway truck ramp eb
74mm	Sideling Hill /exhibit both lanes, full facilities, vending, 1269 ft (seasonal)
74	US 40, Mountain Rd (no return from eb)
73mm	Sideling Hill Creek
72mm	truck ramp wb
72	US 40, High Germany Rd, Swain Rd, **S** Citgo/dsl
68	Orleans Rd, **N** Exxon/dsl
67mm	Town Hill, Town Hill, elevation 940 ft
64	MV Smith Rd, **S** to Green Ridge SF HQ, scenic overlook, 1040 ft
62	US 40, 15 Mile Creek Rd, **N** Billmeyer Wildlife Mgt Area
58.7mm	Polish Mtn, elevation 1246 ft
57mm	Town Creek
56mm	Flintstone Creek
56	MD 144, National Pike, Flintstone, **S** Billi's Gas&Grub
52	MD 144, Pleasant Valley Rd (from eb), National Pike
50	Pleasant Valley Rd, **N** Lakeside Grill, Signature's Grill, Rocky Gap Lodge/golf/rest., to Rocky Gap SP
47	US 220 N, MD 144, Dehaven Rd (from wb), Old National

Exit	Services
46	Continued Pike, Bedford, same as 46
46	US 220 N, Dehaven Rd, Baltimore Pike, Naves Crossroads, **N** Cumberland Motel, Advance Parts, Shop'n Save, vet, **S** Sheetz/dsl, Puccini's Rest.
45	Hillcrest Dr, **S** Sunoco/dsl
44	US 40A, Baltimore Ave, Willow Brook Rd, to Allegany Comm Coll, **S** H, to Allegany Comm Coll
43d	Maryland Ave, **N** Holiday Inn, H, USPO, **S** Gulf/7-11, Chick-fil-A, Papa John's, Quiznos, AT&T, AutoZone, Martin's Foods/gas
43c	downtown, same as 43b
43b	MD 51, Industrial Blvd, **N** McDonald's, Holiday Inn, Family$, **S** Gulf/dsl, Papa John's, Pizza Hut/Taco Bell, Roy Rogers, Wendy's, Fairfield Inn
43a	to WV 28A, Beall St, Industrial Blvd, to Cumberland, Johnson St, **N** Sheetz
42	US 220 S, Greene St, Ridgedale
41	Seton Dr (from wb, no directory turn)
41mm	Haystack Mtn, elev 1240 ft
40	US 220 S, to US 40A, Vocke Rd, La Vale, **N** BP/dsl, Sunoco, Arby's, Asian Garden, Bob Evans, Burger King, D'Atri Rest., DQ, Denny's, Gehauf Rest., Grand China, Henny's Grill, KFC, LJ Silver, McDonald's, Pizza Hut, Rio Grande Mexican, Rita's Custard, Ruby Tuesday, Subway, TX Grill, Wendy's, Best Western/rest, Comfort Inn, Slumberland Motel, Super 8, H, Advance Parts, CVS Drug, $General, Harley-Davidson, Jo-Ann Fabrics, Lowe's, Mr Tire, Staples, st police, **S** Applebee's,

ME
MD

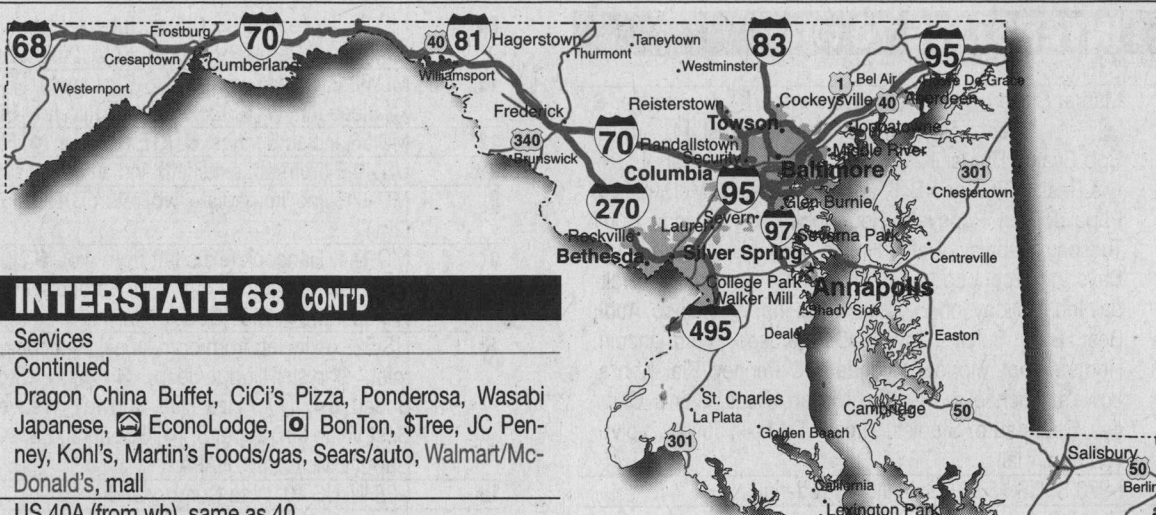

▲ᴇ INTERSTATE 68 CONT'D

F R O S T B U R G

Exit	Services
40	Continued
	Dragon China Buffet, CiCi's Pizza, Ponderosa, Wasabi Japanese, 🏠 EconoLodge, ⊙ BonTon, $Tree, JC Penney, Kohl's, Martin's Foods/gas, Sears/auto, Walmart/McDonald's, mall
39	US 40A (from wb), same as 40
34	MD 36, to Westernport, Frostburg, **N** ⛽ Sheetz, Valero, ⑪ Burger King, Fox's Pizza, McDonald's, Peking House, Pizza Hut, Subway, 🏠 Days Inn, Hampton Inn, ⊙Ⓗ CarQuest, $General, Food Lion, Rite Aid, Save-A-Lot, USPO, **S** to Dans Mtn SP
33	Midlothian Rd, to Frostburg, **N** Ⓗ, **S** to Dans Mt SP
31mm	**weigh sta eb**
30mm	Big Savage Mtn, elevation 2800 ft
29	MD 546, Finzel, **N** ⑪ Hen House Rest., ⊙ Mason-Dixon Camping (4mi/seasonal), **S** Savage River Lodge Rest.
25.8mm	eastern continental divide, elevation 2610 ft
24	Lower New Germany Rd, to US 40A, **S** to New Germany SP, to Savage River SF
23mm	Meadow Mtn, elevation 2780 ft
22	US 219 N, to Meyersdale, **N** ⛽ 🚚/Arby's/dsl/scales/24hr, Sunoco/dsl, ⑪ Burger King, Hilltop Rest., Penn Alps Rest., Subway, ⊙ $Discount, $General, Ford, Hilltop Fruit Mkt, NAPA, Rite Aid, Shop'n Save, TrueValue, **S** ⛽ Valero/dsl, 🏠 Comfort Inn, ⊙ New Germany SP, Savage River SF
20mm	Casselman River
19	MD 495, to US 40A, Grantsville, **N** ⛽ Exxon/Subway/dsl, Sunoco/dsl, 🏠 Casselman Motel/rest., ⊙ CarQuest, Medicine Shoppe, USPO
15mm	Mt Negro, elevation 2740 ft
14mm	Keyser's Ridge, elevation 2880 ft
14b a	US 219, US 40 W, Oakland, **N** ⛽ Liberty/Ridge/rest./dsl, Sunoco/7-11/dsl, ⑪ McDonald's, repair
6mm	Welcome Ctr eb, full ♿ facilities, info, Ⓒ, 🚻, litter barrels, vending, petwalk
4.5mm	Bear Creek
4mm	Youghiogheny River
4	MD 42, Friendsville, **N** ⛽ Liberty/dsl, Marathon/dsl, ⑪ Old Mill Rest., 🏠 Yough Valley Motel, ⊙ S&S Mkt, USPO, **S** 🏠 Sunset Inn, ⊙ to Deep Creek Lake SP, camping
0mm	Maryland/West Virginia state line

▲ᴇ INTERSTATE 70

Exit	Services
	I-70 begins/ends in Baltimore at Cooks Lane.
94	Security Blvd N, **S** ⛽ Shell
91b a	I-695, **N off exit 17** ⛽ Exxon, Sunoco, ⑪ Burger King, 5 Guys Burgers, McDonald's, Panera Bread, Popeye's, Quiznos, 🏠 Best Western, ⊙ Best Buy, Ford, Macy's, Old Navy, Sears/auto, Weis Foods, mall, **S** ⛽ BP/repair, Shell, ⑪ Dunkin Donuts, Subway, Wendy's, 🏠 Days Inn, Leisure Inn, Motel 6, ⊙ Chevrolet, Nissan

B A L T I M O R E

Exit	Services
87b a	US 29 (exits left from wb)to MD 99, Columbia, **2 mi S on US 40** ⛽ BP/dsl, Citgo/Subway, Exxon/dsl, Gulf, Shell, Sunoco, ⑪ Arby's, Baskin-Robbins/Dunkin Donuts, Boston Mkt, Burger King, Checkers, Domino's, Dunkin Donuts, Jerry's Subs, Jimmy John's, McDonald's, Papa John's, Pizza Hut, Qdoba, ⊙ Acura/Infiniti, Advance Parts, Cadillac/Chevrolet, Carmax, CVS Drug, Giant Foods, Goodyear/auto, Home Depot, Honda, Mars Foods, Midas, Mr Tire, NAPA, Nissan, Rite Aid, Safeway Foods, 7-11, Shoppers Foods, Verizon, Walmart
83	US 40, Marriottsville (no EZ wb return), **2 mi S** 🏠 Turf Valley Hotel/Country Club/rest.
82	US 40 E (from eb), same as 83
80	MD 32, Sykesville, **N** golf, **S** ⛽ Shell, ⑪ Subway, Tony's Pizzeria
79mm	**weigh/insp sta wb,** Ⓒ
76	MD 97, Olney, **S** ⛽ High's/dsl, ⑪ Subway
73	MD 94, Woodbine, **N** ⛽ Shell, ⑪ Baskin Robbins, China Yee, Dunkin Donuts, Harvest Chicken, McDonald's, Pizza Hut, Subway, ⊙ $Tree, Food Lion, Ramblin Pines RV Park (6mi), **S** ⛽ BP/dsl, Citgo, ⑪ Town Grill
68	MD 27, Mt Airy, **N** ⛽ Liberty/Blimpie/dsl, 7-11, Shell, ⑪ Arby's, Baskin-Robbns/Dunkin Donuts, Burger King, China Taste, Chipotle, Domino's, 5 Guys Burgers, Jersey Mike' Subs, J&P Pizza, KFC/Taco Bell, Ledo's Pizza, McDonald's, Papa John's, Pizza Hut, Quick Fire Japanese, Starbucks, Subway, TCBY, ⊙ Ace Hardware, Advance Parts, AT&T, Food Lion, GNC, Goodyear, Mr Tire, Radio Shack, Rite Aid, Safeway, Walmart, vet, **S** ⛽ Exxon/dsl, Shell, 🏠 Budget Inn
66mm	truckers parking area eb
64mm	**weigh/insp sta eb**
62	MD 75, Libertytown, **N** ⛽ Classic Fuels, Shell, ⑪ Asian Bistro, Baskin Robbins, Domino's, Dunkin Donuts, McDonald's, Morgan's Grill, ⊙ CVS Drug, Food Lion, vet, New Market Hist Dist
59	MD 144
57mm	Monocacy River
56	MD 144, **N** ⛽ BP, Sheetz, ⑪ Beijing, Burger King, JR's Pizza, McDonald's, Roy Rogers, Taco Bell, Waffle House, Wendy's, ⊙ $General, to Hist Dist, **S** ⊙ Triangle RV Ctr
55	South St **1 mi N** ⛽ BP, Sheetz/dsl

MD

⬆E INTERSTATE 70 CONT'D

Exit	Services
54	Market St, to I-270, **N** 🅖 Costco/gas, 🛏 Travelodge, **S** 🅖 7-11, Sheetz, Shell, Valero, SouStates/dsl, 🍴 Arby's, Bob Evans, Burger King, Checker's, Cracker Barrel, Jerry's Rest., KFC/Taco Bell, Longhorn Steaks, McDonald's, Papa John's, Popeye's, Red Robin, Roy Rogers, Ruby Tuesday, Subway, Waffle House, Wendy's, 🛏 Courtyard, Days Inn, EconoLodge, Fairfield Inn, Hampton Inn, Holiday Inn, Holiday Inn Express, Sleep Inn, 🅞 Aamco, Audi, Best Buy, Buick, Chrysler/Dodge/Jeep, Ford/Lincoln, Home Depot, Honda, Hyundai, JC Penney, Kia, Kohl's, Lowe's, Michael's, Mr Tire, Nissan, Ross, Sam's Club/gas, Sears/auto, Staples, Tires+, TJMaxx, Toyota, Volvo, Walmart, mall
53b a	I-270 S, US 15 N, US 40 W, to Frederick
52b a	US 15 S, US 340 W, Leesburg
49	US 40A, Braddock Heights, **N on US 40** 🅖 Citgo/dsl, Exxon/dsl, Freestate/dsl, GetGo, Shell, Sunoco, 🍴 Arby's, Bob Evans, Boscov's, Boston Mkt, Burger King, Carrabba's, Casa Rico Mexican, City Buffet, Denny's, Dunkin Donuts, Famous Dave's BBQ, Flaming Grill, Fritchie's Rest., Ground Round, HoneyBaked Ham, Hunter's Rest., KFC, Los Trios, McDonald's, Mtn View Diner, Outback Steaks, Pizza Hut, Popeye's, Red Lobster, Roy Rogers, Ruby Tuesday, Starbucks, Subway, Taco Bell, Wendy's, 🛏 Comfort Inn, Motel 6, 🅞 🏥, Advance Parts, Aldi Foods, AT&T, CVS Drug, $General, Ford/Subaru, Giant Eagle Foods, Goodyear/auto, Home Depot, K-Mart, Merchant Tire, Mr Tire, PepBoys, PetCo, 7-11, Tire Pros, Toyota, Verizon, Weis Foods, st police, **S** to Washington Mon SP, camping
48	US 40 E, US 340 (from eb, no return), **1 mi N** same as 49
42	MD 17, Myersville, **N** 🅖 Exxon, Sunoco/dsl, 🍴 Burger King, McDonald's, Old Town Diner, 🅞 to Gambrill SP (6mi); Greenbrier SP (4mi), **S** 🅖 Crown/dsl, 🍴 Subway
39mm	🅁🅂 both lanes, full 🛏 facilities, 🚰 vending, 🗑 litter barrels, petwalk
35	MD 66, to Boonsboro, **S** 🅖 Sheetz/dsl (1mi), 🅞 to Greenbrier SP, camping
32b a	US 40, Hagerstown, **0-3 mi N** 🅖 BP, Exxon/dsl, 7-11, Sheetz/dsl, Sunoco, 🍴 Baskin-Robbins/Dunkin Donuts, Bob Evans, Burger King, Checkers, Denny's, DQ, El Ranchero Mexican, 5 Guys Burgers, Hall of Fame Rest., Hong Kong Chinese, Jimmy John's, KFC, Ledo's Pizza, Little Caesars, McDonald's, Papa John's, Papa Murphy's, Pizza Hut, Popeye's, Quiznos, Sonic, Subway, Super Buffet, Taco Bell, TX Roadhouse, 🛏 Best Western, Clarion, Comfort Suites, Days Inn, Hampton Inn, Super 8, 🅞 🏥, Advance Parts, Aldi Foods, AT&T, AutoZone, Cadillac/Chevrolet, Chrysler/Dodge/Jeep, CVS Drug, $Tree, Family$, Firestone/auto, Martin's Foods, Midas, Mercedes, Mr Tire, Nissan, Tires+, Toyota/Scion, Walgreens, Weis Foods, **S** 🅞 Buick/GMC, Honda, Kia, Subaru, VW
29b a	MD 65, to Sharpsburg, **N** 🅖 Exxon/Subway/dsl, Sheetz, 🍴 FoodCourt, Longhorn Steaks, Starbucks, 🅞 🏥, Prime Outlets/famous brands, st police, **S** 🅖 Liberty/7-11/dsl, 🍴 Burger King, Cracker Barrel, McDonald's, Waffle House, Wendy's, 🛏 Sleep Inn, 🅞 Safari Camping, to Antietam Bfd
28	MD 632, Hagerstown
26	I-81, N to Harrisburg, S to Martinsburg

Exit	Services
24	MD 63, Huyett, **N** 🅖 🚚/Subway/dsl/24hr, Sheetz/dsl (2mi), **S** 🛏 Red Roof Inn, 🅞 KOA (2mi), C&O Canal
18	MD 68 E, Clear Spring, **N** 🅖 BP, Liberty, 🍴 McDonald's, 🛏 Sleep Inn, **S** 🅖 Exxon/dsl, 🍴 Wendy Hill Café
12	MD 56, Indian Springs, **S** 🅖 Exxon/dsl, 🅞 Ft Frederick SP
9	US 40 E (from eb, exits left), Indian Springs
5	MD 615 (no immediate wb return), **N** 🍴 Log Cabin Rest. (2mi)
3	MD 144, Hancock (exits left from wb), **S** 🅖 ACT/Exxon/dsl, Liberty/rest./dsl/24hr, 🍴 Hardee's, Park'n Dine, 🛏 Hilltop Inn, 🅞 Blue Goose Mkt
1b	US 522 (exits left from both lanes), Hancock, **N** 🅞 Chevrolet, Chrysler/Dodge/Jeep, **S** 🅖 PitStop, Mobil/dsl Sheetz/dsl, 🍴 Pizza Hut, Subway, Weaver's Rest., 🛏 Best Value Inn, Super 8, 🅞 $General, Save-A-Lot Foods, Happy Hills Camp, NAPA
1a	I-68 W, US 40, W to Cumberland
0mm	Maryland/Pennsylvania state line Mason-Dixon Line

⬆N INTERSTATE 81

Exit	Services
12mm	Maryland/Pennsylvania state line
10b a	Showalter Rd, E ✈
9	Maugans Ave, **E** 🅖 BP, Sheetz, Shell/Domino's/dsl, 🍴 McDonald's, Papa Murphy's, Pizza Hut, Quiznos, Taco Bell, Waffle House, 🛏 Hampton Inn, 🅞 AutoZone, CVS Drug, $General, Food Lion, Martin's Foods/gas, vet, **W** 🍴 Burger King, 🛏 Microtel, 🅞 Kenworth, Volvo
7b a	MD 58, Hagerstown, same as 6
6b a	US 40, Hagerstown, **E** 🅖 Shell, 🛏 Comfort Inn, Days Inn, Super 8, 🅞 🏥, **W** 🍴 Arby's, Chipotle Mexican, 5 Guys Burgers, IHOP, Jersey Mike's Subs, KFC, McDonald's, Panera Bread, Uno Pizza, Ryan's, Starbucks, Subway, TGIFriday's, Wendy's, 🅞 AT&T, Best Buy, Dick's, $Tree, Home Depot, Marshall's, Petsmart, Walmart
5b a	Halfway Blvd, **E** 🅖 AC&T/dsl, 🍴 Bob Evans, Boston Mkt, Buffalo Wild Wings, Burger King, Café Rio, Chick-fil-A, ChuckECheese's, CiCi's Pizza, Cinco de Mayo, Coldstone, Crazy Horse Steaks, El Ranchero Mexican, Garfield's Rest., Golden Corral, McDonald's, Olive Garden, Orchid Garden, Outback Steaks, Papa John's, Pizza Hut, Popeye's, Quizno's, Red Lobster, Roy Rogers, Ruby Tuesday, Sakura Steaks, Shoney's, Taco Bell, Tilted Kilt, Wendy's, 🛏 Country Inn&Suites, Courtyard, Holiday Inn Express, Homewood Suites, Motel 6, Ramada, SpringHill Suites, 🅞 AT&T, BigLots, BonTon, CVS Drug, $Tree, Firestone/auto, Ford, Hobby Lobby, Hyundai, JC Penney, K-Mart, Lowe's, Macy's, Martin's Foods/gas, Michael's, PetCo, Ross, Sam's Club/gas, Sears/auto, Staples, Target, mall, **W** 🅖 Exxon/dsl/scales/24hr, 🚚/McDonald's/Subway/dsl/scales/24hr, 🛏 Super 8, 🅞 Freightliner
4	I-70, E to Frederick, W to Hancock, to I-68
2	US 11, Williamsport, **E** 🅖 AC&T/dsl, **W** 🅖 Exxon/dsl, Sunoco/dsl, 🍴 China 88, McDonald's, Waffle House, Subway, 🛏 Red Roof Inn, 🅞 KOA (4mi), auto repair
1	MD 63, MD 68, Williamsport, **E** 🅖 Bowman/dsl, 🅞 Jellystone, KOA, to Antietam Bfd, **W** 🅖 Citgo, 🅞 $General, NAPA
0mm	Maryland/West Virginia state line, Potomac River

⬆N INTERSTATE 83

Exit	Services
38mm	Maryland/Pennsylvania state line, Mason-Dixon Line
37	to Freeland

MD

INTERSTATE 83 CONT'D

BALTIMORE

Exit	Services
36	MD 439, Bel Air, W [gas] Sub-Shop, [food] Maryland Line Inn Grill, [other] Holiday Travel Park (5mi), Morris Meadows Camping (5mi)
35mm	**weigh/insp sta sb**
33	MD 45, Parkton, E USPO
31	Middletown Rd, to Parkton, golf
27	MD 137, Mt Carmel, Hereford, E [gas] Exxon/dsl, [food] Subway, [other] Graul's Foods, Hereford Drug, Mt Carmel Drug, NAPA, USPO, vet
24	Belfast Rd, to Butler, Sparks
20	Shawan Rd, Hunt Valley, E [gas] BP, Exxon/dsl, [food] Burger King, Caribou Coffee, Carmine's Pizza, Carrabba's, Chipotle Mexican, McDonald's, Noodles&Co, Outback Steaks, Quizno's, Panera Bread, Subway, Wendy's, Wong's Kitchen, [lodging] Chase Suites, Courtyard, Embassy Suites, Hampton Inn, Hunt Valley Marriott, Ramada Ltd, [other] Giant Foods, Goodyear/auto, Sears/auto, 7-11, Wegman's Foods, mall, vet
18	Warren Rd (from nb, no return), Cockeysville, E [gas] Exxon, [lodging] Residence Inn, services E on York Rd
17	Padonia Rd, Deereco Rd, E [gas] BP/dsl, Hess, Shell, [food] Applebee's, Bob Evans, Chili's, Macaroni Grill, Wendy's, [lodging] Day's Hotel, Extended Stay America, [other] Audi/VW, Chevrolet, Goodyear/auto, Mars Foods, Mr Tire, Porsche, Shopper's Foods, Subaru, Target, USPO, services E on York Rd
16b a	Timonium Rd, E [gas] BP, Petro/Subway, Sunoco/dsl, [food] Baja Fresh, McDonald's, [lodging] Crowne Plaza, Red Roof Inn, [other] Infiniti/Nissan, Rite Aid
14	I-695 N
13	I-695 S, Falls Rd [H], st police
12	Ruxton Rd (from nb, no return)
10b a	Northern Parkway, E [gas] Exxon, Shell, [other] [H]
9b a	Cold Spring Lane
8	MD 25 N (from nb), Falls Rd
7b a	28th St, E [H], W Baltimore Zoo
6	US 1, US 40T, North Ave, downtown
5	MD Ave (from sb), downtown
3	Chase St, Gilford St, downtown
2	Pleasant St (from sb), downtown
1	**Fayette St, I-83 begins/ends**, downtown Baltimore

INTERSTATE 95

Exit	Services
110mm	Maryland/Delaware state line
109b a	MD 279, to Elkton, Newark, E [gas] FLYING J/Patriot Farms/dsl/scales/24hr/@, Shell/dsl, [food] Cracker Barrel, KFC/Taco Bell, McDonald's, Waffle House, [lodging] Days Inn, Elkton Lodge, Hampton Inn, Knights Inn, La Quinta, Motel 6, [other] [H], Blue Beacon, W [gas] TA/Subway/dsl/24hr/@, 7-11, WaWa, [lodging] Comfort Suites, [other] to U of DE
100	MD 272, to North East, Rising Sun, E [gas] FLYING J/Denny's/dsl/LP/24hr, Sunoco/dsl, [food] Burger King, Dunkin Donuts, Empire Rest., Frank's Pizza, McDonald's, Waffle House, Wendy's, [lodging] Comfort Inn, Holiday Inn Express, [other] Advance Parts, AT&T, $General, $Tree, Food Lion, PetCo, Rite Aid, Verizon, Walgreens, Walmart/Subway, auto repair, st police, to Elk Neck SP, W [gas] Citgo, [lodging] Best Western, [other] zoo
96mm	**Chesapeake House service area** (exits left from both

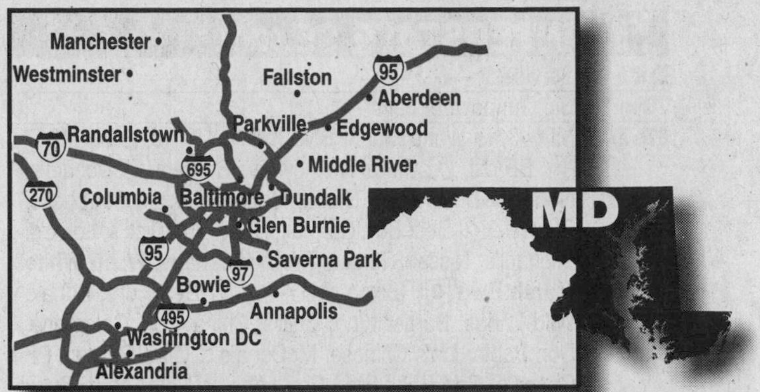

ABERDEEN

Exit	Services
96mm	Continued lanes), Exxon/dsl, Sunoco/dsl, Burger King, Popeye's, Quiznos, Starbucks, gifts
93	MD 275, to Rising Sun, US 222, to Perryville, E [gas] Exxon/dsl, Pilot/Subway/dsl/scales/24hr, [food] Denny's, KFC/Taco Bell, [lodging] Ramada Inn, [other] [H], Perryville Outlets/famous brands, Riverview Camping
92mm	**weigh sta/toll booth**
91.5mm	Susquehanna River
89	MD 155, to Havre de Grace (last nb exit before toll), **1-3 mi** E [food] Burger King, Chesapeake Grill, Dunkin Donuts, MacGregor's Rest., McDonald's, Waffle House, [lodging] Best Budget Inn, Super 8, Van Divers B&B, [other] [H], W to Susquehanna SP
85	MD 22, to Aberdeen, E [gas] BP/dsl, 7-11, Shell/dsl, Royal Farms/dsl, [food] Applebee's, Arby's, Baskin-Robbins/Dunkin Donuts, Bob Evans, Burger King, Durango's, Family Buffet, KFC, Korea House, Little Caesars, Mamie's Cafe, McDonald's, Olive Tree Italian, Panera Bread, Papa John's, Pizza Hut, Rita's Custard, Subway, Taco Bell, Wendy's, [lodging] Clarion, Days Inn, Hilton Garden, Holiday Inn, La Quinta, Red Roof Inn, Super 8, Travelodge, [other] $General, $Tree, Home Depot, Mars Foods, Radio Shack, Rite Aid, ShopRite Foods, Target, Verizon, Walgreens, auto repair, museum, E [lodging] Courtyard, Residence Inn
81mm	**MD House service area** (exits left from both lanes), Exxon/dsl, Sunoco/dsl, Phillips Seafood, Roy Rogers, Sharro's, Starbucks, TCBY, gifts
80	MD 543, to Riverside, Churchville, E [gas] BP/Burger King, 7-11, Shell/Quiznos/dsl, Sunoco, [food] Arby's, China Moon, Cracker Barrel, McDonald's, Pizza Hut, Riverside Crabs, Riverside Grille, Riverside Pizzeria, Ruby Tuesday, Subway, Waffle House, [lodging] Candlewood Suites, Country Inn&Suites, Extended Stay America, Homewood Suites, SpringHill Suites, Wingate Inn, [other] Bar Harbor RV Park (4mi), Rite Aid, ShopRite Foods, Verizon
77b a	MD 24, to Edgewood, Bel Air, E [gas] BP/dsl, Citgo/dsl, Exxon/dsl, Royal Farms/dsl, [food] Denny's, Dimitri's Pizza, El Rodeo, My 3 Sons Rest., Waffle House, [lodging] Best Western, Days Inn, Hampton Inn, Holiday Inn Express, Ramada Inn, Sleep Inn, [other] **Urgent Care**, W [gas] Exxon/dsl, WaWa/dsl, [food] Chick-fil-A, KFC/Taco Bell, McDonald's, Starbucks, [other] [H], BJ's Whse, $Tree, Lowe's, Target, Walmart/Subway, Wegman's Foods
74	MD 152, Fallston, Joppatowne, E [gas] BP/dsl, Citgo/dsl, Exxon/dsl, Sheetz, Shell/dsl, WaWa/dsl, [food] Dunkin Donuts, Friendly's, KFC, Subway, Venitian Palace, Wendy's, [lodging] Edgewood Motel, Super 8, [other] [H], Toyota (1mi), W [gas] Royal Farms/dsl

I-95 **INTERSTATE 95** CONT'D

Exit	Services
70mm	Big Gunpowder Falls
67b a	MD 43, to White Marsh Blvd, US 1, US 40, **E on MD 7** 🅞 BP/dsl, 🍴 Chick-fil-A, 5 Guys Burgers, McDonald's, Noodles&Co, Panera Bread, Qdoba Mexian, Starbucks, Subway, 🅞 Best Buy, Carmax, Chevrolet, Dick's, Lowe's, Michael's, Nissan, Target, Tire Discounters, **W on White Marsh Blvd** 🅞 Exxon/dsl, 7-11, 🍴 Bertucci's, Buffalo Wild Wings, Burger King, Chili's, China Wok, Coldstone, Don Pablo, Lin's Chinese, McDonald's, Olive Garden, PF Chang's, Red Brick Sta., Red Lobster, Red Robin, Ruby Tuesday, Starbucks, Taco Bell, TGIFriday's, Wendy's, Z-Burger, Zack's Hotdogs, 🏠 Fairfield Inn, Hampton Inn, Hilton Garden, Residence Inn, 🅞 AT&T, Barnes&Noble, Giant Foods, JC Penney, Macy's, Old Navy, Sears/auto, Staples, USPO, Verizon, mall, to Gunpowder SP
64b a	I-695 (exits left), E to Essex, W to Towson
62	to I-895 (from sb)
61	US 40, Pulaski Hwy, **E** 🅖 BP, Shell/dsl, 🍴 McDonald's
60	Moravia Rd
59	Eastern Ave, **W** 🅖 BP/dsl, Exxon, Royal Farms/dsl, WaWa, 🍴 Broadway Diner, McDonald's, Subway, Wendy's, 🅞🅷 AT&T, Shoppers Foods
58	Dundalk Ave, (from nb), **E** 🅖 Citgo, Sunoco
57	O'Donnell St, Boston St, **E** 🅖 TA/Buckhorn/Subway/dsl/scales/motel/@, 🍴 McDonald's, 🏠 Best Western
56	Keith Ave
56mm	McHenry Tunnel, toll plaza (north side of tunnel)
55	Key Hwy, to Ft McHenry NM, last nb exit before toll
54	MD 2 S, to Hanover St, **W** downtown, 🅷 Harris Teeter
53	I-395 N, to MLK, **W** downtown, Oriole Park
52	Russell St N, **W** 🅷
51	Washington Blvd
50.5mm	inspection sta nb
50	Caton Ave, **E** 🅖 Citgo, Hess/dsl, Quest, Shell/dsl, 🍴 Caton House, McDonald's, Polock Johnny Sausages, 🏠 Motel 6, 🅞 Aldi Foods, Toyota/Scion, auto repair, **W** 🅷
49b a	I-695, E to Key Bridge, Glen Burnie, W to Towson, to I-70, to I-83
47b a	I-195, to MD 166, to BWI ✈, to Baltimore
46	I-895, to Harbor Tunnel Thruway
43b a	MD 100, to Glen Burnie, **1 mi E on US 1** 🅖 Exxon/Wendy's, Xtra, 🏠 Best Western
41b a	MD 175, to Columbia, **E** 🅖 Citgo, Exxon/dsl, Shell/dsl, TA/Country Pride/Subway/dsl/scales/24hr/@, 🍴 Arby's, Burger King, Fortune Star Chinese, Julia's, McDonald's, Panda Express, Starbucks, 🏠 Comfort Suites, Holiday Inn, La Quinta, Red Roof Inn, Sleep Inn, Super 8, 🅞 Mom's Organic Mkt, **W** 🅖 Exxon, 🍴 Applebee's, Bob Evans, Fat Burger, Houlihan's, Mamma Lucia, McDonald's, Mimi's Cafe, Olive Garden, On the Border, TGIFriday's, 🏠 Homewood Suites, Studio+, 🅞🅷 Best Buy, Costco/gas, Lowe's, Office Depot, Royal Farms, 7-11, Trader Joe's, to Johns Hopkins U, Loyola U
38b a	MD 32, to Ft Meade, **2 mi E on US 1** 🅖 BP, Royal Farms, Shell/dsl, 🍴 Burger King, Dunkin Donuts, McDonald's, Subway, Taco Bell, 🏠 Comfort Inn, Extended Stay America, 🅞 to BWI ✈, **E** 🅞🅷
37mm	**Welcome Ctr both lanes, full ♿ facilities, info, 🕾, vending, 🗑 litter barrels, petwalk, RV Dump**
35b a	MD 216, to Laurel, **E** 🅖 Exxon, Shell/dsl, 🍴 McDonald's,

Exit	Services
35b a	Continued, Subway, 🅞 Weis Food/drug
34mm	Patuxent River
33b a	MD 198, to Laurel, **E** 🅖 Exxon, 🅞🅷 **W** 🅖 Exxon/Blimpie, Shell, 🍴 Outback Steaks, Starbucks, 🏠 Holiday Inn
31	MD 200 (toll)
29	MD 212, to Beltsville, **W** 🅖 Exxon/Blimpie/dsl, 🍴 Baskin-Robbins, Danny's Subs, KFC, McDonald's, Taco Bell, The Villa Rest., Wendy's, 🏠 Comfort Inn, Sheraton, 🅞 Cherry Hill Park, CVS Drug, Giant Foods
27	I-495 S around Washington
25b a	US 1, Baltimore Ave, to Laurel, College Park, **E** 🅖 BP/dsl, Chevron, Exxon/dsl, 7-11, Shell/24hr, 🍴 Arby's, Buffalo Wild Wings, Burger King, Dickey's BBQ, Domino's, El Mexicano, Jerry's Subs, KFC, McDonald's, Moose Creek Steaks, Papa John's, Pizza Hut/Taco Bell, Potbelly's, Quizno's, Subway, 3 Bro's Rest., Wendy's, 🏠 Holiday Inn, 🅞 Urgent Care, Advance Parts, Costco, CVS Drug, PetCo, Radio Shack, Rite Aid, US Agri Library, Verizon, **W** 🅖 BP/24hr, Shell, Xtra, 🍴 Burger King, Dunkin Donuts, China Buffet, College Park Diner, Hard Times Cafe, IHOP, Pizza Hut, Starbucks, Taco Bell, 🏠 Clarion, Comfort Inn, Days Inn, EconoLodge, Hampton Inn, Howard Johnson, Ramada Ltd, Super 8, 🅞 GNC, Home Depot, Honda, Hyundai, Nissan, Shoppers Foods, VW, vet, to U of MD
24	(from sb) to metro
23	MD 201, Kenilworth Ave, **E** 🏠 Marriott/rest., **1 mi W on Greenbelt** 🅖 Shell, 🍴 Atlanta Bread, Boston Mkt, Checker's, Chipotle Mexican, KFC, McDonald's, Popeye's, Quizno's, Silver Diner, TGIFriday's, Wendy's, William's Bistro, 🏠 Courtyard, Hilton Garden, Residence Inn, 🅞 Cadillac, CVS Drug, Giant Food/drug, Jo-Ann Fabrics, Marshall's, Staples, Target
22	Baltimore-Washington Pkwy, **E** to NASA
20b a	MD 450, Annapolis Rd, Lanham, **E** 🍴 Burger King, Jerry's Subs, McDonald's, Red Lobster, 🏠 Best Western, Days Inn/rest., Red Roof Inn, 🅞 Ford/KIA, **W** 🅖 BP, Chevron/dsl, Liberty, 7-11, Shell, Sunoco/24hr, Texaco, 🍴 Bojangles, Domino's, Dunkin Donuts, El Gran Chaparral, 5 Guys Burgers, IHOP, KFC, Manny&Olga's Pizza, Popeye's, Quizno's, Subway, Wendy's, 🏠 Sheraton, 🅞🅷 Aamco, Advance Parts, Chevrolet, Chrysler/Dodge/Jeep, Curves, CVS Drug, $Value, Foodway Foods, Giant Foods, Just-Tires, Lincoln, Lowe's, Office Depot, Radio Shack, Shoppers Foods, Staples
19b a	US 50, to Annapolis, Washington
17	MD 202, Landover Rd, to Upper Marlboro, **E** 🍴 Jasper's Rest., Outback Steaks, Ruby Tuesday, 🏠 Holiday Inn Express, Radisson, **W** 🅞 FedEx Center, Sears/auto
16	Arena Dr, **E** 🍴 Bugaboo Creek Steaks, Carolina Kitchen, Chick-fil-A, ChuckeCheese, 5 Guys Burgers, Golden Corral, Kobe Japanese, Momma Rosa, Panda Express, Qdoba, Quizno's, Stonefish Grill, 🅞 **W** to Arena
15	MD 214, Central Ave, **E** 🏠 Extended Stay America, Hampton Inn, 🅞 to Six Flags, **W** 🅖 Exxon/dsl, Liberty, Shell, Texaco/dsl, 🍴 A&W/LJ Silver, Checker's, Dunkin Donuts, KFC, IHOP, Jerry's Subs, McDonald's, Panda Express, Pizza Hut, Subway, Taco Bell, Wendy's, 🏠 Comfort Inn, Country Inn&Suites, 🅞 Urgent Care, Family$, Goodyear/auto, Home Depot, NTB, Staples, U-Haul
13	Ritchie-Marlboro Rd, Capitol Hgts, **W** 🅖 WaWa, 🍴

BALTIMORE

WASHINGTON DC AREA

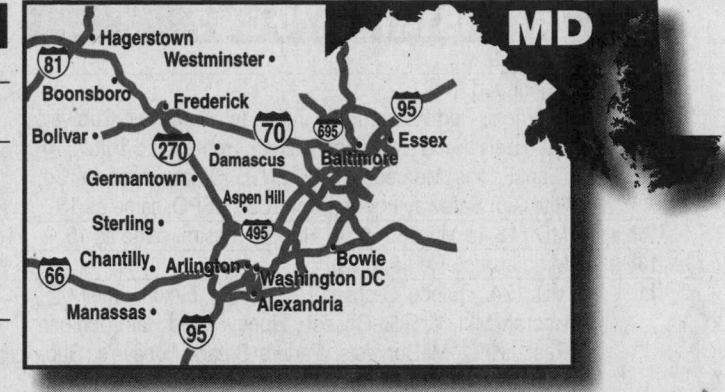

INTERSTATE 95 CONT'D

Exit	Services
13	Continued Chick-fil-A, 🅾 BJ Whse/gas
11	MD 4, Pennsylvania Ave, to Upper Marlboro, **W** 🅖 Exxon, Shell, Sunoco, 🍴 Applebee's, Arby's, Domino's, 5 Guys Burgers, IHOP, LJ Silver, Old Country Buffet, Pizza Hut, Starbucks, Subway, Taco Bell, Wendy's, 🅾 CVS Drug, $Tree, Hancock Fabrics, JC Penney, Marshall's, PetCo, Shoppers Foods, Staples, Target, st police
9	MD 337, to Allentown Rd, **E** 🅖 Shell/repair, Texaco, 🍴 Arby's, Checker's, Dunkin Donuts, McDonald's, Popeye's, 🏠 Days Inn, Quality Inn, Super 8, 🅾 🏨, U-Haul, to Andrews AFB, **W** 🅖 Sunoco
7	MD 5, Branch Ave, to Silver Hill, **E** 🅖 Exxon, Getty, Sunoco, 🍴 Dunkin Donuts, Wendy's, **W** 🅖 Shell/Subway/dsl, 🍴 Red Lobster, 🏠 Holiday Inn Express, 🅾 🏨, BMW, Chrysler/Dodge/Jeep, Ford, KIA, Lincoln, Nissan, Scion/Toyota, VW
4b a	MD 414, St Barnabas Rd, Marlow Hgts, **E** 🅖 Citgo/dsl, Zip-in, 🍴 Burger King, Checker's, IHOP, KFC, McDonald's, Outback Steaks, Wendy's, 🏠 Red Roof Inn, 🅾 CVS Drug, $Tree, GNC, Home Depot, K-Mart, Old Navy, Petsmart, Safeway Foods, Staples, **W** 🅖 Exxon/dsl, Shell/autocare, 🍴 China Best, McDonald's, Subway, 🅾 Family$
3b a	MD 210, Indian Head Hwy, to Forest Hgts, **E** 🅖 Chevron, Shell, Sunoco, 🍴 Dunkin Donuts, Popeye's, Ranch House Rest., Subway, Taco Bell, 🏠 Clarion, Comfort Inn, Red Roof Inn, 🅾 Advance Parts, Aldi Foods, Radio Shack, Sav-A-Lot Foods, Shoppers Foods, USPO, **W** 🅖 BP/dsl/24hr, Pure, Shell, Texaco, 🍴 Burger King, McDonald's, Papa John's, Popeye's, Subway, 🅾 CVS Drug, Family$, Giant Foods, Goodyear/auto, Radio Shack, Rite Aid, 7-11
2b a	I-295, N to Washingon
0mm	Maryland/Virginia state line, Potomac River, Woodrow Wilson Bridge

INTERSTATE 97

Exit	Services
17	I-695. **I-97 begins/ends on I-695.**
16	MD 648, Ferndale, Glen Burnie, **E** 🅖 BP, Shell, 🍴 Hong Kong Cafe, KFC, McDonald's, Rita's Custard, Wendy's, 🅾 $General, Giant Foods, **W** 🅖 Citgo
15b a	MD 176 W, Dorsey Rd, Aviation Blvd, **E** 🅖 BP, Shell, 🍴 KFC, McDonald's, Wendy's, **W** 🅾 to BWI, st police
14b a	MD 100, Ellicott City, Gibson Island
13b a	MD 174, Quarterfield Rd, **E** 🅖 AP/dsl, Gulf, 7-11, 🍴 Subway, The Grill, 🅾 WaWa, **W** 🅖 Shell/dsl, 🍴 Chick-fil-A, Pizza Hut, Quiznos, 🅾 AT&T, Kohl's, Lowe's, Rite Aid, Sam's Club/dsl, Shoppers Foods, Walmart
12	MD 3, New Cut Rd, Glen Burnie, **E on Veterans Hwy** 🅖 BP, Gulf, Royal Farms, WaWa, 🍴 Domino's, KFC, McDonald's, Taco Bell, 🅾 CVS Drug, vet, **E** 🅖 Exxon, Sunoco, 🍴 Burger King, Fortune Cooky, Friendly's, Hardee's, Squisto NY Pizza, Subway, Wendy's, 🅾 🏨, Ace Hardware, Giant Foods, Goodyear/auto, Target, Walgreens
10b a	Benfield Blvd, Severna Park, **E** 🅖 BP/dsl, Exxon/Quiznos/dsl, Transit/dsl/scales, 🍴 Baskin-Robbins/Dunkin Donuts, Hella's Rest., Ledo's Pizza, 🅾 KOA, 7-11, access to same as 12

7	MD 3, MD 32, Bowie, Odenton, **E** motel
5	MD 178 (from sb, no EZ return), Crownsville
0mm	**I-97 begins/ends on US 50/301.**

INTERSTATE 270

Exit	Services
32	**I-270 begins/ends on I-70, exit 53.**
31b a	MD 85, **N** 🅖 Lowest Price/dsl, 7-11, Sheetz/24hr, Shell/24hr, SouStates/dsl, 🍴 Applebee's, Arby's, Bob Evans, Burger King, Checker's, Chick-fil-A, El Ranchero Mexican, Golden Corral, Houlihan's, Jerry's Pizza, KFC, Longhorn Steaks, McDonald's, Olive Garden, Panera Bread, Papa John's, Peking Gourmet, Perkin's, Pizza Hut, Popeye's, Roy Rogers, Ruby Tuesday, Silver Diner, Subway, Taco Bell, UNO Grill, Waffle House, Wendy's, 🏠 Days Inn, EconoLodge, Holiday Inn Express, Sleep Inn, Travelodge, 🅾 Aamco, Audi, Barnes&Noble, Best Buy, Buick/GMC, Chrysler/Dodge/Jeep, Costco/gas, Harley-Davidson, Home Depot, Hyundai, JC Penney, Kohl's, Lincoln, Lowe's, Macy's, Michael's, Mr Tire, Nissan, Office Depot, Ross, Sam's Club, Sears/auto, Staples, Tires+, Volvo, vet, Walmart, mall, **S** 🅖 BP, 🍴 Chipotle Mexican, Cracker Barrel, Firehouse Subs, IHOP, Macaroni Grill, Maggie Moo's, McDonald's, Mediterranean Grill, Mimi's Cafe, Panda Express, Quizno's, Starbucks, TGIFriday's, 🏠 Comfort Inn, Courtyard, Extended Stay America, Fairfield Inn, Hampton Inn, Hilton Garden, MainStay Suites, Residence Inn, 🅾 Honda, Toyota
30mm	Monocacy River
28mm	scenic view, no restrooms (wb only)
26	MD 80, Urbana, **N** 🅖 Exxon, 7-11, 🍴 Buffalo Wild Wings, China Taste, Dunkin Donuts, Foster's Grill, Ledo's Pizza, McDonald's, Waffle House
22	MD 109, to Barnesville, Hyattstown, **N** 🅖 BP/dsl, 🍴 Hyattstown Deli, 🅾 Food+
21mm	weigh/insp sta both lanes
18	MD 121, to Clarksburg, Boyds, **N** Little Bennett Pk, camping, gas, **S** Blackhill Pk
16	MD 27, Father Hurley Blvd, to Damascus, **N** 🅖 Chevron, Exxon, Free State/dsl, Sunoco, 🍴 Applebee's, Bob Evans, Burger King, Jersey Mike's Subs, McDonald's, Starbucks, Subway, 🏠 Extended Stay America, Hampton Inn, 🅾 AT&T, Best Buy, Giant Foods, GNC, Home Depot, Kohl's, Michael's, PepBoys, Petsmart, TJ Maxx, Target, Verizon, Walmart, **S** 🅖 BP, Exxon, 7-11, Shell, Sunoco, 🍴 Bailey's Grill, Baja Fresh, Burger King, Carrabba's, Chick-fil-A, Domino's, Dunkin Donuts, 5 Guys Burgers, Hardtimes Cafe, IHOP, Jerry's Subs, Longhorn Steaks, McDonald's, Mi Rancho, Panera Bread, Pizza Hut,

(Left margin: GLEN BURNIE)
(Right margin: FREDERICK)
(Bottom right: MD)

🅟 = gas 🍽 = food 🛏 = lodging 🅞 = other 🆁🆂 = rest stop Copyright 2014 - The Next Exit ®

INTERSTATE 270 CONT'D

Exit	Services
16	Continued
	Quizno's, Red Robin, Ruby Tuesday, Starbucks, Subway, Taco Bell, Wendy's, 🛏 Fairfield Inn, Homestead Suites, 🅞 Giant Foods, Mercedes, NAPA, NTB, Office Depot, PetCo, Rite Aid, Safeway Foods, SmartCar, USPO, same as 15
15b a	MD 118, to MD 355, **S** 🅞 Honda, Nissan, same as 16
13b a	Middlebrook Rd (from wb)
11	MD 124, Quince Orchard Rd, **N** 🅟 Exxon, Shell, 🍽 Boston Mkt, ChuckeCheese, Honeybaked Ham, Ichiban Rest., KFC, McDonald's, Panera Bread, Popeye's, Subway, 🛏 Hilton, Holiday Inn, TownePlace Suites, Wyndham Garden, 🅞 Aamco, Acura, AT&T, Costco, CVS Drugs, Ford, Hyundai, JC Penney, JustTires, Lincoln, Lord&Taylor, Macy's, Mazda, NAPA, Nissan, Ross, Sam's Club, Sears/auto, Toyota, VW, mall, **S** 🅟 Shell/dsl, 🍽 Chevy's Mexican, CiCi's Pizza, Jerry's Subs, Rita's Ice Cream, Starbucks, 🛏 Motel 6, 🅞 Advance Parts, Chevrolet, Chrysler/Dodge/Jeep, Giant Foods, JoAnn Fabrics, McGruder's Foods, Rite Aid, Staples, Seneca Creek SP
10	MD 117, Clopper Rd (from wb), same as 11
9b a	I-370, to Gaithersburg, Sam Eig Hwy, **S on Washington Blvd** 🅟 Chevron, 🍽 Joe's Crabshack, Macaroni Grill, Pizza Hut, Red Rock Grill, Subway, Uncle Julio's, 🛏 Courtyard, 🅞 Barnes&Noble, Kohl's, Target, Weis Mkt
8	Shady Grove Rd, **N** 🅟 Chevron, Shell/dsl, 🍽 Bugaboo Creek Steaks, Burger King, Red Lobster, 🛏 Sheraton, 🅞 AT&T, Best Buy, Home Depot, Office Depot, 7-11, vet, **S** 🍽 Thatsamore, 🛏 Courtyard, Crowne Plaza, Marriott, Residence Inn, Sleep Inn, SpringHill Suites, 🅞🅗
6b a	MD 28, W Montgomery Ave, **N** 🅞🅗, **S** 🅟 Shell, 🛏 Best Western
5b a	MD 189, Falls Rd
4b a	Montrose Rd, **N** gas, **S** 🍽 Starbucks, 🅞 Harris Teeter, Walgreens st police
2	I-270/I-270 spur diverges eb, converges wb
1	MD 187, Old Georgetown Rd, **S** 🅟 Exxon, 🍽 Hamburger Hamlet, 🅞🅗, Balducci's Foods, Giant Foods, GNC
1b a	(I-270 spur) Democracy Blvd, **E** 🛏 Marriott, **W** 🅟 Exxon/dsl, Shell/dsl, 🅞 Macy's, Nordstrom's, Sears, mall
0mm	**I-270 begins/ends on I-495, exit 35.**

INTERSTATE 495 (DC)

See Virginia Interstate 495 (DC)

INTERSTATE 695 (BALTIMORE)

Exit	Services
48mm	Patapsco River, Francis Scott Key Br
44	MD 695 (from nb)
43mm	**toll plaza**
42	MD 151 S, Sparrows Point (last exit before toll sb), **E** 🅟 Citgo/dsl, 🅞 North Point SP
41	MD 20, Cove Rd, **W** 🅟 Royal Farms, WaWa, 🍽 Burger King, McDonald's, Subway
40	MD 150, MD 151, North Point Blvd, (nb only)
39	Merritt Blvd, **W** 🅟 BP, 🍽 Burger King, McDonald's, 🅞 Aldi Foods, $Tree, Ford, Giant Foods, Honda, Hyundai, JC Penney, Mazda, Mr Tire, Walmart
38b a	MD 150, Eastern Blvd, to Baltimore, **E** 🅟 Royal Farms, **W** 🍽 Applebee's, Arby's, Burger King, Cactus Willy's Steaks, Checker's, Chick-fil-A, Dunkin Donuts, 🅞 AT&T, Kia/Nissan, Sears/auto, Staples, Walgreens, mall

Exit	Services
36	MD 702 S (exits left from sb), Essex
35	US 40, **N** 🅟 WaWa/gas, Sunoco, 🍽 Arby's, Bateman's Bistro, Chipotle Mexican, DQ, Dunkin Donuts, Grand Buffet, Longhorn Steaks, Panda Express, Panera Bread, 🅞 Aldi Foods, Best Buy, Harley-Davidson, Home Depot, NTB, Office Depot, PetCo, Sam's Club/gas, U-Haul, Walmart, same as 34
34	MD 7, Philadelphia Rd, **N** 🍽 McDonald's, Wendy's, 🛏 La Quinta, 🅞🅗, $General, $Tree, Giant Foods, Goodyear/auto, Marshall's, **S** 🅟 Exxon, 🅞 Walgreens, same as 35
33b a	I-95, N to Philadelphia, S to Baltimore
32b a	US 1, Bel Air, **N** 🅟 Exxon, 🍽 Arby's, Bob Evans, Burger King, Denny's, Dunkin Donuts, Golden Corral, IHOP, McDonald's, Taco Bell, 🅞 BJ's Whse, $Tree, Giant Foods, K-Mart, Merchants Tire/auto, Mr Tire/auto, 7-11, Toyota/Scion, Verizon, vet, **S** 🅟 Shell, 🍽 Baskin-Robbins/Dunkin Donuts, Carrabba's, McDonald's, Rita's Custard, Subway, Szechuan Taste, 🅞 Goodyear/auto, 7-11
31c	MD 43 E (from eb, exits left)
31b a	MD 147, Harford Rd, **N** 🅟 BP, CF/dsl, 7-11, Shell/dsl, 🍽 Dunkin Donuts, Wendy's, 🅞 CVS Drug, Chrysler/Jeep, Goodyear/auto, Honda, Mars Foods, VW, Walgreens
30b a	MD 41, Perring Pkwy, **N** 🅟 Shell, 🍽 Burger King, Checker's, Chick-fil-A, Denny's, Dunkin Donuts, 5 Guys Burgers, KFC, McDonald's, Popeye's, Rita's Custard, Subway, Taco Bell, 🅞 Advance Parts, Chevrolet, Ford, Home Depot, JoAnn Fabrics, K-Mart, NTB, Office Depot, Ross, Safeway Foods, Shoppers Foods, Tuesday Morning, Verizon
29b	MD 542, Loch Raven Blvd, **S** 🅟 BP, Gulf, Hess, 🍽 Bel-Loch Diner, Hooters, McDonald's, Pizza Hut, Subway, 🛏 Comfort Inn, Ramada Inn, 🅞 Mr Tire, PepBoys
29a	Cromwell Bridge Rd, **S** 🛏 Best Western
28	Providence Rd, **S** 🅟 Citgo, 🅞 Royal Farms
27b a	MD 146, Dulaney Valley Rd, **N** Hampton NHS, **S** 🅟 Exxon, 🍽 Bahama Breeze, Cheesecake Factory, PF Chang's, Starbucks, Stoney River Steaks, 🛏 Sheraton, 🅞 Barnes&Noble, Fresh Mkt, Macy's, mall
26b a	MD 45, York Rd, Towson, **N** 🅟 BP, Exxon/dsl, Oceanic, Sunoco/dsl, 🍽 Dunkin Donuts, Friendly's, Ocean Pride Rest., Pizza Hut, Subway, 🅞 Best Buy, Kia, Mr Tire, NTB, Rite Aid, **S** 🅟 Exxon, Shell, 🍽 Burger King, 5 Guys Burgers, McDonald's, 🅞 CVS Drug, Goodyear/auto, Honda, Hyundai, Lexus, Safeway Foods, Walgreens, vet
25	MD 139, Charles St, **S** 🅗
24	I-83 N, to York
23b	MD 25, Falls Rd, **N** 🅟 Exxon/dsl
23a	I-83 S, MD 25 N, Baltimore
22	Greenspring Ave
21	MD 129, to Stevenson Rd, Park Hghts Rd
20	MD 140, Reisterstown Rd, Pikesville, **N** 🅟 Exxon/7-11/dsl, 🍽 Chipotle Mexican, 🅞 AT&T, Barnes&Noble, Trader Joe's, **S** 🅟 BP/dsl, Shell/dsl, Sunoco/Subway, 🍽 McDonald's, Olive Branch Italian, 🛏 Hilton, Ramada Inn, 🅞 Target, vet
19	I-795, NW Expswy
18b a	MD 26, Randallstown, Lochearn, **E** 🅟 Shell/dsl, Sunoco/dsl, 🍽 Baskin-Robbins/Dunkin Donuts, KFC, Subway, 🅞 $General, Family$, **W** 🅟 BP, Exxon/dsl Shell, 🍽 Burger King, Dunkin Donuts, McDonald's, Sonic, Subway, Taco Bell, 🅞🅗, Firestone/auto, Giant Foods, 7-11, Shoppers Foods, Walgreens, auto repair
17	MD 122, Security Blvd, **E** 🅟 BP/repair, Shell, 🍽 City

GAITHERSBURG ROCKVILLE

INTERSTATE 695 (BALTIMORE) CONT'D

Exit	Services
17	Continued
	View Grill, Dunkin Donuts, McDonald's, Subway, Wendy's, 🛏 Days Inn, Motel 6, Quality Inn, 🅞 Chevrolet, Family$, Nissan, PriceRite Foods, Rite Aid, **W** 🅖 Exxon/dsl, Sunoco, 🍴 Burger King, 5 Guys Burgers, McDonald's, Panera Bread, Popeye's, Quiznos, Rita's Custard, 🛏 Best Western, 🅞 Best Buy, Ford, Macy's, Old Navy, Rite Aid, Sears/auto, mall
16b a	I-70, E to Baltimore, W to Frederick
15b a	US 40, Ellicott City, Baltimore, **E** 🅖 BP, 🍴 Burger King, Checker's, Chick-fil-A, ChuckECheese's, KFC, McDonald's, Panda Express, Quiznos, Shirley's Diner, Subway, 🛏 Comfort Inn, 🅞 BigLots, CVS Drug, Dodge, $Tree, Firestone/auto, Lowe's, Marshall's, Rite Aid, Ross, Safeway Foods/gas, Sam's Club/gas, Shoppers Foods, U-Haul, Walgreens, **W** 🅖 BP/dsl, Exxon, Gulf, Shell, 🍴 Applebee's, Bob Evans, CiCi's Pizza, McDonald's, Old Country Buffet, Popeye's, Starbucks, Subway, Taco Bell, TT Diner, 🛏 Ramada Ltd, 🅞 Aamco, Chrysler/Jeep, $Tree, Firestone/auto, Giant Foods, Goodyear/auto, Home Depot, Hyundai, Mr Tire, NTB, Office Depot, PepBoys, Petsmart, Staples, Toyota/Scion, Verizon, Walgreens, Walmart/McDonald's
14	Edmondson Ave, **E** 🅖 Sunoco, 🍴 Grilled Cheese&Co, 🅞 Royal Farms, **W** 🅖 CF, 🍴 Papa John's
13	MD 144, Frederick Rd, Catonsville, **W** 🅖 BP, CF, Gulf, 🍴 Baskin-Robbins/Dunkin Donuts, McDonald's, Subway, 🅞 7-11
12c b	MD 372 E, Wilkens, **E** 🎗

11b a	I-95, N to Baltimore, S to Washington
10US 1	Washington Blvd (from wb only), **E** 🅖 Royal Farms/dsl, 🍴 Chick-fil-A, Dunkin Donuts, 3 Bros Pizza, Quiznos, Wendy's, 🛏 Beltway Motel/rest., 🅞 Goodyear/auto, Home Depot, Office Depot, PetCo, Radio Shack, Walmart, **W** 🍴 Burger King
9	Hollins Ferry Rd, Lansdowne, **E** 🅖 BP, Sunoco/7-11/dsl, 🍴 Victor's Deli, 🅞 Royal Farms
8	MD 168, Nursery Rd, **N** 🅖 Exxon, Shell, 🍴 Hardee's, KFC, McDonald's, Taco Bell, Wendy's, 🛏 Motel 6, **S** 🅖 BP, Citgo/dsl, 🍴 G&M Rest., Happy Garden Chinese, Rita's Custard, Seasons Pizza
7b a	MD 295, **N** to Baltimore, **S** BWI ✈
6b a	Camp Mead Rd (from eb)
5	MD 648, Ferndale, **N** 🅖 Shell, Xtra/7-11/dsl, 🍴 Checker's, Dunkin Donuts, Hot Wok, 🛏 Comfort Inn, 🅞 NAPA, police
4b a	I-97 S, to Annapolis
3b a	MD 2, Brooklyn Park, **S** 🅖 Exxon, Hess, Royal Farms/dsl, Shell, Sunoco, 🍴 Best Buffet, Bob Evans, Bone-Fish Grill, Checker's, Chick-fil-A, ChuckECheese's, Coldstone, Denny's, 5 Guys Burgers, Golden Corral, HipHop Fish&Chicken, KFC, McDonald's, Panera Bread, Pappas Rest., Pizza Hut, Qdoba, Quiznos, Starbucks, Subway, Taco Bell, 🛏 Days Inn, Extended Stay America, Hampton Inn, La Quinta, 🅞 Aamco, Advance Parts, Aldi Foods, Best Buy, BigLots, Buick/GMC, Dick's, $Tree, Giant Foods, Hyundai, Just Tires, Lowe's, Office Depot, PetCo, Radio Shack, Salvo Parts, ShopRite Foods, Subaru, Target, Tuesday Morning, Verizon, Walgreens, Walmart
2	MD 10, Glen Burnie
1	MD 174, Hawkins Point Rd, **S** 🅖 Citgo/deli/dsl

MASSACHUSETTS

INTERSTATE 84

Exit	Services
4 (11)	**I-84 begins/ends on I-90, Exit 9.**
3b a (9)	US 20, Sturbridge, **0-2 mi N** 🅖 Citgo, Cumberland Farms, 🍴 Admiral O'Brien's, Burger King, Dunkin Donuts, Empire Village, Friendly's, McDonald's, Rovezzi's Ristorante, Smokehouse BBQ, Thai Place, Village Pizza, 🛏 EconoLodge, Hampton Inn, Quality Inn, Sturbridge Country Inn, Super 8, 🅞 🎗, USPO, vet, **0-2 mi S** 🅖 NE TrkStp/dsl, S&S, Shell/Dunkin Donuts/Subway, 🍴 Applebee's, Cracker Barrel, Uno Pizzaria, Wendy's, 🛏 Comfort Inn, 🅞 Marshall's, Michael's, Staples, Stop&Shop, Verizon, Walmart, vet
2 (5)	MA 131, to Old Sturbridge Village, Sturbridge, **2 mi S** 🛏 Publick House, RV camping
4mm	🍱 wb, litter barrels
1 (3)	Mashapaug Rd, to Southbridge, **S** 🅖 Mobil/dsl, 🅖/deli/dsl/scales/24hr/@, 🍴 Roy Rogers, Sbarro's, 🛏 Days Inn, 🅞 🎗
2mm	**weigh sta both lanes**
.5mm	🍱 eb
0mm	Massachusetts/Connecticut state line

INTERSTATE 90

Exit	Services
37mm	**I-90 begins/ends on I-93, exit 20 in Boston.**
25	to I-93, to downtown Boston
24	to I-93, to downtown Boston
22 (134)	Presidential Ctr, downtown
20 (132)	MA 28, Alston, Brighton, Cambridge, **N** 🛏 Courtyard, Doubletree Inn, 🅞 🎗, **S** 🅖 Sunoco
131mm	**toll plaza**
19 (130)	MA Ave (from eb), **N** 🍴 IHOP, McDonald's, 🛏 Day's Inn
17 (128)	Centre St, Newton, **N** 🛏 Sheraton, 🅞 Cadillac, Chevrolet, Honda, Nissan
16 (125)	MA 16, W Newton, **S** 🅖 Mobil/repair
15 (124)	I-95, **N** 🅖 Marriott
123mm	**toll plaza**
14 (122)	MA 30, Weston
117mm	**Natick Travel Plaza eb**, Gulf/dsl, McDonald's, Dunkin Donuts, info
13 (116)	MA 30, Natick, **S** 🅖 Getty, Gulf, Shell, 🍴 Bickford's, Boston Mkt, Bugaboo Creek Steaks, Burger King, Harvard's Steaks, Lotus Flower Chinese, McDonald's, Papagino's, Panera Bread, Quizno's, 🛏 Best Western, Red Roof Inn, 🅞 🎗, BJ's Whse, Home Depot, Isuzu, Kohl's, Lowe's, Macy's, Marshalls, Target, Walmart, mall, USPO
114mm	**Framingham Travel Plaza wb**, Gulf/dsl, Boston Mkt, McDonald's, info
12 (111)	MA 9, Framington, **N** 🅖 Getty, Hess, 🍴 Acapulco Mexican, Dunkin Donuts, Molly Malone's Grill, Tin Alley Grill, 🛏 Motel 6, Sheraton, 🅞 🎗, **S** 🍴 Chef Orient, 🅞 Chrysler/Isuzu/Jeep, Target, Toyota/Scion, mall
11a (106)	I-495, **N** to NH, S to Cape Cod

⬆🅔 INTERSTATE 90 CONT'D

Exit	Services
105mm	**Westborough Travel Plaza wb**, Gulf/dsl, Boston Mkt, D'angelo, Dunkin Donuts, Papagino's, gifts
11 (96)	MA 122, to Millbury, **N** UMA Med Ctr
10a (95)	MA 146
94mm	Blackstone River
10 (90)	I-395 S, to Auburn, I-290 N, Worcester, **N** 🅖 Shell, 🍴 Piccadilly's, 🛏 Comfort Inn, Holiday Inn Express, **S** 🅖 Shell/repair/24hr, 🍴 Applebee's, D'angelo's, Dunkin Donuts, Friendly's, Wendy's, 🛏 Fairfield Inn, 🅞 🄷, CVS Drug, Hyundai, Park'n Shop, TJ Maxx
84mm	**Charlton Travel Plaza wb**, Gulf/dsl, McDonald's, info
80mm	**Charlton Travel Plaza eb**, Exxon/dsl, McDonald's, info, st police
79mm	**toll plaza**
9 (78)	I-84, to Hartford, NYC, Sturbridge, access to 🄷
67mm	Quaboag River
8 (62)	MA 32, to US 20, Palmer, **S on MA 32** 🅖 Hess/Godfather's, Pride, Shell/dsl, 🍴 Jenny Chan's Chinese, McDonald's, Subway, Wendy's, 🅞 🄷, Big Y Foods, Chevrolet, CVS Drug, Rite Aid, repair/transmissions
58mm	Chicopee River
56mm	**Ludlow Travel Plaza wb**, Gulf/dsl, Boston Mkt, D'angelo
55mm	**Ludlow Travel Plaza eb**, Gulf/dsl, McDonald's
7 (54)	MA 21, to Ludlow, **N** 🅖 Gulf, Pride/dsl, Sunoco, Verizon, 🍴 Burger King, Dunkin Donuts, Friendly's, McDonald's, Subway, 🅞 🄷, Ace Hardware, Big Y Foods, CVS Drug, Jo-Ann Fabrics, NAPA, repair, **S** 🅖 Shell/dsl, 🍴 Dominos, Taco Bell, 🛏 Holiday Inn Express
6 (51)	I-291, to Springfield, Hartford CT, **N** 🅖 Pride/50's Diner/Subway/dsl, 🍴 Dr Deegan's Steaks, Dunkin Donuts, McDonald's, Po's Chinese, 🛏 Econolodge, Motel 6, 🅞 🄷, to Bradley Int 🛪, Basketball Hall of Fame
5 (49)	MA 33, to Chicopee, Westover AFB, **N** 🅖 🍴 Applebee's, Arby's, Chipotle Mexican, Denny's, Dunkin Donuts, Friendly's, 99 Rest., Panera Bread, Popeye's, Royal Buffet, Starbucks, Subway, Wendy's, 🛏 Days Inn, Hampton Inn, Quality Inn, Residence Inn, 🅞 Aldi Foods, BJ's Whse/gas, Big Y Foods, Chrysler/Dodge/Jeep, $Tree, Home Depot, Honda, Marshall's, Monroe, Nissan, Staples, Stop&Shop/gas, TownFair Tire, U-Haul, Walmart, **S** 🅖 Pride/Dunkin Donuts/Subway/dsl, 🅞 Buick/GMC
46mm	Connecticut River
4 (46)	I-91, US 5, to Holyoke, W Springfield, **N on US 5** 🅖 Shell, 🍴 Dunkin Donuts, 🛏 Welcome Inn, **S on US 5** 🅖 Pride/dsl, 🍴 Donut Dip, 5 Guys, Hooters, On the Border, Outback Steaks, Piccadilly's, Subway, 🛏 Knights Inn, Red Roof Inn, Springfield Inn, Super 8, 🅞 AAA, BMW, Honda/Lexus/Toyota/Scion, repair
41mm	st police wb
3 (40)	US 202, to Westfield, **N** 🅖 Mobil, 🍴 Amalfi Pizza, Dunkin Donuts, **S** 🅖 Citgo/Subway/dsl, 🍴 Friendly's, Wendy's, 🛏 EconoLodge, Holiday Inn Express, 🅞 🄷, repair
36mm	Westfield River
35.5mm	runaway truck ramp eb
29mm	**Blandford Travel Plaza both lanes S** Gulf/dsl, McDonalds, gifts, info, vending
20mm	1724 ft, highest point on MA Tpk
14.5mm	Appalachian Trail
2 (11)	US 20, to Lee, Pittsfield, **N** 🅖 Citgo, Shell/dsl, Sunoco, 🍴 Arizona Pizza, Athena's Rest., Dunkin Donuts, Friend

SPRINGFIELD *(left vertical tab)*
PITTSFIELD *(right vertical tab)*

Exit	Services
2 (11)	Continued
	ly's, McDonald's, Red Apple Chinese, Subway, 🛏 Morgan House/rest., Pilgrim Inn, Sunset Motel, Super 8, 🅞 PriceChopper Foods, Rite Aid, True Value, **S** 🍴 Orient Taste, Simply Grillicious, Subway, Villa Pizza, 🅞 Big Y Foods, Lee Outlets/famous brands
10.5mm	Hoosatonic River
8mm	**Lee Travel Plaza both lanes**, Gulf/dsl, McDonald's, atm, info, vending
4mm	**toll booth,** 🅒
1 (2)	MA 41 (from wb, no return), to MA 102, W Stockbridge, the Berkshires, **N** 🅖 Pleasant Valley Motel, 🅞 to Bousquet Ski Area
0mm	Massachusetts/New York state line

⬆🅝 INTERSTATE 91

Exit	Services
55mm	Massachusetts/Vermont state line, call boxes
54mm	parking area both lanes, 🆁🆂
28 (51)	US 5, MA 10, Bernardston, **E** 🍴 Bella Notte Ristorante, 🛏 Fox Inn, **W** 🅖 Sunoco, 🍴 Antonio's II Ristorante, Four-leaf Clover Rest., 🅞 Country Corner Store, RV camping, USPO
27 (45)	MA 2 E (exits left from sb), Greenfield, **US 5 E** 🅖 Gulf, Magic, Sunoco, 🍴 Burger King, Denny's Pantry, Dunkin Donuts, Friendly's, McDonald's, Subway, 🅞 🄷, Aubuchon Hardware, AutoZone, Bond Parts, Buick/GMC, Chrysler/Dodge/Jeep, Honda, Walgreens
26 (43)	MA 2 W, MA 2A E, Greenfield, **E** 🅖 Mobil, Planet/dsl, 🍴 Applebee's, China Gourmet, D'Angelo, Dunkin Donuts, 🛏 Quality Inn, 🅞 🄷, Chevrolet, Ford/Lincoln, Toyota, **W** 🅖 Irving/Circle K, Valero, 🍴 Asian Buffet, Friendly's, KFC, Pizza Hut/Taco Bell, McDonald's, 99 Rest., 🛏 CandleLight Motel, Days Inn, Hampton Inn, 🅞 Big Y Foods, BJ's Whse, $Tree, Family$, Home Depot, Hyundai, Staples, to Mohawk Tr
39mm	Deerfield River
37mm	**weigh sta both lanes**
25 (36)	MA 116 (from sb), S Deerfield hist dist, camping, same as 24
24 (35)	US 5, MA 10, MA 116, Deerfield (no EZ return), **E** 🅖 Irving/Circle K/Dunkin Donuts/Subway/dsl, 🍴 Chandler's Rest., 🛏 Red Roof Inn, 🅞 Yankee Candle Co, vet, **W** 🅖 Roady's Trkstp/diner/dsl/24hr, 🍴 24hr Diner, 🛏 Whatley Inn
34.5mm	parking area both lanes
23 (34)	US 5 (from sb), **E** 🅞 Orchard Trailers, Rainbow Motel/camping
22 (30)	US 5, MA 10 (from nb), **N** Hatfield, **W** Diamond RV Ctr
21 (28)	US 5, MA 10, Hatfield, **W** 🅖 Sunoco, 🛏 Scottish Inn, 🅞 st police
20 (26)	US 5, MA 9, MA 10 (from sb), Northampton, **W** 🅖 Hess/dsl, Pride/Dunkin Donuts/dsl, 🍴 Burger King, D'angelo's, Domino's, KFC, McDonald's, PapaGino's Italian, Sakura, Taco Bell, 🅞 🄷, BigLots, Big Y Food/Drug, CVS Drug, Firestone/auto, Ford, GMC, Honda, NAPA, Radio Shack, Staples, Stop&Shop, Subaru, Toyota/Scion, TownFair Tire, U-Haul, Verizon, VW, Walgreens, Walmart/Subway, transmissions
19 (25)	MA 9, to Amherst, Northampton, **0-2 mi E** 🅖 Getty, Gulf, Phillips 66/Dunkin Donuts, Shell, 🍴 Butterfly Asian, 🛏 Hampton Inn, 🅞 🄷, Nissan, vet, to Elwell SP
18 (22)	US 5, Northampton, **E** 🍴 Page's Loft Rest., 🛏 Clarion,

GREENFIELD *(right vertical tab)*
NORTHAMPTON *(right vertical tab)*

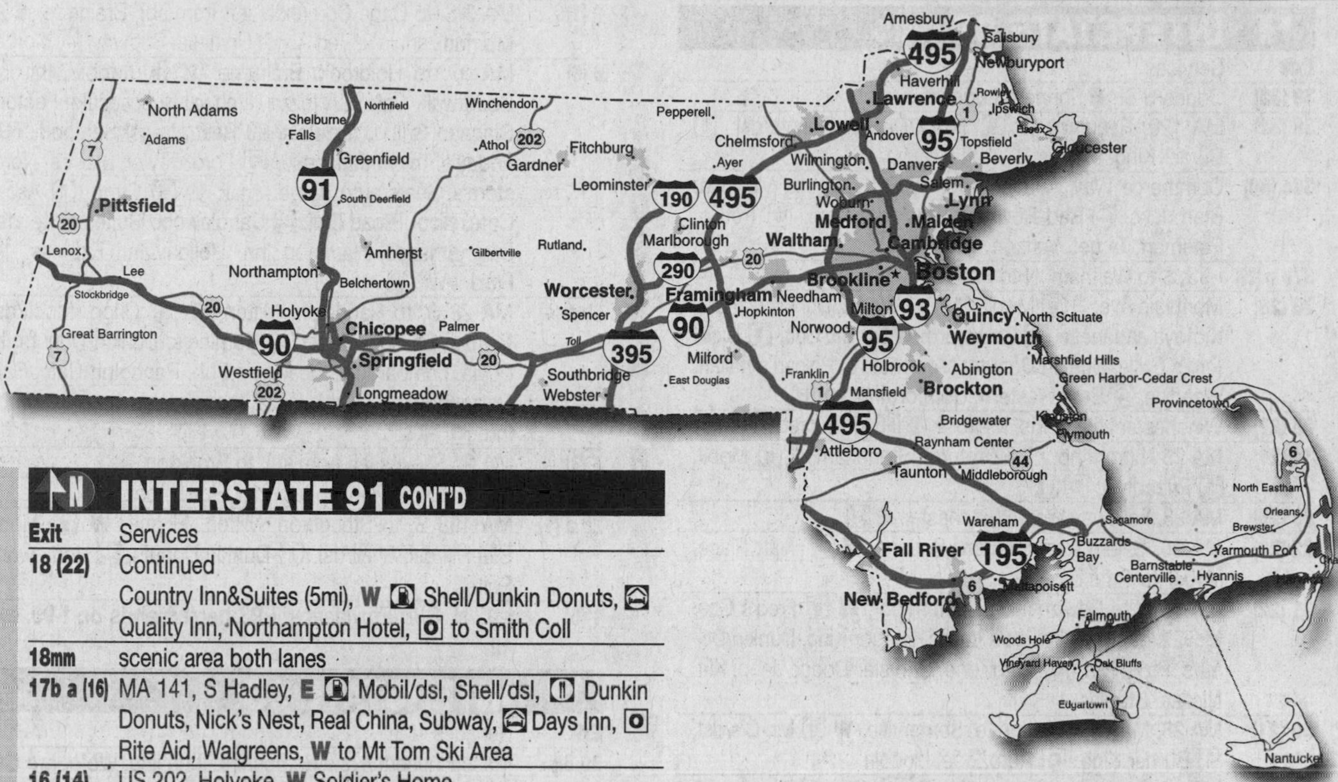

INTERSTATE 91 CONT'D

SPRINGFIELD

Exit	Services
18 (22)	Continued Country Inn&Suites (5mi), W [gas] Shell/Dunkin Donuts, [lodging] Quality Inn, Northampton Hotel, [other] to Smith Coll
18mm	scenic area both lanes
17b a (16)	MA 141, S Hadley, E [gas] Mobil/dsl, Shell/dsl, [food] Dunkin Donuts, Nick's Nest, Real China, Subway, [lodging] Days Inn, [other] Rite Aid, Walgreens, W to Mt Tom Ski Area
16 (14)	US 202, Holyoke, W Soldier's Home
15 (12)	to US 5, Ingleside, E [gas] Shell, [food] Chicago Grill, Cracker Barrel, Friendly's, 99 Rest., Red Robin, Ruby Tuesday, [lodging] Holyoke Hotel, [other] [H], AT&T, Barnes&Noble, Best Buy, JC Penney, Macy's, Old Navy, PetCo, Sears/auto, Target, mall, W [lodging] Homewood Suites
14 (11)	to US 5, to I-90 (Mass Tpk), E to Boston, W to Albany, E [H]
13b a (9)	US 5 N, W Springfield, E [gas] Pride/dsl, [food] Dougnut Dip, Hooters, On-the-Border, Outback Steaks, Piccadilly's, Shallot Thai, Subway, [lodging] Knights Inn, Red Roof Inn, Residence Inn, Springfield Inn, Super 8, [other] BMW, Lexus/Toyota/Scion, W [gas] Mobil/dsl, Pride/dsl, [food] Arby's, Bertucci's, Burger King, Cal's Grill, Carrabba's, Chili's, D'angelo's, Friendly's, Geraldine's Rest., HomeTown Buffet, IHOP, KFC, Longhorn Steaks, McDonald's, 99 Rest., Olive Garden, Panera Bread, Pizza Hut, Tokyo Cuisine, [lodging] Bel Air Inn, Candlewood Suites, Clarion, Days Inn, EconoLodge, Hampton Inn, Quality Inn, Red Carpet Inn, Travelodge, [other] AT&T, Chrysler/Dodge/Jeep, Costco, CVS Drug, Dick's, GNC, Home Depot, Honda, Kohl's, Mazda, Michael's, Nissan, PepBoys, Stop&Shop, Subaru, Town-Fair Tire, Verizon
12 (8.5)	I-391 N, to Chicopee
11 (8)	Birnie Ave (from sb), E [gas] Mobil, [other] [H]
10 (7.5)	Main St (from nb), Springfield, E [gas] Mobil
9 (7)	US 20 W, MA 20A E (from nb), E [food] McDonald's
8 (6.5)	I-291, US 20 E, to I-90, E downtown
7 (6)	Columbus Ave (from sb), E [lodging] Marriott, Sheraton, W [gas] Pride/Subway/dsl, [other] to Basketball Hall of Fame
6 (5.5)	Springfield Ctr, W [gas] Pride/Dunkin Donuts/Subway/dsl, [food] Starbucks
5 (5)	Broad St, E [gas] Mobil/dsl, Shell/dsl, [other] Hyundai, W [gas] Sunoco/dsl, [food] Chicago Grill, Subway, [lodging] Hilton Garden, [other] Buick/GMC, same as 4
4 (4.5)	MA 83, Broad St, Main St, E [gas] Mobil/dsl, [food] Antonio's Grinders, [other] Hyundai, W [gas] Sunoco, [food] Chicago Grill,
4 (4.5)	Continued Subway, [lodging] Hilton Garden, Buick/GMC, Chevrolet, same as 5
3 (4)	US 5 N, to MA 57, Columbus Ave, W Springfield, E [gas] Sunoco, [other] Cadillac, W Chevrolet
2 (3.5)	MA 83 S (from nb), to E Longmeadow, E [food] Friendly's
1 (3)	US 5 S (from sb)
0mm	Massachusetts/Connecticut state line. callboxes begin/end

INTERSTATE 93

METHUEN

Exit	Services
47mm	Massachusetts/New Hampshire state line, callboxes begin/end
48 (46)	MA 213 E, to Methuen, E [H]
47 (45)	Pelham St, Methuen, E [gas] Sunoco/24hr, [food] Dunkin Donuts, McDonald's, Outback Steaks, W [gas] BP, Irving/Circle K/Subway/dsl, [food] Fireside Rest., NE Seafood, [lodging] Day's Hotel/rest., Guesthouse Inn, [other] Chrysler/Jeep
46 (44)	MA 110, MA 113, to Lawrence, E [gas] BP/repair, Mobil, Shell, [food] Burger King, Dunkin Donuts, KFC/Taco Bell, McDonald's/24hr, PapaGino's, Pizza Hut, Taco Bell, [other] [H] $Tree, MktBasket Foods, Rite Aid, W [gas] Citgo, Super, [food] Dunkin Donuts, Irish Cottage Rest., Jackson's Rest., Jay Gee's Ice Cream, Riverside Pizza, [lodging] Passport Inn
45 (43)	Andover St, River Rd, to Lawrence, E [lodging] Courtyard, Homewood Suites, Wyndham, W [gas] Mobil/Dunkin Donuts, [food] Chateu Italian, Chili's, [lodging] La Quinta, Residence Inn, SpringHill Suites, [other] vet
44b a (40)	I-495, to Lowell, Lawrence, E [H]
43 (39)	MA 133, N Tewksbury, E [gas] Mobil/Dunkin Donuts, W [food] 99 Rest
42 (38)	Dascomb Rd, East St, Tewksbury, W [gas] Citgo/dsl, [food] Dunkin Donuts
41 (35)	MA 125, Andover, st police
40 (34)	MA 62, Wilmington

🅖 = gas 🍴 = food 🛏 = lodging 🅞 = other 🆁🆂 = rest stop   Copyright 2014 - The Next Exit ®

🔼Ⓝ INTERSTATE 93 CONT'D

BOSTON AREA

Exit	Services
39 (33)	Concord St, **E** Shriners Auditorium
38 (31)	MA 129, Reading, **W** 🅖 Mobil/Dunkin Donuts/dsl, 🍴 Burger King, 99 Rest.
37c (30)	Commerce Way, Atlantic Ave, **W** 🍴 Chipotle Mexican, Starbucks, 🛏 Red Roof Inn, Residence Inn, 🅞 PetCo, Petsmart, Target, Verizon
37b a (29)	I-95, S to Waltham, N to Peabody
36 (28)	Montvale Ave, **E** 🅖 Mobil, 🍴 Deli Works, Dunkin Donuts, Kiotoya Japanese, 🛏 Courtyard, **W** 🅖 BP, Gulf, 🍴 Bickford's Grille, Dunkin Donuts, McDonald's, Polcari's Italian, Wendy's, 🛏 Best Western, Comfort Inn, 🅞🇭
35 (27)	Winchester Highlands, Melrose, **E** 🇭 (no EZ return to sb)
34 (26)	MA 28 N (from nb, no EZ return), Stoneham, **E** 🅖 Mobil, 🍴 Friendly's, 🅞🇭
33 (25)	MA 28, Fellsway West, Winchester, **E** 🇭
32 (23)	MA 60, Salem Ave, Medford Square, **W** 🛏 Hyatt Place, 🅞🇭, to Tufts U
31 (22)	MA 16 E, to Revere (no EZ return sb), **W** 🅖 Fred's Gas, Mr. C's/dsl, 🍴 Avellino's Italian, Burger King, Dunkin Donuts, Pizza Hut, 🅞 AutoZone, Chrysler/Dodge/Jeep, Kia, Nissan, Staples
30 (21)	MA 28, MA 38, Mystic Ave, Somerville, **W** 🅖 Mr. C's/dsl, 🍴 Burger King, 🅞 AutoZone, Lincoln
29 (20)	MA 28 (from nb), Somerville, **E** 🍴 Dunkin Donuts, 99 Rest., 🛏 La Quinta, 🅞 Home Depot, K-Mart, Staples, TJ Maxx, mall, **W** 🅖 Gulf, Hess, 🅞 Radio Shack, Stop&Shop, same as 30
28 (19)	Sullivans Square, Charles Town, downtown
27	US 1 N (from nb)
26 (18.5)	MA 28 N, Storrow Dr, North Sta, downtown
25	Haymarket Sq, Gov't Center
24 (18)	Callahan Tunnel, **E** 🖥
23 (17.5)	High St, Congress St, **W** 🛏 Marriott
22 (17)	Atlantic Ave, Northern Ave, South Sta, Boston World Trade Ctr
21 (16.5)	Kneeland St, ChinaTown
20 (16)	I-90 W, to Mass Tpk
19 (15.5)	Albany St (from sb), **W** 🅖 Mobil/dsl, 🅞🇭
18 (15)	Mass Ave, to Roxbury, **W** 🇭
17 (14.5)	E Berkeley (from nb), **E** New Boston Food Mkt
16 (14)	S Hampton St, Andrew Square, **W** 🍴 Applebee's, Olive Garden, 🛏 Holiday Inn Express, 🅞 Best Buy, Home Depot, Marshall's, Old Navy, Stop&Shop/gas, Target, TJ Maxx
15 (13)	Columbia Rd, Everett Square, **E** 🛏 DoubleTree, 🅞 JFK Library, to UMA, **W** 🅖 Shell
14 (12.5)	Morissey Blvd (from nb no return), **E** JFK Library, **W** 🅖 Shell
13 (12)	Freeport St, to Dorchester, (from nb), **W** 🅖 BP, 7-11, 🍴 Boston Mkt, D'Angelo's, Deadwood Cafe, Freeport Tavern, 🛏 Comfort Inn, Ramada, 🅞 CVS Drug, Lambert's Mkt, NAPACare, Stop&Shop, Toyota/Scion
12 (11.5)	MA 3A S (from sb, no EZ return), Quincy, **E** 🅖 Shell, repair **W** 🅖 Gulf/Dunkin Donuts, Hess, 🍴 PapaGino's, 🅞 AutoZone, CVS Drug, Lincoln, Staples, Verizon, Walgreens
11b a (11)	to MA 203, Granite Ave, Ashmont
10 (10)	Squantum Ave (from sb), Milton, **W** 🇭
9 (9)	Adams St, Bryant Ave, to N Quincy, **E** 🅖 Milton Fuel, 🍴 Dunkin Donuts, **W** 🅖 Shell/repair
8 (8)	Brook Pkwy, to Quincy, Furnace, **E** 🅖 Gulf/dsl, Mobil/dsl

BOSTON AREA

Exit	Services
7 (7)	MA 3 S, to Cape Cod (exits left from sb), Braintree, **E** 🛏 Marriott
6 (6)	MA 37, to Holbrook, Braintree, **E** 🅖 Mobil/24hr, 🍴 Boardwalk Café, CA Pizza Kitchen, Cheesecake Factory, Chicago Grill, D'angelo's, 99 Rest., Legal Seafood, TGI-Friday's, Tokyo Japanese, 🅞 Lord&Taylor, Macy's, Nordstom's, Sears/auto, Target, mall, **W** 🅖 Citgo, 🍴 Ascari Café, Wood Road Deli, 🛏 Candlewood Suites, Extended Stay America, Hampton Inn, Holiday Inn Express, 🅞 Ford, VW
5b a (4)	MA 28 S, to Randolph, Milton, **E** 🅖 Citgo, Mobil/dsl, Mutual, Shell/dsl/24hr, 🍴 Domino's, Dunkin Donuts, La Scala, Lombardo's, Picadilly's Pub, Randolph Cafe, Sal's Calzone Rest., Stash's Pizza, Wong's Chinese, 🛏 Comfort Inn, 🅞 AT&T
4 (3)	MA 24 S (exits left from sb), to Brockton
3 (2)	MA 138 N, to Ponkapoag Trail, Houghtons Pond
2b a (1)	MA 138 S, to Stoughton, Milton, **E** golf, **W** 🅖 Mobil, BlueHill/dsl, Shell/dsl, 🍴 Dunkin Donuts, 🛏 Homewood Suites
1 (0)	I-95 N, S to Providence. **I-93 begins/ends on I-95, exit 12.**

🔼Ⓝ INTERSTATE 95

AMESBURY

Exit	Services
89.5mm	Massachusetts/New Hampshire state line, **Welcome Ctr/ 🆁🆂 sb, full 🅴 facilities, 🅿 litter barrels**
60 (89)	MA 286, to Salisbury, beaches, **E** 🅖 Mobil/dsl, 🍴 Cosmos Rest., Dunkin Donuts, Lena's Seafood Rest., 🅞 camping (seasonal)
59 (88)	I-495 S (from sb)
58b a (78)	rd 110, to I-495 S, to Amesbury, Salisbury, **E** 🅖 Sunoco/Dunkin Donuts/Subway/dsl, 🍴 China Buffet, Niko's Place, Sylvan St Grille, Winner's Circle Rest., 🅞 A-1 Radiators, U-Haul, **W** 🅖 Irving Gas/Circle K, Mobil, Sunoco, 🍴 Acapulco's Mexican, Burger King, Dunkin Donuts, Friendly's, McDonald's, PapaGino's, 🛏 Fairfield Inn, 🅞 AT&T, Chevrolet, Stop&Shop, Verizon
57 (85)	MA 113, to W Newbury, **E** 🅖 Mobil, Shell/dsl/repair/24hr, Sunoco, 🍴 China One, d'Angelo's, Dunkin Donuts, Giuseppe's Italian, Hana Japan, McDonald's, Panera Bread, PapaGino's, Wendy's, 🅞🇭, GNC, K-Mart, Marshall's, MktBasket Foods, Radio Shack, Rite Aid, 7-11, Shaw's Foods, Verizon, Walgreens
56 (83)	Scotland Rd, to Newbury, **E** st police
55 (82)	Central St, to Byfield, **E** 🍴 Gen Store Eatery, Village Diner, **W** 🅖 Prime/dsl/repair
54b a (78)	MA 133, E to Rowley, W to Groveland
77mm	**weigh sta both lanes**
53b a (76)	MA 97, S to Topsfield, N to Georgetown
52 (74)	Topsfield Rd, to Topsfield, Boxford
51 (72)	Endicott Rd, to Topsfield, Middleton
50 (71)	US 1, to MA 62, Topsfield, **E** 🅖 Gulf/dsl, Mobil/dsl, 🅞 Honda, **W** 🍴 TX Roadhouse, 🛏 Knights Inn, 🅞 CVS Drug, Hyundai, Staples, Stop&Shop, st police
49 (70)	MA 62 (from nb), Danvers, Middleton, **W** same as 50
48 (69)	Hobart St (from sb), **W** 🍴 Italian Rest., 🛏 Comfort Inn, Extended Stay America, Motel 6, 🅞 Home Depot, Kia
47b a (68)	MA 114, to Middleton, Peabody, **E** 🅖 Gulf/Dunkin Donuts, Sunoco, 🍴 Grassfields Grill, Honey Dew Donuts, McDonald's, Olive Garden, Outback Steaks, PapaGino's, 🅞 Audi, BMW, Cadillac/Chevrolet, Chrysler/Dodge/Jeep,

⬆N INTERSTATE 95 CONT'D

Exit	Services

P E A B O D Y

47b a (68) Continued
Fiat, Infiniti, Lexus, Lowe's, Mazda, NTB, Petsmart, Subaru, TJ Maxx, Toyota/Scion, Trader Joe's, Walmart, **W on US 1** ⓖ Hess, 🍴 Chili's, Hardcover Rest., TGIFriday's, 🏠 Motel 6, Residence Inn, TownePlace Suites, ◎ Costco/gas, Home Depot, LandRover, NAPA

46 (67) to US 1, **W** ⓖ Best, Global, Gulf/dsl, Sunoco, 🍴 Dunkin Donuts, ◎ auto repair

45 (66) MA 128 N, to Peabody

44b a (65) US 1 N, MA 129, **E** ⓖ Shell, **W** ⓖ 7-11, Sunoco, 🍴 Bertucci's, Carrabba's, Dunkin Donuts, Santarpio's Pizza, Sonic, Wendy's, 🏠 Carriage House Hotel, Hampton Inn, Holiday Inn, Homewood Suites, SpringHill Suites, ◎ 🏠

43 (61) Walnut St, Lynnfield, **E** to Saugus Iron Works NHS (3mi), **W** 🏠 Sheraton, ◎ golf

42 (62) Salem St, Montrose, **E** ⓖ Irving/Circle K/Subway, Sunoco, 🍴 Dunkin Donuts, **W** 🏠 Sheraton

41 (60) Main St, Lynnfield Ctr, **E** ⓖ Shell

40 (59) MA 129, Wakefield Ctr, N Reading, **E** ⓖ Gulf, 🍴 Bellino's Italian, Honey Dew Donuts, ◎ city park, vet, **W** ⓖ Gulf, 🍴 Dunkin Donuts, Mandarin Chinese, ◎ Chevrolet, Mazda, REI

R E A D I N G

39 (58) North Ave, Reading, **E** ⓖ Citgo/repair, ◎ Volvo, city park, **W** ⓖ Shell/dsl, 🍴 Bertucci's, Chili's, Fuddrucker's, Longhorn Steaks, Oye's Rest., Starbucks, ◎ 🏠, Home Depot, Honda, Mkt Basket Foods, Staples, Stop&Shop Foods, Verizon

38b a (57) MA 28, to Reading, **E** ⓖ Gulf/repair, Hess/dsl, 🍴 Boston Mkt, Burger King, D'Angelo's/PapaGino's, Dunkin Donuts, 5 Guys Burgers, 99 Rest., Subway, ◎ Advance Parts, AutoZone, CVS Drug, Ford, GNC, Marshall's, Radio Shack, Stop&Shop, **W** ⓖ Gulf, Mobil/dsl, Shell, Sunoco, 🍴 Anthony's Roastbeef, Burger King, Calariso's Farm Stand, Domino's, Dunkin Donuts, Harrow's Chicken Pies, McDonald's, Sam's Bistro, Starbucks

37b a (56) I-93, N to Manchester, S to Boston

36 (55) Washington St, to Winchester, **E** ⓖ BP/Dunkin Donuts, 🍴 FarEast Chinese, Fresh City, Munchies, Sal's Pizza, Starbucks, Subway, 🏠 Hilton, ◎ Hogan's Tires, Jaguar, Nissan, Staples, Toyota, **W** ⓖ Sunoco, 🍴 Chicago Grill, d'Angelo's, Joe's Grill, McDonald's, 99 Rest., Panera Bread, Papa Gino's, Qdoba, Sarku Japan, 🏠 Courtyard, Fairfield Inn, Hampton Inn, Red Roof Inn, ◎ AT&T, CVS Drug, Kohl's, Lowe's, Mkt Basket Foods, NTB, Office Depot, Radio Shack, Sullivan's Tire, TJ Maxx, mall

35 (54) MA 38, to Woburn, **E** 🏠 Holiday Inn Select, 🍴 Scoreboard Grill, ◎ 🏠, **W** ⓖ Mobil/dsl, 🍴 Applebee's, Beacon Grille, Dunkin Donuts, 🏠 Extended Stay Delux, ◎ Stop&Shop Foods, city park

34 (53) Winn St, Woburn

33b a (52) US 3 S, MA 3A N, to Winchester, **E** 🍴 Bickford's Grille, Café Escadrille, Capital Grille, ChuckeCheese, Dunkin Donuts, Outback Steaks, Panera Bread, Paparazzi's, Subway, ◎ 🏠, AAA, CVS Drug, Honda, Marshall's, Michael's, Roche Bro's Foods, **W** ⓖ Hess, Prime, 🏠 Marriott, ◎ 🏠 Audi/Porsche, Kia, repair

32b a (51) US 3 N, MA 2A S, to Lowell, **E** ⓖ Mobil, Shell, 🍴 Burger King, d'Angelo's, Dunkin Donuts, McDonald's, Subway, 🏠 Hilton Garden, ◎ Best Buy, Mkt Basket Foods, Old Navy, PetCo, Trader Joe's, Verizon, ◎ **W** 🍴 Border Cafe,

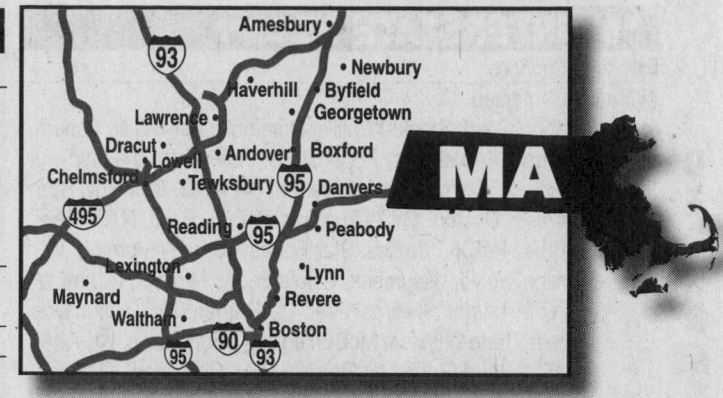

L E X I N G T O N

32b a (51) Continued
Cheesecake Factory, Chicago Grill, Chili's, Legal Seafoods, Macaroni Grill, Pizzaria Regina, 🏠 Candlewood Suites, Homestead Suites, ◎ Barnes&Noble, Macy's, Nordstrom, Sears/auto, Staples, mall

31b a (48) MA 4, MA 225, Lexington, **E** ⓖ Gulf, Mobil/dsl/repair, 🍴 Alexander's Pizza, Starbucks, ◎ Curves, Stop&Shop, Walgreens, **W** ⓖ Gulf, Shell, 🍴 d'Angelo's, Dunkin Donuts, Firebox BBQ, Friendly's, Margarita's, McDonald's, Papa Gino's, 🏠 Bedford Plaza Hotel, Quality Inn, Travelodge, ◎ Staples, TJ Maxx, vet

30b a (47) MA 2A, Lexington, **E** ⓖ Sunoco/Dunkin Donuts/dsl, ◎ 🏠, **W** 🏠 ALoft, Element Hotel, ◎ to MinuteMan NP, Hanscom AFB

46.5mm **travel plaza nb**, Gulf/dsl, Honey Dew Donuts, McDonald's, gifts

29b a (46) MA 2 W, Cambridge

28b a (45) Trapelo Rd, Belmont, **E** ⓖ Gulf/dsl, Mobil/dsl, 🍴 Boston Mkt, Burger King, Dunkin Donuts, Friendly's, McDonald's, Panera Bread, Papa Gino's, ◎ AT&T, Radio Shack, Shaw's Foods/Osco Drugs, city park

27b a (44) Totten Pond Rd, Waltham, **E** ⓖ Shell, 🍴 Naked Fish Rest., 🏠 Best Western, Courtyard, Hilton Garden, Holiday Inn Express, Home Suites, Westin Hotel, **W** 🍴 Bertucci's Rest., Green Papaya Thai, 🏠 Embassy Suites/The Grill, ◎ AT&T, Costco, Home Depot

26 (43) US 20, to MA 117, to Waltham, **E** ⓖ Sunoco/dsl, **W** ⓖ Mobil/dsl, 🍴 Chicago Grill, ◎ NTB, vet

25 (42) I-90, MA Tpk

24 (41) MA 30, Newton, Wayland, **E** ⓖ Hess, 🏠 Marriott/rest.

23 (40) Recreation Rd (from nb), to MA Tpk

22b a (39) Grove St, **E** 🏠 Holiday Inn Express, ◎ golf

38.5mm **travel plaza sb**, Gulf/dsl, HoneyDew Donuts, McDonald's, gifts

N E W T O N

21b a (38) MA 16, Newton, Wellesley, **E** 🏠, **W** ⓖ Sunoco, 🍴 Dunkin Donuts, House of Pizza, Paparazzi, Starbucks

20b a (36) MA 9, Brookline, Framingham

19 (35) Highland Ave, Newton, Needham, **E** ⓖ Hess, 🍴 Acupulcos, Chipotle Mexican, D'Angelo's, Mandarin Cuisine, Mighty Subs, Panera Bread, Pronto Bistro, Starbucks, 🏠 Sheraton/rest., ◎ AAA, CVS Drug, Marshall's, PetCo, Radio Shack, Staples, TJ Maxx, **W** 🍴 Bickford's, ◎ Chevrolet, Ford

18 (34) Great Plain Ave, W Roxbury

33.5mm parking area sb, ◎ litter barrels

17 (33) MA 135, Needham, Wellesley

32mm truck turnout sb

16b a (31) MA 109, High St, Dedham, **W** ⓖ Mobil/dsl

15b a (29) US 1, MA 128, **0-2 mi E** ⓖ Gulf, Monro/service, 🍴 Bug

MA

⬆N INTERSTATE 95 CONT'D

Exit	Services
15b a (29)	Continued
	aboo Creek Steaks, Chili's, Domino's, Joe's Grill, Panera Bread, PapaGino's, PF Chang's, TGIFriday's, ⓛ Fairfield Inn, Holiday Inn, Residence Inn, ⓞ AT&T, Best Buy, BJ's Whse, Costco, CVS Drug, Lincoln, LL Bean, NTB, Pep-Boys, PetCo, Staples, Star Foods, Tuesday Morning, Verizon, Volvo, Walgreens, Whole Foods Mkt, vet, **0-2 mi W** ⓖ Irving/dsl, Shell/dsl/24hr, ⓕ Burger King, Dunkin Donuts, Jade Chinese, McDonald's, ⓛ Budget Inn, ⓞ AAA, AT&T, Audi/Porsche, Buick/GMC, Chevrolet, Chrysler/Dodge/Jeep, Fiat, Honda, Kia, Mercedes, Toyota/Scion
14 (28)	East St, Canton St, **E** ⓛ Hilton
27mm	ⓡs sb, full ⓗ facilities, ⓒ, ⓐ, litter barrels
13 (26.5)	University Ave
12 (26)	I-93 N, to Braintree, Boston, motorist callboxes end nb
11b a (23)	Neponset St, to Canton, **E** ⓖ Citgo/repair, Sunoco, ⓕ Dunkin Donuts, Rosario's Grill, **2 mi W on US 1** ⓖ Gulf, Sunoco, ⓕ Jake&Joe's, ⓛ The Chateau, Hampton Inn, ⓞ ⓗ, Chevrolet, Ferrari, Hyundai, Maserati, Nissan
22.5mm	Neponset River
10 (20)	Coney St (from sb, no EZ return), to US 1, Sharon, Walpole, **1 mi W on US 1** ⓖ Mobil, ⓕ Bertucci's, Chili's, Chipotle Mexican, Dunkin Donuts, 5 Guys Burgers, Friendly's, HoneyDew Donuts, IHOP, McDonald's, 99 Rest., Old Country Buffet, Outback Steaks, Panda Express, Panera Bread, PapaGino's, Pizza Hut, Starbucks, Subway, Taco Bell, TGIFriday's, TX Roadhouse, ⓛ Courtyard, Residence Inn, Sheraton, ⓞ Acura, Advance Parts, Barnes&Noble, CVS Drug, Home Depot, Kohl's, Lexus, Old Navy, PetCo, Radio Shack, Staples, Stop&Shop, TownFair Tire, VW, Walgreens, mall
9 (19)	US 1, to MA 27, Walpole, **W** ⓖ Gulf, Mobil/dsl, ⓕ Applebee's, Asia Treasures, Dunkin Donuts, Starbucks, ⓛ Boston View, EconoLodge, Holiday Inn Express, ⓞ BigY Foods/drug, Stop&Shop, Walmart, same as 10
8 (16)	S Main St, Sharon, **E** ⓕ Dunkin Donuts, ⓞ Rite Aid, Shaw's Foods, whaling museum
7b a (13)	MA 140, to Mansfield, **E** ⓕ Domino's, 99 Rest., Piccadilly's, ⓛ Comfort Inn, Courtyard, Holiday Inn, Red Roof Inn, Residence Inn. **W** ⓖ Shell/HoneyDew Donuts/dsl, ⓕ Dunkin Donuts, PapaGino's, ⓞ AT&T
6b a (12)	I-495, S to Cape Cod, N to NH
10mm	Welcome Ctr/ ⓡs nb, full ⓗ facilities, info, ⓒ, ⓐ, litter barrels, petwalk
9mm	truck parking area sb
5 (7)	MA 152, Attleboro, **E** ⓗ, **W** ⓖ Gulf/dsl, ⓕ Bill's Pizza, Piccadilly Rest., Wendy's, ⓞ Shaw's Foods/Osco Drug
4 (6)	I-295 S, to Woonsocket
3 (4)	MA 123, to Attleboro, **E** ⓖ Shell/dsl, ⓕ Dunkin Donuts, ⓞ ⓗ, zoo
2.5mm	parking area/weigh sta both lanes, no restrooms, litter barrels
2b a (1)	US 1A, Newport Ave, Attleboro, **E** ⓖ Mobil/dsl, Shell, ⓕ Archie's Pizza, HoneyDew Donuts, McDonald's, Olive Garden, Spumoni's Italian, ⓞ Home Depot, K-Mart, Monroe's Service, **W** ⓖ BP
1 (.5)	US 1 (from sb), **E** ⓛ Days Inn, ⓞ Kia, Rite Aid, Volvo, **W** ⓖ Hess
0mm	Massachusetts/Rhode Island state line

⬆N INTERSTATE 195

Exit	Services
22 (41)	I-495 N, MA 25 S, to Cape Cod. **I-195 begins/ends on I-495, exit 1.**
21 (39)	MA 28, to Wareham, **N** ⓖ Maxi/dsl/24hr, ⓕ Longhorn Steaks, Pomodore's Italian, Qdoba Mexican, Red Robin, ⓞ Best Buy, JC Penney, LL Bean, Lowe's, Michaels, Old Navy, PetCo, Staples, Target, TJ Maxx, **S** ⓖ Irving/dsl, Mobil/Dunkin Donuts/dsl, ⓞ ⓗ, repair
37mm	parking area eb, info, boatramp
36mm	Sippican River
20 (35)	MA 105, to Marion, **S** RV camping (seasonal)
19b a (31)	to Mattapoisett, **S** ⓖ Mobil, ⓕ Nick's Pizza, Panino's Rest., Ying Dynasty, ⓞ USPO
18 (26)	MA 240 S, to Fairhaven, **1 mi S** ⓖ 7-11, Valero/dsl, ⓕ Burger King, Dunkin Donuts, Jake's Diner, McDonald's, 99 Rest., PapaGino's, Pasta House, Pizza Hut, Subway, Sweet Ginger Asian, Taco Bell, Wendy's, ⓛ Hampton Inn, ⓞ AutoZone, Brahman Handbags, Buick/GMC, $Tree, GNC, K-Mart, Marshalls, Mazda, Radio Shack, Shaw's Foods, Staples, Stop&Shop/gas, Sullivan Tire, TownFair Tire, Verizon, Walgreens, Walmart
25.5mm	Acushnet River
17 (24)	Coggeshall St, (from wb only), New Bedford, **N** ⓖ Petro, 7-11/gas, Sunoco, ⓕ Dunkin Donuts, HoneyDew Donuts, McDonald's, Papa Johns, Subway, ⓞ Market Basket Foods, same as 16
16 (23)	Washburn St (from eb), **N** ⓖ Sunoco, ⓕ McDonald's, Papa John's
15 (22)	MA 18 S, New Bedford, **S** ⓖ Lukoil, ⓛ Fairfield Inn, ⓞ Whaling Museum, hist dist, to downtown,
14 (21)	Penniman St (from eb), New Bedford, downtown
13b a (20)	MA 140, **N** ⓡ, **S** ⓖ 1 Stop, Sunoco, ⓕ Dunkin Donuts, ⓞ ⓗ, Buttonwood Park/zoo, CVS Drug, Honda, Shaw's Foods, Walgreens
12b a (19)	N Dartmouth, **S** ⓖ Hess, Mobil/dsl, ⓕ Applebee's, Azuma Asian, Burger King, ChuckeCheese, Coldstone, Dunkin Donuts, 5 Guys Burgers, Friendly's, IHOP, Jimmy's Pizza, McDonald's, 99 Rest., Old Country Buffet, Olive Garden, Panera Bread, PapaGino's, Peking Garden, Quiznos, Rose&Vicki's Bistro, Ruby Tuesday, Subway, Taco Bell, TGIFriday's, Tropical Smoothie, TX Roadhouse, Wendy's, ⓛ Residence Inn, ⓞ AT&T, Barnes&Noble, Best Buy, BJ's Whse/gas, Chevrolet, Curves, Dick's, $Tree, Firestone/auto, JC Penney, Kohl's, Lowe's, Macy's, Michael's, Nissan, Old Navy, PetCo, Sears/auto, Stop&Shop/gas, Target, TJ Maxx, TownFair Tire, Toyota/Scion, Verizon, Walgreens, Walmart, USPO, mall, st police
11b a (17)	Reed Rd, to Dartmouth, **2 mi S** ⓖ Shell
10 (16)	MA 88 S, to US 6, Westport, **S** ⓖ Gulf, ⓞ CVS Drug, same as 9
9 (15.5)	MA 24 N (from nb), Stanford Rd, Westport, **S** ⓖ Supreme, Rte 6 Gas, Valero, ⓕ Dunkin Donuts, Galley Grill, ⓛ Hampton Inn, ⓞ White's ⓗ ity
8b	MA 24 N, (exits left from eb)
8a (15)	MA 24 S, Fall River, Westport
7 (14)	MA 81 S, Plymouth Ave, Fall River, **N** ⓖ BP, Hess, ⓕ Boston Mkt, Burger King, D'angelo's Rest., Dunkin Donuts, HoneyDew Donuts, KFC, 99 Rest., Subway, Wendy's, ⓞ ⓗ, CVS Drug, **S** ⓖ Gulf, Shell, ⓕ Applebee's, McDonald's, ⓞ Sullivan Tire, Stop&Shop, Walgreens
6 (13.5)	Pleasant St, Fall River, downtown

DEDHAM

ATTLEBORO

MA

FALL RIVER

⬆N INTERSTATE 195 CONT'D

Exit	Services
5 (13)	MA 79, MA 138, to Taunton, **S** 🅖 Hess, 7-11, 🍴 Dunkin Donuts
12mm	Assonet Bay
4b a (10)	MA 103, to Swansea, Somerset, **N** 🅖 BP, 🍴 Rogers Rest., 🅞 repair, vet, **S** 🅖 Shell/24hr, 🍴 Jillian's Grill, 🛏 Quality Inn, Super 8
3 (8)	US 6, to MA 118, Swansea, Rehoboth, **N** 🅖 Citgo/dsl, Hess, Mobil/Dunkin Donuts, 🍴 Friendly's, McDonald's, Subway, Thai Taste, Wendy's, 🅞 BigLots, CarQuest, $Tree, Firestone/auto, Jo-Ann Fabrics, Macy's, Marshall's, Old Navy, Price Rite Foods, Radio Shack, Sears/auto, Target, mall, **S** 🅖 Gulf, 🍴 Anthony's Seafood, 🛏 Swansea Motel, 🅞 Kia, NAPA
6mm	🆁🆂 eb, full ♿ facilities, 🚻, 🏕 litter barrels, petwalk
5.5mm	parking area wb
2 (5)	MA 136, to Newport, **S** 🅖 Mobil/24hr, Shell/24hr, 🍴 Cathay Pearl Chinese, Dunkin Donuts, McDonald's, Michael's Rest., Subway, 🅞 CVS Drug
3mm	weigh sta both lanes
1 (1)	MA 114A, to Seekonk, **N** 🅖 Citgo, Gulf, Shell/24hr, 🍴 Dunkin Donuts, HoneyDew Donuts, Lums Sandwiches, Newport Creamery, 99 Rest., 🛏 Motel 6, 🅞 vet, **S** 🅖 Hess/dsl, Mobil/24hr, Stop&Shop Gas/repair, 🍴 Applebee's, BigLots, Buca Italian, Burger King, Chili's, D'Angelo's, Dicky's BBQ, Diparma Italian, Dunkin Donuts, 1149 E Rest., 5 Guys Burgers, Friendly's, McDonald's, Old Country Buffet, Outback Steaks, Panera Bread, PapaGino's, Starbucks, Subway, Taco Bell, TGIFriday's, Wendy's, 🛏 Best Western, Comfort Inn, Extended Stay America, Hampton Inn, Knights Inn, Mary's Motel, Ramada Inn, Town&Country Motel, 🅞 Acura, Advance Parts, AT&T, Best Buy, BigLots, Bob's Stores, Dick's, $Tree, Firestone/auto, Home Depot, Kohl's, Lowe's, Michael's, PepBoys, PetCo, Sam's Club, Staples, Stop&Shop Foods, Target, TJMaxx, TownFair Tire, Tuesday Morning, Verizon, Walmart
0mm	**Massachusetts/Rhode Island state line, Exits 8-1 are in RI.**
8 (5)	US 1A N, Pawtucket, **S** 🅖 Mobil/dsl, 🍴 Subway, 🅞 CVS Drug
7 (4)	US 6 E, CT 114 S, to Barrington, Seekonk
6 (3)	Broadway Ave, **N** 🅖 Speedy AutoService, **S** 🅖 Shell, Sunoco/dsl
5 (2.5)	RI 103 E, Warren Ave
4 (2)	US 44 E, RI 103 E, Taunton Ave, Warren Ave, **N** 🅖 Sunoco
3 (1.5)	Gano St, **N** 🅞 Wyndham Garden
2 (1)	US 44 W, Wickenden St, India Pt, downtown, **N** 🅖 Shell/dsl, 🅞 Wyndham Garden
1 (.5)	Providence, downtown
0mm	**I-195 begins/ends on I-95, exit 20 in Providence, RI Exits 1-8 are in RI.**

⬆E INTERSTATE 290

Exit	Services
26b a (20)	**I-495. I-290 begins/ends on I-495, exit 25.**
25b a (17)	Solomon Pond Mall Rd, to Berlin, **N** 🍴 Bertucci's, TGIFriday's, 🍴 Olive Garden, 🛏 Comfort Inn, Residence Inn, 🅞 Best Buy, JC Penney, Macy's, Old Navy, Sears/auto, Target, mall/foodcourt, **S** 🍴 Guiseppe's Grill
24 (15)	Church St, Northborough

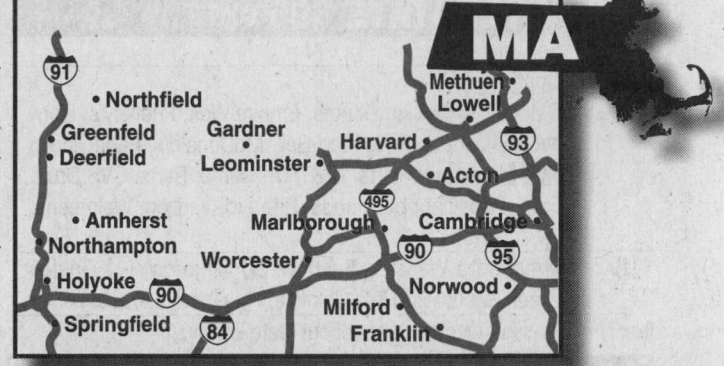

23b a (13)	MA 140, Boylston, **N** 🅖 Citgo/Dunkin Donuts/dsl
22 (11)	Main St, Worchester, **N** 🍴 Dunkin Donuts
21 (10)	Plantation St (from eb), **N** 🍴 Dunkin Donuts, same as 20
20 (8)	MA 70, Lincoln St, Burncoat St, **N** 🅖 Gulf/Subway, 🍴 Crown Chicken, Denny's, Dunkin Donuts, 5&Diner, 5 Guys Burgers, KFC, McDonald's, PapaGino's, Plaza Azteca, Ruby Tuesday, Taco Bell, TX Roadhouse, Wendy's, 🛏 Quality Inn, 🅞 Aldi Foods, AutoZone, Barnes&Noble, CVS Drug, Dick's, $Tree, Lowe's, Radio Shack, Staples, Stop&Shop, Target, Walgreens, USPO
19 (7)	I-190 N, MA 12
18	MA 9, Framington, Ware, Worcester 🍴, **N** 🅷
16	Central St, Worcester, **N** 🍴 99 Rest., Starbucks, 🛏 Crowne Plaza, Hilton Garden, mall
14	MA 122, Barre, Worcester, downtown
13	MA 122A, Vernon St, Worcester, downtown
12	MA 146 S, to Millbury
11	Southbridge St, College Square, **N** 🅖 Shell/dsl, 🍴 Golden House Chinese, Wendy's, 🅞 Family$
10	MA 12 N (from wb), Hope Ave
9	Auburn St, to Auburn, **E** 🅖 BP, Shell, 🍴 Arby's, Auburn Town Pizza, Dunkin Donuts, McDonald's, PapaGino's, Starbucks, Yong Shing, 🛏 Comfort Inn, Holiday Inn Express (1mi), La Quinta, 🅞 Acura, Macy's, Sears/auto, Shaw's Foods, TownFair Tire, mall
8	MA 12 S (from sb), Webster, **W** 🅖 Shell, 🛏 Holiday Inn Express
7	I-90, E to Boston, W to Springfield. **I-290 begins/ends on I-90.**

⬆N INTERSTATE 395

Exit	Services
	I-395 begins/ends on I-90, exit 10.
7 (12)	to I-90 (MA Tpk), MA 12, **E** 🅖 Shell, 🍴 Piccadilly's, 🛏 Holiday Inn Express
6b a (11)	US 20, **E** 🅖 BP, Gulf, 🍴 Frank&Nancy's Cafe, 🅞 NAPA, Honda/VW, truck tires/repair, **W** 🅖 Shell, 🍴 Chuck's Steakhouse, Dunkin Donuts, Friendly's, 🛏 Fairfield Inn, Hampton Inn, 🅞 BJ's Whse, Buick/Cadillac/GMC, Chevrolet, Ford, Home Depot, Nissan, TJ Maxx, transmissions
5 (8)	Depot Rd, N Oxford
4b a (6)	Sutton Ave, to Oxford, **E** 🅞 MktBasket Foods, **W** 🅖 Cumberland Farms, Mobil/24hr, 🍴 Dunkin Donuts, McDonald's, NE Pizza, Subway, Veranda Cafe, 🅞 Cahill's Tire/repair, CVS Drug, Home Depot, MktBasket Foods, Verizon
3 (4)	Cudworth Rd, to N Webster, S Oxford
2 (3)	MA 16, to Webster, **E** 🅞 Subaru, RV Camping, **W** 🅖 BP/ repair, Gulf, Hi-Lo Gas, Sunoco, 🍴 Burger King,

MA

⬆N INTERSTATE 395 CONT'D

Exit	Services
2 (3)	Continued D'angelo's, Dunkin Donuts, Empire Wok, Friendly's, HoneyDew Donuts, KFC/Taco Bell, McDonald's, PapaGino's, 🅞🅗, Advance Parts, AT&T, Consumer Parts, CVS Drug, Ford, PriceChopper Foods, Rite Aid, Verizon, Walgreens, vet
1 (1)	MA 193, to Webster, **E** 🅗, **W** 🅖 Citgo/dsl, 🅘 Golden Greek Rest., Wind Tiki Chinese, 🅞 Goodyear/auto
0mm	Massachusetts/Connecticut state line

⬆N INTERSTATE 495

Exit	Services
I-495 begins/ends on I-95, exit 59.	
55 (119)	MA 110 (from nb, no return), to I-95 S, **E** 🅖 Irving/Circle K, Mobil, Sunoco, 🅘 Acupulco Mexican, Burger King, Dunkin Donuts, Friendly's, McDonald's, PapaGino's, 🅛 Fairfield Inn, 🅞 AT&T, Chevrolet, Stop&Shop, Verizon, **W** 🅖 BP, Gulf, 🅘 Amesbury Pizza, Irene's Pizza, Weiloon Cafe, Whistling Kettle, 🅞 Curves, NAPA
54 (118)	MA 150, to Amesbury, **W** RV camping
53 (115)	Broad St, Merrimac, **W** 🅖 Citgo, 🅘 Dunkin Donuts
114mm	parking area sb, restrooms, 🆎 litter barrels (6AM-8PM)
52 (111)	MA 110, to Haverhill, **E** 🅖 Seafood Etc, 🅞🅗, **W** 🅖 BP, Mobil/dsl, 🅘 Dunkin Donuts
110mm	parking area nb, 🆎 litter barrels
51 (109)	MA 125, to Haverhill, **E** 🅖 Gulf, Mobil, 🅘 Bros Pizza, China King, Dunkin Donuts, Super Buffet, 🅞🅗, Family$, **W** 🅖 Mobil/dsl, 🅘 Dunkin Donuts, Friendly's, Li's Asian, Longhorn Steaks, Lucky Corner Chinese, McDonald's, Mr Mikes Grill, Starbucks, Wendy's, 🅞 Monro Service
50 (107)	MA 97, to Haverhill, **W** 🅞 Ford, Lowe's, Target
49 (106)	MA 110, to Haverhill, **E** 🅖 Gulf, Sunoco/24hr, 🅘 Athens Pizza, Dunkin Donuts, McDonald's, Oriental Garden, 99 Rest., PapaGino's, 🅛 Best Western, Comfort Inn, 🅞 Buick/Chevrolet/GMC, Chrysler/Dodge/Jeep, CVS Drug, MktBasket Foods, Walgreens
105.8mm	Merrimac River
48 (105.5)	MA 125, to Bradford, **E** 🅖 BJ's Whse/gas
47 (105)	MA 213, to Methuen, 1-2 mi **W** 🅘 Bugaboo Steaks, Burger King, ChuckeCheese, McDonald's, Olive Garden, Starbucks, TGIFriday's, Wendy's, 🅞🅗, Home Depot, The Mann Orchards/Bakery, Marshalls, MktBasket Foods, Old Navy, Radio Shack, Stop&Shop, Target, Walmart/Subway
46 (104)	MA 110, **E** 🅖 Pleasant Valley Gas, Sunoco/24hr, 🅖 Giovanni's Deli, 🅞 Lincoln, **W** 🅗
45 (103)	Marston St, to Lawrence, **W** 🅞 Chevrolet, Honda, Kia, VW
44 (102)	Merrimac St, to Lawrence
43 (101)	Mass Ave
42 (100)	MA 114, **E** 🅖 Gulf, Mobil, Wave, 🅘 Bertucci's, Boston Mkt, Burger King, Burtons Grill, Chipotle Mexican, Dunkin Donuts, Friendly's, Lee Chin Chinese, Panera Bread, 🅛 Holiday Inn Express, 🅞 Ace Hardware, CVS Drug, MktBasket Foods, PetCo, Staples, TJ Maxx, Walgreens, **W** 🅖 Gas-N-Go, 🅘 Denny's, KFC, Pizza Hut/Taco Bell, Subway, Wendy's, 🅞🅗, Monroe Service, Rite Aid, Save-a-Lot Foods, VIP Parts/service, vet
41 (99)	MA 28, to Andover, **E** 🅘 Dunkin Donuts, 🅞 Cadillac/

Exit	Services
41 (99)	Continued Chevrolet
40b a (98)	I-93, N to Methuen, S to Boston
39 (94)	MA 133, to Dracut, **E** 🅖 Hess, 🅘 Longhorn Steaks, McDonald's, 🅛 Extended Stay America, **W** 🅖 Mobil/dsl, 🅘 Cracker Barrel, Wendy's, 🅛 Fairfield Inn, Holiday Inn/rest., Residence Inn
38 (93)	MA 38, to Lowell, **E** 🅖 Petroil/dsl, Shell/dsl, 🅘 Applebee's, Burger King, Dunkin Donuts, IHOP, Jade East, 99 Rest., Waffle House, 🅛 Motel Caswell, Motel 6, 🅞 Home Depot, Honda/VW, TownFair Tire, Walmart, **W** 🅖 Citgo, Mobil, Sunoco, USA/dsl, 🅘 Dunkin Donuts, Jillie's Rest., Milan Pizza, McDonald's, Wendy's, 🅞 Buick/GMC, Chevrolet, Chrysler/Dodge/Jeep, CVS Drug, Hannaford Foods, Mazda, MktBasket Foods, Marshalls, Sears Essentials, Staples
37 (91)	Woburn St, to S Lowell, **W** 🅖 Gulf/Dunkin Donuts/Subway
35c (90)	to Lowell SP, Lowell ConX, **0-2 mi W services on US 3** 🅘 Burger King, Chili's, McDonald's, Outback Steaks, Wendy's, 🅛 Courtyard, 🅞 Kia, Lowe's, Shop&Save, Walgreens
35b a (89)	US 3, S to Burlington, N to Nashua, NH
34 (88)	MA 4, Chelmsford, **E** 🅖 Ampet, Mobil, Sunoco, 🅘 Cafe Madrid, Domino's, Dunkin Donuts, Jimmy's Pizza, PapaGino's, 🅛 Radisson, 🅞 CVS Drug, Walgreens, **W** 🅖 Shell, 🅘 Moonstone's Rest., 🅛 Best Western
33	MA 4, N Chelmsford (from nb)
87mm	🆁🆂 both lanes, full ♿ facilities, 🅒, 🆎, litter barrels, vending, (8am-8pm)
32 (83)	Boston Rd, to MA 225, **E** 🅖 Cumberland Farms, Gulf, Mobil, 🅘 Applebee's, British Beer Co Rest., Burger King, Chili's, D'angelo's, Dunkin Donuts, McDonald's, PapaGino's, Starbucks, Subway, Westford Grill, 🅛 Hampton Inn, Residence Inn, 🅞🅗, CVS Drug, Jo-Ann Fabrics, MktBasket Foods, Radio Shack, Rite Aid, Walgreens, to Nashoba Valley Ski Area
31 (80)	MA 119, to Groton, **E** 🅖 Gulf, Mobil/dsl/24hr, Shell, 🅘 Dunkin Donuts, Littleton's Subs, Subway, Tre Amici Ristorante, 🅞 Aubuchon Hardware, CVS Drug, Donelan's Foods, Toyota/Scion, Verizon, vet
30 (78)	MA 110, to Littleton, **1 mi E** 🅖 Shell/Dunkin Donuts, 🅘 CVS Drug, RV Camping, USPO, vet, **W** 🅖 Shell/Dunkin Donuts, 🅞🅗, vet
29b a (77)	MA 2, to Leominster, **E** to Walden Pond St Reserve
28 (75)	MA 111, to Boxborough, Harvard, **E** 🅖 Gulf/Dunkin Donuts, 🅛 Holiday Inn
27 (70)	MA 117, to Bolton, **E** 🅖 Mobil/dsl, 🅘 Subway, **W** 🅘 Bolton Pizza, 🅞 vet
26 (68)	MA 62, to Berlin, **E** 🅖 Gulf/Dunkin Donuts, 🅛 Holiday Inn Express, 🅞🅗, BJ's Whse/gas, Lowe's, **W** 🅖 Shell/dsl, 🅘 Berlin Farms Cafe
66mm	Assabet River
25b (64)	I-290, to Worcester
25a	to MA 85, Marlboro, **1 mi E** 🅖 Gulf, Mobil/dsl, 🅘 Applebee's, Burger King, Checkerboards Rest., Domino's, HoneyDew Donuts, KFC/Taco Bell, 99 Rest., PapaGino's, 🅞 AutoZone, Chevrolet, CVS Drug, $Tree, Family$, Hannaford Foods, PetCo, Stop&Shop/gas, TJ Maxx, Verizon, Walgreens

HAVERHILL *LOWELL*

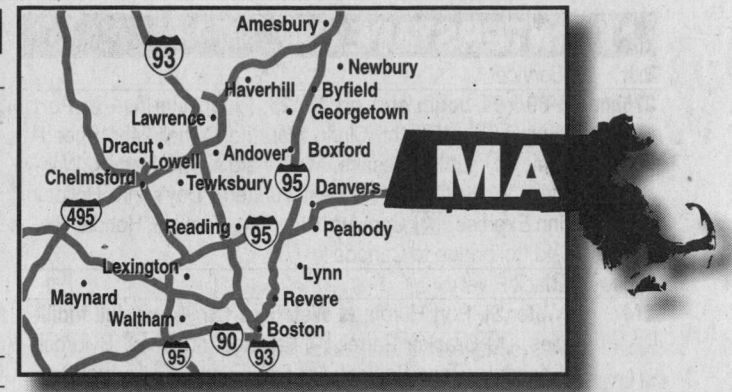

M A R L B O R O	**🔼N INTERSTATE 495 CONT'D**

Exit Services

24b a (63) US 20, to Northboro, Marlboro, **E** 🅖 Mobil, 🍴 Allora Rest., D'angelo's, Dunkin Donuts, Lake Williams Pizza, 🛏 Holiday Inn, **W** 🅖 Gulf, Shell, 🍴 Boston Mkt, China Taste, Chipotle Mexican, 5 Guys Burgers, Japan 1, Longhorn Steaks, McDonald's/playplace, 99 Rest., Panera Bread, PapaGino's, Quiznos, Starbucks, Tandoori Grill, Wendy's, 🛏 Best Western, Courtyard, Embassy Suites, Hampton Inn, Homestead Suites, 🅞 $Tree, GNC, Hannaford Foods

23c (60) Simrano Dr, Marlboro

23b a (59) MA 9, to Shrewsbury, Framingham, **E** 🅖 Cumberland/Dunkin Donuts, Gulf, 🍴 Wendy's, 🛏 Red Roof Inn, **0-2 mi W** 🅖 Mobil/dsl/24hr, Shell, 🍴 Bertucci's, Burger King, Chateau Rest., Chengdu, Chipotle Mexican, D'angelo's, Dunkin Donuts, Friendly's, Harry's Rest., McDonald's, Piccadilly Cafe, Ruby Tuesday, Starbucks, 🛏 Doubletree Inn, Extended Stay America, Extended Stay Deluxe, Residence Inn, 🅞🏥, Buick/GMC, Chrysler/Dodge/Jeep, Marshall's, Staples, Stop&Shop, VW

22 (58) I-90, MA TPK, E to Boston, W to Albany

21b a (54) MA 135, to Hopkinton, Upton, **E** 🅖 Cumberland, Mobil, 🍴 Dino's Pizza, Dynasty Chinese, Golden Spoon Rest.

20 (50) MA 85, to Milford, **W** 🅖 Gulf/dsl/LP, Mobil/dsl, 🍴 99 Rest., Pizza 85/deli, TGIFriday's, Wendy's, 🛏 Comfort Inn, Courtyard, Fairfield Inn, Holiday Inn Express, 🅞🏥, Best Buy, Lowe's, PetCo, Staples, Stop&Shop, Target, TJ Maxx, Toyota/Scion

M I L F O R D	

19 (48) MA 109, to Milford, **W** 🅖 Mobil/Dunkin Donuts/dsl, Shell, 🍴 Alamo Mexican, Applebee's, Bugaboo Cr Steaks, Burger King, D'angelo's, 5 Guys Burgers, Friendly's, KFC/Pizza Hut, Maria's Italian, McDonald's/playplace, Panera Bread, PapaGino's, Subway, 🛏 Doubletree, La Quinta, 🅞 AutoZone, CVS Drug, $Tree, Hannaford Foods, Jo-Ann Fabrics, K-Mart, Kohl's, Radio Shack, Rite Aid, TownFair Tire

18 (46) MA 126, to Bellingham, **E** 🍴 Chili's, Coldstone, McDonald's, 🅞 Barnes&Noble, Michael's, MktBasket Foods, Old Navy, Staples, Verizon, Walmart/Subway, Whole Foods Mkt, **W** 🅖 Hess/dsl, Mobil/24hr, Sunoco/dsl, 🍴 Chicago Grill, DQ, Dunkin Donuts, Outback Steaks, 🅞 Home Depot, Petsmart

17 (44) MA 140, to Franklin, Bellingham, **E** 🅖 Mobil/dsl, Shell, Sunoco, 🍴 Burger King, D'angelo's, Dunkin Donuts, Franklin Cafe, HoneyDew Donuts, Longhorn Steaks, Panera Bread, PapaGino's, Pepper Terrace Thai, Subway, Taco Bell, Tepanyaki Asian, 🅞 AT&T, AutoZone, Buick/GMC, CVS Drug, GNC, Marshalls, Radio Shack, Stop&Shop, **W** 🍴 Encontro Rest., 99 Rest., 🛏 Residence Inn, 🅞🏥, BJ's Whse/Subway/gas

16 (42) King St, to Franklin, **E** 🅖 Sunoco, 🍴 Dunkin Donuts, Joe's Grill, King St Cafe, Spruce Pond Creamery, 🛏 Hampton Inn, **W** 🛏 Hawthorn Inn

15 (39) MA 1A, to Plainville, Wrentham, **E** 🅖 Shell, 🍴 Assisi Pizza, 🅞🏥, **W** 🅖 Mobil/dsl, 🍴 Chicago Grill, Cracker Barrel, Dunkin Donuts, Friendly's, Ruby Tuesday, 🅞 Premium Outlets/famous brands

14b a (37) US 1, to N Attleboro, **E** 🍴 Interstate/D'angelo's/PapaGino's/dsl, 🍴 Luciano's Rest., 🛏 Arbor Motel, 🅞 Bass Pro Shops (4mi), **W** 🅖 Citgo/dsl, Mobil, 🍴 Chili's, Dunkin Donuts, Panera Bread, The Tavern, 🛏 Holiday Inn Ex

14b a (37) Continued press, 🅞 Macdonald's RV Ctr, Stop&Shop, Lowe's, NTB, Stop&Shop, Target, TJ Maxx, vet

13 (32) I-95, N to Boston, S to Providence, access to 🏥

12 (30) MA 140, to Mansfield, **E** 🍴 Asian Grill, Bertucci's Italian, Chipotle Mexican, Friendly's Express, Longhorn Steaks, Qdoba Mexican, Sake Japanese, TGIFriday's, Wendy's, 🅞 AT&T, Best Buy, Home Depot, LL Bean, Michael's, PetCo, Kohl's, Radio Shack, Shaw's Foods, Staples, Verizon

11 (29) MA 140 S (from sb) **1 mi W** 🅖 Gulf, 🍴 Dunkin Donuts, Mandarin Chinese, McDonald's, Subway, 🅞 $Tree

10 (26) MA 123, to Norton, **E** 🍴 Dunkin Donuts, 🅞 QuickStop, **W** 🏥

9 (24) Bay St, to Taunton, **E** 🍴 Chateau Rest., **W** 🍴 Dunkin Donuts, Jaybo Cafe, NE Hotdog, Ruby Tuesday, Subway, Wendy's, 🛏 Extended Stay America, 🅞 BJ's Whse, $Tree, Tadeschi Foods, Watson Pond SP

8 (22) MA 138, to Raynham, **E** 🅖 Hess/dsl, Mobil/dsl, 🍴 Christopher's Pizza, HoneyDew Donuts, Yummyhouse Rest., **W** 🅖 Gulf/dsl, Shell/dsl/repair, Stop'n Go/dsl, 🍴 Brothers Pizza, Cape Cod Cafe, China Garden, D'angelos, Dunkin Donuts, HoneyDew Donuts, Lucky Corner Chinese, McDonald's, Subway, 🅞🏥, Ace Hardware, CVS Drug, Mkt Basket Foods, USPO, vet

7b a (19) MA 24, to Fall River, Boston, **1/2 mi E** 🅖 Mobil/dsl, 🍴 Burger King

18mm weigh sta both lanes

17mm Taunton River

M I D D L E B O R O	

6 (15) US 44, to Middleboro, **E** 🅖 Super/dsl, 🍴 Burger King, Dunkin Donuts, Fireside Grille, Friendly's, Hong Kong Taste, PapaGino's, Subway, **W** 🅖 Mobil/Dunkin Donuts/dsl, 🛏 Fairfield Inn, Holiday Inn Express

5 (14) MA 18, to Lakeville, **E** 🅖 Shell, Super/dsl, 🍴 D'Angelo's, Dave's Diner, Fireside Grille, Harry's Grille, Lorenzo's Rest., PapaGino's, Persy's Place Cafe, 🅞 CVS Drug, Kelly's Tire, Stop&Shop, **W** 🅞 Massasoit SP, RV camping (seasonal)

4 (12) MA 105, to Middleboro, **E** 🅖 Gulf/dsl, Shell/24hr, Sunoco/24hr, 🍴 China Sails, DQ, Dunkin Donuts, McDonald's, Tuttabella Pizza, 🛏 Days Inn, 🅞 AutoZone, Rite Aid

11mm parking area eb

10mm parking area both lanes

3 (8) MA 28, to Rock Village, S Middleboro, **E** 🅖 Irving/dsl, 🅞 Fred's Repair, **W** 🅖 Mobil/Dunkin Donuts/Subway/dsl

2 (3) MA 58, W Wareham, **E** 🅞 RV camping, to Myles Standish SF, **W** 🅖 7-11

2mm Weweantic River

1 (0) **I-495 begins/ends on I-195, MA 25 S.**

MA

Ⓡ = gas Ⓕ = food 🛏 = lodging Ⓞ = other Ⓡˢ = rest stop Copyright 2014 - The Next Exit ®

MI

⬆N INTERSTATE 69

Exit	Services
275mm	**I-69/I-94 begin/end on MI 25, Pinegrove Ave in Port Huron** Ⓡ BP/24hr, Clark, Marathon, Shell/24hr, Speedway, Ⓕ Little Caesar's, McDonald's, Tim Horton, Wendy's, White Castle, 🛏 Best Western, Day's Inn, Holiday Inn Express, Ⓞ Can-Am DutyFree, Family$, Honda, Rite Aid, tollbridge to Canada
275mm	Black River
274	Water St, Port Huron, **N Welcome Ctr/Ⓡˢ wb, full facilities**, Ⓕ Cracker Barrel, 🛏 Ramada Inn, S Ⓡ Bylo/dsl, Speedway/Taco Bell/dsl, Ⓕ Bob Evans, 🛏 Comfort Inn, Fairfield Inn, Hampton Inn, Knight's Inn, Ⓞ Lake Port SP, RV camping
199	Lp 69 (from eb, no return), to Port Huron, **0-2 mi S on Lp 69 S** Ⓡ Mobil/dsl, Speedway, Ⓕ Arby's, Baskin-Robbins, Burger King, Dunkin Donuts, McDonalds, KFC, Quay St Grill, Taco Bell, Wendy's, Ⓞ Advance Parts, AutoZone, Kroger/gas, K-Mart, Sam's Club/gas, repair, to Port Huron
	I-69 E and I-94 E run together into Port Huron. See exits 274-275mm.
198	I-94, to Detroit and Canada
196	Wadhams Rd, **N** Ⓡ Marathon, Speedy Q/dsl, Shell/Wendy's, Ⓕ Hungry Howie's, McDonald's, Peking Kitchen, Subway, Ⓞ Vinckier Foods, Wadham's Drugs, KOA (1mi), **S** golf
194	Taylor Rd, **N** Goodells CP, RV camping
189	Wales Center Rd, to Goodells, **S** golf
184	MI 19, to Emmett, **N** Ⓡ Citgo/Steverino's/dsl/scales/24hr, Ⓞ repair, **S** Ⓡ Marathon/dsl/24hr
180	Riley Center Rd, **N** KOA
176	Capac Rd, **N** Ⓡ BP/McDonald's/dsl/scales, Ⓕ Subway (2mi)
174mm	Ⓡˢ **wb, full ♿ facilities**, Ⓒ, 🚻, **litter barrels, vending, petwalk**
168	MI 53, Imlay City, **N** Ⓡ BP/dsl/24hr, Speedway/dsl, Ⓕ Big Boy, Big Joe's Pizza, Burger King, DQ, Hungry Howie's, John's Country Kitchen, Little Caesar's, Lucky's Steaks, McDonald's, New China, Taco Bell, Wah Wong Chinese, Wendy's/Tim Horton, 🛏 Days Inn, M53 Motel, Super 8, Ⓞ AutoZone, Chevrolet, Chrysler/Dodge/Jeep, $Discount, Ford, GNC, Grocery Outlet, Kroger/gas, NAPA, Pamida, Radio Shack, Sav-On Drug, **S** camping
163	Lake Pleasant Rd, to Attica
160mm	Ⓡˢ **eb, full ♿ facilities**, Ⓒ, 🚻, **litter barrels, vending, petwalk**
159	Wilder Rd
158mm	Flint River
155	MI 24, Lapeer, **1 mi N** Ⓡ BP, Clark/dsl, FS, Speedy Q, Ⓕ Applebee's, Apple Tree Rest., Arby's, Blind Fish Rest., Brian's Rest., Burger King, Checker's, DQ, Farmhouse Rest., Jet's Pizza, Jimmy John's, KFC, Little Caesar's, Mancino's, McDonald's, Mr Pita, Nick's Rest., Sonic, Starbucks, Subway, Taco Bell, Tim Horton, Wah Wong Chinese, Wendy's, 🛏 Best Western, Lapeer Hotel, Ⓞ Ⓗ, AutoZone, $Tree, Home Depot, K-Mart, Kohl's, Kroger, Meijer/dsl, Office Depot, O'Reilly Parts, Radio Shack, Save-a-Lot, Walgreens, st police, vet, **S** Ⓡ Mobil/dsl, Ⓞ Chrylser/Dodge/Jeep
153	Lake Nepessing Rd, **S** to Thumb Correctional, camping, golf
149	Elba Rd, **N** Ⓞ Torzwski CP, **S** Ⓞ Country Mkt, RV/truck repair

L A P E E R

F L I N T

145	MI 15, Davison, **N** Ⓡ Marathon, Shell/dsl, Speedway, Ⓕ Apollo Rest., Applebee's, Arby's, Big Boy, Big John's Rest., Burger King, Chee Kong Chinese, Flag City Diner, Hungry Howie's, Italia Gardens, KFC, Little Caesar's, McDonald's, Pizza Hut, Senor Lucky, Subway, Taco Bell, Tim Horton, 🛏 Comfort Inn, Ⓞ AutoValue Parts, Buick/GMC, GNC, Radio Shack, Rite Aid, Valley Tire, Walgreens, repair, **S** Ⓡ Mobil/dsl
143	Irish Rd, **N** Ⓡ Speedway/dsl, **S** Ⓡ Shell/McDonald's/24hr, Ⓞ Meijer/dsl/e-85, 7-11
141	Belsay Rd, Flint, **N** Ⓡ 1 stop, Shell/Wendy's/dsl/24hr, Ⓕ Country Kitchen, McDonald's, Taco Bell, Ⓞ Curves, K-Mart, Kroger, Walmart/Subway/auto, **S** Ⓡ Sunoco/A&W/LJ Silver/dsl
139	Center Rd, Flint, **N** Ⓡ Speedway/dsl, Ⓕ Applebee's, Cottage Inn Pizza, El Cazumel Mexican, Halo Burger, Old Country Buffet, Olympic Grill, Ponderosa, Quiznos, Starbucks, Subway, Tim Horton, Ⓞ Aldi Foods, Discount Tire, Home Depot, JC Penney, Jo-Ann Fabrics, Lowe's, Staples, **0-2 mi S** Ⓕ Bob Evans, China 1, Coney Island, DQ, Firkin&Fox Rest., Hungry Howie's, McDonald's, Subway, Walli's Rest., 🛏 Super 8, Ⓞ Belle Tire, $Tree, Meijer/dsl, Target, TJ Maxx, Verizon
138	MI 54, Dort Hwy, **N** Ⓡ BP/24hr, Speedway/dsl, Ⓕ Big John's Rest., KFC, Little Caesar's, Tom's Coney Island, YaYa's Chicken, Ⓞ Ⓗ, $General, KanRock Tires, Rite Aid, Save-a-Lot, Walgreens, **0-2 mi S** Ⓡ Marathon, Sunoco, Ⓕ Angelo's Coney Island, Arby's, Burger King, Church's, Empress of China, KFC, McDonald's, Taco Bell, 🛏 Travel Inn, Ⓞ Aamco, Advance Parts, AutoZone, BigLots, $General, Family$, Goodyear, K-Mart, O'Reilly Parts, 7-11, Tuffy Auto, U-Haul, Walgreens
137	I-475, UAW Fwy, to Detroit, Saginaw
136	Saginaw St, Flint, **N** Ⓡ Sunoco, Ⓞ Ⓗ, U MI at Flint
135	Hammerberg Rd, industrial area
133b a	I-75, S to Detroit, N to Saginaw, US 23 S to Ann Arbor
131	MI 121, to Bristol Rd, **1/2 mi N on Miller Rd** Ⓕ Bar Louie, Buffet City, Chili's, ChuckeCheese, Famous Dave's BBQ, Fire Mtn, Golden Moon Chinese, Halo Burger, Leo's Coney Island, LJ Silver, Logan's Roadhouse, Mongolian BBQ, Old Country Buffet, Olive Garden, Outback Steaks, Red Robin, Ruby Tuesday, Subway, Taco Bell, Valley Diner, Ⓞ Barnes&Noble, Best Buy, BigLots, Discount Tire, Firestone/auto, Gander Mtn, Goodyear/auto, Hobby Lobby, JC Penney, Jo-Ann Fabrics, Macy's, Michael's, Old Navy, PetCo, PetsMart, Sears/auto, Target, TJ Maxx, mall
129	Miller Rd, **S** Ⓕ Arby's, Burger King, McDonald's, Subway, Wendy's, Ⓞ Kroger/gas
128	Morrish Rd, **S** Ⓡ Admiral/24hr, BP/dsl/24hr, Ⓞ Sports Creek Horse Racing
126mm	Ⓡˢ **eb, full ♿ facilities, info**, Ⓒ, 🚻, **litter barrels, petwalk**
123	MI 13, to Saginaw, Lennon, **N** Ⓡ Speedway/dsl
118	MI 71, to Corunna, Durand, **N** st police, **S** Ⓡ QuikStop, Shell/dsl, Ⓕ McDonald's, Subway, Wendy's, 🛏 Quality Inn, Ⓞ Ace Hardware, Chevrolet, Family$, Rite Aid, golf
115mm	Shiawassee River
113	Bancroft, **S** Ⓡ BP/dsl, Ⓞ RV camping
105	MI 52, to Owosso, Perry, **S** Ⓡ Mobil, PS/Subway/dsl, 7-11, Sunoco/dsl/scales, Ⓕ Burger King, Café Sports, McDonald's, Taco Bell, 🛏 Heb's Inn, Ⓞ Family$, Ford, IGA Foods, Rite Aid, RV camping, truck repair (1mi)

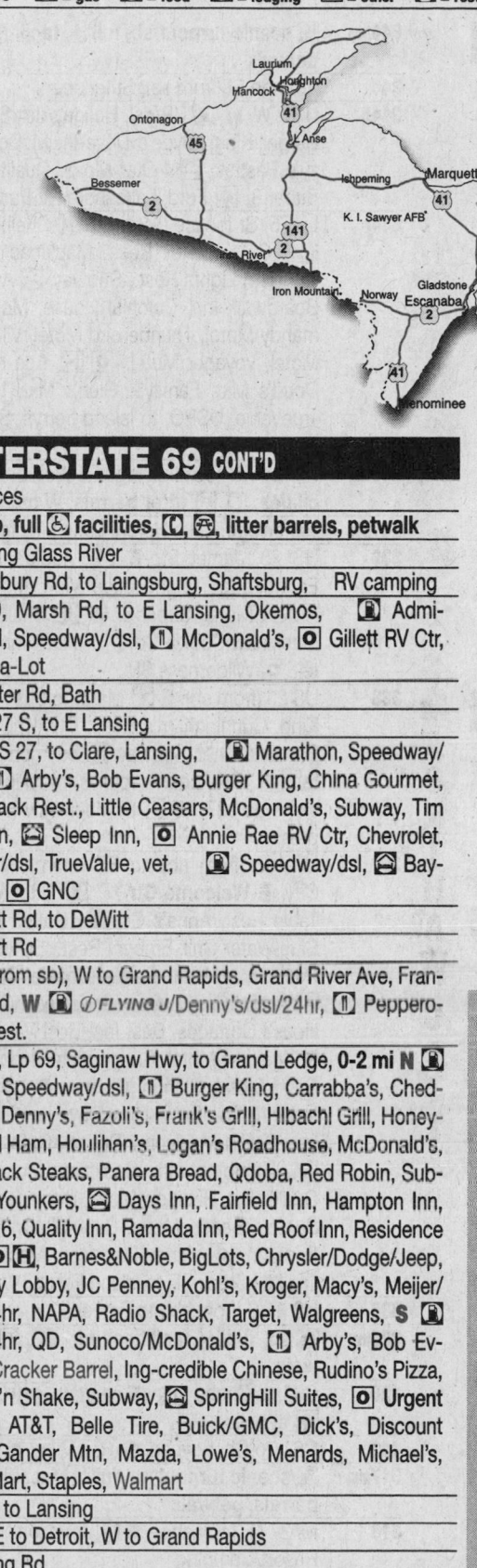

INTERSTATE 69 CONT'D

Exit	Services
101mm	🅿 wb, full ♿ facilities, 🚻, 🪧, litter barrels, petwalk
98.5mm	Looking Glass River
98	Woodbury Rd, to Laingsburg, Shaftsburg, RV camping
94	Lp 69, Marsh Rd, to E Lansing, Okemos, 🅿 Admiral/dsl, Speedway/dsl, 🍽 McDonald's, 🅾 Gillett RV Ctr, Save-a-Lot
92	Webster Rd, Bath
89	US 127 S, to E Lansing
87	Old US 27, to Clare, Lansing, 🅿 Marathon, Speedway/dsl, 🍽 Arby's, Bob Evans, Burger King, China Gourmet, FlapJack Rest., Little Ceasars, McDonald's, Subway, Tim Horton, 🏠 Sleep Inn, 🅾 Annie Rae RV Ctr, Chevrolet, Meijer/dsl, TrueValue, vet, 🅿 Speedway/dsl, 🏠 Baymont, 🅾 GNC
85	DeWitt Rd, to DeWitt
84	Airport Rd
91	I-96 (from sb), W to Grand Rapids, Grand River Ave, Frances Rd, W 🅿 ⓦFLYING J/Denny's/dsl/24hr, 🍽 Pepperoni's Rest.
93b a	MI 43, Lp 69, Saginaw Hwy, to Grand Ledge, 0-2 mi N 🅿 Shell, Speedway/dsl, 🍽 Burger King, Carrabba's, Cheddar's, Denny's, Fazoli's, Frank's Grill, Hibachi Grill, Honeybaked Ham, Houlihan's, Logan's Roadhouse, McDonald's, Outback Steaks, Panera Bread, Qdoba, Red Robin, Subway, Younkers, 🏠 Days Inn, Fairfield Inn, Hampton Inn, Motel 6, Quality Inn, Ramada Inn, Red Roof Inn, Residence Inn, 🅾🏥, Barnes&Noble, BigLots, Chrysler/Dodge/Jeep, Hobby Lobby, JC Penney, Kohl's, Kroger, Macy's, Meijer/dsl/24hr, NAPA, Radio Shack, Target, Walgreens, S 🅿 BP/24hr, QD, Sunoco/McDonald's, 🍽 Arby's, Bob Evans, Cracker Barrel, Ing-credible Chinese, Rudino's Pizza, Steak'n Shake, Subway, 🏠 SpringHill Suites, 🅾 Urgent Care, AT&T, Belle Tire, Buick/GMC, Dick's, Discount Tire, Gander Mtn, Mazda, Lowe's, Menards, Michael's, PetsMart, Staples, Walmart
95	I-496, to Lansing
72	I-96, E to Detroit, W to Grand Rapids
70	Lansing Rd
68mm	🅿 nb, full ♿ facilities, 🚻, 🪧, litter barrels, vending, petwalk
66	MI 100, to Grand Ledge, Potterville, W 🅿 BP, Shell/Subway, 🍽 Charlie's Grill, McDonald's, to Fox Co Park
61	Lansing Rd, E 🍽 Applebee's, 🏠 Comfort Inn, 🅾 AutoZone, Buick/Chevrolet/GMC, $Tree, Walmart/Subway, W 🅿 Speedway/dsl, QD, 🍽 Arby's, Biggby Coffee, Big

LANSING

Exit	Services
61	Continued Boy, Burger King, Jersey Subs, Jet's Pizza, KFC, Little Caesars, McDonald's, Pizza Hut, Rally's, Taco Bell, Tasty Twist, Top Chinese, Wendy's, 🅾🏥, Advance Parts, CarQuest, Charlotte Tires, Family$, Ford, TrueValue, vet
80	MI 50, Charlotte, E 🏠 Holiday Inn Express, 🅾 Meijer/dsl, W 🅿 Admiral, 🏠 Best Value Inn, 🅾🏥, RV camping
57	Lp 69, Cochran Rd, to Charlotte, E RV camping
51	Ainger Rd, 1 mi E gas, food, RV camping
48	MI 78, to Bellevue, Olivet, 1 mi E 🅿 BP/Subway/dsl, 🅾 to Olivet Coll
42	N Drive N, Turkeyville Rd, W 🍽 Cornwell's Rest. (1mi)
41mm	🅿 sb, full ♿ facilities, 🚻, 🪧, litter barrels, petwalk
38	I-94, E to Detroit, W to Chicago
36	Michigan Ave, to Marshall, E 🅿 Admiral, Citgo/dsl/E85, Shell/Subway, 🍽 Applebee's, Arby's, Biggby Coffee, Burger King, Little Caesars, McDonald's, Pizza Hut, Speedy Chick, Taco Bell, Wendy's, Yin Hai Chinese, 🏠 Comfort Inn, 🅾🏥, Ace Hardware, AutoZone, Chevrolet, $General, $Tree, Family Fare Foods, K-Mart, NAPA, Radio Shack, Rite Aid, Save-A-Lot, Tuffy Auto, W 🏠 Arbor Inn, 🅾 Chrysler/Dodge/Jeep
32	F Drive S, E 🅿 Shell (3/4 mi), 🍽 Moonraker Rest. (3mi), W 🅾 RV Camping
25	MI 60, to Three Rivers, Jackson, E 🅿 BP/dsl, TA/Shell/Country Pride/dsl/scales/24hr/@, Sunoco/dsl, 🍽 McDonald's, Subway, 🅾 Auto Value Parts, $General, auto/truck repair, RV camping

MARSHALL

⬆N INTERSTATE 69 CONT'D

COLDWATER

Exit	Services
23	Girard, **W** access to RV camping
16	Jonesville Rd, **W** Waffle Farm Camping (2mi)
13	US 12, to Quincy, Coldwater, **E** 🄡 Speedway/dsl, 🍴 Applebee's, Biggby Coffee, Bob Evans, Buffalo Wild Wings, Grand Buffet, Papa Murphy's, 🛏 Hampton Inn, Red Roof Inn, 🅾 Aldi Foods, AT&T, AutoZone, BigLots, Buick/Chevrolet/GMC, $Tree, Gander Mtn, GNC, Haylett RV Ctr, Home Depot, Meijer/dsl, Radio Shack, Verizon, Walmart/Subway, Younkers, **W** 🄡 Citgo, Speedway/dsl, 🍴 Arby's, Benedict's Steaks, Big Boy, Burger King, Coldwater Garden Rest., Cottage Inn Pizza, Culver's, Jimmy John's, KFC, Little Caesars, McDonald's, Pizza Hut, Ponderosa, Subway, Taco Bell, Wendy's, 🛏 Best Western, Comfort Inn, 🅾 🄷, Advance Parts, Ford/Lincoln, Rite Aid, Walgreens, auto repair, st police
10	Lp 69, Fenn Rd, to Coldwater
8mm	weigh sta nb
6mm	Welcome Ctr nb, full 🅰 facilities, 🄲, 🅰, litter barrels, vending, petwalk
3	Copeland Rd, Kinderhook, **W** 🄡 BP/dsl, 🍴 camping
0mm	Michigan/Indiana state line

⬆N INTERSTATE 75

SAULT STE MARIE

Exit	Services
395mm	US/Canada Border, Michigan state line, **I-75 begins/ends at toll bridge to Canada**
394	Easterday Ave, **E** 🄡 Citgo/dsl, 🍴 McDonald's, 🛏 Holiday Inn Express, 🅾 🄷, to Lake Superior St U, **W** Welcome Ctr/🅰, info, 🄡 Admiral/dsl, Holiday/dsl/currency exchange, 🍴 Freighter's Rest (2mi), 🛏 Ramada Inn (2mi)
392	3 Mile Rd, Sault Ste Marie, **E** 🄡 Admiral/dsl, BP/dsl, Holiday/dsl, Marathon/dsl, Shell/dsl, 🍴 Ang-gio's Italian, Applebee's, Arby's, Buffalo Wild Wings, Burger King, Country Kitchen, DQ, Domino's, Great Wall Chinese, Indo China Garden, Little Caesars, McDonald's, Pizza Hut, Studebaker's Rest., Subway, Taco Bell, Wendy's, 🛏 Best Value Inn, Best Western, Comfort Inn, Days Inn, Park Inn, Plaza Motel, Skyline Motel, Soo Locks Lodge, Super 8, Superior Place Motel, 🅾 🄷, Advance Parts, AT&T, BigLots, Buick/Chevrolet/GMC, $Tree, Family$, Glen's Mkt, Goodyear/auto, JC Penney, Jo-Ann Fabrics, K-Mart, NAPA, Radio Shack, Save-a-Lot, TJ Maxx, Verizon, Walgreens, Walmart/Subway, st police, Soo Locks Boat Tours
389mm	🆁🆂 nb, full 🅰 facilities, info, 🄲, 🅰, litter barrels, petwalk
386	MI 28, **W** 🅾 Clear Lake Camping (5mi), to Brimley SP
379	Gaines Hwy, **E** to Barbeau Area, Clear Lake Camping
378	MI 80, Kinross, **E** 🄡 BP/dsl, 🍴 Frank&Jim's Diner, 🅾 RV Camping, to Kinross Correctional, ⛽, golf
373	MI 48, Rudyard **2 mi W** gas/dsl, food, lodging
359	MI 134, to Drummond Island, **W** National Forest Camping
352	MI 123, to Moran, Newberry
348	H63, to Sault Reservation, St Ignace **0-2 mi E** 🍴 Jose's Cantina, 🛏 Bavarian Haus, Bayview Motel, Bear Cove Inn, Best Value Inn, Birchwood Motel, Comfort Inn, Cedars Motel, Evergreen Motel, Great Lakes Motel, Holiday Inn Express, Kewadin Inn, NorthernAire Motel, Pines Motel, Quality Inn, Tradewinds Motel, 🅾 🄷, Castle Rock Camping, ⛽, st police, to Mackinac Trail, casino, **W** Castle Rock Gifts.

MACKINAW CITY

Exit	Services
346mm	🆁🆂 scenic turnout sb, full 🅰 facilities, 🅰, litter barrels, petwalk
345	Portage St (from sb), St Ignace
344b	US 2 W, **W** 🄡 BP/dsl, Holiday/dsl, Shell/dsl, 🍴 Big Boy, Burger King, Clyde's Drive-In, McDonald's, Subway, Suzy's Pasties, 🛏 4 Star Motel, Quality Inn, Sunset Motel, Super 8, 🅾 Ford, Lakeshore RV Park, golf
344a	Lp 75, St Ignace **0-2 mi E** 🄡 Shell, 🍴 BC Pizza, Bentley's Cafe, Galley Rest., Mackinac Grille, Marina Rest., Northern Lights Rest., Subway, 🛏 Aurora Borealis Motel, Boardwalk Inn, Colonial House, Moran Bay Motel, Normandy Motel, Thunderbird Motel, Village Inn/rest., Vitek's Motel, Voyager Motel, 🅾 🄷, Ace Hardware, Bay Drug, Doud's Mkt, Family$, Glen's Mkt, NAPA, Radio Shack, TrueValue, USPO, to Island Ferrys, Straits SP, public marina, st police
343mm	toll booth to toll bridge, **E** Welcome Ctr nb, full 🅰 facilities, 🄲, 🅰, litter barrels, **W** museum
341mm	toll bridge, Lake Huron, Lake Michigan
339	US 23, Jamet St, **E** 🍴 Audie's Rest., 🛏 Days Inn, EconoLodge, LightHouse View Motel, Parkside Motel, Riviera Motel, Super 8, **W** 🄡 Shell, 🍴 Darrow's Rest., Mackinaw Cookie Co, 🛏 Holiday Inn Express, Vindel Motel, 🅾 Wilderness SP
338	US 23 (from sb), **E** 🄡 Marathon/dsl, 🍴 BC Pizza, Burger King, Cunningham's Rest., DQ, KFC, Mama Mia's Pizza, Pancake Chef, Subway, 🛏 Baymont Inn, Court Plaza Hotel, 🅾 IGA Foods/supplies, Mackinaw Outfitters, USPO, same as 337, **W** 🛏 Ft Mackinaw Motel, Holiday Inn Express
337	MI 108 (from nb, no EZ return), Nicolet St, Mackinaw City, **E** Welcome Ctr 🆁🆂, 🄡 Citgo/dsl/LP, 🍴 Admiral's Table Rest., Anna's Country Buffet, Bell's Melody Motel, Blue Water Grill, Embers Rest., Lakeside Grill, Lighthouse Rest., Mackinaw Pastie&Cookie Co., Mancino's Pizza, 🛏 Anchor Inn, Bayside Inn, BeachComber Motel, Beach House Cottages, Best Inn, Best Value Inn, Best Western, Bridgeview Motel, Bridge Vista Beach Motel, Budget Inn, Capri Motel, Clarion, Clearwater Lakeshore Motel, Comfort Inn, Comfort Suites, Days Inn, EconoLodge, Fairview Inn, Grand Mackinaw Resort, Great Lakes Inn, Hamilton Inn, Hampton Inn, Mackinaw Inn, North Winds Motel, Quality Inn, Rainbow Motel, Ramada Ltd, Sundown Motel, Sunrise Beach Motel, Super 8, Thunderbird Inn, Waterfront Inn, 🅾 Harley-Davidson, Mackinaw Camping (2mi), Old Mill Creek SP, to Island Ferrys, **W** KOA, Wilderness SP
336	US 31 S (from sb), to Petoskey
328mm	🆁🆂 sb, full 🅰 facilities, info, 🄲, 🅰, litter barrels, petwalk
326	C66, to Cheboygan, **E** gas/dsl, 🅾 🄷, Sea Shell City/gifts, 🅾 st police
322	C64, to Cheboygan, **E** 🄷, LP, ⛽, st police
317mm	🆁🆂/scenic turnout nb, full 🅰 facilities, info, 🄲, 🅰, litter barrels, petwalk
313	MI 27 N, Topinabee, **E** 🛏 Johnson Motel, Indian River RV Resort/Camping
311mm	Indian River
310	MI 33, MI 68, **E** 🛏 Hometown Inn, 🅾 Jellystone Park (3mi), **W** 🄡 Marathon, Shell/McDonald's, 🍴 Burger King, DQ, Paula's Cafe, Subway, Wilson's Rest., 🛏 Coach House Motel, Indian River Motel, 🅾 Family$, Ken's Mkt/gas, auto repair, to Indian River Trading Post/RV Resort, to Burt Lake SP

⬆N INTERSTATE 75 CONT'D

Exit	Services

301 C58, Wolverine, **E** 📟 Marathon/dsl, 🍴 Whistle Stop Rest., ⊙ Elkwood Campground (5mi), **W** ⊙ Sturgin Valley Campground (3mi)

297mm Sturgeon River

290 Vanderbilt, **E** 📟 BP/dsl/LP/RV dump, Spirit/dsl, 🍴 Elk Horn Grill, ⊙ Village Mkt Foods, USPO, **W** 📟 Mobil/dsl, ⊙ Black Bear Golf Resort (2mi)

287mm ℞ sb, full ♿ facilities, info, 🚮, 🏕, litter barrels

282 MI 32, Gaylord, **E** 📟 Holiday, Speedway/dsl, 🍴 Arby's, Big Buck Steaks, Burger King, DQ, Gino's Italian, Jet's Pizza, KFC, La Senorita Mexican, McDonald's, Qdoba Mexican, Subway, Wendy's, 🏠 Alpine Lodge, Baymont Inn, Quality Inn, ⊙ Ⓗ, Advance Parts, Ben Franklin, Family$, Glen's Mkt/gas, Harley-Davidson, Rite Aid, st police, **W** 📟 BP/dsl, Marathon/dsl, Mobil/dsl, Shell/dsl, 🍴 Applebee's, BC Pizza, Big Boy, Bob Evans, China 1, Coldstone/Tim Horton, Culver's, El Rancho Mexican, Little Caesars, Mancino's Pizza, Ponderosa, Ruby Tuesday, Taco Bell, 🏠 Hampton Inn, Holiday Inn Express, ⊙ AT&T, BigLots, Chrysler/Dodge/Jeep, $Tree, Hobby Lobby, Home Depot, International RV Ctr, Kenworth, Lowe's, Radio Shack, Save-A-Lot Foods, Verizon, Walgreens, Walmart/Subway, RV camping, tires

279mm 45th Parallel...halfway between the equator and north pole

279 Old US 27, Gaylord, **E** 📟 Marathon/Subway/dsl, Mobil/dsl, Shell, 🍴 Burger King, Mama Leone's, 🏠 Best Value Inn, ⊙ Ace Hardware, Buick/GMC, Chevrolet, Ford, st police, transmissions, **W** 🍴 Bennethums Rest., Stampede Saloon, 🏠 Marsh Ridge Motel (2mi), KOA (3mi)

277mm ℞ nb, full ♿ facilities, info, 🚮, 🏕, litter barrels, petwalk

270 Waters, **E** 📟 BP/dsl, 🍴 Hilltop Rest., **W** 📟 Citgo/dsl, lodging, Waters Inn, ⊙ Waters RV Ctr, USPO, to Otsego Lake SP

264 Lewiston, Frederic, **W** access to food, camping

202mm ℞ sb, full ♿ facilities, 🚮, 🏕, litter barrels, petwalk

259 MI 93, **E** Hartwick Pines SP, **2-4 mi W** on M 93 🏠 Fay's Motel, North Country Lodge, Pointe North Motel, River Country Motel, Woodland Motel, ⊙ Buick/Chevrolet, Chrysler/Dodge/Jeep, Curves, auto/rv repair, rv camping

256 (from sb), to MI 72, Grayling, access to same as 254

254 MI 72 (exits left from nb, no return), Grayling **1 mi W** 📟 Admiral/dsl, Clark, Shell, Speedway, Valero, 🍴 Big Boy, Burger King, DQ, Keg'O'Nails, McDonald's, Pizza Hut, Subway, Taco Bell, Wendy's, 🏠 Days Inn, Ramada, ⊙ Ⓗ, Ace Hardware, Auto Value Parts, $General, Family$, Ford, Glen's Mkt, K-Mart, NAPA, Rite Aid, Save-A-Lot Foods, 7-11, Walgreens

251mm ℞ nb, full ♿ facilities, info, 🚮, 🏕, litter barrels, petwalk, vending

251 4 Mile Rd, **E** Jellystone RV Park (5mi), skiing, **W** 📟 Marathon/Arby's/dsl/scales/RV Dump/24hr, 🏠 Super 8

249 US 127 S (from sb), to Clare

244 MI 18, Roscommon, **3 mi E** 📟 Mobil/dsl, Shell/dsl, 🍴 McDonald's, **W** 📟 Valero/dsl, ⊙ KOA (1mi), Higgins Lake SP, museum

239 MI 18, Roscommon, S Higgins Lake SP, **3 mi E** 📟 Marathon/McDonald's/dsl, ⊙ camping, **W** Higgins Lake SP, camping

235mm ℞ sb, full ♿ facilities, 🚮, info, 🏕, litter barrels, petwalk, vending

227 MI 55 W, rd F97, to Houghton Lake **5 mi W** food

222 Old 76, to St Helen **2-4 mi E** food, lodging, camping

215 MI 55 E, West Branch, **E** 📟 Shell/dsl, 🍴 Wagon Wheel Rest. (6mi), ⊙ Ⓗ

212 MI 55, West Branch, **E** 📟 Citgo/7-11, Murphy USA/dsl, Shell/Subway/dsl, 🍴 Applebee's, Arby's, Big Boy, Burger King, KFC, Lumberjack Rest., McDonald's, Ponderosa, Taco Bell, Tim Horton, Wendy's, 🏠 Quality Inn, Super 8, ⊙ Ⓗ, Home Depot, Tanger Outlet/famous brands, Walmart/Subway, st police, **W** 📟 Jaxx Snaxx/dsl

210mm ℞ nb, full ♿ facilities, info, 🚮, 🏕, litter barrels, petwalk, vending

202 MI 33, to Rose City, Alger, **E** 📟 Narski's Mkt/gas (1/2mi), Mobil/jerky outlet/dsl, Shell/Subway/dsl, ⊙ camping

201mm ℞ sb, full ♿ facilities, 🚮, 🏕, litter barrels, petwalk, vending

195 Sterling Rd, to Sterling **6 mi E** gas, Riverview Camping (seasonal)

190 MI 61, to Standish, **E** ⊙ Ⓗ, Standish Correctional, **W** 📟 Marathon, Mobil/jerky

188 US 23, to Standish **2-3 mi E** gas, food, camping

181 Pinconning Rd, **E** 📟 Shell/McDonald's/dsl, XWay, 🍴 Cheesehouse Diner, 🏠 Pinconning Inn (2mi), ⊙ Pinconning Camping, **W** 📟 Sunoco/pizza/dsl/24hr

175mm ℞ nb, full ♿ facilities, 🚮, 🏕, litter barrels, petwalk, vending

173 Linwood Rd, to Linwood, **E** 📟 Mobil/dsl/jerky, 🍴 Arby's (2mi)

171mm Kawkawlin River

168 Beaver Rd, to Willard, **E** ⊙ to Bay City SRA, **W** 📟 Mobil/jerky

166mm Kawkawlin River

164 to MI 13, Wilder Rd, to Kawkawlin, **E** 🍴 Cracker Barrel, Lucky Steaks, Ponderosa, Uno, 🏠 AmericInn, Holiday Inn Express, ⊙ KanRock Tire, Meijer/dsl, Menards

162b a US 10, MI 25, to Midland

160 MI 84, Delta, **E** 📟 Mobil/Subway, **W** 📟 Citgo/7-11, Speedway, 🍴 Berger's Rest., Burger King, KFC/Taco Bell, McDonald's, ⊙ RV World Super Ctr, to Saginaw Valley Coll

158mm ℞ sb, full ♿ facilities, 🚮, 🏕, litter barrels, vending, petwalk

155 I-675 S, to downtown Saginaw **4 mi W** 🍴 Outback Steaks, 🏠 Hampton Inn

154 to Zilwaukee

153mm Saginaw River

153 MI 13 E Bay City Rd, Saginaw **2-3 mi W** lodging

151 MI 81, to Reese, Caro, **E** 📟 Sunoco/McDonald's/dsl, ⊙ Volvo Trucks, **W** 📟 ⛽FLYING J/Wendy's/dsl/LP/24hr

🔼N INTERSTATE 75 CONT'D

Exit	Services
150	I-675 N, to downtown Saginaw **6 mi W** 🍴 Outback Steaks, 🛏 Hampton Inn
149b a	MI 46, Holland Ave, to Saginaw, **W** 🅖 Speedway/dsl, Sunoco, 🍴 Arby's, Big John's Steaks, Burger King, McDonald's, Subway, Taco Bell, Texan Rest, 🛏 Best Value Inn, Motel 6, Super 7 Inn, 🅞 H, Advance Parts, Save-A-Lot Foods, USPO
144b a	Bridgeport, **E** 🅖 Speedway/dsl, 🅞 Jellystone Camping (9mi), **W** 🅖 Mobil/dsl/e-85, TA/Country Pride/dsl/scales/24hr/@, 🍴 Arby's, Big Boy, Cracker Barrel, Hungry Howie's, McDonald's, Subway, Taco Bell, Wendy's, 🛏 Baymont Inn, Knights Inn, 🅞 Family$, Kroger/gas, Rite Aid, st police, USPO
143mm	Cass River
138mm	pull off both lanes
136	MI 54, MI 83, Birch Run, **E** 🅖 Mobil/dsl/24hr, 🍴 Exit Rest., Halo Burger, KFC, Subway, 🛏 Best Value Inn, Best Western, Comfort Inn, Hampton Inn, Holiday Inn Express, 🅞 CarQuest, General RV Ctr, Meijer/dsl/E-85, Totten Tires, **W** 🅖 Marathon, 7-11, Sunoco/dsl, 🍴 A&W, Arby's, Applebee's, Big Boy, Bob Evans, Culver's, DQ, Little Caesars, McDonald's, Quiznos, Sonic, Starbucks, Taco Bell, Tony's Rest., Uno, Victor&Merek's Pizza, Wendy's, 🛏 Country Inn&Suites, 🅞 Birch Run Drug, Birch Run Outlet/famous brands, Buick/Chevrolet, GNC, Harley-Davidson, Old Navy, USPO
131	MI 57, to Montrose, **E** 🅖 Citgo, Shell, 🍴 Arby's, Big John's Steaks, Burger King, DQ, KFC, McDonald's, Oriental Express, Subway, Taco Bell, Twins Pizza, Tim Horton, Wendy's, 🅞 AutoZone, Chevrolet, Chrysler/Dodge/Jeep, KanRock Tire, K-Mart, Tradewinds RV Ctr, vet, **W** 🅖 BP, Mobil/Rally's/dsl, Murphy USA/dsl, 🍴 Big Boy, Lucky Steaks, 🅞 $Tree, Menards, Walmart/Subway
129mm	Ⓡ🅢 **both lanes, full** ♿ **facilities,** 🚻, 📶 **litter barrels, vending, petwalk**
126	to Mt Morris, **E** 🅖 B&B/Halo Burger/dsl/scales/24hr, **W** 🅖 BP/dsl
125	I-475 S, UAW Fwy, to Flint
122	Pierson Rd, to Flint, **E** 🅖 BP, Marathon/dsl, 🍴 McDonald's, Papa's Coney's, Subway, 🛏 EconoLodge, 🅞 Kroger/gas, Murray's Parts, NW Tire, Tuffy Auto, **W** 🅖 Citgo, Shell/dsl, 🍴 A&W/KFC, Applebee's, Arby's, Big John's Steaks, Bob Evans, Burger King, Cottage Inn Pizza, Cracker Barrel, Denny's, Halo Burger, LJ Silver, Red Lobster, Taco Bell, Tim Horton, Wendy's, YaYa Chicken, 🛏 Baymont Inn, Great Western Inn, 🅞 Aldi Foods, AT&T, Discount Tire, $Tree, Home Depot, Meijer/dsl
118	MI 21, Corunna Rd, **E** 🅖 Sunoco, 🍴 Atlas Coney Island, Badawest Lebanese, Big John's Steaks, Burger King, Halo Burger, Hollywood Diner, Hungry Howie's, Little Caesar's, Taco Bell, Wing Fong Chinese, YaYa Chicken, 🅞 H, CarQuest, $Zone, Family$, Kroger/gas, Rite Aid, **W** 🅖 BP/dsl, Mobil, Shell/Wendy's, Speedway, Valero, 🍴 A&W/KFC, Blue Collar Grill, Burger King, Fazoli's, Happy Valley Rest., McDonald's, Mega Diner, Tim Horton, White Castle, 🛏 Economy Motel, 🅞 Aldi Foods, AutoZone, Buick, Chevrolet, $General, GMC, Home Depot, KanRock Tire, Kroger/gas, Lowe's Whse, Rite Aid, Sam's Club/gas, VG's Foods, Walgreens, Walmart/auto, st police

F L I N T

Exit	Services
117b	Miller Rd, to Flint, **E** 🅖 Speedway/dsl, Sunoco/dsl, 🍴 Applebee's, Arby's, Cottage Inn, Pizza, Don Pablo, Fuddrucker's, KFC, LoneStar Steaks, McDonald's, Qdoba, Sonic, Subway, West Side Diner, 🛏 Comfort Inn, Motel 6, Sleep Inn, 🅞 Urgent Care, Belle Tire, K-Mart, Tuffy Auto, **W** 🅖 BP, Marathon, 🍴 BD's BBQ, Big Boy, Bob Evans, Chili's, ChuckeCheese, Famous Dave's BBQ, Fire Mtn Grill, Happy's Pizza, HoneyBaked Ham, Hooters, Italia Garden, Logan's Roadhouse, Old Country Buffet, Olive Garden, Outback Steaks, Pizza Hut, Rib City, Quizno's, Red Robin, Salvatori's Ristorante, Starbucks, Subway, Taco Bell, Telly's Coney Island, Valley Rest., 🛏 Hometown Inn, Red Roof Inn, Super 8, 🅞 AT&T, Barnes&Noble, Best Buy, Dale's Foods, Discount Tire, Dodge, Gander Mtn, Goodyear, Hobby Lobby, JC Penney, Jo-Ann Fabrics, Macy's, Michael's, Office Depot, Old Navy, PetCo, Radio Shack, Sears/auto, Target, U-Haul, Valley Tire, mall, vet
117a	I-69, E to Lansing, W to Port Huron
116	MI 121, Bristol Rd, **E** 🅖 Citgo, Speedway/dsl, 🍴 Capitol Coney Island, KFC, McDonald's, 🛏 Days Inn, Rodeway Inn, 🅞 AutoZone, **W** 🅖 Mobil/dsl, 🅞 💊
115	US 23 (from sb), **W on Hill Rd** 🅖 Citgo, Mobil, 🍴 Arby's, McDonald's, Redwood Steaks, Subway, Taco Bell, Turkey Farm Deli, 🛏 AmericInn, Best Value Inn, Courtyard, Hampton Inn, Holiday Inn, Residence Inn, 🅞 $Tree, Meijer/dsl
111	I-475 N (from nb), UAW Fwy, to Flint
109	MI 54, Dort Hwy (no EZ return to sb)
108	Holly Rd, to Grand Blanc, **E** 🅖 Sunoco/dsl, 🍴 Big Apple Bagels, Buffalo Wild Wings, Da Edoardo Ristorante, Quiznos, Taco Bell, 🛏 Comfort Inn, Holiday Inn Express, 🅞 BMW/Mercedes/Toyota, Urgent Care, **W** 🅖 BP/McDonald's/dsl, 🍴 Arby's, 🅞 H
106	Dixie Hwy (exits left from sb, no nb return), Saginaw Rd, to Grand Blanc
101	Grange Hall Rd, Ortonville, **E** 🅞 Holly RA, KOA, st police, **W** 🅖 Mobil/dsl, 🅞 to Seven Lakes/Groveland Oaks SP, RV camping
98	E Holly Rd, **E** 🅖 Mobil/Subway/dsl/24hr, 🅞 Ford, golf
96mm	Ⓡ🅢 **nb, full** ♿ **facilities,** 🚻 **litter barrels, info,** 📶 **vending, petwalk**
95mm	Ⓡ🅢 **sb, full** ♿ **facilities,** 🚻 **litter barrels, info,** 📶 **vending, petwalk**
93	US 24, Dixie Hwy, Waterford, **E** 🅖 BP/dsl, 🅞 Chrysler/Dodge/Jeep, Kroger/gas (2mi), Nissan, **1-3 mi W** 🅖 Speedway, 🍴 Big Boy, McDonald's, Subway, Taco Bell, Wendy's, 🅞 Walgreens, to Pontiac Lake RA
91	MI 15, Davison, Clarkston, **E** 🅖 Sunoco/dsl, 🍴 Bullfrog's (5mi), Subway (5mi), 🅞 camping, **W** 🅖 BP, 🍴 Mesquite Creek Café, 🅞 H, Urgent Care
89	Sashabaw Rd, **E** 🅖 Shell/dsl, 🍴 Culvers, Ruby Tuesday, Tropical Smoothie Cafe, 🅞 county park, **W** 🅖 BP, Citgo, 🍴 Caribou Coffee, Chicken Shack, Dunkin Donuts, E Ocean Chinese, Guido's Pizza, Hong Kong Chinese, Hungry Howie's, Jimmy John's, Leo's Coney Island, Little Caesars, McDonald's, Quiznos, Rio Wraps, Subway, Tim Horton, Wendy's, 🅞 CVS Drug, $Tree, Kroger, vet
86mm	weigh sta sb
84b a	Baldwin Ave, **E** 🅖 Shell, 🍴 Arby's, Big Boy, Joe's Crabshack, Longhorn Steaks, Panera Bread, Taco Bell, Wendy's, 🅞 Best Buy, Costco/gas, Discount Tire, $Tree, Kohl's, Michael's, Old Navy, PetCo, Staples, **W** 🅖 Mobil

INTERSTATE 75 CONT'D

Exit	Services

AUBURN HILLS

84b a Continued
🅕 Chili's, 5 Guys Burgers, Jimmy John's, Kerry's Coney Island, Max&Erma's, McDonald's, On-the-Border, Oriental Forest Buffet, Qdoba Mexican, Quiznos, Rainforest Cafe, Starbucks, Steak'n Shake, Subway, 🅞 Hampton Inn, Holiday Inn Express, 🅞 AT&T, Bass Pro Shops, Batteries+, Great Lakes Crossing Outlet/famous brands, Marshall's, TJ Maxx, Vitamin Shoppe, USPO

83b a Joslyn Rd, E 🅖 🅕 Applebee's, Logan's Roadhouse, Olive Garden, 🅞 Belle Tire, Home Depot, Jo-Ann Fabrics, Meijer/dsl, Sam's Club/gas, Target, W 🅖 BP

81 MI 24, Pontiac (no EZ return), E The Palace Arena, to Bald Mtn RA

79 University Dr, E 🅖 BP, 🅕 BD Mongolian, Jimmy John's, Rio Wraps, Spargo Coney Island, Subway, Taste of Thailand, 🅛 Homestead Suites, W 🅖 Mobil, Speedway/dsl, 🅕 A&W/KFC, Burger King, Lelli's Steaks, McDonald's, Taco Bell, Wendy's/Tim Horton, 🅛 Candlewood Suites, Comfort Suites, Courtyard, Crowne Plaza, Extended Stay America, Extended Stay Deluxe, Fairfield Inn, Hampton Inn, Hilton, Hyatt Place, Rodeway Inn, Staybridge Suites, Wingate Inn, 🅞 🅗

78 Chrysler Dr, E 🅞 Chrysler, Chrysler Museum, Oakland Tech Ctr

77b a MI 59, to Pontiac, **2 mi on Adams** E 🅕 5 Guys Burgers, Kerry's Cone Island, McDonald's, 112 Pizza, Panera Bread, 🅞 GNC, Meijer/dsl, Petsmart, Radio Shack, Walmart

75 Square Lake Rd (exits left from nb), to Pontiac, W 🅗, St Mary's Coll

74 Adams Rd

TROY

72 Crooks Rd, to Troy, W 🅕 Cedar Grill, Jimmy John's, Kerby's Coney Island, Loccino Italian, Papa Romano's Pizza, Red Robin, Starbucks, 🅛 Embassy Suites

69 Big Beaver Rd, E 🅕 Champp's Grill, Kona Grill, Shula's Steaks, TGIFriday's, 🅛 Drury Inn, Marriott, W 🅖 BP, 🅕 Benihana, Caribou Coffee, Chipotle Mexican, Granite City Rest, Maggiano's Italian, Melting Pot Rest., Morton's Steaks, Noodles&Co, Papa Romano's Pizza, PF Chang's, Potbelly's, Ruth's Chris Steaks, Starbucks, 🅛 Somerset Inn, 🅞 Macy's, Neiman Marcus, Nordstrom, mall

67 Rochester Rd, to Stevenson Hwy, E 🅖 BP, Shell/dsl, Sunoco, 🅕 Bahama Breeze, Burger King, Caribou Coffee, Dickey's BBQ, Domino's, El Charro, Hills Grille, Hooters, Hungry Howies, Jimmy John's, McDonald's, Mr Pita, Ntl Coney Island, Orchid Cafe, Panera Bread, Papa John's, PeiWei, Picano's Italian, Pizza Hut/Taco Bell, Qdoba, Subway, Tim Hortons, Troy Deli, Wendy's, 🅞 Discount Tire, Nordstrom Rack, Office Depot, Petsmart, Radio Shack, transmissions, vet, W 🅖 BP, 🅛 Courtyard, Quality Inn, Red Roof Inn, 🅞 tires/repair

65b a 14 Mile Rd, Madison Heights, E 🅖 Mobil, Shell, 🅕 Azteca Mexican, Bob Evans, Burger King, Chili's, Chuck-eCheese, CiCi's Pizza, Coldstone, Krispy Kreme, Logan's Roadhouse, McDonald's, Panera Bread, Pizza Papalis, Red Robin, Rio Wraps, Sonic, Steak'n Shake, Taco Bell, Wendy's, 🅛 Motel 6, Red Roof Inn, 🅞 AT&T, Barnes&Noble, Belle Tire, Best Buy, BigLots, CVS Drug, Dick's, Firestone/auto, Ford, JC Penney, Jo-Ann Fabrics, Kohl's, Macy's, Sears/auto, Target, TJ Maxx, Verizon,

65b a Continued
auto repair, W 🅖 Mobil, 🅕 Applebee's, Caribou Coffee, Dolly's Pizza, McDonald's, NY Coney Island, Outback Steaks, 🅛 Courtyard, Days Inn, EconoLodge, Extended Stay America, Fairfield Inn, Hampton Inn, Residence Inn, 🅞 Costco/gas, Value Ctr Foods

63 12 Mile Rd, E 🅖 Marathon/dsl, 🅕 Culver's, Green Lantern Rest., Marinelli's Pizza, McDonald's, Red Lobster, Sero's Rest., Starbucks, TX Roadhouse, Tim Hortons, 🅞 Home Depot, K-Mart/foods, Lowe's, Midas, Radio Shack, Sam's Club/gas, Uncle Ed's Oil, USPO, W 🅖 Marathon/Dunkin Donuts, Speedway, 🅕 Col's Rest., 🅞 Chevrolet, Costco/gas

62 11 Mile Rd, E 🅖 Mobil, 🅕 Albert's Coney Island, Boodles Rest., Happy's Pizza, Jets Pizza, Telway Burgers, 🅞 Advance Parts, CVS Drug, Save-a-Lot, 7-11, Tuffy Auto, Walgreens, repair/tires, vet, W 🅖 BP, Marathon/dsl, Mobil, 🅕 KFC, Taco Bell, Tim Hortons, Tubby's Subs, 🅞 Belle Tire

61 I-696 E, to Port Huron, W to Lansing, to Hazel Park Raceway

60 9 Mile Rd, John R St, E 🅕 Checkers, China 1 Buffet, Coney Craver's Diner, DQ, Hardee's, McDonald's, Subway, Tim Hortons, 🅞 CVS Drug, Kroger/gas, USPO, W 🅖 Exxon, Marathon, Mobil, 🅕 Tubby's Subs, Wendy's, 🅞 Hasting's Parts, repair

DETROIT AREA

59 MI 102, 8 Mile Rd, **3 mi W** st fairgrounds

58 7 Mile Rd, W 🅖 BP/dsl

57 McNichols Rd, E 🅖 Citgo/dsl, Shell/dsl, 🅕 LA Coney Island, 🅞 Auto Parts/Repair

56b a Davison Fwy

55 Holbrook Ave, Caniff St, E 🅖 Mobil/dsl, 🅕 Grandy's Coney Island

54 E Grand Blvd, Clay Ave, W 🅖 BP/dsl

53b I-94, Ford Fwy, to Port Huron, Chicago

53a Warren Ave, E 🅖 Mobil, Shell, W 🅖 BP

52 Mack Ave, E 🅖 Shell, 🅕 McDonald's

51c I-375 to civic center, tunnel to Canada, downtown

51b MI 3 (exits left from nb), Gratiot Ave, downtown

50 Grand River Ave, downtown

49b MI 10, Lodge Fwy, downtown

49a Rosa Parks Blvd, E Tiger Stadium, W 🅖 Mobil/dsl, 🅞 Firestone

48 **I-96 begins/ends**

47b Porter St, E bridge to Canada, MI **Welcome Ctr, DutyFree/24hr**

47a MI 3, Clark Ave, E 🅖 Citgo, W 🅖 Marathon

46 Livernois Ave, to Hist Ft Wayne, E 🅖 Marathon, 🅕 Livernois Coney Island, KFC/Taco Bell

MI

⬆N INTERSTATE 75 CONT'D

Exit	Services
45	Fort St, Springwells Ave, **E** 🅖 BP/dsl, Pure Petro/dsl, **W** 🅖 Mobil, 🍴 McDonald's
44	Deerborn St (from nb)
43b a	MI 85, Fort St, to Schaefer Hwy, **E** 🅖 BP, **W** 🅖 Marathon Refinery, 🅞 to River Rouge Ford Plant
42	Outer Dr, **E** 🅖 Marathon, 🍴 Happy's Pizza, 🅞 Urgent Care, **W** 🅖 BP/Subway/dsl, 🅞 Family$, truck tires
41	MI 39, Southfield Rd, to Lincoln Park, **E** 🍴 A&W, Tim Hortons, White Castle, 🅞 Aldi Foods, O'Reilly Parts, Walgreens, **W** 🅖 Citgo/Tim Hortons, Mobil, 🍴 Burger King, Checker's, Hungry Howie, LJ Silver, McDonald's, Pizza Hut, Starbucks, Taco Bell, Wendy's, 🛏 Sleep Inn, 🅞 AT&T, Belle Tire, Kroger/gas, Radio Shack, Rite Aid, Walgreens
40	Dix Hwy, **E** 🅖 Citgo, Future/A&W/dsl, Marathon/A&W/dsl, Sunoco, Welcome, 🍴 Baskin-Robbins/Dunkin Donuts, Toma's Coney Island, 🅞 CVS Drug, Meijer, 7-11, repair, **Urgent Care**, **W** 🅖 Future, Marathon, 🍴 Big Boy, Burger King, Checker's, DQ, LJ Silver, McDonald's, Pizza Hut, Starbucks, Taco Bell, Wendy's, 🅞 AT&T, Belle Tire, Family$, Kroger/gas, Rite Aid, Sears/auto, Walgreens, auto repair
37	Allen Rd, North Line Rd, to Wyandotte, **E** 🅖 BP, Shell/Tim Hortons, 🛏 Holiday Inn, 🅞 Ⓗ, Sam's Club/gas, **W** 🅖 Mobil, Sunoco, 🍴 Arby's, Burger King, Mallie's Grill, McDonald's, Wendy's, 🛏 Comfort Suites, La Quinta, Motel 6
36	Eureka Rd, **E** 🅖 BP, 🍴 Bob Evans, Denny's, Fire Mtn Grill, Orleans Steaks, 🛏 Ramada Inn, Super 8, 🅞 vet, **W** 🅖 🍴 American Thai Grill, Big Boy, Coldstone, Culver's, HoneyBaked Ham, Hooters, Jimmy John's, Little Daddy's Rest., McDonald's, Ruby Tuesday, Starbucks, Subway, TX Roadhouse, Wendy's, 🛏 Red Roof Inn, 🅞 AT&T, Belle Tire, Best Buy, Discount Tire, Home Depot, JC Penney, Kohl's, Macy's, Meijer/dsl, Petsmart, mall
35	US 24, Telegraph Rd, (from nb, exits left)
34b	Sibley Rd, Riverview, **W** 🅖 Sunoco/Baskin-Robbins/Dunkin Donuts/Subway, 🅞 General RV Ctr
34a	to US 24 (from sb), Telegraph Rd
32	West Rd, to Trenton, Woodhaven, **E** 🅖 ⊕FLYING J/Detroiter/IHOP/dsl/LP/scales/24hr/@, Speedway/dsl, 🍴 Applebee's, Baskin-Robbins/Dunkin Donuts, Blue Margarita Mexican, Bob Evans, Christoff's Rest., Coldstone, 5 Guys Burgers, IHOP, Jersey Subs, Panera Bread, Pizza Hut, Steak'n Shake, Subway, Taco Bell, Tim Hortons, Wendy's, White Castle, 🅞 Aldi Foods, Belle Tire, Chevrolet, Chrysler/Dodge/Jeep, Discount Tire, Ford, Home Depot, K-Mart, Kohl's, Kroger, Lowe's, Meijer/dsl, Michael's, Office Depot, O'Reilly Parts, Petsmart, Radio Shack, Target, Verizon, Walmart, transmissions, **Urgent Care**, **W** 🅖 BP/Tim Hortons, Citgo, Shell, 🍴 Andy's Pizza, Jimmy John's, Little Caesars, McDonald's, Milli's Rest, Subway, 🛏 Best Western/rest., Holiday Inn Express, Westwood Inn, 🅞 Ⓗ, CVS Drug, $Tree, Kroger, SavOn Drug, Walgreens
29	Gilbralter Rd, to Flat Rock, Lake Erie Metropark, **E** 🅖 Citgo/dsl, 🍴 Cottage Inn Pizza, McDonald's, Peking Chinese, Subway, Wendy's, 🅞 Ⓗ, Curves, GNC, Kroger, **W** 🅖 Marathon/dsl, 🛏 Sleep Inn, 🅞 Ford, st police
28	rd 85 (from nb), Fort St, **E** Ⓗ

MONROE

27	N Huron River Dr, to Rockwood, **E** 🅖 Marathon/7-11/dsl, 🍴 Benito's Pizza, Huron River Rest., Marco's Pizza, 🅞 FoodTown Foods, Rite Aid, USPO, **W** 🅖 Speedway/dsl, 🍴 Riverfront Rest.
26	S Huron River Dr, to S Rockwood, **E** 🅖 Sunoco/dsl, 🍴 Dixie Cafe, Drift Inn, 🅞 USPO
21	Newport Rd, to Newport, **E** 🅖 BP/Subway/dsl, 🅞 repair, **W** 🅖 Marathon/Burger King/dsl/24hr
20	I-275 N, to Flint
18	Nadeau Rd, **W** 🅖 ⬛/Taco Bell/dsl/scales/24hr, 🅞 Ⓗ RV camping
15	MI 50, Dixie Hwy, to Monroe, **E** 🅖 Shell, 🍴 Burger King, Red Lobster, 🛏 Best Value Inn, Hampton Inn, Motel 6, Red Roof.Inn, 🅞 to Sterling SP, **W** 🅖 ⬛/Subway/dsl/scales/24hr, TA/BP/Country Pride/Pizza Hut/Popeye's/Tim Hortons/dsl/scales/24hr/@, 🍴 Big Boy, Cracker Barrel, Denny's, El Maguey, McDonald's, Wendy's, 🛏 Knights Inn, Quality Inn, 🅞 Ⓗ, to Viet Vet Mem
14	Elm Ave, to Monroe
13	Front St, Monroe
11	La Plaisance Rd, to Bolles Harbor, **W** 🅖 Marathon/Taco Bell/dsl, Speedway, 🍴 McDonald's, Wendy's, 🛏 Baymont Inn, Comfort Inn, Harbor Town RV Resort, 🅞 Kroger/gas (2mi), st police
10mm	**Welcome Ctr nb, full ♿ services, 📞 info, 🗑 litter barrels, vending, petwalk**
9	S Otter Creek Rd, to La Salle, **W** antiques
7mm	**weigh sta both lanes**
6	Luna Pier, **E** 🅖 Sunoco/dsl/scales, 🍴 Beef Jerky Unltd., Ganders Rest., Roma's Pizza, 🛏 Super 8, **W** 🅞 KOA, st police
5	to Erie, Temperance
2	Summit St
0mm	Michigan/Ohio state line

⬆E INTERSTATE 94

PORT HURON

Exit	Services
275mm	**I-69/I-94 begin/end on MI 25.** Pinegrove Ave in Port Huron 🅖 BP/24hr, Shell, Speedway, 🍴 Jet's Pizza, McDonald's, Tim Horton, Wendy's, 🛏 Days Inn, Quality Inn, 🅞 Buick, Family$, Honda, Rite Aid, tollbridge to Canada
274.5mm	Black River
274	Water St, Port Huron, **N** Welcome Ctr/🆁🆂, full facilities, (from wb only), 🍴 Cracker Barrel, 🛏 Best Western, **S** 🅖 SpeedyQ/dsl, Speedway/dsl, 🍴 Bob Evans, 🛏 Comfort Inn, Fairfield Inn, Hampton Inn, 🅞 Lake Port SP, RV camping
271	I-69 E and I-94 E run together eb, Lp I-69, 0-2 mi **S** on Lp 69 **S** 🅖 Mobil/dsl, Speedway, 🍴 Arby's, Baskin-Robbins, Burger King, Dunkin Donuts, McDonalds, KFC, Quay St Grill, Taco Bell, Wendy's, 🅞 Advance Parts, AutoZone, Kroger/gas, K-Mart, Sam's Club/gas, repair, to Port Huron
269	Dove St, Range Rd, **N** 🅖 Speedway/dsl/24hr, 🍴 Billy Boy's Diner, 🛏 Baymont Inn
266	Gratiot Rd, Marysville, 0-2 mi **S** 🅖 Admiral, BP/dsl/scales/24hr, Marathon/scales/dsl, Speedway, 🍴 Arby's, Big Boy, Burger King, Dairy Boy, Daliono's, KFC, 4 Star Rest., Hungry Howie's, Jimmy John's, Little Caesars, McDonald's, Mr Pita, Pelican Café, Pizza Hut, Seros, Subway, Taco Bell, Tim Horton, 🛏 Super 8, 🅞 Ⓗ, AutoZone, CarQuest, CVS Drug, $General, $Plus, Meijer/dsl, Rite Aid, Wally's Foods, vet

↑E INTERSTATE 94 CONT'D

Exit	Services
262	Wadhams Rd, N camping, S 🅖 Mobil/dsl
257	St Clair, Richmond, S 🅖 BP/dsl, 🄾 st police
255mm	🆁🆂 eb, full ♿ facilities, 🚻, info, 🏕 litter barrels, pet-walk
251mm	🆁🆂 wb, full ♿ facilities, 🚻, info, 🏕 litter barrels, pet-walk
248	26 Mile Rd, to Marine City, N 🍴 McDonald's (2mi), S 🅖 7-11/gas, Speedy Q (1mi), 🍴 Asian Garden, My Place Cafe, Tim Horton, 🄾 Mejier/dsl
247mm	Salt River
247	MI 19 (no eb return), New Haven
243	MI 29, MI 3, Utica, New Baltimore, N 🅖 BP, Marathon/dsl, Sunoco/dsl, 🍴 Applebee's, Arby's, Buffalo Wings, Burger King, Chophouse, Coney Island, Dimitri's Rest., Empire Buffet, Little Caesars, McDonald's, Outback Steaks, Panera Bread, Ruby Tuesday, Starbucks, Subway, Stevie B's Pizza, Tim Horton, Waffle House, Wendy's, White Castle, 🏨 Chesterfield Motel, 🄾 AutoZone, Best Buy, Dick's, Discount Tire, $Tree, GNC, Home Depot, JC Penney, Jo-Ann Fabrics, K-Mart, Kohl's, Lowe's, Meijer/dsl/24hr, Michael's, NAPA, O'Reilly Parts, PetCo, PetsMart, Radio Shack, Rite Aid, Staples, Target, TJ Maxx, Walgreens, S 🅖 Marathon/dsl/24hr, 7-11/gas, Speedway/dsl/24hr, 🍴 Big Boy, Buscemi's Pizza, Hot'n Now Burgers, Taco Bell, 🏨 LodgeKeeper
241	21 Mile Rd, Selfridge, N 🅖 Exxon/dsl, Speedway, 🍴 China King, Hungry Howie's, 🄾 Advance Parts, AT&T, CVS Drug, Verizon, vet, same as 240
240	to MI 59, N 🅖 7-11/gas, Marathon, Mobil, 🍴 Arby's, Bob Evans, Burger King, Coney Island, KFC, McDonald's, O'Charley's, Taco Bell, Tim Horton, 🏨 Hampton Inn, Holiday Inn Express, 🄾 Ford, Harley-Davidson, Tuffy Auto, Walmart
237	N River Rd, Mt Clemens, N 🅖 BP/dsl, Mobil/Subway/dsl, 🍴 McDonald's, 🏨 Victory Inn, 🄾 🄷, General RV Ctr, Gibraltar Trade Ctr
236.5mm	Clinton River
236	Metro Parkway, S 🍴 Big Apple Bagels, Empire Chinese, Little Caesars, McDonald's, Subway, 🄾 🄷, Curves, CVS Drug, GNC, Kroger
235	Shook Rd (from wb)
234b a	Harper Rd, 15 Mile Rd, N 🅖 BP/McDonald's, Marathon/dsl, SpeedyQ, Sunoco/dsl/24hr, 🍴 Dan Good Pizza, Gina's Cafe, 🄾 vet, S 🅖 FL Gas, 🍴 China Moon, Subway, Travis Rest., Winners Grill, 🄾 Urgent Care
232	Little Mack Ave (from wb only), N 🅖 Marathon, 7-11, Shell, Speedway, Sunoco, 🍴 Coldstone, Denny's, Hooters, Longhorn Steaks, McDonald's, Pizza Hut, Red Robin, Sea Breeze Diner, Woody's Grill, 🏨 Holiday Inn Express, Red Roof Inn, Relax Inn, Super 8, Victory Inn, 🄾 Advance Parts, Aldi Foods, Belle Tire, Discount Tire, Firestone, JC Penney, O'Reilly Parts, Sam's Club, Sears/Auto, Staples, Target, S 🅖 Marathon, Speedway/dsl, 🍴 Cracker Barrel, Culvers, IHOP, Izzy's Cafe, 🏨 Baymont Inn, 🄾 Family$, Home Depot, Jo-Ann Fabrics, Meijer/dsl/24hr, PetsMart, same as 231
231	(from eb), MI 3, Gratiot Ave, N 🅖 Marathon, Sunoco, 🍴 Applebee's, Arby's, Big Boy, Bob Evans, Burger King, Chili's, ChuckeCheese, Cici's, Del Taco, Denny's, Famous Dave's BBQ, Logan's Roadhouse, Longhorn Steaks,
231	Continued Marco's Italian, McDonald's, Panera Bread, PetCo, Pizza Hut, Ruby Tuesday, Sajo's Rest., Starbucks, Subway, Tim Horton, TX Roadhouse, 🏨 Best Western, Days Inn, EconoLodge, Extended Stay America, Microtel, 🄾 Best Buy, Discount Tire, Firestone/auto, Honda/Acura, Kia, Kohl's, Kroger, Michael's, Nissan, Radio Shack, Sam's Club/gas, Staples, Toyota, U-Haul, mall
230	12 Mile Rd, N 🅖 Mobil/dsl, Sunoco/dsl, 🍴 BD's Mongolian, Jimmy John's, Noni's Grill, Outback Steaks, Starbucks, Taco Bell, 🄾 AT&T, CVS Drug, $Tree, Marshall's, NAPA, Walmart/Subway
229	I-696 W, Reuther Fwy, to 11 Mile Rd, S 🅖 BP/dsl, Speedway, 🄾 7-11
228	10 Mile Rd, N 🅖 BP/24hr, Mobil, Shell, 🍴 Baskin-Robbins, Coney Island, Eastwind Chinese, Friendly Rest, Jet's Pizza, 🄾 CVS Drug, Save More Drugs
227	9 Mile Rd, N 🅖 Mobil/dsl, Speedway/dsl, Sunoco, 🍴 McDonald's, Papa John's, Pizza Hut/Taco Bell, Subway, Wendy's, 🄾 Aldi Foods, CVS Drug, $Tree, Family$, Fresh Choice Foods, Office Depot, TrueValue, vet, S 🅖 Mobil/dsl, 🏨 Shore Pointe Motel, 🄾 Cadillac, Mercedes
225	MI 102, Vernier Rd, 8 Mile Rd, S 🅖 BP/Subway, Mobil, Sunoco/dsl, 🍴 Coney Island, KFC, Taco Bell, Wendy's, 🄾 Kroger, Walgreens
224b	Allard Ave, Eastwood Ave
224a	Moross Rd, S 🅖 Shell, 🄾 Family Foods, 🄾 🄷
223	Cadieux Rd, S 🅖 BP/Subway, Mobil, Shell, Sunoco, 🍴 McDonald's, Papa's Pizza, Popeye's, Taco Bell, Tubby's Subs, Wendy's, White Castle, 🄾 Rite Aid
222b	Harper Ave (from eb), S 🄾 Hastings Auto
222a	Chalmers Ave, Outer Dr, N 🅖 BP/Subway/dsl, Zoom, 🍴 Coney Island, KFC, Little Caesars, White Castle, 🄾 Family$
220b	Conner Ave, N 🅖 BP, Zoom
220a	French Rd, S 🅖 Marathon
219	MI 3, Gratiot Ave, N 🅖 Marathon/Subway, Speedy, 🍴 Coney Island, KFC, McDonald's, 🄾 Family$, Farmer John's Foods, S 🅖 GasMart, 🍴 Burger King
218	MI 53, Van Dyke Ave, N 🅖 BP, Mobil/dsl
217b	Mt Elliott Ave, S 🅖 Marathon, Sunoco/dsl, 🍴 Royal BBQ
217a	E Grand Blvd, Chene St, S 🅖 Marathon
216b	Russell St (from eb), to downtown
216a	I-75, Chrysler Fwy, to tunnel to Canada
215c	MI 1, Woodward Ave, John R St
215b	MI 10 N, Lodge Fwy
215a	MI 10 S, tunnel to Canada, downtown
214b	Trumbull Ave, to Ford 🄷
214a	(from wb) Grand River Ave

D E T R O I T   A R E A

🚪 = gas 🍴 = food 🛏 = lodging 🅾 = other 🆁🆂 = rest stop   Copyright 2014 - The Next Exit ®

INTERSTATE 94 CONT'D

Exit	Services
213b	I-96 W to Lansing, E to Canada, bridge to Canada, to Tiger Stadium
213a	W Grand (exits left from eb)
212b	Warren Ave (from eb)
212a	Livernois Ave, **S** 🚪 Marathon/Subway/dsl, Sunoco
211b	Cecil Ave (from wb), Central Ave
211a	Lonyo Rd
210	US 12, Michigan Ave, Wyoming Ave, **N** 🚪 Mobil/dsl **S** 🚪 BP/dsl, Sunoco/dsl, Valero
209	Rotunda Dr (from wb)
208	Greenfield Rd, Schaefer Rd, **N** 🚪 Mobil/dsl, 🅾 7-11, **S** River Rouge Ford Plant
207mm	Rouge River
206	Oakwood Blvd, Melvindale, **N** 🚪 Marathon, Shell, 🍴 Applebee's, Carino's, Coney Island, Chili's, Coldstone, Famous Hamburger, Little Caesar's, Longhorn Steaks, Moe's SW Grill, On-the-Border, Panera Bread, Pottbelly, Quizno's, Starbucks, Taco Bell, 🅾 AAA, Barnes&Noble, Best Buy, GNC, Home Depot, Jo-Ann Fabrics, Lowe's, Meijer, Michael's, Old Navy, PetCo, Staples, Target, TJ Maxx, Verizon, Greenfield Village Museum, **S** 🚪 BP/dsl, 🍴 Burger King, McDonald's, Melvindale Coney Island, O'Henry's, Sabina's, Subway, 🛏 Best Western, Holiday Inn Express, 🅾 Curves, CVS Drug, $General, Rite Aid, 7-11
205mm	Largest Uniroyal Tire in the World
204b a	MI 39, Southfield Fwy, Pelham Rd, **N** 🚪 Marathon/dsl, Mobil, Valero/dsl, 🅾 7-11, to Greenfield Village, **S** 🚪 Marathon/dsl, 🍴 Papa's Pizza, 🅾 Walgreens
202b a	US 24, Telegraph Rd, **N** 🚪 Citgo, Shell, Sunoco, 🍴 Burger King, Checkers, Dunkin Donuts, KFC, McDonald's, Pizza Hut, Ram's Horn Rest., Subway, Taco Bell, Wendy's, 🅾 Advance Parts, Aldi Foods, Rite Aid, True Value, Walgreen, **0-2 mi S** 🚪 BP, Marathon/dsl, Valero/dsl, 🍴 Arby's, Big Boy, Burger King, Hungry Howie's, KFC, Leo's Coney Island, Leon's, Rest., Little Caesar's, LJ Silver, Marina's Pizza, McDonald's, New Hong Kong, Old Country Buffet, Pizza Hut, Popeye's, Taco Bell, Subway, Super China, Wendy's, Yum Yum Donuts, 🛏 Comfort Inn, 🅾 AT&T, AutoZone, Curves, $Tree, Family$, Firestone/auto, Radio Shack, Rite Aid, U-Haul, Walgreens, Walmart, st police, USPO
200	Ecorse Rd, (no ez eb return), to Taylor, **N** 🚪 Marathon/Subway/dsl/scales, **S** 🚪 Rich, Speedy/dsl, 🍴 Danny's Pizza, Norm's Subs, Webster's BBQ, 🅾 USPO
199	Middle Belt Rd, **S** 🚪 BP/dsl/24hr, 🍴 Checkers, McDonald's, Wendy's, 🛏 Days Inn, Quality Inn, Super 8
198	Merriman Rd, **N** 🚪 Marathon, Speedway, 🍴 Big Boy, Bob Evans, Leonardo's Italian, McDonald's, Merriman St Grill, Subway, Toramino's Pizza, 🛏 Baymont Inn, Best Western, Clarion, Comfort Inn, Courtyard, Crowne Plaza Hotel, Embassy Suites, Extended Stay America, Fairfield Inn, Hampton Inn, Holiday Inn, Howard Johnson, La Quinta, Lee's Inn, Lexington Motel, Marriott, Metro Inn, Metropolitan Hotel, Ramada Inn, Red Roof Inn, Rodeway Inn, Sheraton, SpringHill Suites, 🅾 USPO, **S** Wayne Co ✈
197	Vining Rd
196	Wayne Rd, Romulus, **N** 🚪 Shell/dsl, 🍴 McDonald's, **S** 🚪 Mobil/dsl, 🍴 Burger King, Subway

DETROIT AREA (vertical sidebar)

Exit	Services
194b a	I-275, N to Flint, S to Toledo
192	Haggerty Rd, **N** 🚪 BP/Tubby's/dsl, Mobil/dsl, **S** Lower Huron Metro Park
190	Belleville Rd, to Belleville, **N** 🚪 BP/dsl, 🍴 Applebee's, Arby's, Big Boy, Coney Island, Cracker Barrel, Culver's, Happy's Pizza, McDonald's, Quiznos, Taco Bell, Tim Horton, Twisted Rooster, Wendy's, 🛏 Holiday Inn Express, Red Roof Inn, 🅾 AT&T, Belle Tire, Camping World RV Ctr, CVS Drug, $Tree, Firestone/auto, Ford, Meijer/dsl, National RV Ctr, O'Reilly Parts, Verizon, Walgreens, Walmart, vet, **S** 🚪 Shell, 🍴 Burger King, China City, Dos Pesos Mexican, Mike's Kitchen, Subway, 🛏 Comfort Inn, Super 8, 🅾 Urgent Care, USPO
189mm	🆁🆂 wb, full ♿ facilities, info, 🅲, 🚻, litter barrels, vending, petwalk
187	Rawsonville Rd, **N** 🅾 Freightliner, **S** 🚪 Mobil/dsl, Speedway/dsl, 🍴 Denny's, KFC, Little Caesars, McDonald's, Pizza Hut, Taco Bell, Tim Horton, Wendy's, 🅾 Detroit Greenfield RV Park, $General, $Tree, GNC, K-Mart
185	US 12, Michigan Ave (from eb, exits left, no return), to frontage rds ✈
184mm	Ford Lake
183	US 12, Huron St, Ypsilanti, **N** 🚪 Marathon/pizza/dsl, 🅾 to E MI U, **S** 🍴 Buffalo Wild Wings, Coney Island, Jet's Pizza, McDonald's, 🛏 Marriott, 🅾 🎃 Kroger/dsl, st police
181b a	US 12 W, Michigan Ave, Ypsilanti, **N** 🚪 Meijer/dsl, Speedway/dsl, 🍴 Coney Island, Dunkin Donuts, Hong Kong Chinese, Roundtree Grill, Taco Bell, Tim Horton/Wendy's, 🅾 🎃 Aamco, BigLots, $Tree, Firestone/auto, GNC, Meijer/dsl, Radio Shack, Rose Mkt, Walmart, **0-2 mi S** 🚪 BP/Circle K, Citgo/Subway/dsl, Sunoco/dsl, 🍴 Harvest Moon Cafe, McDonald's, 🅾 Sam's Club/gas
180b a	US 23, to Toledo, Flint
177	State St, **N** 🚪 BP, Mobil, Shell, 🍴 Burger King, Graham's Steaks, Los Amigos, Macaroni Grill, Max&Erma's, Mediterrano Rest., Olive Garden, Panda Express, Red Robin, Wendy's, 🛏 Comfort Inn, Courtyard, Extended Stay America, Fairfield Inn, Hampton Inn, Hilton Garden, Holiday Inn, Holiday Inn Express, Kensington Court Inn, Red Roof Inn, Sheraton, TownePlace Suites, 🅾 Firestone/auto, Honda, JC Penney, Macy's, Porsche, Sears/auto, Vaun Mar, VW, World Mkt, mall, to UMI, **S** 🚪 Citgo/Subway, Speedway/dsl, 🍴 Coney Island, McDonald's, Taco Bell, 🛏 Motel 6, 🅾 Costco/gas, U-Haul
175	Ann Arbor-Saline Rd, **N** 🚪 Shell, 🍴 Applebee's, Bella Italia, Dibella Subs, Moe's SW Grill, Panera Bread, Subway, 🛏 Candlewood Suites, 🅾 Office Depot, Whole Foods Mkt, vet, to UMI Stadium, **S** 🍴 ChuckECheese's, Godaik Japanese, Jet's Pizza, Joe's Crabshack, McDonald's, Nick's Pancakes, Outback Steaks, TGIFriday's, 🅾 Best Buy, BigLots, Dick's, JoAnn Fabrics, Kohl's, Meijer/dsl/e-85, Petsmart, Target
172	Jackson Ave, to Ann Arbor, **N on Stadium Ave** 🚪 BP, Marathon, Shell, Sunoco/dsl, 🍴 Burger King, McDonald's, Noodles&Co, Quarter Rest., Subway, Taco Bell, Zingerman's Roadhouse, 🅾 🎃 $Tree, Discount Tire, Goodyear/auto, K-Mart, Rite Aid, Staples, Verizon, Walgreens, vet, **S** 🚪 Marathon, 🍴 Weber's Rest., 🛏 Clarion, 🅾 Chevrolet/Cadillac, Ford, Great Lakes Chocolate, Mini
171	MI 14 (from eb, exits left), to Ann Arbor, to Flint by US 23
169	Zeeb Rd, **N** 🚪 BP/dsl, 🍴 Big Boy, Grand Pies Co,

ANN ARBOR (vertical sidebar)

✈ INTERSTATE 94 CONT'D

Exit	Services
169	Continued
	Metzger's Rest., McDonald's, **S** 🅖 Citgo/dsl, 🍴 Arby's, Burger King, Creekside Grill, Culver's, Domino's, Panera Bread, Pizza Hut, Subway, Taco Bell, Wendy's, Westside Grill, 🅞 CVS Drug, Discount Tire, Lowe's, Meijer/dsl, vet
167	Baker Rd, Dexter, **N** 🅖 ▥/Subway/scales/dsl/24hr, **S** 🅖 ▥/Arby's/dsl/scales/24hr, TA/BP/Popeye's/dsl/scales/24hr/@, 🍴 McDonald's, 🅞 Blue Beacon
162	Jackson Rd, Fletcher Rd, **S** 🅖 BP/Subway/dsl/24hr, 🍴 Stiver's Rest.
161mm	🆁🆂 eb, full ♿ facilities, 🅒, 🚮, litter barrels, vending, petwalk
159	MI 52, Chelsea, **N** 🅖 Mobil/dsl, Rich Gas/dsl, Sunoco/dsl, 🍴 Big Boy, Chelsea Grill, China Garden, Chinese Tonite, Jimmy John's, KFC/Taco Bell, McDonald's, Subway, Uptown Coney Island, Wendy's; 🏨 Comfort Inn, Holiday Inn Express, 🅞 🏥, AutoZone, Chrysler/Dodge/Jeep, Country Mkt Foods/drug, CVS Drug, Travel Land RV Ctr, Verizon, USPO, vet, **S** 🅞 Buick/Chevrolet
157	Jackson Rd, Pierce Rd, **N** Gerald Eddy Geology Ctr
156	Kalmbach Rd, **N** to Waterloo RA
153	Clear Lake Rd, **N** 🅖 Marathon/dsl
151.5mm	weigh sta both lanes
150	to Grass Lake, **S** 🅖 Mobil/Subway
150mm	🆁🆂 wb, full ♿ facilities, 🅒, 🚮, litter barrels, vending, petwalk
147	Race Rd, **N** Holiday RV Camp, to Waterloo RA, camping, **S** lodging
145	Sargent Rd, **S** 🅖 BP/dsl, Mobil/145 Rest/dsl/scales/rest./24hr, 🍴 McDonald's, Wendy's, 🏨 Colonial Inn
144	Lp 94 (from wb), to Jackson
142	US 127 S, to Hudson, **3 mi S** 🅖 Meijer/dsl, Speedway, 🍴 Domino's, McDonald's, Wendy's, 🅞 Advance Parts, Kroger, Parts, Rite Aid, to MI Speedway
141	Elm Rd, **N** 🏨 Travelodge, 🅞 Chevrolet, Chrysler/Dodge/Jeep, Ford/Lincoln, Honda, Nissan, **S** 🅞 🏥
139	MI 106, Cooper St, to Jackson, **N** st police/prison, **S** 🅖 Citgo/Subway, 🅞 🍴
138	US 127 N, MI 50, to Lansing, Jackson, **N** 🍴 Red Lobster, 🏨 Baymont Inn, Best Value Inn, Comfort Inn, Country Inn&Suites, Fairfield Inn, Hampton Inn, Super 8, 🅞 vet, **S** 🅖 Admiral, BP, Shell/dsl, 🍴 Arby's, Big Boy, Bob Evans, Burger King, Dunkin Donuts, Fazoli's, Ground Round, Jumbo Buffet, KFC, LJ Silver, Los Tres Amigos, McDonald's, Old Country Buffet, Outback Steaks, Panera Bread, Papa John's, Pizza Hut, Qdoba, Starbucks, Subway, Tim Horton, Wendy's, 🏨 Best Value Inn, 🅞 Advance Parts, Aldi Foods, AT&T, AutoZone, Belle Tire, Best Buy, BigLots, Discount Tire, $Tree, Family$, Home Depot, JoAnn Fabrics, Kohl's, Kroger/gas, Lowe's, Michael's, Midas, Office Depot, O'Reilly Parts, Petsmart, Sears/auto, Target, TJ Maxx, Verizon, Walgreens
137	Airport Rd, **N** 🅖 Marathon, Shell/Taco Bell, 🍴 Burger King, Denny's, McDonald's, Steak'n Shake, Subway, Wendy's, 🏨 Holiday Inn, 🅞 Meijer/dsl, 7-11, **S** 🅖 BP, 🍴 Cracker Barrel, Culvers, Olive Garden, LoneStar Steaks, 🏨 Country Inn&Suites, 🅞 K-Mart, Sam's Club/gas, Save-A-Lot Foods
136	Lp 94, MI 60, to Jackson
135mm	🆁🆂 eb, full ♿ facilities, 🅒, 🚮, litter barrels, vending, petwalk

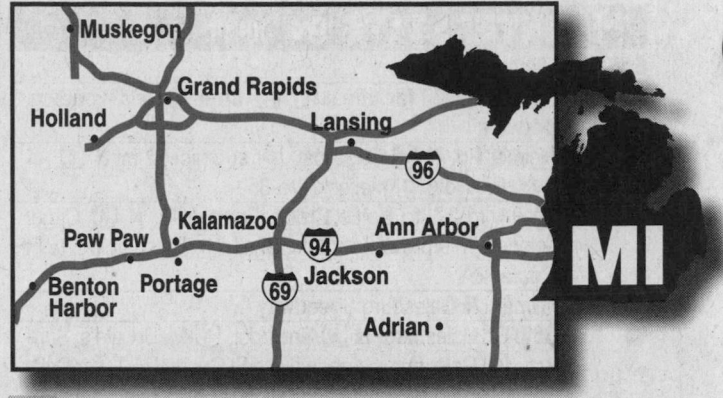

133	Dearing Rd, Spring Arbor, **S** to Spring Arbor U
130	Parma
128	Michigan Ave, **N** 🅖 BP/Burger King/scales/dsl/24hr, Marathon/dsl/24hr, 🅞 RV camping
127	Concord Rd, **N** wineries
124	MI 99, to Eaton Rapids
121	28 Mile Rd, to Albion, **N** 🅖 Mobil/Subway/dsl, 🍴 Arby's, 🏨 Days Inn, **S** 🅖 BP, Clark/dsl, Speedway/dsl, 🍴 Frosty Dan's, KFC, La Casa Mexican, Maria's Garden Rest., McDonald's, Pizza Hut, 🏨 Super 9, 🅞 🏥, AutoZone, Buick/Chevrolet, $General, Family$, Family Fare Foods, Ford, Radio Shack, RV camping, Tire City
119	MI 199, 26 Mile Rd
115	22.5 Mile Rd, **N** 🅖 Citgo/115 Rest./dsl/24hr
113mm	🆁🆂 wb, full ♿ facilities, 🅒, 🚮, litter barrels, vending, petwalk
112	Partello Rd, **S** 🅖 Loves/Hardee's/scales/dsl/24hr, 🍴 Schuler's Rest.
110	Old US 27, Marshall, **N** 🅖 Shell/Country Kitchen/Subway/dsl/24hr, **S** 🅖 Citgo/dsl, 🍴 Denny's, Pizza Hut (2mi), Schuler's Rest. (2mi), 🏨 Hampton Inn, Holiday Inn Express, 🅞 🏥, sheriff
108	I-69, US 27, **N** to Lansing, **S** to Ft Wayne
104	11 Mile Rd, Michigan Ave, **N** 🅖 ▥/McDonald's/dsl/scales/24hr, TA/Country Pride/dsl/scales/24hr/@, **S** 🅖 Citgo/Subway/dsl/e-85, 🏨 Quality Inn/rest., 🅞 casino
103	Lp 94 (from wb, no return), to Battle Creek, **N** 🏥
102mm	Kalamazoo River
100	rd 294, Beadle Lake Rd, **N** 🍴 Moonraker Rest., **S** 🅖 Citgo/dsl/repair, 🅞 Binder Park Zoo
98b	I-194 N, to Battle Creek
98a	MI 66, to Sturgis, **S** 🅖 Citgo/dsl, 🍴 Chili's, Los Aztecas, McDonald's, Ruby Tuesday, Schlotzsky's, Starbucks, Steak'n Shake, 🏨 Holiday Inn, 🅞 AT&T, Best Buy, Discount Tire, Kohl's, Lowe's, Meijer/dsl, Menards, Michael's, PetCo, Sam's Club/gas, Staples, TJ Maxx, Verizon, Walgreens, Walmart/Subway, same as 97
97	Capital Ave, to Battle Creek, **N** 🅖 BP, Marathon, 🍴 Arby's, LoneStar Steaks, Lux Cafe, McDonald's, Old China, Red Lobster, 🏨 Comfort Inn, Knights Inn, **S** 🅖 Citgo/Subway, Shell, 🍴 Applebee's, Bob Evans, Buffalo Wild Wings, Burger King, Canton Buffet, Coney Island, Cracker Barrel, Culver's, Denny's, Don Pablo, Fazoli's, Jimmy John's, La Cocina, Old Country Buffet, Panera Bread, Pizza Hut, Taco Bell, Wendy's, 🏨 Baymont Inn, Best Value Inn, Best Western, Fairfield Inn, Hampton Inn, Howard Johnson, Travelers Inn, Travelodge, 🅞 AAA, Barnes&Noble, Belle Tire, BigLots, $Tree, Firestone/auto, Goodyear/auto, Hobby Lobby, JC Penney, JoAnn Fabrics, Macy's, Sears/auto, Target, mall, vet

MI

	INTERSTATE 94 CONT'D
Exit	**Services**
96mm	🆁🆂 eb, full ♿ **facilities,** 🚻, 🏓, **litter barrels, vending, petwalk**
95	Helmer Rd, **N** 🅿 Citgo/dsl, 🅾 st police, **2 mi N** 🍴 Arby's, Big Boy, 🅾 Meijer/dsl/e-85
92	Lp 94, rd 37, to Battle Creek, Springfield, **N** 🅿 Citgo/Arlene's Trkstp/dsl/rest./24hr, Shell, 🅾 RV camping, to Ft Custer RA
88	Climax, **N** Galesburg Speedway
85	35th St, Galesburg, **N** 🅿 Shell/dsl, 🍴 McDonald's, Subway, 🅾 Galesburg Speedway, to Ft Custer RA, River Oaks CP, **S** 🅾 Colebrook CP, Scottsville CP, Winery Tours, RV camping
85mm	🆁🆂 wb, full ♿ **facilities,** 🚻, 🏓, **litter barrels, vending, petwalk**
81	Lp 94 (from wb), to Kalamazoo
80	Cork St, Sprinkle Rd, to Kalamazoo, **N** 🅿 Marathon/dsl, Speedway/dsl, 🍴 Arby's, Burger King, Chicken Coop, Crew Rest., Denny's, Godfather's, Taco Bell, 🛏 Best Western, Fairfield Inn, Holiday Inn Express, Red Roof Inn, 🅾 vet, **S** 🅿 BP/dsl, Speedway/dsl, 🍴 Derk's Rest., McDonald's, Nob Hill Grill, Subway, Wendy's, 🛏 Candlewood Suites, EconoLodge, Motel 6, Quality Inn
78	Portage Rd, Kilgore Rd, **N** 🅿 BP/Circle K, 🍴 China Hut, Summer Thyme Cafe, Uncle Ernie's Pancakes, 🛏 AmericInn, 🅾 🏥, repair, **S** 🅿 Marathon/dsl, Shell, Speedway, 🍴 Angelo's Italian, Bravo Rest., Brewster's, Café Meli, McDonald's, Pizza King, Quiznos, Taco Bell, Theo&Stacy's Rest., Subway, 🛏 Best Value Inn, Country Inn&Suites, Days Inn, 🅾 AutoValue Parts, Fields Fabrics, museum
76	Westnedge Ave, **N** 🅿 Admiral, Meijer/dsl, Speedway/dsl, 🍴 Arby's, BD BBQ, Burger King, Hibachi Buffet, Hooters, IHOP, Lee's Chicken, McDonald's, Old Chicago Grill, Outback Steaks, Papa John's, Papa Murphy's, Pizza Hut, Root Beer Stand, Steak'n Shake, Stirmax Asian, Subway, Taco Bell, Theo&Stacy's Rest., 🛏 Courtyard, 🅾 Advance Parts, BigLots, Discount Tire, Family$, Firestone/auto, Gander Mtn, Goodyear/auto, Lowe's, Meijer, Midas, Office Depot, **S** 🅿 Shell, 🍴 Applebee's, Bilbo's Pizza, Bob Evans, Burger King, Carrabba's, Chili's, ChuckECheese's, Coldstone, Colonial Kitchen, Culver's, 5 Guys Burgers, HoneyBaked Ham, Jimmy Johns, KFC, Krispy Kreme, Little Caesars, LJ Silver, Logan's Roadhouse, Los Amigos Mexican, MacKenzie's Bakery, McDonald's, Noodles&Co, Old Country Buffet, Olive Garden, Panchero's Mexican, Panera Bread, Penn Sta Subs, Pizza Hut, Qdoba Mexican, Red Lobster, Red Robin, Schlotzsky's, Subway, Taco Bell, TX Roadhouse, Tim Horton, Wendy's, 🛏 Holiday Motel, 🅾 AT&T, AutoZone, Barnes&Noble, Belle Tire, Best Buy, Buick/Cadillac/GMC, Dick's, $Tree, Fannie May Candies, Firestone/auto, Harding's Foods, Hobby Lobby, Home Depot, JoAnn Fabrics, K-Mart, Kohl's, Macy's, Michael's, Old Navy, O'Reilly Parts, PepBoys, Sam's Club, Sears/auto, Target, TJMaxx, Tuesday Morning, Tuffy Auto, Uncle Ed's Oil Shoppe, Verizon, Walgreens, WorldMkt, mall
75	Oakland Dr
74b a	US 131, to Kalamazoo, **N** to W MI U, Kalamazoo Coll
72	9th St, Oshtemo, **N** 🅿 BP, Speedway/dsl, 🍴 Arby's, Culver's, McDonald's, Taco Bell, Wendy's, 🛏 Hampton Inn, **S** 🍴 Cracker Barrel, 🛏 Fairfield Inn, Microtel, Towne Place Suites

66	Mattawan, **N** 🅿 Speedway/Subway/dsl/scales/24hr, 🍴 Main St Grill, Mancino's Italian, 🅾 Family$, Freightliner, Rossman Auto/repair, R&S RV Service, **S** 🅿 Shell/dsl, 🍴 Pizza Hut
60	MI 40, Paw Paw, **N** 🅿 BP, Speedway/dsl, 🍴 Arby's, Burger King, Chicken Coop, Copper Grille, Gallagher's Eatery, McDonald's, Pizza Hut, Root Beer Stand, Subway, Taco Bell, Wendy's, 🛏 Comfort Inn, EconoLodge, Sta-At, 🅾 🏥, Advance Parts, AT&T, Buick/Chevrolet/GMC, Chrysler/Dodge/Jeep, Curves, Family Fare Foods, St Julian Winery, Walgreens
56	MI 51, to Decatur, **N** st police, **S** 🅿 Citgo/dsl, Marathon/dsl/24hr
52	Lawrence, **N** 🍴 Waffle House of America
46	Hartford, **N** 🅿 Shell/dsl, 🍴 McDonald's, Panel Room Rest., Subway, **S** fruit stand
42mm	🆁🆂 wb, full ♿ **facilities,** 🚻, 🏓, **litter barrels, vending, petwalk**
41	MI 140, to Niles, Watervliet, **N** 🅿 Citgo, Marathon/dsl, Shell/dsl, 🍴 Burger King, Chicken Coop, Millcreek Charlie's Rest., Subway, Taco Bell, 🛏 Fairfield Inn, 🅾 🏥, KOA (Apr-Oct)
39	Millburg, Coloma, Deer Forest, **0-1 mi N** 🅿 BP/dsl, Marathon, Speedway/dsl, Wesco/dsl, 🍴 DQ, Diggins Rest., Friendly Grill, J&P Cafe, McDonald's, Subway, 🅾 Family$, Krenek RV Ctr, **S** 🅾 Jollay Mkt, wine tasting
34	I-196 N, US 31 N, to Holland, Grand Rapids
33	Lp I-94, to Benton Harbor, **2-4 mi N** 🔄, sheriff's dept
30	Napier Ave, Benton Harbor, **N** 🅿 🚂/Wendy's/dsl/LP/24hr/@, Shell/dsl, 🛏 Knights Inn, 🅾 🏥, Blue Beacon
29	Pipestone Rd, Benton Harbor, **N** 🍴 Applebee's, Asian Grill, Burger King, IHOP, Isabella's Rest., Mancino's Pizza, McDonald's, Pizza Hut, Sophia's Pancake House, Steak'n Shake, Super Buffet, TX Corral, 🛏 Courtyard, Motel 6, Red Roof Inn, Twin City Inn, 🅾 Aldi Foods, Best Buy, Home Depot, JC Penney, JoAnn Fabrics, Lowe's, Meijer/dsl, Radio Shack, Staples, Walmart/Subway, **S** 🅿 Mobil/dsl/24hr, 🍴 Bob Evans, 🛏 Comfort Suites, Holiday Inn Express
28	US 31 S, MI 139 N, Scottdale Rd, to Niles, **N** 🅿 Citgo/dsl, Marathon/dsl, 🍴 Bejing House, Burger King, Chicken Coop, Country Kitchen, DQ, Henry's Burgers, KFC, Little Caesars, Pizza Hut, Taco Bell, Wendy's, 🛏 Best Value Inn, Rodeway Inn, 🅾 🏥, AutoZone, BigLots, Chevrolet, $Tree, Family$, Kohl's, M&W Tire, Michael's, Midas, NAPA, Office Depot, Old Navy, Petsmart, Rite Aid, Save-A-Lot, Target, TJ Maxx, U-Haul, Walgreens, radiators/repair/transmissions, st police
27mm	St Joseph River
27	MI 63, Niles Ave, to St Joseph, **N** 🅿 BP, 🍴 Nye's Apple Barn, **S** 🍴 Moe's SW Grill, Panera Bread, 🅾 Goodyear
23	Red Arrow Hwy, Stevensville, **N** 🅿 Admiral, BP, Marathon/dsl, Mobil, Shell/dsl, 🍴 Big Boy, Burger King, Cracker Barrel, Culver's, DQ, HoneyBaked Ham, LJ Silver, McDonald's, Papa John's, Popeye's, Quizno's, Subway, 🛏 Baymont Inn, Candlewood Suites, Comfort Suites, 🅾 Honda, Walgreens, **S** 🍴 Five O'Clock Grill, 🛏 Hampton Inn, 🅾 Meijer/dsl
22	John Beers Rd, Stevensville, **N** 🛏 Chalet on the Lake, 🅾 to Grand Mere SP, **S** 🅿 Marathon/dsl, 🍴 Pizza Hut
16	Bridgman, **N** 🅿 BP/Quiznos/dsl, 🅾 camping, to Warren Dunes SP, **S** 🍴 McDonald's, Olympus Rest., Pizza Hut, Roma Pizza, Sammies Rest., Subway, 🛏 Bridgman Inn, 🅾 Chevrolet, auto repair, st police, vet

K A L A M A Z O O

B E N T O N   H A R B O R

INTERSTATE 94 CONT'D

Exit	Services
12	Sawyer, **N** Marathon/deli/dsl/scales/24hr, truck wash, **S** TA/Burger King/Popeye's/Taco Bell/scales/dsl/24hr/@, Super 8, Schlipp's Drug, USPO
6	Lakeside, Union Pier, **N** St Julian's Winery, antiques, **S** RV camping
4b a	US 12, to Three Oaks, New Buffalo, **N** Pizza Hut, Roma Pizza, st police
2.5mm	weigh sta both lanes
1	MI 239, to Grand Beach, New Buffalo, 0-2 mi **N** Shell/Quiznos, Bruster's Italian, Casey's Grille, Hannah's Rest., Jimmy's Grill, McDonald's, Nancy's, Rosie's Rest., Stray Dog Grill, Subway, Wheel Inn Rest., Best Western, Comfort Inn, Fairfield Inn, Holiday Inn Express, Super Inn, $General, **S** Plaza1/rest/dsl/scales/24hr, Harbor Country Kitchen, Wendy's, Obrien's Inn, casino
.5mm	Welcome Ctr eb, full facilities, info, litter barrels, vending, petwalk
0mm	Michigan/Indiana state line

INTERSTATE 96

Exit	Services
	I-96 begins/ends on I-75, exit 48 in Detroit.
191	I-75, N to Flint, S to Toledo, US 12, to MLK Blvd, to Michigan Ave
190b	Warren Ave, **N** BP/dsl, **S** Marathon
190a	I-94 E to Port Huron
189	W Grand Blvd, Tireman Rd, **N** BP/Subway, Mobil
188b	Joy Rd, **N** Church's
188a	Livernois, **N** Mobil, Shell/Subway, Burger King, KFC, McDonald's, Wendy's
187	Grand River Ave (from eb)
186b	Davison Ave, I-96 local and I-96 express divide, no exits from express
186a	Wyoming Ave
185	Schaefer Hwy, to Grand River Ave, **N** BP/24hr, Mobil, Coney Island, McDonald's, CVS Drug, **S** Sunoco
184	Greenfield Rd
183	MI 39, Southfield Fwy, exit from expswy and local
182	Evergreen Rd
180	Outer Dr, **N** BP/dsl/lube
180mm	I-96 local/express unite/divide
179	US 24, Telegraph Rd, **N** BP, Marathon/dsl, Arby's, Baskin-Robbins/Dunkin Donuts, China King, McDonald's, White Castle, Wendy's, Chevrolet, Family$, NAPA, **S** BP, Marathon/dsl
178	Beech Daly Rd, **N** gas
177	Inkster Rd, **N** BP/Tim Horton, Subway, Best Value Inn, Urgent Care, $General, 7-11
176	Middlebelt Rd, **N** Bob Evans, IHOP, Olive Garden, Comfort Inn, 0-1 mi **S** Biggby Coffee, Chili's, Logan's Roadhouse, Noodles&Co, Pottbelly, Qdoba, Red Lobster, Crossland Suites, BigLots, Costco/gas, $Tree, Firestone/auto, Home Depot, Marshall's, Meijer, Michael's, Office Depot, Petsmart, Target, Verizon, Walgreens, Walmart, auto repair/transmissions
175	Merriman Rd, **N** Mobil/dsl, Speedway/dsl, **S** Exxon/dsl, Blimpie, Royal Coney Island
174	Farmington Rd, **N** Mobil/dsl, Sunoco, Looney Baker, **S** BP, KFC

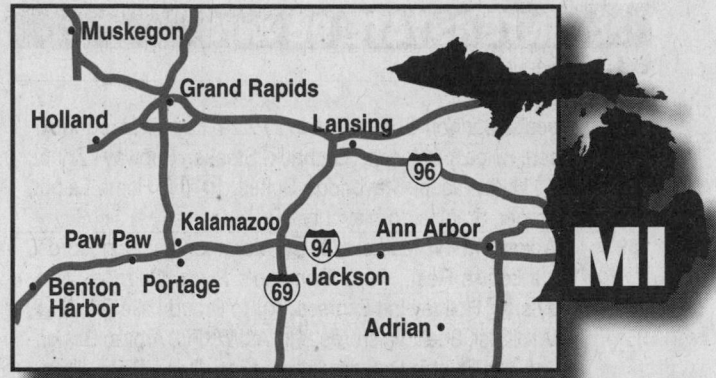

Exit	Services
173b	Levan Rd, **N** H, to Madonna U
173a	Newburgh Rd
171mm	I-275 and I-96 run together 9 miles
170	6 Mile Rd, **N** Big Boy, Buffalo Wild Wings, Jimmy John's, Red Robin, Taco Del Mar, Best Western, Courtyard, Holiday Inn, Marriott, H, ACO Hardware, AT&T, Busch's Foods, GNC, O'Reilly Parts, Rite Aid, Verizon, Walgreens, mall, **S** Marathon, Mobil, Applebee's, Baja Fresh, Brann's Steaks, Bravo Italian, Buca Italian, Charlie's Grill, Claddagh Rest., Flemings, McDonald's, Mitchell's Fishmarket, Panchero's, PF Chang, Potbelly, Subway, Tim Horton, Wendy's, Fairfield Inn, Residence Inn, TownePlace Suites, Barnes&Noble, Kroger, Office Depot, Petsmart
169b a	7 Mile Rd, **N** Big Daddy's, Doc's Grill, Embassy Suites, **S** Alexander's Rest., Andiamo's Cafe, Bahama Breeze Rest., Champp's Rest., Macaroni Grill, Hyatt Place, Home Depot
167	8 Mile Rd, to Northville, **S** BP, Speedway/dsl, Aubree's Pizza, Benihana, Big Boy, Chili's, 5 Guys Burgers, McDonald's, Kerry's Koney Island, On-the-Border, Panera Bread, Qdoba, Starbucks, Taco Bell, TGIFriday's, Extended Stay America, Hampton Inn, Holiday Inn Express, Quality Inn, Sheraton, Best Buy, Costco/gas, Dick's, Firestone/auto, Kohl's, Meijer/dsl, Target, Trader Joe's, Verizon, to Maybury SP
165	I-696, I-275, MI 5, Grand River Ave.
	I-275 and I-96 run together 9 miles
163	I-696 (from eb)
162	Novi Rd, to Walled Lake, Novi, **N** BP, Bar Louie, Black Rock Rest., Buffalo Wild Wings, Carrabba's, Cheesecake Factory, ChuckECheese's, Denny's, Hooters, McDonald's, Novi Chophouse, Red Lobster, Rojo Mexican, Subway, Tilted Kilt Eatery, Crowne Plaza, Hilton Garden, Renaissance, Residence Inn, H, Best Buy, BigLots, Dick's, Gander Mtn, JC Penney, JoAnn Fabrics, Lord&Taylor, Macy's, Marshalls, Michael's, Midas, Nordstrom, Old Navy, Radio Shack, Sears/auto, mall, **S** Mobil/dsl, Sunoco/dsl, Athenian Coney Island, Bagger Dave's Burgers, BD Mongolian BBQ, Big Boy, Biggby Coffee, Blue Fin Rest., Bonefish Grill, Boston Mkt, Famous Dave's, Kim's Chinese, Melting Pot, Olive Garden, Panera Bread, Pei Wei, Potbelly, Qdoba, Red Robin, Steve&Rocky's, TGIFriday's, Tony Sacco Pizza, Wendy's, DoubleTree, Courtyard, Towne Place Suites, Urgent Care, Advance Parts, AT&T, Belle Tire, Better Health Foods, Chevrolet, Discount Tire, Firestone/auto, Kia, NAPA, TJ Maxx, Walmart, vet
160	Beck Rd, 12 Mile Rd, **S** Shell/Tim Horton, Apple

⤴E INTERSTATE 96 CONT'D

Exit	Services
160	Continued

bee's, Caribou Coffee, Guido's Pizza, La Herraduro Mexican, Olga's Kitchen, Outback Steaks, Subway, Zoup!, Ⓛ Hyatt Place, Staybridge Suites, Ⓞ Ⓗ, Home Depot, Kroger, Staples, to Maybury SP

159 Wixom Rd, Walled Lake, **N** Ⓖ Marathon/dsl, Sunoco/dsl, Ⓕ Leon's Rest., Papa Romano's Pizza, Quiznos, Wendy's, Ⓛ Holiday Inn Express, Ⓞ to Proud Lake RA, **S** Ⓖ Mobil/dsl, Shell, Valero/dsl, Ⓕ A&W/KFC, Arby's, Baskin-Robbins/Dunkin Donuts, Burger King, Don's Diner, Jimmy John's, McDonald's, Stinger's Grill, Taco Bell, Ⓛ Comfort Suites, Ⓞ Lincoln, Meijer/dsl, Sam's Club/gas, Target

155b a to Milford, New Hudson, **N** Ⓞ Camp Deerborn (5mi), Ford, to Lyon Oaks CP, **S** Ⓖ Sunoco, Ⓕ Applebee's, Arby's, Jet's Pizza, KG Grill, Leo's Coney Island, McDonald's, Starbucks, Subway, Ⓞ Urgent Care, AT&T, Belle Tire, Chevrolet, Discount Tire, Haws Lake RV Camping (Apr-Oct), Hyundai, Lowe's, Verizon, Walmart

153 Kent Lake Rd, **N** Kensington Metropark, **S** Ⓖ Mobil/dsl, Ⓛ Country Meadows Inn (3mi)

151 Kensington Rd, **N** Kensington Metropark, **S** Island Lake RA, food, lodging

150 Pleasant Valley Rd (no return wb)

148b a US 23, **N** to Flint, **S** to Ann Arbor

147 Spencer Rd, **N** Ⓖ Mobil/dsl, Ⓞ st police, **S** Ⓕ Bagger Dave's Burgers (2mi), Ⓞ to Brighton St RA

145 Grand River Ave, to Brighton, **N** Ⓖ BP, Shell/dsl, Ⓕ Arby's, Baskin-Robbins/Dunkin Donuts, Cracker Barrel, Outback Steaks, Pizza Hut, Ⓛ Courtyard, Ⓞ Ⓗ, Urgent Care, Buick/GMC, $General, Ford, Honda, Mazda, camping, **S** Ⓖ Marathon/Subway, Ⓕ Big Boy, Border Cantina, Burger King, Chili's, Firehouse Subs, IHOP, Jimmy John's, Leo's Coney Island, Lil Chef, McDonald's, Olga's Kitchen, Panera Bread, Pi's Asian, Red Robin, Starbucks, Taco Bell, Tim Horton, Wendy's, Ⓛ Holiday Inn Express, Homewood Suites, Ⓞ AAA, Aldi Foods, Belle Tire, Best Buy, Bob's Tire, CVS Drug, $Tree, Home Depot, JoAnn Fabrics, Marshalls, Meijer/dsl/E85, Michael's, O'Reilly Parts, Radio Shack, Petsmart, Staples, Target, Verizon, Walgreens, USPO, to Brighton Ski Area

141 Lp 96 (from wb, return at 140), to Howell, **0-2 mi N** Ⓖ Shell, Speedway, Sunoco/dsl, Ⓕ Applebee's, Arby's, Biggby Coffee, Bluefin Steaks, Bob Evans, Buffalo Wild Wings, KFC, Little Caesars, McDonald's, New Century Buffet, Subway, Taco Bell, Wendy's, White Castle, Ⓛ Grandview Inn, Ⓞ AT&T, Chevrolet, Discount Tire, $Tree, Home Depot, Kohl's, Lowe's, Meijer, O'Reilly Parts, Staples, TJ Maxx, Walmart

140 S Latson Rd, **N** same as 141

137 D19, to Pinckney, Howell, **N** Ⓖ Mobil, Shell/dsl, Speedway/dsl, Sunoco/Baskin-Robbins/Dunkin Donuts/dsl, Ⓕ Jonna's ToGo, Mario Bros Pizza, Wendy's, Ⓛ Kensington Inn, Ⓞ Ⓗ, Parts+, Spartan Tire, True Value, USPO, vet, **S** Ⓕ Country Kitchen, Ⓛ Best Western

135mm Ⓡ eb, full Ⓗ facilities, vending, Ⓒ, Ⓕ, litter barrels, petwalk

133 MI 59, Highland Rd, **N** Ⓖ Marathon/McDonald's/dsl, Ⓕ Arby's, Leo's Coney Island, Ⓛ Baymont, Holiday Inn Express, Ⓞ Tanger Outlets/famous brands

129 Fowlerville Rd, Fowlerville, **N** Ⓖ BP, Shell/dsl, Sunoco/dsl, Ⓕ A&W/KFC, Great Lakes Rest., McDonald's, Pizza Hut/Taco Bell, Wendy's, Ⓛ Magnuson Hotel, Ⓞ Chevrolet, Walmart, **S** Ⓖ Mobil/dsl, Ⓕ Subway, Ⓞ Chysler/Dodge/Jeep, Ⓞ Ford

126mm weigh sta both lanes

122 MI 43, MI 52, Webberville, **N** Ⓖ Mobil/dsl/24hr, Ⓕ McDonald's, Ⓞ MI Brewing Co

117 to Dansville, Williamston, **N** Ⓖ Marathon/Jersey's Giant Subs/dsl, Ⓕ Spag's Grill (3mi), **S** Ⓖ Sunoco/dsl

111mm Ⓡ wb, full Ⓗ facilities, Ⓒ, Ⓕ, litter barrels, vending, petwalk

110 Okemos, Mason, **N** Ⓖ Marathon/dsl, Sunoco/Dunkin Donuts, Ⓕ Applebee's, Arby's, Backyard BBQ, Biggby Coffee, Big John's Steaks, Coldstone/Tim Horton, Cracker Barrel, Gilbert&Blake's, Grand Traverse Pie Co., Little Caesars, McDonald's, Ozzy Mediterranean, Panchero's Mexican, Starbucks, Stillwater Grill, Subway, Taco Bell, Ⓛ Comfort Inn, Fairfield Inn, Hampton Inn, Holiday Inn Express, Staybridge Suites, Ⓞ BMW/Porsche, Mercedes, 7-11, to stadium

106b a I-496, US 127, to Jackson, Lansing, **N** St Police

104 Lp 96, Cedar St, to Holt, Lansing, **N** Ⓖ Admiral, Speedway/dsl, Ⓕ Applebee's, Arby's, Asia's Finest, Biggby Coffee, Big John's, Blimpie, Bob Evans, Boston Mkt, Burger King, China King, Cici's, Fazoli's, Finley's Rest., Jersey Giant Subs, Happy's Pizza, Hooters, Jet's Pizza, KFC, Los Tres Amigos, Panda Gourmet, Pizza Hut, Steak'n Shake, TX Roadhouse, Tim Horton, Wendy's, Zeus Coney Island, Ⓛ Best Value Inn, Best Western, Magnuson Hotel, Super 8, Ⓞ Ⓗ, Aldi Foods, Belle Tire, Cadillac, Chevrolet, Discount Tire, Dodge, $Tree, Family$, Kia, Lexus, Meijer/dsl, Menards, Sam's Club/gas, Target, Toyota/Scion, Tuffy Auto, Verizon, auto repair, vet, **S** Ⓖ Marathon, Speedway/dsl, Ⓕ Aldaco's Taco Bar, Burger King, Champion's Grill, China East Buffet, Dairy Dan, Famous Dave's BBQ, Flapjack Rest., McDonald's, Ponderosa, Subway, Ⓛ Best Western, Ⓞ AutoZone, Budget Tire, CarQuest, CVS Drug, Family$, Kroger/gas, L&L Foods, Lowe's, Rite Aid

101 MI 99, MLK Blvd, to Eaton Rapids, **0-3 mi N** Ⓖ QD, Ⓕ Arby's, Tim Horton, Ⓞ Kroger/gas, Meijer/dsl, **S** Ⓖ Speedway/Subway/dsl, Sunoco/dsl, Ⓕ Coach's Grill, McDonald's, Wendy's

98b a Lansing Rd, to Lansing, **N** Ⓕ Wendy's, Ⓛ Comfort Inn, Holiday Inn Express, Ⓞ Harley-Davidson, **S** st police

97 I-69, US 27 S, S to Ft Wayne, N to Lansing

95 I-496, to Lansing

93b a MI 43, Lp 69, Saginaw Hwy, to Grand Ledge, **0-2 mi N** Ⓖ Shell, Speedway/dsl, Ⓕ Burger King, Carrabba's, Cheddar's, Denny's, Fazoli's, Frank's Grill, Hibachi Grill, Honeybaked Ham, Houlihan's, Logan's Roadhouse, McDonald's, Outback Steaks, Panera Bread, Qdoba, Red Robin, Subway, Younkers, Ⓛ Days Inn, Fairfield Inn, Hampton Inn, Motel 6, Quality Inn, Ramada Inn, Red Roof Inn, Residence Inn, Ⓞ Ⓗ, Barnes&Noble, BigLots, Chrysler/Dodge/Jeep, Hobby Lobby, JC Penney, Kohl's, Kroger, Macy's, Meijer/dsl/24hr, NAPA, Radio Shack, Target, Walgreens, **S** Ⓖ BP/24hr, QD, Sunoco/McDonald's, Ⓕ Arby's, Bob Evans, Cracker Barrel, Ing-credible Chinese, Rudino's Pizza, Steak'n Shake, Subway, Ⓛ SpringHill Suites, Ⓞ Urgent Care, AT&T, Belle Tire, Buick/GMC, Dick's, Discount Tire, Gander Mtn, Mazda, Lowe's, Menards, Michael's, Petsmart, Staples, Walmart

🅐 = gas 🍽 = food 🛏 = lodging 🅞 = other 🆁🆂 = rest stop

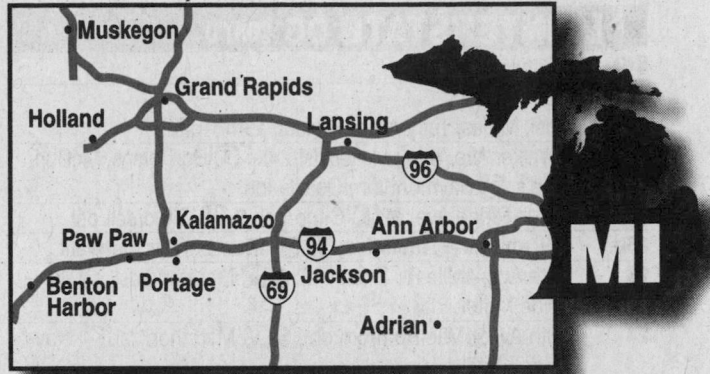

INTERSTATE 96 CONT'D

Exit	Services
92mm	Grand River
91	I-69 N (from wb), US 27 N, to Flint, **S** 🅐 ✈FLYING J/Denny's/dsl/24hr, 🍽 Pepperoni's Rest.
90	Grand River Ave, to ✈ (from wb)
89	I-69 N, US 27 N (from eb), to Flint
87mm	🆁🆂 eb, full ♿ facilities, 🍽, 🛏, litter barrels, vending, petwalk
86	MI 100, Wright Rd, to Grand Ledge, **S** 🅐 Mobil/McDonald's/dsl, Speedway/Subway/24hr
84	to Eagle, Westphalia
79mm	🆁🆂 wb, full ♿ facilities, info, 🍽, 🛏, litter barrels, vending, petwalk
77	Lp 96, Grand River Ave, Portland, **N** 🅐 BP/24hr, Shell/Burger King, Speedway/dsl, 🍽 Arby's, Biggby Coffee, KFC/Taco Bell, Little Caesar's, Hungry Howie's, McDonald's, 🛏 Best Western, 🅞 Curves, Family$, Rite Aid, Tom's Foods, **S** 🍽 Wendy's, 🅞 Ford
76	Kent St, Portland
76mm	Grand River
73	to Lyons-Muir, Grand River Ave
69mm	**weigh sta both lanes**
67	MI 66, to Ionia, Battle Creek, **N** 🅐 ▨▨▨▨/Subway/dsl/scales/24hr, 🍽 Corner Landing Grill, 🛏 Midway Motel, Super 8, 🅞 🏥, Meijer/dsl (4mi), Walmart (4mi), RV camping, st police, truck wash
64	to Lake Odessa, Saranac, **N** Ionia St RA, **S** I-96 Speedway
63mm	🆁🆂 eb, full ♿ facilities, 🍽, 🛏, litter barrels, petwalk, vending
59	Clarksville
52	MI 50, to Lowell, **N** 🅐 Mobil/Subway/dsl, 🅞 fairgrounds, **S** 🅐 Marathon/Noble Roman's/dsl (2mi), 🅞 RV camping
46	rd 6, to rd 37
46mm	Thornapple River
44	36 St, **S** ✈
43b a	MI 11, 28th St, Cascade, **N** 🅐 Marathon/dsl, 🍽 Biggby Coffee, Brann's Steaks, Burger King, Culver's, Jet's Pizza, Jimmy John's, Macaroni Grill, Panera Bread, Papa John's, Pizza Hut, Quizno's, Stabucks, Sundance Grill, Subway, Taco Boy, Wendy's, 🛏 Baymont Inn, Best Western, Country Inn&Suites, Crowne Plaza, EconoLodge, Holiday Inn Express, 🅞 Audi/Porsche/Subaru, Fresh Mkt, GNC, Meijer/dsl, Mercedes/Volvo/VW, True Value, Walmart, **0-3 mi S** 🅐 BP, Citgo, Shell, Speedway/dsl, 🍽 Applebee's, Arby's, Arnie's Rest., Baskin-Robbins/Dunkin Donuts, Burger King, Carabba's, Carlos O'Kelley's, Cantina Mexican, Chili's, Chipotle Mexican, ChuckeCheese, Coldstone, Denny's, Don Julio's, Grand Rapids Brewery, Honey Baked Ham, Hooters, Jimmy John's, Krispy Kreme, Longhorn Steaks, McDonald's, Moe's SW Grill, Noodles&Co, Old Chicago, Olive Garden, Outback Steaks, Panera Bread, Papa Vino's, Perkins, Pizza Hut, Quaker Steak&Lube, Red Lobster, Red Robin, Red Sun Buffet, Ruby Tuesday, Smokey Bones, Starbucks, Steak'n Shake, Subway, Taco Bell, TX Roadhouse, Wendy's, Yin Ching Chinese, 🛏 Clarion, Comfort Inn, Courtyard, Hampton Inn, Hilton, Motel 6, Quality Inn, Ramada, Red Roof Inn, SpringHill Suites, Super 8, 🅞 Belle Tire, Best Buy, CarQuest, Costco/gas, Dick's, $Tree, Ford, Gander Mtn, Hobby Lobby, Home Depot, Honda, Hyundai/KIA, Jo-Ann Fabrics, Lentz Automo

GRAND RAPIDS

Exit	Services
43b a	Continued
	tive, Lowe's, Michael's, Nissan, Office Depot, Old Navy, Petsmart, Radio Shack, Sam's Club/gas, Sears/auto, Staples, Target, TJ Maxx, U-Haul
40b a	Cascade Rd, **N** 🅐 Forrest Hills Fuel, Marathon/dsl, 🍽 Biggby Coffee, China Garden, Forrest Hills Rest, Great Harvest, Little Bangkok, Little Caesar's, Subway, 🅞 7-11, vet, **S** 🅐 Shell/Quizno's/dsl, Speedway/dsl, 🍽 Bonefish Grill, Jimmy John's, Zoup, 🅞 🏥, Keystone Drug
39	MI 21 (from eb), to Flint
38	E Beltline Ave, to MI 21, MI 37, MI 44, **N** 🅐 BP, 🍽 O'Charley's, 🅞 Meijer/dsl, RV camping, **S** 🍽 Uno Pizzaria, 🛏 Country Inn&Suites, 🅞 🏥
37	I-196 (from wb, exits left), Gerald Ford Fwy, to Grand Rapids
36	Leonard St, **2 mi S** 🍽 Arby's, Jimmy John's, McDonald's, 🅞 sheriff's dept
33	Plainfield Ave, MI 44 Connector, **N** 🅐 BP, Speedway/dsl, 🍽 Arby's, Baskin-Robbins, Blimpie, Charley's Grille, Cheers Grill, Fred's Italian, Golden Dragon, KFC, Little Caesar's, LJ Silver, McDonald's, Pizza Hut, Russ' Rest., Subway, Taco Bell, Tokyo Roadhouse, Wendy's, 🛏 Grand Inn, Lazy T Motel, 🅞 AutoZone, Belle Tire, BigLots, Chevrolet, Chrysler/Jeep, Curves, Discount Tire, Dodge, $Tree, Firestone/auto, Ford, Goodyear/auto, K-Mart, Lowe's, Meijer/dsl, NAPA, Nissan/VW, Radio Shack, Save-A-Lot Foods, Toyota, U-Haul, Walgreens, **S** 🅐 BP, 🍽 Denny's
31mm	Grand River
31b a	US 131, N to Cadillac, S to Kalamazoo, **1 mi N** 🅐 BP, 🍽 McDonald's
30b a	Alpine Ave, Grand Rapids, **N** 🅐 BP, Marathon/dsl, 7-11, 🍽 Applebee's, Buffalo Wild Wings, Checkers, ChuckeCheese, Coldstone, Culvers, El Burrito Mexican, Empire Buffet, Fire Mtn Grill, First Wok, Golden Corral, Hibachi Grill, IHOP, Jimmy John's, Little Caesar's, Logan's Roadhouse, Mafia Mike's Pizza, McDonald's, Olive Garden, Outback Steaks, Panera Bread, Perkins, Qdoba, Quizno's, Russ' Rest., Sonic, Starbucks, Steak'n Shake, Subway, Taco Bell, TGIFriday's, Thai Basil, 🛏 Hampton Inn, Holiday Inn Express, SpringHill Suites, 🅞 Aldi Foods, AT&T, AutoZone, Belle Tire, Best Buy, CarQuest, Discount Tire, $Tree, Ford/KIA, GNC, Hobby Lobby, Kohl's, Marshall's, Menards, Michael's, NAPA, Office Depot, PepBoys, PetCo, Radio Shack, Sam's Club/gas, Save-a-Lot Foods, Schuler Books, Target, TJ Maxx, Verizon, Walgreens, Walmart/auto, **S** 🅐 Admiral/dsl, Speedway/dsl, 🍽 Arby's, Burger King, Fazoli's, First 1 Chinese, KFC, LJ Silver, McDonald's, Papa John's, Pizza Hut, Wendy's, 🛏 Motel 6, 🅞 Goodyear/auto, Home Depot, Jo-Ann Fabrics, Meijer/

🅖 = gas 🍴 = food 🛏 = lodging 🅞 = other 🆁🆂 = rest stop Copyright 2014 - The Next Exit ®

▲E INTERSTATE 96 CONT'D

Exit	Services
30b a	Continued
	dsl, Midas, Tuffy Auto, U-Haul, auto repair
28	Walker Ave, **S** 🅖 Meijer/dsl/24hr, 🍴 Bob Evans, McDonald's, 🛏 Baymont Inn, Quality Inn
26	Fruit Ridge Ave, **N** 🅖 Citgo/dsl, **S** 🅖 Citgo/deli/dsl
25mm	🆁🆂 eb, full ♿ facilities, 🅲, 🏛, litter barrels, petwalk
25	8th Ave, 4Mile Rd (from wb), **S** 🅖 Marathon/dsl, 🛏 Wayside Motel
24	8th Ave, 4Mile Rd (from eb), **S** 🅖 Marathon/dsl, 🛏 Wayside Motel
23	Marne, **N** 🅞 tires, **S** 🍴 Depot Café, Rinaldi's Café, 🅞 Ernie's Mkt, USPO, fairgrounds/raceway
19	Lamont, Coopersville, **N** food, **S** 🍴 Sam's Joint Rest., 🅞 LP
16	B-35, Eastmanville, **N** 🅖 BP/Subway/dsl, Speedway/dsl/24hr, Shell/Burger King/dsl, 🍴 Arby's, Hungry Howie's, Little Caesar's, McDonald's, #1 Chinese, Taco Bell, 🛏 Rodeway Inn, 🅞 Buick/Chevrolet/Pontiac, Curves, Family$, Family Fare Foods, Fun 'N Sun RV Ctr, Rite Aid, vet, **S** 🅖 Pacific Pride/dsl, 🅞 RV camping
10	B-31 (exits left from eb), Nunica, **N** 🍴 Turk's Rest., **S** 🅞 Conestoga RV camping, golf course/rest.
9	MI 104 (from wb, exits left), to Grand Haven, Spring Lake, **S** 🅖 Marathon, 🅞 to Grand Haven SP
8mm	🆁🆂 wb, full ♿ facilities, 🅲, 🏛, litter barrels, vending, petwalk
5	Fruitport (from wb, no return)
4	Airline Rd, **N** 🅞 NAPA, **S** 🅖 Speedway/dsl, Wesco/dsl, 🍴 Burger Crest Diner, Dairy Bar, McDonald's, Subway, Village Inn, 🅞 Grover Drug, Orchard Mkt Foods, Water Park (5mi), USPO, auto/tire repair, to PJ Hoffmaster SP
1c	Hile Rd (from eb), **S** 🍴 Arby's, Brann's Grille, Buffalo Wild Wings, ChuckeCheese, Dynasty Buffet, Golden Corral, KFC, Logan's Roadhouse, Perkins, Quizno's, Red Robin, TX Roadhouse, 🛏 Baymont Inn, Fairfield Inn, Hampton Inn, 🅞 AT&T, Barnes&Noble, Best Buy, Hobby Lobby, JC Penney, Jo-Ann Fabrics, Kohl's, Meijer/dsl, Menards, Old Navy, PetCo, Target, TJ Maxx, VW, Younkers, mall
1b a	US 31, to Ludington, Grand Haven, **N** 🛏 Airline Motel, Alpine Motel, Bel-aire Motel, 🅞 All Seasons RV Ctr, **2 mi N on Sherman Blvd** 🅖 Citgo/dsl, 🍴 Applebee's, Arby's, Fazoli's, McDonald's, Pizza Ranch, Red Wok, Subway, Wendy's, 🛏 Comfort Inn/rest., 🅞 🅷 $Tree, GNC, Lowe's, Petsmart, Radio Shack, Sam's Club/gas, Staples, Walmart/24hr, **S** same as 1c
	I-96 begins/ends on US 31 at Muskegon.

▲E INTERSTATE 196 (GRAND RAPIDS)

Exit	Services
81mm	**I-196 begins/ends on I-96**, 37mm in E Grand Rapids.
79	Fuller Ave, **N** sheriff, **S** 🅖 Shell/dsl, Speedway/dsl, 🍴 Biggby Coffee, Bill's Rest., Checkers, Elbow Room, KFC, Subway, Taco Bell, Wendy's, 🅞 🅷, Ace Hardware, Walgreens
78	College Ave, **S** 🅖 Marathon/Circle K, 🍴 McDonald's, Omelette Shop, 🅞 🅷, Ford Museum
77c	Ottawa Ave, downtown, **S** Gerald R Ford Museum
77b a	US 131, S to Kalamazoo, N to Cadillac
76	MI 45 E, Lane Ave, **S** 🍴 El Granjero Mexican, 🅞 Gerald R Ford Museum, John Ball Park&Zoo, auto repair

Exit	Services
75	MI 45 W, Lake Michigan Dr, **N** to Grand Valley St U
74mm	Grand River
73	Market Ave, **N** to Vanandel Arena
72	Lp 196, Chicago Dr E (from eb)
70	MI 11 (exits left from wb), Grandville, Walker, **S** 🅖 BP/dsl, Shell, 🛏 Days Inn, 🅞 Auto Value Parts, USPO
69c	Baldwin St (from wb)
69b a	Chicago Dr, **N** 🅖 Speedway, 🍴 Culver's, Hungry Howie's, KFC, McDonald's, Papa John's, Peppino's Pizza, Perkins, Subway, Taco Bell, Youming Chinese, 🅞 Aldi Foods, AutoZone, Curves, $Tree, Meijer/dsl, Radio Shack, Target, Walgreens, USPO, **S** 🅖 Admiral, Speedway/dsl, 🍴 Adobe Mexican, Arby's, Baskin-Robbins/Dunkin Donuts, Biggby Coffee, Burger King, Little Caesar's, Pizza Hut, Rainbow Grill, Russ' Rest., Subway, Wendy's, 🛏 Best Western, Holiday Inn Express, 🅞 USPO
67	44th St, **N** 🅖 Mobil/dsl, 🍴 Burger King, Cracker Barrel, Panera Bread, Steak'n Shake, 🛏 Comfort Suites, 🅞 Honda, Walmart/auto, 0-2 mi **S** 🍴 Famous Dave's, Jimmy John's, IHOP, Logan's Roadhouse, Max&Erma's, Qdoba, Quizno's, Starbucks, Subway, TX Roadhouse, Wendy's, 🛏 Residence Inn, 🅞 Best Buy, Chrysler/Dodge/Jeep, Costco/gas, Dick's, Discount Tire, $Tree, Fresh Mkt Foods, Gander Mtn., Hobby Lobby, Home Depot, JC Penney, Kohl's, Lowe's, Macy's, Marshall's, Michael's, Old Navy, Petsmart, Sear/auto, World Mkt
64	MI 6 E, to Lansing (exits left from wb)
62	32nd Ave, to Hudsonville, **N** 🅖 BP/dsl/24hr, Citgo/dsl, 🍴 Arby's, Burger King, Hudsonville Grill, Little Caesar's, McDonald's, 🛏 Quality Inn, 🅞 Chevrolet, camping, **S** 🅖 Mobil/Subway/dsl/24hr, 🍴 Rainbow Grill, 🛏 Super 8, 🅞 Harley-Davidson, Harvest Foods
58mm	🆁🆂 eb, full ♿ facilities, 🅲, 🏛, litter barrels, vending, petwalk
55	Byron Rd, Zeeland, **N** 🅖 7-11, 🍴 Blimpie, McDonald's, 3-5 mi **N** 🅷, to Holland SP
52	16th St, Adams St, **2 mi N** 🍴 Wendy's, 🛏 EconoLodge, 🅞 🅷, Meijer/dsl/e-85, **S** 🅖 Mobil/Subway/dsl, 🍴 Burger King
49	MI 40, to Allegan, **N** 🅖 BP/McDonald's/dsl, 🛏 Residence Inn, **S** 🅖 Tulip City/Marathon/Subway/dsl/scales/24hr, 🍴 Rock Island Rest., 🅞 truck repair, truck wash
44	US 31 N (from eb), to Holland 3-5 mi **N** 🛏 Country Inn, 🅞 🅷, gas, food
43mm	🆁🆂 wb, full ♿ facilities, info, 🅲, 🏛, litter barrels, vending, petwalk
41	rd A-2, Douglas, Saugatuck, **N** 🅖 Marathon/dsl, Shell/Subway/dsl, 🍴 Burger King, Spectators Grill, 🛏 Best Western (1mi), Timberline Motel (3mi), 🅞 $General, NAPA, to Saugatuck SP, **S** 🍴 Belvedere Inn, 🅞 Red Barn Gifts
38mm	Kalamazoo River
36	rd A-2, Ganges, **N** 🅖 Shell, 🍴 Christo's Rest., Kalico Kitchen, 🛏 AmericInn
34	MI 89, to Fennville, **N** to West Side CP, **S** 🅖 Shell/24hr, 🅞 Cranes Pie Pantry (4mi, seasonal), Lyons Fruits, Winery Tours
30	rd A-2, Glenn, Ganges, **N** to Westside CP (4mi)
28mm	🆁🆂 eb, full ♿ facilities, 🅲, 🏛, litter barrels, vending, petwalk
26	109th Ave, to Pullman, **N** Dutch Farm Mkt
22	N Shore Dr, **N** 🅞 to Kal Haven Trail SP, Cousin's RV Camping/rest.

↑E INTERSTATE 196 (GRAND RAPIDS) CONT'D

Exit	Services
20	rd A-2, Phoenix Rd, **N** 🅖 BP/dsl, Marathon/dsl, 🍽 Arby's, China Buffet, Taco Bell, 🅞 🅗, AutoZone, $Tree, Walgreens, st police, **S** 🅖 Murphy USA/dsl, Shell/dsl, 🍽 Big Boy, McDonald's, Sherman's Dairybar, Wendy's, 🛏 Comfort Suites, Hampton Inn, Holiday Inn Express, Ramada, 🅞 $General, Menards, Walmart
18	MI 140, MI 43, to Watervliet, **0-2 mi N** 🅖 BP/dsl, Shell/dsl/24hr, Xpress/dsl, 🍽 Burger King, 50's Drive Inn, Hungry Howie's, Little Caesar's, McDonald's, Pizza Hut, Willy O's Pizza, 🛏 Great Lakes Inn, LakeBluff Motel, 🅞 AutoValue Parts, Buick/Cadillac/GMC, Chevrolet, Chrysler/Dodge/Jeep, Ford/Lincoln, Village Mkt Foods, auto repair, st police, **7 mi S** KOA (Apr-Oct),
13	to Covert, **N** to Van Buren SP, RV camping
7	MI 63, to Benton Harbor, **N** 🍽 DiMaggio's Pizza, Vitale's Mkt/subs, 🅞 RV camping
4	to Coloma, Riverside, **S** 🅖 Marathon/dsl, 🅞 KOA (Apr-Oct)
2mm	Paw Paw River
1	Red Arrow Hwy, **N** SW Michigan ✈
0mm	I-94, E to Detroit, W to Chicago

I-196 begins/ends on I-94, exit 34 at Benton Harbor.

↑N INTERSTATE 275 (LIVONIA)

Exit	Services
	I-275 and I-96 run together 9 miles. See Michigan Interstate 96, exits 165-170.
29	I-96 E, to Detroit, MI 14 W, to Ann Arbor
28	Ann Arbor Rd, Plymouth, **E** 🅖 BP/Dunkin Donuts, Mobil, Shell, 🍽 Denny's, Little Caesars, McDonald's, 🛏 Red Roof Inn, 🅞 $Tree, Verizon, **W** 🍽 Burger King, Firehouse Subs, Grand Traverse Pie Co., McDonald's, 🛏 Comfort Inn, 🅞 Cadillac, CVS Drug, K-Mart, Lincoln, vet
25	MI 153, Ford Rd, Garden City, **W** 🅖 BP, Shell, Speedway, Valero, 🍽 Applebee's, Arby's, BD Mongolian BBQ, Bob Evans, Boston Mkt., Buffalo Wild Wings, Carrabba's, Chili's, ChuckeCheese, Coney Island, Dunkin Donuts/Baskin-Robbins, 5 Guys Burgers, KFC, Olga's Kitchen, Outback Steaks, Panera Bread, Potbelly, Quiznos, Roman Forum Rest., Subway, TGIFriday's, Tim Horton, Wendy's, White Castle/Church's, 🛏 Best Value Inn, Comfort Suites, Extended Stay America, Fairfield Inn, Hampton Inn, La Quinta, 🅞 Urgent Care, Advance Parts, Aldi Foods, AT&T, Discount Tire, Firestone/auto, Hobby Lobby, JC Penney, Kohl's, Lowe's, Midas, PetCo, Richardson Drug, Target, Verizon, Walgreens, vet
23	🅡🅢 nb, full 🅗 facilities, 🚻, info, 🪵 litter barrels
22	US 12, Michigan Ave, to Wayne, **E** 🅖 BP/dsl, Shell, Valero/dsl, 🍽 Arby's, Jonathan's Rest., McDonald's, Quiznos, Subway, Wendy's, 🛏 Days Inn, Fellows Cr Motel, Holiday Inn Express, Super 8, Willo Acres Motel, **W** 🅖 Marathon/dsl, 🍽 Jimmy John's, 🅞 Urgent Care, Kia, Nissan
20	Ecorse Rd, to Romulus, **E** 🅖 7-11, **W** 🅖 Mobil/Burger King/scales/dsl/24hr
17	I-94 E to Detroit, W to Ann Arbor, **E** ✈
15	Eureka Rd, **E** 🅖 Shell, 🍽
13	Sibley Rd, New Boston, **W** 🅖 Fusion/Subway/dsl, 🍽 LC's Chicken, 🅞 to Lower Huron Metro Park
11	S Huron Rd, **1 mi W** 🅖 Sunoco/Burger King/dsl, 🍽 Jacob's Rest, 🅞 RV LP (1mi)

Exit	Services
8	Will Carleton Rd, to Flat Rock
5	Carleton, South Rockwood, **W** food
4mm	🅡🅢 sb, full 🅗 facilities, 🚻, 🪵, litter barrels
2	US 24, to Telegraph Rd, **W** 🅖 Marathon/dsl, lodging
0mm	I-275 begins/ends on I-75, exit 20.

↑N INTERSTATE 475 (FLINT)

Exit	Services
17mm	I-475 begins/ends on I-75, exit 125.
15	Clio Rd, **W** 🅖 BP, 🅞 Chevrolet
13	Saginaw St, **E** 🅖 BP, 🍽 McDonald's, Taco Bell, 🅞 Advanced Parts, Family$, Kroger/gas, **W** 🅖 Marathon, 🍽 Burger King, KFC, Little Caesars
11	Carpenter Rd
10	Pierson Rd
9	rd 54, Dort I lwy, Stewart Ave, **E** 🅖 Citgo, 🍽 McDonald's
8mm	Flint River
8b	Davison Rd, Hamilton Ave
8a	Longway Blvd, **W** 🛏 Holiday Inn Express, 🅞 🅗, farmers mkt, USPO
7	rd 21, Court St, downtown Flint
6	I-69, W to Lansing, E to Port Huron
5	Atherton Rd (from sb), **E** 🅖 Marathon/dsl
4	Hemphill Rd, Bristol Rd, **E** 🅖 Speedway/dsl, 🍽 Rally's, Subway, 🅞 Rite Aid, **W** 🅖 Speedway/dsl, 🍽 Little Caesars, Tim Horton/Wendy's, 🅞 Family$, Kroger/dsl, vet
2	Hill Rd, **E** 🅖 Speedway, 🍽 Applebee's, Bob Evans, 🛏 Wingate Inn, 🅞 vet, **W** 🅖 Mobil/Tim Horton, Speedway/dsl, 🍽 Arby's, Bangkok Peppers, Blimpie, Burger King, Burger St Grill, Little Caesars, McDonald's, Wendy's, 🅞 Rite Aid
0mm	I-475 begins/ends on I-75, exit 111.

↑E INTERSTATE 696 (DETROIT)

Exit	Services
	I-696 begins/ends on I-94.
28	I-94 E to Port Huron, W to Detroit, 11 Mile Rd, **E** 🅖 BP/dsl, Speedway, 7-11
27	MI 3, Gratiot Ave, **N** 🅖 BP, Valero, 🍽 Checkers, McDonald's, National Coney Island, Tubby's Subs, 🅞 Costco/gas, 7-11, **S** 🅖 Marathon, Mobil/McDonald's, Shell, 🍽 Biggby Coffee, DQ, 8 China Buffet, Subway, White Castle, 🅞 GNC, Goodyear/auto, K-Mart, Kroger/gas, Radio Shack, Rite Aid, Sav-A-Lot Foods
26	MI 97, Groesbeck Ave, Roseville, **N** 🅖 Shell/dsl, **S** 🍽 Omega Grill
24	Hoover Rd, Schoenherr Rd, **N** 🅖 BP, 🍽 Burger King, KFC, **S** 🅖 BP, Mobil, 🍽 Boston Mkt, Carlito's Pizza, Del Taco, Doc's Rest., Pizza Hut, Quizno's, Red Lobster, Subway, Taco Bell, Tim Horton, 🛏 Holiday Inn Express,

INTERSTATE 696 (DETROIT) CONT'D

Exit	Services
24	Continued
	🅾 Curves, CVS Drug, $Tree, GNC, Home Depot, Kroger, Marshall's
23	MI 53, Van Dyke Ave, **N** 🅡 BP, Mobil/dsl, 🍴 Angelo's Rest., Arby's, Baskin-Robbins/Dunkin Donuts, Juliano's Rest., McDonald's, 🅾 Cadillac, Dodge, $General, Scion/Toyota, **S** 🅡 Citgo, 🍴 Luca's Coney Island, 🅾 Chevrolet, Discount Tire, Ford, Rite Aid, USPO, vet
22	Mound Rd, **N** 🅡 BP/Burger King
20	Ryan Rd, Dequindre Rd, **N** 🅡 BP, Citgo, Marathon, 7-11, Shell, 🍴 Azteca Mexican, Ponderosa, 🏠 Knights Inn, Red Roof Inn, 🅾 BigLots, vet, **S** 🍴 Bob Evans, Chicken Shack, Church's, LA Coney Island, McDonald's, 🏠 Best Value Inn, Comfort Suites, 🅾 Rite Aid, Sears, transmissions
19	Couzens St, 10 Mile Rd, **S** Hazel Park Racetrack
18	I-75 N to Flint, S to Detroit
17	Campbell Ave, Hilton Ave, Bermuda, Mohawk, **S** 🅡 Marathon/dsl
16	MI 1, Woodward Ave, Main St, **N** zoo, **S** 🅡 Sunoco
14	Coolidge Rd, 10 Mile Rd, **S** 🅡 Speedway, 🍴 Hungry Howie's, Jade Palace Chinese, Little Caesar's, Subway, 🅾 CVS Drug, Farm Fresh Foods
13	Greenfield Rd, **N** 🅡 Mobil, Marathon, 🍴 Church's, L George Coney Island, McDonald's, Ponderosa, Popeye's,

Exit	Services
13	Continued
	White Castle, 🅾 Aldi Foods, Family$, K-Mart, Sav-A-Lot Foods, **S** 🅡 Mobil, Sunoco, 🍴 Baskin-Robbins/Dunkin Donuts, Front Page Deli, Pita Cafe, Starbucks, 🅾 Rite Aid
12	MI 39, Southfield Rd, 11 Mile Rd, **N** 🅾 Discount Tire, **S** 🅡 Shell, 🍴 Happy's Pizza, 🅾 AT&T
11	Evergreen Rd, **S** 🏠 Hawthorn Suites
10	US 24, Telegraph Rd, **N** 🅡 Marathon, Mobil, Sunoco, 🍴 Baja Fresh, Copper Canyon Rest., Denny's, Fat Burger, 5 Guys Burgers, Pottbelly, Quizno's, Starbucks, Wendy's, 🏠 Embassy Suites, Hampton Inn, Red Roof Inn, 🅾 AT&T, Belle Tire, Best Buy, Buick/GMC, Chrysler/Dodge/Jeep, Ford, Honda, Hyundai, Lexus, Lincoln, Lowe's, Meijer/dsl, Michael's, Nissan, Office Depot, Petsmart, Subaru, Verizon, mall, **S** 🅡 Mobil, Sunoco, 🍴 Big Boy, Kerry's Koney Island, 🏠 Best Western, Candlewood Suites, Courtyard, Holiday Resort Hotel, Marriott
8	MI 10, Lodge Fwy
7	American Dr (from eb), **S** 🏠 Extended Stay America, Hilton Garden
5	Orchard Lake Rd, Farmington Hills, **N** 🅡 Marathon, Mobil/dsl, Shell, 🍴 Arby's, Camelia's Mexican, Coney Island, Hong Hua Chinese, Jet's Pizza, Jimmy John's, Roberto's Rest., Ruby Tuesday, Starbucks, Steak&Tavern, Subway, Wendy's, 🏠 Comfort Inn, Courtyard, Extended Stay America, Fairfield Inn, 🅾 Discount Tire, to St Mary's Coll
1	(from wb), I-96 W, I-275 S, to MI 5, Grand River Ave

MINNESOTA

INTERSTATE 35

Exit	Services
260mm	I-35 begins/ends on MN 61 in Duluth.
259	MN 61, London Rd, to Two Harbors, North Shore, **W** 🅡 BP, Holiday/dsl, ICO/dsl, 🍴 Blackwoods Grill, Burger King, Dunn Bros Coffee, KFC, McDonald's, Perkins, Pizza Hut, Subway, Taco John's, Wendy's, 🏠 Edgewater Inn, 🅾 vet
258	21st Ave E (from nb), to U of MN at Duluth, same as 259
256b	Mesaba Ave, Superior St, **E** 🅡 ICO/DQ, 🍴 Bellicio's, Caribou Coffee, Famous Dave's BBQ, Grandma's Grill, Grizzly's, Greenmill Rest., Little Angie's Cantina, Old Chicago, Red Lobster, Smokehouse Rest., Subway, Timberlodge Steaks, 🏠 Canal Park Lodge, Comfort Suites, Hampton Inn, Hawthorn Suites, Inn at Lake Superior, Suites Motel, The Inn, **W** 🏠 Holiday Inn, Radisson, Sheraton
256a	Michigan St, **E** waterfront, **W** 🍴, downtown
255a	US 53 N (exits left from nb), downtown, mall, **W** 🅾 Auto Value Parts, Kia
255b	I-535 spur, to Wisconsin
254	27th Ave W, **W** 🅡 Holiday/Burger King/dsl, Spur/dsl, 🍴 Duluth Grill, Little Caesars, Quiznos, Subway, 🏠 Motel 6, 🅾 USPO
253b	40th Ave W, **W** 🅡 BP/dsl/24hr, 🍴 Perkins, 🏠 Comfort Inn, Super 8
253a	US 2 E, US 53, to Wisconsin
252	Central Ave, W Duluth, **W** 🅡 Holiday/dsl, Little Store/dsl, 🍴 China King Buffet, Domino's, Jade Fountain Rest., KFC, McDonald's, Mr D's Grill, Pizza Hut, Sammy's Café, Subway, Taco John's, 🅾 Advance Parts, $Tree, K-Mart, Menards, O'Reilly Parts, Save-a-Lot Foods, Super 1

Exit	Services
252	Continued
	Foods, Walgreens, vet
251b	MN 23 S, Grand Ave
251a	Cody St, **E** 🏠 Allyndale Motel, 🅾 zoo
250	US 2 W (from sb), to Grand Rapids, **1/2 mi W** 🅡 Holiday/dsl, Mobil/dsl/LP, 🍴 Blackwoods Grill, 🏠 AmericInn
249	Boundary Ave, Skyline Pkwy, **E** 🅡 Holiday/McDonald's/dsl, 🏠 Country Inn&Suites, 🅾 to ski area, to Spirit Mtn RA, **W** 🆁🆂 **both lanes, full ♿ facilities, info, 🍴, 🛒 litter barrels, vending,** 🅡 Little Store/dsl/E-85/24hr, 🍴 Blackwoods Grill, 🏠 AmericInn, Best Value Inn
246	rd 13, Midway Rd, Nopeming, **W** 🅡 Armor/dsl, 🍴 Dry Dock Rest.
245	rd 61, **E** 🍴 Buffalo House Rest./camping
242	rd 1, Esko, Thomson, **E** 🅡 BP/dsl
239.5mm	St Louis River
239	MN 45, to Cloquet, Scanlon, **E** 🅾 Jay Cooke SP, KOA (May-Oct), **W** 🅡 Holiday, 🍴 Pantry Rest., Trapper Pete's Steaks, 🏠 Golden Gate Motel, 🅾🍴, camping, dsl repair
237	MN 33, Cloquet, **1 mi W** 🅡 BP, Lemon Tree/dsl, Murphy USA/dsl, 🍴 Applebee's, Arby's, DQ, Erbert&Gerberts, Little Caesars, McDonald's, Papa Murphy's, Perkins, Pizza Hut, South Gate Pizza, Subway, Taco John's/Stake Escape, Wendy's, 🏠 AmericInn, Super 8, 🅾 🍴, AT&T, AutoZone, Chrysler/Dodge/Jeep, $Tree, Family$, Ford, NAPA, Super 1 Foods, Verizon, Walmart/Subway, White Drug
236mm	**weigh sta both lanes**
235	MN 210, to Cromwell, Carlton, **E** 🅡 Armor Fuel, BP/rest./dsl, Spur/dsl/24hr, 🍴 Spirits Rest., 🏠 AmericInn, Royal Pines Motel, 🅾 to Jay Cooke SP, **W** 🅾 Black Bear Casino/Hotel/rest.

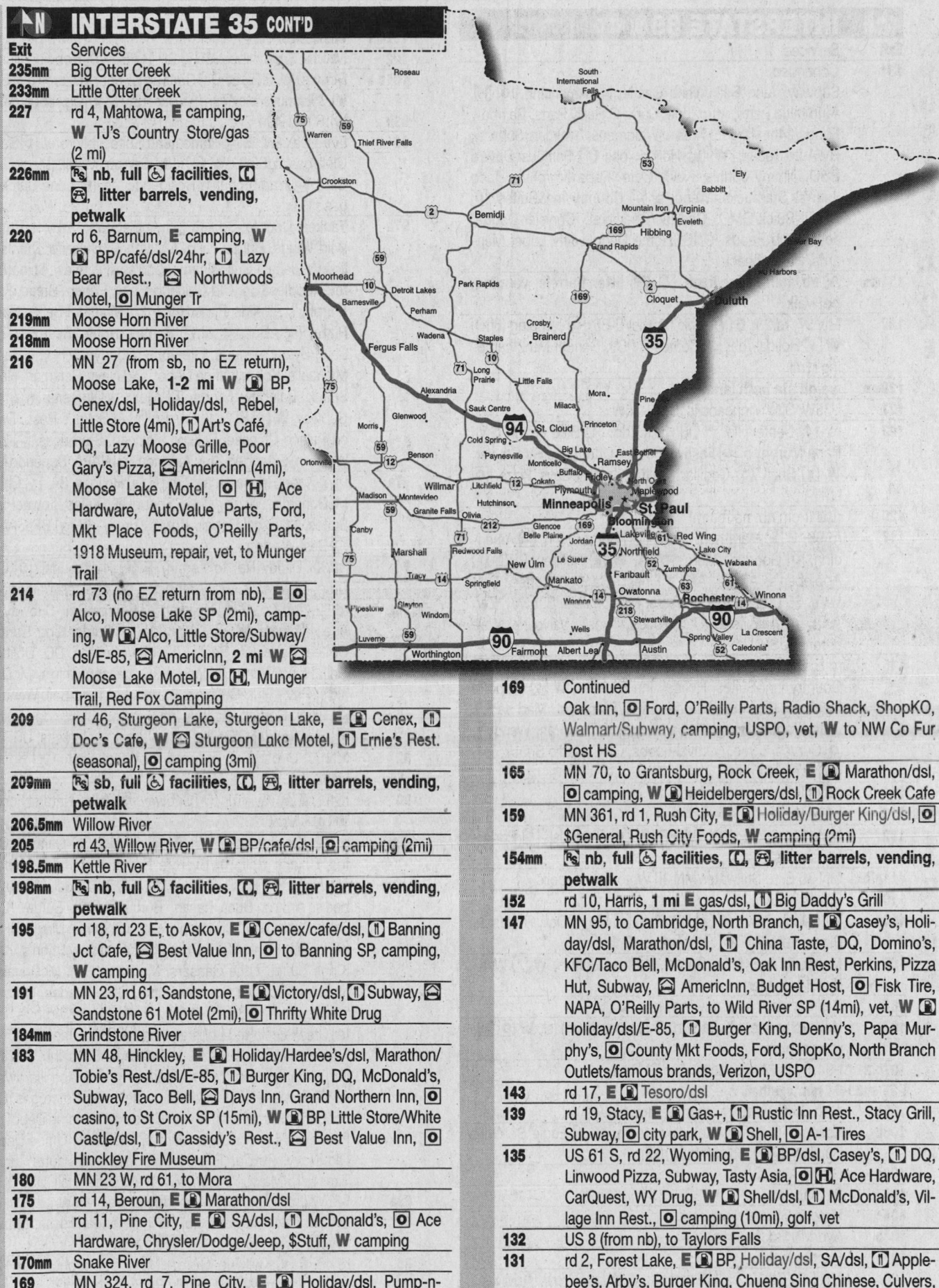

INTERSTATE 35 CONT'D

Exit	Services
235mm	Big Otter Creek
233mm	Little Otter Creek
227	rd 4, Mahtowa, **E** camping, **W** TJ's Country Store/gas (2 mi)
226mm	🆁🆂 nb, full 🚻 facilities, 🅲, 🏞, litter barrels, vending, petwalk
220	rd 6, Barnum, **E** camping, **W** 💷 BP/café/dsl/24hr, 🍴 Lazy Bear Rest., 🏨 Northwoods Motel, 🅾 Munger Tr
219mm	Moose Horn River
218mm	Moose Horn River
216	MN 27 (from sb, no EZ return), Moose Lake, **1-2 mi W** 💷 BP, Cenex/dsl, Holiday/dsl, Rebel, Little Store (4mi), 🍴 Art's Café, DQ, Lazy Moose Grille, Poor Gary's Pizza, 🏨 AmericInn (4mi), Moose Lake Motel, 🅾 🅷 Ace Hardware, AutoValue Parts, Ford, Mkt Place Foods, O'Reilly Parts, 1918 Museum, repair, vet, to Munger Trail
214	rd 73 (no EZ return from nb), **E** 🅾 Alco, Moose Lake SP (2mi), camping, **W** 💷 Alco, Little Store/Subway/dsl/E-85, 🏨 AmericInn, 2 mi **W** 🏨 Moose Lake Motel, 🅾 🅷, Munger Trail, Red Fox Camping
209	rd 46, Sturgeon Lake, Sturgeon Lake, **E** 💷 Cenex, 🍴 Doc's Cafe, **W** 🏨 Sturgeon Lake Motel, 🍴 Ernie's Rest. (seasonal), 🅾 camping (3mi)
209mm	🆁🆂 sb, full 🚻 facilities, 🅲, 🏞, litter barrels, vending, petwalk
206.5mm	Willow River
205	rd 43, Willow River, **W** 💷 BP/cafe/dsl, 🅾 camping (2mi)
198.5mm	Kettle River
198mm	🆁🆂 nb, full 🚻 facilities, 🅲, 🏞, litter barrels, vending, petwalk
195	rd 18, rd 23 E, to Askov, **E** 💷 Cenex/cafe/dsl, 🍴 Banning Jct Cafe, 🏨 Best Value Inn, 🅾 to Banning SP, camping, **W** camping
191	MN 23, rd 61, Sandstone, **E** 💷 Victory/dsl, 🍴 Subway, 🏨 Sandstone 61 Motel (2mi), 🅾 Thrifty White Drug
184mm	Grindstone River
183	MN 48, Hinckley, **E** 💷 Holiday/Hardee's/dsl, Marathon/Tobie's Rest./dsl/E-85, 🍴 Burger King, DQ, McDonald's, Subway, Taco Bell, 🏨 Days Inn, Grand Northern Inn, 🅾 casino, to St Croix SP (15mi), **W** 💷 BP, Little Store/White Castle/dsl, 🍴 Cassidy's Rest., 🏨 Best Value Inn, 🅾 Hinckley Fire Museum
180	MN 23 W, rd 61, to Mora
175	rd 14, Beroun, **E** 💷 Marathon/dsl
171	rd 11, Pine City, **E** 💷 SA/dsl, 🍴 McDonald's, 🅾 Ace Hardware, Chrysler/Dodge/Jeep, $Stuff, **W** camping
170mm	Snake River
169	MN 324, rd 7, Pine City, **E** 💷 Holiday/dsl, Pump-n-Munch/dsl, 🍴 A&W, DQ, KFC, Pizza Hut, Subway, 🏨 Old

Exit	Services
169	**Continued** Oak Inn, 🅾 Ford, O'Reilly Parts, Radio Shack, ShopKO, Walmart/Subway, camping, USPO, vet, **W** to NW Co Fur Post HS
165	MN 70, to Grantsburg, Rock Creek, **E** 💷 Marathon/dsl, 🅾 camping, **W** 💷 Heidelbergers/dsl, 🍴 Rock Creek Cafe
159	MN 361, rd 1, Rush City, **E** 💷 Holiday/Burger King/dsl, 🅾 $General, Rush City Foods, **W** camping (2mi)
154mm	🆁🆂 nb, full 🚻 facilities, 🅲, 🏞, litter barrels, vending, petwalk
152	rd 10, Harris, 1 mi **E** gas/dsl, 🍴 Big Daddy's Grill
147	MN 95, to Cambridge, North Branch, **E** 💷 Casey's, Holiday/dsl, Marathon/dsl, 🍴 China Taste, DQ, Domino's, KFC/Taco Bell, McDonald's, Oak Inn Rest, Perkins, Pizza Hut, Subway, 🏨 AmericInn, Budget Host, 🅾 Fisk Tire, NAPA, O'Reilly Parts, to Wild River SP (14mi), vet, **W** 💷 Holiday/dsl/E-85, 🍴 Burger King, Denny's, Papa Murphy's, 🅾 County Mkt Foods, Ford, ShopKo, North Branch Outlets/famous brands, Verizon, USPO
143	rd 17, **E** 💷 Tesoro/dsl
139	rd 19, Stacy, **E** 💷 Gas+, 🍴 Rustic Inn Rest., Stacy Grill, Subway, 🅾 city park, **W** 💷 Shell, 🅾 A-1 Tires
135	US 61 S, rd 22, Wyoming, **E** 💷 BP/dsl, Casey's, 🍴 DQ, Linwood Pizza, Subway, Tasty Asia, 🅾 🅷 Ace Hardware, CarQuest, WY Drug, **W** 💷 Shell/dsl, 🍴 McDonald's, Village Inn Rest., 🅾 camping (10mi), golf, vet
132	US 8 (from nb), to Taylors Falls
131	rd 2, Forest Lake, **E** 💷 BP, Holiday/dsl, SA/dsl, 🍴 Applebee's, Arby's, Burger King, Chueng Sing Chinese, Culvers, KFC, McDonald's, Papa John's, Perkins, Quack's Cafe,

H I N C K L E Y

🅐 = gas   🍽 = food   🛏 = lodging   🄾 = other   🆁🆂 = rest stop   Copyright 2014 - The NEXT Exit ®

MN

F O R E S T   L A K E

S T   P A U L

INTERSTATE 35 CONT'D

Exit	Services
131	Continued Subway, Taco Bell, White Castle, 🛏 AmericInn, 🄾 🄷, AutoValue Parts, AutoZone, CarX, O'Reilly Parts, Rainbow Foods/24hr, Target, Tires+, Walgreens, Walmart/Subway, RV/Auto repair, **W** 🅐 Holiday/dsl, 🍽 Famous Dave's BBQ, Jimmy John's, Key's Cafe, Papa Murphy's, Taco John's, Starbucks, Wendy's, 🛏 Country Inn&Suites, 🄾 AT&T, Buick/GMC, Cadillac/Chevrolet, Chrysler/Dodge/Jeep, Cub Foods, GNC, Home Depot, Jiffy Lube, Menards, Radio Shack
131mm	🆁🆂 sb, full 🅰 facilities, 🄲, 🄰, litter barrels, vending, petwalk
129	MN 97, rd 23, **E** 🅐 Kwik Trip/dsl/E-85, 🄾 camping (6mi), **W** 🅐 Holiday/dsl, 🄾 Coates RV Ctr, Gander Mtn., camping (1mi)
128mm	weigh sta both lanes
127	I-35W, S to Minneapolis. See I-35W.
123	rd 14, Centerville, **E** 🅐 Kwik Trip, 🍽 Blue Heron Grill, Papa Murphy's, 🄾 Festival Foods, Otter Lake RV Ctr, vet, **W** 🅐 Shell, 🍽 Cadillac Grill, DQ, WiseGuys Pizza, 🄾 NAPA
120	rd J (from nb, no return)
117	rd 96, **E** 🅐 Marathon, SA/dsl, 🍽 Burger King, 🛏 AmericInn, 🄾 Goodyear/auto, NAPA, **W** 🅐 Holiday, PDQ, 🍽 Applebee's, Arby's, Asia's Finest, Caribou Coffee, Culver's, $5 Pizza, Little Caesars, McDonald's, Subway, Zen Asia, 🄾 AutoZone, Cub Foods, Tires+, Valvoline, Walgreens, USPO
115	rd E, **E** 🅐 BP/repair, SA/dsl, 🍽 Jimmy's Rest., Perkins, 🛏 Country Inn&Suites, Holiday Inn Express, **W** 🍽 Chipotle Mexican, Dunn Bros Coffee, KFC/Pizza Hut, Mad Jack's Cafe, Panera Bread, Papa Murphy's, Thai Pan, Wendy's, 🄾 Curves, $Tree, Festival Foods, GNC, Radio Shack, Target, Walmart/auto
114	I-694 E (exits left from sb)
113	I-694 W
112	Little Canada Rd, **E** 🅐 BP, **W** 🅐 Clark/dsl, 🍽 Porterhouse Rest
111a/b	MN 36 E, to Stillwater/MN 36 W, to Minneapolis
110b	Roselawn Ave
110a	Wheelock Pkwy, **E** 🅐 BP, Gulf, 🍽 May's Deli, Roadside Pizza, Subway, **W** 🍽 Champps Grill
109	Maryland Ave, **E** 🅐 SA/dsl, 🍽 Taco John's, **W** 🍽 Wendy's, 🄾 K-Mart
108	Pennsylvania Ave, downtown
107c	University Ave, downtown, **E** 🅐 Marathon/dsl, **W** 🄾 🄷, to st capitol
107b a	I-94, W to Minneapolis, E to St Paul.
I-35 and I-94 run together.	
106c	11th St (from nb), Marion St, downtown
106b	Kellogg Blvd (from nb), downtown, **E** 🍽 Eagle St. Grill, Subway, 🛏 Holiday Inn, 🄾 🄷
106a	Grand Ave, **E** 🄷
105	St Clair Ave
104c	Victoria St, Jefferson Ave
104b	Ayd Mill Rd (from nb)
104a	Randolph Ave
103b	MN 5, W 7th St, **E** 🍽 Burger King, **W** 🅐 SA/dsl, 🄾 Midas, USPO

Exit	Services
103a	Shepard Rd (from nb)
102mm	Mississippi River
102	MN 13, Sibley Hwy, **W** 🅐 BP, Holiday/Subway
101b a	MN 110 W, **E** 🅐 BP, 🍽 Caribou Coffee, McDonald's, Subway, Teresa's Mexican, 🄾 Tuesday Morning, **W** 🅐 SA
99b a	I-494 W/I-494 E
98	Lone Oak Rd, **E** 🛏 Homestead Suites, Microtel, 🄾 Sam's Club/gas, USPO, **W** 🍽 Joe Senser's Grill, Magic Thai Café, 🛏 Hampton Inn, Residence Inn, 🄾 Lone Oak Mkt/gas
97b	Yankee Doodle Rd, **E** 🍽 Applebee's, Arby's, Buffalo Wild Wings, Burger King, Coldstone, Culver's, DQ, Houlihan's, Jake's Grill, Jimmy John's, KFC, New China Buffet, Noodles&Co, Old Chicago Pizza, Panera Bread, Papa Murphy's, Perkins, Pizza Hut, Pizza Man, Pot Bellys, Savoy Pizza, Taco Bell, 🄾 AT&T, Barnes&Noble, Best Buy, BigLots, Byerly's Foods, Firestone, Goodyear, Home Depot, Michael's, Kohl's, Office Depot, Old Navy, Petsmart, Radio Shack, Rainbow Foods, TJ Maxx, Walgreens, Walmart/Subway, **W** 🅐 BP/dsl, SA/dsl, 🍽 Al Baker's Rest., Dragon Palace Chinese, El Loro Mexican, Starbucks, 🛏 Best Western, Extended Stay America, 🄾 NAPA, Superior Auto
97a	Pilot Knob Rd, same as 97b, **E** 🅐 Holiday, SA, 🍽 Chili's, McDonald's, Wendy's, 🛏 SpringHill Suites, TownePlace Suites, 🄾 Excel Repair, Kohl's, Tires+, **W** 🅐 BP, SA/dsl, 🛏 Best Western
94	rd 30, Diffley Rd, to Eagan, **E** 🅐 Holiday/dsl, 🄾 CVS Drug, Kowalski's Mkt/Starbucks, **W** 🅐 Sinclair/Goodyear
93	rd 32, Cliff Rd, **E** 🅐 Holiday, 🍽 Bonfire Grill, Subway, 🄾 Ace Hardware, **W** 🅐 Holiday/dsl, 🍽 Burger King, Caribou Coffee, Caspers's Rest., Chipotle Mexican, DQ, Dolittle's Grill, Hong Wong Chinese, KFC, Leeann Chin's, McDonald's, Pizza Hut, Quiznos, Starbucks, Taco Bell, Wendy's, 🛏 Hilton Garden, Holiday Inn Express, Staybridge Suites, 🄾 Cub Foods, O'Reilly Parts, Target, Walgreens, USPO
92	MN 77, Cedar Ave, **E** Zoo, **1 mi W** access to Cliff Rd services
90	rd 11, **E** 🅐 KwikTrip, 🍽 Subway, 🄾 Valley Natural Foods, **W** 🅐 SA/dsl
88b	rd 42, Crystal Lake Rd, **E** 🅐 SA/dsl, 🍽 Caribou Coffee, Chianti Grill, 🄾 Byerly's Foods, Petsmart, Tuesday Morning, **W** 🅐 BP, Holiday/dsl, PDQ, SA/dsl, 🍽 Applebee's, Arby's, Buca Italian, Burger Jones, Burger King, Cam Ranh Bay, Champp's Grill, Chipotle Mexican, Ernie's Grill, HoneyBaked Ham, IHOP, Jimmy John's, KFC, Kings Buffet, Little Caesars, Macaroni Grill, McDonald's, Noodles&Co, Old Country Buffet, Olive Garden, Outback Steaks, Panera Bread, Papa John's, Papa Murphy's, Porter Creek Grill, Red Lobster, Roasted Pear, Taco Bell, TGIFriday's, Wendy's, 🛏 Best Western, Days Inn, Fairfield Inn, Hampton Inn, InTown Suites, 🄾 🄷, Ace Hardware, AT&T, Barnes&Noble, Cadillac, Chevrolet, Cotco/gas, Cub Foods, Dick's, Discount Tire, Gordman's, Home Depot, JC Penney, K-Mart, Kohl's, Macy's, Michael's, Office Depot, Old Navy, PetCo, Rainbow Foods, Sears/auto, Target, Tires+, TJ Maxx, Verizon, VW, Walgreens, mall, USPO
88a	I-35W (from nb), N to Minneapolis. See I-35W.
87	Crystal Lake Rd (from nb), **W** 🄾 Honda/Nissan, Mazda, Toyota/Scion, to Beaver Mtn ski area
86	rd 46, **E** 🅐 KwikTrip, SA/dsl, 🍽 KFC, Starbucks, 🄾 Harley-Davidson, **W** 🄾 O'Reilly Parts, auto repair
85	MN 50, **E** 🅐 F&F/dsl, SA/dsl, 🍽 Burger King, Caribou

⬆N INTERSTATE 35 CONT'D

Exit	Services
85	Continued
	Coffee, Culver's, DQ, Greenmill Rest., Jimmy John's, Lakeville Chinese, Pizza Hut, Starbucks, Subway, Taco Bell, Wendy's, 🏠 Comfort Inn, 🅞 CVS Drug, $Tree, Goodyear/auto, NTB, O'Reilly Parts, Rainbow Foods, Verizon, Walgreens, **W** 🅖 Holiday/dsl, 🍴 Cracker Barrel, Perkins, Pizza Ranch, 🏠 AmericInn, 🅞 Gander Mtn.
84	185th St W, Orchard Trail, **E** 🍴 Applebee's, Buffalo Wild Wings, Caribou Coffee, Quiznos, SawaJapan, 🅞 Best Buy, Marshall's, Target
81	rd 70, Lakeville, **E** 🅖 Holiday/dsl, 🍴 Baldy's BBQ, McDonald's, Subway, Tacoville, 🏠 Holiday Inn/rest, Motel 6, **W** 🍴 Harry's Cafe, 🅞 Walmart/Subway,
76	rd 2, Elko, **E** gas/dsl **W** 🍴 Endzone Grill, 🅞 Elko Speedway
76mm	🆁🆂 sb, full 🦽 facilities, 🅲, 🅿, litter barrels, vending, petwalk
69	MN 19, to Northfield, New Prague, 7 mi **E** 🅖 KwikTrip, 🍴 Applebee's, Big Steer Rest., Caribou Coffee, McDonald's, Quarterback Rest., Subway, Taco Bell, 🏠 AmericInn, College City Motel, Country Inn&Suites, Super 8, 🅞 🏥, Carleton Coll, St Olaf Coll, **W** 🅖 ⚑FLYING J/Subway/dsl/scales/24hr
68mm	🆁🆂 nb, full 🦽 facilities, 🅲, 🅿, litter barrels, vending, petwalk
66	rd 1, to Dundas, 1 mi **W** 🍴 Boonie's Grill
59	MN 21, Faribault, 0-2 mi **E** 🅖 BP/rest./dsl/scales/24hr, KwikTrip, 🍴 A&W, Arby's, Burger King, DQ, Hardee's, Joe's Cafe, KFC, Pizza Hut, Taco Bell, Taco John's, 🏠 AmericInn, Best Value Inn, Days Inn, Grandstay, 🅞 Aldi Foods, AT&T, Buick/Chevrolet/GMC, Chrysler/Dodge/Jeep, O'Reilly Parts, Satakah St Trail, repair, vet, **W** 🅞 Harley-Davidson, camping
56	MN 60, Faribault, same as 59, **E** 🅖 KwikTrip, 🍴 A&W, Arby's, Burger King, Great China Buffet, Hardee's, Jimmy John's, KFC, Little Caesars, McDonald's, Perkins, Pizza Hut, Subway, Taco John's, 🅞 🏥, Aldi Foods, AutoValue Parts, Buick/Chevrolet/GMC, Chrysler/Dodge/Jeep, Curves, Dodge, $Tree, Family$, Goodyear/auto, Hy-Vee Foods/gas, JC Penney, O'Reilly Parts, Radio Shack, Tires+, TrueValue, Verizon, Walmart, mall, **W** 🅖 Petro/dsl, 🍴 Country Kitchen, DQ, 🏠 Regency Inn, 🅞 Sakatah Lake SP, camping
55	rd 48, (from nb, no return), 1 mi **E** 🅖 KwikTrip, Mobil/dsl, SA/dsl, 🍴 A&W, Arby's, Broaster Rest., Burger King, DQ, KFC, Pizza Hut, Southern China Cafe, Subway, Taco John's, 🏠 AmericInn
48	rd 12, rd 23, Medford, **W** 🍴 McDonald's, 🅞 Outlet Mall/famous brands
45	rd 9, Clinton Falls, **W** 🅖 KwikTrip/dsl, 🍴 Caribou Coffee, Famous Dave's BBQ, Sportsman's Grille, Subway, TimberLodge Steaks, Wendy's, 🏠 Comfort Inn, Holiday Inn, 🅞 Cabela's Sporting Goods, Russell-Stover Candies, museum
43	rd 34, 26th St, Owatonna, **E** 🅞 Noble RV Ctr, **W** 🅞 🏥
42b a	US 14 W, rd 45, to Waseca, Owatonna, **E** 🍴 Kernel Rest., 🏠 Budget Host, 🅞 AutoZone, CashWise Foods, Chrysler/Dodge/Jeep, Ford/Lincoln, O'Reilly Parts, repair, vet, **W** 🅖 KwikTrip/dsl, 🍴 Big 10 Rest., Buffalo Wild Wings, Culver's, Eastwind Buffet, McDonald's, Olivia's Rest., Per

Exit	Services
42b a	Continued
	kins, 🏠 Best Budget Inn, Super 8, 🅞 $Tree, GNC, Kohl's, Lowe's, Radio Shack, Verizon, Walmart/Subway,
41	Bridge St, Owatonna, **E** 🅖 Holiday/dsl, 🍴 Applebee's, Arby's, Asian Kitchen, Burger King, DQ, Jimmy John's, KFC, Papa Murphy's, Quiznos, Starbucks, Subway, Taco Bell, 🏠 AmericInn, Country Inn&Suites, 🅞 🏥, Verizon, **W** 🅖 F&F/dsl, 🏠 Microtel, 🅞 Target
40	US 14 E, US 218, Owatonna, 1 mi **E** on rd 6 🍴 El Tequila Mexican, Godfather's, Taco John's, 🏠 Oakdale Motel, 🅞 🏥, Buick/Chevrolet, Curves, Hy-Vee Foods/dsl, Walgreens, WholesaleTire
38mm	Turtle Creek
35mm	🆁🆂 both lanes, full 🦽 facilities, 🅲, 🅿, litter barrels, vending, petwalk
34.5mm	Straight River
32	rd 4, Hope, 1/2 mi **E** camping, 1 mi **W** gas, food
26	MN 30, to Blooming Prairie, Ellendale, **E** 🅖 Cenex/pizza/dsl
22	rd 35, to Hartland, Geneva, 1 mi **E** gas, food
18	MN 251, to Hollandale, Clarks Grove, **W** 🍴 BP/dsl/LP, 🅞 camping
17mm	weigh sta, both lanes
13b a	I-90, W to Sioux Falls, E to Austin, **W** 🏥
12	US 65 S (from sb), Lp 35, Albert Lea, same as 11
11	rd 46, Albert Lea, **E** 🅖 ❤Loves/Wendy's/dsl/scales/24hr, TA/Coldstone/Pizza Hut/dsl/scales/24hr/@, 🍴 McDonald's, 🏠 Comfort Inn, Holiday Inn Express, 🅞 KOA (may-oct/6mi), dsl repair, **W** 🅖 KwikTrip, Shell/dsl, 🍴 Big John's, Burger King, Casa Zamora Mexican, GreenMill Rest., KFC, Perkins, Pizza Hut, Subway, Taco John's, Trumble's Rest., Wok'n Roll, 🏠 Best Value Inn, Country Inn&Suites, Countryside Inn, Knights Inn, Super 8, 🅞 🏥 Advance Parts, AutoValue Parts, AutoZone, Buick/GMC, CarQuest, Chrysler/Dodge/Jeep, $Tree, Ford, Home Depot, Honda, NAPA, Nissan/VW, O'Reilly Parts, Radio Shack, Volvo, Walmart/Subway, to Myre-Big Island SP
9mm	Albert Lea Lake
8	US 65, Lp 35US 65, Lp 35, Albert Lea, 2 mi **W** 🅖 Freeborn City Co-op/dsl, 🍴 DQ, Hardee's
5	rd 13, to Glenville, Twin Lakes, 3 mi **W** camping
2	rd 5
1mm	Welcome Ctr nb, full 🦽 facilities, 🅲, 🅿, litter barrels, vending, petwalk
0mm	Minnesota/Iowa state line

⬆N INTERSTATE 35 WEST

Exit	Services
41mm	I-35W begins/ends on I-35, exit 127.

☒ = gas ⑪ = food ⌂ = lodging ⊡ = other ℞ = rest stop Copyright 2014 - The NEXT Exit ®

⬆N INTERSTATE 35 WEST CONT'D

Exit	Services
36	rd 23, **E** ☒ Holiday/dsl, ⌂ Country Inn&Suites, **W** ☒ US/dsl, ⑪ Caribou Coffee, DQ, McDonald's, Subway, ⌂ Hampton Inn, ⊡ Discount Tire, Kohl's, Super Target
33	rd 17, Lexington Ave, **E** ☒ F&F/dsl, Holiday, **1 mi E** ⑪ Burger King, McDonald's, **W** ⑪ Applebee's, Arby's, Bonfire Rest., Caribou Coffee, Green Mill Rest., Quizno's, Taco Bell/LJ Silver, Wendy's, Zantigo's Mexican, ⊡ Cub Foods, GNC, Home Depot, Michael's, Radio Shack, Walgreens, Walmart
32	95th Ave NE, to Lexington, Circle Pines, **W** Nat Sports Ctr
31b a	Lake Dr, **E** ☒ Shell/dsl, ⑪ Quizno's, Red Ginger Asian, Steamin Bean Coffee, ⌂ Country Inn&Suites
30	US 10 W, MN 118, to MN 65
29	rd I
28c b	rd 10, rd H, **W** ☒ BP, ⑪ KFC, LJ Silver/Taco Bell, McDonald's, Mermaid Café, RJ Riches Rest., ⌂ AmericInn, Days Inn, ⊡ NAPA, carwash
28a	MN 96
27b a	I-694 E and W
26	rd E2, **W** ☒ Exxon/dsl, ⑪ Jimmy John's, Limu Coffee
25b	MN 88, to Roseville (no EZ return to sb) same as 25a
25a	rd D (from nb), **E** ☒ BP/dsl, ⑪ Blimpie, ⌂ Courtyard, Fairfield Inn, Residence Inn, **W** ☒ PDQ, SA, ⑪ Barley John's, Caribou Coffee, Jake's Café, McDonald's, New Hong Kong, Perkins/24hr, Sarpino's Italian, Subway
24	rd C, **E** ⑪ Burger King, India Palace Rest., Joe Senser's Rest., ⌂ Days Inn, Motel 6, Radisson, ⊡ USPO, **W** ⌂ Holiday Inn Express, ⊡ Chevrolet/GMC, Chrysler/Dodge/Jeep, Volvo
23b	Cleveland Ave, MN 36
23a	MN 280, Industrial Blvd (from sb)
22	MN 280, Industrial Blvd (from nb), **E** ⌂ Ramada Plaza
21b a	Broadway St, Stinson Blvd, **E** Ford/Isuzu Trucks, **W** ⑪ Baja Sol, Burger King, Caribou Coffee, Cousins Subs, Leeann Chin, McDonald's, Pizza Hut/Taco Bell, ⊡ GNC, Home Depot, Old Navy, Rainbow Foods/24hr, Target
19	E Hennepin (from nb)
18	US 52, 4th St SE, University Ave, to U of MN, **E** ☒ BP/repair
17c	11th St, Washington Ave, **E** ⌂ Holiday Inn, **W** ☒ Mobil, ⊡ Ⓗ, Goodyear, to Metrodome
17b	I-94 W (from sb)
17a	MN 55, Hiawatha
16b a	I-94 (from nb), E to St Paul, W to St Cloud, to MN 65
15	31st St (from nb), Lake St, **E** ⑪ McDonald's, Taco Bell, ⊡ Auto Zone, **W** Ⓗ
14	35th St, 36th St
13	46th St
13mm	Minnehaha Creek
12b	Diamond Lake Rd
12a	60th St (from sb), **W** ☒ Mobil, ⊡ Cub Foods
11b	MN 62 E, to 🔄
11a	Lyndale Ave (from sb)
10b	MN 62 W, 58th St
10a	rd 53, 66th St, **E** ☒ SA
9c	76th St (from sb)
9b a	I-494, MN 5, to 🔄
8	82nd St, **E** ⊡ BMW, **W** ⑪ Caribou Coffee, Jimmy Johns, Red Lobster, Sonic, Timberlodge Steaks, Wendy's, ⌂ Embassy Suites, ⊡ Chevrolet, Chrysler/Dodge/Jeep,

MN (side tab)

MINNEAPOLIS (side tab)

Exit	Services
8	Continued Hyundai, Infiniti, Kia, Kohl's, TJ Maxx, Walgreens
7b	90th St
7a	94th St, **E** ⊡ Goodyear/auto, **W** ⌂ Holiday Inn
6	rd 1, 98th St, **E** ☒ Holiday, ⑪ Applebee's, Bakers Square, Burger King, Coldstone, Domino's, Golden Wok, Jimmy John's, Leeann Chen, McDonald's, Starbucks, Wendy's, White Castle, **Urgent Care**, Bloomington Drug, Festival Foods, Ford, Radio Shack, Walgreens, **W** ☒ SA/dsl, ⑪ Denny's
5	106th St
5mm	Minnesota River
4b	113th St, Black Dog Rd
4a	Cliff Rd, **E** Dodge, Subaru, **W** VW
3b a	MN 13, Shakopee, Canterbury Downs, **E** ⌂ Select Inn
2	Burnsville Pkwy, **E** ☒ BP, Marathon, ⑪ Bumpers Grill, **W** ☒ Holiday, ⑪ Gourmet Chinese, Hooters, Perkins, TimberLodge Steaks, ⌂ Best Value Inn, LivInn, Prime Rate Motel, Travelodge, ⊡ Best Buy, Goodyear/auto, vet
1	rd 42, Crystal Lake Rd, **E** ⑪ Chianti Grill, ⊡ Byerly's Foods, PetsMart, Tuesday Morning, **W** ☒ Holiday/dsl, SA, ⑪ Applebee's, Arby's/Sbarro's, Azteca Mexican, Buca Italian, Burger King, Cam Aranh Bay, Champp's Grill, Chili's, Dakota County Grill, HoneyBaked Ham, IHOP, Jimmy John's, KFC, Kings Buffet, Macaroni Grill, McDonald's, Old Country Buffet, Olive Garden, Outback Steaks, Panera Bread, Papa John's, Papa Murphy's, Qdoba Mexican, Red Lobster, Roasted Pear, Starbucks, Taco Bell/Pizza Hut, TGIFriday's, Wendy's, ⌂ Days Inn, Fairfield Inn, Hampton Inn, Holiday Inn, InTown Suites, ⊡ Ⓗ AT&T, Barnes&Noble, Best Buy, Cadillac, Chevrolet, Cub Foods, Discount Tire, Goodyear/auto, Home Depot, JC Penney, K-Mart, Kohl's, Macy's, Michael's, PetCo, Rainbow Foods, Sears/auto, Target, Tires+, Walgreens, mall, USPO
0mm	I-35W begins/ends on I-35, exit 88a.

⬆E INTERSTATE 90

Exit	Services
278mm	Minnesota/Wisconsin state line, Mississippi River
276	US 14, US 61, to MN 16, La Crescent, **N Welcome Ctr wb, full ♿ facilities, info, ⓒ, ☕, litter barrels, vending, petwalk, S** ☒ Kwik Trip (1mi)
273b a	Dresbach
271	Dakota
270	US 14, US 61, to Winona (from wb), **N** to OL Kipp SP/camping
267	rd 12, Nodine, **N** ⊡ Great River Bluffs SP, camping, **S** ☒ Kwik Trip/dsl/Hearty Platter/scales/24hr/@
261mm	weigh sta both lanes
258	MN 76, to Houston, Ridgeway, Witoka, **N** gas, **S** camping
252	MN 43 N, to Winona, **7 mi N** ⑪ Taco Bell, ⌂ Express Inn, Holiday Inn, Holiday Inn Express, Quality Inn, ⊡ Ⓗ
249	MN 43 S, to Rushford, **N** ⊡ Peterbilt Trucks/repair
244mm	℞ eb, full ♿ facilities, ⓒ, ☕, litter barrels, vending, petwalk
242	rd 29, Lewiston
233	MN 74, to Chatfield, St Charles, **N** ☒ Kwik Trip/LP/24hr (2mi), ⑪ A&W (2mi), Subway (2mi), ⊡ Whitewater SP, **S** ☒ BP/Amish Ovens Rest./dsl/RV dump/LP, ⊡ auto/truck repair
229	rd 10, Dover
224	MN 42, rd 7, Eyota, **N** ☒ KwikTrip/dsl/E-85 (3mi), ⑪ Country Cafe

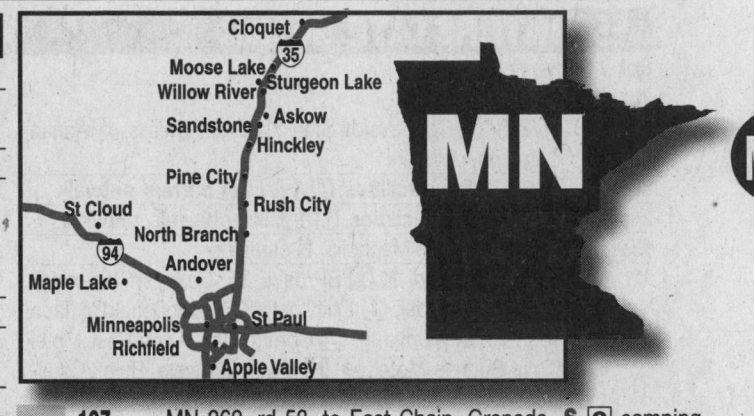

◀▶E INTERSTATE 90 CONT'D

Exit	Services
222mm	🅿️ wb, full 👨‍🦽 facilities, 🚻, 🛢, litter barrels, vending, **petwalk**
218	US 52, to Rochester, **S** 🅶 BP/dsl, 🅾 KOA (Mar-Oct) (1mi)
209b a	US 63, MN 30, to Rochester, Stewartville, **8-10 mi N** 🛏 Clarion, Comfort Inn, EconoLodge, Hampton Inn, Holiday Inn, Relax Inn, **1 mi S** 🅶 KwikTrip/dsl, 🍴 DQ, Subway, 🛏 AmericInn
205	rd 6
202mm	🅿️ eb, full 👨‍🦽 facilities, 🚻, 🛢, litter barrels, vending, **petwalk**
193	MN 16, Dexter, **N** 🅶 BP/Oasis Rest./dsl
189	rd 13, to Elkton
187	rd 20, **S** Jelly Stone Camping
183	MN 56, to Rose Creek, Brownsdale, **S** 🅶 Freeborn County Co-op/dsl/LP
181	28th St NE
180b a	US 218, 21st St NE, to Austin, Oakland Place, **S** 🅶 Shell, 🛏 Rodeway Inn
179	11th Dr NE, to Austin, **N** 🅶 BP/rest./dsl/24hr
178b	6th St NE, to Austin, **S** Spam Museum
178a	4th St NW, **N** 🍴 Culver's, Perkins, Torge's Grille, 🛏 AmericInn, Days Inn, Holiday Inn 🅾 AutoValue Parts, Buick/Chevrolet/GMC, vet, **S** 🅶 KwikTrip/dsl, 🍴 A&W, Burger King, Subway, 🅾 🏥
177	US 218 N, to Owatonna, Austin, Mapleview, **N** 🍴 Applebee's, Arby's, China Star, El Patron Mexican, KFC/LJ Silver, King Buffet, Quiznos, Wendy's, 🅾 Aldi Foods, $Tree, Family$, Hy-Vee Foods/gas, JoAnn Fabrics, O'Reilly Parts, Radio Shack, ShopKO, Staples, Target, Verizon, Walmart/Subway, Younkers, mall, **S** 🅶 Sinclair/McDonald's/dsl, 🛏 Super 8
175	MN 105, rd 46, to Oakland Rd, **N** 🛏 Countryside Inn, **S** 🅶 BP, Shell/dsl, 🅾 Chrysler/Dodge/Jeep, Ford/Lincoln, camping, vet
171mm	🅿️ wb, full 👨‍🦽 facilities, 🚻, 🛢, litter barrels, **petwalk**
166	rd 46, Oakland Rd, **N** 🅾 KOA/LP, golf (par3)
163	rd 26, Hayward, **S** 🅶 Freeborn County Co-op/dsl, 🍴 Pizza Hut (4mi), Trails Rest. (4mi), 🅾 Myre-Big Island SP, camping
161.5mm	🅿️ eb, full 👨‍🦽 facilities, 🚻, 🛢 litter barrels, **petwalk**
159b a	I-35, N to Twin Cities, S to Des Moines
157	rd 22, Albert Lea, **N** 🅾 Kenworth, **S** 🍴 Applebee's, Arby's, DQ, Herberger's, McDonald's, Pizza Ranch, Plaza Morina Mexican, 🛏 AmericInn, Best Western, 🅾 🏥, Ace Hardware, Chevrolet, GNC, Harley-Davidson, Hy-Vee Foods/gas/24hr, ShopKO, Verizon, mall
154	MN 13, to US 69, to Manchester, Albert Lea, **N** 🅶 SA/dsl, **3 mi S** 🛏 BelAire Motel
146	MN 109, to Wells, Alden, **S** 🅶 BP/dsl/rest., Freeborn Co-Op Gas/dsl/E-85, 🅾 truck/dsl repair
138	MN 22, to Wells, Kiester, **S** camping
134	MN 253, rd 21, to Bricelyn, MN Lake
128	MN 254, rd 17, Frost, Easton
119	US 169, to Winnebago, Blue Earth, **S** 🅶 Shell/dsl, Sinclair/dsl, 🍴 Country Kitchen, DQ, McDonald's, Pizza Hut, Subway, 🛏 AmericInn, Super 8, 🅾 🏥, $General, Walmart, Jolly Green Giant, camping
119mm	🅿️ both lanes, full 👨‍🦽 facilities, 🚻, 🛢, litter barrels, **petwalk, playground**
113	rd 1, Guckeen
107	MN 262, rd 53, to East Chain, Granada, **S** 🅾 camping (May-Oct) (1mi), gas/dsl
102	MN 15, to Madelia, Fairmont, **N** 🅶 Verizon, Walmart/Subway, **0-2 mi S** 🅶 BP, Cenex/dsl, ProFuel/dsl, SA/dsl/24hr, 🍴 Arby's, Burger King, China Buffet, DQ, Green Mill Rest., McDonald's, Perkins, Pizza Ranch, Ranch Family Rest., Subway, Taco John's, 🛏 Budget Inn, Comfort Inn, Hampton Inn, Holiday Inn, Super 8, 🅾 🏥, Ace Hardware, CarQuest, Chevrolet, Chrysler/Dodge/Jeep, $Tree, Fareway Foods, Ford, Freightliner, Goodyear/auto, Hy-Vee Foods, JC Penney, NAPA, Radio Shack, Sears, ShopKO, Walgreens, USPO, camping, auto repair
99	rd 39, Fairmont, services **2 mi S**
93	MN 263, rd 27, Welcome, **1/2 mi S** 🅶 Cenex, camping
87	MN 4, Sherburn, **N** 🅾 Everett Park Camping, **S** 🅶 Cenex, Kum&Go/Subway/dsl/E-85
80	rd 29, Alpha
73	US 71, Jackson, **N** 🅶 SA/dsl, 🍴 Burger King, 🛏 EconoLodge, Super 8, 🅾 KOA, to Kilen Woods SP, **S** 🅶 BP/DQ, Casey's, 🍴 Embers Rest., Pizza Ranch, Subway, 🛏 AmericInn, Budget Host, Earth Inn, Prairie Winds Motel, 🅾 🏥, Ace Hardware, Family$, Buick/Chevrolet, Chrysler/Dodge/Jeep, Sunshine Foods, city park, to Spirit Lake
72.5mm	W Fork Des Moines River
72mm	🅿️ wb, full 👨‍🦽 facilities, 🚻, 🛢, litter barrels, vending, **petwalk**
69mm	🅿️ eb, full 👨‍🦽 facilities, 🚻, 🛢, litter barrels, vending, **petwalk**
64	MN 86, Lakefield, **N** 🏥, gas/dsl, food, camping, to Kilen SP (12mi)
57	rd 9, to Heron Lake, Spafford
50	MN 264, rd 1, to Brewster, Round Lake, **S** camping
47	rd 3 (from eb), No return
46mm	weigh sta eb
45	MN 60, Worthington, **N** 🅶 BP/Blueline Cafe/dsl/scales, **S** 🅶 Casey's, Shell/dsl/scales/24hr, 🅾 camping, truckwash
43	US 59, Worthington, **N** 🅶 Mobil/dsl, 🛏 Travelodge, **S** 🅶 Casey's, Cenex/dsl, Shell, 🍴 Arby's, Burger King, DQ, Ground Round, Hardee's, KFC, McDonald's, Perkins, Pizza Hut, Pizza Ranch, Subway, Taco John's, 🛏 AmericInn, Holiday Inn Express, 🅾 🏥, Ace Hardware, CarQuest, Fareway Foods, F&F, Ford, Hy-Vee Foods/dsl, Buick/Cadillac/Chevrolet, $General, $Tree, JC Penney, NAPA, O'Reilly Parts, Radio Shack, ShopKO, Walgreens, Walmart/Subway,
42	MN 266, rd 25, to Reading, **S** 🛏 Days Inn, Super 8
33	rd 13, to Wilmont, Rushmore
26	MN 91, Adrian, **S** 🅶 Cenex/dsl, Kum&Go/Subway/dsl/E-

Side labels: AUSTIN · ALBERT LEA · FAIRMONT · WORTHINGTON

MN

◄► INTERSTATE 90 CONT'D

Exit	Services
26	Continued
	85/24hr, 🍴 Countryside Steaks, Crystal Steaks, 🅾 Adrian Camping, city park
25mm	🆁🆂 wb, full ♿ facilities, 🅲, 🏤, litter barrels, petwalk
24mm	🆁🆂 eb, full ♿ facilities, 🅲, 🏤, litter barrels, petwalk
18	rd 3, Kanaranzi, Magnolia, **N** camping
12	US 75, Luverne, **N** 🅿 BP/dsl/E-85, Casey's, Cenex/dsl, Shell/Subway/dsl, 🍴 ChitChat's Grill, McDonald's, Taco John's, Tasty Drive-In, 🛏 Comfort Inn, Cozy Rest Motel (1mi), Sunrise Motel, 🅾 🅷, Ace Hardware, Buick/Cadillac/Chevrolet/GMC, Chrysler/Dodge/Jeep, $General, Family$, Lewis Drugs, True Value, to Blue Mounds SP, Pipestone NM, **S** 🍴 Magnolia Steaks, 🛏 Super 8, 🅾 Pamida
5	rd 6, Beaver Creek, **N** 🅿 Shell/dsl
3	rd 4 (from eb), Beaver Creek
1	MN 23, rd 17, to Jasper, **N** 🅾 to Pipestone NM, access to gas/dsl
0mm	Minnesota/South Dakota state line, **Welcome Ctr eb, full** ♿ facilities, info, 🅲, 🏤, litter barrels

◄► INTERSTATE 94

Exit	Services
259mm	Minnesota/Wisconsin state line, St Croix River
258	MN 95 N, to Stillwater, Hastings, Lakeland, **N** 🍴 Bungalow Rest.
257mm	**weigh sta wb, Welcome Ctr wb, full** ♿ **facilities,** 🅲, 🏤 **litter barrels, vending, petwalk**
253	MN 95 S, rd 15, Manning Ave, **N** 🅾 StoneRidge Golf, **S** to Afton Alps SP, ski area
251	rd 19, Keats Ave, Woodbury Dr, **S** 🅿 KwikTrip, SA/dsl, 🍴 Applebee's, Arby's, Asia Bistro, Burger King, Caribou Coffee, Chili's, Chipotle Mexican, Dino's Rest, Dunn Bros Coffee, Lakes Grill, Las Margaritas, LeeAnn Chin, McDonald's, Outback Steaks, Quiznos, Ray J's Grill, SmashBurger, Subway, 🛏 Extended Stay America, Holiday Inn Express, 🅾 AT&T, $Tree, Gander Mtn, Hancock Fabrics, Michael's, Sam's Club/gas, Staples, Target, Trader Joe's, Tuesday Morning, Walmart/Subway, Woodbury Lakes Outlets/famous brands
250	rd 13, Radio Dr, Inwood Ave, **N** 🍴 Baja Sol, Buffalo Wild Wings, Caribou Coffee, 5 Guys Burgers, Machine Shed Rest., Milio's Rest., Red Lobster, Olive Garden, 🛏 Hilton Garden, Wild Wood Lodge, 🅾 Best Buy, **S** 🅿 Holiday, 🍴 Champp's, Domino's, DUK Vietnamese, Jamba Juice, Little Caesars, Pei Wei, Starbucks, Taco Bell, Wendy's, Wild Bill's Grill, 🅾 Aldi Foods, BigLots, Cub Foods, CVS Drug, Dick's, Fannie May, GNC, Gordmans, Hepner's Auto Ctr, Home Depot, JC Penney, Jo-Ann, LandsEnd Inlet, Old Navy, Petsmart, Tires+, Verizon, vet
249	I-694 N & I-494 S
247	MN 120, Century Ave, **N** 🍴 Denny's, 🛏 AmericInn, LivInn, 🅾 Harley-Davidson, **S** 🅿 SA, 🍴 GreenMill Rest., 🛏 Country Inn/rest., 🅾 CarQuest, Chevrolet
246c b	McKnight Ave, **N** 3M, **S** 🛏 Holiday Inn
246a	Ruth St (from eb, no return), **N** 🅿 BP, 🍴 Culver's, Domino's, Hoho Chinese, Jimmy John's, 🅾 Cub Foods, $Tree, Firestone/auto, GNC, Radio Shack, TJ Maxx
245	White Bear Ave, **N** 🅿 BP, SA/dsl, 🍴 Subway, 🛏 Super 8, 🅾 Walgreens, **S** 🅿 BP, 🍴 Arby's, Davanni's Pizza/subs,

S T P A U L

Exit	Services
245	Continued
	Los Ocampo, McDonald's, Papa John's, Popeye's, Sonic, Taco Bell, Wendy's, 🅾 Aldi Foods, Byerly's Foods, Family$, NAPA, O'Reilly Parts, Target
244	US 10 E, US 61 S, Mounds/Kellogg
243	US 61, Mounds Blvd, **S** River Centre
242d	US 52 S, MN 3, 6th St, (exits left from wb), **N** 🅿 Holiday, 🍴 Subway
242c	7th St, **S** 🅿 SA
242b a	I-35E N, US 10 W, I-35E S (from eb)
241c	I-35E S (from wb)
241b	10th St, 5th St, to downtown
241a	12th St, Marion St, Kellogg Blvd, **N** 🛏 Best Western Kelly Inn, **S** St Paul's Cathedral
240	Dale Ave
239b a	Lexington Pkwy, Hamline Ave, **N** 🅿 BP, SA, 🍴 Hardee's, Leeann Chin, Popeye's, White Castle, 🅾 🅷, AutoZone, Cub Foods, Discount Tire, Herberger's, O'Reilly Parts, Target
238	MN 51, Snelling Ave, **N** 🍴 Applebee's, Culver's, Jimmy John's, Little Caesars, McDonald's, Perkins, 🅾 CVS Drug, Family$, Radio Shack, Rainbow Foods, Tires+, Walgreens, Walmart, same as 239
237	Cretin Ave, Vandalia Ave, to downtown
236	MN 280, University Ave, to downtown
235b	Huron Blvd
235mm	Mississippi River
235a	Riverside Ave, 25th Ave, **N** 🅿 Tesoro, 🍴 Starbucks, **S** 🍴 Perkins, Taco Bell
234c	Cedar Ave, downtown
234b a	MN 55, Hiawatha Ave, 5th St, **N** 🛏 Courtyard, 🅾 to downtown
233b	I-35W N, I-35W S (exits left from wb)
233a	11th St (from wb), **N** downtown
231b	Hennepin Ave, Lyndale Ave, to downtown
231a	I-394, US 12 W, to downtown
230	US 52, MN 55, 4th St, 7th St, Olson Hwy, **N** Metrodome, **S** 🅷, Int Mkt Square
229	W Broadway, Washington Ave, **N** 🅿 Holiday/dsl, Old Colony/dsl, **S** 🅿 Winner, 🍴 Broadway Pizza, Burger King, Little Caesars, KFC, McDonald's, Subway, Taco Bell, Wendy's, 🅾 AutoZone, Cub Foods, $Tree, Family$, Walgreens
228	Dowling Ave N
226	53rd Ave N, 49th Ave N
225	I-694 E, MN 252 N, to Minneapolis
I-94 & I-494 run together. See Interstate 494/694, exits 28-34	
216	I-94 W and I-494
215	rd 109, Weaver Lake Rd, **N** 🅿 SA/dsl, Shell, 🍴 Anginos, Broadway Pizza, Burger King, Caribou Coffee, Champps, ChuckECheese's, DQ, Domino's, Don Pablo, El Rodeo Mexican, Famous Dave's BBQ, Frankie's Pizza, Great Harvest Bread Co., Jimmy John's, McDonald's, Old Country Buffet, Papa John's, Papa Murphy's, Starbucks, Subway, Taco Bell, Wendy's, 🅾 AT&T, Barnes&Noble, Byerly's Foods, Cub Foods, Gander Mtn, GNC, Goodyear/auto, JC Penney, K-Mart, Kohl's, Michael's, Midas, Old Navy, PetCo, Radio Shack, Tires+, Verizon, Walgreens, mall, USPO, same as 28, **S** 🍴 Applebee's, IHOP
214mm	🆁🆂 eb, full ♿ facilities, 🅲, 🏤, litter barrels
213	rd 30, 95th Ave N, Maple Grove, **N** 🅿 SA/dsl, 🍴 Chipotle Mexican, Subway, 🛏 Cambria Suites, 🅾 🅷, Aldi

M I N N E A P O L I S

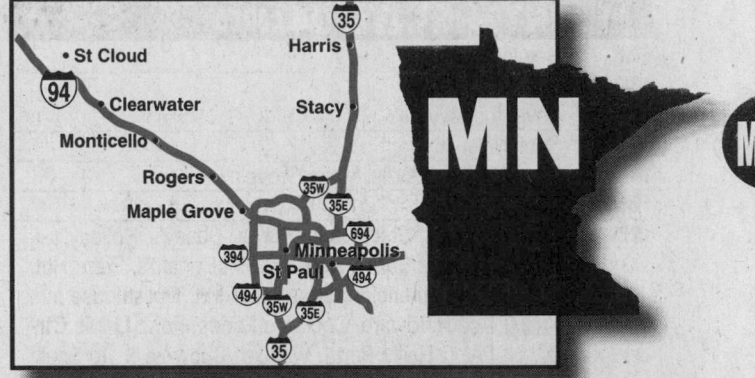

⬆E INTERSTATE 94 CONT'D

Exit	Services
213	Continued
	Foods, GNC, Home Depot, Target, **S** ⛽ Holiday/dsl, 🍴 Culver's, Leeann Chin, Little Caesars, McDonald's, Starbucks, Which Wich, White Castle, ◻ BigLots, Discount Tire, Firestone, Goodyear/auto, Menards, Rainbow Foods, Sam's Club/gas, Verizon, Walgreens, Walmart/Subway, KOA (2mi, Apr-Oct)
207	MN 101, to Elk River, Rogers, **N** ⛽ Holiday, SA/dsl, TA/Country Pride/dsl/scales/24hr/@, 🍴 Applebee's, Arby's, Burger King, China Kitchen, Culver's, DQ, Davanni's Pizza, Denny's, Dickey's BBQ, Domino's, Hardee's, Jimmy John's, Maynard's, McDonald's, Noodles&Co, Starbucks, Subway, Taco Bell, Wendy's, 🏨 Hampton Inn, Holiday Inn Express, Super 8, ◻ AT&T, Cabela's, Camping World, Cub Foods, Discount Tire, $Tree, Gander Mtn, GNC, Kohl's, Lowe's, NAPA, NTB, O'Reilly Parts, Target, Tires+, Verizon, Walgreens, vet, **S** ⛽ BP/Circle K/dsl, Holiday, 🍴 BoBo Asian, Guadalajara Mexican, Harvest Grill, Minne's Diner, 🏨 AmericInn, ◻ **Urgent Care**, Chevrolet, Curves, CVS Drug, TrueValue
205.5mm	Crow River
205	MN 241, rd 36, St Michael, **S** ⛽ QwikTrip/dsl, SA/dsl
202	rd 37, Albertville, **N** ⛽ Shell/dsl, 🍴 Emma Krumbee's Rest., **S** ⛽ BP/dsl, Sunoco/dsl, same as 201
201	rd 19 (from eb), Albertville, St Michael, **N** ⛽ Shell/dsl, 🍴 Andy's Pizza, Burger King, Michael R's Grill, Perkins, Subway, 🏨 Country Inn&Suites, ◻ Albertville Outlets/famous brands, Old Navy, **S** ⛽ BP/dsl, Casey's, Mobil/Subway, Sunoco/dsl, 🍴 Caribou Coffee, China Dragon, Culver's, Little Caesars, Papa Murphy's, Space Aliens Grill, ◻ Ace Hardware, Coburn's/gas, Goodyear/auto, Verizon, auto repair
194	rd 18, rd 39, Monticello, **N** ⛽ Cruiser's/dsl, Marathon/dsl/E85, 🍴 Caribou Coffee, Little Caesars, McDonald's, ◻ 🏨 GNC, Home Depot, Petsmart, Target, Verizon
193	MN 25, to Buffalo, Monticello, Big Lake, **N** ⛽ Holiday/dsl, 🍴 Burger King, Caribou Coffee, 5 Buck Pizza, KFC, Papa Murphy's, Perkins, Poncho Villa Mexican, Quiznos, Rancho Grande Mexican, Taco Bell, 🏨 AmericInn, ◻ AutoValue Parts, Cub Foods, Radio Shack, Walgreens, USPO, **S** ⛽ KwikTrip/dsl, Holiday/dsl, SA/dsl, 🍴 Applebee's, Arby's, Blue Stone Grill, Buffalo Wild Wings, Chatter's Grill, China Buffet, Culver's, DQ, Jimmy John's, McDonald's, Pizza Ranch, Subway, Taco John's, 🏨 Best Western, Days Inn, Super 8, ◻ Buick/GMC, Chevrolet, $Tree, Goodyear/auto, NAPA, O'Reilly Parts, Verizon, Walmart/Subway, vet, Lake Maria SP
187mm	Rs eb, full 🚻 facilities, 🛢, 🏕, litter barrels, vending, petwalk
183	rd 8, to Silver Creek, Hasty, Maple Lake, **S** ⛽ BP/rest./dsl/scales/24hr/@, ◻ to Lake Maria SP, camping
178	MN 24, to Annandale, Clearwater, **N** ⛽ Holiday/Petro/dsl/scales/24hr/@, 🍴 Burger King, DQ, Keith's Kettle, Subway, Taco Gringo, 🏨 Best Value Inn, ◻ Clearwater Hardware, GS Camping (1mi), Coburn's Foods/gas, Parts City, repair, USPO, vet, **S** ◻ A-J Acres RV Camping (Apr-Oct) Recreation Outdoor RV Ctr
178mm	Rs wb, full 🚻 facilities, 🛢, 🏕, litter barrels, petwalk, vending
173	Opportunity Dr

171	rd 7, rd 75, St Augusta, **N** ⛽ ▦/McDonald's/dsl/scales/24hr, Shell, 🍴 Burger King, MadeRite Grill, RJ's Grill, Subway, 🏨 AmericInn, Holiday Inn Express, Travelodge, ◻ 🏨 Goodyear/auto, **S** ◻ Freightliner, Pleasureland RV Ctr
167b a	MN 15, to St Cloud, Kimball, **4 mi N** ⛽ Holiday, SA/dsl, 🍴 Applebee's, Arby's, Bonanza, Boulder Taphouse, Buffalo Wild Wings, Burger King, Caribou Coffee, Chipotle, ChuckECheese's, Domino's, Famous Dave's BBQ, 5 Guys Burgers, Granite City Grill, Grizzly's Grill, IHOP, La Casita Mexican, McDonald's, Noodles&Co, Old Chicago Pizza, Old Country Buffet, Olive Garden, Panda Express, Perkins, Pizza Hut, Pizza Ranch, Qdoba, Red Lobster, Sammy's Pizza, Starbucks, Subway, Taco Bell, Taco John's, TGIFriday's, Wendy's, White Castle, 🏨 Country Inn&Suites, Days Inn, Fairfield Inn, Hampton Inn, Holiday Inn, Homewood Suites, Quality Inn, Super 8, ◻ 🏨, AT&T, Barnes&Noble, Best Buy, BigLots, CashWise Foods, Gander Mtn, Home Depot, JC Penney, Jo-Ann Fabrics, Kohl's, K-Mart, Macy's, Michael's, Office Depot, Old Navy, Petsmart, Sam's Club, Save-A-Lot, Scheel's Sports, Sears/auto, ShopKo, Subaru, Target, Walgreens, Walmart, USPO, **S** ⛽ Shell/dsl (2mi)
164	MN 23, to St Cloud, Rockville, **N** Grande Depot Gourmet Foods, **4-6 mi N** ⛽ Holiday, 🍴 Culver's, IHOP, KFC, Subway, Taco Bell, Wendy's, 🏨 Motel 6, ◻ Discount Tire, Gander Mtn, Hyundai, Kia, Menards, Petsmart, Toyota/Scion, same as 167
162.5mm	Sauk River
160	rd 2, to Cold Spring, St Joseph, **N** ⛽ BP, 🏨 Super 8 (3mi), ◻ Coll of St Benedict
158	rd 75 (from eb exits left), to St Cloud, **3 mi N** same as 160
156	rd 159, St Joseph, **N** St Johns U
153	rd 9, Avon, **N** ⛽ Shell/dsl, Tesoro/McDonald's/dsl, 🍴 Joseph's Rest., Subway, 🏨 Budget Host, ◻ city park, 🏕, USPO, **S** ◻ El Rancho Manana Camping (10mi)
152mm	Rs both lanes, full 🚻 facilities, 🛢, 🏕, litter barrels, vending, petwalk
147	MN 238, rd 10, Albany, **N** ⛽ Holiday/dsl, Shell/A&W/Subway/dsl, 🍴 Chesters, DQ, Hillcrest Rest., 🏨 Norwood Inn&Suites, ◻ 🏨, golf, **S** ◻ Chrysler/Dodge/Jeep, NAPA, vet
140	rd 11, Freeport, **N** ⛽ Cenex/dsl, Clark/dsl, 🍴 Ackie's Pioneer Rest., Charlie's Café, ◻ auto repair, USPO, vet
137	MN 237, rd 65, New Munich
137mm	Sauk River
135	rd 13, Melrose, **N** ⛽ Clark/dsl/repair, Tesoro/Subway/dsl, 🍴 Burger King, Cornerstone Buffet, ◻ 🏨, $General, **S** ⛽ Casey's/dsl, 🍴 DQ, El Portal Mexican, 🏨 Super 8, ◻

(Left margin, vertical text: MONTICELLO)

(Center margin, vertical text: ST CLOUD)

(Right margin: MN)

MN

ALEXANDRIA

⒠ INTERSTATE 94 CONT'D

Exit	Services
135	Continued
	Save Foods, vet
132.5mm	Sauk River
131	MN 4, to Paynesville, Meire Grove
128mm	Sauk River
127	US 71, MN 28, Sauk Centre, **N** 🅿 Casey's, Holiday/dsl, 🍴 DQ, 4 Seas Buffet, Hardee's, McDonald's, Pizza Hut, Subway, 🛏 AmericInn, Best Value Inn, Guesthouse Inn, 🅾 🄷, Ace Hardware, Coborn's Foods, Ford, **Lewis Ctr/** ℞, NAPA, O'Reilly Parts, Walmart/Subway, **S** 🅿 Shell/café/dsl/scales/24hr/@, · 🅾 Buick/Chevrolet/Chrysler/Dodge/Jeep
124	Sinclair Lewis Ave (from eb), Sauk Centre
119	rd 46, West Union
114	MN 27, rd 3, to Westport, Osakis, **3 mi N** 🍴 A&W, Subway, gas, lodging
105mm	℞ wb, full ♿ facilities, Ⓒ, 🛢, litter barrels, vending, petwalk
103	MN 29, to Glenwood, Alexandria, **N** 🅿 F&F/dsl, Holiday, Tesoro, 🍴 Arby's, Burger King, Caribou Coffee, China Buffet, Culver's, Dolittle's Grill, Dunn Bros Coffee, Godfather's Pizza, Great Hunan, Hardee's, Jimmy John's, KFC, McDonald's, Perkins, Subway, Taco Bell, TN Roadhouse, Wendy's, 🛏 AmericInn, Best Western, Days Inn, Hampton Inn, Super 8, 🅾 🄷, AT&T, Cadillac/Chevrolet/Mazda, County Mkt Foods, Goodyear/auto, Harley-Davidson, Jeep, Jo-Ann Fabrics, K-Mart, Menards, Radio Shack, Target, Tires+, Verizon, Walmart/Subway, **S** 🅿 Holiday/dsl, 🛏 Country Inn&Suites, Holiday Inn, 🅾 Alexandria RV Ctr
100	MN 27, **N** 🅿 ⒽⒾⓁⒾⓉⒺ/Subway/dsl/scales/24hr/@, 🛏 Best Inn/Alexandria RV Park, 🅾 🄷, **S** camping
100mm	Lake Latoka
99mm	℞ eb, full ♿ facilities, Ⓒ, 🛢, litter barrels, vending, petwalk
97	MN 114, rd 40, to Lowry, Garfield
90	rd 7, Brandon, **S** camping, ski area
82	MN 79, rd 41, to Erdahl, Evansville, **2 mi N** 🅿 BP/dsl, **S** 🅾 🄷, camping
77	MN 78, rd 10, to Barrett, Ashby, **N** gas/dsl, 🅾 Prairie Cove Camping (May-Sept), **S** camping
69mm	℞ wb, full ♿ facilities, Ⓒ, 🛢, litter barrels, petwalk, vending
67	rd 35, Dalton, **N** camping, **S** camping
61	US 59 S, rd 82, to Elbow Lake, **N** 🅿 Tesoro/café/dsl/LP/24hr, 🅾 🄷, Pine Plaza RV Ctr, camping (4mi), **S** camping

FERGUS FALLS

57	MN 210 E, rd 25, Fergus Falls, **N** 🄷
55	rd 1, to Wendell, Fergus Falls, **N** antiques
54	MN 210 W, Lincoln Ave, Fergus Falls, **N** 🅿 Cenex/dsl, F&F/dsl, Tesoro/dsl, 🍴 Applebee's, Arby's, Burger King, Debbie's Kitchen, Family Diner, Hunan Spring Buffet, KFC, McDonald's, Papa Murphy's, Perkins, Pizza Hut, Pizza Ranch, Subway, 🛏 AmericInn, Best Value Inn, Best Western, Comfort Inn, Motel 7, Super 8, 🅾 🄷, AT&T, Chrysler/Dodge/Jeep, $Tree, Ford/Lincoln, GMC, Herbergers, Home Depot, K-Mart, NAPA, O'Reilly Parts, SunMart Foods, Target, Tires+, Toyota, museum, **S** 🍴 Mabel Murphy's Rest., 🅾 Walmart
50	rd 88, rd 52, to US 59, to Fergus Falls, Elizabeth, **N** camping

MOORHEAD

38	rd 88, Rothsay, **S** 🅿 Tesoro/cafe/dsl/24hr, 🍴 Ole&Lena's Pizza, 🛏 Comfort Zone Inn, 🅾 tires
32	MN 108, rd 30, to Pelican Rapids, Lawndale, **19 mi N** Maplewood SP
24	MN 34, Barnesville, **N** 🍴 Renee's Drive-in, **1 mi S** 🅿 Cenex/dsl, Tesoro/dsl, 🍴 DQ, Subway, 🛏 motel, 🅾 Wagner Park Camping (May-Oct), city park
22	MN 9, Barnesville, **1 mi S** 🅿 Cenex/dsl, Tesoro/dsl, 🍴 DQ, Subway, 🛏 motel
15	rd 10, Downer
8mm	Buffalo River
6	MN 336, rd 11, to US 10, Dilworth, **N** to Buffalo River SP
5mm	**Red River weigh sta eb**
2b a	rd 52, Moorhead, **N** 🅿 Holiday/dsl/e-85, 🅾 Menards, **2 mi N** 🅿 Tesoro, 🍴 Arby's, McDonald's, Perkins, Pizza Ranch, Subway, Taco Bell, 🛏 Travelodge, 🅾 🄷, CVS Drug, K-Mart, KOA, Radio Shack, Target, Walmart, **S** antiques
2mm	**Welcome Ctr eb, full** ♿ **facilities, info,** Ⓒ, 🛢, **litter barrels, vending**
1b	20th St, Moorhead (from eb, no return)
1a	US 75, Moorhead, **N** 🅿 Clark/dsl, 🍴 Burger King, Crave Burger Co., Little Caesars, Papa Murphy's, Qdoba, Sarpinos Pizza, Starbucks, Village Inn, 🛏 Courtyard, 🅾 Curves, SunMart Foods, Verizon, **S** 🅿 Casey's, Orton's Gas, 🍴 DQ, Panchero's Mexican, Snapdragon Asian, Speak Easy Rest., Subway, 🛏 Days Inn, Grand Inn, Super 8, 🅾 CVS Drug, Walgreens, vet
0mm	Minnesota/North Dakota state line, Red River

⒠ INTERSTATE 494/694

Exit	Services
I-494/I-694 loops around Minneapolis/St Paul.	
71	rd 31, Pilot Knob Rd, **N** 🛏 Courtyard, Fairfield Inn, **S** 🛏 Best Western, Crowne Plaza, 🍴 LoneOak Café
70	I-35E, **N** to St Paul, **S** to Albert Lea
69	MN 149, MN 55, Dodd Rd, **N** 🍴 Ziggy's Deli, **S** 🍴 Caribou Coffee, McDonald's, Subway, 🛏 Budget Host, Country Inn&Suites,
67	MN 3, Roberts St, **1 mi N** 🅿 BP, Mobil, Holiday, 🍴 Acre's Rest., Arby's/Sbarro's, Baker's Square, Buffalo Wings, Burger King, Chipotle Mexican, ChuckeCheese, Culver's, Grand Buffet, KFC, Old Country Buffet, Pizza Hut, Taco Bell, Timber Lodge Steaks, White Castle, 🅾 Aamco, Best Buy, Buick, Checker Parts, Chevrolet, Cub Foods, Dodge, Ford, Jo-Ann Fabrics, Kia, K-Mart, Lincoln, Mazda, NAPA, Nissan, Rainbow Foods/24hr, Target, Tires+, Toyota, VW, Walmart, **S** 🅿 PDQ
66	US 52, **S** 🅿 SA, 🍴 Old World Pizza, Outback Steaks, 🛏 Country Inn&Suites, Microtel
65	7th Ave, 5th Ave
64b a	MN 56, Concord St, **N** 🅿 Conoco/dsl, 🛏 Best Western Drovers, 🅾 Ford Trucks, Goodyear, Peterbilt, **S** 🅿 EZ Stop, 🅾 Chrysler/Jeep/Dodge, Parts+
63mm	Mississippi River
63c	Maxwell Ave
63b a	US 10, US 61, to St Paul, Hastings, **S** 🅿 BP, SA, 🍴 Burger King, Subway, 🛏 Boyd's Motel, 🅾 NAPA
60	Lake Rd, **E** 🅿 SA/dsl, **W** 🛏 Country Inn&Suites
59	Valley Creek Rd, **E** 🅿 BP/repair, SA/dsl/LP, 🍴 America's Burger, Applebees, Broadway Pizza, Chipotle Mexican, DQ, Old Country Buffet, Papa Murphy's, Perkins, Potbelly's Rest., Yang's Chinese, 🛏 Red Roof Inn, 🅾

ST PAUL

⬆⬇E　INTERSTATE 494/694 CONT'D

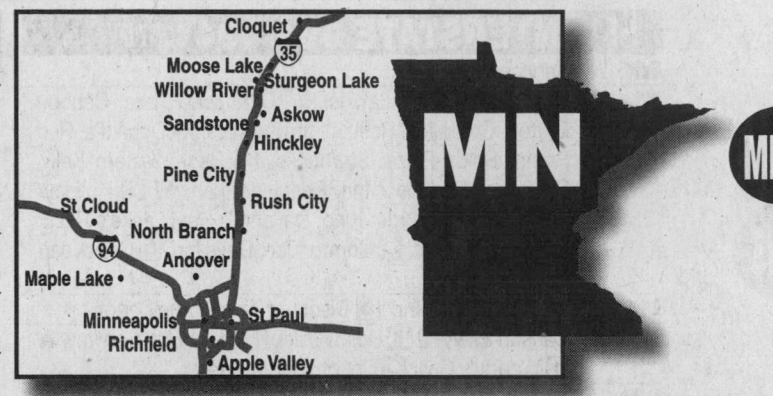

Exit	Services
59	Continued Barnes&Noble, Kohl's, Marshall's, Office Depot, PetCo, Rainbow Foods, Target, Walgreens, USPO, **W** 🅖 PBQ, 🍴 Bonfire Rest., Burger King, McDonald's, Pizza Hut, Subway, 🛏 Hampton Inn, 🅞 🅗, Ace Hardware, Goodyear
58c	Tamarack Rd, **E** 🍴 Paisano's Cafe, Woodbury's Cafe, 🛏 Sheraton
58b a	I-94, E to Madison, W to St Paul. **I-494 S begins/ends, I-694 N begins/ends**
57	rd 10, 10th St N, **E** 🅖 SA 🍴 IHOP, Quizno's, 🛏 Wingate Inn, **W** 🅖 Holiday, 🍴 Burger King, Hunan Buffet, KFC, 🅞 $Tree, K-Mart, Rainbow Foods/24hr, mall, vet
55	MN 5, **E** 🅞 Target, **W** 🅖 Holiday/dsl, 🍴 Subway, 🅞 Menards, st patrol
52b a	MN 36, N St Paul, to Stillwater, **W** 🅖 F&F/dsl
51	MN 120, **E** 🅖 BP, SA/dsl, 🍴 Jethro's, Starbucks, **W** 🅖 Kellie's Corner/gas
50	White Bear Ave, **E** 🅖 SA, 🅞 K-Mart, Sam's Club/gas, **W** 🅖 BP, Shell, 🍴 Acupulco Chicken, Arby's, Bakers Square, Buffalo Wild Wings, Caribou Coffee, Chili's, Denny's, Great Moon Buffet, IHOP, Jake's Grill, Jimmy John's, KFC, McDonald's, Noodles&Co, North China, Old Country Buffet, Outback Steaks, Peiwei Asian, Perkins/24hr, Red Lobster, Taco Bell, TGI Friday, Wendy's, 🛏 Emerald Inn, 🅞 Aamco, Best Buy, Goodyear/auto, JC Penney, Jo-Ann Fabrics, Kohl's, Macy's, Marshall's, Michael's, PetCo, Sears/auto, Tires+, Tuesday Morning, Walgreens, mall
48	US 61 (from wb), **E** 🅞 Acura, Chrysler/Dodge/Jeep, Ford, Honda, Hyundai, Isuzu/Subaru, Lincoln, **W** 🍴 Chili's, Gulden's Rest., McDonald's, Olive Garden, 🛏 Best Western, 🅞 🅗, Audi/Porsche, Lexus, Mercedes, Toyota, Venburg Tire, Volvo
47	I-35E, N to Duluth
46	I-35E, US 10, S to St Paul
45	rd 49, Rice St, **N** 🅖 Gas+, Marathon/dsl, 🍴 Papa John's, Subway, Taco Bell, 🅞 Checker Parts, **S** 🅖 Marathon/dsl, 🍴 A&W, Burger King, Caribou Coffee, Taco John's, 🅞 Kath Parts
43b	Victoria St, **S** Bill's Foods
43a	Lexington Ave, **N** 🍴 Greenmill Rest., Red Robin, 🛏 Hampton Inn, Hilton Garden, **S** 🅖 Exxon, Sinclair, 🍴 Blue Fox Grill, Burger King, Davanni's Pizza, Papa Murphy's, Perkins, Subway, Wendy's, 🛏 Holiday Inn, Super 8, 🅞 Cub Foods, Goodyear/auto, Target, transmissions
42b	US 10 W (from wb), to Anoka
42a	MN 51, Snelling Ave, **1 mi S** 🅖 Shell, 🍴 Flaherty's Grill, Lindey's Steaks, McDonald's, 🛏 Country Inn&Suites, Holiday Inn
41b a	I-35W, S to Minneapolis, N to Duluth
40	Long Lake Rd, 10th St NW
39	Silver Lake Rd, **N** 🅖 BP, 🍴 Acupulco Mexican, Champps, McDonald's, Subway, 🅞 Fairview Drug, Ford, U-Haul
38b a	MN 65, Central Ave, **N** 🅖 Holiday/dsl, 🍴 Subway, **S** 🅖 SA, SuperStop, 🍴 A&W/KFC, Applebee's, Asia Rest., Big Marina Deli, Buffalo Wild Wings, Flameburger Rest., La Casita Mexican, McDonald's, Mr BBQ, Papa John's, Ricky's, Sonic, Subway, Taco Bell, Wendy's, White Castle, 🛏 LivInn Hotel, 🅞 Advance Parts, AutoZone, $General, Discount Tire, Menards, O'Reilly Parts, PetCo, Rainbow Foods, Target, Tires+, Walgreens, vet
37	rd 47, University Ave, **N** 🅖 Holiday, SA/dsl, 🍴 Burger King, McDonald's, Papa Murphy's Pizza, Zantigo's Rest., 🅞 Cub Foods, CVS Drug, Goodyear, Home Depot, **S** 🅖 Bona Bros/repair, Shell
36	E River Rd
35mm	**I-494 W begins/ends, I-694 E begins/ends**
35c	MN 252, **N** 🅖 Holiday, SA
35b a	I-94 E to Minneapolis
34	to MN 100, Shingle Creek Pkwy, **N** 🍴 Denny's, Mr BBQ, Oak City Rest., 🛏 AmericInn, Comfort Inn, Country Inn&Suites, Crowne Plaza, Days Inn, Extended Stay America, Motel 6, Super 8, **S** 🍴 C1 Buffet, Global Kitchen, Ocean Buffet, Panera Bread, 🛏 Embassy Suites, 🅞 🅗, AT&T, Curves, Kohl's, PepBoys, Target, Tires+, Walmart
33	rd 152, Brooklyn Blvd, **N** 🅖 SA/dsl, Shell, 🍴 Culver's, Slim's Café, Subway, 🅞 Buick/GMC, Chevrolet, Honda, Toyota/Scion, USPO, **S** 🅖 BP, 🍴 Applebee's, Arby's, IHOP, McDonald's, Popeye's, Starbucks, Subway, Taco Bell, Wendy's, 🅞 AutoZone, Cub Foods, CVS Drug, Family$, NTB, Sun Foods, Walgreens
31	rd 81, Lakeland Ave, **N** 🅖 SA/dsl, 🍴 Chipotle Mexican, Wagner's Drive-In, Wendy's, 🅞 Target, U-Haul, **S** 🛏 Northstar Inn
30	Boone Ave, **N** 🛏 La Quinta, Marriott, **S** 🅞 Discount Tire, Home Depot
29b a	US 169, to Hopkins, Osseo
28	rd 61, Hemlock Lane, **N on Elm Crook** 🍴 Arby's, Benihana, Biaggi's Italian, Boston's Grill, Buca Italian, CA Pizza Kitchen, Chick-fil-A, Chipotle Mexican, Coldstone, Dave&Buster's, Dickey's BBQ, 5 Guys Burgers, Granite City Rest., Houlihan's, Leeann Chin, Malone's Grill, Mongo's Grill, Noodles&Co, Olive Garden, Panera Bread, PF Chang's, Pittsburgh Blue, Potbelly's, Red Lobster, Redstone Grill, Starbucks, Subway, TGIFriday's, Wild Bill's Café, 🛏 Courtyard, Hampton Inn, Holiday Inn, Staybridge Suites, 🅞 Urgent Care, Best Buy, Costco/gas, Dick's, $Tree, Jo-Ann Fabrics, Marshalls, Lowe's, Office Depot, Old Navy, Whole Foods Mkt, **S** 🅖 BP, 🍴 Perkins, 🛏 Asteria Suites
27	I-94 W to St Cloud, I-94/694 E to Minneapolis
26	rd 10, Bass Lake Rd, **E** 🅖 Freedom, 🍴 Caribou Coffee, Culver's, McDonald's, Subway, 🛏 Extended Stay America, 🅞 mall, vet, **W** 🅖 BP, Marathon/dsl, 🍴 Dunn Bro's Cofee, Milio's Sandwiches, Pancake House, Pizza Hut, 🛏 Hilton Garden, 🅞 CVS Drug
23	rd 9, Rockford Rd, **E** 🅖 Holiday, 🍴 Chili's, Peony's Chinese, 🅞 GNC, O'Reilly Parts, PetsMart, Rainbow Foods, Target, TJ Maxx, Walgreens, vet, **W** 🅖 PDQ, 🍴 Cousins Subs, DQ, LeAnn Chin, Panchero's, Subway

Map labels: Cloquet, 35, Moose Lake, Sturgeon Lake, Willow River, Sandstone, Askow, Hinckley, Pine City, St Cloud, Rush City, North Branch, 94, Andover, Maple Lake, Minneapolis, Richfield, St Paul, Apple Valley

MN

MINNEAPOLIS

MN
MS

➤E INTERSTATE 494/694 CONT'D

Exit	Services
22	MN 55, E 🅖 Holiday/dsl, 🍴 Broadway Pizza, Caribou Coffee, Green Mill Rest., Jimmy John's, McDonald's, Red Robin, Solos Pizza, Starbucks, 🏠 Best Western Kelly, Radisson, Red Roof Inn, Residence Inn, W 🅖 Holiday/dsl, 🍴 Arby's, Burger King, Davanni's Rest., Jake's Rest., Perkins, Wendy's, 🏠 Comfort Inn, Days Inn, 🅞 Goodyear/auto, Tires+
21	rd 6, E 🅖 KwikTrip, 🅞 Discount Tire, Home Depot
20	Carlson Pkwy, E 🅖 Holiday/dsl, 🍴 Pizza Hut, Subway, W 🍴 Woody's Grill, 🏠 Country Inn&Suites
19 b a	I-394 E, US 12 W, to Minneapolis, **1 mi E off of I-394** 🍴 Applebee's, Wendy's, 🅞 Barnes&Noble, Best Buy, Byerly's Foods, Ford, JC Penney, Jo-Ann Fabrics, Mazda, Mazerati, Mercedes, Sears/auto, Subaru, Target, Tires+, **1/2 mi W** 🅖 BP, Holiday, 🍴 KFC, McDonald's, 🅞 BMW, Chevrolet, Lexus, Mitsubishi, Nissan
17 b a	Minnetonka Blvd, W 🅖 US Gas, 🍴 Cousin's Subs, Dunn Bros Coffee
16 b a	MN 7, **1 mi W** 🅖 Marathon, 🍴 Christo's Rest., Davanni's Rest., Famous Dave's BBQ, Taco Bell, 🅞 Goodyear
13	MN 62, rd 62
12	Valleyview Rd, rd 39 (from sb)
11c	MN 5 W, same as 11 a b
11 b a	US 169 S, US 212 W, N 🍴 Don Pablo, Subway, 🏠 Courtyard, Fairfield Inn, Hampton Inn, Hyatt Place, Residence Inn, S 🅖 BP, Marathon, Holiday, 🍴 Caribou Coffee, Davanni's Rest., Fuddruckers, Jake's Grill, Jason's Deli, KFC, Leeann Chin, Old Chicago, Panera Bread, Papa John's, Qdoba, Starbucks, 🏠 Best Western, Discount Tire, Homestead Suites, SpringHill Suites, JC Penney, Office Depot, Sears/auto, Target, Walgreens, Walmart
10	US 169 N, to rd 18
8	rd 28 (from wb, no return), E Bush Lake Rd, same as 7 a b
7 b a	MN 100, rd 34, Normandale Blvd, N 🅖 Shell/dsl, 🍴 Burger King, Caribou Coffee, Chili's, DQ, Subway, TGIFriday, 🏠 Days Inn, Sheraton, Sofatel, S 🍴 Oak City Rest., 🏠 Country Inn&Suites, Crowne Plaza, Hilton Garden, La Quinta, Staybridge Inn
6b	rd 17, France Ave, N 🅖 Mobil, 🍴 Cattle Co Rest., Chuck-eCheese, Fuddrucker's, Hot Wok, Macaroni Grill, McDonald's, Perkins, Quizno's, 🏠 Best Western, Le Bourget, Park Plaza Hotel, 🅞 H, Michael's, Office Depot, S 🍴 Denny's, Joe Senser's Grill, Olive Garden, 🏠 Hampton Inn, Hilton, 🅞 Buick/GMC, Ford, Mercedes, Nissan, Toyota/Scion
6a	Penn Ave (no EZ eb return), N 🏠 Residence Inn, 🅞 Best Buy, Buick, Hyundai, Isuzu, S 🍴 Applebee's, Atlantic Buffet, McDonald's, Starbucks, Steak&Ale, Subway, 🏠 Embassy Suites, 🅞 Chevrolet, Chrysler/Jeep/Plymouth, Dodge, Hancock Fabrics, Herberger's, Kohl's, Rainbow Foods, Target, TJ Maxx
5 b a	I-35W, S to Albert Lea, N to Minneapolis
4b	Lyndale Ave, N 🍴 Boston Mkt, Chipotle Mexican, Don Pablo's, DQ, Eddie Cheng's, Papa John's, Subway, 🏠 Candlewood Suites, Hampton Inn, Ramada Inn, 🅞 Best Buy, Honda, Lands End, PetsMart, Tires+, S 🏠 Extended Stay America, 🅞 Lincoln, Mazda, Subaru
4a	MN 52, Nicollet Ave, N 🅖 SA/dsl, 🍴 Burger King, Ember's, Rest, Jumbo Chinese, 🏠 Candlewood Suites, 🅞 Honda, Menards, S 🅖 Mobil, Shell, 🍴 Culver's, Kwik Mart, Big Boy, McDonald's, 🏠 La Quinta, Super 8, 🅞 Home Depot, Sam's Club
3	Portland Ave, 12th Ave, N 🅖 Phillips 66, Sinclair, PDQ Mart, 🍴 Arby's, 🏠 AmericInn, S 🅖 BP, 🍴 Denny's, Outback Steaks, Subway, 🏠 Comfort Inn/rest., Holiday Inn Express, Microtel, Quality Inn, Residence Inn, Travelodge, 🅞 Walgreens, Walmart
2c b	MN 77, N 🏠 Motel 6, S 🅖 BP, SA, 🏠 AmeriSuites, Best Western, Courtyard, Embassy Suites, Exel Inn, Fairfield Inn, Grand Motel, Marriott, Sheraton, 🅞 Nordstrom's, Sears, Mall of America
2a	24th Ave, same as 2c b
1b	34th Ave, Nat Cemetary, S 🏠 Embassy Suites, Hilton, Holiday Inn
1a	MN 5 E, N ➤
0mm	Minnesota River. **I-494/I-694 loops around Minneapolis/St Paul.**

MISSISSIPPI

M O S S   **P O I N T**

➤E INTERSTATE 10

Exit	Services
77mm	Mississippi/Alabama state line, **weigh sta wb**
75	Franklin Creek Rd
75mm	**Welcome Ctr wb, full ♿ facilities, 🍴, 🅿, litter barrels, petwalk, RV dump, weigh sta eb**
74mm	Escatawpa River
69	MS 63, to E Moss Point, N 🅖 Raceway, Texaco/Domino's/dsl/24hr, 🍴 Waffle House, 🏠 Best Value, Deluxe Inn, La Quinta, S 🅖 Chevron/dsl, Cone/dsl, Exxon/Subway/24hr, Shell, 🍴 Barnhill's Buffet, Burger King, Cracker Barrel, Hardee's, KFC, McDonald's, Pizza Hut, Ruby Tuesday, San Miguel Mexican, Waffle House, Wendy's, 🏠 Best Western, Comfort Inn, Days Inn, Hampton Inn, Holiday Inn Express, Quality Inn, Shular Inn, 🅞 H
68	MS 613, to Moss Point, Pascagoula, N 🅖 BP, Chevron/dsl, 🍴 Coco Loco, 🏠 Super 8, S 🅖 BP/dsl, 🅞 H
64mm	Pascagoula River
63.5mm	🆁🆂 **both lanes, full ♿ facilities, 🍴, 🅿, litter barrels, petwalk, RV dump, 24hr security**
61	to Gautier, N 🅞 MS Nat Golf Course, **1-3 mi S** 🅖 BP/dsl, 🍴 Hardee's, KFC, McDonald's, Pizza Hut, Wendy's, 🏠 Best Western, Suburban Lodge, 🅞 Shephard Camping, Sandhill Crane WR
57	MS 57, to Vancleave, N 🅖 Chevron/dsl, 🍴 Shed BBQ, 🅞 Journey's End Camping, tires, S 🅖 Exxon, 🅞 H
50	MS 609 S, Ocean Springs, N 🅖 Texaco/Domino's/dsl, 🍴 Waffle House, 🏠 Best Western, Comfort Inn, Country Inn&Suites, Motel 6, Ramada Ltd, Scottish Inn, Super 8, 🅞 Martin Lake Camping (1mi), S 🅖 BP/dsl, Chevron/McDonald's, Kangaroo/Subway/dsl, 🍴 Denny's, Lil Italy, Waffle House, Wendy's, 🏠 Comfort Inn, Days Inn, Hampton Inn, Holiday Inn Express, Howard Johnson, Quality Inn, 🅞 $General, Family$, Nat Seashore, vet
46b a	I-110, MS 15 N, to Biloxi, N 🍴 Beef O'Brady's, Beijing Chinese, Buffalo Wild Wings, Chick-fil-A, Chili's, China

INTERSTATE 10 CONT'D

BILOXI

Exit	Services
46b a	Continued

Town, 5 Guys Burgers, Fox's Pizza, Logan's Roadhouse, Moe's SW Grill, Olive Garden, Outback Steaks, Papa John's, Red Lobster, Ruby Tuesday, Samurai, Sonic, Strami's Italian, Subway, Waffle House, Wendy's, Whataburger, 🏠 Courtyard, Regency Inn, Wingate Inn, ◎ AT&T, Best Buy, Dick's, Kohl's, Lowe's, Marshall's, Office Depot, Petsmart, Radio Shack, Target, Tire Kingdom, Verizon, Walgreens, Walmart, **S** Ⓗ, to beaches

44 Cedar Lake Rd, to Biloxi, **N** ⓖ ♥Loves/ Subway/dsl/scales/24hr, ◎ Chevrolet, **S** ⓖ Chevron/dsl, Shell/dsl, 🍴 Applebee's, El Saltillo, KFC/LJ Silver, McDonald's, Red Eye Grill, Sonic, Subway, Waffle House, Wow Cafe, 🏠 La Quinta, ◎ Ⓗ, $General, Harley-Davidson, Home Depot, O'Reilly Parts, to Jeff Davis Shrine (Beauvoir), Biloxi Nat Cem

41 MS 67 N, to Woolmarket, **N** ⓖ Chevron/dsl, Texaco/dsl, ◎ golf (6mi), **S** Mazalea RV Prk, Parkers Landing RV Prk

39.5mm Biloxi River

38 Lorraine-Cowan Rd, **N** ⓖ Exxon/Subway, Kangaroo/dsl, 🍴 Capt Al's Cafe, Domino's, McDonald's, Sonic, ◎ Toyota/Scion, **S** ⓖ Pure/dsl, ◎ Ⓗ, Baywood RV Park (3mi), Foxes RV Park (8mi), to beaches

34b a US 49, to Gulfport, **N** ⓖ Exxon, Kangaroo/dsl, Texaco/dsl, 🍴 Backyard Burger, Barnhill's Buffet, Beef O'Brady's, Burger King, Cane's Chicken, Chick-fil-A, Chili's, ChuckeCheese, CiCi's Pizza, Cracker Barrel, Domino's, Golden Corral, Hardee's, KFC, Krystal, Little Caesars, Logan's Roadhouse, Longhorn Steaks, McDonald's, Newk's Cafe, O'Charley's, Panda Palace, Papa John's, Pizza Hut, Pepper's Deli, Popeye's, Sonic, Starbucks, Subway, Taco Bell, Taco Sombrero, TGIFriday's, Waffle House, Wendy's, Whataburger, ◎ Advance Parts, Barnes&Noble, Belk, Best Buy, Buick/Cadillac/Chevrolet, CVS Drug, $General, Foley's RV Ctr, Food Giant/gas, Fred's Store, Goodyear/auto, Honda, K-Mart, Michael's, Office Depot, Old Navy, Petsmart, Radio Shack, Rite Aid, Ross, Sam's Club/gas, Tire Kingdom, TJ Maxx, USPO, Walgreens, Winn-Dixie, **Urgent Care**, **S** ⓖ Chevron, Kangaroo/dsl, Murphy USA, RaceTrac, RaceWay/dsl, Shell/dsl, 🍴 Applebee's, Arby's/24hr, Burger King, Choung's Garden, Hooters, IHOP, KFC/LJ Silver, Krispy Kreme, Los Tres Amigos, McAlister's Deli, McDonald's, Morelia's Mexican, Sonic, Subway, Waffle House, Wendy's, 🏠 Best Value, Best Western, Comfort Suites, Days Inn, EconoLodge, Fairfield Inn, Hampton Inn, Holiday Inn, Motel 6, Quality Inn, Ramada, Sun Suites, Value Place, ◎ Ⓗ Ford/Lincoln, Freightliner, Home Depot, Kia, Mazda, Michael's, Nissan, Premium Outlets/famous brands, Verizon, Walmart/McDonald's, transmissions

31 Canal Rd, to Gulfport, **N** ⓖ Clarks/Subway/dsl, ◎ Bayberry RV Park, **S** ⓖ ⊕FLYING J/Denny's/dsl/LP/

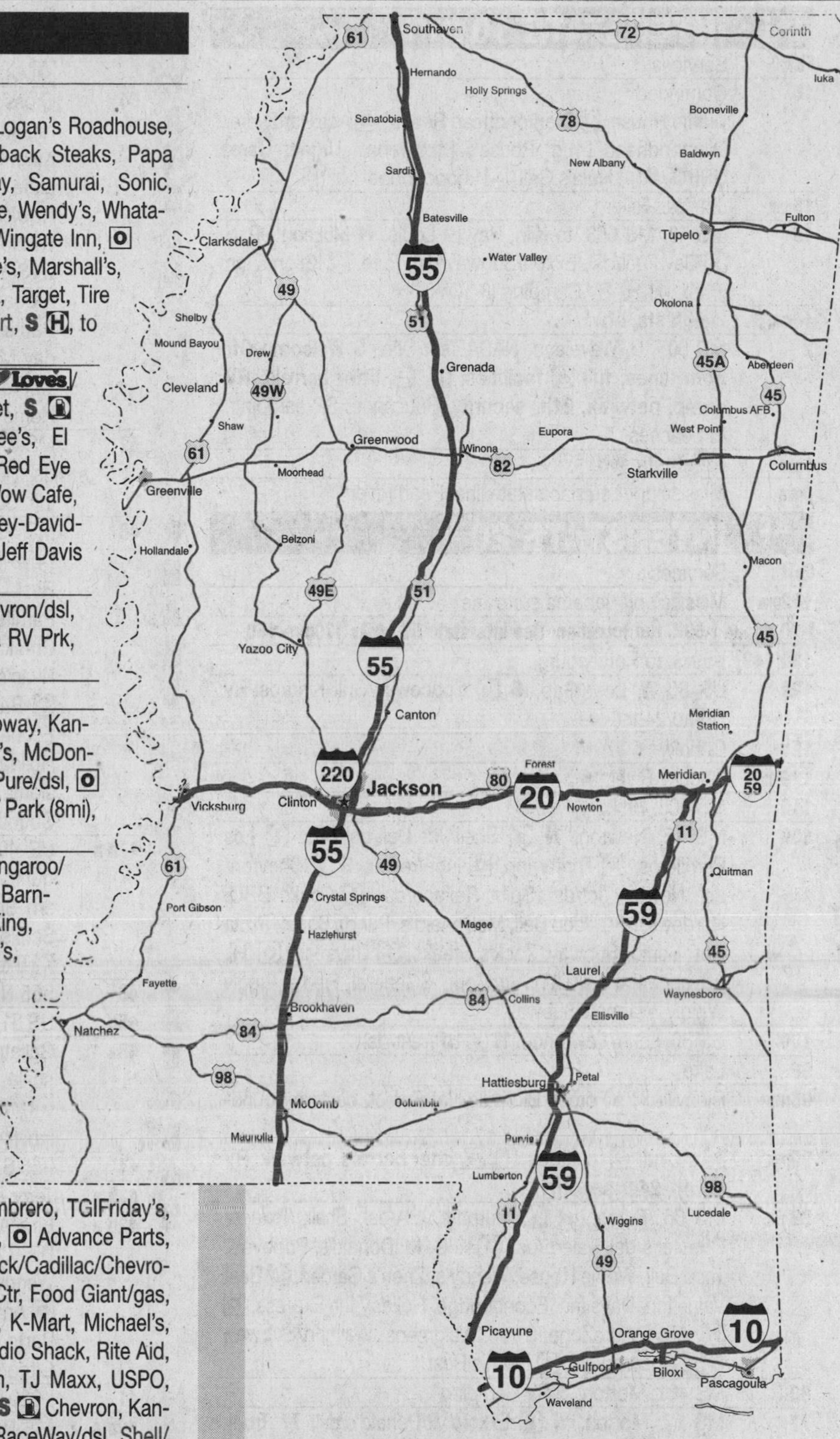

GULFPORT

31 Continued
scales/24hr, Shell/McDonald's/dsl/24hr, 🍴 Waffle House, Wendy's, 🏠 Legacy Inn, Magnolia Bay Inn, ◎ Plantation Pines RV Prk

28 to Long Beach, **S** ⓖ Chevron/dsl, Shell/dsl, 🍴 Subway, ◎ RV camping, tires

27mm Wolf River

24 Menge Ave, **N** ⓖ Chevron/Subway/dsl/scales, ◎ $General, **S** ⓖ Texaco, ◎ flea mkt/RV Park, golf, to beaches

20 to De Lisle, to Pass Christian, **N** ⓖ Kin-Mart

16 Diamondhead, **N** ⓖ Chevron/dsl, Shell/Domino's, 🍴 Burger King, DQ, Lenny's Subs, Red Zone Grill, Subway,

MS

🔁 INTERSTATE 10 CONT'D

Exit	Services
16	Continued
	Waffle House, 🏨 Diamondhead Resort, 🅾 Ace Hardware, Diamondhead Drug, Rouse's Mkt, repair, **Urgent Care**, USPO, **S** 🍽 Hula's Grill, 🏨 EconoLodge
15mm	Jourdan River
13	MS 43, MS 603, to Kiln, Bay St Louis, **N** McLeod SP, **S** 🅰 Bay Fuel/dsl, Exxon/Subway/dsl, Pure, 🏨 Knights Inn (6mi), 🅾 🏥, RV Camping (8-13mi)
10mm	**weigh sta, eb**
2	MS 607, to Waveland, NASA Test Site, **S Welcome Ctr both lanes, full** ♿ **facilities,** 📞 🏞, **litter barrels, RV dump, petwalk, 24hr security,** Buccaneer SP, camping, to beaches
1mm	**weigh sta, wb**
0mm	Mississippi/Louisiana state line, Pearl River

🔁 INTERSTATE 20

Exit	Services
172mm	Mississippi/Alabama state line
	I-20 W and I-59 S run together. See Interstate 59, exits 170mm-150
130[149]	I-59 S, to Hattiesburg.
129	US 80 W, Lost Gap, **S** 🅰 Spaceway/Grill King/dsl/RV Dump/24hr
121	Chunky
119mm	Chunky River
115	MS 503, Hickory
109	MS 15, Newton, **N** 🅰 Shell/Jct Deli/dsl/24hr, 🍽 Los Parrilleros, 🏨 Thrifty Inn, 🅾 lube/repair, **S** 🅰 Chevron/dsl, Newton Jct/dsl, Spirit, Texaco/dsl, 🍽 Cooks BBQ, Hardee's, KFC/Taco Bell, McDonald's, Panda Buffet, Pizza Hut, Sonic, Subway, Zack's Steaks, 🏨 Days Inn, 🅾 🏥, Advance Parts, AT&T, AutoZone, $General, Fred's, Piggly Wiggly, Walmart/Subway,
100	US 80, Lake, Lawrence, **N** 🅰 BP/rest/dsl
96	Lake
95mm	Bienville Nat Forest, Bienville Nat Forest, eastern boundary
90mm	🆁🆂 eb, **full** ♿ **facilities,** 📞 🏞, **litter barrels, petwalk, RV dump, 24hr security**
88	MS 35, Forest, **N** 🅰 Murphy USA/dsl, Shell, Texaco/Chester's/dsl, Valero/dsl, 🍽 KFC, McDonald's, Popeye's, Taco Bell, Waffle House, Wendy's, Zhen's Garden, 🏨 Best Value Inn, Days Inn, EconoLodge, Holiday Inn Express, 🅾 🏥, AT&T, AutoZone, $Tree, Walgreens, Walmart/Subway, **S** 🅰 Chevron/dsl, 🍽 Penn's Rest.
80	MS 481, Morton, **S** RV Camping
77	MS 13, Morton, **N** 🅰 Exxon/McDonald's/dsl, 77 Truck Ctr/dsl, Texaco/dsl, 🅾 🏥, RV camping, to Roosevelt SP, **S** 🅰 Shell/Subway/dsl
76mm	Bienville NF, western boundary
75mm	🆁🆂 wb, **full** ♿ **facilities,** 📞 🏞, **litter barrels, petwalk, RV dump, 24hr security**
68	MS 43, Pelahatchie, **N** 🅰 Chevron/Subway/dsl/24hr, Texaco/rest./dsl/24hr, 🅾 Jellystone Camping, **S** 🅰 BP/dsl
59	US 80, E Brandon, **2 mi** **S** 🅰 Shell
56	US 80, Brandon, **N** 🅰 Shell/dsl, 🍽 Heart&Soul Diner, Krystal, Sonny's BBQ, Taco Bell, 🏨 Microtel, 🅾 AT&T, AutoZone, O'Reilly Parts, Verizon, USPO, **S** 🅰 BP, Chevron, Mac's Gas, Texaco, 🍽 DQ, Penn's Rest., Sonic,

B R A N D O N

56	Continued
	Waffle House, Wendy's, 🏨 Best Value Inn, Red Roof Inn, 🅾 Auto+, vet, to Ross Barnett Reservoir
54	Crossgates Blvd, W Brandon, **N** 🅰 BP, Exxon, Kangaroo, Murphy USA, 🍽 Abner's Chicken, Applebee's, Burger King, Chick-fil-A, China Buffet, Fernando's Mexican, KFC, Little Caesars, Mazzio's, McAlister's Deli, McDonald's, Newk's Rest, Papa John's, Pizza Hut, Popeye's, Subway, Waffle House, 🅾 🏥, BigLots, Buick/GMC, Chevrolet, CVS Drug, $Tree, Ford, Fred's, GNC, Hancock Fabrics, Kroger/dsl, Lincoln, Nissan, Office Depot, Piggly Wiggly, Radio Shack, Scotty's Tire/repair, Toyota/Scion, Tuesday Morning, Walgreens, Walmart/Subway, **S** 🅰 Exxon, Valero/Domino's, Valero/dsl, 🍽 Wendy's, 🏨 La Quinta, 🅾 Home Depot, Honda, Tire Pros

P E A R L

52	MS 475, **N** 🅰 RaceWay/dsl, Texaco/dsl, Valero/Subway/dsl, 🍽 Waffle House, 🏨 Quality Inn, Ramada Ltd, Sleep Inn, Super 8, 🅾 Peterbilt, to Jackson 🖕
48	MS 468, Pearl, **N** 🅰 Exxon, Texaco, 🍽 Arby's, Bumpers Drive-In, Cracker Barrel, Domino's, Dunkin Donuts, Jose's Rest., KFC, Logan's Roadhouse, LoneStar Steaks, Los Parrilleros, McAlister's Deli, McDonald's, Mikado, Moss Creek Fishouse, O'Charley's, Popeye's, Ruby Tuesday, Ryan's, Shoney's, Sonic, Subway, Waffle House, Wendy's, 🏨 Baymont Inn, Best Western, Comfort Inn, Days Inn, EconoLodge, Fairfield Inn, Hampton Inn, Hilton Garden, Holiday Inn Express, Motel 6, 🅾 AT&T, CarCare, transmissions, **S** 🅰 Exxon/dsl, Valero/dsl, 🏨 Candlewood Suites, Country Inn&Suites, La Quinta, 🅾 $General
47b a	US 49 S, Flowood, **N** 🅰 🛢FLYING J/Denny's/dsl/LP/RV dump/24hr, 🛢Loves/Subway/dsl/scales/24hr, 🍽 Western Sizzlin, 🏨 🖕 Inn, Holiday Inn, 🅾 Bass Pro Shop, Sam's Club/dsl, SpeedCo, **2-3 mi** **S** 🍽 DQ, Waffle House, 🏨 Executive Inn, 🅾 Freightliner, Kenworth, tires
46	I-55 N, to Memphis
45b	US 51, State St, to downtown
45a	Gallatin St, to downtown, **N** 🅰 BP/dsl, Petro/rest./dsl/scales/24hr/@, Shell, 🅾 Blue Beacon, tires/truck repair, vet, **S** 🅰 🛢/McDonald's/dsl/scales/24hr, 🏨 Hilltop Inn, 🅾 Nissan
44	I-55 S (exits left from wb), to New Orleans
43b a	Terry Rd, **N** 🅰 Exxon/dsl, Jasco
42b a	Ellis Ave, Belvidere, **N** 🅰 BP, Citgo/dsl, Shell, 🍽 Capt D's, Church's, McDonald's, Pizza Hut, Popeye's, Rally's, Wendy's, 🏨 Best Inn, Metro Inn, Scottish Inn, Super 8, 🅾 Advance Parts, AutoZone, Family$, Firestone, O'Reilly Parts, Sav-a-Lot Foods, U-Haul, transmissions, zoo, **S** 🅰 Citgo/dsl, Exxon/dsl, 🍽 DQ
41	I-220 N, US 49 N, to Jackson
40b a	MS 18 W, Robinson Rd, **N** 🅰 Exxon/dsl, Jasco/dsl, Shell/dsl, 🍽 Arby's, El Mezquite, Krystal, Mazzio's, Picadilly's, Popeye's, 🅾 AT&T, Office Depot, auto repair, USPO, **S** 🅰 Chevron, Citgo/dsl, Murphy USA, Shell/Church's/dsl, 🍽 Chan's Garden, IHOP, McDonald's, Subway, Waffle House, Wendy's, 🏨 Comfort Inn, 🅾 🏥, $Tree, GNC, Lowes, Radio Shack, Walmart/Subway,
36	Springridge Rd, Clinton, **N** 🅰 Chevron/Burger King, Citgo/dsl, Murphy USA/dsl, Shell, 🍽 Capt D's, Chick-fil-A, China Buffet, DQ, El Sombrero, KFC, Little Ceasars, Mazzio's, McAlister's, McDonald's, Newk's Cafe, Sonic, Starbucks, Subway, Taco Bell, Waffle House, Wendy's, Zaxby's, 🏨 Clinton Inn, Comfort Inn, Days Inn, 🅾 Ad

J A C K S O N

N E W T O N

INTERSTATE 20 CONT'D

Exit	Services
36	Continued
	vance Parts, AT&T, BigLots, CVS Drug, $Tree, Family$, Home Depot, Kroger/gas, O'Reilly Parts, Radio Shack, Walgreens, Walmart (2mi), **S** ⓖ Exxon/Baskin-Robbins/Quiznos, Valero/dsl, 🍴 Applebee's, Bonsai, Egg Head Grill, Pizza Hut, Popeye's, Salsa's Mexican, Shoney's, 🏠 Best Western, Econolodge, Hampton Inn, Holiday Inn Express, Quality Inn, Super 8, Ⓞ Curves, Davis Tire, $General, Springridge RV Park, vet
35	US 80 E, Clinton, **N** ⓖ Chevron/dsl, Shell/dsl, Valero/dsl
34	Natchez Trace Pkwy
31	Norrell Rd
27	Bolton, **S** ⓖ Chevron/dsl
19	MS 22, Edwards, Flora, **N** Ⓞ Askew's Landing Camping (2mi), **S** ⓖ Exxon/dsl, Shell/dsl, 🏠 Relax Inn
17mm	Big Black River
15	Flowers
11	Bovina, **N** ⓖ Texaco/Subway/dsl/24hr, Ⓞ RV camping
10mm	weigh sta wb
8mm	weigh sta eb
6.5mm	parking area eb
5b a	US 61, MS 27 S, **N** ⓖ Exxon/dsl, Kangaroo/dsl, 🍴 Sonic, **S** same as 4a
4b a	Clay St, **N** ⓖ Valero/Kangaroo, 🏠 Battlefield Inn, Hampton Inn, Motel 6, Quality Inn, Ⓞ 🅷, RV Park, to Vicksburg NP, **S** ⓖ Texaco, Valero/dsl, 🍴 Bumper's Drive-In, China Buffet, Cracker Barrel, Pizza Inn, McAlister's deli, Rowdy's Rest., Waffle House, Wendy's, 🏠 Baymont Inn, Beechwood Inn/rest., Comfort Suites, Courtyard, Econolodge, Holiday Inn Express, La Quinta, Scottish Inn, Ⓞ $General, Outlet Mall/famous brands/deli, Toyota, same as 5
3	Indiana Ave, **N** ⓖ Valero/Subway/dsl, 🍴 China King, McDonald's, Papa John's, Waffle House, 🏠 Best Western, Deluxe Inn, Ⓞ Chevrolet, Chrysler/Dodge/Jeep, Corner Mkt Foods, Ford/Lincoln, Honda, Mazda, Nissan, Rite Aid, **S** ⓖ Kangaroo/dsl, 🍴 KFC, Goldie's BBQ, 🏠 Best Inn, Ⓞ Buick/Cadillac/GMC, Family$,
1c	Halls Ferry Rd, **N** ⓖ Exxon, 🍴 Burger King, Sonic, 🏠 Travel Inn, Ⓞ 🅷, Durst Drugs, **S** ⓖ Kangaroo/dsl, 🍴 Asian Kitchen, Capt D's, El Sombrero Mexican, Goldie's BBQ, Pizza Hut, Popeye's, Shoney's, Subway, Taco Bell, Taco Casa, Wendy's, Whataburger, 🏠 Candlewood Suites, Fairfield Inn, Holiday Inn, Rodeway Inn, Super 8, Ⓞ Advance Parts, AT&T, Belk, BigLots, Dillard's, $General, Home Depot, Fred's, JC Penney, Kroger/dsl, TJ Maxx, Walgreens, USPO, mall
1b	US 61 S, **S** ⓖ Kangaroo/Domino's, Murphy Express/dsl, 🍴 McDonald's, Panda Buffet, Waffle House, Ⓞ $Tree, Radio Shack, Verizon, Walmart/Subway, same as 1c
1a	Washington St, Vicksburg, **N Welcome Ctr both lanes, full 🅗 facilities,** 🄯, ⓖ Kangaroo/dsl, Shell/Subway/dsl, 🏠 AmeriStar Hotel/Casio/RV Park, **S** 🍴 Waffle House, 🏠 Best Value Inn, Days Inn
0mm	Mississippi/Louisiana state line, Mississippi River

INTERSTATE 22 (FUTURE)

Exit	Services
118mm	Alabama/Mississippi State Line
115mm	**Welcome Ctr/🆁🆂 wb, 🏞, litter barrels, petwalk, vending, RV dump**

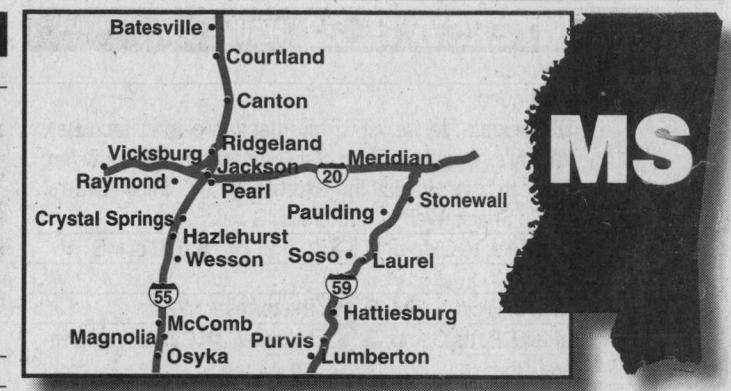

113	rd 23, Tremont, Smithville
108	rd 25 N, Belmont, Iuka
106mm	**weigh sta, both lanes**
104	rd 25 S, Fulton, Amory, **N** ⓖ Shell/cafe/dsl/scales, Texaco/dsl, 🍴 Baskin-Robbins/Huddle House, Burger King, Hardee's, McDonald's, Sonic, Subway, 🏠 Days Inn, Holiday Inn Express, Ⓞ AutoZone, $General, Food Giant/gas, Fred's, O'Reilly Parts, RV camping, Whitten HS, **S** ⓖ Murphy USA/dsl, Ⓞ KFC, Los Compadres Mexican, Pizza Hut, Wendy's, Ⓞ Walmart
104mm	Tombigbee River/Tenn-Tom Waterway
101	rd 178, rd 363, Peppertown, Mantachie, **N** ⓖ Exxon, **S** ⓖ Dorsey Fuel/dsl (2mi)
97	Fawn Grove Rd
94	rd 371, Mantachie, Mooreville, **N** ⓖ Woco/Pizza Inn/dsl
90	Auburn Rd, **N** ⓖ Dee's Oil/dsl
87	Veterans Blvd, **N** ⓖ Shell/Chix Rest/dsl, 🍴 Huddle House, 🏠 Wingate Inn, Ⓞ E. Presley Campground/Park, **S** Tombigbee SP
86	US 45 N, Tupelo, to Corinth, **1 exit N** ⓖ BP, Shell, Texaco, 🍴 Abner's Rest., Applebee's, Burger King, Capt D's, Chick-fil-A, Chili's, ChuckECheese, Cici's Pizza, Cracker Barrel, IHOP, Kyoto Japanese, Lenny's Subs, Logan's Roadhouse, McDonald's, New China, O'Charley's, Olive Garden, Pizza Hut, Red Lobster, Ryan's, Sonic, Subway, Taco Bell, Wendy's, 🏠 Baymont Inn, Best Inn, Comfort Inn, Days Inn, Fairfield Inn, Hampton Inn, Jameson Inn, La Quinta, Ⓞ AutoZone, Barnes&Noble, Belk, Best Buy, Books-A-Million, Dick's, $General, Ford/Lincoln, Hobby Lobby, Home Depot, Hyundai, JC Penney, Kohl's, Kroger/gas, Lowe's, Mazda, NAPA, Old Navy, Petsmart, Ross, Sam's Club/gas, Sears, Staples, Toyota, Tuesday Morning, Walgreens, Walmart
85	Natchez Trace Pkwy
81	rd 178, McCullough Blvd, **N** ⓖ Loves/McDonald's/dsl/scales/24hr, **S** ⓖ Exxon/dsl, Shell/dsl, Texaco/dsl, 🍴 Old Venice Pizza, Sonic, 🏠 Super 8, Ⓞ $General, USPO
76	rd 9 S, Sherman, Pontotoc, **N** ⓖ Wild Bill's/dsl, Ⓞ Sherman RV Ctr
73	rd 9 N, Blue Springs
64	rd 15, rd 30 E, Pontotoc, Ripley, **N** ⓖ Eagle/dsl, **S** ⓖ Pilot/Arby's/scales/dsl/24hr, Shell/dsl
63	New Albany, **N** ⓖ Dee's Oil/dsl, Ⓞ Buick/Chevrolet/GMC, Ford
62mm	Tallahatchie River
61	rd 30 W, W New Albany, **N** ⓖ Gas Express, 🍴 China Buffet, McAlister's Deli, McDonald's, Pizza Hut, Subway, Wendy's, 🏠 Hampton Inn, Ⓞ 🅷, Rite Aid, Walgreens, **S** ⓖ Exxon, Murphy USA/dsl, Shell, 🍴 Burger King, Capt

MS

INTERSTATE 22 (FUTURE) CONT'D

Exit	Services
61	Continued D's, Huddle House, KFC, Mi Pueblo Mexican, Taco Bell, Wendy's, Western Sizzlin, 🏨 Comfort Inn, Economy Inn, Hallmarc Inn, Holiday Inn Express, ⊙ 🄷, $Tree, Lowe's, Radio Shack, Walmart, to U of MS
60	Glenfield, to Oxford, N 🏨 Budget Inn, S to U of MS
55	Myrtle
48	rd 178, Hickory Flat, S gas:Trkstp/rest/dsl/24hr
41	rd 346, Potts Camp, S 🅰 Flicks/dsl, ⊙ CarQuest, $General
41mm	Tippah River
37	Lake Center, N Chewalla Lake/RV camping
30	rd 7, rd 4, Holly Springs, Oxford, N 🅰 Exxon, Shell/Chester's/BBQ, 🍴 Capt D's, El Nopalito, Huddle House, KFC, McDonalds, Panda Buffet, Pizza Hut, Popeye's, Sonic, Subway, Taco Bell, Wendy's, 🏨 Magnolia Inn, ⊙ 🄷, AutoZone, $General, Libby's Drug, Save-a-Lot, Wall Doxey SP/RV camping, S 🅰 Exxon, 🏨 Days Inn, Le Brooks Inn, ⊙ Walmart
26	W Holly Springs
21	Red Banks, N 🅰 Dee's Oil/dsl, Texaco/dsl
18	Victoria, E Byhalia, N 🅰 BP
14	rd 309, Byhalia, N 🅰 Exxon, Shell/Chester's/dsl, 🏨 Best Value Inn
10	W Byhalia
6	Bethel Rd, Hacks Crossroad, N 🅰 BP, ⊛FLYING J/Denny's/dsl/scales/LP/RV dump/24hr, Shell/Chesters/dsl, 🍴 JR's Grill, Tops BBQ, 🏨 Best Western, Super 8, ⊙ truck repair
6mm	parking area both lanes
4	rd 305, Olive Branch, Independence, N 🅰 BP/dsl, Mobil/Huddle House, Shell/Circle K, 🍴 Old Style BBQ, Pizza Hut, 🏨 Holiday Inn Express, S 🅰 BP/Quiznos, ⊙ CVS Drug
3.5mm	weigh sta, both lanes
2	rd 302, Olive Branch, N 🍴 Abbay's Rest., Baskin-Robbins, Buffalo Wild Wings, Chick-fil-A, Chili's, Colton's Steaks, IHOP, Krystal, Lenny's Subs, McAlisters Deli, O'Charley's, Starbucks, Subway, Wendy's, 🏨 Candlewood Suites, Comfort Suites, ⊙ $Tree, Ford, Home Depot, Lowe's, Radio Shack, Walmart, S 🅰 Chevron/dsl, Shell/Circle K, 🍴 Applebees, Backyard Burger, Burger King, Casa Mexicana, McDonald's, Steak Escape, Subway, Taco Bell, Waffle House, Zaxby's, 🏨 Comfort Inn, Hampton Inn, ⊙ AutoZone, CVS Drug, GNC, Goodyear/auto, Kroger/gas
1	Craft Rd, N ⊙ American RV Ctr, Chevrolet, Hyundai, Suzuki
0mm	Mississippi/Tennessee state line, I-22 (future) begins/ends. US 78 continues wb.

INTERSTATE 55

Exit	Services
291.5mm	Mississippi/Tennessee state line
291	State Line Rd, Southaven, E 🅰 Exxon, RaceWay/dsl, Shell/dsl, 🍴 Interstate BBQ, Little Caesars, Subway, Tops BBQ, Waffle House, 🏨 Days Inn, Holiday Inn Express, Quality Inn, Southern Inn, Super 8, ⊙ Family$, Firestone/auto, Goodyear/auto, Kroger/dsl, Southaven RV Park, Walgreens, W 🅰 Exxon, 🍴 Capt D's, Checker's, China Wok, Dales Rest, El Patron Mexican, Lucky China,

OLIVE BRANCH

SOUTHAVEN

Exit	Services
291	Continued Mainstreet Pizza, Sonic, Taco Bell, Wendy's, ⊙ BigLots, Fred's, Mainstreet Automotive, Rite Aid, USPO, tires
289	MS 302, to US 51, Horn Lake, E 🅰 BP/Circle K, Shell, 🍴 Abbays Rest., Backyard Burger, Baskin-Robbins, Brusters, Buffalo Wild Wings, Burger King, Chick-fil-A, Chili's, Dunkin Donuts, Fazoli's, Firehouse Subs, Fox&Hound, IHOP, Haru Japanese, Huey's Rest., Hunan Buffet, Krystal, Kublai Khan, La Hacienda, Lenny's Subs, Logan's Roadhouse, Longhorn Steaks, Maria's Cantina, McDonald's, Mi Pueblo, Nagoya Japanese, O'Charley's, Olive Garden, On-the-Border, Outback Steaks, Red Lobster, Sonic, Starbucks, Steak'n Shake, Subway, TGIFriday's, Wendy's, 🏨 Comfort Suites, Courtyard, Fairfield Inn, Hampton Inn, Hilton Garden, Holiday Inn, Home2Suites, Residence Inn, ⊙ 🄷, Urgent Care, Aldi Foods, AT&T, Best Buy, Books-A-Million, Buick/GMC, Chevrolet, Chrysler/Dodge/Jeep, CVS Drug, Dillards, $Tree, Ford, GNC, Gordman's, Hancock Fabrics, JC Penney, Jo-Ann Fabrics, Kroger/dsl, Lowe's, Marshall's, Nissan, Office Depot, Old Navy, PetCo, Radio Shack, Sam's Club/gas, Tuesday Morning, Verizon, Walmart/Subway, W 🅰 BP/Circle K, Phillips 66/dsl, Shell/Circle K/dsl, 🍴 Applebee's, Arby's, Country Home Buffet, ChuckECheese's, Cracker Barrel, Grand Buffet, Holiday Deli, Hooters, KFC, McDonald's, Memphis BBQ, Mrs Winner's, Papa John's, Pizza Hut, Popeye's, Ryan's, Sekisui Japan, Taco Bell, TX Roadhouse, Waffle House, Wendy's, Zaxby's, 🏨 Best Western, Comfort Inn, Drury Inn, EconoLodge, La Quinta, Motel 6, Ramada Ltd, Sleep Inn, ⊙ CVS Drug, Family$, Gateway Tires/repair, Home Depot, Kroger, Meineke, Save-a-Lot Foods, Target, Verizon, Walgreens
287	Church Rd, E 🅰 Citgo/dsl, 🍴 Domino's, Wadford's Grill, ⊙ AutoZone, W 🅰 Citgo/dsl, Shell/Circle K/dsl, 🍴 Boiling Point Seafood, Casa Mexicana, McDonald's, Sonic, Subway, Taco Bell, 3 Guys Pizza, Waffle House, 🏨 Keywest Inn, Magnolia Inn, ⊙ El Daze RV Camping (1mi), Family$, Fred's, Harley-Davidson, Jellystone Camping, Southaven RV Ctr, Walgreens
285mm	weigh sta both lanes
284	to US 51, Nesbit Rd, W 🅰 Shell, 🍴 Happy Daze Dairybar, ⊙ USPO
283	I-69, MS 304, Tunica
280	MS 304, US 51, Hernando, E 🅰 Exxon, Murphy USA/dsl, 🍴 Arby's, Asian Buffet, Capt D's, Dominos, Fins Grill, Guadalajara Mexican, KFC, Sonic, Steak Escape, Taco Bell, Zaxby's, 🏨 Days Inn, Hampton Inn, ⊙ Urgent Care, AT&T, $Tree, Ultimate Tires/repair, Walmart, Walgreens, W 🅰 Mobil, Shell/Circle K/dsl, 🍴 Brick Oven Rest., Coleman's BBQ, Lenny's Subs, Little Caesars, McDonald's, Mi Pueblo, Mr Chen's, Papa John's, Pizza Hut, Subway, Taco Felix, Waffle House, Wendy's, 🏨 Super 8, ⊙ AutoZone, Bryant Repair, Desoto Museum, Family$, Fred's, Kroger/gas, Memphis S Camping (2mi), NAPA, USPO, to Arkabutla Lake
279mm	Welcome Ctr sb, full ♿ facilities, 🄲, 🄵, litter barrels, petwalk, RV dump, 24hr security
276mm	🆁🆂 nb, full ♿ facilities, 🄲, 🄵, litter barrels, petwalk, RV dump, 24hr security
273mm	Coldwater River
271	MS 306, Coldwater, W 🅰 Shell/dsl, 🍴 Subway, ⊙ Memphis S RV Park, Lake Arkabutla

⬆N INTERSTATE 55 CONT'D

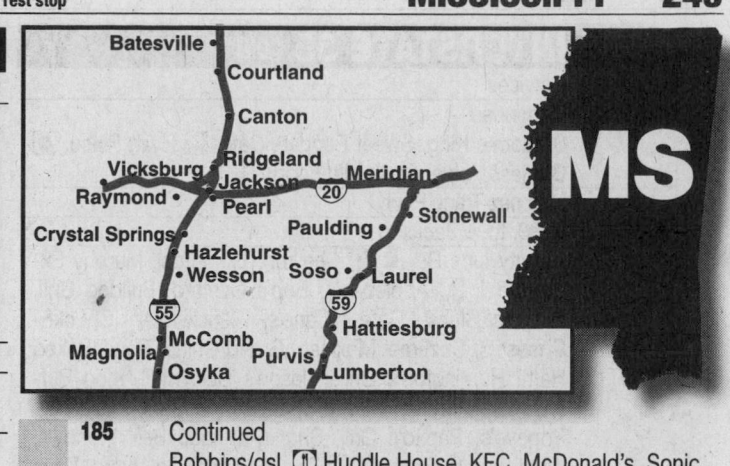

Exit	Services
265	MS 4, Senatobia, **W** 🅖 BP/dsl, Exxon, ⬛/Huddle House/dsl/scales/24hr, Shell/dsl, 🍴 Backyard Burger, Coleman's BBQ, Domino's, KFC, McDonald's/playplace, New China Buffet, Pizza Hut, Popeye's, Rio Lindo Mexican, Sonic, Subway, Taco Bell, Waffle House, Wendy's, 🏠 Best Value Inn, Days Inn, 🅞 H, AT&T, CarQuest, City Drug, Curves, Fred's, Kaye Mkt, transmissions, truck repair, USPO
263	rd 740, S Senatobia
257	MS 310, Como, **E** 🅖 Dee's Oil, 🅞 N Sardis Lake, **W** 🅖 Citgo/dsl, 🍴 Windy City Grille (1mi)
252	MS 315, Sardis, **E** 🅖 Chevron/dsl, Local/dsl, 🍴 McDonald's, 🏠 Lake Inn, Super 8, 🅞 NAPA, to Kyle SP, Sardis Dam, repair, RV camping, **W** 🅖 BP/Chester's/dsl, Shell/dsl, 🍴 Sonic, 🅞 H, $General, Family$, Fred's
246	MS 35, N Batesville, **E** to Sardis Lake, **W** 🅖 ❤Loves/McDonald's/Subway/dsl/scales/24hr, Shell/dsl
243b a	MS 6, to Batesville, **E** 🅖 BP/dsl, Murphy USA/dsl, Shell/dsl, 🍴 Backyard Burger, Chili's, Mi Pueblo Mexican, Zaxby's, 🏠 Comfort Suites, 🅞 H, $Tree, Lowe's, Walmart/Subway, to Sardis Lake, U of MS, **W** 🅖 BP, Exxon/dsl, Phillips 66/dsl, Shell/dsl, Valero/Kangaroo/dsl, 🍴 Burger King, Burn's BBQ, Cafe Ole, Capt D's, Cracker Barrel, Domino's, Hardee's, Huddle House, KFC, McDonald's, New China, Pizza Hut, Popeye's, Sonic, Subway, Taco Bell, Waffle House, Wendy's, Western Sizzlin, 🏠 Days Inn, EconoLodge, Hampton Inn, Holiday Inn, Quality Inn, Ramada Ltd, 🅞 H, **Urgent Care**, AT&T, AutoZone, Curves, $General, Factory Stores/famous brands, Family$, Fred's, Kroger, O'Reilly Parts, Piggly Wiggly, Save-a-Lot, Walgreens, USPO
240mm	🆁🆂 both lanes, full ♿ facilities, 🚻, 🛢, litter barrels, petwalk, RV dump, 24hr security
237	to US 51, Courtland, **E** 🅖 Pure/dsl, **W** 🅞 $General
233	to Enid Dam, **E** to Enid Lake, RV camping
227	MS 32, Oakland, **E** to Cossar SP, Sunrise RV Park, **W** 🅖 Exxon/Chester's/dsl, Shell/dsl, 🅞 $General, antiques
220	MS 330, Tillatoba, **E** 🅖 Conoco/rest./dsl/@
211	MS 7 N, to Coffeeville, **E** Frog Hollow RV Park, **W** 🅖 Shell/Chester's/dsl
208	Papermill Rd, **E** Grenada 🅞
206	MS 8, MS 7 S, to Grenada, **E** 🅖 Exxon/dsl, Shell/dsl, 🍴 Burger King, China Buffet, Church's, Clubhouse Rest., Domino's, Great Wall Chinese, Jake&Rip's Café, La Cabana Mexican, Lost Pizza Co., McAlister's Deli, McDonald's, Pizza Hut, Pizza Inn, Shoney's, Subway, Taco Bell, Wendy's, Western Sizzlin, 🏠 Baymont Inn, Best Value Inn, Days Inn, EconoLodge, Hampton Inn, Holiday Inn Express, Quality Inn, Relax Inn, Super 8, 🅞 H, Advance Parts, AT&T, AutoZone, Chrysler/Dodge/Jeep, Curves, CVS Drug, $General, $Tree, GNC, O'Reilly Parts, Radio Shack, USPO, Walmart/McDonald's, to Grenada Lake/RV camping, **W** 🅖 Exxon/Huddle House, 🍴 Waffle House, 🏠 Comfort Inn, Motel 6, 🅞 Ford/Lincoln, Nissan, Toyota, repair
204mm	parking area sb, 🚻, litter barrels
202mm	parking area nb, 🚻, litter barrels
199	Troutt Rd, S Grenada, **E** to camp McCain
195	MS 404, Duck Hill, **E** to Camp McCain, **W** 🅖 Conoco/dsl
185	US 82, Winona, **E** 🅖 Exxon, Shell/Kangaroo/Baskin-
185	Continued Robbins/dsl, 🍴 Huddle House, KFC, McDonald's, Sonic, Subway, Waffle House, 🏠 Best Value Inn, Holiday Inn Express, Magnolia Lodge, Relax Inn, 🅞 H, **W** 🅖 ⬛/Taco Bell/dsl/scales/24hr/@
174	MS 35, MS 430, Vaiden, **E** 🅖 Chevron/dsl, 35-55 Trkstp/Chester's/dsl/scales/24hr, Shell, 🅞 NAPA, Vaiden Camping, **W** 🅖 Exxon/dsl
173mm	🆁🆂 sb, full ♿ facilities, 🚻, 🛢, litter barrels, petwalk, RV dump, 24hr security
164	to West, **W** 🅖 West Trkstp/dsl
163mm	🆁🆂 nb, full ♿ facilities, 🚻, 🛢, litter barrels, petwalk, RV dump, 24hr security
156	MS 12, Durant, **E** 🅖 Shell/Chester's/dsl, 🍴 Subway, 🏠 Durant Motel/rest. (3mi), Super 8, **W** H (7mi)
150	**E** Holmes Co SP, RV camping
146	MS 14, Goodman, **W** to Little Red Schoolhouse
144	MS 17, to Pickens, **W** 🅖 BP/Baskin-Robbins/dsl/24hr, 🅞 to Little Red Schoolhouse
139	MS 432, to Pickens
133	Vaughan, **E** to Casey Jones Museum
128mm	Big Black River
124	MS 16, to N Canton
119	MS 22, to MS 16 E, Canton, **E** 🅖 Canton Jct/dsl, Exxon, Kangaroo/Subway/dsl, Shell/Domino's, Valero/dsl, 🍴 El Sombrero Mexican, McDonald's, Pizza Hut, Popeye's, Sonic, Waffle House, Wendy's, Western Sizzlin, 🏠 Best Value Inn, Best Western, Brentwood Inn, Hampton Inn, Holiday Inn Express, La Quinta, Relax Inn, Studio 9, 🅞 H, $General Mkt, Family$, O'Reilly Parts, to Ross Barnett Reservoir, **W** 🅖 Chevron/KFC/dsl, Citgo, ❤Loves/Arby's/dsl/scales/24hr/@, Texaco/Penn's/dsl, 🍴 Bumpers Drive-In, 2 Rivers Steaks
118a b	Nissan Parkway, **E** to Nissan
114a b	Sowell Rd
112	US 51, Gluckstadt, **E** 🅖 Exxon/Krystal/dsl, 🍴 Sonic, 🏠 Super 8, 🅞 Goodyear/auto, **W** Camper Corral RV Ctr
108	MS 463, Madison, **E** 🅖 Shell/dsl, Valero/dsl, 🍴 Applebee's, Backyard Burger, Burger King, Chick-Fil-A, Chili's, Coldstone, Corner Bakery Café, Dickey's BBQ, El Potrillo, Haute Pig Café, Little Caesars, 🅞 AT&T, Best Buy, Dick's, $Tree, GNC, Lowe's, Michael's, Office Depot, PetCo, SteinMart, Walmart **W** 🅖 Exxon/KFC/dsl, 🍴 BoneFish Grill, Nagoya Japanese, Papito's Grill, PieWorks, Pizza Inn, Subway, Tay's BBQ, Wendy's, 🏠 Hilton Garden, 🅞 H, CVS Drug, Home Depot, Kroger
105c b	Old Agency Rd, **E** 🅖 Chevron/dsl, 🏠 Home2Suites, 🅞 Honda, Hyundai, **W** 🍴 Biaggi's Ristorante, 5 Guys Burgers, Maggie Moo's, PF Changs, Ruth's Chris Steaks,

Left margin (vertical): **BATESVILLE**   **GRENADA**

Right/center margin (vertical): **CANTON**   **MADISON**

Map locations: Batesville, Courtland, Canton, Ridgeland, Vicksburg, Jackson, Meridian, Raymond, Pearl, Crystal Springs, Paulding, Stonewall, Hazlehurst, Wesson, Soso, Laurel, Magnolia, McComb, Hattiesburg, Osyka, Purvis, Lumberton, 20, 55, 59, **MS**

⬆N INTERSTATE 55 CONT'D

Exit	Services
105c b	Continued Smoothie King, Sweet Peppers Cafe, 🛏 Hyatt Place, ⊙ Barnes&Noble, Fresh Mkt Foods
105a	Natchez Trace Pkwy
104	I-220, to W Jackson
103	County Line Rd, E 🕭 Chevron, Exxon/dsl, Murphy Express/dsl, 🍴 Applebee's, Bop's Custard, Bulldog Grill, Burgers&Blues Cafe, Cane's, Chick-fil-A, ChuckE-Cheese's, Cozumel Mexican, Grand China, HoneyBaked Ham, Huntington's Grille, Jason's Deli, KFC, King Buffet, Krispy Kreme, Mazzio's, Peachtree Cafe, Pizza Hut, Popeye's, Papito's Grill, Shoney's, Taco Bell, Wendy's, Whataburger, Zaxby's, 🛏 Cabot Lodge, Courtyard, Days Inn, EconoLodge, Hilton, Quality Inn, Red Roof Inn, ⊙ Acura, Belk, Best Buy, BigLots, Cadillac, Dillard's, $Tree, JC Penney, Lowe's, Marshall's, Office Depot, Old Navy, Radio Shack, Sam's Club/gas, TJ Maxx, Tuesday Morning, Verizon, Walgreens, Walmart, to Barnett Reservoir, W 🍴 Nagoya Japanese, Olive Garden, Red Lobster, Logan's Roadhouse, Subway, 🛏 Drury Inn, Holiday Inn Express, Motel 6, Studio 7, ⊙ Fred's, Home Depot, Jo-Ann Fabrics, Office Depot, Petsmart, Target, Upton Tire
102b	Beasley Rd, Adkins Blvd, E 🍴 Cracker Barrel, Outback Steaks, Twin Peaks Rest., 🛏 Super 8, ⊙ Chevrolet, Ford, Nissan, Toyota/Scion, W 🕭 Exxon/dsl, Shell/dsl, 🍴 Baskin-Robbins, Burger King, Chili's, IHOP, McDonald's, 🛏 Baymont Inn, Best Western, Fairfield Inn, Hampton Inn, Harmony Court, Howard Johnson, InTown Suites, ⊙ Car-Max, Mercedes, Save-A-Lot Foods, frontage rds access 102a
102a	Briarwood, E 🛏 La Quinta, ⊙ Buick/GMC, W 🍴 Capt D's, Popeye's, 🛏 Clarion, Hampton Inn, ⊙ Chrysler/Dodge/Jeep, Porsche/Smart
100	North Side Dr W, E 🕭 BP/dsl, Chevron, Sprint, 🍴 Burger King, Char Rest., Charokee Drive-In, McAlister's Deli, Papa John's, Piccadilly's, Pizza Hut, Starbucks, Subway, Wendy's, 🛏 Extended Stay America, ⊙ AT&T, Audi, Books-A-Million, CVS Drug, $Tree, Firestone/auto, Goodyear/auto, Jaguar/LandRover, Kroger/gas, Office Depot, SteinMart, VW, Walgreens, vet, W 🕭 Exxon/dsl FastLane, Shell, 🍴 Domino's, Hooters, Waffle House, 🛏 Select Motel, USA Inn
99	Meadowbrook Rd, Northside Dr E (from nb), E 🍴 Newk's Eatery
98c b	MS 25 N, Lakeland Dr, E 🕭 Shell/dsl, 🛏 Parkside Inn, ⊙ LaFleur's Bluff SP, museum, W 🅗, ⊙
98a	Woodrow Wilson Dr (exits left from nb), downtown
96c	Fortification St, E 🛏 Studio 6 Suites, W 🅗, Bellhaven College
96b	High St, Jackson, E ⊙ BMW, Chevrolet, Infiniti, Lexus, W 🕭 Shell/Subway/dsl, Valero/Kangaroo/dsl, 🍴 Arby's, Chimneyville Cafe, Domino's, Popeye's, Shoney's, Taco Bell, Waffle House, Wendy's, Whataburger, 🛏 Best Western, Comfort Inn, Days Inn, Jackson Hotel, Hampton Inn, Red Roof Inn, Regency Hotel, Travelodge, ⊙ 🅗, Honda, Subaru/Volvo, fairgrounds, museum, st capitol
96a	Pearl St (from nb), Jackson, W downtown, access to same as 96b
94	(46 from nb), I-20 E, to Meridian, US 49 S
45b[I-20]	US 51, State St, to downtown, N 🕭 BP, Petro, Shell, S 🕭 Pilot
45a	Gallatin St (from sb), N 🕭 BP, Petro/dsl, Shell, S 🍴 🚂 /McDonald's/dsl, ⊙ Nissan
92c	(44 from sb), I-20 W, to Vicksburg, US 49 N
92b	US 51 N, State St, Gallatin St
92a	McDowell Rd, E 🕭 Petro/dsl, 🚂/McDonald's/dsl, W 🕭 BP/dsl, BJ's/dsl, Citgo/dsl, Exxon, Shell, 🍴 McDonald's, Subway, Waffle House, ⊙ Food Depot, Fred's, Rite Aid, Roses
90b	Daniel Lake Blvd (from sb), W 🕭 Shell, ⊙ Harley-Davidson
90a	Savanna St, E ⊙ transmissions, W 🕭 BP, ⊙ Caney Creek RV Ctr
88	Elton Rd, W 🕭 Exxon/dsl, Shell/Subway/dsl
85	Byram, E 🕭 Blue Sky/dsl, BP/Burns Grill/dsl, 🍴 Krystal, Mexican Grill, Tin Shed BBQ, 🛏 Comfort Inn, ValuePlace, ⊙ Swinging Bridge RV Park, W 🕭 Byram/dsl, Chevron, Exxon/dsl, Valero/Kangaroo/dsl, 🍴 Backyard Burger, Burger King, Capt D's, Domino's, KFC, Mazzio's, McAlister's Deli, McDonald's, New China, Newk's Eatery, Papa John's, Pizza Hut, Popeye's, Sonic, Subway, Taco Bell, Waffle House, Wendy's, 🛏 Days Inn, Holiday Inn Express, ⊙ AutoZone, $General, Family$, Mkt Place Foods, NAPA, O'Reilly Parts, Tire Depot, Walgreens
81	Wynndale Rd, E ⊙ repair, W 🕭 Chevron/dsl
78	Terry, E 🕭 Citgo/dsl, Texaco/Subway/dsl, ⊙ Buick/Chevrolet/GMC (1mi), Fred's, USPO, W 🕭 Mac's, ⊙ $General
72	MS 27, Crystal Springs, E 🕭 Exxon/Subway/dsl, Phillips 66/dsl, 🍴 Louise's Pit BBQ, McDonald's, Popeye's, ⊙ Ford, vet
68	to US 51, S Crystal Springs, gas/dsl, ⊙ Red Barn Produce, vet
65	to US 51, Gallman, E 🕭 Stuckey's/dsl
61	MS 28, Hazlehurst, E 🕭 BP, Exxon/Circle K/Subway/dsl, Murphy Express/dsl, Phillips 66/dsl, Pump&Save, 🍴 Bumpers Drive Inn, Burger King, China Buffet, KFC/Taco Bell, McDonald's, Pizza Hut, Sonic, Waffle House, Wendy's, 🛏 Best Value Inn, Claridge Inn, Western Inn, ⊙ 🅗, Advance Parts, $General, $Tree, Family$, Fred's, Walgreens, Walmart
59	to S Hazlehurst
56	to Martinsville
54mm	🆁🆂 both lanes, full ♿ facilities, 🅲, 🛏, litter barrels, petwalk, RV dump, vending, 24hr security
51	to Wesson, E ⊙ Lake Lincoln SP, W 🕭 Country Jct Trkstp/rest/dsl
48	Mt Zion Rd, to Wesson
42	to US 51, N Brookhaven, E 🕭 Exxon/Subway, Shell/Gridiron Grill/dsl/scales/24hr, ⊙ 🅗, W 🛏 Super 8
40	to MS 550, Brookhaven, E 🕭 BP/Domino's/dsl, Blue Sky, Exxon/Subway, Murphy USA/dsl, Shell/dsl, 🍴 Bowie BBQ, Burger King, China Buffet, Cracker Barrel, DQ, Hudgey's Rest., KFC, Krystal, El Sombrero Little Caesars, McDonald's, Mitchell's Steaks, Pizza Hut, Popeye's, Sonic, Taco Bell, Waffle House, Wards Burgers, Wendy's, Western Sizzlin, 🛏 Best Inn, Best Value Inn, Comfort Inn, Hampton Inn, Holiday Inn Express, Lincoln Inn, Spanish Inn, ⊙ 🅗, AT&T, AutoZone, Buick/Cadillac/Chevrolet/GMC, CarQuest, $General, $Tree, Family$, Ford/Lincoln, Fred's, Gene's Tires, Honda, Nissan, O'Reilly Parts, Rite Aid, Save-A-Lot Foods, Toyota, Walgreens, Walmart, W ⊙ Home Depot
38	US 84, S Brookhaven, W 🕭 Chevron/dsl

JACKSON

BROOKHAVEN

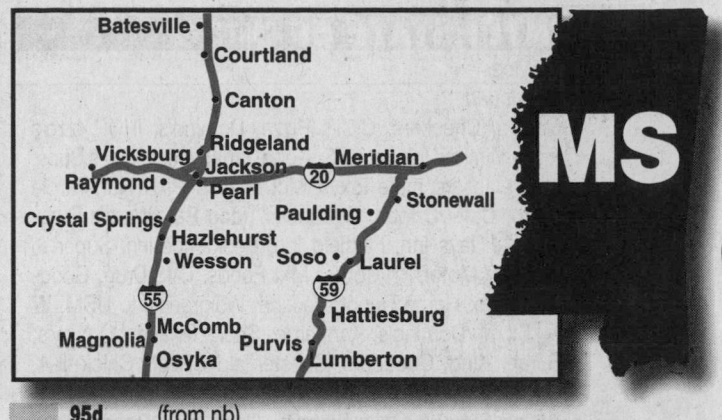

INTERSTATE 55 CONT'D

Exit	Services
30	Bogue Chitto, Norfield, E ⓖ Shell/BogueChitto/dsl, W 🅞 Bogue Chitto RV Park
24	Johnston Station, E to Lake Dixie Springs
20b a	US 98 W, to Natchez, Summit, E ⓖ BP/dsl, Shell/dsl, Stop'n Shop/dsl, W ⓖ Exxon/Subway/dsl, ShawnMart/dsl
18	MS 570, Smithdale Rd, N McComb, E ⓖ BP, 🍴 Burger King, McDonald's, Piccadilly's, Ruby Tuesday, 🏨 Holiday Inn Express, 🅞 Ⓗ, AT&T, Belk, JC Penney, Kia, Lowe's, Radio Shack, Walgreens, Walmart/Subway, mall, W ⓖ Chevron/Mr Whiskers/dsl, 🍴 Applebee's, Arby's, El Dorado Mexican, Santa Fe Steaks, 🏨 Deerfield Inn, Hampton Inn, Ramada, 🅞 Ford/Lincoln
17	Delaware Ave, McComb, E ⓖ BP/Subway, Blue Sky, Chevron/dsl, Exxon/Penn's Rest., Pump&Savor, RaceWay/dsl, 🍴 Backyard BBQ, Burger King, Domino's, Golden Corral; Kyoto Steaks, Papa's Pizza, Popeye's, Smoothie King, Sonic, Taco Bell, Waffle House, Wendy's, 🏨 Best Western, Comfort Inn, Executive Inn, 🅞 Ⓗ, AutoZone, CVS Drug, $General, Family$, Fred's, Kroger, Office Depot, O'Reilly Parts, Rite Aid, Verizon, W 🏨 Days Inn, 🅞 Chrysler/Dodge/Jeep
15b a	US 98 E, MS 48 W, McComb, 1 mi E ⓖ BP, Citgo, Exxon/Subway, Presley QuikStop/dsl, Shell, 🍴 Church's, KFC, 🏨 Camellian Motel, 🅞 Advance Parts, $General, Family$, tires, vet; W ⓖ BP/dsl
13	Fernwood Rd, E truck repair, W ⓖ Loves/Chester's/McDonald's/dsl/scales/24hr/@, 🅞 golf, to Percy Quin SP
10	MS 48, Magnolia, 1 mi E ⓖ Exxon, Shell/dsl, 🍴 Subway, 🅞 RV camping
8	MS 568, Magnolia
4	Chatawa
3mm	Welcome Ctr nb, full 🚻 facilities, 🍴, 🅿️, litter barrels, petwalk, RV dump, 24hr security
2mm	weigh sta nb
1	MS 584, Osyka, Gillsburg
0mm	Mississippi/Louisiana state line

INTERSTATE 59

Exit	Services
172mm	Mississippi/Alabama state line
149mm	I-59 and I-20 run together to AL state line. See Interstate 20, exits 170mm-150
142	to US 11, Savoy, W to Dunns Falls
137	to N Enterprise, to Stonewall
134	MS 513, S Enterprise
126	MS 18, to Rose Hill, Pachuta, E ⓖ BB/dsl, Pachuta TP/dsl
118	to Vossburg, Paulding
113	MS 528, to Heidelberg, E ⓖ Chevron/dsl, Exxon/Subway/dsl, Shell, 🍴 Ward's Burgers
109mm	parking area sb, litter barrels, no restrooms
106mm	parking area nb, litter barrels, no restrooms
104	Sandersville, E Lucky's Rest. (4mi)
99	US 11, E 🅞 Sleepy Hollow RV Park (1mi)
97	US 84 E, E ⓖ Exxon/Huddle House/dsl/scales, Kangaroo/Subway/dsl, 🍴 Hardee's, Ward's Burgers, W ⓖ Shell, 🍴 KFC, Vic's Rest.
96b	MS 15 S, Cook Ave
96a	Masonite Rd, 4th Ave

Exit	Services
95d	(from nb)
95c	Beacon St, Laurel, W 🍴 Burger King, Cane's, Church's, DQ, Little Caesars, McDonald's, Popeye's, Tokyo Grill, 🏨 TownHouse Motel, 🅞 AT&T, Expert Tire, Family$, Grocery Depot, JC Penney, NAPA, Winn-Dixie, museum of art
95b a	US 84 W, MS 15 N, 16th Ave, Laurel, 0-2 mi W ⓖ Alliance/dsl, Chevron, Exxon/dsl, Murphy Express/dsl, Pure, Shell, 🍴 Applebee's, Arby's, Buffalo Wild Wings, Buffet City, Burger King, Capt D's, Checkers, China Town, China Wok, Dickey's BBQ, Domino's, Eatza Pizza, Hardee's, KFC, Laredo Grill, McDonald's, Mi Casita, Papa John's, Pizza Hut, Popeye's, Shipley's Donuts, Shoney's, Sonic, Subway, Sweet Peppers Deli, Taco Bell, Waffle House, Ward's Burgers, Wendy's, Western Sizzlin, 🏨 Best Western, Comfort Suites, EconoLodge, Hampton Inn, Holiday Inn Express, Rodeway Inn, Super 8, 🅞 Ⓗ, Advance Parts, AutoZone, BigLots, Buick/GMC, Chevrolet, Chrysler/Dodge/Jeep, CVS Drug, $General, $Tree, Ford/Lincoln, Grocery Depot, Kia, Kroger/dsl; Lowe's, New South Tires, Nissan, Office Depot, O'Reilly Parts, Piggly Wiggly, Roses, Toyota, Tuesday Morning, Verizon, Walgreens, Walmart/Subway,
93	US 11, S Laurel, W ⓖ Exxon/Subway/dsl, Shell/dsl, 🍴 Hardee's, 🅞 Southern Tires
90	US 11, Ellisville Blvd, E ⓖ Texaco/dsl, 🍴 Huddle House, W ⓖ Dixie/dsl
88	MS 588, MS 29, Ellisville, E ⓖ Chevron/dsl, Fast Mkt/dsl, Shell, 🍴 Domino's, KFC, McDonald's, Pizza Hut, Sonic, Subway, Ward's Burgers, 🅞 Urgent Care, AutoZone, $General, Ellisville Drug, Food Tiger, Family$, NAPA, O'Reilly Parts, W ⓖ Exxon/dsl, 🏨 Best Western
85	MS 590, to Ellisville, W auto repair
80	to US 11, Moselle, E ⓖ Chevron/dsl
78	Sanford Rd
76	W to Hattiesburg-Laurel Reg 🛬
73	Monroe Rd, to Monroe
69	MS 42 E, Gandy Pkwy, to Petal, Eatonville
67b a	US 49, Hattiesburg, E ⓖ Exxon, Shell, Texaco, Valero/Kangaroo/dsl/scales, 🍴 Arby's, Burger King, Cracker Barrel, DQ, Krystal, McDonald's, Pizza Hut, Waffle House, 🏨 Budget Inn, Comfort Inn, EconoLodge, Executive Inn, Howard Johnson, La Quinta, Motel 6, Quality Inn, Red Carpet Inn, Regency Inn, Sleep Inn, Sunset Inn, Super 8, 🅞 $General, Hattiesburg Cycles, W ⓖ Chevron, MapleLeaf/dsl, Pure/dsl, Shell/Subway, Stuckey's Express/dsl, Texaco, 🍴 Sonic, Waffle House, Ward's Burgers, Wendy's, 🏨 Candlewood Suites, Holiday Inn, Northgate Inn
65b a	US 98 W, Hardy St, Hattiesburg, E ⓖ Shell/dsl, 🍴 Applebee's, Bop's Custard, Buffalo Wild Wings, Caliente Grille,

MS 3 MO

HATTIESBURG

⬆N   INTERSTATE 59 CONT'D

Exit	Services
65b a	Continued
	Cane's, Checkers, CiCi's Pizza, Domino's, IHOP, Izzo's Pizza, Jimmy John's, KFC, Kobe Japanese, Lenny's Subs, Little Caesars, Little Tokyo, McDonald's, Pizza Hut, Purple Parrot Cafe, Qdoba, Starbucks, Taco Bell, Ward's Burgers, 🛏 Days Inn, Fairfield Inn, Residence Inn, Super 8, Western Motel, 🅞 Corner Mkt Foods, CVS Drug, Goodyear/auto, Home Depot, Verizon, Walgreens, to USM, **W** 🅖 Exxon/Domino's, Kangaroo, Shell, Texaco, 🍴 Arby's, Burger King, Cheddars, Chesterfield's Rest., Chick-fil-A, Chili's, China Buffet, ChuckECheese's, Coldstone, FireHouse Subs, 5 Guys Burgers, Gatti Town Pizza, Grand China, Hardee's, HoneyBaked Ham, Hooters, Krispy Kreme, Logan's Roadhouse, Longhorn Steaks, McDonald's, Mellow Mushroom, Newk's Eatery, O'Charley's, Olive Garden, Outback Steaks, Papa Murphy's, Peking Garden, Pepper's Deli, Pizza Inn, Popeye's, Red Lobster, Subway, Super King Asian, Taco Bell, TGIFriday's, Waffle House, Ward's Burgers, Wendy's, Yamato Japan, Zaxby's, 🛏 Baymont Inn, Comfort Suites, Hampton Inn, Hilton Garden, Microtel, Sun Suites, 🅞 🏥, Aamco, Advance Parts, AT&T, AutoZone, Belk, Best Buy, BigLots, Books-A-Million, Dick's, Dillard's, Firestone/auto, Gander Mtn, Goodyear/auto, Hobby Lobby, JC Penney, Kohl's, Lowe's, Michael's, Midas, Nissan, Office Depot, Old Navy, PetCo, Petsmart, Radio Shack, Ross, Sam's Club/gas, Sears/auto, SteinMart, Target, TJ Maxx, Tuesday Morning, Verizon, Walgreens, Walmart, Winn-Dixie, mall
60	US 11, S Hattiesburg, **E** 🅖 Shell/dsl, **W** 🅖 Kangaroo/Subway/dsl/24hr, Texaco, 🍴 Huddle House, 🅞 Freightliner, Peterbilt
59	US 98 E, to US 49, Lucedale, MS Gulf Coast, No facilites
56mm	parking area both lanes, litter barrels, no restrooms
51	rd 589, to Purvis, **W** 🅖 Chevron/dsl, Pinebelt Oil/dsl, Shell/dsl (2mi), 🍴 McDonald's (2mi), Pizza Hut (2mi), to Little Black Cr Water Park
48mm	Little Black Creek
41	MS 13, to Lumberton, **W** 🅞 $General, to Little Black Cr Water Park
35	Hillsdale Rd, **E** 🅖 Pitstop/dsl, 🛏 to Kings Arrow Ranch, to Lake Hillside Resort
32mm	Wolf River
29	rd 26, to Poplarville, **W** 🅖 Pure/dsl, 🍴 Burger King (2mi)
27	MS 53, to Poplarville, Necaise, **W** 🅖 Shell/dsl, 🍴 McDonald's, 🅞 RV Camping (2mi)
19	to US 11, Millard
15	to McNeill, **W** 🅖 McNeill Trkstop/rest./dsl
10	to US 11, Carriere, **E** 🅖 Texaco/Huddle House/dsl, 🅞 Clearwater RV Camp (5mi), repair/tires
6	MS 43 N, N Picayune, **E** 🍴 Marble Slab, Paul's Pastries, **W** 🅖 Chevron/dsl, 🍴 Dockside Rest. (1mi), McDonald's, Sonic, Subway, 🛏 Picayune Motel (1mi), 🅞 🏥, CVS Drug, Family$, Walgreens, Winn-Dixie, vet
4	MS 43 S, to Picayune, **E** 🅖 Murphy USA/dsl, RaceTrac/dsl, 🍴 McDonald's, Ryan's, Subway, Wow Wingery, 🅞 AT&T, Buick/Cadillac/Chevrolet/GMC, $Tree, GNC, Home Depot, Nissan, Sun Roamers RV Park (1mi), Verizon, Walgreens, Walmart, **W** 🅖 Chevron/dsl, Exxon/dsl, Shell/dsl, 🍴 Applebee's, Burger King, Domino's, Golden Dragon Buffet, Hardee's, IHOP, KFC, New Buffet City, Pizza Hut, Popeye's, Subway, Taco Bell, Waffle House, Wendy's, 🛏

PICAYUNE

Exit	Services
4	Continued
	Days Inn, Heritage Inn, Holiday Inn Express, 🅞 🏥, Urgent Care, Advance Parts, AutoZone, $General, Family$, Firestone, Ford/Lincoln, Fred's, Midas, O'Reilly Parts, Paw Paw's RV Ctr, Radio Shack, Rite Aid, Winn-Dixie
3mm	**Welcome Ctr nb, full ♿ facilities, 🚻, vending, 🏞, litter barrels, petwalk, RV dump**
1.5mm	**weigh sta both lanes**
1	US 11, MS 607, **E** NASA, **W** 🅖 Chevron/dsl, Shell/Subway/dsl
0mm	Mississippi/Louisiana state line, Pearl River. **Exits 11-1 are in Louisiana**
11	Pearl River Turnaround. Callboxes begin sb.
5b	Honey Island Swamp
5a	LA 41, Pearl River, **E** 🅖 Riverside TrvlCtr/dsl
3	US 11 S, LA 1090, Pearl River 0-1 mi **W** 🅖 Chevron/dsl, Shell/Subway/dsl, Texaco, 🍴 McDonald's, Sonic, Waffle House, 🛏 Microtel, 🅞 AutoZone, Family$, Jubilee Foods/drug, NAPA
1.5mm	**Welcome Ctr sb, full ♿ facilities, info, 🚻, 🏞, litter barrels, petwalk, RV dump**
1c b	I-10, E to Bay St Louis, W to New Orleans
1a	I-12 W, to Hammond. **I-59 begins/ends on I-10/I-12. Exits 1-11 are in Louisiana.**

⬆N   INTERSTATE 220 (JACKSON)

Exit	Services
11mm	**I-220 begins/ends on I-55, exit 104.**
9	Hanging Moss Rd, County Line Rd, **E** 🅖 BP
8	Watkins Dr, **E** 🅖 Exxon/Subway, Shell/Chester's/dsl
5b a	US 49 N, Evers Blvd, to Yazoo City, **E** 🅖 BP, 🍴 KFC, Sonic, 🛏 Star Motel, 🅞 Family$, Food Depot/gas, **W** 🅖 BP, Exxon/Burger King, Gas+, Shell/Subway/dsl
3	Industrial Dr
2b a	Clinton Blvd, Capitol St, **E** to Jackson Zoo, **W** 🅖 RaceWay, Shell, 🍴 McDonald's, Popeye's, Sonic, 🅞 Family$
1b a	US 80, **E** 🅖 BP, Citgo/dsl, Shell, 🍴 Capt D's, Hunan Garden, KFC, McDonald's, Pizza Hut, Popeye's, Sonny's BBQ, Taco Bell, Wendy's, 🛏 Best Inn, Scottish Inn, Super 8, 🅞 Mr Transmission, **W** 🅖 Exxon/dsl, 🍴 Arby's, Krystal, 🅞 $General
0mm	**I-220 begins/ends on I-20, exit 41.**

MISSOURI

⬆N   INTERSTATE 29

Exit	Services
124mm	Missouri/Iowa state line
123mm	Nishnabotna River
121.5mm	**weigh sta both lanes**
116	rd A, rd B, to Watson, **W** fireworks
110	US 136, Rock Port, Phelps City, **E** 🅖 Shell/dsl, 🛏 Rockport Inn, fireworks, to NW MO St U, **W** 🅖 BP/dsl/24hr, Phillips 66/Stuckey's/Subway/dsl/24hr, 🍴 Black Iron Grill, McDonald's, Trails End Rest., 🛏 Super 8, 🅞 KOA, fireworks, truck repair
109.5mm	**Welcome Ctr sb, full ♿ facilities, info, 🚻, 🏞, litter barrels, petwalk**
107	MO 111, to Rock Port

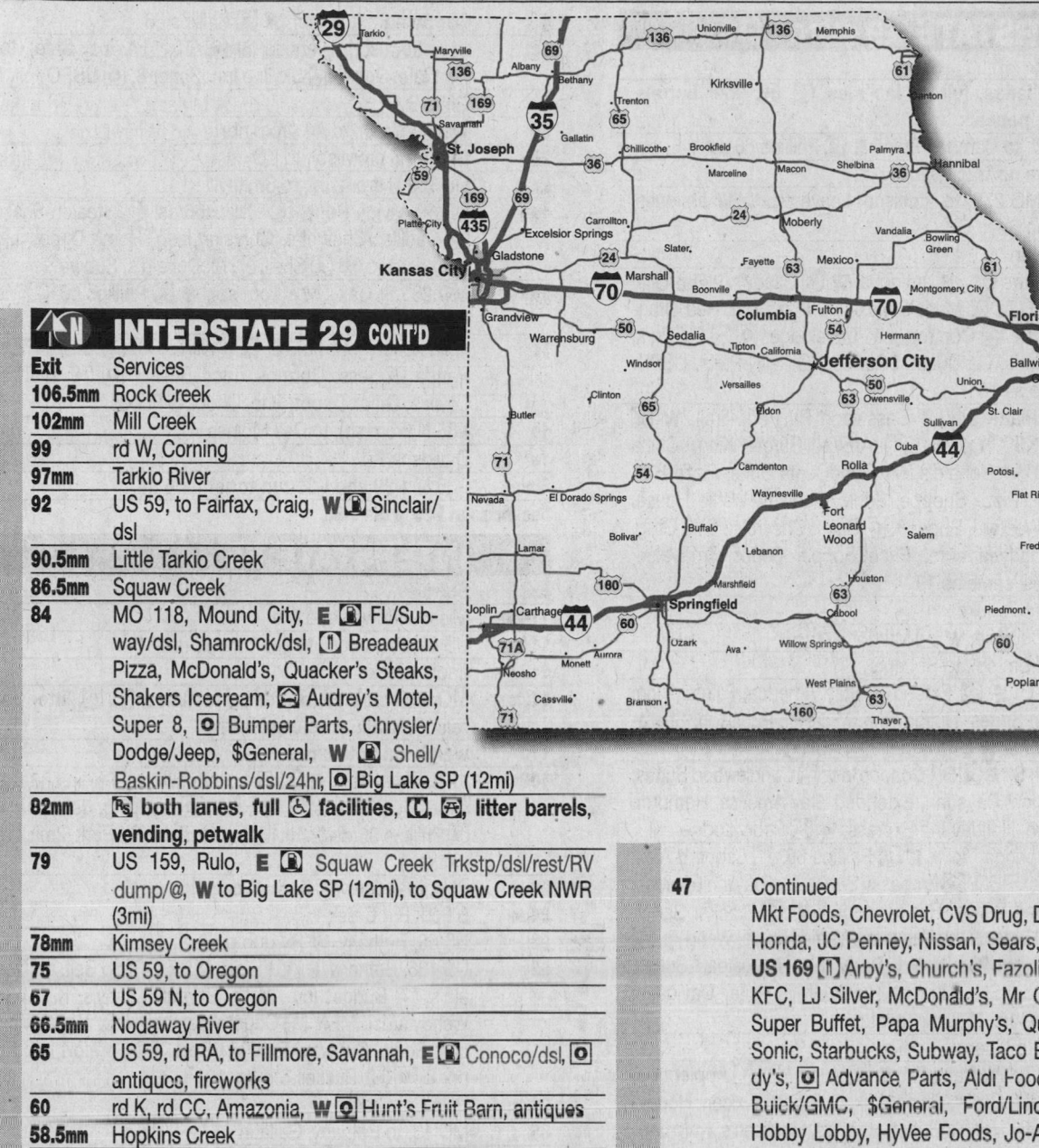

INTERSTATE 29 CONT'D

Exit	Services
106.5mm	Rock Creek
102mm	Mill Creek
99	rd W, Corning
97mm	Tarkio River
92	US 59, to Fairfax, Craig, W [gas] Sinclair/dsl
90.5mm	Little Tarkio Creek
86.5mm	Squaw Creek
84	MO 118, Mound City, E [gas] FL/Subway/dsl, Shamrock/dsl, [food] Breadeaux Pizza, McDonald's, Quacker's Steaks, Shakers Icecream, [lodging] Audrey's Motel, Super 8, [other] Bumper Parts, Chrysler/Dodge/Jeep, $General, W [gas] Shell/Baskin-Robbins/dsl/24hr, [other] Big Lake SP (12mi)
82mm	**[rest stop] both lanes, full [handicapped] facilities, [phone], [picnic], litter barrels, vending, petwalk**
79	US 159, Rulo, E [gas] Squaw Creek Trkstp/dsl/rest/RV dump/@, W to Big Lake SP (12mi), to Squaw Creek NWR (3mi)
78mm	Kimsey Creek
75	US 59, to Oregon
67	US 59 N, to Oregon
66.5mm	Nodaway River
65	US 59, rd RA, to Fillmore, Savannah, E [gas] Conoco/dsl, [other] antiques, fireworks
60	rd K, rd CC, Amazonia, W [other] Hunt's Fruit Barn, antiques
58.5mm	Hopkins Creek
56b a	I-229 S, US 71 N, US 59 N, to St Joseph, Maryville
55mm	Dillon Creek
53	US 59, US 71 bus, to St Joseph, Savannah, E AOK Camping, fireworks, W [gas] Phillips 66/dsl, [other] antiques
50	US 169, St Joseph, King City, **1-3 mi W on Belt Hwy** [gas] BP, Conoco, Phillips 66, Shell, Sinclair, [food] Bob Evans, Buffalo Wild Wings, Cheddar's, Chick-fil-A, Chili's, Chipotle Mexican, Coldstone, Culver's, Famous Dave's, 54th St Grill, Hardee's, IHOP, KFC, McDonald's, Olive Garden, Panda Express, Ryan's, Sonic, Subway, Taco Bell, [other] Advance Parts, Best Buy, Home Depot, Kohl's, Lowe's, Michael's, Old Navy, Sam's Club/gas, Target, Tires+, TJ Maxx, Walgreens, Walmart
47	MO 6, Frederick Blvd, to Clarksdale, St Joseph, E [gas] Conoco, [food] Bandanas BBQ, Basil's Italian, [lodging] Days Inn, Drury Inn, W [gas] Phillips 66/dsl, Sinclair, [food] Applebee's, Burger King, Carlos O'Kelly's, Cracker Barrel, Denny's, Dunkin Donuts, Ground Round, Hazel's Coffee, Panera Bread, Perkins, Pizza Hut, Red Lobster, Taco Bell, Whiskey Creek Steaks, [lodging] Comfort Suites, Hampton Inn, Motel 6, Ramada, Stoney Creek Inn, Super 8, [other] [H], Apple
47	Continued Mkt Foods, Chevrolet, CVS Drug, Dillard's, Firestone/auto, Honda, JC Penney, Nissan, Sears, Walgreens, **1 mi W on US 169** [food] Arby's, Church's, Fazoli's, El Maguey Mexican, KFC, LJ Silver, McDonald's, Mr Goodcents, New China Super Buffet, Papa Murphy's, Quiznos, Rib Crib BBQ, Sonic, Starbucks, Subway, Taco Bell, Taco John's, Wendy's, [other] Advance Parts, Aldi Foods, AutoZone, BigLots, Buick/GMC, $General, Ford/Lincoln, Hastings Books, Hobby Lobby, HyVee Foods, Jo-Ann Fabrics, Office Depot, Radio Shack, Toyota/Scion, U-Haul, vet
46b a	US 36, to Cameron, St Joseph, **1 mi W on US 169** [gas] BP/dsl, FL, Murphy USA/dsl, Roadstar/dsl, Shell, Sinclair/dsl, [food] Burger King, Godfather's, Jimmy John's, Pizza Hut, Taco John's, [other] **Urgent Care**, Ace Hardware, AT&T, $General, KIA, Klein RV Ctr, O'Reilly Parts, Suzuki, Walgreens, Walmart, to MO W St Coll
44	US 169, to Gower, St Joseph, E [gas] Phillips 66, Love's/Arby's/dsl/scales/24hr, [food] Nelly's Mexican, Subway, [lodging] Best Western, [other] dsl repair, W [gas] Murphy USA/dsl, Shell/dsl/24hr, [food] DQ, McDonald's, Mr Goodcents, San Jose Steaks, Sonic, Taco Bell, Waffle House, [other] Apple Mkt Foods, Chrysler/Dodge/Jeep, $Tree, Goodyear, Harley-Davidson, Hyundai, K-Mart, Menards, Walmart
43	I-229 N, to St Joseph
39.5mm	Pigeon Creek
35	rd DD, Faucett, W [gas] Farris Trkstp/dsl/motel/rest/24hr/@
33.5mm	Bee Creek
30	rd Z, rd H, Dearborn, New Market, E [gas] Conoco/Subway/dsl/24hr
29.5mm	Bee Creek

ST JOSEPH

ST JOSEPH

🏚 INTERSTATE 29 CONT'D

Exit	Services
27mm	🆁🆂 both lanes, full ♿ facilities, 🚻, 🚮, litter barrels, vending, petwalk
25	rd E, rd U, to Camden Point, **E** ⛽ Phillips 66/dsl
24mm	weigh sta nb/truck parking sb
20	MO 92, MO 273, to Atchison, Leavenworth, **W** antiques, to Weston Bend SP
19.5mm	Platte River
19	rd HH, Platte City, **E** antiques, **W** ⛽ Casey's, Platte-Clay Fuel/dsl, 🍽 DQ, Maria's Mexican, Pizza Hut, Red Dragon Chinese, 🛏 Comfort Inn, Travelodge, 🅾 ⊛ RV Park, ALPS Foods, CarQuest, $General, O'Reilly Parts, USPO, vet, same as 18
18	MO 92, Platte City, **E** Basswood RV Park (5mi), **W** ⛽ Conoco/KFC, QT/dsl, 🍽 Arby's, Burger King, China Wok, DQ, McDonald's, Mr GoodCents Subs, Pizza Hut/Taco Bell, Pizza Shoppe, Sonic, Subway, Waffle House, 🛏 Best Western, Super 8, 🅾 Buick/Chevrolet, Ford, Goodyear/auto, PriceChopper Foods, TrueValue, Walgreens, same as 19
17	I-435 S, to Topeka
15	Mexico City Ave, **W** 🛏 Marriott, 🅾 ⊛
14	I-435 E (from sb), to St Louis
13	to I-435 E, **E** 🛏 Extended Stay America, Fairfield Inn, Hawthorn Suites, Holiday Inn, Microtel, Radisson, Sheraton, Super 8, **W** 🛏 Marriott, 🅾 KCI ⊛
12	NW 112th St, **E** ⛽ BP, Conoco/dsl, 🛏 Candlewood Suites, Comfort Inn, Days Inn, Extended Stay America, Hampton Inn, Hilton, Holiday Inn Express, **W** 🛏 EconoLodge
10	Tiffany Springs Pkwy, **E** ⛽ Phillips 66, 🍽 Cirque d'Alex, SmokeBox BBQ, 🛏 Embassy Suites, Holiday Inn Express, Homewood Suites, Residence Inn, **W** 🍽 Cracker Barrel, Marco's Pizza, Ruby Tuesday, Waffle House, Wendy's, 🛏 Chase Suites, Courtyard, Drury Inn, Homestead Suites, Hyatt Place, Sleep Inn, 🅾 Buick/GMC, Harley-Davidson, Honda, Lexus, Nissan, Toyota
9b a	MO 152, to Liberty, Topeka
8	MO 9, rd T, NW Barry Rd, **E** ⛽ Valero/dsl, 🍽 Applebee's, Boston Mkt, Chili's, China Wok, Chipotle Mexican, Honeybaked Cafe, Hong's Buffet, Hooters, Houlihan's, Kato Japanese, LoneStar Steaks, On the Border, Panda Express, Panera Bread, Pizza Hut/Taco Bell, Sheradon's Custard, Starbucks, Subway, Wendy's, Winstead's Rest., 🅾 🏥, Best Buy, $Tree, Ford, Hobby Lobby, Home Depot, HyVee Foods, JC Penney, Lowe's, SteinMart, Target, Walmart, **W** ⛽ Phillips 66, QT/dsl, 🍽 A&W/LJSilver, Arby's, BoLings Chinese, 54th St Grill, Jimmy John's, McDonald's, Mimi's Cafe, Minsky's Pizza, Outback Steaks, Quiznos, Rainbow Oriental, Smokehouse BBQ, Sonic, Stone Canyon Pizza, Taco Bueno, 🛏 La Quinta, Motel 6, Super 8, 🅾 AT&T, Barnes&Noble, CVS Drug, Dick's, Dillard's, Marshall's, Old Navy, Staples
6	NW 72nd St, Platte Woods, **E** ⛽ Sinclair/dsl, 🅾 vet, **W** ⛽ Phillips 66, 🍽 Iron Wok, KFC, Papa John's, Tasty Thai, 🅾 K-Mart
5	MO 45 N, NW 64th St, **W** ⛽ Shell/dsl, 🍽 All-star Pizza&Subs, Bonefish Grill, Caribou Coffee, Chamas Brazilian Grill, Goodcents Subs, IHOP, Mazatlan Mexican, McDonald's, O'Quigley's Grill, Papa Murphy's, Quiznos, Starbucks, Subway, Taco Bell, 🅾 CVS Drug, $General, GNC, Radio Shack

Exit	Services
4	NW 56th St (from nb), **W** ⛽ Phillips 66
3c	rd A (from sb), Riverside, **W** ⛽ QT, 🍽 Argosy Café, Corner Café, Sonic, 🛏 Skyline Inn, Super 8, 🅾 USPO
3b	I-635 S
3a	Waukomis Dr, rd AA (from nb)
2b	US 169 S (from sb), to KC
2a	US 169 N (from nb), to Smithville
1e	US 69, Vivion Rd, **E** ⛽ Phillips66/dsl, 🍽 Steak'n Shake, 🅾 Cadillac/Chevrolet, Chrysler/Jeep, Home Depot, Lincoln, Suzuki, **W** ⛽ Shell, 🍽 McDonald's, Subway
1d	MO 283 S, Oak Tfwy (from sb), **W** ⛽ Phillips 66, 🍽 McDonald's
1c	Gladstone (from nb), **E** ⛽ Phillips 66, 🍽 CiCi's Pizza, Panda Express, Quiznos, Taco Bueno, 🅾 🏥, BigLots, Lowe's, Office Depot, PriceChopper Foods
1b	I-35 N (from sb), to Des Moines
1a	Davidson Rd
8mm	I-35 N. **I-29 and I-35 run together 6 mi.**

See Missouri I-35, exits 3-8a.

🏚 INTERSTATE 35

Exit	Services
114mm	Missouri/Iowa state line
114	US 69, to Lamoni, **W** ⛽ Conoco/dsl/24hr
113.5mm	Zadie Creek
112mm	MO welcome ctr sb, full ♿ facilities, 🚻, 🚮, litter barrels, petwalk, wireless internet
110	weigh sta both lanes
106	rd N, Blythedale, **E** ⛽ Conoco/fireworks, Phillips 66/Dinner Bell Cafe/motel/dsl/24hr/@, 🅾 camping, dsl repair, **W** ⛽ Phillips 66/dsl/24hr, 🅾 Eagle Ridge RV Park (2mi), fireworks
99	rd A, to Ridgeway, 5 mi **W** camping
94mm	E Fork Big Creek
93	US 69, Bethany, **W** RV dump
92	US 136, Bethany, **E** ⛽ FL/dsl, 🍽 KFC/Taco Bell, McDonald's, 🛏 Budget Inn, **W** ⛽ BP/dsl, Casey's, Kum&Go/Wendy's/dsl, MFA, 🍽 Country Kitchen, DQ, Nopal Mexican, Sonic, Subway, TootToot Rest., 🛏 Comfort Inn, Super 8, 🅾 🏥, Russell Stover, Walmart
90mm	Pole Cat Creek
88	MO 13, to Bethany, Gallatin
84	rds AA, H, to Gilman City, **E** Crowder SP (24mi)
81mm	truck parking, limited facilities
80	rds B, N, to Coffey
78	rd C, Pattonsburg, **W** ⛽ Phillips 66/dsl
74.5mm	Grand River
72	rd DD
68	US 69, to Pattonsburg
64	MO 6, to Maysville, Gallatin
61	US 69, Winston, Gallatin, **E** ⛽ Shell/rest/dsl/24hr
54	US 36, Cameron, **E** ⛽ Shell/Baskin-Robbins/Wendy's/dsl/24hr, Sinclair/dsl/scales/24hr, 🍽 McDonald's, Subway, 🛏 Best Western, Budget Inn, Comfort Inn, 🅾 Crossroads RV Park, **W** ⛽ Valero/dsl, 🍽 Burger King, Chinese Chef, Domino's, DQ, El Maguey Mexican, Ma&Pa's Kettle Rest., KFC/Taco Bell, Pizza Hut, Sonic, 🛏 Best Value Inn, Comfort Inn, Days Inn, EconoLodge, Super 8, 🅾 🏥, Advance Parts, Buick/Chevrolet/GMC, CountryMart Foods, O'Reilly Parts, Radio Shack, Twin Creeks Tire, Verizon, Walmart, antiques, tires, USPO
52	rd BB, Lp 35, to Cameron, **E** 🅾 🏥, **W** ⛽ Casey's, same as 54

(left margin, vertical) MO

(left margin, vertical) PLATTE CITY

(left margin, vertical) KANSAS CITY

(right margin, vertical) BETHANY

(right margin, vertical) CAMERON

INTERSTATE 35 CONT'D

Exit	Services
49mm	Brushy Creek
48.5mm	Shoal Creek
48	US 69, Cameron, **E** to Wallace SP (2mi), **W** 🅖 Shamrock, 🅞 fireworks
40	MO 116, Lathrop, **E** 🅞 antiques
34.5mm	🆁🆂 **both lanes, full** ♿ **facilities,** 🍴, 🚻, **litter barrels, vending, petwalk**
33	rd PP, Holt, **E** 🍴 Hilltop Grill, **W** 🅖 BP, Conoco/dsl, 🛏 American Eagle Inn
30mm	Holt Creek
26	MO 92, Kearney, **E** 🅖 Casey's, Phillips 66/dsl, Shell/dsl, 🍴 China Wok, McDonald's, Pizza Hut, Sonic, 🛏 Comfort Inn, Super 8, 🅞 CountryMart Foods, CVS Drug, Kramer Hardware, Red Cross Drug, to Watkins Mill SP, **W** 🅖 🍴/Taco Bell/dsl/scales/24hr, 🍴 Arby's, Burger King, Hunan Garden Chinese, Pizza Shoppe, Stables Grill, Subway, 🛏 EconoLodge, Quality Inn, 🅞 Curves, Goodyear/auto, John's Foods, O'Reilly Parts, to Smithville Lake
22mm	**weigh sta nb**, parking area sb
20	US 69, MO 33, to Excelsior Springs, **E** 🅗
17	MO 291, rd A, **1 mi** **E** 🅖 BP, QT, 🍴 A&W, Arby's, CiCi's, LJ Silver, McDonald's, Minsky's Pizza, Papa John's, Papa Murphy's, Perkins, Sonic, Subway, Taco Bell, 🅞 Days Inn, 🅞 Chevrolet, $General, Firestone, Lifestyle RV Ctr, O'Reilly Parts, Walgreens, same as 16, **W** 🅖 Phillips 66/dsl, QT, 🍴 McDonald's, Nicky's Pizza, Sonic, Subway, Wasabi Japanese, 🛏 Sleep Inn, ValuePlace Inn, 🅞 Price Chopper Foods, Walgreens, **Urgent Care**, to KCI ✈
16	MO 152, Liberty, **E** 🅖 Phillips 66, 🍴 Baskin-Robbins, Chick-fil-A, CiCi's Pizza, Culver's, 5 Guys Burgers, IHOP, Jimmy John's, Margarita's, Olive Garden, Perkins, Pizza Hut, Planet Sub, Red Robin, Starbucks, TX Roadhouse, Wendy's, 🛏 Days Inn, Super 8, 🅞🅗, Advance Parts, AutoZone, Chevrolet, CVS Drug, Dick's, Firestone/auto, Ford, Hy-Vee Foods, K-Mart, Lowe's, Walgreens, **Urgent Care**, **W** 🅖 Phillips 66/Circle K/dsl, 🍴 Applebee's, Arby's, Bob Evans, Buffalo Wild Wings, Burger King, Chili's, Chipotle Mexican, Corner Cafe, Cracker Barrel, 54th St Grill, Freddy's Burgers, Golden Corral, Jose Peppers, KFC, Long-Horn Steaks, McDonald's, Panera Bread, Panda Express, Schlotzsky's, SmokeBox BBQ, Steak'n Shake, Subway, Taco Bell, Waffle House, 🛏 Comfort Suites, Fairfield Inn, Hampton Inn, Holiday Inn Express, 🅞 Aldi Foods, AT&T, Best Buy, Christian Bros Auto, Ford, Home Depot, JC Penney, Jiffy Lube, Kohl's, Michael's, NAPA, NTB, Office Depot, Petsmart, Radio Shack, Target, TJ Maxx, Verizon, Walmart/Subway,
14	US 69 (exits left from sb), Liberty Dr, to Glenaire, Pleasant Valley, **E** 🅖 Phillips 66, Sinclair, Shell, 🅞 I-35 RV Ctr, **W** 🅖 QT/dsl
13	US 69 (from nb), to Pleasant Valley, **E** 🅖 Phillips 66/dsl, Shell, Sinclair/24hr, 🍴 KFC, McDonald's, 🅞 auto repair, **W** 🅖 QT/dsl
12b a	I-435, to St Louis
11	US 69 N, Vivion Rd, **E** 🅖 BP/dsl, Shell/dsl, 🍴 Church's, McDonald's, **W** 🅖 QT, 🍴 Sonic, Stroud's Rest.
10	N Brighton Ave (from nb), **E** 🍴 Church's, McDonald's
9	MO 269 S, Chouteau Trfwy, **E** 🅖 Phillips 66, 🍴 IHOP, McDonald's, Ming Garden, Outback Steaks, Papa Murphy's, Popeye's, Subway, Wing Stop, 🅞 AT&T, Food Festival,

Side tabs: **KEARNEY**, **LIBERTY**

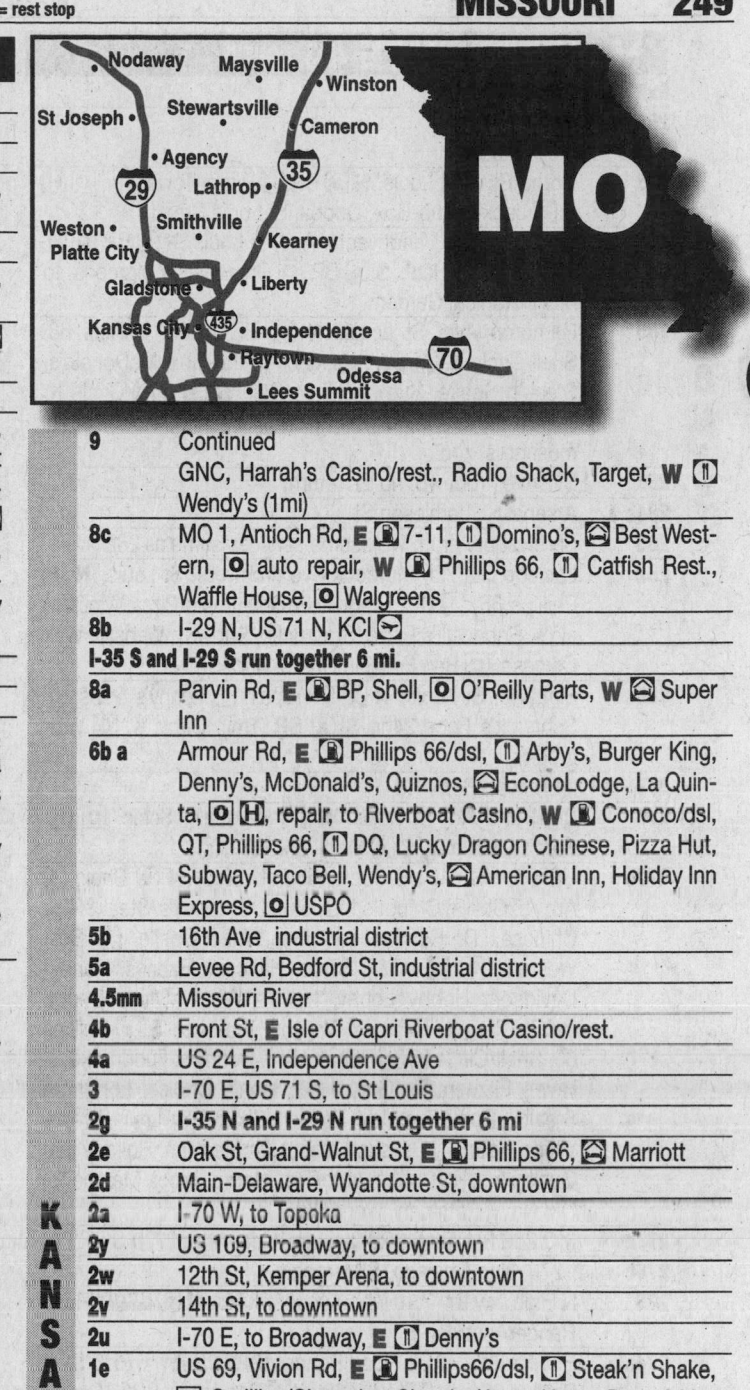

Map showing cities: Nodaway, Maysville, Winston, St Joseph, Stewartsville, Cameron, Agency, Lathrop, 35, 29, Weston, Smithville, Kearney, Platte City, Gladstone, Liberty, Kansas City, 435, Independence, Raytown, Odessa, 70, Lees Summit. MO.

Exit	Services
9	**Continued** GNC, Harrah's Casino/rest., Radio Shack, Target, **W** 🍴 Wendy's (1mi)
8c	MO 1, Antioch Rd, **E** 🅖 7-11, 🍴 Domino's, 🛏 Best Western, 🅞 auto repair, **W** 🅖 Phillips 66, 🍴 Catfish Rest., Waffle House, 🅞 Walgreens
8b	I-29 N, US 71 N, KCI ✈
	I-35 S and I-29 S run together 6 mi.
8a	Parvin Rd, **E** 🅖 BP, Shell, 🅞 O'Reilly Parts, **W** 🛏 Super Inn
6b a	Armour Rd, **E** 🅖 Phillips 66/dsl, 🍴 Arby's, Burger King, Denny's, McDonald's, Quiznos, 🛏 EconoLodge, La Quinta, 🅞🅗, repair, to Riverboat Casino, **W** 🅖 Conoco/dsl, QT, Phillips 66, 🍴 DQ, Lucky Dragon Chinese, Pizza Hut, Subway, Taco Bell, Wendy's, 🛏 American Inn, Holiday Inn Express, 🅞 USPO
5b	16th Ave industrial district
5a	Levee Rd, Bedford St, industrial district
4.5mm	Missouri River
4b	Front St, **E** Isle of Capri Riverboat Casino/rest.
4a	US 24 E, Independence Ave
3	I-70 E, US 71 S, to St Louis
2g	**I-35 N and I-29 N run together 6 mi**
2e	Oak St, Grand-Walnut St, **E** 🅖 Phillips 66, 🛏 Marriott
2d	Main-Delaware, Wyandotte St, downtown
2a	I-70 W, to Topeka
2y	US 169, Broadway, to downtown
2w	12th St, Kemper Arena, to downtown
2v	14th St, to downtown
2u	I-70 E, to Broadway, **E** 🍴 Denny's
1e	US 69, Vivion Rd, **E** 🅖 Phillips66/dsl, 🍴 Steak'n Shake, 🅞 Cadillac/Chevrolet, Chrysler/Jeep, Home Depot, Lincoln, Suzuki, **W** 🅖 Shell, 🍴 McDonald's, Subway
1d	20th St (from sb), **W** 🅖 Phillips 66, 🍴 McDonald's
1c	27th St, SW Blvd, W Pennway (from nb), **E** 🅖 Phillips 66, 🍴 CiCi's Pizza, Panda Express, Quiznos, Taco Bueno, 🅞🅗, BigLots, Lowe's, Office Depot, PriceChopper Foods
1b	I-29 (from nb), to Des Moines
1a	SW Trafficway (from sb)
0mm	Missouri/Kansas state line

INTERSTATE 44

Exit	Services
290mm	**I-44 begins/ends on I-55, exit 207 in St Louis.**
290a	I-55 S, to Memphis
290c	Gravois Ave (from wb), 12th St, **S** 🍴 McDonald's
290b	18th St (from eb) downtown
289	Jefferson Ave, St Louis, **N** 🅖 Phillips 66, 🛏 Holiday Inn Express, Residence Inn, **S** 🅖 Conoco, 🍴 Lee's Chicken,

Side tab: **KANSAS CITY**

MO

ST LOUIS

🔺E INTERSTATE 44 CONT'D

Exit	Services
289	Continued
	McDonald's
288	Grand Blvd, St Louis, N 🅖 BP, 🛏 Water Tower Inn, 🅞 🅗 S 🍴 Jack-in-the-Box, Qdoba, St Louis Bread
287b a	Kingshighway, Vandeventer Ave, St Louis, N 🅖 BP, 🅞 🅗 Jiffy Lube, U-Haul, S 🅖 BP, 🅞 Chevrolet, Walgreens, to MO Botanical Garden
286	Hampton Ave, St Louis, N 🅖 BP, Mobil, Phillips 66, Shell/Circle K, 🍴 Denny's, Jack-in-the-Box, McDonald's, Steak'n Shake, Subway, Taco Bell, S 🅖 Shell/Circle K, 🍴 Hardee's, 🛏 Drury Inn, Holiday Inn, Red Roof Inn, 🅞 museums, zoo
285	SW Ave (from wb, no EZ return)
284b a	Arsenal St, Jamieson St
283	Shrewsbury (from wb), some services same as 282
282	Laclede Sta Rd, Murdock Ave (from eb), St Louis, N 🅖 Phillips 66, 🍴 DQ, Front Row Grill, Imo's Pizza, McDonald's, Racanelli's Pizza, Starbucks, Subway, Webster Wok Chinese, 🅞 Ben Franklin Crafts, Subaru, vet
280	Elm Ave, St Louis, N 🅖 BP/repair, 🍴 Lenny's Subs, 🅞 Schnuck's Food/24hr, S 🅖 BP (1mi), Circle K, 🅞 Walgreens
279	(from wb), Berry Rd
278	Big Bend Rd, St Louis, N 🍴 Hardee's, Sonic, 🅞 🅗 Sam's Club/gas, S 🅖 Mobil/dsl, QT
277b	US 67, US 61, US 50, Lindbergh Blvd, N 🅖 Shell, 🍴 Arby's, Chili's, Chipotle Mexican, O'Charley's, Steak&Rice Chinese, TX Roadhouse, Uno, White Castle, 🛏 Best Western, 🅞 🅗 AT&T, $Tree, Hancock Fabrics, Harley-Davidson, Hobby Lobby, Lowe's Whse, Office Depot, PetCo, Target, TJ Maxx, Verizon, Walmart, S 🅖 Phillips 66, Shell/Circle K, 🍴 Burger King, Denny's, Fuddrucker's, Helen Fitzgerald's Grill, IHOP, Lion's Choice, Longhorn Steaks, Ruby Tuesday, Steak'n Shake, St Louis Bread, Viking Rest, 🛏 Days Inn/rest., Hampton Inn, Holiday Inn, Quality Inn, 🅞 Dobb's Auto/Tire, Home Depot, Marshall's, Old Navy, Petsmart, WorldMkt
277a	MO 366 E, Watson Rd, access to same as 277b S
276b a	I-270, N to Chicago, S Memphis
275	N Highway Dr (from wb), Soccer Pk Rd, N 🅖 🚛/Road Ranger/rest/dsl
274a b	Bowles Ave, N 🅖 Road Ranger/🚛/Subway/dsl, S 🅖 Phillips 66/dsl, QT/dsl, ZX/dsl, 🍴 Bandana's BBQ, Cracker Barrel, Denny's, Jack-in-the-Box, Krispy Kreme, Mandarin Cuisine, McDonald's, Quiznos, Sonic, White Castle, 🛏 Drury Inn, Fairfield Inn, Holiday Inn Express, Motel 6, PearTree Inn, Rodeway Inn, Stratford Inn, Super 8, TownePlace Inn, 🅞 Goodyear
272	MO 141, Fenton, Valley Park, N 🅖 Motomart, S 🅖 Phillips 66/dsl, 🍴 Bob Evans, Burger King, Dickey's BBQ, Hardee's, Jimmy John's, McDonald's, Ruby Tuesday, Starbucks, Steak'n Shake, Subway, Taco Bell, 🛏 Drury Inn, Hampton Inn, 🅞 AT&T, Curves, Save-A-Lot Foods
269	Antire Rd, Beaumont
266	Lewis Rd, N 🅞 Rte 66 SP, golf
266mm	Meramec River
265	Williams Rd (from eb)
264	MO 109, rd W, Eureka, N 🅖 Phillips 66/dsl, 🍴 Arby's, Burger King, Culver's, Domino's, El Nopal Mexican, McDonald's, Pizza Hut, Ponderosa, Smokers BBQ, St Louis

S U L L I V A N

C U B A

Exit	Services
264	Continued Bread, Subway, Taco Bell, White Castle, 🛏 Best Value Inn, 🅞 AT&T, Byerly RV Ctr, O'Reilly Parts, Schnuck's Foods, Valvoline, to Babler SP, S 🅖 QT, 🅞 Walgreens
261	Lp 44, to Allenton, N 🅖 Motomart/McDonald's/dsl, 🍴 Applebee's, China King, Denny's, Imo's Pizza, Lion's Choice, Steak'n Shake, White Castle, 🛏 Best Inn, Holiday Inn, Super 8, 🅞 AutoZone, $Tree, GNC, Jellystone RV Camping, Radio Shack, Verizon, Walmart, to Six Flags, same as 264, S 🅖 Shell/Circle K/dsl, 🅞 KOA, Long's RV Ctr
257	Lp 44, Pacific, N 🅖 Phillips 66, 🚛/Subway/dsl/scales/24hr, 🍴 Huddle House, 🛏 Comfort Inn, 🅞 fireworks, S 🅖 BP/dsl, Mobil/dsl, Motomart, 🍴 Hardee's, KFC, McDonald's, New China, Pizza Hut, Taco Bell, 🛏 Quality Inn, 🅞 Chrysler/Dodge/Jeep, $General, O'Reilly Parts, Queen's Foods, vet
253	MO 100 E, to Gray Summit, S 🅖 Phillips 66/dsl, 🛏 Gardenway Motel, Travelodge, 🅞 CarQuest, fireworks
251	MO 100 W, to Washington, N 🅖 BP/dsl, Mr Fuel/dsl/scales, Phillips 66/Burger King/dsl, 🍴 Domino's, 🅞 🅗 $General, antiques
247	US 50 W, rd AT, rd O, to Union, N 🅞 Harley-Davidson, S to Robertsville SP
247mm	Bourbeuse River
242	rd AH, to Hist Rte 66
240	MO 47, St Clair, N 🅖 Phillips 66/Taco Bell/dsl, 🍴 Burger King, Los Cabos, 🅞 NAPA, Reed RV Ctr, S 🅖 Mobil/dsl, 🍴 McDonald's, Subway, 🛏 Budget Lodge, Super 8, 🅞 $General, Save-A-Lot Foods, USPO
239	MO 30, rds AB, WW, St Clair, N repair
238mm	**weigh sta both lanes**
235mm	🆁🆂 **both lanes (both lanes exit left), full ♿ facilities, 🍴, 🅿, litter barrels, vending, petwalk**
230	rds W, Stanton, S 🅖 Shell/fireworks, 🅞 KOA, Meramec Caverns Camping (3mi)
226	MO 185 S, Sullivan, N 🅖 ⭐FLYING J/Denny's/dsl/LP/scales/24hr, 🅞 vet, S 🅖 Phillips 66/Burger King, 🍴 Applebee's, Arby's, DQ, Imo's Pizza, KFC, McDonald's, Steak'n Shake, Subway, Taco Bell, 🅞 AutoZone, $General, Lowe's, O'Reilly Parts, Verizon, Walmart, to Meramec SP, same as 225
225	MO 185 N, rd D, Sullivan, N 🅖 Mobil, Phillips 66/dsl, 🍴 Domino's, 🛏 Baymont Inn, Best Value Inn, Family Inn, Super 8, 🅞 Chrysler/Dodge/Jeep, Ford, S 🅖 BP/Fas-Trip/dsl/café, ZX, 🍴 China Buffet, Cracker Barrel, Jack-in-the-Box, Lion's Choice, Pizza Hut, Sonic, 🛏 Comfort Inn, 🅞 🅗 Aldi Foods, AT&T, Goodyear, city park, same as 226
218	rds N, C, J, Bourbon, N 🅖 ZX/dsl, 🛏 Budget Inn, S 🅖 Mobil, 🍴 Barn&Grill Rest, 🅞 Bourban RV Ctr, Blue Sprgs Camping (6mi), Riverview Ranch Camping (8mi)
214	rd H, Leasburg, N 🅖 Mobil/dsl, S 🅞 to Onandaga Cave SP (7mi)
210	rd UU, N 🅞 Meremac Valley Resort, S 🍴 MO Hick BBQ (2mi), 🅞 winery
208	MO 19, Cuba, N 🅖 BP/Dotty's Rest/dsl/scales/24hr/@, Phillips 66, 🍴 Country Kitchen, Huddle House, Pizza Hut, 🛏 Best Western, Super 8, 🅞 Blue Beacon, antiques, S 🅖 Casey's, Mobil, 🍴 Domino's, East Sun Chinese, Hardee's, Jack-in-the-Box, McDonald's, Sonic, Subway, 🛏 Chateau Inn, 🅞 $General, Mace Foods, O'Reilly Parts, Walmart, to Ozark Nat Scenic Riverways, vet

INTERSTATE 44 CONT'D

Exit	Services
203	rds F, ZZ, **N** Ladybug RV Park, **S** Rosatti Winery (2mi)
195	MO 8, MO 68, St James, Maramec Sprg Park, **N** 🅿 Mobil/dsl, Shell/dsl, 🍴 McDonald's, Pizza Hut, Sonic, Subway, 🛏 Days Inn, Economy Inn, 🅾 Ford, NAPA, O'Reilly Parts, Ray's Tires, tours ctr, to Maremac Winery, **S** 🅿 Delano/dsl, Phillips 66/dsl, 🍴 Burger King, 🛏 Finn's Motel, 🅾 CountryMart Foods
189	rd V, Industrial Park Dr, Hypoint, **N** 🅿 Loves/McDonald's/Subway/dsl/scales/24hr, 🅾 Mule Trading Post
186	US 63, MO 72, Rolla, **N** 🅿 Sinclair, 🍴 Steak'n Shake, 🛏 Drury Inn, Hampton Inn, Sooter Inn, 🅾 Big O Tire, Kia, Kohl's, Nissan, Lowe's, Plaza Tire, **S** 🅿 BP, Mobil/dsl, Phillips 66, 🍴 Colton's Steaks, Domino's, Donut King, Koi Chinese, Lee's Chicken, Panera Bread, 🛏 Budget Motel, 🅾 🏥
185	rd E, to Rolla, **N** hwy patrol, **S** 🅿 Delano, Phillips 66, 🍴 Arby's, DQ, Gordoz Steaks, Hardee's, Huddle House, Jimmy John's, Kyoto Japanese, LJ Silver, Papa John's, Subway, Taco Bell, Wendy's, 🅾 🏥, Ford/Lincoln, Kroger, Walgreens, UMO at Rolla
184	US 63 S, to Rolla, **N** 🛏 Comfort Suites, Holiday Inn Express, **S** 🅿 Delano, MotoMart, Route 66, 🍴 Arby's, Burger King, Little Caesars, LJ Silver, Lucky House Chinese, Maid-Rite, McDonald's, Pizza Hut, Pizza Inn, Shoney's, Sirloin Stockade, Waffle House, Wendy's, 🛏 Baymont Inn, Best Value Inn, Best Way Inn, Best Western, Days Inn, EconoLodge, Quality Inn, Sunset Inn, Super 8, 🅾 🏥 Buick/Cadillac/GMC, Chevrolet, Goodyear/auto, Kroger, city park
179	rds T, C, to Doolittle, Newburg, **S** 🅿 Phillips 66, 🍴 Cookin' From Scratch Rest.
178mm	truck parking both lanes, restrooms
176	Sugar Tree Rd, **N** 🛏 Vernelle's Motel, **S** 🅾 Arlington River Resort Camping (2mi)
172	rd D, Jerome, **N** camping
169	rd J
166	to Dig Piney
164mm	Big Piney River
163	MO 28, to Dixon, **N** 🅿 🛢/Road Ranger/Chesters/Subway/dsl/scales/24hr, **S** 🅿 Phillips 66/dsl, 🍴 Country Café, Sweetwater BBQ, 🛏 Best Western, Country Hearth Inn, Days Inn, 🅾 RV Park
161b a	rd Y, to Ft Leonard Wood, **N** 🅿 Mobil/dsl, Shell/dsl, 🍴 Aussie Jack's, Cracker Barrel, Domino's, Home Cookin' Diner, Kyoto Japanese, Miller's Grill, Papa Murphy's, Pizza Hut, Ruby Tuesday, Ryan's, Subway, Wendy's, 🛏 Baymont Inn, Best Value Inn, Candlewood Suites, Comfort Inn, Fairfield Inn, Hampton Inn, Mainstay Suites, Red Roof Inn, ValuePlaceother: AT&T, $Tree, Kwik Kar, Lowe's, Toyota/Scion, Walmart/Subway, visitors ctr, **S** 🅿 Cenex/dsl, Conoco, Kum&Go/dsl, 🍴 Arby's, Buffalo Wild Wings, China Buffet, Colton's Steaks, Culver's, El Sombrero, KFC, Luigi's Italian, McDonald's, Panera Bread, Papa John's, Subway, Taco Bell, Waffle House, 🛏 Budget Inn, EconoLodge, Holiday Inn Express, Motel 6, Quality Inn, 🅾 AutoZone, Chrysler/Dodge/Jeep, $General, Family$, Ford/Lincoln, Goodyear/auto, Mazda, NAPA, O'Reilly Parts, Radio Shack, Verizon, U-Haul
159	Lp 44, to Waynesville, St Robert, **N** 🅿 Gas City/dsl, 🍴 DQ, Sonic, 🛏 All Star Motel, Super 8, 🅾 O'Reilly Parts,

Exit	Services
159	Continued auto repair, **S** 🅿 Phillips 66/dsl, 🍴 Pepper's Grill, 🛏 Alliance Inn, 🅾 Big O Tire, Cadillac/GMC, TrueValue
158mm	Roubidoux Creek
156	rd H, Waynesville, **N** 🅿 BP, Casey's, Conoco/dsl/E-85, Kum&Go/dsl, 🍴 McDonald's, Starbucks, Subway, 🅾 Chevrolet, $General, Price Cutter+, vet
153	MO 17, to Buckhorn, **N** 🅿 Whitmor Farms/dsl, 🛏 Ft Wood Inn, **S** 🅿 Shell/dsl, 🅾 Glen Oaks RV Park
150	MO 7, rd P to Richland, **S** 🍴 Roadhouse Steaks
145	MO 133, rd AB, to Richland, **N** 🅿 Sinclair/Oasis/cafe/dsl/24hr, **S** camping
143mm	Gasconade River
140	rd N, to Stoutland, **S** 🅿 Phillips 66/pizza/dsl
139mm	Bear Creek
135	rd F, Sleeper
130	rd MM, **N** 🅿 Conoco/dsl, Phillips 66, 🍴 Napoli's Italian, 🛏 Best Western, Budget Inn, Munger Moss Inn, **S** 🅿 Kum&Go, 🅾 🏥
129	MO 5, MO 32, MO 64, to Hartville, Lebanon, **N** 🍴 Applebee's, Arby's, Bamboo Garden, Burger King, DQ, Elm St Eatery, KFC, LJ Silver, Little Caesars, McDonald's, Papa John's, Shoney's, Sonic, Steak'n Shake, Subway, Taco Bell, Wendy's, Western Sizzlin, 🅾 Aldi Foods, AT&T, AutoZone, Chevrolet, Ford, O'Reilly Parts, Rte 66 Museum, Smitty's Foods, Verizon, Walgreens, Walnut Bowl Factory, repair, to Bennett Sprgs SP, **S** 🅿 Conoco/dsl, Phillips 66/dsl, 🍴 Capt D's, Domino's, Hardee's, Pizza Hut, T's Steaks, 🅾 🏥, $General, $Tree, FSA/Famous Brands, Goodyear, Lowe's, O'Reilly Parts, Walmart/Subway, vet, to Lake of the Ozarks
127	Lp 44, Lebanon, **N** 🅿 B&D/rest/dsl/scales/24hr, Phillips 66, 🍴 Dowd's Catfish&BBQ, El Sombrero Mexican, Great Wall Chinese, Waffle House, 🛏 Best Value Inn, Days Inn, Hampton Inn, Holiday Inn Express, Midwest Inn, Super 8, 🅾 Cutlery/Walnut Bowl Outlet, Chrysler/Dodge/Jeep, Firestone/auto, **S** 🅿 Conoco/McDonald's/dsl, Phillips 66/dsl, 🍴 Dickey's BBQ, 🅾 Buick/Cadillac/GMC, Harley-Davidson, Russell Stover
123	County Rd, **S** 🅾 Happy Trails RV Ctr, Happy Trails RV Park, antiques
118	rds C, A, Phillipsburg, **S** 🅿 Phillips 66, 🅾 Redmond's Gifts, tourist info
113	rds J, Y, Conway, **N** 🅿 Conoco/dsl, Phillips 66, 🍴 Rockin Chair Café, 🛏 Budget Inn, 🅾 to Den of Metal Arts, **S** 🅿 Sinclair/dsl, 🅾 $General, SummerFresh Foods, USPO
111mm	🆁🆂 **both lanes, full** 🛏 **facilities,** 🍴**, vending, litter barrels,** 🐾 **petwalk, playground**
108mm	Bowen Creek

↑E INTERSTATE 44 CONT'D

Exit	Services
107	Sparkle Brooke Rd, Sampson Rd
106mm	Niangua River
100	MO 38, rd W, Marshfield, **N** 🛢️ Murphy USA/dsl, Phillips 66, ⊙ AT&T, Chevrolet, Ford, Radio Shack, Walmart/Subway, auto repair, **S** 🛢️ Conoco/dsl, Kum&Go/dsl, Phillips 66/dsl, 🍽️ DQ, El Charro, Golden China, Grillos Cafe, KFC/Rib Crib, McDonald's, Pizza Hut, Pizza Inn, Sonic, Subway, Taco Bell, 🛏️ Holiday Inn Express, ⊙ AutoZone, $General, O'Reilly Parts, PriceCutter Foods, RV Express RV Park, Walgreens, antiques
96	rd B, Northview, **N** Paradise RV Park (2mi)
89mm	**weigh sta both lanes**
88	MO 125, to Fair Grove, Strafford, **N** 🛢️ 💛Loves/Hardee's/dsl/scales/rv dump/24hr, Shell/scales, TA/Country Pride/Subway/Taco Bell/dsl/scales/24hr/@, 🍽️ McDonald's, ⊙ Camping World RV Ctr, truckwash, vet, **S** 🛢️ Conoco/dsl, Kum&Go, 🍽️ Fox's Pizza, Pizza Hut, 🛏️ Motel 8, ⊙ $Station, Strafford RV Park
84	MO 744, **S** Peterbilt
82b a	US 65, to Branson, Fedalia, **S** 🛢️ Kum&Go, Phillips 66/dsl, 🍽️ Waffle House, ⊙ Bass Pro Shops, Kenworth, st patrol, to Table Rock Lake, Bull Shoals Lake
80b a	rd H to Pleasant Hope, Springfield, **N** 🛢️ Conoco/rest/dsl/24hr, 🍽️ Waffle House, 🛏️ Budget Lodge, Days Inn, Microtel, Super 8, ⊙ to SWSU, **S** 🛢️ Casey's, Kum&Go/dsl, Phillips 66/dsl, Shell, 🍽️ Andy's Custard, Applebee's, Backyard Burger, Bob Evans, Braum's, Buckingham BBQ, Burger King, Chicago Gyros, China Garden, Cracker Barrel, Culver's, El Maguey Mexican, Fazoli's, Hardee's, Hong Kong Garden, Houlihan's, Jade East Chinese, Kyoto Japanese, Krispy Kreme, La Mision Mexican, Little Tokyo, LJ Silver, McDonald's, Pizza Hut, Rib Crib, Ruby Tuesday, Schlotzsky's, Shanghai Chicken, Shoney's, Sonic, Steak'n Shake, Subway, Taco Bell, Ziggies Cafe, 🛏️ Best Value Inn, Best Western, Budget Inn, Candlewood Suites, Comfort Inn, Dogwood Park Inn, Doubletree Hotel, Drury Inn, EconoLodge, Economy Inn, Flagship Motel, Hampton Inn, Holiday Inn, Homestay Inn, Lamplighter Hotel, La Quinta, Motel 6, Ozark Inn, Plaza Inn, Quality Inn, Ramada, Rancho Motel, ⊙ ⊞, Aamco, Aldi Foods, AutoZone, $General, Goodyear/auto, K-Mart, O'Reilly Parts, PriceCutter Foods, U-Haul, Walmart/Subway, antiques, **Urgent Care**, vet
77	MO 13, KS Expswy, **N** 🛢️ Kum&Go/dsl/e-85, ⊙ Lowe's, **S** 🛢️ Casey's, Gas+, Phillips 66/dsl, 🍽️ Arby's, Buffalo Wild Wings, Braum's, CiCi's, El Charro, Golden Corral, IHOP, Jimmy John's, McAlister's Deli, McDonald's, Mr Goodcents, Panera Bread, Papa John's, Papa Murphy's, Pizza Inn, Subway, Taco Bell, Waffle House, ⊙ AT&T, BigLots, Dillon's Foods, $Tree, Drug Mart, GNC, Goodyear/auto, Hobby Lobby, O'Reilly Parts, Radio Shack, ShopKO, Staples, Verizon, Walgreens, Walmart
75	US 160 W byp, to Willard, Stockton Lake, **S** 🛢️ Kum&Go/dsl, 🍽️ Quiznos, Wendy's, 🛏️ Courtyard, La Quinta
72	MO 266, to Chesnut Expwy, **1-2 mi S** 🛢️ Casey's, Cenex, Kum&Go, 🍽️ Alli's Rest, Arby's, Hardee's, KFC, La Hacienda Mexican, LJ Silver, McDonald's, Sonic, Subway, Taco Bell, Taco Bueno, Waffle House, 🛏️ Best Budget Inn, Ramada Ltd, Redwood Motel, ⊙ AutoZone, Curves, $General, city park

Exit	Services
70	rds MM, B, **N** antiques, fireworks, **S** ⊙ Wilson's Creek Nat Bfd (5mi), KOA (1mi)
69	to US 60, Springfield
67	rds N, T, Bois D' Arc, to Republic, **S** 🛢️ Shell/dsl, 🛏️ AmericInn (5mi), ⊙ art glass
66mm	Pond Creek
64.6mm	Dry Branch
64.5mm	Pickerel Creek
61	rds K, PP, **N** 🛢️ Cenex/Hoods/dsl/scales/LP/24hr, Phillips 66, 🛏️ Hood I-44 Motel
58	MO 96, rds O, Z, to Carthage, Halltown, **S** 🛢️ Shell/dsl, ⊙ antiques, truck/auto parts
57	to rd PP (from wb)
56.5mm	Turnback Creek
56mm	Goose Creek
52.5mm	Ⓡˢ **both lanes, full** ♿ **facilities,** 🍽️, 🐾, **litter barrels, vending, petwalk**
49	MO 174E, rd CCW, Chesapeake
46	MO 39, MO 265, Mt Vernon, Aurora, **N** 🛢️ Casey's/dsl, Kum&Go/dsl, Phillips 66/dsl, TA/Conoco/Country Pride/dsl/scales/24hr/@, 🍽️ Bamboo Garden Chinese, KFC, LJ Silver, Mazzio's, McDonald's, Red Barn Cafe, Sonic, Subway, Taco Bell, TJ's BBQ, 🛏️ Super 8, USA Inn, ⊙ $General, Family$, Hometown Drug, O'Reilly Parts, Summer Fresh Foods, True Value, **S** 🛢️ Conoco/dsl, 🛏️ Relax Inn, ⊙ to Table Rock Lake, Stockton Lake, antiques
44	rd H, to Monett, Mt Vernon, **N** 🍽️ Subway (1mi), ⊙ Mid-America Dental/Hearing, RV Camping
43.5mm	Spring River
38	MO 97, to Stotts City, Pierce City, **N** gas/dsl/repair/tires, **S** U of MO SW Ctr
33	MO 97 S, to Pierce City, **S** 🍽️ Hungry House Cafe
29	rd U, to La Russell, Sarcoxie, **N** Ozark Village Gifts, Beagle Bay RV Camping, antiques, **S** 🛢️ Casey's (1mi), Kum&Go/Subway/dsl
29mm	Center Creek
26	MO 37, to Reeds, Sarcoxie, **N** Bill's Truck/trailer repair
22	rd 100 N, **N** Colaw RV Ctr, **S** Consignment RV Sales
21mm	Jones Creek
18b a	US 71 N, MO 59 S, to Carthage, Neosho, **N** ⊙ Big Barn Camping, Coachlight RV Ctr/Camping
15	MO 66 W, Lp 44 (from wb), Joplin, **N** 🛏️ Tara Motel
15mm	Grove Creek
14mm	Turkey Creek
11b a	US 71 S, MO 249 N, to Neosho, Ft Smith, **S** 🛢️ ⊕FLYING J/Denny's/dsl/LP/scales/24hr/@, Phillips 66, Speedco, ⊙ Blue Beacon, Kenworth
8b a	US 71, to Neosho, Joplin, **N** 🛢️ Conoco/dsl, Kum&Go/dsl, Phillips 66/dsl, 🍽️ Applebee's, Backyard Burger, Bob Evans, Braum's, Cabo del Sol, Carino's Italian, Casa Montez Mexican, Cheddar's, Chick-fil-A, ChuckeCheese, Denny's, Domino's, Garfield's, Golden Corral, Golden Dragon, Hardee's, IHOP, Jimmy John's, KFC, King Palace, Logan's Roadhouse, Mazzio's, McAlister's, McDonald's, Noodle&Grill, Ocean Rest, Olive Garden, Outback Steaks, Pitcher's Grill, Pizza Hut, Quiznos, Red Hot&Blue Grill, Red Lobster, Rib Crib, Ruby Tuesday, Ryan's, Schlotzsky's, Sonic, Starbucks, Steak'n Shake, Subway, Taco Bell, Waffle House, Wendy's, 🛏️ Baymont Inn, Best Western, Candlewood Suites, Comfort Inn, Days Inn, Drury Inn, Fairfield Inn, Hallmark Inn, Hampton Inn, Hilton Garden, Holiday Inn, Homewood Suites, La Quinta, Motel 6, Qual

MARSHFIELD · SPRINGFIELD · JOPLIN

MO

INTERSTATE 44 CONT'D

Exit	Services
8b a	Continued
	ity Inn, Residence Inn, Sunrise Inn, Aldi Foods, AT&T, AutoZone, Best Buy, Books-A-Million, Cadillac/Chevrolet, Dillon's Foods, $Tree, Firestone/auto, Food4Less, Ford, Freightliner, Goodyear/auto, Hasting's, Hobby Lobby, Home Depot, Honda, Hyundai, JC Penney, Jo-Ann Fabrics, Kohl's, Lowe's, Macy's, Mercedes, Michael's, Nissan, Office Depot, O'Reilly Parts, Petsmart, Ross, Sam's Club/ gas, Sears, Target, TJ Maxx, Toyota/Scion, Verizon, Walgreens, Walmart/Subway, **S** Casey's, Cracker Barrel, Fazoli's, Microtel, TownePlace Suites, Wheelen RV Ctr
6	MO 86, MO 43 N, to Racine, Joplin, **N** Phillips 66, KFC (1mi), Schlotzsky's (1mi), Walgreens (2mi), **S** H, Harley-Davidson
5.5mm	Shoal Creek
4	MO 43 to Seneca, **N** Loves/Hardee's/dsl/ scales/24hr, Peterbilt, antiques, **S** Conoco/Subway/ dsl, Petro/Iron Skillet/dsl/scales/24hr/@, Wendy's/ dsl/scales/24hr, McDonald's, Sleep Inn, $General, IA 80 Truckomat, KOA, fireworks
3mm	weigh sta both lanes
2mm	Welcome Ctr eb, full facilities, litter barrels, vending. truck parking wb, restrooms
1	US 400, US 166W, to Baxter Springs, KS, **N** Downstream/dsl, Red Oak Steaks, Downstream Casino/ RV Park, **S** Sandstone Gardens
0mm	Missouri/Oklahoma state line

INTERSTATE 55

Exit	Services
209mm	Missouri/Illinois state line at St. Louis, Mississippi River
209b	I 70 W to Kansas City
209a	to Arch, Busch Stadium
208	Park Ave, 7th St, **W** BP, Rally's, Taco Bell, White Castle, Hilton
207c b	Truman Pkwy, **W** I-44 W, to Tulsa
207a	Gravois St (from nb), **E** Midwest Petroleum, **W** A-1 Chinese Wok, Jack-in-the-Box
206c	Arsenal St, **E** Anheuser-Busch Tour Ctr, **W** Shell
206b	Broadway (from nb)
206a	Potomac St (from nb)
205	Gasconade, **W** H
204	Broadway, **E** Phillips 66/repair, **W** Sinclair/dsl, Hardee's, McDonald's, Subway, Radio Shack, Walgreen/24hr
203	Bates St, Virginia Ave, **W** BP, 7-11
202c	Loughborough Ave, **W** St Louis Bread Co, Starbucks, Lowe's Whse, Schnuck's Foods
202b	Germania (from sb)
202a	Carondelet (from nb)
201b	Weber Rd
201a	Bayless Ave, **E** BP, McDonald's, **W** Mobil, 7-11/ gas, China Wok, DQ, Jack-in-the-Box, Pizza Hut/Taco Bell, Subway, Taco Bell, Walgreens, auto repair
200	Union Rd (from sb)
199	Reavis Barracks Rd, **E** Shell, Pennie's BBQ, Hancock Fabrics
197	US 50, US 61, US 67, Lindbergh Blvd, **E** Phillips 66, Arby's, Buffalo Wild Wings, ChuckeCheese, Dillard's,

Exit	Services
197	Continued
	HoneyBaked Ham, Hooters, KFC, Krispy Kreme, Macaroni Grill, Noodles&Co, Qdoba, Quiznos, Station Subs, Steak'n Shake, St Louis Bread Co, Subway, Tucker's Place, Holiday Inn, Advance Parts, Best Buy, Dillard's, Discount Tire, Dodge, Ford, Home Depot, JC Penney, Jo-Ann Fabrics, Kia, K-Mart, Macy's, Marshall's, NTB, Sears/auto, Tuesday Morning, mall, **W** QT, Bob Evans, Casa Gallardo, Culvers, Denny's, Lenny's Subs, O'Charley's, Ponderosa, Best Value Inn, Motel 6, Aldi Foods, AT&T, Costco/gas, Ford/Lincoln, Honda, Hyundai, Mazda, Office Depot, Target
196b	I-270 W, to Kansas City
196a	I-255 E, to Chicago
195	Butler Hill Rd, **E** Phillips 66, Hampton Inn, Holiday Inn/rest., Advance Parts, Walgreens, **W** Phillips 66, Burger King, Hardee's, Pizza Hut/Taco Bell, Subway, Waffle House, Schnuck's Foods, tires/repair
193	Meramec Bottom Rd, **E** Mobil/dsl, QT, Cracker Barrel, Best Western, Midwest RV Ctr
191	MO 141, Arnold, **E** QT, Applebee's, Arby's, Bandana's BBQ, Capt D's, Casa Mexicana, Chick-fil-A, CiCi's Pizza, China King, Denny's, Fazoli's, 54th St Grill, 5 Guys Burgers, Jack-in-the-Box, Lee's Chicken, Lion's Choice, LJ Silver, McDonald's, Pizza Hut, Rally's, Steak'n Shake, Super China Buffet, Taco Bell, Terrazza Grill, Drury Inn, Pear Tree Inn, Aldi Foods, AT&T, Dobbs Tire, Hobby Lobby, Kohl's, NAPA, O'Reilly Parts, PetCo, Shop'n Save Foods, Walgreens, Walmart, vet, **W** Phillips 66/dsl, Chili's, Pasta House, Qdoba, St Louis Bread, TX Roadhouse, ValuePlace Hotel, Dierberg's Foods, $Tree, GNC, Lowe's, Office Depot, Petsmart, Verizon
190	Richardson Rd, **E** Phillips 66/dsl, QT, Shell/Circle K/ dsl, Culver's, DQ, Domino's, Pizza Hut, Ponderosa, Quiznos, Roly-Poly Sandwiches, Sonic, Taco Bell, White Castle, Advance Parts, Auto Tire, $Tree, Firestone, Ford, Save-A-Lot Foods, Urgent Care, **W** Phillips 66/ dsl, 7-11, Shell/Circle K/dsl, Burger King, Happy Wok, Imo's Pizza, McDonald's/playplace, Mr. Goodcents Subs, Pizza Den, Ruby Tuesday, Waffle House, Comfort Inn, Aamco, AutoZone, GNC, Home Depot, Plaza Tire, Radio Shack, Schnuck's Foods, Target, Walgreens
186	Imperial, Kimmswick, **E** Mobil, Shell/Circle K, Blue Owl (1mi), Main St BBQ, auto repair, **W** Phillips 66/ Jack-in-the-Box/dsl, China Wok, Domino's, Gianno's Grill, O'aces Grill, Papa John's, Subway, USPO, to Mastodon SP
185	rd M, Barnhart, Antonia, **E** BP/dsl, Ginny's Kitchen, **W** BP, Phillips 66/dsl, 7-11, Walgreens

🅽 INTERSTATE 55 CONT'D

Exit	Services
184.5mm	weigh sta both lanes
180	rd Z, to Hillsboro, Pevely, **E** 🅶 Mobil/dsl, 🍽 Burger King, China House, Domino's, Main St BBQ, Subway, Taco Bell, The Kitchen, Ⓞ $General, Queens Foods, **W** 🅶 Mr Fuel, Phillips 66/McDonald's/dsl/scales, 🛏 Super 8, Ⓞ auto repair, rv camping
178	Herculaneum, **E** 🅶 QT/Wendy's/dsl/scales, Shell/Circle K, 🍽 Cracker Barrel, DQ, Dog House Diner, Jack-in-the-Box, La Pachanga Mexican, Ⓞ Toyota/Scion, **W** Buick/GMC, Cadillac/Chevrolet, Ford, vet
175	rd A, Festus, **E** 🅶 Mobil, Murphy USA/dsl, Phillips 66/dsl, 🍽 Arby's, Bob Evans, Burger King, Capt D's, China 1, Fazoli's, Imo's Pizza, Jack-in-the-Box, McDonald's/playplace, Papa John's, Ryan's, Sonic, St. Louis Bread Co, Steak'n Shake, Subway, Taco Bell, Tanglefoot Steaks, White Castle, 🛏 Best Western, Drury Inn, Ⓞ Advance Parts, Aldi Foods/dsl, AutoZone, $Tree, GNC, Home Depot, K-Mart, Plaza Tire, Radio Shack, Schnuck's Foods, Verizon, Walgreens, Walmart, **Urgent Care**, **W** 🅶 Phillips 66/Domino's/dsl, 7-11/dsl, 🍽 Hardee's, Jimmy John's, Ruby Tuesday, Waffle House, Whittaker's Pizza, 🛏 Comfort Inn, Holiday Inn Express, Ⓞ Chrysler/Dodge/Jeep, Lowe's
174b a	US 67, Lp 55, Festus, Crystal City, **E** 🅶 Phillips 66/dsl
170	US 61, **W** 🅶 BP/dsl/LP, 🍽 Laddie Boy Rest
165	rd TT (from sb)
162	rds DD, OO
160mm	🅿ˢ **both lanes, full** ♿ **facilities,** 🚮 **litter barrels,** 🚻 **s, vending, petwalk**
157	rd Y, Bloomsdale, **E** 🅶 Phillips 66, **W** 🅶 ❤Loves/Chester's/McDonald's/dsl/scales/24hr
154	rd O, to St Genevieve
150	MO 32, rds B, A, to St Genevieve, **E** 🅶 BP, 🍽 DQ, Ⓞ 🅷 Hist Site (6mi), **W** 🅶 Phillips 66/dsl, Ⓞ Hawn SP (11mi)
143	rds J, M, N, Ozora, **W** 🅶 Shell/dsl, 🍽 Zone Grill, 🛏 Regency Inn, Ⓞ truckwash
141	rd Z, St Mary
135	rd M, Brewer, **E** propane depot
129	MO 51, to Perryville, **E** 🅶 MotoMart/McDonald's/dsl, Phillips 66/dsl, 🍽 Burger King, KFC, Ponderosa, Taco Bell, Ⓞ 🅷, Ford, **W** 🅶 Rhodes/dsl, 🍽 China Buffet, 5 Star Chinese, 🛏 Comfort Inn, Days Inn, Super 8, Ⓞ AT&T, Buick/Chevrolet, Chrysler/Dodge/Jeep, Walmart
123	rd B, Biehle, **W** 🅶 Rhodes/dsl, 🍽 Missy's Country Kettle
119mm	Apple Creek
117	rd KK, to Appleton, **E** 🍽 Terri's Cafe, Ⓞ Ron's Grocery
111	rd E, Oak Ridge
110mm	🅿ˢ **both lanes, full** ♿ **facilities,** 🚮 **litter barrels,** 🚻 **s, vending, petwalk**
105	US 61, Fruitland, **E** 🅶 Casey's, Phillips 66/dsl, Rhodes/dsl, Ⓞ $General, Percull Tires/repair, Trail of Tears SP (11mi), **W** 🅶 D-Mart/dsl, 🍽 Bavarian Halle, DQ, Pizza Inn, 🛏 Drury Inn
102	LaSalle Ave, E Main St
99	US 61, MO 34, to Jackson, **E** RV camping, **W** 🛏 Comfort Suites, Ⓞ McDowell South RV Ctr
96	rd K, to Cape Girardeau, **E** 🅶 Phillips 66, 🍽 Applebee's, Blimpie, Bob Evans, Buffalo Wild Wings, Burger King, Chick-fil-A, CiCi's Pizza, Cracker Barrel, DQ, Denny's, Dexter BBQ, El Acapulco, Great Wall Chinese, Honey

CAPE GIRARDEAU

96	Continued Baked Ham, Logan's Roadhouse, O'Charley's, Olive Garden, Panera Bread, Papa Murphy's, Pizza Hut, Pizza Inn, Popeye's, Qdoba, Red Lobster, Ruby Tuesday, Ryan's, Schnucks, Starbucks, Steak'n Shake, Subway, Taco Bell, TX Roadhouse, Wendy's, 🛏 Auburn Place, Drury Lodge/rest., Holiday Inn Express, PearTree Inn, Ⓞ 🅷, AT&T, Barnes&Noble, Best Buy, BigLots, Hancock Fabrics, Hobby Lobby, JC Penney, Macy's, Old Navy, Schnuck's Foods, Verizon, to SEMSU, **W** 🅶 Shell, 🍽 McDonald's/playplace, Outback Steaks, Penn Sta Subs, Sonic, Subway, White Castle, 🛏 Drury Suites, Hampton Inn, Ⓞ $Tree, Honda, Hyundai, Kohl's, Lowe's, Mazda, Nissan, PetCo, Plaza Tire, Sam's Club, Sears Grand, Staples, Target, TJ Maxx, Toyota, Walmart/Subway, USPO
95	MO 74 E, **E** 🛏 Candlewood Suites, **W** Ⓞ Menards
93a b	MO 74 W, Cape Girardeau, **E** 🛏 Townhouse inn, Ⓞ diesel repair
91	rd AB, to Cape Girardeau, **E** 🅶 Rhodes/dsl, 🍽 Huddle House, Ⓞ Harley-Davidson, tire repair, vet, **W** Ⓞ Capetown RV Ctr, Youngbloods RV Ctr, 📧
89	US 61, rds K, M, Scott City, **E** 🅶 Rhodes, Store 24, 🍽 Burger King, Ice Cream Corner, Las Brisas Mexican, Pizza Pro, Ⓞ Bob's Foods, $General, Medicap Drug, NAPA, Plaza Tires, repair
80	MO 77, Benton, **E** 🅶 Express/dsl, **W** 🅶 Phillips 66/McDonald's/dsl/fireworks, Ⓞ antiques, winery (8mi)
69	rd HH, to Sikeston, Miner, **E** Ⓞ Peterbilt, **W** 🅶 Sinclair/dsl (1mi), Ⓞ 🅷, golf

MINER

67	US 60, US 62, Miner, **E** 🅶 Breaktime/dsl, 🛏 Best Value Inn, Holiday Inn Express, Motel 6, Ⓞ Hinton RV Park, **0-2 mi W** 🅶 Cenex, Hucks, Jasper's Gas, QuickCheck, 🍽 Bo's BBQ, Buffalo Wild Wings, Burger King, Dexter BBQ, El Tapatio Mexican, Lambert's Rest., Little Caesars, McDonald's, Pizza Hut, Pizza Inn, Ruby Tuesday, Sonic, Subway, Taco John's, Wendy's, 🛏 Comfort Inn, Country Hearth Inn, Drury Inn, PearTree Inn, Super 8, Thrifty Inn, Ⓞ 🅷, AutoZone, Buick/Chevrolet, Cadillac/GMC, $General, Family$, Food Giant, Raben Tires, Sikeston Outlets/famous brands, Verizon, Walgreens, vet
66b	US 60 W, to Poplar Bluff, **3 mi W on US 61/62** 🅶 Breaktime/E-85, Sinclair, 🍽 A&W/LJ Silver, Applebee's, Arby's, China Buffet, DQ, El Bracero Mexican, Hardee's, KFC, McDonald's, Sonic, Subway, Taco Bell, 🛏 Days Inn, Ⓞ Aldi Foods, AT&T, Chrysler/Dodge/Jeep, $Tree, Ford/Lincoln, GNC, JC Penney, Lowe's, O'Reilly Parts, Radio Shack, Walmart
66a	I-57 E, to Chicago, US 60 W
59mm	St Johns Bayou
58	MO 80, Matthews, **E** 🅶 TA/Taco Bell/dsl/scales/24hr/@, Ⓞ to Big Oak Tree SP (24mi), truck repair, **W** 🅶 ✈FLYING J/Denny's/dsl/LP/RV dump/scales/24hr, ❤Loves/Chester's/Subway/dsl/scales/24hr, Ⓞ truckwash/repair
52	rd P, Kewanee, **E** 🅶 BJ Trvl Ctr/BBQ/dsl
49	US 61, US 62, New Madrid, **E** Ⓞ Hunter-Dawson HS (3mi)
44	US 61, US 62, Lp 55, New Madrid, **E** Ⓞ hist site
42mm	**truck parking nb, restrooms;** 🅿ˢ **sb, full** ♿ **facilities,** 🚮 **litter barrels,** 🚻 **s, vending, petwalk**
40	rd EE, St Jude Rd, Marston, **E** 🅶 ▥▥▥/Subway/dsl/scales/24hr, 🛏 Super 8, **W** 🅶 MFA, 🛏 Moore's Landing Suites
32	US 61, MO 162, Portageville, **W** 🅶 Phillips 66/dsl,

MO

	▲N **INTERSTATE 55** CONT'D
Exit	Services
32	Continued
	Casey's, 🍴 China King, McDonald's, Sonic, ⊡ $General, dsl repair
27	rds K, A, BB, to Wardell, **E** ⊡ KOA (2mi), **W** ⊡ Delta Research Ctr
20mm	**Welcome Ctr, ℞ₛ nb, full ♿ facilities, 🚻 litter barrels, Ⓒ vending, petwalk**
19	MO 84, Hayti, **E** ⓖ Double Nickel/dsl, 🚚/Arby's/dsl/scales/24hr, Shell, 🍴 McDonald's, KFC/Taco Bell, Pizza Hut, 🛏 Comfort Inn/rest., M Motel, ⊡ Ⓗ, KOA (6mi), Lady Luck Casino/camping, **W** ⓖ BP/dsl, Hayti Trvl Ctr/Subway/dsl, R&P/dsl, 🍴 Apple Barrel, Chubby's BBQ, Los Portales, Patty Ann's BBQ, 🛏 Drury Inn, ⊡ Ⓗ, CarQuest, $General, Fred's Store, Goodyear/auto, Hay's Foods, repair, USPO
17b a	I-155 E, US 412, to TN
14	rds J, H, U, to Caruthersville, Braggadocio
10mm	**weigh sta nb**
8	US 61, MO 164, Steele, **W** ⓖ BP/Chester's/Subway/dsl/scales, 🛏 Deerfield Inn, ⊡ truck repair
4	rd E, to Holland, Cooter
3mm	truck parking, restrooms
1	US 61, rd O, Holland, **W** ⓖ Shell/dsl/24hr
0mm	Missouri/Arkansas state line

	▲N **INTERSTATE 57**
Exit	Services
22mm	Missouri/Illinois state line, Mississippi River
18.5mm	**weigh sta both lanes**
12	US 62, MO 77, Charleston, **E** ⓖ Exxon/Cheers/Quiznos/dsl/scales/24hr, 🛏 Eagle Inn, **W** ⓖ ⓕFLYING J/Huddle House/dsl/scales/24hr, 🍴 Las Brisas Mexican, 🛏 EconoLodge
10	MO 105, Charleston, **E** ⓖ Conoco/Boomland/dsl, 🚚/Subway/dsl/scales/24hr, 🍴 Wally's Eatery, ⊡ Boomland RV Park, **W** ⓖ Casey's, 🍴 China Buffet, McDonald's, Pizza Hut, 🛏 Quality Inn, ⊡ Alco, CountryMart Foods, Plaza Tire, Verizon, city park
4	rd B, Bertrand
1b a	I-55, N to St Louis, S to Memphis. **I-57 begins/ends on I-55**

	▲E **INTERSTATE 64**
Exit	Services
41mm	Missouri/Illinois state line, Mississippi River
40b a	Broadway St, to Stadium, to the Arch, **N** 🛏 Hilton, Sheraton, stadium, **S** ⊡ Dobb's Tire
40c	(from wb), I-44 W, I-55 S
39c	11th St (exits left), downtown
39b	14th St, downtown, **N** 🛏 Sheraton, **S** ⓖ BP
39a	21st St, Market St (from wb), **N** 🛏 Drury Inn, Hampton Inn
38d	Chestnut at 20th St, **N** 🛏 Drury Inn, Hampton Inn
38c	Jefferson Ave, St Louis Union Sta, **N** ⊡ Joplin House, **S** 🛏 Residence Inn
38a	Forest Park Blvd (from wb), **N** ⓖ Shell
37b a	Market St, Bernard St, Grand Blvd, **N** ⓖ Shell, 🍴 Del Taco, 🛏 Courtyard, Hampton Inn, Hyatt, Drury Inn, Adam's Mark Hotel, Marriott
36d	Vandeventer Ave, Chouteau Ave

36b a	Kingshighway, **N** ⊡ Ⓗ, **S** ⓖ BP
34d c	Hampton Ave, Forest Park, **N** museums, zoo, **S** ⓖ BP, Mobil, Phillips 66, 🍴 Courtesy Diner, Hardee's, Imo's Pizza, Jack-in-the-Box, Smokin' Al's BBQ, Steak'n Shake, Subway, Taco Bell, 🛏 Hampton Inn
34a	Oakland Ave, **N** ⓖ BP, 🍴 Del Taco, Subway, ⊡ Ⓗ
33d	McCausland Ave, **N** ⓖ BP, 🍴 Del Taco
33c	Bellevue Ave, **N** Ⓗ
33b	Big Bend Blvd
32b a	Eager Rd, Hanley Rd, **S** ⓖ Shell, 🍴 Lion's Choice, Macaroni Grill, McDonald's, St Louis Bread Co, Subway, ⊡ Best Buy, Dierberg's Foods, Home Depot, Target, Whole Foods Mkt
31b a	I-170 N, **N** ⓖ Shell, 🍴 Burger King, DQ, IHOP, KFC, Steak'n Shake, TGIFriday, Dillard's, ⊡ mall, **S** ⓖ BP, 🍴 Macaroni Grill, Subway, ⊡ Dierberg's Foods, Goodyear, Target
30	McKnight Rd
28c	Clayton Rd (from wb)
28b a	US 67, US 61, Lindbergh Blvd, **S** ⓖ BP, 🍴 Brio Grill, Fleming's Rest., Schneithouse Rest., Starbucks, 🛏 Hilton, ⊡ Honda, Shnuck's Foods, mall
27	Spoede Rd
26	rd JJ, Ballas Rd, **N** Ⓗ, **S** Ⓗ
25	I-270, N to Chicago, S to Memphis
24	Mason Rd, **N** 🛏 Courtyard, Marriott, ⊡ LDS Temple, hwy patrol
23	Maryville Centre Dr (from wb), **N** 🛏 Courtyard, Marriott
22	MO 141, **N** 🍴 Rogatta Grille, ⊡ Ⓗ, **S** 🍴 5 Guys Burgers, Pizza Hut
21	Timberlake Manor Pkwy
20	Chesterfield Pkwy (from wb), same as 19b a
19b a	MO 340, Chesterfield Pkwy, Olive Blvd, **N** ⓖ BP, Shell, 🍴 Applebee's, Pizzaria Uno, Sheridan's Custard, Taco Bell, Yaya's Cafe, 🛏 DoubleTree Hotel, Hampton Inn, Homewood Suites, Residence Inn, ⊡ USPO, Dobb's Tire, Schnucks Foods, Walgreens, **S** ⓖ Mobil, 🍴 Bahama Breeze Rest., Bacana Cafe, Casa Gallardo's, California Pizza Kitchen, Chili's, Houlihans, Macaroni Grill, PF Chang's, 🛏 Drury Plaza Hotel, ⊡ Dillard's, mall
17	Boones Crossing, Long Rd, Chesterfield ↗ Rd, **1 mi S** ⓖ Mobil, 🍴 Bob Evans, Chick-fil-A, Coldstone, Cousins Subs, Culver's, East Coast Pizza, Emperor's Buffet, Fox&Hound, Golden China, Hardee's, Hometown Buffet, IHOP, IMO's Pizza, Joe's Crabshack, Kaldi's Coffee, Lion's Choice, Longhorn Steaks, Matador Cafe., McDonald's, Mimi's Cafe, O'Charley's, Old Country Buffet, Old Spaghetti Factory, Olive Garden, Original Pancakes, Qdoba Mexican, Quiznos, Red Lobster, Red Robin, SmokeHouse

MO

⬆E INTERSTATE 64 CONT'D

Exit	Services
17	Continued
	Rest., Sonic, Starbucks, Steak'n Shake, Subway, Taco Bell, 🛏 Hampton Inn, Hilton Garden, ⊙ Best Buy, Dick's, Dobb's Tire, $Tree, Firestone, Ford, Home Depot, KIA, Lowe's, Michael's, Petsmart, Radio Shack, Sam's Club, Target, Walmart, WorldMkt, vet
14	Chesterfield 🔄 Rd (from eb), S 🚹 Phillips 66, 🛏 Comfort Inn
13mm	Missouri River
11	Research Park Ctr Dr
10	MO 94, St. Charles, N 🚹 Mobil, QT, Shell, 🍴 Jack-in-the-Box, McDonald's, ⊙ Mercedes, Busch Wildlife Area
9	rd k, O'Fallon, N 🚹 Mobil, QT, 🍴 Cracker Barrel, Ruby Tuesday, Starbucks, 🛏 Holiday Inn Express, Residence Inn, Staybridge Suites, ⊙ Chevrolet, Honda, Volvo
6	rd DD, Wing Haven Blvd, N 🚹 Phillips 66, 🍴 Bristol Seafood, Hunan King, Massa's Italian, Outback Steaks, Subway, VA BBQ, 🛏 Hilton Garden
4	rd N, N 🚹 PetroMart, Phillips 66, 🍴 McDonald's, Qdoba Mexican, Red Robin, Steak'n Shake, St. Louis Bread Co., ⊙ JC Penney, Shop'n Save, Target, S 🚹 Murphy USA/dsl, Phillips 66, 🍴 Dragon Buffet, El Maguay, Jack-in-the-Box, McDonald's, Sonic, Starbucks, Subway, Taco Bell, Wendy's, White Castle, ⊙ Aldi Foods, AutoZone, Dobb's Tire, $Tree, Firestone, GNC, Lowe's, Radio Shack, Walmart
2	Lake St. Louis Blvd, N 🍴 BC's Rest., Max&Erma's, ⊙ Old Navy, Schnuck's Foods, Von Maur, Walgreens
1	Prospect Rd, N 🚹 Shell
0mm	I-70 E to St Louis, W to Kansas City

⬆E INTERSTATE 70

Exit	Services
252mm	Missouri/Illinois state line, Mississippi River
251a	I-55 S, to Memphis, to I-44, to downtown/no return
250b	Memorial Dr, downtown, Stadium, S 🚹 Shell, 🍴 McDonald's, 🛏 Days Inn
250a	Arch, Riverfront, N ⊙ The Arch, S 🛏 Drury Inn, Hampton Inn, Hilton, Hyatt, Millineal Hotel, Renaissance, ⊙ Edward Jones Dome
249c	6th St (from eb)
249a	Madison St, 10th St
248b	St Louis Ave, Branch St
248a	Salisbury St, McKinley Br, N truck repair/24hr, S 🚹 BP, Phillips 66
247	Grand Ave, N 🚹 BP, Phillips 66/Subway/dsl, 🛏 Western Inn
246b	Adelaide Ave
246a	N Broadway, O'Fallon Park, N 🚹 Love's/McDonald's/Subway/dsl/scales/24hr, Mobil/dsl, ⊙ Freightliner
245b	W Florissant
245a	Shreve Ave, S 🚹 BP
244b	Kingshighway, 3/4 mi S 🍴 Burger King, McDonald's, Subway
244a	Bircher Blvd, Union Blvd
243b	(243c from eb) Bircher Blvd
243a	Riverview Blvd
243	Goodfellow Blvd, N 🚹 Shell
242b a	Jennings Sta Rd, S 🛏 Western Inn
241b	Lucas-Hunt Rd, N 🚹 Shell/Circle K, 3/4 mi S 🍴 Lee's Chicken, McDonald's

S T   L O U I S

Exit	Services
241a	Bermuda Rd, S 🅷
240b a	Florissant Rd, N 🚹 BP/McDonald's, 🍴 DQ, Sonic, Taco Bell, ⊙ Schnuck's Foods, Walgreens
239	N Hanley Rd, N 🍴 Jack-in-the-Box, 🛏 Hilton Garden, S 🚹 BP, Mobil, 🍴 McDonald's
238c b	I-170 N, I-170 S, no return
238a	N Lambert-St Louis ✈, S 🛏 Renaissance Hotel
237	Natural Bridge Rd (from eb), S 🚹 BP, Phillips 66, Shell, 🍴 Diner, Arby's, Burger King, Denny's, Jack-in-the-Box, KFC, Pizza Hut, Steak'n Shake, Waffle House, Wendy's, DoubleTree, 🛏 Best Western, Days Inn, Double Tree, Holiday Inn, Renaissance, Travelodge
236	Lambert-St Louis ✈, S 🚹 BP, 🍴 BBQ, Big Boy, Coco's, Golden Pancake, Grone Cafeteria, Hardee's, Lombardo's Café Rafferty's Rest., Tiffany's Rest., 🛏 ✈ Inn, Best Western, Days Inn, Drury Inn/rest., Hampton Inn, Hilton, Holiday Inn, Marriott, Motel 6, Peartree Inn
235c	Cypress Rd, rd B W, N to ✈
235b a	US 67, Lindbergh Blvd, N 🛏 Best Western, S 🚹 Shell, 🍴 Lion's Choice Rest., Steak'n Shake, TGIFriday's, 🛏 Crowne Plaza, Embassy Suites, Homestead Studios, ⊙ Chevrolet, Dillard's, Firestone, JC Penney, Sears/auto, mall
234	MO 180, St Charles Rock Rd, N 🚹 Phillips 66/dsl, 🍴 Applebee's, Arby's, Fazoli's, HomeTown Buffet, Imo's Pizza, Jack-in-the-Box, LoneStar Steaks, McDonald's, New China Buffet, Ponderosa, Red Lobster, St Louis Bread, Subway, Wendy's, White Castle, ⊙ 🅷, Aldi Foods, AutoZone, Best Buy, $Tree, Kohl's, Lowe's, Meineke, NTB, Office Depot, Petsmart, Save-A-Lot Foods, Target, Tuesday Morning, Verizon, Walgreens, Walmart, S 🚹 QT, 🍴 IHOP, ⊙ Chrysler/Dodge/Jeep, Home Depot, Schucks, Walgreens, tires/repair
232	I-270, N to Chicago, S to Memphis
231b a	Earth City Expwy, N 🚹 Motomart, Phillips 66/Jack-in-the-Box/dsl, 🍴 McDonald's, Quiznos, 🛏 Candlewood Suites, Courtyard, Holiday Inn, Residence Inn, SpringHill Suites, Studio+, S 🚹 Mobil, 🍴 Burger King, Dave&Buster's, 🛏 Holiday Inn Express, Homewood Suites, Wingate Inn, ⊙ Harrah's Casino/Hotel, Riverport Ampitheatre
230mm	Missouri River

S T   C H A R L E S

Exit	Services
229b a	5th St, St Charles, N 🚹 BP, Mobil/dsl, 🍴 Bellacino's Italian, Buffalo Wild Wings, Denny's, El Tio Pepe, Jack-in-the-Box, KFC, Lee's Chicken, McDonald's, Waffle House, 🛏 Best Value Inn, Best Western, Comfort Suites, Quality Inn, ⊙ Aldi Foods, Ameristar Casino, Bass Pro Shops, Gordman's, Walgreens, S 🚹 QT/dsl, 🍴 Cracker Barrel, 🛏 Embassy Suites, Fairfield Inn, ⊙ malls
228	MO 94, to Weldon Springs, St Charles, N 🚹 Phillips 66, ZX/dsl, 🍴 Arby's, Chinatown Express, DQ, Imo's Pizza, Papa John's, Steak'n Shake, ⊙ Advance Parts, Chevrolet, NAPA, Walgreen, Valvoline, S 🚹 QT, 🍴 Chinese Express, ChuckECheese, Fazoli's, Gingham's Rest., Grappa Grill, McAlister's Deli, Outback Steaks, Pizza Hut, 🛏 Days Inn, Intown Suites, ⊙ Dobb's Tire, vet, access to 227
227	Zumbehl Rd, N 🚹 Phillips 66/dsl, ZX, 🍴 Culpepper's Grill, 🛏 Super 8, ⊙ Lowe's, Sav-A-Lot Foods, S 🚹 BP, Hucks/dsl, 🍴 Applebee's, Bob Evans, Boston Mkt, Capt D's, Chevy's Mexican, Chirco's Grill, CiCi's Pizza, El Mariachi Mexican, Fazoli's, Gingham's Rest., Golden Corral, Great Wall Chinese, Hardee's, Hoho Chinese, Jack-in-the-Box, McCalister's, McDonald's, Quiznos, Subway, Taco

🔼E INTERSTATE 70 CONT'D

Exit	Services
227	Continued Bell/Pizza Hut, Wiliker's Cafe, 🛏 Days Inn, Red Roof Inn, TownePlace Suites, Travelodge, 🄾 BigLots, Dierberg's Foods, $Tree, GNC, Jiffy Lube, Michael's, NTB, Petsmart, Radio Shack, Sam's Club/gas, Schnuck's Foods, Walmart/Blimpie, Walgreens, vet, access to 228
225	Truman Rd, to Cave Springs, **N** 🅰 BP, Casey's, Shell, ZX Gas, 🛏 Hampton Inn, Motel 6, 🄾 Buick/GMC, Cadillac, Kenworth, Mazda, Subaru, U-Haul, VW, **S** 🅰 Conoco, Mobil, QT, 🍴 Bandanas BBQ, Big Boy, Burger King, China Wok, Culver's, DQ, Denny's, El Tio Pepe, Hooters, IHOP, Jack-in-the-Box, Longhorn Steaks, Lion's Choice Rest., LJ Silver, McDonald's, O'Charley's, Pasta House, Pizza Hut, Pizza St, Red Lobster, Steak'n Shake, Subway, Taco Bell, Thai Kitchen, White Castle, 🛏 Country Inn&Suites, 🄾 H, Batteries+, Chrysler/Dodge/Jeep, Firestone, Home Depot, Kia, Office Depot, Shop'n Save, Target, TJ Maxx
224	MO 370 E
222	Mid-Rivers Mall Dr, rd C, St Peters, **N** 🅰 QT/dsl/24hr, 🍴 Burger King, 🄾 Chevrolet, Honda, Lincoln, Toyota/Scion, **S** 🅰 Mobil, ZX Gas/dsl, 🍴 Arby's, Bob Evans, Buffalo Wild Wings, Chili's, China Wok, Domino's, HoneyBaked Ham, Jack-in-the-Box, Joe's Crabshack, Macaroni Grill, Max & Erma's, McDonald's/playplace, Olive Garden, Pizza Hut/Taco Bell, Qdoba, Red Robin, Ruby Tuesday, Steak'n Shake, Subway, Wendy's, 🛏 Drury Inn, Extended Stay America, 🄾 Aldi Foods, AutoZone, Barnes&Noble, Best Buy, BigLots, Costco/gas, Dick's, Dillard's, Discount Tire, Hancock Fabrics, Hyundai/Nissan/VW, JC Penney, Jo-Ann Fabrics, Marshall's, NTB, Sears/auto, Tuesday Morning, Walgreens
220	MO 79, to Elsberry, **N** Cherokee Lakes Camping (7mi), **S** 🅰 BP, Phillips 66/dsl, 7-11/gas, 🍴 Caleco's Rest., El Mezon, Jack-in-the-Box, McDonald's/playplace, Pirrone's Pizzaria, Quiznos, Roly Poly Sandwiches, Sonic, Subway, 🛏 Days Inn, 🄾 Curves, Dierberg's Foods, O'Reilly Parts, Walgreens
219	T R Hughes Blvd, **S** 🅰 QT, 🍴 Ethyl's Smokehouse, 🛏 Comfort Inn
217	rds K, M, O'Fallon, **N** 🅰 Hucks/dsl, 🍴 Baskin-Robbins, Burger King, Jack-in-the-Box, Rally's, Piggy's BBQ, Pizza Hut/Taco Bell, Sonic, Waffle House, 🄾 Firestone, Jiffy Lube, O'Reilly Parts, Radio Shack, **S** 🅰 Phillips 66/dsl, QT, ZX, 🍴 Applebee's, Arby's, Bob Evans, Chick-fil-A, Domino's, Fazoli's, IHOP, KFC, Krieger's Grill, Lion's Choice Rest., McDonald's/playplace, Pantera's Pizza, Papa John's, Pizza Hut, Red Robin, Stefanina's Pizza, Subway, 🄾 Advance Parts, Aldi Foods, Auto Tire, AutoZone, GNC, Home Depot, K-Mart/drugs, Lowe's, Schnuck's Foods, Shop'n Save Foods, TrueValue, Walgreens, Walmart, camping
216	Bryan Rd, **N** 🛏 Super 8, 🄾 CarQuest, Ford, Peterbilt, **S** 🅰 Conoco, Phillips 66/Jack-in-the-Box/dsl, QT, 🍴 DQ, Cappuccino's, Mr. Goodcents, Wendy's
214	Lake St Louis, **N** 🅰 Phillips 66/McDonald's/dsl, Q-Stop, 🍴 McDonald's, **S** 🅰 Phillips 66/dsl, Shell/Circle K, 🍴 Denny's, El Maguey Mexican, Hardee's, Subway, 🛏 Days Inn, 🄾 H, Wharf Drug
212	rd A, **N** 🛏 Economy Inn, **S** 🅰 Mobil, 🍴 Imo's Pizza, 🛏 Motel 6, 🄾 Chrysler/Dodge/Jeep

Exit	Services
210b a	to I-64, US 40 E, US 61 S, **S** 🅰 Shell, 🄾 H
209	rd Z, Church St, New Melle, **N** 🍴 DQ, **S** 🅰 Phillips 66/dsl
208	Pearce Blvd, Wentzville Pkwy, Wentzville, **N** 🅰 Mobil, Phillips 66, QT/dsl, 🍴 Applebee's, Arby's, Bob Evans, Buffalo Wild Wings, China Buffet, Culver's, Domino's, 54th St Grill, Fritz's Custard, Hardee's, Imo's Pizza, Jack-in-the-Box, Jimmy John's, KFC, Lion's Choice, McDonald's, Mr Goodcents, Olive Garden, Papa John's, Penn Sta., Pizza Hut, Pizza Pro, Qdoba, Ruby Tuesday, Starbucks, Steak'n Shake, St Louis Bread, Subway, Taco Bell, Waffle House, Wendy's, White Castle, 🄾 H, AT&T, AutoZone, Best Buy, Chevrolet, Dierberg's Foods, Dobb's Tire, $General, Family$, Home Depot, Hyundai, Kohl's, Lowe's, Michael's, O'Reilly Parts, Petsmart, Radio Shack, Save-A-Lot, Schnuck's Food, Target, Walgreens, Walmart, **Urgent Care**, **S** 🅰 BP, 🍴 Bandana's BBQ, IHOP, 🛏 Super 8, 🄾 Thomas RV Ctr
204mm	weigh sta both lanes
203	rds W, T, Foristell, **N** 🅰 TA/BP/Pizza Hut/Popeye's/Taco Bell/dsl/scales/24hr/@, Mr Fuel/dsl/scales, 🛏 Best Western, 🄾 Freightliner, **S** 🅰 Phillips 66/McDonald's/dsl, 🄾 dsl repair
200	rds J, H, F (from wb), Wright City, **N** 🅰 Midwest/dsl, 🍴 Ruiz Castillo's Mexican (1mi), **S** 🅰 Phillips 66, 🍴 New China, 🛏 Super 7 Inn
199	rd J, H, F, Wright City, **N** 🅰 Shell/McDonald's/dsl, 🄾 $General, **S** 🛏 Super 7 Inn, 🄾 Volvo Trucks
198mm	℞ both lanes, full ♿ facilities, 🍴, 🅰, litter barrels, pet-walk
193	MO 47, Warrenton, **N** 🅰 Phillips 66/dsl, ZX Gas/dsl, 🍴 Applebee's, Burger King, China House, Dominos, Jack-in-the-Box, KFC, McDonald's, Pizza Hut, Subway, Waffle House, 🛏 Best Value Inn, Holiday Inn Express, Super 8, 🄾 Mosers Foods, Radio Shack, Walmart, USPO, **S** 🅰 BP, Conoco/dsl, Phillips 66/dsl, 🍴 Denny's, Taco Bell, 🛏 Comfort Inn, 🄾 Aamco, AutoZone, CarQuest, Chevrolet/GMC, Walgreens, Warrenton Outlets/famous brands
188	rds A, B, to Truxton, **S** 🅰 *FLYING J*/Denny's/dsl/LP/RV Dump/scales/24hr, 🛏 Budget Inn
183	rds E, NN, Y, Jonesburg, **1 mi N** Jonesburg Gardens Camping, **S** 🅰 Phillips 66/dsl, 🄾 USPO
179	rd F, High Hill, **S** 🛏 Budget Motel, Colonial Inn
175	MO 19, New Florence, **N** 🅰 BP/Hardee's/dsl, Shell/dsl/24hr, 🍴 JJ's BBQ, McDonald's, 🛏 Best Inn, Best Value Inn, Days Inn, 🄾 Stone Hill Winery/gifts (15mi), auto repair
170	MO 161, rd J, Danville, **N** 🅰 Sinclair/dsl, 🄾 to Graham Cave SP, Kan-Do RV Park, **S** Lazy Day RV Park
169.5mm	truck parking

St Peters · O' Fallon · WENTZVILLE · WARRENTON

■ = gas   ⑪ = food   ☒ = lodging   ◉ = other   Ⓡ = rest stop   Copyright 2014 - The NEXT Exit ®

MO

COLUMBIA

⧫Ε **INTERSTATE 70** CONT'D

Exit	Services
168mm	Loutre River
167mm	truck parking eb
161	rds D, YY, Williamsburg, **N** ■ Cranes/mkt, ⑪ Marlene's Rest, ◉ USPO
155	rds A, Z, to Calwood, **N** antiques
148	US 54, Kingdom City, **N** ■ BP/dsl, ⑪ Taco Bell, ◉ MO Tourism Ctr, to Mark Twain Lake, **S** ■ Conoco/Subway/dsl/scales/24hr, Petro/Mobil/Iron Skillet/dsl/scales/24hr/@, Phillips 66/dsl, Shell/Gasper's/Arby's/dsl/scales/@, ⑪ Denny's, McDonald's, ☒ Comfort Inn, Days Inn, Super 8, ◉ Ozarkland Gifts, Wheeler's Truckwash
144	rds M, HH, to Hatton, **S** ◉ fireworks
137	rds DD, J, to Millersburg, Stephens, **S** Freightliner, antiques, to Little Dixie WA (4mi)
133	rd Z, to Centralia, **N** ◉ Loveall's RV
131	Lake of the Woods Rd, **N** ■ BP, Phillips 66/Subway/dsl, ⑪ George's Rest, Sonic, ☒ Super 8, ◉ Harley-Davidson, **S** ■ Conoco/dsl, ⑪ Jimmy John's, ☒ Holiday Inn
128a	US 63, to Jefferson City, Columbia, **N** ■ Mobil/dsl, QT, ⑪ Bandanas BBQ, Bob Evans, Burger King, China Garden, Cracker Barrel, Golden Corral, Hooters, KFC, Lee's Chicken, Lonestar Steaks, McDonald's, Pizza Hut, Ruby Tuesday, Steak'n Shake, Taco Bell, Waffle House, Wendy's, White Castle, ☒ Comfort Inn, Fairfield Inn, Hampton Inn, Hilton Garden, Residence Inn, Super 8, ◉ Bass Pro Shop, Home Depot, Pine Grove RV Park, **S** ■ BreakTime/dsl, ⑪ Applebee's, Baskin-Robbins, Chili's, Chipotle Mexican, CiCi's, Culver's, El Magueay, 5 Guys Burgers, Good Cents Subs, Houlihan's, IHOP, Kobe Japanese, Longhorn Steaks, Quiznos, Sonic, Starbucks, Subway, TGIFriday's, ☒ Baymont Inn, Best Western, Candlewood Suites, Country Inn&Suites, Howard Johnson, Motel 6, Ramada, Staybridge Suites, Wingate Inn, ◉ Ⓗ, AT&T, $Tree, HyVee Foods, Lowe's, Patricia's Foods, Sam's Club, Staples, Verizon, Walmart/McDonald's
128	Lp 70 (from wb), Columbia, **N** ⑪ Hardee's, **S** ⑪ Capt D's, ☒ Eastwood Motel, ◉ Ⓗ, Big O Tire, same as 128a
127	MO 763, to Moberly, Columbia, **N** ■ BreakTime/dsl, ⑪ Waffle House, ☒ Budget Host, ◉ Chrysler/Dodge/Jeep, $General, Fiat, Hyundai, Mazda, Mercedes, Toyota/Scion, transmissions, **S** ■ Phillips 66/dsl, ☒ Super 7 Motel
126	MO 163, Providence Rd, Columbia, **N** ■ Phillips 66/dsl, ⑪ Chop Sticks, Country Kitchen, ☒ Best Value Inn, Quality Inn, Red Roof Inn, ◉ CarQuest, Honda, McKnight Tire, same as 127, **S** ■ BreakTime/dsl, ⑪ Burger King, Carlito's Mexican, Church's, DQ, LJ Silver, McDonald's, Pizza Hut, Sonic, Subway, Taco Bell, ◉ Ⓗ, AutoZone, Buick/Cadillac/Chevrolet/GMC, Nissan, O'Reilly Parts, Transmissions+
125	Lp 70, West Blvd, Columbia, **N** ☒ Comfort Suites, **S** ■ Phillips 66/dsl, Shell/dsl, ⑪ Cheddar's, Domino's, Fazoli's, JJ's Cafe, Olive Garden, Outback Steaks, Teppanyaki Grill, ☒ EconoLodge, ◉ Aldi Foods, BMW, Firestone/auto, Kia, Mosers Foods, Subaru, U-Haul, same as 124
124	MO 740, rd E, Stadium Blvd, Columbia, **N** ☒ Extended Stay America, **S** ■ BreakTime, Phillips 66/dsl, ⑪ Applebee's, ChuckECheese, Denny's, 5 Guys Burgers, Hardee's, Jazz Kitchen, KFC, Lee's Chicken, Macaroni Grill, McDonald's, Panera Bread, Pizza Hut, Quiznos, Red Lobster, Ruby Tuesday, Steak'n Shake, Subway, Taco Bell, TX

BOONVILLE

CONCORDIA

Exit	Services
124	Continued Roadhouse, Wendy's, ☒ Days Inn, Drury Inn, Holiday Inn, La Quinta, Motel 6, ◉ Barnes&Noble, Best Buy, Dick's, Dillard's, $Tree, Ford, Hobby Lobby, Macy's, Marshalls, Michael's, Natural Grocers, Old Navy, PetCo, Petsmart, Radio Shack, Sears/auto, Target, Verizon, mall, to U of MO, same as 125
122mm	Perche Creek
121	US 40, rd UU, Midway, **N** ■ Conoco/dsl/rest., Phillips 66, ☒ Budget Inn, ◉ tires/repair, **S** golf
117	rds J, O, to Huntsdale, Harrisburg
115	rd BB N, Rocheport, **N** to Katy Tr SP, winery
114.5mm	Missouri River
111	MO 98, MO 179, to Wooldridge, Overton, **S** ■ Phillips 66/dsl/repair, ◉ RV Park
106	MO 87, Bingham Rd, to Boonville, **S** ■ Phillips 66/dsl
104mm	Ⓡ **both lanes, full** ♿ **facilities,** ⧂, 🅿, **litter barrels, vending, petwalk**
103	rd B, Main St, Boonville, **N** ■ Breaktime, Murphy USA/dsl, Phillips 66/dsl, ⑪ Happy China, KFC/LJ Silver, La Hacienda Mexican, McDonald's, Pizza Hut, Sonic, Subway, Taco Bell, ☒ Days Inn, Super 8, ◉ Ⓗ, Dave's Mkt, Radio Shack, RV Express Camping, Walmart/Subway, to Katy Tr SP, **S** ■ Cenex/dsl, ☒ QT Inn
101	US 40, MO 5, to Boonville, **N** ■ ⬚⬚/Wendy's/dsl/24hr, ⑪ Arby's, ☒ Comfort Inn, Holiday Inn Express, Isle of Capri Hotel (3mi), ◉ Buick/Cadillac/Chevrolet/GMC, Ford, Russell Stover Candies, **S** ■ Loves/Hardee's/scales/dsl/24hr, to Lake of the Ozarks
98	MO 41, MO 135, Arrow Rock, **N** to Arrow Rock HS (13mi), tires, **S** ■ Conoco/Dogwood Rest./dsl, Phillips 66/dsl, ◉ repair
93mm	Lamine River
89	rd K, to Arrow Rock, **N** to Arrow Rock HS
84	rd J, **N** ■ Valero/DQ/Stuckey's, truck repair
78b a	US 65, to Marshall, **N** ■ Conoco/dsl, ◉ RV Park, fireworks
77mm	Blackwater River
74	rd YY, **N** ■ Shell/Betty's/cafe/dsl/repair/24hr, ☒ Welcome Motel
71	rds EE, K, to Houstonia
66	MO 127, Sweet Springs, **N** Ⓗ, **S** ■ BreakTime/dsl, Casey's/dsl, ⑪ Mi Pueblo, ☒ Rodeway Inn, ◉ $General, NAPA
65.5mm	Davis Creek
62	rds VV, Y, Emma
58	MO 23, Concordia, **N** ■ TA/Country Pride/Subway/dsl/scales/24hr/@, ⑪ KFC/Taco Bell, McDonald's, ◉ $General, Patricia's Foods, truck/RV wash, **S** ■ Breaktime/dsl, Casey's, Conoco/dsl, Phillips 66 ⑪ Biffle's BBQ, Hardee's, Pizza Hut, ☒ Budget Inn, Days Inn, Travelodge, ◉ NAPA
57.5mm	Ⓡ **both lanes, full** ♿ **facilities,** ⧂, 🅿, **litter barrels, vending, petwalk**
52	rd T, Aullville
49	MO 13, to Higginsville, **N** ■ Casey's, ⬚⬚/McDonald's/Subway/dsl/scales/24hr, ☒ Camelot Inn/rest, ◉ to Confederate Mem, **S** ☒ Super 8, ◉ Great Escape RV Park, Interstate RV Park
45	rd H, to Mayview
43mm	**weigh sta both lanes**
41	rds O, M, to Lexington, Mayview

INTERSTATE 70 CONT'D

O D E S S A

Exit	Services
38	MO 131 (from wb), Odessa, S 🅖 BP/dsl, Phillips 66/dsl, Shell, Sinclair, 🍴 McDonald's, Morgan's Rest., Pizza Hut, Sonic, Subway, Taco John's, 🅞 $General, O'Reilly Parts, camping, same as 37
37	MO 131, Odessa, N 🅞 Country Gardens RV Park/dump, S 🅖 BP/dsl, Shell, Sinclair, 🍴 El Camino Real, McDonald's, Pizza Hut, Sonic, Subway, Taco John's, 🛏 Parkside Inn, 🅞 $General, O'Reilly Parts, Patricia's Foods, fireworks, same as 38
35mm	truck parking both lanes
31	rds D, Z, to Bates City, Napoleon, N 🅞 Bates City RV Camping, S 🅖 Valero/dsl, 🍴 Bates City BBQ, 🅞 fireworks
29.5mm	Horse Shoe Creek
28	rd H, rd F, Oak Grove, N 🅖 TA/Country Pride/Popeye's/dsl/scales/24hr/@, 🛏 Days Inn, 🅞 Blue Beacon, KOA, S 🅖 Casey's, Petro/BP/DQ/Wendy's/scales/dsl/@, QT/dsl, 🍴 China Buffet, Hardee's, KFC/Taco Bell, McDonald's, Pizza Hut, PJ's Rest., Subway, Waffle House, 🛏 EconoLodge, 🅞 Cash Saver Foods, Lake Paradise RV/Camping (9mi), O'Reilly Parts, SpeedCo Lube, Verizon, Walgreens, Walmart
24	US 40, rds AA, BB, to Buckner, N 🅖 McShop/dsl, 🛏 Best Value Inn, Comfort Inn, 🅞 LifeStyle RV Ctr, auto/dsl repair, S 🅖 Conoco/Subway/dsl/scales/24hr, 🍴 Sonic, 🅞 Trailside RV Park/Ctr
21	Adams Dairy Pkwy, N 🛏 Days Inn, 🅞 Nationwide RV Ctr (1mi), S 🅖 Murphy USA/dsl, Phillips 66/Burger King/dsl, 🍴 Arby's, Buffalo Wild Wings, Chick-fil-A, Chipotle Mexican, Olive Garden, Panda Express, Panera Bread, Planet Sub, Sonic, Taco Bell, TX Roadhouse, 🛏 Courtyard, 🅞 AT&T, GNC, Gordman's, Home Depot, Kohl's, Michael's, NTB, PetCo, Ross, Staples, Target, TJ Maxx, Verizon, Walmart

B L U E   S P G S

Exit	Services
20	MO 7, Blue Springs, N 🅖 Phillips 66/dsl, QT/dsl, 🍴 Backyard Burger, Bob Evans, China 1, Minsky's Pizza, Papa Murphy's, Pizza Shoppe, Pizza St, Rancho Grande, Sonic, Subway, 🛏 Best Value Inn, Days Inn, Motel 6, 🅞 Ace Hardware, CVS Drug, $General, O'Reilly Parts, PriceChopper Foods, Walgreens, S 🅖 BP/dsl, QT/dsl, Shell, Valero, 🍴 Applebee's, Arby's, Cinco de Mayo, Denny's, Godfather's, Jack-in-the-Box, Jimmy John's, KFC, LJ Silver, McDonald's, Original Pizza, Sheridan's Custard, Starbucks, Subway, Taco Bueno, Wendy's, Winsteads Cafe, Zarda's BBQ, 🛏 Hampton Inn, Quality Inn, 🅞 🅗, Urgent Care, Advance Parts, Aldi Foods, AutoZone, BigLots, Chevrolet, Firestone/auto, Goodyear/auto, Hobby Lobby, Hy-Vee Foods/gas, NAPA, Office Depot, Russell Stover
18	Woods Chapel Rd, N 🅖 BP, 🛏 American Inn, La Quinta, Night's Inn, Super 8, 🅞 Harley-Davidson, S 🅖 Conoco/dsl, Phillips 66/dsl, QT, 🍴 China Kitchen, KFC/Taco Bell, Las Playas Mexican, McDonald's, Pizza Hut, Sonic, Subway, Taco John's, Waffle House, 🅞 Ford/Lincoln, Hyundai, Nissan, same as 20
17	Little Blue Pkwy, 39th St, N 🍴 Buffalo Wild Wings, Coldstone, Hereford House, Jimmy John's, Joe's Crabshack, On the Border, Sonic, 🛏 Hilton Garden, 🅞 🅗, World Mkt, mall entrance, S 🅖 QT, 🍴 Arby's, BD Mongolian, Carrabba's, Chipotle Mexican, Corner Cafe, Culver's, El Maguey Mexican, Golden Corral, Hooters, IHOP, Kobe Steaks,

I N D E P E N D E N C E

Exit	Services
17	Continued Outback Steaks, Red Robin, Rib Crib, Subway, Wendy's, 🛏 Comfort Suites, Drury Inn, Holiday Inn Express, 🅞 Carmax, Costco/gas, Lowe's
16mm	Little Blue River
15b	MO 291 N, Independence, **1 exit** N on 39th St 🅖 QT, Phillips 66, 🍴 Applebee's, Bob Evans, Burger King, Chick-fil-A, Chili's, ChuckECheese, 54th St Grill, Fazoli's, Logan's Roadhouse, Longhorn Steaks, McDonald's, Noodles&Co, Perkins, Smokehouse BBQ, Taco Bell, Zio's Italian, 🛏 Fairfield Inn, Staybridge Suites, 🅞 🅗, AT&T, Barnes&Noble, Best Buy, Dick's, Dillard's, JC Penney, Kohl's, Macy's, Marshalls, NTB, Petsmart, Ross, Sam's Club/gas, Sears/auto, Target, Verizon, Walmart, mall
15a	I-470 S, MO 291 S, to Lee's Summit
14	Lee's Summit Rd, **1 mi** N 🍴 Bob Evans, Longhorn Steaks, S 🍴 Cheddar's, Cracker Barrel, 🅞 Bass Pro Shops, Hobby Lobby, Home Depot
12	Noland Rd, Independence, N 🅖 Conoco/dsl, QT, Shell, 🍴 China Town, Denny's, Domino's, Hardee's, Mr Goodcents, Pizza St, Sheridan's Custard, Sonic, 🛏 Best Western, Super 8, 🅞 Advance Parts, Buick/Chevrolet, Chrysler/Jeep, CVS Drug, $General, Firestone/auto, Hancock Fabrics, Honda, K-Mart, Office Depot, TrueValue, Walgreens, to Truman Library, S 🅖 Phillips 66/Circle K, 🍴 Arby's, Bandana's BBQ, Burger King, HoneyBaked Ham, KFC/Taco Bell, Krispy Kreme, McDonald's, Olive Garden, Pizza Hut, Quiznos, Red Lobster, Ruby Tuesday, Steak'n Shake, Wendy's, 🛏 American Inn, Best Value Inn, EconoLodge, Quality Inn, Super 6 Motel, 🅞 BigLots, $Tree, Gordman's, HyVee Foods/gas, Meineke, Savers, Tires+, U-Haul
11	US 40, Blue Ridge Blvd, Independence, N 🅖 QT, 🍴 A&W/LJ Silver, Benny's BBQ, Sonic, Subway, V's Italian, S 🅖 7-11, Sinclair, 🍴 Applebee's, Big Boy, Chipotle Mexican, Church's, East Buffet, Firehouse Subs, IHOP, McDonald's, Papa John's, Samurai Chef, Starbucks, Subway, Taco Bell, 🅞 Cadillac, Family$, GNC, Lowe's, O'Reilly Parts, Radio Shack, Verizon, Walmart/Subway, vet
10	Sterling Ave (from eb), same as 11
9	Blue Ridge Cutoff, N 🍴 Denny's, 🛏 Drury Inn, Holiday Inn, 🅞 🅗, S 🅖 BP, Conoco/Subway, 🍴 Taco Bell, 🛏 Clarion, 🅞 Sports Complex
8b a	I-435, N to Des Moines, S to Wichita
7b	Manchester Trafficway
7mm	Blue River
7a	US 40 E, 31st St
6	Van Brunt Blvd, N 🅖 Phillips 66/dsl, S 🅖 BP, 🍴 McDonald's, Pizza Hut, 🅞 VA, 🅗, NAPA
5c	Jackson Ave (from wb)

🔼E INTERSTATE 70 CONT'D

Exit	Services
5b	31st St (from eb)
5a	27th St (from eb)
4c	23rd Ave
4b	18th St
4a	Benton· Blvd (from eb), Truman Rd, N 🅖 Super Stop/ Wendy's/dsl, 🍴 Subway, 🅞 Advance Parts, Save-A-Lot Foods
3c	Prospect Ave, N 🅖 BP, 🍴 Bryant's BBQ, Church's, S 🍴 McDonald's
3b	Brooklyn Ave (from eb), N 🍴 Gates BBQ, S 🍴 Bryant's, Church's, McDonald's
3a	Paseo St, S 🅖 BP/dsl, 🅞 tires
2m	US 71 S, downtown
2l	I-670, to I-35 S
2j	11th St, downtown
2g	I-29/35 N, US 71 N, to Des Moines
2h	US 24 E, downtown
2e	MO 9 N, Oak St, S 🅖 Phillips 66, Valero, 🏠 Marriott
2d	Main St, downtown
2c	US 169 N, Broadway, S 🅖 Phillips 66, 🏠 Marriott
2b	Beardsley Rd
2a	I-35 S, to Wichita
0mm	Missouri/Kansas state line, Kansas River

🔼N INTERSTATE 270 (ST LOUIS)

Exit	Services
15b a	I-55 N to Chicago, S to St Louis. **I-270 begins/ends in Illinois on I-55/I-70, exit 20.**
12	IL 159, to Collinsville, **1 mi** N 🅖 Conoco, Phillips 66, 🍴 Applebee's, China Rest., DQ, Denny's, Hardee's, Jack-in-the-Box, KFC, Papa John's, Ponderosa, Quizno's 🅞 Aldi Foods, Buick/GMC, Chrysler/Dodge/Jeep, Home Depot, Lowes Whse, PetsMart, Radio Shack, Walgreens, Walmart, S 🅗
9	IL 157, to Collinsville, N 🍴 Comfort Inn, S 🅖 Phillips 66/24hr, 🏠 Hampton Inn
7	I-255, to I-55 S to Memphis
6b a	IL 111, N 🅖 BP, 🌀FLYING J/Denny's/dsl/scales/24hr, 🍴 Hen House Rest., 🏠 Magnuson Hotel, 🅞 Blue Beacon/ scales, Speedco, truck/trailer repair, S 🅖 Mobil/dsl, 🍴 Denny's, McDonald's/playplace, La Mexicana Rest., Taco Bell, 🏠 Days Inn, Holiday Inn Express, Sleep Inn, Super 8, 🅞🅗, to Pontoon Beach
4	IL 203, Old Alton Rd, to Granite City
3b a	IL 3, N Riverboat Casino, S 🅖 Phillips 66, 🍴 Hardee's, Waffle House, 🏠 Budget Motel, EconoLodge, Sun Motel, 🅞 KOA, MGM Camping
2mm	Chain of Rocks Canal
0mm	Illinois/Missouri state line, Mississippi River, motorist callboxes begin eb
34	Riverview Dr, to St Louis, N 🅖 Moto Mart/Subway, **Welcome Ctr/🆁🆂 both lanes, full** ♿ **facilities, info,** 🚮, **litter barrels,** 🚻 **s**
33	Lilac Ave, N USPO, S 🅖 Phillips 66/Jack-in-the-Box/dsl, QT/dsl/scales/24hr, 🍴 Hardee's
32	Bellefontaine Rd, N 🅖 Mobil, QT, Shell, 🍴 China King, KFC, McDonald's, Pizza Hut, Steak'n Shake, 🏠 Economy Inn, Motel 6, 🅞 Advance Parts, Firestone, Schnuck's Foods, S 🅖 BP, 🍴 White Castle, 🅞 Aldi Foods
31b a	MO 367, N 🅖 BP, QT/dsl, 🍴 Jack-in-the-Box, McDon

Exit	Services
31b a	Continued alds, Subway, 🅞 🅗, Chevrolet, $General, Shop'n Save Foods, U-Haul, Walgreens
30b a	Hall's Ferry Rd, rd AC, N 🅖 Mobil/dsl, Phillips 66/dsl, QT, ZX, 🍴 Applebee's, Capt. D's, Popeye's, Waffle House, White Castle, 🏠 Knights Inn, 🅞 Ford/Lincoln, S 🅖 BP/ dsl, Conoco, Phillips 66, 🍴 China Wok, Church's, CiCi's Pizza, Cracker Barrel, IHOP, Steak'n Shake, Subway, 🅞 AutoZone, $Buster, Family$, Home Depot, JoAnn Fabrics, O'Reilly Parts, Shop'n Save Foods
29	W Florissant Rd, N 🍴 Jack-in-the-Box, Lion's Choice, Pasta House, 🅞 Dobb's Tire/auto, $General, K-Mart, Firestone, Office Depot, S 🅖 Phillips 66, 🍴 Arby's, Burger King, Krispy Kreme, Malone's Grill, McDonald's, Pantera's Pizza, Sonic, 🅞 BigLots, $Tree, Mazda, NTB, Radio Shack, Sam's Club/gas, Walmart, Walgreens
28	Elizabeth Ave, Washington St, N 🅖 Phillips 66/dsl, 🍴 Jack-in-the-Box, Jerome's Pizza, Pizza Hut/Taco Bell, Subway, 🅞 Chevrolet, Schnuck's Foods, Walgreens, S 🅖 BP
27	New Florissant Rd, rd N, N 🅖 BP, Shell/Circle K
26b	Graham Rd, N Hanley, N 🅖 7-11/dsl 🍴 Arby's, LJ Silver, Starbucks, 🏠 Hampton Inn, Motel 6, 🅞 🅗, S 🅖 QT, 🍴 McDonald's, 🏠 Days Inn, 🅞 $General, Hancock Fabrics
26a	I-170 S
25b a	US 67, Lindbergh Blvd, N 🅖 BP, Phillips 66, QT, 🍴 Bandana's BBQ, Burger King, China Wok, Church's, Del Taco, IHOP, Imo's Pizza, Jack-in-the-Box, McDonald's, Outback Steaks, Papa John's, Pizza Hut/Taco Bell, Pueblo Nuevo Mexican, Quiznos, Rally's, Sonic, Starbucks, Waffle House, Wendy's, 🏠 Comfort Inn, InTown Suites, La Quinta, Ramada Inn, 🅞 AutoZone, Cadillac, Dierberg's Deli, Family$, Firestone/auto, Ford, GNC, Goodyear, NAPA, Nissan, Radio Shack, Sav-a-Lot Foods, Schnuck's Foods, Toyota/Scion, Walgreens, S 🅖 7-11, 🍴 Subway, 🏠 Budget Inn, EconoLodge, Extended Stay America, Studio+, 🅞 Honda, VW, transmissions, USPO
23	McDonnell Blvd, E 🍴 Denny's, Quiznos, 🏠 La Quinta, W 🅖 BP, QT, ZX, 🍴 Arby's, Jack-in-the-Box, Lion's Choice, McDonald's, Starbucks, Steak'n Shake, 🅞 Buick/GMC
22b a	MO 370 W, to MO Bottom Rd
20c	MO 180, St Charles Rock Rd, E 🅖 Phillips 66/dsl, 🍴 A&W/LJ Silver, Arby's, Casa Gallardo's, Hometown Buffet, Fazoli's, Jack-in-the-Box, Lonestar Steaks, McDonald's, Ponderosa, Red Lobster, St. Louis Bread, Subway, Taco Bell, Wendy's, White Castle, 🏠 Economy Inn, 🅞 🅗 Aldi Foods, AutoZone, Best Buy, $Tree, K-Mart, Kohl's, Lowe's, NTB, Office Depot, Petsmart, Target, Tuesday Morning, Verizon, Walgreens, vet, W 🅖 QT, ZX, 🍴 Bob Evans, Olive Garden, Waffle House, 🏠 Best Value Inn, Motel 6, Super 8
20b a	I-70, E to St Louis, W to Kansas City
17	Dorsett Rd, E 🅖 BP, QT, 🍴 BBQ, Syberg's Grill, 🏠 Best Western, Drury Inn, Hampton Inn, W 🅖 Mobil, Phillips 66, Shell, 🍴 Arby's, Denny's, Fuddrucker's, McDonald's, Steak'n Shake, Subway, 🏠 Baymont Inn
16b a	Page Ave, rd D, MO 364 W, E 🅖 BP, CFM, Citgo/7-11, QT, Sinclair, 🍴 Blimpie, Copperfield's Rest., Hardee's, Hooters, Malone's Grill, McDonald's, Stazio's Café, 🏠 Comfort Inn, Courtyard, DoubleTree, Holiday Inn, Homestead Suites, Red Roof Inn, Residence Inn, Sheraton
14	MO 340, Olive Blvd, E 🅖 BP, Mobil, 🍴 Applebee's, Bristol

K A N S A S   C I T Y

MO

S T   L O U I S

S T   L O U I S

INTERSTATE 270 (ST LOUIS)

Exit	Services
14	Continued
	Cafe, Denny's, Domino's, KFC, McDonald's, Lion's Choice Rest., Pasta House, Steakout, 🏠 Courtyard, Drury Inn, ⊡ �H, BMW/Land Rover/Cadillac, Chevrolet, Crysler/Jeep, Lexus, W ⓡ Schnucks, 🍴 Coldstone Creamery, Culpepper's Café, House of Wong, Subway, TGIFriday, ⊡ Dierberg's Foods, Kohl's, Walgreens
13	rd AB, Ladue Rd
12b a	I-64, US 40, US 61, E to St Louis, W to Wentzville, E �H
9	MO 100, Manchester Rd, E ⓡ BP, 🍴 Café America, Houlihan's Rest, IHOP, Lion's Choice Rest., McDonald's, ⊡ Famous Barr, Galyan's, Lord&Taylor, Nordstrom's, mall, W ⓡ Phillips 66, Shell, 🍴 Applebee's, Casa Gallardo's Mexican, Olive Garden, Red Robin
8	Dougherty Ferry Rd, S ⓡ Citgo/7-11, Mobil, 🍴 McDonald's, ⊡ �H
7	Big Ben Rd, N �H
5b a	I-44, US 50, MO 366, E to St Louis, W to Tulsa
3	MO 30, Gravois Rd, N ⓡ BP, Phillips 66, 🍴 Bandana BBQ, Olive Garden, Outback Steaks, 🏠 Days Inn, Quality Inn, ⊡ Ford
2	MO 21, Tesson Ferry Rd, N ⓡ BP, 🍴 El Muguey Mexican, Jimmy John's, Panda Chinese, Pizza Hut, ⊡ Acura, AutoZone, Buick, Dobb's Auto, O'Reilly Parts, Scion/Toyota, vet, N on Lindbergh ⓡ Mobil, 🍴 Burger King, Church's, 54th St Grill, Jack-in-the-Box, Olive Garden, Outback Steaks, Quizno's, Red Lobster, Subway, Taco Bell, TGIFriday's, Waffle House, White Castle, ⊡ Buick/GMC, Honda, Schnuck's Foods, Shop'n Save, Walgreens, S ⓡ Shell/Circle K/dsl, 🍴 Little Caesar's, other Dierberg's Foods
1b a	I-55 N to St Louis, S to Memphis

INTERSTATE 435 (KANSAS CITY)

Exit	Services
83	I-35, N to KS City, S to Wichita
82	Quivira Rd, Overland Park, N 🍴 Burger King, Old Chicago Pizza, Pizza Hut, Ponderosa, Taco Bell, ⊡ �H, CVS Drug, S 🍴 McDonald's, Subway, Wendy's, 🏠 Extended Stay America
81	US 69 S, to Ft Scott
80	Antioch Rd
79	Metcalf Ave, N ⓡ Conoco/7-11, 🍴 Carrabba's, D'Bronx Pizza, Denny's, Hardee's, Hooters, Jack-in-the-Box, Jose Peppers, Krispy Kreme, Winstead's, 🏠 Clarion, Comfort Inn, Days Inn, Embassy Suites, Hampton Inn, Super 8, ⊡ �H, AAA, Office Depot, Walmart Mkt, S 🍴 Applebee's, McDonald's, Panera Bread, 🏠 Drury Inn, Marriott, PearTree Inn
77b a	Nall Ave, Roe Ave, N ⓡ BP, QT, 🍴 DQ, Mr Goodcents, Sonic, Winstead's Grill, 🏠 Best Value Inn, S 🍴 McDonald's, Wendy's, 🏠 Courtyard, Hilton Garden, Holiday Inn, Homestead Suites, Hyatt Place, Sheraton
75b	State Line Rd, N ⓡ Phillips 66, 🍴 Applebee's, Gate's BBQ, McDonald's, Taco Bell, Waid's Rest., Wendy's, ⊡ Goodyear/auto, Lexus, Midas, O'Reilly Parts, PriceChopper Foods, Volvo, S ⓡ BP, ⊡ �H, city park
75a	Wornall Rd, N ⓡ QT, 🍴 Applebee's, China King, Coach's Grill, Dunkin Donuts, Fuzzy's Taco Shop, McDonald's, Pizza Hut, Subway, ⊡ Urgent Care, Acura, Audi, Chevrolet, Honda, Infiniti, Nissan, Toyota/Scion, Volvo, VW

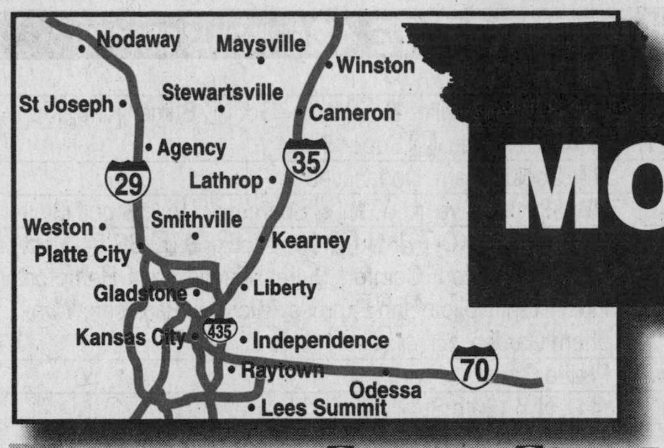

74	Holmes Rd, N ⓡ Phillips 66/dsl, 🍴 Subway, Thai House, S 🏠 Courtyard, Extended Stay America
73	103rd St (from sb)
71b a	I-470, US 71 S, US 50 E
70	Bannister Rd, E ⓡ Phillips 66, 🍴 McDonalds, Wendy's, ⊡ K-Mart, W 🍴 A&W/LJ Silver, Taco Bell, ⊡ Firestone/auto, Home Depot
69	87th St., E ⓡ Conoco/dsl, QT, 🏠 A-1 Motel, Capital Inn, ⊡ Meineke, Suzuki, W 🏠 Baymont Inn
67	Gregory Blvd (same as 66a b), E ⓡ Shell, 🍴 Applebee's, Niece's Rest., Wendy's, ⊡ BigLots, $General, PriceChopper Foods, W Nature Ctr, zoo
66	MO 350 E, 63rd st
65	Eastwood Tfwy, W ⓡ Conoco, 🍴 Church's, McDonald's, Peachtree Rest, Pizza Hut
63c	Raytown Rd, Stadium Dr (nb only), E to Sports Complex
63b a	I-70, W to KC, E to St Louis
61	MO 78, 1 mi E Church's Chicken
60	MO 12 E, Truman Rd, 12th St, E ⓡ BP/dsl, Shamrock, W ⓡ QT
59	US 24, Independence Ave, E ⓡ QT, 🍴 Hardee's, ⊡ to Truman Library, W ⊡ CarQuest, Waffle House
57	Front St, E ⓡ Ⓕ FLYING J/Conoco/rest/dsl/scales/24hr, ⊡ Blue Beacon, Freightliner, Kenworth, W ⓡ Phillips 66/dsl, QT, 🍴 Denny's, McDonald's, Smugglers Rest, Subway, Taco Bell, Waffle House, Wendy's, 🏠 Ramada, ⊡ Walgreens, Urgent Care
56mm	Missouri River
55b a	MO 210, E 🏠 Ameristar Hotel/Casino, Red Roof Inn, ⊡ Riverboat Casino, Ford/Volvo/GMC/Mercedes Trucks, W 🍴 Arby's, Burger King, Denny's, 🏠 La Quinta
54	48th St, Parvin Rd, E ⓡ Phillips 66, ⊡ RV Park, W ⓡ QT, 🍴 Subway, Waffle House, Wendy's, 🏠 Candlewood Suites, Crossland Suites, Days Inn, Fairfield Inn, Funpark Inn, Hampton Inn, Holiday Inn, Super 8
52a	US 69, E ⓡ Phillips 66, Shell, Sinclair, W ⓡ Fuel Outlet, 🍴 McDonald's, Pizza Hut, Subway, Taco Bell, ⊡ CVS Drug, $General, Save-A-Lot Foods
52b	I-35, S to KC
51	Shoal Creek Dr
49b a	MO 152 E, to I-35 N, Liberty, E 🍴 Applebee's, Bob Evans, Buffalo Wild Wings, Cracker Barrel, 54th St Grill, Longhorn Steaks, Steak'n Shake, 🏠 Best Western, Comfort Inn, Fairfield Inn, Hampton Inn, Holiday Inn Express, Super 8
47	NE 96th St
46	NE 108th St
45	MO 291, NE Cookingham Ave, E to I-35 N
42	N Woodland Ave

MO / **MT**

KANSAS CITY

⬆N INTERSTATE 435 (KANSAS CITY) CONT'D

Exit	Services
41b a	US 169, Smithville, N Kum&Go, Burger King, McDonald's, Sonic, Super 8
40	NW Cookingham, No facilties
37	NW Skyview Ave, rd C, N Shamrock (1mi), S golf (3mi)
36	to I-29 S, to KCI , N Shamrock, S BP, Best Western, Clarion, Comfort Suites, Fairfield Inn, Hampton Inn, Hilton, Holiday Inn Express, Microtel, Radisson, Wyndham Garden
31mm	Prairie Creek
29	rd D, NW 120th St
24	MO 152, rd N, NW Berry Rd
22	MO 45, Weston, Parkville
20mm	Missouri/Kansas state line, Missouri River
18	KS 5 N, Wolcott Dr, E to Wyandotte Co Lake Park
16	Donohoo Rd, new exit
15b a	Leavenworth Rd, E Conoco/Subway/dsl, Comfort Suites, Woodlands Racetrack
14b a	Parallel Pkwy, E Honda, Toyota/Scion, W Phillips 66/Subway/dsl, Applebee's, Arby's, Bob Evans, Bryant's BBQ, Carino's Italian, Cheeseburger Paradise, Chili's, Chipotle Mexican, Culver's, Dave&Buster's, Granite City Rest, Hooters, IHOP, Jack-in-the-Box, Logan's Roadhouse, McDonald's, Olive Garden, Panda Express, Red Lobster, Sheridan's Custard, Sonic, Taco Bell, Taco Bueno, Wendy's, Candlewood Suites, Country Inn&Suites, Holiday Inn Express, AT&T, Kohl's, NTB, Old Navy, Sam's Club/dsl, Target, TJ Maxx, Walmart

SHAWNEE MISSION

Exit	Services
13b a	US 24, US 40, State Ave, E Frontier Steaks, W Famous Dave's BBQ, Lonestar Steaks, Best Western, Great Wolf Lodge, Hampton Inn, Cabela's, KS Race Track, Russell Stovers
12b a	I-70, KS Tpk, to Topeka, St Louis
11	Kansas Ave
9	KS 32, KS City, Bonner Springs, W Phillips 66/dsl
8b	Woodend Rd, E Peterbilt, W Shell/food court/dsl/scales
8.8mm	Kansas River
8a	Holliday Dr, to Lake Quivira
6c	Johnson Dr
6b a	Shawnee Mission Pkwy, E McDonald's, Subway, Home Depot, Kohl's, Lowe's, Michael's, Old Navy, Petsmart, Radio Shack, Target, Walmart/Subway, museum
5	Midland Dr, Shawnee Mission Park, E Conoco, Phillips 66/Subway/dsl, Barley's Brewhaus, Chen's Kitchen, Eggct, Jose Pepper's Grill, Minsky's Pizza, Paula&Bill's Ristorante, Wendy's, Hampton Inn, vet, W Hereford House, Courtyard
3	87th Ave, E BP, Phillips 66/dsl, McDonald's, Panera Bread, Panzon's Rest, Papa John's, Papa Murphy's, Sonic, Taco Bell, Ace Hardware, Aldi Foods, Tuesday Morning, Walgreens
2	95th St
1b	KS 10, to Lawrence
1a	Lackman Rd, N Phillips 66, Suburban Lodge
0mm	**I-435 begins/ends on I-35.**

MONTANA

SHELBY

⬆N INTERSTATE 15

Exit	Services
398mm	Montana/US/Canada Border
397	Sweetgrass, W both lanes, full facilities, , litter barrels, petwalk, , Gastrak, Glocca Morra Motel/cafe, Duty Free
394	ranch access
389	MT 552, Sunburst, W CFN/dsl, Prairie Mkt/Chester Fried, Sunburst RV Park, USPO
385	Swayze Rd
379	MT 215, MT 343, to Kevin, Oilmont, W Four Corners Café
373	Potter Rd
369	Bronken Rd
366.5mm	weigh sta sb
364	Shelby, E Lewis&Clark RV Park, W
363	US 2, Shelby, to Cut Bank, 0-1 mi E Cenex, /Exxon/Country Skillet/dsl/scales/24hr, Sinclair/dsl, Cowloon Chinese, Dash Drive-In, Dixie Inn Steaks, Pizza Hut, Subway, The Griddle, Comfort Inn, Crossroads Inn, Glacier Motel/RV Park, O'Haire Motel, , Albertsons, CarQuest, Mark's Tire, Parts+, TrueValue, city park, USPO, visitor info, W Best Western, ShopKo, to Glacier NP
361mm	parking area nb
358	Marias Valley Rd, to Golf Course Rd, E camping
357mm	Marias River
352	Bullhead Rd
348	rd 44, to Valier, W Lake Frances RA (15mi)

Exit	Services
345	MT 366, Ledger Rd, E to Tiber Dam (42mi)
339	Conrad, E /weigh sta, both lanes, full facilities, litter barrels, , W Calumet/dsl, Cenex/dsl, Exxon/Subway/dsl, A&W/Chester's, Home Cafe, Main Drive-In, Pizza House, Northgate Motel, Super 8, , Buick/Chevrolet/GMC, Conrad Tire/repair, IGA Foods, Olson's Drug, Radio Shack, Ford, Pondera RV Park, TrueValue, Westco RV Ctr, museum, vet, USPO
335	Midway Rd, Conrad, 4 mi W , gas, food, , lodging, RV camping
328	MT 365, Brady, W Mtn View Co-op/dsl, city park, USPO
321	Collins Rd
319mm	Teton River, both lanes, full facilities, , , litter barrels, petwalk
313	MT 221, MT 379, Dutton, W Cenex/dsl, Café Dutton, city park, USPO
302	MT 431, Power
297	Gordon
290	US 89 N, rd 200 W, to Choteau, W Conoco/dsl, Sinclair/dsl/LP/RV dump, USPO
288mm	parking area both lanes
286	Manchester, W livestock auction, same as 290 (2mi)
282	US 87 N (from sb), NW bypass, 2-3 mi E Conoco/dsl, Holiday/dsl, Arby's, Burger King, Little Caesars, McDonald's, New Peking, Pizza Hut, Subway, Taco Bell, Taco John's, Days Inn, Albertsons/Osco, $Tree, K-Mart, O'Reilly Parts, Sam's Club/gas, ShopKo, Staples, Tire-Rama, Walgreens, Walmart

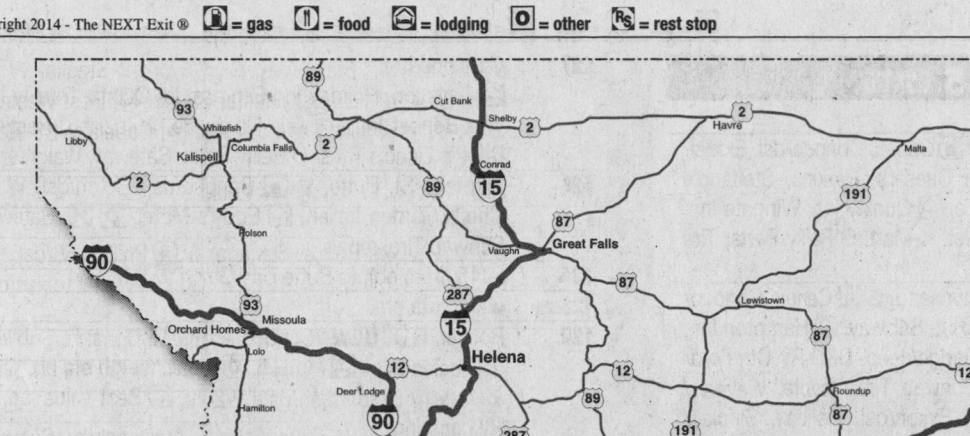

MT

INTERSTATE 15 CONT'D

GREAT FALLS

Exit	Services
280	US 87 N, Central Ave W, Great Falls, **E** Loaf 'N Jug, A&W/KFC, Ford's Drive-In, Lippi's Kitchen, Papa John's, Alberta Inn, Central Motel, Days Inn (3mi), Staybridge Suites, U-Haul/LP, Whalen Tire, to Giant Sprgs SP, city park, vet
280mm	Sun River
278	US 89 S, rd 200 E, 10th Ave, Great Falls, **E** Chili's, Classic 50s Diner/casino, Coldstone, Golden Corral, McDonald's, Moonshine Grill, On-the-Border Mexican, Pizza Hut, Comfort Inn, Hampton Inn, Hilton Garden, Holiday Inn Express, AT&T, Barnes&Noble, Home Depot, Michael's, Old Navy, PetCo, Smith's/dsl, **1-3 mi E** Calumet/dsl, Cenex/dsl, Conoco/dsl, Exxon/dsl, Holiday/Subway/dsl, Sinclair/dsl, Applebee's, Arby's, Baskin-Robbins, Beef'O'Brady's, Best Wok, Boston's Pizza, Burger King, Café Rio, China Buffet, DQ, Fiesta Jalisco, 4B's Rest., Fuddrucker's, Hardee's, Jaker's Rest., JB's Rest., Jimmy John's, KFC, Little Caesars, MacKenzie River Pizza, McDonald's, Ming's Chinese, Noodle Express, Papa John's, Papa Murphy's, Plta Plt, Pizza Hut, PrimeCut Rest., Quiznos, Sonic, Starbucks, Subway, Taco Bell, Taco John's, Taco Treat, Wendy's, Wheat MT, Best Western, Comfort Inn, Extended Stay America, Fairfield Inn, Holiday Inn, La Quinta, Motel 6, Plaza Inn, Super 8, Townhouse Inn, Western Motel, H, Ace Hardware, Albertsons/Osco, AT&T, AutoZone, BigLots, Cadillac/Chevrolet/Toyota, CarQuest, Chrysler/Dodge/Jeep, CVS Drug, Dick's RV Park, Discount Drug, $Tree, Firestone/auto, Ford, Harley-Davidson, Hastings Books, Herberger's, Honda, Hyundai, JC Penney, Jo-Ann Fabrics, KOA, Midas, NAPA, Nissan, O'Reilly Parts, Pierce RV Ctr, Ross, Scheels Sports, Sears/auto, Target, Tire-Rama, Travel Time RV Ctr, Van's/IGA, Verizon, VW, Walgreens, USPO, transmissions, vet, to Malmstrom AFB
277	Airport Rd, **E** FLYING J/Denny's/dsl/scales/24hr, /Conoco/Subway/casino/dsl/scales/24hr, Crystal Inn **W**
275mm	weigh sta nb
270	MT 330, Ulm, **E** Conoco/dsl/LP, USPO, **W** Beef'n Bone Steaks, to Ulm SP

256	rd 68, Cascade, **1/2 mi E** Sinclair, Badger Cafe, Tom's Foods, USPO
254	rd 68, Cascade, **1/2 mi E** same as 256
250	local access
247	Hardy Creek, **W** to Tower Rock SP, food, RV camping
246.5mm	Missouri River
245mm	scenic overlook sb
244	Canyon Access, **2 mi W** MO Inn Rest., Prewett Creek Camping, RV camping, rec area
240	Dearborn, **E** RV park
239mm	**both lanes, full facilities, , , litter barrels, petwalk**
238mm	Stickney Creek
236mm	Missouri River
234	Craig, **E** Izaak's Cafe, Trout Shop Café/lodge, rec area, boating, camping
228	US 287 N, to Augusta, Choteau
226	MT 434, Wolf Creek, **E** Exxon/dsl, Oasis Café, MT River Outfitters/lodge/flyshop, camping, to Holter Lake, **W** Frenchman&Me Café, USPO
222mm	parking area both lanes
219	Spring Creek, Recreation Rd (from nb) boating, camping
218mm	Little Prickly Pear Creek
216	Sieben
209	**E** to Gates of the Mtns RA
205mm	turnout both directions
202mm	**weigh sta sb**
200	MT 279, MT 453, Lincoln Rd, **W** Sinclair/Bob's Mkt/dsl, GrubStake Rest., Lincoln Rd RV Park, to ski area
194	Custer Ave, **E** Conoco/dsl, Chili's, Hardee's, IHOP, Macaroni Grill, Moonshine Grill, Comfort Suites, Residence Inn, Costco/gas, Helena RV Park (5mi), Home Depot, Staples, TJMaxx, Whalen Tire, **W** Cenex, Conoco/dsl, Exxon/dsl, Arby's, Applebee's, Buffalo Wild Wings, Burger King, DQ, Jade Garden, McDonald's, Panda Express, Pizza Hut, Quiznos, Taco Bell, Taco Del Mar, Holiday Inn Express, Albertson's, AT&T, AutoZone, CVS Drug, $Tree, Hastings Books, Macy's, Murdoch's, Natural Grocers, PetCo, Lowe's, Office Depot, Ross, ShopKo, Target, Verizon

[R] = gas [food] = food [lodging] = lodging [O] = other [Rs] = rest stop   Copyright 2014 - The NEXT Exit ®

↑N INTERSTATE 15 CONT'D

Exit	Services
193	Cedar St, Helena, E [🍴], W [R] Cenex, Conoco/dsl, Exxon/dsl, [food] Godfather's, Little Caesars, Perkins, Steffano's Pizza, Subway, Taco John's, [lodging] Quality Inn, Wingate Inn, [O] Ace Hardware, Chevrolet, K-Mart, O'Reilly Parts, Tire Rama, USPO, vet
192b a	US 12, US 287, Helena, Townsend, E [R] Cenex, Conoco/dsl, [food] Burger King, Pizza Hut, Subway, [lodging] Hampton Inn, [O] Buick/GMC, Chrysler/Dodge/Jeep, D&D RV Ctr, Ford/Lincoln, Honda, Nissan, Schwab Tire, Toyota, Walmart/Subway, st patrol, W [R] Exxon/dsl, Holiday, Sinclair/dsl, [food] A&W/KFC, DQ, Hunan Chinese, Jimmy John's, L&D Chinese, McDonald's, Overland Express Rest., Papa John's, Papa Murphy's, Quiznos, Starbucks, Steve's Cafe, Taco John's, Taco Treat, Village Inn Pizza, Wendy's, [lodging] Comfort Inn, Days Inn, Fairfield Inn, Howard Johnson, Jorgenson's Inn, La Quinta, Motel 6, Red Lion Inn, Shilo Inn, Super 8, [O] H, AAA, Albertsons, CVS Drug, GNC, JC Penney, Safeway/dsl, Tire Factory, Verizon, Walgreens
190	S Helena, W [H]
187	MT 518, Montana City, Clancy, E [food] Hugo's Pizza/casino, W [R] Cenex/dsl, [food] Jackson Creek Cafe, MT City Grill, [lodging] Elkhorn Inn
182	Clancy, E RV camping, W [food] Chubby's Grill, [O] USPO, to NF
178mm	[Rs] both lanes, full & facilities, (C), 🪑, litter barrels, pet-walk
176	Jefferson City, NF access
174.5mm	chain up area both lanes
168mm	chainup area both lanes
164	rd 69, Boulder, E [R] Exxon/dsl/casino, [food] Elkhorn Cafe, Gator's Pizza Parlour, Mtn Good Rest., The River Café, [O] L&P Foods, Parts+, USPO, RC RV camping, auto repair
161mm	parking area nb
160	High Ore Rd
156	Basin, E [O] Merry Widow Health Mine/RV camping, W [O] Basin Cr Pottery, camping, USPO
154mm	Boulder River
151	to Boulder River Rd, Bernice, W camping, 🪑
148mm	chainup area both lanes
143.5mm	chainup area both lanes
138	Elk Park, W [O] Sheepshead 🪑, wildlife viewing
134	Woodville
133mm	continental divide, elev 6368
130.5mm	scenic overlook sb
129	I-90 E, to Billings
I-15 S and I-90 W run together 8 mi	
127	Harrison Ave, Butte, E [R] Cenex/dsl, Conoco/dsl, Exxon/dsl, [food] A&W/KFC, Arby's, Burger King, 4B's Rest., McDonald's, MacKenzie River Pizza, MT Club Rest., Perkins, Pizza Hut, Silver Bow Pizza, Starbucks, Subway, Taco Bell, Wendy's, [lodging] Best Western, Comfort Inn, Copper King Hotel, Hampton Inn, Super 8, [O] American Car Care, CarQuest, Buick/Chevrolet/GMC, Chrysler/Dodge/Jeep, $Tree, Ford, Hart's RV Ctr, Herberger's, Honda, JC Penney, Jo-Ann Fabrics, Kia, K-Mart, Murdoch's, NAPA, Rocky Mtn RV Ctr, Staples, Subaru, Toyota/Scion, Verizon, Walmart/Subway, casinos, W [R] Cenex/dsl, Conoco/dsl, [food] DQ, Derby Steaks, Domino's, El Taco Mexican, Hanging 5 Rest., John's Rest., L&D Chinese, Papa John's, Papa Murphy's, Quiznos, Royse's Burgers, Taco John's,

Exit	Services
127	Continued [lodging] Days Inn, Holiday Inn Express, La Quinta, Quality Inn, War Bonnet Inn, [O] Ace Hardware, AutoZone, Hastings Books, Lisac's Tires, O'Reilly Parts, Safeway, Walgreens
126	Montana St, Butte, E [R] Conoco/dsl, Exxon/dsl, W [food] Chef's Garden Italian, [lodging] Eddy's Motel, [O] H, Safeway, Schwab Tire, repair
124	I-115 (from eb), to Butte City Ctr
123mm	weigh sta sb
122	Rocker, E [R] [food]/Conoco/Arby's/McDonald's/Subway/dsl/scales/24hr, [lodging] Motel 6, [O] repair, weigh sta nb, W [R] ✈FLYING J/Exxon/rest./dsl/LP/24hr, [lodging] Best Value Inn, [O] RV camping
I-15 N and I-90 E run together 8 mi	
121	I-90 W, to Missoula, W 2 Bar Lazy-H RV Camping
119	Silver Bow, Port of MT Transportation Hub
116	Buxton
112mm	Continental Divide, elevation 5879
111	Feely
109mm	[Rs] both lanes, full & facilities, (C), 🪑, litter barrels, pet-walk
102	rd 43, to Wisdom, Divide, W [O] rv camping (2mi), to Big Hole Nat Bfd (62mi)
99	Moose Creek Rd
93	Melrose, W [food] Melrose Café/grill/dsl, Hitchin Post Rest., [lodging] Great Waters Inn (5mi), Pioneer Mtn Cabins, [O] Sportsman Motel/RV Park, Sunrise Flyshop, USPO
85.5mm	Big Hole River
85	Glen, E [O] Willis Sta RV camping
74	Apex, Birch Creek
64mm	Beaverhead River
63	Lp 15, rd 41, Dillon, Twin Bridges, E [R] Cenex/dsl/LP/RV Dump, Exxon/KFC/dsl/24hr, Phillips 66/dsl, [food] Lions Den, McDonald's, Pizza Hut, Subway, [lodging] Best Value Inn, Best Western/rest., Comfort Inn, GuestHouse Inn, Motel 6, Sundowner Motel, [O] H, Buick/Chevrolet, CarQuest, Family$, KOA, Les Schwab Tire, Murdoch's, NAPA, O'Reilly Parts, Safeway/dsl, auto repair/tires, city park, museum, W MT U
62	Lp 15, Dillon, E [food] DQ, El Toro Mexican, Sparky's Rest., Taco John's, [lodging] Creston Motel, Flyshop Inn, [O] H, KOA, Van's/IGA Foods, Southside RV Park, to W MT U
60mm	Beaverhead River
59	MT 278, to Jackson, W [O] Bannack SP, Countryside RV Park/LP
56	Barretts, E RV camping
52	Grasshopper Creek
51	Dalys (from sb, no return)
50mm	Beaverhead River
46mm	Beaverhead River
45mm	Beaverhead River
44	MT 324, E [lodging] Buffalo Lodge, [O] Armstead RV Park, W [O] Clark Cyn Reservoir/RA, RV camping
38.5mm	Red Rock River
37	Red Rock
34mm	parking area both lanes, litter barrels, restrooms
29	Kidd
23	Dell, E [R] Cenex/dsl, [food] Yesterdays Calf-a, [O] USPO
16.5mm	weigh sta both lanes
15	Lima, E [R] Exxon/dsl, [food] Jan's Café, [lodging] Mtn View Motel/RV Park, [O] Big Sky Tire/auto, USPO, ambulance, [Rs], both lanes, & facilities, litter barrels, petwalk

HELENA / BUTTE / DILLON

MT

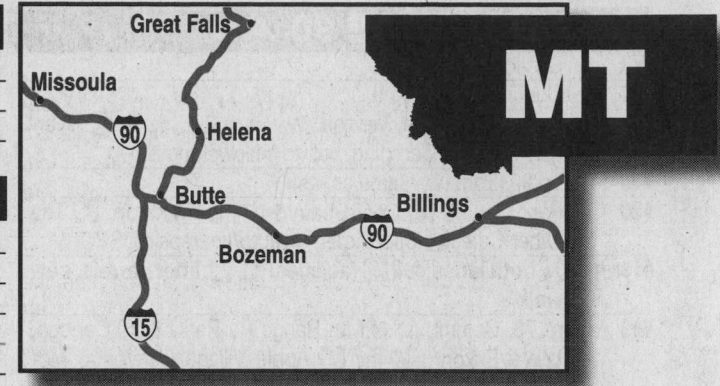

INTERSTATE 15 CONT'D

Exit	Services
9	Snowline
0	Monida, E 🅾, to Red Rock Lakes
0mm	Montana/Idaho state line, Monida Pass, elevation 6870

INTERSTATE 90

Exit	Services
559.5mm	weigh sta both lanes
554.5mm	Montana/Wyoming state line
549	Aberdeen
544	Wyola
530	MT 463, Lodge Grass, **1 mi** S 🅿 gas, dsl, food, lodging
517.5mm	Little Bighorn River
514	Garryowen, N 🅿 Conoco/Subway, 🅾 Custer Bfd Museum, S 🅾 7th Ranch RV camp
511.5mm	Little Bighorn River
510	US 212 E, N 🅿 Exxon/café/dsl/gifts, 🍽 Crows Nest Café, 🅾 🏥, to Little Bighorn Bfd, casino, S 🅾 Little Bighorn RV Camp/dump
509.5mm	weigh sta, both lanes exit left
509.3mm	Little Bighorn River
509	Crow Agency, N 🅿 Conoco, S to Bighorn Canyon NRA
503	Dunmore
498mm	Bighorn River
497	MT 384, 3rd St, Hardin, S 🏥, Bighorn Cty Museum, **2 mi** S 🛏 Western Motel, 🅾 Casino Rest./lounge
495	MT 47, City Ctr, Hardin, N 🅿 Cenex/dsl, 🍽 Purple Cow Rest., 🅾 KOA, S 🅿 Cenex/dsl, *FLYING J*/Conoco/Subway/dsl/LP/24hr, Exxon/dsl, Soco/dsl, 🍽 DQ, Farwest Rest., McDonald's, Pizza Hut, Taco John's, 🛏 Rodeway Inn, Super 8, Western Motel, 🅾 🏥, Chevrolet, Grand View Camping/RV Park, Sunset Village RV Park, casinos
484	Toluca
478	Fly Creek Rd
477mm	🆁🆂 both lanes, full ♿ facilities, 🍽🅿, litter barrels, petwalk
469	Arrow Creek Rd
462	Pryor Creek Rd
456	I-94 E, to Bismarck, ND
455	Johnson Lane, N 🅿 🚚/Conoco/McDonald's/dsl/scales/24hr, S 🅿 Exxon/A&W/dsl, *FLYING J*/dsl/LP/scales/24hr, 🍽 Burger King, Domino's, DQ, Jin's Chinese, Subway, 🛏 Holiday Inn Express, 🅾 Bretz RV Ctr (1mi), Verizon, Whalen Tire
452	US 87 N, City Ctr, Billings, N 🅿 Conoco/Arby's/dsl/LP, Exxon, 🛏 Best Western, 🅾 American Spirit RV Ctr, Metra Rv Ctr, transmissions, **2-4 mi N on US 87** 🅿 Cenex/dsl, Conoco/dsl, Holiday/dsl, 🍽 Applebee's, Arby's, Bugz Rest./casino, Burger King, Domino's, DQ, Fuddrucker's, Golden Phoenix, Jimmy John's, KFC, Little Caesars, McDonald's, MT Jack's, Panda Express, Papa John's, Papa Murphy's, Pizza Hut, Shanghai Buffet, Sonic, Subway, Taco Bell, Taco John's, Wendy's, 🛏 Country Inn&Suites, Foothills Inn, Heights Motel, 🅾 Ace Hardware, Albertsons/Osco, AT&T, AutoZone, BigLots, CarQuest, CVS Drug, $Tree, GNC, O'Reilly Parts, Office Depot, Radio Shack, Target, Tire Rama, U-Haul, Verizon, Walgreens, Walmart, vet, S 🅿 Cenex/dsl, 🅾 RV Camping
451.5mm	Yellowstone River
450	MT 3, 27th St, Billings, N 🅿 Conoco/dsl, Sinclair, 🍽 Blondy's Cafe, Pizza Hut, 🛏 Crowne Plaza, Vegas Motel,

Exit	Services
450	Continued 🅾 🏥, CarQuest, city park, USPO, visitor ctr, S KOA, Yellowstone River Camping
447	S Billings Blvd, N 🅿 Conoco/Subway/dsl, Holiday/dsl, 🍽 Burger King, DQ, El Corral Mexican, McDonald's, 🛏 Best Western/Kelly, Days Inn, Extended Stay America, Hampton Inn, Sleep Inn, Super 8, Cabela's Sporting Goods, NAPA, Sam's Club/gas, S 🅾 Billings RV Park (2mi), Freightliner, Kenworth, KOA (2mi), Yellowstone River Campground
446	King Ave, Billings, **N on King Ave** 🅿 Exxon, Conoco/dsl, Holiday/dsl/LP/RV dump, 🍽 Applebee's, Arbys, Bruno's Italian, Burger King, Cactus Creek Steaks, Café Rio, Carino's Italian, City Brew Coffee, Coldstone, DQ, Del Taco, Denny's, Dos Machos, Emporium Rest., Famous Dave's, Fuddrucker's, Gusicks Rest., HuHot Mongolian, IHOP, Jade Palace, Jake's Grill, Japanese Steaks, Lemongrass Thai, MooYah Burgers, Olive Garden, Old Chicago, Outback Steaks, Perkins, Pizza Hut, Pizza Ranch, Qdoba, Red Lobster, Subway, Taco John's, TX Roadhouse, 🛏 C'Mon Inn, Comfort Inn, Fairfield Inn, Hilton Garden, Lexington Inn, Quality Inn, Residence Inn, SpringHill Suites, Western Executive Inn, 🅾 Best Buy, Chevrolet, Chrysler/Dodge/Jeep, Costco/gas, Ford, Home Depot, JoAnn Fabrics, Lisac's Tire, Lowe's, Mercedes, Michael's, Nissan, Office Depot, Old Navy, O'Reilly Parts, Petsmart, Ross, ShopKo, Suzuki, Toyota, Verizon, Walmart/Subway, World Mkt, USPO, **N on 24th** 🅿 Conoco/dsl, Exxon/Subway, 🍽 Buffalo Wild Wings, ChuckECheese's, Golden Corral, Hardee's, KFC, Little Caesars, McDonald's, Papa John's, Rendezvous Grill, Starbucks, Taco Bell, Wendy's, 🅾 Albertsons/Osco, AutoZone, Barnes&Noble, Cadillac/GMC, Dillards, Hancock Fabrics, Hobby Lobby, JC Penney, Kia, K-Mart, Natural Grocers, Subaru, mall, S 🅿 Conoco/dsl, 🍽 Cracker Barrel, Emporium Rest., 🛏 Billings Hotel, EconoLodge, Holiday Inn, Howard Johnson, Kelly Inn, Motel 6, 🅾 Volvo/Mack Trucks, water funpark
443	Zoo Dr, to Shiloh Rd, N 🅿 Holiday/dsl, 🍽 MT Rib/Chophouse, 🛏 Bighorn Resort/waterpark, Hampton Inn, Holiday Inn Express, Homewood Suites, 🅾 Honda, Pierce RV Ctr, zoo, S 🅾 Harley-Davidson, vet
439mm	weigh sta both lanes
437	E Laurel, S 🅿 Sinclair/rest./dsl/scales/casino/motel/RV Park/24hr
434	US 212, US 310, to Red Lodge, Laurel, N 🅿 Cenex/dsl, Conoco/dsl, Exxon/dsl, 🍽 City Brew Coffee, Hardee's, McDonald's, Pitts Pizza, Pizza Hut, Subway, Taco John's, 🛏 Best Western, Locomotive Inn, 🅾 Ace Hardware, AutoZone, Chevrolet, CVS Drug, Ford, IGA Foods, O'Reilly

MT

INTERSTATE 90 CONT'D

Exit	Services
434	Continued
	Parts, Rapid Tire, Verizon, Walmart/Subway, S 🄾 Riverside Park/RV Camping, vet, to Yellowstone NP
433	Lp 90 (from eb), same as 434
426	Park City, S 🄐 Cenex/café/dsl/24hr, KwikStop, 🅵 The Other Cafe, 🄰 CJ's Motel, 🄾 auto/tire repair, USPO
419mm	🆁🆂 both lanes, full ♿ facilities, 🄲, 🛒, litter barrels, petwalk
408	rd 78, Columbus, N Mtn Range RV Park, S 🄐 Conoco, 🚂/Exxon/dsl/24hr, 🅵 Apple Village Café/gifts, McDonald's, Subway, 🄰 Big Sky Motel, Super 8, 🄾 🄷, IGA Foods, casino, city park, museum, tires/repair, to Yellowstone
400	Springtime Rd
398mm	Yellowstone River
396	ranch access
392	Reed Point, N 🄾 Old West RV Park, USPO
384	Bridger Creek Rd
381mm	🆁🆂 both lanes, full ♿ facilities, 🄲, 🛒, litter barrels, petwalk
377	Greycliff, S 🄾 Prairie Dog Town SP, KOA
370	US 191, Big Timber, 1 mi N 🄐 Cenex/dsl, Sinclair/dsl, 🄰 Grand Hotel, Lazy J Motel, 🄾 🄷, Spring Creek RV Ranch (4mi), USPO, vet
369mm	Boulder River
367	US 191 N, Big Timber, N 🄐 Exxon/dsl, Conoco/dsl, 🅵 Country Skillet, 🄰 River Valley Inn, Super 8, 🄾 CarQuest, Spring Creek Camping (3mi), historic site/visitor info
362	De Hart
354	MT 563, Springdale
352	ranch access
350	East End access
343	Mission Creek Rd, N Ft Parker HS
340	US 89 N, to White Sulphur Sprgs, S 🛩🄰
337	Lp 90, to Livingston, 2 mi N services
333mm	Yellowstone River
333	US 89 S, Livingston, N 🅵 Clark's Rest., DQ, Mark's In&Out, Pizza Hut, Taco John's, 🄰 Best Western, Budget Host, Livingston Inn, Quality Inn, Rodeway Inn, 🄾 🄷, Chrysler/Dodge/Jeep, Radio Shack, ShopKo, RV Park, Town&Country Foods, Verizon, Western Drug, S 🄐 Cenex/dsl, Conoco/dsl, Exxon/dsl, 🅵 Arby's, McDonald's, Rosa's Pizza, Subway, 🄰 Comfort Inn, Super 8, 🄾 Albertsons/Osco, KOA (10mi), Osen's RV Park, LP, vet, to Yellowstone
330	Lp 90, Livingston, 1 mi N 🄐 Cenex/Yellowstone Trkstp/dsl/rest./24hr
326.5mm	chainup/chain removal area both lanes
324	ranch access
323mm	chainup/chain removal area wb
322mm	Bridger Mountain Range
321mm	turnouts/hist marker both lanes
319	Jackson Creek Rd
319mm	chainup area both lanes
316	Trail Creek Rd
313	Bear Canyon Rd, S 🄾 Bear Canyon Camping
309	US 191 S, Main St, Bozeman, N 🄾 Subaru, Sunrise RV Park, VW, S 🄐 Cenex/dsl, Exxon/dsl, 🅵 MT AleWorks, 🄰 Continental Motel, Ranch House Motel, Western Heritage Inn, 🄾 🄷, Heeb's Foods, Tire Rama, to Yellowstone, repair, vet

LIVINGSTON

306	MT 205, N 7th, to US 191, Bozeman, N 🄐 Cenex, 🅵 McDonald's, Panda Buffet, 🄰 Fairfield Inn, La Quinta, Microtel, Motel 6, Ramada Ltd, Super 8, TLC Inn, 🄾 Merdoch's, Whalen Tire, ski area, S 🄐 Conoco/Arby's/dsl, Exxon, 🅵 Applebee's, Bar-3 BBQ, Dominos, DQ, Famous Dave's BBQ, Papa John's, Santa Fe Red's Cafe, Taco John's, Tarintino's Pizza, The Wok Chinese, 🄰 Best Western, Bozeman Inn, Comfort Inn, Days Inn, Hampton Inn, Holiday Inn, Homewood Suites, Royal 7 Inn, 🄾 Big O Tire, Firestone/auto, K-Mart, U-Haul, Walmart/McDonald's, Museum of the Rockies
305	MT412, N 19th Ave, N 🄐 Exxon, 🄰 Mountainview Inn, 0-2 mi S 🄐 Conoco/dsl, 🅵 A&W/KFC, Baja Fresh, Buffalo Wild Wings, Canyons Grill, Carino's Italian, City Brew Coffee, Clarks Fork Rest., IHOP, Jimmy John's, Mongolian BBQ, Old Chicago Pizza, Olive Garden, Outback Steaks, Papa Murphy's, Starbucks, Subway, Wasabi Grill, Wendy's, 🄰 C'mon Inn, Comfort Suites, Hilton Garden, Holiday Inn Express, My Place Extended Stay, Residence Inn, 🄾 AT&T, Costco/gas, Ford/Lincoln/RV Ctr, Home Depot, Lowe's, Michaels, Office Depot, Petsmart, Target, Radio Shack, REI, Ross, Smith's Foods, Staples, TJMaxx, UPS, Verizon, World MKT, USPO, vet, 🆁🆂, full ♿ facilities, 🛒/litter barrels, petwalk

BOZEMAN

298	MT 291, rd 85, Belgrade, N 🄐 Cenex/dsl, Exxon/Subway/dsl, 🅵 Burger King, DQ, McDonald's, Papa Murphy's, Pizza Hut, Rosa's Pizza, Starbucks, Taco Time, 🄰 Holiday Inn Express, 🄾 Albertson's/Osco, Lee&Dad's Foods, NAPA, Verizon, Whalen Tire, S 🄐 🅵LYING J/Conoco/dsl/scales/LP, 🄰 La Quinta, Quality Inn, Super 8, 🄾 Freightliner, Harley-Davidson, KOA (9mi), Tire Factory, TrueValue, repair, truckwash, to Yellowstone NP
292.5mm	Gallatin River
288	MT 288, MT 346, Manhattan, N 🄐 Conoco/Subway/dsl, 🄾 RV camping
283	Logan, S 🄾 Madison Buffalo Jump SP (7mi)
279mm	Madison River
278	MT 205, rd 2, Three Forks, Trident, N Missouri Headwaters SP, 1 mi S 🄐 Conoco/dsl, 🄰 Broken Spur Motel, Lewis&Clark Motel, Sacajawea Hotel, 🄾 CarQuest, camping, 🄲
277.5mm	Jefferson River
274	US 287, to Helena, Ennis, N 🄐 Conoco/dsl, 🅵 Wheat MT Bakery/deli, 🄰 Ft 3 Forks Motel, 🄾 KOA (2mi), to Canyon Ferry SP, dsl repair, S 🄐 🚂/Exxon/Subway/dsl/scales/24hr, 🄾 Camp 3 Forks, Lewis&Clark Caverns SP, to Yellowstone NP
267	Milligan Canyon Rd
261.5mm	chain-up area
257mm	Boulder River
256	MT 359, Cardwell, S 🄐 Cenex/dsl/RV Park, 🄾 to Yellowstone NP, Lewis&Clark Caverns SP, RV camping
249	rd 55, to rd 69, Whitehall, S 🄐 Exxon/dsl, 🅵 A&W/KFC, Subway, 🄰 Rodeway Inn, 🄾 Virginia City NHS, camping, casino
241	Pipestone
240.5mm	chainup/chain removal area both lanes
238.5mm	runaway ramp eb
237.5mm	pulloff eb
235mm	truck parking both lanes, litter barrels, rest rooms
233	Homestake, Continental Divide, elev 6393
230mm	chain-up area both lanes

BELGRADE

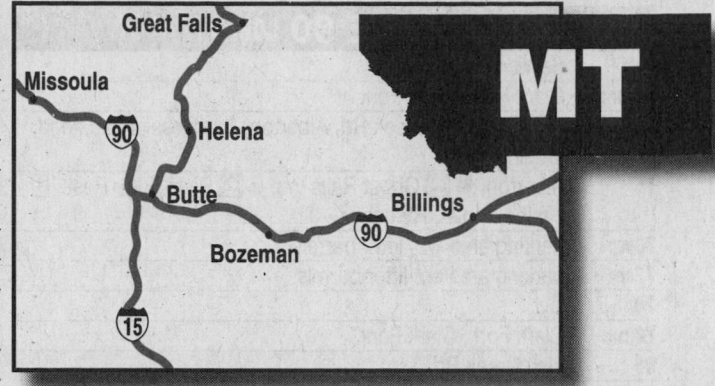

INTERSTATE 90 CONT'D

Exit	Services
228	MT 375, Continental Dr, **S** 🅖 Conoco/dsl, Ⓞ Harley-Davidson, 3 Bears Foods
227	I-15 N, to Helena, Great Falls
	I-90 and I-15 run together 8 mi. See Montana Interstate 15, exits 122-127.
219	I-15 S, to Dillon, Idaho Falls
216	Ramsay
211	MT 441, Gregson, **3-5 mi S** food, lodging, Fairmont RV Park (Apr-Oct)
210.5mm	parking area wb, Pintlar Scenic route info
208	rd 1, Pintler Scenic Loop, Georgetown Lake RA, Opportunity, Anaconda, **S** Ⓞ 🅷, gas, food, lodging, RV camp/dump, ski area, ℞ **both lanes, full** ♿ **facilities,** 🚮, **litter barrels, petwalk**
201	Warm Springs, to Anaconda, **S** MT ST 🅷
197	MT 273, Galen, **S** to MT ST 🅷
195	Racetrack, **S** Ⓞ dsl repair
187	Lp 90, Deer Lodge (no wb return), **2 mi S** 🍴 Monty's Subs, 🛏 Budget Inn, Downtowner Motel, Scharf's Motel/rest., Ⓞ 🅷, KOA (seasonal), Radio Shack, Valley Foods, Old MT Prison, Tow Ford Museum, same as 184
184	Deer Lodge, **0-1 mi S** 🅖 Exxon/dsl/casino, Conoco/dsl/casino, Sinclair/dsl, 🍴 A&W, 4B's Rest., McDonald's, Pizza Hut, Yak Yak Cafe, 🛏 Downtowner Motel, Rodeway Inn, Western Big Sky Inn, Ⓞ 🅷, Indian Creek Camping, Keystone Drug, KOA, Safeway/deli, Schwab Tire, city park, Grant-Kohrs Ranch NHS, USPO
179	Beck Hill Rd
175	US 12 E, Garrison, **N** Ⓞ RiverFront RV Park, 🚻, hist site
175mm	Little Blackfoot River
174	US 12 E (from eb), **S** 🍴 Ranch House Cafe/RV Park, same as 175
170	Phosphate
168mm	℞ **both lanes, full** ♿ **facilities,** 🚻, 🚮, **litter barrels, petwalk, hist site**
166	Gold Creek, **S** Ⓞ Camp Mak-A-Dream
162	Jens
154	to MT 1 (from wb), Drummond, **S** 🅖 Conoco/dsl, Mtn West/dsl, Sinclair/dsl, 🍴 Parker's Rest., Wagon Wheel Café, 🛏 Drummond Motel, Sky Motel, Wagon Wheel Motel, Ⓞ Front St Mkt, Pintler Scenic Lp, Georgetown Lake RA, Goodtime RV Park (3mi)
153	MT 1 (from eb), **N** Ⓞ Garnet GhostTown, Goodtime RV Park (3mi) **S** same as 154
150.5mm	**weigh sta both lanes**
143mm	℞ **both lanes, full** ♿ **facilities,** 🚻, 🚮, **litter barrels, petwalk**
138	Bearmouth Area, **N** Ⓞ Chalet Bearmouth Camp/rest., to gas, food, lodging
130	Beavertail Rd, **S** Ⓞ to Beavertail Hill SP, rec area, camping (seasonal)
128mm	parking area both lanes, litter barrels/restrooms
126	Rock Creek Rd, **S** 🛏 Rock Creek Lodge/gas/casino, Ⓞ rec area
120	Clinton, **N** 🅖 Sinclair/dsl, 🍴 Poor Henry's Café (1mi W in on frtg rd), Ⓞ Clinton Market, **S** Ⓞ USPO
113	Turah, **S** Turah RV Park/gas
109.5mm	Clark Fork
109mm	Blackfoot River
109	MT 200 E, Bonner, **N** 🅖 🍴 /Exxon/Arby's/Subway/dsl

Exit	Services
109	Continued scales/casino/LP/24hr, Sinclair/dsl, 🍴 River City Grill, Ⓞ USPO, hist site
108.5mm	Clark Fork
107	E Missoula, **N** 🅖 Ole's Mkt/Conoco/diner/dsl, Sinclair/Chester's, 🍴 Reno Cafe 🛏 Aspen Motel, Ⓞ dsl repair, **2 mi S** 🛏 Holiday Inn Express
105	US 12 W, Missoula, **S** 🅖 Cenex/dsl, Conoco/dsl, Sinclair/dsl, 🍴 Burger King, 5 Guys Burgers, McDonald's, Pizza Hut, Quiznos, Subway, Taco Bell, 🛏 Campus Inn, Days Inn, DoubleTree, Family Inn, Holiday Inn, Holiday Inn Express, Motel 6, Ponderosa Motel, Thunderbird Motel, Ⓞ Ace Hardware, Albertson's, Kingfisher Flyshop, O'Reilly Parts, Verizon, U of MT, Vietnam Vet's Mem
104	Orange St, Missoula, **S** 🅖 Conoco/dsl, 🍴 Pagoda Chinese, Subway, Taco John's, 🛏 Mountain Valley Inn, Red Lion Inn, Ⓞ 🅷, Curves, TireRama, to City Ctr
101	US 93 S, Reserve St, **N** 🅖 Conoco/dsl, 🍴 Cracker Barrel, MacKenzie River Pizza, Starbucks, 🛏 Best Western, C'Mon Inn, Motel 6, Ⓞ ski area, **0-2 mi S** 🅖 Cenex/dsl/LP, Conoco, Exxon/dsl, Sinclair, 🍴 Arby's, Blue Canyon Rest., Burger King, Carino's, China Bowl, Coldstone, DQ, Famous Dave's BBQ, Fuddrucker's, HoagiVille, Hooters, IHOP, Little Caesars, McDonald's, MT Club rest./casino, Outback Steaks, Perkins, Quiznos, Rowdy's Mexican, Stone Of Accord, Taco Bell, Taco Time/TCBY, Wendy's, 🛏 AmericInn, Courtyard, EconoLodge, Hampton Inn, Hilton Garden, Holiday Inn Express, La Quinta, Ruby's Inn/rest., Staybridge Suites, Super 8, Travelers Inn, Ⓞ Albertson's, AT&T, Barnes&Noble, Best Buy, Bretz RV/Marine, Chevrolet, Costco/gas, Firestone/auto, Home Depot, Lowe's, Michael's, Old Navy, Petsmart, Radio Shack, Ross, Staples, Target, TJ Maxx, Walgreens, Walmart, casinos, dsl repair
99	Airway Blvd, **S** 🅖 Mobil/dsl/24hr, Sinclair/dsl, 🛏 Hawthorn Suites, Wingate Inn, Ⓞ Chrysler/Dodge, Harley-Davidson, 🚲
96	US 93 N, MT 200W, Kalispell, **N** 🅖 Conoco/rest./dsl/scales/24hr/@, 🛏 Days Inn/rest., Ⓞ Freightliner, Peterbilt, Jellystone RV Park (1mi), Jim&Mary's RV Park (1mi), to Flathead Lake&Glacier NP, **S** 🅖 CrossroadsTC/Sinclair/rest/dsl/24hr, 🛏 Redwood Lodge, Ⓞ Kenworth, RV repair
92.5mm	**inspection sta both lanes**
89	Frenchtown, **S** 🅖 Conoco/dsl/café, 🍴 Alcan Grill, French Connectino Grill, Quiznos, Ⓞ Frenchtown Drug, USPO, to Frenchtown Pond SP
85	Huson, **S** gas, cafe, 🚲
82	Nine Mile Rd, **N** 🍴 Mile House Rest., Ⓞ Hist Ranger Sta/info, food, 🚲
81.5mm	Clark Fork

Ⓐ = gas 🍴 = food 🛏 = lodging Ⓞ = other Ⓡ = rest stop   Copyright 2014 - The NEXT Exit ®

⬆E INTERSTATE 90 CONT'D

Exit	Services
80mm	Clark Fork, Clark Fork
77	MT 507, Petty Creek Rd, Alberton, **S** access to gas, food, lodging, Ⓒ
75	Alberton, **N** 🛏 Ghost Rails Inn, **S** 🛏 River Edge Rest, Ⓞ casino, motel, RV camp
73mm	parking area wb, litter barrels
72mm	parking area eb, litter barrels
70	Cyr
70mm	Clark Fork, Clark Fork
66	Fish Creek Rd
66mm	Clark Fork, Clark Fork
61	Tarkio
59mm	Clark Fork, Clark Fork
58mm	Ⓡ **both lanes, full ♿ facilities, Ⓒ, 🛋, litter barrels, petwalk, NF camping (seasonal)**
55	Lozeau, Quartz
53.5mm	Clark Fork, Clark Fork
49mm	Clark Fork, Clark Fork
47	MT 257, Superior, **N** Ⓐ Conoco/dsl, Mtn West/LP, Sinclair/Durango's Rest., 🍴 Jackie's Rest., 🛏 Budget Host, Hilltop Motel, Ⓞ Ⓗ, Family Foods, Mineral Drug, NAPA, USPO, **S** Ⓐ ▥/Exxon/dsl/casino/24hr, Ⓞ repair
45mm	Clark Fork, Clark Fork
43	Dry Creek Rd, **N** NP camping (seasonal)
37	Sloway Area
34mm	Clark Fork, Clark Fork
33	MT 135, St Regis, **N** Ⓐ Conoco/rest/dsl/gifts, Exxon, Sinclair, 🍴 Frosty Drive-In, Huck's Grill, Jasper's Rest., OK Café/casino, Subway, 🛏 Little River Motel, Super 8, Ⓞ Nugget Camground, St Regis Campground, USPO, antiques, to Glacier NP
30	Two Mile Rd, **S** fishing access
29mm	fishing access, wb
26	Ward Creek Rd (from eb)
25	Drexel
22	Camels Hump Rd, Henderson, **N** Ⓞ camping (seasonal), antiques (1mi)
18	DeBorgia, **N** 🍴 Billy Big Riggers, O'aces Rest., Ⓞ Black Diamond Guest Ranch
16	Haugan, **N** Ⓐ Exxon/dsl/24hr, 🛏 50,000 Silver $/motel/rest./casino/RV park
15mm	weigh sta both lanes, exits left from both lanes
10	Saltese, **N** 🍴 MT Grill, 🛏 Mangold's Motel, Ⓞ antiques
10mm	St Regis River
5	Taft Area, access to Hiawatha Trail
4.5mm	Ⓡ **both lanes, full ♿, 🛋, litter barrels, petwalk, chain-up/removal**
0	Lookout Pass, Ⓞ access to Lookout Pass ski area/lodge, info
0mm	Montana/Idaho state line, Central/Pacific time zone, Lookout Pass elev 4680

⬆E INTERSTATE 94

Exit	Services
250mm	Montana/North Dakota state line
248	Carlyle Rd
242	MT 7 (from wb), Wibaux, **S** Ⓡ **both lanes, full ♿ facilities, Ⓒ, 🛋, litter barrels, Ⓐ** Amsler's/dsl, Cenex/dsl/service, 🍴 Tastee Hut, 🛏 Beaver Creek Inn, Ⓞ RV camping
241	MT 261 (from eb), to MT 7, Wibaux, **S** same as 242

240mm	weigh sta both lanes
236	ranch access
231	Hodges Rd
224	Griffith Creek, frontage road
222.5mm	Griffith Creek
215	MT 335, Glendive, City Ctr, **N** Ⓐ Cenex, 🍴 C's Family Café, 🛏 Astoria Suites, Comfort Inn, Days Inn, Holiday Inn Express, Super 8, Yellowstone River Inn, Ⓞ Glendive Camping (apr-oct), Running's Hardware, museum, **S** Ⓐ Exxon/dsl, Holiday/dsl, 🍴 Mexico Lindo, Subway, Taco John's, 🛏 El Centro Motel, Glendive Inn, Guesthouse Inn, Ⓞ Ⓗ, Radio Shack, to Makoshika SP
215mm	Yellowstone River
213	MT 16, to Sidney, Glendive, **N** Ⓞ Green Valley Camping, st patrol, **S** Ⓐ Cenex/dsl, Conoco/dsl, Sinclair/dsl, 🍴 Dickey's BBQ, Pizza Hut, 🛏 Riverside Inn, Ⓞ Albertson's/Osco, Ford, K-Mart, NAPA, Reynolds Mkt
211	MT 200S (from wb, no EZ return), to Circle
210	Lp 94, to rd 200 S, W Glendive, **S** Ⓐ Cenex/dsl, Ⓞ Buick/Chevrolet, I-94 RV Park, Tire Rama, Makoshika SP
206	Pleasant View Rd
204	Whoopup Creek Rd
198	Cracker Box Rd
192	Bad Route Rd, **S** Ⓡ/weigh sta both lanes, full ♿ facilities, weather info, Ⓒ, 🛋, litter barrels, camping, petwalk
187mm	Yellowstone River
185	MT 340, Fallon, **S** café, Ⓒ
184mm	O'Fallon Creek
176	MT 253, Terry, **N** Ⓐ Conoco/dsl, 4Corners/dsl, 🍴 Dizzy Diner, 🛏 Kempton Hotel, Ⓞ Ⓗ, Terry RV Oasis, museum
170mm	Powder River
169	Powder River Rd
159	Diamond Ring
148	Valley Access
141	US 12 E, Miles City, to Baker, **N** Ⓞ RV Camping
138	rd 59, Miles City, **N** Ⓐ Cenex/dsl, Conoco/dsl, ▥/Exxon/dsl/24hr, 🍴 Arby's, Boardwalk Rest., DQ, 4B's Rest., Gallagher's Rest., Little Caesars, McDonald's, Mexico Lindo, Pizza Hut, R&B Chophouse, Subway, Taco John's, Wendy's, 🛏 Best Western, EconoLodge, Motel 6, Sleep Inn, Ⓞ Ⓗ, Ace Hardware, Albertsons/Osco, Meadows RV Park, Murdoch's, O'Reilly Parts, Verizon, Walmart, casinos, **S** 🍴 New Hunan Chinese, 🛏 Comfort Inn, Guesthouse Inn, Holiday Inn Express, Super 8
137mm	Tongue River
135	Lp 94, Miles City, **N** Ⓞ KOA (Apr-Oct)
128	local access
126	Moon Creek Rd
117	Hathaway
114mm	Ⓡ **eb, full ♿ facilities, Ⓒ, 🛋, litter barrels, petwalk**
113mm	Ⓡ **wb, full ♿ facilities, Ⓒ, 🛋, litter barrels, petwalk, overlook**
106	Butte Creek Rd, to Rosebud, **N** food, Ⓒ
103	MT 446, MT 447, Rosebud Creek Rd, **N** food, Ⓒ
98.5mm	weigh sta both lanes
95	Forsyth, **N** Ⓐ Exxon/dsl, Kum&Go, 🍴 DQ, M&M Café, 🛏 Magnuson Hotel, Ⓞ Ⓗ, Ford, NAPA, Van's/IGA, Yellowstone Drug, museum, to Rosebud RA, **S** Wagon Wheel Camping
93	US 12 W, Forsyth, **N** Ⓐ Exxon/dsl, Kum&Go, 🍴 Fitzgerald's Rest., Top That Eatery, 🛏 Rails Inn, Restwel Inn,

GLENDIVE · MILES CITY · FORSYTH

🧭 INTERSTATE 94 CONT'D

Exit	Services
93	Continued WestWind Motel, 🅞 🅗, Tire Factory/repair, museum, RV camping
87	rd 39, to Colstrip
82	Reservation Creek Rd
72	MT 384, Sarpy Creek Rd
67	Hysham, **1-2 mi** N gas, food, 🅞
65mm	🆁🆂 **both lanes, full** ♿ **facilities,** 🅞, 🚮, **litter barrels, pet-walk**
63	ranch access
53	Bighorn, access to 🅞

52mm	Bighorn River
49	MT 47, to Hardin, Custer, S 🍴 Ft Custer Café, 🅞 to Little Bighorn Bfd, camping
47	Custer, S 🅖 Custer Sta/dsl, 🍴 Jct City Saloon/café, 🅞 USPO
41.5mm	🆁🆂 **wb, full** ♿ **facilities,** 🅞, 🚮, **litter barrels, petwalk**
38mm	🆁🆂 **eb, full** ♿ **facilities,** 🅞, 🚮, **litter barrels, petwalk**
36	frontage rd, Waco
23	Pompeys Pillar, N 🅞 Pompeys Pillar Nat Landmark
14	Ballentine, Worden, S 🍴 Long Branch Café/casino
6	MT 522, Huntley, N gas/🅞, 🍴 Pryor Creek Café/casino, S golf
0mm	I-90, E to Sheridan, W to Billings. **I-94 begins/ends on I-90, exit 456.**

NEBRASKA

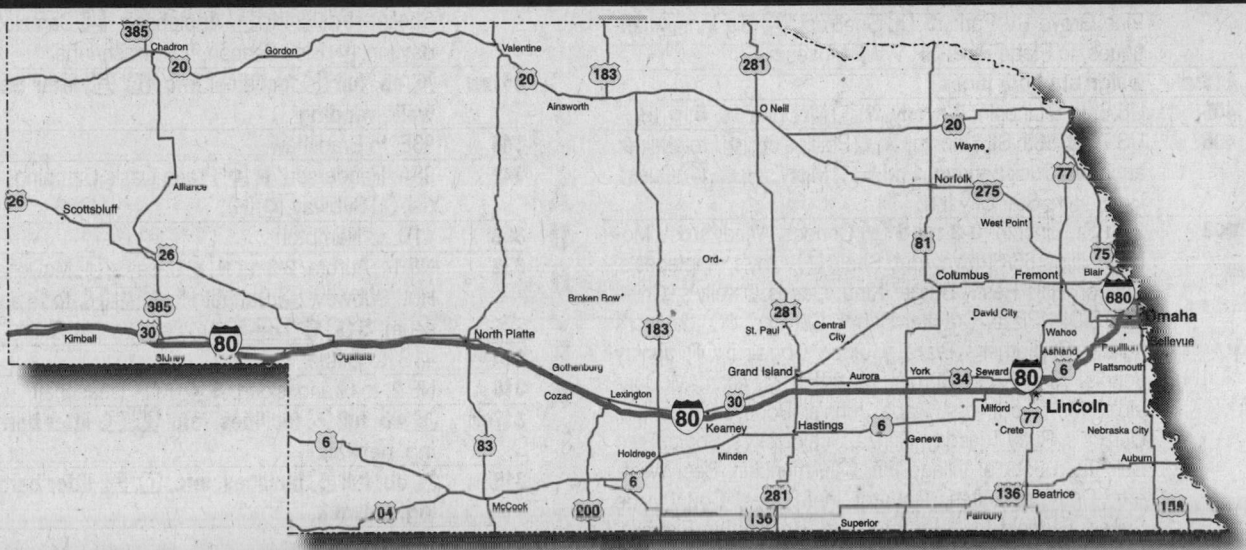

🧭 INTERSTATE 80

Exit	Services
455mm	Nebraska/Iowa state line, Missouri River
454	13th St, N 🅖 BP/dsl, Midtown, Valero, 🍴 Big Horn BBQ, Burger King, McDonald's/playplace, 🛏 Comfort Inn, 🅞 Family$, tires/repair, S 🍴 King Kong Burgers, 🅞 Doorly Zoo, Imax, stadium
453	24th St (from eb)
452b	I-480 N, US 75 N, to Henry Ford's Birthplace, Eppley Airfield
452a	US 75 S
451	42nd St, N 🅖 BP/dsl, S 🅖 Phillips 66, 🍴 Burger King, McDonald's, Taco Bell, 🅞 🅗, Pitstop Lube
450	60th St, N 🅖 Phillips 66, 🅞 NAPA, to U of NE Omaha, S 🅖 Omaha 66/dsl, 🅞 transmissions
449	72nd St, to Ralston, N 🅖 BP, QT, 🍴 Arby's, Burger King, Margarita's Mexican, Perkins, Spezia Italian, 🛏 Comfort Inn, DoubleTree, Holiday Inn/rest., Omaha Executive Inn, Quality Inn, Super 8, Travelodge, 🅞 🅗, S 🅖 Cenex/dsl, 🍴 Anthony's Steaks
448	84th St, N 🍴 Arby's, Denny's, Farmhouse Café, Husker Hounds, McDonald's, Subway, Taco Bell, Top of the World, 🛏 Motel 6, 🅞 Ace Hardware, Advance Parts, Curves, Hancock Fabrics, Jensen's Tire/auto, Jo-Ann Fabrics, Mangelson's Crafts, ShopKO, USPO, S 🅖 QT, Shell/dsl, 🍴 Wendy's, 🅞 Chevrolet, Kia

446	I-680 N, to Boystown
445	US 275, NE 92, I thru L St, N 🅖 Cenex, 🍴 Famous Dave's BBQ, Hardee's, Jason's Deli, Smash Burger, Wendy's, 🛏 Carol Hotel, 🅞 Best Buy, Book-A-Million, Buick/GMC, Home Depot, Michael's, Nelsen's RV Ctr, PetCo, Sam's Club/gas, Super Target, Verizon, Walmart/24hr S 🍴 Brew Burgers, Perkins, Village Inn, 🛏 Baymont Inn, Best Western, Carlisle Hotel, Comfort Inn, Days Inn, EconoLodge, Hawthorn Suites, Holiday Inn Express, Howard Johnson, La Quinta, Motel 6, Super 8, 🅞 Goodyear, NE Beef Co, **S on 108th** 🅖 BP, QT/dsl, 🍴 Arby's, Burger King, Godfather's Pizza, Hong Kong Café, Jimmy John's, LJ Silver, McDonald's, Pizza Hut/Taco Bell, Quizno's, Runza, Sonic, Subway, Valentino's, Wongs Hunan Garden, 🅞 Bag'n Save Foods, O'Reilly Parts
444	Q St, N 🅖 Cenex/dsl
442	126th St, Harrison St, N 🅞 Chrysler/Dodge/Jeep, Toyota, VW, S 🅖 Phillips 66, 🍴 Burger King, Jimmy John's, Pizza Gourmet, Runza, 🛏 Courtyard, Embassy Suites, Hampton Inn, ValuePlace Hotel, 🅞 Cabela's
440	NE 50, to Springfield, N 🅖 Phillips 66, Shell/Sapp Bros/Subway/dsl/24hr/@, 🍴 Azteca Mexican, Cracker Barrel, Hardee's, McDonald's, 🛏 Comfort Inn, Countryside Suites, Hometowne Lodge, Motel 6, Quality Inn, Red Carpet Inn, 🅞 🅗, Ford, truckwash, S 🅖 BP/dsl, to Platte River SP
439	439 NE 370, to Gretna, N 🅖 Kum&Go/Quiznos/dsl, Phil

MT
NE

INTERSTATE 80 CONT'D

NE

LINCOLN

Exit	Services
439	Continued lips 66/dsl, 🏨 Holiday Inn Express, ⊙ Walmart/Subway, S 🅷 Volvo Trucks, museum
432	US 6, NE 31, to Gretna, N ⛽ Sinclair/rest/dsl/24hr, 🍴 McDonald's, 🏨 Super 8, ⊙ Curves, Nebraska X-ing/famous brands, S ⛽ FLYING J/Denny's/dsl/LP/24hr, ⊙ KOA, to Schramm SP
431mm	🅿️ wb, full ♿ facilities, info, 📞, 🗑, litter barrels, petwalk
427mm	Platte River
426	NE 66, to Southbend, N to Mahoney SP, museum, rv camping
425.5	🅿️ eb, full ♿ facilities, 📞, 🗑, litter barrels, petwalk, vending
420	NE 63, Greenwood, N ⛽ Cenex/cafe/dsl/scales/24hr, ⊙ Pine Grove RV Park, S ⛽ Shell/dsl, 🏨 Big Inn, ⊙ antiques, to Platte River SP, WWII Museum
416mm	weigh sta both lanes
409	US 6, to E Lincoln, Waverly, N 🍴 McDonald's, S ⊙ 🅷
405	US 77 N, 56th St, Lincoln, S ⛽ Phillips 66, ⊙ Freightliner, antiques, truck parking, 1 mi S 🍴 Misty's Rest., 🏨 GuestHouse Inn, Star City Inn
403	27th St, Lincoln, 0-3 mi S ⛽ Conoco/Wendy's/dsl, Mobil, Phillips 66/Subway/dsl, Shell, 🍴 Arby's, Applebee's, Beacon Hills Rest., Burger King, Carlos O'Kelly's, China Inn, CiCi's Pizza, Cracker Barrel, Culver's, DQ, daVinci's Italian, Godfather's Pizza, Golden Corral, IHOP, Jimmy John's, King Kong Burger, Mazatlan Mexican, McDonald's, Mr Goodcents, Papa John's, Popeye's/Taco Inn, Quizno's, Ruby Tuesday, Runza, Schlotzsky's, Sonic, Taco Bell, Taco John's, Village Inn, 🏨 AmericInn, Best Western, Comfort Suites, Country Inn&Suites, Countryside Suites, Fairfield Inn, Hampton Inn, Holiday Inn Express, La Quinta, Microtel, Settle Inn, Staybridge Suites, Super 8, ValuePlace Inn, ⊙ Urgent Care, AutoZone, BMW, Cadillac/Chevrolet/GMC, Chrysler, Curves, Dodge/Jeep, $Tree, Ford/Lincoln, GNC, Haas Tire, Home Depot, Hy-Vee Foods, Lexus, Mazda, Menards, Mercedes, Petsmart, Sam's Club/gas, ShopKO, Super Saver Foods, Toyota, Verizon, Walmart, to U NE, st fairpark
401b	US 34 W, S RV camping
401a	I-180, US 34 E, to 9th St, Lincoln
399	Lincoln, N ⛽ BP/dsl, Phillips 66, 🍴 Baskin-Robbins, McDonald's, Perkins, Quiznos, 🏨 Comfort Inn, Days Inn, Hampton Inn, Holiday Inn Express, Horizon Inn, Luxury Inn, Motel 6, Quality Inn, Ramada Inn, Sleep Inn, ⊙ to 🅷 S ⛽ Casey's, 🍴 Subway, 🏨 EconoLodge, Economy Lodge
397	US 77 S, to Beatrice
396	US 6, West O St (from eb), S ⛽ Sinclair/dsl, 🏨 Rodeway Inn, Super 8
395	US 6, NW 48th St, S ⛽ Phillips 66/dsl, Shoemaker's/Shell/dsl/scales/@, 🏨 Cobbler Inn, ⊙ Harley-Davidson, truck repair
388	NE 103, to Crete, Pleasant Dale
382	US 6, Milford, S ⛽ Phillips 66/dsl
381mm	🅿️ eb, full ♿ facilities, 📞, 🗑, litter barrels, petwalk, vending
379	NE 15, to Seward, N ⊙ Buick/Chevrolet/GMC, Ford, 2-3 mi N 🍴 McDonald's, 🏨 Super 8, ⊙ 🅷 antiques, S ⛽ Shell/dsl,

YORK

AURORA

KEARNEY

Exit	Services
375mm	truck parking (wb)
373	80G, Goehner, N ⛽ Sinclair
369	80E, Beaver Crossing, Friend, 3 mi S 🅷, food, RV camping
366	80F, to Utica
360	93B, to Waco, N ⛽ Phillips 66/Waco Rest/dsl/24hr, S 🏨 Double Nickel Camping
355mm	🅿️ wb, full ♿ facilities, info, 📞, 🗑, litter barrels, vending, petwalk
353	US 81, to York, N ⛽ Byco Fuel, Pump-N-Pantry, SappBros/Sinclair/Subway/scales/dsl, Shell/dsl, 🍴 Arby's, Burger King, Chinese Buffet, Country Kitchen, Golden Gate Chinese, KFC/Taco Bell, McDonald's, Runza, Starbucks, Taco John's, Wendy's, 🏨 Comfort Inn, Days Inn, Hampton Inn, New Victorian Inn, Super 8, Yorkshire Motel, ⊙ 🅷, Buick/GMC, Chevrolet, rv park, Walmart/Subway, S ⛽ Petro/Phillips 66/Iron Skillet/Pizza Hut/dsl/24hr/@, Shell/rest/dsl/24hr, 🍴 Applebee's, 🏨 Camelot Inn, Holiday Inn, ⊙ Blue Beacon, tires/wash/lube
351mm	🅿️ eb, full ♿ facilities, info, 📞, 🗑, litter barrels, petwalk, vending
348	93E, to Bradshaw
342	93A, Henderson, N ⊙ Prarie Oasis Camping, S ⛽ Fuel/dsl, 🍴 Subway, ⊙ 🅷
338	41D, to Hampton
332	NE 14, Aurora, 2-3 mi N ⛽ Casey's, 🍴 McDonald's, Pizza Hut, Subway, 🏨 Budget Host, ⊙ 🅷, to Plainsman Museum, S ⛽ Loves/Arby's/dsl/scales/24hr
324	41B, to Giltner
318	NE 2, to Grand Island, S ⊙ KOA (seasonal)
317mm	🅿️ wb, full ♿ facilities, info, 📞, 🗑, litter barrels, vending, petwalk
315mm	🅿️ eb, full ♿ facilities, info, 📞, 🗑, litter barrels, vending, petwalk
314mm	Platte River
314	Locust Street, to Grand Island, 4-6 mi N gas, food, lodging
312	US 34/281, to Grand Island, N ⛽ Bosselman/Sinclair/Little Caesar's/Max's/Subway/scales/dsl/24hr, Phillips 66, 🏨 Motel 6, USA Inn, ⊙ 🅷, Mormon Island RA, to Stuhr Pioneer Museum, S ⛽ Sinclair/Arby's/dsl, 🏨 Holiday Inn Express/rest, ⊙ Peterbilt, Hastings Museum (15mi)
305	40C, to Alda, N ⛽ Sinclair/dsl, TA/Country Pride/dsl/scales/24hr/@, S ⊙ Crane Meadows Nature Ctr/🅿️
300	NE 11, Wood River, N to Cheyenne SRA, S ⛽ Loves/Subway/dsl/scales/24hr, 🏨 motel/RV park
291	10D, Shelton, N ⊙ War Axe SRA
285	10C, Gibbon, N ⛽ Petro Oasis/dsl, ⊙ Windmill SP, RV camping, S 🏨 Country Inn
279	NE 10, to Minden, N ⛽ Shell/dsl, S ⊙ Pioneer Village Camping
276mm	new exit
275mm	The Great Platte River Road Archway Monument
272	NE 44, Kearney, N ⛽ Casey's, Cenex/Subway/dsl, Gas Stop, Shell/dsl, Sinclair, Valero, 🍴 Amigo's, Arby's, Burger King, Carlos O'Kelly's, DQ, Egg&I, Gourmet House Japanese, Hunan's Rest., King's Buffet, LJ Silver, McDonald's, Old Chicago Rest, Perkins, Pizza Hut, Quiznos, Red Lobster, Ruby Tuesday, Runza, Taco Bell, Taco John's, USA Steaks, Wendy's, Whiskey Creek, 🏨 AmericInn, Best Western, Comfort Inn, Country Inn&Suites, Days Inn, EconoLodge, Fairfield Inn, Hampton Inn, Holiday Inn, Microtel, Midtown Western Inn, Motel 6, Quality Inn, Ramada

⬆E INTERSTATE 80 CONT'D

Exit	Services
272	Continued
	Inn, Rodeway Inn, Super 8, Western Inn South, Wingate Inn, 🅞 🅷, Big Apple Foods, Boogaart's Foods, Buick/Cadillac, Chevrolet, Chrysler/Dodge/Jeep, $General, NAPA, Verizon, Walmart (3mi), to Archway Mon, U NE Kearney, Museum of NE Art, **S** 🅖 Qwest/dsl, 🍴 Grandpa's Steaks, Runza, Skeeter's BBQ, 🛏 Best Western, Holiday Inn Express
271mm	🆁🆂 wb, full ♿ facilities, info, 🅒, 🆐, litter barrels, petwalk
269mm	🆁🆂 eb, full ♿ facilities, info, 🅒, 🆐, litter barrels, petwalk
263	Rd 10 b; Odessa, **N** 🅖 Sapp Bros./Shell/rest/dsl, 🅞 motel, UP Wayside
257	US 183, Elm Creek, **N** 🅖 ▓▓▓/Subway/dsl/scales/24hr, 🛏 1st Interstate Inn, 🅞 Antique Car Museum, Nebraska Prarie Museum, Sunny Meadows Camping
248	Overton
237	US 283, Lexington, **N** 🅖 Casey's, Cenex/dsl, Conoco/dsl, Shell, 🍴 Arby's, Baskin-Robbins, Burger King, DQ, Delight Donuts, Hong Kong Buffet, KFC/Taco Bell, Little Caesar's, McDonald's, Pizza Hut, San Pedro Mexican, Sonic, Wendy's, 🛏 Comfort Inn, Days Inn, 1st Interstate Inn, Gable View Inn, Holiday Inn Express, Minute Man Motel, 🅞 🅷, Advance Parts, Buick/Cadillac/Chevrolet, $General, Plum Creek Foods, Walmart/Subway, Military Vehicle Museum, **S** 🅖 Sinclair/dsl/@, 🍴 Kirk's Café, 🛏 Super 8, 🅞 to Johnson Lake RA
231	Darr Rd, **S** truckwash/24hr
227mm	🆁🆂 both lanes, full ♿ facilities, info, 🅒, 🆐, litter barrels, vending, petwalk
222	NE 21, Cozad, **N** 🅖 Cenex/dsl, Casey's/dsl, 🍴 Burger King, DQ, El Paraiso Mexican, Pizza Hut, Runza, Subway, 🛏 Circle S Motel, Rodeway Inn, 🅞 🅷, Alco, museum
211	NE 47, Gothenburg, **N** 🅖 Shell/dsl/24hr, Sinclair/dsl, 🍴 China Cafe, Lasso Espresso, McDonald's, Mi Ranchito Mexican, Pizza Hut, Randazzle Cafe, Runza, 🛏 Comfort Suites, Pony Express Inn, Super 8, Travel Inn, 🅞 🅷, Buick/Chevrolet, Pony Express Sta Museum (1mi), NAPA, Pamida, truck permit sta, **S** KOA/Sinclair
199	Brady, **N** 🅖 Brady 1 Stop/DQ/dsl
194mm	🆁🆂 both lanes, full ♿ facilities, 🅒, 🆐, litter barrels, vending, petwalk
190	Maxwell, **N** 🅖 Sinclair/dsl, **S** 🅞 to Ft McPherson Nat Cemetary, RV camping
181mm	weigh sta both lanes, 🅒
179	to US 30, N Platte, **N** 🅖 Sinclair, 🛏 La Quinta, 🅞 RV camping, **S** 🅖 *FLYING J*/Denny's/dsl/scales/LP/RV dump /24hr, 🅛🅞🅥🅔🅢/McDonald's/Subway/dsl/scales/24hr, 🅞 tire/lube/repair, truckwash
177	US 83, N Platte, **N** 🅖 Cenex/dsl, Shell/dsl, Sinclair/Quiznos/dsl, 🍴 A&W, Amigo's Rest., Applebee's, Arby's, Burger King, Coldstone, DQ, Hong Kong Chinese, Jimmy John's, KFC, King Buffet, Little Caesar's, LJ Silver/Taco Bell, McDonald's, Penny's Diner, Perkins, Pizza Hut, Roger's Diner, Ruby Tuesday, Runza, San Pedro Mexican, Sonic, Starbucks, Subway, Valentino's, Village Inn, Wendy's, Whiskey Creek Steaks, 🛏 Blue Spruce Motel, Fairfield Inn, Hampton Inn, Howard Johnson, Knights Inn, Motel 6, Oak Tree Inn, Quality Inn, Royal Colonial Inn, 🅞

Nebraska state map showing I-80 route with cities: Sioux City, Biencoe, Fremont, Omaha, Pine Bluffs, Lodgepole, Lorenzo, North Platte, Gothenburg, Grand Island, Kearney, Westmark, Hastings, Lincoln; routes 29, 680, 80.

NE

Exit	Services
177	Continued
	🅷 Advance Parts, $General, $Tree, Goodyear/auto, Harley-Davidson, Holiday RV Park, JC Penney, ShopKO, Staples, SunMart Foods, Walgreens, Walmart, mall, museum, to Buffalo Bill's Ranch, vet, **S** 🅖 Cenex, Conoco/Taco Bell/dsl/24hr, U-Fillem/dsl/RV dump, 🍴 Hunan Chinese, Taco John's, 🛏 Comfort Inn, Days Inn, Holiday Inn Express, Ramada Ltd, Super 8, 🅞 Cadillac, Chevrolet, Chrysler/Dodge/Jeep, Ford/Lincoln, Honda, Menards, Nissan, Toyota, truck permit sta, to Lake Maloney RA, antiques, dsl repair, veterans memorial/info, vet
164	56C, Hershey, **N** 🅖 Western/Western Cafe/dsl/24hr/@, 🅞 Rivers Edge Ranch Store
160mm	🆁🆂 both lanes, full ♿ facilities, info, 🅒, 🆐, litter barrels, petwalk
158	NE 25, Sutherland, **N** 🛏 Park Motel (1mi), **S** 🅖 Sinclair/Godfather's Pizza/dsl, 🅞 RV camping
149mm	Central/Mountain time zone
145	51C, Paxton, **N** 🅖 Shell/dsl/24hr, 🛏 Days Inn, 🅞 RV camping
133	51B, Roscoe
132mm	🆁🆂 wb, full ♿ facilities, info, 🅒, 🆐, litter barrels, petwalk
126	US 26, NE 61, Ogallala, **N** 🅖 Cenex/dsl, Petro, Sapp Bros/Shell/dsl/24hr, Sinclair, 🍴 Arby's, Country Kitchen, Denny's, Front Street Cafe, McDonald's, Mi Ranchito, Peking Chinese, Pizza Hut, Runza, Taco John's, Valentino's, 🛏 Best Western, Days Inn, Gray Goose Lodge, Holiday Inn Express, Quality Inn, 🅞 🅷, Alco, Cadillac/GMC, Chrysler/Dodge/Jeep, Firestone/auto, Ford/Lincoln, NAPA, SunMart Foods, TrueValue, U-Save Drug, to Lake McConaughy, **S** 🅖 Conoco/Subway/dsl, TA/Country Pride/dsl/scales/24hr/@, 🍴 DQ, KFC/Taco Bell, Wendy's, 🛏 Comfort Inn, Rodeway Inn, Super 8, 🅞 $General, Corral RV Park, Countryview Camping, Pamida
124mm	🆁🆂 eb, full ♿ facilities, info, 🅒, 🆐, litter barrels, petwalk
117	51A, Brule, **N** 🅖 Sinclair/dsl, 🅞 Riverside RV camping
107	25B, Big Springs, **N** 🅖 Big Springs/dsl, *FLYING J*/Grandma Max's/Subway/dsl/scales/24hr/@, 🍴 Sam Bass' Steaks, 🛏 Motel 6, 🅞 truckwash, **S** 🅞 McGreer's Camping
102	I-76 S, to Denver
102mm	S Platte River
101	US 138, to Julesburg, **S** truck parking
99mm	scenic turnout eb
95	NE 27, to Julesburg
85	25A, Chappell, **N** 🅖 Cenex/dsl/repair, Shell, Sinclair/dsl, 🅞 Creekside RV Park/Camping, Super Foods, USPO,

Ⓖ = gas Ⓕ = food Ⓛ = lodging Ⓞ = other Ⓡˢ = rest stop Copyright 2014 - The NEXT Exit ®

INTERSTATE 80 CONT'D

Exit	Services
85	Continued
	wayside park
82mm	truck parking (eb only)
76	17F, Lodgepole, **1 mi N** gas/dsl, lodging
69	17E, to Sunol
61mm	Ⓡˢ **wb, full** Ⓗ **facilities,** Ⓒ, Ⓐ, **litter barrels, vending, petwalk**
59	US 385, 17J, Sidney, **N** Ⓖ Conoco/dsl, Bell/dsl, Sapp Bros/Shell/dsl/24hr, Ⓕ Arby's, Buffalo Point Rest., China 1 Buffet, DQ, McDonald's, Mi Ranchito Mexican, Perkins, Pizza Hut, Runza, Subway, Ⓛ AmericInn, Comfort Inn, Days Inn, Hampton Inn, Motel 6, Ⓞ Cabela's Outfitters/RV Park, Chrysler/Dodge/Jeep, Ford, Radio Shack, Walmart, auto/dsl repair, RV camping (2mi), golf, truck permit sta, visitor ctr, **S** Ⓖ Shamrock/dsl, Ⓛ Holiday Inn/WheatRidge Grille, Ⓞ truckwash, auto tire/truck repair
55	NE 19, to Sterling, Sidney
51.5mm	Ⓡˢ/hist marker eb, **full** Ⓗ **facilities,** Ⓒ, Ⓐ, **litter barrels, vending, petwalk**
48	to Brownson
38	rd 17 b, Potter, **N** Ⓖ Cenex/dsl/LP, Ⓞ repair
29	53A, Dix, **1/2 mi N** gas, food
22	53E, Kimball, **1-2 mi N** Ⓖ Sinclair, Vince's/dsl, Ⓕ DQ, Pizza Hut, Subway, Ⓛ Days Inn, Motel Kimball, Sleep-4Less Motel, Ⓞ Co-op Foods, Family$, Kimball RV Park (seasonal), city park, golf
20	NE 71, Kimball, **0-2 mi N** Ⓖ Cenex/dsl, Sinclair, Vince's/dsl, Ⓕ DQ, O'Henry's Diner, Pizza Hut, Subway, Ⓛ Days Inn, 1st Interstate Inn, Motel Kimball, Sleep4Less Motel, Super 8, Ⓞ Co-op Foods, Family$, Kimball RV Park (seasonal), Pamida, city park, golf
18mm	parking area eb, litter barrel
8	53C, to Bushnell
1	53B, Pine Bluffs, **1 mi N** RV camping
0mm	Nebraska/Wyoming state line

INTERSTATE 680 (OMAHA)

Exit	Services
	I-680 begins/ends on I-80, exit 27.
29b a	I-80, W to Omaha, E to Des Moines.
28	IA 191, to Neola, Persia
21	L34, Beebeetown
19mm	Ⓡˢ **wb, full** Ⓗ **facilities, info,** Ⓒ, Ⓐ, **litter barrels, pet-walk**

16mm	Ⓡˢ **eb, full** Ⓗ **facilities, info,** Ⓒ, Ⓐ, **litter barrels, pet-walk**
15mm	scenic overlook
71	I-29 N, to Sioux City
66	Honey Creek, **W** Ⓖ Sinclair/dsl/rest., Ⓕ Iowa Feed&Grain Co Rest.
3b a	(61 b a from wb), I-29, S to Council Bluffs, IA 988, to Crescent, **E** Ⓖ Phillips 66, Ⓞ to ski area
1	County Rd
14mm	Nebraska/Iowa state line, Missouri River, Mormon Bridge
13	US 75 S, 30th St, Florence, **E** Ⓖ Shell/dsl, Ⓕ Jimmy C's Cafe, Zesto Diner, Ⓛ Mormon Trail Motel, Ⓞ HyVee Drug, LDS Temple, Mormon Trail Ctr, vet, **W** Ⓖ Florence
12	US 75 N, 48th St, **E** Ⓖ Cenex/dsl, Ⓕ Burger King (2mi), Taco Bell (2mi)
9	72nd St, **1-2 mi E** Ⓖ QuikShop, Ⓕ Applebee's, Burger King, Famous Dave's BBQ, IHOP, Jimmy John's, Sonic, Taco Bueno, Village Inn, Ⓞ Ⓗ, **W** Cunningham Lake RA
6	NE 133, Irvington, **E** Ⓖ Phillips 66, Ⓕ Burger King, Jimmy John's, Wings'n Things, Ⓞ Walmart/Subway/drugs/24hr, **W** Ⓕ Legend's Grill, Zesto Cafe, Ⓛ Holiday Inn Express
5	Fort St, **W** Ⓖ KwikShop, Ⓞ Urgent Care, CVS Drug, Goodyear/auto, HyVee Foods, Walgreens, USPO
4	NE 64, Maple St, **E** Ⓖ BP, **W** Ⓖ Kum&Go/dsl, Shell, Ⓕ Burger King, China 1, Godfather's Pizza, Jimmy John's, KFC, La Mesa Mexican, McDonald's, Pizza Hut, Runza, Subway, Taco Bell, Taco John's, Ⓛ Comfort Suites, La Quinta, Ⓞ Bag'n Save, $General, O'Reilly Parts, vet
3	US 6, Dodge St, **E** Ⓕ Cheesecake Factory, Granite City Rest., JC Manderin Chinese, Panera Bread, PF Chang's, TGIFriday's, Ⓛ Hampton Inn, Marriott, Ⓞ AAA, Audi/VW, BMW, Hynundai, Jaguar/Land Rover, JC Penney, Mazda, Mini, Subaru, Whole Foods Mkt, Von Maur, Younkers, mall, **W** Ⓖ BP, Phillips 66, Ⓕ Boston Mkt, Burger King, DQ, Grand China Buffet, Grisanti's, McDonald's, Starbucks, Ⓛ Best Western, Crowne Plaza Motel, Holiday Inn, Super 8, TownPlace Suites, Ⓞ Bag'n Save Foods, Cadillac, Chevrolet, Costco/gas, Ford, Hummer, Menards, Nissan, Toyota
2	Pacific St, **E** Ⓖ BP, Ⓛ Regency Lodge
1	NE 38, W Center Rd, **E** Ⓖ Cenex/dsl, Ⓕ Don Carmelo's, Don&Millie's Rest., **W** Ⓖ Phillips 66, Ⓕ Arby's, Burger King, Godfather's Pizza, Krispy Kreme, Ozark BBQ, Taco Bell, Wendy's, Ⓞ Baker's Foods, $Tree, Haas Tire, TJ Maxx
0mm	**I-680 begins/ends on I-80, exit 446**

NEVADA

INTERSTATE 15

Exit	Services
123mm	Nevada/Arizona state line, Pacific/Mountain time zone
122	Lp 15, Mesquite, **E** NV Welcome Ctr both lanes, **full** Ⓗ **facilities, petwalk,** Ⓖ Maverik, Shell/DQ/dsl, Sinclair/Arby's, Ⓕ Canton Chinese, Dominos, Golden West Rest./casino, Home Plate Diner, Jack-in-the-Box, KFC, Los Cazadores, Los Lupes, Panda Garden, Taco Bell, Ⓛ Best Western, Ⓞ Ace Hardware, AutoZone, Big O Tire, CarQuest, Radio Shack, Smith's/Subway/dsl, The Ranch Mkt, Walgreens, USPO, **W** Ⓖ Rebel/dsl/LP/RV park, Ⓕ Mc\

122	Continued
	Donald's, Starbucks, Ⓛ Eureka Motel/casino, Virgin River Hotel/casino
120	Lp 15, Mesquite, Bunkerville, **E** Ⓖ Chevron/dsl, Shell/dsl, Terrible's, Ⓕ McDonald's, Ⓛ Casablanca Resort/casino/RV Park, Oasis Resort/casino/RV Park, Ⓞ USPO, **W** Ⓖ Chevron/dsl, Ⓕ Del Taco, Little Caesars, Mia's Mexican, Papa Murphy's, Popeye's, Ⓛ Holiday Inn Express, Ⓞ Ⓗ, Beall's, $Tree, Ford, Verizon, Walmart/Subway,
112	NV 170, Riverside, Bunkerville
110mm	truck parking both lanes, litter barrels
100	to Carp, Elgin

◤N INTERSTATE 15 CONT'D

Exit	Services
96mm	truck parking nb, litter barrels
93	NV 169, to Logandale, Overton, **E** 🅐 Chevron (3mi), 🅞 Lake Mead NRA, Lost City Museum
91	NV 168, Glendale, **W** 🅐 Arco/dsl, 🍴 Muddy River Rest., 🅞 USPO
90.5mm	Muddy River
90	NV 168 (from nb), Glendale, Moapa, **W** gas, 🅞 Moapa Indian Reservation, USPO
88	Hidden Valley
88mm	parking area both lanes, litter barrels
84	Byron
80	Ute
75	Valley of Fire SP, Lake Mead NRA, **E** 🅐 Sinclair/dsl, 🅞 casino, fireworks
64	US 93 N, Great Basin Hwy, to Ely, Great Basin NP, **W** 🅐 Loves/Subway, Godfather's/dsl/scales/24hr
60mm	livestock check sta sb
58	NV 604, Las Vegas Blvd, to Apex, Nellis AFB
54	Speedway Blvd, Hollywood Blvd, **E** 🅐 Va, 🍴 Shelby Cafe/museum, 🅞 Las Vegas Speedway
52	rd 215 W
50	Lamb Ave, **1-2 mi E** 🅐 Shell/dsl, 🛏 Comfort Inn, 🅞 Hitchin Post RV Park
48	Craig Rd, **E** 🅐 Arco, 🛏/KFC, scales/24hr, 7-11, Shell, Sinclair/Subway/dsl, 🍴 Burger King, Jack-in-the-Box, Zapata's Cantina, 🅞 Firestone, to Nellis AFB, **W** 🅐 7-11, 🍴 Cannery Grill, Carl's Jr, Chipotle Mexican, Del Taco, Jamba Juice, Famous Dave's BBQ, In-N-Out, Marble Slab, Mulligan's, Panda Express, Poppa's Grill, Quiznos, Sonic, Starbucks, Subway, 🛏 Best Western, Hampton Inn, 🅞 Freightliner, Just Brakes, Lowe's, Sam's Club/gas, dsl repair
46	Cheyenne Ave, **E** 🅐 Arco/24hr, 🍴 CiCi's Pizza, Lucy's Grill, Marianna's Mkt, Panda Express, Starbucks, Subway, 🅞 $Tree, NAPA, 7-11, vet, **W** 🅐 FLYIN LP/rest./24hr, 7-11, Sinclair/Jack-in-the-Box, 🍴 Denny's, McDonald's, 🛏 Comfort Inn, 🅞 Blue Beacon, Kenworth, Mack, SpeedCo, Volvo, dsl repair, tires
45	Lake Mead Blvd, **E** 🅐 Chevron, Rebel/dsl, 🍴 Burger King, Carl's Jr., Jack-in-the-Box, McDonald's, 🅞 Pep-Boys, 7-11, **W** 🅐 Arco/dsl, 🍴 Jack-in-the-Box, McDonald's, 🅞 CVS Drug
44	Washington Ave (from sb), **E** casinos
43	D St (from nb, same as 44)
42b a	I-515 to LV, US 95 N to Reno, US 93 S to Phoenix
41b a	NV 159, Charleston Blvd, **E** 🅐 Arco/dsl, 7-11, 🅞 Walgreens, antiques, **W** 🅐 Rebel, Terrible's/E-85/dsl/casino, 🍴 Bentley's Coffee, Carl's Jr, Del Taco, McDonald's, Wendy's, 🅞 🅗, CVS Drug, Smith's Foods
40	Sahara Ave, **E** The Strip, 🛏 Artisan Hotel, Vagabond Inn, 🅞 KOA, NV Tire/Repair, multiple casinos/hotels, **W** 🅐 Chevron, Rebel/dsl, 7-11, Shell, 🍴 Carl's Jr, Chipotle Mexican, El Pollo Loco, In-N-Out, Jack-in-the-Box, Jimmy Johns, KFC, Landry's Seafood, Los Tacos, Macaroni Grill, McDonald's, Panda Express, Pizza Hut, Shilla BBQ, Starbucks, TGIFriday's, Wendy's, 🛏 Palace Sta. Hotel/Casino, 🅞 CVS Drug, Food4Less, Office Depot, Ross,
40	Continued TJ Maxx, Von's Foods, Walgreens, casinos
39	Spring Mtn Rd (from sb), **E** 🅞 multiple hotels/casinos **W** 🍴 Multiple Asian Cuisine, Quiznos, Starbucks, 🅞 Firestone/auto
38b a	Flamingo Rd, **E** The Strip, to UNLV, multiple casinos/hotels, **W** 🅐 Chevron, 🍴 Burger King, McDonald's, Sonic, Starbucks, Subway, Taco Bell, TGIFriday's, Wendy's, 🛏 Gold Coast Hotel, Palms Hotel, Rio Hotel, 🅞 Discount Tire
37	Tropicana Ave, **E** 🅐 Rebel, 🍴 Coco's Rest., McDonald's, 🛏 Bellagio, Excaliber Hotel, Hooters Hotel/casino, Mandalay Bay, MGM Grand, Monte Carlo, Motel 6, Tropicana Hotel, 🅞 ✈, multiple hotels/casinos, **W** 🅐 Rebel/dsl, Shell/Subway, Standard, Texaco, 🍴 Burger King, Dennys, In-N-Out, Jack-in-the-Box, McDonald's, Taco's Mexico, Wendy's, 🛏 Budget Suites, Days Inn, Hampton Inn, La Quinta, Motel 6, Orleans Hotel, Siegel Suites
36	Russell Rd, **E** 🅞 multiple hotels/casinos, to ✈, **W** 🅐 Chevron/Herbst/dsl, 🛏 Courtyard, Fairfield Inn, Holiday Inn Express, Residence Inn, Staybridge Suites
34	to I-215 E, Las Vegas Blvd, to The Strip McCarran
33	NV 160, to Blue Diamond, Death Valley, **E** 🅐 Chevron, Rebel/dsl, 7-11/dsl, 🍴 Bootlegger Bistro, Burger King, Buffalo Wild Wings, Chili's, Cane's Rest, Chipotle Mexican, Dickey's BBQ, Dunkin Donuts, IHOP, McDonald's,

⛽ = gas   🍴 = food   🛏 = lodging   Ⓞ = other   Ⓡˢ = rest stop   Copyright 2014 - The NEXT Exit ®

⮕ Ⓝ INTERSTATE 15 CONT'D

Exit	Services
33	Continued
	Outback Steaks, Panda Express, Popeyes, Quizno's, Starbucks, Subway, Wienerschnitzel, 🛏 Budget Suites, Carib Resort, Crestwood Suites, Hilton Garden, Microtel, Ⓞ CVS Drug, Food4Less, Oasis RV Resort, Verizon, factory outlet/famous brands, **W** ⛽ Chevron/dsl, Fills/dsl, Shell, TA/Burger King/Subway/TacoTime/dsl/LP/scales/24hr/@, 🍴 Bilbo's Grill, Cafe Rio, Carl's Jr, Del Taco, Famous Dave's BBQ, In-N-Out, Jack-in-the-Box, Panda Express, Quiznos, Taco Bell, 🛏 Silverton Lodge/Casino, Ⓞ Albertson's, Bass ProShops, BigLots, Discount Tire, $Tree, GNC, Kohl's, Office Depot, PetCo, Radio Shack, Ross, Target, Verizon, Walgreens, WorldMkt
31	Silverado Ranch Blvd, **E** 🍴 Steak'n Shake, 🛏 South Point Hotel/Casino
27	NV 146, to Henderson, Lake Mead, Hoover Dam, **0-2 mi E** ⛽ Arco, Chevron, Shell, 🍴 Jack-in-the-Box, Starbucks, Subway, 🛏 Hampton Inn, Wingate Inn, Ⓞ Camping World, casino, USPO, **W** vet
25	NV 161, Sloan, **1 mi E** Camping World
24mm	bus/truck check sta nb
12	NV 161, to Goodsprings, Jean, **E** ⛽ Shell/dsl, Ⓞ Gold Strike Casino/hotel, NV Correctional, NV HP, USPO, skydiving, **W** ⛽ Shell
1	Primm, **E** ⛽ Chevron/dsl, Texaco/dsl, 🍴 Carl's Jr, Dennys, KFC, Mad Greek Cafe, McDonald's, Panda Express, Starbucks, Taco Bell, Tony Roma, Ⓞ Buffalo Bill's Resort/casino, Primm Valley Resort/casino, factory outlets, **W** ⛽ Chevron/dsl/scales, 🛏 Whiskey Pete's Hotel/casino
0mm	Nevada/California state line

⮕ Ⓔ INTERSTATE 80

Exit	Services
411mm	Nevada/Utah state line
410	US 93A, to Ely, W Wendover, **S NV Welcome Ctr/info, full ♿ facilities,** 🍴, ⛽ Chevron/dsl, 🛢Arby's/dsl/scales/24hr, Shell/Taco Time/dsl, 🍴 Burger King, McDonald's, Pizza Hut, Subway, 🛏 Best Value Inn, Days Inn, Knights Inn, Motel 6, Nugget Hotel/casino, Peppermill Hotel/casino/RV parking, Rainbow Hotel/casino, Red Garter Hotel/casino, Ⓞ Best Hardware, Smith's Foods/dsl, KOA, city park
407	Ola, W Wendover
405mm	Pacific/Mountain time zone
398	to Pilot Peak
390mm	Silverzone Pass, Silverzone Pass, elev 5940
387	to Shafter
378	NV 233, to Montello, Oasis
376	to Pequop
373mm	Pequop Summit, elev 6967, Ⓡˢ **both lanes,** 🚮, **litter barrels, rest rooms**
365	to Independence Valley, **N** prison camp
360	to Moor
354mm	parking area eb
352b a	US 93, Great Basin Hwy, E Wells, **N** ⛽ Sinclair/dsl/café/casino, Shell/Quiznos/dsl/LP, 🍴 Bella's Diner, Burger King/Subway, 🛏 LoneStar Motel, Motel 6, Rest Inn Motel, Sharon Motel, Super 8, Ⓞ Crossroads RV Park, 4-Way Casino/Rest., Schwab Tire, repair, truckwash, **S** ⛽ FLYING J/dsl/scales/LP/casino/RV Dump/24hr,

Exit	Services
352b a	Continued
	💙Loves/McDonalds/dsl/scales/24hr, Ⓞ Great Basin NP
351	W Wells, **N** ⛽ Wells/dsl/LP, Ⓞ Mtn. Shadows RV Park, NAPA, Roy's Foods, Well's Hardware, USPO, **S** Ⓞ Angel Lake RV Park, to Angel Lake RA
348	to Beverly Hills, **N** RV camping
343	to Welcome, Starr Valley, **N** Welcome RV Park, 🍴, food
333	Deeth, Starr Valley
328	to River Ranch
321	NV 229, Halleck, Ruby Valley
318mm	N Fork Humboldt River
317	to Elburz
314	to Ryndon, Devils Gate, **N** ⛽ Sinclair/cafe/dsl, **S** RV camping
312mm	check sta both lanes
310	to Osino, **4 mi S** Valley View RV Park
303	E Elko, **N** ⛽ CFN/dsl, Sinclair/Arctic Circle/dsl/24hr, 🍴 Wingers, 🛏 TownePlace Suites, **S** ⛽ Chevron/dsl, Conoco/dsl, Maverik/dsl, Sinclair/dsl, Tesoro/dsl, 🍴 Burger King, Chef Cheng's Chinese, DQ, Grilled Pepper Mexican, J Ossies Rest., King Buffet, McDonald's/playplace, Monkey Sun Chinese, Pizza Barn, Pizza Hut, Subway, Taco Time, Toki Ona Diner, Wendy's, 🛏 Best Value Inn, Best Western, Budget Inn, Comfort Inn, Days Inn, EconoLodge, High Desert Inn, Hilton Garden, Holiday Inn Express, Holiday Motel, Motel 6, Red Lion Inn/casino, Super 8, Travelodge, Ⓞ ♿, Albertson's, AT&T, Big O Tires, Buick/Cadillac/Chevrolet/GMC, Cal Store, Curves, Double Dice RV Park, Ford, Gold Country RV Park, Goodyear/auto, Iron Horse RV Park, JC Penney, Valley View RV Park, auto repair, city park, USPO
301	NV 225, Elko, **N** ⛽ Maverik/dsl, 🍴 Arby's, Burger King, Coffee Mug Rest., Greatwall Chinese, Mattie's Grill, McDonald's/playplace, 9 Beans/Burrito, Papa Murphy's, Port of Subs, 🛏 OakTree Inn, Shilo Inn Suites, Ⓞ AT&T, GNC, Home Depot, JoAnn Fabrics, K-Mart, Raley's Foods, Ross, Verizon, Walmart/Subway, **S** ⛽ Shell, 🍴 Cimarron West Rest., Dominos, Dos Amigos, KFC, Little Caesar's, Sergio's Mexican, Starbucks, Taco Bell, 🛏 American Inn, Centre Motel, Economy Inn, Elko Inn, Esquire Inn, Key Motel, Manor Inn, Midtown Motel, Rodeway Inn, Stampede Motel, Stockmen's Hotel/casino, Thunderbird Motel, Ⓞ ♿, CarQuest, CVS Drug, Family$, O'Reilly Parts, Smith's Foods/dsl, Verizon, casino/rest., 🔜
298	W Elko, No facilites
292	to Hunter
285mm	Humboldt River, tunnel
282	NV 221, E Carlin, **N** prison area
280	NV 766, Carlin, **N** Ⓞ Desert Gold RV Park, dsl repair, **S** ⛽ 🛢/Subway/dsl/scales/24hr, Texaco/Burger King/dsl, 🍴 Chin's Cafe, Rigobertos Mexican, State Café/casino, 🛏 Cavalier Motel, Comfort Inn, Ⓞ Ace Hardware, USPO, tires
279	NV 278 (from eb), to W Carlin, **1 mi S** gas/dsl
271	to Palisade
270mm	Emigrant Summit, elev 6114, truck parking both lanes, litter barrels
268	to Emigrant
261	NV 306, to Beowawe, Crescent Valley
258mm	Ⓡˢ **both lanes, full** ♿ **facilities,** 🚮, **litter barrels, petwalk**
257mm	Humboldt River

Ⓝⱽ

J E A N

W E N D O V E R

W E L L S

E L K O

C A R L I N

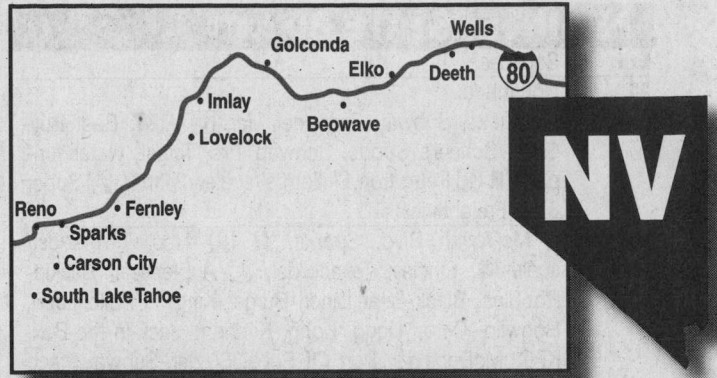

◄►E INTERSTATE 80 CONT'D

Exit	Services
254	to Dunphy
244	to Argenta
233	NV 304, to Battle Mountain, N 🅰 Conoco/dsl, 🍴 Mama's Pizza/deli, 🏠 Best Value Inn, 🅾 🅷, FoodTown, Royal Hardware
231	NV 305, Battle Mountain, N 🅰 Chevron/dsl, Quickmart/pizza, 🍴 Hide-a-way Steaks, McDonald's, 🏠 Super 8, 🅾 Family$, Mills Drug, NAPA, USPO, **1 mi N** 🅰 ⊕FLYING J /76/Blimpie/dsl/casino/24hr, 🍴 El Aguila Real, Ming Dynasty, Owl Rest., 🏠 Big Chief Motel, Nevada Hotel, Owl Motel, 🅾 🅷, NAPA Care, Tire Factory
229	NV 304, W Battle Mountain, N 🅰 ⊕FLYING J/76/Blimpie/dsl/casino/scales/24hr, Shell/dsl, 🏠 Battle Mtn. Inn, Big Chief Motel, 🅾 Colt RV camping, NAPA Care
222	to Mote
216	Valmy, N 🅰 Shell/USPO/dsl, S 🅿️ **both lanes, full** ♿ **facilities,** 🅲, 🏠, **litter barrels, petwalk, RV dump**
212	to Stonehouse
205	to Pumpernickel Valley
203	to Iron Point
200	Golconda Summit, elev 5145, truck parking area both lanes, litter barrels
194	Golconda, N 🍴 Waterhole #1 Cafe, 🅾 USPO
187	to Button Point, N 🅿️ **both lanes, full** ♿ **facilities,** 🅲, 🏠 **litter barrels, petwalk, RV dump**
180	NV 794, E Winnemucca Blvd
178	NV 289, Winnemucca Blvd, Winnemucca, S 🅰 Maverik/dsl, Sinclair/dsl, 🍴 Las Margaritas, Rte 66 Grill, 🏠 Budget Inn, Cozy Motel, Frontier Motel, Valu Motel, 🅾 🅷, CarQuest, carwash
176	US 95 N, Winnemucca, N 🅰 Pacific Pride/dsl, S 🅰 Chevron/dsl/24hr, ⊕FLYING J/dsl/LP/RV dump/24hr, KwikServ, Shell/dsl, Texaco, 🍴 Arby's, Burger King, Dos Amigos Mexican, Griddle Rest., Jack-in-the-Box, KFC/LJ Silver, McDonald's/playplace, Pig BBQ, Pizza Hut, RoundTable Pizza, Sid's Rest., Subway, Taco Time, Wonderful House Chinese, 🏠 Best Western, Days Inn, Economy Inn, Holiday Inn Express, Holiday Motel, Motel 6, Park Hotel, Pyrenees Motel, Quality Inn, Regency Inn, Santa Fe Inn, Scott Motel, Scottish Inn, Winnemucca Inn/casino, Winner Hotel/casino, Super 8, 🅾 🅷, AutoZone, Ford, Freightliner, O'Reilly Parts, Raley's Foods, Schwab Tire, Verizon, Walmart/Subway, RV camping, auto/truck repair, casino
173	W Winnemucca, N 🅰 ⬛/Subway/dsl/scales/24hr, S 📠
168	to Rose Creek, **S** prison area
158	to Cosgrave, S 🅿️ **both lanes, full** ♿ **facilities,** 🅲, 🏠, **litter barrels, petwalk**
151	Mill City, N 🅰 TA/Subway/Taco Bell/Fork/dsl/casino/24hr/@
149	NV 400, Mill City, **1 mi N** 🅰 TA/Subway/Taco Bell/Fork/dsl/24hr/@, **S** Star Point Gen. Store/RV camping
145	Imlay
138	Humboldt
129	Rye Patch Dam, N 🍴 Oasis Pizza, 🅾 to Rye Patch SRA, S 🅰 Rye Patch Trkstp/dsl
119	to Rochester, Oreana
112	to Coal Canyon, **S** to correctional ctr
107	E Lovelock (from wb), same as 106
106	Main St, Lovelock, N 🅰 Chevron/dsl/LP, PJ's Gas/subs/

Exit	Services
106	Continued dsl, 2 Stiffs, 🍴 Cowpoke Cafe, Las Palomas Mexican, McDonald's, Pizza Factory, Ricardo's BBQ, 🏠 Cadillac Inn, Covered Wagon Motel, Royal Inn, Sturgeons Motel/rest., Super 10 Motel, 🅾 🅷, Ace Hardware, Lazy K Camping, Safeway Foods, city park/playground/restrooms, dsl repair
105	W Lovelock (from eb), N 🅰 Shell/dsl, Shop'n Go/dsl, 🍴 La Casita Mexican, 🅾 🅷, Brookwood RV Park, NAPA, museum, same as 106
93	to Toulon, S 📠
83	US 95 S, to Fallon, S 🅿️ **both lanes, full** ♿ **facilities,** 🅲, 🏠, **litter barrels**
78	to Jessup
65	to Hot Springs, Nightingale
50	NV Pacific Pkwy, Fernley
48	US 50A, US 95A, to Fallon, E Fernley, S 🅰 Shell/dsl, Silverado/dsl, 🍴 Burger King, Domino's, Jack-in-the-Box, KFC, Louie's China, McDonald's, Papa Murphy's, Pizza Factory, Pizza Hut, Port Of Subs, Silverado Rest./casino, Starbucks, Taco Bell, 🏠 Best Western, Super 8, 🅾 Urgent Care, AutoZone, Curves, $Tree, Lowe's, O'Reilly Parts, Radio Shack, Scolari's Foods, Walgreens, Walmart/Subway, USPO, casinos, tires, to Great Basin NP
46	US 95A, W Fernley, N 🅰 ⬛Loves/Arby's/dsl/scales/24hr, S 🅰 ⬛/DQ/Wendy's/dsl/scales/24hr, 🍴 Chukars Grill/Casino, 🏠 Comfort Suites, 🅾 Blue Beacon, SpeedCo
45mm	Truckee River
43	to Pyramid Lake, Wadsworth, N 🅰 Pyramid Lake gas/dsl/RV camping
42mm	🅿️ wb, full ♿ facilities, 🅲, 🏠, litter barrels, petwalk, wireless internet, check sta eb
40	Painted Rock
38	Orchard
36	Derby Dam
32	USA Pkwy, Tracy, Clark Station
28	NV 655, Waltham Way, Patrick
27mm	scenic view, eb
25mm	check sta wb
23	Mustang, S 🅰 Chevron/dsl, truck repair
22	Lockwood
21	Vista Blvd, Greg St, Sparks, N 🅰 Chevron/McDonald's, QwikStop, 🍴 Del Taco, 🏠 Fairfield Inn, 🅾 🅷, S 🅰 Petro/Iron Skillet/dsl/24hr/@, 🏠 Super 8, 🅾 Peterbilt, truckwash
20	Sparks Blvd, Sparks, N 🅰 7-11, Shell/dsl, 🍴 BJ's Rest., Carl's Jr, Fuddruckers, Grimaldi's Pizza, Jamba Juice, Olive Garden, Outback Steaks, Panda Express, Popeye's,

Side labels: BATTLE MTN, WINNEMUCCA (left column); LOVELOCK, SPARKS (right column)

Ⓖ = gas Ⓕ = food Ⓛ = lodging Ⓞ = other Ⓡˢ = rest stop   Copyright 2014 - The NEXT Exit ®

▲Ⓔ INTERSTATE 80 CONT'D

Exit	Services
20	Continued starbucks, Subway, Taco del Mar, Ⓞ AT&T, Best Buy, GNC, Scheel's Sports, Schwab Tire, Target, water fun-park, **S** Ⓖ Petro/Iron Skillet/dsl/scales/24hr/@, Ⓛ Super 8, Ⓞ Freightliner
19	**E** McCarran Blvd, Sparks, **N** Ⓖ Arco, TA/rest/dsl/scales/@, Sinclair, Texaco/dsl, Ⓕ Applebee's, Baskin-Robbins, Black Bear Diner, Burger King, El Pollo Loco, Hogwild Cafe, Hong Kong Kitchen, Jack-in-the-Box, KFC, McDonald's, Port Of Subs, Sizzler, Subway, Taco Bell, Wendy's, Wienerschnitzel, Ⓛ Aloha Inn, Sunrise Motel, Windsor Inn, Ⓞ BigLots, CVS Drug, $Tree, Good-year/auto, O'Reilly Parts, Pep Boys, Radio Shack, Ross, Savemart Foods, Victorian RV Park, **S** Ⓕ Denny's, Super Burrito, Ⓛ Holiday Inn, Ⓞ NAPA
18	NV 445, Pyramid Way, Sparks, **N** Ⓖ 7-11, Ⓕ In-N-Out, Starbucks, Ⓛ Nugget Courtyard, Silver Club Hotel/casino, **S** Ⓛ Nugget Hotel/casino
17	Rock Blvd, Nugget Ave, Sparks, **N** Ⓖ Arco, Chevron, V/dsl, Ⓛ Safari Motel, Victorian Inn, Wagon Train Motel, Ⓞ O'Reilly Parts, casinos, **S** Ⓛ Nugget Hotel/casino
16	B St, E 4th St, Victorian Ave, **N** Ⓖ Arco, KwikServ, Ⓕ Jack's Cafe, Ⓛ Motel 6, Ⓞ Rail City Casino, **S** Ⓖ Chevron/repair
15	US 395, to Carson City, Susanville, **1 mi N on McCarran Blvd** Ⓖ Shell/dsl, Ⓕ Arby's, Burger King, Del Taco, Fat Burger, Littel Caesar's, Port Of Subs, Sonic, Wendy's, Ⓞ CVS Drug, Home Depot, Office Depot, O'Reilly Parts, Pet-Co, Ross, Tires+, WinCo Foods, **0-1 mi S** Ⓛ Holiday Inn Express, Hyatt Place, La Quinta, Ⓞ Costco/gas, Grand Sierra Resort
14	Wells Ave, Reno, **N** Ⓛ Motel 6, **S** Ⓖ Chevron/dsl, Ⓕ Car-row's Rest., Denny's, Ⓛ America's Best Inn, Days Inn, Ra-mada Inn, Ⓞ Goodyear, auto repair
13	US 395, Virginia St, Reno, **N** Ⓖ Shell/dsl, Ⓕ Giant Burger,

Exit	Services
13	Continued **S** Ⓖ Shell/dsl, Ⓞ Ⓗ, Circus Circus, NAPA, Walgreens, to downtown hotels/casinos, to UNVReno
12	Keystone Ave, Reno, **N** Ⓖ Arco, Ⓕ Pizza Hut, Rose Gar-den Asian, Starbucks, Ⓛ Gateway Inn, Motel 6, Ⓞ CVS Drug, Raley's Foods, 7-11, **S** Ⓖ Chevron/dsl, Texaco/dsl, Ⓕ Burger King, Jack-in-the-Box, KFC, Little Caesar's, McDonald's, Port of Subs, Round Table Pizza, Taco Bell, Wendy's, Ⓞ Keystone RV Park, Meineke, NAPA, O'Reilly Parts, Radio Shack, SaveMart/drug, casinos
10	McCarran Blvd, Reno, **N** Ⓖ Arco, 7-11/dsl, Ⓕ Arby's, Asian Wok, Baskin-Robbins, Burger King, Bully's Grill, Carl's Jr, Chili's, Del Taco, DQ, El Pollo Loco, Hacienda Mexican, IHOP, Jack-in-the-Box, KFC, Keva Juice, Mc-Donald's, Papa Murphy's, Qdoba Mexican, RoundTable Pizza, Starbucks, Subway, Taco Bell, Ⓞ AT&T, AutoZone, Big O Tire, Curves, $Tree, Kohl's, O'Reilly Parts, Petsmart, Ross, Safeway/dsl, SaveMart Foods, Staples, Tires+, Ve-rizon, Walgreens, Walmart/McDonald's, **S** Ⓖ 7-11, Ⓞ Ur-gent Care, Home Depot, vet
9	Robb Dr, **N** Ⓖ Chevron/dsl, Maverik/dsl, Ⓕ Bully's Grill, Domino's, Jimmy John's, Moxie's Cafe, Papa John's, Port Of Subs, Starbucks, Subway, Tahoe Burger, Ⓞ CVS Drug, Raley's Foods, Scolari's Foods
8	W 4th St (from eb), Robb Dr, Reno, **S** RV camping
7	Mogul
6.5mm	truck parking/hist marker/scenic view both lanes
5	to E Verdi (from wb no return), **N** Backstop Grill
4.5mm	scenic view eb
4	Garson Rd, Boomtown, **N** Ⓖ Chevron/Boomtown Hotel/dsl/casino, Ⓕ Cassidy's Rest., Denny's, Peet's Rest., Ⓞ Cabela's, KOA/RV dump
3.5mm	check sta eb
3	Verdi (from wb)
2.5mm	Truckee River
2	Lp 80, to Verdi, **N** Ⓖ Terribles/Chevron/dsl/24hr, Ⓕ Jack-in-the-Box, Taco Bell, Ⓛ Gold Ranch RV Resort/casino
0mm	Nevada/California state line

NEW HAMPSHIRE

▲Ⓝ INTERSTATE 89

Exit	Services
61mm	New Hampshire/Vermont state line, Connecticut River
20 (60)	NH 12A, W Lebanon, **E** Ⓖ Sunoco/24hr, Ⓕ Benning St Grill, Brick Oven Pizza, Chili's, Domino's, Dunkin Donuts, KFC/Taco Bell, 99 Rest., Oriental Wok, Parthenon Pizza, Subway, Ⓞ GNC, Hannaford Foods, Jo-Ann Fabrics, K-Mart, LL Bean, Rite Aid, Shaw's Foods, TJ Maxx, **W** Ⓕ Applebee's, Burger King, D'angelo's, Denny's, Friendly's, Koto Japanese, McDonald's, Panera Bread, Pizza Hut, 7 Barrel Rest., Weathervane Seafood, Wendy's, Ⓛ Bay-mont Inn, Fireside Inn, Ⓞ AT&T, Best Buy, BJ's Whse, CVS Drug, $Tree, Home Depot, JC Penney, Kohl's, PriceChop-per Foods, Radio Shack, Sears, Shaw's Foods, Staples, Verizon, Walgreens, Walmart
19 (58)	US 4, NH 10, W Lebanon, **E** Ⓖ Gulf/dsl, Shell, Ⓕ China Station, Ⓞ AutoZone, Family$, Ford, Harley-Davidson, Honda, Pricechopper Foods, **W** Ⓖ Irving, Sunoco
57mm	**Welcome Ctr/Ⓡˢ/weigh sta sb, full Ⓛ facilities, Ⓒ, Ⓐ, litter barrels, vending, petwalk, weigh sta nb**
18 (56)	NH 120, Lebanon, **E** Ⓛ Courtyard (3mi), Days Inn, Resi

Exit	Services
18 (56)	Continued dence Inn (2mi), Ⓞ Ⓗ, Cadillac/Chevrolet, Chrysler/Dodge/Jeep, Freightliner, Nissan, Volvo/VW, Wilson Tire/repair, to Dartmouth Coll, **W** Ⓖ Mobil/Subway/dsl, Shell, Ⓞ U-Haul
17 (54)	US 4, to NH 4A, Enfield, **E** Ⓕ Riverside Grill, Shaker Mu-seum, Ⓞ Northern States Tire, RV Camping, vet
16 (52)	Eastman Hill Rd, **E** Ⓖ Gulf/Subway/dsl, **W** Ⓖ Mobil/Dunkin Donuts/dsl, Ⓞ Whaleback Ski Area
15 (50)	Montcalm
14 (47)	NH 10 (from sb), N Grantham
13 (43)	NH 10, Grantham, **E** Ⓖ Irving/Gen Store/dsl, **W** Ⓖ Irving/Circle K, Ⓕ Dunkin Donuts, Pizza Chef, Ⓞ repair
40mm	Ⓡˢ **nb, full Ⓛ facilities, info, Ⓒ, Ⓐ, litter barrels, vend-ing, petwalk**
12A (37)	Georges Mills, **W** Ⓞ to Sunapee SP, food, Ⓒ, lodging, RV camping
12 (34)	NH 11 W, New London, **2 mi E** Ⓖ Irving/dsl, Ⓕ McKenna Rest., Ⓛ Maple Hill Country Inn, New London Inn, Ⓞ Ⓗ
11 (31)	NH 11 E, King Hill Rd, New London, **2-3 mi E** Ⓕ Hole in the Fence Cafe, Ⓛ Fairway Motel, New London Inn, ski area

WARNER

▲N INTERSTATE 89 CONT'D

Exit	Services
10 (27)	to NH 114, Sutton, **E** to Winslow SP, **1 mi W** lodging, to Wadleigh SB
26mm	🆁🆂 sb, full 🛏 facilities, info, 🍴, 🗑, litter barrels, vending, petwalk
9 (19)	NH 103, Warner, **E** 🅖 Irving/Circle K/Dunkin Donuts/dsl, Shell/Subway/pizza, 🍴 McDonald's, Ⓞ Aubuchon Hardware, MktBasket Foods, Rollins SP, **W** to Sunapee SP, ski area
8 (17)	NH 103 (from nb, no EZ return), Warner, **1 mi W** gas, food, museum, to Rollins SP
15mm	Warner River
7 (14)	NH 103, Davisville, **E** camping, **W** Pleasant Lake Camping
12mm	Contoocook River
6 (10)	NH 127, Contoocook, **1 mi E** 🅖 Sunoco, **W** Ⓞ Elm Brook Park, Sandy Beach Camping (3mi)
5 (8)	US 202 W, NH 9 (exits left from nb), Hopkinton, **W** food, RV camping (seasonal)
4 (7)	NH 103, Hopkinton (from nb, no EZ return), **E** HorseShoe Tavern, gas
3 (4)	Stickney Hill Rd (from nb)
2 (2)	NH 13, Clinton St, Concord, **E** 🏥, **W** NH Audubon Ctr
1 (1)	Logging Hill Rd, Bow, **E** 🅖 Mobil/24hr, 🍴 Chen Yang Li Chinese, 🛏 Hampton Inn
0mm	I-93 N to Concord, S to Manchester. **I-89 begins/ends on I-93, 36mm.**

▲N INTERSTATE 93

Exit	Services
2 (11)	I-91, N to St Johnsbury, S to White River Jct. **I-93 begins/ends on I-91, exit 19.**
1 (8)	VT 18, to US 2, to St Johnsbury, **2 mi E** gas, food, lodging, camping
1mm	Welcome Ctr nb, full 🛏 facilities, info, 🍴, 🗑, litter barrels, vending, petwalk, WiFi
131mm	Vermont/New Hampshire state line, Connecticut River. **Exits 1-2 are in VT.**
44 (130)	NH 18, NH 135, **W** Welcome Ctr (8am-8pm)/scenic vista both lanes, full 🛏 facilities, info, 🍴, 🗑, litter barrels, petwalk
43 (125)	NH 135 (from sb), to NH 18, Littleton, **1-2 mi W** 🏥, same as 42
42 (124)	US 302 E, NH 10 N, Littleton, **E** 🅖 Citgo/Quiznos, Gulf, Irving, Sunoco/24hr, 🍴 Burger King, Deluxe Pizza, Dunkin Donuts, Littleton Diner, Pizza Hut, Subway, 🛏 Beal House, Littleton Motel, Ⓞ Bond Parts, Rite Aid, Verizon, Walgreens, USPO, **W** 🅖 Mobil, 🍴 Applebee's, Asian Garden Chinese, Dunkin Donuts, McDonald's, 99 Rest., Oriental Cafe, 🛏 Hampton Inn, Ⓞ Aubuchan Hardware, Buick/Chevrolet, Chrysler/Dodge/Jeep, $Tree, Home Depot, KOA (5mi), Lowe's, Shaw's Foods/Osco Drug, Staples, Tire Whse, TJ Maxx, VIP Parts/service, Walmart/drug, camping
41 (122)	US 302, NH 18, NH 116, Littleton, **E** 🅖 Irving/Circle K/dsl/24hr, 🛏 Eastgate Motel/rest., Travel Inn, Ⓞ food co-op, **W** Ⓞ NE Tire
40 (121)	US 302, NH 10 E, Bethlehem, **E** 🛏 Adair Country Inn/Rest., Ⓞ to Mt Washington
39 (119)	NH 116, NH 18 (from sb), N Franconia, Sugar Hill, **W** lodging
38 (117)	NH 116, NH 117, NH 142, NH 18, Sugar Hill, **E** 🍴 Shaw's

38 (117)	Continued Rest., 🛏 Best Western, **W** 🅖 Citgo, 🍴 DutchTreat Rest., Wendell's Deli, Ⓞ Franconia Hardware, Franconia Village Store, Frost Museum, Mac's Mkt, USPO, camping, gifts, info
37 (115)	NH 142, NH 18 (from nb), Franconia, Bethlehem, **W** 🛏 Cannon Mtn View Motel, Hillwinds Lodge, Stonybrook Motel, Ⓞ Franstead Camping
36 (114)	NH 141, to US 3, S Franconia, **W** golf, food, lodging
35 (113)	US 3 N (from nb), to Twin Mtn Lake
112mm	S Franconia, Franconia Notch SP begins sb
34c (111)	NH 18, S Franconia Echo Beach Ski Area, view area, info
34b	Cannon Mtn Tramway, **W** Ⓞ Boise Rock, Old Man Viewing, Lafayette Place Camping
109mm	trailhead parking
108mm	Lafayette Place Camping, trailhead parking
107mm	The Basin
34a	US 3, The Flume Gorge, info, camping (seasonal)
104mm	Franconia Notch SP begins nb
33 (103)	US 3, N Woodstock, **E** 🅖 Irving/dsl, 🍴 Dad's Rest., Fresolones Pizza, Longhorn Palace Rest., Notchview Country Kitchen, 🛏 EconoLodge, Green Village Cottages, Lin

LITTLETON

▲N INTERSTATE 93 CONT'D

Exit	Services
33 (103)	Continued
	coln Inn, Mt Coolidge Motel, Pemi Motel, Profile Motel, Rodeway Inn, Woodward's Resort/Rest., ⊙ Indian Head viewing, to Franconia Notch SP, waterpark, **W** 🍴 Sunny Day Diner, 🛏 Country Bumpkin Cottages/Camping, Cozy Cabins, Mt Liberty Cabins, White Mtn Motel/Cottages, ⊙ Arnold's NAPACare, Clark's Trading Post, Cold Springs Camping, Tim's Repair
32 (101)	NH 112, Loon Mtn Rd, N Woodstock, **E** ⛽ Irving, Mobil, Munce's/dsl, Shell/dsl, 🍴 Bill&Bob's Roast Beef, Cheng Garden Chinese, Common Man Rest., Dunkin Donuts, Elvio's Pizza, Flapjack's Pancakes, George's Rest., GH Pizza, Gordi's Fish&Steaks, Hamburger Heaven, McDonald's, Mr. W's Pancakes, Mtn View Pizza, Nacho's Mexican Grill, Subway, 3 Cultures Deli, White Mtn Bagel Deli, 🛏 Comfort Inn, Inn Season Resorts, Kancamagu's Lodge, Lincoln Sta. Lodge, Nordic Inn, ⊙ Aubuchan Hardware, CarQuest, Family$, PriceChopper Foods, Rite Aid, Village Shops, USPO, to North Country Art Ctr, **W** ⛽ Sunoco, 🍴 Imperial Palace Japanese, Landmark II Rest., Lafayette Dinner Train, Peg's Café, Truant's Rest., Woodstock Inn Rest., 🛏 Alpine Lodge, Autumn Breeze Motel, Cascade Lodge, Carriage Motel, ⊙ NAPA, USPO, candy/fudge/gifts
31 (97)	to NH 175, Tripoli Rd, **E** RV camping (seasonal), **W** KOA (2mi)
30 (95)	US 3, Woodstock, **E** 🍴 Lanterns End Grill, Tony's Rest., 🛏 Jack-O-Lantern Inn/rest., ⊙ golf, **W** flea mkt, camping (seasonal)
29 (89)	US 3, Thornton, **E** Pemi River RV Park/LP, **W** 🛏 Gilcrest Motel
28 (87)	NH 49, Campton, **E** ⛽ Gulf, Mobil, 🍴 Dunkin Donuts, Exit 28 Pizza, ⊙ Handy Man Hardware, USPO, to ski area, RV camping, **W** ⛽ Irving/dsl, 🍴 Sunset Grill, ⊙ Branch Brook Camping, Chesley's Glory Sta., Mtn Vista RV Park
27 (84)	Blair Rd Beebe River, **E** 🍴 Country Cow Rest., 🛏 Days Inn, Red Sleigh Condos
26 (83)	US 3, NH 25, NH 3A, Tenney Mtn Hwy **W on US 3** 🍴 McDonald's, 🛏 Common Man Inn, Pilgrim Inn, Red Roof Inn, ⊙ 🏥
25 (81)	NH 175 (from nb), Plymouth, **W** ⛽ Citgo/dsl, Irving/Circle K/dsl, 🍴 Annie's Rest., College Town Pizza, Downtown Pizza, HongKong Garden, Lucky Dog Grill, Mark's Cafe, Subway, Thai Smile, ⊙ 🏥, Chase St Mkt, USPO, Plymouth State U
24 (76)	US 3, NH 25, Ashland, **E** ⛽ Gulf, Irving/Circle K/dsl, Mobil/dsl, 🍴 Ashland Pizza, Bullwinkle's Grill, Burger King, Common Man Diner, Dunkin Donuts, John's Cafe, Lucky Dragon Chinese, Village Grill, 🛏 Comfort Inn, ⊙ AutoValue Parts, Bob's Mkt, Jellystone RV Camp (4mi), TrueValue, USPO, repair
23 (71)	NH 104, NH 132, to Mt Washington Valley, New Hampton, **E** ⛽ Citgo/dsl, Irving/Circle K/dsl, 🍴 Dunkin Donuts, Rossi Italian, Subway, ⊙ Clearwater Campground, Jellystone, New Hampton Parts, info, USPO, **W** 🍴 Homestead Rest. (2mi), ⊙ RV Park (2mi), ski area
22 (62)	NH 127, Sanbornton, **1-5 mi W** ⊙ 🏥, gas/dsl, food, 🏧
61mm	🅿 sb, full ♿ facilities, info, 🏧, 🗑 litter barrels, vending, petwalk
20 (57)	US 3, NH 11, NH 132, NH 140, Tilton, **E** ⛽ Irving/Circle

Exit	Services
20 (57)	Continued
	K/dsl/24hr, Shell/Subway/dsl, 🍴 Applebees, Burger King, Chicago Grill, Dunkin Donuts, Green Ginger Chinese, KFC, McDonald's, 99 Rest., Starbucks, Thai Cuisine, Tilt'n Diner, UpperCrust Pizza, Wendy's, 🛏 Hampton Inn, Holiday Inn Express, Super 8, ⊙ BJ's Whse/gas, Home Depot, Old Navy, Shaw's Foods/Osco Drug, Staples, Tanger Outlet/famous brands, VIP Auto, Walgreens, **W** 🍴 Chili's, Pizza Hut, ⊙ Chrysler/Dodge/Jeep, Ford, Kohl's, Lowe's, MktBasket Foods, Nissan, VW, Walmart/auto, USPO
56mm	Winnipesaukee River
19 (55)	NH 132 (from nb no ez return), Franklin, **W** ⛽ Gulf, ⊙ 🏥 NH Vet Home, antiques
51mm	🅿 nb, full ♿ facilities, 🏧, info, 🗑 litter barrels, vending, petwalk
18 (49)	to NH 132, Canterbury, **E** ⛽ Sunoco, ⊙ to Shaker Village HS
17 (46)	US 4 W, to US 3, NH 132, Boscawen, **4 mi W** gas
16 (41)	NH 132, E Concord, **E** ⛽ Mobil/dsl, ⊙ Quality Cash Mkt
15W (40)	US 202 W, to US 3, N Main St, Concord, **W** ⛽ Citgo, Cumberland/Dunkin Donuts, Hess, 🍴 Domino's, Friendly's, 🛏 Courtyard/café
15E	I-393 E, US 4 E, to Portsmouth
14 (39)	NH 9, Loudon Rd, Concord, **E** ⛽ Shell/dsl, 🍴 Boloco Burritos, Chicago Grill, Moritomo Japanese, Outback Steaks, Panera Bread, Wok Inn, ⊙ AAA, Ace Hardware, AutoZone, $Tree, GNC, Hannaford Foods, LLBean, Lowe's, Mkt Basket Foods, PetCo, Radio Shack, Rite Aid, Shaws Foods/24hr, Staples, TJ Maxx, Verizon, USPO, **1-2 mi E on Loudon Rd** ⛽ Irving/Circle K/Subway/dsl, Mobil, 7-11, Shell/dsl, Sunoco, 🍴 Applebee's, Arnie's Place, Burger King, D'angelo's, Dunkin Donuts, Friendly's, KFC, LJ Silver/Taco Bell, Longhorn Steaks, McDonald's, Newick's Lobster House, 99 Rest., Olive Garden, PapaGino's, Pizza Hut, Red Apple Buffet, Ruby Tuesday, Starbucks, Sunshine Oriental, TGIFriday's, Wendy's, Windmill Rest., ⊙ Advance Parts, Best Buy, BonTon, Dick's, Home Depot, JC Penney, Michael's, Petsmart, Sam's Club/gas, Sears/auto, Shaw's Foods/Osco Drug, Target, TownFair Tire, Verizon, Walgreens, city park, Walmart, **W** ⛽ Citgo, Gulf/dsl, Hess, 🍴 Domino's, Gas Lighter Rest., Nonni's Rest., Siam Orchid, Tea Garden Rest., 🛏 Holiday Inn, ⊙ Pill MktPlace, to state offices, hist sites, museum
13 (38)	to US 3, Manchester St, Concord, **E** ⛽ Gulf, Sunoco/dsl/deli, 🍴 Beefside Rest., Cityside Grille, Dunkin Donuts, Ichiban Japanese, Kaylen's Pizza, Red Blazer Rest., ⊙ Buick/GMC, Cadillac/Chevrolet, Chrysler/Dodge/Jeep, Harley-Davidson, Kia, Lincoln, Nissan, Outdoor RV Ctr Subaru, Tire Whse, VIP Auto, Volvo, **W** ⛽ Hess, Mobil/dsl, 🍴 Burger King, Common Man Diner, D'angelo's, KFC, McDonald's, 🛏 Best Western, Comfort Inn, Fairfield Inn, Residence Inn, ⊙ 🏥, Aubuchon Hardware, CVS Drug, Firestone, Goodyear/auto, NAPA
12N (37)	NH 3A N, S Main, **E** ⛽ Gulf, Irving/Subway/dsl/24hr, 🍴 Dunkin Donuts, 🛏 Days Inn, ⊙ Ford, Honda, Hyundai, Mazda, Toyota/Scion, **W** ⊙ 🏥
12S	NH 3A S, Bow Junction
36mm	I-89 N to Lebanon, **toll road begins/ends**
31mm	🅿 both lanes, full ♿ facilities, info, 🏧, vending
11 (28)	NH 3A, to Hooksett **toll plaza**, 🏧, **4 mi E** ⛽ Trkstp/dsl/rest.
28mm	I-293, Everett Tpk

WOODSTOCK

NH

CONCORD

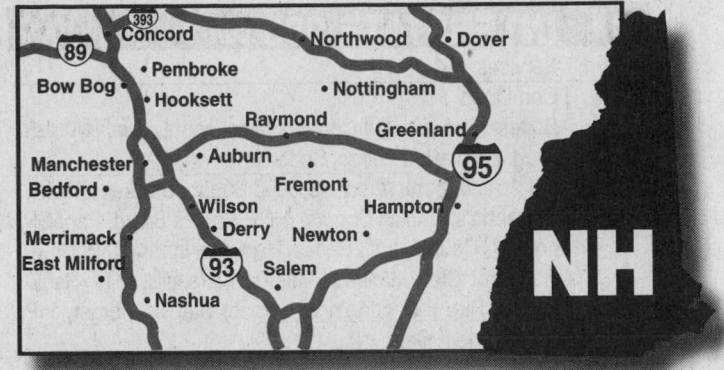

⬆N INTERSTATE 93 CONT'D

Exit	Services
10 (27)	NH 3A, Hooksett, **E** ⛽ Irving/Circle K/dsl, 🍴 Dunkin Donuts, Subway, Wendy's, ⦿ BJ's Whse, Home Depot, Kohl's, Staples, Target, **W** ⛽ Irving/Circle K/Dunkin Donuts/dsl, ⦿ Lowe's, Walmart
26mm	Merrimac River
9N S (24)	US 3, NH 28, Manchester, **E** 🏠 Fairfield Inn, **W** ⛽ Manchester/dsl, Sunoco/dsl, 🍴 Burger King, Cheng Du Chinese, D'Angelo's, Happy Garden Chinese, KFC, La Carreta Mexican, Lusia's Italian, PapaGino's, Puritan Rest., Shogun Japanese, Shorty's Mexican, Subway, ⦿ 🅷, Chrysler/Dodge/Jeep, Ford, Hannaford Foods, Kia, Lincoln, U-Haul, VIP Auto, city park
8 (23)	to NH 28a, Wellington Rd, **W** VA 🅷, Currier Gallery
7 (22)	NH 101 E, to Portsmouth, Seacoast
6 (21)	Hanover St, Candia Rd, Manchester, **E** 🍴 Dunkin Donuts, Wendy's, ⦿ vet, **W** ⛽ Citgo/dsl, Mobil/dsl, Shell, 🍴 McDonald's, Subway, ⦿ Hannaford Foods, repair
19mm	I-293 W, to Manchester (from nb), to 🛈
5 (15)	NH 28, to N Londonderry, **E** ⛽ Sunoco/Dunkin Donuts/dsl, 🍴 Poor Boy's Diner, **W** ⛽ Shell/dsl, 🍴 Subway, 🏠 Sleep Inn
4 (12)	NH 102, Derry, **E** ⛽ Citgo/dsl, Mobil, Rte 102 Gas, Shell/24hr, Sunoco/dsl, 🍴 Burger King, Cracker Barrel, Derry Rest., Poorboys Drive-In, Subway, ⦿ 🅷, R. Frost Farm, **W** ⛽ Global, Gulf/dsl/repair, Hess, 7-11, 🍴 Avandi's Rest., Dunkin Donuts, KFC, McDonald's, 99 Rest., PapaGino's, Taco Bell, Wendy's, ⦿ AT&T, Curves, Ford, Hannaford Foods, Home Depot, Mkt Basket Foods, Radio Shack, Shaw's Foods, Staples, TJ Maxx, USPO, Verizon, VIP Auto
7mm	**weigh sta both lanes**
3 (6)	NH 111, Windham, **E** ⛽ Mobil/McDonald's, 🍴 House of Plzza, Windham Rest., ⦿ vet, **W** ⛽ B&H, 🍴 Capri Pizza, Clemm's Bakery, Gourmet Grille, ⦿ Castleton Conference Ctr, CVS Drug, Osco Drug, Shaw's Foods, USPO
2 (3)	to NH 38, NH 97, Salem, **E** 🍴 Tuscan Kitchen, 🏠 Red Roof Inn, **W** 🍴 A&A Rest., Dunkin Donuts, Margarita's Cafe, 🏠 Holiday Inn, La Quinta
1 (2)	NH 28, Salem, **E** ⛽ BP/dsl, Citgo/dsl, Gulf, 🍴 Bickfords, Burger King, Chili's, Denny's, Grand China, LJ Silver, McDonald's, 99 Rest., Taco Bell, T-Bones, 🏠 Park View Inn, ⦿ AT&T, Barnes&Noble, Best Buy, Home Depot, JC Penney, Kohl's, K-Mart, Lord&Taylor, Macy's, Marshall's, MktBasket Foods, Michael's, NTB, PetCo, Radio Shack, Sears/auto, Shaw's Foods, Staples, Target, TJ Maxx, TownFair Tire, mall, racetrack
1mm	**Welcome Ctr nb, full** ♿ **facilities, info,** 🚻, 🗑 **litter barrels, vending, petwalk**
0mm	New Hampshire/Massachusetts state line

⬆N INTERSTATE 95

Exit	Services
17mm	New Hampshire/Maine state line, Piscataqua River
7 (16)	Market St, Portsmouth, Port Authority, waterfront hist sites, **E** 🏠 Sheraton, **0-2 mi W** ⛽ BP, Gulf, Mobil, 🍴 Applebee's, D'Angelo's, Dunkin Donuts, Panera Bread, Ruby Tuesday, Wendy's, 🏠 Courtyard, Hampton Inn, Homewood Suites, ⦿ BJ's Whse/gas, Chevrolet, $Tree, K-Mart, Marshall's, MktBasket Foods, PepBoys, PetCo, Rite Aid, Shaw's Foods, TJ Maxx, Verizon
6 (15)	Woodbury Ave (from nb), Portsmouth, **E** 🏠 Best Inn, **W** same as 7
5 (14)	US 1, US 4, NH 16, The Circle, Portsmouth, **E** ⛽ Citgo/dsl, Gulf, Shell/dsl, 🍴 Roudabout Diner, 🏠 Anchorage Inn, Best Inn, Best Western, Fairfield Inn, Holiday Inn, Port Inn, ⦿ 🅷, Buick/Cadillac/GMC, U-Haul, **W** ⛽ Gulf, 🍴 D'Angelo's, Longhorn Steaks, McDonald's, 🏠 Hampton Inn, Motel 6, Residence Inn, ⦿ Barnes&Noble, Best Buy, Dick's, Ford, Home Depot, Kohl's, Mazda, Michael's, Nissan, Old Navy, Staples
4 (13.5)	US 4 (exits left from nb), to White Mtns, Spaulding TPK, **E** 🅷, **W** to Pease Int Trade Port
3a (13)	NH 33, Greenland
3b (12)	NH 33, to Portsmouth, **E** 🅷, **0-2 mi W** ⛽ Sunoco/dsl, TA/dsl/rest./scales/24hr/@, 🍴 Dunkin Donuts, McDonald's, ⦿ Lowe's, Mercedes, Target, VW
6.5mm	**toll plaza**
2 (6)	NH 101, to Hampton, **E** 🅷
4mm	Taylor River
1 (1)	NH 107, to Seabrook, **toll rd begins/ends**, **E** ⛽ BP, Irving/Circle K/dsl, 1 Stop, Prime, Richdale, Sunoco/Subway/dsl, Xtra, 🍴 Applebees, Chili's, Dunkin Donuts, HoneyDew Donuts, KFC/Taco Bell, McDonald's, 99 rest., PapaGino's, Pizza Hut, Sal's Pizza, Starbucks, Wendy's, 🏠 Hampshire Inn, Holiday Inn Express, ⦿ Advance Parts, AutoZone, CVS Drug, $Tree, GNC, Home Depot, Jo-Ann Fabrics, Kohl's, Lowe's, MktBasket Foods, NTB, Radio Shack, Shaw's Foods, Staples, Sullivan Tire, TJ Maxx, TownFair Tire, Walmart, to Seacoast RA, **W** ⛽ Citgo, 🍴 McGrath's Dining, 🏠 Best Western, ⦿ NAPA, Sam's Club
.5mm	**Welcome Ctr nb, full** ♿ **facilities,** 🚻, **vending,** 🗑 **litter barrels, petwalk**
0mm	New Hampshire/Massachusetts state line

⬆N INTERSTATE 293

Exit	Services
8 (9)	I-93, N to Concord, S to Derry. **I-293 begins/ends on I-93, 28mm.**
7 (6.5)	NH 3A N, Dunbarton Rd (from nb)
6 (6)	Amoskeag Rd, Goffstown, **E** ⛽ Sunoco/dsl, **W** ⛽ Mobil, Shell/dsl, 🍴 Dunkin Donuts, Hot Stone Pizza, ⦿ 🅷
5 (5)	Granite St, Manchester, **E** 🏠 Radisson, **W** ⛽ Gulf, 7-11, 🍴 Dunkin Donuts, ⦿ 🅷, Walgreens, tires
4 (4)	US 3, NH 3A, NH 114A, Queen City Br, **E** ⛽ 7-11, Mobil/dsl, Sunoco, 🍴 Emperial Kitchen, 🏠 Elliott Hotel, **W on US 3** ⛽ Hess/dsl, Mobil, Z1 Gas/dsl, 🍴 Applebee's, Burger King, Chen's Garden, CJ's Grill, Clam King, D'angelo's, DQ, Dunkin Donuts, KC's Rib Shack, KFC, Little Caesars, McDonald's, Outback Steaks, Panera Bread, Taco Bell, T-

Manchester · Derry · Salem · Seabrook

⬆N INTERSTATE 293 CONT'D

Exit	Services
4 (4)	Continued
	Bones, Wendy's, 🛏 Comfort Inn, EconoLodge, ⊙ CVS Drug, Hannaford Foods, Subaru
3 (3)	NH 101, **0-2 mi W on US 3** 🅖 Bugaboo Creek Steaks, Carrabba's, Dunkin Donuts, IHOP, Panera Bread, PapaGino's, 🛏 Country Inn& Suites, Hampton Inn, ⊙ CVS Drug, House of Cloth, Lowe's, Macy's, Marshalls, Mini, Radio Shack, Rite Aid, Stop'n Shop/gas, Staples, Target, VIP Auto, **Urgent Care**, vet
2.5mm	Merrimac River
2 (2)	NH 3A, Brown Ave, **S** 🅖 Mobil/dsl, 7-11, Shell/Subway/dsl, 🍴🔧 Diner, Dunkin Donuts, McDonald's, 🛏 Holiday Inn, Super 8, ⊙ Manchester ✈
1 (1)	NH 28, S Willow Rd, **N** 🅖 Irving, Mobil/dsl, Sunoco/dsl, 🍴 Boston Mkt, Burger King, Cactus Jack's, Chili's, Chipotle Mexican, Coldstone, D'angelo's, Dunkin Donuts, 5 Guys Burgers, Friendly's, McDonald's, Panera Bread,

1 (1)	Continued
	PapaGino's, Papa John's, Pizza Hut, Quiznos, Sal's Pizza, Starbucks, Taco Bell, Wendy's, Yee Dynasty Chinese, 🛏 Fairfield Inn, Holiday Inn Express, Sheraton, ⊙ 🅗, AT&T, AutoZone, Batteries+, Buick/GMC, Chevrolet, CVS Drug, $Tree, GMC, Harley-Davidson, Hannaford Foods, Home Depot, Michael's, PepBoys, PetCo, Petsmart, Mazda, Radio Shack, Sam's Club, Shaw's Foods/Osco Drug, Stop'n Shop, Sullivan Tire/repair, Tire Whse, TJ Maxx, Town-Fair Tire, U-Haul, Verizon, Volvo, VW, vet, **S** 🅖 Shell, 🍴 Bertucci's, ChuckeCheese, D'angelo's, Dunkin Donuts, Famous Dave's, FoodCourt, Great Buffet, La Carreta, Longhorn Steaks, 99 Rest., Olive Garden, Ruby Tuesday, TGIFriday's, 🛏 Courtyard, TownePlace Suites, ⊙ 🅗 Barnes&Noble, Best Buy, Ford, Hobby Lobby, Honda, Hyundai, JC Penney, Lexus, LL Bean, Lowe's, Nissan, Macy's, NTB, Old Navy, Sears/auto, Staples, Toyota/Scion, Walmart, mall
0mm	I-93, N to Concord, S to Derry. **I-293 begins/ends on I-93.**

NEW JERSEY

⬆E INTERSTATE 78

Exit	Services
58b a	US 1N, US 9N, NJ Tpk
57	US 1S, US 9S, **N** 🛏 Holiday Inn, Ramada Inn, Sheraton, **S** 🛏 Courtyard, Fairfield Inn, SpringHill Suites, ⊙ to Newark ✈
56	Clinton Ave (exits left from eb)
55	Irvington (from wb), **N** 🅖 Delta, 🍴 Wendy's, ⊙ 🅗, Goodyear
54	Hillside, Irvington (from eb), **N** 🅖 Delta, 🍴 Wendy's, ⊙ 🅗 Goodyear
52	Garden State Pkwy
50b a	Millburn (from wb), **N** 🅖 BP, Exxon, Lukoil, 🍴 Manny's Wieners, ⊙ Best Buy, Firestone/auto, Ford/Lincoln, Home Depot Superstore, Target, USPO, Whole Foods Mkt
49b a	NJ 124 (from eb), to Maplewood, same as 50b a
48	to NJ 24, to I-287 N, (exits left from eb), Springfield
48mm	I-78 eb divides into express & local
45	NJ 527 (from eb), Glenside Ave, Summit
44	(from eb), to Berkeley Heights, New Providence
43	to New Providence, Berkeley Heights
41	to Berkeley Heights, Scotch Plains
40	NJ 531, The Plainfields, **S** 🅖 Valero, ⊙ 🅗
36	NJ 651, to Warrenville, Basking Ridge, **N** 🅖 Exxon/repair, 🍴 Dunkin Donuts, ⊙ A&P, **S** 🅖 Exxon
33	NJ 525, to Martinsville, Bernardsville, USGA Golf Museum, **N** 🍴 Ciao Italian, LingLing Chinese, Starbucks, 🛏 Courtyard, Hotel Indigo, Somerset Hills Inn, **S** 🅖 Exxon/7-11, 🍴 Panera Bread
32mm	scenic overlook wb
29	I-287, to US 202, US 206, I-80, to Morristown, Somerville, **S** 🅗
26	NJ 523 spur, to North Branch, Lamington
24	NJ 523, to NJ 517, to Oldwick, Whitehouse, **2-3 mi S** 🅖 Exxon/dsl, 🍴 McDonald's, Readington Diner, Starbucks
20b a	NJ 639 (from wb), to Cokesbury, Lebanon, **S** 🅖 Exxon, Shell, Sunoco, 🍴 Bagelsmith Deli, Dunkin Donuts, Kirst

20b a	Continued
	en's Italian Grill, 🛏 Courtyard, ⊙ to Round Valley RA
18	US 22 E, Annandale, Lebanon, **N** 🅗, same as 17, **S** Honda
17	NJ 31 S, Clinton, **N** 🅖 Exxon, Hess, Valero/dsl, 🍴 Baskin-Robbins/Dunkin Donuts, Blimpie, Country Griddle, Finnigan's, McDonald's, ⊙ to Voorhees SP
16	NJ 31 N (from eb), Clinton, **N** same as 17
15	NJ 173 E, to Pittstown, Clinton, **N** 🅖 Express/repair, Shell/dsl, 🍴 Subway, 🛏 Holiday Inn Select, ⊙ museum, **S** 🍴 Cracker Barrel, Frank's Italian, Hunan Wok, Quiznos, 🛏 Hampton Inn, ⊙ 🅗, GNC, ShopRite Foods, TJMaxx, Verizon, Walmart/McDonald's
13	NJ 173 W (from wb), **N** 🍴 Clinton Sta Diner, same as 12
12	NJ 173, to Jutland, Norton, **N** 🅖 Clinton/dsl, Exxon, Dunkin Donuts/dsl, 🚛/Subway/dsl/scales/24hr, 🍴 Grand Colonial Rest., ⊙ vet, to Spruce Run RA, **S** 🅖 Shell/dsl, 🍴 Bagelsmith Deli, Perryville Inn Rest.
11	NJ 173, West Portal, Pattenburg, **N** 🅖 Mobil, Shell/pizza/dsl, 🍴 Chalet Rest., Landslide Rest., ⊙ Jugtown Camping, st police
8mm	🅡ⓢ **both lanes, 🗑, litter barrels, no restrooms**
7	NJ 173, to Bloomsbury, West Portal, **N** RV camping, **S** 🅖 Citgo/deli, 🚛/Subway/dsl/scales/24hr, TA/Burger King/Country Pride/dsl/scales/24hr/@
6mm	**weigh sta both lanes**
6	Warren Glen, Asbury (from eb)
4	Warren Glen, Stewartsville (from wb)
3	US 22, NJ 173, to Phillipsburg, **0-2 mi N** 🅖 Getty/dsl, Hess/dsl, Penn Jersey Trkstp/dsl/scales/24hr, US/dsl, 🍴 Applebee's, Burger King, Friendly's, Key City Diner, McDonald's, Panera Bread, Perkins, Pizza Hut, Ruby Tuesday, Sammy's Drive-in, Sonic, Taco Bell, 🛏 Phillipsburg Inn, ⊙ 🅗, Advance Parts, Best Buy, BonTon, $Tree, Home Depot, Honda, JC Penney, Kohl's, Lowe's, Michael's, Old Navy, PetCo, ShopRite Foods, Staples, Stop&Shop, Target, Walmart, **S** ⊙ Chevrolet
0mm	New Jersey/Pennsylvania state line, Delaware River

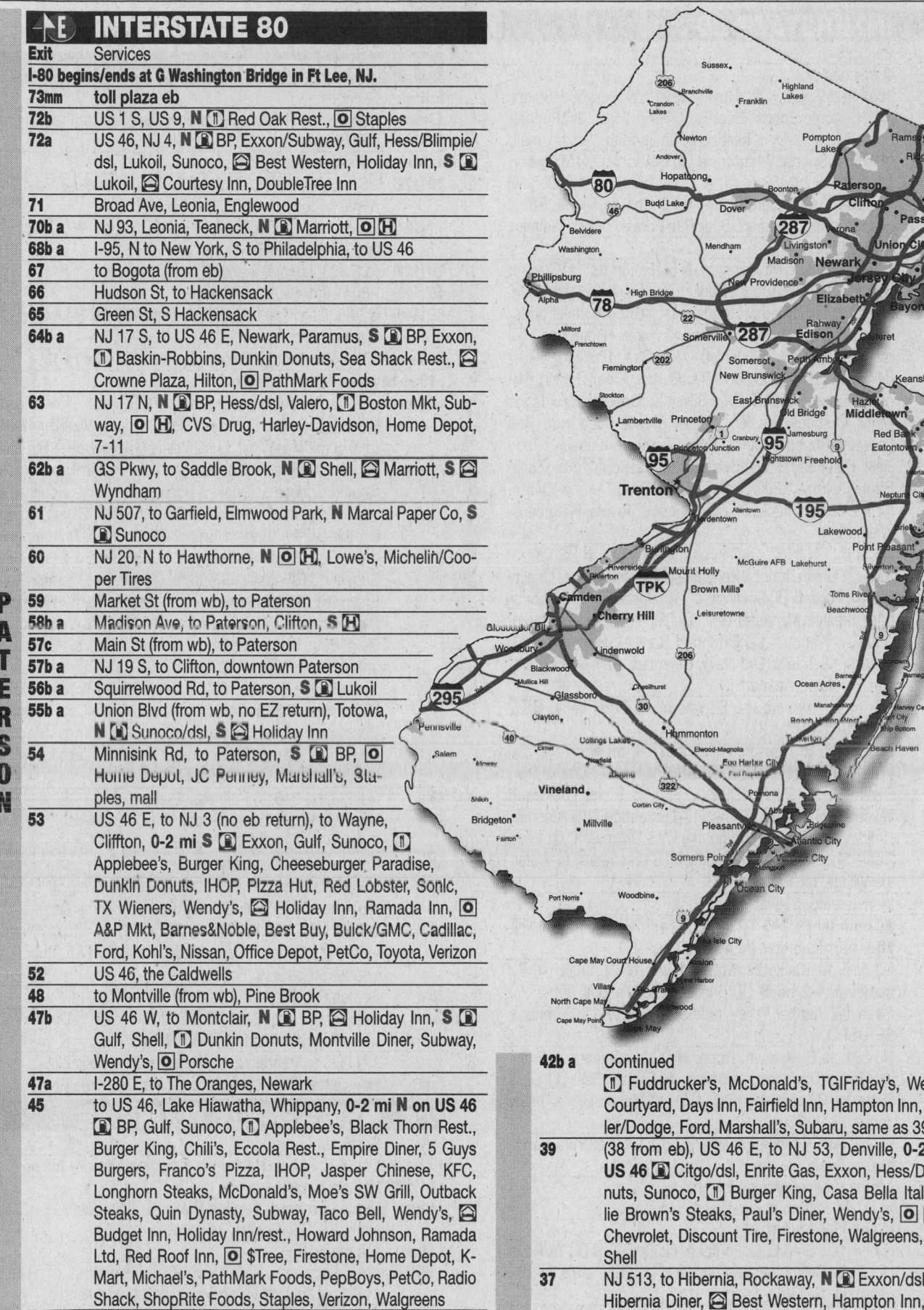

INTERSTATE 80

Exit	Services
	I-80 begins/ends at G Washington Bridge in Ft Lee, NJ.
73mm	toll plaza eb
72b	US 1 S, US 9, **N** 🍴 Red Oak Rest., 🅾 Staples
72a	US 46, NJ 4, **N** 🅿 BP, Exxon/Subway, Gulf, Hess/Blimpie/dsl, Lukoil, Sunoco, 🛏 Best Western, Holiday Inn, **S** 🅿 Lukoil, 🛏 Courtesy Inn, DoubleTree Inn
71	Broad Ave, Leonia, Englewood
70b a	NJ 93, Leonia, Teaneck, **N** 🛏 Marriott, 🅾 🏥
68b a	I-95, N to New York, S to Philadelphia, to US 46
67	to Bogota (from eb)
66	Hudson St, to Hackensack
65	Green St, S Hackensack
64b a	NJ 17 S, to US 46 E, Newark, Paramus, **S** 🅿 BP, Exxon, 🍴 Baskin-Robbins, Dunkin Donuts, Sea Shack Rest., 🛏 Crowne Plaza, Hilton, 🅾 PathMark Foods
63	NJ 17 N, **N** 🅿 BP, Hess/dsl, Valero, 🍴 Boston Mkt, Subway, 🅾 🏥, CVS Drug, Harley-Davidson, Home Depot, 7-11
62b a	GS Pkwy, to Saddle Brook, **N** 🅿 Shell, 🛏 Marriott, **S** 🛏 Wyndham
61	NJ 507, to Garfield, Elmwood Park, **N** Marcal Paper Co, **S** 🅿 Sunoco
60	NJ 20, N to Hawthorne, **N** 🅾 🏥, Lowe's, Michelin/Cooper Tires
59	Market St (from wb), to Paterson
58b a	Madison Ave, to Paterson, Clifton, **S** 🏥
57c	Main St (from wb), to Paterson
57b a	NJ 19 S, to Clifton, downtown Paterson
56b a	Squirrelwood Rd, to Paterson, **S** 🅿 Lukoil
55b a	Union Blvd (from wb, no EZ return), Totowa, **N** 🅿 Sunoco/dsl, **S** 🛏 Holiday Inn
54	Minnisink Rd, to Paterson, **S** 🅿 BP, 🅾 Home Depot, JC Penney, Marshall's, Staples, mall
53	US 46 E, to NJ 3 (no eb return), to Wayne, Cliffton, **0-2 mi S** 🅿 Exxon, Gulf, Sunoco, 🍴 Applebee's, Burger King, Cheeseburger Paradise, Dunkin Donuts, IHOP, Pizza Hut, Red Lobster, Sonic, TX Wieners, Wendy's, 🛏 Holiday Inn, Ramada Inn, 🅾 A&P Mkt, Barnes&Noble, Best Buy, Buick/GMC, Cadillac, Ford, Kohl's, Nissan, Office Depot, PetCo, Toyota, Verizon
52	US 46, the Caldwells
48	to Montville (from wb), Pine Brook
47b	US 46 W, to Montclair, **N** 🅿 BP, 🛏 Holiday Inn, **S** 🅿 Gulf, Shell, 🍴 Dunkin Donuts, Montville Diner, Subway, Wendy's, 🅾 Porsche
47a	I-280 E, to The Oranges, Newark
45	to US 46, Lake Hiawatha, Whippany, **0-2 mi N on US 46** 🅿 BP, Gulf, Sunoco, 🍴 Applebee's, Black Thorn Rest., Burger King, Chili's, Eccola Rest., Empire Diner, 5 Guys Burgers, Franco's Pizza, IHOP, Jasper Chinese, KFC, Longhorn Steaks, McDonald's, Moe's SW Grill, Outback Steaks, Quin Dynasty, Subway, Taco Bell, Wendy's, 🛏 Budget Inn, Holiday Inn/rest., Howard Johnson, Ramada Ltd, Red Roof Inn, 🅾 $Tree, Firestone, Home Depot, K-Mart, Michael's, PathMark Foods, PepBoys, PetCo, Radio Shack, ShopRite Foods, Staples, Verizon, Walgreens
43b a	I-287, to US 46, Boonton, Morristown
42b a	US 202, US 46, to Morris Plains, Parsippany, **0-1 mi N on US 46** 🅿 Delta/Dunkin Donuts/dsl, Exxon, Shell, Sunoco,
42b a	Continued 🍴 Fuddrucker's, McDonald's, TGIFriday's, Wendy's, 🛏 Courtyard, Days Inn, Fairfield Inn, Hampton Inn, 🅾 Chrysler/Dodge, Ford, Marshall's, Subaru, same as 39
39	(38 from eb), US 46 E, to NJ 53, Denville, **0-2 mi N on US 46** 🅿 Citgo/dsl, Enrite Gas, Exxon, Hess/Dunkin Donuts, Sunoco, 🍴 Burger King, Casa Bella Italian, Charlie Brown's Steaks, Paul's Diner, Wendy's, 🅾 🏥, BMW, Chevrolet, Discount Tire, Firestone, Walgreens, vet, **S** 🅿 Shell
37	NJ 513, to Hibernia, Rockaway, **N** 🅿 Exxon/dsl, Shell, 🍴 Hibernia Diner, 🛏 Best Western, Hampton Inn, **S** 🅿 BP, 🅾 🏥
35b a	to Dover, Mount Hope, **S** 🅿 Exxon, 🍴 Coldstone, Dunkin Donuts, Fat Burger, La Salsa Mexican, Olive Garden, Quiz-

P A T E R S O N (vertical text, left margin)

🅟 = gas 🍴 = food 🛏 = lodging 🅾 = other 🆁🆂 = rest stop   Copyright 2014 - The NEXT Exit ®

◀E INTERSTATE 80 CONT'D

Exit	Services
35b a	Continued
	nos, Red Robin, 🛏 Hilton Garden, Homewood Suites, 🅾 Ⓗ, Acme Foods, Best Buy, FoodWorks, JC Penney, Lord&Taylor, Macy's, Michael's, Sears/auto, Verizon, mall
34b a	NJ 15, to Sparta, Wharton, **N** 🅟 Exxon/dsl, 🍴 Ming Buffet, Subway, 🅾 Rite Aid, **S** 🍴 Dunkin Donuts, Good 5 Chinese, Townsquare Diner, 🅾 Ⓗ, Costco, Dick's, $Tree, Home Depot, Petsmart, ShopRite Foods, Target, Walmart
32mm	truck 🆁🆂 wb
30	Howard Blvd, to Mt Arlington, **N** 🅟 Exxon/dsl, 🍴 Cracker Barrel, Davy's Hotdogs, Dunkin Donuts, IHOP, Wingman, 🛏 Courtyard, Holiday Inn Express, 🅾 QuickChek Foods
28	US 46, to NJ 10, to Ledgewood, Lake Hopatcong, **1-2 mi S on US 46, NJ 10** 🅟 Delta Gas, Gas&Go, Hess/dsl, Sunoco, 🍴 Boston Mkt, Burger King, Dunkin Donuts, Fuddruckers, KFC/LJ Silver, McDonald's, Muldoons Diner, Outback Steaks, Panera Bread, Pizza Hut, Red Lobster, Roxbury Diner, Ruby Tuesday, Subway, Taco Bell, TGIFriday's, Wendy's, White Castle, 🅾 AutoZone, Barnes&Noble, BJ's Whse, CVS Drug, Home Depot, Kohl's, Radio Shack, ShopRite Foods, Toyota, Walgreens, Walmart
27	US 206 S, NJ 182, to Netcong, Somerville, **N** 🅟 Valero/dsl, 🍴 Dunkin Donuts, Perkins, 🛏 Comfort Suites, Quality Inn, 🅾 Ford, **S** 🅟 Shell/dsl, 🍴 Applebee's, Chili's, Longhorn Steaks, Macaroni Grill, McDonald's, Panera Bread, Subway, Wendy's, 🛏 Extended Stay America, 🅾 AT&T, Lowe's, Michael's, Old Navy, Petsmart, Sam's Club, Staples, TJMaxx, Walmart
26	US 46 W (from wb, no EZ return), to Budd Lake, **S** 🅟 Shell/dsl, same as 27
25	US 206 N, to Newton, Stanhope, **1-2 mi N on US 206** 🅟 Exxon, Shell/dsl, 🍴 Blackforest Rest., Byram Diner, Byram Pizza, Dunkin Donuts, Frank's Pizza, Lockwood Tavern, McDonald's, Subway, 🛏 Extended Stay America, Holiday Inn, Residence Inn, 🅾 CVS Drug, GNC, Nissan, Radio Shack, ShopRite Foods, STS tires/repair, to Waterloo Village, Int Trade Ctr, vet
23.5mm	Musconetcong River
21mm	🆁🆂 both lanes, NO TRUCKS, scenic overlook (eb), 🛅, litter barrels, petwalk, no facilities
19	NJ 517, to Hackettstown, Andover, **N** 🅟 Shell, 🅾 RV camping, **1-2 mi S** 🅟 Shell, 🍴 Foxy's Grill, Terranova Pizza, 🛏 Panther Valley Inn/rest., 🅾 Ⓗ, 7-11, Stephen's SP, USPO
12	NJ 521, to Blairstown, Hope, **N** 🍴 Mediterranean Diner, 🅾 Harley-Davidson, st police, **S** 🅟 US Gas, 🍴 Gio's Pizza, 🅾 RV camping (5mi), Land of Make Believe, Jenny Jump SF, USPO
7mm	🆁🆂 eb, full ♿ facilities, info, 🄲, 🛅, litter barrels, vending, petwalk
6mm	scenic overlook wb, no trailers
4c	to NJ 94 N (from eb), to Blairstown
4b	to US 46 E, to Buttzville
4a	NJ 94, to US 46 E, to Portland, Columbia, **N** 🅟 TA/Pizza Hut/Taco Bell/dsl/scales/24hr/@, 🍴 McDonald's, 🅾 RV camping, **S** USPO
3.5mm	Hainesburg Rd (from wb), accesses services at 4
1mm	Worthington SF, **S** 🆁🆂 both lanes, restrooms, info, 🛅, litter barrels, petwalk

(side tab: STANHOPE)

Exit	Services
1	to Millbrook (from wb), **N** Worthington SF
0mm	New Jersey/Pennsylvania state line, Delaware River

▲N INTERSTATE 95

Exit	Services
124mm	New Jersey/New York state line, Geo Washington Br, Hudson River
123mm	Palisades Pkwy (from sb)
72 (122)	US 1, US 9, US 46, Ft Lee, **E** 🅟 Mobil, Shell, 🛏 Courtesy Motel, Hilton
71 (121)	Broad Ave, Leonia, Englewood, **E** 🅟 Shell, **W** 🅟 Gulf, 🛏 Day's Inn, Executive Inn
70 (120)	to NJ 93, Leonia, Teaneck, **W** 🛏 Marriott
69 (119)	I-80 W (from sb), to Paterson
68 (118)	US 46, Challenger Blvd, Ridgefield Park, **E** 🅟 Exxon, 🛏 Hampton Inn

I-95 and NJ Turnpike run together sb. See NJ TPK, exits 7a-18

I-95 nb becomes I-295 sb at US1

Exit	Services
67b a	US 1, to Trenton, New Brunswick, **E** 🅟 Shell, 🍴 Michael's Diner, 🛏 Howard Johnson, Sleepy Hollow Motel, 🅾 Acura, **0-3 mi W** 🅟 Gulf, LukOil/dsl, 🍴 Applebee's, Big Fish Bistro, Cheeburger Cheeburger, Chevy's Mexican, Chili's, ChuckECheese's, Dunkin Donuts, Hooters, Houlihan's, Joe's Crabshack, Macaroni Grill, NY Deli, Olive Garden, On-the-Border, Panera Bread, PF Chang's, Princetonian Diner, Pure Rest., Red Lobster, Rita's Custard, Starbucks, Subway, TGIFriday's, Wendy's, 🛏 Clarion, Comfort Inn, Extended Stay America, Hyatt Place, Hyatt Regency, Red Roof Inn, Residence Inn, 🅾 AT&T, Barnes&Noble, Best Buy, Buick/Cadillac, Chevrolet, Dick's, Firestone/auto, Home Depot, JC Penney, Jo-Ann Fabrics, Kohl's, Lord&Taylor, Lowe's, Macy's, Marshall's, Michael's, Mini, NTB, Office Depot, Old Navy, PepBoys, PetCo, Petsmart, Ross, Sam's Club, Sears/auto, ShopRite Foods, Staples, Target, TJ Maxx, Trader Joe's, Verizon, Walmart, Wegman's Foods, Whole Foods Mkt, malls
8b a	NJ 583, NJ 546, to Princeton Pike
7b a	US 206, **W** 🍴 Tastee Subs, **W** 🅟 LukOil/dsl, 🍴 Fox's Pizza
5b a	Federal City Rd (sb only)
4b a	NJ 31, to Ewing, Pennington, **E** 🅟 Citgo/repair, Exxon/repair, LukOil/Dunkin Donuts/dsl, 🅾 Robbins Drug, 7-11, USPO, 🛏 SpringHill Suites, **W** 🅟 Exxon, LukOil/Blimpie/dsl, 🍴 Mizuki Asian, Starbucks, 🅾 AT&T, ShopRite Foods, Stop&Shop Foods
3b a	Scotch Rd, **E** 🛏 Courtyard, **W** Ⓗ
2	NJ 579, to Harbourton, **E** 🅟 LukOil (1mi), 🍴 Dunkin Donuts, Red Star Pizza, 🅾 7-11, **W** 🅟 BP
1	1 NJ 29, to Trenton, **2 mi W** museum, st police
0mm	New Jersey/Pennsylvania state line, Delaware River

(side tab: TRENTON)

▲N NEW JERSEY TURNPIKE

Exit	Services
18 (117)	US 46 E, Ft Lee, Hackensack, **last exit before toll sb**
17 (116)	Lincoln Tunnel
115mm	**Vince Lombardi Service Plaza nb** Sunoco/dsl, Big Boy, Nathan's, Roy Rogers, TCBY, gifts
114mm	**toll plaza**, 🄲
16W (113)	NJ 3, Secaucus, Rutherford, **E** 🅟 Hess, Shell, 🛏 Hilton, M Plaza Hotel, **W** 🛏 Sheraton, 🅾 Meadowlands
112mm	**Alexander Hamilton Service Area sb** Sunoco, Roy Rogers, gifts
16E (112)	NJ 3, Secaucus, **E** Lincoln Tunnel

NEW JERSEY TURNPIKE CONT'D

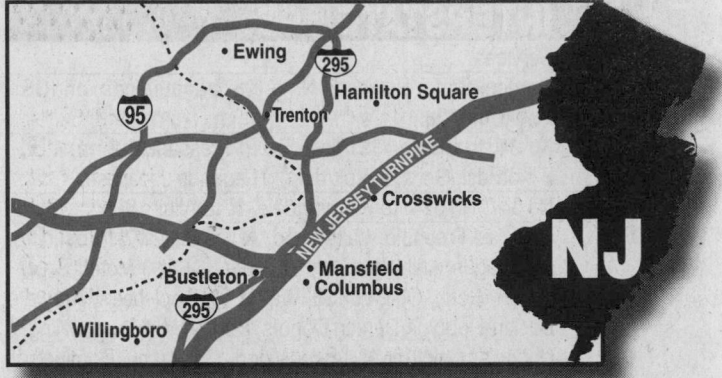

Exit	Services
15W (109)	I-280, Newark, The Oranges
15E (107)	US 1, US 9, Newark, Jersey City, **E** Lincoln Tunnel
14c	Holland Tunnel
14b	Jersey City
14a	Bayonne
14 (105)	I-78 W, US 1, US 9, **2 mi** **W** 🏠 Fairfield Inn, Holiday Inn, SpringHill Suites, 🅾 ✈
102mm	**Halsey Service Area,** Sunoco, Roy Rogers, other services in Elizabeth
13a (102)	Elizabeth, **E** 🏠 Courtyard, Extended Stay America, Residence Inn, **W** 🍴 McDonald's, 🏠 DoubleTree, Econolodge, Hilton, Sheraton, Wyndham Garden, services on US1/US9
13 (100)	I-278, to Verrazano Narrows Bridge
12 (96)	Carteret, Rahway, **E** 🍴 McDonald's, 🏠 Holiday Inn, **W** 🍴 Radisson
93mm	**Cleveland Service Area nb** 🍴 Nathans, Roy Roger's, Starbucks, **T Edison Service Area sb** 🅶 Sunoco/dsl, 🍴 Burger King, Dunkin Donuts, Popeye's, Sbarro's, Starbucks
11 (91)	US 9, Garden State Pkwy, to Woodbridge, **E** 🏠 Hampton Inn, Homestead Suites, 🅾 Home Depot
10 (88)	I-287, NJ 514, to Perth Amboy, **E** 🏠 Courtyard, **W** 🅶 Hess/dsl, 🏠 Holiday Inn
9 (83)	US 1, NJ 18, to New Brunswick, E Brunswick, **E** 🅶 Gulf, Hess/dsl, 🍴 Bone Fish Grill, Boston Mkt, Burger King, Carrabba's, Dunkin Donuts, Grand Buffet, KFC, Perkins, Starbucks, 🏠 Days Inn, Motel 6, 🅾 Best Buy, Goodyear/auto, Lowe's, Office Depot, Petsmart, Rite Aid, Sam's Club, Shopper's World Foods, ShopRite Foods, Staples, TJ Maxx, **W** 🅶 Exxon, 🍴 Fuddruckers, 🏠 Hilton, Holiday Inn Express, Howard Johnson
79mm	**Kilmer Service Area nb** 🅶 Sunoco/dsl, 🍴 Burger King, Cookies and Creamery, Sbarro, Starbucks
8a (74)	to Jamesburg, Cranbury, **W** 🏠 Courtyard, Crowne Plaza
72mm	**Pitcher Service Area sb** 🅶 Sunoco/dsl, 🍴 Arthur Treacher's, Cinnabon, Dick Clark's AB Grill, Nathan's, Roy Rogers, Starbucks
8 (67)	NJ 33, NJ 571, Hightstown, **E** 🅶 Hess/dsl, Petro/dsl, RaceWay, Shell/Dunkin Donuts, 🍴 Prestige Diner, 🏠 Days Inn, Hampton Inn, Holiday Inn, 🅾 CVS Drug, vet, **W** 🏠 Quality Inn
7a (60)	I-195 W to Trenton, E to Neptune
59mm	**Richard Stockton Service Area sb** 🅶 Sunoco/dsl, 🍴 Burger King, Pizza Hut, Quiznos, Starbucks, TCBY, **Woodrow Wilson Service Area nb** 🅶 Sunoco, 🍴 Nathan's, Roy Rogers
7 (54)	US 206, to Bordentown, to Ft Dix, McGuire AFB, to I-295, Trenton, **Services W on US 206** 🅶 Citgo, Delta/dsl, Exxon, Gulf, 🅻Loves/Wendy's/dsl/scales/24hr, Petro/Iron Skillet/dsl/scales/24hr/@, Sunoco, Valero/dsl, 🍴 Denny's, Dunkin Donuts, McDonald's, Wendy's, 🏠 Best Western, Comfort Inn, Days Inn, Hampton Inn, Ramada Inn, 🅾 WaWa
6 (51)	I-276, to PA Tpk
5 (44)	to Mount Holly, Willingboro, **E** 🅶 US Gas/dsl, 🍴 Applebee's, Charlie Brown's Steaks, Cracker Barrel, McDonald's, Recovery Grill, 🏠 Best Western, Hampton Inn, Hilton Garden, Quality Inn, **W** 🅶 BP, Exxon/dsl, Valero/dsl, 🍴 Burger King, China House, ChuckECheese's, Dunkin Donuts, IHOP, Subway, TGIFriday's, Quiznos, 🏠 Court
5 (44)	Continued yard, Holiday Inn Express, 🅾 $Tree, Home Depot, JC Penney, Kohl's, Sears/auto, Target, vet
39mm	**James Fenimore Cooper Service Area nb** 🅶 Sunoco/dsl, 🍴 Burger King, Cinnabon, Popeye's, Roy Rogers, TCBY, 🅾 gifts
4 (34)	NJ 73, to Philadelphia, Camden, **E** 🅶 Exxon, WaWa/dsl, 🍴 Chick-fil-A, Cracker Barrel, Chili's, Denny's, Dunkin Donuts, Macaroni Grill, McDonald's, On-the-Border, Sage Rest., TGIFriday's, Wendy's, 🏠 Candlewood Suites, Comfort Inn, Extended Stay America, Hampton Inn, Hilton Garden, Hyatt Place, Knights Inn, Rodeway Inn, Staybridge Suites, Wingate Inn, Wyndham Hotel, 🅾 BMW, Cadillac, Lexus, Rite Aid, 7-11, Toyota/Scion, Verizon, Whole Foods Mkt, **W** 🅶 Gulf/dsl, Hess, Lukoil, Shell, 🍴 Bob Evans, Burger King, Dunkin Donuts, KFC, Pizza Hut, 🏠 aLoft, Courtyard, DoubleTree Motel, Fairfield Inn, Marriott, Motel 6, Ramada Inn, Red Roof Inn, Super 8, 🅾 Lincoln, Mazda, transmissions, to st aquarium
30mm	**Walt Whitman Service Area, Walt Whitman Service Area sb** 🅶 Sunoco, 🍴 Cinnabon, Roy Rogers, Nathan's, TCBY, 🅾 gifts
3 (26)	NJ 168, Atlantic City Expwy, Walt Whitman Br, Camden, Woodbury, **E** 🅶 Pioneer, 7-11, WaWa, 🍴 Antonietta's, Bella Rizzo's Pizza, Luigi's Pizza, Pat's Pizza, Phily Diner, Rita's Custard, 🏠 Comfort Inn, Runnymead Suites, 🅾 CVS Drug, Toyota/Scion, Walgreens, **W** 🅶 Citgo, Gulf/repair, Shell/dsl, Shamrock/dsl, 🍴 Burger King, Club Diner, Dunkin Donuts, Italia Pizza, Wendy's, 🏠 Bellmawr Motel, Comfort Inn, EconoLodge, Holiday Inn, Howard Johnson, Motel 6, Red Roof Inn, Super 8, 🅾 CVS Drug, Walgreens, transmissions
2 (13)	US 322, to Swedesboro, **W** 🅶 Shell/Dunkin Donuts/dsl
5mm	**Barton Service Area sb** 🅶 Sunoco, Burger King, Nathan's, Pizza Hut, Starbucks, TCBY, **Fenwick Service Area nb** 🅶 Sunoco, 🍴 TCBY
1 (1.2)	Deepwater, **W** 🅶 Gulf, 🚛Subway/dsl/scales/24hr, 🏠 Comfort Inn, Friendship Motor Inn, Holiday Inn Express, Wellesley Inn
1mm	**toll road begins/ends**
2 (I-295)	I-295 N divides from toll road, I-295 S converges with toll road, **W** 🅶 Shell/Dunkin Donuts/dsl
1 (I-295)	NJ 49, to Pennsville, **E** 🅶 Exxon/dsl/repair, 🍴 Applebees, Burger King, Cracker Barrel, Dunkin Donuts, KFC/Taco Bell, McDonald's, Subway, 🏠 Hampton Inn, Super 8, 🅾 Peterbilt, **W** 🅶 Gulf, 🚛Subway/dsl/scales/24hr, 🏠 Best Value, Comfort Inn, Friendship Motor Inn, Quality Inn, Seaview Motel
0mm	New Jersey/Delaware state line, Delaware River, Delaware Memorial Bridge

🅰 = gas 🍴 = food 🛏 = lodging 🅾 = other 🆁🆂 = rest stop Copyright 2014 - The NEXT Exit ®

INTERSTATE 195

Exit	Services
36	Garden State Parkway N. **I-195 begins/ends on GS Pkwy, exit 98.**
35b a	NJ 34, to Brielle, GS Pkwy S., Pt Pleasant, **0-2 mi S** 🅰 Exxon/dsl, Getty, Lukoil/dsl, 🍴 Legends Japanese
31b a	NJ 547, NJ 524, to Farmingdale, **N** to Allaire SP
28b a	US 9, to Freehold, Lakewood, **N** 🅰 LukOil/7-11/dsl, 🍴 Ivy League Grill, Stewart's Drive-In, 🛏 At 9 Motel, **S** 🅰 Exxon, Getty, Gulf, LukOil, WaWa, 🍴 Applebee's, Arby's, Baskin-Robbins/Dunkin Donuts, Boston Mkt, Burger King, Carino's, Chick-fil-A, China Moon, Coldstone, Domino's, 5 Guys Burgers, Jersey Mike's Subs, Longhorn Steaks, Luigi's Pizza, McDonald's, Panera Bread, Pizza Hut, Rojo Loco, Ruby Tuesday, Sonic, Starbucks, Taco Bell, 🛏 Capri Inn, 🅾 Barnes&Noble, Best Buy, GNC, K-Mart, Kohl's, Lowe's, Michael's, PathMark Foods, PepBoys, PetCo, Petsmart, Radio Shack, Staples, Stop&Shop, Target, TJ Maxx, Verizon, Walgreens, Walmart/McDonald's, repair, USPO
22	to Jackson Mills, Georgia, **N** to Turkey Swamp Park, **2 mi S** 🍴 McDonald's, 🅾 ShopRite Foods
21	NJ 526, NJ 527, to Jackson, Siloam
16	NJ 537, to Freehold, **N** 🅰 Remington/dsl/LP, Sunoco, 🍴 DQ, FoodCourt, GianMarco's Pizza, Java Moon Café, 🅾 H, Jackson Outlets/famous brands, **S** 🅰 WaWa/dsl, 🍴 BellaV Pizzaria, Burger King, Chicken Holiday, Dunkin Donuts, KFC/LJ Silver, McDonald's, McGinns Pizzaria, Rio Grande Mexican, Tommy's Rest., 🅾 6Flags Themepark
11	NJ 524, Imlaystown, **S** to Horse Park of NJ
8	NJ 539, Hightstown, Allentown, **S** 🅰 Shell (1mi), Valero/repair, 🍴 American Hero Deli, 🅾 Crosswicks HP, vet
7	NJ 526 (no eb return), Robbinsville, Allentown, **1 mi S** 🍴 La Piazza Ristorante
6	NJ Tpk, **N** to NY, **S** to DE Memorial Br
5b a	US 130, **N** 🅰 Delta/dsl/repair, Valero/dsl, 🍴 Domino's, Dunkin Donuts, Rusert's Deli, ShrimpKing Rest., 🅾 AAA, Harley-Davidson, vet, **S** 🅰 GS Fuel/dsl, 🍴 Chick-fil-A, Chili's, China Grill, Cracker Barrel, DQ, Jersey Mike's Subs, Longhorn Steaks, McDonald's, Outback Steaks, Panera Bread, Red Robin, Ruby Tuesday, Subway, TGIFriday's, Wendy's, 🛏 Hilton Garden, 🅾 AT&T, Barnes&Noble, BJ's Whse, $Tree, GNC, Hamilton Shops/famous brands, Harry's Army Navy, Home Depot, Kohl's, Lowe's, Michael's, Old Navy, Petsmart, Ross, ShopRite Foods, Staples, USPO, Verizon, Walmart, mall, to state aquarium
3b a	Hamilton Square, Yardville, **N** 🅾 H
2	US 206 S, S Broad St, Yardville, **N** 🍴 Rosa's Ristorante, **S** 🅰 Shell, Valero, 🍴 Subway, 🅾 CVS Drug, Rite Aid, 7-11
1b a	US 206 (eb only), **N** 🍴 Circle Deli, Taco Bell, 🅾 Advance Parts, **S** 🍴 Papa John's, 🅾 ShopRite Foods
0mm	I-295, **I-195 begins/ends.**

INTERSTATE 287

Exit	Services
68mm	New Jersey/New York state line
66	NJ 17 S, Mahwah, **1-3 mi E** 🅰 Getty, Gulf, [Hess]/dsl, Royal, Sunoco, Valero/Subway/dsl, 🍴 Boston Mkt, Burger King, Dunkin Donuts, McDonald's, State Line Diner, Wendy's, 🛏 Best Western, Comfort Suites, Courtyard, Doubletree, Homewood Suites, Holiday Inn Express, Sheraton, Super 8, 🅾 Aamco, Chrysler/Jeep, GMC,
66	Continued Home Depot, Hyundai, Mini
59	NJ 208 S, Franklin Lakes, **W** 🍴 Blimpie, 🅾 Super Stop'n Shop Foods
58	US 202, Oakland, **E** 🅰 Gulf/dsl, Lukoil, 🍴 Dunkin Donuts, Mike's Doghouse, Jr's Pizza, Ruga Rest., 🅾 ShopRite Foods, Walgreens, **W** 🅰 Exxon/24hr
57	Skyline Dr, Ringwood
55	NJ 511, Pompton Lakes, **E** 🍴 Frank's Pizza, Quizno's, Wendy's, 🅾 A&P, **W** 🅰 Getty/dsl, 🍴 Baskin-Robbins, Burger King, Dunkin Donuts, 🛏 Holiday Inn Express, 🅾 Stop'n Shop
53	NJ 511A, rd 694, Bloomingdale, Pompton Lakes, **E** 🅰 Sunoco, Valero, 🍴 Blimpie, 🅾 USPO
52b a	NJ 23, Riverdale, Wayne, Butler, **0-3 mi E** 🅰 BP, Lukoil, United/dsl, 🍴 Baskin-Robbins, Dunkin Donuts, Friendly's, Fuddrucker's, McDonald's, Pompton Queen Diner, 23 Buffet, 🛏 Best Western, La Quinta, 🅾 H, A&P, Buick/GMC, Goodyear/auto, Honda, TJ Maxx, Toyota/Scion, **W** 🅰 Getty, Lukoil, 🍴 Applebees, Chili's, Ruppert's Rest., Subway, Wendy's, 🅾 BJ's Whse, Harley-Davidson, Home Depot, Lowes Whse, Staples, Target, Walmart
47	US 202, Montville, Lincoln Park, **E** 🅰 Exxon/24hr, 🍴 Harrigan's Rest.
45	Myrtle Ave, Boonton, **W** 🅰 Hess, Shell, 🍴 Dunkin Donuts, IHOP, McDonald's, Subway, 🅾 A&P/24hr, Buick/Chevrolet, Drug Fair
43	Intervale Rd, to Mountain Lakes, **E** 🅰 Valero, **W** Dodge
42	US 46, US 202 (from sb only), **W** 🅰 Exxon, Shell, Sunoco, 🍴 Applebees, Dunkin Donuts, Fuddrucker's, Longhorn Steaks, McDonald's, Subway, Wendy's, 🛏 Courtyard, Day's Inn, Embassy Suites, Fairfield Inn, Hampton Inn, 🅾 Ford, GNC, Marshall's, Michael's, Subaru, USPO
41b a	I-80, **E** to New York, **W** to Delaware Water Gap
40	NJ 511, Parsippany Rd, to Whippany, **W** 🅰 BP, Shell/dsl, Woroco Gas, 🍴 Fuddrucker's (2mi), Marco's Pizza, Wok's Chinese, Subway, 🛏 Embassy Suites (1mi)
39b a	NJ 10, Dover, Whippany, **E** 🅰 Exxon, Shell, 🍴 Bensi Italian, Brookside Diner, Capriccio's Italian, Dunkin Donuts, Melting Pot, Nikko's Japanese, Pancake House, 🅾 CVS Drug, PathMark Foods, Tuesday Morning, **W** 🅰 Lukoil, Raceway, 🍴 Atlanta Bread, Chevy's Mexican, Ruth Criss Steak, Subway, Wendy's, 🛏 Candlewoods Suites, Hilton, Marriott, Red Carpet Inn, Residence Inn, Welsley Motel, 🅾 Barnes&Noble, Buick/GMC, GNC, Kohl's, Shoprite, Stop'n Shop
37	NJ 24 E, Springfield
36b a	rd 510, Morris Ave, Lafayette
35	NJ 124, South St, Madison Ave, Morristown, **E** 🍴 Friendly's, **W** 🍴 Brick Oven, Calaloo Cafe, 🛏 Best Western, 🅾 H, Rite Aid, Walgreens
33	Harter Rd
33mm	🆁🆂 **nb, full** 🚻 **facilities,** 🅲, 🅿, **litter barrels, vending, petwalk**
30b a	to US 202, N Maple Ave, Basking Ridge, **E** 🍴 Bamboo Grill, 🛏 Dolce Resort, **W** 🅰 Gulf, 🍴 Burger King, Friendly's, GrainHouse Rest., 🛏 Olde Mill Inn/rest.
26b a	rd 525 S, Mt Airy Rd, Liberty Corner, **3 mi E** 🅰 Exxon/24hr, 🛏 Courtyard, Somerset Hotel, 🅾 Kwik-Pik Foods
22b a	US 202, US 206, Pluckemin, Bedminster, **E** 🅰 Exxon, 🍴 Burger King, Golden Chinese, 🅾 King's Foods, **W** 🅰 Shell, 🍴 Dunkin Donuts

⬆N INTERSTATE 287 CONT'D

Exit	Services
21b a	I-78, E to NY, W to PA
17	US 206 (from sb), Bridgewater, **E** 🅾 Buick, **W** 🅿 Exxon, Hess, 🍴 Chipotle Mexican, Dunkin Donuts, Friendly's, KFC, Lonestar Steaks, Maggino's Italian, McDonald's, Red Town Diner, Starbucks, TGIFriday, Wendy's, 🛏 Marriott, 🅾 Best Buy, Bloomingdale's, Lord&Taylor, Macy's, TJ Maxx, mall
14b a	US 22, to US 202/206, **E** 🅿 Hess/dsl, 🅾 Chevrolet/Lexus, **W** 🍴 Fuddrucker's, Houlihan's, Red Lobster, 🛏 Day's Inn, 🅾 Acura, Buick/Cadillac, Infiniti, Mercedes
13b a	NJ 28, Bound Brook, **E** 🅿 BP/24hr, Sunoco, 🍴 Amazing Hot Dog, Burger King, Dunkin Donuts, Frank's Pizza, Girasole Rest., Joey's Grill, Rosinas Rest., Subway, 🅾 Radio Shack, Rite Aid, 7-11, ShopRite Foods, Walgreens, **W** 🍴 Applebees, ChuckeCheese, McDonald's, 🛏 Hilton Garden, 🅾 🅷, Costco, Home Depot, Marshall's, Michael's, Old Navy, PepBoys, PetsMart, Target
12	Weston Canal Rd, Manville, **E** 🅾 ShopRite (3mi), USPO, **W** 🍴 SportsTime Rest., 🛏 Ramada Inn
10	NJ 527, Easton Ave, New Brunswick, **E** 🛏 Crowne Plaza, **W** 🅿 Exxon, 🍴 Burger King (2mi), Dunkin Donuts, McDonald's (2mi), Ruby Tuesday, 🛏 Courtyard, Holiday Inn, Doubletree, Hampton Inn, Madison Suites, Quality Inn, Staybridge Suites, 🅾 🅷, Drug Fair, Garden State Exhibit Ctr
9	NJ 514, River Rd, **W** 🅿 Delta, 🛏 Embassy Suites, Radisson
8.5mm	**weigh sta nb**
8	Possumtown Rd, Highland Park
7	S Randolphville Rd, Piscataway, **E** 🅿 Lukoil/dsl
6	Washington Ave, Piscataway, **E** 🅿 Shell, **W** 🍴 Applebees, Burger King, Friendly's, KFC, McDonald's, TGIFriday, Johnny Carino's, Longhorn Steaks, Panera Bread, Ray's Pizza, Red Lobster, White Castle, 🅾 GNC, Lowes Whse, PetCo, ShopRite Foods, same as 5
5	NJ 529, Stelton Rd, Dunellen, **E** 🅿 Gulf/dsl, Lukoil, Shell, 🍴 Banzai Japanese, KFC, 🛏 Ramada Ltd., 🅾 Home Depot, Stop'n Shop, **W** 🅿 Exxon, 🍴 Baja Fresh, Burger King, Chicago Grill, Dunkin Donuts, Friendly's, Gianni Pizza, IHOP, Fontainbleu Diner, Gabrieles Grill, Grand Buffet, McDonald's, New York Deli, Red Lobster, Red Robin, Quiznos, Starbucks, Taco Bell, Wendy's, 🛏 Best Western, Motel 6, Hampton Inn, Holiday Inn, 🅾 Burlington Coats, $Tree, Kohl's, Lowes Whse, Macy's, Marshall's, PathMark Foods, Pep Boys, Radio Shack, Sears Essentials/auto, Staples, Target, Walmart/auto
4	Durham Ave (no EZ nb return), S Plainfield, **E** 🅿 Lukoil, 🅾 🅷
3	New Durham Rd (from sb), **E** 🅿 Shell, **W** 🍴 Dunkin Donuts, 🛏 Fairfield Inn, Red Roof Inn, 🅾 Walgreens
2b a	NJ 27, Metuchen, New Brunswick, **W** 🅿 BP, Lukoil, 🍴 Dunkin Donuts, 🅾 Costco, USPO, Walmart
1b a	US 1, **1-2 mi N on US 1** 🅿 Exxon/dsl, Getty, Gulf, RaceWay/dsl, 🍴 Bone Fish Grill, Cheese Burger Paradise, China Cafe, Dunkin Donuts, Famous Dave's BBQ, KFC, Macaroni Grill, McDonald's, Menlo Park Diner, Panera Bread, Pollo Tropical, Red Lobster, Ruby Tuesday, TGI Friday, Uno, White Castle, 🛏 Woodbridge Hotel, 🅾 A&P Foods, Best Buy, Goodyear/auto, Macy's, Marshall's, Nordstrom's, Rite Aid, Sears/auto, 7-11, mall, **S** 🅿 Shell, 🍴

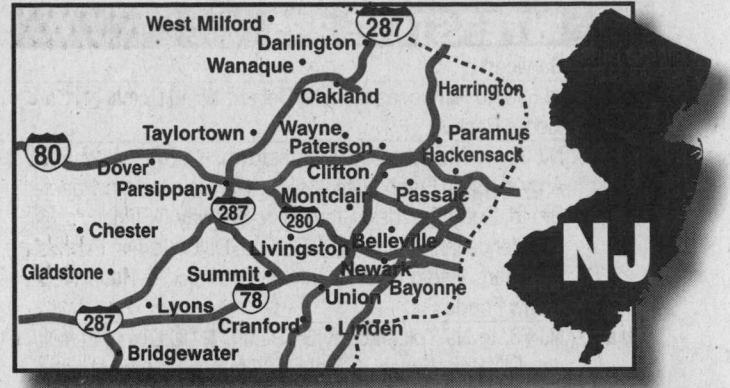

1b a	**Continued** Applebees, Boston Mkt, ChuckeCheese, Grand Buffet, McDonald's, Quizno's, 🛏 Holiday Inn Express, 🅾 Astin Martin/Jaguar/Porche, BJ's Whse, BMW, Home Depot, Infiniti, Mercedes, Office Depot, PepBoys, PetCo, Sam's Club/gas, Staples, Stop'n Shop Foods
0mm	**I-287 begins/ends on NJ 440, I-95, NJ Tpk.**

⬆N INTERSTATE 295

Exit	Services
67b a	US 1. **I-295 nb becomes I-95 sb at US 1. See NJ I-95, exit 67b a.**
65b a	Sloan Ave, **E** 🅿 Exxon, 🍴 Burger King, Dunkin Donuts, New China Buffet, Subway, Taco Bell, Uno Grill, 🅾 Goodyear/auto, Rizoldi's Mkt
64	NJ 535 N (from sb), to NJ 33 E, same as 63
63b a	NJ 33 W, rd 535, Mercerville, Trenton, **E on rd 33** 🅿 Hess/dsl, Lukoil, Valero, 🍴 Applebee's, Asia Buffet, McDonald's, Pizza Hut, Popeye's, Stewart's Rootbeer, Subway, Vincent's Pizza, 🅾 Ace Hardware, CVS Drug, Ford/Subaru, Rite Aid, Staples, auto repair, USPO, **W** 🅿 Exxon, 🍴 Dunkin Donuts, Hamilton Diner, Szechuan House, 🅾 Advance Parts, Family$, Walgreens, WaWa, transmissions
62	Olden Ave N (from sb, no return), **W** 🅿 Delta
61b a	Arena Dr, White Horse Ave, **W** 🅿 7-11
60b a	I-195, to I 95, W to Trenton, E to Neptune
58mm	scenic overlook both lanes
57b a	US 130, to US 206, **E** 🅿 Shell, Valero, 🍴 Denny's, McDonald's, 🛏 Best Western, Comfort Inn, Days Inn, EconoLodge, Hampton Inn, 🅾 Blue Beacon, **W** 🛏 Candlewood Suites, 🅾 st police
56	to US 206 S (from nb, no return), to NJ Tpk, Ft Dix, McGuire AFB, **E** 🅿 ❤Loves/Wendy's/dsl/scales/24hr, Petro/Iron Skillet/dsl/scales/24hr/@, 🛏 Days Inn, Hampton Inn, same as 57, **W** 🛏 Candlewood Suites, 🅾 st police
52b a	rd 656, to Columbus, Florence, **3 mi E** 🅿 Petro/Iron Skillet/dsl/scales/24hr/@, ❤Loves/Wendy's/dsl/scales/24hr
47b a	NJ 541, to Mount Holly, NJ Tpk, Burlington, **E** 🅿 BP, Exxon/dsl, Valero/dsl, 🍴 Applebee's, Burger King, China House, ChuckECheese's, Coldstone, Cracker Barrel, Dunkin Donuts, IHOP, Quiznos, Recovery Grill, TGIFriday's, 🛏 Best Western, Budget Inn, Courtyard, Hampton Inn, Hilton Garden, Holiday Inn Express, Quality Inn, 🅾 AT&T, Dick's, $Tree, Home Depot, JC Penney, Kohl's, Sears/auto, Target, mall, vet, **W** 🅿 Citgo/dsl, US Gas, WaWa/dsl, 🍴 Checker's, Friendly's, Subway, Villa Pizza, Wedgewood Farms Rest., Wendy's, 🅾 🅷, Acme Foods, AutoZone, Marshall's, Walmart
45b a	to Mt Holly, Willingboro, **W** 🅿 LukOil, 🅾 🅷, auto repair

T R E N T O N

NJ

◤N INTERSTATE 295 CONT'D

Exit	Services
43b a	rd 636, to Rancocas Woods, Delran, **W** 🅐 Exxon, 🍴 Carlucci's Rest.
40b a	NJ 38, to Mount Holly, Moorestown, **W** 🅐 Shell/dsl, 🍴 Arby's, Baja Fresh, Chick-fil-A, Dunkin Donuts, Panera Bread, Ruby Tuesday, Starbucks, Subway, TGIFriday's, 🛏 Residence Inn (4mi), 🅞 🅗, Costco, GNC, Jo-Ann Fabrics, Petsmart, Radio Shack, Target, TJ Maxx, U-Haul, Wegman's Foods
36b a	NJ 73, to NJ Tpk, Tacony Br, Berlin, **E** 🅐 Exxon, LukOil/dsl, 🍴 Bob Evans, 🛏 aLoft, Courtyard, EconoLodge, Fairfield Inn, Red Roof Inn, Super 8, **W** 🅐 Citgo, Shell, 🍴 Bertucci's, Boscov's, Boston Mkt, Chick-fil-A, Chipotle Mexican, Don Pablo, Dunkin Donuts, 5 Guys Burgers, Friendly's, Mikado Japanese, Old Town Buffet, Panera Bread, PeiWei, Perkins, PJ Whelahin's, Popeye's, Uno Grill, Wendy's, 🛏 Bel-Air Motel, Crossland Suites, Homewood Suites, Motel 6, Quality Inn, 🅞 Acura, AT&T, AutoZone, Barnes&Noble, Best Buy, Chevrolet, Dick's, $Tree, Fiat, Firestone/auto, Ford/Lincoln, Home Depot, Infiniti, K-Mart, Lord&Taylor, Lowe's, Macy's, Marshall's, Michael's, Old Navy, PepBoys, Petsmart, Ross, Sears/auto, ShopRite Foods, Staples, mall
34b a	NJ 70, to Camden, Cherry Hill, **E** 🅐 BP, Exxon, WaWa, 🍴 Big John's Steaks, Burger King, Dunkin Donuts, PJ Whelihans, 🛏 Extended Stay America, 🅞 Curves, Tires+, **W** 🅐 Exxon, Gulf/dsl, LukOil, US Gas, 🍴 Dunkin Donuts, Famous Dave's BBQ, McDonald's, Mirabella Cafe, Norma's Cafe, Ponzio's Rest, Qdoba, Salad Works, Seasons Pizza, Steak&Ale, Starbucks, Subway, 🛏 Crowne Plaza (3mi), 🅞 🅗, AT&T, CVS Drug, $Tree, Goodyear/auto, Rite Aid, WaWa, vet
32	NJ 561, to Haddonfield, Voorhees, **3 mi E** 🅐 LukOil/dsl, 🍴 Applebee's, 5 Guys Burgers, Olive Garden, Panera Bread, Vito's Pizza, 🛏 Hampton Inn, Wingate Inn, 🅞 🅗, USPO, **W** 🅐 Pioneer/dsl, Sunoco, 🍴 Burger King, Dunkin Donuts, Subway, 🅞 Ford, 7-11, vet
31	Woodcrest Station
30	Warwick Rd (from sb)
29b a	US 30, to Berlin, Collingswood, **E** 🅐 Astro/dsl, Citgo/dsl, Exxon, LukOil/dsl, 🍴 Arby's, Church's, Dunkin Donuts, McDonald's, Popeye's, Subway, Wendy's, 🅞 AutoZone, Home Depot, Lowe's, PathMark Foods, Petsmart, Sears Essentials
28	NJ 168, to NJ Tpk, Belmawr, Mt Ephraim, **E** 🅐 Citgo, Gulf/repair, Shell/dsl, Shamrock/dsl, 🍴 Burger King, Club Diner, Dunkin Donuts, Italia Pizza, Wendy's, 🛏 Bellmawr Motel, Comfort Inn, EconoLodge, Holiday Inn, Howard Johnson, Motel 6, Red Roof Inn, Super 8, 🅞 CVS Drug, Walgreens, transmissions, **W** 🅐 BP, Exxon/LP, Hess/dsl, WaWa, 🍴 Applebee's, Arby's, Black Horse Diner, Chick-fil-A, Domino's, Dunkin Donuts, 5 Guys Burgers, Golden Corral, McDonald's, Sonic, Subway, 🅞 Acme Foods, AutoZone, Chrysler/Dodge, CVS Drug, Firestone, Harley-Davidson, PepBoys, Staples, Walgreens, Walmart, USPO
26	I-76, NJ 42, to I-676 (exits left from sb), Walt Whitman Bridge
25b a	NJ 47, to Westville, Deptford
24b a	NJ 45, NJ 551 (no EZ sb return), to Westville, **E** 🅞 🅗, AutoZone, repair, **W** 🅐 WaWa 🅞 Chevrolet, Family$

Exit	Services
23	US 130 N, to National Park
22	NJ 644, to Red Bank, Woodbury, **E** 🅐 LukOil, **1 mi W** 🅐 Crown Point Trkstp/dsl/@, WaWa, 🍴 Wendy's
21	NJ 44 S, Paulsboro, Woodbury, **W** 🍴 WaWa, Wendy's, 🛏 Westwood Motor Lodge
20	NJ 44, rd 643, to National Park, Thorofare, **E** 🛏 Best Western, **W** 🛏 Red Bank Inn
19	to NJ 44, rd 656, Mantua
18b a	rd 667, to rd 678, Clarksboro, Mt Royal, **E** 🅐 BP/dsl, TA/Exxon/Buckhorn Rest./dsl/scales/@, 🍴 Dunkin Donuts, KFC/Taco Bell, McDonald's, Wendy's, 🅞 RV camping, **W** 🅐 Valero, WaWa/dsl
17	rd 680, to Mickleton, Gibbstown, **W** 🍴 Burger King, Domino's, 🛏 Motel 6, 🅞 Advance Parts, Family$, GNC, Rite Aid, ShopRite Foods, WaWa
16b	rd 551, to Gibbstown, Mickleton
16a	rd 653, to Paulsboro, Swedesboro
15	rd 607, to Gibbstown
14	rd 684, to Repaupo
13	US 130 S, US 322 W, to Bridgeport (from sb, no return)
11	US 322 E, to Mullica Hill
10	Ctr Square Rd, to Swedesboro, **E** 🅐 BP/dsl, WaWa/dsl, 🍴 Applebee's, Dunkin Donuts, McDonald's, Subway, Wendy's, 🛏 Hampton Inn, Holiday Inn, 🅞 Acme Foods/Sav-On, Firestone/auto, Rite Aid, **W** 🅞 Camping World RV Supplies/service
7	to Auburn, Pedricktown
4	NJ 48, Woodstown, Penns Grove
3mm	**weigh sta nb**
2mm	🆁🆂 nb, full 🅗 facilities, info, 🍴, 🅐, litter barrels, rv dump, vending
2c	to US 130 (from sb), Deepwater, **E** same as 2b, **W** 🅐 ⚑FLYING J/Denny's/dsl/scales/LP/24hr, Sunoco/Dunkin Donuts/dsl/scales/24hr, 🅞 🅗
2b	US 40 E, to NJ Tpk, **E** 🅐 Gulf, 🍴/Subway/dsl/scales/24hr, 🛏 Best Value, Comfort Inn, Friendship Motor Inn, Knights Inn, Quality Inn, **W** same as 2c
2a	US 40 W (from nb), to Delaware Bridge
1c	NJ 551 S, Hook Rd, to Salem, **E** 🛏 White Oaks Motel, **W** 🅗
1b	US 130 N (from nb), Penns Grove
1a	NJ 49 E, to Pennsville, Salem, **E** 🅐 Exxon/dsl/repair, 🍴 Applebees, Burger King, Cracker Barrel, Dunkin Donuts, KFC/Taco Bell, McDonald's, Subway, 🛏 Hampton Inn, Super 8, 🅞 Peterbilt, **W** 🅐 Coastal/dsl, 🛏 Seaview Motel
0mm	New Jersey/Delaware state line, Delaware River, Delaware Memorial Bridge

NEW MEXICO

◤E INTERSTATE 10

Exit	Services
164.5mm	New Mexico/Texas state line
164mm	**Welcome Ctr wb, full 🅗 facilities, 🍴, 🅐, litter barrels, petwalk**
162	NM 404, Anthony, **S** 🅐 Alon/dsl, 🅞 Family$, RV camping
160mm	**weigh sta wb**
155	NM 227 W, to Vado, **N** Western Sky's RV Park, **S** 🅐 NTS/dsl/scales/24hr/@, Texaco/El Viajero/dsl/scales/24hr, 🅞 $General, El Camino Real HS
151	Mesquite

CHERRY HILL

NJ NM

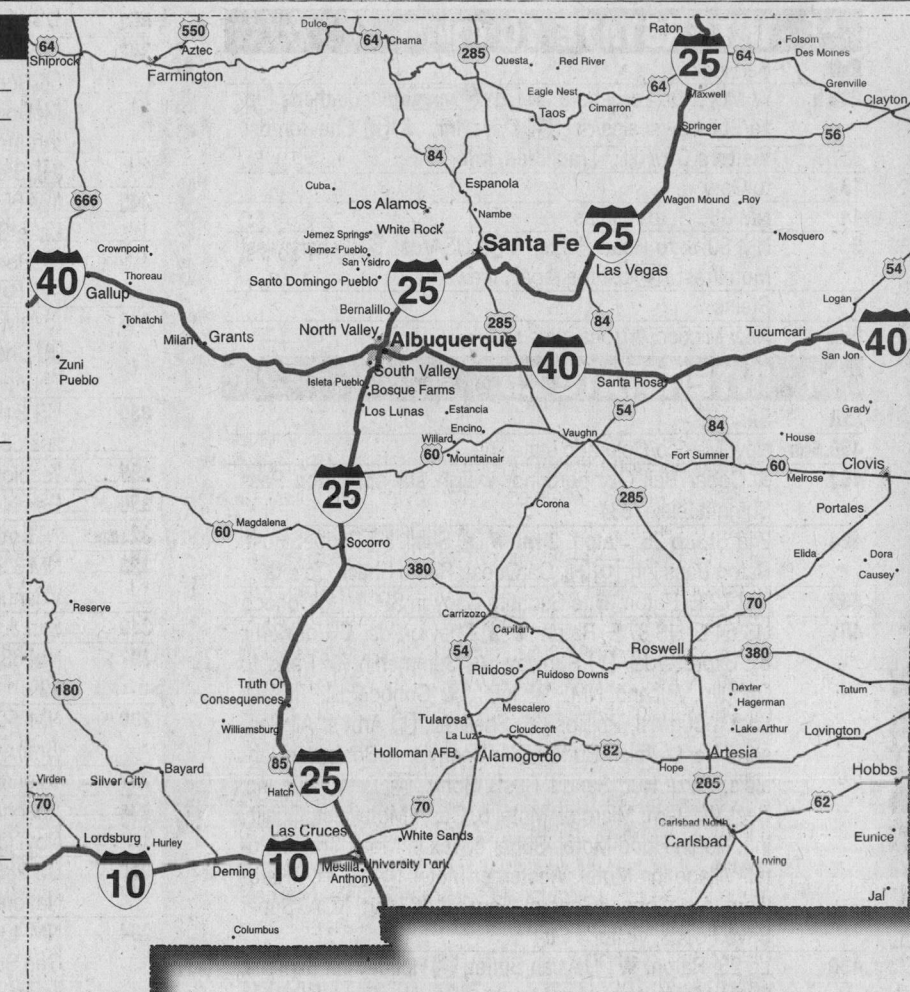

LAS CRUCES

Exit	Services
INTERSTATE 10 CONT'D	
144	I-25 N, to Las Cruces
142	Rd 188, Rd 101, Valley Dr, Las Cruces, **N** 🅖 Chevron/dsl, 🍴 Chilito's Mexican, Dick's Cafe, Whataburger, 🏨 Best Western, EconoLodge, Holiday Inn Express, Motel 6, Quality Inn, Ramada Inn, Super 8, Teakwood Inn, 🅞 Ⓗ Cadillac/Chevrolet, Dalmont's RV Camping, Ford/Lincoln, Honda, Hyundai, Mazda, Nissan, auto/RV repair/tires, NMSU, vet, **S** 🅖 Alon/dsl, 🅞 USPO
140	NM 28, to Mesilla, Las Cruces, **N** 🅖 Fina/dsl, Murphy Express/dsl, Shamrock/dsl, 🍴 Applebee's, Blake's Lotaburger, BurgerTime, Cracker Barrel, Dickey's BBQ, Domino's, McDonald's, Murry Express, Starbucks, Subway, 🏨 Best Value Inn, Days Inn, Drury Inn, La Quinta, SpringHill Suites, 🅞 Buick/GMC, Kia, Radio Shack, Toyota/Scion, VW, Walmart/McDonald's, **S** 🍴 LunaRossa Pizza, 🏨 Comfort Inn, 🅞 Harley-Davidson, Siesta RV Park, Sunland RV Ctr, United RV Ctr
139	NM 292, Amador Ave, Motel Blvd, Las Cruces, **N** 🅖 Ⓟ/Subway/dsl/scales/24hr, TA/Burger King/Pizza Hut/Taco Bell/dsl/24hr/scales/@, **S** 🍴 PitStop Café, 🏨 Coachlight Inn/RV Park, 🅞 NAPACare
138mm	Rio Grande River
135.5mm	🆁🆂 eb, full ♿ facilities, 🅿 litter barrels, petwalk, scenic view, RV dump
135	US 70 E, to W Las Cruces, Alamogordo, 1 mi **N** 🅞 KOA
132	**N** to 🏨, fairgrounds, **S** 🅖 Loves/Subway/dsl/scales/24hr
127	Corralitos Rd, **N** 🅖 Exxon, 🅞 Bowlin's Trading Post, to fairgrounds
120.5mm	insp sta wb
116	NM 549
111mm	parking area wb, litter barrels
102	Akela, **N** 🅖 Exxon/dsl/gifts

DEMING

Exit	Services
85	East Motel Dr, Deming, **S** 🅖 Chevron/dsl, Save Gas/dsl, 🏨 Hampton Inn, Holiday Inn, La Quinta, Motel 6, 🅞 Buick/Cadillac/Chevrolet/GMC, Chrysler/Dodge/Jeep, Escapee's RV Park
82b	Railroad Blvd, Deming, **N** 🅖 Chevron/dsl, **S** 🅖 Fina/dsl, 🍴 DQ, Empire Buffet, KFC, Little Caesars, Wendy's, 🏨 Days Inn, Grand Motel, 🅞 AutoZone, Big O Tire, $General, $Tree, Ford/Lincoln, K-Mart, Little Vinyard RV Park, NAPA, O'Reilly Parts, Roadrunner RV Park, Sunrise RV Park, Wagon Wheel RV Park, Walmart/Subway, to Rock Hound SP, Deming Visitors Ctr, st police
82a	US 180, NM 26, NM 11, Deming, **N** 🅖 Chevron/dsl, 🍴 Blake's Lotaburger, **S** 🅖 Exxon, Mimbres/dsl, Phillips 66, 🍴 Burger King, Denny's, Domino's, Golden Start Chinese, KFC, Palma's Italian, Pizza Hut, Rancher's Grill, Si Senor, 🏨 Butterfield Stage Motel, 🅞 Budget Tire, CarQuest, Radio Shack, museum, to Pancho Villa SP, Rockhound SP
81	NM 11, W Motel Dr, Deming, 🅖 Shamrock/dsl, 🍴 Benji's Rest, Burger Time, El Camino Real, McDonald's, Sonic, Subway, Taco Bell, 🏨 Best Western, Comfort Inn, Deming Motel, Executive Motel, Grand Motor Inn, Super 8, Western Motel, 🅞 81 Palms RV Park, Hitchin Post RV Park, city park, to Pancho Villa SP, Rock Hound SP
68	NM 418, **S** 🅖 Savoy/rest/dsl/24hr, tires/repair
62	Gage, **S** 🅖 Butterfield Station/Exxon/DQ/dsl
61mm	🆁🆂 wb, full ♿ facilities, 🅿 litter barrels, vending, petwalk
55	Quincy
53mm	🆁🆂 eb, full ♿ facilities, 🅿 litter barrels, vending, petwalk
51.5mm	Continental Divide, elev 4585
49	NM 146 S, to Hachita, Antelope Wells
42	Separ, **S** Bowlin's Continental Divide Trading Post/Gifts, truck/auto repair
34	NM 113 S, Muir, Playas
29	no services

LORDSBURG

Exit	Services
24	US 70, E Motel Dr, Lordsburg, **N** 🅖 FLYING J/Denny's/dsl/LP/scales/RV Dump/24hr, Ⓟ/Arby's/dsl/scales/24hr, 🏨 American Motel, 🅞 Horseman RV Park
23.5mm	weigh sta both lanes
22	NM 494, Main St, Lordsburg, **N** 🍴 Don Juan Mexican, McDonald's, 🏨 Comfort Inn, Hampton Inn, 🅞 Family$, Saucedo's Foods, USPO, **S** 🅖 Valero, 🍴 Kranberry's Rest., 🏨 Best Value Inn, Best Western, EconoLodge, Plaza Inn, 🅞 KOA

NM

⬅🅴	**INTERSTATE 10** CONT'D
Exit	**Services**
20b a	W Motel Dr, Lordsburg, **N** 🅶 Loves/Godfather's Pizza/Subway/scales/dsl, 🛏 Days Inn, **S** 🅶 Chevron/dsl, **Visitors Ctr/full** 🛇 **facilities, info**
15	to Gary
11	NM 338 S, to Animas
5	NM 80 S, to Road Forks, **S** 🅶 USA/dsl, 🛏 Desert West Motel/rest., 🄾 dsl/tire repair, fireworks
3	Steins
0mm	New Mexico/Arizona state line

⬆🅽	**INTERSTATE 25**
Exit	**Services**
460.5mm	New Mexico/Colorado state line
460	**E** Cedar Rail Campground, **weigh sta sb**, Raton Pass Summit, elev 7834
454	2nd St, Lp 25, Raton, **2 mi W** 🅶 Shell, 🛏 Budget Host, Raton Pass Inn, 🄾 🄷 CarQuest, Radio Shack, Toyota
452	NM 72 E, Raton, **E** to Sugarite Canyon SP, **W** 🅶 Conoco
451	US 64 E, US 87 E, Raton, **E** 🅶 Chevron/dsl, CR/dsl/24hr, 87 Express/dsl, 🍴 Subway, 🄾 Summerlin RV Park, to Capulin Volcano NM, **W** info, 🅶 Conoco/dsl, CR/dsl, Loaf'n Jug/dsl, Phillips 66, Shell/dsl, 🍴 Arby's, All Seasons Rest., Asian Buffet, DQ, Denny's, K-Bob's, McDonald's, Pizza Hut, Sand's Rest., Sonic, 🛏 Best Value Inn, Best Western, Microtel, Motel 6, Oasis Motel/rest, Quality Inn, Robin Hood Motel, Super 8, Texan Motel, Travel Motel, Village Inn Motel, Westerner Motel, 🄾 🄷 Ace Hardware, AutoZone, $General, Family$, K-Mart, KOA, Super Save Foods, Visitor's Ctr
450	Lp 25, Raton, **W** 🍴 Asian Buffet, 🛏 Holiday Inn Express, Oasis Motel, Westerner Motel, 🄾 🄷 AutoZone, KOA, vet
446	US 64 W, to Cimarron, Taos, **4 mi W** NRA Whittington Ctr, camping
440mm	Canadian River
435	Tinaja
434.5mm	🆁ₛ **both lanes, full** 🛇 **facilities, weather info,** 🄿, **litter barrels, petwalk**
426	NM 505, Maxwell, **W** 🅶 LC OneStop/dsl, 🄾 USPO, to Maxwell Lakes
419	NM 58, to Cimarron, **E** 🅶 Shell/Russell's/Subway/dsl/scales/24hr/@
414	US 56, Springer, **1 mi E** 🅶 Conco/dsl, Shell/dsl, 🛏 Oasis Motel, 🄾 Old Santa Fe Trail RV Park
412	US 56 E, US 412 E, NM 21, NM 468, Springer, **1 mi E** 🅶 Fina, 🛏 Brown Hotel/cafe, 🄾 CarQuest, Springer Foods, USPO
404	NM 569, Colmor, Charette Lakes
393	Levy
387	NM 120, to Roy, Wagon Mound, **E** 🅶 Conoco/dsl, Phillips 66/dsl
376mm	🆁ₛ **sb, full** 🛇 **facilities,** 🍴, 🄿, **litter barrels, petwalk, RV camp**
374mm	🆁ₛ **nb, full** 🛇 **facilities,** 🍴, 🄿, **litter barrels, petwalk, RV camp**
366	NM 97, NM 161, Watrous, Valmora, **W** Santa Fe Trail, Ft Union NM
364	NM 97, NM 161, Watrous, Valmora
361	No Services
360mm	🆁ₛ **both lanes, litter barrels**
356	Onava

352	**E** RV camping, **W** ✈
347	to NM 518, Las Vegas, **0-2 mi W** 🅶 Pino/dsl/rest., Phillips 66/Burger King, 🍴 Arby's, Hillcrest Rest., K-Bob's, KFC, McDonald's, Subway, 🛏 Best Western, Budget Inn, Comfort Inn, Days Inn, Palamino Inn, Regal Motel, Super 8, 🄾 🄷, Storrie Lake SP
345	NM 65, NM 104, University Ave, Las Vegas, **E** to Conchas Lake SP, **W** 🅶 Allsups, Chevron, Shell/dsl, 🍴 DQ, KFC, McDonald's, Subway, Wendy's, 🛏 El Fidel, Sante Fe Trail Inn, 🄾 🄷, Hist. Old Town Plaza
343	to NM 518 N, Las Vegas, **E** 🄾 Garcia Tires, **0-2 mi W** 🅶 Chevron, Fina, Phillips 66/dsl, 🛏 Holiday Inn Express, Thunderbird Motel
339	US 84 S, to Santa Rosa, Romeroville, **E** KOA, **W** 🅶 Phillips 66/Subway/dsl
335	Tecolote
330	Bernal
325mm	🆁ₛ **both lanes,** 🄿, **litter barrels, no restrooms**
323	NM 3 S, Villanueva, **E** 🅶 Sunshine, 🍴 La Risa (1mi), 🄾 to Villanueva SP/rv camping, Madison Winery (6mi)
319	San Juan, San Jose, **W** 🅶 Pecos River Sta.
307	NM 63, Rowe, Pecos, **W** Pecos NM, Hist Rte 66, same as 299
299	NM 50, Glorieta, Pecos, **W** 🅶 Conoco/dsl (4mi), Shell (6mi), 🄾 Glorieta Conf Ctr
297	Valencia
294	Apache Canyon, **W** 🄾 KOA, Rancheros Camping (Mar-Nov) (3mi)
290	US 285 S, to Lamy, S to Clines Corners, **W** 🍴 Real Food Nation, 🄾 KOA (2mi), Rancheros Camping (Mar-Nov)
284	NM 466, Old Pecos Trail, Santa Fe, **W** 🅶 Chevron/Sunset Gen Store/dsl, Shell/dsl, 🍴 Harry's Roadhouse, 🄾 🄷 museums
282	US 84, US 285, St Francis Dr, **W** 🅶 Conoco/Wendy's/dsl, Giant/dsl, 🍴 Church's
278	NM 14, Cerrillos Rd, Santa Fe, **0-4 mi W** 🅶 Giant/dsl, Phillips 66/dsl, Shell, 🍴 Adelita's Mexican, Applebee's, Arby's, Bumble Bee's Baja Grill, Burger King, China Star, Denny's, Domino's, El Campanaro Mexican, Flying Tortilla, IHOP, KFC, LJ Silver, Lotaburger, McDonald's, Olive Garden, Outback Steaks, Panda Express, Pizza Hut, Quizno's, Red Lobster, Schlotzsky's, Sonic, Starbucks, Taco Bell, Tortilla Flats, Village Inn, 🛏 Best Western, Comfort Inn, Comfort Suites, Courtyard, Days Inn, EconoLodge, Fairfield Inn, Hampton Inn, Holiday Inn, Holiday Inn Express, Hyatt Place, La Quinta, Luxury Inn, Motel 6, Park Inn, Quality Inn, Red Roof Inn, Santa Fe Inn, Super 8, 🄾 Albertson's, AT&T, Best Buy, BigLots, BMW, Buick/GMC, Cadillac/Chevrolet, Chrysler/Dodge/Jeep, Dillard's, Discount Tire, Dodge, Firestone/auto, Ford/Lincoln, Harley-Davidson, Home Depot, Honda, Hyundai, JC Penney, JoAnn Fabrics, Kohl's, Land Rover, Lowe's, Lexus, Mazda, Michael's, Midas, NAPA, Natural Grocers, Peerless Tire, PepBoys, Petsmart, Ross, Sam's Club/gas, Sears/auto, Staples, Subaru/VW, Target, TJ Maxx, Verizon, Volvo, Walgreens, Walmart/Subway, rv camping, transmissions, Santa Fe Outlets/famous brands
276b a	NM 599, to NM 14, to Madrid, **E** 🄾 Santa Fe Skies RV Park, **4 mi W** 🅶 Shell, 🄾 Sunrise Springs
271	CR 50F, La Cienega
269mm	🆁ₛ **nb, full** 🛇 **facilities,** 🍴, 🄿, **litter barrels, petwalk**
267	Waldo Canyon Rd, **insp sta., access to nb** 🆁ₛ

LAS VEGAS

RATON

SANTA FE

INTERSTATE 25 CONT'D

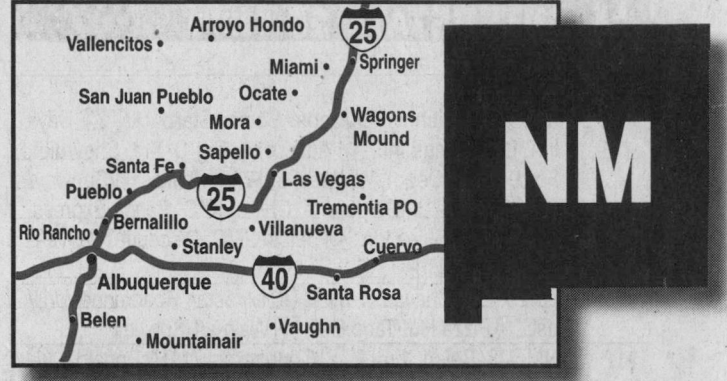

Exit	Services
264	NM 16, Pueblo, **W** to Cochiti Lake RA
263mm	Galisteo River
259	NM 22, to Santo Domingo Pueblo, **W** ⓡ Phillips 66/cafe/dsl, 🅾 to Cochiti Lake RA
257	Budaghers, **W** Mormon Battalion Mon
252	San Felipe Pueblo, **E** ⓡ Phillips 66/dsl, 🍴 San Felipe Casino/rest.
248	Rte 66, Algodones
242	US 550, NM 44 W, NM 165 E, to Farmington, Aztec, **0-2 mi W** ⓡ Chevron/dsl, Circle K, Conoco/dsl, M&M/Burger King/dsl, Phillips 66/dsl, 🍴 Coronado Rest., Denny's, Domino's, Guang Dong Chinese, IHOP, KFC, Lotaburger, McDonald's, Papa Murphy's, Pizza Hut, Quizno's, Sonic, Starbucks, Subway, Taco Bell, Twisters, Wendy's, 🏨 Days Inn, Holiday Inn Express, Quality Inn, Super 8, 🅾 Albertsons, AutoZone, Casino, Curves, $General, $Tree, Home Depot, KOA, O'Reilly Parts, Walgreens, Walmart, to Coronado SP
240	NM 473, to Bernalillo, **W** ⓡ Tri-H/dsl, 🍴 Abuelita's Mexican, Range Café, 🅾 KOA, vet, to Coronado SP
234	NM 556, Tramway Rd, **E** ⓡ Valero, 🅾 casino, **W** ⓡ Phillips 66/dsl
233	Alameda Blvd, **E** ⓡ Chevron, 🍴 Burger King, 🏨 Comfort Suites, Motel 6, Staybridge Suites, 🅾 Audi/Porsche, Lincoln, Mercedes, Scion/Toyota, Volvo, **W** ⓡ Phillips 66/Circle K/dsl, 🍴 Carl's Jr, 🏨 Holiday Inn Express, Ramada Ltd, 🅾 Balloon Fiesta Park, CarMax
232	Paseo del Norte, **E** 🍴 Chick-fil-A, China Luck, Jason's Deli, McDonald's, Red Brick Pizza, Starbucks, Subway, Tomato Cafe, Wendy's, 🏨 Clarion, Howard Johnson, 🅾 Aloha RV Ctr, AutoZone, Kohl's, Lowe's, Office Depot, Target, Verizon, Walgreens, **W** ⓡ Shell/Circle K, 🍴 Arby's, 🏨 Courtyard
231	San Antonio Ave, **E** ⓡ Fina/7-11, 🍴 Cracker Barrel, Denny's, 🏨 Hilton Garden, Homewood Suites, La Quinta, Quality Suites, 🅾 H, USPO, **W** 🏨 Crossland Suites, Hampton Inn, La Quinta, 🅾 Mazda, VW
230	San Mateo Blvd, Osuna Rd, Albuquerque, **E** ⓡ Chevron, Circle K, Giant/dsl, Phillips 66/Circle K, Shell, 🍴 Applebee's, Arby's, Azuma Grill, Bob's Burgers, Burger King, Chili's, Cici's Pizza, Furrs Buffet, Hooters, KFC, McDonald's, Olive Garden, Pizza Hut/Taco Bell, Schlotzsky's, Sonic, Souper Salad, Starbucks, Subway, SweetTomatoes, Taco Bueno, Taco Cabana, Teriyaki Chicken, TX Roadhouse, Village Inn, Wendy's, Wienerschnitzel, 🏨 Nativo Lodge, 🅾 H, AT&T, AutoZone, Brake Masters, Cadillac, Curves, CVS Drug, $Tree, Firestone/auto, GNC, Hummer, Just Brakes, Midas, NAPA, PepBoys, PetCo, Ross, Subaru/Isuzu, Sunflower Mkt, Suzuki, Tires-4-less, Tuesday Morning, U-Haul Verizon, Walgreens, **W** ⓡ Chevron, Valero/dsl, 🍴 Cajun Kitchen, McDonald's, Oasis Cafe, Quizno's, Whataburger, 🏨 Studio 6, 🅾 BMW/Mini
229	Jefferson St, **E** 🍴 Carrabba's, Landry's Seafood, Outback Steaks, 🏨 Holiday Inn, 🅾 H, same as 230, **W** 🍴 Boston's Pizza, Chama River Rest., Coldstone Creamery, Food Ct, Fox&Hound, Fuddrucker's, Genghis Grill, Jersey Jack's, Mimi's Café, Nick&Jimmy's Grill, Pappadeaux, PF Chang's, Red Robin, Subway, TX Land&Cattle Steaks, Twin Peaks Rest., 🏨 Drury Inn, Residence Inn 🅾 Lexus
228	Montgomery Blvd, **E** ⓡ Chevron/dsl, Conoco/dsl, Fina/7-

228	Continued 11, 🍴 Fiestas Cantina, Lotaburger, 🏨 Best Western, 🅾 H, Discount Tire, **W** ⓡ Shell/Circle K, 🍴 Arby's, Carl's Jr, IHOP, McDonald's, Panda Express, Starbucks, Wendy's, 🏨 InTowne Suites, 🅾 Acura, Ford, Costco/gas, Home Depot, Infiniti, Office Depot, Petsmart, Sam's Club/gas, Sportsman's Whse
227b	Comanche Rd, Griegos Rd, **E** UPS Depot
227a	Candelaria Rd, Albuquerque, **E** ⓡ Circle K/dsl, Pump'n'Save/dsl, Shell, TA/dsl/scales/24hr/@, 🍴 Applebee's, Little Anita's, Mesa Grill, Range Cafe, Subway, Village Inn, 🏨 Candlewood Suites, Clubhouse Inn, Days Inn, Elegante Hotel, Fairfield Inn, Hilton, Holiday Inn Express, La Quinta, Ramada, Rodeway Inn, Motel 1, Motel 76, Super 8, Travelodge, 🅾 Kenworth, **W** ⓡ Chevron, 🏨 Ambassador Inn, Red Roof Inn, 🅾 Volvo
226b a	I-40, E to Amarillo, W to Flagstaff
225	Lomas Blvd, **E** ⓡ Chevron, 7-11, 🍴 JB's, 🏨 Plaza Inn/rest., 🅾 Chevrolet, **W** ⓡ Chevron, Shell/Circle K/McDonald's, 🍴 Burger King, Starbucks, 🏨 Embassy Suites 🅾 H
224	Lead Ave, Coal Ave, Grand Ave, Central Ave, **E** 🅾 7-11, 🍴 66 Diner, Souper Salad, 🏨 Crossroads Motel, 🅾 H **W** ⓡ M&M, 🍴 Milton's Rest, 🏨 Best Value Inn, EconoLodge, Stardust Inn
223	Chavez Ave, **E** 🏨 Motel 6, 🅾 sports arena
222b a	Gibson Blvd, **E** ⓡ Phillips 66/dsl, 🍴 Applebee's, Burger King, Fuddrucker's, IHOP, Subway, Waffle House, Village Inn, 🏨 Best Western, Comfort Inn, Country Inn&Suites, Courtyard, Days Inn, EconoLodge, Extended Stay Deluxe, Fairfield Inn, Hampton Inn, Hawthorn Suites, Hilton Garden, Holiday Inn Express, La Quinta, Quality Suites, Residence Inn, Sleep Inn, TownePlace Suites, Vagabond Inn, 🅾 H, Kirtland AFB, museum, vet, **W** ⓡ Fina/7-11, 🍴 Church's, Lotaburger
221	Sunport, **E** 🏨 Holiday Inn, Homewood Suites, Hyatt Place, Staybridge Suites, 🅾 USPO, 🛬
220	Rio Bravo Blvd, Mountain View, **E** 🅾 golf, **1-2 mi W** ⓡ Shell/dsl, Valero, 🍴 A&W, Bob's Burgers, Burger King, Church's, KFC, McDonald's, Pizza Hut, Subway, Super China, Taco Bell, 🅾 Albertsons/Sav-On, Family$, Walgreens, 🅾 vet
215	NM 47, **E** ⓡ Conoco/dsl, Phillips 66/dsl, 🅾 to Isleta Lakes RA/RV Camping, casino, golf, st police
214mm	Rio Grande
213	NM 314, Isleta Blvd, **W** ⓡ Chevron/Subway/dsl/24hr
209	NM 45, to Isleta Pueblo
203	NM 6, to Los Lunas, **E** ⓡ Chevron/dsl, Shell/Circle K/Wendy's/dsl/24hr, Valero/dsl, 🍴 Benny's, Del Taco, Den

🅿 = gas 🍴 = food 🛏 = lodging Ⓞ = other 🆁🆂 = rest stop Copyright 2014 - The NEXT Exit ®

⬆N INTERSTATE 25 CONT'D

Exit	Services
203	**Continued** ny's, Papa John's, Quiznos, Sonic, Starbucks, 🛏 Days Inn, Los Lumas Inn, Ⓞ AutoZone, Big O Tire, Chevrolet, Ford, Home Depot, Walgreens, **W** 🅿 Phillips 66/Subway/dsl, 🍴 Carl's Jr, Coldstone, Chili's, KFC, Panda Express, 🛏 Western Skies Inn, Ⓞ Buick/GMC, Discount Tire, Verizon, Walmart
195	Lp 25, Los Chavez, **1 mi E** 🅿 Mirastar, Roadrunner/grill/dsl, 🍴 Pizza Hut/Taco Bell, Ⓞ Walmart/Subway,
191	NM 548, Belen, **1 mi E** 🅿 Conoco/dsl, 🍴 McDonald's, 🛏 Super 8, Ⓞ $General, **W** 🍴 Rio Grande Diner, 🛏 Holiday Inn Express, La Mirada Hotel/RV park
190	Lp 25, Belen, **1-2 mi E** 🅿 Conoco/dsl, Phillips 66, 🍴 A&W, Arby's, Casa de Pizza, McDonald's, 🛏 Super 8, Ⓞ AutoZone, Big O Tire
175	US 60, Bernardo, **E** Salinas NM, **W** Ⓞ Kiva RV Park
174mm	Rio Puerco
169	**E** La Joya St Game Refuge, Sevilleta NWR
167mm	🆁🆂 **both lanes, full** ♿ **facilities,** 🚮 **litter barrels, vending, petwalk**
166mm	Rio Salado
165mm	**weigh sta**/parking area both lanes
163	San Acacia
156	Lemitar, **W** Phillis 66/dsl/24hr
152	Escondida, **W** to st police
150	US 60 W, Socorro, **W** 🅿 Chevron, Exxon/dsl, Phillips 66/dsl, Valero/dsl, 🍴 Burger King, China Best, Denny's, K-Bob's, Lotaburger, McDonald's, Pizza Hut, RoadRunner Steaks, Socorro Springs Rest., Sonic, Subway, Taco Bell, 🛏 Best Western, Comfort Inn, Days Inn, Economy Inn, EconoLodge, Holiday Inn Express, Howard Johnson, Sands Motel, Super 8, Ⓞ Ace Hardware, AutoZone, Brooks Foods, CarQuest, $General, Family$, Ford, NAPA, Radio Shack, Smith's Foods, TrueValue, Verizon, Walmart, vet, to NM Tech
147	US 60 W, Socorro, **W** 🅿 Conoco/dsl/LP, Pump N Save/dsl, Shell/Circle K/dsl, 🍴 Arby's, 🛏 Motel 6, Ⓞ 🅷, Socorro RV Park, repair/transmissions, to ⬇
139	US 380 E, to San Antonio, **E** gas/food, to Bosque Del Apache NWR
124	to San Marcial, **E** Ⓞ to Bosque del Apache NWR, Ft Craig
115	NM 107, **E** 🅿 Truck Plaza/dsl/rest./24hr, to Camino Real Heritage Ctr
114mm	🆁🆂s **both lanes, full** ♿ **facilities,** 🚮 **litter barrels, petwalk, RV parking, vending**
107mm	Nogal Canyon
100	Red Rock
92	Mitchell Point
90mm	La Canada Alamosa, La Canada Alamosa
89	NM 181, to Cuchillo, to Monticello, **4 mi E** Monticello RV Park
83	NM 52, NM 181, to Cuchillo, **3 mi E** 🍴 Ivory Tusk Inn& Tavern, 🛏 Elephant Butte Inn/rest., Ⓞ RV Park, Elephant Lake Butte SP
82mm	**insp sta nb**
79	Lp 25, to Truth or Consequences, **E** 🅿 Chevron/dsl, Circle K, Phillips 66/dsl, 🍴 Denny's, Hilltop Café, K-Bob's, KFC/Taco Bell, La Cocina Mexican, Los Arcos Steaks, McDonald's, Pizza Hut, Sonic, Subway, 🛏 Ace Lodge, Comfort Inn, Desert View Motel, Hot Springs Inn, Motel

Exit	Services
79	**Continued** 6, Oasis Motel, Ⓞ 🅷, AutoZone, $General, IGA Foods, O'Reilly Parts, Radio Shack, Walmart, USPO, to Elephant Butte SP
76	(75 from nb), Lp 25, to Williamsburg, **E** 🅿 Chevron/24hr, Conoco/dsl, Phillips 66/dsl, Shell/dsl, 🍴 Big-A-Burger, 🛏 Rio Grande Motel, Ⓞ Alco, Buick/Chevrolet/GMC, Cielo Vista RV Park, NAPA, RJ RV Park, Shady Corner RV Park, USPO, auto/tire repair, city park
71	Las Palomas
63	NM 152, to Hillsboro, Caballo, **E** Ⓞ Lakeview RV Park/dsl/LP
59	rd 187, Arrey, Derry, **E** to Caballo-Percha SPs
58mm	Rio Grande,
51	rd 546, to Arrey, Garfield, Derry
41	NM 26 W, Hatch, **1 mi W** 🅿 Fina/Subway/dsl, 🍴 Burgers&More, 🛏 Village Plaza Motel, Ⓞ Chile Pepper Outlets, Franciscan RV Ctr, USPO
35	NM 140 W, Rincon
32	Upham
27mm	scenic view nb, 🚮, litter barrels
26mm	**insp sta nb**
23mm	🆁🆂 **both lanes, full** ♿ **facilities,** 🚮 **litter barrels, vending, petwalk**
19	Radium Springs, **W** Leasburg SP, Fort Selden St Mon, RV camping
9	Dona Ana, **W** 🅿 Circle K/dsl, Chucky's/dsl, Texaco, 🍴 Alejandro's Mexican, Jake's Cafe, Ⓞ Family$, RV camping, USPO
6	US 70, to Alamogordo, Las Cruces, **E** 🅿 Fina/dsl, Shell, 🍴 Chicago Grill, Coldstone Creamery, IHOP, Outback Steaks, Papa Johns, Peter Piper Pizza, Pizzaria Uno, Red Brick Pizza, Ruby Tuesday, Starbucks, 🛏 Fairfield Inn, Motel 6, Staybridge Suites, Towneplace Suites, Ⓞ 🅷, AT&T, Curves, K-Mart, Sam's Club/gas, USPO, **W** 🅿 Chevron, Chucky's/dsl, Fina, Shell, Valero, 🍴 Burger King, BurgerTime, DQ, Domino's, KFC, Little Caesar's, Lotaburger, McDonald's, Quizno's, Sonic, Spanish Kitchen, Subway, Taco Bell, Whataburger/24hr, Ⓞ Albertson's, AutoZone, $General, Family$, Kohl's, Jiffy Lube, Lowe's, O'Reilly Parts, Radio Shack, Verizon, Walgreens, golf, vet
3	Lohman Ave, Las Cruces, **E** 🅿 Fina, Shell, 🍴 Applebee's, Buffalo Wild Wings, Burger King, Cattle Baron Steaks, Chili's, ChuckeCheese, Farley's Grill, Fidencio's Mexican, Golden Corral, Hooters, Jack-in-the-Box, KFC, McAlister's Deli, Olive Garden, Pecan Grill, Red Lobster, Sonic, Starbucks, Village Inn, Whataburger, 🛏 Hotel Encanto, Ⓞ Albertsons, AutoZone, Barnes&Noble, Dillard's, Discount Tire, Home Depot, JC Penney, Marshalls, PetCo, Ross, Sears/auto, Target, mall, **W** 🍴 Arby's, Carl's Jr, Furr's Buffet, McDonald's, Mesilla Valley Kitchen, Papa Murphy's, Si Senor, Subway, Taco Bell, TX Roadhouse, Wendy's, Wienerschnitzel, 🛏 Hampton Inn, Ⓞ Best Buy, Big Lots, Brake Masters, Hastings Books, Hobby Lobby, Martin Tires, NAPA, Old Navy, PepBoys, Petsmart, Staples, Verizon, Walgreens, Walmart/24hr, **Urgent Care**, vet
1	University Ave, Las Cruces, **E** 🅿 Fina/Subway/dsl, 🛏 Hilton Garden, Ⓞ 🅷, golf, museum, st police, **W** 🅿 Western/dsl, 🍴 DQ, Dublin's Cafe, Lorenzo's Italian, McDonald's, 🛏 Comfort Suites, Sleep Inn, ValuePlace, Ⓞ $Tree, Jo-Ann Fabrics, NMSU
0mm	**I-25 begins/ends on I-10, exit 144 at Las Cruces.**

BELEN

SOCORRO

NM

LAS CRUCES

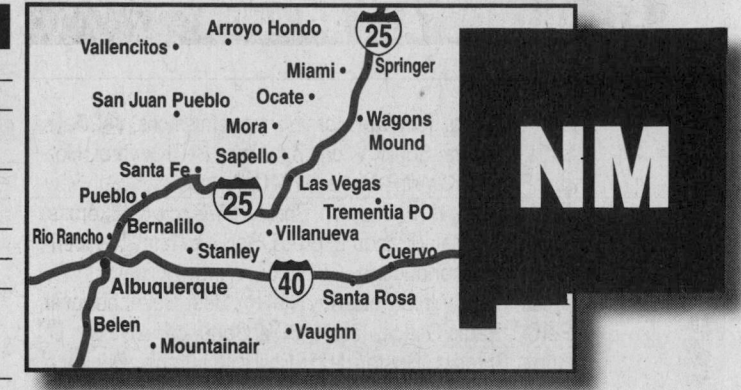

⬆E   INTERSTATE 40

Exit	Services
373.5mm	New Mexico/Texas state line, Mountain/Central time zone
373mm	**Welcome Ctr wb, full ⬜ facilities, ⬜, ⬜ litter barrels, petwalk**
369	NM 93 S, NM 392 N, Endee, **N** ⬜ Chevron/Russell's Truck&Travel/Subway/dsl/scales/24hr
361	Bard
358mm	**weigh sta both lanes**
356	NM 469, San Jon, **N** ⬜ Dhillon/cafe/dsl, ⬜ repair, to Ute Lake SP, **S** ⬜ Valero/dsl, ⬜ San Jon Motel, ⬜ USPO, city park
343	no services
339	NM 278, **N** ⬜
335	Lp 40, E Tucumcari Blvd, Tucumcari, **N** ⬜ Conoco/dsl, Phillips 66, ⬜ EconoLodge, Gateway Inn, Hampton Inn, Motel 6, Quality Inn, Rodeway Inn, Super 8, ⬜ Empty Saddle RV Park, to Conchas Lake SP, **S** ⬜ KOA
333	US 54 E, Tucumcari, **0-1 mi N** ⬜ ⬛*FLYING J*/Denny's/dsl/LP/scales/RV Dump/24hr, ⬛*Loves*/Arbys/Chester's/Godfather's/dsl/scales, ⬜ Rockin Y's Roadhouse, ⬜ Tucumcari Inn, ⬜ K-Mart, Mtn Rd RV Park, city park, truckwash, truck repair
332	NM 209, NM 104, 1st St, Tucumcari, **0-2 mi N** ⬜ Phillips 66/Allsups, Shell/Circle K/Subway/dsl, ⬜ Blake's Lotaburger, K-Bob's, McDonald's, Pizza Hut, Sonic, ⬜ Best Western, Days Inn, Desert Inn, Holiday Inn Express, La Quinta, ⬜ ⬜, Ace Hardware, $General, Family$, Lowe's Foods, Dinosaur Museum, st police, to Conchas Lake SP
331	Camino del Coronado, Tucumcari
329	US 54, US 66 E, W Tucumcari Ave
321	Palomas, **S** ⬜ Shell/DQ/Stuckey's/dsl
311	Montoya
302mm	**⬜ both lanes, full ⬜ facilities, ⬜, ⬜ litter barrels, petwalk, RV dump**
300	NM 129, Newkirk, **N** ⬜ Rte 66/dsl, ⬜ USPO, to Conchas Lake SP
291	to Rte 66, Cuervo, **N** Cuervo Gas/repair
284	No Services
277	US 84 S, to Ft Sumner, **N** ⬜ Phillips 66/dsl, ⬜ DQ, Denny's, Silver Moon Café, ⬜ Best Western, Budget Inn, Comfort Inn, Hampton Inn, Holiday Inn Express, Motel 6, Quality Inn, ⬜ NAPACare, Rte 66 Car Museum, RV/auto repair, **S** ⬜ ⬛*Loves*/Carl's Jr/dsl/24hr, TA/Shell/Subway/dsl/24hr/@, ⬜ truck/tire repair
275	US 54 W, Santa Rosa, **N** ⬜ Phillips 66, ⬜ KFC/LJ Silver, McDonald's, Rte 66 Rest., Santa Fe Grill, ⬜ Best Western, Days Inn, La Quinta, Travelodge, ⬜ Santa Rosa Camping, st police, **S** ⬜ Shell/Circle K/dsl, ⬜ Joseph's Grill, Papo's Pizza, ⬜ American Inn, Laloma Motel/RV Park, Sun'n Sand Motel/rest., Super 8, Tower Motel, ⬜ ⬜, CarQuest, $General, Family$, NAPA, USPO, city park
273.5mm	Pecos River
273	US 54 S, Santa Rosa, **N** ⬜ Santa Rosa Lake SP, **S** ⬜ Phillips 66, ⬜ Best Value Inn, ⬜ NAPACare, to Carlsbad Caverns NP
267	Colonias, **N** ⬜ Shell/Stuckey's/dsl/rest.
263	San Ignacio
256	US 84 N, NM 219, to Las Vegas
252	No Services
251.5mm	**⬜ both lanes, full ⬜ facilities, ⬜, ⬜ litter barrels, petwalk, RV dump**

Exit	Services
243	Milagro, **N** ⬜ Phillips 66/dsl
239	no services
234	**N** ⬜ Exxon/Flying C/DQ/dsl/gifts
230	NM 3, to Encino, **N** ⬜ to Villanueva SP
226	no services
220mm	parking area both lanes, litter barrels
218b a	US 285, Clines Corners, **N** ⬜ Conoco/dsl/24hr, Phillips 66/dsl, ⬜ Clines Corners Rest., Subway, **S** ⬜ to Carlsbad Caverns NP
208	Wagon Wheel
207mm	**⬜ both lanes, full ⬜ facilities, ⬜, litter barrels, petwalk**
203	**N** RV Park
197	to Rte 66, Moriarty, **S** ⬜ Lisa's TC/dsl/rest./@, ⬜ auto/RV repair, **1-2 mi S** Glider Museum, same as 194, 196
196	NM 41, Howard Cavasos Blvd, **S** ⬜ Phillips 66/Circle K/dsl, ⬜ Blakes Lotaburger, SuperChina Buffet, ⬜ Comfort Inn, Sunset Motel, ⬜ Family$, NAPA, USPO, to Salinas NM (35mi), auto repair, city park
194	NM 41, Moriarty, **S** ⬜ Conoco, Pump'n Save, TA/Shell/Burger King/Country Pride/Pizza Hut/dsl/24hr/scales/@, ⬜ Arby's, El Comedor, KFC/Taco Bell, McDonald's, Subway, ⬜ Best Value Inn, Best Western, Motel 6, Ponderosa Motel, Super 8, ⬜ Urgent Care, Alco, Chevrolet/GMC, $General, Moriarty Foods, RV Ctr
187	NM 344, Edgewood, **N** ⬜ Conoco/DQ/dsl, ⬜ Walmart/McDonald's, **S** ⬜ Phillips 66/dsl, ⬜ Chili Hills Mexican, China Chef, Domino's, McDonald's, Pizza Barn, Sonic, Subway, ⬜ AutoZone, Family$, Ford, Smith's Foods/dsl, Walgreens, USPO, auto/rv repair, RV Camping, vet
181	NM 217, Sedillo, **S** ⬜ Route 66/dsl
178	Zuzax, **S** ⬜ Shelby's/dsl, ⬜ Hidden Valley RV Park, Leisure Mtn RV Park
175	NM 337, NM 14, Tijeras, **N** ⬜ to Cibola NF, Turquoise Trail RV Park, **S** ⬜ Subway
170	Carnuel
167	Central Ave, to Tramway Blvd, **S** ⬜ Alon/7-11, Phillips 66, Valvoline, ⬜ Blakes Lotaburger, Carl's Jr, KFC, McDonald's, Pizza Hut/Taco Bell, Starbucks, Subway, Waffle House, ⬜ Best Value, Budget Host, Comfort Inn, Deluxe Inn, EconoLodge, Edgwood Studios, Travelodge, Value Place, ⬜ Albertsons, $Tree, Rocky Mtn RV/marine, Smith's/gas, to Kirtland AFB
166	Juan Tabo Blvd, **N** ⬜ Phillips 66/Circle K, Texaco, ⬜ AA Buffet, China King, Dominos, Fedrico's Mexican, Lin's Chinese, McDonald's, Olive Garden, Paul's Rest., Pizza Hut/Taco Bell, Twisters Diner, Village Inn Rest., Wendy's, ⬜ Best Value, Super 8, ⬜ Albertson's, Big O Tire, Discount Tire, $General, Hastings Books, Hobby Lobby, Family$,

NM

🅟 = gas   🍴 = food   🏨 = lodging   🅞 = other   ⛺ = rest stop   Copyright 2014 - The NEXT Exit ®

🅔 INTERSTATE 40 CONT'D

Exit	Services
166	Continued Sav-On Drug, Tuesday Morning, transmissions, vet, **S** 🍴 Little Caesars, Sonic, Wienerschnitzel, 🅞 $General, Holiday RV Ctr, KOA/LP, Meyer's RV Ctr, repair
165	Eubank Blvd, **N** 🅟 Chevron, Phillips 66/Circle K, 🍴 Applebee's, Owl Cafe, Panda Express, Sadie's Rest., Sonic, 🏨 Days Inn, EconoLodge, Guesthouse Inn, Holiday Inn Express, Quality Inn, Rodeway Inn, 🅞 Best Buy, CarQuest, PetCo, Radio Shack, Target, **S** 🅟 Conoco/dsl, Valero, 🍴 Bob's Burgers, Boston Mkt, Chili's, Church's, Del Taco, Golden Corral, IHOP, Jack-in-the-Box, Pizza Hut, Starbucks, Subway, Taco Bell, Taco Cabana, Twister's Burritos, Wendy's, 🅞 AutoZone, Costco/gas, Home Depot, Office Depot, O'Reilly Parts, Peerless Tires, Petsmart, Sam's Club/gas, Toyota, Walgreens, Walmart, repair
164	Lomas Blvd, Wyoming Blvd, **N** 🅟 Circle K/dsl, Phillips 66/dsl, 🍴 Dominos, Eloy's Mexican, South China, Wandy's, 🅞 🅗, NAPA, Walgreens, vet, **S** 🅞 Dodge, Ford, Honda, Hyundai, Kia, transmissions, Kirtland AFB
162b a	Louisiana Blvd, **N** 🍴 Bravo Italian, Buca Italian, CA Pizza Kitchen, Chili's, Elephant Bar Rest., Fuddrucker's, Garduno's, Jasons Deli, LePeep, Macaroni Grill, Marcello's, McAlister's Diner, Peiwei Asian, Shoney's, Starbucks, 🏨 Homewood Suites, Hilton Garden, Hyatt Place, Marriott, Sheraton, 🅞 Barnes&Noble, Big O Tire, Dillard's, Firestone, JC Penney, Kohl's, Macy's, Sears/auto, Trader Joe's, Verizon, **S** 🅟 Shell, 🍴 Burger King, 🅞 atomic museum
161b a	San Mateo Blvd, Albuquerque, **N** 🅟 Giant/dsl, Shell, 🍴 Bob's Burgers, Boston Mkt, Carl's Jr., Denny's, KFC, Pizza Hut, Starbucks, Subway, Taco Bell, Wendy's, 🏨 La Quinta, 🅞 $Tree, Office Depot, Old Navy, **S** 🅟 Chevron/dsl
160	Carlisle Blvd, Albuquerque, **N** 🅟 Circle K/gas, Premier, Pump'n Save, Shell, 🍴 Applebee's, Blakes Lotaburger, Cheesecake Factory, China Wok, Little Anita's, McDonald's, Pizza Hut, Range Cafe, Rudy's BBQ, Sonic, Subway, Twisters Grill, Village Inn Rest., Whataburger, 🏨 Candlewood Suites, Days Inn, EconoLodge, Elegante Hotel, Hampton Inn, Hilton, Holiday Inn Express, La Quinta, Motel 6, Radisson, Residence Inn, Rodeway Inn, Suburban Motel, Super 8, 🅞 Firestone/auto, JC Penney, Smith's Foods, Walgreens, **S** 🅟 Chevron/Subway/dsl, 🍴 Burger King, 🅞 🅗, K-Mart, Whole Foods Mkt
159b c	I-25, S to Las Cruces, N to Santa Fe
158	6th St, 8th St, 12th St, Albuquerque, **N** 🅟 Loves/Subway/dsl, 🅞 U-Haul, **S** 🅟 Chevron, 🏨 Quality Inn
157b	12th St (from eb), **N** 🅟 Alon/Arby's/dsl, 🏨 Holiday Inn Express, 🅞 Lowe's, Walgreens
157a	Rio Grande Blvd, Albuquerque, **N** 🅟 Chevron, **S** 🅟 Shell, 🍴 Ben Michaels, Blakes Lotaburger, Little Anita's, Starbucks, 🏨 Best Western/grill, Hotel Albuquerque, 🅞 repair
156mm	Rio Grande River
155	Coors Rd, Albuquerque, **N** 🅟 Chevron, Circle K, Duke City/dsl, Giant Gas/dsl, 🍴 Applebee's, Arby's, Baskin-Robbins, Burger King, Chili's, Cracker Barrel, Golden Corral, IHOP, Krispy Kreme, McDonald's, Mimmo's Pizza, Panda Express, Papa Murphy's, Quiznos, Red Brick Pizza, Sonic, Subway, Taco Cabana, Twisters Burritos, Wendy's, Wing Stop, 🅞 AutoZone, Brake Masters, Brook's Foods, $Tree, Family$, Firestone, GNC, Home Depot, Jiffy Lube, Midas, Radio Shack, Staples, Verizon, Walgreens,

Exit	Services
155	Continued Walmart, vet, **S** 🅟 Phillips 66, Shell, Valero, 🍴 Altimar's Mexican, Blakes Lotaburger, Del Taco, Denny's, Federico's Mexican, McDonald's, New China, Papa John's, Pizza Hut/Taco Bell, Subway, Twisters Burritos, Village Inn Rest., 🏨 Days Inn, EconoLodge, Hampton Inn, La Quinta, Motel 6, Motel 76, Quality Inn, Rodeway Inn, Super 8, 🅞 BigLots, Discount Tire, O'Reilly Parts, dsl repair
154	Unser Blvd, **N** 🅟 Valero, 🅞 to Petroglyph NM
153	98th St, **S** 🅟 ⓕFLYING J/Denny's/dsl/LP/24hr, Valero, 🍴 Burger King, Little Caesars, McDonald's, Subway, 🏨 Microtel, 🅞 AutoZone, $Tree, truckwash/tire/lube
149	Central Ave, Paseo del Volcan, **N** 🅞 Camping World, Enchanted Trails RV Camping, Freightliner, LaMesa RV Ctr, to Shooting Range SP, **S** 🅞 American RV Park, High Desert RV Park
140.5mm	Rio Puerco River, **N** 🅟 66 Pit Stop
140	Rio Puerco, **N** 🅟 66 Pit Stop/dsl, **S** 🅟 Rte 66 TC/DQ/Road Runner Cafe/hotel/casino/dsl/@
131	To'Hajiilee
126	NM 6, to Los Lunas
120mm	Rio San Jose, Rio San Jose
117	Mesita
114	NM 124, Laguna, **1/2 mi N** 66 Pit Stop/dsl
113.5mm	scenic view both lanes, litter barrels
108	Casa Blanca, Paraje, **S** 🅟 Dancing Eagle TC/DQ/dsl/24hr, 🅞 Ace Hardware, casino, RV park
104	Cubero, Budville
102	Sky City Rd, Acomita, **N** 🅟 Sky City/McDonald's/hotel/casino/dsl, 🍴 Huwak'a Rest., 🅞 RV Park/laundry, casino, **S** ⛺ **both lanes, full** ♿ **facilities,** 🅒**,** 🚿**, litter barrels, petwalk,** 🅗
100	San Fidel
96	McCartys
89	NM 117, to Quemado, **N** 🅟 Skyway/Shell/Subway/dsl/gifts, **S** El Malpais NM
85	NM 122, NM 547, Grants, **N** 🅟 Alon/dsl, Phillips 66/dsl, Shell/dsl, 🍴 Asian Buffet, Blakes Lotaburger, Canton Cafe, Denny's, Pizza Hut, Subway, Taco Bell, 🏨 Comfort Inn, Days Inn, Holiday Inn Express, Motel 6, Quality Inn, Red Lion Motel, Sands Motel, Super 8, Travelodge, 🅞 🅗 AutoZone, Delta Tire, O'Reilly Parts, $Tree, Walmart, repair/transmissions/towing, **S** Lavaland RV Park,
81b a	NM 53 S, Grants, **N** 🅟 Phillips 66, 🍴 Domino's, KFC, McDonald's, 🅞 🅗, Ford, NAPA, USPO, **S** 🅞 Blue Spruce RV Park, KOA/Cibola Sands RV Park, El Malpais NM
79	NM 122, NM 605, Milan, **N** 🅟 Chevron/dsl, Loves/Chester's/Subway/dsl/scales/24hr, 🍴 DQ, 🏨 Crossroads Motel, 🅞 Bar-S RV Park, **S** 🅟 Petro/Iron Skillet/dsl/scales/24hr/@, 🅞 Speedco Lube, st police
72	Bluewater Village, **N** 🅟 Exxon/DQ/dsl
63	NM 412, Prewitt, **S** to Bluewater Lake SP (7mi)
53	NM 371, NM 612, Thoreau, **N** 🅟 Giant/Blimpie/dsl, 🅞 Family$, NAPA, USPO
47	Continental Divide, 7275 ft, **N** 🅟 Phillips 66, 🅞 Continental Divide Trdg Post, towing/repair, **S** USPO
44	Coolidge
39	Refinery, **N** 🅟 ▨▨▨/Subway/Dennys/dsl/scales/24hr/@
36	Iyanbito
33	NM 400, McGaffey, Ft Wingate, **N** 🅞 to Red Rock SP, RV camping, museum
26	E 66th Ave, E Gallup, **N** 🅟 Shell/Subway/dsl, 🍴 Denny's,

🔼E INTERSTATE 40 CONT'D

Exit	Services
26	Continued
	🛏 Comfort Suites, Holiday Inn Express, La Quinta, Sleep Inn, 🄾 Red Rock Camping, to Red Rock SP, museum, st police, **S on Rte 66** 🅟 Alon/dsl, Conoco/dsl, Giant, Shell/Ortega Gifts, 🍴 Aurelie's Diner, Blakes Lotaburger, Burger King, KFC, McDonald's, Sonic, Wendy's, 🛏 Days Inn, Hacienda Motel, Roadrunner Motel, 🄾 H, $General
22	Montoya Blvd, Gallup, **N** 🆁🆂 **both lanes, full facilities, info, S on Rte 66** 🅟 Duke City, Gas Up, Phillips 66, 🍴 Big Cheese Pizza, Church's, DQ, Domino's, Earl's Rest., Hong Kong Buffet, LJ Silver, Panz Alegra, Papa John's, Pizza Hut, Subway, Taco Bell, 🛏 Blue Spruce Motel, El Capitan Motel, El Rancho Motel/rest., 🄾 Albertson's, Giant/dsl, O'Reilly Parts, Radio Shack, Walgreens
20	US 491, to Shiprock, Gallup, **N** 🅟 Alon/dsl, Giant/dsl, 🍴 Applebee's, Arby's, Big Cheese Pizza, Blakes Lotaburger, Burger King, Canton Chinese, Carl's Jr., Church's, Cracker Barrel, DQ, Denny's, Furr's Café, Golden Corral, KFC, King Dragon Chinese, Little Caesars, McDonald's, Pizza Hut, Sizzler, Sonic, Super Buffet, Taco Bell, Wendy's, 🛏 Comfort Inn, Hampton Inn, Quality Inn, 🄾 AT&T, AutoZone,

Exit	Services
20	Continued
	Beall's, Big Lots, CarQuest, Chrysler/Dodge/Jeep, $Tree, Family$, Home Depot, JC Penney, Midas, NAPA, Nissan, O'Reilly Parts, PepBoys, Radio Shack, Safeway, Walmart, mall, **$ on Rte 66** 🅟 Phillips 66/dsl, 🍴 Blakes Lotaburger, Don Diego's, El Dorado Rest., El Sombrero Mexican, Garcia's Rest., Rte 66 Diner, Sonic, McDonald's, 🛏 Ambassador Motel, Best Value Inn, Days Inn, Desert Skies, Golden Desert Motel, Rodeway Inn, Royal Holiday Motel, Super 8, 🄾 H, Ford/Lincoln, Tire Factory, RV camping
16	NM 118, W Gallup, Mentmore, **N** 🅟 ❤Loves/Chester's/Subway/dsl/24hr, Navajo/dsl/24hr, TA/Country Pride/dsl/scales/24hr/@, USave Trkstp/dsl, 🄾 Blue Beacon, dsl repair, **S** 🅟 Alon, Conoco, Phillips 66/Allsup's, Thrift Way, 🍴 Ranch Kitchen, Taco Bell, 🛏 Baymont, Budget Inn, EconoLodge, Gallup Inn, Hampton Inn, Microtel, Motel 6, Red Lion, Red Roof Inn, Travelodge, 🄾 USA RV Park
12mm	**inspection/weigh sta eb**
8	to Manuelito
3mm	**Welcome Ctr eb, full** ♿ **facilities, 🚻, 🏕, litter barrels, petwalk**
0mm	New Mexico/Arizona state line

NEW YORK

🔼N INTERSTATE 81

Exit	Services
184mm	US/Canada border, New York state line. **I-81 begins/ends.**
183.5mm	US Customs (sb)
52 (183)	Island Rd, to De Wolf Point, last US exit nb, **E** food
51 (180)	Island Rd, to Fineview, Islands Parks, **2-3 mi E** 🛏 Seaway Island Resort, Thousand Islands Club/rest, 🄾 Nature Ctr, camping, golf, USPO, **W** 🅟 Sunoco/dsl
179mm	St Lawrence River
178.5mm	Thousand Islands **Toll Bridge Booth, NY Welcome Ctr/** 🆁🆂 **sb, full** ♿ **facilities, 🚻, 🏕, litter barrels, petwalk**
50NS (178)	NY 12, **E** to Alexandria Bay, 🅟 Mobil/dsl, 🍴 Kountry Kottage Rest., Subway, 🛏 Bonnie Castle Resort, Otter Creek Inn, PineHurst Motel, River Edge Inn, 🄾 H, funpark (seasonal), st police, to Thousand Island Region, **W** to Clayton, 🅟 Mobil, 🛏 Bridgeview Motel, PJ's Motel, 🄾 **NY Welcome Ctr/**🆁🆂, to RV camping
174mm	🆁🆂 **nb, full** ♿ **facilities, 🚻, vending, 🏕, litter barrels, petwalk, st police**
49 (171)	NY 411, to Theresa, Indian River Lakes, **E** 🅟 Mobil/dsl (4mi), Sunoco/dsl, **W** 🍴 Trickey's Diner
168mm	parking area sb, 🏕
161mm	parking area nb
48a (159)	new exit
48 (158)	US 11, NY 37, **1-4 mi E** 🅟 Mobil/dsl, Nice'n Easy/dsl, Sunoco/dsl, 🍴 Arby's, McDonald's, Longway's Diner, Papa John's, Subway, 🛏 Allen's Budget Motel, Candlewood Suites, Fort Drum Studio-Tels, Microtel, Royal Inn, 🄾 Sugar Creek Stores, st police
156.5mm	parking area both lanes
47 (155)	NY 12, Bradley St, Watertown, **E** 🅟 Nice'n Easy/Subway/dsl, Valero, 🍴 Frosty Dairy Bar, 🄾 H, **W** 🛏 Rainbow Motel
154.5mm	Black River

Exit	Services
46 (154)	NY 12F, Coffeen St, Watertown, **E** 🅟 Mobil, 🍴 Cracker Barrel, Shorty's Diner, 🄾 Home Depot, **Urgent Care**
45 (152)	NY 3, to Arsenal St, Watertown, **E** 🅟 Mobil, Sunoco, 🍴 American Grill, Applebee's, Arby's, Buffalo Wild Wings, Burger King, Chipotle Mexican, CiCi's Pizza, Coldstone, Denny's, Dunkin Donuts, 5 Guys Burgers, Friendly's, Jreck Subs, KFC, McDonald's, Panda Buffet, Ponderosa, Ruby Tuesday, Starbucks, Taco Bell, Tilted Kilt, 🛏 Best Value Inn, Comfort Inn, EconoLodge, Fairfield Inn, Hampton Inn, Hilton Garden, Holiday Inn Express, Rodeway Inn, 🄾 Advance Parts, Aldi Foods, AT&T, AutoZone, BigLots, $General, $Tree, Jo-Ann Fabrics, Kost Tire, Mavis Discount Tire, Michael's, Monro, PriceChopper Foods/24hr, Radio Shack, Staples, TJ Maxx, USPO, Walgreens, **W** 🅟 Fastrac, 🍴 Bob Evans, Olive Garden, Panera Bread, Pizza Hut, Red Lobster, Subway, Teriyaki Experience, TX Roadhouse, TGIFriday's, 🛏 Ramada Inn, 🄾 Best Buy, BonTon, Dick's, Gander Mtn, Hannaford Foods, JC Penney, K-Mart, Kohl's, Lowe's, Michael's, Old Navy, PetCo, Sam's Club, Sears/auto, Target, Verizon, Walmart, mall, to Sackets Harbor
149mm	parking area nb, 🚻
44 (148)	NY 232, to Watertown Ctr, **3 mi E** 🅟 Mobil, 🍴 Subway, 🛏 Best Western, 🄾 H
147mm	🆁🆂 **sb, full** ♿ **facilities, 🚻, 🏕, litter barrels, vending, petwalk**
43 (146)	US 11, to Kellogg Hill
42 (144)	NY 177, Adams Center, **E** 🅟 Nice'n Easy/Mama Mia's Pizza/dsl, Sunoco/dsl, 🍴 Depot Cafe, 🄾 Harley-Davidson, Tugger's Camping (12mi)
41 (140)	NY 178, Adams, **E** 🅟 Sunoco/dsl, 🍴 Dunkin Donuts, McDonald's, Subway, 🄾 KOA, Willows on the Lake RV Park, st police
138mm	South Sandy Creek
40 (135)	NY 193, to Ellisburg, Pierrepont Manor

🅖 = gas   🍴 = food   🛏 = lodging   🅾 = other   🆁🆂 = rest stop   Copyright 2014 - The NEXT Exit ®

⬆N INTERSTATE 81 CONT'D

PULASKI

Exit	Services
134mm	parking area/ 🆁, both lanes
39 (133)	Mannsville
38 (131)	US 11
37 (128)	Lacona, Sandy Creek, **E** 🍴 J&R Diner, 🛏 Harris Lodge, **W** 🅖 Mobil, Valero, 🍴 Sandy Creek Diner, 🛏 Anglers Roost B&B, 🅾 CarQuest, Colonial Court Camping, Sandy Island Beach SP, USPO
36 (121)	NY 13, Pulaski, **E** 🅖 Byrne Dairy/dsl, Valero, 🍴 Ponderosa, 🛏 Travelodge, **W** 🅖 KwikFill/dsl, Mobil/dsl, Nice'n Easy/Subway/dsl, Valero, 🍴 Arby's, Burger King, Dunkin Donuts, Eddy's Place, Jreck Subs, McDonald's, Paulanjo's Pizza, River House Rest., Stefano's Rest., 🛏 1880 House B&B, Super 8, 🅾 Aldi Foods, Buick/Chevrolet, Family$, Kinney Drug, NAPA, Rite Aid, Top's Foods, Verizon, to Selkirk Shores SP, camping, fish hatchery
35 (118)	to US 11, Tinker Tavern Rd, **E** Streamside RV Park
34 (115)	NY 104, to Mexico, **E** 🅖 Mobil/Maple View Rest./dsl/scales, **W** 🅖 Sunoco, 🛏 Feeder Creek Lodge (5mi), 🅾 J&J (4mi), Jellystone Camping (9mi)
33 (111)	NY 69, Parish, **E** 🅖 Sunoco/dsl/24hr, 🍴 Grist Mill Rest., 🛏 E Coast Resort (4mi), 🅾 Up Country RV Park (8mi), **W** 🅖 Gulf, Mirabito/Dunkin Donuts/dsl, 🍴 Candlelight Rest, G&F Pizza, 🛏 Parish Motel, 🅾 USPO
32 (103)	NY 49, to Central Square, **E** 🅖 Mirabito/dsl, Sunoco/Subway/dsl, 🍴 Good Golly's Rest., 🅾 Murphy's Auto, **W** 🅖 Fastrac/gas, 🍴 Burger King, Dunkin Donuts, McDonald's, 🅾 Advance Parts, $Tree, Ford, NAPA, Rite Aid, Walmart/Subway, st police
31 (99)	to US 11, Brewerton, **E** Oneida Shores Camping, **W** 🅖 Mirabito/Tim Hortons/dsl, Mobil/dsl, Nice'n Easy/dsl, 🍴 Castaway's Cafe, Dunkin Donuts, Little Caesars, McDonald's, Subway, 🛏 Days Inn, 🅾 AT&T, $General, Kinney Drugs, vet
30 (96)	NY 31, to Cicero, **0-1 mi E** 🅖 Fastrac/dsl, Hess/dsl, KwikFill, 🍴 Arby's, Cracker Barrel, Dunkin Donuts, McDonald's, 🛏 Comfort Suites, Holiday Inn Express, 🅾 Gander Mtn, **W** 🅖 Kwikfill, 🍴 Cicero Diner, Cicero Pizza, Frank's Café, 🅾 70's RV Ctr
29 (93)	I-481 S, NY 481, to Oswego, Syracuse, **1 mi W on US 11** 🅖 Hess, 🍴 Buffalo Wild Wings, Burger King, Copper Top Tavern, Denny's, Dunkin Donuts, KFC, Kyoto Buffet, Little Caesars, Moe's SW Grill, Panera Bread, Pizza Hut, Subway, Taco Bell, Tim Hortons, Tully's Rest., Wendy's, 🛏 Budget Inn, 🅾 Advance Parts, AT&T, Audi/Porsche/VW, Chrysler/Dodge/Jeep, $General, $Tree, Dunn Tire, Firestone/auto, GNC, Home Depot, Hyundai, Kia, Lexus, Lincoln, Lowe's, Marshall's, NAPA, Nissan, PepBoys, PriceChopper Foods, Radio Shack, Rite Aid, Suzuki, Target, Toyota/Scion, Verizon, Wegman's Foods, Walmart
28 (91)	N Syracuse, Taft Rd, **E** 🅖 KwikFill, Sunoco/dsl, 🅾 U-Haul, **W** 🅖 Sunoco, 🅾 Auto Value Parts, USPO
27 (90)	N Syracuse, **E** 🍴
26 (89)	US 11, Mattydale, **E** 🅖 Mobil, 🍴 Hofmann Rest., Pizza Hut, 🛏 Red Carpet Inn, 🅾 BigLots, $Tree, GNC, Goodyear/auto, K-Mart, Michael's, PetCo, Rite Aid, Staples, TJ Maxx, vet, **W** 🅖 Delta Sonic/dsl, 🍴 Arby's, Burger King, Denny's, Dunkin Donuts, Gino&Joe's, Jreck Subs, Julie's Diner, McDonald's, Ponderosa, Subway, Taco Bell, Tim Hortons, Wendy's, 🛏 Candlewood Suites, EconoLodge, Holiday Inn Express, 🅾 Advance Parts, Aldi Foods, Kost Tire, Monro Auto, Rite Aid, Top's Foods

SYRACUSE

Exit	Services
25a (88)	I-90, NY Thruway
25 (87.5)	7th North St, **E** 🅖 🚂/McDonald's/dsl/scales/24hr, 🅾 NAPA, repair, **W** 🅖 Sunoco/dsl, 🍴 Burger King, Denny's, Dunkin Donuts, La Pizzeria, North Buffet, Subway, Tim Hortons, Tully's Rest., 🛏 Comfort Inn, Hampton Inn, Maplewood Inn/cafe, Quality Inn, Ramada Inn, Super 8
24 (86)	NY 370 W, to Liverpool, same as 23
23 (86)	NY 370 E, Hiawatha Blvd, **E** 🍴 Wendy's, **W** 🅖 Hess, 🍴 PF Chang's, 🅾 Best Buy, Dick's, JC Penney, Macy's, mall
22 (85)	NY 298, Court St
21 (84.5)	Spencer St, Catawba St (from sb), industrial area
20 (84)	I-690 W (from sb), Franklin St, West St
19 (84)	I-690 E, Clinton St, Salina St, to E Syracuse
18 (84)	Harrison St, Adams St, **E** 🛏 Crowne Plaza, 🅾 🅷, to Syracuse U, Civic Ctr
17 (82)	Brighton Ave, S Salina St, **W** 🅖 KwikFill, Valero/Chicken Basket
16a (81)	I-481 N, to DeWitt
16 (78)	US 11, to Nedrow, Onondaga Nation, **1-2 mi W** 🍴 Fire Keepers Diner, McDonald's, Pizza Hut
15 (73)	US 20, La Fayette, **E** 🅖 Sunoco/dsl, 🍴 La Fayette Inn, Old Tymes Rest., 🅾 $General, NAPA, USPO, st police, vet, **W** 🍴 McDonald's
71mm	truck insp sta both lanes, 🔧 s

CORTLAND

Exit	Services
14 (67)	NY 80, Tully, **E** 🅖 Nice'n Easy/deli/dsl, 🍴 Elm St Cafe, 🛏 Best Western, 🅾 Chevrolet, Kinney Drug, **W** 🍴 Burger King
13 (63)	NY 281, Preble, **E** 🅖 Mirabito/Dunkin Donuts/Subway/dsl, 🅾 to Song Mtn Ski Resort
60mm	🆁🆂/truck insp nb, full ♿ facilities, 🔧, 🆁, litter barrels, vending, petwalk
12 (53)	US 11, NY 281, to Homer, **W** 🅖 KwikFill, Sunoco/dsl, Valero, 🍴 Applebee's, Burger King, Doug's Fishfry, Fabio's Italian, Little Italy, Ponderosa, 🛏 Country Inn&Suites, 🅾 🅷, st police, to Fillmore Glen SP
11 (52)	NY 13, Cortland, **E** 🍴 Perkins, 🛏 Comfort Inn, Holiday Inn Express, Quality Inn, **W** 🅖 Mobil/Dunkin Donuts/dsl, 🍴 Arby's, China Moon, Crown City Rest., Friendly's, McDonald's, Subway, Taco Bell, Tim Hortons, Wendy's, 🛏 Hampton Inn, Ramada Inn, 🅾 Advance Parts, Family$, Jo-Ann Fabrics, Kost Tire, P&C Foods, museum
10 (50)	US 11, NY 41, to Cortland, McGraw, **W** 🅖 Citgo/Dunkin Donuts/Quiznos/dsl, Sunoco/Subway/dsl/24hr, 🛏 Cortland Motel, Days Inn
9 (38)	US 11, NY 221, **W** 🅖 Sunoco/XtraMart/dsl/24hr, Valero, 🍴 NY Pizzaria, 🛏 3 Bear Inn/rest., Greek Peak Lodge, 🅾 Gregg's Mkt, Country Hills Camping, Maple Museum, Robinson's Repair, antiques, city park, st police, USPO
33mm	🆁🆂 sb, full ♿ facilities, 🔧, 🆁, litter barrels, vending, petwalk
8 (30)	NY 79, to US 11, NY 26, NY 206 (no EZ return), Whitney Pt, **E** 🅖 Hess, Kwikfill, Sunoco, 🍴 Aiello's Ristorante, Arby's, Country Kitchen, McDonald's, Subway, 🛏 Hotel Griffin, 🅾 $General, Gregg's Mkt, NAPA, Parts+, Radio Shack, USPO, to Dorchester Park
7 (21)	US 11, Castle Creek, **W** 🅖 Mirabito/Subway/Tim Hortons/dsl
6 (16)	US 11, to NY 12, I-88E, Chenango Bridge, **E on US 11** 🅖 Gulf/dsl, Hess/dsl, Sunoco/Tim Hortons/dsl, 🍴 Arby's, Burger King, Denny's, Dunkin Donuts, Pizza Hut, Ponderosa, Subway, Tokyo Buffet, Wendy's, 🅾 Advance Parts, Chrysler/Dodge/Jeep, CVS Drug, Kost Tire, Lowe's,

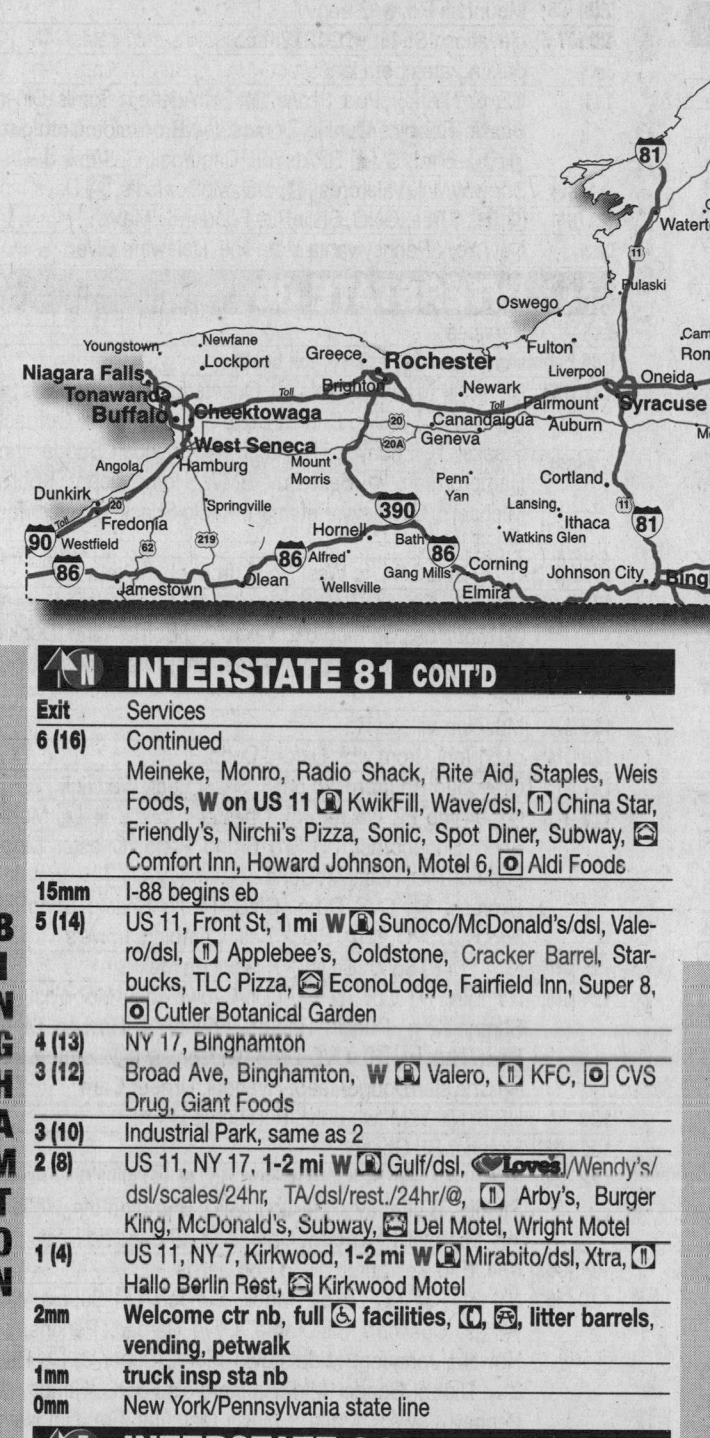

⬆N INTERSTATE 81 CONT'D

Exit	Services
6 (16)	Continued
	Meineke, Monro, Radio Shack, Rite Aid, Staples, Weis Foods, **W on US 11** 🅖 KwikFill, Wave/dsl, 🍴 China Star, Friendly's, Nirchi's Pizza, Sonic, Spot Diner, Subway, 🏨 Comfort Inn, Howard Johnson, Motel 6, 🄾 Aldi Foods
15mm	I-88 begins eb
5 (14)	US 11, Front St, **1 mi W** 🅖 Sunoco/McDonald's/dsl, Valero/dsl, 🍴 Applebee's, Coldstone, Cracker Barrel, Starbucks, TLC Pizza, 🏨 EconoLodge, Fairfield Inn, Super 8, 🄾 Cutler Botanical Garden
4 (13)	NY 17, Binghamton
3 (12)	Broad Ave, Binghamton, **W** 🅖 Valero, 🍴 KFC, 🄾 CVS Drug, Giant Foods
3 (10)	Industrial Park, same as 2
2 (8)	US 11, NY 17, **1-2 mi W** 🅖 Gulf/dsl, ♥Loves/Wendy's/dsl/scales/24hr, TA/dsl/rest./24hr/@, 🍴 Arby's, Burger King, McDonald's, Subway, 🏨 Del Motel, Wright Motel
1 (4)	US 11, NY 7, Kirkwood, **1-2 mi W** 🅖 Mirabito/dsl, Xtra, 🍴 Hallo Berlin Rest, 🏨 Kirkwood Motel
2mm	**Welcome ctr nb, full** 🅰 **facilities,** 🅲, 🏨**, litter barrels, vending, petwalk**
1mm	**truck insp sta nb**
0mm	New York/Pennsylvania state line

⬆E INTERSTATE 84

Exit	Services
71.5mm	New York/Connecticut state line
21 (69)	US 6, US 202, NY 121 (from wb), N Salem, same as 20
20N (67.5)	NY 22, Palling, **N** 🅖 Mobil, Shell/dsl, Valero, 🍴 Dunkin Donuts, Portofinos, 🄾 Cadillac/Chevrolet, Ford, Honda, Subaru
20S	I-684, to NYC
20S	I-684, to NYC
19 (65)	NY 312, Carmel, **N** 🄾 st police, **S** 🍴 Applebee's, Dunkin Donuts, Eveready Diner, Gaetano's Deli, 🄾 🄷 DeCicco's Mkt, Home Depot, Kohl's, Marshall's, Michael's, Verizon
18 (62)	NY 311, Lake Carmel, **S** 🍴 Lakeview Pizza
17 (59)	Ludingtonville Rd, **S** 🅖 Hess/Blimpie/dsl, Sunoco/dsl, 🍴 Cacciatore's Pizzaria, Cutiloo's Rest., Dunkin Donuts,

	Gappy's Pizza, Lou's Deli
56mm	elevation 965 ft
55mm	🆁🆂 **both lanes, full** 🅰 **facilities,** 🅲**, vending,** 🏨**, litter barrels, petwalk**
16 (53)	Taconic Parkway, N to Albany, S to New York
15 (51)	Lime Kiln NY, **3 mi N** 🅖 Mobil, 🍴 Dunkin Donuts, 🏨 Arbor Ridge Inn
13 (46)	US 9, to Poughkeepsie, **N** 🅖 Flory's/deli, Mobil/dsl, Shell/dsl, 🍴 A&W/KFC, Boston Mkt, Charlie Brown Steaks, Coldstone, Cracker Barrel, Fishkill Grill, 5 Guys, Hudson Buffet, Izumi Japanese, Little Asia, Panera Bread, Pizza Shop, Red Line Diner, Ruby Tuesday, Starbucks, Subway, Taco Bell, Wendy's, 🏨 Comfort Inn, Courtyard, Days Inn, Extended Stay America, Hampton Inn, Hilton Garden, Holiday Inn Express, Hyatt House, Ramada Inn, Residence Inn, 🄾 AT&T, Sam's Club, Verizon, Walmart, **S** 🅖 Hess/Blimpie/dsl, 🍴 Maya Cafe, McDonald's, 🄾 Home Depot
12 (45)	NY 52 E, Fishkill, **N** 🅖 Valero, 🍴 Golden Buddha, Green Garden, Sal's Pizza, 🄾 CVS Drug, **S** 🅖 Mobil, Sunoco/dsl, 🍴 84 Diner, Hometown Deli, 🏨 Quality Inn
11 (42)	NY 9D, to Wappingers Falls, **1 mi N** 🅖 Mobil/dsl, Shell
41mm	**toll booth**
40mm	Hudson River
10 (39)	US 9W, NY 32, to Newburgh, **N** 🅖 Citgo, Sunoco, 🍴 Alexis Diner, Andiamo Rest., Bonura's Little Italy, Burger King, Dunkin Donuts, Great Wall, Green Garden Chinese, KFC, McDonald's, New China, Pizza Hut, Subway, 🄾 Advance Parts, BigLots, $Tree, Family$, Firestone/auto, Monroe, PriceChopper Foods, Rite Aid, Shop Rite Foods, Walgreens, **S** 🅖 Citgo/dsl, Sunoco, 🄾 🄷
8 (37)	NY 52, to Walden, **N** 🅖 Shell/dsl

⛽ = gas ‖ = food 🛏 = lodging 🄾 = other 🅁🅂 = rest stop Copyright 2014 - The NEXT Exit ®

🆖 INTERSTATE 84 CONT'D

Exit	Services
7b (36)	NY 300, Newburgh, **N** ⛽ Mobil, ‖ Daddy Grill, DQ, Dunkin Donuts, Leo's Pizzaria, McDonald's, Newburgh Buffet, Perkins, Taco Bell, Wendy's, 🄾 AT&T, AutoZone, BonTon, $Tree, Marshall's, Mavis Tire, Midas, Office Depot, Sears/auto, Stop&Shop Foods, **S** ⛽ Hess/dsl, Sunoco/dsl, ‖ Applebee's, Burger King, Chili's, China City, Cosimos Ristorante, Denny's, 5 Guys Burgers, Gateway Diner, IHOP, Johnny D's, Longhorn Steaks, Neptune Diner, Panera Bread, Pizza Mia, Sonic, Starbucks, Steak'n Stein, Subway, TGIFriday's, Union Sq Rest., 🛏 Days Inn, Hampton Inn, Hilton Garden, Howard Johnson, Ramada Inn, Super 8, 🄾 Adam's Farm Mkt, Aldi Foods, Associated Foods, Barnes&Noble, Buick/GMC, Cadillac/Chevrolet, Chrysler/Dodge/Jeep, Ford/Lincoln, Home Depot, Honda, Kohl's, Lowe's, Meineke, Michael's, Nissan, Orange County Choppers/cafe, PetsMart, Radio Shack, Target, Verizon, Walmart
7a (35)	I-87, NY Thruway, Albany, to NYC
6 (34)	NY 17K, to Newburgh, **N** ⛽ Mobil, 🚛/Arby's/dsl/scales/24hr, ‖ 🍽 Diner, 🛏 Comfort Inn, **S** ⛽ Shell/dsl, 🛏 Courtyard, **3 mi** **S** 🛏 Days Inn, Hilton Garden, Howard Johnson
5a (33)	NY 747, International Blvd, to Stewart ✈ **S** 🛏 Homewood Suites
5 (29)	NY 208, Maybrook, **N** ⛽ Mobil/dsl, Sunoco/dsl, ‖ Burger King, Dunkin Donuts, McDonald's, 🄾 NAPA, Rite Aid, ShopRite Foods, Walgreens, Winding Hills Camping, **S** ⛽ Hess/dsl, TA/Valero/Country Pride/Pizza Hut/dsl/scales/24hr/@, ‖ Prima's Deli, Renee's Deli, Subway, 🛏 Super 8, 🄾 Advance Parts, Blue Beacon, auto/truck repair, st police
24mm	🅁🅂 wb, full ♿ facilities, ⛽ vending, 🗑 litter barrels, petwalk
4 (19)	NY 17, Middletown, **N** ⛽ Mobil/24hr, ‖ Americana Diner, Applebee's, Arby's, Baskin-Robbins/Dunkin Donuts, Boston Mkt, Burger King, Cheeseburger Paradise, ChuckeCheese, Denny's, Friendly's, KFC, McDonald's, Olive Garden, Panera Bread, Papa John's, Perkins, Pizza Hut, Red Lobster, Ruby Tuesday, Starbucks, Subway, Taco Bell, Wendy's, Youyou Japanese, 🛏 Howard Johnson, Middletown Motel, Super 8, 🄾 🄷 Aldi Foods, AutoZone, Best Buy, Big Lots, $Tree, Firestone/auto, Gander Mtn, Hannaford Foods, Home Depot, Honda, JC Penney, Jo-Ann Fabrics, Kohl's, Lowe's, Marshall's, Michael's, Old Navy, PetCo, PetsMart, PriceChopper Foods, Rite Aid, Sam's Club/gas, Sears/auto, ShopRite Foods, Staples, Tire Discount, TJ Maxx, U-Haul, Verizon, Walmart/24hr, mall, Urgent Care, vet, **S** ⛽ Citgo/dsl, ‖ Chili's, El Bandido Mexican, Outback Steaks, TGIFriday, 🛏 Courtyard, Hampton Inn, Holiday Inn, Microtel, 🄾 st police
17mm	🅁🅂 eb, full ♿ facilities, ⛽ vending, 🗑 litter barrels, petwalk
3 (15)	US 6, to Middletown, **N** ⛽ Citgo/dsl, Mobil, QuickChek/dsl, Shell, Valero, ‖ Bro Bruno's Pizza, Dunkin Donuts, IHOP, McDonald's, NY Buffet, Peking Chinese, Rita's Custard, Subway, Taco Bell, Wendy's, 🄾 🄷 Acura, AutoZone, Buick/Chevrolet, CarQuest, Family$, Goodyear, Mavis Discount Tire, Mazda, Meineke, Radio Shack, Rite Aid, ShopRite Foods, Subaru, Verizon, VW, **S** ⛽ Citgo/dsl, Geo/Dunkin Donuts/dsl, 🛏 Days Inn, Global Budget Inn, 🄾 Kia, Nissan, Toyota/Scion

2 (5)	Mountain Rd, **S** Greenville's Deli
4mm	elevation 1254 ft wb, 1272 ft eb
3mm	parking area both lanes
1 (1)	US 6, NY 23, Port Jervis, **N** ‖ Arlene'n Tom's Diner, Baskin-Robbins/Dunkin Donuts, 🛏 Brookside Cottages, 🄾 🄷, Ford, **S** ⛽ BP/dsl/LP, Citgo/dsl, Gulf/dsl, 🚛/Subway/dsl, Valero/dsl, ‖ DQ, McDonald's, 🛏 Days Inn, 🄾 🄷, $Tree, GNC, ShopRite Foods, TJ Maxx
0mm	New York/Pennsylvania state line, Delaware River

🆖 INTERSTATE 86

Exit	Services
I-86 begins/ends on I-87, exit 16, toll booth	
131 (379)	NY 17, **N** ‖ Applebee's, 🄾 Outlets/famous brands, **S** ⛽ Gulf/dsl, ‖ Chili's, Dunkin Donuts, McDonald's, Outback Steaks, TGIFriday's, Uno Grill, 🛏 American Budget Inn, Hampton Inn, 🄾 Best Buy, BMW, Home Depot, Kohl's, Michael's, Old Navy, Petsmart, Radio Shack, Staples, Target, TJMaxx
130a (378)	US 6, Bear Mtn, to West Point (from eb, no return)
130 (377)	NY 208, Monroe, Washingtonville, **N** ‖ Rambler's Rest, **S** ⛽ Mobil/dsl, Sunoco/dsl, Valero, ‖ Burger King, Dunkin Donuts, Monroe Diner, 🄾 $Tree, ShopRite Foods, st police
129 (375)	Museum Village Rd
128 (374)	rd 51 (only from wb), Oxford Depot
127 (373)	Greycourt Rd (from wb only), Sugar Loaf, Warwick
126 (372)	NY 94 (no EZ wb return), Chester, Florida, **N** ⛽ Mobil, Shell, Sunoco/dsl, ‖ Bro Bruno Pizza, Chester Diner, Lobster Pier Rest, McDonald's, Wendy's, 🛏 Holiday Inn Express, 🄾 CVS Drug, GNC, Radio Shack, ShopRite Foods, USPO, **S** 🄾 Black Bear Camping, Lowe's
125 (369)	NY 17M E, South St, **N** ‖ Hacienda Mexican
124 (368)	NY 17A, NY 207, **N** ⛽ Gulf/Subway/dsl, Mobil/dsl, ‖ Burger King, Dunkin Donuts, Friendly's, Goshen Diner, Pizza Hut, 🄾 🄷, CVS Drug, Verizon, **S** 🛏 Comfort Inn, 🄾 Chrysler/Dodge/Jeep, Hyundai, Urgent Care
123	US 6, NY 17M (wb only), Port Jervis
122a (367)	Fletcher St, Goshen
122 (364)	rd 67, E Main St, Crystal Run Rd, **N** ‖ Chili's, Outback Steaks, TGIFriday's, 🛏 Courtyard, Hampton Inn, Holiday Inn, Microtel, 🄾 Urgent Care, **S** ‖ El Bandido Rest.
121 (363)	I-84, E to Newburgh, W to Port Jervis
120 (363)	NY 211, **N** ⛽ Lukoil, Mobil, Sunoco, ‖ Buffalo Wild Wings, Cosimo's Ristorante, Olive Garden, Perkins, 🛏 Howard Johnson, Middletown Motel, Super 8, 🄾 Best Buy, Dick's, Gander Mtn, Hannaford's Foods, Honda, JC Penney, Lowe's, Macy's, Mavis Discount Tire, Old Navy, PetCo, Sam's Club/gas, Sears, Target, vet, **S** ⛽ Mobil, ‖ Americana Diner, Applebee's, Arby's, Boston Mkt, Burger King, Cheeseburger Paradise, Denny's, Dunkin Donuts, 5 Guys Burgers, Franko Di Roma Italian, Friendly's, KFC, McDonald's, Panera Bread, Papa John's, Pizza Hut, Red Lobster, Ruby Tuesday, Starbucks, Subway, Taco Bell, TX Roadhouse, Wendy's, YouYou Chinese, 🄾 Aldi Foods, AT&T, AutoZone, BigLots, $General, $Tree, Firestone/auto, Hobby Lobby, Home Depot, Kohl's, Marshall's, Michael's, Midas, Petsmart, PriceChopper, Rite Aid, ShopRite Foods, Staples, Tire Discount Ctr, TJMaxx, U-Haul, Verizon, Walmart/Subway,
119 (360)	NY 309, Pine Bush, **S** ⛽ Citgo/dsl, Valero/Dunkin Donuts/dsl, ‖ Subway
118a (358)	NY 17M, Fair Oaks

NY

MIDDLETOWN

🅴 INTERSTATE 86 CONT'D

Exit	Services
118 (358)	Circleville, **N** Economy Inn, **S** 🅖 Citgo/dsl, Mobil/dsl
116 (355)	NY 17K, Bloomingburg, **N** 🍴 Mtn View Rest, **S** 🅖 Citgo/dsl, 🍴 Quickway Diner
115	Burlingame Rd
114	Wurtsboro, Highview (from wb)
113 (350)	US 209, Wurtsboro, Ellenville, **N** 🅖 Mobil/dsl, Stewarts/gas, 🍴 Custar's Last Stand, Danny's Steaks, 🛏 Gold Mtn Chalet, Days Inn, Honors Haven Resort, Valley Brook Motel, 🄾 G-Mart Foods, Spring Glen Camping, **S** Giovanni's Café (2mi)
112 (347)	Masten Lake, Yankee Lake, **N** 🛏 Days Inn, ValleyBrook Motel, 🄾 Catskill Mtn Ranch Camping, Yankee Lake
111 (344)	(eb only), Wolf Lake, **S** 🅖 Citgo/dsl
110 (343)	Lake Louise Marie
109 (342)	Rock Hill, Woodridge, **N** 🅖 Citgo/dsl, 🍴 Angelo's Kitchen, Dutch's Cafe, Krust Italian, Pizza Rock, RockHill Diner, 🛏 Sullivan Hotel, 🄾 Ace Hardware, Hilltop Farms Camping, Super Mkt Trading Post, auto repair, USPO, **S** 🅖 Mobil/dsl, 🍴 Dragon Garden Chinese
108 (341)	Bridgeville, same as 109
107 (340)	Thompsonville, **S** 🍴 Old Homestead Diner, 🄾 Chevrolet, Chrysler/Dodge/Jeep, Toyota
106 (339)	(wb only), E Broadway, **N** Ford/Lincoln, **S** 🅖 Mobil/dsl, 🛏 Super 8 (2 mi), 🄾 GMC Trucks, Hyundai
105 (337)	NY 42, Monticello, **N** 🅖 Mobil, Valero, 🍴 Bro Bruno's Pizza, Blue Horizon Diner, Burger King, China 1, Dunkin Donuts, Giovanni's Rest, KFC, McDonald's, Subway, 🄾 AutoZone, Home Depot, Radio Shack, ShopRite Foods, Staples, Walmart/McDonald's, museum, **S** 🅖 Citgo/dsl, Sunoco/dsl, 🍴 Pizza Hut, Miss Monticello Diner, Nugget Rest, Pizza Hut, Stewart's, Wendy's, 🛏 EconoLodge, Heritage Inn, Super 8, 🄾 Advance Parts, Family$, NAPA, Rite Aid
104 (336)	NY 17B, Raceway, Monticello, **S** 🅖 Citgo/dsl, Mobil/dsl, 🍴 Albella Rest, Bean Bag Cafe, Colosseo Rest., 🛏 Best Western, Raceway Motel, Travel Inn, 🄾 AT&T, Swinging Bridge Camp, Woodstock Camping
103	Rapp Rd (wb only)
102 (332)	Harris, **N** 🄾 🄷
101 (327)	Ferndale, Swan Lake, **S** 🅖 Mobil/dsl, 🄾 Swan Lake Camping (5mi)
100 (327)	NY 52 E, Liberty, **N** 🅖 Citgo, Sam's, Sunoco, 🍴 Albert's Diner, Burger King, Dunkin Donuts, Last Licks Cafe, Liberty Diner, McDonald's, Piccolo Italian, Pizza Hut, Subway, Taco Bell, Wendy's, 🛏 Days Inn, Howard Johnson, 🄾 Ace Hardware, Advance Parts, $Tree, Rite Aid, ShopRite Foods, USPO, **S** 🅖 XtraMart, 🛏 Lincoln Motel, 🄾 Buick/Cadillac, Chrysler/Dodge/Jeep, Ford/Lincoln, Southend Parts, Swan Lake Camping (5mi)
100a	NY 52 W (no wb return), Liberty, **S** 🍴 McCabe's Rest, 🄾 K&K Drug, st police
99 (325)	NY 52 W, to NY 55, Liberty, **S** 🅖 Sunoco, 🛏 Catskill Motel
98 (321)	Cooley, Parksville, **N** 🅖 Mobil/dsl, 🍴 Dari-King
97 (319)	Morsston
96 (316)	Livingston Manor, **N** 🄾 Covered Bridge Camping, **S** 🅖 Citgo, Sunoco, 🍴 Lazy Beagle Grill, Robinhood Diner, 🛏 Lanza's Country Inn, 🄾 Covered Bridge Camping, Mongaup Pond Camping, Peck's Mkt, USPO, to Covered Bridge

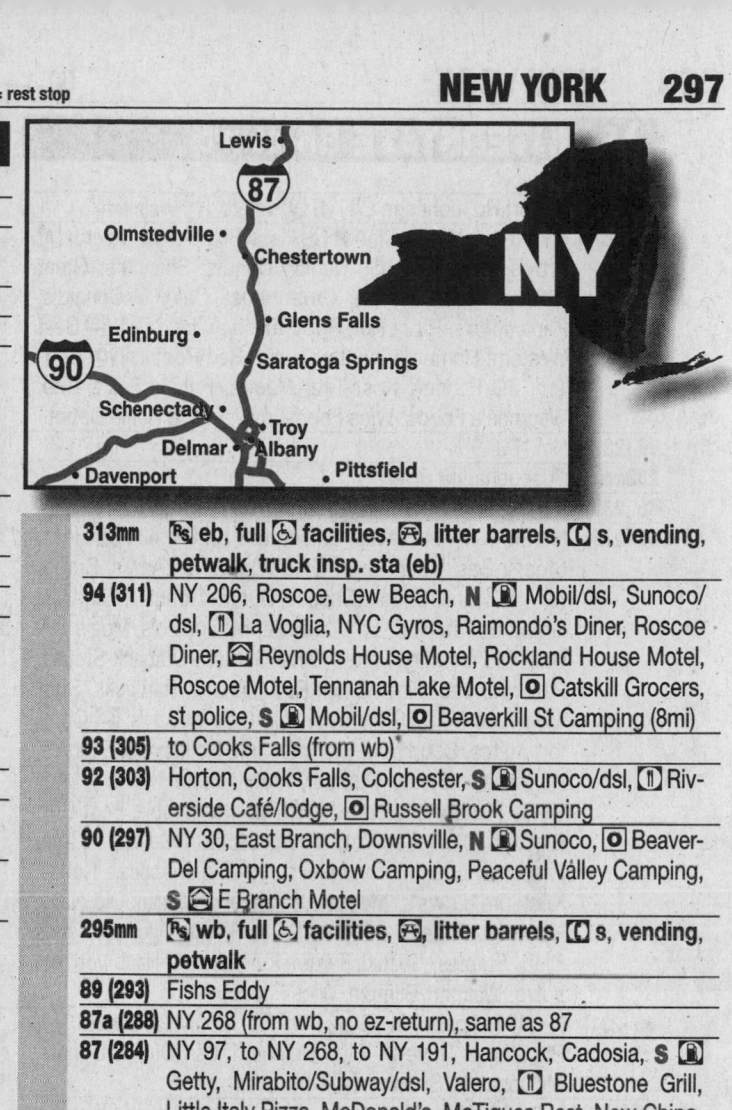

313mm	🆁🆂 eb, full ♿ facilities, 🗑 litter barrels, 🅲 s, vending, petwalk, truck insp. sta (eb)
94 (311)	NY 206, Roscoe, Lew Beach, **N** 🅖 Mobil/dsl, Sunoco/dsl, 🍴 La Voglia, NYC Gyros, Raimondo's Diner, Roscoe Diner, 🛏 Reynolds House Motel, Rockland House Motel, Roscoe Motel, Tennanah Lake Motel, 🄾 Catskill Grocers, st police, **S** 🅖 Mobil/dsl, 🄾 Beaverkill St Camping (8mi)
93 (305)	to Cooks Falls (from wb)
92 (303)	Horton, Cooks Falls, Colchester, **S** 🅖 Sunoco/dsl, 🍴 Riverside Café/lodge, 🄾 Russell Brook Camping
90 (297)	NY 30, East Branch, Downsville, **N** 🅖 Sunoco, 🄾 Beaver-Del Camping, Oxbow Camping, Peaceful Valley Camping, **S** 🛏 E Branch Motel
295mm	🆁🆂 wb, full ♿ facilities, 🗑 litter barrels, 🅲 s, vending, petwalk
89 (293)	Fishs Eddy
87a (288)	NY 268 (from wb, no ez-return), same as 87
87 (284)	NY 97, to NY 268, to NY 191, Hancock, Cadosia, **S** 🅖 Getty, Mirabito/Subway/dsl, Valero, 🍴 Bluestone Grill, Little Italy Pizza, McDonald's, McTigues Rest, New China, 🛏 Capra Inn, Colonial Motel, Starlight Lake Inn, 🄾 Family$, Grand Union Foods, NAPA, Rite Aid
276mm	parking area wb
84 (274)	Deposit, **N** 🅖 Citgo/dsl, 🍴 BC Pizza, Grand Stand Rest., Pines Rest., Wendy's, 🛏 Deposit Motel, Laurel Bank Motel, 🄾 Family$, st police
83 (272)	Deposit, Oquaga Lake
82 (270)	NY 41, McClure, Sanford, **N** 🍴 Cornerstone Cafe, 🄾 Kellystone Park, **S** 🅖 Sun/dsl, 🛏 Scott's Family Resort, 🄾 Guestward Camping (3mi), Oquaga Creek SP
265mm	parking area eb, 🗑 litter barrels
81 (263)	E Bosket Rd
80 (261)	Damascus, **N** 🅖 Gulf/Manley's/dsl, 🄾 Forest Hill Lake Park Camping, auto repair
79 (259)	NY 79, Windsor, **N** 🅖 Extra, Sunoco/dsl, 🍴 McBride's Rest, Subway, **S** 🍴 Marian's Pizza/Subs, 🄾 Lakeside Camping (8mi)
78 (256)	Dunbar Rd, Occanum
77 (254)	W Windsor, **N** 🅖 Sunoco/dsl, 🍴 McDonald's
76 (251)	Haskins Rd, to Foley Rd
75 (250)	I-81 S, to PA (exits left from wb)
I-86/I-81 run together 4 miles	
3	Colesville Rd (from eb), **S** 🅖 ❤Loves/Wendy's, TA/dsl/scales/24hr
I-86/I-81 run together 4 miles	
3	Broad Ave (from wb, no return)
4ns	NY 7
72 (244)	I-81 N, US 11, Front St, Clinton St, (no wb re-entry), **S** 🄾 Aamco

W I N D S O R

▲E INTERSTATE 86 CONT'D

Exit	Services
71 (242)	Airport Rd, Johnson City, S 🅿 Valero, 🅾 Walmart
70sn (241)	NY 201, Johnson City, N 🅿 Hess/Blimpie/dsl, Valero, 🍴 Arby's, Christy's Grill, Dunkin Donuts, Friendly's, Great China, Ground Round, Grub House Cafe, McDonald's, Papa John's, Pizza Hut, Ruby Tuesday, Taco Bell, 🏠 Best Western, Hampton Inn, La Quinta, Red Roof Inn, 🅾 Bon-Ton, JC Penney, Kost Tire, Macy's, PetCo, Sears/auto, Wegman's Foods, Wies Foods, mall, vet, S Home Depot
69 (239)	NY 17C
238mm	Susquehanna River
68 (237)	NY 17C, Old Vestal Rd, (from eb, no re-entry)
67 (236)	NY 26, NY 434, Vestal, Endicott, S on NY 434 🅿 Hess, Stop'N Gas, Valero/dsl, 🍴 A&W/LJ Silver, Arby's, Burger King, CA Grill, ChuckECheese, Dunkin Donuts, Friendly's, Grand Buffet, KFC, La Vita Bella, McDonald's, Moe's SW Grill, Old Country Buffet, Olive Garden, Outback Steaks, Panera Bread, Plaza Diner, Red Lobster, Starbucks, Subway, Taco Bell, TGIFriday's, Uno Grill, Wendy's, 🏠 Comfort Suites, Courtyard, Hampton Inn, Holiday Inn Express, Homewood Suites, Parkway Motel, Vestal Motel, 🅾 Advance Parts, Aldi Foods, AT&T, Barnes&Noble, Best Buy, BigLots, CarQuest, CVS Drug, Dick's, $General, $Tree, Firestone/auto, Ford/Lincoln, Jo-Ann Fabrics, Kohl's, Kost Tire, Lowe's, Meineke, Michael's, Nissan, Old Navy, Petsmart, Price Rite Foods, Radio Shack, Rite Aid, Sam's Club, Staples, Suzuki, Target, TJ Maxx, U-Haul, Verizon, Volvo, Walmart/Blimpie, Wies Foods, vet
66 (231)	NY 434, Apalachin, S 🅿 KwikFill, Mobil/dsl, Sunoco, 🍴 Big Dipper Drive-In, Blue Dolphin Diner, Dunkin Donuts, McDonald's, Subway, 🏠 Quality Inn
65 (225)	NY 17C, NY 434, Owego, N 🅿 Sunoco, 🍴 A&W/KFC, Arby's, Panda Wok, Pizza Hut, Subway, Wendy's, 🏠 Hampton Inn, Holiday Inn Express, Treadway Inn/rest., 🅾 Buick/GMC, $General, Hickories Park Camping, Kost Tire, Verizon, Top's Foods, S st police
64 (223)	NY 96, Owego, N 🍴 Dunkin Donuts, 🅾 AutoZone, CVS Drug, USPO, S 🅿 Valero
222mm	🆁🆂 wb, full 🚻 facilities, 💧, vending, 🏕 litter barrels, petwalk
63 (218)	Lounsberry, S 🅿 Valero/rest./dsl/24hr
62 (214)	NY 282, Nichols, S 🅿 Citgo/pizza/dsl, 🅾 Jim's RV Ctr, Tioga Downs Race Track (2mi)
212mm	🆁🆂 eb, full 🚻 facilities, 🏕 litter barrels, 💧, vending, petwalk
208mm	Susquehanna River
61 (206)	NY 34, PA 199, Waverly, Sayre, N 🅾 $General, Goodyear/gas, S 🅿 Gulf, Sunoco/dsl, 🏠 Best Western/rest., 🅾 Chrysler/Dodge/Jeep, Joe's RV Ctr, Kia, Nissan
60 (204)	US 220, to Sayre, Waverly, N 🏠 O'brien's Inn, 🅾 Clark's Foods, S 🅿 Citgo/dsl, Xtra/dsl, 🍴 Wendy's (3mi), 🏠 Hampton Inn, 🅾 Advance Parts, Aldi Foods, K-Mart, Rite Aid, Top's Foods
59a (202)	Wilawana, S 🅿 Sunoco/Subway/dsl
59 (200)	NY 427, Chemung, N 🅿 Dandy/dsl
58a (197)	to NY 60
58 (195)	rd 2, Lowman, Wellsburg, N USPO S 🅾 Gardiner Hill Campsites (4mi), st police
56 (190)	Jerusalem Hill, S 🅿 Citgo/dsl, KwikFill, Sunoco/Pizza Hut/Subway/dsl, 🍴 Hilltop Rest., McDonalds, 🏠 Coachman Motel, Holiday Inn, Mark Twain Motel

Exit	Services
54 (186)	NY 13, to Ithaca
53 (185)	Horseheads, S 🅿 Mobil, Sunoco, 🍴 Burger King, Dunkin Donuts, Guiseppe's Pizza, Lin Buffet, McDonald's, Subway, Wendy's, 🏠 Motel 6, Red Carpet Inn, 🅾 Advance Parts, Family$, K-Mart, Radio Shack, Rite Aid, Save-A-Lot Foods
52b (184)	NY 14, to Watkins Glen, N 🍴 Friendly's, 🏠 Holiday Inn Express, Knights Inn, Landmark Inn, S 🍴 Denny's
52a (183)	Commerce Ctr, S 🍴 Buffalo Wild Wings, CiCi's Pizza, Cracker Barrel, Empire Buffet, TX Roadhouse, 🅾 Aldi Foods, AT&T, Dick's, Jo-Ann Fabrics, Kohl's, Mavis Discount Tire, Petsmart, Walmart/McDonald's
51ba (182)	Chambers Rd, N 🅿 Sunoco/Subway/dsl, 🍴 Bon Ton, Chili's, Dunkin Donuts, McDonald's, Olive Garden, Outback Steaks, Red Lobster, Ruby Tuesday, 🏠 Candlewood Suites, Country Inn&Suites, Hampton Inn, Hilton Garden, 🅾 Firestone/auto, JC Penney, Macy's, Nissan, Sears/auto, mall, S 🍴 Applebee's, Charley's Subs, 5 Guys Burgers, Mt Fuji Japanese, Old Country Buffet, Panera Bread, Taco Bell, TGIFriday's, Wendy's, 🏠 EconoLodge, 🅾 Barnes&Noble, Best Buy, Buick/GMC, $Tree, Hobby Lobby, Hyundai, Kost Tire, Lowe's, Michael's, Old Navy, PetCo, Sam's Club, Staples, Subaru/Suzuki, Target, TJ Maxx, Top's Foods, Toyota/Scion, Verizon, museum, Urgent Care
50 (180)	Kahler Rd, N to 🛏
49 (178)	Olcott Rd, Canal St, Big Flats, N 🛏, antiques, S 🅿 Sunoco, 🍴 Picnic Pizza, 🅾 USPO
48 (171)	NY 352, E Corning, N 🅿 Citgo, 🏠 Budget Inn, Gate House Motel
47 (174)	NY 352, Gibson, Corning, N 🏠 Budget Inn, Gate House Motel
46 (171)	NY 414, to Watkins Glen, Corning, N 🅾 Ferenbaugh Camping (5mi), KOA (14mi), Watkins Glen Camping, S 🅿 Sunoco, 🏠 Comfort Inn, Days Inn, Radisson, Staybridge Suites, 🅾 🏠, Corning Glass Museum
45 (170)	NY 352, Corning, S 🅿 Fastrac, 🍴 Bob Evans, EnEn Chinese, Friendly's, Subway, Wendy's, 🏠 Fairfield Inn, 🅾 AT&T, AutoZone, CarQuest, Rite Aid
44ba (168)	US 15 S, NY 417 W, Gang Mills, N 🅿 Sunoco, 🍴 McDonald's, S 🅿 Citgo, Sunoco, 🍴 Applebee's, Arby's, 🏠 Best Value Inn, Corning Inn, Ramada Inn, 🅾 Aldi Foods, Buick/GMC, Chevrolet, Harley-Davidson, Home Depot, Walmart
43 (167)	NY 415, Painted Post, N 🅿 Citgo, 🍴 Burger King, 🅾 AutoValue Parts, $General, Firestone/auto, Verizon, S 🅿 Sunoco, 🍴 Denny's, 🏠 Hampton Inn
167mm	parking area wb, litter barrels
42 (165)	Coopers Plains, N st police
41 (161)	rd 333, Campbell, N 🅾 Camp Bell Camping (1mi), S 🅿 Sunoco, 🅾 Cardinal Campsites (6mi), antiques
160mm	🆁🆂 eb, full 🚻 facilities, 🏕 litter barrels, 💧, vending, petwalk
40 (156)	NY 226, Savona, N 🅿 Mobil/dsl, 🍴 Savona Diner, Subway
39 (153)	NY 415, Bath, N 🍴 Chat-a-Whyle Rest. (3mi), 🏠 Holland American Country Inn, National Hotel, S 🅾 Babcock Hollow Camping (2mi)
38 (150)	NY 54, to Hammondsport, Bath, N 🅿 Citgo, KwikFill, Mobil, Sunoco/dsl, 🍴 Arby's, Burger King, Dunkin Donuts, Ling Ling Chinese, McDonald's/playplace, Pizza Hut, Ponderosa, Rico's Pizza, Subway, 🏠 Budget Inn, Days Inn, Microtel, Super 8, 🅾 🏠, Advance Parts, AT&T, Campers

Side tabs: NY · VESTAL · OWEGO · ELMIRA · CORNING · BATH

🔼E INTERSTATE 86 CONT'D

Exit	Services
38 (150)	Continued
	Haven Camping, Camping World RV Ctr, $General, Family$, Hickory Hill Camping (3mi), K-Mart, Rite Aid, Top's Foods/gas, Walgreens, museum, st police, winery, to Keuka Lake
147mm	🆁🆂 wb, full ♿ facilities, 🚻, 🛍, litter barrels, vending, petwalk
37 (146)	NY 53, to Prattsburg, Kanona, S 🅖 📷/Subway/dsl/scales/24hr/@, Sunoco/Smokey's/dsl/scales, 🅾 Wilkin's RV Ctr (1mi), st police, USPO
36 (145)	I-390 N, NY 15, to Rochester
35 (138)	Howard, S to Lake Demmon RA, 🍴
34 (130)	NY 36, Hornell, Arkport, 0-2 mi S 🅖 KwikFill, Sunoco/dsl, 🍴 Applebee's, Country Kitchen, Dunkin Donuts, McDonald's, Subway, 🏨 Days Inn, EconoLodge, Sunshine Motel, 🅾 Advance Parts, Aldi Foods, Chrysler/Dodge/Jeep, $General, $Tree, Ford, GNC, Lowe's, NAPA, Radio Shack, Verizon, Walmart/Subway, Wegman's Foods
125mm	scenic overlook eb, litter barrels
33 (124)	NY 21, to Alfred, Almond, Andover, S 🅖 Wilson Farms, 🅾 Lake Lodge Camping (8mi), Kanakadea Camping, USPO
117mm	highest elevation on I-86, elev 2110 ft eb, 2080 ft wb
32 (116)	W Almond
31 (108)	Angelica, N 🅖 Valero/dsl, 🏨 Angelica Inn B&B
30 (104)	NY 19, Belmont, Wellsville, N 🅾 6-S Camping (3mi), Letchworth SP (27mi), S 🍴 Iron Kettle Rest., 🅾 🏥 st police
101mm	🆁🆂 eb, full ♿ facilities, 🚻, 🛍, litter barrels, vending, petwalk
29 (99)	NY 275, to Bolivar, Friendship, S 🅖 Mobil/Subway/dsl, Miller&Brandes Gas
28 (92)	NY 305, Cuba, N 🍴 Moonwink's Rest., 🏨 EconoLodge, 🅾 $General, Maple Lane RV Park, S 🅖 Sunoco/dsl, Valero/dsl, 🍴 Charlie's Chicken Pizza, McDonald's, Subway, 🅾 🏥 Cuba Cheese Shop, Cuba Drug, Family$, Giant Foods
27 (84)	NY 16, NY 446, Hinsdale, N food, S gas, lodging
26 (79)	NY 16, Olean, S 🅖 Sunoco, 🍴 Burger King, Wendy's, 🅾 🏥
25 (77)	Buffalo St, Olean, S 🅖 Citgo/dsl, 🍴 Country Fare, 🅾 🏥 2 mi S on NY 417 🅖 KwikFill, 🍴 Applebee's, Burger King, Coldstone/Tim Hortons, Domino's, Dunkin Donuts, Friendly's, Little Caesars, McDonald's, Perkins, Ponderosa, Subway, 🏨 Best Western, Country Inn&Suites, Microtel, 🅾 🏥 Advance Parts, Aldi Foods, AT&T, BJ's Whse/gas, $Tree, GNC, Home Depot, Jo-Ann Fabrics, K-Mart, NAPA, Old Navy, Radio Shack, Staples, Tops Foods/gas, Verizon, Walmart/Subway, St Bonaventure U
24 (74)	NY 417, Allegany, 1 mi S 🅖 Mobil/7-11/dsl, 🅾 to St Bonaventure U
73mm	🆁🆂 wb, full ♿ facilities, 🛍, litter barrels, petwalk
23 (68)	US 219 S, N 🅖 Allegany Jct./Subway/dsl
66mm	Allegheny River
21 (61)	US 219 N, Salamanca, S 🍴 Red Garter Rest
20 (58)	NY 417, NY 353, Salamanca, N 🅖 Antone's Gas, Nafco Quickstop/Burger King/24hr, Seneca OneStop/dsl/24hr, VIP Gas, 🍴 McDonald's, 🏨 Holiday Inn Express, Hotel Westgate, 🅾 AutoZone, Rail Museum, Seneca-Iroquis Museum, S casino
19 (54)	S 🅾 Allegany SP, Red House Area

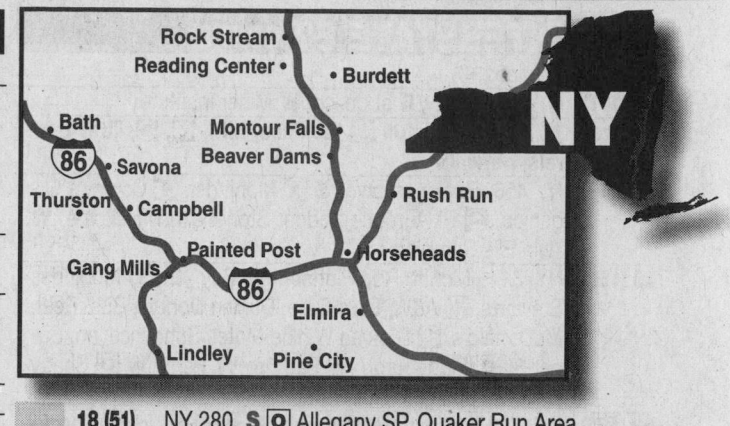

Exit	Services
18 (51)	NY 280, S 🅾 Allegany SP, Quaker Run Area
17 (48)	NY 394, Steamburg, N gas, 🅾 RV camping, S 🅖 Seneca, WW/dsl, 🅾 RV camping
16 (41)	W Main St, Randolph, N 🅖 Mobil/dsl, 🍴 R&M Rest., 🅾 RV camping
40mm	parking area, 🛍
15 (39)	School House Rd
39mm	parking area, 🛍
14 (36)	US 62, Kennedy, 1 mi N 🅖 Keystone Gas, 🍴 Office Pizza/Subs, S RV camping
32mm	Cassadaga Creek
13 (31)	NY 394, Falconer, S 🅖 Mobil/dsl, Sunoco, 🍴 Burger King, McDonald's, Tim Hortons, Wendy's, 🏨 Budget Inn, Red Roof Inn, 🅾 CVS Drug, Sugar Creek Stores, Harley-Davidson
12 (28)	NY 60, Jamestown, N 🅖 KwikFill/Dunkin Donuts/dsl, S 🅖 Mobil/McDonald's/dsl, 🍴 Bob Evans, 🏨 Comfort Inn, Hampton Inn, 🅾 🏥 st police
11 (25)	to NY 430, Jamestown, S gas, dsl, food, lodging
22mm	welcome ctr/🆁🆂 eb, full ♿ facilities, 🛍, litter barrels, petwalk, vending
10 (21)	NY 430 W, Bemus Point
9 (20)	NY 430 E (no EZ eb return), N 🅖 Mobil, S gas, food, lodging
19mm	Chautauqua Lake
8 (18)	NY 394, Mayville, N 🅖 Mobil/dsl, lodging, 🅾 RV camping, USPO
7 (15)	Panama
6 (9)	NY 76, Sherman, N 🅖 Keystone Gas, 🍴 Main Street Diner, Murdock's Rest., 🏨 Morse Hotel, Plum B&B, 🅾 NAPA, Sherman Drug, city park, USPO
4 (1)	NY 430, Findley Lake, N 🏨 Holiday Inn Express, S gas, food, 🏨 Peek'n Peak Conference Ctr, 🅾 RV camping, to Peek'n Peak Ski Area
0mm	New York/Pennsylvania state line. **Exits 3-1 are in PA.**
3	PA 89, North East, Wattsburg, N gas, food
1b a	I-90, W to Erie, E to Buffalo.

I-86 begins/ends on I-90, exit 37. I-390 begins/ends on I-86, exit 36.

🔼N INTERSTATE 87

Exit	Services
176mm	US/Canada Border, NY state line, **I-87 begins/ends.**
43 (175)	US 9, Champlain, E World Duty Free, W 🅖 Peterbilt Trkstp/deli/dsl/scales/24hr/@, 🅾 repair
42 (174)	US 11 S, to Rouse's Point, Champlain, E 🅖 Irving/dsl, 🍴 J-reck Subs, Pizza+, Subway, 🅾 Ace Hardware, Chevrolet (3mi), Kinney Drug, PriceChopper, Rite Aid, USPO, W 🅖 Mobil/dsl, Valero, 🍴 Dunkin Donuts, McDonald's, Papa John's

⬛N INTERSTATE 87 CONT'D

Exit	Services
41 (167)	NY 191, Chazy, **E** st police, **W** Miner Institute
162mm	🆁 **both lanes, full** ♿ **facilities, info,** 🅒, 🚮, **litter barrels, petwalk**
40 (160)	NY 456, Beekmantown, **E** 🅖 Mobil/dsl, 🍴 Conroy's Organics, 🛏 Pt Auroche Lodge, Stonehelm Motel/café, **W** Twin Ells Camping
39 (158)	NY 314, Moffitt Rd, Plattsburgh Bay, **E** 🅖 Mobil/dsl, Stewarts, 🍴 A&W, Bill's Cafe, Dunkin Donuts, Gus' Rest., McDonald's, 🛏 Rip van Winkle Motel, Sundance Inn, Super 8, 🅞 Plattsburgh RV Park, to VT Ferry, **W** 🅞 Shady Oaks Camping, to Adirondacks
38 (154)	NY 22, NY 374, to Plattsburgh, **E** 🅖 Mobil/dsl, 🍴 Checker Hill Farm Cafe, 🅞 Kinney Drug
37 (153)	NY 3, Plattsburgh, **E** 🅖 Mobil/dsl, Stewarts, Sunoco, 🍴 Burger King, China Buffet, Domino's, Dunkin Donuts, Guiseppe's Pizza, Jade Buffet, KFC, Koto Japanese, Legends Cafe, Mangia Pizza, McDonald's, #1 Chinese, Panera Bread, Papa John's, Perkins, Pizza Hut, Quiznos, Starbucks, Subway, Taco Bell, Wendy's, 🛏 Comfort Inn, Holiday Inn, 🅞 🅗, BigLots, Buick/Cadillac/GMC, Family$, Ford, Kinny Drug, Michael's, Petsmart, PriceChopper Foods, Radio Shack, Rite Aid, Sam's Club, Staples, TJ Maxx, TrueValue, Verizon, Walgreens, Walmart, vet, **W** 🅖 Mobil, Shell, Sunoco/Jreck Subs, 🍴 Anthony's Rest., Applebee's, Butcher Block Rest., Dunkin Donuts, Friendly's, Ground Round, Moe's SW Grill, 99 Rest., Uno, 🛏 Best Value Inn, Best Western, Days Inn, EconoLodge, Hampton Inn, La Quinta, Microtel, 🅞 Advance Parts, AT&T, AutoZone, Best Buy, Dick's, $Tree, Gander Mtn, Hannaford Foods, Harley-Davidson, Honda, JC Penney, Kinny Drug, K-Mart, Lowe's, Prays Mkt, Sears/auto, Suzuki, Target, vet
151mm	Saranac River
36 (150)	NY 22, Plattsburgh 🚆, **E** 🅖 Mobil/dsl/24hr, 🅞 U-Haul, st police, **E** 🅖 Shell/dsl, 🍴 Bluff Point Rest.
146mm	**truck insp sta both lanes,** 🆁 **nb full** ♿ **facilities,** 🚮, **litter barrels,** 🅒 **petwalk**
35 (144)	NY 442, to Port Kent, Peru, **2-8 mi E** 🅞 Iroquois/Ausable Pines Camping, to VT Ferry, **W** 🅖 Mobil/Dunkin Donuts/Subway/dsl, Wilson Farms, 🍴 Cricket's Rest., McDonald's, Pasquale's Rest., 🅞 Auchuban Hardware, USPO, vet
143mm	emergency 🅒 s at **2 mi** intervals begin sb/end nb
34 (137)	NY 9 N, Ausable Forks, **E** 🅖 Sunoco/dsl, 🍴 Pleasant Corner Rest., Mac's Drive-in, 🅞 vet, **W** 🅞 Prays Mkt, Ausable River RV Camping, auto repair
136mm	Ausable River
33 (135)	US 9, NY 22, to Willsboro, **E** gas/dsl, food, lodging, RV camping, to Essex Ferry
125mm	N Boquet River
32 (124)	Lewis, **E** 🅞 RV Camping, **W** 🅖 Lukoil/dsl, 🍴 Trkstp Diner, 🅞 RV Camping, st police
123mm	🆁 **sb, full** ♿ **facilities, info,** 🅒, 🚮, **petwalk,** 🆁 **nb, no restrooms**
120mm	Boquet River
31 (117)	NY 9 N, to Elizabethtown, Westport, **E** 🅖 Mobil, 🛏 HillTop Motel, 🅞 RV camp/dump, **W** 🅞 🅗, st police, vet
111mm	**trk insp sta both lanes,** 🆁 **nb only, full** ♿ **facilities,** 🅒, 🚮, **litter barrels, vending, petwalk**
30 (104)	US 9, NY 73, Keene Valley
99mm	**trk insp sta,** 🆁 **both lanes, full** ♿ **facilities,** 🅒, 🚮, **litter barrels, petwalk**

Exit	Services
29 (94)	N Hudson, **E** 🅞 Jellystone Camping, USPO, **W** Blue Ridge Falls Camping
28 (88)	NY 74 E, to Ticonderoga, Schroon Lake, **E** 🍴 Mt Severance Country Store, Sunoco/dsl, 🛏 Maple Leaf Motel, Schroon Lake B&B, 🅞 RV camp/dump, st police, services on US 9
83mm	🆁 **both lanes, full** ♿ **facilities,** 🅒, 🚮, **litter barrels, petwalk, vending**
27 (81)	US 9 (from nb, no EZ return), Schroon Lake, to gas/dsl, food, lodging
26 (78)	US 9 (no EZ return), Pottersville, Schroon Lake, (from sb) **E** 🍴 Cafe Adirondack, 🛏 Lee's Corner Motel, 🅞 RV Camping, (from nb) **W** 🅖 Valero, 🍴 Black Bear Diner
25 (73)	NY 8, Chestertown, **E** 🅖 Crossroads Country Store, 🅞 Riverside Pines Camping **W** 🅖 Mobil/dsl
24 (67)	Bolton Landing, **E** RV camping
67mm	Schroon River
66mm	parking area sb, 🚮
64mm	parking area nb, 🚮
23 (58)	to US 9, Diamond Point, Warrensburg, **W** 🅖 Citgo/dsl, Cumberland, Mobil/Dunkin Donuts/e85, Stewarts, 🍴 Geroge Henry's Rest., Gino's Pizza, McDonald's, Subway, 🛏 Season's B&B, Super 8, 🅞 Family$, Family Mkt Foods, Ford, Central Adirondack Tr, Riverview Camping, Schroon River Camping (3mi), ski area
22 (54)	US 9, NY 9 N, to Diamond Pt, Lake George, **E on US 9** 🍴 Gino&Tony's, Guiseppe's Pizza, John Barleycorn, KFC, Mario's Italian, Monte Cristo's, Moose Tooth Grill, Paolini's, 🛏 Admiral Motel, Balsam Motel, Barberry Ct, Best Value Inn, Blue Moon Motel, Brookside Motel, EconoLodge, Georgian Lakeside Resort, Heritage Motel, Lake Crest Inn, Lake Motel, Lake George Inn, Lake Haven Motel, Marine Village Resort, Motel Montreal, Nordick's Motel, Oasis Motel, O'Sullivan's Motel, Park Lane Motel, 7 Dwarfs Motel, Sundowner Motel, Surfside Motel, multiple services, 🅞 PriceChopper Foods, same as 21, **W** parking area both lanes
21 (53)	NY 9 N, Lake Geo, Ft Wm Henry, **E on US 9** 🅖 Stewarts, Sunoco, Valero, 🍴 Adirondack Brewery, A&W, Barnsider BBQ, Dining Room, DJ's Cafe, Gourmet Subs, Howard Johnson's Rest., Jasper's Steaks, Lobster Pot, Mama Riso's Italian, McDonald's, Mezzaluna's, Pizza Hut, Smokey Joe's Grill, Sub City, 🛏 Best Western, Country Hearth Inn, Ft William Henry Inn, Hampton Inn, Holiday Inn Resort, HollyTree Hotel, Lake Crest Hotel, Lakeview Hotel, Lincoln Log Motel, Marine Village Resort, Quality Inn, Travelodge, Tiki Hotel, Super 8, Villager Motel, Windsor Hotel, Wingate Inn, 🅞 Harley-Davidson, King Phillip/Lake George Camping (2mi), Rite Aid, USPO, city park, waterpark, multiple services, same as 22, **W** 🅖 Mobil/dsl/LP, 🛏 Kathy's Cottages
51mm	Adirondack Park
20 (49)	NY 149, to Ft Ann, **E N on US 9** 🅖 Mobil/Dunkin Donuts/dsl, Sunoco/dsl, 🍴 Frank's Pizza, Logjam Rest., Montcalm Rest., Olde Post Grille, 🛏 Clarion, Comfort Suites, Mohican Motel, Rodeway Inn, 🅞 Ledgeview RV Park (3mi), Factory Outlets/famous brands, st police, **E S on US 9** 🍴 Blue Moose Rest., Johnny Rocket's, 🛏 Country Inn&Suites, 🅞 6 Flags Funpark, waterpark
19 (47)	NY 254, Glens Falls, **E** 🅖 Getty, Hess, Mobil, Sunoco, 🍴 A&W/KFC, Burger King, Chicago Grill, Dunkin Donuts, 5 Guys Burgers, Friendly's, Gavano's, Golden Corral, LJ

NY (side tab)

PLATTSBURGH (side tab)

LAKE GEORGE (side tab)

INTERSTATE 87 CONT'D

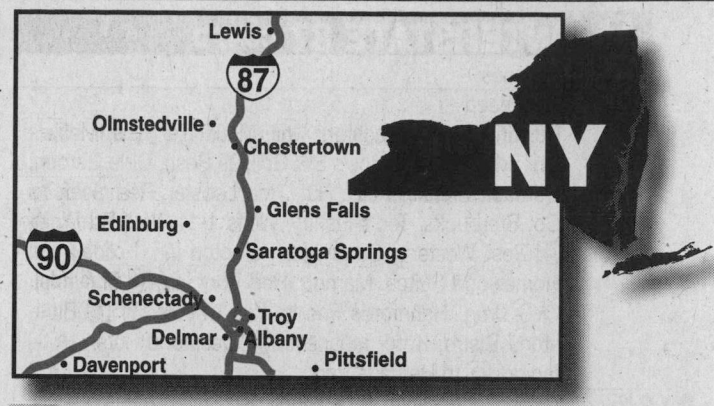

Exit	Services
19 (47)	**Continued**
	Silver, McDonald's, Moe's SW Grill, Mr B's Rest., Old China Buffet, Olive Garden, Outback Steaks, Panera Bread, Papa John's, Pizza Hut, Red Lobster, Silo Rest., Starbucks, Subway, Taco Bell, Wendy's, ☐ Alpen Haus, Budget Inn, EconoLodge, Quality Inn, Red Roof Inn, Sleep Inn, ☐ Ace Hardware, AT&T, AutoZone, Bon Ton, Firestone/auto, Goodyear, Home Depot, JC Penney, Jo-Ann Fabrics, PriceChopper Foods, Radio Shack, Rite Aid, Sears, Staples, Target, TJ Maxx, Verizon, Walmart, mall, **W** ☐ Mobil/Dunkin Donuts/Subway/dsl, Stewarts, ☐ Ramada/rest., st police
18 (45)	Glens Falls, **E** ☐ Gulf/Subway/e-85, Hess/dsl/24hr, Sunoco, ☐ Carl R's Café, Dunkin Donuts, Pizza Hut, Steve's Place Rest., ☐ Best Inn, Queensbury Hotel, ☐ ☐ CVS Drug, Hannaford Foods, Toyota/Scion, U-Haul, Walgreens, **W** ☐ Stewarts, ☐ McDonald's, ☐ Super 8
43mm	☐ **both lanes, full** ☐ **facilities,** ☐ **litter barrels,** ☐ **vending, petwalk**
42mm	Hudson River
17 (40)	US 9, S Glen Falls, **E** ☐ Citgo/dsl, Gulf, Hess/Blimpie/Dunkin Donuts, Sunoco/dsl, Valero/Subway/dsl/24hr, ☐ Fitzgerald's Steaks, ☐ Budget Inn, Landmark Motel (1mi), Sara-Glen Motel, Town&Country Motel, ☐ Adirondack RV Camp, Suzuki, auto/truck repair/transmissions, vet, **W** Moreau Lake SP
16 (36)	Ballard Rd, Wilton, **E** ☐ Coldbrook Campsites, golf, **W** ☐ Mobil, Stewart's, Sunoco/Scotty's Rest./dsl/scales/24hr, ☐ Mt View Acres Motel, ☐ Alpin Haus RV Ctr
15 (30)	NY 50, NY 29, Saratoga Springs, **E** ☐ Hess/dsl, Sunoco, ☐ Applebee's, Burger King, Chicago Grill, Chipotle Mexican, Denny's, Dunkin Donuts, 5 Guys Burgers, Friendly's, Giavanno's Pizza, Golden Corral, KFC/Taco Bell, McDonald's, Moe's SW Grill, 99 Rest., Osaka, Panera Bread, Ruby Tuesday, Subway, Sunny Wok, TGIFriday's, ☐ Comfort Inn, ☐ AT&T, Barnes&Noble, Best Buy, BJ's Whse, BonTon, Dick's, Ford, Hannaford Foods, Home Depot, JC Penney, Kohl's, Lowe's, Mazda, Old Navy, Petsmart, PriceChopper Foods, Rite Aid, Sears/auto, Staples, Subaru, Target, TJ Maxx, Toyota/Scion, Walgreens, Walmart, **W** ☐ Residence Inn, ☐ ☐
14 (38)	NY 9P, Schuylerville, **2 mi W** ☐ Hampton Inn, Holiday Inn, ☐ HOPSITAL, museum, racetrack
13 (25)	US 9, Saratoga Springs, **E** ☐ Bentley's Rest., DeLucia's Deli, Saratoga Pizza Place, ☐ Budget Inn, Locust Grove Motel, Maggiore's Motel, ☐ Nissan, Ballston Spa SP, **W** ☐ Mobil/Dunkin Donuts/dsl, Stewarts, ☐ Finish Line Rest., Hibachi Grill, PJ's BBQ, ☐ Best Western, Hilton Garden (4mi), Roosevelt Inn/rest., Top Hill Hotel, ☐ Saratoga SP, vet
12 (21)	NY 67, Malta, **E** ☐ Getty/dsl, Sunoco/dsl, ☐ Bentley's Rest., Dunkin Donuts, KFC, Malta Diner, McDonald's, Subway, Taco Bell, ☐ Cocca's Motel, Fairfield Inn, ☐ CVS Drug, GNC, PriceChopper Foods, Stewart's, Verizon, Saratoga NHP, st police, **W** ☐ Hyatt Place
11 (18)	Round Lake Rd, Round Lake, **W** ☐ Gulf/dsl, Sunoco/dsl, ☐ Lake Ridge Rest., Mulligan's Rest., ☐ Rite Aid, Stewarts
10 (16)	Ushers Rd, **E** ☐ Hess/Dunkin Donuts/dsl, Xtra/dsl, ☐ Ferretti's Rest., ☐ auto repair, **W** ☐ Stewarts
14mm	☐ nb, full ☐ facilities, info, ☐, ☐, litter barrels, vending, petwalk
9 (13)	NY 146, Clifton Park, **E** ☐ Hess/Dunkin Donuts/dsl, USA, ☐ Burger King, Caputo's Pizza, Chili's, Cracker Barrel, Giffy's BBQ, Harborhouse Fish Fry, Peddler's Grill, Red Robin, Snyder's Rest., Subway, ☐ Comfort Suites, Holiday Inn Express, ☐ Advance Parts, Aldi Foods, BigLots, Goodyear/auto, Home Depot, Kohl's, Lowe's, Michael's, NAPA, Rite Aid, Target, vet, **W** ☐ Mobil, Sunoco/dsl, ☐ Arizona Pizza, Bellini's Italian, Buffalo Wild Wings, Chipotle Mexican, Domino's, Dunkin Donuts, East Palace, East Wok, 5 Guys Burgers, Friendly's, IHOP, La Fiesta, LJ Silver/Taco Bell, McDonald's, Moe's SW Grill, 99 Rest., Outback Steaks, Panera Bread, Pasta Pane, Ruby Tuesday, Salad Creations, Shane's Rib Shack, Starbucks, Subway, TGIFriday's, Wendy's, ☐ Best Western, Hampton Inn, ☐ AT&T, Chevrolet, CVS Drug, $Tree, GNC, Hannaford Foods, JC Penney, Jo-Ann Fabrics, K-Mart, Marshall's, Petsmart, PriceChopper Foods, Staples, Toys-R-Us, Verizon, Walgreens, st police
8a (12)	Grooms Rd, to Waterford
8 (10)	Crescent, Vischer Ferry, **E** ☐ Hess/Blimpie/Godfather's/dsl/24hr, ☐ McDonald's, **W** ☐ Gulf/dsl, Sunoco, ☐ Pancho's Mexican, Tufan Pizza, ☐ CVS Drug, Stewarts
8mm	Mohawk River
7 (7)	NY 7, Troy, **E on US 9 N** ☐ Hess/dsl, ☐ Century House, ☐ Clarion, Holiday Inn Express, Ramada Inn, Sycamore Motel, Stay Inn, ☐ Acura, $General, Ford, Infiniti, Lexus, Lincoln, Nissan, Rite Aid, Volvo, **E on US 9 S** ☐ Mobil, ☐ Dunkin Donuts, McDonald's, Red Robin, Subway, ☐ Hobby Lobby, Marshall's
6 (6)	NY 2, to US 9, Schenectady, **E on US 9** ☐ Hess, ☐ Boston Mkt, Circle Diner, Dakota Steaks, Friendly's, KFC, Red Robin, Wendy's, ☐ Cocca's Inn, La Quinta, Travelodge, ☐ CVS Drug, JC Penney, Mavis Discount Tire, Lowe's, PriceChopper Foods, Toyota/Scion, same as 7, **E** ☐ Mobil, ☐ Applebee's, Chicago Grill, ChuckeCheese, Panera Bread, Starbucks, ☐ GNC, Hannaford Foods, Home Depot, Michael's, Petsmart, Sam's Club, Staples, VW, Walmart, **W** ☐ Mobil/dsl, ☐ Carrabba's, Chipotle Mexican, DiBella's Subs, Dunkin Donuts, Fillet 7, Friendly's, Kings Buffet, Ruby Tuesday, Subway, ☐ Fairfield Inn, Microtel, Quality Inn, Super 8, ☐ Goodyear/auto, Target, TJ Maxx, Verizon
5 (5)	NY 155 E, Latham, **E** ☐ DeeDee's Rest., Philly's Grill, Vintage Pizza, ☐ EconoLodge, ☐ USPO
4 (4)	NY 155 W, Wolf Rd, **E on Wolf Rd** ☐ Hess/dsl, Mobil/Subway, Sunoco, ☐ Arby's, Buffalo Wagon, Burger King, Capital Buffet, Chipotle Mexican, CiCi's Pizza, Denny's,

Map labels: Lewis, 87, Olmstedville, Chestertown, Glens Falls, Edinburg, Saratoga Springs, Schenectady, 90, Troy, Delmar, Albany, Davenport, Pittsfield, **NY**

🅖 = gas 🍽 = food 🛏 = lodging 🅞 = other 🆁🆂 = rest stop Copyright 2014 - The NEXT Exit ®

⬆N INTERSTATE 87 CONT'D

ALBANY

Exit	Services
4 (4)	Continued Dunkin Donuts, Macaroni Grill, Maurice's Subs, Maxie's Grill, McDonald's, Moe's SW Grill, 99 Rest., Olive Garden, Outback Steaks, Pizza Hut, Red Lobster, Reel Seafood Co, Starbucks, Ted's Fishfry, Wolfs 1-11, Wolf Rd Diner, 🛏 Best Western, Courtyard, Hampton Inn, Holiday Inn, Homewood Suites, Marriott, Red Roof Inn, 🅞 Chevrolet, CVS Drug, Hannfords Foods, Kia, Lincoln, **W** 🍽 Bluestone Bistro, Koto Japanese, 🛏 Desmond Hotel, Hotel Indigo, 🅞 to Heritage Park
2 (2)	NY 5, Central Ave, **E** 🅖 Mobil/dsl, Sunoco, 🍽 Wendy's, 🛏 Cocca's Inn, Scottish Inn, SpringHill Suites, 🅞 BJ's Whse, Jo-Ann Fabrics, Kost Tire, Marshall's, Lowe's, PetCo, Staples, Target, E on Wolf Rd...gas: Mobil/Subway/dsl, 🍽 Bucca Italian, Cheesecake Factory, Chili's, Dunkin Donuts, Emperor Chinese, Friendly's, Honeybaked Ham, Hooters, IHOP, LJ Silver/Taco Bell, Panera Bread, PF Chang's, Starbucks, 🛏 Days Inn, Travelodge, 🅞 Barnes&Noble, Firestone/auto, Goodyear/auto, LL Bean, Macy's, Sears/auto, mall, **W** 🅖 Gulf/dsl, Mobil, 🍽 Blue Spice Thai, Central Steak, Delmonico's Steaks, Domino's, Dunkin Donuts, La Fiesta, McDonald's, Moe's SW Grill, Mr Subb, Smokey Bones BBQ, Subway, Truman's Grill, Wendy's, 🛏 Baymont Inn, EconoLodge, Green Park Inn, Howard Johnson, Motel 6, Quality Inn, Super 8, 🅞 Advance Parts, AT&T, Buick/GMC, Cadillac, Krause's Candy, PepBoys, Subaru, Verizon
1W (1)	NY State Thruway (from sb), I-87 S to NYC, I-90 W to Buffalo
1E (1)	I-90 E (from sb), to Albany, Boston
1S (1)	to US 20, Western Ave, **E** on US 20 🅖 Getty, 🍽 Burger King, Chipotle Mexican, Coldstone, Creo, Dunkin Donuts, 5 Guys Burgers, 99 Rest., Starbucks, TGIFriday's, 🛏 Best Western, Days Inn, Holiday Inn Express, other AT&T, CVS Drug, Verizon, **W** on US 20 🅖 Mobil/Subway, USA, 🍽 Capital City Diner, Chicago Grill, Friendly's, Hana Grill, Ichyban Japanese, McDonald's, Starbucks, 🅞 Adirondack Tires, Best Buy, Dick's, Home Depot, JC Penney, Macy's, Michael's, Old Navy, Petsmart, PriceChopper Foods, Walmart, mall, USPO, vet
1N (1)	I-87 N (from nb), to Plattsburgh, NY State Thruway goes west to Buffalo (I-90), S to NYC (I-87), I-87 N to Montreal
24 (148)	I-90 and I-87 N
23 (142)	I-787, to Albany, US 9 W, **E** on US 9 **W** 🅖 Cumberland Farms/Dunkin Donuts/dsl, Sunoco/dsl, 🛏 Comfort Inn, Regency Inn, 🅞 transmissions, to Knickerbocker Arena, **W** 🅖 Stewarts, 🛏 EconoLodge
139mm	parking area sb, 🅒, 🛏, litter barrel
22 (135)	NY 396, to Selkirk
21a (134)	I-90 E, to MA Tpk, Boston
127mm	**New Baltimore Travel Plaza both lanes**, Mobil/dsl, Famous Famiglia, Quiznos, Roy Rogers, Starbucks, TCBY, atm, info, wi-fi
21b (124)	US 9 W, NY 81, to Coxsackie, **W** 🅖 Trvl Plaza/Citgo/rest./dsl/scales/24hr, Sunoco/dsl, 🍽 McDonald's (5mi), 🛏 Best Western, Budget Inn, Holiday Inn Express, Red Carpet Inn, 🅞 Boat'n RV Whse, repair, vet
21 (114)	NY 23, Catskill, **E** 🅖 Mobil, Sunoco/dsl, 🛏 Catskill Motel/rest. (2mi), Pelokes Motel (2mi), Quality Inn, 🅞 Home Depot, transmissions, visitors ctr, to Rip van Winkle Br,

NY

Exit	Services
21 (114)	Continued **W** 🍽 Anthony's Rest, Koch's Rest., Southside Rest., 🛏 Astoria Motel, Budget Inn (3mi), Rip Van Winkle Motel, 🅞 to Hunter Mtn/Windham Ski Areas
103mm	**Malden Service Area nb**, Mobil/dsl, Carvel Ice Cream, Hotdogs, McDonald's, atm, 🅒, parking area sb
20 (102)	NY 32, to Saugerties, **E** 🅖 Citgo, Mobil/dsl, Stewarts, Sunoco, 🍽 Dunkin Donuts, Emiliani Italian, Giordano's Pizza, McDonald's, Pizza Star, Starway Café, Subway, 🅞 CarQuest, Chrysler/Dodge/Jeep, Curves, CVS Drug, Family$, NAPA, PriceChopper Foods, vet, **W** 🅖 Hess/Blimpie/Dunkin Donuts/dsl, Sunoco/dsl, 🍽 Johnny G's Diner, Land&Sea Grill, 🛏 Comfort Inn, Howard Johnson/rest., 🅞 Blue Mtn Campground (5mi), Brookside Campground (10mi), KOA (2mi), Rip Van Winkle Campground (3mi), to Catskills
99mm	parking area nb, 🅒, 🛏, litter barrels
96mm	**Ulster Travel Plaza sb**, Sunoco/dsl, Arthur Treacher's Fish&Chips, Nathan's, Pizza Hut, Roy Rogers, Starbucks, TCBY, atm, 🅒, wi-fi
19 (91)	NY 28, Rhinecliff Br, Kingston, **E** 🅖 Mobil, QuickChek/dsl, 🍽 Blimpie, Friendly's, Olympic Diner, Picnic Pizza, 🛏 Holiday Inn, Super 8, 🅞 Advance Parts, CVS Drug, Hannaford Foods, Radio Shack, Walgreens, access to I-587 E, **W** 🍽 Family Diner, Lorenzo's Pizza, Roudigan's Steaks, Skytop Steaks, 🛏 Motel 19, Quality Inn, Rodeway Inn, SuperLodge, 🅞 Camper's Barn RV Ctr, Ford, Nissan, access to US 209
18 (76)	NY 299, to Poughkeepsie, New Paltz, **E** 🅖 Cumberland Farms, Mobil, Shell/dsl, 🍽 College Diner, Genesis Rest., Village Grill, 🛏 EconoLodge, 87 Motel, 🅞 repair, to Mid-Hudson Br, **W** 🅖 Sunoco, 🍽 Burger King, Dunkin Donuts, Gabaletos Seafood, McDonald's, Pasquale's Pizza, Plaza Diner, Rino's Pizza, Rococo's Pizza, Subway, TCBY, 🛏 Super 8, 🅞 Advance Parts, AT&T, Midas, Radio Shack, Rite Aid, ShopRite Foods, Stop'n Shop, Jellystone (9mi), KOA (10mi), vet
66mm	**Modena service area sb**, 🅖 Sunoco/dsl, 🍽 Carvel's Ice Cream, Chicago Grill, McDonald's, Moe's SW Grill, 🅞 atm, UPS, wi-fi
65mm	**Plattekill Travel Plaza nb**, 🅖 Sunoco/dsl, 🍽 Nathan's, Roy Rogers, Starbucks, 🅞 atm, info, wi-fi
17 (60)	I-84, NY 17K, to Newburgh, **E** on NY 300 **N** 🅖 Mobil, 🍽 DQ, Dunkin Donuts, Green Olive Grill, Joe's Deli, King Buffet, McDonald's, Newburgh Buffet, Old Town Buffet, Perkins, Subway, Taco Bell, Wendy's, 🅞 AT&T, AutoZone, BonTon, $Tree, Marshall's, Mavis Tire, Midas, Office Depot, Old Navy, Radio Shack, Sears/auto, Stop&Shop, mall, E on NY 300 **S** 🅖 Getty, Hess/dsl, Sunoco/dsl, 🍽 Applebee's, Burger King, Chili's, Cosimos Ristorante, Denny's, Gateway Diner, Johnny D's Diner, Longhorn Steaks, Neptune Diner, Panera Bread, Sonic, Steak&Stein, Subway, TGIFriday's, Union Sq Rest., 🛏 Days Inn, Hampton Inn, Howard Johnson, Knights Inn, Ramada Inn, Super 8, 🅞 Adam's Food Mkt, Aldi Foods, Barnes&Noble, Buick/GMC, Cadillac/Chevrolet, Chrysler/Dodge/Jeep, Ford/Lincoln, Home Depot, Honda, Kohl's, Lowe's, Michael's, Nissan, Petsmart, Target, Verizon, Walmart/McDonald's, **W on NY 17K** 🛏 Hilton Garden
16 (45)	US 6, NY 17, to West Point, Harriman, **W** 🅖 Gulf/dsl, 🍽 Applebee's, Chicago Grill, Chili's, Dunkin Donuts, KFC, Outback Steaks, Taco Bell, TGIFriday's, Wendy's, 🛏

NEWBURGH

↑N INTERSTATE 87 CONT'D

Exit	Services
16 (45)	Continued
	American Budget Inn, Hampton Inn, 🅾 Best Buy, BJ's Whse, BMW, $Tree, GNC, Home Depot, Kohl's, Petsmart, Radio Shack, Staples, Target, TJ Maxx, Walmart/Subway, (1mi), Woodbury Outlet/famous brands, st police
34mm	**Ramapo Service Area sb**, 🅐 Sunoco/dsl, 🍴 Carvel, McDonald's, Uno Pizza, 🅾 atm, wi-fi
33mm	**Sloatsburg Travel Plaza nb**, 🅐 Sunoco/dsl, 🍴 Burger King, Dunkin Donuts, Quiznos, Sbarro's, 🅾 atm, gifts, info
15a (31)	NY 17 N, NY 59, Sloatsburg
15 (30)	I-287 S, NY 17 S, to NJ. **I-87 S & I-287 E run together.**
14b (27)	Airmont Rd, Montebello, **E** 🛏 Crowne Plaza, **W on NY9** 🅐 Gulf/Dunkin Donuts/dsl, 🍴 Airmont Diner, Applebee's, Bagel Boys Cafe, Friendly's, Pasta Cucina, Starbucks, Subway, Sutter's Mill Rest., Water Wheel Cafe, 🛏 Howard Johnson, 🅾 🅷 DrugMart, ShopRite Foods, Tall Man Tires, Walgreens, Walmart, vet
14a (23)	Garden State Pkwy, to NJ, Chestnut Ridge
14 (22)	NY 59, Spring Valley, Nanuet, **E** 🅐 Citgo/dsl, Shell/dsl, Valero/dsl, 🍴 Burger King, Deliziosa Pizza, IHOP, McDonald's, Planet Wings, 🛏 Fairfield Inn, 🅾 BMW/Ferrarl, CarQuest, Maserati, Michael's, Target, TJ Maxx, Verizon, **W** 🅐 Citgo, Gulf, 🍴 Baskin-Robbins/Dunkin Donuts, ChuckeCheese, Franko's Pizza, KFC, Nanuet Diner, Panera Bread, Red Lobster, Starbucks, Taco Bell, White Caotlo, 🛏 Days Inn, Hampton Inn, Hilton Garden, 🅾 AT&T, Barnes&Noble, $Tree, Home Depot, Hyundai, Macy's, Marshall's, PetCo, Sears/auto, Staples, Stop&Shop Foods, Verizon, transmissions
13 (20)	Palisades Pkwy, N to Bear Mtn, S to NJ
12 (19)	NY 303, Palisades Ctr Dr, W Nyack, **W** 🅐 Mobil, 🍴 Cheesecake Factory, Dunkin Donuts, Tony Roma's, 🛏 Nyack Motel, 🅾 Barnes&Noble, Best Buy, BJ's Whse, Dave&Buster's, Macy's, Home Depot, JC Penney, Lord&Taylor, Old Navy, Staples, ShopRite Foods, STS Tires, Target, mall
11 (18)	US 9W, to Nyack, **E** 🅐 Gulf, Mobil, Shell, 🛏 Best Western, **W** 🅐 Shell/dsl, 🍴 Dunkin Donuts, McDonald's, 🛏 Super 8, 🅾 🅷 J&L Repair/tire, Old World Food Mkt
10 (17)	Nyack (from nb), same as 11
14mm	Tappan Zee Br, Hudson River
13mm	**toll plaza**
9 (12)	to US 9, to Tarrytown, **E** 🅐 Hess/dsl, 🅾 Stop&Shop, **W** 🅐 Mobil, 🍴 El Dorado West Diner, 🛏 DoubleTree Hotel, 🅾 Honda, Mavis Tire
8 (11)	I-287 E, to Saw Mill Pkwy, White Plains, **E** 🛏 Hampton Inn, Marriott
7a (10)	Saw Mill River Pkwy S, to Saw Mill River SP, Taconic SP
7 (8)	NY 9A (from nb), Ardsley, **W** 🛏 Ardsley Acres Motel, 🅾 🅷
6mm	**Ardsley Travel Plaza nb**, Sunoco/dsl, Burger King, Popeye's, vending
5.5mm	**toll plaza**, 🅒
6ba (5)	Stew Leonard Dr, to Ridge Hill, **W** 🅾 Costco, Home Depot, Stew Leonard's Farmfresh Foods
6 (4.5)	Tuckahoe Dr, Yonkers, **E** 🅐 Getty/repair, 🍴 Marcellino's Pizza, McDonald's, Subway, 🛏 Tuckahoe Motel, 🅾 ShopRite Foods/drug, **W** 🅐 Gulf, Mobil/dsl, 🍴 Domino's, Dunkin Donuts, Kim Wei Chinese, 🛏 Ramada Inn, Royal Regency Hotel

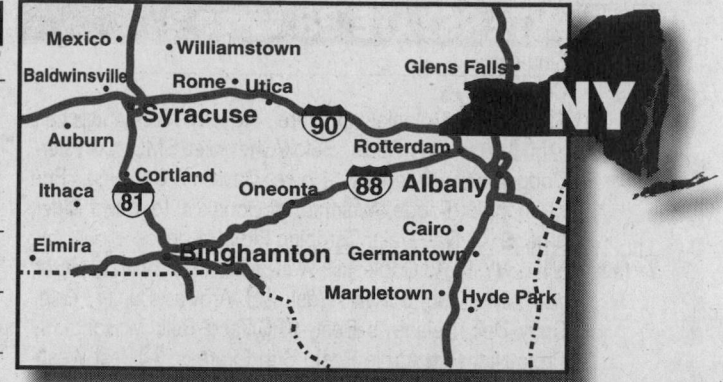

Exit	Services
5 (4.3)	NY 100 N (from nb), Central Park Ave, White Plains
4 (4)	Cross Country Pkwy, Mile Sq Rd, **E** 🅐 Lukoil, 🅾 Ford/Lincoln/Subaru, Macy's, Marshll's, Sears/auto, TJ Maxx, **W** 🅐 Getty, Shell/Dunkin Donuts/dsl, 🍴 Burger King, 🅾 Chevrolet, Mavis Tire
3 (3)	Mile Square Rd, **E** 🅾 GNC, Stop&Shop, Thriftway Drug, mall, **W** 🅐 Getty, Shell
2 (2)	Yonkers Ave (from nb), Westchester Fair, **E** 🅐 Mobil, 🅾 Yonkers Speedway
1 (1)	Hall Place, McLean Ave, **E** 🅾 A&P Foods/Subway, 🍴 Dunkin Donuts
0mm	**New York St Thruway and I-87 N run together to Albany**
14 (11)	McLean Ave, **E** 🅐 A&P/dsl, 🍴 Dunkin Donuts, Subway
13 (10)	E 233rd. **NE Tollway, service plaza both lanes**/Mobil
12 (9.5)	Hudson Pkwy (from nb), Sawmill Pkwy
11 (9)	Van Cortlandt Pk S
10 (8.5)	W 230th St (from sb), W 240th (from nb), **E** 🅐 Lukoil, **W** 🅐 Getty, 🍴 Dunkin Donuts, 🅾 🅷 Marshall's, Target
9 (8)	W Fordham Rd, **E** 🅐 BP/dsl, 🍴 Dallas BBQ, 🅾 🅷
8 (7)	W 179th (from nb), **W** Roberto Clemente SP
7 (6)	I-95, US 1, S to Trenton, NJ, N to New Haven, CT
6 (5)	E 153rd t, River Ave, Stadium Rd, **E** 🅾 Yankee Stadium
5 (5)	E 161st, Macombs Dam Br, (exit 4 from nb), **E** 🅾 AT&T, Best Buy, Michael's, Target, Yankee Stadium
3 (3)	E 138th St, Madison Ave Br, **E** 🅐 BP/dsl
2 (2)	Willis Ave, 3rd Ave Br, **E** 🅐 Mobil/dsl, **W** 🍴 McDonald's
1 (1)	Brook Ave, Hunts Point, **E** 🅐 BP, Hess
0mm	**I-87 begins/ends on I-278.**

↑E INTERSTATE 88

Exit	Services
25a	I-90/NY Thruway. **I-88 begins/ends on I-90, exit 25a.**
117mm	**toll booth** (to enter or exit NY Thruway)
25 (116)	NY 7, to Rotterdam, Schenectady, **S** 🅐 ⛽/Dunkin Donuts/Subway/dsl/scales/24hr, **3 mi S** 🅐 Gulf, 🍴 Burger King, McDonald's, Peppino's Pizza, Top's Diner, Wagon Train BBQ, 🛏 L&M Motel, Quality Inn, 🅾 Frosty Acres Camping
24 (112)	US 20, NY 7, to Duanesburg, **N** 🅐 Mobil, Stewarts, 🍴 Dunkin Donuts, 🅾 st police, **S** 🍴 Duanesburg Diner, 🅾 USPO
23 (101)	NY 30, to Schoharie, Central Bridge, **N** 🅐 Apple Food/dsl, 🛏 Holiday Motel, 🅾 Hideaway Camping, Locust Park Camping, **S** 🅐 Mobil/Subway/dsl, 🍴 Dunkin Donuts, 🛏 Days Inn, Hyland House B&B (2mi), Wedgewood B&B (2mi)
22 (95)	NY 7, NY 145, to Cobleskill, Middleburgh, **2-5 mi N** 🅐 Hess/dsl, Mobil, Sunoco, 🍴 Dunkin Donuts, Pizza Hut,

N Y A C K / **N Y C A R E A** (left margin)
N Y C A R E A (right margin)

🄴 INTERSTATE 88 CONT'D

Exit	Services
22 (95)	Continued Subway, 🅛 Colonial CT Motel, Holiday Motel, Super 8, 🅞 🄷, Advance Parts, Buick/Chevrolet/GMC, Chrysler/Dodge/Jeep, $General, Howe Caverns Camping, PriceChopper Foods, Walmart/McDonald's to Howe Caverns, S 🅞 Twin Oaks Camping (5mi), st police
21 (90)	NY 7, NY 10, to Cobleskill, Warnerville, **2-3 mi N** 🅖 Hess/dsl, Mobil/dsl, Stewart's/dsl, 🅕 Arby's, Burger King, Dairy Deli, Delaney's Rest, KFC/Taco Bell, McDonald's, Pizza Hut, Red Apple Rest., Sub Express, 🅛 Best Western, Gables B&B, 🅞 🄷, Ace Hardware, CarQuest, CVS Drug, $General, NAPA, PriceChopper Foods, TrueValue, Walmart/McDonald's
20 (87)	NY 7, NY 10, to Richmondville, S 🅖 Mobil/dsl, Sunoco/dsl, 🅕 Reinhardt's Deli, Sub Express, 🅛 Red Carpet Inn, 🅞 USPO
79mm	🆁🆂 wb, full 🅫 facilities, 🄲, vending, 🄿, litter barrels, petwalk
19 (76)	to NY 7, Worcester, N 🅖 Stewarts, Sunoco/dsl
18 (71)	to Schenevus, N 🅖 Citgo, 🅕 Schenevus Rest.
17 (61)	NY 7, to NY 28 N, Colliersville, Cooperstown, **2 mi N** 🅖 Sunoco, 🅛 Best Western (14mi), Red Carpet Inn, 🅞 to Baseball Hall of Fame
16 (59)	NY 7, to Emmons, N 🅕 Arby's, Brooks BBQ, Farmhouse Rest., Morey's Rest., Pizza Hut, Sonny's Pizza, 🅛 Amber Life Motel, Rainbow Inn, 🅞 PriceChopper Foods, Rite Aid
15 (56)	NY 28, NY 23, Oneonta, N 🅖 Citgo, Hess, KwikFill, 🅕 Dunkin Donuts, Friendly's, KFC, 🅛 Clarion, Townhouse Inn, 🅞 🄷, Advance Parts, to Soccer Hall of Fame, S 🅖 Hess/Dunkin Donuts, Mirabito/dsl, 🅕 Applebee's, Burger King, Denny's, McDonald's, Neptune Diner/24hr, Quiznos, Sabatini's Italian, Subway, Taco Bell, Wendy's, 🅛 Budget Inn, Christopher's Lodge/rest., Holiday Inn, Sun Lodge, Super 8, 🅞 Aldi Foods, BJ's Whse/gas, Dick's, $Tree, Ford, Hannaford Foods, Home Depot, JC Penney, Kost Tire, TJ Maxx, Verizon, Walmart
14 (55)	Main St (from eb), Oneonta, N 🅖 Citgo, Stewarts, Sunoco, 🅕 Alfresco's Italian, 🅞 CarQuest
13 (53)	NY 205, **1-2 mi N** 🅖 Citgo, Hess, Valero/dsl, 🅕 DQ, Dunkin Donuts, McDonald's, 🅛 Celtic Motel, Hampton Inn, Motel 88, 🅞 Buick/Cadillac/Chevrolet/GMC, Family$, Honda, Jellystone Park Camping, Kia, NAPA, Nissan, Rite Aid, Subaru, to Susquehanna Tr, Gilbert Lake SP (11mi), camping, st police
12 (47)	NY 7, to Otego, S 🅖 Mirabito/Subway/Tim Hortons/dsl/24hr
11 (40)	NY 357, to Unadilla, Delhi, N KOA
39mm	🆁🆂 eb, full 🅫 facilities, 🄲, 🄿, litter barrels, vending, petwalk
10 (38)	NY 7, to Unadilla, **2 mi N** 🅖 KwikFill, Mirabito, 🅛 Country Motel (4mi), 🅞 Great American Foods, USPO, st police
9 (33)	NY 8, to Sidney, N 🅖 Hess/dsl, Mobil/dsl, Sunoco, 🅕 China Buffet, Little Caesars, McDonald's, Pizza Hut, Subway, 🅛 Algonkin Motel, Country Motel, Super 8, 🅞 🄷, Advance Parts, $General, K-Mart, PriceChopper Foods, Tall Pines Camping, USPO
8 (29)	NY 206, to Bainbridge, N 🅖 Sunoco, 🅕 Bob's Family Diner, Deli Joe's, Dunkin Donuts, 🅛 Algonkin Motel, Susquehanna Motel, 🅞 Chevrolet/GMC, Riverside RV Park, Parts+, USPO, to Oquage Creek Park
7 (22)	NY 41, to Afton, **1-2 mi N** 🅖 Mobil, Sunoco/dsl, 🅕 RiverClub Rest., Vincent's Rest., 🅞 Afton Golf/rest., Kellystone Park, Smith-Hale HS
6 (16)	NY 79, to NY 7, Harpursville, Ninevah, S 🅖 Mirabito/dsl, 🅕 Gramma's Country Cafe, Tim Hortons, 🅞 USPO, to Nathanial Cole Park
5 (12)	Martin Hill Rd, to Belden, N 🅖 Manley's Trstp/dsl, 🅞 Belden Manor Camping
4 (8)	NY 7, to Sanitaria Springs, S 🅖 Hess/dsl
3 (4)	NY 369, Port Crane, N to Chenango Valley SP, S 🅖 Fastrac/dsl, KwikFill
2 (2)	NY 12a W, to Chenango Bridge, N 🅖 Mirabito, 🅞 USPO
1 (1)	NY 7 W (no wb return), to Binghamton
0mm	I-81, N to Syracuse, S to Binghamton.

i-88 begins/ends on I-81.

🄴 INTERSTATE 90

Exit	Services
B24.5mm	New York/Massachusetts state line
B3 (B23)	NY 22, to Austerlitz, New Lebanon, W Stockbridge, N 🅖 Citgo/dsl/scales/24hr, S 🅖 Sunoco/dsl, 🅛 Berkshire Travel Lodge, 🅞 Woodland Hills Camp
B18mm	toll plaza, 🄲
B2 (B15)	NY 295, Taconic Pkwy, **1-2 mi S** gas
B1 (B7)	US 9, NY Thruway W, to I-87, **toll booth**, 🄲
12 (20)	US 9, to Hudson, N 🅖 🄶🄰🅂/McDonald's/Subway/dsl/scales/24hr, **0-3 mi S** 🅞 to Van Buren NHS
18.5mm	🆁🆂/weigh sta wb, full 🅫 facilities, 🄲, 🄿, litter barrels, vending, petwalk
11 (15)	US 9, US 20, E Greenbush, Nassau, N 🅖 Hess/dsl, Sunoco/dsl, 🅕 Dunkin Donuts, 🅞 st police, S 🅖 Mobil (2mi), Stewarts, 🅕 Lighthouse Rest., 🅛 Host Field Inn, Knights Inn, 🅞 Rite Aid, repair, vet
10 (10)	Miller Rd, to E Greenbush, S 🅖 Mobil/dsl, Stewarts, 🅕 Dunkin Donuts, 🅛 Comfort Inn
9 (9)	US 4, to Rensselaer, Troy, N 🅖 Mobil, 🅕 Applebee's, Domino's, Dunkin Donuts, 5 Guys Burgers, McDonald's, OffShore Pier Rest., Panera Bread, Starbucks, Subway, The Sports Grill, 🅛 Holiday Inn Express, Residence Inn, 🅞 $Tree, Home Depot, PetsMart, Radio Shack, Staples, Target, Walmart, S 🅖 Mobil/dsl, Stewart's, 🅕 Cracker Barrel, Denny's, Dunkin Donuts, 🅞 Fairfield Inn
8 (8)	NY 43, Defreestville
7 (7)	Washington Ave (from eb), Rensselaer
6.5mm	Hudson River
6a	I-787, to Albany
6 (4.5)	US 9, Northern Blvd, to Loudonville, N 🅖 Stewarts, 🅕 Forbidden City, Mr Subb, NY Pizza, 🅛 Red Carpet Inn, 🅞 🄷
5a (4)	Corporate Woods Blvd
5 (3.5)	Everett Rd, to NY 5, **S on NY 5**, **Central Ave** 🅖 Hess/dsl, ShopRite, 🅕 Bob&Ron's Fishfry, Dunkin Donuts, Gateway Diner, Little Caesars, Mama Buffet, McDonald's, Popeye's, Subway, Taco Bell, 🅞 🄷, Aamco, Advance Parts, Chevrolet, Chrysler/Dodge/Jeep, CVS Drug, $Tree, Fiat, Ford, Hannaford's Foods, Home Depot, Honda, Hyundai, Kia, Mavis Tire, Mazda, Monroe, Nissan, PepBoys, PriceChopper Foods, Radio Shack, ShopRite Foods, Rite Aid
4 (3)	NY 85 S, to Slingerlands
3 (2.5)	State Offices
2 (2)	Fuller Rd, Washington Ave, **S on Washington** 🅖 Sunoco/Subway, 🅕 Dunkin Donuts, 🅛 Courtyard, CrestHill Suites, Extended Stay America, Fairfield Inn, Hilton Garden, Red Carpet Inn, TownePlace Suites, same as 1S

Side labels: COBLESKILL · ONEONTA (left column), ALBANY (right column), NY

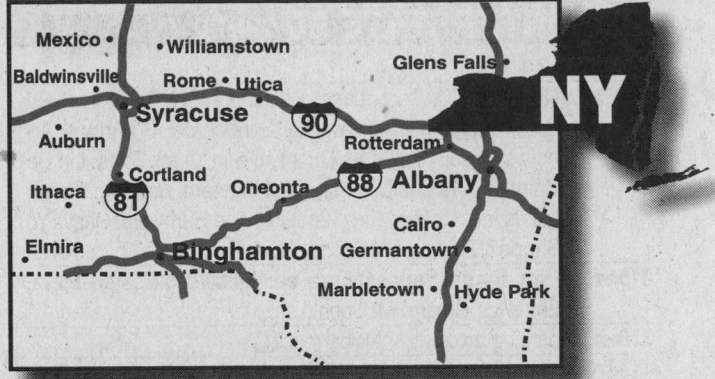

🅔 INTERSTATE 90 CONT'D

Exit	Services
1N (1)	I-87 N, to Montreal, to Albany ✈
1S (1)	US 20, Western Ave, **S** 🅖 Mobil, 🍴 Burger King, Capital City Diner, Chipotle Mexican, Dunkin Donuts, 5 Guys Burgers, Hana Grill, Ichiban Japanese, McDonald's, Moe's SW Grill, 99 Rest., Panera Bread, Peaches Cafe, Starbucks, TGIFriday's, Uno Grill, Wendy's, 🛏 Holiday Inn Express, Residence Inn, 🅾 AT&T, Best Buy, CVS Drug, Dick's, Home Depot, JC Penney, Macy's, Michael's, Old Navy, PetsMart, PriceChopper Foods, Verizon, Walmart, mall, USPO, vet
24 (149)	I-87 N to Albany, Montreal, S to NYC
153mm	**Guilderland Service Area eb**, Mobil/dsl, McDonald's
25 (154)	I-890, NY 7, NY 146, to Schenectady
25a (159)	I-88 S, NY 7, to Binghamton, **S** 🅖 🚃/Dunkin Donuts/Subway/dsl/scales/24hr
26 (162)	I-890, NY 5 S, Schenectady
168mm	**Pattersonville Service Area wb**, Mobil/dsl, Hershey's, Quiznos, Roy Rogers, Starbucks, atm, wi-fi
172mm	**Mohawk Service Area eb**, Mobil/dsl, McDonald's,
27 (174)	NY 30, Amsterdam, **N** 🅖 Mobil/dsl, Valero, 🛏 Super 8, Valleyview Motel, **1 mi N** 🛏 Best Value Inn, 🅾 Alpin Haus RV Ctr (3mi)
28 (182)	NY 30A, Fonda, **N** 🅖 Citgo/rest/dsl/motel/24hr, Mobil (1mi), Sunoco/dsl, TA/Buck Hill Rest/dsl/motel/scales/24hr/@, 🍴 Dunkin Donuts, McDonald's, 🛏 Holiday Inn (7ml), Microtel, Riverside Motel, Super 8 (8ml), 🅾 Ⓗ, st police, truck repair
184mm	**parking area/truck insp area both lanes**, 🚻 s, **litter barrels**
29 (194)	NY 10, Canajoharie, **N** 🅖 Gulf, Stewarts, 🍴 McDonald's, Subway, 🅾 Ace Hardware, BigLots, $General, NAPA, Rite Aid, Riverfront Park, USPO, **S** 🅖 Citgo/dsl, Lukoll/dsl; Sunoco, 🍴 Mercato Pizza, Village Rest., 🛏 Rodeway Inn, 🅾 NAPACare, USPO
210mm	**Indian Castle Service area eb** 🅖 Mobil/dsl, 🍴 Hershey's Ice Cream, Roy Rogers, Starbucks, 🅾 atm, gifts, wi-fi. **Iroquois Service Area wb** 🅖 Mobil/dsl, Burger King, Dunkin Donuts, wi-fi
29a (211)	NY 169, to Little Falls, **N** 🛏 Knights Inn (3mi), 🅾 Ⓗ, to Herkimer Home
30 (220)	NY 28, to Mohawk, Herkimer, **N** 🅖 FasTrac/dsl, Mobil/Subway/dsl, Stewarts, 🍴 Applebee's, Burger King, Denny's, Dunkin Donuts, KFC/Taco Bell, McDonald's, Pizza Hut, Tony's Pizzaria, Vinny's Pizza, 🛏 Best Inn, Budget Motel, Herkimer Motel, Inn Towne Motel, 🅾 Advance Parts, Aubuchon Hardware, AutoZone, $General, $Tree, Goodyear, Rite Aid, Verizon, Walmart, **S** 🅖 FasTrac, 🍴 Little Caesars, Red Apple Chinese, 🛏 Red Carpet Inn (2mi), 🅾 Factory Depot, Family$, to Cooperstown (Baseball Hall of Fame)
227mm	**Schuyler Service Area wb**, Mobil/dsl, Breyer's, Fresh Fudge, McDonald's, atm, st police
31 (233)	I-790, NY 8, NY 12, to Utica, **N** 🅖 Citgo/dsl, Fastrac, Sunoco, 🍴 Burger King, Franco's Pizza, Good Friend Chinese, 🅾 BigLots, Curves, $Tree, PriceChopper Foods, Rite Aid, **1 mi N on frontage rd** 🍴 Applebees, 🅾 BJ's Whse/gas, Lowe's, Walmart/McDonald's, **S** 🅖 Hess/dsl, 🍴 Babe's Grill, Delmonico's Steaks, Denny's, Dunkin Donuts, Friendly's, Knock-Out Pizza, McDonald's, Pizza Hut, Romeo's Italian, Subway, Taco Bell, Wendy's, 🛏 Best

Exit	Services
31 (233)	Continued Western, Days Inn, Hampton Inn, Happy Journey Motel, Red Roof Inn, Scottish Inn, Super 8, 🅾 AT&T
236mm	I-790 (from eb), to Utica
237.5mm	Erie Canal
238mm	Mohawk River
32 (243)	NY 232, Westmoreland, **N** 🛏 Scottish Inn, 4-8 mi **N** 🛏 EconoLodge, Quality Inn, Red Carpet Inn, 5 mi **S** 🛏 Hampton Inn
244mm	**Oneida Service Area eb**, Sunoco/dsl, Burger King, Sbarro's, Starbucks, atm, gifts
250mm	parking area eb, 🚻 s, 🗑, litter barrel
33 (253)	NY 365, to Vernon Downs, Verona, **N** 🅖 SavOn Gas/dsl, 🍴 Joel's Frontyard Steaks, 🛏 Inn at Turning Stone, **S** 🅖 SavOn Gas/LP/repair, 🍴 Dunkin Donuts, Recovery Grill, 🛏 Fairfield Inn, La Quinta, 🅾 Ⓗ, Turning Stone Casino
256mm	parking area wb, 🚻 s, 🗑, litter barrel
34 (262)	NY 13, to Canastota, **S** 🅖 KwikFill, SavOn/dsl, Sunoco, 🍴 Dunkin Donuts, McDonald's, 🛏 Days Inn, Graziano Motel/rest., Super 8, 🅾 Boxing Hall of Fame, Verona Beach SP Camping
266mm	**Chittenango Service Area wb**, Sunoco/dsl, Sbarro's, Starbucks atm, wi-fi
34a (277)	I-481, to Syracuse, Chittenango
35 (279)	NY 298, The Circle, Syracuse, **S** 🅖 Mobil, Valero/dsl, 🍴 Burger King, Denny's, Dunkin Donuts, East Wok, Green Onion Rest., Grimaldi's, Joey's Italian, Jreck Subs, Justin's Grill, McDonald's, Ruby Tuesday, Weigh Look Cafe, 🛏 Candlewood Suites, Comfort Inn, Courtyard, Cresthill Suites, Days Inn, Doubletree Inn, Embassy Suites, Extended Stay America, Hampton Inn, Hilton Garden, Holiday Inn, John Milton Inn, Microtel, Motel 6, Quality Inn, Ramada Ltd, Red Roof Inn, Residence Inn, Super 8, 🅾 Goodyear/auto
280mm	**Dewitt Service Area eb**, Sunoco/dsl, Edy's Ice Cream, McDonald's
36 (283)	I-81, N to Watertown, S to Binghamton
37 (284)	7th St, Electronics Pkwy, to Liverpool, **N** 🛏 Best Western, **S** 🅖 Hess/Blimpie/Dunkin Donuts/Godfather's, 🍴 KFC/Taco Bell, 🛏 Holiday Inn, Homewood Suites, Knights Inn, Staybridge Suites, 🅾 Kinny Drug
38 (286)	NY 57, to Liverpool, Syracuse, **N** 🅖 Fastrac/dsl, Hess, KwikFill, 🍴 Bangkok Thai, Hooligan's, Kirby's Rest., Pier 57 Diner, Pizza Hut, Quiznos, Salsarita's Grill, 🛏 Hampton Inn (7mi), Super 8, 🅾 Aldi Foods, $Tree, NAPA, Rite Aid
39 (290)	I-690, NY 690, Syracuse, **N** 🛏 Comfort Inn/rest., 🅾 Camping World RV Ctr, **S** 🍴 Quaker Steak&Lube, 🛏 Holiday Inn Express
292mm	**Warners Service Area wb**, Mobil/dsl, Boston Pizza, Edy's Ice Cream, McDonald's

SYRACUSE

UTICA

⛏ INTERSTATE 90 CONT'D

Exit	Services
40 (304)	NY 34, to Owasco Lake, Weedsport, **N** Riverforest RV Park, **S** 🅖 Fastrac, KwikFill, Sunoco/dsl, 🍴 Arby's, Arnold's Rest., Cj's Rest., DB's Drive-In, Jreck Subs, Lin Bo Chinese, Old Erie Diner, 🛏 Best Western, Days Inn, Finger Lakes Inn, Holiday Inn (12mi), Ⓞ Ace Hardware, Bass Pro Shops (12mi), Big M Foods, $General, Kinney Drug, NAPA
310mm	**Port Byron Service Area eb**, 🅖 Mobil/dsl, Boston Pizza, Edy's Ice Cream, McDonald's
318mm	parking area wb, litter barrels, 🆁🆂 s
41 (320)	NY 414, to Cayuga Lake, Waterloo, **S** 🅖 Nice'n Easy/dsl, Petro/Iron Skillet/dsl/scales/24hr/@, 🍴 MaGee Country Diner, 🛏 Hampton Inn (4mi), Holiday Inn (4mi), Microtel (4mi), Ⓞ Cayuga Lake SP/camping, Waterloo Outlets/famous brands (3mi)
324mm	**Junius Ponds Service Area wb**, Sunoco/dsl, Dunkin Donuts, Roy Rogers, atm, wi-fi
42 (327)	NY 14, to Geneva, Lyons, **N** RV camping, **S** 🅖 Mobil/dsl/scales, 🛏 Red Carpet Inn, Ⓞ Waterloo Outlets/famous brands (3mi), Junius Ponds RV Camping, **6 mi S** 🛏 Belherst, Best Value Inn, Days Inn, Hampton Inn, Ramada Inn
337mm	**Clifton Springs Service Area eb**, Sunoco/dsl, Roy Rogers, Sbarro's, Starbucks, atm, gifts
43 (340)	NY 21, to Palmyra, Manchester, **N** Hill Cumorah LDS HS (6mi), **S** 🅖 Sunoco/dsl, 🍴 Lehigh Valley Rest., McDonald's, 🛏 Scottish Inn, Ⓞ KOA
44 (347)	NY 332, Victor, **S** 🅖 Getty/Subway/dsl, Sunoco/dsl, 🍴 Dairy-Ann, Dunkin Donuts, KFC, King's Wok, McDonald's, NY Pizza, 🛏 Best Value Inn, Budget Inn, Comfort Inn, Travelodge, Ⓞ Aldi Foods, CVS Drug, KOA (4mi), Wade's Foods, casino, st police
350mm	**Seneca Service Area wb**, 🅖 Mobil/dsl, 🍴 Checker's, Tim Hortons, Villa Pizza, Ⓞ atm, wi-fi
45 (351)	I-490, NY 96, to Rochester, **N** 🅖 Mobil/dsl, 🍴 Biaggi's Rest., BoneFish Grill, Champp's Grill, Distillery Rest., Longhorn Steaks, Moe's SW Grill, Olive Garden, PF Chang's, Starbucks, Subway, TGIFriday's, Uno Grill, 🛏 Hampton Inn, Springdale Farm B&B, Ⓞ Best Buy, BJ's Whse/gas, Bonton, Dick's, $Tree, Home Depot, JC Penney, K-Mart, Kohl's, Lord&Taylor, Macy's, Michael's, Old Navy, Petsmart, Rite Aid, Sears/auto, Staples, Target, Verizon, Walmart, **S** 🅖 KwikFill, 🍴 Burger King, Chili's, Denny's, Wendy's, 🛏 Best Western, Holiday Inn Express, Homewood Suites, Microtel, Royal Inn, Ⓞ Ballantyne RV Ctr
353mm	parking area eb, 🆁🆂, litter barrels
46 (362)	I-390, to Rochester, **N on NY 253 W** 🅖 Gulf/dsl, Hess, Sunoco/dsl, 🍴 Lehigh Rest., McDonald's, Peppermint's Rest., Tim Hortons, Wendy's, 🛏 Country Inn&Suites, Days Inn, Fairfield Inn, Microtel, Red Carpet Inn, Red Roof Inn, Super 8 Ⓞ Buick/GMC
366mm	**Scottsville Service Area eb**, 🅖 Mobil/dsl, 🍴 Arby's, Tim Horton, Ⓞ atm, info, wi-fi
376mm	**Ontario Service Area wb**, 🅖 Sunoco/dsl, 🍴 Boston Pizza, Edy's Ice Cream, McDonald's, atm, wi-fi
47 (379)	I-490, NY 19, to Rochester, **N** Timberline Camping
48 (390)	NY 98, to Batavia, **N** 🛏 Comfort Inn, Hampton Inn, Holiday Inn Express, **S** 🅖 Citgo, 🍴 Applebee's, Bob Evans, Peking Buffet, 🛏 Best Western, Budget Inn, Clarion, Days Inn, Quality Inn, Red Roof Inn, Super 8, Ⓞ AT&T,
48 (390)	Continued AutoZone, BJ's Whse, Home Depot, K-Mart, Michael's, PetCo, Radio Shack, Target, Walmart
397mm	**Pembroke Service Area eb**, 🅖 Sunoco/dsl, 🍴 Checker's, Tim Hortons, Ⓞ atm, gifts, 🆁🆂, wi-fi
48a (402)	NY 77, Pembroke, **S** 🅖 ⭑FLYING J/Denny's/Subway/dsl/LP/scales/24hr, TA/Valero/dsl/scales/24hr/@, 🍴 Subway, 🛏 Darien Lake Lodge/camping, EconoLodge, Ⓞ Sleepy Hollow Camping (8mi)
412mm	**Clarence Service Area wb, full 🅰 facilities**, 🅖 Sunoco/dsl, 🍴 Arby's, Tim Hortons, Ⓞ atm, info, wi-fi
49 (417)	NY 78, Depew, **0-3 mi N** 🅖 Delta Sonic, Mobil/dsl, Sunoco, 🍴 Applebee's, Arby's, Burger King, Carmen's Rest., Chili's, Coldstone, Cracker Barrel, Denny's, Dibella's Subs, DQ, Dunkin Donuts, Friendly's, Frog Hair Grille, Just Pizza, KFC, La Tolteca, McDonald's, Mighty Taco, Moe's SW Grill, Mr Pita, Old Country Buffet, Panera Bread, Perkins, Picasso's Pizza, Pizza Hut, Pizza Plant, Pomegranate, Protocol Rest., Quaker Steak&Lube, Quiznos, Red Lobster, Russel's Steaks, Salsarita's, Spilio's Rest., Starbucks, Subway, Taco Bell, Ted's HotDogs, TGIFriday's, Tim Horton, Tully's Rest., Wendy's, 🛏 Clarion, Microtel, Motel 6, Rodeway Inn, Salvatore's Hotel, Staybridge Suites, Super 8, Ⓞ Acura, Aldi Foods, AT&T, Barnes&Noble, Best Buy, BigLots, BJ's Whse/gas, BonTon, Buick/GMC, Chrysler/Dodge/Jeep, Dick's, $Tree, Dunn Tire, Firestone/auto, Ford, Goodyear, Home Depot, Honda, JC Penney, Jo-Ann Fabrics, Kohl's, Lowe's, Michael's, PetCo, PetsMart, Rite Aid, Sears/auto, SteinMart, Suzuki, Target, TJ Maxx, Top's Food/deli, Tuesday Morning, Walgreens, Walmart, Wegman's Foods, mall, vet, **S** 🅖 Kwikfill, Mobil, 🍴 Bob Evans, China 1, Dunkin Donuts, John&Mary's Cafe, McDonald's, Salvatore's Italian, Subway, Tim Horton, 🛏 Garden Place Hotel, Hospitality Inn, La Quinta, Red Roof Inn, Ⓞ Aamco, CarQuest, $Tree, Top's Foods
419mm	**toll booth**
50 (420)	I-290 to Niagara Falls
50a (421)	Cleveland Dr (from eb)
51 (422)	NY 33 E, Buffalo, **S** 🆁🆂, st police
52 (423)	Walden Ave, to Buffalo, **N** 🍴 Applebees, Burger King, Famous Dave's BBQ, IHOP, McDonald's, Ruby Tuesday, Starbucks, Subway, TGIFriday's, Tim Horton, 🛏 Hampton Inn, Residence Inn, Ⓞ Aldi Foods, AT&T, $Tree, Firestone, Ford, Goodyear/auto, Home Depot, Michael's, Office Depot, PetsMart, PriceRight, Target, Top's Foods, Walmart, **S** 🅖 Delta Sonic, Jim's Trk Plaza/Sunoco/dsl/rest./scales/24hr, KwikFill, 🍴 Alton's Rest., Bar Louie's, Bravo Italiano, Cheesecake Factory, Dunkin Donuts, Fuddrucker's, Hyde Park Steaks, Jack Astor's Grill, McDonald's, Melting Pot, Mighty Taco, Milton's Rest., Olive Garden, PF Chang's, Pizza Hut, Smokey Bones BBQ, Zahng's Buffet, 🛏 Millenium Hotel, Oak Tree Inn, Ⓞ Best Buy, Burlington Coats, Dick's, Dunn Tire, Lord&Taylor, Macy's, JC Penney, K-Mart, NAPA, Niagara Hobby, Old Navy, Sears, mall
52a (424)	William St
53 (425)	I-190, to Buffalo, Niagara Falls, **N** 🛏 Best Western
54 (428)	NY 400, NY 16, to W Seneca, E Aurora
55 (430)	US 219, Ridge Rd, Orchard Park, to Wilson Stadium, **S** 🅖 Delta Sonic, Valero, 🍴 Denny's, Mighty Taco, Subway, Tim Horton, Wendy's, 🛏 Country Inn&Suites, Hampton Inn, Staybridge Suites, Ⓞ Aldi Foods, BigLots, $General, Goodyear/auto, Home Depot, K-Mart, Mr Tire, Pepboys, Tops Foods, Wegman's Foods

ROCHESTER

NY

DEPEW

BUFFALO

⬆🄴 INTERSTATE 90 CONT'D

Exit	Services
431mm	**toll booth**
56 (432)	NY 179, Mile Strip Rd, **N** 🅖 Sunoco, Valero, 🍴 Blasdale Pizza, China King, DiPallo's Rest., Odyssey Rest., Whse Rest., 🛏 EconoLodge, 🄾 CarQuest, CVS Drug, $General, Family$, Jubilee Foods, Rite Aid, repair, USPO, **S** 🍴 Applebee's, Boston Mkt, Buffalo Wild Wings, ChuckeCheese, Friendly's, McDonald's, Mongolian Buffet, Olive Garden, Outback Steaks, Panera Bread, Pizza Hut, Red Lobster, Ruby Tuesday, Starbucks, Subway, TGIFriday's, Wasabi Japanese, Wendy's, 🛏 Best Western, McKinley's Hotel, Red Carpet Inn (2mi), 🄾 Aldi Foods, Barnes&Noble, Best Buy, BJ's Whse, BonTon, Dick's, $Tree, Firestone/auto, Home Depot, JC Penney, Jo-Ann Etc, Macy's, Old Navy, PepBoys, Sears, TJ Maxx, Wegman's Foods, mall
57 (436)	NY 75, to Hamburg, **N** 🅖 Mobil/Dunkin Donuts/dsl, 🍴 Anthony's Diner, Bozanna's Pizza, Denny's, McDonald's, Tim Horton, Uncle Joe's Diner, Wendy's, 🛏 Comfort Inn, Holiday Inn Express, Motel 6, Red Roof Inn, 🄾 Chevrolet, Chrysler/Dodge/Jeep, Ford, Lowe's, Walmart (3mi), repair, transmissions, **S** 🅖 Go Gas, Kwikfill/dsl, Stop&Gas, 🍴 Arby's, Burger King, Hideaways Rest., Pizza Hut, Subway, Tim Horton, 🛏 Quality Inn, Super 8, 🄾 AutoZone, $General, Goodyear/auto, USPO, vet
442mm	parking area both lanes, 🍴, litter barrels
57a (445)	to Eden, Angola, **2 mi N** 🅖 Sunoco/dsl
447mm	**Angola Service Area both lanes**, Sunoco/dsl, McDonald's, Moe's SW Grill, Subway, atm, gifts, wi-fi
58 (456)	US 20, NY 5, to Silver Creek, Irving, **N** 🅖 Citgo, Kwikfill, 🍴 Burger King, Colony Rest., Millie's Rest., Primo's Rest., Subway, Sunset Bay, Tim Hortons, Tom's Rest., 🛏 Lighthouse Inn, 🄾 🄷, to Evangola SP
59 (468)	NY 60, Fredonia, Dunkirk, **N** 🛏 Clarion (2mi), Dunkirk Motel (4mi), 🄾 Lake Erie SP/camping (7mi), **S** 🅖 Country Fair, Fuel Ctr/dsl, Kwikfill/dsl, Mobil/dsl, 🍴 Applebee's, Arby's, Azteca Mexican, Best Buffet, Bob Evans, Burger King, Denny's, Dunkin Donuts, KFC/Taco Bell, McDonald's, Pizza Hut, Subway, Tim Hortons, Wendy's, Wing City Grille, 🛏 Best Western, Comfort Inn, Days Inn, 🄾 Advance Parts, Aldi Foods, AutoZone, BigLots, $General, $Tree, Ford/Lincoln, GMC, GNC, Home Depot, Radio Shack, Rite Aid, Tops Foods/gas, TJ Maxx, Walmart
60 (485)	NY 394, Westfield, **N** 🛏 Webb's Motel, 🄾 Brookside Beach Camping, KOA, to Lake Erie SP/camping, **S** 🛏 Holiday Motel, 🄾 🄷
494mm	**toll booth**
61 (495)	Shortman Rd, to Ripley, **N** 🄾 Lakeshore RV Park
496mm	New York/Pennsylvania state line

⬆🄽 INTERSTATE 95

Exit	Services
32mm	New York/Connecticut state line
22 (30)	Midland Ave (from nb), Port Chester, Rye, **W** 🍴 Subway, 🄾 🄷, Home Depot, Staples
21 (29)	I-287 W, US 1 N, to White Plains, Port Chester, Tappan Zee
20 (28)	US 1 S (from nb), Port Chester, **E** 🅖 Shell, 🄾 CVS Drug, Ford, Subaru, USPO
19 (27)	Playland Pkwy, Rye, Harrison
18b (25)	Mamaroneck Ave, to White Plains, **E** 🅖 Hess, Shell, 🍴

18b (25)	Continued Domino's, 🄾 A&P Foods, Mavis Tire
18a (24)	Fenimore Rd (from nb), Mamaroneck, **E** 🅖 Sunoco/dsl
17 (20)	Chatsworth Ave (from nb, no return), Larchmont
19.5mm	**toll plaza**
16 (19)	North Ave, Cedar St, New Rochelle, **E** 🍴 Applebee's, Buffalo Wild Wings, 🛏 Residence Inn, 🄾 ShopRite, Toyota, USPO, **W** 🄷
15 (16)	US 1, New Rochelle, The Pelhams, **E** 🅖 Getty/dsl, SuperGas, 🄾 AutoZone, Costco, CVS Drug, Harley-Davidson, Home Depot, NAPA, Walgreens, **W** auto repair
14 (15)	Hutchinson Pkwy (from sb), to Whitestone Br
13 (16)	Conner St, to Mt Vernon, **E** 🅖 Gulf/dsl, 🛏 Ramada Inn, **W** 🅖 BP, 🍴 McDonald's, 🛏 Exit 13 Motel, Holiday Motel, 🄾 🄷
12 (15.5)	Baychester Ave (exits left from nb)
11 (15)	Bartow Ave, Co-op City Blvd, **E** 🅖 Mobil, 🍴 Applebee's, Baskin-Robbins, Barto Pizza, Burger King, Checker's, Genarro's Pizza, Little Caesars, McDonald's, Panera Bread, Popeye's, Red Lobster, Zinhi Chinese, 🄾 Barnes&Noble, JC Penney, K-Mart, Marshall's, Old Navy, PathMark Foods, Pay Half, Staples, Verizon, **W** 🅖 Gulf, Shell/mart, Sunoco/dsl, 🍴 ChuckeCheese, Dunkin Donuts, Eastern Wok, Pizza Hut, Subway, TGIFriday's, 🄾 Home Depot
10 (14.5)	Gun Hill Rd (exits left from nb), **W** 🛏 Pelham Bay Hotel/diner
9 (14)	Hutchinson Pkwy
8c (13.5)	Pelham Pkwy W
8b (13)	Orchard Beach, City Island
8a (12.5)	Westchester Ave (from sb)
7c (12)	Pelham Bay Park (from nb), Country Club Rd
7b (11.5)	E Tremont (from sb), **W** 🄾 Super FoodTown
7a (11)	I-695 (from sb), to I-295 S, Throgs Neck Br
6b (10.5)	I-278 W (from sb), I-295 S (from nb)
6a (10)	I-678 S, Whitestone Bridge
5b (9)	Castle Hill Ave, **W** 🅖 Sunoco, 🍴 McDonald's, 🄾 GNC
5a (8.5)	Westchester Ave, White Plains Rd
4b (8)	Bronx River Pkwy, Rosedale Ave, **E** 🅖 BP, Getty
4a (7)	I-895 S, Sheridan Expsy
3 (6)	3rd Ave, 🄷
2b (5)	Webster Ave, **E** 🄷
2a (4)	Jerome Ave, to I-87
1c (3)	I-87, Deegan Expswy, to Upstate
1b (2)	Harlem River Dr
1a (1)	US 9, NY 9A, H Hudson Pkwy, 178th St, downtown
0mm	New York/New Jersey state line, Hudson River, Geo Washington Br

🅟 = gas   🍴 = food   🛏 = lodging   🅞 = other   🆁🆂 = rest stop   Copyright 2014 - The NEXT Exit ®

⬆N INTERSTATE 190 (BUFFALO)

Exit	Services
25.5mm	US/Canada Border US Customs
25b a	R Moses Pkwy, NY 104, NY 265, Lewiston, **E** 🏥
24	NY 31, Witmer Rd, **E** 🏥, st police
23	NY 182, Porter Rd, Packard Rd, **E** 🅟 Sunoco, 🍴 Applebees, Burger King, DQ, Mighty Taco, Perkins, Subway, Tim Horton, 🅞 Big Lots, CarQuest, Chrysler/Jeep, Firestone/auto, Jo-Ann Fabrics, K-Mart, NAPA, Prime Outlets/famous brands, U-Haul, **W** 🍴 Wendy's, 🅞 Aldi Foods, Sam's Club, Walmart/Subway,
22	US 62, Niagara Falls Blvd, **E** 🅟 Sunoco, 🍴 Bob Evans, Burger King, Denny's, Dunkin Donuts, KFC, McDonald's, Pizza Hut, Taco Bell, Wendy's, 🛏 Budget Host, Caravan Motel, Holiday Motel, Howard Johnson, Knight's Inn, Pelican Motel, Quality Inn, Red Carpet Inn, Super 8, Swiss Cottage Inn, 🅞 Advance Parts, Ford, Radio Shack, Rite Aid, Target, Top's Foods/gas, Toyota, **W** 🛏 Econolodge, Sunrise Inn, 🅞 Home Depot
21a	NY 384, Buffalo Ave, R Moses Pkwy, **W** 🅟 Getty, 🅞 casino, to NY SP, American Falls
21	La Salle Expswy
20.5mm	Niagara River East, **toll booth sb**
20b a	Long Rd, **E** 🛏 Budget Motel
19	Whitehaven Rd, **E** 🅟 Getty, Noco Gas, 🍴 McDonald's, Subway, 🛏 Chateu Motel (2mi), Holiday Inn (4mi), 🅞 $Tree, Top's Foods/gas, KOA (1mi), funpark, **W** 🅞 Chevrolet, Toyota/Scion, vet
18b a	NY 324 W, Grand Island Blvd, **E** 🍴 Asian Buffet, Burger King, Tim Horton, Wendy's, 🛏 Chateu Motel, Grand Suites, 🅞 NAPA, **W** Beaver Island SP
17.5mm	Niagara River East, **toll booth**
17	NY 266, last free exit nb
16	I-290 E, to I-90, Albany
15	NY 324, Kenmore Ave, **E** 🅟 7-11, **W** 🅞 U-Haul
14	Ontario St, **E** 🅟 KwikFill, 🍴 McDonald's, Tim Horton, 🅞 Advance Parts, Family$, **W** 🍴 Harry's Grille
13	(from nb) same as 14
12	Amherst St, (from nb), downtown
11	NY 198, Buffalo, **E** 🅟 Sunoco
9	Porter Ave, to Peace Bridge, Ft Erie
8	NY 266, Niagara St, downtown, **E** 🛏 Adam's Mark Hotel
7	NY 5 W, Church St, Buffalo, downtown
6	Elm St, **E** 🏥, downtown, **W** HSBC Arena
5	Louisiana St, Buffalo, downtown
4	Smith St, Fillmore Ave, Buffalo, downtown
3	NY 16, Seneca St, from sb, **W** 🅞 CarQuest
2	US 62, NY 354, Bailey Ave, Clinton St
1	Ogden St, **E** 🅟 Sunoco, 🍴 Wendy's, 🛏 Comfort Inn, Holiday Inn Express, 🅞 CVS Drug, Tops Foods, Volvo/GMC Trucks
.5mm	**toll plaza nb**
0mm	I-90. I-190 begins/ends on I-90, exit 53.

⬆E INTERSTATE 287 (NEW YORK CITY)

Exit	Services
	I-287 begins/ends on I-95, exit 21.
12	I-95, N to New Haven, S to NYC.
11	US 1, Port Chester, Rye, **N** 🅟 BP, Mobil, Sunoco, 🍴 Burger King, Domino's, Dunkin Donuts, KFC, McDonald's, Port Chester Diner, Subway, Wendy's, 🅞 🏥, Goodyear/auto, Kohl's, Mavis Discount Tire, Nissan, Petsmart, Staples, Verizon

Exit	Services
10	Bowman Ave, Webb Ave
9N S	Hutchinson Pkwy, Merritt Pkwy, to Whitestone Br
9a	I-684, Brewster
8	Westchester Ave, to White Plains, **S** 🅟 BP, Mobil, Cheesecake Factory, Morton's Steaks, PF Chang's, Westchester Burger Co, White Plains Diner, 🅞 Chrysler/Dodge/Jeep, Hyundai, Neiman Marcus, Nordstrom, Stop&Shop Foods, Westchester Mall Place, Whole Foods Mkt
7	Taconic Pkwy (from wb), to N White Plains
6	NY 22, White Plains
5	NY 100, Hillside Ave, **S** 🅟 Citgo, Gulf, Lukoil, 🍴 Applebee's, Dunkin Donuts, Papa John's, Planet Pizza, Subway, 🅞 Aamco, AutoZone, Barnes&Noble, GNC, K-Mart, Lexus, Mazda, Radio Shack, vet
4	NY 100A, Hartsdale, **N** 🅟 Shell, 🅞 🏥, **S** 🍴 Bamboo Garden Chinese, Burger King, 🅞 BMW/Mini, Jaguar, Staples, Volvo
3	Sprain Pkwy, to Taconic Pkwy, NYC
2	NY 9A, Elmsford, **N** 🅟 BP, Citgo, Mobil, Sunoco, 🍴 Dunkin Donuts, KFC/Taco Bell, Subway, 🅞 Mavis Discount Tire, NAPA, Sam's Club, **S** 🅟 Shell, 🍴 Wendy's
1	NY 119, Tarrytown, **N** 🅟 Gulf/dsl, 🍴 Ruth's Chris Steaks, 🛏 Marriott, Sheraton, **S** 🅟 Gulf/dsl, 🍴 El Dorado Diner, 🛏 Extended Stay America, Hampton Inn

I-287 runs with I-87 N.

⬆E INTERSTATE 290 (BUFFALO)

Exit	Services
8	I-90, NY Thruway, **I-290 begins/ends on I-90, exit 50.**
7b a	NY 5, Main St, **N** 🅟 Mobil, Sunoco, 🍴 La Nova Pizza/Wings, McDonald's, Pizza Plant, Subway, Tim Horton, Wendy's, 🅞 Quality Mkt Foods, Walgreens, **S** 🅟 Valero, 🍴 Sonoma Grille, 🛏 Amherst Motel, 🅞 vet
6	NY 324, NY 240, **N** 🅟 Getty, 🛏 Courtyard, **S** 🅟 Valero, 🍴 China Star, ChuckeCheese, Subway, 🅞 Chrysler/Jeep, CVS Drug, Hyundai/Subaru, KIA/Mazda, Lexus, Nissan
5b a	NY 263, to Millersport, **N** 🍴 Houlihan's, 🛏 Comfort Inn, Marriott, Red Roof Inn, **S** 🅟 Mobil, 🛏 Homewood Suites, 🅞 Scion/Toyota, VW, Walgreens
4	I-990, to St U
3b a	US 62, to Niagara Falls Blvd, **N** 🅟 Citgo, Valero, 🍴 Bob Evans, Dunkin Donuts, Just Pizza, Max's Grill, Pancake House, Ted's Hot Dogs, 🛏 Blvd Inn, Econolodge, Extended Stay America, Holiday Inn, Knight's Inn, Red Carpet Inn, Sleep Inn, 🅞 Buick/GMC, CarQuest, Dodge, Home Depot, Honda, Walmart/auto, vet, **S** 🅟 Delta Sonic, Mobil, 🍴 Applebee's, Arby's, BoneFish Grill, Burger King, Carrabba's, Chili's, Denny's, Dibella's Subs, John's Pizza, McDonald's, Moe's SW Grill, Montana's Grill, Outback Steaks, Panera Bread, Pizza Hut, Starbucks, Subway, Swiss Chalet Grill, TGIFriday, Tim Horton, Tulley's, 🛏 Days Inn, Royal Inn, 🅞 Barnes&Noble, Best Buy, $Tree, Firestone, Goodyear/auto, JC Penney, Jo-Ann Fabrics, Lowes Whse, Macy's, Michael's, PetCo, PetsMart, Sears/auto, Target, mall
2	NY 425, Colvin Blvd, **N** 🍴 Athena's Rest., KFC, McDonald's, Subway, Texas Roadhouse, Tim Horton, Wendy's, 🅞 🏥, Big Lots, BJ's Whse/gas, Family$, Gander Mtn, Goodyear/auto, Top's Foods/gas, **S** 🅟 KwikFill
1b a	Elmwood Ave, NY 384, NY 265, **N** 🅟 KwikFill, 🍴 John's Pizza/Subs, Sam's Cafe, 🛏 Microtel, 🅞 🏥, $Tree, NAPA, Rite Aid, **S** 🅟 Mobil/dsl, 🍴 Arby's
0mm	I-190. I-290 begins/ends on I-190 in Buffalo.

NIAGARA FALLS **BUFFALO** (left margin)

NY (left margin)

NYC AREA **BUFFALO** (right margin)

N INTERSTATE 390 (ROCHESTER)

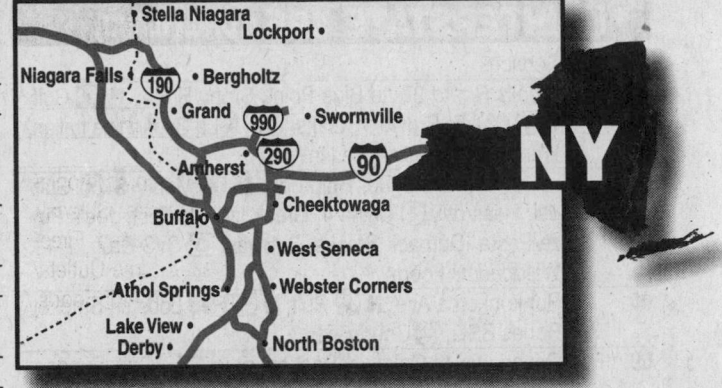

Exit	Services
20a b (76)	I-490. **I-390 begins/ends on I-490 in Rochester**
19 (75)	NY 33a, Chili Ave, **N** 🍴 Wishing Well Rest., **S** 🅖 Sunoco, 🍴 Burger King, Pizza Hut, Subway, 🛌 Motel 6, Quality Inn, 🅞 $General
18a b (74)	NY 204, Brooks Ave, **N** 🛌 Holiday Inn, **S** 🛌 Fairfield Inn, 🅞 🚗
17 (73)	NY 383, Scottsville Rd, **W** 🅖 Sunoco/Subway/dsl
16 (71)	NY 15a, to E Henryetta, **S** 🍴 Basil's Rest., 🛌 Courtyard, Hampton Inn, 🅞 🅗
15 (70)	I-590, Rochester
14 (68)	NY 15a, NY 252, **E** 🍴 Domino's, Gray's Cafe, McDonald's, Outback Steaks, Papa John's, Perkins, Tully's Rest., 🛌 Extended Stay America, 🅞 Staples, **W** 🅖 Mobil/dsl, 🍴 Boston Mkt, Dunkin Donuts, Starbucks, Subway, Taco Bell, 🛌 Best Western, DoubleTree Inn, 🅞 Big Lots, Office Depot, Radio Shack, Top's Foods
13 (67)	Hylan Dr, **E** 🍴 Cracker Barrel, 🛌 Comfort Suites, Homewood Suites, **W** 🅖 Mobil/dsl,food: Bonton, ChuckE-Cheese, IHOP, McDonald's, Olive Garden, Panera Bread, Tim Hortons, Uno Grill, Wendy's, 🅞 Aldi Foods, Best Buy, BJ's Whse, Gander Mtn, Goodyear/auto, JC Penney, Lowe's, Macy's, Michael's, Old Navy, PepBoys, PetCo, Sam's Club/gas, Sears, Target, Walmart, Wegman's Foods
12 (66)	I-90. NY Thruway, NY 253, **W** 🅖 Gulf/dsl/scales, Hess, Sunoco/dsl, 🍴 Lehigh Rest., McDonald's, Peppermint's Rest., Tim Hortons, Wendy's, 🛌 Country Inn&Suites, Days Inn, Fairfield Inn, Microtel, Red Carpet Inn, Red Roof Inn, Super 8 🅞 Buick/GMC
11 (62)	NY 15, NY 251, Rush, Scottsville, **2 mi N** 🍴 McDonald's, Tim Hortons, Wendy's, 🛌 Days Inn, Fairfield Inn, Red Roof Inn, RIT Inn
10 (55)	US 20, NY 5, Avon, Lima, **N** 🅖 Exxon, 🍴 Countryside Diner, 🛌 CrestHill Inn, Stratford Inn, **S** 🅖 Sugar Creek/dsl, 🅞 Chrysler/Dodge/Jeep, Ford, **3 mi S** 🍴 Avon Cafe, Dutch Hollow Cafe, McDonald's, Tom Wahls Cafe, Subway, 🛌 Avon Cedar Lodge, 🅞 Sugar Creek Camping
9mm	scenic area wb
9 (52)	NY 15, **N** 🅖 Mobil/Dunkin Donuts/dsl, 🍴 Fratelli's Rest., Lakeville Rest., McDonald's, Tee&Gee Cafe, 🛌 Conesus Motel, 🅞 Chevrolet
8 (48)	US 20a, Geneseo, **N** 🛌 Oak Valley Inn, 🅞 Conesus Lake Camping, **S** 🍴 Denny's, Dunkin Donuts, KFC/Taco Bell, McDonald's, Wendy's, 🛌 Quality Inn
7 (39)	NY 63, NY 408, Geneseo, **S** st police, **S** 🅖 Mobil, KwikFill, Sunoco/dsl, 🍴 Brian's Diner, McDonald's, 🛌 Alligence B&B, Country Inn&Suites, Geneseo River Hotel/Rest., Greenway Motel, 🅞 Bonadonna Auto, Family$, Letchworth SP, NAPA, Ridge Camping, Rite Aid, Save-A-Lot Foods
38mm	🆁🆂 both lanes, full ♿ facilities, 🛋 litter barrels, vending, petwalk
6 (33)	NY 36, Mt Morris, Sonyea
5 (26)	NY 36, Dansville, **N** 🅖 KwikFill, Mobil/Subway, 🍴 Arby's, Burger King, Dunkin Donuts, McDonald's, Pizza Hut, Subway, 🅞 Advance Parts, BigLots, Chevrolet, Chrysler/Dodge/Jeep, CVS Drug, $Tree, Radio Shack, Rite Aid, Save-A-Lot Foods, Top's Foods/gas, Verizon, **S** 🅖 TA/Valero/Country Pride/dsl/scales/24hr/@, 🛌 TA Motel
4 (23)	NY 36, Dansville, **N** 🅖 Sunoco/dsl, 🛌 Logan's Inn, 🅞 🅗

Exit	Services
4 (23)	Continued vet, **S** 🅖 Skybrook Camping, Stonybrook Park Camping, Sugar Creek Camping, Sunvalley Camping
3 (17)	NY 15, NY 21, Wayland, **N** 🍴 Farmer's Kitchen Rest. (1mi), 🅞 CarQuest (1mi), Holiday Hill Campground (7mi), st patrol
2 (11)	NY 415, Cohocton, Naples, **N** 🅖 Mobil (2mi), 🅞 Tumble Hill Camping (3mi)
1 (2)	NY 415, Avoca, **N** truck/auto repair, USPO (2mi), **S** 🅖 Mobil, 🛌 Caboose Motel (3mi)

E INTERSTATE 495 (LONG ISLAND)

Exit	Services
	I-495 begins/ends on NY 25.
73	rd 58, Old Country Road, to Greenport, Orient, **0-2 ml S** 🅖 Gulf, Hess/dsl, Lukoil/7-11, Mobil/dsl, 🍴 Applebees, Boulder Creek Steaks, Panera Bread, TGIFridays, Taco Bell, Wendy's, 🛌 Hilton Garden, Holiday Inn Express, 🅞 AutoZone, Best Buy, Buick/GMC, Chevrolet, Chrysler/Jeep, Curves, CVS Drug, Ford/Lincoln, Harley-Davidson, Home Depot, Honda, Kia/Mazda, Lowe's, Michael's, Nissan/Hyundai, PetCo, Stop&Shop, Subaru/VW, Tanger/famous brands, Target, Toyota/Scion, Volvo, Waldbaum's, Walgreens
72	NY 25, (no ez eb return), Riverhead, Calverton, **N** funpark, **S** 🅖 Hess, 🛌 Hotel Indigo, 🅞 Tanger/famous brands/foodcourt
71	NY 24, to Hampton Bays (no ez eb return), Calverton, **N** 🅖 Hess/Subway/dsl
70	NY 111, to Eastport, Manorville, **S** 🅖 Mobil/dsl, 7-11, 🍴 McDonald's, Michelangelo's Rest., Starbucks, 🅞 King Kullen Food/drug, Verizon
69	Wading River Rd, Center Moriches, to Wading River
68	NY 46, to Shirley, Wading River, **S** 🅞 7-11, golf
67	Yaphank Ave
66	NY 101, Sills Rd, Yaphank, **N** 🅖 Shell/24hr
65.5mm	parking area
65	Horse Block Rd, **N** 🍴 Baskin-Robbins/Dunkin Donuts, Kings Buffet, 🅞 Ford/Kenworth/Mack, LI RV Ctr, **S** funpark
64	NY 112, to Coram, Medford, **N** 🅖 Citgo/dsl, Hess, 🍴 Subway, 🅞 Lowe's, Michael's, Radio Shack, Sam's Club, 7-11, Staples, Target, Walgreens, **S** 🅖 BP, Gulf, USA/dsl, 🍴 J&R Steaks, Quiznos, Rita's Custard, Starbucks, 🛌 Comfort Inn, Fairfield Inn, 🅞 Aid Parts, 7-11
63	NY 83, N Ocean Ave, **N** 🅖 Hess/dsl, 🍴 Applebee's, Burger King, McDonald's, Taco Bell, TGIFriday's, 🅞 Hampton Inn, 🅞 CVS Drug, K-Mart, 7-11, Stop'n Shop, **S** 🅖 Gulf/dsl, Lukoil/dsl, 🍴 Yogi's Grill, 🛌 Crowne Plaza

Side labels: ROCHESTER, RIVERHEAD, MEDFORD, NY

INTERSTATE 495 (LONG ISLAND)

Exit	Services
62	Nicolls Rd, rd 97, to Blue Point, Stony Brook, N ⓡ Gulf, S ⓕ Charlie Brown's Steaks, Chili's, La Capannina Italian, Wendy's, ⌂ Residence Inn
61	rd 19, to Patchogue, Holbrook, N ⓡ Mobil, S ⓡ Gulf/dsl, Hess/dsl, ⓕ China 4, Greek Islands Rest, Joe's Pizza/Pasta, Outback Steaks, Subway, ⓞ CVS Drug, 7-11, Waldbaums Foods
60	Ronkonkoma Ave, N ⓡ Gulf, S ⓕ Red Lobster, Smokey Bones BBQ, ⌂ Courtyard
59	Ocean Ave, to Oakdale, Ronkonkoma, S ⓡ Gulf, Sunoco, ⌂ Hilton Garden (2mi), ⓞ 7-11
58	Old Nichols Rd, Nesconset, N ⓡ Gulf, ⓕ Hooters, ⌂ Marriott, ⓞ BJ's Whse, S ⓡ BP
57	NY 454, Vets Hwy, to Hauppauge, N ⓡ Exxon/dsl, ⓕ TGIFriday's, S ⓡ Getty's, Gulf/dsl, Shell, Sunoco, ⓕ Dave&Buster's, Subway, ⌂ Hampton Inn, ⓞ Radio Shack, Rite Aid, 7-11, Stop&Shop Foods, TJ Maxx, Walmart
56	NY 111, Smithtown, Islip, N ⓡ Gulf/Subway/Domino's/dsl, Mobil, S ⓡ Mobil, ⓕ Café La Strada, ⌂ Holiday Inn Express
55	Central Islip, N ⓡ Mobil, S ⓡ Exxon/dsl
54	Wicks Rd, N ⓡ BP, ⌂ Sheraton, S ⓡ Mobil
53	Sunken Meadow Pkwy, to ocean beaches, Bayshore
52	rd 4, Commack, N ⓡ Mobil/dsl, Shell/repair, ⓕ Conca d'Oro Pizza, Ground Round, ⌂ Hampton Inn, ⓞ Costco
51.5mm	parking area both lanes, ⓒ, litter barrels
51	NY 231, to Northport, Babylon
50	Bagatelle Rd, to Wyandanch
49N	NY 110 N, to Huntington, N ⌂ Marriott
49S	NY 110 S, to Amityville
48	Round Swamp Rd, Old Bethpage, S ⓡ Mobil/dsl, ⓕ Old Country Pizza/deli, ⌂ Homewood Suites, Palace Hotel, Sheraton, ⓞ USPO
46	Sunnyside Blvd, Plainview, N ⌂ Holiday Inn
45	Manetto Hill Rd, Plainview, Woodbury
44	NY 135, to Seaford, Syosset
43	S Oyster Bay Rd, to Syosset, Bethpage, N ⓡ Mobil
42	Northern Pkwy, rd N, Hauppauge
41	NY 106, NY 107, Hicksville, Oyster Bay, S ⓡ BP, Mobil, Sunoco, ⓕ Boston Mkt, Boulder Creek Steaks, Broadway Diner, Burger King, Dunkin Donuts, McDonald's, On the

HAUPPAUGE

NY NC

HICKSVILLE

41	Continued Border, ⓞ Goodyear/auto, Sears/auto
40	NY 25, Mineola, Syosset, S ⓡ BP, Exxon, Hess/dsl, Shell, ⓕ A&W, Burger King, Friendly's, IHOP, McDonald's, Wendy's, ⌂ Howard Johnson, ⓞ Home Depot, Kohl's, 7-11, Staples
39	Glen Cove Rd, N ⓡ Mobil
38	Northern Pkwy E, Meadowbrook Pkwy, to Jones Beach
37	Willis Ave, to Roslyn, Mineola, N ⓡ Gulf, Shell, ⓕ Dunkin Donuts, Skinny Pizza, S ⓡ Mobil/dsl, ⓕ Tofu Chinese
36	Searingtown Rd, to Port Washington, S ⌂
35	Shelter Rock Rd, Manhasset, S ⌂
34	New Hyde Park Rd
33	Lakeville Rd, to Great Neck, N ⌂
32	Little Neck Pkwy, N ⓡ Gulf, ⓕ Centre Pizza, Jain Rest., KFC/Taco Bell, Panera Bread, Starbucks
31	Douglaston Pkwy, S ⓡ BP/service, ⓕ Burger King, Grimaldi's Pizza, Pinecourt Chinese, Subway, ⓞ DR Drug, Macy's, USPO, Verizon, Waldbaum's Foods
30	E Hampton Blvd, Cross Island Pkwy
29	Springfield Blvd, S ⓡ Citgo, Gulf/Dunkin Donuts, ⓕ McDonald's
27	I-295, Clearview Expswy, Throgs Neck, N ⓡ Gulf, 7-11, ⓕ Blue Bay Diner, ⓞ drugstore
26	Francis Lewis Blvd
25	Utopia Pkwy, 188th St, N ⓡ Citgo, Gulf, S ⓡ Mobil, Quality/dsl, Savvy, Shell, ⓕ Arby's, Baskin-Robbins, Dunkin Donuts, 5 Guys Burgers, Subway, ⓞ Radio Shack, USPO
24	Kissena Blvd, N ⓡ Gulf/dsl, ⓕ Baskin-Robbins, Dunkin Donuts, S ⓡ Mobil
23	Main St, N ⓕ Palace Diner
22	Grand Central Pkwy, to I-678, College Pt Blvd, N ⌂ Holiday Inn Express
21	108th St, N ⓡ BP/7-11, Mobil
19	NY 25, Queens Blvd, Woodhaven Blvd, to Rockaways, N ⓕ McDonald's, ⓞ JC Penney, Macy's, mall, S ⓡ BP, ⓕ Applebees, Burger King, Dallas BBQ, 5 Guys Burgers, Moe's SW Grill, Subway, ⓞ Aldi Foods, Costco, Kohl's, Marshall's, Old Navy, Rite Aid, Sears, TJ Maxx
18.5	69th Ave, Grand Ave (from wb)
18	Maurice St, N ⓡ Exxon S ⓡ BP, ⓕ McDonald's, ⌂ Holiday Inn Express, ⓞ dsl repair
17	48th St, to I-278, N ⌂ Queensboro Hotel, ⓞ ⚡
16	**I-495 begins/ends in NYC.**

NORTH CAROLINA

INTERSTATE 26

Exit	Services
71mm	North Carolina/South Carolina state line
69mm	N Pacolet River
67.5mm	**Welcome Ctr wb, full ♿ facilities, ⓒ, 🚻, litter barrels**
67	US 74 E, to NC 108, Columbus, Tryon, N ⓡ Shell/Burger King/dsl, Vgo, ⓕ Cocula Mexican, McDonald's, Subway, Waffle House, Wendy's, ⓞ Advance Parts, CVS Drug, Family$, Food Lion, S ⓡ Exxon/dsl, ⓕ KFC/Taco Bell, Mtn View Deli, ⌂ Days Inn, ⓞ ⌂ , Bi-Lo, $General
59	Saluda, N ⌂ Saluda Motel, S ⓡ BP/dsl, Marathon/Subway/dsl, ⓕ Mama Locas, ⌂ B&B, ⓞ camping, repair, vet
56mm	Green River

54	US 25 (from eb), to Greenville, E Flat Rock, to Carl Sandburg Home
53.5mm	Eastern Continental Divide, 2130 ft
53	Upward Rd, Hendersonville, N ⓡ Marathon/Dunkin Donuts, ⓕ Waffle House, Zaxby's, ⌂ Mtn Inn&Suites, ⓞ Bloomfields Giftshop, Lakewood RV Park, S ⓡ Exxon/McDonald's/dsl, Shell/Pizza Inn/dsl, ⓕ Cracker Barrel, Subway, ⌂ Holiday Inn Express, ⓞ Twin Ponds RV Park, to Carl Sandburg Home
49b a	US 64, Hendersonville, N ⓡ Marathon/dsl, Shell/dsl, Sunoco/dsl, ⓕ Asaka Japanese, Atlanta Bread Co, Chick-fil-A, Golden Corral, Jack-in-the-Box, O'Charley's, Sonic, Starbucks, Waffle House, Zaxby's, ⌂ Best Western, Hampton Inn, Quality Inn, Ramada Inn, ⓞ ⌂ , Advance

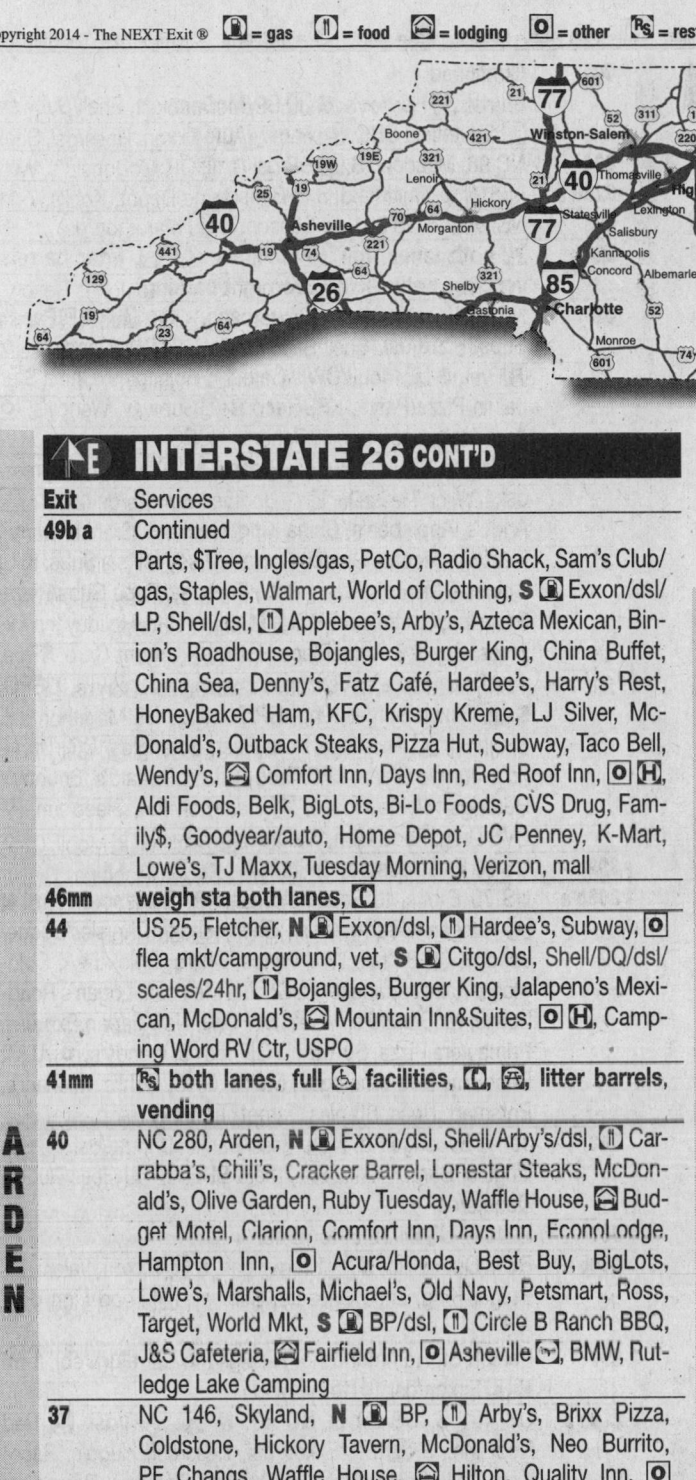

⤙E INTERSTATE 26 CONT'D

Exit	Services
49b a	**Continued**
	Parts, $Tree, Ingles/gas, PetCo, Radio Shack, Sam's Club/gas, Staples, Walmart, World of Clothing, **S** 🅿 Exxon/dsl/LP, Shell/dsl, 🍴 Applebee's, Arby's, Azteca Mexican, Binion's Roadhouse, Bojangles, Burger King, China Buffet, China Sea, Denny's, Fatz Café, Hardee's, Harry's Rest, HoneyBaked Ham, KFC, Krispy Kreme, LJ Silver, McDonald's, Outback Steaks, Pizza Hut, Subway, Taco Bell, Wendy's, 🛏 Comfort Inn, Days Inn, Red Roof Inn, ⚙ 🅷, Aldi Foods, Belk, BigLots, Bi-Lo Foods, CVS Drug, Family$, Goodyear/auto, Home Depot, JC Penney, K-Mart, Lowe's, TJ Maxx, Tuesday Morning, Verizon, mall
46mm	**weigh sta both lanes, 🅒**
44	US 25, Fletcher, **N** 🅿 Exxon/dsl, 🍴 Hardee's, Subway, ⚙ flea mkt/campground, vet, **S** 🅿 Citgo/dsl, Shell/DQ/dsl/scales/24hr, 🍴 Bojangles, Burger King, Jalapeno's Mexican, McDonald's, 🛏 Mountain Inn&Suites, ⚙ 🅷, Camping Word RV Ctr, USPO
41mm	🅿ₛ **both lanes, full 🦽 facilities, 🍴, 🛏, litter barrels, vending**
40	NC 280, Arden, **N** 🅿 Exxon/dsl, Shell/Arby's/dsl, 🍴 Carrabba's, Chili's, Cracker Barrel, Lonestar Steaks, McDonald's, Olive Garden, Ruby Tuesday, Waffle House, 🛏 Budget Motel, Clarion, Comfort Inn, Days Inn, EconoLodge, Hampton Inn, ⚙ Acura/Honda, Best Buy, BigLots, Lowe's, Marshalls, Michael's, Old Navy, Petsmart, Ross, Target, World Mkt, **S** 🅿 BP/dsl, 🍴 Circle B Ranch BBQ, J&S Cafeteria, 🛏 Fairfield Inn, ⚙ Asheville ➤, BMW, Rutledge Lake Camping
37	NC 146, Skyland, **N** 🅿 BP, 🍴 Arby's, Brixx Pizza, Coldstone, Hickory Tavern, McDonald's, Neo Burrito, PF Changs, Waffle House, 🛏 Hilton, Quality Inn, ⚙ Barnes&Noble, CVS Drug, Ingles/gas
34mm	French Broad River
33	NC 191, Brevard Rd, **N** ⚙ Toyota/Scion, **2 mi N** ⚙ Asheville Farmers Mkt, Bear Creek RV Camp, **S** 🅿 Citgo, HotSpot/dsl, 🍴 Apollo Flame, Chick-fil-A, Harbor Inn Seafood, LJ Silver, McDonald's, Papa's Mexican, Ryan's, Shogun Buffet, Stoneridge Grill, Taco Bell, Waffle House, 🛏 Comfort Suites, Country Inn&Suites, Fairfield Inn, Hampton Inn, Holiday Inn Express, Rodeway Inn, ⚙ Belk, Dillards, $Tree, Kia, K-Mart, Ingles Foods, PetCo, mall, to Blue Ridge Pkwy
31b a	I-40, E to Statesville, W to Knoxville
27mm	I-240 E, Patton Ave
	I-26 and I-240 run together 3 mi. See NC Interstate 240 exits 1-4
25	rd 251, to UNCA

ASHEVILLE

Exit	Services
24	Elk Mtn Rd, Woodfin
23	Merrimon Ave, N Asheville, **N** 🅿 BP/dsl, HotSpot, 🍴 Bellagio Bistro, Frank's Pizza, Magnolia Ray Rest., 🛏 Days Inn, ⚙ camping, vet
21	New Stock Rd, **N** 🅿 Citgo/dsl, Shell, 🍴 Granny's Kitchen, Pizza Hut, ⚙ Campfire Lodge RV Park, CVS, $General, Ingles/gas
19a b	N US 25, W US 70, Marshall, **N** 🅿 Shell/dsl, 🍴 Arby's, Bojangles, Burger King, Chapala Mexican, KFC, La Carreta Mexican, Little Caesars, McDonald's, Subway, TCBY, Waffle House, Zaxby's, ⚙ Ace Hardware, Advance Parts, AutoZone, BigLots, Kerr Drug, Ingles/dsl, Roses, **Urgent Care**, **S** 🅿 Shell/DQ/dsl, 🍴 Steak'n Shake, ⚙ CVS, $Tree, Lowe's, Walmart/Subway
18	Weaverville (no EZ return from eb)
17	to Flat Creek
15	rd 197, to Jupiter, Barnardsville
13	Forks of Ivy, **N** 🅿 Mkt Ctr/dsl, **S** 🅿 Shell/dsl
11	rd 213, to Mars Hill, Marshall, **N** tires, **S** 🅿 Exxon//Hardee's/dsl, Shell/dsl, TriCo, 🍴 Osaka Japanese, Subway, Waffle House, Wagon Wheel Rest., 🛏 Comfort Inn, ⚙ CVS, $General, Ingles/dsl, NAPA, Radio Shack
9	Burnsville, Spruce Pine to Mt Mitchell SP
7mm	scenic overlook wb, runaway truck ramp eb
6mm	**Welcome Ctr/🅿ₛ eb, full 🦽 facilities**
5.5mm	**runaway truck ramp eb**
5mm	Buckner Gap, elev. 3370
3	to US 23 A, Wolf Laurel, **N** 🅿 Exxon/dsl, 🍴 Little Creek Cafe, ⚙ to ski areas
2.5mm	**eb runaway truck ramp**
.5mm	**eb brake insp sta**
0mm	North Carolina/Tennessee state line

⤙E INTERSTATE 40

Exit	Services
420mm	**I-40 begins/ends at Wilmington, Services on US 17, N** 🛏 Hampton Inn, ⚙ Ford/Lincoln, Hyundai, Home Depot, Kia, Land Rover, Mazda, Nissan, Subaru, Suzuki, Toyota/Scion, Volvo, **S** 🅿 BP, Carolina Petro, Exxon/dsl, Hess, Hugo's, Murphy USA/dsl, 🍴 Arby's, Bojangles, Bonefish Grill, Carrabba's, Chick-fil-A, ChopStix, Church's, Cracker Barrel, Dunkin Donuts, Elizabeth's Pizza, Hardee's, Hooters, IHOP, Jason's Deli, Marlin&Ray's Seafood, McDonald's, Olive Garden, Sonic, Subway, Tokyo Grill, Waffle House, 🛏 Best Western, Budgetel, Comfort Suites, Days

ARDEN

WILMINGTON

◆E INTERSTATE 40 CONT'D

Exit	Services
420mm	Continued
	Inn, EconoLodge, Extended Stay America, Holiday Inn, MainStay Suites, Quality Inn, Ramada Inn, Red Roof Inn, Sleep Inn, Travelodge, Travel Inn, Wingate Inn, 🅞 Advance Parts, AutoZone, Black's Tires/auto, Cadillac, Costco/gas, Batteries+, Family$, Marshall's, Petsmart, Radio Shack, Rite Aid, Target, Walgreens, Walmart, **Services 2-4 mi S on US 117/NC 132** 🅖 BP/dsl, Exxon/dsl, 🅕 Applebee's, Bojangles, Burger King, Carolina Ale House, Checker's, Chili's, CiCi's Pizza, College Diner, Cookout, Domino's, Golden Corral, Hardee's, HoneyBaked Ham, KFC, Little Caesars, McAlister's Deli, McDonald's, Okami Japanese, Outback Steaks, Starbucks, Taco Bell, Wendy's, 🅛 Baymont Inn, Comfort Inn, Courtyard, Holiday Inn Express, 🅞 **Urgent Care**, Acura/Honda, AT&T, Best Buy, Buick/GMC, Chevrolet, Chrysler/Dodge/Jeep, Dick's, $Tree, Fiat, Harris-Teeter, K-Mart, Lowe's Foods, Lowe's Whse, Mercedes, Old Navy, PetCo, Sam's Club, Staples, TJ Maxx, Tuesday Morning, Verizon, to UNCW
420b a	Gordon Rd, NC 132 N, **2 mi N** 🅖 Hess/dsl, Kangaroo/dsl, 🅕 Andy's, Domino's, Hardee's, KFC, McDonald's, Smithfield's BBQ, Waffle House, Zaxby's, 🅞 CVS Drug, KOA (4mi), Rite Aid, Walgreens, vet, **S** 🅖 BP/dsl, Kangaroo/dsl, Go Gas/dsl, 🅕 Carolina BBQ, China Wok, Subway, 🅞 Family$, Lowe's Foods, Rite Aid
416b a	I-140, US 17, to Topsail Island, New Bern, & Myrtle Beach
414	Holly Shelter Rd, to Brunswick Co beaches, Castle Hayne, **S** 🅖 BP, GoGas/dsl, Kangaroo/dsl, 🅕 Carolina Cafe, Hardee's, Subway, 🅞 Bo's Foods, CVS Drug, $General, USPO
413mm	NE Cape Fear River
408	NC 210, **N** Mack/Volvo/Isuzu, **S** 🅖 Hess/Wendy's/dsl/cafe/scales/24hr, Phoenix TC/dsl/scales, Shell/Noble Roman's, 🅕 Hardee's, McDonald's, Subway, 🅞 Food Lion, USPO, to Moore's Creek Nat Bfd/camping
398	NC 53, Burgaw, **2 mi S** 🅕 CW's Cafe, Hardee's, McDonald's, Subway, 🅛 Burgaw Motel, 🅞 🅗, camping
390	to US 117, Wallace
385	NC 41, Wallace, **N** 🅖 Exxon/Village Subs, 🅕 Mad Boar Rest., 🅛 Holiday Inn Express, 🅞 camping, **1.5 mi S** 🅖 Hess/dsl, Murphy USA/dsl, 🅕 Burger King, Taco Bell, 🅞 $General, $Tree, Food Lion, O'Reilly Parts, Verizon, Walgreens, Walmart/Subway,
384	NC 11, Wallace
380	Rose Hill, **S** 🅖 BP/dsl (1mi), Pure
373	NC 24 E, NC 903, Magnolia, **N** 🅖 BP/dsl, Exxon/dsl/e-85, 🅞 🅗, Cowan Museum
369	US 117, Warsaw
364	NC 24, to NC 50, Clinton, 🆁🆂 **both lanes, full** 🅗 **facilities, 🚻, 🛒, litter barrels, vending, petwalk, N** 🅖 Wilco/Hess/Arby's/Dunkin Donuts/Stuckey's/dsl/24hr, **S** 🅖 BP/dsl, Kangaroo/dsl, Marathon, Sunoco/Bojangles, 🅕 KFC, McDonald's, Smithfield's BBQ, Subway, Waffle House, Wendy's, 🅛 Days Inn, Quality Inn
355	NC 403, to US 117, Goldsboro, Faison, **3 mi N** 🅖 Exxon
348	Suttontown Rd
343	US 701, Newton Grove, **1 mi N** 🅖 Exxon/dsl, to Bentonville Bfd
341	NC 50, NC 55, to US 13, Newton Grove, **1.5 mi N** 🅖 Exx

NC

Exit	Services
341	Continued
	on/dsl, 🅕 Hardee's, **S** 🅖 BP/McDonald's, Shell/Subway, 🅕 Smithfield BBQ, 🅞 Family Auto/tire
334	NC 96, Meadow, **S** 🅖 BP/dsl (1mi)
328b a	I-95, N to Smithfield, S to Benson
325	NC 242, to US 301, to Benson, **S** 🅖 Marathon/dsl
324mm	🆁🆂 **both lanes, full** 🅗 **facilities, 🚻, 🛒, litter barrels, vending, petwalk, no overnight parking**
319	NC 210, McGee's Crossroads, **N** 🅖 BP/Papa's Subs&Pizza/dsl, Shell/BBQ/dsl/24hr, 🅕 McDonald's, 🅞 🅗, vet, **S** 🅖 Mobil/CW's Cafe, 🅕 Bojangles, China Star, Italian Pizza/Pasta, KFC/Taco Bell, Subway, Wendy's, 🅞 AutoZone, Food Lion, $General, USPO
312	NC 42, to Clayton, Fuquay-Varina, **N** 🅖 Murphy Express/dsl, Wilco/Hess/Dunkin Donuts/Wendy's/dsl/24hr, 🅕 Andy's, Applebee's, China King, Cookout, Cracker Barrel, Fiesta Mexicana, Golden Corral, Jersey Mike's Subs, King Chinese, Marco's Pizza, Ruby Tuesday, Papa Subs/Pizza, Pizza Inn, Smithfield BBQ, 🅛 Comfort Inn, Holiday Inn Express, Super 8, ValuePlace Hotel, 🅞 **Urgent Care**, $Tree, JustTires, Lowe's, Verizon, Walmart/McDonald's, USPO, **S** 🅖 Exxon/Burger King, BP/Subway/dsl, Marathon/dsl, Shell/dsl, 🅕 American Hero Rest, Bojangles, DQ, Domino's, Jumbo China, KFC/Taco Bell, McDonald's, Snoopy's Hotdogs, Waffle House, 🅛 Hampton Inn, Sleep Inn, 🅞 CVS Drug, Food Lion, Walgreens, vet
309	US 70 E, Goldsboro, Smithfield
306b a	US 70 E bus, to Smithfield, Garner, Goldsboro, **1 mi N** 🅖 Kangaroo/Subway/dsl, Shell/dsl, 🅞 Chrysler/Dodge/Jeep, **S** 🅕 Buffalo Wild Wings, Chili's, Chick-fil-A, Coldstone, Kaze Japanese, La Cocina Mexican, Logan's Roadhouse, McDonald's, Moe's SW Grill, New Japan Express, Prima Vera Pizza, Subway, TGIFriday's, Wendy's, 🅞 AT&T, Best Buy, BJ's Whse/gas, Dick's, GNC, Kohl's, Michael's, Petsmart, Ross, Staples, Target, TJ Maxx
303	Jones Sausage Rd, **N** 🅖 Hess/Dunkin Donuts/dsl, 🅕 Bojangles, Burger King, Smithfield BBQ, **S** 🅖 Hess/Dunkin Donuts/dsl
301	I-440 E, US 64/70 E, to Wilson
300b a	Rock Quarry Rd, **N** 🅞 Kroger/gas, **S** 🅖 Exxon, Valero, 🅕 Burger King, Little Caesars, Subway, 🅞 Food Lion, Rite Aid
299	Person St, Hammond Rd, Raleigh (no EZ return eb), **1 mi N** 🅖 Exxon/dsl, 🅞 to Shaw U
298b a	US 401 S, US 70 E, NC 50, **N** 🅖 Shell/dsl, 🅛 Red Roof Inn, **S** 🅖 BP, Exxon/dsl, Hess/dsl, Hugo's, Raceway, 🅕 Baskin-Robbins/Dunkin Donuts, Bojangles, Cinco de Mayo Mexican, Cook-Out, Domino's, Golden Seafood&Chicken, Taco Bell, Wendy's, 🅛 Claremont Inn, Super 8, 🅞 AutoZone, CarQuest, Family$, Meineke, Sam's Club/gas
297	Lake Wheeler Rd, **N** 🅖 Exxon, 🅕 Subway, 🅞 🅗, Farmer's Mkt, **S** 🅖 Marathon
295	Gorman St, **1 mi N** 🅖 Exxon/dsl, 🅕 Hardee's, McDonald's, Subway, 🅛 Holiday Inn Express, 🅞 to NCSU, **S** 🅖 Kangaroo
293	to I-440, US 1, US 64 W, Raleigh, **S** 🅖 Exxon, Shell, 🅕 Astor's Grill, Bob Evans, Chick-fil-A, China King, Coldstone, Cook-Out, Golden Corral, Dickey's BBQ, HoneyBaked Ham, Jason's Deli, Jersey Mike's Subs, McDonald's, Moe's SW Grill, Noodles&Co, Olive Garden, Panera Bread, Qdoba, Red Lobster, Red Robin, Remington Grill,

RALEIGH

🔀 INTERSTATE 40 CONT'D

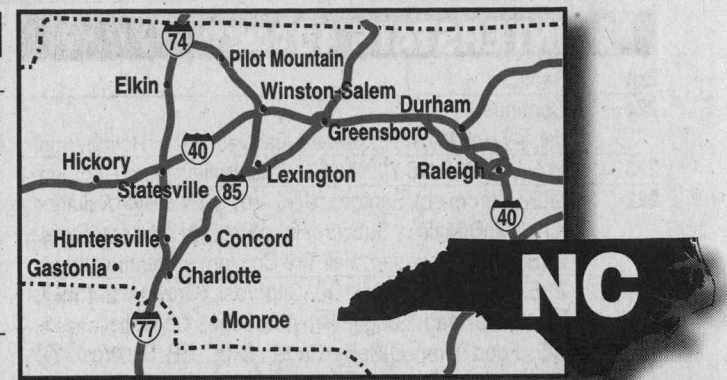

Exit	Services

R A L E I G H

293 Continued
Ruby Tuesday, Starbucks, Subway, Taco Bell, Waffle House, Wild Wing Cafe, 🛏 Best Western, DoubleTree, Hilton Garden, Holiday Inn, Red Roof Inn, 🅾 Best Buy, BJ's Whse, Dick's, Ford, GNC, Home Depot, Jo-Ann Fabrics, Kohl's, Lincoln, Lowe's, Marshalls, Mazda, Michael's, NTB, Office Depot, Old Navy, PetCo, Petsmart, SteinMart, Target

C A R Y

291 Cary Towne Blvd, Cary, **1 mi S** ⛽ Circle K, 🍴 Burger King, China 1, DQ, 5 Guys Burgers, Jersey Mike's, Macaroni Grill, McDonald's, Mimi's Cafe, On-the-Border, Pei Wei, Ragazzi's, S ´Asian, Starbucks, Tomyum Thai, 🅾 AT&T, Barnes&Noble, Belk, Dillard's, Firestone, Harris Teeter, JC Penney, Macy's, Sears, TJ Maxx

290 NC 54, Cary, **N** ⛽ Sheetz/dsl, 🍴 McDonald's, 🅾 Hyatt Place, Wingate Inn, **S** ⛽ Exxon (1mi), 🛏 Hampton Inn

289 to I-440, Wade Ave, to Raleigh, **N** 🅾 🏥, Carter-Finley Stadium, museum, **S** to fairgrounds

287 Harrison Ave, Cary, **N** to Wm B Umstead SP, **S** ⛽ BP/dsl, 🍴 An Cuisine, Bonefish Grill, Burger King, BurgerFi, Carolina Cafe, Chick-fil-A, Maggie Moo's, McDonald's, Moe's SW Grill, NY Pizza, Ruth's Chris Steaks, Starbucks, Subway, Thai Cuisine, Wendy's, 🛏 Embassy Suites, Studio+, TownePlace Suites, Umstead Hotel, 🅾 Colony Tire

285 Aviation Pkwy, to Morrisville   Raleigh/Durham ✈, **N** ⛽ Sheetz/dsl, 🛏 Hilton Garden

284 ✈ Blvd, **N** 🍴 Capital City Chophouse, 🛏 Cambria Suites, Country Inn&Suites, Hyatt Place, 🅾 to RDU ✈, **S** ⛽ BP/dsl, Mobil, 🍴 Bojangles, Cracker Barrel, Hooters, KFC/Taco Bell, TX Steaks, Waffle House, Wendy's, 🛏 Courtyard, Days Inn, Extended Stay America, Fairfield Inn, Hampton Inn, Holiday Inn, Holiday Inn Express, La Quinta, Microtel, Residence Inn, Sheraton, Staybridge Suites, 🅾 Morrisville Outlets/famous brands/food court

283 I-540 E, **toll** I-540 W, to US 70, Aviation Pkwy

282 Page Rd, **S** 🍴 Arby's, Bojangles, Jimmy John's, McDonald's, Mez Cafe, Starbucks, 🛏 Comfort Suites, Hilton, Sheraton, Sleep Inn, Wingate Inn

281 Miami Blvd, **N** 🛏 Extended Stay Deluxe, Hilton Garden, Marriott, **S** ⛽ BP, Shell, 🍴 Arby's, Bojangles, Burger King, McDonald's, Quiznos, Randy's Pizza, Rudino's Grill, Subway, Tropical Smoothie, Wendy's, Wok'n Grill, 🛏 Extended Stay Deluxe, Holiday Inn Express, Homewood Suites, Hotel Indigo, 🅾 Office Depot

280 Davis Dr, **N** to Research Triangle, **S** 🛏 Radisson

279b a NC 147 N, Triangle Expwy, to Durham, **N** 🏥

278 NC 55, to NC 54, Apex, **N** ⛽ Marathon, 🍴 Sansui Grill, Waffle House, 🛏 Comfort Inn, DoubleTree, EconoLodge, La Quinta, Red Roof Inn, **S** ⛽ BP, Exxon/dsl, Mobil/dsl, 🍴 Arby's, Backyard BBQ, Bojangles, Chick-fil-A, Capt D's, El Agave Mexican, El Dorado Mexican, Golden Corral, Hardee's, Little Caesars, Papa John's, Pizza Hut, Quiznos, Sal's Italian, Starbucks, Subway, Taco Bell, Thai China, Wendy's, William's Kitchen, 🛏 Candlewood Suites, Courtyard, Crossland Suites, Homestead Suites, Residence Inn, 🅾 AAA, Aamco, Advance Parts, AutoZone, BigLots, Colonial Tire, CVS Drug, $Tree, Firestone, Food Lion, Jiffy Lube, Just Tires, Lube N'Tune, Meineke, O'Reilly Parts, Walgreens

---

C H A P E L   H I L L

276 Fayetteville Rd, **N** ⛽ Circle K/dsl, Exxon/dsl, Shell/Circle K, 🍴 China Cafe, McDonald's, Orient Garden, Quiznos, Ruby Tuesday, Rudino's Pizza, Souper Salad, Waffle House, Wendy's, Wing Stop, 🅾 GNC, Harris-Teeter, Kroger/dsl, Walgreens, to NC Central U, **S** 🍴 Bufflo Wild Wings, CA Pizza Kitchen, Champp's Rest, Cheesecake Factory, Chili's, Firebird's, Fork-in-the-Road Cafe, Los Portales Mexican, Maggiano's, McAlister's Deli, Melting Pot, Moe's SW Grill, PF Chang's, Rockfish Rest, Ruth's Chris Steaks, Starbucks, Ted's MT Grill, 🛏 Hilton Garden, 🅾 AT&T, Belk, Best Buy, JC Penney, Macy's, Nordstrom, Old Navy, Sears/auto, World Mkt, mall

274 NC 751, to Jordan Lake, **N** ⛽ BP, Marathon, 🍴 Burger King, Char Grill, Dunkin Donuts, Jimmy John's, KFC, McDonald's, Taco Bell, Waffle House, Wendy's, 🅾 Urgent Care, Advance Parts, CVS Drug, Harris Teeter, Honda, Lexus, Rite Aid, Walgreens, **S** ⛽ BP, 🍴 Bonefish Grill, Chick-fil-A, Subway, 🛏 Sheraton, 🅾 Aldi Foods, Michael's, PetCo, Target

273 NC 54, to Durham, UNC-Chapel Hill, **N** ⛽ BP/dsl, **S** ⛽ BP, Shell/dsl, 🍴 Hardee's, Nantucket Grill, 🛏 Courtyard (2mi), Hampton Inn, Holiday Inn Express, 🅾 Urgent Care, vet

270 US 15, US 501, Chapel Hill, Durham, **N** 🍴 Applebee's, Bob Evans, Carrabba's, Dickey's BBQ, Firehouse Subs, Jason's Deli, Lonestar Steaks, Longhorn Steaks, McAlister's, Moe's SW Grill, NY Pizza, Outback Steaks, Panera Bread, Philly Steaks, Red Robin, Starbucks, Xank's Japanese, 🛏 Comfort Inn, Homewood Suites, SpringHill Suites, Staybridge Suites, 🅾 🏥 S, AT&T, Barnes&Noble, Best Buy, Dick's, $Tree, Home Depot, Kohl's, Kroger, Marshalls, Michael's, Old Navy, Petsmart, Verizon, Walmart/Subway, to Duke U, **S** ⛽ BP, Exxon, 🍴 Boston Mkt, Chick-fil-A, Hardee's, K&W Cafeteria, La Hacienda Mexican, McDonald's, Subway, Wendy's, 🛏 Days Inn, Quality Inn, Red Roof Inn, Sheraton, 🅾 Acura, Advance Parts, BMW, Chevrolet, Dillard's, Food Lion, Harris Teeter, Kia, Lowe's, Subaru, Trader Joe's

266 NC 86, to Chapel Hill, **2 mi S** ⛽ BP, Exxon, Hess/dsl, 🍴 Pop's Pizza, Subway

263 New Hope Church Rd

261 Hillsborough, **1.5 mi N** ⛽ BP, Citgo/dsl, Shell, 🍴 Hardee's, KFC/Taco Bell, McDonald's, Subway, Waffle House, Wendy's, 🛏 Holiday Inn Express, Microtel

259 I-85 N, to Durham,

I-40 and I-85 run together 30 mi. See Interstate 85, exits 131-161.

227 to I-85 S, to I-73 N, to US 421, Highpoint, Charlotte

226 McConnell Rd, **S** ⛽ Exxon

224 E Lee St, to US 29 N, to US 220 N, **N** gas:BP/dsl, Shell/

 Copyright 2014 - The NEXT Exit ®

INTERSTATE 40 CONT'D

GREENSBORO

Exit	Services
224	Continued dsl, [lodging] Holiday Inn Express, Quality Inn
223	to N US 29, E US 70, N US 20, Reidsville
222	MLK Jr (from eb), Sanford, S [food] Arby's, Biscuitville, Burger King, McDonald's, Subway, Taco Bell, [other] Advance Parts, CVS Drug, Food Lion, Hall Tire Co, Tom's Tire/auto
221	S Elm-Eugene St, N [gas] Citgo/dsl, Crown/dsl, Shell, [lodging] Homestead Lodge, [other] AutoZone, CarQuest, Family$, Food Lion, O'Reilly Parts, S [gas] BP, Shell/dsl, [lodging] EconoLodge, Super 8, [other] Home Depot
220	Randleman Rd, US 220 S, to Greensboro, Ashboro, N [gas] BP, Solo, [food] Biscuitville, Church's, KFC, McDonald's, Pizza Hut, Sub Sta 2, [lodging] Budget Inn, [other] Harley-Davidson, Rite Aid, Save-A-Lot, S [gas] BP, Kangaroo, [food] Cook-Out, Mayflower Seafood, Waffle House, Wendy's
219	US 29 S, W US 70, Highpoint (exits left from wb), Charlotte
218	US 220, Freeman Mill Rd, Ashboro
217	Highpoint Rd, Koury Blvd (from wb), N [gas] Exxon, Shell/dsl, [food] Biscuitville, Burger King, Chili's, China King, Fatz Cafe, Ham's Rest, Hooters, Little Caesars, Lonestar Steaks, Olive Garden, Sakura Japanese, Subway, Taco Bell, [lodging] DoubleTree Hotel, Hampton Inn, Park Lane Hotel, Quality Inn, Red Roof Inn, Super 8, [other] $General, Office Depot, S [gas] Shell, [food] Bonefish Grill, Carrabba's, Jimmy John's, Krispy Kreme, McDonald's, Smokey Bones BBQ, Waffle House, Wendy's, [lodging] Baymont Inn, Comfort Suites, Drury Inn, Ramada Inn, Sheraton, Studio 6, [other] Dillard's, Discount Tire, Gander Mtn, JC Penney, O'Reilly Parts
216	(from eb), Greensboro, coliseum
214	Wendover Ave, N [gas] Sheetz, [food] Burger King, China Buffet, Coldstone, Mario's Pizza, Moe's SW Grill, Panera Bread, Penn Sta Subs, Waffle House, [lodging] Extended Stay, Fairfield Inn, Hilton Garden, Holiday Inn Express, Microtel, [other] Audi, Costco/gas, CVS Drug, Fiat, Ford, Nissan, PetCo, Staples, Verizon, VW, S [food] Applebee's, Arby's, Biscuitville, Bojangles, Chick-fil-A, Chipotle Mexican, Cracker Barrel, Elizabeth's Pizza, Fuddrucker's, Golden Corral, Golden Wok, IHOP, Jimmy John's, Kabuto Japanese, La Hacienda Mexican, Logan's Roadhouse, Longhorn Steaks, McDonald's, O'Charley's, Panda Express, Papa John's, Red Lobster, Steak'n Shake, Subway, TGIFriday's, Taco Bell, Tripp's Rest., Wendy's, [lodging] Comfort Inn, Courtyard, Days Inn, Hyatt Place, La Quinta, Lodge America, SpringHill Suites, Studio+, Wingate Inn, [other] AT&T, Best Buy, Buick/GMC, Chevrolet, Dick's, $Tree, GNC, Goodyear, Hobby Lobby, Home Depot, Kohl's, K-Mart/gas, Lowe's, Macy's, Mazda, Meineke, Michael's, Petsmart, Radio Shack, Ross, Sam's Club/gas, Target, Walmart
213	Guilford College Rd, N [gas] BP/dsl, [lodging] Clarion, S [gas] Sheetz, same as 214
212b a	I-73, US 241 S, to I-85, to Bryan Blvd, Ashboro, N to [airport]
211	Gallimore Dairy Rd, N [other] Freightliner
210	NC 68, to High Point, Piedmont Triad, N [gas] Shell, [food] Arby's, Carolina's Diner, [lodging] Days Inn, Embassy Suites, Fairview Inn, Homewood Suites, Sleep Inn, Wyndham Garden, [other] Ford Trucks, Kenworth, to [airport], S [gas] Exxon/dsl, [food] Bojangles, Fatz Cafe, McDonald's, Pizza Hut/Taco Bell, Pollo Pizza/Pasta, Ruby Tuesday, Shoney's, Subway, Wendy's, [lodging] Best Western, Candlewood Suites, Comfort

NC

WINSTON • SALEM

Exit	Services
210	Continued Suites, Courtyard, Extended Stay Deluxe, Fairfield Inn, Hampton Inn, Holiday Inn Express, Motel 6, Quality Inn, Red Roof Inn, Residence Inn
208	Sandy Ridge Rd, N [gas] Exxon/Subway/dsl, Hess/dsl, [other] Camping World RV Ctr, S [gas] Shell/Circle K/dsl, [other] Out Of Doors Mart
206	Lp 40 (from wb), to Kernersville, Winston-Salem, downtown
203	NC 66, to Kernersville, N [gas] Citgo/McDonald's/dsl, Hess/dsl, QM/Subway/dsl, [food] Capt Tom's Seafood, Clark's BBQ, Wendy's, [lodging] Sleep Inn, [other] [H], Curves, Ford, Merchant Tire/repair, S [gas] Shell/dsl, [lodging] Holiday Inn Express
201	Union Cross Rd, N [gas] Citgo/dsl, QM/dsl, [food] Blue Naples Pizza, Burger King, China Café, Subway, [other] CVS Drug, $Mart, Food Lion
196	US 311 S, to High Point
195	US 311 N, NC 109, to Thomasville, S [gas] Citgo, Hess/dsl, [other] Family$
193b a	US 52, NC 8, to Lexington, S [gas] Hess/dsl, Shell, [food] Hardee's
193c	Silas Creek Pkwy (from eb), same as 192
192	NC 150, to Peters Creek Pkwy, N [gas] Giant, Hess, Shell, [food] Bojangles, Burger King, China Wok, Hero House Rest, Hong Kong Buffet, IHOP, KFC, Little Caesars, Monterrey Mexican, Mr BBQ, Sonic, Subway, Taco Bell, Tokyo Japanese, Tomo'E Steaks, [lodging] Innkeeper, [other] Acura/Subaru, Audi, AutoZone, BigLots, $General, $Tree, Ford, Hamrick's, Hyundai, Infiniti, Mazda, Office Depot, Radio Shack, Rite Aid, VW, S [gas] BP, QM, [food] Arby's, Baskin-Robbins/Dunkin Donuts, Cook-Out, McDonald's, K&W Cafeteria, Papa John's, Pizza Hut, Waffle House, Wendy's, [lodging] Holiday Inn Express, [other] Advance Parts, Aldi Foods, BMW/Mini, CVS Drug, Family$, Food Lion, Hancock Fabrics, Honda, K-Mart, Mock Tire, Toyota/Scion
190	Hanes Mall Blvd (from wb, no re-entry), N [food] Chipotle Mexican, Coldstone, Elizabeth's Pizza, Jimmy John's, McDonald's, Ruby Tuesday, TGIFriday's, Tripp's Rest., [lodging] Quality Inn, [other] [H], Belk, Dick's, Dillard's, Firestone/auto, JC Penney, Macy's, Marshalls, Sears/auto, mall, same as 189, S [food] Burger King, ChuckECheese, Outback Steaks, Starbucks, Subway, [lodging] Comfort Suites, Microtel, [other] Office Depot
189	US 158, Stratford Rd, Hanes Mall Blvd, N [food] Bojangles, Chili's, Golden Corral, Olive Garden, Red Lobster, Taco Bell, TX Roadhouse, [lodging] Courtyard, Fairfield Inn, [other] [H], Belk, Buick/GMC, Cadillac, Chevrolet, Dillard's, JC Penney, Jo-Ann Fabrics, Macy's, Sears/auto, Walgreens, mall, S [gas] BP, Shell, [food] Applebee's, Bleu Rest., Brixx Pizza, Buffalo Wild Wings, Chick-fil-A, Firebirds Grill, 5 Guys Burgers, Fuddruckers, Hooters, Jason's Deli, KFC/LJ Silver, Lonestar Steaks, Longhorn Steaks, Macaroni Grill, Moe's SW Grill, Nuke's Cafe, Panera Bread, Qdoba, Subway, Village Tavern, Which Wich, [lodging] Extended Stay America, Hampton Inn, Hilton Garden, La Quinta, Sleep Inn, SpringHill Suites, [other] AT&T, Barnes&Noble, Best Buy, Costco/gas, CVS Drug, Discount Tire, $Tree, Food Lion, Home Depot, Kohl's, Lowe's, Michael's, Petsmart, Ross, Sam's Club/gas, Target, Verizon
188	US 421, to Yadkinville, to WFU (no EZ wb return), Winston-Salem, **1/2mi N off US 421** [gas] BP, Exxon, Kangaroo, Shell, [food] Arby's, Burger King, Cook-Out, Dickey's BBQ,

INTERSTATE 40 CONT'D

C L E M M O N S

Exit	Services
188	Continued
	McDonald's, Starbucks, Subway, Waffle House, Wendy's, 🅾 CarMax, Mercedes, Walmart, vet
184	to US 421, Clemmons, **N** 🅶 Mobil, Shell, 🍴 Applebee's, Dunkin Donuts, IHOP, KFC, K&W Cafe, Panera Bread, Steak Escape, 🛏 Holiday Inn Express, **S** 🅶 BP/dsl, Hess, Kangaroo, 🍴 Arby's, Biscuitville, Brick Oven Pizza, Burger King, Cozumel Mexican, Cracker Barrel, Domino's, Kimono Japanese, Little Richard's BBQ, McDonald's, Mi Pueblo Mexican, Mtn Fried Chicken, Pizza Hut, Sonic, Starbucks, Subway, Taco Bell, Time to Eat Cafe, Waffle House, Wendy's, 🛏 Super 8, 🅾 Advance Parts, BigLots, CVS Drug, $Tree, GNC, K-Mart, Lowe's Foods, Meineke, Merchant Tire, O'Reilly Parts, Staples, Verizon, Walgreens, USPO, vet
182	Bermuda Run, Tanglewood, **S** 🍴 Chang Thai, Lee's Chinese, Monte De Rey Mexican, Papa John's, Subway, 🅾 Harris-Teeter, Tanglewood Camping
182mm	Yadkin River
180	NC 801, Tanglewood, **N** 🍴 Capt's Galley Seafood, Chilo's Mexican, Domino's, Subway, 🛏 Hampton Inn, 🅾 Lowe's Foods/dsl, Rite Aid, **S** 🅶 BP/McDonald's/dsl, Hess/dsl, 🍴 Bojangles, Jimmy's Greek, Miyabi Japanese, Venezia Italian, Wendy's, 🅾 Ace Hardware, CVS Drug, $General, Food Lion, Radio Shack, Walgreens
177mm	🅿ⓢ both lanes, full ♿ facilities, ☎, vending, 🛢 litter barrels, petwalk
174	Farmington Rd, **N** 🅶 Shell/dsl, 🅾 antiques, **S** 🅾 vineyards

M O C K S V I L L E

170	US 601, Mocksville, **N** 🅶 Citgo/dsl, Horn's TC/Marathon/DQ/Jersey Mike's/dsl/scales/24hr, Murphy USA/dsl, 🍴 JinJin Chinese, La Carreta Mexican, Moe's Cafe, Subway, 🅾 Campers Inn RV Ctr, $Tree, Verizon, Walmart, **S** 🅶 Exxon, Hess/Taco Bell, Sheetz/dsl, 🍴 Arby's, Blackbeard's Seafood Shack, Bojangles, Burger King, China Grill, Dunkin Donuts, Dynasty Chinese, KFC, Marco's Pizza, McDonald's, Papa John's, Pier 601, Pizza Hut, Sagebrush Steaks, Shiki Japanese, Wendy's, 🛏 Days Inn, HighWay Inn, Quality Inn, Scottish Inn, 🅾 🏥, Advance Parts, $General, Lowe's, Mocksville Tire/auto, Walgreens, USPO, vet
168	US 64, to Mocksville, **N** 🅶 Exxon/dsl, 🅾 Lake Myers RV Resort (3mi), **S** 🅶 BP/dsl, 🅾🏥
162	US 64, Cool Springs, **N** 🅾 Lake Myers RV Resort (5mi), **S** 🅶 Shell/dsl, 🅾 KOA
161mm	S Yadkin River
154	to US 64, Old Mocksville Rd, **N** 🏥, **S** 🅶 Citgo/dsl, 🍴 Jaybee's Hotdogs, 🅾 repair/tires
153	US 64 (from eb), 1/2 mi **S** 🅶 Citgo/dsl, 🍴 Jaybee's Hotdogs, 🅾 repair/tires
152b a	I-77, S to Charlotte, N to Elkin
151	US 21, E Statesville, **N** 🅶 Hess/dsl, Marathon/DQ/dsl, 🍴 Applebee's, Baskin-Robbins/Dunkin Donuts, Bojangles, Chick-fil-A, Chili's, Cook-Out, Cracker Barrel, Golden Corral, KFC, K&W Cafeteria, Logan's Roadhouse, McDonald's, Mi Pueblo Café, Pizza Hut/Taco Bell, Red Lobster, Ruby Tuesday, Shiki Japanese, Wendy's, Zaxby's, 🛏 Days Inn, Sleep Inn, 🅾 Urgent Care, Advance Parts, Aldi Foods, AutoZone, BigLots, Chevrolet, CVS Drug, $Tree,

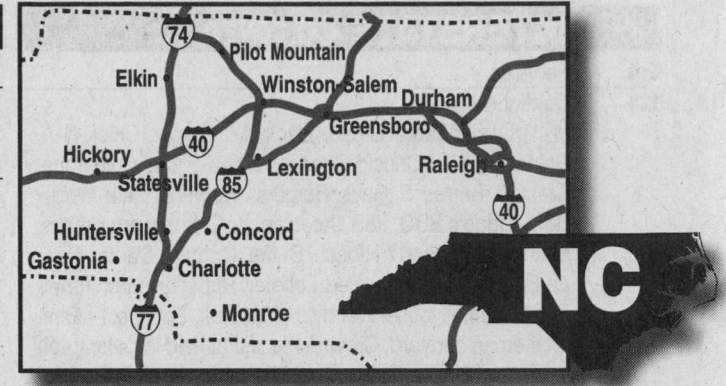

S T A T E S V I L L E

151	Continued
	GNC, Home Depot, Lowe's, Meineke, Michael's, Petsmart, Radio Shack, Staples, Tire Kingdom, TJ Maxx, Verizon, Walmart, **S** 🅶 Exxon, food:lodging: Holiday Inn Express, Masters Inn, Quality Inn, 🅾🏥, Urgent Care, $General
150	NC 115, Statesville, **N** 🅶 BP/dsl, Citgo, Sheetz/dsl, Shell/Subway, 🍴 Amalfi's Italian, Little Caesars, Ol'Bob's BBQ, Waffle Shop, 🅾 CVS Drug, $General, Food Lion, Fred's, museum
148	US 64, NC 90, W Statesville, **N** 🅶 Citgo/dsl, Shell, 🍴 Arby's, BoxCar Grille, Burger King, McDonald's, Shiki Japanese, Subway, Village Inn Pizza, 🛏 Economy Inn, 🅾 CVS Drug, $General, Ingles Foods
146	Stamey Farm Rd, **N** truck repair
144	Old Mountain Rd, **N** 🅶 BP/dsl/repair, 🍴 Troy's Rest., **S** 🅶 BP/dsl, Shell/dsl
143mm	weigh sta both lanes
141	Sharon School Rd, **N** 🅶 Citgo/dsl
140mm	Catawba River
138	NC 10 W, Oxford School Rd, to Catawba, **N** 🅶 Exxon/dsl
136mm	🅿ⓢ both lanes, full ♿ facilities, ☎, 🛢, vending, litter barrels, petwalk
105	Claremont, **S** 🅶 Shell, 🍴 BoxCar Grille, Burger King, Hannah's BBQ, Hardee's, New Panda, Subway, 🛏 Super 8, 🅾 Carolina Coach RV Ctr, $General, Lowe's Foods
133	Rock Barn Rd, **N** 🅶 Shell/dsl, **S** 🅶 Wilco/Hess/Godfather's/Stuckey's/Subway/dsl/scales/24hr
132	to NC 16, Taylorsville, **N** 🅶 BP, Shell/dsl, 🍴 Burger King, JinJin's Buffet, Subway, Zaxby's, 🛏 Holiday Inn Express, 🅾 $Tree, Verizon, Walmart
130	Old US 70, **N** 🍴 Jack-in-the-Box, Subway, 🅾 $General, K-Mart, Verizon, repair, vet, **S** 🅶 Citgo, Pure, 🅾 USPO
128	US 321, Fairgrove Church Rd, Hickory, **N** 🅶 BP, Marathon/dsl, Shell, 🍴 McDonald's, Waffle House, 🅾🏥, to Catawba Valley Coll, **S** 🅶 Citgo/dsl, 🍴 Wendy's, Yukio Japanese, 🛏 Days Inn, La Quinta, 🅾 Chrysler/Dodge/Jeep, GMC/Volvo Trucks
126	to US 70, NC 155, **S** 🅶 Exxon, Marathon/dsl, 🍴 Applebee's, Buffalo Wild Wings, Chili's, East Coast Wings, IHOP, Jason's Deli, Libby Hill Seafood, McDonald's, O'Charley's, Olive Garden, Taco Bell, 🛏 Holiday Inn Express, 🅾 Barnes&Noble, Discount Tire, $Tree, Hickory Furniture Mart, Lowe's, Michael's, Office Depot, PetCo, Ross, Sam's Club/gas, Walmart/McDonald's
125	Hickory, **N** 🅶 RaceWay/dsl, 🍴 Biscuitville, Bojangles, Dickey's BBQ, Golden Corral, Mamatown Buffet, Mellow Mushroom, Starbucks, TX Roadhouse, Tripp's Rest., 🛏 Red Roof Inn, 🅾 Aamco, Advance Parts, BMW/Mercedes, $General, Firestone/auto, **S** 🅶 Hess/dsl, Shell/dsl,

H I C K O R Y

⊞ = gas 🍴 = food ⌂ = lodging ⊙ = other ℞s = rest stop Copyright 2014 - The NEXT Exit ®

⬆E INTERSTATE 40 CONT'D

Exit	Services
125	Continued
	🍴 Arby's, Atlanta Bread, Backyard Burger, Chick-fil-A, China Garden, ChuckECheese, CiCi's Pizza, Coldstone, Cracker Barrel, 5 Guys Burgers, Hooters, Jack-in-the-Box, Judge's BBQ, J&S Cafeteria, KFC, Longhorn Steaks, Mamma's Pizza, NY Hibachi Buffet, Outback Steaks, Panda Express, Quiznos, Red Lobster, Ruby Tuesday, Tony's Pizza, Waffle House, Wendy's, Wild Wok, Zaxby's, ⌂ Best Western, Courtyard, Crowne Plaza, Fairfield Inn, Hampton Inn, Motel 6, Quality Inn, ⊙ Aldi Foods, AT&T, Belk, Best Buy, Carmax, Dick's, Dillard's, $Tree, Food Lion, Ford, Hamrick's, Hancock Fabrics, Harley-Davidson, Home Depot, Honda, JC Penney, Kohl's, Mazda, NAPA, Nissan, Office Depot, Old Navy, O'Reilly Parts, PetCo, Petsmart, Porsche/VW, Sears/auto, Sunrise Camping Ctr, Suzuki, Target, Tire Kingdom, TJ Maxx, Toyota/Scion, Verizon, mall
123	US 70/321, to NC 127, Hickory
121	Long View, N ⊙ Kenworth
119b a	Hildebran, N ⊞ Shell, 🍴 Bojangles, Hardee's, ⊙ $General
118	Old NC 10, N ⊞ Pure, Shell/dsl
116	Icard, S ⊞ Marathon/McDonald's/dsl, 🍴 Burger King, Granny's Kitchen, ⌂ Icard Inn/rest.
113	Connelly Springs, N ⊞ Citgo/dsl, 🍴 Patsy Ann's Rest., Subway, ⊙ �H, CVS Drug, Ford/Hyundai, Walgreens
112	Mineral Springs Mtn Rd, Valdese
111	Valdese
107	NC 114, to Drexel
106	Bethel Rd, S ⊞ Exxon/dsl, ⌂ Economy Inn
105	NC 18, Morganton, N ⊞ Hess/Dunkin Donuts/dsl, 🍴 Abele's Rest., Arby's, Capt D's, Fatz Café, Harbor Inn Seafood, Las Salsas, McDonald's, Sonic, Wendy's, Zaxby's, Zeko's Italian, ⌂ Hampton Inn, ⊙ �H, Cadillac/Chevrolet/GMC, S ⊞ Shell/dsl, Marathon/dsl, 🍴 Sagebrush Steaks, Waffle House, ⌂ Budget Inn, Plaza Inn, Quality Inn, Sleep Inn, ⊙ to South Mtns SP
104	Enola Rd, S 🍴 Chen's Garden, Jersey Mike's Subs, ⊙ Belk, BigLots, $Tree, Food Lion, Staples
103	US 64, Morganton, N ⊞ Citgo/dsl, Exxon/dsl, 🍴 Allison's Rest., Cook-Out, Village Inn Pizza, ⌂ Days Inn, S ⊞ Marathon, RaceWay/dsl, 🍴 Bojangles, Butch's BBQ, Denny's, Dragon Garden, Hardee's, KFC, Subway, Taco Bell, Tokyo Diner, ⌂ Comfort Inn, ⊙ Clarks Tire, $General, Food Lion, Goodyear/auto, GNC, Ingles Foods, Lowe's, Walmart
100	Jamestown Rd, N ⊞ BP/dsl, 🍴 Waffle Shop, ⊙ Chrysler/Dodge/Jeep, Ford/Lincoln, **2 mi N** 🍴 KFC, Taco Bell, ⌂ Eagle Motel
98	Causby Rd, to Glen Alpine, S B&B/food
96	Kathy Rd
94	Dysartsville Rd, Lake James, N Lake James SP
90	Lake James, Nebo, N ⊞ Nebo/dsl, ⊙ to Lake James SP, S ⊞ Marathon/dsl, ⊙ Springs Creek RV Ctr
86	NC 226, to Spruce Pine, Marion, N ⊞ Exxon, ❤Love's /Subway/Godfather's/dsl/scales/24hr, 🍴 Hardee's, KFC, Waffle House, ⊙ Jellystone RV Park (1mi)
85	US 221, Marion, N ⌂ Hampton Inn, ⊙ to Mt Mitchell SP, S ⊞ Marathon/dsl, ⌂ Days Inn, Super 8, ⊙ $General

Exit	Services
83	Ashworth Rd
82mm	℞s both lanes, full ♿ facilities, 🕿, 🛢, vending, litter barrels, petwalk
81	Sugar Hill Rd, to Marion, N ⊞ BP/dsl, Murphy Express/dsl, 🍴 Andy's Burgers, New China, Nopale's Mexican, TX Pizza, ⊙ �H, Chrysler/Dodge/Jeep, $Tree, Walmart/Subway, S ⊞ Marion Travel Plaza/dsl
76mm	Catawba River
75	Parker Padgett Rd, S ⊞ Exxon/Stuckey's/DQ/dsl
73	Old Fort, N ⊞ BP/dsl, 🍴 Hardee's, ⌂ B&B, ⊙ Auto+, Mtn Gateway Museum, S ⊞ Sunoco/dsl, 🍴 McDonald's
72	US 70 (from eb), Old Fort, N B&B
71mm	Pisgah Nat Forest, eastern boundary
67.5mm	truck ℞s eb
66	Ridgecrest, N ⌂ B&B
65	(from wb), to Black Mountain, Black Mtn Ctr
64	NC 9, Black Mountain, N ⊞ Exxon, Shell/Subway, 🍴 Pizza Hut, ⊙ BiLo/café, S ⊞ BP/dsl, 🍴 Denny's, Huddle House, KFC, McDonald's, Phil's BBQ, Starbucks, Taco Bell, Wendy's, ⌂ Comfort Inn, ⊙ Ingles Foods/gas, Rite Aid
63mm	Swannanoa River
59	Swannanoa, N ⊞ BP/Subway, Shell/dsl, 🍴 Athens Pizza, Burger King, ⊙ Ace Hardware, CVS Drug, Harley-Davidson, Ingles Foods/gas, KOA (2mi), Miles RV Ctr/Park, to Warren Wilson Coll, USPO, vet, S ⊙ Mama Gertie's Camping
55	US 70, E Asheville, N ⊞ BP, Citgo/Subway, Mobil, 🍴 Arby's, Bojangles, Cocula Mexican, Dominos, Zaxby's, ⌂ B&B, Days Inn, Holiday Inn, Motel 6, Quality Inn, ⊙ VA �H, Family$, Go Groceries, Top's RV park, to Mt Mitchell SP, Folk Art Ctr
53b a	I-240 W, US 74 a, to Asheville, Bat Cave, N 🍴 China Buffet, KFC, La Posada Mexican, Little Caesars, McDonald's, Subway, ⊙ Advance Parts, BiLo, CVS Drug, $General, Hamrick's, Hancock Fabrics, Meineke, **N on Fairview Rd** ⊞ Citgo, 🍴 Pizza Hut, ⌂ Ramada Inn, ⊙ Home Depot, S ⊞ BP/dsl/LP, 🍴 Sonic, Subway, ⊙ CVS Drug, Ingles, to Blue Ridge Pkwy
51	US 25A, Sweeten Creek Rd, S 🍴 Depot Diner, Subway, ⌂ Brookstone Lodge, ⊙ Fun Depot
50	US 25, Asheville, N ⊞ Market Ctr, Shell/dsl, 🍴 Arby's, Asaka Japanese, Chapala Mexican, Hardee's, LJ Silver, McDonald's, Moe's SW Grill, Ruth's Chris Steaks, Starbucks, Subway, TX Roadhouse, TGIFriday's, Wendy's, Zoe's Kitchen, ⌂ Baymont Inn, Doubletree Inn, Grand Bohemian Hotel, Guesthouse Inn, Howard Johnson, Residence Inn, Sleep Inn, ⊙ �H, to Biltmore House, S ⊞ Hess/dsl, 🍴 Apollo Flame Rest., Atl Bread Co, Huddle House, Juicy Lucy's, ⌂ Forest Manor Inn
47mm	French Broad River
47	NC 191, W Asheville, N ⊙ Bear Creek RV Camping, S ⊞ BP/Subway, 🍴 Moose Cafe, ⊙ Audi/Porsche/VW, Farmer's Mkt, Ford, Nissan, **2 mi S** ⌂ Comfort Inn, Country Inn&Suites, Fairfield Inn, Hampton Inn, Holiday Inn Express, Rodeway Inn
46b a	I-26 & I-240 E, **2 mi N** multiple services from I-240
44	US 19, US 23, W Asheville, N ⊞ BP, Hess/dsl, Shell/DQ/dsl, 🍴 Applebee's, Asiana Buffet, Burger King, Dunkin Donuts, Cracker Barrel, El Chapala Mexican, Fatz Cafe, Hardee's, IHOP, Pizza Hut, Waffle House, Wendy's, ⌂ Comfort Inn, Country Inn&Suites, Ramada Inn, Red Roof

HICKORY — **MORGANTON** — **ASHEVILLE**

NC

◀E INTERSTATE 40 CONT'D

Exit	Services
44	Continued
	Inn, Rodeway Inn, Sleep Inn, Whispering Pines Motel, 🅞 Chevrolet, Chrysler/Dodge/Jeep, Family$, Ingles Foods, Lowe's, Mazda/Mercedes, **S** 🍴 McDonald's, Shoney's, 🛏 Budget Motel, Holiday Inn, ValuePlace Inn, 🅞 Bi-Lo Foods, CVS Drug, Home Depot
41mm	**weigh sta both lanes**
37	Candler, **N** 🅡 BP, TA/Buckhorn Rest./dsl/scales/24hr/@, 🅞 Goodyear, tires, **S** 🅡 Exxon/dsl, 🛏 Days Inn, Plantation Motel, 🅞 KOA
33	Newfound Rd, to US 74, **S** gas
31	Rd 215, Canton, **N** 🍴 Sagebrush Steaks, 🛏 Days Inn, **S** 🅡 BP/dsl, Marathon/DQ, Shell/dsl, 🍴 Arby's, Bojangles, Burger King, McDonald's, Subway, Taco Bell, Waffle House, 🛏 Comfort Inn, 🅞 Ford, Ingles Foods/gas, RV/truck repair
27	US 19/23, to Waynesville, Great Smokey Mtn Expswy, **3 mi S** 🅡 Shell/Burger King, 🍴 Shoney's, Subway, Taco Bell, 🛏 Super 8, 🅞 🅷 $Tree, Food Lion, GNC, Lowe's, to WCU (25mi)
24	NC 209, to Lake Junaluska, **N** 🅡 🅡/Subway/dsl/scales/24hr/@, 🛏 Midway Motel, **S** 🅡 Shell/cafe dsl/24hr, 🅞🅷
20	US 276, to Maggie Valley, Lake Junaluska, **S** 🅡 BP/dsl, Exxon/dsl, Marathon (2mi), 🅞 Creekwood RV Park, Pride RV Resort, Winngray RV Park
16mm	Pigeon River
15	Fines Creek
13mm	Pisgah NF eastern boundary
10mm	🆁🆂 **both lanes, full** 🦽 **facilities,** 🅒 **vending,** 🗑 **litter barrels, petwalk**
7	Harmon Den
4mm	tunnel both lanes
0mm	North Carolina/Tennessee state line

▲N INTERSTATE 77

Exit	Services
105mm	North Carolina/Virginia state line
105mm	**Welcome Ctr sb, full** 🦽 **facilities, info,** 🅒 **vending,** 🗑 **litter barrels, petwalk**
103mm	**weigh sta both lanes**
101	I-74 E, to Mt Airy, Winston-Salem, Greensboro, **E** 🛏 Hampton Inn, 🅞🅷 (12mi)
100	NC 89, to Mt Airy, **E** 🅡 BP/Brintle's/rest/dsl/scales/24hr/@, Marathon/Subway/dsl, Shell/Circle K/dsl, 🍴 Copper Pot Rest., 🛏 Best Western, 🅞🅷 (12mi), **E** dsl repair
93	to Dobson, Surry, **E** 🅡 BP/DQ/dsl, Marathon/dsl, 🍴 BelloVino Italian, 🛏 Hampton Inn, Surry Inn, 🅞 camping
85	NC 118, CC Camp Rd, to Elkin, **1-3 mi W** 🅡 Murphy Express/dsl, Neighbor's, Shell/Blimpie/Stuckey's/dsl, Wilco/Hess/dsl, 🍴 Burger King, KFC, Mazzini's Italian, McDonald's, Sonic, 🛏 Elk Inn, Fairfield Inn, 🅞 AT&T, BigLots, $Tree, Food Lion, Lowe's, Rite Aid, Walmart/Subway,
83	US 21 byp, to Sparta (from nb)
82.5mm	Yadkin River
82	NC 67, Elkin, **E** 🅡 BP/Subway/dsl, Citgo/Case Outlet/dsl, Exxon/dsl, 🍴 Arby's, Cracker Barrel, Pop-Pops Grill, 🛏 Best Western, 🅞 Holly Ridge Camping (8mi), **W** 🅡 Wilco/Hess/Dunkin Donuts/dsl, 🍴 Bojangles, Capt Galley, McDonald's, Valentino's Pizza, Waffle House, Wendy's, 🛏

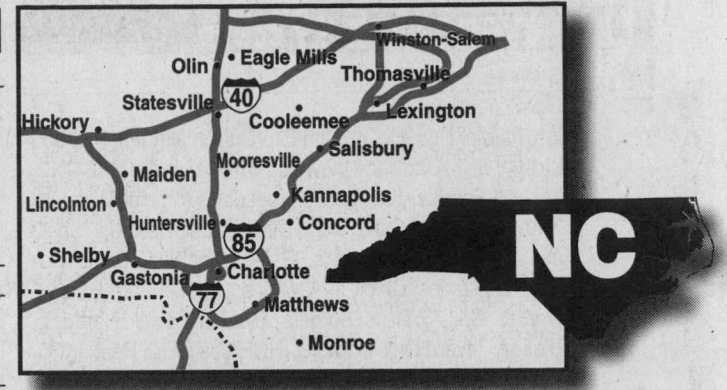

Exit	Services
82	Continued
	Comfort Inn, Days Inn, Hampton Inn, Rose's Motel, 🅞 D-Rex Drug, Food Lion, vet
79	US 21 S, to Arlington, **E** 🅡 Citgo/Subway/dsl, 🛏 Super 8, **W** 🅡 BP/dsl, 🍴 Glenn's BBQ, 🛏 Best Value Inn
73b a	US 421, to Winston-Salem (20mi), **E** 🅡 Shell/Subway/dsl (1mi), USPO
72mm	🆁🆂 **nb, full** 🦽 **facilities,** 🅒 **vending,** 🗑 **litter barrels, petwalk**
65	NC 901, to Union Grove, Harmony, **E** 🅞 Van Hoy Farms Camping, **W** 🅡 BP/dsl, Shell/Subway/dsl/24hr, 🍴 Burger Barn, 🛏 B&B, 🅞 Ace Hardware, Fiddler's Grove Camping (2mi), auto/tire repair
63mm	🆁🆂 **sb, full** 🦽 **facilities,** 🅒 **vending,** 🗑 **litter barrels, petwalk**
59	Tomlin Mill Rd, **W** 🅡 Valero/dsl
56.5mm	S Yadkin River
54	US 21, to Turnersburg, **E** 🅡 Citgo, **W** 🅡 Shell/dsl, 🍴 Arby's, **2 mi W** 🍴 Baskin-Robbins/Dunkin Donuts, Chick-fil-A, CookOut, Golden Corral, Zaxby's
51b a	I-40, E to Winston-Salem, W to Hickory
50	E Broad St, Statesville, **E** 🅡 Citgo, Kangaroo/dsl, Shell, 🍴 Arby's, Bojangles, Burger King, Charanda Mexican, Domino's, Golden Dragon, IHOP, Jack-in-the-Box, Little Caesar's, McDonald's, Papa John's, Pizza Hut, Shanghai Buffot, Shoney's, Starbucks, Subway, Taco Bell, Wendy's, 🛏 Brookwood Inn, Red Roof Inn, 🅞 Ace Hardware, AT&T, Belk, Bi-Lo, $General, $Tree, Food Lion, JC Penney, JR Outlet, K-Mart, Rite Aid, Urgent Care, USPO
49b a	US 70, G Bagnal Blvd, to Statesville, **E** 🅡 BP, Citgo/dsl, Kangaroo, Shell, Solo, 🍴 KFC, Outback Steaks, Rice Fun Chinese, Subway, Waffle House, 🛏 Best Value Inn, Best Western, Comfort Inn, Courtyard, Hampton Inn, Motel 6, Ramada Inn, 🅞 Camping World RV Ctr, Ford/Lincoln, Harley-Davidson, Honda, Nissan, Toyota/Scion, auto repair, **W** 🅡 Citgo/dsl, Exxon/dsl, 🛏 Microtel, 🅞 Buick/GMC, Chrysler/Dodge/Jeep
45	to Troutman, Barium Springs, **E** 🅞 KOA, RV Repair, **W** 🅡 4 Bros (3mi)
42	US 21, NC 115, to Troutman, Oswalt, **E** 🅡 Hess/Wilco/Subway/dsl/scales/24hr, 🍴 McDonald's, Wendy's, 🅞 AutoZone, Lowe's, **W** 🅡 Citgo/dsl, 🍴 Arby's, 🅞 to Lake Norman SP, camping
39mm	🆁🆂 **both lanes, full** 🦽 **facilities,** 🅒, 🗑, **litter barrels, petwalk, vending**
36	NC 150, Mooresville, **E** 🅡 Circle K/dsl, Exxon, Shell/dsl, 🍴 Applebee's, China Buffet, CiCi's Pizza, CookOut, Denny's, FatBoy's Cafe, Pomodoro's, Italian, Pizza Hut, Sonny's BBQ, Taco Bell, Waffle House, Wendy's, 🛏 Days

Sidebar (left): **ELKIN**

Sidebar (right): **STATESVILLE**

Sidebar tab: **NC**

⬆N INTERSTATE 77 CONT'D

MOORESVILLE

Exit	Services
36	Continued
	Inn, Fairfield Inn, Holiday Inn Express, Quality Inn, Ramada Ltd, 🅾 Belk, Cadillac/Chevrolet, $Tree, Gander Mtn, GNC, Jo-Ann Fabrics, Kia, Kohl's, Tuesday Morning, Walmart/Subway, **Urgent Care**, W 🅿 Circle K/dsl, Hess/dsl, Shell/dsl, Valero/dsl, 🍴 Arby's, Baskin-Robbins/Dunkin Donuts, Bojangles, Chick-fil-A, Chili's, Cracker Barrel, Duckworth's Grill, 5 Guys Burgers, Golden Corral, Hardee's, Hickory Tavern Grill, Hooters, IHOP, Joe's Fish Rest., KFC, Kyoto Japanese, LoneStar Steaks, McAlister's Deli, McDonald's, Monterrey Mexican, O'Charley's, Panera Bread, Pizza Vito, Portofino's, Queen's Pizza, Red Robin, Rita's Custard, Showmar's, Smoothie King, Sonic, Starbucks, Steak'n Shake, Subway, TX Roadhouse, 🛏 Hampton Inn, Sleep Inn, Super 8, Wingate Inn, 🅾 Advance Parts, AT&T, AutoZone, Best Buy, BJ's Whse/gas, CVS Drug, Dick's, Discount Tire, Food Lion, Lowe's, Michael's, Old Navy, PetCo, Petsmart, Ross, Staples, Target, Tire Kingdom, TJ Maxx, Verizon, Walgreens
35	Brawley School Rd
33	US 21 N, E 🅿 Shell, 🍴 Big League Hotdogs, China Express, DQ, Jeffrey's Rest, McDonald's, Quiznos, Starbucks, Subway, 🛏 Candlewood Suites, Hilton Garden, SpringHill Suites, TownePlace Suites, 🅾 🏩, AT&T, W 🅿 BP, Citgo/dsl, 🍴 Arby's, Baskin-Robbins/Dunkin Donuts, Sauza's Mexican, 🅾 Food Lion, Lake Norman RV Resort (13mi), vet
31	Langtree Rd, W 🅿 Shell/dsl
30	Davidson, E 🅿 Exxon/dsl, Liberty, 🍴 Char-Grill, Subway, 🛏 Homewood Suites, 🅾 Harris-Teeter, to Davidson College, W 🍴 North Harbor Rest
28	US 21 S, NC 73, Cornelius, Lake Norman, E 🅿 Cashion/dsl, Citgo, 🍴 Acropolis Cafe, 🛏 Days Inn, Hampton Inn, 🅾 NAPA, W 🅿 Kangaroo, 🍴 Asiana, Bojangles, Chicago Dog, Drifter's Grill, KFC, Kobe Japanese, Mac's BBQ, McAlister's Deli, McDonald's, Pizza Hut, Starbucks, Subway, Taco Bell, Waffle House, Wendy's, 🛏 Clarion, Comfort Inn, EconoLodge, Microtel, 🅾 Chrysler/Dodge/Jeep, CVS Drug, $Tree, Fresh Mkt, Hyundai, Rite Aid, SteinMart, Walgreens, USPO

CONCORD

| 25 | NC 73, Concord, Lake Norman, E 🅿 Shell/dsl, 🍴 Burger King, Chick-fil-A, Chili's, Donato's Pizza, IHOP, Longhorn Steaks, McDonald's, Melting Pot, Moe's SW Grill, O'Charley's, Panda Express, Papa John's, Starbucks, 🛏 Country Inn&Suites, Holiday Inn Express, Quality Inn, 🅾 AAA, Advance Parts, AT&T, GNC, Harris-Teeter, Home Depot, Kohl's, Lowe's, Marshall's, PetCo, Radio Shack, Staples, Target, Tuffy Auto, Verizon, vet, W 🅿 Shell/Circle K/dsl, 🍴 Arby's, Bob Evans, Bojangles, Carrabba's, ColdStone, DQ, Fox&Hound, Jason's Deli, Hickory Tavern Grill, House of Tei Pei, Kabuto Japanese, Outback Steaks, Qdoba, Red Rock's Cafe, Starbucks, Subway, Taco Mac, 🛏 Candlewood Suites, Courtyard, Residence Inn, Sleep Inn, 🅾 Barnes&Noble, Dick's, Food Lion/deli, Office Depot, Walgreens, to Energy Explorium |
| 23 | Gilead Rd, to US 21, Huntersville, E 🅿 BP, Citgo/dsl, Shell/24hr, 🍴 Baskin-Robbins/Dunkin Dounuts, Capt's Galley, Chico's Mexican, CookOut, Hardee's, Little Caesar's, Subway, Taco Bell, Waffle House, Wendy's, 🛏 Best |

CHARLOTTE

23	Continued
	Western, Comfort Suites, Hampton Inn, Ramada Inn, 🅾 AutoZone, Buick/GMC, Food Lion, Ford, Goodyear/auto, Hancock Fabrics, O'Reilly Parts, Rite Aid, Toyota, Tuesday Morning, VW, USPO, vet, W 🅿 Shell, 🍴 Domino's, Firehouse Subs, 5 Guys Burgers, McDonald's, Salsarita's, Starbucks, 🅾 🏩, Batteries+, Bi-Lo, CVS Drug, Earth Fare, Harris-Teeter, Walgreens, **Urgent Care**
19 b a	S I-485 Outer, Rd 115, to Spartanburg
18	Harris Blvd, Reames Rd, E 🅿 BP/Arby's, Shell/dsl, 🍴 Azteca Mexican, Bob Evans, Hickory Tavern, Jack-in-the-Box, Lin's Buffet, Subway, Waffle House, 🛏 Comfort Suites, Fairfield Inn, Hilton Garden, Suburban Lodge, 🅾 🏩, Advance Parts, Staples, **Urgent Care**, to UNCC, Univ Research Park, W 🍴 Bravo Italian, Chick-fil-A, Chili's, Coldstone, Edomae Grill, Firebirds, Firehouse Subs, 5 Guys Burgers, Fox&Hound, Mimi's Cafe, Moe's SW Grill, Olive Garden, On-the-Border, Panera bread, PF Chang's, Red Robin, Shane's Rib Shack, TGI Friday's, Wendy's, 🛏 Drury Inn, 🅾 AT&T, Belk, Best Buy, Dick's, Dillard's, $Tree, Lowe's, Macy's, Old Navy, Petsmart, Target, Verizon, mall
16 b a	US 21, Sunset Rd, E 🅿 Circle K, QT/dsl, Shell, 🍴 Capt D's, Hardee's, KFC, McDonald's, Papa John's, Subway, Taco Bell, Wendy's, 🛏 Days Inn, Super 8, 🅾 AutoZone, NAPA, W 🅿 Circle K/dsl, Citgo/dsl, Shell/dsl/scales/24hr, 🍴 Baskin-Robbins/Dunkin Donuts, Bojangles, Bubba's BBQ, CookOut, Denny's, Domino's, Jack-in-the-Box, Subway, Waffle House, 🛏 Microtel, Sleep Inn, 🅾 Advance Parts, Aldi Foods, CVS Drug, Family$, Food Lion, Walgreens
13 b a	I-85, S to Spartanburg, N to Greensboro
12	La Salle St, W 🅿 Marathon/dsl, Shell/dsl
11 b a	I-277, Brookshire Fwy, NC 16
10b	Trade St, 5th St, E 🅾 to Discovery Place, W 🅿 Marathon, 🍴 Bojangles
10a	US 21 (from sb), Moorhead St, downtown
9	I-277, US 74, to US 29, John Belk Fwy, downtown, E 🏩, stadium
8	Remount Rd (from nb, no re-entry)
7	Clanton Rd, E 🅿 Marathon/dsl, 🛏 EconoLodge, Super 8, 🅾 Family$, W 🅿 BP, Shell/dsl
6 b a	US 521, Billy Graham Pkwy, E 🅿 BP, Citgo, Shell/dsl, Sunoco/dsl, 🍴 Arby's, Azteca Mexican, Bojangles, Capt D's, Carolina Prime Steaks, Domino's, Dragon House, Firehouse Subs, HoneyBaked Ham, IHOP, KFC, Papa John's, Tres Pesos Grill, Waffle House, 🛏 Best Western, Days Inn, Howard Johnson, Ramada Ltd, Sheraton, 🅾 CVS Drug, Family$, Home Depot, TJ Maxx, Walgreens, to Queens Coll, W 🅿 Kangaroo, 🍴 Omaha Steaks, 🛏 Courtyard, Embassy Suites, Homestead Suites, Hyatt House, InTown Suites, La Quinta, Sleep Inn, 🅾 ⛽
5	Tyvola Rd, E 🅿 Kangaroo, Shell, 🍴 Chili's, China King, Kabuto Japanese, McDonald's, Sonny's BBQ, Subway, 🛏 Candlewood Suites, Comfort Inn, Hilton, Marriott, Quality Inn, Residence Inn, Studio+, 🅾 Aldi Foods, Costco/gas, Jaguar, Verizon, services 1 mi E, W 🛏 Extended Stay America, Wingate Inn
4	Nations Ford Rd, E 🅿 Citgo, Shell/Circle K/24hr, 🍴 New England Seafood, 🛏 Knights Inn, La Casa Inn, W 🅿 Shell/Burger King
3	Arrowood Rd, E 🍴 Jack-in-the-Box, Sonic, Starbucks, Wendy's, 🛏 Courtyard, Fairfield Inn, Holiday Inn Express,

NC

▲N INTERSTATE 77 CONT'D

Exit	Services
3	Continued
	Hyatt Place, Mainstay Suites, Staybridge Suites, Towne-Place Suites, **W** 🍴 Ruby Tuesday, 🏠 Hampton Inn
2	I-485
1.5mm	**Welcome Ctr nb, full ♿ facilities, info, 🚻, vending, 🏠, litter barrels, petwalk**
1	Westinghouse Blvd, to I-485 (from nb), **E** ⓖ BP/dsl, 🍴 Jack-in-the-Box, Subway, Waffle House, 🏠 Super 8, **W** ⓖ Shell/dsl, 🍴 Burger King
0mm	North Carolina/South Carolina state line

▲N INTERSTATE 85

Exit	Services
234mm	North Carolina/Virginia state line
233	US 1, to Wise, **E** 🍴 Budget Inn
231mm	**Welcome Ctr sb, full ♿ facilities, 🚻, 🏠, litter barrels, petwalk**
229	Oine Rd, to Norlina, **E** ⓖ BP, **W** SRA
226	Ridgeway Rd, **W** ⊙ to Kerr Lake, to SRA
223	Manson Rd, **E** ⓖ BP/dsl, ⊙ camping, **W** to Kerr Dam
220	US 1, US 158, Flemingtown Rd, to Middleburg, **E** ⓖ Mobil/dsl, **W** ⓖ Exxon/dsl/scales/truck wash, 🏠 Chex Motel/rest.
218	US 1 S (from sb exits left), to Raleigh
217	Nutbush Bridge, **E** ⊙ auto repair, **W** ⓖ Exxon/dsl, ⊙ Kerr Lake RA
215	US 158 BYP E, Henderson (no EZ return from nb), **E** ⓖ Hess/dsl, Shell, Sunoco, 🍴 Burger King, Forsyth's BBQ, Nunnery-Freeman BBQ, Subway, 🏠 Budget Host, EconoLodge, Scottish Inn, ⊙ $General, Food Lion, Roses, repair/tires, services on US 158
214	NC 39, Henderson, **E** ⓖ BP, 🍴 Waffle House, ⊙ Verizon, **W** ⓖ Mobil/dsl, Shell, ⊙ to Kerr Lake RA
213	US 158, Dabney Dr, to Henderson, **E** ⓖ Marathon, Valero, 🍴 Bamboo Garden, Big Cheese Pizza, Bojangles, Denny's, Ichibar Chinese, KFC, McDonald's, Papa John's, Pino's Italian, Subway, Wendy's, ⊙ Family$, Food Lion, Radio Shack, Roses, Save-a-Lot Foods, **W** ⓖ Shell, 🍴 Chick-fil-A, Golden Corral, Mayflower Seafood, Pizza Hut, Ruby Tuesday, Smithfields BBQ, Taco Bell, 🏠 Holiday Inn Express, ⊙ Advance Parts, BigLots, Buick/Chevrolet/GMC, Chrysler/Dodge/Jeep, Ford/Lincoln, Lowe's, Rite Aid, Staples, Verizon
212	Ruin Creek Rd, **E** ⓖ Shell/dsl, 🍴 Cracker Barrel, Mazatlan Mexican, Ribeye's, Waffle House, 🏠 Knight's Inn, ⊙ Toyota/Scion, **W** ⓖ Exxon/Burger King, Sheetz/dsl, 🏠 Baymont Inn, Hampton Inn, Sleep Inn, ⊙ 🅗, Belk, $Tree, JC Penney, Walmart
209	Poplar Creek Rd, **W** Vance-Granville Comm Coll
206	US 158, Oxford, **W** ⓖ BP/dsl, ⊙ 🚻
204	NC 96, Oxford, **E** ⓖ BP/dsl, 🏠 Comfort Inn, King's Inn, ⊙ Buick/Chevrolet/GMC, Ford, Honda, **W** ⓖ Hess, Shell, Valero, 🍴 Burger King, China Wok, Cookout, Domino's, KFC/Taco Bell, McDonald's, Pizza Hut, Subway, Wendy's, ⊙ 🅗, GNC, Just Save
202	US 15, Oxford, **W** ⓖ Murphy Express/dsl, 🍴 Bojangles, Hibachi, HWY 55, 🏠 Crown Motel (2mi), ⊙ $Tree, Verizon, Walmart
199mm	℞ both lanes, full ♿ facilities, 🚻, 🏠, litter barrels, petwalk

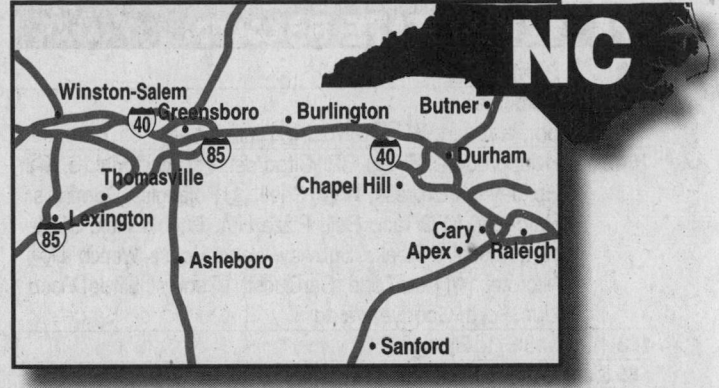

198mm	Tar River
191	NC 56, Butner, **E** ⓖ BP/dsl, Hess/dsl, 🍴 Betty Lue's Rest., Bob's BBQ, Bojangles, Domino's, El Rio Mexican, KFC/Taco Bell, McDonald's, Pizza Hut, Pizza Mia, Sonic, Subway, Taste of China, Wendy's, 🏠 Creedmor Inn, ⊙ Advance Parts, AutoZone, $General, $Tree, Food Lion, M&H Tires, Rite Aid, vet, to Falls Lake RA, **W** ⓖ Exxon, Shell/dsl, 🍴 Hardee's, Ribeye's, 🏠 Best Western, EconoLodge, Ramada Ltd, ⊙ auto repair
189	Butner, 1 mi **W** ⓖ BP/dsl, Citgo, Valero, 🍴 Subway, ⊙ repair
186b a	US 15, to Creedmoor, **E** ⓖ Variety Mart/dsl
185mm	Falls Lake
183	Redwood Rd
182	Red Mill Rd, **E** ⓖ Exxon/dsl, ⊙ Kenworth/Isuzu Trucks
180	Glenn School Rd
179	E Club Blvd, **E** ⓖ Exxon
178	US 70 E, to Raleigh, Falls Lake RA, Research Triangle, RDU 🛧
177	Avondale Dr, NC 55, **W** gas BP, Shell, 🍴 American Hero, Arby's, Hong Kong Buffet, Los Comales, McDonalds, Subway, ⊙ Advance Parts, Family$
176b a	Gregson St, US 501 N, **E** ⓖ Hugo's, 🍴 Biscuitville, Burger King, PanPan Diner, Randy's Pizza, Ruby Tuesday, Tripp's Diner, 🏠 Hampton Inn, ⊙ Macy's, Museum of Life&Science, Sears/auto, mall, **W** ⊙ 🅗, museum
175	Guess Rd, **E** ⓖ Citgo, 🍴 Doghouse Cafe, Hog Heaven BBQ, 🏠 Holiday Inn Express, Super 8, ⊙ Rite Aid, **W** ⓖ BP/dsl, Puro/dsl, 🍴 Bojangles, Honey's Diner, IHOP, TX Roadhouse, 🏠 Red Roof Inn, ⊙ Family Dollar, GNC, Home Depot, Kroger, PetsMart, Ross, Verizon, vet
174a	Hillandale Rd, **W** ⓖ BP, 🍴 Blue Olive, China King, El Corral, Pomodoro Italian, 🏠 Comfort Inn, Courtyard, ⊙ Urgent Care, Kerr Drug
174b	US 15 S, US 501 S
173	US 15, US 501, US 70, Colemill Rd, W Durham, **E** ⓖ BP, Exxon/dsl, Mobil, Shell, 🍴 Arby's, Biscuitville, Bojangles, Chick-fil-A, Cookout, Cracker Barrel, DogHouse Rest., Domino's, Japan Express, KFC/Taco Bell, McDonald's, Shanghai Chinese, Subway, Waffle House, Wendy's, 🏠 Days Inn, Hilton, Motel 6, Quality Inn, ⊙ 🅗, Advance Parts, Autozone, CVS Drug, $General, Hancock Fabrics, Kroger, O'Reilly Parts, Rite Aid
172	NC 147 S, to US 15 S, US 501 S, Durham, from nb
170	to NC 751, to Duke U (no EZ return from nb), **E** 🏠 Durham Skyland Inn, Scottish Inn, **W** to Eno River SP
165	NC 86, to Chapel Hill, **E** ⓖ Eagles/Burger King/dsl, 🍴 China Fuji, Hwy 55, Papa John's, Subway, ⊙ Home De

(Side tabs: HENDERSON, OXFORD, BUTNER, DURHAM; NC)

⬆N INTERSTATE 85 CONT'D

Exit	Services
165	Continued
	pot, Walmart, **W** 🅖 BP/dsl, 🅞 auto repair
164	Hillsborough, **E** 🅖 BP, Citgo/dsl, 🍽 McDonald's, 🏨 Holiday Inn Express, **W** 🅖 Shell, 🍽 Bojangles, Domino's, Hardee's, KFC/Taco Bell, Pizza Hut, Pueblo Viejo Mexican, Russell's Steaks, Subway, Waffle House, Wendy's, 🏨 Microtel, 🅞 AutoZone, CarQuest, $General, $Tree, Food Lion, Ford, Goodyear/auto
163	I-40 E, to Raleigh.
	I-85 S and I-40 W run together 38 mi.
161	to US 70 E, NC 86 N
160	to NC 86 N, Efland, **W** 🅖 Exxon/dsl, 🅞 Andrew's Repair
158mm	**weigh sta both lanes**
157	Buckhorn Rd, **E** 🅖 BP/dsl, Petro/Valero/Dunkin Donuts/Iron Skillet/dsl/scales/24hr/@, **W** 🅖 Citgo
154	Mebane-Oaks Rd, **E** 🅖 Murphy USA/dsl, Sheetz/dsl, 🍽 China Garden, Ciao Pizza, Subway, Wendy's, Zaxby's, 🅞 $Tree, GNC, Radio Shack, Walmart/Subway, **W** 🅖 BP, Hess/dsl, Shell/dsl, 🍽 Biscuitville, Blue Ribbon Diner, Bojangles, La Fiesta Mexican, McDonald's, Roma Pizza, Sake Japanese, Waffle House, 🏨 Budget Inn, 🅞 Advance Parts, AutoZone, CVS Drug, Lowe's Foods, Tanger Outlets/famous brands, Verizon, Walgreens, vet
153	NC 119, Mebane, **E** 🅖 BP/KFC/Pizza Hut/Taco Bell, 🍽 Anna Maria's Pizza, Cracker Barrel, Jersey Mike's, Moe's SW Grill, Ruby Tuesday, Sakura Japanese, Smithfield's BBQ, Yogurt Café, 🏨 Hampton Inn, Holiday Inn Express, 🅞 $General, Lowe's, O'Reilly Parts, vet, **W** 🅖 Exxon/Burger King, 🍽 Domino's, La Cocina Mexican, Papa John's, Sonic, Subway, YumYum Chinese, 🅞 Curves, Food Lion
152	Trollingwood Rd, **E** 🅖 🚛/McDonald's/dsl/scales/24hr
150	to Roxboro, Haw River, **W** 🅖 Hess/Wilco/DQ/Wendy's/dsl/scales/24hr, *FLYING J*/Denny's/dsl/LP/scales/24hr, SpeedCo, 🏨 Days Inn, 🅞 Blue Beacon
148	NC 54, Graham, **E** 🅖 BP/dsl, Marathon/dsl, Shell/dsl, 🍽 Waffle House, 🏨 Homestay Suites, **W** 🍽 AmMex 2 Cafe
147	NC 87, to Pittsboro, Graham, **E** 🅖 BP, Sheetz/dsl, 🍽 AnnaMaria's Pizzeria, Arby's, Bojangles, Burger King, Domino's, Great Wall Chinese, Guerrero Mexican, Lucky Bamboo, Pizza Hut, Subway, Wendy's, 🅞 Advance Parts, AutoZone, Champion Tire/Repair, Curves, Family$, Food Lion, Ford, Just Save, O'Reilly Parts, Rite Aid, vet, **W** 🅖 Citgo/dsl, Exxon/dsl, Shell/dsl, 🍽 Biscuitville, Cook-Out, Golden China, McDonald's, Taco Bell, Zaxby's, 🅞 H, CVS Drug, $General, Verizon, Walgreens
145	NC 49, Burlington, **E** 🅖 Marathon/dsl, Shell/dsl, 🍽 Capt D's, 🏨 EconoLodge, Microtel, Motel 6, 🅞 Harley-Davidson, **W** 🅖 BP/dsl, 🍽 Biscuitville, Bojangles, Burger King, China Inn, Hardee's, KFC, Subway, 🏨 Quality Inn, Red Carpet Inn, Royal Inn, 🅞 Chrysler/Dodge/Jeep, $General, Family$, Food Lion, Radio Shack, Rite Aid
143	NC 62, Burlington, **E** 🅖 Sav-Way, 🍽 Hardee's, Waffle House, Wendy's, 🅞 JR Outlet, to Alamance Bfd, **W** 🅖 Marathon, Sheetz/dsl, 🍽 Biscuitville, Cutting Board Rest, K&W Cafeteria, 🏨 Ramada Inn, 🅞 Cadillac, Chevrolet, $General, Food Lion, Ford, Home Depot, Mazda, auto repair, vet
141	Huffman Mill Rd, Burlington, **E** 🅖 BP, Marathon/Kanga\

Exit	Services
141	Continued
	roo, 🍽 IHOP, Mayflower Seafood, Outback Steaks, 🏨 Hampton Inn, Holiday Inn Express, 🅞 Nissan, **W** 🅖 Raygo, 🍽 Andy's, Applebee's, Arby's, Biscuitville, Bojangles, Cancun Mexican, Chick-fil-A, China Gate, Cook-Out, Cracker Barrel, 5 Guys Burgers, Golden Corral, Good Times Cafe, Grill 584, Hibachi Buffet, HoneyBaked Ham, Hooters, KFC, La Cocina Mexican, Longhorn Steaks, Mellow Mushroom, O'Charley's, Panera Bread, Ruby Tuesday, Sal's Italian, Starbucks, Steak'n Shake, Subway, Taco Bell, Village Grill, Wholly Guacamole, 🏨 Best Western, Country Inn&Suites, Courtyard, Super 8, 🅞 H, $Tree, Hamrick's, Harris Teeter, Hyundai, K-Mart/gas, Lowe's, Radio Shack, Sears/auto, TJ Maxx, Verizon, Walgreens, Walmart/McDonald's, mall, to Elon Coll
140	University Ave, **E** 🅞 H, Toyota/Scion, **W** 🍽 Brixx Pizza, Buffalo Wing Wings, Burger King, Chick-fil-A, Chili's, Coldstone, Jimmy John's, Little Italy, McDonald's, Mimi's Cafe, Moe's SW Grill, Olive Garden, Peking House, Qdoba, Red Bowl Asian, Red Lobster, Red Robin, Starbucks, TX Roadhouse, 🅞 AT&T, Barnes&Noble, Belk, Best Buy, BJ's Whse/gas, Dick's, Dillard's, Discount Tire, GNC, Hobby Lobby, JC Penney, Kohl's, Michael's, Old Navy, Petsmart, Ross, Target, Verizon
139mm	📶 **both lanes, full** ♿ **facilities,** 🚻, 🍴 **,litter barrels, vending**
138	NC 61, Gibsonville, **W** 🅖 TA/BP/Burger King/Popeye's/dsl/scales/24hr/@, 🅞 truckwash
135	Rock Creek Dairy Rd, **W** 🅖 Citgo, Marathon/Kangaroo, 🍽 Bojangles, Ciao Italian, China 1, Domino's, Guacamole Mexican, Jersey Mike's Subs, McDonald's, Pizza Hut/Taco Bell, Subway, 🏨 Comfort Suites, 🅞 Curves, CVS Drug, $General, Food Lion, Midtown Drug, Verizon
132	Mt Hope Church Rd, **E** 🅖 Citgo/Subway/dsl, 🍽 McDonald's, Pascali's Pizza, **W** 🅖 Exxon/dsl, Hess/Wendy's/dsl/24hr, 🏨 Hampton Inn
131	to I-85 S, to I-73 N, to US 421, Highpoint, Charlotte
129	Youngsmill Rd, **W** Greensboro Camping (4mi)
128	Alamance Church Rd, **E** 🅖 Citgo/Subway/dsl
126b a	US 421, to Sanford, **E** 🅖 Exxon/dsl, Kangaroo/dsl, 🅞 Hagan Stone Park Camping
124	S Elm, Eugene St, **W** 🅖 Murphy Express/dsl, 🍽 Andy's, Bamboo Grill, Bojangles, Cracker Barrel, McDonald's, Mi Casa, Smithfield's BBQ, Starbucks, Subway, Waffle House, Wendy's, 🅞 AT&T, Lowe's, Verizon, Walmart/McDonald's
122c b a	US 220, to Greensboro, Asheboro (from sb)
121	I-40 W, I-73 N, to Winston-Salem
120	N US 29, E US 70, to I-40 W
119	Groometown Rd, from nb, **W** 🅖 Citgo/dsl
118	US 29 S, US 70 W, to High Point, Jamestown, **W** 🏨 Grandover Resort, 🅞 H
115mm	Deep River
113bc	I-74, US 311, Ashboro, to Winston-Salem
113a	NC 62, Archdale, **E** 🅖 Citgo/dsl, **W** 🅖 BP/dsl, 🏨 Quality Inn
111	US 311, to High Point, Archdale, **E** 🅖 Sheetz/dsl, 🍽 Bamboo Garden, Bojangles, Hardee's, Pizza Hut, Subway, Wendy's, 🏨 Days Inn, 🅞 CVS Drug, $General, Food Lion, Lowe's Foods/24hr, **W** 🅖 Citgo, Exxon/McDonald's, Marathon/dsl, Shell/Circle K/dsl, 🍽 Biscuitville, J&S Cafe, Rancho Rest, Waffle House, 🏨 Comfort Inn, Country

Side markers: **MEBANE**, **BURLINGTON**, **NC**, **GREENSBORO**

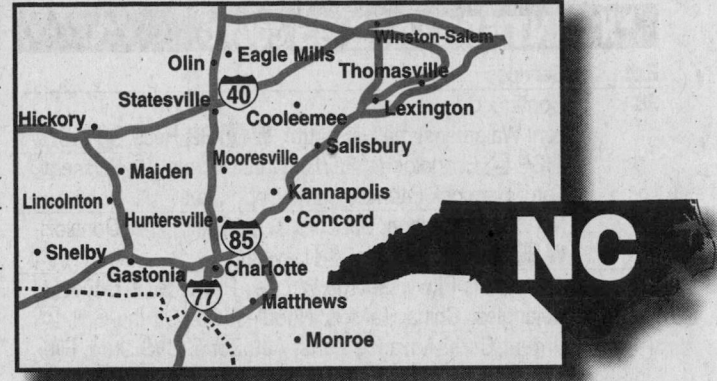

⬛N INTERSTATE 85 CONT'D

Exit	Services
111	Continued
	Inn&Suites, Fairfield Inn, Hampton Inn, Holiday Inn Express, ⊙ 🛏, O'Reilly Parts, USPO, tires, vet
108	Hopewell Church Rd, Trinity
106	Finch Farm Rd, **E** █ BP/dsl, **W** █ Sheetz/dsl, 🍴 Smokey T's BBQ, Subway (1mi)
103	NC 109, to Thomasville, **E** █ Marathon/dsl, Murphy USA/dsl, Shell, 🍴 Arby's, Chen's Kitchen, Cookout Burgers, Elizabeth's Pizza, Taco Bell, 🛏🛏ity Suites, ⊙ CVS Drug, $Tree, Ingles Foods, K-Mart, Radio Shack, Walmart/McDonald's, **W** █ Exxon/Subway/dsl, RaceWay, Hess/Wilco/dsl, Shell, 🍴 BBQ Shack, Biscuitville, Bojangles, Burger King, Captain Tom's, China Garden, Denny's, E Coast Grill, Hardee's, Hunan Chinese, KFC, La Carreta Mexican, Little Caesars, Mandarin Express, Mazatlan Mexican, McDonald's, Mr Gatti's, Papa John's, Pizza Hut, Ruby Tuesday, Sonic, Sunrise Diner, Waffle House, Wendy's, 🛏 Davidson Lodge, Quality Inn, ⊙ Advance Parts, Aldi Foods, AutoZone, $General, Family$, Food Lion, Merchant's Tire, Mighty$, NAPA, O'Reilly Parts, Peebles, Rite Aid, Verizon, Walgreens
102	Lake Rd, **W** █ Marathon/dsl, Sunoco/dsl, 🛏 Comfort Inn, Microtel, ⊙ 🛏
100mm	℞ both lanes, full ♿ facilities, 🍴 vending, 🗑 litter barrels, petwalk
96	US 64, to Asheboro, Lexington, **E** █ Exxon/dsl, ⊙ Modern Tire, NC Zoo, **W** █ Citgo/dsl, Gulf/dsl, 🍴 Randy's Rest., ⊙ to Davidson Co Coll
94	Old US 64, **E** █ Shell, **W** ⊙ Timberlake Gallery
91	NC 8, to Southmont, **E** █ BP/dsl, Mobil/7-11, Shell/dsl, 🍴 Biscuit King, Chrissy's Doghouse, Christo Rest., Hunan Express, Jimmy's BBQ, Kabuki, KFC, McDonald's, Ocean View Seafood, Subway, Wendy's, 🛏 Days Inn, Hwy 8 Motel, ⊙ Food Lion, High Rock Lake Camping (7mi), Kerr Drug, Mock Tire, **W** █ Exxon/dsl, QM/dsl, 🍴 Applebee's, Arby's, Burger King, Cagmey's Kitchen, Cracker Barrel, Golden Corral, La Carreta Mexican, Little Ceasars, Mi Pueblo, Pizza Hut (1mi), Subway, Taco Bell, Zaxby's, 🛏 Country Hearth Inn, Quality Inn, ⊙ 🛏, Belk, $Tree, GNC, Lowe's (1mi), Radio Shack, Walmart (1mi)
88	Linwood, **W** █ Gulf/dsl, ⊙ 🛏
87	US 29, US 70, US 52 (from nb), High Point, **W** ⊙ 🛏, ↩
86	Belmont Rd, **W** █ Bill's Trkstp/dsl/scales/24hr/@
84	US 29 S, US 70 W, NC 150 (from nb), to Spencer
82	US 29, US 70 (from sb), to Spencer
81.5mm	Yadkin River
81	Long Ferry Rd, Spencer, **E** █ Liberty/dsl
79	Spencer Shops SHS, Spencer, E Spencer, **1 mi W** █ Citgo, 🍴 Bojangles, Subway, ⊙ $General, Food Lion, Kerr Drug
76b a	US 52, to Albemarle, Salisbury, **E** █ BP, Citgo, Pop Shoppe, 🍴 Applebee's, Capriano's, ColdStone, E Coast Grill, Grand Asian, IHOP, Mr Gatti's Pizza, Pancho Villa Mexican, Top China, Zaxby's, 🛏 Days Inn, Economy Inn, Happy Traveler Inn, ⊙ Aldi Foods, AT&T, CVS Drug, $Tree, Food Lion, GNC, Harley-Davidson, Lowe's, Marshall's, Old Navy, Petsmart, Radio Shack, Rite Aid, Staples, Tire Kingdom, Verizon, Walgreens, vet, **W** █ Murphy Express/dsl, Shell/Circle K/dsl, Wilco/Hess/dsl, 🍴 Blue Bay Sea

SALISBURY

Exit	Services
76b a	Continued
	food, Bojangles, Burger King, Capt D's, Chick-fil-A, China Buffet, Christo's Rest., Cookout, Cracker Barrel, Hardee's, HoneyBaked Ham, KFC, McDonald's, O'Charley's, Outback Steaks, Papa John's, Pizza Hut, Starbucks, Subway, Taco Bell, Tokyo Express, Wendy's, 🛏 Comfort Suites, Courtyard, ⊙ 🛏, Advance Parts, AutoZone, BigLots, Family$, Firestone/auto, Goodyear/auto, K-Mart, Office Depot, USPO, Walmart/Subway,
75	US 601, Jake Alexander Blvd, **E** █ Sheetz/dsl, 🍴 Arby's, Farmhouse Rest., 🛏 EconoLodge, ⊙ NAPA, to Dan Nicholas Park, **W** █ BP, Citgo, Shell/dsl, 🍴 Casa Grande Mexian, CiCi's Pizza, Ichiban Japanese, Nyoshi Japanese, Ryan's, Waffle House, Wendy's, 🛏 Hampton Inn, Holiday Inn, Quality Inn, ⊙ Buick, Cadillac/Chevrolet, Chrysler/Dodge/Jeep, Ford, GMC, Honda, Kia, Magic Mart, Nissan, Toyota/Scion
74	Julian Rd, **W** 🍴 Longhorn Steaks, Los Arcos, Olive Garden, Subway, ⊙ Belk, $Tree, Kohl's, Michael's
72	Peach Orchard Rd
71	Peeler Rd, **E** █ ⬤Loves/Chester's/McDonald's/dsl/scales/24hr, **W** █ Hess/Wilco/Bojangles/Subway/dsl/scales/24hr, ⊙ dsl repair
70	Webb Rd, **E** flea mkt, **W** █ Shell/dsl, 🍴 Bebops BBQ, ⊙ st patrol
68	US 29, US 601, to Rockwell, China Grove, **1 mi W** on US 29 █ BP, 🍴 Domino's, Gary's BBQ, Hardee's, Jimmie's Rest., Pizza Hut, Subway, ⊙ AutoZone, $General, Family$, Food Lion, Rite Aid
63	Kannapolis, **E** █ ⬤/Subway/dsl/scales, 🍴 Waffle House, 🛏 Motel 6
60	Earnhardt Rd, Copperfield Blvd, **E** █ Exxon/dsl, Marathon, 🍴 Bojangles, Cracker Barrel, Waffle House, 🛏 Country Inn&Suites, Hampton Inn, Sleep Inn, ⊙ 🛏, Discount Tire, **W** █ Marathon/Kangaroo/dsl, 🍴 Carino's Italian, Casa Grande Mexican, Dragon Wok, Firehouse Subs, Logan's Roadhouse, McDonald's, Ruby Tuesday, Steak'n Shake, Subway, Taco Bell, Wendy's, 🛏 Holiday Inn Express, ⊙ Urgent Care, Hobby Lobby, Kohl's, Lowe's, Sam's Club/gas, Walmart

CONCORD

Exit	Services
59mm	℞ both lanes, full ♿ facilities, 🍴 vending, 🗑 litter barrels, petwalk
58	US 29, US 601, Concord, **E** █ BP, Marathon/dsl, Shell/dsl, 🍴 Applebee's, Capt D's, Chick-fil-A, Chili's, El Vallarta Mexican, Golden Corral, Jimmy John's, Mayflower Seafood, McDonald's, Moe's SW Grill, Mr C's Rest., O'Charley's, Popeye's, Starbucks, Subway, Wendy's, 🛏 Best Value Inn, Howard Johnson, Rodeway Inn, ⊙ 🛏, Belk, Harris Teeter, JC Penney, Sears/auto, Staples, Veri

NC

= gas = food = lodging = other = rest stop Copyright 2014 - The NEXT Exit ®

INTERSTATE 85 CONT'D

Exit	Services
58	Continued
	zon, Walgreens, mall, st patrol, W BP, Hess, CiCi's, IHOP, Econolodge, Fairfield Inn, Microtel, $General, Ford, Hancock Fabrics, Home Depot, vet
55	NC 73, to Davidson, Concord, E Shell, McDonald's, W Shell/Circle K/dsl, Days Inn
54	Kannapolis Pkwy, George W Lyles Pkwy, E Citgo, Bojangles, China Garden, Noodles&Co, Off-the-Grill, Urgent Care, Advance Parts, AutoZone, CVS Drug, Firestone, Food Lion, Harris Teeter, Walgreens, vet, W Marathon/Kangaroo, Arby's, Asian Cafe, Buffalo Wild Wings, Chick-fil-A, Fatz Cafe, Jersey Mike's, McDonald's, Mi Pueblo, Starbucks, Best Buy, Dick's, $Tree, Goodyear/auto, Marshall's, Steinmart, Super Target
52	Poplar Tent Rd, E Shell/7-11/dsl, R&R BBQ, to Lowe's Speedway, museum, W Exxon/7-11/dsl
49	Bruton Smith Blvd, Concord Mills Blvd, E BP/McDonalds, Shell/7-11/dsl, Bojangles, Camila's Mexican, Carrabbas, ChuckECheese, Cinco de Mayo Mexican, Cookout, Cracker Barrel, Firehouse Subs, 5 Guys Burgers, Hooters, KFC/Taco Bell, Quaker Steak, Jack-in-the-Box, Ruby Tuesday, Sonic, Starbucks, Subway, Sonny's BBQ, Taco Bell, TX Land&Cattle Steaks, TX Roadhouse, Waffle House, Wendy's, Zaxby's, Comfort Suites, Courtyard, Embassy Suites, Great Wolf Lodge, Hampton Inn, Hilton Garden, Holiday Inn Express, Residence Inn, Sleep Inn, SpringHill Suites, Suburban Lodge, Wingate Inn, BJ's Whse/gas, Fleetwood RV camping (1.5mi), Harley-Davidson, Honda, Tom Johnson RV Ctr (1.5mi), Toyota/Scion, to Lowe's Motor Speedway, W Marathon/dsl, Texaco, Applebee's, Burger King, Charanda Mexican, Chick-fil-A, Foster's Grille, Jimmy John's, Mayflower Seafood, McAlisters Deli, Olive Garden, On-the-Border, Panera Bread, Razzoo's Cafe, Red Lobster, Steak'n Shake, Sticky Fingers, TGI Friday's, Urgent Care, AT&T, BassPro Shops, Best Buy, BooksAMillion, Discount Tire, $Tree, Concord Mills Mall, Goodyear/auto, Lowe's, PetCo, Radio Shack, Ross, TJ Maxx, Verizon, Walmart/Subway
48	I-485, to US 29, to Rock Hill
46	Mallard Creek Church Rd, E Exxon/7-11, Hess/dsl, Kangaroo, China Cafe, Giacomos Pizza, Hibachi Buffet, Jack-in-the-Box, Wild Wing Cafe, Research Park, Tire Kingdom, W Shell/Circle K, 5 Guys Burgers, Hickory Tavern, Rita's, Starbucks, Thai Taste, PetCo, Trader Joes
45b a	Harris Blvd, E Applebee's, Bikini's Grill, Bojangles, Buffalo Wild Wings, Burger King, Cheddar's, Chick-fil-A, Chili's, China Buffet, Chipotle, Fuse Buffet, IHOP, Jersey Mike's Subs, Jimmy John's, Los Arcos, McDonald's, Nakato's, Panera Bread, Papa John's, Picasso's Pizza, Qdoba, Quiznos, Shane's Rib Shack, Shoney's, Showmar's Rest, Smokey Bones, Starbucks, Taco Bell, Taco Mac, TGIFriday's, Country Inn&Suites, Courtyard, Drury Inn, Extended Stay America, Hampton Inn, Hilton, Holiday Inn Express, Homewood Suites, Microtel, Residence Inn, Sleep Inn, , AT&T, Dick's, Food Lion, Kohl's, Michael's, Office Depot, Ross, Sam's Club, TJ Maxx, Verizon, Walgreens, Walmart/McDonald's, to UNCC, to Miz Scarlett's, U Research Park, 0-2 mi W Longhorn

Exit	Services
45b a	Continued
	Steaks, Macaroni Grill, Red Robin, Tony's Pizza, SpringHill Suites, TownePlace Suites, Harris Teeter, Rite Aid
43	University City Blvd
42	US 29 (nb only)
41	Sugar Creek Rd, E RaceWay, Shell/dsl, Bojangles, McDonald's, Taco Bell, Wendy's, Brookwood Inn, Continental Inn, Economy Inn, Garden Inn, Motel 6, Travel Inn, W Shell/Circle K, Chicken Box Rest, Cookout, Sugar Creek Rest., TX Ranch Steaks, Days Inn, Ramada Inn, Red Roof Inn, Rodeway Inn, Sunset Inn, Super 8
40	Graham St, E Exxon/7-11/dsl, Budget Inn, UPS, Volvo, Western Star, W Marathon/dsl, Freightliner
39	Statesville Ave, E /Subway/dsl/scales/24hr, CarQuest, W Citgo/dsl, Shell/dsl, Bojangles, Family$
38	I-77, US 21, N to Statesville, S to Columbia
37	Beatties Ford Rd, E Marathon, Shell/Chester's/dsl, Burger King, McDonald's, Subway, CVS Drug, Family$, Food Lion, USPO, W BP
36	NC 16, Brookshire Blvd, E Brookshire Inn, repair, W Hari/dsl, RaceWay, Shell/dsl, Sunoco, Burger King, Jack-in-the-Box, Kennedy Chicken/Pizza, La Unica Mexican, Subway, Family$, Griffin Tire
35	Glenwood Dr, E Knights Inn, W Shell/dsl
34	NC 27, Freedom Dr, E Shell, Walkers, Beauregard's Rest, Bojangles, Capt D's, Cookout, KFC, McDonald's, Mr C's Rest, Pizza Hut, Showmar's, Subway, Taco Bell, Wendy's, Advance Parts, Aldi Foods, AutoZone, $Tree, Family$, Goodyear, K-Mart, Rite Aid, Save-A-Lot Foods, Walgreens, Urgent Care, vet, W Charlotte Express, JiffyLube
33	US 521, Billy Graham Pkwy, E Shell, Bojangles, KFC/Taco Bell, McDonald's, Wendy's, Comfort Suites, Days Inn, Royal Inn, Sheraton, SpringHill Suites, , W Exxon/dsl, Cracker Barrel, Ichiban, Waffle House, Best Value Inn, EconoLodge, La Quinta, Microtel, Motel 6, Quality Inn, Red Roof Inn
32	Little Rock Rd, E Shell/dsl, Inn, Courtyard, Hampton Inn, Holiday Inn, W Citgo, Exxon/dsl, Shell/dsl, Arby's, Hardee's, Showmar's Rest., Shoney's, Subway, Country Inn&Suites, Ramada Inn, Wingate Inn, Family$, Food Lion, Griffin Tire, Rite Aid
30	I-485, to 1-77, Pineville
29	Sam Wilson Rd, E BP (1mi), camping, W Shell/dsl
28mm	weigh sta both lanes
27.5mm	Catawba River
27	NC 273, Mt Holly, E Exxon/Dunkin Donuts/dsl, Murphy USA/dsl, Chick-fil-A, KFC, Pizza Hut, Sake Japanese, Subway, Taco Bell, Waffle House, Wendy's, CVS Drug, Family$, Firestone, Food Lion, Lowe's, NAPA, Rite Aid, Walgreens, Walmart/Subway, W Citgo/dsl, Holiday Inn Express
26	NC 7, E BP, Marathon/dsl, Bojangles, Hardee's, King Buffet, McDonald's, New China, Papa John's, Hampton Inn, Advance Parts, Aldi Foods, BiLo, Curves, Ford, Verizon, W Belmont Abbey Coll
24mm	South Fork River
23	NC 7, McAdenville, W Exxon/dsl, Shell/Subway, Hardee's, Hillbilly's BBQ/Steaks
22	Cramerton, Lowell, E Hess, Marathon, Applebee's,

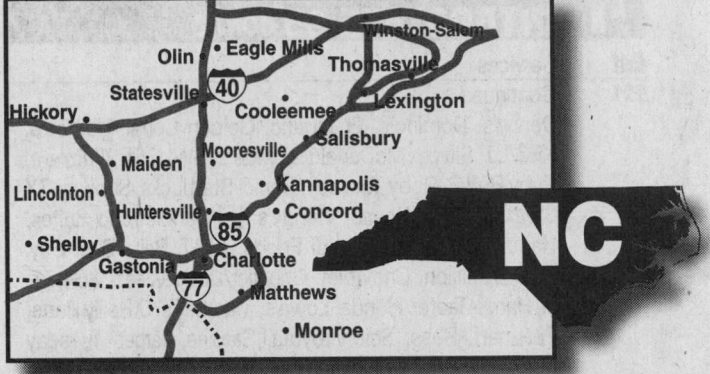

↑N INTERSTATE 85 CONT'D

Exit	Services
22	Continued
	Burger King, Chick-fil-A, Gator's Rest., Hooters, Jack-in-the-Box, Jersey Mike's Subs, Moe's SW Grill, Portofino's, Saurka Japanese, Schlotzsky's, Thai House, Zaxby's, 🅞 Books-A-Million, Buick/Cadillac/Chevrolet/GMC, Honda, Kia, K-Mart, Kohl's, Lowe's, Old Navy, Petsmart, Sam's Club/gas, U-Haul
21	Cox Rd, E 🅖 Marathon, 🍴 Akropolis Cafe, Buffalo Wild Wings, Chili's, ChuckeCheese, Cookout, Dynasty Buffet, Golden Corral, Krispy Kreme, La Fuente, Logan's Roadhouse, Longhorn Steaks, McAlister's Deli, McDonald's, Olive Garden, On-the-Border, Panera Bread, Peking Garden, Ruby Tuesday, Qdoba, Quiznos, Ryan's, Ruby Tuesday, Steak'n Shake, 🅞 AAA, AT&T, Best Buy, Chrysler/Dodge/Jeep, Dick's, Discount Tire, $Tree, Ford/Subaru, GNC, Harris-Teeter, Home Depot, Office Depot, Mary Jo's Cloth, Michael's, Nissan, O'Reilly Parts, PepBoys, Ross, Target, Tire Kingdom, TJ Maxx, Verizon, Walgreens, Walmart/Subway, vet, W 🅖 Marathon, 🍴 Arby's, Brixx Pizza, IHOP, 🛏 Super 8, 🅞 🅗, $General, Medical Ctr Drug
20	NC 279, New Hope Rd, E 🅖 World Gas, 🍴 Capt D's, McDonald's, O'Charley's, Pizza Hut, Red Lobster, Sake Japanese, Showmar's Rest, Taco Bell, Wendy's, 🛏 Knights Inn, 🅞 Advance Parts, AutoZone, Belk, Dillard's, Family$, Firestone, Hobby Lobby, JC Penney, Office Depot, Sears/auto, Target, Tuesday Morning, W 🍴 Bojangles, Cracker Barrel, KFC, Outback Steaks, TX Roadhouse, Waffle House, 🛏 Best Western, Comfort Suites, Courtyard, Fairfield Inn, Hampton Inn, 🅞 🅗, CarMax
19	NC 7, E Gastonia, E 🅖 Shell
17	US 321, Gastonia, E 🅖 Citgo/dsl/LP, 🍴 Los Arcos Mexican, 🛏 Days Inn, ValuePlace, 🅞 Family$, W 🅖 Marathon/dsl, 🍴 Hardee's, 🛏 Holiday Inn Express, Motel 6, Red Carpet Inn
14	NC 274, E Bessemer, W 🅖 BP/Subway, Citgo/dsl, 🍴 Bojangles, Waffle House, 🛏 Express Inn
13	Edgewood Rd, Bessemer City, E to Crowders Mtn SP, W 🅖 Exxon/dsl, 🛏 Best Inn
10b a	US 74 W, US 29, Kings Mtn
8	NC 161, to Kings Mtn, E 🛏 Holiday Inn Express, 🅞 camping, W 🅖 BP, 🍴 Big E BBQ, McDonald's, Subway, Taco Bell, Waffle House, Wendy's, 🛏 Quality Inn, 🅞🅗
5	Dixon School Rd, E 🅖 Citgo/Subway/dsl/24hr, 🅞 truck/tire repair
4	US 29 S (from sb)
2.5mm	Welcome Ctr nb, full 🚻 facilities, info, 🅲, vending, 🏞, litter barrels, petwalk
2	NC 216, Kings Mtn, E to Kings Mtn Nat Military Park
0mm	North Carolina/South Carolina state line

↑N INTERSTATE 95

Exit	Services
181mm	North Carolina/Virginia state line, **Welcome Ctr sb, full** 🚻 **facilities,** 🅲, 🏞, **litter barrels, vending, petwalk**
180	NC 48, to Gaston, to Lake Gaston, Pleasant Hill, W 🅖 ⬛/Subway/dsl/scales/24hr
176	NC 46, to Garysburg, W 🅖 Shell, 🍴 Burger King, 🛏 Super 8

ROANOKE RAPIDS

Exit	Services
174mm	Roanoke River
173	US 158, Roanoke Rapids, Weldon, E 🅖 BP/dsl, Shell/dsl, 🍴 Frazier's Rest., Ralph's BBQ, Waffle House, 🛏 Days Inn, Orchard Inn, 🅞 🅗, W 🅖 BP/dsl, Exxon/DQ/Stuckey's, Murphy USA/dsl, Shell, 🍴 Applebee's, Arby's, Burger King, Chick-fil-A, Cookout, Cracker Barrel, Hardee's, Ichiban, KFC, Little Caesar's, Logan's Roadhouse, Mayflower Seafood, McDonald's, New China, Pizza Hut, Ruby Tuesday, Ryan's, Starbucks, Subway, Taco Bell, TX Steaks, Waffle House, Wendy's, 🛏 Comfort Suites, Hampton Inn, Jameson Inn, Motel 6, Quality Inn, Sleep Inn, 🅞 Urgent Care, Advance Parts, AutoZone, Belk, BigLots, Buick/GMC, $General, $Tree, Firestone/auto, Food Lion, GNC, Harley-Davidson, Lowe's, O'Reilly Parts, Radio Shack, Rite Aid, Save a Lot Foods, Staples, Toyota, Verizon, Walgreens, Walmart
171	NC 125, Roanoke Rapids, E 🛏 Hilton Garden, 🅞 Carolina Crossroads RV Resort, Roanoke Rapids Theater, W 🅖 Shell/dsl, 🛏 Holiday Inn Express, 🅞 st patrol
168	NC 903, to Halifax, E 🅖 Exxon/Subway/dsl, Shell/Burger King/dsl, W 🅖 Oasis/Dunkin Donuts/LP/dsl
160	NC 561, to Brinkleyville, E 🅖 Exxon, W 🅖 Shell/dsl
154	NC 481, to Enfield, 1 mi W 🅞 KOA
151mm	weigh sta both lanes
150	NC 33, to Whitakers, E golf, W 🅖 BP/Subway/DQ/Stuckey's/dsl
145	NC 4, to US 301, Battleboro, E 🅖 BP/dsl, Exxon/DQ/Marathon/dsl, Shell, 🍴 Denny's, Hardee's, Shoney's, Waffle House, 🛏 Ashburn Inn, Best Value Inn, Best Western, Comfort Inn, Days Inn, Deluxe Inn, Gold Rock Inn, Howard Johnson, Quality Inn, Red Carpet Inn
142mm	🆁🆂 both lanes, full 🚻 facilities, 🅲, 🏞, litter barrels, vending, petwalk
141	NC 43, Red Oak, E 🅖 BP/dsl, Exxon/dsl/LP, 🅞 $General, Smith's Foods, W 🛏 Red Carpet Inn
138	US 64, 1 mi E on Winstead 🅖 Hess/dsl, 🍴 Bicuitville, Bojangles, Cracker Barrel, Gardner's BBQ, Hardee's, Highway Diner, KFC, Outback Steaks, TX Steaks, 🛏 Candlewood Suites, Comfort Inn, Country Inn&Suites, Courtyard, Doubletree, Hampton Inn, Holiday Inn, Residence Inn, 🅞 🅗, Buick/GMC, Harley-Davidson, Honda, to Cape Hatteras Nat Seashore
132	to NC 58, E 🅖 Pitstop/dsl, 1 mi W 🅖 BP/dsl
128mm	Tar River
127	NC 97, to Stanhope, E 🅞 🍴
121	US 264a, Wilson, 0-4 mi E 🅖 BP, Citgo/Subway/dsl, Exxon, Hess/dsl, Kangaroo/dsl/LP, Marathon, Murphy USA/dsl, Shell, 🍴 Applebee's, Arby's, Buffalo Wild Wings, Burger King, Chick-fil-A, Chili's, CiCi's Pizza, Cookout,

⬆N INTERSTATE 95 CONT'D

WILSON / KENLY / SMITHFIELD

Exit	Services
121	Continued Denny's, Domino's, El Tapatio, Golden Corral, Hardee's, KFC/LJ Silver, McDonald's, Moe's SW Grill, Quizno's, Ruby Buffet, Ruby Tuesday, Sonic, Starbucks, Subway, TX Steaks, Waffle House, Wendy's, 🅛 Candlewood Suites, Hampton Inn, 🅞 🏥, Aldi Foods, AT&T, Belk, Best Buy, BooksAMillion, Chevrolet, Chrysler/Dodge/Jeep, $General, Harris-Teeter, Honda, Lowe's, Marshall's, O'Reilly Parts, Petsmart, Ross, Scion/Toyota, Staples, Target, Tuesday Morning, Verizon, Walmart, White's Tires, **W** 🅖 BP/dsl, 🍴 Bojangles, Burger King, Cracker Barrel, McDonald's, Pino's Pizza, 🅛 Comfort Suites, Country Inn&Suites, Fairfield Inn, Hampton Inn, Holiday Inn Express, Jameson Inn, Microtel, Sleep Inn, 🅞 to Country Dr Museum
119 b a	US 264, US 117
116	NC 42, to Clayton, Wilson, **E** 🅖 Shell/dsl, 🅞 🏥, **W** 🅖 BP/dsl, 🅞 Rock Ridge Camping
107	US 301, Kenly, **E** 🅖 BP/dsl, Exxon/McDonald's/dsl, Fuel Doc, PitStop, 🍴 Andy's Cafe, Golden China, Nik's Pizza, Norman's BBQ, Subway, 🅛 Budget Inn, Deluxe Inn, Quality Inn, 🅞 CarQuest, $General, Food Lion, Ford, Family$, Piggly Wiggly, Tobacco Museum
106	Truck Stop Rd, Kenly, **E** 🅖 ✈FLYING J/Denny's/dsl/LP/scales/24hr, **W** 🅖 Petro/Subway/Wendy's/dsl/scales/24hr/@, Wilco/Hess/Arby's/dsl/scales/24hr, 🍴 Waffle House, 🅛 Days Inn, EconoLodge, 🅞 Blue Beacon, Speedco Lube, Truck-o-Mat
105.5mm	Little River
105	Bagley Rd, Kenly, **E** 🅖 Big Boys/Shell/105 Pizza/dsl/scales/24hr, 🍴 Lowell Mill Rest.
102	Micro, **W** 🅖 Shop'N-Go, 🍴 Backdoor Cafe, 🅞 $General, city park, USPO
101	Pittman Rd
99mm	🆁🆂 both lanes, full ♿ facilities, vending, 🔌, 🚻, litter barrels, petwalk, hist marker
98	to Selma, **E** 🅞 RVacation
97	US 70 A, to Pine Level, Selma, **E** 🅖 Kings/dsl/24hr, Mobil/dsl, 🍴 Denny's, 🅛 Days Inn, 🅞 J&R Outlet, **W** 🅖 BP/dsl, Exxon/dsl/24hr, Shell/dsl, 🍴 Bojangles, Cookout, Golden China, KFC, McDonald's, Shoney's, Waffle House, 🅛 Hampton Inn, Masters Inn, Quality Inn, Regency Inn, Royal Inn, 🅞 🏥
95	US 70, Smithfield, **E** 🅛 Best Value Inn, Log Cabin Motel/rest., Village Motel, 🅞 Ava Gardner Museum, **W** 🅖 Hess/dsl, Sunoco, 🍴 Bob Evans, Burger King, Checker's, CiCi's Pizza, Coldstone, Cracker Barrel, Golden Corral, El Sombrero Mexican, Outback Steaks, Ruby Tuesday, Smithfield BBQ (2mi), Subway, TX Steaks, Waffle House, Zaxby's, 🅛 Best Western, Comfort Inn, Jameson Inn, Sleep Inn, Super 8, 🅞 Harley-Davidson, Carolina Premium Outlets/famous brands
93	Brogden Rd, Smithfield, **W** 🅖 BP/dsl, Citgo
91.5mm	Neuse River
90	US 301, US 701, to Newton Grove, **E** 🅖 BP/dsl, Citgo/dsl, 🅛 Travelers Inn, 🅞 KOA, Ronnie's Tires, to Bentonville Bfd, **W** 🅖 Exxon/dsl, 🅛 Four Oaks Motel/RV Park
87	NC 96, Four Oaks, **W** 🅖 BP/dsl, 🍴 Subway
81 b a	I-40, E to Wilmington, W to Raleigh
79	NC 50, to NC 27, to NC 242, Benson, Newton Grove, **E**

DUNN / FAYETTEVILLE

Exit	Services
79	Continued 🅖 BP/dsl, Citgo, 🍴 Waffle House, 🅞 auto repair, **W** 🅖 Exxon/Burger King, Mule City/dsl, Pure, 🍴 China 8, Domino's, El Charro Mexican, KFC, McDonald's, Pizza Hut, Subway, 🅛 Days Inn, 🅞 Advance Parts, Family$, Food Lion, Kerr Drug, auto repair
78 mm	Neuse River
77	Hodges Chapel Rd, **E** 🅖 Loves/Subway/dsl/scales/RV dump/24hr
75	Jonesboro Rd, **W** 🅖 Exxon/Milestone Diner, 🍴/Shell/DQ/Quiznos/dsl/scales/24hr/@
73	US 421, NC 55, to Dunn, Clinton, **E** 🍴 Cracker Barrel, Panda House Chinese, Wendy's, 🅞 Buick/Chevrolet, Chrysler/Dodge/Jeep, Family$, Food Lion, **W** 🅖 Exxon/dsl, Hess/dsl, Shell, 🍴 Bojangles, Burger King, Dairy Freeze, El Charro Mexican, Hot Dog&Hamburger Heavan, Sagebrush Steaks, Subway, Taco Bell, Triangle Waffle, 🅛 Baymont Inn, Hampton Inn, Holiday Inn Express, Quality Inn, Super 8, 🅞 IGA Foods, to Campbell U., museum
72	Pope Rd, **E** 🅖 Atex, 🅛 Comfort Inn, Royal Inn, **W** 🅖 BP, Pure/dsl, 🍴 Brass Lantern Steaks, 🅛 Valley Motor Inn, 🅞 Cadillac/GMC
71	Longbranch Rd, **E** 🅖 🍴/Kangaroo/Hardee's/dsl/scales/24hr, 🅞 dsl repair, **W** to Averasboro Bfd
70	SR 1811
65	NC 82, Godwin, **E** Falcon Children's Home, **W** 🅖 Epco/dsl
61	to Wade, **E** 🅖 61 Trkstp/dsl, 🅞 KOA (1mi), **W** 🅖 Exxon/dsl/24hr
58	US 13, to Newton Grove, I-295 to Fayetteville, **E** 🅖 Eastgate, Shell, 🍴 Quiznos, Waffle House, 🅛 Days Inn
56	Lp 95, to US 301 (from sb), Fayetteville, **W** 🅖 Epco/dsl, Kangaroo/24hr, 🅛 Easterner Inn, 🅞 🏥, to Ft Bragg, Pope AFB
55	NC 1832, Murphy Rd, **W** 🅖 Epco/dsl, Kangaroo/24hr, 🅛 Easterner Inn
52	NC 24, Fayetteville, **W** 🅞 to Ft Bragg, Pope AFB, botanical gardens, museum
49	NC 53, NC 210, Fayetteville, **E** 🅖 BP, Exxon, Kangaroo/dsl, Marathon, 🍴 Burger King, McDonald's, Pizza Hut, Taco Bell, Waffle House, 🅛 Days Inn, Deluxe Inn, Motel 6, Travelers Inn, **W** 🅖 BP/Subway/dsl, Exxon/dsl, Shell/dsl, 🍴 Cracker Barrel, Ruby Tuesday, Shoney's, 🅛 Comfort Inn, Country Hearth Inn, Doubletree, EconoLodge, Fairfield Inn, Hampton Inn, Holiday Inn, Quality Inn, Red Roof Inn, Sleep Inn, Super 8
48mm	🆁🆂 both lanes, full ♿ facilities, 🔌, 🚻, litter barrels, vending, petwalk
47mm	Cape Fear River
46 b a	NC 87, to Fayetteville, Elizabethtown, **W** 🅞 🏥, museum, Civic Ctr, to Agr Expo Ctr
44	Claude Lee Rd, **W** 🅞 Lazy Acres Camping, to 🐾
41	NC 59, to Hope Mills, Parkton, **E** 🅖 Kangaroo/24hr, **W** 🅖 BP/dsl, 🅞 Lake Waldo's Camping, Spring Valley RV Park
40	Lp 95, to US 301 (from nb), to Fayetteville, Services on US 301 (5-7mi)
33	US 301, St Pauls, **E** 🅖 BP/dsl/repair/24hr
31	NC 20, to St Pauls, Raeford, **E** 🅖 BP, Marathon/Huddle House/Quiznos/dsl, Mobil/McDonald's, Pit Row, 🍴 Burger King, Hardee's, 🅛 Days Inn, 🅞 Volvo Trucks, **W** 🅖 Exxon/dsl, Sunoco, 🍴 Taco Bell, 🅞 Food Lion
25	US 301, **E** 🅖 BP/dsl

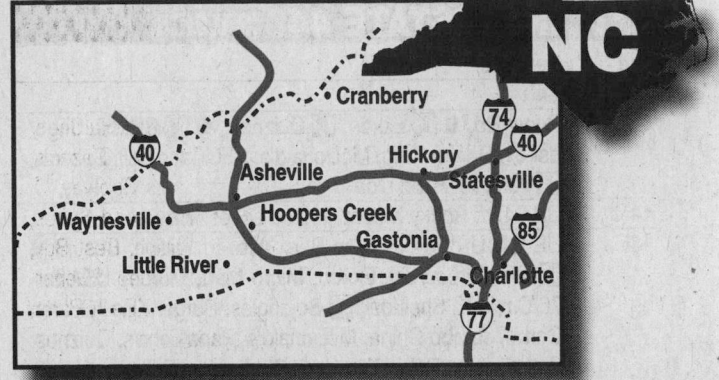

⬆N INTERSTATE 95 CONT'D

Exit	Services
24mm	**weigh sta both lanes**
22	US 301, **E** 🅖 Exxon, Marathon, Shell/DQ, 🍴 Burger King, China Wok, DQ, Denny's, Friendly's, Golden Corral, Hardee's, Huddle House, Outback Steaks, Papa John's, Pizza Hut, Quiznos, Ruby Tuesday, Shogun, Smithfield BBQ, Subway, TX Steaks, Waffle House, Wendy's, Zaxby's, 🛏 Best Western, Comfort Suites, Hampton Inn, Holiday Inn, Redwood Inn, Super 8, 🅞 Urgent Care, Chrysler/Dodge/ Jeep, $Tree, Goodyear, Honda, Lowe's Foods, Lowe's, Office Depot, Toyota, Verizon, Walmart, st patrol, **W** 🅖 Quality, Sun-Do/dsl, Sunoco/dsl, 🍴 Bojangles, Uncle George's Rest., 🅞 Ford/Lincoln, Sam's Club/gas
20	NC 211, to NC 41, Lumberton, **E** 🅖 Citgo, Exxon/dsl, Liberty/dsl, 🍴 Arby's, Bojangles, Buger King, Capt D's, CiCi's Pizza, Cook Out, Del Sol Mexican, Golden City Chinese, Hardee's, Hong Kong Chinese, Kami Japanese, KFC, Little Caesar's, McDonald's, Pizza Inn, Shoney's, Sonic, Subway, Taco Bell, Tokyo Japanese, 2 Guys Grille, Village Sta. Rest., Waffle House, 🛏 Deluxe Inn, Howard Johnson, Ramada Inn, 🅞 🅷, Advance Parts, AutoZone, Belk, CVS Drug, Food Lion/deli, JC Penney, K-Mart, Nissan, O'Reilly Parts, Walgreens, city park, **W** 🅖 Marathon, Sun-do/dsl, 🍴 Cracker Barrel, Fuller's BBQ Buffet, San Jose Mexican, 🛏 Best Value Inn, Comfort Inn, Country Inn&Suites, Days Inn/rest., Fairfield Inn, Quality Inn
19	Carthage Rd, Lumberton, **E** 🅖 BP/dsl, 🛏 Travelers Inn, **W** 🅖 Exxon/dsl, 🛏 Knights Inn, Motel 6
18mm	Lumber River
17	NC 72, Lumberton, Pembroke, **E** 🅖 Atkinson's/dsl, BP/ dsl, Dobb's/Stuckey's/Wendy's, Go-Gas/dsl, Mobil/dsl, 🍴 Burger King, Hardee's, Huddle House, McDonald's, Ruby Tuesday, Subway, Waffle House, 🛏 Atkinson Inn, Budget Inn, Economy Inn, Southern Inn, 🅞 Advance Parts, AutoZone, CVS Drug, Food Lion, $General, Family$, **W** 🅞 Sleepy Bear's RV Park (3mi)
13	I-74, US 74, Rockingham, Wilmington, **E** 🅞 U.S.S. Wilmington, SE NC Beaches
10	US 301, to Fairmont
7	to McDonald, Raynham
5mm	**Welcome Ctr nb, full ♿ facilities, 🍴 🛏, litter barrels, vending, petwalk**
2	NC 130, to NC 904, Rowland
1b a	US 301, US 501, Dillon, **E** 🅖 Exxon, Mobil, 🍴 Hot Tamale Rest., Peddler Steaks, Pedro's Diner, Porky's Truckstp, 🛏 Budget Motel, South-of-the-Border Motel, 🅞 Pedro's Campground, **W** 🅖 Shell/dsl, 🍴 Waffle House, 🛏 Knights Inn, Super 8
0mm	North Carolina/South Carolina state line

⬆E INTERSTATE 240 (ASHEVILLE)

Exit	Services
9mm	**I-240 begins/ends on I-40, exit 53b a.**
8	Fairview Rd, **N** 🅖 Shell/dsl, 🍴 Burger King, Cheddar's, China Buffet, J&S Cafeteria, KFC, La Posada Mexican, Little Caesar's, Little Venice, McDonald's, Subway, 🛏 Ramada Inn, 🅞 Advance Parts, Aldi Foods, Bi-Lo Foods, CVS Drug, $General, Hamrick's, Hancock Fabrics, Kohl's, Petsmart, U-Haul, Walmart, **S** 🅖 Citgo, 🍴 Pizza Hut, 🅞 Home Depot

Exit	Services
7.5mm	Swannanoa River
7	US 70, **N** 🛏 Best Western, 🅞 KIA, Subaru, Suzuki, **S** 🅖 Shell/dsl, 🍴 Applebee's, Bonefish Grill, Buffalo Wild Wings, Burger King, Cancun Mexican, Chick-fil-A, Chili's, China Palace, ChuckeCheese, Cici's Pizza, Cook Out, Cornerstone Rest., Cracker Barrel, DQ, East Buffet, Firehouse Subs, Guadalajara Mexican, Hooters, IHOP, Longhorn Steaks, McAlister's Deli, McDonald's, Mikado, Mike's Subs, Mountaineer Inn, O'Charley's, Olive Garden, Outback Steaks, Red Lobster, Subway, Taco Bell, Waffle House, 🛏 Country Inn&Suites, Courtyard, Days Inn, EconoLodge, Hampton Inn, Holiday Inn, Homewood Suites, InTown Motor Inn, SpringHill Suites, Super 8, 🅞 Barnes&Noble, Belk, Best Buy, BigLots, Books-A-Million, Dick's, Dillards, $General, $Tree, Ingles Foods/gas, JC Penney, K-Mart, Lowe's, Michael's, Mtn View Tire, Office Depot, Old Navy, Radio Shack, Ross, Sears/auto, Target, TJ Maxx, Tuesday Morning, Verizon, Walgreens
6	Tunnel Rd (from eb) same as 7
5b	US 70 E, US 74A, Charlotte St, **N** 🅖 BP, Pure, 🍴 Charlotte St. Grill, Fuddruckers, Starbucks, Two Guys Hogi, 🛏 B&B, 🅞 vet, **S** 🍴 Chop House Rest., Tripp's Rest., 🛏 Renaissance Hotel, Sheraton, 🅞 Civic Ctr
5a	US 25, Merrimon Ave, **N** 🅖 Exxon/dsl, Shell/dsl, 🍴 Bojangles, La Carreta, 🅞 Green Life Foods, Staples
4c	Haywood St (no EZ return to eb), Montford, **S** 🍴 3 Bros Rest., 🛏 B&B
4b	Patton Ave (from eb), downtown
4a	US 19 N, US 23 N, US 70 W, to Weaverville
3b	Westgate, **N** 🍴 Jason's Deli, Oriental Pavillion, Tomato Latina, 🛏 Crowne Plaza, 🅞 CVS Drug, EarthFare Foods, NTB, Sam's Club/gas
3a	US 19 S, US 23 S, W Asheville, **N** 🅖 BP, 🍴 A&W/LJ Silver, Arby's, Bojangles, Burger King, Denny's, Green Tea Japanese, KFC, Krispy Kreme, Little Caesar's, McDonald's, New 1 China, Nona Mia Italian, Pizza Hut, Ryan's, Sonic, Subway, Taco Bell, Vera Cruz Mexican, Wendy's, Yoshida Japanese, 🅞 Advance Parts, Aldi Foods, AutoZone, Buick/Cadillac/GMC, Curves, $General, Family$, Ingles Foods, Kerr Drug, K-Mart, Mtn View Tire, Radio Shack, Sav-Mor Foods, vet
2	US 19, US 23, W Asheville, **N** 🅞 B&B Drug, **S** 🅖 Haywood Quickstop/dsl
1c	Amboy Rd (from eb)
1b	NC 191, to I-40 E, Brevard Rd, **S** 🅞 farmers mkt, camping
1a	I-40 W, to Knoxville
0mm	**I-240 begins/ends on I-40, exit 46b a.**

🔼E INTERSTATE 440 (RALEIGH)

Exit	Services
16	I-40
15	Poole Rd, E 🅖 Exxon, 🅕 Quiznos, W 🅖 BP/dsl, Citgo/dsl, 🅕 Burger King, McDonald's, KFC/Taco Bell, Subway, 🅕 Family$, Food Lion
14	US 64, to Rocky Mount, limited access hwy
13b a	US 64, US 264 E, New Bern Ave, to Wilson, 0-2 mi E 🅖 BP, Caroco/dsl, Exxon, Micro Mart, Murphy USA/dsl, 76/Circle K, Shell/dsl, 🅕 Bojangles, Burger King, Golden Corral, Jumbo China, McDonald's, Papa John's, Quiznos, Roh Buffet, Ruby Tuesday, Starbucks, Subway, Waffle House, Wendy's, 🅛 Best Western, Comfort Suites, Holiday Inn Express, Microtel, Super 8, 🅞 Advance Parts, AutoZone, CVS Drug, Firestone/auto, Food Lion, Kroger, Office Depot, O'Reilly Parts, RV Ctr, U-Haul, Walgreens, Walmart, W 🅗
12	Yonkers Rd, Brentwood Rd
11b a	US 1, US 401, Capital Blvd N, N 🅖 BP, Citgo, Exxon, Kangaroo/dsl, Mobil, Shell, 🅕 Baskin-Robbins/Dunkin Donuts, Buffalo Bro's, Burger King, ChuckeCheese, Cici's, Cookout, IHOP, Mayflower Seafood, McDonald's, Outback Steaks, Perkins, Taco Bell, Vallerta Mexican, Waffle House, 🅛 Best Western, Days Inn, EconoLodge, Holiday Inn, Lodge America, Quality Inn, Sleep Inn, Super 8, Wingate Inn, 🅞 Aamco, AutoZone, Food Lion, Pepboys, Rite Aid, Walgreens, U-Haul
10	Wake Forest Rd, N 🅕 Bahama Breeze, Denny's, 🅛 Days Inn, Hilton, Homestead Suites, Hyatt Place, 🅞 🅗, CVS Drug, S 🅖 BP, 🅕 Applebee's, Arby's, Biscuitville, Burger King, Courtney's Cafe, Jersey Mike's, Jimmy John's, Jumbo China, KFC/Taco Bell, McDonald's, Melting Pot Rest., Papa John's, Pizza Hut, Qdoba, Quiznos, Subway, 🅛 Courtyard, Extended Stay America, Hampton Inn, Studio+, 🅞 Advance Parts, AutoZone, Buick/GMC, Costco/gas, Curves, Discount Tire, Hancock Fabrics, Hyundai, Mazda, Nissan, Staples, Subaru, Trader Joe's, VW
8b a	6 Forks Rd, North Hills, N 🅖 Exxon/repair, 🅕 Bonefish Grill, Chick-fil-A, Firebirds Grill, 5 Guys Burgers, Fox&Hound Grille, Moe's SW Grill, Panera Bread, Pig Shack, Ruths Chris Steaks, Starbucks, Tiola Pizza, Zoe's Kitchen, 🅛 Renaissance, 🅞 AT&T, GNC, Harris Teeter, JC Penney, Kerr Drug, Target
7b a	US 70, NC 50, Glenwood Ave, Crabtree Valley, N 🅖 BP, Shell, 🅕 Brio Grill, Cheesecake Factory, Fleming's, McDonald's, PF Chang's, 🅛 Crabtree Inn, Embassy Suites, Holiday Inn, Marriott, Residence Inn, Windsor Inn, 🅞 Barnes&Noble, Belk, Best Buy, Macy's, McCormick&Shmicks, Just Tires, Old Navy, Sears/auto, mall
6	Ridge Rd (from nb), same as 7
5	Lake Boone Tr, W 🅖 Circle K, 🅕 McDonald's, Starbucks, Subway, Wendy's, 🅞 🅗, Food Lion, Tuesday Morning
4b a	to I-40 W, Wade Ave, W to I-40, RDU 🛬
3	NC 54, Hillsboro St, E 🅖 BP, Exxon, Hugo's, Pure, 🅕 Applebee's, Arby's, Bean Sprout Chinese, Burger King, Marco's Pizza, Quiznos, Snoopy's Hotdogs, Subway, Waffle House, Zaxby's, 🅞 USPO, to Meredith Coll, to St Mary's
2b a	Western Blvd, E 🅖 Hess, Hugo's, 76/Circle K, 🅕 Bojangles, Cookout, Dunkin Donuts, Greek Fiesta, McDonalds,

Exit	Services
2b a	Continued Pizza Hut, Subway, Taco Bell, Ten Ten Chinese, Wendy's, 🅞 Advance Parts, BigLots, Food Lion, to NCSU, Shaw U, W 🅞 K-Mart
1d	Melbourne Rd (from sb)
1c	Jones-Franklin Rd
1b a	I-40. **I-440 begins on I-40. 1-2 mi** W **on Walnut St** 🅖 Exxon, Shell, 🅕 Astor's Grill, Bob Evans, Chick-fil-A, China King, Coldstone, Cookout, Golden Corral, Dickey's BBQ, HoneyBaked Ham, Jasmin Bistro, McDonald's, Moe's SW Grill, Noodles&Co, Olive Garden, Panera Bread, Qdoba, Red Lobster, Red Robin, Remington Grill, Ruby Tuesday, Starbucks, Subway, Taco Bell, Waffle House, 🅛 Best Western, Red Roof Inn, 🅞 BJ's Whse, Ford, GNC, Home Depot, Jo-Ann Fabrics, Kohl's, Lowe's, Marshall's, Michael's, NTB, Office Depot, Old Navy, PetsMart, Steinmart, mall

🔼N INTERSTATE 485 (CHARLOTTE)

Exit	Services
61	US 251, Johnston Rd, N 🅕 Eddie's Place Rest, Global Rest, Hickory Tavern, Quizno's, Red Robin, Ruby Tuesday, Sticky Fingers, 🅛 SpringHill Suites, 🅞 Earth Fare Foods, S 🅖 Texaco/dsl, 🅕 Buffalo's SW Cafe, 5 Guys Burgers, Flat Rock Grille, Moe's SW Grill, Smoothie King, Tony's Pizza, 🅛 Ballantyne Hotel, Courtyard, Staybridge Suites, 🅞 CVS Drug
64b a	Rd 51, N 🅖 Exxon, Shell/Circle K, 🅕 Bojangles, Donato's Pizza, KFC/Pizza Hut, McDonald's, Pier 57 Seafood, Wendy's, 🅛 Extended Stay America, Extended Stay Deluxe, 🅞 🅗, Bi-Lo, Firestone/auto, S 🅖 Shell, 🅕 Applebee's, Buca Italian, Burger King, China Buffet, IHOP, Jason's Deli, Red Lobster, Subway, Taco Bell, Tony Roma's, 🅛 Holiday Inn Express, Quality Inn, 🅞 Belk, Dillard's, $General, Food Lion, Home Depot, JC Penney, K-Mart, Office Depot, Petsmart, Rite Aid, Sear/auto, SteinMart, TJ Maxx
65	South Blvd, N 🅖 Texaco, 🅕 Chick-fil-A, Golden Corral, Hooters, McDonald's, Rafferty's, Sonny's BBQ, Steak'n Shake, TX Roadhouse, Wendy's, 🅞 Advance Parts, Chevrolet, Discount Tire, $Tree, Kohl's, Nissan, Old Navy, PetCo, Ross, Target, VW, World Mkt, S 🅞 Cadillac, CarMax, Pineville Tires, vet
67	I-77, US 21, to Charlotte, Columbia, **I-485 begins/ends**
61b a	US 521 S, Johnston Rd, E 🅖 Exxon, 🅕 Applebee's, Chick-fil-A, China Bistro, 1511 Cantina, JoJo China Bistro, Firebird's Grill, Marble Slab, Miro Spanish Grill, Noodles Rest, Pizza Inn, Starbucks, Wendy's, 🅛 Residence Inn, 🅞 GNC, Goodyear/auto, Harris-Teeter, Radio Shack, Target, vet
59	Rea Rd
57	Providence Rd, Rd 16, E 🅖 Texaco/Wendy's, 🅕 Hickory Tavern, Penn Sta, The Wok, 🅞 Curves, Harris-Teeter, USPO, W 🅖 Exxon, Shell, 🅕 BBQ Shack, Cold Stone, Macaroni Grill, Red Bowl Rest, Starbucks, 🅞 CVS Drug, Home Depot, Lowes Foods, Rite Aid, Staples, SteinMart, vet
52	to Matthews
51b a	US 74, to Charlotte, Monroe, E 🅖 76/Circle K/dsl, Shell, Sunoco/dsl, 🅛 Country Inn&Suites, Holiday Inn Express, InTown Suites, 🅞 Country Camping RV Ctr, Scion/Toyota, W 🅖 Exxon, Shell, 🅕 Bojangles, Pizza Hut, Taco Bell, Wendy's, 🅛 Courtyard, EconoLodge, Microtel, other: 🅗,

NC

CHARLOTTE

C H A R L O T T E

↑N INTERSTATE 485 (CHARLOTTE) CONT"D

Exit	Services
51b a	Continued
	Aamco, AutoZone, Firestone/auto, Goodyear/auto, Radio Shack, Tuesday Morning
49	Idlewild Rd, **E** 🅖 Exxon/dsl, 🍴 China Cafe, El Maguey Mexican, Mama's Pizza, 🅾 Lowe's Foods, Rite Aid
47	Lawyers Rd, **E** 🅖 Gate, 🍴 Aladdin's, Bellacino's Pizza, Best China, Domino's, McDonald's, 🅾 CVS Drug, Harris-Teeter, vet, **2 mi W** 🍴 Dunkin Donuts, Wendy's
44	Rd 218, to Mint Hill, **W** 🅖 BP/dsl
43	Rd 51, to Mint Hill
41	Rd 24, Rd 27, to Albemarle, **2 mi W** 🍴 Chick-fil-A, Taco Bell
39	Harrisburg Rd, **W** 🅖 BP, 🍴 China Garden, Papa John's, Wendy's, 🅾 Food Lion
36	Rocky River Rd, **N** 🅖 Citgo/dsl, Gate, 🍴 Best China, Bojangles, Capriccio's Pizza, Subway, 🅾 CVS Drug, Discount Tire, Harris-Teeter, Tuffy Auto
33	Rd 49, to Harrisburg, **N** 🅖 Hess/dsl, 🍴 Cici's Pizza, 🅾 Food Lion, **S** 🅖 BP, Exxon, 76/Circle K, Sunoco, 🍴 Little Caesar's, Wendy's, 🅾 Family$
32	US 29, **N** 🅾 CVS Drug, **S** 🅖 Texaco, 🍴 Jack-in-the-Box, 🅾 🅷
23c	Rd 115, to Huntersville.
I-485 begins/ends on I-85	
23b a	I-77, to Charlotte, Statesville

21	Rd 24, Harris Blvd, **S** 🍴 Bravo Italian, Chick-fil-A, Chili's, Cold Stone, Edomae Grill, Firehouse Subs, 5 Guys Burgers, Fox&Hound, Mimi's Cafe, Moe's SW Grill, Olive Garden, On-the-Border, Panera bread, PF Chang's, Red Robin, Shane's Rib Shack, TGI Friday's, Wendy's, 🛏 Drury Inn, 🅾 AT&T, Belk, Best Buy, Dillard's, Lowe's Whse, Macy's, Old Navy, Petsmart, Target, mall
16	Rd 16, to Newton, Brookshire Blvd, **W** 🍴 Bojangles, Bull&Barrister Rest, Chick-fil-A, CiCi's Pizza, McDonald's, Pizza Hut, Red Bowl Asian, Subway, Wendy's 🅾 Harris-Teeter, Rite Aid, Walmart
14	Rd 27, to Mt Holly Rd, **W** 🅖 BP (2mi)
12	Moores Chapel Rd, **E** 🍴 Jin Jin Chinese, 🅾 Advance Parts, CVS Drug, Food Lion
10	I-85, to Spartanburg, Greensboro
9	US 29, US 74, Wilkinson Blvd, **S** 🅖 BP
4	Rd 160, to Fort Mill, **N** 🅖 Exxon/dsl, 🅾 CVS Drug
3	Arrowood Rd, **S** 🅖 Quizno's
1	S Tryon St, Rd 49, **N** 🅖 Exxon, Shell, Texaco, 🍴 Bojangles, Dragon Buffet, McDonald's, O'Charley's, Panera Bread, Qdoba, 🅾 Bi-Lo, Lowe's Whse, Walmart, **S** 🅖 Texaco/dsl, 🍴 Applebee's, Baskin-Robbins/Dunkin Donuts, Burger King, Domino's, Don Pedro Mexican, Firehouse Subs, Fortune Cookie, Hungry Howie's, McAlister's Deli, Moe's SW Grill, Pan China, Starbucks, Subway, Wild Wing Cafe, 🛏 Hilton Garden, Yorkshire Inn, 🅾 AT&T, AutoZone, Discount Tire, $Tree, Food Lion, NAPA, Office Depot, Tire Kingdom, Tuffy Auto

NORTH DAKOTA

G R A N D   F O R K S

↑N INTERSTATE 29

Exit	Services
218mm	North Dakota state line, US/Canada border
217mm	US Customs sb
216mm	historical site nb, tourist info sb
215	ND 59, rd 55, Pembina, **E** 🅖 Gastrak/DutyFree Store/dsl, Gastrak/pizza/dsl/scales/24hr, 🅾 Pembina State Museum/info
212	no services
208	rd 1, to Bathgate
203	US 81, ND 5, to Hamilton, Cavalier, **W** to Icelandic SP (25 mi), **weigh sta both lanes**
200	no services
196	rd 3, Bowesmont
193	no services
191	rd 11, to St Thomas
187	ND 66, to Drayton, **E** 🅖 Cenex/pizza/dsl/E-85, Tesoro/dsl, 🛏 Motel 66, 🅾 Drayton Drug, USPO, city park
184	to Drayton, **2 mi E** gas/dsl, USPO
180	rd 9
179mm	🆁🆂 both lanes (both lanes exit left), full ♿ facilities, 🚹, 🚮, litter barrels, vending, petwalk
176	ND 17, to Grafton, **10 mi W** 🅷, gas, food, 🛏 AmericInn
172	no services
168	rd 15, to Minto, Warsaw
164	no services
161	ND 54, rd 19, to Ardoch, Oslo
157	no services
152	US 81, to Gilby, Manvel, **W** 🅖 Manvel/dsl/food
145	US 81 bus, N Washington St, to Grand Forks
141	US 2, Gateway Dr, Grand Forks, **E** 🅖 Cenex, Loaf'N Jug/

141	Continued
	dsl, Univ. Sta/dsl, 🍴 Al's Grill, Burger King, Greatwall Buffet, McDonald's, Northside Cafe, Papa Murphy's, 🛏 Best Value Inn, Budget Inn, Clarion, EconoLodge, Howard Johnson, Ramada Inn, Select Inn, Super 8, 🅾 AT&T, Ford/Lincoln, Freightliner, O'Reilly Parts, transmissions, to U of ND, **1 mi E** 🍴 DQ, Little Caesars, Subway, Taco John's, 🅾 🅷, Hugo's Foods, Kia, Subaru, U-Haul, auto repair, **W** 🅖 Simonson/café/dsl/24hr, StaMart/Tesoro/dsl/RV dump/scales/24hr/@, 🍴 Perkins, 🛏 Settle Inn, 🅾 Budget RV Ctr, Mack/Volvo, NW Tire, 🔧 dsl repair, to AFB
140	DeMers Ave, **E** 🅖 Cenex, Loaf'N Jug, Valley Dairy, 🍴 Red Pepper Cafe, 🛏 Canada Inn, Hilton Garden, Sleep Inn, Staybridge Suites, 🅾 🅷, Alerus Ctr, to U of ND
138	US 81, 32nd Ave S, **E** 🅖 Cenex, Holiday/dsl, 🍴 Arby's, Buffalo Wild Wings, Burger King, China Garden, Cherry Berry Yogurt, Coldstone, Culver's, 5 Guys Burgers, Golden Corral, Ground Round, IHOP, Jimmy John's, McDonald's, Noodles&Co, Olive Garden, Papa Murphy's, Pizza Hut, Pizza Ranch, Qdoba Mexican, Quiznos, Red Lobster, Ruby Tuesday, Space Alien's Rest, Starbucks, Subway, TX Roadhouse, Village Inn, Wendy's, 🛏 C'mon Inn, Country Inn&Suites, Days Inn, Fairfield Inn, Holiday Inn Express, Lakeview Inn, Quality Inn, Roadking Inn, SpringHill Suites, 🅾 AT&T, Best Buy, Chrysler/Dodge/Jeep, CVS Drug, $Tree, Ford/Lincoln, Gordman's, Hugo's Foods, JC Penney, Jo-Ann Fabrics, Kohl's, Lowe's, Macy's, Menards, Michael's, Old Navy, PetCo, Sam's Club/gas, Super 1 Foods, Target, Tire 1, Tires+, TJ Maxx, Toyota/Scion, Verizon, Walmart/Subway, White Drug, vet, **W** 🅖 ⊘FLYING J/Subway/dsl/LP/scales/RV dump/24hr, 🅾 Grand Forks Camping

NC

ND

⬆N INTERSTATE 29 CONT'D

Exit	Services
130	ND 15, rd 81, Thompson, **1 mi W** gas, food
123	to Reynolds, **E** to Central Valley School
118	to Buxton
111	ND 200 W, to Cummings, Mayville, **W** 🅞 Big Top Fireworks, to Mayville St U
104	Hillsboro, **E** 🅡 Cenex/Burger King/dsl/LP/24hr, Tesoro/Stop-n-Go/dsl/24hr, 🍴 Country Hearth Rest., Pizza Ranch, Subway, 🛌 Hillsboro Inn, 🅞 🏩 RV park, USPO
100	ND 200 E, ND 200A, to Blanchard, Halstad
99mm	🆁🆂 **both lanes, full** ♿ **facilities,** 🚻, 🏬, **litter barrels, vending, petwalk**
92	rd 11, Grandin, **W** 🅡 Stop&Shop/dsl
86	Gardner
78	Argusville
74.5mm	Sheyenne River
72	rd 17, rd 22, Harwood, **E** 🅡 Cenex/pizza/dsl/LP/café/24hr
69	rd 20
67	US 81 bus, 19th Ave N, **1 mi E** 🍴 Applebee's, Buffalo Wild Wings, Burger King, McDonald's, Subway, Taco Bell, 🛌 Candlewood Suites, Days Inn, Homewood Suites, 🅞 VA 🏩, CVS Drug, Hector Int ✈
66	12th Ave N, **E** 🅡 StaMart/Tesoro/dsl/24hr/scales, Stop'n Go, 🅞 🏩, tuck wash, to ND St U, **W** 🅡 Cenex/dsl, 🍴 Arby's, 🛌 Super 8,
65	US 10, Main Ave, W Fargo, **E** 🅡 Tesoro/dsl, 🅞 NAPA, OK Tire, True Value, vet, **W** 🅡 Cenex/Subway/dsl, Simonson/dsl, 🍴 Hardee's, O'Kelly's Rest, Season Buffet Chinese, 🛌 Kelly Inn, 🅞 CarQuest, Honda, Lincoln, Mac's Hardware, Mazda, O'Reilly Parts, Recreation RV Ctr, Subaru, Toyota/Scion
64	13th Ave, Fargo, **E** 🅡 All-Stop, Don's, Kum&Go/dsl, PetroServe/dsl, 🍴 Acapulco Mexican, Applebee's, Arby's, Buck's Rest, Burger King, ChuckeCheese, DQ, Dickey's BBQ, Erbert&Gerbert's Subs, Giant Panda Chinese, GreenMill Rest., Ground Round, Hooters, Little Caesars, Perkins, Quiznos, Subway, Taco John's, Wendy's, 🛌 AmericInn, Best Western, Comfort Inn, Comfort Suites, Country Inn&Suites, Days Inn, EconoLodge, Grand Inn, Motel 6, Super 8, 🅞 AT&T, CashWise Foods/drug/gas, CVS Drug, Family$, Goodyear/auto, O'Reilly Parts, Tires+/transmissions, Tuesday Morning, White Drug, auto repair, **W** 🅡 All-Stop/dsl, Cenex, Tesoro, 🍴 Applebee's, Arby's, Buffalo Wild Wings, Chili's, Culver's, DQ, Denny's, Domino's, Happy Joe's Pizza, KFC, Kobe Japanese, Kroll's Diner, LoneStar Steaks, Longhorn Steaks, McDonald's, Olive Garden, Osaka Japanese, Panchero's Mexican, Paradiso Mexican, Pizza Hut, Red Lobster, Ruby Tuesday, Santa Lucia Cafe, Schlotzsky's, Spitfire Grill, Subway, Taco Bell, Taco John's, TX Roadhouse, TGIFriday's, 🛌 Days Inn, EconoLodge, Fairfield Inn, Fargo Inn, Holiday Inn, Holiday Inn Express, Kelly Inn, Ramada Inn, Red River Lodge, 🅞 Audi/VW, Barnes&Noble, Best Buy, BigLots, Cadillac/Chevrolet, Chrysler/Dodge/Jeep, $Tree, GNC, Gordman's, Herberger's, Hobby Lobby, Hornbacher's Foods, Hyundai, JC Penney, Jo-Ann Fabrics, Kohl's, Lowe's, Macy's, Menards, Michael's, Nissan, Office Depot, Old Navy, PetCo, Petsmart, Sam's Club/gas, Sears/auto, SunMart Foods, Target, TJ Maxx, Walmart/Subway, Walgreens, USPO
63b a	I-94, **W** to Bismarck, **E** to Minneapolis

Exit	Services
62	32nd Ave S, Fargo, **E** 🅡 F&F/dsl, Holiday, Tesoro, 🍴 Arby's, Country Kitchen, Culver's, Jimmy John's, KFC, Little Caesars, Moe's SW Grill, Papa John's, Quiznos, Starbucks, Subway, Taco John's, Village Inn, 🅞 🏩, Buick/GMC, Ford, Freightliner, JiffyLube, SunMart Foods, Verizon, **W** 🅡 ⛽FLYING J/dsl/LP/scales/24hr/@, 💚Loves/McDonald's/Subway/dsl/scales/24hr, 🛌 Motel 6, 🅞 Fargo Tire/repair, Peterbilt, Volvo
60	52nd Ave S, to Fargo, **W** 🅞 Walmart/Subway,
56	to Wild Rice, Horace
54	rd 16, to Oxbow, Davenport
50	rd 18, Hickson
48	ND 46, to Kindred
44	to Christine, **1 mi E** gas
42	rd 2, to Walcott
37	rd 4, to Abercrombie, Colfax, **E** to Ft Abercrombie HS, **3 mi W** gas
31	rd 8, Galchutt
26	to Dwight
24mm	**weigh sta both lanes exit left**
23b a	ND 13, to Wahpeton, Mooreton, **10 mi E** 🏩, ND St Coll of Science
15	rd 16, to Mantador, Great Bend
8	ND 11, to Hankinson, Fairmount, **E** 🅡 Tesoro/dsl, **3 mi W** camping
3mm	**Welcome Ctr nb, full** ♿ **facilities,** 🚻, 🏬, **litter barrels, petwalk**
2	rd 22
1	rd 1E, **E** Dakota Magic Casino/Hotel/rest./gas/dsl
0mm	North Dakota/South Dakota state line

⬆E INTERSTATE 94

Exit	Services
352mm	North Dakota/Minnesota state line, Red River
351	US 81, Fargo, **N** 🅡 Loaf'n Jug, Stop'n Go, 🍴 Duane's Pizza, Great Harvest Breads, Great Wall Chinese, Taco Shop, 🅞 🏩, Hornbacher's Foods, Medicine Shoppe, Verizon, vet, **S** 🅡 Stop'n Go, Tesoro/dsl, 🍴 A&W/LJ Silver, Burger King, Happy Joe's Pizza, McDonald's, Pepper's Café, Randy's Diner, Subway, Taco Bell, 🛌 Rodeway Inn, Vista Inn, 🅞 Hornbacher's/gas, K-Mart, O'Reilly Parts, USPO
350	25th St, Fargo, **N** 🅡 Stop'n Go, **S** 🅡 Cenex/dsl, Loaf'n Jug/dsl, 🍴 Dolittle's Grill, Ruby Tuesday
349b a	I-29, **N** to Grand Forks, **S** to Sioux Falls, **Services 1 mi N, exit 64**
348	45th St, **0-2 mi N Visitor Ctr/full facilities, litter barrels,** 🏬 🅡 Holiday/dsl, Petro/dsl/LP/24hr/@, 🍴 Carino's, Coldstone, Culver's, Denny's, Dunn Bros Coffee, Huhot Chinese, IHOP, Kroll's Diner, Little Caesars, Longhorn Steaks, McDonald's, Noodles&Co, Pizza Hut, Qdoba, Quaker Steak&Lube, Quiznos, Papa Murphy's, Smash Burger, Space Aliens Grill, Subway, Wendy's, 🛌 Best Western, C'mon Inn, Expressway Suites, Hilton Garden, MainStay Suites, Ramada Inn, Red Roof Inn, Staybridge Suites, Wingate Inn, 🅞 Blue Beacon, Hobby Lobby, Home Depot, Kohl's, Office Depot, Old Navy, NAPA, Sam's Club, Scheel's Sports, Target, Tuffy Auto, Verizon, Walmart, **S** 🅡 Holiday, Stop'n Go, Tesoro/DQ/dsl, 🍴 Applebee's, Famous Dave's BBQ, 5 Guys Burgers, Golden Corral, Hardee's, Korean BBQ, Mexican Village, Old Chicago Pizza, Pizza Ranch, Taco John's, Taco Shop, 🛌 Arbuckle Lodge,

ND

FARGO

FARGO

🅴 INTERSTATE 94 CONT'D

Exit	Services
348	Continued
	Comfort Suites, Hampton Inn, La Quinta, Residence Inn, Sleep Inn, 🅞 AT&T, Gander Mtn, Red River Zoo
347	9th St E, Veterans Blvd, **S** 🅖 Stop-N-Go/dsl, 🍽 Taco Bell, 🅞 Costco/gas
346b a	to Horace, W Fargo, **S** 🅖 Tesoro/dsl, repair
343	US 10, Lp 94, W Fargo, **N** 🅖 Cenex/dsl, 🛏 Sunset Motel, 🅞 Adventure RV Ctr, Harley-Davidson, Pioneer Village
342	no services
342mm	weigh sta wb
340	to Kindred
338	Mapleton, **N** 🅖 Tesoro/dsl
337mm	truck parking wb, litter barrels
331	ND 18, to Leonard, Casselton, **N** 🅖 Tesoro/Subway/dsl, 🍽 Country Kitchen, 🛏 Days Inn/RV park, 🅞 NAPA, repair
328	to Lynchburg
327mm	truck parking eb, litter barrels
324	Wheatland, to Chaffee
322	Absaraka
320	to Embden
317	to Ayr
314	ND 38 N, to Alice, Buffalo, **3 mi N** gas, food
310	no services
307	to Tower City, **N** 🅖 Cenex/café/dsl/RV Park/24hr, motel
304mm	🆁🆂 both lanes (both lanes exit left), full ♿ facilities, info, 🅒, 🔥, litter barrels, vending, petwalk
302	ND 32, to Fingal, Oriska, **1 mi N** city park
298	no services
296	no services
294	Lp 94, to Kathryn, Valley City, **N** 🅗, camping
292	Valley City, **N** 🅖 Tesoro/café/dsl, 🍽 Sabir's Rest., 🛏 AmericInn, Super 8, Wagon Wheel Inn/rest., 🅞 🅗, to Bald Hill Dam, camping, **S** 🅞 Ft Ransom SP (35mi)
291	Sheyenne River
290	Lp 94, Valley City, **N** 🅖 Tesoro/dsl, 🍽 Burger King, Kenny's Rest., Roby's Rest., Subway, 🅞 🅗, Chrysler/Dodge/Jeep, Family$, Firestone/auto, Ford, NAPA, Radio Shack, ShopKo
288	ND 1 S, to Oakes, **S** Fort Ransom SP (36 mi)
283	ND 1 N, to Rogers

Exit	Services
281	to Litchville, Sanborn, **1-2 mi N** gas, food, lodging
276	Eckelson, **S** 🅞 Prairie Haven Camping/gas/dsl
275mm	continental divide, elev 1490
272	to Urbana
269	Spiritwood
262	Bloom, **N** ✈
260	Jamestown, **N** 🅖 Stop'n Go, Tesoro/café/dsl/@, 🛏 Starlite Motel, 🅞 to St 🅗, camping
259mm	James River
258	US 52 W, US 281, Jamestown, **N** 🅖 Clark/TCBY/dsl, Tesoro/dsl, 🍽 Arby's, DQ, Hardee's, McDonald's, Pizza Ranch, Subway, Taco Bell, 🛏 Comfort Inn, Days Inn, Holiday Inn Express, Jamestown Motel, 🅞 🅗, Buffalo Herd/museum, Buick/Chevrolet/GMC, Firestone/auto, NW Tire, O'Reilly Parts, Toyota, vet, **S** 🅖 Shell/dsl, 🍽 Applebee's, Burger King, Grizzly's Rest., Hong Kong Buffet, La Carreta Mexican, Paradiso Mexican, Perkins, 🛏 EconoLodge, Hampton Inn, Quality Inn, Super 8, 🅞 AT&T, Chrysler/Dodge/Jeep, $Tree, Ford/Lincoln, GNC, Harley-Davidson, JC Penney, Mac's Hardware, Radio Shack, Sears, Walmart, mall, USPO, vet
257	Lp 94 (from eb, exits left), to Jamestown, **N** dsl repair
256	US 52 W, US 281 N, **S** 🅞 Wiest truck/trailer repair, **1 mi S** Jamestown Campground/RV dump
254mm	🆁🆂 both lanes, full ♿ facilities, 🅒, 🔥, litter barrels, petwalk, vending
251	Eldridge
248	no services
245	no services
242	Windsor
238	to Gackle, Cleveland
233	no services
230	Medina, **1 mi N** 🅖 Famer's Union/dsl/LP, 🍽 DairyTreat, 🅞 Medina RV Park, USPO, city park
228	ND 30 S, to Streeter
224mm	🆁🆂 wb, full ♿ facilities, 🅒, 🔥, litter barrels, vending, petwalk
221	Crystal Springs
221mm	🆁🆂 eb, full ♿ facilities, 🅒, 🔥, litter barrels, vending, petwalk
217	Pettibone
214	Tappen, **S** gas/dsl/food
208	ND 3 S, Dawson, **N** RV camping, **1/2 mi S** gas, food, to

JAMESTOWN

ND

⬆E INTERSTATE 94 CONT'D

Exit	Services
208	Continued Camp Grassick, RV camping
205	Robinson
200	ND 3 N, to Tuttle, Steele, **S** 🛢 Cenex/dsl, 🍴 Beary Tweet&Tasty, 🛏 OK Motel, ⊙ truckwash
195	no services
190	Driscoll, **S** food
182	US 83 S, ND 14, to Wing, Sterling, **S** 🛢 Cenex/dsl, 🛏 Top's Motel (1mi)
176	McKenzie
170	Menoken, **S** to McDowell Dam, RV Park
168mm	🅿 **both lanes, full** 🦽 **facilities,** Ⓒ, 🗑, **litter barrels, vending, petwalk, wifi**
161	Lp 94, Bismarck Expswy, Bismarck, **N** 🛢 Cenex/dsl/LP/24hr, Clark/dsl, 🛏 My Place, ⊙ Peterbilt, Toyota/Scion, **S** 🛢 Tesoro/Marlin's Rest./dsl/scales/24hr, 🍴 McDonald's, 🛏 Ramada Ltd, ⊙ Capital RV Ctr, Dakota Zoo, Freightliner, Kenworth, OK Tires, Volvo, dsl repair, truckwash
159	US 83, Bismarck, **N** 🛢 Holiday/dsl, Simonson/dsl, 🍴 Applebee's, Arby's, China Star, China Town, Golden Corral, Hooters, KFC, Kroll's Diner, Little Caesars, MacKenzie River Pizza, McDonald's, Olive Garden, Paradiso Mexican, Perkins, Pita Pit, Red Lobster, Ruby Tuesday, Space Alien Grill, Subway, Taco Bell, TCBY, Wendy's, 🛏 AmericInn, Candlewood Suites, Comfort Inn, Comfort Suites, Country Suites, Fairfield Inn, Hampton Inn, Holiday Inn Express, Mainstay Suites, Motel 6, Residence Inn, Sleep Inn, Staybridge Suites, Wingate Inn, ⊙ AT&T, Chevrolet, CVS Drug, Dan's Foods, Hancock Fabrics, Hobby Lobby, Jo-Ann Fabrics, K-Mart, Menards, NW Tire, Sears/auto, UHaul, Verizon, Walmart/Subway, mall, USPO, **S** 🛢 PetroServe/dsl, Shell/dsl, Tesoro, 🍴 Caspars Rest., DQ, Hardee's, Minerva's Rest., Pizza Hut, Schlotzsky's, Starbucks, Subway, Taco John's, Woodhouse Rest., 🛏 Best Value Inn, Days Inn, Kelly Inn, La Quinta, Ramada Inn, Super 8, ⊙ Ⓗ, O'Reilly Parts
157	Divide Ave, Bismarck, **N** 🛢 Shell/dsl, 🍴 Carino's, Coldstone, 5 Guys Burgers, Cracker Barrel, Goodtimes Grill/Taco John's, Jimmy John's, McDonald's, Pancheros Mexican, Starbucks, Subway, TX Roadhouse, Wendy's, ⊙ AT&T, Best Buy, $Tree, GNC, Kohls, Lowe's, Old Navy, Petsmart, TJ Maxx, Verizon, visitor ctr, **S** 🛢 Cenex/dsl/E85/LP/RV Dump, 🍴 Stadium Café, 🛏 Hampton Inn, ⊙ Central Mkt Foods
156mm	Missouri River
156	I-194, Bismarck Expswy, Bismarck City Ctr, **1/2 mi S** Dakota Zoo
155	to Lp 94 (exits left from wb), Mandan, City Ctr, same as 153
153	ND 1806, Mandan Dr, Mandan, **1/2 mi S** 🛢 Cenex/dsl, PetroServe/dsl, Tesoro, 🍴 Bonanza, Burger King, Dakota Farms Rest., DQ, Domino's, Hardee's, Papa Murphy's, Pizza Hut, Pizza Ranch, Subway, Taco John's, 🛏 North Country Inn, ⊙ Central Mkt Foods, Chevrolet, Family$, Goodyear/auto, NAPA, NW Tire, O'Reilly Parts, Subaru, Verizon, Dacotah Centennial Park, Ft Lincoln SP (5mi)
152	Sunset Dr, Mandan, **N** 🛢 Tesoro, 🍴 MT Mike's Steaks, 🛏 Best Western, Walmart, **S** 🛢 Tesoro/RV dump, 🍴 Fried's Rest., ⊙ Ⓗ

Exit	Services
152mm	scenic view eb
147	ND 25, to ND 6, Mandan, **S** 🛢 Tesoro/Subway/cafe/dsl/scales/24hr
140	to Crown Butte
135mm	scenic view wb, litter barrel
134	to Judson, Sweet Briar Lake
127	ND 31 N, to New Salem, **N** Knife River Indian Village (35mi), **S** 🛢 Cenex/dsl, Tesoro/dsl, 🍴 Sunset Cafe, 🛏 Arrowhead Inn/café, ⊙ DFC/dsl, Food Pride, Gaebe Drug, World's Largest Cow, vet
123	to Almont
120	no services
119mm	🅿 **both lanes, full** 🦽 **facilities,** Ⓒ, 🗑, **litter barrels, petwalk**
117	no services
113	no services
110	ND 49, to Glen Ullin
108	to Glen Ullin, Lake Tschida, **3 mi S** gas, food, lodging, camping
102	Hebron, to Glen Ullin, to Lake Tschida, **3 mi S** gas, food, lodging, camping
97	Hebron, **2 mi N** gas, food, lodging
96.5mm	central/mountain time zone
90	no services
84	ND 8, Richardton, **N** 🛢 Cenex/dsl, ⊙ Ⓗ, to Assumption Abbey, Schnell RA
78	to Taylor
72	to Enchanted Hwy, Gladstone
64	Dickinson, **S** 🛢 Cenex/Tiger Truckstop/rest./dsl/24hr, 🍴 Dakota Diner, ⊙ Ford/Lincoln, Honda, NW Tire, Toyota/Scion, dsl repair
61	ND 22, Dickinson, **N** 🛢 Cenex/dsl/LP, Simonson/dsl, 🍴 Applebee's, Arby's, Bonanza, Burger King, DQ, El Sombrero Mexican, Papa Murphy's, Pizza Ranch, Sakura Japanese, Sanford's Rest., Taco Bell, Taco John's, Wendy's, 🛏 AmericInn, Astoria Suites, Best Western, Comfort Inn, Hampton Inn, Holiday Inn Express, Microtel, My Place, Ramada, Savannah Suites, ⊙ AT&T, Chevrolet, Dan's Foods, Goodyear/auto, Herberger's, JC Penney, K-Mart, Midas, O'Reilly Parts, Runnings Hardware, Verizon, Walmart/Subway, White Drug, USPO, **S** 🛢 Cenex/dsl, Conoco/repair, Holiday/dsl, Tesoro/dsl, 🍴 A&W/KFC, Country Kitchen, Domino's, Don Pedro's Mexican, King Buffet, McDonald's, Perkins, Subway, 🛏 La Quinta, Quality Inn, Relax Inn, Select Inn, Super 8, ⊙ Ⓗ, Mac's Hardware, museum, visitor info
59	Lp 94, to Dickinson, **N** 🛏 Extended Stay, ValuePlace, **S** to Patterson Lake RA, camping, **3 mi S** services in Dickinson
51	South Heart
42	US 85, to Grassy Butte, Belfield, Williston, **N** gas:MVP/dsl, ⊙ T Roosevelt NP (52mi), **S** 🛢 Cenex/dsl/24hr, Conoco/dsl, 🍴 DQ, Trapper's Kettle Rest., 🛏 Trapper's Inn, ⊙ NAPA, info
36	Fryburg
32	T Roosevelt NP, **Painted Canyon Visitors Ctr, N** 🅿 **both lanes, full** 🦽 **facilities,** Ⓒ, 🗑, **litter barrels, petwalk**
27	Lp 94, Historic Medora (from wb), T Roosevelt NP
24.5mm	Little Missouri Scenic River
24	Medora, Historic Medora, Chateau de Mores HS, T Roosevelt NP, **S** visitors ctr
23	West River Rd (from wb)
22mm	scenic view eb

BISMARCK

ND

HEBRON

DICKINSON

INTERSTATE 94 CONT'D

Exit	Services
18	Buffalo Gap, **N** Buffalo Gap Camping (seasonal), food/lodging
10	Sentinel Butte, Camel Hump Lake, **S** gas
7	Home on the Range

OHIO

INTERSTATE 70

Exit	Services
225.5mm	Ohio/West Virginia state line, Ohio River
225	US 250 W, OH 7, Bridgeport, **N** 🛢 Marathon, StarFire, Sunoco/dsl, 🍴 DQ, Papa John's, Pizza Hut, Wendy's (1mi), 🅾 Advance Parts, AutoZone, Family$, Meineke, NAPA, **S** 🛢 Clark, Exxon, Gulf, 🍴 Domino's
220	US 40, rd 214, **N** 🛢 Marathon, Sunoco/dsl, 🍴 Mehlman Cafe, 🏨 Comfort Inn, **S** 🏨 Days Inn, 🅾 vet
219	I-470 E, to Bel-Aire, Washington PA, (from eb)
218	Mall Rd, to US 40, to Blaine, **N** 🛢 BP, Exxon/dsl, 🍴 Applebee's, Arby's, Buffalo Wild Wings, Burger King, DeFelice Pizza, Denny's, Eat'n Park, HoneyBaked Ham, King Buffet, Little Caesars, Outback Steaks, Pizza Hut, Red Lobster, Starbucks, Steak'n Shake, Taco Bell, Tlaquepaque Mexican, Wendy's, W Texas Steaks, 🏨 Best Value Inn, EconoLodge, Hampton Inn, Holiday Inn Express, Microtel, Red Roof Inn, Super 8, 🅾 Urgent Care, AAA, Aldi Foods, AT&T, AutoZone, Buick/Cadillac/Chevrolet, $General, $Tree, Kroger, Lowe's, Sam's Club, Staples, Stewarts RV Ctr, Verizon, Walmart/McDonald's, **S** 🍴 Bob Evans, Bonanza, Cracker Barrel, Garfield's Rest., KFC/LJ Silver, Longhorn Steaks, McDonald's, Osaka Steaks, Panera Bread, Starbucks, 🏨 Fairfield Inn, 🅾 Chrysler/Dodge/Jeep, Elder-Beerman, JC Penney, JoAnn Fabrics, K-Mart, Macy's, NTB, Sears/auto, mall
216	OH 9, St Clairsville, **N** 🛢 BP
215	National Rd, **N** 🍴 Burger King, Domino's, WenWu Chinese, 🅾 NAPA, Riesbeck's Foods, USPO
213	OH 331, Flushing, **S** 🛢 BP, Marathon/Subway/dsl, Sunoco/dsl
211mm	🆁🆂 both lanes, full ♿ facilities, 📞, 🛢, litter barrels, petwalk, vending
208	OH 149, Morristown, **N** 🛢 Exxon/McDonald's/dsl, 🍴 Schlepp's Rest., 🏨 Arrowhead Motel (1mi), Holiday Inn Express, 🅾 Cannonball Speedway, $General, Ford/Lincoln, **S** 🛢 Marathon/Quiznos/dsl, 🅾 Harley-Davidson, Barkcamp SP
204	US 40 E (from eb, no return), National Rd
202	OH 800, to Barnesville, **S** 🛢 202 Gas/dsl, 🅾 🏥
198	rd 114, Fairview
193	OH 513, Middlebourne, **N** 🛢 BP, FuelMart/dsl, 🅾 fireworks
189mm	🆁🆂 eb, full ♿ facilities, 📞, 🛢, litter barrels, petwalk, vending
186	US 40, OH 285, to Old Washington, **N** 🛢 BP, **S** 🛢 GoMart/dsl, Speedway/dsl/scales/24hr
180b a	I-77 N, to Cleveland, to Salt Fork SP, I-77 S, to Charleston
178	OH 209, Cambridge, **0-1 mi N** 🛢 Marathon/dsl, Sheetz/dsl, Starfire/dsl, 🍴 Bob Evans, China Village, Coldstone/Tim Hortons, Cracker Barrel, Denny's, DQ, Forum

Exit	Services
1	ND 16, **S** 🛢 Cenex/dsl/LP/24hr, ⭐FLYING J/Subway/dsl/scales/LP/24hr, 🏨 Buckboard Inn, 🏥 Beach RV Park, **Welcome/Visitor Ctr, full** ♿ **facilities, litter barrels, petwalk,** 🚌
1mm	**weigh sta eb,** litter barrel
0mm	North Dakota/Montana state line

CAMBRIDGE / ZANESVILLE

Exit	Services
178	**Continued** Rest, KFC, McDonald's, Papa John's, Pizza Hut, Ruby Tuesday, Subway, Wendy's, 🏨 Comfort Inn, Days Inn, EconoLodge, Hampton Inn, Holiday Inn Express, Microtel, Southgate Hotel, 🅾 🏥, Advance Parts, AutoZone, Big-Lots, Buick/Cadillac/GMC, $General, Family$, Riesbecks Foods, Verizon, **S** 🛢 Murphy USA/dsl, 🚛/Subway/dsl/scales/24hr, 🍴 Arby's, Burger King, Great Chinese, Little Caesars, Taco Bell, Tlaquepaque Mexican, 🏨 Baymont Inn, 🅾 Aldi Foods, $Tree, $Zone, K-Mart/gas, Radio Shack, Spring Valley RV Park, Verizon, Walmart/Subway,
176	US 22, US 40, to Cambridge, **N** 🛢 Sunoco/dsl, 🏨 Budget Inn, 🅾 Western Shop, RV camping, st patrol
173mm	**weigh sta both lanes**
169	OH 83, to Cumberland, New Concord, **N** 🅾 John&Annie Glen Historic Site, RV camping, to Muskingum Coll
164	US 22, US 40, Norwich, **N** 🛢 BP, 🏨 Baker's Motel, Zane Gray Museum, **S** 🅾 antiques, pottery
163mm	🆁🆂 wb, full ♿ facilities, 📞, 🛢, litter barrels, petwalk, vending
160	OH 797, Airport Rd 🔧, **N** 🛢 ❤Love's/Arby's/dsl/scales/24hr, **S** 🛢 BP, Exxon/Subway/dsl, 🍴 Denny's, McDonald's, Wendy's, 🏨 Best Value Inn, Best Western, Ramada Inn, 🅾 🔧, st patrol
157	OH 93, Zanesville, **N** 🛢 BP, **S** 🛢 Marathon, Shell/dsl, st patrol
155	OH 60, OH 146, Underwood St, Zanesville, **N** 🍴 Bob Evans, Olive Garden, Oriental Buffet, Red Lobster, Steak'n Shake, Tumbleweed Grill, 🏨 Comfort Inn, Fairfield Inn, Hampton Inn, Holiday Inn Express, 🅾 🏥, Pick'n Save Foods, USPO, visitor info, **S** 🛢 Exxon/dsl, 🍴 Adornetto Pizza, Cracker Barrel, Subway, Wendy's, 🏨 Baymont Inn, EconoLodge, Travelodge, 🅾 Rite Aid
154	5th St (from eb)
153b	Maple Ave (no EZ return from wb), **N** 🛢 BP, 🍴 DQ, Italian Eatery, Papa John's, Tee Jaye's Rest., 🅾 🏥, CVS Drug, Family$
153a	State St, **N** 🛢 Speedway/dsl, 🅾 to Dillon SP (8mi), **S** 🛢 Marathon
153mm	Licking River
152	US 40, National Rd, **N** 🛢 Exxon/A&W/Blimpie/dsl, Starfire/dsl, 🍴 McDonald's, 🏨 Super 8
142	US 40 (from wb, no EZ return), Gratiot, **N** RV camping
141	OH 668, US 40 (from eb, no return), to Gratiot, same as 142
132	OH 13, to Thornville, Newark, **N** Dawes Arboretum (3mi), **S** 🛢 BP, Shell, 🍴 Subway (2mi), 🅾 RV camping
131mm	🆁🆂 both lanes, full ♿ facilities, 📞, 🛢, litter barrels, petwalk, vending
129b a	OH 79, to Buckeye Lake, Hebron, **N** 🏨 Best Western, **S** 🛢 BP, Valero, 🍴 Donato's Pizza, McDonald's, Pizza Hut/Taco Bell, Wendy's, 🏨 Super 8, 🅾 CarQuest, KOA (2mi),

BLAINE

ND OH

🚏 INTERSTATE 70 CONT'D

Exit	Services
129b a	Continued Blue Goose Marina (2mi)
126	OH 37, to Granville, Lancaster, N ⓡ Marathon/dsl, ▨ /Chester's/Subway/dsl/scales/24hr, Sunoco/dsl, S ⓡ TA/ BP/Popeye's/Sbarro's/dsl/scales/24hr/@, Valero/dsl, 🏠 Deluxe Inn, Red Roof Inn, ⓞ IA 80 Truckomat/truckwash, KOA
122	OH 158, to Baltimore, Kirkersville, N 🏠 Regal Inn, S ⓡ ⦿FLYING J/Denny's/dsl/LP/scales/24hr, ⓞ fireworks
118	OH 310, to Pataskala, N ⓡ BP/McDonald's, Shell/dsl, Speedway/dsl, ⓕ DQ, S ⓡ BP/Duke's/Subway/dsl, ⓞ RCD RV Ctr
112c	OH 204, to Blecklick Rd (from eb)
112	OH 256, to Pickerington, Reynoldsburg, N ⓡ BP, Shell/ McDonald's, ⓕ Chipotle Mexican, Culver's, 5 Guys Burgers, IHOP, Logan's Roadhouse, Noodles&Co, O'Charley's, Olive Garden, Panera Bread, Penn Sta, Rotolo's Pizza, Smokey Bones BBQ, Subway, TGIFriday's, Tim Horton's, 🏠 Fairfield Inn, Holiday Inn Express, ⓞ AT&T, Best Buy, Gander Mtn, Jo-Ann Fabrics, Marshall's, NTB, Radio Shack, Sam's Club/gas, Staples, Target, Tire Discounters, Verizon, Walgreens, Walmart/Subway, S ⓡ Speedway/ dsl, ⓕ Arby's, Bob Evans, CiCi's Pizza, Classic's Diner, Cold Stone, Cracker Barrel, Dragon China, Feta Greek Cafe, Graffiti Burger, Iron Chef, KFC, La Fogata Mexican, LJ Silver, Longhorn Steaks, Skyline Chili, Steak'n Shake, Uno, Wendy's, 🏠 Best Western, Comfort Inn, Hampton Inn, ⓞ Barnes&Noble, Kohl's, Kroger/E85, Tuesday Morning, **Urgent Care**
110	Brice Rd, to Reynoldsburg, N ⓡ Speedway, Sunoco, ⓕ Burger King, Donato's, Genji Japanese, Golden China, Popeye's, Subway, TeeJaye's Rest., Tim Horton's, Waffle House, 🏠 Days Inn, Extended Stay America, La Quinta, Red Roof Inn, Super 8, ⓞ BigLots, Goodyear/ auto, Home Depot, O'Reilly Parts, S ⓡ BP, Speedway/ dsl, ⓕ Applebee's, Arby's, Asian Star, Big Boy, Boston Mkt, Burger King, Chipotle Mexican, Ichiban Steaks, KFC, McDonald's, Ruby Tuesday, Starbucks, Taco Bell, Waffle House, White Castle, 🏠 Best Value Inn, Comfort Suites, EconoLodge, Motel 6, ⓞ Acura, Advance Parts, Aldi Foods, Discount Tire, Family$, Fiat, Firestone/auto, GNC, Hobby Lobby, Honda, Lowe's, Michael's, NTB, Old Navy, Toyota/Scion, Walgreens
108b a	I-270 N to Cleveland, access to Ⓗ, I-270 S to Cincinnati
107 ba	OH 317, Hamilton Rd, to Whitehall, S ⓡ Shell/dsl, Valero/ dsl, ⓕ Arby's, Burger King, Capt D's, ChuckECheese, Eastland Buffet, Ichiban Japanese, McDonald's, Papa John's, Pizza Hut, Red Lobster, Steak'n Shake, Taco Bell, 🏠 Fort Rapids Resort, Hampton Inn, Hawthorn Inn, In-Town Suites, Knights Inn, ⓞ AT&T, $General, JC Penney, Kohl's, Macy's, PepBoys, Staples
105a	US 33, to Lancaster, **2 mi** N ⓕ Tat Italian
105b	US 33, James Rd, Bexley, N ⓕ Tat Italian
103b a	Livingston Ave, to Capital University, N ⓡ Exxon, Speedway/dsl, ⓕ Mr Hero Subs, Peking Dynasty, Popeye's, Subway, Taco Bell, Wendy's, ⓞ auto repair, S ⓡ Marathon, Shell, ⓕ McDonald's, Rally's, White Castle
102	Kelton Ave, Miller Ave
101a	I-71 N, to Cleveland

Exit	Services
100b	US 23, to 4th St, downtown
99c	Rich St, Town St (exits left from eb), N ⓡ Sunoco, ⓞ Ford
99b	OH 315 N, downtown
99a	I-71 S, to Cincinnati
98b	Mound St (from wb, no EZ return), S ⓡ Speedway, ⓕ Little Caesars, McDonald's, Rally's, ⓞ Aldi Foods
98a	US 62, OH 3, Central Ave, to Sullivant same as 98b
97	US 40, W Broad St, N ⓡ Valero/dsl, ⓕ Arby's, Burger King, KFC, McDonald's, Pizza Hut/Taco Bell, Subway, Tim Horton's, Wendy's, White Castle, 🏠 Knights Inn, ⓞ Aamco, CVS Drug, U-Haul, USPO
96	I-670 (exits left from eb) to 🛫
95	Hague Ave (from wb), S ⓡ Sunoco
94	Wilson Rd, N ⓡ Marathon/Circle K/Subway/dsl, Mobil, S ⓡ BP, ▨/Wendy's/dsl/scales/24hr, Shell/dsl, Speedway, ⓕ McDonald's, Waffle House, White Castle, 🏠 EconoLodge
93b a	I-270, N to Cleveland, S to Cincinnati
91b a	to Hilliard, New Rome, N ⓡ GetGo, Shell, Speedway/dsl, ⓕ AA China, Applebee's, Arby's, Big Boy, Buffalo Wild Wings, Burger King, Cracker Barrel, Chick-fil-A, Cold Stone/Tim Horton's, Culver's, Donato's Pizza, El Vaquero Mexican, Fazoli's, 5 Guys Burgers, Golden Chopsticks, Hooters, KFC, McDonald's, Outback Steaks, Panera Bread, Perkins, Pizza Hut/Taco Bell, Red Robin, Ruby Tuesday, Salvi's Bistro, Skyline Chili, Smoothie King, TX Roadhouse, White Castle, Wendy's, 🏠 Best Value Inn, Comfort Suites, Fairfield Inn, Hampton Inn, Hawthorn Inn, Holiday Inn, La Quinta, Motel 6, Red Roof Inn, ⓞ Advance Parts, AT&T, Dick's, Discount Tire, Firestone/auto, Ford, Gander Mtn, Giant Eagle Foods/gas, GNC, Kohl's, Marshall's, Meijer/dsl, Michael's, Midas, Old Navy, Petsmart, Sam's Club/gas, Radio Shack, Target, Verizon, Walmart/ Subway, **Urgent Care**, S ⓡ BP/dsl, Marathon/dsl, ⓕ Bob Evans, Handel's Icecream, Steak'n Shake, 🏠 Best Western, Country Inn&Suites, Super 8
85	OH 142, to Plain City, W Jefferson, N ⓞ Prairie Oaks SP, S ⓞ Battelle Darby SP
80	OH 29, to Mechanicsburg, S hwy patrol
79	US 42, to London, Plain City, N ⓡ ▨/Arby's/dsl/ scales/24hr, ⓕ Waffle House, ⓞ Raber's RV Ctr, truck/ auto repair, S ⓡ Speedway/Subway/dsl, TA/BP/Pizza Hut/Popeye's/dsl/scales/24hr/@, ⓕ McDonald's, Taco Bell, Wendy's, 🏠 Holiday Inn Express, Motel 6, ⓞ Ⓗ, truckwash
72	OH 56, to London, Summerford, N ⓡ Marathon, **4 mi** S Ⓗ, lodging
71mm	℞ both lanes, full 🏠 facilities, ⓕ, 🔵, litter barrels, vending, petwalk
66	OH 54, to Catawba, South Vienna, N ⓡ Fuelmart/dsl/ scales, S ⓡ Speedway/dsl
62	US 40, Springfield, N 🏠 Harmony Motel, ⓞ Harmony Farm Mkt, antiques, auto repair, to Buck Creek SP, S Beaver Valley Camping
59	OH 41, to S Charleston, N ⓞ Ⓗ, Harley-Davidson, st patrol, S ⓡ BP, Clark/dsl, antiques
54	OH 72, to Cedarville, Springfield, N ⓡ BP/dsl, Shell, Speedway/dsl, Sunoco/dsl, ⓕ A&W/LJ Silver, Arby's, Bob Evans, Cassano's Pizza/subs, Cracker Barrel, Domino's, El Toro Mexican, Hardee's, Lee's Chicken, Little Caesars, McDonald's, Panda Chinese, Rally's, Rudy's Smokehouse, Subway, Taco Bell, Wendy's, 🏠 Comfort Suites,

(margin labels: COLUMBUS AREA, OH, COLUMBUS AREA, SPRINGFIELD)

⬆️E   INTERSTATE 70 CONT'D

Exit	Services
54	Continued Days Inn, Hampton Inn, Quality Inn, Ramada Ltd, Red Roof Inn, Super 8, 🅾 🅷, Advance Parts, Big-Lots, Family$, Kroger/deli, Rite Aid, Walgreens, **S** 🅿 Marathon/dsl, Swifty
52b a	US 68, to Urbana, Xenia, **S** to John Bryan SP
48	OH 4 (from wb), to Enon, Donnelsville, **N** 🅿 Speedway, 🅾 camping
47	OH 4 (from eb), to Springfield, **N** 🅿 Speedway, 🅾 RV Camping
44	I-675 S, Spangler Rd, to Cincinnati
43mm	Mad River
41b a	OH 4, OH 235, to Dayton, New Carlisle, **1 mi N** 🅿 BP/dsl, 🍴 KFC/LJ Silver, McDonald's, Wendy's, 🅾 Freightliner, Kenworth
38	OH 201, Brandt Pike, **N** 🅿 Marathon/dsl, 🅾 Meijer/dsl/E85, **S** 🅿 Shell, UDF/dsl, 🍴 Bob Evans, Sonic, Tim Horton's, Waffle House, Wendy's, 🏠 Best Value Inn, Comfort Inn, 🅾 Walmart/McDonald's, vet
36	OH 202, Huber Heights, **N** 🅿 Speedway/dsl, 🍴 Applebee's, Big Boy, Dragon City, El Toro Grill, Fazoli's, Steak'n Shake, Taco Bell, Waffle House, 🏠 Baymont Inn, 🅾 AT&T, Dick's, $Tree, Elder Beerman, Gander Mtn., GNC, Hobby Lobby, Kia, Kohl's, Lowe's, Marshall's, Petsmart, Target, Verizon, **Urgent Care**, vet, **S** 🅿 BP/dsl, Marathon/dsl, 🍴 Arby's, Buffalo Wild Wings, Burger King, Cadillac Jack's, Chipotle Mexican, CiCi's Pizza, El Dorado Mexican, La Rosa's Pizza, McDonald's, Skyline Chili, Subway, TGIFriday's, TX Roadhouse, White Castle, 🏠 Days Inn, Hampton Inn, Holiday Inn Express, 🅾 Kroger/gas
33b a	I-75, N to Toledo, S to Dayton
32	to US 40, Vandalia, **N** to Dayton Intn'l ✈
29	OH 48, to Dayton, Englewood, **N** 🅿 BP, Speedway/dsl, Sunoco/dsl, Valero, 🍴 Arby's, Big Boy, Bob Evans, Company BBQ, Hot Head Burrito, KFC, Lee's Chicken, Perkins, Ponderosa, Skyline Chili, Taco Bell, Tim Horton's, Tony's Italian, Wendy's, Yen Ching Chinese, 🏠 Best Value Inn, Best Western, Hampton Inn, Holiday Inn, Super 8, 🅾 Advance Parts, Aldi Foods, BigLots, Family$, O'Reilly Parts, vet, **S** 🍴 McDonald's, Steak'n Shake, Tumbleweed SW Grill, Waffle House, 🏠 Comfort Inn, Motel 6, 🅾 🅷, Meijer/dsl/E85
26	OH 49 S, **N** 🅿 Murphy USA/dsl, 🍴 Bob Evans, La Rosa's Pizza, Sonic, 🅾 Radio Shack, Walmart/Subway, **Urgent Care**, **S** 🍴 Wendy's
24	OH 49 N, to Greenville, Clayton, **N** 🅿 Sunoco/dsl, 🅾 KOA (seasonal)
21	Arlington Rd, Brookville, **N** 🅿 GA/Subway, **S** 🅿 Speedway/dsl, Swifty, 🍴 Arby's, Brookville Grill, DQ, Great Wall

Exit	Services
21	Continued Chinese, K's Rest., KFC/Taco Bell, McDonald's, Pizza Hut, Rob's Rest., Subway, Waffle House, Wendy's, 🏠 Best Value Inn, Holiday Inn Express, 🅾 Brookville Parts, Chevrolet, Curves, $General, Family$, IGA Foods, Rite Aid
14	OH 503, to West Alexandria, Lewisburg, **N** 🅿 Marathon/Subway/dsl, 🍴 Dari Twist, 🏠 Super Inn, 🅾 IGA Foods, **S** 🅿 Valero/dsl
10	US 127, to Eaton, Greenville, **N** 🅿 TA/BP/Burger King/Subway/dsl/scales/24hr/@, st patrol, **S** 🅿 🚚/Subway/dsl/scales/24hr, 🏠 Budget Inn
3mm	Welcome Ctr eb/🆁🆂 both lanes, full ♿ facilities, 🅲, vending, 🚮, litter barrels, petwalk
1	US 35 E (from eb), to Eaton, New Hope
0mm	Ohio/Indiana state line, Welcome Arch, **weigh sta eb**

⬆️N   INTERSTATE 71

Exit	Services
	I-71 begins/ends on I-90, exit 170 in Cleveland.
247b	I-90 W, I-490 E.
247a	W 14th, Clark Ave
246	Denison Ave, Jennings Rd (from sb)
245	US 42, Pearl Rd, **E** 🅿 BP, Gas&Go, 🅾 🅷, zoo
244	W 65th, Denison Ave (exits left from nb)
242b a	W 130th, to Bellaire Rd, **W** 🅿 Sunoco
240	W 150th, **E** 🅿 Marathon, Speedway/dsl, Sunoco, 🍴 Burger King, Denny's, 🏠 Marriott, 🅾 AutoZone, Goodyear/auto, Marc's Foods, **W** 🅿 BP/Subway/dsl, 🍴 Nana's Italian, Somers Rest., 🏠 Holiday Inn, La Quinta

DAYTON (vertical left margin)

OH (right margin tab)

🅖 = gas   🍽 = food   🛏 = lodging   🅞 = other   🆁🆂 = rest stop   Copyright 2014 - The NEXT Exit ®

🧭N INTERSTATE 71 CONT'D

Exit	Services
239	OH 237 S (from sb), **W** to ⊝
238	I-480, Toledo, Youngstown, **W** ⊝
237	Snow Rd, Brook Park, **E** 🅖 BP, Marathon/Circle K, Shell, 🍽 Bob Evans, Burger King, Dunkin Donuts, Goody's Rest., KFC, McDonald's, Rally's, Reddi's Pizza, Subway, Taco Bell, 🛏 Best Western, Holiday Inn Express, Howard Johnson, 🅞 Advance Parts, AutoZone, Conrad Tire/repair, $General, O'Reilly Parts, Rite Aid, **W** to ⊝
235	Bagley Rd, **E** 🍽 Bob Evans, 🅞 Mr Tire, vet, **W** 🅖 BP/dsl, Shell, Speedway/dsl, 🍽 Baskin-Robbins/Dunkin Donuts, Burger King, Caribou Coffee, Chipotle, Denny's, 5 Guys Burgers, Friendly's, Jimmy John's, Max&Erma's, McDonald's, Olive Garden, Panera Bread, Perkins, Pizza Hut, Roadhouse Grill, Taco Bell, 🛏 Comfort Inn, Courtyard, Crowne Plaza, Days Inn, Motel 6, Red Roof Inn, Residence Inn, TownePlace Suites, 🅞 🏥, Aldi Foods, K-Mart
234	US 42, Pearl Rd, **E** 🅖 Shell/dsl, Sunoco/dsl, 🍽 Katherine's Rest., 3 Bros Pizza, Wendy's, 🅞 Audi/Porsche, Honda, **W** 🅖 Gas&Food/dsl, 🍽 Buffalo Wild Wings, Jennifer's Rest., 🛏 Kings Inn, La Siesta Motel, Metrick's Motel, 🅞 Circle K, Home Depot, Lowe's, Walmart
233	I-80 and Ohio Tpk, to Toledo, Youngstown
231	OH 82, Strongsville, **E** 🅖 Shell, 🛏 Holiday Inn, Super 8, 🅞 Chevrolet, **W** 🅖 BP/7-11/dsl, Marathon/dsl, 🍽 Applebee's, Buca Italian, Chick-fil-A, DiBella's Subs, Houlihan's, Longhorn Steaks, Macaroni Grill, Panera Bread, Red Lobster, Rock Me's Grill, Rosewood Grill, Starbucks, 🅞 Best Buy, Costco/gas, Dick's, Dillard's, Giant Eagle Foods, JC Penney, Kohl's, Macy's, Midas, NTB, PetCo, Sears/auto, Target, Verizon, mall
226	OH 303, Brunswick, **E** 🅖 Shell/dsl, 🍽 Pizza Hut, 🅞 Chrysler/Dodge/Jeep, Hyundai, Subaru, Toyota/Scion, VW, **W** 🅖 BP, Speedway, Sunoco/dsl, 🍽 Applebee's, Arby's, Bob Evans, Burger King, Chipotle, CiCi's Pizza, McDonald's, Panera Bread, Panini's Grill, Sonic, Starbucks, Steak'n Shake, Subway, Taco Bell, Wendy's, 🛏 Quality Inn, 🅞 Buehler's Foods, $General, Ford, Giant Eagle Food, Home Depot, K-Mart, Radio Shack, Verizon
225mm	🆁🆂 nb, full ♿ facilities, 🍽, 🏞, litter barrels, petwalk
224mm	🆁🆂 sb, full ♿ facilities, 🍽, 🏞, litter barrels, petwalk
222	OH 3, Medina, Hinckley, **W** st patrol
220	I-271 N, (from nb) to Erie, Pa
218	OH 18, to Akron, Medina, **E** 🅖 BP/dsl, Marathon/dsl, Sunoco/dsl, 🍽 Alexandri's Rest., Ay Carumba, Baskin-Robbins/Dunkin Donuts, Burger King, DQ, 🛏 Quality Inn, Rodeway Inn, Super 8, 🅞 Kia, Nissan, **W** 🅖 Speedway/dsl, 🍽 Arby's, Bob Evans, Buffalo Wild Wings, Denny's, McDonald's, Pizza Hut, Rocknes Rest., Waffle House, Wendy's, 🛏 Hampton Inn, Motel 6, Red Roof Inn, 🅞 🏥, Aldi Foods, Buehler's Foods, Buick/Cadillac/GMC, Dodge, Harley-Davidson, Honda, NTB
209	I-76 E, to Akron, US 224, **W** 🅖 🚚/Subway/dsl/scales/24hr, TA/Country Pride/Burger King/Popeye's/dsl/scales/24hr/@, 🍽 Arby's, McDonald's, Starbucks, 🛏 Super 8, 🅞 Blue Beacon, Chippewa Valley Camping (1mi), SpeedCo
204	OH 83, Burbank, **E** 🅖 BP/dsl, Duke/dsl, ♥Love's/Hardee's/dsl/scales/24hr, 🛏 Plaza Motel, **W** 🅖 🚚/Wendy's/dsl/scales/24hr, 🍽 Bob Evans, Burger King, KFC/Taco Bell, McDonald's, 🅞 🏥, Lodi Outlets/famous brands

198	OH 539, W Salem
196mm	🆁🆂 both lanes, full ♿ facilities, 🍽, vending, 🏞, litter barrels, petwalk
196	OH 301 (from nb, no re-entry), W Salem
186	US 250, Ashland, **E** 🅖 Marathon, 🍽 Perkins, Grandpa's Village/cheese/gifts, 🅞 Hickory Lakes Camping (7mi), **W** 🅖 Goasis/BP/Pizza Hut/Popeye's/Starbucks/Taco Bell/dsl/24hr, Marathon, 🍽 Brian Buffet, Denny's, Donato's Pizza, Jake's Rest., McDonald's, Wendy's, 🛏 Ashland Inn, Days Inn, Holiday Inn Express, Super 8, 🅞 🏥, Aldi Foods, Buehler's Foods, GNC, Home Depot, Walmart, st patrol, to Ashland U
176	US 30, to Mansfield, **E** 🛏 Heritage Inn, 🅞 fireworks
173	OH 39, to Mansfield
169	OH 13, Mansfield, **E** 🅖 Marathon/dsl, Murphy USA/dsl, 🍽 Applebee's, Cracker Barrel, Steak'n Shake, Subway, Wendy's, 🛏 Best Western, La Quinta, 🅞 Walmart/Subway, Mohican SP, **W** 🅖 Marathon, 🍽 Arby's, Bob Evans, Burger King, El Compasino Mexican, McDonald's, Taco Bell, 🛏 Hampton Inn, Super 8, Travelodge, 🅞 🏥, st patrol
165	OH 97, to Bellville, **E** 🅖 BP, Speedway/dsl, Shell/dsl, 🍽 Burger King, Dutch Heritage Rest., KC's Rib House, McDonald's, 🛏 Days Inn, Comfort Inn, Economy Inn, Quality Inn, 🅞 to Mohican SP, **W** 🍽 Wendy's
151	OH 95, to Mt Gilead, **E** 🅖 Duke/BP/deli, Marathon, 🍽 Gathering Place Rest., McDonald's, Wendy's, 🛏 Best Western, 🅞 st patrol, **W** 🅖 Shell/dsl, Sunoco/dsl/E85, 🍽 Subway, 🛏 Knights Inn, 🅞 🏥, Mt Gilead SP (6mi)
149mm	truck parking both lanes
140	OH 61, Mt Gilead, **E** 🅖 🚚/Arby's/dsl/scales/24hr, **W** 🅖 BP/Taco Bell, Marathon/Subway, 🍽 Farmstead Rest., 🅞 Cardinal Ctr Camping
131	US 36, OH 37, to Delaware, **E** 🅖 ✈FLYING J/Denny's/dsl/LP/scales/24hr/@, 🚚/Subway/dsl/scales/24hr, 🍽 Burger King, 🅞 Harley-Davidson, **W** 🅖 BP/dsl, Shell/Tim Hortons, 🍽 Arby's, Bob Evans, Cracker Barrel, KFC/LJ Silver, McDonald's, Starbucks, Taco Bell, Waffle House, Wendy's, White Castle, 🛏 Best Value Inn, Hampton Inn, Holiday Inn Express, 🅞 🏥, Alum Cr SP, Cross Creek Camping (6mi)
128mm	🆁🆂 both lanes, full ♿ facilities, 🍽, vending, 🏞, litter barrels, petwalk
121	Polaris Pkwy, to Gemini Pl, **E** 🅖 BP, Mobil, Shell, 🍽 Bonefish Grill, Buffalo Wild Wings, Canes, Carfagna's, 5 Guys Burgers, McDonald's, Mellow Mushroom Pizza, Pei Wei, Polaris Grill, Skyline Chili, Starbucks, Steak'n Shake, 🛏 Best Western, Fairfield Inn, Hampton Inn, Holiday Inn Express, Wingate Inn, 🅞 Firestone/auto, Polaris Amphitheatre, **W** 🅖 BP, Marathon/Circle K, Shell/Tim Horton, 🍽 Applebee's, Arby's, Benihana, BJ's Rest., Brio Grille, Caribou Coffee, Carrabba's, Charley Subs, CheeseCake Factory, Chick-fil-A, Chipotle Mexican, City BBQ, Claddagh Rest., Coldstone, Cosi Cafe, Dave&Buster's, Domino's, El Vaquero Mexican, Hoggy's Grill, Honey Baked Ham, Hooters, House of Japan, Jimmy John's, Krispy Kreme, Marcella's Italian, Max&Erma's, McDonald's, Merlot's Rest., MiMi's Cafe, Mitchell Steaks, Noodles&Co, O'Charley's, Olive Garden, Panera Bread, Papa John's, Penn Sta Subs, Pizza Hut/Taco Bell, Planet Smoothie, Potbelly, Qdoba, Quaker Steak, Red Lobster, Red Robin, Rudedog Grill, Smokey Bones BBQ, Sonic, Starbucks, Subway, Tequilas

Side tab (left): STRONGSVILLE

Side tab (right): MANSFIELD

Left margin tab: OH

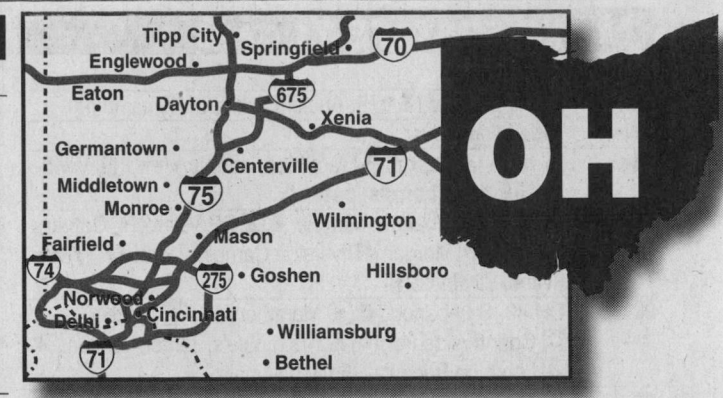

ⓝ INTERSTATE 71 CONT'D

Exit	Services
121	Continued
	Mexican, TGIFriday's, TX Roadhouse, Waffle House, Wendy's, ⓛ Cambria Suites, Candlewood Suites, Comfort Inn, Extended Stay Deluxe, Hilton, Hilton Garden, Residence Inn, ⓞ Urgent Care, AutoZone, Barnes&Noble, Best Buy, BigLots, Cabela's, Costco/gas, Dick's, Earth Fare, GNC, JC Penney, Jo-Ann Etc, Kroger/gas, Lowe's, Macy's, NTB, Old Navy, Petsmart, Sears/auto, Target, TireDiscounters, TJ Maxx, Walgreens, Walmart (3mi), World Mkt, funpark, mall
119b a	I-270, to Indianapolis, Wheeling
117	OH 161, to Worthington, E ⓖ BP/dsl, Shell, Speedway/dsl, Sunoco/dsl, ⓕ Burger King, Carfagna's, China Dynasty, Chipotle, KFC, LJ Silver, Max&Erma's, McDonald's, Rally's, Red Lobster, Subway, Super Seafood Buffet, Wendy's, White Castle, ⓛ Comfort Inn, Days Inn, Knights Inn, Motel 6, Red Roof Inn, ⓞ Urgent Care, CVS Drug, Family$, Staples, TireDiscounters, Walgreens, auto repair, vet, W ⓖ GetGo, Shell, Speedway/dsl, ⓕ Bob Evans, China Jade, Domino's, McDonald's, Pizza Hut, Skyline Chili, Starbucks, Subway, Tim Hortons, Waffle House, Wendy's, ⓛ Baymont Inn, Best Western, Clarion, Columbus Inn, Country Inn&Suites, Crowne Plaza, Extended Stay America, Hawthorn Suites, Rodeway Inn, Super 8, Travelodge, ValuePlace, ⓞ Advance Parts, Chevrolet, Family$, Giant Eagle Foods, NTB, Walgreens
116	Morse Rd, Sinclair Rd, E ⓖ BP, Marathon/dsl, Shell, Speedway, Turkey Hill/dsl, ⓕ Chipotle, Jimmy John's, Little Caesars, McDonald's, Papa John's, Subway, Taco Bell, Tim Horton, ⓛ Extended Stay America, ⓞ AT&T, Buick/GMC, CVS Drug, $General, Family$, Firestone/auto, Ford, Kroger, Menards, PepBoys, Save-A-Lot Foods, W ⓖ Sunoco, ⓛ Best Value Inn, Motel 6, Ramada, ⓞ NTB
115	Cooke Rd
114	N Broadway, W ⓖ Sunoco, ⓕ Broadway Mkt Cafe, Subway
113	Weber Rd, W ⓖ Speedway/dsl, ⓞ CarQuest
112	Hudson St, E ⓖ Marathon, Shell/dsl, ⓕ Wendy's, ⓛ Holiday Inn Express, W ⓕ Big Boy, ⓞ Aldi Foods, Lowe's, NTB
111	17th Ave, W ⓕ McDonald's, ⓛ Comfort Inn, Days Inn
110b	11th Ave
110a	5th Ave, E ⓖ Sunoco, ⓕ Royal Fish&Chicken, White Castle, W ⓖ Valero, ⓕ Church's, KFC, Popeye's, Rally's, Wendy's, ⓞ AutoZone
109a	I-670
109b	OH 3, Cleveland Ave
109c	Spring St (exits left from sb)
108b	US 40, Broad St, downtown
108 a	Main St
101a[70]	I-70 E, US 23 N, to Wheeling
100ba[70]	US 23 S, Front St, High St, downtown
106a	I-70 W, to Indianapolis
106b	OH 315 N, Dublin St, Town St
105	Greenlawn, E ⓖ BP, ⓕ White Castle, W ⓖ Shamrock
104	OH 104, Frank Rd
101b a	I-270, Wheeling, Indianapolis
100	Stringtown Rd, E ⓖ BP, ⓕ Bob Evans, Charley's Grilled Subs, Chick-fil-A, Chipotle, CiCi's Pizza, Coldstone, DQ, 5 Guys Burgers, Jalapeno's Mexican, Longhorn Steaks,
100	Continued
	O'Charley's, Olive Garden, Panda Express, Red Robin, Roosters Grill, Smokey Bones BBQ, Sonic, Starbucks, Steak'n Shake, White Castle, ⓛ Best Western, Drury Inn, Hampton Inn, Holiday Inn Express, Hilton Garden, La Quinta, Microtel, Red Roof Inn, ⓞ Best Buy, Dick's, Firestone/auto, Home Depot, Michael's, Petsmart, Staples, Target, TJ Maxx, Walmart, W ⓖ GetGo, Speedway/dsl, Sunoco/dsl, Turkey Hill/dsl, ⓕ Applebee's, Arby's, Burger King, Cane's Chicken Fingers, China Bell, Cracker Barrel, Donato's Pizza, El Mesquite Mexican, Fazoli's, Golden Corral, KFC, Mariachi Mexican, McDonald's, Papa John's, Rally's, Ruby Tuesday, Starbucks, Taco Bell, TeeJaye's Rest., Tim Horton, Waffle House, Wendy's, ⓛ Comfort Inn, Days Inn, Motel 6, Travelodge, ⓞ Ace Hardware, Advance Parts, Aldi Foods, AutoZone, BigLots, CVS Drug, Giant Eagle Foods, Goodyear/auto, K-Mart, Kroger, PetCo, Radio Shack, Tuffy Auto, Walgreens
97	OH 665, London-Groveport Rd, E ⓖ Marathon/Circle K, ⓕ Arby's, McDonald's, Peking House, Quiznos, Sunny St Cafe, Tim Horton/Wendy's, ⓞ ⓗ, Urgent Care, CVS Drug, Kroger/gas/E85, Meijer/E85, TireDiscounters, to Scioto Downs, W ⓞ Eddie's Repair
94	US 62, OH 3, Orient, W ⓖ Sunoco/dsl
84	OH 56, Mt Sterling, E ⓖ BP/Subway, ⓛ Royal Inn, ⓞ to Deer Creek SP (9mi)
75	OH 38, Bloomingburg, E fireworks, W ⓖ Sunoco/dsl
69	OH 41, OH 734, Jeffersonville, E ⓖ ⓕLYING J/Denny's/dsl/scales/LP/24hr, ⓞ ⓗ, Walnut Lake Camping, W ⓖ BP, Shell/Subway, ⓕ Arby's, Wendy's, ⓛ Quality Inn, ⓞ Family$
68mm	ⓡs both lanes, full ♿ facilities, ⓒ, vending, 🗑 litter barrels, petwalk
65	US 35, Washington CH, E ⓖ Shell, TA/BP/Pizza Hut/Popeye's/dsl/scales/24hr/@, ⓕ A&W/KFC, Bob Evans, Chipotle Mexican, LJ Silver/Taco Bell, McDonald's, Subway, Waffle House, Wendy's, Werner's BBQ, ⓛ Baymont Inn, Fairfield Inn, Hampton Inn, ⓞ ⓗ, AT&T, Tanger Outlets/famous brands, W ⓖ ♥Love's/Hardee's/dsl/scales/24hr, ⓛ EconoLodge
58	OH 72, to Sabina
54mm	weigh sta sb
50	US 68, to Wilmington, E ⓞ ⓗ, W ⓖ BP/dsl, ⓕ Subway/dsl/scales/24hr, Shell/dsl, ⓕ Max&Erma's, McDonald's, Wendy's, ⓛ Budget Inn, Holiday Inn, Robert's Center, repair/tires
49mm	weigh sta nb
45	OH 73, to Waynesville, E ⓖ BP, Shell/dsl, ⓕ 73 Grill, ⓞ ⓗ, camping (3mi), RV Park, W flea mkt, Caesar Creek SP (5mi)

C
O
L
U
M
B
U
S

A
R
E
A

OH

= gas = food = lodging = other = rest stop Copyright 2014 - The NEXT Exit ®

INTERSTATE 71 CONT'D

Exit	Services
36	Wilmington Rd, **E** to Ft Ancient St Mem, RV camping
35mm	Little Miami River
34mm	both lanes, full facilities, scenic view, , vending, , litter barrels, petwalk
32	OH 123, to Lebanon, Morrow, **E** BP, Valero, Country Kitchen, Morgan's Riverside Camping, **3 mi W** Bob Evans, Skyline Chili
28	OH 48, S Lebanon, **E** Marathon/dsl, White Castle, Countryside Inn, Kohl's, Lowe's, Target, Verizon, **W** Lebanon Raceway (6mi), hwy patrol
25	OH 741 N, Kings Mills Rd, **E** Shell/Popeye's, Speedway/dsl, McDonald's, Ruby Tuesday, Taco Bell, Outback Steaks, Comfort Suites, Great Wolf Lodge, Kings Island Resort, Harley-Davidson, **W** BP, Exxon/Subway, Arby's, Big Boy, Bob Evans, Burger King, Chipotle, Perkins, Pizza Hut, Skyline Chili, Tabby's Grill, Waffle House, Wendy's, Baymont Inn, Hampton Inn, Microtel, Super 8, CarX, CVS Drug, GNC, Kroger
24	Western Row, King's Island Dr (from nb), **E** Sunoco, Fantastic Wok, MVPizza, King's Island Resort, Jellystone Camping, funpark
19	US 22, Mason-Montgomery Rd, **E** Speedway/dsl, Arby's, Asian Fusion, Big Boy, Boston Mkt, Burger King, Cracker Barrel, Fiesta Brava, Firehouse Subs, Golden Corral, HoneyBaked Ham, Iron Chef Grill, KFC, McDonald's, Olive Garden, Quiznos, Taco Bell, Taz Mediterranean Grill, TGIFriday's, Wendy's, White Castle, Clarion, Comfort Inn, SpringHill Suites, TownePlace Suites, Aldi Foods, AT&T, AutoZone, Barnes&Noble, Best Buy, BigLots, Buick/GMC, Chevrolet, Chrysler/Dodge/Jeep, Costco/gas, Firestone/auto, Ford, GNC, Goodyear/auto, Hobby Lobby, Honda, Infiniti, JC Penney, Kia, Kohl's, Kroger, Lexus, Lincoln, Mazda, Meijer/dsl, Michael's, Nissan, Old Navy, O'Reilly Parts, Porsche, Radio Shack, Sam's Club/gas, Target, TireDiscounters, Toyota/Scion, Tuffy Auto, Verizon, Walgreens, USPO, vet, **W** BP/dsl, Marathon/dsl/24hr, Abuelo's Mexican, Applebee's, BD Mongolian Grill, Bravo Italian, Burger King, Claddagh Irish, Carrabba's, Chipotle Mexican, China City, Dao Asian, 5 Guys Burgers, Fox&Hound Grill, Graeter's Cafe, IHOP, Jimmy John's, LoneStar Steaks, McAlister's Deli, MiMi's Cafe, O'Charley's, Panera Bread, Polo Grill, Qdoba, Red Robin, River City Grill, Steak'n Shake, Skyline Chili, Subway, Waffle House, Wendy's, Best Western, Days Inn, Hilton Garden, Holiday Inn Express, Hyatt Place, La Quinta, Marriott, Motel 6, Red Roof Inn, Bigg's Foods, Dick's, Home Depot, Lowe's, NAPA, Staples, Walmart, Whole Foods Mkt, vet
17b a	I-275, to I-75, OH 32
15	Pfeiffer Rd, **E** , **W** BP, Shell/dsl, Sunoco/dsl/24hr, Applebee's, Bob Evans, Buffalo Wild Wings, Subway, Watson Bro's Bistro, Courtyard, Crowne Plaza, Embassy Suites, Hampton Inn, Holiday Inn Express, Red Roof Inn, Office Depot
14	OH 126, Reagan Hwy, Blue Ash
12	US 22, OH 3, Montgomery Rd, **E** BP/dsl, Shell/24hr, Arby's, Bob Evans, Chipotle Mexican, Ember's, Jalapeno Cafe, KFC, LJ Silver, Outback Steaks, Panera Bread, Red Lobster, Ruby Tuesday, Subway, Taco Bell, TGIFriday, Wendy's, Best Western, Dodge, Firestone, Good

Exit	Services
12	Continued year, Hyundai, PepBoys, Staples, Tuesday Morning, **W** Chevron, Cheesecake Factory, IHOP, KFC, Johnny Rocket's, Macaroni Grill, Max&Erma's, McDonald's, Potbelly's, Starbucks, Wendy's, , Barnes&Noble, Dillard's, Firestone/auto, Fresh Mkt Foods, Macy's, Old Navy, Staples, mall
11	Kenwood Rd, (from nb), **W** , same as 12
10	Stewart Rd (from nb), to Silverton, **W** Marathon/dsl
9	Redbank Rd, to Fairfax, (no ez sb return), **E** Mobil, Speedway, BMW
8	Kennedy Ave, Ridge Ave W, **E** Meijer/dsl, IHOP, Motel 6, Dodge, Sam's Club/gas, Target, **W** Marathon/dsl, Shell/Subway, Speedway, Denny's, Golden Corral, Gold Star Chili, KFC, LJ Silver, McDonald's, Old Country Buffet, Pizza Hut, Rally's, Taco Bell, White Castle, Wendy's, Bigg's Foods, Big Lots, Ford, Goodyear, Home Depot, Lowes Whse, Office Depot, Tire Discounter, Walmart, transmissions
7b a	OH 562, Ridge Ave E, Norwood, **E** BP, Ponderosa, AutoZone
6	Edwards Rd, **E** BP, Shell, Speedway, Boston Mkt, Buca Italian, Donato's, Don Pablo, Fuddrucker's, GoldStar Chili, J Alexander's Rest., Longhorn Steaks, Max&Erma's, Noodles, PF Chang's, Starbucks, GNC, SteinMart, **W** Shell
5	Dana Ave, Montgomery Rd, **W** Xavier Univ, Zoo
3	Taft Rd (from sb), U of Cincinnati
2	US 42, Reading Rd, Gilbert ave (from sb), **W** , art Museum, ballpark stadium arena, downtown
1k j	I-471 S
1d	Main St, downtown
1c b	Pete Rose Way, Fine St, stadium, downtown
1a	I-75 N, US 50, to Dayton
I-71 S and I-75 S run together	
0mm	Ohio/Kentucky state line, Ohio River

INTERSTATE 74

Exit	Services
20	I-75 (from eb), N to Dayton, S to Cincinnati, **I-74 begins/ends on I-75.**
19	Gilmore St, Spring Grove Ave
18	US 27 N, Colerain Ave
17	Montana Ave (from wb), **N** Circle K
14	North Bend Rd, Cheviot, **N** Shell, Speedway/dsl, DQ, Dunkin Donuts, McDonald's, Papa John's, Perkins, Skyline Chili, Subway, Wendy's, White Castle, Curves, Family$, Kroger, Sam's Club/gas, Tire Discounters, Walgreens, **S** BP, Bob Evans, vet
11	Rybolt Rd, Harrison Pike, **S** BP, Longhorn Steaks, Marco's Pizza, McDonald's, Sakura Steaks, Skyline Chili, Wendy's, White Castle, Holiday Inn Express, Kohl's, Meijer/gas,
9	I-275 N, to I-75, N to Dayton, (exits left from eb)
8mm	Great Miami River
7	OH 128, to Hamilton, Cleves, **N** BP/dsl, Marathon/dsl, Wendy's
5	I-275 S, to Kentucky
3	Dry Fork Rd, **N** BP, **S** Marathon/dsl, Shell/Dunkin Donuts/dsl
2mm	**weigh sta eb**
1	New Haven Rd, to Harrison, **N** BP/dsl, Buffalo Wild Wings, China Garden, Chipotle Mexican, Cracker Barrel,

↗E INTERSTATE 74 CONT'D

Exit	Services
1	Continued
	GoldStar Chili, Little Caesars, O'Charley's, Subway, 🅞 Biggs Foods, Ford, Home Depot, Kia, Staples, Tires+, Verizon, S 🅖 Shell/Circle K, Speedway/dsl, Sunoco/White Castle, 🍴 A&W/KFC, Arby's, Burger King, DQ, Domino's, Happy Garden, El Mariachi, McDonald's, Penn Sta Subs, Pizza Hut, Skyline Chili, Taco Bell, Waffle House, Wendy's, 🏠 Holiday Inn Express, 🅞 Advance Parts, AT&T, AutoZone, BigLots, CVS Drug, $General, $Tree, Family$, Firestone/auto, GNC, K-Mart, Kroger/dsl, Meineke, NAPA, O'Reilly Parts, Radio Shack, Tire Discounters, Walgreens
0mm	Ohio/Indiana state line

↗N INTERSTATE 75

Exit	Services
211mm	Ohio/Michigan state line
210	OH 184, Alexis Rd, to Raceway Park, W 🅖 BP/Circle K/dsl, 🚚/Subway/dsl/scales/24hr, 🍴 Arby's, Bob Evans, Burger King, McDonald's, Taco Bell, Wendy's, 🏠 Fairfield Inn, Hampton Inn, Holiday Inn Express, 🅞 AutoZone, Meijer/dsl, Menards, **Urgent Care**
210mm	Ottawa River
209	Ottawa River Rd (from nb), E 🅖 BP, Sunoco, 🍴 China King, Little Caesars, Marco's Pizza, River Diner, 🅞 Family$, Kroger/E85, Rite Aid, vet
208	I-280 S, to I-80/90, to Cleveland
207	Stickney Ave, Lagrange St, E 🅖 BP, 🍴 Arby's, McDonald's, Wendy's, 🅞 Family$, K-Mart, Rite Aid, Save-A-Lot Foods, USPO
206	to US 24, Phillips Ave, W transmissions
205b	Berdan Ave, E 🅗, W 🅖 Marathon/dsl, 🍴 Burger King, Subway
205a	to Willys Pkwy, to Jeep Pkwy
204	I-475 W, to US 23 (exits left fom nb), to Maumee, Ann Arbor
203b	US 24, to Detroit Ave, W 🅖 AP/dsl, BP, 🍴 KFC, McDonald's, Rally's, Wendy's, 🅞 Rite Aid, Save-A-Lot Foods, U-Haul
203a	Bancroft St, downtown
202	Washington St, Collingwood Ave (from sb, no E7 return), E 🅖 BP, 🅞 🅗, Art Museum, W 🍴 McDonald's
201b a	OH 25, Collingwood Ave, W Toledo Zoo
200	South Ave, Kuhlman Dr
200mm	Maumee River
199	OH 65, Miami St, to Rossford, E 🏠 Days Inn
198	Wales Rd, Oregon Rd, to Northwood, E 🅖 Shell/Subway/dsl, Sunoco/dsl, 🍴 Arby's, China Wok, Coney Is. 🏠 Baymont Inn, Comfort Inn
197	Buck Rd, to Rossford, E 🅖 Shell/dsl, 🍴 Tim Horton's, Wendy's, W 🅖 BP, Sunoco/dsl, 🍴 Denny's, McDonald's, 🏠 American Inn, Knights Inn
195	to I-80/90, OH 795, OH Tpk (**toll**), Perrysburg, E 🅖 BP/Subway/dsl, 🏠 Country Inn&Suites, Courtyard, Hampton Inn, 🅞 Bass Pro Shops
193	US 20, US 23 S, Perrysburg, E 🅖 BP/dsl, GetGo, Sunoco, 🍴 Arby's, Big Boy, Bob Evans, Burger King, Chili's, China City, Coldstone, Cracker Barrel, 1st Wok, 5 Guys Burgers, Dragon Chef, Fricker's, IHOP, Jimmy John's, KFC, Mancino's Pizza, Ok Patron, Panera Bread, Penn Sta Subs, Sonic, Subway, Taco Bell, 🏠 Candlewood

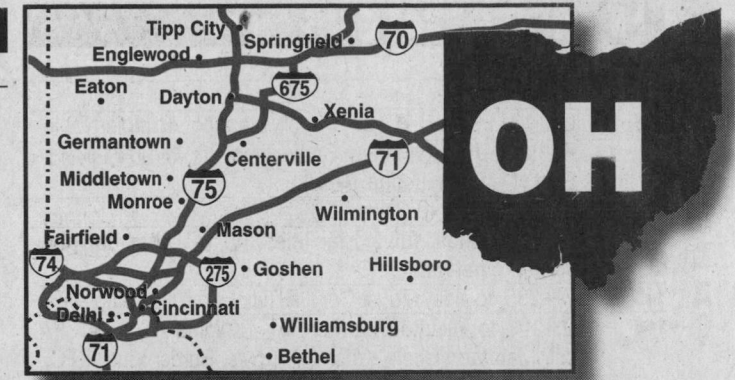

Exit	Services
193	Continued
	Suites, Comfort Suites, EconoLodge, Holiday Inn, Holiday Inn Express, Quality Inn, 🅞 Belle Tire, Best Buy, Discount Tire, $Tree, Giant Eagle Foods, GNC, Hobby Lobby, Home Depot, Kohl's, Kroger/gas/E85, KOA (7mi), Lowe's, Meijer/dsl, Michael's, Petsmart, Radio Shack, Target, TJ Maxx, Tuffy, Walgreens, Walmart/Subway, W 🅖 Speedway/dsl, 🏠 La Quinta, 🅞 AutoZone, Harley-Davidson
192	I-475, US 23 N (exits left from nb), to Maumee, Ann Arbor
187	OH 582, to Luckey, Haskins
181	OH 64, OH 105, to Pemberville, Bowling Green, E 🏠 Holiday Inn Express, 🅞 Meijer/dsl/E85, W 🅖 BP/Circle K/Subway/dsl, Speedway, 🍴 Big Boy, Bob Evans, Buffalo Wild Wings, Burger King, Chipotle Mexican, Cinco de Mayo, Coldstone/Tim Horton's, Domino's, El Zarape Mexican, Fricker's Rest., Hunan Buffet, Jimmy John's, McDonald's, Padrone's Pizza, Starbucks, Waffle House, Wendy's, 🏠 Best Western, Days Inn, Hampton Inn, Quality Inn, Victory Inn, 🅞 🅗, Verizon, USPO, to Bowling Green State U
179	US 6, to Fremont, Napoleon, W museum
179mm	🆁🆂 both lanes, full ♿ facilities, 🍴, 🏠, litter barrels, vending, petwalk
175mm	weigh sta nb
171	OH 25, Cygnet
168	Eagleville Rd, Quarry Rd, E 🅖 FuelMart/dsl
167	OH 18, to Fostoria, North Baltimore, E 🅖 Petro/BP/Iron Skillet/dsl/scales/24hr/@, 🍴 McDonald's, 🅞 Blue Beacon, truck repair, W 🅖 Loves/Arby's/dsl/scales/24hr, Sunoco, 🏠 Crown Inn, 🅞 $General, Great Scot Mkt
165mm	Rocky Ford River
164	OH 613, to McComb, Fostoria, E 🅞 KOA, Van Buren SP, W 🅖 🚚/Subway/Taco Bell/dsl/scales/24hr
162mm	weigh sta sb, 🍴
161	rd 99, E 🅖 Speedway/dsl, Shell/Subway, 🏠 Comfort Suites, 🅞 Ford/Lincoln, Kia, hwy patrol, W antiques
159	US 224, OH 15, Findlay, E 🅖 BP/dsl, Speedway/dsl, Swifty, 🍴 Archie's Ice Cream, Burger King, Culver's, Dakota Grill, Fin's Seafood Grill, Jimmy John's, KFC/LJ Silver, McDonald's, Ming's Great Wall, Pizza Hut, Ralphie's, Spaghetti Shop, Steak'n Shake, Subway, Taco Bell, Wendy's, 🏠 Drury Inn, Red Roof Inn, Rodeway Inn, Motel 6, 🅞 🅗, auto/truck repair, W 🅖 Murphy USA/dsl, Shell/dsl, 🍴 Bob Evans, China Garden, Coldstone/Tim Horton's, Cracker Barrel, Denny's, Hokkaido Steaks, Jac&Do's Pizza, Landing Pad, Max&Erma's, Outback Steaks, Tony's Rest., TX Roadhouse, Waffle House, 🏠 Country Inn&Suites, Hampton Inn, Holiday Inn Express, Quality Inn, 🅞 Best 1 Tires/repair, Chrysler/Dodge/Jeep, Peterbilt, Verizon, Walmart/Subway,

OH

(side margin: TOLEDO, PERRYSBURG, FINDLAY)

Ⓖ = gas   Ⓕ = food   Ⓛ = lodging   Ⓞ = other   Ⓡˢ = rest stop   Copyright 2014 - The NEXT Exit ®

🆖 INTERSTATE 75 CONT'D

Exit	Services
158mm	Blanchard River
157	OH 12, Findlay, **E** Ⓖ GA/dsl, Marathon/Blimpie/Noble Roman's/dsl, Ⓞ Findlay Convention Ctr, **W** Ⓕ Fricker's Rest., Ⓛ EconoLodge, Ⓞ vet
156	US 68, OH 15, to Carey, **E** Ⓗ
153mm	Ⓡˢ **both lanes, full** Ⓗ **facilities,** Ⓒ, Ⓟ, **litter barrels, vending, petwalk**
145	OH 235, to Ada, Mount Cory, **E** TwinLakes Camping
142	OH 103, to Arlington, Bluffton, **E** Ⓛ Knights Inn, **W** Ⓖ BP/dsl, Marathon/Circle K/dsl, Ⓕ Arby's, Burger King, KFC, McDonald's/rv parking, Subway, Taco Bell, Ⓛ Comfort Inn, Ⓞ $General, auto repair, vet, to Bluffton Coll
140	Bentley Rd, to Bluffton, **W** Ⓗ
135	OH 696, to US 30, to Delphos, Beaverdam, **E** Ⓖ Speedway/dsl/24hr, **W** Ⓖ ⒻLYING J/Denny's/dsl/scales/LP/24hr/@, ▣/McDonald's/Subway/dsl/24hr/@, Ⓕ Waffle House, Ⓞ Blue Beacon, SpeedCo, tires, truck repair
134	Napolean Rd (no nb re-entry), to Beaverdam
130	Bluelick Rd, **E** Ⓛ Best Value Inn
127b a	OH 81, to Ada, Lima, **W** Ⓖ BP/dsl, Marathon/Subway/dsl, Ⓕ Waffle House, Ⓛ Comfort Inn, Days Inn/rest., Ⓞ Best 1 Tires/repair
126mm	Ottawa River
125	OH 309, OH 117, Lima, **E** Ⓖ BP/dsl, Murphy USA/dsl, Speedway/dsl, Ⓕ Applebee's, Arby's, Bob Evans, Burger King, Capt D's, China Buffet, Cracker Barrel, Hunan Garden, J's Grill, McDonald's, Olive Garden, Panera Bread, Pizza Hut, Ralphie's, Red Lobster, Skyline Chili, Subway, Taco Bell, TX Roadhouse, Wendy's, Ⓛ Courtyard, Hampton Inn, Howard Johnson, Motel 6, Ⓞ BigLots, Ford, K-Mart, Radio Shack, Ray's Foods, Sam's Club/gas, Verizon, Walgreens, Walmart/McDonald's, **W** Ⓖ Shell, Ⓕ Kewpee Hamburger's, Yamato Steaks, Ⓛ Country Inn&Suites, Holiday Inn, Travelodge, Ⓞ Ⓗ, Advance Parts, Best 1 Tires/repair, Curves, $General, Rite Aid, Save-A-Lot Foods
124	4th St, **E** hwy patrol
122	OH 65, Lima, **E** Ⓖ Speedway/dsl, **W** Ⓖ Marathon/Subway/dsl, Ⓞ Freightliner, GMC, Mack, Volvo, truck repair, vet
120	Breese Rd, Ft Shawnee, **W** Ⓖ AP Trkstp/dsl, Ⓞ Harley-Davidson
118	to Cridersville, **W** Ⓖ Fuelmart/Subway/dsl, Speedway/dsl, Ⓕ Dixie Ley Diner, Ⓞ $General
114mm	Ⓡˢ **both lanes, hadicapped facilities,** Ⓟ, **litter barrels, pet walk,** Ⓒ s, **vending**
113	OH 67, to Uniopolis, Wapakoneta
111	Bellefontaine St, Wapakoneta, **E** Ⓖ TA/Marathon/rest./dsl/scales/@, Ⓕ Country Charm Rest., Ⓛ Knights Inn, Ⓞ KOA, truck tires, **W** Ⓖ BP/dsl, Murphy USA/dsl, Shell, Ⓕ Arby's, Bob Evans, Burger King, Capt D's, Comfort Zone, DQ, El Azteca, King Buffet, Lucky Steer Rest., McDonald's, Pizza Hut, Taco Bell, Waffle House, Wendy's, Ⓛ Best Western, Comfort Inn, Super 8, Western Inn, Ⓞ Advance Parts, Aldi Foods, CVS Drug, Lowe's, Neil Armstrong Museum, O'Reilly Parts, Radio Shack, Verizon, Walmart, st patrol
110	US 33, to St Marys, Bellefontaine, **E** KOA, hwy patrol
104	OH 219, **W** Ⓖ Marathon/dsl, Shell/Circle K/Subway/dsl, Ⓕ Larry's Pizza, Ⓛ Budget Host
102	OH 274, to Jackson Ctr, New Breman, **E** bicycle museum, **W** air stream tours

Exit	Services
99	OH 119, to Minster, Anna, **E** Ⓖ 99/dsl, **W** Ⓖ GA/Taco Bell, Shell, Ⓕ Subway, Wendy's, Ⓞ lube/wash/repair
94	rd 25A, Sidney, **E** Ⓖ Marathon/deli
93	OH 29, to St Marys, Sidney, **W** Lake Loramie SP, RV camping
92	OH 47, to Versailles, Sidney, **E** Ⓖ Shell, Speedway/dsl, Ⓕ Arby's, China Garden, Coldstone, Subway, Time Horton, Wendy's, Ⓞ Ⓗ, AutoZone, CVS Drug, $General, DM, NAPA, Save-A-Lot Foods, Walgreens, **Urgent Care**, **W** Ⓖ Murphy USA/dsl, Sunoco/dsl, Valero, Ⓕ A&W/LJ Silver, Applebee's, Bob Evans, Buffalo Wild Wings, Burger King, Cazadores Mexican, Culver's, Highmarks Rest., KFC, McDonald's, Perkins, Pizza Hut, Quiznos, Smokin Joe's BBQ, Sonic, Taco Bell, Waffle House, Ⓛ Comfort Inn, Country Hearth Inn, Days Inn, Travel Inn, Ⓞ Aldi Foods, AT&T, Best 1 Tires/repair, Buick/Cadillac/Chevrolet/GMC, Chrysler/Dodge/Jeep, $Tree, Ford/Lincoln, Kroger/dsl, Lowe's, Menards, Radio Shack, Staples, Walmart/McDonald's
90	Fair Rd, to Sidney, **E** Ⓖ Sunoco/dsl, **W** Ⓖ Marathon/DQ/dsl, Ⓛ Hampton Inn
88mm	Great Miami River
83	rd 25A, Piqua, **W** Ⓖ Marathon/MaidRite Cafe/Noble Roman's/dsl, Ⓛ Red Carpet Inn, Ⓞ Chrysler/Dodge/Jeep, Sherry RV Ctr, to Piqua Hist Area
82	US 36, to Urbana, Piqua, **E** Ⓖ Murphy USA/dsl, Valero, Ⓕ A&W/LJ Silver, Arby's, China East, China Garden, DQ, KFC, Pizza Hut/Taco Bell, Subway, Waffle House, Wendy's, Ⓞ Aldi Foods, BigLots, $Tree, Harley-Davidson, Home Depot, JoAnn Fabrics, Radio Shack, Verizon, Walmart/Subway, st patrol, vet, **W** Ⓖ Speedway, Ⓕ Bob Evans, Cracker Barrel, El Tapatio Mexican, McDonald's, Red Lobster, Ⓛ Comfort Inn, Knights Inn, La Quinta, Ⓞ JC Penney
81mm	Ⓡˢ **both lanes, full** Ⓗ **facilities,** Ⓒ s, Ⓟ, **litter barrels, vending**
78	rd 25A, **E** Ⓗ
74	OH 41, to Covington, Troy, **E** Ⓖ BP/dsl, Ⓕ Al's Pizza, China Garden, Donato's Pizza, Fox's Pizza, Little Caesars, McDonald's, Pizza Hut, Subway, Taco Bell, Ⓞ Ⓗ, Radio Shack, Super Petz, to Hobart Arena, **W** Ⓖ Shell, Speedway/dsl, Ⓕ Applebee's, Big Boy, Bob Evans, Buffalo Wild Wings, Burger King, Chipotle Mexican, Culver's, Fazoli's, Friendly's, KFC, Logan's Roadhouse, Los Pitayos Mexican, Outback Steaks, Panera Bread, Penn Sta Subs, Ruby Tuesday, Sakai Japanese, Skyline Chili, Sonic, Steak'n Shake, Ⓛ Best Inn, Comfort Suites, Fairfield Inn, Hampton Inn, Holiday Inn Express, Residence Inn, Ⓞ AT&T, AutoZone, $General, $Tree, GNC, Goodyear, Kohl's, Lowe's, Meijer/dsl, Staples, Tire Discounters, Verizon, Walmart/Subway,
73	OH 55, to Ludlow Falls, Troy, **E** Ⓖ BP, Shell, Ⓕ Boston Stoker Coffee House, Hot Head Burrito, Lincoln Sq Rest., Papa John's, Subway, Waffle House, Wendy's, Ⓛ Quality Inn, Royal Inn, Super 8, Ⓞ Ⓗ, $General, Kroger/e85
69	rd 25A, **E** Ⓖ BP/Circle K/Subway/dsl, Starfire/dsl, Ⓞ Arbogast RV Ctr, Buick/GMC, Chrysler/Dodge/Jeep, Ford
68	OH 571, to West Milton, Tipp City, **E** Ⓖ BP/dsl, Shell, Speedway/dsl, Ⓕ Burger King, Cassano's Pizza, Hickory River BBQ, Hong Kong Kitchen, McDonald's, Subway, Taco Bell, Ⓞ AutoValue Parts, CVS Drug, Family$, FoodTown, Goodyear, Honda, Verizon, **W** Ⓖ Speedway/dsl, Ⓕ Arby's, Big Boy, Bob Evans, Tipp' O the Town Rest.,

OH

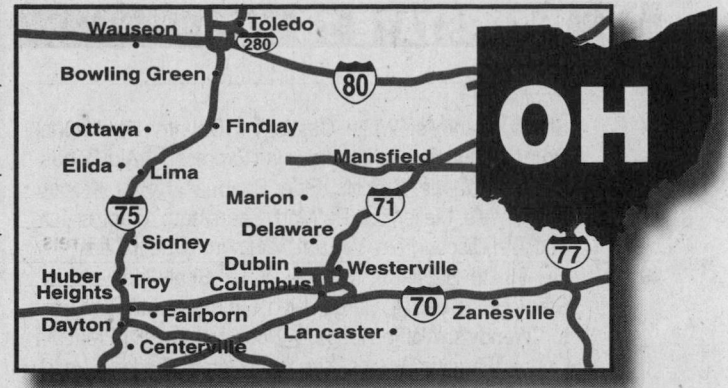

INTERSTATE 75 CONT'D

Exit	Services
68	Continued Wendy's, 🛏 Holiday Inn Express, La Quinta, ⊡ Main St Parts, Menards, vet
64	Northwoods Blvd, **E** 🍴 El Toro Mexican, Emperial Palace, ⊡ $Tree, Kroger/dsl
63	US 40, to Donnelsville, Vandalia, **E** 🅿 Speedway/dsl, 🍴 Bunker's Grill, Dragon China, Fricker's, ⊡ repair, **W** 🅿 BP/dsl, Shell, Speedway/dsl, 🍴 Arby's, Burger King, Domino's, Hot Head Burrito, KFC/LJ Silver, McDonald's, Pizza Hut, Rib House, Subway, Taco Bell, Waffle House, Wendy's, 🛏 Super 8, ⊡ Goodyear/auto, Rexall Drug, Rite Aid
61b a	I-70, E to Columbus, W to Indianapolis, to Dayton Int ✈
59	Wyse Rd, Benchwood Rd, **E** 🍴 El Rancho Grande, Little York Pizza, Mr Lee's, 🛏 Dayton Inn, Hawthorn Suites, ⊡ BMW/Volvo/VW, Discount Tire, **W** 🅿 Speedway/dsl, Valero, 🍴 Arby's, Asian Buffet, Big Boy, Bob Evans, Cassano's Pizza, Chick-fil-A, Chipotle Mexican, Coldstone, Cracker Barrel, Fricker's, Golden Corral, Hooters, LoneStar Steaks, Max&Erma's, McDonald's, O'Charley's, Olive Garden, Outback Steaks, Panera Bread, Pop's Diner, Red Lobster, Ruby Tuesday, Sake Japanese, Skyline Chili, SmashBurger, SmokeyBones BBQ, Steak'n Shake, Subway, Tim Horton, 🛏 Best Value Inn, Comfort Inn, Country Inn&Suites, Courtyard, Days Inn, Drury Inn, Extended Stay America, Fairfield Inn, Hampton Inn, Knights Inn, Red Roof Inn, Residence Inn, Rodeway Inn, TownePlace Suites, ⊡ Batteries+, Office Depot, Radio Shack, Sam's Club/gas, Verizon, Walmart/Subway,
58	Needmore Rd, to Dayton, **E** 🅿 BP/dsl, Shell/McDonald's, 🍴 Hardee's, 🛏 ⊡ Goodyear/auto, to AF Museum, **W** 🅿 Marathon/dsl, Speedway/dsl, Sunoco/dsl, Swifty, 🍴 A&W/LJ Silver, Church's, Domino's, Subway, Tim Horton, Waffle House, Wendy's, ⊡ Advance Parts, AutoZone, $Tree, Kroger/gas, O'Reilly Parts, Walgreens, USPO, repair/transmissions
57b	Wagner Ford Rd, Siebenthaler Rd, Dayton, **E** 🅿 Sunoco, 🛏 Ramada Inn
57a	Neva Rd
56	Stanley Ave, Dayton, **E** 🅿 Shell, **W** 🅿 Clark, 🍴 Dragon City Chinese, Gold Star Chili, McDonald's, Taco Bell, 🛏 Dayton Motel, ⊡ truck repair
55b a	Keowee St, Dayton, downtown
54c	OH 4 N, Webster St, to Springfield, downtown
54mm	Great Miami River
54b	OH 48, Main St, Dayton, **E** 🅿 Cadillac, Chevrolet, Honda, **W** 🅿 BP, ⊡ 🅷
54a	Grand Ave, Dayton, downtown
53b	OH 49, 1st St, Salem Ave, Dayton, downtown
53a	OH 49, 3rd St, downtown
52b a	US 35, E to Dayton, W to Eaton
51	Edwin C Moses Blvd, Nicholas Rd, **E** 🅿 Loves/Hardee's/dsl/scales/24hr, 🛏 Courtyard, ⊡ 🅷, to U of Dayton, **W** 🅿 BP/dsl, 🍴 McDonald's, Wendy's, 🛏 EconoLodge, ⊡ SunWatch Indian Village
50b a	OH 741, Kettering St, Dryden Rd, **E** 🅷, vet, **W** 🅿 Marathon/dsl, 🛏 Days Inn, Super 8, ⊡ U-Haul
47	Dixie Dr, Kettering, Moraine, **E** 🅿 Sunoco, Valero, 🍴 Big Boy, Waffle House, ⊡ auto repair, transmissions, **W** 🅿 Shell, Speedway/dsl, 🍴 Ele Cake Co., El Mason, KFC,

Exit	Services
47	Continued McDonald's, Pizza Hut, Sonic, Taco Bell, Wendy's, ⊡ $General, USPO
44	OH 725, to Centerville, Miamisburg, **E** 🅿 BP/dsl, Shell, Speedway, 🍴 Applebee's, Baskin-Robbins, Big Boy, Bonefish Grill, Bravo Italiana, Burger King, Dunkin Donuts, El Toro Mexican, Fazoli's, Friendly's, Golden Corral, Hardee's, Jimmy John's, KFC, Logan's Roadhouse, Lonestar Steaks, McDonald's, O'Charley's, Olive Garden, Panera Bread, PF Chang's, Red Lobster, Rooster's Grill, Rusty Bucket Grill, Sake Japanese, Skyline Chili, SmashBurger, Starbucks, Steak'n Shake, Subway, Taco Bell, TGIFriday's, Waffle House, Wendy's, 🛏 Comfort Suites, Courtyard, DoubleTree Suites, Garden Inn, Hornewood Suites, InTowne Suites, SpringHill Suites, Studio 6, ⊡ 🅷 Advance Parts, Aldi Foods, AT&T, Barnes&Noble, Best Buy, Cub Foods, Dick's, $Tree, Elder Beerman, Hobby Lobby, Home Depot, Honda/Nissan/Mazda, JC Penney, JoAnn Fabrics, Kia, Lowe's, Macy's, Michael's, NTB, Office Depot, PepBoys, Petsmart, Sears/auto, Super Petz, Target, Tire Discounters, TJ Maxx, Toyota/Scion, Verizon, Walmart, mall, **Urgent Care**, **W** 🅿 BP, Marathon, Shell/dsl, 🍴 Bob Evans, LJ Silver, Perkins, Tim Horton, 🛏 Knights Inn, Quality Inn, Red Roof Inn, Super 8, ⊡ 🅷, Aamco, CarMax, Chevrolet, $General, Ford, NAPA
43	I-675 N, to Columbus
41	Austin Blvd, **E** Kohl's
38	OH 73, Springboro, Franklin, **E** 🅿 Shell, Speedway, 🍴 Applebee's, Arby's, Bob Evans, Burger King, China Garden, Chipotle Mexican, KFC, LJ Silver, McDonald's, Papa John's, Pizza Hut, Skyline Chili, Subway, Taco Bell, Tim Horton, Wendy's, 🛏 Comfort Inn, Hampton Inn, ⊡ K-Mart, Kroger, Radio Shack, Tire Discounters, vet, **W** 🅿 Murphy USA/dsl, Road Ranger, Shell, Swifty, 🍴 A&G Pizza, Big Boy, Cazadore's Mexican, Domino's, GoldStar Chili, Lee's Chicken, McDonald's, 🛏 EconoLodge, Holiday Inn Express, Knights Inn, ⊡ Advance Parts, AutoZone, Clark's Drug, $General, $Tree, Kemper Auto, Main St Mkt, NAPA, Walgreens, Walmart, USPO
36	OH 123, to Lebanon, Franklin, **E** 🅿 BP, 🍴/Subway/Pizza Hut/dsl/scales/24hr/@, Shell, 🍴 McDonald's, Waffle House, 🛏 Quail Inn, **W** 🅿 Marathon/White Castle/dsl, Sunoco
32	OH 122, Middletown, **E** 🍴 McDonald's, 🛏 Best Value Inn, Days Inn, Super 8, Reyton Inn, ⊡ 🅷, CVS Drug, **W** 🍴 Applebee's, Arby's, Big Boy, Bob Evans, Cracker Barrel, El Rancho Grande, Golden Corral, GoldStar Chili, Hot Head Burrito, KFC, La Rosa's Pizza, LoneStar Steaks, O'Charley's, Olive Garden, Schlotzsky's, Sonic, Steak'n

DAYTON / **MIDDLETOWN**

OH

🅖 = gas 🍴 = food 🛏 = lodging 🄾 = other 🆁🆂 = rest stop   Copyright 2014 - The NEXT Exit ®

↙N INTERSTATE 75 CONT'D

Exit	Services
32	Continued
	Shake, Wendy's, White Castle, 🛏 Country Hearth Inn, Drury Inn, Fairfield Inn, Holiday Inn Express, 🄾 Aldi Foods, AT&T, AutoZone, BigLots, Elder Beerman, Kohl's, Kroger/dsl, Lowe's, Meijer/dsl, PetMart, Sears/auto, Staples, Target, Tire Discounters, Verizon, Walmart, **Urgent Care**
29	OH 63, to Hamilton, Monroe, **E** 🅖 Shell/Popeye's/dsl, Stony Ridge/dsl, 🍴 Burger King, GoldStar Chili, Tim Horton/Wendy's, Waffle House, 🛏 Comfort Inn, 🄾 Premium Outlets/Famous Brands, Tire Discounters, Trader's World, **W** 🅖 Speedway/dsl, 🍴 Froggy Blue's, McDonald's, Richard's Pizza, Sara Jane's Rest., Subway, 🛏 Hampton Inn, Howard Johnson, 🄾 Honda
27.5mm	🆁🆂 both lanes, full ♿ facilities, info, 🚻, 🛐, litter barrels, vending, petwalk
24	OH 129 W, to Hamilton, **W** Cincinnati Gardens
22	Tylersville Rd, to Mason, Hamilton, **E** 🅖 Sunoco, Thornton's/dsl, 🍴 Arby's, Bob Evans, BoneFish Grill, Burger King, Caribou Coffee, Chick-fil-A, Chopsticks, City BBQ, Firehouse Subs, 5 Guys Burgers, Geisha, GoldStar Chili, IHOP, Jimmy John's, KFC, LJ Silver, Longhorn Steaks, McAlister's Deli, McDonald's, Noodles&Co, Panera Bread, Perkins, Pizza Hut, Qdoba, Ruby Tuesday, Skyline Chili, SmashBurger, Soho Japanese, Starbucks, Subway, Taco Bell, TGIFriday's, Twin Dragon, Wendy's, 🛏 Economy Inn, 🄾 🄷, AT&T, BigLots, Firestone, GNC, Goodyear/auto, Home Depot, Kohl's, Kroger, Michael's, Office Depot, Petsmart, Radio Shack, Target, Tires+, TJ Maxx, Verizon, Walgreens, **W** 🅖 Shell, Speedway/dsl, 🍴 O'Charley's, 🛏 Wingate Inn, 🄾 Aldi Foods, CarX, Lowe's, Meijer/dsl, Tire Discounters
21	Cin-Day Rd, **E** 🍴 Big Boy, 🛏 Holiday Inn Express, **W** 🅖 Marathon/dsl, Mobil/Subway/dsl, Speedway/dsl, 🍴 Arby's, Domino's, Guenther's Steaks, La Rosa's Pizza, Las Copas Mexican, Papa John's, Sonic, Waffle House, Wendy's, White Castle, 🄾 Ace Hardware, AutoZone, Curves, PetMart, Walgreens, Walmart/Subway,
19	Union Centre Blvd, to Fairfield, **E** 🍴 Bravo Italiana, Champps Rest., Mitchell's Fish Mkt, Original Pancakes, Panera Bread, PF Chang's, Red Robin, Smokey Bones BBQ, Steak'n Shake, 🄾 Barnes&Noble, Verizon, **W** 🅖 BP/Subway/dsl, Marathon/Circle K, Shell, 🍴 Aladdin's Eatery, Applebee's, Bob Evans, Buffalo Wild Wings, Burger King, Chipotle Mexican, Jag's Steaks, Jimmy John's, McDonald's, Qdoba, Quiznos, Rafferty's, Skyline Chili, Starbucks, Tazza Mia, Uno, Wendy's, 🛏 Comfort Inn, Courtyard, Hampton Inn, Marriott, Residence Inn, Staybridge Suites, 🄾 Mercedes, Volvo
16	I-275 to I-71, to I-74
15	Sharon Rd, to Sharonville, Glendale, **E** 🅖 Sunoco, Thornton's/dsl, 🍴 Big Boy, Bob Evans, Cracker Barrel, Jim Dandy BBQ, Ruby Tuesday, Skyline Chili, Subway, Waffle House, 🛏 Baymont Inn, Country Inn&Suites, Drury Inn, Hawthorn Suites, Hilton Garden, Holiday Inn Express, La Quinta, Red Roof Inn, Travel Inn, Travelodge, Wyndham, **W on Kemper** 🅖 Sunoco, 🍴 Burger King, Chick-fil-A, Chili's, ChuckeCheese, 5 Guys Burgers, IHOP, LJ Silver, Macaroni Grill, McDonald's, Panera Bread, Pizza Hut, Taco Bell, Subway, Tokyo Japanese, Vincenzo's, Wendy's, 🛏 Crowne Plaza, EconoLodge, Extended Stay Deluxe,

C I N C I N N A T I   A R E A

15	Continued
	Extended Stay America, Fairfield Inn, LivInn Suites, Residence Inn, 🄾 Best Buy, Costco/gas, Dick's, Lowe's, Nissan, Sam's Club, Sears, Target
14	OH 126, to Woodlawn, Evendale, **E** GE Plant, 🛏 Wingate Inn (3mi), **W** 🅖 Swifty
13	Shepherd Lane, to Lincoln Heights, **E** GE Plant, **W** 🍴 Taco Bell, Wendy's, 🄾 Advance Parts
12	Wyoming Ave, Cooper Ave, to Lockland, **W** 🅖 Marathon, 🍴 DQ, Subway
10a	OH 126, Ronald Reagan Hwy
10b	Galbraith Rd (exits left from nb), Arlington Heights
9	OH 4, OH 561, Paddock Rd, Seymour Ave, **E** to Cincinnati Gardens, **W** fairgrounds
8	Towne St, Elmwood Pl (from nb)
7	OH 562, to I-71, Norwood, Cincinnati Gardens
6	Mitchell Ave, St Bernard, **E** 🅖 Marathon, Shell, Sunoco, 🍴 White Castle, 🛏 Holiday Inn Express, 🄾 Walgreens, to Cincinnati Zoo, to Xavier U, **W** 🅖 BP/Subway/dsl, 🍴 McDonald's, Rally's, 🄾 Advance Parts, Family$, Ford, Honda, Hyundai, Kia, Kroger, Tires+
4	I-74 W, US 52, US 27 N, to Indianapolis
3	to US 27 S, US 127 S, Hopple St, U of Cincinnati, **E** 🅖 BP/Subway/dsl, 🍴 Camp Washington Chili, Isador Italian, White Castle, 🄾 🄷, Family$, **W** 🅖 Shell, 🍴 Wendy's
2b	Harrison Ave, industrial district, **W** 🅖 BP, 🍴 McDonald's
2a	Western Ave, Liberty St (from sb)
1g	Ezzard Charles Dr, **W** 🛏 Ramada Inn
1f	US 50W, Freeman Ave, **W** 🅖 Sunoco, 🍴 Big Boy, Pizza Hut/Taco Bell, Wendy's, White Castle, 🛏 Ramada Inn, 🄾 Ford, GMC, NAPA, USPO
1e	7th St (from sb), downtown
1c	5th St, downtown, **E** 🛏 Crowne Plaza, Hyatt, Millenial Hotel, Sheraton, 🄾 Macy's, to Duke Energy Center
1a	I-71 N, to Cincinnati, downtown, to stadium
0mm	Ohio/Kentucky state line, Ohio River

↙E INTERSTATE 76

Exit	Services
Ohio/Pennsylvania state line, See OH TPK exits 232-234	
60mm	I-76 eb joins Ohio TPK **(toll)**
57	to OH 45, Bailey Rd, to Warren
54	OH 534, to Newton Falls, Lake Milton, **N** RV camping, **S** 🅖 BP, 🄾 to Berlin Lake, camping
52mm	Lake Milton
48	OH 225, to Alliance, **N** to W Branch SP, camping, **S** to Berlin Lake, to Lake Milton SP
45mm	🆁🆂 both lanes, full ♿ facilities, 🚻, 🛐, litter barrels, petwalk
43	OH 14, to Alliance, Ravenna, **N** to W Branch SP, **S** 🅖 Marathon/dsl, 🄾 fireworks
38b a	OH 5, OH 44, to Ravenna, **N** 🅖 BP, Speedway/dsl, 🍴 Arby's, McDonald's/rv parking, Wendy's, 🄾 🄷, **S** 🅖 Marathon/Circle K/Subway, 🍴 Cracker Barrel, 🄾 $General, Giant Eagle Foods, auto repair/parts, RV camping
33	OH 43, to Hartville, Kent, **N** 🅖 BP/dsl, Sunoco, 🍴 Salsita's Mexican, 🛏 Best Value Inn, Comfort Inn, Days Inn, EconoLodge, Hampton Inn, Holiday Inn Express, Super 8, 🄾 to Kent St U, **S** 🅖 Speedway/dsl, 🍴 Gemini Pizza, Giomino's Pizza, McDonald's, Pizza Hut, Subway, Wendy's, 🄾 Curves, $General, vet
31	rd 18, Tallmadge, **N** 🍴 Applebee's, Arabica/Strickland's Cafe, Beef'O'Brady's, La Terraza Mexican, 🄾 AT&T, $Tree,

OH

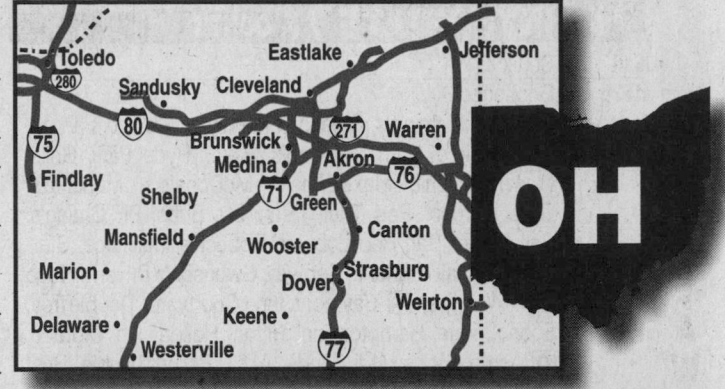

⬆️E INTERSTATE 76 CONT'D

Exit	Services
31	Continued
	GNC, Kohl's, Lowe's, Verizon, Walmart/Subway
29	OH 532, Tallmadge, Mogadore
27	OH 91, Canton Rd, Gilchrist Rd, **N** 🍴 Bob Evans, **S** 💵 Marathon/Subway/dsl, 🍴 Hardee's, 🛏 Quality Inn
26	OH 18, E Market St, Mogadore Rd, **N** 💵 Marathon/dsl, 🔲 Goodyear/auto, **S** 🍴 Arby's, McDonald's, Subway, Wendy's, 🔲 $General
25b a	Martha Ave, General St, Brittain, **N** 💵 Circle K, 🔲 Goodyear HQ, Mercedes, Toyota/Scion
24	Arlington St, Kelly Ave, **N** Goodyear HQ
23b	OH 8, Buchtell Ave, to Cuyahoga (exits left from eb) to U of Akron
23a	I-77 S, to Canton
22b	Grant St, Wolf Ledges, Akron, downtown, **S** 💵 BP, 🍴 McDonald's, 🔲 Family$
22a	Main St, Broadway, downtown
21c	OH 59 E, Dart Ave, **N** 🏥
21b	Lakeshore St, Bowery St (from eb)
21a	East Ave (from wb)
20	I-77 N (from eb), to Cleveland
19	Battles Ave, Kenmore Blvd
18	I-277, US 224 E, to Canton, Barberton
17b a	OH 619, Wooster Rd, State St, to Barberton (no eb return), **S** 💵 Sunoco/dsl, 🔲 🏥, NAPA, tires/repair
16	Barber Rd, **S** 💵 Rocky's/dsl/E85, 🍴 Tomaso's Italian, 🔲 Chrysler/Dodge/Jeep, Nissan, Suzuki
14	Cleve-Mass Rd, to Norton, **S** 💵 BP, Marathon/Circle K, 🍴 Subway, 3 Sons Rest. 🔲 Ace Hardware, Advance Parts, Acme Mkt, CVS Drug, $General, Radio Shack, Ritzman Drug
13b a	OH 21, N to Cleveland, S to Massillon
11	OH 261, Wadsworth, **N** 💵 Speedway/dsl, **S** 💵 Giant Eagle, GetGo/E85, 🍴 Arabica Cafe, Beef'O'Brady's, 🔲 GNC, Kohl's, Lowe's, MC Sports, PetCo, Target, Verizon
9	OH 94, to N Royalton, Wadsworth, **N** 💵 Marathon/Circle K, 🍴 Applebee's, Arby's, Bob Evans, Burger King, China Buffet, China Express, Chipotle Mexican, Galaxy Rest., KFC, Marie's Cafe., McDonald's, Panera Bread, Pizza Hut, Subway, Taco Bell, Wendy's, 🛏 Holiday Inn Express, Rodeway Inn, 🔲 AT&T, BigLots, Buehler's Foods, $General, $Tree, DrugMart, Goodyear/auto, Home Depot, NTB, Radio Shack, Verizon, Walmart, **S** 💵 Convenient/gas, Marathon/DQ/dsl, Sunoco/dsl, 🍴 Casa Del Rio, Dunkin Donuts, 🛏 Legacy Inn, 🔲 Advance Parts, AutoZone, CVS Drug, NAPA, Rite Aid, auto repair, vet
7	OH 57, to Rittman, Medina, **N** 💵 Marathon/dsl, **S** 🔲 🏥, 🍴
6mm	**weigh sta both lanes**
2	OH 3, to Medina, Seville, **N** 💵 Marathon/Circle K, 🍴 DQ, Hardee's, Huddle House, Pizzazo's, Subway, 🛏 Comfort Inn, Hawthorn Suites, 🔲 Maple Lakes Camping (seasonal), **S** 💵 Shell/dsl, Sunoco, 🍴 E of Chicago Pizza, El Patron Mexican, #1 Chinese, 🔲 Curves, $General, Ritzman Drug
1	I-76 E, to Akron, US 224, **W** on US 224 💵 🚛/Subway/dsl/scales/24hr, TA/BP/Burger King/Popeye's/dsl/scales/24hr/@, 🍴 Arby's, McDonald's, 🛏 Super 8, 🔲 Blue Beacon, SpeedCo, Chippewa Valley Camping (1mi), SpeedCo
0mm	**I-76 begins/ends on I-71, exit 209.**

⬆️N INTERSTATE 77

Exit	Services
I-77 begins/ends on I-90 exit 172, in Cleveland.	
163c	I-90, E to Erie, W to Toledo
163b	E 9th St, Tower City
162b	E 22nd St, E 14th St (from nb)
162a	E 30th St, Woodland Ave, Broadway St (from nb), **W** USPO
161b	I-490 W, to I-71, E 55th, **E** 🏥
161a	OH 14 (from nb), Broadway St
160	Pershing Ave (from nb), **W** 🏥
159b	Fleet Ave, **E** 💵 BP/Subway/dsl
159a	Harvard Ave, Newburgh Heights, **W** 💵 BP/Subway/dsl
158	Grant Ave, Cuyahoga Heights
157	OH 21, OH 17 (from sb), Brecksville Rd
156	I-480, to Youngstown, Toledo
155	Rockside Rd, to Independence, **E** 💵 Shell, Sunoco/dsl, 🍴 Aladdin's, Bob Evans, Bonefish Grill, Del Monico's Steaks, DiBella's Subs, Denny's, Jimmy John's, McDonald's, Melt Grill, Outback Steaks, Panera Bread, Red Robin, Shula's Steaks, Starbucks, Wendy's, Zoup, 🛏 Comfort Inn, Doubletree, Embassy Suites, Holiday Inn, La Quinta, Red Roof Inn, 🔲 Drugmart, Verizon, Walgreens, to Cuyahoga Valley NP, **W** 💵 BP/dsl, 🍴 Applebee's, Longhorn Steaks, 🛏 Courtyard, Crowne Plaza, Hampton Inn, Hyatt Place, Residence Inn
153	Pleasant Valley Rd, to Independence, 7 Hills
151	Wallings Rd
149	OH 82, to Broadview Heights, Brecksville, 1 mi **E** 💵 BP, Shell, 🍴 Austin's Grille, McDonald's, Panera Bread, Sakura Japanese, Starbucks, Subway, 🔲 CVS Drug, vet, **W** 💵 BP, GetGo, 🔲 Giant Eagle Foods
147	to OH 21, Miller Rd (from sb)
146	I-80/Ohio Tpk, to Youngstown Toledo
145	OH 21 (from nb), **E** 💵 🚛/Wendy's/dsl/scales, 🍴 DQ, Memories Rest., Richfield Rest., Subway, 🛏 Days Inn, Hampton Inn, Holiday Inn Express, Motel 6, Super 8
144	I-271 N, to Erie
143	OH 176, to I-271 S, **W** 💵 Sunoco, 🍴 McDonald's, Panda Chinese, Richfield Cafe, Subway, Teresa's Pizza
141mm	🅿️ **both lanes, full ♿ facilities, 🍴, 🚮, litter barrels, vending, petwalk**
138	Ghent Rd, **W** 💵 Circle K/dsl, 🍴 Gasoline Ally, Lanning's Rest.
137b a	OH 18, to Fairlawn, Medina, **E** 💵 BP, GetGo, Shell, Speedway, 🍴 Applebee's, A-Wok, Bob Evans, Boston Mkt, Chick-fil-A, Chili's, Chipotle Mexican, Coldstone, Cracker Barrel, Cusina Italian, Donato's Pizza, 5 Guys

OH

FAIRLAWN / AKRON

⬆N INTERSTATE 77 CONT'D

Exit	Services
137b a	Continued Burgers, Fleming's Steaks, Friendly's, Gionino's Pizza, HoneyBaked Ham, Hudson's Rest., Hyde Park Grille, Macaroni Grill, Max&Erma's, McDonald's, Menchie's, Olive Garden, Pad Thai, Penn Sta Subs, PF Chang's, Rail Burger Bar, Red Lobster, Robeck's FruitJuice, Starbucks, Steak'n Shake, Subway, Swenson's Drive-In, Taco Bell, Wendy's, 🛏 Baymont Inn, Courtyard, DoubleTree, EconoLodge, Hampton Inn, Hilton, Holiday Inn, Motel 6, Ⓞ Acme Foods, Aldi Foods, AT&T, Barnes&Noble, Best Buy, Ford, Dick's, Dillard's, $Tree, Earth Fare Foods, Giant Eagle Foods, Goodyear/auto, Hobby Lobby, Home Depot, JC Penney, Jo-Ann Fabrics, Lowe's, Macy's, Michael's, NTB, Old Navy, Petsmart, Sam's Club, Staples, TJ Maxx, Verizon, Walmart, World Mkt, W 🍴 Burger King, Don Pablo, Longhorn Steaks, Nicolinni's, Outback Steaks, Steak on a Stone, TGIFriday's, Tres Patrilios, Wasabi Grill, 🛏 Best Western, Comfort Inn, Radisson, StayPlace Suites, Studio+, Ⓞ Ⓗ
136	(exits left from nb), OH 21S, to Massillon
135	Cleveland-Massillon Rd (from nb, no return)
133	Ridgewood Rd, Miller Rd, E ⛽ Circle K/dsl, W 🍴 Tiffany's Bakery, Old Carolina BBQ
132	White Pond Dr, Mull Ave
131	OH 162, Copley Rd, E ⛽ Circle K, 🍴 Church's, Ⓞ Save-A-Lot Foods, Walgreens, USPO, W ⛽ BP/dsl/24hr, 🍴 McDonald's, Pizza Hut
130	OH 261, Wooster Ave, E ⛽ Circle K, Marathon/dsl, Valero, 🍴 Ann's Place, Burger King, Church's, New Ming Chinese, Rally's, Subway, Ⓞ Acme Foods, Advance Parts, AutoZone, Family$, O'Reilly Parts, W Ⓞ Chevrolet, Toyota/Scion, U-Haul
129	I-76 W, to I-277, to Kenmore Blvd, Barberton
I-77 and I-76 run together 3.5 mi. See Interstate 70, exits 19b a - 20	
125b	I-76 E, to Youngstown, I-77 and I-76 run together
125a	OH 8 N, to Cuyahoga Falls, U of Akron
124b	Lover's Lane, Cole Ave
124a	Archwood Ave, Firestone Blvd (from sb), E BP
123b	OH 764, Wilbeth Rd, E 🍴 DQ, Ⓞ to 🖥
123a	Waterloo Rd (from sb), W ⛽ GetGo, Marathon, 🍴 Burger King, Hungry Howies, Papa John's, Rally's, Subway, Ⓞ $Tree, Giant Eagle Foods, Goodyear/auto, Rite Aid, Walgreens
122b a	I-277, US 224 E, to Barberton, Mogadore
120	Arlington Rd, to Green, E ⛽ Speedway/dsl, 🍴 Applebee's, Church's/White Castle, Denny's, Friendly's, Golden Corral, IHOP, Starbucks, Waffle House, 🛏 Comfort Inn, Quality Inn, Red Roof Inn, Ⓞ AutoZone, $General, Home Depot, Kohl's, Staples, Walmart, W ⛽ BP, 🍴 Bob Evans, Burger King, Chipotle Mexican, CiCi's Pizza, Lion Garden, Mariachi Mexican, McDonald's, Panera Bread, Subway, Taco Bell, Wendy's, 🛏 Fairfield Inn, Hampton Inn, Holiday Inn Express, ValuePlace Inn, Ⓞ Acura, Buick/GMC, Chevrolet, GNC, Goodyear/auto, Honda, Hyundai, Lexus, Lowe's, Mazda, Meineke, Nissan, Sirpilla RV Ctr/Camping World, Subaru, Target
118	OH 241, to OH 619, Massillon, E ⛽ Sheetz, Speedway/dsl, 🍴 Gionino's Pizza, Handel's Icecream, Subway, W ⛽ BP/Circle K, GetGo, 🍴 Arby's, DQ, Grille 39, Hungry Howie's, Lucky Star Chinese, McDonald's, Menche's

CANTON

Exit	Services
118	Continued Rest., Quiznos, Subway, 🛏 Cambria Suites, Super 8, Ⓞ Ⓗ, Advance Parts, AT&T, Curves, $General, Giant Eagle Foods, Verizon, vet
113	Akron-Canton ✈, W 🛏 Hilton Garden, Ⓞ General RV Ctr (2mi)
112	Shuffel St
111	Portage St, N Canton, E ⛽ Circle K, Marathon, Sunoco/dsl, TA/Country Pride/dsl/scales/24hr/@, 🍴 Burger King, Geisen Haus, Jimmy's Rest., KFC, Palombo's Italian, Quaker Steak, Subway, Sylvester's Italian, Ⓞ TrueValue, W ⛽ BP/dsl, Speedway/dsl, 🍴 Baskin-Robbins/Dunkin Donuts, Bonefish Grill, Carrabba's, ChuckeCheese, Coldstone, Cracker Barrel, Donato's Pizza, Don Pablo, Dunkin Donuts/Baskin-Robbins, 5 Guys Burgers, Heavenly Ham, Hungry Howie's, IHOP, Longhorn Steaks, Lucky Star Chinese, McDonald's, Panera Bread, Philly Connection, Pizza Hut, Red Robin, Rockne's Cafe, Samantha's Rest., Subway, Taco Bell, Wasabi Japanese, Wendy's, 🛏 Best Western, Microtel, Motel 6, Ⓞ At&T, Best Buy, BJ's Whse, Chevrolet, DrugMart, Gander Mtn, Giant Eagle Foods, GNC, Goodyear/auto, Harley-Davidson, Home Depot, Lowe's, Marshall's, Old Navy, Sam's Club/gas, Walgreens, Walmart/Subway/auto
109b a	Everhard Rd, Whipple Ave, E ⛽ Marathon/Subway, Speedway/dsl, 🍴 Denny's, Fazoli's, McDonald's, Taco Bell, Waffle House, 🛏 Comfort Inn, Fairfield Inn, Hampton Inn, La Quinta, Residence Inn, Ⓞ Ford, W ⛽ Marathon, 🍴 Applebee's, Arby's, Bob Evans, Bravo Italian, Buffalo Wild Wings, Buffet Dynasty, Chick-fil-A, Chili's, Chipotle Mexican, Chips&Salsa Mexican, Cheeseburger Paradise, CiCi's Pizza, Damon's, Fox&Hound Grill, Friendly's, Golden Corral, HomeTown Buffet, HoneyBaked Ham, Jimmy John's, KFC, LoneStar Steaks, Macaroni Grill, Manchu Cafe, Max&Erma's, Mulligan's, Olive Garden, Outback Steaks, Panera Bread, Panini's Grill, Papa Bear's, Papa Gyros, Penn Sta. Subs, Perkin's, Red Lobster, Rita's Custard, Roadhouse Cafe, Robek's Cafe, Ruby Tuesday, Sahara Grill, Starbucks, Steak'n Shake, TGIFriday's, Wendy's, 🛏 Courtyard, Holiday Inn, Knights Inn, Magnuson Hotel, Red Roof Inn, Ⓞ Aamco, Advance Parts, Aldi Foods, AT&T, Dick's, Dillard's, $Tree, Firestone/auto, Goodyear/auto, Jo-Ann Fabrics, Kohl's, Macy's, Marc's Foods, NTB, Petsmart, Radio Shack, Sears/auto, Target, TJ Maxx, Tuesday Morning, Verizon, World Mkt, mall, USPO
107b a	US 62, OH 687, Fulton Rd, to Alliance, E ⛽ Marathon/Circle K/Subway, Ⓞ city park, W ⛽ Circle K, Ⓞ Pro Football Hall of Fame
106	13th St NW, E Ⓗ
105b	OH 172, Tuscarawas St, downtown
105a	6th St SW (no EZ return from sb), E ⛽ Sunoco, 🍴 McDonald's, W 🍴 Subway, Ⓞ Ⓗ, AutoZone
104b a	US 30, US 62, to E Liverpool, Massillon
103	OH 800 S, E ⛽ Marathon/Subway/dsl, Speedway, 🍴 Arby's, DQ, Italo's Pizza, McDonald's, Peking Chinese, Taco Bell, Waffle House, Ⓞ Advance Parts, Family$, Goodyear/auto, Rite aid, Save-A-Lot Foods, auto repair
101	OH 627, to Faircrest St, E ⛽ ▭▭▭/Subway/dsl/scales/24hr, Speedway/McDonald's, 🍴 Wendy's
99	Fohl Rd, to Navarre, W ⛽ Sunoco, Ⓞ KOA (4mi)
93	OH 212, to Zoar, Bolivar, E ⛽ Speedway/Subway/dsl, 🍴

⬆N INTERSTATE 77 CONT'D

Exit	Services
93	Continued
	McDonald's, Pizza Hut, Wendy's, 🏠 Sleep Inn, ⊡ $General, Giant Eagle Foods, NAPA, Zoar Tavern HS (3mi), vet, to Lake Atwood Region, W 🗒 Marathon/DQ, ⊡ KOA
87	US 250W, to Strasburg, W 🗒 Marathon/dsl, 🍴 Hardee's, Manor Rest., McDonald's, Subway, 🏠 Ramada Ltd, ⊡ Verizon
85	Schneiders Crossing Rd, to Dover, E 🗒 Marathon, 🍴 Arby's, Subway
83	OH 39, OH 211, to Sugarcreek, Dover, E 🗒 BP, Speedway/Subway/dsl, 🍴 Bob Evans, KFC, McDonald's, Shoney's, Wendy's, 🏠 Best Value Inn, ⊡ H, Chrysler/Dodge/Jeep, Flynn's Tires, Ford, Honda, Lincoln, Nissan, W 🏠 Comfort Inn, Country Inn&Suites
81	US 250, to Uhrichsville, OH 39, New Philadelphia, E 🗒 KwikFill, Sheetz/dsl, Speedway, 🍴 Burger King, Denny's, El San Jose Mexican, Hog Heaven BBQ, LJ Silver, McDonald's, Pizza Hut, Taco Bell, TX Roadhouse, 🏠 Best Western, Hampton Inn, Holiday Inn Express, Knights Inn, Motel 6, Schoenbrunn Inn, ⊡ Advance Parts, Aldi Foods, BigLots, $General, $Tree, Walmart/Subway, W 🗒 Auto TP/rest./dsl/scales/24hr, ⊡ Harley-Davidson
73	OH 751, to rd 53, Stone Creek, W 🗒 Marathon/dsl
65	US 36, Port Washington, Newcomerstown, W 🗒 BP, Duke TP/rest./dsl, Speedway/Wendy's, 🍴 McDonald's, 🏠 Hampton Inn, Super 8
64mm	Tuscarawas River
54	OH 541, rd 831, to Plainfield, Kimbolton, W 🗒 BP, 🍴 Jackie's Rest.
47	US 22, to Cadiz, Cambridge, E to Salt Fork SP (6mi), lodging, RV camping, W 🗒 BP/repair, ⊡ H, to Glass Museum, info
46b a	US 40, to Old Washington, Cambridge, W 🗒 Clark, Marathon/Wendy's/dsl, Speedway/dsl, 🍴 Burger King, Hunan Chinese, Lee's Rest., LJ Silver, McDonald's, ⊡ Family$, Riesbeck's Food
44b a	I-70, E to Wheeling, W to Columbus
41	OH 209, OH 821, Byesville, W 🗒 Circle K, Starfire, 🍴 McDonald's, Subway, ⊡ Byesville Drug, $General, Family$, museum, to Glenn HS
39mm	🅿️ nb, full 🚻 facilities, ⊡, 🏕️, litter barrels, petwalk, vending
37	OH 313, Buffalo, E 🗒 BP, 🍴 Coutos Pizza, Subway, ⊡ truck repair, to Senecaville Lake, UPSO
36mm	🅿️ sb, full 🚻 facilities, ⊡, 🏕️, litter barrels, petwalk, vending
28	OH 821, Belle Valley, E 🗒 Sunoco/dsl, ⊡ USPO, to Wolf Run SP, RV camping
25	OH 78, Caldwell, Woodsfield, E 🗒 BP, 🚛/Arby's/dsl/scales/24hr, Sunoco/Subway/dsl, 🍴 DQ, Lori's Rest., McDonald's, 🏠 Best Western
16	OH 821, Macksburg, E food, ⊡ antiques
6	OH 821, to Devola, E 🗒 Exxon/dsl, W 🗒 Marathon/dsl/LP, ⊡ H, RV camping
3mm	🅿️ nb, full 🚻 facilities, info, ⊡, vending, 🏕️, litter barrels, petwalk
1	OH 7, to OH 26, Marietta, E 🗒 GoMart/dsl/24hr, 🍴 Black Smith Grill, China Wind, DQ, Subway, 🏠 Comfort Inn, Fairfield Inn, Holiday Inn, ⊡ Aldi Foods, Buick/GMC, Cadillac/Chevrolet, Chrysler/Dodge/Jeep, $Tree, Ford/Lin-

M A R I E T T A

1	Continued
	coln, Lowe's, Radio Shack, Toyota/Scion, Walmart/McDonald's, W 🗒 BP/dsl, Duke/dsl, GetGo/dsl, Marathon/dsl; Speedway/dsl, 🍴 Applebee's, Arby's, Bar-B-Cutie, Bob Evans, Burger King, Capt D's, China Fun, E Chicago Pizza, Empire Buffet, KFC, Little Caesar's, LJ Silver, McDonald's, Napoli's Pizza, Papa John's, Pizza Hut, Shoney's, Subway, Taco Bell, Tim Horton, Wendy's, 🏠 Hampton Inn, Microtel, Super 8, ⊡ Advance Parts, AT&T, AutoZone, BigLots, Curves, CVS Drug, Family$, Food-4Less, JoAnn Fabrics, K-Mart, Kroger, Rite Aid, Save-A-Lot Foods, TrueValue, Verizon, Walgreens, museum, st patrol
0mm	Ohio/West Virginia state line, Ohio River

⬆E INTERSTATE 80

Exit	Services
237mm	Ohio/Pennsylvania state line
237mm	**Welcome Ctr wb, full 🚻 facilities, info, ⊡, 🏕️, litter barrels, vending, petwalk**
234b a	US 62, OH 7, Hubbard, to Sharon, PA, N 🗒 ⓕFLYING J/Denny's/dsl/LP/scales/24hr, Shell/rest./dsl/scales/motel/ 24hr/@, 🍴 Arby's, Burger King, McDonald's, Waffle House, 🏠 Best Western, ⊡ Blue Beacon, Homestead RV Ctr., RV camping (2mi), tire/dsl repair, S 🗒 ♥Loves/Chester's/Subway/dsl/scales/24hr, ⊡ Chevrolet
232mm	**weigh sta wb**
229	OH 193, Belmont Ave, to Youngstown, N 🗒 GetGo, Speedway/dsl, 🍴 Handl's Ice Cream, Rotelli Italian, Subway, 🏠 Hampton Inn, Motel 6, Super 8, ⊡ Giant Eagle Foods, Verizon, S 🗒 BP/dsl, Shell, 🍴 Antone's Italian Grille, Arby's, Armondo's Rest., Arthur Treacher's, Bob Evans, Casa Ramirez Mexican, Charley's Subs, Denny's, Golden Hunan Chinese, Ianazones Pizza, Jimmy's Italian, KFC, Little Caesars, LJ Silver, McDonald's, Papa John's, Pizza Hut, Subway, Taco Bell, Uptown Pizza, Wendy's, Westfork Steaks, Youngstown Crab Co, 🏠 Days Inn, Quality Inn, ⊡ Advance Parts, Aldi Foods, AT&T, AutoZone, BigLots, $General, Family$, Firestone/auto, Goodyear/auto, Radio Shack, Rite Aid, Walgreens, Walmart/Subway, vet
228	OH 11, to Warren (exits left from eb), Ashtabula
227	US 422, Girard, Youngstown, N 🗒 Shell/dsl, 🍴 Burger King, DQ, JibJab Hotdogs, Subway
226	Salt Springs Rd, to I-680 (from wb), N 🗒 BP/Dunkin Donuts/dsl, Sheetz, 🍴 McDonald's, Waffle House, ⊡ vet, S 🗒 Mr Fuel/Road Rocket Diner/dsl/24hr, Petro/rest./dsl/scales/24hr/@, 🚛/Subway/dsl/scales/24hr, ⊡ Blue Beacon, SpeedCo, dsl repair
224b	I-680 (from eb), to Youngstown

OH

 Copyright 2014 - The NEXT Exit ®

INTERSTATE 80 CONT'D

Exit	Services
224a	OH 11 S, to Canfield
223	OH 46, to Niles, **N** [gas] Country Fair, Pilot/McDonald's/dsl/scales/24hr, [food] Bob Evans, Burger King, Dunkin Donuts, IceHouse Rest., Salsita's Mexican, [lodging] Comfort Inn, Economy Inn, Holiday Inn Express, **S** [gas] BP/dsl, Fuel-Mart/dsl/scales, Sunoco/Subway, TA/Counry Pride/dsl/scales/24hr/@, [food] Arby's, Cracker Barrel, LJ Silver/Taco Bell, Quaker Steak&Lube, Perkins, Starbucks, Wendy's, [lodging] Best Western, Country Inn&Suites, EconoLodge, Fairfield Inn, Hampton Inn, Sleep Inn, Super 8, [other] Blue Beacon, Freightliner/24hr, Harley-Davidson
221mm	Meander Reservoir
219mm	I-80 wb joins Ohio Tpk **(toll)**

For I-80 exits 2-218, see Ohio Turnpike.

INTERSTATE 90

Exit	Services
244mm	Ohio/Pennsylvania state line
242mm	**[rest stop]/weigh sta wb, full [handicapped] facilities, info, [phone], [picnic], litter barrels, petwalk**
241	OH 7, to Andover, Conneaut, **N** [food] Burger King, McDonald's (2mi), [lodging] Days Inn, [other] [H], AutoZone, Evergreen RV Park, K-Mart, **S** [gas] Love's/McDonald's/Subway/dsl/scales/24hr, [food] Beef&Beer Café
235	OH 84, OH 193, to Youngstown, N Kingsville, **N** [gas] Grab&Go/gas, Marathon/Circle K, [lodging] Dav-Ed Motel, [other] Village Green Camping (2mi), **S** [gas] Circle K/Subway/dsl, TA/BP/Burger King/dsl/scales/24hr/@, [food] Kay's Place Diner, [lodging] Kingsville Motel, [other] tire repair
228	OH 11, to Ashtabula, Youngstown, **N** [H] (4mi)
223	OH 45, to Ashtabula, **N** [gas] FLYING J/Denny's/Shell/dsl/LP/scales/24hr, [food] Mr C's Rest., [lodging] Best Value Inn, Holiday Inn Express, Ramada, Sleep Inn, [other] Buccaneer Camping, **S** [gas] Pilot/Subway/dsl/scales/24hr, SpeedCo, [food] Burger King, McDonald's, Quinn's Grille, Waffle House, [lodging] Hampton Inn, [other] auto repair
218	OH 534, Geneva, **N** [gas] GetGo, [food] Best Friend's Grill, Chop's Grille, McDonald's, Pizza Hut, Wendy's, [lodging] Motel 6, [other] [H], Goodyear/repair, Indian Creek Camping (8mi), to Geneva SP, **S** [gas] KwikFill/Subway/dsl/scales/24hr, [other] Kenisse's Camping
212	OH 528, to Thompson, Madison, **N** [food] Cornerstone Rest, McDonald's, [other] Mentor RV Ctr, **S** [gas] Marathon/dsl, [other] Heritage Hills Camping (4mi), radiator repair
205	Vrooman Rd, **0-2 mi S** [gas] BP/dsl, Marathon/dsl, [food] Capps Eatery, Subway, [other] Indian Point Park, Masons Landing Park
200	OH 44, to Painesville, Chardon, **S** [gas] BP/Subway/dsl, Sunoco/dsl, [food] Bellacino's, CK Steakhouse, McDonald's, Palmer's Bistro, Paninis, Red Hawk Grille, Teresa's Pizzaria, Waffle House, [lodging] Baymont Inn, Quail Hollow Resort, [other] [H], Curves, Reider's Foods, hwy patrol, **Urgent Care**
198mm	**[rest stop] both lanes, full [handicapped] facilities, [phone], [picnic], litter barrels, vending, petwalk**
195	OH 615, Center St, Kirtland Hills, Mentor, **1-2 mi N** [gas] BP, [food] El Rodeo Mexican, Yours Truly Rest., [lodging] Best Western
193	OH 306, to Mentor, Kirtland, **0-2 mi N** [gas] BP/Subway, Shell, Speedway, [food] Chipotle Mexican, McDonald's, [lodging] Best Value Inn, Comfort Inn, Super 8, **S** [gas] Speedway/dsl, [food] Burger King, [lodging] Days Inn, Red Roof Inn, [other] [H], Kirtland
193	Continued Temple LDS Historic Site
190	Express Lane to I-271 (from wb)
189	OH 91, to Willoughby, Willoughby Hills, **N** [gas] BP/dsl, Shell, [food] Arby's (1mi), Bob Evans, Café Europa, Cracker Barrel, Eat'n Park, Peking Chef, Subway, TX Roadhouse, Wendy's, [lodging] Courtyard, Motel 6, Radisson (2mi), Travelodge, [other] [H], CVS Drug, Walgreens, **S** [other] BMW/Mini, Lexus
188	I-271 S, to Akron
187	OH 84, Bishop Rd, to Wickliffe, Willoughby, **S** [gas] BP/dsl, Shell, [food] Baker's Square, McDonald's, Golden Mtn Chinese, Mr Hero, Subway, Tony's Pizza, [lodging] Ramada Inn, [other] [H], AT&T, Curves, CVS Drug, Chevrolet, Giant Eagle Foods, Marc's Foods, Mazda/VW, NTB, Verizon
186	US 20, Euclid Ave, **N** [gas] Sunoco, [food] McDonald's, [lodging] Mosley Suites, Quality Inn, [other] Ford, Subaru, Suzuki, radiators/transmissions, **S** [gas] Shell, [food] Arby's, KFC, Popeye's, R-Ribs, Sidewalk Cafe, Taco Bell, [other] Advance Parts, $General, Family$, Firestone/auto, Save-a-Lot Foods
185	OH 2 E (exits left from eb), to Painesville
184b	OH 175, E 260th St, **N** [gas] Shell, [other] USPO, **S** [other] auto/tire repair, vet
184a	Babbitt Rd, **N** Buick/GMC
183	E 222nd St, **N** [gas] Sunoco/dsl, tires, **S** [gas] BP, Sunoco, [other] vet
182b a	185 St, 200 St, **N** [food] Subway [other] Home Depot, Honda, Hyundai, **S** [other] Marathon/dsl, Shell/dsl, Speedway/dsl
181b a	E 156th St, **S** [gas] BP
180b a	E 140th St, E 152nd St
179	OH 283 E, to Lake Shore Blvd
178	Eddy Rd, to Bratenahl
177	University Circle, MLK Dr, **N** [other] Cleveland Lake SP, **S** [other] [H], Rockefeller Park
176	E 72nd St
175	E 55th St, Marginal Rds
174b	OH 2 W, to Lakewood, downtown, Rock&Roll Hall of Fame, Browns Stadium
174a	Lakeside Ave
173c	Superior Ave, St Clair Ave, downtown, **N** [gas] BP
173b	Chester Ave, **S** [gas] BP
173a	Prospect Ave (from wb), downtown
172d	Carnegie Ave, downtown, **S** [food] Burger King, [other] Cadillac
172c b	E 9th St, **S** [other] [H], to Cleveland St U
172a	I-77 S, to Akron
171b a	US 422, OH 14, Broadway St, Ontario St, **N** [gas] BP, [lodging] Hilton Garden, [other] to Browns Stadium
171	Abbey Ave, downtown
170c b	I-71 S, to I-490
170a	US 42, W 25th St, **S** gas
169	W 44th St, W 41st St, **N** [H]
167b a	OH 10, West Blvd, 98th St, to Lorain Ave, **N** [H], **S** [gas] BP/dsl, [other] CVS Drug
166	W 117th St, **N** [gas] BP/dsl, Get Go, Shell, [food] KFC, [other] Advance Parts, Giant Eagle Foods, Home Depot, Staples, Target, **S** [food] Church's/White Castle
165	W 140th St, Bunts Rd, Warren Rd, **N** [gas] Marathon, [other] [H]
164	McKinley Ave, to Lakewood
162	Hilliard Blvd (from wb), to Westway Blvd, Rocky River, **S** [gas] BP, Shell
161	OH 2, OH 254 (from eb, no EZ return), Detroit Rd, Rocky River
160	Clague Rd (from wb), **S** [other] [H], same as 159

EUCLID

CLEVELAND

🛣 INTERSTATE 90 CONT'D

Exit	Services
159	OH 252, Columbia Rd, **N** 🍴 Carrabba's, Clubhouse Grille, Dave&Busters, Manero's, Outback Steaks, 🛏 Courtyard, TownePlace Suites, Super 8, 🅞 🅷, **S** 🅖 BP, 🍴 Houlihan's, KFC, McDonald's, Taco Bell, 🅞 Chevrolet, NTB
156	Crocker Rd, Bassett Rd, Westlake, Bay Village, **N** 🅖 BP, Shell, 🛏 Extended Stay Deluxe, Holiday Inn, Red Roof Inn, Residence Inn, **S** 🅖 BP, Speedway, 🍴 Applebee's, Baskin-Robbins, Blake's Seafood, Bob Evans, Cabin Club Steaks, Caribou Coffee, Cheesecake Factory, Chicago Grill, Chipotle Mexican, El Rodeo Mexican, 5 Guys Burgers, Max&Erma's, McDonald's, Starbucks, Subway, TGI-Friday's, Vieng's Asian, Wendy's, 🛏 Hampton Inn, 🅞 🅷 Aldi Foods, CVS Drug, Giant Eagle, GNC, Marc's Foods, Radio Shack, Sears Grand, Trader Joes, mall
155	Nagel Rd
153	OH 83, Avon Lake, **N** 🅖 GetGo/dsl, Marathon/Dunkin Donuts/dsl, 🍴 Arby's, Bubba's BBQ, Buffalo Wild Wings, Perkins, 🅞 AutoZone, Best Buy, Firestone/auto, JC Penney, Lowe's, PetCo, Walmart/auto, **S** 🍴 Applebees, Bob Evans, Burger King, Caribou Coffee, CiCi's Pizza, Coldstone, 5 Guys Burgers, Hot Dog Heaven, IHOP, Mandarin House, Moe's SW Grill, Panera Bread, Quiznos, Red Robin, Subway, Wendy's, 🅞 AT&T, Costco/gas, Curves, CVS Drug, GNC, Home Depot, Kohl's, Marc's Foods, Marshall's, Michael's, Old Navy, Radio Shack, Target, World Mkt
151	OH 611, Avon, **N** 🅖 BP/dsl, 🏪Subway/dsl/24hr, 🍴 McDonald's, 🛏 Fairfield Inn, Value Place Hotel, 🅞 Chevrolet, Goodyear/repair, Harley-Davidson, **S** 🅖 BJ's Whse/gas, 🍴 Mulligan's Grille
148	OH 254, Sheffield, Avon, **N** 🍴 Quaker Steak&Lube, 🅞 Ford, GMC, KIA, Mazda, Mitsubishi, Nissan, **S** 🅖 BP, GetGo, Sheetz, Speedway, 🍴 Arby's, Burger King, China Star, Cracker Barrel, KFC, McDonald's, Pizza Hut, Ruby Tuesday, Steak'n Shake, Subway, Taco Bell, Wendy's, 🅞 Aldi Foods, CVS Drug, $General, $Tree, Drug Mart, Gander Mtn, Giant Eagle, NTB, Sam's Club/gas
147mm	Black River
145	OH 57, to Lorain, I-80/Ohio Tpk E, Elyria, **N** 🅖 Speedway, 🍴 George's Rest., Hunan King, Red Lobster, Wendy's, 🛏 Country Inn&Suites, 🅞 Chevrolet, Save-a-Lot, U-Haul, vet, **S** 🅖 Speedway, 🍴 Applebee's, Arby's, Bob Evans, Buffalo Wild Wings, Burger King, Chipotle Mexican, Denny's, Eat'n Park, Golden Corral, Harry Buffalo, McDonald's, #1 Buffet, Old Century Buffet, Olive Garden, Red Lobster, Subway, Wasabi Grill, Wendy's, 🛏 Best Western, Comfort Inn, Country Inn&Suites, EconoLodge, Red Carpet Inn, Red Roof Inn, Super 8, 🅞 AT&T, Best Buy, Curves, Dick's, $General, Firestone/auto, Giant Eagle, Home Depot, Honda, Hyundai, JC Penney, Jo-Ann Fabrics, Lowe's, Macy's, Marc's Foods, NTB, Petsmart, Radio Shack, Sears, Staples, Target, Tuffy Repair, Verizon, Walmart/auto
144	OH 2 W (from wb, no return), to Sandusky, **1 mi N** on **Broadway Ave E** 🅖 Marathon, Shell/24hr, 🍴 McDonald's, 🅞 🅷
143	**I-90 wb joins Ohio Tpk, WB exits to Ohio/Indiana state line are on Ohio Turnpike. Exits 142-0.**
142	I-90 (from eb), OH 2, to W Cleveland
139mm	**Middle Ridge Service Plaza wb, Vermilion Service Plaza eb**, Sunoco/dsl/24hr, FoodCourt, gifts, 🅞, RV parking

Exit	Services
135	rd 51, Baumhart Rd, to Vermillion
132mm	Vermilion River
118	US 250, to Norwalk, Sandusky, **N** 🅖 DM/dsl, Marathon, Speedway, 🍴 4Monks Italian, McDonald's, Subway, 🛏 Comfort Inn, Day's Inn, Hampton Inn, Motel 6, Ramada Ltd, Super 8, 🅞 Oulet/famous brands, **5 mi N** 🍴 Perkins, Roadhouse Grill, 🛏 Econolodge, Fairfield Inn, Red Roof Inn, **S** 🛏 Colonial Inn, Homestead Inn/rest., 🍴 Race Café, 🅞 Chevrolet, to Edison's Birthplace
110	OH 4
100mm	**Erie Islands Service Plaza wb, Commodore Perry Service Plaza eb**, 🅖 Sunoco/dsl/24hr, 🍴 Burger King, Cinnabon, Max&Erma's, Sbarro's, Starbucks, 🅞 🅒
93mm	Sandusky River
91	OH 53, to Fremont, Port Clinton, **N** 🍴 Z's Diner, 🛏 Best Budget Inn, Day's Inn, **S** 🅖 Shell/dsl/24hr, 🍴 Applebee's (2mi), 🛏 Fremont Tpk Motel, Holiday Inn, 🅞 🅷
81	OH 51, Elmore, Woodville, Gibsonburg
80.5mm	Portage River
77mm	**Blue Heron Service Plaza wb, Wyandot Service Plaza eb**, Sunoco/dsl/24hr, Hardee's/chicken, 🅒
71	I-280, OH 420, to Stony Ridge, Toledo, **N** 🅖 Petro/Mobil/dsl/rest./24hr/@, FLYING J/Denny's/dsl/24hr/LP/@, 🍴 Charter House Rest., Country Diner, 🛏 Howard Johnson, Pizza Hut, Knight's Inn, Ramada Ltd, Stony Ridge Inn/truck plaza/dsl/@, 🅞 Blue Beacon, **S** 🅖 FuelMart/dsl/@, 🏪/dsl/24hr/@, TA/BP/Burger King/Taco Bell/dsl/24hr/@, 🍴 McDonald's, Wendy's, 🅞 truckwash
64	I-75 N, to Toledo, Perrysburg
63mm	Maumee River
59	US 20, to I-475, Maumee, Toledo, **N** 🅖 Amoco, BP/dsl, Speedway/dsl, 🍴 Arby's, Bob Evans, China Gate Rest., Church's, Dominic's Italian, Indian Cuisine, Max's Diner, McDonald's, Pizza Hut, 🛏 Budget Inn, Econolodge, Holiday Inn, Motel 6, Quality Inn, 🅞 Advance Parts, Goodyear/auto, Jo-Ann Fabrics, K-Mart/Little Caesar's, NAPA, Radio Shack, Savers Foods, Sears/auto, to Toledo Stadium, **S** 🅖 Meijer/dsl/24hr, Speedway, 🍴 Big Boy's, Fazoli's, Fricker's, Friendly's, Ralphie's Burgers, Red Lobster, Schlotsky's, Taco Bell, 🛏 Best Western, Comfort Inn, Cross Country Inn, Day's Inn, Hampton Inn, Red Roof Inn, Super 8, 🅞 Ames, Chevrolet, Ford/Lincoln, Honda, Toyota
52	OH 2, to Toledo, **S** 🛏 Days Inn, Quality Inn (6mi), Super 8, 🅞 RV/truck repair
49mm	**service plaza both lanes**, Valero/dsl/24hr, gifts/ice cream
39	OH 109, Delta, **N** 🅖 Valero, 🍴 Country Lion's
34	OH 108, to Wauseon, **S** 🅖 Shell/Subway/dsl/24hr, 🍴 Smith's Rest., 🛏 Arrowhead Motel, Best Western, Holiday Inn Express, Super 8, 🅞 🅷, Toledo RV Ctr, Woods

OH (vertical side labels: AVON, TOLEDO)

⛽ = gas 🍴 = food 🛏 = lodging ⊙ = other 🅿️ = rest stop Copyright 2014 - The NEXT Exit ®

INTERSTATE 90 CONT'D

Exit	Services
34	Continued
	Trucking/repair (1mi), **2 mi S on US 20A** ⛽ BP/Circle K, 🍴 Burger King, DQ, McDonald's, Pizza Hut, Taco Bell, Wendy's, ⊙ Ace Hardware, Rite Aid, Walmart/dsl
25	OH 66, Burlington, **3 mi S** ⊙ Sauder Village Museum
24.5mm	Tiffin River
13	OH 15, to Bryan, Montpelier, **S** ⛽ Marathon/Subway/dsl, Sunoco, 🍴 Country Fair Rest., 🛏 Econolodge, Holiday Inn Express, Rainbow Motel, Ramada Inn, ⊙ Hutch's dsl Repair
11.5mm	St Joseph River
3mm	**toll plaza,** 🍴
2	OH 49, to US 20, **N** 🍴 Burger King, ⊙ tire repair
0mm	Ohio/Indiana state line

INTERSTATE 270 (COLUMBUS)

Exit	Services
55	I-71, to Columbus, Cincinnati
52b a	US 23, High St, Circleville, **N** ⛽ Marathon/Circle K, Speedway/dsl, 🍴 A&W/KFC, Arby's, Bob Evans, Burger King, China Town, LJ Silver, Los Campero's, McDonald's, Pizza Hut, Ponderosa, Roadhouse Grill, Skyline Chili, Subway, Taco Bell, Tim Horton, Waffle House, Wendy's, White Castle, 🛏 Kozy Inn, ⊙ AutoZone, Curves, $General, Firestone, Kroger/gas, Lowe's, Walgreens, Walmart, **S** ⛽ BP/dsl, 🛏 Budget Inn, ⊙ Kioto Downs
49	Alum Creek Dr, **N** ⛽ Duke/dsl, Sunoco/dsl, 🍴 Donato's Pizza, KFC/LJ Silver, Subway, **S** ⛽ BP/dsl, 🍴 Arby's, McDonald's, Taco Bell, Wendy's, 🛏 Comfort Inn, Sleep Inn
46b a	US 33, Bexley, Lancaster
43b a	I-70, E to Cambridge, W to Columbus
41b a	US 40, **E** ⛽ BP, Shell, 🍴 Bob Evans, Boston Mkt, Hooters, McDonald's, Outback Steaks, Rally's, Steak'n Shake, Texas Roadhouse, ⊙ Walgreens, **W** ⛽ Mobil, Shell, Speedway, 🍴 Fuddruckers, Golden Corral, Hunan Chinese, LoneStar Steaks
39	OH 16, Broad St, **E** ⛽ Meijer/dsl, Speedway/dsl, 🍴 Arby's, Chipotle Grill, Church's, Quizno's, Waffle House, White Castle, 🛏 Country Inn&Suites, ⊙ H, **W** ⛽ Shell, 🍴 Applebee's, 🛏 Ramada Inn
37	OH 317, Hamilton Rd, **E** ⛽ BP/dsl, Marathon, Speedway/dsl, 🍴 Big Boy, Bob Evans, Burger King, Chinese Express, Damon's, Donato's Pizza, Hickory House, KFC, Pizza Hut/Taco Bell, Starbucks, 🛏 Holiday Inn Express, SpringHill Suites, ⊙ Firestone, GNC, Kroger, **2 mi W** 🛏 Comfort Suites, Hampton Inn, Hilton Garden
35b a	I-670W, US 62, **E** ⛽ Speedway/dsl, 🍴 City BBQ, Donato's Pizza, McDonald's, Tim Horton, ⊙ CVS Drug, **W** I-670
33	no services
32	Morse Rd, **E** ⛽ Marathon/DM, Speedway/dsl, 🍴 Donato's Pizza, ⊙ Mazda, Toyota, **W** ⛽ BP, Mobil/dsl, Shell/Subway, 🍴 Applebee's, Champp's Grill, HomeTown Buffet, Kobe Japanese, Logan's Roadhouse, McDonald's, On-the-Border, Pizza Hut/Taco Bell, Steak'n Shake, Wendy's, 🛏 Extended Stay America, Hampton Inn, ⊙ Best Buy, BMW, Cadillac, Carmax, Discount Tire, Jo-Ann Fabrics, Lexus, Lowe's Whse, Macy's, Mercedes, Nordstrom's, NTB, Sam's Club, Target, Walmart/24hr, mall
30	OH 161 E to New Albany, W to Worthington

Exit	Services
29	OH 3, Westerville, **N** ⛽ BP/dsl, Shell, 🍴 Applebee's, Arby's, Chipotle Mexican, McDonald's, Fazoli's, Pizza Hut, Tim Horton, 🛏 Baymont Inn, Knight's Inn, ⊙ CarQuest, Firestone/auto, Kroger, **S** ⛽ Speedway/dsl, Sunoco/dsl, 🍴 Carsoni's Italian, China House, Domino's, Subway, ⊙ Aldi Foods, Family$, Midas
27	OH 710, Cleveland Ave, **N** ⛽ Speedway, 🍴 Subway, Tim Horton, Wendy's, 🛏 Quality Inn, Ramada Inn, Signature Inn, ⊙ CVS Drug, NAPA, Tuffy, **S** 🍴 Bob Evans, McDonald's, O'Charley's, Steak'n Shake, 🛏 Embassy Suites, ⊙ Home Depot
26	I-71, S to Columbus, N to Cleveland
23	US 23, Worthington, **N** 🍴 Alexander's, Amazon Grill, Bob Evans, Bravo Italian, Buffalo Wild Wings, Champp's Grill, Chipotle Mexican, Columbus Fish Mkt, El Acapulco, Gilbert's Steaks, Lotus Grill, Mitchell's Steaks, Panera Bread, Quizno's, Ruth's Chris Steaks, Starbucks, Sushiko Japanese, Tutt's Italian, 🛏 AmeriSuites, Courtyard, Days Inn, DoubleTree, Extended Stay America, Motel 6, Homewood Suites, Red Roof Inn, Residence Inn, Sheraton, **S** ⛽ BP, 🍴 Buca Italian, Cosi Grill, Jimmy John's, McDonald's, 🛏 Econolodge, Holiday Inn
22	OH 315, **N** ⛽ Marathon/dsl
20	Sawmill Rd, **N** ⛽ BP, Marathon/dsl, 🍴 Burger King, McDonald's, Olive Garden, Subway, Taco Bell, Wendy's, ⊙ Buick/GMC, CVS Drug, Ford, Hyundai, Lincoln, Mazda, NTB, Subaru, Tire Kingdom, **S** ⛽ Meijer, Shell, Speedway, 🍴 Applebee's, Asian Star, Arby's, BajaFresh, Bob Evans, Boston Mkt, Burger King, Charlie's Subs, Chili's, Chipotle Mexican, Cosi Grill, Don Pablo, Golden Corral, HoneyBaked Cafe, Joe's Crabshack, KFC, Krispy Kreme, McDonald's, Mongolian BBQ, Steak'n Shake, Red Lobster, Ruby Tuesday, Ted's MT Grill, 🛏 Hampton Inn, Quality Inn, Woodfin Suites, ⊙ Barnes&Noble, Big Lots, Cadillac/Honda, Discount Tire, $Tree, Firestone, Jo-Ann Fabrics, Kohl's, Lowe's Whse, PetCo, Sam's Club, Staples, SteinMart, Target, Toyota/Scion, Trader Joe's
17b a	US 33, Dublin-Granville Rd, **E** ⛽ Marathon, Sunoco, 🍴 Bob Evans, Donato's, Max&Erma's, McDonald's, Subway, 🛏 Best Value Inn, Courtyard, Crowne Plaza, Embassy Suites, Hilton Garden, Red Roof Inn, Residence Inn, ⊙ BMW/Mini, CVS Drug, Kroger, Mitsubishi, Mr Tire, USPO
15	Tuttle Crossing Blvd, **E** ⛽ BP, Mobil, 🍴 Bob Evans, Boston Mkt, Chipotle Mexican, Cozymel's, Longhorn Steaks, Macaroni Grill, McDonald's, PF Chang's, Pizza Hut/Taco Bell, River City Grill, TGIFriday, Wendy's, 🛏 Drury Inn, Homewood Suites, Hyatt Place, La Quinta, Marriott, ⊙ JC Penney, Macy's, Sears/auto, mall, **W** ⛽ Exxon/Subway/dsl, Shell, 🍴 Quizno's, Steak'n Shake, Uno Pizzaria, 🛏 Staybridge Suites, ⊙ Best Buy, NTB, Walmart/auto, World Mkt
13	Cemetery Rd, Fishinger Rd, **E** ⛽ Shell/Subway, Speedway, 🍴 Burger King, CheeseBurger Paradise, Chili's, Chipotle Mexican, Damon's, Dave&Buster's, Donato's Pizza, KFC, Panera Bread, Quizno's, Skyline Chili, Spaghetti's, TGIFriday, Tropical Bistro, 🛏 Comfort Suites, Homewood Suites, ⊙ CVS Drug, Home Depot, Lowe's Whse, Radio Shack, Staples, Target, Tire Dicounters, **W** ⛽ BP, Mobil, Speedway, Sunoco, 🍴 Bob Evans, Max&Erma's, McDonald's, Tim Horton, Wendy's, 🛏 Hampton Inn, Motel 6, ⊙ Nissan
10	Roberts Rd, **E** ⛽ Marathon, Thornton's/dsl, 🍴 Subway,

COLUMBUS

OH

INTERSTATE 270 (COLUMBUS) CONT'D

Exit	Services
10	Continued
	Tim Horton, Wendy's, **W** 🅖 Speedway, 🍴 Waffle House, 🏨 Courtyard, Quality Inn, Royal Inn, 🅞 Kroger/gas
8	I-70, E to Columbus, W to Indianapolis
7	US 40, Broad St, **E** 🅖 BP, Speedway, 🍴 Bob Evans, Boston Mkt, Burger King, McDonald's, Popeye's, TeeJay's, Wendy's, White Castle, 🅞 Buick/GMC, Chevrolet, Chrysler/Jeep, Family$, Firestone/auto, Kohl's, NTB, Pepboys, Sears/auto, Staples, Suzuki, Target, Tuffy, **W** 🅖 GetGo, Speedway/dsl, Thornton's, 🍴 A&W/LJ Silver, Arby's, Big Boy, KFC, Papa John's, Waffle House, 🏨 Holiday Inn Express, Hometown Inn, 🅞 🏥 CVS Drug, Giant Eagle Foods, Goodyear, Home Depot, Jo-Ann Fabrics
5	Georgesville, **E** 🅖 Marathon, Mobil, Sunoco/dsl, 🅞 Walmart, **W** 🍴 Applebee's, Arby's, Bob Evans, Buffalo Wild Wings, Chipotle Mexican, DQ, Fazoli's, Fiesta Mariachi, KFC/LJ Silver, LoneStar Steaks, McDonald's, O'Charley's, Red Lobster, Steak'n Shake, Subway, Wendy's, White Castle, 🅞 Advance Parts, GNC, Hyundai/Isuzu/Subaru, KIA, Kroger/gas, Lowe's Whse, NTB, Toyota/Scion, VW
2	US 62, OH 3, Grove City, **N** 🅖 BP, **S** 🅖 Shell, Speedway, Sunoco, 🍴 Big Boy, Brewster's, Burger King, Domino's, Donato's Pizza, McDonald's, Quizno's, Subway, Tim Horton/Wendy's, Waffle House, 🏨 Knight's Inn
0mm	I-71

▲N INTERSTATE 271 (CLEVELAND)

Exit	Services
39mm	**I-271 begins/ends on I-90, exit 188**
38mm	**I-271/I-480, Express Lanes**
36	Wilson Mills Rd, Highland Hts, Mayfield, **E** 🅖 Shell, 🍴 Austin's Steaks, 🏨 Hilton Garden, Holiday Inn, 🅞 CVS Drug, vet, **W** 🅖 BP, Marathon/dsl, 🍴 Denny's, Hibachi Steaks, Panera Bread, Qdoba, 🅞 Dick's, DrugMart, Home Depot, Kohl's, Tuesday Morning, Verizon
34	US 322, Mayfield Rd, **E** 🅖 BP/7-11, Sunmart, 🍴 DiBella's Subs, 5 Guys Burgers, Fox&Hound Grille, Hotl Iead Burritos, Jimmy John's, Potbelly, Starbucks, Subway, Wendy's, 🅞 🏥 CVS Drug, Marc's Foods, Michael's, Mr Tire, Old Navy, Rite Aid, Target, Walgreens, Walmart, **W** 🅖 Marathon, Shell, Speedway, 🍴 Arby's, Bob Evans, Burger King, El Rio Grande, McDonald's, Panera Bread, Panini's Grill, Penn Sta Subs, Sonic, Subway, TGI Friday's, 🏨 Comfort Inn, 🅞 🏥 Advance Parts, AT&T, Best Buy, Costco/gas, CVS Drug, Ford/Lincoln, Giant Eagle Foods, GNC, JoAnn Fabrics, Marshalls, Midas, Nissan, NTB, Petsmart, O'Reilly Parts, Radio Shack, Staples, Verizon, World Mkt, vet
32	Brainerd Rd, **E** 🍴 Champp's Rest., J Alexander's, 🅞 🏥
29	US 422 W, OH 87, Chagrin Blvd, Harvard Rd, **E** 🅖 Shell, Speedway, Sunoco, 🍴 Bahama Breeze, Bob Evans, Bravo Italian, Corky&Lenny's Rest., Firehouse Subs, Flemings, McDonald's, Mitchell's Fish Mkt, Paladar Latin Kitchen, Red Lobster, Starbucks, Stone Oven, Wasabi Japanese, Wendy's, 🏨 Courtyard, Extended Stay America, Fairfield Inn, Hampton Inn, Homestead Suites, Super 8, 🅞 🏥 AT&T, Barnes&Noble, CVS Drug, Rite Aid, TJ Maxx, Trader Joe's, Verizon, Whole Foods Mkt, **W** 🅖 BP/Subway, Shell, 🍴 Hyde Park Steaks, PF Chang's, The

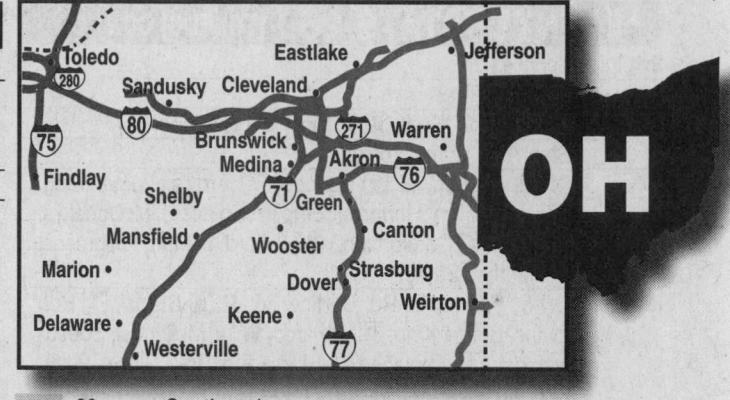

Exit	Services
29	Continued
	Pit Steaks, Yours Truly, 🏨 Clarion, DoubleTree, Embassy Suites, Homewood Suites, Residence Inn, 🅞 Buick/GMC, Cadillac, NTB, Porsche
28b	Harvard Rd, **E** 🍴 Red Robin, **W** 🍴 Abuelo's, Buffalo Wilds Wings, Chick-fil-A, Chipotle, DiBella's Subs, 5 Guys Burgers, Olive Garden, Panera Bread, River City Grille, Robeks Cafe, Zoup!, 🏨 Aloft, Marriott, 🅞 🏥
28a	OH 175, Richmond Rd, Emery Rd, **E** 🅖 BP, GetGo, Marathon/Circle K/Subway/dsl, 🍴 Baskin-Robbins/Dunkin Donuts, Jimmy John's, Marianne's Bakery, McDonald's, Quiznos, **W** 🍴 BJ's Whse
27b	I-480 W
27a	US 422 E, **E** 🅞 Lowe's
26	Rockside Rd, **E** 🅖 Speedway/dsl, Sunoco, 🍴 Burger King, Subway
23	OH 14 W, Forbes Rd, Broadway Ave, **E** 🅖 Sunoco, 🍴 Double Dragon Chinese, McDonald's, Subway, Wendy's, 🏨 Holiday Inn Express, 🅞 Sam's Club/gas, **W** 🅖 Marathon/Circle K/dsl, 🅞 🏥
21	I 480 E, OH 14 E (from sb), to Youngstown
19	OH 82, Macedonia, **E** 🅖 Speedway/dsl/E85, 🍴 Papa John's, Penn Sta Subs, **W** 🅖 Sunoco, 🍴 Applebee's, Arby's, Chick-fil-A, Chili's, Chipotle, Coldstone, Fuji Japanese, Golden Corral, KFC, McDonald's, Outback Steaks, Panera Bread, Pizza Hut, Popeye's, Steak'n Shake, Subway, Taco Bell, Wendy's, 🅞 Best Buy, Chevrolet, Discount Tire, Giant Eagle Foods, GNC, Hobby Lobby, Home Depot, Kohl's, Lowe's, NTB, PetCo, Petsmart, O'Reilly Parts, Radio Shack, Target, Verizon, Walgreens, Walmart
18b a	OH 8, Boston Hts, to Akron, (exits left from sb), **E** 🅖 BP/dsl, GetGo, Speedway/dsl, 🍴 Bob Evans, Dos Coronas Mexican, Pacific Chinese, 🏨 Country Inn&Suites, Days Inn, Knights Inn, La Quinta, Motel 6, **W** same as 19
12	OH 303, Richfield, Peninsula
10	I-77, to I-80, OH Tpk (from nb), to Akron, Cleveland
9	I-77 S, OH 176 (from nb), to Richfield
8mm	🆁🆂 both lanes, full ♿ facilities, 🍴, 🏨, litter barrels, petwalk
3	OH 94, to I-71 N, Wadsworth, N Royalton, **W** 🅖 Marathon/dsl
0mm	**I-271 begins/ends on I-71, exit 220.**

▲N INTERSTATE 280 (TOLEDO)

Exit	Services
13	**I-280 begins/ends on I-75, exit 208**
12	Manhattan Blvd, **E** 🅖 Sunoco, 🏨 Classic Inn, **W** 🅖 Sunoco, 🍴 Arby's, McDonald's
11	OH 25 S, Eerie St, **W** 🅞 Huntington Ctr

CLEVELAND (vertical left margin)

MACEDONIA (vertical right margin)

OH (tab)

⬆N INTERSTATE 280 (TOLEDO) CONT'D

Exit	Services
10mm	Maumee River
9	OH 65, Front St, **E** 🅖 Sunoco, **W** 🅖 Sunoco
8	Starr Ave, (from sb only)
7	OH 2, Oregon, **E** 🅖 Sunoco, 🅕 Arby's, Burger King, Coldstone/Tim Horton's, Empire Chinese, McDonald's, Wendy's, 🛏 Comfort Inn, 🅞 🅗, Ford, K-Mart, Walgreens, to Maumee Bay SP
6	OH 51, Woodville Rd, Curtice Rd, **E** 🅖 BP/dsl, 🅕 Bob Evans, Burger King, 🅞 Menards, **W** 🅖 Meijer/dsl, Speedway/dsl, 🅕 Applebee's, Arby's, Big Boy, Gino's Pizza, KFC, LJ Silver, McDonald's, Pizza Hut, Subway, Taco Bell, 🛏 Sleep Inn, 🅞 🅗, Advance Parts, $General, $Tree, Jo-Ann Fabrics, O'Reilly Parts, Rite Aid, Tires+
4	Walbridge
2	OH 795, Perrysburg, **W** 🅖 Sunoco/Subway/dsl
1b	Bahnsen Rd, **E** 🅖 ⊕FLYING J/Denny's/dsl/LP/scales/24hr, 🛏 Crown Inn, Executive Inn, Regency Inn, **W** 🅖 ♥Loves/Arby's/dsl/scales/24hr, Petro/BP/Iron Skillet/dsl/scales/24hr/@, 🅕 McDonald's, 🅞 Super 8, 🅞 Blue Beacon, SpeedCo
1a	**I-280 begins/ends on I 80/90, Ohio Tpk, Exit 71. services S** 🅖 FuelMart/Subway/dsl/scales, 🅕🅕🅕/McDonald's/dsl/scales/24hr, TA/BP/Burger King/Taco Bell/dsl/scales/24hr/@, 🅕 Sunrise Cafe

INTERSTATE 275 (CINCINNATI)

See Kentucky Interstate 275

⬆N INTERSTATE 475 (TOLEDO)

Exit	Services
20	I-75. **I-475 begins/ends on I-75, exit 204.**
19	Jackman Rd, Central Ave, **S** 🅕 Subway, 🅞 🅗
18b	Douglas Rd (from wb)
18a	OH 51 W, Monroe St
17	Secor Rd, **N** 🅖 Shell/dsl, Valero, 🅕 Applebee's, Bob Evans, Boston Mkt, Burger King, China Crown, Famous Dave's BBQ, Hooters, Penn Sta. Subs, Red Robin, Rudy's Hot Dogs, Tim Horton, 🅞 🅗, AT&T, Best Buy, Kohl's, Kroger/dsl, O'Reilly Parts, Verizon, Walgreens, **S** 🅖 BP, 🅕 Big Boy, Chipotle Mexican, Del Taco, El Nuevo Vallarta, El Vaquero, 5 Guys Burgers, McDonald's, Original Pancakes, Pizza Hut, Popeye's, Ritter's Custard, Sonic, Starbucks, Subway, Taco Bell, Uncle John's Pancakes, 🛏 Comfort Inn, Ramada Inn, 🅞 Batteries+, Costco/gas, Fresh Mkt, Home Depot, Radio Shack, Rite Aid, Sears/auto, Steinmart, U of Toledo
16	Talmadge Rd (from wb, no return), **N** 🅖 BP/dsl, Speedway/dsl, 🅕 Aladdin's Eatery, Bravo Italiana, Coldstone, J Alexander's Rest., Jimmy John's, Longhorn Steaks, Panera Bread, Potbelly, 🅞 Dick's, JC Penney, Kohl's, Macy's, Old Navy, mall
15	Corey Rd (from eb, no return)
14	US 23 N, to Ann Arbor
13	US 20, OH 120, Central Ave, **E** 🅖 Speedway/dsl, 🅕 Bob Evans, Magic Wok, McDonald's, Rally's, Subway, 🅞 BMW, Cadillac, Chrysler/Dodge/Jeep, Fiat, Ford, Honda, Kia, Nissan, Radio Shack, Subaru, Toyota/Scion, Walmart, **W** 🅖 BP, Shell, Speedway, 🅞 Lowe's
8b a	OH 2, **E** 🅖 BP/dsl, 🅕 Don Pablo, TX Roadhouse, TGIFriday's, 🛏 Extended Stay America, Hawthorn Suites,

Exit	Services
8b a	Continued Knights Inn, Red Roof Inn, 🅞 🅗, Gander Mtn, Home Depot, Kohl's, Old Navy, PetCo, to OH Med Coll, **W** 🅖 BP, Speedway/dsl, Sunoco/dsl, 🅕 Arby's, Bob Evans, Boston Mkt, Burger King, Chili's, Chipotle Mexican, DQ, IHOP, Little Caesar's, Mancino's Pizza, McDonald's, Subway, Wendy's, 🛏 Courtyard, EconoLodge, Quality Inn, 🅞 Best Buy, BigLots, Dick's, Firestone/auto, Kroger, Petsmart, Rite Aid, Sam's Club/gas, Target, TJ Maxx, Verizon, Walmart/Subway,
6	Dussel Dr, Salisbury Rd, to I-80-90/tpk, **E** 🅖 BP, Speedway, 🅕 Applebee's, Arby's, Bankok Kitchen, Bluewater Grill, Buffalo Wild Wings, Coldstone, Cracker Barrel, El Camino Royal, Gino's Pizza, Jimmy John's, Longhorn Steaks, Marie's Diner, Max&Erma's, McDonald's, Outback Steaks, Panera Bread, Salsarita's Cantina, Smokey Bones BBQ, Subway, Tim Horton, Yoko Japanese, 🛏 Country Inn&Suites, Courtyard, Fairfield Inn, Homewood Suites, Residence Inn, Studio+, Super 8, **W** 🅖 BP, 🅕 Abuelo's, Bob Evans, Briarfield Café, Carraba's, 🛏 Baymont Inn, 🅞 Churchill's Foods, vet
4	US 24, to Maumee, Napolean, **N** 🅞 🅗, Toledo Zoo
3mm	Maumee River
2	OH 25, to Bowling Green, Perrysburg, **N** 🅖 BP/dsl, Circle K/dsl, Shell, 🅕 American Table Rest., Buffalo Wild Wings, Beaner's Coffee, Charlie's Rest., El Vaquero, Gino's Pizza, Lee Garden Chinese, Marco's Pizza, McDonald's, Subway, Wendy's, 🅞 Auto Value, Churchill's Mkt, Goodyear/auto, GMC, Hyundai, Toms Tire/auto, Volvo, VW, **S** 🅖 Exxon, Speedway/dsl, 🅕 Bar Louie's, Biaggi's, Blue Pacific Grill, Bob Evans, JB's Shoppe, Marie's Scrambler, Max&Erma's, Starbucks, Tea Tree Asian, Waffle House, 🛏 Economy Inn, Hilton Garden, 🅞 AT&T, Books-A-Million, GNC, Tireman, Verizon, Urgent Care, vet
0mm	**I-475 begins/ends on I-75, exit 192.**

⬆E INTERSTATE 480 (CLEVELAND)

Exit	Services
42	I-80, PA Tpk, **I-480 begins/ends, 0-2 mi S** 🅖 BP, Marathon/Circle K, Sheetz/24hr, Shell, Speedway, 🅕 Applebees, Arby's, Baskin Robbins/Dunkin Dounts, Big Boy, Bob Evans, Brown Derby Roadhouse, Buffalo Wild Wings, Burger King, CiCi's Pizza, Denny's, DQ, Eat'n Park, KFC, McDonald's, Mr Hero, New Peking Chinese, Pizza Hut, Quizno's, Rockney's Grill, Ruby Tuesday, Sonic, Steak'n Shake, Taco Bell, Wendy's, Zeppe's Pizza, 🛏 Best Value Inn, Comfort Inn, Econolodge, Fairfield Inn, Hampton Inn, Holiday Inn Express, Microtel, TownePlace Suites, Wingate Inn, 🅞 🅗, Aldi Foods, AutoZone, Buick/GMC, Curves, Defer Tire, $General, Giant Eagle, Home Depot, Honda, Hyundai, K-Mart, Lowes Whse, Midas, NAPA, NTB, Save-a-Lot Foods, Staples, Target, U-Haul, Van's Tires, Walgreens, Walmart, mall, USPO, vet, to Kent St U
41	Frost Rd, Hudson-Aurora
37	OH 91, Solon, Twinsburg, **N** 🅕 Arby's, Pizza Hut, Taco Bell, 🅞 Comfort Suites, 🅞 Giant Eagle, **S** 🅖 BP
36	OH 82, Aurora, Twinsburg, **N** 🅖 BP/dsl, Get'n Go, 🅕 Burger King, 🛏 Super 8, **S** 🅖 Marathon, Bob Evans, Cracker Barrel, Damon's, Donato's Pizza, McDonald's, Wendy's, 🛏 Hilton Garden
26	I-271, to Erie, PA
25a b c	OH 8, OH 43, Northfield Rd, Bedford, **N** 🅞 Harley-Davidson, **S** 🅕 McDonald's, Rally's, White Castle

OH

T O L E D O

▲E INTERSTATE 480 (CLEVELAND) CONT'D

Exit	Services
23	OH 14, Broadway Ave, N 🅖 Gulf/dsl, 🍴 Burger King, KFC
22	OH 17, Garanger, Maple Hts, Garfield Hts
21	Transportation Blvd, to E 98th St, S 🅞 Giant Eagle Foods, JoAnn Fabrics, Walmart
20b a	I-77, Cleveland
17	OH 176, Cleveland
16	OH 94, to OH 176 S, State Rd, N 🅞 Convenient Mart, transmissions, S 🅖 BP, Sunoco/dsl, 🅞 KIA
15	10 US 42, Ridge Rd, N 🅖 BP, 🍴 Applebee's, Baskin-Robbins/Dunkin Donuts, Boston Mkt, CiCi's Pizza, Coldstone Creamery, Hong Kong Buffet, McDonald's, Quizno's, Rockney's Rest., Starbucks, TX Roadhouse, 🅞 Chevrolet, GNC, Lowe's, Marc's Foods, Radio Shack, TJMaxx, S 🅖 Speedway, 🍴 Arby's, DQ, Denny's, Wendy's, 🅞 K-Mart, Best Buy, $Tree, Hyundai, Staples
13	Teideman Rd, Brooklyn, S 🅖 BP, Speedway, 🍴 Burger King, Carrabba's, Chipotle Mexican, Cracker Barrel, Don Pablo's, IHOP, LJ Silver, Panera Bread, Perkin's, Pizza Hut, Steak 'n Shake, TGIFriday's, Wild Ginger China Bistro, 🏠 Extended Stay America, Hampton Inn, 🅞 Aldi Foods, Home Depot, Jaguar, LandRover, Mazda, Sam's Club/gas, Volvo, Walmart
12	W 150th, W130th, Brookpark, N 🍴 Subway, S 🅖 Marathon, Shell, 🍴 Arby's, Big Boy, Bob Evans, 🏠 Best Value Inn, Park Brook Inn, 🅞 Acura, Lexus, Infiniti, Toyota, U-Haul
11	I-71, Cleveland, Columbus
10	S rd 237, Airport Blvd, (wb only)
9	OH 17, Brookpark Rd, N 🏠 Hilton Garden, 🅞 H, S 🏠 Sheraton, 🔲
7	(wb only)Clague Rd, to WestLake
6	OH 252, Great Northern Blvd, to N Olmsted, N 🅖 BP, Shell, Speedway, 🍴 Applebee's, Arby's, Bamboo Garden, Boston Mkt, Brown Bag Burgers, Burger King, Chick-fil-A, Chili's, ChuckeCheese, Daishin Japanese, Great Wall Buffet, Famous Dave's, Fat Burger, Harry Buffalo, Jimmy John's, Lonestar Steaks, Macaroni Grill, Moe's SW Grill, Olive Garden, Panera Bread, Penn Sta Subs, Red Lobster, Red Robin, Ruby Tuesday, Smokey Bones BBQ, Wendy's, 🏠 Candlewood Suites, Courtyard, Homestead Suites, La Quinta, Radisson, Studio ı, 🅞 Aldi Foods, AT&T, Best Buy, Chipotle Mexican, Dillard's, $Tree, Firestone/auto, Home Depot, JC Penney, Jo-Ann Etc, Macy's, Marc's Foods, Mr Tire, NTB, Petsmart, Radio Shack, Sears/auto, Target, TJ Maxx, Toyota, Walmart, mall
3	Stearns Rd, N 🅗, 2 mi S 🍴 Razzle's Cafe
2	OH 10, Lorain Rd, to OH Tpk, S 🅖 BP, Sheetz/24hr, Speedway/dsl, 🍴 Ace's Grille, Gourme Rest., McDonald's, Pizza Pan, 🏠 Motel 6, Super 8
2	OH 10, Lorain Rd, to OH Tpk, S 🅖 BP, Sheetz/24hr, Speedway/dsl, 🍴 Ace's Grille, Gourme Rest., McDonald's, Pizza Pan, 🏠 Motel 6, Super 8
1	OH 10 W, to US 20 (from wb), Oberlin
0mm	OH 10, to Cleveland, **I-480 begins/ends on exit 151, OH Tpk**

▲E INTERSTATE 680 (YOUNGSTOWN)

Exit	Services
14	OH 164, to Western Reserve Rd, **I-680 begins/ends on OH Tpk, exit 234,** S 🅖 Shell/Subway/dsl, 🍴 Dunkin Donuts, McDonald's, Pizza Hut, Wendy's, 🅞 🅗

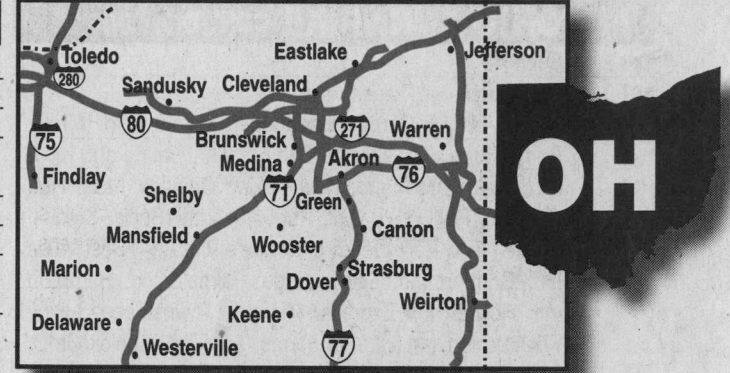

11b a	US 224, S 🅖 BP, GetGo, Shell, 🍴 Applebee's, Burger King, Carabba's, Dunkin Donuts, KFC, LJ Silver, Longhorn Steaks, McDonald's, O'Charley's, Olive Garden, Outback Steaks, Papa John's, Red Lobster, Springfield Grill, Starbucks, Subway, Taco Bell, TGIFriday's, 🏠 Days Inn, Fairfield Inn, Hampton Inn, Holiday Inn, Red Roof Inn, Residence Inn, 🅞 🅗, Giant Eagle, K-Mart, Lowe's, Marc's Foods, Radio Shack, Sam's Club/gas, Walmart/Subway, **Urgent Care**
9b a	OH 170, Midlothian Blvd, Struthers, S 🍴 McDonald's
8	Shirley Rd, downtown
7	US 62, OH 7, South Ave, downtown
6b a	US 62, OH 7, Mkt St, downtown
5	Glenwood Ave, Mahoning Ave, downtown
4b a	OH 193, to US 422, Salt Springs Rd, S 🅗, museum
3c b	Belle Vista Ave, Connecticut Ave
3a	OH 711 E, to I-80 E
2	Meridian Rd, S 🅖 Marathon, 🅞 Ford
1	OH 11

▲E OHIO TURNPIKE

Exit	Services
241mm	Ohio/Pennsylvania state line
239mm	**toll plaza, 🔲**
237mm	**Mahoning Valley Travel Plaza eb, Glacier Hills Travel Plaza wb,** Sunoco/dsl/24hr, McDonald's, gifts, 🔲
234	I-680 (from wb), to Youngstown
232	OH 7, to Boardman, Youngstown, N 🅖 Sheetz, Valero/dsl, 🍴 DQ, Los Gallos Mexican, Rita's Custard, Steamer's Stonewall Tavern, 🏠 Best Value Inn, Budget Inn, Holiday Inn Express, Super 8, 🅞 antiques, S 🅖 🔲/McDonald's/dsl/scales/24hr, Sunoco/dsl, 🍴 Ambrozini's Rest., Road House Diner, 🏠 Davis Motel, Liberty Inn, 🅞 truck repair
218	I-80 E, to Youngstown. **OH Tpk runs with I-76 eb, I-80 wb, to Niles, services S on Mahoning**
216	Lordstown (from wb), N GM Plant
215	Lordstown (from eb), N GM Plant
210mm	Mahoning River
209	OH 5, to Warren, N 🏠 Rodeway Inn, S 🅖 Marathon/dsl, 🏠 EconoLodge, Holiday Inn Express
197mm	**Portage Service Plaza wb, Bradys Leap Service Plaza eb,** Sunoco/dsl/24hr, Au Bon Pain, McDonald's, Sbarro's, Starbucks, gifts, 🔲
193	OH 44, to Ravenna
192mm	Cuyahoga River
187	OH 14 S, I-480, to Streetsboro, 0-2 mi S 🅖 BP, Marathon/Circle K, Sheetz, Shell, Speedway, 🍴 Applebee's, Arby's, Baskin Robbins/Dunkin Dounts, Big Boy, Bob Evans,

🅿 = gas 🍴 = food 🛏 = lodging ⦿ = other ℞ₛ = rest stop   Copyright 2014 - The NEXT Exit ®

OHIO TURNPIKE CONT'D

Exit	Services
187	**Continued** Evans, Brown Derby Roadhouse, Buffalo Wild Wings, Burger King, CiCi's Pizza, Denny's, DQ, Eat'n Park, KFC, McDonald's, Mr Hero, New Peking Chinese, Pizza Hut, Quiznos, Rockney's Grill, Ruby Tuesday, Sonic, Steak'n Shake, Taco Bell, Wendy's, Zeppe's Pizza, 🛏 Best Value Inn, Comfort Inn, EconoLodge, Fairfield Inn, Hampton Inn, Holiday Inn Express, Microtel, TownePlace Suites, Wingate Inn, ⦿ 🅷, Aldi Foods, AutoZone, Buick/GMC, Curves, Defer Tire, $General, Giant Eagle Foods, Home Depot, Honda, Hyundai, K-Mart, Lowe's, Midas, NAPA, NTB, Save-a-Lot Foods, Staples, Target, U-Haul, Van's Tires, Walgreens, Walmart, mall, USPO, vet, to Kent St U
180	OH 8, to I-90 E, **N** 🛏 Comfort Inn, Holiday Inn, ⦿ Harley-Davidson, **S** 🅿 BP/dsl, ⦿ to Cuyahoga Valley NRA
177mm	Cuyahoga River
173	OH 21, to I-77, **N** 🅿 ▦/Wendy's/dsl/scales, 🛏 Holiday Inn Express, Motel 6, **S** 🍴 DQ, Memories Rest., Richfield Rest., Subway, 🛏 Days Inn, Hampton Inn, Super 8
170mm	**Towpath Service Plaza eb**, Great Lakes **Service Plaza wb**, 🅿 Sunoco/dsl/24hr, 🍴 Burger King, FoodCourt, Panera Bread, Pizza Hut, Starbucks, ⦿ gifts, ℂ
161	US 42, to I-71, Strongsville, **N on US 42** 🅿 AP/dsl, 🍴 Buffalo Wild Wings, Jennifer's Rest, Mad Cactus Mexican, 🛏 Days Inn, Kings Inn, La Siesta Motel, Metrick's Motel, Village Motel, ⦿ Circle K, Home Depot, Lowe's, Walmart, vet, **S on US 42** 🍴 Burger King, DQ, J-Bella Rest., KFC, La Volte Grill, Marco's Pizza, Olympia's Cafe, 🛏 Elmhaven Motel, ⦿ Dodge, NAPA, Staples
152	OH 10, to Oberlin, I-480, Cleveland, **N** 🅿 BP, Sheetz, Speedway/dsl, 🍴 Ace's Grille, Gourme Rest., McDonald's, Pizza Pan, 🛏 Motel 6, Super 8
151	I-480 E (from eb), to Cleveland 🖝
146mm	Black River
145	OH 57, to Lorain, to I-90, Elyria, **N** 🅿 Speedway 🍴 Applebee's, Arby's, Bob Evans, Buffalo Wild Wings, Burger King, Chipotle Mexican, Denny's, Eat'n Park, Golden Corral, Harry Buffalo, Hunan King, Old Century Buffet, Olive Garden, McDonald's, Qdoba Mexican, Red Lobster, Subway, Wasabi Grill, Wendy's, 🛏 Best Western, Comfort Inn, Country Inn&Suites, EconoLodge, Holiday Inn, Red Carpet Inn, Red Roof Inn, ⦿ AT&T, Best Buy, Curves, $Tree, $General, Firestone/auto, Home Depot, Honda, JC Penney, Jo-Ann Fabrics, Lowe's, Macy's, Marc's Foods, NTB, Petsmart, Radio Shack, Sears/auto, Staples, Target, Walmart/auto, **S** 🅿 Shell, Speedway, 🛏 Howard Johnson
142	I-90 (from eb, exits left), OH 2, to W Cleveland
140	OH 58, Amherst, **0-2 mi N** 🅿 BP, GetGo, Speedway, Sunoco/Subway/dsl, 🍴 Blue Sky Rest., Bob Evans, DQ, Donato's Pizza, KFC, Marco's Pizza, McDonald's, Moosehead Grill, Mr Hero, Taco Bell, Wendy's, 🛏 Days Inn, Motel 6, ⦿ Advance Parts, Aldi Foods, Chevrolet, Chrysler/Dodge, Drug Mart, Giant Eagle Foods, K-Mart, Rite Aid, VW, Walgreens, repair, USPO, **S** ⦿ Ford
139mm	**Service Plaza both lanes**, 🅿 Sunoco/dsl/24hr, 🍴 Burger King, Great Steak&Potato, Hershey's, Panera Bread, Popeye's, Starbucks, ⦿ gifts, ℂ, RV parking

135	rd 51, Baumhart Rd, to Vermilion
132mm	Vermilion River
118	US 250, to Norwalk, Sandusky, **N** 🅿 BP/Circle K/Dunkin Donuts, Marathon/dsl, 🍴 Italian Gardens, McDonald's, Subway, 🛏 Days Inn, Hampton Inn, Motel 6, Quality Inn, Red Roof Inn, Super 8, ⦿ Milan RV Park, to Edison's Birthplace, **S** 🛏 Colonial Inn
110	OH 4, to Bellevue
100mm	**Service Plaza both lanes**, 🅿 Sunoco/dsl/24hr, 🍴 Burger King, Cinnabon, Einstein Bros. Bagels, Sbarro's, Starbucks, ⦿ ℂ
93mm	Sandusky River
91	OH 53, to Fremont, Port Clinton, **N** 🛏 Days Inn, **0-2 mi S** 🅿 BP/Subway/dsl/24hr, Murphy USA/dsl, 🍴 Applebee's, Bob Evans, Burger King, Fricker's, Hibachi Buffet, McDonald's, Pizza Hut, Subway, Taco Bell, 🛏 Clarion, Comfort Inn, Delux Inn, Hampton Inn, ⦿ 🅷, Aldi Foods, $Tree, Ford/Lincoln, Lowe's, Staples, Verizon, Walmart, Rutherford B. Hayes Library, USPO, vet
81	OH 51, Elmore, Woodville, Gibsonburg
80.5mm	Portage River
77mm	**Service Plaza both lanes**, 🅿 Sunoco/dsl/24hr, 🍴 Hardee's, Mancino's, Red Burrito, ℂ
71	I-280, OH 420, to Stony Ridge, Toledo, **N** ⦿ ⚡FLYING J/Denny's/dsl/scales/LP/24hr, 🅿Loves/Arby's/dsl/scales/24hr, Petro/BP/Iron Skillet/dsl/scales/24hr/@, 🛏 Budget Inn, Crown Inn, Super 8, Travel Inn, ⦿ Blue Beacon, KOA, SpeedCo, **S** 🅿 FuelMart/Roadeez Rest./dsl/scales, ▦/McDonald's/dsl/scales/24hr, TA/BP/Burger King/Taco Bell/dsl/scales/24hr/@, 🍴 Sunrise Grill, ⦿ truckwash
64	I-75 N, to Toledo, Perrysburg, **S** ⦿ BP/Subway/dsl, 🛏 Country Inn&Suites, Courtyard, Hampton Inn, ⦿ Bass Pro Shops
63mm	Maumee River
59	US 20, to I-475, Maumee, Toledo, **N** 🅿 BP, Shell, Speedway/dsl, 🍴 Bob Evans, Golden Lily, McDonald's, Olive Garden, Pizza Hut, Steak'n Shake, Subway, Waffle House, 🛏 Clarion, Motel 6, ⦿ Family$, Goodyear/auto, Jo-Ann Fabrics, K-Mart, NAPA, O'Reilly Parts, Radio Shack, Rite Aid, Savers, Walgreens, to Toledo Stadium, **S** 🅿 Speedway/dsl, 🍴 Big Boy, Chipotle Mexican, Donato's Pizza, El Azteca, Fricker's, Friendly's, Jed's BBQ, La Fiesta Mexican, Red Lobster, Schlotzsky's, Taco Bell, 🛏 Best Value Inn, Budget Inn, Comfort Inn, Hampton Inn, Holiday Inn, Red Roof Inn, ⦿ AT&T, Ford, Honda, Meijer/gas, Toyota/Scion
52	OH 2, to Toledo, **N** 🅿 Shamrock/dsl, 🍴 Loma Linda Mexican, **S** 🛏 Days Inn, ⦿ RV/truck repair, 🖝
39	OH 109, **S** 🅿 Country Corral/Valero/Winchesters Rest/dsl/scales/wi-fi/24hr
34	OH 108, to Wauseon, **S** 🅿 Shell/Subway/dsl/24hr, 🍴 Smith's Rest., 🛏 Arrowhead Motel, Best Western, Holiday Inn Express, Super 8, ⦿ 🅷, Woods Trucking/repair (1mi), **2 mi S on US 20A** 🅿 BP/Circle K, Circle K, Marathon, Murphy USA/dsl, Valero, 🍴 A&W/KFC, Arby's, Burger King, DQ, Grasshopper Rest., Kamwa Chinese, McDonald's, Pizza Hut, Subway, Taco Bell, Wendy's, ⦿ Ace Hardware, AutoZone, $General, O'Reilly Parts, Rite Aid, Walmart, Wood Trucking

LORAIN

TOLEDO

OH

🗲E OHIO TURNPIKE CONT'D

Exit	Services
25	OH 66, Burlington, **N** 🄾 Harrison Lake SP, 3 mi **S** 🄾 Sauder Village Museum
24.5mm	Tiffen River
21 mm	**Indian Meadow Service Plaza both lanes,** 🗲 Sunoco/dsl, 🍴 Burger King, Sbarro's, Starbucks

OKLAHOMA

🗲N INTERSTATE 35

Exit	Services
236mm	Oklahoma/Kansas state line
235mm	**weigh sta, sb only**
231	US 177, Braman, **E** 🗲 Conoco/deli/dsl
230	Braman Rd
229mm	Chikaskia River
225mm	**Welcome Ctr sb, full ♿ facilities, 🍴 s, 🗑, litter barrels, vending, petwalk**
222	OK 11, to Blackwell, Medford, Alva, Newkirk, **E** 🗲 Conoco/dsl, Shell/dsl, 🍴 Braum's, KFC/Taco Bell, Los Potros Mexican, McDonald's, Plains Man Rest., Subway, 🛏 Best Way Inn, Best Western, Comfort Inn, 🄾 🄷
218	Hubbard Rd
217mm	**weigh sta both lanes**
214	US 60, to Tonkawa, Lamont, Ponca City, N OK Coll, **W** 🗲 Casey's/dsl, Shell/dsl, 🛏 New Western Inn, 🄾 RV Park
213mm	Salt Fork of Arkansas River
211	Fountain Rd, **E** 🗲 ❤Loves/Chester's/Subway/dsl/scales/24hr/RV Dump
209mm	parking area, litter barrels
203	OK 15, to Marland, Billings, **E** 🗲 Phillips 66/DQ/dsl/scales/24hr
199mm	Red Rock Creek
195mm	parking area both lanes, litter barrels
194b a	US 412, US 64 W, **E** Cimarron Tpk (eb), to Tulsa, **W** to Enid, Phillips U
193	Airport Rd (from nb, no return)
191mm	Black Bear Creek
186	US 64 E, to Fir St, Perry, **E** 🗲 Mobil/Subway/dsl, 🍴 Braum's, McDonald's, Taco Mayo, 🛏 Super 8, 🄾 🄷, museum, **W** 🗲 Exxon/dsl, 🛏 Comfort Suites, Holiday Inn Express, Regency Inn
185	US 77, to Covington, Perry, **E** 🛏 American Inn, **W** 🗲 Phillips 66/rest/motel/dsl/24hr, 🄾 RV camping
180	Orlando Rd
174	OK 51, to Stillwater, Hennessey, **E** 🗲 Conoco/dsl, 🍴 Smokey Pokey Cafe, 🛏 Fairfield Inn (12mi), Hampton Inn (12mi), Motel 6 (12mi), 🄾 Lake Carl Blackwell RV Park, to OSU
173mm	parking area sb, litter barrels, parking only
171mm	parking area nb, litter barrels, parking only
170	Mulhall Rd
166mm	Cimarron River
157	OK 33, to Cushing, Guthrie, **W** 🗲 K&L/dsl, ❤Loves/Subway/dsl, Road Star, Shell/dsl, Valero, 🍴 Arby's, Braum's, El Rodeo Mexican, KFC (2mi), LJ Silver, Mazzio's, McDonald's (3mi), Pizza Hut, Sonic, The Ribshack, 🛏 Best Western, Holiday Inn Express, Interstate Motel, Sleep Inn, 🄾 🄷, OK Terr Museum, Langston U, RV camping

13	OH 15, to Bryan, Montpelier, **S** 🗲 Marathon/dsl, Sunoco, 🍴 4Seasons Rest., 🛏 EconoLodge, Holiday Inn Express, Rainbow Motel, Ramada Inn, 🄾 Hutch's dsl Repair
11.5mm	St Joseph River
3mm	**toll plaza,** 🍴
2	OH 49, to US 20, **N** 🍴 Burger King, Subway, 🄾 info, truck tires
0mm	Ohio/Indiana state line

153	US 77 N (exits left from nb), Guthrie, **W** 🍴 McDonald's (3mi), Taco Bell (3mi), 🄾 Buick/Cadillac/GMC, Chevrolet, Chrysler/Dodge/Jeep
151	Seward Rd, **E** 🗲 Shell/cafe/dsl, 🄾 Lazy E Arena (4mi), Pioneer RV park
149mm	**weigh sta both lanes**
146	Waterloo Rd, **E** 🗲 Shell/Subway/dsl
143	Covell Rd
142	Danforth Rd (from nb)
141	US 77 S, OK 66E, to 2nd St, Edmond, Tulsa, **W** 🗲 Conoco/dsl, Phillips 66/dsl, 🛏 Best Western, Comfort Suites, Fairfield Inn, Hampton Inn, Holiday Inn Express, 🄾🄷, vet
140	SE 15th St, Spring Creek, Arcadia Lake, Edmond Park, **W** 🗲 Phillips 66/Circle K/Subway, 🍴 Braum's, McDonald's, 🄾 Walmart/McDonald's
139	SE 33rd St
138d	Memorial Rd
138c	Sooner Rd (from sb)
138b	Kilpatrick Tpk
138a	I-44 Tpk E to Tulsa
I-35 S and I-44 W run together 8 mi.	
137	NE 122nd St, to OK City, **E** 🗲 Shamrock/dsl, Shell/dsl, 🍴 Charly's Rest., IHOP, 🛏 Knights Inn, Sleep Inn, **W** 🗲 ⊘FLYING J/Huddle House/dsl/scales/LP/24hr, ❤Loves/Godfathers/Subway/dsl/24hr, Phillips 66/dsl/scales, 🍴 Cracker Barrel, McDonald's, Sonic, Waffle House, 🛏 Comfort Inn, Days Inn, EconoLodge, Economy Inn, Holiday Inn Express, Motel 6, Red Carpet Inn, Super 8, 🄾 Abe's RV Park, Frontier City Funpark, Oklahoma Visitors Ctr/info/restrooms, truckwash
136	Hefner Rd, **W** 🗲 Conoco/dsl, same as 137
135	Britton Rd
134	Wilshire Blvd, **W** 🛏 Executive Inn, 🄾 Blue Beacon
I-35 N and I-44 E run together 8 mi	
133	I-44 W, to Amarillo, **W** st capitol, Cowboy Hall of Fame
132b	NE 63rd St (from nb), **1/2 mi E** 🗲 Conoco/dsl, 🍴 Braum's, 🛏 Remington Inn
132a	NE 50th St, Remington Pk, **W** 🄾 funpark, info, museum, zoo
131	NE 36th St, **W** 🗲 Phillips 66/dsl/24hr, 🄾 45th Inf Division Museum
130	US 62 E, NE 23rd St, **E** 🗲 Shell/dsl, **W** to st capitol
129	NE 10th St, **E** 🗲 Conoco/McDonald's/dsl
128	I-40 E, to Ft Smith
127	Eastern Ave, OK City, **W** 🗲 Petro/rest/dsl/24hr/@, JR's Trvl Ctr/Wendy's/dsl/scales/24hr/@, 🍴 Waffle House, 🛏 Brick-Town Hotel, Best Western, Central Plaza Hotel, EconoLodge, Quality Inn, 🄾 Blue Beacon, Lewis RV Ctr
126a	I-40, W to Amarillo, I-235 N, to st capitol
126b	I-35 S to Dallas
125d	SE 15th St, **E** 🗲 Conoco/dsl

GUTHRIE

OH OK

⬆N INTERSTATE 35 CONT'D

Exit	Services
125b	SE 22nd St (from nb)
125a	SE 25th, same as 124b
124b	SE 29th St, E 🍴 China Queen, Denny's, McDonald's, Sonic, Taco Bell, 🛏 Best Value Inn, Days Inn, Plaza Inn, Royal Inn, W 🅖 Phillips 66/Circle K, 🍴 Mama Lou's Rest., 🛏 Executive Inn, same as 125a
124a	Grand Blvd, E 🛏 Studio 6, Super 8, W 🛏 Drover's Inn
123b	SE 44th St, E 🅖 Shell, 🍴 Domino's, Sonic, 🛏 Best Value Inn, Courtesy Inn, Motel 6, W 🅖 Phillips 66, 🍴 Subway, Taco Mayo, 🅞 $General, Family$, USPO
123a	SE 51st St, E 🅖 Conoco/dsl, 🛏 Best Value Inn
122b	SE 59th St, E 🅖 Phillips 66/dsl, W 🅖 Shell, Valero/dsl, 🅞 U-Haul
122a	SE 66th St, E 🍴 Burger King, Luby's, McDonald's, Subway, TX Roadhouse, Zeke's Rest., 🛏 Fairfield Inn, Ramada Inn, Residence Inn, 🅞 Tires+, W 🅖 7-11, 🍴 Arby's
121b	US 62 W, I-240 E
121a	SE 82nd St, (from sb), W 🛏 Baymont Inn, Days Inn
120	SE 89th St, E 🅖 Valero/dsl/scales, 🛏 Ford, W 🅖 ♥Loves/Subway/dsl/24hr, 🅞 Classic Parts
119b	N 27th St, E 🅖 Shell/Circle K/dsl, W 🍴 Pickles Rest.
119a	Shields Blvd (exits left from nb)
118	N 12th St, E 🍴 Mazzio's, Peking Buffet, 🛏 Super 8, W 🅖 Shell, 🍴 A&W/LJ Silver, Arby's, Braum's, Grandy's, KFC, La Fajitas, Mamma Lou's, McDonald's, Papa John's, Subway, Taco Bell, Wendy's, Western Sizzlin, 🛏 Best Western, Candlewood Suites, Comfort Inn, SpringHill Suites, 🅞 AutoZone, $General, Family$, 7-11, vet
117	OK 37, S 4th St, W 🅖 7-11, 🍴 Van BBQ, 🅞 USPO
116	S 19th St, E 🅖 Conoco, Shell, 🍴 Braum's, Genghis Grill, McDonald's, Ricky's Cafe, Taco Bell, Waffle House, Whataburger, 🅞 AT&T, Best Buy, Firestone/auto, GNC, Hobby Lobby, JC Penney, Office Depot, Petsmart, Ross, W 🅖 Murphy USA, 🍴 Alfredo's Mexican, Applebee's, Arby's, Buffalo Wild Wings, Burger King, Cane's, Carl's Jr, Chicken Express, Chick-fil-A, Chili's, China House, Earl's Ribs, 5 Guys Burgers, Freddy's Custard, Furr's Buffet, Harry Bears, Hollies Steaks, IHOP, Jack-in-the-Box, Jersey's Mike's Subs, Jimmy's Egg, Mazzio's, McAlister's Deli, Panda Express, Poblano Grill, Qdoba Mexican, Quiznos, Schlotzsky's, Sonic, Starbucks, Subway, Taco Mayo, 🛏 La Quinta, 🅞 Aldi Foods, AT&T, Discount Tire, $Tree, Gordman's, Harley-Davidson, Home Depot, Kohl's, Lowe's, Radio Shack, Target, Tires+, Walmart
114	Indian Hill Rd, E 🛏 ValuePlace Hotel, E 🍴 Double Dave's Pizza, 🅞 Cadillac, funpark
113	US 77 S (from sb, exits left), Norman
112	Tecumseh Rd, E 🅞 Nissan, Toyota/Scion, W 🍴 McDonald's, Sonic, 🅞 H, CVS Drug, **Urgent Care**
110b a	Robinson St, E 🍴 Carl's Jr, Cheddar's, 5 Guys Burgers, Logan's Roadhouse, Panda Express, Pei Wei, Qdoba Mexican, Taco Bell, Wing Stop, Zio's Italian, 🛏 Embassy Suites, Motel 6, 🅞 H, AT&T, Buick/GMC, Discount Tire, $Tree, Ford, GMC, Homeland Foods/gas, Honda, Hyundai, Kohl's, Lincoln, Mazda, Office Depot, PetCo, Target, Tires+, TJ Maxx, Verizon, VW, W 🅖 Conoco/Subway, 🍴 Arby's, Braum's, Cafe Escondido, Chuy's Mexican, Cracker Barrel, Domino's, Jersey Mike's, Outback Steaks, Papa John's, Papa Murphy's, Pizza Hut, Rib Crib, Saltgrass Steaks, Waffle House, Yamato Steaks, 🛏 Comfort

N O R M A N

O K L A H O M A   C I T Y

OK

110b a	Continued Inn, Courtyard, Hilton Garden, Holiday Inn, 🅞 Kia, 7-11, Suzuki
109	Main St, E 🅖 Murphy USA, Phillips 66/dsl, Shell/Circle K, Sinclair, 🍴 Chick-fil-A, Golden Corral, Panera Bread, Prairie Kitchen, Taco Cabana, Waffle House, Wendy's, Whataburger, 🛏 EconoLodge, Guest Inn, Motel 6, Super 8, Travelodge, 🅞 AT&T, AutoZone, Best Buy, BigLots, Cadillac, Chevrolet, Chrysler/Dodge/Jeep, Hastings Books, Hobby Lobby, Kwik Kar, Lowe's, Nissan, Tires+, Walmart/McDonald's, W 🅖 Conoco/Circle K/dsl, 🍴 Applebee's, BJ's Brewhouse, Burger King, Charleston's Rest. Chili's, McDonald's, Olive Garden, On the Border, Red Lobster, 🛏 Fairfield Inn, Hampton Inn, La Quinta, 🅞 Barnes&Noble, Dillard's, JC Penney, Michael's, Old Navy, Sam's Club, Sears/auto
108b a	OK 9 E, Norman, E 🅖 Conoco/Circle K, 🍴 Arby's, Braum's, Del Rancho Steaks, Schlotzsky's, Taco Bell, 🛏 Sooner Legends Inn/rest, 🅞 $General, NAPA, O'Reilly Parts, to U of OK, W 🍴 Cajun King Buffet, Carino's Italian, IHOP, Interurban Grill, Jasons Deli, Red Robin, 🛏 Country Inn&Suites, La Quinta, 🅞 Chevrolet, Home Depot, Petsmart, Ross
107mm	Canadian River
106	OK 9 W, to Chickasha, E 🅞 Casino, W 🅖 ♥Loves/Subway/dsl/24hr, Shell, 🍴 McDonald's, Sonic, 🛏 Sleep Inn, 🅞 casino, vet
104	OK 74 S, Goldsby, E 🅞 Floyd's RV Ctr, W 🅖 Shamrock/dsl, 🍴 Libby's Cafe
101	Ladd Rd
98	Johnson Rd, E 🅖 Shamrock/dsl, 🅞 Sooner RV Ctr
95	US 77 (exits left from sb), Purcell, **1-3 mi** E 🅖 Shell, 🍴 Braum's, KFC, Mazzio's, Pizza Hut, Subway, 🅞 H, Ford
91	OK 74, to OK 39, Maysville, E 🅖 Conoco/dsl, Murphy USA/dsl, Phillips 66/dsl, 🍴 Braum's, McDonald's, New China, Subway, Taco Mayo, 🛏 EconoLodge, Executive Inn, Ruby's Inn/rest., 🅞 AT&T, Walmart/Subway, W 🅖 Shell/dsl, 🍴 A&W/LJ Silver, Taco Bell
86	OK 59, Wayne, Payne, E 🅞 American RV Park
79	OK 145 E, Paoli, E 🅖 Phillips 66
76mm	Washita River
74	Kimberlin Rd, to OK 19
72	OK 19, Paul's Valley, E 🅖 Conoco/dsl, Murphy USA/dsl, Valero/dsl/rest/24hr, 🍴 Arby's, Braum's, Chicken Express, Green Tea Chinese, Happy Days Diner, KFC/Taco Bell, McDonald's, Sonic, Stevenson BBQ, Subway, Taco Mayo, Tio's Mexican, 🛏 American Inn, Best Value Inn, Comfort Inn, Days Inn, Holiday Inn Express, Relax Inn, 🅞 AT&T, Buick/Cadillac/GMC, Chrysler/Dodge/Jeep, Ford/Lincoln, Walmart, W 🅖 Phillips 66/dsl/24hr, 🅞 truckwash
70	🅞 Rd, E 🅖 ♥Loves/Burger King/dsl/LP/scales/24hr/@, 🅞 H
66	OK 29, Wynnewood, E 🅖 Kent's Motel, W 🅖 Shell/dsl
64	OK 17A E, to Wynnewood, E GW Exotic Animal Park
60	Ruppe Rd
59mm	🆁🆂 both lanes, full ♿ facilities, 🅲, 🔁, litter barrels, pet-walk, RV dump
55	OK 7, Davis, E 🅖 Conoco, Phillips 66/A&W/dsl/24hr, 🅞 Treasure Valley Casino/Inn, to Chickasaw NRA, W 🅞 **Chickasaw Nation Welcome Ctr**, to Arbuckle Ski Area
54.5mm	Honey Creek Pass
53mm	**weigh sta both lanes**

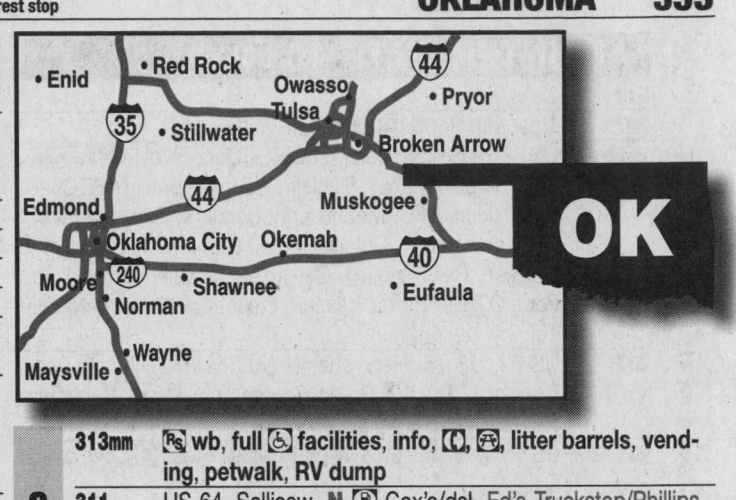

⬆️N INTERSTATE 35 CONT'D

Exit	Services
51	US 77, Turner Falls, **E** 🛏 Arbuckle Mtn Motel, Mtnview Inn (3mi), 🅞 to Arbuckle Wilderness, RV camping, **W** 🅖 Sinclair/rv park, 🍴 Cliff Steaks, 🅞 Botanic Gardens
49mm	scenic turnout both lanes
47	US 77, Turner Falls Area
46mm	scenic turnout both lanes
42	OK 53 W, Springer, Comanche, **W** 🅖 Exxon/dsl
40	OK 53 E, Gene Autry, **E** 🅖 Shell/dsl/café/24hr, 🍴 Broaster Rest, 🅞 Gene Autry Museum (8mi)
33	OK 142, Ardmore, **E** 🅖 Phillips 66/dsl, 🍴 IHOP, Jimmy's Egg Cafe, 🛏 Guest Inn, Holiday Inn, La Quinta, SpringHill Suites, Super 8, 🅞 tires, regional park, **W** 🅖 ⊕FLYING J/Huddle House/dsl/LP/scales/24hr
32	12th St, Ardmore, **E** 🅖 Conoco/dsl, Shell, 🍴 Braum's, CiCi's Pizza, Cotton Patch Cafe, Quiznos, Santa Fe Steaks, Starbucks, Whataburger, 🛏 Candlewood Suites, Holiday Inn, La Quinta, 🅞 $Tree, Hyundai, Lowe's, PetCo, Ross, Toyota, **W** 🅖 Loves/Godfather's/Subway/dsl/24hr/@, 🍴 McDonald's, 🛏 Microtel
31b a	US 70 W, OK 199 E, Ardmore, **E** 🅖 Shell/dsl, Valero/dsl, 🍴 Applebee's, Burger King, Cattle Rustlers, Denny's, El Chico, El Tapatio, Interurban Grill, Jack-in-the-Box, KFC, Mazzio's, McDonald's, Papa John's, Pizza Hut, Prairie Kitchen, 2Frogs Grill, 🛏 Best Western, Comfort Inn, Days Inn, Motel 6, Quality Inn, Rodeway Inn, 🅞 AutoZone, Honda, O'Reilly Parts, **W** 🅖 Conoco/dsl, 🅞 Ardmore RV Park, Chrysler/Dodge/Jeep, Ford/Lincoln, Nissan, vet
29	US 70 E, Ardmore, **E** 🅞 to Lake Murray SP/lodge (8mi), **W** 🅞 Hidden Lake RV Park
24	OK 77 S, **E** 🅞 Red River Livestock Mkt, to Lake Murray SP
22.5mm	Hickory Creek
21	Oswalt Rd, **W** 🅞 Lazy Man's Corner RV Park, **W** 🅖 Valero/dsl, 🅞 Ardmore Marietta RV Park
15	OK 32, Marietta, **E** 🅖 Valero/dsl/24hr, 🍴 Carl's Jr, McDonald's, Pizza Hut, Robertson's Sandwiches, Sonic, Subway, 🅞 🅷, $General, to Lake Texoma SP, **W** 🅖 Phillips 66, 🍴 Hickory House BBQ
5	OK 153, Thackerville, **W** 🅞 Shorty's Foods/gas, Red River Ranch RV Park
3.5mm	**Welcome Ctr nb, full** ♿ **facilities,** 🚻🚻, 📵, **litter barrels, vending, petwalk**
1	US 77 N, **E** 🅖 Phillips 66/dsl, 🛏 Best Western, The Inn, 🅞 Winstar Casino, RV park, **W** 🅞 Red River RV Resort (3mi)
0mm	Oklahoma/Texas state line, Red River

⬆️E INTERSTATE 40

Exit	Services
331mm	Oklahoma/Arkansas state line
330	OK 64D S (from eb), Ft Smith
325	US 64, Roland, Ft Smith, **N** 🅖 Cherokee Trkstp/Valero/Subway/dsl/scales/24hr, 🍴 Four Star Diner, 🛏 Cherokee Inn, Travelodge, 🅞 casino, **S** 🅖 🚛/Wendy's/dsl/scales/24hr, Shell/dsl/scales, Valero/dsl, 🍴 Arby's, El Celaya Mexican, McDonald's, Mazzio's, Sonic, Subway, Taco Bell, 🛏 Interstate Inn, 🅞 $General, Marvin's Foods
321	OK 64b N, Muldrow, **N** 🍴 Sonic (1mi), **S** 🅖 Shell/dsl, 🛏 Best Value Inn, 🅞 auto/dsl repair
316mm	🆁🆂 **eb, full** ♿ **facilities, info,** 📵, 🚻🚻, **litter barrels, vending, petwalk**

Exit	Services
313mm	🆁🆂 **wb, full** ♿ **facilities, info,** 📵, 🚻🚻, **litter barrels, vending, petwalk, RV dump**
311	US 64, Sallisaw, **N** 🅖 Cox's/dsl, Ed's Truckstop/Phillips 66/diner/dsl, 🍴 Hardee's, KFC/Taco Bell, Pizza Hut, Taco Mayo, 🛏 Motel 6, Sallisaw Inn, 🅞 🅷, AutoZone, Brushy Lake SP (10mi), $General, NAPA, Sequoya's Home (12mi), city park, USPO
308	US 59, Sallisaw, **N** 🅖 Murphy USA/dsl, Phillips 66/dsl, 🍴 A&W/LJ Silver, Arby's, Braum's, China Panda, Gino's Pizza, Mazzio's, McDonald's, Roma's Italian, Sonic, Subway, Taco Pronto, Western Sizzlin, 🛏 Best Value Inn, Blue Ribbon Inn, Days Inn, Golden Spur Motel, Super 8, 🅞 🅷, AT&T, $General, $Tree, Verizon, Walmart, antiques, casino, **S** 🅖 Shell/dsl, 🍴 Emma B's Diner, 🅞 Buick/Chevrolet/GMC, Chrysler/Dodge/Jeep, Ford, KOA, to Kerr Lake, truck/tire repair
303	Dwight Mission Rd
297	OK 82 N, Vian, **N** 🅖 FL/dsl, 🍴 Subway, 🅞 Cherokee Landing SP (24 mi), IGA Foods, to Tenkiller Lake RA (12 mi), USPO, **S** 🅞 Sequoia NWR
291	OK 10 N, to Gore, **N** 🅞 Greenleaf SP (10mi), Tenkiller SP (21mi)
290mm	Arkansas River
287	OK 100 N, to Webbers Falls, **N** 🅖 Loves/Burger King/Subway/dsl/24hr, 🍴 Charlie's Chicken, Godfather's Pizza, 🛏 Sleepy Traveler Motel, 🅞 Greenleaf SP, Tenkiller SP, parts/tires/repair
286	Muskogee Tpk, to Muskogee
284	Ross Rd
283mm	parking area both lanes, litter barrels
278	US 266, OK 2, Warner, **N** 🅖 Conoco, Phillips 66/dsl, Sinclair/McDonald's/dsl, 🍴 Duke's Diner, Simon's Pizza, Sonic, Subway, 🛏 Sleepy Traveler Motel, 🅞 $General, Parts+, city park
270	Texanna Rd, to Porum Landing, **S** 🅖 Sinclair
265	US 69 bus, Checotah, **N** 🅖 Quick'n Easy, 🍴 Pizza Hut, Sonic, **S** 🅖 Shell/dsl, 🛏 Budget Inn, 🅞 Chevrolet/Chrysler/Dodge/Jeep
264b a	US 69, to Eufaula, **1 mi N** 🅖 ⊕FLYING J/dsl/LP/scales/24hr, Phillips 66/dsl/24hr, 🍴 Charlie's Chicken, El Jarocho Pizza, McDonald's, Simple Simon's Pizza, Subway, 🛏 Best Value Inn, 🅞 Ace Hardware, $General, O'Reilly Parts, TrueValue, Walmart/Subway, repair
262	to US 266, Lotawatah Rd, **N** 🅖 Sinclair
261mm	Lake Eufaula
259	OK 150, to Fountainhead Rd, **S** 🅖 Shell, 🛏 Lake Eufaula Inn, 🅞 to Lake Eufaula SP
255	Pierce Rd, **N** KOA
251mm	🆁🆂 both lanes

OK

INTERSTATE 40 CONT'D

Exit	Services
247	Tiger Mtn Rd, **S** 🅞 Quilt Barn/antiques
240b a	US 62 E, US 75 N, Henryetta, **N** 🅟 Conoco/dsl, ♥Love's/dsl, Phillips 66, Shell, Sinclair, 🍴 Arby's, Braum's, El Charro Mexican, KFC, Mazzio's, McDonald's, Sonic, Subway, 🛏 Best Value Inn, Colonial Motel, Economy Inn, Henryetta Inn/rest., Relax Inn, 🅞 Chevrolet, Chrysler/Dodge/Jeep, Ford, O'Reilly Parts, Walmart, tires/repair, **S** Indian Nation Tpk
237	US 62, US 75, Henryetta, **N** 🅟 Shell/dsl/24hr, 🍴 Char Crushers BBQ, 🛏 Green Country Inn, 🅞 🏥, Henryetta RV Park (2mi), **S** 🛏 Super 8
231	US 75 S, to Weleetka, **N** 🅟 Phillips 66/dsl, 🍴 Cowpoke's Cafe
227	Clearview Rd, **S** casino
221	US 62, OK 27, Okemah, **N** 🅟 Phillips 66/McDonald's, Valero/Subway/dsl/24hr, 🍴 Mazzio's, Sonic, 🛏 Days Inn, 🅞 🏥, Chevrolet, $General, Homeland Foods, NAPA, TrueValue, **S** 🅟 ♥Love's/Chester Fried/dsl/24hr, Shell/dsl, 🍴 Kellogg's Rest, 🅞 casino, truck repair
217	OK 48, to Bristow, Bearden, **S** gas
216mm	N Canadian River
212	OK 56, to Cromwell, Wewoka, **N** 🅞 auto/tire repair, **S** 🅟 Shell/cafe/dsl, to Seminole Nation Museum
208mm	Gar Creek
202mm	Turkey Creek
200	US 377, OK 99, to Little, Prague, **N** 🅟 Bar H Bar TC/Shell/dsl/RV park, **S** 🅟 Conoco/dsl, ♥Love's/Subway/dsl/24hr, Sinclair/dsl, 🍴 Robertson's Ham Sandwiches, Roundup Rest/RV Park, 🅞 🏥
197mm	🆁🆂 both lanes, full 🛏 facilities, 🄲, 🛠, litter barrels, petwalk
192	OK 9A, Earlsboro, **S** 🅟 Shell/dsl, 🍴 Biscuit Hill
189mm	N Canadian River
186	OK 18, to Shawnee, **N** 🅟 Phillips 66, Sinclair, 🍴 Denny's, 🛏 American Inn, Best Value Inn, Comfort Inn, Days Inn, La Quinta, Motel 6, Super 8, **S** 🍴 Sonic, Van's BBQ, 🅞 Cadillac/Chevrolet/GMC, Chrysler/Dodge/Jeep, Ford, Homeland Foods, vet
185	185 OK 3E, Shawnee Mall Dr, to Shawnee, **N** 🅟 Murphy USA/dsl, 🍴 Buffalo Wild Wings, Chili's, KFC, Red Lobster, Santa Fe Steaks, Taco Bueno, Wendy's, 🛏 Holiday Inn Express, 🅞 AT&T, Dillard's, $Tree, JC Penney, Old Navy, Radio Shack, Ross, Sears/auto, Walgreens, Walmart/McDonald's, mall, **S** 🅟 Phillips 66/Circle K/Quiznos/dsl, 🍴 Braum's, Burger King, Cracker Barrel, Delta Cafe, Garfield's Rest., IHOP, Mazzio's, McAlister's Deli, McDonald's, Popeye's, Sonic, Starbucks, Subway, Taco Bell, Whataburger, 🛏 Hampton Inn, 🅞 CVS Drug, Kwik Kar, Lowe's, Staples
181	US 177, US 270, to Tecumseh, **S** 🛏 Budget Inn
180mm	N Canadian River
178	OK 102 S, Dale, **N** 🅟 Firelake/dsl/casino
176	OK 102 N, McLoud Rd, **S** 🅟 ♥Love's/Subway/dsl/24hr, Sinclair/dsl, 🍴 Curtis Watson Rest.
172	Newalla Rd, to Harrah
169	Peebly Rd
166	Choctaw Rd, to Woods, **N** 🅞 KOA, **S** 🅟 ♥Love's/McDonald's/Subway/dsl/scales/24hr, ⛽/Wendy's/dsl/scales/24hr, 🍴 Sonic, 🅞 to Lake Thunderbird SP (11mi)
165	I-240 W (from wb), to Dallas

162	Anderson Rd, **N** Leisure Time RV Ctr, LP
159b	Douglas Blvd, **N** 🅟 Conoco, Shell, 🍴 Denny's, LJ Silver, McDonald's, Sonic, Subway, Taco Bell, 🅞 Eastland Hills RV Park, **S** 🅞 Tinker AFB, 🏥
159a	Hruskocy Gate, **N** 🅟 Shell, 🍴 Cheddar's, Denny's, McDonald's, Taco Bell, 🅞 Dodge, Family$, Nissan, U-Haul, same as 157, **S** Gate 7, Tinker AFB
157c	Eaker Gate, Tinker AFB, same as 159
157b	Air Depot Blvd, **N** 🅟 Shell/Circle K, 🍴 Chick-fil-A, Chili's, Jack-in-the-Box, Logans Roadhouse, Old Chicago Grill, Panda Express, Pizza Inn, Qdoba Grill, Santa Fe Steaks, Starbucks, Steak&Shake, 🛏 Super 8, 🅞 Best Buy, Dick's, Firestone, JC Penney, Kohl's, Lowe's, Marshall's, O'Reilly Parts, Petsmart, Target, **S** Gate 1, Tinker AFB
157a	SE 29th St, Midwest City, **N** 🅟 Conoco/dsl, Shell, 🛏 Best Western, Traveler's Inn, 🅞 O'Reilly Parts, **S** 🅞 Ford, Sam's Club/gas
156b a	Sooner Rd, **N** 🅟 Conoco/Circle K, 🍴 Primo's Rest., Waffle House, 🛏 Comfort Inn, Hampton Inn, Hawthorn Suites, Holiday Inn Express, La Quinta, Sheraton, Studio 6, 🅞 Home Depot, Nissan, Radio Shack, Walmart/Subway, **S** 🍴 Buffalo Wild Wings, Carl's Jr, 🛏 Candlewood Suites, Motel 6, 🅞 Chevrolet/GMC, Discount Tire, Tires+, Toyota/Scion
155b	SE 15th St, Del City, **N** 🅟 Shell, 🅞 Family$, **S** 🍴 Madison's Kitchen
155a	Sunny Lane Rd, Del City, **N** 🅟 Conoco/dsl, 🅞 Hyundai, U-Haul, **S** 🅟 Shell, Shamrock, 🍴 Braum's, Dunkin Donuts, Sonic, 🅞 Ace Hardware, $General
154	Reno Ave, Scott St, **N** 🅟 Sinclair, 🅞 Value Place Motel, **S** 🅟 7-11
152	(153 from wb)I-35 N, to Wichita
127	Eastern Ave (from eb), Okla City, **N** 🅟 Petro/Mobil/dsl/scales/rest./@, JR's Trvl Crt/Corky's Grill/dsl/24hr, Shamrock, 🍴 Waffle House, 🛏 Bricktown Hotel, Econolodge, Quality Inn, 🅞 Blue Beacon, Lewis RV Ctr
151b c	I-35, S to Dallas, I-235 N, to downtown, st capitol
151a	Lincoln Blvd, **N** 🅟 Conoco/Subway/Circle K/dsl, 🍴 Earl's Rib Palace, Falcon's Pizza, IHOP, Sonic, 🛏 Residence Inn, Hampton Inn, 🅞 Bass Pro Shop, Bricktown Stadium
150c	Robinson Ave (from wb), OK City, **N** 🍴 Spaghetti Whse, Zio's Italian, 🛏 Courtyard, Residence Inn, Westin Hotel, 🅞 U-Haul, Ford Ctr
150b	Harvey Ave (from eb), downtown, **N** 🛏 Courtyard, Renaissance Hotel, Sheraton, Westin Hotel, 🅞 Ford
150a	Walker Ave (from eb), **N** 🍴 La Luna Mexican, 🅞 Ford, Lincoln, **S** transmissions
149b	Classen Blvd (from wb), same as 149a, to downtown
149a	Western Ave, Reno Ave, **N** 🅟 Valero/Subway/dsl, 🍴 China Queen, McDonald's, Sonic, Taco Bell, **S** 🅟 Conoco/dsl, Shell, 🍴 Sweis Gyros
148c	Virginia Ave (from wb), to downtown
148b	Penn Ave (from eb), **N** 🅟 Shamrock, **S** 🅞 Isuzu Trucks
148a	Agnew Ave, Villa Ave, **N** 🅟 Phillips 66/dsl
147c	May Ave
147b a	I-44, E to Tulsa, W to Lawton
146	Portland Ave (from eb, no return), **N** 🅟 Conoco/Subway/dsl, 🅞 water funpark
145	Meridian Ave, OK City, **N** 🅟 Conoco/Circle K/dsl, Shell/Circle K/dsl, 🍴 Cimarron Steakhouse, Denny's, Jin Wei Aisan, Louie's Grill, Mango's, McDonald's, On the Border, Portofinos Italian, Shorty Small's Rest., Trapper's Rest.,

Vertical left margin: **HENRYETTA** / **SHAWNEE** / **OK**

Vertical right margin: **OKLAHOMA CITY**

INTERSTATE 40 CONT'D

Exit	Services
145	Continued
	⌂ Best Western, Biltmore Hotel, Days Inn, Extended Stay America, Howard Johnson, Red Roof Inn, Residence Inn, Super 8, □ USPO, S □ Phillips 66/Circle K/dsl, Sinclair, □ Arby's, Burger King, Charleston Rest., Chili's, Cracker Barrel, El Sombrero, Golden Palace Chinese, IHOP, Kona Ranch Steaks, Mackie's Steaks, Panera Bread, Pearl's Fish House, Poblano's, Quiznos, Rib Crib, Riggin's Grill, Sonic, Subway, Taco Bell, Taco Bueno, Waffle House, Whataburger, Zapata's, Zio's Italian, ⌂ Baymont Inn, Best Value Inn, Candlewood Suites, Clarion Hotel, Comfort Suites, Caountry Inn&Suites, Courtyard, Embassy Suites, Fairfield Inn, Governors Suites, Hampton Inn, Hilton Garden, Holiday Inn, Holiday Inn Express, Hyatt Place, La Quinta, Meridian Inn, Motel 6, Oak Tree Inn, Ramada Ltd, Regency Inn, Sleep Inn, Staybridge Suites, Wingate Inn, Wyndham Garden, □ Celebration Sta., Shepler's
144	MacArthur Blvd, N □ Shell/Circle K/dsl, □ Applebee's, Coldstone, Golden Corral, Jack-in-the-Box, KFC, Lin's Buffet, McDonald's, Panda Express, Quiznos, Sonic, Starbucks, Steak'n'Shake, Taco Cabana, TX Roadhouse, ⌂ SpringHill Suites, □ AT&T, $Tree, GNC, Hobby Lobby, Office Depot, Petsmart, Radio Shack, Ross, Walmart, S ⌂ Comfort Inn, Green Carpet Inn, Microtel, Super 10 Motel, Travelers Inn, □ Kenworth, Sam's Club/gas, dsl repair
143	Rockwell Ave, N □ Shell/dsl, □ Buffalo Wild Wings, Mike's Subs, Taco Bell, ⌂ Homewood Suites, Rodeway Inn, □ Best Buy, Dick's, Discount Tire, Harley Davidson, Home Depot, McClain's RV Ctr, Tires+, S ⌂ Sands Motel/RV Park/LP, □ Rockwell RV Park, A-OK RV Park
142	Council Rd, N □ Shell, Sinclair, □ BJ's Rest, Braum's, McDonald's, Subway, Taco Bell, ⌂ Super 40 Inn, □ Goodyear/auto, S □ TA/Country Pride/dsl/scales/24hr/@, ⌂ EconoLodge, □ Council Rd RV Park, Ford/Peterbilt, dsl repair, truckwash
140	Morgan Rd, N □ ▢/McDonald's/dsl/24hr/@, TA/Popeye's/dsl/24hr/@, □ Blue Beacon, S □ FLYING J/dsl/LP/scales/24hr, ▢Loves/Subway/dsl/scales/24hr, □ Ricky's Cafe, Sonic, □ Speedco
139	Kilpatrick Tpk
138	OK 4, to Yukon, Mustang, N □ Best Value Inn, Comfort Suites, □ Chrysler/Dodge/Jeep, S □ Conoco/Circle K/dsl, □ Braum's, Burger King, Hunan Express, IHOP, Interurban Grill, McDonald's, Sonic, Subway, Taco Bell, ⌂ Best Western, La Quinta, □ Urgent Care, CVS Drug, Homeland Food/drug, Cottman Transmissions
137	Cornwell Dr, Czech Hall Rd, N Homeland Food/drug
136	OK 92, Garth Brooks Blvd, Yukon, N □ Murphy USA/dsl, Shell/Circle K, □ A&W/LJ Silver, Braum's, CiCi's Pizza, Harry's Rest., KFC, McDonald's, Primo's Italian, Subway, Taco Mayo, Waffle House, Wendy's, Yukon Buffet, ⌂ Hampton Inn, □ AutoZone, Big Lots, Big O Tire, $Tree, GNC, Hancock Fabrics, Hastings Books, Radio Shack, Tuesday Morning, Verizon, Walmart, Walgreens, USPO, repair, S □ Alfredo's, Carino's Italian, Chick-fil-A, Chili's, Jimmy's Egg Café, Logan's Roadhouse, Louie's Grill, Mike's Subs, Pizza Hut, Quiznos, Rib Crib, Santa Fe Steaks, Starbucks, Taco Bueno, ⌂ Holiday Inn Express, □ H, Discount Tire, Ford, Kohl's, Kwik Kar, Lowe's, PetsMart, Staples, Target, Tires+

Exit	Services
132	Cimarron Rd, S ▢
130	Banner Rd, N □ Shell/dsl/rest.
129mm	weigh st both lanes
125	US 81, to El Reno, N □ Conoco/dsl, ▢Loves/Subway/dsl, □ China King, Serapio's Mexican, Taco Mayo, ⌂ Deluxe Inn, Economy Express, Super 8, □ Buick/GMC, Chevrolet, Chrysler/Dodge/Jeep, $General, Ford/Lincoln, S truck repair
123	Country Club Rd, to El Reno, N □ Phillips 66, Murphy USA/dsl, Shell, Valero, □ Arby's, Braum's, Burger King, Greatwall Chinese, KFC, Little Caesar's, Mazzio's, McDonald's, Pizza Hut, Subway, Taco Bell, ⌂ Motel 6, □ H AutoZone, Radio Shack, Walmart, Walgreens, S □ □ □ Denny's, MT Mikes Steaks, ⌂ Baymont Inn, Best Western/RV Park, Days Inn, Regency Motel
119	Lp 40, to El Reno
115	US 270, to Calumet
111mm	▢ eb, ▢, litter barrels
108	US 281, to Geary, N □ Shell/Subway/dsl/24hr, □ KOA Indian Trading Post, to Roman Nose SP, S □ Phillips 66/dsl
105mm	S Canadian River
104	Methodist Rd
101	US 281, OK 8, Hinton, N to Roman Nose SP, S □ ▢Loves/Chester's/Godfather's/Sonic/dsl/scales, □ Subway, ⌂ Hinton Travel Inn, □ Chevrolet, casino, ▢, to Red Rock Canyon SP
95	Bethel Rd
94.5mm	▢ wb, ▢, litter barrels
88	OK 58, to Hydro, Carnegie
84	Airport Rd, N □ Phillips 66/dsl/scales/24hr, □ Lucille's Roadhouse, ⌂ Holiday Inn Express, Travel Inn, □ H, Buick/Cadillac/Chevrolet/GMC, Chrysler/Dodge/Jeep, S Stafford Aerospace Museum
82	E Main St, Weatherford, N □ Conoco/dsl, Phillips 66/dsl, Shell/dsl, Sinclair, Valero/dsl, □ Arby's, Braum's, Carl's Jr, Jerry's Rest., KFC/Taco Bell, Little Caesars, Mark Rest., Mazzio's, McDonald's, Pizza Hut, Quiznos, Sonic, Subway, Taco Mayo, T-Bone Steaks, Vinicio's Mexican, ⌂ Best Western, Comfort Inn, Fairfield Inn, Scottish Inn, □ H, Ace Hardware, $General, GNC, O'Reilly Parts, Walgreens, to SW OSU, S □ Walmart
80a	(from eb), N □ Conoco, □ Ford
80	W Main St, Mountainview, Thomas, N ⌂ Best Value Inn
71	Custer City Rd, N □ ▢Loves/Subway/dsl/24hr, □ Cherokee Trading Post/rest.
69	Lp 40 (from wb), to Clinton, 2 mi N □ DQ, ⌂ Travel Inn
67.5mm	Washita River
66	US 183, Clinton, S □ Shell/dsl, □ Buick/Chevrolet/GMC, Ford

OK

OK

🅿 = gas 🍴 = food 🛏 = lodging 🅾 = other 🆁🆂 = rest stop Copyright 2014 - The NEXT Exit ®

I▶E INTERSTATE 40 CONT'D

Exit	Services
65a	10th St, Neptune Dr, Clinton, **N** 🍴 Branding Iron Rest., China King, Oakwood Steaks, Picante Grille, Pizza Hut, 🛏 Days Inn, Relax Inn, Super 8, 🅾 United Foods, **S** 🛏 EconoLodge, 🅾 Hargus RV Park
65	Gary Blvd, Clinton, **N** 🅿 Conoco, Shell/dsl, 🍴 Braum's, Del Rancho, KFC/Taco Bell, LJ Silver, Mazzio's, McDonald's, MT Mike's, Placio Mexican, Subway, Taco Mayo, 🛏 Budget Inn, Hampton Inn, Ramada Inn, Tradewinds Inn, 🅾 🅷, $General, K-Mart, Rte 66 Museum, **S** 🛏 Holiday Inn Express
62	Parkersburg Rd, **S** Hargus RV Ctr
61	Haggard Rd
57	Stafford Rd
53	OK 44, Foss, **N** to Foss SP, **S** gas/dsl
50	Clinton Lake Rd, **N** 🅾 KOA/LP/dsl
47	Canute, **S** 🅿 Shell, 🛏 Sunset Inn
41	OK 34 (exits left from eb), Elk City, **N** 🅿 ❤Loves/Subway/dsl, Shell, 🍴 Home Cooking Rest., 🛏 Best Value Inn (3mi), Best Western (3mi), Economy Express, Elk City Motel, HomeTowne Inn, La Quinta, Motel 6, Sleep Inn, Super 8, Travel Inn, 🅾 🅷, Elk Run RV Park, Rte 66 Museum
40	E 7th St, Elk City, **N** 🍴 Portobello Grill, 🛏 Holiday Inn Express, **S** 🅿 Hutch's/dsl/CNG, 🍴 Huddle House, 🛏 Hampton Inn, 🅾 Walmart, same as 41
38	OK 6, Elk City, **N** 🅿 Conoco/dsl, Phillips 66/dsl, 🍴 Arby's, China Super Buffet, Denny's, LJ Silver, McDonald's, Quizno's, Western Sizzlin, 🛏 Bedford Inn, Days Inn, 🅾 Ace Hardware, Elk Creek RV Park, tires, vet, **S** 🅿 Phillips 66/dsl, 🛏 Clarion Inn, Comfort Inn, Ramada Inn, Rodeway Inn, 🅾 to Quartz Mtn SP
34	Merritt Rd
32	OK 34 S (exits left from eb), Elk City
26	Cemetery Rd, **N** 🅿 Shell/dsl, 🅾 dsl repair, **S** 🅿 TA/Taco Bell/Subway/dsl/scales/24hr/@
25	Lp 40, Sayre, **1 mi N** 🅿 Shell/dsl, 🛏 Western Motel, 🅾 🅷, Chevrolet/GMC, Deep Creek RV Park, $General, Ford
23	OK 152, Sayre, **S** 🅿 Shell/dsl
22.5mm	N Fork Red River
20	US 283, Sayre, **N** 🅿 ⊕FLYING J/Denny's/dsl/LP/RV dump/scales/24hr, 🛏 AmericInn, 🅾 truckwash, to Washita Bfd Site (25mi)
14	Hext Rd
13.5mm	check sta both lanes, litter barrels
11	Lp 40, to Erick, Hext
10mm	**Welcome Ctr/🆁🆂 both lanes, full 🛏 facilities,** 🅲, 🔄, **litter barrels, petwalk, RV dump**
7	OK 30, Erick, **N** 🛏 Premier Inn, **S** 🅿 ❤Loves/Subway/dsl/scales, 🍴 Simple Simon's Pizza, 🛏 Days Inn
5	Lp 40, Honeyfarm Rd
1	Texola, **S** 🅿 gas/dsl/rest., 🅾 RV camping
0mm	Oklahoma/Texas state line

I▶E INTERSTATE 44

Exit	Services
329mm	Oklahoma/Missouri state line
321mm	Spring River
314mm	**Oklahoma Welcome Ctr wb, full 🛏 facilities, info, restrooms**
313	OK 10, Miami, **N** 🅿 Conoco, ❤Loves/dsl, Phillips 66, 🍴 Donut Palace, Okie Burger, 🛏 Best Value Inn, Deluxe

Exit	Services
313	Continued Inn, EconoLodge, Hampton Inn, Holiday Inn Express, Legacy Inn, Microtel, 🅾 🅷, Miami RV Park, to NE OK A&M Coll, auto repair, **S** 🅾 Chrysler/Dodge/Jeep, casino
312mm	Neosho River
302	US 59, US 69, Afton, **S** 🅿 Buffalo Ranch/Subway/dsl, 🛏 Rte 66 Motel (3mi)
289	US 60, Vinita, **N** 🅿 Murphy USA/dsl, 🍴 Braum's, Clanton's Cafe, McDonald's, Pizza Hut, Sonic, Subway, Woodshed Deli, 🛏 Holiday Inn Express, Vinita Inn, 🅾 🅷, Ace Hardware, Chevrolet, $General, O'Reilly Parts, Radio Shack, Walmart, st patrol, USPO
288mm	**service plaza both lanes**, Phillips 66/dsl/24hr, McDonald's, 🅲
286mm	**toll plaza**
283	US 69, Big Cabin, **N** 🅿 Big Cabin/dsl/rest./scales/24hr/@, 🛏 Super 8, 🅾 Cabin RV Park, trk repair
269	OK 28 (from eb, no re-entry), to Adair, Chelsea, **S** 🅿 Sinclair
255	OK 20, to Pryor, Claremore, **0-2 mi N** 🅿 Kum&Go/dsl/e-85, Murphy USA/dsl, QT/dsl, 🍴 Carl's Jr, Chili's, Red's Coney Island, 🛏 Clairmore Inn, Super 8, Travel Inn, Will Rogers Inn, 🅾 🅷, Walgreens, Walmart, to Rogers U, Will Rogers Memorial, museum
248	to OK 266, Port of Catoosa, **N** 🅿 QT, 🛏 Comfort Inn, Will Rogers Inn, 🅾 Dave's RV Ctr
244mm	Kerr-McClellan Navigation System
241mm	Will Rogers Tpk begins eb, ends wb 🅲
241	OK 66 E, to Catoosa
240b	US 412 E, Choteau
240a	OK 167 N, 193rd E Ave, **N** 🍴 IHOP, McDonald's, Taco Bueno, Waffle House, Wendy's, 🛏 Cherokee Inn/Casino, Hampton Inn, Hardrock Hotel/Casino, La Quinta, 🅾 KOA, Walgreens, **S** 🅿 QT, 🍴 Mazzio's, PortCity Diner, Sonic, Subway, 🛏 Holiday Inn Express, 🅾 $General, O'Reilly Parts, tires/repair
238	161st E Ave, **N** 🅿 Sinclair/rest/dsl/scales/24hr, 🅾 Goodyear Trk Tires, truckwash, **S** 🅿 QT/dsl/scales/24hr, 🍴 Arby's, Burger King, 🛏 Microtel, 🅾 **OK Welcome Ctr**, truckwash
236b	I-244 W, to downtown Tulsa 🔄
236a	129th E Ave, **N** 🅿 ⊕FLYING J/Denny's/dsl/LP/24hr, **S** 🍴 McDonald's
235	E 11th St, Tulsa, **N** 🍴 Big Daddy's BBQ, Mazzio's, Rioberto's Mexican, Sonic, Subway, 🛏 Economy Inn, Executive Inn, Knights Inn, Super 8, 🅾 $General, Drug Whse, O'Reilly Parts, **S** 🅿 QT, 🍴 Braum's, Taco Bueno, 🛏 EconoLodge, 🅾 Whse Mkt
234b a	US 169, N to Owasso, to 🔄, S to Broken Arrow
233	E 21st St, **S** 🍴 El Chico, 🛏 Comfort Suites, 🅾 K-Mart, Dean's RV Ctr, vet
231	(232 from wb), US 64, OK 51, to Muskogee, E 31st St, Memorial Dr, **N** 🍴 Speedy Gonzales Mexican, Whataburger, 🛏 Days Inn, Ramada Inn, Tulsa Inn, **S** 🅿 Shell, 🍴 Cracker Barrel, IHOP, McDonald's, Pizza Hut, Ruby Tuesday, Village Inn, 🛏 Best Value Inn, Best Western, Comfort Suites, Courtyard, EconoLodge, Embassy Suites, Extended Stay America, Fairfield Inn, Hampton Inn, Holiday Inn Express, Quality Inn, Sleep Inn, Studio+, Super 8, 🅾 Cavender's Boots, Chevrolet, Harley-Davidson, Nissan, **Urgent Care**
230	E 41st St, Sheridan Rd, **N** 🅿 Shell, 🍴 Carl's Jr, Desi Wok, On-the-Border, Panera Bread, Schlotzsky's, Subway, TGI

E INTERSTATE 44 CONT'D

TULSA

Exit	Services
230	Continued Friday's, Whataburger, [other] AT&T, Barnes&Noble, Curves, Dillard's, JC Penney, Jo-Ann Fabrics, Michael's, Old Navy, Petco, Petsmart, Reasor's Foods, Ross, Verizon, **S** [food] Buffalo Wild Wings, Carino's Italian, [lodging] La Quinta, [other] Batteries+, Home Depot
229	Yale Ave, Tulsa, **N** [gas] Shell, [food] McDonald's, Subway, [other] Firestone, JC Penney, Macy's, PetCo, mall, **S** [gas] Phillips 66/dsl, QT, [food] Applebee's, Arby's, Braum's, Charlie Mitchell's Grill, Delta Cafe, Jack-in-the-Box, Outback Steaks, Qdoba, Red Lobster, Smoothie King, Sonic, Taco Bell, Village Inn, [lodging] Baymont Inn, Hilton Garden, Red Roof Inn, Tulsa Select Hotel, [other] [H], Kia, vet
228	Harvard Ave, Tulsa, **N** [food] El Tequila Mexican, NYC Pizza, [lodging] Tradewinds Motel, **S** [gas] Express, [food] A&W/LJ Silver, Chili's, Chimi's Mexican, Freckle's Frozen Custard, Jamil's Rest, Mario's Pizza, Osaka Steaks, Papa John's, Starbucks, Subway, [lodging] Stratford House Hotel, Wingate Inn, [other] $Tree, Food Pyramid, Hobby Lobby, K-Mart, SteinMart
227	Lewis Ave, Tulsa, **S** [food] Goldie's Grill, [other] Walgreens
226b	Peoria Ave, Tulsa, **N** [gas] Kum&Go, QT/dsl, [food] Arby's, Burger St., CiCi's, Egg Roll Express, Jimmy's Egg, La Hacienda Mexican, Little Caesars, Mazzio's, KFC, Pizza Hut, Ron's Burgers/Chili, Sonic, Subway, Super Buffet, Taco Bell, Taco Bueno, [lodging] Peoria Inn, [other] Advance Parts, Food Pyramid, Harley-Davidson, O'Reilly Parts, Robertson Tire, Verizon, Walmart Mkt, Whole Foods Mkt, **S** [food] Braum's, Corner Cafe, Golden Palace, [other] AutoZone, $General, Drug Whse, Family$
226a	Riverside Dr
225mm	Arkansas River
225	Elwood Ave, **N** [other] Chevrolet, Ford, **S** [lodging] Budget Inn
224b a	US 75, to Okmulgee, Bartlesville, **N** [gas] QT/dsl, [food] KFC, Mazzio's, Sonic, Subway, [other] $General, Whse Mkt, **S** [lodging] Royal Inn, [other] RV park
223c	33rd W Ave, Tulsa, **N** [food] Braum's, Domino's, **S** [gas] Conoco, [food] Rib Crib BBQ
223b	51st St (from wb)
223a	I-244 E, to Tulsa, downtown
222c	(from wb), **S** [lodging] Value Inn
222b	55th Place, **N** [lodging] Capri Motel, Crystal Motel, **S** [lodging] Days Inn, Economy Inn
222a	49th W Ave, Tulsa, **N** [food] Carl's Jr, Kelly's Country Cooking, Monterey Mexican, Subway, [lodging] Gateway Motel, Interstate Inn, Motel 6, Rest Inn, [other] BigLots, $General, Mack Trucks, **S** [gas] QT/Wendy's/dsl/scales/24hr, [food] Arby's, McDonald's, Taco Bueno, Village Inn, Waffle House, [lodging] Super 8, [other] Buick/GMC, Freightliner, Kenworth, Peterbilt, Volvo Trucks
221a	57th W Ave, (from wb), **S** [food] Go West Rest, [other] Buick/GMC
221mm	Turner Tkp begins wb, ends eb
218	Creek Tpk E (from eb)
215	OK 97, to Sand Sprgs, Sapulpa, **S** [gas] Kum&Go, [food] Arby's, Freddy's, Subway, Whataburger, [lodging] Super 8, [other] [H], Hunter RV Ctr, Route 66 RV Park
211	OK 33, to Kellyville, Drumright, **S** [gas] Shell/dsl, [other] Heyburn Lake SP
207mm	**service plaza wb,** [gas] Phillips 66/dsl
197mm	**service plaza eb,** [food] McDonald's
196	OK 48, Bristow, **S** [gas] Conoco/dsl, Phillips 66, [food] Mazzio's, McDonald's, Pizza Hut, Sonic, Steak'nEgg Rest, Taco

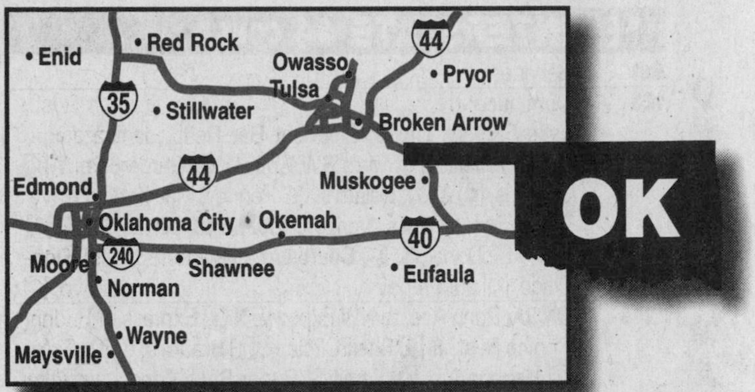

Exit	Services
196	Continued Mayo, [lodging] Carolyn Inn, [other] [H], Buick/Chevrolet, Ford, O'Reilly Parts, Walmart
182mm	**toll plaza**
179	OK 99, to Drumright, Stroud, **N** [lodging] Best Western/rest, **S** [gas] Kids/dsl, Phillips 66/Subway/dsl, [food] 5Star BBQ, Mazzio's, McDonald's, Mi Casa Mexican, Sonic, Vallarta's Rest, [lodging] Skyliner Motel, Sooner Motel, [other] [H], auto/tire repair, USPO
178mm	**Hoback Plaza both lanes** (exits left), [gas] Phillips 66/dsl, [food] McDonald's
171mm	[rest stop] eb, litter barrels
167mm	**service plaza** (from eb), **S** [gas] Phillips 66/dsl
166	OK 18, to Cushing, Chandler, **N** [other] Chrysler/Dodge/Jeep, **S** [gas] Phillips 66/dsl, [food] B's Rest, Sonic, [lodging] EconoLodge, Lincoln Motel, [other] Chandler Tire, Ford
158	OK 66, to Wellston, **N** [gas] Kum&Go/Subway/dsl/24hr, [other] $General
146	Luther-Jones (from eb, no return)
138d	to Memorial Rd, to Enterprise Square
138a	I-35, I-44 E to Tulsa, Turner Tpk
I-44 and I-35 run together 8 mi.	
137	NE 122nd St, to OK City, **E** [gas] Shamrock/dsl, Shell/dsl, [food] Charly's Rest., IHOP, [lodging] Knights Inn, Sleep Inn, **W** [gas] FLYING J/Huddle House/dsl/scales/LP/24hr, Love's /Godfathers/Subway/dsl/24hr, Phillips 66/dsl/scales, [food] Cracker Barrel, McDonald's, Sonic, Waffle House, [lodging] Comfort Inn, Days Inn, EconoLodge, Economy Inn, Holiday Inn Express, Motel 6, Red Carpet Inn, Super 8, [other] Abe's RV Park, Frontier City Funpark, Oklahoma Visitors Ctr/info/restrooms, truckwash
136	Hefner Rd, **W** [gas] Conoco/dsl, same as 137
135	Britton Rd, **E** [gas] Drivers/dsl
135mm	Turner Tpk begins eb, ends wb
134	Wilshire Blvd, **E** [gas] Drivers/dsl, [food] Braum's, [other] Gordon Inland Marine, **W** [lodging] Executive Inn, [other] Blue Beacon
I-44 and I-35 run together 8 mi.	
130	I-35 S, to Dallas, access to services on I-35 S
129	MLK Ave, Remington Park, **N** [lodging] Park Hill Inn, [other] Cowboy Museum, **S** [food] McDonald's, Sonic, [other] Family$
128b	Kelley Ave, OK City, **N** [gas] Conoco, Valero/Subway/dsl, [food] 44 Diner
128a	Lincoln Blvd, st capitol, **S** [gas] Lincoln Mart/dsl, [lodging] Lincoln Inn/Express, Oxford Inn
127	I-235 S, US 77, City Ctr, Broadway St, **N on 63rd St** [gas] Conoco/Circle K, Shell/Circle K, [lodging] Best Western, Clarion
126	Western Ave, **N** [food] Camille's Cafe, Sonic, Flip's Rest, **S** [lodging] Sleep Inn
125c	NW Expressway (exits left from sb)
125	Classen Blvd, (exits left from wb), OK City, **N** [food] Cheese

O K L A H O M A   C I T Y

🔼E INTERSTATE 44 CONT'D

Exit	Services
125	Continued
	cake Factory, Chili's, Elephant Bar Rest., Jamba Juice, Milegro Mexican, Moe's SW Grill, Olive Garden, Pei Wei, Quiznos, Ⓞ AT&T, Dillard's, JC Penney, Macy's, Old Navy, Radio Shack, Ross, Verizon, Walmart/McDonald's, **S** 🍴 IHOP, McDonald's, 🛏 Courtyard, Hawthorn Suites, Hyatt Place, Ⓞ auto repair
125a	OK 3A, Penn Ave, to NW Expswy, **N** 📶 Express, 🍴 Lion's Choice Rest., **S** 📶 Shell/Circle K, 🍴 Braum's, Coit's Cafe, 🛏 Habana Inn, Ⓞ Family$, Super Save Foods, auto/tire repair
124	N May, **W** 📶 Shell/Circle K/Subway, 🍴 San Marco's Mexican, 🛏 Days Inn, Motel 6, Super 8, Ⓞ O'Reilly Parts, **S** 📶 Shell, 🍴 Jersey Mike's Subs, Starbucks, Wendy's, Ⓞ Aamco, Advance Parts, Ford, Lowe's
123b	OK 66 W, NW 39th, to Warr Acres, **N** 📶 7-11, Shell, Valero/McDonald's/dsl, 🍴 Braum's, Carl's Jr, Jimmy's Egg, Los Mariachi's, Sonic, Taco Bueno, 🛏 Carlyle Motel, Ⓗ ity Inn, Ⓞ Advance Parts, $General, U-Haul
123a	NW 36th St, **S** Value Place Hotel
122	NW 23rd St, **N** 📶 7-11, 🍴 Church's, EggRoll King, Taco Mayo, Ⓞ Tires+, **S** 📶 Conoco, 🍴 Arby's, Sonic, Ⓞ Family$
121b a	NW 10th St, **N** 📶 Shell, **S** 📶 7-11, Sinclair, Ⓞ $General, Family$, Whittaker's Foods, antiques, fairgrounds
120b a	I-40, W to Amarillo, E to Ft Smith
119	SW 15th St
118	OK 152 W, SW 29th St, OK City, **E** 📶 7-11, 🍴 A&W/LJ Silver, Burger King, CiCi's Pizza, KFC/Taco Bell, McDonald's, Pizza Hut, Sonic, Subway, Taco Bueno, Ⓞ Advance Parts, AutoZone, Buy-4-Less Foods, $General, $Tree, O'Reilly Parts, Walgreens, city park, **W** 📶 Shell, Ⓞ U-Haul/LP, city park, transmissions
117	SW 44th St, **W** auto repair
116b	Airport Rd (exits left from nb), **W** 🚻
116a	SW 59th St, **E** 📶 Conoco/Circle K, 🍴 Pizza Inn, Taco Mayo, Ⓞ Family$, **W** Will Rogers 🚻
115	I-240 E, US 62 E, to Ft Smith
114	SW 74th St, OK City, **E** 📶 Valero, 🍴 Braum's, Burger King, Perry's Rest., 🛏 Cambridge Inn, Ramada Ltd, Ⓞ $General
113	SW 89th St, **E** 📶 Loves/Subway/dsl, OG, 7-11, Valero/dsl, 🍴 Sonic, Ⓞ Ⓗ, CVS Drug
112	SW 104th St, **E** 📶 Valero
111	SW 119th St, **E** 🍴 Sonic, Ⓞ General Store RV Ctr
110	OK 37 E, to Moore, **E** Ⓗ
109	SW 149th St, **E** 🍴 JR's Grill
108mm	S Canadian River
108	OK 37 W, to Tuttle, **W** 📶 Conoco/dsl, Phillips 66, 🍴 Arby's, Braum's, Carlito's Mexican, Jimmy's Egg, Little Caesars, Mazzio's, McDonald's, New China, Sonic, Taco Bell, Ⓞ AT&T, $General, O'Reilly Parts, Walgreens, Walmart/Subway, **Urgent Care**
107	US 62 S (no wb return), to Newcastle, **E** casino/gas, 🛏 Newcastle Motel, Ⓞ Newcastle RV
99	H E Bailey Spur, rd 4, to Blanchard, Tuttle, Norman
97mm	**toll booth**, Ⓒ
96mm	🚻 wb, 🚻, litter barrels
85.5mm	**service plaza**, both lanes exit left, Phillips 66/dsl, McDonald's

C H I C K A S H A

Exit	Services
83	US 62, Chickasha, **W** 🍴 Jay's/dsl, Valero/dsl, Ⓞ Indian Museum
80	US 81, Chickasha, **E** 📶 Phillips 66/dsl, Shell/dsl, 🍴 Eduardo's Mexican, La Fiesta Mexican, Western Sizzlin, 🛏 Best Value Inn, Hampton Inn, Holiday Inn Express, Maverick Inn, Super 8, Ⓞ Ⓗ, Buick/GMC, Cadillac/Chevrolet, Chrysler/Dodge/Jeep, $Tree, vet, **W** 📶 Griffith's, Loves/dsl, Murphy USA/dsl, Valero, 🍴 Arby's, Braum's, Chicken Express, China Moon, Domino's, KFC, LJ Silver, Little Caesars, Mazzio's Pizza, McDonald's, Napoli's Rest., New China, Pizza Hut, Quiznos, Sonic, Taco Bell, Taco Mayo, 🛏 Best Western, Budget Inn, Ranch House Motel, Ⓞ Ace Hardware, AT&T, AutoZone, Chickasha RV Park, CVS Drug, $General, Family$, Ford, O'Reilly Parts, Ralph&Son's Tires/repair, Save-A-Lot Foods, Staples, Verizon, Walgreens, Walmart/Subway,
78mm	**toll plaza**, Ⓒ
63mm	🚻 wb, 🚻, litter barrels
62	to Cyril (from wb)
60.5mm	🚻 eb, tables, litter barrels
53	US 277, Elgin, Lake Ellsworth, **E** 📶 Shamrock, Valero/McDonald's/dsl, 🍴 Billy Sim's BBQ, China Garden, Sonic, Subway, Ⓞ Family$, tires, **W** 📶 Fina/dsl
46	US 62 E, US 277, US 281, to Elgin, Apache, Comanche Tribe, last free exit eb
45	OK 49, to Medicine Park, **W** 📶 Loves/Subway/dsl/24hr, 🍴 Burger King, Sonic, Ⓞ Whichita NWR
41	to Ft.Sill, Key Gate, **W** Ft Sill Museum
40c	Gate 2, to Ft Sill
40a	to Cache
39	US 62 W, to Cache, **E** 📶 Alon/dsl, **W** 🛏 Super 8
39b	US 281 (from sb), **W** 🍴 Pizza Hut, 🛏 Super 9 Motel, Ⓞ U-Haul, transmissions
39a	US 281, Cache Rd (exits left from nb), Lawton, **1-3 mi W** 📶 Valero/dsl, 🍴 Bianco's Italian, Pizza Hut, 🛏 Best Value Inn, Super 9 Motel, Ⓞ Family$, Nissan, U-Haul, transmissions
38	Cache Rd (exits left from nb)
37	Gore Blvd, Lawton, **E** 🍴 Braum's, Los Tres Amigos, Papa John's, Sonic, Taco Mayo, 🛏 Best Western, Ⓞ Curves, casino, USPO, **W** 🍴 Cracker Barrel, Mike's Grille, 🛏 Fairfield Inn, Holiday Inn Express, Homewood Suites, Sleep Inn, SpringHill Suites, Ⓞ Harley-Davidson, Nissan
36a	OK 7, Lee Blvd, Lawton, **E** 📶 Phillips 66, **W** 📶 Alon/dsl/repair, Shamrock/dsl, 🍴 Big Chef Rest., Braum's, Burger King, KFC/Taco Bell, Leo&Ken's Rest., McDonald's, Salas Mexican, Sonic, 🛏 Motel 6, Ⓞ Ⓗ, 🚻, vet
33	US 281, 11th St, Lawton, **W** 🚻
30	OK 36 (last free exit sb), Gerónimo
20.5mm	**Elmer Graham Plaza**, both lanes exit left, Phillips 66/dsl, McDonald's, info
20	OK 5, to Walters
19.5mm	**toll plaza**
5	US 277 N, US 281, Randlett, last free exit nb
1	OK 36, to Grandfield
0mm	Oklahoma/Texas state line, Red River

🔼E INTERSTATE 240 (OKLAHOMA CITY)

Exit	Services
16mm	I-240 begins/ends on I-40.
14	Anderson Rd, **S** 📶 Conoco
11b a	Douglas Blvd, **N** Tinker AFB

OK

INTERSTATE 240 (OKLAHOMA CITY) CONT'D

Exit	Services
9	Air Depot Blvd
8	OK 77, Sooner Rd, N ⓖ Shell/dsl, 🍴 Sonic, S ⓖ Phillips 66/Popeye's/dsl, Valero/McDonald's/dsl, ⓞ H
7	Sunnylane Ave, S ⓖ Valero/Subway/dsl, 🏠 Value Place Motel
6	Bryant Ave
5	S Eastern Ave
4c	Pole Rd, N 🍴 Burger King, Subway, TX Roadhouse, Zeke's Grill, 🏠 Fairfield Inn, Ramada Inn, Residence Inn, ⓞ Urgent Care, Best Buy, Tires+
4b a	I-35, N to OK City, S to Dallas, US 77 S, US 62/77 N
3b	S Shields, N ⓖ Valero/dsl, ⓞ Dodge, Home Depot, S ⓞ Discount Tire, Nissan, Subaru
3a	S Santa Fe, S ⓖ Murphy USA/dsl, Shell, 🍴 Chili's, IHOP, Mike's Subs, ⓞ Buick, Staples, Lowe's, Walmart
2b	S Walker Ave, N ⓖ 7-11, Shell/Circle K, 🍴 Rib Crib, S 🍴 Carino's, ChuckeCheese, City Bites, Coach's Grill, Jimmy's Egg Grill, On-the-Border, Primo's Italian, ⓞ Urgent Care, PepBoys
2a	S Western Ave, N ⓖ Conoco, 7-11, 🍴 Burger King, Ci

2a	Continued Ci's Pizza, House of Szechwan, Nino's Mexican, Taste of China, ⓞ Advance Parts, $General, Hyundai, Tires+, vet, S ⓖ 7-11, Valero/dsl, 🍴 A&W/LJ Silver, Arby's, Grandy's, Hibachi Buffet, KFC, Krispy Kreme, McDonald's, Red Lobster, 🏠 Best Western, Comfort Inn, Hampton Inn, Quality Inn, ⓞ Big O Tire, Chevrolet, Home Depot, Honda, Office Depot, Tire Factory
1c	S Penn Ave, N ⓖ Conoco, 🍴 Carl's Jr, Charleston's Rest., Denny's, Golden Corral, Harrigan's Rest., Hooters, Old Chicago Pizza, Olive Garden, Outback Steaks, Pioneer Pies, SaltGrass Steaks, Santa Fe Grill, Schlotsky's, ⓞ AT&T, BigLots, GNC, Hobby Lobby, Marshall's, Michaels, Old Navy, Radio Shack, Ross, Verizon, S ⓖ Shell/Circle K, 🍴 August Moon, Hunan Buffet, Joe's Crabshack, Mazzio's, Pancho's Mexican, Papa John's, Starbucks, Subway, Taco Bueno, Wendy's, Western Sizzlin, ⓞ $Tree, Hancock Fabrics
1b	S May Ave, N ⓖ 7-11/gas, 🍴 Abel's Mexican, Durango Mexican, Taco Bell, Waffle House, ⓞ O'Reilly Parts, S ⓖ Valero, 🍴 Burger King, Perry's Rest., 🏠 Cambridge Inn, Ramada Ltd, ⓞ $General
1a	I-44, US 62, I-240 begins/ends on I-44.

OREGON

INTERSTATE 5

Exit	Services
308.5mm	Oregon/Washington state line, Columbia River
308	Jansen Beach Dr, E ⓖ Chevron/dsl, 🍴 Burger King, Hooters, Starbucks, Taco Bell, 🏠 Oxford Suites, Red Lion, ⓞ Safeway, W 🍴 BJ's Rest., Bradley's Grill, Denny's, McDonald's, Original Joe's, Stanford's Rest., Starbucks, Subway, ⓞ Barnes&Noble, Best Buy, Home Depot, Jansen Beach RV Park, Michael's, Office Depot, Old Navy, PetCo, Ross, Michael's, Staples, Target
307	OR 99E S, MLK Blvd, Union Ave, Marine Dr (sb only), E ⓖ Jubitz Trvl Ctr/rest/dsl/@, 76/dsl, 🍴 Portland Cascade Grill, 🏠 Courtyard, Fairfield Inn, Portlander Inn, Residence Inn, ⓞ Blue Beacon, Expo Ctr, truck repair
306b	Interstate Ave, Delta Park, E ⓖ 76, 🍴 Burger King, Elmer's, Mars Meadows Chinese, Shari's, 🏠 Best Western, Days Inn, Motel 6, ⓞ Baxter Parts, Dick's, Lowe's, Portland Meadows
306a	Columbia (from nb), same as 306b
305b a	US 30, Lombard St (from nb, no return), E 🍴 Little Caesar's, ⓞ Knecht's Parts, W ⓖ Astro/dsl, Shell/dsl, 🍴 Panda Express, Subway, Wendy's, ⓞ Fred Meyer
304	Rosa Parks Way, U of Portland, W ⓖ Arco, 76/dsl, 🍴 Nite Hawk Cafe, Taco Time, 🏠 Viking Motel
303	Alberta St, Swan Island, E H, W 🍴 Subway, Taco Bell, 🏠 Monticello Motel, Westerner Motel, ⓞ CarQuest
302b	I-405, US 30 W, W to ocean beaches, zoo
302a	Rose Qtr, City Ctr, E ⓖ 76/Circle K/dsl, Shell/dsl, 🍴 Bellagio's Pizza, Burger King, Chipotle Mexican, McDonald's, Qdoba Mexican, Starbucks, Taco Bell, Wendy's, 🏠 Crowne Plaza, Shiloh Inn, ⓞ H, KIA, Toyota/Scion, Schwab Tire, 7-11, Walgreens, W ⓞ coliseum
301	I-84 E, US 30 E, Services E off I-84 exits
300	US 26 E (from sb), Milwaukie Ave, W 🏠 Hilton, Marriott
299b	I-405, US 26 W, to city ctr

299a	US 26 E, OR 43 (from nb), City Ctr, to Lake Oswego
298	Corbett Ave
297	Terwilliger Blvd, W 🍴 Baja Fresh, KFC, La Costita, Starbucks, ⓞ H, Fred Meyer, to Lewis and Clark Coll.
296b	Multnomah Blvd (from sb), same as 296a
296a	(from sb), Barbur, W ⓖ Chevron, 76/dsl, 🍴 Bellagio's Pizza, Original Pancake House, Subway, Taco Del Mar, 🏠 Aladdin Inn, Budget Lodge, Capitol Hill Motel, ⓞ 7-11, Schwab Tire
295	Capitol Hwy (from sb), Taylors Ferry Rd (from nb), E ⓖ Shell/dsl, 🍴 Juan Colorado Mexican, Koji Japanese, McDonald's, RoundTable Pizza, Starbucks, 🏠 H ity Inn, W 🍴 Taco Time, Wendy's
294	Barbur Blvd, OR 99W, to Tigard, E Comfort Suites, W ⓖ Chevron, Shell, 🍴 Arby's, Baja Fresh, Banning's Rest., Baskin-Robbins, Burger King, Buster's BBQ, Chang's Mongolian Grill, Gators Eatery, King's Buffet, Little Caesar's, Mazatlan Mexican, McDonald's, Newport Bay Rest., Quiznos, Starbucks, Subway, Taco Bell, TCBY, 🏠 Quality Inn, Regency Inn, ⓞ Americas Tire, Baxter Parts, Costco, Fred Meyer, JoAnn Fabrics, NAPA, PetCo, Radio Shack, Schwab Tire, U-Haul, Winco Foods, transmissions, vet
293	Haines St, W ⓞ Ford/Lincoln
292	OR 217, Kruse Way, Lake Oswego, E ⓖ Shell/dsl, 🍴 Applebee's, Chevy's Mexican, Olive Garden, Oswego Grill, Quiznos, Stanford's Rest., Starbucks, Taco Del Mar, 🏠 Crowne Plaza, Fairfield Inn, Hilton Garden, Phoenix Inn, Residence Inn, ⓞ AAA, Curves, LDS Temple, W 🏠 Homestead Suites, ⓞ Lowe's
291	Carman Dr, W ⓖ Chevron, 76/dsl, 🍴 Burgerville, Domino's, El Sol De Mexico, Starbucks, Subway, Sweet Tomatoes, 🏠 Courtyard, Holiday Inn Express, ⓞ Home Depot, Office Depot
290	Lower Boonsferry Rd, Lake Oswego, E ⓖ Chevron/dsl, Space Age/dsl/LP, 🍴 Arby's, Baja Fresh, Baskin-Robbins, Burger King, Carl's Jr., Fuddruckers, Miller's Rest., Panda

= gas = food = lodging = other = rest stop   Copyright 2014 - The NEXT Exit ®

INTERSTATE 5 CONT'D

Exit	Services
290	**Continued**
	Express, Starbucks, Subway, Taco Bell, Wu's Kitchen, Motel 6, Dick's, Safeway Foods, Walgreens, **W** CA Pizza Kitchen, Claim Jumper, Jamba Juice, Jimmy John's, Macaroni Grill, McCormick&Schmick's, Pastini Pastaria, PF Chang's, Qdoba Mexican, Royal Panda, Starbucks, Village Inn, Grand Hotel, Verizon, Whole Foods Mkt
289	Tualatin, **E** 76, Shell/dsl, Chipotle Mexican, Famous Dave's BBQ, McDonald's, Panera Bread, Subway, Best Buy, GNC, Old Navy, Petsmart, Portland RV Park, 7-11, **W** Applebee's, Coldstone, Hayden's Grill, Jack-in-the-Box, Outback Steaks, Pizza Hut, Quiznos, Starbucks, Taco Bell, Thai Bistro, Wendy's, Century Hotel, H, Fred Meyer, Haggen's Foods, K-Mart, Michael's, O'Reilly Parts, Radio Shack, camping
288	I-205, to Oregon City
286	Elligsen Rd, Boonsferry Rd, Stafford, **E** 76/dsl, Burger King, Moe's SW Grill, Panda Express, Pizza Schmizza, Starbucks, Subway, La Quinta, Super 8, Costco/gas, Mercedes, Office Depot, Petsmart, Pheasant Ridge RV Resort, Target, Verizon, **W** Chevron, Big Town Hero, Holiday Inn/rest., Audi, Camping World RV Ctr, Chevrolet, Dodge, Nissan, Toyota/Scion
283	Wilsonville, **E** 76/dsl, Abella Italian, Arby's, Bellagio's Pizza, Boston's Grill, Denny's, Jamba Juice, Juan Colorado, McDonald's, Papa Murphy's, Red Robin, Shari's, Starbucks, Subway, Taco Bell, Taco Del Mar, Wanker's Café, Wendy's, Wong's Chinese, GuestHouse Inn, Quality Inn, SnoozInn, AT&T, Fry's Electronics, GNC, Honda, Lamb's Foods, NAPA, Rite Aid, Schwab Tire, USPO, funpark, **W** Chevron, Baskin-Robbins, Burger King, Domino's, Hunan Kitchen, Sonic, Starbucks, Wilsonville Grill, Wilsonville Inn, Albertson's, Fred Meyer, 7-11, Walgreens, auto repair
282.5mm	Willamette River
282	Charbonneau District, **E** Langdon Farms Rest., Langdon Farms Golf
281.5mm	both lanes, full facilities, info, litter barrels, petwalk, vending, coffee
278	Donald, **E** 76/dsl/LP, Aurora Acres RV Park, **W** Shell/dsl, TA/Country Pride/Popeye's/dsl/scales/24hr/@, SpeedCo Lube, truckwash, to Champoeg SP
274mm	weigh sta both lanes
271	OR 214, Woodburn, **E** Arco/dsl, Chevron, 76/repair, Burger King, Country Cottage Rest., DQ, Denny's, KFC, McDonald's/playplace, Subway, Taco Bell, Best Western, Super 8, Fairway Drug, Walgreens, Walmart/McDonald's, vet, **W** Shell, Arby's, Elmer's, Jack-in-the-Box, Jamba Juice, Quiznos, Starbucks, La Quinta, Ford, Tire Factory, Woodburn RV Park, Woodburn Outlets/famous brands
263	Brooks, Gervais, **E** 76/dsl, Brooks Mkt/deli, **W** /Subway/Taco Bell/dsl/LP/scales/24hr, Chalet Rest., Freightliner, Willamette Mission SP (4mi)
260b a	OR 99E, Chemawa Rd, Keizer, **2 mi E** camping, **W** Burger King, Jamba Juice, Panda Express, RoundTable Pizza, Starbucks, Subway, Taco Del Mar, AT&T, Lowe's, Marshall's, Michael's, Old Navy, PetCo, Ross, Staples, Target, Verizon, World Mkt
259mm	45th parallel, halfway between the equator and N Pole
258	N Salem, **E** 76/Circle K, Figaro's Italian, Guesthouse Rest., McDonald's, Original Pancake House, Best Western, Rodeway Inn, Al's RV Ctr, 5 RV Park, Hwy RV Ctr, Roth's Foods, **W** Arco, 76/Circle K, Pacific Pride/dsl, Shell/dsl, Don Pedro Mexican, Jack-in-the-Box, LumYuen Chinese, Budget Lodge, Travelers Inn, Stuart's Parts, to st capitol
256	to OR 213, Market St, Salem, **E** Alberto's Mexican, Chalet Rest., Denny's, Elmer's, Cozzzy Inn, Days Inn, Fred Meyer/dsl, **E on Lancaster** 76/dsl, Arby's, Baja Fresh, Blue Willow Rest., Carl's Jr, China Buffet, El Mirador Mexican, 5 Guys Burgers, Izzy's Rest., Jack-in-the-Box, Olive Garden, Outback Steaks, Quiznos, Sizzler, Skipper's, Subway, Taco Bell, Americas Tire, BigLots, Sears/auto, Schwab Tires, Walgreens, **W** Arco, Pacific Pride/dsl, Shell/dsl, Texaco/dsl, Almost Home Rest., Baskin-Robbins, DQ, McDonald's, Newport Bay Seafood, Pietro's Pizza, Rockin-Rogers Diner, Subway, Comfort Inn, Holiday Lodge, Motel 6, Phoenix Inn, Red Lion Hotel, Shilo Inn, Super 8, Mazda, Nissan, Save-A-Lot Foods
253	OR 22, Salem, Stayton, **E** Chevron/repair, Shell/dsl, Space Age/dsl, Burger King, Carls Jr, Las Polomas Mexican, McDonalds/playplace, Shari's, Subway, $Tree, Home Depot, ShopKO, Salem Camping/RV Park, WinCo Foods, to Detroit RA, **W** Shell/dsl, DQ, Denny's, Jack-in-the-Box, Panda Express, Sybil's Omelette, Taco Del Mar, Best Western, Comfort Suites, La Quinta, Residence Inn, H, AAA, Cadillac/Chevrolet/Subaru, Chrysler/Jeep, Costco/gas, K-Mart, Lowe's, Schwab Tire, Toyota/Scion, Walmart, st police
252	Kuebler Blvd
249	to Salem, **2 mi W** Arco, 76, Arby's, Burger King, Carl's Jr, Kwan's Cuisine, Phoenix Inn, Safeway
248	Sunnyside, **E** Enchanted Forest Themepark, Willamette Valley Vineyards, **W** Pacific Pride/dsl
244	to N Jefferson, **E** Emerald Valley RV Park
243	Ankeny Hill
242	Talbot Rd
241mm	both lanes, full facilities, info, litter barrels, petwalk
240.5mm	Santiam River
239	Dever-Conner
238	S Jefferson, to Scio
237	Viewcrest (from sb)
235	Viewcrest (from nb), Millersburg, **E** Harley-Davidson
234	OR 99E, Albany, **E** Comfort Suites, Holiday Inn Express, Knox Butte Camping/RV dump, , **W** Chevron, Burger King, Carl's Jr, China Buffet, DQ, McDonald's, Subway, Taco Bell, Budget Inn, La Quinta, Motel 6, Super 8, H, Costco/gas, K-Mart, Kohl's, to Albany Hist Dist
233	US 20, Albany, **E** Chevron/dsl/LP, 76/dsl, Denny's, LumYuen Chinese, EconoLodge, Phoenix Inn, Quality Inn, Chevrolet, Home Depot, Honda, RV camping, Toyota/Scion, st police, **W** 76/dsl, Shell, Abby's Pizza, Arby's, Baskin-Robbins, Burgerville, Carl's Jr, Elmer's, Figaro's, Fox Den Pizza, Jack-in-the-Box, Los Dos Amigos, Los Tequilos Mexican, Original Breakfast Cafe, Skipper's, Starbucks, Sweetwaters Rest., Taco Time, Wendy's, Valu Inn, H, Albertson's, Bi-Mart, CarQuest, Chrysler/Dodge/Hyundai/Jeep/Subaru, Curves, Fred Meyer/dsl, JoAnn Fabrics, Knechts's Parts, NAPA, O'Reilly Parts,

Side labels: **WILSONVILLE** · **OR** · **SALEM** · **ALBANY**

N   INTERSTATE 5 CONT'D

Exit	Services
233	Continued PetCo, Rite Aid, Schwab Tires, Staples, Target, Walgreens
228	OR 34, to Lebanon, Corvallis, E 🅖 Leather's/dsl, 76/dsl, 🅕 Pine Cone Cafe, 🅞 Mallard Creek Golf/RV Resort, W 🅖 Arco/dsl, Chevron/CFN/A&W/dsl, Shell/dsl, 🅞 to OSU, KOA (5mi)
222mm	Butte Creek
216	OR 228, Halsey, Brownsville, E 🅕 Pioneer Villa Trk Stp/76/Blimpie/dsl/24hr/@, 🅛 Travelodge, 🅞 parts/repair/towing, W 🅖 Shell/dsl
209	to Jct City, Harrisburg, W 🅞 Diamond Hill RV Park
206mm	🆁🆂 both lanes, full ♿ facilities, info, 🅲, 🅐, litter barrels, petwalk
199	Coburg, E 🅖 Fuel'n Go/dsl, 🅞 Premier RV Resort, W 🅖 Shell/dsl, TA/Country Pride/Truck'n'Travel Motel/dsl/scales/24hr/@, 🅞 Armitage Park Camping, Evert RV Ctr, Freightliner, Volvo, dsl repair, hist dist
197mm	McKenzie River
195b a	N Springfield, E 🅖 Arco, Chevron, 🅕 Applebee's, Cafe Yummi, Carl's Jr, China Sun, Ciao Pizza, ChuckeCheese, Denny's, Elmer's Rest., FarMan Chinese, 5 Guys Burgers, Gateway Chinese, HomeTown Buffet, IHOP, Jack-in-the-Box, Jimmy John's, KFC, McDonald's, Outback Steaks, Quiznos, Roadhouse Grill, Shari's, Sizzler, Starbucks, Subway, Taco Bell, Taco Time, 🅛 Best Western, Comfort Suites, Courtyard, Hilton Garden, Holiday Inn Express, Holiday Inn, Motel 6, Quality Inn, Shilo Inn/rest., Super 8, 🅞 🅗 Best Buy, Cabela's, Kohl's, Michael's, Sears/auto, Staples, Target, USPO, mall, st police, W 🅕 Taco Bell, 🅞 Costco/gas, Office Depot, Petsmart, ShopKO, to 🆁🆂
194b a	OR 126 E, I-105 W, Springfield, Eugene, 1 mi W 🅖 Chevron, 76/repair, 🅕 Carl's Jr, PF Chang's, Quiznos, Starbucks, 🅛 La Quinta, Red Lion Inn, Residence Inn, 🅞 Albertson's/gas, Nissan, Subaru, Trader Joe's, U Of O
193mm	Willamette River
192	OR 99 (from nb), to Eugene, W 🅖 76, 🅕 Boulevard Grill, House Of Chen, Subway, Wendy's, 🅛 Best Western, Days Inn, Holiday Inn Express, University Inn, 🅞 Mkt Of Choice, to U of O
191	Glenwood, W 🅖 Shell/dsl/LP, 🅕 Denny's, 🅛 Comfort Suites, Motel 6
189	30th Ave S, Eugene, E 🅖 Shell/dsl/LP, 🅞 Harley-Davidson, Shamrock RV Park, marine ctr, W 🅖 76/dsl
188b	OR 99 S (nb only), Goshen
188a	OR 58, OR 99 S to Oakridge, E 🅞 Deerwood RV Park, W 🅖 Pacific Pride/dsl, 🅞 tires
186	Dillard Rd, to Goshen (from nb)
182	Creswell, E 🅕 Subway, 🅛 Comfort Inn, 🅞 Bi Mart, OR RV Ctr, Ray's Foods/drug, golf, W 🅖 Arco, 76/dsl, 🅕 China Wok, Dari Mart, Figaro's Pizza, Hawaiian BBQ, TJ's Rest., 🅛 Super 8, 🅞 Knecht's Parts, Sherwood Forest RV Park
180mm	Coast Fork of Willamette River
178mm	🆁🆂 both lanes, full ♿ facilities, 🅲, 🅐, litter barrels, petwalk, coffee
176	Saginaw
175mm	Row River
174	Cottage Grove, E 🅖 Chevron/dsl/repair, Pacific Pride, 🅕 El Paraiso Mexican, Subway, Taco Bell, 🅛 Village Resort/RV park, 🅞 🅗 Brad's RV Ctr, Chevrolet/GMC, Chrys
174	Continued ler/Dodge/Jeep, Walmart, W 🅖 Chevron/dsl/LP, 76/dsl, Shell/dsl, 🅕 Arby's, Burger King, Carl's Jr, Figaro's Pizza, KFC, McDonald's/RV parking, Torero's Mexican, Vintage Rest., 🅛 Best Western, City Ctr Motel, Comfort Inn, Relax Inn, 🅞 🅗 Bi-Mart Foods, $Tree, Save-A-Lot Foods, Village Green Motel/RV Park
172	6th St (from sb), Cottage Grove Lake, 2 mi E Cottage Grove RV Village
170	to OR 99, London Rd (nb only), Cottage Grove Lake, 6 mi W Cottage Grove RV Village

EUGENE

SPRINGFIELD

OR

⬆N INTERSTATE 5 CONT'D

Exit	Services
163	Curtin, Lorane, **E** 🏠 Stardust Motel, ⊙ antiques, **W** ⊙ Pass Creek RV Park,
162	OR 38, OR 99, to Drain, Elkton
161	Anlauf (from nb)
160	Salt Springs Rd
159	Elk Creek, Cox Rd
154	Yoncalla, Elkhead
150	OR 99, to OR 38, Yoncalla, Red Hill, **W** ⊙ Trees of Oregon RV Park
148	Rice Hill, **E** ⛽ Chevron/LP, Pacific Pride/dsl, 🏨/Denny's/Subway/dsl/scales/24hr, 🍴 Peggy's Rest., Ranch Rest., 🏠 Motel 6, Ranch Motel, ⊙ Rice Hill RV Park, towing/dsl repair, **W** 🍴 K-R Drive-In
146	Rice Valley
144mm	🅿️ **sb, full** ♿ **facilities,** 🍴, 🚮, **litter barrels, petwalk**
143mm	🅿️ **nb, full** ♿ **facilities,** 🍴, 🚮, **litter barrels, petwalk**
142	Metz Hill
140	OR 99 (from sb), Oakland, **E** 🍴 Tolly's Rest., ⊙ Oakland Hist Dist
138	OR 99 (from nb), Oakland, **E** 🍴 Tolly's Rest., ⊙ Oakland Hist Dist
136	OR 138W, Sutherlin, **E** ⛽ Chevron/A&W/dsl, 76/dsl, 🍴 Abby's Pizza, Apple Peddler Rest., Burger King, Hong Kong Chinese, McDonald's, Papa Murphy's, Pedotti's Italian, 🏠 Best Western, Microtel, Relax Inn, ⊙ CarQuest, I-5 RV Ctr, vet, **W** ⛽ Shell, 🍴 Dakota St Pizza, DQ, Si Casa Flores, Subway, Taco Bell, ⊙ Hi-Way Haven RV Camp, Umpqua RV Park, auto repair
135	Wilbur, Sutherlin, **E** ⛽ CFN/dsl, Shell/dsl/LP, muffler repair
129	OR 99, Winchester, **E** gas, food, camping, dsl repair, RV Ctr (1mi)
129mm	N Umpqua River
127	Stewart Pkwy, Edenbower Rd, N Roseburg, **E** ⛽ Shell, 🍴 Shari's Rest., 🏠 Motel 6, Super 8, ⊙ Home Depot, Lowe's, Mt Nebo RV Park, **W** ⛽ Texaco/Taco Maker/dsl, 🍴 Applebee's, Jack-in-the-Box, McDonald's/playplace, Red Robin, Subway, 🏠 EconoLodge, ⊙ 🅷 Albertson's/gas, Big O Tire, K-Mart, Macy's, Office Depot, Sherm's Foods, Walmart, vet
125	Garden Valley Blvd, Roseburg, **E** ⛽ Texaco, 🍴 Brutke's Rest., Casey's Rest., Elmer's, Friday BBQ, Gilberto's Mexican, Jack-in-the-Box, KFC, Los Dos Amigo's Mexican, McDonald's, Papa Murphy's, Sonic, Subway, Taco Bell, 🏠 Comfort Inn, Quality Inn, Windmill Inn/rest., ⊙ AT&T, BigLots, Buick/Chevrolet/GMC, Ford/Lincoln, NAPA, Safeway/dsl, Toyota, U-Haul, Verizon, Walgreens, transmissions, **W** ⛽ Chevron/dsl, Shell/LP/repair, 🍴 Arby's, Burger King, Carl's Jr, Fox Den Pizza, Quiznos, Rodeo Steaks, RoundTable Pizza, Si Casa Flores Mexican, Sizzler, Starbucks, TomTom Rest., Wendy's, 🏠 Best Value Inn, Best Western, ⊙ 🅷 Bi-Mart Foods, $Tree, Fred Meyer, JC Penney, JoAnn Fabrics, Michael's, O'Reilly Parts, PetCo, Rite Aid, Ross, Sears/auto, Staples, Walgreens, mall
124	OR 138, Roseburg, City Ctr, **E** ⛽ 76/dsl, Texaco/dsl, 🍴 Chi's Chinese, Denny's, 🏠 Dunes Motel, Holiday Inn Express, Travelodge, ⊙ Honda, Rite Aid, **W** ⛽ 76/dsl, Shell/dsl, 🍴 Charley's BBQ, Gay 90's Deli, KFC/LJ Silver, Pete's Drive-In, Subway, Taco Time, ⊙ Grocery Outlet, Harvard

Exit	Services
124	Continued Ave Drug, Hometown Drug
123	Roseburg, **E** ⊙ to Umpqua Park, camping, museum
121	McLain Ave
120.5mm	S Umpqua River
120	OR 99 N (no EZ nb return), Green District, Roseburg, **E** 🏠 Shady Oaks Motel, **W** ⊙ auto repair
119	OR 99 S, OR 42 W, Winston, **E** ⊙ Ingram Dist., **W** ⛽ Chevron/A&W/dsl, 💚Loves/Arby's/dsl/scales/LP/24hr, Shell/dsl, 🍴 McDonald's, Ocampos Mexican, Papa Murphy's, Rae's Diner, Subway, ⊙ Ray's Foods, Rising River RV Park, Western Star RV Park
113	Clarks Branch Rd, Round Prairie, **W** 🏠 Quikstop Motel, ⊙ On the River RV Park (2mi), Quikstop Mkt, dsl repair
112.5mm	S Umpqua River
112	OR 99, OR 42, Dillard, **E** ⊙ Rivers West RV Park
111mm	**weigh sta both directions**
110	Boomer Hill Rd
108	Myrtle Creek, **E** ⛽ Chevron, 🍴 DQ, El Azteca, Golf Course Cafe, Myrtle Creek Cafe, Subway, ⊙ Myrtle Creek RV Park
106	Weaver Rd
103	Tri City, Myrtle Creek, **E** ⊙ Tri-City RV Park, **W** ⛽ Chevron/A&W/dsl, Pacific Pride, 🍴 McDonald's
102	Gazley Rd, **E** Surprise Valley RV Park (1mi)
101.5mm	S Umpqua River, S Umpqua River
101	Riddle, Stanton Park, **W** camping
99	Canyonville, **E** ⛽ Penny Pincher, 🍴 Burger King, El Paraiso, 🏠 Riverside Motel, 7 Feathers Hotel/casino, Valley View Motel, ⊙ Canyon Mkt, **W** ⛽ 7 Feathers Trkstp/café/dsl/scales/24hr/@, 🍴 Creekside Rest., 🏠 Holiday Inn Express, ⊙ 7 Feathers RV Resort, **rest stop**
98	OR 99, Canyonville, Days Creek, **E** ⛽ Arco/dsl, Shell/dsl, 🍴 Canyon Cafe, Ken's Cafe, Marla Kay's Cafe, Serafino's Italian, 🏠 Leisure Inn, ⊙ Ace Hardware, NAPA, Ray's Foods, auto repair, vet, **W** ⊙ Bill's Tire/repair, museum
95	Canyon Creek
90mm	Canyon Creek Pass, elev 2020
88	Azalea
86	Barton Rd, Quine's Creek, **E** ⊙ Heaven on Earth Rest./rest., Meadow Wood RV Park (3mi)
83	Barton Rd (from nb), **E** ⊙ Meadow Wood RV Park/camping
80	Glendale, **W** ⛽ Country Jct./LP, 🍴 Village Inn Rest.
79.5mm	Stage Road Pass, elev 1830
78	Speaker Rd (from sb)
76	Wolf Creek, **W** ⛽ Pacific Pride/dsl, 76/deli/dsl, Texaco/dsl, 🍴 Wolf Creek Inn Rest., ⊙ Creekside RV park, auto repair
74mm	Smith Hill Summit, elev 1730
71	Sunny Valley, **E** 🏠 Sunny Valley Motel, ⊙ Covered Bridge Store/gas, **W** ⊙ Sunny Valley RV Park
69mm	Sexton Mtn Pass, elev 1960
66	Hugo, **E** ⊙ Joe Creek Waterfalls RV Park, **W** ⊙ Pottsville Museum
63mm	🅿️ **both lanes, full** ♿ **facilities,** 🍴, **info,** 🚮, **litter barrels, vending, petwalk**
61	Merlin, **W** ⛽ Shell/dsl, ⊙ Almeda RV Park, Beaver Creek RV Resort (2mi), OR RV Ctr, Ray's Foods, Rouge Valley RV Ctr, repair
58	OR 99, to US 199, Grants Pass, **W** ⛽ CFN/dsl, Chevron, 76/dsl/RV dump, Shell/dsl/repair, Texaco/dsl, TownePump

Vertical side labels: **S U T H E R L I N**, **R O S E B U R G**, **O R**, **C A N Y O N V I L L E**

⬆N INTERSTATE 5 CONT'D

Exit	Services

58 Continued
Gas, 🍴 Angela's Mexican, Beacon Cafe, Black Bear Diner, Burger King, Carl's Jr, China Hut, Della's Rest., DQ, Denny's, Jack-in-the-Box, McDonald's, Muchas Gracias Mexican, Papa Murphy's, Sizzler, Subway, Taco Bell, Wendy's, 🛏 Best Way Inn, Comfort Inn, Hawks Inn, La Quinta, Motel 6, Redwood Motel, Royal Vue Motel, Shilo Inn, Sunset Inn, Super 8, SweetBreeze Inn, Travelodge, Wild River Inn, 🅞 🅷, AutoZone, Chevrolet/Honda, Chrysler/Dodge/Jeep, Curves, $Tree, Jack's RV Resort, NAPA, Nissan, Radio Shack, Ray's Foods, Rouge Valley RV Park, Schwab Tire, st police, towing

55 US 199, Redwood Hwy, E Grants Pass, **W** 🅖 Arco/dsl, CFN/dsl, 🍴 Applebee's, Abby's Pizza, Carl's Jr, Elmer's, JJ North's Grand Buffet, Las Fajitas, McDonald's, Quiznos, Shari's, Si Casa Flores Mexican, Subway, Taco Bell, 🛏 Best Western, Holiday Inn Express, 🅞 🅷, Albertson's/gas, AT&T, BigLots, $Tree, Fred Meyer/dsl, Grocery Outlet, Moon Mtn RV Park (2mi), RiverPark RV Park (4mi), Ross, Schuck's Parts, Siskiyou RV Ctr, Tehama Tire, Walmart

48 Rogue River, **E** 🅖 Chevron/dsl, 🍴 Abby's Pizza, Homestead Rest., Tarasco Mexican, 🅞 Ace Hardware, Rogue River RA, auto repair, **W** 🍴 🛏 Bella Rosa Inn, Best Western, Weasku Inn, 🅞 Chinook Winds RV Park, Bridgeview RV Park, Whispering Pines RV Park, visitors ctr/info

45b **W** 🅞 Valley of the Rogue SP/🅟🆂 **both lanes, full 🦽 facilities, 🚻, 🛋, litter barrels, petwalk, camping**

45mm Rogue River

45a OR 99, Savage Rapids Dam, **E** 🅞 Cypress Grove RV Park

43 OR 99, OR 234, to Crater Lake, Gold Hill, **E** 🛏 Lazy Acres Motel/RV Park, RoadRiver B&B

40 OR 99, OR 234, Gold Hill, **E** 🍴 Figaro's Pizza, Patti's Kitchen, 🅞 Gold Hill Auto Ctr/gas, KOA, Lazy Acres Motel/RV Park, Running Salmon RV Park, USPO, to Shady Cove Trail, **W** Dardanelle's RV Ctr/gas, Dardanelle's Trailer Park

35 OR 99, Blackwell Rd, Central Point, **2-4 mi W** gas, food, lodging, st police, Jacksonville Nat Hist Landmark

33 Central Point, **E** 🅖 Chevron, 🏪/Subway/Taco Bell/dsl/scales/24hr, 🍴 Burger King, KFC, Quiznos, Shari's Rest., Sonic, 🛏 Candlewood Suites (2mi), Courtyard (2mi), Fairfield Inn, Holiday Inn Express, Super 8, 🅞 funpark, **W** 🅖 76/Circle K/dsl, Shell/dsl, 🍴 Abby's Pizza, Mazatlan Grill, McDonald's, 🅞 Albertson's, USPO

30 OR 62, to Crater Lake, Medford, **E** 🅖 Chevron, Witham Trkstp/rest./dsl/24hr/@, 🍴 Abby's Pizza, Applebee's, Asian Grill, Burger King, Carl's Jr, DQ, Del Taco, Elmer's, Marie Callender's, McDonald's, Olive Garden, Outback Steaks, Panda Express, Papa John's, Pizza Hut, Quiznos, Red Robin, Si Casa Flores Mexican, Sizzler, Sonic, Starbucks, Subway, Taco Bell, Taco Delite, Thai Bistro, Wendy's, 🛏 Comfort Inn, Hampton Inn, Motel 6, Quality Inn, Ramada, Rogue Regency Hotel, Shilo Inn, 🅞 Ace Hardware, Affordable RV Ctr, AT&T, Barnes&Noble, Best Buy, BigLots, BiMart Foods, Costco/gas, $Tree, Ford/Lincoln, Fred Meyer/dsl, Food4Less, JoAnn, Lowe's, Mazda, Mercedes, Michael's, Office Depot, Old Navy, Petsmart, Ross, Safeway, Schuck's Parts, Schwab Tire, Sears/auto,

30 Continued
TJ Maxx, USPO, Verizon, Walmart, st police, vet, **W** 🅖 76/dsl, Shell/dsl, Spirit/dsl, 🍴 Jack-in-the-Box, KFC, King-Wah Chinese, Red Lobster, Wendy's, 🅞 🅷, CarQuest, JC Penney, Kohl's, Macy's, Target, Toyota/Scion, mall

27 Barnett Rd, Medford, **E** 🍴 Blackbear Diner, DQ, 🛏 Best Western, Days Inn/rest., Homewood Suites, Motel 6, Travelodge, 🅞 🅷, **W** 🅖 Chevron, 76/Circle K/dsl, Shell/dsl, Texaco/dsl, 🍴 Abby's Pizza, Arby's, Burger King, Carl's Jr, HomeTown Buffet, Jack-in-the-Box, KFC, McDonald's, McGrath's FishHouse, Pizza Hut, Quiznos, Rooster's Rest., Senor Sam's Mexican, Shari's, Starbucks, Subway, Taco Bell, Wendy's, 🛏 Capri Motel, Comfort Inn, Holiday Inn Express, Medford Inn, Royal Crest Motel, SpringHill Suites, TownePlace Suites, 🅞 Fred Meyer/dsl, Grocery Outlet, Harry&David's, Office Depot, Radio Shack, Schucks Parts, Staples, Walgreens, WinCo Foods

24 Phoenix, **E** 🅖 Petro/Iron Skillet/dsl/scales/RV dump/24hr/@, 🛏 Best Inn/PearTree RV park, 🅞 Home Depot, Peterbilt, **W** 🅖 76/Circle K/dsl, 🍴 Angelo's Pizza, Debby's Diner, Jack-in-the-Box, McDonald's, Si Casa Flores Mexican, Taste of Orient, 🛏 Bavarian Inn, 🅞 Ray's Foods, Holiday RV Park

22mm 🅟🆂 sb, full 🦽 facilities, 🚻, 🛋, litter barrels, vending, petwalk

21 Talent, **W** 🅖 Chevron/dsl, 🍴 Avalon Grill, Figaro's Italian, 🛏 GoodNight Inn, 🅞 American RV Resort, Walmart/auto, repair

19 Valley View Rd, Ashland, **W** 🅖 Pacific Pride/dsl, 76/dsl, Shell/dsl/LP, 🍴 Burger King, El Tapatio Mexican, 🛏 EconoLodge, La Quinta, 🅞 Acura, Chevrolet, Ford, Suzuki

18mm weigh sta both lanes

14 OR 66, to Klamath Falls, Ashland, **E** 🅖 Chevron/dsl, 76/dsl/LP, Shell/dsl, 🍴 El Pariso Mexican, OakTree Rest., 🛏 Best Western, Holiday Inn Express, Relax Inn, Windmill Inn, 🅞 Emigrant Lake Camping (3mi), Glenyan RV Park (3mi), Nat Hist Museum, **W** 🅖 Arco, Texaco, 🍴 Korean BBQ, Panda Garden Chinse, Subway, Taco Bell, Wendy's, Wild Goose Cafe, Yuan Yuan Chinese, 🛏 Knights Inn/rest., Rodeway Inn, Super 8, 🅞 🅷, Albertson's, Bi-Mart, NAPA, Radio Shack, Rite Aid, Schwab Tire, U-Haul, vet

11 OR 99, Siskiyou Blvd (nb only, no return) **services 2-4 mi W**

6 to Mt Ashland, **E** 🛏 Callahan's Siskiyou Lodge/rest., 🅞 🚻, ski area

4mm Siskiyou Summit, elev 4310, brake check both lanes

1 to Siskiyou Summit (from nb, no return)

0mm Oregon/California state line

OR

↑E INTERSTATE 84

OR

Exit	Services
378mm	Oregon/Idaho state line, Snake River
377.5mm	**Welcome Ctr wb, full ♿ facilities, info, 🍽, 🕭, litter barrels, vending, petwalk**
376b a	US 30, to US 20/26, Ontario, Payette, **N** 🅖 Chevron/dsl, 🍽 A&W/KFC, Burger King, Carl's Jr, China Buffet, Country Kitchen, DQ, Denny's, Domino's, McDonald's, Quiznos, Taco Del Mar, Taco Time, Wingers, 🛏 Best Value Inn, Best Western, Clarion, Colonial Inn, Motel 6, Sleep Inn, Super 8, 🅞 $Tree, GNC, Home Depot, K-Mart, Staples, Toyota/Scion, Verizon, Walgreens, Walmart/Subway, st police, **S** 🅖 ▨/Arby's/dsl/scales/24hr, Shell/dsl, 🍽 DJ's, East Side Cafe, Far East Chinese, Gandolfo's Deli, Ogawa's Japanese, Rusty's Steaks, Sizzler, Subway, Taco Bell, 🛏 Economy Inn, Holiday Inn Express, OR Trail Motel, Rodeway Inn, Stockman's Motel, 🅞 🅗, Commercial Tire, Les Schwab Tire, NAPA, Radio Shack, 4 Wheeler Museum
374	US 30, OR 201, to Ontario, **N** to Ontario SP, **S** 🅖 ❤Loves/Chester's/Subway/dsl/scales/24hr/@, Pacific Pride, 🛏 Budget Inn, 🅞 🅗
373.5mm	Malheur River
371	Stanton Blvd, **2 mi S** to correctional institution
362	Moores Hollow Rd
356	OR 201, to Weiser, IDm **3 mi N** Catfish Junction RV Park, Oasis RV Park
354.5mm	**weigh sta eb**
353	US 30, to Huntington, **N weigh sta wb**, 🅞 to Farewell Bend SP, RV camping, info
351mm	Pacific/Mountain time zone
345	US 30, Lime, Huntington, **1 mi N** gas, food, lodging, to Snake River Area, Van Ornum BFD
342	Lime (from eb)
340	Rye Valley
338	Lookout Mountain
337mm	Burnt River
335	to Weatherby, **N 🆁🆂 both lanes, full ♿ facilities, Oregon Trail Info, 🕭, litter barrels, vending, petwalk**
330	Plano Rd, to Cement Plant Rd, **S** cement plant
329mm	pulloff eb
327	Durkee, **N** 🅖 Co-op/dsl/LP/café
325mm	Pritchard Creek
321mm	Alder Creek
317	to Pleasant Valley (from wb)
315	to Pleasant Valley (from wb)
313	to Pleasant Valley (from eb)
306	US 30, Baker, **2-3 mi S** 🅖 Chevron/dsl, 🍽 DQ, 🛏 Baker City Motel/RV Park, Bridge Street Hotel, OR Trail Motel/rest., 🅞 🅗, Les Schwab Tire, to st police, same as 304
304	OR 7, Baker, **N** 🅖 Chevron/dsl, 🛏 Super 8, Welcome Inn, **S** 🅖 Maverik/dsl, Shell/dsl, Sinclair/rest./dsl/scales/24hr, USA/dsl, 🍽 Arceo's Mexican, DQ, Golden Crown, McDonald's, Papa Murphy's, Pizza Hut, Raceo's Mexican, Rising Sun Chinese, Starbucks, Subway, Sumpter Jct Rest., Taco Time, 🛏 Best Western, Budget Inn, Eldorado Inn, Geyser Grand Motel, Rodeway Inn, Western Motel, 🅞 🅗, Albertson's/gas, Bi-Mart, CarQuest, $Tree, Ford, Mtn View RV Park/LP (3mi), Paul's Transmissions/repair, Rite Aid, Safeway Foods, Verizon, city park, museum, to hist dist
302	OR 86 E to Richland, **S** 🅞 🅗, OR Tr RV Park/LP, st police

ONTARIO / **BAKER**

Exit	Services
298	OR 203, to Medical Springs
297mm	Baldock Slough
295mm	🆁🆂 **both lanes, full ♿ facilities, info, 🍽, 🕭, litter barrels, vending, petwalk**
289mm	Powder River
287.5mm	45th parallel...halfway between the equator and north pole
286mm	N Powder River
285	US 30, OR 237, North Powder, **N** 🛏 North Powder Motel/cafe, **S** 🅞 to Anthony Lakes, ski area
284mm	Wolf Creek
283	Wolf Creek Lane
278	Clover Creek
273	Frontage Rd
270	Ladd Creek Rd (from eb, no return)
269mm	🆁🆂 **both lanes, full ♿ facilities, info, 🍽, 🕭, litter barrels, vending, petwalk**
268	Foothill Rd
265	OR 203, LaGrande, **N** 🅞 Eagles Hot Lake RV Park, ▨ **S** 🅖 Ⓕ/FLYING J/Shell/res./dsl/scales/24hr, 🍽 SmokeHouse Rest. (2mi), 🅞 Freightliner
261	OR 82, LaGrande, **N** 🅖 Chevron/dsl, Shell/dsl, 🍽 Denny's, Pizza Hut, Primo's Pizza, Quiznos, Starbucks, Taco Bell, 🛏 LaGrande Inn, 🅞 Chrysler/Dodge/Jeep, Ford/Lincoln, Grocery Outlet, Les Schwab Tire, Thunder RV Ctr, Verizon, Walmart/Subway, st police, vet, **S** 🅖 Chevron, 76/Baskin-Robbins/Subway/dsl, Texaco/dsl, 🍽 Bear Mtn. Pizza, China Buffet, DQ, Dutch Bro's Coffee, KFC, La Fiesta Mexican, McDonald's, Moy's Dynasty, Nell's Steakburger, Papa Murphy's, Taco Time, Wendy's, 🛏 Best Value Inn, Best Western, Royal Motel, Sandman Inn, Super 8, 🅞 🅗 Ace Hardware, Albertson's, $General, $Tree, Rite Aid, Safeway/gas, Schwab Tire, vet, E OR U, Wallowa Lake
260mm	Grande Ronde River
259	US 30 E (from eb), to La Grande, **1-2 mi S** 🅖 Chevron, Shell/dsl, 🍽 Burger King, KFC, 🛏 Greenwell Motel/rest., Rodeway Inn, Royal Motel, same as 261
257	Perry (from wb)
256.5mm	**weigh sta eb**
256	Perry (from eb)
255mm	Grande Ronde River
254mm	scenic wayside
252	OR 244, to Starkey, Lehman Springs, **S** 🅞 Hilgard SP, camping, chainup area
251mm	Wallowa-Whitman NF, eastern boundary
248	Spring Creek Rd, to Kamela, **3 mi N** Oregon Trail Visitors Park
246mm	Wallowa-Whitman NF, western boundary
243	Summit Rd, Mt Emily Rd, to Kamela, Oregon Trail info, **2 mi N** 🅞 Emily Summit SP
241mm	Summit of the Blue Mtns, elev 4193
238	Meacham
234	Meacham, **S** 🅞 Emigrant Sprs SP, RV camping
231.5mm	Umatilla Indian Reservation, eastern boundary
228mm	Deadman Pass, Oregon Trail info, 🆁🆂 **both lanes, full ♿ facilities, 🍽 (wb), picnic table, litter barrel, petwalk, vending, RV Dump (wb)**
227mm	**weigh sta wb, brake check area**
224	Poverty Flats Rd, Old Emigrant Hill Rd, to Emigrant Springs SP
223mm	wb viewpoint, no restrooms
221.5mm	eb viewpoint, no restrooms
220mm	wb runaway truck ramp

LA GRANDE

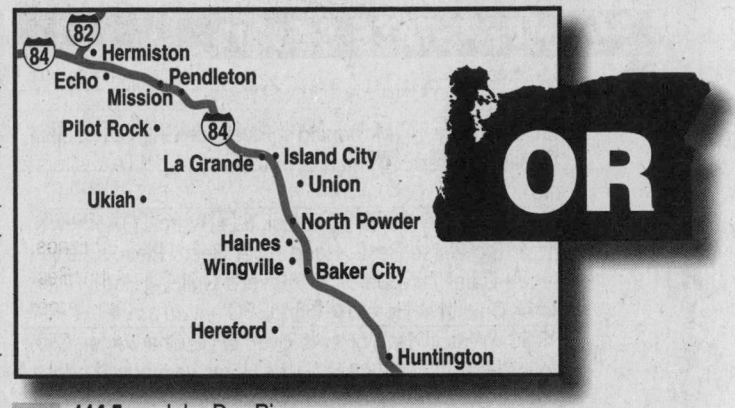

INTERSTATE 84 CONT'D

Exit	Services
216	Mission, McKay Creek, **N** 🅐 Arrowhead Trkstp/Pacific Pride/McDonald's/dsl/24hr, 🅞 Wildhorse Casino/RV Park
213	US 30 (from wb), Pendleton, **3-5 mi N** 🅐 Chevron/dsl, Shell, 🛏 Travelers Inn, 🅞 H, Pendleton NHD
212mm	Umatilla Indian Reservation western boundary
210	OR 11, Pendleton, **N** 🅞 H, museum, st police, **S** 🅐 Chevron/Circle K/dsl, Shell/dsl/LP, 🍴 Shari's/24hr, 🛏 Best Western, Hampton Inn, Holiday Inn Express, Motel 6, Red Lion Inn/rest., Super 8, 🅞 KOA
209	US 395, Pendleton, **N** 🅐 Arco, 🍴 Jack-in-the-Box, KFC, Little Caesars, Pizza Hut, Quiznos, Taco Bell, 🛏 Oxford Suites, Travelodge, 🅞 Dean's Mkt, $Tree, O'Reilly Parts, Radio Shack, Rite Aid, Safeway/dsl, Verizon, Walmart/Subway, **S** 🅐 Astro/dsl, 76/dsl, 🍴 Abby's Pizza, Burger King, Denny's, McDonald's, Rooster's Rest., Starbucks, Subway, Wendy's, 🛏 EconoLodge, 🅞 Les Schwab, Thompson RV Ctr
208mm	Umatilla River
207	US 30, W Pendleton, **N** 🅐 Shell/dsl/LP, 🅞 Lookout RV Park, truck repair
202	Barnhart Rd, to Stage Gulch, **N** Woodpecker Truck Repair, **S** 🛏 Rodeo City Inn, 🅞 Oregon Trail info
199	Stage Coach Rd, Yoakum Rd
198	Lorenzen Rd, McClintock Rd, **N** 🅞 trailer/reefer repair
190	Echo Rd, to Echo Oregon Trail Site
188	US 395 N, Hermiston, **N** 🅐 Chevron/dsl (1mi), 🍴 /Subway/McDonald's/dsl/24hr/RV park, **5 mi N** 🍴 Denny's/24hr, Jack-in-the-Box, McDonald's, Shari's/24hr, 🛏 Best Western, Economy Inn, Oak Tree Inn, Oxford Suites, 🅞 H, **S** 🅞 Henrietta RV Park (1mi), Echo HS
187mm	🆁 **both lanes, full ♿ facilities, 🛢, info, 🚮, litter barrels, petwalk**
182	OR 207, to Hermiston, **N** 🅐 Space Age/A&W/dsl/LP/24hr, 🛏 Comfort Inn
180	Westland Rd, to Hermiston, McNary Dam, **N** 🅞 Freightliner, trailer repair
179	I-82 W, to Umatilla, Kennewick, WA
177	Umatilla Army Depot
171	Paterson Ferry Rd, to Paterson
168	US 730, to Irrigon, **8 mi N** 🅞 Green Acres RV Park, Oasis RV Park, Oregon Trail info
165	Port of Morrow, **S** 🅐 Pacific Pride/dsl
164	Boardman, **N** 🅐 Chevron/Circle K/dsl, Shell/dsl, 🍴 C&D Drive-In, Lynard's Cafe, Sunrise Café, 🛏 Fair Deal Inn, Riverview Motel, 🅞 Boardman RV/Marina Park, city park, USPO, **S** 🅐 Shell/dsl, 🛏 Rodeway Inn, 🅞 Michael's Repair, NAPA, Oregon Trail Library, Select Mkt
161mm	🆁 **both lanes, full ♿ facilities, 🛢, 🚮, litter barrels, vending, petwalk**
159	Tower Rd
151	Threemile Canyon
147	OR 74, to Ione, Blue Mtn Scenic Byway, Heppner, Oregon Trail Site
137	OR 19, Arlington, **S** 🅐 Shell/Circle K/dsl, 🍴 Happy Canyon Cafe, Village Inn, 🛏 Village Inn Motel, 🅞 Ace Hardware, Arlington RV Park, Thrifty Foods, city park, USPO
136.5mm	view point wb, 🚮 litter barrels
131	Woelpern Rd (from eb, no return)
129	Blalock Canyon, Lewis&Clark Trail
123	Philippi Canyon, Lewis&Clark Trail
114.5mm	John Day River
114	**S** LePage Park
112	parking area, both lanes, litter barrels, **N** John Day Dam
109	Rufus, **N** John Day Visitor Ctr, **S** 🅐 Shell/dsl, 🍴 Bob's T-Bone, 🛏 Hillview Motel, Tyee Motel, 🅞 Ed's RV Park, Rufus RV Park
104	US 97, Biggs, **N** 🅞 Des Chutes Park Bridge, **S** 🅐 76/Circle K/Noble Roman's/dsl/24hr, 🛢/McDonald's/dsl/scales/24hr, Shell/Subway/dsl, 🍴 Linda's Rest., 🛏 Biggs Motel/café, Dinty's Motel, 3 Rivers Inn, 🅞 Dinty's Mkt, Maryhill Museum, dsl repair
100mm	Deschutes River, Columbia River Gorge Scenic Area
97	OR 206, Celilo, **N** 🅞 Celilo SP, restrooms, **S** 🅞 Deschutes SP, Indian Village
92mm	pullout, eb
88	**N** to The Dalles Dam
87	US 30, US 197, to Dufur, **N** 🅐 Chevron, 76/dsl/24hr, 🍴 McDonald's, Portage Grill, 🛏 Comfort Inn, Shilo Inn/rest., 🅞 Columbia Hills RV Park, Lone Pine RV Park, st police, **S** 🍴 Big Jim's Drive-In, 🛏 Celilo Inn
85	The Dalles, **N** Riverfront Park, restrooms, 🛢, 🚮, litter barrels, playground, marina, **S** 🅐 Chevron, 76/dsl, Shell, 🍴 Burgerville, Clock Tower Rest., Domino's, Taco Del Mar, 🛏 Dalles Inn, Oregon Motel, 🅞 H, AJ's Radiators, Dalles Parts, NAPA, TrueValue, Verizon, camping, USPO, vet, to Nat Hist Dist
83	(84 from wb) W The Dalles, **N** 🍴 Casa El Mirador, 🅞 Tire Factory, **S** 🅐 Astro/dsl, Shell/dsl, 🍴 Arby's, Burger King, Denny's, DQ, Dutch Bro's Coffee, Ixtapa Mexican, KFC, McDonald's, Papa Murphy's, Quiznos, Shari's Rest., Skipper's, Starbucks, Subway, Taco Bell, Taco Time, The BBQ, Wendy's, 🛏 Cousin's Inn/rest., Motel 6, Super 8, 🅞 H AT&T, Buick/Chevrolet/GMC, Chrysler/Dodge/Jeep, $Tree, Ford, Fred Meyer/gas, Grocery Outlet, Honda, Jo-Ann Fabrics, K-Mart, Nissan, Oil Can Henry's, O'Reilly Parts, PetCo, Radio Shack, Rite Aid, Save-a-Lot Foods, Safeway/dsl, Staples, Subaru, Toyota/Scion, Walgreens
82	Chenowith Area, **S** 🅐 76/dsl, 🍴 Spooky's Café, 🅞 Bi-Mart Foods, Columbia Discovery Ctr, Home Depot, museum, same as 83
76	Rowena, **N** 🅞 Mayer SP, Memaloose SP, Lewis & Clark info, windsurfing
73mm	Memaloose SP, 🆁 **both lanes, full ♿ facilities, 🚮, litter barrels, 🛢, petwalk, RV dump, camping**
69	US 30, Mosier, **S** 🍴 10 Speed East Rest., Thirsty Woman, 🅞 USPO
66mm	**N** Koberg Beach SP, 🆁 **wb, full facilities, picnic table, litter barrels**
64	US 30, OR 35, to White Salmon, Hood River, **N** 🅐 Chev

PENDLETON

BOARDMAN

THE DALLES

OR

HOOD RIVER

🛫E INTERSTATE 84 CONT'D

Exit	Services
64	Continued ron, Shell/24hr, 🍴 McDonald's, Riverside Grill, Starbucks, 🏨 Best Western, 🄾 marina, museum, st police, visitors info
63	Hood River, City Ctr, **N** Ⓖ 76/dsl, **S** Ⓖ Astro, 🍴 Andrew's Pizza, Big Horse Rest., Hood River Rest., Pietro's Pizza, Sage's Cafe, Taco Del Mar, 3 River's Grill, 🏨 Hood River Hotel, Oakstreet Hotel, 🄾 Ⓗ, USPO, same as 64
62	US 30, Westcliff Dr, W Hood River, **N** 🍴 Charburger, Cliff House Rest., 🏨 Columbia Gorge Hotel, Vagabond Lodge, **S** Ⓖ Chevron/dsl/LP, 76/dsl, 🍴 Domino's, DQ, Egg River Cafe, HoHo Chinese, McDonald's, Pizzicato, Quiznos, Red Carpet Cafe, Starbucks, Subway, Taco Bell, 🏨 Comfort Suites, Lone Pine Motel, Prater's Motel, Riverview Lodge, Sunset Motel, 🄾 Ⓗ, AT&T, Les Schwab, Oil Can Henry's, Rite Aid, Safeway, Walmart
61mm	pulloff wb
60	service rd wb (no return)
58	Mitchell Point Overlook (from eb)
56	**N** 🄾 Viento SP, RV camping, 🚻
55	Starvation Peak Tr Head (from eb), restrooms
54mm	**weigh sta wb**
51	Wyeth, **S** camping
49mm	pulloff eb
47	Forest Lane, Hermon Creek (from wb), camping
45mm	**weigh sta eb**
44	US 30, to Cascade Locks, **N** Ⓖ CFN, Chevron/dsl, Shell/dsl, 🍴 Cascade Inn Rest., Charburger, Pacific Crest Pub, Waterfront Cafe, 🏨 Best Western, Bonneville Hot Spring Hotel, Bridge of the Gods Motel, Cascade Motel, Columbia Gorge Inn, Rodeway Inn, Skamania Springs Hotel, 🄾 Columbia Mkt, KOA, Stern Wheeler RV Park, USPO, to Bridge of the Gods
41	Eagle Creek RA (from eb), to fish hatchery
40	**N** 🄾 Bonneville Dam NHS, info, to fish hatchery
37	Warrendale (from wb)
35	Historic Hwy, Multnomah Falls, **S** 🄾 Ainsworth SP, scenic loop highway, waterfall area, Fishery RV Park
31	Multnomah Falls (exits left from both lanes), **S** Multnomah Falls Lodge/Rest. (hist site), camping
30	**S** Benson SRA (from eb)
29	Dalton Point (from wb)
28	to Bridal Veil (7 mi return from eb), **S** USPO
25	**N** Rooster Rock SP
23mm	viewpoint wb, hist marker
22	Corbett, **2 mi S** Ⓖ Corbett Mkt, 🍴 View Point Rest., 🄾 Crown Point RV Camping
19mm	Columbia River Gorge scenic area
18	Lewis&Clark SP, to Oxbow SP
17.5mm	Sandy River
17	Marine Dr, Troutdale, **N** 🏨 Holiday Inn Express, **S** Ⓖ Chevron/24hr, 💗Loves/Chester's/dsl/LP/scales/24hr, TA/Shell/Buckhorn Rest./Popeye's/Subway/dsl/scale24hr/@, 🍴 Arby's, McDonald's, Shari's/24hr, Subway, Taco Bell, 🏨 Comfort Inn, Motel 6, 🄾 Premium Outlets/famous brands, Sandy Riverfront RV Resort
16	238th Dr, Fairview, **N** Ⓖ Arco/dsl/24hr, 🍴 Bronx Eatery, Burger King, Jack-in-the-Box, Taco Del Mar, 🏨 Travelodge, 🄾 Camping World, Walmart/Subway, **S** Ⓖ 76, 🏨 Best Western, 🄾 Ⓗ

OR

PORTLAND

Exit	Services
14	207th Ave, Fairview, **N** Ⓖ Shell/dsl, 🍴 Europa Grill, 🄾 American Dream RV Ctr, NAPACare, Portland RV Park, Rolling Hills RV Park, auto repair
13	181st Ave, Gresham, **N** Ⓖ Chevron/dsl, 🏨 Hampton Inn, **S** Ⓖ Arco, Texaco, 🍴 Burger King, Carl's Jr, Jung's Chinese, McDonald's, Quiznos, RoundTable Pizza, Shari's/24hr, Starbucks, Tom's Pizza, Wendy's, Xavier's, 🏨 Days Inn, Extended Stay America, Guesthouse Suites, Rodeway Inn, Sheraton, 🄾 Albertson's, Curves, Rite Aid, Safeway, 7-11, auto repair, vet
10	122nd Ave (from eb)
9	I-205, S to Salem, N to Seattle, to ✈, (to 102nd Ave from eb)
8	I-205 N (from eb), **N** to ✈
7	Halsey St (from eb) Gateway Dist
6	I-205 S (from eb)
5	OR 213, to 82nd Ave (eb only), **N** 🏨 Days Inn, **S** 🍴 Eastern Cathay, 🏨 Comfort Inn
4	68th Ave (from eb), to Halsey Ave
3	58th Ave (from eb), **S** Ⓖ Shell, 🄾 Ⓗ, Fred Meyer
2	43rd Ave, 39th Ave, Halsey St, **N** Ⓖ Chevron, 76, Shell, Texaco, 🍴 Baja Fresh, Burger King, China Kitchen, McDonald's, Panera Bread, Quizno's, Poor Richard's Rest., Subway, 🏨 Banfield Motel, Rodeway Inn, 🄾 Radio Shack, Rite Aid, Trader Joe's, **S** 🄾 Ⓗ, Buick/Jeep, same as 1
1	33rd Ave, Lloyd Blvd (eb only), downtown, same as 2, **N** 🍴 Applebee's, 🏨 DoubleTree Inn, Residence Inn, 🄾 $Tree, Macy's, Marshall's, JC Penney, Sears, **S** 🍴 Pizza Hut, 🄾 Cadillac
1	to downtown (wb only)
0mm	**I-84 begins/ends on I-5, exit 301.**

🛣N INTERSTATE 205 (PORTLAND)

Exit	Services
37mm	**I-205 begins/ends on I-5. Exits 36-27 are in Washington.**
36	NE 134th St (from nb), **E** Ⓖ Arco, 7-11, 76, TrailMart/dsl, 🍴 Applebee's, Billygan's Roadhouse, Booster Juice, Burger King, Burgerville, Jack-in-the-Box, McDonald's, Muchas Gracias, Panda Express, Round Table Pizza, Starbucks, Subway, Taco Bell, Taco Del Mar, 🏨 Comfort Inn, Holiday Inn Express, Olympia Motel, Red Lion, Salmon Creek Inn, Shilo Inn, 🄾 Ⓗ, Albertson's/gas, Long's Drugs, Safeway/gas, Zupan's Mkt, 99 RV Park, to Portland ✈, **W** Ⓖ Shell, 🍴 Baskin-Robbins, Coldstone, El Tapatio, Papa Murphy's, PizzaSchmitzza, Quizno's, Starbucks, The Great Impasta, 🏨 La Quinta, 🄾 Fred Meyer
32	NE 83rd St, Anderson Rd, Battle Ground, **W** Ⓖ Shell/dsl/24hr, 🍴 Burger King, Emporor Chinese, Krispy Kreme, Panda Express, Starbucks, Subway, Wendy's, Weinerschnitzel, 🄾 Costco/gas, Home Depot
30c b a	WA 500, Orchards, Vancouver, **E** Ⓖ 76, Shell/24hr, 🍴 ABC Buffet, Applebee's, Burger King, Burgerville, DQ, Imperial Palace, McDonald's, Papa Murphy's, Starbucks, Subway, Wendy's, 🄾 Jo-Ann Crafts, Office Depot, PetCo, Sportsman's Whse, Toyota, Tuesday Morning, Walgreens, **W** Ⓖ Chevron/24hr, Shell/dsl, 🍴 A&W, Azteca Mexican, Buffet City, Burgerville, Chevy's Mexican, ChuckeCheese, Elmer's Rest., Golden Tent BBQ, IHOP, Jamba Juice, Muchas Gracias, Newport Bay Seafood, Olive Garden, Outback Steaks, Red Lobster, Red Robin, RoundTable Pizza, Shari's/24hr, Starbucks, Subway, Taco Bell, TCBY,

⬆N INTERSTATE 205 (PORTLAND) CONT'D

Exit	Services
30c b a	Continued TGIFriday, 🛏 Best Western, Comfort Suites, Ramada, Residence Inn, Rodeway Inn, Staybridge Inn, 🅞 Americas Tire, Big Lots, $Tree, Ford, JC Penney, Lincoln, Macy's, Old Navy, Ross, Sears/auto, Target, VW, mall, RV park
28	Mill Plain Rd, **E** 🅖 Chevron, 76/Circle K, Shell/dsl, 🍴 Baskin-Robbins, Burger King, Burgerville, DQ, Elmer's Rest., Irishtown Grill, Kings Buffet, McDonald's, Muchas Gracias Mexican, Pizza Hut, Quiznos, Shari's, Starbucks, Taco Bell, 🛏 Best Western, Extended Stay America, Motel 6, 🅞 $Tree, Fred Meyer, PetCo, Schuck's Parts, Schwab Tire, 7-11, **W** 🅖 Arco, 76, 7-11, 🍴 Arby's, Jack-in-the-Box, Subway, Taco Del Mar, 🅞 🄷 Chevrolet, Walmart, Walgreens, auto/tire repair, vet, transmissions
27	WA 14, Vancouver, Camas, Columbia River Gorge
25mm	Oregon/Washington state line. Columbia River. Exits 27-36 are in Washington.
24	122nd Ave, 🔄 Way, **E** 🍴 Burger King, China Wok, CoffeeHouse, Jack-in-the-Box, McDonald's, Shari's, Subway, 🛏 Clarion, Comfort Suites, Courtyard, Fairfield Inn, Hilton Garden, Holiday Inn Express, La Quinta, Residence Inn, Shilo Inn/rest., SpringHill Suites, Staybridge Suites, Super 8, 🅞 Home Depot, **W** 🛏 Embassy Suites, Hampton Inn, Loft Hotel, Sheraton/rest., 🅞 Best Buy, PetsMart, Ross, Staples, 🔄
23b a	US 30 byp, Columbia Blvd, **E** 🅖 Leather's Fuel/dsl, Shell/dsl, 🍴 Bill's Steaks, Elmer's Rest., 🛏 Best Western, Carolina Motel, Comfort Inn, Econolodge, Quality Inn, Rodeway Inn, 🅞 🄷, **W** 🅖 Shell, 🛏 Best Value Inn, Holiday Inn, Radisson, Ramada Inn, 🅞 camping
22	I-84 E, US 30 E, to The Dalles
21b	I-84 W, US 30 W, to Portland
21a	Glisan St, **E on NE 102nd St** 🅖 Arco, 76, 🍴 Applebee's, Carl's Jr, Jamba Juice, Quizno's, McDonald's, 🅞 Fred Meyer, Kohl's, Office Depot, Ross, WinCo Foods
20	Stark St, Washington St, **E** 🅖 Chevron/dsl, 🍴 Arby's, Baja Fresh, Burger King, Denny's, Elmer's Rest., Jack-In-the-Box, McMenamin's Rest., Old Chicago Pizza, Olive Garden, Panda Express, Pizza Shmizza, Red Robin, Saylor's, Starbucks, Village Inn, 🛏 Chestnut Tree Inn, Holiday Inn Express, 🅞 Big Lots, Home Depot, Target, Tuesday Morning, mall, **W** 🍴 Stark St Pizza, Taco Bell, 🛏 Motel 6, 🅞 7-11
19	US 26, Division St, **E** 🅖 Space Age/dsl, 🅞 🄷, **W** 🅖 76, 🍴 Burgerville, Campbell's BBQ, ChuckeCheese, McDonald's, Subway, 🅞 Jo-Ann Fabrics, 7-11, Walmart
17	Foster Rd, **1 mi W** 🅖 Chevron, 76, Shell, 🍴 Arby's,

Exit	Services
17	Continued Burger King, IHOP, McDonald's, Wendy's, 🛏 Econolodge, Home Depot, 🅞 U-Haul
16	Johnson Creek Blvd, **W** 🅖 76, 🍴 Applebee's, Arby's, Bajio, Burger King, Carl's Jr, Jack-in-the-Box, Krispy Kreme, McDonald's, Outback Steaks, Pizza Shmizza, Quizno's, Ron's Café, RoundTable Pizza, Starbucks, Subway, Taco Bell, WeiWei, 🅞 Best Buy, Fred Meyer/gas, Home Depot, Knecht's Parts, PetsMart, RV Ctrs, Schuck's Parts, 7-11, Trader Joe's, Walgreens, Wal-Mart
14	Sunnyside Rd, **E** 🅖 76, 🍴 A&W/KFC, Baja Fresh, Chen's Kitchen, Domino's, Gustav's Grill, Izzy's Pizza, KFC, McMenamin's, Quizno's, Starbucks, Subway, TCBY, 🛏 Days Inn, Howard Johnson, 🅞 🄷, Office Depot, **W** 🅖 Texaco/dsl/24hr, 🍴 Burger King, CA Pizza Kitchen, Chevy's Mexican, Chili's, Claim Jumper, Denny's, DQ, Macaroni Grill, McDonald's, Noodles&Co, Old Spaghetti Factory, Olive Garden, Pizza Hut, Red Robin, Stanford's Rest., Taco Time, Wendy's, 🛏 Courtyard, Monarch Hotel/rest., 🅞 America's Tire, Barnes&Noble, JC Penney, Kohl's, Macy's, Nordstroms, Old Navy, PetCo, Sears/auto, Target, U-Haul, Walgreens, World Mkt, mall
13	OR 224, to Milwaukie, **W** 🅞 K-Mart, Lowe's
12	OR 213, to Milwaukie, **E** 🅖 Chevron/24hr, Pacific Pride, Shell, 🍴 Denny's, Elmer's, KFC, McDonald's, Subway, Taco Bell/24hr, Wendy's, 🛏 Clackamas Inn, Hampton Inn, 🅞 Fred Meyer, 7-11, **W** 🛏 Comfort Suites
11	82nd Dr, Gladstone, **W** 🅖 Arco/24hr, Chevron, 🍴 McDonald's, Starbucks, Subway, 🛏 Oxford Suites, 🅞 Harley-Davidson, Safeway
10	OR 213, Park Place, **E** 🅖 76/Pacific Pride/dsl, 🅞 🄷, Home Depot, to Oregon Trail Ctr
9	OR 99E, Oregon City, **E** 🅖 Chevron/dsl, 76, 🍴 KFC, 🅞 🄷, Subaru, repair, **W** 🍴 La Hacienda Mexican, McDonald's, Shari's, Starbucks, Subway, Thai Rest., 🛏 Best Western/rest., 🅞 AT&T, $Tree, Firestone/auto, Michael's, Rite Aid, Urgent Care
8.5mm	Willamette River
8	OR 43, W Linn, Lake Oswego, **E** 🅖 76, 🅞 museum, **W** 🅖 76/dsl, Shell/dsl/24hr, 🍴 BJ Willy's Pizza, Coldstone, Starbucks, Taco Del Mar, 🅞 Mkt of Choice, USPO
7mm	viewpoint nb, hist marker
6	10th St, W Linn St, **E** 🅖 Chevron/LP, 76, 🍴 5 Guys Burgers, Ixtapa Mexican, McDonald's, McMenamin's Rest., Papa Murphy's, Shari's/24hr, Shenanigan's Rest., Wilamet Coffee House, 🅞 Les Schwab, Oil Can Henry's, **W** 🍴 Biscuit's Cafe, Jack-in-the-Box, Starbucks, Subway, 🅞 Albertsons/Sav-On
4mm	Tualatin River
3	Stafford Rd, Lake Oswego, **W** 🍴 Corner Saloon, 🅞 🄷
0mm	**I-205 begins/ends on I-5, exit 288.**

PENNSYLVANIA

⬆E INTERSTATE 70

Exit	Services
Exit	Services
171mm	Pennsylvania/Maryland state line. **Welcome Ctr wb, full** 🦽 **facilities, info,** 🚽 **vending,** 🗑 **litter barrels, petwalk**
168	US 522 N, Warfordsburg, **N** 🅖 Exxon/dsl, **S** fireworks
163	PA 731 S, Amaranth
156	PA 643, Town Hill, **N** 🛏 Days Inn, 🅞 NAPA

Exit	Services
153mm	🆁🆂 eb, full 🦽 facilities, 🚽, 🗑 litter barrels, vending, petwalk
151	PA 915, Crystal Spring, **N** 🅞 auto repair, **S** 🅞 Country Store/USPO
149	US 30 W, to Everett, **S** Breezewood (no immediate wb return), **3 mi S** 🍴 McDonald's, 🛏 Penn Aire Motel, Redwood Motel, Wildwood Motel

INTERSTATE 70 CONT'D

BREEZEWOOD / FAYETTE CITY (vertical margin text)

Exit	Services
147	US 30, Breezewood, **Services on US 30** 🚗 Exxon/dsl, ✈FLYING J/Perkins/dsl/scales/24hr, Sheetz/dsl, Shell/Dunkin Donuts/Subway/dsl, Sunoco/café/dsl, TA/Gateway Rest/dsl/scales/24hr/@, Valero/dsl, 🍴 Bob Evans, DQ, Denny's, Hardee's, McDonald's, Pizza Hut, Quiznos, Starbucks, Taco Bell, Wendy's, 🏨 Best Western, EconoLodge, Holiday Inn Express, Howard Johnson, Penn Aire Motel, Quality Inn, Village Motel, Wiltshire Motel, 🅾 Blue Beacon, Radio Shack, camping, museum, truck/auto repair.
	I-70 and I-76/PA Tpk run together 71 mi. For I-70 and I-76/PA Tpk exits 148mm - 75, see Pennsylvania I-76/PA Tpk
57b a	I-70 W, US 119, PA 66 **(toll)**, New Stanton, N 🚗 Exxon, Sheetz, 🍴 Bob Evans, Campy's Pizza, Eat'n Park, McDonald's, Pagano's Rest., Pizza Hut, Subway, Szechuan Wok, Wendy's, 🏨 Budget Inn, Comfort Inn, Days Inn, EconoLodge, Express Inn, Fairfield Inn, Howard Johnson, Super 8, S 🚗 BP/dsl, Sunoco/dsl, 🍴 Cracker Barrel, La Tavola Risorante, TJ's Rest., 🅾 USPO
54	Madison, N KOA S truck repair
53	Yukon
51b a	PA 31, West Newton, S Volvo/Mack
49	Smithton, N 🚗 Citgo/rest./dsl/scales/@, ✈FLYING J/Denny's/dsl/LP/scales/24hr/@
46b a	PA 51, Pittsburgh, N 🚗 Sunoco/dsl, 🍴 Burger King, 🏨 Comfort Inn, 🅾 Buick/Cadillac/Chevrolet, Ford/Kia, S 🚗 GetGo/dsl, PP/dsl, 🍴 Clubhouse Grille, 🏨 Belle Vernon Hotel, Budget Inn, 🅾 golf
44	Arnold City
43b a	(43 from eb) PA 201, to PA 837, Fayette City, S 🚗 Exxon/dsl, 🍴 A&W/LJ Silver, Burger King, Denny's, Eat'n Park, Hibachi Buffet, Hoss' Rest., Italian Village Pizza, KFC, Little Bamboo, McDonald's, Old Mexico, Pizza Hut, Rita's Custard, Starbucks, Subway, Taco Bell, Wendy's, 🏨 Hampton Inn, Holiday Inn Express, 🅾 Advance Parts, Aldi Foods, AT&T, BigLots, CVS Drug, $General, $Tree, Giant Eagle Foods, GNC, JoAnn Fabrics, K-Mart, Lowe's, Radio Shack, Rite Aid, Staples, Verizon, Walmart
42a	Monessen
42	N Belle Vernon, S 🚗 BP/McDonald's/7-11, Sunoco/dsl, 🍴 DQ
41	PA 906, Belle Vernon
40mm	Monongahela River
40	PA 88, Charleroi, N 🚗 BP/dsl, Gulf, Sunoco, 🍴 McDonald's, My Girl's Rest., Subway/TCBY, 🅾 H, Rite Aid, Save-A-Lot Foods, Valley Tire
39	Speers, N 🍴 Lorraine's Rest., S 🚗 Exxon/dsl
37b a	PA 43 **(toll)**, N to Pittsburgh, S to CA
36	Lover (from wb, no re-entry)
35	PA 481, Centerville
32b a	PA 917, Bentleyville, N 🍴 King of the Hill Steaks, S 🚗 BP/dsl, ▦▦▦/DQ/Subway/dsl/scales/24hr, 🍴 Burger King, King Rest., McDonald's, Pizza Hut, 🏨 Best Western, Holiday Inn Express, 🅾 Advance Parts, Blue Beacon, $General, Giant Eagle Foods, Rite Aid
31	to PA 136, Kammerer, N 🏨 Carlton Motel
27	Dunningsville, S 🏨 Avalon Motel
25	PA 519, to Eighty Four, S 🚗 BP/7-11 Diner/dsl/24hr, Sunoco/dsl

WASHINGTON / PHILADELPHIA (vertical margin text)

Exit	Services
21	I-79 S, to Waynesburg.
	I-70 W and I-79 N run together 3.5 mi.
20	PA 136, Beau St, S to Washington&Jefferson Coll
19b a	US 19, Murtland Ave, N 🚗 GetGo, 🍴 Applebee's, Arby's, Bruster's, Cracker Barrel, Fusion Steaks, Jimmy John's, Krispy Kreme, Max&Erma's, McDonald's, Moe's SW Grill, Outback Steaks, Panera Bread, Ponderosa, Quiznos, Red Lobster, Red Robin, Rita's Custard, Starbucks, Subway, TX Roadhouse, TGIFriday's, Wong's Wok, 🏨 SpringHill Suites, 🅾 Aldi Foods, AT&T, Dick's, $Tree, Ford, Giant Eagle Foods, GNC, Honda, Hyundai, Kohl's, Lowe's, Mercedes, Michael's, Nissan, PetCo, Petsmart, Radio Shack, Sam's Club/gas, Save-A-Lot Foods, Target, Toyota/Scion, Walmart/McDonald's, **Urgent Care**, vet, S 🚗 BP/dsl, Exxon/dsl, Sunoco, Valero; 🍴 A&W/LJ Silver, Bob Evans, CiCi's Pizza, Donut Connection, Eat'n Park, Evergreen Chinese, Grand China, KFC, Old Mexico, Papa John's, Pizza Hut, Waffle House, 🏨 Hampton Inn, Motel 6, 🅾 H BigLots, Buick/GMC, Chevrolet, Curves, Firestone/auto, Home Depot, JC Penney, Jo-Ann Fabrics, Mazda, Pepboys, Staples, Subaru
18	I-79 N, to Pittsburgh.
	I-70 E and I-79 S run together 3.5 mi.
17	PA 18, Jefferson Ave, Washington, N 🚗 GetGo/dsl, 🍴 DQ, McDonald's, 🅾 Family$, Rite Aid, S 🚗 Valero/dsl, 🍴 Burger King, China Express, DeFelice Bros Pizza, Domino's, 4Star Pizza, Little Caesars, Subway, 🅾 Advance Parts, AutoZone, CVS Drug, $General, Shop'n Save Foods, Walgreens, USPO
16	Jessop Place, N 🚗 Citgo, S auto/truck repair
15	US 40, Chesnut St, Washington, N 🍴 USA Steaks, 🅾 Food Land, S 🚗 BP, Exxon, Sunoco/dsl, Valero, 🍴 Bob Evans, Denny's, El Paso Mexican, Garfield's Rest., LJ Silver, McDonald's, Pizza Hut, Taco Bell, Wendy's, 🏨 Best Value Inn, Comfort Suites, Days Inn, Ramada Inn, Red Roof Inn, 🅾 BonTon, Gander Mtn, Macy's, Marshalls, Rite Aid, Sears/auto, mall
11	PA 221, Taylorstown, N 🚗 BP/dsl, 🅾 truck repair
6	PA 231, to US 40, Claysville, N 🚗 Exxon, S 🚗 Petro/Sunoco/Huddle House/Subway/dsl/scales/24hr/@
5mm	**Welcome Ctr/weigh sta eb, full ♿ facilities, 🍴, vending, 🗑 litter barrels, petwalk**
1	W Alexander
0mm	Pennsylvania/West Virginia state line

INTERSTATE 76

Exit	Services
354mm	Pennsylvania/New Jersey state line, Delaware River, Walt Whitman Bridge
351	Front St, I-95 (from wb), N to Trenton, S to Chester
350	Packer Ave, 7th St, to I-95 (fromeb), S 🏨 Holiday Inn, 🅾 to sports complex
349	to I-95, PA 611, Broad St, N 🚗 Citgo
348	PA 291, W to Chester (exits left from wb)
347a	to I-95 S (exits left from wb)
347b	Passyunk Ave, Oregon Ave, N 🍴 Burger King, McDonald's, 🅾 BJ's Whse, Home Depot, Ross, ShopRite, S 🅾 sports complex
346c	28th St, Vare Ave, Mifflin St (from wb)
346b	Grays Ferry Ave, University Ave, N 🍴 Little Caesars, McDonald's, 🅾 PathMark Foods, Radio Shack, USPO, S 🚗 Citgo, Hess/dsl, 🅾 H
346a	South St (exits left from wb)

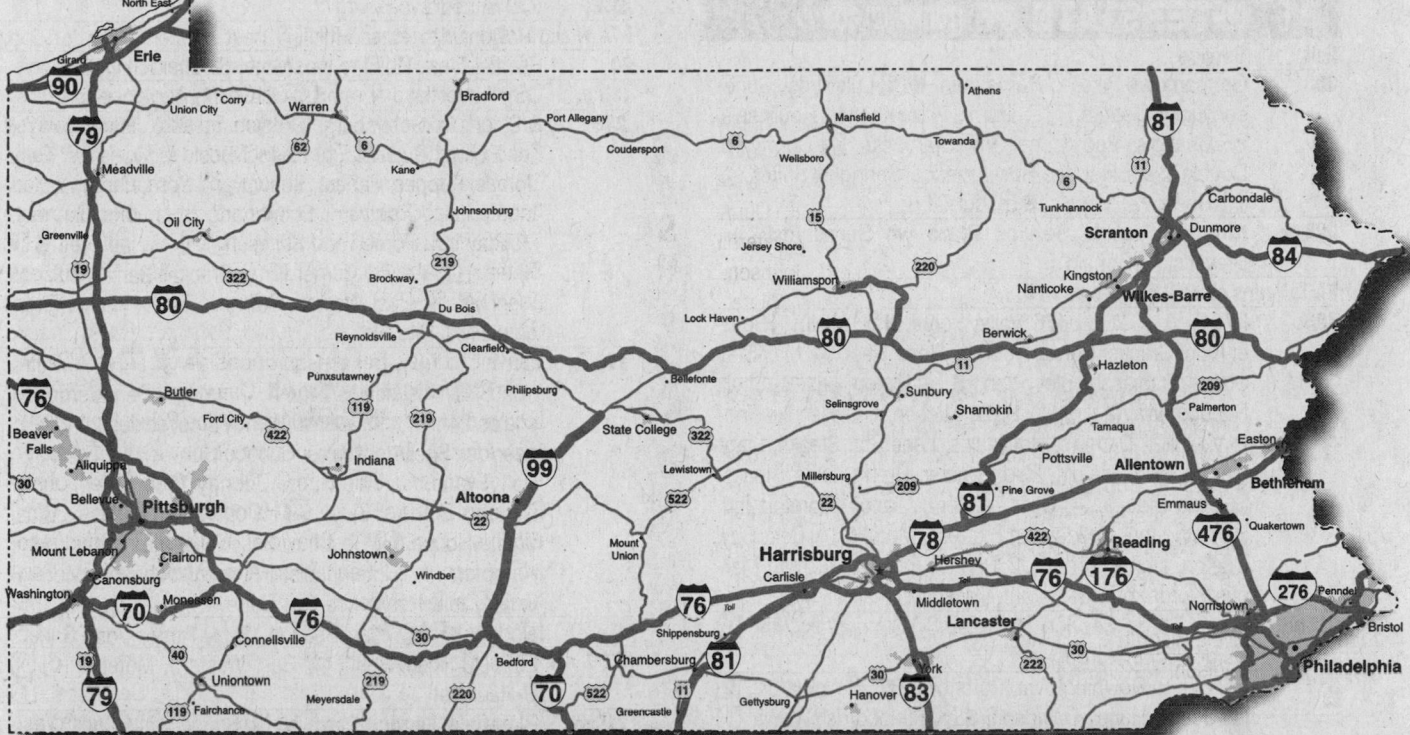

INTERSTATE 76 CONT'D

Exit	Services
345	30th St, Market St, downtown
344	I-676 E, US 30 E, to Philadelphia (no return from eb)
343	Spring Garden St, Haverford
342	US 13, US 30 W, Girard Ave, **S** Philadelphia Zoo, E Fairmount Park
341	Montgomery Dr, W River Dr, **S** W Fairmount Park
340b	US 1 N, Roosevelt Blvd, to Philadelphia
339	US 1 S, **S** 🍴 CA Pizza Kitchen, Chipotle Mexican, Houlihans, PeiWei Asian, Potbelly's, Starbucks, TGIFriday's, 🛏 Crowne Plaza, 🅾 Target, Verizon
340a	Lincoln Dr, Kelly Dr, to Germantown
338	Belmont Ave, Green Lane, **S** 🅿 Sunoco, 🅾 WaWa, St Police
337	Hollow Rd (from wb), Gladwyne
332	PA 23 (from wb), Conshohocken, **N** 🛏 Marriott
331 b a	I-476, PA 28 (from eb), to Chester, Conshohocken
330	PA 320, Gulph Mills, **S** to Villanova U
329	Weadley Rd (from wb), **N** 🅿 Exxon
328b a	US 202 N, to King of Prussia, **N** 🅿 Citgo, Exxon/dsl, Lukoil, Shell, Sunoco, WaWa, 🍴 Bahama Breeze, Baja Fresh, Burger King, CA Pizza Kitchen, Capital Grille, Champp's, Cheesecake Factory, Chili's, Fox&Hound, Gino's, Joe's Crabshack, Lonestar Steaks, Maggiano's, Morton's Steaks, Panera Bread, Red Lobster, Ruby's Diner, Sullivan's Steaks, TGIFriday's, Uno Grill, 🛏 Best Western, Clarion, Comfort Inn, Crowne Plaza, Fairfield Inn, Hampton Inn, Holiday Inn, Hotel Sierra, Motel 6, 🅾 Acme Foods, Best Buy, Bloomingdale's, Costco, Home Depot, JC Penney, Lord&Taylor, Macy's, Neiman Marcus, Nordstrom, Old Navy, Sears/auto, mall, vet
327	US 202 S, to US 420 W, Goddard Blvd Valley Forge Park
326	I-76 wb becomes I-76/PA Tpk to Ohio
For I-76 westbound to Ohio, see I-76/PA Turnpike.	

INTERSTATE 76 (TURNPIKE)

Exit	Services
PA Tpk runs wb as I-276.	
359	I-276 continues to NJ, connecting with NJ TPK, Pennsylvania/New Jersey state line, Delaware River Bridge
358	US 13, Delaware Valley, **N** 🅿 BP, WaWa, 🍴 Dallas Diner, 🛏 Comfort Inn, Day's Inn, Ramada Inn, 🅾 auto repair, 7-11, U-Haul, vet, **S** 🅿 LukOil/dsl, Sunoco/dsl, Valero, 🍴 Burger King, Gigi's Pizza, Golden Eagle Diner, Italian Family Pizza, 🛏 Villager Lodge, 🅾 Buick, $General, Mr. Transmission
352mm	**Neshaminy Service Plaza, wb Welcome Ctr,** 🅿 Sunoco/dsl/24hr, 🍴 Burger King, Nathan's, 🅾 Starbucks, eb 🅿 Sunoco/dsl, 🍴 Breyer's, HotDog Co, McDonald's, Nathan's
351	US 1, to I-95, to Philadelphia, **N** 🍴 Bob Evans, Chick-fil-A, Cracker Barrel, Longhorn Steaks, On The Border, 99, Red Robin, Ruby Tuesday, Starbucks, Wendy's, 🛏 Courtyard, Hampton Inn, Holiday Inn Select, 🅾 Buick/GMC, Home Depot, Lowes Whse, Macy's, Sears/auto, Target, Walmart, mall, **S** 🅿 Exxon/Subway, LukOil, Sunoco/dsl, 🍴 Dunkin Donuts, 🛏 Comfort Inn, Howard Johnson, Knight's Inn, Neshaminy Inn, Radisson, Red Roof Inn, Sunrise Inn, 🅾 Toyota/Scion
343	PA 611, Willow Grove, **N** 🅿 Shell, 🍴 Carrabba's, 🛏 Candlewood Suites (5mi), Courtyard, 🅾 🏨 **S** 🅿 Hess/dsl, Shell, Sunoco, 🍴 Bonefish Grill, China Garden, Domino's, Dunkin Donuts, Friendly's, McDonald's, Nino's Pizza, Ooka Japanese, Starbucks, Williamson Rest., 🛏 Hampton Inn, 🅾 Audi/Infiniti, Best Buy, PepBoys, 7-11, Staples, repair, transmissions
340	to VA Dr EZ tagholder only, no trucks, no return eb
339	PA 309, Ft Washington, **N** 🅿 Gulf, LukOil/dsl, 🍴 Dunkin Donuts, Friendly's, Subway, 🛏 Best Western, Hilton Garden, Holiday Inn, 🅾 BMW, Mercedes, Volvo, WaWa
334	PA Tpk NE Extension, I-476, **S** to Philadelphia, **N** to Allentown

PA

🅖 = gas 🍴 = food 🛏 = lodging 🅞 = other 🆁🆂 = rest stop   Copyright 2014 - The NEXT Exit ®

◆E	INTERSTATE 76 (TURNPIKE) CONT'D
Exit	**Services**
333	Germantown Pike, to Norristown, **N** 🅖 LukOil/dsl, Sunoco/Dunkin Donuts, 🍴 California Pizza Kitchen, Houlihan's, PF Chang's, Red Stone Grill, Starbucks, 🛏 Courtyard, DoubleTree, Extended Stay America, SpringHill Suites, 🅞 🅷, Boscov's, Macy's, **S** 🅖 LukOil
328mm	**King of Prussia Service Plaza wb** Sunoco/dsl/24hr, Breyer's, McDonald's
	PA Tpk runs eb as I-276, wb as I-76.
326	I-76 E, to US 202, I-476, Valley Forge, **N** 🅖 Shell, 🍴 Burger King, Cracker Barrel, Hooters, Hoss' Rest., 🛏 MainStay Suites, Radisson, Sleep Inn, **S** 🅖 Exxon, LukOil, Shell, Sunoco, WaWa, 🍴 CA Pizza Kitchen, Cheesecake Factory, Chili's, Denny's, Houlihan's, Lone Star Steaks, Maggiano's, McDonald's, Red Lobster, Ruth's Chris Steaks, Sullivan Steaks, 🛏 Best Western, Clarion, Comfort Inn, Hampton Inn, Holiday Inn Express, Motel 6, 🅞 Best Buy, Costco, Home Depot, JC Penney, Macy's, Neiman Marcus, Nordstrom, Sears/auto, Walmart, mall
325mm	**Valley Forge Service Plaza eb** 🅖 Sunoco/dsl/24hr, 🍴 Burger King, Starbucks
312	PA 100, to Downingtown, Pottstown, **N** 🅖 WaWa/dsl, 🅞 CarSense, Harley-Davidson, **S** 🅖 Sunoco/dsl, WaWa, 🍴 Applebee's, Chick-fil-A, Hoss's, Isaac's Deli, Red Robin, Starbucks, Uno Grill, 🛏 Comfort Suites, Extended Stay America, Fairfield Inn, Hampton Inn, Residence Inn, 🅞 🅷, Genuardi's Foods, Giant Foods, Walgreens
305mm	**Camiel Service Paza wb** Sunoco/dsl/24hr, Roy Rogers, Sbarro's, Starbucks
298	I-176, PA 10, to Reading, Morgantown, **N** 🍴 Arby's, DQ, Dunkin Donuts, Sonic, Subway, 🛏 Economy Lodge, Heritage Motel/rest., 🅞 🅷, $Tree, GNC, Lowe's, Verizon, Walmart, **S** 🅖 Exxon, Sheetz, 🍴 Heritage Rest., McDonald's, Rita's Custard, 🛏 Holiday Inn, 🅞 Chevrolet, Rite Aid
290mm	**Bowmansville Service Plaza eb** 🅖 Sunoco/dsl/24hr, 🍴 Burger King, Hershey's, Starbucks
286	US 322, PA 272, to Reading, Ephrata, **N** 🅖 Citgo/dsl, Turkey Hill, 🍴 Baskin-Robbins/Dunkin Donuts, Subway, 🛏 Black Horse Inn/rest., Comfort Inn, Red Carpet Inn, Red Roof Inn, 🅞 **S** 🛏 Hampton Inn (11mi)
266	PA 72, to Lebanon, Lancaster, **N** 🅖 Hess/Blimpie/dsl, Sunoco/Chester's, 🍴 Farmer's Hope Inn Rest., 🛏 Holiday Inn Express (17 mi), Penns Woods Inn, Red Carpet Inn, 🅞 🅷, Harley-Davidson, NAPA, auto repair, **S** 🍴 Hitz Mkt/deli, 🛏 Hampton Inn, 🅞 Mt Hope Winery, Pinch Pond Camping
259mm	**Lawn Service Plaza wb** 🅖 Sunoco/dsl/24hr, 🍴 Burger King, Starbucks, 🅞 RV dump
250mm	**Highspire Service Plaza eb** 🅖 Sunoco/dsl/24hr, 🍴 Hershey's Ice Cream, Sbarro's, Starbucks
247	I-283, PA 283, to Harrisburg, Harrisburg East, Hershey, **N** 🅖 Exxon/dsl, Sunoco, 🍴 Bob Evans, Capitol Diner, Eat'n Park, McDonald's, Taco Bell, Wendy's, 🛏 Best Western, Courtyard, Days Inn, EconoLodge, Holiday Inn Express, Howard Johnson, La Quinta, Red Roof Inn, Rodeway Inn, Sheraton, Super 8, Travelodge, Wingate Inn, Wyndham, 🅞 Harrisburg East Camping, JC Penney, Kia, Target
246mm	Susquehannah River
242	I-83, Harrisburg West, **N** 🅖 Shell/dsl, Hess/Dunkin Donuts, 🍴 Bob Evans, Doc Holliday's Rest., John's Diner,

242	Continued
	McDonald's, Pizza Hut, 🛏 Best Western, Comfort Inn, Fairfield Inn, Holiday Inn, Motel 6, Quality Inn, Rodeway Inn, Travel Inn, 🅞 vet, **S** 🛏 Days Inn, Keystone Inn
236	US 15, to Gettysburg, Gettysburg Pike, Harrisburg, **N** 🅖 Exxon, Gulf/dsl, 🍴 Isaac's Rest, McDonald's, Papa John's, Peppermill Rest., Subway, 🛏 Comort Inn, Country Inn&Suites, Courtyard, EconoLodge, Hampton Inn/rest., Holiday Inn, Homewood Suites, 🅞 🅷, U-Haul, vet, **S** 🅖 Sheetz, 🍴 Arby's, Burger King, Cracker Barrel, Quiznos, Wendy's, 🛏 Best Western, Wingate Inn, 🅞 Giant Food/gas, GNC, Rite Aid
226	US 11, to I-81, to Harrisburg, Carlisle, **N** 🅖 Gulf, Petro/Iron Skillet/dsl/scales/24hr/@, ⬧FLYING J/Denny's/dsl/LP/scales/24hr/@, ♥Love's/Wendy's/dsl/scales/24hr, Pioneer/dsl, Shell/dsl/scales, Sunoco/Subway/dsl, 🍴 Arby's, Bob Evans, Carelli's Subs, Country Club Diner, Dunkin Donuts, Embers Steaks, McDonald's, Middlesex Diner, Waffle House, 🛏 Best Inn, Best Value Inn, EconoLodge, Hampton Inn, Hotel Carlisle, Howard Johnson, Motel 6, Quality Inn, Residence Inn, Rodeway Inn, Super 8, Travelodge, 🅞 🅷, Blue Beacon, **S** 🅖 Rutter's/dsl, Sheetz, E85, 🍴 Hoss' Rest., 🛏 Best Western, Motel 6, 🅞 🅷, U-Haul, vet
219mm	**Plainfield Service Plaza eb** 🅖 Sunoco/dsl/24hr, 🍴 Hershey's Ice Cream, Roy Rogers, 🅞 gifts
203mm	**Blue Mtn Service Plaza wb** 🅖 Sunoco/dsl/24hr, 🍴 Hershy's Ice Cream, Nathan's, Roy Rogers, Uno
201	PA 997, to Shippensburg, Blue Mountain, **S** 🛏 Johnnie's Motel/rest., Kenmar Motel
199mm	Blue Mountain Tunnel
197mm	Kittatinny Tunnel
189	PA 75, Willow Hill, **S** 🛏 Willow Hill Motel/rest.
187mm	Tuscarora Tunnel
180	US 522, Mt Union, Ft Littleton, **N** 🅖 Gulf/dsl, Noname/dsl, 🍴 The Family Rest., 🛏 Downes Motel, 🅞 🅷, st police
172mm	Sideling Hill Service Plaza both lanes **S** 🅖 Sunoco/dsl, 🍴 Burger King, Famiglia Pizza, Hershey's Ice Cream, Popeye's, Starbucks, 🅞 gifts, RV dump
161	US 30, Breezewood, **Services on US 30** 🅖 Exxon/dsl, ⬧FLYING J/Perkins/dsl/scales/24hr, Sheetz/dsl, Shell/Dunkin Donuts/Subway/dsl, Sunoco/café/dsl, TA/Gateway Rest/dsl/scales/24hr/@, Valero/dsl, 🍴 Bob Evans, DQ, Denny's, Hardee's, McDonald's, Pizza Hut, Quiznos, Starbucks, Taco Bell, Wendy's, 🛏 Best Western, EconoLodge, Holiday Inn Express, Howard Johnson, Penn Aire Motel, Quality Inn, Village Motel, Wiltshire Motel, 🅞 Blue Beacon, Radio Shack, camping, museum, truck/auto repair
161mm	**I-70 W and I-76/PA Turnpike W run together**
148mm	**Midway Service Plaza both lanes** Sunoco/dsl/24hr, Hershey's Ice Cream, Quiznos, Sbarro's, Starbucks, gifts
146	I-99, US 220, Bedford, **N** 🅖 Gulf/dsl, PP/dsl, Sheetz/dsl/24hr, Shell/Subway/dsl, 🍴 Arena Rest., Bedford Diner, Carriage House Rest., Denny's, Ed's Steaks, Hoss' Rest., LJ Silver, McDonald's, Pizza Hut, Wendy's, 🛏 Best Value Inn, Best Western, Budget Host, Fairfield Inn, Hillcrest Motel, Quality Inn, Relax Inn, 🅞 to Shawnee SP (10mi), Blue Knob SP (15mi), **S** 🛏 Hampton Inn
123mm	Allegheny Tunnel
112mm	**Somerset Service Plaza both lanes** Sunoco/dsl/24hr, 🍴 Famiglia Pizza, Hershey's Ice Cream, Quiznos, Roy Rogers, Starbucks, 🅞 gifts

🅴 INTERSTATE 76 (TURNPIKE) CONT'D

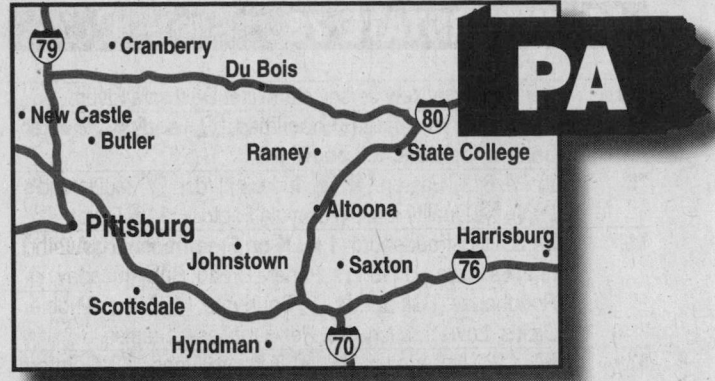

Exit	Services
110	PA 601, to US 219, Somerset, **N** 🅖 KwikFill/dsl, Sheetz, 🅕 Hog Father's BBQ, Hoss' Rest., King's Rest., Pizza Hut, 🅛 $Inn, Economy Inn, 🅞 Advance Parts, Chrysler/Jeep, Ford, tires, **S** 🅖 Somerset TravelCtr/dsl/@, Turkey Hill, 🅕 Arby's, Bruster's Ice Cream, DQ, Donut Connection, Eat'n Park, KFC, LJ Silver, Maggie Mae's Café, McDonald's, Pine Grill, Ruby Tuesday, Starbucks, Subway, Summit Diner, Wendy's, 🅛 Best Value Inn, Best Western, Budget Host, Budget Inn, Comfort Inn, Days Inn, Hampton Inn, Holiday Inn, Quality Inn, Super 8, 🅞 Dodge, Harley-Davidson, Volvo
91	PA 711, PA 31, to Ligonier, Donegal, **N** 🅕 Tall Cedars Rest., **S** 🅖 BP/McDonald's, Exxon/Subway/dsl, Sunoco/dsl, 🅕 DQ, 🅛 Days Inn, 🅞 camping, golf
78mm	**New Stanton Service Plaza wb** 🅖 Sunoco/dsl/24hr, 🅕 Burger King, Hershey's Ice Cream, Quiznos, Starbucks

I-70 E runs with I-76/PA Turnpike eb.

Exit	Services
75	I-70 W, US 119, PA 66 (**toll**), New Stanton, **S** 🅖 BP/7-11/dsl, Exxon, Sheetz, Sunoco, 🅕 Bob Evans, Campy's Pizza, Cracker Barrel, Eat'n Park, La Tavola Risorante, McDonald's, Pagano's Rest., Pizza Hut, Subway, Szechuan Wok, TJ's Rest., Wendy's, 🅛 Best Value Inn, Budget Inn, Comfort Inn, Days Inn, EconoLodge, Fairfield Inn, Howard Johnson, Super 8, 🅞 USPO
74.6mm	**Hemphill Service Plaza eb** 🅖 Sunoco/dsl/24hr, 🅕 Breyer's, McDonald's, 🅞 atm
67	US 30, to Greensburg, Irwin, **N** 🅖 BP/dsl, Sheetz/24hr, 🅞 🅗, Ford, tires, vet, **S** 🅖 Marathon/7-11, Sunoco/24hr, 🅕 Arby's, Bob Evans, Burger King, CiCi's Pizza, Denny's, DQ, Dunkin Donuts, Eat'n Park, KFC, LJ Silver, Los Campesinos Mexican, McDonald's, Panera Bread, Pizza Hut, Subway, Taco Bell, Teddy's Rest., Wendy's, 🅛 Conley Inn, Holiday Inn Express, 🅞 Advance Parts, Aldi Foods, CarQuest, $Tree, Giant Eagle Foods/24hr, GNC, Kohl's, Radio Shack, Rite Aid, Target
61mm	parking area eb
57	I-376, US 22, to Pittsburgh, Monroeville, **S** 🅖 Citgo/dsl, Exxon, Sheetz, Sunoco, 🅕 A&W/LJ Silver, Arby's, Baskin-Robbins, Bob Evan's, Chick-fil-A, China Palace, Chuck-eCheese, CiCi's Pizza, Damon's, Denny's, Golden Corral, Honeybaked Ham, Max&Erma's, McDonald's, Olive Garden, Outback Steaks, Panera Bread, Park Diner, Pizza Hut, Primanti Bro's, Quizno's, Red Lobster, Starbucks, Taco Bell, TGIFridays, Wendy's, 🅛 Comfort Suites, Courtyard, Day's Inn, Extended Stay America, Hampton Inn, Holiday Inn, Radisson Inn, Red Roof Inn, Springhill Suites, 🅞 🅗, Aamco, Big Lots, Firestone/auto, Honda, Jaguar/Land Rover, Jo-Ann Fabrics, Marshall's, Michael's, Lowes Whse, NTB, Office Depot, Old Navy, PetCo, Pet Land, Radio Shack, Rite Aid, to Three Rivers Stadium
49mm	**Oakmont Service Plaza eb** Sunoco/dsl/24hr, FoodCourt, 🅡🅢, litter barrels, 🅲
48.5mm	Allegheny River
48	PA 28, to Pittsburgh, Allegheny Valley, New Kensington, **N** 🅖 Shell/24hr, Sunoco, 🅕 Pizza Hut, Subway, 🅞 CarQuest, Rite Aid, **S** 🅖 Exxon/dsl, GetGo, 🅕 Bob Evans, Bruster's, Denny's, Gino Bro's Pizza, KFC, King's Rest., McDonald's, Ponderosa, Primanti Bro's, Subway, Taco Bell, Wendy's, 🅛 Comfort Inn, Day's Inn, Holiday Inn Express, Super 8, Valley Motel, 🅞 Advance Parts, Ford, Target

Exit	Services
41mm	parking area/call box eb
39	PA 8, to Pittsburgh, Butler Valley, 0-1 mi **N** 🅖 Exxon/7-11/dsl, GetGo, Sheetz/24hr, Sunoco, 🅕 Applebees, Atria's Rest., Bruno's Pizza, Buffalo Wild Wings, Eat'n Park, King's Rest., Max&Erma's, McDonald's, Sonic, Starbucks, Taco Bell, Wendy's, 🅛 Comfort Inn, Pittsburgh N Motel/rest, 🅞 Advance Parts, Curves, Dodge, $Tree, Giant Eagle Foods, GNC, Kohl's, Lowes Whse, Rite Aid, Shop'n Save Foods, Target, TJ Maxx, Walmart/auto/drugs, **S** 🅖 BP, Sunoco/dsl, 🅕 Arby's, Brusters, Burger King, China Bistro, KFC, McDonald's, Pasquales Pizza, Panera Bread, Pizza Hut, Subway, Vocelli Pizza, Wendy's, 🅞 🅗, AutoZone, Firestone/auto, Goodyear/auto, Home Depot, Mr. Tire, Radio Shack, Rite Aid, USPO
31mm	**Toll Plaza wb**
28	to I-79, to Cranberry, Pittsburgh, **N** 🅖 BP/dsl, Exxon/dsl/24hr, GetGo, Sheetz, Sunoco/dsl, 🅕 A&W/LJ Silver, Adrian's Pizza, Arby's, Bob Evans, Boston Mkt, Bravo Italian, Burger King, Chipotle Mexican, CiCi's Pizza, DQ, Denny's, Dominichi's Rest., Dunkin Donuts, Dynasty, Eat'n Park, 5 Guys Burgers, Hartner's Rest., HotDog Shoppe, Houlihan's, Ichiban Steakhouse, King's Rest., Krispy Kreme, LoneStar Steaks, Mad Mex, Max&Erma's, McDonald's, Montecello's Grill, Panera Bread, Perkins, Pizza Hut, Pizza Roma, Primanti Bros, Quaker Steak, Saga Steaks, Subway, UNO, Vocelli Pizza, Wendy's, 🅛 Comfort Inn, Fairfield Inn, Hampton Inn, Holiday Inn Express, Hyatt Place, Motel 6, Red Roof Inn, Residence Inn, Sheraton, Super 8, 🅞 Barnes&Noble, Best Buy, Costco/gas, Dick's, $Tree, GNC, Giant Eagle Foods, Home Depot, Jo-Ann Fabrics, Kuhn's Foods, Marshall's, Michael's, NAPA, Old Navy, PepBoys, PetCo, Radio Shack, Rite Aid, Toyota/Scion, Tuesday Morning, Walgreens, Walmart, mall, transmissions, USPO, vet
23.5mm	pulloff eb
22mm	**Zelienople Service Plaza eb Welcome Ctr**, 🅖 Sunoco/dsl/24hr, 🅕 FoodCourt, 🅞 crafts, gifts
17mm	parking area eb
13.4mm	parking area eb
13mm	Beaver River
13	PA 8, to Ellwood City, Beaver Valley, **N** 🅖 Al's Corner, 🅕 Subway, 🅛 Alpine Inn, Beaver Falls Motel, HillTop Motel, Holiday Inn, Lark Motel, 🅞 🅗, **S** 🅛 Super 8
10	PA 60 (**toll**), to New Castle, Pittsburgh, **S** services (6mi), to ✈
6mm	pulloff eb
2mm	pulloff eb
1mm	**toll plaza eb**, 🅲, call boxes located at 1 mi intervals
0mm	Pennsylvania/Ohio state line

Vertical text in margin: PITTSBURGH

Map labels: 79, Cranberry, Du Bois, New Castle, Butler, Ramey, 80, State College, Pittsburg, Altoona, Harrisburg, Johnstown, Saxton, 76, Scottsdale, Hyndman, 70

PA

Ⓖ = gas Ⓕ = food Ⓛ = lodging Ⓞ = other Ⓡˢ = rest stop Copyright 2014 - The NEXT Exit ®

▶Ｅ INTERSTATE 78

Exit	Services
77mm	Pennsylvania/New Jersey state line, Delaware River
76mm	**Welcome Ctr wb, full** Ⓗ **facilities,** Ⓒ, **vending,** Ⓟ, **litter barrels, petwalk, toll booth wb**
75	to PA 611, Easton, **N** Ⓖ TurkeyHill/dsl, Ⓕ McDonald's (1mi), Ⓛ Quality Inn, Ⓞ Crayola Factory, **S** Ⓖ Exxon
71	PA 33, to Stroudsburg, **1 mi N on Freemansburg Ave** Ⓕ Frank's Pizza, JJ Wong's, Panera Bread, Ruby Tuesday, TX Roadhouse, TGIFriday's, Ⓛ Courtyard, Ⓞ Barnes&Noble, Dick's, Lowe's, Michael's, Pet Supplies+, Staples
67	PA 412, Hellertown, **N** Ⓖ TurkeyHill/gas, Ⓛ Comfort Suites (3mi), Ⓕ Wendy's, Ⓞ Ⓗ, Chevrolet, **S** Ⓖ Citgo, Exxon/dsl, Lukoil, Sunoco, Ⓕ Antonio's Brick Oven, Rocco's Pizza, Rita's Shakes, Vassi's Drive-In, Waffle House, Ⓛ Holiday Inn Express, Ⓞ CVS Drug, Firestone, 7-11, repair
60b a	PA 145 N, PA 309 S, South Fort St, Quakertown
59	to PA 145 (from eb), Summit Lawn
58	Emaus St (from wb), **S** Ⓖ Gulf, Sunoco
57	Lehigh St, **N** Ⓖ Hess/dsl, WaWa, Ⓕ Arby's, Dragon Pond Chinese, IHOP, Palumbo Pizza, Queen City Diner, Subway, Willy Joe's Rest., Ⓛ Best Value Inn, Ⓞ BigLots, CVS Drug, $Tree, Family$, Ford/Lincoln, Home Depot, Kia, NSA Mkt, Radio Shack, Redner's Whse, STS Tires/repair, Toyota/Scion, VW, **S** Ⓖ Lukoil, Pipeline/dsl, Sunoco, TurkeyHill, Ⓕ Brass Rail Rest., Domino's, Dunkin Donuts, McDonald's, Papa John's, Perkins, Pizza Hut/Taco Bell, Rossi's Pizza, Starbucks, Subway, Wendy's, Ⓞ Acura, AT&T, Audi/Mercedes/Porsche, BonTon, Buick/GMC, Cadillac/Chevrolet, Chrysler/Dodge/Jeep, Honda, Hyundai, Mazda, PetCo, Staples, SteinMart, Verizon, Volvo
55	PA 29, Cedar Crest Blvd, **N** Ⓖ Shell, **S** Ⓗ
54b a	US 222, Hamilton Blvd, **N** Ⓖ Hess, Ⓕ Baskin-Robbins/Dunkin Donuts, Boston Mkt, Burger King, Cali Burrito, Carrabba's, Friendly's, Ice Cream World, King George Rest., Mango's Rest., McDonald's, Perkins, Subway, Teppan Steaks, TGIFriday's, Wendy's, Ⓛ Comfort Suites/rest., Holiday Inn Express, Howard Johnson, Ⓞ Dorney Funpark, Dorneyville Drug, Office Depot, Rite Aid, Weis Foods, **S** Ⓖ WaWa, Ⓕ Dunkin Donuts, Pizza Hut, Ⓛ Wingate Inn, Ⓞ Queen City Tire, Subaru, repair
53	PA 309 (wb only)
51	to I-476, US 22 E, PA 33 N (eb only), Whitehall
49b a	PA 100, Fogelsville, **N** Ⓕ Arby's, Cracker Barrel, Joe's Pizza, LJ Silver, Panda&Fish Chinese, Pizza Hut, Ⓛ Comfort Inn, Hawthorn Inn, Ⓞ KOA, Rite Aid, STS Tire/repair, **S** Ⓖ Shell, Sunoco, WaWa, Ⓕ Boston's Grill, Burger King, Florence Italian, Starlite Diner, Taco Bell, Yocco's Hotdogs, Ⓛ Hampton Inn, Hilton Garden, Holiday Inn, Sleep Inn, Staybridge Suites, Ⓞ Clover Hill Winery, Toyota/Scion, st police
45	PA 863, to Lynnport, **N** Ⓖ Exxon/Subway/dsl, Sunoco/New Smithville Diner/dsl, **S** Ⓛ Super 8
40	PA 737, Krumsville, **N** Ⓞ Pine Hill Campground, Robin Hill RV Park (4mi), **S** Ⓖ Shell/dsl, Ⓛ Skyview Rest.
35	PA 143, Lenhartsville, **3 mi S** Robin Hill Park
30	Hamburg, **S** Ⓕ Hamburg Mkt
29b a	PA 61, to Reading, Pottsville, **N** Ⓖ Shell/dsl, WaWa/dsl, Ⓕ Baskin-Robbins/Dunkin Donuts, Burger King, Campfire Rest., Cracker Barrel, JA Buffet, LJ Silver/Taco Bell, Logan's Roadhouse, McDonald's, Pappy T's, Pizza Hut, Red

Robin, Wendy's, Ⓛ Microtel, Ⓞ AT&T, Boat'n RV Ctr RV, Cabela's Outdoor, GNC, Harley-Davidson (8mi), Hyundai, Lowe's, Pet Supplies+, Toyota/Scion, Verizon, Walmart/Subway

23	Shartlesville, **N** Ⓖ ◆Loves/McDonald's/Subway/dsl/scales/24hr, Ⓛ Dutch Motel, Ⓞ Appalachian Campsites, **S** Ⓕ Blue Mtn Family Rest., Ⓛ Scottish Inn, Ⓞ Dutch Haus/gifts, antiques, camping, USPO
19	PA 183, Straussstown, **N** Ⓖ Lukoil, Ⓛ Sheepskin Motel, **S** Ⓖ Power/dsl
17	PA 419, Rehrersburg, **N** truck/tire repair
16	Midway, **N** Ⓖ Exxon/dsl, Sunoco/dsl, Ⓕ Midway Diner, Ⓛ Comfort Inn, **S** auto/truck repair
15	Grimes
13	PA 501, Bethel, **N** Ⓖ Shell/dsl, **S** Ⓖ Exxon/dsl, Ⓞ dsl repair
10	PA 645, Frystown, **S** Ⓖ Pilot/rest./dsl/scales/24hr/@, Gulf/dsl, Ⓛ Travel Inn
6	(8 from wb, US 22)PA 343, Fredricksburg, **1 mi S** Ⓖ PP/dsl, Redner's Whse/mkt, Ⓕ Esther's Rest., Ⓞ KOA (5mi)
1	I-81. **I-78 begins/ends on I-81, exit 89.**

▲Ｎ INTERSTATE 79

Exit	Services
183b a	PA 5, 12th St, Erie, **E** Ⓞ Ⓗ, Valley Tire, **W** Ⓖ Country Fair/dsl, Sunoco/dsl, Ⓕ Applebee's, Bob Evans, Dominos, Eat'n Park, El Canelo Mexican, 5 Guys, Hibachi Japanese, KFC, McDonald's, Panera Bread, Pizza Hut, Taco Bell, Taki Rest., Tim Hortons, Wendy's, Ⓛ Comfort Inn (2mi), Ⓞ Aamco, Advance Parts, Aldi Foods, BigLots, CVS Drug, $General, $Tree, Dunn Tire, Family$, Giant Eagle Foods, GNC, Monro, NAPA, Rite Aid, Save-a-Lot Foods, Tires-4-Less, Tuesday Morning, U-Haul, vet, to Presque Isle SP
182	US 20, 26th St, **E** Ⓖ Country Fair, KwikFill, Ⓕ Subway, Ⓞ Ⓗ, CVS Drug, Family$, Tops Foods/gas/24hr, **W** Ⓖ Country Fair, GetGo/dsl, Ⓕ Applebee's (2mi), Arby's, Burger King, DQ, Hong Kong Chinese, Hoss's Steaks, LJ Silver, McDonald's, Pizza Pete's, Subway, Tim Hortons, Ⓛ Glass House Inn, Ⓞ Urgent Care, AT&T, AutoZone, $General, Family$, Ford, Giant Eagle Foods, K-Mart/Little Caesar's, Meineke, Shack, TrueValue, Volvo, vet
180	US 19, to Kearsarge, **E** Ⓕ Aoyama Japanese, Arby's, Buffalo Wild Wings, Cheddars, Coldstone, Firebirds Grill, Fox&Hound, KFC, Max&Erma's, McDonald's, Moe's SW Grill, O'Charley's, Olive Garden, Outback Steaks, Red Lobster, Ruby Tuesday, Smokey Bones BBQ, Starbucks, Wendy's, Ⓛ Fairfield Inn, Homewood Suites, SpringHill Suites, TownePlace Suites, Ⓞ Ⓗ, Audi/Cadillac, Barnes&Noble, Bon-Ton, Chrysler/Dodge/Jeep, Dick's, Firestone/auto, Gander Mtn, JC Penney, Macy's, Michael's, Old Navy, PetCo, Ross, Sears/auto, TJ Maxx, Toyota/Scion, Verizon, mall, **W** Ⓖ Country Fair/dsl, Ⓞ camping
178b a	I-90, E to Buffalo, W to Cleveland
174	to McKean, **E** access to gas/dsl, **W** camping
166	US 6N, to Edinboro, **E** Ⓖ Country Fair/dsl, Sheetz, Ⓕ McDonald's (3mi), Perkins (2mi), Subway, Wendy's, Ⓛ Comfort Suites, Ⓞ Advance Parts, Verizon, Walmart, vet
163mm	Ⓡˢ **both lanes, full** Ⓗ **facilities,** Ⓒ, **vending,** Ⓟ, **litter barrels, petwalk**
154	PA 198, to Saegertown, Conneautville, **E** Erie NWR (17mi)
147b a	US 6, US 19, US 322, to Meadville, **E** Ⓖ All American

PA

ALLENTOWN (side tab)

ERIE (side tab)

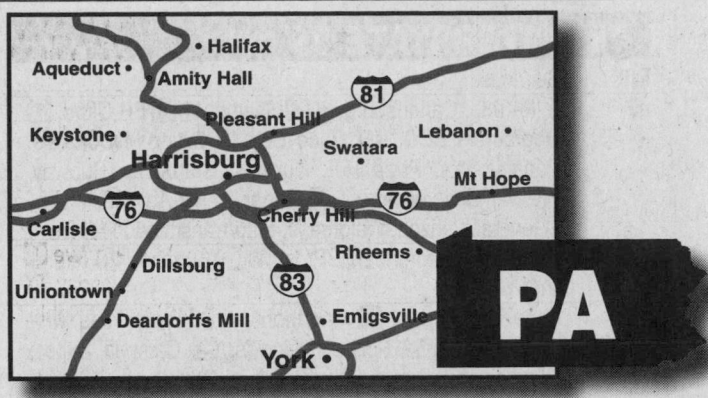

⬆N INTERSTATE 79 CONT'D

MEADVILLE

Exit	Services
147b a	Continued
	Gas/wash, Country Fair, GetGo, Sheetz/dsl, 🍴 Applebee's, Arby's, Chovy's Italian, Cracker Barrel, DQ, 5 Guys Burgers, Hoss's Rest., KFC, Perkins, Pizza Hut, Super Buffet, Taco Bell, 🛏 Days Inn/rest., EconoLodge, Holiday Inn Express, 🅾 🅷, Advance Parts, Eddie's Hotdogs, Family$, Giant Eagle Foods, Jo-Ann Fabrics, Home Depot, Radio Shack, Save-a-Lot Foods, W 🅶 Sheetz/dsl, 🍴 Burger King, Compadres Mexican, King's Rest., McDonald's, Red Lobster, Subway, Tim Hortons, Yuen's Garden, 🛏 Hampton Inn, Quality Inn, 🅾 Urgent Care, Aldi Foods, AutoZone, Buick/Cadillac/GMC, Chevrolet, $Tree, GNC, K-Mart, Staples, Toyota/Scion, Verizon, Walmart, to Pymatuning SP, st police, visitor info
141	PA 285, to Geneva, E to Erie NWR (20mi), W 🅶 Aunt Bee's Rest./dsl, Citgo/dsl
135mm	🆁🆂/weigh sta both lanes, full ♿ facilities, 🅲 vending, 🚮 litter barrels, petwalk
130	PA 358, to Sandy Lake, W 🅾 🅷 (13mi), to Goddard SP
121	US 62, to Mercer, E 🅾 Valley Tire, W 🅶 Sunoco/dsl, 🅾 st police
116b a	I-80, E to Clarion, W to Sharon
113	PA 208, PA 258, to Grove City, E 🅶 BP, Country Fair/dsl, 🍴 Compadres Mexican, 🅾 🅷, W 🅶 KwikFill/Subway, Sheetz/dsl, 🍴 Eat'n Park, Elephant&Castle Rest., Hoss' Rest., King's Rest., McDonald's, My Bro's Place, Primanti Bros, Taco Bell, Wendy's, 🛏 Best Western, Comfort Inn, Hampton Inn, Holiday Inn Express, Microtel, Super 8, 🅾 KOA (3mi), Premium Outlets/famous brands, tires
110mm	🆁🆂/weigh sta sb, full ♿ facilities, 🅲 vending, 🚮 litter barrels, petwalk
107mm	🆁🆂/weigh sta nb, full ♿ facilities, 🅲 vending, 🚮 litter barrels, petwalk
105	PA 108, to Slippery Rock, E 🍴 DQ, 🛏 Evening Star Motel, 🅾 Slippery Rock Camping, to Slippery Rock U
99	US 422, to New Castle, E to Moraine SP, W 🅶 📻/McDonald's/Subway/dsl/scales/24hr, 🅾 Coopers Lake Camping, to Rose Point Camping
96	PA 488, Portersville, E Bear Run Camping, Moraine SP, W 🍴 Brown's Country Kitchen, McConnell's Mill SP (3mi), gas/dsl
88	(87 from nb) US 19, PA 68, Zelienople, E 🍴 Log Cabin Inn Rest., W 🅶 BiLo/dsl, 🍴 Burger King, Pizza Hut
85	(83 from nb), PA 528 (no quick return), to Evans City, W 🅾 Buick
80mm	weigh sta both lanes
78	(76 from nb, exits left from nb), US 19, PA 228, to Mars, access to I-76, PA TPK, E 🅶 GetGo/dsl, Gulf/7-11/dsl, 🍴 Applebee's, Chick-fil-A, Coldstone, DiBella's Subs, Echo Rest., Jimmy Wan's Chinese, Longhorn Steaks, McDonald's, Moe's SW Grill, Noodles&Co, Olive Garden, On-the-Border, Red Robin, Smokey Bones BBQ, Starbucks, Subway, 🛏 Courtyard, Hilton Garden, Marriott, 🅾 🅷, AT&T, Dick's, GNC, Kohl's, Lowe's, Petsmart, Staples, Target, TJ Maxx, W on US 19 🅶 BP/dsl, GetGo, Marathon/dsl, Sheetz, Sunoco/dsl, 🍴 A&W/LJ Silver, Alladin's Eatery, Arby's, Bob Evans, Boston Mkt, Bravo Italian, Buffalo Wild Wings, Burger King, Chipotle Mexican, DQ, Denny's, Dunkin Donuts, Dynasty, Eat'n Park, Emiliano's Mexican, Firehouse Subs, 5 Guys Burgers, HotDog

CRANBERRY

PITTSBURGH

Exit	Services
78	Continued
	Shoppe, Houlihan's, Ichiban Steakhouse, Jimmy John's, LoneStar Steaks, Mad Mex, Max&Erma's, McDonald's, Monte Cello's Grill, Panera Bread, Perkins, Pizza Roma, Primanti Bros, Quaker Steak, Saga Steaks, Sports Grille, Subway, Wendy's, 🛏 Candlewood Suites, Comfort Inn, Fairfield Inn, Hampton Inn, Holiday Inn Express, Hyatt Place, Motel 6, Red Roof Inn, Residence Inn, Sheraton, Super 8, 🅾 AAA, AT&T, Autozone, Barnes&Noble, Best Buy, Costco/gas, $Tree, Firestone/auto, GNC, Giant Eagle Foods, Home Depot, Jo-Ann Fabrics, Kuhn's Foods, Marshall's, Michael's, NAPA, Old Navy, PepBoys, PetCo, Radio Shack, Rite Aid, Toyota/Scion, Tuesday Morning, Verizon, Walgreens, Walmart, mall, transmissions, USPO, vet
77	I-76/Tpk, to Youngstown
75	US 19 S (from nb), to Warrendale, services on US 19
73	PA 910, to Wexford, E 🅶 BP, 🍴 Eat'n Park, King's Family Rest., Starbucks, 🛏 EconoLodge, 🅾 W 🅶 Exxon/Subway/dsl, 🍴 Carmody's Rest.
72	I-279 S (from sb, exits left), to Pittsburgh
68	Mt Nebo Rd, E 🅶 Sheetz/dsl, W 🅷
66	to PA 65, Emsworth
65	to PA 51, Coraopolis, Neville Island, E 🍴 Kings Grille, 🛏 Fairfield Inn, 🅾 Penske Trucks, W 🍴 Subway
64.5mm	Ohio River
64	PA 51 (from nb), to Coraopolis McKees Rocks
60	PA 60, Crafton, E 🍴 King's Rest, Primanti Bros, 🛏 Comfort Inn, EconoLodge, Motel 6, Travelodge, 🅾 🅷, W 🍴 Juliano's Rest., 🅾 Meineke
59b	I-376 W, US 22 W, US 30 (from nb), W ✈
59a	I-376 E, to Pittsburgh
57	to Carnegie
55	PA 50, to Heidelberg, E on PA 50 🅶 BP, Marathon, Sunoco, 🍴 Arby's, Bob Evans, ChuckeCheese, Damon's, Eat'n Park, KFC, LJ Silver, McDonald's, Pizza Hut, Firestone/auto, Sonic, Starbucks, Taco Bell, TX Roadhouse, Wendy's, 🅾 BigLots, $Tree, Ford, Giant Eagle Foods, GNC, Home Depot, Jo-Ann Fabrics, K-Mart/Little Caesar's, Lowe's, Mr Tire, Pepboys, Radio Shack, Rite Aid, TJ Maxx, Walgreens, Walmart
54	PA 50, to Bridgeville, E 🅶 BP/dsl, Fuel Stop/dsl, GetGo, 🍴 King's Rest., McDonald's, 🛏 Holiday Inn Express, 🅾 🅷, Chevrolet, Midas, Monro, NAPA, Rite Aid, USPO, W 🅶 Sunoco/dsl, 🛏 Hampton Inn, Knights Inn
50mm	🆁🆂/weigh sta both lanes, full ♿ facilities, 🅲 vending, 🚮 litter barrels, petwalk
48	South Pointe, W 🍴 Jackson's Rest., 🛏 Hilton Garden, Homewood Suites

Ⓖ = gas　Ⓕ = food　Ⓛ = lodging　Ⓞ = other　Ⓡˢ = rest stop　Copyright 2014 - The NEXT Exit ®

⬆N INTERSTATE 79 CONT'D

Exit	Services
45	to PA 980, Canonsburg, E Ⓖ Sheetz, W Ⓖ BP, Citgo, Ⓕ Hogfathers BBQ, KFC/Taco Bell, LJ Silver, McDonald's, Papa John's, Pizza Hut, Quiznos, Starbucks, Subway, WaiWai Grill, Wendy's, Ⓛ Super 8, Ⓞ Advance Parts, $General, Verizon, Walgreens, auto/transmission repair
43	PA 519, Houston, E Ⓖ BP/dsl, W Ⓖ Sunoco, Ⓞ Freightliner
41	Race Track Rd, E Ⓖ Marathon/dsl, Ⓕ Buger King, McDonald's, Waffle House, Wendy's, Ⓛ Cambria Suites, Candlewood Suites, Comfort Inn, Country Inn&Suites, Courtyard, Doubletree, Hampton Inn, Holiday Inn, Ⓞ Audi, Old Navy, Tanger Outlets/famous brands, racetrack, W Ⓖ BP/dsl, Ⓛ Microtel, Ⓞ Trolley Museum
40	Meadow Lands, W Ⓞ Trolley Museum (3mi), golf, racetrack
38	I-70 W, to Wheeling
	I-79 and I-70 run together 3.5 mi. See Interstate 70, exits 19ba - 20.
34	I-70 E, to Greensburg
33	US 40, to Laboratory, W Ⓞ KOA
31mm	**weigh sta sb**
30	US 19, to Amity, W Ⓖ Exxon/Subway/dsl
23	to Marianna, Prosperity
19	US 19, to PA 221, Ruff Creek, W Ⓖ BP/dsl
14	PA 21, to Waynesburg, E Ⓖ BP, Ⓕ Bob Evans, Ⓛ Comfort Inn, Microtel, Ⓞ Walmart/Subway, W Ⓖ BP/7-11/dsl, Exxon/dsl, GetGo, Marathon, Sheetz, Sunoco, Ⓕ Burger King, DQ, Golden Wok, Hardee's, KFC, Little Caesars, McDonald's, Pizza Hut, Scotty's Pizza, Subway, Vocelli Pizza, Wendy's, Ⓛ EconoLodge, Hampton Inn, Super 8, Ⓞ Ⓗ, Ace Hardware, Advance Parts, Aldi Foods, AT&T, AutoZone, BigLots, Cadillac/Chevrolet/Subaru, Chrysler/Dodge/Jeep, CVS Drug, $General, $Tree, Giant Eagle Foods, Family$, Radio Shack, Rite Aid, Verizon, Walgreens, st police
7	to Kirby
6mm	**Welcome Ctr/weigh sta nb, full** Ⓗ **facilities,** Ⓒ, Ⓑ, **litter barrels, vending, petwalk**
1	Mount Morris, E Ⓖ Sunoco/Huddle House/dsl/scales /24hr, Ⓞ Honda/Mazda, W Ⓖ BFS/dsl, Ⓞ Mt Morris Campground
0mm	Pennsylvania/West Virginia state line

⬆E INTERSTATE 80

Exit	Services
311mm	Pennsylvania/New Jersey state line, Delaware River
310.5	**toll booth wb,** Ⓒ
310	PA 611, Delaware Water Gap, S **Welcome Ctr/**Ⓡˢ, **full services, info,** Ⓖ Fuel On, Gulf/repair, Ⓕ Doughboys Pizza, Village Farmer Bakery, Water Gap Diner
309	US 209 N, PA 447, to Marshalls Creek, N Ⓖ Exxon/dsl, Gulf, Ⓕ Blue Tequila Mexican, DQ, Dunkin Donuts, Landmark Cafe, Wendy's (2mi), Ⓛ Days Inn, ⓄⒽ
308	East Stroudsburg, N Ⓖ Exxon/Subs Now, Ⓞ Ⓗ, WaWa, vet, S Ⓕ JR's Grill, Ⓛ Budget Motel, Super 8, **1 mi** S Ⓕ Arby's, Burger King, CiCi's, Friendly's, Holy Guacamole, KFC, McDonald's, Ⓞ K-Mart, NAPA, Radio Shack, ShopRite Foods, Walmart/McDonald's
307	PA 191, Broad St, N Ⓛ Hampton Inn, Ⓞ Ⓗ, S Ⓖ Sunoco, Ⓕ Compton's Rest., Ⓛ Budget Host
306	Dreher Ave (from wb, no EZ return), N Ⓖ WaWa

Exit	Services
305	US 209, Main St, N Ⓖ Gulf, Shell, Ⓕ Perkins, Ⓛ Quality Inn, S Ⓖ Exxon/dsl
304	US 209, to PA 33, 9th St (from wb), same as 303
303	9th St, (from eb), N Ⓖ Ⓕ Burger King, Dunkin Donuts, 5 Guys Burgers, Fulay Chinese, Garfield's Rest., McDonald's, Olive Garden, Panera Bread, Pizza Hut, Popeye's, Ruby Tuesday, Starbucks, TX Roadhouse, Ⓞ Best Buy, Buick/GMC, Cadillac, Chevrolet, Chrysler/Dodge, CVS Drug, $Tree, JC Penney, Old Navy, Petsmart, Subaru, Walgreens, Weis Foods/gas
302	PA 611, to Bartonsville, N Ⓖ Exxon/dsl, Ⓕ Big Daddy's BBQ, Chili's, Dunkin Donuts, Frank's Pizza, Ichiban Steaks, Longhorn Steaks, Moe's SW Grill, Red Lobster, Red Robin, Sonic, Subway (2mi), Ⓛ Comfort Inn, Howard Johnson, Knights Inn, Ⓞ Advance Parts, AT&T, $Tree, Giant Foods/gas, Kohl's, Lowe's, Nissan, Peterbilt, Verizon
299	PA 715, Tannersville, N Ⓖ Chohan, Shell, Turkey Hill, Ⓕ Pocono Diner, Ⓛ Ramada Ltd, Ⓞ CVS Drug, The Crossing Factory Outlet/famous brands, Weis Foods, **1-4 mi** N Ⓕ Barley Creek Brewing, 5 Guys Burgers, Friendly's, Subway, Wendy's, Ⓞ camping, S Ⓖ Sunoco, Ⓕ Tannersville Diner, Ⓛ Days Inn, Summit Resort, Ⓞ to Camelback Ski Area, to Big Pocono SP
298	PA 611 (from wb), to Scotrun, N Ⓖ Sunoco/dsl, Ⓕ Brick Oven Pizza, Plaza Deli, Ⓛ Great Wolf Lodge, Scotrun Diner/motel, Ⓞ to Mt Pocono
295mm	Ⓡˢ **eb, full** Ⓗ **facilities,** Ⓒ, Ⓑ, **litter barrels, vending, petwalk**
293	I-380 N, to Scranton, (exits left from eb)
284	PA 115, to Wilkes-Barre, Blakeslee, N Ⓖ WaWa (1mi), Ⓛ Best Western, Blakeslee Inn (2mi), Ⓞ Fern Ridge Camping, st police, S Ⓖ Exxon/dsl, Ⓞ to Pocono Raceway
277	PA 940, to PA Tpk (I-476), to Pocono, Lake Harmony, Allentown, N Ⓖ WaWa, Ⓕ A&W/LJ Silver, Arby's, McDonald's, Ⓛ Comfort Inn, EconoLodge, Holiday Inn Express, Knights Inn, Mtn Laurel Resort, Pocono Inn/Resort, Split Rock Resort
274	PA 534, N Ⓖ Fuel On/Subs Now/dsl/24hr, Hickory Run/Valero/rest./dsl/scales/24hr, Ⓞ towing/repair, S Ⓞ to Hickory Run SP (6mi)
273mm	Lehigh River
273	PA 940, PA 437, to Freeland, White Haven, N Ⓖ Exxon, Fuel On, S Ⓕ Powerhouse Eatery, Ⓞ Sandy Valley Campground
270mm	Ⓡˢ **eb, full** Ⓗ **facilities, info,** Ⓒ, Ⓑ, **litter barrels, vending, petwalk**
262	PA 309, to Hazleton, Mountain Top, N Ⓖ Safari, Ⓕ Mary's Rest., Wendy's, Ⓛ EconoLodge, Ⓞ auto/truck repair, S Ⓛ Holiday Inn Express, Ⓞ Nescopeck SP (5mi)
260b a	I-81, N to Wilkes-Barre, S to Harrisburg
256	PA 93, to Nescopeck, Conyngham, N Ⓖ ▥▥▥/Subway/dsl/scales/24hr, Sunoco/repair, Ⓛ Lookout Motel, S Ⓕ Tom's Kitchen (2mi), Ⓛ Best Value Inn, Hampton Inn (4mi), Ⓞ Ⓗ, towing/truck repair
251mm	Nescopeck River
246mm	Ⓡˢ/**weigh sta both lanes, full** Ⓗ **facilities, weather info,** Ⓒ, Ⓑ, **litter barrels, vending, petwalk**
242	PA 339, to Mainville, Mifflinville, N Ⓖ Loves/Arby's/dsl/scales/24hr, Sunoco/Subway/dsl, Ⓕ McDonald's, Ⓛ Super 8, S Ⓖ Universal/dsl, Ⓛ Comfort Inn
241mm	Susquehanna River
241b a	US 11, to Berwick, Lime Ridge, Bloomsburg, N Ⓛ Red

🅴 INTERSTATE 80 CONT'D

Exit	Services
241b a	Continued Maple Inn (2mi), 🅞 🅷, S 🅖 Exxon, 🍴 Morris Rest., Taste of Italy, 🛏 Budget Host, **2-5 mi** S 🅖 Sheetz/dsl, 🍴 Applebee's, Arby's, Burger King, China Queen, Domino's, Dunkin Donuts, McDonald's, New China Buffet, Pizza Hut, Playa Cancun, Rita's Custard, Subway, Taco Bell, Terrapins Cantina, Wendy's, 🅞 Ace Hardware, Advance Parts, BigLots, Cadillac/Chevrolet, CVS Drug, $Tree, Ford/Honda, Giant Foods/gas, Kost Tire, Rite Aid, Staples, U-Haul, Weis Foods/gas
236	PA 487, to Bloomsburg, Lightstreet, S 🅖 Sunoco, 🍴 Denny's, 🛏 Hampton Inn, Tennytown Motel (2mi), Turkey Hill Inn, 🅞 🅷, to Bloomsburg U
232	PA 42, Buckhorn, **N** 🅖 Exxon, TA/Subway/dsl/scales/24hr/@, 🍴 Burger King, Cracker Barrel, KFC, Perkins, Quaker Steak&Lube, Ruby Tuesday, Wendy's, 🛏 EconoLodge, Holiday Inn Express, 🅞 AT&T, BonTon, Home Depot, JC Penney, Sears/auto, mall, S 🍴 Carini's Italian, Gourmet Buffet, Panera Bread, 🛏 Comfort Suites, 🅞 $Tree, Indian Head Camping (3mi), Lowe's, PetCo, Verizon, Walmart/McDonald's
224	PA 54, to Danville, **N** 🅖 Shell/Subway/dsl, 🛏 Quality Inn, **S** 🍴 Friendly's, McDonald's, Mom's Dutch Kitchen, 🛏 Best Western, Days Inn, Hampton Inn, Red Roof Inn, Super 8, 🅞 🅷
219mm	🆁🆂 both lanes, full ♿ facilities, info, 🅲, 🛢, litter barrels, vending, petwalk
215	PA 254, Limestonevill, **N** 🅖 Milton 32 Trkstp/rest./dsl/24hr, **S** 🅖 Penn 80/Shell/Subway/dsl/scales/24hr/@
212b a	I-180 W, PA 147 S, to Muncy, Williamsport, **S** 🅖 Sunoco (1mi)
210.5mm	Susquehanna River
210b a	US 15, to Williamsport, Lewisburg, **S** 🅖 Citgo, 🍴 Bonanza, 🛏 Comfort Inn, Holiday Inn Express, 🅞 🅷, KOA (5mi)
199	Mile Run
194mm	🆁🆂/weigh sta both lanes, full ♿ facilities, 🅲, 🛢, litter barrels, vending, petwalk
192	PA 880, to Jersey Shore, **N** 🅖 Citgo/dsl, 🍴 Pit-Stop Rest., **S** 🅖 Valero/dsl, 🅞 🅷, towing/truck repair
185	PA 477, Loganton, **N** 🅖 Valero, 🅞 camping, **S** 🍴 Twilight Diner, RB Winter SP (12mi)
178	US 220, Lock Haven, **5 mi N** 🅖 KwikFill/dsl, Sheetz, 🍴 Ruby Tuesday, Subway, 🅞 Advance Parts, K-Mart, Lowe's, Walmart
173	PA 64, Lamar, **N** 🅖 ▦/Subway/dsl/scales/24hr, 🍴 Cottage Rest., McDonald's, Perkins, 🛏 Comfort Inn/rest., Hampton Inn, **S** 🅖 Citgo, *FLYING J*/Denny's/dsl/LP/scales, TA/Country Pride/Subway/dsl/scales/24hr/@, 🍴 DQ, 🅞 auto repair
161	I-99, US 220 S, PA 26, to Bellafonte, **N** 🅞 KOA (2mi), **S** 🅞 to PSU
158	US 220 S, PA 150, to Altoona, Milesburg, **N** 🅖 Bestway/rest./dsl/motel/24hr/@, B&B Mkt/dsl, TA/dsl/scales/24hr/@, 🍴 Buckhorn Rest., McDonald's, Subway, 🛏 Quality Inn, **S** st police
147	PA 144, to Snow Shoe, **N** 🅖 Citgo/dsl/24hr, Exxon/dsl/repair/24hr, 🍴 Snow Shoe Sandwich Shop, Subway, 🅞 Hall's Foods, repair
146mm	🆁🆂 both lanes, full ♿ facilities, 🅲, 🛢, litter barrels, vending, petwalk

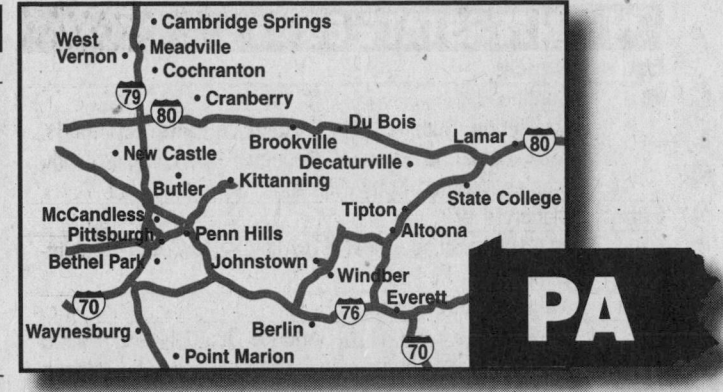

Exit	Services
138mm	Moshannon River
133	PA 53, to Philipsburg, Kylertown, **N** 🅖 KwikFill/motel/dsl/scales, Sunoco/dsl, 🍴 Roadhouse Rest., 🅞 USPO, dsl repair, Black Moshannon SP (9mi), **S** 🅞 🅷
123	PA 970, to Shawville, Woodland, **S** 🅞 Woodland Camping, **S** 🅖 Gio's BBQ/dsl (2mi), RP/dsl, 🅞 st police, USPO
120mm	Susquehanna River, W Branch
120	PA 879, Shawville, Clearfield, **N** 🅖 Sapp Bros/rest./dsl/scales/24hr/@, 🛏 Country Hearth Inn, **S** 🅖 BP, Sheetz, Snappy's, 🍴 Arby's, Burger King, Dunkin Donuts, Dutch Pantry, KFC/Taco Bell, McDonald's, 🛏 Comfort Inn, Days Inn, Hampton Inn, Holiday Inn Express, Super 8, 🅞 🅷, Lowe's, Walmart/Subway
111mm	highest point on I-80 east of Mississippi River, 2250 ft
111	PA 153, to Penfield, **N** to Parker Dam, to SB Elliot SP, **S** 🅷
101	PA 255, Du Bois, **N** 🅖 Snappy's/Quiznos/dsl, 🅞 camping, **S** 🅞 🅷, st police, **1-2 mi S** 🅖 Sheetz/dsl, 🍴 A&W/LJ Silver, Arby's, Burger King, Domino's, Eat'n Park, Italian Oven, KFC, McDonald's, Perkins, Pizza Hut, Ponderosa, Red Lobster, Ruby Tuesday, Subway, Taco Bell, Valley Dairy Rest., Wendy's, 🛏 Best Western, Hampton Inn, 🅞 Aldi Foods, BigLots, BonTon, CVS Drug, $General, $Tree, Hyundai, JC Penney, Jo-Ann Fabrics, K-Mart, Lowe's, Old Navy, PetCo, Radio Shack, Rite Aid, Ross, Sears/auto, Shop'n Save Foods, Staples, Walmart/Subway, mall
97	US 219, to Brockway, Du Bois, **S** 🅖 ▦/Arby's/dsl/scales/24hr, Sheetz/dsl/24hr, 🍴 Dutch Pantry Rest., 🛏 Clarion, Holiday Inn Express, 🅞 🅷, Freightliner, st police, **2 mi S** 🍴 Hoss' Rest., Pizza Hut, 🛏 Best Western, 🅞 Advance Parts
90	PA 830 E, **N** Du Bois Regional 🛩
87.5mm	🆁🆂 both lanes, full ♿ facilities, 🅲, 🛢, litter barrels, vending, petwalk
86	PA 830, to Reynoldsville
81	PA 28, to Brookville, Hazen, **S** Brookville, hist dist (2mi)
78	PA 36, to Sigel, Brookville, **N** 🅖 *FLYING J*/Denny's/dsl/LP/scales/24hr, TA/BP/Taco Bell/dsl/scales/Howard Johnson/24hr/@, 🍴 DQ, KFC, McDonald's, Pizza Hut, 🛏 Super 8, 🅞 NAPA, to Cook Forest SP, **S** 🅖 Country Fair, Sheetz, USA, 🍴 Arby's, Burger King, China Wok, Plyler's Buffet, Subway, 🛏 Budget Host, Quality Inn, Travelodge, 🅞 Chrysler/Dodge/Jeep, Family$
73	PA 949, Corsica, **N** 🅞 to Clear Creek SP, **S** USPO
70	US 322, to Strattanville
64	PA 66 S, to New Bethlehem, Clarion, **N** to Clarion U
62	PA 68, to Clarion, **N** 🅖 BP, KwikFill/dsl, 🍴 A&W/LJ Silver, Applebee's, Arby's, Eat'n Park, Hunan King, McDonald's, Perkins, Pizza Hut, RRR Roadhouse, Subway, Taco Bell, 🛏 Comfort Inn, Hampton Inn, Holiday Inn/rest., Microtel,

Vertical side labels: **DU BOIS**, **BROOKVILLE**, **LAMAR**

↑E INTERSTATE 80 CONT'D

Exit	Services
62	Continued
	Quality Inn, Super 8, 🅾 H, Advance Parts, Aldi Foods, AT&T, AutoZone, $Tree, JC Penney, K-Mart, Radio Shack, Staples, Walmart/Subway, mall
61mm	Clarion River
60	PA 66 N, to Shippenville, N 🍴 Jiffy, 🅾 to Cook Forest SP, camping
56mm	**weigh sta both lanes**
53	to PA 338, to Knox, N 📻 Satterlee Gas/dsl (cardlock), 🍴 BJ's Eatery, 🅾 Countryside Crafts/Quilts, Wolf's Camping Resort, S 🅾 Good Tire Service
45	PA 478, to St Petersburg, Emlenton, **4 mi S** 🅾 Golf Hall of Fame
44.5mm	Allegheny River
42	PA 38, to Emlenton, N 📻 Exxon/Subway/dsl, Roady's Trkstp/rest./dsl/scales/24hr, 🍴 Fat Chaps Rest., 🛏 Deluxe Motel, 🅾 Gaslight RV Park, truck/RV repair
35	PA 308, to Clintonville
30.5mm	🅿️ₛ **both lanes, full** ♿ **facilities,** 🚻, 🛏, **litter barrels, vending, petwalk**
29	PA 8, to Franklin, Barkeyville, N 🍴 Arby's, Burger King, King's Rest., 🛏 Comfort Inn, Motel 6, 🅾 Freightliner, S 📻 Citgo, KwikFill/dsl/scales/motel/24hr, TA/BP/Subway/dsl/scales/24hr/@, 🅾 truckwash, to Slippery Rock U
24	PA 173, to Grove City, Sandy Lake, S 🅾 H, Grove City Coll, Wendell August Forge/gifts (3mi), truck repair
19b a	I-79, N to Erie, S to Pittsburgh
15	US 19, to Mercer, N 📻 BP, PP/dsl, 🍴 Charlie B's Rest., Burger King, McDonald's/rv parking, 🛏 Comfort Inn, 🅾 st police, **2 mi S** 🍴 Iron Bridge Rest., 🅾 KOA (4mi)
4b a	I-376, PA 60, to PA 18, to Sharon-Hermitage, New Castle, N 📻 Sheetz, Sunoco/Subway/dsl, 🛏 EconoLodge, Holiday Inn Express, Quality Inn, Park Inn, Red Roof Inn, Super 8, S 🍴 DQ, MiddleSex Diner, 🅾 $General
2.5mm	Shenango River
1mm	**Welcome Ctr eb, full** ♿ **facilities,** 🚻, 🛏, **litter barrels, vending, petwalk**
0mm	Pennsylvania/Ohio state line

↑N INTERSTATE 81

Exit	Services
233mm	Pennsylvania/New York state line
232mm	**Welcome Ctr/weigh sta sb, full** ♿ **facilities,** 🚻, 🛏, **litter barrels, petwalk**
230	PA 171, Great Bend, E 📻 Valero, 🅾 Lakeside Camping (5mi), W 📻 Exxon/Tim Hortons/dsl, Sunoco/dsl, 🍴 Burger King, Dobb's Country Kitchen, Dunkin Donuts, Golden China, McDonald's, Subway, 🛏 Colonial Brick Motel, 🅾 Family$, Reddon's Drugs, Rob's Foods
223	PA 492, New Milford, E 🅾 East Lake Camping/RV Park (3mi), W 📻 Gulf/dsl, Sunoco, Valero, 🍴 Green Gables Rest., 🛏 Blue Ridge Motel, Lynn Lee B&B
219	PA 848, to Gibson, E 📻 Sunoco/dsl, W 📻 Exxon/McDonald's/dsl/24hr, ✈FLYING J/Denny's/dsl/scales/24hr, 🛏 Holiday Inn Express, st police
217	PA 547, Harford, E 📻 Exxon/Subway/dsl/24hr, Mobil/dsl/24hr
211	PA 92, Lenox, E Elk Mtn Ski Area, Shady Rest Camping (3mi), W 📻 Pump-N-Pantry/dsl, Shell/dsl, 🍴 Bingham's Rest., 🅾 Lenox Drug

Exit	Services
209mm	🅿️ₛ **sb, full** ♿ **facilities,** 🚻, 🛏, **litter barrel, vending, petwalk**
206	PA 374, to Glenwood, Lenoxville, E 📻 Sunoco/dsl, 🅾 to Elk Mountain Ski Resort
203mm	🅿️ₛ **nb, full** ♿ **facilities,** 🚻, 🛏, **litter barrels, vending, petwalk**
202	PA 107, to Fleetville, Tompkinsville
201	PA 438, East Benton, W 📻 Duchniks/dsl/repair, 🍴 B&B Rest
199	PA 524, Scott, E 📻 Delta/Eat'n Go Rest/dsl, Mobil/dsl, W 📻 Exxon/Subway, 🛏 Motel 81, 🅾 to Lackawanna SP
197	PA 632, Waverly, E 🅾 Rite Aid, Weis Foods, W 📻 Sunoco/Doc's Deli, 🛏 Camelot Inn/rest
194	US 6, US 11, to I-476/PA Tpk, Clarks Summit, W 📻 Exxon/dsl, Sheetz/dsl, Sunoco/dsl, 🍴 Burger King, Damon's, Dino&Francesco's, Domino's, Dunkin Donuts, Gourmet Rest., Hibachi Steaks, Krispy Kreme, Kyoto, La Tonalteca, McDonald's, Moe's SW Grill, New Century Chinese, Pizza Hut, Starbucks, Taco Bell, Waffle House, Wendy's, 🛏 Comfort Inn, EconoLodge, Hampton Inn, Nichols Village Inn, Ramada Inn, 🅾 Ace Hardware, Advance Parts, Kost Tire, Monro, Radio Shack, Rite Aid
191b a	US 6, US 11, to Carbondale, E 📻 Sheetz/dsl, Sunoco, 🍴 A&W/LJ Silver, Applebee's, Burger King, China Palace, ChuckECheese, Denny's, Dunkin Donuts, Eastern Buffet, 5 Guys Burgers, HoneyBaked Ham, La Tonalateca, Masaru Japanese, McDonald's, Old Country Buffet, Olive Garden, Panera Bread, Perkins, Quaker Steak&Lube, Red Lobster, Red Robin, Rita's Custard, Royal Buffet, Ruby Tuesday, Starbucks, Subway, TCBY, TX Roadhouse, TGIFriday's, Uno Grill, Viewmont Diner, 🛏 Days Inn, Holiday Inn Express, 🅾 Aldi Foods, AT&T, Books-A-Million, Dick's, $Tree, Firestone/auto, Harley-Davidson, Hobby Lobby, Home Depot, Hyundai, JC Penney, Jo-Ann Crafts, K-Mart, Kohl's, Macy's, Marshall's, Michael's, Old Navy, PepBoys, Petsmart, Rite Aid, Sears/auto, Target, TJ Maxx, Verizon, Walmart, William's Tires, mall, W 🅾 to Anthracite Museum
190	Main Ave, Dickson City, E 🍴 Teppanyaki Buffet, Wendy's, 🛏 Fairfield Inn, Microtel, Residence Inn, 🅾 Best Buy, Gander Mtn, Lowe's, Sam's Club/gas, Staples, auto repair, vet, W 🅾 Schiff's Foods, Toyota/Scion
188	PA 347, Throop, E 📻 Sheetz, Sunoco/dsl, 🍴 China Buffet, McDonald's, Wendy's, 🛏 Dunmore Inn, Quality Inn, Scottish Inn, Sleep Inn, 🅾 Advance Parts, BigLots, Kost Tire, Monro, PriceChopper Foods, st police, Urgent Care, W 📻 Exxon/Subway/dsl, 🍴 Burger King, Dunkin Donuts, Friendly's
187	to I-84, I-380, US 6 (no return from nb)
186	PA 435, Drinker St (from nb), E 📻 Valero/dsl, 🛏 Best Western, W 📻 Exxon
185	Central Scranton Expwy (exits left from nb), W H
184	to PA 307, River St, W 📻 Exxon/Subway/dsl, Valero, Vamco, 🍴 Dunkin Donuts, House of China, 🛏 Clarion, 🅾 H, CVS Drug, $Tree, Gerrity Foods
182	Davis St; Montage Mtn Rd, E 📻 Exxon/Coldstone/Subway/dsl, 🍴 Doc's Oyster House, Johnny Rockets Cafe, Longhorn Steaks, Panchero's Mexican, Panera Bread, Quiznos, Ruby Tuesday, Starbucks, 🛏 Comfort Suites, Courtyard, Hampton Inn, Springhill Suites, TownePlace Suites, 🅾 AT&T, GNC, W 📻 Sunoco, 🍴 Dunkin Donuts, Waffle House, Wendy's, 🛏 EconoLodge, 🅾 CVS Drug, USPO

C L A R I O N

PA

S C R A N T O N

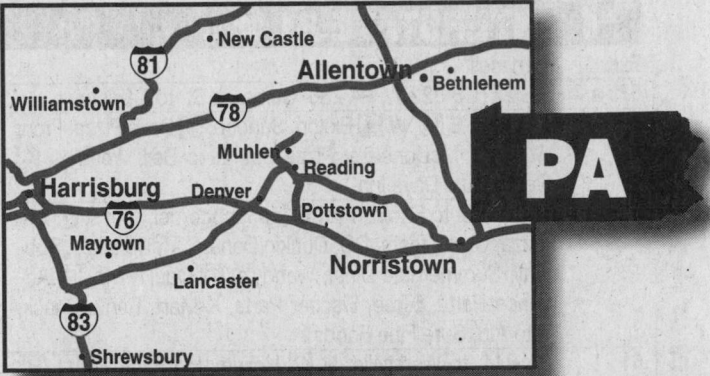

INTERSTATE 81 CONT'D

Exit	Services
180	to US 11, PA 502, to Moosic, (exits left from nb), **W on US 11** 🅖 Exxon, Sunoco, 🍴 McDonalds, Subway, 🛏 Rodeway Inn
178b a	to US 11, Avoca, **E** 🛏 Holiday Inn Express, **W** 🅖 Petro/Valero/Iron Skillet/dsl/scales/24hr/@
175b a	PA 315 S, to I-476, Dupont, **E** 🅖 Exxon/Subway/dsl, Sunoco, 🍴 Arby's, McDonald's, Perkins, 🛏 Knights Inn, Super 8, 🅾 Volvo, **W** 🅖 🚛/Wendy's/dsl/scales/24hr, 🍴 🛏 Best Value, 🅾 Walmart/Subway, truck repair
170b a	PA 115, PA 309, Wilkes-Barre, **E** 🅖 Exxon/Subway/dsl, Sunoco/dsl, 🛏 Best Western, 🅾 to Pocono Downs, **W** 🅖 Citgo, Sunoco/dsl, 🍴 Burger King, Denny's, Friendly's, LJ Silver, Lonestar Steaks, McDonald's, Pizza Hut, Red Lobster, Sonic, TGIFriday's, Wendy's, 🛏 Days Inn, Extended Stay America, Fairfield Inn, Holiday Inn Express, Quality Inn, Red Roof Inn, 🅾 🏥, BonTon, Chevrolet, $General, Harley-Davidson, JC Penney, Goodyear, Macy's, Sears/auto, mall
168	Highland Park Blvd, Wilkes-Barre, **W** 🅖 Sheetz, Sunoco, TurkeyHill, 🍴 Applebee's, Arby's, Bob Evans, Chili's, ChuckeCheese, Cracker Barrel, King's Buffet, La Tolteca Mexican, Logan's Roadhouse, Lucky's SportHouse, Olive Garden, Outback Steaks, Panera Bread, Red Robin, Smokey Bones BBQ, Subway, Starbucks, Wendy's, 🛏 Hampton Inn, Hilton Garden, 🅾 Urgent Care, AT&T, Barnes&Noble, Best Buy, Dick's, Firestone/auto, Kohl's, Kost Tire, Lowe's, Marshall's, Michael's, Nissan, Old Navy, PepBoys, PetCo, Petsmart, PriceChopper, Radio Shack, Ross, Sam's Club/gas, Staples, Target, TJ Maxx, U-Haul, Verizon, Walgreens, Walmart, Wegman's Foods
165b a	PA 309 S, (exits left from nb), Wilkes-Barre, **W** 🅖 Citgo/dsl, Gulf, 🍴 Dunkin Donuts, McDonald's, Perkins, Taco Bell, 🛏 Comfort Inn, EconoLodge, 🅾 Advance Parts, $Tree, K-Mart
164	PA 29, to Nanticoke, Ashley
159	Nuangola, **W** 🅖 UniMart, 🅾 camping (10mi)
157mm	🆁🆂/weigh sta sb, full ♿ facilities, vending, 🅒, 🏓, litter barrels, petwalk
156mm	🆁🆂/weigh sta nb, full ♿ facilities, vending, 🅒, 🏓, litter barrels, petwalk
155	to Dorrance, **E** 🅖 Sunoco/dsl, 🛏 EconoLodge (2mi), **W** 🅖 Blue Ridge Plaza/dsl
151b a	I-80, E to Mountaintop, W to Bloomsburg
145	PA 93, W Hazleton, **E** 🅖 Sunoco/dsl, TurkeyHill/dsl, 🍴 Arby's, Bonanza, Damon's, 5 Stars Chinese, Friendly's, LJ Silver, McDonald's, Perkins, Pizza Hut, Taco Bell, Wendy's, 🛏 Best Western (2mi), Comfort Inn, Fairfield Inn, Forest Hill Inn, Ramada Inn (2mi), 🅾 🏥, Aldi Foods, Buick/Cadillac/GMC, Chrysler, $Tree, JC Penney, K-Mart, Mazda, Old Navy, Radio Shack, Staples, st police, **W** 🍴 Shell, Top of the 80's, 🛏 Candlewood Suites, Hampton Inn
143	PA 924, to Hazleton, **W** 🅖 Fuelon/Subs Now/dsl, Shell/Subway, TurkeyHill/dsl, 🍴 Burger King, Sonic, 🛏 Residence Inn
141	PA 424, S Hazleton Beltway, **E** 🛏 Mt Laurel Motel
138	PA 309, to McAdoo, **2 mi E** 🛏 Pines Motel
134	to Delano
132mm	parking area/weigh sta both lanes
131b a	PA 54, Mahanoy City, **E** 🅾 to Tuscarora/Locust Lake SP, **W** 🅖 Shell/dsl, Sunoco/dsl

Exit	Services
124b a	PA 61, to Frackville, **E** 🍴 Cracker Barrel, McDonald's, 🛏 Holiday Inn Express, 🅾 BigLots, BonTon, K-Mart, Sears/auto, mall, **W** 🅖 Exxon, Gulf, Hess, 🍴 Anthony's Pizza, Dutch Kitchen, Subway, 🛏 EconoLodge, Granny's Motel, Rodeway Inn, 🅾 🏥, Rite Aid, st police
119	High Ridge Park Rd, to Gordon, **E** 🛏 Country Inn&Suites, 🅾 🏥
116	PA 901, to Minersville, **E** 🍴 901 Rest.
112	PA 25, to Hegins, **W** 🅾 camping
107	US 209, to Tremont
104	PA 125, Ravine, **E** 🅖 Exxon/Burger King/dsl/scales/24hr, 🅾 Echo Valley Campground
100	PA 443, to Pine Grove, **E** 🅖 Exxon/dsl, 🍴 Arby's, McDonald's, 🛏 Comfort Inn, EconoLodge, 🅾 $General, **W** 🅖 🚛/DQ/Subway/dsl/scales/24hr, 🍴 Gooseberry Farms Diner, 🛏 Hampton Inn, 🅾 KOA (5mi), truckwash
90	PA 72, to Lebanon, **E** 🅖 Exxon/Subway, Hess/Blimpie/Dunkin Donuts/dsl, Loves/McDonald's/dsl/scales/24hr, 🍴 DQ, Sbarro's, Wendy's, 🛏 Best Western, Days Inn, 🅾 KOA, repair, st police, **W** 🛏 Quality Inn
89	I-78 E, to Allentown
85b a	PA 934, to Annville, **2 mi W** 🅖 Exxon/dsl, 🍴 Funck's Rest., 🅾 to IndianTown Gap Nat Cem
80	PA 743, Grantville, **E** 🅖 Shell/dsl, 🛏 Days Inn, Hampton Inn, **W** 🅖 Exxon/dsl, 🍴 Italian Delight, 🛏 Comfort Suites, Holiday Inn, 🅾 camping, racetrack
79mm	🆁🆂/weigh sta both lanes, full ♿ facilities, 🅒, vending, 🏓, litter barrels, petwalk
77	PA 39, to Hershey, **E** 🅖 Exxon/dsl, 🚛/Pizza Hut/dsl/scales/24hr, Valero/dsl, 🍴 Hershey Rd Rest., 🛏 Country Inn&Suites, EconoLodge, La Quinta, Motel 6, Scottish Inn, 🅾 to Hershey Attractions, st police, **W** 🅖 Exit 77 TP/dsl, TA/Country Pride/dsl/scales/24hr/@, Wilco/Hess/Perkins/Stuckey's/dsl/24hr/@, 🍴 McDonald's, 🛏 Holiday Inn Express, 🅾 Goodyear, SpeedCo
72	to US 22, Linglestown, **E** 🅖 Hess/dsl, Sheetz, Sunoco/dsl, 🍴 Bro Joe's Pizza, Burger King, Chipotle Mexican, 5 Guys Burgers, McDonald's, Red Robin, Starbucks, Subway, Tonino's Pizza, 🛏 Comfort Inn, Quality Inn, 🅾 Advance Parts, Chrysler/Dodge/Jeep, Costco/gas, CVS Drug, Giant Foods, Harley-Davidson, Karn's Foods, Target, Toyota/Scion, U-Haul, **W** 🍴 Mikado Japanese, Mtn Rd Diner, 🛏 Candlewood Suites, Ramada Inn
70	I-83 S, to York 🔄
69	Progress Ave, **E** 🍴 Cracker Barrel, Fox&Hound, Macaroni Grill, Starbucks, Tonino's Grill, 🛏 Hampton Inn, 🅾 AT&T, CVS Drug, Susquehanna Shoppes, st police, **W** 🅖 Turkey Hill/dsl, 🍴 Arby's, YP Rest., 🛏 EconoLodge, Red Roof Inn, SpringHill Suites

PA

▶N INTERSTATE 81 CONT'D

Exit	Services
67b a	US 22, US 322 W, PA 230, Cameron St, to Lewistown
66	Front St, **E** 🍴, **W** 🅖 Exxon, Sunoco, 🍴 Bro's Pizza, Front St Diner, McDonald's, Pizza Hut, Taco Bell, Wendy's, 🛏 Best Value, Days Inn
65	US 11/15, to Enola, **1 mi E** 🅖 Sunoco/dsl, Tom's, 🍴 Al's Pizza, China Taste, DQ, Dunkin Donuts, McDonald's, Subway, Summerdale Diner, Wendy's, 🛏 Quality Inn, 🅞 Advance Parts, $Tree, Fischer Parts, K-Mart, Radio Shack, Rite Aid, Sure Fine Foods
61	PA 944, to Wertzville, **E** 🛏 Holiday Inn Express, 🅞 🍴, Weiss Mkt, **W** 🅖 Turkey Hill/dsl, 🛏 Microtel
59	PA 581, to US 11, to I-83, Harrisburg, **3 mi E on Carlisle Pk E** 🅖 Sunoco, 🍴 Bob Evans, Burger King, Carrabba's, Dunkin Donuts, Denny's, McDonald's, Outback Steaks, TGIFriday's, 🛏 Comfort Inn, Park Inn, 🅞 AutoZone, Buick/GMC, Dick's, GNC, Home Depot, Hyundai, K-Mart, Lowe's, Nissan, Pepboys, Petsmart, Radio Shack, Staples, TJ Maxx
57	PA 114, to Mechanicsburg, **2 mi E** 🅖 Sheetz/dsl, 🍴 Alfredo's Pizza, Arby's, Great Wall Chinese, Isaac's Rest., KFC/LJ Silver, McDonald's, Olive Garden, Pizza Hut, Red Robin, Silver Spring Diner, Subway, Taco Bell, 🛏 Ramada Ltd, 🅞 Giant Foods/gas, Marshall's, Verizon, Walmart
52b a	US 11, to I-76/PA Tpk, Middlesex, **E** 🅖 FLYING J/Denny's/dsl/scales/24hr/@, 🍴 Bob Evans, Dunkin Donuts, Ember's Steaks, Middlesex Diner, 🛏 Best Value Inn, Days Inn, Hotel Carlisle, Red Roof Inn, Super 8, 🅞 🍴, **W** 🅖 Gulf, Love's/Wendy's/dsl/24hr, Petro/dsl/24hr/@, Sunoco/Subway, 🍴 Arby's, Carelli's Subs, McDonald's, Rte 11 Diner, Waffle House, 🛏 Best Western, EconoLodge, Hampton Inn, Holiday Inn Express, Howard Johnson, Motel 6, Quality Inn, Residence Inn, Rodeway Inn, Travelodge, 🅞 🍴, Blue Beacon, truckwash
49	PA 74 (no EZ sb return), **E** 🅖 Sheetz, same as 48, **W** 🅖 Citgo, 🍴 Trindle Grill, 🅞 AAA
48	PA 74, York Rd (no EZ nb return), **E** 🍴 Red Robin, Starbucks, Subway, 🅞 Aldi Foods, $Tree, Kohl's, Michael's, Old Navy, Petsmart, Rite Aid, Target, Verizon, **W** 🅖 Gulf/dsl, Hess, 🍴 Burger King, Little Caesars, Mama Sprigg's Rest., McDonald's, Pizza Hut, Taco Bell, 🅞 BonTon, CVS Drug, Dunkin Donuts, Ford, Lowe's, Midas, Radio Shack, Weis Foods
47	PA 34, Hanover St, **E** 🍴 Chili's, Cracker Barrel, 🛏 Sleep Inn, 🅞 Home Depot, **W** 🍴 Applebee's, Bruster's/Nathan's, DQ, Palace China, Panera Bread, Papa John's, Rita's Custard, Subway, Super Buffet, Vinny's Rest, Wendy's, 🅞 AT&T, CVS Drug, Rite Aid, Ross, Staples, TJ Maxx, Walmart
45	College St, **E** 🅖 Gulf/dsl, 🍴 Alfredo Pizza, Arby's, Bonanza, Great Wall Buffet, McDonald's, Subway, 🛏 Days Inn, Super 8, 🅞 🍴, K-Mart, Nell's Foods, Tire Pros, Verizon
44	PA 465, Allen Rd, to Plainfield, **E** 🛏 Country Inn&Suites, Fairfield Inn, 🅞 st police, **W** 🅖 Sheetz, 🍴 Subway
38.5mm	🆁🆂 **both lanes, full** ♿ **facilities,** 🍴, 🛏, **litter barrels, petwalk**
37	PA 233, to Newville, **E** Pine Grove Furnace SP, **W** Col Denning SP
29	PA 174, King St, **E** 🅖 Sunoco/dsl, 🛏 Rodeway Inn, **W** 🅖 Gulf, Rutter's/dsl, 🍴 Bro's Pizza, Burger King, China House, Domino's, KFC, Subway, Taco Bell, Wendy's, 🛏

Exit	Services
29	Continued Best Western, Theo's Motel, 🅞 Advance Parts, Cadillac/Chevrolet, CVS Drug, $General, Ford, Lowe's, Verizon, Walmart, vet
24	PA 696, Fayette St, **W** 🅖 Pacific Pride
20	PA 997, Scotland, **E** 🅖 Citgo/dsl, 🍴 Bonanza, McDonald's, 🛏 Comfort Inn, Super 8, 🅞 BonTon, Gander Mtn, JC Penney, Sears/auto, mall, **W** 🅖 Sunoco, 🛏 Sleep Inn
17	Walker Rd, **W** 🅖 Sheetz, 🍴 Aki Steaks, Bruster's/Nathan's, Chipotle Mexican, Fuddrucker's, Longhorn Steaks, Moe's SW Grill, Olive Garden, Panera Bread, Pizza Boxx, Red Robin, Sonic, Subway, TGIFriday's, TX Roadhouse, 🛏 Candlewood Suites, Country Inn&Suites, 🅞 AT&T, Buick/Chevrolet/GMC, Ford, Giant Foods/gas, Kohl's, Michael's, Petsmart, Staples, Target, Verizon
16	US 30, to Chambersburg, **E** 🅖 Fuel Ctr, Sheetz, 🍴 Arby's, Benny's Italian, Broadway Deli, Bro's Pizza, Burger King, Chris' Country Kitchen, Hoss's Rest., KFC, Little Caesars, Meadow's Custard, Montezuma Mexican, Perkins, Popeye's, Rita's Custard, Ryan's, Supreme Buffet, Waffle House, Wendy's, 🛏 Days Inn, 🅞 AAA, Aldi Foods, AT&T, Curves, $Tree, Harley-Davidson, Hobby Lobby, Jo-Ann Fabrics, Lowe's, Midas, NAPA, Nissan/Toyota/Scion, U-Haul, Verizon, Walmart/Subway, st police, transmissions, vet, **W** 🅖 Hess/dsl, 🍴 Big Oak Cafe, Burger King, Chambersburg Diner, Copper Kettle, Hardee's, LJ Silver, McDonald's, Pat&Carla Italian, Ruby Tuesday, Starbucks, Subway, Taco Bell, 🛏 Best Western, La Quinta, Sheraton, Travelodge, 🅞 🍴, **Urgent Care**, Advance Parts, AutoZone, Lincoln, Walgreens
14	PA 316, Wayne Ave, **E** 🅖 Sheetz/dsl, 🍴 Bob Evans, Cracker Barrel, 🛏 Fairfield Inn, Hampton Inn, Red Carpet Inn, **W** 🅖 KwikFill, Sheetz, Shell, 🍴 Applebee's, Arby's, China Buffet, China Wok, Denny's, Mario's Italian, Montezuma Mexican, Papa John's, Red Lobster, SteviB's Pizza, Subway, Twin Dragon Chinese, Wendy's; 🛏 Best Value, Holiday Inn Express, Quality Inn, 🅞 AT&T, CVS Drug, $Tree, Giant Foods/gas, GNC, K-Mart, Mr Tire, Save-a-Lot Foods, Verizon, Weis Foods
12mm	**weigh sta sb**
10	PA 914, Marion
7mm	**weigh sta nb**
5	PA 16, Greencastle, **E** 🅖 Shell/dsl, Sunoco/dsl, TA/Country Pride/dsl/scales/24hr/@, Sunoco/grill/dsl, 🍴 Arby's, McDonald's, Subway, 🛏 Star Inn, TA Motel, 🅞 Whitetail Ski Resort, **W** 🅖 Exxon/dsl, Sheetz/dsl, 🛏 Castle Green Motel/rest
3	US 11, **E** 🅖 Sunoco/dsl, 🍴 Bro's Pizza, 🛏 Comfort Inn, 🅞 Goodyear/auto
2mm	**Welcome Ctr nb, full** ♿ **facilities,** 🍴, 🛏, **litter barrels, vending, petwalk**
1	PA 163, Mason-Dixon Rd, **W** 🛏 Stateline Inn, Stateline Motel, 🅞 Keystone RV Ctr
0mm	Pennsylvania/Maryland state line, Mason-Dixon Line

▶N INTERSTATE 83

Exit	Services
51b a	**I-83 begins/ends on I-81, exit 70.**
50b a	US 22, Jonestown Rd, Harrisburg, **E** 🅖 Hess/dsl, Sunoco/dsl, USA, 🍴 Applebee's, Arby's, Atlanta Bread, Chipotle Mexican, Cold Stone, Colonial Park Diner, Domino's, El Rodeo Mexican, 5 Guys Burgers, Gilligan's Grill, Grand Buffet, LJ Silver, McDonald's, Old Country Buffet, Olive

HARRISBURG

CARLISLE

CHAMBERSBURG

PA

N INTERSTATE 83 CONT'D

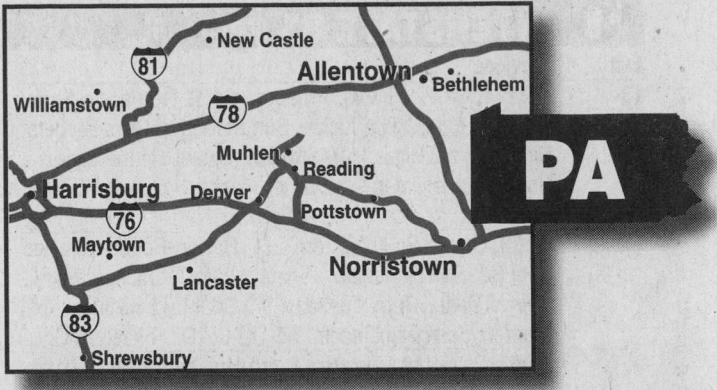

HARRISBURG

Exit	Services
50b a	Continued Garden, Pizza Hut, Red Lobster, Red Robin, Starbucks, Subway, Taco Bell, Tonino's Pizza, Wendy's, 🅞 Aamco, Advance Parts, Best Buy, BonTon, Boscov's, Coscto/gas, CVS Drug, Dick's, Ford, Gander Mtn, Giant Foods, Goodyear/auto, Home Depot, K-Mart, Kohl's, Marshall's, Michael's, NAPA, NTB, Old Navy, PepBoys, PetCo, Radio Shack, Ross, Sears/auto, Super Petz, Target, Tires+, U-Haul, Verizon, Weis Foods, William's Tires/repair, mall, **Urgent Care**, W 🅖 Capital, 🍴 DQ, Dunkin Donuts, Friendly's, Gabriella's Italian, KFC, Roberto's Pizza, 🅞 Rite Aid
48	Union Deposit Rd, E 🅖 Sunoco, 🍴 Arby's, Burger King, Evergreen Chinese, Panera Bread, 🏠 Best Western, Hampton Inn, 🅞 🄷, $Tree, Giant Foods/gas, Rite Aid, Staples, mall, W 🅖 Gulf/dsl, 🍴 ChuckeCheese, Empire Asian Bistro, Great Wall Chinese, Jimmy John's, JoJo's Pizza, Maple's Pizza, McDonald's, Mulligan's Grill, New China, Outback Steaks, Rita's Ice Cream, Starbucks, Subway, TX Roadhouse, TGIFriday's, Waffle House, Wendy's, YP Rest., 🏠 Country Inn&Suites, Fairfield Inn, Holiday Inn Express, Motel 6, 🅞 BigLots, Curves, $Tree, Family$, Hancock Fabrics, Lowe's, PriceRite Foods, Tuesday Morning, Weis Foods
47	(46b from nb), US 322 E, to Hershey, Derry St, E 🅖 Hess, 🍴 Papa John's, 🅞 Home Depot, Petsmart
46b a	I-283 S, to I-76/PA Tpk, **services E off I-283 S** 🅖 Exxon/dsl, Sunoco, 🍴 Bob Evans, Capitol Diner, Doc Holliday's Steaks, Domino's, Eat'n Park, McDonald's, Waffle House, 🏠 Courtyard, EconoLodge, Holiday Inn, Howard Johnson, La Quinta, Red Roof Inn, Sheraton, Super 8, Travelodge, Wyndham, 🅞 Buick, JC Penney, LandRover, Target, VW/Audi, W 🅖 Sunoco, 🍴 Taco Bell, Wendy's, 🏠 Best Western, Days Inn
45	Paxton St, E 🅖 Sheetz/dsl, 🍴 Applebees, Burger King, Dunkin Donuts, Fuddrucker's, Isaac's Rest., Pizza Hut, Ruby Tuesday, Starbucks, Wendy's, 🏠 Hilton Garden, Homewood Suites, Towneplace Suites, 🅞 Bass Pro Shops, Barnes&Noble, JC Penney, Macy's, Mazda/Subaru/Toyota, Nissan, mall
44b	17th St, 19th St, E 🅖 Sunoco, 🍴 Bankok Thai Cuisine, Benihana Japanese, Dunkin Donuts, Hardee's, 🅞 Advance Parts, AutoZone, Buick/GMC, Firestone/auto, Honda, Hyundai/Suzuki, Nissan, Tires+
44a	PA 230, 13th St, Harrisburg, downtown, W 🅞 Chevrolet
43	2nd St, Harrisburg, downtown, st capitol, W 🏠 Crowne Plaza, Hilton, 🅞 🄷
42.5mm	Susquehanna River
42	Lemoyne
41b	Highland Park, E 🅖 Hess, Turkey Hill, 🍴 Burger King, KFC, E 🅖 Sunoco, 🍴 Ciao Pizza, 🅞 Ace Hardware, Family$, Weis Foods
41a	US 15, PA 581 W, to Gettysburg
40b	New Cumberland, W 🅖 Gulf/dsl, 🍴 JoJo's Pizza, McDonald's, New China, Sidoti's Italian, Subway, 🅞 CVS Drug, $General
40a	Limekiln Rd, to Lewisberry, E 🅖 Shell/dsl, Tom's, 🍴 Bob Evans, Doc Holliday's, John's Diner, McDonald's, Pizza Hut, 🏠 Comfort Inn, Fairfield Inn, Holiday Inn/rest, Quality Inn, Rodeway Inn, W 🅖 Hess, 🏠 Best Western, Motel 6, Travel Inn, 🅞 vet

LEWISBERRY / YORK

Exit	Services
39b	I-76/PA Tpk
39a	PA 114, Lewisberry Rd, E 🅖 Rutter's/dsl, 🏠 Days Inn, Highland Inn, Keystone Inn, Red Carpet Inn
38	Reesers Summit
36	PA 262, Fishing Creek, E 🅖 Hess/Dunkin Donuts, 🍴 Bruster's, Mamma's Pizza, 🅞 CVS Drug
35	PA 177, Lewisberry, E 🍴 Hillside Café, W 🅖 Exxon, 🍴 Francescos, Summit Rest., 🏠 Alpine Inn
34mm	parking area/**weigh sta sb**
34	Valley Green (from nb), same as 33
33	PA 392, Yocumtown, E 🅖 Hess/Dunkin Donuts/dsl, Rutter's, 🍴 Burger King, Hong Kong Buffet, KFC/Taco Bell, Maple Donuts, McDonald's, NewBerry Diner, New China Buffet, 2 Bro's Pizza, 🏠 Super 8, 🅞 $Tree, Family$, GNC, Radio Shack, Rite Aid, Verizon, Walmart/Subway
33mm	parking area/**weigh sta nb**
32	PA 382, Newberrytown, E 🅖 Rutter's/deli/dsl/24hr, W 🅖 Exxon/dsl
28	PA 295, Strinestown, W 🅖 Rutter's/24hr, 🍴 83 Diner, Wendy's
24	PA 238, Emigsville, W 🅖 Tom's, 🍴 4 Bro's Rest.
22	PA 181, N George St, E 🅖 Rutter's, 🏠 Comfort Inn, Homewood Suites, W same as 21b
21b a	US 30, Arsenal Rd, to York, E 🅖 Sheetz, 🍴 Clock Diner, San Carlo's Rest., Starbucks, 🏠 Days Inn, Motel 6, Sheraton, Yorkview Hotel, 🅞 Buick/GMC, W 🅖 Citgo, Rutter's/dsl, 🍴 Arby's, Bob Evans, Burger King, Chili's, China Kitchen, DQ, Denny's, Domino's, Dunkin Donuts, El Rodeo Mexican, 5 Guys Burgers, Friendly's, Hardee's, Hooters, Hoss's, KFC, Little Caesars, Logan's Roadhouse, LJ Silver, McDonald's, Old Country Buffet, Olive Garden, Panera Bread, Pizza Hut, Popeye's, Quiznos, Rita's Custard, Ruby Tuesday, Smokey Bones BBQ, Subway, Taco Bell, TGIFriday's, Wendy's, 🏠 Best Western, Red Roof Inn, Rodeway Inn, Super 8, Wingate Inn, 🅞 Acura, Advance Parts, AT&T, AutoZone, BJ's Whse, BMW, BonTon, Cadillac/Chevrolet, Chrysler/Dodge/Jeep, Curves, CVS Drug, Dick's, $General, $Tree, Giant Foods/gas, Harley-Davidson, Honda, Kia, Kohl's, Lowe's, Macy's, NTB, Office Depot, Old Navy, PepBoys, PetCo, Petsmart, Radio Shack, Ross, Staples, Subaru, Target, TJ Maxx, Verizon, Walmart/McDonald's, Weis Foods/gas, transmissions
19	PA 462, Market St, E 🅖 Hess, 🍴 Applebee's, Arby's, ChuckECheese's, Coldstone, DQ, Fuddruckers, Outback Steaks, Papa John's, Perkins, Rita's Custard, Taco Bell, Tokyo Diner, Wendy's, 🏠 Quality Inn, 🅞 🄷, Advance Parts, Aldi Foods, $General, $Tree, Giant Foods, Home Depot, Lowe's, Nissan, NTB, Sam's Club, Walgreens, Walmart, Weis Foods

PA

⬆N INTERSTATE 83 CONT'D

Exit	Services
18	PA 124, Mt Rose Ave, Prospect St, **E** 🅿 Pacific Pride, Rutters, 🍽 Al Dente Italian, Burger King, 5 Guys Burgers, Nino's Pizza, Pizza Hut, Subway, Sweet House Chinese, Uncle Nick's Diner, 🛏 Budget Host, ⊙ Curves, K-Mart, Nello Tire
16b a	PA 74, Queen St, **E** 🅿 Tom's, 🍽 Baskin-Robbins/Dunkin Donuts, Bella's Italian, China Buffet, Cracker Barrel, Isaac's Rest., Ruby Tuesday, 🛏 Country Inn&Suites, ⊙ Giant Foods/gas, Lincoln, **W** 🅿 LukOil, Sheetz, 🍽 Infinito's Pizza, McDonald's, Pizza Hut/Taco Bell, Quiznos, S Yorke Diner, Subway, ⊙ BonTon, CVS Drug, $General, $Tree, Jo-Ann Fabrics, Price Rite Foods, Tuesday Morning, Walgreens
15	S George St, I-83 spur into York, **W** Ⓗ
14	PA 182, Leader Heights, **E** 🍽 Domino's, First Wok, Subway, ⊙ vet, **W** 🅿 Rutter's, 🍽 McDonald's, 🛏 Holiday Inn Express, ⊙ Rite Aid
10	PA 214, Loganville, **W** 🍽 Elsie's Rest., Mamma's Pizza, 🛏 Midway Motel, ⊙ TrueValue, st police
8	PA 216, Glen Rock, **E** 🛏 Rocky Ridge Motel, **W** ⊙ Amish Farmers Mkt (2mi)
4	PA 851, Shrewsbury, **E** 🅿 Tom's/dsl/24hr, 🍽 Cracker Barrel, Ruby Tuesday, 🛏 Hampton Inn, ⊙ Home Depot, TrueValue, **W** 🅿 Exxon/dsl, 🍽 Arby's, Chick-fil-A, Coachlight Rest., Emerald Garden Chinese, KFC/Taco Bell, McDonald's, Quiznos, Rita's Custard, Starbucks, Subway, Szechuan Chinese, Wendy's, ⊙ Advance Parts, Curves, $Tree, Giant Foods, GNC, Mr Tire, Radio Shack, Sauble's Foods, Walmart
2mm	**Welcome Ctr nb, full ♿ facilities, 🚰 vending, 🛆 litter barrels, petwalk**
0mm	Pennsylvania/Maryland state line

⬆E INTERSTATE 84

Exit	Services
54mm	Pennsylvania/New York state line, Delaware River
53	US 6, PA 209, Matamoras, **N Welcome Ctr/both lanes, full ♿ facilities, 🚰 vending, 🛆 litter barrels, petwalk,** 🅿 Go24, Shell, TurkeyHill/dsl, 🍽 Polar Bear Rest., Stewart's Drive-Inn, The Grill, 🛏 Appl Inn, ⊙ AutoZone, PriceChopper, auto repair, fireworks, **S** 🅿 Sunoco/dsl, 🍽 Dunkin Donuts, McDonald's, Perkins, Roma Pizza, Subway, Village Diner, Wendy's, 🛏 Best Western, Hampton Inn, Scottish Inn, ⊙ Advance Parts, $Tree, Home Depot, K-Mart, Lowe's, Staples, Tristate RV Park, Walmart/Subway
46	US 6, to Milford, **N** 🅿 Sunoco/dsl, **0-2 mi S** 🅿 Exxon/dsl, Gulf, TurkeyHill, Xtra, 🍽 Apple Valley Rest., Chang Mao Chinese, China Buffet, 🛏 Black Walnut B&B, Red Carpet Inn, ⊙ Grand Union Foods, NAPA, Rite Aid, USPO
34	PA 739, to Lords Valley, Dingmans Ferry, **S** 🅿 Sunoco/Dunkin Donuts/dsl, Xtra/dsl, 🍽 Bruno's Pizza, McDonald's, Panda Chinese, Subway, ⊙ Family$, Rite Aid, Weis Foods, USPO
30	PA 402, to Blooming Grove, **N** st police, to Lake Wallenpaupack
26	PA 390, to Tafton, **N** Exxon/dsl, Tanglewood Ski Area (4mi), to Lake Wallenpaupack, **S** ⊙ to Promised Land SP
26mm	🆁🆂/weigh sta both lanes, full ♿ facilities, 🚰 vending, 🛆 litter barrels, petwalk

20	PA 507, Greentown, **N** 🅿 Exxon/dsl, Shell/Subway, 🍽 John's Italian, ⊙ Animal Park (5mi)
17	PA 191, to Newfoundland, Hamlin, **N** 🅿 Howe's/Exxon/dsl/scales/24hr, 🍽 Twin Rocks Diner, 🛏 Comfort Inn, ⊙ dsl repair
8	PA 247, PA 348, Mt Cobb, **N** 🅿 Gulf/dsl, Sunoco/Burger King/Tim Hortons/dsl, **S** 🅿 Exxon/Subway/dsl
4	I-380 S, to Mount Pocono
2	PA 435 S, to Elmhurst
1	Tigue St, **N** 🛏 Best Western, **S** 🅿 Valero/dsl
0mm	**I-84 begins/ends on I-81, exit 54.**

⬆E INTERSTATE 90

Exit	Services
46mm	Pennsylvania/New York state line, **Welcome Ctr/weigh sta wb, full ♿ facilities, 🚰 vending, 🛆 litter barrels, petwalk**
45	US 20, to State Line, **N** 🅿 **KwikFill/dsl/scales,** 🍽 McDonald's, **S** 🅿 BP/Subway/dsl, 🛏 Red Carpet Inn, ⊙ Niagara Falls Info, fireworks
41	PA 89, North East, **N** 🅿 Shell/repair, 🍽 New Harvest Rest., 🛏 Holiday Inn Express, Super 8, Vineyard B&B, **S** ⊙ Family Affair Camping (4mi), winery
37	I-86 E, to Jamestown
35	PA 531, to Harborcreek, **N** 🅿 TA/Country Pride/Pizza Hut/Subway/dsl/scales/24hr/@, 🛏 Rodeway Inn, ⊙ Blue Beacon, dsl repair
32	PA 430, PA 290, to Wesleyville, **N** 🅿 Country Fair, st police, **S** ⊙ camping
29	PA 8, to Hammett, **N** 🅿 Country Fair, 🍽 Wendy's, ⊙ Ⓗ, **S** 🛏 Best Value, ⊙ Peterbilt, dsl repair
27	PA 97, State St, Waterford, **N** 🅿 Country Fair/dsl, Kwikfill, 🍽 Arby's, Barbato's Italian, Doc Holiday's Grill, McDonald's, 🛏 Days Inn, La Quinta, Red Roof Inn, Tallyho Inn, ⊙ Ⓗ, **S** 🅿 🚂/Subway/dsl/scales/24hr, Shell/Tim Hortons/dsl, 🛏 Quality Inn, Super 8, ⊙ casino
24	US 19, Peach St, to Waterford, **N** 🅿 Country Fair, Kwik-Fill, 🍽 Applebee's, Burger King, Chick-fil-A, Chipotle Mexican, ChuckeCheese, Cracker Barrel, Dunkin-Donuts, Eat'n Park, Famous Dave's BBQ, 5 Guys Burgers, Golden Corral, KFC, Krispy Kreme, Longhorn Steaks, McDonald's, Old Country Buffet, Olive Garden, Panera Bread, Qdoba, Quaker Steak&Lube, Quiznos, Safari Grill, S&S Buffet, Steak'n Shake, Subway, Taco Bell, TX Roadhouse, TGIFriday's, Tim Hortons, 🛏 Courtyard, Hilton Garden, ⊙ Ⓗ, Advance Parts, AT&T, Best Buy, $Tree, Giant Eagle Foods, Hobby Lobby, Home Depot, Jo-Ann Fabrics, Kohl's, Lowe's, Marshall's, Petsmart, Sam's Club/gas, Staples, Target, Verizon, Walmart/Subway, Wegman's Foods, **Urgent Care, S** 🅿 BP/dsl, Country Fair, Shell/dsl, 🍽 Bob Evans, Boston's Rest., 🛏 Comfort Inn, Country Inn&Suites, EconoLodge, Hampton Inn, Holiday Inn Express, Microtel, Residence Inn, Wingate Inn, ⊙ waterpark
22b a	I-79, N to Erie, S to Pittsburgh, **3-5 mi N** services in Erie
18	PA 832, Sterrettania, **N** 🅿 Marathon/dsl, 🍽 Burger King, ⊙ Presque Passage RV Park, Waldameer Park (8mi), to Presque Isle SP, **S** 🍽 Beechwood Rest., 🛏 Quality Inn, ⊙ KOA, golf
16	PA 98, to Franklin Center, Fairview, **S** ⊙ Follys Camping (2mi), Mar-Da-Jo-Dy Camping (5mi)
9	PA 18, to Girard, Platea, **N** Fiesler's Service/repair/tires, st police, **S** 🛏 Green Roof Inn (2mi)

⬆ INTERSTATE 90 CONT'D

Exit	Services
6	PA 215, to Albion, E Springfield, **N lodging**
3	US 6N, to Cherry Hill, West Springfield, **N lodging on US 20, S** 🅕 State Line/deli/dsl/scales/24hr
2.5mm	🆁🆂/weigh sta eb, full ♿ facilities, info, 🅒, 🚻, litter barrels, vending, petwalk
0mm	Pennsylvania/Ohio state line

⬆ INTERSTATE 95

Exit	Services
51mm	Pennsylvania/New Jersey state line, Delaware River
51	PA 32, to New Hope, **W** Washington Crossing Hist Park
50mm	Welcome Ctr sb, full ♿ facilities, vending, 🅒, 🚻, litter barrels, petwalk
49	PA 332, to Yardley, Newtown, **W** 🅕 Dunkin Donuts, 🛏 Hampton Inn, 🅞 🇭, to Tyler SP
46b a	US 1 to I-276, PA TPK, Langhorne, Oxford Valley, **E** 🇭
44	US 1, PA 413, to Penndel, Levittown, **E** 🅖 Shell/7-11/dsl, 🅕 Arrano Hibachi Steaks, Blue Fountain Diner, Buffalo Wild Wing, ChuckECheese's, Dunkin Donuts, Friendly's, Great American Diner, Hong Kong Pearl, Langhorne Ale House, Ming's Asian, Olive Garden, Panera Bread, Red Lobster, Ruby Tuesday, Subway, Wendy's, 🛏 Sheraton, 🅞 🇭, Acura, Chrysler/Dodge/Jeep, $Tree, Firestone/auto, Ford, Goodyear/auto, Harley-Davidson, Honda, Hyundai/Suzuki, Kia, K-Mart, Lincoln, Lowe's, Marshall's, Mazda, PepBoys, Redner's Whse Mkt, Sam's Club, Staples, Subaru, Target, TJ Maxx, VW/Volvo, **W** 🅖 LukOil/dsl, 🅕 Denny's, McDonald's, 🅞 Toyota/Scion, U-Haul
40	PA 413, I-276, to Bristol Bridge, Burlington, **E** 🅖 Hess/Dunkin Donuts/dsl, WaWa, 🅕 Fish Factory Rest., Golden Eagle Diner, KFC, McDonald's, 🅞 🇭, Chevrolet
37	PA 132, to Street Rd, **W** 🅖 BP/dsl, Sunoco/dsl, 🅕 Burger King, Chili's, China Sun Buffet, Dunkin Donuts, Gino's Burgers/Chicken, Golden Corral, IHOP, McDonald's, Old Country Buffet, Popeye's, Sonic, TX Roadhouse, Wendy's, 🅞 Advance Parts, Aldi Foods, $Tree, Giant Foods, GNC, Goodyear/auto, K-Mart, Kohl's, PepBoys, Radio Shack, Ross, Save-A-Lot, 7-11, U-Haul, Walgreens, WaWa
35	PA 63, to US 13, Woodhaven Rd, Bristol Park, **W** 🅖 Liberty, 🅕 Bob Evans, Champs Pizza, Dunkin Donuts, McDonald's, Old Haven Pizza, Rita's Custard, 🛏 Hampton Inn, 🅞 🇭, Acme Foods, Home Depot, Verizon, WaWa, **1 mi W** 🅖 BP, Exxon, LukOil, Sunoco/dsl, 🅕 Arby's, Boston Mkt, Burger King, Dave&Buster's, Dynasty Rest., Grand China Buffet, Hibachi Buffet, Joe Santucci's, KFC, McDonald's, Mr V's Steaks, Panda King, Pizza Hut, Ruby Tuesday, Supreme Buffet, Taco Bell, Uno, Wendy's, 🅞 BigLots, Burlington Coats, Dick's, $Tree, Marshall's, NTB, Old Navy, Pathmark Foods, Rite Aid, Sam's Club, Tires+, Walmart
32	Academy Rd, **W** 🅞 🇭, K-Mart
30	PA 73, Cottman Ave, **W** 🅖 Sunoco
27	Bridge St, **W** 🅖 BP, Exxon, LukOil, 7-11, 🅕 Dunkin Donuts, 🅞 🇭, Rite Aid
26	to NJ 90, Betsy Ross Brdg, **W** 🅖 BP, Hess, Sunoco/dsl, 🅕 Applebee's, Burger King, KFC, McDonald's, Wendy's, 🅞 Home Depot, Lowe's, ShopRite Foods, Target
25	Allegheny Ave, **W** 🅖 Sunoco, 🅞 🇭, WaWa
23	Lehigh Ave, Girard Ave, **E** casino, **W** 🅖 Exxon, 🅕 Applebee's, Arby's, Coldstone, Dunkin Donuts, Pizza Hut, Rita's Custard, 🅞 🇭, AutoZone, CVS Drug, Family$, GNC, Pep

Exit	Services
23	Continued Boys, Radio Shack, Rite Aid, WaWa
22	I-676, US 30, to Central Philadelphia, Independence Hall
20	Columbus Blvd, Penns Landing, **1-2 mi E on Columbus** 🅖 BP, Liberty/WaWa/dsl, LukOil/dsl, 🅕 Burger King, Dave&Buster's, Champp's Rest., ChartHouse Rest., Chick-fil-A, Famous Dave's BBQ, IHOP, La Veranda Italian, Longhorn Steaks, McDonald's, Moshulu Rest., Ruby Buffet, Wendy's, 🛏 Comfort Inn, Sheraton, Hyatt Hotel (1mi), 🅞 Best Buy, $Tree, Home Depot, Lowe's, Marshall's, PepBoys, ShopRite Foods, Staples, Target, Verizon, Walmart
19	I-76 E, to Walt Whitman Bridge, **E** 🛏 Holiday Inn, to stadiums, **W on Front St E** 🅖 BP, Exxon/dsl, Sunoco, 🅕 Burger King, Dunkin Donuts, KFC, Little Caesars, McDonald's, Pizza Hut, 🅞 Aldi Foods
17	PA 611, to Broad St, Pattison Ave, **W** 🅞 🇭, to Naval Shipyard, to stadium
15mm	Schuykill River
15	Enterprise Ave, Island Ave (from sb)
14	Bartram Ave, Essington Ave (from sb)
13	PA 291, to I-76 W (from nb), to Central Philadelphia, **E** 🅖 Exxon/dsl, 🛏 Days Inn, Guest Quarters, Hilton, Marriott, Renaissance Inn, Residence Inn, Sheraton, Sheraton Suites, Westin Suites
12	**E** Philadelphia Intl ✈, services same as 10
10	PA 291, Bartrom Ave, (from nb), Cargo City, **E** 🛏 Marriott, Renaissance Hotel, **W** 🅖 WaWa/dsl, 🅕 Ruby Tuesday, 🛏 Courtyard, Embassy Suites, Extended Stay America, Extended Stay Deluxe, Fairfield Inn, Hampton Inn, Microtel, Studio+, 🅞 Heins NWR
9b a	PA 420, to Essington, Prospect Park, **E** 🅖 Sunoco/dsl, Valero/dsl, 🅕 Denny's, Lehmans Rest., Mel's Diner, Philly Diner, 🛏 Comfort Inn, Motel 6, Ramada Inn, Red Roof Inn, Residence Inn, SpringHill Suites, Wyndham Garden, 🅞 USPO, WaWa
8	to Chester Waterfront, Ridley Park, **W on US 13** 🅕 Stargate Diner
7	I-476 N, to Plymouth, Meeting
6	PA 352, PA 320, to Edgmont Ave, **1 mi E on US 13** 🅕 McDonald's, Popeye's, 🅞 Radio Shack, Walmart/Subway, **W** 🛏 Days Inn/Dawn's Diner
5	Kerlin St (from nb), **E** 🅖 Gulf
4	US 322 E, to NJ, to Barry Bridge, **W** 🛏 Highland Motel
3	(from nb, no EZ return) US 322 W, Highland Ave, **E** 🅖 Sunoco/dsl, 🅞 Ford, Goodyear
2	PA 452, to US 322, Market St, **E W** 🅖 Exxon, 🅕 McDonald's, Subway
1	Chichester Ave, **E** 🅖 Sunoco, 🅞 fireworks, **W** 🅖 BP, 🅞 WaWa, transmissions

LEVITTOWN

PHILADELPHIA AREA

PA

= gas   = food   = lodging   = other   = rest stop   Copyright 2014 - The NEXT Exit ®

INTERSTATE 95 CONT'D

Exit	Services
0mm	Pennsylvania/Delaware state line, **Welcome Ctr/weigh sta nb, full** ♿ **facilities,** 🚻, 🗑, litter barrels, petwalk

INTERSTATE 99

Exit	Services
83	PA 350, **(I-99 begins/ends on I-80, exit 161)**, Bellafonte, **E** 🅿 Weis Foods, **W** 🅿 Lyken's Mkt, 🍴 Bonfatto's Rest., Burger King, Pizza Hut, 🅾 Rite Aid, TrueValue
81	PA 26 S, to PA 64, to Pleasant Gap
80	Harrison Rd (no re-entry nb)
78b a	PA 150, to Bellafonte, **W** 🅿 Sheetz/dsl, 🍴 Bro's Pizza, EconoLodge, 🅾 Bumper Parts, Ford, auto repair, Vistors Ctr
76	Shiloh Rd, **E** 🅿 Sheetz, 🍴 Garfields, LJ Silver, McDonald's, Rey Azteca, 🛏 Best Western, 🅾 Barnes&Noble, BigLots, BonTon, Chevrolet, JC Penney, Jo-Ann Fabrics, Macy's, Office Depot, Ross, Sam's Club, Sears, Subaru, Walmart/Subway
74	Innovation Park, Penn State U, Beaver Stadium
73	US 322 E, Lewiston State College
71	Woodycrest, Tofftrees, **E** 🍴 Applebee's, Chick-fil-A, Cracker Barrel, Eat'n park, Hoss', KFC, McDonald's, Olive Garden, Outback Steaks, TX Roadhouse, Wendy's, 🛏 Hampton Inn, Holiday Inn Express, Quality Inn, SpringHill Suites, 🅾 Dick's, Kohl's, Michael's, PetCo, Target, Wegman's Foods, Walmart
69	US 322 E, Valley Vista Dr, **E** 🅿 Exxon
68	Skytop Mtn Rd, Grays Woods, Waddle
62	US 322 W, to Phillipsburg (from sb)
61	US 322 W, Port Matilda, **E** 🅿 Best, 🍴 Brother's Pizza, Subway, 🛏 Port Matilda Hotel, 🅾 USPO
52	PA 350, **E** 🅿 BP/Subway
48	PA 453, Tyrone, **W** 🅿 Choice, 🍴 Burger King, 🅾 🏥, Rite Aid
45	Tipton, Grazierville, **W** 🍴 Pizza Hut (2mi), Sammy's BBQ, 🅾 🏥, DelGrosso's Funpark
41	PA 865 N, Bellwood, **E** Ft Roberdeau HS, **W** 🅿 Martin Gen Store/dsl, Sheetz/dsl, 🅾 DelGrosso's Funpark
39	PA 764 S, Pinecroft, **W** Oak Spring Winery
33	17th St, Altoona, **E** same as 32, **W** 🅿 Sheetz, 🍴 Hoss' Rest., Subway (2mi), 🅾 Lowe's, Railroader Museum, U-Haul
32	PA 36, Frankstown Rd, Altoona, **E** 🅿 GetGo, 🍴 Chili's, Panera Bread, 🅾 Barnes&Noble, Best Buy, Boscov's, Giant Eagle Foods, GNC, Home Depot, Kohl's, Michael's, PetCo, Ross, Staples, Canoe Cr SP, **W** 🅿 Gulf, Sheetz, 🍴 ChuckeCheese, Dunkin Donuts, HongKong Buffet, McDonald's, Olive Garden, Papa John's, Perkins, Pizza Hut, Red Lobster, Subway, Uno, Wendy's, 🛏 EconoLodge, Holiday Inn Express, Quality Inn, Super 8, 🅾 🏥, AutoZone, Cadillac, CVS Drug, Dodge, $Tree, Jo-Ann Fabrics, NAPA, Nissan, Rite Aid, Save-A-Lot, Walgreens, USPO
31	Plank Rd, Altoona, **E** 🍴 Cici's Pizza, Friendly's, Hoss' Rest, Jethro's Rest., King's Rest., Krispy Kreme, Outback Steaks, Ruby Tuesday, TGIFriday's, 🛏 Comfort Inn, Ramada Inn, 🅾 Firestone/auto, Radio Shack, Sam's Club/gas, Target, TJ Maxx, Walmart, st police, **W** 🅿 Shell/Subway, 🍴 Applebee's, Arby's, Burger King, Cracker Barrel, Denny's, Eat'n Park, Hooters, KFC, Little Ceasars, LJ Sil

Exit	Services
31	Continued ver, Ponderosa, Taco Bell, 🛏 Hampton Inn, Motel 6, 🅾 Advance Parts, BigLots, $General, Giant Eagle Foods, JC Penney, K-Mart, Macy's, PharMor, Sears/auto, Weis Foods
28	US 22, to Ebensburg, Holidaysburg
23	PA 36, PA 164, Roaring Spring, Portage, **E** 🅿 GetGo/dsl, Sheetz/24hr, Turkey Hill, 🍴 Backyard Burger, 🅾 🏥 Walmart, truck repair
15	Claysburg, King, **W** 🍴 Subway, gas
10	to Imler, **W** gas, food, Blue Knob SP (8mi)
7	PA 869, Osterburg, St Clairsville, **W** gas, food, Blue Knob SP
3	PA 56, Johnstown, Cessna, **E** 🅾 truck parts
1	I-70/76. **I-99 begins/ends on US 220.**, **E** 🅿 BP/dsl, Pacific Pride, Sheetz/dsl, 🍴 Arena Rest., Denny's, Ed's Steaks, Hoss' Rest, LJ Silver, McDonald's, Pizza Hut, Subway, Wendy's, 🛏 Best Western, Budget Host, Hampton Inn, Hillcrest Motel, Holiday Inn Express, Quality Inn, Relax Inn, Super 8

INTERSTATE 476

Exit	Services
131	US 11, US 6. **I-476 begins/ends on I-81.** Services same as I-81, exit 194.
122	Keyser Ave, Old Forge, Taylor
121mm	**toll plaza**
115	I-81, PA 315, Wyoming Valley, Pittston, **W** 🅿 Mobil, 🚛/Wendy's/dsl/scales/24hr, Sunoco, 🍴 Arby's, McDonald's, Perkins, 🛏 Knight's Inn, Ramada Inn, 🅾 Chevrolet
112mm	**toll plaza**
105	PA 115, Wilkes-Barre, Bear Creek, **E** 🅿 BP, Exxon, PSC
97mm	parking areas both lanes
95	I-80, PA 940, Pocono, Hazleton, **W** 🅿 WaWa, 🍴 A&W/LJ Silver, Arby's, McDonald's, 🛏 Comfort Inn, EconoLodge, Holiday Inn Express, Knights Inn, Mtn Laurel Resort, Pocono Inn/Resort, Split Rock Resort
90mm	parking area sb
86mm	**Hickory Run Service Plaza both lanes,** 🅿 Sunoco/dsl, 🍴 Breyer's, McDonald's, hot dogs
74	US 209, Mahoning Valley, Lehighton, Stroudsburg, **W** 🅿 Shell/Subway/dsl, 🍴 Trainer's Inn Rest., 🛏 Country Inn&Suites, Hampton Inn
71mm	Lehigh Tunnel
56	I-78, US 22, PA 309, Lehigh Valley, **E** 🅿 Gulf, 🍴 Dunkin Donuts, Quiznos, Red Robin, Trivet Diner, Wendy's, 🛏 Comfort Inn, Days Inn, McIntosh Inn, 🅾 BMW, CVS Drug, Infiniti, Jaguar, K-Mart, Land Rover, Staples, **W on US 22** 🅿 Mobil, Sunoco, 🍴 Chris Rest., Parma Pizza, 🛏 Best Western, 🅾 CVS Drug
56mm	**Allentown Service Plaza both lanes,** 🅿 Sunoco/dsl, 🍴 Big Boy, Hershey's Ice Cream, Pizza Hut, Roy Rogers
44	PA 663, Quakertown, Pottstown, **E** 🅿 BP, Mobil/dsl, 🍴 Avanti Grill, Faraco's Pizza, 🛏 Best Western (3mi), Comfort Suites, Hampton Inn, Holiday Inn Express, Rodeway Inn, 🅾 🏥
37mm	parking area sb
31	PA 63, Lansdale, **E** 🅿 Exxon, Lukoil, WaWa 🍴 Bones Grill, 🛏 Best Western, Courtyard, Lansdale Motel, Residence Inn, 🅾 🏥
20	Germantown Pike W, to I-276 W, PA Tpk W
19	Germantown Pike E
18b a	(18 from sb), Conshohocken, Norristown, **E** 🅿 Lukoil

S T A T E   C O L L E G E

A L T O O N A

PA

🏁E INTERSTATE 476 CONT'D

Exit	Services
18b a	Continued
	Sunoco, 🍴 Andy's Diner, Baja Fresh, Burger King, Domino's, Dunkin Donuts, Illiano's Pizza, McDonald's, Outback Steaks, Panera Bread, Rita's Ice Cream, Salad Works, Starbucks, 🅞 Giant Foods, Genuradi's Foods, Marshall's, Toyota/Scion, **E on Chemical Rd** 🍴 Cracker Barrel, Ruby Tuesday, 🏠 Hampton Inn, 🅞 Barnes&Noble, Best Buy, Dick's, Giant Foods, Lowe's, Office Depot, Old Navy, Petsmart, Ross, Target, **W** 🍴 Papa John's, Uno, Wendy's, 🅞 BJ's Whse, Ford, Home Depot, Honda, Hyundai, Kia, Mazda, Michael's, Nissan, Porsche

16b a	(16 from sb), I-76, PA 23, to Philadelpia, Valley Forge
13	US 30, **E** 🅖 Shell, 🍴 Campus Pizza, Nova Grill, Winger's, 🅞 🏨 Staples, USPO, to Villanova U
9	PA 3, Broomall, Upper Darby, **E** 🍴 Barnaby's Rest, 🅞 🏨
5	US 1, Lima, Springfield, **E** 🍴 Dragon Garden, Mesa Mexican, 🅞 AT&T, Giant Foods, Jo-Ann Fabrics, Marshall's, Old Navy, Petsmart, Verizon, Walmart
3	Baltimore Pike, Media, Swarthmore, **E** 🅖 Lukoil, 🍴 Ruby Tuesday, 🅞 🏨 Macy's, Target, Swarthmore Coll
1	McDade Blvd, **E** 🅖 Exxon, 🍴 Dunkin Donuts, KFC, McDonald's, Panda Chinese, 🅞 CVS Drug, Rite Aid
0mm	I-476 begins/ends on I-95, exit 7.

RHODE ISLAND

🏁N INTERSTATE 95

Exit	Services
43mm	Rhode Island/Massachusetts state line
30 (42)	East St, to Central Falls, **E** 🍴 Dunkin Donuts, Subway
29 (41)	US 1, Cottage St, **W** 🍴 d'Angelo's
28 (40)	RI 114, School St, **E** 🅖 Sunoco, 🅞 🏨 Car Pros, Yarn Outlet, to hist dist
27 (39)	US 1, RI 15, Pawtucket, **W** 🅖 Shell/repair, Sunoco/dsl/24hr, 🍴 Burger King, Dunkin Donuts, Ground Round, 🏠 Comfort Inn
26 (38)	RI 122, Lonsdale Ave (from nb), **E** 🅞 U-Haul
25 (37)	US 1, RI 126, N Main St, Providence, **E** 🅖 Gulf, Hess, Shell, 🍴 Chili's, Dunkin Donuts, Gregg's Rest., Subway, 🅞 🏨 PepBoys, Rite Aid, Walgreens, **Urgent Care**, **W** 🅖 Gulf/dsl, Hess, 🍴 Burger King, Chelo's Rest., 🅞 AAA, Aamco, Suzuki
24 (36.5)	Branch Ave, Providence, downtown, **W** 🅖 Mobil, 🍴 Wendy's, 🅞 Stop&Shop, Walmart/Subway, **Urgent Care**
23 (36)	RI 146, RI 7, Providence, **E** 🅖 Mobil/dsl, 🏠 Marriott, 🅞 🏨, **W** USPO
22 (35.5)	US 6, RI 10, Providence, **E** 🍴 Cheesecake Factory, Dave&Buster's, 🅞 CVS Drug, JC Penney, Macy's, Nordstrom's, mall
21 (35)	Broadway St, Providence, **E** 🏠 Hilton, Regency Plaza
20 (34.5)	I-195, to E Providence, Cape Cod
19 (34)	Eddy St, Allens Ave, to US 1, **W** 🍴 Wendy's, Dunkin Donuts, 🏨
18 (33.5)	US 1A, Thurbers Ave, **W** 🅖 Shell/dsl, 🍴 Burger King, 🅞 🏨
17 (33)	US 1 (from sb), Elmwood Ave, **W** 🅞 Cadillac, Tires Whse
16 (32.5)	RI 10, Cranston, **W** Williams Zoo/park
15 (32)	Jefferson Blvd, **E** 🅖 Mobil, 🍴 Bugaboo Creek Steaks, Dunkin Donuts, Shogun Steaks, 🏠 Courtyard, La Quinta, Motel 6, **W** 🅞 Ryder Trucks
14 (31)	RI 37, Post Rd, to US 1, **W** 🅖 Shell, Sunoco 🍴 Burger King, 🅞 🏨 CVS Drug, Ford/Lincoln, Mazda, Volvo
13 (30)	1 mi **E** TF Green ✈, 🅖 Shell, Sunoco/Dunkin Donuts, 🍴 Chelo's Grill, Legal Seafood, Wendy's, 🏠 Best Western, Comfort Inn, Hampton Inn, Hilton Garden, Holiday Inn Express, Homestead Suites, Homewood Suites, Radisson, Residence Inn
12b (29)	RI 2, I-295 N (from sb)
12a	RI 113 E, to Warwick, **E** 🅖 Shell/Dunkin Donuts/dsl, 🏠 Crowne Plaza Hotel, 🅞 Lowe's, Stop&Shop, **W** 🅖 Su

Side label: **PROVIDENCE**

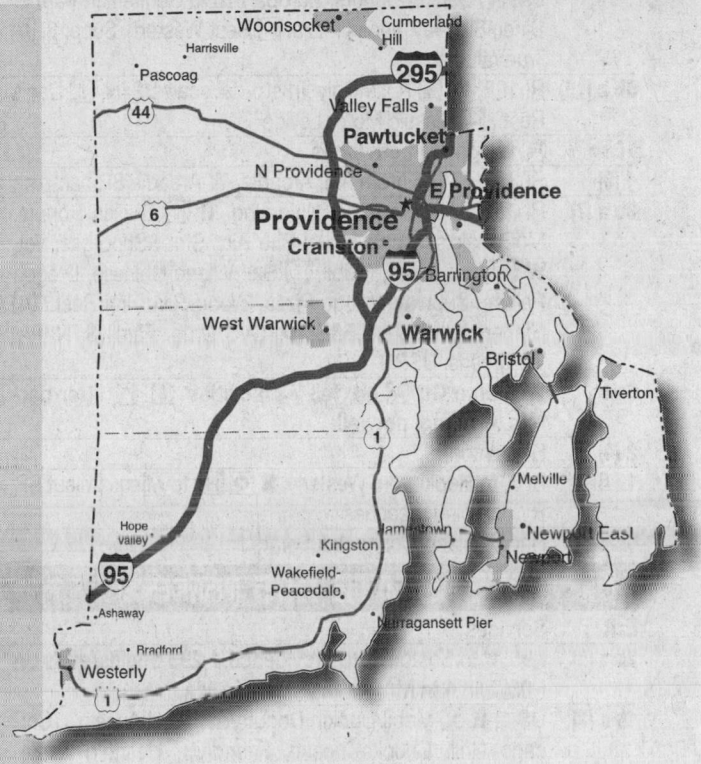

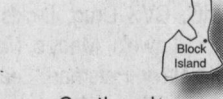

Map labels: Woonsocket, Cumberland Hill, Harrisville, 295, Pascoag, 44, Valley Falls, Pawtucket, N Providence, 6, E Providence, Providence, Cranston, 95, Barrington, West Warwick, Warwick, Bristol, Tiverton, Hope Valley, Kingston, Jamestown, Melville, Newport East, Newport, 95, Wakefield-Peacedale, Narragansett Pier, Ashaway, Bradford, Westerly, 1, Block Island

Side label: **E GREENWICH**

12a	Continued
	noco, 🍴 ChuckeCheese, Wendy's, 🅞 Kohl's, Sears/auto, Walmart/Subway, mall
11 (29)	I-295 N (exits left from nb), to Woonsocket
10ba (28)	RI 117, to Warwick, **W** 🏨
9 (25)	RI 4 S, E Greenwich
8b a (24)	RI 2, E Greenwich, **E** 🅖 Shell/dsl, 🍴 China Buffet, Coldstone, Dunkin Donuts, McDonald's, Outback Steaks, Panera Bread, Ruby Tuesday, TX Roadhouse, 🏠 Extended Stay America, 🅞 AT&T, CVS Drug, Dave's Mkt, Walgreens, **0-2 mi W** 🅖 Citgo, Sunoco/dsl, 🍴 Agave's Mexican, Applebee's, Carrabba's, Chili's, Denny's, 5 Guys Burgers, KFC, Olive Garden, PapaGino's Pizza, Smokey Bones BBQ, TGIFriday's, Wendy's, 🏠 SpringHill Suites, 🅞 Acura, Aldi Foods, Arlington RV Ctr, Audi/Bentley/

⬆N INTERSTATE 95 CONT'D

Exit	Services
8b a (24)	Continued
	BMW/Inifinti/Lexus/Mini/Porsche/Smart, Barnes&Noble, Best Buy, Cadillac, Dick's, GNC, Goodyear/auto, Home Depot, Honda, Hyundai, Jaguar, Jo-Ann Fabrics, Land Rover, Lowe's, Mercedes, Michael's, Nissan, PepBoys, Petco, Petsmart, Staples, Stop&Shop, Target, VW, mall, vet
7 (21)	to Coventry, E 🅡 Mobil/dsl, W 🍽 Applebee's, Cilantro Mexican, Cracker Barrel, Denny's, Dunkin Donuts, Honeydew Donuts, Riccotti's Subs, Wendy's, 🏨 Fairfield Inn, Hampton Inn, Residence Inn, 🅞 BJ's Whse/gas, CVS Drug, GNC, Home Depot, Radio Shack, Walmart/Subway
6a (20)	Hopkins Hill Rd, W 🍽 Dunkin Donuts, 🅞 park&ride
6 (18)	RI 3, to Coventry, W 🅡 Lukoil, Shell/dsl/24hr, Sunoco/dsl, 🍽 Dunkin Donuts, Europa Pizza, Gentleman Farmer Diner, Subway, Venus Pizza, 🏨 Best Western, Super 8, 🅞 TrueValue
5b a (15)	RI 102, W 🅡 R.I.'s Only Trkstp/dsl/scales/24hr, 🍽 Dan's Rest., 🏨 Classic Motor Lodge
10mm	🅡ₛ/weigh sta both lanes
4 (9)	RI 3, to RI 165 (from nb), Arcadia, W Arcadia SP, camping
3b a (7)	RI 138 E, to Kingston, Wyoming, E 🍽 Dunkin Donuts, McDonald's, Wendy's, 🅞 Rite Aid, Stop&Shop/gas, vet, W 🅡 Gulf, Hess, Mobil, 🍽 Bali Village Chinese, Dragon Palace, Subway, Village Pizza, Wood River Inn Rest., 🏨 Stagecoach House B&B, 🅞 CVS Drug, Family$, NAPA, Walgreens, USPO
6mm	Welcome Ctr/🅡ₛ nb, full ♿ facilities, 🔌, 🔦, litter barrels, vending, petwalk
2 (4)	Hopkinton
1 (1)	RI 3, to Hopkinton, Westerly, E 🅞 🄷, to Misquamicut SP, RV camping, beaches
0mm	Rhode Island/Connecticut state line

⬆N INTERSTATE 295 (PROVIDENCE)

Exit	Services
2b a (4)	I-95, N to Boston, S to Providence. **I-295 begins/ends on I-95, exit 4 in MA. Exits 2-1 are in MA.**
1b a (2)	US 1, E 🅡 Mobil/Dunkin Donuts/dsl, 🍽 d'Angelo's, Chicago Grill, ChuckeCheese, Friendly's, Hearth'n Kettle, Longhorn Steaks, 99 Rest., Panera Bread, PapaGino's Italian, Ruby Tuesday, TGIFriday's, 🅞 Best Buy, BJ's Whse, Buick/Chevrolet/GMC, CVS Drug, Dick's, $Tree, JC Penney, Jo-Anne Fabrics, Lowe's, Macy's, Marshalls, Michael's, Office Depot, Old Navy, Petsmart, Sears/auto, Staples, Stop&Shop, Target, TJMaxx, Walmart, mall, W 🅡 Emerald/dsl, Gulf, Shell/dsl, 🍽 Applebee's, Dunkin Donuts, 🏨 Holiday Inn Express, Pineapple Inn, Super 8, 🅞 CVS Drug, Nissan, Toyota/Scion
0mm	Rhode Island/Massachusetts state line. **Exits 1-2 are in MA.**
11 (24)	RI 114, to Cumberland, E 🅡 Shell/dsl, Sunoco, 🍽 Dunkin Donuts, HoneyDew Donuts, 🅞 CVS Drug, Dave's Foods, USPO, W 🍽 J's Deli, Pizza Pasta&More, Saki's Pizza/subs, 🅞 Diamond Hill SP
10 (21)	RI 122, E 🅡 Gulf, Lukoil, 🍽 Burger King, Dunkin Donuts, Forno Pizza, Jacky's Rest., McDonald's, Ronzio Pizza, 🅞 Verizon, W 🍽 Forno Pizza, Fortune House Chinese, Pamfilios Deli, Subway, 🅞 Ace Hardware, Curves, CVS Drug, Rite Aid, Seabra Foods, **Urgent Care**

P R O V I D E N C E

20mm	Blackstone River
19.5mm	**weigh sta/🅡ₛ (full facilities) nb,** Baskin-Robbins/Dunkin Donuts
9b a (19)	RI 146, Woonsocket, Lincoln, E 🏨 Courtyard
8b a (16)	RI 7, N Smithfield, E 🍽 European Cafe, W 🅡 7-11/dsl, Shell, 🍽 Decarlo's Italian, Dunkin Donuts, House of Pizza, Parentes Rest., 🏨 Comfort Suites, Hampton Inn, Holiday Inn Express, 🅞 Smith-Appleby House
7b a (13)	US 44, Centerdale, E 🅡 Hess, Valero, 🍽 Ball's Grill, Cancun Mexican, La Cocina Italian, 🅞 🄷, NAPA, CarQuest, repair, W 🅡 Gulf/dsl, Mobil, Shell, 🍽 A&W, Applebee's, Burger King, Chelo's Grill, Chicago Grill, Chili's, D'angelo's, Dominos, Dunkin Donuts, KFC/Taco Bell, McDonald's, Panera Bread, PapaGino's, Subway, TinTsin Chinese, Wendy's, Yamato Steaks, 🅞 AAA, AT&T, Barnes&Noble, Curves, CVS Drug, Dave's Foods, Dick's, $Tree, Home Depot, Kohl's, Michael's, Old Navy, Radio Shack, Rite Aid, Staples, Stop&Shop, Target, TJ Maxx, Verizon, **Urgent Care,** to Powder Mill Ledges WR
6b c (10)	US 6, to Providence, E 🅡 7-11, Shell, 🍽 Atwood Grill, Burger King, D'Angelo's, Dunkin Donuts, Jacky's Rest., KFC, Newport Creamery, Noble House Chinese, Ruby Tuesday, Subway, Wendy's, 🅞 AT&T, BJ's Whse, Buick/Chevrolet/GMC, Chrysler/Dodge/Jeep, CVS Drug, Honda, Kia, Office Depot, PetsMart, Rite Aid Stop&Shop, USPO
6a (9)	US 6 E Expswy, **1 mi** E 🍽 McDonald's, Ribs&Co, Ruby Tuesday, Taco Bell, 🅞 BJ's Whse, Home Depot, Petsmart
5 (8)	RI Resource Recovery Industrial Park
4 (7)	RI 14, Plainfield Pk, E 🅡 Hess, W 🅡 Gulf, Mobil/dsl/24hr, 🍽 Dunkin Donuts, Palmieri Pizza, 🅞 CVS Drug, repair
3b a (4)	rd 37, Phenix Ave, E TF Green ✈
2 (2)	RI 2 S, to Warwick, E 🍽 Chicago Grill, Longhorn Steaks, Red Robin, 🅞 JC Penney, Macy's, Marshalls, Old Navy, Verizon, Walgreens, mall, W 🅡 Mobil, Sunoco, 🍽 Burger King, Chili's, Chipotle Mexican, ChuckeCheese, Dunkin Donuts, Hometown Buffet, McDonald's/playplace, Olive Garden, On-the-Border, Panera Bread, Starbucks, Taco Bell, Subway, Wendy's, 🅞 AT&T, Barnes&Noble, Best Buy, Chrysler/Dodge/Keep/Kia, Home Depot, Jaguar, Kohl's, Price Rite Foods, PetsMart, Rite Aid, Sears/auto, Staples, Subaru, Target, TJMaxx, TownFair Tire, Trader Joe's, Verizon, Walmart/Subway, mall
1 (1)	RI 113 W, to W Warwick, same as 2
0mm	**I-295 begins/ends on I-95, exit 11.**

SOUTH CAROLINA

⬆E INTERSTATE 20

Exit	Services
141b a	I-95, N to Fayetteville, S to Savannah. **I-20 begins/ends on I-95, exit 160. See Interstate 95, exit 160a for services.**
137	SC 340, to Timmonsville, Darlington, N 🅡 BP (1mi), S 🅡 Marathon
131	US 401, SC 403, to Hartsville, Lamar, N 🅡 Exxon/dsl, to Darlington Int Raceway, S 🅡 Shell/Markette/dsl
129mm	parking area no facilities both lanes, commercial vehicles only
123	SC 22, N camping, Lee SP
121mm	Lynches River

RI
SC

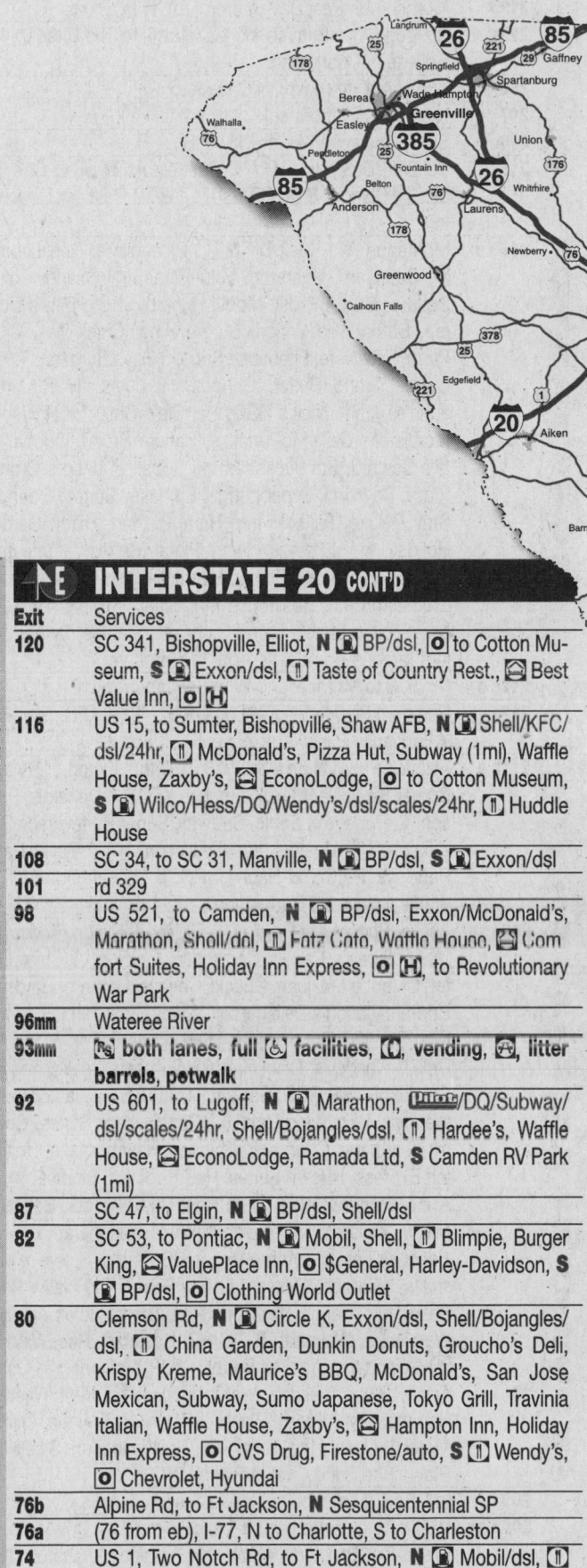

⟋E INTERSTATE 20 CONT'D

Exit	Services
120	SC 341, Bishopville, Elliot, **N** 🅐 BP/dsl, 🅾 to Cotton Museum, **S** 🅐 Exxon/dsl, 🍴 Taste of Country Rest., 🏨 Best Value Inn, 🅾 🕀
116	US 15, to Sumter, Bishopville, Shaw AFB, **N** 🅐 Shell/KFC/dsl/24hr, 🍴 McDonald's, Pizza Hut, Subway (1mi), Waffle House, Zaxby's, 🏨 EconoLodge, 🅾 to Cotton Museum, **S** 🅐 Wilco/Hess/DQ/Wendy's/dsl/scales/24hr, 🍴 Huddle House
108	SC 34, to SC 31, Manville, **N** 🅐 BP/dsl, **S** 🅐 Exxon/dsl
101	rd 329
98	US 521, to Camden, **N** 🅐 BP/dsl, Exxon/McDonald's, Marathon, Shell/dsl, 🍴 Fatz Cafe, Waffle House, 🏨 Comfort Suites, Holiday Inn Express, 🅾 🕀, to Revolutionary War Park
96mm	Wateree River
93mm	🆁🆂 **both lanes, full** ♿ **facilities,** 🍴 **vending,** 🗑 **litter barrels, petwalk**
92	US 601, to Lugoff, **N** 🅐 Marathon, ▨▨▨/DQ/Subway/dsl/scales/24hr, Shell/Bojangles/dsl, 🍴 Hardee's, Waffle House, 🏨 EconoLodge, Ramada Ltd, **S** Camden RV Park (1mi)
87	SC 47, to Elgin, **N** 🅐 BP/dsl, Shell/dsl
82	SC 53, to Pontiac, **N** 🅐 Mobil, Shell, 🍴 Blimpie, Burger King, 🏨 ValuePlace Inn, 🅾 $General, Harley-Davidson, **S** 🅐 BP/dsl, 🅾 Clothing World Outlet
80	Clemson Rd, **N** 🅐 Circle K, Exxon/dsl, Shell/Bojangles/dsl, 🍴 China Garden, Dunkin Donuts, Groucho's Deli, Krispy Kreme, Maurice's BBQ, McDonald's, San Jose Mexican, Subway, Sumo Japanese, Tokyo Grill, Travinia Italian, Waffle House, Zaxby's, 🏨 Hampton Inn, Holiday Inn Express, 🅾 CVS Drug, Firestone/auto, **S** 🍴 Wendy's, 🅾 Chevrolet, Hyundai
76b	Alpine Rd, to Ft Jackson, **N** Sesquicentennial SP
76a	(76 from eb), I-77, N to Charlotte, S to Charleston
74	US 1, Two Notch Rd, to Ft Jackson, **N** 🅐 Mobil/dsl, 🍴 Chili's, Fazoli's, Hooters, IHOP, Lizard's Thicket, Outback Steaks, Waffle House, 🏨 Best Western, Comfort Suites, EconoLodge, Fairfield Inn, Hampton Inn, La Quinta, Microtel, Motel 6, Red Roof Inn, 🅾 Home Depot, USPO, to

C O L U M B I A

Exit	Services
74	Continued Sesquicentennial SP, **S** 🅐 BP, Exxon, Shell/dsl, 🍴 Applebee's, Bojangles, Capt D's, China Garden, Church's, Jasmine Buffet, Harbor Inn Seafood, Hardee's, Honeybaked Ham, Maurice's BBQ, McDonald's, Monterrey Mexican, Nick's Gyros, Substaion II, 🏨 Days Inn, 🅾 Advance Parts, AutoZone, Best Buy, Firestone/auto, K-Mart, Lowe's, Macy's, Marshalls, Sears/auto, Verizon, mall
73b	SC 277 N, to I-77 N
73a	SC 277 S, to Columbia, **S** 🕀
72	SC 555, Farrow Rd
71	US 21, N Main, to Blythewood, Columbia, **N** 🅐 Citgo/dsl, TravelPlaza/Pizza Hut/Subway/dsl/scales/24hr/@, Save-a-Ton/dsl, 🍴 McDonald's, 🏨 Days Inn, 🅾 truckwash, tires, **S** 🅐 Shell
70	US 321, Fairfield Rd, **S** 🅐 Exxon, ⟫FLYING J/Denny's/dsl/LP/24hr, 🍴 Hardee's, 🏨 Super 8, 🅾 Blue Beacon
68	SC 215, Monticello Rd, to Jenkinsville, **N** 🅐 Exxon/dsl, Shell/dsl, **S** 🅐 Shell/dsl
66mm	Broad River
65	US 176, Broad River Rd, to Columbia, **N** 🅐 BP, El Cheapo, Exxon, Shell/Circle K, 🍴 Applebee's, Bojangles, Rush's BBQ, Sonic, Subway, Waffle House, 🏨 Economy Inn, 🅾 Aamco, CVS Drug, $Tree, U-Haul, Walgreens, **S** 🅐 Hess/Godfather's Pizza, RaceWay/dsl, 🍴 Arby's, Baskin-Robbins/Dunkin Donuts, Chick-fil-A, Church's, KFC, Lizard's Thicket, McDonald's, Ocean View Seafood, Ruby Tuesday, Sandy's HotDogs, Scholtzsky's, Taco Bell, Wendy's, Zaxby's, 🏨 American Inn, InTown Suites, Quality Inn, Ramada Ltd, Royal Inn, 🅾 Advance Parts, Belk, $General, Office Depot, PepBoys, Rite Aid

SC

🅖 = gas 🍴 = food 🛏 = lodging 🅞 = other 🆁🆂 = rest stop   Copyright 2014 - The NEXT Exit ®

COLUMBIA

▲E INTERSTATE 20 CONT'D

Exit	Services
64b a	I-26, US 76, E to Columbia, W to Greenville, Spartanburg
63	Bush River Rd, **N** 🅖 Shell/Circle K/dsl, 🍴 Burger King, Cracker Barrel, Real Mexican, Subway, 🛏 Travelodge, 🅞 CVS Drug, **S** 🅖 Marathon, Murphy USA/dsl, RaceWay, Sunoco/dsl, 🍴 El Chico, Fuddrucker's, The Villa, 🛏 Best Western, DoubleTree, Knights Inn, Sleep Inn, 🅞 Hamrick's, Walmart
61	US 378, W Columbia, **N** 🅖 Exxon/Hardee's, 🍴 Chili's, McDonald's, Taco Bell, 🛏 Wingate Inn, 🅞 Honda, **S** 🅖 BP/dsl, Shell/Burger King/dsl, 🍴 Waffle House
58	US 1, W Columbia, **N** 🅖 Exxon, Shell/Subway/dsl, 🍴 Waffle House, **S** 🅖 Murphy Express/dsl, 🍴 Bojangles, San Jose Mexican, 🛏 ValuePlace Inn
55	SC 6, to Lexington, **N** 🅖 Shell, 🛏 Hampton Inn (2mi), 🅞 CarQuest, John's RV Ctr, **S** 🅖 BP/dsl, Kangaroo/DQ/dsl, Pops, 🍴 Bojangles, Dunkin Donuts, Great Wall Chinese, Maurice's BBQ, McDonald's, Waffle House, Wendy's, 🛏 Ramada Ltd, 🅞 CVS Drug, $General, Piggly Wiggly
52.5mm	**weigh sta wb**
51	SC 204, to Gilbert, **N** 🅖 Exxon/dsl, Shell/Stuckey's/Subway/dsl/24hr, 🍴 Burger King, **S** 🅖 ♥Loves/Chester's/McDonald's/dsl/scales/24hr, 🅞 $General
44	SC 34, to Gilbert, **N** 🅖 BP/Blimpie/dsl, 44Trkstp/rest/dsl/24hr
39	US 178, to Batesburg, **N** 🅖 Exxon/dsl, 🍴 Hillview Rest. **S** 🅖 Marathon/dsl
35.5mm	**weigh sta eb**
33	SC 39, to Wagener, **N** 🅖 Cheapway/dsl, **S** 🅖 KK/Huddle House/dsl/scales
29	SC 49, Wire Rd
22	US 1, to Aiken, **S** 🅖 BP/dsl, RaceWay, Shell/Circle K/dsl, 🍴 Baynham's, Hardee's, McDonald's, Waffle House, 🛏 Days Inn, Quality Inn, 🅞 $General, Palmetto Lake RV Camping, to USC Aiken
20mm	parking area, both lanes (commercial vehicles only)
18	SC 19, to Aiken, **S** 🅖 Exxon/Subway/dsl, Shell/dsl, 🍴 Waffle House, 🛏 Deluxe Inn, Guesthouse Inn, 🅞 🅗
11	Bettis Academy Rd, SC 144, Graniteville, **N** 🅖 BP/Huddle House/dsl/scales/24hr, **S** 🅖 Wilco/Hess/Dunkin Donuts/Subway/dsl/scales/24hr
6	I-520 to N Augusta
5	US 25, SC 121, **N** 🅖 BP/Circle K/dsl, Circle K/DQ, Shell/Circle K/Bojangles/dsl, 🍴 Burger King, Checkers, McDonald's, Sonic, Subway, 🅞 Advance Parts, $General, Food Lion, **S** 🅖 Marathon, 🍴 Waffle House, 🛏 Sleep Inn
1	SC 230, Martintown Rd, N Augusta, **N** 🅖 Gas+/dsl, **S** 🅖 Shell/Circle K/Subway/dsl, 🍴 Waffle House, 🅞 to Garn's Place
.5mm	**Welcome Ctr eb, full 🅗 facilities, 🅒, 🛏, litter barrels, vending, petwalk**
0mm	South Carolina/Georgia state line, Savannah River

▲E INTERSTATE 26

Exit	Services
221	Meeting St, Charleston, **2 mi E** 🍴 Church's, KFC, 🛏 Hampton Inn, 🅞 Visitors Ctr, Family$, Piggly Wiggly
221b	US 17 N, to Georgetown
I-26 begins/ends on US 17 in Charleston, SC.	
221a	US 17 S, to Kings St, to Savannah, **N** 🅗
220	Romney St (from wb)

CHARLESTON

219b	Morrison Dr, East Bay St (from eb), **N** 🅖 Exxon
219a	Rutledge Ave (from eb, no EZ return), to The Citadel College of Charleston
218	Spruill Ave (from wb), N Charleston
217	N Meeting St (from eb)
216b a	SC 7, Cosgrove Ave, to US 17 S
215	SC 642, Dorchester Rd, N Charleston, **N** 🅖 El Cheapo/dsl, 🛏 Clarion, **S** 🅖 BP/dsl, 🍴 Alex's Rest, 🅞 Rodeway Inn
213b a	Montague Ave, Mall Dr, **N** 🍴 Piccadilly's, Red Lobster, 🛏 Courtyard, Sheraton, ValuePlace, 🅞 Charles Towne Square, **S** 🅖 BP/dsl, Mobil, 🍴 Arby's, Big Billy's Burgers, Bufflo Wild Wings, Burger King, Chick-fil-A, CiCi's Pizza, Fatz Cafe, Firehouse Subs, 5 Guys Burgers, Golden Corral, Grand Buffet, Gringos, Hardee's, IHOP, Jimmy John's, Jim'N Nick's BBQ, Kamille's Cafe, La Hacienda, McAlister's Deli, McDonald's, Panera Bread, Qdoba, Rita's Custard, Starbucks, Waffle House, 🛏 ALoft, Crowne Plaza, Days Inn, EconoLodge, Embassy Suites, Extended Stay Deluxe, Fairfield Inn, Hampton Inn, Hilton Garden, Holiday Inn Express, HomePlace Suites, Homestead Suites, Homewood Suites, Hyatt Place, InTown Suites, N Charleston Inn, Residence Inn, Sleep Inn, 🅞 AT&T, Old Navy, Radio Shack, Sam's Club/gas, Staples, Tanger Outlet/Framous Brands, Verizon, Walmart, vet
212c b	I-526, E to Mt Pleasant, W to Savannah 🔄
212a	Remount Rd, Hanahan, **N on US 52/78** 🍴 KFC, Taco Bell, 🅞 Advance Parts, AutoZone, Ford, Suzuki
211b a	Aviation Pkwy, **N on US 52/78** 🅖 Citgo, Exxon, 🍴 Arby's, Burger King, Capt D's, Church's, KFC, McDonald's, Papa John's, Popeye's, Sonic, Subway, Super Buffet, Taco Bell, Zaxby's, 🛏 Masters Inn, Radisson, 🅞 O'Reilly Parts, PepBoys, PetCo, U-Haul, USPO, **S** 🅖 Kangaroo/dsl, 🍴 Waffle House, 🛏 Budget Inn
209	Ashley Phosphate Rd, to US 52, **N** 🅖 Exxon, Kangaroo, 🍴 Applebee's, Cane's, Carrabba's, Chick-fil-A, China Buffet, Chipotle Mexican, ChuckECheese, Denny's, Hardee's, Hooters, Jason's Deli, Jersey Mike's Subs, Jimmy John's, King Street Grill, Longhorn Steaks, Los Reyes, Moe's SW Grill, O'Charley's, Olive Garden, Outback Steaks, Perkins, Smokey Bones BBQ, Starbucks, Taco Bell, Waffle House, Wendy's, Wild Wing Cafe, 🛏 Candlewood Suites, Country Hearth Inn, Country Inn&Suites, Hawthorn Inn, Holiday Inn Express, InTown Suites, Red Roof Inn, Studio+, 🅞 🅗 AT&T, Barnes&Noble, Belk, Best Buy, BigLots, Books-A-Million, Dillard's, $General, $Tree, Firestone/auto, GNC, Hancock Fabrics, Home Depot, JC Penney, Lowe's, Marshalls, Michael's, Nissan, Office Depot, Old Navy, Ross, Sears/auto, Target, Tire Kingdom, Toyota/Scion, Verizon, Walgreens, Walmart, **S** 🅖 BP, Hess/dsl, RaceWay/dsl, 🍴 Bojangles, Cracker Barrel, IHOP, McDonald's, Osaka Asian, Ruby Tuesday, Waffle House, 🛏 Best Western, Hampton Inn, Hyatt Place, InTown Suites, La Quinta, Motel 6, Quality Inn, Relax Inn, Residence Inn, Sleep Inn, Staybridge Suites, Value Place Inn
209a	to US 52 (from wb), to Goose Creek, Moncks Corner
205b a	US 78, to Summerville, **N** 🅖 BP, Hess/dsl, 🍴 Arby's, Atl Bread Co, Bruster's, Cook-Out, Dunkin Donuts, Fortune Garden, Sonic, Subway, Waffle House, Wendy's, Zaxby's, 🛏 Fairfield Inn, Hampton Inn, Holiday Inn Express, Wingate Inn, 🅞 🅗, CVS Drug, Charleston Southern U, **S** 🅖 Hess/dsl, Sunoco/dsl, 🍴 Burger King, KFC, 🅞 Advance

NORTH CHARLESTON

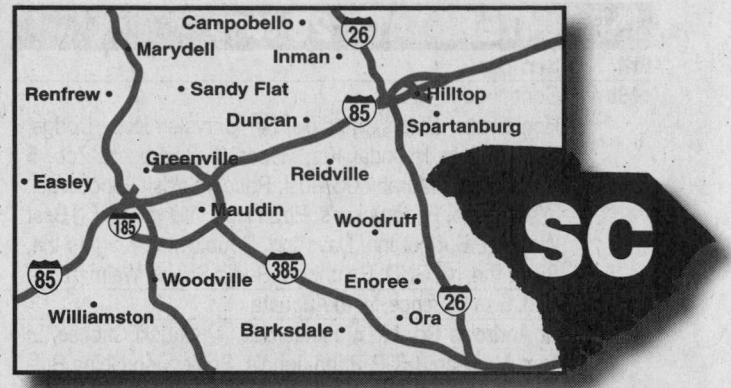

⬆️ E INTERSTATE 26 CONT'D

Exit	Services
205b a	Continued Parts, KOA, Piggly Wiggly
204mm	🆁🆂 eb, full 🅰 facilities, vending, 🅲, 🅰, litter barrels, petwalk
203	College Park Rd, Ladson, N 🅰 BP, Sunoco/dsl, 🍴 Mc-Donald's, Waffle House, 🏨 Best Western, Days Inn, S 🅾 KOA (2mi)
202mm	🆁🆂 wb, full 🅰 facilities, vending, 🅲, 🅰, litter barrels, petwalk
199b a	US 17 A, to Moncks Corner, Summerville, N 🅰 BP, Hess/Dunkin Donuts/Godfather's Pizza/dsl, Kangaroo/dsl, 🅻🅾🆅🅴🆂/McDonald's/dsl/scales/24hr, Shell, 🍴 China Chef, China Wok, KFC, Subway, 🅾 Advance Parts, AutoZone, BiLo, Buick/GMC, CVS Drug, $General, Family$, O'Reilly Parts, vet, S 🅰 Shell/Circle K, 🍴 Applebee's, Arby's, Atlanta Bread, Bojangles, Burger King, Chick-fil-A, China Token, Cracker Barrel, Domino's, Firewater Grille, 5 Guys Burgers, Hardee's, IHOP, Jersey Mike's Subs, La Hacienda, Logan's Roadhouse, Marble Slab, McAlisters Deli, Mc-Donald's, Moe's SW Grill, O'Charleys, Panera Bread, Papa John's, Perkins, Ruby Tuesday, Ryan's, Santi's Taqueria, Shoney's, Starbucks, Sticky Fingers, Waffle House, Ye Ole Fashioned Cafe, Zaxby's, 🏨 Comfort Suites, Country Inn&Suites, EconoLodge, Economy Inn, Hampton Inn, Holiday Inn Express, Quality Inn, Sleep Inn, 🅾 AT&T, Best Buy, Belk, Chrysler/Jeep, Dick's, GNC, Home Depot, Kohl's, Lowe's, Petsmart, Radio Shack, Ross, Staples, Target, Tire Kingdom, TJ Maxx, Verizon, Walgreens, Walmart, World Mkt
194	SC 16, to Jedburg, access to Foreign Trade Zone 21
187	SC 27, to Ridgeville, St George, N 🅰 Shell, S 🅰 BP/dsl, 🅾 Francis Beidler Forest (10mi)
177	SC 453, to Holly Hill, Harleyville, S 🅰 Shell/dsl, 🏨 Ashley Lodge
174mm	weigh sta both lanes
172b a	US 15, to Santee, St George, S 🅰 Horizon/Domino's/Subway/dsl/e-85/scales/24hr
169b a	I-95, N to Florence, S to Savannah
165	SC 210, to Bowman, N 🅰 Exxon/dsl, S 🅰 BP/dsl
159	SC 36, to Bowman, N 🅰 🅻🅾🆅🅴🆂/McDonald's/dsl/scales/24hr/@, N 🅰 Exxon
154b a	US 301, to Santee, Orangeburg, N 🍴 Cook-Out, 🏨 Days Inn, S 🅰 Exxon/dsl, Loves/Chesters/Subway/dsl/scales/24hr, Shell/dsl, 🍴 Waffle House
152mm	🆁🆂 wb, full 🅰 facilities, vending, 🅲, 🅰, litter barrels, petwalk
150mm	🆁🆂 eb, full 🅰 facilities, vending, 🅲, 🅰, litter barrels, petwalk
149	SC 33, to Cameron, to SC State Coll, Edisto Gardens Claflin Coll
145b a	US 601, to Orangeburg, St Matthews, S 🅰 BP, Citgo/dsl, Exxon, Shell, Sunoco/dsl, 🍴 Burger King, Chick-fil-A, Cracker Barrel, Fatz Café, Hardee's, KFC, McDonald's, Ruby Tuesday, Seafood Academy, Subway, Waffle House, Wendy's, Zaxby's, 🏨 Carolina Lodge, Comfort Inn, Country Inn&Suites, Fairfield Inn, Hampton Inn, Holiday Inn Express, Howard Johnson, Quality Inn, Sleep Inn, Southern Lodge, Travelers Inn, 🅾 🅷, Cadillac/Chevrolet, Chrysler/Dodge/Jeep, $General, Ford, Nissan, Toyota/Scion
139	SC 22, to St Matthews, S 🅰 Horizon/e-85, Mobil, Wilco/

Exit	Services
139	Continued Hess/Arby's/dsl/scales/24hr, 🅾 Sweetwater Lake Camping (2.5mi)
136	SC 6, to North, Swansea, N 🅰 Exxon/dsl
129	US 21, N 🅰 Shell/dsl
125	SC 31, to Gaston, N 🅾 Wolfe's Truck/trailer repair
123mm	🆁🆂 both lanes, full 🅰 facilities, vending, 🅲, 🅰, litter barrels, petwalk
119	US 176, US 21, to Dixiana, S 🅰 BP/Subway/dsl, Exxon/dsl
116	I-77 N, to Charlotte, US 76, US 378, to Ft Jackson
115	US 176, US 21, US 321, to Cayce, N 🅰 BP, Gulf, Race-Way, Shell, 🍴 Pizza Hut, Waffle House, 🅾 Advance Parts, Bi-Lo, CVS Drug, $General, $Tree, Harley-Davidson, Reid's Foods, S 🅰 🅻🅾🆅🅴🆂/DQ/Wendy's/dsl/scales/24hr, Shell, 🍴 Bojangles, Great China, Hardee's, McDonald's, Subway, 🏨 Country Hearth Inn, 🅾 Firestone, Piggly Wiggly
113	SC 302, Cayce, N 🅰 Exxon, Mobil/Burger King, Sunoco/dsl, 🍴 Waffle House, 🏨 Inn, Knights Inn, Masters Inn, 🅾 AutoZone, $General, O'Reilly Parts, Rite Aid, Save-A-Lot, Toyota/Scion, Walgreens, S 🅰 BP, RaceWay/dsl, Shell/Circle K, 🍴 Lizard's Thicket, Shoney's, Subway, Waffle House, 🏨 Carolina Lodge, Country Inn&Suites, Days Inn, Sleep Inn, Travelers Inn, 🅾 NAPA, 🏨
111b a	US 1, to W Columbia, N 🅰 Murphy USA/dsl, RaceWay/dsl, Shell/Circle K, 🍴 Carolina Wings, Chick-fil-A, Domino's, Dragon City Chinese, Hardee's, Little Caesars, Maurice's BBQ, Moe's SW Grill, Ruby Tuesday, Sonic, Subway, Tokyo Grill, Waffle House, Zaxby's, 🏨 Clarion, Quality Inn, 🅾 AT&T, Bi-Lo, $General, $Tree, GNC, Hobby Lobby, Pet Supplies+, Radio Shack, Walgreens, Walmart, to USC, S 🅰 Hess/dsl, 🍴 Applebee's, Popeye's, Wendy's, 🅾 Aldi Foods, BigLots, Family$, Lowe's, U-Haul
110	US 378, to W Columbia, Lexington, N 🍴 Burger King, Grecian Gardens, Happy China, Lizard's Thicket, McDonald's, Rush's Rest., Subway, Waffle House, 🏨 America's Inn, Best Value Inn, Hampton Inn, Holiday Inn, 🅾 CVS Drug, Family$, Food Lion, S 🅰 Mobil/dsl, Shell/Circle K, 🍴 Atlanta Bread, Bojangles, China Dragon, Firehouse Subs, La Fogata, Pizza Hut, 🏨 Executive Inn, 🅾 🅷, Urgent Care
108b a	I-126 to Columbia, Bush River Rd, N 🅰 Shell/dsl, 🍴 Capt D's, Chick-fil-A, Hardee's, Ruby Tuesday, Schlotzsky's, Shoney's, Wendy's, Zaxby's, 🏨 Comfort Inn, Western Inn, 🅾 Advance Parts, Belk, $General, Firestone/auto, Office Depot, Rite Aid, Verizon, **Multiple services 1-3 mi N off I-126**, Greystone Blvd, N 🅰 BP, Exxon/dsl, 🍴 Waffle House, 🏨 Embassy Suites, Extended Stay America,

CAYCE

COLUMBIA

SC

🅿 = gas 🍴 = food 🛏 = lodging 🅾 = other 🅿ⓢ = rest stop   Copyright 2014 - The NEXT Exit ®

↗🅔 INTERSTATE 26 CONT'D

Exit	Services
108b a	Continued Homewood Suites, Studio+, 🅾 Chrysler/Jeep, Dodge, Ford/Lincoln, Hyundai, Kia, Mazda, S Riverbanks Zoo, S 🅿 City Gas, Murphy USA/dsl, RaceWay/dsl, Sunoco/dsl, 🍴 El Chico, Fuddrucker's, Pizza Hut, Villa Italian, 🛏 Best Western, Budget Inn, Days Inn, DoubleTree, Knights Inn, Sleep Inn, 🅾 GNC, Hamrick's, Radio Shack, Walmart
107b a	I-20, E to Florence, W to Augusta
106b a	St Andrews Rd, N 🅿 Exxon/dsl, 🍴 ChuckECheese, El Toro Mexican, IHOP, Papa John's, Sonic, Top China Buffet, 🛏 Motel 6, 🅾 Bi-Lo, Camping World RV Ctr, CVS Drug, $Tree, Infiniti, Jaguar, Nissan, Walgreens, S 🅿 BP/dsl, Hess/Dunkin Donuts/dsl, Shell, 🍴 Domino's, King Buffet, Maurice's BBQ, McDonald's, Pizza Hut, Substation II, Waffle House, WG's Wings, Zaxby's, 🛏 EconoLodge, Red Roof Inn, 🅾 $General, Food Lion, Fred's, Tire Kingdom, vet
104	Piney Grove Rd, N 🅿 Sunoco/dsl, 🍴 Hardee's, San Jose Mexican, Waffle House, 🛏 Quality Inn, 🅾 Sportsmans Whse, S 🅿 Exxon, Shell/dsl, 🛏 Country Inn&Suites, Microtel, 🅾 Carmax, Land Rover
103	Harbison Blvd, N 🍴 Applebee's, Hooters, Wendy's, 🛏 Hampton Inn, 🅾 Chevrolet, Home Depot, Lowe's, funpark, S 🅿 Hess/Dunkin Donuts/dsl, Shell, 🍴 Bailey's Grille, Bojangles, BoneFish Grill, Bruster's, Buffalo Wild Wings, Carolina Alehouse, Carrabba's, Casa Linda, Chili's, Chick-fil-A, China Buffet, Chiptle Mexican, Coldstone, Copper River Grill, Denny's, Fazoli's, Firehouse Subs, 5 Guys Burgers, Food Court, Huhot Mongolian, Huller's Rest, Jimmy John's, Longhorn Steaks, Macaroni Grill, Marble Slab, McAlister's Deli, McDonald's, Miyabi Japanese, Miyo's, Monterrey Mexican, O'Charley's, Olive Garden, Outback Steaks, Panera Bread, Ruby Tuesday, Rush's BBQ, Ryan's, Sonic, Subway, TX Roadhouse, Tokyo Grill, Tsunami Steaks, Which Wich, Wild Wing Cafe, Yamato Japanese, 🛏 Comfort Suites, Fairfield Inn, Hilton Garden, Holiday Inn Express, InTown Suites, TownePlace Suites, Wingate Inn, 🅾 AT&T, Barnes&Noble, Belk, Best Buy, Books-A-Million, Buick/GMC, Dick's, Dillard's, $Tree, Firestone/auto, Goodyear/auto, Hancock Fabrics, JC Penney, Kohl's, Marshalls, Michael's, Midas, Office Depot, Old Navy, Petsmart, Publix, Ross, Sam's Club/gas, Sears/auto, Staples, SteinMart, Target, Tire Kingdom, TJ Maxx, Verizon, Walmart, mall
102	SC 60, Ballentine, Irmo, N 🍴 Cracker Barrel, 🛏 Extended Stay Deluxe, Hyatt Place, S 🅿 JP/dsl, Shell, 🍴 Arby's, Atlanta Bread Co, Bellacino's Pizza, Maurice's BBQ, Moe's SW Grill, New China, Taco Bell, TCBY, Zaxby's, 🛏 Residence Inn, 🅾 AAA, CVS Drug, Jiffy Lube, tires, same as 103
101b a	US 76, US 176, to N Columbia, 1/2 mi N 🅿 Exxon/Subway/dsl, 🍴 China House, Fatz Café, Fuji Cafe, HotDog Heaven, Jersey Mike's Subs, Zorba's, 🅾 AutoZone, $General, Food Lion, Harley-Davidson, Publix, Rite Aid, Walgreens, S 🅿 BP, Hickory Point/dsl, Mobil, 🍴 Burger King, Lucky's BurgerShack, Waffle House, 🅾 Bi-Lo, $General, Toyota/Scion
97	US 176, to Ballentine, Peak, N 🍴 China 1, Subway, 🅾 Food Lion, S 🅿 Exxon/dsl
94mm	weigh sta wb

Exit	Services
91	SC 48, to Chapin, S 🅿 BP/dsl, Exxon/Taco Bell/dsl, Shell/dsl, 🍴 Bojangles, Farm Boys BBQ, McDonald's, Waffle House, 🅾 Urgent Care, to Dreher Island SP
85	SC 202, Little Mountain, Pomaria, S to Dreher Island SP
82	SC 773, to Prosperity, Pomaria, N 🅿 Marathon/Kangaroo/Subway/dsl/24hr, Wilco/Hess/Wendy's/dsl/scales/24hr, 🍴 Waffle House, 🅾 Flea Mkt Campground
81mm	weigh sta eb
76	SC 219, to Pomaria, Newberry, N 🅿 ❤Loves/McDonald's/Chester's/dsl/scales/24hr, 0-2 mi S 🅿 BP, Murphy USA, 🍴 Burger King, Wendy's, 🛏 Hampton Inn (4mi), Holiday Inn Express, 🅾 Walmart, to Newberry Opera House
74	SC 34, to Newberry, N 🅿 BP, Shell/dsl, 🍴 Bill&Fran's Café, 🛏 Best Value Inn, S 🅿 Citgo/dsl, 🍴 Waffle House, 🛏 Days Inn, 🅾 Ⓗ, to NinetySix HS, 2-4 mi S 🍴 Arby's, Capt D's, Hardee's, McDonald's, 🛏 Comfort Inn, Economy Inn, Holiday Inn Express
72	SC 121, to Newberry, S 🅿 Citgo/dsl, 🅾 Ⓗ, to Newberry Coll
66	SC 32, to Jalapa
63.5mm	🅿ⓢ both lanes, full ♿ facilities, 🍴 vending, 🗑 litter barrels, petwalk
60	SC 66, to Joanna, S 🅿 BP/dsl, 🅾 Magnolia RV Park
54	SC 72, to Clinton, N 🅿 BP/dsl, S 🅿 Citgo/dsl/24hr, 🍴 Fatz Cafe, 🛏 Hampton Inn, 🅾 Ⓗ, to Presbyterian Coll
52	SC 56, to Clinton, N 🅿 🚚/Subway/dsl/scales/24hr, 🍴 Blue Ocean Rest., McDonald's, 🛏 Comfort Suites, Quality Inn, S 🅿 Citgo/dsl, 🍴 Hardee's, Waffle House, Wendy's, 🛏 Days Inn, Howard Johnson, 🅾 Ⓗ
51	I-385, to Greenville (from wb)
45.5mm	Enoree River
44	SC 49, to Cross Anchor Union
41	SC 92, to Enoree, N 🅿 Valero
38	SC 146, to Woodruff, N 🅿 HotSpot/Shell/Hardee's/Stuckey's/dsl/scales/24hr
35	SC 50, Walnut Grove Rd, to Woodruff, S 🅿 BP/dsl
33mm	S Tyger River
32mm	N Tyger River
28	US 221, to Spartanburg, N 🅿 Kangaroo/Quiznos/dsl/24hr, Shell/Subway/dsl, 🍴 Bojangles, Burger King, J-Bones BBQ, Waffle House, 🅾 Ⓗ, Pine Ridge Camping (3mi), to Walnut Grove Plantation
22	SC 296, Reidville Rd, to Spartanburg, N 🅿 Marathon/Kangaroo/dsl, Exxon, Spinx, 🍴 Arby's, Blue Bay Rest., Bruster's, Carolina BBQ, Chief's Rest., Fatz Cafe, Fuddrucker's (1mi), Little Caesars, McDonald's, Outback Steaks, Quiznos, Waffle House, Wasabi Japanese, Zaxby's, 🅾 Advance Parts, $General, USPO, vet, to Croft SP, S 🅿 Hickory Point/dsl, Sunoco/dsl, 🍴 Apollo's Pizza, Burger King, Clock Rest., Denny's, Domino's, Hardee's, Hong Kong Express, Papa John's, Subway, 🛏 Sleep Inn, Southern Suites, Super 8, 🅾 Bi-Lo, BMW, CVS Drug, $General, Hyundai, Midas, Rite Aid, Toyota/Scion, VW, Walgreens, vet
21b a	US 29, to Spartanburg, N 🅿 BP, Spinx, 🍴 A&W/LJ Silver, Blue Fin Grill, Bojangles, Buffalo Wild Wings, Burger King, Chick-fil-A, Chipotle Mexican, City Range Steaks, ChuckECheese, CiCi's, City Range Grill, Corona Mexican, DQ, Cowboy Steaks, Firehouse Subs, FoodCourt, Fuji Japanese, Golden Corral, Jack-in-the-Box, Jason's Deli, Kanpai Tokyo, KFC, La Taverna Italian, Longhorn

COLUMBIA

SPARTANBURG

SC

S P A R T A N B U R G

⬆🄴 INTERSTATE 26 CONT'D

Exit	Services
21b a	Continued Steaks, McAlister's Deli, Moe's SW Grill, O'Charley's, Olive Garden, Panera Bread, Pizza Hut, Red Lobster, Ruby Tuesday, Ryan's, Substation II, Subway, Wendy's, 🛏 Comfort Suites, Hampton Inn, Holiday Inn Express, 🅞 AT&T, Barnes&Noble, Belk, Best Buy, Costco/gas, Curves, Dick's, Dillard's, Discount Tire, $General, Firestone/auto, Hamrick's, Home Depot, JC Penney, Jo-Ann Fabrics, Lowe's, Meineke, Michael's, Office Depot, Old Navy, Petsmart, Rite Aid, Ross, Sears/auto, TJ Maxx, Verizon, Walmart/McDonald's, mall, USPO, **S** 🅖 Marathon/dsl, Shell/dsl, 🍴 Apollo's Pizza, Applebee's, Compadre's TexMex, IHOP, McDonald's, Piccadilly Cafe, Pizza Inn, Shogun Japanese, Starbucks, Taco Bell, Waffle House, 🅞 Advance Parts, CarQuest, $Tree, Hobby Lobby, Ingles Foods/gas, Kohl's, Sam's Club/gas, Target, TrueValue
19b a	Lp I-85, Spartanburg, **N** 🅖 Valero, 🍴 Cracker Barrel, Subway, 🛏 Residence Inn, **S** 🛏 Brookwood Inn
18b a	I-85, N to Charlotte, S to Greenville
17	New Cut Rd, **S** 🅖 Sunoco/dsl, 🍴 Burger King, Fatz Café, McDonald's, Waffle House, 🛏 Days Inn, EconoLodge, Howard Johnson, Red Roof Inn
16	John Dodd Rd, to Wellford, **N** 🅖 Marathon/Kangaroo/Aunt M's/dsl, 🅞 Camping World RV Ctr
15	US 176, to Inman, **N** 🅖 Breakers, Shell/Circle K/dsl, 🍴 Waffle House, 🅞 🄷 **S** 🅖 Citgo/dsl
10	SC 292, to Inman, **N** 🅖 Shell/Subway/dsl/24hr
7.5mm	Lake William C. Bowman
5	SC 11, Foothills Scenic Dr, Chesnee, Campobello, **N** 🅖 Kangaroo/🅻🅾🆅🅴🆂/Subway/dsl/scales/24hr, **S** 🅖 Marathon/Li'l Cricket/dsl
3mm	**Welcome Ctr eb, full** 🅰 **facilities, info,** 🄲, 🄰, **litter barrels, vending, petwalk, wi fi**
1	SC 14, to Landrum, **S** 🅖 Shell/Burger King/dsl, 🍴 Bojangles, China Cafe, Pizza Hut (1mi), Stone Soup Rest, Subway, 🅞 Bi-Lo Foods, $General, Ingles/café/gas, Verizon, vet
0mm	South Carolina/North Carolina state line

⬆🄽 INTERSTATE 77

Exit	Services
91mm	South Carolina/North Carolina state line
90	US 21, Carowinds Blvd, **E** 🅖 Gulf/dsl, Kangaroo, 🍴 Bojangles, McDonald's, 🅞 🄷, Carowinds Camping (4mi), fireworks, **W** 🅖 Exxon/café, Kangaroo/Subway, Shell/Circle K/Wendy's/dsl, 🍴 Cracker Barrel, El Cancun Mexican, KFC, Shoney's, 🛏 Best Western, Comfort Inn, Motel 6, Plaza Motel, Quality Inn, Sleep Inn, 🅞 Carowinds Funpark
89.5mm	**Welcome Ctr sb, full** 🅰 **facilities, info,** 🄲, **vending,** 🄰, **litter barrels, petwalk/weigh sta nb**
88	Gold Hill Rd, to Pineville, **E** 🅞 Urgent Care, **W** 🅖 Shell/dsl, Valero, 🅞 Chrysler/Dodge/Jeep, Ford, Hyundai, KOA
85	SC 160, Ft Mill, Tega Cay, **E** 🅖 Exxon, 🍴 Subway, 🅞 Bi-Lo, Ft Mill Drug, **W** 🅖 BP/dsl, Shell/7-11, 🍴 Beef O'Brady's, Burger King, Charanda Mexican, Chick-fil-A, Fish Mkt Grill, Fratelli's Italian, LiuLiu's Chinese, Papa John's, Pizza Hut, Starbucks, Wendy's, Zaxby's, 🛏 Fairfield Inn, 🅞 AutoZone, CVS Drug, Firestone/auto, Goodyear/auto, Harris-Teeter, Lowe's, Walgreens, vet
84.5mm	**weigh sta sb**

R O C K   H I L L

83	SC 49, Sutton Rd, **W** 🅖 🅻🅾🆅🅴🆂/Chester/Subway/dsl/scales/24hr
82.5mm	Catawba River
82c	US 21, SC 161, Rock Hill, Ft Mill, **E** 🅖 Exxon, 🍴 IHOP, Sonny's BBQ, Steak'n Shake, Zaxby's, 🅞 Home Depot, Petsmart, museum, **W** 🅖 Citgo, Kangaroo/dsl, Shell/Circle K, 🍴 Empire Grill, Hooters, Outback Steaks, Sonic, Starbucks, 🛏 Courtyard, 🅞 🄷, $General, Food Lion, Tuffy Auto
82b a	**E** 🅖 Exxon, 🛏 Ramada Inn, **W** 🅖 Kangaroo, RaceWay, Sunoco/dsl, 🍴 Arby's, Bojangles, Burger King, Burk's BBQ, Chick-fil-A, CiCi's Pizza, Cookout, Del Taco, HoneyBaked Ham, Jack-in-the-Box, Little Caesar's, McDonald's, Penn Sta. Subs, Pizza Hut, Sake Express, Sakura Japanese, Subway, Taco Bell, Waffle House, Wendy's, 🛏 Dest Value Inn, Dest Way, Country Inn&Suites, Days Inn, EconoLodge, Microtel, Quality Inn, Regency Inn, 🅞 Advance Parts, Aldi Foods, AutoZone, BigLots, Bi-Lo, Cadillac/Chevrolet, Compare Mkt, $General, Family$, Firestone/auto, Hancock Fabrics, K-Mart, NAPA, Nissan, Office Depot, O'Reilly Parts, PepBoys, Verizon, city park
79	SC 122, Dave Lyle Blvd, to Rock Hill, **E** 🅖 BP, Murphy USA/dsl, 🍴 Amber Buffet, Applebee's, Charanda Mexican, Chick-fil-A, Cracker Barrel, DQ, Hardee's, Longhorn Steaks, Maurice's BBQ, O'Charley's, Ryan's, Ruby Tuesday, 🛏 Comfort Suites, Hampton Inn, Holiday Inn, Towne Place Suites, Wingate Inn, 🅞 Belk, Discount Tire, $Tree, Food Lion, Hobby Lobby, Honda, JC Penney, Kohl's, Lowe's, Meineke, Nissan, Sears/auto, Staples, Tire Kingdom, Toyota, Verizon, Walmart, mall, **W** 🅖 Kangaroo/dsl, 🍴 Baskin-Robbins/Dunkin Donuts, Bob Evans, Chili's, DQ, Fast Lane Grill, Jack-in-the-Box, McAlister's Deli, McDonald's, Olive Garden, Panera Bread, Pizza Cafe, Quiznos, Subway, Taco Bell, Wendy's, 🛏 Hilton Garden, 🅞 Best Buy, Books-A-Million, Dick's, Ford/Lincoln, Michael's, Ross, Target, TJ Maxx, Urgent Care, visitor ctr
77	US 21, SC 5, to Rock Hill, **E** 🅖 BP/Subway/dsl, Citgo/dsl, Wilco/Hess/dsl, 🅞 to Andrew Jackson SP (12mi), **W** 🅖 Exxon/dsl, Pride/dsl/scales, 🍴 Bojangles, Waffle House, 🅞 to Winthrop Coll
75	Porter Rd, **E** 🅖 Sunoco/dsl
73	SC 901, to Rock Hill, York, **E** 🅖 Exxon/dsl, 🅵🅻🆈🅸🅽🅶 🅹/Denny's/dsl/scales/LP/24hr, **W** 🄷
66mm	🆁🆂 both lanes, full 🅰 facilities, 🄲, 🄰, litter barrels, vending, petwalk
65	SC 9, to Chester, Lancaster, **E** 🅖 BP/24hr, Citgo/dsl, Liberty/Subway/dsl, 🍴 Bojangles, China Wok, Waffle House, 🛏 Days Inn, EconoLodge, Relax Inn, 🅞 $General, IGA Foods/gas, **W** 🅖 Exxon/dsl, 🍴 Burger King, Country

🅖 = gas 🍴 = food 🛏 = lodging 🄾 = other 🆁🆂 = rest stop   Copyright 2014 - The NEXT Exit ®

⬆️N INTERSTATE 77 CONT'D

Exit	Services
65	Continued Omelette, Front Porch Cafe, KFC/Taco Bell, McDonald's, 🛏 Comfort Inn, Motel 6, Super 8, 🄾 🗓, vet
62	SC 56, to Fort Lawn, Richburg
55	SC 97, to Chester, Great Falls, **E** 🅖 Exxon/dsl, **W** 🗓, to Chester SP
48	SC 200, to Great Falls, **E** 🅖 Shell/Grand Central Rest./dsl/@, **W** 🅖 Wilco/Hess/DQ/Wendy's/dsl
46	SC 20, to White Oak
41	SC 41, to Winnsboro, **E** to Lake Wateree SP
34	SC 34, to Winnsboro, Ridgeway, **E** 🅖 ampm, 🛏 Ridgeway Motel (1mi), 🄾 camping (1mi), **W** 🅖 Exxon/dsl, 🍴 Waffle House, 🛏 Ramada Ltd.
32	Peach Rd, Ridgeway, **E** Little Cedar Creek Camping (2mi)
27	Blythewood Rd, **E** 🅖 BP/dsl, Exxon/Bojangles/dsl/24hr, 🍴 Carolina Wings, Hardee's, KFC/Pizza Hut, McDonald's, San Jose Mexican, Subway, Waffle House, Wendy's, 🛏 Comfort Inn, Days Inn, Holiday Inn Express, 🄾 Curves, $General, IGA Foods, repair/tires, USPO, vet, **W** 🍴 Lizard's Thicket, 🄾 Food Lion, Groucho's Deli
24	US 21, to Wilson Blvd., **E** 🅖 BP, Shell/Subway/dsl, 🄾 auto repair, vet
22	Killian Rd, **E** 🅖 Mobil/Burger King/dsl, Murphy Express/dsl, 🍴 Bojangles, Taco Bell, Zaxby's, 🄾 Acura, Aldi Foods, AutoZone, CVS Drug, Firestone, Honda, Kia, Lowe's, Mazda, Rite Aid, Toyota/Scion, VW, Walgreens, **W** 🍴 China Dragon, Monterrey's Mexican, 🄾 AT&T, Lexus, Verizon, Walmart/McDonald's
19	SC 555, Farrow Rd, **E** 🅖 BP, Exxon, Shell, 🍴 Bojangles, Cracker Barrel, Sonic, Wendy's, 🛏 Courtyard, Hilton Garden, Residence Inn, 🄾 🗓, Longs Drug, **W** 🅖 Shell/dsl, 🍴 Waffle House, 🄾 SC Archives
18	to SC 277, to I-20 W (from sb), Columbia
17	US 1, Two Notch Rd, **E** 🅖 BP, Citgo, Kangaroo, Shell/Circle K, 🍴 Arby's, Burger King, TX Roadhouse, Waffle House, 🛏 Holiday Inn, InTown Suites, Quality Inn, Wingate Inn, 🄾 Bi-Lo, Rite Aid, U-Haul, USPO, Walgreens, to Sesquicentennial SP, vet, **W** 🅖 Mobil, 🍴 Chili's, Fazoli's, Hooters, IHOP, Lizard's Thicket, Outback Steaks, Waffle House, 🛏 Comfort Suites, EconoLodge, Fairfield Inn, Hampton Inn, Jameson Suites, La Quinta, Microtel, Motel 6, Red Roof Inn, 🄾 Home Depot
16b a	I-20, **W** to Augusta, **E** to Florence, Alpine Rd
15b a	SC 12, to Percival Rd, **W** 🅖 El Cheapo/gas, Shell, 1/2 mi **W** 🅖 Exxon
13	Decker Blvd (from nb), **W** 🅖 El Cheapo
12	Forest Blvd, Thurmond Blvd, **E** to Ft Jackson, **W** 🅖 BP/dsl, 76/dsl, Shell/dsl/24hr, 🍴 Bojangles, Chick-fil-A, Fatz Café, Golden Corral, Hardee's, McDonald's, RedBone Rest., Steak&Ale, Subway, Wendy's, 🛏 Extended Stay America, Marlboro Inn, Super 8, 🄾 🗓, $Tree, Sam's Club/gas, Walmart/24hr, museum
10	10 SC 760, Jackson Blvd, **E** to Ft Jackson, 2 mi **W** 🅖 BP, 🍴 Applebee's, Bojangles, Burger King, Maurices BBQ, Ruby Tuesday, Subway, 🛏 EconoLodge, Liberty Inn
9b a	US 76, US 378, to Sumter, Columbia, 0-2 mi **E** 🅖 BP, Citgo, Murphy USA/dsl, Shell/Burger King, Sunoco/dsl, United, 🍴 Arby's, Bojangles, Capt D's, Chick-fil-A, Domino's, Hibachi Grill, KFC, Lizard's Thicket, McDonald's, Pizza Hut, Popeye's, Ruby Tuesday, Rush's Rest., Shon

Exit	Services
9b a	Continued ey's, Subway, Taco Bell, Waffle House, 🛏 Best Western, Candlewood Suites, Comfort Inn, Country Inn&Suites, Days Inn, Hampton Inn, Holiday Inn Express, La Quinta, Microtel, Quality Inn, Sleep Inn, TownePlace Suites, 🄾 Advance Parts, Aldi Foods, AutoZone, Buick/Cadillac/GMC, CVS Drug, $Tree, Family$, Firestone/auto, Interstate Batteries, Lowe's, NAPA, O'Reilly Parts, Tire Kingdom, USPO, Walgreens, Walmart, **W** 🅖 Circle K, Shell, 🍴 CiCi's Pizza, Eric's Mexican, Hardee's, Jimmy John's, Panera Bread, Sonic, Starbucks, Wendy's, 🛏 Best Value Inn, 🄾 🗓, BigLots, $General, Radio Shack, Rite Aid, Sav-A-Lot Foods, Target
6b a	Shop Rd, **W** to USC Coliseum, fairgrounds
5	SC 48, Bluff Rd, 1 mi **E** 🅖 76, **W** 🅖 Shell/Burger King/dsl, 🍴 Bojangles (2mi)
3mm	Congaree River
2	Saxe Gotha Rd
1	US 21, US 176, US 321 (from sb), Cayce, **W** accesses same as SC I-26, exit 115.
0mm	I-77 begins/ends on I-26, exit 116.

⬆️N INTERSTATE 85

Exit	Services
106.5mm	South Carolina/North Carolina state line
106	US 29, to Grover, **E** 🅖 BP/dsl, **W** 🅖 Exxon/dsl, Hickory Point/gas, Wilco/Hess/DQ/Wendy's/dsl/scales/24hr
104	SC 99, Tribal Rd, **E** 🅖 Loves/McDonald's/Subway/dsl/scales/24hr, **W** fireworks
103mm	Welcome Ctr sb, full ♿ facilities, info, 🄲, 🛏, litter barrels, vending, petwalk
102	SC 198, to Earl, **E** 🅖 BP/dsl, Shell, 🍴 Hardee's, **W** 🅖 Citgo/dsl, ➡FLYING J/Denny's/dsl/scales/LP/24hr, 🍴 McDonald's, Waffle House
100mm	Buffalo Creek
100	SC 5, to Blacksburg, Shelby, **W** 🅖 Citgo, Sunoco/Subway/dsl/scales/24hr
98	Frontage Rd (from nb), **E** 🍴 Broad River Café
97mm	Broad River
96	SC 18, **E** 🅖 Kangaroo/Krystal/dsl
95	SC 18, to Gaffney, **E** 🅖 Kangaroo/Aunt M's Rest/dsl, PetroMax/dsl, 🛏 Gaffney Inn, Shamrock Inn, 🍴 Mr Waffle, 🄾 🗓, to Limestone Coll
92	SC 11, to Gaffney, **E** 🅖 Marathon/Subway, Murphy USA/dsl, 🍴 Aegean Pizza, Applebee's, Bojangles, Burger King, Chick-fil-A, Daddy Joe's BBQ, Domino's, Fuji, KFC, King Buffet, Little Caesars, McDonald's, Olive Garden, Papa John's, Pizza Hut, Santiago's Mexican, Sonic, Taco Bell, Waffle House, Wendy's, Zaxby's, 🛏 Jameson Inn, Super 8, 🄾 Advance Parts, Aldi Foods, Belk, BigLots, BiLo, $General, $Tree, Ingles Foods, Lowe's, O'Reilly Parts, Radio Shack, Rite Aid, Walgreens, Walmart, USPO, to Limestone Coll, **W** 🅖 BP, 🍴 Fatz Cafe, 🛏 Homestead Lodge, Quality Inn, 🄾 to The Peach, Foothills Scenic Hwy
90	SC 105, SC 42, to Gaffney, **E** 🅖 BP/DQ/dsl, Loves/Arby's/dsl/scales/24hr, 🍴 Bronco Mexican, Clock Rest., Starbucks, Subway, Waffle House, 🛏 Red Roof Inn, Sleep Inn, **W** 🅖 Citgo/dsl, Kangaroo/Burger King, 🍴 Cracker Barrel, FoodCourt, Outback Steaks, 🛏 Hampton Inn, 🄾 Hamrick's, Prime Outlets/famous brands, fruit stand
87	SC 39, **E** 🄾 KOA, **W** 🄾 Rug Outlet, fruit stand/peaches/fireworks
83	SC 110, **E** 🅖 Hot Spot/dsl, 🄾 NAPA, fruit stand, truck re

⬆N INTERSTATE 85 CONT'D

Exit	Services
83	Continued
	pair, **W** 🅖 Auto Trkstp/Mr Waffle/dsl/24hr/@, ⊙ to Cowpens Bfd, fruitstand
82	Frontage Rd (from nb)
80.5mm	Pacolet River
80	SC 57, to Gossett, **E** 🅖 Hot Spot/Shell/dsl
78	US 221, Chesnee, **E** 🅖 Citgo/dsl, 🍴 Hardee's, 🏠 Motel 6, ⊙ fruit stand, **W** 🅖 BP/Subway, QT/dsl, RaceWay/dsl, Sunoco/Burger King/dsl, 🍴 Arby's, Bojangles, McDonald's, Southern BBQ, Subway, Waffle House, Wendy's, 🏠 Hampton Inn, Holiday Inn Express, ⊙ Advance Parts, $General, Harley-Davidson, Ingles Foods/cafe/dsl
77	Lp 85, Spartanburg, services along Lp 85 exits E
75	SC 9, Spartanburg, **E** 🍴 Denny's, 🏠 Best Value Inn, **W** 🅖 BP/Burger King/dsl, Pure, QT/dsl, RaceWay/dsl, 🍴 Bruster's, Capri's Italian, Copper River Grill, Fatz Café, Grapevine Rest, Jade House Asian, La Paz Mexican, McDonald's, Pizza Hut, Waffle House, Zaxby's, 🏠 Days Inn, Comfort Inn, ⊙ CVS Drug, Ingles/cafe/gas, USPO
72	US 176, to I-585, **E** ⊙ to USCS, Wofford/Converse Coll, **W** 🅖 Kangaroo, RaceWay, 🍴 Subway, Waffle House, ⊙ $General, Ingles Foods/cafe/gas, Masters RV Ctr
70b a	I-26, E to Columbia, W to Asheville
69	Lp 85, SC 41 (from nb), to Fairforest
68	SC 129, to Greer
67mm	N Tyger River
66	US 29, to Lyman, Wellford, **E** 🅖 Exxon/Subway/dsl, 🍴 Waffle House
63	SC 290, to Duncan, **E** 🅖 Circle K/dsl, Citgo/dsl, Spinx/Dunkin Donuts/dsl, 🍴 Arby's, Clock Rest., Cracker Barrel, Firehouse Subs, KFC, Paisanos Italian, Pizza Inn, Sake Japanese, Taco Bell, Thai Cuisine, Waffle House, Zaxby's, 🏠 Hampton Inn, Jameson Inn, Microtel, ⊙ Curves, **W** 🅖 BP, Marathon/dsl, 🛢️/Wendy's/dsl/scales/24hr, TA/BP/DQ/rest./dsl/scales/24hr/@, 🍴 Bojangles, Hardee's, La Molcajete Mexican, McDonald's, Waffle House, 🏠 Holiday Inn Express, Quality Inn, Sheridan Inn, ValuePlace Inn, ⊙ Blue Beacon, Speedco
62.5mm	S Tyger River
60	SC 101, to Greer, **E** 🅖 Grand/dsl, Marathon, Sunoco/dsl, 🍴 Senor Garcia's Mexican, Subway, Theo's Rest, **W** 🅖 Exxon/Burger King, 🍴 Waffle House, 🏠 Super 8, ⊙ BMW Visitor Ctr
58	Brockman-McClimon Rd
57	**W** ⊙ Greenville-Spartanburg ✈
56	SC 14, to Greer, **E** 🅖 Citgo/dsl, **W** 🅖 Spinx/dsl, ⊙ 🄷 Goodyear, Outdoor World RV Ctr
55mm	Enoree River
54	Pelham Rd, **E** 🅖 Marathon/Kangaroo, Stop-A-Minute/dsl, 🍴 Burger King, Corona Mexican, Skin's Hotdogs, Waffle House, 🏠 Best Western, **W** 🅖 BP/dsl, 🍴 Acapulcos Mexican, Acropolis Rest, Atlanta Bread Co, Bellacino's, Bojangles, Bertolos Pizza, Chick-fil-A, China Kitchen, Chophouse 47, Dunkin Donuts, Firehouse Subs, 5 Guys Burgers, Hardee's, Jack-in-the-Box, Joe's Crabshack, Joy of Tokyo, Logan's Roadhouse, Macaroni Grill, McDonald's, Moe's SW Grill, On the Border, Palmett Alehouse, Papa Murphy's, Ruby Tuesday, Schlotzsky's, Starbucks, Subway, Tony's Pizza, 🏠 Courtyard, EconoLodge, Extended Stay America, Fairfield Inn, Hampton Inn, Holi-

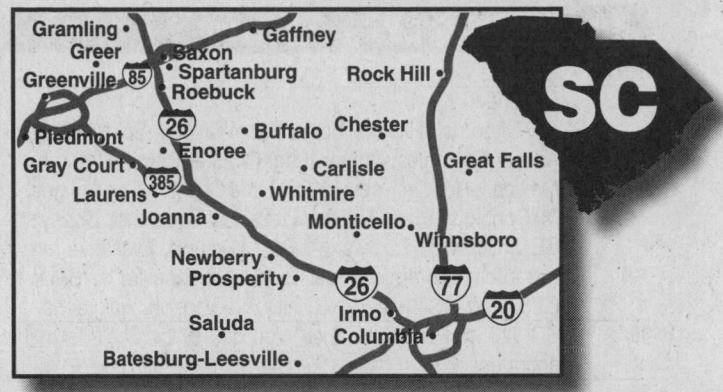

Exit	Services
54	Continued
	day Inn Express, Marriott, Residence Inn, Wingate Inn, ⊙ Advance Parts, Bi-Lo, CVS Drug, EarthFare Foods, Goodyear/auto, Radio Shack, Verizon, Walgreens, Walmart
51	I-385, SC 146, Woodruff Rd, **E** 🅖 Blue Jay/dsl, 🍴 Brixx Pizza, Buffalo Wild Wings, Chipotle Mexican, Coldstone, Cracker Barrel, Fatz Café, Fuddrucker's, IHOP, Lieu's Bistro, Longhorn Steaks, Mimi's Cafe, Monterrey Mexican, Nihao Buffet, Oriental House, Panera Bread, PF Chang's, Red Robin, Sticky Fingers, Wasabi, 🏠 Drury Inn, Hampton Inn, Hilton Garden, Homewood Suites, Staybridge Suites, ⊙ Barnes&Noble, Best Buy, Dick's, Goodyear/auto, Hamrick's Outlet, Lowe's, Marshalls, PetCo, Petsmart, Ross, Verizon, Whole Foods Mkt, vet, **W** 🅖 Marathon/Kangaroo, QT/dsl, RaceWay/dsl, 🍴 Capri's Italian, Carolina Alehouse, Carrabba's, Cheddars, El Patron Mexican, Krystal, McDonald's, MidTown Deli, Ruby Tuesday, Ruth's Chris Steaks, Subway, TGIFriday's, Twin Peaks Rest, Waffle House, 🏠 Crowne Plaza, Days Inn, Embassy Suites, Holiday Inn Express, La Quinta, Marriott (3mi), Vintel, ⊙ AT&T, Cabela's, Costco/gas, Firestone/auto, Home Depot, Old Navy, Target, Trader Joe's
48b a	US 276, Greenville, **E** 🍴 Waffle House, 🏠 Red Roof Inn, ⊙ CarMax, to ICAR, **W** 🅖 Exxon/dsl, 🍴 Arby's, Bojangles, Burger King, Happy China, Hooters, McDonald's, Olive Garden, Pizza Hut/Taco Bell, Ryan's, Subway, 🏠 Comfort Inn, Embassy Suites, Relax Inn, ⊙ Acura, Audi/Porsche/VW, Bi-Lo, Books-A-Million, Buick/GMC, Chevrolet, Chrysler/Dodge/Jeep, CVS Drug, $Tree, Ford/Lincoln, Hancock Fabrics, Infiniti, Jaguar, Kia, Lexus, Mazda, Meineke, Mercedes, Michael's, Nissan, Office Depot, Old Time Pottery, PepBoys, Petsmart, SteinMart, Subaru, Toyota, Volvo
46c	rd 291, Pleasantburg Rd, Mauldin Rd, **W** 🅖 BP, Citgo/dsl, 🍴 Jack-in-the-Box, Papa John's, Subway, 🏠 InTown Suites, Quality Inn, Super Lodge, ValuePlace, ⊙ Aamco, Advance Parts, Bi-Lo/gas, CVS Drug, Home Depot, Tire Kingdom, same as 46ba
46b a	US 25 bus, Augusta Rd, **E** 🅖 Mike&Jack/dsl, QT/dsl, Spinx/dsl, Sunoco, Vgo, 🍴 Burger King, Waffle House, 🏠 Camelot Inn, Country Hearth Inn, Holiday Inn, Southern Suites, **W** 🏠 Economy Inn, Traveler's Inn, ⊙ Home Depot, same as 46c
44	US 25, White Horse Rd, **E** 🅖 Spinx/Subway/dsl, **W** 🅖 Citgo/McDonald's, RaceWay/dsl, 🍴 Waffle House, ⊙ 🄷 Freightliner
44a	SC 20 (from sb), to Piedmont
42	I-185, to Greenville, I-185 S **(toll)**, Columbia, **W** 🄷
40	SC 153, to Easley, **E** 🅖 BP/dsl, 🍴 Waffle House, **W** 🅖

🅖 = gas 🍴 = food 🛏 = lodging 🄾 = other 🆁🆂 = rest stop   Copyright 2014 - The NEXT Exit ®

⬆N INTERSTATE 85 CONT'D

Exit	Services
40	Continued
	BP, Citgo/dsl, Hickory Point, RaceWay/dsl, Spinx/dsl, 🍴 Arby's, Bojangles, Burger King, Cracker Barrel, El Sureno Mexican, Huddle House, KFC, Little Caesars, Los Amigos, McDonald's, Pizza House, Pizza Hut/Taco Bell, Sonny's BBQ, Subway, Zaxby's, 🛏 Best Western, Executive Inn, Hampton Inn (4mi), Super 8, 🄾 Advance Parts, Bi-Lo, CVS Drug, $General, GNC, Rite Aid, Verizon, Walgreens
39	SC 143, to Piedmont, **E** 🅖 Vgo/dsl, **W** 🅖 Shell/dsl, 🄾 antiques
35	SC 86, to Easley, Piedmont, **E** 🅖 🚚/McDonald's/dsl/scales/24hr, 🍴 Hardee's (1.5mi), Mozzerelli's Pizza, Ole Carolina Smokehouse, Subway (1.5mi), 🄾 repair/tires, **W** 🅖 Spinx/Pete's Grill/dsl
34	US 29 (from sb), to Williamston
32	SC 8, to Pelzer, Easley, **E** 🅖 Hickory Point/dsl, Shell/dsl
27	SC 81, to Anderson, **E** 🅖 BP/dsl, Exxon, Zooms, 🍴 Arby's, KFC/Pizza Hut, McDonald's, Waffle House, 🛏 Hampton Inn, Holiday Inn Express, 🄾 🄷, **W** 🍴 Charlie's Wings
23mm	🆁🆂 sb, full 🅰 facilities, 🄲, vending, 🗑, litter barrels, petwalk
21	US 178, to Anderson, **E** 🅖 QT/dsl, Shell/dsl, 🍴 Waffle House, **2 mi E** 🍴 Applebee's, Chick-fil-A, Chili's, Longhorn Steaks, O'Charley's, 🛏 HomeTowne Suites, Quality Inn, 🄾 Publix/deli
19b a	US 76, SC 28, to Anderson, **E** 🅖 Exxon/dsl, 🍴 Fuddruckers, Hardee's, 🛏 Days Inn, Hilton Garden, Royal American Motel, 🄾 Russell Stover, **2 mi E** 🅖 QT/dsl, Shell, 🍴 Applebee's, Chick-fil-A, Chili's, CookOut, 5 Guys Burgers, Golden Corral, Grand China, Hardee's, Jack-in-the-Box, Logan's Roadhouse, Longhorn Steaks, O'Charley's, Olive Garden, Panera Bread, Red Lobster, Rita's Custard, Ryan's, Sonny BBQ, TX Roadhouse, Zaxby's, 🛏 Best Value Inn, Holiday Inn, La Quinta, Super 8, 🄾 Advance Parts, Aldi Foods, AT&T, Best Buy, Chrysler/Dodge/Jeep, Dick's, $General, $Tree, Ford/Mazda, Goodyear, Hancock Fabrics, Harley-Davidson, Hobby Lobby, Home Depot, Honda, K-Mart, Kohl's, Lowe's, Michael's, Nissan, Office Depot, Old Navy, O'Reilly Parts, Petsmart, Publix/deli, Ross, Sam's Club/gas, Staples, Target, Toyota/Scion, Verizon, Walmart, vet, **W** 🅖 HotSpot/McDonald's, RaceWay/dsl, 🍴 Arby's, Cracker Barrel, Fatz Cafe, Hooters, Outback Steaks, Subway, Waffle House, Wendy's, Wild Wing Cafe, 🛏 Comfort Suites, Country Inn&Suites, Fairfield Inn, Hampton Inn, Holiday Inn Express, Jameson Inn, Microtel, 🄾 to Clemson U
18mm	🆁🆂 nb, full 🅰 facilities, 🄲, vending, 🗑, litter barrels, petwalk
15mm	Lake Hartwell
14	SC 187, to Clemson, Anderson, **E** 🅖 Marathon/dsl, 🍴 Huddle House, 🄾 camping (1mi), **W** 🅖 Hickory Point/dsl, 🍴 Famous Pizza Grill, 🛏 Budget Inn, 🄾 to Clem Research Pk
12mm	Seneca River, Lake Hartwell
11	SC 24, SC 243, to Townville, **E** 🅖 Exxon/dsl, Sunoco/dsl/24hr, 🍴 Subway, 🄾 to Savannah River Scenic Hwy, **W** 🅖 Shell/dsl, 🍴 Townville Cafe, 🄾 RV camping
9mm	weigh sta nb
4	SC 243, to SC 24, Fair Play, **E** 🅖 ♥Love's/Arby's/dsl/scales/24hr, Mobil/dsl/scales/LP/24hr

---

2	SC 59, to Fair Play, **W** fireworks
1	SC 11, to Walhalla, **W** 🍴 Gazebo Rest., 🄾 fireworks, to Lake Hartwell SP
.5mm	**Welcome Ctr nb, full 🅰 facilities, info, 🄲, 🗑, litter barrels, vending, petwalk**
0mm	South Carolina/Georgia state line, Lake Hartwell, Tagaloo River

⬆N INTERSTATE 95

Exit	Services
198mm	South Carolina/North Carolina state line
196mm	**Welcome Ctr sb, full 🅰 facilities, info, 🄲, vending, 🗑, litter barrels, petwalk**
195mm	Little Pee Dee River
193	SC 9, SC 57, to N Myrtle Beach, Dillon, **E** 🅖 Exxon, Mobil/dsl, Murphy Express/dsl, Sunoco/dsl, 🍴 B&C Steak/BBQ, Burger King, Huddle House, Pizza Hut, Shoney's, Subway, Tokyo Cafe, Waffle House, Wendy's, Zaxby's, 🛏 Best Value Inn, Comfort Inn, Days Inn, Quality Inn, Royal Regency Inn, 🄾 🄷, Advance Parts, CVS Drug, $General, $Tree, Food Lion, O'Reilly Parts, Walgreens, Walmart, fireworks, **W** 🅖 BP/dsl, 🛏 EconoLodge, Super 8, 🄾 Bass Lake RV Camp/LP
190	SC 34, to Dillon, **W** 🅖 ♥Love's/Arby's/dsl/scales/24hr
181	SC 38, Oak Grove, **E** 🅖 BP/Subway/dsl/24hr, ⊕FLYING J/Subway/dsl/LP/scales/24hr, Shell/McDonald's/dsl/24hr, 🄾 fireworks, **W** 🅖 Wilco/Hess/DQ/Wendy's/dsl/scales/24hr, 🛏 Best Western, 🄾 auto/truck repair
175mm	Pee Dee River
170	SC 327, **E** 🅖 BP, 🚚/Wendy's/dsl/scales/24hr, 🍴 McDonald's, Waffle House, Zaxby's, 🛏 Holiday Inn Express, 🄾 to Myrtle Beach, Missile Museum
169	TV Rd, to Florence, **E** 🄾 Florence RV Park, dsl repair, **W** 🅖 BP/dsl, ⊕FLYING J/Shell/rest./dsl/scales/24hr/@, 🛏 Best Value Inn, 🄾 Blue Beacon, Peterbilt, dsl repair
164	US 52, to Darlington, Florence, **E** 🅖 Exxon/dsl, RaceWay/24hr, Shell/Huddle House/dsl, 🍴 Angelo's Seafood Rest., Cracker Barrel, Hardee's, McDonald's, Quincy's, Quiznos, Ruby Tuesday, Waffle House, Wendy's, 🛏 Baymont Inn, Best Western, EconoLodge, Motel 6, Ramada Inn, Suburban Lodge, Super 8, Travel Inn, 🄾 🄷 Chrysler/Dodge/Jeep, Hyundai, **W** 🅖 TA/BP/Popeye's/dsl/scales/@, 🚚/Subway/Taco Bell/dsl, 🍴 Arby's, Bojangles, Fatz Café, Krispy Kreme, La Fogata Mexican, Shoney's, Young's Pecans, Zaxby's, 🛏 Comfort Suites, Country Inn&Suites, Days Inn, Hampton Inn, Howard Johnson, Microtel, Sleep Inn, Thunderbird Inn, Travel House Inn, Wingate Inn, 🄾 transmissions, to Darlington Raceway
160b	I-20 W, to Columbia
160a	Lp 20, to Florence, **E** 🍴 Arby's, Bruster's Ice Cream, Burger King, Chick-fil-A, Chili's, ChuckeCheese, IHOP, Indigo Joe's Rest., Longhorn Steaks, Olive Garden, Outback Steaks, Percy & Willy, Red Lobster, Ruby Tuesday, Shoney's, Waffle House, Western Sizzlin, 🛏 Courtyard, Fairfield Inn, Hampton Inn, Hilton Garden, Holiday Inn Express, Quality Inn, Red Roof Inn, Residence Inn, SpringHill Suites, 🄾 Barnes&Noble, Belk, Best Buy, $Tree, Hobby Lobby, Hamricks, Home Depot, JC Penney, Kohl's, Lowes Whse, Sam's Club, Sears/auto, Target, Walmart, mall
157	US 76, Timmonsville, Florence, **E** 🅖 BP/dsl/repair, Exxon/McDonald's/dsl, Kangaroo/dsl, Marathon, 🍴 La Palmas Mexican, Waffle House, 🛏 Day's Inn, Howard Johnson

Side markers: DILLON, ANDERSON, FLORENCE

SC

INTERSTATE 95 CONT'D

MANNING

SANTEE

Exit	Services
157	Continued Express, Swamp Fox Inn, Travelodge, **W** [gas] Sunoco, [lodging] Ramada/rest., Tree Top Inn, Swamp Fox Camping (1mi)
153	Honda Way, **W** [gas] Exxon, [food] Hardees (2mi), [other] Honda Plant
150	SC 403, to Sardis, **E** [gas] BP/scales/dsl, [food] Hotplate Cafe, [lodging] Econolodge, **W** [gas] Exxon/dsl
147mm	Lynches River
146	SC 341, to Lynchburg, Olanta, **E** [gas] Moneysaver/dsl, [lodging] Relax Inn
141	SC 53, SC 58, to Shiloh, **E** [gas] Exxon/dsl, [other] DonMar RV Ctr, to Woods Bay SP, **W** [gas] Shell
139mm	**[RS] both lanes, full [handicapped] facilities, [phone], vending, [picnic], litter barrels, petwalk**
135	US 378, to Sumter, Turbeville, **E** [gas] BP, Citgo/dsl/24hr, [food] Compass Rest., [lodging] America's Inn, Day's Inn, **W** [gas] Exxon/Subway/dsl, [other] Pineland Golf Course
132	SC 527, to Sardinia, Kingstree
130mm	Black River
122	US 521, to Alcolu, Manning, **W** [gas] Exxon/dsl, [food] Paradise Cafe
119	SC 261, to Paxville, Manning, **0-1 mi E** [gas] Mobil, Murphy USA/dsl, Shell/dsl, TA/BP/Pizza Hut/Popeye's/dsl/scales/24hr/@, [food] Arby's, Bojangles, Huddle House, KFC, Mariachi's Mexican, McDonald's, Shoney's, Sonic, Subway, Waffle House, Wendy's, Yucatan Mexican, Zaxby's, [lodging] Baymont Inn, Days Inn, Hampton Inn, Quality Inn, Ramada Inn, [other] [H], AutoZone, Chrysler/Dodge/Jeep, CVS Drug, $General, Ford, O'Reilly Parts, Radio Shack, Verizon, Walmart, **W** [gas] Horizon/dsl/e-85, Paxville, [lodging] Super 8, [other] auto repair
115	US 301, to Summerton, Manning, **W** [gas] Shell/dsl, [food] Georgio's Rest, [lodging] Executive Inn, Knights Inn
108	rd 102, Summerton, **E** [gas] BP/DQ/Stuckey's, Travel Depot/dsl, [other] TawCaw Camping (6m), **W** [lodging] Days Inn, Deluxe Inn
102	US 15, US 301 N, to N Santee, **E** [gas] StopSpot/dsl, [food] Arista Rest., [lodging] Santee Resort/Motel, [other] Bigwater RV Camping, Santee Lakes Camping, **W** [gas] Horizon/dsl/e-85, [other] to Santee NWR
100mm	Lake Marion
99mm	**[RS] both lanes, full [handicapped] facilities, [phone], info, vending, [picnic], litter barrels, petwalk**
98	SC 6, to Eutawville, Santee, **E** [gas] BP/Bojangles, Citgo, Exxon, Mobil, [food] Captains Quarters Rest., Coaster's Seafood, Huddle House, KFC, Pizza Hut, Shoney's, Subway, [lodging] Best Value Inn, Best Western, Hampton Inn, Howard Johnson, Super 8, Whitten Inn, [other] $General, IGA Foods, Russell Stover Candy, **W** [gas] Hess/dsl, Horizon/dsl/e-85, Shell, [food] Burger King, Cracker Barrel, Domino's, Maurice's BBQ, McDonald's, Peking Chinese, Waffle House, Wendy's, [lodging] Clark Inn/rest., Comfort Inn, Fairway Inn, Holiday Inn, Lake Marion Inn, Quality Inn, [other] CarQuest, CVS Drug, Family$, Food Lion, USPO, to Santee SP (3mi)
97	US 301 S (from sb, no return), to Orangeburg
93	US 15, to Santee, Holly Hill
90	US 176, to Cameron, Holly Hill, **W** [gas] Exxon/dsl
86b a	I-26, W to Columbia, E to Charleston
82	US 178, to Bowman, Harleyville, **E** [gas] BP, Wilco/Hess/Stuckey's/Wendy's/DQ/dsl/scales/24hr, [lodging] Peachtree Inn, **W** [gas] Shell/dsl, [other] tires/truck repair

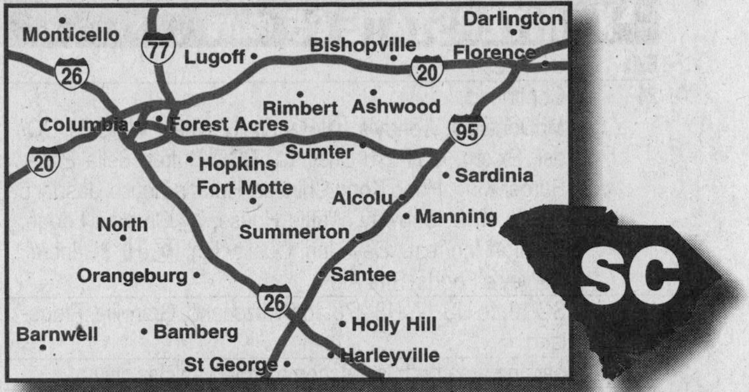

WALTERBORO

Exit	Services
77	US 78, to Bamberg, St George, **E** [gas] FLYING J/Denny's/dsl/scales/24hr, Horizon/Subway/dsl/e-85, Monoco, Sunoco, [food] Georgio's Rest., Hardee's, KFC, McDonald's, Pizza Hut, Skynyrd's Grill, Waffle House, [lodging] Best Value Inn, Comfort Inn/RV Park, EconoLodge, Quality Inn, [other] Ace Hardware, CarQuest, Chevrolet/GMC, CVS Drug, $General, Family$, Ford, Reid's Foods, St George RV Park, USPO, **W** [gas] BP, Shell/Taco Bell/dsl, [lodging] Country Hearth Inn, Days Inn, Southern Inn, Super 8
74mm	**weigh sta nb**, parking area commercial vehicles only sb
68	SC 61, Canadys, **E** [gas] BP, Circle C/scales, Shell/Subway/dsl, [other] truck lube/repair, to Colleton SP (3mi)
62	McLeod Rd
57	SC 64, Lodge, Walterboro, **E** [gas] Horizon/e-85, Shell/DQ, Mobil/dsl, Sunoco/dsl, [food] Arby's, Bojangles, Burger King, Capt D's, Dimitrio's Rest., Domino's, Hardee's, Huddle House, KFC, McDonald's, Olde House Café, Quiznos, Subway, Taco Bell, Waffle House, Wendy's, [lodging] Carolina Lodge, Sleep Inn, Southern Inn, [other] [H], Ace Hardware, Advance Parts, AutoZone, Belk, $General, Ford, GNC, O'Reilly Parts, Reid's Foods, Rite Aid, **W** [gas] BP, Murphy USA/dsl, [food] China Buffet, Zaxby's, [lodging] Super 8, [other] $Tree, PetCo, Radio Shack, Verizon, Walmart
53	SC 63, to Varnville, Walterboro, Hampton, **E** [gas] BP/McDonald's, El Cheapo, Exxon, Petro Express/dsl, Shell/DQ, [food] Glasshouse Rest., KFC, Ruby Tuesday, Shoney's, Waffle House, [lodging] Best Western, Comfort Inn, EconoLodge, Motel 6, Palms Inn, Quality Inn, Ramada Inn, Rice Planter's Inn, [other] fireworks, **W** [gas] Horizon/dsl, [food] Cracker Barrel, [lodging] Country Hearth Inn, Days Inn, Hampton Inn, Holiday Inn Express, Microtel, [other] Green Acres Camping
47mm	**[RS] both lanes, full [handicapped] facilities, [phone], vending, [picnic], litter barrels, petwalk**
42	US 21, to Yemassee, Beaufort
40mm	Combahee River
38	SC 68, to Hampton, Yemassee, **E** [gas] Horizon/dsl/e-85, [other] Family$, **W** [gas] BP/Subway/TCBY, Exxon/dsl, Shell/dsl, [lodging] Palmetto Lodge/rest., Super 8
33	US 17 N, to Beaufort, **E** [gas] BP/dsl, Exxon/McDonald's, Marathon/Subway/TCBY, Shell, [food] Denny's, Waffle House, Wendy's, [lodging] Baymont Inn, Best Western, EconoLodge, Hampton Inn, Knights Inn, [other] Confederate Railroad Museum, Encore RV Camping, KOA
30.5mm	Tullifinny River
29mm	Coosawhatchie River
28	SC 462, to Coosawhatchie, Hilton Head, Bluffton, **W** [gas] Citgo, El Cheapo, Exxon/Chester Fried/dsl
22	US 17, Ridgeland, **W** [gas] Sunoco, [lodging] Ridgeland Inn, [other] [H]
21	SC 336, to Hilton Head, Ridgeland, **E** [gas] Liberty/dsl, [food]

⬆N INTERSTATE 95 CONT'D

Exit	Services
21	Continued
	McDonald's, Wendy's, ⊙ Boat'n RV Whse, W 🅿 BP/DQ/dsl, Exxon, Gulf/dsl, Shell, 🍴 BBQ Buffet, Bella Pizza, Burger King, Hong Kong Chinese, Huddle House, Jasper's Porch, KFC, Subway, Waffle House, 🛏 Carolina Lodge, Comfort Inn/rest., Days Inn, Quality Inn, ⊙ H, $General, Harvey's Foods, Rite Aid
18	SC 13, to US 17, US 278, to Switzerland, Granville, Ridgeland
17mm	parking area both lanes, commercial vehicles only
8	US 278, to Bluffton, Hardeeville, E 🅿 BP/Huddle House/Wendy's/dsl/scales, Exxon, Kangaroo/McDonald's, 🍴 Dunkin Donuts, ⊙ H, Hilton Head info, W 🅿 Horizon/Domino's/Krispy Kreme/Subway/dsl, 🛏 Holiday Inn Express, Motel 6
5	US 17, US 321, to Savannah, Hardeeville, E 🅿 Citgo/dsl, Exxon/Blimpie, Gulf/dsl, Shell, 🍴 Mi Tierrita Mexican, Waffle House, 🛏 Days Inn, Economy Inn, Sleep Inn, ⊙ fireworks, to Savannah NWR, W 🅿 Butlers/dsl/repair, Marathon/dsl, Octane/dsl, Sunoco/dsl, 🍴 Burger King, New China, Wendy's, 🛏 Clean Stay USA, Country Hearth Inn, Deluxe Inn, Knights Inn, Magnolia Motel, Quality Suites, Red Roof Inn, Super 8, Travelodge, ⊙ $General, NAPA, fireworks
4.5mm	**Welcome Ctr nb, full 🚻 facilities, info, 🅒, 🛀, litter barrels, vending, petwalk, wi-fi**
4mm	**weigh sta both lanes**
0mm	South Carolina/Georgia state line, Savannah River

⬆N INTERSTATE 385 (GREENVILLE)

Exit	Services
42	US 276, Stone Ave, to Travelers Rest., to Greenville Zoo, E 🍴 Pete's Gyros, ⊙ CarQuest, W 🅿 Spinx/dsl, **1-2 mi W** multiple services on US 276, **I-385 begins/ends on US 276.**
40b a	SC 291, Pleasantburg Dr, E 🅿 Sunoco, 🍴 Jack-in-the-Box, Little Caesar's, Olive Tree, S&S Cafeteria, Sonic, Starbucks, Subway, Taco Casa, Wendy's, ⊙ CVS Drug, $Tree, Walgreens, to BJU, Furman U, W 🅿 Citgo/dsl, 🍴 Domino's, Krispy Kreme, 🛏 Quality Inn, Phoenix Inn/Rest., Sleep Inn, ⊙ Cottman Transmissions
39	Haywood Rd, E 🅿 BP, Spinx, 🍴 Noodleville, Outback Steaks, Portofino's, Tony's Pizzeria, 🛏 Clarion, Courtyard, Hawthorn Inn, Hilton, Hyatt Place, La Quinta, ⊙ Firestone/auto, TJ Maxx, W 🅿 BP, Pumpers, 🍴 Arby's, Applebee's, Backyard Burger, Burger King, Chick-fil-A, Chili's, ChuckeCheese, CiCi's Pizza, CityRange Steaks, Copper River Grill, Don Pablo, Fried Green Tomatoes, Harbor Inn Seafood, Honeybaked Ham, Italian Mkt/grill, Jason's Deli, Jimmy John's, Kanpai Tokyo, McAlister's Deli, Miabi Japanese, Moe's SW Grill, Monterrey Mexican, Panera Bread, Quiznos, Rafferdi's, Starbucks, Steak'n Shake, Waffle House, 🛏 Studio+, ⊙ AT&T, Barnes&Noble, Belk, Dillard's, Discount Tire, JC Penney, Macy's, NTB, Sears/auto, mall
37	Roper Mtn Rd, W 🅿 BP/dsl, RaceWay/dsl, 🍴 Atl Bread Co, Capri's Italian, Carrabba's, Cracker Barrel, El Patron Mexican, 5 Guys Burgers, FlatRock Grille, Harry&Jean's Rest., Krystal, McDonald's, Ruby Tuesday, Ruths Chris Steaks, Steak'n Shake, Strossner's Cafe, Subway, TGI

Exit	Services
37	Continued
	Friday's, Waffle House, 🛏 Days Inn, Comfort Inn, Crowne Plaza, Embassy Suites, Holiday Inn Express, La Quinta, Vintel, ⊙ AT&T, Costco/gas, Firestone/auto, Home Depot, Hyundai, Lincoln, Lowe's, Old Navy, Target, Trader Joe's
36b a	I-85, N to Charlotte, S to Atlanta
35	SC 146, Woodruff Rd, **0-2 mi E** 🅿 BP, Spinx, 🍴 Applebee's, AZ Steaks, Bojangles, Bone Fish Grill, Boston Pizzeria, Bruster's, Burger King, Chick-fil-A, Chili's, Chin Chin Chinese, China Buffet, Dunkin Donuts, Great Harvest Bread, Green Tomato, Hardee's, Hibachi Grill, Jersey Mike's, KFC, Little Caesar's, McAlister's Deli, McDonald's, Mimi's Japanese Steaks, Moe's SW Grill, Perkins, Pizza Inn, Quiznos, Sonic, Starbucks, Stevi B's, Subway, Taco Bell, Topper's Rest., Travinia Italian, Waffle House, Wendy's, Zaxby's, ⊙ **Urgent Care**, Ace Hardware, Aldi Foods, Bi-Lo Foods, BigLots, Curves, Discount Tire, $Tree, GNC, Hobby Lobby, Kohl's, Publix, Radio Shack, Rite Aid, Sam's Club/gas, Save-a-Lot Foods, Staples, Tire Kingdom, USPO, Walmart, W 🅿 Blue Jay/dsl, 🍴 Brixx Pizza, Buffalo Wild Wings, Chipotle Mexican, Coldstone, Cracker Barrel, Fatz Café, Fuddrucker's, IHOP, Lieu's Bistro, Longhorn Steaks, Mimi's Cafe, Monterrey Mexican, Nihao Buffet, Oriental House, Panera Bread, PF Chang's, Red Robin, Sticky Fingers, Wasabi, 🛏 Drury Inn, Hampton Inn, Hilton Garden, Homewood Suites, Staybridge Suites, ⊙ Barnes&Noble, Best Buy, Dick's, Goodyear/auto, Hamrick's Outlet, Lowe's, Marshall's, Petsmart, Ross, Verizon, Whole Foods Mkt, vet
34	Butler Rd, Mauldin, E 🅿 Exxon, 🍴 Arby's, ⊙ CVS Drug, W 🍴 Dino's Rest., Moretti's Pizzeria, Sub Sta. 2, ⊙ $General
33	Bridges Rd, Mauldin
31	I-185 **toll**, SC 417, to Laurens Rd, E 🅿 BP, 🍴 Hardee's, McDonald's
30	I-185 **toll**, US 276, Standing Springs Rd
29	Georgia Rd, to Simpsonville, W 🛏 ValuePlace Inn
27	Fairview Rd, to Simpsonville, E 🍴 Carolina Rest., Coach-House Rest., Little Caesar's, McDonald's, Milano Pizzeria, Mojo's Burgers, New China Buffet, Subway, 🛏 Palmetto Inn, ⊙ H, Advance Parts, AutoZone, CVS Drug, $General, O'Reilly Parts, W 🅿 Exxon, Murphy USA, Spinx, 🍴 Anthony's Pizza, Applebee's, Arby's, AZ Steaks, Baskin-Robbins, Bellacino's, Bruster's, Burger King, Chick-fil-A, Cracker Barrel, Dragon Den Chinese, 5 Guys Burgers, Hungry Howie's, Jack-in-the-Box, Jersey Mike's, KFC, La Fogata Mexican, McDonald's, Moe's SW Grill, O'Charley's, Panera Bread, Pizza Hut, Quiznos, Ruby Tuesday, Ryan's, Sonic, Starbucks, Subway, Taco Bell, Tequila's Mexican, Waffle House, Wendy's, Zaxby's, 🛏 Comfort Suites, Days Inn, Hampton Inn, Holiday Inn Express, Quality Inn, ⊙ AT&T, Belk, Bi-Lo, CVS Drug, $Tree, GNC, Goodyear/auto, Home Depot, Ingles Foods, Kohl's, Lowe's, Publix, Radio Shack, Ross, Target, Tire Kingdom, TJ Maxx, Verizon, Walgreens, Walmart, USPO
26	Harrison Bridge Rd, **W** same as 27
24	Fairview St, E 🅿 Marathon, 🍴 Hardee's, Waffle House, ⊙ carwash
23	SC 418, to Fountain Inn, Fork Shoals, E 🅿 Exxon/pizza/subs, ⊙ $General, USPO, W 🅿 Sunoco/dsl
22	SC 14 W, Old Laurens Rd, to Fountain Inn
19	SC 14 E, to Gray Court, Owings

INTERSTATE 385 (GREENVILLE) CONT'D

Exit	Services
16	SC 101, to Woodruff, Gray Court
10	rd 23, Barksdale, Ora
9	US 221, to Laurens, Enoree, **E** 🅿 Citgo/Subs/dsl, 🍴 Waffle House, 🛏 Budget Lodge, **W** Walmart Dist Ctr
6mm	🆁🆂 both lanes (both lanes exit left), full ♿ facilities, 🍴, vending, 🚮 litter barrels, petwalk
5	SC 49, to Laurens, Union
2	SC 308, to Clinton, Ora, **W** ⊙ 🏥, to Presbyterian Coll in Clinton
0mm	I-26 S to Columbia, **I-385 begins/ends on I-26 at 52mm.**

INTERSTATE 526 (CHARLESTON)

Exit	Services
33mm	**I-526 begins/ends.**
32	US 17, **0-1 mi N** 🅿 Hess/dsl, Shell, 🍴 Benito's Pizza, Burger King, Chili's, IHOP, LongHorn Steaks, Mama Fu's Asian, On The Border, Starbucks, TGIFriday, 🛏 Courtyard, ⊙ Advance Parts, Barnes&Noble, Belk, Chevrolet, CVS Drug, Firestone, Lowes Whse, Midas, Old Navy, Rite Aid, Tire Kingdom, TrueValue, Walgreens, **0-1 mi S** 🅿 Exxon/Dunkin Donuts, Mobil, Shell/Circle K, Sunoco, 🍴 Applebees, Arby's, Chick-fil-A, Cici's, Domino's, Hardee's, Huddle House, KFC, La Hacienda Mexicana, McDonald's, Outback Steaks, Papa John's, Sticky Fingers, Subway, Wendy's, Zeus Grill, 🛏 Best Western, Day's Inn, Extended Stay America, Hampton Inn, Holiday Inn, Masters Inn, Quality Inn, Red Roof Inn, River Inn, ⊙ Aamco, Bi-Lo, Cadillac, $General, Ford, Harris Teeter, Jiffy Lube, K-Mart, Marshall's, Office Depot, Radio Shack, Staples, TJ Maxx, USPO, VW, Walmart, Whole Foods Mkt, vet
30	Long Point Rd, **N** 🅿 BP, Exxon, 🍴 Bamboo Garden, Beef'o Brady's, McAlister's, Moe's SW Grill, Sonic, Starbucks, Subway, Waffle House, Wendy's, ⊙ CVS Drug, Food Lion, Harris Teeter Foods, PetsMart, Ross, Steinmart, Charles Pinckney NHS
26mm	Wando River
24	Daniel Island, **S** 🅿 Texaco, 🍴 Dragon Palace, Lana's Mexican, Queen Anne's Steaks/seafood, Subway, 🛏 Hampton Inn, ⊙ Publix

CHARLESTON

Exit	Services
23b a	Clements Ferry Rd
21mm	Cooper River
20	Virginia Ave (from eb), **S** 🅿 Hess Depot
19	N Rhett Ave, **N** 🅿 Hess, Kangaroo/Subway/dsl, 🍴 Hardee's, ⊙ Family$, Food Lion, Rite Aid, **S** 🅿 BP
18b a	US 52, US 78, Rivers Ave, **N** 🅿 BP/dsl, Hess, Kangaroo/dsl, 🍴 KFC, Peking Gourmet, Pizza Hut/Taco Bell, ⊙ AutoZone, Dodge, Family$, Ford, H&L Foods, auto repair, **S** 🅿 Exxon
17b a	I-26, E to Charleston, W to Columbia
16	Montague Ave, 🛏 Rd, **S** 🅿 Sunoco, 🍴 Chili's, La Hacienda, Panera Bread, Quizno's, Starbucks, Wendy's, 🛏 Comfort Inn, Embassy Suites, Extended Stay America, Hilton Garden, Holiday Inn, Homewood Suites, Quality Inn, Residence Inn, Wingate Inn, ⊙ Sam's Club, Staples, Tanger Outlet/famous brands, Walmart
15	SC 642, Dorchester Rd, Paramount Dr, **N** 🅿 BP, 🍴 Pizza Roma (1mi), Wendy's (1mi), **S** 🅿 Citgo/dsl, Sunoco, 🍴 Burger King, Checker's, Domino's, East Bay Deli, Huddle House, Pizza Hut, 🛏 🛏 Inn, ⊙ Bi-Lo Foods, CVS Drug, Family$, Food Lion, Harley-Davidson, U-Haul
14	Leeds Ave, **S** 🛏 Value Place Inn, ⊙ 🏥, boat marina
13mm	Ashley River
11b a	SC 61, Ashley River Rd, **N** 🍴 Chick-fil-A, McDonald's, O'Charley's, Subway, ⊙ 🏥, Food Lion, Home Depot, Lowes Whse, Rite Aid
10	US 17, SC 7, **Services from US 17**, **E** 🅿 BP, 🍴 Alex's Rest., Burger King, Capt D's, Checker's, CiCi's, Dunkin Donuts, 5 Guys Burgers, Hopsing's, IHOP, McDonald's, Messengers BBQ, Pizza Hut, Red Lobster, Ruby Tuesday, Shoney's, Taco Bell, 🛏 Best Western, Holiday Inn Express, Motel 6, Sleep Inn, ⊙ Buick/GMC, Chevrolet, Dillards, Ford, Honda, Hyundai, Jaguar, Kerr Drug, K-Mart, Mazda, Mini, Mitsubishi, Nissan, Dodge, Pepboys, Piggly Wiggly, Sears/auto, Tire Kingdom, vet, **W** 🅿 Exxon, Hess, Shell/Circle K, 🍴 Halligan's Rest., Hardees, Subway, Waffle House, 🛏 Econolodge, Hampton Inn, InTown Suites, ⊙ Acura, Audi, Advance Parts, Carmax, Chrysler/Jeep, Costco/gas, CVS Drug, Family$, Food Lion, KIA, Subaru, Toyota

I-526 begins/ends on US 17.

SOUTH DAKOTA

INTERSTATE 29

Exit	Services
253mm	South Dakota/North Dakota state line
251mm	**Welcome Ctr sb, full ♿ facilities, info, 🍴, 🚮, litter barrels, petwalk**
246	SD 127, to Rosholt, New Effington, **3 mi W** gas, food, RV camping, Sica Hollow SP (24mi)
242	No Services
235mm	**weigh sta sb**
232	SD 10, Sisseton, **E** 🅿 Dakota Connection/dsl/casino/24hr, 🍴 Crossroads Cafe, **1-3 mi W** 🅿 Amstar/dsl, FuelMax/dsl, Sinclair/dsl/E-85, Tesoro, 🍴 Cottage Rest, DQ, Pizza Hut, Subway, Taco John's, 🛏 Holiday Motel, I-29 Motel, Super 8, ⊙ 🏥, Alco, Camp Dakotah, Buick, Family$, NAPA, ShopKO, SuperValu Foods/gas, Teals Mkt, to Roy Lake SP (25mi), Ft Sisseton SP (35mi)

WATERTOWN

Exit	Services
224	Peever, Sioux Tribal Hqtrs, **E** 🅿 I-29 Food'n Fill/dsl, **W** Pickerel Lake (16mi)
213	SD 15, to Wilmot 🆁🆂 **both lanes, full ♿ facilities, 🍴 🚮 litter barrels, petwalk, RV dump, st patrol, 7 mi E** gas, food, to Hartford Beach SP (17mi)
207	US 12, Summit, **E** 🅿 Sinclair/dsl/24hr, 🍴 County Line Rest (1mi), **W** Blue Dog Fish Hatchery (15mi), Waubay NWR (19mi)
201	to Twin Brooks
193	SD 20, to South Shore, Stockholm
185	to Waverly, **4 mi W** ⊙ Dakota Sioux Casino/rest.
180	US 81 S, to Watertown, **5 mi W** 🅿 Sinclair, ⊙ Bramble Park Zoo, 🛏
177	US 212, Watertown, **E** 🅿 Tesoro/Grainery Cafe/dsl/24hr, 🛏 Holiday Inn Express, ⊙ WW Tires, fireworks, truck repair, truck wash, **0-2 mi W** 🅿 Cenex/Subway/dsl, Clark/dsl, Freedom/dsl, Sinclair/dsl, Tesoro/dsl, 🍴 Applebee's,

🅖 = gas 🍴 = food 🛏 = lodging 🅞 = other 🆁🆂 = rest stop Copyright 2014 - The NEXT Exit ®

SD

WATERTOWN · BROOKINGS

▶N INTERSTATE 29 CONT'D

Exit	Services
177	Continued
	Arby's, Buffalo Wild Wings, Burger King, China Buffet, Culver's, Domino's, DQ, Godfather's, Guadalajara Mexican, Italian Garden, Jimmy John's, KFC, McDonald's, Papa Murphy's, Perkins, Pizza Hut, Quiznos, Senor Max's Mexican, Starbucks, Subway, Taco John's, 🛏 Days Inn, Hampton Inn, Quality Inn, Rodeway Inn, Travelers Inn, 🅞 Advance Parts, AT&T, Chrysler/Dodge/Jeep, $Tree, Ford/Lincoln, Goodyear/auto, Harley-Davidson, Herberger's, Hy-Vee Foods, JC Penney, Menards, NAPA, O'Reilly Parts, Radio Shack, ShopKO, Target, Tires+, Verizon, Walgreens, Walmart/Subway, to Sandy Shore RA (10mi)
164	SD 22, to Castlewood, Clear Lake, **9 mi E** 🅖 Cenex/dsl, 🅞 🅗
161mm	🆁🆂 **both lanes, full** ♿ **facilities,** ☕, 🖼, **litter barrels, vending, petwalk**
157	to Brandt
150	SD 28, SD 15 N, to Toronto, **7 mi W** gas, food, lodging, **24 mi W** Lake Poinsett RA, SD Amateur Baseball Hall of Fame
140	SD 30, to White, Bruce, **W** Oakwood Lakes SP (12mi)
133	US 14 byp, Brookings, **E** 🅞 WW Tires, **W** to SD St U, museums, Laura Ingalls Wilder Home
132	US 14, Lp 29, Brookings, **E** 🅖 Cenex/dsl, 🍴 Applebee's, 🛏 Fairfield Inn, Hampton Inn, Holiday Inn Express, Super 8, **W** 🅖 BP, 🍴 Arby's, Buffalo Wild Wings, Burger King, Culver's, DQ, Ground Round, Guadalajara Mexican, Hardee's, Jimmy John's, KFC, King's Wok, McDonald's, Papa John's, Papa Murphy's, Perkins, Pizza Ranch, Qdoba Mexican, Subway, 🛏 Comfort Inn, Days Inn, Staurolite Inn, 🅞 🅗, Advance Parts, CarQuest, Buick/Chevrolet/GMC, Lowe's, Radio Shack, Walmart/Subway, city park
127	SD 324, to Elkton, Sinai
124mm	Big Sioux River
121	to Nunda, Ward, **E** 🆁🆂 **both lanes, full** ♿ **facilities,** ☕, 🖼 **litter barrels, vending, petwalk, RV dump,** st patrol, **W** food, RV camping
114	SD 32, to Flandreau, **7 mi E** 🅖 Cenex, 🍴 Subway, 🛏 Sioux River Motel/RV park, 🅞 Royal River Casino/hotel, Santee Tribal Hqtrs
109	SD 34, to Madison, Colman, **W** 🅖 BP/rest/dsl, Shell/rest/dsl, **20 mi W** 🅞 to Lake Herman SP, Dakota St U, museum
104	to Trent, Chester
103mm	parking area both lanes
98	SD 115 S, Dell Rapids, **E** Chevrolet, **3 mi E** 🅖 Cenex, Shell, 🍴 DQ, Pizza Ranch, 🛏 Bilmar Inn, 🅞 🅗
94	SD 114, to Baltic, **10 mi E** 🅞 to EROS Data Ctr, US Geological Survey
86	to Renner, Crooks
84b a	I-90, W to Rapid City, E to Albert Lea
83	SD 38 W, 60th St, **E** 🅖 ⓕFLYING J/Denny's/dsl/LP/scales/24hr/@, 🛏 Quality Suites, 🅞 Freightliner, Harley-Davidson, repair, **W** 🅞 fireworks, hwy patrol
82	Benson Rd
81	SD 38 E, Russell St, Sioux Falls, **E** 🅖 BP, Food'n Fuel/Quiznos, 🍴 Roll'n Pin Rest., 🛏 Arena Motel, Best Western/Ramkota, Brimark Inn, Guesthouse Inn, Knights Inn, Motel 6, Ramada Inn, Sheraton, Sleep Inn, 🅞 AAA, Schaap's RV Ctr, golf, **W** 🍴 Subway

SIOUX FALLS

Exit	Services
80	Madison St, **E** 🅖 Sinclair/dsl, 🅞 to fairgrounds
79	SD 42, 12th St, **E** 🅖 BP, Freedom, 🍴 Burger King, Burger Time, Fry'n Pan, Golden Harvest Chinese, KFC, McDonald's, Pizza Hut, Subway, Taco Bell, Taco John's, Tomacelli's Pizza, Wendy's, 🛏 Ramada, ValuePlace Inn, 🅞 🅗, Ace Hardware, BMW/Cadillac/Mercedes, Chevrolet, $General, K-Mart, Lewis Drug, NAPA, Nissan, Toyota/Scion, Walgreens, city park, USPO, to Great Plains Zoo/museum, **W** 🅖 BP/dsl, Cenex/Chester's/dsl, Food'n Fuel, 🅞 Meineke, Tower RV Park
78	26th St, Empire St, **E** 🅖 BP/dsl/E85, 🍴 Buffalo Wild Wings, Carino's Italian, Carnaval Brazillian Grill, Coldstone, Chevy's Mexican, ChuckeCheese, Cracker Barrel, Culver's, Domino's, Granite City Rest, Outback Steaks, Puerto Vallarta, Ruby Tuesday, Sonic, 🛏 ClubHouse Suites, Hampton Inn, Holiday Inn Express, StayBridge Suites, 🅞 BigLots, Home Depot, Michael's, Petsmart, Sam's Club/gas, USPO, World Mkt, **W** 🍴 DQ, Papa John's, Quiznos, Starbucks, 🛏 TownePlace Suites, 🅞 Hy-Vee Foods/gas, Lowe's, Tuffy Auto
77	41st St, Sioux Falls, **E** 🅖 BP, Shell, Sinclair/dsl, SA/dsl, 🍴 Applebee's, Arby's, Burger King, Chili's, Fry'n Pan Rest., Fuddrucker's, HuHot Mongolian, KFC, Lonestar Steaks, McDonald's, Old Chicago Pizza, Olive Garden, Pancake House, Papa Murphy's, Perkins, Pizza Hut, Pizza Ranch, Qdoba Mexican, Red Lobster, Royal Fork Buffet, Starbucks, Subway, Szechwan Chinese, Taco Bell, Taco John's, TX Roadhouse, Valentino's, Wendy's, 🛏 Best Western, Comfort Suites, Courtyard, Fairfield Inn, Microtel, Red Rock Inn, Residence Inn, SpringHill Suites, Super 8; 🅞 Advance Parts, Barnes&Noble, Best Buy, Ford/Lincoln, Goodyear/auto, Gordman's, Hy-Vee Foods/dsl, Hyundai, JC Penney, Kohl's, Macy's, Mazda, Menards, Old Navy, PetCo, Radio Shack, Sears/auto, ShopKO, Target, Tires+, TJ Maxx, Verizon, Walgreens, Walmart/Subway, Younkers, **W** 🅖 Shell/dsl, 🍴 Burger King, Godfather's, IHOP, Little Caesars, Perkins, Subway, 🛏 AmericInn, Baymont Inn, Days Inn, Red Roof Inn, 🅞 Lewis Drug, USPO
75	I-229 E, to I-90 E
73	Tea, **E** 🅖 Sinclair/dsl, 🍴 Marlin's Rest, **1.5 mi W** Red Barn Camping
71	to Harrisburg, Lennox, **E** repair, **W** RV camping
68	to Lennox, Parker
64	SD 44, Worthing, **W** 🅞 Buick/Chevrolet, Great Plains RV Ctr
62	US 18 E, to Canton, **E** 🅖 Shell/pizza/dsl, 🛏 Countryside RV park/motel
59	US 18 W, to Davis, Hurley
56	to Fairview, **E** to Newton Hills SP (12mi)
53	to Viborg
50	to Centerville, Hudson
47	SD 46, to Irene, Beresford, **E** 🅖 BP/Burger King, Casey's/dsl, Sinclair/dsl, 🍴 Emily's Café, Subway, 🛏 Crossroads Motel, Super 8, 🅞 Chevrolet, $General, Fiesta Foods, Jet Auto Repair, **W** 🅖 Clark/Godfather's/dsl/scales/24hr
42	to Alcester, Wakonda
41mm	truck check (from sb)
38	to Volin, **E** to Union Grove SP (3mi)
31	SD 48, to Akron, Spink
26	SD 50, to Vermillion, **E** Welcome Ctr/🆁🆂 both lanes, full ♿ facilities, info, ☕, 🖼, litter barrels, petwalk, **W** 🅖 BP/dsl, **6-7 mi W** 🍴 Burger King, Godfather's Pizza, Red

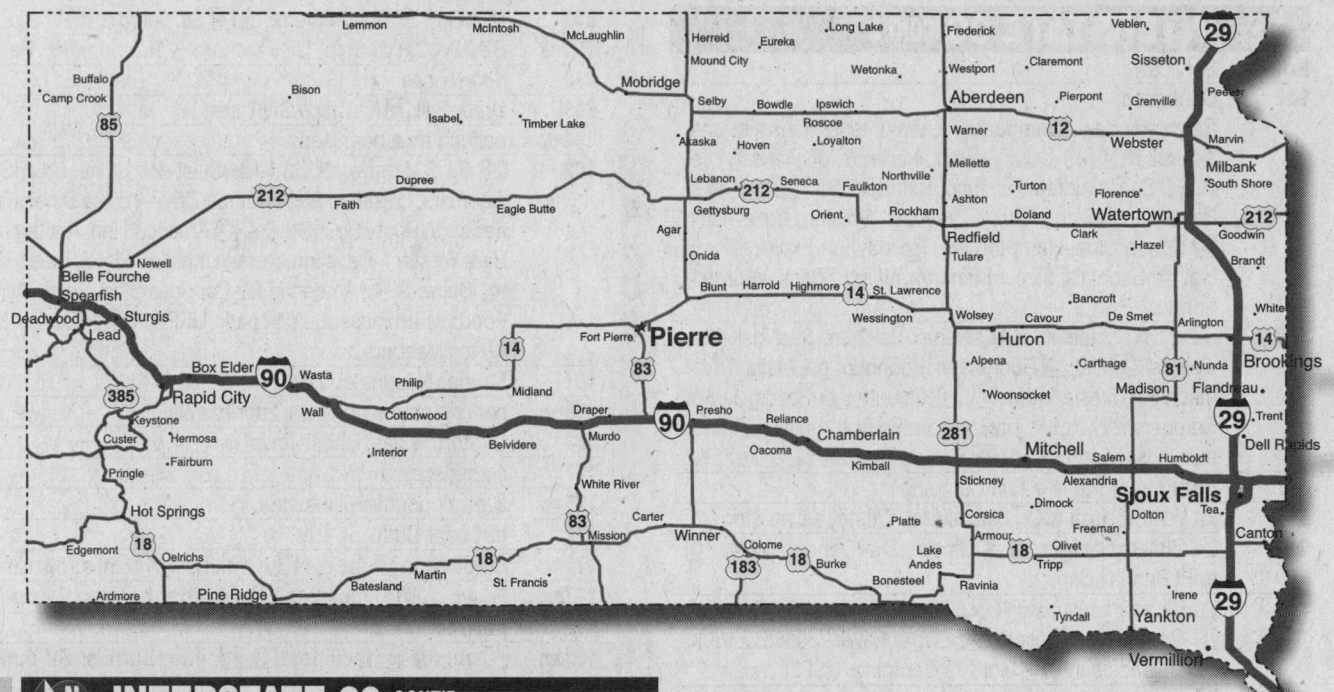

SD

⬆️N INTERSTATE 29 CONT'D

Exit	Services
26	Continued
	Steakhouse, Subway, Taco John's, 🛏 Comfort Inn, Holiday Inn Express, Prairie Inn, Super 8, Westside Inn, 🅞 🅗 Hy-Vee Foods, Walmart/deli, to U of SD, to Lewis & Clark RA
18	Lp 29, to Burbank, Elk Point, E 🅖 A-1/dsl, Casey's, 🛏 HomeTowne Inn
15	to Elk Point, E 🅖 Kum&Go/Subway/dsl, W fireworks
13mm	**weigh sta nb**, parking area sb
9	SD 105, Jefferson, E 🅖 BP/Choice Cut Rest.
4	McCook, **1 mi W** 🅞 KOA (seasonal), Adams Homestead/nature preserve
2	N Sioux City, E 🅖 Goode/casino/dsl/E10/20/30, 🍴 McDonald's, Subway, Taco John's, 🅞 USPO, fireworks, W 🅖 Casey's, Clark, 🛏 Days Inn, Hampton Inn, Red Carpet Inn, Super 8, 🅞 KOA, to Sodrac Dogtrack
1	E 🅞 Dakota Dunes Golf Resort, W 🅖 Dunes Gen. Store/dsl, 🍴 Graham's Grill, 🛏 Country Inn&Suites
0mm	South Dakota/Iowa state line, Big Sioux River

⬆️E INTERSTATE 90

Exit	Services
412.5mm	South Dakota/Minnesota state line
412mm	**Welcome Ctr wb/🆁🆂 eb, full ♿ facilities, info, 🅒, 🅐, litter barrels, petwalk, RV dump (wb), weigh sta (wb)**
410	Valley Springs, N Palisades SP (7mi), S Beaver Creek Nature Area, gas, food
406	SD 11, Brandon, Corson, N Palisades SP (10mi), S 🅖 BP/dsl, Shell, Sinclair/McDonald's/dsl, 🍴 Brandon Steaks, DQ, Great Wall, Pizza Ranch, Subway, Taco John's, Tailgater's Grill, 🛏 Comfort Inn, Holiday Inn Express, 🅞 Curves, Lewis Drug, Sunshine Foods, TrueValue, Verizon, to Big Sioux RA (4mi)
402	EROS Data Ctr, N 🅞 Jellystone RV Park, tires
400	I-229 S
399	SD 115, Cliff Ave, Sioux Falls, N 🅖 TC's/BP/dsl, 🅞 Spader RV Ctr, KOA, S 🅖 BP, Holiday/dsl/E-85, 💙Love's/Grandma Max's/Subway/dsl/scales/24hr/@, Shell/dsl,

S I O U X   F A L L S

Exit	Services
399	Continued
	Sinclair, 🍴 Arby's, Burger King, McDonald's/truck parking, Perkins, Taco Bell, Taco John's, 🛏 Cloud Nine Motel, Days Inn, EconoLodge, Super 8, 🅞 🅗 Blue Beacon, Graham Tire, Kenworth, Peterbilt, Volvo
398mm	Big Sioux River
396b a	I-29, N to Brookings, S to Sioux City
395	Marion
390	SD 38, Hartford, N 🍴 Pizza Ranch, 🅞 Camp Dakota RV Park, Goos RV Ctr, S 🅖 Cowboy Town/dsl
387	rd 17, Hartford, N 🅖 BP/dsl, 🍴 Pizza Ranch
379	SD 19, Humboldt, N 🅖 Mobil/dsl, Shell/Town&Country Store/dsl (1mi), 🅞 USPO
375mm	E Vermillion River
374	to SD 38, Montrose, **5 mi S** 🅞 Battle Creek Res., Lake Vermillion RA, RV camping
368	Canistota, **4 mi S** 🛏 Best Western
364	US 81, to Yankton, Salem, **4 mi N** 🅖 Cenex, 🛏 Home Motel, 🅞 Camp America
363.5mm	W Vermillion River
363mm	🆁🆂 **both lanes, full ♿ facilities, 🅒, 🅐, litter barrels, vending, petwalk, RV dump, st patrol**
357	to Bridgewater, Canova
353	Spencer, Emery, S 🅖 FuelMart/Subway/dsl/casino/24hr
352mm	Wolf Creek
350	SD 25, Emery, Farmer, N to DeSmet, Home of Laura Ingalls Wilder
344	SD 262, to Fulton, Alexandria, S 🅖 Shell/dsl
337mm	parking area both lanes
335	Riverside Rd, N KOA (1mi)
334.5mm	James River
332	SD 37 S, to Parkston, Mitchell, N 🅖 Cenex/DQ/dsl, Clark, Mobil, 🔲Shell/Marlin's Rest./Subway/dsl/scales/24hr, Sinclair, 🍴 Arby's, Corona Village Mexican, McDonald's, Perkins, Pirogue's BBQ, Pizza Hut, Pizza Ranch, Twin Dragon Chinese, 🛏 AmericInn, Best Western, Days Inn, Quality Inn, Super 8/truck parking, Thunderbird Motel, 🅞 🅗 Advance Parts, Chrysler/Dodge/Jeep, K-Mart, O'Reilly

M I T C H E L L

INTERSTATE 90 CONT'D

Exit	Services
332	Continued
	Parts, Rondee's Campground, Walgreens, transmissions, **1-2 mi N** ⦿ to Corn Palace, Museum of Pioneer Life, **S** 🍴 Shell/Godfather's/Taco Bell/dsl/24hr, 🍴 Culver's, Hardee's, Quiznos, Ruby Tuesday, Whiskey Creek Grill, ⌂ Comfort Inn, Hampton Inn, Holiday Inn Express, Kelly Inn, ⦿ Cabela's, $Tree, Menards, Radio Shack, Walmart/Subway
330	SD 37 N, Mitchell, **N** ℝ Cenex/dsl/24hr, Shell/dsl, Sinclair/dsl, 🍴 DQ, ⌂ Budget Inn, EconoLodge, Motel 6, Ramada Inn, Siesta Motel, ⦿ Ⓗ, County Fair Foods, Jack's Campers/RV Ctr, Mr. Tire, to Corn Palace, museum, transmissions, **weigh sta, S** ⦿ Dakota RV Park
325	Betts Rd, **S** Famil-e-Fun Camping
319	Mt Vernon, **1 mi N** ℝ Sinclair/dsl, Westey's One Stop
310	US 281, to Stickney, **S** ℝ Sinclair/Deli Depot/dsl/24hr, ⦿ to Ft Randall Dam
308	Lp 90, to Plankinton, **N** ℝ Cenex, Sinclair/Al's Cafe/dsl, 🍴 Commerce St Grille, ⌂ Cabin Fever Motel/RV Park, Smart Choice Inn, ⦿ Gordy's Camping, USPO, repair
301.5mm	🅁ₛ **both lanes, full** ♿ **facilities,** 🅒 **s,** 🛆 **litter barrels, RV dump**
296	White Lake, **1 mi N** ℝ A-Z Gas, Cenex/dsl, ⌂ A-Z Motel, ⦿ USPO, **S** ⦿ Siding 36 Motel/RV Park
294mm	Platte Creek
289	SD 45 S, to Platte, **S** ⦿ to Snake Cr/Platte Cr RA (25mi)
284	SD 45 N, Kimball, **N** ℝ Clark, Ditty's/Diner/dsl, ⌂ Dakota Winds Motel, Super 8, ⦿ Parkway Campground, repair/tires, **S** ⦿ tractor museum
272	SD 50, Pukwana, **2 mi N** gas, food, lodging, **S** ⦿ Snake/Platte Creek Rec Areas (25mi)
265	SD 50, Chamberlain, **N** ℝ Cenex/DQ/dsl, ⌂ AmericInn, ⦿ Ⓗ, Alco, St Joseph Akta Lakota Museum (4mi), vet, **S** ℝ SA/dsl, ⦿ Happy Camper Campground
264mm	🅁ₛ **both lanes, full** ♿ **facilities, scenic view, info,** 🅒 **s,** 🛆 **litter barrels**
263	Chamberlain, **N** ℝ Sinclair/dsl, 🍴 Casey's Café, McDonald's, Pizza Hut, Subway (1mi), Taco John's, ⌂ Best Western (1mi), Bel Aire Motel (1mi), Riverview Inn, Super 8, ⦿ Crow Creek Sioux Tribal Hqtrs, SD Hall of Fame
262mm	Missouri River
260	SD 50, Oacoma, **N** ℝ Cenex/Arby's/dsl, Clark/dsl, Shell/dsl, ⌂ Al's Oasis/Motel/Camping/cafe/mkt, Cedar Shore Motel/Camping (3mi), Days Inn, Howard Johnson, Quality Inn, ⦿ Buick/Chevrolet, Old West Museum, antiques
251	SD 47, to Winner, Gregory
248	SD 47, Reliance, **N** ℝ Cenex (1mi), Farmer's Union/dsl (1mi), ⦿ Sioux Tribal Hqtrs, to Big Bend RA
241	to Lyman
235	SD 273, Kennebec, **N** ℝ Clark/dsl, 🍴 Hot Rods Steaks, ⌂ Budget Host, Kings Inn, ⦿ KOA
226	US 183 S, Presho, **N** ℝ Cenex/dsl, Sinclair/dsl, ⌂ Hutch's Motel/café, ⦿ New Frontier RV Park, repair, vet
225	lp 90, Presho, same as 226
221mm	🅁ₛ **wb, full** ♿ **facilities, info,** 🅒, 🛆 **litter barrels, RV dump, petwalk**
220	No Services
218mm	🅁ₛ **eb, full** ♿ **facilities, info,** 🅒, 🛆 **litter barrels, RV dump, petwalk**
214	Vivian

Exit	Services
212	US 83 N, SD 53, to Pierre, **N** ℝ Sinclair/dsl, 🍴 Vivian Jct Rest., ⦿ Ⓗ (34mi)
208	no services
201	Draper, **N** ℝ Farmer's Oil/Cafe
194mm	parking area both lanes
192	US 83 S, Murdo, **N** ℝ HHH/Shell/dsl, Pioneer/dsl, Sinclair/dsl, 🍴 Buffalo Rest., Murdo Drive-In, The Diner, Prairie Pizza, Rusty Spur Steaks, ⌂ American Inn, Anchor Inn, Best Western, Days Inn, Iversen Inn, Lee Motel, Sioux Motel, Super 8, ⦿ American RV Park/camping, Ford, Murdo Foods, auto museum, city park, USPO, **S** ⌂ Country Inn, ⦿ to Rosebud
191	Murdo, **N** same as 192
188mm	parking area both lanes, litter barrels
183	Okaton, **S** gas, Ghost Town
177	no services
175mm	central/mountain timezone
172	to Cedar Butte
170	SD 63 N, to Midland, **N** ℝ Shell/dsl, ⦿ 1880's Town, KOA
167mm	🅁ₛ **wb, full** ♿ **facilities,** 🅒, 🛆 **litter barrels, RV dump, petwalk**
165mm	🅁ₛ **eb, full** ♿ **facilities,** 🅒, 🛆 **litter barrels, RV dump, petwalk**
163	SD 63, Belvidere, **S** ℝ Belvidere Store/dsl, 🍴 JR's Grill
152	Lp 90, Kadoka, **N** ℝ Conoco/rest./dsl/24hr, **S** ⦿ Badlands Petrified Gardens, camping
150	SD 73 S, Kadoka, **N** ℝ Dakota Inn/rest., **S** ℝ Clark, Sinclair/pizza/dsl, ⌂ Best Value Inn, Budget Host, Ponderosa Motel/RV Park, Rodeway Inn, Wagon Wheel Motel, ⦿ Kadoka Kampground, to Buffalo Nat Grasslands, repair
143	SD 73 N, to Philip, **15 mi N** Ⓗ
138mm	scenic overlook wb
131	SD 240, **S** ℝ Conoco, ⌂ Badlands Inn (9mi), Cedar Pass Lodge/rest. (9mi), ⦿ Circle 10 Camping, Prairie Home NHS, KOA (11mi), to Badlands NP
129.5mm	scenic overlook eb
127	no services
121	Bigfoot Rd
116	239th St
112	US 14 E, to Philip
110	SD 240, Wall, **N** ℝ Conoco/dsl, Exxon, Phillips 66/Subway, 🍴 DQ, Elkton House Rest., Red Rock Rest., Wall Drug Rest., ⌂ Ann's Motel, Best Value Inn, Best Western, Days Inn, EconoLodge, Fountain Hotel, Motel 6, Sunshine Inn, Super 8, The Wall Motel, Welsh Motel, ⦿ Ace Hardware, Arrow Campground, NAPA, National Grasslands Visitor Ctr, Sleepy Hollow RV Park/Camping, Wall Drug, Wall Foods, Wounded Knee Museum, **S** to Badlands NP, RV camping
109	W 4th Ave, Wall, **1-2 mi N** access to same as 110
107	Cedar Butte Rd
101	Jensen Rd, to Schell Ranch
100mm	🅁ₛ **both lanes, full** ♿ **facilities, info,** 🅒, 🛆 **litter barrels, RV dump, vending, petwalk**
99.5mm	Cheyenne River
98	Wasta, **N** ℝ Mobil/dsl, ⌂ Redwood Motel, ⦿ 24 Express RV Camping, USPQ
90	173rd Ave, to Owanka
88	171st Ave (from eb, no re-entry)
84	167th Ave, **N** Olde Glory Fireworks
78	161st Ave, New Underwood, **1/2 mi S** ⦿ Boondocks Camping, Steve's General Store/dsl/motel/rest.

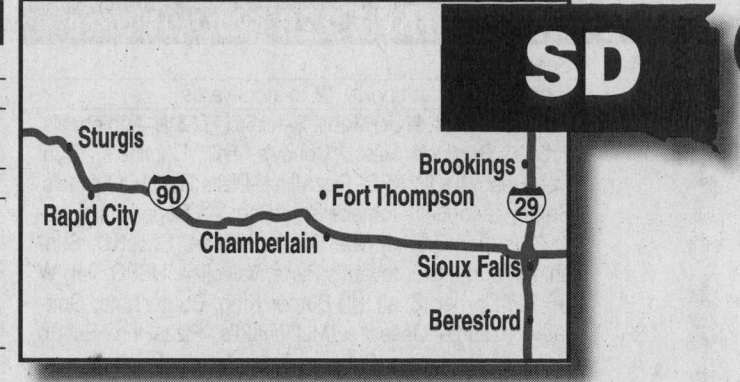

INTERSTATE 90 CONT'D

Exit	Services
69mm	parking area both lanes
67	to Box Elder, Ellsworth AFB, N 🅖 Loaf'n Jug, 🅞 Air&Space Museum
63	(eb only) to Box Elder, Ellsworth AFB
61	Elk Vale Rd, N 🅖 *FLYING J*/Conoco/CountryMkt/dsl/e-85/LP/RV dump/scales/24hr/@, 🅞 Cabela's, Dakota RV Ctr, S 🅖 Conoco, Mobil/dsl, 🍴 Arby's, McDonalds, 🛏 Comfort Inn, Fairfield Inn, La Quinta, Sleep Inn, 🅞 I-90 RV Ctr, KOA (2mi, seasonal), transmissions
60	Lp 90, to Mt Rushmore, Rapid City, S 🍴 Pizza Ranch, Qdoba Mexican, 🅞 🅗 $Tree, Gordman's, Menards, Michael's, PetCo, Sam's Club/gas, Scheel's Sports, Target, TJ Maxx, Verizon, Nat Coll of Mines/Geology
59	La Crosse St, Rapid City, N 🅖 Mobil/24hr, Phillips 66, 🍴 Boston's Rest, Burger King, Denny's, Fuddrucker's, Minerva's Rest., Outback Steaks, Starbucks, TGIFriday's, 🛏 Best Western, Country Inn&Suites, EconoLodge, Hilton Garden, Holiday Inn Express, Super 8, 🅞 Hobby Lobby, Sears/auto, mall, st patrol, S 🅖 Exxon/24hr, Sinclair, 🍴 Arnold's Diner, China Wok, Golden Corral, Mongolian Grill, MillStone Rest., Perkins/24hr, Schlotzsky's, Subway, 🛏 AmericInn, Comfort Inn, Days Inn, Fair Value Inn, Foothills Inn, Grand Gateway Hotel, Hampton Inn, Microtel, Motel 6, Quality Inn, Thrifty Motel, Travelodge, 🅞 Walgreens, Walmart/McDonald's
58	Haines Ave, Rapid City, N 🅖 SPF, 🍴 Applebee's, Chili's, Hardee's, IHOP, Olive Garden, Red Lobster, 🛏 Best Value Inn, Grand Stay Motel, 🅞 Best Buy, $Discount, Hancock Fabrics, Herbergers, JC Penney, Kohl's, Lowe's, Petsmart, Sewing Ctr/Bernina, Tires+, to Rushmore Mall, S 🅖 Loaf'n Jug, 🍴 ChuckeCheese, Dickey's BBQ, Jimmy John's, Papa John's, Taco John's, Wendy's, 🅞 🅗 Family$, ShopKO
57	I-190, US 16, to Rapid City, Mt Rushmore, **1 mi S on North St** 🅖 Exxon, 🛏 Holiday Inn, Howard Johnson, Radisson, 🅞 Ace Hardware, Family Thrift Foods, Office Depot
55	Deadwood Ave, N 🅞 Dakota RV Ctr, Harley-Davidson/cafe, S 🅖 📷/Sinclair/Subway/dsl/scales/24hr/@, 🍴 Marlin's Rest., Windmill Rest., 🅞 Cadillac/Chevrolet, dsl repair
52	Peaceful Pines Rd, Black Hawk, N 🅞 Three Flags Camping (1mi), S 🍴 BJ's/dsl, 🍴 Godfather's Pizza, Longhorn Rest., Pizza Hut, 🅞 Curves, Family$, USPO
48	Stagebarn Canyon Rd, N 🅞 RV camping, S 🅖 PitStop/dsl, Sinclair/Haggar's Mkt/food, 🍴 Pizza Hut, Sacora Sta Rest., Summerset Bistro, 🛏 Ramada, 🅞 Mid-States RV Ctr, auto repair
46	Piedmont Rd, Elk Creek Rd, N 🅞 Elk Creek RV Park, to Petrified Forest, camping, S 🅖 Conoco/Country Corner Cafe/dsl, 🍴 Sacora Sta Rest.
44	Bethlehem Rd, S 🅞 Jack's RV Ctr (2mi)
42mm	🆁🆂 both lanes, full ♿ facilities, info, 🅒, 🚮, litter barrels, RV dump, petwalk, vending
40	Tilford, S RV Park
39mm	weigh sta eb
37	Pleasant Valley Rd, N 🅞 Elkview Camp, S 🅞 Bulldog Camping, Rush-No-More Camping
34	S 🅞 Black Hills Nat Cemetary, No Name City RV Park
32	SD 79, Jct Ave, Sturgis, N 🅖 Conoco/dsl, Exxon/dsl, 🍴 Si Senor Mexican, Taco John's, 🛏 Best Western, StarLite

Exit	Services
32	Continued Motel, 🅞 🅗 Ford, Grocery Mart, NAPA, Rodney RV Park, motorcycle museum, vet, to Bear Butte SP
30	US 14A W, SD 34E, to Deadwood, Sturgis, N 🅖 Cenex/dsl, Fresh Start/dsl, 🍴 McDonald's, Pizza Hut, Sturgis Doghouse, 🅞 Back to Nature Foods, CarQuest, Famliy$, Mr Tire, O'Reilly Parts, Pamida/drug, Radio Shack, Day's End Camping, S 🅖 Conoco/dsl, RanchMart, 🍴 Burger King, DQ, Pizza Ranch, Subway, 🛏 Holiday Inn Express, Days Inn, Super 8, 🅞 Chevrolet
23	SD 34 W, to Belle Fourche, Whitewood, N 🅞 Northern Hills RV Ctr, S 🅖 Howdy's/dsl, 🍴 Whitewood Rest., 🛏 Iron Horse Inn, Tony's Motel, 🅞 USPO
17	US 85 S, to Deadwood, 9-17 mi S in Deadwood 🍴 Brown Rock, Deadwood Grill, Silverado Café, 🛏 AmericInn, Deadwood Lodge, Elkhorn Ridge Motel, Franklin Motel, Holiday Inn Express, Mineral Palace Motel, Super 8, 🅞 Deadwood NLH, Elkhorn Ridge RV Resort, Whistler Gulch Camping
14	US 14A, Spearfish Canyon, N 🅖 FreshStart/dsl, 🍴 Applebee's, Culver's, Subway, 🛏 Comfort Suites, Fairfield Inn, Holiday Inn/rest., Quality Inn, 🅞 Walmart/Papa John's, S 🅖 Phillips 66/dsl, 🍴 KFC/LJ Silver, Perkins, Pizza Ranch, Roma's Rest., 🛏 Howard Johnson, Rodeway Inn, Super 8, 🅞 Ace Hardware, Ford/Lincoln, K-Mart, auto museum, camping
12	Jackson Blvd, Spearfish, S 🅖 Conoco/dsl, Exxon, Loaf'n Jug, Phillips 66/dsl, 🍴 Arby's, Barbacoa's, Domino's, Emperial China, McDonald's, Millstone Rest., Papa John's, Papa Murphy's, Pizza Hut, Quiznos, Taco John's, 🛏 Best Western, Travelodge, 🅞 🅗 CarQuest, Chrysler/Dodge/Jeep, Curves, Radio Shack, Black Hills St U, historic fish hatchery, same as 10
10	US 85 N, to Belle Fourche, S 🍴 Burger King, Cedar House Rest., Golden Dragon Chinese, McDonald's, Subway, Taco Bell, 🛏 Days Inn, 🅞 🅗 Buick/Chevrolet, Cadillac/GMC, KOA, Safeway/drug/gas, Walgreens, USPO, same as 12
8	McGuigan Rd, W Spearfish, S KOA (1mi)
2	**1 mi N** McNenny St Fish Hatchery
1mm	**Welcome Ctr eb, full** ♿ **facilities, info,** 🅒, 🚮, **litter barrels, RV dump, petwalk**
0mm	South Dakota/Wyoming state line

INTERSTATE 229 (SIOUX FALLS)

Exit	Services
10b a	I-90 E and W. **I-229 begins/ends on I-90, exit 400.**
9	Benson Rd, W 🅖 BP/pizza, 🍴 Marlin's Rest., 🅞 Ford Trucks, Western Star
7.5mm	Big Sioux River

SD
TN

SIOUX FALLS

🔼N INTERSTATE 229 (SIOUX FALLS) CONT'D

Exit	Services
7	Rice St, **E** winter sports, **W** to stockyards
6	SD 38, 10th St, **E** 🅿 Mobil, Sinclair, 🍴 A&W, Applebee's, Arby's, Boston's Rest., Denny's, DQ, Domino's, Fryn' Pan Rest., IHOP, KFC, Pizza Hut, Pizza Ranch, Quizno's, Sonic, Taco Bell, Tomacelli's Italian, 🛏 Super 8, 🅾 AutoZone, Family$, Hy-Vee Foods, K-Mart, ShopKO, Sunshine Foods, Sturdevant's Parts, Valvoline, USPO, vet, **W** 🅿 BP, Corner, Shell, 🍴 Burger King, BurgerTime, Godfather's, Little Caesar's, McDonald's, Pizza Inn, Puerto Vallarta, Steak-Out, Subway, Taco John's, 🛏 Rushmore Motel, 🅾 Lewis Drug, vet
5.5mm	Big Sioux River
5	26th St, **E** 🅿 Shell/dsl, 🍴 Burger King, Cherry Creek Grill, Dario's Pizza, McDonald's, SaiGon Panda, 🅾 city park, **W** 🅾 H
4	Cliff Ave, **E** 🅿 BP/dsl
3	SD 115, Lp 229, Minnesota Ave, **E** city park, **W** 🅿 BP, Sinclair, 🍴 Burger King, Camilles Cafe, Culver's, DQ, Fa

3	Continued mous Dave's BBQ, Golden Bowl Chinese, Little Caesar's/ TCBY, McDonald's, Subway, Z'kota Grille, 🅾 Ace Hardware, Buick/GMC, $Tree, Hy-Vee Foods/gas, Kia, Lewis Drug, Staples, tire, USPO
2	Western Ave, **E** 🅿 Shell/dsl, 🍴 Bracco Cafe, DQ, Joey's Grill, Nucci Italian, Scooters Coffee, Starbucks, **W** 🅿 Cenex/dsl, Shell, 🍴 Buck's Roadhouse, Burger King, Champp's Café, China Buffet, Huhot Mongolian, Papa Murphy's, Qdoba Mexican, Quizno's, Redrossa Pizza, Scheell's, 🅾 H, Advance Parts, Best Buy, Goodyear/ auto, Hancock Fabrics, Radio Shack
1.5mm	Big Sioux River
1c	Louise Ave, **E** 🛏 Homewood Suites, 🅾 H, Dodge, **W** 🅿 BP, Phillips 66/dsl, 🍴 Applebee's, Arby's, Burger King, Cici's Pizza, Jimmy John's, McDonald's, Panera Bread, Qdoba Mexican, Red Lobster, Royal Palace, Spezia's Rest., Taco John's, Wendy's, 🛏 Hilton Garden Inn, 🅾 Barnes&Noble, Honda, Hy-Vee Foods/gas, JC Penney, Jo-Ann Fabrics, Kohl's, Target, Walgreens, mall
1b a	I-29 N and S. **I-229 begins/ends on I-29, exit 75.**

TENNESSEE

CHATTANOOGA

🔼E INTERSTATE 24

Exit	Services
185b a	I-75, N to Knoxville, S to Atlanta.
I-24 begins/ends on I-75, exit 2 in Chattanooga.	
184	Moore Rd, **S** 🍴 Chef Lin's Buffet, Provino's Italian, 🅾 $Tree, Radio Shack
183	(183a from wb), Belvoir Ave, Germantown Rd
181a	US 41 S, to East Ridge (from eb), **S** 🍴 Sugar's Ribs, 🛏 King's Lodge, 🅾 Ford Trucks
181	Fourth Ave, to TN Temple U, Chattanooga, **N** 🅿 Citgo/ dsl, Exxon/dsl, Hi-Tech Fuel, Stop'n Save, 🍴 Bojangles, Burger King, Capt D's, Hardee's, Krystal, Subway, Waffle House, 🛏 Chatt Inn, 🅾 BiLo, $General, Mack/Volvo Trucks, O'Reilly Parts, repair, vet, **S** 🅿 Mystik
180b a	US 27 S, TN 8, Rossville Blvd, **N** 🅾 U-Haul, tires, to UT Chatt, **S** 🅿 Mapco/dsl, RaceWay/dsl, 🛏 Hamilton Inn, 🅾 Family$, NTB, auto repair, to Chickamauga Battlefield
178	US 27 N, Market St, to Lookout Mtn, Chattanooga, **N** 🅿 BP/dsl, Citgo, 🛏 Country Hearth Inn, La Quinta, Marriott, Staybridge Suites, 🅾 Chevrolet, Ford/Lincoln, Midas, Nissan, U-Haul, to aquarium, to Chattanooga ChooChoo, **S** 🅿 RaceWay/dsl, 🍴 KFC, 🛏 Comfort Suites, Motel 6
175	Browns Ferry Rd, to Lookout Mtn, **N** 🅿 BP, Exxon/dsl, 🍴 China Gourmet, 🛏 Best Value Inn, 🅾 CVS Drug, $General, vet, **S** 🅿 Mapco/dsl, 🍴 Hardee's, McDonald's, 🛏 Comfort Inn, EconoLodge, Quality Inn
174	US 11, US 41, US 64, Lookout Valley, **N** 🍴 Waffle House, 🛏 Days Inn, 🅾 Racoon Mtn Camping (1mi), **S** 🅿 BP/ dsl, Kangaroo, 🍴 Cracker Barrel, Logan's Roadhouse, Los 3 Amigos, New China, Taco Bell, Waffle House, Wendy's, 🛏 Baymont Inn, Best Western, Budget Motel, Country Inn&Suites, Fairfield Inn, Hampton Inn, Holiday Inn Express, Knights Inn, Ramada Ltd, Super 8, 🅾 Ace Hardware, AT&T, $Tree, Lookout Valley Camping, Verizon, Walmart/Subway, st patrol
172mm	🆁🆂 eb, full 🚻 facilities, 🅲, 🐾, litter barrels, vending, petwalk

MONTEAGLE

171mm	Tennessee/Georgia state line
169	GA 299, to US 11, **N** 🅿 Mapco/dsl, **S** gas, BP/Krispy Chicken/dsl/24hr, 🅛🅞🅥🅔🅢/Subway/dsl/scales/24hr, RaceWay, 🍴 Granny's Rest., 🅾 repair
167	I-59 S, to Birmingham
167mm	Tennessee/Georgia state line, Central/Eastern time zone
161	TN 156, to Haletown, New Hope, **N** 🅿 BP/dsl (1mi), 🅾 Hales Bar RV Park, **S** 🅿 Chevron/fireworks
160mm	Tennessee River/Nickajack Lake
159mm	**Welcome Ctr wb/🆁🆂 eb, full 🚻 facilities, 🅲, vending, 🐾 litter barrels, petwalk**
158	US 41, TN 27, Nickajack Dam, **N** 🅿 ❤Love's/McDonald's/Subway/dsl/scales/24hr, **S** 🅿 BP/dsl/fireworks, 🅾 Shellmound Camping (2.5mi)
155	TN 28, Jasper, **N** 🅿 BP/dsl (1mi), Hi-Tech, 🍴 DQ (1mi), Hardee's, Western Sizzlin, **S** 🅿 BP/Quiznos/dsl, 🅾 H
152	US 41, US 64, US 72, Kimball, S Pittsburg, **N** 🅿 BP/fireworks, RaceWay/dsl, Shell/dsl, 🍴 A&W/LJ Silver, Arby's, China Buffet, Cracker Barrel, Domino's, El Toril, KFC, Krystal, Los Amigos, McDonald's, Pizza Hut, Shoney's, Subway, Taco Bell, Waffle House, Wendy's, 🛏 Best Value Inn, Comfort Inn, Holiday Inn Express, Super 8, 🅾 H, Buick/Chevrolet/GMC, $Tree, GNC, Lowe's, Radio Shack, Walmart, to Russell Cave NM, **3 mi S** 🅾 Lodge Cast Iron
143	Martin Springs Rd, **N** 🅿 Chevron/dsl/fireworks
135	US 41 N, Monteagle, **N** 🅿 BP/dsl, Wilco/Hess/Wendy's/ dsl/scales/24hr, 🍴 Shan Chinese, Smok'n B's BBQ, 🅾 Family$, Laurel Trails Camping, USPO, **S** Days Inn
134	US 64, US 41A, to Sewanee, Monteagle, **N** 🅿 Mapco/McDonald's, 🍴 Sonic, 🛏 American Eagle Inn, 🅾 CVS Drug, to S Cumberland SP, **S** 🅿 Marathon/Kangaroo, Shell/dsl, 🍴 Hardee's, Monteagle Diner, Pizza Hut, Smokehouse BBQ, Subway, Waffle House, 🛏 Best Western, Mtn Inn, Super 8, 🅾 $General, Fred's, Monteagle Winery, Piggly Wiggly, to U of The South
133mm	🆁🆂 both lanes, full 🚻 facilities, 🅲, 🐾, litter barrels, vending, petwalk
128mm	Elk River

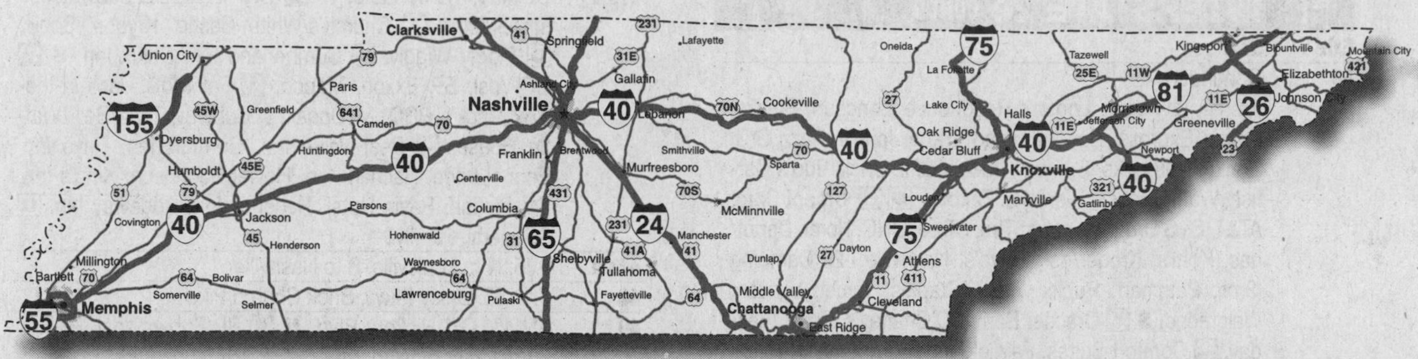

INTERSTATE 24 CONT'D

MANCHESTER

Exit	Services
127	US 64, TN 50, to Winchester, Pelham, N BP, Phillips 66, S Gulf/dsl, to Tims Ford SP/RV camping
119mm	trucks only parking area both lanes
117	to Tullahoma, USAF Arnold Ctr, UT Space Institute
116mm	**weigh sta both lanes**
114	US 41, Manchester, N BP/24 Truckers/scales/dsl, Marathon/dsl, Murphy USA/dsl, Shell/dsl, El Potrillo, Great Wall Chinese, Logan's Roadhouse, O'Charley's, Starbucks, Comfort Suites, Holiday Inn Express, Motel 6, Quality Inn, Scottish Inn, Sleep Inn, Truckers Inn, Country Cabin Camping, $Tree, Home Depot, KOA, Nissan, Toyota, Verizon, Walmart/Subway, S Marathon, RaceWay/dsl, Arby's, Baskin-Robbins, Burger King, Capt D's, Hong Kong Buffet, KFC, Krystal, McDonald's/playplace, Pizza Hut, Shoney's, Subway, Taco Bell, Waffle House, Wendy's, Best Value Inn, Country Inn&Suites, Days Inn, Microtel, Royal Inn, Advance Parts, AutoZone, Family$, Ford/Lincoln, O'Reilly Parts, Russell Stover, USPO
111	TN 55, Manchester, N BP/dsl, Co-op gas/dsl, Marathon/Kangaroo, to Rock Island SP, S BP, Hardee's, J&G Pizza/Steaks, Sonic, H, Gateway Auto, Rite Aid, Walgreens, vet, to Jack Daniels Dist HS, Old Stone Fort
110	TN 53, Manchester, N BP, Marathon, Shell/dsl, Cracker Barrel, Emma's Rest., Oak Rest., Ambassador Inn, Economy Inn, Super 8, S Shell/dsl/24hr, Los 3 Amigos, Waffle House, H
110mm	Duck River
105	US 41, N BP/dsl, Shell/dsl, S Whispering Oaks Camping, tire/repair, to Normandy Dam, Dickle HS
97	TN 64, to Shelbyville, Beechgrove, S BP/dsl
89	Buchanan Rd, N /McDonald's/dsl/scales/24hr, S Shell/dsl, Fiesta Grill, $General
84	Joe B. Jackson Pkwy, N Subway
81	US 231, Murfreesboro, N BP/dsl, Exxon, Shell, Cathay Asian, Cracker Barrel, Krystal, Parthenon Grille, Sal's Pizza, Shoney's, Waffle House, Wendy's, Best Value Inn, Knights Inn, Quality Inn, Ramada Ltd, Regal Inn, H, Chrysler/Dodge/Jeep, Honda, antiques, S Kangaroo, Mapco/dsl, Marathon, /Arby's/scales/dsl/24hr, Bojangles, Burger King, Dick's Hamburgers, La Siesta Mexican, McDonald's/playplace, Pizza Hut/Taco Bell, Sonic, Starbucks, Subway, Waffle House, Zaxby's, Safari Inn, Select Inn, Vista Suites, Advance Parts, AutoZone, Discount Tire, Gateway Auto, Kroger/gas, Rite

MURFREESBORO

Exit	Services
81	Continued Aid, Toyota/Scion, U-Haul, vet
80	New Salem Hwy, rd 99, S Domino's, Subway
78	TN 96, to Franklin, Murfreesboro, N BP, Marathon, Murphy USA/dsl, Phillips 66/Church's/White Castle/dsl, Shell/Jack-in-the-Box, Arby's, Baskin-Robbins, Bonefish Grill, Buffalo Wild Wings, Carrabba's, Cheddar's, Chick-fil-A, ChuckECheese, Coconut Bay Cafe, Cracker Barrel, Fazoli's, IHOP, Jason's Deli, Jimmy John's, Jim'n Nick's BBQ, KFC, McDonald's, Mi Patria, Old Chicago, Olive Garden, Outback Steaks, Panda Express, Panera Bread, Red Lobster, Red Robin, Sam's Grill, Samurai's Cuisine, SmashBurger, Starbucks, Steak'n Shake, Subway, TGIFriday's, Waffle House, Wendy's, Zaxby's, Baymont Inn, Best Western, Candlewood Suites, Clarion, Comfort Suites, Country Inn&Suites, Days Inn, DoubleTree, EconoLodge, Fairfield Inn, Hampton Inn, Holiday Inn Express, Microtel, Motel 6, Red Roof Inn, Sleep Inn, Super 8, Aldi Foods, AT&T, Books-A-Million, Dillard's, Discount Tire, $Tree, Firestone, Hobby Lobby, Home Depot, JC Penney, Jo-Ann Fabrics, Lowe's, Marshalls, NTB, Petsmart, Ross, Sears/auto, Staples, Target, Thornton's/dsl, TJ Maxx, Verizon, Walgreens, Walmart, vet, to Stones River Bfd, S Kangaroo, Mapco, Marathon/dsl, Shell, Capt D's, China Garden, China Garden, Hardee's, Jersey Mike's Subs, Las Palmas, Little Caesars, McDonald's, O'Charley's, Papa Murphy's, Pizza Hut, Sonic, Subway, Taco Bell, Waffle House, Wasabi Japanese, ValuePlace Inn, AutoZone, $General, Kohl's, Kroger/dsl, Old Time Pottery, O'Reilly Parts, Rite Aid, Sam's Club/gas, Walgreens
76	Fortress Blvd, Manson Pike, Medical Center Pkwy, N Bar Louie, Chili's, Culver's, Genghis Grill, Longhorn Steaks, Macaroni Grill, Mimi's Cafe, Subway, Which Wich, Embassy Suites, H, Barnes&Noble, Belk, Best Buy, Dick's, Michael's, Old Navy, Thornton's/dsl, World Mkt, to Stones River Nat. Bfd, S Exxon/dsl

NASHVILLE

Exit	Services
74b a	TN 840, to Lebanon, Franklin
70	TN 102, Lee Victory Pkwy, Almaville Rd, to Smyrna, N Shell/dsl/scales, S BP, Kangaroo/Quiznos/dsl, Mapco, McDonald's, Mi Camino Mexican, Legends Steaks, Sonic, Subway, Deerfield Inn, $General, Tennessee Expo
66	TN 266, Sam Ridley Pkwy, to Smyrna, N Shell/dsl, Arby's, A&W/LJ Silver, Buffalo Wild Wings, Catfish House, Cheddar's, Chick-fil-A, Chili's, CiCi's Pizza, Famous Dave's BBQ, 5 Guys Burgers, Golden China, Hickory Falls Cafe, IHOP, Jersey Mike's Subs, Jim'n Nick's BBQ, Krispy

📱 = gas   🍴 = food   🏨 = lodging   Ⓞ = other   🆁🆂 = rest stop   Copyright 2014 - The NEXT Exit ®

TN

➤Ⓔ INTERSTATE 24 CONT'D

Exit	Services
66	Continued
	Kreme, La Fiesta, Logan's Roadhouse, Longhorn Steaks, Panda Express, Panera Bread, Papa John's, Razz Grill, Sonic, Starbucks, Subway, Tody's Grill, Uncle Bud's Catfish, Waffle House, Wendy's, Zaxby's, Ⓞ Ⓗ **Urgent Care**, AT&T, CVS Drug, Discount Tire, $Tree, GNC, Home Depot/gas, Kohl's, Kroger/dsl, Lowe's, Nashville I-24 Camping (3mi), Petsmart, Publix, Ross, Staples, Target, Verizon, Walgreens, **S** 🍴 Cracker Barrel, O'Charley's, Ruby Tuesday, 🏨 Comfort Suites, Fairfield Inn, Hampton Inn, Hilton Garden, Holiday Inn Express, La Quinta, Sleep Inn
64	Waldron Rd, to La Vergne, **N** 📱 Kangaroo, Kwik Sak, 🚂/Subway/dsl/scales/24hr, 🍴 Arby's, Hardee's, Krystal, McDonald's, Waffle House, 🏨 Comfort Inn, Quality Inn, Ramada Inn, Ⓞ RV ctr, **S** 📱 Mapco/dsl
62	TN 171, Old Hickory Blvd, **N** 📱 Citgo/Subway/dsl, Shell/dsl, TA/BP/Burger King/Popeye's/dsl/scales/24hr@, 🍴 Acapulco Burrito, 🏨 Best Western
60	Hickory Hollow Pkwy, **N** 📱 BP, Exxon/dsl, Mapco, 🍴 Applebee's, Burger King, ChuckECheese, El Patron, KFC/LJ Silver, Logan's Roadhouse, McDonald's/Playplace, O'Charley's, Red Lobster, Starbucks, Subway, Taco Bell, Wendy's, Zaxby's, 🏨 Country Inn&Suites, Hampton Inn, Nashville Hotel, Ⓞ Chevrolet, Chrysler/Dodge/Jeep, $Tree, Family$, Firestone/auto, Kroger/gas, Mazda, NTB, Office Depot, TJ Maxx, **S** 📱 BP/Quiznos/dsl, Shell/Dunkin Donuts, 🍴 Camino Royale Mexican, Casa Fiesta Mexican, Evergreen Chinese, Fox's Pizza, IHOP, Olive Garden, Shoney's, Steak'n Shake, 🏨 Knights Inn, Super 8, Ⓞ Home Depot, Kia, Target, vet
59	TN 254, Bell Rd, same as 60
57	Haywood Lane, **N** 📱 Kwik Sak/dsl, 🍴 Hardee's, Pizza Hut, Whitt's BBQ, Ⓞ CarQuest, $General, Walgreens, **S** 📱 Kangaroo, Shell
56	TN 255, Harding Place, **N** 📱 Exxon, Mapco, Shell/dsl, 🍴 Applebee's, Bar-B-Cutie, Dunkin Donuts, Hardee's, KFC, McDonald's, Pizza Hut/Taco Bell, Subway, Waffle House, Wendy's, 🏨 Executive Inn, Harding Inn, M Motel, Stay Lodge, Thrifty Inn, Ⓞ Sam's Club/gas, **S** 📱 Mapco, Shell/dsl, 🍴 Burger King, Hooters, Jack-in-the-Box, La Fiesta, 🏨 Best Value Inn, Travelodge, Ⓞ Ⓗ
54b a	TN 155, Briley Pkwy to Opryland
53	I-440 W, to Memphis
52	US 41, Murfreesboro Rd, **N** 📱 Mapco, Phillips 66/dsl, Shell, 🍴 Picadilly's, Pizza Hut, Taco Bell, Waffle House, 🏨 Days Inn, Executive Inn, Holiday Inn Express, Rodeway Inn, Super 8, Ⓞ AutoZone, Family$, Wagreens, **S** NAPA
52b a	I-40, E to Knoxville, W to Memphis
I-24 and I-40 run together 2 mi. See I-40 exits 212-213.	
50b	I-40 W
49	Shelby Ave, (from wb only), to LP Field
48	James Robertson Pkwy, **N** 📱 Citgo, **S** 📱 Exxon, TA/Subway/dsl/24hr/@, 🍴 Shoney's, 🏨 Ramada, Stadium Inn, Ⓞ LP Stadium, st capitol
47a	US 31E
47	N 1st St, Jefferson St, **N** 📱 BP/Subway, Phillips 66, Ⓞ Family$, **S** 📱 Mystic Gas, 🏨 Days Inn, Knights Inn, Ⓞ U-Haul
I-24 and I-65 run together. See I-65 exit 87 b a.	

NASHVILLE (vertical)

CLARKSVILLE (vertical)

Exit	Services
87b a	US 431, Trinity Lane, **N** 📱 BP, ♥Loves/Subway/dsl/scales/24hr, 🍴 Church's/White Castle, Krystal, Sonic, Ⓞ Piggly Wiggly, 🏨 Cumberland Inn, Delux Inn, **S** 📱 BCP/dsl, BP, Exxon, Mapco, 🍴 Fat Mo's, Jack-in-the-Box, Jack's BBQ, McDonald's, Subway, Taco Bell, Waffle House, 🏨 Best Value Inn, Comfort Inn, Days Inn, EconoLodge, Halmark Inn, Howard Johnson, King's Inn, Quality Inn, Ravin Hotel, Regency Inn, Rodeway Inn, Ⓞ $General, Family$
44b a	I-65, N to Louisville, S to Nashville
43	TN 155, Briley Pkwy, Brick Church Pike
40	TN 45, Old Hickory Blvd, **N** 📱 BP/Subway/dsl, Phillips 66/dsl/24hr, Shell/dsl, 🏨 Super 8
35	US 431, to Joelton, Springfield, **N** Ⓗ, **S** 📱 Heritage TC/DQ/Subway/dsl, Shell, 🍴 Family Rest., Mazatlan Mexican, McDonald's, 🏨 Days Inn, Ⓞ Curves, Family$, OK Camping, auto repair
31	TN 249, New Hope Rd, **N** 📱 Shell/Taco Tico/dsl, **S** 📱 BP/dsl, Shell/dsl/24hr
24	TN 49, to Springfield, Ashland City, **N** 📱 BP/dsl, Mapco/dsl/24hr, Phillips 66/dsl/24hr, Ⓞ Ⓗ, repair, **S** 📱 Shell/dsl, SS/Dunkin Donuts/Wendy's, 🍴 Dragon Buffet, KFC/Taco Bell, Sonic, Subway, Ⓞ $General, Hill Foods, USPO, city park, vet
19	TN 256, Maxey Rd, to Adams, **N** 📱 BP/dsl, **S** 📱 Shell
11	TN 76, to Adams, Clarksville, **N** 📱 Shell/dsl/24hr, **S** 📱 BP/dsl/24hr, 🍴 McDonald's, Subway, Waffle House, 🏨 Days Inn, Holiday Inn Express, Quality Inn, Super 8, Ⓞ Ⓗ
9mm	Red River
8	TN 237, Rossview Rd, **S** Dunbar Cave SP
4	US 79, to Clarksville, Ft Campbell, **N** 📱 BP/dsl/24hr, Exxon/dsl, 🍴 Cracker Barrel, 🏨 Hilton Garden, Ⓞ Sam's Club/gas, Spring Creek Camping (2mi), **S** 📱 BP/dsl/24hr, Murphy USA/dsl, Shell/dsl, 🍴 Applebee's, Arby's, Baskin-Robbins, Buffalo Wild Wings, Burger King, Capt D's, Chili's, Chopsticks, ChuckeCheese, Church's/White Castle, DQ, Fazoli's, Golden Corral, Harbor Cafe, IHOP, KFC, Krystal, Logan's Roadhouse, LJ Silver, Longhorn Steaks, McDonald's, O'Charley's, Old Chicago Pizza, Olive Garden, Outback Steaks, Papa Murphy's, Quiznos, Rafferty's, Red Lobster, Ryan's, Shogun Japanese, Shoney's, Starbucks, Steak'n Shake, Subway, Taco Bell, Waffle House, Wendy's, Zaxby's, 🏨 AT&T, Best Inn, Best Value Inn, Best Western, Candlewood Suites, Comfort Inn, Country Inn&Suites, Courtyard, Days Inn, EconoLodge, Fairfield Inn, Guesthouse Inn, Hampton Inn, Hawthorn Suites, Hometowne Suites, Mainstay Suites, Microtel, Quality Inn, Ramada Ltd, Red Roof Inn, Super 8, ValuePlace Hotel, Wingate Inn, Ⓞ Ⓗ, Advance Parts, Belk, Best Buy, Books-A-Million, Buick/GMC, Dick's, Dillard's, $Tree, Firestone/auto, Goodyear/auto, Hancock Fabrics, Hobby Lobby, Home Depot, Hyundai, JC Penney, Kohl's, Kroger/dsl, K-Mart, Lowe's, Mazda, Office Depot, Petsmart, Sears/auto, Subaru, Target, TJ Maxx, Verizon, U-Haul, Walmart, mall, winery, to Austin Peay St U, to Land Between the Lakes
1	TN 48, to Clarksville, Trenton, **N** 📱 Shell/dsl, Ⓞ Clarksville RV Camping, **S** 📱 BP, 🍴 Coldstone, El Tapatio Mexican, Gatti's Pizza, Sonic, Wendy's, Ⓞ AutoZone, $General, Walgreens
.5mm	**Welcome Ctr eb, full 🚻 facilities, 🍴, vending, ♻ litter barrels, petwalk**
0mm	Tennessee/Kentucky state line

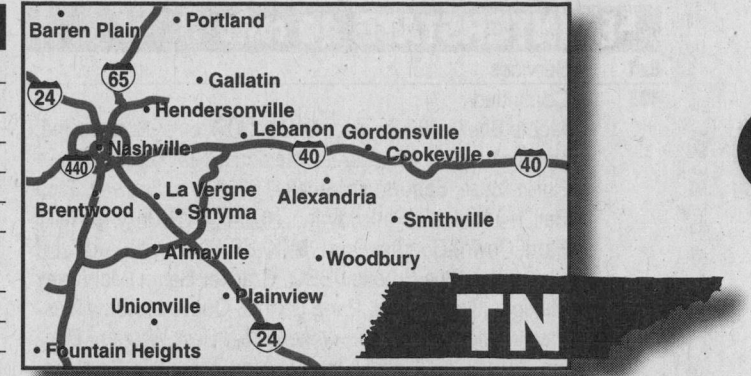

🛣E INTERSTATE 26

Exit	Services
54.5mm	Tennessee/North Carolina state line
54mm	runaway truck ramp wb
52mm	scenic overlook eb, (no trucks), runaway truck ramp wb
50	Flag Pond Rd
47.5mm	scenic overlook wb, (no trucks),
46mm	**N Welcome Ctr/🆁🆂 both lanes, full ♿ facilities, 🄾, litter barrels, 🐾 petwalk**
44mm	Higgins Creek
43	US 19 W, rd 352, Temple Hill Rd
42mm	S Indian Creek

ERWIN

40	Jackson-Love Hwy, Erwin, Jonesborough, **N** 🄶 Valero/dsl, 🛏 Mtn Inn, 🄾 🄷, Nolichucky Gorge Camping (2mi)
37	TN 81, rd 107, Erwin, Jonesborough, **N** 🄶 Shell, 🍴 Huddle House, McDonald's, 🄾 🄷, Walgreens, USPO, **S** 🛏 Super 8, 🄾 River Park Camping (5mi), A. Johnson NHS
36	Main St, Erwin, **N** 🄶 BP/dsl, Exxon/dsl/e-85, 🍴 Azteca Mexican, Hardee's, KFC, Little Caesars, Pizza Hut, Subway, Wendy's, 🄾 Advance Parts, AutoZone, $General, Firestone, IGA Foods, Rite Aid
34	Tinker Rd, **N** 🄶 Murphy USA/dsl, 🍴 Los Jalapenos, Primo's Pizza, 🄾 Walmart
32	rd 173, Unicoi Rd, to Cherokee NF, **N** 🄶 Unicoi Mkt, 🍴 Clarence's Drive-In, Maple Grove Café, 🄾 Grandview Ranch Camping (7mi), **S** Woodsmoke Camping
27	rd 359 N, Okolona Rd, **N** 🄶 BP, 🍴 Kozy Kitchen, 🛏 Budget Inn (3mi), 🄾 truck repair
24	US 321, TN 67, Elizabethton, **N** 🄶 Shell/dsl, **S** 🄶 BP/dsl, 🍴 Arby's, Burger King, Fox's Pizza, Little Caesars, LJ Silver, Subway, 🛏 Comfort Inn, 🄾 🄷, Advance Parts, CVS, Food City/gas, Price Less Foods, Walgreens, to ETSU, Roan Mtn SP
23	rd 91, Market St, **N** 🍴 DQ, McDonald's, **S** 🄾 museum
22	rd 400, Unaka Ave, Watauga Ave

JOHNSON CITY

20 b a	US 11 E, US 19 N, to Roan St, **N** 🄶 Shell/dsl, Sunoco, 🍴 Arby's, Cootie Brown's Rest., El Rancon, Empire Buffet, Fred's, Harbor House Seafood, Hardee's, Hibachi Grill, Little Caesars, LJ Silver, Mellow Mushroom Pizza, Moto Japanese, Papa John's, Peerless Rest., Perkins, Popeye's, Rainbow Asian, Sonic, 🛏 Best Western, Holiday Inn, Ramada Ltd, Super 8, 🄾 Acura, Advance Parts, AT&T, AutoZone, BigLots, Ford, Honda, Hyundai, Mazda, O'Reilly Parts, Subaru, Tuesday Morning, VW, **S** 🍴 Applebees, Bailey's Grille, Bonefish Grill, Fazoli's, 5 Guys Burgers, Hooters, Jack's City Grill, Jersey Mike's Subs, KFC, Longhorn Steaks, McAlister's Deli, McDonald's, O'Charley's, Olive Garden, Papa Murphy's, Red Lobster, Red Pig BBQ, Shoney's, Smokey Bones BBQ, Starbucks, Subway, Taco Bell, TX Roadhouse, Zaxby's, 🛏 Motel 6, Red Roof Inn, 🄾 Belk, Books-A-Million, CVS, Dick's, $General, $Tree, Hancock Fabrics, JC Penney, Kroger, Office Depot, Sears/auto, Target, TJ Maxx, Verizon, Walgreens
19	TN 381, to St of Franklin Rd, to Bristol, **N** 🄶 Murphy USA/dsl, Valero/McDonald's, 🍴 Golden Corral, Honeybaked Ham, Logan's Roadhouse, Outback Steaks, Subway, 🛏 Comfort Suites, 🄾 Hyundai, Radio Shack, VW, Walmart, **0-2 mi S** 🍴 Atlanta Bread, Barberito's Grille, Buffalo Wild Wings, Carrabba's, Cheddar's, Chick-fil-A, Chili's, Chuck-E-Cheese's, Cocula Mexi, Fuddruckers, IHOP, Marble Slab, Ming's Asian, Panera Bread, Rita's Custard, Wendy's, Which Wich, 🛏 Courtyard, Hampton Inn, Sleep Inn, 🄾

KINGSPORT

19	Continued 🄷, AT&T, Barnes&Noble, Best Buy, Home Depot, K-Mart, Kohl's, Lowe's, Michael's, Natural Foods Mkt, Old Navy, PetsMart, Ross, Sam's Club/gas, Steinmart, USPO, Verizon, vet
17	Boone St, **N** 🄶 BP, 🍴 Beef'o Brady's, Bob Evans, Burger King, Giovanni's Italian, McDonald's, Pal's Drive-in, Pizza+, 🄾 Ingles Foods, **S** 🄶 Exxon/e-85, Shell/Subway, 🍴 Cracker Barrel, Domino's, Poblano's Mexican, Waffle House, Wendy's, 🛏 Holiday Inn Express, Quality Inn, Value Place
13	rd 75, Bobby Hicks Hwy, **N** 🄶 BP, Shell, 🍴 Burger King, China Luck, DQ, Gino's Italian, La Carreta, McDonald's, Papa John's, Pizza Hut, Subway, Taco Bell, Yong Asian, 🄾 Advance Parts, $General, Food City/gas, O'Reilly Parts, Walgreens, USPO, **S** 🄶 Exxon/dsl
10	Eastern Star Rd, **N** 🍴 Phil's Dream Pit
8 b a	I-81, to Bristol, Knoxville
6	rd 347, Rock Springs Rd, **S** 🄶 Rite Quik
5	Pond Springs Rd
4	TN 93, Wilcox Dr, **N** 🄶 BP/Subway, Shell/McDonald's/dsl, 🍴 Burger King, Hardee's, La Carrota Mexican, Pizza Hut, Wendy's, 🛏 Comfort Suites, Hampton Inn, Holiday Inn Express, Quality Inn, 🄾 Cave's Drug, $General, Price Less Foods, **S** 🄶 BP, Zoomerz/Arby's/dsl/e-85, 🍴 Pizza+
3	Meadowview Pkwy, **N** 🛏 Marriott
1	US 11 W, West Stone Dr, **N** 🄶 Shell, 🍴 Little Caesars, Molcajete's Mexican, 🛏 Super 8, 🄾 🄷, Walgreens, **S** 🄶 Exxon, Murphy USA, 🍴 Bojangles, China Star, Fatz Cafe, Sonic, Subway, 🄾 $Tree, Lowe's, Walmart
0mm	I-26 begins/ends on US 23.

🛣E INTERSTATE 40

Exit	Services
451mm	Tennessee/North Carolina state line
451	Waterville Rd
447	Hartford Rd, **N** 🄶 Citgo/dsl, **S** 🄶 BP/dsl, 🍴 Bean Tree Cafe, Pigeon River Smokehouse, 🄾 Foxfire Camping, Shauan's Riverside RV Park, whitewater rafting
446mm	**Welcome Ctr wb, full ♿ facilities, 🐾, vending, 🄾, litter barrels, petwalk, NO TRUCKS**
443	Foothills Pkwy, to Gatlinburg, Great Smoky Mtns NP, **S** camping
443mm	Pigeon River
440	US 321, to Wilton Spgs Rd, Gatlinburg, **S** 🄶 BP, 🍴 Krispy Krunchy Chicken, 🄾 Arrow Creek Camping (14mi), Crazy Horse Camping (14mi), Jellystone Camping (12mi)
439mm	Pigeon River
435	US 321, to Gatlinburg, Newport, **N** 🄶 Exxon/Biodsl/e-85,

◢E INTERSTATE 40 CONT'D

TN / NEWPORT / DANDRIDGE

Exit	Services
435	Continued
	Mobil, Shell/dsl/24hr, Stop'n Go, 🍴 Arby's, Burger King, Hardee's, KFC, La Carreta Mexican, McDonald's, Pizza Hut, Pizza+, SageBrush Steaks, Shoney's, Subway, Taco Bell, 🛏 Motel 6, Parkway Inn, 🅾 H, CVS Drug, O'Reilly Parts, Town&Country Drug, **S** 🅿 BP, Murphy USA/dsl, 🍴 Bojangles, Blue Smokey BBQ, Cracker Barrel, Monterrey Mexican, New China, Papa John's, Quiznos, Ruby Tuesday, Waffle House/24hr, Wendy's, 🛏 Best Western, Days Inn, Family Inn, Holiday Inn Express, Mountain Crest Inn, 🅾 $General, $Tree, Lowe's, Save-A-Lot Foods, Verizon, Walmart
432b a	US 70, US 411, US 25W, to Newport, **N** 🅿 BP/dsl, Exxon/dsl/24hr, TimeOut Travel Ctr/Huddle House/dsl/scales/, Phillips 66, 🍴 Country Kitchen, Osaka Japanese, 🛏 Comfort Inn, Relax Inn, 🅾 Buick/Chevrolet, Chrysler/Dodge/Jeep, Ford, KOA (2mi), TMC Camping, Westgate Tire, **S** 🅿 BP/pizza/dsl, Citgo/dsl/24hr, Marathon, Shell, 🛏 Family Inn/rest.
426mm	℞ wb, full 🚻 facilities, 🅲, vending, 🛋 litter barrels, petwalk
425mm	French Broad River
424	TN 113, Dandridge, **N** 🅿 BP/dsl
421	I-81 N, to Bristol
420mm	℞ eb, full 🚻 facilities, 🅲, vending, 🛋 litter barrels, petwalk
417	TN 92, Dandridge, **N** 🅿 BP, 🚛/Subway/dsl/scales/24hr/@, 🍴 Capt's Galley, Hardee's, McDonald's, Perkins, Ruby Tuesday, 🛏 EconoLodge, **S** 🅿 Shell/Wendy's/dsl, Marathon/KFC/dsl, Weigel's, 🍴 Arby's, LJ Silver/Taco Bell, Shoney's, Waffle House, 🛏 Hampton Inn, Holiday Inn Express, Jefferson Inn, Quality Inn, Super 8, 🅾 Advance Parts
415	US 25W, US 70, to Dandridge, **S** 🅿 Marathon/dsl, 🍴 Sonic (3mi)
412	Deep Sprgs Rd, to Douglas Dam, **N** 🅿 ♥Loves♥/Chester's/Subway/dsl/scales/24hr, **S** 🅿 TR Trkstp/rest/dsl/scales/24hr/@
407	TN 66, to Sevierville, Pigeon Forge, Gatlinburg, **N** 🅿 Shell/Huddle House/dsl, 🍴 Chophouse, Cracker Barrel, Marble Slab, McDonald's, 🛏 Fairfield Inn, Hampton Inn, Holiday Inn Express, Motel 6, 🅾 Bass Pro Shops, RV Camping, Smoky Mtn Visitor's Ctr, **S** 🅿 BP/Dunkin Donuts, Exxon/Subway/dsl, Shell/Krystal/dsl, 🍴 FlapJack's, Wendy's, 🛏 Comfort Suites, Days Inn, Knights Inn, Quality Inn, 🅾 Chrysler/Dodge/Jeep, Russell Stover, RV Camping, USPO, flea mkt, **3-10 mi S** multiple services/outlets
402	Midway Rd
398	Strawberry Plains Pk, **N** 🅿 BP/dsl, Exxon/dsl, Shell/dsl, 🍴 McDonald's, Outback Steaks, Quality Inn, Ruby Tuesday, Waffle House, Wendy's, 🛏 Baymont Inn, EconoLodge, Hampton Inn, Holiday Inn Express, Quality Inn, Ramada Ltd, Red Roof Inn, Super 8, 🅾 Camping World/TN RV Ctr, **S** 🅿 🚛/Subway/dsl/scales/24hr, Weigel's, 🍴 Arby's, Burger King, Cracker Barrel, Golden Wok Chinese, KFC, Krystal, Puleo's Grille, Taco Bell, 🛏 Best Western, Comfort Suites, Fairfield Inn, La Quinta, Motel 6
395mm	Holston River
394	US 70, US 11E, US 25W, Asheville Hwy, **N** 🅿 Marathon, Mobil/dsl, 🚛/dsl, 🍴 Subway, Wendy's, 🛏 Gate

Exit	Services
394	Continued
	way Inn, 🅾 Advance Parts, AutoZone, city park, **S** 🅿 Exxon, Shell/dsl, 🍴 Penson Rest., Scott's Place, Waffle House/24hr, 🛏 Days Inn, 🅾 CVS Drug, Family$, Kroger/gas, Walgreens, vet
393	I-640 W, to I-75 N
392	US 11W, Rutledge Pike, **N** 🅿 Citgo/dsl, 🅾 $General, U-Haul, truck repair, **S** 🅿 BP, 🍴 Buddy's BBQ, Hardee's, Shoney's, 🛏 Family Inn, 🅾 NAPA, Sav-A-Lot Foods, transmissions, to Knoxville Zoo
390	Cherry St, Knoxville, **N** 🅿 Marathon/dsl, Top Fuel Mart, Weigel's/Subway, 🍴 Country Table Rest., Happy Garden Chinese, 🛏 Red Carpet Inn, 🅾 tires, **S** 🅿 Exxon, 🍴 Arby's, KFC, Little Caesar's, LJ Silver, McDonald's, WishBone's Wings, 🛏 Regency Inn, 🅾 Advance Parts, Family$, O'Reilly Parts, Walgreens, vet
389	US 441 N, Broadway, 5th Ave, **N** 🅿 BP, 🚛/dsl, Star, 🍴 Burger King, Capt D's, KFC, Krystal, McDonald's, Sonic, Subway, Taco Bell, Wendy's, 🅾 Belew Drug, CVS Drug, $General, Family$, Firestone/auto, Kroger/gas, Radio Shack, Save-A-Lot Foods, Walgreens/24hr, USPO
388	US 441 S (exits left from wb) downtown, **S** 🛏 Hilton, Holiday Inn, Crowne Plaza, 🅾 to Smokey Mtns, to U of TN
387b	TN 62, 17th St, **N** 🅿 Gas'N Go, 🚛/dsl, 🛏 Economy Inn, Royal Inn, 🅾 $General, Food City/gas
387a	I-275 N, to Lexington
386b a	US 129, University Ave, to UT
385	I-75 N, I-640 E
I-40 W and I-75 S run together 17 mi.	
383	Papermill Rd, **N** 🛏 Red Roof Inn, **S** 🅿 BP, Citgo, 🚛/dsl, Spur Gas, 🍴 Buddy's BBQ, Burger King, 5 Guys Burgers, Krispy Kreme, Sonic, TGIFriday's, Waffle House, 🛏 Super 8, 🅾 Food City, Walgreens, same as 380
380	US 11, US 70, West Hills, **S** 🅿 Shell, Weigel's, 🍴 Applebee's, Arby's, Chick-fil-A, Chili's, Brazeiro's Brazilian Steaks, Brixx Pizza, Dunkin Donuts, Firehouse Subs, Hardee's, Honeybaked Ham, Jet's Pizza, Macaroni Grill, McAlister's Deli, McDonald's, Mr Gatti's, O'Charley's, Olive Garden, Papa John's, Petro's Chili, PF Chang's, Pizza Hut, PlumTree Chinese, Puleo's Grille, Qdoba Mexican, Ray's Grille, Red Lobster, Salsarita's Cantina, Spice Rack Grill, Starbucks, Subway, Taco Bell, TX Roadhouse, Tropical Smoothie Cafe, Wishbone Wings, 🛏 Extended Stay America, Magnuson Hotel, Ramada Inn, 🅾 AT&T, Barnes&Noble, Belk, Dillards, $Tree, Food City, JC Penney, Kohl's, NTB, Office Depot, Old Navy, O'Reilly Parts, Petsmart, Ross, Sears/auto, Staples, Steinmart, Target, TJ Maxx, U-Haul, Walgreens, mall, st patrol
379	Bridgewater Rd, **N** 🅿 Exxon/Subway, 🚛/McDonald's, Shell, 🍴 McDonald's, Taco Bell, 🅾 Sam's Club/gas, Walmart, **S** 🅿 BP/dsl, Citgo/dsl, Conoco, 🍴 Buddy's BBQ, Burger King, China Buffet, ChuckeCheese, CiCi's Pizza, Krystal, Makino's Japanese, Shoney's, Sonic, Wendy's, 🛏 InTown Suites, 🅾 Aamco, Advance Parts, AutoZone, Books-A-Million, Buick/GMC, Chrysler/Dodge/Jeep, Firestone/auto, Ford/Lincoln, Hyundai, Mazda, Nissan Subaru, Tire Barn, Transmission World
378	Cedar Bluff Rd, **N** 🅿 🚛/Taco Bell, Shell, Weigel's, 🍴 Arby's, Burger King, Cracker Barrel, Dunkin Donuts, KFC, Little Caesar's, McDonald's, Old Mill Bread Co., Papa John's, Quiznos, Starbucks, Subway, Waffle House, Wendy's, 🛏 Country Inn&Suites, Days Inn, Hampton Inn,

KNOXVILLE

INTERSTATE 40 CONT'D

Exit	Services
378	**Continued**
	Holiday Inn, Ramada Inn, Sleep Inn, [o] [H], $General, **S** [gas] Exxon, Phillips 66, [food] Applebee's, Bob Evans, Carrabba's, Corky's Ribs/BBQ, Denny's, Fazoli's, Famous Dave's BBQ, Firehouse Subs, Friendly's, Fuddrucker's, Grady's Grill, IHOP, Krystal, Outback Steaks, Panera Bread, Parkside Grill, Peerless Grill, Penn Sta. Subs, Pizza Hut, Puleo's Grill, Rafferty's, Rubio's Grill, Sunny's BBQ, [lodging] Best Western, Clubhouse Inn, Comfort Inn, Courtyard, Extended Stay America, Guesthouse Suites, Hilton Garden, Jameson Inn, La Quinta, Microtel, Red Roof Inn, Residence Inn, Signature Inn, Towne Place Suites, [o] Best Buy, Cadillac, Celebration Sta, Chevrolet, Chrysler, CVS Drug, Dick's, Food City, Ford, Jo-Ann Fabrics, KIA, Lowe's, Michael's, Staples, Tuesday Morning, Walgreens
376	I-140 E, TN 162 N, to Maryville, **N** to Oak Ridge Museum
374	TN 131, Lovell Rd, **N** [gas] Shell/dsl, TA/Country Pride/dsl/scales/24hr/@, [food] Bojangles, McDonald's, Subway, Waffle House, [lodging] Guesthouse Inn, Travelodge, [o] Harley-Davidson, **S** [gas] [wendys]/Wendy's/dsl/24hr, [food] Arby's, Baskin-Robbins, Bonefish Grill, Brixx Pizza, Buffalo Wild Wings, Calhoun's Rest., Chick-fil-A, Connor's Rest., Flemings, Genghis Grill, Jim'N Nick's BBQ, IHOP, Jimmy John's, Kabuki Japanese, Krystal, Mangia Pizza, Marble Slab, McAlister's Deli, McDonald's, Mike's Subs, Mimi's Cafe, Noodles&Co, O'Charley's, Olive Garden, Pei Wei, Pimento's Cafe, Red Robin, Salsarita's Cantina, Shoney's, Smokey Mtn Brewery, Sonic, Starbucks, Steak'n Shake, Subway, TX Roadhouse, Wasabai Japanese, [lodging] Candlewood Suites, Homewood Suites, Motel 6, SpringHill Suites, [o] Advance Parts, Belk, Best Buy, BMW/Mini, CarMax, $Tree, EarthFare Foods, GNC, Hobby Lobby, Honda, Lexus, Marshall's, Mercedes, Old Navy, Petsmart, Radio Shack, Ross, Target, Toyota/Scion, Walgreens, Walmart
373	Campbell Sta Rd, **N** [gas] Shell/dsl, Marathon/dsl, [lodging] Comfort Suites, Country Inn&Suites, Holiday Inn Express, Super 8, [o] Buddy Gregg RV Ctr, **S** [gas] BP, [wendys], Weigel's, [food] Border Tacos, Capt Ernie's Fishouse, Cracker Barrel, Dunkin Donuts, Gatti's Pizza, Hardee's, Kasumi Japanese, Mellow Mushroom, Newk's Grill, Vietnamese Bistro, Wild Wings Cafe, [lodging] Baymont Inn, EconoLodge, Hampton Inn, [o] AT&T, Gander Mtn, JC Penney, Verizon, Walgreens
372mm	**weigh sta both lanes**
369	Watt Rd, **N** [gas] /FLYING J/Denny's/dsl/LP/scales/RV dump/24hr, Speedco, **S** [gas] Exxon/dsl, Petro/Iron Skillet/dsl/scales/24hr/@, TA/BP/Burger King/Pizza Hut/Popeye's/Subway/dsl/24hr/@, [o] Blue Beacon, Knoxville Coach/RV
	I-40 E and I-75 N run together 17 mi.
368	I-75 and I-40
364	US 321, TN 95, Lenoir City, Oak Ridge, **N** [gas] Melton Hill Mkt/gas, [o] Crosseyed Cricket Camping (2mi), **S** [gas] [Loves]/McDonald's/Subway/dsl/24hr, **4-5 mi S** [food] KFC, Krystal, Ruby Tuesday, [lodging] Comfort Inn, Days Inn, EconoLodge, Hampton Inn, Holiday Inn Express, Ramada Ltd
362	Industrial Park Rd
360	Buttermilk Rd, **N** Soaring Eagle RV Park
356	TN 58 N, Gallaher Rd, to Oak Ridge, **N** [gas] BP/dsl, Weigels/dsl, [food] Gallaher Grill, [lodging] Budget Inn, Motel 6, [o] 4 Seasons Camping

HARRIMAN

Exit	Services
355	Lawnville Rd, **N** [gas] [wendys]/Subway/dsl
352	TN 58 S, Kingston, **N** [lodging] Knights Inn, **S** [gas] Exxon/dsl, RaceWay, Shell, [food] Buddy's BBQ, Hardee's, McDonald's, Sonic, Subway, Taco Bell, [lodging] Super 8, [o] Family$, Marina RV Park, Piggly Wiggly, USPO, to Watts Bar Lake
351mm	Clinch River
350	US 70, Midtown, **N** [H], **S** [food] Gondolier Italian, [o] Caney Creek Camping (3mi), Kroger, Lowe's, Patterson RV Supplies, Walgreens
347	US 27, Harriman, **N** [gas] Phillips 66/dsl, [food] Hardee's, KFC, Los Primos Mexican, LJ Silver, McDonald's, Pizza Hut, Ruby Tuesday, Subway, Taco Bell, Wendy's, [lodging] Days Inn, [o] Verizon, to Frozen Head SP, Big S Fork NRA, **S** [gas] BP, Shell/Krystal/dsl/24hr, Sunoco/dsl, [food] Cancun Mexican, Cracker Barrel, Shoney's, [lodging] Comfort Inn, Holiday Inn Express, Quality Inn, Rodeway Inn, **2-3 mi S** [gas] Murphy USA/dsl, [food] Capt D's, China King, Domino's, Sonic, [o] [H] Ace Hardware, BigLots, Radio Shack, Walmart/Subway, vet
340	TN 299 N, Airport Rd
339.5mm	eastern/central time zone line eastern/central time zone line
338	TN 299 S, Westel Rd, **N** [gas] BP/dsl, **S** [gas] Shell/dsl, [o] Boat-N-RV Ctr/Park
336mm	parking area/**weigh sta eb**, litter barrel
329	US 70, Crab Orchard, **N** [gas] BP/dsl, Liberty/dsl, [o] KOA (4mi), **S** [o] Cumberland Trails SP, Wilson SP
327mm	[rest stop] wb, full [handicap] facilities, [phone], [picnic], litter barrels, petwalk, vending
324mm	[rest stop] eb, full [handicap] facilities, [phone], [picnic], litter barrels, petwalk, vending
322	TN 101, Peavine Rd, Crossville, **N** [gas] BP/Bean Pot Rest., Exxon/dsl, Volunteer/dsl, [food] Hardee's, McDonald's, Quiznos, Subway, [lodging] Holiday Inn Express, [o] Deer Run RV Resort, KOA Camping, Roam-Roost RV Campground, to Fairfield Glade Resort, **S** [gas] Phillips 66/dsl, [food] Cancun Mexican, Taco Bell, [lodging] Comfort Suites, Hampton Inn, Super 8, [o] [H], Chestnut Hill Winery, Cumberland Mtn SP, RV Camping, Vallyhoo
320	TN 298, Crossville, **N** [gas] [wendys]/Wendy's/dsl/scales/24hr, [food] Halcyon Days Rest., [o] antiques, golf, winery, **S** [gas] BP/DQ/Pizza*Hut/dsl, Shell/dsl, [o] [H], Crossville Outlet/famous brands, Save-A-Lot Foods, antiques, auto repair/tires
318mm	Obed River
317	US 127, Crossville, **N** [gas] Exxon/dsl/24hr, Shell/dsl, [food] Shoney's, Subway, [lodging] Best Western, La Quinta, Motel 6, [o] repair, to Big South Fork RA, to York SP, **0-2 mi S** [gas] Citgo/dsl, Jiffy, Marathon, Murphy USA/dsl, Shell,

CROSSVILLE

🅖 = gas 🍽 = food 🛏 = lodging 🅞 = other 🆁🆂 = rest stop Copyright 2014 - The NEXT Exit ®

◆E INTERSTATE 40 CONT'D

Exit	Services
317	Continued
	🍽 Arby's, Burger King, Cancun Mexican, Cracker Barrel, La Costa Mexican, McDonalds, Papa John's, Peking Buffet, Ruby Tuesday, Ryan's, Sonic, Subway, Taco Bell, Vegas Steaks, Waffle House, Zaxby's, 🛏 Best Value Inn, Days Inn, Economy Inn, 🅞 🄷 AT&T, Buick/Cadillac/Chevrolet/GMC, Chrysler/Dodge/Jeep, $General, $Tree, GNC, Lowe's, Rite Aid, Shadden Tires, Staples, Verizon, Walmart, Walgreens, vet, to Cumberland Mtn SP.
311	Plateau Rd, N 🅖 Sunoco/Papa Lorenzo's Pizza/dsl, S 🅖 BP/dsl, Exxon/Hunt Bro's Pizza, 🅞 rv service
307mm	parking area/weigh sta wb, litter barrels
301	US 70 N, TN 84, Monterey, N 🅖 Phillips 66, Shell, 🍽 Burger King, DQ, Subway, 🛏 Super 8
300	US 70, Monterey, N 🅖 Citgo/dsl, 🍽 DQ, Hardee's
291mm	Falling Water River
290	US 70, Cookeville, N 🍽 BP (1mi), S 🅖 Citgo, 🛏 Alpine Suites
288	TN 111, to Livingston, Cookeville, Sparta, N Hull SP, S 🅖 Sunoco/dsl, TN TravelCtr/dsl/24hr, 🍽 Mona's Rest., 🛏 Knights Inn
287	TN 136, Cookeville, N 🅖 BP, Exxon, Murphy USA, 🍽 Applebee's, Arby's, Baskin-Robbins, Bully's Rest., Burger King, Capt D's, Cheddars, Chick-fil-A, Chili's, Cracker Barrel, DQ, Fazoli's, Golden Corral, IHOP, King Buffet, Krystal, LJ Silver, Logan's Roadhouse, Longhorn Steaks, Mandarin Palace, McDonald's, Mike's Subs, Nick's Rest., O'Charley's, Olive Garden, Outback Steaks, Papa Murphy's, Pizza Hut, Puleo's Grill, Quiznos, Red Lobster, Ruby Tuesday, Shoney's, Sonic, Starbucks, Steak'n Shake, Subway, Taco Bell, Wendy's, 🛏 Best Value Inn, Best Western, Clarion, Comfort Inn&Suites, Days Inn, Hampton Inn, Red Roof Inn, Super 8, 🅞 Aldi Foods, BigLots, Firestone/auto, Harley-Davidson, JC Penney, K-Mart, Kroger/gas, Lowe's, Nissan, Radio Shack, Verizon, Walmart, st patrol, transmissions, S 🅖 Marathon/dsl, 🄻🄾🅅🄴🅂/dsl, 🍽 Gondola, KFC, Waffle House, 🛏 Baymont Inn, Country Hearth Inn, Country Inn&Suites, Fairfield Inn, Holiday Inn Express, 🅞 Urgent Care, Sam's Club/gas
286	TN 135, Burgess Falls Rd, N 🅖 BP, Exxon, RaceWay/dsl, Shell/dsl, 🍽 Arby's, Beef'O'Brady's, Christy's Cafe, Hardee's, Waffle House, 🅞 🄷 Chrysler/Dodge/Jeep, Ford/Lincoln, Goodyear/auto, Hyundai, KIA, Toyota/Scion, USPO, to TTU, vet, S 🅖 Sunoco/dsl, 🛏 Star Motor Inn, 🅞 Burgess Falls SP (8mi)
280	TN 56 N, Baxter, N 🅖 ◆Loves/McDonalds/Subway/dsl/scales/24hr, 🍽 Huddle House, 🅞 Camp Discovery (2mi), Twin Lakes RV Park (2mi)
276	Old Baxter Rd
273	TN 56 S, to Smithville, S 🅖 BP/dsl, Phillips 66, 🍽 Rose Garden Rest., 🅞 USPO
268	TN 96, Buffalo Valley Rd, N Grandville Marina Camping (11mi), S to Edgar Evins SP/RV camping
267mm	Caney Fork River
267mm	🆁🆂 both lanes, full ♿ facilities, info, 🅲, 🚮, litter barrels, petwalk, vending
266mm	Caney Fork River
263mm	Caney Fork River
258	TN 53, Gordonsville, N 🅖 Exxon/KFC/Taco Bell, Shell/dsl, 🍽 McDonald's, Timberloft Café, Waffle House,

Exit	Services
258	Continued
	Comfort Inn, 🅞 to Cordell Hull Dam, S 🅖 Hess/Wendy's/dsl/scales/24hr, Mobil/dsl, 🍽 Arby's, Cornerstone Cafe, El Corral Mexican, 🅞 $General
254	TN 141, to Alexandria
252mm	parking area/truck sta both lanes, 🚮 litter barrels
245	Linwood Rd, N 🅖 BP/dsl
239	US 70, Lebanon, N 🅖 Citgo/dsl, RaceWay, S 🅖 Phillips 66/Uncle Pete's/dsl/scales, 🍽 Jalisco Mexican
238	US 231, Lebanon, N 🅖 Exxon, Mapco, Shell, 🍽 Applebee's, Arby's, Cici's Pizza, Cracker Barrel, Demo's Steaks, El Molino Mexican, Gondola Rest., Hardee's, Jack-in-the-Box, KFC, King Buffet, McDonald's, Pizza Hut, Ponderosa, Ryan's, Shoney's, Sunset Rest., Subway, Taco Bell, Waffle House, Wendy's, White Castle, Whitt's BBQ, Zaxby's 🛏 Best Value Inn, EconoLodge, Executive Inn, Holiday Inn Express, Quality Inn, Ramada, 🅞 🄷 Aldi Foods, $Tree, Discount Tire, Lowe's, Walgreens, Walmart, to Bledsoe SP, S 🅖 Citgo/Pizza Inn/Quiznos/dsl, 🄻🄾🅅🄴🅂/Chester's/Subway/dsl/scales/24hr, Shell/dsl, 🍽 O'Charley's, Sonic, 🛏 Comfort Suites, Country Inn&Suites, Days Inn, Knights Inn, Super 8, 🅞 Family RV Ctr, Lebanon Outlets/famous brands, Shady Acres Camping, Timberline Campground, to Cedars of Lebanon SP, RV camping
236	S Hartmann Dr, N 🅖 Mapco, Shell/dsl, 🍽 Chili's, Outback Steaks, Pizza Inn, Ruby Tuesday, Sonic, Subway, 🅞 Hampton Inn, 🅞 🄷 Home Depot, Rose Tire
235	TN 840 W, to Murfreesboro
232	TN 109, to Gallatin, N 🅖 Citgo, Mapco/Quiznos/dsl, Shell/McDonald's/dsl/24hr, Thornton's/dsl, 🍽 Bellacino's Pizza, Coach's Grill, Sonic, Subway, Waffle House, Wendy's, 🛏 Sleep Inn, ValuePlace Inn, 2 mi S 🅞 Countryside Resort Camping
228mm	truck sta, wb only
229b a	Beckwitch Rd
226mm	truck sta
226	TN 171, Mt Juliet Rd, N 🅖 BP/McDonald's/dsl, Exxon/dsl, Shell/dsl/24hr, 🍽 Arby's, Capt D's, Cheddars, Don Pancho Mexican, Far East Buffet, 5 Guys Burgers, Subway, 🛏 Comfort Suites, 🅞 Aldi Foods, $Tree, Lowe's, NTB, Walmart, S 🅖 Mapco/Quiznos/dsl, 🍽 Buffalo Wild Wings, Chick-fil-A, Cori's Dog House, Cracker Barrel, Fulin's Asian, Hacienda Del Sol, Logan's Roadhouse, NY Pizza, O'Charley's, Olive Garden, Panera Bread, Red Lobster, Red Robin, Ruby Tuesday, Salsarita's Cantina, Sonic, Steak'n Shake, Taco Bell, Waffle House, Wasabi Steaks, Wendy's, Zaxby's, 🛏 Hampton Inn, Holiday Inn Express, Quality Inn, 🅞 AT&T, Belk, Best Buy, Books-A-Million, Curves, Dick's, Discount Tire, Ford, GNC, JC Penney, JoAnn Fabrics, Kroger/dsl, Old Navy, Petsmart, Publix, Ross, Staples, Target, TJ Maxx, Verizon, Walgreens, to Long Hunter SP
221	TN 45 N, Old Hickory Blvd, to The Hermitage, 0-2 mi N 🅖 BP, Exxon, Mapco/dsl, RaceWay/dsl, Shell/24hr, 🍽 Applebee's, Baskin-Robbins/Dunkin Donuts, Buffalo Wild Wings, Burger King, Chick-fil-A, Chili's, DQ, Famous Dave's, Fazoli's, Firehouse Subs, Golden Corral, Hardee's, IHOP, Jack-in-the-Box, Mike's Subs, O'Charley's, Outback Steaks, Panera Bread, Qdoba Mexican, Starbucks, Steak'n Shake, Subway, Waffle House, 🛏 Best Value Inn, Suburban Lodge, Super 8, Vista Inn, 🅞 🄷 Hobby Lobby, Home Depot, Kroger, Lowe's, PetCo, Staples, Walgreens,

Side labels: COOKEVILLE, LEBANON, NASHVILLE

TN

🅖 = gas 🅕 = food 🏠 = lodging 🅞 = other 🆁🆂 = rest stop

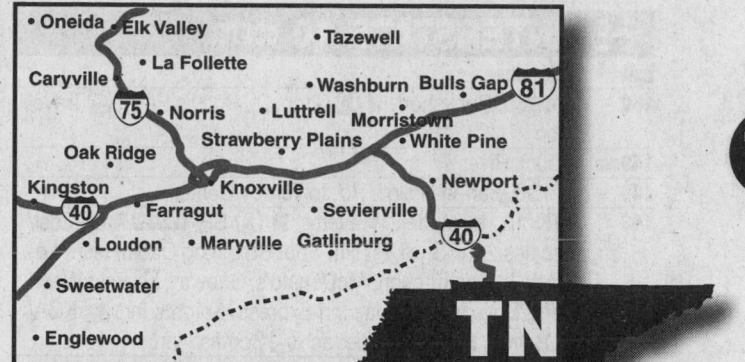

▲Ｅ INTERSTATE 40 CONT'D

Exit	Services
221	Continued **S** 🅖 Phillips 66/White Castle, Shell/McDonald's, Qwik-sak/dsl
219	Stewart's Ferry Pike, **N** 🅖 Mapco, **S** 🅖 Mapco/dsl, Shell/dsl, Thornton's/dsl, 🅕 China King, Cracker Barrel, Epic Pizza, La Hacienda Mexican, Sal's Pizza, Subway, Waffle House, 🏠 Best Western, Comfort Suites, Country Inn&Suites, Days Inn, EconoLodge, Family Inn, Sleep Inn, 🅞 $General, Food Lion, Fred's, vet
216	(216 c from eb)TN 255, Donaldson Pk, **N** 🅖 BP/dsl, Mapco, RaceWay/dsl, Shell/dsl/24hr, 🅕 Arby's, Backyard Burger, Bar-B-Cutie, Darfon's, Domino's, Jalisco Mexican, KFC, McDonald's, New China, Pizza Hut/Taco Bell, Ruby Tuesday, Shoney's, Subway, Waffle House, Wendy's, 🏠 Country Inn&Suites, Drury Inn, Fairfield Inn, Hampton Inn, Holiday Inn Express, Hyatt Place, La Quinta, Radisson, Red Roof Inn, SpringHill Suites, Super 8, Wingate Inn, 🅞 Advance Parts, K-Mart, Walgreens, USPO, **S** 🛬
216b a	(from eb), **S** Nashville Intn'l 🛬
215b a	TN 155, Briley Pkwy, to Opryland, **N on Elm Hill** 🅖 Citgo, Mapco, 🅕 Casta Fiesta Mexican, Jack-in-the-Box, Waffle House, 🏠 Alexis Inn, Baymont Inn, Comfort Suites, Courtyard, Embassy Suites, Extended Stay, Hilton Garden, Holiday Inn, Homestead Suites, Homewood Suites, La Quinta, Marriott, Ramada, Residence Inn, Sheraton, Studio+, **S** 🅖 Phillips 66/dsl, 🅕 Dunkin Donuts, Mazatlan Mexican, Panda House, Subway, 🏠 Hamilton Inn, Hotel Preston
213b	I-24 W
213a	I-24 E/I-440, E to Chattanooga
213	US 41 (from wb no return), to Spence Lane, **N** 🅞 Kenworth, **S** 🅖 Phillips 66/dsl, Shell, 🅕 Waffle House, 🏠 Days Inn, Holiday Inn Express, Rodeway Inn, Super 8, same as 212
212	Fessler's Lane (from eb, no return), **N** 🅞 Freightliner, Harley-Davidson, **S** 🅖 Mapco/dsl, Shell/Dunkin Donuts, 🅕 Burger King, McDonald's, Sonic, Wendy's, 🏠 Scottish Inn, 🅞 Chevrolet, same as 213
211mm	Cumberland River
211b	I-24 W
211a	I-24E, I-40 W
210c	US 31 S, US 41A, 2nd Ave, 4th Ave, **N** 🏠 Hilton, Sheraton, Stouffer Hotel, **S** museum
210b a	I-65 S, to Birmingham
209b a	US 70 S, Charlotte Ave, Nashville, **N** 🅖 Exxon, 🅕 McDonald's, 🏠 Sheraton, 🅞 Firestone, Country Music Hall of Fame, Conv Ctr, transmissions, **S** 🅖 Exxon, 🅕 Burger King, Krystal, Sonic, Subway, White Castle, 🏠 Comfort Inn, Guesthouse Inn, 🅞 Walgreens, Urgent Care
208b a	I-65, N to Louisville, S to Birmingham
207	28th Ave, Jefferson St, Nashville, **N** 🅖 BP, Citgo, 🅕 Subway, Wendy's, Wing Zone, 🅞 🄷, Family$, to TN St U
206	I-440 E, to Knoxville
205	46th Ave, W Nashville, **N** 🅞 Harley-Davidson, **S** 🅖 Mapco, Shell, 🅕 McDonald's, Mrs. Winners
204	TN 155, Briley Pkwy, **S** 🅖 BP/dsl, Citgo, 🅕 Burger King, China Buffet, Church's/White Castle, Cinco De Mayo, Domino's, Jack-in-the-Box, KFC, Krystal, Las Palmas, Papa John's, Shoney's, Subway, Waffle House, 🏠 Baymont Inn, Best Western, Comfort Inn, Days Inn, 🅞 CarQuest, CVS Drug, Firestone/auto, Kroger/gas, NTB, O'Reilly Parts, PepBoys, Sav-a-lot Foods, Walgreens

Exit	Services
201b a	US 70, Charlotte Pike, **N** 🅖 Exxon, Shell/dsl/24hr, 🅕 Bojangles, China Buffet, Cracker Barrel, Jim 'N Nick's BBQ, Krystal, Subway, Waffle House, Wendy's, 🏠 Super 8, 🅞 $Tree, GNC, Kwik Kar, Lowe's Whse, Radio Shack, Walmart, **S** 🅖 BP, Mapco, Shell, 🅕 Arby's, McDonald's, Pizza Hut, Red Robin, Taco Bell, 🅞 Best Buy, Big Lots, Books-A-Million, BigLots, Costco/gas, Firestone/auto, Marshall's, Old Navy, PetsMart, Ross, Staples, Target, Uhaul, World Mkt
199	rd 251, Old Hickory Blvd, **N** 🅖 Shell, **S** 🅖 BP, Mapco, 🅕 Sonic, Subway, 🅞 Sam's Club/gas
196	US 70, to Bellevue, Newsom Sta, **N** 🅖 Mapco/dsl, 🅕 Shoney's, **S** 🅖 BP, Mapco/dsl, Shell/dsl/24hr, 🅕 Arby's, Asihi Asian, O'Charley's, Pizza Hut, Sir Pizza, Sonic, Subway, Taco Bell, Waffle House, Wendy's, 🏠 Hampton Inn, Microtel, 🅞 $Tree, Firestone/auto, Home Depot, Michael's, PetCo, Publix, Sears/auto, Staples, USPO, Walgreens
195mm	Harpeth River
192	McCrory Lane, to Pegram, **N** 🅖 Eddie's Mkt (1mi), **4 mi S** 🅕 Loveless Cafe, 🅞 Natchez Trace Pkwy
190mm	Harpeth River
188mm	Harpeth River
188	rd 249, Kingston Springs, **N** 🅖 BP, Mapco/Quiznos/dsl, Shell/Arby's/dsl, 🅕 El Jardin Mexican, McDonald's/playplace, Sonic, Subway, 🏠 Best Western, Mid-Town Inn, Relax Inn, 🅞 CB Foods, USPO, **S** 🅖 Petro/BP/Quick Skillet/dsl/scales/showers/24hr/@, 🅞 vet
182	TN 96, to Dickson, Fairview, **N** 🅖 BP/dsl, 🏠 Fairview Inn, 🅞 M Bell SP (16mi), **S** 🅖 /⊕FLYING J/Denny's/dsl/LP/scales/24hr, Shell/Backyard Burger/Dunkin Donuts/dsl, 🏠 Deerfield Inn
176	TN 840
172	TN 46, to Dickson, **N** 🅖 Citgo/Subway, Exxon, 🚛/Wendy's/dsl/scales/24hr, Shell, 🅕 Arby's, Cracker Barrel, Farmer's Rest., Logan's Roadhouse, McDonald's, Ruby Tuesday, Waffle House/24hr, Wang's China, 🏠 Best Western, Comfort Inn, EconoLodge, Hampton Inn, Motel 6, Quality Inn, South-Aire Inn, Super 8, 🅞 🄷, Chappell's Foods, Chevrolet, Dickson RV Park, Ford, Nissan, truck repair, to M Bell SP, **S** 🅖 BP, Shell/dsl, 🅕 O'Charley's, Sonic, 🏠 Days Inn, Dickson Inn, Holiday Inn Express
170	🆁🆂 **both lanes, full ♿ facilities, 🅕, 🏠, litter barrels, vending, petwalk**
166mm	Piney River
163	rd 48, to Dickson, **N** 🅖 ❤Loves/McDonald's/Subway/dsl/scales/24hr, Phillips 66/dsl, 🅞 tire repair, **S** 🅖 Shell, 🅞 Pinewood Camping (7mi), Tanbark Camping

D I C K S O N

TN

⮕E INTERSTATE 40 CONT'D

Exit	Services
152	rd 230, Bucksnort, N 🅶 Citgo, 🍴 Rudy's Rest., 🏠 Travel Inn
149mm	Duck River
148	rd 50, Barren Hollow Rd, to Turney Center
143	TN 13, to Linden, Waverly, N 🅶 BP, 🍴/Arby's/dsl/scales/24hr, Shell, 🍴 Hot Spot BBQ, Log Cabin Rest., Loretta Lynn's Kitchen, McDonald's, Subway, 🏠 Best Western, Days Inn, Holiday Inn Express, Knights Inn, 🅾 KOA/LP, tires, S 🅶 Fast Fuel/dsl 🏠 Scottish Inn
141mm	Buffalo River
137	Cuba Landing, N 🅾 TN River RV Park, S 🍴 Cuba Landing Rest./gas
133mm	Tennessee River
133	rd 191, Birdsong Rd, 9 mi N 🏠 Birdsong RV Resort/marina, Good Sam RV Park
131mm	🆁🆂 both lanes, full ♿ facilities, 🍴, vending, 🎴, litter barrels, petwalk
126	US 641, TN 69, to Camden, N 🅶 Marathon/Subway/dsl, Phillips 66/North 40/dsl, Shell/dsl, 🅾 Paris Landing SP, tire/truck repair, to NB Forrest SP, S 🅶 BP/dsl, Shell/dsl, 🏠 Days Inn, 🅾 H, Mouse-tail Landing SP (24mi)
116	rd 114, S 🅾 to Natchez Trace SP, RV camping
110mm	Big Sandy River
108	TN 22, to Lexington, Parkers Crossroads, N 🅶 BP/McDonald's/24hr/dsl, Citgo/dsl/24hr, Phillips 66/dsl, 🍴 Bailey's Rest., DQ, Subway, 🏠 Knights Inn, 🅾 USPO, city park, S 🅶 Exxon, 🍴 Po' Boys Pizza, 🏠 Best Value Inn, 🅾 H, RV camping, Parkers Crossroads Bfd Visitors Ctr, to Shiloh NMP (51mi)
103mm	parking area/truck sta eb, litter barrels
102mm	parking area/truck sta wb, litter barrels
101	rd 104, N 🅶 101 TP/rest/dsl/tires/24hr, 🅾 golf (3mi)
93	rd 152, Law Rd, N 🅶 Phillips 66/deli/dsl/24hr, S 🅶 BP/dsl, Super Way/dsl
87	US 70, US 412, Huntingdon, McKenzie, N 🅶 Coastal/dsl, S 🅶 BP/dsl, ♥Loves/Hardee's/dsl/scales/24hr
85	Christmasville Rd, to Jackson, N 🅶 BP/dsl, Exxon/dsl/24hr, 🍴/Denny's/dsl/scales/24hr, 🏠 Comfort Inn, 🅾 $General, S 🅶 Horizon/Baskin-Robbins/Pizza Pro, 🍴 Jiang Jun Chinese, Lenny's Subs, Los Portales, McDonald's, Reggi's BBQ, Sonic, Sparky's, Taco Bell, 🏠 Holiday Inn Express, 🅾 $Tree, Food Giant
83	Campbell st, N 🅶 Exxon/Old Madina Mkt/dsl, 🏠 Residence Inn, S 🏠 Courtyard, Hampton Inn
82b a	US 45, Jackson, N 🅶 BP, 🍴 Cracker Barrel, 🏠 Knights Inn, Microtel, 🅾 Batteries+, Curves, Smallwoods RV Ctr (4mi), S 🅶 BP, Clark/dsl, Exxon, 🍴 Baskin-Robbins, Burger King, Catfish Galley, ChuckeCheese, DQ, KFC, Krystal, Little Caesar's, LJ Silver, McDonald's/playplace, Niko's Creek, Pizza Hut, Popeye's, Sakura Japanese, Shoney's, Sonic, Subway, Taco Bell, Tulum Mexican, Waffle House, Wendy's, 🏠 Executive Inn, La Quinta, Ramada Ltd, Super 8, Travellers Motel, 🅾 Advance Parts, AT&T, AutoZone, BigLots, $General, $Tree, Firestone/auto, Fred's, Goodyear/auto, JC Penney, Kroger/24hr, Macy's, Office Depot, Radio Shack, Sears/auto, TJ Maxx, mall, vet
80b a	US 45 Byp, Jackson, 0-2 mi N 🅶 BP, Exxon, 🍴 Arby's, Asahi Japanese, Backyard Burger, Baskin-Robbins, Buffalo Wild Wings, Capt D's, Chili's, Chick-fil-A, El Comal Mexican, Fazoli's, Fujiyama Japanese, HoneyBaked Ham,

J A C K S O N

Exit	Services
80b a	Continued IHOP, Jason's Deli, KFC, Lenny's Subs, Longhorn Steaks, Los Portales, Maggie Moo's, McAlisters Deli, Moe's SW Grill, Olive Garden, Outback Steaks, Panera Bread, Peking Chinese, Perkins, Popeye's, Quiznos, Red Robin, Ruby Tuesday, Sonic, Starbucks, Steak'n Shake, Subway, TGIFriday's, Wendy's, Zaxby's, 🏠 Baymont Inn, Jameson Inn, SigNature Hotel, 🅾 AT&T, Best Buy, Books-A-Million, Buick/Cadillac/Chevrolet/GMC, Dick's, Firestone/auto, Gateway Tires/repair, Hobby Lobby, Home Depot, JoAnn Fabrics, Kohl's, Lowe's, Marshall's, Mazda, Nissan, Old Navy, Petsmart, Ross, Sam's Club/gas, Steinmart, Target, Verizon, Walmart/gas, S 🅶 BP/Circle K, G/dsl, Phillips 66/dsl, 🍴 Arby's, Asia Garden, Barnhill's Buffet, Burger King, Double D Ranch Rest., Heavenly Ham, Logan's Roadhouse, McDonald's, Mrs Winner's, O'Charley's, Old Hickory Steakhouse, Old Town Spaghetti, Red Bones Grill, Subway, Taco Bell, Waffle House, 🏠 Best Western, Casey Jones Motel, Comfort Suites, Days Inn, DoubleTree, EconoLodge, Guesthouse Inn, Holiday Inn, Motel 6, Old Hickory Inn, Quality Inn, 🅾 H, Chrysler/Dodge/Jeep, $General, Ford/Lincoln, Harley-Davidson, Honda, Hyundai, K-Mart, Toyota/Scion, Tuesday Morning, to Pinson Mounds SP, Chickasaw SP
79	US 412, Jackson, N 🅾 Gander Mtn., S 🅶 BP/dsl, Citgo/dsl, Exxon, 🏠 Days Inn, 🅾 Jackson RV Park
78mm	Forked Deer River
76	rd 223, S 🍴 McKenzie BBQ, 🅾 McKellar-Sites 🛩, Whispering Pines RV Park
74	Lower Brownsville Rd
73mm	🆁🆂 both lanes, full ♿ facilities, info, 🍴, 🎴, litter barrels, vending, petwalk
68	rd 138, Providence Rd, N 🅶 BP/dsl, 🏠 Ole South Inn, S 🅶 TA/Citgo/Subway/dsl/scales/24hr/@, Valero/dsl, 🅾 Joy-O RV Park
66	US 70, to Brownsville, N 🅾 Ft Pillow SHP (51mi), S 🅶 Exxon/dsl, 🏠 Motel 6
60	rd 19, Mercer Rd
56	TN 76, to Brownsville, N 🅶 BP, Shell/dsl/24hr, 🍴 DQ, KFC, McDonald's/playplace, Pizza Hut/Taco Bell, 🏠 Best Value Inn, Comfort Inn, Days Inn, Econolodge, S 🅶 Exxon/Huddle House/dsl/24hr
55mm	Hatchie River
52	TN 76, rd 179, Koko Rd, to Whiteville, S 🅶 Koko/dsl
50mm	weigh sta both lanes, 🍴
47	TN 179, to Stanton, Dancyville, S 🅶 Exit 47 Trkstp/dsl
42	TN 222, to Stanton, N 🏠 Best Value Inn, S 🅶 Exxon/dsl, 🍴/Chester's/Subway/dsl/scales/24hr, 🏠 Deerfield Inn
35	TN 59, to Somerville, S 🅶 BP/dsl/scales, 🍴 Longtown Rest.
29.5mm	Loosahatchie River
25	TN 205, Airline Rd, to Arlington, N 🅶 Shell/dsl, S 🅶 Exxon/Backyard Burger/dsl, 🅾 vistor ctr
24	TN 385, rd 204, to Arlington, Millington, Collierville
20	Canada Rd, Lakeland, N 🅶 BP/McDonald's, Shell, 🍴 Cracker Barrel, Waffle House, 🏠 Motel 6, Relax Inn, Super 8, S 🅶 Exxon/Subway/dsl, 🍴 TCBY, 🅾 Memphis East Camping
18	US 64, to Bartlett, N 🅶 Shell, 🍴 Abuelo's, Bob Evans, Buffalo Wild Wings, El Porton Mexican, Firebird's Grill, Hooters, McAlister's Deli, Longhorn Steaks, O'Charley's, Olive Garden, Steak'n Shake, TGI Friday's, TX Road

🅔 INTERSTATE 40 CONT'D

Exit	Services
18	Continued

house, 🛏 Best Western, Fairfield Inn, Holiday Inn, La Quinta, SpringHill Suites, 🅞 Buick/GMC, Firestone/auto, Goodyear/auto, Lowe's, Sam's Club/gas, Walmart, same as 16, **S** 🅖 BP/Circle K, Citgo/dsl, 🍴 Backyard Burger, KFC, Lenny's Subs, Papa John's, Pizza Hut, Subway, Zaxby's, 🅞 Kroger, Schnuck's Foods/gas, Walgreens, Zaxby's

16b a TN 177, to Germantown, **N** 🅖 BP/Circle K, Shell/Circle K, 🍴 Abuelo's, Arby's, Bahama Breeze, Burger King, Casa Mexicana, Chili's, Chick-fil-A, Danver's, IHOP, J. Alexander's, Joe's Crabshack, Logan's Roadhouse, Macaroni Grill, McDonald's/playplace, On-the-Border, Red Lobster, Taco Bell, TCBY, Tellini's Italian, Waffle House, Wendy's, 🛏 Extended Stay Deluxe, Hampton Inn, Hyatt Place, 🅞 🅗, Barnes&Noble, Best Buy, BigLots, Chevrolet, Chrysler/Dodge/Jeep, Dillard's, $Tree, Ford, Hancock Fabrics, Hobby Lobby, Home Depot, Honda, JC Penney, Macy's, Michael's, Nissan, Office Depot, Old Navy, Petsmart, Sears/auto, Target, TJ Maxx, Walgreens, mall, **0-2 mi S** 🅖 BP/Circle K, Shell/Circle K, 🍴 Abbay's Rest., Arby's, Backyard Burger, Burger King, ChuckeCheese, Corky's BBQ, El Porton Mexican, Genghis Grill, Honeybake Ham, Howard's Doughnuts, Jason's Deli, Jim'n Nick's BBQ, Jimmy John's, Lenny's Subs, McDonald's, Newk's Cafe, Pei Wei Chinese, Qdoba Mexican, Shogun Japanese, Slim Skillets, Smoothie King, Waffle House, Wendy's, 🛏 Comfort Suites, Microtel, Quality Inn, Quality Suites, Studio+, Wingate Inn, 🅞 Aldi Foods, AT&T, AutoZone, Costco/gas, Dick's, GNC, Gordman's, Kroger/gas, Kohl's, Marshall's, Rite Aid, Ross, Steinmart, Toyota/Scion, Tuesday Morning, Verizon, vet

15b a Appling Rd, **N** 🅖 BP/Circle K/dsl, Shell/dsl, 🅞 🅗

14 Whitten Rd, **N** 🅖 Citgo/dsl, Mapco, Shell/Burger King, 🍴 McDonald's, Sidecar Café, 🅞 Harley-Davidson, **S** 🅖 BP/Circle K, Shell/Backyard Burger/dsl, 🍴 Dunkin Donuts, Subway, Supreme Hot Wings, 🅞 Walgreens

12 Sycamore View Rd, **N** 🅖 Citgo/dsl, Texaco/dsl, 🍴 Cajun Catfish Co., Capt D's, Church's, Cracker Barrel, IHOP, McDonald's, Mrs Winner's, Perkins, Ruby Tuesday, Shoney's, Sonic, Starbucks, Taco Bell, Waffle House, 🛏 Baymont Inn, Best Value Inn, Clarion, Drury Inn, EconoLodge, Extended Stay America, Memphis Plaza, Red Roof Inn, 🅞 AutoZone, $General, Family$, Fred's, Walgreens, **S** 🅖 BP/Circle K/dsl, Exxon, Mapco, 🍴 Beijing Chinese, Burger King, Popeye's, Subway, Tops BBQ, Wendy's, 🛏 Best Western, Budgetel, Comfort Inn, Days Inn, Fairfield Inn, La Quinta, Memphis Inn, Motel 6, Super 8, 🅞 Bass Pro Shops, Parts+

10.5mm Wolf River

10b a (from wb)I-240 W around Memphis, I-40 E to Nashville

12c (from eb)I-240 W, to Jackson, I-40 E to Nashville

12b Sam Cooper Blvd (from eb)

12a US 64/70/79, Summer Ave, **N** 🅖 Mapco/dsl, Shell, 🍴 Asian Palace, Waffle House, 🛏 Welcome Inn, 🅞 U-Haul, **S** 🅖 Exxon, 🍴 Arby's, McDonald's, 🅞 $Tree, Firestone/auto, Fred's, Goodyear/auto, Sav-A-Lot Foods

10 TN 204, Covington Pike, **N** 🅖 BP/Circle K, 🍴 McDonald's, Wendy's, 🅞 Audi/VW, Buick/GMC, Chevrolet, Chrysler/Dodge/Jeep, Honda, Hyundai, KIA, Mazda, Nis

M E M P H I S

10 Continued
san, Sam's Club, Subaru, Suzuki, SuperLo Food/gas, Volvo

8b a TN 14, Jackson Ave, **N** 🅖 Citgo/dsl, Shell, 🛏 Motel 6, Sleep Inn, 🅞 Raleigh Tire, vet, **S** 🅖 Citgo/dsl, Mapco, 🅞 AutoZone, Family$, O'Reilly Parts, transmissions

6 Warford Rd

5 Hollywood St, **N** 🅖 BP, Q-Mart/dsl, 🍴 Burger King, Mother's Rest., **S** 🅞 Memphis Zoo

3 Watkins St, **N** 🅖 BP, Chevron/dsl, Coastal/dsl, Oil City USA/dsl, Texaco/dsl, 🅞 Family$, U-Haul

2a rd 300, to US 51 N, Millington, **N** 🅞 Meeman-Shelby SP

2 Smith Ave, Chelsea Ave, **N** 🅖 Citgo, **S** 🅖 BP

1e I-240 E

1d c b US 51, Danny Thomas Blvd, **N** 🅖 Exxon, 🍴 KFC, Wendy's, 🅞 Ronald McDonald House, St Jude Research Ctr

1a 2nd St (from wb), downtown, **S** 🛏 Crowne Plaza, Holiday Inn, Marriott, Sheraton, Wyndham Garden, 🅞 Conv Ctr

1 Riverside Dr, Front St (from eb), Memphis, **S** 🛏 Comfort Inn, 🅞 Conv Ctr, Riverfront, **Welcome Ctr**

0mm Tennessee/Arkansas state line, Mississippi River

🅝 INTERSTATE 55

Exit	Services
13mm	Tennessee/Arkansas state line, Mississippi River

12c Delaware St, Memphis

12b Riverside Dr, downtown Memphis, **E** TN Welcome Ctr

12a E Crump Blvd (from nb), **E** 🅖 Exxon, 🍴 Capt D's, KFC, LJ Silver, Taco Bell, Wendy's, 🅞 Family$, museum

11 McLemore Ave, Presidents Island, industrial area

10 S Parkway, **1/2 mi E** 🅖 BP/dsl

9 Mallory Ave, industrial area

8 Horn Lake Rd (from sb)

7 US 61, 3rd St, **E** 🅖 BP, Exxon, 🍴 Church's, Interstate BBQ, 🅞 AutoZone, $Tree, Family$, Kroger, NAPA, Rose's, Save-A-Lot Foods, Walgreens, **W** 🅖 BP/dsl, MapCo, 🍴 KFC, McDonald's, Subway, 🛏 Rest Inn, 🅞 Fuller SP, Indian Museum

6b a I-240

5b US 51 S, Elvis Presley Blvd, to Graceland, **0-2 mi W on US 51** 🅖 BP, Citgo/dsl, Dodge's/dsl, Exxon, Shell/dsl, 🍴 Baskin-Robbins, BJ's Wings, Burger King, Checker's, Exline Pizza, KFC, Krispy Kreme, Little Caesars, McDonald's, Piccadilly's, Subway, Taco Bell, 🛏 American Inn, Days Inn, EconoLodge, Heartbreak Hotel/RV Park, Value Place Inn, 🅞 🅗, Advance Parts, Aldi Foods, D&N RV Ctr, $General, $Tree, Family$, Presley RV Park, Radio Shack, Walgreens, Memphis Visitors Ctr, to Graceland

5a Brooks Rd, **E** 🅖 BP, Exxon, Mapco/dsl, 🍴 Blimpie,

⛽ = gas 🍴 = food 🛏 = lodging ⓞ = other Ⓡˢ = rest stop   Copyright 2014 - The NEXT Exit ®

TN

🏕N INTERSTATE 55 CONT'D

Exit	Services
5a	Continued
	Burger King, Popeye's, 🛏 Airport Inn, Best Value Inn, Budget Lodge, Clarion, Motel 6, ⓞ Freightliner, Peterbilt
2b a	TN 175, Shelby Dr, Whitehaven, **E** ⛽ BP/dsl, Citgo/Subway, Exxon, Shell/dsl, Texaco, 🛏 Colonial Inn, **W** ⛽ BP, Exxon/dsl, Shell/dsl, 🍴 Burger King, Dixie Queen Burgers, IHOP, McDonald's, Popeye's, ⓞ $General, Family$, Goodyear/auto, Kroger/gas, Macy's, Save-a-Lot Foods, Sears/auto, Toyota/Scion, U-Haul, Walgreens
0mm	Tennessee/Mississippi state line

🏕N INTERSTATE 65

Exit	Services
121.5mm	Tennessee/Kentucky state line
121mm	**Welcome Ctr sb, full** ♿ **facilities,** 🚻, 🅿, **litter barrels, vending, petwalk**
119mm	**weigh/insp sta both lanes**
117	TN 52, Portland, **E** ⛽ BP/Godfather's/Quiznos/dsl, Shell/dsl/fireworks, 🛏 Comfort Suites, ⓞ 🅷 Bledsoe Cr SP, **W** ⛽ BP/dsl, 🛏 Budget Host, ⓞ fireworks
116mm	Red River
113mm	Red River
112	TN 25, Cross Plains, **E** ⛽ BP/dsl, 🍴 Sad Sam's Deli, ⓞ Bledsoe Cr SP, antiques, fireworks **W** ⛽ Mapco/dsl, Shell/Godfather's/dsl, 🍴 Sweet&Savory Diner
108	TN 76, White House, **E** ⛽ Nervous Charlie's/dsl, Shell, 🍴 A&W/KFC, China Spring, Cracker Barrel, Hardee's, Little Caesars, Los Agave's, McDonald's, Mr Wok, Sonic, Subway, Taco Bell, Waffle House, Wendy's, 🛏 Best Western, Comfort Inn, Holiday Inn Express, Quality Inn, ⓞ Ace Hardware, $Tree, Kroger/gas, O'Reilly Parts, Rite Aid, Walgreens, Walmart/Subway, USPO, city park/playground, **W** ⛽ BP/dsl, 🍴 Greek Gyro, 🛏 Days Inn
104	rd 257, Bethel Rd, **E** ⛽ BP/rest./dsl, **W** ⛽ Shell/dsl, ⓞ Owl's Roost Camping
98	US 31 W, Millersville, **E** ⛽ Citgo/dsl, RaceWay, Shell/dsl, 🍴 Subway, Waffle House, ⓞ $General, Nashville Country RV Park, auto repair, **W** ⛽ BP, 🛏 Economy Inn, ⓞ fireworks
97	rd 174, Long Hollow Pike, **E** ⛽ BP/dsl, Exxon, Mapco, 🍴 Arby's, Capt D's, China Express, Cracker Barrel, Domino's, Kabuto Japanese, KFC, McDonald's, Papa Murphy's, Quiznos, Shoney's, Subway, Waffle House, Wendy's, 🛏 Best Western, Courtyard, Days Inn, Executive Inn, Hampton Inn, Quality Inn, Red Roof Inn, ⓞ K-Mart, Kroger, Walgreens, **W** ⛽ Shell/dsl, 🍴 Buck's BBQ, DQ, Hardee's, Krystal, Poncho Villa Grill, Sonic, 🛏 Holiday Inn Express, Motel 6, ⓞ Rite Aid, Walgreens, vet
96	Rivergate Pky, **E** ⛽ Citgo/dsl, Shell/dsl, 🍴 Bailey's Grill, Dougie Ray's Grill, El Chico, Fuji Steaks, HoneyBaked Ham, Hooters, Las Palmas Mexican, McDonald's, Pizza Hut, Subway, Waffle House, Wendy's, 🛏 Baymont Inn, Best Value Inn, Comfort Suites, Rodeway Inn, ⓞ 🅷 Best One Tires, Dillard's, Macy's, JC Penney, Sears/auto, mall, **E on Gallatin N** 🍴 A&W/LJ Silver, Arby's, Bar-B-Cutie, Burger King, Calhoun's Cafe, Checker's, Chick-fil-A, Chili's, ChuckeCheese, Fazoli's, IHOP, Krispy Kreme, Las Fiestas, Logan's Roadhouse, Longhorn Steaks, Olive Garden, Outback Steaks, Panera Bread, Popeye's, Rafferty's, Ryan's, Sonic, Starbucks, Steak'n Shake, TGI Friday's,

NASHVILLE

Exit	Services
96	Continued
	Taco Bell, ⓞ AAA, AT&T, Best Buy, Books-A-Million, CarMax, Chevrolet, Chrysler/Dodge/Jeep, CVS Drug, Dick's, Discount Tire, $General, Firestone/auto, Goodyear/auto, Harley-Davidson, Hobby Lobby, Home Depot, Honda, Jo-Ann's Etc, Kia, Lexus, Lincoln, Lowe's, Mazda, Michael's, Nissan, Office Depot, Old Navy, PepBoys, Petsmart, Sam's Club/gas, Staples, Target, TJ Maxx, Toyota/Scion, Verizon, VW, Walgreens, Walmart, **Urgent Care, W** ⛽ Marathon, Volunteer
95	TN 386, Vietnam Veterans Blvd (from nb)
92	rd 45, Old Hickory Blvd, **E** ⓞ 🅷, to Old Hickory Dam
90 b	TN 155 E, Briley Pkwy, **E** to Opreyland
90a	US 31W, US 41, Dickerson Pike, **E** ⛽ Citgo/dsl, Exxon/dsl, Mapco/dsl, Shell, 🍴 Arby's, Capt D's, Chicago Gyros, China King, Church's, Domino's, Jay's Rest., KFC, McDonald's, Pizza Hut, Subway, Taco Bell, Waffle House, Wendy's, 🛏 Days Inn, EconoLodge, Sleep Inn, Super 8, ⓞ Advance Parts, AutoZone, CVS Drug, $General, Family$, Kroger, O'Reilly Parts, Walgreens, **W** ⓞ Lowe's, Walmart
88b a	I-24, W to Clarksville, E to Nashville
87b a	US 431, Trinity Lane, **E** ⛽ BP, 🔴Loves/Subway/dsl/scales/24hr, 🍴 Church's/White Castle, Krystal, Sonic, ⓞ Piggly Wiggly, 🛏 Cumberland Inn, Delux Inn, **W** ⛽ BCP/dsl, BP, Exxon, Mapco, 🍴 Fat Mo's, Jack-in-the-Box, Jack's BBQ, McDonald's, Subway, Taco Bell, Waffle House, 🛏 Best Value Inn, Comfort Inn, Days Inn, EconoLodge, Halmark Inn, Howard Johnson, King's Inn, Quality Inn, Ravin Hotel, Regency Inn, Rodeway Inn, ⓞ $General, Family$
86	I-24 E, to I-40 E, to Memphis
86mm	Cumberland River
85	US 41A, 8th Ave, **E** ⛽ BP, ⓞ O'Reilly Parts, tires, to st capitol, **W** ⛽ Exxon, 🍴 Arby's, Jersey Mike's, McDonald's, Pizza Hut, Starbucks, Subway, Taco Bell, Wendy's, Wise Burger, 🛏 Millennium Hotel, SpringHill Suites, ⓞ Cadillac/Honda
84b a	I-40, E to Knoxville, W to Memphis
209[I-40]	US 70, Charlotte Ave, Church St, **E** ⛽ Exxon, 🍴 McDonald's, ⓞ Firestone, **W** ⛽ Exxon, Shell, 🍴 Burger King, Krystal, Sonic, Subway, White Castle, 🛏 Comfort Inn, ⓞ Walgreens, **Urgent Care**
82b a	I-40, W to Memphis, E to Nashville
81	Wedgewood Ave, **W** ⛽ BP, Exxon, Shell, 🍴 Burger King, Subway ⓞ $General, U-Haul
80	I-440, to Memphis, Knoxville
79	Armory Dr, **E on Powell** ⛽ Shell, 🍴 Applebee's, Jersey Mike's, Logan's Roadhouse, Panda Express, Panera Bread, Rafferty's, Subway, Wendy's, ⓞ BMW, CarMax, Home Depot, Michael's, Petsmart, Ross, Staples, TJ Maxx
78b a	rd 255, Harding Place, **E** ⛽ Mapco, Pure, Shell, 🍴 Beijing Chinese, Cracker Barrel, Mama Mia's Italian, Sub House, Waffle House, 🛏 La Quinta, Red Roof Inn, Traveler's Rest Hist Home, ⓞ CVS Drug
74	TN 254, Old Hickory Blvd, to Brentwood, **E** 🍴 Capt D's, Coldstone, Longhorn Steaks, Panera Bread, Qdoba Mexican, Shoney's, Waffle House, 🛏 Best Western, Holiday Inn Express, Hyatt Place, Sheraton, ⓞ GNC, Target, **W** ⛽ BP, Gulf, Shell/dsl, 🍴 Backyard Burger, Chick-fil-A, Chili's, Chipotle Mexican, Church's, Corky's BBQ, 5 Guys

NASHVILLE

🅖 = gas 🍴 = food 🛏 = lodging 🄾 = other 🆁🆂 = rest stop

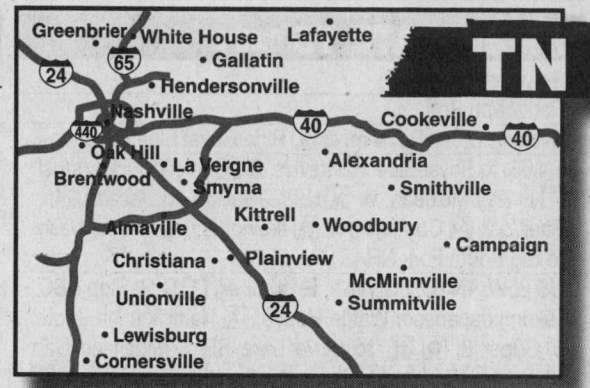

INTERSTATE 65 CONT'D

BRENTWOOD

Exit	Services
74	Continued
	Burgers, Jimmy John's, Maggie Moo's, Mazatlan Mexican, McAlister's Deli, McDonald's, Moe's SW Grill, Mrs Winner's, O'Charley's, Papa John's, Pei Wei, Pizza Hut, Ruby Tuesday, Starbucks, Subway, Taco Bell, Wendy's, 🛏 Courtyard, Extended Stay America, Hampton Inn, Hilton Suites, Homestead Suites, Studio+, 🄾 Cadillac, CVS Drug, Fresh Mkt Foods, Harris-Teeter, Land Rover, Office Depot, PetCo, Publix, Rite Aid, SteinMart, TJ Maxx, USPO, Walgreens
71	TN 253, Concord Rd, to Brentwood
69	rd 441, Moores Lane, Galleria Blvd, E 🅖 MapCo/dsl, Shell, 🍴 Amerigo's Grill, Baskin-Robbins, Cozymel's, Dunkin Donuts, Fuji Japanese, Greek Cafe, Outback Steaks, Papa Murphy's, Shogun Japanese, Sonic, Starbucks, 🛏 Hilton Garden, Hyatt Place, Red Roof Inn, Wingate Inn, 🄾 Acura/Lexus, CVS Drug, Home Depot/gas, Michael's, Petsmart, Publix, Walgreens, W 🅖 BP, Shell/dsl, 🍴 Backyard Burger, Buca Italian, Burger King, Capt D's, Chili's, Cracker Barrel, Famous Dave's, HoneyBaked Ham, J Alexander's Rest., Krispy Kreme, Logan's Roadhouse, Macaroni Grill, McDonald's, Peking Palace, Pizza Hut/Taco Bell, Red Lobster, Schlotzsky's, Stoney River Steaks, 🛏 Sleep Inn, 🄾 Barnes&Noble, Belk, Best Buy, Costco/gas, Dillard's, Discount Tire, $Tree, JC Penney, Macy's, NTB, Old Navy, Ross, Sears/auto, Target, mall
68b a	Cool Springs Blvd, E 🍴 Jersey Mike's, 🛏 Courtyard, Embassy Suites, Marriott, Residence Inn, W 🅖 Exxon, Shell, 🍴 BoneFish Grill, Bread&Co, Canton Buffet, Carrabba's, Chick-fil-A, ChuckeCheese, Chuy's Mexican, 5 Guys Burgers, Genghis Grill, Golden Corral, Greek Cafe, Jack-in-the-Box, Jason's Deli, J Christopher's, Jersey Mike's, KFC, McAlister's Deli, McDonald's, Moe's SW Grill, Newk's Cafe, Omikoshi Japanese, Otter's Chicken Tenders, Panera Bread, PF Chang's, Pizza Hut, Quiznos, Royal Thai, Starbucks, Subway, TGIFriday's, Wendy's, 🛏 ALoft, Country Inn&Suites, Hampton Inn, 🄾 Acura, AT&T, Dick's, GNC, Harley-Davidson, Jo-Ann Fabrics, Kohl's, Kroger, Lowe's, Marshall's, Office Depot, Sam's Club/gas, Staples, TJ Maxx, Verizon, Walgreens, to Galleria Mall
67	McEwen Dr, W 🍴 Blue Coast Burrito, Brick Top's, Little Caesars, Marco's Pizza, Sonic, Subway, Tazikis Mediterranean Cafe, 🛏 Drury Inn, 🄾 Toyota/Scion, Walmart/Blimpie, Whole Food Mkt

FRANKLIN

65	TN 96, to Murfreesboro, Franklin, E 🅖 Mapco, Shell/Krystal, 🍴 Cracker Barrel, Sonic, Steak'n Shake, 🛏 Best Value Inn, Comfort Inn, Days Inn, Holiday Inn Express, La Quinta, Ramada Inn, 🄾 Chevrolet, Honda, Kia, Subaru, Volvo, Walgreens, auto repair, **Urgent Care**, W 🅖 BP/dsl, Shell/dsl, 🍴 Arby's, Backyard Burger, Hardee's, KFC, McDonald's, Nashville Pizza, O'Charley's, Papa John's, Poncho's Mexican, Shoney's, Starbucks, Subway, Taco Bell, Waffle House, Wendy's, Zaxby's, 🛏 Best Western, Quality Inn, 🄾 Aldi Foods, BigLots, Chrysler/Dodge/Jeep, Discount Tire, $General, Ford, Hobby Lobby, Home Depot, Kroger, K-Mart, Publix/gas, Radio Shack, Rite Aid, SteinMart, USPO, Verizon, Walgreens, to Confederate Cem at Franklin, vet

Exit	Services
64mm	Harpeth River
61	TN 248, Peytonsville Rd, to Spring Hill, E 🅖 TA/BP/rest./dsl/scales/24hr/@, W 🅖 Mapco, Shell/dsl, 🄾 Goose Creek Inn/rest.
59b a	TN 840, to Nashville
58mm	W Harpeth River
53	TN 396, Saturn Pkwy, Spring Hill, Columbia, TN Scenic Pkwy
48mm	truck insp/weigh sta nb, litter barrels
46	US 412, TN 99, to Columbia, Chapel Hill, E 🅖 BP/dsl, 🅻🅾🆅🅴🆂/Arbys/dsl/scales/24hr, 🄾 Harley-Davidson, Henry Horton SP, W 🅖 Citgo/dsl, Phillip 66/Subway/dsl, Shell, TJ's/Burger King, 🍴 Cracker Barrel, Waffle House, Wendy's, 🛏 Best Value Inn, Comfort Inn, Hampton Inn, Holiday Inn Express, Relax Inn, Super 8, 🄾 🄷
40.5mm	Duck River
37	TN 50, to Columbia, Lewisburg, E 🄾 🄷, TN Walking Horse HQ, W 🅖 Shell/dsl, 🄾 to Polk Home
32	rd 373, to Lewisburg, Mooresville
27	rd 129, to Lynnville, Cornersville, E 🄾 Texas T Camping
25mm	parking area sb, litter barrels
24mm	parking area nb, litter barrels
22	US 31A, to Pulaski, E 🅖 Tennesseean Trkstp/Exxon/Pop's BBQ/dsl/scales/24hr/@, 🍴 McDonald's, Subway, 🛏 EconoLodge, W 🅖 🅻🅾🆅🅴🆂/dsl/scales/24hr, Shell/dsl
14	US 64, to Pulaski, E 🅖 BP/dsl, Shell/dsl, 🍴 Sarge's Shack Rest., 🛏 Super 8, 🄾 to Jack Daniels Distillery, W HOSPTIAL, to David Crockett SP
6	rd 273, Bryson, E 🅖 Phillips 66/rest./dsl, 🛏 Best Value Inn, 🄾 dsl repair, W 🅖 Marathon (2mi)
5mm	weight sta nb
4mm	Elk River
3mm	Welcome Ctr nb, full ♿ facilities, info, 🄲, 🍽, litter barrels, petwalk
1	US 31, rd 7, Ardmore, E 🅖 Chevron/dsl, Exxon/Chicken Express/dsl, 1-2 mi E 🅖 Shell/repair, 🍴 DQ, Hardee's, McDonald's, Subway
0mm	Tennessee/Alabama state line

INTERSTATE 75

Exit	Services
161.5mm	Tennessee/Kentucky state line
161mm	Welcome Ctr sb, full ♿ facilities, 🄲, vending, 🍽, litter barrels, petwalk
160	US 25W, Jellico, E 🅖 BP, Exxon/dsl, Marathon/dsl, 🛏 Jellico Motel, W 🅖 BP/Wendy's, Shell/Arby's/dsl, 🍴 Hardee's, Heritage Pizza, Subway, 🛏 Best Value Inn, Days Inn/rest., 🄾 🄷, camping, fireworks, to Indian Mtn SP

🅖 = gas   🍴 = food   🛏 = lodging   🅞 = other   🆁🆂 = rest stop   Copyright 2014 - The NEXT Exit ®

⬆N INTERSTATE 75 CONT'D

Exit	Services
156	Rarity Mtn Rd
144	Stinking Creek Rd, **4 mi E** 🅖 Ride Royal Blue Camping
141	TN 63, to Royal Blue, Huntsville, **E** 🅖 Shell/Stuckey's/dsl, 🍴 El Rey Mexican, **W** 🅖 ▦/Subway/dsl/scales/24hr, Shell/dsl, 🛏 Comfort Inn, 🅞 fireworks, repair/truckwash, to Big South Fork NRA
134	US 25W, TN 63, Caryville, **E** 🅖 Shell, 🍴 Quik Stop BBQ, Takumi Japanese, Waffle House, 🛏 Hampton Inn, Motel 6, Super 8, 🅞 🏥, to Cove Lake SP, Cumberland Gap NHP, **W** 🅖 BP/dsl, 🍴 Shoney's, Scotty's Hamburgers, 🛏 Budget Host, 🅞 USPO
129	US 25W S, Lake City, **W** 🅖 BP/Sonic, Exxon/dsl, ▦/dsl, Shell/dsl, 🍴 Cracker Barrel, Domino's, Glen's Pizza, KFC/Taco Bell, La Fiesta Mexican, McDonald's, Subway, 🛏 Days Inn, Blue Haven Motel, Lamb's Inn/rest., Scottish Inn, 🅞 $General, Family$, fireworks, same as 128
128	US 441, to Lake City, **E** 🅖 BP, Sunoco, 🅞 Mtn Lake Marina Camping (4mi), **W** 🅖 Exxon/dsl, Marathon, Weigel's/dsl, 🛏 Blue Haven Motel, 🅞 Advance Parts, $General, Family$, antique cars, to Norris Dam SP, same as 129
126mm	Clinch River
122	TN 61, Bethel, Norris, **E** 🅖 Shell/dsl, Wiegel's/dsl, 🍴 Shoney's, 🅞 Fox Inn Camping, Suzuki, Toyota/Scion, Museum of Appalachia, antiques, **W** 🅖 BP, Exxon/Burger King/Subway/dsl, Git'n Go, Phillips 66, Shell/Baskin-Robbins, 🍴 Arby's, Golden Girls Rest., Hardee's, Harrison's Grill, Krystal, LJ Silver, McDonald's, Waffle House, Wendy's, Zaxby's, 🛏 Comfort Inn, Country Inn&Suites, Holiday Inn Express, Red Roof Inn, Super 8, Travelodge, 🅞 Ford, Verizon, Walgreens, Walmart/McDonald's, Big Pine Ridge SP
117	rd 170, Racoon Valley Rd, **E** 🅖 ▦/dsl/scales/24hr, **W** 🛏 Valley Inn, 🅞 Volunteer RV Park
112	rd 131, Emory Rd, to Powell, **E** 🅖 BP/Buddy's BBQ/dsl, ▦/DQ/Taco Bell/dsl, 🍴 Arby's, Aubrey's Rest., Bruster's, Firehouse Subs, 5 Guys Burgers, McDonald's/playplace, Krystal, Ruby Tuesday, Starbucks, Steak'n Shake, Subway, 3 Amigos Mexican, Wendy's, Zaxby's, 🛏 Comfort Inn, Country Inn&Suites, Holiday Inn Express, 🅞 🏥, CVS Drug, Family$, Ingles/gas, O'Reilly Parts, Rigg's Drug, Verizon, **W** 🅖 Exxon/dsl, Shell/dsl, Weigel's/dsl, 🍴 Hardee's, Shoney's, Waffle House, 🛏 Super 8
110	Callahan Dr, **E** 🅖 Weigel's, 🍴 Asian Cafe, 🛏 Express Inn, Quality Inn/rest., 🅞 Honda, **W** 🅖 BP, 🛏 Scottish Inn, 🅞 Kia, Mack/Volvo
108	Merchants Dr, **E** 🅖 BP/dsl, Citgo/dsl, ▦/dsl, Shell/dsl, 🍴 Applebee's, Cracker Barrel, El Chico's, Hooters, Monterrey Mexican, O'Charley's, Pizza Hut, Puelo's Grill, Ramsey's Rest., Starbucks, Waffle House, Wok Hay Asian, 🛏 Best Western, Comfort Suites, Days Inn, Hampton Inn, Mainstay Suites, Quality Inn, Red Roof Inn, Sleep Inn, 🅞 Ingles, Valvoline, **W** 🅖 Conoco/dsl, Exxon/dsl, ▦/dsl, 🍴 Baskin-Robbins, Burger King, Capt D's, Great American Steaks, IHOP, Mandarin House, McDonald's, Nixon's Deli, Outback Steaks, Quaker Steak, Red Lobster, Subway, 🛏 Best Value Inn, Clarion Inn, EconoLodge, Motel 6, Super 8, 🅞 CVS Drug, Radio Shack, Walgreens
107	I-640 & I-75
3b [I-640]	US 25W, (from nb), **W** 🅞 Chevrolet, Dodge, Ford, Nissan
1 [I-640]	rd 62, Western Ave, **E** 🍴 Hardee's, Krystal, 🅞 Advance

1 [I-640]	Continued
	Parts, O'Reilly Parts, **W** 🅖 Exxon/dsl, Marathon/dsl, RaceWay/dsl, 🍴 Central Park, KFC, Little Caesars, LJ Silver, McDonald's, Panda Chinese, Shoney's, Subway, Taco Bell, Wendy's, 🅞 CVS Drug, Kroger/gas, Walgreens

I-75 and I-40 run together 17 mi. See Interstate 40, exits 369 - 385.

84ba [368]	I-40, W to Nashville, E to Knoxville
81	US 321, TN 95, to Lenoir City, **E** 🅖 BP/Buddy's BBQ/TCBY/dsl, Exxon/Subway/dsl, Marathon/dsl, Mobil, Murphy USA/dsl, Shell/dsl, 🍴 Angelo's Brick Oven, Bojangles, Burger King, Capt D's, Chili's, China Buffet, Cracker Barrel, Dunkin Donuts, 5 Guys Burgers, Hardee's, KFC, McDonald's, Monterrey Mexican, Panda Buffet, Pizza Hut, Quiznos, Shoney's, Snappy Tomato Pizza, Taco Bell, Waffle House, Wendy's, Zaxby's, 🛏 Days Inn, Hampton Inn, Holiday Inn Express, King's Inn/rest., 🅞 Advance Parts, AutoZone, AT&T, CVS Drug, $General Mkt, $Tree, Food City/gas, Ford, Home Depot, Lazy Acres RV Park (7mi), O'Reilly Parts, Radio Shack, Verizon, Walmart/Subway, Great Smokies NP, Ft Loudon Dam, **W** 🅖 Citgo/dsl, Shell/dsl, 🍴 Krystal, Ruby Tuesday, 🛏 Comfort Inn, EconoLodge, Knights Inn, 🅞 Crosseyed Cricket Camping (6mi), Matlock Tires/Repair
76	rd 324, Sugar Limb Rd, **W** to TN Valley Winery
74mm	Tennessee River
72	TN 72, to Loudon, **E** 🅖 BP/McDonald's, Shell/Wendy's, 🍴 Cabin Rest., KFC, Taco Bell, 🛏 Country Inn&Suites, Super 8, 🅞 Weigel's/dsl, to Ft Loudon SP, **W** 🅖 Marathon, 🛏 Best Value Inn, 🅞 Express RV Park
68	rd 323, to Philadelphia, **E** 🅖 BP/dsl, Sunoco (2mi), 🍴 cheese factory/store (2mi)
62	RD 322, Oakland Rd, to Sweetwater, **E** 🍴 Dinner Bell Rest., **W** 🅞 KOA
60	TN 68, Sweetwater, **0-2 mi E** 🅖 BP, RaceWay, Shell/dsl, 🍴 A&W/LJ Silver, Bradley's BBQ, Burger King, Hardee's, KFC, McDonald's, Pizza Hut, Sonic, Subway, Taco Bell, 🛏 Comfort Inn, Days Inn, EconoLodge, Economy Inn, Hilltop Motel, 🅞 🏥, Ace Hardware, Advance Parts, $General, O'Reilly Parts, $General, Family$, Ford/Lincoln, K-Mart, Verizon, Walgreens, to Lost Sea Underground Lake, **W** 🅖 Marathon, Kangaroo/dsl, 🛏 Magnuson Hotel, Quality Inn, 🅞 flea mkt, to Watts Bar Dam, tires/repair, vet
56	rd 309, Niota, **E** 🅖 Wilco/Stuckey's/Wendy's/dsl/scales/24hr, 🅞 TN Country Camping, **W** tires
52	rd 305, Mt Verd Rd, to Athens, **E** 🅖 Marathon/dsl (2mi), 🍴 Subway (2mi), 🅞 Overniter RV Park, **W** 🅖 BP, 🛏 Athens Lodge
49	TN 30, to Athens, **E** 🅖 BP, Marathon, Murphy USA/dsl, Kangaroo, RaceWay, Shell/dsl, 🍴 Applebee's, Arby's, Buddy's BBQ, Burger King, Capt D's, China Wok, Firehouse Subs, Hardee's, KFC, Krystal, McDonald's, Monterrey Mexican, Papa John's, Pizza Hut, Ruby Tuesday, Shoney's, Sonic, Subway, Taco Bell, Waffle House, Wendy's, Western Sizzlin, Zaxby's, 🛏 Days Inn, Hampton Inn, Holiday Inn Express, Homestead Inn, Motel 6, Scottish Inn, Super 8, 🅞 🏥, Advance Parts, Athens I-75 Camping, BigLots, $General, Food Lion, K-Mart, Lowe's, Russell Stover, Staples, Verizon, Walgreens, Walmart/Subway, to TN Wesleyan Coll, **W** 🅖 Shell, 🍴 Cracker Barrel, 🛏 Best Value Inn, Comfort Inn
45mm	🆁🆂s, both lanes, full ♿ facilities, 🏕 litter barrels, 🍴 petwalk, vending

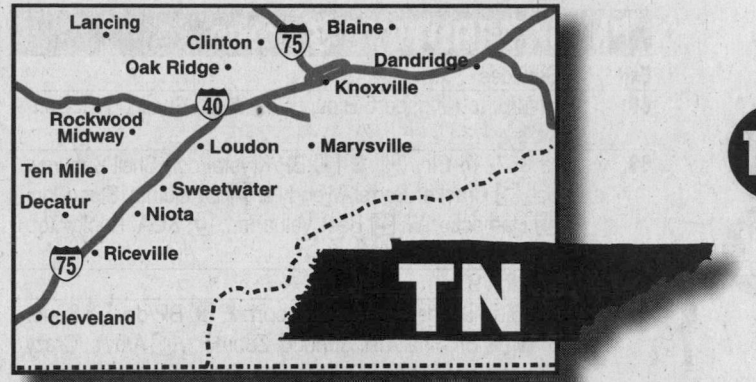

🔼N INTERSTATE 75 CONT'D

Exit	Services
42	rd 39, Riceville Rd, **E** 📱 Citgo/dsl, 🛏 Relax Inn, Rice Inn (2mi)
36	rd 163, to Calhoun, **E** 🍴 Hardee's (3mi), ⭕ Hiwassee/Ocoee River SP
35mm	Hiwassee River
33	rd 308, to Charleston, **E** 📱 Marathon/dsl, **W** 📱 **Loves** /McDonald's/Subway/dsl/scales/24hr, Shell, rest./dsl
27	Paul Huff Pkwy, **1 mi E** 📱 Murphy USA, Phillips 66, 🍴 Applebee's, Capt D's, Chili's, CiCi's, DQ, Fazoli's, Firehouse Subs, 5 Guys Burgers, Golden Corral, IHOP, McDonald's, O'Charley's, Outback Steaks, Panera Bread, Pizza Hut, Ryan's, Sonic, Steak'n Shake, Taco Bell, Takoyaki, 🛏 Jameson Inn, ⭕ Aldi Foods, AutoZone, Belk, Buick/Cadillac/GMC, CVS Drug, $Tree, Food Lion, Hobby Lobby, Home Depot, JC Penney, K-Mart, Lowe's, PetCo, Radio Shack, Rite Aid, Sears, Staples, TJ Maxx, Verizon, Walgreens, Walmart, auto repair/tires, mall, **W** 📱 BP/dsl, Exxon/dsl, Shell/Subway, 🍴 Denny's, Fulin's Asian, Hardee's, Shane's Ribshack, Stevi B's Pizza, Waffle House, Wendy's, 🛏 Classic Suites, Hampton Inn, Quality Inn, Ramada Ltd, Royal Inn, Super 8, ⭕ AT&T, Books-A-Million, Kohl's, Michael's, Ross, Target
25	TN 60, Cleveland, **E** 📱 Chevron/dsl, RaceWay/dsl, Shell/dsl, 🍴 Bojangles, Burger King, Checker's, Cracker Barrel, Hardee's, McDonald's, Sonic, Waffle House, Wendy's, Zaxby's, 🛏 Colonial Inn, Days Inn, Douglas Inn, EconoLodge, Economy Inn, Fairfield Inn, Howard Johnson, Knights Inn, Travel Inn, ⭕ 🅷 Ace Hardware, BigLots, Cherokee Drug, $General, Tuesday Morning, vet, to Lee Coll, **W** 📱 Shell, 🛏 Comfort Inn, Mtn View Inn, Wingate Inn
23mm	**truck/weigh sta nb**
20	US 64 byp, to Cleveland, **1-4 mi E** 📱 FuelMart, ⭕ Ford, Honda, **W** 📱 BP/DQ/Pizza Hut/dsl, Exxon/dsl, 🍴 McDonald's, ⭕ KOA (1mi), Toyota/Scion, fireworks
16mm	scenic view sb
13mm	**truck/weigh sta, litter barrels sb**
11	US 11 N, US 64 E, Ooltewah, **E** 📱 BP, Murphy USA/dsl, RaceWay/dsl, Shell, 🍴 Arby's, Bojangles, Burger King, Cracker Barrel, Capt D's, China Rose, El Matador Mexican, Hardee's, Little Caesars, McDonald's, Sonic, Subway, Taco Bell, Wendy's, Zaxby's, 🛏 Hampton Inn, Holiday Inn Express, ⭕ Ace Hardware, Bi-Lo, GNC, O'Reilly Parts, Verizon, Walgreens, Walmart/Subway, **W** 📱 BP/Quiznos/dsl, 🍴 Krystal, Waffle House, 🛏 Super 8, ⭕ Publix, to Harrison Bay SP
9	Volkswagon Dr
7b a	US 11, US 64, Lee Hwy, **E** 📱 Exxon/dsl, **W** 📱 Shell, 🍴 City Cafe, Waffle House, 🛏 Best Inn, Best Value Inn, Best Western, Comfort Inn, EconoLodge, Motel 6, ⭕ Harley-Davidson, Jaguar/Land Rover/Porsche, repair
5	Shallowford Rd, **E** 🍴 Alexander's, Arby's, Capt D's, Chili's, Chophouse Rest., CiCi's, Country Place Rest., DQ, Famous Dave's, J. Alexanders, Krystal, Logan's Roadhouse, Macaroni Grill, McAlister's Deli, McDonald's/playplace, Outback Steaks, Smokey Bones BBQ, Starbucks, Steak'n Shake, Souper Salad, Taco Bell, Zaxby's, 🛏 Courtyard, Quality Inn, Wingate Inn, ⭕ AAA, Barnes&Noble, Best Buy, Books-A-Million, Firestone/auto, Ford, FreshMkt Foods, Hobby Lobby, Home Depot, Lowe's, Office Depot, Old Navy, Petsmart, SteinMart, Tar

Exit	Services
5	Continued get, Walgreens, Walmart/Subway, World Mkt, **W** 📱 BP, Citgo/dsl, Exxon, Shell, 🍴 Applebee's, Blimpie, Cracker Barrel, Fazoli's, Fuji Steaks, GlenGene Deli, O'Charley's, Papa John's, Shoney's, Sonic, Subway, TX Roadhouse, Waffle House, Wendy's, 🛏 Clarion, Comfort Inn, Country Inn&Suites, Fairfield Inn, Guesthouse Inn, Hampton Inn, Hilton Garden, Homewood Suites, Knights Inn, La Quinta, MainStay Suites, Microtel, Ramada Ltd, Red Roof Inn, Residence Inn, Sleep Inn, Staybridge Suites, Super 8, ⭕ 🅷 Bi-Lo, CVS Drug, Goodyear/auto, U of TN/Chatt, same as 4a
4a	(from nb) Hamilton Place Blvd, **E** 🍴 Abuelo's, Acropolis, Big River Grille, BoneFish Grill, Carraba's, DQ, El Mason, Firehouse Subs, 5 Guys Burgers, Fox&Hound Grill, Golden Corral, Jason's Deli, Moe's SW Grill, Olive Garden, Outback Steaks, Panera Bread, PF Chang's, Piccadilly's, Red Lobster, Ruby Tuesday, Salsarita's Mexican, Shogun Japanese, Starbucks, Sticky Fingers BBQ, Kampai Of Tokyo, 🛏 InTown Suites, ⭕ AAA, Belk, Dillard's, Firestone, JC Penney, Kohl's, Marshall's, Michael's, Ross, Sears/auto, Staples, Target, TJ Maxx, mall, same as 5
4	TN 153, Chickamauga Dam Rd, 🚐
3b a	TN 320, Brainerd Rd, **E** 📱 BP, 🍴 Baskin-Robbins, Subway, **W** ⭕ BMW
2	I-24 W, to I-59, to Chattanooga, Lookout Mtn
1.5mm	**Welcome Ctr nb, full ♿ facilities, 🕾, vending, 🗑, litter barrels, petwalk**
1b a	US 41, Ringgold Rd, to Chattanooga, **E** 📱 BP, Texaco/dsl, 🍴 Wendy's, 🛏 Best Value Inn, Best Western, Clarion, Knights Inn, Motel 6, ⭕ Bi-Lo, Camping World RV Ctr/park, Family$, **W** 📱 Conoco/dsl, Mapco/Quiznos/dsl, 🍴 A&W/LJ Silver, Arby's, Baskin-Robbins, Burger King, Central Park Burger, Cracker Barrel, Hardee's, Krystal, McDonald's, PortoFino Italian, Subway, Taco Bell, Teriyaki House, Waffle House, Wally's Rest., 🛏 Days Inn, Fairfield Inn, Holiday Inn Express, Super 8, Superior Creek Lodge, Waverly Motel, ⭕ O'Reilly Parts, U-Haul
0mm	Tennessee/Georgia state line

🔼N INTERSTATE 81

Exit	Services
75mm	Tennessee/Virginia state line, **Welcome Ctr sb, full ♿ facilities, info, 🕾, vending, 🗑 litter barrels, petwalk**
74b a	US 11W, to Bristol, Kingsport, **E** 📱 Hampton Inn, ⭕ 🅷 **W** 📱 Valero, 🛏 Super 8, Travelodge
69	TN 394, to Blountville, **E** 📱 BP/Subway/dsl, 🍴 Arby's, Domino's, ⭕ Advance Parts, Bristol Int Speedway, Lakeview RV Park (8mi)

⬆N   INTERSTATE 81 CONT'D

Exit	Services
66	rd 126, to Kingsport, Blountville, **W** 🚪 Shell, 🍴 McDonald's
63	rd 357, Tri-City ✈, **E** 🚪 BP/Krystal/dsl, Shell/Subway/dsl, 🍴 Cracker Barrel, Wendy's, 🛏 La Quinta, Sleep Inn, ⊙ Hamricks, **W** 🛏 Best Value Inn, ⊙ KOA, Rocky Top Camping, dsl repair
60mm	Holston River
59	rd 36, to Johnson City, Kingsport, **E** 🚪 BP/dsl, 🛏 Super 8, **W** 🚪 BP, Shell/dsl, Sunoco, Zoomerz, 🍴 Arby's, Crazy Tomato, Domino's, Fisherman's Dock Rest., Hardee's, HotDog Hut, Jersey Mike's Subs, La Carreta Mexican, Little Caesars, McDonald's, Moto Japanese, Pal's Drive-Thru, Perkins, Pizza Hut, Raffaele's Pizza, Subway, The Shack BBQ, 🛏 Colonial Inn, Comfort Inn, ⊙ Urgent Care, Advance Parts, Curves, CVS Drug, $General, $Tree, Firestone/auto, Ingles/deli, O'Reilly Parts, Verizon, Walgreens, USPO, vet, to Warrior's Path SP
57b a	I-26
56	Tri-Cities Crossing, **E** regional shopping complex
50	TN 93, Fall Branch, **W** ⊙ auto auction, st patrol
44	Jearoldstown Rd, **E** 🚪 Marathon
41mm	🅿️ sb, full ♿ facilities, 🚻, vending, 🛉 litter barrels, petwalk
38mm	🅿️ nb, full ♿ facilities, 🚻, vending, 🛉 litter barrels, petwalk
36	rd 172, to Baileyton, **E** 🚪 🏪/Subway/dsl/scales/24hr, **W** 🚪 BP/dsl, Shell/Subway/dsl/24hr, TA/Country Pride/dsl/scales/24hr/@, 🍴 Pizza+, 🛏 36 Motel, ⊙ Around Pond RV Park, Baileyton Camp (2mi), $General, Family$
30	TN 70, to Greeneville, **E** 🚪 Exxon/DQ/Stuckey's/dsl
23	US 11E, to Greeneville, **E** 🚪 Marathon/Wendy's, Zoomerz/Subway, ⊙ Tri-Am RV Ctr, to Andrew Johnson HS, Crockett SP, **W** 🚪 Exxon/DQ/dsl, Phillips 66/dsl/rest./scales, 🍴 McDonald's, Pizza+, Taco Bell, Tony's BBQ, 🛏 Best Western, Super 8
21mm	weigh sta sb
15	rd 340, Fish Hatchery Rd
12	TN 160, to Morristown, **E** 🚪 Phillips 66, **W** 🚪 Shell/dsl, 🛏 Days Inn (6mi), Hampton Inn (12mi), Holiday Inn Ex

Exit	Services
12	Continued press (5mi), Super 8 (5mi), ⊙ to Crockett Tavern HS
8	US 25E, to Morristown, **E** 🍴 Sonic (2mi), **W** 🚪🍴 Fastop/dsl, Cracker Barrel, Hardee's, 🛏 Best Western, Parkway Inn, Super 8, ⊙ to Cumberland Gap NHP
4	rd 341, White Pine, **E** 🚪 🏪/McDonald's/dsl/scales/24hr, **W** 🚪 Wilco/Hess/Wendy's/dsl/scales/24hr, 🛏 Days Inn, ⊙ to Panther Cr SP
2.5mm	🅿️ sb, full ♿ facilities, 🚻, 🛉, litter barrels, vending, petwalk
1b a	I-40, E to Asheville, W to Knoxville.
I-81 begins/ends on I-40, exit 421.	

⬆E   INTERSTATE 640 (KNOXVILLE)

Exit	Services
9mm	**I-640 begins/ends on I-40, exit 393.**
8	Millertown Pike, Mall Rd N, **N** 🚪 Exxon/DQ/24hr, Shell, 🍴 Applebee's, Burger King, Don Pablos, Gunthor's, KFC, Krystal, McDonald's, Pizza Hut, Taco Bell, TX Roadhouse, Wendy's, ⊙ Belk, $General, Food City, JC Penney, Kohl's, Marshall's, NTB, Old Navy, Ross, Sam's Club, Sears/auto, Target, Walmart, mall, **S** 🚪 Shell, 🍴 Cracker Barrel, Little Caesars, O'Charley's, Subway, ⊙ Food Lion, Home Depot, Lowe's Whse, PepBoys
6	US 441, to Broadway, **N** 🚪 Citgo, Phillips 66, 🏪/dsl, Shell, 🍴 Arby's, Austin's Steaks, Cancun Mexican, Chop House, CiCi's, Fazoli's, Hardee's, Krispy Kreme, Lenny's Subs, LJ Silver, Marble Slab, McDonald's, Panera Bread, Papa John's, Ruby Tuesday, Sonic, Subway, Taco Bell, ⊙ Advance Parts, AutoZone, BigLots, CVS Drug, $General, Firestone, Food City/gas, Kroger/24hr, Walgreens, repair/tires, **S** 🍴 Buddy's BBQ, Little Caesars, Shoney's, ⊙ $General, Food City, K-Mart, Office Depot
3a	I-75 N to Lexington, I-275 S to Knoxville
3b	US 25W, Clinton Hwy, (from eb), **N** ⊙ Chevrolet, Dodge, Ford, Nissan, services on frontage rds
1	TN 62, Western Ave, **N** 🚪 Exxon/dsl, Marathon/dsl, Raceway/dsl, 🍴 Central Park, KFC, Little Caesars, LJ Silver, McDonald's, Panda Chinese, Shoney's, Subway, Taco Bell, Wendy's, ⊙ CVS Drug, Kroger/gas, Walgreens, **S** 🍴 Hardee's, Krystal, ⊙ Advance Parts, O'Reilly Parts,
0mm	**I-640 begins/ends on I-40, exit 385.**

TEXAS

⬆E   INTERSTATE 10

Exit	Services
880.5mm	Texas/Louisiana state line, Sabine River
880	Sabine River Turnaround, RV camping
870mm	**Welcome Ctr wb, full** ♿ **facilities,** 🚻, 🛉, **litter barrels, vending, petwalk**
878	US 90, Orange, **N** 🚪 Mobil/dsl, ⊙ airboat rides, RV Park, **S** ⊙ Western Store
877	TX 87, 16th St, Orange, **N** 🚪 Exxon/dsl, Shamrock/dsl, 🍴 Pizza Hut, Subway, 🛏 Hampton Inn, ⊙ Ace Hardware, $General, Market Basket/deli, **S** 🚪 Exxon, Kwik Stop, Shell/dsl, Valero/dsl, 🍴 Casa Ole, Church's, DQ, General Wok, Jack-in-the-Box, McDonald's, Popeye's, Sonic, Taco Bell, 2 Amigo's Mexican, ⊙ CVS Drug, Goodyear/auto, HEB Foods, Kroger/dsl, Modica Tires, O'Reilly Parts, Verizon, Walgreens
876	Adams Bayou, frontage rd, Adams Bayou, **N** 🚪 Mobil/dsl, 🍴 Cajun Cookery, Gary's Café, Taste of Orange Rest., Waffle House, 🛏 Best Value, Days Inn, EconoLodge, Executive Inn, Ramada Inn, Super 8, ⊙ Toyota, **S** 🚪 Chevron/dsl, 🛏 Holiday Inn Express, same as 877
875	FM 3247, MLK Dr, **S** ⊙ 🅷, Chrysler/Dodge/Jeep
874	US 90, Womack Rd, to Orange, **S** 🅷
873	TX 62, TX 73, to Bridge City, **N** 🚪 Exxon/dsl/24hr, / ⊕FLYING J/Denny's/dsl/LP/scales/24hr, 🛏 Studio 6, ⊙ Oak Leaf RV Park, **S** 🚪 🏪/Subway/Wendy's/dsl/scales/24hr, Shell/Church's/dsl, Valero, 🍴 Jack-in-the-Box, McDonald's, Sonic, Waffle House, Whataburger, 🛏 Comfort Inn, La Quinta, Sleep Inn
872	N Mimosa Ln, Jackson Dr, from wb
870	FM 1136
869	FM 1442, to Bridge City, **S** 🚪 Chevron, ⊙ Lloyd's RV Ctr

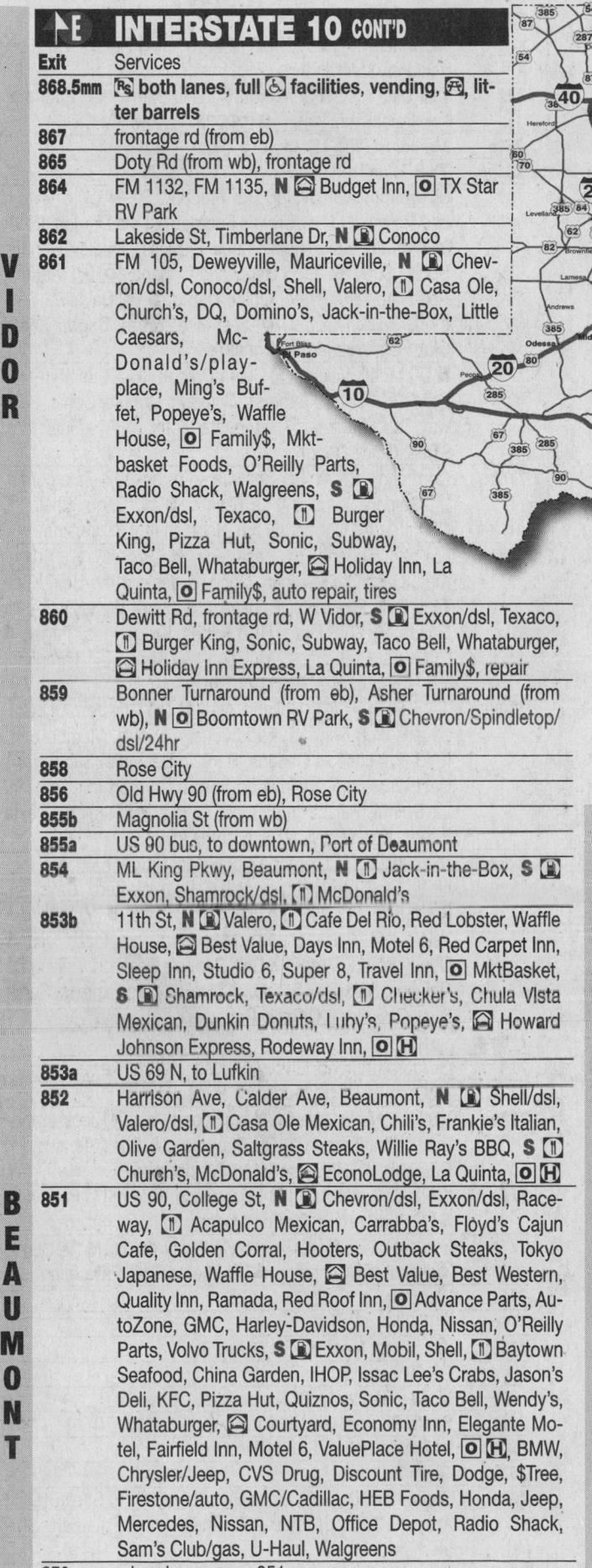

INTERSTATE 10 CONT'D

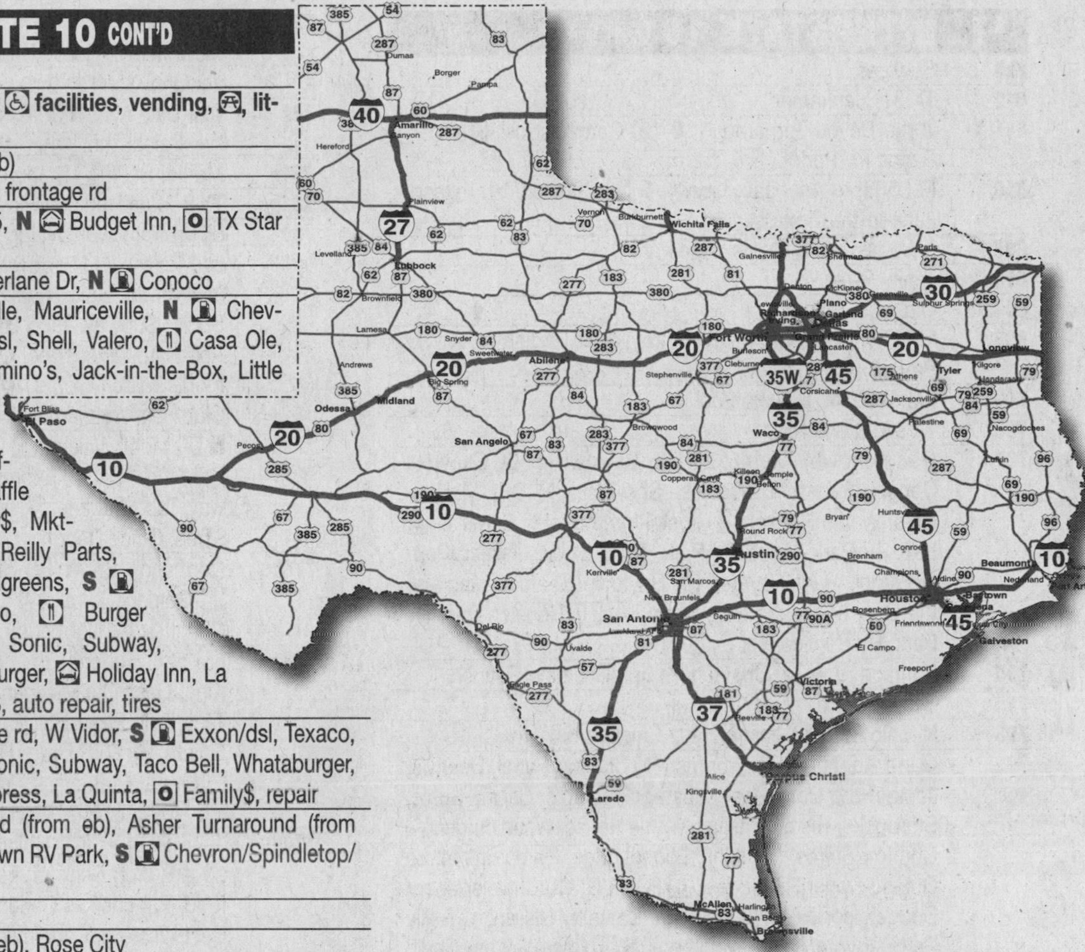

Exit	Services
868.5mm	🅁🅂 both lanes, full ♿ facilities, vending, ⛾ litter barrels
867	frontage rd (from eb)
865	Doty Rd (from wb), frontage rd
864	FM 1132, FM 1135, **N** 🛏 Budget Inn, Ⓞ TX Star RV Park
862	Lakeside St, Timberlane Dr, **N** ⛽ Conoco
861	FM 105, Deweyville, Mauriceville, **N** ⛽ Chevron/dsl, Conoco/dsl, Shell, Valero, 🍴 Casa Ole, Church's, DQ, Domino's, Jack-in-the-Box, Little Caesars, McDonald's/playplace, Ming's Buffet, Popeye's, Waffle House, Ⓞ Family$, Mktbasket Foods, O'Reilly Parts, Radio Shack, Walgreens, **S** ⛽ Exxon/dsl, Texaco, 🍴 Burger King, Pizza Hut, Sonic, Subway, Taco Bell, Whataburger, 🛏 Holiday Inn, La Quinta, Ⓞ Family$, auto repair, tires
860	Dewitt Rd, frontage rd, W Vidor, **S** ⛽ Exxon/dsl, Texaco, 🍴 Burger King, Sonic, Subway, Taco Bell, Whataburger, 🛏 Holiday Inn Express, La Quinta, Ⓞ Family$, repair
859	Bonner Turnaround (from eb), Asher Turnaround (from wb), **N** Ⓞ Boomtown RV Park, **S** ⛽ Chevron/Spindletop/dsl/24hr
858	Rose City
856	Old Hwy 90 (from eb), Rose City
855b	Magnolia St (from wb)
855a	US 90 bus, to downtown, Port of Beaumont
854	ML King Pkwy, Beaumont, **N** 🍴 Jack-in-the-Box, **S** ⛽ Exxon, Shamrock/dsl, 🍴 McDonald's
853b	11th St, **N** ⛽ Valero, 🍴 Cafe Del Rio, Red Lobster, Waffle House, 🛏 Best Value, Days Inn, Motel 6, Red Carpet Inn, Sleep Inn, Studio 6, Super 8, Travel Inn, Ⓞ MktBasket, **S** ⛽ Shamrock, Texaco/dsl, 🍴 Checker's, Chula Vista Mexican, Dunkin Donuts, Luby's, Popeye's, 🛏 Howard Johnson Express, Rodeway Inn, Ⓞ Ⓗ
853a	US 69 N, to Lufkin
852	Harrison Ave, Calder Ave, Beaumont, **N** ⛽ Shell/dsl, Valero/dsl, 🍴 Casa Ole Mexican, Chili's, Frankie's Italian, Olive Garden, Saltgrass Steaks, Willie Ray's BBQ, **S** 🍴 Church's, McDonald's, 🛏 EconoLodge, La Quinta, Ⓞ Ⓗ
851	US 90, College St, **N** ⛽ Chevron/dsl, Exxon/dsl, Raceway, 🍴 Acapulco Mexican, Carrabba's, Floyd's Cajun Cafe, Golden Corral, Hooters, Outback Steaks, Tokyo Japanese, Waffle House, 🛏 Best Value, Best Western, Quality Inn, Ramada, Red Roof Inn, Ⓞ Advance Parts, AutoZone, GMC, Harley-Davidson, Honda, Nissan, O'Reilly Parts, Volvo Trucks, **S** ⛽ Exxon, Mobil, Shell, 🍴 Baytown Seafood, China Garden, IHOP, Issac Lee's Crabs, Jason's Deli, KFC, Pizza Hut, Quiznos, Sonic, Taco Bell, Wendy's, Whataburger, 🛏 Courtyard, Economy Inn, Elegante Motel, Fairfield Inn, Motel 6, ValuePlace Hotel, Ⓞ Ⓗ, BMW, Chrysler/Jeep, CVS Drug, Discount Tire, Dodge, $Tree, Firestone/auto, GMC/Cadillac, HEB Foods, Honda, Jeep, Mercedes, Nissan, NTB, Office Depot, Radio Shack, Sam's Club/gas, U-Haul, Walgreens
850	wb only, same as 851
849	US 69 S, Washington Blvd, to Port Arthur ✈
848	Walden Rd, **N** ⛽ Shell, 🍴 Pappadeaux Seafood, Sonic, 🛏 Comfort Suites, Holiday Inn/rest., La Quinta, Ⓞ USPO, **S** ⛽ Petro/Mobil/dsl/scales/24hr/@, Shell, 🍴 Carino's Italian, Cheddar's, Cracker Barrel, Jack-in-the-Box, Joe's Crabshack, Waffle House, 🛏 Candlewood Suites, Courtyard, Hampton Inn, Homewood Suites, Hilton Garden, Knights Inn, Residence Inn, Super 8, Ⓞ Blue Beacon
847	Brooks Rd (from wb), (845 from eb), **S** Ⓞ Gulf Coast RV Resort
843	Smith Rd
838	FM 365, Fannett, **N** 🍴 Alligator Park/Rest., Bar-H BBQ, Ⓞ T&T RV Park
837.5mm	cmv sta wb
833	Hamshire Rd, **N** ⛽ Chevron/dsl, 🍴 Bergerons Rest.
829	FM 1663, Winnie, **N** ⛽ Exxon/dsl, Shell/dsl/24hr, Texaco/Burger King/dsl, 🍴 McDonald's, Taco Bell, Whataburger/24hr, 🛏 Days Inn, Ⓞ RV Park, **S** ⛽ Chevron/Chester's/dsl, Mobil/Pizza Hut/Subway/dsl/scales, 🍴 Al-T's Seafood, Hart's Chicken, Jack-in-the-Box, Subway, Waffle House, 🛏 Comfort Inn, EconoLodge, Hampton Inn, Holiday Inn Express, Home Suites, La Quinta, Motel 6, Studio 6, Winnie Inn/RV Park, Ⓞ Ⓗ
828	TX 73, TX 124 (from eb), to Winnie, **S** Ⓗ same as 829
827	FM 1406
822	FM 1410
819	Jenkins Rd, **S** ⛽ Exxon/Stuckey's/Chester's/dsl
817	FM 1724
814	frontage rd, from eb
813	TX 61 (from wb), Hankamer, **N** ⛽ Shell/dsl, 🛏 Days Inn, **S** ⛽ Exxon/DJ's Diner/dsl, 🍴 McDonald's, same as 812

VIDOR (vertical left margin, rows 861–860)

BEAUMONT (vertical left margin, rows 851)

WINNIE (vertical margin, right column)

TX (tab, right edge)

➍Ⓔ INTERSTATE 10 CONT'D

TX

B A Y T O W N

Exit	Services
812	TX 61, Hankamer
811	Turtle Bayou Turnaround, **S** 🛢 Gator Jct/dsl, ⊡ Turtle Bayou RV Park
810	FM 563, to Anahuac, Liberty, **S** 🛢 Chevron/dsl, Texaco/Jack-in-the-Box/dsl
807	to Wallisville, **S** ⊡ Heritage Park
805.5mm	Trinity River
804mm	Old, Lost Rivers
803	FM 565, Cove, Old River-Winfrey, **N** ⊡ Paradise Cove RV Park, **S** 🛢 Valero/dsl
800	FM 3180, **N** 🛢 Exxon/dsl
799	TX 99, Grand Pkwy
797	(798 from wb) TX 146, 99 **toll**, Baytown, **N** 🛢 Chevron, Conoco/Subway/dsl/scales, Shell/dsl, ⅱ DQ, McDonald's, Waffle House, 🛏 Crystal Inn, Motel 6, Super 8, ⊡ L&R RV Park, Value RV Park, **S** 🛢 Exxon, Texaco/Popeye's/dsl, RaceWay/dsl, ⅱ Baytown Seafood, Jack-in-the-Box, KFC/Taco Bell, Sonic, ⊡ Ⓗ, Houston East RV Park, RV Service, vet
796	frontage rd, **N** 🛢 Chevron/Phillips/Chemical Refinery
795	Sjolander Rd
793	N Main St, **S** 🛢 Valero/Hartz Chicken/dsl/24hr
792	Garth Rd, **N** 🛢 Chevron/dsl, ⅱ Cracker Barrel, Denny's, Jack-in-the-Box, Red Lobster, Richard's Cajun, Sonic, Starbucks, Tuscany Italian, Waffle House, Whataburger, 🛏 Comfort Suites, Days Inn, EconoLodge, Hampton Inn, La Quinta, SpringHill Suites, ⊡ Buick/GMC, Chrysler/Jeep/Dodge, Honda, Hyundai, Kia, Lincoln, Nissan, O'Reilly Parts, Toyota/Scion, Walgreens, **S** 🛢 RaceWay/dsl, Shell/dsl, ⅱ Bravos's Mexican, Buffalo Wild Wings, Carino's Italian, Chili's, Chinese Buffet, McDonald's, Olive Garden, Outback Steaks, Pizza Hut/Taco Bell, Popeye's, Subway, Tortuga Mexican, Wendy's, 🛏 Candlewood Suites, Palace Inn, Sleep Inn, ValuePlace Hotel, ⊡ Ⓗ, $General, JC Penney, Kohl's, Macy's, Marshall's, Michael's, Sears/auto, Tuesday Morning, Verizon
791	John Martin Rd, **S** ⅱ Cheddars, ⊡ Cadillac/Chevrolet, Ford
790	Ellis School Rd, **N** 🛏 Super 8
789	Thompson Rd, **N** 🛢 ❤Loves/McDonald's/dsl/scales/@, Valero/dsl, **S** 🛢 ⚜FLYING J/Denny's/dsl/LP/scales/RV dump/24hr, TA/SpeedCo Lube/dsl/rest./24hr/scales/@, ⊡ Blue Beacon
788.5mm	🆁🆂 eb, full 🚻 facilities, ⅱ, 🚶, litter barrels, petwalk
788	sp 330 (from eb), to Baytown
787	sp 330, Crosby-Lynchburg Rd, to Highlands, **N** 🛢 Texaco/Domino's/dsl, ⊡ RV Camping (1mi), **S** 🛢 Phillips 66/dsl, ⅱ Four Corners BBQ, ⊡ to San Jacinto SP, camping
786.5mm	San Jacinto River
786	Monmouth Dr
785	Magnolia Ave, to Channelview, **N** 🛢 Shell/dsl, **S** 🛢 Exxon/dsl, truckwash
784	Cedar Lane, Bayou Dr, **N** 🛢 Valero/dsl, 🛏 Budget Lodge, Knights Inn
783	Sheldon Rd, **N** 🛢 Shell, Texaco/dsl, Valero, ⅱ Burger King, Church's, Jack-in-the-Box, Pizza Hut, Popeye's, Subway, Taco Bell, Whataburger, 🛏 Best Value, Days Inn, Economy Inn, Holiday Inn, Leisure Inn, Parkway Inn, Travelers Inn, ⊡ Advance Parts, AutoZone, Discount Tire, Family$, FoodFair, USPO, **S** 🛢 Chevron, Texaco/dsl, ⅱ

H O U S T O N

Exit	Services
783	Continued
	McDonald's, Scottish Inn, Wendy's, 🛏 Deluxe Inn, Fairfield Inn, Scottish Inn
782	Dell-Dale Ave, **N** 🛢 Exxon, 🛏 Dell-Dale Motel, Economy Inn, Palace Inn, ⊡ Ⓗ, **S** ⊡ Channelview RV Ctr
781b	Market St, **N** 🛏 Clarion, ⊡ Ⓗ
781a	TX 8, Sam Houston Pkwy
780	(779a from wb) Uvalde Rd, Freeport St, **N** 🛢 Chevron/dsl, Texaco, ⅱ Capt Tom's Seafood, China Dragon, IHOP, Jack-in-the-Box, KFC, Panda Express, Shipley Donuts, Sonic, Subway, Taco Bell, Taco Cabana, ⊡ Ⓗ, Aamco, Ace Hardware, $Tree, Office Depot, **S** ⅱ Baytown Seafood, Golden Corral, ⊡ Firestone, Home Depot, Sam's Club/gas, Walmart/McDonald's
779b	**N** 🛢 Mobil, Valero, ⅱ China Dragon, IHOP, Jack-in-the-Box, KFC, Panda Express, Shipley's Donuts, Sonic, Subway, Taco Cabana, 🛏 Interstate Motel, ⊡ Ace Hardware, $Tree, Office Depot
778b	Normandy St, **N** 🛢 Shell/Jack-in-the-Box, Texaco/dsl, ⅱ Golden Corral, 🛏 La Quinta, **S** 🛢 Citgo, Shell, ⅱ Church's, 🛏 Normandy Inn, Scottish Inn, ⊡ Verizon
778a	FM 526, Federal Rd, Pasadena, **N** 🛢 Shell, ⅱ Burger King, Casa Ole Mexican, Denny's, Jack-in-the-Box, KFC/Taco Bell, Pizza Hut, Popeye's, Subway, Wendy's, 🛏 La Quinta, ⊡ CVS Drug, HEB Foods, Kroger/gas, Target, **S** ⅱ Joe's Crabshack, McDonald's, Sonic, 🛏 Lamplight Inn, ⊡ AutoZone, Discount Tire
776b	John Ralston Rd, Holland Ave, **N** 🛢 Chevron, ⅱ Chinese Buffet, Denny's, Fuddruckers, Luby's, Mambo Seafood, Pappasito's Cantina, Rancho Del Viejo, Subway, 🛏 Best Western, Candlewood Suites, Comfort Inn, Day Inn, La Quinta, Palace Inn, Regency Inn, ⊡ Family$, Fiesta Foods, Kroger/deli, NTB, **S** same as 778
776a	Mercury Dr, **N** ⅱ Aranda's Mexican, Burger King, McDonald's, TX Grill, 🛏 Baymont Inn, Best Western, Days Inn, Premier Inn, Quality Inn, ⊡ Volvo Trucks, **S** 🛢 Shell/dsl, Valero, ⅱ Chili's, Chula's Mexican, Cici's Pizza, James Coney Island, Murphy's Deli, Pappa's Seafood, Peking Bo Chinese, Saltgrass Steaks, 🛏 Holiday Inn Express, Super 8, ⊡ CVS Drug, O'Reilly Parts
775b a	I-610
774	Gellhorn (from eb) Blvd, Anheuser-Busch Brewery
773b	McCarty St, **N** 🛢 Mobil/dsl, Shell
773a	US 90A, N Wayside Dr, **N** 🛢 Speedy/dsl, ⅱ Jack-in-the-Box, Whataburger, **S** 🛢 Chevron/dsl, Shell, Texaco, ⅱ Church's, ⊡ HEB Foods, NAPA, dsl repair
772	Kress St, Lathrop St, **N** 🛢 Conoco, Exxon, ⅱ Popeye's, **S** ⅱ Burger King, Seafood Rest.
771b	Lockwood Dr, **N** 🛢 Chevron/Subway/dsl, ⅱ McDonald's, ⊡ Family$, Walgreens, **S** 🛢 Shell/dsl, 🛏 Palace Inn
771a	Waco St
770c	US 59 N
770b	Jenson St, Meadow St, Gregg St
770a	US 59 S, to Victoria
769c	McKee St, Hardy St, Nance St downtown
769a	Smith St (from wb), to downtown
768b a	I-45, N to Dallas, S to Galveston
767b	Taylor St
767a	Studemont Dr, Yale St, Heights Blvd, **S** 🛢 Shell/dsl, ⅱ Arby's, Chili's, Jason's Deli, Subway, ⊡ Petsmart, Staples, Target
766	(from wb), Heights Blvd, Yale St

⌖ INTERSTATE 10 CONT'D

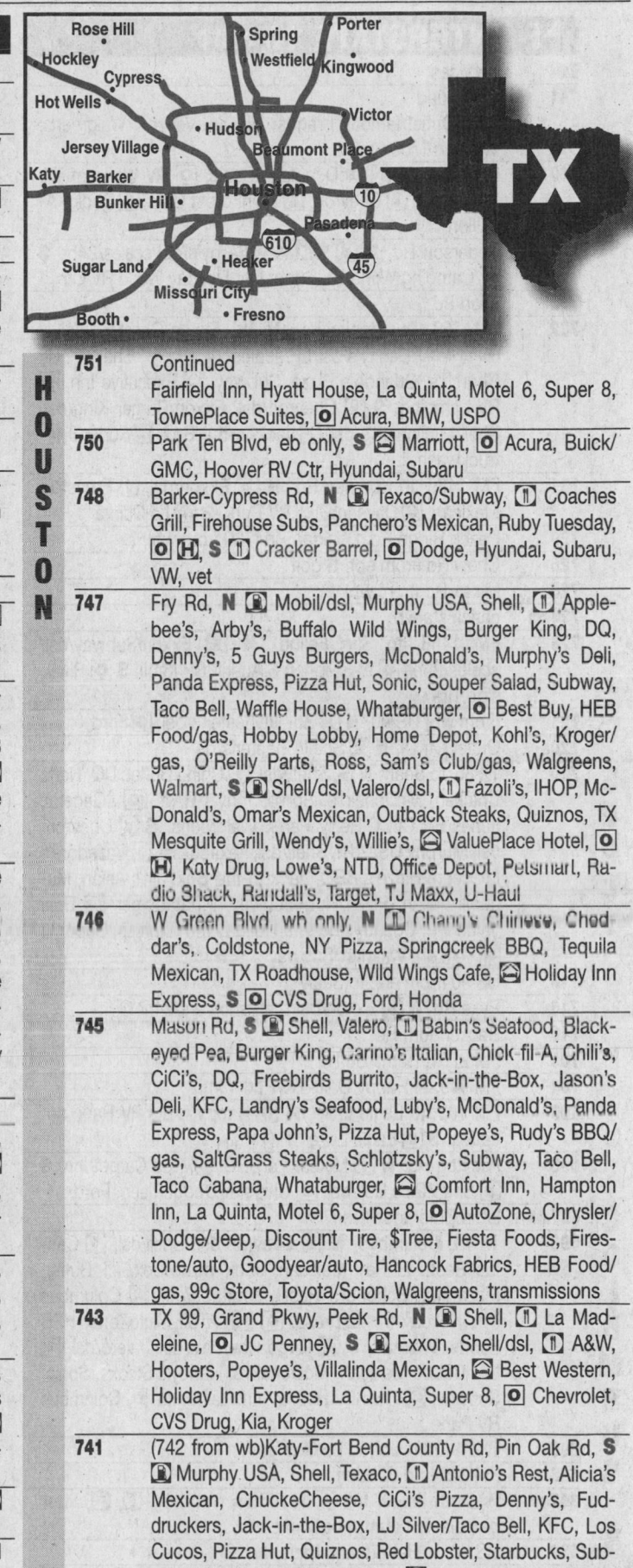

Exit	Services
765b	N Durham Dr, N Shepherd Dr, **N** 🅖 Shell/dsl, 🍴 Wendy's, 🏨 Howard Johnson, 🅞 vet, **S** 🅖 Valero/dsl
765a	TC Jester Blvd, **N** 🍴 Wendy's, **S** 🅖 Exxon/dsl, Texaco/dsl, 🍴 Quiznos, Starbucks
764	Westcott St, Washington Ave, Katy Rd, **N** 🍴 Denny's, 🏨 Comfort Inn, **S** 🅖 Chevron, 🍴 IHOP, 🏨 Scottish Inn
763	I-610
762	Silber Rd, Post Oak Rd, **N** 🍴 Cafe Adobe, Panda Express, Quiznos, Red Robin, SteaKountry, Wings&More, 🅞 Dodge, Firestone/auto, **S** 🍴 Jack-in-the-Box, 🏨 Crowne Plaza, Holiday Inn Express, Plaza Hotel
761b	Antoine Rd, **N** 🍴 Hunan Chinese, **S** 🅖 Exxon, 🍴 Subway, 🅞 CVS Drug
761a	Wirt Rd, Chimney Rock Rd, **S** 🅖 Exxon/TCBY, Shell/dsl, 🅞 CVS Drug
760	Bingle Rd, Voss Rd, **N** 🍴 Hunan Chef, Starbucks, Subway, 🅞 AT&T, Home Depot, **S** 🅖 Citgo/dsl, 🍴 Avalon Diner, Goode's TX BBQ, Mason Jar Rest., Pappy's Café, SaltGrass Steaks, Sweet Tomatoes, 🅞 🏥, vet
759	Campbell Rd (from wb), same as 758b
758b	Blalock Rd, Campbell Rd, **N** 🍴 Ciro's Italian, Sonic, 🅞 Adam's Automotive, Lowe's, LubeStop, Mail It, cleaners, **S** 🅖 Chevron/McDonald's/dsl, 🅞 🏥 Kroger, Walgreens
758a	Bunker Hill Rd, **N** 🅖 Exxon, 🍴 Arby's, Boudreaux's Cajun, CiCi's, Dennys, Five Guys Burgers, Olive Garden, Panda Express, Quiznos, 🅞 Best Buy, Costco/gas, HEB Foods, Lowe's, Michael's, PepBoys, Radio Shack, **S** 🍴 Baskin-Robbins, Ciro's Italian, Denis Seafood, Firehouse Subs, Guadalajara Mexican, Kobe Japanese, Lupe Tortilla, Subway, 🏨 Memorial Inn, 🅞 Marshall's, Ross
757	Gessner Rd, **N** 🍴 Chili's, Cici's, DQ, McDonald's, Olive Garden, Schlotsky's, Taco Bell, SteaKountry, Wendy's, Whataburger, 🅞 CVS Drug, Hobby Lobby, Home Depot, NAPA, Petsmart, Radio Shack, Sam's Club/gas, U-Haul, **S** 🍴 Cheesecake Factory, 59 Diner, Fuddrucker's, Goode Co. Seafood, Jason's Deli, La Peep, Pappasito's, Pappadeaux Seafood, Perry's Steaks, Smoothie King, Starbucks, Taste of TX, 🏨 Westin Hotel, 🅞 🏥, Firestone/auto, Ford, Macy's, Office Depot, Target, mall
756	TX 8, Sam Houston **Tollway**
755	Willcrest Rd, **N** 🅞 Buick, Discount Tire, Mazda, Lincoln, NTB, U-Haul, **S** 🅖 Citgo/dsl, Exxon, Phillips 66/dsl, 🍴 Brenner's Steaks, Brunch Kafe, Carabbas, Denny's, IHOP, McDonald's, Subway, 🏨 Extended Stay America, Hampton Inn, La Quinta, Sheraton
754	Kirkwood Rd, **N** 🏨 Embassy Suites, 🅞 Lexus, Lincoln, Toyota/Scion, same as 753b, **S** 🅖 Shell, 🍴 Carrabba's, La Fiesta, Murphy's Deli, Shipley Do-Nuts, Spicy Pickle, Starbucks, Taco Cabana, Whataburger, 🅞 Chevrolet
753b	Dairy-Ashford Rd, **N** 🅞 Buick, Chrysler/Dodge, Infiniti, Lexus, Nissan, Toyota, Volvo, **S** 🅖 Exxon/dsl, 🍴 Beck's Prime Rest., Hibachi Grill, Subway, TX Cattle Steaks, 🏨 Courtyard, Hilton Garden, Holiday Inn Express, 🅞 Cadillac, Chevrolet, Urgent Care
753a	Eldridge Pkwy, **N** 🅖 Conoco/dsl, 🏨 Omni Hotel, **S** 🅖 Valero/dsl, 🅞 Kwik Kar
751	TX 6, to Addicks, **N** 🅖 Shell, 🍴 Bro.'s Pizza, Cattlegard Rest., Waffle House, 🏨 Crowne Plaza, Drury Inn, Homewood Suites, Red Roof Inn, Studio 6, 🅞 Sam's Club/gas, **S** 🍴 North China, Subway, 🏨 Extended Stay Deluxe,

Exit	Services
751	Continued Fairfield Inn, Hyatt House, La Quinta, Motel 6, Super 8, TownePlace Suites, 🅞 Acura, BMW, USPO
750	Park Ten Blvd, eb only, **S** 🏨 Marriott, 🅞 Acura, Buick/GMC, Hoover RV Ctr, Hyundai, Subaru
748	Barker-Cypress Rd, **N** 🅖 Texaco/Subway, 🍴 Coaches Grill, Firehouse Subs, Panchero's Mexican, Ruby Tuesday, 🅞 🏥, **S** 🍴 Cracker Barrel, 🅞 Dodge, Hyundai, Subaru, VW, vet
747	Fry Rd, **N** 🅖 Mobil/dsl, Murphy USA, Shell, 🍴 Applebee's, Arby's, Buffalo Wild Wings, Burger King, DQ, Denny's, 5 Guys Burgers, McDonald's, Murphy's Deli, Panda Express, Pizza Hut, Sonic, Souper Salad, Subway, Taco Bell, Waffle House, Whataburger, 🅞 Best Buy, HEB Food/gas, Hobby Lobby, Home Depot, Kohl's, Kroger/gas, O'Reilly Parts, Ross, Sam's Club/gas, Walgreens, Walmart, **S** 🅖 Shell/dsl, Valero/dsl, 🍴 Fazoli's, IHOP, McDonald's, Omar's Mexican, Outback Steaks, Quiznos, TX Mesquite Grill, Wendy's, Willie's, 🏨 ValuePlace Hotel, 🅞 🏥, Katy Drug, Lowe's, NTD, Office Depot, Petsmart, Radio Shack, Randall's, Target, TJ Maxx, U-Haul
746	W Green Blvd, wb only, **N** 🍴 Chang's Chinese, Cheddar's, Coldstone, NY Pizza, Springcreek BBQ, Tequila Mexican, TX Roadhouse, Wild Wings Cafe, 🏨 Holiday Inn Express, **S** 🅞 CVS Drug, Ford, Honda
745	Mason Rd, **S** 🅖 Shell, Valero, 🍴 Babin's Seafood, Black-eyed Pea, Burger King, Carino's Italian, Chick-fil-A, Chili's, CiCi's, DQ, Freebirds Burrito, Jack-in-the-Box, Jason's Deli, KFC, Landry's Seafood, Luby's, McDonald's, Panda Express, Papa John's, Pizza Hut, Popeye's, Rudy's BBQ/gas, SaltGrass Steaks, Schlotzsky's, Subway, Taco Bell, Taco Cabana, Whataburger, 🏨 Comfort Inn, Hampton Inn, La Quinta, Motel 6, Super 8, 🅞 AutoZone, Chrysler/Dodge/Jeep, Discount Tire, $Tree, Fiesta Foods, Firestone/auto, Goodyear/auto, Hancock Fabrics, HEB Food/gas, 99c Store, Toyota/Scion, Walgreens, transmissions
743	TX 99, Grand Pkwy, Peek Rd, **N** 🅖 Shell, 🍴 La Madeleine, 🅞 JC Penney, **S** 🅖 Exxon, Shell/dsl, 🍴 A&W, Hooters, Popeye's, Villalinda Mexican, 🏨 Best Western, Holiday Inn Express, La Quinta, Super 8, 🅞 Chevrolet, CVS Drug, Kia, Kroger
741	(742 from wb)Katy-Fort Bend County Rd, Pin Oak Rd, **S** 🅖 Murphy USA, Shell, Texaco, 🍴 Antonio's Rest, Alicia's Mexican, ChuckeCheese, CiCi's Pizza, Denny's, Fuddruckers, Jack-in-the-Box, LJ Silver/Taco Bell, KFC, Los Cucos, Pizza Hut, Quiznos, Red Lobster, Starbucks, Subway, TGIFriday's, Whataburger, 🏨 Best Western, Comfort Suites, Hilton Garden, Residence Inn, SpringHill Suites, 🅞 🏥, BassPro Shops, Discount Tire, HEB/dsl, Katy

gas = gas   food = food   lodging = lodging   other = other   Rs = rest stop   Copyright 2014 - The NEXT Exit

TX

INTERSTATE 10 CONT'D

Exit	Services
741	Continued
	Mills Outlet/famous brands, Nissan, Verizon, Walgreens, Walmart/McDonald's
740	FM 1463, N food McDonald's, Sonic, other RV World of TX, Yamaha, S gas Chevron, food RainForest Café, other Books-A-Million
737	Pederson Rd, N gas Loves/Arby's/dsl/scales/24hr, S other Camping World RV Super Ctr, Holiday World RV Ctr
735	Igloo Rd
732	FM 359, to Brookshire, N gas Exxon/Chester's/dsl, / FLYING J/Denny's/dsl/LP/scales/24hr/@, Shell, food Church's, Orlando's Pizza, Subway, lodging Executive Inn, other RV camping, S gas Chevron/dsl, Exxon/Burger King/dsl, Shell/McDonald's/dsl, food Jack-in-the-Box, lodging Super 8, other truckwash
731	FM 1489, to Koomey Rd, N gas Exxon/dsl, food Ernesto's Mexican, lodging Days Inn, other RV Park, S lodging La Quinta
729	Peach Ridge Rd, Donigan Rd (730 from wb)
726	Chew Rd (from eb), S golf
725	Mlcak Rd (from wb)
724mm	check sta wb
723	FM 1458, to San Felipe, N gas Exxon/Subway/dsl/scales/24hr, other to Stephen F Austin SP (3mi), S other Riverside Tire
721	(from wb) US 90, N gas Shell/Chester's/dsl, other Ford
720a	Outlet Ctr Dr, N gas Shell/Chester's/dsl
720	TX 36, to Sealy, N gas Shell/dsl, food China Buffet, DQ, Hartz Chicken, McDonald's, Sonic, Tony's Rest., other $General, Jones RV Ctr, O'Reilly Parts, Walgreens, S gas Chevron/dsl, Murphy USA/dsl, Shell/dsl, Texaco/dsl, food Cazadore's Mexican, Hinze's BBQ, Jack-in-the-Box, Jin's Asian, Maribelli Italian, Pizza Hut, Subway, Whataburger, lodging Best Value Inn, Countryside Inn, Holiday Inn Express, Super 8, other Verizon, Walmart/Subway
718	US 90 (from eb), to Sealy
716	Pyka Rd, N gas Exxon/dsl/rest./showers/24hr/@
713	Beckendorff Rd
709	FM 2761, Bernardo Rd
704	FM 949, N Happy Oaks RV Park (3mi)
699	FM 102, to Eagle Lake, N other Happy Oaks RV Park, antiques, S other Eagle Lake SP (14mi)
698	Alleyton Rd, N food Mikeska's BBQ, lodging Red Carpet Inn, S gas Shell/Taco Bell/dsl, other Chrysler/Dodge/Jeep, Ford
697mm	Little Colorado River
696	TX 71, Columbus, N gas Chevron/dsl, Shell/dsl, food Cantus Rest., El Ray Mexican, Jack-in-the-Box, #1 Buffet, Pizza Hut, Schobel's Rest., Whataburger, lodging Columbus Inn, Holiday Inn Express, other H, AT&T, AutoZone, HEB Foods, Walmart, S gas Citgo/Church's/dsl, Valero/dsl, food Los Cabos Mexican, McDonald's, Nancy's Steaks, Sonic, Subway, lodging Country Hearth Inn, LaQuinta, other Columbus RV Park
695	TX 71 (from wb), to La Grange
693	FM 2434, to Glidden
692mm	Rs both lanes, full facilities, vending, litter barrels, RV dump, petwalk
689	US 90, to Hattermann Lane, N KOA
682	FM 155, to Wiemar, N gas Exxon/dsl, Shell/BBQ/dsl, food DQ, McDonald's, Subway/Texas Burger, lodging Days Inn, other H, $General, Tire Pros, S gas Chevron/dsl/24hr, Loves
682	Continued
	/Chester's/Wendy's/dsl/scales/24hr, other Buick/Chevrolet/GMC
678mm	E Navidad River
677	US 90
674	US 77, Schulenburg, N gas Chevron/dsl, Exxon/dsl, food McDonald's, Oak Ridge Smokehouse, lodging Executive Inn, Oak Ridge Motel, other Ford, Potter Country Store, S gas Citgo, Shell/dsl, Valero/Subway, food DQ, Frank's Rest., Guadalajara Mexican, Paddy's TX Kitchen, Whataburger, lodging Best Western, other $General, Schulenberg RV Park
672mm	W Navidad River
668	FM 2238, to Engle
661	TX 95, FM 609, to Flatonia, N gas Citgo/dsl, food Joel's BBQ, San Jose Mexican, other Flatonia RV Ranch (1mi), S gas Exxon/dsl, Shell/McDonald's/Grumpy's Rest./motel/dsl, Valero, food DQ, lodging Carefree Inn, other $General, NAPA
658mm	Rs both lanes, tables, litter barrels
653	US 90, Waelder, N gas Shell/dsl/cafe
649	TX 97, to Waelder
642	TX 304, to Gonzales
637	FM 794, to Harwood
632	US 90/183, to Gonzales, N gas Loves/Subway/dsl/scales/24hr, lodging Coachway Inn (2mi), S gas Shell/Buc-ee's/dsl, other to Palmetto SP, camping
630mm	San Marcos River
628	TX 80, to Luling, N gas Exxon (2mi), Valero/Church's/dsl/24hr, food DQ (2mi), other H, Riverbend RV Park
625	Darst Field Rd
624.5mm	Smith Creek
621mm	weigh sta, both lanes
620	FM 1104
619mm	Rs both lanes, full facilities, petwalk
617	FM 2438, to Kingsbury
615	New exit
614.5mm	Mill Creek
612	US 90
611mm	Geronimo Creek
610	TX 123, to San Marcos, N gas Exxon/dsl, Shell/Subway/dsl, food Bella Sera Italian, Chili's, IHOP, Los Cucos Mexican, lodging Comfort Inn, Days Inn, Hampton Inn, Holiday Inn Express, other Carters Tires, S gas Valero/dsl, food Taco Cabana, other H
609	TX 123, Austin St, S gas Phillips 66/dsl, other Chevrolet, Home Depot
607	TX 46, FM 78, to New Braunfels, N gas Valero/Jack-in-the-Box/dsl, lodging Motel 6, S gas Chevron/dsl, Exxon/DQ/dsl, Valero/dsl, food Bill Miller BBQ, Dixie Grille, McDonald's, Whataburger, lodging La Quinta, Super 8, other Chrysler/Dodge
605	FM 464, N other Twin Palms RV Park
605mm	Guadalupe River
604	FM 725, to Lake McQueeney, N gas Loves/Arby's/dsl/scales/24hr, other Explore USA RV Ctr, Twin Palms RV Park
603	US 90 E, US 90A, to Seguin, N other Explore USA RV Sales
601	FM 775, to New Berlin, N gas Chevron/Subway/dsl/scales/24hr
600	Schwab Rd
599	FM 465, to Marion
599mm	Santa Clara Creek
597	Santa Clara Rd, N auto racetrack
595	Zuehl Rd
594mm	Cibolo Creek

INTERSTATE 10 CONT'D

Exit	Services
593	FM 2538, Trainer Hale Rd, **N** 🅶 Texaco/dsl, 🅾 tires, **S** 🅶 Exxon/Lucille's Rest./dsl/24hr
593mm	Woman Hollering Creek
591	FM 1518, to Schertz, **N** Alamo Trvl Ctr/Shell/dsl, 🅾 repair
589	Pfeil Rd, Graytown Rd
589mm	Salatrillo Creek
587	LP 1604, Randolph AFB, to Universal City
585.5mm	Escondido Creek
585	FM 1516, to Converse, **N** 🅶 Shell/Church's/dsl/scales/24hr, 🛏 Best Western, **S** 🅾 Kenworth, Peterbilt/GMC/Freightliner
585mm	Martinez Creek
583	Foster Rd, **N** 🅶 ⓕFLYING J/Denny's/dsl/LP/scales/24hr/@, Valero/Subway/dsl/24hr, 🍴 Jack-in-the-Box, 🛏 La Quinta, 🅾 Blue Beacon, Speedco Lube, T&W Tire, Tire Mart, **S** 🅶 TA/Chevron/Burger King/Pizza Hut/Popeye's/dsl/24hr/@
582.5mm	Rosillo Creek
582	Ackerman Rd, Kirby, **N** 🅶 🚉/Subway/dsl/scales/24hr, 🅾 Blue Beacon, **S** 🅶 Petro/Iron Skillet/dsl/scales/24hr/@, 🍴 El Rodeo Mexican, 🛏 Knights Inn, 🅾 Petrolube, Blue Beacon
581	I-410
580	LP 13, WW White Rd, **N** 🅶 Chevron/dsl, Fina/dsl, 🍴 El Jacalito, La Playa Seafood, Wendy's, 🛏 Motel 6, Red Roof Inn, Rodeway Inn, 🅾 RV camping, tires, **S** 🅶 Exxon/dsl, 🍴 Bill Miller BBQ, La Vina Mexican, Lazaritas Mexican, McDonald's, Popeye's, Pizza Hut, Sonic, Subway, 🛏 EconoLodge, Quality Inn, Rosepark Inn, Super 8, 🅾 $General, Ford/Volvo Trucks, tires/repair
579	Houston St, **N** 🅶 Valero/dsl, 🛏 Travelodge, **S** 🅶 Chevron, 🛏 Comfort Inn, Days Inn, Passport Inn
578	Pecan Valley Dr, ML King Dr, **N** gas
577	US 87 S, to Roland Ave, **S** 🍴 Whataburger, 🛏 Super 8
576	New Braunfels Ave, Gevers St, **S** 🅶 Valero, 🍴 McDonald's
575	Pino St, Hackberry St, **S** 🍴 Little Red Barn Steaks, Pizza Hut
574	I-37, US 281
573	Probandt St, **N** 🍴 Jack-in-the-Box, Miller's BBQ, **S** 🅶 Valero, 🅾 to SA Missions HS, tires
572	**I-10 and I-35 run together 3 mi. See Interstate 35, exits 156-154a**
570	no services
569c	Santa Rosa St, downtown, to Our Lady of the Lake U
568	spur 421, Culebra Ave, Bandera Ave, **S** to St Marys U
567	Lp 345, Fredericksburg Rd (from eb upper level accesses I-35 S, I-10 E, US 87 S, lower level accesses I-35 N)
566b	Fresno Dr, **S** 🅶 Exxon, 🛏 Galaxy Inn
566a	West Ave, **N** 🅶 Exxon, 🍴 DQ, Subway, Whataburger, 🅾 CarCare
565c	(from wb), access to same as 565 a b, **S** 🅶 Shell, 🍴 Guadalahara Mexican, Starbucks, 🛏 La Quinta
565b	Vance Jackson Rd, **N** 🅶 Murphy USA, 🍴 Bill Miller BBQ, IHOP, 🛏 Comfort Inn, Days Inn, EconoLodge, 🅾 Walmart, **S** 🅶 Shell, 🛏 La Quinta
565a	Crossroads Blvd, Balcone's Heights, **N** 🅶 Exxon, Shell/dsl, 🍴 Denny's, Whataburger, 🛏 Comfort Suites, Howard Johnson, Rodeway Inn, **S** 🍴 Dave&Buster's, El Pollo Loco, McDonald's, 🛏 SpringHill Suites, Super 8, 🅾 Fire

565a	Continued stone/auto, Mazda, Office Depot, RV Ctr, Target, Toyota, mall, transmissions
564b a	I-410, services off of I-410 W, Fredericksburg Rd
563	Callaghan Rd, **N** 🅶 Valero, 🍴 Las Palapas Mexican, Philly Connection, Subway, 🛏 Embassy Suites, Marriott, 🅾 $General, Ford, Lexus, Mazda, Sun Harvest Foods, Toyota, **S** 🅶 Exxon, 🍴 Mamacita's Rest., 🅾 Lowe's
561	Wurzbach Rd, **N** 🅶 Texaco/dsl, 🍴 Bolo's Grille, County Line BBQ, Egg&I, Fuddrucker's, Honeybaked Ham, Jason's Deli, Pappasito's Cantina, Popeye's, Quiznos, Sea Island Shrimphouse, Taste Of China, TX Land&Cattle, Wasabi Grill, 🛏 Homewood Suites, Hyatt Place, Knights Inn, Omni Hotel, Staybridge Suites, Studio+, 🅾 AutoZone, BigLots, Ford, HEB Food/gas, Office Depot, Toyota/Scion, **S** 🅶 Shell/dsl, 🍴 Alamo Café, Arby's, Benihana, Chester's Burgers, China Sea, Church's, Denny's, El Taco Tote, IHOP, Jack-in-the-Box, Mamma Margie's Mexican, McDonald's, Pizza Hut, Taco Bell, Wendy's, 🛏 Baymont Inn, Best Western, Candlewood Suites, Drury Inn, Holiday Inn Express, La Quinta, Motel 6, Residence Inn, Sloop Inn, 🅾 🄷, CarMax
560b	frontage rd (from eb), **N** 🍴 Water St Seafood
560a	Huebner Rd, **N** 🍴 Carrabba's, Champp's, La Madeleine, Macaroni Grill, On the Border, Panera Bread, SaltGrass Steaks, 🅾 Acura, Cadillac/Hummer, Chrysler/Jeep/Dodge, Old Navy, Ross, Smart Car, **S** 🅶 Chevron, Exxon, 🍴 Burger King, Cracker Barrel, Jim's Rest., 🛏 Days Inn, Hampton Inn, Homestead Village
559	Lp 335, US 87, Fredericksburg Rd, **N** 🍴 Brew Wok, La Madeleine, Macaroni Grill, On-the-Border, Outback Steaks, Panera Bread, Pearl Inn, Saltgrass Steaks, Starbucks, 🅾 Acura, Ross Old Navy, **S** 🅶 Shell, Texaco, 🍴 Cracker Barrel, Jack-in-the-Box, Krispy Kreme, 🛏 Days Inn, Hampton Inn, HomeGate Studios, Motel 6, SpringHill Suttes, 🅾 Infinity
558	De Zavala Rd, **N** 🅶 Chevron, Shell/Subway, 🍴 Bill Miller BBQ, Burger King, Carrabba's, Chick-fil-A, Chili's, Joe's Crabshack, KFC/Taco Bell, Logan's Roadhouse, McDonald's, Outback Steaks, Papa Murphy's, Sonic, Taco Cabana, The Earl of Sandwich, Wendy's, 🛏 Super 8, 🅾 GNC, HEB Food/gas, Home Depot, Hyundai, Marshall's, PetCo, Petsmart, Steinmart, Target, **S** 🍴 Cracker Barrel, IHOP, Schlotzsky's, 🛏 Hampton Inn, Sleep Inn, SpringHill Suites, Studio6, 🅾 Buick, Discount Tire, Sam's Club, Walmart
557	Spur 53, Univ of TX at San Antonio, **N** 🅶 Exxon/dsl, 🛏 Best Western, EconoLodge, Howard Johnson, Super 8, 🅾 Audi, Chevrolet, Hyundai, Jaguar/Mazerati/Ferrari, **S**

vertical side labels: KIRBY, SAN ANTONIO, SAN ANTONIO

TX

SAN ANTONIO

⭧🅴 INTERSTATE 10 CONT'D

Exit	Services
557	Continued
	🍽 A&W/LJ Silver, Cici's Pizza, Huhot Chinese, IHOP, Matamoro's Cantina, My Sam Chinese, Quiznos, TGIFriday's, Zio's Italian, Whataburger, 🅞 Costco/gas, Land Rover, Sams Club/gas, Walmart
556b	frontage rd
556a	to Anderson Lp, S 🛏 Comfort Inn, 🅞 to Seaworld
555	La Quintera Pkwy, N 🍽 Chick-fil-A, Little Italy, McDonald's/playplace, Mimi's Cafe, Red Robin, 🛏 Courtyard, Residence Inn, 🅞 Bass Pro Shops, Best Buy, Dick's, JC Penney, Lowe's, Ross, Target, S 🍽 Olive Garden, RedLobster, 🛏 Drury Inn, La Quinta, Motel 6, 🅞 Honda, to La Cantera Pkwy
554	Camp Bullis Rd, N 🅖 Citgo, 🍽 TGIFriday's, 🅞 Lowe's, Old Navy, Russell CP, TJ Maxx, S 🅖 Shell, 🛏 Rodeway Inn
551	Boerne Stage Rd (from wb), to Leon Springs, N 🅖 Shamrock/dsl, 🍽 Rudy's BBQ, Sonic, S 🍽 Las Palapas Mexican, Longhorns Rest., Pappa Nacho's, Quiznos, Starbucks, 🅞 GNC, HEB Foods/gas, vet
550	FM 3351, Ralph Fair Rd, N 🅖 Exxon/McDonald's/dsl, Valero/dsl, 🍽 Leon Creek Steaks, 🛏 La Quinta, S 🅖 Shell/Domino's/dsl
546	Fair Oaks Pkwy, Tarpon Dr, N 🍽 Papa John's, 🅞 American Dream RV Ctr, Harley-Davidson, vet, S 🅖 Chevron/dsl/café, Exxon/dsl/café, 🅞 Goodyear/auto, Hoover RV Ctr
543	Boerne Stage Rd, to Scenic LP Rd, N 🅖 Valero/Subway/dsl, 🛏 Caverns Inn/rest., Fairfield Inn, 🅞 Ancira RV Ctr, Buick/GMC, Chevrolet, Chrysler/Dodge/Jeep, Ford, NAPA, Buick/GMC, W&W Tires, to Cascade Caverns, S 🅞 Explore USA RV Ctr, Mercedes, Toyota/Scion
542	(from wb), N 🅖 Shamrock, 🍽 Domino's, Pizza Hut, Wendy's, 🅞 Alamo Fiesta RV Park, $Tree, same as 540
540	TX 46, to New Braunfels, N 🅖 Exxon/Taco Bell/dsl, Murphy USA, Shell/dsl/24hr, 🍽 Baskin-Robbins, Burger King, Church's, DQ, Denny's, El Rio Mexican, Guadalajara Mexican, Little Caesars, Marble Slab Creamery, Margarita's Café, Pizza Hut, Quiznos, Shanghai Chinese, Sonic, Taco Cabana, Wendy's, 🛏 Best Value, Comfort Inn, Key to the Hills Motel, 🅞 AutoZone, HEB Food/gas, Radio Shack, Walgreens, Walmart, S 🍽 Chili's, Starbucks, Whataburger, 🛏 Hampton Inn, 🅞 Home Depot
539	Johns Rd, N 🛏 La Quinta, S 🅖 Valero/dsl/LP
538mm	Cibolo Creek
538	Ranger Creek Rd
537	US 87, to Boerne
533	FM 289, Welfare, N 🍽 Po-Po Family Rest., 🅞 Top of the Hill RV Park (1mi)
532mm	Little Joshua Creek
531mm	🆁🆂 wb, tables, litter barrels
530mm	Big Joshua Creek
529.5mm	🆁🆂 eb, tables, litter barrels
527	FM 1621 (from wb), to Waring
526.5mm	Holiday Creek
524	TX 27, FM 1621, to Waring, N vet, S 🅖 Shell
523.5mm	Guadalupe River
523	US 87 N, to Comfort, N 🅖 Chevron/dsl, ❤Loves/McDonald's/Subway/dsl/scales/24hr, S 🅖 Exxon/dsl, 🍽 Comfort BBQ, DQ, 🛏 Executive Inn, 🅞 $General, RV Park/LP

KERRVILLE

Exit	Services
521.5mm	Comfort Creek
520	FM 1341, to Cypress Creek Rd
515mm	Cypress Creek
514mm	🆁🆂 both lanes, full ♿ facilities, vending, 🍽, 🅖, litter barrels, RV dump, petwalk, playground, wireless internet
508	TX 16, Kerrville, N 🅖 Exxon/dsl, 🅞 Buick/Cadillac/Chevrolet, RV camping, 0-2 mi S 🅖 Exxon, Shell/McDonald's/dsl/24hr, Stripes/dsl, Valero/dsl, 🍽 Acapulco Mexican, Bamboo Asian, Cracker Barrel, DQ, IHOP, KFC, Jack-in-the-Box, Little Caesars, McDonald's, Santo Coyote, Schlotzsky's, Sonic, Taco Bell, Taco Casa, 🛏 Best Value Inn, Best Western, Big Texas Inn, Comfort Inn, Days Inn, Hampton Inn, Holiday Inn Express, La Quinta, Motel 6, Super 8, Yo Ranch Hotel, 🅞 🏥, Advance Parts, AT&T, BigLots, $Tree, Hastings Books, Home Depot, Kerrville RV Ctr, Lowe's, NAPA, O'Reilly Parts, Walgreens, vet
505	FM 783, to Kerrville, S 🅖 Exxon/dsl, 3 mi S on TX 27 🅖 Chevron/dsl, Exxon, Phillips 66/dsl, Stripes/dsl, 🍽 Chili's, CiCi's, Culver's, DQ, Fuddruckers, Mamcita's, McDonald's, Pizza Hut, Quiznos, Starbucks, Sonic, Subway, Taco Casa, Wendy's, Whataburger, 🛏 Inn of the Hills, 🅞 AutoZone, Chrysler/Dodge/Jeep, Curves, CVS Drug, Discount Tire, $General, HEB Foods/gas, Walmart/McDonald's
503.5mm	scenic views both lanes, litter barrels
501	FM 1338, N 🅞 Buckhorn RV Resort, S 🅞 KOA (2mi)
497mm	🆁🆂 both lanes, tables, litter barrels
492	FM 479
490	TX 41
488	TX 27, to Ingram, Mountain Home
484	Midway Rd
477	US 290, to Fredericksburg
476.5mm	service rd eb
472	Old Segovia Rd
465	FM 2169, to Segovia, S 🅖 Phillips 66/rest./dsl, 🛏 EconoLodge/RV park
464.5mm	Johnson Fork Creek
462	US 83 S, to Uvalde
461mm	🆁🆂 eb, tables, litter barrels
460	(from wb), to Junction
459mm	🆁🆂 wb, tables, litter barrels
457	FM 2169, to Junction, N 🅖 Shell/dsl, S 🛏 Days Inn, 🅞 RV camping, S. Llano River SP
456.5mm	Llano River

JUNCTION

Exit	Services
456	US 83/377, Junction, N 🅖 Chevron/dsl, Fina/dsl, Valero/McDonald's/dsl/24hr, 🍽 Cooper's BBQ, JR's Rest., Tia Nina's Mexican, 🛏 Motel 6, S 🅖 Big Star/dsl, Exxon, Church's, Shell/dsl, 🍽 DQ, Isaack Rest., La Familia Mexican, Lum's BBQ, Sonic, Subway, 🛏 Best Western, Lazy T Motel, Legends Inn, Rodeway Inn, The Hills Motel, 🅞 🏥, Best Hardware, CarQuest, $General, Family$, KOA (.5mi), Plumley's Store, Radio Shack, Super S Foods, to S Llano River SP
452.5mm	Bear Creek
451	RM 2291, to Cleo Rd
448mm	North Creek
445	RM 1674, S camping
444.5mm	Stark Creek
442mm	Copperas Creek
442	RM 1674, to Ft McKavett, N to Ft McKavett SHS
439mm	N Llano River

➤🄴 INTERSTATE 10 CONT'D

Exit	Services
438	Lp 291 (from wb), to Roosevelt, same as 437
437	Lp 291 (from eb, no EZ return), to Roosevelt, **1 mi N** 🅖 Simon Bros Mercantile/dsl, 🅞 USPO
429	RM 3130, to Harrell
423mm	parking area both lanes, litter barrels
420	RM 3130, to Baker Rd
412	Allison Rd, RM 3130
404	RM 3130, RM 864, **N** to Ft McKavett St HS, **3 mi S** 🅖 Stripes/dsl, 🛏 Holiday Host Motel, 🅞 🄷
400	US 277, Sonora, **N** 🅖 Shell/dsl, 🍴 Sutton Co Steaks, 🛏 Days Inn, 🅞 vet, **S** 🅖 Chevron/dsl, Exxon/dsl, Fina/7-11/dsl, Stripes/dsl, 🍴 DQ, La Mexicana Rest., Pizza Hut, Sonic, Taco Grill, 🛏 Best Western, Comfort Inn, Economy Inn, 🅞 Alco, CarQuest, Family$, NAPA, USPO
399	(from eb) LP 467, Sonora, **N** 🛏 Days Inn, **S** 🅖 Chevron/dsl, Fina, Exxon/dsl, Stripes, 🍴 DQ, Subway, 🅞 🄷, RV camping
394mm	🆁🆂 both lanes, full ♿ facilities, 🄲, 🄰, litter barrel, pet-walk, RV dump
392	RM 1989, Caverns of Sonora Rd, **8 mi S** 🅞 Caverns of Sonora Camping, 🄲
388	RM 1312 (from wb)
381	RM 1312 (from eb)
372	Taylor Box Rd, **N** 🅖 Exxon/rest./dsl/scales/24hr, 🛏 Super 8, 🅞 Circle Bar RV Park, auto museum
368	LP 466, **N** same as 365 & 363
365	TX 163, Ozona, **N** 🅖 Chevron/dsl, Stripes/Godfather's/Taco Co/dsl, 🍴 DQ, Sonic, Subway, 🛏 Best Value Inn, Best Western, Economy Inn/RV Park, Hillcrest Inn, Holiday Inn Express, 🅞 🄷, Best Hardware, $General, NAPA, to David Crockett Mon, **S** 🅖 Chevron, 🍴 El Chato's
363	Lp 466, to Ozona
361	RM 2083, Pandale Rd
357mm	Eureka Draw
351mm	Howard Draw
350	FM 2398, to Howard Draw
349mm	parking area wb, litter barrels
346mm	parking area eb, litter barrels
343	TX 290 W, **S** Ft. Lancaster Historic Site
337	Live Oak Rd
336.5mm	Live Oak Creek
328	River Rd, Sheffield
327.5mm	Pecos River
325	TX 290, TX 349, to Iraan, Sheffield, **N** 🄷
320	frontage rd
314	frontage rd
309mm	🆁🆂 both lanes, full ♿ facilities, 🄲, 🄰, litter barrels, pet-walk, wireless internet
307	US 190, FM 305, to Iraan, **N** 🄷
298	RM 2886
294	FM 11, Bakersfield, **N** 🅖 Exxon, **S** 🅖 Chevron/café/dsl, 🅞 🄲
288	Ligon Rd, **N** many windmills
285	McKenzie Rd, **S** 🅞 Domaine Cordier Ste Genevieve Winery
279mm	🄰 eb, tables, litter barrels
277	FM 2023
273	US 67/385, to McCamey, 🄰 wb, tables, litter barrels
272	University Rd
264	Warnock Rd, **N** 🅞 Fort Stockton RV Park/BBQ/cafe

Exit	Services
261	US 290 W, US 385 S, **N** 🅖 Exxon/dsl, **1-2 mi S** 🅖 Stripes/dsl, 🛏 Budget Inn, Deluxe Inn, EconoLodge, 🍴 DQ, Pizza Hut, Sonic, Subway, 🅞 🄷, RV camping, to Big Bend NP
259b a	(259 from eb) TX 18, FM 1053, Ft Stockton, **N** 🅖 Apache Fuel Ctr/dsl, Fina/dsl, Shell/Burger King/dsl, 🅞 I-10 RV Park, tires
257	US 285, to Pecos, Ft Stockton, **N** 🅞 Comanche Land RV Park, golf, **S** 🅖 Chevron/dsl, Exxon/rest./dsl, Fina/dsl, Shell, 🍴 DQ, IHOP, KFC/Taco Bell, McDonald's, Pizza Hut, Pizza Pro, Sonic, Steak House, Subway, 🛏 Atrium Inn, Candlewood Suites, Days Inn, Hampton Inn, Quality Inn, Texan Inn, 🅞 Ace Hardware, AutoZone, Buick/Chevrolet, $General, Firestone/auto, Lowe's Foods, McKissick Tires, O'Reilly Parts, Radio Shack
256	to US 385 S, Ft Stockton, **N** 🅞 HillTop RV, **1 mi S** 🅖 Shell/dsl, 🍴 Dragon Buffet, Howard's Drive-In, K-Bob's Steaks, Subway, 🛏 Comfort Suites, Holiday Inn Express, Motel 6, Sleep Inn, Super 8, Swiss Clock Inn, 🅞 🄷, Ford, Walmart, to Ft Stockton Hist Dist, Big Bend NP, auto/RV repair, vet
253	FM 2037, to Belding
248	US 67, FM 1776, to Alpine, **S** to Big Bend NP
246	Firestone
241	Kennedy Rd
235	Mendel Rd
233mm	🆁🆂 both lanes, full ♿ facilities, 🄲, 🄰, litter barrels, pet-walk
229	Hovey Rd
222	Hoefs Rd
214	(from wb), FM 2448
212	TX 17, FM 2448, to Pecos, **N** 🄰, litter barrels, **S** 🅖 I-10 Fuel/café/dsl, Saddleback RV Camping
209	TX 17, **S** 🅞 to Balmorhea SP, to Davis Mtn SP, Ft Davis NHS
206	FM 2903, to Balmorhea, Toyah, **S** to Balmorhea SP
192	FM 3078, to Toyahvale, **S** 🅞 to Balmorhea SP
188	Giffin Rd
187	I-20, to Ft Worth, Dallas
186	I-10, E to San Antonio (from wb)
185mm	🄰 both lanes, tables, litter barrels
184	Springhills
181	Cherry Creek Rd, **S** 🅖 Chevron/dsl
176	TX 118, FM 2424, to Kent, **S** 🅞 to McDonald Observatory, Davis Mtn SP, Ft Davis
173	Hurd's Draw Rd
166	Boracho Sta
159	Plateau, **N** 🅖 Exxon/rest./dsl/24hr
153	Michigan Flat
146	Wild Horse Rd

SONORA · OZONA · FT STOCKTON

▲E INTERSTATE 10 CONT'D

TX **VAN HORN**

Exit	Services
146mm	weigh sta wb
145mm	[Rs] both lanes, full [&] facilities, [🏠] litter barrels, pet-walk, wireless internet
140b	Ross Dr, Van Horn, N [Q] Chevron/dsl, Exxon/dsl, ♥Loves/Subway/dsl/scales/24hr, [🏠] Days Inn, Desert Inn, Sands Motel/rest., [O] El Campo RV Park, repair, S [O] Mountain View RV Park/dump
140a	US 90, TX 54, Van Horn Dr, N [🏠] Hotel El Capitan, [O] [H] NAPA, S [Q] Exxon, ▦/Wendy's/dsl/scales/24hr, [↑] Papa's Pantry, [O] KOA, RV Dump, dsl/tire repair
138	Lp 10, to Van Horn, N [↑] Chuy's Rest., [🏠] Best Value Inn, Budget Inn, EconoLodge, King's Inn, Knights Inn, Motel 6, Ramada Ltd, Value Inn, [O] $General, Eagles Nest RV Park, Pueblo Foods, auto/dsl repair, city park, UPSO, visitor info, S [Q] Chevron/dsl/24hr, [↑] McDonald's, [🏠] Hampton Inn, Holiday Inn Express, Super 8, [O] tires/repair
137mm	weigh sta eb
136mm	scenic overlook wb, [🏠] litter barrels
135mm	Mountain/Central time zone line, Mountain/Central time zone line
133	(from wb)frontage rd
129	to Hot Wells, Allamore
108	to Sierra Blanca (from wb), same as 107
107	FM 1111, Sierra Blanca Ave, N [Q] Exxon/Subway/dsl/24hr, [O] truck/tire repair, USPO, to Hueco Tanks SP, S [Q] Chevron/dsl, [🏠] Americana Inn, [O] Stagecoach Trading Post
105	(106 from wb) Lp 10, Sierra Blanca, same as 107
102.5mm	insp sta eb
99	Lasca Rd, N [O][🏠] both lanes, [🏠] litter barrels, no restrooms
98mm	[🏠] eb, tables, litter barrels, no restrooms
95	frontage rd (from eb)
87	FM 34
85	Esperanza Rd
81	FM 2217
78	TX 20 W, to McNary
77mm	truck parking area wb
72	spur 148, to Ft Hancock, S [Q] Shell/dsl, [↑] Angie's Rest., [🏠] Ft Hancock Motel, [O] USPO
68	Acala Rd
55	Tornillo
51mm	[Rs] both lanes, full [&] facilities, [🏠] litter tables, petwalk
49	FM 793, Fabens, S [Q] FastTrac/dsl, [↑] Church's, Little Caesars, McDonald's, Subway, [🏠] Fabens Inn/Cafe, [O] Family$, San Eli Foods
42	FM 1110, to Clint, S [Q] Express/dsl, [↑] Cotton Eyed Joe's, Mamacita's Rest., [🏠] Adobe Inn, Cotton Valley Motel/RV Park/rest./dump, Super 8
37	FM 1281, Horizon Blvd, N [Q] ◆FLYING J/Denny's/dsl/scales/24hr/@, ♥Loves/Chester's/Subway/dsl/scales/24hr/@, [🏠] Americana Inn, [O] Freightliner, Speedco Lube, RV Camping, S [Q] Petro/Valero/Iron Skillet/Subway/dsl/scales/24hr/@, [↑] McDonald's, [🏠] Deluxe Inn, [O] Blue Beacon
35	Eastlake Blvd.
34	TX 375, Americas Ave, N [Q] Chevron/dsl, Valero/dsl, [🏠] Microtel, ValuePlace, [O] GMC, Mission RV Camping, Peterbilt, S [O] El Paso Museum of Hist
32	FM 659, Zaragosa Rd, N [Q] Fina/7-11, [↑] Arby's, Barrigos

EL PASO

32	Continued
	Mexican, BJ's Grill, Cheddar's, Chico's Tacos, Famous Daves, Furr's Buffet, Great American Steaks, IHOP, Krispy Kreme, LJ Silver/Taco Bell, Logan's Roadhouse, Macaroni Grill, Outback Steaks, Pei Wei, Peter Piper Pizza, San Francisco Oven, Sonic, Starbucks, Subway, Taco Bell, Village Inn, Whataburger, [🏠] Holiday Inn Express, [O] Chevrolet, Discount Tire, Kohl's, Lowe's, Michael's, Nissan, Office Depot, Ross, Walgreens, World Mkt, S [Q] Valero/dsl, [↑] Gallego's Mexican, [O] Volvo/Mack, city park, vet
30	Lee Trevino Dr, N [Q] Circle K, Exxon, [↑] Chili's, Denny's, Jack-in-the-Box, La Ganadas Mexican, Taco Cabana, Whataburger, [🏠] La Quinta, Motel 6, Red Roof Inn, Studio 6, [O] Discount Tire, Firestone, Ford, Isuzu, Home Depot, Lexus, Mazda, NTB, Sears/auto, Toyota/Scion, mall, S [O] Chrysler/Dodge/Jeep
29	Lomaland Dr, N [↑] Denny's, [🏠] Hyatt Place, S [Q] Fina/7-11, [🏠] Ramada, [O] Harley-Davidson
28b	Yarbrough Dr, El Paso, N [Q] Murphy USA, Shell/Coldstone, [↑] Beijing Lili, Buffalo Wild Wings, Burger King, Grandy's, Dunkin Donuts, El Ciro's, Hong Kong Buffet, LJ Silver, McDonald's, Peter Piper Pizza, Quiznos, Sonic, Subway, TX Roadhouse, Wendy's, Whataburger, Wienerschnitzel, [🏠] Days Inn, [O] Marshall's, PepBoys, Petsmart, Radio Shack, Ross, Walmart, S [Q] Rudy's BBQ, Valero/dsl, [↑] Applebee's, Fuddrucker's, Julio's Cafe, La Malinche Mexican, Lin's Buffet, Pizza Hut, Rudy's BBQ/gas, Shangri-La, Villa Del Mar, [🏠] Comfort Inn, InTown Suites, La Quinta, [O] [H]
28a	FM 2316, McRae Blvd, N [Q] Texaco/dsl, Valero, [↑] ChuckECheese, Grand China, Jack-in-the-Box, KFC, La Hacienda, Pizza Hut, Red Barrel Grill, Taco Bell, Taco Campero, [🏠] La Quinta, [O] [H], Barnes&Noble, Best Buy, BigLots, $General, $Tree, Family$, Firestone/auto, Goodyear/auto, Jo-Ann Fabrics, K-Mart, Michael's, Office Depot, Walgreens, S [Q] Circle K/dsl, [↑] Fuddruckers, Gabriel's Mexican, Pizza Hut, [🏠] Comfort Inn, La Quinta, [O] NAPA, Tuesday Morning, vet
27	Hunter Dr, Viscount Blvd, N [Q] Fina/7-11, Valero, [↑] Carrow's Rest., Grand China Buffet, K-Bob's, Red Lobster, Taco Bell, [🏠] La Quinta, [O] Barnes&Noble, Best Buy, Firestone, S [Q] Alon/7-11, Exxon/dsl, [↑] Whataburger, [O] Family$, Food City
26	Hawkins Blvd, El Paso, N [Q] Chevron, Murphy USA, Shamrock, Shell, [↑] Anadele Rest., Arby's, Burger King, Country Kitchen, DQ, Golden Corral, IHOP, Landry's Seafood, Luby's, Olive Garden, Red Lobster, Taco Cabana, Wyatt's Cafeteria, [🏠] Howard Johnson, [O] Dillard's, JC Penney, Macy's, Office Depot, Pennzoil, Sam's Club/gas, Sears/auto, Walmart, S [Q] Valero/dsl, [↑] McDonald's, Village Inn, [🏠] Super 8, [O] Tony Lama Boots
25	Airway Blvd, El Paso [↗], N [Q] Shell/dsl, [↑] Jack-in-the-Box, Landry's Seafood, Starbucks, Whataburger, [🏠] Courtyard, Hampton Inn, Holiday Inn, Radisson, Residence Inn, [O] VW/Volvo/Mercedes, S [Q] Chevron/Subway/dsl/24hr, [🏠] Holiday Inn Express, Staybridge Suites
24b	Geronimo Dr, N [↑] El Taco Tote, Taco Cabana, [🏠] Wingate Inn, [O] Costco/gas, Dillard's, Kohl's, Office Depot, Marshall's, Ross, Target, Walgreens, mall, S [Q] Alon/7-11/dsl, Circle K, [↑] IHOP, Denny's, El Nido Mexican, La Cebolla Roja, [🏠] Embassy Suites, Hilton Garden, Homewood Suites, Hyatt Place, La Quinta, [O] Urgent Care

▶E INTERSTATE 10 CONT'D

EL PASO

Exit	Services
24a	Trowbridge Dr, **N** 🅖 Fina, Thunderbird Gas, 🍴 Alexandrio's Mexican, Luby's, McDonald's, Steak&Ale, Whataburger, 🏨 Budget Inn, 🅞 Ford, Nissan, Toyota
23b	US 62/180, to Paisano Dr, **N** 🍴 Jack-in-the-Box, McDonald's, Whataburger, 🏨 Budget Inn, Sleep Inn, 🅞 Ford, U-Haul, to Carlsbad
23a	Raynolds St, **S** 🍴 Arby's, 🏨 Motel 6, Super 8, 🅞 🏥
22b	US 54, Patriot Fwy
22a	Copia St, El Paso, **N** 🅖 Shamrock, 🍴 KFC
21	Piedras St, El Paso, **N** 🍴 Burger King, McDonald's, 🅞 Family$
20	Dallas St, Cotton St, **N** 🅖 Valero, 🍴 Church's, Subway
19	TX 20, El Paso, downtown, **N** 🅖 Chevron, **S** 🏨 Camino Real Hotel, DoubleTree Inn, Holiday Inn Express
18b	Franklin Ave, Porfirio Diaz St
18a	Schuster Ave, **N** Sun Bowl, **S** to UTEP
16	Executive Ctr Blvd, **N** 🅖 Valero, 🏨 Best Value Inn
13b a	US 85, Paisano Dr, to Sunland Park Dr, **N** 🅖 Shamrock, 🍴 Barrigo's Café, Carino's Italian, ChuckECheese, 5 Guys Burgers, Grand China, IHOP, Olive Garden, PF Chang's, Quiznos, Red Lobster, Sonic, Whataburger, 🅞 Barnes&Noble, Best Buy, Dillard's, JC Penney, K-Mart, Macy's, Michael's, Office Depot, Old Navy, Petsmart, Sears/auto, Target, Verizon, mall, **S** 🅖 Shamrock/dsl, Shell, 🍴 Bob-O's Rest., La Malinche Mexican, Little Caesars, McDonald's, Sonic, State Line BBQ, Subway, 🏨 Best Western, Comfort Suites, Holiday Inn, Sleep Inn, Studio+, 🅞 Buick/GMC, Chrysler/Dodge/Jeep, Family$, Fiat, Sunland Park RaceTrack, Vista Mkt, funpark
12	Resler Dr (from wb)
11	TX 20, to Mesa St, Sunland Park, **N** 🅖 Chevron/dsl, Circle K, Mobil, Valero, 🍴 AJ's Diner, Aloha BBQ, Chili's, CiCi's, Coldstone, Cracker Barrel, El Taco Tote, Famous Dave's BBQ, Fuddruckers, Golden Corral, Jaxon's Rest/brewery, Krispy Kreme, Leo's Mexican, PacoWong's Chinese, Papa John's, Pei Wei, Popeye's, Rancher's Grill, Subway, Taco Bell, TX Roadhouse, Wienerschnitzel, Wendy's, 🏨 Comfort Suites, EconoLodge, Fairfield Inn, La Quinta, Red Roof Inn, SpringHill Suites, 🅞 Albertson's, BigLots, Curves, $General, Family$, Firestone/auto, GNC, Goodyear/auto, Home Depot, PepBoys, SteinMart, Verizon, Walmart/McDonald's, USPO, **S** 🅖 Chevron/dsl, Valero/dsl, 🍴 Ay Caramba Mexican, Burger King, Church's, Domino's, Golden Buddha, Jack-in-the-Box, KFC, McDonald's, Peter Piper Pizza, Pizza Hut, Starbucks, Subway, Taco Cabana, Village Inn, 🏨 Days Inn, Motel 6, Super 8, Travelodge, 🅞 AutoZone, Big 8 Foods, $General, $Tree, Hobby Lobby, Martin Tires, Radio Shack, Sam's Club/gas, Walgreens
9	Redd Rd, **N** 🅖 Valero, 🍴 Applebee's, Baskin-Robbins, Burger King, Double Dave's Pizza, Pizza Hut, Starbucks, Subway, 🅞 Albertson's/gas, Ford, Kohl's, Lowe's, O'Reilly Parts, **S** 🅖 Circle K/dsl, Shamrock, 🅞 Chevrolet, Honda, Mazda
8	Artcraft Rd, **S** 🅖 Shell/dsl, 🍴 Carl's Jr, Church's, Rudy's BBQ/gas, 🏨 Hampton Inn, Holiday Inn Express, Microtel
6	Lp 375, to Canutillo, **N** 🅖 Shell/DQ/dsl, 🅞 to Trans Mountain Rd, Franklin Mtns SP, **S** 🅖 Chevron/McDonald's, Shorty's/Mama's Mexican/dsl, 🍴 Starbucks, Whataburger, 🅞 Discount Tire, El Paso Shops/Famous Brands, RV camping

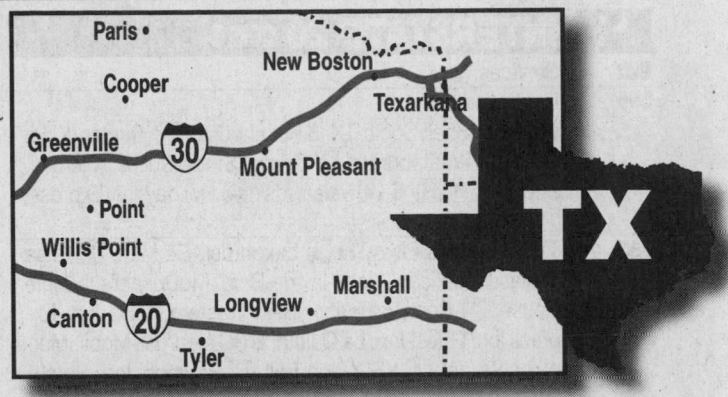

ANTHONY

Exit	Services
5mm	truck check sta eb
2	Westway, Vinton, **N** 🅖 Petro/Valero/Subway/dsl/scales/24hr/@, 🅞 American RV Park, Camping World (1mi), PetroLube/tires, **S** 🅖 gas, 🅞 Mack, truck repair/tires
1	**Welcome Ctr eb, full** 🅢 **facilities, info, 🅒, 🅿, litter barrels, petwalk, weigh sta wb**, **S** 🍴 Great American Steaks, 🅞 Fun Country RV Ctr
0	FM 1905, Anthony, **N** 🅖 ⭐FLYING J/Denny's/dsl/LP/RV dump/24hr, Loves/Chester's/McDonald's/dsl/scales/24hr, 🍴 Carl's Jr, 🏨 Super 8, **S** 🅖 Alon/7-11/dsl, 🅖/Subway/Wendy's/dsl/24hr/@, 🍴 Burger King, KFC/Taco Bell, 🏨 Best Western, 🅞 Anthony RV Ctr, Big 8 Foods, $General, $Tree, Walgreens, funpark, truckwash, tires
0mm	Texas/New Mexico state line

▶E INTERSTATE 20

MARSHALL

Exit	Services
636mm	Texas/Louisiana state line
635.5mm	**Welcome Ctr/🆁🆂 wb, full** 🅢 **facilities, 🅒, 🅿, litter barrels, petwalk**
635	TX 9, TX 156, to Waskom, **N** 🅖 Chevron/Burger King/dsl, Exxon/dsl, 🍴 DQ, Jim's BBQ, 🅞 Family$, USPO
633	US 80, FM 9, FM 134, to Waskom, **N** 🅖 Shell, 🍴 Catfish Village Rest., **S** 🅞 Miss Ellie's RV Park
628	to US 80, to frontage rd
624	FM 2199, to Scottsville
620	FM 31, to Elysian Fields, **N** Marshall RV Park (2mi)
617	US 59, Marshall, **0-2 mi N** 🅖 Exxon/dsl, Shell, 🍴 Applebee's, Burger King, Cafe Italia, Catfish Express, Golden Corral, IHOP, In Japan Steaks, KFC, LJ Silver, Little Caesars, McDonald's, Pizza Hut, Porky's Smokehouse, Sonic, Subway, Taco Bell, Waffle House, Wendy's, Whataburger, 🏨 Baymont Inn, Best Western, Comfort Suites, Days Inn, Fairfield Inn, Hampton Inn, Quality Inn, 🅞 Chevrolet, Chrysler/Dodge/Jeep, $General, Ford/Lincoln, JC Penney, NAPA, Save-A-Lot Foods, Toyota/Scion, **S** 🅖 Chevron/dsl, Conoco/Pony Express/dsl/scales/@, Rudy's/dsl, Valero/dsl, 🍴 JW's Diner, 🏨 Best Value Inn, EconoLodge, Holiday Inn Express, La Quinta, Motel 6, Super 8, 🅞 Holiday Springs RV Park (2mi)
614	TX 43, to Marshall, **S** to Martin Creek Lake SP
610	FM 3251
604	FM 450, Hallsville, **N** 🅖 Valero/dsl, 🅞 450 Hitchin' Post RV Park, to Lake O' the Pines
600mm	Mason Creek
599	FM 968, Longview, **N** 🅞 Kenworth Trucks, truck/rv wash, **S** 🅖 Exxon/Sonic/dsl, Natl TrkStp/dsl, 🅞 Goodyear, truck repair
596	US 259 N, TX 149, to Lake O' Pines, **N** 🅖 Exxon/Gran

TX

INTERSTATE 20 CONT'D

Exit	Services
596	**Continued** dy's/dsl, Shell/Sonic/TX Smokehouse, 🍴 Burger King, Denny's, Whataburger, 🛏 Center Stone Suites, Microtel, Super 8, 🅾 🎗, **S** 📟 Valero/dsl, 🛏 Holiday Inn Express, 🅾 to Martin Lake SP
595b a	TX 322, Estes Pkwy, **N** 📟 Exxon/dsl, EZ Mart, 🍴 Casa Tomasa Mexican, Jack-in-the-Box, McDonald's, Waffle House, 🛏 Best Value Inn, Best Western, Days Inn, Express Inn, Guest Inn, La Quinta, **S** 📟 Alon/dsl, Mobil, Murphy USA/dsl, 🍴 KFC/Taco Bell, 🛏 Baymont Inn, Hampton Inn, Motel 6, 🅾 Walmart/Subway, auto repair
593mm	Sabine River
591	FM 2087, FM 2011, **S** 🅾 Fernbrook RV Park (2mi)
589b a	US 259, TX 31, Kilgore (exits left from both lanes), **1-3 mi S** 📟 Chevron/dsl, Exxon, 🍴 Chili's, Kilgore Café, Mazzio's, McDonald's, Taco Bueno, 🛏 Best Value Inn, Comfort Suites, Hampton Inn, Holiday Inn Express, Homewood Suites, 🅾 AutoZone, Ford, O'Reilly Parts, **S** 🅾 E Texas Oil Museum
587	TX 42, Kilgore, **N** 📟 Exxon/dsl, 🍴 Bodacious BBQ, **S** 📟 Shell/Wendy's/dsl, 🍴 Denny's, 🛏 Days Inn, 🅾 Big Rig Lube, E TX Oil Museum, **3 mi S** 🅾 Walmart
583	TX 135, to Kilgore, Overton, **N** 📟 Exxon/dsl, 🅾 Shallow Creek RV Resort
582	FM 3053, Liberty City, **N** 📟 Mobil/Subway/dsl, Shell/Whataburger/dsl, 🍴 Bob's BBQ, DQ, Sonic
579	Joy-Wright Mtn Rd
575	Barber Rd
574mm	🆂🆂 both lanes, 🗑 litter barrels, ♿ accessible
571b	FM 757, Omen Rd, to Starrville
571a	US 271, to Gladewater, Tyler, **S** 📟 Shell/Sonic/Texas Smokehouse/dsl/scales/24hr
567	TX 155, Winona, **N** 📟 Valero/dsl/24hr, **S** 🍴 DQ (2mi), 🛏 Best Value Inn, 🅾 🎗, Freightliner
565	FM 2015, to Driskill-Lake Rd
562	FM 14, **N** 🍴 Bodacious BBQ, 🅾 to Tyler SP, **S** 📟 🏕 McDonald's/dsl/scales/24hr, 🅾 Northgate RV Park (4mi)
560	Lavender Rd, **S** 🅾 5 Star RV Park (2 mi)
557	Jim Hogg Rd, **N** 📟 Shell/dsl
556	US 69, to Tyler, **N** 📟 Murphy USA/dsl, RaceWay/dsl, Shamrock/dsl, 🍴 Burger King, Chicken Express, Chili's, Dixie Pig's BBQ, Domino's, Eastern Buffet, IHOP, KFC\LJ Silver, Juanita's Mexican, Lincoln's Rest, McDonald's, Pizza Hut, Pizza Inn, Posado's Cafe, Sonic, Subway, Taco Bell, 🛏 Best Western, Comfort Suites, Days Inn, Hampton Inn, La Quinta, 🅾 $General, Family$, Fred's, Kwik-Kar, Lowe's, Verizon, Walmart/Subway, **S** 📟 Chevron/DQ, Exxon, 🍴 Cracker Barrel, Wendy's, 🛏 Best Value Inn
554	Harvey Rd
553	New exit
552	FM 849, **N** 📟 Chevron/Subway/dsl, 🍴 Collin St Bakery
548	TX 110, to Grand Saline, **N** 📟 Exxon/dsl, **S** 📟 Valero/dsl
546mm	cmv insp sta eb
544	Willow Branch Rd, **N** 🅾 Willow Branch RV Park
540	FM 314, to Van, **N** 📟 Love's/Carl's Jr/dsl/scales/24hr, 🍴 DQ, Farmhouse Rest, Sonic, Soul Mans BBQ, 🛏 Van Inn
538mm	🆁🆂 both lanes, full ♿ facilities, 🍴, vending, 🗑 litter barrels, petwalk
537	FM 773, FM 16

TYLER

536	Tank Farm Rd
533	Oakland Rd, to Colfax, **N** 📟 Shell/A&W/LJ Silver/dsl
530	FM 1255, Canton
528	FM 17, to Grand Saline
527	TX 19, **N** 📟 Exxon/dsl, 🍴 Burger King, Denny's, Papadales Grill, Whataburger, 🛏 Motel 6, Quality Inn, Super 8, **S** 📟 Circle K/dsl/24hr, Mobil, Shell/Subway/dsl, 🍴 DQ, Dairy Palace, Juanita's Mexican, KFC/Taco Bell, McDonald's, Senorita's Mexican, 🛏 Best Western, Days Inn, 🅾 Ford, Mill Creek Ranch RV Resort, to First Monday SP, LP
526	FM 859, to Edgewood, **N** water park
523	TX 64, Wills Point, **N** 📟 Shell/dsl/24hr, 🍴 Duke's BBQ, Taco Casa
521	Myrtle Springs Rd, **S** 🅾 Explore USA RV Ctr, repair, RV camp/dump
519	Turner-Hayden Rd, **S** Canton RV Park
516	FM 47, to Wills Point, **N** to Lake Tawakoni, **S** 📟 Texaco/dsl, 🍴 Robertson's Café/gas, 🛏 Interstate Motel
512	FM 2965, Hiram-Wills Point Rd
512mm	**cmv inspection sta both lanes**
509	Hiram Rd, **S** 📟 Shell/dsl/cafe/24hr
506	FM 429, FM 2728, College Mound Rd, **N** Blue Bonnet Ridge RV Park
503	Wilson Rd, **S** 📟 TA/Shell/Country Fare/Pizza Hut/Subway/dsl/LP/24hr/@
501	TX 34, to Terrell, **N** 📟 Exxon/dsl, Shell/Subway/dsl, 🍴 Church's, Schlotzsky's, Sonic, Starbucks, Steak&Grill, Taco Shack, Waffle House, 🛏 Best Value Inn, Best Western, Comfort Inn, Days Inn, La Quinta, Motel 6, 🅾 🎗, Home Depot, **S** 📟 Circle K/dsl, Valero/dsl/24hr, 🍴 Applebee's, Carmona's Cantina, IHOP, McDonald's, Wendy's, 🛏 Holiday Inn Express, Super 8, 🅾 Old Navy, Tanger Outlet/famous brands
499b	Rose Hill Rd, to Terrell
499a	to US 80, W to Dallas, same as 498
498	FM 148, to Terrell, **N** 📟 Exxon/Denny's/Subway/dsl, Shell/dsl, 🍴 Soulman's BBQ, **S** 📟 Terrell RV Park
493	FM 1641, **S** 📟 Exxon/Sonic/Taco Mayo/dsl
491	FM 2932, Helms Tr, to Forney, **N** 📟 Shell/Subway/dsl
490	FM 741, to Forney
487	FM 740, to Forney, **S** Forney RV park
483	Lawson Rd, Lasater Rd
482	Belt Line Rd, to Lasater, **N** 📟 Exxon/dsl, 🍴 Smokehouse, Sonic, **S** 📟 Shell/KFC/Pizza Hut/Subway, 🅾 RV park
481	Seagoville Rd, **N** 📟 Valero/dsl, Shell/Church's/Dickey's BBQ, 🛏 La Quinta, **S** 🍴 Lindy's Rest.
480	I-635, N to Mesquite
479b a	US 175, **S** 📟 Shell/dsl
477	St Augustine Rd, **S** 📟 Shell/dsl, 🍴 Sonic
476	Dowdy Ferry Rd
474	TX 310 N, Central Expsy
473b a	JJ Lemmon Rd, I-45 N to Dallas, S to Houston
472	Bonnie View Rd, **N** 📟 /🏕 FLYING J/Denny's/dsl/LP/24hr, Shell, 🍴 Jack-in-the-Box, 🛏 Ramada Ltd, 🅾 Blue Beacon, Kenworth, Speedco Lube, **S** 📟 TA/Exxon/Burger King/Taco Bell/dsl/scales/24hr/@
470	TX 342, Lancaster Rd, **N** 📟 Chevron, USA/Texaco/Popeye's/dsl/scales/24hr, 🍴 Big Bruce's BBQ, **S** 📟 🏕 /Wendy's/dsl/scales/24hr, Shell, 🍴 LJ Silver/Taco Bell, McDonald's, Sonic, Subway, Whataburger, William's Chicken, 🛏 Days Inn
468	Houston School Rd, **S** 📟 Exxon/dsl, 🍴 Whataburger

CANTON

TERRELL

DALLAS

INTERSTATE 20 CONT'D

Exit	Services
467b a	I-35E, N to Dallas, S to Waco, **1 mi N** off of I-35E, Ⓖ Shell, Ⓕ McDonald's
466	S Polk St, **N** Ⓖ Exxon, Texaco, Ⓕ DQ, Sonic, Subway, Ⓞ Family$, **S** Ⓖ 〈Loves〉/Carl's Jr/dsl/scales/24hr
465	Wheatland/S Hampton Rds, **N** Ⓕ Chick-fil-A, Chili's, Ⓞ CVS Drug, Target, **S** Ⓖ Chevron/McDonald's, Murphy USA, RaceWay, Ⓕ Arby's, Cheddar's, Jack-in-the-Box, Popeye's, Sonic, Spring Creek BBQ, Taco Bell, Wendy's, 🏨 Super 8, Ⓞ Ⓗ, Buick/GMC, Home Depot, Honda, Hyundai, Kia, Lincoln, Lowe's, Mazda, Petsmart, Sam's Club/gas, Suzuki, Toyota, Walmart
464b a	US 67, Love Fwy
463	Camp Wisdom Rd, **N** Ⓖ Chevron, Exxon, Ⓕ Catfish King Rest., Denny's, Taco Bell/LJ Silver, Taco Cabana, 🏨 Hotel Suites of America, Motel 6, Royal Inn, Suburban Lodge, Ⓞ Nissan, **S** Ⓖ Shamrock, Ⓕ Burger King, Chubby's Rest., Dave's BBQ, Jack-in-the-Box, McDonald's, Olive Garden, Red Lobster, Subway, Tortilla Factory, Wendy's, Ⓞ K-Mart
462b a	Duncanville Rd (no EZ wb return), **S** Ⓖ Exxon, QT, Shell/dsl, Ⓕ Arby's, Church's, KFC, Los Lupes Mexican, Mr Gatti's, Popeye's, Whataburger, 🏨 Hilton Garden, Motel 6, Ⓞ Goodyear, Kroger, Radio Shack
461	Cedar Ridge Rd
460	TX 408
458	Mt Creek Pkwy
457	FM 1382, to Grand Prairie, **N** Ⓖ Shell/7-11/dsl, Valero/dsl, Ⓕ Waffle House, **S** Ⓖ RaceTrac, Ⓕ Jack-in-the-Box, Ⓞ to Joe Pool Lake
456	Carrier Pkwy, to Corn Valley Rd, **N** Ⓖ QT, Ⓕ Chick-fil-A, Don Pablo, Starbucks, Taco Cabana, Whataburger, Ⓞ Home Depot, Kohl's, Radio Shack, Target, **S** Ⓖ Shell, Ⓕ Baskin-Robbins, Boston Mkt, Chapp's Cafe, Cheddar's, Chili's, Denny's, IHOP, Little Caesar's, McDonald's, Spring Creek BBQ, Subway, 🏨 Holiday Inn Express, Ⓞ Albertsons/gas, CVS Drug, GNC, Tom Thumb Foods/gas, Walgreens, vet
455	TX 151
454	Great Southwest Pkwy, **N** Ⓖ Chevron, Conoco/dsl, Exxon, Ⓕ Beto's, Carino's Italian, China Dragon, Chuck-eCheese, Golden Corral, KFC, McDonald's, Taco Bell, Taco Bueno, TX Roadhouse, Waffle House, Wendy's, Wienerschnitzel, 🏨 Heritage Inn, La Quinta, Quality Inn, Ⓞ Ⓗ Goodyear, Harley-Davidson, U-Haul, **S** Ⓖ 7-11, Shell/Subway/dsl, Valero/dsl, Ⓕ Applebee's, Arby's, Buffalo Wild Wings, Burger King, Schlotzsky's, Sonic, 🏨 Comfort Inn, La Quinta, Super 8, Ⓞ AT&T, Discount Tire, Dodge, $Tree, Kroger, Office Depot, Petsmart, Sam's Club/gas, Walgreens, Walmart, to Joe Pool Lake
453b a	TX 360
452	Frontage Rd
451	Collins St, New York Ave, **N** Ⓖ Exxon/dsl, RaceTrac, Ⓕ Jack-in-the-Box, Whataburger, Ⓞ Acura, Chrysler/Dodge/Jeep, Kia/Mazda/VW, Subaru, **S** Ⓖ E-Z, QT, Valero, Ⓕ Chicken Express, KFC, McDonald's, Sonic, Subway, Taco Bell, Taco Bueno, 🏨 Hampton Inn, Ⓞ Buick/GMC, Lincoln, Nissan
450	Matlock Rd, **N** Ⓖ QT, Ⓕ BJ's Rest., Bone Daddy's, Boudreaux's Cajun, Chey's Mexican, Coldstone Creamery, Dave&Buster's, Fat Fish Blue, Genghis Grill, Gloria's

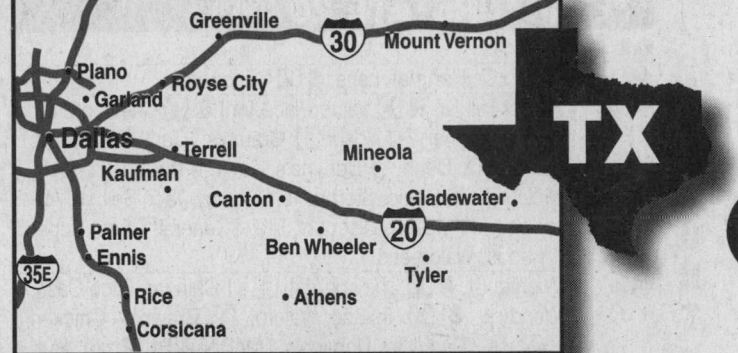

Exit	Services
450	Continued Cafe, Hoffbrau Steaks, Houlihan's, IHOP, In-N-Out, Jamba Juice, Kincade's Burgers, India Grill, Italian Mkt, Keg Steaks, Melting Pot, Mendela's Italian, Mercado Juarez, Mimi's Cafe, PF Changs, Pluckers's Wings, Pot Belly, Ralph's BBQ, Red Robin, Sweet Tomatoes, Wendy's, 🏨 Quality Inn, Ⓞ Ⓗ, AT&T, Costco/gas, Jo-Ann Fabrics, Lowe's, Michael's, Old Navy, Petsmart, Staples, **S** Ⓖ 7-11, RaceTrac, Shamrock, Shell/7-11, Ⓕ Joe's Pizza, Starbucks, Ⓞ Fry's Electronics, NTB
449	FM 157, Cooper St, **N** Ⓖ Mobil, Shell, 7-11, Texaco, Ⓕ Abuelo's Mexican, Atlanta Bread, Blackeyed Pea, Cheesecake Factory, Chili's, China Café, CiCi's, Corner Bakery, Don Pablo, Golden Corral, Grandy's, Hong Kong Cafe, Jason's Deli, KFC, McDonald's, On-the-Border, Outback Steaks, Razzoo's Cajun Café, Red Lobster, Rock Fish Grill, Salt Grass Steaks, Schlotsky's, Souper Salad, Spaghetti Whse, Starbucks, Thai Cuisine, Wendy's, Whataburger, 🏨 Best Western, Days Inn, Holiday Inn Express, Homestead Village, La Quinta, Studio 6, Ⓞ Barnes&Noble, Best Buy, Dillard's, Discount Tire, Hancock Fabrics, Hyundai, JC Penney, Office Depot, PetCo, Sears/auto, Subaru, Target, TJ Maxx, mall, **S** Ⓖ Chevron, Conoco, Shell, Ⓕ Applebee's, Arby's, Boston Mkt, Burger King, Burger St, Chick-fil-A, Denny's, El Fenix Mexican, LJ Silver, Luby's, Macaroni Grill, McDonald's, Olive Garden, Panda Express, Popeye's, Ryan's, Sonic, Subway, Taco Bueno, TGIFriday, 🏨 InTown Suites, Ⓞ Acura, $Tree, Ford, GMC, Hobby Lobby, Home Depot, Honda, Hyundai, Isuzu, Kia, K-Mart, Kroger, Ross, Suzuki, Toyota, Walmart/24hr
448	Bowen Rd, **N** Ⓖ QT, RaceTrac, Ⓕ Cracker Barrel, **S** Ⓖ Shell
447	Kelly-Elliott Rd, Park Springs Blvd, **N** Ⓖ Lonestar Express, 7-11, **S** Ⓖ Exxon, Fina/Blimpie, Ⓞ camping
445	Green Oaks Blvd, **N** Ⓖ Conoco/dsl, Shell, Ⓕ Arby's, Boston Mkt, Braum's, Burger St, Church's, Colter's BBQ, Hooters, Jack-in-the-Box, KFC, Mac's Grill, Papa John's, Popeye's, Quizno's, Schlotzsky's, Starbucks, Taco Bell, Taco Cabana, Whataburger, Ⓞ Ace Hardware, Albertsons, CVS Drug, Firestone, Office Depot, Radio Shack, **S** Ⓖ Chevron/24hr, Murphy Express/dsl, 7-11, Valero, Ⓕ Cheddar's, IHOP, Fazoli's, Khaki's, McDonald's, Pancho's Mexican, Panda Express, Sonic, Subway, Taco Bueno, Waffle House, Ⓞ AutoZone, BigLots, Discount Tire, $General, NTB, O'Reilly Parts, Walmart, vet
444	US 287 S, to Waxahatchie, same as 445, from eb
443	Bowman Springs Rd (from wb)
442b a	I-820, to Ft Worth, US 287 bus, **N** Ⓖ Valero, 🏨 Great Western Inn, Super 8, **S** Ⓖ Chevron/dsl

F T W O R T H

TX

➤E INTERSTATE 20 CONT'D

Exit	Services
441	Anglin Dr, Hartman Lane, **S** 🅖 Conoco/dsl
440b	Forest Hill Dr, **N** 🅖 Value Place Inn, **S** 🅖 Chevron/24hr, Conoco, Shell/7-11/dsl, 🍴 Braum's, Capt D's, CiCi's Pizza, DQ, Denny's, Domino's, Jack-in-the-Box, Luby's, McDonald's, Sonic, Starbucks, Subway, Taco Bell, Ⓞ AutoZone, CVS Drug, Discount Tire, $General, $Tree, Super 1 Foods, Walgreens
440a	Wichita St, **N** 🅖 Chevron/dsl, 🍴 #1 Chinese, Taco Casa, Wendy's, **S** 🅖 Texaco, Valero, 🍴 Braum's, Chicken Express, Denny's, Domino's, McDonald's, Pizza Hut, Schlotzsky's, Taco Bueno, Whataburger, 🛏 Hampton Inn
439	Campus Dr, **N** Ⓞ Chrysler/Jeep, Ford, **S** Ⓞ Sam's Club/gas
438	Oak Grove Rd, **1 mi N** 🅖 Shell, 🍴 Burger King, Denny's, Jack-in-the Box, McDonald's, Whataburger, 🛏 Days Inn, **S** 🅖 Valero
437	I-35W, N to Ft Worth, S to Waco
436b	Hemphill St, **N** 🅖 Shell/dsl, **S** Ⓞ Chevrolet
436a	FM 731 (from eb), to Crowley Ave, **N** 🅖 Valero, Ⓞ $General, Sav-a-Lot Foods, **S** 🍴 BurgerBox, Pizza Hut/Taco Bell, Subway, Ⓞ transmissions
435	McCart St, **N** 🅖 Shell, **S** 🅖 Mobil
434b	Trail Lakes Dr, **S** 🅖 Shell, 🍴 Sonic, Starbucks, Ⓞ CVS Drug
434a	Granbury rd, **S** 🍴 Pancho's Mexican, Wendy's, Ⓞ Jo-Ann Fabrics
433	Hulen St, **N** 🅖 Shell/dsl, 🍴 ChuckECheese, Grady's Grill, Hooters, Olive Garden, Souper Salad, Subway, TGIFriday's, 🛏 TownePlace Suites, Ⓞ Albertsons, Home Depot, Office Depot, Petsmart, TJ Maxx, **S** 🅖 Shamrock, Valero, 🍴 Denny's, Jack-in-the-Box, In-N-Out, McDonald's, Red Lobster, Taco Bell, 🛏 Hampton Inn, Ⓞ Dillard's, Macy's, Ross, mall
431	(432 from wb), TX 183, Bryant-Irvin Rd, **N** 🅖 Chevron, Valero, 🍴 Chipotle Mexican, Genghis Grill, Mimi's Café, On-the-Border, Taste of Asia, Ⓞ Best Buy, Cavender's Boots, Kohl's, Lowe's, Petsmart, Sam's Club/gas, **S** 🅖 Chevron, Exxon, QT, Shell, Texaco, 🍴 Blackeyed Pea, Chicken Express, Chick-fil-A, Cousin's BBQ, Fuddruckers, IHOP, Lonestar Oysters, Outback Steaks, Quizno's, Razzoo's Cajun, Rio Mambo, SaltGrass Steaks, Schlotzsky's, Sonic, Starbucks, Subway, 🛏 Courtyard, Extended Stay America, Holiday Inn Express, Hyatt Place, La Quinta, Ⓞ Ⓗ, AT&T, Buick, Costco/gas, Ford, Goodyear/auto, Lexus, Mazda, PetCo, Suzuki, Staples, Target, Tom Thumb/gas, Verizon, Walgreens, transmissions/repair
430mm	Clear Fork Trinity River
429b	Winscott Rd, **N** 🅖 Circle K/dsl 🍴 Cracker Barrel, 🛏 Best Western, Comfort Suites
429a	US 377, to Granbury, **S** 🅖 RaceTrac, Valero, 🍴 Arby's, Burger King, Chicken Express, Domino's, DQ, Jack-in-the-Box, KFC/Taco Bell, McDonald's, Sonic, Starbucks, Waffle House, Whataburger, 🛏 Motel 6, Ⓞ Albertsons, AutoZone, $General, Walgreens
428	I-820, N around Ft Worth
426	RM 2871, Chapin School Rd
425	Markum Ranch Rd
421	I-30 E (from eb), to Ft Worth
420	FM 1187, Aledo, Farmer, parking & ride
419mm	**weigh sta eb**

W E A T H E R F O R D

Exit	Services
418	Ranch House Rd, Willow Park, Willow Park, **N** 🅖 Exxon/Taco Casa, Shell/dsl, 🍴 Pizza Hut, Sonic, Subway, Whataburger, **S** 🅖 Shell/ChickenExpress/dsl, 🍴 Domino's, McDonald's, Milano's Italian, Mr Jim's Pizza, Railhead BBQ, 🛏 Knights Inn, Ⓞ Ace RV Ctr., Brookshire Foods, Cowtown RV Park, $General
417mm	no services
415	FM 5, Mikus Rd, Annetta, **S** 🅖 Chevron/dsl, Shell/dsl, 🍴 Drivers Diner, Ⓞ 415 RV Ctr
413	(414 from wb), US 180 W, Lake Shore Dr, **N** 🅖 Murphy USA/dsl, RaceTrac/dsl, Shell/dsl, 🍴 DQ, Golden Chick, McDonald's, Sonic, Subway, Taco Bell, Waffle House, Ⓞ Buick/Cadillac/Chevrolet/GMC, Ford, Hyundai, Lincoln, Nissan, Suzuki, Toyota/Scion, Walgreens, Walmart/Subway, **S** 🅖 Valero/dsl
410	Bankhead Hwy, **S** 🅖 Loves/Subway/dsl/24hr
409	FM 2552 N, Clear Lake Rd, **N** 🅖 Petro/Valero/rest/dsl/24hr/@, 🍴 Antonio's Mexican, Granny's Kitchen, Jack-in-the-Box, 🛏 Best Western, Sleepgo, Ⓞ Ⓗ, Blue Beacon, **S** 🅖 Shell/dsl
408	TX 171, FM 1884, FM 51, Tin Top Rd, Weatherford, **N** 🅖 Exxon, Mobil, Murphy USA/dsl, 🍴 Applebee's, Baker's Ribs, Braum's, Buffalo Wild Wings, Chicken Express, China Harbor, CiCi's Pizza, Cotton Patch Cafe, Denny's, IHOP, Kincade's Burgers, LJ Silver, Logan's Roadhouse, McAlister's Deli, McDonald's, MT Rest., Olive Garden, Rosa's Cafe, Schlotzsky's, Starbucks, Subway, Taco Bell, Taco Bueno, Taco Cabana, Whataburger, Wild Mushroom Steaks, 🛏 La Quinta, Sleep Inn, Super 8, Ⓞ AT&T, AutoZone, Belk, Christian Bro's Auto, Discount Tire, $Tree, Firestone/auto, JC Penney, Just Brakes, Michael's, Radio Shack, TJ Maxx, Verizon, Walgreens, Walmart/Subway, **S** 🅖 Exxon/Subway/dsl, Shell/Burger King/dsl, 🍴 Chick-fil-A, Chili's, Cracker Barrel, Honey Bee Ham, On-the-Border, Waffle House, Whataburger, 🛏 Candlewood Suites, Comfort Suites, Fairfield Inn, Hampton Inn, Holiday Inn Express, Motel 6, Quality Inn, Super Value Inn, Ⓞ Urgent Care, Best Buy, Kohl's, Lowe's, NTB, Petsmart, Ross, Target
407	Tin Top Rd (from eb), **N** Ⓞ Home Depot, **S** Ⓞ KOA, same as 408
406	Old Dennis Rd, **N** 🅖 Truck&Travel/dsl, 🍴 Chuck Wagon Rest., 🛏 Quest Inn, **S** 🅖 🚚/Wendy's/dsl/scales/24hr, 🛏 EconoLodge, Quality 1 Motel, Ⓞ Boss Shop Repair
402	(403 from wb), TX 312, to Weatherford
397	FM 1189, to Brock, **N** 🅖 Valero/dsl, Ⓞ Oak Creek RV Park
394	FM 113, to Millsap
393mm	Brazos River
391	Gilbert Pit Rd
390mm	🅡ₛ **both lanes, full** ♿ **facilities,** 🍴, **vending,** 🐾 **litter barrels, petwalk**
386	US 281, to Mineral Wells, Stephenville, **N** 🅖 Shell/Subway/dsl, **S** 🅖 Chevron/Maverick TC/Taco Casa/dsl, 🍴 DQ
380	FM 4, Santo-Liban, **S** 🍴 Sunday Creek Rest
376	Blue Flat Rd, Panama Rd
373	TX 193, Gordon
370	TX 108 S, FM 919, Gordon, **N** 🅖 Texaco/Bar-B/dsl, **S** 🅖 Exxon/dsl, Ⓞ Cactus Rose RV Park, Longhorn Inn/Country Store
367	TX 108 N, Mingus, **N** 🍴 Smoke Stack Café, Ⓞ Thurber Sta, **S** 🍴 NY Hill Rest.

📍 INTERSTATE 20 CONT'D

Exit	Services
364mm	Palo Pinto Creek
363	Tudor Rd 🅿️, tables, litter barrels
362mm	Bear Creek, 🅿️ both lanes, tables, litter barrels
361	TX 16, to Strawn
358	(from wb), frontage rd
356mm	Russell Creek
354	Lp 254, Ranger
351	(352 from wb), College Blvd
349	FM 2461, Ranger, **N** ⛽ *Loves*/Godfather's/Subway/dsl/scales/24hr, 🍴 DQ, 🛏 Best Value Inn, Ⓞ RL RV Park, **S** ⛽ Shell/dsl, repair
347	FM 3363 (from wb), Olden, **S** Ⓞ TX Steakhouse
345	FM 3363 (from eb), Olden, **S** 🍴 TX Steakhouse
343	TX 112, FM 570, Eastland, Lake Leon, **N** ⛽ Alon/7-11/Subway, Murphy USA/dsl, Shell/dsl, 🍴 Chicken Express, DQ, Golden Chick, La Familia, McDonald's, Pizza Heaven, Sonic, Taco Bell, 🛏 Holiday Inn Express, La Quinta, Super 8/RV park, Ⓞ AT&T, AutoZone, Buick/Cadillac/Chevrolet/GMC, Chrysler/Dodge/Jeep, $General, Ford, O'Reilly Parts, TrueValue, Walmart, **S** ⛽ Exxon/dsl, 🍴 Pulido's Mexican, 🛏 Budget Host, Days Inn
340	TX 6, Eastland, **N** ⛽ Chevron/dsl, Ⓞ 🏥, **S** ⛽ Shell/dsl
337	spur 490, **N** Ⓞ The Wild Country RV Park
332	US 183, Cisco, **N** ⛽ Alon/Allsups/dsl, Cow Pokes/dsl, 🍴 Chicken Express, DQ, Pizza Heaven, Sonic, Subway, 🛏 Cisco Inn, Executive Inn/RV Park, Ⓞ $General, Hilton Mon (1mi), NAPA
330	TX 206, Cisco, **N** 🛏 Best Value Inn, Ⓞ 🏥
329mm	🅿️ wb, tables, litter barrels, ♿ accessible
327mm	🅿️ eb, tables, litter barrels, ♿ accessible
324	Scranton Rd
322	Cooper Creek Rd
320	FM 880 N, FM 2945 N, to Moran
319	FM 880 S, Putnam, **N** ⛽ Fillin Sta/café, Ⓞ USPO
316	Brushy Creek Rd
313	FM 2228
310	Finley Rd
308	Lp 20, Baird
307	US 283, Clyde, **N** 🍴 DQ, 🛏 Baird Motel/RV park/dump, **S** ⛽ Alon/Allsups/7-11, Conoco/dsl, 🍴 Robertson's Café
306	FM 2047, Baird, **N** Ⓞ Chevrolet/GMC, Hanner RV Ctr
303	Union Hill Rd
301	FM 604, Cherry Lane, **N** ⛽ Exxon/Subway/dsl, 🍴 Sonic, Whataburger, **S** ⛽ Alon/7-11/dsl, Shell/dsl, 🍴 Chicken Express, Pizza House, Ⓞ Family$, Lawrence Bro's Mkt
300	FM 604 N, Clyde, **N** Ⓞ Chrysler/Dodge/Jeep, **S** ⛽ Conoco/dsl, Ⓞ White's RV Park/dump
299	FM 1707, Hays Rd
297	FM 603, Eula Rd
296.5mm	🅿️ both lanes, full ♿ facilities, 📞, 🅿️, litter barrels, petwalk, wireless internet
294	Buck Creek Rd, **N** Big Counry RV Ctr, RV Dump, **S** Abeline RV Park
292b	Elmdale Rd
292a	Lp 20 (exits left from wb)
290	TX 36, Lp 322, **S** 🏞, zoo
288	TX 351, **N** ⛽ Alon/Allsups/dsl, Alon/7-11/dsl, Murphy USA/dsl, 🍴 Chick-fil-A, Chili's, Cracker Barrel, DQ, Jason's Deli, Oscar's Mexican, Subway, Taco Casa, Wendy's, 🛏 Comfort Suites, Days Inn, Executive Inn, Holiday

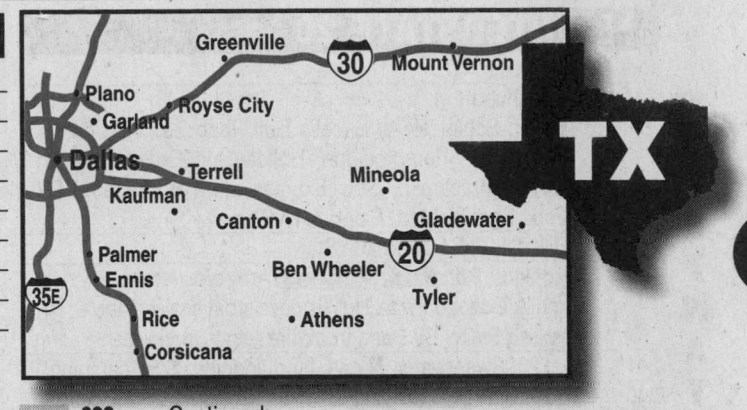

A B I L E N E

Exit	Services
288	Continued Inn Express, Quality Inn, Residence Inn, Whitten Inn, Ⓞ $Tree, Lowe's, Radio Shack, Walmart/Subway, **S** 🛏 Super 8, Ⓞ 🏥
286c	FM 600, Abilene, **N** ⛽ Alon/Allsups/dsl, Alon/7-11/dsl, 🍴 Denny's, 🛏 Best Western, Hampton Inn, La Quinta, **S** ⛽ Alon/7-11/dsl, 🛏 Sleep Inn, Ⓞ Russell Stover Candies
286	US 83, Pine St, Abilene, **S** ⛽ Alon/Allsups, 🛏 Frontier Inn, Ⓞ 🏥
285	Old Anson Rd, **S** ⛽ Alon/Allsups/dsl, 🛏 Best Value Inn
283b	N US 277, U83, Anson
283a	US 277 S, US 83 (exits left from wb)
282	FM 3438, Shirley Rd, **S** 🛏 Motel 6, Ⓞ KOA
280	Fulwiler Rd, to Dyess AFB
279	US 84 E, to Abilene, **1-3 mi S** access to facilities
278	Lp 20, **N** ⛽ Conoco/dsl/24hr, Ⓞ dsl repair, **S** ⛽ Westgo TC/Conoco/rest/dsl/scales/24hr/@, Ⓞ Mack Trucks/Volvo
277	FM 707, Tye, **N** ⛽ ⛽FLYING J/Denny's/dsl/LP/24hr, Peterbilt, Tye RV Park, truck lube, **S** ⛽ Alon/7-11/dsl, Ⓞ USPO
274	Wells Lane
272	Wimberly Rd
270	FM 1235, Merkel, **N** ⛽ Conoco/dsl, Shell/dsl/24hr
269	FM 126, **N** 🍴 Sonic, Subway, 🛏 Scottish Inn, **S** ⛽ Alon/7-11/dsl, Shell/dsl, 🍴 DQ, Skeet's BBQ, Ⓞ CarQuest, Family$
267	Lp 20, Merkel, **1 mi S** access to gas, food, lodging, 266 Derstine Rd
264	Noodle Dome Rd
263	Lp 20, Trent, **N** RV Park
262	FM 1085, **S** ⛽ Alon/7-11/dsl
261	Lp 20, Trent
259	Sylvester Rd
258	White Flat Rd, oil wells
257mm	🅿️ both lanes, full ♿ facilities, 📞, vending, 🅿️, litter barrels, petwalk
256	Stink Creek Rd
255	Adrian Rd
251	Eskota Rd
249	FM 1856, **N** Ⓞ Lonestar RV Park
247	TX 70 N, Sweetwater, **N** 🍴 Whataburger
246	Alabama Ave, Sweetwater
245	Arizona Ave (from wb), same as 244
244	TX 70 S, Sweetwater, **N** ⛽ Alon/7-11/dsl/24hr, Chevron/Subway/dsl, Murphy USA/dsl, 🍴 DQ, Domino's, Golden Chick, Little Panda, McDonald's, Subway, Wendy's, 🛏 Best Western, Budget Inn, La Quinta, Ⓞ 🏥, AutoZone, Medicine Place Drug, Verizon, Walmart, **S** ⛽ Shell/dsl, 🍴 Big Boy's BBQ, Buck's BBQ, Golden Chick, Great Wall

S W E E T W A T E R

Ⓟ = gas Ⓕ = food 🛏 = lodging Ⓞ = other Ⓡˢ = rest stop Copyright 2014 - The NEXT Exit

INTERSTATE 20 CONT'D

SWEETWATER

Exit	Services
244	Continued
	Buffet, Schlotzsky's, Skeet's Grill, Taco Bell, 🛏 Country Hearth Inn, Hampton Inn, Holiday Inn Express, Ranch House Motel/rest., Stay Express Inn, Ⓞ Chaparral RV Park, Ford, K-Mart, Rainbolt RV Park
243	Hillsdale Rd, Robert Lee St
242	Hopkins Rd, **N** Ⓟ ❤Loves/Arby's/dsl/scales/24hr, **S** Ⓟ TA/Conoco/Pizza Hut/Popeye's/dsl/scales/24hr/@, Ⓞ Rolling Plains RV Park, truck/tire repair, truck wash
241	Lp 20, Sweetwater, **N** gas, food, lodging, **S** RV camping
240	Lp 170, **N** 🔄, camping
239	May Rd
238b a	US 84 W, Blackland Rd
237	Cemetery Rd
236	FM 608, Roscoe, **N** Ⓟ Shell, Stripes/Country Cookin/dsl, Ⓞ NAPA, **S** Ⓕ Retta Mae's Rest
235	to US 84, Roscoe, **S** repair
230	FM 1230, many wind turbines
229mm	🛏 wb, tables, litter barrels, ♿ accessible
228mm	🛏 eb, tables, litter barrels, ♿ accessible
227	Narrell Rd
226b	Lp 20 (from wb), Loraine
226a	FM 644 N, Wimberly Rd
225	FM 644 S, **1 mi S** access to gas, food
224	Lp 20, to Loraine, **1 mi S** gas, food
223	Lucas Rd, **S** Ⓞ 223 RV Park
221	Lasky Rd
220	FM 1899
219	Lp 20, Country Club Rd, Colorado City
217	TX 208 S
216	TX 208 N, **N** Ⓟ Chevron/Subway/dsl, Ⓕ DQ, 🛏 Days Inn, **S** Ⓟ Stripes/Country Cookin/dsl, Ⓕ Pizza Hut, Sonic, 🛏 American Inn, Western Suites, Ⓞ 🅷 Alco, $General, Health Mart Drugs, Parts+
215	FM 3525, Rogers Rd, **2 mi S** 🅷 access to gas, food
214.5mm	Colorado River
213	Lp 20, Enderly Rd, Colorado City
212	FM 1229
211mm	FM 1229 Morgan Creek
210	FM 2836, **S** Ⓟ Just Stop/dsl, Ⓞ to Lake Colorado City SP, 🛏, camping
209	Dorn Rd
207	Lp 20, Westbrook
206	FM 670, to Westbrook
204mm	Ⓡˢ **wb, full** ♿ **facilities,** Ⓕ, 🛏, **litter barrels, petwalk**
200	Conaway Rd
199	Iatan Rd
195	frontage rd (from eb)
194a	E Howard Field Rd
192	FM 821, many oil wells
191mm	Ⓡˢ **eb, full** ♿ **facilities,** Ⓕ, 🛏, **litter barrels, petwalk**
190	Snyder Field Rd
189	McGregor Rd
188	FM 820, Coahoma, **N** Ⓟ Stripes/Country Cookin/dsl, Ⓕ DQ, Vickie's Cafe, Ⓞ USPO
186	Salem Rd, Sand Springs
184	Moss Lake Rd, Sand Springs, **N** Ⓟ Alon/dsl, **S** RV camping
182	Midway Rd
181b	Refinery Rd, **N** Ⓟ Fina Refinery

BIG SPRING / **MIDLAND** / **ODESSA**

181a	FM 700, **N** 🔄, RV camping, **2 mi S** 🅷
179	US 80, Big Spring, **S** Ⓟ Fina/7-11, Ⓕ DQ, Denny's, 🛏 Camlot Inn, Quality Inn, Super 8, Ⓞ Buick/Cadillac/Chevrolet, $General
178	TX 350, Big Spring, **N** Ⓟ Shell/dsl, **S** Ⓞ truck repair
177	US 87, Big Spring, **N** Ⓟ Exxon/dsl, TA/Country Fare/Popeye's/dsl/scales/24hr/@, Ⓕ Texas Cajun Cafe, 🛏 Advantage Inn, La Quinta, Motel 6, Plaza Inn, **S** Ⓟ Chevron/dsl, Fina/dsl, Ⓕ Casa Blanca Mexican, DQ, 🛏 Best Western, Hampton Inn, Holiday Inn Express
176	TX 176, Andrews
174	Lp 20 E, Big Spring, **S** Ⓟ Shell/dsl, Ⓞ 🅷, Big Spring SP, 🔄
172	Cauble Rd
171	Moore Field Rd
169	FM 2599
168mm	🛏 both lanes, tables, littter barrels
165	FM 818
158	Lp 20 W, to Stanton, **N** RV camping
156	TX 137, Lamesa, **S** Ⓟ Phillips 66/Stripes/Subway/dsl/24hr, Ⓕ Sonic, 🛏 Comfort Inn
154	US 80, Stanton, **2 mi S** access to gas, food, lodging
151	FM 829 (from wb)
144	Loop 250, **2-3 mi N** facilities in Midland
143mm	frontage rd (from eb)
142mm	🛏 both lanes, tables, litter barrels, hist marker
140	FM 307 (from eb)
138	TX 158, FM 715, Greenwood, **N** Ⓟ Shell/dsl, United/dsl, Ⓕ KD's BBQ, Whataburger, **S** Ⓟ Stripes/Subway/dsl
137	Old Lamesa Rd
136	TX 349, Midland, **N** Ⓟ Murphy USA, Stripes/tacos/dsl, Ⓕ Cici's Pizza, Domino's, IHOP, Jack-in-the-Box, Little Caesars, McAlister's Deli, Sonic, Starbucks, 🛏 Best Western, Comfort Inn, Country Inn&Suites, West Texas Inn, Ⓞ Advance Parts, AutoZone, Chavez Tires, Discount Tire, $General, $Tree, Family$, Petroleum Museum, Verizon, Walmart, **S** Ⓟ Exxon/Burger King/dsl, Daves Gas/NAPA, Stripes/tacos
135	Cotton Flat Rd, **S** 🅷
134	Midkiff Rd, **0-1 mi** (Wall St) **N** Ⓟ Fina/7-11, Exxon/dsl, Shell, Stripes/Subway/dsl, Ⓕ Denny's, DQ, 🛏 Best Value Inn, Bradford Inn, Days Inn, Executive Inn, Knights Inn, La Quinta, Studio 6, Super 8, Ⓞ 🅷, Bo's RV Ctr, Chevrolet, Chrysler/Dodge/Jeep, Honda, Ford, Mercedes/Volvo, Midland RV Park, Nissan, Subaru, Toyota/Scion
131	TX 158, Midland, **N** 🛏 Travelodge, **S** Ⓞ Midland RV Park
126	FM 1788, **N** Ⓟ Chevron/Stripes/tacos/dsl, ▦/McDonald's/dsl/scales/24hr, Warfield/Texaco/Subway/dsl/scales/@, Ⓞ Western Auto, museum, 🔄
121	Lp 338, Odessa, **0-3 mi** (TX 191) **N** Ⓟ Alon/7-11, Stripes/tacos/dsl, Ⓕ Buffet King, Carino's, Casa Ole, Cheddar's, Chili's, Domino's, Fazoli's, Fuddruckers, Golden Corral, Harigan's Grill, Hooters, IHOP, Jack-in-the-Box, KFC, Logan's Roadhouse, McDonald's, Pizza Hut, Red Lobster, Schlotzsky's, Sonic, Subway, Twin Peaks Rest, Wendy's, Wienerschnitzel, Whataburger, 🛏 Days Inn, Comfort Suites, Elegante Hotel, Fairfield Inn, Hampton Inn Express, Hilton Garden, Holiday Inn, Holiday Inn Express, La Quinta, Parkway Inn, Quality Inn, Studio 6, Super Inn, TownePlace Suites, Ⓞ Albertsons, AT&T, Buick/GMC, Chevrolet, Dillard's, $Gerneral, $Tree, Hobby Lobby, Home

⬆E INTERSTATE 20 CONT'D

Exit	Services
121	Continued
	Depot, Honda, Hyundai, JC Penney, Lowe's, Mazda, Nissan, Sears/auto, Sam's Club/gas, Staples, Target, Toyota/Scion, Verizon, Walmart/Subway, USPO, U of TX Permian Basin
120	JBS Pkwy, **N** 🛏 Super 8, Comfort Inn, ◎ Mack/Volvo
118	FM 3503, Grandview Ave, **N** 🅿 Alon/dsl, ◎ Freightliner/Peterbilt
116	US 385, Craine, Andrews, **N** 🅿 Chevron/dsl, Stripes/tacos, 🍴 DQ, La Margarita, 🛏 Best Western, Delux Inn, Villa West Inn, ◎ H $General, Family$, city park, **S** 🅿 Alon/dsl, Shell/dsl, 🛏 Motel 6
115	FM 1882, **N** 🅿 Stripes/tacos/dsl/24hr, **S** 🅿 ♥Loves/McDonald's/Subway/dsl/scales/24hr
113	TX 302, Odessa
112	FM 1936, Odessa
108	Moss Ave, Meteor Crater
104	FM 866, Meteor Crater Rd, Goldsmith, **N** RV park
103.5mm	**weigh sta both directions**
101	FM 1601, Penwell
93	FM 1053
86	TX 41, **N** Monahans Sandhills SP, camping
83	US 80, Monahans, **2 mi N** ◎ H, RV camping
80	TX 18, Monahans, **N** 🅿 Chevron/dsl, 🍴 Bar-H Steaks, DQ, Great Wall Buffet, McDonald's, Pappy's BBQ, Pizza Hut, Sonic, ◎ H, Aloo, $General, Family$, Lowe's Foods, O'Reilly Parts, Verizon, RV Park, repair/tires, **S** 🅿 Alon/dsl, Texaco/Huddle House/dsl/24hr, Stripes/Subway/dsl, 🍴 Huddle House, 🛏 Best Value Inn, Best Western, Comfort Inn, Texan Inn, ◎ Buick/Chevrolet/GMC, Chrysler/Dodge/Jeep
79	Lp 464, Monahans
76	US 80, Monahans, **2 mi N** ◎ to Million Barrel Museum, RV camping
73	FM 1219, Wickett, **N** 🅿 Phillips 66/Allsup's/dsl, **S** 🅿 Texaco/Subway/dsl/24hr
70	TX 65
69.5mm	🆁🆂 both lanes, full ♿ facilities, 🆁, 🗑, litter barrels, pet-walk, wi-fi
66	TX 115, FM 1927, to Pyote
58	frontage rd, multiple oil wells
52	Lp 20 W, to Barstow
49	FM 516, to Barstow
48mm	Pecos River
44	Collie Rd
42	US 285, Pecos, **N** 🅿 Alon, ✈FLYING J/Denny's/dsl/scales/24hr, ♥Loves/Chesters/Subway/dsl/scales/24hr, Shell/dsl, Stripes, 🍴 Alfredo's Mexican, DQ, El Rodeo Mexican, Golden Palace Chinese, Pizza Hut, 🛏 Holiday Inn Express, Motel 6, Quality Inn, OakTree Inn, ◎ AutoZone, Walmart, museum, tire repair
40	Country Club Dr, **N** 🛏 Comfort Suites, ◎ st patrol, **S** 🅿 Stripes/Subway, 🍴 Alpine Lodge Rest, 🛏 Best Western/rest., ◎ Pecos Park/Zoo, RV camping, municipal park
39	TX 17, Pecos, **S** 🛏 Hampton Inn, ◎ H, Buick/Chevrolet/GMC, Pecos Tire, Trapark RV Park
37	Lp 20 E, **2 mi N** 🍴 Sonic, 🛏 Pecos Economy Inn
33	FM 869
29	Shaw Rd, **S** to TX AM Ag Sta

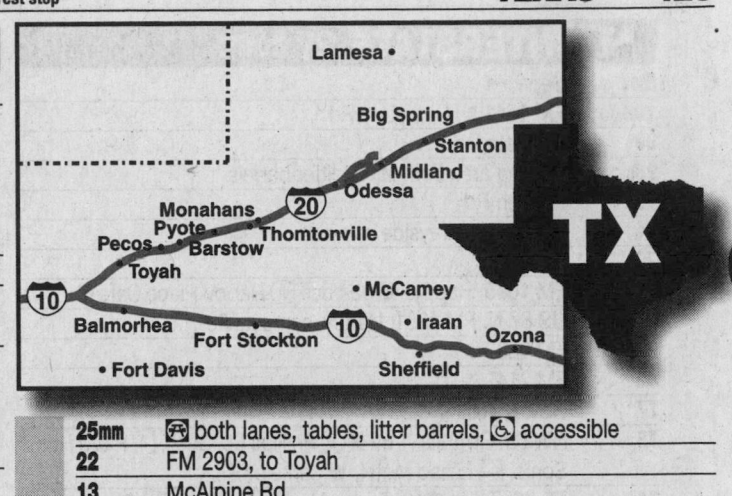

25mm	🆁 both lanes, tables, litter barrels, ♿ accessible
22	FM 2903, to Toyah
13	McAlpine Rd
7	Johnson Rd
3	Stocks Rd
0mm	I-20 begins/ends on I-10, 187mm.

⬆N INTERSTATE 27

Exit	Services
I-27 begins/ends on I-40, exit 70 in Amarillo.	
123b	I-40, W to Albuquerque, E to OK City
123a	26th Ave, **E** 🅿 Discount Gas, **W** 🍴 DJ Burgers
122c	from sb only
122a	34th Ave, Tyler St, **E** 🅿 Shell, Valero, 🍴 Sonic
122b	FM 1541, Washington St, Parker St, Moss Lane, **W** 🍴 Hungry Howie's, Taco Bell, Thai Express
121a	Hawthorne Dr, Austin St, **E** 🛏 Amarillo Motel, **W** ◎ Scottie's Transmissions
121b	Georgia St, **E** 🅿 Murphy USA/dsl, ◎ Buick/GMC, Honda, Subaru, Walmart/McDonald's
120b	45th Ave, **E** 🍴 Waffle House, ◎ O'Reilly Parts, repair, **W** 🅿 Shell, Valero, 🍴 Abuelo's Mexican, Burger King, Donut Stop, Gatti's Pizza, GJ's Cafe, McDonald's, Whataburger, ◎ Advance Parts, Dodge, $General, Drug Emporium, Walgreens, vet
120a	Republic Ave
119b a	(from sb), Western St, 58th Ave, **E** 🅿 Phillips 66, 🍴 Sonic, Subway, ◎ $General, **W** 🅿 Shell/dsl, Valero, 🍴 Arby's, Braum's, LJ Silver, Pizza Hut, Thai Palace, Wendy's, ◎ Aamco, U-Haul, Walgreens, USPO
119a	(from nb), **W** Hillside
117	Bell St, Arden Rd, **W** 🅿 Shell, 🍴 Popeye's, Sonic, ◎ $General
116	Lp 335, Hollywood Rd, **E** 🅿 ♥Loves/Subway/dsl/scales/24hr, Phillips 66/dsl, 🍴 McDonald's, Waffle House, Whataburger, 🛏 Canyon View Motel, Comfort Suites, **W** 🛏 Holiday Inn Express, ◎ H (8mi)
115	Sundown Lane
113	McCormick Rd, **E** ◎ $General, Ford, **W** ◎ Family Camping Ctr
112	FM 2219, **E** ◎ Stater's RV Ctr
111	Rockwell Rd, **W** ◎ Buick/GMC
110	(from sb), US 87 S, US 60 W, Canyon
109	Buffalo Stadium Rd, **W** stadium
108	FM 3331, Hunsley Rd
106	TX 217, to Palo Duro Cyn SP, Canyon, **E** ◎ Palo Duro Canyon SP (10mi), Palo Duro RV Park, **3 mi W** 🍴 McDonald's, 🛏 Buffalo Inn, Holiday Inn Express, ◎ Plains Museum, to WTA&M

TX

⬆N INTERSTATE 27 CONT'D

Exit	Services
103	FM 1541 N, Cemetery Rd
99	Hungate Rd
98mm	parking area both lanes, litter barrels
96	Dowlen Rd
94	FM 285, to Wayside
92	Haley Rd
90	FM 1075, Happy, **W** gas/dsl, 🍴 Happy Place Cafe
88b a	US 87 N, FM 1881, Happy, same as 90
83	FM 2698
82	FM 214
77	US 87, Tulia
75	NW 6th St, Tulia, **1 mi E** 🅖 Phillips 66, Shell, 🍴 Pizza Hut, Sonic, 🏠 Lasso Motel, **W** same as 74
74	TX 86, Tulia, **E** 🏠 Lasso Motel, 🄾 🄷, **W** 🅖 Rip Griffin/Shell/Subway/dsl/scales/24hr, 🏠 Executive Inn
70mm	parking area both lanes, litter barrels
68	FM 928
63	FM 145, Kress, **1 mi E** gas/dsl, food, 🅲
61	US 87, County Rd
56	FM 788
54	FM 3183, to Plainview
53	Lp 27, Plainview, **E** 🄾 🄷, access to gas, camping, food, lodging
51	Quincy St
50	TX 194, Plainview, **E** 🅖 Phillips 66, 🄾 🄷, to Wayland Bapt U, **W** 🏠 Reddy Hotel
49	US 70, Plainview, **E** 🅖 Allstar/dsl, Conoco, Fina/dsl, Shell/dsl, 🍴 A&W/LJ Silver, Carlito's Mexican, China Dragon, Cotton Patch Café, Domino's, Furr's Café, Leal's Mexican, Pizza Hut, 🏠 Best Western, Comfort Suites, Days Inn, 🄾 AutoZone, Beall's, $Tree, Ford/Lincoln, GNC, NAPA, O'Reilly Parts, Radio Shack, Toyota, United Foods, **W** 🅖 Chevron, Murphy USA/dsl, Phillips 66/dsl, 🍴 Burger King, Chicken Express, Chili's, Empire Buffet, IHOP, McDonald's, Monterrey Mexican, Sonic, Subway, Taco Bell, Wendy's, 🏠 Holiday Inn Express, Knights Inn, Super 8, 🄾 Verizon, Walmart/McDonald's
48	FM 3466, Plainview (from nb)
45	Lp 27, to Plainview
43	FM 2337
41	County Rd
38	Main St
37	FM 1914, Cleveland St, **E** 🅖 Co-op, **W** 🅖 Conoco, 🄾 🄷, Lowe's Foods, city park
36	FM 1424 Hale Center
32	FM 37 W
31	FM 37 E
29mm	🅁🆂 both lanes, full 🅯 facilities, 🅲, 🚮, litter barrels, petwalk, tornado shelter, vending
27	County Rd
24	FM 54, **W** RV park/dump
22	Lp 369, Abernathy
21	FM 597, Main St, Abernathy, **W** 🅖 Conoco/dsl, 🍴 DQ, 🄾 $General, USPO
20	FM 597, Abernathy (from nb)
17	CR 53
15	Lp 461, to New Deal, same as 14
14	FM 1729, **E** 🅖 Fina/rest/dsl/scales/24hr
13	Lp 461, to New Deal
12	access rd (from nb)

PLAINVIEW

11	FM 1294, Shallowater
10	Keuka St, **E** 🄾 Fed Ex
9	🅖 Rd, **E** 🅖, **W** 🄾 Lubbock RV Park/LP/dump
8	FM 2641, Regis St, **E** 🅖
7	Yucca Lane, **E** Pharr RV Ctr
6b a	Lp 289, Ave Q, Lubbock, **E** 🄾 Pharr RV
5	B. Holly Ave, Municipal Dr, **E** 🄾 Mackenzie Park, **W** 🄾 Civic Ctr
4	US 82, US 87, 4th St, to Crosbyton, **E** funpark, **W** 🅖 ✈FLYING J/Subway/dsl/LP/scales/24hr, 🄾 to TTU
3	US 62, TX 114, 19th St, Floydada
2	34th St, **E** 🅖 Phillips 66, 🍴 Pete's Drive Inn, **W** 🅖 Valero, 🍴 Simple Simon's Pizza, Subway, 🄾 AutoZone, Raff&Hall Drug, U-Haul
1c	50th St, **E** 🅖 Buddy's, 🍴 El Jalapeno Café, **W** 🅖 Bolton Fuel/dsl, Fina/7-11, Valero, 🍴 A&W/LJ Silver, Bryan's Steaks, Burger King, China Star, Church's, Domino's, KFC, McDonald's, Pizza Hut/Taco Bell, Subway, Taco Villa, Tech Cafe, Whataburger, Wienerschnitzel, 🏠 Travelodge, 🄾 $General, Family$, O'Reilly Parts, United Food/gas, Walgreens, USPO
1b	US 84, **E** 🏠 Best Value Inn, Days Inn, **W** 🏠 Best Western, Comfort Inn, Holiday Inn Express, Motel 6, Quality Inn, Red Roof Inn, Super 8, Value Place
1a	Lp 289
1	82nd St, **W** 🅖 Phillips 66/dsl, **I-27 begins/ends on US 87 at 82nd St in S Lubbock.**

LUBBOCK

⬆E INTERSTATE 30

Exit	Services
223mm	Texas/Arkansas state line
223b a	US 59, US 71, State Line Ave, Texarkana, **N** 🅖 EZ Mart, Mobil/dsl, Shell/dsl, 🍴 Denny's, IHOP, Pizza Inn, Waffle House, 🏠 Baymont Inn, Best Western, Clarion, Holiday Inn Express, Howard Johnson, LaCrosse Hotel, La Quinta, Quality Inn, Ramada Inn, Regency Inn, Super 8, Wyndham Garden, 🄾 Cooper Tire, Firestone, KOA, **S** 🅖 Chevron/dsl, Conoco, Exxon, RaceWay/dsl, Shell, 🍴 Burger King, Cattleman's Steaks, China Inn, China King, Fuzzy's Tacos, Hooters, Joe's Pizza, KFC, Little Caesars, LJ Silver, Marble Slab, McDonald's, Papa John's, Pizza Hut, Popeye's, Quiznos, Schlotzsky's, Subway, Taco Bell, Taco Tico, Wendy's, Whataburger, 🏠 Ambassador Inn, Best Value Inn, Days Inn, EconoLodge, Economy Inn, La Quinta, Rodeway Inn, 🄾 Albertson's/Sav-On, AutoZone, Chevrolet, CVS Drug, $General, $Tree, Hancock Fabrics, Kia, O'Reilly Parts, Radio Shack, Walgreens, Walmart, city park
223mm	**Welcome Ctr wb, full 🅯 facilities, info, 🅲, 🚮, litter barrels, vending, petwalk**
222	TX 93, FM 1397, Summerhill Rd, **N** 🅖 EZ Mart, Shell, Valero/Subway/dsl, 🍴 Applebee's, McDonald's, Shogun Steaks, Waffle House, 🏠 Motel 6, 🄾 AT&T, Freightliner, Goodyear/auto, Hyundai, **S** 🅖 Shell, 🍴 Bryce's Rest., Catfish King, 🄾 Discount Wheel&Tire, Ford, Gateway Tires, Nissan
220b	FM 559, Richmond Rd, **N** 🅖 Chevron, Exxon, Shell, 🍴 Asian Grill, Buffalo Wild Wings, Burger King, Carino's Italian, Cracker Barrel, Chick-fil-A, CiCi's Pizza, Coldstone Creamery, Domino's, Genghis Grill, Jason's Deli, Jimmy John's, Little Caesars, Longhorn Steaks, McAlister's Deli, On-the-Border, Osaka Japanese, Pizza Hut, Red Lobster, Ruby Tuesday, Sonic, Starbucks, Taco Bell, TaMolly's

TEXARKANA

↑E INTERSTATE 30 CONT'D

Exit	Services
220b	Continued
	Mexican, TX Roadhouse, Wendy's, Wing Stop, 🏠 Comfort Suites, Courtyard, TownePlace Suites, 🅾 AT&T, Best Buy, Chevrolet, Discount Tire, $Tree, Home Depot, Honda, Kohls, Kwik Kar, Old Navy, Petsmart, Sam's Club/gas, Staples, Super 1 Food/gas, Target, TJ Maxx, Verizon, **S** 🅟 Valero/dsl, 🍴 Arby's, Chili's, ChuckeCheese, Firehouse Subs, Golden Corral, Grandy's, McDonald's, Olive Garden, Outback Steaks, Quiznos, Subway, Taco Bueno, 🏠 Candlewood Suites, Fairfield Inn, Hampton Inn, Hilton Garden/Conv Ctr, Holiday Inn Express, 🅾 AT&T, Albertson's/Sav-On, Books-A-Million, Buick/GMC, Cadillac, Cavender's Boots, CVS Drug, Dillard's, Hobby Lobby, JC Penney, Jeep, Mazda, Michael's, Office Depot, Ross, Sears/auto, Tuesday Morning, Walgreens, mall
220a	US 59 S, Texarkana
219	Pecan St, University Ave, **S** 🅟 Exxon, Murphy USA, 🍴 Subway, Wendy's, 🏠 Country Inn&Suites, 🅾 Buick/GMC, Cadillac, Chrysler/Dodge/Jeep, Gander Mtn, Harley-Davidson, Lowe's, Mazda, Mercedes, Radio Shack, Walmart, vet
218	FM 989, Nash, **N** 🅟 Road Runner/dsl, 🍴 Dixie Diner, **S** 🅟 Exxon/Burger King/dsl, 🍴 Sonic, 🅾 GMC/Peterbilt, Toyota/Scion, USPO, to Lake Patman
213	FM 2253, Leary, **S** 🅟 ❤Loves/McDonald's/Subway/dsl/scales/24hr
212	spur 74, Lone Star Army Ammo Plant, **S** 🅟 Shell
208	FM 560, Hooks, **S** 🅟 Texaco/Subway/dsl/scales/24hr, 🍴 DQ, Sonic, TasteeHouse Rest., 🅾 $General, Family$, Hooks Tire
207	no services
206	TX 86, **S** 🅾 Red River Army Depot
201	TX 8, New Boston, **N** 🅟 Shell/dsl, Valero/dsl, 🍴 Pitt Grill, 🏠 Tex Inn, 🅾 Chevrolet, Chrysler/Dodge/Jeep, **S** 🅟 Murphy USA/dsl, Shell/dsl, 🍴 Catfish King, Church's, DQ, Domino's, KFC/Taco Bell, McDonald's, Pizza Hut, Randy's BBQ, Sonic, 🏠 Best Value Inn, Bostonian Inn, Holiday Inn Express, 🅾 🅷, Brookshire's Foods/gas, Ford, O'Reilly Parts, Verizon, Walmart/Subway, RV park
199	US 82, DeKalb, **1/2 mi N** 🅟 Shell
198	TX 98, **1/2 mi N** 🅟 Shell
193mm	Anderson Creek
192	FM 990, **N** 🅟 FuelStop/Culpeppers Rest/dsl
186	FM 561
181mm	Sulphur River
178	US 259, to DeKalb, Omaha
174mm	White Oak Creek
170	FM 1993
165	FM 1001, **S** 🅟 Exxon/dsl
162b a	US 271, FM 1402, FM 2152, Mt Pleasant, **N** 🅟 Exxon/dsl, 🍴 Applebee's, Blalock BBQ, 🏠 Holiday Inn Express, Super 8, 🅾 KOA, **S** 🅟 Shell/Chester's/Pizza Inn/dsl, Valero/Subway/dsl, 🍴 Burger King, McDonald's, Sonic, 🏠 Best Western, 🅾 🅷, Cadillac/Chevrolet,Chrysler/Dodge/Jeep, Family$, Ford, vet
160	US 271, FM 1734, Mt Pleasant, **N** 🅟 Texaco/dsl, 🍴 Senorita's Mexican, 🏠 La Quinta, 🅾 Buick/GMC (1mi), Lowe's, Ramblin Fever RV Park (2mi), Toyota, **S** 🅟 Exxon/dsl, Shell/dsl, 🍴 El Chico, HideOut Rest, IHOP, Varsity Diner, 🏠 Days Inn, Executive Inn, Hampton Inn, Quality Inn, 🅾 Sandlin SP

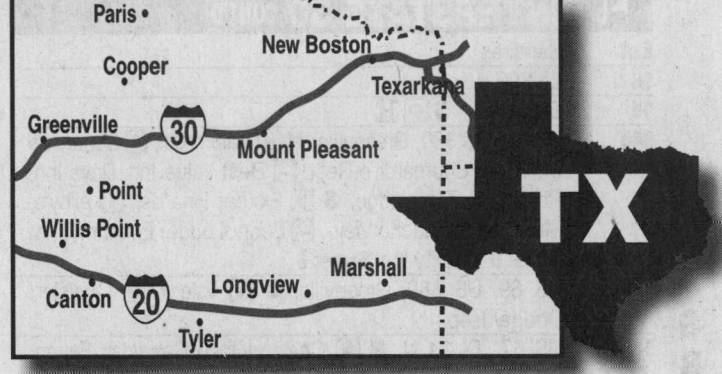

158mm	weigh sta both lanes
156	frontage rd
153	spur 185, to Winfield, Millers Cove, **N** 🅟 Phillips 66, Winfield/dsl, **S** 🅟 Shamrock/dsl
150	Ripley Rd, **N** 🅾 Lowe's Distribution
147	spur 423, **N** 🅟 ❤Loves/Chester's/Subway/dsl/scales /24hr, 🏠 American Inn, Economy Inn, 🅾 tires/repair
146	TX 37, Mt Vernon, **N** 🅟 Shell/dsl, 🍴 Sonic, 🅾 Alco, auto repair, 🅾 🅷, **S** 🅟 Exxon/dsl, 🍴 Burger King, DQ, Mi Casita, Mt Vernon Cafe, TX BBQ Corral, 🏠 Super 8, 🅾 to Lake Bob Sandlin SP
143	🆁🆂 both lanes, full ♿ facilities, 🍴, 🏠, litter barrels, vending, petwalk
142	County Line Rd (from eb)
141	FM 900, Saltillo Rd
136	FM 269, Weaver Rd
135	US 67 N
131	FM 69
127	US 67, Lp 301, **N** 🏠 Comfort Suites, Days Inn, Ferrari Inn, Motel 6, 🅾 🅷, **S** 🅟 Shell, 🍴 Burton's Rest, 🏠 Best Western
126	FM 1870, College St, **S** 🅟 Shell, 🏠 Best Western, 🅾 Firestone/auto, same as 127
125	Bill Bradford Rd, same as 124
124	TX 11, TX 154, Sulphur Springs, **N** 🅟 Exxon, 🍴 Bodacious BBQ, Chicken Express, Juan Pablo's Mexican, Lakeside Buffet, Pizza Hut, San Remo Italian, Subway, 🏠 Hampton Inn, Holiday Inn Express, La Quinta, Royal Inn, 🅾 🅷, AutoZone, CVS Drug, $General, Family$, Ford/Lincoln, FSA Outlet/famous brands, O'Reilly Parts, VF Outlet/famous brands, Walgreens, USPO, **S** 🅟 Exxon/dsl, Murphy USA/dsl, Shell, 🍴 Braum's, Burger King, Chili's, China House, Domino's, Furr's Rest., H-H Steaks, Jack-in-the-Box, LJ Silver/Taco Bell, McDonald's, Sonic, Whataburger, 🅾 Cody Drug, Discount Wheel&Tire, Lowe's, Radio Shack, Verizon, Walmart/Subway
123	FM 2297, League St, **N** 🅟 Shamrock/dsl, Shell
122	TX 19, to Emory, **N** 🅟 Shamrock, 🅾 🅷, Chrysler/Dodge/Jeep, **S** 🅟 ❤/Arby's/dsl/scales/24hr, 🅾 dsl repair, RV Park, vet, to Cooper Lake SP
120	US 67 bus
116	FM 2653, Brashear Rd
112	FM 499 (from wb)
110	FM 275, Cumby, **N** 🅟 Phillips 66/dsl, **S** 🅟 Shell
104	FM 513, FM 2649, Campbell, **S** to Lake Tawakoni
101	TX 24, TX 50, FM 1737, to Commerce, **N** 🅟 Valero/dsl, 🅾 to E TX St U, **S** 🍴 TX Beach Club Grill
97	Lamar St, **N** 🅟 Exxon/dsl, 🏠 Budget Inn, Dream Lodge Motel, **S** 🅾 vet

Left margin (vertical): NEW BOSTON   MT PLEASANT   SULPHUR SPGS

INTERSTATE 30 CONT'D

Exit	Services
96	Lp 302
95	Division St, S 🅞 🄷
94b	US 69, US 380, Greenville, N 🅡 Valero/dsl, 🍴 Senorita's Mexican, Shumardii's Rest, 🏠 Best Value Inn, Days Inn, Royal Inn, Travelodge, S 🅡 Exxon, Fina/dsl, 🍴 Arby's, McDonald's, Racho Viejo, 🏠 EconoLodge, Economy Inn, Motel 6, Quality Inn, Super 8
94a	US 69, US 380, Greenville, S 🅡 Valero, 🅞 Chrysler/Dodge/Jeep
93b a	US 67, TX 34 N, N 🅡 Chevron/Taco Casa/dsl, Exxon, Shell/dsl, Texaco, 🍴 Applebee's, Chick-fil-A, Chicken Express, CiCi's, DQ, Grandy's, IHOP, Jack-in-the-Box, KFC, Little Caesars, Pizza Hut, Schlotzsky's, Sonic, Starbucks, Subway, Taco Bell, Taco Bueno, Tony's Italian, Wendy's, Whataburger, 🏠 Hampton Inn, 🅞 🄷, AT&T, Beall's, Belk, BigLots, Braum's, Brookshire's Foods, Discount Tire, JC Penney, Kwik Kar, Lowe's, O'Reilly Parts, Staples, Verizon, Walgreens, USPO, mall, transmissions, S 🅡 Exxon/dsl, Valero/dsl, 🍴 Chili's, Cracker Barrel, Jersey's Grill, Molino's Mexican, Paesano Italian, Papa Murphy's, Red Lobster, Soulman's BBQ, Subway, TaMolly's Mexican, 🏠 Best Western, Holiday Inn Express, 🅞 Buick/GMC, $Tree, Ford/Lincoln, Home Depot, Hyundai, Mitsubishi, Nissan, NTB, Radio Shack, RV Ctr, Walmart
92	Stratton Pkwy
90mm	Farber Creek
89	FM 1570, S 🏠 Luxury Inn
89mm	E Caddo Creek
87	FM 1903, N 🅡 Chevron/dsl, 🅞 fireworks, S 🅡 🆁🆂/McDonald's/dsl/scales/24hr, Texaco/Huddle House/dsl, 🍴 Baker's Ribs, 🅞 tire repair
87mm	Elm Creek
85	FM 36, Caddo Mills, N KOA
85mm	W Caddo Creek
83	FM 1565 N, N 🅡 Exxon/dsl
79	FM 2642, N Budget RV Ctr, S vet
77b	FM 35, Royse City, N 🅡 Exxon/dsl, Texaco/Subway/dsl/scales/24hr, 🍴 Soulman's BBQ, 🅞 Family$
77a	TX 548, Royse City, N 🅡 Shell/dsl, 🍴 Jack-in-the-Box, McDonald's, 🏠 Royse Inn, 🅞 AutoZone, tires, S 🅡 Exxon/KFC/Quiznos, 🍴 Denny's, Rice Express, Sonic, 🏠 Holiday Inn Express
73	FM 551, Fate
70	FM 549, N 🅞 Happy Trails RV Ctr, Hyundai, McLains RV Ctr, S 🅡 Loves/Carl's Jr./dsl/scales/24hr
69	(from wb), frontage rd, N 🏠 Super 8, S 🅞 Toyota/Scion
68	TX 205, to Rock Wall, N 🅡 RaceWay, Shell, 🍴 Braum's, DQ, Jowilly's Grill, KFC, Luigi's Italian, Pizza Hut, Pizza Inn, Subway, Taco Casa, Whataburger, 🏠 Best Western, Super 8, Value Place, 🅞 Buick/GMC, Chevrolet, Dodge, Ford, Hobby Lobby, S 🅡 RaceTrac, TA/Burger King/Starbucks/dsl/24hr/scales/@, Valero/dsl, 🍴 Firehouse Subs, Freebird Burritos, In-N-Out, 🅞 Belk, Costco/gas, Jo-Ann Fabrics, Toyota/Scion
67	FM 740, Ridge Rd, N 🅡 Chevron, Murphy USA/dsl, 🍴 Arby's, Burger King, Carabba's, Culver's, Domino's, Grandy's, IHOP, Logan's Roadhouse, McDonald's, Popeye's, Schlotzsky's, Smoothie King, Starbucks, Steak'n Shake, Taco Bueno, Taco Cabana, Trevino's Mexican, Waffle House, Wendy's, 🏠 Hampton Inn, 🅞 Firestone/auto,

Exit	Services
67	Continued Goodyear/auto, Kwik Kar, Walmart, S 🅡 Exxon, Shell, Valero, 🍴 Applebee's, Bahama Buck's Ice Cream, Black-eyed Pea, Buffalo Wild Wings, Carino's Italian, Chick-fil-A, Chili's, Chipotle Mexican, ChuckeCheese, CiCi's, Cotton Patch Cafe, El Chico, 5 Guys Burgers, Jack-in-the-Box, La Madelein, McDonald's, Mi Cocina, Olive Garden, On-the-Border, Pizza Hut/Taco Bell, Quiznos, Shogun Steaks, Sonic, Soulman's BBQ, Starbucks, Subway, TGIFriday's, 🏠 La Quinta, 🅞 Albertson's, AT&T, Belk, Best Buy, CVS Drug, Dick's, Discount Tire, $Tree, GNC, Home Depot, JC Penney, Kohl's, Lowe's, Michael's, Office Depot, Old Navy, PetCo, Petsmart, Radio Shack, Ross, Staples, SteinMart, Target, TJ Maxx, Verizon, Walgreens, to Lake Tawakoni, vet
67a	Horizon Rd, Village Dr, N 🍴 Genghis Grill, Kyoto Japanese, Saltgrass Steaks, Snuffer's Rest, Starbucks, 🏠 Hampton Inn, S 🍴 Culpepper Steaks, Oar House, 🏠 Hilton, 🅞 Office Depot
66mm	Ray Hubbard Reservoir
64	Dalrock Rd, Rowlett, N 🅡 Shell/dsl, Valero/dsl, 🍴 Church's, Dickey's BBQ, 🏠 Comfort Suites, 🅞 🄷, Express Drug
63mm	Ray Hubbard Reservoir
62	Bass Pro Dr, N 🏠 Best Western, 🅞 to Hubbard RA, S 🅡 Shell/dsl, Texaco, Valero/dsl, 🍴 CiCi's Pizza, Flying Saucer Grill, Primo's Grill, Sonic, TexMex, TX Land&Cattle, Whataburger, 🅞 Bass Pro Shops
61	Zion Rd (from wb), N 🅡 Exxon/dsl, 🏠 Discovery Inn
60b	Bobtown Rd (eb only), N 🅡 Texaco/7-11, 🍴 Jack-in-the-Box, 🏠 La Quinta, S 🅡 Shell, 🍴 Subway
60a	Rose Hill Dr
59	Beltline Rd, Garland, N 🅡 QT, 7-11, 🍴 Chili's, China City, Denny's, IHOP, India Garden, KFC, McDonald's, Papa John's, Pizza Hut/Taco Bell, Quiznos, Starbucks, Subway, Taco Casa, Taco Cabana, Whataburger, Wendy's, 🅞 Albertson's, Discount Tire, GNC, Radio Shack, Tuesday Morning, Walgreens, Walmart, S 🍴 Baker's Ribs, Buffet King, Carl's Jr, DQ, Sonic, Waffle House, Williams Chicken, 🏠 Best Value Inn, Motel 6, Super 8, 🅞 Kroger
58	Northwest Dr, N 🅡 Shell, Valero/dsl, 🅞 Hyundai, Nissan, S 🅡 Fina, Texaco, 🍴 Jack-in-the-Box, 🅞 Lowe's
56c b	I-635 S-N
56a	Galloway Ave, Gus Thomasson Dr (from eb), N 🅡 Texaco, Valero, 🍴 KFC, McDonald's, Sonic, 🅞 AutoZone, Hyundai, USPO, S 🅡 Chevron, 7-11, 🍴 Church's, Dicky's BBQ, El Fenix, Grandy's, Hooters, Jack-in-the-Box, Luby's, Olive Garden, Outback Steaks, Razzoo's Cajun, Red Lobster, Sports City Cafe, Subway, TGIFriday's, Tops Buffet, Wendy's, 🏠 Courtyard, Crossland Suites, Delux Inn, Fairfield Inn, 🅞 🄷, Aldi Foods, BigLots, Celebration Sta Funpark, Firestone/auto, Kroger/dsl, Nichols RV Ctr, NTB
55	Motley Dr, N 🅡 Shell/dsl, 🏠 Astro Inn, Executive Inn, S 🅡 Chevron, 🏠 Microtel, 🅞 🄷, to Eastfield Coll
54	Big Town Blvd, N 🅡 Valero/dsl, 🏠 Mesquite Inn, S 🅞 Explore RV Ctr, Holiday World RV Ctr, dsl repair
53b	US 80 E (from eb), to Terrell
53a	Lp 12, Buckner, N 🅡 RaceTrac, Texaco, 🍴 Burger King, Circle Grill, 🏠 Holiday Inn Express, Luxury Inn, Super 8, 🅞 Chevrolet, Toyota/Scion, S 🍴 Pizza Hut, Taco Cabana, Whataburger, 🅞 $Tree, Radio Shack, Sam's Club/gas, Staples, Walmart

Side labels: TX, GREENVILLE, ROCK WALL, GARLAND, DALLAS

⬆E INTERSTATE 30 CONT'D

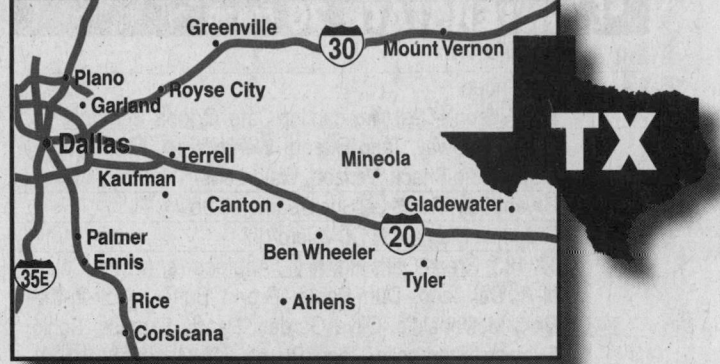

Exit	Services
51	(52 a from wb), Highland Rd, Jim Miller Blvd, **N** 🅖 Exxon, 🅕 Country China, Denny's, JP's Cafe, McDonald's, 🅛 Holiday Inn Express, La Quinta, **S** 🅖 RaceWay/dsl, Shell/dsl, 🅕 Burger King, Capt D's, CiCi's Pizza, Furr's Cafe, Grandy's, KFC, Subway, Taco Bell, Wendy's, 🅛 Motel 6, Super 7 Inn, 🅞 AutoZone, CVS Drug, O'Reilly Parts
50b a	Longview, Ferguson Rd, **N** 🅖 Texaco, **S** 🅞 Brake-O, U-Haul
49b	Dolphin Rd, Lawnview Ave, Samuell Ave, **N** 🅖 Shell, 🅛 Best Value Inn
49a	Winslow St, **N** 🅖 Circle K, Shell/dsl/repair, 🅕 Jack-in-the-Box, McDonald's, **S** 🅖 Circle K, Shell, 🅞 tires
48b	TX 78, E Grand, **S** fairpark, arboretum
48a	Carroll Ave, Central Ave, Peak St, Haskell Ave, **N** 🅖 7-11, Shamrock, Valero, 🅞 🅷 Hamm's Tires, **S** 🅕 Joe's Rest
47	2nd Ave, **S** 🅖 Shell, 🅕 McDonald's, 🅞 Cotton Bowl, fairpark
46b	I-45, US 75, to Houston
46a	Central Expswy, downtown
45	I-35E, N to Denton, to Commerce St, Lamar St, Griffin St, **S** 🅖 Gulf/dsl, 🅕 McDonald's, 🅛 Ambassador Inn
44b	I-35E S, Industrial Blvd
44a	I-35E N, Beckley Ave (from eb)
43b a	Sylvan Ave (from wb), **N** 🅖 Valero/dsl, 🅞 🅷 Family$, USPO
42	Hampton Rd
41	Westmoreland Ave
39	Cockrell Hill Rd, **N** 🅖 Shell/dsl, 🅕 Grand China, KFC/Taco Bell, IHOP, Pollo Campero, Sonic, Wing Stop, 🅛 Comfort Suites, Hampton Inn, 🅞 Staples, **S** 🅖 Murphy USA, 🅕 Chili's, Del Taco, Dickey's BBQ, Golden Corral, Lucky Rice, McDonald's, Panda Express, Starbucks, Subway, Taco Cabana, Wendy's, Whataburger, 🅛 Holiday Inn Express, 🅞 Best Buy, $Tree, Lowe's, Radio Shack, Ross, Walmart/McDonald's
38	Lp 12, **1 mi N** 🅖 Exxon/7-11, Whip-In/dsl, 🅕 Burger King, Popeye's
36	MacArthur Blvd, **S** 🅞 U-Haul
34	Belt Line Rd, **N** 🅖 Chevron, RaceTrac, 🅛 Studio 6, Super 8, 🅞 Ford, Ripley's Museum, **S** 🅖 RaceTrac/dsl, Shell/Subway, Valero, 🅕 Burger King, Popeye's, Schlotzsky's, Starbucks, 🅞 city park, vet
32ba	George Bush Tpk, **toll**, **N** 🅖 Shamrock
30	TX 360, Six Flags Dr, Arlington Stadium, **N** 🅖 Mobil/dsl, Shell, 🅕 Boston's, Cracker Barrel, Grand Buffet, Saltgrass Steaks, Steak'n Shake, TrailDust Steaks, Wendy's, 🅛 Best Inn, Budget Suites, Candlewood Suites, Crowne Plaza, Extended Stay America, Fairfield Inn, Hawthorn Suites, Hilton, Hilton Garden, Residence Inn, Studio 6, Wingate Inn, **S** 🅖 Shell/7-11/dsl, Valero, 🅕 Denny's, Jack-in-the-Box, McDonald's, Mariano's Mexican, Pancho's Mexican, Red Neck Heaven Rest, Subway, 🅛 Baymont Inn, Holiday Inn Express, Homewood Suites, Hyatt Place, Knight's Inn, La Quinta, Ranger Inn, Sleep Inn, 🅞 Ford/Lincoln, Six Flags Funpark
29	Ball Park Way, **N** 🅖 Chevron, QT, Valero, 🅕 Dicky's BBQ, Sonic, 🅛 Hampton Inn, Springhill Suites, Towneplace Suites, 🅞 Toyota/Scion, USPO, **S** 🅕 On-the-Border, 🅛 Howard Johnson, Sheraton, 🅞 Six Flags Funpark
28ba	FM 157, Collins St, **N** 🅖 Chevron/dsl, 🅕 Arby's, Chipotle,

Exit	Services
28ba	Continued IHOP, Waffle House, 🅞 Cadillac, Chrysler/Dodge/Jeep, 🅛 EconoLodge, Holiday Inn, 🅞 BMW, Whole Foods Mkt, **S** 🅕 Asian Buffet, Blackeyed Pea, Chick-fil-A, Chili's, Colter's BBQ, El Fenix, Hooters, Jason's Deli, Joe's Crab Shack, Panera Bread, Pappasito's Cantina, Poppadeaux, Souper Salad, Taco Bueno, TGIFriday's, Wendy's, 🅛 Comfort Suites, Courtyard, 🅞 Barnes&Noble, Best Buy, $Tree, Home Depot, Michael's, PepBoys, Petsmart, Save-A-Lot Foods, SteinMart, TX Stadium
27	Lamar Blvd, Cooper St, **N** 🅖 Texaco, 🅕 Jack-in-the-Box, 🅞 BigLots, Family$, Kroger/dsl, vet, **S** 🅖 7-11, Shell, 🅕 Burger King, Denny's, Tom's Burgers
26	Fielder Rd, **S** 🅞 to Six Flags (from eb)
25mm	Village Creek
24	Eastchase Pkwy, **N** 🅕 Jack-in-the-Box, Panda Express, 🅞 CarMax, Lowe's, Sam's Club/gas, Verizon, Walmart/McDonald's, **S** 🅖 Chevron/dsl, RaceTrac, Shell/7-11/dsl, 🅕 Burger King, Chicken Express, CiCi's Pizza, IHOP, McDonald's, No Frills Grill, Schlotzsky's, Subway, Taco Bell, Wendy's, Whataburger, 🅞 AT&T, GNC, Office Depot, Radio Shack, Ross, Target
23	Cooks Lane, **S** 🅖 Shell
21c b	I-820
21a	Bridgewood Dr, **N** 🅖 Chevron, 🅕 Braums, Church's, KFC, Jack-in-the-Box, Luby's, Subway, Wendy's, 🅞 Albertson's, Discount Tire, $General, Firestone, Home Depot, U-Haul, **S** 🅖 Conoco, Phillips 66, QT, 🅕 Domino's, Taco Bueno, Whataburger/24hr
19	Brentwood Stair Rd (from eb), **N** 🅖 Shell, **S** 🅖 Shamrock, Texaco, 🅞 Family$
18	Oakland Blvd, **N** 🅖 Circle K, Shell/dsl, 🅕 Taco Bell, Waffle House, 🅛 Motel 6
16c	Beach St, **S** 🅖 7-11, 🅛 Ambassador Hotel, Inn Suites
16b a	Riverside Dr (from wb), **S** 🅛 Great Western Inn
15b a	I-35W N to Denton, S to Waco
14b	Jones St, Commerce St, Ft Worth, downtown
14a	TX 199, Henderson St, Ft Worth, downtown
13b	TX 199, Henderson St, **N** 🅛 Omni, Sheraton
13a	8th Ave, **N** 🅛 Holiday Inn Express
12b	Forest Park Blvd, **N** 🅕 Pappa's Burgers, Pappadeaux Café, Pappasito's, **S** 🅞 🅷 Urgent Care
12a	University Dr, City Parks, **S** 🅛 SpringHill Suites
11	Montgomery St, **S** 🅖 Shell/7-11/dsl, 🅕 Taco Bell, Whataburger, 🅞 visitor info
10	Hulen St, Ft Worth, **S** 🅕 Chick-fil-A, McDonald's, Smoothie King, Starbucks, 🅞 Central Mkt, WorldMkt
9b	US 377, Camp Bowie Blvd, Horne St, **N** 🅕 Uncle Julio's Mexican, **S** 🅖 Exxon, 7-11, Texaco/dsl, 🅕 Jack-in-the-

TX

⟵E INTERSTATE 30 CONT'D

Exit	Services
9b	Continued
	Box, Jason's Deli, Mexican Inn Cafe, Qdoba, Schlotzsky's, Sonic, Subway, Taco Bueno, Wendy's, ⊙ AT&T, Batteries+, Radio Shack, Verizon, Walgreens
9a	Bryant-Irvin Rd, S 🖩 Shell, same as 9b
8b	Ridgmar, Ridglea, N 🖩 Valero/dsl
8a	TX 183, Green Oaks Rd, N 🍴 Applebee's, Arby's, Chick-fil-A, Del Taco, Don Pablo, Grand Buffet, Jack-in-the-Box, McDonald's, Olive Garden, Panda Express, Sonic, Subway, Starbucks, Taco Bueno, 🛏 Courtyard, ⊙ Albertson's, Aldi Foods, AT&T, Best Buy, BigLots, $Tree, Dillard's, Firestone/auto, JC Penney, Jo-Ann Fabrics, Lowe's, Macy's, Neiman Marcus, NTB, Office Depot, Old Navy, PetCo, Petsmart, Radio Shack, Ross, Sam's Club/gas, Sears/auto, Target, U-Haul, Verizon, Walmart/Subway, S 🛏 Fairfield Inn, Hampton Inn
7b a	Cherry Lane, TX 183, spur 341, to Green Oaks Rd, N 🖩 Shell/7-11, Texaco/dsl, Valero/dsl, 🍴 ChuckECheese, IHOP, Popeye's, Ryan's, Subway, Wendy's, 🛏 La Quinta, Motel 6, ⊙ O'Reilly Parts, U-Haul, same as 8a, S 🛏 Holiday Inn Express, Quality Inn, Super 8
6	Las Vegas Trail, N 🖩 Chevron/McDonald's/dsl, Conoco/dsl, 🍴 Jack-in-the-Box, Waffle House, 🛏 Days Inn, ⊙ Hyundai, Suzuki, S 🖩 Alon, Shell/7-11/dsl, Valero/dsl, 🛏 Best Value Inn, Knights Inn, Relax Inn, ⊙ AutoZone, Kia
5b c	I-820 N and S
5a	Alemeda St (from eb, no EZ return)
3	RM 2871, Chapel Creek Blvd, S 🖩 Exxon/Church's/Subway, 🍴 Sonic
2	spur 580 E
1b	Linkcrest Dr, S 🖩 Gulf/dsl
0mm	I-20 W. I-30 begins/ends on I-20, exit 421.

⟵N⟶ INTERSTATE 35

Exit	Services
504mm	Texas/Oklahoma state line, Red River
504	frontage rd, access to **Texas Welcome Ctr**
503mm	parking area both lanes
502mm	Welcome Ctr sb, full ♿ facilities, TX Tourist Bureau/info, 🍴, 🅡🅢, litter barrels, wireless internet
501	FM 1202, Prime Outlets Blvd, E ⊙ Chrysler/Dodge/Jeep, Ford, W 🖩 Conoco/café/dsl, 🍴 Applebee's, Cracker Barrel, Serna's Mexican, 🛏 Hampton Inn, La Quinta, ⊙ Prime Outlets/famous brands, Western Outfitter, RV camping
500	FM 372, Gainesville, W 🖩 Hitchin' Post/Shell/dsl
498b a	US 82, to Wichita Falls, Gainesville, Sherman, E 🖩 Exxon, Chevron/dsl, Shell/dsl, Valero/dsl, 🍴 TX Border Rest, Waffle Inn, 🛏 Bed&Bath Inn, Budget Host, Super 8, 12 Oaks Inn, ⊙ 🖈, W 🖩 Exxon/dsl, 🛏 Atria Inn, Comfort Suites, Days Inn
497	frontage rd, W 🖩 Valero/dsl
496b	TX 51, FM 51, California St, Gainesville, E 🍴 Arby's, Braum's, Fera's Mexican, IHOP, McDonald's, Starbucks, Taco Bell, Taco Casa, Sonic, Starbucks, Wendy's, 🛏 Holiday Inn Express, Quality Inn, ⊙ Goodyear/auto, N Central TX Coll, W 🖩 Valero, 🍴 Chili's
496a	to Weaver St
496mm	Elm Fork of the Trinity River
495	frontage rd
494	FM 1306

GAINESVILLE

Exit	Services
492mm	🅡🅢 sb, tables, litter barrels
491	Spring Creek Rd
490mm	🅡🅢 nb, 🅡🅢, litter barrels
489	(488 from nb), FM 1307, to Hockley Creek Rd
487	FM 922, Valley View, W 🖩 Valero/dsl/24hr, 🍴 DQ, ⊙ USPO
486	Fm 1307, W 🖩 Texaco/dsl, 🛏 Motel 6, ⊙ $General
485	frontage rd (from sb)
483	FM 3002, Lone Oak Rd, E Shell/Church's/Subway/dsl, ⊙ Roberts Lake SP
482	Chisam Rd
481	View Rd, W ⊙ McClain's RV Ctr
480	Lois Rd, E ⊙ Walmart Dist Ctr
479	Belz Rd, Sanger, same as 478
478	FM 455, to Pilot Pt, Bolivar, E 🖩 QuickTrack, Shell, 🍴 DQ, Fuzzy's Tacos, Miguelitos, Sonic, Subway, Taco Bell, 🛏 Sanger Inn, ⊙ RV park, USPO, W 🖩 Chevron/dsl, Fuel 4 TX/Chicken Express/dsl, 🍴 Jack-in-the-Box, McDonald's, ⊙ Chevrolet, Family$, IGA Foods, Kwik Kar Lube, O'Reilly Parts, RV Park, Ray Roberts Lake and SP
477	Keaton Rd, E 🖩 Exxon, ⊙ Curves
475b	Rector Rd
475a	FM 156, to Krum (from sb)
474	Cowling rd (from nb)
473	FM 3163, Milam Rd, E 🖩 Loves/Subway/dsl/scales/24hr
472	Ganzer Rd, W Best Value RV Ctr, Crandell RV Ctr
471	US 77, FM 1173, Lp 282, to Denton, Krum, E 🖩 TA/Pizza Hut/Taco Bell/dsl/scales/24hr/@, ⊙ 🖈, W ⊙ Foster's Western Shop, truckwash, to Camping World RV Supply
470	Lp 288, same services as 469 from sb
469	US 380, University Dr, to Decatur, McKinney, E 🖩 Chevron/Subway, RaceTrac/dsl, 🍴 Braum's, Catfish King, Chick-fil-A, ChinaTown Café, Cowboy Chicken, Cracker Barrel, Freebird's Burrito, Luigi's Pizza, McDonald's, Panda Express, Taco Casa, Villa Grande, Whataburger, Which Wich, Wing Stop, 🛏 Best Western, Fairfield Inn, ⊙ Albertson's/Sav-On, AT&T, GNC, Jo-Ann Fabrics, Kohl's, Kwik Kar, PetCo, Ross, Sam's Club/gas, Walmart/McDonald's, W 🖩 QT/dsl, Shell/dsl, 🍴 DQ, Denny's, Sonic, Waffle House, 🛏 Comfort Inn, Days Inn, Holiday Inn Express, Howard Johnson, La Quinta, Motel 6, ValuePlace Inn, ⊙ 🖈, Camping World RV Supply, I-35 RV Ctr, to TX Woman's U
468	FM 1515, ⊙ Rd, W Oak St, E 🖈
467	I-35W, S to Ft Worth
I-35 divides into E and W sb, converges into I-35 nb. See Texas I-35 W.	
466b	Ave D, E 🖩 Exxon/dsl, 🍴 IHOP, McDonald's, Pancho's Mexican, Taco Cabana, 🛏 Comfort Suites, ⊙ $General, Sack'n Save Foods, to NTSU
466a	McCormick St, E 🖩 EKon, Shell/7-11/dsl, 🍴 Poncho's Mexican, Taco Cabana, 🛏 Comfort Suites, Royal Inn, ⊙ Sack&Save, W 🖩 Fina/dsl
465b	US 377, Ft Worth Dr, E 🖩 RaceTrac/dsl, Valero, 🍴 Michael's Kitchen, Taco Bell, Taco Bueno, Whataburger, 🛏 La Quinta, W 🖩 EKon, QuickTrack, 🍴 Outback Steaks, Sonic, 🛏 Knights Inn
465a	FM 2181, Teasley Ln, E 🖩 7-11, 🍴 Applebee's, Braum's, Carino's, ChuckECheese, Domino's, Hooters, KFC, Little Caesars, Pizza Hut, 🛏 Hampton Inn, Holiday Inn, Quality Inn, ⊙ Brookshires Foods, PepBoys, U-Haul, bank, W 🖩 Exxon, Shell, 🍴 La Milpa Mexican, Rudy's BBQ/gas, 🛏

DENTON

⬆N   INTERSTATE 35 CONT'D

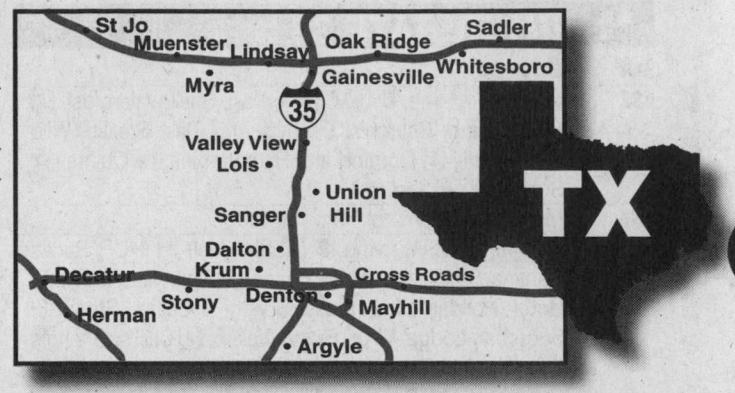

Exit	Services
465a	Continued
	Best Value Inn, Super 8, 🅞 vet
464	US 77, Pennsylvania Dr, Denton, same as 463
463	Lp 288, to McKinney, E 🍴 Arby's, Buffet King, Burger King, CiCi's Pizza, El Chico, El Fenix, Golden Corral, Grandy's, Jason's Deli, McAlister's Deli, Olive Garden, On-the-Border, Pizza Hut/Taco Bell, Red Lobster, Starbucks, TX Roadhouse, Wendy's, 🏠 Best Western, Courtyard, Hilton Garden, 🅞 AT&T, Barnes&Noble, BigLots, Burlington Coats, Dillards, Discount Tire, $Tree, Goodyear, Hastings Books, Hobby Lobby, Home Depot, JC Penney, Macy's, Office Depot, Old Navy, PetCo, Ross, Sears/auto, Staples, Target, Verizon, W 🅖 Chevron/dsl, 🍴 Blackeyed Pea, Chili's, Chuy's Mexican, Genghis Grill, Italia Cafe, Jack-in-the-Box, Schlotzsky's, 🏠 Homewood Suites, 🅞 vet, same as 464
462	State School Rd, Mayhill Rd, E 🅖 QT, 🍴 Dickey's BBQ, 🅞 🏥, Urgent Care, W 🅖 Exxon, 🍴 Shogun Japanese, Sonic, 🅞 Buick/GMC, Cadillac, Chevrolet, Curves, Dodge, Honda, Toyota/Scion
461	Sandy Shores Rd, Post Oak Dr, E 🅞 Explore USA RV Ctr, Ford, Hyundai, vet, W 🅞 Christian Bros Auto, Chrysler/Dodge/Jeep, Kia, Mazda, Nissan, Subaru
460	Corinth Pkwy, E 🅖 Chevron/dsl, 🅞 McClains RV Ctr, camping, W 🅞 Harley-Davidson
459	frontage rd, W 🅞 Destiny RV Resort
458	FM 2181, Swisher Rd, E 🅖 Circle K, QT/dsl, Shell, 🏠 Best Western, Comfort Inn, 🅞 O'Reilly Parts, W 🅖 Chevron/McDonald's, Exxon/7-11, Murphy USA/dsl, 🍴 Burger King, Chicken Express, Chick-fil-A, IHOP, Jack-in-the-Box, KFC/Taco Bell, IHOP, Little Caesars, McDonald's, Sonic, Starbucks, Subway, Wendy's, Whataburger, 🅞 Albertson's, AutoZone, Discount Tire, GNC, Kwik Kar, Radio Shack, Walgreens, Walmart, Urgent Care
457b	Denton Rd, Hundley Dr, Lake Dallas, W 🍴 Chili's, Hickory Creek BBQ, TX L&C Steaks
457a	Hundley Dr (from nb), Lake Dallas
456	Highland Village
456mm	Lewisville Lake
454b	Garden Ridge Blvd, W 🅖 Fuel4TX, 🅞 city park
454a	FM 407, Justin, E 🅖 Valero, 🍴 Old House BBQ, W 🅖 QT, Valero, 🍴 McDonald's
453	Valley Ridge Blvd, E 🅞 Ford, May's RV, W 🅖 Chevron, 🍴 Burger King, Subway, 🅞 Home Depot, Kohl's, Lowe's, Staples
452	FM 1171, to Flower Mound, E 🍴 IHOP, Taco Bueno, 🏠 Select Inn, 🅞 🏥, W 🅖 Shell, 🍴 Buffet Palace, Cane's, Chick-fil-A, Chipotle Mexican, CiCi's Pizza, Corner Cafe, Grandy's, McDonald's, Panda Express, Taco Bell, Taco Cabana, Whataburger, 🅞 Albertson's, Midas, PetCo, Radio Shack, Sam's Club/gas, Staples, U-Haul, Walmart, transmissions, Urgent Care, same as 451
451	Fox Ave, E 🅖 Shell/dsl, 🍴 Braum's, W 🅖 Chevron, 🍴 Cracker Barrel, 🏠 EconoLodge, Hampton Inn, 🅞 Family$, VW
450	TX 121, Lewisville, E 🅖 7-11, 🏠 Texan Inn, 🅞 Chrysler/Dodge/Jeep, $General, Oliver's Automotive, W 🅖 Chevron, Conoco/dsl, Fina/dsl, 🍴 Burger King, Church's, LJ Silver, McDonald's, Subway, Taco Bell, Waffle House, 🅞

Exit	Services
450	Continued
	Firestone/auto, Kroger, Kwik Kar, Nissan, Toyota/Scion, transmissions
449	Corporate Drive, E 🅖 Valero/dsl, 🍴 Awshucks Oyster Bar, Fox&Hound, Hooters, On-the-Border, Wild Ginger Steaks, 🏠 Extended Stay America, Motel 6, 🅞 Cavender's Boots, Chevrolet, Honda, Just Brakes, transmissions, W 🅖 Valero, 🍴 Cantina Loredo, Chili's, Denny's, El Fenix, Outback Steaks, 🏠 Best Western, La Quinta, 🅞 $Tree, Jo-Ann Fabrics, Marshall's, NTB, Petsmart
448b a	FM 3040, Round Grove Rd, E 🅖 Citgo, 7-11, 🍴 Abuelo's Mexican, A&W, Cane's, ChuckeCheese, Dickey's BBQ, Frankie's Grill, Jack-in-the-Box, Joe's Crabshack, LJ Silver, Mimi's Cafe, Olive Garden, Pei Wei, Saltgrass Steaks, Souper Salad, Starbuks, Subway, Tilted Kilt, 🏠 Homewood Suites, 🅞 Honda, Radio Shack, Ross, Target, W 🅖 Exxon/7-11, RaceTrac, 🍴 Applebee's, BJ's Grill, Buffalo Wild Wings, Carino's Italian, Chick-fil-A, Chipotle Mexican, Cotton Patch Rest, Denny's, Firehouse Subs, 5 Guys Burgers, IHOP, Jason's Deli, La Madeline Bakery, Logan's Roadhouse, Macaroni Grill, McDonald's, Panda Express, Red Lobster, Redneck Heaven BBQ, Schlotzsky's, Sonic, Spring Creek BBQ, Starbucks, Steak'n Shake, Taco Bueno, Taco Cabana, TGIFriday's, Twin Peaks, 🏠 Comfort Suites, Country Inn&Suites, Courtyard, Fairfield Inn, Hampton Inn, Hilton Garden, Holiday Inn Express, Old Country Inn, 🅞 AT&T, Barnes&Noble, Best Buy, Costco/gas, Dillard's, Discount Tire, JC Penney, Macy's, Michael's, Office Depot, Old Navy, Sears/auto, Verizon, mall
446	Frankford Rd, E 🅖 RaceTrac, 🍴 La Hacienda Ranch Grill, 🅞 Volvo
445b a	Pres Geo Bush Tpk
444	Whitlock Lane, Sandy Lake Rd, E 🅖 Shell, 🍴 Bros Pizza, El Paisa, La Hacienda, 🏠 Rodeway Inn, 🅞 Buick/GMC, Kia, RV camping, W 🍴 McDonald's, Starbucks, 🏠 Delux Inn, 🅞 Harley-Davidson
443	Belt Line Rd, Crosby Rd, E 🅖 RaceTrac, 🅞 Ford, Hyundai, NTB, W 🅖 Shell, 🅞 Chevrolet, U-Haul
442	Valwood Pkwy, E 🅖 Chevron/Subway, 🍴 Abby's Mexican, DQ, Grandy's, Jack-in-the-Box, Redline Burgers, Taco Bueno, Waffle House, 🏠 Guest Inn, LoneStar Inn, Royal Inn, Super 8, 🅞 Hill Tire, W 🅖 Fina/dsl, 🅞 transmissions
441	Valley View Lane, W 🅖 Chevron, Shell, 🍴 Michael's Rest., 🏠 Best Value Inn, Days Inn, La Quinta
440b	I-635 E
440c	I-635 W, to DFW ✈
439	Royal Lane, E 🅖 Shamrock, Shell, 🍴 McDonald's, W 🅖 Chevron, Exxon/dsl, 🍴 Jack-in-the-Box

Left margin (top to bottom): LEWISVILLE

Left margin (bottom): DALLAS

TX

⬆N INTERSTATE 35 CONT'D

DALLAS

Exit	Services
438	Walnut Hill Lane, **E** 🅖 Chevron/dsl, Shell, Valero/dsl, 🍴 Burger King, Church's, Denny's, Trail Dust Steaks, Wild Turkey Grill, 🛏 Comfort Inn, Hampton Inn, La Quinta, 🅞 Suzuki, **W** 🅖 Shell/dsl
437	Manana Rd (from nb), same as 438
436	TX 348, to DFW, Irving, **E** 🅖 Shell/dsl, 🍴 IHOP, Rucas Cantina, Starbucks, Waffle House, 🛏 Courtyard, Elegante Hotel, Holiday Inn Express, SpringHill Suites, Studio 6, Suburban Lodge, **W** 🅖 Exxon, Valero, 🍴 Chili's, Ghengis Grill, Humperdinks, Jack-in-the-Box, Jason's Deli, Joe's Crabshack, McDonald's, Olive Garden, Papadeaux Seafood, Pappa's BBQ, Pappasito's Mexican, Red Lobster, Taco Bell/Pizza Hut, TX L&C, Wendy's, 🛏 Best Value Inn, Budget Suites, Century Inn
435	Harry Hines Blvd (from nb)
434b	Regal Row, **E** 🅖 Texaco/Grandy's, 🍴 Denny's, Whataburger, 🛏 Motel 6, **W** 🛏 Ramada Inn
434a	Empire, Central, **E** 🅖 Shell/McDonald's, 🍴 Kay's Rest, Sonic, Wendy's, 🛏 Budget Suites, Candlewood Suites, InTown Suites, Wingate Inn, 🅞 Office Depot, **W** 🅖 Texaco, 🍴 Burger King, Pizza Hut/Taco Bell, Schlotzsky's
433b	Mockingbird Lane, Love Field 🛬, **E** 🅖 Shell/dsl, 🍴 Jack-in-the-Box, 🛏 Budget Suites, Comfort Inn, Crowne Plaza, Park Inn, Radisson, Residence Inn, Sheraton
433a	(432b from sb)TX 356, Commonwealth Dr, **W** 🛏 Delux Inn
432a	Inwood Rd, **E** 🅖 Exxon/7-11, 🅞 🏥, Chevrolet, **W** 🅖 Texaco/Subway/dsl, Shell, 🍴 Whataburger, 🛏 Embassy Suites, Holiday Inn Express, Homewood Suites
431	Motor St, **E** 🅖 Chevron, 🍴 Denny's, 🅞 🏥, **W** 🅖 Shell/7-11, 🍴 Alamo Rest, 🛏 Marriott Suites
430c	Wycliff Ave, **E** 🍴 JoJo's Rest., 🛏 Holiday Inn, Renaissance Hotel, 🅞 Intn'l Apparel Mart, **W** 🛏 Hilton Anatole, Hilton Garden
430b	Mkt Ctr Blvd, **E** 🅞 World Trade Ctr, **W** 🅖 Shell, 🍴 Denny's, 🛏 Courtyard, DoubleTree, Fairfield Inn, Ramada Inn, Sheraton Suites, Wyndham Garden
430a	Oak Lawn Ave, **E** 🛏 Holiday Inn, **W** 🅖 Shell, Texaco/dsl, 🍴 Denny's, Medieval Times Rest., 🅞 to Merchandise Mart
429c	HiLine Ave (from nb)
429b	Continental Ave, Commerce St W downtown, **E** 🍴 Hooters, **W** 🅖 Exxon, Shell, 🍴 McDonald's
429a	to I-45, US 75, to Houston
428e	Commerce St E, Reunion Blvd, Dallas, downtown
428d	I-30 W, to Ft Worth
428a	I-30 E, to I-45 S
428b	Industrial Blvd, **E** 🅖 Exxon, **W** 🅖 Gulf/dsl, Shamrock
427b	I-30 E
427a	Colorado Blvd, **E** 🏥
426c	Jefferson Ave, **E** 🅖 Shell/dsl
426b	TX 180 W, 8th St, **E** 🅖 Shell/dsl
426a	Ewing Ave, **E** 🍴 McDonald's, Popeye's
425c	Marsalis Ave, **W** 🅖 Chevron, Valero, 🍴 Jack-in-the-Box
425b	Beckley Ave, 12th St, sb only, **W** 🅖 Shell, Valero, 🍴 Wendy's
425a	Zang Blvd same as 425b
424	Illinois Ave, **E** 🅖 Chevron, 🍴 William's Chicken, 🅞 🏥 **W** 🅖 Exxon/7-11, 🍴 Church's, Jack-in-the-Box, Pancake House, Sonic, Subway, Taco Bell, 🛏 Oak Tree Inn, 🅞 Kroger, Ross, Walgreens

Exit	Services
423b	Saner Ave
423a	(422b from nb)US 67 S, Kiest Blvd, **W** 🅖 Shell/repair, 🍴 McDonald's, Subway, Taco Del Mar, 🛏 Dallas Inn
421b	Ann Arbor St, **W** 🅖 Exxon/dsl, 🅞 L&L Repair
421a	Lp 12E W, **E** 🅖 RaceWay, 🛏 Delux Inn
420	Laureland, **W** 🅖 Exxon/dsl, Texaco, 🛏 Linfield Inn
419	Camp Wisdom Rd, **E** 🅖 Exxon, 🍴 Jack-in-the-Box, 🛏 Oak Cliff Inn, **W** 🅖 Chevron, Shell, 🍴 McDonald's, 🛏 Grand Inn, 🅞 U-Haul
418c	Danieldale Rd (from sb)
418b	I-635/I-20 E, to Shreveport
418a	I-20 W, to Ft Worth
417	Wheatland Rd (from nb)
416	Wintergreen Rd, **E** 🅞 repair, **W** 🅖 7-11, 🍴 Cracker Barrel, Waffle House, 🛏 Days Inn, Grande Hotel, Hampton Inn, Holiday Inn Express
415	Pleasant Run Rd, **E** 🅖 Chevron, Shell/dsl, 🍴 Bienvenidos Mexican, Chili's, Chubby's, CiCi's Pizza, Grandy's, Evergreen Buffet, IHOP, In-N-Out, Logan's Roadhouse, Subway, Taco Cabana, Waffle House, 🛏 Great Western Inn, Hwy Express Inn, Motel 6, Royal Inn, Spanish Trails Motel, 🅞 Home Depot, Kia, NAPA, **W** 🅖 Chevron, 🍴 Burger King, Dicky's BBQ, El Chico, KFC, LJ Silver, Luby's, McDonald's, On the Border, Outback Steaks, Starbucks, Taco Bueno, Wendy's, 🛏 Best Value Inn, Best Western, La Quinta, 🅞 🏥, AT&T, Chevrolet, Discount Tire, Firestone/auto, Ford, Kroger, Office Depot, Ross
414	FM 1382, Desoto Rd, Belt Line Rd, **E** 🅖 Murphy USA/dsl, 🍴 Taco Bell, Whataburger, 🅞 Radio Shack, Walmart/McDonald's, **W** 🅖 QT, Shell
413	Parkerville Rd, **W** 🅖 Exxon/Subway, 🅞 U-Haul
412	Bear Creek Rd, **W** 🅖 Shell/dsl, 🍴 Jack-in-the-Box, Whataburger, 🅞 HiHo RV Ctr, transmissions, vet
411	FM 664, Ovilla Rd, **E** 🅖 Exxon, RaceTrac, 🍴 DQ, Denny's, LJ Silver/Taco Bell, McDonald's, Whataburger, 🛏 Comfort Inn, 🅞 Brookshire's Foods, CVS Drug, Walmart, **W** 🅖 Exxon/Subway, Shamrock
410	Red Oak Rd, **E** 🅖 Shell/Pizza Inn/Subway/dsl, Valero, 🛏 Best Value Inn, **W** 🅞 Hilltop Travel Trailers
408	US 77, TX 342, to Red Oak, **E** golf
406	Sterrett Rd, **E** fireworks
405	FM 387, **E** 🅖 Phillips 66/dsl
404	Lofland Rd, industrial area
403	US 287, to Ft Worth, **E** 🅖 RacTrac, Valero, 🍴 A&W/LJ Silver, Carino's, Chick-fil-A, Chili's, DQ, El Fenix, IHOP, Jack-in-the-Box, KFC, Logan's Roadhouse, McDonald's, Panda Express, Pizza Hut, Taco Bell, Taco Bueno, Waffle House, Wendy's, 🛏 Comfort Suites, Hampton Inn, Holiday Inn Express, 🅞 Belk, Best Buy, Cadillac/Chevrolet, Discount Tire, Home Depot, Lowe's, Office Depot, Ross, Target, Walmart, **W** 🅞 Buick/GMC, Chrysler/Dodge/Jeep, Ford
401b	US 287 bus, Waxahatchie, **E** 🛏 Best Value Inn, Super 8
401a	Brookside Rd, **E** 🛏 American Suites, Executive Inn, **W** vet
399b	FM 1446
399a	FM 66, FM 876, Maypearl, **E** 🛏 Texas Inn, **W** 🅖 Exxon/dsl
397	to US 77, to Waxahachie
393mm	🆁🆂 both lanes, full 🛏 facilities, 🍴, 🅖, litter barrels, vending, petwalk
391	FM 329, Forreston Rd
386	TX 34, Italy, **E** gas Shell/Smokehouse BBQ/dsl, 🍴 Son

WAXAHATCHIE

⬆N INTERSTATE 35 CONT'D

Exit	Services
386	Continued
	ic, ⊙ $General, W ⑪ Exxon/Grandy's/McDonald's/dsl/scales, ⑪ Pizza Inn, Subway, ⌂ Italy Inn, ⊙ truckwash
384	Derrs Chapel Rd
381	FM 566, Milford Rd
377	FM 934
374	FM 2959, Carl's Corner, W ⑪ Petro/Exxon/Dunkin Donuts/Iron Skillet/dsl/scales/24hr
371	I-35 W. I-35 divides into E and W nb, converges sb. See Texas I-35 W.
370	US 77 N, FM 579, Hillsboro
368b	FM 286 (from sb), E ⑪ LoneStar Café, Taco Bell, Wendy's, ⌂ Hampton Inn, W ⑪ Exxon, Valero/dsl, ⑪ Braum's, El Conquistador Mexican, El Taco Jalisco, Pizza Hut, ⌂ Best Value Inn, Comfort Inn, EconoLodge, La Quinta, ⊙ H
368a	TX 22, TX 171, to Whitney, E ⑪ 7-11, ♥Loves/Chester's/Subway/dsl/scales/24hr, ⑪ Arby's, Blackeyed Pea, DQ, Harvest Buffet, IHOP, McDonald's, Starbucks, ⌂ Comfort Suites, Days Inn, Holiday Inn Express, Motel 6, Super 8, ⊙ Hillsboro Outlets/Famous Brands, W ⑪ Chevron/dsl, Mobil, Murphy USA/dsl, 7-11, ⑪ Chicken Express, Jack-in-the-Box, KFC, Schlotzsky's, Whataburger, ⌂ Thunderbird Motel/rest., ⊙ Chrysler/Dodge/Jeep, Ford, Walmart/Subway
367	Old Bynum Rd (from nb), same as 368
364b	TX 81 N, to Hillsboro (from nb, exits left)
364a	FM 310 (from sb)
362	CR 3111
361mm	Rs both directions, full facilities, ⊞, litter barrels, petwalk
359	FM 1304, W ⑪ Mobil/dsl/24hr, ⊙ truckwash
358	FM 1242 E, Abbott, E ⑪ Up in Smoke BBQ
356	Co Rd 3102
355	County Line Rd, E ⊙ Waco North RV Park
354	Marable St, E ⊙ Waco North RV Park
353	FM 2114, West, E ⑪ Chevron/dsl, Shell/Czech Bakery, ⑪ Bush's Chicken, Sonic, Subway, ⊙ Ford, W ⌂ Czech Inn, ⊙ Chevrolet, auto repair
351	FM 1858, E tires/repair
349	Wiggins Rd
347	FM 3149, Tours Rd
346	Ross Rd, W ⑪ Exxon/Church's/dsl/24hr, ⊙ I-35 RV Park/LP, antiques
345	Old Dallas Rd, E ⊙ antiques, W ⊙ I-35 RV Park/LP
345a	frontage rd, same as 345
343	FM 308, Elm Mott, E ⑪ Exxon/DQ, Shell/Jct Cafe/dsl/scales/24hr, W ⊙ $General
342b	US 77 bus, W North Crest RV Park
342a	FM 2417, Crest Dr, W ⑪ Valero/dsl, ⑪ Bush's Chicken, DQ, ⌂ Everyday Inn, ⊙ Family$, auto repair
341	Craven Ave, Lacy Lakeview, W ⑪ Chevron, Shell
340	Myers Lane (from nb)
339	to TX 6 S, FM 3051, Lake Waco, E ⑪ Valero/dsl, ⑪ Casa Ole, Cici's Pizza, Domino's, El Conquistador, Jack-in-the-Box, Luby's, Pizza Hut, Popeye's, Sonic, Subway, Wendy's, Whataburger, WingStop, ⌂ Holiday Inn, ⊙ Advance Parts, Discount Tire, $General, Home Depot, Walmart, W ⑪ Chevron, Shell, ⑪ Burger King, Cracker Barrel, Heitmiller Steaks, KFC, McDonald's, Starbucks, Taco Bell, ⌂ Fairfield Inn, Hampton Inn, ⊙ AT&T, Urgent Care, to ✈

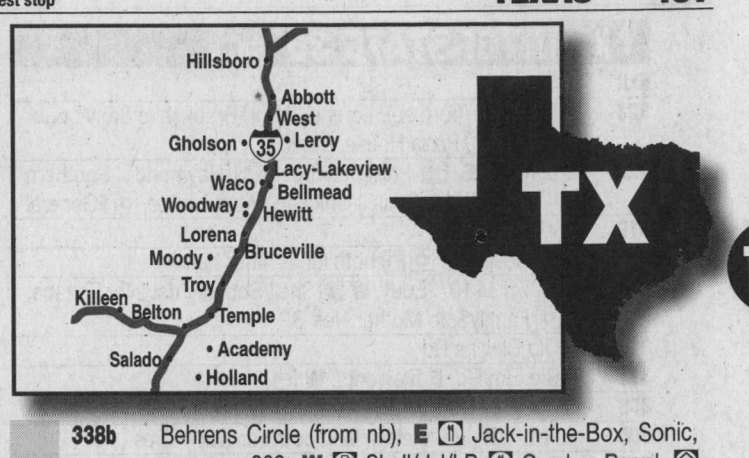

Exit	Services
338b	Behrens Circle (from nb), E ⑪ Jack-in-the-Box, Sonic, same as 339, W ⑪ Shell/dsl/LP, ⑪ Cracker Barrel, ⌂ Comfort Inn, Country Inn&Suites, Days Inn, Delta Inn, Hampton Inn, Knights Inn, Motel 6
338a	US 84, to TX 31, Waco Dr, E ⑪ Phillips 66, ⑪ Subway, ⌂ Value Place Suites, ⊙ AutoZone, Family$, HEB Food/gas, O'Reilly Parts, Sam's Club/gas, W ⌂ Orchid Hotel, ⊙ H
337	US 77 business
335c	Lake Brazos Dr, MLK Blvd, W ⑪ Buzzard Billy's, ⌂ Scottish Inn, Victorian Inn, ⊙ H
335mm	Brazos River
335b	FM 434, University Parks Dr, E ⑪ Chili's, Starbucks, ⊙ Baylor U, TX Ranger Museum, W ⑪ Arby's, Jack-in-the-Box, Magic China, ⌂ Best Value Inn, Residence Inn
335a	4th St, 5th St, E ⑪ Exxon/Subway/dsl, ⑪ Denny's, IHOP, Pizza Hut, ⌂ Best Western, La Quinta, ⊙ Baylor U, W ⑪ Chevron/dsl, Valero/dsl, ⑪ Fazoli's, LJ Silver, McDonald's, Taco Bell, Taco Bueno, Taco Cabana, Wendy's, Whataburger, ⌂ Clarion
334b	US 77 S, 17th St, 18th St, E ⑪ Phillips 66, Shell/dsl, ⑪ Burger King, Popeye's, Schlotzsky's, Vitek's BBQ, ⌂ Budget Inn, Magnuson Hotel, Super 8, W ⑪ Phillips 66/dsl, Shell, ⑪ Arranda's Mexican, ⊙ H
333a	Lp 396, Valley Mills Dr, E ⑪ El Chico, Elite Café, Rudy's BBQ, TX Roadhouse, Trujillo's Mexican, ⌂ Comfort Suites, La Quinta, Motel 6, ⊙ Kia, Mazda, Suzuki, W ⑪ RaceWay, Valero, ⑪ Bush's Chicken, Catfish King, Church's, Jack-in-the-Box, Little Caesars, Papa John's, Sonic, Subway, ⊙ Aamco, Advance Parts, AutoZone, CVS Drug, Family$, HEB Foods, Lincoln, Walgreens
331	New Rd, E ⑪ Phillips 66, ⌂ New Road Inn, Relax Inn, Rodeway Inn, W ⑪ ⊕FLYING J/Denny's/dsl/scales/24hr, ⑪ Burger King, Carl's Jr, Hooters, IHOP, ⌂ Quality Inn, ⊙ Harley Davidson
330	Lp 340, TX 6, 0-2 mi W ⑪ Chevron, ⑪ Bush's Chicken, Chuy's Mexican, Coldstone, Don Carlo's Mexican, Logan's Roadhouse, Outback Steaks, Panda Express, Panera Bread, Sonic, Subway, TGIFriday's, ⌂ Extended Stay America, Fairfield Inn, Hampton Inn, Homewood Suites, ⊙ H, Belk, Best Buy, Books-A-Million, Ford, Honda, Hyundai, Kohl's, Lowe's, Marshall's, Nissan, Office Depot, Ross, Old Navy, Toyota/Scion, Verizon, Walmart, Urgent Care
328	FM 2063, FM 2113, Moody, E ⑪ ▥▥/Subway/Wendy's/dsl/scales/24hr/@, ⑪ McDonald's, ⌂ Days Inn, ⊙ Kenworth, W ⑪ Shell, Valero/dsl, ⑪ DQ, ⌂ Ramada Inn, Sleep Inn
325	FM 3148, Moonlight Dr, W ⑪ Smiley's/dsl, ⊙ FunTown RV Ctr

H I L L S B O R O

W A C O

P = gas   ⊓ = food   △ = lodging   ⊙ = other   ⧖ = rest stop   Copyright 2014 - The NEXT Exit

TX

⭢ INTERSTATE 35 CONT'D

Exit	Services
323	FM 2837 (from sb), Lorena, **W** P Brookshire Bros/Conoco/dsl, ⊓ Pizza House, Sonic
322	Lorena, **E** P Phillips 66/dsl, ⊓ Raymond's Southern Kitchen, **W** ⊓ Bush's Chicken, Pizza House, ⊙ $General
319	Woodlawn Rd
318b a	Bruceville, **E** ⊙ ⧖ both lanes, litter barrels
315	TX 7, FM 107, Eddy, **W** P Shell/Subway/dsl/24hr, Texaco, ⊙ Family$, to Mother Neff SP
314	Old Blevins Rd
311	Big Elm Rd, **E** fireworks, **W** ⧖
308	FM 935, Troy, **W** P Exxon, ⊙ dsl repair
306	FM 1237, Pendleton, **W** Goodyear Truck Tires
305	Berger Rd, **W** ⊙ Lucky's RV Park, repair
304	Lp 363, Dodgen Loop, **W** P Shell/Wendy's/dsl, ⊙ Freightliner
303	spur 290, N 3rd St, Temple, **E** P S-2 Gas, △ Texas Inn, **W** △ Continental Inn
302	Nugent Ave, **E** P Exxon/dsl, Texaco, △ Baymont Inn, Best Value Inn, EconoLodge, Quality Inn, **W** P Pay Less Gas, Shell/dsl, ⊓ Denny's, △ Days Inn, Knights Inn, Motel 6, Stratford House Inn
301	TX 53, FM 2305, Adams Ave, **E** P Valero, ⊓ Arby's, Chick-fil-A, KFC, LJ Silver, Mad Mongo's Grill, McDonald's, Pizza Hut, Starbucks, Subway, Taco Bell, Wendy's, Whataburger, △ La Quinta, ⊙ H, Advance Parts, Ford/Lincoln, HEB Foods, **W** ⊓ TX Roadhouse, △ Best Western, ⊙ Hyundai
300	Ave H, 49th –57th Sts, **E** ⊓ Clem Mikeskas BBQ
299	US 190 E, TX 36, **E** P Shell, ⊓ Cracker Barrel, Jack-in-the-Box, Luby's, Olive Garden, △ Budget Inn, Residence Inn, Travelodge, ⊙ H, AT&T, Chrysler/Dodge/Jeep, NTP, Verizon, **W** ⊓ BJ's Rest, Chili's, Chipotle Mexican, 5 Guys Burgers, IHOP, McDonald's, Subway, Taco Cabana, ⊙ Best Buy, GNC, Home Depot, Michael's, Petsmart, Target
298	nb only, to frontage rd, **E** △ Residence Inn
297	FM 817, Midway Dr, **E** P Phillips 66/dsl, △ Holiday Inn, Super 8/rest., ⊙ Nissan, **W** P Valero, ⊙ Meineke, VW
294b	FM 93, 6th Ave, **E** P Shell/dsl, ⊓ McDonald's, ⊙ Chevrolet, Toyota/Scion, **W** ⊓ Subway, △ River Forest Inn, ⊙ Harley-Davidson, U of Mary Hardin Baylor
294a	Central Ave, **W** P Shell/dsl, ⊓ Burger King, El Mexicano Grill, Pizza Hut, Schlotzsky's, Sonic, Taco Bell, Whataburger, △ Knights Inn, ⊙ AutoZone, O'Reilly Parts, Parts+, city park, USPO
293b	TX 317, FM 436, Main St
293a	US 190 W, to Killeen, Ft Hood
292	Lp 121 (same as 293a), **E** P Valero/rest./dsl/24hr, △ Budget Host, **W** P Mobil/dsl, ⊓ Oxbow Steaks, △ La Quinta, ⊙ Belton RV Park, Sunbelt RV Ctr
290	Shanklin Rd
289	Tahuaya Rd
287	Amity Rd
286	FM 2484, **E** △ Best Western, Holiday Inn Express, **W** ⊙ Tranquil RV Park (2mi), to Stillhouse Hollow Lake
285	FM 2268, Salado, **E** ⊓ Subway, △ Holiday Inn Express, ⊙ Brookshire Foods/gas, **W** P Pay Less, ⊓ Cowboys BBQ, Robertson's Rest., Rush's Chicken, Sonic
284	Stagecoach Rd, **E** P Exxon/Arby's, △ Stagecoach Inn, **W** ⊙ ⊓ DQ, Johnny's Steaks
283	FM 2268, FM 2843, to Holland, Salado, **E** △ Stagecoach Inn

TEMPLE (vertical)

282	FM 2115, **E** P Valero/dsl, ⧖ sb, full ♿ facilities, ⊓, picnic table, litter barrels, vending, petwalk, RV dump
281mm	⧖ nb, full ♿ facilities, ⊓, picnic table, litter barrels, vending, petwalk, RV dump
280	Prairie Dell
279	Hill Rd
277	Rd 305
275	FM 487, to Florence, Jarrell, **E** P Exxon/dsl, ⊙ $General, **W** P Shell, ⊙ USPO
274	Rd 312, **E** P Chevron/dsl, Exxon/Subway/dsl, ⊛ FLYING J /Burger King/Denny's/dsl/scales, ⊓ McDonald's
271	Theon Rd, Rd 311, **W** P Shell/Subway/dsl/24hr
268	fm 972, Walburg, **E** ⊙ Crestview RV Ctr
266	TX 195, **E** P Phillips 66/dsl, **W** P Shell/dsl
265	TX 130 **Toll** S, to Austin
264	Lp 35, Georgetown
262	RM 2338, Lake Georgetown, **E** P Valero, ⊓ Chipotle Mexican, Duke's Smokehouse, KFC, McDonald's, Papa John's, Pizza Hut, Sonic, Starbucks, Subway, ⊙ CVS Drug, $Tree, Parts+, Radio Shack, Urgent Care, **W** P Shell, ⊓ DQ, La Tapatia, Placa Greek, Whataburger, △ Candlewood Suites, Georgetown Inn, Holiday Inn Express, La Quinta
261	TX 29, Georgetown, **E** P Shell/dsl, ⊓ Applebee's, Burger King, Chili's, KFC, Luby's, McDonald's, Schlotzsky's, Taco Bell, △ Comfort Suites, Country Inn&Suites, ⊙ Albertson's, HEB Foods, Hobby Lobby, Midas, Tuesday Morning, same as 262, **W** P Murphy USA/dsl, ⊓ Casa Ole, Chick-fil-A, CiCi's, Genghis Grill, Ichyban Buffet, IHOP, Longhorn Steaks, Mama Fu's, McAlister's Deli, MT Mike's, Panda Express, Souper Salad, Subway, Taco Cabana, Wendy's, Zio's Italian, ⊙ AT&T, Beall's, Best Buy, Discount Tire, Home Depot, Kohl's, Michael's, Office Depot, Old Navy, Petsmart, Ross, Target, TJ Maxx, Verizon, Walgreens, Walmart, antiques
260	RM 2243, Leander, **E** ⊙ H, USPO, **W** P Chevron, Exxon, Texaco, ⊓ Jack-in-the-Box, △ Quality Inn
259	Lp 35, **W** ⊙ RV Outlet Ctr, to Interspace Caverns
257	Westinghouse Rd, **E** ⊙ Buick/Chevrolet, Chrysler/Dodge/Jeep, Ford/Lincoln, Mazda, Subaru/Volvo, VW
256	RM 1431, Chandler Rd, **E** ⊓ BJ Rest, Chili's, Jamba Juice, La Madeline, Mimi's Cafe, Panda Express, ⊙ Round Rock Outlet/famous brands, Mazda, JC Penney, Jo-Ann Fabrics, Mazda, Petsmart, REI, Ross, Volvo
254	FM 3406, Round Rock, **E** P Chevron, ⊓ Arby's, Gatti's Pizza, La Tapatia, McDonald's, △ Best Western, ⊙ CVS Drug, $General, Firestone/auto, Harley-Davidson, Honda, Hyundai, Smart Car, Toyota/Scion, **W** P Phillips 66/dsl, Shell, ⊓ Blue Oak Grill, Carino's Italian, Chuy's Mexican, Cracker Barrel, Dave's Pizza, Denny's, Mesa Rosa Mexican, Rudy's BBQ/gas, SaltGrass Steaks, △ Country Inn&Suites, Courtyard, Hilton Garden, Holiday Inn Express, La Quinta, Red Roof Inn, SpringHill Suites, ValuePlace, ⊙ CVS Drug, GMC, Nissan
253b	US 79, to Taylor, **E** P Chevron, Shell, Texaco, ⊓ Arby's, Baskin-Robbins, Casa Garcia's, DQ, Fuddrucker's, KFC, LJ Silver, Pizza Hut, Short Stop Dogs, Sirloin Stockade, △ Best Western, Wingate Inn, ⊙ H, AutoZone, Beall's, CarQuest, Cottman Transmissions, $General, Just Brakes, vet, **W** P Exxon/dsl, Shell/dsl, ⊓ Gatti's Pizza, Hunan Lion, IHOP, La Margarita, Popeye's, Starbucks, Taco Bell, Westside Ale House, △ Best Value Inn, Country

GEORGETOWN (vertical)

ROUND ROCK (vertical)

INTERSTATE 35 CONT'D

Exit	Services
253b	**Continued** Inn&Suites, Fairfield Inn, La Quinta, Red Roof Inn, Sleep Inn, ValuePlace, 🅾 CVS Drug, $Tree, USPO
253a	Frontage Rd, same as 253 b
252b a	RM 620, **E** 🅖 Shell/dsl, 🛏 Candlewood Suites, Extended Stay America, 🅾 NAPA, **W** 🅖 Texaco/dsl, 🍴 Freddy's Steakburgers, Little Caesars, McDonald's, Starbucks, Wendy's, 🛏 Comfort Suites, Staybridge Suites
251	Lp 35, Round Rock, **E** 🅖 Valero, 🍴 CiCi's Pizza, Outback Steaks, Whataburger, 🛏 Residence Inn, 🅾 Aamco, BigLots, Brake Check, $General, Tuesday Morning, **W** 🅖 Shell, 🍴 Burger King, China Wall, Jack-in-the-Box, Lucky Dog Grill, Luby's, Taco Cabana, 🛏 Days Inn, Mariott, Sleep Inn, 🅾 GNC, NTB, Walgreens, transmissions
250	FM 1325, **E** 🍴 Chick-fil-A, Chili's, 5 Guys Burgers, Jason's Deli, Joe's Crabshack, Macaroni Grill, McDonald's, Panda Express, Subway, Twin Peaks Rest., 🛏 Hampton Inn, Homewood Suites, Residence Inn, 🅾 AT&T, Best Buy, Discount Tire, $Tree, Home Depot, Michael's, Petsmart, Radio Shack, Ross, Steinmart, Target, Walmart, Urgent Care, **W** 🅖 Shell, 🍴 Antonio's Cantina, ChuckeCheese, Fast Eddie's, Hooters, Jimmy John's, Mongolian Grill, Olive Garden, Schlotzsky's, Starbucks, 🛏 Extended Stay America, La Quinta, 🅾 Barnes&Noble, Hobby Lobby, Kohl's, Lowe's, Marshall's, Old Navy, PetCo, Ross, Sam's Club, World Mkt
248	Grand Ave Pkwy, **E** 🅖 Citgo, Shell, Texaco/Subway/dsl, 🍴 Chucho's Mexican, Posados Cafe, Thundercloud Subs, TX Roadhouse, 🛏 Comfort Suites, 🅾 Firestone, Urgent Care, **W** 🅖 Chevron/McDonald's
247	FM 1825, Pflugerville, **E** 🅖 Texaco, 🍴 Cheddar's, Fish Daddy's Grill, Jack-in-the-Box, Sonic, Subway, Taco Cabana, Wendy's, 🛏 Comfort Suites, 🅾 Firestone/auto, HEB Foods/gas, **W** 🅖 Exxon, Shell/Church's, 🍴 KFC, Miller's BBQ, Sonic, 🛏 Holiday Inn Express, 🅾 Goodyear, Tires4Less
246	Howard Lane, **E** 🅖 Citgo, Shell/dsl, 🍴 Arby's, Baby Acapulco, McDonald's, Subway, Wings'n More, 🅾 Home Depot, Kohl's, NTB, **W** 🅖 Valero/dsl, 🍴 IHOP, Whataburger, 🛏 Sleep Inn
245	FM 734, Parmer Lane, to Yager Lane (244 from nb), **E** 🍴 Carino's, Chick-fil-A, Chili's, Golden Wok, Jimmy John's, Pei Wei, Schlotzsky's, Souper Salad, Subway, Zed's Rest, 🛏 Courtyard, 🅾 $Tree, HEB Food/E-85, Hobby Lobby, JC Penney, Kohl's, Office Depot, PetCo, Petsmart, Ross, Sears Grand, Target, Verizon, **W** 🅖 Conoco/dsl, Exxon, Murphy USA/dsl, 🍴 Buffalo Wild Wings, Golden Corral, Hoho Chinese, Red Robin, Starbucks, 🛏 Courtyard, Fairfield Inn, Hilton Garden, Residence Inn, SpringHill Suites, 🅾 AT&T, CarMax, Discount Tire, Lowe's, Walmart
243	Braker Lane, **E** 🅖 Valero, 🍴 Jack-in-the-Box, Whataburger, 🅾 U-Haul, **W** 🅖 Citgo, Shell/dsl, 🛏 Austin Motel, ValuePlace, 🅾 $General
241	Rundberg Lane, **E** 🅖 Exxon, 🍴 Grand China Buffet, Jack-in-the-Box, Mr Gatti's, Old San Francisco Steaks, 🛏 Extended Stay Deluxe, Ramada Inn, 🅾 Albertson's, Chevrolet, $General, U-Haul, Walmart, **W** 🅖 Chevron, Conoco, Shell, Texaco, 🛏 Austin Suites, Budget Inn, Budget Lodge, Economy Inn, Holiday Inn Express, Motel 6, Red Roof Inn, Super 8, Wingate Inn
240a	US 183, Lockhart, **E** 🅖 Exxon, 🍴 DQ, Jack-in-the-Box, Old San Francisco Steaks, 🛏 Days Inn, Ramada Inn, **W** 🅖 Chevron/dsl, Texaco/dsl, 🛏 Motel 6, Red Roof Inn, Super 8, Wingate Inn
239	St John's Ave, **E** 🅖 Shell, 🍴 Burger King, Chili's, Japon Japanese, Pappadeaux, Pappasito's Mexican, 🛏 Crowne Plaza, Days Inn, DoubleTree, Drury Inn, Hampton Inn, North Austin Plaza, Studio 6, 🅾 USPO, **W** 🅖 Conoco/dsl, Exxon, Valero/dsl, 🍴 Antonio's Texmex, Applebee's, Buffalo Wild Wings, Carrabba's, Denny's, IHOP, Panda Express, Quiznos, Verona Italian, Wendy's, 🛏 Baymont Inn, Best Value Inn, Comfort Inn, Country Inn&Suites, Courtyard, Holiday Inn Express, Hyatt Place, La Quinta, Radisson, Ramada Inn, Sheraton, Sumner Suites, 🅾 Ford, Office Depot
238b	US 290 E, RM 222, same as 238a, frontage rds connect several exits
238a	51st St, **E** 🅖 Exxon, Chevron/dsl, Shell, 🍴 Buffet King, Burger King, Church's, McDonald's, TX Steaks, 🛏 DoubleTree Hotel, Drury Inn, EconoLodge, Embassy Suites, North Austin Suites, 🅾 Advance Parts, AutoZone, Best Buy, $Tree, Firestone, FoodLand, Home Depot, Jo-Ann Crafts, Marshall's, Old Navy, Petsmart, Ross, Staples, Target, Walgreens, **W** 🍴 Baby Acapulco, Capt Benny's Seafood, 🛏 Capital Inn, Courtyard, Fairfield Inn, Hilton, Motel 6, Super 8, 🅾 Dillard's
237b	51st St, same as 238a
237a	Airport Blvd, **E** 🍴 BBQ, **W** 🍴 Jack-in-the-Box, Quiznos, Wendy's, 🅾 GNC, Goodyear, HEB Foods, Old Navy, PetCo, Sears/auto, upper level is I-35 thru, lower level accesses downtown
236b	39th St, **E** 🅖 Chevron/dsl, 🍴 Short Stop Burgers, Subway, 🅾 Fiesta Foods, O'Reilly Parts, U-Haul, **W** 🅖 Shell/dsl, 🅾 Tune&Lube, tires, to U of TX
236a	26th-32nd Sts, **E** 🍴 Los Altos Mexican, Subway, 🛏 Days Inn, **W** 🛏 Rodeway Inn, 🅾 🅷
235b	Manor Rd same as 236a, **E** 🍴 Denny's, 🛏 DoubleTree, **W** 🛏 Rodeway Inn, 🅾 U of TX, st capitol, vet
235a	MLK, 15th St, **W** 🅷, upper level is I-35 thru, lower level accesses downtown
234c	11th St, 12th St, downtown, **E** 🅖 Chevron/dsl, Shell/dsl, 🍴 Denny's, Wendy's, 🛏 DoubleTree Hotel, Super 8, 🅾 CVS Drug, **W** 🅖 Chevron, Shell, Texaco, 🍴 Wendy's, 🛏 Crowne Plaza, Marriott, Hilton Garden, La Quinta, Omni Motel, Radisson, Sheraton, 🅾 🅷, museum, st capitol
234b	8th-3rd St, **W** 🍴 IHOP
234a	Cesar Chavez St, Holly St, downtown
233	Riverside Dr, Town Lake, **E** 🅖 Shell/dsl, **W** 🅖 Chevron/dsl, 🛏 Holiday Inn

AUSTIN

⬆N INTERSTATE 35 CONT'D

Exit	Services
232mm	Little Colorado River
232b	Woodland Ave
232a	Oltorf St, **E** 🅟 Gulf, Shell/dsl, 🍴 Luby's, Sonic, 🏨 Country Garden Inn, Garden West, Howard Johnson, La Quinta, Motel 6, Parkwest Inn, **W** 🅟 Conoco/dsl, Exxon, 🍴 Denny's, Starbucks, 🏨 Clarion
231	Woodward St, **E** 🅟 Shell/dsl, 🏨 Wyndham Garden, same as 232, **W** 🅾 Home Depot
230b a	US 290 W, TX 71, Ben White Blvd, St Elmo Rd, **E** 🅟 Shell, 🍴 Domino's, Jim's Rest., McDonald's, Sigon Kitchen, Subway, Western Choice Steaks, 🏨 Baymont Inn, Best Western, Comfort Suites, Courtyard, Fairfield Inn, Hampton Inn, Marriott, Omni Hotel, Red Roof Inn, Residence Inn, SpringHill Suites, 🅾 Acura, **W** 🍴 Burger King, Furr's Cafeteria, IHOP, Pizza Hut, 🏨 Candlewood Suites, Days Inn, La Quinta, 🅾 🄷, Audi, CarMax, Chrysler/Dodge/Jeep, Ford, Hyundai, Kia, Mazda, Nissan, NTB, Suzuki, Toyota/Scion
229	Stassney Lane, **W** 🍴 Buffalo Wild Wings, Chili's, Krispy Kreme, Logan's Roadhouse, Macaroni Grill, Pizza Hut, Rockfish Grill, TX Cattle Co Steaks, Twin Peaks Rest., 🅾 Albertson's/gas, Fiesta Foods/gas, Kia, Lowe's
228	Wm Cannon Drive, **E** 🅟 Exxon, Valero, 🍴 Applebee's, McDonald's, Taco Bell, 🅾 Brake Check, Chrysler, Discount Tire, HEB Foods, Mitsubishi, Nissan, Radio Shack, Target, **W** 🅟 Texaco, Shell/dsl, 🍴 Arby's, Burger King, China Harbor, Gatti's Pizza, Jack-in-the-Box, KFC, LJ Silver, Peter Piper Pizza, Taco Cabana, Wendy's, Whataburger, 🅾 Advance Parts, BigLots, Chevrolet, CVS Drug, $General, Firestone, Hyundai/Subaru
227	Slaughter Lane, Lp 275, S Congress, **E** 🅟 Shell/dsl, 🍴 Don Dario's, IHOP, 🅾 Home Depot, Lone Star RV Resort, U-Haul, **W** 🅟 Murphy USA/dsl, Texaco, Valero/dsl, 🍴 Carino's, Chick-fil-A, Chili's, Chipotle Mexican, Gatti's, Jason's Deli, Longhorn Steaks, Mama Fu's, Miller BBQ, Panda Express, Sonic, Starbucks, Steak'n Shake, Subway, Jack-in-the-Box, Taco Bell, TGIFriday's, TX Roadhouse, Wendy's, Whataburger, 🅾 Best Buy, Firestone/auto, GNC, Hobby Lobby, JC Penney, Marshall's, Petsmart, Ross, Sam's Club/gas, Target, Walgreens, Walmart
226	Slaughter Creek Overpass
225	FM 1626, Onion Creek Pkwy, **E** 🅟 Texaco, Valero, 🍴 Subway, 🅾 Harley-Davidson
224	frontage rd (from nb)
223	FM 1327, rd 45 **toll**
221	Lp 4, Buda, **E** 🅟 Chevron/McDonald's, Shell/dsl, 🍴 Starbucks, 🏨 Best Value Inn, Comfort Suites, Holiday Inn Express, 🅾 Ford, Kenworth, **W** 🅟 Chevron, Murphy USA/dsl, Shell, 🍴 Arby's, Chili's, Cracker Barrel, Dan's Burgers, Jack-in-the-Box, KFC/LJ Silver, Little Caesars, Logan's Roadhouse, Miller BBQ, Papa John's, Pizza Hut, Sonic, Subway, Taco Bell, Whataburger, loding: Hampton Inn, Microtel, 🅾 AT&T, Cabela's, HEB Food/dsl/E-85, O'Reilly Parts, Radio Shack, Walgreens, Walmart, USPO
220	FM 2001, Niederwald, **E** 🅟 Shell, 🅾 Camper Clinic RV Ctr, Marshall's RV Park, **W** 🅾 Crestview RV Ctr/Park, Peterbilt
217	Lp 4, Buda, **E** 🅟 Conoco/dsl/24hr, 🏨 La Quinta, 🅾 Mack/Volvo, **W** 🅟 Valero/dsl, 🍴 Burger King, 🏨 Best Western, 🅾 Christian Bros Auto, Home Depot

SAN MARCOS

Exit	Services
215	Bunton Overpass, **E** 🅟 Exxon/KFC/LJ Silver, 🅾 🄷, AT&T, Discount Tire, Lowe's, Walgreens, **W** 🅟 Shell/dsl, 🍴 Jack-in-the-Box, McDonald's, Papa Murphy's, Starbucks, Subway, Whataburger, 🅾 $Tree, Explore USA RV Ctr, GNC, HEB Foods/dsl, Kohl's, PetCo, Target
213	FM 150, Kyle, **E** 🅟 Valero/dsl, 🍴 DQ, 🅾 AutoZone, Goodyear/auto, **W** 🅟 Conoco/dsl, 🍴 Casa Maria Mexican, 🅾 CVS Drug, repair
210	Yarrington Rd, **E** 🅾 Hyundai, **W** 🅾 Buick/Chevrolet/GMC, Plum Creek RV Park
209	**weight sta (sb only)**
208mm	Blanco River
208	Frontage Rd, Blanco River Rd, **W** 🅾 Buick/Chevrolet/GMC
206	Lp 82, Aquarena Springs Rd, **E** 🅟 Conoco, Valero, 🅾 San Marcos RV Park, **W** 🅟 Citgo/dsl, Exxon/dsl, Shell, Texaco, 🍴 Pancake House, Popeye's, Sonic, 🏨 Best Value Inn, Howard Johnson, La Quinta, Motel 6, Ramada Ltd, Rodeway Inn, Summit Inn, Super 8, Travelodge, 🅾 to SW TX U
205	TX 80, TX 142, Bastrop, **E** 🅟 Exxon, Quix, RaceWay, Shell/dsl, Valero/dsl, 🍴 Arby's, China Palace, DQ, Fazoli's, Jason's Deli, Subway, Wing Stop, 🏨 Executive Inn, 🅾 AutoZone, CVS Drug, $General, Hastings Books, Hobby Lobby, Kwik Kar, Verizon, Walmart, vet, **W** 🅟 Valero, 🍴 A&W/LJ Silver, Burger King, Church's, KFC, Kobe Japanese, Logan's Roadhouse, McDonald's, Pizza Hut, Taco Cabana, Wendy's, 🏨 Best Western, Budget Inn, Days Inn, Gateway Inn, Knights Inn, Red Roof Inn, Rodeway Inn, 🅾 Brake Check, GNC, HEB Foods, JC Penney, Office Depot, Radio Shack, Walgreens, city park
204mm	San Marcos River
204b	CM Allen Pkwy, **W** 🅟 Shell/dsl, Spirit, 🍴 DQ, Krispy Kreme, La Fonda Rest, Mazatlan Mexican, Plucker's Grill, Sonic, 🏨 Best Western, EconoLodge, 🅾 AutoZone, O'Reilly Parts, transmissions
204a	Lp 82, TX 123, to Seguin, **E** 🅟 Conoco, Exxon/dsl, Valero, 🍴 Burger King, Carino's, Chicken Express, Chili's, Golden Corral, Luby's, McDonald's, Red Lobster, Whataburger, 🏨 Comfort Suites, Hampton Inn, Holiday Inn Express, 🅾 🄷 Aamco, Ford
202	FM 3407, Wonder World Dr, **E** 🅟 Exxon, Shell/Church's, 🍴 Carl's Jr, Chick-fil-A, Fuschaks BBQ, Jack-in-the-Box, Taco Bueno, Taste of China, Wienerschnitzel, 🅾 🄷, Best Buy, Discount Tire, $Tree, Lowe's, Marshall's, Petsmart, Ross, Sams Club/gas, **W** 🅟 Valero/dsl, 🍴 TX Roadhouse, 🏨 Candlewood Suites, Country Inn&Suites, 🅾 repair
201	McCarty Lane, **E** 🏨 Embassy Suites, **W** 🍴 Panda Express, Sonic, 🅾 AT&T, Beall's, Chrysler/Dodge/Jeep, Firestone/auto, JC Penney, Nissan, Target
200	Centerpoint Rd, **E** 🍴 Cracker Barrel, Food Court, Outback Steaks, River City Grill, Subway, Taco Bell, Wendy's, 🅾 GNC, Old Navy, San Marcos Outlets/famous brands, Tanger Outlet/famous brands, VF Outlets/famous brands, **W** 🅟 Valero/dsl, 🍴 McDonald's, Quiznos, Starbucks, Whataburger, 🏨 Baymont Inn, 🅾 Honda
199	Posey Rd, **E** 🅾 Tanger Outlets/famous brands, Toyota/Scion, same as 200
196	FM 1106, York Creek Rd, **W** 🅾 Canyon Trail RV Park
195	Watson Lane, Old Bastrop Rd
193	Conrads Rd, Kohlenberg Rd, **W** 🅟 TA/Country Fare Rest/

INTERSTATE 35 CONT'D

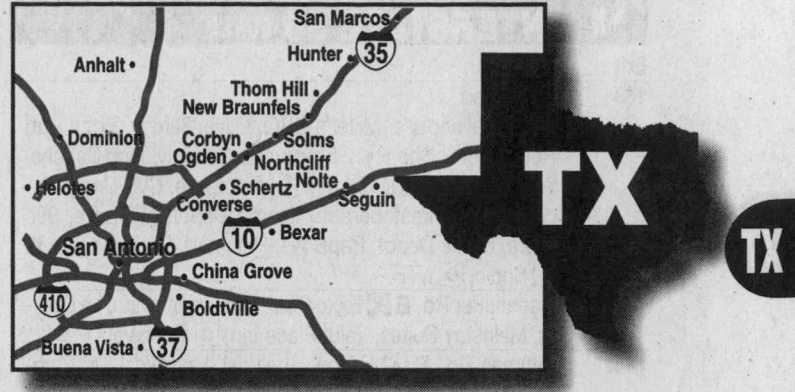

Exit	Services
193	Continued
	Popeye's/Subway/dsl/scales/24hr/@, 🄾 Camping World RV Ctr
191	FM 306, FM 483, Canyon Lake, E 🅖 Buc-ee's, 🄵 BJ's Rest, Longhorn Steaks, Subway, Whataburger, 🄾 AT&T, Best Buy, Dick's, I-35 RV Camping, JC Penney, Petsmart, Ross, Target, Verizon, Walmart Dist Ctr, Urgent Care, W 🅖 Chevron, Exxon/dsl, 🄵 Burger King, Quiznos, 🛏 Wingate Inn, 🄾 transmissions
190c	Post Rd
190b	frontage rd
190a	frontage rd, same as 189
189	TX 46, Seguin, E 🅖 Shell/dsl, 🄵 Chili's, Denny's, Golden Corral, Logan's Roadhouse, Olive Garden, Peter Piper Pizza, Taco Bueno, 🛏 Best Value Inn, EconoLodge, Hampton Inn, La Quinta, Super 8, 🄾 Discount Tire, Home Depot, Kohl's, Office Depot, vet, W 🅖 Texaco, Valero, 🄵 Applebee's, Chili's, Chipotle Mexican, El Tapatio, IHOP, Mama Fu's, McDonald's, MT Mike's, Pizza Hut, Subway, Taco Bell, Taco Cabana, TJ's Burgers, Wendy's, 🛏 Baymont, Best Western, Comfort Suites, Days Inn, Edelweiss Inn, Fairfield Inn, Hilton Garden, Howard Johnson, Microtel, Motel 6, Ramada Inn, Rodeway Inn, Quality Inn, Sleep Inn, 🄾 🄷, Walgreens
188	Frontage Rd, W 🄵 Garden Buffet, HoneyBaked Ham, Mamacita's Rest., 🛏 River Ranch Resort, 🄾 Hastings Books, Tuesday Morning
188mm	Guadalupe River
187	FM 725, Lake McQueeny Rd, E 🄵 A&W/LJ Silver, Arby's, Burger King, CiCi's, Schobell's Rest., Subway, Whataburger, 🄾 Aamco, BigLots, Chevrolet, Family$, Ford/Lincoln, Hobby Lobby, Jeep, Meineke, W 🄵 Adobe Café, DQ, Jack-in-the-Box, Jason's Deli, Steaks to Go, 🛏 Budget Inn, 🄾 🄷, CVS Drug, River Ranch RV Resort
186	Walnut Ave, E 🅖 Exxon/Subway, Murphy USA/dsl, Valero, 🄵 Carl's Jr, Chick-fil-A, McDonald's, Popeye's, Schlotzsky's, Taco Bell, 🛏 Red Roof Inn, 🄾 Lowe's, Walmart, W 🅖 Shell/dsl, 🄵 Baskin-Robbins, Bonzai Japanese, KFC, Mr Gatti's, Panda Express, Papa John's, Starbucks, 🄾 AT&T, AutoZone, Brake Check, $Tree, Ford/Lincoln, GNC, HEB Foods/gas, Radio Shack, U-Haul, Walgreens
185	FM 1044
184	FM 482, Lp 337, Ruekle Rd, E 🅖 Shell/dsl, 🄾 Kia, Mazda, RV Camping, W 🅖 /McDonald's/Subway/dsl/scales, 🄵 Jack-in-the-Box, 🄾 Suzuki
183	Solms Rd, W 🅖 Exxon/dsl
182	Engel Rd, E 🄾 Stamann RV Ctr
180	Schwab Rd
179mm	🆁🆂 both lanes, full ♿ facilities, 🄵, 🅿, litter barrels, vending, petwalk
178	FM 1103, Cibolo Rd, Hubertus Rd, E 🅖 Shell/dsl, 🄾 Walgreens
177	FM 482, FM 2252, W 🄾 Stone Creek RV Park
176	Weiderstein Rd, same as 175
175	FM 3009, Natural Bridge, E 🅖 Valero/dsl, 🄵 Chili's, IHOP, La Pasadita Mexican, McDonald's, Miller's BBQ, Schlotzsky's, Sonic, Taco Cabana, 🛏 Fairfield Inn, Hampton Inn, 🄾 HEB Food/dsl/E-85, Lowe's, Radio Shack, Verizon, W 🅖 Murphy USA/dsl, Shell/dsl, Valero/Subway/
175	Continued
	dsl, 🄵 Abel's Diner, Arby's, Denny's, Domino's, Jack-in-the-Box, KFC/Pizza Hut/Taco Bell, McDonald's, Panda Express, Quiznos, Starbucks, Wendy's, Whataburger, Wing Stop, 🛏 Atrium Inn, La Quinta, 🄾 AT&T, Walmart/McDonald's, Urgent Care
174b	Schertz Pkwy, E 🅖 Shell, E 🄾 Crestview RV Ctr
174a	FM 1518, Selma, E 🅖 Phillips 66/dsl, 🄵 Ruddy's BBQ, 🄾 Honda, Subaru, W 🛏 Comfort Inn, 🄾 Crestview RV Ctr
173	Old Austin Rd, Olympia Pkwy, E 🄵 Baskin Robbins, Charlie's Subs, Cheddar's, Chick-fil-A, Chili's, Chipotle Mexican, CiCi's, Firehouse Subs, 5 Guys Burgers, Freddy's Custard, Freddy's Steakburgers, Genghis Grill, Hooters, IHOP, Las Palapas, Outback Steaks, Panda Express, Panera Bread, Papouli's Greek, Peter Piper Pizza, Red Robin, Sea Island Srimp, Starbucks, Subway, Taste of China, Wendy's, 🛏 Holiday Inn Express, 🄾 AT&T, Beall's, Best Buy, Costco/gas, Discount Tire, GNC, Hobby Lobby, Home Depot, Kohl's, Michael's, NTB, Old Navy, Petsmart, Ross, Verizon, Target, TJ Maxx, WorldMkt, W 🄵 Chuck-eCheese, Chuy's Mexican, Freebirds Burritos, Houlihan's, 🛏 Hampton Inn, 🄾 Office Depot
172	TX 218, Anderson Lp, P Booker Rd, E 🄵 Buffalo Wild Wings, Coldstone, IHOP, Krystal, On-the-Border, TX Roadhouse, Zio's, 🛏 Comfort Inn, ValuePlace, 🄾 Nissan, to Randolph AFB, W to SeaWorld
171	Topperwein Rd, same as 170
170	Judson Rd, to Converse, E 🄵 Carl's Jr, Denny's, Subway, Whataburger, 🛏 Great Value Inn, La Quinta, 🄾 🄷 Buick/GMC, Chevrolet, Ford, Hyundai, Nissan, GMC, W 🅖 Exxon, 🛏 Best Western, 🄾 Kia, Mazda, Sam's Club/gas
169	O'Conner Rd, Wurzbach Pkwy, E 🅖 Exxon/dsl, 🄵 McDonald's, Quiznos, Subway, Taco Cabana, 🛏 Comfort Suites, 🄾 CarMax, Chrysler/Dodge/Jeep, Lowe's, Walgreens, W 🅖 Shell/dsl, Valero, 🄵 Jack-in-the-Box, Jim's Rest., Mi Casa Mexican, Sonic, 🄾 Mazda
168	Weidner Rd, E 🅖 Citgo/dsl, 🛏 Days Inn, Comfort Suites, W 🅖 Chevron, 🛏 Quality Inn, Super 8, 🄾 Harley-Davidson, Volvo Trucks
167b	Thousand Oaks Dr, Starlight Terrace, E 🅖 Valero/dsl
167a	Randolph Blvd, E 🅖 Valero, W 🛏 Days Inn, Midtowne Suites, Motel 6, Ruby Inn
166	I-410 W, Lp 368 S, W 🄾 to Sea World
165	FM 1976, Walzem Rd, E 🅖 Shell, Valero/dsl, 🄵 Applebee's, Burger King, China Harbor, Church's, Firehouse Grill, IHOP, Jack-in-the-Box, KFC/Taco Bell, Las Palapas Mexican, Little Caesars, LJ Silver, Luby's, McDonald's,

🅝 INTERSTATE 35 CONT'D

Exit	Services
165	Continued
	Marie Callender's, Miller's BBQ, Olive Garden, Pizza Hut, Red Lobster, Shoney's, Starbucks, Subway, Taco Cabana, Whataburger, 🛏 Drury Inn, 🅞 AutoZone, CVS Drug, Discount Tire, Firestone/auto, Home Depot, Michael's, 99c Store, Office Depot, PepBoys, Petsmart, Radio Shack, **W** 🍽 Sonic, 🅞 NTB
164b	Eisenhauer Rd, **E** 🅖 Exxon/dsl, 🛏 Hampton Inn, La Quinta, Mainstay Suites, ValuePlace Inn, 🅞 $General
164a	Rittiman Rd, **E** 🅖 Exxon, Shell/dsl, Valero/dsl, 🍽 Burger King, Church's, Cracker Barrel, Denny's, Guadalajara Mexican, Jack-in-the-Box, McDonald's, Taco Cabana, Whataburger, 🛏 Best Western, Comfort Suites, La Quinta, Motel 6, Rittiman Inn, Travel Inn, ValuePlace Inn, 🅞 HEB Foods, dsl repair, **W** 🅖 Chevron/dsl, Valero, 🍽 Bill Miller BBQ, Popeye's, Sonic, Subway
163	I-410 S (162 from nb, exits left from sb)
161	Binz-Engleman Rd (from nb) same as 160
160	Splashtown Dr, **E** 🅖 Valero/Subway/dsl/24hr, 🛏 Delux Inn, 🅞 funpark, **W** 🍽 Grady's BBQ, 🛏 Best Value Inn, Days Inn, Howard Johnson, Microtel, Super 8, Travelodge
159b	Walters St, **E** 🍽 McDonald's, **W** 🛏 EconoLodge, 🅞 to Ft Sam Houston
159a	New Braunfels Ave, **E** 🅖 Shell/dsl, Texaco/Burger King, **W** 🅖 Chevron, Valero/dsl, 🍽 Miller BBQ, Sonic, 🛏 Antonian Suites, 🅞 to Ft Sam Houston
158c	N Alamo St, Broadway
158b	I-37 S, US 281 S, to Corpus Christi, to Alamo
158a	US 281 N (from sb), to Johnson City
157b a	Brooklyn Ave, Lexington Ave, N Flores, downtown, **E** 🛏 Super 8, 🅞 🎗, **W** 🍽 Luby's
156	I-10 W, US 87, to El Paso
155b	Durango Blvd, downtown, **E** 🛏 Best Western, Courtyard, Fairfield Inn, Holiday Inn, La Quinta, Residence Inn, Woodfield Suites, 🅞 🎗, **W** 🍽 McDonald's, 🛏 Motel 6, Radisson
155a	South Alamo St, **E** 🅖 Exxon, Shell, 🍽 Church's, Denny's, McDonald's, Piedras Negras Mexican, Pizza Hut, Wendy's, 🛏 Best Western, Comfort Inn, Days Inn, Holiday Inn, La Quinta, Ramada Ltd, Residence Inn, 🅞 USPO, **W** 🅖 Conoco, 🛏 Microtel
154b	S Laredo St, Ceballos St, same as 155b
154a	Nogalitos St
153	I-10 E, US 90 W, US 87, to Kelly AFB, Lackland AFB
152b	Malone Ave, Theo Ave, **E** 🍽 Taco Cabana/24hr, **W** 🅖 Shamrock, Shell
152a	Division Ave, **E** 🅖 Chevron, 🍽 Bill Miller BBQ, Las Cazuelas Mexican, Whataburger/24hr, 🛏 Quality Inn, **W** 🍽 Sonic, 🅞 transmissions
151	Southcross Blvd, **E** 🅖 Exxon, Shell, **W** 🅖 Shell/dsl, 🍽 Mazatlan Mexican
150b	Lp 13, Military Dr, **E** 🅖 Valero, 🍽 Applebee's, Arby's, Denny's, Don Pedro Mexican, KFC, Pizza Hut, Sonic, Starbucks, Subway, Taco Cabana, 🛏 La Quinta, 🅞 AutoZone, Discount Tire, U-Haul, **W** 🅖 Exxon, 🍽 Chili's, Coyote Canyon, Freddy's Custard, Hungry Farmer Rest, Jack-in-the-Box, KFC, LJ Silver, Luby's, Moma Margie's Mexican, McDonald's, Mr Gatti, Olive Garden, Panda Express, Pizza Hut, Sea Island Shrimp House, Wendy's, Whataburger, 🛏 La Quinta, 🅞 AT&T, Best Buy, $Tree, Firestone/auto, Ford,
150b	Continued
	HEB Foods, Home Depot, JC Penney, Lowe's, Macy's, Office Depot, Old Navy, Sears/auto, Walgreens, mall,
150a	Zarzamora St (149 fom sb), same as 150b
149	Hutchins Blvd (from sb), **E** 🅖 Valero/dsl, 🛏 Motel 6, ValuePlace, 🅞 🎗, **W** 🅞 Chevrolet, Ford, Honda, Hyundai, Kia
148b	Palo Alto Rd, **W** 🅖 Valero
148a	TX 16 S, spur 422 (from nb), Poteet, **E** 🅖 Chevron, 🛏 Days Inn, **W** 🅖 Phillips 66, 🅞 $General
147	Somerset Rd, **E** 🅖 Shell/dsl, **W** 🅞 Chrysler/Dodge/Jeep
146	Cassin Rd (from nb)
145b	Lp 353 N
145a	I-410, TX 16
144	Fischer Rd, **E** 🅖 Valero/Subway/dsl/scales/24hr, 🛏 D&D Motel, 🅞 lube, RV camping, **W** 🍽 Loves/Carl's Jr/dsl/scales/24hr/@, 🅞 Toyota/Scion
142	Medina River Turnaround (from nb)
141	Benton City Rd, Von Ormy, **E** 🅞 USPO, **W** 🅖 Shell/dsl/Parador Café
140	Anderson Lp, 1604, **E** 🅖 Exxon/dsl/24hr, 🍽 Burger King, **W** 🅖 Valero/Church's/dsl/scales/24hr, 🅞 Alamo River RV Resort, to Sea World
139	Kinney Rd
137	Shepherd Rd, **E** truck repair, **W** gas/dsl, dsl repair
135	Luckey Rd
133	TX 132 S (from sb), Lytle, same as 131
131	FM 3175, FM 2790, Benton City Rd, **E** 🛏 Best Western, 🅞 Chuck's Repair, NAPA, **W** 🅖 Pico/dsl/24hr, 🍽 Bill Miller BBQ, McDonald's, Sonic, Subway, Whataburger, 🛏 Days Inn/cafe, 🅞 AutoZone, Crawford Drug, $General, Family$, HEB Food/dsl, USPO
129mm	🆁🆂 both lanes, full 🎗 facilities, 🍽, 🚻, litter barrels, vending, petwalk
127	FM 471, Natalia, **W** 🅖 Loves/Subway/Wendy's/dsl/scales/24hr/@
125	FM 770
124	FM 463, Bigfoot Rd, **E** Ford
122	TX 173, Devine, **E** 🅖 Exxon/dsl, 🅞 Chevrolet, Chrysler/Dodge/Jeep, **W** 🅖 Chevron/McDonald's/Subway/dsl, Exxon, Shell/dsl, 🍽 CCC Steaks, Church's, Pizza Inn, Sonic, Viva Zapatas Mexican, 🛏 Country Corner Inn
121	TX 132 N, Devine
118.5mm	weigh sta both lanes
114	FM 462, Yancey, Bigfoot, **E** 🅖 Lucky/dsl, **W** 🅖 Shell/Subway/dsl, 🅞 USPO
111	US 57, to Eagle Pass, **W** 🅖 Valero/dsl
104	Lp 35, **E** 🅞 Gilendo RV Park
101	FM 140, Pearsall, **E** 🅖 Chevron/dsl, 🍽 Cowpokes BBQ, 🛏 Best Western, Pearsall Inn, Rio Frio Motel, Royal Inn, 🅞 HEB Foods/dsl, **W** 🅖 Exxon/Subway/dsl/24hr, Valero/Porter House Rest/dsl/scales/24hr, 🍽 Hungry Hunter Grill, 🛏 Holiday Inn Express, La Quinta, Southern Inn, 🅞 🎗
99	FM 1581, to Divot, Pearsall
93mm	parking/🚻 both lanes, litter barrels, 🎗 accessible
91	FM 1583, Derby
90mm	Frio River
86	Lp 35, Dilley
85	FM 117, **E** 🍽 Garcia Café, 🛏 Relax Inn, Super 8, **W** 🅖 Exxon, 🍽 DQ, 🛏 Budget Inn, Sona Inn, 🅞 RV park
84	TX 85, Dilley, **E** 🅖 Conoco/Burger King/dsl, 🅞 🎗,

(vertical marginal text between columns): **PEARSALL**

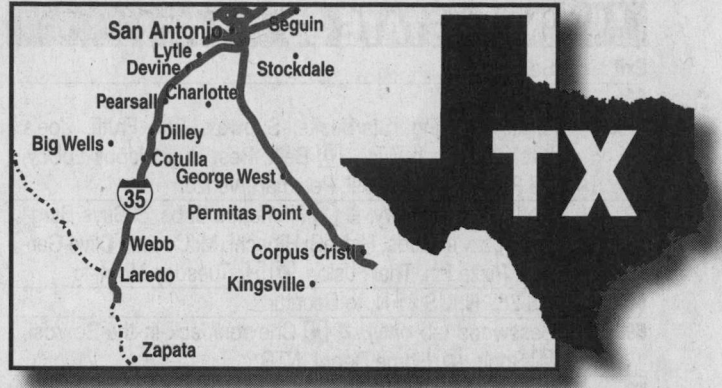

⬆N INTERSTATE 35 CONT'D

Exit	Services
84	Continued
	Chevrolet, Super S Foods/dsl, **W** ⓖ Shell/Pollo Grande/dsl/24hr, Valero/Subway/dsl/24hr, 🛏 Executive Inn
82	County Line Rd, to Dilley
77	FM 469, Millett
74	Gardendale, 68 (69 from sb) Lp 35, Cotulla, **E** ⓖ Phillips 66, Ⓞ Family$, Super S Foods
67	FM 468, to Big Wells, **E** ⓖ Exxon/Wendy's/dsl/24hr, JJ's/dsl, Valero/deli/dsl/24hr, 🍴 DQ, Golden Chick, Subway, Taco Palenque, 🛏 Executive Inn, Extended Stay, Holiday Inn Express, Village Inn, Ⓞ tire repair, **W** ⓖ Chevron/McDonald's/dsl/scales/24hr, 🛏 Best Western, Ⓞ rv park
65	Lp 35, Cotulla
63	Elm Creek Interchange
59mm	ⓡ both lanes, full 🛏 facilities, ⓖ, 🍴, litter barrels, vending, petwalk
56	FM 133, Artesia Wells
48	Caiman Creek Interchange
39	TX 44, Encinal, **E** ⓖ ♥Love's/Chester Fried/Subway/dsl/scales/24hr, **W** ⓖ Exxon/dsl
38	TX 44 (from nb), Encinal
32	San Roman Interchange
29mm	inspection sta nb
27	Callaghan Interchange
24	255 **toll**, Camino Colombia **toll rd**, to Monterrey
22	Webb Interchange
18	US 83 N, to Carrizo Springs, **E** **TX Travel Info Ctr (8am-5pm)**/ⓡ, **full facilities**, 🍴, **litter barrels, petwalk, wireless internet, W** RV Camping
14mm	parking area, sb
12b	(13 from sb), Uniroyal Interchange, **E** ⓖ 🛢/McDonald's/Subway/dsl/scales/24hr, Ⓞ Blue Beacon, **W** ⓖ /⊕FLYING J/Denny's/dsl/scales/24hr, TA/Burger King/Subway/Taco Bell/dsl/scales/24hr/@
12a	Port Loredo
10	Port Laredo Carriers Dr (from nb)
9	Industrial Blvd, to Bob Bullock Lp (from sb only)
9	Industrial Blvd, to Bob Bullock Lp (from sb only)
8b	Lp 20 W, to Solidarity Bridge
8a	Lp 20 W, to to World Trade Bridge, Mllo
5	San Isidro Pkwy
4b	Las Cruces Dr, **E** ⓖ Valero/dsl, 🍴 El Pescador
4a	FM 1472 new exit
4	FM 1472, Del Mar Blvd, **E** ⓖ Exxon/Burger King/dsl, 🍴 Applebee's, Carino's Italian, CiCi's, IHOP, Jack-in-the-Box, McDonald's, Quiznos, Whataburger, 🛏 Extended Stay America, Hampton Inn, Ⓞ Best Buy, BigLots, HEB Foods/gas, Marshall's, Old Navy, Radio Shack, Target, **W** ⓖ Shell/dsl, 🛏 Days Inn, Ⓞ Harley-Davidson
3b	Mann Rd, **E** 🍴 Buffalo Wild Wings, Krispy Kreme, Lin's Chinese, 🛏 Residence Inn, Ⓞ Urgent Care, Buick/Cadillac/GMC, Ford/Lincoln, Honda, Kia, Lowe's, Mazda, mall, **W** 🍴 Chili's, Danny's Rest, Golden Corral, Hayashi Japanese, Kettle Pancake House, Subway, Taco Palenque, TX Roadhouse, Whataburger, 🛏 Best Value, Family Garden Inn, Gateway Inn, La Hacienda Motel, Monterey Inn, Motel 6, Red Roof Inn, SpringHill Suites, Ⓞ AT&T, $Tree, Home Depot, Kohl's, Michael's, Office Depot, PetCo, Ross, Verizon, Walmart/McDonald's
3a	San Bernardo Ave, **E** ⓖ Shell, 🍴 Chick-fil-A, Chuck

L A R E D O

3a	Continued
	eCheese, El Taco Tote, Emperor Garden, Fuddrucker's, LJ Silver, Logan's Roadhouse, Luby's, Olive Garden, Peter Piper Pizza, Red Lobster, Sirloin Stockade, Tony Roma's, 🛏 Fairfield Inn, Ⓞ Advance Parts, Dillards, HEB Foods/gas, K-Mart, Macy's, NAPA, PepBoys, Sears/auto, SteinMart, mall, **W** ⓖ Valero, 🍴 Arby's, Burger King, DQ, McDonald's, Pizza Hut, Popeye's, Taco Bell, Taco Palenque, Wendy's, Ⓞ O'Reilly Parts, Sam's Club/gas
2	US 59, Saunders Rd, **E** ⓖ Conoco, Shell, 🍴 Jack-in-the-Box, Ⓞ 🏥, **W** ⓖ Exxon/Burger King/dsl, Shell, 🍴 Church's, Denny's, 🛏 Courtyard, Holiday Inn, La Quinta, Super8, Ⓞ Advance Parts, AutoZone, Mexico Insurance
1b	Park St, to Sanchez St, **W** ⓖ Conoco/dsl, 🍴 La Mexicana Rest., Pizza Hut, Popeye's
1a	Victorla St, Scott St, Washington St (from sb), **E** ⓖ Shell, Valero, **W** ⓖ Exxon/dsl, Valero, 🍴 Mariachi Express, McDonald's, Wendy's, Ⓞ Firestone/auto

I-35 begins/ends in Laredo at Victoria St...access to multiple services

⬆N INTERSTATE 35 (WEST)

Exit	Services
	I-35W begins/ends on I-35, exit 467.
85b	W Oak St, **E** 🏥
85a	I-35E S
84	FM 1515, Bonnie Drae St, **E** 🏥
82	FM 2449, to Ponder
79	Crawford Rd
76	FM 407, to Justin, Argyle, **W** ⓖ Exxon/dsl, Ⓞ Paradise Mkt, Paradise RV Park
76mm	ⓡ both lanes, litter barrels, 🛏
74	FM 1171, to Lewisville
72	Dale Earnhardt Way, **W** 🛏 Marriott, Ⓞ TX Motor Speedway
70	TX 114, to Dallas, Bridgeport, **E** ⓖ Shell/Subway/dsl, Valero/dsl, 🛏 Motel 6, Sleep Inn, Ⓞ North Lake RV Park, to DFW ✈, **W** 🛏 Marriott, Ⓞ TX Motor Speedway
68	Eagle Pkwy, **W** ✈
67	Alliance Blvd, **W** Ⓞ to Alliance ✈, FedEx
66	to Westport Pkwy, Keller-Haslet Rd, **E** 🛏 Hampton Inn, Hilton Garden, Residence Inn, **W** ⓖ 7-11/Wendy's/dsl, 🍴 Bryan's BBQ, Schlotzsky's, Snooty Pig, Subway, Taco Bueno, Ⓞ USPO
65	TX 170 E, **E** ⓖ 🛢/McDonald's/dsl/scales/24hr, 🍴 IHOP, Ⓞ Cabela's/cafe
64	Golden Triangle Blvd, to Keller-Hicks Blvd, **E** Ⓞ Chrysler/Dodge/Jeep
63	Heritage Trace, **E** ⓖ 7-11, 🍴 BJ's, Cheddar's, Chick-fil-A, Free Birds Burritos, Houlihan's, Jason's Deli, McDonald's,

TX

⬆N INTERSTATE 35 (WEST) CONT'D

Exit	Services
63	Continued Smoothie King, Starbucks, Subway, Tutti Frutti, Zoe's Kitchen, Which Wich, 🄾 Belk, Best Buy, Hobby Lobby, JC Penney, Kroger/dsl, Petsmart, Verizon
62	North Tarrant Pkwy, **E** 🍴 Firehouse Subs, 5 Guys Burgers, Fuzzy's Tacos, HaNaBi Hibachi, Mi Cocina, Olive Garden, Pizza Inn, Thai Fusion, 🄾 🛏, Tuesday Morning
60	US 287 N, US 81 N, to Decatur
59	Basswood (sb only), **E** 🛢 Chevron/Jack-in-the-Box/dsl, 🍴 Sonic, 🄾 Home Depot, NTB
58	Western Ctr Blvd, **E** 🛢 7-11, Shell/Church's, 🍴 Braum's, Casa Rita, Chili's, Denny's, Dublin Square Rest., Flips Grill, Genghis Grill, Jimmy John's, Macaroni Grill, On-the-Border, Posados Cafe, SaltGrass Steaks, Shady Oak Grill, Wendy's, Which Wich, Wing Stop, Zio's Italian, 🛏 Best Western, Residence Inn, 🄾 AT&T, Kauffman Tire, **W** 🍴 Boston's, Firehouse Subs, Joe's Crabshack, McDonald's, Popeye's, Rosa's Cafe, Salad Bowl, Smoothie King, Starbucks, Subway, Waffle House, Whataburger, 🛏 Comfort Inn, Holiday Inn Express, 🄾 Urgent Care, repair
57b a	I-820 E&W
56b	Melody Hills Dr
56a	Meacham Blvd, **E** 🛢 Shell/7-11, 🛏 Hilton Garden, Knights Inn, La Quinta, **W** 🛢 Texaco/dsl, 🍴 Cracker Barrel, McDonald's, Subway, 🛏 Holiday Inn, Quality Inn, Radisson, Super 8, 🄾 USPO
55	Pleasantdale Ave (from nb)
54c	33rd St, Long Ave (from nb), **W** 🛢 Conoco/dsl, Valero/dsl, 🛏 Motel 6
54b a	TX 183, NE 28th St, **E** Lisa's Chicken/dsl, **W** 🛢 QT/dsl, 🛏 Stockyards Inn
53	North Side Dr, Yucca Dr, **E** 🛢 Shell/7-11/dsl, **W** 🍴 Mercado Juarez Café, 🛏 Country Inn&Suites
53mm	Trinity River
52e	Carver St (from nb)
52d	Pharr St (exits left from nb)
52b	US 377N, Belknap
52a	US 377 N, TX 121, to DFW
51a	I-30 E, to Avalene (from nb), downtown Ft Worth
50c a	I-30 W, E to Dallas
50b	TX 180 E (from nb)
49b	Rosedale St, **E** gas 7-11/dsl, 🍴 Jack-in-the-Box, **W** 🛏
49a	Allen Ave, **E** 🛢 Valero, **W** 🛏
48b	Morningside Ave (from sb), same as 48a
48a	Berry St, **E** 🛢 Chevron/McDonald's, 🄾 Autozone, El Rio Grande Foods, Family$, **W** 🛢 RaceTrac/dsl, 🄾 U-Haul, zoo
47	Ripy St, **E** 🄾 transmissions, **W** 🛏 Astro Inn
46b	Seminary Dr, **E** 🛢 RaceWay, 🍴 Grandy's, Jack-in-the-Box, Taco Cabana, Whataburger, 🛏 Days Inn, Delux Inn, Regency Inn, Super 7 Inn, 🄾 NAPA, **W** 🛢 Shell, Valero, 🍴 Denny's, Sonic, Wendy's, 🄾 Firestone/auto, Pepboys
46a	Felix St, **E** 🛢 Valero, 🛏 Dalworth Inn, **W** 🍴 Cesar's Tacos, McDonald's, 🄾 Family$
45b a	I-20, E to Dallas, W to Abilene
44	Altamesa, **E** 🛏 Radisson, **W** 🛢 Prism, 🍴 Rig Steaks, Waffle House, 🛏 Baymont Inn, Best Western, Comfort Suites, Motel 6, South Lp Inn
43	Sycamore School Rd, **W** 🛢 Exxon, 🍴 Chicken Express, Jack-in-the-Box, Sonic, Subway, Whataburger, 🄾 $General, Home Depot, Radio Shack, repair

Exit	Services
42	Everman Pkwy, **W** gas QT/dsl/scales, Shell
41	Risinger Rd, **W** 🄾 Camping World RV Service/Supplies, McClain's RV Ctr
40	Garden Acres Dr, **E** 🛢 💙Loves/Subway/dsl/scales/24hr, 🛏 Microtel, 🄾 🛏, **W** 🍴 Taco Bell
39	FM 1187, McAlister Rd, **E** 🛏, **W** 🛢 Shamrock/dsl/24hr, Shell, 🍴 Buffalo Wild Wings, Firehouse Subs, Logan's Roadhouse, Olive Garden, Panda Express, Red Lobster, TGIFriday's, Waffle House, 🛏 Howard Johnson, 🄾 Best Buy, Kohl's, Staples, Verizon
38	Alsbury Blvd, **E** 🛢 Chevron/24hr, Mobil/dsl, 🍴 Chili's, Cracker Barrel, Hibachi Japanese, IHOP, McDonald's, Mexican Inn Cafe, On-the-Border, Outback Steaks, Over Time Grill, Spring Creek BBQ, 🛏 Hampton Inn, Holiday Inn Express, La Quinta, Super 8, 🄾 Discount Tire, Ford, Lowe's Whse, **W** 🛢 RaceTrac, Shamrock, Shell/24hr, 🍴 Applebees, Arby's, Burger King, Chick-fil-A, Coldstone Creamery, Cotton Patch Cafe, Denny's, Pancho's Mexican, Sonic, Taco Cabana, Wendy's, 🄾 Albertson's, Chevrolet, JC Penney, Kwik Kar, Michael's, PetsMart, Radio Shack, Ross, vet
37	TX 174, Wilshire Blvd, to Cleburne, **W** Walmart Super Ctr/24hr (2mi), from sb, same as 36
36	FM 3391, TX 174S, Burleson, **E** 🛢 Chevron, Mobil, 🍴 Miranda's Cantina, Sonic, Waffle House, 🛏 Best Western, Comfort Suites, Days Inn, **W** 🄾 Curves, $General, transmissions
35	Briaroaks Rd (from sb), **W** RV camping
33mm	Ⓡs sb, full 🛁 facilities, 🄲, 🛒, litter barrels
32	Bethesda Rd, **E** 🛢 Valero, 🛏 Best Value Inn, 🄾 RV Ranch Park, **W** 🄾 Mockingbird Hill RV Park
31mm	Ⓡs nb, full 🛁 facilities, 🄲, 🛒, litter barrels
30	FM 917, Mansfield, **E** 🛢 Shell/Sonic/dsl, **W** 🛢 Shell/dsl, 🍴 RanchHouse Rest.
27	Rd 604, Rd 707
26b a	US 67, Cleburne, **E** 🛢 Chevron/KFC/dsl, 🍴 Chicken Express, DQ, McDonald's, Pizza Hut, Sonic, Waffle House, Whataburger, 🛏 Best Western, Days Inn, La Quinta, Super 8, 🄾 Ancira RV Ctr, AutoZone, Brookshire Foods, $General, Family$, Motor Home Specialist, Parts+, Walmart
24	FM 3136, FM 1706, Alvarado, **E** 🛢 Shell/Grandy's/dsl/scales/24hr, 🍴 Longhorn Grill
21	Rd 107, to Greenfield
17	FM 2258
16	TX 81 S, Rd 201, Grandview
15	FM 916, Maypearl, **W** 🛢 Chevron/dsl, Mobil/dsl, 🍴 Subway
12	FM 67
8	FM 66, Itasca, **E** 🛢 Valero/dsl/café/24hr, **W** 🍴 DQ, 🄾 Ford, 🛒, litter barrels
7	FM 934, **E** 🛒, litter barrels, **W** 🛢 Exxon/dsl, 🍴 Golden Chick Cafe
3	FM 2959, **E** to Hillsboro 🛬

I-35W begins/ends on I-35, 371mm.

⬆N INTERSTATE 37

Exit	Services
142b a	I-35 S to Laredo, N to Austin. **I-37 begins/ends on I-35 in San Antonio.**
141c	Brooklyn Ave, Nolan St (from sb), downtown
141b	Houston St, **E** 🛏 Comfort Suites, Red Roof Inn, 🄾 tires, **W** 🛢 Shell, 🍴 Denny's, 🛏 Crockett Hotel, Crowne Plaza, Days Inn, Drury Inn, Fairfield Inn, Hampton Inn, Hyatt Ho

⬆N INTERSTATE 37 CONT'D

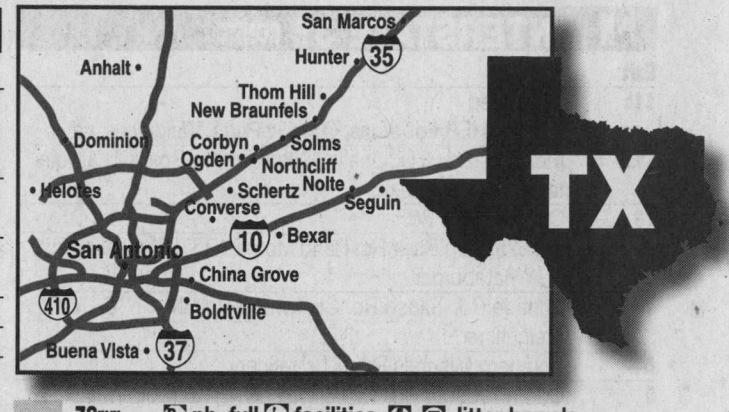

Exit	Services
141b	Continued tel, Marriott, La Quinta, Residence Inn, SpringHill Suites, 🅾 Macy's, to The Alamo
141a	Commerce St, E 🅖 Staybridge Suites, W 🍴 Denny's, 🛏 La Quinta, Marriott, 🅾 Macy's
140b	Durango Blvd, downtown, E 🍴 Bill Miller BBQ, 🅾 to Alamo Dome
140a	Carolina St, Florida St, E 🅖 Shell/dsl
139	I-10 W, US 87, US 90, to Houston, W 🅾 to Sea World
138c	Fair Ave, Hackberry St, E 🍴 DQ, Jack-in-the-Box, La Tapatia Mexian, Las Margarita's, Popeye's, 🅾 Brake Check, Family$, Home Depot, W 🅖 Exxon, Shell
138b	E New Braunfels Ave (from sb), E 🍴 IHOP, Little Caesars, McDonald's, Taco Cabana, Whataburger, Wendy's, 🅾 Beall's, HEB/dsl, Marshall's, W 🅖 Exxon, 🍴 Sonic
138a	Southcross Blvd, W New Braunfels Ave, E 🅖 McDonald's, Taco Cabana, Wendy's, W 🅖 Exxon, 🍴 Sonic
137	Hot Wells Blvd, W 🍴 IHOP, 🛏 Motel 6, Super 8
136	Pecan Valley Dr, E 🅖 Citgo/dsl, 🍴 KFC/Taco Bell, Pizza Hut, 🛏 Pecan Valley Inn, 🅾 AutoZone, O'Reilly Parts, W 🛗
135	Military Dr, Lp 13, E 🅖 Shell, Valero, 🍴 Jack-in-the-Box, 🛏 Quality Inn, 🅾 Mission Trail RV park, W 🅖 Valero/Subway/dsl, 🍴 A&W/LJ Silver, Buffalo Wild Wings, Burger King, Carino's Italian, Chaba Thai, Chick-fil-A, Chili's, Cracker Barrel, IHOP, Little Caesars, Longhorn Cafe, Panda Express, Papa John's, Peter Piper Pizza, Sonic, Starbucks, Subway, Whataburger, 🛏 La Quinta, 🅾 🛗, Advance Parts, AT&T, Best Buy, BigLots, Discount Tire, $Tree, Hancock Fabrics, HEB Food/gas, Home Depot, Lowe's, Office Depot, PetCo, Radio Shack, Ross, Target, Walgreens, Walmart/McDonald's, to Brooks AFB
133	I-410, US 281 S
132	US 181 S, to Floresville, E 🅖 Shell, 🅾 $General
130	Donop Rd, Southton Rd, E 🅖 Valero/dsl, 🍴 Tom's Burgers, 🛏 Days Inn, 🅾 Braunig Lake RV Resort, W 🅖 Shell/dsl, 🅾 car/truckwash
127	San Antonio River Turnaround (from nb), Braunig Lake
127mm	San Antonio River
125	FM 1604, Anderson Lp, E 🅖 Conoco/dsl/24hr, 🍴 Burger King, 🅾 fireworks, W 🅖 Exxon/dsl, Shell/dsl, 🍴 Miller's BBQ, Whataburger, 🅾 fireworks, tires
122	Priest Rd, Mathis Rd, E 🅖 Valero
120	Hardy Rd
117	FM 536
113	FM 3006
112mm	🆁🆂 both lanes, tables, litter barrels
109	TX 97, to Floresville, E 🅖 Chevron/dsl, 🍴 Portrillo's Mexican, 🅾 Chrysler/Dodge/Jeep
106	Coughran Rd
104	spur 199, Leal Rd, to Pleasanton (no immediate sb return) same as 103
103	US 281 N, Leal Rd, to Pleasanton, E 🅖 Valero/dsl, 🍴 DQ, K&K Cafe, 🛏 Kuntry Inn
98	TX 541, McCoy
92	US 281A, Campbellton
88	FM 1099, to FM 791, Campbellton
83	FM 99, Whitsett, Peggy, E 🅖 Shell/cafe/dsl, W 🅖 Chevron/dsl, Exxon/dsl, 🍴 Choke Canyon BBQ
82mm	🆁🆂 sb, full 🛗 facilities, 🍴, 🚮 litter barrels
78mm	🆁🆂 nb, full 🛗 facilities, 🍴, 🚮 litter barrels
76	US 281A, FM 2049, Whitsett
75mm	truck weigh sta sb
74mm	truck weigh sta nb
72	US 281 S, Three Rivers, W 🅖 ❤Loves/McDonald's/Subway/dsl/scales/24hr/@, 4 mi W 🅖 Valero, 🍴 DQ, Staghorn Rest, Van's BBQ, 🛏 Best Western, EconoLodge, 🅾 to Rio Grande Valley
69	TX 72, Three Rivers, W 🅖 Valero/café/dsl/24hr, 🅾 RV park, tires, to Choke Cyn SP
65	FM 1358, Oakville, E 🍴 Van's BBQ
59	FM 799
56	US 59, George West, E 🅖 Valero/dsl/24hr, W 🅖 Shell/Subway/dsl/24hr, Valero/Burger King/dsl/24hr
51	Hailey Ranch Rd
47	FM 3024, FM 534, Swinney Switch Rd, W 🍴 Swinney Switch Cafe, 🅾 Mike's Mkt/gas (1mi), to KOA (4mi)
44mm	parking area sb
42mm	parking area nb
40	FM 888
36	TX 359, to Skidmore, Mathis, W 🅖 Citgo/Subway/dsl, Shell/McDonald's/dsl, Valero/dsl (1mi), 🍴 Pizza Hut, 🛏 Mathis Inn, 🅾 Lake Corpus Christi SRA
34	TX 359 W, E 🅾 Adventure TX RV Ctr/LP, W 🅖 Shell, Valero/dsl, 🛏 DQ, Pizza Hut, 🅾 $General, O'Reilly Parts, to Lake Corpus Christi SP
31	TX 188, to Sinton, Rockport
22	TX 234, FM 796, to Odem, Edroy
20b	Cooper Rd
19.5mm	🆁🆂 both lanes, 🛗 accessible, tables, litter barrels
17	US 77 N, to Victoria
16	LaBonte Park, W info, 🚮 litter barrels
15	Sharpsburg Rd (from sb), Redbird Ln
14	I-69, US 77 S, Redbird Ln, to Kingsville, Robstown, 1 mi W on FM 624 🅖 RaceWay/dsl, Valero/Burger King/dsl, Shell/dsl, 🍴 Chili's, CiCi's, Denny's, Good'n Crisp Chicken, Miller's BBQ, Papa John's, Pizza Hut, Popeye's, Sonic, Subway, Whataburger, Wienerschnitzel, 🛏 Comfort Inn, Holiday Inn Express, 🅾 🛗, AT&T, AutoZone, Beall's, CVS Drug, Discount Tire, $General, $Tree, Firestone/auto, GNC, Hobby Lobby, Home Depot, O'Reilly Parts, Radio Shack, Walmart/McDonald's
13b	Sharpsburg Rd (from nb)
13a	FM 1694, Callicoatte Rd, Leopard St
11b	FM 24, Violet Rd, Hart Rd, E 🅖 Citgo/Subway/dsl, 🍴 Chicken Shack, W 🅖 Exxon/dsl, Valero/dsl, 🍴 DQ, Fliz Amancer Mexican, KFC/LJ Silver, Little Caesars, McDonald's, Pizza Hut, Schlotzsky's, Sonic, Subway, Taco Bell, Whataburger, 🛏 Best Western, Hampton Inn, 🅾 Au

🅖 = gas   🍴 = food   🏠 = lodging   🅞 = other   🅡ₛ = rest stop   Copyright 2014 - The NEXT Exit

⬆N INTERSTATE 37 CONT'D

Exit	Services
11b	Continued
	toZone, HEB Food/gas, O'Reilly Parts, Walgreens, vet
11a	McKinzie Rd, **E** 🅖 Shell, 🍴 Jack-in-the-Box, 🏠 La Quinta, **W** 🅖 Valero/dsl
10	Carbon Plant Rd
9	FM 2292, Up River Rd, Rand Morgan Rd, **W** 🅖 Valero/dsl, 🍴 Whataburger
7	Suntide Rd, Tuloso Rd, Clarkwood Rd, **W** 🅞 CC RV Ctr, Freightliner
6	Southern Minerals Rd, **E** 🅖 refinery
5	Corn Products Rd, Valero Way, **E** 🅞 Kenworth/Mack, **W** 🅖 PetroFleet, 🍴 Jalisco II Rest., 🏠 Howard Johnson, Travelodge, ValStay
4b	Lantana St, McBride Lane (from sb), **W** 🏠🛏 Inn, Motel 6
4a	TX 358, to Padre Island, **W** 🏠 Holiday Inn, Plaza Inn, Quality Inn, 🅞 Walmart (4mi)
3b	McBride Lane (from nb), **W** 🅞 Gulf Coast Racing
3a	Navigation Blvd, **E** 🅖 Valero/dsl, 🏠 Rodeway Inn, **W** 🅖 Exxon/dsl, 🍴 Denny's, La Milpas, Miller BBQ, 🏠 Days Inn, Hampton Inn, Holiday Inn Express, La Quinta, Super 8, 🅞 CarQuest
2	Up River Rd, **E** refinery
1e	Lawrence Dr, Nueces Bay Blvd, **E** refinery, **W** 🅖 Valero, 🍴 Church's, 🏠 Red Roof Inn, 🅞 Aamco, AutoZone, HEB Foods, Firestone, USPO
1d	Port Ave (from sb), **W** 🅖 Coastal, Shell, 🍴 Vick's Burgers, Whataburger, 🏠 EconoLodge, 🅞 Radio Shack, Port of Corpus Christi
1c	US 181, TX 286, Shoreline Blvd, Corpus Christi, **W** 🅗
1b	Brownlee St (from nb), **W** Shell
1a	Buffalo St (from sb) **0-1 mi W on Shoreline** 🅖 Valero/dsl, 🍴 Burger King, Joe's Crabshack, Landry's Seafood, Subway, Waterstreet Seafood, Whataburger, 🏠 Bayfront Inn, Best Western, Omni Hotel, Super 8, 🅞 U-Haul, USPO,

I-37 begins/ends on US 181 in Corpus Christi.

⬆E INTERSTATE 40

Exit	Services
177mm	Texas/Oklahoma state line
176	spur 30 (from eb), to Texola
169	FM 1802, Carbon Black Rd
167	FM 2168, Daberry Rd
165mm	check sta wb
164	Lp 40 (from wb), to Shamrock, **1 mi S** 🏠 EconoLodge, 🅞 🅗, museum, check sta eb
163	US 83, to Wheeler, Shamrock, **N** 🅖 Chevron/Taco Bell/dsl, 🍴 Mitchell's Rest., 🏠 Best Western, Motel 6, 🅞 Ace Hardware, **S** 🅖 Conoco/dsl, Phillips 66/Subway/dsl, 🍴 DQ, McDonald's, 🏠 EconoLodge, Holiday Inn Express, Sleep Inn, Western Motel, 🅞 Family$
161	Lp 40, Rte 66 (from eb), to Shamrock
157	FM 1547, Lela, **1 mi S** 🅞 West 40 RV Camping
152	FM 453, Pakan Rd
148	FM 1443, Kellerville Rd
146	County Line Rd
143	Lp 40 (from wb), to McLean, to Shell/dsl
142	TX 273, FM 3143, to McLean, **N** 🅖 Shell/dsl, 🍴 Red River Steaks, 🏠 Cactus Inn, 🅞 RV Camping/dump, USPO
141	Rte 66 (from eb), McLean, same as 142
135	FM 291, Rte 66, Alanreed, **S** 🅖 Conoco/motel/café/RV park/dump, 🅞 USPO

Exit	Services
132	Johnson Ranch Rd ranch access
131mm	🅡ₛ wb, full 🚻 facilities, 🄲, 🏚, litter barrels, petwalk
129mm	🅡ₛ eb, full 🚻 facilities, 🄲, 🏚, littler barrels, petwalk, playground
128	FM 2477, to Lake McClellan, **N** 🅞 Lake McClellan RA/RV Dump
124	TX 70 S, to Clarendon, **S** RV camping/dump
121	TX 70 N, to Pampa
114	Lp 40, Groom, **N** dsl repair
113	FM 2300, Groom, **S** 🅖 Phillips 66/dsl, 🍴 DQ, 🏠 Chalet Inn
112	FM 295, Groom, **S** 🅞 Biggest Cross, **1 mi S** gas
110	Lp 40, Rte 66
109	FM 294
108mm	parking area wb, litter barrels
106mm	parking area eb, 🏚, litter barrels
105	FM 2880, grain silo
98	TX 207 S (from wb), to Claude
96	TX 207 N, to Panhandle, **N** 🅖 💙Loves/Subway/dsl/24hr, **S** 🏠 Conway Inn/cafe, Executive Inn,
89	FM 2161, to Rte 66
87	FM 2373
87mm	🅡ₛs both lanes, litter barrels
85	Amarillo Blvd, Durrett Rd, access to camping
81	FM 1912, **N** 🅖 Phillips 66/dsl
80	FM 228, **N** 🅞 AOK RV Park
78	US 287 S (from eb), FM 1258, Pullman Rd, Travel Plaza/dsl/scales/24hr
77	FM 1258, Pullman Rd, **N** 🅖 Travel Plaza/dsl/scales/24hr
76	spur 468, **N** 🅖 /⊕FLYING J/Denny's/dsl/LP/RV dump/scales/24hr, Shell/dsl, 🍴 Buffalo Wild Wings, 🏠 Fairfield Inn, Holiday Inn Express, 🅞 Mack/Volvo Trucks, tourist info, **S** 🅖 Speedco, 🅞 Custom RV Ctr, TX info
75	Lp 335, Lakeside Rd, **N** 🅖 Pilot/McDonald's/dsl/scales/24hr/@, 🍴 Waffle House, 🏠🛏 Plaza Hotel, Best Value Inn, Super 8, 🅞 UPS, Peterbilt Trucks, KOA (2mi), **S** 🅖 Petro/dsl/rest./scales/@, 🅞 Blue Beacon
74	Whitaker Rd, **N** 🍴 Big Texan Inn, 🅞 RV camping, **S** 🅖 💙Loves/Subway/dsl/scales/@, TA/Exxon/FoodCourt/dsl/scales/24hr/@, 🏠 Budget Inn, 🅞 Blue Beacon
73	Eastern St, Bolton Ave, Amarillo, **N** 🅖 Shell/dsl, 🏠 Dean Motel, Motel 6, Value Place, **S** 🅖 Chevron/dsl, 🏠 Best Western
72b	Grand St, Amarillo, **N** 🅖 Shell, 🍴 Henk's BBQ, 🏠 Value Inn, 🅞 Family$, O'Reilly Parts, **S** 🅖 Murphy USA/dsl, Phillips 66, Valero, 🍴 Braum's, Chicken Express, McDonald's, Pizza Hut, Sonic, Starbucks, Subway, Taco Villa, Whataburger, 🏠 Motel 6, 🅞 Urgent Care, Advance Parts, Amigo's Foods, AutoZone, BigLots, $General, Walmart, same as 73
72a	Nelson St, **N** 🍴 Cracker Barrel, 🏠 La Kiva Hotel, Luxury Inn, Sleep Inn, Super 8, Travelodge, 🅞 Qtrhorse Museum, **S** 🅖 Shell/dsl, 🏠 Camelot Suites, 🅞 transmissions
71	Ross St, Osage St, Amarillo, **N** 🅖 Shell/dsl, Valero, 🍴 A&W/LJ Silver, Burger King, IHOP, KFC, McDonald's, Schlotsky's, Subway, Wienerschnitzel, 🏠 Comfort Inn, Days Inn, Holiday Inn, Microtel, Quality Inn, **S** 🍴 Arby's, Denny's, Fiesta Grande Mexican, Sonic, Taco Bell, Wendy's, 🏠 Hampton Inn, La Quinta, Magnuson Hotel, 🅞 Chevrolet, Ford Trucks, Hyundai, Sam's Club/gas, USPO
70	I-27 S, US 60 W, US 87, US 287, to Canyon, Lubbock, to downtown Amarillo

TX (side tab)

CORPUS CHRISTI (side tab)

SHAMROCK (side tab)

AMARILLO (side tab)

▶E INTERSTATE 40 CONT'D

Exit	Services
69b	Washington St, Amarillo, **S** ■ DQ, Subway, ■ CVS Drug
69a	Crockett St, access to same as 68b
68b	Georgia St, **N** ■ Shell/Subway, ■ Schlotzky's, TGIFriday, ■ Ambassador Hotel, **S** ■ Valero, ■ Baker Bro's Deli, Burger King, Church's Chicken, Coldstone, Denny's, Furr's Café, LJ Silver, Pizza Hut, Red Lobster, Sonic, Starbucks, Taco Bueno, TX Roadhouse, Whataburger, ■ Baymont Inn, Holiday Inn Express, Quality Inn, Travelodge, ■ ■ Hastings Books, Home Depot, Office Depot, Radio Shack, Walgreens
68a	Julian Blvd, Paramount Blvd, **N** ■ Shell, ■ Arby's, Chili's, Nick's Rest., Pizza Hut, Schlotzsky's, TGIFriday's, Wendy's, ■ Ambassador Inn, same as 67, **S** ■ Valero, ■ Baker Bro's Deli, Burger King, Furr's Buffet, Kushiyama, Red Lobster, Ruby Tequila's Mexican, TX Roadhouse, ■ Best Value, Comfort Suites, Holiday Inn Express, Motel 6, Super 8, Travelodge, ■ Home Depot, Office Depot
67	Western St, Amarillo, **N** ■ Phillips 66, Shell, ■ Braum's, Burger King, Cattle Call BBQ, Chili's, McDonald's, Rosa's Cafe, Sonic, Taco Bell, Wendy's, **S** ■ Rudy's/BBQ/dsl, Valero, ■ Blue Sky Rest., Cheddar's, IHOP, Olive Garden, Waffle House, Willy's Grill, ■ Baymont Inn, ■ Discount Tire, Firestone, Michael's, Petco, same 68
66	Bell St, Amarillo, **N** ■ Shell/dsl, Valero/dsl, ■ Fairfield Inn, Quality Inn, Relax Inn, Residence Inn, ■ Harley-Davidson, **S** ■ Doughnut Stop, King & I Chinese, Taco Bueno, ■ Albertson's/Sav-On
65	Coulter Dr, Amarillo, **N** ■ Phillips 66/dsl, ■ Arby's, Carino's Italian, Country Barn BBQ, Golden Corral, Kabuki Japanese, SaltGrass Steaks, Subway, Taco Bell, Waffle House, ■ Courtyard, Days Inn, Executive Inn, La Quinta, ■ ■ Cadillac/Chevrolet, Cavender's Boots, Discount Tire, Dodge, Firestone/auto, Nissan, **S** ■ Chevron/Chicken Express/dsl, Shell, ■ ChinaStar, CiCi's, Hoffbrau Steaks, Jason's Deli, McDonald's, Outback Steaks, Pizza Hut, Wendy's, Whataburger, ■ Hampton Inn, 5th Season Inn, Sleep Inn, ■ AT&T, Goodyear/auto, Verizon
64	Soncy Rd, to Pal Duro Cyn, **N** ■ Famous Dave's BBQ, Furr's Buffet, Jimmy John's, Red Robin, Lin's Chinese, Logan's Roadhouse, Plaza Rest., ■ Comfort Inn, Country Inn&Suites, Drury Inn, Extended Stay America, Hilton Garden, Holiday Inn, Holiday Inn Express, Homewood Suites, ■ USPO, **S** ■ Valero/dsl/24hr, ■ Applebee's, Baker Bros Deli, ChuckeCheese, DQ, Fazoli's, Hooters, Jake's Grill, Marble Slab Creamery, McAlisters Deli, McDonald's, On-the-Border, Pei Wei, Ruby Tequila's Mexican, Starbucks, Subway, ■ Barnes&Noble, Best Buy, Dillard's, $Tree, Ford, Home Depot, JC Penney, Jo-Ann Fabrics, Kohl's, Lincoln, Old Navy, PetsMart, Ross, Sears/auto, Target, World Mkt, mall
62b	Lp 40, Amarillo Blvd, **N** ■ Gander Mtn, **S** ■ Sundown RV Resort
62a	Hope Rd, Helium Rd, **S** ■ RV camping, antiques
60	Arnot Rd, **S** ■ Love's/Subway/dsl, ■ Oasis RV Resort/dump
57	RM 2381, Bushland, **N** grain silos, **S** ■ Phillips 66/dsl, ■ BBQ Barn, ■ USPO, RV camping/dump (1mi)
55mm	parking area wb, litter barrels
54	Adkisson Rd
53.5mm	parking area eb, litter barrels

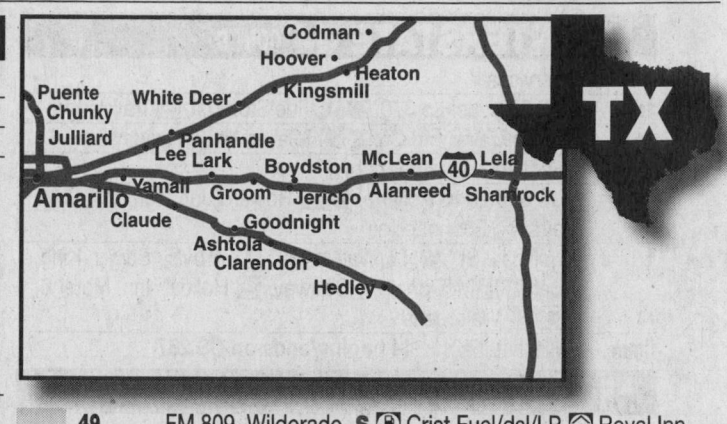

Exit	Services
49	FM 809, Wildorado, **S** ■ Crist Fuel/dsl/LP, ■ Royal Inn
42	Everett Rd
37	Lp 40 W, to Vega, **1 mi N** ■ Bonanza Motel, ■ Walnut RV Park, same as 36
36	US 385, Channing, Hereford, **N** ■ Conoco/dsl/24hr, Alon/dsl, Shamrock, ■ Boothill Grill, DQ, Wooden Spoon Cafe, ■ Days Inn, ■ RV Park, **S** ■ Shell/cafe/dsl
35	to Rte 66, to Vega, **N** ■ Best Western, Bonanza Motel (1mi), ■ Walnut RV Park (1mi), same as 36
32mm	■ both lanes, litter barrels
28	to Rte 66, Landergin
23	to Adrian, Vega, same as 22
22	TX 214, Adrian, **N** ■ Midpoint Cafe, ■ USPO, auto repair, **S** ■ Phillips 66/dsl/Tommy's Café
18	FM 2858, Gruhlkey Rd, **S** ■ Shell/Stuckey's/cafe/dsl
15	Ivy Rd
13mm	■ both lanes, ■ litter barrels
5.5mm	turnout
0	Lp 40, to Glenrio
0mm	Texas/New Mexico state line, Central/Mountain time zone

▶E INTERSTATE 44

Exit	Services
15mm	Texas/Oklahoma state line, Red River
14	Lp 267, E 3rd St, **W** ■ Burk RV Park, historical marker
13	Glendale St, **W** ■ Subway, ■ Beall's
12	Burkburnett, **E** ■ Hampton Inn, **W** ■ Fina/7 11/dsl, ■ Braum's, Chicken Express, Feedlot Rest., Lite Pan Asian, Mazzio's, McDonald's, Whataburger, ■ CarQuest, Chevrolet, Ford
11	FM 3429, Daniels Rd
9mm	■ both lanes, picnic table, litter barrels, petwalk
7	East Rd
6	Bacon Switch Rd
5a	FM 3492, Missile Rd, **E** ■ El Mejicano Rest., Hunan Chinese, Marco's Pizza, ■ st patrol, **W** ■ Exxon/dsl
5	Access Rd
4	City Loop St
3c	FM 890, **W** ■ Murphy USA/dsl, ■ Cracker Barrel, Jack-in-the-Box, KFC/Taco Bell, Papa Murphy's, Subway, ■ Walmart/Subway, vet
3b	sp 325, Sheppard AFB
3a	US 287 N, to Amarillo, **W** ■ Shell, ■ Carl's Jr, ■ Ramada Ltd
2	Maurine St, **E** ■ Fina/7-11/dsl, Shell/dsl, ■ Best Value Inn, Executive Inn, Quality Inn, ■ Chevrolet, Mazda, **W** ■ Fina/7-11, ■ China Star, Denny's, El Chico, LJ Silver, Whataburger, ■ Candlewood Suites, Comfort Inn, La Quinta, Red Roof Inn, Super 8

Vertical labels: AMARILLO, VEGA

TX

◆E INTERSTATE 44 CONT'D

Exit	Services
1d	US 287 bus, Lp 370, **W** 🅖 FuelStop/dsl, 🛏 Travelodge
1c	Texas Travel Info Ctr, **E** 🅖 $Saver, **W** 🛏 Holiday Inn
1b	Scotland Park (from nb)
1a	US 277 S, to Abilene, **E** 🛏 Howard Johnson, **W** 🍴 Arby's, 🛏 EconoLodge
1	Holliday St, **W** 🅖 Valero/dsl, 🍴 Arby's, Burger King, Carl's Jr, McDonald's, Subway, 🛏 Holiday Inn, Motel 6, ⊙ H, Walgreens
0mm	Witchita Falls, **I-44 begins/ends on US 287**

◆N INTERSTATE 45

Exit	Services
286	to I-35 E, to Denton. **I-45 begins/ends in Dallas.**
285	Bryan St E, US 75 N
284b a	I-30, W to Ft Worth, E to Texarkana, access to H
283b	Pennsylvania Ave, to MLK Blvd, **E** 🅖 Shamrock
283a	Lamar St
281	Overton St (from sb), **W** 🅖 Chevron
280	Illinois Ave, Linfield St, **E** 🛏 Star Motel, **W** 🅖 Exxon, Shell/dsl
279b a	Lp 12
277	Simpson Stuart Rd, **W** ⊙ to Paul Quinn Coll
276b a	I-20, W to Ft Worth, E to Shreveport
275	TX 310 N (from nb, no re-entry)
274	Dowdy Ferry Rd, Hutchins, **E** 🅖 Exxon/Subway/dsl, Shell/McDonald's/dsl, 🛏 Gold Inn, La Quinta, Motel 6, ⊙ auto repair, **W** 🍴 DQ, Jack-in-the-Box, Whataburger
273	Wintergreen Rd, **W** 🅖 QT/dsl/scales/24hr
272	Fulghum Rd, **E** 🅖 ♥Love's/Carl's Jr/dsl/scales/24hr, **W** weigh sta, both lanes
271	Pleasant Run Rd
270	Belt Line Rd, to Wilmer, **E** 🅖 Texaco/Pizza Inn/dsl, **W** 🅖 Exxon/Sonic/dsl, Shell/Church's/Subway/dsl, ⊙ $General, Family$, USPO
269	Mars Rd
268	Malloy Bridge Rd
267	Frontage Rd
266	FM 660, **E** 🍴 Jack-in-the-Box, **W** 🅖 Shamrock/dsl, 🍴 DQ, Pizza Hut
265	Lp 45, Ferris, Nb only
263a b	Lp 561
262	frontage rd
260	Lp 45, **E** 🍴 Trailor RV Park, **W** 🅖 Shell/Sonic/dsl
259	FM 813, FM 878, Jefferson St, **W** ⊙ Goodyear
258	Lp 45, Palmer, **E** 🅖 Chevron/Subway/dsl/scales/24hr, ⊙ golf
255	FM 879, Garrett, **E** 🅖 Exxon/dsl, **W** 🅖 Chevron/dsl
253	Lp 45, **W** 🅖 Shell/Subway/dsl
251b	TX 34, Ennis, **E** 🅖 Fina/dsl, Shell/dsl, Valero/dsl, 🍴 Bubba's BBQ, McDonald's, 🛏 Baymont Inn, Comfort Suites, Days Inn, Holiday Inn Express, ⊙ Ford, **W** 🅖 Chevron/dsl, Exxon/dsl/24hr, Murphy USA/dsl, Valero, 🍴 Braum's, Burger King, Chili's, Denny's, DQ, Domino's, Golden Chick, Grand Buffet, Hilda's Kitchen, IHOP, Jack-in-the-Box, Jungle Jack's Pizza, KFC, Little Caesars, Sonic, Starbucks, Subway, Taco Bell, Taco Cabana, Waffle House, Wall Chinese, Wendy's, Whataburger, 🛏 Ennis Inn, Quality Inn, ⊙ H, AutoZone, Beall's, Chevrolet, Chrysler/Dodge/Jeep, $Tree, Radio Shack, Walmart/McDonald's, RV camping

Exit	Services
251a	Creechville Rd, FM 1181, **W** H
249	FM 85, Ennis, **E** 🛏 Budget Inn, **W** 🅖 Exxon/Subway, ⊙ Blue Beacon, repair
247	US 287 N, to Waxahatchie
246	FM 1183, Alma, **W** 🅖 Chevron
244	FM 1182
243	Frontage Rd
242	Calhoun St, Rice, **W** 🅖 Shell/Sonic/dsl
239	FM 1126, **W** 🅖 45 Kwik Stop, ⊙ Rendell RV Ctr
238	FM 1603, **E** 🅖 Exxon/rest/dsl/24hr, ⊙ Casita RV Trailers
237	Frontage Rd
235b	Lp I-45 (from sb), to Corsicana
235a	Frontage Rd
232	Roane Rd, E 5th Ave
231	TX 31, Corsicana, **E** 🅖 Phillips 66/dsl, 🍴 Jack-in-the-Box, 🛏 Best Western, Colonial Inn, La Quinta, ⊙ Buick/Cadillac/Chevrolet/GMC, **W** 🅖 Exxon/Subway/dsl, Shell/Arby's, 🍴 Bill's Fried Chicken, DQ, McDonald's, 🛏 Comfort Inn, ⊙ H, Chrysler/Dodge/Jeep, Ford/Lincoln, to Navarro Coll
229	US 287, Palestine, **E** 🅖 Exxon/Wendy's/dsl, Shell/dsl, 🍴 Applebee's, Chili's, Collin St Bakery, Denny's, Sonic, Subway, Taco Bell, 🛏 Hampton Inn, Holiday Inn Express, ⊙ Corsicana Outlets, Gander Mtn, Home Depot, Office Depot, Russell Stover Candies, **W** 🍴 Waffle House, 🛏 Corsicana Inn, EconoLodge, Motel 6, Traveler's Inn
228b	Lp 45 (exits left from nb), Corsicana, **2 mi W services in Corsicana**
228a	15th St, Corsicana, **W** ⊙ Scion/Toyota
225	FM 739, Angus, **E** 🅖 Conoco/dsl, ⊙ to Chambers Reservoir, RV park
221	Frontage Rd
220	Frontage Rd
219b	Frontage Rd
219a	TX 14 (from sb), to Mexia, Richland, **W** 🅖 Shell
218	FM 1394 (from nb), Richland, **W** 🅖 Shell
217mm	Rs **both lanes, full** ♿ **facilities,** C, 🛢, **litter barrels, vending, petwalk**
213	TX 75 S, FM 246, to Wortham, **W** 🅖 Exxon/dsl
211	FM 80, to Streetman, Kirvin
206	FM 833, **3 mi W on frntge rd** ⊙ I-45 RV Park
198	FM 27, to Wortham, **E** 🅖 Shell/Cole's BBQ, 🍴 Gilberto's Mexican, 🛏 La Quinta, ⊙ H, **W** 🅖 Cooper Farms/dsl, ♥Love's/Burger King/dsl/scales/24hr, 🛏 Budget Inn, ⊙ I-45 RV Park (4mi)
197	US 84, Fairfield, **E** 🅖 Chevron/dsl, Exxon/dsl, Shell/dsl, 🍴 Bush's Chicken, DQ, Jack-in-the-Box, McDonald's, Sam's Rest., Something Different Rest, Sonic, Subway/TX Burger, 🛏 Days Inn, Holiday Inn Express, Super 8, ⊙ Brookshire Foods/gas, Chevrolet, Chrysler/Dodge/Jeep, Fred's Store, **W** 🅖 Exxon/dsl, Shell/dsl, Texaco/dsl, 🍴 I-45 Rest., KFC/Taco Bell, Lonestar Grill, Pizza Hut, Ponte's Diner, 🛏 Best Value Inn, Regency Inn, ⊙ Ace Hardware, Ford
189	TX 179, to Teague, **E** 🅖 Exxon/Dinner Bell Rest/dsl, Citgo/Shirley's Cafe/dsl
180	TX 164, to Groesbeck
178	US 79, Buffalo, **E** 🅖 Chevron, Conoco/dsl, Shell/dsl, 🍴 Pizza Hut, Subway/TX Burger, ⊙ Brookshire Foods/gas, $General, Family$, **W** 🅖 Exxon/Church's/Subway/dsl/scales, Shamrock/dsl/24hr, Texaco/dsl, 🍴 Dickey's BBQ, DQ, Pitt Grill, Rancho Viejo, Mexican, Sonic, 🛏 Craig's Inn, Comfort Inn, Economy Inn, Hampton Inn

(Left margin vertical labels: DALLAS, ENNIS. Right margin vertical labels: CORSICANA, FAIRFIELD.)

INTERSTATE 45 CONT'D

Exit	Services
175mm	Bliss Creek
166mm	**weigh sta sb**
164	TX 7, Centerville, **E** 🅿️ Chevron, Shell/Woody's BBQ/dsl, 🍴 Country Cousins BBQ, Subway/TX Burger, 🏨 Days Inn, **W** 🅿️ Exxon/dsl, Shell/Woody's BBQ/dsl, 🍴 DQ, Jack-in-the-Box, Roble's Mexican
160mm	🆁🆂 sb, tables, litter barrels
159mm	Boggy Creek
156	FM 977, to Leona, **W** 🅿️ Exxon/dsl
155mm	🆁🆂 nb, 🆁🆂 litter barrels
152	TX OSR, to Normangee, **W** 🅿️ Chevron/dsl, Shell/Arby's/dsl
146	TX 75
142	US 190, TX 21, Madisonville, **E** 🅿️ Exxon/BBQ/dsl, Shell/Buc-ees/dsl, 🏨 Best Western, Carefree Inn, **W** 🅿️ Chevron/Church's/dsl, Shell/Subway, 🍴 Castanedas Mexican, Jack-in-the-Box, Lakeside Rest, McDonald's, Pizza Hut, Sonic, Taco Bell, TX Burger, 🏨 Budget Motel, Western Lodge, 🅾️ 🇭 Ford, Toyota
136	spur 67, **E** 🍴 Shrimpy's Seafood, 🅾️ Home on the Range RV camping/LP (3mi)
132	FM 2989
124mm	🆁🆂 **both lanes, full** ♿ **facilities,** 🍴, 🆁🆂, **litter barrels, vending, petwalk**
123	FM 1696
118	TX 75, **E** 🅿️ Shell/Hitchin Post/dsl/24hr/@, 🅾️ Texas Prison Museum, truckwash, **W** 🅿️ 🚍/Wendy's/dsl/scales/24hr, Shell/Dickey's BBQ/Subway/dsl, 🍴 Chicken Express
116	US 190, TX 30, **E** 🅿️ Conoco/dsl, Phillips 66/dsl, Valero/dsl, 🍴 Arby's, Bandera Grill, Church's, El Chico, Golden Corral, Imperial Garden Chinese, Jct Steaks, McDonald's, Popeye's, Schlotzsky's, Sonic, Whataburger, 🏨 Days Inn, EconoLodge, Holiday Inn Express, La Quinta, Motel 6, 🅾️ 🇭, AutoZone, Brookshire Foods/gas, Buick/Cadillac/Chevrolet/GMC, Cavander's Boots, Chrysler/Dodge/Jeep, CVS Drug, Family$, Firestone/auto, Hastings Books, O'Reilly Parts, Walgreens, vet, **W** 🅿️ Exxon/dsl, Murphy USA/dsl, Shell, 🍴 Bob Luby's Seafood, Burger King, Chili's, Denny's, 5 Guys Burgers, Grand Buffet, IHOP, Jack-in-the-Box, Little Caesars, Olive Garden, Pizza Hut, Starbucks, Subway, Taco Bell, Tinsley's Chicken, Wing Stop, 🅾️ AT&T, Discount Tire, $Tree, GNC, Home Depot, JC Penney, Kroger, Marshall's, Office Depot, Radio Shack, Target, Verizon, Walmart, USPO
114	FM 1374, **E** 🅿️ Exxon/dsl, Shell, 🍴 DQ, Margaritas Rest., 🏨 Gateway Inn, Super 8, **W** 🅿️ Texaco/dsl, Valero/dsl, 🍴 Country Inn Steaks, 🏨 Best Value Inn, Comfort Suites, 🅾️ 🇭, Ford, Hyundai
113	TX 19 (from nb), Huntsville
112	TX 75, **E** 🅿️ Citgo, 🏨 Baker Motel, 🅾️ Houston Statue, to Sam Houston St U, museum
109	Park 40, **W** 🅾️ to Huntsville SP
103	FM 1374/1375 (from sb), to New Waverly, **W** 🅿️ Chevron/Burger King/dsl
102	FM 1374/1375, TX 150 (from nb), to New Waverly, **E** 🅿️ Valero/dsl (1mi), **W** 🅿️ Chevron/Burger King/dsl (1mi), 🍴 Waverly Rest.
101mm	**weigh sta nb**
98	TX 75, Danville Rd, Shepard Hill Rd, **E** 🅾️ Convenience RV Ctr/repair

HUNTSVILLE

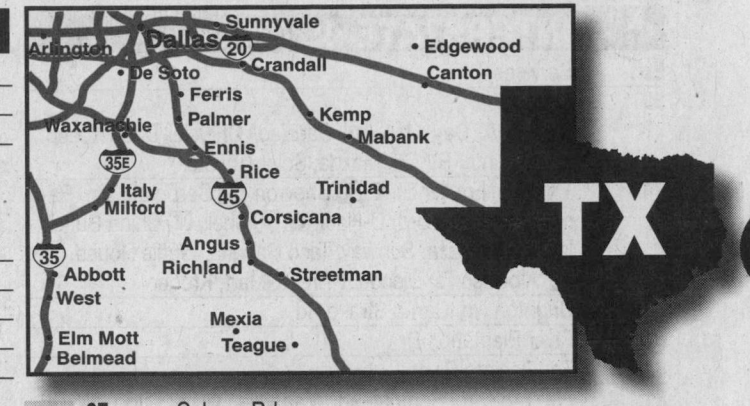

Exit	Services
97	Calvary Rd
95	Longstreet Rd, Calvary Rd, Willis, **W** 🅿️ ❤️Loves/Subway/Wendy's/dsl/scales/24hr
94	FM 1097, Longstreet Rd, to Willis, **E** 🅿️ Kwik Stop/dsl, 🍴 Jack-in-the-Box, Sonic, Taco Bell, 🅾️ AutoZone, $General, **W** 🅿️ Chevron/Popeye's, Shell/dsl, 🍴 Burger King, Chick-fil-A, Little Caesars, McDonald's, Pizza Hut, Rico's Grill, Scholtzsky's, Subway, Whataburger, 🏨 Best Western, 🅾️ Kroger/dsl, Walgreens, vet
92	FM 830, Seven Coves Dr, **W** 🅾️ Omega Farms RV Park, RV Park on the Lake (3mi), Thousand Trails Resort
91	League Line Rd, **E** 🅿️ Chevron/McDonald's, Shell/dsl, 🍴 Mamma Juanita's Mexican, Waffle House, Wendy's, 🏨 Comfort Inn, Days Inn, La Quinta, 🅾️ Conroe Outlets/famous brands, **W** 🅿️ Shell/Jack-in-the-Box, 🍴 Cracker Barrel
90	FM 3083, Teas Nursery Rd, Montgomery Co Park, **E** 🅿️ Exxon/dsl, 🍴 Applebee's, Buffalo Wild Wings, Popeye's, Red Lobster, Smokey Mo's BBQ, 🏨 Fairfield Inn, 🅾️ AT&T, Kohl's, Old Navy, Petsmart, Ross, TJ Maxx, convention center (4mi), **W** 🍴 Firehouse Subs, Olive Garden, Subway, Wings Wok, 🏨 ValuePlace Inn, 🅾️ Vorizon, JC Penney
88	Lp 336, to Cleveland, Navasota, **E** 🅿️ Mobil/Chester's/dsl, Shell/dsl, Valero/dsl, 🍴 Arby's, A&W/LJ Silver, Burger King, Chili's, China Delight, Denny's, Domino's, Los Cucos Mexican, Marble Slab Creamery, Margarita's Mexican, McDonald's, Papa John's, Pizza Hut, Quizno's, Sonic, TX Roadhouse, Whataburger, Wing Stop, 🏨 Hampton Inn, Holiday Inn Express, 🅾️ Advance Parts, Buick, CVS Drug, Discount Tire, $Tree, GNC, HEB Foods/gas, Hobby Lobby, Just Brakes, Kroger/gas, Michael's, Walgreens, vet, **W** 🅿️ Chevron/24hr, 🍴 Blackeyed Pea, Casa Ole Mexican, Culver's, Dickie's BBQ, El Bosque Mexican, Jack-in-the-Box, KFC, Ryan's, Subway, 🅾️ Hancock Fabrics, Lowe's, 99Cent Store, PetCo, Sam's Club/gas, Tuesday Morning, Walmart
87	TX 105, Conroe, **E** 🍴 Burger King, Jack-in-the-Box, Kettle, Luther's BBQ, McDonald's, Outback Steaks, Popeye's, Sonic, Saltgrass Steaks, Taco Bell, Tast of China, 🏨 Super 8, 🅾️ 🇭, CVS Drug, $General, Firestone/auto, Hyundai, Kia, NTB, **W** 🅿️ Exxon, 🍴 Chick-fil-A, Coney Island, Luby's, Panda Express, Panera Bread, Quizno's, Schlotzsky's, Shogun Japanese, Smoothie King, Starbucks, Subway, Taco Bell, Taco Bueno, Whataburger, 🅾️ Best Buy, Buick/GMC, Hastings Books, Home Depot, Office Depot, Radio Shack, Target, Tiremaxx
85	FM 2854, Gladstell St, **E** 🅿️ Citgo/dsl, 🏨 Motel 6, 🅾️ 🇭, Honda, Nissan, **W** 🅿️ Shell/dsl, Valero, 🍴 IHOP, 🏨 Bay

CONROE

🅖 = gas   🍴 = food   🛏 = lodging   ◉ = other   🅡🅢 = rest stop   Copyright 2014 - The NEXT Exit

⬆N INTERSTATE 45 CONT'D

Exit	Services
85	Continued
	mont Inn, Days Inn, ◉ Cadillac, Chrysler/Dodge/Jeep, Fun Country RV Ctr, Mazda, Scion/Toyota
84	TX 75 N, Frazier St, E 🅖 Chevron, 🛏 Corporate Inn, Ramada Ltd, ◉ Ford, U-Haul, W 🅖 Shell, 🍴 China Buffet, Incredible Pizza, Subway, Taco Cabana, Waffle House, ◉ H, Albertson's, Discount Tire, K-Mart, Kroger
83	Crighton Rd, Camp Strake Rd
82	River Plantation Dr
82mm	San Jacinto River
81	FM 1488, to Hempstead, Magnolia, E 🅖 Citgo, W 🅖 Valero/Subway, ◉ CamperLand RV Ctr
80	Needham Rd (from sb)
79	TX 242, Needham, E 🅖 Shell/McDonald's, 🍴 Mama Juanita's Mexican, Quizno's, 🛏 Best Western, ◉ Batteries+, W 🅖 Chevron, Murphy USA/dsl, 🍴 Adobe Cafe, Arby's, Burger King, ChuckeCheese, Domino's, Outback Steaks, Popeye's, Sonic, Subway, Taco Cabana, Wendy's, Whataburger, Willie's Grill, Wings'N More, 🛏 Country Suites, Fairfield Inn, TownPlace Suites, ◉ H, BMW/Mini, Firestone/auto, Kohl's, Lowe's Whse, Walgreens, Walmart
78	Needham Rd (from sb), Tamina Rd, access to same as 77
77	Woodlands Pkwy, Robinson, Chateau Woods, E 🅖 Chevron, Conoco/dsl, 🍴 Babin's Seafood, Buca Italian, Buffalo Wild Wings, Church's, Chuy's, Hooters, Lupe Tortilla, Melting Pot, Pancho's Mexican, Pappa's BBQ, Pappadeaux, PeiWei, Pizza Hut, Red Robin, Saltgrass Steaks, Subway, Tom's Steaks, 🛏 Best Value Inn, Budget Inn, ◉ Discount Tire, Home Depot, Jo-Ann Fabrics, Michael's, NTB, Office Depot, Old Navy, Petsmart, Sam's Club/gas, SteinMart, Walgreens, funpark, vet, W 🅖 Exxon, Shell, Texaco, Valero/dsl, 🍴 A&W/KFC, Blackeyed Pea, Cane's, Chick-fil-A, Chili's, Chipotle Mexican, Culver's, Denny's, El Bosque Mexican, Guadalajara Mexican, Jack-in-the-Box, Jason's Deli, Jimmy John's, Kabab House, Kirby's Steakhouse, La Madeliene, Landry's Seafood, Luby's, Macaroni Grill, Olive Garden, Red Lobster, Sweet Tomatos, TGIFriday's, 🛏 Comfort Suites, Days Inn, Drury Inn, Hampton Inn, Homewood Suites, La Quinta, Marriott, Shenandoa Inn, ◉ H, Best Buy, Dillard's, HEB Foods, Macy's, Marshall's, Sears, Ross, Target, World Mkt, auto repair, mall
76	Research Forest Dr, Tamina Rd, E 🅖 Chevron/dsl, 🍴 LJ Silver, Pappa's BBQ, ◉ Urgent Care, Firestone/auto, JustBrakes, Tiremaxx, vet, W 🅖 Shell, 🍴 Carrabba's, Denny's, El Chico, IHOP, Jack-in-the-Box, Kyoto Japanese, Macaroni Grill, Olive Garden, TGIFriday's, Tortuga Mexican, 🛏 Crossland Suites, Courtyard, Residence Inn, ◉ Goodyear/auto, JC Penney, Sears/auto, Woodlands Mall
73	Rayford Rd, Sawdust Rd, E 🅖 Conoco, Shell, Valero, 🍴 Hartz Chicken, Jack-in-the-Box, McDonald's, Popeye's, Sonic, Taqueria Arandas, Thomas BBQ, 🛏 Holiday Inn Express, La Quinta, ◉ Aamco, AutoZone, O'Reilly Parts, U-Haul, W 🅖 Mobil/dsl, Shell, Texaco, 🍴 Carrabba's, Cici's Pizza, Grand Buffet, IHOP, Subway, Taipei Chinese, Tortuga, 🛏 Extended Stay America, Red Roof Inn, Super 8, ◉ Brake Check, Discount Tire, GNC, Goodyear/auto, Harley-Davidson, HEB Foods, Kroger, Walgreens
72a	Spring Crossing Dr, W 🅖 Texaco/dsl
72b	to Hardy **Toll Rd** from sb

70b	Spring-Stuebner Rd, E 🅖 Vaughn RV Ctr
70a	FM 2920, to Tomball, E 🅖 Exxon, Murphy USA/dsl, Rudy's BBQ/dsl, Shell, 🍴 Arby's, Chick-fil-A, El Palenque Mexican, Godfather's Pizza, Golden Jade Chinese, Hartz Chicken, McDonald's, Pizza Hut, Subway, Quizno's, Taco Cabana, Wendy's, Whataburger, ◉ BigLots, $General, $Tree, Kohl's, Kroger, Lincoln, Michael's, O'Reilly Parts, Radio Shack, Ross, Scion/Toyota, Vaughn's RV Ctr, Walmart/24hr, transmissions, W 🅖 Chevron, RaceTrac, Texaco, 🍴 Burger King, Taco Bell, Tuscan Sun Coffee, Whataburger/24hr, 🛏 Travelodge, ◉ Ford, U-Haul
68	Holzwarth Rd, Cypress Wood Dr, E 🅖 Texaco/dsl, 🍴 Burger King, Pizza Hut/Taco Bell, Sonic, Starbucks, Wendy's, ◉ Albertson's, AT&T, Gander Mtn, GNC, Tiremaxx, W 🅖 Chevron/dsl, 🍴 Cheddar's, Denny's, Jack-in-the-Box, Lenny's Subs, Pizza Hut, Popeye's, Starbucks, 🛏 Motel 6, Spring Lodge, ◉ Advance Parts, Best Buy, Chrysler/Dodge/Jeep, Firestone/auto, Ford, Home Depot, Lowe's Whse, Office Depot, PetCo, Target, Walgreens
66	FM 1960, to Addicks, E 🅖 Chevron, RaceTrac, Shell, 🍴 Hick's Rest., Jack-in-the-Box, Sonic, Subway, TX Roadhouse, ◉ Acura, AT&T, BMW, Chevrolet, Honda, Mercedes, Mistubishi, Petsmart, Radio Shack, Subaru, W 🅖 Exxon, Shell/dsl/24hr, Texaco/dsl, Valero, 🍴 Cici's Pizza, Hooters, Jack-in-the-Box, James Coney Island, McDonald's, Outback Steaks, Panda Express, Red Lobster, Subway, Taco Bell, Taquiera Arendas, 🛏 Baymont Inn, Comfort Suites, Fairfield Inn, Hampton Inn, Studio 6, ◉ H, Audi, Infiniti, Jaguar/LandRover, Lexus, NTB, U-Haul, mall
64	Richey Rd, E 🍴 Atchafalaya River Café, 🛏 Best Value Inn, Holiday Inn, Lexington Suites, Rmada, ◉ CarMax, Discount Tire, Sam's Club/gas, W 🅖/⊕FLYING J/Denny's/dsl/scales/24hr, 🍴 Cracker Barrel, House of Creole, Jack-in-the-Box, Joe's Crabshack, Lupe Tortilla, Mamacita's Mexican, Michoacan Rest, SaltGrass Steaks, Tokyohana, Whataburger, Wings'n More, Zio's Italian, ◉ Jones RV Ctr
63	Airtex Dr, E 🅖 Texaco/Subway, Valero/Church's, 🍴 China Bear, Pappasito's Cantina, 🛏 ValuePlace Inn, ◉ Acura, Cadillac, LoneStar RV Ctr, Nissan, W 🍴 Cracker Barrel, Jack-in-the-Box, Whataburger, 🛏 Best Western, Guesthouse Suites
62	Rankin Rd, Kuykendahl, E 🛏 Best Classic Inn, Scottish Inn, W 🅖 Chevron/McDonald's, RaceTrac, Shell, 🍴 Luby's, Shiply Donuts, 🛏 Palace Inn, Studio+, SunSuites, ◉ Buick/GMC, Demontrono RV Ctr, Hummer, Hyundai, Kia, Lamborghini, Mercedes, Volvo, VW
61	Greens Rd, E 🅖 Texaco, 🍴 Brown Sugar's BBQ, IHOP, Imperial Dragon, Luna's, 🛏 Knights Inn, ◉ Dillard's, JC Penney, Macy's, Sears/auto, mall, W 🍴 Burger King, Luby's, Subway, 🛏 Baymont Inn, Comfort Inn, ◉ Burlington Coat Factory, $General, Kroger
60c	Beltway E
60	(b a from nb), TX 525, W 🍴 Pappas Seafood, ◉ U-Haul
59	FM 525, West Rd, E 🅖 Shell/dsl, 🍴 A&W/LJ Silver, Burger King, China Border, Denny's, Domino's, Mambo Seafood, McDonald's, Michoacan Rest, Moon Palace Chinese, Pizza Hut, Taco Cabana, ◉ CarQuest, Chrysler/Dodge/Jeep, Firestone, Honda, Office Depot, W 🅖 Exxon, Shell, 🍴 Chili's, Jalisco's Mexican, Panda Express, Papa John's Pizza, Quizno's, Starbucks, Subway, Taco Bell, Taco Cabana, Wendy's, Whataburger, Wing Stop, 🛏 Best Value Inn, Best Western, ◉ AT&T, Best Buy, Discount Tire,

INTERSTATE 45 CONT'D

Exit	Services
59	Continued $Tree, Fry's Electronics, Home Depot, Office Depot, NTB, PepBoys, Radio Shack, Ross, Verizon, Walmart/24hr
57	(b a from nb), TX 249, Gulf Bank Rd, Tomball, **E** 🅟 Chevron, Mobil/dsl, Texaco/Church's, 🍴 Wings'n More, **W** 🅟 Shell, 🍴 Sonic, Tombico Seafood, 🛏 Greenchase Motel, La Quinta, Quality Inn, 🅞 CVS Drug, Family$, Giant$, Mas Club/dsl
56	Canino Rd, **E** 🛏 Taj Inn Suites, **W** 🅟 Shell, Texaco, 🍴 Capt D's, Denny's, Jack-in-the-Box, KFC, Luby's, 🛏 Best Value Inn, EconoLodge, Gulfwind Motel, Passport Inn, 🅞 Ford, Isuzu, USPO
55	(b a from nb), Little York Rd, Parker Rd, **E** 🅟 Chevron, Texaco, 🍴 Burger King, China Panda, McDonald's, Whataburger, 🅞 Advance Parts, Family$, FoodTown, **W** 🅟 Shell, 🍴 Popeye's, 🛏 Symphony Inn, 🅞 🅗, Family$, Walgreens
54	Tidwell Rd, **E** 🅟 Exxon/dsl, 🍴 Aunt Bea's Rest, Burger King, Chacho's Mexican, China Border, Frenchys, Pancho's Mexican, Subway, Thomas BBQ, Wings'N More, 🅞 CVS Drug, Discount Tire, Radio Shack, transmissions, **W** 🅟 Chevron, 🍴 McDonald's, 🛏 Guest Motel, Scottish Inn, Southwind Motel, Town Inn, 🅞 U-Haul
53	Airline Dr, **E** 🅟 Citgo, 🍴 Popeye's, 🅞 Fiesta Foods/drug, **W** 🅟 Citgo, Shell, 🍴 Little Mexico, Wendy's, 🛏 Luxury Inn, Palace Inn
52	(b a from nb), Crosstimbers Rd, **E** 🍴 Baskin-Robbins, Burger King, Chick-fil-A, China Star, ChuckeCheese, Cici's, IHOP, Jack-in-the-Box, James Coney Island, KFC, Pappas BBQ, Pizza Hut, Pollo Rico, Sonic, Subway, Taco Bell, 🅞 AT&T, CVS Drug, Discount Tire, $Tree, Firestone, GNC, Marshall's, Office Depot, Ross, Verizon, Walmart, mall, **W** 🅟 Chevron/dsl, 🍴 Whataburger/24hr, 🛏 Texan Inn
51	I-610
50	(b a from nb), Patton St, Calvacade St, Link Rd, **E** 🅟 Citgo, Exxon, ♥Loves/Wendy's/dsl/scales/24hr, Shell, 🛏 Best Value Inn, Luxury Inn, **W** 🛏 Astro Inn, 🅞 NAPA
49b	N Main St, Houston Ave, **E** 🅟 Citgo, 🍴 Casa Grande Mexican, 🛏 Best Value Inn, Luxury Inn, **W** 🅟 Exxon/dsl, 🍴 Domino's, McDonald's, Subway, Whataburger/24hr, 🛏 Sleep Inn, 🅞 O'Reilly Parts
48b a	I-10, E to Beaumont, W to San Antonio
47d	Dallas St, Pierce St (from sb), **E** 🅞 🅗
47c	McKinney St (from sb, exits left)
47b	Houston Ave, Memorial Dr, downtown, **W** 🛏 Double Tree Hotel
47a	Allen Pkwy (exits left from sb)
46b a	US 59, N to Cleveland, S to Victoria, **E** 🅟 Chevron, **W** 🅟 Texaco, 🍴 McDonald's, Taco Bell, 🅞 BMW
45b a	South St, Scott St, Houston, **E** 🅟 Shell/Blimpie, to TSU
44	Cullen Blvd, Houston, **E** 🅟 Valero/dsl, to U of Houston
43b	Tele 🍴 Rd, Houston
43a	Tellepsen St, **E** 🍴 Luby's, **W** 🅞 U of Houston
41b	US 90A, Broad St, S Wayside Dr, **E** 🅟 Phillips 66, 🍴 Aranda's Mexican, 🛏 Houston Inn, Red Carpet Inn, **W** 🅟 Chevron, Exxon, Mobil, 🍴 Jack-in-the-Box, McDonald's, Monterrey Mexican, Subway, Taquiera Mexican, Wings and More, 🅞 $Tree, K-Mart, Sellars Foods
41a	Woodridge Dr, **E** 🅟 Shell, 🍴 Bonnie's Rest., China Star,
41a	Continued Denny's, James Coney Island, McDonald's, Pappa's Seafood House, Schlotsky's, 🅞 King$, **W** 🅟 Citgo, 🍴 Bone-Break BBQ, IHOP, Pappas BBQ, Sonic, Subway, Whataburger, Wendy's, 🅞 Chevrolet/Buick, Dillard's, HEB Food/gas, Home Depot, Lowe's, Marshall's, Office Depot, Old Navy, Radio Shack, Ross, mall
40c	I-610 W
40b	I-610 E, to Pasadena
40a	Frontage Rd (from nb)
39	Park Place Blvd, Broadway Blvd, **E** 🅟 Shell/dsl, **W** 🅟 Shell, 🍴 Kelley's Rest., Papa John's, Red Panda, Subway, 🅞 Chevrolet/Dodge/Jeep, Family$, transmissions
38b	Howard Dr, Bellfort Dr (from sb), **E** 🅟 Shell, 🍴 Jack-in-the-Box, Wendy's, **W** 🅟 Citgo, Shell, Texaco, 🍴 Chilo's Seafood, 🛏 Camelot Inn, Moonlight Inn, Mustang Inn, Palace Inn, 🅞 PepBoys
38	TX 3, Monroe Rd, **E** 🅟 Chevron/dsl, Shell/dsl, Valero, 🍴 DQ, Jack-in-the-Box, Ninfa, Starbucks, Wendy's, 🅞 Family$, Firestone, NTB, TX Campers, U-Haul, **W** 🅟 Chevron/dsl, Texaco/dsl, 🍴 Manny's Seafood, Pappa's BBQ, Subway, 🛏 Holiday Inn Express, Sheraton, 🅞 Firestone, U-Haul
36	College Ave, 🚐 Blvd, **E** 🅟 Valero, 🍴 Arranda's Bakery, Burger House, DQ, Jack-in-the-Box, Shipley Do-Nuts, Waffle House, 🛏 Knights Inn, **W** 🅟 Shell/dsl, Valero/dsl, 🍴 Denny's, Paco Joe's, Taco Cabana, 🛏 Baymont Inn, Comfort Suites, Courtyard, Days Inn, Drury Inn, Hampton Inn, La Quinta, Marriott, Motel 6, SpringHill Suites, Super 8, Travel Inn, 🅞 Discount Tire
35	Edgebrook Dr, **E** 🅟 Chevron, RaceWay, 🍴 Arranda's Mexican, Burger King, Chilo's Rest., Jack-in-the-Box, KFC, Popeye's, Subway, Taco Bell, 🛏 🚐 Inn, 🅞 Family$, Fiesta Foods, Firestone, Office Depot, vet, **W** 🅟 Mobil, 🍴 James Coney Island, Mambo Seafood, McDonald's, Pizza Hut, Whataburger, 🅞 Verizon
34	S Shaver Rd, **E** 🅟 Conoco, 🍴 McDonald's, 🛏 Island Suites, 🅞 Ford, Kia, Nissan, Toyota/Scion, **W** 🅟 MurphyUSA/dsl, 🍴 Arby's, China Star Buffet, Chopstix, KFC, Pancho's Mexican, Piccadilly's, Pizza Patron, Starbucks, Subway, Taco Bell, Wendy's, 🅞 AT$T, Discount Tire, Firestone, GNC, Honda, Macy's, Marshall's, PetsMart, Ross, Staples, Walmart/McDonald's
33	Fuqua St, **E** 🍴 Denny's, Chili's, Fuddrucker's, Las Haciendas, Luby's, Olive Garden, Schlotzky's, TGIFriday's, 🛏 Studio 6, Sun Suites, 🅞 Hyundai, Lincoln, Volvo, **W** 🍴 Bayou City Wings, Boudreaux's, Blackeyed Pea, Casa Ole, Cici's Pizza, Fox&Hound, Golden Corral, Gringo's Mexican, IHOP, Joe's Crabshack, Kimhai Asian, McDon

TX

▲N INTERSTATE 45 CONT'D

Exit	Services
33	Continued
	ald's, Murphy's Deli, Outback Steaks, Subway, Taco Cabana, TX Land&Cattle Steaks, Whataburger, Wings&More, Ⓞ Buick/GMC, CarMax, Chevrolet, Home Depot, JC Penney, Old Navy, Radio Shack, Sam's Club/gas, Subaru, mall
32	**Sam Houston Tollway**
31	FM 2553, Scarsdale Blvd, W Ⓞ Chevrolet
30	FM 1959, Dixie Farm Rd, Ellington Field, E Ⓖ Shell/dsl, Ⓕ El Nopalito, Subway, Ⓛ Howard Johnson, Ⓞ Ⓗ, Chrysler/Dodge/Jeep, Fiat, Infiniti, W Ⓖ RaceWay, Shell/dsl, Ⓕ McDonald's, Popeye's, Ⓛ Palace Inn, Ⓞ Lonestar RV, VW
29	FM 2351, Clear Lake City Blvd, to Clear Lake RA, Friendswood, W Ⓞ Hyundai
27	El Dorado Blvd, E Ⓖ Exxon, Shell, Ⓕ Taco Bell, Ⓞ Home Depot, W Ⓕ Sonic, TX Roadhouse, Whataburger, Ⓞ Cadillac, Kohl's, Lexus, Radio Shack, Sam's Club/gas, Walmart/McDonald's
26	Bay Area Blvd, E Ⓖ Chevron, Ⓕ Chick-fil-A, Panera Bread, Peiwei, Potbelly's, Red Lobster, TGIFriday's, Zio's Kitchen, Ⓞ Ⓗ, Barnes&Noble, Best Buy, Lowe's, Michael's, Staples, World Mkt, to Houston Space Ctr, W Ⓕ Cafe Adobe, Chick-fil-A, ChuckeCheese, Denny's, 5 Guys, McDonald's, Olive Garden, Panda Express, Ⓛ Holiday Inn Express, Ⓞ AT&T, Dillard's, JC Penney, Jo-Ann Fabrics, Macy's, Marshall's, Office Depot, Old Navy, Sears/auto, Target, Verizon, U of Houston, mall
25	FM 528, NASA rd 1, E Ⓖ Chevron, Conoco, Ⓕ Big Ben Rest., Cheddar's, Chili's, Chuy's Mexican, Las Hacienda Mexican, Marble Slab, McAlister's Deli, Michiru Asian, Pappa's Seafood, Pappasito's Cantina, Rudy's BBQ/gas, Saltgrass Steaks, Steak'n Shake, Twin Peaks Rest., Waffle House, Vito's, Ⓛ Motel 6, Springhill Suites, Ⓞ Ⓗ BigLots, Fry's Electronics, Hobby Lobby, Home Depot, Honda, Mazda, Volvo, W Ⓕ Cici's Pizza, Floyd's Cajun, Han's BBQ, Hooters, Hot Wok Chinese, James Coney Island, Pappa's Cafe, Subway, Ⓞ Tuesday Morning
23	FM 518, League City, E Ⓖ RaceWay/dsl, Ⓕ Center Buffet, KFC, La Brisa, Subway, Sudie's Seafood, Ⓞ Just Brakes, Kroger, W Ⓖ Chevron/dsl, Valero, Ⓕ Cracker Barrel, McDonald's, Taco Bell, Waffle House, Wendy's, Ⓛ Super 8, Ⓞ Discount Tire, Space Ctr RV Park, U-Haul
22	Calder Dr, Brittany Bay Blvd, E Ⓕ Wings'n More, Ⓞ BMW/Mini, Mercedes, Nissan, Toyota/Scion, **Urgent Care**, W Ⓞ Acura, Holiday World RV Ctr
20	FM 646, Santa Fe, Bacliff, E Ⓖ MurphyUSA/dsl, Ⓕ Chick-fil-A, Cici's Pizza, Denny's, 5 Guys, Jack-in-the-Box, Logan's Roadhouse, Marble Slab, McDonald's, Panda Express, Schlotzky's, Spring Creek BBQ, Subway, Whataburger, Ⓛ Candlewood Suites, Hampton Inn, Ⓞ Best Buy, $Tree, Hobby Lobby, Home Depot, JC Penney, Lowe's, Michael's, NTB, PetsMart, Radio Shack, Ross, Staples, Target, TJ Maxx, Walmart/McDonald's, W Ⓖ Chevron/dsl, Ⓕ Badabing, Chili's, Chinese Rest., Subway, Taco Cabana, Ⓞ HEB Foods/gas, Kohl's, PetCo, Verizon
19	FM 517, Dickinson Rd, Hughes Rd, E Ⓕ Jack-in-the-Box, Monterey Mexico, Shipley Do-Nuts, Ⓞ Buick/GMC, CVS Drug, Due's RV Ctr, Family$, Kia, W Ⓖ Conoco/dsl, Shell/dsl, Ⓕ Burger King, Dickenson's Seafood, KFC, Mc

LEAGUE CITY

Exit	Services
19	Continued
	Donald's, Pizza Hut, Sonic, Subway, Taco Bell, Wendy's, Whataburger/24hr, Ⓛ Days Inn, Economy Inn, Ⓞ Chrysler/Dodge/Jeep, Curves, Ford, Kroger, Walgreens
17	Holland Rd, W Tanger Outlets/Famous Brands, to Gulf Greyhound Park
16	FM 1764 E (from sb), Texas City, same as 15
15	FM 2004, FM 1764, Hitchcock, E Ⓖ Shell, Ⓕ Gringo's Cafe, Jack-in-the-Box, Olive Garden, Popeye's, Ryan's, Uncle Chan's, Ⓛ Best Western, Fairfield Inn, Hampton Inn, Holiday Inn Express, Value Place Inn, Ⓞ Ⓗ, Chevrolet/Toyota/RV Ctr, DeMontrond RV Ctr, Dillard's, JC Penney, Lowe's, Macy's, Sam's Club/gas, Sears/auto, Toyota/Scion, mall, W Ⓖ Gulf/Subway, MurphyUSA/dsl, Shell, Ⓕ IHOP, Little Caesars, Pizza Hut, Sonic, Waffle House, Wendy's, Whataburger, WingStop, Ⓞ AT&T, Gulf Greyhound Park, Radio Shack, Verizon, Walmart/McDonald's
13	Century Blvd, Delany Rd, W Ⓕ Barcema's Mexican, Ⓛ Best Value Inn, Super 8, Ⓞ VF Factory Outlet/famous brands, Lazy Days RV Park
12	FM 1765, La Marque, E Ⓖ Chevron/24hr, Ⓕ Domino's, Jack-in-the-Box, Kelley's Rest., Sonic, W Ⓖ Texaco, Ⓞ Little Thicket RV Park
11	Vauthier Rd
10	E Ⓖ Exxon, Valero, Ⓕ KFC, McDonald's, PitStop BBQ, Subway, W Ⓖ Shell/dsl, Ⓞ Hoover RV Ctr, Oasis RV Park
9	Frontage Rd (from sb, no return/turnaround)
8	Frontage Rd (from nb)
7c	Frontage Rd
7b	TX 146, TX 6 (exits left from nb), Texas City
7a	TX 146, TX 3
6	Frontage Rd (from sb)
5	Frontage Rd
4	Frontage Rd, Village of Tiki Island, W Ⓖ Valero Ⓞ **Welcome Ctr**, public boat ramp
4mm	West Galveston Bay
1c	TX 275, FM 188 (from nb), Port Ind Blvd, Teichman Rd, Port of Galveston, E Ⓖ Citgo, Exxon, Valero, Ⓛ Motel 6, Ⓞ Buick/Chevrolet/GMC, Ford, Toyota/Scion
1b	71st St (from sb), E Ⓖ EZ Mart/gas, same as 1c
1a	TX 342, 61st St, to W Beach, E Ⓕ WingStop, Ⓛ Candlewood Suites, Ⓞ BigLots, Home Depot, NTB, PetsMart, Target, **0-2 mi** W Ⓖ Chevron, Citgo, Exxon, RaceWay, Valero, Ⓕ Cici's Pizza, Happy Buddah, Healthy Chinese, Hibachi Grill, Jack-in-the-Box, KFC, Little Caesars, Mario's, McDonald's, Pizza Hut, Popeye's, Quiznos, Sonic, Starbucks, Subway, Taco Bell, Taco Cabana, Wafflehouse, Whataburger, Yamato Japanese, Ⓛ Best Western, Comfort Inn, Days Inn, Quality Inn, Springhill Suites, Super 8, Ⓞ AT&T, AutoZone, CVS Drug, $Tree, Family$, Firestone, KwikCar, Kroger/dsl, Marshall's, Office Depot, O'Reilly Parts, Randall's Food/gas, Ross, Tuesday Morning, Verizon, USPO

GALVESTON

I-45 begins/ends on TX 87 in Galveston.

▲N INTERSTATE 410 (SAN ANTONIO)

Exit	Services
53	I-35, S to Laredo, N to San Antonio
51	FM 2790, Somerset Rd
49	TX 16 S, spur 422, N Ⓖ Chevron, Texaco/dsl, Ⓕ Church's, Domino's, Sonic, Subway, Whataburger, Ⓛ Days Inn, Ⓞ Ⓗ, to Palo Alto Coll, S Ⓖ Valero/dsl, Ⓕ Jack-in-the-Box, Ⓛ Best Western
48	Zarzamora St

⬆N INTERSTATE 410 (SAN ANTONIO) CONT'D

Exit	Services
47	Turnaround (from eb)
46	Moursund Blvd
44	US 281 S, spur 536, Roosevelt Ave, N ® Shell/McDonald's/dsl, Valero/dsl, S 🏠 Holiday Inn Express
43	Espada Rd (from eb)
42	spur 122, S Presa Rd, to San Antonio Missions Hist Park, S ® Citgo/dsl
41	I-37, US 281 N
39	spur 117, WW White Rd
37	Southcross Blvd, Sinclair Rd, Sulphur Sprs Rd, N ® Valero, ⑪ Capparelli's Pizza, 🄾 🄷
35	US 87, Rigsby Ave, E ® Exxon, Murphy USA/dsl, Valero/dsl, ⑪ A&W, BorderTown Mexican, Cici's Pizza, Denny's, Jack-in-the-Box, LJ Silver, McDonald's, Subway, Taco Bell, 🄾 $Tree, Radio Shack, Walmart/24hr, W ® Chevron, ⑪ Barnacle Bill's Seafood, Bill Miller BBQ, Domino's, El Tapito Mexican, Luby's, Sonic, Taco Cabana, Whataburger, 🏠 Days Inn, 🄾 Aamco, Advance Parts, $General, O'Reilly Parts, U-Haul, Walgreens, auto/dsl repair, vet
34	FM 1346, E Houston St, W ® Valero/dsl
33	I-10 E, US 90 E, to Houston, I-10 W, US 90 W, to San Antonio
32	Dietrich Rd (from sb), FM 78 (from nb), to Kirby
31b	Lp 13, WW White Rd
31a	FM 78, Kirby, E ® Citgo, Valero/dsl, 🄾 Family$
30	Binz-Engleman, Space Center Dr (from nb)
	I-410 and I-35 run together 7 mi. See Interstate 35 exits 161-105.
27	I-35, N to Austin, S to San Antonio
26	Lp 368 S, Alamo Heights
25b	FM 2252, Perrin-Beitel Rd, N ® Chevron/dsl, Valero, ⑪ Carl's Jr, KFC/Taco Bell, Quizno's, Schlotsky's, Tastee-Freez/Wienerschnitzel, Wendy's, 🏠 Best Value Inn, 🄾 Brake Check, S ⑪ Jim's Rest.
25a	Starcrest Dr, N ® Valero, ⑪ Jack-in-the-Box, Los Patios Mexican, 🄾 🄷, Toyota
24	Harry Wurzbach Hwy, N ⑪ Taco Cabana, S ® Chevron, ⑪ BBQ Sta., 🄾 VW
23	Nacogdoches Rd, N ® Shell, ⑪ Bill Miller BBQ, Church's, IHOP, Jack-in-the-Box, Luby's, Mamma's Cafe, Pizza Hut, Sonic, Wendy's, 🏠 Crowne Plaza, S ® Chevron
22	Broadway St, N ® Shell/dsl, ⑪ Chili's, Las Palapas, McDonald's, 🏠 Cambria Suites, Courtyard, 🄾 vet, S ® Citgo, Valero, ⑪ Chesters Hamburgers, Jim's Rest., Little Caesar's, Martha's Mexican, Quizno's, Taco Palenque, Whataburger, 🏠 Residence Inn, TownHouse Motel
21	US 281 S, ✈ Rd, Jones Maltsberger Rd, N ⑪ Applebee's, Bubba's Rest, 🏠 Best Western, Drury Suites, Hampton Inn, Holiday Inn, Holiday Inn Express, PearTree Inn, S ® Murphy USA/dsl, ⑪ Pappadeaux, Red Lobster, Texas Land&Cattle, Whataburger, 🏠 Best Western, Courtyard, Days Inn, Fairfield Inn, La Quinta, Renaissance Hotel, Staybridge Suites, TownePlace Suites, 🄾 Hyundai/Kia, Mitsubishi, Subaru, Target, TJ Maxx, Walmart/McDonald's/24hr
20	TX 537, N ® Valero, ⑪ Arby's, Chick-fil-A, Jack-in-the-Box, Jason's Deli, McDonald's, Subway, TGIFriday's, 🏠 DoubleTree Hotel, Hilton, 🄾 Barnes&Noble, Bealls, Best Buy, Brake Check, Cavender's Boots, Chevrolet, Honda, Jo-Ann Fabrics, Lexus, Lincoln, Marshall's, Mazda, Office Depot, PetCo, Ross, WorldMkt, S ⑪ Cheesecake Fac

Exit	Services
20	Continued
	tory, El Pollo Loco, Luby's, La Madeleine, Taco Cabana, 🄾 AT&T, CVS Drug, Dillard's, Dodge, JC Penney, Macy's, Saks 5th, Sears/auto, Target, Verizon, mall
19b	FM 1535, FM 2696, Military Hwy, N ⑪ Guajillos Mexican, Souper Salad, S ⑪ Denny's, Jim's Rest.
19a	Honeysuckle Lane, Castle Hills
17b	(18 from wb), S ® Shell, ⑪ Bill Miller BBQ, Subway, 🄾 Firestone/auto, HEB Foods/gas
17	Vance Jackson Rd, N ® Valero/dsl, ⑪ Jack-in-the-Box, McDonald's, Sonic, Taco Cabana, Whataburger, 🏠 Embassy Suites, Marriott, 🄾 Aamco, Discount Tire, S ® Citgo, Shell, ⑪ Church's, Subway, 🄾 U-Haul
16b a	I-10 E, US 87 S, to San Antonio, I-10 W, to El Paso, US 87 N
15	Lp 345, Fredericksburg Rd, E ® Citgo, ⑪ Church's, Dave&Buster's, Denny's, El Pollo Loco, Jack-in-the-Box, Jim's Rest., Luby's, McDonald's, Taco Cabana, Wendy's, Whataburger, 🏠 Best Value Inn, SpringHill Suites, 🄾 AT&T, Family$, Firestone/auto, Hobby Lobby, Jo-Ann Fabrics, SteinMart, Target, transmissions, W ® Chevron/dsl, 🄾 CVS Drug
14	(c b a from sb), Callaghan Rd, Babcock Ln, E ® Chevron/dsl, Valero, ⑪ Marie Callender's, Popeye's, 🏠 Comfort Inn, Hampton Inn, Travelodge Suites, 🄾 AT&T, GMC, Hyundai, W ® Shell, Valero, ⑪ Burger King, Chili's, ChopSticks Chinese, DingHow Chinese, Golden Corral, Henry's Tacos, IHOP, Jack-in-the-Box, Jim's Rest, Joe's Crabshack, Las Palapas Mexican, McDonald's, Quizno's, Red Lobster, Taco Cabana, Wendy's, 🄾 🄷, Cavander's Boots, Chevrolet, Home Depot, NTB, Petsmart, Sam's Club/gas, Walmart/Subway/24hr, vet
13	(b a from sb), TX 16 N, Bandera Rd, Evers Rd, Leon Valley, E ⑪ Outback Steaks, Panda Express, 🄾 Audi, HEB Foods/dsl, Office Depot, Old Navy, Toyota, U-Haul, W ⑪ Bill Miller BBQ, Henry's Tacos, Jim's Rest., Schlotzsky's, Sea Island Rest, Taco Cabana, 🄾 BigLots, Chevrolet
12	(from sb), W ⑪ Fortune Cookie Chinese, Jason's Deli, Sea Island Shrimp House, Starbucks, 🄾 AT&T, Barnes&Noble, Best Buy, $Tree, Marshall's, Michael's, Ross
11	Ingram Rd, E ® Shell/dsl, ⑪ KFC/Taco Bell, Krystal, Panda Buffet, TX Roadhouse, 🏠 Days Inn, Comfort Suites, Courtyard, EconoLodge, Holiday Inn Express, Red Roof Inn, Residence Inn, 🄾 Aamco, BrakeCheck, Chrysler/Dodge/Jeep, Mazda, W ⑪ Applebee's, Casa Real Mexican, Chick-fil-A, ChuckeCheese, Denny's, Fuddrucker's, Jack-in-the-Box, Whataburger, 🏠 Best Western, 🄾 Dillard's, Firestone/auto, JC Penney, Macy's, Sears/auto, mall

San Marcos
Hunter 35
Anhalt
Thom Hill
New Braunfels
Dominion
Corbyn   Solms
Ogden   Northcliff
Helotes   Schertz Nolte
Converse   Seguin
San Antonio   10   Bexar
China Grove
410   Boldtville
Buena Vista   37

TX

Ⓖ = gas Ⓕ = food Ⓛ = lodging Ⓞ = other Ⓡₛ = rest stop   Copyright 2014 - The NEXT Exit

▲N INTERSTATE 410 (SAN ANTONIO) CONT'D

Exit	Services
10	FM 3487, Culebra Rd, **E** Ⓕ Bill Miller BBQ, Denny's, J Anthony's Seafood, McDonald's, Wendy's, Ⓛ La Quinta, Ramada Ltd, Ⓞ Harley-Davidson, to St Mary's U, **W** Ⓖ Phillips 66, Ⓞ Ford, Mitsubishi
9	(b a from sb), TX 151, **W** gas Murphy USA/dsl, Ⓕ Buffalo Wild Wings, Carino's Italian, Cheddar's, Chili's, Chipotle Mexican, IHOP, McAlister's Deli, Panda Express, Starbucks, Taco Bueno, TGIFriday's, Cracker Barrel, Ⓛ Alamo City Hotel, Quality Inn, Sleep Inn, Ⓞ Home Depot, Lowe's Whse, Office Depot, Petsmart, Ross, Target, Verizon, Walmart/24hr, to Sea World
7	(8 from sb), Marbach Dr, **E** Ⓖ Exxon, Ⓕ Church's, IHOP, Ⓞ PepBoys, **W** Ⓖ Chevron/dsl, Shell, Ⓕ Acadiena Café, Asia Kitchen, Burger King, Coyote Canyon, Golden Wok, Jack-in-the-Box, Jim's Rest., KFC, LJ Silver, McDonald's, Mr Gatti's, Pancho's Mexican, Peter Piper Pizza, Pizza Hut, Red Lobster, Sonic, Subway, Taco Bell, Taco Cabana, Whataburger/24hr, Ⓛ Motel 6, Super 8, Ⓞ Advance Parts, Bealls, BigLots, BrakeCheck, Discount Tire, $General, $Tree, Firestone/auto, HEB Foods/gas
6	US 90, to Lackland AFB, **E** Ⓛ Country Inn Motel, **W** Ⓖ Shell/dsl, Valero/dsl, Ⓕ Andrea's Mexican, Ⓛ Best Western, Ⓞ Explore USA RV Ctr
4	Valley Hi Dr, to Del Rio, San Antonio, **E** Ⓖ Valero, Ⓕ Burger King, Church's, McDonald's, Pizza Hut, Sonic, Ⓞ AutoZone, HEB Food/gas, Radio Shack, **W** Ⓖ Valero, Ⓕ Jack-in-the-Box, Ⓞ Walgreens, to Lackland AFB
3	(b a from sb), Ray Ellison Dr, Medina Base, **E** Ⓖ Chevron/dsl, **W** Ⓖ Valero/Subway/dsl
2	FM 2536, Old Pearsall Rd, **E** Ⓖ Shell/dsl, Valero/dsl, Ⓕ Bill Miller BBQ, Church's, Mexico Taqueria, McDonald's, Sonic, Subway, Ⓞ O'Reilly Parts
1	Frontage Rd, **S** Scion/Toyota

▲N INTERSTATE 610 (HOUSTON)

Exit	Services
38c a	TX 288 N downtown, access to zoo
37	Scott St, **N** Ⓖ Citgo, Valero
36	FM 865, Cullen Blvd, **N** Ⓛ Crystal Inn, **S** Ⓖ Chevron/McDonald's, Mobil, Shell, Valero, Ⓕ Timmy Chan, Ⓛ Crown Inn, Cullen Inn
35	Calais Rd, Crestmont St, MLK Blvd, **N** Ⓖ Exxon, Valero, Ⓕ Burger King
34	S Wayside Dr, Long Dr, **N** Ⓖ Chevron, Phillips 66, Shell, Ⓕ Church's, Wendy's, **S** Ⓖ Valero, Shell, Ⓞ NAPA
33	Woodridge Dr, Tele Ⓖ Rd, **N** Ⓖ Shell/dsl, Ⓕ ChuckeCheese, Cici's Pizza, IHOP, KFC/Taco Bell, McDonald's, Papa John's, Starbucks, Wendy's, Ⓛ South Lp Inn, Ⓞ Best Buy, Brake Check, HEB Foods, Lowe's, Marshall's, Old Navy, Ross, Staples, **S** Ⓖ Texaco/dsl, Ⓕ Burger King, Gabby's BBQ, KFC, Piccadilly's Cafeteria, Spanky's Pizza, Whataburger, Ⓞ Dodge, Ford, mall
32b a	I-45, S to Galveston, N to Houston, to ✈
31	Broadway Blvd, **S** Ⓖ Valero/dsl, Texaco/dsl
30c b	TX 225, to Pasadena, San Jacinto Mon
29	Port of Houston Main Entrance
28	Clinton Dr to Galina Park
27	Turning Basin Dr, industrial area
26b	Market St
26a	I-10 E, to Beaumont, I-10 W, to downtown

Exit	Services
24	(b a from sb), US 90 E, Wallisville Rd, **E** Ⓖ Citgo/dsl, ♥Love's/Arby's/dsl/scales/24hr, Pilot/McDonald's/dsl/scales, Texaco/dsl, Valero/Heart's Chicken/dsl/scales/24hr, Ⓕ Luby's, Wendy's, Ⓞ Blue Beacon, **W** Ⓖ Citgo/dsl
23b	N Wayside, **N** Ⓖ Valero
23a	Kirkpatrick Blvd
22	Homestead Rd, Kelley St, **N** Ⓖ Shell/dsl, Ⓕ Whataburger, Ⓛ Super 8, **S** Ⓖ Chevron/Subway/dsl/scales
21	Lockwood Dr, **N** Ⓖ Chevron/McDonald's, Shell, Ⓕ Church's, Popeye's, Timmy Chan Chinese, Ⓞ Ⓗ, Family$, Fiesta Foods
20a b	US 59, to downtown
19b	**Hardy Toll Rd**
19a	Hardy St, Jensen Dr (from eb)
18	Irvington Blvd, Fulton St, **N** Ⓖ Chevron, **S** Ⓖ Shell/dsl
17b c	I-45, N to Dallas, S to Houston
17a	(eb only) Airline Dr, **S** Ⓖ Shell, Ⓕ Jack-in-the-Box, Ⓛ Western Inn
16	(b a from eb), Yale St, N Main St, Shamrock, **N** Ⓖ Exxon, Ⓞ Harley-Davidson, **S** Ⓖ Texaco, Ⓕ Burger King, Church's, KFC/Taco Bell, Starbucks
15	TX 261, N Shepherd Dr, **N** Ⓕ Sonic, Taco Cabana, **S** Ⓖ Chevron, Shell, Ⓕ Wendy's, Whataburger, Ⓞ Home Depot, PepBoys
14	Ella Blvd, **N** Ⓖ Exxon, Texaco, Ⓕ A&W, KFC, McDonald's, Popeye's, Taco Bell, **S** Ⓖ Shell, Ⓕ Thomas BBQ, Ⓞ Ⓗ, BrakeCheck, Lowe's Whse, Office Depot
13c	TC Jester Blvd, **N** Ⓖ Mobil, Shell, Ⓕ Denny's, Juanita's Mexican, Po' Boys Sandwiches, Ⓛ Courtyard, SpringHill Suites, **S** Ⓖ Phillips 66/dsl
13b a	US 290 (exits left from nb)
12	W 18th St, **E** Ⓕ Applebee's, Whataburger, **W** Ⓖ Shell, Ⓕ Burger King, Ⓛ Sheraton
11	I-10, W to San Antonio, E to downtown Houston
10	Woodway Dr, Memorial Dr, **W** Ⓖ Chevron/Pizza Inn/dsl, Shell/dsl, Ⓞ Goodyear
9b	Post Oak Blvd, **E** Ⓛ Drury Inn, Hampton Inn, La Quinta, **W** Ⓕ Champp's Rest., McCormick&Schmick's Café
9a	San Felipe Rd, Westheimer Rd, FM 1093, **E** Ⓖ Mobil, Shell, Ⓕ Omaha Steaks, Ⓛ Courtyard, Extended Stay America, Hampton Inn, La Quinta, Ⓞ CVS Drug, NTB, Target, **W** Ⓖ Shell, Ⓕ Jamba Juice, Luke's Burgers, Ⓛ Crowne Plaza Hotel, HomeStead Suites, Marriott, Sheraton, Ⓞ Best Buy, Dillard's, Nieman-Marcus
8a	US 59, Richmond Ave, **E** Ⓛ Holiday Inn, Extended Stay America, Ⓞ CVS Drug, **W** Ⓖ Shell, Ⓞ Dillards,
7	Bissonet St, West Park Dr, Fournace Place, **E** Ⓕ Beudreax's Kitchen, Ⓛ Candlewood Suites, Ⓞ Home Depot, **W** Ⓖ Shell/dsl/repair
6	Bellaire Blvd
5b	Evergreen St
5a	Beechnut St, **E** Ⓖ Chevron, Ⓕ Boston Mkt, IHOP, Lowe's, McDonald's, Outback Steaks, **W** Ⓖ Citgo, Shell, Ⓕ Escalante Mexican Grill, James Coney Island, Saltgrass Steaks, Smoothie King, Ⓞ GNC, Marshall's, Ross, mall
4a	S Post Oak Rd, Brasswood, **E** Ⓖ Citgo, Ⓕ Outback Steaks, Ⓛ Days Inn, **W** Ⓞ Target, Walmart
3	Stella Link Rd, **N** Ⓖ Chevron, Ⓕ Jack-in-the-Box, Ⓞ Discount Tire, Food City, Radio Shack, **S** Ⓖ Exxon, Phillips 66/dsl, Shell, Valero, Ⓞ Brake Check
2	US 90A, **N** Ⓖ Chevron, Conoco, Valero, Ⓕ Arby's, Burger

HOUSTON

🔼N INTERSTATE 610 (HOUSTON) CONT'D

Exit	Services
2	Continued King, Church's, Denny's/24hr, KFC, McDonald's, Shoney's, Taco Bell, Wendy's, 🏠 Grand Plaza Hotel, Howard Johnson, Villa Motel, 🅾 CVS Drug, Discount Tire, Ford, Honda, Walgreen, **S** 🅿 Chevron, Shell, 🍴 Golden Corral, Pizza Hut/Taco Bell, Whataburger/24hr, 🏠 Candlewood Suites, CareFree Inn, La Quinta, Motel 6, Speedway Inn, Super 8, 🅾 Chevrolet, Firestone, Mazda, Nissan, Toyota,

2	Continued U-Haul, to Buffalo Speedway
1c	Kirby Dr (from eb), **N** 🍴 Shell, 🍴 Burger King, 🏠 Crowne Plaza, Holiday Inn, Radisson, **S** 🍴 Joe's Crabshack, Pappadeaux Seafood, Pappasito's Cantina, 🅾 Cavender's Boots, Chevrolet, NTB, Toyota/Scion
1b a	FM 521, Almeda St, Fannin St, **N** 🅿 Chevron, Shell, 🍴 Burger King, 🏠 Scottish Inn, 🅾 Astro Arena, **S** 🅿 Shell, 🍴 McDonald's, 🅾 Aamco, Chrysler/Dodge/Jeep, Sam's Club, to Six Flags

UTAH

🔼N INTERSTATE 15

Exit	Services
400.5mm	Utah/Idaho state line
398	Portage
392	UT 13 S, Plymouth, **E** 🅿 Sinclair/Subway/dsl
385	UT 30 E, to Riverside, Fielding, **1 mi E** 🅿 Sinclair/Riverside Grill/dsl
381	Tremonton, Garland, **2 mi E** 🅾 H, gas, food, lodging
379	I-84 W, to Boise
376	UT 13, to Tremonton, **E** 🅿 Texaco/Arby's/dsl/24hr, **2-3 mi E** 🍴 Arctic Circle, Crossroads Rest., El Parral Mexican, JC'S Diner, Subway, Taco Time, 🏠 Marble Motel, Sandman Motel
372	UT 240, to UT 13, to rec area, Honeyville, **E** 🅾 Crystal Hot Springs Camping
370mm	🆁🆂 sb, full 🚻 facilities, info, 🅲, 🅿, litter barrels, vending, petwalk
365	UT 13, Brigham City, **W** 🅾 to Golden Spike NHS
363	Forest St, Brigham City, **W** 🅾 Bear River Bird Refuge
362	US 91, to US 89, Brigham City, Logan, **E** 🅿 Chevron/dsl, ✈FLYING J/dsl/24hr, 7-11, USA, Sinclair, 🍴 Arby's, Beto's Mexican, Burger King, Hunan Chinese, KFC/Taco Bell, Little Caesar's, McDonald's, Old Grist Mill Bread, Pizza Hut, Pizza Press, Sonic, Subway, Taco Time, Wendy's, Wingers, 🏠 Crystal Inn, Howard Johnson Express, 🅾 H AutoZone, Buick/Cadillac/Chevrolet, Chrysler/Dodge/Jeep, $Tree, Golden Spike RV Park, KOA, Smith's, O'Reilly Parts, Radio Shack, ShopKO, Walmart/Subway, to Yellowstone NP via US 89, **W** 🅿 DQ/dsl/scales/24hr, 🏠 Days Inn
361mm	🆁🆂 nb, full 🚻 facilities, 🅲, 🅿, litter barrels, vending, petwalk
359	Port of Entry both lanes
357	UT 315, to Willard, Perry, **E** 🅿 ✈FLYING J/Denny's/dsl/LP/scales/24hr, 🅾 KOA (2mi)
351	UT 126, to US 89, to Utah's Fruit Way, Willard Bay, **W** 🅾 Smith & Edwards Hardware
349	UT 134, N Ogden, Farr West, **E** 🅿 Exxon/Wendy's, Maverik, 7-11, 🍴 Arby's, Domino's, Jumbo Burger, McDonald's, Bella's Mexican, Subway, 🏠 Comfort Inn, 🅾 Kwik Lube, **W** 🅿 Conoco/dsl
346	to Harrisville, **W** 🅿 Chevron/dsl, Maverik, Cal Store, dsl repair
344	UT 39, 12th St, Ogden, **E** 🅿 Chevron, Phillips 66, Shell/dsl, 🏠 Best Western/rest., **1-2 mi E** 🅿 Chevron, 🍴 Denny's, KFC, McDonald's, Sizzler, Village Inn Rest., 🏠 Motel 6, 🅾 to Ogden Canyon RA, **W** 🅿 DQ/Subway/Taco Bell/dsl/24hr, 🍴 Iron Pan Bistro, 🏠 Sleep Inn, Western Inn

OGDEN

Exit	Services
343	UT 104, 21st St, Ogden, **E** 🅿 Chevron/Arby's/dsl, / ✈FLYING J/Denny's/dsl/LP/24hr, Phillips 66/dsl, 🍴 Cactus Red's Rest., McDonalds, Outlaw Rest., 🏠 Best Western, Comfort Suites, Holiday Inn Express, ValuePlace Inn, 🅾 Justus RV Ctr, RV Repair, **W** 🅿 Texaco, 🏠 Super 8, 🅾 Century RV Park
342	(from nb), UT 53, 24th St, Ogden, **E** 🅿 Sinclair/dsl
341b a	UT 79 W, 31st St, Ogden, **1-2 mi E on Wall St** 🅿 7-11, 🍴 Arby's, Golden Corral, JJ North's Buffet, Sizzler, 🏠 Day's Inn, Hampton Inn, Marriott, 🅾 H Dillard's, Chevrolet, Ford/Lincoln, RV Ctr, mall, to Weber St U, **W** ⊡
340	I-84 E (from sb), to Cheyenne, Wyo
339	UT 26 (from nb), to I-84 E, Riverdale Rd, **E** 🅿 Conoco/dsl, Sinclair, 🍴 Applebee's, Arby's, Boston Mkt, Carl's Jr, Chili's, La Salsa Mexican, McDonald's, 🏠 Motel 6, 🅾 Buick/GMC, Chrysler/Jeep, Harley-Davidson, Home Depot, Honda/Nissan, Isuzu, Jo-Ann Fabrics, Lincoln/Kia, Mazda, Sam's Club/gas, Target, Toyota, Walmart, Wilderness RV
338	UT 97, Roy, Sunset, **E** 🅾 Air Force Museum, **W** 🅿 Exxon/dsl, Phillips 66, 7-11, Sinclair, 🍴 Arby's, Arctic Circle, Blimpie, Burger King, DQ, KFC, McDonald's, Panda Express, Pizza Hut, Ponderosa, Sonic, Subway, Taco Bell, Village Inn Rest., Wendy's, 🏠 Quality Inn, Motel 6, 🅾 AutoZone, BrakeWorks, Citte RV Ctr, Discount Tire, Early Tires, Firestone, Goodyear, O'Reilly Parts, Radio Shack, RiteAid, Schwab Tires, Smith's/gas, Walgreen, transmissions
335	UT 103, Clearfield, **E** Hill AFB, **W** 🅿 Chevron, Conoco, PetroMart, 7-11, Texaco, Circle K, 🍴 Arby's, Carl's Jr, KFC, McDonald's, Skipper's, Subway, Taco Bell, Winger's, 🏠 Days Inn, The Cottage Inn, 🅾 Big O Tire, Sierra RV Ctr
334	UT 193, Clearfield, to Hill AFB, **E** 🅿 Chevron, Maverik, **W** 🅿 Chevron/dsl, 🍴 Wendy's
332	UT 108, Syracuse, **E** 🅿 Chevron, Phillips 66/dsl, Circle K, 🍴 Applebee's, Brick Oven, Carl's Jr., Cracker Barrel, Famous Dave's, Golden Corral, JB's, Marie Callender's, Outback Steaks, Quizno's, Red Robin, Tepanyaki, TimberLodge Steaks, 🏠 Courtyard, Fairfield Inn, Hampton Inn, Hilton Garden, Holiday Inn Express, La Quinta, TownePlace Suites, 🅾 Barnes&Noble, Lowe's Whse, Office Depot, Old Navy, Target, **W** 🅿 Conoco, 7-11, 🍴 Arby's, McDonald's, 🅾 H, to Antelope Island
331	UT 232, UT 126, Layton, **E** 🅿 Mobil, Phillips 66, Texaco, 🍴 Buffalo Wild Wings, Denny's, Garcia's, McDonald's, Olive Garden, Red Lobster, Sizzler, TX Roadhouse, Training Table Rest., Wendy's, 🏠 Comfort Inn, Hilton Garden, 🅾 Dick's, JC Penney, Tuesday Morning, mall, to Hill AFB

TX
UT

⬆N INTERSTATE 15 CONT'D

Left column (KAYSVILLE / N SALT LAKE)

Exit	Services
331	Continued
	S Gate, **W** 🅶 Common Cents/dsl, 🍴 Blimpie, Burger King, China Buffet, ChuckeCheese, IHOP, KFC, Krispy Kreme, LoneStar Steaks, McGrath's FishHouse, Taco Bell, Ⓞ Batteries+, Cadillac/GMC, Chevrolet, Discount Tire, Dodge, Home Depot, NTB, Jeep, Ream's Foods, Sam's Club/gas, ShopKO, Staples, Walmart
330	Layton Pkwy, to UT 126, Layton, **E** 🍴 Little Orient Chinese, Ⓞ repair, **W** 🅶 Texaco, Ⓞ Jensen's RV
328	UT 273, Kaysville, **E** 🅶 Chevron/McDonald's, 7-11, Sinclair, 🍴 Arby's, Cutler's Sandwiches, DQ, Joanie's Rest., Gandolfo's, KFC, Quizno's, Subway, Taco Maker, Taco Time, Wendy's, Winger's, Ⓞ Fresh Mkt Foods, O'Reilly Parts, Schwab Tire, Walgreens, **W** Ⓞ Camping World/Jensen RV Ctr, Kia
325mm	parking area both lanes
325	UT 225, Lagoon Dr, Farmington (from sb), **E** 🍴 Subway, Ⓞ funpark, camping, **W** Ⓞ Kohls
324	US 89 N, UT 225, Legacy Pkwy (from sb), **1 mi E** 🅶 Conoco/Smith's Foods/dsl, Maverik/gas, 🍴 Arby's, Burger King, Little Caesar's, Subway, Ⓞ Aunt Pam's, Goodyear/auto, RV Park, to I-84
322	UT 227 (from nb), Lagoon Dr, to Farmington, **E** 🍴 Subway, Ⓞ Lagoon Funpark/RV Park
319	Centerville, **E** 🅶 Chevron/dsl, Phillips 66/dsl, 🍴 Arby's, Arctic Circle, Burger King, Carl's Jr, Chili's, DQ, Del Taco, Fusion of Asia, Gandolfo's, IHOP, In-N-Out, Jake's Shakes, McDonald's, Subway, Taco Bell, TacoMaker, Wendy's, Ⓞ Albertson's, Big O Tire, Checker Parts, Curves, Home Depot, Kohl's, Land Rover, Radio Shack, Schwab Tire, Target/foods, Walmart, **W** Ⓞ RV Ctr
317	US 89 S (exits left from sb), UT 131, 500W, S Bountiful, **E** 🅶 Chevron, Exxon/dsl, Sinclair/dsl, 🍴 Alicia's Rest., Starbucks, 🛏 Country Inn Suites, Ⓞ Chrysler/Dodge/Jeep, Costco/gas, Office Depot, Parts+, PetCo, Goodyear, Jiffy Lube, tires
316	UT 68, 500 S, W Bountiful, Woods Cross, **E** 🅶 Exxon, Texaco, 🍴 Applebee's, Blimpie, Burger King, Cafe Rio, Carl's Jr, Christopher's Steaks, ChuckaRama, Coldstone, Del Taco, HogiYogi, KFC, La Frontera Mexican, McDonald's, Panda Express, Pizza Hut, Rinny's Rest., Sizzler, Subway, SuCasa Mexican, Taco Bell, Winger's, Ⓞ H, AutoZone, Barnes&Noble, Big O Tire, Costco/gas, Firestone/auto, Michael's, O'Reilly Parts, Radio Shack, Ross, ShopKO, TJ Maxx, Walgreens, **W** 🅶 Phillips 66/A&W/dsl, 🛏 InTown Suites
315	26th S, N Salt Lake, **E** 🅶 Chevron/dsl, Sinclair, Tesoro, 🍴 Apollo Burger, Arby's, Atlantis Burger, Empire Chinese, McDonald's, Subway, Taco Time, Village Inn, Wendy's, 🛏 Best Western, Comfort Inn, Ⓞ Ace Hardware, Chevrolet/Buick/Kia, Discount Tire, Dodge, Ford/Lincoln, Honda, K-Mart, Mazda, Nissan, Schwab Tire, Smith's Foods, Toyota, Tunex, U-Haul, **W** 🅶 Conoco, 🍴 Denny's, Lorena's Mexican, 🛏 Hampton Inn, Motel 6, Ⓞ Goodyear
314	Center St, Cudahy Lane (from sb), N Salt Lake, **E** gas
313	I-215 W (from sb), to ✈
312	US 89 S, to Beck St, N Salt Lake
311	2300 N
310	900 W, **W** 🍴 Tia Maria's Mexican, 🛏 Regal Inn, Salt City Motel, Ⓞ 7-11, Self's conv/rest.

Right column (SALT LAKE / SANDY / DRAPER)

Exit	Services
309	600 N, **E** Ⓞ H, LDS Temple, downtown, to UT State Fair-Park
308	I-80 W, to Reno ✈
307	400 S, downtown
306	600 S, SLC City Ctr, **1 mi E** 🅶 Chevron, Phillips 66/dsl, Circle K, 🍴 Burger King, DQ, Denny's, McDonald's, Wendy's, 🛏 Embassy Suites, Hampton Inn, Little America, Motel 6, Quality Inn, Ramada Inn, Residence Inn, Super 8, Ⓞ Ford, Toyota, to Temple Square, LDS Church Offices
305c-a	1300 S, 2100 S UT 201 W, West Valley, **E** 🅶 Phillips 66, Texaco, 🍴 Atlantis Burgers, Carl's Jr, McDonald's, Wienerschnitzel, Ⓞ Costco/gas, Home Depot, PetsMart, U-Haul, Walmart, **W** 🅶 /⊕FLYING J/Denny's/dsl/LP/24hr, 🍴 Wendy's, Ⓞ Best Buy, Blue Beacon, Cadillac, Chevrolet, $Tree, Ford, Goodyear, NAPA, Office Depot
304	I-80 E, to Denver, Cheyenne
303	UT 171, 3300 S, S Salt Lake, **E** 🅶 7-11, Phillips 66, 🍴 Apollo Diner, Burger King, McDonald's, Taco Bell, 🛏 Bonneville Inn, Day's Inn, Roadrunner Motel, **W** 🅶 Maverik/dsl, Ⓞ Sam's Club/gas, GMC
301	UT 266, 4500 S, Murray, Kearns, **E** 🍴 McDonald's, Ⓞ UpTown Tire, **W** 🅶 Chevron, Conoco, Shell/dsl, Sinclair, Burger King/dsl, Texaco, 🍴 Burger King, Denny's, Wendy's, 🛏 Fairfield Inn, Hampton Inn, Holiday Inn Express, Quality Inn, Ⓞ InterMtn RV Ctr, Lowe's Whse
300	UT 173, 5300 S, Murray, Kearns, **E** H, **W** 🅶 Chevron, Conoco, Sinclair, 7-11, 🍴 KFC, Schlotsky's, 🛏 Reston Hotel, Ⓞ Smith's Foods, FunDome, Jenson's RV Ctr
298	I-215 E and W
297	UT 48, 7200 S, Midvale, **E** 🅶 Chevron, Conoco, Phillips 66, Sinclair, Texaco/LP, 🍴 Chili's, Denny's, John's Place, KFC, McDonald's, Midvale Mining Café, Sizzler, South Seas Café, Taco Bell, Village Inn Rest., 🛏 Best Western, Day's Inn, Discovery Inn/café, Executive Inn, La Quinta, Motel 6, Rodeway Inn, Sandman Inn, Super 8, Ⓞ Cadillac/Buick, carwash, to Brighton, Solitude Ski Areas, Walgreens, **W** 🅶 Sinclair/Subway/dsl
295	UT 209, 9000 S, Sandy, **E** 🅶 Chevron, Sinclair, 🍴 Arby's, Burger King, Fuddrucker's, Hardee's, Johanna's Kitchen, Schlotzky's, Sconecutter's Rest., Sweet Tomato, 🛏 Comfort Inn, Majestic Rockies Motel, Ⓞ Discount Tire, Early Tires, Firestone, Ford, NAPA, to Snowbird, Alta Ski Areas, **W** 🅶 Maverik, Tesoro, 🍴 KFC, Village Inn Ⓞ H, Aamco
293	106th S, Sandy, S Jordan, **E** 🅶 Conoco, Phillips 66, Tesoro, 🍴 Bennett's BBQ, Carver's Prime Rib, Chili's, Eat a Burger, HomeTown Buffet, Jim's Rest., Johanna's Rest., Subway, TGIFriday, Village Inn, Wendy's, 🛏 Best Western, Courtyard, Extended Stay America, Hampton Inn, Hilton Garden, Hyatt Summerfield, Marriott, Residence Inn, TownePlace Suites, Ⓞ Best Buy, Chevrolet, Chrysler/Jeep, Costco/gas, Dillard's, Goodyear, Honda, JC Penney, Nissan, Target, Toyota, mall, **W** 🍴 Denny's, 🛏 Country Inn Suites, Sleep Inn, Super 8, Ⓞ Buick/GMC, CarMax, Sam's Club/gas, VW, Walmart
291	UT 71, 12300 S, Draper, Riverton, **E** 🅶 Chevron, Common Cents/dsl, 🍴 Arby's, Arctic Circle, Café Rio Mexican, Carl's Jr, Del Taco, Fazoli's, Guadalahonky's Mexican, In-N-Out, Jamba Juice, KFC, McDonald's, Panda Express, Pizza Hut, Quizno's, Ruby Tuesday, Sonic, Teriyaki Express, Wendy's, Wienerschnitzel, Wingers Diner, 🛏 Comfort Inn, Fairfield Inn, Ramada Ltd, Ⓞ Brown RV, Camping World RV Supplies (1mi), Discount Tire, Goodyear/auto,

⬆N   INTERSTATE 15 CONT'D

Exit	Services
291	Continued Greenbax, Kohl's, Mountain Shadows Camping, Smith's Foods, FSA Outlets/famous brands **W** gas Phillips 66, Ⓞ Sam's Club/gas, Walmart
289	Bangerter Hwy, **W** gas Exxon, 7-11, 🍴 Quizno's
288	UT 140, Bluffdale, **E** 🅟 Chevron/dsl, Ⓞ Kohl's, Camping World RV Supplies (2mi), Quality RV Ctr, **W** 🅟 Common Sense/gas, 7-11, Ⓞ st prison
284	UT 92, to Alpine, Highland, **E** Ⓞ Cabela's, **W** 🅟 Chevron/Iceberg Café/dsl, Maverik/dsl, 🍴 Del Taco, JCW Burgers, 🛏 Hampton Inn, SpringHill Suites, Ⓞ Lone Peak RV Ctr, Thanksgiving Point/café, to Timpanogas Cave
282	US 89 S, 12th W, to UT 73, Lehi, **W** 🅟 Chevron
279	UT 73, to Lehi, **E** 🅟 Texaco/dsl, 🍴 Applebee's, 1 Man Band Diner, Panda Express, TX Roadhouse, Wienerschnitzel, 🛏 Motel 6, Ⓞ Costco/gas, Lowe's Whse, Home Depot, Petsmart, Schwab Tire, Walgreens, Walmart, **W** 🅟 Chevron/dsl, Phillips 66/Wendy's, 🍴 Arctic Circle, KFC/Pizza Hut, McDonald's, Papa Murphy's, Subway, Tepanyki Japanese, Wingers, 🛏 Best Western, Comfort Inn, Day's Inn, Super 8, Ⓞ Big O Tire, Checker Parts, GNC, Dave's Chiropractic, Macey's, USPO, museum
278	Main St, American Fork, **E** 🅟 Phillips 66/dsl, Texaco, 🍴 Chili's, Cobblestone Pizza, Del Taco, In-N-Out, Ottavio's Italian, Pier 49, Sonic, Wendy's, Ⓞ Ⓗ Chevrolet, Chrysler/Dodge/Jeep, $Tree, Home Depot, K-Mart, Kohl's, Office Depot, Old Navy, Smith's Foods, Subaru/Suzuki, Target, Walmart, **W** 🛏 Value Place
276	5th E, Pleasant Grove, **E** 🅟 Conoco/Blimpie, 🍴 Carl's Jr, Denny's, McDonald's, Taco Bell, 🛏 Quality Inn, Ⓞ Stewart's RV Ctr, **1-2 mi E** 🅟 Circle K, Phillips 66, Texaco, 🍴 Arby's, Del Taco, Golden Corral, Hardee's, KFC, Subway, Wendy's, Ⓞ Ⓗ, American Camping, Chevrolet, **W** Ⓞ Buick/GMC, Ford, Land Rover
275	Pleasant Grove, **E** 🍴 Bajio Grill, Panda Express, Sonic, Wienerschnitzel, Ⓞ BMW, Macey's Foods
273	Orem, Lindon, **E** 🅟 Exxon/dsl, Holiday, 🍴 Costa Vida Mexican, Del Taco, Ⓞ Discount Tire, Home Depot, Lexus, Mercedes, Schwab Tire, **W** Ⓞ Harley-Davidson
272	UT 52, to US 189, 8th N, Orem, **E** 🅟 Maverik, Phillips 66, 🛏 La Quinta, **1 mi E** 🍴 Arby's, Cafe Rio, DQ, Denny's, Sonic, Ⓞ to Sundance RA
271	Center St, Orem, **E** 🅟 Conoco, 7-11, Ⓞ Ⓗ, funpark, **1-2 mi E** 🍴 Burger King, Cafe Rio, KFC, Panda Express, Taco Bell, Wendy's, **W** 🅟 Tesoro, 🍴 La Casita Blanca Mexican, 🛏 Econolodge, Ⓞ LP
269	272 UT 265, 12th St S, University Pkwy, **E** 🅟 Texaco/Wendy's/dsl, Sinclair, 🍴 HoneyBaked Ham, IHOP, Krispy Kreme, McDonald's, Subway, Thai Evergreen, 🛏 Comfort Inn, Hampton Inn, La Quinta, Ⓞ Ford, JiffyLube, Mazda

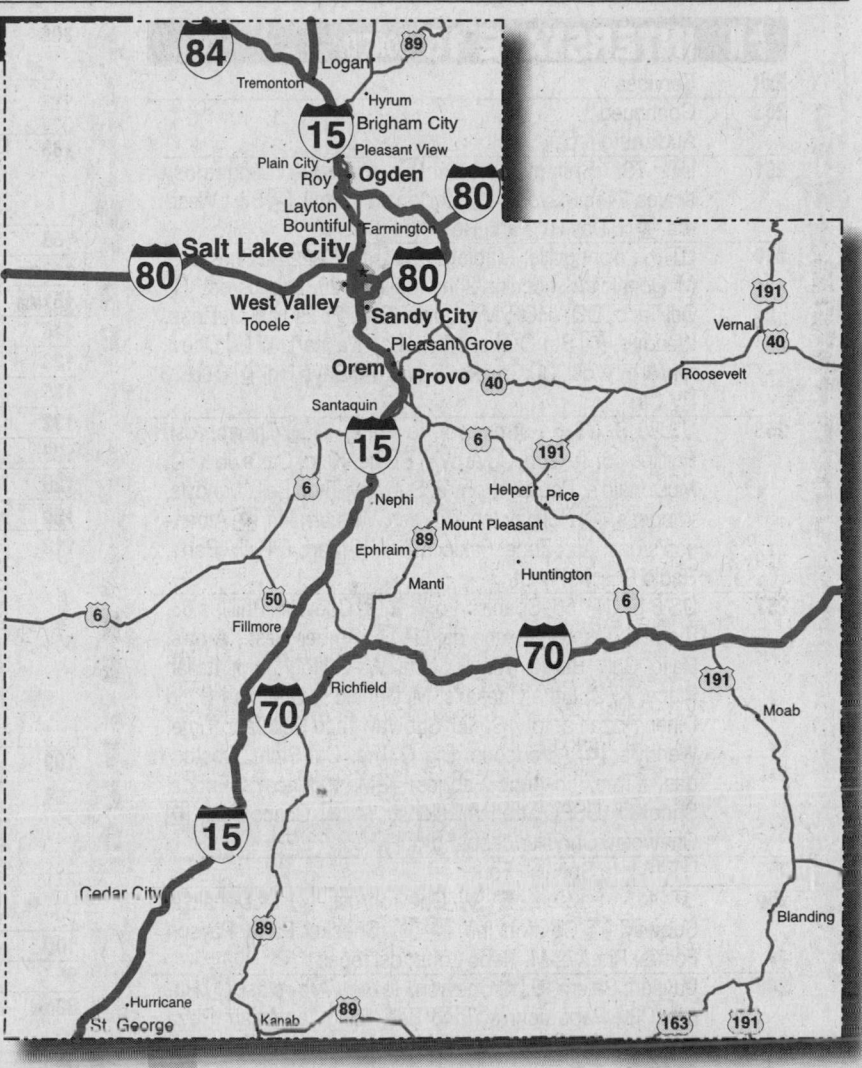

269	Continued Toyota/Scion, Walmart, **1-3 mi E** 🅟 Chevron, 🍴 Applebee's, Arby's, Carrabba's, Chili's, Fuddrucker's, Golden Corral, Noodles & Co., Outback Steaks, Pizza Hut, Sakura Japanese, Sizzler, Starbucks, Village Inn, 🛏 Best Western, Courtyard, Ⓞ Barnes&Noble, Best Buy, Honda, JC Penney, Jo-Ann Fabrics, Lowe's Whse, Mazda, Michael's, Nissan, Office Depot, Old Navy, Petsmart, Ross, Subaru, TJ Maxx, VW, mall, to BYU, many services on US 89, **W** 🅟 Chevron
265b a	UT 114, Center St, Provo, **E** 🅟 Conoco, Phillips 66/Wendy's, Shell, Sinclair/dsl, 7-11, Ⓞ Ⓗ, Albertson's, Checker Parts, Firestone/auto, auto repair, **1 mi E** 🛏 Marriott, Travelers Inn, Travelodge, **W** 🅟 Chevron, Shell/dsl, 🍴 Great Steak Rest., Subway, 🛏 Econolodge, Ⓞ KOA, Lakeside RV, to Utah Lake SP
263	US 189 N, University Ave, Provo, **E** 🅟 Chevron, Conoco/dsl, Maverik, Sinclair, 🍴 A&W/KFC, Arby's, Burger King, ChuckaRama, Fazoli's, Hogi Yogi, McDonald's, Papa Murphy's, Ruby River Steaks, Sizzler, Taco Bell, Taco Time, Village Inn Rest., Wendy's, 🛏 Best Western, Colony Inn, Fairfield Inn, Hampton Inn, La Quinta, Motel 6, National 9 Inn, Sleep Inn, Super 8, Ⓞ Curves, Dillard's, GoodEarth Foods, Home Depot, JC Penney, K-Mart, Les Schwab, NAPA, Sam's Club/gas, Sears/auto, Staples, Silver Fox RV Camping, mall, to BYU, **1 mi E** 🍴 Los Three Amigos Mexican, 🛏 Safari Motel, Western Inn, Ⓞ CarQuest, VW/

Vertical labels (left margin): **LEHI**, **OREM**

Vertical labels (right column margin): **PROVO**

🅖 = gas 🍴 = food 🛏 = lodging 🅞 = other · 🆁🆂 = rest stop   Copyright 2014 - The NEXT Exit

INTERSTATE 15 CONT'D

SPRINGVILLE

Exit	Services
263	Continued
	Audi, auto repair
261	UT 75, Springville, **E** 🅖 ⓕ*FLYING J*/Denny's/dsl/scales/24hr, Maverik, 🍴 McDonald's (1mi), 🛏 Best Western, 🅞 E Bay RV Park, RestStop
260	UT 77, Springville, Mapleton, **E** 🅖 🅛*Loves*/Chester's/McDonald's/dsl/scales/24hr, Phillips 66/Quiznos/dsl, 🍴 Del Taco, DQ, IHOP, Mongolian Grill, Pizza Hut, Quiznos, Wendy's, 🅞 Big O Tire, JiffyLube, Walmart, **W** 🅖 Chevron/Arby's/dsl, 🍴 Cracker Barrel, 🛏 Days Inn, 🅞 Quality RV Ctr
258	US 89 S, US 6 E (from sb), to Price, **E** 🅖 Chevron/dsl, Phillips 66, Texaco, 🍴 Arby's, Burger King, Carl's Jr, KFC, McDonald's, Papa Murphy's, Subway, Taco Bell, Wendy's, Winger's, 🛏 Holiday Inn Express, Western Inn, 🅞 Albertson's/gas, AutoZone, Fakler's Tire, K-Mart, O'Reilly Parts, Radio Shack, RV Ctr
257	US 6 E, UT 156, Spanish Fork, **E** 🅖 Chevron, Phillips 66, Sinclair, Tesoro, Texaco/dsl/LP, 🍴 Amber Rest., Arby's, Bajio Grill, Burger King, China Wok, Hogi Yogi, Italian Place, KFC, Little Caesar's, McDonald's, One Man Band Diner, Pizza Factory, Sonic, Subway, Taco Bell, Taco Time, Wendy's, 🅞 Albertsons, Big O Tire, Cal Store, Costco/gas, $Tree, Jo-Anne Fabrics, K-Mart, Macey's Foods, ShopKO, USPO, transmissions, **W** 🅖 Conoco/dsl, 🅞 Chevrolet, Chrysler/Jeep, Ford, RV Ctr
253	UT 164, to Spanish Fork
250	UT 115, Payson, **E** 🅖 Chevron/dsl, 🍴 McDonald's, Subway, 🛏 Comfort Inn, 🅞 🅷 Checker Parts, Payson Foods, RiteAid, Mt Nebo Loop, dsl repair
248	Payson, Salem, **E** 🅖 Chevron, Texaco/Arby's/dsl, 🍴 Hunan City, Papa John's, Taco Bell, Tsing Tao Asian, Pizza Hut, Subway, 🅞 AutoZone, $Tree, Walmart, **W** 🅖 Phillips 66/Wendy's/dsl
244	US 6 W, Santaquin, **E** 🅖 Maverik/dsl, 🍴 DQ, 🅞 Tire Factory, TrueValue, **W** 🅖 Conoco/dsl, Sinclair, 🍴 Family Tree Rest., One Man Band Diner, Santa Queen Burgers, Subway, Taco Time, 🅞 Family$, Ford, Main St Mkt, Nat Hist Area, USPO, auto/tire care
242	to S Santaquin, **W** Chevron/dsl
233	UT 54, Mona
228	UT 28, to Nephi, **2-4 mi W** services
225	UT 132, Nephi, **E** 🅖 Tesoro/dsl/LP, 🍴 Quizno's, Salt Creek Steaks, Taco Time, One Man Band Rest., 🅞 Burn's Bros RV Park (5mi), **W** 🅖 Chevron/Arby's/dsl, Phillips 66/Wendy's/dsl, 🛏 Economy Inn, 🅞 🅷 Big O Tire
222	UT 28, to I-70, Nephi, **E** 🅖 Chevron/dsl, Sinclair/Hogi Yogi/scales/dsl/24hr, Texaco/dsl/24hr, 🍴 Burger King, Mickelson's Rest., Subway, 🛏 Motel 6, Roberta's Cove Motel, Super 8, 🅞 dsl repair, **W** 🅖 ⓕ*FLYING J*/Denny's/dsl/LP/scales/24hr, 🍴 Lisa's Country Kitchen, 🛏 Best Western, Safari Motel, 🅞 🅷 Hi-Country RV Park
207	to US 89, Mills
202	Yuba Lake, 🄫, access to boating, camping, rec services
188	US 50 E, to I-70, Scipio, **E** 🅖 Chevron/Subway/dsl, Texaco, 🛏 Scipio Hotel, **W** 🅖 ⓕ*FLYING J*/DQ/dsl/rest stop/24hr
184	ranch exit
178	US 50, to Delta, **W** gas, 🄫, to Great Basin NP
174	to US 50, Holden, to great Basin NP
167	Lp 15, Fillmore, **0-3 mi E** 🅖 Chevron/dsl, Shell, Sinclair/dsl, 🛏 Best Western/rest., 🅞 🅷 CarQuest, Goodyear,

NEPHI

FILLMORE

167	Continued
	KOA (3mi), WagonsWest RV Park, city park, golf, **W** 🅖 Chevron/Subway/rest stop, Texaco/dsl, 🍴 Carl's Jr, 🅞 tires/repair
163	Lp 15, to UT 100, Fillmore, **E** 🅖 Chevron/Burger King/dsl, Maverik/dsl, 🍴 Hong Kong Chinese, Larry's Drive-In, 🛏 Comfort Inn, 🅞 🅷, KOA, **W** 🅖 Texaco/dsl, 🛏 motel
158	UT 133, Meadow, **E** 🅖 Conoco/dsl, Shell/dsl
153mm	view area sb
151mm	view area nb
146	Kanosh, **2 mi E** gas, chainup area
138	ranch exit
135	Cove Fort Hist Site, **E** 🅖 Chevron/Subway, 🅞 rest stop
132	I-70 E, to Denver, Capitol Reef NP, Fremont Indian SP
129	Sulphurdale, chainup area
125	ranch exit
120	Manderfield, chainup area nb
112	to UT 21, Beaver, Manderfield, **E** 🅖 Chevron/dsl, Sinclair/dsl, Conoco/dsl, 🍴 Arby's, Arshel's Café, Crazy Cow Cafe, Hunan Chinese, McDonald's, Subway, 🛏 Beaver Lodge, Best Western, Country Inn, De Lano Motel/RV Park, Motel 6, 🅞 🅷, Alco, Family$, KOA (1mi), auto repair, **W** 🅖 ⓕ*FLYING J*/cafe/dsl/scales/24hr, 🍴 Wendy's, 🛏 Days Inn, Super 8, 🅞 to Great Basin NP
109	to UT 21, Beaver, **E** 🅖 Phillips 66/dsl, Shell/Burger King/dsl/24hr, 🍴 Taco Shop, 🛏 Best Western, Comfort Inn, 🅞 🅷, Cache Valley Cheese, Mike's Foodtown, NAPA, auto repair, **W** 🅖 Chevron/DQ/dsl/24hr, 🍴 KanKun Mexican, Timberline Rest., 🛏 Quality Inn, 🅞 truck wash, to Great Basin NP
100	ranch exit
95	UT 20, to US 89, to Panguitch Bryce Canyon NP
88mm	🆁🆂 **both lanes, full ♿ facilities, 🄫, picnic table, litter barrel, petwalk, hist site**
82	UT 271, Paragonah
78	UT 141, **1 mi E** 🅖 Chevron/dsl, Maverik, 🛏 Days Inn, 🅞 NAPA, ski areas, **W** 🅖 TA/Subway/Taco Bell/LP/dsl/scales/24hr/@
75	UT 143, **2 mi E** 🅖 Chevron, Maverik, 🛏 Days Inn, 🅞 Foodtown, to Brian Head/Cedar Breaks Ski Resorts
71	Summit
62	UT 130, Cedar City, **E** 🅖 🅛*Loves*/Carl's Jr/Subway/dsl/scales/24hr, Phillips 66/dsl, 🍴 Arctic Circle, Allberto's Mexican, MaggieMoo's, 🅞 🅷, Country Aire RV Park, KOA (2mi), st patrol, **W** 🅖 Maverik/dsl, Shell/dsl/24hr/dsl repair, 🛏 Travelodge
59	UT 56, Cedar City, **0-2 mi E** 🅖 Chevron/dsl, Maverik, Phillips 66/dsl/LP, Texaco, 🍴 A&W/KFC, Arby's, Burger King, China Kitchen, Denny's, Great Harvest Bread Co., Hermie's Drive-In, Hong Kong Buffet, IHOP, Jimmy John's, Little Caesars, McDonald's/playplace, Papa Murphy's, Pizza Factory, Roberto's Tacos, Sizzler, Sonny Boy's BBQ, Subway, Taco Bell, Wendy's, 🛏 Abbey Inn, Best Value Inn, Best Western, Quality Inn, Stratford Hotel, 🅞 Buick/Chevrolet, $Tree, Goodyear/auto, Lin's Mkt, NAPA, Tire Co., USPO, Verizon, **W** 🅖 Maverik/dsl, Sinclair/dsl, 🍴 Bard's Cafe, Subway, 🛏 Crystal Inn, Motel 6, Super 8
57	Lp 15, to UT 14, Cedar City, **0-2 mi E** 🅖 Chevron/repair/24hr, Maverik, Phillips 66/dsl, Shell, Sinclair/dsl, 🍴 DQ, Mi Pueblo, Pizza Hut, Subway, Taco Time, 🛏 Comfort Inn, Days Inn, Holiday Inn Express, Knights Inn, SpringHill Suites, 🅞 🅷, AutoZone, BigLots, Big O Tire, Cadillac/

BEAVER

CEDAR CITY

⬆N INTERSTATE 15 CONT'D

Exit	Services
57	Lp
	GMC, CAL Ranch, $Tree, Family$, Jo-Ann Fabrics, KOA, NAPACare, O'Reilly Parts, Parts+, Smith's Food/gas, Staples, Verizon, to Cedar Breaks, Navajo Lake, Bryce Cyn, Duck Crk, **W** 🅖 Chevron/dsl, USA, 🍴 Applebee's, Cafe Rio, Chili's, Costa Vida, Del Taco, 5 Buck Pizza, Lupita's Mexican, Ninja Japanese, Panda Express, Papa John's, Quiznos, Starbucks, Subway, Winger's, 🏨 Hampton Inn, 🅞 GNC, Home Depot, Jiffy Lube, Radio Shack, Tunex, Verizon, Walgreens, Walmart/McDonald's
51	Kanarraville, Hamilton Ft
44mm	🆁ˢ **both lanes, full ♿ facilities, 🅲, 🚮, litter barrels, pet-walk, hist site**
42	New Harmony, Kanarraville, **W** 🅖 Texaco/dsl
40	to Kolob Canyon, **E** 🅞 Zion's NP, tourist info/🅲, scenic drive
36	Black Ridge
33	Snowfield
31	Pintura
30	Browse
27	UT 17, Toquerville, **E** 🅞 to Zion NP, Grand Canyon, Lake Powell
23	Leeds, Silver Reef (from sb), **3 mi E** 🅞 Leed's RV Park/gas, hist site, museum
22	Leeds, Silver Reef (from nb), same as 23
16	UT 9, to Hurricane, **E** 🅖 Texaco/dsl, 🏨 Holiday Inn Express, 🅞 Harley-Davidson, Walmart Dist Ctr
13	Washington Pkwy, **E** 🅖 Maverik/dsl
10	Middleton Dr, Washington, **E** 🅖 Phillips 66/dsl, Sinclair/dsl, USA, 🍴 Alvero's Mexican, Arby's, Arctic Circle, Benja's Thai, Bishop's Cafe, Burger King, Costa Vida, Del Taco, Don Pedro's Mexican, El Pollo Loco, IHOP, In-N-Out, Jack-in-the-Box, Jimmy John's, Little Caesars, Mad Pita, McDonald's, Pizza Factory, Pizza Hut, Port of Subs, Royal Thai, Sonic, Steak&Seafood, Subway, TX Roadhouse, Toro Moro Mexican, Wendy's, 🏨 Country Inn&Suites, Red Cliffs Inn, 🅞 AAA, Albertsons/Sav-On, AT&T, AutoZone, Barnes&Noble, Best Buy, BigLots, Costco/gas, Dillard's, Discount Tire, Home Depot, Kohl's, JC Penney, Jo-Ann Fabrics, O'Reilly Parts, PetCo, Radio Shack, Sears/auto, Tunex, Walmart/Subway, vet, **W** 🅖 Chevron/dsl/LP, Texaco/dsl, 🅞 auto repair
8	St George Blvd, St George, **E** 🅖 Chevron/Subway/dsl, Texaco/dsl, 🍴 Applebee's, Brick Oven, Carl's Jr, Chili's, ChuckaRama, Coldstone, Don Jose Mexican, Fazoli's, 5 Guys Burgers, Golden Corral, Jimmy John's, Mongolian BBQ, Olive Garden, Outback Steaks, Pachanga's, Panda Express, Papa John's, Quiznos, Red Lobster, Sharky's Mexican, Starbucks, Village Inn Rest., Winger's, 🏨 Best Inn, Courtyard, Hampton Inn, Ramada Inn, TownePlace Suites, 🅞 🅷 Dick's, $Tree, Harmon's Foods, Lowe's, Michael's, Old Navy, Petsmart, Ross, Staples, Sunrise Tire, Target, TJ Maxx, Verizon, same as 10, **W** 🅖 Conoco/dsl, Maverik/dsl, Shell, Sinclair/Domino's/LP/dsl, Texaco/dsl, 🍴 A&W/KFC, Burger King, Cafe Rio, Denny's, Fairway Grill, Iceberg Drive-In, Jimmy John's, Larsen's Drive-In, Mandarin Buffet, McDonald's, Panda Garden, Roberto's, Taco Bell, Taco Time, Wendy's, 🏨 Best Western, Coronada Inn, Days Inn, EconoLodge, Economy Inn, Motel 6, Rodeway Inn, Sands Motel, SunTime Inn, Super 8, 🅞

S T G E O R G E (vertical, left margin)

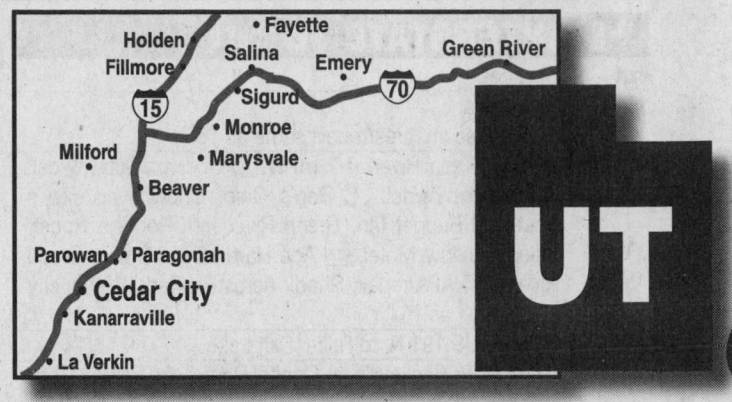

UT

8	Continued
	Aamco, Big O Tire, O'Reilly Parts, Desert Coach RV Ctr, NAPA, Rite Aid, St Geo RV, to LDS Temple
6	UT 18, Bluff St, St George, **E** 🅖 Chevron/dsl/24hr, Texaco/dsl, 🍴 Cracker Barrel, Jack-in-the-Box, Player's Grill, Subway, 🏨 Ambassador Inn, Comfort Inn, Fairfield Inn, Hilton Garden, 🅞 Buick/GMC, Firestone/auto, Hyundai, U-Haul, **W** 🅖 Shell, Texaco, 🍴 Arby's, Burger King, Claimjumper Steaks, DQ, Denny's, JB's, Jimmy John's, McDonald's, Pizza Hut, SF Pizza, 🏨 Best Value Inn, Best Western, Budget Inn, Claridge Inn, Comfort Suites, Crystal Inn, Desert Palms, Holiday Inn, Howard Johnson, Knight's Inn, Quality Inn, 🅞 🅷 Albertson's, AutoZone, Big O Tire, Cadillac/Chevrolet, Camping World RV Ctr, Chrysler/Dodge/Jeep, Ford/Lincoln, Goodyear/auto, Honda, Jo-Ann Fabrics, K-Mart, KwikLube, Mazda, NAPA, Nissan, Parts+, Radio Shack, Staples, Subaru, TempleView RV Park, Toyota, funpark
4	Brigham Rd, Bloomington, **E** 🅖 🚛/Burger King/dsl/scales/24hr, 🏨 La Quinta, **W** 🅖 Chevron/Taco Bell, Mirastar/dsl, 🍴 Hungry Howie's, Subway, Taco Time, Wendy's, 🏨 Wingate Inn, 🅞 Walmart
2	UT 7 E, Southern Pkwy, **E** 🚻
1	**Port of Entry/weigh sta both lanes**
0mm	Utah/Arizona state line

⬆E INTERSTATE 70

Exit	Services
232mm	Utah/Colorado state line
228mm	view area wb, litter barrels
227	Westwater
221	ranch exit
214	to Cisco
204	UT 128, to Cisco
193	Yellowcat Ranch Exit
190mm	**Welcome Ctr wb, full ♿ facilities, vending, info, 🚮, litter barrels**
187	Thompson Springs, **N** 🅖 Shell/dsl, 🅞 café, camping, lodging
185mm	parking area eb
182	US 191 S, Crescent Jct, to Moab, **N** 🅖 Papa Joe's, **S** to Arches/Canyonlands NP
181mm	🆁ˢ **eb, full ♿ facilities, scenic view, 🚮, litter barrels**
175	ranch exit
164	UT 19, Green River, **1-3 mi N** 🅖 Phillips 66/Burger King/dsl, 🚛/Westwinds/rest/dsl/scales/24hr, Silver Eagle/Blimpie/dsl, 🍴 Tamarisk Rest., 🏨 Bookcliff Motel/rest., Comfort Inn, Holiday Inn Express, Knights Inn, Motel 6, Super 8, Ramada Ltd, River Terrace Inn, 🅞 KOA, Powell

🅖 = gas   🍴 = food   🛏 = lodging   🅞 = other   🆁🆂 = rest stop   Copyright 2014 - The NEXT Exit

UT

🔺E	**INTERSTATE 70** CONT'D	

Exit	Services
164	Continued
	River Museum, tires/repair, same as 160
160	UT 19, Green River, **0-2 mi N** 🅖 Chevron/Subway/dsl, Conoco/Arby's/dsl, 🍴 Ben's Cafe, Chowhound, Ray's Rest., 🛏 Budget Inn, Green River Inn, Robbers Roost, Sleepy Hollow Motel, 🅞 Ace Hardware, AG Mkt, Green River SP, NAPA/repair, Shady Acres RV Park, USPO, city park, same as 164
157	US 6 W, US 191 N, to Price, Salt Lake
149	UT 24 W, to Hanksville, to Capitol Reef, Lake Powell, Goblin Valley SP
146	view area, restrooms wb
144mm	runaway truck ramp eb
143mm	view area both lanes, restrooms
142mm	runaway truck ramp eb
138mm	brake test area, restrooms eb
131	Temple Mt Rd
122mm	Ghost Rock View Area both lanes, restrooms
116	to Moore, **N** view area both lanes
115	**N** view area eb
108	ranch exit
105mm	Salt Wash View Area both lanes
99	ranch exit
91	UT 10 N, UT 72, to Emery, Price, **12 mi N** gas, **S** to Capitol Reef NP
86mm	**S** 🆁🆂 **both lanes, full ♿ facilities, litter barrels, petwalk**
73	ranch exit
63	Gooseberry Rd
56	US 89 N, to Salina, US 50 W, to Delta, **0-1 mi N** 🅖 Conoco/dsl, Maverik, Phillips 66/dsl, Sinclair/Burger King/dsl, 🍴 Denny's, El Mexicano Mexican, Losta Motsa Pizza, Mom's Cafe, Subway, 🛏 EconoLodge, Rodeway Inn, Super 8, 🅞 Barretts Foods, Butch Cassidy RV Camp, NAPA, truck/RV/auto repair, **NEXT SERVICES 109 MI EB**
48	UT 24, to US 50, Sigurd, Aurora, **1-2 mi S** gas, food, to Fishlake NF, Capitol Reef NP
40	Lp 70, Richfield, **0-2 mi S** 🅖 Chevron, ✈FLYING J/Pepperoni's/dsl/LP/rest./24hr, Maverik, Texaco/dsl, 🍴 Arby's, Frontier Village Rest., South China Rest., Subway, Taco Time, 🛏 Best Western, Budget Host, Days Inn/rest., Holiday Inn Express, Super 8, 🅞 🎗, Big O Tire, Buick/Cadillac/Chevrolet/GMC, Chrysler/Dodge/Jeep, Family$, Fresh Mkt, IFA Store, NAPA, city park, USPO, RV/truck repair
37	Lp 70, Richfield, **S** 🅖 Phillips 66/Wendy's/dsl, 🍴 KFC/Taco Bell, Wingers, 🛏 Comfort Inn, Fairfield Inn, Hampton Inn, 🅞 Home Depot, golf, **1-2 mi S** 🅖 Silver Eagle/Burger King/dsl, 🍴 JB's Rest., Lotsa Motsa Pizza, McDonald's, Pizza Hut, Rice King Chinese, 🛏 New West Motel, Quality Inn, Royal Inn, Travelodge, 🅞 Ace Hardware, AutoZone, $Tree, Ford, K-Mart, KOA, O'Reilly Parts, Pearson Tire, Verizon, Walmart/Subway, to Fish Lake/Capitol Reef Parks, st patrol
31	Elsinore, Monroe, **S** 🅖 Silver Eagle/gas
25	UT 118, Joseph, Monroe, **S** 🅖 Diamond D Travel Plaza, 🅞 Flying U Country Store/dsl/RV park
23	US 89 S, to Panguitch, Bryce Canyon, Zion
17	**N** 🅞 Fremont Indian SP, museum, info, 🎗, camping, chain-up area (WB)
13mm	brake test area eb
7	Ranch Exit

Exit	Services
3mm	Western Boundary Fishlake NF
1	Historic Cove Fort, **N** 🅖 Chevron/Subway/rest stop (2mi)
0mm	I-15, N to SLC, S to St George.
	I-70 begins/ends on I-15, exit 132.

🔺E	**INTERSTATE 80**	

Exit	Services
197mm	Utah/Wyoming state line
193	Wahsatch
189	ranch exit
185	Castle Rock
182mm	**Port of Entry/weigh sta wb**
180	Emery (from wb)
170	**Welcome Ctr wb/🆁🆂 eb, full ♿ facilities, 🎗, vending, 🚻 litter barrels, petwalk, RV dump**
169	Echo
168	I-84 W, to Ogden, I-80 E, to Cheyenne
166	view area both lanes, litter barrels
162	Coalville, **N** 🅖 Phillips 66/dsl/mart, 🛏 Best Western, 🅞 Holiday Hills RV Camp/LP, CamperWorld RV Park, **S** 🅖 Chevron/dsl, Sinclair, 🅞 Griffith's Foods, NAPA, USPO, to Echo Res RA
155	UT 32 S, Wanship, **N** 🍴 Spring Chicken Café, **S** 🅖 Sinclair/dsl, 🅞 to Rockport SP
150	**toll gate promontory**
146b a	US 40 E, to Heber, Provo, **N** 🅖 Sinclair/Blimpie/dsl, **S** 🅞 Home Depot
145	UT 224, Kimball Jct, to Park City, **N** 🅞 Chevrolet, Ford, RV camping, **S** 🅖 Chevron, 🍴 Arby's, Bajio Grill, Coldstone Creamery, Gandalfo's Deli, Ghidottis Italian, Loco Lizard Cantina, McDonald's, Panda Express, Quizno's, Starbucks, Subway, Ruby Tuesday, Taco Bell, Wendy's, Wild Oats Cafe, Wingers, 🛏 Best Western, Hampton Inn, Holiday Inn Express, 🅞 GNC, Smith's Foods, USPO, Walmart, Outlet Mall/famous brands, RV camping, to ski areas
144mm	view area eb
141	ranch exit, **N** 🅖 Phillips 66/Blimpie, 🍴 Pizza Hut, 🅞 to Jeremy Ranch, **S** 🍴 Booster Juice, Cafe Sabor, Oh Shucks Grill, 🅞 Albertson's, camping, ski area
140	Parley's Summit, **S** 🅖 Sinclair/dsl, 🍴 No Worries Café
137	Lamb's Canyon
134	UT 65, Emigration Canyon, East Canyon Mountaindale RA
133	utility exit (from eb)
132	ranch exit
131	(from eb) Quarry
130	I-215 S (from wb)
129	UT 186 W, Foothill Dr, Parley's Way, **N** 🎗
128	I-215 S (from eb)
127	UT 195, 23rd E St, to Holladay
126	UT 181, 13th E St, to Sugar House, **N** 🅖 Chevron, Texaco, 🍴 Olive Garden, Red Lobster, Sizzler, Training Table Rest., Wendy's, 🅞 ShopKO
125	UT 71, 7th E St. 🅖 Texaco, 🅞 Firestone, **N** 🍴 McDonald's
124	US 89, S State St, **N** 🅖 Chevron, 7-11, Texaco/dsl, 🍴 Burger King, Skipper's, Taco Bell, Uncle Sid's Rest., Wendy's, Woody's Drive-In, 🅞 Buick, Chrysler/Jeep, Discount Tire, Dodge, Honda, Suzuki, transmissions, **S** 🍴 KFC, Pizza Hut, 🛏 Ramada Inn
123mm	I-15, N to Ogden, S to Provo
	I-80 and I-15 run together approx 4 mi. See Interstate 15, exits 308-310.

GREEN RIVER

RICHFIELD

KIMBALL JCT

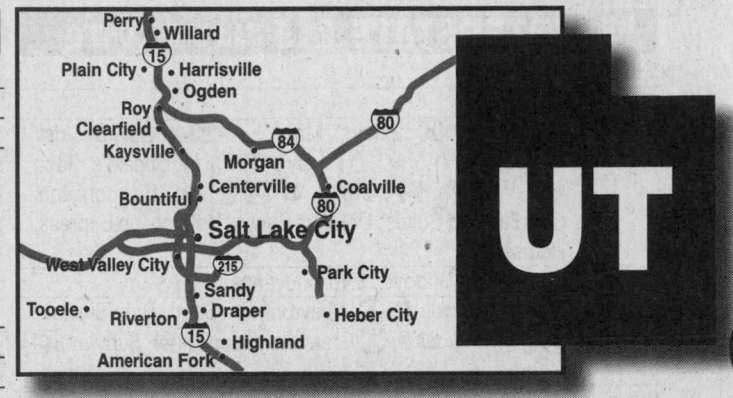

SALT LAKE

⬆️E INTERSTATE 80 CONT'D

Exit	Services
121	600 S, to City Ctr
120	I-15 N, to Ogden
118	UT 68, Redwood Rd, to N Temple, **0-1 mi N on N Temple E** 🅖 Chevron/Subway/dsl, Maverik, ❤️Loves/Arby's/dsl/scales/24hr, Tesoro, 🅕 A&W/KFC, Burger King, Carls Jr, Denny's, Taco Bell, Wendy's, 🅛🔜 Inn, Candlewood Suites, Comfort Suites, Day's Inn, Holiday Inn Express, Motel 6, Quality Inn, Radisson, Utah St Fairpark, **S** 🅷
117	I-215, N to Ogden, S to Provo
115b a	Bangerter Hwy, **N** to Salt Lake 🔜
114	Wright Bros Dr (from wb), **N** same as 113
113	5600 W (from eb), **N** 🅖 Phillips 66/dsl, 🅕 Perkins, Subway, Wingtips Bistro, 🅛 Comfort Inn, Courtyard, Fairfield Inn, Hampton Inn, Hilton, Holiday Inn, Hyatt Place, La Quinta, Microtel, Ramada Inn, Residence Inn, SpringHill Suites, Super 8
111	7200 W
104	UT 202, Saltair Dr, to Magna, **N** 🅞 Great Salt Lake SP, beaches
102	UT 201 (from eb), to Magna
101mm	view area wb
99	UT 36, to Tooele, **S** 🅖 Chevron/Subway/dsl, ⊕FLYING J/Denny's/dsl/scales/LP/24hr, TA/Burger King/Taco Bell/dsl/scales/24hr/@, Texaco/dsl, 🅕 Del Taco, McDonald's, 🅛 Comfort Inn/Suites, Oquirrh Motel/RV Park, 🅞 🅷, Blue Beacon, Mamie's Place, SpeedCo
88	to Grantsville
84	UT 138, to Grantsville, Tooele
77	UT 196, to Rowley, Dugway
70	to Delle, **S** 🅖 Delle/Sinclair/café/dsl
62	to Lakeside, Eagle Range, military area
56	to Aragonite
55mm	🆁🆂 both lanes, full ♿ facilities, 🅕, 🔜, litter barrels, pot walk, vending
49	to Clive
41	Knolls
26mm	architectural point of interest
10mm	🆁🆂 both lanes, full ♿ facilities, 🅕, 🔜, litter barrels, vending, petwalk, observation area
4	Bonneville Speedway, **N** 🅖 Sinclair/dsl/café/24hr
3mm	**Port of Entry, weigh sta both lanes**
2	UT 58 (no EZ wb return), Wendover, **S** 🅖 Sinclair/dsl, Shell/Taco Time/dsl, 🅕 Subway, 🅛 Best Western, Bonneville Inn, Days Inn, Knights Inn, Motel 6, Nugget Hotel/casino, Quality Inn, Western Ridge Motel, 🅞 Family$, Fred's Foods, Bonneville Speedway Museum, Montego Bay Hotel/Casino, KOA, USPO, auto repair
0mm	Utah/Nevada state line, Mountain/Pacific time zone

⬆️E INTERSTATE 84

Exit	Services
120	**I-84 begins/ends on I-80, exit 168 near Echo, Utah.**
115	Ut 65 S, to Henefer, Echo, **1/2 mi S** 🅞 Grump's Gen Store, USPO, to E Canyon SP
112	UT 86 E, Henefer, **S** gas, food, lodging
111	Croydon
111mm	Devil's Slide Scenic View
108	Taggart
106	ranch exit
103	UT 66, Morgan, E Canyon SP, **N** Ford, **S** 🅖 Phillips 66/7-

Exit	Services
103	Continued 11, Texaco/dsl, 🅕 Luise's Mexican, Spring Chicken Café, Steph's Drive-In, Subway, 🅞 Ace Hardware, Ridley's Mkt, USPO, city park
96	Peterson, **N** 🅖 Sinclair (3mi), 🅞 to Snow Basin, Powder Mtn, Nordic Valley Ski Areas, **S** 🅖 Phillips 66/dsl
94mm	🆁🆂 wb, full ♿ facilities, 🔜 litter barrels, petwalk
92	UT 167 (from eb), to Huntsville, **N** 🅖 Sinclair/dsl (2mi), 🅞 trout farm (1mi), to ski areas
91mm	🆁🆂 eb, full ♿ facilities, 🔜 litter barrels, petwalk
87b a	US 89, to Ogden, Layton, **N** 🅕 McDonald's (2mi), 🅛 Best Western, 🅞 Cheese Outlet, Goodyear/auto **S** to Hill AFB
85	S Weber, Uintah
81	to I-15 S, UT 26, Riverdale Rd, **N** 🅖 Conoco/dsl, Sinclair, 🅕 Applebee's, Arby's, Carl's Jr, Chili's, Del Taco, IHOP, Jamba Juice, Lucky Buffet, McDonald's, Starbucks, 🅞 AT&T, Best Buy, Buick/GMC, Cadillac, $Tree, Good Earth Foods, Harley-Davidson, Home Depot, Honda, Jo-Ann, Kia, Lowe's Whse, Mazda, Nissan, PepBoys, Petsmart, Sam's Club/gas, Schwab Tire, Target, Toyota/Scion, Walmart/McDonald's, **S** 🅛 Motel 6, 🅞 Chrysler/Dodge/Jeep
	I-84 and I-15 run together. See interstate 15, exits 344-379.
41	I-15 N to Pocatello
40	UT 102, Tremonton, Bothwell, **N** 🅖 Chevron/Quiznos/dsl/wash/24hr, Sinclair/Burger King/dsl/scales/@, 🅕 Denny's, McDonald's, Wendy's, 🅛 Hampton Inn, Western Inn, 🅞 🅷 (4mi), RV/truck/tire repair, **1 mi N** 🅖 Maverik, Tesoro/dsl, 🅞 Alco, **S** 🅞 to Golden Spike NHS
39	to Garland, Bothwell, **N** 🅷
32	ranch exit
26	UT 83 S, to Howell, **S** to Golden Spike NSH
24	to Valley
20	to Blue Creek
17	ranch exit
16	to Hansel Valley (from wb)
12	ranch exit
7	Snowville, **N** 🅖 ⊕FLYING J/Pepperoni's/dsl/LP/24hr, 🅕 Mollie's Café, Ranch House Diner, 🅛 Outsiders Inn, 🅞 Lotti-Dell RV camping, city park, USPO
5	UT 30, to Park Valley
0mm	Utah/Idaho state line

⬆️N INTERSTATE 215 (SALT LAKE)

Exit	Services
29	**I-215 begins/ends on I-15.**
28	UT 68, Redwood Rd, **W** 🅖 ⊕FLYING J/dsl/rest./mart/24hr/@, Maverik/24hr, 🅕 Subway
26	Legacy Pkwy

🛢 = gas 🍴 = food 🛏 = lodging 🅾 = other 🆁🆂 = rest stop   Copyright 2014 - The NEXT Exit

⬆N INTERSTATE 215 (SALT LAKE) CONT'D

Exit	Services
25	22nd N
23	7th N, **E** 🛢 Exxon, Maverik, ♥Love's/Arbys/dsl/scales/24hr (1.5 mi), 🍴 Arby's, KFC, McDonald's, Taco Bell, Wendy's, 🛏 Motel 6, **W** 🛏 ✈ Inn, Baymont Inn, Candlewood Suites, Comfort Suites, Holiday Inn Express, Radisson
22b a	I-80, W to Wendover, E to Cheyenne
21	California Ave, **E** 🛢 Chevron/dsl, Sapp Bros/Sinclair/Burger King/dsl/@, 🍴 Great American Diner, Subway, 🅾 Goodyear
20b a	UT 201, W to Magna, 21st S, **W** 🅾 Goodyear, Kenworth
18	UT 171, 3500 S, W Valley, **E** 🛢 Sinclair, 🍴 Applebee's, Chili's, Costa Vida Mexican, Cowloon Moon, Cracker Barrel, Denny's, IHOP, Training Table, 🛏 Baymont Inn, Country Inn Suites, Crystal Inn, Extended Stay America, La Quinta, Ruby Tuesday, Sleep Inn, 🅾 ⒽPepBoys, **W** 🍴 Olive Garden, Pizza Hut, Red Robin, Starbucks, TGIFriday's, Winger's, 🅾 Big O Tire, Costco/gas, JC Penney, Jubilee Foods, Macy's, Staples, Verizon
15	UT 266, 47th S, **E** 🛢 Conoco/dsl, 🍴 Dee's Rest., KFC, Pizza Hut, Taco Time, Taco Bell, Village Inn, Wendy's, 🅾 Albertson's, Goodyear/auto, Marie Callender's, Rite Aid, Walgreens, **W** 🛢 Chevron, 🍴 Arby's
13	UT 68, Redwood Rd, **E** 🛢 Chevron, Tesoro, 🍴 Applebee's, Apollo Burger, Arby's, Bajio Grill, Burger King, Carl's Jr, Golden China, Great Harvest Bread, Honey Baked Ham, McDonald's/playplace, Old Spaghetti Factory,

<table>
<tr><td>S
A
L
T

L
A
K
E

C
I
T
Y</td><td></td></tr>
</table>

Exit	Services
13	Continued Panda Express, Papa John's, Souper Salad, Starbucks, Subway, TX Roadhouse, Tuesday Morning, 🛏 Homestead Suites, 🅾 $Tree, Harmon's, Jo-Ann Fabrics, PetsMart, Radio Shack, Ross, ShopKO, Walmart/auto
12	I-15, N to SLC, S to Provo
11	same as 10 (from eb)
10	UT 280 E, **E** 🅾 Sam's Club, **W** 🍴 Applebee's, Arby's, Hooters, Jason's Deli, La Salsa Mexican, Macaroni Grill, Olive Garden, Red Lobster, Taco Bell, Wendy's, Village Inn, 🅾 Ⓗ
9	Union Park Ave, **E** 🍴 Black Angus, Carl's Jr, Chili's, Denny's, Famous Dave's BBQ, LaSalsa Mexican, Marie Callender's, Outback Steaks, Sweet Tomato, Tony Roma, 🛏 Best Western, Crystal Inn, Extended Stay America, Homewood Suites, 🅾 Albertson's, Barnes&Noble, Home Depot, Old Navy, Ross, Smith's Foods, Target, Walmart/auto, **W** 🛢 Tesoro, 🛏 Crystal Inn, Motel 6, Super 8
8	UT 152, 2000 E, **E** 🛢 Chevron, 🍴 KFC, Panda Express, Taco Bell, **W** 🍴 Wendy's
6	6200 S, **E** 🍴 Loco Lizards Café, Mikado Café, Quizno's, 🅾 Alta, Brighton, Snowbird, Solitude/ski areas
5	UT 266, 45th S, Holladay, **W** 🛢 Tesoro
4	39th S, **E** 🛢 Chevron, Sinclair, 🍴 Barbacoa Grill, Rocky Mtn Pizza, 🅾 Ace Hardware, Dan's Foods, **W** Ⓗ
3	33rd S, Wasatch, **W** 🛢 Tesoro, 🍴 Burger King, KFC, McDonald's, Taco Bell, Wendy's
2	I-80 W

I-215 begins/ends on I-80, exit 130.

VERMONT

⬆N INTERSTATE 89

Exit	Services
130mm	I-89 Begins/Ends, US/Canada Border, Vermont state line
22 (129)	US 7 S, Highgate Springs, **E** 🅾 DutyFree, **3 mi E** 🛢 Irving/dsl
129mm	Latitude 45 N, midway between N Pole and Equator
128mm	Rock River
21 (123)	US 7, VT 78, Swanton, **E** 🛢 Shell/dsl, **W** 🛢 Mobil/dsl, Shell, Sunoco/dsl, 🍴 Dunkin Donuts, Jacob's Rest., McDonald's, Pam's Pizza, Shaggy's Snack Bar, 🅾 Hannaford Foods, NAPA
20 (118)	US 7, VT 207, St Albans, **W** 🛢 Mobil/dsl, Shell/dsl, Sunoco, 🍴 Burger King, Dunkin Donuts, KFC/Taco Bell, McDonald's, Oriental Kitchen, Panda China, Pizza Hut, Thai House, 🅾 Ⓗ, Advance Parts, AT&T, Aubuchon Hardware, Chevrolet, Ford, Hannaford Foods, Jo-Ann Fabrics, Kinney Drug, PriceChopper Foods, Radio Shack, Sears, Staples, TJ Maxx, Verizon
19 (114)	US 7, VT 36, VT 104, St Albans, **W** 🛢 Mobil/dsl, Shell, 🛏 La Quinta, 🅾 Ⓗ, st police, vet
111mm	🆁🆂 both lanes, full ♿ facilities, info, Ⓒ, ✉, litter barrels, vending, petwalk, wifi
18 (107)	US 7, VT 104A, Georgia Ctr, **E** 🛢 Mobil/dsl, Shell, 🍴 GA Farmhouse Rest., 🅾 GA Auto Parts, Homestead RV Park, USPO, repair
17 (98)	US 2, US 7, Lake Champlain Islands, **E** 🛢 Mobil, Shell/dsl, 🅾 camping (4mi), **W** 🅾 to NY Ferry, camping (6mi)
96mm	weigh sta both lanes

<table>
<tr><td>S
T

A
L
B
A
N
S</td><td></td></tr>
</table>

Exit	Services
16 (92)	US 7, US 2, Winooski, **E** 🛢 Mobil, 🍴 Friendly's, T-Bones Rest., 🛏 Hampton Inn, 🅾 Costco, Osco Drug, Shaw's Foods, **W** 🛢 Citgo, Irving, Shell/dsl, 🍴 Beyo Cafe, Burger King, Jr's Italian, Libby's Diner, McDonald's, Subway, 🛏 Motel 6, Quality Inn
15 (91)	VT 15 (from nb no return), Winooski, **E** 🛏 Days Inn, Handys Extended Stay Suites, 🅾 to St Michael's Coll., **W** 🛢 Mobil/dsl, Shell, 🅾 USPO
90mm	Winooski River
14 (89)	US 2, Burlington, **E** 🛢 Citgo/repair, Gulf, Mobil, Shell/dsl, Sunoco, 🍴 Al's Cafe, Applebee's, Burger King, CheeseTrader, Chicken Charlie's, Dunkin Donuts, Friendly's, Leonardo's Pizza, Marco's Pizza, McDonald's, Moe's SW Grill, Outback Steaks, Quiznos, Starbucks, Trader Dukes, Wind Jammer Rest., Zachary's Pizza, 🛏 Anchorage Inn, Best Western, Comfort Inn, DoubleTree Hotel, Holiday Inn, La Quinta, University Inn, 🅾 Barnes&Noble, BonTon, Healthy Living Mkt, JC Penney, Jo-Ann Fabrics, Kohl's, PriceChopper, Rite Aid, Sears/auto, mall, USPO, **W** 🛢 Mobil/dsl, Shell, 🛏 Sheraton, 🅾 Ⓗ, Advance Parts, Michael's, PetCo, Staples, Verizon, to UVT
13 (87)	I-189, to US 7, Burlington, **2 mi W on US 7 N** 🛢 Citgo, Gulf, 🍴 Buffalo Wild Wings, China Express, Dunkin Donuts, KFC, Mamma Mia's Pizza, Starbucks, Subway, 🛏 Liberty Inn, 🅾 Bond Parts, Hyundai/Subaru, Kinney Drug, PriceChopper Foods, Radio Shack, Shaw's Foods, TJ Maxx, Walgreens, USPO, **2 mi W on US 7 S** 🛢 Gulf, Mobil, Sunoco, Shell, 🍴 Burger King, Burlington Cafe, Chicago Grill, Denny's, Koto Japanese, Lakeview House

<table>
<tr><td>B
U
R
L
I
N
G
T
O
N</td><td></td></tr>
</table>

🔼🔽 INTERSTATE 89 CONT'D

Exit	Services
13 (87)	Continued Rest., McDonald's, Olive Garden, Pauline's Cafe, Pizza Hut, Quiznos, Zen Garden, 🛏 Comfort Suites, Ho-Hum Hotel, Holiday Inn Express, Maple Leaf Motel, North Star Motel, Quality Inn, Rodeway Inn, Ⓞ Acura/Audi/VW, Advance Parts, Buick/Cadillac/GMC, Chevrolet, Country Curtains, Dodge, Ford, Hannaford Foods, Jeep, K-Mart, Lowe's, Nissan, Tire Whse, Toyota/Scion, repair, vet
12 (84)	VT 2A, to US 2, to Essex Jct, Williston, **E** ⛽ Mobil/24hr, Sunoco/dsl/24hr, 🍴 Chili's, Friendly's, Longhorn Steaks, Moe's SW Grill, 99 Rest., Ponderosa, Starbucks, TX Roadhouse, VT Sandwich, 🛏 Fairfield, TownePlace Suites, Ⓞ Best Buy, Dick's, Hannaford Foods, Home Depot, Marshall's, Natural Provisions Mkt, Old Navy, Osco Drug, Petsmart, Shaws Foods, Staples, Walmart, st police, **W** 🛏 Courtyard, Residence Inn
82mm	Ⓡ both lanes (7am-11pm), full ♿ facilities, 🚻, 🚮 litter barrels, vending, petwalk, WiFi
11 (79)	US 2, to VT 117, Richmond, **E** 🛏 Kitchen Table Rest., **W** ⛽ Mobil/dsl
67mm	parking area/**weigh sta sb**
66mm	**weigh sta nb**
10 (64)	VT 100, to US 2, Waterbury, **E** ⛽ Mobil/dsl/24hr, Shell/dsl, 🍴 Pizza Shoppe, 🛏 Best Western/rest, Thatcher Brook Inn/rest., Ⓞ Shaws Foods/Osco Drug, TrueValue, **W** ⛽ Citgo/dsl, 🍴 Maxi's Rest., Zachary's Pizza, Ⓞ USPO
9 (59)	US 2, to VT 100B, Middlesex, **W** 🍴 Red Hen Baking Co, Ⓞ museum, st police
8 (53)	US 2, Montpelier, **1 mi E** ⛽ Citgo, Gulf/dsl, Mobil, Shell/dsl, Sunoco/repair, 🍴 Al Portego Italian, China Star, Dunkin Donuts, Julio's, Sarducci's Rest., Subway, 🛏 Capitol Plaza Hotel, Montpelier Inn, Ⓞ Aubuchon Hardware, Bond Parts, Rite Aid, Shaw's Foods, camping (6mi), to VT Coll
7 (50)	VT 62, to US 302, Barre, **E** ⛽ Irving/dsl, 🍴 Applebee's, 🛏 Comfort Suites, Ⓞ Honda, Shaw's Foods, Staples, **1 mi E** 🛏 Hilltop Inn, Ⓞ 🏥 JC Penney, Jo-Ann Fabrics, Subaru, Toyota/Scion, camping (7mi)
6 (47)	VT 63, to VT 14, S Barre, **4 mi E** gas, food, lodging, camping, info
5 (43)	VT 64, to VT 12, VT 14, Williamstown, **6 mi E** gas/dsl, food, lodging, camping, **W** to Norwich U
41mm	highest elevation on I-89, 1752 ft
34.5mm	**weigh sta both lanes**
4 (31)	VT 66, Randolph, **E** Ⓞ RV camping (seasonal 1mi), **W** ⛽ Mobil/dsl, 🍴 McDonald's, lodging (3mi), Ⓞ 🏥 RV camping (5mi)
30mm	parking area sb
3 (22)	VT 107, Bethel, **E** ⛽ Mobil/dsl, 🍴 Eaton's Rest., Village Pizza, Ⓞ to Jos Smith Mon (8mi), **1 mi W** ⛽ Irving/dsl/LP, Ⓞ Rite Aid, st police, vet

Exit	Services
14mm	White River
2 (13)	VT 14, VT 132, Sharon, **W** ⛽ Gulf/dsl, 🍴 Dixie's Kitchen, Sandy's Drive Inn, Ⓞ Sharon Country Store, USPO, Jos Smith Mon (6mi)
9mm	Ⓡ/weigh sta both lanes (7am-11pm), full ♿ facilities, 🚻, info, 🚮 litter barrels, vending, wi-fi
7mm	White River
1 (4)	US 4, to Woodstock, Quechee, **3 mi E** ⛽ Irving, 🛏 Hampton Inn, Holiday Inn Express, Super 8
1mm	I-91, N to St Johnsbury, S to Brattleboro
0mm	Vermont/New Hampshire state line, Connecticut River

🔼🔽 INTERSTATE 91

Exit	Services
178mm	**I-91 begins/ends.** US/Canada Border, Vermont state line, US Customs
29 (177)	US 5, Derby Line, **E** Dutyfree, **1 mi W** ⛽ Irving/Circle K/dsl, Ⓞ city park
176.5mm	**Welcome Ctr sb**, full ♿ facilities, info, 🚮 litter barrels,

B U R L I N G T O N

VT

🅖 = gas   🍴 = food   🛏 = lodging   🅞 = other   🆁🆂 = rest stop   Copyright 2014 - The NEXT Exit

⬆⬇🇳 INTERSTATE 91 CONT'D

VT

DERBY CTR

Exit	Services
176.5mm	**Continued**
	🄲, **petwalk, wi-fi,** Midpoint between the Equator and N Pole
28 (172)	US 5, VT 105, Derby Ctr, **E** 🅖 Gulf, Shell/dsl, Sunoco/repair, 🍴 Cow Palace Rest., 🛏 Border Motel, 🅞 Ace Hardware, USPO, **W** 🅖 Irving/Hoagie's Pizza, Mobil/dsl, 🍴 McDonald's, Roasters Cafe, Sub Sta./Village Pizza, 🛏 4 Seasons, Pepin's Motel, 🅞 🅷 Advance Parts, Bond Parts, Chrysler/Dodge/Jeep, $Tree, Kinney Drug, Parts+, PriceChopper Foods, Rite Aid, Shaw's Foods, Verizon, RV camping, st police
27 (170)	VT 191, to US 5, VT 105, Newport, **3 mi W** 🅞 🅷, Border Patrol, camping, info
167mm	parking area/**weigh sta both directions**
26 (161)	US 5, VT 58, Orleans, **E** 🅖 Irving, Sunoco, 🍴 Subway, 🅞 Austin's Drugs, Family$, Thibaults Mkt, TrueValue, USPO, **W** camping (5mi)
156.5mm	Barton River
25 (156)	VT 16, Barton, **1 mi E** 🅖 Gulf, Irving/Circle K/dsl, 🍴 Ming's Chinese, Parson's Corner Rest., Step Back Cafe, 🅞 Barton Drug, Bond Parts, C&C Foods, USPO, camping (2mi), repair
154mm	parking area nb
150.5mm	highest elevation on I-91, 1856 ft
143mm	scenic overlook nb
141mm	🆁🆂 **sb, full** 🚻 **facilities, info,** 🗑 **litter barrels,** 🄲
24 (140)	VT 122, Wheelock, **2 mi E** gas, food, lodging
23 (137)	US 5, to VT 114, Lyndonville, **E** 🅖 Gulf/dsl, Mobil/Dunkin Donuts, Valero, 🍴 China Moon, Hoagie's Pizza, McDonald's, Miss Lyndonville Diner, Pizza Man, 🛏 Colonnade Inn, 🅞 $General, NAPA, Kinney Drug, Rite Aid, TrueValue, White Mkt Foods, **W** 🛏 Lyndon Motel
22 (132)	to US 5, St Johnsbury, **1-2 mi E** 🅖 Sunoco/dsl, 🍴 KFC/Taco Bell, Kham's Cuisine, Pizza Hut, 🅞 🅷, Aubuchon Hardware, Bond Parts, Buick/GMC, Kinney Drug, PriceChopper Foods, Subaru, repair, **3 mi E on US 5** 🅖 Irving, 🅞 AT&T, Firestone, JC Penney, Radio Shack, Sears
21 (131)	US 2, to VT 15, St Johnsbury, **1-2 mi E** services
20 (129)	US 5, to US 2, St Johnsbury, **E** 🅖 Irving/dsl, Mobil, Shell/dsl, 🍴 Anthony's Diner, Dunkin Donuts, East Garden Chinese, McDonald's, Subway, Winegate Rest., 🅞 Family$, Kevin's Repair, Mkt St, Rite Aid, TrueValue, museum, **welcome ctr, W** 🛏 Comfort Inn, 🅞 st police
19 (128)	I-93 S to Littleton NH
122mm	scenic view nb
18 (121)	to US 5, Barnet, **E** 🅞 camping (5mi), **W** 🅞 camping (5mi)
115mm	parking area sb
113mm	parking area nb
17 (110)	US 302, to US 5, Wells River, NH, **E** 🍴 Warner's Rest., **W** 🅖 P&H Trkstp/rest./dsl/scales/24hr, 🅞 🅷 (5mi), camping (9mi)
100mm	nb 🆁🆂, **full** 🚻 **facilities,** 🄲, **info,** 🗑 **litter barrels, petwalk, sb parking area**
16 (98)	VT 25, to US 5, Bradford, **E** 🅖 Mobil/dsl/LP/café, 🍴 Hungry Bear Grill, 🛏 Bradford Motel, 🅞 Bond Parts, Hannafords Foods, Kinney Drug, NAPA, Pierson Farm Mkt, **W** st police

ST JOHNSBURY

Exit	Services
15 (92)	Fairlee, **E** 🅖 Citgo/dsl, Gulf, Irving/dsl, Shell/dsl/LP, 🍴 Baileys Tavern, Fairlee Diner, Subway, 🅞 Ace Hardware, Wings Mkt/deli, USPO, camping, **W** 🅞 golf
14 (84)	VT 113, to US 5, Thetford, **1 mi E** 🅞 food, camping, **W** 🅞 camping
13 (75)	US 5, VT 10a, Hanover, NH, **E** 🅞 🅷, to Dartmouth, **W** 🅖 Citgo, 🍴 Norwich Inn Rest., 🅞 Subaru, USPO
12 (72)	US 5, White River Jct, Wilder, **E** 🅖 Gulf/dsl, Mobil
11 (71)	US 5, White River Jct, **E** 🅖 Mobil/dsl, Shell/Subway/dsl, Sunoco, 🍴 China Moon, Crossroads Country Café, McDonald's, 🛏 Comfort Inn, Regency Inn, 🅞 Ford/Lincoln, Hyundai, Jct Mktplace, Toyota, USPO, **W** 🅖 Citgo, Irving/Dunkin Donuts, Lukoil/dsl, 🛏 Fairfield Inn, Hampton Inn, Holiday Inn Express, Super 8, White River Inn, 🅞 🅷
10N (70)	I-89 N, to Montpelier
10S	I-89 S, to NH, 🄬
68mm	**weigh sta both lanes**
9 (60)	US 5, VT 12, Hartland, **E** 🅷, **W** 🅖 Mobil (1mi), info
8 (51)	US 5, VT 12, VT 131, Ascutney, **E** 🅖 Citgo/dsl, Gulf/dsl, Irving/Circle K, Sunoco/Dunkin Donuts/dsl, 🍴 Ascutney House Rest., RedBarn Cafe, 🛏 Yankee Village Motel, 🅞 🅷, Getaway Camping (2mi), USPO, **W** auto repair/tires
7 (42)	US 5, VT 106, VT 11, Springfield, **W** 🅖 Irving/Circle K/Subway/dsl/scales/24hr, 🛏 Holiday Inn Express, 🅞 🅷 (5mi), camping
39mm	**weigh sta sb**
6 (34)	US 5, VT 103, to Bellows Falls, Rockingham, **E** 🅖 Shell/dsl, 🍴 Leslie's Rest., 🛏 Every Day Inn, **W** 🅖 Sunoco/dsl, 🅞 st police (6mi)
5 (29)	VT 121, to US 5, to Bellows Falls, Westminster, **3 mi E** gas, food, 🄲, lodging
24mm	parking area both lanes
22mm	**weigh sta sb**
20mm	parking area nb
4 (18)	US 5, Putney, **E** 🛏 Putney Inn/rest., **W** 🅖 Rod's/repair, Sunoco/dsl/LP/24hr, 🅞 Putney Grocery/deli, camping (3mi)
3 (11)	US 5, VT 9 E, Brattleboro, **E** 🅖 Agway/dsl, Citgo/dsl, Mobil/dsl, Sunoco, 🍴 China Buffet, Dunkin Donuts, Fast Eddy Cafe, Friendly's, House of Pizza, KFC, McDonald's, 99 Rest., Panda North, Pizza Hut, Steak-Out, Taco Bell, Village Pizza, Wendy's, 🛏 Best Inn, Colonial Motel, Hampton Inn, Holiday Inn Express, Motel 6, Quality Inn, Super 8, 🅞 Advance Parts, Bond Parts, Buick/Chevrolet/GMC, $Tree, Ford, Hannaford Foods, Radio Shack, Rite Aid, Staples, Subaru, TrueValue, Verizon, USPO
2 (9)	VT 9 W, to rd 30, Brattleboro, **W** 🅖 Shell, 🍴 VT Country Deli, 🅞 to Marlboro Coll, st police
1 (7)	US 5, Brattleboro, **E** 🅖 Gulf/dsl, Irving/Circle K/dsl, Mobil/Dunkin Donuts, Shell/Subway/dsl, 🍴 Burger King, FC Chinese, Millenium Pizzaria, VT Inn Pizza, 🛏 EconoLodge, 🅞 🅷, PriceChopper Foods, Rite Aid, Walgreens, vet, to Ft Dummer SP
6mm	**Welcome Ctr nb, full** 🚻 **facilities, info,** 🄲, 🗑, **litter barrels, vending, petwalk, playground, wi-fi**
0mm	Vermont/Massachusetts state line

BRATTLEBORO

⬆⬇🇳 INTERSTATE 93

See New Hampshire Interstate 93.

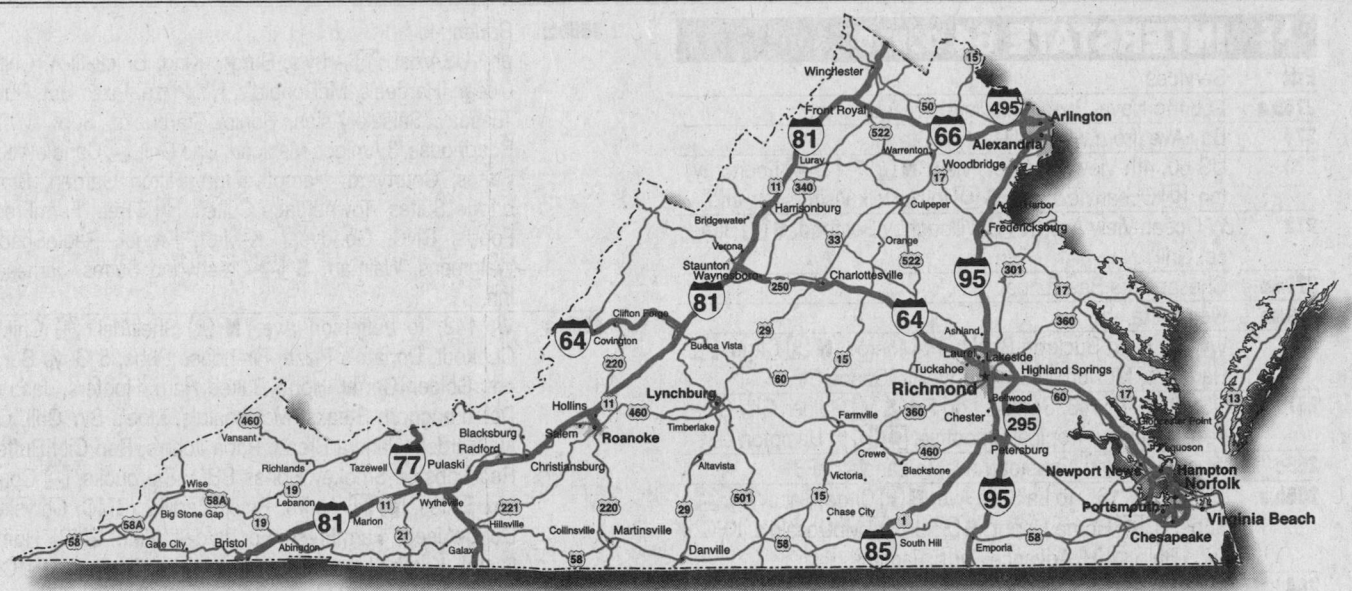

VA

	INTERSTATE 64
Exit	**Services**
299b a	I-264 E, to Portsmouth. **I-64 begins/ends on I-264.**
297	US 13, US 460, Military Hwy, N 🅿 Exxon, 7-11, 🍴 McDonald's
296b a	US 17, to Portsmouth, N 🅿 7-11, 🍴 Hardee's, McDonald's, Papa John's, Subway, Zino's Cafe, 🛏 Comfort Inn, 🅾 $General, Food Lion, USPO, vet
294mm	S Br Elizabeth River
292	VA 190, to VA 104 (from eb, no EZ return), Dominion Blvd, S 🅿 7-11, 🍴 Burger King, #1 China, Royal China, Subway, 🅾 Family$, Food Lion
291b a	I-464 N, VA 104 S, to Elizabeth City, Outer Banks, same services as 292
290b a	VA 168, Battlefield Blvd, to Nag's Head, Manteo, N 🍴 Burger King, 🛏 ValuePlace, 🅾 BigLots, $General, Hancock Fabrics, K-mart, Merchant's Auto Ctr, NAPA, S 🅿 BP/DQ, 7-11, Shell, 🍴 Applebee's, Baskin-Robbins, Burger King, Carrabba's, Chick-fil-A, ChuckECheese's, Denny', Dunkin Donuts, Firehouse Subs, 5 Guys Burgers, Golden Corral, Grand China Buffet, Hardee's, Hunan Wok, Jade Garden, McDonald's, Salsarita's Cantina, Sonic, Starbucks, Taco Bell, TX Roadhouse, TGIFriday's, Tropical Smoothie Café, Waffle House, Wendy's, Wildwing Café, Woodchick's BBQ, 🛏 Days Inn, Hampton Inn, Quality Inn, Savannah Suites, 🅾 Ⓗ $Tree, Goodyear/auto, Home Depot, Kohl's, Lowe's, Nissan, Rite Aid, Sam's Club/gas, Walgreens, Walmart, USPO, vet
289b a	Greenbrier Pkwy, N 🅿 Citgo, 7-11, WaWa, 🍴 Burger King, Cugini's Pizza, McDonald's, Taco Bell, Subway, Wendy's, 🛏 Cedar Tree Inn, Extended Stay, Hampton Inn, Marriott, Red Roof Inn, Staybridge Suites, Wingate Inn, 🅾 Acura, Chevrolet, Chrysler/Jeep, Dodge, Ford, Hyundai, JoAnn Fabrics, Kia, Lincoln, Mazda, Scion/Toyota, U-Haul, auto repair, vet, S 🅿 7-11, 🍴 Abuelo's Mexican, Baker's Crust, Boston Mkt, Buffalo Wild Wings, Chipotle, Coldstone, Cracker Barrel, Fazoli's, Firehouse Subs, Friendly's, Greenbrier Buffet, Hooters, Jason's Deli, Jersey Mike's Subs, Jimmy John's, Joe's Crabshack, Kyoto Japanese, LoneStar Steaks, McDonald's, Olive Garden, Panera Bread, Paradocks Grill, Pizza Hut, Pop's Diner, Qdoba, Red Robin, Ruby Tuesday, Smokey Bones

289b a	Continued
	BBQ, Starbucks, Subway, Zero's Subs, Zoot's Cafe, 🛏 Aloft Hotel, Comfort Suites, Courtyard, Extended Stay America, Fairfield Inn, Hilton Garden, Homewood Suites, Residence Inn, SpringHill Suites, Sun Suites, 🅾 AT&T, Barnes&Noble, Best Buy, Dillard's, Food Lion, Harris Teeter, Macy's, Marshall's, Michael's, Office Depot, Old Navy, Petsmart, Ross, Sears/auto, Steinmart, Target, TJ Maxx, Verizon, Walgreens, mall
286b a	Indian River Rd, N 🅿 BP/dsl, Gulf, Hess/dsl, SkyMart/dsl, 🍴 Dunkin Donuts, Golden China, Hardee's, 🅾 CVS, S 🅿 Sunoco/dsl, 🍴 Capt D's, Oriental Cuisine, Shoney's, Top's China, Waffle House, 🅾 7-11
285mm	E Branch Elizabeth River
284a	I-264, to Norfolk, to VA Beach (exits left from eb)
284b	Newtown Rd
282	US 13, Northampton Blvd, N 🛏 Quality Inn, Sleep Inn, 🅾 to Chesapeake Bay Br Tunnel
281	VA 165, Military Hwy (no EZ eb return), N 🅿 Shell/dsl, 🛏 EconoLodge, 🅾 Aamco, Chysler/Dodge/Jeep, Fiat, S 🅿 Citgo, 7-11, 🍴 Burger King, Chick-fil-A, Cook-Out, Frank'n Bubba's BBQ, Hooters, IHOP, Jersey Mike's Subs, Jimmy John's, KFC, Logan's Roadhouse, Max&Erma's, Panera Bread, Qdoba, Sonic, Starbucks, Taco Bell, Wendy's, 🛏 Candlewood Suites, Hampton Inn, Hilton, Holiday Inn Express, Holiday Inn, La Quinta, Ramada, Residence Inn, Savannah Suites, 🅾 BJ's Whse, FarmFresh Foods, Firestone/auto, Food Lion, Home Depot, Lowe's, Nissan, Pep Boys, Petco, Petsmart, Target, TJ Maxx, Verizon, Walgreens, Walmart/Subway
279	Norview Ave, N 🅿 K Express, Shell/repair, WaWa, 🍴 China House, Franco's Italian, Golden Corral, Pizza Hut, Wendy's, 🅾 $General, $Tree, Food Lion, K-Mart/gas, 7-11, Tire City, to 🌳 & botanical garden
278	VA 194 S (no EZ return)
277b a	VA 168, to Tidewater Dr, N 🅿 7-11, Shell, 🍴 Bojangles, Hardee's, Ruby Tuesday, 🅾 Advance Parts, Food Lion, Radio Shack, Walmart/Subway, S 🅿 BP
276c	to US 460 W, VA 165, Little Creek Rd, (from wb only), N 🅿 Race Coast Gas, S 🅿 BP, Shell, 🍴 McDonald's, KFC, Papa John's, Pizza Hut, Starbucks, Taco Bell, Wendy's, 🅾 AutoZone, FarmFresh Foods, Kroger, Rite Aid, Walgreens, USPO

NORFOLK

◮E INTERSTATE 64 CONT'D

Exit	Services
276b a	I-564 to Naval Base (exits left from wb)
274	Bay Ave (from wb), to Naval Air Sta
273	US 60, 4th View St, Oceanview, N ◻ 7-11, ◻ Economy Inn, ◻ Oceanview Pier, S ◻ to Norfolk Visitors Ctr, info
272	W Ocean View Ave, N ◻ Willoughby Seafood, S ◻ Sunset Grill
270mm	Chesapeake Bay Tunnel
269mm	**weigh sta eb**
268	VA 169 E, to Buckroe Beach, Ft Monroe, N ◻ Citgo, ◻ Hardee's, McDonald's, ◻ to VA Air&Space Ctr
267	US 60, to VA 143, Settlers Ldg Rd, S ◻ Golden City Chinese, Subway, Tropical Smoothie, ◻ Ⓗ to Hampton U
265c	(from eb), N ◻ Armistead Ave, to Langley AFB
265b a	VA 134, VA 167, to La Salle Ave, N ◻ Citgo, RaceWay, ◻ Super 8, ◻ Home Depot, S ◻ BP, ◻ McDonald's, KFC/Taco Bell, ◻ Ⓗ Advance Parts, Family$
264	I-664, to Newport News, Suffolk
263b a	US 258, VA 134, Mercury Blvd, to James River Br, N ◻ BP, Exxon/dsl, 7-11, Shell, ◻ Abuelo's Mexican, Applebee's, Bojangles, Boston Mkt, Burger King, Chick-fil-A, Chili's, China Wok, Chipotle Mexican, Denny's, Dog House, El Azteca, Firehouse Subs, 5 Guys Burgers, Golden Corral, Hooters, IHOP, Jason's Deli, KFC, McDonald's, New Garden Buffet, Olive Garden, Outback Steaks, Panera Bread, Parklane Rest., Pizza Hut, Quizno's, Rally's, Red Lobster, Starbucks, Subway, Taco Bell, Tokyo Japanese, Waffle House, Wendy's, ◻ Comfort Inn, Courtyard, Days Inn, Embassy Suites, Holiday Inn Express, Quality Inn, Red Roof Inn, Rodeway Inn, ◻ AT&T, Chevrolet/Mazda, $Tree, FarmFresh Foods, Food Lion Ford, GNC, Goodyear/auto, JC Penney, Jo-Ann Fabrics, Macy's, Marshall's, Michael's, NAPA, Nissan, Office Depot, PetCo, Ross, Target, U-Haul, Verizon, Volvo, USPO, Walgreens, Walmart, S ◻ Citgo/dsl, Miller's, ◻ Chick-fil-A, CiCi's Pizza, Coldstone, Cracker Barrel, Domino's, Joe's Crabshack, Lonestar Steaks, Longhorn Steaks, Pizza Hut, Rita's, Sonic, Sports Grill, Waffle House, Zaxby's, ◻ Hampton Bay Suites, Hilton Garden, La Quinta, Relax Inn, Savannah Suites, SpringHill Suites, ◻ Aamco Advance Parts, BassPro Shop, BigLots, BJ's Whse/Subway/gas, CVS Drug, Firestone/auto, Hancock Fabrics, Lowe's, PepBoys, Radio Shack, Toyota/Scion, 7-11
262	VA 134, Magruder Blvd (from wb, no EZ return), N ◻ Exxon, 7-11, ◻ Country Inn&Suites, Suburban Lodge, ◻ Hyundai, Mercedes
261b a	Center Pkwy, to Hampton Roads, N ◻ Hampton Inn (2mi), S ◻ 7-11, Shell, ◻ Anna's Italian, ChuckECheese's, Fortune Garden Chinese, McDonald's, Peking Chinese, Pizza Hut/Taco Bell, Plaza Azteca, Ruby Tuesday, Subway, ◻ $Tree, FarmFresh Foods, Food Lion, GNC, Rite Aid, TJ-Maxx
258b a	US 17, J Clyde Morris Blvd, N ◻ BP, Shell/dsl, ◻ Domino's, Fiorello Italian, New China, Waffle House, ◻ BudgetLodge, Country Inn&Suites, Holiday Inn, Host Inn, PointPlaza Hotel, Quality Inn, ◻ Advance Parts, Family$, Food Lion, 7-11, S ◻ BP, Kangaroo, WaWa, ◻ Angelo's Steaks, Burger King, DQ, KFC/Taco Bell, McDonald's, Papa John's, Starbucks, Subway, Vinny's Pizza, Wendy's, ◻ Motel 6, ◻ Ⓗ Rite Aid, Subaru, VW, museum
256b a	Victory Blvd, Oyster Point Rd, N ◻ BP, Citgo/dsl, Mur

256b a	Continued phy USA/dsl, ◻ Arby's, Burger King, Chick-fil-A, China Ocean, Hardee's, McDonald's, NY Pizza, Pizza Hut, Ruby Tuesday, Saisaki Asian, Sonic, Starbucks, Subway, TX Roadhouse, 3 Amigos Mexican, Uno Grill, ◻ CandleWood Suites, Courtyard, Hampton Inn, Hilton Garden, Staybridge Suites, TownePlace Suites, ◻ $Tree, FarmFresh Foods, GNC, Goodyear, K-Mart, Kroger, RadioShack, Walgreens, Walmart, S ◻ Crestwood Suites, Jameson Inn
255b a	VA 143, to Jefferson Ave, N ◻ Shell/dsl, ◻ Chili's, Cookout, Donato's Pizza, Firehouse Subs, 5 Guys Burgers, Golden Corral, HoneyBaked Ham, Hooters, Jason's Deli, Longhorn Steaks, McDonald's, Moe's SW Grill, Olive Garden, Panera Bread, Papa John's, Red City Buffet, Red Lobster, Smokey Bones BBQ, Starbucks, ◻ Comfort Suites, ◻ Ⓗ Acura, Buick/Cadillac/GMC, Chrysler/Dodge/Jeep, FarmFresh Foods/deli, Fiat, GNC, Home Depot, Kohl's, Lincoln, Lowe's, Michael's, Ross, PetCo, Sam's Club/gas, TJ Maxx, Trader Joe's, Tuesday Morning, Walmart, ◻ S ◻ BP/dsl, Citgo/dsl, Exxon/dsl, ◻ Applebee's, Bailey's Grille, Buffalo Wild Wings, Carrabba's, Cheddar's, Cheeseburger Paradise, Chick-fil-A, Chipotle Mexican, Coldstone, Cracker Barrel, KFC, McDonald's, Outback Steaks, Red Robin, Starbucks, Subway, Taco Bell, TGIFriday's, Waffle House, Wendy's, ◻ Best Western, Comfort Inn, Courtyard, Extended Stay America, Hampton Inn, Microtel, Residence Inn, ◻ Barnes&Noble, Best Buy, Costco, Dick's, Dillard's, Fresh Mkt, JC Penney, Macy's, Petsmart, Sears Auto Ctr, 7-11, Target, Verizon, World Mkt, mall
250b a	to US Army Trans Museum, N ◻ Dodge's Store, Exxon/dsl, 7-11/gas, Sunoco, ◻ China Dragon, Hardee's, Little Italy, Subway, ◻ B&L Auto Repair, to Yorktown Victory Ctr, S ◻ Ft Eustis Inn, Holiday Inn Express, Mulberry Inn, ◻ Newport News Campground/Park (1mi), 7-11
247	VA 143, to VA 238 (no EZ return wb), N ◻ 7-11/gas, ◻ to Yorktown, S ◻ to Jamestown Settlement
243	VA 143, to Williamsburg, exits left from wb, S same as 242a
242b a	VA 199, to US 60, to Williamsburg, N ◻ Day's Hotel/rest., ◻ Best Buy, Dick's, JC Penney, Kohl's, Target, water funpark, to Yorktown NHS, **1 mi** S ◻ 7-11/gas, Shell, Sunoco, ◻ China's Cuisine, Doraldo's Italian, KFC, McDonald's, Sportsmans Grille, Starbucks, Subway, Taco Bell, Wendy's, Whaling Co Rest., ◻ Country Inn&Suites, Courtyard, Marriott/rest., Quality Inn, ◻ camping, to William&Mary Coll, Busch Gardens, to Jamestown NHS
238	VA 143, to Colonial Williamsburg, Camp Peary, **2-3 mi** S on US 60 ◻ 7-11/gas, Shell, Sunoco, ◻ Aberdeen Barn Rest., Applebee's, Arby's, Chili's, Chipotle Mexican, Cracker Barrel, DQ, Firehouse Subs, 5 Guys Burgers, Golden Corral, Hooters, IHOP, Jefferson Steaks, KFC, Kyoto, McDonald's, Pancake House, Pizza Hut, Plaza Azteca, Red Hot&Blue, Ruby Tuesday, Sal's Rest., Seafare Rest., Smokehouse Grill, Subway, Taco Bell, Uno Grille, Wendy's, ◻ America's Inn, Best Western, Comfort Inn, Comfort Suites, Country Inn&Suites, Days Inn, EconoLodge, Embassy Suites, Fairfield Inn, Hampton Inn, Hilton Garden, Holiday Inn/rest., Holiday Inn Express, Homewood Suites, La Quinta, Quality Inn, 1776 Hotel, Sleep Inn, SpringHill Suites, Travelodge, ◻ Ⓗ Anvil Camping (4mi), CVS Drug, Goodyear, K-Mart

VA

HAMPTON

WILLIAMSBURG

◆E INTERSTATE 64 CONT'D

Exit	Services
234	VA 646, to Lightfoot, **1-2 mi N** ⊙ KOA, **2-3 mi S** ⛽ BP/dsl, Exxon/dsl, Shell/dsl, 🍴 Burger King, Chick-fil-A, China Wok, Hardee's, IHOP, McDonald's, Quiznos, Sonic, Starbucks, Subway, 🛏 Greatwolf Lodge, Holiday Inn Express, Super 8, ⊙ H $Tree, Ford, Home Depot, Lowe's, PetCo, Pottery Camping (3mi), Ross, Toyota/Scion, Walmart, USPO
231b a	VA 607, to Norge, Croaker, **N** ⛽ 7-11/gas, ⊙ to York River SP, **1-3 mi S on US 60** ⛽ Shell/dsl, 🍴 Candle Light Kitchen, China Star, Daddy-O's Pizza, Jimmy's Grill, Pizza Hut, 🛏 EconoLodge, ⊙ American Heritage RV Park, CVS Drug, FarmFresh Deli/gas, Food Lion, Honda, Hyundai, USPO
227	VA 30, to US 60, to West Point, Toano, **S** ⛽ BP/dsl (2mi), Shell/dsl, Star/Subway/dsl, 🍴 McDonald's
220	VA 33 E, to West Point, **N** ⛽ Exxon/dsl, Mobil/Circle K/dsl
214	VA 155, to New Kent, Providence Forge, **S** ⛽ Exxon/DQ/dsl, 🍴 Antonio's Pizza, Tops China, ⊙ Colonial Downs Racetrack, camping (8mi)
213mm	🅿 both lanes, full ♿ facilities, 🍴 vending, 🗑 litter barrels, petwalk
211	VA 106, to Talleysville, to James River Plantations, **S** ⛽ ☰☰☰/Subway/dsl/scales/24hr
205	VA 33, VA 249, to US 60, Bottoms Bridge, Quinton, **N** ⛽ Exxon/dsl, Star Express, Valero, 🍴 Julio's Mexican, Maria's Italian, Panda Garden, Pizza Hut, Subway, Wendy's, ⊙ Food Lion, **S** ⛽ FasMart, Shell/dsl, 🍴 Bojangle's, McDonald's, 🛏 Star Motel (3mi), ⊙ Food Lion, Rite Aid
204mm	Chickahominy River
203mm	weigh sta both lanes
200	I-295, N to Washington, S to Rocky Mount, to US 60
197b a	VA 156, Airport Dr, to Highland Springs, **N** ⛽ Shell/dsl, Valero, 🍴 Antonio's Pizza, Domino's, Hardee's, Subway, Tops China, ⊙ Advance Parts, CVS Drug, Farmers Foods, 7-11, **S** ⛽ BP, Chubby's/dsl, 7-11, WaWa, 🍴 Arby's, Aunt Sarah's Pancakes, Burger King, Mexico Rest., Pizza Hut, The Patron, Waffle House, 🛏 Best Value Inn, Best Western, Comfort Inn, Courtyard, EconoLodge, Hampton Inn, Hilton Garden, Holiday Inn, Holiday Inn Express, Homewood Suites, Microtel, Motel 6, Quality Inn, Red Roof Inn, Super 8, ⊙ $General, to ✈
195	Laburnum Ave, **N** ⛽ Citgo, ⊙ auto repair, **S** ⛽ BP, Exxon, 7-11, WaWa, 🍴 Applebee's, Capt D's, Chick-fil-A, China King, CiCi's Pizza, Cracker Barrel, Firehouse Subs, 5 Guys Burgers, Hardee's, IHOP, KFC, Little Caesars, Longhorn Steaks, McDonald's, Olive Garden, Panera Bread, Papa John's, Qdoba Mexican, Red Lobster, Steak'n Shake, Subway, Taco Bell, Tepanyaki Grill, TGIFriday's, Wendy's, 🛏 Hyatt Place, Sheraton, Wyndham Hotel, ⊙ AT&T, CarQuest, CVS Drug, $General, $Tree, GNC, JC Penney, Kroger, Lowe's, Martin's Foods, Michael's, Petsmart, Radio Shack, Sam's Club/gas, Target, Walgreens
193b a	VA 33, Nine Mile Rd, **N** ⛽ Exxon/Subway/dsl, Sunoco/dsl, ⊙ PepBoys, **S** H
192	US 360, to Mechanicsville, **N** ⛽ Citgo/dsl, Shell, 🍴 McDonald's, ⊙ Tuffy Repair, **S** ⛽ Citgo, Shell, 🍴 Church's
190	I-95 S, to Petersburg, 5th St, **N** ⊙ Richmond Nat Bfd Park, **S** 🛏 Hilton Garden, Marriott, ⊙ st capitol, coliseum.

I-64 and I-95 run together. See Interstate 95, exits 76-78

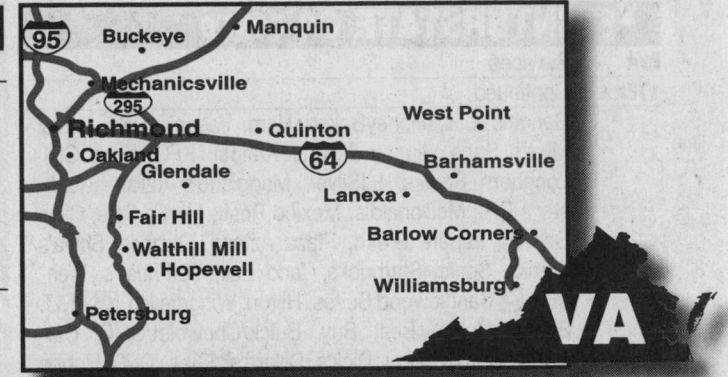

187	I-95 N (exits left from eb), to Washington.
186	I-195, to Powhite Pkwy, from wb, Richmond
185b a	US 33, Staples Mill Rd, Dickens Rd
183c	from wb, US 250 W, Broad St, Glenside Dr N, same as exit 183
183b a	US 250, Broad St E, Glenside Dr S, **N** ⛽ Chevron, Sheetz, 🍴 Bob Evans, Famous Dave's, McDonald's, Olive Garden, Pizza Hut, Taco Bell, TGIFriday's, Waffle House, 🛏 Baymont Inn, Best Western, Embassy Suites, Hampton Inn, Super 8, ValuePlace, ⊙ AutoZone, Honda, Hyundai, K-Mart, Volvo, vet, same as 181, **S** 🍴 Denny's, Plaza Azteca, 🛏 Courtyard, Sheraton, Westin, ⊙ H Home Depot, Target, to U of Richmond
181b a	Parham Rd, **2 mi N on Broad** ⛽ BP/dsl, Citgo, Exxon, Hess, Shell, Wawa, 🍴 Arby's, Bailey's Grill, Buffalo Wild Wings, Burger King, Casa Grande Mexican, Chick-fil-A, ChuckeCheese, CiCi's Pizza, Coldstone, Domino's, Friendly's, Gyros & Subs, Hooters, KFC, LoneStar Steaks, Ma Ma Wok, McDonald's, Nanking Rest., Outback Steaks, Penn Sta Subs, Piccadilly, Quaker Steak, Red Lobster, Shoney's, Starbucks, Superking Buffet, Valacino's, Wendy's, Zorba's Rest., 🛏 Country Inn&Suites, EconoLodge, Quality Inn, Rodeway Inn, Suburban Lodge, ⊙ H Aamco, Acura, Audi/VW, BigLots, BMW/Mini, Books-A-Million, Cadillac, Chrysler/Dodge/Jeep, CVS Drug, $General, $Tree, Food Lion, Hancock Fabrics, Infiniti, Jo-Ann Fabrics, KIA, Marshall's, Merchant's Tire, Mercedes, NAPA, PepBoys, Scion/Toyota, Subaru, Steinmart, TJ Maxx, Tuffy Repair, Verizon, Walgreens
180	Gaskins Rd, **N** ⛽ BP, Shell/dsl, 🍴 Cracker Barrel, O'Charley's, Starbucks, 🛏 Fairfield Inn, Holiday Inn Express, SpringHill Suites, **N on Broad.** ⛽ East Coast, Exxon, 7-11, 🍴 Applebee's, Golden Corral, IHOP, McDonald's, Pizza Hut, Qdoba, Ruby Tuesday, Subway, Taco Bell, Tripp's Rest., ⊙ Advance Parts, AutoZone, Costco/gas, $Tree, Goodyear/auto, Kroger/gas, Lowe's, Martin's Foods, Mazda, Michael's, Sam's Club/gas
178b a	US 250, Broad St, Short Pump, **N** ⛽ Exxon, 7-11, Wawa, 🍴 BurgerWorks, Capital Alehouse, Chipotle Mexican, DQ, Firehouse Subs, 5 Guys Burgers, Hondo's Rest., Joey's Hotdogs, Leonardo's Pizza, Moe's SW Grill, Panera Bread, Silver Diner, Starbucks, 🛏 Comfort Suites, Courtyard, Extended Stay America, Hampton Inn, Hilton Garden, Homestead Suites, Hyatt Place, Marriott, Residence Inn, ⊙ CarMax, CVS Drug, Firestone/auto, Ford, Kia, Marshall's, Ross, Verizon, **S** ⛽ 7-11, Shell, 🍴 Arby's, Bertucci's, Bonefish Grill, Buffalo Wild Wings, Burger King, Capt D's, Cheesecake Factory, Chick-fil-A, Chili's, Chipotle Mexican, Chuy's Mexican, Dave&Buster's, Domino's,

RICHMOND

⛽ = gas   🍴 = food   🛏 = lodging   ⊡ = other   🆁🆂 = rest stop   Copyright 2014 - The NEXT Exit ®

INTERSTATE 64 CONT'D

Exit	Services
178b a	Continued
	Genghis Grill, HoneyBaked Ham, Jason's Deli, Jersey Mike's Subs, Jimmy John's, Kanpai, KFC, Kona Grill, Longhorn Steaks, LJSilver, Maggiano's Italian, McAlister's Deli, McDonald's, Mexico Rest., Mimi's Cafe, Olive Garden, Panera Bread, Plaza Azteca, Quiznos, Shula's Steaks, Sonic, Starbucks, Taco Bell, TGIFriday's, Wendy's, 🛏 Candlewood Suites, Hilton, Wingate Inn, ⊡ AT&T, Barnes&Noble, Best Buy, Buick/Chevrolet/GMC, CarQuest, Crate&Barrel, Dick's, Dillard's, $Tree, GNC, Hobby Lobby, Home Depot, Kohl's, Kroger, Lowe's, Macy's, Martin's Foods, Merchant's Tires, Nissan, Nordstrom, Petco, Petsmart, Radio Shack, Staples, Steinmart, Target, Trader Joe's, Tom Leonard's Mkt, Verizon, Walmart, Whole Foods Mkt, World Mkt
177	I-295, to I-95 N to Washington, to Norfolk, VA Beach, Williamsburg
175	VA 288, Chesterfield
173	VA 623, to Rockville, Manakin, **0-2 mi S** ⛽ Exxon/dsl, Shell/dsl, Valero/Subway/dsl, 🍴 BBQ, Sunset Grill, ⊡ $General, Food Lion
169mm	🆁🆂 both lanes, full ♿ facilities, vending, 🍴🖼 litter barrels, petwalk
167	VA 617, to Goochland, Oilville, **N** ⛽ Exxon/dsl, **S** ⛽ BP/Bullets/dsl
159	US 522, to Goochland, Gum Spring, **N** ⛽ Exxon/dsl, **S** ⛽ BP/DQ/dsl, Citgo
152	VA 629, Hadensville, **1 mi S** ⛽ BP, Liberty, ⊡ repair
148	VA 605, Shannon Hill
143	VA 208, to Louisa, Ferncliff, **7 mi N** ⊡ Small Country Camping, **S** ⛽ Citgo/dsl, Exxon/dsl
136	US 15, to Gordonsville, Zion Crossroads, **N** ⛽ Sheetz/dsl, 🍴 Arby's, Subway, 🛏 Best Western, 🍴 IHOP, ⊡ Lowe's, Walmart, **S** ⛽ BP/McDonald's/dsl/24hr, Exxon/Burger King/dsl, Shell/Blimpie/dsl/scales, 🍴 Crescent Rest.
129	VA 616, Keswick, Boyd Tavern
124	US 250, to Shadwell, **2 mi N** ⛽ BP, Exxon, Hess, Shell, 🍴 Applebee's, Burger King, Guadalajara Mexican, Hardee's, McDonald's, Quiznos, Starbucks, Taco Bell, TipTop Rest., Topeka's Steaks, 🛏 Hilton Garden, ⊡ H Audi/VW, BMW, CarMax, Ford, Giant Foods, KIA, Mercedes, Porsche, Rite Aid, Toyota/Scion, **S** 🛏 Comfort Inn
123mm	Rivanna River
121	VA 20, to Charlottesville, Scottsville, **N** ⛽ BP/Blimpie, **S** ⊡ KOA (10mi), to Monticello
120	VA 631, 5th St, to Charlottesville, **N** ⛽ Exxon/dsl, 🍴 Burger King, Domino's, Hardee's, Pizza Hut/Taco Bell, Waffle House, 🛏 Holiday Inn, Sleep Inn, ⊡ CVS Drug, Food Lion, vet
118b a	US 29, to Lynchburg, Charlottesville, **N** ⛽ BP, ⊡ H to UVA, **services N on US 220**
114	VA 637, to Ivy
113mm	🆁🆂 wb, full ♿ facilities, 🍴 vending, 🖼 litter barrels, petwalk
111mm	Mechum River
108mm	Stockton Creek
107	US 250, Crozet, **1 mi N** ⛽ Citgo, Shell/dsl, **1 mi S** ⊡ Misty Mtn Camping
105mm	🆁🆂 eb, full ♿ facilities, 🍴 vending, 🖼 litter barrels, petwalk

---

104mm	scenic area eb, litter barrels, no truck or buses
100mm	scenic area eb, litter barrels, hist marker, no trucks or buses
99	US 250, to Waynesboro, Afton, **N** 🛏 Colony Motel, ⊡ to Shenandoah NP, Skyline Drive, ski area, to Blue Ridge Pkwy, **S** 🛏 Afton Inn
96	VA 622, to Lyndhurst, Waynesboro, **3 mi N** ⛽ Hess, Shell, 🍴 Tastee Freez 🛏 Quality Inn, ⊡ Waynesboro Camping
95mm	South River
94	US 340, to Stuarts Draft, Waynesboro, **N** ⛽ Exxon/dsl, 7-11/dsl, 🍴 Applebee's, Buffalo Wild Wings, Cracker Barrel, Giovanni's Pizza, Golden Corral, KFC, King Garden, Logan's Roadhouse, Outback Steaks, Panera Bread, Plaza Azteca, Ruby Tuesday, Shoney's, Sonic, Starbucks, Waffle House, Wendy's, 🛏 Best Western, Comfort Inn, Days Inn, Holiday Inn Express, Residence Inn, Super 8, ⊡ H Home Depot, Lowe's, Martin's Food/Drug, Radio Shack, Waynesboro **N** 340 Camping (9mi), Walmart, vet, **S** ⛽ Shell/dsl, 🍴 Chick-fil-A, McAlister's Deli, McDonald's, ⊡ Books-A-Million, GNC, Kohl's, Michael's, Petsmart, Ross, Target, Verizon, museum
91	Va 608, to Stuarts Draft, Fishersville, **N** ⛽ Exxon/Subway (1mi), Shell/dsl, 🛏 Hampton Inn, ⊡ H Eaver's Tires, **S** ⛽ Sheetz/dsl, 🍴 McDonald's, Wendy's, ⊡ Shenadoah Acres Camping (8mi), Walnut Hills Camping (9mi)
89mm	Christians Creek
87	I-81, **N** to Harrisonburg, **S** to Roanoke
I-64 and I-81 run together 20 miles. See Interstate 81, exits 195-220.	
55	US 11, to VA 39, **N** ⛽ Exxon, 🍴 Burger King, Crystal Chinese, Naples Pizza, Ruby Tuesday, Waffle House, 🛏 Best Western, Sleep Inn, Super 8, Wingate Inn, ⊡ $Tree, Radio Shack, Stonewall Jackson Museum, Lowe's, Verizon, Walmart, **S** ⛽ BP/DQ, Marathon/7-11/Subway, 🍴 Applebee's, Country Cookin, Redwood Rest., 🛏 Best Western, Comfort Inn, Country Inn&Suites, Holiday Inn Express, Motel 6, ⊡ Cool Spring Mkt/cafe
50	US 60, rd 623, to Kerrs Creek, Lexington, **5 mi S** 🛏 Days Inn
43	rd 780, to Goshen
35	VA 269, rd 850, Longdale Furnace
33mm	truck 🆁🆂 eb
29	VA 269, VA 42 E, **S** ⛽ Sunoco/dsl
27	US 60 W, US 220 S, VA 629, Clifton Forge, **N** ⊡ to Douthat SP, **S** ⛽ BP/dsl, Exxon, 🍴 Bella Pizza, Pizza Hut (2mi), ⊡ Alleghany Highlands Arts/crafts
24	US 60, US 220, Clifton Forge, **1 mi S** ⛽ Shell/dsl, 🍴 DQ, Hardee's, Vick's Cafe
21	to rd 696, Low Moor, **S** ⛽ Exxon, 🍴 Penny's Diner, Quiznos, 🛏 Oak Tree Inn, ⊡ H
16	US 60 W, US 220 N, to Hot Springs, Covington, **N** ⛽ BP/Subway, Exxon/dsl, Shell, 🍴 Burger King, Cucci's, Mtn View Rest., Western Sizzlin, 🛏 Best Value Inn, Best Western, Holiday Inn Express, Pinehurst Hotel, ⊡ to ski area, **S** 🍴 McDonald's, 🛏 Compare Inn, ⊡ K-Mart, Radio Shack
14	VA 154, to Hot Springs, Covington, **N** ⛽ Exxon/Arby's, Sunoco, 🍴 Hong Kong Chinese, KFC, Little Caesars, LJ Silver, Subway, Wendy's, ⊡ Advance Parts, AutoZone, CVS Drug, $General, Family$, Food Lion, **S** 🍴 Applebee's, China House, Petron Mexican, Trani's Grille, ⊡ $Tree, Walmart
10	US 60 E, VA 159 S, Callaghan, **S** ⛽ Marathon/dsl/LP
7	rd 661

Side labels (vertical): VA / CHARLOTTESVILLE / WAYNESBORO / LEXINGTON / COVINGTON

⬆️E INTERSTATE 64 CONT'D

Exit	Services
2.5mm	Welcome Ctr eb, full ♿ facilities, 🅾🗑 litter barrels, petwalk, no trucks
1	Jerry's Run Trail, **N** to Allegheny Trail
0mm	Virginia/West Virginia state line

⬆️E INTERSTATE 66

Exit	Services
77mm	Constitution Ave, to Lincoln Mem. **I-66 begins/ends in Washington, DC.**
76mm	Potomac River, T Roosevelt Memorial Bridge
75	US 50 W (from eb), to Arlington Blvd, G Wash Pkwy, I-395, US 1, **S** Iwo Jima Mon
73	US 29, Lee Hwy, Key Bridge, to Rosslyn, **N** 🏨 Marriott, **S** 🏨 Holiday Inn
72	to US 29, Lee Hwy, Spout Run Pkwy (from eb, no EZ return), **N** 🅿 Shell, 🏨 Virginia Inn, **S** 🍴 Starbucks, Tarbouch Grill, 🅾 CVS Drug, Starbucks, Giant Foods, Rite Aid, Walgreens
71	VA 120, Glebe Rd (no EZ return from wb), **N** 🅷 **S** 🅿 Sunoco, 🍴 Booeymonger Grill, IHOP, Melting Pot, PF Chang's, 🏨 Comfort Inn, Holiday Inn
69	US 29, Sycamore St, Falls Church, **N** 🅿 Exxon/7-11, **S** 🍴 Rock Cafe, 🏨 EconoLodge
68	Westmoreland St (from eb), same as 69
67	to I-495 N (from wb), to Baltimore, Dulles 🔜
66b a	VA 7, Leesburg Pike, to Tysons Corner, Falls Church, **N** 🅿 Exxon, Sunoco, 🍴 Jason's Deli, Ledo's Pizza, Olive Garden (2mi), Starbucks, Subway, Tara Thai, 🅾 7-11, Trader Joe's, Whole Foods Mkt, **S** 🅿 Citgo, 🍴 Baja Fresh, LJ Silver, McDonald's, Starbucks, 🅾 CVS Drug, Giant Foods, GNC, Kia, Staples, Volvo, vet
64b a	I-495 S, to Richmond
62	VA 243, Nutley St, to Vienna, **S** 🅿 Citgo, 🍴 Starbucks, 🅾 CVS Drug, Michael's, Safeway Foods/gas, Walgreens, **1 mi S** on Lee Hwy. 🅿 Citgo, Liberty, Shell, Sunoco/dsl, 🍴 Chick-fil-A, Dunkin Donuts, IHOP, McDonald's, 🅾 Advance Parts, Chrysler/Dodge/Jeep, Harley-Davidson, Home Depot, Jeep, Radio Shack, 7-11, Subaru
60	VA 123, to Fairfax, **S** 🅿 Exxon, Shell, Sunoco, 🍴 Denny's, Fuddruckers, Hooters, KFC, Outback Steaks, Panera Bread, Red Lobster, 29 Diner, 🏨 Best Western, Hampton Inn, Residence Inn, 🅾 Chevrolet, CVS Drug, Kia, Mazda, NAPA, Rite Aid, Toyota/Scion, to George Mason U
57b a	US 50, to Dulles 🔜 **N** 🍴 Cheesecake Factory, 🏨 Extended Stay America, Marriott, 🅾 JC Penney, Lord&Taylor, Macy's, Sears/auto, mall, access to same as 55, **S** 🅿 BP, Shell/dsl, 🍴 Ruby Tuesday, Wendy's, 🏨 Comfort Inn/rest., Courtyard, SpringHill Suites, 🅾 Ford, Giant Foods, Honda, K-Mart, NRA Museum, Volvo, VW, Walmart
55	Fairfax Co Pkwy, to US 29, **N** 4 Lakes Mall, 🅿 Exxon, Sunoco, 🍴 Applebees, Blue Iguana Café, Burger King, Cantina Italiana, Cooker Rest., Joe's Crabshack, Logan's Roadhouse, Malibu Grill, Olive Garden, Pizza Hut/Taco Bell, Red Robin, Sakura Japanese, Starbucks, Wendy's, 🏨 Hyatt Hotel, Residence Inn, 🅾 🅷 Best Buy, BJ's Whse, Bloom's Foods, GNC, Kohl's, Michael's, Petsmart, Radio Shack, Target, Walmart, Whole Foods Mkt, World Mkt
53b a	VA 28, to Centreville Dulles 🔜 Manassas Museum, **S** same as 52
52	US 29, to Bull Run Park, Centreville, **N** 🅿 Sunoco/dsl, 🅾

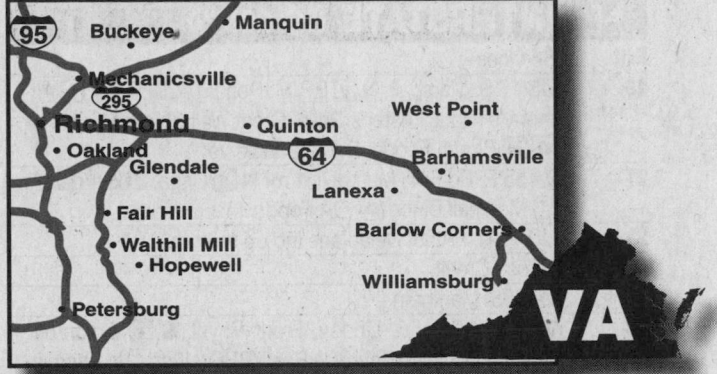

Exit	Services
52	Continued Bull Run Park/RV Dump, Goodyear/auto, **S** 🅿 Exxon, Sunoco/dsl, 🍴 5 Guys Burgers, IHOP, Panda Express, Pizza Hut, Starbucks, Subway, Thai Rest., Tien Asia, 🅾 SpringHill Suites, 🅾 Advance Parts, AT&T, $Tree, Giant Foods, Grand Mart, Radio Shack, Trader Joe's, Walgreens, vet
49mm	🆁🆂 both lanes, full ♿ facilities, 🅾🗑 litter barrels, petwalk
47b a	VA 234, to Manassas, **N** 🅿 Shell/dsl, 🍴 Cracker Barrel, 5 Guys Burgers, Golden Corral, Hershey's Ice Cream, Jerry's Subs, Uno, Wendy's, 🏨 Courtyard, Fairfield Inn, Holiday Inn Express, Sheraton, 🅾 Kohl's, Old Navy, Manassas Nat Bfd, **S** 🅿 BP, Exxon, RaceWay/dsl, 7-11, Shell/repair, Sunoco, 🍴 Arby's, Backyard Grill, Baja Fresh, Bob Evans, Burger King, Cafe Rio, CA Tortilla, Casa Chimayo, Checker's, Chick-fil-A, Chili's, China Jade, Chipotle Mexican, ChuckECheese's, City Grille, Coldstone, Denny's, Domino's, Don Pablo's, El Tolteca, Firehouse Subs, Great American Buffet, Hibachi Buffet, Hooters, KFC, Logan's Roadhouse, Marlin Ray's Grill, McDonald's, Olive Garden, Panda Express, Panera Bread, Papa John's, Pizza Hut, Pollo Campero, Popeye's, Potbelly's, Red Hot&Blue BBQ, Red Lobster, Starbucks, Subway, Taco Bell, TGIFriday's, Wendy's, Wok'n Roll, 🏨 Best Western, Comfort Suites, Hampton Inn, Holiday Inn, Quality Inn, Red Roof Inn, Residence Inn, Super 8, 🅾 Advance Parts, Aldi Foods, AT&T, AutoZone, Barnes&Noble, Best Buy, Bottom$ Foods, Buick/GMC, Burlington Coats, Costco/gas, CVS Drug, Chevrolet, Dick's, $Tree, Family$, Giant Foods, Macy's, Home Depot, Honda, Jo-Ann Fabrics, K-Mart, Lowe's, Macy's, Marshall's, Merchant Auto Ctr, Michael's, NTB, Office Depot, PepBoys, PetCo, Petsmart, Radio Shack, Reines RV Ctr, Ross, Sears/auto, Shopper's Foods, Staples, Toyota, Tuesday Morning, Verizon, Walgreens, Walmart, vet
44	VA 234 S, Manassas, **N** to Bristoe Sta Bfd SP
43b a	US 29, to Warrenton, Gainesville, **N** 🅿 WaWa, **S** 🅿 7-11, Sunoco/dsl, WaWa, 🍴 Burger King, Chick-fil-A, Chili's, Coldstone, Domino's, 5 Guys Burgers, IHOP, Joe's Pizza/Subs, KFC/Pizza Hut/Taco Bell, McDonald's, Mimi's Cafe, MVP Grill, Papa John's, PeiWei, Potbelly, Qdoba, Subway, Wendy's, 🏨 Hampton Inn, ValuePlace, 🅾 Best Buy, CVS Drug, Giant Food/drug, GNC, Goodyear/auto, Lowe's, Petsmart, Target/food, Walgreens
40	US 15, Haymarket, **N** 🅾 Greenville Farms Camping, **S** 🅿 Sheetz/dsl, 🍴 Foster's Grill, Giuseppe's Italian, McDonald's, Papa John's, Subway, Young Chow Cafe, 🅾 Bloom Foods, CVS Drug
31	VA 245, to Old Tavern, **1 mi N** 🅿 BP, 🅾 USPO

◆E INTERSTATE 66 CONT'D

Exit	Services
28	US 17 S, Marshall, **N** 🅿️ BP/McDonald's/dsl, 7-11, 🍴 Anthony's Pizza, Foster's Grille, Great Wall Chinese, Subway, Ⓞ 🅷 Bloom Foods, Radio Shack, vet
27	VA 55 E, Rd 647, Marshall, **1 mi N** 🅿️ Citgo, Exxon/dsl/LP, 🍴 Marshall Diner, Ⓞ IGA Foods
23	US 17 N, VA 55, Delaplane (no eb re-entry)
20mm	Goose Creek
18	VA 688, Markham
13	VA 79, to VA 55, Linden, Front Royal, **S** 🅿️ Exxon/dsl, Shell/7-11, 🍴 Applehouse Rest./BBQ/gifts, Ⓞ to Shenandoah NP, Skyline Drive
11mm	Manassas Run
7mm	Shenandoah River
6	US 340, US 522, to Winchester, Front Royal, **N** 🅿️ Quarle's/Bullet's/dsl, 7-11, 🍴 Applebee's, Checkers, Cracker Barrel, Foster's Grille, Ledo's Pizza, Los Potrillo's, McAlister's Deli, Mikado, Panda Express, Quiznos, Starbucks, TGIFriday's, Vocelli Pizza, Ⓞ Buick/GMC, $Tree, Ford, GNC, Lowe's, PetCo, Staples, Target, Walmart, **S** 🅿️ Exxon/Dunkin Donuts, 7-11, Shell, 🍴 McDonald's, 🛏️ Hampton Inn, Ⓞ Poe's Southfork Camping (2mi)
1b a	I-81, N to Winchester, S to Roanoke
0mm	**I-66 begins/ends on I-81, exit 300.**

◆◆N INTERSTATE 77

Exit	Services
67mm	Virginia/West Virginia state line, East River Mtn
66	VA 598, to East River Mtn
64	US 52, VA 61, to Rocky Gap
62	VA 606, to South Gap
62mm	**Welcome Ctr sb, full** ♿ **facilities, info,** Ⓒ **vending,** 🗑️ **litter barrels, petwalk**
59mm	**🆁🆂 nb, full** ♿ **facilities,** Ⓒ **vending,** 🗑️ **litter barrels, petwalk**
58	US 52, to Bastian, **E** 🅿️ BP/pizza/dsl, **W** 🅿️ Citgo/dsl, Kangaroo
56mm	runaway ramp nb
52	US 52, VA 42, Bland, **E** 🅿️ Citgo, 🍴 Subway, Ⓞ $General, IGA Foods, **W** 🅿️ Kangaroo/DQ/dsl, 🛏️ Big Walker Motel
51.5mm	**weigh sta both lanes**
48mm	Big Walker Mtn
47	VA 717, **6 mi W** Ⓞ to Deer Trail Park/NF Camping
41	VA 610, Peppers Ferry, Wytheville, **E** 🍴 Sagebrush Steaks, 🛏️ Best Western, Sleep Inn, Super 8, **W** 🅿️ Kangaroo/dsl/scales/24hr, TA/BP/Country Pride/Popeye's/Subway/Taco Bell/dsl/scales/24hr/@, 🍴 Southern Diner, 🛏️ Comfort Suites, Country Inn&Suites, Fairfield Inn, Hampton Inn, Ramada Inn
40	I-81 S, to Bristol, US 52 N
	I-77 and I-81 run together 9 mi. See Interstate 81, exits 73-80.
32	I-81 N, to Roanoke
26mm	New River
24	VA 69, to Poplar Camp, **E** 🅿️ Pure, Ⓞ to Shot Tower HP, New River Trail Info Ctr, **W** 🅿️ Marathon/Kangaroo/Subway/dsl
19	VA 620, 🛏️
14	US 58, US 221, to Hillsville, Galax, **E** 🅿️ Citgo/Subway, 🍴 Peking Palace, 🛏️ Red Carpet Inn, Ⓞ 🅷 LakeRidge RV Resort (14mi), **W** 🅿️ BP, Exxon/dsl, Gulf/dsl/24hr, 🍴 Countryside Rest., McDonald's, Pizza Inn, Shoney's,

Exit	Services
14	Continued TCBY, Wendy's, 🛏️ Best Western, Comfort Inn, Hampton Inn, Holiday Inn Express, Quality Inn, Super 8, Ⓞ Chevrolet
8	VA 148, VA 775, to Fancy Gap, **E** 🅿️ Gulf, Marathon/dsl, 🍴 Fancy Gap Cafe (2mi), 🛏️ Lakeview Motel/rest., Ⓞ Chance's Creek RV Ctr, $General, to Blue Ridge Pkwy, **W** 🅿️ BP, Marathon/Kangaroo/dsl, 🛏️ Countryview Inn, Days Inn, Ⓞ KOA (2mi)
6.5mm	runaway truck ramp sb
4.5mm	runaway truck ramp sb
3mm	runaway truck ramp sb
1	VA 620, **E** 🅿️ ♥Love's/McDonald's/Subway/dsl/scales/24hr
.5mm	**Welcome Ctr nb, full** ♿ **facilities, info,** Ⓒ 🗑️ **litter barrels, petwalk**
0mm	Virginia/North Carolina state line

◆N INTERSTATE 81

Exit	Services
324mm	Virginia/West Virginia state line
323	rd 669, to US 11, Whitehall, **E** 🅿️ Exxon, **W** 🅿️ ⨁FLYING J/Denny's/Subway/dsl/LP/scales/24hr
321	rd 672, Clearbrook, **E** 🅿️ Citgo/Old Stone Cafe/dsl, Ⓞ vet
320mm	**Welcome Ctr sb, full** ♿ **facilities,** Ⓒ **vending,** 🗑️ **litter barrels, petwalk**
317	US 11, Stephenson, **E** 🍴 Chick-fil-A, Guan's Garden, Las Trancas, McDonald's, Subway, TX Roadhouse, Tropical Smoothie Café, Ⓞ AT&T, Lowe's, Target, Verizon, **W** 🅿️ Exxon/dsl, 7-11/Burger King, Sheetz, Sunoco/dsl, 🍴 Denny's, Pizza Hut/Taco Bell, 🛏️ Comfort Inn, EconoLodge, Holiday Inn Express (3mi), Ⓞ 🅷 Candy Hill Camping
315	VA 7, Winchester, **E** 🅿️ Exxon, Sheetz, 🍴 Bamboo Garden, Ledo's Pizza, Little Caesars, Sansui Japanese, Sonic, Starbucks, Waffle House, 🛏️ TownePlace Suites, Ⓞ Urgent Care, Chrysler/Dodge/Jeep, $Tree, Goodyear/auto, Martin's Foods/gas, PetCo, Walgreens, **W** 🅿️ Exxon/Dunkin Donuts/Subway, Liberty/dsl, Shell/dsl, 🍴 Arby's, Bros Pizza, Camino Real Mexican, 5 Guys Burgers, KFC, McDonald's, Pizza Hut, Shoney's, Wendy's, 🛏️ Best Value Inn, Hampton Inn, Ⓞ CVS Drug, Family$, Food Lion, Food Maxx, TrueValue
314mm	Abrams Creek
313	US 17/50/522, Winchester, **E** 🅿️ Exxon/Baskin-Robbins/Dunkin Donuts/Subway, Liberty/dsl, Shell/dsl, 🍴 Asian Garden, Chinatown, Cracker Barrel, Golden Corral, Hibachi Grill, IHOP, Los Tolteco's Mexican, TX Steaks, 🛏️ Aloft Hotel, Candlewood Suites, Holiday Inn, Fairfield Inn, Red Roof Inn, Sleep Inn, Super 8, Travelodge, Ⓞ BigLots, Costco/gas, Food Lion, Jo-Ann Fabrics, Nissan, **W** 🅿️ Sheetz, 🍴 Bob Evans, Chick-fil-A, Chili's, China Jade, China Wok, Chipotle Mexican, ChuckECheese's, CiCi's Pizza, 5 Guys Burgers, Glory Days Grill, Jimmy John's, KFC, Longhorn Steaks, McDonald's, Olive Garden, Panera Bread, Perkins, Pizza Hut/Taco Bell, Rancho Mexican, Red Lobster, Ruby Tuesday, TGIFriday's, Waffle House, Wendy's, 🛏️ Best Western, Hampton Inn, Hilton Garden, Wingate Inn, Ⓞ Urgent Care, Belk, Best Buy, Books-A-Million, $Tree, Hobby Lobby, Home Depot, JC Penney, K-Mart, Kohl's, Lowe's, Martin's Foods, Merchants Tire, Michael's, Old Navy, PepBoys, Petsmart, Radio Shack, Ross, Sears/auto, Staples, Target, TJ Maxx, Verizon, Walgreens, Walmart, mall, to Shenandoah U

VA   **WYTHEVILLE**   **WINCHESTER**

⬆N INTERSTATE 81 CONT'D

Exit	Services
310	VA 37, to US 50W, **W** 🅶 Citgo/dsl, Shell/7-11/dsl, 🍴 Carrabba's, McDonald's, Outback Steaks, Subway, 🛏 Best Value Inn, Budget Motel, Country Inn&Suites, Motel 6, 🅾 🄷 Aldi Foods, Camping World, Candy Hill Camping (6mi), CarQuest, Gander Mtn, Honda, NAPA, Volvo, VW
307	VA 277, Stephens City, **E** 🅶 Gulf, 7-11, Shell/Subway/dsl, 🍴 Arby's, Burger King, Butcher Block Cafe, China House, Del Rio Mexicna, Domino's, Ginger Asian, KFC/Taco Bell, McDonald's, Pizza Hut, Roma Italian, Waffle House, Wendy's, 🛏 Comfort Inn, Holiday Inn Express, 🅾 Advance Parts, AutoZone, Curves, Food Lion, Martin's Foods/gas, Rite Aid, vet, **W** 🅶 Exxon/Dunkin Donuts, Sheetz
304mm	**weigh sta both lanes**
302	rd 627, Middletown, **E** 🅶 Exxon/dsl, **W** 🅶 Liberty/dsl, 7-11, 🅾 $General, to Wayside Theatre
300	I-66 E, to Washington, Shenandoah NP, Skyline Dr
298	US 11, Strasburg, **E** 🅶 Exxon/McDonald's/dsl/LP, Shell/7-11/dsl, 🍴 Anthony's Pizza, Arby's, Burger King, Castiglia Italian, Ciro's Pizza, Denny's, Great Wall Buffet, Golden China, 🛏 Fairfield Inn, Hotel Strasburg/rest., Ramada Inn, 🅾 Family$, Food Lion, vet, **W** 🅾 Battle of Cedar Grove Camping, to Belle Grove Plantation
296	US 48, VA 55, Strasburg, **E** 🅾 museums
291	rd 651, Toms Brook, **E** 🛏 Budget Inn (3mi), **W** 🅶 Loves/Arby's/dsl/scales/24hr, Wilco/Hess/DQ/Stuckey's/Subway/dsl/scales/24hr, 🅾 truckwash/repair
283	VA 42, Woodstock, **E** 🅶 Liberty/7-11, Sheetz, Shell/Dunkin Donuts, 🍴 Arby's, Burger King, China Wok, KFC, Las Trancas, McDonald's, Pizza Hut, Taco Bell, Wendy's, 🛏 Comfort Inn, Hampton Inn, Holiday Inn Express, 🅾 🄷 CVS Drug, Family$, Food Lion, Rite Aid, to Massanutten Military Academy, **W** 🅶 Exxon/dsl, Sunoco, 🍴 China Wok, Cracker Barrel, Domino's, Subway, 🅾 $Tree, Ford, Lowe's, NAPA Care, Radio Shack, Walmart
279	VA 185, rd 675, Edinburg, **E** 🅶 Exxon/dsl, Shell/dsl, 🍴 Sal's Italian Bistro, 🅾 Creekside Camping (2mi), auto repair, USPO
277	rd 614, Bowmans Crossing
273	VA 292, RD 703, Mt Jackson, **E** 🅶 Exxon/dsl, Liberty/dsl/scales/24hr, 7-11, Sheetz/dsl/scales/24hr, 🍴 Burger King, China King, Denny's, Subway, 🛏 Super 8, 🅾 $General, Food Lion, USPO, to Mt Jackson Hist Dist
269	rd 730, to US 11, Shenandoah Caverns, **E** 🅶 Shell/dsl
269mm	N Fork Shenandoah River
264	US 211, New Market, **E** 🅶 Exxon/Subway/dsl, Liberty/dsl, Mobil/dsl, Shell/dsl, 🍴 Appleseed's Rest., Burger King, Italian Job, McDonald's, Publick House Rest., 🛏 Budget Inn, Quality Inn, 🅾 Endless Caverns Camping, NAPA Care, USPO, to Shenandoah NP, Skyline Dr, **W** 🅶 7-11, 🛏 Days Inn, 🅾 to New Market Bfd SHP
262mm	🅁 both lanes, full ♿ facilities, 🍴 vending, 🐾 litter barrels, petwalk
257	US 11, VA 259, to Broadway, **E** 🅶 Liberty/7-11/Burger King/dsl, **3-5 mi E** 🛏 KOA, Endless Caverns Camping
251	US 11, Harrisonburg, **W** 🅶 Exxon/dsl, ⛽/Subway/dsl/scales/24hr 🛏 Economy Inn
247b a	US 33, Harrisonburg, **E** 🅶 Citgo/dsl, Exxon/dsl, Royal/dsl, Sheetz/dsl, Shell/dsl, Walmart, 🍴 Applebee's, Aroma Buffet, Bob Evans, Bruster's, Burger King, Chick-fil-A, Chili's, China Jade, Chipotle, CiCi's Pizza, Cook Out,

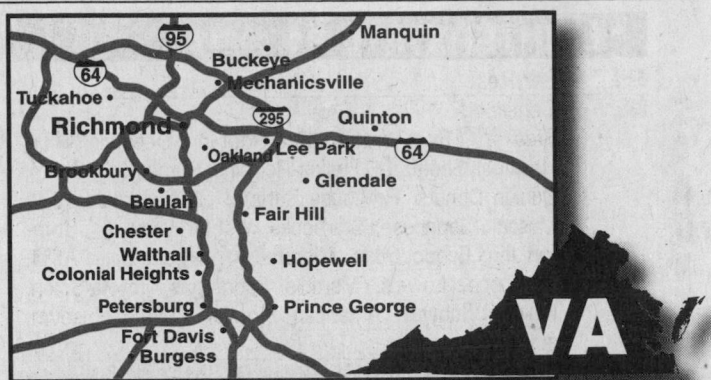

Exit	Services
247b a	Continued Country Cookin, Domino's, El Charro Mexican, Firehouse Subs, 5 Guys Burgers, Golden Corral, Great Wok, IHOP, Jess' Lunch, Jimmy John's, LJ Silver, McAlister's Deli, O'Charley's, Outback Steaks, Panera Bread, Qdoba, Quaker Steak&Lube, Red Lobster, Ruby Tuesday, Shoney's, Subway, Taco Bell, TX Roadhouse, Tilted Kilt, Waffle House, Wendy's, Wood Grill Buffet, 🛏 Best Western, Candlewood Suites, Comfort Inn, Courtyard, EconoLodge, Fairfield Inn, Hampton Inn, Holiday Inn, Motel 6, Quality Inn, Residence Inn, Sleep Inn, 🅾 AT&T, Barnes&Noble, Belk, Best Buy, Books-A-Million, Cadillac/Chevrolet, Costco/gas, Dick's, $Tree, Firestone/auto, Home Depot, JC Penney, K-Mart, Kohl's, Kroger, Lowe's, Martin's Foods/gas, Michael's, Nissan, Old Navy, PetCo, Petsmart, Ross, Staples, Target, TJ Maxx, Verizon, Walmart/McDonald's, to Shenandoah NP, Skyline Dr, **W** 🅶 Exxon/dsl, Liberty, Sheetz, 🍴 Arby's, DQ, Dragon Palace, El Rancho Mexican, Golden China, Hardee's, KFC, Kyoto, Little Caesars, McDonald's, Sam's Hotdogs, Subway, 🅾 🄷 Advance Parts, BigLots, CVS Drug, Food Lion
245	VA 659, Port Republic Rd, **E** 🅶 Campus Corner, Exxon/dsl, Liberty/dsl, Royal/dsl, 🍴 El Charro, Log Cabin BBQ, McDonald's, Subway, 🛏 Days Inn, 🅾 CVS Drug, Food Lion, **W** 🍴 Asian City, Jimmy John's, Starbucks, 🅾 🄷 to James Madison U
243	US 11, to Harrisonburg, 0-2 mi **W** 🅶 BP/dsl, Exxon/dsl, Harrisonburg Travel Ctr/diner/dsl/scales, Liberty, Sheetz/dsl, Shell/7-11/dsl, 🍴 Burger King, Cracker Barrel, McDonald's, Pano's Rest., Pizza Hut, Subway, Taco Bell, 🛏 Come On Inn, Hampton Inn, Holiday Inn Express, Microtel, Ramada Inn, Super 8, 🅾 Advance Parts, AutoZone, CarMax, $General, Family$, Ford, Honda, Hyundai, Kia, Lincoln, Subaru, Toyota/Scion
240	VA 257, rd 682, Mount Crawford, **E** 🅶 Shell/7-11/dsl, 🍴 McDonald's, **W** 🅶 Exxon/Burger King/dsl (1mi)
235	VA 256, Weyers Cave, **E** 🅶 Shell/dsl, **W** 🅶 BP/Subway/dsl, Exxon/dsl, 🅾 Freightliner, antiques, to Grand Caverns
232mm	🅁 both lanes, full ♿ facilities, 🍴 vending, 🐾 litter barrels, petwalk
227	rd 612, Verona, **E** 🅶 BP/Subway/dsl, 🍴 Waffle Inn, **W** 🅶 Citgo/Wendy's/dsl, Exxon/Dunkin Donuts, Shell/dsl, 🍴 Burger King, China City, Ciro's Pizza, Hardee's, McDonald's, 🛏 Knights Inn, 🅾 $General, Food Lion, Good Sam RV Park (3mi), Rite Aid, antiques
225	VA 262, Woodrow Wilson Pkwy, **E** 🛏 Motel 6, **W** 🛏 Days Inn, Holiday Inn/rest.
222	US 250, Staunton, **E** 🅶 BP, Royal/dsl, 🍴 Cracker Barrel, Hometown Grill, McDonald's, Mrs Rowe's Rest., TX

(side margin vertical text) **HARRISONBURG**
(side margin) **VA**

INTERSTATE 81 CONT'D

Exit	Services
222	Continued Steaks, Best Western, Red Roof Inn, Sleep Inn, **W** Hess/dsl, Sheetz, Baskin-Robbins, Burger King, Chili's, Dunkin Donuts, Firehouse Subs, 5 Guys Burgers, KFC, Massaki Japanese, Starbucks, Waffle House, Comfort Inn, EconoLodge, Microtel, Urgent Care, AT&T, AutoZone, Lowe's, Martin's Foods/gas, Toyota/Scion, Walmart/Subway, American Frontier Culture Museum, auto repair
221	I-64 E, to Charlottesville, Skyline Dr, Shenandoah NP.

I-81 and I-64 run together 20 mi.

220	VA 262, to US 11, Staunton, **1 mi W** Citgo, Exxon, Shell, A&W/LJ Silver, Applebee's, Arby's, Burger King, CiCi's Pizza, 88 Buffet, El Puerto, Jimmy John's, Kathy's Rest., Kline's Dairy Bar, Maria's Italian, McDonald's, Papa John's, Red Lobster, Sam's HotDogs, Subway, Taco Bell, Wendy's, Budget Inn, Hampton Inn, Advance Parts, Belk, Buick/GMC, Cadillac/Chevrolet, Chrysler, CVS Drug, Dodge/Jeep, $General, $Tree, Food Lion, Ford, Harley-Davidson, Honda, Hyundai, JC Penney, Kia/Mazda, Kroger, Merchant's Tire/auto, Nissan, Obaugh RV Ctr, Petco, Staples, Subaru, TJ Maxx, Verizon, VW, vet
217	Rd 654, to Mint Spring, Stuarts Draft, **E** BP/Subway/ dsl, Days Inn, **W** Liberty/LP, Marathon/Kangaroo/ dsl/24hr, Relax Inn, KOA
213b a	US 11, US 340, Greenville, **E** BP/Subway, /Arby's/scales/dsl/24hr, Shell, Edelweiss Rest., Hometown Inn, KOA
205	Rd 606, Raphine, **E** Fuel City/Smiley's BBQ/dsl/24hr, Petro/Exxon/Burger King/dsl/scales/24hr/@, Sunoco/dsl, **W** Wilco/Hess/Wendy's/dsl/scales/24hr, Days Inn/ rest., Peterbilt
200	RD 710, Fairfield, **E** BP/McDonald's/dsl, Pure, **W** Exxon/Subway/dsl, Shell/dsl
199mm	**sb, full** **facilities,** **vending,** **litter barrels, petwalk**
195	US 11, Lee Hwy, **E** Maple Hall Country Inn, **W** Exxon/dsl, TA/Shell/Berky's Rest./dsl/scales/24hr/@, Days Inn, Howard Johnson, Quality Inn, Lee-Hi Camping, repair
191	I-64 W (exits left from nb), US 60, to Charleston.

I-81 and I-64 run together 20 mi.

188b a	US 60, to Lexington, Buena Vista, **3-5 mi E** BP, Exxon, Burger King, Hardee's, Buena Vista Inn, $General, Family$, Food Lion, to Glen Maury Park, to Stonewall Jackson Home, Marshall Museum, to Blue Ridge Pkwy, **W** Exxon/dsl, to Washington&Lee U, VMI
180	US 11, Natural Bridge, **E** Relax Inn, Cave Mtn NF, Jellystone Camping, **W** Shell/dsl, Pink Cadillac Diner, Budget Inn, KOA, (180a exits left from sb)
175	US 11 N, to Glasgow, Natural Bridge, **E** Exxon, Natural Bridge Hotel/rest. (2mi), to James River RA, Jellystone Camping
168	VA 614, US 11, Blue Ridge Pkwy, Arcadia, **E** Shell, Mtn View Rest., Wattstull Inn, Middle Creek Camping (6mi), **2 mi W** Exxon, Burger King, Rancho Veijo
167	US 11 (from sb), Buchanan
162	US 11, Buchanan, **E** Exxon/dsl, to BR Pkwy, **W** Citgo/Subway
158mm	**sb, full** **facilities,** **vending,** **litter barrels, petwalk**

156	RD 640, to US 11, **E** Exxon/Brugh's Mill/dsl
150	US 11/220, to Fincastle, **E** Dodge's/dsl, Marathon/ Kangaroo/dsl/24hr, /Subway/dsl/24hr, TA/BP/ Country Pride/dsl/scales/24hr/@, Bella Pizza, Country Cookin, Cracker Barrel, Hardee's, McDonald's, Shoney's, Taco Bell, Waffle House, Comfort Inn, Holiday Inn Express, Quality Inn, Red Roof Inn, Travelodge, Berglund RV Ctr, $General, truckwash, **W** BP/dsl, Exxon/dsl, Sunoco, Bojangles, Little Caesars, Pizza Hut, Rancho Viejo Mexican, 3 Lil Pigs BBQ, Wendy's, Howard Johnson, Super 8, Curves, Kroger/gas, Verizon, vet
149mm	**weigh sta both lanes**
146	VA 115, Cloverdale, **E** BP, Exxon, Shell/dsl, El Rodeo Mexican, Hardees, McDonald's, Subway, Country Inn&Suites, Days Inn/rest., Fairfield Inn, Hampton Inn, Camping World, CVS, Gander Mtn, to Hollins U
143	I-581, US 220, to Roanoke, Blue Ridge Pkwy (exits left from sb) **1 mi E** Kroger Gas/dsl, El Toreo, Subway, Waffle House, Howard Johnson, Quality Inn, Super 8, Honda, **2-3 mi E on Hershberger** Exxon, Murphy USA/dsl, Shell, Abuelo's Mexican, Applebee's, Buffalo Wild Wings, Carrabba's, Cheddar's, Chick-fil-A, Coldstone, Hardee's, IHOP, Logan's Roadhouse, Longhorn Steaks, O'Charley's, Olive Garden, Panera Bread, Penn Sta Subs, Red Palace Chinese, Red Robin, Ruby Tuesday, Shaker's, Smokey Bones BBQ, Starbucks, TGI- Friday's, Zaxby's, Best Western, Comfort Inn, Courtyard, Extended Stay America, Hampton Inn, Holiday Inn, Hyatt Place, MainStay Suites, Residence Inn, Sheraton, AT&T, Barnes&Noble, Belk, Best Buy, BigLots, Dick's, $Tree, Home Depot, JC Penney, Macy's, NTB, Old Navy, Petsmart, Sears/auto, Staples, Target, U-Haul, Verizon, Walmart, mall
141	VA 419, Salem, **E** BP, Liberty/7-11/dsl, Marathon/Burger King, Hardee's, IHOP, Starbucks, Subway, Days Inn, Holiday Inn Express, La Quinta, Quality Inn, Chevrolet, GNC, Kroger/gas, **W** BP/Subway/dsl, Citgo
140	VA 311, Salem **1 mi E** Mac&Bob's Cafe, **1 mi W** Hanging Rock Grill/golf
137	VA 112, VA 619, Salem, **E** BP, Citgo/dsl, Exxon/dsl, Go- Mart, Marathon, Sheetz, Anthony's Cafe, Applebees, Arby's, Bojangles, Burger King, Chick-fil-A, Denny's, Dynasty Buffet, El Rodeo Mexican, Firehouse Subs, Hardee's, K&W Cafeteria, KFC, Mamma Maria Italian, McDonald's, Omelette Shoppe, Pizza Hut, Quiznos, Rancho Veijo, Shoney's, Starbucks, Subway, Taco Bell, Tokyo Express, Wendy's, Zaxby's, Comfort Suites, EconoLodge, Quality Inn, Super 8, Aamco, Advance Parts, AutoZone, BigLots, $General, $Tree, Food Lion, Goodyear, K-Mart, Kroger/gas, Lowe's, Merchant's Tire, O'Reilly Parts, Snyder's RV, Verizon, Walgreens, Walmart/Subway, vet, **W** Holiday Inn, Howard Johnson
132	VA 647, to Dixie Caverns, **E** Shell (2mi), Blue Jay Hotel, Dixie Caverns Camping, st police
129mm	**nb, full** **facilities,** **vending,** **litter barrels, petwalk**
128	US 11, VA 603, Ironto, **E** Shell, **W** Exxon/Dixie's/ Subway/dsl/24hr
118c b a	US 11/460, Christiansburg, **E** Shell/dsl, Denny's, Cracker Barrel, Days Inn, Fairfield Inn, Holiday Inn Express, Quality Inn, Super 8, **W** Exxon/dsl, Liberty/7-11/ dsl, Shell, Country Cookin, Hardee's, McDonald's,

INTERSTATE 81 CONT'D

Exit	Services
118c b a	Continued
	Pizza Hut, Ruby Tuesday, Waffle House, Wendy's, 🏠 EconoLodge, Rodeway Inn, ⊙ Ⓗ Advance Parts, Chevrolet, Chrysler/Dodge/Jeep, $General, Food Lion, Ford, Honda, Hyundai, Kia, Subaru, Toyota/Scion, to VA Tech
114	VA 8, Christiansburg, **E** to Blue Ridge Pkwy, 0-1 mi **W** ⓖ Citgo/dsl, 🍴 Burger King, Pizza Inn, Subway, 🏠 Budget Inn, ⊙ $General Mkt, Family$, tires, USPO
109	VA 177, VA 600, **E** ⊙ Ⓗ 0-2 mi **W** ⓖ Marathon, Sunoco/dsl, 🏠 Best Western, Comfort Inn, La Quinta, Super 8 (2mi), ⊙ Buick/Cadillac/Chevrolet
107mm	🅁🅂 both lanes, full ♿ facilities, Ⓒ vending, 🗑 litter barrels, petwalk
105	VA 232, RD 605, to Radford, **W** ⓖ Marathon/dsl, 2-4 mi **W** ⓖ Citgo, 🍴 Sal's Italian, 🏠 Executive Motel, ⊙ museum
101	RD 660, to Claytor Lake SP, **E** 🏠 Claytor Lake Inn, Sleep Inn, ⊙ repair, **W** ⓖ Marathon/DQ/dsl, Shell/Omelette Shoppe/Taco Bell/dsl/scales/@
98	VA 100 N, to Dublin, **E** ⓖ Exxon/Subway/dsl, Marathon, 🍴 Bojangles, Shoney's, 🏠 Comfort Inn, Hampton Inn, Holiday Inn Express, **W** ⓖ Liberty/Blimpie/dsl, Marathon/dsl, 🍴 Arby's, Burger King, El Ranchero Mexican, Fatz Cafe, McDonald's, Subway, Waffle House, Wendy's, 🏠 Super 8, ⊙ Ⓗ $General, O'Reilly Parts, Walmart/Subway, vet, to Wilderness Rd Museum
94b a	VA 99 N, to Pulaski, 0-3 mi **W** ⓖ BP, Exxon/dsl, Hess, 🍴 China Wall, Compadre's Mexican, Domino's, Hardee's, KFC, Kimono Japanese, Little Caesars, McDonald's, Pizza Hut, Sonic, Subway, Taco Bell, Wendy's, ⊙ Ⓗ Advance Parts, CVS, Curves, $General, Family$, Food Lion, Goodyear/auto, O'Reilly Parts, Rite Aid
92	Rd 658, to Draper, **E** ⓖ BP, ⊙ to New River Trail SP
89b a	US 11 N, VA 100, to Pulaski, **E** auto/truck repair
86	Rd 618, Service Rd, **W** ⓖ Sunoco/Appletree Rest./dsl, ⊙ repair
84	Rd 619, to Grahams Forge, **W** ⓖ Kangaroo/DQ/dsl/24hr, 🛢Loves/Chester Fried/Subway/dsl/scales/24hr, 🍴 Italian Garden, 🏠 Fox Mtn Inn, Trail Motel
81	I-77 S, to Charlotte, to Blue Ridge Pkwy, Galax
I-81 S and I-77 N run together 9 mi.	
80	US 52 S, VA 121 N, to Ft Chiswell, **E** ⓖ BP/Burger King/dsl, ✈FLYING J/Denny's/dsl/scales/24hr/@, 🍴 Wendy's, 🏠 Hampton Inn, Super 8, ⊙ Blue Beacon, Ft Chiswell RV Park, NAPA, **W** ⓖ Kangaroo/dsl, Marathon/dsl, Valero, 🍴 McDonald's, 🏠 Comfort Inn, ⊙ Speedco
77	Service Rd, **E** ⓖ ✈FLYING J/Denny's/dsl/scales/LP/RV Dump/24hr, Kangaroo/Subway/dsl/24hr, Wilco/Hess/dsl/LP, 🍴 Burger King, ⊙ KOA, **W** ⓖ Exxon/dsl, Wilco/Hess/Arby's/DQ/dsl/scales/24hr, ⊙ Truck'o Mat, st police
73	US 11 S, Wytheville, **E** ⓖ BP, Citgo/Quiznos/dsl, Go-Mart, Kangaroo/dsl, 🍴 Applebee's, Bob Evans, Cracker Barrel, El Puerto Mexican, Hardee's, LJ Silver, Ocean Bay Rest., Papa John's, Peking Chinese, Pizza Hut, Shoney's, Smokey's BBQ, Sonic, Waffle House, Wendy's, 🏠 Budget Host, Days Inn, EconoLodge, Knights Inn, La Quinta, Motel 6, Quality Inn, Red Roof Inn, Travelodge, ⊙ Ⓗ AutoZone, Buick/Chevrolet/GMC, CVS Drug, $General, Food Lion, Ford, Goodyear/auto, Harley-Davidson, K-Mart, Nissan, Rite Aid, Subaru

WYTHEVILLE *(side tab)*

I-81 N and I-77 S run together 9 mi

72	I-77 N, to Bluefield, 1 mi N, I-77 exit 41 **E** 🍴 Sagebrush Steaks, 🏠 Best Western, Sleep Inn, Super 8, **W** ⓖ Kangaroo/dsl/24hr, TA/Country Pride/Popeye's/Subway/Taco Bell/dsl/scales/24hr/@, 🍴 Southern Diner, 🏠 Comfort Suites, Country Inn&Suites, Fairfield Inn, Hampton Inn, Ramada/rest.
70	US 21/52, Wytheville, **E** ⓖ BP/dsl, Sheetz/dsl, 🍴 Bojangles, China Wok, El Patio Mexican, KFC/Taco Bell, Little Caesars, McDonald's, Ruby Tuesday, Starbucks, Subway, Tokyo Japanese, Wendy's, ⊙ Ⓗ AT&T, $Tree, Food Lion, Lowe's, PetCo, Verizon, Walmart/Subway, **W** ⓖ Kangaroo, 🏠 Comfort Inn
67	US 11 (from nb, no re-entry), to Wytheville
61mm	🅁🅂 nb, full ♿ facilities, Ⓒ vending, 🗑 litter barrels, petwalk, NO TRUCKS
60	VA 90, Rural Retreat, **E** ⓖ Shell/dsl, Spirit/dsl, 🍴 Dutch Pantry, El Ranchero, McDonald's, ⊙ $General, to Rural Retreat Lake, camping
54	rd 683, to Groseclose, **E** ⓖ Sunoco/dsl, 🍴 The Barn Rest., 🏠 Relax Inn, ⊙ Settler's Museum
53.5mm	🅁🅂 sb, full ♿ facilities, Ⓒ vending, 🗑 litter barrels, petwalk
50	US 11, Atkins, **W** ⓖ Marathon/Subway/dsl/24hr, Exxon, 🏠 Comfort Inn, ⊙ NAPA Care
47	US 11, to Marion, **W** ⓖ Gas'N Go, Shell/dsl, Valero/Subway, 🍴 Arby's, KFC/Taco Bell, Little Caesars, LJ Silver, McDonald's, Pizza Hut, Puerto Mexican, Sonic, Wendy's, 🏠 Best Value Inn, EconoLodge, Travel Inn, ⊙ Ⓗ Advance Parts, AutoZone, Buick/Chevrolet/GMC, CVS Drug, $General, $Tree, Family$, Food City, Food Lion, Ford, Ingles, Marion Drug, O'Reilly Parts, Rite Aid, Walgreens, Walmart, to Hungry Mother SP (4mi)
45	VA 16, Marion, **E** ⓖ Valero/dsl, 🍴 AppleTree Rest., ⊙ to Grayson Highlands SP, Mt Rogers NRA, **W** ⓖ Sunoco, 🍴 Hardee's, ⊙ NAPA, USPO
44	US 11, Marion, **W** ⓖ Marathon/dsl
39	US 11, rd 645, Seven Mile Ford, **E** 🏠 Budget Inn, **W** ⊙ Interstate Camping
35	VA 107, Chilhowie, **E** 🍴 Chilhowie Pizza, Hardees, 🏠 Knights Inn, **W** ⓖ Exxon/dsl, Gas'N Go, Shell/dsl, 🍴 McDonald's, Riverfront Rest., Subway, 🏠 Budget Inn (1mi), ⊙ Curves, $General, Food City, Greever's Drugs, USPO
32	US 11, to Chilhowie
29	VA 91, to Damascus, Glade Spring, **E** ⓖ Marathon/Subway/dsl, Petro/rest./dsl/24hr/@, Valero/Wendy's, 🍴 Giardino's Italian, Pizza+, 🏠 EconoLodge, Super 8, ⊙ $General, Peterbilt, **W** ⓖ Exxon, Shell/dsl, Spirit, ⊙ CarQuest, vet

MARION *(side tab)*

🅖 = gas 🍴 = food 🛏 = lodging 🅞 = other 🆁🆂 = rest stop Copyright 2014 - The NEXT Exit ®

⬆️N INTERSTATE 81 CONT'D

Exit	Services
26	rd 737, Emory, **W** 🍴 Mikado's (1mi), 🅞 to Emory&Henry Coll
24	VA 80, Meadowview Rd, **W** auto repair
22	rd 704, Enterprise Rd, **E** 🅖 Brown's Pantry/dsl, 🅞 🅷
19	US 11/58, to Abingdon, **E** 🅖 Shell/Subway/dsl, 🍴 DQ, McDonald's, Pizza+, 🅞 Urgent Care, Lowe's, vet, to Mt Rogers NRA, **W** 🅖 BP/dsl, Citgo/Huddle House, Exxon/dsl, 🍴 Bella's Pizza, Burger King, Cracker Barrel, DaVinci's Cafe, Harbor House Seafood, Wendy's, 🛏 Alpine Motel, Best Value Inn, Holiday Inn Express, Quality Inn
17	US 58A, VA 75, Abingdon, **E** 🍴 Domino's, LJ Silver, 🛏 Hampton Inn, **W** 🅖 Exxon, Gas'n Go, 🍴 Arby's, Charley's Subs, China Wok, Hardee's, KFC, Los Arcos, McDonald's, Papa John's, Pizza Hut, Shoney's, Subway, Taco Bell, Wendy's, 🛏 Super 8, 🅞 🅷 Advance Parts, Food City, GNC, Kroger, K-Mart, Radio Shack
14	US 19, VA 140, Abingdon, **W** 🅖 BP/dsl, Exxon, Shell/dsl, 🍴 McDonald's, Milano's Italian, Moon Dog Cafe, Subway, 🛏 Comfort Inn, Comfort Suites, 🅞 Chevrolet, Ford/Lincoln, Riverside Camping (10mi)
13.5mm	**Truckers Only** 🆁🆂 nb, full ♿ facilities, 🚻 vending, 🗑 litter barrels
13	VA 611, to Lee Hwy, **W** 🅖 Shell/dsl, 🅞 Kenworth, Mack, Volvo
10	US 11/19, Lee Hwy, **W** 🅖 BP/dsl, Exxon, Shell/dsl, 🛏 Deluxe Inn, Economy Inn, Evergreen Inn, Red Carpet Inn
7	Old Airport Rd, **E** 🅖 Shell/dsl, 🍴 Bojangles, Cheddar's, Cracker Barrel, Sonic, 🛏 La Quinta, **W** 🅖 Marathon, Sunoco/Wendy's, Valero/dsl, 🍴 Bellecino's, Charley's Subs, Chick-fil-A, Chili's, Cook-Out, DQ, Domino's, El Patio Mexican, Golden Corral, IHOP, Jersey Mike's Subs, Kobe Japanese, Logan's Roadhouse, Los Arcos, Mellow Mushroom, O'Charley's, Olive Garden, Outback Steaks, Pal's Drive-In, Perkins, Pizza Hut, Red Lobster, Ruby Tuesday, Starbucks, Subway, Taco Bell, 🛏 Courtyard, Holiday Inn, Microtel, Motel 6, 🅞 Advance Parts, AutoZone, Best Buy, Books-A-Million, $Tree, $General, Food City, Home Depot, Lowe's, Office Depot, Old Navy, Petsmart, Ross, Sam's Club/gas, Target, TJ Maxx, Verizon, Walmart, Sugar Hollow Camping
5	US 11/19, Lee Hwy, **E** 🅖 BP, Shell, 🍴 Arby's, Burger King, Hardee's, KFC, LJ Silver, McDonald's, Shoney's, 🛏 Budget Inn, Super 8, 🅞 Family$, Harley-Davidson, USPO, **W** 🅖 Exxon/dsl, 🛏 Comfort Inn, 🅞 Blevins Tire, Buick/GMC, Lee Hwy Camping
3	I-381 S, to Bristol, **1 mi E** 🅖 Shell/dsl, Zoomers/dsl, 🍴 Applebee's, Arby's, Krystal, 🛏 EconoLodge
1b a	US 58/421, Bristol, **1 mi E** 🅖 Exxon, 5 Mart, Shell, Zoomers, 🍴 Burger King, Capt D's, Chick-fil-A, Chinese Family Buffet, KFC, McDonald's, Pizza Hut, Sonic, Subway, Taco Bell, Wendy's, 🛏 Knights Inn, 🅞 🅷 Urgent Care, Belk, Chrysler/Dodge/Jeep, CVS Drug, Family$, JC Penney, K-Mart, Kroger/dsl, Sears/auto, Toyota/Scion, Verizon, Walgreens, mall, vet
0mm	Virginia/Tennessee state line, **Welcome Ctr nb, full** ♿ **facilities, info,** 🚻 **vending,** 🗑 **litter barrels, petwalk, No Trucks**

⬆️N INTERSTATE 85

Exit	Services
69mm	**I-85 begins/ends on I-95.**
69	US 301, I-95 N, Wythe St, Washington St, Petersburg

Exit	Services
68	I-95 S, US 460 E, to Norfolk, Crater Rd
65	Squirrel Level Rd, **E** 🅞 to Richard Bland Coll, **W** 🅖 BP
63b a	US 1, to Petersburg, **E** 🅖 Chubby's/dsl, Exxon/KFC/dsl, Shell/Burger King/dsl, 🍴 Hardee's, Waffle House, 🛏 Holiday Inn Express, **W** 🅖 BP, 🍴 McDonald's
61	US 460, to Blackstone, **E** 🅖 EastCoast/Subway/dsl/LP/e85, 🍴 Huddle House, **W** 🍴 Giuseppe's Pizza, 🅞 🗑 auto repair
55mm	🆁🆂 both lanes, full ♿ facilities, 🚻 🗑 litter barrels, vending, petwalk
53	VA 703, Dinwiddie, **W** 🅖 Exxon/dsl, 🍴 Fats BBQ, 🅞 to 5 Forks Nat Bfd
52mm	Stony Creek
48	VA 650, DeWitt
42	VA 40, McKenney, **W** 🅖 Citgo, Exxon, 🅞 auto repair
40mm	Nottoway River
39	VA 712, to Rawlings, **W** 🅖 Davis TC/Exxon/Dunkin Donuts/Subway/dsl/scales/24hr, Racine, 🛏 Nottoway Motel/rest.
34	VA 630, Warfield, **W** 🅖 Exxon/dsl
32mm	🆁🆂 both lanes, full ♿ facilities, 🚻 🗑 litter barrels, vending, petwalk
28	US 1, Alberta, **W** 🅖 Exxon, 🅞 Family Dollar
27	VA 46, to Lawrenceville, **E** 🅞 to St Paul's Coll
24	VA 644, to Meredithville
22mm	**weigh sta both lanes**
20mm	Meherrin River
15	US 1, to South Hill, **E** 🅖 Citgo, **W** 🅖 Loves/Subway/McDonald's/dsl/scales/24hr, Valero/dsl, 🍴 Kahill's Rest.
12	US 58, VA 47, to South Hill, **E** 🅖 BP/Quizno's/Stucky's/dsl, RaceWay, Shell/dsl, 🍴 Applebee's, Arby's, Bojangles, Domino's, Glass House Grill, Sonic, 🛏 Best Western, Comfort Inn, Fairfield Inn, Hampton Inn, 🅞 $Tree, Verizon, Walmart/Subway, **W** 🅖 Exxon/dsl, Kangaroo/dsl, 🍴 Brian's Steaks, Burger King, Cracker Barrel, Down Home Buffet, Hardee's, KFC/Taco Bell, McDonald's, New China, Pizza Hut, Subway, Wendy's, 🛏 Quality Inn, 🅞 🅷 AutoZone, CVS Drug, $General, Family$, Food Lion, Home Depot, Roses
4	VA 903, to Bracey, Lake Gaston, **E** 🅖 BP/Subway/dsl, Exxon/Simmon's/dsl/scales/24hr/@, 🍴 K St. Café, Huddle House, 🅞 Americamps Camping (5mi), **W** 🅖 Shell/Pizza Hut/Quizno's, 🛏 Lake Gaston Inn
3mm	Lake Gaston
1mm	**Welcome Ctr nb, full** ♿ **facilities,** 🚻 🗑 🚻**, litter barrels, vending, petwalk**
0mm	Virginia/North Carolina state line

⬆️N INTERSTATE 95

Exit	Services
178mm	Virginia/Maryland state line, Potomac River, **W** Wilson Mem Br
177c b a	US 1, to Alexandria, Ft Belvoir, **E** 🍴 Great American Steaks, 🛏 Budget Host, Hampton Inn, Red Roof Inn, Relax Inn, 🅞 Chevrolet, Chrysler/Dodge/Jeep, **W** 🅖 Hess, Liberty/repair
176b a	VA 241, Telegraph Rd, **E** 🅖 Hess/dsl, **W** 🛏 Courtyard, Holiday Inn, Homestead Suites, 🅞 Staples
174	Eisenhower Ave Connector, to Alexandria
173	rd 613, Van Dorn St, to Franconia, **E** 🛏 Comfort Inn, **1 mi W** 🅖 Exxon, Shell, 🍴 Dunkin Donuts, Jerry's Subs, McDonald's, Quizno's, Red Lobster, 🅞 Aamco, Giant Foods, NTB

Side labels: **A B I N G D O N** · **VA** · **P E T E R S B U R G** · **S O U T H   H I L L** · **D C   A R E A**

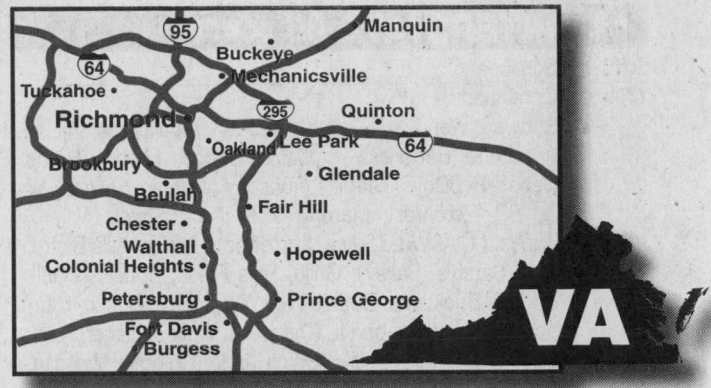

INTERSTATE 95 CONT'D ⬆N

Exit	Services
170a	I-495 N, **I-495 & I-95 N run together to MD., to Rockville**
170b	I-395 N, to Washington
169b a	rd 644, Springfield, Franconia, **E** 🍴 Bertucci's, Dunkin Donuts, Silver Diner, Starbucks, Subway, TGIFriday's, 🏨 Best Western, Courtyard, Extended Stay America, Hampton Inn, Hilton, 🅞 🅷 AT&T, Barnes&Noble, Best Buy, Family$, Firestone/auto, Ford, Home Depot, JC Penney, Macy's, Michael's, Nissan, Old Navy, Petsmart, Staples, Subaru, Target, mall, **W** 🅖 BP, Shell, Sunoco, 🍴 Bob Evans, Chipotle Mexican, Deliah's Grill, Domino's, Dunkin Donuts, 5 Guys Burgers, KFC, McDonald's, Outback Steaks, Quizno's, Starbucks, Subway, Tokyo Japanese, 🏨 Holiday Inn Express, Motel 6, Residence Inn, TownePlace Suites, 🅞 CarQuest, CVS Drug, Dodge/Jeep, Giant Foods, Goodyear/auto, K-Mart, Mr Tire, Toyota/Scion, Verizon, VW, vet
167	VA 617, Backlick Rd (from sb), **W** 🅖 InterFuel/dsl
166b a	VA 7100, Newington, to Ft Belvoir, **E** 🅖 Pkwy Express, 🍴 Wendy's, 🅞 NTB, U-Haul, **W** 🅖 Exxon, 🅞 Costco
163	VA 642, Lorton, **E** 🅖 Shell, Sunoco, **W** 🅖 Shell, 🍴 Antoneli's Pizza, Burger King, McDonald's, 🏨 Comfort Inn
161	US 1 S (exits left from sb, no reentry nb), to Ft Belvoir, Mt Vernon, Woodlawn Plantation, Gunston Hall
160.5mm	Occoquan River
160b a	VA 123 N, Woodbridge, Occoquan, **E** 🅖 BP, Sunoco, 🍴 Dixie Bones BBQ, Subway, Taco Bell, 🏨 EconoLodge, Hampton Inn, Quality Inn, Rodeway Inn, 🅞 Aldi Foods, Radio Shack, **W** 🅖 Exxon/dsl, Fast Fuels, Shell, 🍴 KFC, McDonald's, VA Grill, Wendy's, 🅞 7-11, same as 161
158b a	VA 294, Prince William Pkwy, Woodbridge, **W** 🅖 Exxon, Shell, 7-11, Sunoco, WaWa, 🍴 Boston Mkt, Chick-fil-A, Chipotle Mexican, ChuckeCheese, Coldstone, Famous Dave's BBQ, Hooters, IHOP, Macaroni Grill, McDonald's, Old Country Buffet, On-the-Border, Panda Express, Panera Bread, Quiznos, Red Lobster, Smokey Bones BBQ, Starbucks, Taco Bell, TGIFriday's, UNO Grill, Wendy's, 🏨 Country Inn&Suites, Courtyard, Fairfield Inn, Holiday Inn Express, Residence Inn, Sleep Inn, SpringHill Suites, 🅞 Advance Parts, Best Buy, CarMax, $Tree, Lowe's, Michael's, Office Depot, Petsmart, Sam's Club/gas, Shopper's Foods, Target, Verizon, Walmart/Subway
156	VA 784, Potomac Mills, **E** 🅖 Shell, 🍴 Zoe's Kitchen, 🅞 🅷 AT&T, Wegmans, to Leesylvania SP, **W** 🅖 Mobil, Shell, Sunoco, 🍴 Bamboo Buffet, Bob Evans, Burger King, Char Broil Grill, Chili's, China King Buffet, Denny's, DQ, El Charro Mexican, Guapo's, La Azteca Latina, McDonald's, Olive Garden, Outback Steaks, Popeye's, Silver Diner, Subway, Wendy's, 🏨 Best Western, Wytestone Suites, 🅞 Books-A-Million, Costco/gas, Family$, Firestone/auto, JC Penney, Jo-Ann Fabrics, K-Mart, Marshalls, NAPA, Nordstrom's, NTB, Potomac Mills Outlets/Famous Brands, Staples, TJ Maxx, Tuesday Morning, U-Haul, vet
154mm	🆁🆂/weigh sta both lanes
152	VA 234, Dumfries, to Manassas, **E** 🅖 BP/dsl, Shell/dsl, Texaco/Subway, 🍴 Applebee's, China One, 5 Guys Burgers, Joe's Place Pizza, KFC, McDonald's, Ruby Tuesday, Taco Bell, 🏨 Sleep Inn, Super 8, 🅞 AutoZone, $Tree, NAPA, Weems-Botts Museum, **W** 🅖 Exxon, 7-11, 🍴 Cracker Barrel, IHOP, Jerry's Subs, MontClair Rest.,
152	Continued Panera Bread, Subway, Tiziano Italian, Waffle House, 🏨 Comfort Inn, Days Inn, EconoLodge, Hampton Inn, Holiday Inn, 🅞 Prince William Camping, Rite Aid, Shoppers Foods, Target
150	VA 619, Quantico, to Triangle, **E** 🅖 7-11, 🍴 Dunkin Donuts, 🏨 Ramada Inn, 🅞 to Marine Corps Base, **W** Prince William Forest Park
148	to Quantico, **2 mi E** 🅖 Gulf/dsl, 🏨 Spring Lake Motel, 🅞 to Marine Corps Base
143b a	to US 1, VA 610, Aquia, **E** 🅖 7-11, Valero, 🍴 Carlos O'Kelly's, El Gran Charro, KFC, McDonald's, Mick's Rest., Pizza Hut, Ruby Tuesday, 🏨 Best Western, Hampton Inn, Staybridge Suites, Towne Place Suites, 🅞 Tires+, **W** 🅖 Exxon, Kangaroo, 7-11/dsl, WaWa, 🍴 Amici Italian, Applebee's, Baskin-Robbins/Dunkin Donuts, Bob Evans, Bruster's, Buffalo Wild Wings, Burger King, Chick-fil-A, Chili's, China Wok, Firehouse Subs, 5 Guys Burgers, Hardee's, IHOP, Jerry's Subs, Jimmy the Greek, Little Caesar's, Maggie Moo's, McDonald's, Moe's SW Grill, Outback Steaks, Pancho Villa, Panera Bread, Popeye's, Quiznos, Ruby Tuesday, Starbucks, Taco Bell, Wendy's, 🏨 Comfort Inn, Country Inn, Holiday Inn Express, Super 8, Wingate Inn, 🅞 **Urgent Care**, Aldi Foods, AutoZone, Best Buy, CVS Drug, $General, $Tree, Giant Foods, GNC, Home Depot, Kohl's, Lowe's, Merchant's Tire, Michael's, PetCo, Petsmart, Radio Shack, Ross, Shopper's Foods, Staples, Target, TJ Maxx, Toyota/Scion, Verizon, Walmart/McDonald's, Aquia Pines Camping
140	VA 630, Stafford, **E** 🅖 7-11, Sunoco/dsl, Valero, 🍴 McDonald's, **W** 🅖 Exxon, Shell/dsl
137mm	Potomac Creek
136	rd 8900, Centreport, **E** 🅖 Valero/dsl, **W** ✈ 🛬
133b a	US 17 N, to Warrenton, **E** 🅖 Exxon/dsl, Gulf/dsl, 🍴 Arby's, 🏨 Howard Johnson Express, Motel 6, 🅞 CarQuest, 7-11, auto/truck repair, **W** 🅖 EastCoast/Subway/dsl, Shell/dsl, WaWa/dsl, 🍴 Burger King, Foster's Grille, Hardee's, McDonald's, Perkin's, Pizza Hut, Ponderosa, Taco Bell, Waffle House, 🏨 Comfort Inn, Country Inn&Suites, Days Inn, Holiday Inn, Quality Inn, Sleep Inn, Super 8, Super Value Inn, Travelodge, Wingate Inn, 🅞 **Urgent Care**, Advance Parts, Blue Beacon, Honda, Petsmart, Target
132.5mm	Rappahannock River
132mm	🆁🆂 sb, full ♿ facilities, 🍴 🚶 litter barrels, petwalk, vending
130b a	VA 3, to Fredericksburg, **E** 🅖 BP/dsl, Gulf, Shell, Wawa, 🍴 Arby's, Bob Evans, Carlos O'Kelly's, Dunkin Donuts, Friendly's, Honeybaked Ham, KFC, King Buffet, Lonestar Steaks, Mexico Lindo, Popeye's, Shoney's, Starbucks,

Left margin vertical text: **DUMFRIES**   Right margin vertical text: **FREDERICKSBURG** **VA**

🅝 INTERSTATE 95 CONT'D

Exit	Services
130b a	Continued

Subway, Wendy's, 🛏 Best Western, Quality Inn, ⭕ Ⓗ AutoZone, Batteries+, BigLots, Hancock Fabrics, Home Depot, PepBoys, Staples, Tuesday Morning, U-Haul, **W** ⛽ BP, Exxon/dsl, Murphy USA, 7-11, Sheetz, Valero, WaWa, 🍴 A&W/LJ Silver, Applebee's, Arby's, Asia Bistro, Aunt Sarah's, Bailey's Grille, Baja Fresh, BoneFish Grill, Bridges Brickoven, Buffalo Wild Wings, Burger King, Caribou Coffee, Carrabba's, Checker's, Cheeseburger Paradise, Chick-fil-A, Chili's, China Jade, Chipotle Mexican, ChuckeCheese, CiCi's Pizza, Cracker Barrel, Denny's, Dunkin Donuts, El Paso Mexican, 5 Guys Burgers, Firehouse Subs, Fuddrucker's, IHOP, Joe's Crabshack, Krispy Kreme, Logan's Roadhouse, Margarita Grill, McDonald's, Melting Pot, Noodles&Co, O'Charley's, Old Country Buffet, Olive Garden, Outback Steaks, Pancho Villa, Panda Express, Panera Bread, Piccadilly, Poncho Villa Mexican, Qdoba, Quizno's, Red Lobster, Rodango's Steaks, Ruby Tuesday, Ryan's, Sam's Pizza, Santa Fe Grill, Smokey Bones BBQ, Starbucks, Subway, Taco Bell, TGIFriday's, 🛏 Best Western, Hampton Inn, Hilton Garden, Homewood Suites, Hospitality House, Ramada Inn, Residence Inn, Super 8, ⭕ Advance Parts, AT&T, AutoZone, Belk, Best Buy, BJ's Whse, Bloom Foods, Costco, CVS Drug, $General, $Tree, Gander Mtn, Giant Foods, JC Penney, Kohl's, K-Mart, Lowe's, Macy's, Merchants Tire, Michael's, NTB, Office Depot, Old Navy, Petsmart, Radio Shack, Ross, Sears/auto, Shopper's Foods, Target, Walmart, Wegman's Foods, Yankee Candle, mall

Exit	Services
126	US 1, US 17 S, to Fredericksburg, **E** ⛽ BP, Citgo, Exxon, Shell/dsl, 🍴 Arby's, Denny's, Friendly's, Golden Corral, Hardee's, Hooters, McDonald's, Pizza Hut, Poncho Villa Mexican, Ruby Tuesday, Subway, Taco Bell, Waffle House, 🛏 Country Inn&Suites, Days Inn/rest., EconoLodge, Fairfield Inn, Hampton Inn, Motel 6, Ramada Inn, Royal Inn, Super 8, TownePlace Suites, ⭕ Ⓗ Advance Parts, Aldi Foods, AutoZone, BMW, Buick/GMC, Cadillac, CVS Drug, Dodge, $General, $Tree, Family$, Nissan, Hyundai, KIA, Mazda, Rite Aid, Subaru, Suzuki, VW, White Tires, **W** ⛽ Exxon, 7-11, Sunoco/dsl, WaWa, 🍴 Applebee's, Arby's, Bob Evans, Burger King, Chick-fil-A, Chili's, China Jade, Chipotle Mexican, Coldstone Creamery, Cracker Barrel, El Charro Mexican, Famous Dave's BBQ, Firehouse Subs, 5 Guys Burgers, Foster's Grill, Glory Days Grill, Golden China, KFC, Lenny's Subs, Longhorn Steaks, McDonald's, Mimi's Cafe, Ozeki Japanese, Panera Bread, Papa John's, Red Robin, Sonic, Starbucks, Steak'n Shake, Subway, Sully's Seafood, Tony's Pizza, Wendy's, 🛏 Comfort Inn, Sleep Inn, WyteStone Suites, ⭕ AT&T, Best Buy, Carmax, CVS Drug, $Plus, Firestone/auto, Jo-Ann Fabrics, Kohl's, Lowe's, Marshalls, Petsmart, Radio Shack, Rite Aid, Ross, Staples, Target, Verizon, Walmart, World Mkt, USPO, vet
118	VA 606, to Thornburg, **E** ⛽ Shell/dsl, ⭕ Safford RV Ctr, to Stonewall Jackson Shrine, **W** ⛽ Citgo/dsl, Exxon, Shell/DQ, Valero, 🍴 Angela's Rest., Burger King, McDonald's, Subway, 🛏 Holiday Inn Express, Lamplighter Motel, Quality Inn, ⭕ KOA (7mi), to Lake Anna SP, USPO
110	VA 639, to Ladysmith, **E** ⛽ Citgo, Shell/dsl, **W** ⛽ Citgo/dsl, Exxon/dsl, 🍴 Domino's, Guiseppe's Rest., Lin's Gormet, Subway, Timbers Rest., VA BBQ, ⭕ Curves, Express Tire/repair, Family$, Food Lion, Lady Smith Drug

Exit	Services
108 mm	Ⓡⓢ both lanes, full ♿ facilities, 🏕 litter barrels, pet walk, Ⓥ vending
104	VA 207, to US 301, Bowling Green, **E** ⛽ Exxon/dsl, Mr Fuel/dsl, Ruther Glen TP/dsl/scales/24hr/@, 💙Loves/DQ/Subway/dsl/scales/24hr, Shell/dsl, Valero/dsl, 🍴 Arby's, McDonald's, Wendy's, 🛏 Howard Johnson, Super 8, ⭕ Blue Beacon, Russell Stover Candies, SpeedCo, to Ft AP Hill, **W** ⛽ Exxon/dsl, ✈FLYING J/Denny's/dsl/scales/RV dump/24hr, 🍴 Aunt Sarah's, Waffle House, 🛏 Comfort Inn, Days Inn/rest., EconoLodge, Quality Inn, ⭕ CarQuest, USPO
98	VA 30, Doswell, **E** to King's Dominion Funpark, ⛽ All American Plaza/Subway/dsl/scales/24hr/@, Exxon, 7-11, 🍴 Burger King, Denny's, 🛏 Best Western, Comfort Suites, Country Inn&Suites, Days Inn, Quality Inn, ⭕ Camp Wilderness, King's Dominion Camping, truckwash
92	VA 54, Ashland, **E**⛽ Sunoco, **W**⛽BP/dsl, TA/dsl/rest./@, EC/Blimpie/Krispy Kreme/dsl, Exxon/Subway, 7-11, Shell/dsl, Valero, 🍴 Anthony's Pizza, Applebee's, Arby's, Brickoven Rest., Burger King, Capt D's, China Wok, Cracker Barrel, DQ, El Azteca, Hardee's, Jersey Mike's Subs, KFC/LJ Silver, McDonald's, New China Buffet, Perkin's, Pizza Hut, Ponderosa, Quiznos, Ruby Tuesday, Starbucks, Taco Bell, Waffle House, Wendy's, 🛏 Apple Garden Motel, Days Inn, EconoLodge, Hampton Inn, Holiday Inn Express, Howard Johnson, Motel 6, Quality Inn, Sleep Inn, ⭕ Ace Hardware, Advance Parts, AutoZone, CarQuest, CVS Drug, Family$, Food Lion, Radio Shack, Rite Aid, Tuesday Morning, Ukrop's Foods, Walmart
89	VA 802, to Lewistown Rd, **E** ⛽ Shell, TA/Pizza Hut/Popeye's/dsl/scales/24hr/@, ⭕ Americamps RV Camp, **W** 🛏 Cadillac Motel, ⭕ Bass Pro Shops, Kosmo Village Camping, Rolling Hills RV Ctr
86b a	VA 656, Elmont, to Atlee, **E** ⛽ Sheetz, Valero, 🍴 Burger King, McDonald's, ⭕ CVS Drug, Food Lion, **W** 🍴 CiCi's Pizza, Jade Chinese, Jersey Mike's Subs, ⭕ Gander Mtn, Home Depot, **W on US 1** ⛽ 7-11, Shell/dsl, 🍴 Applebee's, Arby's, Buffalo Wild Wings, Burger King, Chick-fil-A, Chili's, Chipotle Mexican, Chophouse, Coldstone Creamery, Famous Dave's BBQ, McDonald's, NY Grill, O'Charley's, Panera Bread, Papa John's, Pizzaro, Quizno's, Red Robin, Roda Japanese, Ruby Tuesday, Shoney's, Sonic, Starbucks, Subway, TX Roadhouse, Vinny's Grill, Wendy's, 🛏 Candlewood Suites, Comfort Suites, Courtyard, Hampton Inn, SpringHill Suites, ⭕ AT&T, Barnes&Noble, Best Buy, Dillard's, $Tree, Firestone/auto, Goodyear/auto, JC Penney, Macy's, Merchant's Tire, Michael's, Petsmart, Sears/auto, Target, Tire America, Ukrop's Foods, Walgreens, mall
84b a	I-295 W, to I-64, to Norfolk
83b a	VA 73, Parham Rd, **W** ⛽ Exxon/DQ, 7-11, Shell/dsl, Wawa, 🍴 Aunt Sarah's, Burger King, Firehouse Subs, Frida's Cafe, Hardee's, Hawks BBQ, KFC, McDonald's, River City Diner, Starbucks, Stuffy's Subs, Subway, Taco Bell, Waffle House, Wendy's, 🛏 Best Western, Broadway Motel, Clarion, EconoLodge, Guest Inn, Knights Inn, Sleep Inn, ⭕ BigLots, CVS Drug, Family$, Food Lion, Kroger, Lowe's, Verizon, Walmart
82	US 301, Chamberlayne Ave, **E** ⛽ Exxon/dsl, Sunoco, Texaco, WaWa, 🍴 Arby's, Friendly's, McDonald's, Subway, 🛏 Days Inn, Super 8, ⭕ Food Lion, USPO
81	US 1, Chamberlayne Ave (from nb), same as 82

FREDERICKSBURG

ELMONT

⬆N INTERSTATE 95 CONT'D

Exit	Services
RICHMOND	
80	Hermitage Rd, Lakeside Ave (from nb, no return), W ⛽ EC/Subway, ⊙ Goodyear/auto, Ginter Botanical Gardens
79	I-64 W, to Charlottesville, I-195 S, to U of Richmond
78	Boulevard (no EZ nb return), E ⛽ BP, 🛏 Clarion, W ⛽ Citgo/dsl, 🍴 Bill's BBQ, 🛏 EconoLodge, ⊙ H to VA HS, stadium
76	Chamberlayne Ave, Belvidere, E ⊙ H VA Union U
75	I-64 E, VA Beach, to Norfolk 🅿️
74c	US 33, US 250 W, to Broad St, W ⊙ H st capitol, Museum of the Confederacy
74b	Franklin St, E ⊙ Richmond Nat Bfd Park
74a	I-195 N, to Powhite Expswy, downtown
73.5mm	James River
73	Maury St, to US 60, US 360, industrial area
69	VA 161, Bells Rd, E Port of Richmond, W ⛽ Exxon/dsl, Shell/dsl; 🍴 McDonald's, Subway, 🛏 Candlewood Suites, Hampton Inn, Holiday Inn, Red Roof Inn
67b a	VA 895 (**toll E**), VA 150, to Chippenham Pkwy, Falling Creek, W ⛽ BP/dsl, RaceWay, Shell/dsl, 🍴 Burger King, Hardee's, ⊙ Food Lion, U-Haul
64	VA 613, to Willis Rd, E ⛽ BP, Exxon, 🍴 Waffle House, 🛏 Best Value Inn, EconoLodge, W ⛽ Chubby's, Citgo, 7-11, Shell/dsl, Sunoco, 🍴 Bandito's Mexican, Burger King, McDonald's, Subway, 🛏 Country Inn&Suites, Economy House Motel, La Quinta, Sleep Inn, VIP Inn, ⊙ Drewry's Bluff Bfd, flea mkt
62	VA 288 N, to Chesterfield, Powhite Pkwy, to 🅿️
CHESTER 61b a	VA 10, Chester, E ⛽ RaceWay, 🍴 Don Jose Mexican, Hardee's, 🛏 Comfort Inn, Courtyard, Hampton Inn, Holiday Inn Express, Homewood Suites, Quality Inn, ⊙ H to James River Plantations, City Point NHS, Petersburg NBF, W ⛽ BP, Citgo, Exxon/dsl, Gulf, 7-11, 🍴 Applebee's, Burger King, Capt D's, Chili's, CiCi's Pizza, Cracker Barrel, Denny's, Don Paba Mexican, 5 Guys Burgers, Friendly's, Hardee's, Hooters, IHOP, KFC, McDonald's, O'Charley's, Panera Bread, Peking Chinese, Pizza Hut, Quiznos, Shoney's, Sonic, Starbucks, Subway, Taco Bell, UNO, Waffle House, Wendy's, 🛏 Clarion, Country Inn&Suites, Days Inn, Fairfield Inn, InTowne Suites, Suburban Lodge, Super 8, ⊙ Aamco, Chevrolet, CVS Drug, $General, $Tree, Food Lion, GNC, Home Depot, K Mart, Kohl's, Kroger/gas, Lowe's, NAPA, PetCo, Radio Shack, Rite Aid, Target, Tuesday Morning, Ukrops Foods, to Pocahontas SP
58	VA 746, to Ruffinmill Rd, E ⛽ 🍴/Wendy's/dsl/scales/24hr, ⊙ Honda, Hyundai, Kia, Nissan, Toyota/Scion, VW, W ⛽ Exxon, 7-11, 🍴 Dunkin Donuts, McDonald's, Subway, 🛏 Candlewood Suites
54	VA 144, Temple Ave, Hopewell, to Ft Lee, E ⛽ BP, Exxon, Subway, Sheetz, Shell/Burger King, 🍴 Applebee's, Arby's, Buffalo Wild Wings, China Min's Buffet, CiCi's Pizza, Denny's, El Caporal Mexican, 5 Guys Burgers, Golden Corral, Great China, LoneStar Steaks, McDonald's, Olive Garden, Outback Steaks, Panera Bread, Picadilly, Pizza Hut, Quiznos, Red Lobster, Ruby Tuesday, Sagebrush Steaks, Sonic, Starbucks, Taco Bell, Wendy's, 🛏 Comfort Suites, Hampton Inn, Hilton Garden, Holiday Inn, ValuePlace Inn, ⊙ AT&T, Best Buy, BooksAMillion, Dick's, Dillard's, $Tree, Macy's, Home Depot, JC Penney, Jo-Ann Fabrics, KIA, K-Mart, Macy's, Marshall's, Merchant's Tire, Michael's, Nissan, Old Navy, Petsmart, Radio Shack, Sam's Club/gas,

Exit	Services
54	Continued Sears/auto, Staples, Target, Verizon, Walmart, mall, W ⛽ Kangaroo/dsl, 🍴 DQ, Hardee's, Waffle House, ⊙ U-Haul, to VSU
53	S Park Blvd (from nb), E same as 54
52.5mm	Appomattox River
52	Washington St, Wythe St, E ⛽ Exxon/dsl, Valero/dsl, 🍴 Jade Garden, 🛏 Best Value Inn, Red Carpet Inn, Royal Inn, Super 8, Travelodge, ⊙ Petersburg Nat Bfd, W ⛽ Liberty, 🛏 Broadway Inn, Fort Lee Regency, ⊙ H
51	I-85 S, to South Hill, US 460 W
50d	Wythe St, (from nb) same as 52
50 b c	E ⛽ 7-11, 🛏 Flagship Inn
50a	US 301, US 460 E, to Crater Rd, County Dr, E ⛽ BP, RaceWay, Star Express, 🍴 Hardee's, 🛏 American Inn, Budget Inn, California Inn, EconoLodge, ⊙ H
48b a	Wagner Rd, W on Crater Rd ⛽ Gulf, Wawa, 🍴 Arby's, Bettos, Bojangles, Burger King, Capt D's, KFC, Pizza Hut, Subway, Taste of China, Taco Bell, 🛏 Country Inn&Suites, Super 8, ⊙ Advance Parts, $Tree, $General, PepBoys, Radio Shack, Walgreens, Walmart, USPO
47	VA 629, to Rives Rd, W ⛽ Shell, 🛏 Heritage Motel, **1-2 mi W** 🍴 Mad Italian, Subway, Taco Bell, 🛏 Country Inn&Suites, Crater Inn, ⊙ Softball Hall of Fame Museum, same as 48 on US 301
46	I-295 N (exits left from sb), to Washington
45	US 301, E ⛽ Shell/dsl, W ⛽ Exxon/dsl, 🍴 Lighthouse Rest., Nanny's Rest., Steven Kent Rest., 🛏 Comfort Inn, Days Inn, Hampton Inn, Holiday Inn Express, Howard Johnson, Quality Inn
41	US 301, VA 35, VA 156, E ⛽ US/Exxon/dsl/scales/24hr, 🛏 EconoLodge, ⊙ South 40 camp resort, W 🛏 Travelers Inn
40mm	weigh sta both lanes
37	US 301, Carson, W ⛽ BP/dsl, Shell/dsl
36mm	🅿️ nb, full 🚻 facilities, 🍴 vending, 🗑 litter barrel, petwalk
33	VA 602, W ⛽ Davis/Exxon/Subway/Starbucks/dsl/scales/24hr, 🍴 Burger King, Denny's, Little Italy, 🛏 Hampton Inn, Sleep Inn
31	VA 40, Stony Creek, to Waverly, W ⛽ Shell/dsl, Sunoco, 🍴 Tastee Hut, ⊙ Family$
24	VA 645
20	VA 631, Jarratt, W ⛽ Exxon/Blimpie/dsl/24hr, Race-in/dsl, ⊙ Ford
17	US 301, **1 mi E** 🛏 Knights Inn, Reste Motel, ⊙ Jellystone Park Camping
13	VA 614, to Emporia, E ⛽ Exxon/Chester's/dsl, Shell/dsl
12	US 301 (from nb)

PETERSBURG

Map labels: Chancellor • Fredericksburg • 95 • Bowling Green • Beaverdam • Tappahannock • Dunnsville • Ashland • Hanover • Tuckahoe • Mechanicsville • Richmond • New Kent • Glochester • 295 • Chester • Colonial Heights • Hopewell • Petersburg • Prince George • **VA**

VA

📱 = gas   🍴 = food   🛏 = lodging   ⊙ = other   Ⓡ = rest stop   Copyright 2014 - The NEXT Exit ®

⬆N INTERSTATE 95 CONT'D

Exit	Services
11b a	US 58, Emporia, to South Hill, **E** 📱 BP/Subway/dsl, Citgo/Burger King, Exxon/Blimpie/LJ Silver, Shell/dsl, 🍴 Applebee's, Arby's, Carolina BBQ, Cracker Barrel, Domino's, Hardee's, KFC, McDonald's, Pizza Hut, Taco Bell, Wendy's, Wong's Garden, 🛏 Country Inn&Suites, Fairfield Inn, Rodeway Inn, ⊙ Ⓗ Advance Parts, CVS Drug, $Tree, Family$, Food Lion, Lowe's, NAPA, O'Reilly Parts, Radio Shack, Rite Aid, Verizon, Walmart, **W** 📱 Exxon, Race-In/Quiznos/dsl, 🅿️/Sadler/5 Guys Burgers/dsl/scales/24hr/@, 🍴 Bojangles, Pueblo Viejo, Shoney's, 🛏 Best Western, Days Inn, Hampton Inn, Holiday Inn Express, Quality Inn, Sleep Inn
8	US 301, **E** 📱 Citgo, Exxon/Huddle House/Simmon's/dsl/scales/24hr, 🛏 Deluxe Inn, Red Carpet Inn, ⊙ truck repair
4	VA 629, to Skippers, **E** 📱 Love's/McDonald's/dsl/scales/24hr, 🍴 Subway, **W** 📱 Shell/dsl, 🛏 EconoLodge, ⊙ camping (3mi)
3.5mm	Fountain's Creek
.5mm	**Welcome Ctr nb, full** ♿ **facilities,** 🍴 **vending,** 🗑 **litter barrels, petwalk**
0mm	Virginia/North Carolina state line

⬆E INTERSTATE 264 (NORFOLK)

Exit	Services
23mm	**I-264 begins/ends, BP, Shell, convention ctr**
22	Birdneck Rd, **I-264 begins/ends**, **S** 📱 Shell/dsl, 🍴 LJ Silver, Max&Erma's, McDonald's/playplace, Subway, 🛏 Double Tree, ⊙ Family$, Food Lion, museum
21	VA Beach Blvd, First Colonial Rd, **N** 📱 BP, Shell, 🍴 Applebee's, Arby's, Burger King, Burton's Grill, Chick-fil-A, China Wok, DQ, 5 Guys Burgers, IHOP, KFC, McDonald's, Moe's SW Grill, Otani Japanese, Outback Steaks, Panera Bread, Pizza Hut, Plaza Azteca, Qdoba, Schlotzsky's, Shogun Japanese, Sonic, Starbucks, Subway, Taco Bell, Wendy's, Virginian Steaks, ⊙ Advance Parts, CVS, GNC, Infiniti, JoAnn Fabrics, K-Mart, Kroger/dsl, Michael's, Office Depot, Petsmart, Radio Shack, Rite Aid, SteinMart, Target, Toyota/Scion, Trader Joe's, Whole Foods Mkt, vet, USPO, **S** 📱 Shell, Wawa/dsl, ⊙ CarQuest, 7-11, NAPA
20	US 58 E, to VA Beach Blvd (eb only), **N** 📱 Citgo, Kangaroo, Wawa, 🍴 Bojangle's, Capt. George's Seafood, China Moon, Hardee's, Ruby Tuesday, Subway, ⊙ Family$, Food Lion, KIA/Lincoln, Lowe's, PepBoys, 7-11, TJ Maxx, Tuesday Morning, vet
19	Lynnhaven Pkwy, **N** 📱 7-11, Wawa, 🍴 Ensenda Mexican, Iggle's, Lucky Express, Subway, ⊙ Urgent Care, Audi, Chevrolet, FarmFresh Foods, Ford, Hyundai, Jaguar, Porsche, Subaru, VW, **S** 🍴 McDonald's
18	Rosemont, **N** 📱 Exxon, 🍴 Bonefish Grill, Burger King, Denny's, Hardee's, Jade Garden, KFC, LJ Silver, McDonald's, Mi Casita Mexican, Papa John's, Starbucks, Taco Bell, Wendy's, Zero's Subs, 🛏 EconoLodge, ⊙ Acura, AutoZone, BJ's Whse/gas, CarMax, Chrysler/Dodge/Jeep, $Tree, Food Lion, Harris Teeter, Home Depot, Honda, Kroger, Merchant's Tire/Auto, Nissan, Petsmart, Radio Shack, Rite Aid, Sam's Club/gas, Walgreens, **S** 📱 Hess/dsl, Wawa, 🍴 4 Seasons Chinese, ⊙ CVS, $General
17.5mm	**wb only inspection sta**
17a b	Independance Blvd, **N** 📱 Exxon, 🍴 Cheesecake Factory, Chipotle, IHOP, Jason's Deli, Macaroni Grill, Max&Erma's,

Exit	Services
17a b	Continued McDonald's, Panera Bread, PF Chang's, Ruby Tuesday, Smokey Bones BBQ, Starbucks, Taco Bell, Tripps Rest., Wendy's, Village Inn, 🛏 Candlewood Suites, Crowne Plaza, Days Inn, Extended Stay, Hilton Garden, Motel 6, Westin, ⊙ Barnes&Noble, Best Buy, Dick's, K-Mart, Kohl's, Michael's, Old Navy, Sears/auto, Steinmart, Target, Walgreens, **S** 📱 Exxon, 7-11, Wawa, 🍴 Arby's, Azteca Mexican, Domino's, Firehouse Subs, Golden Corral, Hardee's, KFC, Panda China, Quiznos, Starbucks, Subway, TX Roadhouse, Zero Subs, 🛏 InTown Suites, ⊙ $General, Food Lion, Mazda, Rite Aid, auto repair, vet
16	Witchduck Rd
15a b	Newtown Rd, **N** 📱 BP, Citgo, 🍴 McDonald's, Shoney's, Wendy's, 🛏 Homewood Suites, TownePlace Suites, ⊙ AutoZone, **S** 📱 BP, Shell, 🍴 Denny's, Ruby Tuesday, 🛏 Courtyard, Hampton Inn, Holiday Inn, La Quinta, Red Roof Inn, SpringHill Suites ⊙ Rite Aid, 7-11
14b a	I-64. US 13, to Military Hwy
13	US 13, Military Hwy, **N** 📱 Shell, 🍴 Arby's, Boston Mkt, Lonestar Steaks, Mongolian BBQ, Norfolk Garden Korean, Piccadilly, Schlotzsky's, 🛏 Days Inn, EconoLodge, Motel 6, Ramada Ltd, ⊙ CVS, Firestone/auto, JC Penney, Macy's, Ross
12	Ballentine Blvd, **N** ⊙ Ⓗ Norfolk SU
11b a	US 460, VA 166/168, Brambleton Ave, Campostello Rd, **N** 📱 7-11, Shell
10	Tidewater Dr, City Hall Ave, exits left from eb, **N** 📱 7-11, Shell
9	St Paul's Blvd, Waterside Dr, to Harbor Park Stadium
8	I-464 S, to Chesapeake
7.5mm	tunnel
7b a	VA 141, Effingham St, Crawford St, **N** 📱 Shell, ⊙ Naval Ⓗ **S** ⊙ Shipyard
6.5mm	**weigh sta eb**
6	Des Moines Ave (from eb)
5	US 17, Frederick Blvd, Midtown Tunnel, **N** Ⓗ **S** 📱 BP, ⊙ Harley-Davidson
4	VA 337, Portsmouth Blvd
3	Victory Blvd, **N** 📱 Exxon, 7-11, Shell, WaWa, 🍴 Bojangles, Capt D's, DQ, Domino's, Firehouse Subs, KFC, McDonald's, Pizza Hut, Ruby Tuesday, Taco Bell, Wendy's, ⊙ Advance Parts, AutoZone, BigLots, $Tree, Lowe's, PepBoys, Radio Shack, Walgreens, **S** 📱 Valero/dsl
2b a	Greenwood Dr
0mm	**I-264 begins/ends on I-64, exit 299**

⬆N INTERSTATE 295 (RICHMOND)

Exit	Services
53b a	I-64, **W** to Charlottesville, **E** to Richmond, to US 250, **I-295 begins/ends.**
51b a	Nuckols Rd, **1 mi N** 📱 Miller's/dsl, Valero, 🍴 Bruster's, Casa Grande, Cheeburger, Chen's Chinese, Home Team Grill, McDonald's, Nonna's Pizzaria, Rico's Mexican, Samurai Japanese, Starbucks, Subway, Tropical Smoothie Cafe, ⊙ CVS Drug, Food Lion, Walgreens, vet, **S** 📱 Exxon/Mkt Cafe, ⊙ USPO
49b a	US 33, Richmond, **2 mi S** 🍴 Carvel's Ice Cream, Little Szechuan, Quiznos, ⊙ Martin's Foods, 7-11
45b a	Woodman Rd, **1-2 mi S** 📱 7-11, Valero, 🍴 Little Caesar's, ⊙ CVS Drug, $General, Meadow Farm Museum
43	I-95, US 1, **N** to Washington, **S** to Richmond (exits left from nb) **N on US 1** 📱 BP, Shell/dsl, 🍴 Applebee's, Ar

EMPORIA (vertical tab, left margin)

VA (vertical tab, left margin)

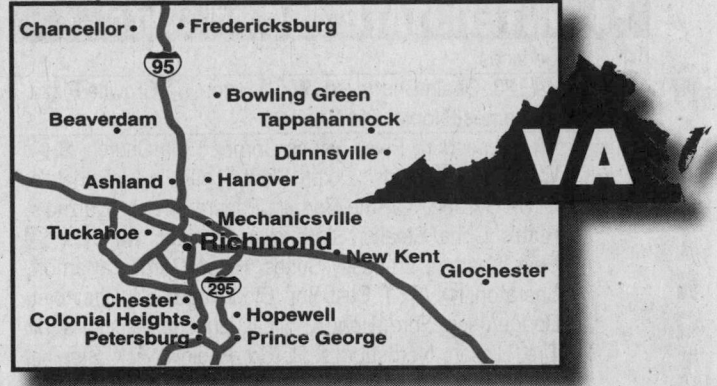

INTERSTATE 295 (RICHMOND) CONT'D

Exit	Services
43	Continued

by's, Buffalo Wild Wings, Burger King, Chick-fil-A, Chili's, Chipotle Mexican, Chophouse, Famous Dave's BBQ, McDonald's, O'Charley's, Panera Bread, Papa John's, Pizzaro, Quizno's, Red Robin, Ruby Tuesday, Shoney's, Subway, TX Roadhouse, Vinny's Grill, Wendy's, 🛏 Candlewood Suites, Comfort Suites, Courtyard, Hampton Inn, SpringHill Suites, 🅾 Barnes&Noble, Best Buy, Dillard's, Firestone/auto, Goodyear/auto, Home Depot, JC Penney, Macy's, Martin's Foods, Merchant's Tire, Michael's, Old Navy, PetsMart, Sears/auto, 7-11, Target, Tire America, Walgreens, mall, **1-2 mi** S 🅿 Exxon, EC/Subway/dsl, 7-11, Sheetz, Shell, WaWa/dsl, 🍴 Aunt Sarah's, Burger King, Cesaer's El Pa,so Mexican, Hardee's, McDonald's, Subway, Waffle House, Wendy's, Wings Pizza & Things, 🛏 Broadway Motel, Cavalier Motel, EconoLodge, GuestHouse Inn, Howard Johnson, Knights Inn, Residence Inn, 🅾 Aamco, CVS Drug, Food Lion, Firestone, Lowe's, Rite Aid, Walmart

41b a	US 301, VA 2; E 🅿 BP/dsl, Valero/dsl, WaWa/dsl, 🍴 Burger King, McDonald's, Popeye's, Tropical Smoothie Cafe, Zheng's Chinese, 🅾 $General, Kroger/gas, Walgreens, **0-4 mi** W 🅿 Exxon/dsl, 🍴 Friendly's, 🛏 Holiday Inn, Super 8, Travelodge
38b a	VA 627, Pole Green Rd, **0-1 mi** E 🅿 BP/Miller's Mkt/dsl, Exxon, 7-11, 🍴 Antonio's Pizza, Bruster's, Chen's Rest., Coffee Lane, Mimmo's Rest., Plaza Tapatia, Subway, 🅾 Curves, Food Lion, vet, W 🅿 7-11, Valero, 🍴 Padon's Hams
37b a	US 360, **1 mi** E 🅿 BP, Shell/dsl, Valero, 🍴 Applebee's, Arby's, Buffalo Wild Wings, Burger King, Chick-fil-A, China Buffet, Cracker Barrel, DQ, Gus' Italian, IHOP, KFC, McDonald's, Mexico Rest., Moe's SW Grill, Noodles&Co, Outback Steaks, Panera Bread, Papa John's, Pizza Hut, Ruby Tuesday, Shoney's, Starbucks, Taco Bell, Waffle House, Wendy's, 🛏 Hampton Inn, Holiday Inn Express, 🅾 AT&T, Best Buy, BJ's Whse/gas, $Tree, GNC, Home Depot, Kohl's, Marshall's, Martin's Foods, Old Navy, Petsmart, Radio Shack, Target, Verizon, Walmart, W 🅿 7-11, Sunoco/dsl, Valero/dsl, 🅾 $General, to Mechanicsville
34b a	VA 615, Creighton Rd, E 🅿 7-11, Valero
31b a	VA 156, E 🅿 Citgo/dsl, 🅾 to Cold Harbor Bfd, **4 mi** W 🅿 Shell, Valero, 🍴 Hardee's, 🛏 Courtyard, EconoLodge, Holiday Inn Express, Motel 6
28	I-64, to US 60, W 🅾 museum
25	Rd 895 W (toll), to Richmond
22b a	VA 5, Charles City, E 🅿 Exxon/dsl, 🍴 DQ, 🅾 Shirley Plantation, W 🅿 Valero/dsl, 🍴 China Taste, Portabella's Cafe, 🅾 Food Lion, Rite Aid, Richmond Nat Bfd
18mm	James River
16	Rivers Bend Blvd
15b a	VA 10, Hopewell, E 🅿 BP/dsl, 🅾 🏥 James River Plantations, W 🅿 EC/Subway/dsl, Exxon/McDonald's/dsl, Sheetz, WaWa, 🍴 Cesare's Ristorante, Chen's Rest., Jalapeno's, Wendy's, Wing's Pizza, 🛏 Hyatt Place, Residence Inn, 🅾 Curves, CVS Drug, Food Lion, 7-11
13mm	Appomattox River
9b a	VA 36, Hopewell, E 🅿 Gulf, Petrol, WaWa, 🍴 A&W, Bojangles, El Nopal Mexican, Hardee's, Hong Kong's Rest.,

9b a	Continued

Huddle House, KFC, Little Caesar's, LJ Silver, McDonald's, Rosa's Italian, 🛏 Best Western, EconoLodge, Fairfield Inn, StayOver Suites, 🅾 Advance Parts, AutoZone, Family$, O'Reilly Parts, Walgreens, vet, W 🅿 BP/dsl/24hr, Shell, Valero/dsl, 🍴 Burger King, DQ, Denny's, Dragon Express, Dunkin Donuts, Kanpai Japanese, McDonald's, Papa John's, Pizza Hut, Ruby Tuesday, Shoney's, Subway, Taco Bell, Top's China, Waffle House, Wendy's, 🛏 Baymont Inn, Candlewood Suites, Hampton Inn, Quality Inn, 🅾 Chevrolet, $General, Family$, Farmer's Foods, Food Lion, Rite Aid, U-Haul, US Army Museum, to Petersburg Nat Bfd

5.5mm	Blackwater Swamp
3b a	US 460, Petersburg, to Norfolk, E 🅿 EC/Subway/dsl, Wilco/Hess/Wendy's/dsl/scales/24hr, 🍴 Prince George BBQ, **1-2 mi** W 🅿 BP/dsl, 🍴 McDonald's
1	I-95, N to Petersburg, S to Emporium, **I-295 begins/ends**.

INTERSTATE 495 (DC)

Exit	Services
27	I-95, N to Baltimore, S to Richmond. **I-495 & I-95 S run together. See MD Interstate 95, exits 25b a - 2b a.**
28b a	MD 650, New Hampshire Ave, N 🅿 Citgo, Exxon/dsl, Shell/repair, 🍴 Domino's, Quizno's, Starbucks, Urban BBQ, 🅾 CVS Drug, Radio Shack, Safeway Foods, 7-11
29b a	MD 193, University Blvd
30b a	US 29, Colesville, N 🅿 BP, Getty, Oceanic, Shell, 🍴 McDonald's, Papa John's, Starbucks, Subway, 🅾 CVS Drug, Safeway Foods, 7-11/Jerry's Subs, Tuesday Morning
31b a	MD 97, Georgia Ave, Silver Springs, N 🏥 S 🅿 C&G, Chevron, Exxon/dsl, Shell, 🍴 Armand's Pizza, Domino's, Mayflower Chinese, 🅾 CVS Drug, Snider's Foods, Staples, vet
33	MD 185, Connecticut Ave, N 🅾 LDS Temple, S 🅿 Citgo/repair, Liberty, Sunoco, 🍴 Starbucks, 🍴 Chevy Chase Foods
34	MD 355, Wisconsin Ave, Bethesda
35	(from wb), I-270
36	MD 187, Old Georgetown Rd, S 🅾 🏥
38	I-270, to Frederick
39	MD 190, River Rd, Washington, Potomac
40	Cabin John Pkwy, Glen Echo (from sb), no trucks
41	Clara Barton Pkwy, Carderock, Great Falls, no trucks
42mm	Potomac River, Virginia/Maryland state line. **Exits 41-27 are in Maryland.**
43	G Washington Mem Pkwy, no trucks
44	VA 193, Langley
45b a	VA 267 W (toll), to I-66 E, to Dulles 🅿

MECHANICSVILLE

HOPEWELL

VA

INTERSTATE 495 (DC) CONT'D

Exit	Services
46b a	VA 123, Chain Bridge Rd, W 🛏 Hilton, 🛏 Crowne Plaza, 🅞 Barnes&Noble, Old Navy
47b a	VA 7, Leesburg Pike, Tysons Corner, Falls Church, E 🛏 Westin, W 🅖 BP/dsl, Exxon, Shell, 🍴 Chili's, McDonald's, Olive Garden, On-the-Border, Panera Bread, Quizno's, Ruth's Chris Steaks, Starbucks, Subway, Wendy's, 🛏 Best Western, Embassy Suites, Hilton Garden, Marriott, Sheraton, 🅞 AT&T, Best Buy, Bloomingdale's, Chevrolet, Dodge/Jeep, Ford, Honda, Infiniti, Lincoln, Marshall's, Mr Tire, Nissan, Nordstrom's, PetCo, Radio Shack, Staples, Subaru/VW, TJ Maxx, mall
49c b a	I-66 (exits left from both lanes), to Manassas, Front Royal,
50b a	US 50, Arlington Blvd, Fairfax, Arlington, E 🛏 Marriott, W 🅖 Shell, Sunoco, 🍴 Chevy's Mexican, 5 Guys Burgers, Jasmine Garden, KFC, McDonald's, Panda Express, Papa John's, Starbucks, UNO Grill, Wendy's, 🛏 Residence Inn, Sweet Water Tavern Inn, 🅞 🅗 CVS Drug, vet
51	VA 657, Gallows Rd, W 🅖 Exxon, 🅞 🅗 7-11
52b a	VA 236, Little River Tpk, Fairfax, E 🅖 Citgo, Sunoco/repair, 🍴 Chicken Loco, McDonald's, Wendy's, 🅞 Safeway Foods, 7-11
54b a	VA 620, Braddock Rd, Ctr for the Arts, Geo Mason U, S 🅖 Sunoco, 🅞 Curves, NTB, Rite Aid, Safeway Foods, 7-11
57	I-95 S, I-395 N

I-495 and I-95 N run together. See Virginia I-95, exits 173-177

INTERSTATE 664 (NORFOLK)

Exit	Services
15b a	I-64 to Chesapeake, I-264 E to Portsmouth & Norfolk **I-664 begins/ends on I-64, exit 299.**
13b a	US 13, US 58, US 460, Military Hwy, E 🅖 Shell/dsl, 🛏 Bowers Hill Inn
12	VA 663, Dock Landing Rd
11b a	VA 337, Portsmouth Blvd, E 🅖 Citgo, Exxon/dsl, Hess, 7-11, Shell/dsl, 🍴 Applebee's, Arby's, Buffet City, Burger King, Chick-fil-A, ChuckECheese, 5 Guys Burgers, Golden Corral, IHOP, Jalapeno's, McDonald's, Olive Garden, Outback Steaks, Piccadilly, Pizza Hut, Plaza Azteca, Red Lobster, Red Robin, Rita's Custard, Subway, Taco Bell, Wen

11b a	Continued dy's, 🛏 Extended Stay 4 Less, Hampton Inn, Holiday Inn Express, 🅞 AutoZone, Best Buy, BJ's Whse/gas, Buick, $Tree, $Tree Mkt, Firestone Auto, Food Lion, Ford, Home Depot, JC Penney, K-Mart, Macy's, Merchant's Auto Ctr, Michael's, Old Navy, Petsmart, Ross, Sam's Club/gas, Sears/auto, Target, Tuesday Morning, Walmart, W 🅖 7-11, 🍴 Burger King, Cracker Barrel, Subway, Waffle House, 🛏 Baymont Inn, Candlewood Suites, 🅞 Lowe's
10	VA 659, Pughsville Rd, E 🅖 7-11, Shell, 🅞 Food Lion, Rite Aid
9b a	US 17, US 164, E 🅖 Hess, 7-11, Wawa, 🍴 Burger King, Capt D's, DQ, Domino's, Dunkin Donuts, Great Wall Chinese, KFC, McDonald's, Pizza Hut, Sonic, Taco Bell, Waffle House, Wendy's, 🛏 Best Western, Budget Lodge, Extended Stay America, Sleep Inn, Super 8, 🅞 Advance Parts, Chevrolet, $Tree, FarmFresh Foods, Honda, Hyundai, NAPA, Nissan, O'Reilly Parts, Toyota/Scion, tires, W 🍴 Buffalo Wild Wings, Subway, 🛏 Comfort Suites, Hilton Garden, 🅞 🅗 Harris Teeter, to James River Br, museum
8b a	VA 135, College Dr, E 🅖 Exxon, 7-11, 🍴 Applebee's, Arby's, Chick-fil-A, Firehouse Subs, McDonald's, Panera Bread, Ruby Tuesday, Subway, Wendy's, 🅞 Dick's, Food Lion, GNC, Kohl's, Petsmart, Radio Shack, TJ Maxx, Walmart, W 🍴 Riverstone Chophouse, 🛏 Courtyard, TownePlace Suites
11.5mm	insp sta nb
9mm	James River
8mm	tunnel
7	Terminal Ave
6	25th St, 26th St, E 🅖 7-11, 🍴 McDonald's
5	US 60 W, 35th St, Jefferson Ave, E 🅖 Fast&Easy, 🍴 Church's, King's Pizza, #1 Chinese, 🅞 Hornsby Tire
4	Chesnut Ave, Roanoke Ave
3	Aberdeen Rd, W 🅖 7-11, 🍴 Hardee's, McDonald's, Wendy's
2	Powhatan Pkwy, E 🅖 7-11, **1-2 mi** W 🍴 Coldstone, Joe's Crabshack, Lonestar Steaks, 🛏 Hilton Garden, SpringHill Suites, 🅞 Bass Pro Shop, BJ's Whse/gas, Lowe's
1b a	I-64, W to Richmond, E to Norfolk. **I-664 begins/ends on I-64.**

WASHINGTON

INTERSTATE 5

Exit	Services
277mm	USA/Canada Border, Washington state line, customs
276	WA 548 S, Blaine, E 🅖 Shell/dsl, Texaco/dsl, USA/dsl, 🍴 Big Al's Diner, 🅞 Duty Free, NAPA, to Peace Arch SP, W 🅖 Chevron/dsl/repair, 🍴 Chada Thai, Little Red Caboose Cafe, Pizza Factory, Pasa Del Norte, Seaside Bakery Cafe, Subway, Tony's Cafe, 🛏 Anchor Inn, Bay Side Motel, Cottage by the Bay B&B, International Motel, Sunset Inn, 🅞 Blaine Marine Park, USPO
275	WA 543 N (from nb, no return) truck customs, E 🅖 Chevron/dsl, Mkt/dsl, Shell/dsl, 🍴 Burger King, Little Caesars, Subway, 🅞 Ace Hardware, CostCutter Foods, $Tree, Rite Aid, vet
274	Peace Portal Drive (from nb, no return), Blaine, W 🅖 Shell/dsl, 🍴 Hot Spot Burgers, 🅞 Semi-ah-moo Resort, camping
270	Birch Bay, Lynden, W 🅖 Shell/Domino's/Subway/dsl, 🍴 Bob's Burgers, Jack-in-the-Box, 🛏 Semi-ah-moo Resort, 🅞 Birch Bay Mkt, Curves, Thousand Trails Camping, vet
269mm	Welcome Ctr sb, full ♿ facilities, info, 🅒, 🚮 litter barrels, petwalk, vending
267mm	🆁🆂 nb, full ♿ facilities, info, 🅒, 🚮 litter barrels, petwalk, vending
266	WA 548 N, Grandview Rd, Custer, W 🅖 Arco, 🅞 Birch Bay SP
263	Portal Way, E 🅖 Pacific Pride/dsl, Shell/dsl, 🅞 Cedars RV Park
263mm	Nooksack River
262	Main St, Ferndale, E 🅖 76/dsl, Texaco/dsl, 🍴 Denny's, McDonald's, Subway, 🛏 Super 8, 🅞 RV Park, TDS Tires, W 🅖 Gull/dsl, 76, Shell/Pizza Hut/dsl, 🍴 Bob's Burgers, DQ, Domino's, Quiznos, Sonic, Starbucks, 🛏 Scottish Lodge, 🅞 Costcutter Foods, $Tree, Haggen's Foods, NAPA, Schwab Tire, Walgreens, vet

🅖 = gas   🍴 = food   🛏 = lodging   🅾 = other   🆁🆂 = rest stop

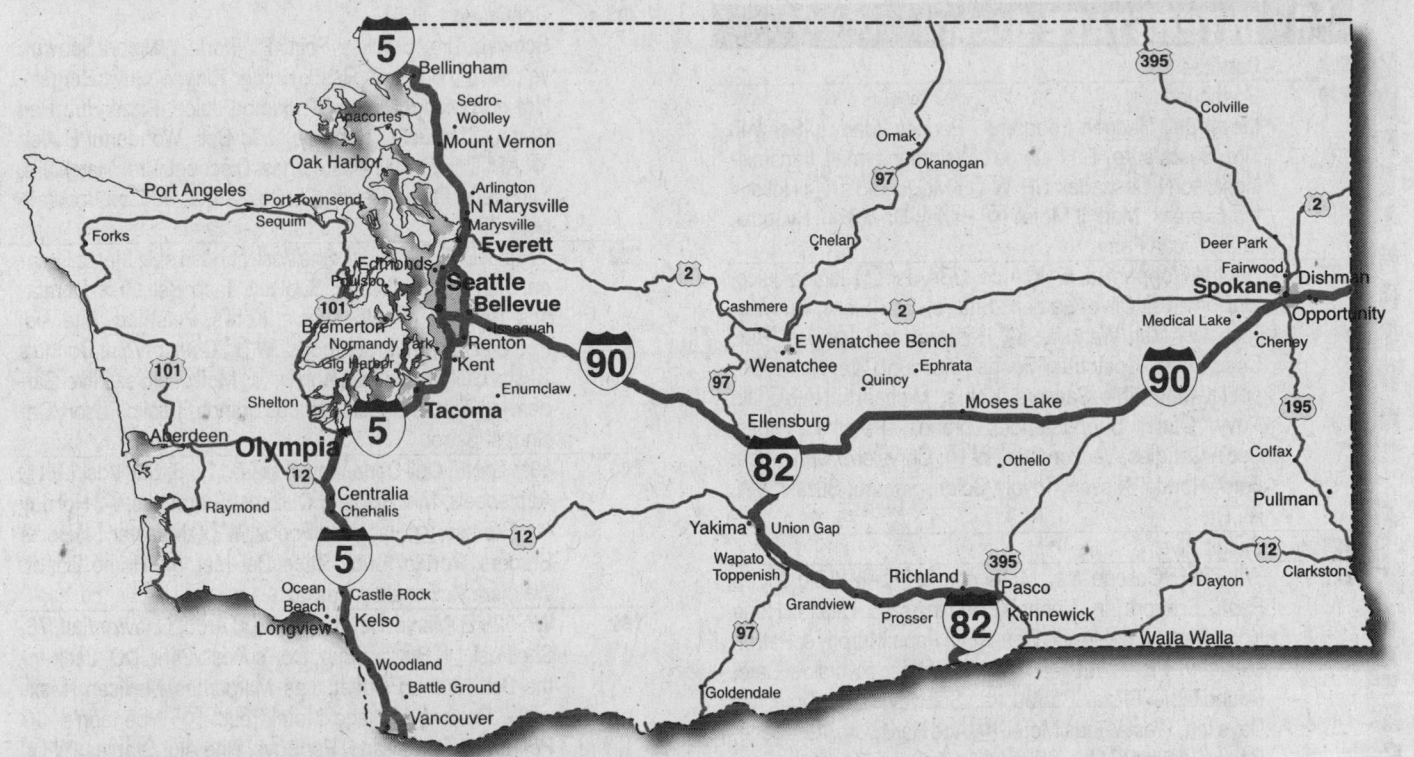

WA

## ⬆N INTERSTATE 5 CONT'D	**254** Continued
	Ford/Lincoln, NAPA, O'Reilly Parts, repair
Exit Services	**253** Lakeway Dr, Bellingham, E 🍴 Lychee Buffet, Little Cae-
260 Slater Rd, Lummi Island, E 🅖 Arco, 🅾 El Monte RV Ctr,	sars, Papa Murphy's, Port of Subs, Sol de Mexico, Sub-
antiques, **4 mi** W 🅖 76, Shell/dsl, 🛏 Silver Reef Hotel/	way, 🛏 Best Western, Guesthouse Inn, 🅾 Discount Tire,
Casino, 🅾 Lummi Ind Res	Fred Meyer/dsl, Radio Shack, 7-11, W same as 252
258 Bakerview Rd, E 🍴 Baskin-Robbins, Chilli Mexican, 5	**252** Samish Way, Bellingham, E same as 253, W 🅖 Chevron,
Guys Burgers, Papa Murphy's, Subway, 🅾 Fred Meyer/	76, Shell/dsl, SuperGas/dsl, 🍴 Arby's, Boomers Drive-In,
dsl, Verizon, W 🅖 Arco, Mkt/dsl, 76, 🍴 Jack-in-the-Box,	Diego's Mexican, El Agave, Kyoto Steaks, McDonald's,
Mykono's Greek Rest., 🛏 Hampton Inn, Shamrock Motel,	Pizza Hut, Pizza Pipeline, Quiznos, Starbucks, Subway,
🅾 Bellingham RV Park, 🆁🆂 st patrol	Taco Time, Thai Cuisine, Wendy's, 🛏 Aloha Motel, Bay
257 Northwest Ave, E 🅾 Urgent Care, Cadillac/Chevrolet	City Motel, Cascade Inn, Coachman Inn, Days Inn, Motel
256b Bellis Fair Mall Pkwy, E 🅾 JC Penney, Sears, Target, mall	6, Travelodge, Villa Inn, 🅾 Haggen Foods, Rite Aid
256a WA 539 N, Meridian St, E 🅖 Shell/dsl, Super Gas/dsl, 🍴	**250** WA 11 S, Chuckanut Dr, Bellingham, Fairhaven Hist Dist,
Arby's, Asian 1, Boston's Rest., Burger King, China Palace,	W 🅖 Arco, Chevron/repair, 🅾 Fairhaven Mkt, to Larrabee
Coldstone, Denny's, Lorenzo's Mexican, McHale's Rest.,	SP, to Alaska Ferry
Mi Mexico, Old Country Buffet, Olive Garden, Quiznos,	**246** N Lake Samish, W 🅖 Shell/dsl, 🅾 Lake Padden RA, RV
Red Robin, Shari's, Subway, Taco Bell, Taco Time, Thai	camping
House Rest., Wendy's, Wonderful Buffet, 🛏 Best West-	**242** Nulle Rd, S Lake Samish
ern, Comfort Inn, Holiday Inn Express, La Quinta, Quality	**240** Alger, E 🅖 Shell/dsl/LP/RV dump, 🍴 Alger Grille, 🛏
Inn, 🅾 AAA, AT&T, Barnes&Noble, Best Buy, Costco/gas,	Whispering Firs Motel/RV Parking
Costcutter Foods, $Tree, Home Depot, JC Penney, Kohl's,	**238mm** 🆁🆂 both lanes, full ♿ facilities, 🚻, 🛒 litter barrels,
Macy's, Michael's, Office Depot, O'Reilly Parts, PetCo,	vending, petwalk
Petsmart, Rite Aid, Ross, Schwab Tire, Sears/auto, Tar-	**236** Bow Hill Rd, E Skagit Hotel Casino/rest./dsl/LP
get, TJ Maxx, U-Haul, Walgreens, Walmart/McDonald's,	**235mm** weigh sta sb
mall, st patrol, to Nooksack Ind Res, W 🍴 Slopitch Grill,	**234mm** Samish River
🛏 EconoLodge, Rodeway Inn	**232** Cook Rd, Sedro-Woolley, E 🅖 76/Subway/dsl, Shell/dsl,
255 WA 542 E, Sunset Dr, Bellingham, E 🅖 Chevron/dsl, 76,	**232** Continued
Shell/Subway/Domino's/dsl, 🍴 A&W/KFC, Applebee's,	🍴 Bob's Burgers, Jack-in-the-Box, Starbucks, 🛏 Fair-
Hawaii BBQ, Jack-in-the-Box, Panda Express, RoundTa-	field Inn, 🅾 🏥, KOA
ble Pizza, Taco Bell, 🅾 Costcutter Foods, Jo-Ann Fabrics,	**231** WA 11 N, Chuckanut Dr, E 🅾 Camping World RV Ctr, KIA,
K-Mart, Lowe's, Rite Aid, Tuesday Morning, Walgreens,	st patrol, W to Larrabee SP (14mi)
repair, USPO, to Mt Baker, W 🅾 🏥	**230** WA 20, Burlington, E 🅖 Shell/dsl, 🍴 Applebee's, Carino's
254 Iowa St, State St, Bellingham, E 🅖 76, Valero, 🅾 Audi/	Italian, China Wok, El Cazador, Jack-in-the-Box, Krispy
VW, Buick/GMC, Chrysler/Dodge/Jeep, Honda, Hyundai,	Kreme, Outback Steaks, Papa Murphy's, Pizza Factory,
KIA, Mercedes, Nissan, Subaru, Toyota/Scion, Volvo, W	Pizza Hut/Taco Bell, Popeye's, Quiznos, Red Robin, 🛏
🅖 Chevron/dsl, Shell, 🍴 DQ, McDonald's, Subway, 🅾	Cocusa Motel, Sterling Motel, 🅾 🏥, AutoZone, Fred

B E L L I N G H A M

⬆N INTERSTATE 5 CONT'D

Exit	Services
230	Continued
	Meyer/dsl, Haggen Foods, JC Penney, Macy's, Schwab Tire, Sears/auto, 7-11, Target, Walgreens, mall, transmissions, to N Cascades NP, **W** 🍴 McDonald's, 🛏 Holiday Inn Express, Mark II Motel, ⊡ Harley-Davidson, Hyundai, to San Juan Ferry
229	George Hopper Rd, **E** ⓡ Arco, USA/dsl, 🍴 Jamba Juice, McDonald's, Olive Garden, Shari's, Starbucks, Subway, Taco Del Mar, Wendy's, 🛏 Hampton Inn, ⊡ Best Buy, Costco/gas, Costcutter Foods, Discount Tire, Home Depot, K-Mart/Little Caesars, Kohl's, Michael's, NAPA, Old Navy, Outlet Shops/famous brands, Petsmart, Ross, See's Candies, Verizon, vet, **W** ⊡ Chrysler/Jeep/Dodge, Ford, Honda, Nissan, Toyota/Scion, Subaru, Suzuki, VW, RV Ctr
228mm	Skagit River
227	WA 538 E, College Way, Mt Vernon, **E** 🍴 A&W, Big Scoop Rest., Dragon Inn, Denny's, Domino's, El Gitano, Hong Kong Rest., Jack-in-the-Box, KFC, Papa Murphy's, Patron Mexican, Pizza Hut/Taco Bell, Quiznos, Riverside Cafe, RoundTable Pizza, Starbucks, Subway, Taco Time, 🛏 Days Inn, West Winds Motel, ⊡ Ace Hardware, AutoZone, Buick/Cadillac/GMC, $Plus, $Tree, Goodyear/auto, Grocery Outlet, Jo-Ann Fabrics, Office Depot, O'Reilly Parts, PetCo, Rite Aid, Safeway/dsl, **W** ⓡ APP/dsl, Shell/dsl, 🍴 Arby's, Burger King, Cranberry Tree Rest., DQ, Forks&Knives Steaks, Fortune Chinese, Royal Star Buffet, 🛏 Best Western, Quality Inn, Tulip Inn, ⊡ Blade RV Ctr, Chevrolet, Lowe's, Riverbend RV Park, Walmart/Subway
226	WA 536 W, Kincaid St, City Ctr, **E** ⊡ Ⓗ, RV camping, **W** 🍴 Old Towne Grainery Rest., Skagit River Brewing Co, ⊡ NAPA, Red Apple Mkt, Valley RV Ctr, antiques
225	Anderson Rd, **E** ⓡ Fuel Express/dsl, 76/dsl, ⊡ Country Motorhomes, **W** ⓡ Truck City Trkstp/dsl, Valero, 🍴 Long Haul Cafe, ⊡ Freightliner, Poulsbo RV Ctr, Valley RV Ctr
224	WA 99 S (from nb, no return), S Mt Vernon, **E** gas/dsl, food
221	WA 534 E, Conway, Lake McMurray, **E** ⓡ 76/dsl, ⊡ farmers mkt, **W** ⓡ 76/dsl, Texaco/dsl/LP, 🍴 Conway Deli, 🛏 Channel Lodge/Rest. (11mi), ⊡ Blake's RV Park/marina (6mi)
218	Starbird Rd
215	300th NW, **W** ⓡ Interstate/dsl
214mm	weigh sta nb
212	WA 532 W, Stanwood, Bryant, **W** ⓡ 76/dsl, Shell/Burger Stop/dsl, ⊡ Camano Island SP (19mi)
210	236th NE, **E** ⊡ Angel of the Winds Casino/Watershed Rest.
209mm	Stillaguamish River
208	WA 530, Silvana, Arlington, **E** ⓡ Arco/dsl, 76/Circle K, Shell, Tesoro/dsl, 🍴 Denny's, Patty's Eggnest&Turkeyhouse, 🛏 Arlington Motel, ⊡ Ⓗ, to N Cascades Hwy, **W** ⓡ 76/dsl
207mm	ⓡ **both lanes, full** ♿ **facilities,** 🚻, 🏕, **litter barrels, coffee, vending, RV dump, petwalk**
206	WA 531, Lakewood, **E** ⓡ Arco, Shell, 7-11, 🍴 Alfy's Pizza, Buzz Inn Steaks, Domino's, Jack-in-the-Box, KFC, McDonald's, Moose Creek BBQ, Olympia Pizza, Starbucks, Subway, Taco Del Mar, Taco Time, Wendy's, 🛏 Medallion Hotel, Smokey Point Motel, ⊡ AT&T, Buick/GMC, Chrysler/Dodge/Jeep, $Tree, Harley-Davidson, Jo-Ann Fabrics, Lowe's, O'Reilly Parts, Rite Aid, Safeway/gas,

Exit	Services
206	Continued
	Schwab Tire, Smokey Point RV Park, Walmart/Subway, vet, **W** 🍴 Boston's Rest., Burger King, 5 Guys Burgers, Hot Iron Mongolian, IHOP, Jamba Juice, Pizza Hut, Red Robin, Starbucks, Subway, Taco Bell, Wonderful Buffet, ⊡ AT&T, Best Buy, Costco/gas, Discount Tire, Marshall's, Michael's, Office Depot, PetCo, Target, Verizon, to Wenburg SP
202	116th NE, **E** ⓡ 76/dsl, Shell/dsl, 🍴 Carl's Jr, Magic Dragon Chinese, Starbucks, Subway, Taco Bell, Tres Hermanos Mexican, ⊡ Albertson's, Kohl's, Petsmart, Rite Aid, Ross, Verizon, WinCo Foods, **W** ⓡ Chevron/dsl, Donna's Trkstp/Gull/dsl/scales/24hr/@, 🍴 McDonald's, Olive Garden, ⊡ Seattle Outlets/famous brands, Tulalip Resort/Casino, st patrol
200	88th St NE, Quil Ceda Way, **E** ⓡ 7-11, 76, Shell/dsl/LP, 🍴 Applebee's, Mkt St Cafe, Quiznos, Starbucks, 🛏 Holiday Inn Express, ⊡ Haggen's Foods, **W** ⓡ Mirastar, 🍴 Bob's Burgers, Port of Subs, Taco Del Mar, ⊡ Home Depot, Walmart/McDonald's, casino
199	WA 528 E, Marysville, Tulalip, **E** ⓡ Arco, Chevron/dsl, 76, Shell/dsl, 🍴 Burger King, Don's Rest./24hr, DQ, Jack-in-the-Box, Jumbo Buffet, Las Margaritas Mexican, Maxwell's Rest., 🛏 Village Motel/Rest., ⊡ Albertson's, JC Penney, O'Reilly Parts, PepBoys, Rite Aid, Staples, **W** ⓡ 76, 🍴 Arby's, McDonald's, Taco Time, Wendy's, 🛏 Best Western/rest., Comfort Inn, ⊡ Chevrolet/Subaru, Robinson RV Ctr, to Tulalip Indian Res
198	Port of Everett (from sb), Steamboat Slough, st patrol
195mm	Snohomish River
195	Port of Everett (from nb), Marine View Dr
194	US 2 E, Everett Ave City Ctr, **W** ⓡ Shell/dsl, ⊡ Schwab Tire
193	WA 529, Pacific Ave (from nb), **W** ⓡ Chevron, 76, 🍴 Denny's, 🛏 Best Western, Holiday Inn, Travelodge, ⊡ Ⓗ Lowe's
192	Broadway, to 41st St, City Ctr, **W** ⓡ Arco, Chevron, 76/dsl, Shell, 🍴 Buzz Inn Steaks, IHOP, Iver's Seafood, La Cuesta Mexican, Little Caesars, McDonald's, Quiznos, Starbucks, Subway, 🛏 Days Inn, Travelodge
189	WA 526 W, WA 527, Everett Mall Way, Everett, **E** ⓡ Arco, Chevron, Shell/dsl, 🍴 Alfy's Pizza, Burger King, Buzz Inn Steaks, Subway, Wendy's, 🛏 Travelodge, ⊡ Costco/gas, WinCo Foods, vet, **W** ⓡ Shell, 🛏 Best Western, Days Inn, Extended Stay America, Motel 6, ⊡ Goodyear/auto, Macy's, mall
188mm	ⓡ/weigh sta sb, full ♿ facilities, info, 🚻, 🏕, litter barrels, coffee, RV dump
186	WA 96, 128th SW, **E** ⓡ 76/dsl, Shell/dsl, Texaco, 🍴 O'Donnells Rest., 🛏 Quality Inn, ⊡ Lakeside RV Park, **W** ⓡ Arco, Chevron, 7-11, Shell, 🍴 A&W/KFC, Acropolis Pizza, DQ, Denny's, McDonald's, Ming Dynasty, Pizza Hut, Skipper's, Subway, Taco Bell, Taco Time, 🛏 Holiday Inn Express, La Quinta, Motel 6, ⊡ Albertson's/Sav-on, $Tree, Goodyear/auto, Maple RV Park, transmissions, vet
183	164th SW, **E** ⓡ Arco, Shell/dsl, 🍴 Jack-in-the-Box, Panda Express, Quiznos, Starbucks, Subway, Taco Del Mar, Taco Time, ⊡ Curves, Walgreens, Walmart, **W** ⓡ Chevron/dsl, 🍴 5 Guys Burgers, ⊡ Fred Meyer/dsl
182	WA 525, Alderwood Mall Blvd, to Alderwood Mall, **E** I-405 S, to Bellevue, **W** ⓡ Arco, 🍴 Fatburger, Jersey Mike's, Keg Steaks, Macaroni Grill, Panera Bread, PF Chang's,

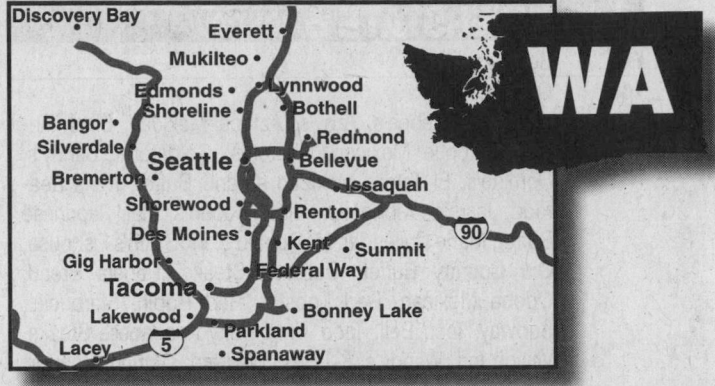

⬆N INTERSTATE 5 CONT'D

Exit	Services
182	Continued

SEATTLE

182 — Qdoba Mexican, Red Robin, Subway, TCBY, 🛏 Residence Inn, 🅾 JC Penney, Kohl's, Macy's, Marshall's, Nordstrom, Rite Aid, Ross, Sears/auto, See's Candies, Target, vet

181 — 44th Ave W, to WA 524, Lynnwood, **E** 🅰 Arco, 76/dsl, Shell, 🍴 Jimmy John's, McDonald's/playplace, Old Spaghetti Factory, Starbucks, 🛏 Embassy Suites, Extended Stay America, Hampton Inn, Holiday Inn Express, 🅾 Barnes&Noble, Best Buy, Jaguar, Land Rover, Lowe's, Old Navy, PetCo, Staples, Verizon, **W** 🅰 Arco, Chevron, 76/dsl, Shell/repair, 🍴 Alfy's Pizza, Applebee's, Arby's, Black Angus, Buca Italian, Celtic Bayou, Chevy's Mexican, Chipotle Mexican, ChuckeCheese, Denny's, Herfy's Burgers, IHOP, Jack-in-the-Box, KFC, McDonald's, Old Country Buffet, Olive Garden, Panda Express, Quiznos, Red Lobster, Rock Woodfire Pizza, Silver Spoon Rest., Starbucks, Subway, Taco Bell, Taco Time, Todo Mexico, Wendy's, 🛏 Best Western, Courtyard, Days Inn, La Quinta, 🅾 Urgent Care, Fred Meyer/dsl, Goodyear/auto, Radio Shack, Schwab Tire, 7-11, Tuesday Morning, USPO, vet

179 — 220th SW, Mountlake Terrace, Mountlake Terrace, **W** 🅰 Shell/dsl, 🍴 Azteca Mexican, Port of Subs, Subway, 🅾 🏥

178 — 236th St SW (from nb), Mountlake Terrace

177 — WA 104, Edmonds, **E** 🅰 Chevron/dsl, Shell/dsl, 🍴 Mazatlan Mexican, McDonald's/playplace, Starbucks, Subway, Tagalicci Pizza, Todo Mexico, 🛏 Motel 6, 🅾 Office Depot, O'Reilly Parts, RiteAid, Thriftway Foods, **1-2 mi W on WA 99** 🅰 76/dsl, 🍴 A&W/KFC, Arby's, Barlee's Rest., Scott's Grill, Starbucks, 🛏 Days Inn, 🅾 Costco, Discount Tire, Home Depot, Nissan, PetCo, Radio Shack, Verizon, VW

176 — NE 175th St, Aurora Ave N, to Shoreline

175 — WA 523, NE 145th, 5th Ave NE

174 — NE 130th, Roosevelt Way

173 — 1st Ave NE, Northgate Way, **E** 🅰 76, 🍴 Azteca Mexican, CA Pizza Kitchen, Chipotle Mexican, 5 Guys Burgers, Macaroni Grill, Marie Callender's, Panera Bread, Quiznos, Ram Rest., Red Robin, Stanford's Rest., Super Buffet, 🅾 Barnes&Noble, Best Buy, JC Penney, Macy's, Nordstrom, Ross, Target, Verizon, mall, **W** 🅰 Chevron, 76, Shell/dsl, 🍴 McDonald's, Pizza Xpress, Saffron Grill, Starbucks, 🛏 Hotel Nexus, 🅾 7-11

172 — N 85th, Aurora Ave

171 — WA 522, Lake City Way, Bothell

170 — (nb only) Ravenna Blvd, **E** 🅰 Shell/dsl

169 — NE 45th, NE 50th, **E** 🅰 76, Shell, 🍴 Subway, 🅾 🏥, PetCo, U of WA, **W** 🅾 to Seattle Pacific U, zoo

168b — WA 520, to Bellevue

168a — Lakeview Blvd, downtown

167 — Mercer St (exits left from nb), Fairview Ave, Seattle Ctr, **W** 🅰 Shell, 🛏 Silver Cloud Inn

166 — Olive Way, Stewart St, **E** 🅾🏥, **W** 🛏 SpringHill Suites, 🅾 Honda

165a — Seneca St (exits left from nb), James St, **E** 🅾 🏥

165b — Union St, **E** 🛏 Homewood Suites, **W** 🍴 Ruth's Chris Steaks, 🛏 Renaissance Inn

164b — 4th Ave S, to Kingdome, downtown

164a — I-90 E, to Spokane, downtown

163 — 6th Ave, S Spokane St, W Seattle Br, Columbian Way, **1**

SEATTLE

163 — Continued
mi W on 4th Ave S 🅰 Arco/dsl, Gull/dsl, Shell, 🍴 Arby's, Burger King, Denny's, Jack-in-the-Box, KFC, McDonald's, Quiznos, Starbucks, Subway, Taco Bell, 🅾 Costco/gas, Pepboys, USPO

162 — Corson Ave, Michigan St (exits left from nb), same as 161

161 — Swift Ave, Albro Place, **W** 🅰 Shell/dsl, 🍴 Starbucks, Thai Rest., 🛏 Georgetown Inn

158 — Pacific Hwy S, E Marginal Way, **W** 🅰 Chevron, 🅾 NAPA

157 — ML King Way

156 — WA 539 N, Interurban Ave (no EZ return to sb), Tukwila, **E** 🅰 Pacific Pride/dsl, 🍴 Billy Baroos Rest., **W** 🅰 76/dsl, Shell/dsl, 🍴 Emerald Green, Jack-in-the-Box, Quiznos, Starbucks, 🛏 Days Inn

154b — WA 518, Burien, **W** 🛏 Extended Stay America

154a — I-405, N to Bellevue

153 — S Center Pkwy, (from nb), **E** 🅰 Chevron/dsl, 🍴 Applebee's, Azteca Mexican, Bahama Breeze, BJ's Rest., Cheesecake Factory, Chipotle Mexican, Famous Dave's, IHOP, Jamba Juice, McDonald's, Olive Garden, Outback Steaks, Panda Express, Panera Bread, Qdoba Mexican, Quiznos, Red Robin, Simply Thai, Sizzler, Starbucks, Stanford's Rest., Subway, Zoopa, 🛏 DoubleTree Inn, 🅾 Acura, AT&T, Barnes&Noble, Best Buy, $Tree, JC Penney, Jo-Ann Fabrics, Kohl's, Macy's, Michael's, Nordstrom, Office Depot, Old Navy, PetCo, Petsmart, Ross, Sears/auto, See's Candies, Target, Tuesday Morning, Verizon, World Mkt, mall

152 — S 188th, Orillia Rd, **W** 🅰 76/dsl, 🛏 Motel 6, 🅾 city park, **1 mi W** 🅰 Shell, 🍴 Dave's Diner, Denny's, Jack-in-the-Box, Taco Bell, 🛏 DoubleTree Hotel, La Quinta, 🅾 to 🆁🆂

151 — S 200th, Military Rd, **E** 🅰 Shell/dsl, 🛏 Motel 6, **W** 🅰 Chevron, 7-11, 76, 🍴 Bob's Burger, IHOP, 🛏 Best Value Inn, Best Western, Days Inn, Comfort Inn, EconoLodge, Fairfield Inn, Hampton Inn, Holiday Inn Express, Quality Inn, Sleep Inn, Super 8, 🅾 NAPA, O'Reilly Parts, U-Haul, city park

149 — WA 516, to Kent, Des Moines, **E** 🛏 Century Motel, 🅾 Poulsbo RV Ctr, **W** 🅰 Arco, Chevron, Shell/dsl, 🍴 Burger King, Church's, McDonald's, Pizza Hut, Starbucks, Subway, 🛏 Garden Suites, Kings Arms Motel, New Best Inn, 🅾 $Tree, Lowe's, Radio Shack, 7-11, Walgreens, to Saltwater SP

147 — S 272nd, **E** 🅰 76/Circle K/dsl, **W on Pacific Hwy** 🅰 Arco, Shell/dsl, 🍴 Jack-in-the-Box, Little Caesars, McDonald's, Quiznos, Papa Murphy's, Starbucks, Subway, Taco Bell, 🅾 Ace Hardware, AutoZone, Bartell Drug, Firestone/auto, Safeway

143 — S 320th, Federal Way, **W** 🅰 Arco, 76/Circle K/dsl, Shell/

🏧 = gas   🍴 = food   🛏 = lodging   🅾 = other   Rs = rest stop   Copyright 2014 - The NEXT Exit ®

INTERSTATE 5 CONT'D

Exit	Services
143	Continued
	dsl, 🍴 Applebee's, Arby's, Azteca Mexican, Black Angus, Chipotle Mexican, Church's, Coldstone, Denny's, Domino's, El Torero Mexican, Grand Buffet, Ivar's Seafood, Jasmine Mongolian, Jimmy John's, Main Japanese Buffet, Marie Callender, McDonald's, McGrath's Fishouse, Old Country Buffet, Outback Steaks, Panera Bread, Qdoba Mexican, Red Lobster, Red Robin, Starbucks, Subway, Taco Bell, Taco Time, Tokyo Japanese Steaks, Village Inn, Wendy's, 🛏 Best Western, Clarion, Comfort Inn, Courtyard, Extended Stay America, Hampton Inn, 🅾 AT&T, Barnes&Noble, Best Buy, BigLots, Discount Tire, Jo-Ann Fabrics, Macy's, Michael's, O'Reilly Parts, PetCo, Petsmart, Radio Shack, Rite Aid, Ross, Safeway, See's Candies, Sears/auto, Target, TJ Maxx, Top Foods, Trader Joe's, Verizon, Walmart/McDonald's, mall, to Dash Point SP
142b a	WA 18 E, S 348th, Enchanted Pkwy, E 🅾 funpark, W 🏧 Chevron, Shell/dsl, 🍴 Arby's, Burger King, Del Taco, Denny's, Fatburger, Jack-in-the-Box, Jamba Juice, Jimmy Mac's Roadhouse, KFC, LJ Silver, McDonald's, Olive Garden, Panda Express, Popeye's, Puerta Vallarta, RoundTable Pizza, Shari's, Starbucks, Subway, Taco Bell, Taco Del Mar, The Rock Pizza, Time Out Grill, 🛏 Quality Inn, Super 8, 🅾 🅷 Chevrolet, Costco/gas, Discount Tire, Home Depot, Lowe's, Office Depot, Schwab Tire, Verizon, Walmart/Subway
140mm	**weigh sta, both lanes. Rs, nb, full ♿ facilities, litter barrels, 🐾, petwalk, RV dump**
137	WA 99, Fife, Milton, E 🏧 Arco, Chevron/dsl, 76/dsl, Shell, 🍴 DQ, Johnny's Rest., 🛏 Motel 6, 🅾 Acura, Cadillac, Hummer W 🏧 76/Circle K/dsl, Shell/dsl, 🍴 Arby's, A&W/KFC, Baskin-Robbins, Denny's, Fife Rest., Herfy's Burgers, McDonald's, Mitzel's Kitchen, Pizza Hut/Taco Bell, Poodle Dog, Quiznos, Starbucks, Taco Time, Wendy's, 🛏 Baymont Inn, Days Inn, EQC Motel/casino, Kings Motel, 🅾 Emerald RV Ctr, Holiday RV Ctr, Infiniti, NAPA, O'Reilly Parts, Schwab Tire
136b a	Port of Tacoma, E 🏧 CFN/dsl, 🅾 Baydos RV Ctr, BMW, Costco, Honda, I-5 Motors, Mercedes, Mini, Peterbilt, Tacoma RV Ctr, W 🏧 Chevron/dsl, ♥Loves/Chester's/Subway/dsl/scales/LP/RV dump/24hr, Gull/dsl, 🍴 Jack-in-the-Box, Subway, 🛏 Best Night Inn, Extended Stay America, Howard Johnson, Rodeway Inn, Sunshine Motel, Travelodge, 🅾 Goodyear/biodsl, Harley-Davidson, Land Rover/Jaguar/Lexus, Nissan, Volvo, truck repair
135	Bay St, Puyallup, E 🏧 Shell, 🅾 Majestic RV Park (4mi), W 🏧 Arco, 🛏 La Quinta, 🅾 to Tacoma Dome
134	Portland Ave (from nb), same as 135
133	WA 7, I-705, City Ctr, W 🛏 Best Western, Courtyard, 🅾 Tacoma Dome, museum
132	WA 16 W, S 38th, Gig Harbor, to Bremerton, W 🍴 Adriatic Grill, Jamba Juice, Jimmy John's, Krispy Kreme, Panera Bread, Quiznos, Red Robin, Subway, Wendy's, 🅾 Best Buy, Costco/gas, $Tree, Firestone/auto, Ford/Toyota, Goodyear/auto, JC Penney, JoAnn Fabrics, Macy's, Nordstrom, PetCo, Sears/auto, Verizon, to Pt Defiance Pk/Zoo, mall
130	S 56th, Tacoma Mall Blvd, W 🏧 Shell/dsl, 🍴 Azteca Mexican, ChuckeCheese, Jack-in-the-Box, Subway, Wingers,

130	Continued
	🛏 Extended Stay America
129	S 72nd, S 84th, E 🏧 Chevron, Valero, 🍴 Applebee's, Burger King, DQ, Elmer's, Famous Dave's, IHOP, Jack-in-the-Box, Mongolian Grill, Olive Garden, Red Lobster, RoundTable Pizza, Shari's, Starbucks, Subway, 🛏 Motel 6, Shilo Inn, 🅾 Lowe's, WinCo Foods, W 🍴 Hooters, 🛏 Days Inn, 🅾 Home Depot, to Steilacoom Lake
128	S 84th St (from nb)same as 129, E 🏧 76, Shell/dsl, 🍴 Denny's, Greatwall Chinese, Neo Woodfire Pizza, Subway, 🛏 American Lodge, Comfort Inn, Crossland Suites, Hampton Inn, Holiday Inn Express, King Oscar Motel, Red Lion Hotel, Rodeway Inn, Rothem Inn, Tacoma Inn, W 🏧 Shell, 🅾 Discount Tire
127	WA 512, S Tacoma Way, Puyallup, Mt Ranier, W 🏧 Arco, 7-11, 76/Circle K, 🍴 DQ, Ivar's Seafood, Mazatlan Mexican, McDonald's, Sizzler, Starbucks, Subway, Taco Guaynas, Taco Time, Wendy's, 🛏 Best Value Inn, Candlewood Suites, 🅾 Grocery Outlet, O'Reilly Parts, transmissions
125	to McChord AFB, Lakewood, W 🏧 Chevron, 76/Circle K/dsl, 🍴 A&W/KFC, Carr's Rest., Church's, Denny's, Greek Cafe, Pizza Hut, Wendy's, 🛏 La Quinta, 🅾 🅷 Aamco, Ford, NAPA, O'Reilly Parts, 7-11, U-Haul, tires/repair, vet
124	Gravelly Lake Dr, W 🏧 Arco/repair, 76/Circle K, 🍴 El Toro Mexican, Pizza Casa, Red Robin (2mi), same as 125
123	Thorne Lane, Tillicum Lane
122	Berkeley St, Camp Murray, E 🅾 🅷, W 🏧 Chevron/repair, 🍴 BBQ Inn, Gertie's Grill, Happy Wok, KFC, McDonald's, Papa John's, Pizza Hut, Subway, Taco Bell, Teryaki Hut, 🅾 AutoZone, 7-11
120	Ft Lewis, E 🅾 Ft Lewis Military Museum
119	Du Pont Rd, Steilacoom, E to Ft Lewis, W 🏧 Chevron, 76, 🍴 Jack-in-the-Box, Starbucks, Subway
118	Center Dr, W 🏧 Chevron/dsl, 🍴 Domino's, Farrelli's Pizza, Fortune Cookie Chinese, Jack-in-the-Box, Koko's Wok, McNamara's Eatery, McDonald's, Quiznos, Starbucks, Subway, Super Buffet, Viva Mexico, 🛏 GuestHouse Inn, Liberty Inn
117mm	weigh sta nb
116	Mounts Rd, Old Nisqually, E Lacy Creek Cafe, golf
115mm	Nisqually River
114	Nisqually, E 🏧 Chevron/repair, Shell/dsl/LP, 🍴 Nisqually Grill, Norma's Burgers, Shipwreck Café, 🅾 Nisqually RV Park, River Bend RV Park (3mi), WLYH RV Park (2mi)
111	WA 510 E, Marvin Rd, to Yelm, E 🏧 Chevron, 76/Circle K, Shell/dsl, 🍴 Burger King, Coldstone, Hawk's Prairie Rest./casino, Jack-in-the-Box, Jamba Juice, KFC/LJ Silver, McDonald's, Panda Express, Panera Bread, Papa Murphy's, Puerto Vallarta, Quiznos, RoundTable Pizza, Starbucks, Super Buffet, Taco Del Mar, Taco Time, 🛏 Best Western, King Oscar Motel, 🅾 Best Buy, BigLots, Costco/gas, $Tree, Harley Davidson, Home Depot, O'Reilly Parts, Radio Shack, Safeway/gas, Schwab Tire, Verizon, Walgreens, Walmart/Subway, WLYH RV Park (2mi), W 🏧 Pacific Pride/dsl, 🍴 Mayan Mexican, 🅾 Cabela's, Tolmie SP (5mi), RV camping
109	Martin Way, Sleator-Kenny Rd, E 🍴 Main Chinese Buffet, Taco Bell, The Rock Pizza, 🅾 Discount Tire, ShopKO, Top Food, W 🏧 Shell/dsl, 🍴 Casa Mia, Denny's, El Serape Mexican, Red Lobster, Shari's, Subway, 🛏 Comfort Inn, La Quinta, Ramada Inn, Super 8, 🅾 🅷 Tire Factory
108	Sleater-Kinney Rd, E 🏧 Shell/dsl, 🍴 Applebee's, Arby's,

🅝 INTERSTATE 5 CONT'D

OLYMPIA

Exit	Services
108	Continued McDonald's/playplace, Starbucks, Wendy's, 🅾 $Tree, Firestone/auto, Fred Meyer, Kohl's, Marshall's, Michael's, Office Depot, Petsmart, Radio Shack, Rite Aid, Sears/auto, Target, Tuesday Morning, Verizon, **W** 🅖 Shell, 🍴 Casa Mia, Coldstone, Dirty Dave's, El Sarape Mexican, Jack-in-the-Box, Panda Express, Subway, 🛏 Ramada Inn, 🅾 🅷 K-Mart, Lowe's, Safeway/gas, Tire Factory, same as 109
107	Pacific Ave, **E** 🅖 Shell/dsl/E-85, 🍴 DQ, Izzy's Pizza, Shari's, Sizzler, Subway, Taco Time, 🅾 🅷 Albertson's/Sav-on, Home Depot, Ross, vet, **W** 🅾 Coumbs RV Ctr, Ford
105	St Capitol, **W** 🅖 Chevron/dsl, Shell/Subway/dsl, 🛏 Quality Inn, 🅾 to St Capitol
104	US 101 N, W Olympia, to Aberdeen, **W** 🅖 Arco, Chevron, 7-11, 🍴 Jack-in-the-Box, Oly Burgers, 🛏 Extended Stay America, Red Lion Hotel, 🅾 🅷 to Capitol Mall
103	2nd Ave, Deschutes Ave, to hist dist
102	Trosper Rd, Black Lake, **E** 🅖 Shell/dsl, 🍴 Arby's, Brewery City Pizza, Burger King, El Sarape Mexican, Happy Teriyaki, Jack-in-the-Box, KFC, McDonald's, Plaza Jalisco Mexican, Starbucks, Subway, Taco Bell, Taco Time, 🛏 Best Western, Motel 6, 🅾 Ace Hardware, Goodyear/auto, O'Reilly Parts, **W** 🅖 Chevron, 76/Circle K, 🍴 Georglo's Subs, Nickelby's Rest., Panda Express, Papa Murphy's, Port of Subs, Starbucks, Subway, Taco Del Mar, The Brick Rest., 🅾 Albertson's/gas, Alderbrook RV Park, AutoZone, Costco/gas, Fred Meyer, GNC, Home Depot, MegaFoods, Radio Shack, Walmart
101	Tumwater Blvd, **E** 🅖 Chevron, Shell/dsl, 🍴 DQ (1mi), Inferno's Pizza, Quiznos, Teriyaki Wok, 🛏 Comfort Inn, GuestHouse Inn, Olympia Camping, 🅾 USPO
99	WA 121 S, 93rd Ave, Scott Lake, **E** 🅖 ⛽ McDonald's/Subway/dsl/scales/24hr, 🅾 Ace Hardware, American Heritage Camping, Olympia Camping, **W** 🅖 Shell/Michael's Rest./dsl/LP, 🛏 Restover Motel
95	WA 121, Littlerock, **3 mi E** 🅾 Millersylvania SP, RV camping, **W** 🅖 Chevron/dsl, 🍴 Farmboy Drive-In
93.5mm	🆁🆂 sb, full ♿ facilities, info, 🚻, 🛆, litter barrels, vending, coffee, petwalk
91mm	🆁🆂 nb, full ♿ facilities, info, 🚻, 🛆, litter barrels, vending, coffee, petwalk
88	US 12, Rochester, **E** 🅾 I-5 RV Ctr/Service, **W** 🅖 Arco, CFN, Chevron/dsl, 76/dsl, Shell/McDonald's, 🍴 Burger Claim, DQ, Figaro's Pizza, Little Red Barn Rest., Quiznos, The Grill, 🛏 Great Wolf Lodge, 🅾 Curves, Outback RV Park (2mi), truck wash

CENTRALIA

Exit	Services
82	Harrison Ave, Factory Outlet Way, Centralia, **E** 🅖 Arco, Shell/dsl, 🍴 Burger King, Burgerville, Casa Ramos Mexican, Centralia Deli, DQ, Panda Chinese, Papa Pete's Pizza, Peking House Chinese, Pizza Hut, Quiznos, Thai Dish, Wendy's, 🛏 Ferryman's Inn, King Oscar Motel, Rodeway Inn, 🅾 🅷 VF/famous brands, **W** 🅖 Chevron, Shell, Texaco/Circle K, 🍴 Arby's, Bill&Bea's, Country Cousin Rest., Denny's, Domino's, Jack-in-the-Box, McDonald's, Papa Murphy's, Starbucks, Subway, Taco Bell, 🛏 Motel 6, 🅾 Centralia Outlets/famous brands, Midway RV Park, O'Reilly Parts, Rite Aid, Safeway/dsl, Schwab Tire
82mm	Skookumchuck River

Exit	Services
81	WA 507, Mellen St, **E** 🅖 Chevron, Shell, 🍴 PJ's Rest., Subway, 🛏 Empress Inn, Pepper Tree Motel/RV Park/dump, Travel Inn, **W** 🅷
79	Chamber Way, **E** 🅖 Shell/dsl, 🍴 Jalisco Mexican, 🅾 Goodyear/auto, museum, visitor info, **W** 🅖 Texaco/dsl/LP, 🍴 Applebee's, Coldstone, McDonald's, Roobucks Pizza, Starbucks, Subway, Taco Del Mar, Wendy's, 🅾 $Tree, Ford, GNC, Grocery Outlet, Home Depot, K-Mart/Little Caesar's, Michael's, Radio Shack, Toyota/Scion, Verizon, Walgreens, Walmart/McDonald's, st patrol
77	WA 6 W, Chehalis, **E** 🅖 Cenex/dsl/LP, 76/dsl, 🍴 Dairy Bar, 🛏 Holiday Inn Express, 🅾 NAPA, Schwab Tire, USPO, **W** 🅾 Rainbow Falls SP (16mi), truck parts, veterans museum
76	13th St, **E** 🅖 Arco, Chevron/dsl, 🍴 Denny's, Jack-in-the-Box, Kit Carson Rest., South Pacific Bistro, Subway, 🛏 Best Western, Chehalis Inn, Relax Inn, 🅾 Baydo's RV Ctr, Uhlmann's I-5 RV Ctr/RV dump, **W** RV park/dump
74	Labree Rd
72	Rush Rd, Napavine, **E** 🅖 Shell/dsl/scales, 🍴 Burger King, McDonald's, RibEye Rest., Subway, 🅾 Dave's RV Ctr/repair, RV park, **W** 🅖 Loves/Carl's Jr/dsl/scales/24hr, Shell/dsl
72mm	Newaukum River
71	WA 508 E, Onalaska, Napavine, **E** 🅖 76/dsl, 🅾 KC Truck Parts
68	US 12 E, Morton, **E** 🅖 Arco/dsl, Texaco/dsl, 🍴 Spiffy's Rest., 🅾 RV Park, to Lewls&Clark SP, Mt Ranier NP, **W** 🅖 76/rest./dsl, 🍴 Jammer's Rest.
63	WA 505, Winlock, **W** 🅖 Shell/Chesters/dsl/LP
60	Toledo Vader Rd
59	WA 506 W, Vader, **E** 🅖 Shell/dsl, 🍴 Beesley's Cafe, **W** 🅖 Chevron/Subway/dsl, 🍴 Country House Rest.
59mm	Cowlitz River
57	Jackson Hwy, Barnes Dr, **E** 🅾 R&R Tires, **W** 🅖 GeeCee's/café/dsl/scales/24hr/@, 🅾 repair, RV camping
55mm	🆁🆂 both lanes, full ♿ facilities, 🚻, 🛆, litter barrels, vending, petwalk
52	Barnes Dr, Toutle Park Rd, **E** 🅾 Paradise Cove RV Park/general store, **W** 🅾 Toutle River RV Resort
50mm	Toutle River
49	WA 504 E, Castle Rock, **E** 🅖 Shell/dsl, Texaco/dsl/LP, 🍴 Burger King, C&L Burgers, El Compadre Mexican, 49er Diner, Papa Pete's Pizza, RoseTree Rest., Subway, 🛏 Mt St Helens Motel, 7 West Motel, Silver Lake Motel/RV resort, Timberland Inn, 🅾 Seaquest SP (5mi)
48	Castle Rock, **W** 🍴 Hattie's Rest. (2mi), 🅾 Cedars RV Park/dump
46	Pleasant Hill Rd, Headquarters Rd, **E** 🅾 Cedars RV Park/dump

🅖 = gas 🍴 = food 🛏 = lodging 🅞 = other 🆁🆂 = rest stop Copyright 2014 - The NEXT Exit ®

WA

🔼 INTERSTATE 5 CONT'D

Exit	Services
44mm	**weigh sta sb**, 🅲
42	Bridge Dr, Lexington, **W** 🅖 Chevron/dsl
40	to WA 4, Kelso-Longview
39	WA 4, Kelso, to Longview, **E** 🅖 Arco, Shell, 🍴 Denny's, Grinder Rest., McDonald's, Shari's, Subway, Taco Time, 🛏 Motel 6, Red Lion Hotel, 🅞 Brook Hollow RV Park, Rite Aid, city park, **W** 🍴 Azteca Mexican, Burger King, ChuckeCheese, DQ, Izzy's Pizza, Red Lobster, Starbucks, Taco Bell, 🛏 Comfort Inn, GuestHouse Inn, 🅞 JC Penney, Macys, Safeway/dsl, Sears/auto, Target, mall, museum
36	WA 432 W, to WA 4, to US 30, Kelso, **E** 🅞 U-Neek RV Ctr, **W** 🅞 Toyota/Scion, RV Camping
32	Kalama River Rd, **E** 🍴 Fireside Café, 🅞 Camp Kalama RV Park/camping/gifts
31mm	Kalama River
30	Kalama, **E** 🅖 Chevron/dsl, 🍴 Burger Bar, Columbia Rest., Lucky Dragon Chinese, Playa Azul Mexican, Poker Pete's Pizza, Subway, 🛏 Columbia Motel, Kalama River Inn, 🅞 Godfrey's Drug, USPO, antiques, **W** 🅖 Spirit/dsl, 🅞 RV camping
27	Todd Rd, Port of Kalama, **E** 🅖 Rebel/Shell/café/dsl/24hr
22	Dike Access Rd, **E** 🅞 tires, transmissions, **W** 🅖 CFN/dsl, 🅞 Columbia Riverfront RV Park
21	WA 503 E, Woodland, **E** 🅖 Arco, Chevron, Pacific Pride, Shell/LP/dsl, 🍴 America's Diner, Burgerville, Casa Tapatia, DQ, Fat Moose Grill, Figaro's, Guilliano's Pizza, Mali Thai, OakTree Rest., Rosie's Rest., 🛏 Lewis River Inn, Motel 6, Woodland Inn, 🅞 Ace Hardware, Hi-School Drug, Radio Shack, Woodland Shores RV Park, **W** 🅖 Astro, Shell, 🍴 Guadalajara Mexican, McDonald's, Papa Murphy's, Quiznos, Starbucks, Subway, 🛏 Hansen's Motel, Scandia Motel, 🅞 NAPA, Oil Can Henry's, Safeway/dsl, repair
20mm	N Fork Lewis River
18mm	E Fork Lewis River
16	NW La Center Rd, La Center, **E** 🅖 Shell/dsl, 🍴 Twin Dragons Rest., 🅞 Paradise Point SP, Tri-Mountain Golf/rest.
15mm	**weigh sta nb**
14	WA 501 S, Pioneer St, Ridgefield, **E** 🅖 Arco, 76/Circle K/dsl, 🍴 Country Café, Papa Pete's Pizza, Subway, 🅞 to Battleground Lake SP (14mi), Big Fir RV Park (4mi), Ridgefield WR, Tri-Mountain RV Park, **W** 🅖 Chevron/dsl
13mm	🆁🆂 sb, full 🚻 facilities, info, 🅲, 🗑, litter barrels, vending, petwalk, **RV dump**
11	WA 502, Battleground, 🆁🆂 nb, full 🚻 facilities, info, 🅲, 🗑, litter barrels, vending, petwalk, **RV dump**
9	NE 179th St, **E** 🍴 Jollie's Rest., **W** 🅖 Chevron/dsl, 🅞 RV Park
7	I-205 S (from sb), to I-84, WA 14, NE 134th St, **E** 🅖 Arco, 7-11, 76, TrailMart/dsl, 🍴 Applebee's, Billygan's Roadhouse, Booster Juice, Burger King, Burgerville, Jack-in-the-Box, McDonald's, Muchas Gracias, Panda Express, Round Table Pizza, Starbucks, Subway, Taco Bell, Taco Del Mar, 🛏 Comfort Inn, Holiday Inn Express, Olympia Motel, Red Lion, Salmon Creek Inn, Shilo Inn, 🅞 🅷, Albertson's/gas, Long's Drugs, Safeway/gas, Zupan's Mkt, 99 RV Park, to Portland 🍴, **W** 🅖 Shell, 🍴 Baskin-Robbins, Coldstone, El Tapatio, Papa Murphy's, PizzaSchmizza, Quizno's, Starbucks, The Great Impasta, 🛏 La Quinta, 🅞 Fred Meyer

VANCOUVER

Exit	Services
5	NE 99th St, **E** 🅖 7-11, 🍴 Burgerville, Carl's Jr, Del Taco, Domino's, Fat Dave's Rest., Quiznos, 🅞 Harley-Davidson, Nissan/Kia, Walgreens, Walmart/Subway, Winco Foods/gas, **W** 🅖 Arco/dsl, Chevron/dsl, 🍴 Applebee's, Bortolami's Pizza, McDonald's, Papa John's, Primo's Subs, Subway, Taco Del Mar, 🅞 $Tree, Kohl's, Office Depot, PetCo, Target
4	NE 78th St, Hazel Dell, **E** 🅖 76, 7-11, 🍴 Baja Fresh, Burger King, Don Pedro Mexican, Dragon Buffet, KFC, McDonald's, Pizza Hut, PeachTree Rest., Skipper's, Smokey's Pizza, Steakburger, Subway, Taco Bell, 🛏 Quality Inn, 🅞 Aamco, CarQuest, CostLess Parts, Firestone, Fred Meyer, Dodge, Ford, Mazda, Nissan, Radio Shack, Save-A-Lot Foods, Schuck's Parts, Tire Factory, U-Haul, **W** 🅖 Shell/dsl/LP, 🍴 Jack-in-the-Box, Nick&Willy's Pizza, Panda Express, RoundTable Pizza, Starbucks, Tully's Coffee, Wendy's, 🅞 Petsmart, Ross, Safeway, Tuesday Morning
3	NE Hwy 99, Main St, Hazel Dell, **E** 🅖 7-11, 🍴 Muchas Gracias Mexican, Pizza Hut, Skippers, 🅞 🅷, Schwab Tire, vet, **W** 🅖 Arco/dsl, 76/dsl, 🅞 Safeway, transmissions
2	WA 500 E, 39th St, to Orchards
1d	E 4th, Plain Blvd W, to WA 501, Port of Vancouver
1c	Mill Plain Blvd, City Ctr, **W** 🅖 Chevron, 🍴 Black Angus, Burgerville, 🛏 Comfort Inn, 🅞 Clark Coll, st patrol
1b	6th St, **E** 🍴 Joe's Crabshack, **W** 🛏 EconoLodge, Hilton
1a	WA 14 E, to Camas, **E** 🅷, **W** 🛏 EconoLodge, Hilton
0mm	Washington/Oregon state line, Columbia River

🔼 INTERSTATE 82

Exit	Services
11mm	**I-82 Oregon begins/ends on I-84, exit 179.**
10	Westland Rd, **E** 🅞 to Umatilla Army Depot
5	Power Line Rd
1.5mm	Umatilla River
1	US 395/730, Umatilla, **E** 🍴 Jack-in-the-Box (5mi), 🛏 Best Western (8mi), Desert Inn/rest. (2mi), Motel 6 (8mi), Oxford Inn (5mi), 🅞 Hatrock Camping (8mi), to McNary Dam, **W** 🅖 Shell/Crossroads Trkstp/dsl/rest./24hr, Tesoro/Subway/dsl, Texaco/dsl, 🛏 Tillicum Motel, Umatilla Inn, 🅞 Harvest Foods, USPO, st police, Umatilla Marina/RV Park, **Welcome Ctr, weigh sta**
132mm	Washington/Oregon state line, Columbia River
131	WA 14 W, Plymouth, **N** 🅞 RV camping, to McNary Dam
130mm	**weigh sta wb**
122	Coffin Rd
114	Locust Grove Rd
113	US 395 N, to I-182, Kennewick, Pasco, **2-4 mi N** 🅖 Chevron, Exxon, Mirastar/dsl, Tesoro/dsl, 🍴 A&W/KFC, Azteca Mexican, Bob's Burgers, Burger King, Carl's Jr, DQ, Denny's, Jack-in-the-Box, Little Caesars, McDonald's, Panda Express, Starbucks, Subway, Taco Bell, 🛏 Baymont Inn, Best Western, Days Inn, EconoLodge, La Quinta, 🅞 🅷 AT&T, $Tree, Fred Meyer/dsl, GNC, Harley-Davidson, Home Depot, PetCo, Radio Shack, Rite Aid, Safeway/dsl, Traveland RV Ctr, Verizon, Walgreens, Walmart/Blimpie, st patrol
109	Badger Rd, W Kennewick, **N** 🅖 Shell/Subway/dsl, 🍴 Chico's Tacos, **3 mi N** 🛏 Guesthouse Suites, Quality Inn, Red Lion Hotel, Super 8
104	Dallas Rd, **3 mi N** 🅖 Conoco/dsl

KELSO KALAMA

KENNEWICK

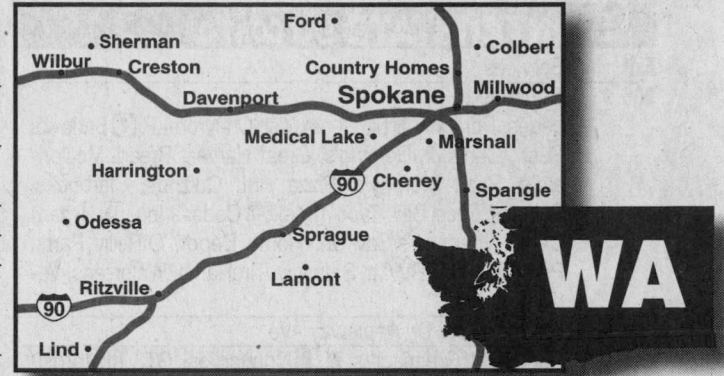

🚏 INTERSTATE 82 CONT'D

Exit	Services
102	I-182, US 12 E, to US 395, Spokane, 🅗, services in Richland, Pasco
96	WA 224 E, Benton City, **N** 🅖 Conoco/cafe/dsl, 🅞 Beach RV Park
93	Yakitat Rd
88	Gibbon Rd
82	WA 22, WA 221, Mabton, **S** 🅖 Conoco, **2 mi S** 🛏 Prosser Motel, 🅞 🅗, to WAS U Research, to Wine Tasting, museum
82mm	Yakima River
80	Gap Rd, **S** 🅖 Chevron/dsl, Pacific Pride/dsl, Shell/dsl/scales, 🍽 Burger King, El Rancho Alegre, Golden Horse Chinese, KFC/Taco Bell, McDonald's, Starbucks, Subway, 🛏 Barn Motel/RV Park/rest., Best Western, Prosser Motel, 🅞 🅗, Ford, Wine Country RV Park, 🅟ₛ **both lanes, full** 🚻 **facilities,** 🅒, 🛒, **litter barrels, rv dump**
76mm	**weigh sta eb**
75	County Line Rd, Grandview, **S** 🅖 Cenex/dsl, Conoco/dsl (1mi)
73	Stover Rd, Wine Country Rd, Grandview, **S** 🅖 Chevron/Subway/dsl, Conoco/dsl, 🍽 DQ, Eli&Kathy's Rest., New Hong Kong, 10-4 Café, 🛏 Apple Valley Motel, Grandview Motel, 🅞 Chrysler/Dodge/Jeep, Grandview Mkt, Safeway, Schwab Tire, auto repair, RV park/dump
69	WA 241, Vernita Bridge, to Sunnyside, **N** 🅖 Arco/dsl, Mirastar, Shell/TacoMaker/dsl/scales/24hr, 🍽 A&W, Burger King, China Buffet, China Grove, El Charrito Mexican, KFC, Little Caesars, McDonald's, Mongolian Grill, Papa Murphy's, Pizza Hut, Skipper's, Subway, Taco Bell, 🛏 Best Western, Rodeway Inn, 🅞 AT&T, AutoZone, Buick/Chevrolet, $Tree, Fiesta Foods, GNC, JC Penney, O'Reilly Parts, Radio Shack, Rite Aid, Walmart/Subway
67	Sunnyside, Port of Sunnyside, **N** 🅖 Chevron/CFN/dsl, Conoco/dsl/e85, 🍽 Jack-in-the-Box, 🅞 🅗, BiMart Foods, **S** 🅞 DariGold Cheese
63	Sunnyside, Outlook **3 mi N** 🍽 Snipe's Rest., 🛏 Country Inn&Suites, Travel Inn, 🅞 RV camping
58	WA 223 S, to Granger, **S** 🅖 Arco/dsl, Conoco/dsl
54	Division Rd, Yakima Valley Hwy, to Zillah, **S** 🅞 Teapot Dome NHS
52	Zillah, Toppenish, **N** 🅖 Chevron/dsl, Shell/dsl, 🍽 El Porton Mexican, McDonald's, Pizza Hut, Subway, Tuscan Sans Rest., 🛏 Comfort Inn
50	WA 22 E, to US 97 S, Toppenish, **3-4 mi S** 🍽 Legends Buffet/casino, McDonald's, 🛏 Days Inn, Quality Inn, 🅞 🅗 Murals Museum, RV Park, to Yakima Nation Cultural Ctr
44	Wapato, **N** 🅖 Shell/dsl
40	Thorp Rd, Parker Rd, Yakima Valley Hwy, **N** 🅞 Sagelands Vineyard/Winery, **S** 🅞 Windy Point Vineyard
39mm	Yakima River
38	Union Gap (from wb), **1 mi S** 🅞 gas, lodging, museum
37	US 97 (from eb), **1 mi S** 🅖 Shell
36	Valley Mall Blvd, Yakima, **S** 🅖 Arco/dsl, Cenex/dsl, Shell/Gearjammer/Subway/dsl/scales/24hr/@, 🍽 Applebee's, A&W/KFC, Burger King, Coldstone, Denny's, El Porton Mexican, IHOP, McDonald's, Miner's Drive-In, Old Country Buffet, Outback Steaks, SeaGalley Rest., Shari's, Starbucks, Subway, Taco Bell, 🛏 Best Western, Quality Inn, Super 8, 🅞 Best Buy, Canopy RV Ctr, Gap Autoparts, Kohl's, Lowe's, Office Depot, Old Navy, Macy's, PetCo,

Exit	Services
36	Continued Rite Aid, Ross, Sears/auto, ShopKO, Tire Factory, TJ Maxx, Verizon, dsl/repair, mall, st patrol
34	WA 24 E, Nob Hill Blvd, Yakima, **N** 🅞 K-Mart, Sportsman SP, dsl/repair, **S** 🅖 Arco/dsl, CFN/dsl, 76/dsl, 7-11, Time/dsl, 🍽 McDonald's, 🅞 🅗, 19th Hole RV Park, Freightliner, Kenworth, 19th Hole RV Park, O'Reilly Parts, Peterbilt, Volvo
33	Yakima Ave, Yakima, **N** 🅖 Chevron/dsl, Shell/Chester's/dsl, 🍽 Burger King, El Mirador Mexican, 🛏 Oxford Inn&Suites, 🅞 Chevrolet, Honda, Walmart/McDonald's, **S** 🅖 Arco, 7-11, 🍽 Bob's Burgers, DQ, Pizza Hut, Taco Bell, 🛏 Cedars Suites, Fairfield Inn, Holiday Inn, Holiday Inn Express, Howard Johnson, Ledgestone Hotel, Red Lion Hotel, 🅞 BigLots, Schwab Tire, Target
31b a	US 12 W, N 1st St, to Naches, **S** 🅖 Arco/dsl, Shell, 🍽 Arctic Circle, Black Angus Steaks, Golden Moon Chinese, Goody's Rest., Jack-in-the-Box, Mel's Diner, NY Teryaki, Peking Palace, Red Lobster, Subway, Waffle's Cafe, Wendy's, 🛏 All Star Motel, Best Western, Clarion, Days Inn, EconoLodge, Knights Inn, Motel 6, Red Apple Motel, Rodeway Inn, Sun Country Inn, Sunshine Motel, Yakima Inn, 🅞 Harley-Davidson, Trailer Inns RV Park
30	WA 823 N, Rest Haven Rd, to Selah
29	E Selah Rd, **N** 🅞 fruits/antiques
26	WA 821 N, to WA 823, Canyon Rd, **N** 🅖 Shell/Noble Romans/Subway/dsl
24mm	🅟ₛ eb, full 🚻 facilities, 🛒 litter barrels, RV dump
23mm	Selah Creek
22mm	🅟ₛ wb, full 🚻 facilities, 🛒 litter barrels, RV dump
21mm	S Umptanum Ridge, 2265 elev
19mm	Burbank Creek
17mm	N Umptanum Ridge, 2315 elev
15mm	Lmuma Creek
11	Military Area
8mm	view point both lanes, Manastash Ridge, 2672 elev
3	WA 821 S, Thrall Rd
0mm	I-90, E to Spokane, W to Seattle. **I-82 begins/ends on I-90, exit 110.**

🚏 INTERSTATE 90

Exit	Services
300mm	Washington/Idaho state line, Spokane River
299	State Line, Port of Entry, **N** Welcome Ctr/🅟ₛ both lanes, full 🚻 facilities, 🅒, 🛒, litter barrels, petwalk, **N** 🅞 Cabela's, Walmart
298mm	weigh sta wb
296	Otis Orchards, Liberty Lakes, **N** 🅖 Conoco/dsl, 🍽 Legend's Grill, 🛏 Best Western, 🅞 Buick/GMC, Kia, Mer

(Side label: YAKIMA)
(Side label: SUNNYSIDE)

WA | **VERADALE** | **SPOKANE**

🅴 INTERSTATE 90 CONT'D

Exit	Services
296	Continued cedes, Porsche, S 🅰 Cenex/dsl, Chevron/LP, 🍴 Barlow's Rest., Carl's Jr, Domino's, Great Harvest Bread, McDonald's, Papa Murphy's, Pizza Hut, Quiznos, Starbucks, Subway, Taco Bell, Taco Time, 🛏 Cedar's Inn, 🅾 Urgent Care, Albertson's/Sav-On, Home Depot, O'Reilly Parts, Peterbilt, RNR RV Ctr, Safeway, TireRama, Walgreens, Verizon, vet
294	Country Vista Dr, Appleway Ave
293	Barker Rd, Greenacres, N 🅰 Conoco/dsl, GTS Trkstp/dsl/scales, 🍴 Roadside Grill, Wendy's, 🅾 Freedom RV Ctr, Harley-Davidson, S 🅰 Exxon/Subway/dsl, Mobil/dsl, 🅾 NW RV Ctr, repair, USPO
291b	Sullivan Rd, Veradale, N 🍴 Arby's, Hooters, Krispy Kreme, Outback Steaks, 🛏 Hampton Inn, Oxford Suites, Residence Inn, 🅾 AT&T, Avocado Buffet, Barnes&Noble, Best Buy, Jo-Ann Fabrics, Staples, mall, S 🅰 Cenex, Chevron/dsl, Conoco/dsl, Tesoro, 🍴 A&W, DQ, 5 Guys Burgers, Jack-in-the-Box, KFC, Little Caesars, McDonald's, Mongolian BBQ, Noodle Express, Panda Express, Pizza Hut, Schlotzsky's, Shari's, Starbucks, Subway, Taco Bell, Wendy's, 🛏 Mirabeau Park Hotel, Ramada Inn, 🅾 Ace Hardware, $Tree, Fred Meyer/dsl, Hancock Fabrics, Hastings Books, Kohl's, Lowe's, Michael's, NAPA, PetCo, Petsmart, Ross, Schwab Tire, Verizon, Walgreens, Walmart, USPO
291a	Evergreen Rd, N 🍴 Azteca Mexican, Black Angus, Boston's Rest, IHOP, Red Robin, Wingers, 🅾 Hobby Lobby, JC Penney, Macy's, Old Navy, Sears/auto, TJ Maxx, mall, S 🅰 Exxon/dsl
289	WA 27 S, Pines Rd, Opportunity, N 🅰 7-11, 🍴 Black Pearl Rest., Subway, S 🅰 Cenex, Conoco/dsl, Holiday, 🍴 Applebee's, DQ, Jack-in-the-Box, Old Country Buffet, Qdoba Mexican, Quiznos, 🛏 Pheasant Hill Inn, 🅾 🅷, Walgreens, repair
287	Argonne Rd, Millwood, N 🅰 Holiday/dsl, 🍴 Burger King, Denny's, Domino's, DQ, Jack-in-the-Box, Longhorn BBQ, Marie Callender's, McDonald's, Panda Express, Papa Murphy's, Pizza Hut, Starbucks, Subway, Taco Time, Timber Creek Grill, Wendy's, 🛏 Motel 6, Super 8, 🅾 Albertson's/gas, $Tree, O'Reilly Parts, Savon, Walgreens, Yoke's Foods, S 🅰 Cenex/dsl, Conoco, 🍴 Casa de Oro Mexican, Little Caesars, Perkins, Starbucks, 🛏 Holiday Inn Express, Quality Inn, 🅾 Curves, Rite Aid, Safeway
286	Broadway Ave, N 🅰 Chevron, ✈FLYING J/Conoco/rest./dsl/LP/scales/24hr/@, 🍴 Smacky's Cafe, Zip's Burgers, Goodyear, 🛏 Rodeway Inn, 🅾 International Trucks, Volvo, Kenworth, Schwab Tire, S 🅾 7-11
285	Sprague Ave, N 🍴 Dragon Garden Chinese, IHOP, Jack-in-the-Box, McDonald's, Subway, Wendy's, 🛏 ParkLane Motel/RV Park, 🅾 AutoZone, Costco/gas, Grocery Outlet, Freightliner, Home Depot, K-Mart/Little Caesars, Lowe's, O'Reilly Parts, Radio Shack, S 🅰 Conoco, 🍴 Cottage Cafe, Puerta Vallarta Mexican, Starbucks, Stop&Go Rest., Taco Time, Zip's Burger, 🅾 Chrysler/Dodge, Nissan, Tirerama, Trailer Inn RV Park, transmissions, vet
284	Havana St (from eb, no EZ return), N 🅰 Tesoro/dsl, 🍴 Jack-in-the-Box, McDonald's, Wolf Lodge Steaks, S 🅰 Conoco/dsl, 🅾 Fred Meyer/dsl
283b	Freya St, Thor St, N 🅰 Tesoro/dsl, 🍴 Jack-in-the-Box, McDonald's, Wolf Lodge Steaks, S 🅰 Conoco/dsl, 🅾 Fred Meyer/dsl

CHENEY

Exit	Services
283a	Altamont St, S 🅰 Cenex
282b	2nd Ave, N 🅰 Conoco/dsl, 🛏 Comfort Inn, 🅾 Office Depot
282a	WA 290 E, Trent Ave, Hamilton St, N 🅰 Conoco/dsl, 🛏 Comfort Inn, 🅾 Office Depot
281	US 2, US 395, to Colville, N 🅰 Conoco, Exxon, 7-11, Tesoro/dsl, 🍴 Arby's, Dick's Hamburgers, Frankie Doodles Rest., Ichiban Buffet, Starbucks, Subway, Taco Time, 🛏 Days Inn, FairBridge Inn, 🅾 Firestone/auto, Schwab Tire, U-Haul, S 🛏 Quality Inn, 🅾 🅷
280b	Lincoln St, N 🅰 Conoco/dsl, 🍴 Carl's Jr, Domino's, Jack-in-the-Box, McDonald's, Molly's Rest., Taco Bell, Taste of Asia, Thai Cuisine, Zip's Burgers, 🛏 Tradewinds Motel, 🅾 Honda, Lexus, Toyota/Scion, Troy's Tire, S 🅷
280a	Spokane, downtown, N 🅰 Chevron/McDonald's/dsl, Conoco/dsl, 🍴 Frank's Diner, 🛏 Select Motel, 🍴 Pizza Hut, Subway, 🅾 AAA, Jaguar, Land Rover, Volvo
279	US 195 S, Pullman, to Colfax
277b a	US 2 W (no ez wb return), to Grand Coulee Dam, Fairchild AFB, N 🛏 Best Value Inn, Blvd Motel, EconoLodge, Hampton Inn, Motel 6, Sunset Motel, West Wynn Motel
276	Geiger Blvd, N 🅰 ✈FLYING J/dsl/LP/24hr, 🍴 Denny's, Subway, 🛏 Airway Express Inn, Best Western, 🅾 st patrol, S 🅰 Conoco/dsl, 🅾 Hideaway RV Park
272	WA 902, Medical Lake, N 🅰 Mobil/dsl, 🅾 Overland Sta/RV Park, S 🅰 Exxon/Subway/dsl, Petro/Iron Skillet/dsl/scales/24hr/@, 🍴 McDonald's, 🛏 Super 8, 🅾 Freightliner, Ponderosa Falls RV Resort, truck repair
270	WA 904, Cheney, Four Lakes, S 🅰 Exxon, 🛏 Holiday Inn Express (4mi), Willow Springs Motel (6mi), 🅾 Peaceful Pines RV Park (7mi), E WA U
264	WA 902, Salnave Rd, to Cheney, Medical Lake, **2 mi N** camping
257	WA 904, Tyler, to Cheney, S 🅾 Peaceful Pines RV Park (10mi), Tyler Store/RV Park, to Columbia Plateau Trail SP
254	Fishtrap, S 🅾 Fishtrap RV camping/tents
245	WA 23, Sprague, S 🅰 Chevron/dsl, 🍴 Viking Drive-In, 🛏 Sprague Motel, 🅾 4 Seasons RV Park (6mi), Sprague Lake Resort/RV Park
242mm	🆁 **both lanes, full ♿ facilities, 📞, 🚮, litter barrels, tourist/weather info, petwalk, RV dump (eb)**
231	Tokio, **S weigh sta both lanes**, 🅰 Templin's Café/CFN/dsl, 🅾 RV Park
226	Schoessler Rd
221	WA 261 S, Ritzville, City Ctr, N 🅰 Conoco/dsl, Chevron/McDonald's, Shell/Subway/dsl, 🍴 Perkins, Starbucks, Taco Del Mar, Zip's Rest., 🛏 Best Western, Cedars Inn, The Cottage/RV Park, Empire Motel, Top Hat Motel, 🅾 🅷 Cow Creek Merchantile, hist dist, S 🅰 ♥Love's/Carl's Jr/dsl/scales/24hr
220	to US 395 S, Ritzville, N 🅰 Pacific Pride/dsl, Texaco/Jake's Rest./dsl, 🍴 Casuela's Grill, 🛏 Top Hat Motel, 🅾 Cedars Inn RV Park, Harvest Foods, Schwab Tire, st patrol
215	Paha, Packard
206	WA 21, Odessa, to Lind
199mm	🆁 **both lanes, full ♿ facilities, 📞, 🚮, litter barrels, vending, RV dump, petwalk**
196	Deal Rd, to Schrag
188	U Rd, to Warden, Ruff
184	Q Rd
182	O Rd, to Wheeler
179	WA 17, Moses Lake, N 🅰 Conoco/Subway/dsl, Ernie's

🅷🅴 INTERSTATE 90 CONT'D

Exit	Services
179	**Continued**
	Trkstp/Chevron/café/dsl/24hr, Texaco/dsl, 🍴 Arby's, Bob's Cafe, Burger King, Denny's, McDonald's, Shari's, Starbucks, Taco Bell, 🛏 Comfort Suites, Holiday Inn Express, Moses Lake Inn, Ramada Inn, Shilo Inn, 🅞 🎗, Chevrolet, Chrysler/Dodge/Jeep, Lowe's, Nissan, Toyota/Scion, vet, **1 mi N** 🍴 DQ, Subway, 🛏 El Rancho Motel, 🅞 $Tree, Ford/Lincoln, Honda, vet, **S** 🅞 I-90 RV, Mardon RV Park (15mi), Willows RV Park (2mi), Potholes SP (22mi)
177mm	**Moses Lake**
176	WA 171, Moses Lake, **N** 🅖 Cenex/dsl, Chevron/dsl, Conoco, Exxon/dsl, 76/dsl, Shell/dsl, 🍴 El Rodeo Mexican, Michael's Rest., Perkins, Subway, Taco Del Mar, 🛏 Best Western/rest., Interstate Inn, Motel 6, Oasis Motel, Super 8, 🅞 🎗, AAA RV Park, Ace Hardware, Harvest Foods, Lake Front RV Park, auto repair, transmissions, vet, **S** 🛏 Lakeshore Motel
175	Westshore Dr (from wb), **N** 🅞 Moses Lake SP, to Mae Valley, **S** 🅞 st patrol
174	Mae Valley, **N** 🅞 Suncrest Resort/RV, **S** 🅖 Conoco/dsl, 🅞 Pier 4 RV Park, st patrol
169	Hiawatha Rd
164	Dodson Rd, **N** 🅞 Sunbasin RV park/camp (1mi)
162mm	🆁🆂 **wb, full** ♿ **facilities,** 🄲, 🄿, **litter barrels, petwalk, RV dump**
161mm	🆁🆂 **eb, full** ♿ **facilities,** 🄲, 🄿, **litter barrels, petwalk, RV dump**
154	Adams Rd
151	WA 281 N, to Quincy, **N** 🅖 Shell/pizza/subs/dsl, 🅞 🎗 (12mi), Shady Grove RV park, to Grand Coulee Dam
149	WA 281 S, George, **N** 🎗 (12mi), **S** 🅖 Cenex/dsl, 76/Subway/dsl, 🅞 RV camp
143	Silica Rd to The Gorge Ampitheatre
139mm	Wild Horses Mon, scenic view both lanes
137	WA 26 E, to WA 243, Othello, Richland
137mm	Columbia River
136	Huntzinger Rd, Vantage, **N** 🅖 Spirit, Texaco/dsl, 🍴 Blustory's Burger Drive-in, Golden Harvest Rest., 🅞 Riverstone Vantage Resort/RV Park, Vantage Gen. Store, to Ginkgo SP, auto repair, **S** 🅞 to Wanapum SP (3mi)
126mm	Ryegrass, elev 2535, 🆁🆂 **both lanes, full** ♿ **facilities,** 🄲, 🄿, **litter barrels, petwalk**
115	Kittitas, **N** 🅖 Shell/dsl/LP, 🅞 Olmstead Place SP
110	I-82 E, US 97 S, to Yakima
109	Canyon Rd, Ellensburg, **N** 🅖 Astro/dsl, Chevron, Circle K, Eagle/dsl, 76, Shell, 🍴 Arby's, Baskin Robbins, BoxcCar Burgers, Burger King, East Chinese Buffet, Fiesta Mexican, Golden Dragon Chinese, KFC, Los Cabos Mexican, McDonald's, Papa Murphy's, RanchHouse Rest., Roadhouse Grill, Rodeo City BBQ, Starbucks, Subway, Taco Bell, Taco Del Mar, Wendy's, 🛏 Best Western, Comfort Inn, Goose Creek Inn, Holiday Inn Express, Quality Inn, Super 8, 🅞 🎗, AutoZone, CarQuest, Chevrolet, NAPA, O'Reilly Parts, Rite Aid, Schwab Tire, Super 1 Foods, TrueValue, vet, **S** 🅖 *FLYING J*/Sak's/dsl/scales/LP/24hr, 🍴 Buzz Inn Steaks, 🛏 Days Inn/RV park
106	US 97 N, to Wenatchie, **N** 🅖 Chevron/dsl, Conoco/dsl, ♥*Loves*/Subway/dsl/scales/24hr, 76/dsl, 🍴 DQ, Perkins, 🛏 Hampton Inn, I-90 Inn, Thunderbird Motel, 🅞 Buick/Cadillac/GMC, Canopy Country RV Ctr, Chrysler/Jeep, Truck/RV Wash, **S** 🅞 KOA, st patrol

Exit	Services
101	Thorp Hwy, **N** 🅖 Arco/dsl, 🅞 antiques/fruits/vegetables
93	Elk Heights Rd, Taneum Creek
92.5mm	Elk Heights, elev 2359
89mm	Indian John Hill, elev 2141, 🆁🆂 **both lanes, full** ♿ **facilities,** 🄲, 🄿, **litter barrels, RV dump, petwalk, vending**
85	WA 970, WA 903, to Wenatchie, **N** 🅖 Gas Save/dsl, 76/dsl, Shell/dsl, 🍴 Cottage Café, Giant Burger, Homestead Rest., 🛏 Aster Inn, Cascade Mtn Inn, Chalet Motel, Cle Elum Traveler's Inn, 🅞 vet
84	Cle Elum (from eb, return at 85), **N** 🅖 Chevron/dsl, Pacific Pride/dsl, Shell/Subway/dsl, 🍴 Beau's Pizza, Burger King, Caboose Grill, DQ, El Caporal Mexican, Lentine's Italian, MaMa Vallones, McDonald's, New Cam Chinese, Quiznos, Sahara Pizza, Sunset Café, Taco Del Mar, 🛏 Best Western Snowcap, Timber Lodge Inn, Stewart Lodge, 🅞 🎗, Cle Elum Drug, Cle Elum Hardware, NAPA AutoCare, Radio Shack, Safeway/dsl, Trailer Corral RV Park, museum
81mm	Cle Elum River
80	Roslyn, Salmon la Sac
80mm	**weigh sta both lanes**
78	Golf Course Rd, **S** 🅞 Sun Country Golf/RV Park
74	W Nelson Siding Rd
71	Easton, **S** 🅖 CB's Store/dsl/LP, 🅞 John Wayne Tr, Iron Horse SP, USPO
71mm	Yakima River
70	Sparks Rd, Easton, Lake Easton SP, **N** 🅖 Shell/RV Town/dsl/café, 🍴 Mtn High Burger, 🅞 Silver Ridge Ranch RV Park, repair, **S** 🅞 Easton Ridge RV Camping, Lake Easton SP
63	Cabin Creek Rd
62	Stampede Pass, elev 3750, to Lake Kachess, **N** Lake Kachess Lodge
54	Hyak, Gold Creek, **S** Ski Area
53	Snoqualmie Pass, elev 3022 info, **S** 🅖 Chevron, 🍴 Red Mtn Coffee, Xanadu Rest., 🛏 Summit Lodge, 🅞 to rec areas
52	W Summit (from eb), same as 53
47	Tinkham Rd, Denny Creek, Asahel Curtis, **N** 🅞 chain area, **S** 🅞 RV camping/dump
45	USFS Rd 9030, **N** 🅞 to Lookout Point Rd
42	Tinkham Rd
38	**N** 🅞 fire training ctr
35mm	S Fork Snoqualmie River
34	468th Ave SE, Edgewick Rd, **N** 🅖 76/BBQ/dsl, Shell/cafe/dsl, TA/Country Pride/dsl only/24hr/@, 🛏 Edgewick Inn, 🅞 Norwest RV Park
32	436th Ave SE, Snoqualmie Ranger Sta, **1 mi N** gas, food, lodging, **S** Iron Horse SP (3mi)
31	WA 202 W, North Bend, Snoqualmie, **N** 🅖 Chevron/dsl,

🅡 = gas 🍴 = food 🏠 = lodging 🅞 = other 🆁🆂 = rest stop   Copyright 2014 - The NEXT Exit ®

◥E INTERSTATE 90 CONT'D

Exit	Services
31	Continued Shell/dsl, 🍴 Arby's, Baskin-Robbins, Blimpie, Burger King, Los Cabos, McDonald's, Mongolian Grill, Papa Murphy's, Starbucks, Subway, Taco Time, 🏠 North Bend Motel, Sallish Lodge, Sunset Motel, 🅞 🄷, NorthBend Outlets/famous brands, O'Reilly Parts, Safeway/dsl, museum, st patrol
27	North Bend, Snoqualmie (from eb, no return), N 🅡 76/dsl, 🍴 Woodman's Steaks, 🅞 🄷
25	WA 18 W, Snoqualmie Pkwy, Tacoma, to Auburn, N 🅡 Shell/dsl/e85 (1.5mi), 🅞 weigh sta
22	Preston, N 🅡 Shell/dsl, 🍴 Burgers& Teriyaki, Subway, 🅞 LP, NAPA, Snoqualmie River RV Park (4mi), USPO, S 🅞 Blue Sky RV Park
20	High Point Way
18	E Sunset Way, Issaquah, S 🅡 Shell (1mi), 🍴 Flying Pie Pizza, Front St Mkt, Issaquah Brewhouse, Jack's Grill, Mandarin Garden, Shanghai Garden Chinese, Stan's BBQ, Sunset Alehouse, 🅞 Curves
17	E Sammamish Rd, Front St, Issaquah, N 🅡 76, 🍴 Coho Café, Coldstone, Fatburger, Jamba Juice, Krispy Kreme, McDonald's, Qdoba Mexican, Quiznos, Papa John's, Starbucks, Subway, 🅞 Urgent Care, AT&T, Bartell Drug, Best Buy, Fred Meyer, Home Depot, Verizon, Walgreens, S 🅡 Arco/dsl, Chevron/dsl, Shell/dsl, 🍴 Boehms Chocolates, Domino's, Extreme Pizza, La Costa Mexican, Las Margaritas, Pogacha Rest., Shanghai Garden Rest., Stan's BBQ, Subway, 🅞 Staples, transmissions
15	WA 900, Issaquah, Renton, N 🅡 Arco, 🍴 Cocina Cocina, Georgio's Subs, IHOP, O'Char Thai, Red Robin, Tully's Coffee, 🏠 Holiday Inn, Motel 6, 🅞 Barnes&Noble, Costco/gas, Lowe's, Michael's, Office Depot, Petsmart, Trader Joe's, to Lk Sammamish SP, vet, S 🅡 Shell/dsl, 🍴 Baskin-Robbins, Burger King, Cascade Garden Chinese, Chipotle Mexican, Denny's, Franky's Pizza, Georgio's Subs, Issaquah Cafe, Jack-in-the-Box, Jamba Juice, KFC/Taco Bell, Lombardi's Italian, McDonald's, Panera Bread, Papa Murphy's, RoundTable Pizza, Starbucks, Subway, Taco Time, Tuttabella Pizza, 🏠 Hilton Garden, 🅞 Chevrolet, Firestone/auto, Ford, GNC, O'Reilly Parts, PetCo, QFC Foods, Radio Shack, Rite Aid, Ross, Safeway, See's Candies, Target, Verizon, USPO
13	SE Newport Way, W Lake Sammamish
11	SE 150th, 156th, 161st, Bellevue, N LDS Temple, 🅡 Shell, 🍴 DQ, Greenwood Mandarin Chinese, Lil' Jon's Rest., McDonald's, Starbucks, Subway, Tulley's Coffee, 🏠 Days Inn, Embassy Suites, Hotel Sierra, Silver Cloud Inn, 🅞 Ford, 7-11, Subaru/VW, Safeway, Toyota/Scion, S 🅡 Chevron, 76, Shell/dsl, Standard, 🍴 Baskin-Robbins, Domino's, Outback Steaks, Pizza Hut, 🏠 Homestead Suites, 🅞 Albertson's, Honda, Larkspur Landing, O'Reilly Parts, Rite Aid, RV Park
10	I-405, N to Bellevue, S to Renton, facilities located off I-405 S, exit 10
9	Bellevue Way
8	E Mercer Way, Mercer Island
7c	80th Ave SE (exits left from wb)
7b a	SE 76th Ave, 77th Ave, Island Crest Way, Mercer Island, S 🅡 Chevron, 76/repair, Shell/dsl/repair, 🍴 McDonald's, Starbucks, Subway, Thai Rest., Tully's Coffee, 🏠 Travelo

Exit	Services
7b a	Continued dge, 🅞 Island Foods, TrueValue, Walgreens
6	W Mercer Way (from eb), same as 7
5mm	Lake Washington
3b a	Ranier Ave, Seattle, downtown, N 🅡 Shell/dsl, 🅞 VET
2c b	I-5, N to Vancouver, S to Tacoma
2a	4th Ave S, to King Dome

I-90 begins/ends on I-5 at exit 164.

◥E INTERSTATE 182 (RICHLAND)

Exit	Services
14b a	US 395 N, WA 397 S, or Ave, N 🅡 ✈FLYING J/dsl/scales/24hr, King City/Shell/rest/dsl/@, 🍴 Burger King, Subway, 🅞 Freightliner, Peterbilt, RV Park, S 🏠 Motel 6, **I-182 begins/ends on US 395 N.**
13	N 4th Ave, Cty Ctr, N 🍴 CFN/dsl, 🏠 👁 Motel, Starlite Motel, S 🅡 76/dsl, 🅞 🄷, RV park, museum
12b	N 20th Ave, N 🏠 Best Western, Red Lion Hotel
12a	US 395 S, Court St, **S on Court St.** 🅡 Chevron/Domino's, Conoco, Exxon/Jack-in-the-Box, Shell, Tesoro, Texaco, 🍴 Asian Express, A&W/KFC, Baskin-Robbins, Burger King, DQ, Little Caesars, McDonald's, Oriental Express, Papa Murphy's, Pizza Hut, Quiznos, RoundTable Pizza, Subway, Super China Buffet, Taco Bell, Wendy's, 🅞 Albertson's/gas, AutoZone, Cadillac/Chevrolet, Chief RV Ctr, $Tree, Ford, Hyundai, Mazda, Nissan, Rite Aid, Save-A-Lot Foods, Subaru, U-Haul, Walgreens
9	rd 68, Trac, N 🅡 Maverik/dsl, Shell, Tesoro/dsl, 🍴 Antonio's Pizza, Applebee's, Arby's, Bruchi's, Cousin's Rest., Eatza Pizza, Fiesta Mexican, Figaro's Pizza, Hacienda Mexican, IHOP, Jack-in-the-Box, McDonald's, Panda Express, Pier 39 Seafood, Pita Pit, Sonic, Starbucks, Subway, Taco Bell, Teryaki Grill, 🏠 Holiday Inn Express, 🅞 AT&T, Discount Tire, Firestone/auto, Franklin County RV Park, Lowe's, O'Reilly Parts, Schwab Tire, Verizon, Walgreens, Walmart/Subway, Yokes Foods
7	Broadmoor Blvd, N 🏠 Sleep Inn, 🅞 Broadmoor Outlets/famous brands, GNC, S 🅡 Shell/dsl, 🅞 Broadmoor RV Ctr, KOA
6.5mm	Columbia River
5b a	WA 240 E, Geo Washington Way, to Kennewick, N 🅡 Conoco/dsl, 🍴 Applebee's, Jack-in-the-Box, Starbucks, 🏠 Clarion, Courtyard, Days Inn, Economy Inn, Hampton Inn, Red Lion Hotel, Shilo Inn, 🅞 AT&T, $Tree, Winco Foods/gas
4	WA 240 W, N 🅡 Shell/dsl, 🍴 McDonald's, Rancho Bonito, 🅞 BMW, Fred Meyer/dsl
3.5mm	Yakima River
3	Keene Rd, Queensgate, N 🅡 Mirastar/dsl, Shell, 🍴 A&W/KFC, Burger King, El Rancho Alegre, LJ Silver, McDonald's, Panda Express, Starbucks, Subway, Taco Bell, 🅞 GNC, Home Depot, PetCo, Target, Walmart/Subway, S 🅞 RV Park (3mi)
0mm	**I-182 begins/ends on I-82, exit 102.**

◥N INTERSTATE 405 (SEATTLE)

Exit	Services
30	I-5, N to Canada, S to Seattle, **I-405 begins/ends on I-5, exit 182.**
26	WA 527, Bothell, Mill Creek, E 🍴 Canyon's Rest., McDonald's, 🏠 Extended Stay Deluxe, 🅞 Lake Pleasant RV Park, W 🅡 Shell/dsl, 🍴 Applebee's, Arby's, Bamboo House, Baskin-Robbins, Bonefish Grill, Crystal Creek

⬆N INTERSTATE 405 (SEATTLE) CONT'D

Exit	Services
26	Continued
	Cafe, D.Thai, Denny's, Fortune Cookie Chinese, Grazie Ristorante, Imperial Wok, Jack-in-the-Box, Mongolian Grill, Outback Steaks, Papa Murphy's, Qdoba Mexican, Quiznos, Starbucks, Subway, Taco Bell, Taco Time, Tully's Coffee, Wendy's, 🛏 Comfort Inn, Extended Stay America, Hilton Garden, Holiday Inn Express, 🅞 Albertson's, Bartell Drug, Goodyear/auto, QFC Foods, Radio Shack, Rite Aid, 7-11, Verizon
24	NE 195th St, Beardslee Blvd, **E** 🅖 Shell/Quiznos/dsl, 🍴 Subway, Teryaki Etc., 🛏 Country Inn&Suites, Residence Inn
23b	WA 522 W, Bothell
23a	WA 522 E, to WA 202, Woodinville, Monroe
22	NE 160th St, **E** 🅖 Chevron, Shell/dsl, 🍴 Denice's Cafe
20	NE 124th St, **E** 🅖 Chevron, Shell/dsl, 🍴 Denny's, Jack-in-the-Box, KFC, Pizza Hut, Santa Fe Mexican, Subway, Taco Bell, Thai Kitchen, Zaburo's Grill, 🛏 Baymont Inn, Comfort Inn, Motel 6, 🅞 🅷 Big O Tire, Chrysler/Dodge/Jeep, Discount Tire, Fiat, Firestone/auto, Ford, Hyundai, Infiniti, O'Reilly Parts, Radio Shack, Rite Aid, Ross, Schwab Tire, 7-11, Toyota/Scion, Verizon, **W** 🅖 Arco, 76, 🍴 Azteca Mexican, Burger King, Hunan Wok, McDonald's, Papa Murphy's, Romio's Pizza, Olive Garden, Starbucks, Subway, Taco Del Mar, Taco Time, Wendy's, 🛏 Courtyard, 🅞 AT&T, Buick/GMC, Fred Meyer, GNC, QFC Foods
18	WA 908, Kirkland, Redmond, **E** 🅖 Chevron, 76/Circle K/dsl, Shell/dsl, 🍴 Baskin-Robbins, Garlic Jim's, McDonald's, Outback Steaks, Starbucks, Subway, Valhalla Grill, 🅞 Chevrolet, Costco, Goodyear/auto, Hancock Fabrics, Honda, KIA, Mazda, O'Reilly Parts, PetCo, Safeway, 7-11, U-Haul, Walgreens, vet, **W** 🅖 Chevron, Shell/dsl, 🍴 Acropolis Pizza, Crab Cracker, Papa John's, Subway, Taco Del Mar, Wendy's, 🅞 QFC Foods, Tire Factory, Verizon
17	NE 70th Pl
14b a	WA 520, Seattle, Redmond
13b	NE 8th St, **E** 🅖 Arco, Chevron/dsl, Shell/dsl, 🍴 Burger King, Denny's, Hunan Garden, 🛏 Coast Hotel, 🅞 🅷 Bartell Drugs, Cadillac, Chevrolet, Chrysler/Dodge/Jeep, Ford/Lincoln, Home Depot, Lexus, Mercedes, Nissan, Porsche, Volvo, Whole Foods Mkt, **W** 🍴 Starbucks, Subway, 🛏 Courtyard, Hyatt

13a	NE 4th St, **E** 🛏 Extended Stay America, Residence Inn, 🅞 Ford, Lexus, **W** 🛏 Best Western, Doubletree Hotel, Hilton, Ramada Ltd., Red Lion/Bellevue Inn, Sheraton
12	SE 8th St, **W** 🛏 Residence Inn
11	I-90, E to Spokane, W to Seattle
10	Cold Creek Pkwy, Factoria, **E on Factoria Blvd** 🅖 Chevron, 76, 🍴 Applebee's, Burger King, Coldstone, El Tapatio Mexican, Goldberg's Rest., Great Harvest Bread, Jamba Juice, Keg Steaks, McDonald's, Old Country Buffet, Panda Express, Panera Bread, Quiznos, Red Robin, Ricardo's Mexican, Romio's Pizza, Starbucks, Subway, Taco Bell, Taco Time, Thai Ginger, 🅞 AT&T, Bartell Drug, Old Navy, O'Reilly Parts, PetCo, QFC Foods, Radio Shack, Rite Aid, Safeway, 7-11, Target, Verizon, vet
9	112th Ave SE, Newcastle, 🅞
7	NE 44th St, **E** 🍴 Denny's, McDonald's, Subway, 🛏 EconoLodge
6	NE 30th St, **E** 🅖 Arco, **W** 🅖 Chevron, Shell, 🅞 7-11
5	WA 900 E, Park Ave N, Sunset Blvd NE, **W** 🅞 Fry's Electronics
4	WA 169 S, Wa 900 W, Renton, **E** 🍴 Shari's, 🛏 Quality Inn, 🅞 Aqua Barn Ranch Camping, **W** 🍴 Burger King, Stir Rest., 🛏 Renton Inn, 🅞 7-11,
2	WA 167, Rainier Ave, to Auburn, **E** 🛏 Hilton Garden, Larkspur Landing, SpringHill Suites, TownePlace Suites, 🅷, **W** 🅖 Chevron, 76/dsl, Shell, USA/dsl, 🍴 A&W/KFC, Applebee's, Arby's, Baskin-Robbins, Georgio's Subs, IHOP, Jack-in-the-Box, Jimmy Mack's, King Buffet, Mazatlan Mexican, McDonald's, PanAsia, Panda Express, Papa Murphy's, Pizza Hut, Popeye's, Qdoba Mexican, Starbucks, Subway, Taco Bell, Taco Time, Torero's Mexican, Wendy's, Yankee Grill, 🛏 Holiday Inn, 🅞 Aamco, Buick/Cadillac/GMC, Chevrolet, Chrysler/Jeep, Discount Tire, Dodge, Ford, Fred Meyer, Firestone/auto, Honda/Hyundai/Kia/Mazda, Isuzu, O'Reilly Parts, Radio Shack, Rite Aid, Safeway/gas, Sam's Club/gas, Schwab Tire, Subaru, Toyota/Scion, Walgreens, Walmart, vet
1	WA 181 S, Tukwila, **E** 🅖 Chevron/dsl, 76/dsl, Shell/dsl, 🍴 Barnaby's Rest., Jack-in-the-Box, McDonald's, Sushi&Grill, Taco Bell, Teriyaki Wok, Wendy's, 🛏 Best Western, Courtyard, Embassy Suites, Hampton Inn, Homestead Suites, Residence Inn, 🅞 7-11, mall, **W** 🅖 Shell, 🛏 Comfort Suites, Homewood Suites, 🅞 fun center
0mm	I-5, N to Seattle, S to Tacoma, WA 518 W.

I-405 begins/ends on I-5, exit 154.

WEST VIRGINIA

⬆E INTERSTATE 64

Exit	Services
184mm	West Virginia/Virginia state line
183	VA 311, (from eb, no reentry), Crows
181	US 60, WV 92 (no ez wb return), White Sulphur Springs, **0-2 mi N** 🅖 BP/Godfather's, Exxon/Quiznos, Shell, 🍴 April's Pizzaria, Hardee's, 🛏 Budget Inn, Greenbrier Resort, Old White Motel, 🅞 Family$, Food Lion, Rite Aid, USPO, to Midland Trail, ski area, **S** 🛏 Black Bear Lodge, 🅞 Twilight Camping
179mm	**Welcome Ctr wb, info, full 🛏 facilities, 🅲, 🛋, litter barrels, petwalk**
175	US 60, WV 92, Caldwell, **N** 🅖 Exxon, Mountaineer Mart/

175	Continued
	dsl, Shell/Subway/dsl, 🍴 Carlitos, McDonald's, Wendy's, 🛏 Village Inn, 🅞 $General, **S** 🅞 Greenbrier SF, Mountainaire Camping
173mm	Greenbrier River
169	US 219, Lewisburg, Hist Dist, **N** 🅖 Shell, 🍴 Biscuit World, 🅞 Federated Parts, **S** 🅖 Exxon/dsl, Gomart, Shell, 🍴 Applebee's, Arby's, Bob Evans, China Palace, Hardee's, Papa John's, Ruby Tuesday, Shoney's, Subway, Taco Bell, 🛏 Fairfield Inn, Hampton Inn, Holiday Inn Express, Quality Inn, Super 8, 🅞 🅷, Urgent Care, AT&T, AutoZone, Buick/Chevrolet, $Tree, Ford, Lowe's, Verizon, Walmart
161	WV 12, Alta, **S** 🅖 Citgo/dsl, 🍴 Alta Sta/cafe, 🅞 Green

🅿 = gas 🍴 = food 🛏 = lodging 🅾 = other 🆁🆂 = rest stop Copyright 2014 - The NEXT Exit ®

INTERSTATE 64 CONT'D

Exit	Services
161	Continued
	brier River Camping (14mi)
156	US 60, Midland Trail, Sam Black Church, N 🅿 Citgo/dsl, Shell/dsl
150	rd 29, rd 4, Dawson, S 🅿 Exxon, 🍴 Cheddar's Cafe, 🛏 Dawson Inn, 🅾 RV camping
147mm	runaway truck ramp wb
143	WV 20, Green Sulphur Springs, N 🅿 Liberty/dsl
139	WV 20, Sandstone, Hinton, S 🅿 Citgo/dsl, 🅾 Blue Stone SP (16mi), Richmonds Store/USPO, to Pipestem Resort Park (25 mi)
138mm	New River
136mm	eb runaway truck ramp
133	WV 27, Pluto Rd, Bragg, Sandstone Mtn (Elev. 2765), mandatory truck stop eb, S RV camping
129	WV 9, Shady Spring, N 🅾 to Grandview SP, S 🅿 Exxon/dsl, Shell/dsl, 🍴 Subway, 🅾 Little Beaver SP
125	WV 307, 🚉 Rd, Beaver, N 🅿 Shell/dsl, 🍴 Biscuit World, 🛏 Sleep Inn, 1 mi S 🅿 BP/dsl, GoMart/gas, Sheetz/dsl, 🍴 Bellacino's, DQ, El Mariachi, Hardee's, KFC, Little Caesars, LJ Silver, McDonald's, Pizza Hut, Subway, Wendy's, 🅾 Advance Parts, Adventure RV Ctr, CVS Drug, Family$, Kroger, Radio Shack, Walgreens, USPO
124	US 19, Eisenhower Dr, E Beckley, 1-2 mi N 🅿 GoMart/gas, 🍴 Capt D's, Huddle House, 🛏 Green Bank Motel, Microtel, 🅾 H, $General, last exit before toll rd wb
121	I-77 S, to Bluefield
	I-64 and I-77 run together 61 mi. See I-77, exits 42 through 100.
59	I-77 N (from eb), to I-79
58c	US 60, Washington St, N 🅿 BP, Exxon, GoMart/dsl, 🍴 Arby's, 🅾 Lincoln, S 🍴 5th Quarter Steaks, LJ Silver, Shoney's, Wendy's, 🛏 Embassy Suites, Hampton Inn, Holiday Inn Express, Marriott, 🅾 H, Sears, civic ctr, mall
58b	US 119 N (from eb), Charleston, same as 58c, downtown
58a	US 119 S, WV 61, MacCorkle Ave, S 🅿 Exxon/7-11, 🍴 Domino's, 🅾 vet
56	Montrose Dr, N 🅿 Exxon/dsl, Marathon, Speedway, 🍴 Hardee's, Los Agaves Mexican, 🛏 Holiday Inn, Microtel, Wingate Inn, 🅾 Acura, Advance Parts, Chevrolet, Dodge, $General, Hyundai, KIA, NAPA, Rite Aid, VW
55	Kanawha Tpk (from wb)
54	US 60, MacCorkle Ave, N 🍴 Burger King, Krispy Kreme, Subway, 🅾 $Tree, Kroger/dsl, TJ Maxx, S 🍴 Bob Evans, Husson's Pizza, LJ Silver, McDonald's, Pizza Hut, Schlotzsky's, Taco Bell, Wendy's, 🅾 H, Urgent Care, Aamco, Family$, Harley-Davidson, Honda, Mazda
53	Roxalana Rd, to Dunbar, S 🅿 GoMart/gas, 🍴 Biscuit-World, Capt D's, Gino's Pizza, McDonald's, Shoney's, Subway, Wendy's, 🛏 Super 8, Travelodge, 🅾 Advance Parts, Aldi Foods, CVS Drug, Jo-Ann Fabrics, Kroger, NTB, Rite Aid
50	VW 25, Institute, S 🅿 GoMart/gas
47b a	WV 622, Goff Mtn Rd, N 🅿 Chevron, Exxon, GoMart, Speedway/dsl, 🍴 BiscuitWorld, Bob Evans, Capt D's, Cozumel Mexican, Domino's, Gino's Pizza, McDonald's, Papa John's, Pizza Hut, Rice Bowl, Subway, Taco Bell, Tim Horton, Wendy's, 🛏 Motel 6, 🅾 Urgent Care, Advance Parts, Kroger/gas, Rite Aid, Walgreens, S 🍴 Arby's, Buffalo Wild Wings, Burger King, Coco's Chinese, Cracker Barrel, Fazoli's, Golden Corral, HoneyBaked Ham, La

Exit	Services
47b a	Continued
	Roca Mexican, Subway, TGIFriday's, 🛏 Comfort Inn, Holiday Inn Express, Sleep Inn, 🅾 $Tree, Freightliner, Lowe's, Radio Shack, Staples, Walmart
45	WV 25, Nitro, N 🅿 🍴/Arby's/dsl/scales/24hr, 🅾 Chevrolet, S 🅿 Exxon/dsl, Shell, Speedway/dsl, 🍴 BiscuitWorld, Checker's, DQ, Gino's Pizza, McDonald's, Subway, Wendy's, 🛏 EconoLodge, Economy Inn, 🅾 Marty's Tires
44.3mm	Kanawha River
44	US 35, St Albans, S 🅿 Shell/dsl, 🅾 7-11
40	US 35 N, Winfield, Pt Pleasant, S 🅿 Sheetz, Speedway, 🍴 DQ
39	WV 34, Winfield, N 🅿 BP/Arby's, GoMart/dsl, 🍴 Applebee's, Bob Evans, Rio Grande Mexican, Taste of Asia, 🛏 Days Inn, Holiday Inn Express, Red Roof Inn, 🅾 Advance Parts, BigLots, $General, Elder-Beerman, GNC, Home Depot, Radio Shack, Urgent Care, USPO, S 🅿 Exxon/7-11/dsl, GoMart/gas, TA/dsl/rest./scales/24hr/@, 🍴 Biscuit World, Burger King, Capt D's, China Chef, El Rancho Grande, Fat Patty's, Gino's Pizza, Graziano's Pizza, KFC, McDonald's, Penn Sta., Subway, Taco Bell, TCBY, Wendy's, 🛏 Hampton Inn, 🅾 AT&T, AutoZone, K-Mart, Kroger/gas, Rite Aid, Verizon
38mm	weigh sta both lanes
35mm	🆁🆂 both lanes, full ♿ facilities, 🚻, vending, 🚮, litter barrels, petwalk
34	WV 19, Hurricane, N 🍴 Arby's, KFC, Taco Bell, 🅾 Chevrolet, Chrysler/Dodge/Jeep, $Tree, Ford, Martin RV Ctr, Walmart/Subway, S 🅿 Exxon/7-11, Go-Mart, Sheetz, 🍴 BiscuitWorld/Gino's Pizza, Little Caesar's, McDonald's, Mi Pueblito, Pizza Hut, Subway, Wendy's, 🛏 American Inn, 🅾 Rite Aid, Walgreens, vet
28	US 60, Milton, 0-2 mi S 🅿 Exxon, Go-Mart, Marathon/dsl, Sheetz, 🍴 Biscuit World, DQ, Gino's Pizza, Jin Long Chinese, McDonald's, Pizza Hut, Subway, Wendy's, 🅾 Advance Parts, AutoZone, Curves, $General, Family$, Foodland, Jim's Camping (2mi), KOA (3mi), NAPA, Rite Aid, Save-A-Lot foods, USPO
20	US 60, Mall Rd, Barboursville, N 🍴 Alexander's Steaks, Applebee's, Arby's, Bob Evans, Burger King, Chick-fil-A, Chili's, Cici's Pizza, IHOP, Logan's Roadhouse, McDonald's, Old Chicago, Olive Garden, Panera Bread, Qdoba Mexican, Ruby Tuesday, Super China, Wendy's, 🛏 Comfort Inn, 🅾 Best Buy, Drug Emporium, Elder-Beerman, Firestone/auto, Hobby Lobby, JC Penney, Jo-Ann Fabrics, Kohl's, Lowe's, Macy's, Michael's, NTB, Old Navy, Sears/auto, Walmart, mall, S 🅿 BP/dsl, Sheetz/dsl, 🍴 Cracker Barrel, 3 Amigos, Famous Dave's BBQ, Johnny's Pizza, Outback Steaks, Shogun Japanese, Sonic, Steak&Shake, Subway, Taco Bell, TCBY, 🛏 Best Western, Hampton Inn, Holiday Inn, 🅾 Toyota/Scion
18	US 60, to WV 2, Barboursville, N 🍴 Bellacino's, O'Charley's, Starbucks, 🅾 $Tree, Home Depot, Marshall's, Office Depot, Target, S 🅿 Shell/7-11, 🍴 Biscuit World, Gino's, Giovanni's Pizza, Hardee's, Hooters, Papa John's, Pizza Hut, 🅾 Curves, Food Land, Honda, Kia, Kroger/gas, NAPA, PetCo, Rite Aid, Walgreens
15	US 60, 29th St E, N 🅿 GoMart/dsl, Shell, Speedway/dsl, 🍴 Arby's, Biscuit World, Pizza Hut, Subway, Wendy's, Waffle House, 🅾 H, AT&T, BigLots, Curves, $General, NAPA, Save-a-Lot Foods, Verizon, Walmart/McDonald's,

Vertical margins: WV · CHARLESTON · HUNTINGTON

INTERSTATE 64 CONT'D

Exit	Services
15	Continued
	st police, **S** 🗵 Exxon, 🍴 Fazoli's, Golden Corral, KFC, Little Caesar's, McDonald's, Penn Sta., Taco Bell, 🛏 Days Inn, Red Roof Inn, 🅾 Buick/Cadillac/GMC, CVS Drug, Honda, K-Mart, Nissan, Subaru, VW
11	WV 10, Hal Greer Blvd, **0-2 mi N** 🗵 BP/dsl, Go-Mart, Marathon, 🍴 Arby's, Baskin-Robbins, Biscuit World, Bob Evans, Frostop Drive-In, Gino's, McDonald's, Papa John's, Ritzy's Cafe, Wendy's, 🛏 Hampton Inn, Ramada Ltd, Super 8, TownePlace Suites, 🅾 🅗, AutoZone, Rite Aid, **S** 🅾 Beech Fork SP (8mi)
10mm	**Welcome Ctr eb, full ♿ facilities, 🚻 vending, 🍴 litter barrels, petwalk**
8	WV 152 S, WV 527 N, **N** Urgent Care, **S** 🗵 Speedway
6	US 52 N, W Huntington, Chesapeake, **N** 🗵 GoMart, Sheetz/dsl, Speedway, 🍴 Pizza Hut, Shoney's, Wendys, 🅾 🅗, AutoZone, BigLots, $General, Family$, Save-A-Lot Foods
1	US 52 S, Kenova, **0-1 mi N** 🗵 Exxon, Shell/dsl, 🍴 Burger King, Evaroni's Pizza, Gino's Pizza, McDonald's, Pizza Hut, Stewart's Hotdogs, Taco Bell, 🛏 Hollywood Motel, 🅾 Advance Parts, $General, NAPA, Save-A-Lot
0mm	West Virginia/Kentucky state line, Big Sandy River

INTERSTATE 68

Exit	Services
32mm	West Virginia/Maryland state line
31mm	**Welcome Ctr wb, full ♿ facilities, 🚻 litter barrels, 🍴 vending, petwalk**
29	rd 5, Hazelton Rd, **N** 🗵 Sunoco/dsl, 🛏 Microtel (1mi), **S** 🅾 Big Bear Camping (3mi), Pine Hill RV Camp (4mi)
23	WV 26, Bruceton Mills, **N** 🗵 BFS/Subway/dsl/24hr, Sunoco/Little Sandy's Rest./dsl/24hr, 🍴 Mills Rest., 🛏 Maple Leaf Motel, 🅾 Family$, Hostetler's Store, USPO, antiques
18mm	Laurel Run
17mm	runaway truck ramp eb
16mm	weigh sta wb
15	WV 73, WV 12, Coopers Rock, **N** 🅾 Chestnut Ridge SF, Sand Springs Camping (2mi)
12mm	runaway truck ramp wb
10	WV 43 N, to rd 857, Fairchance Rd, Cheat Lake, **N** 🗵 BFS/Charlie's/Little Ceasars/dsl, Exxon/dsl, 🍴 Anthony's Pizza, China Kitchen, Subway, 🛏 Lakeview Resort, 🅾 USPO, vet, **S** 🍴 Burger King
9mm	Cheat Lake
7	rd 705, Pierpont Rd, **N** 🗵 BFS/Little Ceasars/Subway/TCBY, Exxon/Taco Bell/dsl, 🍴 Bob Evans, Fujiyama Steaks, Honeybaked Ham, IHOP, Outback Steaks, Ruby Tuesday, Wendy's, 🛏 Euro Suites, Hilton Garden (3mi), Holiday Inn Express, Residence Inn, Super 8, 🅾 🅗 Books-A-Million, Family$, GNC, Harley-Davidson, Lowe's, Michael's, Shop'n Save Foods, Verizon, to WVU Stadium,

Exit	Services
7	Continued
	S 🗵 Sunoco/dsl, 🍴 Don Patron Mexican, Fox's Pizza Den, Rita's Custard, 🅾 Chrysler/Dodge, Fiat
4	rd 7, to Sabraton, **N** 🗵 BFS/Subway/dsl, Sheetz/dsl, 🍴 Arby's, Burger King, Dunkin Donuts, Hardee's, KFC, LJ Silver, McDonald's, Wendy's, 🛏 SpringHill Suites, Suburban Lodge, 🅾 Advance Parts, AutoZone, CVS Drug, $General, Ford/Lincoln, Kroger/dsl, NAPA, Save-A-Lot Foods, Walgreens, USPO, **S** 🗵 Marathon/Circle K, Sunoco/dsl, 🍴 China City
3mm	Decker's Creek
1	US 119, Morgantown, **N** 🗵 Go-Mart/dsl, 🛏 Comfort Inn, Ramada Inn/rest., 🅾 tires, **S** 🍴 Mariachi Loco, Subway, 🅾 $Tree, Walmart, to Tygart L SP
0mm	I-79, N to Pittsburgh, S to Clarksburg.

I-68 begins/ends on I-79, exit 148.

INTERSTATE 70

Exit	Services
14mm	West Virginia/Pennsylvania state line
13.5mm	**Welcome Ctr wb, full ♿ facilities, 🚻 vending, 🍴 litter barrels, petwalk**
11	WV 41, Dallas Pike, **N** 🗵 TA/Country Pride/dsl/scales/24hr/@, 🛏 Comfort Inn, **S** 🗵 Exxon, Marathon/DQ/dsl, 🛏 EconoLodge, 🅾 RV camping
10	rd 65, to Cabela Dr, **N** 🗵 Sheetz/dsl, 🍴 Applebee's, Bob Evans, Cheddar's, Coldstone, Cracker Barrel, Eat'n Park, El Paso Mexican, Fusion Steaks, Logan's Roadhouse, McDonald's, Olive Garden, Panera Bread, Quaker Steak, Wendy's, 🛏 Hampton Inn, Microtel, 🅾 AT&T, Best Buy, Books-A-Million, Cabela's, JC Penney, Kohl's, Michael's, Old Navy, PetCo, Russell Stover Candies, Target, TJ Maxx, Verizon, Walmart/Subway, WV travel info, **S** 🛏

WV

INTERSTATE 70 CONT'D

WHEELING

Exit	Services
10	Continued Holiday Inn Express, Suburban Lodge, [other] Buick/GMC, Chevrolet, Ford, Honda, Hyundai, Nissan, Toyota/Scion
5	US 40, WV 88 S, Tridelphia, **N** [gas] Marathon/dsl, [food] Pizza Hut, Subway, Wendy's, [lodging] Super 8, [other] **Urgent Care**, Chrysler/Dodge/Jeep, Family$, Riesbeck's Foods, Rite Aid, Subaru, vet, **S** [gas] Drive/dsl, Marathon/dsl, [food] Arby's, DQ, McDonald's, Undo's Rest., [other] Advance Parts, AT&T, Rite Aid, museum
5a	I-470 W, to Columbus
4	WV 88 N (from eb), Elm Grove, same as 5
3.5mm	**weigh sta eb**
2b	Washington Ave, **N** [gas] Marathon, **S** [food] Dino's Pizza, Figaretti's Italian, [other] [H]
2a	rd 88 N, to Oglebay Park, **N** [gas] Marathon/dsl, Sheetz, [food] AC Buffet, Bob Evans, DeFelice Bros Pizza, Hardee's, Little Caesars, LJ Silver, Papa John's, Perkins, Subway, Tim Hortons, TJ's Rest, [lodging] Hampton Inn, SpringHill Suites, [other] Advance Parts, CVS Drug, Kroger/gas, NTB, Radio Shack, Verizon
1b	US 250 S, WV 2 S, S Wheeling
1mm	tunnel
1a	US 40 E, WV 2 N, Main St, downtown, **S** [lodging] Wheeling Inn
0	US 40 W, Zane St, Wheeling Island, **N** [gas] Marathon/dsl, [food] Burger King, KFC
0mm	West Virginia/Ohio state line, Ohio River

INTERSTATE 77

PARKERSBURG

Exit	Services
186mm	West Virginia/Ohio state line, Ohio River
185	WV 14, WV 31, Williamstown, **W** [gas] GoMart/dsl, Shell, [food] Dutch Pantry, Subway (1mi), [lodging] Magnuson Inn, [other] Glass Factory Tours, **WV Welcome Ctr/[rest stop], full facilities, info, [picnic], litter barrels**
179	WV 2 N, WV 68 S, to Waverly, **E** [gas] Exxon, [other] [airport], **W** [gas] BP, OneStop, [food] Burger King, Hardee's (3mi), [lodging] Red Carpet Inn, [other] [H]
176	US 50, 7th St, Parkersburg, **E** to North Bend SP, **W** [gas] BP, GoMart, 7-11, [food] Bob Evans, Burger King, Domino's, DQ, LJ Silver, McDonald's, Mountaineer Rest./24hr, Omelette Shoppe, Wendy's, [lodging] Economy Inn, Knights Inn, Red Roof Inn, Travelodge, [other] Advance Parts, CVS Drug, Family$, Ford, Hyundai, Kroger/dsl, Lincoln, Mercedes, NAPA, Rite Aid, Toyota, to Blennerhassett Hist Park, vet
174	WV 47, Staunton Ave, **1 mi E** [gas] GoMart/Sub Express/dsl, [food] Subway, [other] $General, **W** [gas] 47 Carry Out
174mm	Little Kanawha River
173	WV 95, Camden Ave, **E** [gas] Marathon/dsl, **1-4 mi W** [gas] BP, [food] Hardee's, [lodging] Blennerhassett Hotel, [other] [H]
170	WV 14, Mineral Wells, **E** [gas] BP/dsl/repair/24hr, GoMart/Taco Bell/dsl, Liberty Trkstp/dsl/24hr, [food] McDonald's, Taco Bell, Wendy's, [lodging] Comfort Suites, Hampton Inn, **W** [food] Cracker Barrel, [lodging] Holiday Inn Express, Knights Inn, Mineral Wells Inn
169mm	**weigh sta both lanes, [phone]**
166mm	**[rest stop] both lanes, full [handicapped] facilities, [phone], [picnic], litter barrels, vending, petwalk, RV dump**
161	WV 21, Rockport, **W** [gas] Marathon
154	WV 1, Medina Rd
146	WV 2 S, Silverton, Ravenswood, **E** [other] Ruby Lake Camping (4mi), **W** [gas] BP/dsl, Exxon, Marathon/dsl, [food] DQ, Gino's Pizza, McDonald's (3mi), Wendy's (3mi), Subway (4mi), [lodging] Scottish Inn
138	US 33, Ripley, **E** [gas] BP/dsl, Exxon, Marathon/dsl, [food] Arby's, KFC, Las Trancas Mexican, LJ Silver, McDonald's, Pizza Hut, Taco Bell, Wendy's, [lodging] Fairfield Inn, Holiday Inn Express, McCoy's Inn/rest, Super 8, [other] $Tree, Family$, Kroger/dsl, NAPA, Rite Aid, Sav-A-Lot Foods, Verizon, Walmart/Subway, vet, **W** [gas] Exxon/dsl, [food] Bob Evans, Ponderosa, Shoney's, Subway, [lodging] Quality Inn, [other] [H]
132	WV 21, Fairplain, **E** [gas] BP/7-11/dsl, GoMart/dsl, [food] Burger King, Fratello's Italian, Village Pizza, [other] Curves, $General, Ford, Statts Mills RV Park (6mi), **W** [gas] Love's/Chester's/McDonald's/dsl/scales/24hr
124	WV 34, Kenna, **E** [gas] Exxon
119	WV 21, Goldtown, same as 116
116	WV 21, Haines Branch Rd, Sissonville, **4 mi E** [other] Rippling Waters Camping
114	WV 622, Pocatalico Rd, **E** [gas] BP/dsl, [other] FasChek Foods/drug, Tom's Hardware
111	WV 29, Tuppers Creek Rd, **W** [gas] BP/Subway/dsl, [food] Gino's (2mi), Tudor's Biscuit World, Wendy's (2mi)
106	WV 27, Edens Fork Rd, **W** [gas] Marathon/dsl/country store, [lodging] Sunset Motel (3mi)
104	I-79 N, to Clarksburg
102	US 119 N, Westmoreland Rd, **E** [gas] BP/7-11, GoMart, [food] Hardee's, [other] Foodland
101	I-64, E to Beckley, W to Huntington
100	Broad St, Capitol St, **W** [lodging] Best Western, Fairfield Inn, Marriott, [other] [H], Cadillac/GMC, CVS Drug, Family$, Firestone, Rite Aid
99	WV 114, Capitol St, **E** [airport], **W** [gas] BP/7-11, Exxon/Noble Roman's, [food] Domino's, McDonald's, Wendy's, [other] to museum, st capitol
98	35th St Bridge (from sb), **W** [food] Husson's Pizza, McDonald's, Steak Escape, Shoney's, Subway, Taco Bell, Wendy's, [other] [H], Rite Aid, to U of Charleston
97	US 60 W (from nb), Kanawha Blvd
96	US 60 E, Midland Trail, Belle, **W** [food] Biscuit World, Gino's, [lodging] Budget Host
96mm	**W Va Turnpike begins/ends**
95.5mm	Kanawha River
95	WV 61, to MacCorkle Ave, **E** [gas] BP/Subway/dsl, GoMart/dsl/24hr, [food] Bellacino's, Bob Evans, El Patron Mexican, IHOP, Lonestar Steaks, McDonald's, TX Steaks, Wendy's, [lodging] Country Inn&Suites, Days Inn, Holiday Inn Express, Knights Inn, Motel 6, Red Roof Inn, [other] Advance Parts, AutoZone, K-Mart, **W** [gas] Exxon/dsl, GoMart, Shell, [food] Applebee's, Arby's, Burger King, Capt D's, China Buffet, Cracker Barrel, Hooters, Little Caesar's, Piro Pizza, Pizza Hut/Taco Bell, [other] AT&T, $Tree, Drug Emporium, Foodland, Kroger/dsl, Lowe's, Radio Shack, Tire World, **Urgent Care**, vet
89	WV 61, WV 94, to Marmet, **E** [gas] Exxon/Subway/dsl/24hr, GoMart, Sunoco/dsl, [food] BiscuitWorld, Gino's Pizza, Hardee's, LJ Silver, Wendy's, [other] $General, Family$, Kroger/dsl, NAPA, Rite Aid, USPO
85	US 60, WV 61, East Bank, **E** [gas] Exxon, GoMart, [food] Gino's Pizza, McDonald's, Shoney's, [other] Chevrolet, $General, Kroger, Rite Aid, Walmart/Subway, tire repair, USPO
82.5mm	**toll booth**
79	Cabin Creek Rd, Sharon

CHARLESTON

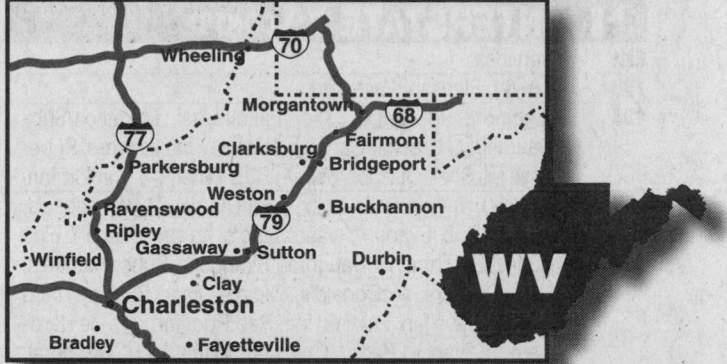

🔼N INTERSTATE 77 CONT'D

Exit	Services
74	WV 83, Paint Creek Rd
72mm	**Morton Service Area nb**, 🅖 Exxon/dsl, 🍴 Burger King, Hershey's Ice Cream, KFC, Pizza Hut, Starbucks, atm
69mm	🅡ₛ **sb, full** ♿ **facilities**, 🅒, 🗑 **litter barrels**
66	WV 15, to Mahan, **1/2 mi W** 🅖 Sunoco/dsl/24hr
60	WV 612, to Mossy, Oak Hill, **1/2 mi E** 🅖 Exxon/dsl/repair/24hr, 🅞 RV camping
56.5mm	**toll plaza**, 🅒
54	rd 2, rd 23, Pax, **E** 🅖 Citgo/dsl
48	US 19, N Beckley, **1-4 mi E on US 19/WV 16** 🅖 Exxon/Subway, 🍴 Bob Evans, Burger King, Chick-fil-A, Chili's, Garfield's Rest., Logan's Roadhouse, LoneStar Steaks, LJ Silver, McDonald's, Peking Buffet, Rally's, Ryan's, Sonic, Starbucks, Taco Bell, Tumbleweed Grill, Wendy's, ⛺ Days Inn, 🅞 Advance Parts, AT&T, Belk, BigLots, Cadillac/Chevrolet, CVS Drug, $General, $Tree, Food Lion, Goodyear/auto, Hobby Lobby, Honda, Hyundai, JC Penney, Jo-Ann Fabrics, Kia/Subaru, K-Mart, Kohl's, Kroger/gas, Lowe's, NAPA, Nissan, Radio Shack, Rite Aid, Sam's Club/gas, Sears, Staples, Suzuki, TJ Maxx, Toyota, U-Haul, Walgreens, Walmart, RV Ctr
45mm	**Tamarack Service Area both lanes, W** 🅖 Exxon/dsl, 🍴 Burger King, Hershey's Ice Cream, Quiznos, Sbarro's, Starbucks, 🅞 gifts
44	WV 3, Beckley, **E** 🅖 Exxon, Marathon/dsl, Shell/Hardee's/24hr, 🍴 Applebee's, Campestre Mexican, DQ, Hibachi Japanese, Hooters, IHOP, McDonald's, Omelette Shoppe, Outback Steaks, Pizza Hut, ⛺ Best Value Inn, Courtyard, EconoLodge, Fairfield Inn, Howard Johnson, Quality Inn/rest., Super 8, 🅞 🅗, Advance Parts, CVS Drug, Kroger/gas, Rite Aid, Tires, Urgent Care, **W** 🅖 BP/Subway/dsl, Go-Mart/dsl, 🍴 Bob Evans, Cracker Barrel, Pasquale Mira Italian, Ruby Tuesday, Sam's Hotdogs, TX Steaks, Wendy's, ⛺ Baymont Inn, Comfort Inn, Country Inn&Suites, Hampton Inn, Holiday Inn, Microtel
42	WV 16, WV 97, to Mabscott, **2 mi E** 🍴 BiscuitWorld, ⛺ Budget Inn, 🅞 🅗, **W** 🅖 BP/dsl, Go-Mart, 🍴 Godfather's Pizza, Subway, 🅞 AutoValue Repair, Walmart, USPO
40	I-64 E, to Lewisburg
30mm	**toll booth**, 🅒
28	WV 48, to Ghent, **E** 🅖 Exxon/dsl, Marathon/dsl, 🍴 Subway, ⛺ Glade Springs Resort (1mi), Appalachian Resort Inn (12mi), 🅞 to ski area, **W** ⛺ Knight's Inn
26.5mm	Flat Top Mtn, elevation 3252
20	US 19, to Camp Creek, **E** 🅖 Exxon/dsl, **W** 🅞 Camp Creek SP/RV camping
18.5mm	scenic overlook/parking area/**weigh sta sb**, Bluestone River
17mm	**Bluestone Service Area/weigh sta nb, full** ♿ **facilities, scenic view**, 🗑 Exxon/dsl, Blimpie, Hershey's Ice Cream, Starbucks, Uno Pizza, atm/fax
14	WV 20, Athens Rd, **E** 🅞 Pipestem Resort SP, to Concord U
9mm	**WV Turnpike begins/ends**
9	US 460, Princeton, Pearisburg, **E** 🍴 Campestre Mexican, Kimono Japanese, Outback Steaks, Ryan's, Subway, ⛺ Country Inn&Suites, 🅞 **Welcome Ctr**/🅡ₛ, 🗑, **litter barrels**, 🅒 **s, full facilities**, AT&T, $Tree, Radio Shack, Verizon, Walmart/Subway, **Urgent Care, W** 🅖 BP/dsl, Exxon, Marathon, Sheetz/dsl, Shell/Subway, 🍴 Apple

PRINCETON (vertical)

Exit	Services
9	**Continued** bee's, Arby's, Bob Evans, Capt D's, Chili's, Cracker Barrel, DQ, Hardee's, McDonald's, Omelette Spot, Shoney's, Starbucks, Taco Bell, TX Steaks, Wendy's, ⛺ Budget Inn, Comfort Inn, Days Inn, Eden Rock Motel, Hampton Inn, Holiday Inn Express, Microtel, Sleep Inn, Turnpike Motel, 🅞 🅗, Hyundai, Lowe's, Suzuki
7	WV 27, Twelve Mile Rd
5	WV 112 (from sb, no re-entry), to Ingleside
3mm	East River
1	US 52 N, to Bluefield, **4 mi W** 🍴 KFC/LJ Silver, Wendy's, ⛺ EconoLodge, Knights Inn, Quality Inn, 🅞 🅗, to Bluefield St Coll
0mm	West Virginia/Virginia state line East River Mtn

🔼N INTERSTATE 79

MORGANTOWN (vertical)

Exit	Services
160mm	West Virginia/Pennsylvania state line
159	**Welcome Ctr sb, full** ♿ **facilities, info**, 🗑, **litter barrels**, 🅒, **vending, petwalk**
155	US 19, WV 7, **0-3 mi E** 🅖 GetGo, Sheetz/dsl, 🍴 Cheddars, Chili's, CiCi's Pizza, Cracker Barrel, Evergreen Buffet, Golden Corral, Longhorn Steaks, McDonald's, Olive Garden, Red Lobster, Shoney's, TX Roadhouse, ⛺ Best Western, EconoLodge, Fairfield Inn, HM Hotel, 🅞 🅗 Barnes&Noble, Best Buy, Buick/Chevrolet/GMC, CVS Drug, Dick's, $Tree, Giant Eagle Foods, Old Navy, PetCo, Sam's Club/gas, Target, TJ Maxx, Walmart, to WVU, **W** 🅞 Harley-Davidson
152	US 19, to Morgantown, **E** 🅖 BFS/dsl, Exxon, Getty, 🍴 Arby's, China Wok, McDonald's, Pizza Hut, Subway, Taco Bell, ⛺ EconoLodge, 🅞 Urgent Care, Advance Parts, BigLots, Monro, **W** 🍴 Bob Evans, Burger King, Garfield's Rest., ⛺ Microtel, 🅞 Belk, Elder-Beerman, JC Penney, K-Mart, Lowe's, Sears/auto, mall
150mm	Monongahela River
148	I-68 E, to Cumberland, MD, **1 mi E** 🅖 Go-Mart/dsl, 🍴 Mariachi Loco, Subway, ⛺ Comfort Inn, Morgantown Motel, Ramada Inn, 🅞 $Tree, Walmart, to Tygart Lake SP, tires
146	WV 77, to Goshen Rd, **W** 🅖 🍴 /deli/dsl/scales/24hr
141mm	**weigh sta both lanes**
139	WV 33, E Fairmont, **E** 🅖 Sunoco, **W** 🅖 Exxon, K&T/BP/dsl/scales (1 mi), 🅞 RV camping, repair, to Prickett's Ft SP
137	WV 310, to Fairmont, **E** 🅖 Exxon/dsl, Sunoco, ⛺ Clarion, 🅞 to Valley Falls SP, vet, **W** 🅖 Shell/dsl, 🍴 Domino's, KFC, McDonald's, Subway, Wendy's, 🅞 🅗, Advance Parts, $General, Family$, Shop'n Save Foods
136	rd 273, Fairmont

INTERSTATE 79 CONT'D

Exit	Services
135	WV 64, Pleasant Valley Rd
133	Kingmont Rd, **E** Exxon/Fazoli's/dsl, Marathon/Subway/dsl, Cracker Barrel, Holiday Inn Express, Super 8, **W** Shell/Quiznos/dsl, DJ's Diner, Comfort Inn
132	US 250, S Fairmont, **E** BFS/DQ/dsl, Applebee's, Arby's, Bob Evans, Colasessano's Italian, Grand China Buffet, Dutchman's Daughter, Firehouse Subs, Hardee's, Little Caesars, McDonald's, Oldie's Diner, Subway, Taco Bell, Days Inn, Fairfield Inn, Red Roof Inn, Ace Hardware, Advance Parts, Chrysler/Dodge/Jeep, $General, GNC, NAPA, Sav-A-Lot Foods, Shop'n Save, Walmart, mall, to Tygart Lake SP, **W** Exxon/dsl, GoMart/dsl, Sunoco/dsl, Steak Escape, Country Club Motel (4mi), , Buick/GMC, Ford/Lincoln, Toyota/Scion, Trailer City RV Ctr
125	WV 131, Saltwell Rd, to Shinnston, **E** Oliverio's Rest. (4mi), **W** Exxon/Circle K/Dunkin Donuts/Subway/dsl
124	rd 279, Jerry Dove Dr, **E** BFS, Exxon/Dunkin Donuts/dsl, Buffalo Wild Wings, DQ, Little Caesars, Microtel, Wingate Inn, **W** Sheetz/dsl, IHOP, Subway, Courtyard, Holiday Inn Express,
123mm	**both lanes, full facilities, info, , , litter barrels, vending, petwalk, RV dump**
121	WV 24, Meadowbrook Rd, **E** GoMart, Sheetz, Biscuit World, Bob Evans, Gino's Pizza, Hampton Inn, Urgent Care, Hyundai/Subaru, **W** Exxon/dsl, Burger King, Garfield's Rest., Outback Steaks, Super 8, Dick's, JC Penney, Jo-Ann Fabrics, Marshall's, NTB, Old Navy, Sears/auto, Target, mall
119	US 50, to Clarksburg, **E** A&W/LJ Silver, Brickside Grille, Chick-fil-A, Coldstone, Denny's, Eat'n Park, Grand China, Hank's Deli, KFC, Las Trancas, Little Caesar's, Maxey's Rest., McDonald's, Panera Bread, Pizza Hut, Red Hot Buffet, Starbucks, Taco Bell, TX Roadhouse, Wendy's, Best Western, Days Inn, Sleep Inn, Sutton Inn, Townplace Suites, Travelodge, , Advance Parts, Autozone, Big-Lots, Family$, GNC, Home Depot, K-Mart, Kohl's, Kroger/dsl, Lowe's, Monro, Radio Shack, Sam's Club/gas, Walgreens, USPO
117	WV 58, to Anmoore, **E** BFS/dsl, Applebee's, Arby's, Burger King, Honeybaked Ham, Ruby Tuesday, Ryan's, Subway, Hilton Garden, Aldi Foods, AT&T, Kia, Staples, Walmart
115	WV 20, Nutter Fort, to Stonewood, **E** BP/7-11/dsl, Exxon/dsl, Stonewood Bulk Foods, **W** Greenbrier Motel (5mi)
110	Lost Creek, **E** BP/dsl
105	WV 7, to Jane Lew, **E** Jane Lew Trkstp/dsl/rest., Valero/dsl/rest., Plantation Inn, **W** GoMart, Shell, $General, Kenworth/Mack/Volvo, glass factory tours
99	US 33, US 119, to Weston, **E** Marathon/DQ/Little Caesars/dsl, Sheetz/dsl, Burger King, Gino's Pizza, McDonald's, Patron Mexican, Peking Buffet, Steer Steakhouse, Subway, Comfort Inn/rest., Hampton Inn (9mi), Holiday Inn Express, Super 8, Advance Parts, Curves, Family$, GNC, Kroger/dsl, Radio Shack, Walmart, **0-2 mi** **W** Exxon, Go-Mart, Shell/7-11, Domino's, Giovanni's, Hardee's, KFC, LJ Silver, Pizza Hut, Subway, Wendy's, , Chrysler/Dodge, CVS Drug, $General, Ford, NAPA, NAPACare, Rite Aid, Save-a-Lot, to Canaan Valley Resort, Blackwater Falls

96	WV 30, to S Weston, **E** Broken Wheel Camping, to S Jackson Lake SP
91	US 19, to Roanoke, **E** Marathon/dsl, Stillwaters Rest., to S Jackson Lake SP, camping
85mm	**both lanes, full facilities, info, , litter barrels, vending, petwalk, RV dump**
79.5mm	Little Kanawha River
79	WV 5, Burnsville, **E** Exxon, 79er Motel/rest., Burnville Dam RA, **W** GoMart, Cedar Cr SP
76mm	Saltlick Creek
67	WV 4, to Flatwoods, **E** BP/Arby's/dsl, Exxon, Go-Mart/dsl, Shell/dsl, Custard Stand, KFC/Taco Bell, McDonald's, Subway, Day's Hotel, Sutton Lake Motel, Buick/Chevrolet, to Sutton Lake RA, antiques, camping, **W** /Moe's SW Grill/dsl/scales/24hr, Sunoco, China Buffet, Shoney's, Wendy's, Bulk Foods, Flatwood Factory Stores, farmer's mkt
62	WV 4, Gassaway, to Sutton, **E** Elk Motel, Sutton Lake Camping, **W** GoMart, LJ Silver, Pizza Hut, Microtel, , Chrysler/Dodge/Jeep, CVS Drug, Ford, Kroger/deli
57	US 19 S, to Beckley
52mm	Elk River
51	WV 4, to Frametown, **E** antiques, food
49mm	**both lanes, full facilities, , , litter barrels, vending, petwalk, RV dump**
46	WV 11, Servia Rd
40	WV 16, to Big Otter, **E** GoMart/dsl, **W** Exxon/dsl
34	WV 36, to Wallback, **10 mi E** BiscuitWorld, Gino's Diner, Subway
25	WV 29, to Amma, **E** Exxon/dsl
19	US 119, VW 53, to Clendenin, **E** BP/dsl, BiscuitWorld, Gino's Diner, 7-11, Shafer's Superstop
9	WV 43, to Elkview, **E** GoMart/dsl, Burger King, AutoZone, **W** Exxon/Arby's/dsl, Speedway/dsl, Bob Evans, La Carreta, McDonald's, Pizza Hut, Ponderosa, Subway, Inn&Suites, Advance Parts, CVS Drug, $Tree, K-Mart, Kroger/dsl, Radio Shack
5	WV 114, to Big Chimney, **1 mi E** Exxon, Hardee's, Rite Aid, Smith's Foods
1	US 119, Mink Shoals, **E** Harding's Family Rest., Sleep Inn
0	I-77, S to Charleston, N to Parkersburg.

I-79 begins/ends on I-77, exit 104.

INTERSTATE 81

Exit	Services
26mm	West Virginia/Maryland state line, Potomac River
25mm	**Welcome Ctr sb, full facilities, info, , , litter barrels, petwalk**
23	US 11, Marlowe, Falling Waters, **E** Exxon/AC&T/Subway/dsl, Kings Rest., Red Lantern Chinese, $General, Food Lion, Falling Waters Camping (1mi), **W** BP/dsl, Outdoor Express RV Ctr, 7-11
20	WV 901, Spring Mills Rd, **E** Sheetz, Barney's Rest., China Spring, Cinco de Mayo, McDonald's, Pizza Montese, Tokyo Cafe, Motel 6, Advance Parts, AT&T, $Tree, Walmart/Subway, **W** Shell/dsl, Burger King, Domino's, Holiday Inn Express
16	WV 9, N Queen St, Berkeley Springs, **E** Crown/dsl, Exxon/Subway/dsl, Sheetz, American Icecream, Arby's, Casa Gonzales Mexican, China King, DQ, Domino's, Dunkin Donuts, East Moon Asian, Hibachi Grill, Hoss's,

WV

CLARKSBURG

CHARLESTON

INTERSTATE 81 CONT'D

MARTINSBURG

Exit	Services
16	Continued KFC, LJ Silver, McDonald's, Pizza Hut, Rita's Custard, Subway, Waffle House, Comfort Inn, Knights Inn, Rodeway Inn, Super 8, URGENT CARRE, Advance Parts, Aldi Foods, AT&T, AutoZone, BigLots, CVS Drug, Family$, Food Lion, Walgreens, USPO, **W** Shell/Subway/dsl
14	rd 13, Dry Run Rd, **E** H, **W** Butler's Farm Mkt (1mi)
13	rd 15, Kings St, Martinsburg, **E** BP/Subway/dsl, Sheetz/dsl, Applebee's, Buffalo Wild Wings, Burger King, Cracker Barrel, Daily Grind, Jerry's Subs, Kobe Japanese, Las Trancas, Outback Steaks, Pizza Hut, Wendy's, Days Inn, Holiday Inn/rest., H, Chevrolet/Scion/Toyota, Walmart
12	WV 45, Winchester Ave, **E** Sheetz/dsl, Shell/dsl, Arby's, Asian Garden, Bob Evans, Chick-fil-A, China City
12	Continued Buffet, McDonald's, Olive Garden, Papa John's, Ryan's, Ruby Tuesday, Taco Bell, TX Steaks, Waffle House, Hampton Inn, Advance Parts, AutoZone, BonTon, Food Lion, JC Penney, K-mart/Little Caesars, Lowe's, Martin's Foods/gas, Nahkeeta Camping, **W** Ledo's Pizza, Logan's Roadhouse, Subway, AT&T, Best Buy, Books-A-Million, Dick's, $Tree, GNC, Michael's, Petsmart, Staples, Target, TJ Maxx
8	rd 32, Tablers Sta Rd
5	WV 51, Inwood, to Charles Town, **E** BP, Liberty, 7-11, Sheetz/dsl, Shell/dsl, Burger King, DQ, Domino's, KFC, McDonald's, Pizza Hut, Pizza Oven, Subway, Waffle House, Hampton Inn, Advance Parts, CVS Drug, Family$, Food Lion, NAPA, Rite Aid, **W** Lazy-A Camping (9mi)
2mm	**Welcome Ctr/weigh sta nb, full facilities, info, vending, litter barrels, petwalk**
0mm	West Virginia/Virginia state line

WISCONSIN

INTERSTATE 39

WAUSAU

Exit	Services
211	US 51, rd K, Merrill, **2 mi W** Cenex, Chip's Burgers, Hardee's, Pizza Hut,
208	WI 64, WI 17, Merrill, **E** KFC, Taco Bell, **W** Cenex/dsl, KwikTrip/dsl, Mobil/dsl, Culver's, Los Mezcales, McDonald's, Pine Ridge Rest., Pizza Now, Subway, 3's Company Rest., Americinn, Best Inn, EconoLodge, H, Chrysler/Dodge/Jeep, $Tree, O'Reilly Parts, Piggly Wiggly, Walmart, to Council Grounds SP
206mm	Wisconsin River
205	US 51, rd Q, Merrill, **E** BP/Hwy 51/rest./dsl/24hr, Buick/Cadillac/Chevrolet, fireworks
197	rd WW, to Brokaw
194	US 51, rd U, rd K, Wausau, **E** F&F/dsl, KwikTrip/dsl, McDonald's, Taco Bell, **W** BP/Arby's, Ford, Nissan, Subaru, Toyota/Scion
193	Bridge St, **E** CVS Drug, **W** H
192	WI 29 W, WI 52 E, Wausau, to Chippewa Falls, **W** same as 191 b
191b	Sherman St, **E** BP, Applebee's, Dickey's BBQ, Great Dane Rest., Hudson's Grill, Jimmy John's, King Buffet, Little Caesars, McDonald's, Noodles&Co, Panera Bread, Papa Murphy's, Qdoba, Starbucks, Subway, Toppers Pizza, Courtyard, Days Inn, Hampton Inn, La Quinta, Plaza Hotel, Super 8, County Mkt Foods, ShopKo, Trig's Foods, Walgreens, **W** KwikTrip/dsl, Hardee's, 2510 Deli, H, Cadillac, Home Depot, Honda, Menards
191a	WI 29, Chippewa Falls
190mm	Rib River
190	rd NN, **E** Mobil/Burger King, Bo-Jo's Grill, IHOP, Krumbee's Bakery, Howard Johnson, **W** The Store/Subway/dsl, Best Western, Granite Mtn Ski Area, Rib Mtn Ski Area, st patrol
188	rd N, **E** BP/dsl/scales/24hr, KwikTrip/dsl, Phillips 66/dsl, Burracho's Mexican, Fazoli's, Hibachi Buffet, McDonald's, Olive Garden, Rococo Pizza, Ropa Pizza, Starbucks, TX Roadhouse, Wendy's, Days Inn, Aldi Foods, AT&T, Barnes&Noble, Best Buy, Chevrolet,
188	Continued $Tree, GNC, Gordman's, Hobby Lobby, Hyundai, JoAnn Fabrics, King's RV Ctr, Kohl's, Michael's, Old Navy, PetCo, Petsmart, Radio Shack, Sam's Club/gas/dsl, TJ Maxx, Tires+, Tuesday Morning, Volvo, Walmart/Subway, **W** Rib Mtn SP
187mm	**I-39 begins/ends. Freeway continues N as US 51.**
187	WI 29 E, to Green Bay
186mm	Wisconsin River
185	US 51, Rothschild, Kronenwetter, **E** BP/dsl, Arby's, Culver's, Denny's, Green Mill Rest., Master Buffet, Subway, Candlewood Suites, Cedar Creek Lodge, EconoLodge, Holiday Inn, Motel 6, Stoney Creek Inn, Cedar Creek Factory Stores/famous brands, Gander Mtn, Harley-Davidson, Pick'n Save Foods, mall, visitor ctr
181	Maple Ridge Rd, Kronenwetter, Mosinee, **E** Peterbilt, Volvo, vet, **W** Kenworth
179	WI 153, Mosinee, **W** BP/Subway/dsl, KwikTrip, Shell/dsl, McDonald's, StageStop Rest., Quality Inn
175	WI 34, Knowlton, to WI Rapids, **1 mi W** Mullins Cheese Factory
171	rd DB, Knowlton, **E** Rivers Edge Camping, **W** to gas, food, lodging, camping
165	US 10 W, to Marshfield (no nb re-entry)
163	Casimir Rd

STEVENS PT

Exit	Services
161	US 51, Stevens Point, **W** BP, Quik Mart/dsl, Shell/dsl/E85, The Store, China Wok, Coldstone, Cousins Subs, Culver's, Dosirak Korean, Hardee's, Jimmy John's, KFC, McDonald's, Michele's Rest., Natalie's Rest., Noodles&Co, Perkins, Rococo's Pizza, Starbucks, Subway, Taco Bell, Tokyo Steaks, Topper's Pizza, Comfort Suites, Country Inn&Suites, Days Inn, Point Motel, AT&T, $Tree, K-Mart, Radio Shack, Trig's Foods, visitors ctr
159	WI 66, Stevens Point, **W** KwikTrip/dsl, H, Ford, Honda, Hyundai, Nissan, VW
158	US 10, Stevens Point, **E** F&F/dsl, KwikFill/dsl, Mobil/dsl, The Store/Subway/dsl, Amber Grille, Applebee's, Arby's, Buffalo Wild Wings, Culver's, DQ, El Mezcal Mexican, Fazoli's, Grazie's Italian, Hibachi Buffet, McDonald's, Taco Bell, Wendy's, Fairfield Inn, Holiday Inn Express,

⮙N INTERSTATE 39 CONT'D

Exit	Services
158	Continued 🅞 Aldi Foods, Copp's Foods, Frank's Hardware, Hancock Fabrics, Target, vet, **W** 🅖 BP/dsl, 🍴 Hilltop Grill, Parkridge Rest., 🏨 EconoLodge, La Quinta
156	rd HH, Whiting, **E** 🅖 The Store/Subway/dsl, 🍴 Charcoal Grill, Chili's, Denny's, Golden Corral, McDonald's, Starbucks, 🅞 Best Buy, $Tree, GNC, JoAnn Fabrics, Kohl's, Lowe's, Michael's, PetCo, Staples, TJ Maxx, Walmart/Subway
153	rd B, Plover, **W** 🅖 BP, Fueling Depot, Mobil/Dunkin Donuts/dsl, 🍴 Bamboo House, Burger King, Happy Wok, IHOP, KFC, McDonald's, Subway, Taco Bell, Tempura House Asian, 🏨 AmericInn, Comfort Inn, Hampton Inn, 🅞 Copp's Foods, Menards, NAPA, ShopKo, Toyota/Scion, Younkers, city park, dsl repair, vet
151	WI 54, to Waupaca, **E** 🅖 KwikTrip/rest./dsl/scales/24hr, 🍴 4Star Family Rest., Shooter's Rest., 🏨 Best Western, Elizabeth Inn/Conv Ctr, 🅞 tires/repair
143	rd W, Bancroft, to WI Rapids, **E** 🅖 Citgo/dsl, 🍴 Area 51 Rest.
139	rd D, Almond
136	WI 73, Plainfield, to WI Rapids, **E** 🅖 BP/dsl, 🍴 Hooligan's Grill, 🅞 NAPA Care, **W** 🅖 Citgo/dsl
131	rd V, Hancock, **E** 🅖 Citgo, 🍴 Country Kettle
127mm	**weigh sta both lanes (exits left)**
124	WI 21, Coloma, **E** 🅖 Mobil/A&W/dsl, 🍴 Subway, 🏨 Mecan Inn, 🅞 Buick/Chevrolet, Caloma Camping, **W** 🅖 BP/dsl
120mm	📷 sb, **full** ♿ **facilities**, 🚻, 🏕, **vending, litter barrels, petwalk**
118mm	📷 nb, **full** ♿ **facilities**, 🚻, 🏕, **vending, litter barrels, petwalk**
113	rd E, rd J, Westfield, **W** 🅖 BP/Burger King, Marathon, Mobil/dsl, 🍴 McDonald's, Subway, 🏨 Pioneer Motel/rest., 🅞 Curves, Family$, city park
106	WI 82 W, WI 23 E, Oxford, **E** 🏨 Crossroads Motel, **W** 🅖 Citgo/dsl
104	(from nb, no EZ return)rd D, Packwaukee
100	WI 23 W, rd P, Endeavor, **E** 🅖 BP/dsl, 🍴 KW's Grill
92	US 51 S, Portage, **E** 🅖 KwikTrip/dsl, Mobil, 🍴 Chi-pan Asian, Culver's, Dino's Rest., Golden Cup 2 Cafe, Jimmy John's, KFC, La Tolteca Mexican, McDonald's, Papa Murphy's, Pizza Ranch, Subway, Suzy's Steaks, Taco Bell, World Buffet, 🏨 Best Western, Ridge Motel, Sunset Motel, Super 8, 🅞 🅗, Ace Hardware, AutoZone, Chrysler/Dodge/Jeep, Curves, $Tree, Ford/Lincoln, GNC, K-Mart, Pierce's Foods, Radio Shack, Staples, Verizon, Walgreens, Walmart
89b a	WI 16, to WI 127, Portage, **E** 🅖 BP/dsl, 🍴 Hitching Post Eatery, Murph's Chop Shop
88.5mm	Wisconsin River
87	WI 33, Portage, **W** ski area
86mm	Baraboo River
85	Cascade Mt Rd
84	I-39, **I-90 & I-94 run together sb/eb**

⮙N INTERSTATE 43

Exit	Services
192mm	**I-43 begins/ends at Green Bay on US 41.**
192b	US 41 S, US 141 S, to Appleton, services on Velp Ave, **1 mi S** 🅖 BP/A&W/dsl, Express/dsl, Mobil/Arby's, Shell/

P O R T A G E (vertical text)

Exit	Services
192b	Continued dsl, 🍴 Burger King, Gilligan's Rest, Julie's Cafe, McDonald's, Riverstreet Rest, Subway, Taco Bell, Watering Hole Rest, 🏨 AmericInn, 🅞 Bay Parts, Bumper Parts, Family$, Good Wrench Auto, Harley-Davidson
192a	US 41 N, US 141 N
189	Atkinson Dr, to Velp Ave, Port of Green Bay
188mm	Fox River
187	East Shore Dr, Webster Ave, **W** 🅖 Shell/dsl/24hr, 🍴 McDonald's, Mi Pueblo Mexican, Wendy's, 🏨 Clarion, Hyatt, 🅞 🅗
185	WI 54, WI 57, University Ave, to Algoma, **W** 🅖 Mobil, Shell/A&W, 🍴 Green Bay Pizza, Subway, Taco Bell, 🅞 Family$, University Foods, Walgreens, U of WI GB
183	Mason St, rd V, **E** 🍴 Culver's, Makinaw's Grill, 🏨 Country Inn&Suites, Super 8, 🅞 🅗, **1 mi W** 🅖 BP, Mobil/dsl, Shell, 🍴 Applebee's, Arby's, Burger King, China Buffet, Fazoli's, Grand Buffet, Great Lakes Sandwiches, KFC, Little Caesars, McDonald's, Papa John's, Papa Murphy's, Perkins, Pizza Hut, Pizza Ranch, Sonic, Starbucks, Taco Bell, 🅞 Advance Parts, Aldi Foods, AT&T, AutoZone, Batteries+, Copps Foods, $General, Family$, Goodyear/auto, Hobby Lobby, Kohl's, Mazda, O'Reilly Parts, PetCo, ShopKO, Subaru, Tires+, Verizon, Walgreens, Walmart/Subway
181	Eaton Rd, rd JJ, **E** 🅖 BP/McDonald's/dsl, 🍴 Hardee's, Jimmy John's, Luigi's, Taco John's, 🅞 Ford/Kia, Harley-Davidson, Home Depot, **W** 🅖 Mobil/Subway/dsl, Shell, 🍴 A&W, Ravine Grill, 🏨 AmericInn, 🅞 Farm&Fleet/gas, Festival Foods, Menards
180	WI 172 W, to US 41 1 exit **W** 🅖 BP/Taco Bell/24hr, Citgo/Country Express/dsl/scales/24hr, KwikTrip, Shell/Subway, 🍴 Burger King, McDonald's, Tuscon's Rest., 🏨 Holiday Inn Express, 🅞 🅗, Copps Foods, Target, Walgreens, to stadium, **5 mi W** multiple services
178	US 141, to WI 29, rd MM, Bellevue, **E** 🅖 Shell/Arby's/dsl, **W** repair
171	WI 96, rd KB, Denmark, **E** 🅖 BP/dsl, 🍴 deGrande Rest. McDonald's, Smurava Cafe, Steve's Cheese, Subway, 🅞 Shady Acres Camping
168mm	📷 both lanes, **full** ♿ **facilities**, 🚻, vending, 🏕, litter barrels, petwalk
166mm	Devils River
164	WI 147, rd Z, Maribel, **W** 🅖 BP/dsl, 🍴 Ridge Rest
160	rd K, Kellnersville
157	rd V, Hillcrest Rd, Francis Creek, **E** 🅖 Citgo/Subway/dsl, Marathon/diner/dsl
154	US 10 W, WI 310, Two Rivers, to Appleton, **E** 🅖 Mobil, 🅞 🅗, **W** 🅖 Cenex
153mm	Manitowoc River
152	US 10 E, WI 42 N, rd JJ, Manitowoc, **E** 🍴 TimeOut Grill, 🅞 🅗, antiques, maritime museum
149	US 151, WI 42 S, Manitowoc, **E** 🅖 BP, Exxon, Grand Central Sta, KwikTrip/dsl, Mobil/dsl, Shell/dsl, 🍴 A&W, Applebee's, Arby's, Burger King, Charcoal Grill, China Buffet, Culver's, DQ, Fork&Knife Rest., 4 Seasons Rest., Frier Tuck's Sandwiches, Jimmy John's, Las Carretas Mexican, Little Caesars, McDonald's, Papa Murphy's, Perkins, Pizza Ranch, Starbucks, Taco Bell, Wendy's, 🏨 Birch Creek Inn, Comfort Inn, Holiday Inn, Super 8, 🅞 🅗, Advance Parts, Aldi Foods, AutoZone, Buick/Cadillac/Chevrolet/GMC, Chrysler/Dodge/Jeep, Copps Foods, $Tree, Family$, Festival Foods, GNC, Hobby Lobby, Kohl's, Lowe's,

G R E E N   B A Y (vertical text)

M A N I T O W A C (vertical text)

WI (tab marker)

INTERSTATE 43 CONT'D

Exit	Services
149	Continued

O'Reilly Parts, PetCo, Radio Shack, Shop-KO, Tires+, Verizon, Walgreens, Walmart/Subway, museum, USPO, vet, **W** 🅖 Express/McDonald's, 🅗 Subway, 🅛 AmericInn, 🅞 Harley-Davidson, Menards

144 rd C, Newton, **E** 🅖 Mobil/dsl, 🅞 antiques

142mm weigh sta sb, 🅒

137 rd XX, Cleveland, **E** 🅖 Citgo/Subway/dsl, 🅗 Cleveland Family Rest., 🅛 Kessler's Old World Guesthouse, 🅞 Wagner's RV Ctr

128 WI 42, Howards Grove, **E** 🅖 BP/dsl/24hr, KwikTrip, 🅗 Culver's, Hardee's, Harry's Diner, Shuff's Rest, TX Roadhouse, 🅛 Quality Inn, 🅞 Gander Mtn, Pomp's Tire, **W** 🅖 Mobil/dsl, 🅞 Menards, Walmart/Subway

126 WI 23, Sheboygan, **E** 🅖 BP, KwikTrip, 🅗 Applebee's, Cousins Subs, Culver's, McDonald's, New China, Pizza Hut/Taco Bell, Pizza Ranch, 🅛 La Quinta, 🅞 🅗, Aldi Foods, Batteries+, BigLots, Festival Foods, Firestone/auto, Ford/Kia, Goodyear/auto, Hobby Lobby, Honda/Mazda, Kohl's, NAPA, Sears/auto, ShopKO, Subaru, Toyota/Scion

123 WI 28, rd A, Sheboygan, **E** 🅖 Citgo/dsl/24hr, Mobil/McDonald's/dsl, 🅗 Coldstone, Jimmy John's, Perkins, Starbucks, Wendy's, 🅛 AmericInn, Holiday Inn Express, 🅞 Harley-Davidson/Cruisers Burgers, Walmart/Subway, **W** 🅗 Arby's, Century Buffet, Chili's, 🅞 AT&T, Best Buy, Boston's Store, $Tree, GNC, Home Depot, Jo-Ann Fabrics, Petsmart, Radio Shack, Target, TJ Maxx

120 rds OK, V, Sheboygan, **E** 🅖 Citgo/dsl, 🅗 Hwy Ridge Rest, 🅛 Sleep Inn, 🅞 Nissan, VW, to Kohler-Andrae SP, camping, **1 mi W** 🅞 Horn's RV Ctr

116 rd AA, Foster Rd, Oostburg, **1 mi W** 🅗 Judi's Place Rest, Pizza Ranch, Subway

113 WI 32 N, rd LL, Cedar Grove, **W** 🅖 Citgo/dsl/repair, Fueling Depot, Mobil, 🅗 Country Grove Rest, Cousins Subs, 🅛 Lakeview Motel

107 rd D, Belgium, **E** 🅛 Lake Church Inn/grill, 🅞 Harrington Beach SP, **W** 🅖 BP/McDonald's/dsl/24hr, How-Dea Trkstp/Hobo's Korner Kitchen/dsl/scales, Mobil/dsl/24hr, 🅗 Bic's Place, Say Cheese Outlet, Subway, 🅛 Regency Inn, 🅞 repair, USPO

100 WI 32 S, WI 84 W, Port Washington, **E** 🅖 Citgo/dsl, Mobil, 🅗 Arby's, McDonald's, Pizza Hut, Subway, 🅛 Country Inn&Suites, Holiday Inn, 🅞 Allen-Edmonds Shoes, Goodyear/auto, Sentry Foods, ShopKO Express, True Value, **W** 🅛 Nisleit's Country Rest.

97 (from nb, exits left), WI 57, Fredonia

96 WI 33, to Saukville, **E** 🅖 Citgo, 🅗 Culver's, KFC/LJ Silver, 🅞 Best Hardware, Buick/Cadillac/Chevrolet, Chrysler/Dodge/Jeep, Ford, Pick'n Save Foods, Piggly Wiggly, Walgreens, Walmart, **W** 🅖 Exxon/McDonald's, 🅗 DQ, Domino's, La Chimenea, Lam's Chinese, Papa Murphy's, Subway, Taco Bell, 🅛 Super 8, 🅞 repair/tires

93 WI 32 N, WI 57 S, Grafton, **1-2 mi E** 🅖 BP, 🅗 George Webb Rest, Mamma Mia's Cafe, **W** 🅗 Flannery's Cafe

92 WI 60, rd Q, Grafton, **E** 🅖 BP, 🅗 GhostTown Rest.,

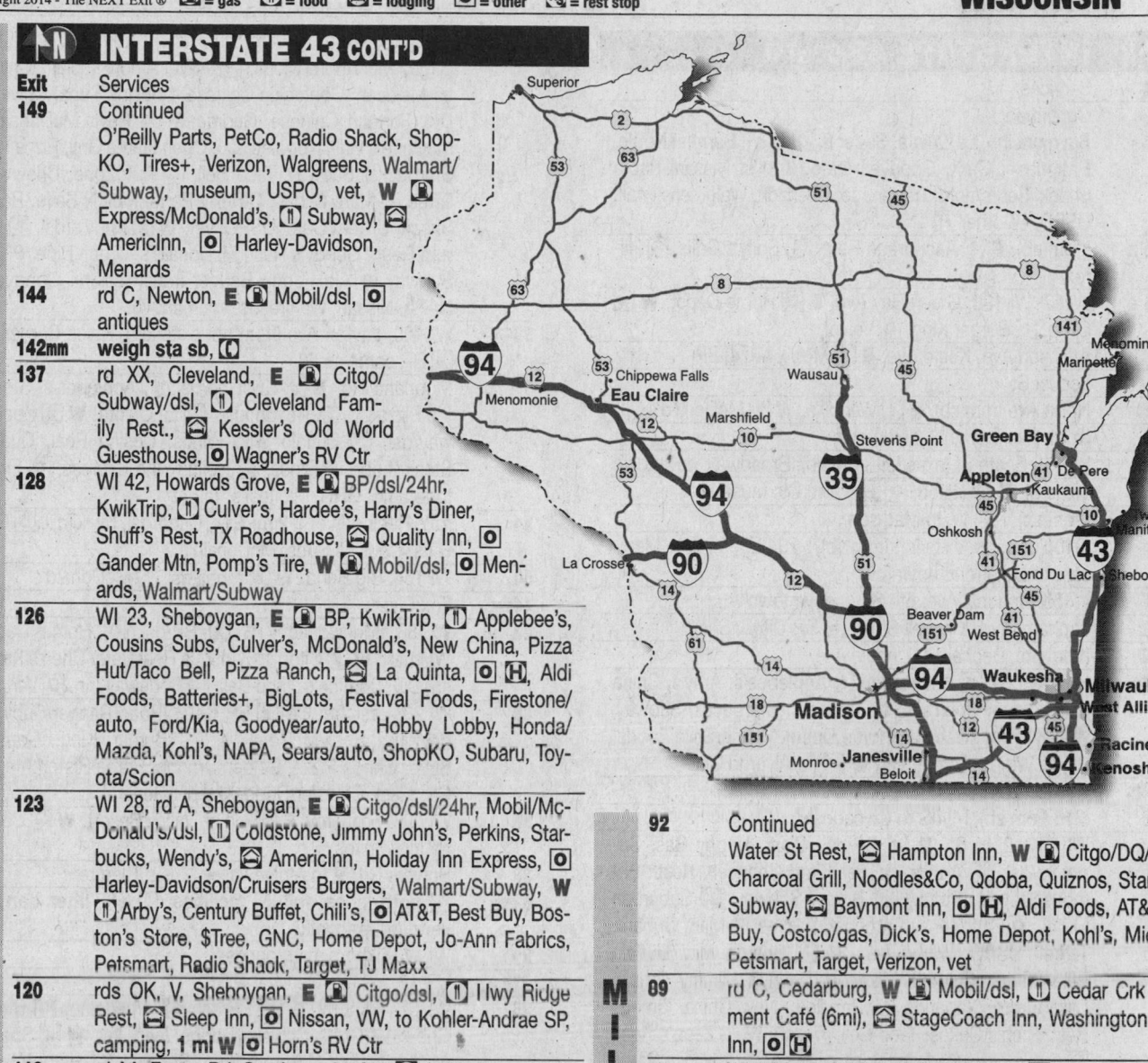

(sidebar vertical text) **MILWAUKEE**

92 Continued
Water St Rest, 🅛 Hampton Inn, **W** 🅖 Citgo/DQ/dsl, 🅗 Charcoal Grill, Noodles&Co, Qdoba, Quiznos, Starbucks, Subway, 🅛 Baymont Inn, 🅞 🅗, Aldi Foods, AT&T, Best Buy, Costco/gas, Dick's, Home Depot, Kohl's, Michael's, Petsmart, Target, Verizon, vet

89 rd C, Cedarburg, **W** 🅖 Mobil/dsl, 🅗 Cedar Crk Settlement Café (6mi), 🅛 StageCoach Inn, Washington House Inn, 🅞 🅗

85 WI 57 S, WI 167 W, Mequon Rd, **W** 🅖 BP, Citgo/dsl, Mobil, Shell, 🅗 Caribou Coffee, Chancery Rest., Cousins Subs, Culver's, DQ, Hong Palace Chinese, Jimmy John's, Leonardo's Pizza, McDonald's, Panera Bread, Papa Murphy's, Pizza Hut, Starbucks, Subway, 🅛 Best Western, Chalet Motel, 🅞 🅗, Ace Harware, Kohl's, Office Depot, Sendik's Foods, Verizon, Walgreens, vet

83 rd W, Port Washington Rd (from nb only)

82b a WI 32 S, WI 100, Brown Deer Rd, **E** 🅖 BP, Sendik's/dsl, 🅗 Baskin-Robbins, Benji's Deli, Jimmy John's, La Paisa Mexican, Maxfield's Pancakes, McDonald's, Noodles&Co, Peking Chef, Qdoba, Starbucks, Subway, Toppers Pizza, 🅞 Best Buy, CVS Drug, Fresh Mkt, GNC, Land's Inlet, Verizon, Walgreens

80 Good Hope Rd, **E** 🅖 BP, 🅗 Jimmy John's, King's Wok, Nick-n-Willy's Pizza, Samurai Japanese, 🅛 Radisson, Residence Inn, 🅞 Pick'n Save Foods, to Cardinal Stritch U

78 Silver Spring Dr, **E** 🅖 BP, Citgo, 🅗 Applebee's, Bar Louie, BD Mongolian, Boston Mkt, Bravo Italian, Buffalo Wild Wings, Burger King, CA Pizza Kitchen, Carabou Coffee, Cheesecake Factory, COA Mexican, Cousins Subs, Devon Steaks, 5 Guys Burgers, Food Court, McDonald's, Panera Bread, Perkins, Pizza Hut, Qdoba, Taco Bell, 🅛

(sidebar tab) **WI**

⬆N INTERSTATE 43 CONT'D

Exit	Services
78	Continued
	Baymont Inn, La Quinta, Super 8, 🅞 AT&T, Barnes&Noble, Batteries+, CarX, Goodyear/auto, Kohl's, Nissan, Radio Shack, Sears/auto, Trader Joe's, Verizon, Walgreens, mall, USPO, **W** other 🅷
77b a	(from nb), **E** 🍴 Anchorage Rest., 🍴 Solly's Grille, 🏠 Hilton
76b a	WI 57, WI 190, Green Bay Ave, **E** 🅞 Home Depot, **W** 🅖 CTrip, 🍴 Burger King, 🅞 Volvo
75	Atkinson Ave, Keefe Ave, **E** 🅖 Mobil, **W** 🅖 BP
74	Locust St
73c	North Ave (rom sb), **E** 🍴 Wendy's, **W** 🍴 McDonald's
73b	North Ave (from nb) downtown
73a	WI 145 E, 4th St (exits left from sb), Broadway, downtown
72c	Wells St, **E** 🏠 Hilton, 🅞 🅷, Civic Ctr, museum
72b	(from sb), I-94 W, to Madison
72a	(310c from nb, exits left from sb), I-794 E, I-94 W to Madison, to Lakefront, downtown
311	WI 59, National Ave, 6th St downtown
312a	Lapham Blvd, Mitchell St, **W** 🅖 BP, Citgo, Shell
312b	(from nb), Becher St, Lincoln Ave
314a	Holt Ave, **E** 🅖 Andy's/dsl, 🍴 Applebee's, Arby's, China King, Jimmy John's, Little Caesars, Starbucks, Subway, Wendy's, 🅞 $General, Home Depot, Pick'n Save Foods, Piggly Wiggly, Target, vet, **W** 🅷, to Alverno Coll
314b	Howard Ave
10b	(316 from sb), I-94 S to Chicago ✈
9b a	WI 241, 27th St, **E** 🅖 BP/dsl, Clark, Happy Gas, Supreme/dsl, 🍴 Arby's, Burger King, Chancery Rest., Famous Dave's, Pizza Hut, Sonic, Subway, 🏠 Suburban Motel, 🅞 AutoZone, Carquest, Curves, K-Mart, Subaru, Target, USPO, Walgreens, **W** 🍴 Boston Mkt, Buffalo Wild Wings, Chipotle Mexican, Denny's, Jimmy John's, Los Burritos Tapatios, McDonald's, New China, Omega Rest., Rich's Cakes, Taco Bell, Wong's Wok, Zebb's Rest., 🏠 Quality Inn, Rodeway Inn, 🅞 🅷, AAA, Advance Parts, CarX, Chevrolet, CVS Drug, $Tree, Firestone/auto, Ford, Goodyear/auto, Kohl's, Marshall's, Michael's, Pick'n Save Foods, Radio Shack, Save-A-Lot Foods, Walmart
8a	WI 36, Loomis Rd, **E** 🅖 BP, Citgo, 🍴 Los Mariachi's, 🅞 Aldi Foods, Walgreens, **W** 🍴 Griddler's Cafe, 🅞 to Alverno Coll
7	60th St, **E** 🅖 Speedway/dsl, 🍴 Subway, Wendt's Grille, 🅞 Harley-Davidson, **W** 🅖 Speedway
5b	76th St (from sb, no EZ return), **E** 🍴 Applebee's, Bakers Square, Breadsmith, Burger King, Carrabba's Italian, Cousins Subs, El Beso, Griddler's Cafe, Hooters, Kopp's Burgers, Kyoto Japanese, McDonald's, Noodles&Co, Old Country Buffet, Olive Garden, Outback Steaks, Panera Bread, Qdoba, Red Lobster, Red Robin, Ruby Tuesday, Starbucks, TGIFriday's, Topper's Pizza, Traditional Pancake House, Wendy's, 🅞 AT&T, Barnes&Noble, Best Buy, CarX, $Tree, F&F Tire, Firestone/auto, Goodyear, Jo-Ann Fabrics, Office Depot, PetCo, Petsmart, Sears/auto, Sendik's Food, Tuesday Morning, Valvoline, Verizon, **W** 🍴 Arby's, Pizza Hut, Popeye's, 🅞 Pick'n Save Foods, TJ Maxx, Walgreens, USPO
5a	WI 24 W, Forest Home Ave, **E** 🅖 Citgo, 🅞 Boerner Botanical Gardens, Welk's Auto
61	(4 from sb), I-894/US 45 N, I-43/US 45 S

Exit	Services
60	US 45 S, WI 100, 108th St (exits left from sb), **E** 🅖 BP, Citgo, Marathon, Mobil, 🍴 A&W, Amore Italian, Chipotle Mexican, Confucius Chinese, Cousins Subs, Culver's, DQ, Fortune Chinese, George Webb Rest., McDonald's, McGuire's Grill, Noodles&Co, Open Flame Grill, Pizza Hut, Starbucks, Subway, Taco Bell, 🅞 AutoZone, Chevrolet, $Tree, K-Mart, Midas, O'Reilly Parts, Pick'N Save, Radio Shack, **Urgent Care**, USPO, vet, **W** 🅖 Andy's/dsl, 🍴 Forum Rest., Goody's Rest., McDonald's, Organ Piper Pizza, Subway, 🅞 Aldi Foods, Badger Transmissions, Goodyear, NAPA, Nissan, Walgreens, Walmart, vet
59	WI 100, Layton Ave (from nb, exits left), Hales Corner, **W** 🅖 BP, same as 60
57	Moorland Rd, **E** 🅖 KwikTrip/dsl, 🍴 Applebee's, Stonefire Pizza Co, TX Roadhouse, 🏠 La Quinta, **W** 🅖 Speedway/dsl, 🍴 Buffalo Wild Wings, Cosina Real, Quaker Steak&Lube, Quiznos, 🏠 Holiday Inn Express, 🅞 Firestone/auto, GNC, Michael's, Target
54	rd Y, Racine Ave, **1-2 mi E** 🅖 Citgo/dsl, KwikTrip, 🅞 Culver's, Cousins Subs, McDonald's
50	WI 164, Big Bend, **W** 🅖 Mobil/dsl, 🍴 McDonald's
44mm	Fox River
43	WI 83, Mukwonago, **E** 🅖 BP/dsl, 🅞 Home Depot, Walmart, **W** 🅖 Citgo, 🍴 Antigua Real Cafe, Chen's Kitchen, DQ, Domino's, Taco Bell, 🏠 Rodeway Inn, 🅞 Verizon
38	WI 20, East Troy, **W** 🅖 BP, 🚚/Road Ranger/Subway/dsl/24hr, Shell/McDonald's, 🍴 Burger King, Cousins Subs, Genoa Pizza, Golden Dragon, Roma Ristorante, 🅞 Carquest, Chrysler/Dodge/Jeep, $General
36	WI 120, East Troy, **E** 🏠 Alpine Valley Resort, **W** 🏠 Country Inn&Suites
33	Bowers Rd, **E** to Alpine Valley Music Theatre
32mm	🆁🆂 **both lanes, full** ♿ **facilities, 🅲, 🏠, litter barrels, vending, petwalk**
29	WI 11, Elkhorn, fairgrounds
27b a	US 12, to Lake Geneva, **E** 🅷
25	WI 67, Elkhorn, **E** 🅖 BP/dsl, 🏠 AmericInn, 🅞 Buick/Chevrolet/GMC, Chrysler/Dodge/Jeep, vet, **W** 🅖 Speedway/dsl/24hr, 🍴 Burger King, Subway, 🏠 Hampton Inn (2mi), 🅞 Dehaan Auto/RV Ctr
21	WI 50, Delavan, **E** 🍴 Brodie's Beef, Chili's, China 1, Culvers, Domino's, Panera Bread, Papa Murphy's, Starbucks, Subway, Yoshi Japanese, 🅞 Aldi Foods, AT&T, F&F Tires, Kohl's, Lowe's, Petsmart, Radio Shack, Staples, Verizon, Walmart, golf, **W** 🅖 Mobil, Speedway/dsl, 🍴 KFC, McDonald's, Perkins, Pizza Hut, Taco Bell, Wendy's, 🏠 Comfort Suites, Super 8, 🅞 Ace Hardware, AutoZone, Cadillac/Chevrolet, $Tree, Ford/Lincoln, GNC, NAPA, Piggly Wiggly, ShopKO, Walgreens
17	rd X, Delavan, Darien, **W** 🅖 BP/dsl
15	US 14, Darien, **E** 🅖 Mobil/dsl, 🍴 West Wind Diner
6	WI 140, Clinton, **E** 🅖 Citgo/Subway/TCBY/dsl, 🅞 Ford
2	rd X, Hart Rd, **E** 🍴 Butterfly Fine Dining
1b a	I-90, E to Chicago, W to Madison, **S** 🅖 BP, Mobil/McDonald's, 🚚/Taco Bell/dsl/scales/24hr, Shell, Speedway/dsl, 🍴 Applebee's, Arby's, Asia Buffet, Atlanta Bread, Burger King, Culver's, Jimmy John's, Little Caesars, Papa Murphy's, Road Dawg Rest, Starbucks, Subway, Wendy's, 🏠 Comfort Inn, EconoLodge, Fairfield Inn, Hampton Inn, Holiday Inn Express, Rodeway Inn, 🅞 Aldi Foods, Buick/GMC, Cadillac/Chevrolet, $Tree, GNC, Menards, NTB, O'Reilly Parts, Radio Shack, Staples, Walmart

I-43 begins/ends on I-90, exit 185 in Beloit.

INTERSTATE 90

Exit	Services
187mm	Wisconsin/Illinois state line, **I-90 & I-39 run together nb**
187mm	**Welcome Ctr wb, full** 🅗 **facilities, info,** 🅒, 🚻, **litter barrels, vending, petwalk**
185b	I-43 N, to Milwaukee
185a	WI 81, Beloit, **S** 🅖 BP, Mobil/McDonald's, ▯▯▯/Taco Bell/dsl/scales/24hr, Shell, Speedway/dsl, 🅕 Applebee's, Arby's, Asia Buffet, Atlanta Bread, Burger King, Culver's, Jimmy John's, Little Caesars, Papa Murphy's, Road Dawg Rest, Starbucks, Subway, Wendy's, 🅗 Comfort Inn, EconoLodge, Fairfield Inn, Hampton Inn, Holiday Inn Express, Rodeway Inn, 🅞 Aldi Foods, Buick/GMC, Cadillac/Chevrolet, $Tree, GNC, Menards, NTB, O'Reilly Parts, Radio Shack, Staples, Walmart
183	Shopiere Rd, rd S, to Shopiere, **S** 🅖 BP/Rollette/dsl/24hr, 🅞 🅗, camping, repair
181mm	**weigh sta, wb**
177	WI 11 W, Janesville, **2 mi S** 🅖 BP, KwikTrip, 🅕 Bobble Heads Grill, El Jardin Mexican, 🅞 to Blackhawk Tec Coll, Rock Co 🚲
175b a	WI 11 E, Janesville, to Delavan, **N** 🅖 BP/Subway/dsl/24hr, 🅕 Denny's, 🅗 Baymont Inn, 🅞 🅗, **S** 🅖 BP, Mobil, 🅕 DQ, 🅗 Lannon Stone Motel, 🅞 city park
171c b	US 14, WI 26, Janesville, **N** 🅖 TA/Mobil/Wendy's/dsl/scales/24hr, 🅕 Coldstone, Cozumel Mexican, Fuddruckers, IHOP, Old Country Buffet, Starbucks, Subway, TX Roadhouse, 🅗 Holiday Inn Express, Microtel, 🅞 Best Buy, Gander Mtn, GNC, Home Depot, Michael's, NTB, Old Navy, PetCo, Staples, TJ Maxx, **S** 🅖 Citgo, Exxon, Kwik Trip/dsl/24hr, 🅕 Applebee's, Arby's, Buffalo Wild Wings, Burger King, ChuckeCheese, Cousin's Subs, Culver's, Famous Dave's, Fazoli's, Fuji Steaks, Ground Round, Hacienda Real, Hardee's, Hooters, Jimmy John's, KFC, La Tolteca Mexican, McDonald's, Noodles&Co, Olive Garden, Papa Murphy's, Peking Chinese, Perkins, Pizza Hut, Prime Quarter Steaks, Red Robin, Subway, Taco Bell, Taco John's, World Buffet, 🅗 EconoLodge, Super 8, 🅞 🅗, Aldi Foods, AutoZone, CarQuest, $Tree, F&F, Ford/Lincoln, Harley-Davidson, Hobby Lobby, JC Penney, KIA, Kohl's, K-Mart, Menards, O'Reilly Parts, Sears/auto, ShopKO, Subaru, Target, Toyota, Verizon, mall, USPO
171a	WI 26, **N** 🅖 BP/dsl, Phillips 66/dsl, 🅕 Cracker Barrel, 🅗 Best Western/rest., Hampton Inn, Motel 6, 🅞 Chrysler/Dodge/Jeep, Sam's Club, VW, Walmart, Walgreens, **S** same as 171c b
168mm	🆁🆂 **eb, full** 🅗 **facilities,** 🅒, 🚻, **litter barrels, vending, petwalk**
163.5mm	Rock River
163	WI 59, Edgerton, to Milton, **N** 🅖 Mobil/Subway/dsl, Shell, Dunkin Donuts/Taco John's, 🅕 Culver's, McDonald's, WI Cheese Store, 🅗 Comfort Inn, 🅞 marina
160	US 51S, WI 73, WI 106, Oaklawn Academy, to Deerfield, **N** 🅞 Hickory Hills Camping, **S** 🅖 BP/dsl/scales/24hr/@, 🅞 🅗
156	US 51N, to Stoughton, **S** 🅗 Coachman's Inn/rest., 🅗
147	rd N, Cottage Grove, to Stoughton, **S** 🅖 BP/Arby's/24hr, Road Ranger/▯▯▯/Subway/dsl/scales, 🅞 Lake Kegonsa SP, fireworks
146mm	**weigh sta eb**
142b a	(142a exits left from wb) US 12, US 18, Madison, to Cambridge, **N** 🅖 BP/dsl, 🅕 Roadhouse Rest, 🅗 Best Value

Exit	Services
142b a	Continued Inn, Magnuson Grand Hotel, 🅞 Harley-Davidson, **S** 🅖 Cenex/dsl, Phillips 66/Arby's/dsl, Shell, 🅕 Culver's, Denny's, Quiznos, 🅗 Days Inn, Sleep Inn, 🅞 🅗, Menards, UWI
138a	I-94, E to Milwaukee, W to La Crosse, **I-90 W and I-94 W run together for 93 miles** (exits left from eb)
138b	WI 30, Madison, **S** 🚲
135c b	US 151, Madison, **N** 🅖 BP, 🅕 Erin's Cafe, Happy Wok, Subway, Uno Grill, 🅗 Cambria Suites, Courtyard, Fairfield Inn, GrandStay Suites, Holiday Inn, Staybridge Suites, 🅞 Buick/GMC, Chrysler/Dodge/Jeep, Ford, Honda, Hyundai, Kia, Mazda, Nissan, Subaru, Toyota/Scion
135a	US 151, Madison, **S** 🅖 BP, Citgo, Mobil, Shell, 🅕 Applebee's, Arby's, Buffalo Wild Wings, Chili's, Chipotle Mexican, Cracker Barrel, Culver's, Denny's, Dickey's BBQ, Fazoli's, Hardee's, Hometown Buffet, Hooters, IHOP, Imperial Garden, KFC, McDonald's, Milio's, Noodles&Co, Old Country Buffet, Olive Garden, Outback Steaks, Panera Bread, Perkins, Pizza Hut, Potbelly, Qdoba, Red Lobster, Red Robin, Rocky's Pizza, Starbucks, Taco Bell, Takumi Japanese, TGIFriday's, Toppers's Pizza, TX Roadhouse, Wendy's, 🅗 Baymont Inn, Best Western, Comfort Inn, Crowne Plaza Hotel/rest., EconoLodge, Hampton Inn, Howard Johnson, Microtel, Motel 6, Red Roof Inn, Residence Inn, Rodeway Inn, Super 8, 🅞 Urgent Care, Aldi Foods, AT&T, Barnes&Noble, Best Buy, Dick's, $Tree, Firestone/auto, Gander Mtn, Goodyear/auto, Home Depot, Hy-Vee Foods, JC Penney, JoAnn Fabrics, Kohl's, Marshalls, Menards, Office Depot, Old Navy, Petsmart, Savers, Sears/auto, ShopKO, Target, Verizon, city park, mall, st patrol, vet
132	US 51, Madison, De Forest, **N** 🅖 Shell/Pinecone Rest/dsl/24hr, 🅞 Camping World RV Ctr, Gander Mtn, **S** 🅖 TA/BP/Subway/Taco Bell/dsl/scales/24hr/@, 🅞 Goodyear, Peterbilt, Freightliner/GMC/Volvo/White, WI RV World, camping
131	WI 19, Waunakee, **N** 🅖 Kwik Trip, Mobil/dsl, Speedway/dsl, 🅕 A&W, McDonald's, Rodeside Grill, 🅗 Best Value Inn, Days Inn, 🅞 Mousehouse Cheesehaus, Kenworth, truckwash, fireworks
126	rd V, De Forest, to Dane, **N** 🅖 Phillips 66/Arby's/dsl, 🅕 Burger King, Culver's, McDonald's, Subway, 🅗 Holiday Inn Express, 🅞 Cheese Chalet, KOA, **S** 🅖 Exxon, Shell, 🅗 Comfort Inn, 🅞 dsl repair
119	WI 60, Arlington, to Lodi, **S** 🅖 Mobil/Cousins Subs/dsl, 🅕 A&W, Rococo's Pizza, 🅗 Quality Inn, 🅞 dsl/tire repair
115	rd CS, Poynette, to Lake Wisconsin, **N** 🅖 BP/dsl, 🅕 McDonald's, Subway, 🅞 Smokey Hollow Camping, dsl truck/

◫ = gas   ⊓ = food   ⌂ = lodging   ◉ = other   Rs = rest stop   Copyright 2014 - The NEXT Exit ®

⌖ INTERSTATE 90 CONT'D

Exit	Services
115	Continued trailer repair, motel, trout fishing
113mm	Rs both lanes, full ♿ facilities, ⊓, 🚻, litter barrels, vending, petwalk
111mm	Wisconsin River
108b a	I-39 N, WI 78, to US 51 N, Portage, N ◉⊔, to WI Dells, S ◫ BP, Petro/DQ/Subway/dsl/24hr/@, ⌂ Comfort Suites, Days Inn, Devil's Head Resort/Conv Ctr, ◉ Blue Beacon
106mm	Baraboo River
106	WI 33, Portage, N ◉⊔, S ◫ BP, ◉ Kamp Dakota, Sky-High Camping, to Cascade Mtn Ski Area, Devil's Lake SP, Circus World Museum, Wayside Park, motel
92	US 12, to Baraboo, N ◫ BP/dsl, Exxon, Mobil/Dunkin Donuts/dsl/24hr, Sinclair/Subway/dsl, ⊓ Buffalo Phil's Grille, Burger King, Cracker Barrel, Cheese Factory Rest, Culver's, Damon's, Denny's, Domino's, Famous Dave's BBQ, Field's Steaks, Marley's Rest., Mark's Rest, McDonald's, Monk's Grill, Ponderosa, R Place Italian, Sarento's Italian, Wintergreen Grill, Uno, ⌂ Alakai Hotel, Country Squire Motel, Dell Creek Motel, Grand Marquis Inn, Great Wolf Lodge, Holiday Motel, Holiday Inn Express, Kalahari Resort, Lake Delton Motel, Ramada, Wilderness Hotel, Wintergreen Hotel, ◉ Urgent Care, Broadway Dinner Theater, Kalahari Conv Ctr, Mkt Square Cheese, Tanger Outlets Famous Brands, museum, S ⌂ Motel 6, ◉ ⊔, Scenic Traveler RV Ctr, Jellystone Camping, Red Oak Camping, Mirror Lake SP
89	WI 23, Lake Delton, N ◫ Phillips 66, Shell/dsl, ⊓ Brathouse Grill, Denny's Diner, Howie's Rest., KFC, Moosejaw Pizza, ⌂ EconoLodge, Hilton Garden, Kings Inn, Malibu Inn, Olympia Motel, ◉ Crystal Grand Music Theatre, Springbrook Camping, Jellystone Camping, USPO, S ⊓ McDonald's, ◉ Home Depot, Kohl's, Walmart/Subway, Country Roads RV Park
87	WI 13, Wisconsin Dells, N ◫ Citgo, Mobil/Arby's/dsl, Shell, ⊓ Applebee's, Bunyan's Rest., Burger King, Coldstone, Country Kitchen, Culver's, Denny's, IHOP, Jimmy John's, McDonald's, Mexicali Rose Rest., Perkins, Starbucks, Taco Bell, Wendy's, ⌂ AmericInn, Best Western, Comfort Inn, Days Inn, Dells Island Resort, Polynesian Hotel, Super 8, ◉ KOA, Sherwood Forest Camping, Walgreens, golf, waterpark, info
85	US 12, WI 16, Wisconsin Dells, 0-3 mi N ⊓ Crabby's Seafood, Culver's, Starbucks, ⌂ Days Inn, Mayflower Motel, ◉ American World RV Park/Hotel, KOA, Sherwood Forest Camping, Standing Rock Camping, to Rocky Arbor SP, S ◫ BP, ⊓ Piccadilly's, ⌂ Arrowhead Camping, Edge-O-the-Dell RV Camping, Summer Breeze Resort
79	rd HH, Lyndon Sta, S ◫ BP/Subway/dsl/24hr
76mm	Rs wb, full ♿ facilities, ⊓, 🚻, litter barrels, vending, petwalk
74mm	Rs eb, full ♿ facilities, ⊓, 🚻, litter barrels, vending, petwalk
69	WI 82, Mauston, N ◫ Mauston TP/BP/Taco Bell/24hr, ▦/Wendy's/dsl/scales/24hr, Shell/24hr, ⊓ China Buffet, ⌂ Best Western Oasis, Country Inn, Super 8, ◉ Carr Valley Cheese, to Buckhorn SP, S ◫ KwikTrip/Hearty Platter Rest/dsl/scales/24hr, Mobil, ⊓ Culver's, Garden Valley Rest., McDonald's, Pizza Hut, Roman Castle Rest., Subway, ⌂ Alaskan Inn, Best Value Inn, ◉⊔, Buckhorn

Exit	Services
69	Continued SP, Buick/Chevrolet, $General, Family$, Festival Foods, K-Mart, Walgreens, vet
61	WI 80, New Lisbon, to Necedah, N ◫ Mobil/A&W/Subway/dsl/scales/24hr, ⌂ Edge O' the Woods Motel, Travelers Inn, ◉ Buckhorn SP, Chrysler/Jeep, Ford, fireworks, S ◫ KwikTrip/24hr, ◉ True Value, Elroy-Sparta ST Tr, city park, USPO
55	rd C, Camp Douglas, N ◉ wayside, to Camp Williams, Volk Field, S ◫ BP/dsl, Mobil/Subway/dsl, ⊓ German Haus Rest., ⌂ K&K Motel, ◉ to Mill Bluff SP
49mm	weigh sta both lanes
48	rd PP, Oakdale, N ◫ Road Ranger/▦/Subway/dsl/scales/24hr, ◉ Granger's Camping, KOA, truck/car wash, antiques, S ◫ ♥Love's/Hardee's/dsl/scales/24hr, ◉ Mill Bluff SP, repair
45	I-94 W, to St Paul
	I-90 E and I-94 E run together for 93 miles
43	US 12, WI 16, Tomah, N ◫ BP, KwikTrip/dsl/24hr, ⊓ Burnstadt's Café, DQ, ⌂ Daybreak Inn, Rest Well Motel, ◉⊔, Burnstadt's Mkt, vet
41	WI 131, Tomah, to Wilton, N ◫ BP, Mobil/dsl, KwikTrip/dsl/24hr, ⊓ Burnstadts Cafe, ⌂ Daybreak Inn, ◉ vet, S st patrol
28	WI 16, Sparta, Ft McCoy, N ◫ BP/diner/dsl/scales, KwikTrip/dsl, ⌂ Best Western, ◉⊔
25	WI 27, Sparta, to Melvina, N ◫ Casey's, Cenex/dsl, KwikTrip/dsl, Mobil/Taco Bell, Shell/dsl, ⊓ Burger King, Culver's, DQ, KFC, McDonald's, Pizza Hut, Subway, ⌂ Country Inn, Super 8, ◉⊔, Buick/Chevrolet, $General, Family$, Ford, O'Reilly Parts, Piggly Wiggly, Walgreens, Walmart, S camping
22mm	Rs wb, full ♿ facilities, ⊓, 🚻, litter barrels, vending, petwalk
20mm	Rs eb, full ♿ facilities, ⊓, 🚻, litter barrels, vending, petwalk
15	WI 162, Bangor, to Coon Valley, N gas, S ◉ Chevrolet
12	rd C, W Salem, N ◫ Cenex/cafe/dsl/24hr, ◉ Coulee Region RV Ctr, NAPA, Neshonoc Camping, S ◫ BP/Quiznos/dsl, ⌂ AmericInn
10mm	weigh sta eb
5	WI 16, La Crosse, N ⊓ Buffalo Wild Wings, Coldstone, Manny's Mexican, Outback Steaks, Quiznos, ⌂ Baymont Inn, Hampton Inn, Microtel, ◉ Aldi Foods, $Tree, Freightliner, Home Depot, Walmart/Subway, Woodman's Foods/gas/lube, S ◫ Kwik Trip/dsl/24hr, ⊓ Burracho's Mexican Grill, Carlos O'Kelly's, ChuckeCheese, Culver's, Fazoli's, Jimmy John's, McDonald's, Hong Kong Buffet, Old Country Buffet, Olive Garden, Perkins, Starbucks, TGIFriday's, ⌂ Holiday Inn Express, ◉⊔, Barnes&Noble, Best Buy, F&F, Ford/Lincoln, Hobby Lobby, JC Penney, Kohl's, Macy's, Michael's, Sears/auto, ShopKO, Target, Walgreens, mall
4	US 53 N, WI 16, to WI 157, La Crosse, N ◉ Harley-Davidson, S ◫ Kwik Trip, TO, ⊓ Applebee's, Burger King, Caribou Coffee, China Inn, El Charro Mexican, Cousins Subs, Famous Dave's BBQ, Grizzly's Rest, Panera Bread, Papa Murphy's, Red Lobster, Rococo's Pizza, Subway, Taco Bell, Wendy's, ⌂ Comfort Inn, ◉⊔, AT&T, Festival Food/24hr, Gander Mtn, GNC, Goodyear/auto, Hancock Fabrics, Office Depot, Old Navy, PetCo, Petsmart, Sam's Club, Tires+, TJ Maxx, Verizon, La Crosse River St Trail

WI

WISCONSIN DELLS

T O M A H

L A C R O S S E

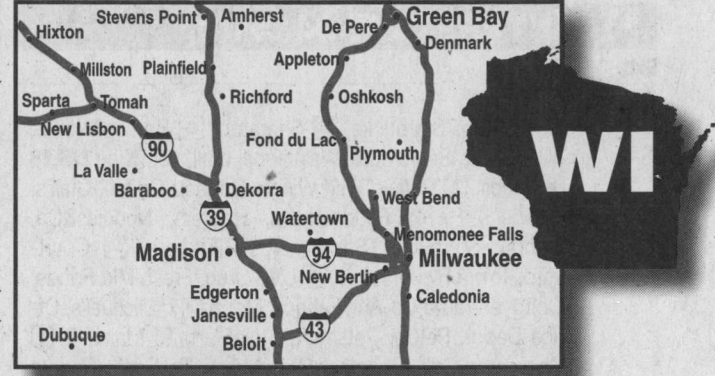

◆E INTERSTATE 90 CONT'D

Exit	Services
3	US 53 S, WI 35, to La Crosse, **S** 🅶 Citgo, Kwik Trip, 🍴 Burger King, Coney Island, Edwardo's Pizza, Hardee's, KFC, La Crosse Rest., McDonald's, North Country Steaks, Perkins, Pizza Hut, Subway, 🏨 Best Value Inn, Best Western, Brookstone Inn, EconoLodge, Howard Johnson, Settle Inn, Super 8, 🅾 ShopKo, U-Haul, Walgreens, to Great River St Trail, Viterbo Coll
2.5mm	Black River
2	rd B, French Island, **N** 🅾 ☕, **S** 🅶 BP/dsl, Kwik Trip, 🏨 Days Hotel/rest, 🅾 IGA Foods
1mm	**Welcome Ctr eb, full ♿ facilities, info, 🚻, 🏭, litter barrels, vending, petwalk**
0mm	Wisconsin/Minnesota state line, Mississippi River

◆E INTERSTATE 94

Exit	Services
349mm	Wisconsin/Illinois state line, **weigh sta nb**
347	WI 165, rd Q, Lakeview Pkwy, **E** 🅶 BP/dsl, 🍴 Chancery Rest., Culver's, McDonald's, 🏨 Radisson, 🅾 Old Navy, Prime Outlets/famous brands, **Welcome Ctr, full facilities**
345	rd C, **E** 🏨 Holiday Inn Express (1mi)
345mm	Des Plaines River
344	WI 50, Lake Geneva, to Kenosha, **E** 🍴 Citgo/dsl, Shell/dsl, Woodman's/gas, 🍴 Buffalo Wild Wings, Dickey's BBQ, Nick-N-Willy's, Noodles&Co, Perkins, Pizza Hut, Sparti's Gyros, Starbucks, TX Roadhouse, Tuscany Bistro, White Castle, 🏨 La Quinta, Super 8, 🅾 Best Buy, Chevrolet, Gander Mtn, Walgreens, **1 mi E** 🍴 Cheddar's, Cousins Subs, Famous Dave's, Olive Garden, Panda Express, 🏨 Candlewood Suites, Holiday Inn Express, 🅾 🏥, AT&T, Dick's, GNC, JC Penney, Petsmart, Target, Verizon, **W** 🅶 BP, Speedway/dsl, 🍴 Arby's, Birchwood Grill, Cracker Barrel, KFC, McDonald's, Phoenix Rest., Wendy's, 🏨 Best Western, Country Inn&Suites, Quality Inn, Value Inn, 🅾 BratStop Cheese Store, CarMax, Honda, Nissan, Toyota/Scion
342	WI 158, to Kenosha, **E** Harley-Davidson, **W** antiques
340	WI 142, rd S, to Kenosha, **E** 🅶 Kenosha TP/BP/Subway/dsl/E85/LP/scales/24hr, 🅾 🏥, **W** 🍴 Mars Cheese Castle Rest., 🏨 Oasis Inn, 🅾 Fun Time RV Ctr, to Bong RA
339	rd E
337	rd KR, to Mt Pleasant, **W** 🍴 Apple Holler Rest/orchard
335	WI 11, to Mt Pleasant, Burlington, to Racine
333	WI 20, Waterford, to Racine, **E** 🅶 KwikTrip/dsl/24hr, Shell/Cousins Subs/dsl, 🍴 Burger King, McDonald's, 🏨 Days Inn, Holiday Inn Express, 🅾 🏥, **W** 🅶 Citgo/Wendy's/dsl/24hr, Petro/Mobil/Iron Skillet/dsl/scales/24hr/@, 🍴 Culver's, Route 20 Outhouse Grill, Subway, 🏨 Travelodge, 🅾 Burlington RV Ctr, visitor info
329	rd K, Thompsonville, to Racine, **E** 🅶 🍔Loves/Arby's/Subway/dsl/scales/24hr, **W** 🍴 A&W, 🅾 dsl repair
328mm	**weigh sta eb**
327	rd G, **W** fireworks
326	7 Mile Rd, **E** 🅶 BP, Mobil/dsl, 🅾 Jellystone Park, **W** 🅾 antiques
325	WI 241 N (from wb), to 27th St
322	WI 100, to Ryan Rd, **E** 🅶 KwikTrip/dsl, 🍴 McDonald's, Wendy's, 🅾 dsl repair, **W** 🅶 🍔Loves/Denny's/dsl/LP/scales/RV dump/24hr, Mobil, 🍔Subway/dsl/LP/scales/24hr, Shell/A&W/KFC/dsl, 🍴 Arby's, Cousins

Exit	Services
322	Continued Subs, Perkins, Yen Hwa Chinese, 🏨 Staybridge Suites, Value Inn, 🅾 AutoZone, Blue Beacon, Freightliner/repair, Pick'n Save, Walgreens, vet
321	Drexel Ave
320	rd BB, Rawson Ave, **E** 🅶 BP, Mobil, 🍴 Applebee's, Burger King, 🏨 La Quinta
319	rd ZZ, College Ave, **E** 🅶 Shell/Subway, Speedway/dsl, 🍴 Branded Steer Rest., McDonald's, 🏨 Candlewood Suites, Comfort Suites, Country Inn&Suites, Crowne Plaza, Days Inn, EconoLodge, Fairfield Inn, Hampton Inn, Holiday Inn Express, MainStay Suites, Ramada, Red Roof Inn, **W** 🅶 BP, FoodMart
318	WI 119, **E** ☕
317	I-43, I-894 (from wb)
316	I-43 S, I-894 W (I-94 exits left from eb), to Beloit
314b	Howard Ave, to Milwaukee, **W** to Alverno Coll
314a	Holt Ave, **E** 🅶 Andy's/dsl, 🍴 Applebee's, Arby's, China King, Little Caesars, Quiznos, Starbucks, Subway, Wendy's, 🅾 $General, Home Depot, Pick'n Save Foods, Sentry Foods, Target, vet, **W** 🏥, to Alverno Coll
312b a	Becher St, Mitchell St, Lapham Blvd, **W** 🅶 BP, Citgo, Shell
311	WI 59, National Ave, 6th St, downtown
310a	13th St (from eb), **E** 🏥
310b	I-43 N, to Green Bay
310c	I-794 E, **E** 🏨 Hilton, Holiday Inn, 🅾 to downtown, Lake Michigan Port of Entry
309b	26th St, 22nd St, Clybourn St, St Paul Ave, **N** 🅾 🏥, to Marquette U
309a	35th St, **N** 🅶 BP, Speedway, 🅾 Urgent Care
308c b	US 41
308a	VA Ctr, **N** 🅾 Miller Brewing, **S** 🅾 Miller Park
307b	68th-70th St, Hawley Rd
307a	68th-70th St
306	WI 181, to 84th St, **N** 🏥, **S** 🅾 Olympic Training Facility
305b	US 45 N, to Fond du Lac, **N** 🏥
305a	I-894 S, US 45 S, to Chicago to ☕
304b a	WI 100, **N** 🅶 BP, Clark/dsl, 7-11, Shell/dsl, 🍴 Cousins Subs, Edwardo's Pizza, Ghenghis Khan BBQ, Habanero's Mexican, HoneyBaked Cafe, Jimmy John's, Mo's Irish Grill, Peony Chinese, Qdoba, Rococo's, Starbucks, Subway, Taco Bell, 🏨 Days Inn, 🅾 🏥, zoo, **S** 🅶 MiniMart 100, Mobil, Speedway/dsl, 🍴 Culver's, DQ, Fazoli's, McDonald's, Pallas Rest., Starbucks, Wendy's, 🏨 Days Inn, 🅾 Midas, O'Reilly Parts, Sam's Club, U-Haul, Walgreens
301b a	Moorland Rd, **N** 🍴 Bakers Square, Bravo Italiano, Claim Jumper, Culver's, Firehouse Subs, Fleming's Rest., McDonald's, Mitchell's Fish Mkt, Original Pancake House,

= gas   = food   = lodging   = other   = rest stop   Copyright 2014 - The NEXT Exit ®

INTERSTATE 94 CONT'D

Exit	Services
301b a	Continued

Red Robin, Starbucks, ☒ Sheraton, ◙ Barnes&Noble, JC Penney, Sears/auto, Walgreens, mall, vet, **N on US 18** ☒ Mobil, ⒧ Buffalo Wild Wings, Caribou Coffee, Chili's, Cooper's Hawk, Fuddrucker's, Hooters, Noodles&Co, Qdoba, Starbucks, Stir Crazy, TGIFriday's, ☒ Court-yard, TownePlace Suites, ◙ CVS Drug, Fresh Mkt Foods, Goodyear/auto, Jo-Ann Fabrics, Metro Mkt, Michael's, Office Depot, PetCo, Petsmart, SteinMart, TJ Maxx, **S** ⒧ Champp's Grill, Charcoal Grill, Maxwell's Rest., Panera Bread, Outback Steaks, ☒ Best Western Midway, Brookfield Suites, Country Inn&Suites, Residence Inn, ◙ Pick'n Save Foods, Walgreens, golf

297 WI 164 S, US 18, rd JJ, Blue Mound Rd, Barker Rd **0-2 mi** **N** ☒ Clark, ⒧ Applebee's, BoneFish Grill, Boston Mkt, Brookfield Rest., Bullwinkle's Rest., Carrabba's, Chuck-ECheese's, Cousins Subs, George Webb Rest., Honey-Baked Ham, Jose's Mexican, KFC, Kopp's Custard, Loredos Mexican, McDonald's, Melting Pot, Olive Garden, Perkins, Potbelly, Subway, ☒ DoubleTree, Extended Stay America, Hampton Inn, La Quinta, Motel 6, Quality Inn, ◙ Acura, Advance Parts, Aldi Foods, Best Buy, $Tree, GNC, K-Mart, Lexus/Mazda/VW, Meineke, Metro Mkt, **S** ☒ Clark, F&F/dsl, PDQ, ⒧ Arby's, Burger King, Cousin's Subs, Culver's, Famous Dave's BBQ, McDonald's, Milio's, New China, Oscar's Burgers, Papa Murphy's, Sonic, Starbucks, Taco Bell, TX Roadhouse, Topper's Pizza, Wendy's, ☒ Ramada Ltd, Super 8, ◙ AT&T, Buick/GMC, Cadillac, CarMax, CarX, Chevrolet, Firestone/auto, Ford, Gander Mtn, Home Depot, Honda, Hyundai, Infiniti/Maserati/Mercedes/Porsche, Jaguar/Land Rover/Volvo, Kia, Kohl's, Menards, Midas, Nissan, Pick'n Save Foods, Radio Shack, Sam's Club, Target, Tires+, Volvo, Walgreens, st patrol

295 rd F, to WI 74, Waukesha, **N** ☒ KwikTrip/dsl, ⒧ Jimmy John's, ☒ Marriott, **S** ◙ Ⓗ, to Carroll Coll

294 WI 164, rd J S, to Waukesha, **N** ☒ Mobil/Subway/dsl, ⒧ Machine Shed Rest., Thunder Bay Grille, ☒ Holiday Inn, Wildwood Lodge, **S** ◙ Expo Ctr, Peterbilt

293c WI 16 W, Pewaukee (from wb), **N** ◙ GE Plant

293b a rd T, Wausheka, Pewaukee, **S** ☒ Mobil, KwikTrip, ⒧ Arby's, Asian Fusion, Canyon City Wood Grill, Caribou Coffee, Cousins Subs, Culver's, Denny's, Dunkin Donuts, Feng's Kitchen, Jimmy John's, McDonald's, Mr. Wok, Papa Murphy's, Peking House, Primos Pizza, Qdoba, Rococo's Pizza, Rox Grill, Spring City Rest., Subway, Taco Amigo, Topper's Pizza, Weissgerber's Gasthaus Rest., Wendy's, ☒ Best Western, ◙ AT&T, AutoZone, CVS Drug, $Tree, Firestone/auto, GNC, Goodharvest Mkt, JoAnn Fabrics, Office Depot, Pick'n Save Foods, Radio Shack, Verizon, Walgreens

291 rd G, rd TT, **N** ☒ Country Springs Inn

290 rd SS, Pewaukee

287 WI 83, Hartland, to Wales, **N** ⒧ Applebee's, 5 Guys Burgers, Hardee's, McDonald's, Noodles&Co, Panera Bread, Perkins, Qdoba, Starbucks, Water St Brewery/rest., ☒ Country Pride Inn, Holiday Inn Express, ◙ Albrecht's Mkt, Amish Barn Gifts, Best Buy, GNC, Kohl's, Marshalls, Radio Shack, Verizon, Walgreens, **S** ☒ BP/dsl, PDQ/dsl/24hr, ⒧ Burger King, Coldstone, DQ, Jimmy John's,

---

287 Continued

Marty's Pizza, Pacific Asian Bistro, Pizza Hut, StoneCreek Coffee, Subway, ☒ La Quinta, ◙ Ace Hardware, $Tree, Home Depot, PetCo, Target, Tires+, Walmart, vet

285 rd C, Delafield, **N** ☒ BP/dsl, Mobil/deli, ☒ Delafield Hotel, ◙ to St John's Military Academy, **S** ◙ to Kettle Moraine SF

283 rd P, to Sawyer Rd

282 WI 67, Dousman, to Oconomowoc, **0-2 mi N** ☒ KwikTrip/dsl, Mobil, ⒧ Chili's, Cousins Subs, Culver's, Feng's Kitchen, Jimmy John's, Pizza Hut, Quiznos, Rococo's Pizza, Rosati's Pizza, Sammy's Taste Of Chicago, Schlotzsky's, Starbucks, Stone Creek Coffee, Subway, ☒ Hilton Garden, Olympia Resort, ◙ Ace Hardware, Aldi Foods, AT&T, Brennan's Mkt, Ford, GNC, K-Mart, Pick'n Save, Radio Shack, Walgreens, vet, **S** ☒ Staybridge Suites, ◙ Ⓗ, Harley-Davidson, to Kettle Moraine SF (8mi), Old World WI HS (13mi)

277 Willow Glen Rd (from eb, no return)

275 rd F, Ixonia, to Sullivan, **N** ☒ Mobil/dsl, ◙ Concord Gen Store, **S** camping

267 WI 26, Johnson Creek, to Watertown, **N** ☒ BP/McDonald's/dsl, Shell/dsl/rest./scales/24hr, ⒧ Arby's, Hwy Harry's Cafe, ☒ Days Inn, Comfort Suites, ◙ Goodyear/auto, Johnson Creek Outlet Ctr/famous brands, Old Navy, **S** ☒ KwikTrip/dsl, ⒧ Culver's, Subway, ◙ Ⓗ, Kohl's, Menards, to Aztalan SP

266mm Rock River

264mm ☒ wb, full ♿ facilities, Ⓒ, ♨, litter barrels, vending, petwalk

263mm Crawfish River

261mm ☒ eb, full ♿ facilities, Ⓒ, ♨, litter barrels, vending, petwalk

259 WI 89, Lake Mills, to Waterloo, **N** ☒ Mobil/rest/dsl/24hr, ☒ Best Value Inn, ◙ truck repair, **S** ☒ BP/dsl/E85, KwikTrip/dsl, ⒧ Jimmy John's, McDonald's, Pizza Pit, Subway, ☒ Pyramid Motel/RV park, ◙ Urgent Care, Ace Hardware, Buick/Chevrolet, Walgreens, vet, to Aztalan SP

250 WI 73, Deerfield, to Marshall

244 rd n, Sun Prairie, Cottage Grove, **N** ☒ BP, **S** ☒ BP, KwikTrip, ⒧ Arby's, Subway

240 I-90 E.

I-94 and I-90 run together 93 miles. See Interstate 90 exits 48-138

138a I-94, E to Milwaukee, W to La Cross (exits left from eb)

138b WI 30, to Madison, **S** ◙ ☒

135c b US 151, Madison, **N** ☒ BP, ⒧ Erin's Cafe, Happy Wok, Subway, Uno Grill, ☒ Cambria Suites, Courtyard, Fairfield Inn, GrandStay Suites, Holiday Inn, Staybridge Suites, ◙ Buick/GMC, Chrysler/Dodge/Jeep, Ford, Honda, Hyundai, Kia, Mazda, Nissan, Subaru, Toyota/Scion

135a **S** ☒ BP, Citgo, Mobil, Shell, ⒧ Applebee's, Arby's, Buffalo Wild Wings, Chili's, Chipotle Mexican, Cracker Barrel, Culver's, Denny's, Dickey's BBQ, Fazoli's, Hardee's, Hometown Buffet, Hooters, IHOP, Imperial Garden, KFC, McDonald's, Milio's, Noodles&Co, Old Country Buffet, Olive Garden, Outback Steaks, Panera Bread, Perkins, Pizza Hut, Potbelly, Qdoba, Red Lobster, Red Robin, Rocky's Pizza, Starbucks, Taco Bell, Takumi Japanese, TGIFriday's, Topper's Pizza, TX Roadhouse, Wendy's, ☒ Baymont Inn, Best Western, Comfort Inn, Crowne Plaza Hotel/rest., EconoLodge, Hampton Inn, Howard

⤴E INTERSTATE 94 CONT'D

Exit	Services

135a Continued

Johnson, Microtel, Motel 6, Red Roof Inn, Residence Inn, Rodeway Inn, Super 8, ⊡ Urgent Care, Aldi Foods, AT&T, Barnes&Noble, Best Buy, Dick's, $Tree, Firestone/auto, Gander Mtn, Goodyear/auto, Home Depot, Hy-Vee Foods, JC Penney, JoAnn Fabrics, Kohl's, Marshalls, Menards, Office Depot, Old Navy, Petsmart, Savers, Sears/auto, ShopKO, Target, Verizon, city park, mall, st patrol, vet

132 US 51, Madison, De Forest, **N** 🏪 Shell/Pinecone Rest/dsl/24hr, ⊡ Camping World RV Ctr, Gander Mtn, **S** 🍴🏪 TA/BP/Subway/Taco Bell/dsl/scales/24hr/@, ⊡ Goodyear, Peterbilt, Freightliner/GMC/Volvo/White, WI RV World, camping

131 WI 19, Waunakee, **N** 🏪 Kwik Trip, Mobil/dsl, Speedway/dsl, 🍴 A&W, McDonald's, Rodeside Grill, 🛏 Best Value Inn, Days Inn, ⊡ Mousehouse Cheesehaus, Kenworth, truckwash, fireworks

126 rd V, to Dane, De Forest, **N** 🏪 Phillips 66/Arby's/dsl, 🍴 Burger King, Culver's, McDonald's, Subway, 🛏 Holiday Inn Express, ⊡ Cheese Chalet, KOA, **S** 🏪 Exxon, Shell, 🛏 Comfort Inn, ⊡ dsl repair

119 WI 60, to Lodi, Arlington, **S** 🏪 Mobil/Cousins Subs/dsl, 🍴 A&W, Rococo's Pizza, 🛏 Quality Inn, ⊡ dsl/tire repair

115 rd CS, to Lake Wisconsin, Poynette, **N** 🏪 BP/dsl, 🍴 McDonald's, Subway, ⊡ Smokey Hollow Camping, dsl truck/trailer repair, motel, trout fishing

113mm Ⓡ both lanes, full ♿ facilities, 🍴, 🛏, litter barrels, vending, petwalk, RV dump

111mm Wisconsin River

108b a I-39 N, WI 78, to US 51 N, Portage, **N** ⊡ 🏥, to WI Dells, **S** 🏪 BP, Petro/DQ/Subway/dsl/24hr/@, 🛏 Comfort Suites, Days Inn, Devil's Head Resort/Conv Ctr, ⊡ Blue Beacon

106mm Baraboo River

106 WI 33, Portage, **N** 🏪 Mobil/dsl/rest, ⊡ 🏥, **S** 🏪 BP, ⊡ Kamp Dakota, SkyHigh Camping, to Cascade Mtn Ski Area, Devil's Lake SP, Circus World Museum

92 US 12, to Baraboo, **N** 🏪 BP/dsl, Exxon, Mobil/Dunkin Donuts/dsl/24hr, Sinclair/Subway/dsl, 🍴 Buffalo Phil's Grille, Burger King, Cracker Barrel, Cheese Factory Rest, Culver's, Damon's, Denny's, Domino's, Famous Dave's BBQ, Field's Steaks, Marley's Rest., Mark's Rest, McDonald's, Monk's Grill, Ponderosa, R Place Italian, Sarento's Italian, Wintergreen Grill, Uno, 🛏 Alakai Hotel, Country Squire Motel, Dell Creek Motel, Grand Marquis Inn, Great Wolf Lodge, Holiday Motel, Holiday Inn Express, Kalahari Resort, Lake Delton Motel, Ramada, Wilderness Hotel, Wintergreen Hotel, ⊡ Urgent Care, Broadway Dinner Theater, Kalahari Conv Ctr, Mkt Square Cheese, Tanger Outlets Famous Brands, museum, **S** 🛏 Motel 6, ⊡ 🏥, Scenic Traveler RV Ctr, Jellystone Camping, Red Oak Camping, Mirror Lake SP

89 WI 23, Lake Delton, **N** 🏪 Phillips 66, Shell/dsl, 🍴 Brathouse Grill, Denny's Diner, Howie's Rest., KFC, Moosejaw Pizza, 🛏 EconoLodge, Hilton Garden, Kings Inn, Malibu Inn, Olympia Motel, ⊡ Crystal Grand Music Theatre, Springbrook Camping, Jellystone Camping, USPO, **S** 🍴 McDonald's, ⊡ Home Depot, Kohl's, Walmart/Subway, Country Roads RV Park

87 WI 13, Wisconsin Dells, **N** 🏪 Citgo, Mobil/Arby's/dsl,

---

87 Continued

Shell, 🍴 Applebee's, Bunyan's Rest., Burger King, Coldstone, Country Kitchen, Culver's, Denny's, IHOP, Jimmy John's, McDonald's, Mexicali Rose Rest., Perkins, Starbucks, Taco Bell, Wendy's, 🛏 AmericInn, Best Western, Comfort Inn, Days Inn, Dells Island Resort, Polynesian Hotel, Super 8, ⊡ KOA, Sherwood Forest Camping, Walgreens, golf, waterpark, info

85 US 12, WI 16, Wisconsin Dells, 0-3 mi **N** 🍴 Crabby's Seafood, Culver's, Starbucks, 🛏 Days Inn, Mayflower Motel, ⊡ American World RV Park/Hotel, KOA, Sherwood Forest Camping, Standing Rock Camping, to Rocky Arbor SP, **S** 🏪 BP, 🍴 Piccadilly's, 🛏 Arrowhead Camping, Edge-O-the-Dell RV Camping, Summer Breeze Resort

79 rd HH, Lyndon Sta, **S** 🏪 BP/Subway/dsl/24hr

76mm Ⓡ wb, full ♿ facilities, 🍴, 🛏, litter barrels, vending, petwalk

74mm Ⓡ eb, full ♿ facilities, 🍴, 🛏, litter barrels, vending, petwalk

69 WI 82, Mauston, **N** 🏪 Mauston TP/BP/Taco Bell/24hr, 🏪Pilot/Wendy's/dsl/scales/24hr, Shell/24hr, 🍴 China Buffet, 🛏 Best Western Oasis, Country Inn, Super 8, ⊡ Carr Valley Cheese, to Buckhorn SP, **S** 🏪 KwikTrip/Hearty Platter Rest/dsl/scales/24hr, Mobil, 🍴 Culver's, Garden Valley Rest., McDonald's, Pizza Hut, Roman Castle Rest., Subway, 🛏 Alaskan Inn, Best Value Inn, ⊡ 🏥, Buckhorn SP, Buick/Chevrolet, $General, Family$, Festival Foods, K-Mart, Walgreens, vet

61 WI 80, to Necedah, New Lisbon, **N** 🏪 Mobil/A&W/Subway/dsl/scales/24hr, 🛏 Edge O' the Woods Motel, Travelers Inn, ⊡ Buckhorn SP, Chrysler/Jeep, Ford, fireworks, **S** 🏪 KwikTrip/24hr, ⊡ True Value, Elroy-Sparta ST Tr, city park, USPO

55 rd C, Camp Douglas, **N** ⊡ wayside, to Camp Williams, Volk Field, **S** 🏪 BP/dsl, Mobil/Subway/dsl, 🍴 German Haus Rest., 🛏 K&K Motel, ⊡ to Mill Bluff SP

51mm weigh sta eb

48 rd PP, Oakdale, exits 48-138 are I-90 exit numbers, **N** 🏪 Road Ranger/Pilot/Subway/dsl/scales/24hr, ⊡ Granger's Camping, KOA, truck/car wash, antiques, **S** 🏪 Loves/Hardee's/dsl/scales/24hr, ⊡ Mill Bluff SP, repair

147 I-90 W, to La Crosse

I-94 and I-90 run together 93 miles

143 US 12, WI 21, Tomah, **N** 🏪 Mobil/dsl, 🍴 A&W/LJ Silver, Perkins, 🛏 AmericInn, Best Western, Microtel, Super 8, ⊡ Humbird Cheese/gifts, truckwash, **S** 🏪 BP, KwikTrip/rest./dsl/scales/24hr, 🍴 Arby's, China Buffet, Culver's, Ground Round, KFC, McDonald's, Pizza Hut, Subway,

🅰 = gas 🍴 = food 🏠 = lodging 🅾 = other 📷 = rest stop   Copyright 2014 - The NEXT Exit ®

INTERSTATE 94 CONT'D

TOMAH

Exit	Services
143	Continued Taco Bell, 🏠 Cranberry Lodge, EconoLodge, Hampton Inn, Quality Inn, 🅾🅷 Advance Parts, Aldi Foods, $Tree, U-Haul, Verizon, Walmart/Subway, to Ft McCoy (9mi), **S on US 12** 🍴 Burger King, 🅾 Ace Hardware, Chrysler/Dodge/Jeep, Firestone/auto, Ford, GMC, NAPA, O'Reilly Parts
135	rd EW, Warrens, **N** 🅰 Cenex/dsl, 🏠 3 Bears Resort, 🅾 Jellystone Camping, **S** 🍴 Bog Rest.
128	rd O, Millston, **N** 🅾 Black River SF, camping, **S** 🅰 Cenex/dsl, 🅾 USPO
123mm	📷/scenic view both lanes, full ♿ facilities, 🅲, 🚻, litter barrels, vending, petwalk
116	WI 54, **N** 🅰 Cenex/Subway/Taco Johns/dsl/LP, 🍴 Perkins, 🏠 Best Western Arrowhead/rest., Comfort Inn, Super 8, 🅾 Black River RA, Parkland Camp, casino, **S** 🅰 ⓕFLYING J/Denny's/dsl/24hr/@, KwikTrip/dsl, 🍴 Burger King, Culver's, McDonald's, Oriental Kitchen, Pizza Hut, 🏠 Days Inn, 🅾 Buick/Chevrolet/GMC, $General, Walmart/Subway
115mm	Black River
115	US 12, WI 27, Black River Falls, to Merrillan, **S** 🅰 BP, Holiday/dsl, 🍴 Hardee's, KFC, Subway, Sunrise Rest., 🅾🅷 Ace Hardware, Harley-Davidson, vet
105	to WI 95, Hixton, to Alma Center, **N** 🏠 Motel 95/camping, 🅾 KOA (3mi), **S** 🅰 Cenex/dsl, Clark/dsl/24hr, 🍴 Timber Valley Rest., 🅾 city park
98	WI 121, Northfield, Pigeon Falls, to Alma Center, **S** 🅰 Cenex/dsl, 🍴 Crazy Jerry's Burgers
88	US 10, Osseo, to Fairchild, **N** 🅰 BP/DQ, Exxon/Webb Rest./dsl/scales/24hr, Mobil/dsl, 🍴 Hardee's, Moe's Diner, 🏠 10-7 Inn, Super 8, 🅾 Chevrolet, Ford, Stoney Cr RV Park, **S** 🅰 SA/dsl, 🍴 McDonald's, Subway, Taco John's, 🏠 Osseo Inn, 🅾🅷 Family$
81	rd HH, rd KK, Foster, **S** 🅰 BP/dsl/LP, 🍴 Foster Cheesehaus

EAU CLAIRE

Exit	Services
70	US 53, Eau Claire, **N off Golf Rd** 🅰 Mobil/dsl, 🍴 Applebee's, Asia Palace, Buffalo Wild Wings, Burracho's Mexican, Caribou Coffee, Chipotle, Coldstone, Culver's, Fazoli's, Firehouse Subs, Fuji Steaks, Grizzly's Grill, HuHot Chinese, Jade Garden, Jimmy John's, Mancino's, Manny's Grill, McDonald's, Noodles&Co, Olive Garden, Panera Bread, TX Roadhouse, TGIFriday's, 🏠 Baymont Inn, Country Inn&Suites, Grandstay, Holiday Inn, 🅾 Aldi Foods, AT&T, Bam!, Best Buy, $Tree, Hancock Fabrics, JC Penney, Jo-Ann Fabrics, Kohl's, Macy's, Menards, Michael's, Office Depot, PetCo, Petsmart, Sam's Club, Scheel's Sports, Sears/auto, Target, TJ Maxx, Tuesday Morning, Verizon, Walmart/Subway, Younkers, mall, **S** 🅾 Gander Mtn, st police
68	WI 93, to Eleva, **N** 🅰 Holiday, KwikTrip/dsl, 🍴 Burger King, Cousins Subs, DQ, Famous Dave's BBQ, Quiznos, Red Robin, 🏠 EconoLodge, 🅾 BigLots, Chrysler/Dodge/Jeep, County Mkt Foods, Festival Foods, Firestone/auto, Goodyear/auto, Kia, NAPA, Nissan, Subaru, Suzuki, transmissions, vet, **S** 🅰 Holiday/dsl, 🏠 Metropolis Resort, 🅾 Audi/VW, Ford/Lincoln, Honda, Hyundai
65	WI 37, WI 85, Eau Claire, to Mondovi, **N** 🅰 Exxon, Holiday/dsl, KwikTrip/dsl, 🍴 Arby's, Godfather's Pizza, Green Mill Rest., Hardee's, Jimmy John's, Mancino's, McDonald's, Pizza Hut, Randy's Rest., Red Lobster, Starbucks, Subway, Taco Bell, 🏠 Best Value Inn, Best Western, Clarion, Comfort Inn, Days Inn/rest., Hampton Inn, Highlander

MENOMONIE

Exit	Services
65	Continued Inn, Plaza Hotel, Super 8, 🅾🅷 County Mkt Foods, Radio Shack, ShopKo, Verizon, Walgreens, dsl repair
64mm	Chippewa River
59	to US 12, rd EE, to Eau Claire, **N** 🅰 Holiday/Burger King/dsl/24hr, Holiday/Subway/dsl/24hr, 🍴 Dana's Grill, El Mariachi, McDonald's, 🏠 AmericInn, Days Inn, Knights Inn, 🅾🅷 Freightliner, Mack/Volvo Trucks, Peterbilt, auto repair/towing, **S** 🅾 dsl repair
52	US 12, WI 29, WI 40, Elk Mound, to Chippewa Falls, **S** 🅰 U-Fuel/E85
49mm	weigh sta wb
45	rd B, Menomonie, **N** 🅰 Cenex/Subway/dsl/scales/24hr, **S** 🅰 KwikTrip/dsl/scales/24hr, 🍴 Red Cedar Steaks, 🏠 Quality Inn, 🅾🅷 AOK RV Ctr, Kenworth, Walmart Dist Ctr, dsl repair, truckwash
44mm	Red Cedar River
43mm	📷s both lanes, full ♿ facilities, 🅲, 🚻, litter barrels, vending, petwalk, weather info
41	WI 25, Menomonie, **N** 🅰 Cenex/E85, 🍴 Applebee's, Caribou Coffee, China Buffet, Los Cabos Mexican, Pizza Hut, Subway, 🅾🅷 Aldi Foods, AT&T, $Tree, Radio Shack, Walmart/Subway, Twin Springs Camping, **S** 🅰 F&F/dsl, Holiday, SA/dsl, 🍴 Arby's, Denny's, Dickey's BBQ, Jimmy John's, McDonald's, Perkins, Taco Bell, Taco John's, Wendy's, 🏠 AmericInn, Country Inn&Suites, EconoLodge, Motel 6, Super 8, 🅾 Advance Parts, Buick/GMC, Chevrolet, Chrysler/Dodge/Jeep, K-Mart, Mkt Place Foods, O'Reilly Parts, Walgreens, to Red Cedar St Tr
32	rd Q, to Knapp
28	WI 128, Wilson, Elmwood, to Glenwood City, **N** 🅰 KwikTrip/rest./dsl/24hr, **S** 🅾 Eau Galle RA, camping, dsl repair
24	rd B, to Baldwin, **N** 🅰 BP, 🏠 Woodville Motel, **S** 🅾 Eau Galle RA, camping
19	US 63, Baldwin, to Ellsworth, **N** 🅰 Freedom/dsl, KwikTrip/Subway/dsl, 🍴 A&W, DQ, Hardee's, McDonald's, 🏠 AmericInn, 🅾🅷 🅰 Mobil/rest./dsl, 🏠 Super 8, 🅾 fireworks
16	rd T, Hammond
10	WI 65, Roberts, to New Richmond, **N** 🅰 BP/dsl (2mi), ⓕFLYING J/McDonald's/dsl/scales/24hr, 🍴 Barnboard Rest. (2mi), **S** Freightliner
8mm	weigh sta eb
4	US 12, rd U, Somerset, **N** 🅰 BP/dsl, TA/Country Pride/dsl/scales/24hr/@, 🏠 Regency Inn, 🅾 vet, to Willow River SP
3	WI 35 S, to River Falls, U of WI River Falls
2	rd F, Carmichael Rd, Hudson, **N** 🅰 BP/repair, Freedom/dsl, Holiday/dsl, 🍴 Applebee's, Caribou Coffee, Culver's, Domino's, Fiesta Loca, Jimmy John's, KFC, Papa Murphy's, Taco John's, 🏠 Royal Inn, 🅾 $Tree, Family Fresh Foods, GNC, Radio Shack, Target, Verizon, Walgreens, repair, **S** 🅰 F&F/dsl, Holiday, KwikTrip/dsl, Shell, 🍴 Arby's, Buffalo Wild Wings, Burger King, Chipotle Mexican, Coldstone, Denny's, Green Mill Rest., Kingdom Buffet, Little Caesars, McDonald's, Noodles&Co, Perkins, Pizza Hut, Starbucks, Subway, Taco Bell, Wendy's, 🏠 Comfort Suites, Fairfield Inn, Holiday Inn Express, Hudson House Hotel, Super 8, 🅾🅷 Aldi Foods, Chevrolet/GMC, Chrysler/Dodge/Jeep, County Mkt Foods, Ford, Home Depot, Menards, NAPA, O'Reilly Parts, TirePros, Tires+, Verizon, Walmart, USPO, to Kinnickinnic SP
1	WI 35 N, Hudson, **1 mi N** 🅰 Freedom/dsl, Holiday, 🍴 Carbones Pizzeria, DQ
0mm	Wisconsin/Minnesota state line, St Croix River

HUDSON

⬆N INTERSTATE 25

Exit	Services
300	I-90, E to Gillette, W to Billings. **I-25 begins/ends on I-90, exit 56.**
299	US 16, Buffalo, **E** 🗋 Cenex, Exxon/dsl, Maverik/dsl, 🍴 Winchester Steaks, 🏠 Comfort Inn, Hampton Inn, Holiday Inn Express, Motel 6, 🅾 Bighorn Tire, Deer Park Camping, KOA, NAPA, vet, **W** 🗋 Cenex/rest/dsl/24hr, 🍴 Bozeman Tr Steaks, Dash Inn Rest., Hardee's, McDonald's, Pizza Hut, Sub Shop, Subway, Taco John's, 🏠 Crossroads Inn, Days Inn, WYO Motel, Super 8, 🅾 🅷 Ace Hardware, Family$, Indian RV Camp, Verizon, to Yellowstone

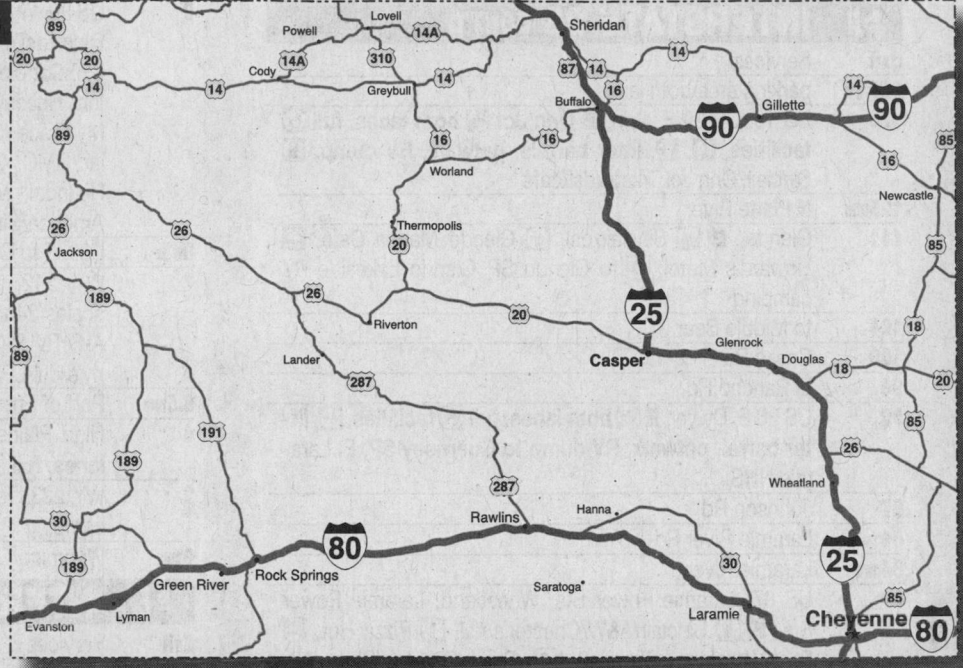

298	US 87, Buffalo, **W** Nat Hist Dist Info
291	Trabing Rd
280	Middle Fork Rd
274mm	parking area both lanes, litter barrels
265	Reno Rd
254	Kaycee, **E** 🗋 Exxon/dsl, 🍴 Country Inn Diner, Invasion Rest., 🏠 Cassidy Inn Motel, Siesta Motel, 🅾 Kaycee Gen. Store, NAPA Repair, Powder River RV Park, USPO, museum, **W** 🆁🆂 both lanes, full 🔥 facilities, 🍴, 🚻, litter barrels, petwalk, 🗋 Sinclair/pizza/subs/dsl/LP/motel, 🅾 KC RV Park
249	I I I Rd
246	Powder River Rd
235	Tisdale Mtn Rd
227	WY 387 N, Midwest, Edgerton, **E** Oil Field Museum
223	no services
219mm	parking area both lanes, litter barrels
216	Ranch Rd
210	Horse Ranch Creek Rd, Midwest, Edgerton
197	Ormsby Rd
191	Wardwell Rd, to Bar Nunn, **W** 🗋 Loaf'N Jug/dsl, 🅾 KOA
189	US 20, US 26 W, to Shoshone Port of Entry, 📵
188b	WY 220, Poplar St, **E** 🍴 Godfather's Pizza, 🏠 Best Western, Hampton Inn, Hilton Garden, La Quinta, Motel 6, Quality Inn, **W** 🗋 Exxon, 🍴 Burger King, Casper's Rest., DQ, 🅾 Harley-Davidson, to Ft Casper HS
188a	Center St, Casper, **E** 🗋 Conoco/dsl, Shell/dsl, 🍴 Poor Boys Steaks, Taco John's, 🏠 National 9 Inn, Ramada, Showboat Motel, **W** 🍴 Subway, 🏠 Days Inn, Parkway Plaza Motel, 🅾 USPO
187	McKinley St, Casper, **E** 🗋 Loaf'N Jug/dsl, 🏠 Ranch House Motel, 🅾 repair/transmissons
186	US 20, US 26, US 87, Yellowstone St, **E** 🅾 city park, dsl repair, transmissions, **W** 🗋 Exxon, 🅾 🅷 Chevrolet/Subaru, Kia, O'Reilly Parts, Toyota, auto repair
185	WY 258, Wyoming Blvd, E Casper, **E** 🗋 Kum&Go/dsl, Loaf'n Jug/dsl, 🍴 Applebee's, HQ BBQ, IHOP, Outback Steaks, 🏠 Baymont Inn, C'mon Inn, Shilo Inn, Super 8, 🅾 Smith RV Ctr, RV camping, **W** 🗋 Exxon/dsl, ⊕FLYING J

185	Continued /Conoco/Subway/dsl/LP/scales/24hr, Loaf'n Jug, 🍴 Arby's, Burger King, DQ, Hardee's, HomeTown Buffet, KFC/LJ Silver, McDonald's, Old Chicago Grill, Olive Garden, On The Border, Perkins, Pizza Hut, Sanford's Cafe, Starbucks, Taco Bell, Taco John's, Village Inn, Wendy's, 🏠 Coutyard, 1st Interstate Motel, Holiday Inn Express, 🅾 AutoZone, Best Buy, Home Depot, JC Penney, K-Mart, Macy's, PetCo, Plains Tire, Safeway Foods/gas, Sam's Club/gas, Sears/auto, Staples, Target, Verizon, Walgreens, Walmart, to Oregon Tr, mall
182	WY 253, Brooks Rd, Hat Six Rd, **E** 🗋 Sinclair/Lou's Rest/dsl, 🍴 Sonic, 🏠 Sleep Inn, 🅾 Rivers Edge Camping, to Wilkins SP, **W** 🍴 Famous Dave's BBQ, FireRock Rest., Golden Corral, Keg&Cork Rest., 🏠 Holiday Inn, Mainstay Suites, 🅾 🅷 Buick/Cadillac/GMC, Chrysler/Dodge/Jeep, Kohl's, Menards, VW
171mm	parking area both lanes, litter barrels
165	Glenrock, **E** dinosaur museum, same as 160
160	US 87, US 20, US 26, E Glenrock, **E** 🍴 G-Rock's, Paisley Shawl, 🏠 All American Inn, Hotel Higgins B&B, 🅾 Deer Creek Village Camping, to Johnston Power Plant
156	Bixby Rd
154	Barber Rd
153mm	parking area both lanes, litter barrels
151	Natural Bridge
150	Inez Rd
146	La Prele Rd
140	WY 59, Douglas, **E** 🗋 Conoco/Subway/dsl, Maverik/dsl, 🍴 Arby's, La Costa Mexican, McDonald's, Taco John's, 🏠 Douglas Inn, Holiday Inn Express, Sleep Inn, Super 8, 🅾 🅷, Chrysler/Dodge/Jeep, Ford, KOA, Lone Tree Village RV Park, NAPA, Pioneer Museum, WY St Fair, city park
135	US 20, US 26, US 87, Douglas, **E** 🗋 Sinclair/dsl/rest., 🏠 1st Interstate Inn, 🅾 auto repair, **1-2 mi E** 🗋 Loaf'n Jug/dsl, Sinclair/dsl, 🍴 4 Seasons Chinese, KFC, Pizza Hut, Plains Trading Post Rest., Village Inn, 🏠 4 Winds Motel, 🅾 🅷, Douglas Hardware, Family$, O'Reilly Parts, Safeway Foods, Shopko, Verizon

WY

Left margin vertical labels: **BUFFALO** / **CASPER**

Right margin vertical label: **DOUGLAS**

⬆🅝 INTERSTATE 25 CONT'D

Exit	Services
129mm	parking area both lanes
126	US 18, US 20 E, Orin, **E** Orin Jct 🆁🆂 **both lanes, full** 🛁 **facilities,** 🅒, 🚻, **litter barrels, petwalk, RV dump,** 🅖 Sinclair/Orin Jct Trkstp/dsl/café
125mm	N Platte River
111	Glendo, **E** 🅖 Sinclair/dsl, 🍴 Glendo Marina Café, 🛏 Howard's Motel, 🅞 to Glendo SP, Glendo Lakeside RV camping
104	to Middle Bear
100	Cassa Rd
94	El Rancho Rd
92	US 26 E, Dwyer, **E** 🆁🆂 **both lanes, full** 🛁 **facilities,** 🚻, **litter barrel, petwalk, RV dump to Guernsey SP**, Ft Laramie NHS
87	Johnson Rd
84	Laramie River Rd
84mm	Laramie River
80	US 87, Laramie Power Sta, Wheatland, Laramie Power Sta, **E** 🅖 Sinclair/A&W/Chester's/dsl, 🍴 Pizza Hut, 🛏 Best Western, Super 8, 🅞 Buick/Cadillac/Chevrolet, Chrysler/Dodge/Jeep, Family$, Ford, Safeway Foods, ShopKo, Arrowhead RV Park, museum, same as 78
78	US 87, Wheatland, **E** 🅖 Cenex/dsl, Maverik/dsl, Shell/dsl, 🍴 Arby's, Burger King, Subway, Taco John's, Western Sky's Diner, 🛏 All American Motel, Motel 6, West Winds Motel, WY Motel, 🅞 🅷, Wheatland Country Store, visitors ctr, **W** 🅖 Exxon/dsl, Pitstop/dsl, 🅞 Radio Shack, Mtn View RV Park
73	WY 34 W, to Laramie
70	Bordeaux Rd
68	Antelope Rd
66	Hunton Rd
65.5mm	parking area both lanes, litter barrels
65	Slater Rd
64mm	Richeau Creek
57	TY Basin Rd, Chugwater
54	Lp 25, Chugwater, **E** 🅖 Sinclair/dsl, 🛏 Buffalo Lodge/Grill, 🅞 RV camping, 🆁🆂 **both lanes, full** 🛁 **facilities,** 🅒, 🚻, **litter barrels, petwalk, RV dump**
47	Bear Creek Rd
39	Little Bear Community
36mm	Little Bear Creek
34	Nimmo Rd
33mm	Horse Creek
29	Whitaker Rd
25	ranch exit
21	Ridley Rd
17	US 85 N, to Torrington, **W** 🍴 Little Bear Rest. (2mi)
16	WY 211, Horse Creek Rd
13	Vandehei Ave, **E** 🅖 Loaf'n Jug/Subway, 🍴 Mr Gem's Pizza, Silvermine Subs, **W** 🅖 Shamrock/dsl
12	Central Ave, Cheyenne, **E** 🅖 Exxon/dsl, 🛏 Rodeway Inn, 🅞 🅷, Frontier Days Park, museum, **E on Yellowstone Rd** 🅖 Loaf'n Jug, 🍴 Arby's, Godfather's, Great Harvest Bread, McDonald's, Pizza Hut, Starbucks, Taco John's, 🅞 Albertsons, Big O Tire
11b	Warren AFB, Gate 1, Randall Ave, **E** 🅞 to WY St Capitol, museum
10b d	Warren AFB, Gate 2, Missile Dr, WY 210, HappyJack Rd, **W** 🅞 to Curt Gowdy SP

Exit	Services
9	US 30, W Lincolnway, Cheyenne, **E** 🅖 Exxon/Downhome Diner/dsl, 🍴 Outback Steaks, Village Inn, 🛏 Best Value Inn, Candlewood Suites, Days Inn, Fairfield Inn, Hampton Inn, Holiday Inn Express, La Quinta, Luxury Inn, Motel 6, My Place, Super 8, Towne Place Suites, 🅞 Buick/Cadillac/GMC, Chevrolet, Ford/Lincoln, Home Depot, Honda, Hyundai, Mazda, Nissan, Subaru, Toyota, **W** 🅖 Little America/Sinclair/dsl/rest./motel/@
8d b	I-80, E to Omaha, W to Laramie
7	WY 212, College Dr, **E** 🅖 💙Love's/Wendy's/dsl/scales/24hr/@, Shamrock/Subway/dsl/24hr, 🍴 Arby's, 🅞 A-B RV Park (2mi), Truck Repair, **W** 🅖 ✈FLYING J/Denny's/dsl/LP/scales/24hr/@, 🍴 McDonald's, 🛏 Quality Inn
6.5mm	Port of Entry, nb
4	High Plains Rd, **WY Welcome Ctr, rest/info ctr, both lanes, full** 🛁 **facilities,** 🅒, 🚻, **litter barrels, petwalk**
2	WY 223, Terry Ranch Rd, **2 mi E** Terry Bison Ranch RV camping
0mm	Wyoming/Colorado state line

⬆🅔 INTERSTATE 80

Exit	Services
402mm	Wyoming/Nebraska State line
401	WY 215, Pine Bluffs, **N** 🅖 Conoco/Subway/dsl, Sinclair/A&W/dsl/24hr/@, 🍴 Rikachee's Cafe, Rock Ranch Grill, 🛏 Gator's Motel, 🅞 NAPA, USPO, Pine Bluff RV Park, **S Welcome Ctr/**🆁🆂 **both lanes, full** 🛁 **facilities, info,** 🅒, **playground, nature trail,** 🚻, **litter barrels, petwalk**
391	Egbert
386	WY 213, WY 214, Burns, **N** Antelope Trkstp/dsl/cafe
377	WY 217, Hillsdale, **N** 🅖 TA/Burger King/Taco Bell/dsl/scales/24hr/@, 🅞 Wyo RV Camping
372mm	**Port of Entry wb, truck insp**
370	US 30 W, Archer, **N** 🅖 Sapp Bros/Spirit/T-Joe's Rest./dsl/scales/24hr/@, 🅞 fireworks, repair, RV park
367	Campstool Rd, **N** gas 🅖/Subway/dsl/scales/24hr, 🛏 Sleep Inn, 🅞 KOA (seasonal), **S** 🅞 to Wyoming Hereford Ranch
364	WY 212, to E Lincolnway, Cheyenne, **1-2 mi N on Lincoln way** 🅖 Exxon, Loaf'n Jug/Subway, Valero, 🍴 Burger King, IHOP, KFC, McDonald's, Shari's Rest., Subway, Taco Bell, Wendy's, 🅞 🅷, AutoZone, BigLots, Big O Tire, $Tree, Family$, Harley-Davidson, Hobby Lobby, Sierra Trading Post, Walgreens, **S** 🅞 AB Camping (4mi), Peterbilt
362	US 85, I-180, to Central Ave, Cheyenne, Greeley, **1 mi N** 🅖 Kum&Go/dsl, Sinclair, 🍴 Arby's, Carls' Jr, Guadalajara Mexican, Hacienda Mexican, Jimmy John's, Papa John's, Quiznos, Village Inn, 🅞 CarQuest, museum, st capitol, **S** 🅖 Exxon/Domino's/dsl, Shamrock/dsl, 🍴 Burger King, Taco John's, Little Caesar's, Pizza Hut, Sonic, Subway, 🛏 Holiday Inn, Roundup Motel, SpringHill Suites, 🅞 🅷, Family$, Safeway Foods/gas, RV camping, transmissions
359c a	I-25, US 87, N to Casper, S to Denver
358	US 30, W Lincolnway, Cheyenne, **N** 🅖 Exxon/dsl/24hr, Little America/Sinclair/dsl/motel/@, 🍴 Denny's, Outback Steaks, Pizza Inn, Village Inn, 🛏 Days Inn, EconoLodge, Express Inn, Hampton Inn, Hitching Post Inn, Holiday Inn Express, La Quinta, Luxury Inn, Motel 6, Super 8, 🅞 🅷, Chevrolet, Home Depot, Honda
357	Wy 222, Roundtop Rd
348	Otto Rd
345	Warren Rd, **N** truck parking

⬆️E INTERSTATE 80 CONT'D

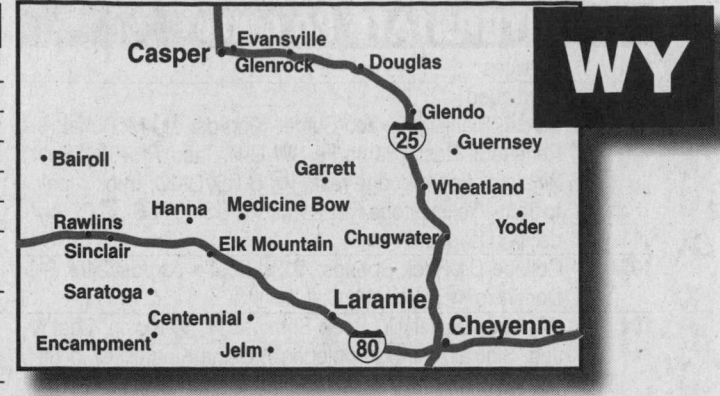

Exit	Services
342	Harriman Rd
341mm	parking area both lanes
339	Remount Rd
335	Buford
333mm	point of interest, parking area both lanes
329	Vedeauwoo Rd, N camping, S to Ames Monument, Nat Forest RA
323	WY 210, Happy Jack Rd, N 🆁🆂 both lanes, full ♿ facilities, 🅒, 🏠, litter barrels, petwalk, Lincoln Monument, elev. 8640, to Curt Gowdy SP
322mm	chain up area both lanes

LARAMIE

316	US 30 W, Grand Ave, Laramie, 0-2 mi N 🅖 Exxon/dsl, Loaf'N Jug, 🍴 Applebee's, Arby's, Burger King, Chili's, Hong Kong Buffet, Jimmy John's, McAlister's Deli, McDonald's, Papa Murphy's, Perkins, Quiznos, Sonic, Subway, Taco Bell, Taco John's, Village Inn, Wendy's, 🏠 AmericInn, Comfort Inn, Hampton Inn, Hilton Garden, Holiday Inn, 🄾 🏥, Albertsons/Osco/gas, AT&T, Buick/Chevrolet/GMC, $Tree, Ford/Lincoln, GNC, Staples, Toyota, Verizon, Walmart/24hr, **Urgent Care**, to UW
313	US 287, to 3rd St, Laramie, Port of Entry, N 🅖 GasaMat, Loaf'N Jug, Exxon, Phillips 66/dsl, Shell/dsl, 🍴 Chuck Wagon Rest., Corona Village Mexican, 🏠 Express Inn, Motel 8, Sunset Inn, 🄾 🏥, Honda, Laramie Plains Museum, NAPA, Nissan, S 🏠 Motel 6, Ramada Inn, 🄾 USPO
312mm	Laramie River
011	WY 130, WY 230, Snowy Range Rd, Laramie, S 🅖 Conoco/dsl, Phillips 66, Sinclair/dsl/LP, 🍴 McDonald's, Subway, 🏠 Best Value Inn, Snowy Range Inn, to Snowy Range Ski Area, WY Terr Park, repair/tires
310	Curtis St, Laramie, N 🅖 🍴/Wendy's/dsl/scales/24hr/@, Shamrock/café/dsl, 🏠 Best Western, Days Inn, EconoLodge, Super 8, 🄾 🏥, KOA, repair, S 🅖 Petro/Iron Skillet/dsl/scales/24hr/@, Blue Beacon, 🏠 Fairfield Inn, Quality Inn
307mm	parking area both lanes, litter barrels
297	WY 12, Herrick Lane
290	Quealy Dome Rd, S 🅖 A&C Truckstop/dsl
279	Cooper Cove Rd
272mm	Rock Creek
272	WY 13, to Arlington, N gas, RV camping
267	Wagonhound Rd, S 🆁🆂 both lanes, full ♿ facilities, 🅒, 🏠, litter barrels, petwalk
262mm	parking area both lanes
260	CR 402
259mm	Medicine Bow River, E Fork
257mm	Medicine Bow River
255	WY 72, Elk Mtn, to Hanna, N 🅖 Conoco/dsl, S 🏠 Elk Mtn Hotel/rest
238	Peterson Rd
235	WY 130, S US 30/87, N 🅖 Shell/dsl
229mm	N Platte River
228	Ft Steele HS, N 🆁🆂 both lanes, full ♿ facilities, 🅒, 🏠, litter barrels, petwalk
221	E Sinclair, N 🅖 Phillips 66/rest/dsl/24hr, 🄾 to Seminoe SP, camping
219	W Sinclair, N 🄾 to Seminoe SP, camping
215	Cedar St, Rawlins, N 🅖 Conoco/dsl, Phillips 66/dsl, Shell/KFC/Taco Bell/dsl, Sinclair, 🍴 Burger King, China House, McDonald's, Pizza Hut, Subway, Taco John's, 🏠 Comfort

RAWLINGS

215	Continued Inn, Days Inn, 1st Choice Inn, Hampton Inn, Holiday Inn Express, Quality Inn, OakTree Inn, The Key Motel, 🄾 Alco, Buick/Chevrolet/GMC, CarQuest, Checker Parts, Chrysler/Dodge/Jeep, City Mkt Food/gas, Do-It Hardware, Firestone/auto, Pamida, TDS Tire, museum, Frontier Prison NHS, to Yellowstone/Teton NP
214	Higley Blvd, Rawlins, N 🏠 Microtel, 🄾 KOA, S 🅖 TA/Shell/Subway/dsl/scales/24hr/@, 🏠 Best Value Inn
211	WY 789, to US 287 N, Spruce St, Rawlins, N 🅖 Conoco/dsl, Exxon/dsl, Loaf'n Jug, Phillips 66/dsl, Sinclair/dsl, 🍴 Cappy's Rest., 🏠 Best Western, Budget Inn, EconoLodge, Express Inn, Knights Inn, La Bella, Super 8, Sunset Motel, Travelodge, 🄾 🏥, Family$, Ford/Lincoln, Golden Eagle RV Park, RV World Camping, V1/LP
209	Johnson Rd, N 🅖 FLYING J/Denny's/dsl/LP/scales/24hr
206	Hadsell Rd (no return)
205.5mm	continental divide, elev 7000
204	Knobs Rd
201	Daley Rd
196	Riner Rd
190mm	parking area wb, litter barrels
189mm	parking area eb, 🏠, litter barrels
187	WY 789, Creston, Baggs Rd
184	Continental Divide Rd
173	Wamsutter, N 🅖 Loves/Chester's/Subway/dsl/24hr/@, S 🅖 Conoco/dsl/repair/café/24hr, Phillips 66/dsl, 🍴 Broadway Café, 🏠 Wamsutter Motel
165	Red Desert
158	Tipton Rd continental divide, elev 6930
156	GL Rd
154	BLM Rd
152	Bar X Rd
150	Table Rock Rd
146	Patrick Draw Rd
144mm	🆁🆂 both lanes, full ♿ facilities, 🅒, 🏠, litter barrels, petwalk
143mm	parking area both lanes, litter barrels
142	Bitter Creek Rd
139	Red Hill Rd
136	Black Butte Rd
133mm	parking area both lanes
130	Point of Rocks, N 🅖 Conoco/dsl, 🄾 RV Park
122	WY 371, to Superior
111	Airport Roads, Baxter Rd, S 🆁🆂
107	Pilot Butte Ave, Rock Springs, S 🅖 Kum&Go, Mobil/dsl, 🍴 Pizza Hut, 🏠 Sands Inn/café, Springs Motel
104	US 191 N, Elk St, Rock Springs, N 🅖 Conoco/dsl, Exxon, FLYING J/Denny's/dsl/LP/24hr, Kum&Go/gas, Phillips

= gas   = food   = lodging   = other   = rest stop   Copyright 2014 - The NEXT Exit ®

↑E INTERSTATE 80 CONT'D

Exit	Services
104	Continued 66/dsl, Sinclair, Texaco/Burger King/dsl, McDonald's, Renegade Rest., Santa Fe SW Grill, Taco Time, Best Western, EconoLodge/rest., Buick/GMC, truck repair, to Teton/Yellowstone Nat Parks via US 191, S Exxon/dsl, Days Inn
103	College Dr, Rock Springs, S Loaf'n Jug/dsl/24hr, Domino's H, W WY Coll
102	WY 430, Dewar Dr, Rock Springs, N Exxon, Loaf'N Jug, Sinclair/dsl, Applebee's, China King, KFC/LJ Silver, Taco Time, Best Value Inn, Comfort Inn La Quinta, Motel 6, Cadillac/Chevrolet, Chrysler/Dodge, $Tree, Harley-Davidson, Herberger's, Home Depot, JC Penney, K-Mart, Smith's Foods, S Kum&Go, Loaf'N Jug, Mirastar/dsl, Mobil, Arby's, Bonsai Chinese, Burger King, Golden Corral, IHOP, McDonald's, Pizza Hut, Quizno's, Sonic, Starbucks, Subway, Taco Bell, Village Inn, Wendy's, Wiki Hawaiian BBQ, Winger's, Wonderful House Chinese, Budget Host, Hampton Inn, Holiday Inn, Holiday Inn Express, Homewood Suites, Motel 8, Quality Inn, Super 8, Western Inn, H, Albertsons/Sav-on, AutoZone, Big O Tire, Checker Parts, Curves, Ford/Lincoln, Hastings Books, NAPA, Nissan, Radio Shack, Staples, Walgreens, Walmart
99	US 191 S, E Flaming Gorge Rd, N KOA (1mi), S Sinclair/dsl/rest./24hr/@, Ted's Rest., fireworks, transmissions
94mm	Kissing Rock
91	US 30, to WY 530, Green River, **2 mi S** Gasamat, Loaf'N Jug, Arctic Circle, Don Pedro's Mexican, McDonald's, Pizza Hut, Subway, Taco Time, Coachman Inn, Mustang Inn, Super 8, Expedition NHS, to Flaming Gorge NRA, same as 89
89	US 30, Green River, S Exxon/dsl, Sinclair/dsl, Penny's Diner, Pizza Hut, Hampton Inn, OakTree Inn, Super 8, Western Inn, Adam's RV Service, Tex's RV Camp, to Flaming Gorge NRA
87.5mm	Green River
85	Covered Wagon Rd, S Adams RV parts/service, Tex's Travel Camp
83	WY 372, La Barge Rd, N to Fontenelle Dam
78	(from wb)
77mm	Blacks Fork River
72	Westvaco Rd
71mm	parking area both lanes
68	Little America, N Sinclair/Little America Hotel/rest./dsl/24hr@, RV camping
66	US 30 W, to Teton, Yellowstone, Fossil Butte NM, Kemmerer
61	Cedar Mt Rd, to Granger
60mm	parking area both lanes, litter barrels
54mm	parking area eb, litter barrels
53	Church Butte Rd
49mm	parking area wb, litter barrels
48	Lp 80, Lyman, Ft Bridger, Hist Ft Bridger
45mm	Blacks Fork River
41	WY 413, Lyman, **N** Gas'n Go/cafe/dsl, **S** **both lanes, full facilities, , , litter barrels, petwalk,** Taco Time, Gateway Inn (2mi), KOA (1mi)
39	WY 412, WY 414, to Carter, Mountain View
34	Lp 80, to Ft Bridger, S Wagon Wheel Motel, Ft Bridger RV Camp, Ft Bridger NHS, to Flaming Gorge NRA
33.5mm	parking area eb, litter barrels
33	Union Rd
30	Bigelow Rd, N TA/Tesoro/Burger King/Taco Bell/Fork In the Road/dsl/scales/24hr/@, S fireworks
28	French Rd
28mm	French Rd, parking area both lanes
24	Leroy Rd
23	Bar Hat Rd
21	Coal Rd
18	US 189 N, to Kemmerer, to Nat Parks, Fossil Butte NM
15	Guild Rd (from eb)
14mm	parking area both lanes
13	Divide Rd
10	Painter Rd, to Eagle Rock Ski Area, to Eagle Rock Ski Area
6	US 189, Bear River Dr, Evanston, N /Subway/dsl/scales/24hr, Sinclair/dsl, Bear Town Rest., Don Pedro Mexican, Best Value Inn, Motel 6, Prairie Inn, Vagabond Motel, Bear River RV Park, Wyo Downs Racetrack, repair/tires, S **Welcome Ctr both lanes, full facilities, , , litter barrels, petwalk, RV dump (seasonal), playground,** Bear River SP
5	WY 89, Evanston, N Chevron/Taco Time/dsl, Maverik/dsl, Arby's, DragonWall Chinese, McDonald's, Papa Murphy's, Subway, Wendy's, EconoLodge, H, AutoZone, Buick/Chevrolet, $Tree, Family$, Jiffy Lube, Murdoch's, NAPA, Verizon, Walmart/Subway, S WY St H
3	US 189, Harrison Dr, Evanston, N Chevron/dsl, / FLYING J/Subway/dsl/scales/24hr, Gasamat, Sinclair, JB's, Lotty's Rest., Wally's Burgers, Best Western/rest., Comfort Inn, Days Inn, Hampton Inn, HighCountry Inn, HillCrest Motel, Holiday Inn Express, Howard Johnson, Super 8, Cadillac/GMC, Chrysler/Jeep, USPO, S KFC/Taco Bell, H, fireworks
.5mm	**Port of Entry eb, weigh sta wb**
0mm	Wyoming/Utah state line

↑E INTERSTATE 90

Exit	Services
207mm	Wyoming/South Dakota state line
205	Beulah, N Shell/dsl/LP, Buffalo Jump Rest., The Mill, Sand Creek Camping, USPO, S Ranch A NHP (5mi)
204.5mm	Sand Creek
199	WY 111, to Aladdin, N **Welcome ctr (both directions) full facilities, , litter barrels, , petwalk,** Re Water Creek RV Park, to Devil's Tower NM, to Vore Buffalo Jump NHP
191	Moskee Rd
189	US 14 W, Sundance, N Conoco/dsl/24hr, Best Western, H, Mt View Camping, to Devil's Tower NM, museum, S **both lanes, full facilities, info, , , litter barrels, playground, petwalk, RV dump, port of entry/weigh sta**
187	WY 585, Sundance, N Fresh Start/dsl, Sinclair/dsl, Aro Rest., Subway, Bear Lodge, Best Western, Budget Host Arrowhead, Pineview Motel, Rodeway Inn, H, Decker's Foods, NAPA, to Devil's Tower
185	to WY 116, to Sundance, S Conoco/dsl/service, **2 mi** same as 187
178	Coal Divide Rd
177mm	parking area both lanes
172	Inyan Kara Rd
171mm	parking area eb, litter barrels
165	Pine Ridge Rd, to Pine Haven, N Cedar Ridge RV Park (10mi), to Keyhole SP

⬆E INTERSTATE 90 CONT'D

Exit	Services
163mm	parking area both lanes
160	Wind Creek Rd
154	US 14, US 16, **S** 🅶 Cenex/dsl, 🍴 Donna's Diner, Subway, 🛏 Cozy Motel, Moorcourt Motel, Rangerland Motel/RV Park, Wyo Motel, 🅾 Diehl's Foods/gas, USPO, museum, city park
153	US 16 E, US 14, W Moorcroft, **N** 🆁🆂 **both lanes, full** ♿ **facilities,** 🚻, 🏕, **litter barrels, petwalk, S** same as 154
152mm	Belle Fourche River
141	Rozet
138mm	parking area both lanes
132	Wyodak Rd
129	Garner Lake Rd, **S** 🛏 Settle Inn, 🅾 Crazy Woman Camping, Harley-Davidson, High Plains Camping, auto repair
128	US 14, US 16, Gillette, Port of Entry, **N** 🅶 Conoco, Kum&Go, Maverik/dsl, 🍴 Mona's American/Mexican, Taco John's, Village Inn, 🛏 Howard Johnson, Mustang Motel, National 9 Inn, Smart Choice Inn, 🅾 Crazy Woman Camping (2mi), East Side RV Ctr., **S** 🛏 Settle Inn, 🅾 High Plains Camping
126	WY 59, Gillette, **N** 🅶 Cenex/dsl, Conoco/dsl, Loaf'N Jug, 🍴 China King Buffet, Hardee's, Maria's Mexican, McDonald's, Pokey's BBQ, Prime Rib Rest., Starbucks, Subway, 🛏 Best Value Inn, 🅾 Family$, Radio Shack, Smith's Foods, Tire Factory, city park, **S** 🅶 Exxon, ⭕FLYING J /dsl/24hr, Loaf'N Jug, 🍴 A&W/LJ Silver, Applebee's, Arby's, Aztec Buffet, Burger King, DQ, Goodtimes Grill/Taco John's, Great Wall Chinese, KFC, Papa Murphy's, Perkins/24hr, Pizza Hut, Quiznos, Taco Bell, Wendy's, 🛏 Candlewood Suites, Clarion, Country Inn&Suites, Days Inn, Fairfield Inn, Holiday Inn Express, Wingate Inn, 🅾 Urgent Care, Ace Hardware, Albertson's, Big O Tire, $Tree, Goodyear/auto, Hastings Books, Home Depot, K-Mart, Office Depot, O'Reilly Parts, Osco Drug, Tire-O-Rama, Verizon, Walgreens, Walmart/Subway, city park
124	WY 50, Gillette, **N** 🅶 Conoco/dsl/24hr, Shell/Burger King/dsl, 🍴 Granny's Kitchen, Hong Kong Rest., Los Compadres Mexican, Pizza Hut, Subway, 🛏 Best Western/rest., Budget Inn, Comfort Inn, Hampton Inn, Motel 6, Super 8, 🅾 🏥, Don's Foods, **S** 🅶 Kum&Go/dsl, 🅾 Bighorn Tire, Buick/Chevrolet/GMC, Chrysler/Dodge/Jeep
116	Force Rd
113	Wild Horse Creek Rd
110mm	no services
106	Kingsbury Rd
102	Barber Creek Rd
91	Dead Horse Creek Rd
89mm	Powder River
88	Powder River Rd, **N** 🅶 RV Park, 🆁🆂 **both lanes, full** ♿ **facilities,** 🚻, 🏕, **litter barrels, petwalk**
82	Indian Creek Rd
77	Schoonover Rd
73.5mm	Crazy Woman Creek
73	Crazy Woman Creek Rd
69	Dry Creek Rd
68.5mm	parking area both lanes, litter barrels (wb only)
65	Red Hills Rd, Tipperary Rd
60mm	parking area both lanes, litter barrels
58	US 16, to Ucross, Buffalo, **0-3 mi S** 🅶 Cenex/rest/dsl/24hr, Maverik/dsl, 🍴 Bozeman Tr Steaks, Dash Inn Rest., Hardee's, McDonald's, Pizza Hut, Sub Shop, Subway, Taco John's, Winchester Steaks, 🛏 Crossroads Inn,

Wyoming state map showing cities including Casper, Evansville, Glenrock, Douglas, Glendo, Guernsey, Wheatland, Yoder, Chugwater, Laramie, Cheyenne, Rawlins, Sinclair, Saratoga, Centennial, Encampment, Jelm, Bairoll, Garrett, Hanna, Medicine Bow, Elk Mountain, with Interstates 25 and 80.

WY

BUFFALO

Exit	Services
58	Continued Comfort Inn, Days Inn, Hampton Inn, Holiday Inn Express, Motel 6, Super 8, WYO Motel, 🅾 🏥, Ace Hardware, Bighorn Tire, Deer Park Camping, Family$, Indian RV Camp, KOA, NAPA, Verizon, Nat Hist Dist, vet
56b	I-25 S, US 87 S, to Buffalo
56a	25 Bus, 90 Bus, to Buffalo, **Services 2 mi S** (from eb)
53	Rock Creek Rd
51	Lake DeSmet, **1 mi N** Lake Stop gas/motel/cafe, Lake De Smet RV park
47	Shell Creek Rd
44	US 87 N, Piney Creek Rd, to Story, Banner, **N** 🅾 Ft Phil Kearney, museum, **5 mi S** Wagon Box Cabins/Rest.
39mm	scenic turnout wb
37	Prairie Dog Creek Rd, to Story
33	Meade Creek Rd, to Big Horn
31mm	parking area eb
25	US 14 E, Sheridan, **N** 🛏 Quality Inn, 🅾 Dalton's RV Ctr, **S** 🅶 Exxon/dsl, Holiday/dsl, Loaf'n Jug/dsl, Maverik/dsl, 🍴 Arby's, Burger King, Goodtimes/Taco John's, JB's, Jimmy John's, Los Agaves, McDonald's, Ole's Pizza, Papa John's, Papa Murphy's, Perkins, Qdoba, Starbucks, Subway, Taco Bell, Wendy's, 🛏 Candlewood Suites, Days Inn, Holiday Inn, Holiday Lodge, Mill Inn, 🅾 Ace Hardware, Albertson's/Osco Drug, Buick/GMC, Chrysler/Dodge/Jeep, $Tree, Firestone/auto, Ford/Lincoln, Goodyear/auto, Home Depot, Jeep, Meineke, Midas, NAPA, O'Reilly Parts, Tire-Rama, Toyota, Walgreens, Walmart/Subway, ✈, to Hist Dist, Sheridan Coll, vet
23	WY 336, 5th St, Sheridan, **N** 🅶 Rock Stop/Subway/dsl, 🛏 Wingate Inn, 🆁🆂 **both lanes, full** ♿ **facilities, info,** 🚻, 🏕, **litter barrels, petwalk, RV dump, 1-2 mi S** 🅶 Cenex, Holiday/dsl, 🍴 DQ, El Tapatio Dos, Olivia's Kitchen, Quiznos, WYO Rib&Chop House, 🛏 Alamo Motel, Best Value Inn, Best Western, Hampton Inn, Motel 6, Sheridan Inn, 🅾 🏥, Honda, Peter D's RV Park, Sheridan Cty Museum, park, radiators
20	Main St, Sheridan, **S** 🅶 Exxon/dsl/scales/24hr, Gasamat/dsl, Maverik, 🍴 Country Kitchen, Domino's, Firewater Grill, Kim's Rest., Little Ceasars, McDonald's, Pizza Hut, 🛏 Aspen Inn, Bramble Motel, Budget Host, Rodeway Inn, Stage Stop Motel, Super 8, Super Saver Motel, Trails End Motel/rest., 🅾 🏥, K-Mart, KOA, Peerless Tires
16	to Decker, Montana, port of entry
15mm	Tongue River
14	WY 345, Acme Rd
9	US 14 W, Ranchester, **1 mi S** 🅶 Cenex/dsl, 🅾 Western Motel, 🅾 Foothills Campground, Lazy R Campground, to Yellowstone, Teton NPs, Conner Bfd NHS, Ski Area
1	Parkman
0mm	Wyoming/Montana state line

SHERIDAN

ssist A Fellow Traveler with...

the Next EXIT®

Published annually,

the Next EXIT®

provides the best

USA Interstate Highway Information available.

Use this form to order another copy of the Next EXIT®

for yourself or someone special.

Please send _____ copies of the Next Exit® to the address below.

I've enclosed my check or money order for $20.95 US/$25.95 Canadian per copy.

Name:_____

Address: _____ Apt./Suite # _____

City: _____ State: _____ Zip:_____

THREE EASY ORDER OPTIONS:

1. **MAIL ORDER FORM TO:**
   the Next EXIT®, Inc.
   PO Box 888
   Garden City, Utah 84028

2. **ORDER ON THE WEB AT:**
   www.theNextExit.com

3. **Give Us A Call & Use Your Charge Card**
   1-800-NEX-EXIT or 1-800-639-3948

the Next EXIT® is available online at:
www.theNextExit.com
iPhone App FREE with your subscription.